THIRD EDITION

Handbook of Social Psychology

VOLUME II
Special Fields and Applications

Gardner Lindzey
Center for Advanced Study in the Behavioral Sciences

Elliot Aronson
University of California, Santa Cruz

 RANDOM HOUSE

New York

Distributed exclusively by
Lawrence Erlbaum Associates, Inc., Publishers
Hillsdale, New Jersey, and London

Third Edition

987654321

Copyright © 1985 by Newbery Award Records, Inc.

Library of Congress Cataloging in Publication Data
Main entry under title:

The Handbook of social psychology.

Includes index.
Contents: v. 1. Theory and method—v. 2. Special fields and applications.
1. Social psychology. I. Lindzey, Gardner.
II. Aronson, Elliot.
HM251.H224 1985   302   84-18509
ISBN 0-394-35049-9 (v. 1)
ISBN 0-394-35050-2 (v. 2)

Manufactured in the United States of America

The editors wish to thank a number of publishers and copyright holders for permission to reproduce tables, figures, and excerpts from the following sources:

Reprinted with permission from Baker, C., "The Vroom-Yetton Model of leadership—Model, theory, or technique." *Omega, 8.,* 9-10. Copyright © 1980, Pergamon Press, Ltd.

Burgess, R. L., and T. L. Huston, Eds. *Social Exchange in Developing Relationships.* New York: Academic Press. P. 8. Copyright © 1979. Reprinted by permission.

Clark, H. H., and J. W. French. *Language in Society.* Cambridge: Cambridge University Press. Pp. 1-19. Copyright © 1981. Reprinted by permission.

Cook, S. W., and J. L. Berrenberg, "Approaches to encouraging conservation behavior: A review and conceptual framework." *Journal of Social Issues, 37.* Table 1, p. 100. Copyright © 1981. Reprinted by permission.

Garvey, C., "The contingent query: A dependent act in conversation." In M. Lewis and L. Rosenblum (Eds.), *Interaction, conversation, and the development of language: The origins of behavior.* New York: Wiley. Copyright © 1977. Reprinted by permission.

Harrington, C., and J. W. M. Whiting, "Socialization process and personality." In F. L. K. Hsu (Ed.) *Psychological anthropology.* Cambridge, Mass.: Schenkman. P. 471. Copyright © 1972. Reprinted by permission.

Krauss, R. M., and S. Weinheimer, "Changes in reference phrases as a function of frequence of usage in social interaction: A preliminary study." *Psychonomic Science, 1,* 113. Copyright © 1964. Reprinted by permission.

Lane, R. E., *Political Ideology.* New York: The Free Press. Copyright © 1962. Reprinted with permission of Macmillan, Inc.

Reprinted by permission of the Linguistic Society of America excerpts from: Linde, C., and W. Labov, "Spatial networks as a site for the study of language and thought," *Language, 51,* 924-939, copyright © 1975. Sacks, H., E. A. Schegloff, and G. Jefferson, "A simplest systematics for the organization of turn-taking in conversation," *Language, 53,* 696-735, copyright © 1974. Schegloff, E. A., G. Jefferson, and H. Sacks, "The preference for self-correction in the organization of repair in conversation," *Language, 53,* 361-382, copyright © 1977.

Schegloff, F. and H. Sacks, "Opening up closings." *Semiotica, 8,* 289-327. Copyright © 1973. Reprinted by permission.

Secord, P. F., and C. W. Backman, "An interpersonal approach to personality." In B. Maher, Ed., *Progress in experimental personality research.* Vol. 2. Copyright © 1965. Reprinted by permission.

Vonnegut, K., "A truly modern hero." *Psychology Today, 15,* 10. Copyright 1981 by Kurt Vonnegut Jr. Reprinted by permission of Mr. Vonnegut's attorney Donald C. Farber.

Preface to the Third Edition

This is the fourth *Handbook of Social Psychology*—the third involving one or both of the current editors. To examine these four *Handbooks* for constancy and change is a revealing exercise.

In introducing his 1935 *Handbook* Carl Murchison remarked, "The social sciences at the present moment stand naked and feeble in the midst of the political uncertainty of the world. The physical sciences seem so brilliant, so clothed with power by contrast. Either something has gone all wrong in the evolution of the social sciences, or their great day in court has not yet arrived. It is with something akin to despair that one contemplates the piffling, trivial, superficial, damnably unimportant topics that some social scientists investigate with agony and sweat. And at the end of all these centuries, no one knows what is wrong with the world or what is likely to happen to the world" (p. ix). A mere decade later this paragraph already seemed to many observers archaic and poorly informed. Even more remarkable is the fact that more than one-third the chapters in the 1935 *Handbook* dealt with the social psychology of bacteria, plants, and lower animals. Moreover, four chapters dealt with the social history of the negro, the red man, the white man, and the yellow man—labels that if used today would create a wave of revulsion. These chapters and others not

mentioned, strike no note of resonance with contemporary social psychology.

Are there any traces in Murchison's *Handbook* of what has emerged as social psychology fifty years later? Clearly, the answer is yes, although the number of such continuities is not large. Perhaps the most dramatic example of anticipating the future is Gordon Allport's chapter on attitudes. In the 1954 *Handbook* there were to be two chapters on attitudes—one on measurement, and the other on attitude theory and research—and it was a last-minute withdrawal that led to omission of the chapter on attitude theory and research. In subsequent volumes we have observed a very heavy emphasis on attitude research as a cornerstone of social psychology. A second line of continuity is represented by Esper's chapter on language, which has been reflected and elaborated on in each of the subsequent editions. Moreover, Dashiell's chapter on human social experiments remarkably anticipates the industrious experimental social psychologists who to date have played an increasingly dominant role in American social psychology. Chapters on gender differences and the behavior of children in social situations are also reflected in subsequent *Handbooks*.

The 1954 edition fell naturally into two volumes: Volume I was devoted to prominent theories and major methods; Volume II dealt entirely with the most active substantive research areas of the time. The theoretical positions represented in the 1954 edition were almost identical to those in the 1968–1969 edition. In 1954, separate chapters were devoted to S-R theory (including reinforcement and contiguity), cognitive theory, psychoanalytic theory, field theory, and role theory. In the 1968–1969 edition each of those theoretical positions was again represented, and in addition, separate chapters were devoted to organization theory and mathematical models. In the current edition we have reverted to five theoretical positions. We retained S-R theory but broadened it to include the wider issues implied by the title "learning theory." Our chapter on cognitive theories acknowledges the continuing development of exciting systematic positions in that area. Similarly, our decision to retain a chapter on organization theory indicates the continued impact of that position. Our chapter on role theory has now been expanded to include symbolic interactionism in order to provide stronger representation of sociological perspectives. Although we have dropped specific chapters on mathematical models and field theory, work in these areas is very much in evidence in our new chapters on decision theory and cognitive theories. Our decision not to include a chapter on psychoanalytic theory was difficult. Although we appreciate the riches that social psychologists have extracted from this particular mine of ideas, it seems clear that over the past two decades very little research by social psychologists has been directly stimulated by this theory.

With regard to methods, we find few changes in chapter titles over the past thirty years. Social psychologists are still interested primarily in experimentation, attitude and opinion measurement, survey research, systematic observation, and quantitative analysis. Needless to say, the *content* of the chapters has changed dramatically over the years as our colleagues have become increasingly sophisticated in their use of these methods. The one new chapter that has been added concerns evaluation—reflecting a body of techniques that has become increasingly important since the late 1960s and has resulted in a new psychological specialty.

It is particularly interesting to compare the substantive research areas across the three modern editions of the handbook. Some areas have been a major focus of social psychological research since World War II and seem destined to remain so for the foreseeable future. Thus since the war all three handbooks have included chapters on attitude change, leadership, the media, prejudice and racism, anthropological social psychology, psycholinguistics, and political behavior.

Some content areas have undergone a shift in emphasis over the years that has been great enough to require a major change in the title of the chapter. Thus our current chapter on social influence covers some of the same issues and kinds of research contained in chapters from earlier editions on group problem solving, but with a much wider range. Similarly, social psychologists have been interested in the socialization process for a very long time. The title of the current chapter emphasizes that the socialization process is not confined to infants, children, and adolescents, and reflects the increase in research on socialization throughout the life cycle. Likewise, the new chapter on social factors in cognition combines and expands earlier chapters on person perception and social and cultural factors in perception. The current edition also continues some trends that were initiated in the 1968–1969 edition. These include a special emphasis on interpersonal attraction and on the interaction between personality and social psychology.

Finally, there are some substantive chapters that are either totally new to this edition or that bear only slight resemblance to anything that has appeared in previous editions. These include chapters on sex roles, environmental psychology, social deviance, prosocial and antisocial behavior, and applications of social psychology. The chapters on sex roles and environmental psychology reflect issues and interests that were simply not factors in 1954, were barely on the horizon in 1968–1969, but are very much a part of our lives in the 1980s. Social psychologists have been playing a major role in increasing our understanding of these issues. In one sense, the handbook has been involved with applied social psychology throughout its existence. Thus the 1954 edition included a chapter on industrial social psychology; the 1968 edition included a revised version of that chapter but also included separate chapters on the social psychology of education, social psychological aspects of international relations, the social psychology of mental health, and others. But in another sense, the current chapter is innovative in that its focus is not on "applied social psychology" but on the broader issue of "the application" of social psychological knowledge and methods to a wide variety of contemporary problems such as health care, the legal system, and the classroom.

The only author to appear in all four *Handbooks* is Allport, who has written both on attitudes (1935) and on the history of social psychology (1954, 1968, 1985). His contribution to the present volume appears posthumously and is a slightly abridged version of the chapter that appeared in the last edition. No other author has appeared in more than two editions, although one was involved with four chapters in the 1954 and 1968–1969 editions, and a substantial number (twenty-five) have contributed to two editions. There are forty-five contributors to the current edition only seven of whom contributed to the last edition. As these figures indicate, the current volumes represent a decidedly fresh perspective on the field of social psychology. Many of our colleagues continued to find the 1954 edition useful after the appearance of the 1968–1969 edition, and we have little doubt that both the previous editions will continue to be of utility even with the appearance of this revision.

Because the *Handbook* is generally regarded as a kind of "standard," it is sometimes used to gauge current interests in social psychology or even to predict the health and direction of social psychology. For this reason we feel the editors have an obligation to make certain that our decisions (implicit and explicit) are not misinterpreted. For example one reviewer, in noting that the 1954 edition did not contain a chapter on "Attitude Theory and Research," concluded that social psychologists were losing interest in the concept of attitude. As noted earlier, the absence of that chapter was no more meaningful than the delinquency of one of our contributors! A final *Handbook* is almost never a precise reflection of the intentions of the editors and their advisors, and consequently readers should be cautious in interpreting trends or the current state of the field from the contents of the various editions.

With these concerns in mind, it is clearly important to discuss changes we have made in the format of the *Handbook*. The 1954 edition consisted of two volumes. The 1968–1969 edition was expanded to five volumes. For the current edition we decided to return to the two-volume format. A facile (but incorrect) interpretation might be that social psychology reached its peak in the 1960s and is now declining. We do not hold this view. We believe social psychology is as vital today as it was twenty years ago. Our decisions regarding format were based on more mundane issues—utility, convenience, and cost. Specifically, in 1967–1968 we believed that the five-volume format would make it easier for social psychologists interested in specific topics to purchase one or two

small volumes rather than the entire set. This proved to be a poor prediction: sales figures indicated that most users purchased all five volumes simultaneously. Moreover, we noted with dismay that the five-volume format changed the way the *Handbook* was being used. Apparently there is a tendency for a work in five volumes to be seen and used as if it were an encyclopedia. That is, our graduate students and colleagues tended to place their *Handbooks* on a shelf and to pull down a volume only when they needed a reference book. This was not the case with the 1954 edition, which was used both as a text and as a portable companion. Moreover, the cost of producing a five-volume set today would place the *Handbook* beyond the financial grasp of all but libraries and the very well-to-do. In short, our decision to return to a two-volume format was made because we believe the *Handbook* is more vital if it is off the shelf and priced at the lowest possible level.

The current volumes had their beginnings in May 1978, when we sent more than 130 letters to well-known social psychologists, including all contributors to the previous edition of the *Handbook*. We enclosed a tentative outline for the current *Handbook* and asked for comments about both topics and potential authors. We also pointed to a reorganization that in both number of volumes and chapters implied a product that would be more like the 1954 volumes than the 1968–1969 *Handbook*. We received more than seventy-five replies. All but one of the respondents felt a revision was timely. All but one respondent also approved, explicitly or implicitly, the reduction in number of volumes from five to two. Virtually all had suggestions for changes in our outline and roster of potential authors. The outline was substantially altered as a result of these suggestions, and in October 1978 we began to solicit authors. We will not take you through the tortuous path of changing deadlines, authors, and (very slightly) chapters. Actually, of the thirty-two chapters included in our outline, only two have been lost through attrition.

Some readers may be surprised to discover that these volumes have been published by Random House rather than Addison-Wesley. Certainly the editors were surprised when informed in the late stages of production that Addison-Wesley was transferring all of its social science publications to Random House. We were assured that there would be no delay in the appearance of the volumes and that Random House was looking forward eagerly to the production and promotion of the *Hand-*

book. We see no reason to doubt these statements and look forward to an amicable and rewarding relationship with Random House.

The facilities of the Center for Advanced Study in the Behavioral Sciences played a very significant role in the production of these volumes. In particular, the pa-tience and skill of Joyce McDonald were indispensable and are deeply appreciated.

September 1984
Stanford, California   G. L.
Santa Cruz, California   E. A.

Preface to the Second Edition

In the fourteen years that have elapsed since the last edition of this *Handbook,* the field of social psychology has evolved at a rapid rate. The present volumes are intended to represent these changes as faithfully as possible and at a level appropriate for the beginning graduate student as well as the fully trained psychologist.

The reader familiar with the previous *Handbook* will realize that we have employed the same general outline in the present volumes. The many new chapters reflect the increased quantitative and methodological sophistication of social psychologists, the development of certain specialized areas of research, and the increased activity in a variety of applied areas. In some instances we have attempted to compensate for known deficiencies in the coverage of the previous edition.

One can never be certain of portraying adequately the changes in a large and diverse area of scholarship, but we can be certain that this *Handbook* is very different from its predecessor. It is substantially larger—instead of one million words, two volumes, and 30 chapters, there are now approximately two-and-one-half million words, five volumes, and 45 chapters. We are convinced that our decision to present this material in five volumes will increase its utility for those who have specialized interests linked to either teaching or research activities. But the difference goes beyond mere size. The list of contributors has a decidedly new flavor—of the 45 authors in the previous edition, only 22 have contributed to this volume. Viewed from another vantage, of the 68 authors contributing to the current volume, 46 are represented in the *Handbook* for the first time. Only one chapter is reprinted without a thorough revision, and this, an essay (Hebb and Thompson) presenting a point of view that seems little affected by recent research and formulation. There are 15 chapters that are completely new and, in addition, a number of the replacements bear little resemblance to the chapter of the same, or similar, title that appeared earlier.

Plans for the current revision were begun in January of 1963. By July of that year a tentative chapter outline had been prepared and distributed to an array of distinguished social scientists, including the previous contributors to the *Handbook.* We benefited materially from the advice of dozens of persons in regard to both the chapter outline and the nomination of potential authors; we are grateful for their efforts on behalf of the *Handbook.* By fall of 1963 we had succeeded in constructing a final outline and a list of contributors. Our initial letters of invitation asked that completed manuscripts be submitted by January 1, 1965. We managed to obtain the bulk of the chapters eighteen months and several dead-lines later, and the first two volumes were sent to the publishers early in 1967. The final chapters were secured the following July, when the remaining volumes went to press.

In selecting contributors we made every effort, within the general constraints of technical competence and availability, to obtain scholars of diverse professional and institutional backgrounds. Thus we take special pleasure in the fact that almost all areas of the country are well represented, that six of the contributors are affiliated with institutions outside the United States, and that the authors include political scientists, sociologists, and anthropologists as well as psychologists.

We consider it extremely fortunate that of the chapters listed in our working outline, all of those that we regarded as "key" or central chapters are included here. Indeed, there are only three chapters from that list that are not a part of the present volumes; this includes one (attitude change) that was deliberately incorporated within another chapter because such an arrangement

seemed to offer a greater likelihood of satisfactory integration and coverage. It should be noted that this success is in marked contrast to the previous *Handbook,* where such essential areas as attitudes and social perception were omitted because of last-minute delinquencies. Although a few invited contributors did withdraw from the present *Handbook* after initially having agreed to prepare a chapter, in all cases we were fortunate in being able to find equally qualified replacements who were willing to take on this assignment on relatively short notice. To these individuals we owe a special debt of gratitude.

We wish to acknowledge the indispensable assistance of Judith Hilton, Shirley Cearley, and Leslie Segner in connection with the final preparation of the manuscript. Finally, we would like to express our gratitude to Mary Jane Whiteside for her tireless efforts in the final indexing of all volumes of the *Handbook.*

February 1968   G. L.
Austin, Texas   E. A.

Preface to the First Edition

The accelerating expansion of social psychology in the past two decades has led to an acute need for a source book more advanced than the ordinary textbook in the field but yet more focused than scattered periodical literature. Murchison's *Handbook of Social Psychology* (1935), the only previous attempt to meet this need, is out of date and out of print. It was this state of affairs that led us to assemble a book that would represent the major areas of social psychology at a level of difficulty appropriate for graduate students. In addition to serving the needs of graduate instruction, we anticipate that the volumes will be useful in advanced undergraduate courses and as a reference book for professional psychologists.

We first considered the possibility of preparing a *Handbook* three years ago. However, a final decision to proceed with the plan was not reached until the fall of 1951. During the interval we arranged an outline of topics that represented our convictions concerning the present state of social psychology. We then wrote to a large number of distinguished social psychologists asking them whether they felt our venture was likely to be professionally valuable and asking for criticisms of the outline we had prepared. The response to these letters was immensely gratifying—social psychologists as a group appear sufficiently altruistic to spend large amounts of

time criticizing and commenting on a project of which they approve even though they may be unable to participate in it themselves. We also asked for specific recommendations of people who seemed best qualified to prepare the various chapters. After receiving answers we drastically revised our outline and proceeded to invite authors to prepare the various chapters. It was not until the spring of 1952 that we completed our list of contributors and even this list later underwent change. We first suggested (tongue in cheek) that the manuscripts be submitted by September 15, 1952. However, as we secretly expected, we were forced to change this due date to January 1, 1953. This "deadline" we tried hard to meet. But of course we failed and shifted our aspiration to June 15, 1953. Again we failed, although by now we were making substantial progress. By early in the fall of 1953 we had all the chapters excepting two, and the first volume was completed and in the hands of the publishers. The last two chapters were not received until early in 1954, when the second volume went to press.

Something should be said concerning the basis for the organization of the subject matter of these volumes. It became apparent early that there are many ways to subdivide social psychology but very little agreement concerning just which is best. Although we sought the advice of others, we found for almost every compelling suggestion an equally compelling countersuggestion. Thus, in the end, it was necessary to make many arbitrary decisions. So much for our knowledge that the *Handbook* could have been organized in many different ways. There is no single scheme that would satisfy all readers.

We early discovered that the subject matter was too voluminous to be contained in a single volume. Given this decision it seemed quite natural to present in one volume the chapters that dealt primarily with theoretical convictions or systematic positions, and also the methods and procedures commonly employed in social psychology. Likewise it seemed wise to present in one volume those chapters that focus upon the substantive findings and applications of social psychology. The decision to place the historical introduction, theory, and method chapters in the first volume reflects a bias in favor of investigation that begins with an awareness of the message of the past, an attempt at theoretical relevance, and finally with a full knowledge of the procedural or measurement alternatives. All of the content of the first volume is seen, at least by the editor, as a necessary preparation for good investigation. These are the things the social psychologist should know before he lifts a single empirical finger. The second volume, then, can be seen as a justification of the contents of the first volume. Here are the empirical fruits stemming from the theories and methods summarized in the first volume.

But does this ideal scheme mirror common practice? Are the major empirical advances summarized in the second volume in reality a legitimate by-product of theoretical conceptions and sophisticated method? In fairness to science in action (as opposed to science on the books) we are afraid the answer is No. Social psychology has made its advances largely on the shoulders of random empiricists and naive realists. Inability to distinguish between analytic and synthetic and a tendency toward reification of concepts has accompanied many of the most significant advances in this field. Who would say that those who view an attitude as a "construct" created by the investigator have made more of a contribution to this area of psychology than those who naively view attitudes as real and concrete entities? Thus we sorrowfully admit the organization we have imposed upon the *Handbook* may bear little relation to the path thus far trod in the development of social psychology. Nevertheless, it stands as a suggestion of the manner in which future development may well take place and as a reminder that the powerful weapon of systematic theory is now more nearly within the grasp of the wise psychologist than formerly. Where yesterday the theoretically oriented investigator and the random realist may have been on even terms, recent developments within the field may well have destroyed this equality. An approach efficient in the wilderness may be foolish in a more carefully mapped region. In summary, the precedence we give to theoretical positions reflects our conviction of the importance of theories as spurs to research, but may also represent a program for the future rather than a reflection of the past.

It must be conceded that not all areas of social psychology are covered in these volumes with equal thoroughness. Some gaps are due to the blind spots of the editor while others are the result of contributors failing to cover an area they originally agreed to cover and, in a few cases, to contributors who withdrew altogether. In spite of these shortcomings, the volumes in their present state provide the most comprehensive picture of social psychology that exists in one place today.

While deficiencies of the final product are my own responsibility, they exist in spite of a number of advisors who gave their time and energy generously throughout the venture. Of these collaborators none was nearly so important as Gordon Allport. In fairness he should be co-editor of the volume, as he contributed immeasurably both in matters of policy and in matters of detail. I owe a very special debt of gratitude to my wife Andrea for her tolerance, encouragement, and detailed assistance. Likewise of great importance is the contribution of Shirley H. Heinemann, who has been of constant help throughout the editorial process and in preparing the Index. Crucial to the success of this work were various additional colleagues who served as referees, reading individual chapters and suggesting changes and deletions. On this score I express my gratitude to Raymond Bauer, Anthony Davids, Edward E. Jones, Kaspar Naegele, David Schneider, and Walter Weiss. In addition, many of the contributors served as referees for chapters other than their own. I am indebted to E. G. Boring, S. S. Stevens, and Geraldine Stone for many helpful suggestions based on their experience in arranging the *Handbook of Experimental Psychology*. Mrs. Olga Crawford of Addison-Wesley played an indispensable role in final preparation of the manuscripts.

April 1954   G. L.

Contents

VOLUME II: SPECIAL FIELDS AND APPLICATIONS

CHAPTER 14

Altruism and Aggression

Dennis L. Krebs
Simon Fraser University

Dale T. Miller
Simon Fraser University

INTRODUCTION

Although impossible to prove, it is safe to assume that all people everywhere engage in behaviors considered both altruistic and aggressive by their fellows. Wherever you go, whatever culture or society of people you encounter, you will find both incidents of murder, assault, and rape, and incidences of sharing, aiding, self-sacrifice, and heroism. The purpose of this chapter is to consider the reasons why individuals behave altruistically and aggressively.

ON THE DEFINITION OF ALTRUISM AND AGGRESSION

Like many of the constructs employed by people in their everyday lives, altruism and aggression are fuzzy. Although they supply a rough indication of the nature of an act, they mean different things to different people. The criteria employed by people when they classify a behavior as altruistic or aggressive stem from their naive theories concerning human nature and morality. Because the majority of the experience on which implicit theories about the nature of altruism and aggression are constructed is similar for most people, the theories concerning these two kinds of behavior are also similar. However, when pressed to define altruism and aggression precisely, and to distinguish them from other closely related kinds of behavior, people inevitably differ in their definitions (see Krebs, 1982b; 1982c; 1982d, for an analysis of conceptual problems concerning the definition of altruism).

There is considerable diversity in the definitions of altruism and aggression supplied by social scientists (see Berkowitz, 1962; Eisenberg, 1982; Krebs and Wispé, 1974; Rule and Nesdale, 1976). The central sources of difference among definitions lie in their tendency to focus on (1) observable behaviors versus motives and intentions, (2) immediate versus long-term consequences, (3) gross versus net gains and losses, and (4) physical versus psychological effects. Is carelessly killing someone a more aggressive act than attempted murder? Is giving money to beggars an altruistic act if it perpetuates the recipients' dependency on others? Is an act of helping more altruistic if it is costly to the benefactor than if it is not? Are you behaving aggressively toward children when you discipline them? Is hitting someone a more aggressive action than talking behind his or her back?

From the perspective of operational simplicity, it would be most convenient to define altruism and aggression phenotypically, that is, on the basis of their appearance. The problem with this practice, however, is that it causes behaviors whose function and purpose are quite different to be construed similarly. Knocking someone out in order to save his life is not the same as knocking him out in order to steal his money. Because of the plasticity of human behavior, almost any act may serve an altruistic or aggressive purpose. Indeed, doing nothing may be among either the most benevolent or malicious of all behaviors.

Focusing on the consequences of social acts, a number of investigators have endowed those acts that benefit others with the label "altruistic" and those that harm others with the label "aggressive." There are a number of problems with this strategy, however. One is that it neglects the important distinction between accidental and intentional benefits and damage. Although few would agree that unintentionally injuring another driver in an automobile accident is an inherently aggressive act, most people would consider ineffective attempts to help or harm another to be less altruistic or aggressive than effective attempts. Indeed, the more benefit extended or the more damage caused by similarly intentioned behaviors, the more responsible for the outcome the perpetrators of the behavior may seem. Another problem with focusing exclusively on consequences is that the same act may simultaneously benefit one party and harm another. For example, a Kamakasi suicide may be viewed as either altruistic or aggressive depending upon one's political position (see Krebs, 1982b, for an elaboration of arguments against behavior-based definitions; and Rushton, 1982, for a defense of them).

As suggested by Krebs and Wispé (1974), problems surrounding the definition of social behaviors may lend themselves to empirical research. At least two approaches are available:

1. Investigating the basis on which the average person makes attributions of altruism and aggression—studying people's implicit theories of these phenomena.

2. Studying the development of these ideas in children.

What little research exists on attributions of altruism and aggression indicates that the average person attends both to the intentions underlying the acts and to their consequences (see, for example, Tesser, Gatewood, and Driver, 1968). Cognitive-developmental research suggests that internal, subjective factors such as intentions assume increasing importance with development (see Krebs, 1982d).

It is appropriate to say that the subject matter of this chapter is behaviors that have been called atruistic and aggressive by those who have investigated them. Because the immediate purpose of most social scientific research is to determine the effect of an independent variable on a dependent variable, it could be argued that it doesn't matter much what the behaviors are called. However, investigators must be careful to avoid two pitfalls: (1) assessing qualitatively different behaviors and calling them the same thing and (2) coopting the connotative power of constructs like aggression and altruism inappropriately, leading their readers to believe that they have investigated phenomena they have not. A cursory glance at the literature reveals a wide array of operational definitions of altruism and aggression. Aggression has been defined in terms of behaviors ranging from the number or intensity of relatively innocuous electric shocks to fantasy themes evoked by a projective test. Similarly, behaviors as diverse as making boxes for a supervisor, donating a kidney, and intervening in an emergency have been classified as altruistic. There is good reason to question the assumption that the factors that have been found to affect one type of behavior also affect the others in a comparable way. For example, Underwood and Moore (1982) found that rescue behavior followed a different developmental course from generosity and assistance in nonemergencies and also bore a different relationship to the sex, level of moral reasoning, and degree of nurturance of the people who displayed the behaviors.

Although investigators have the right to use the construct of altruism loosely to describe "other-oriented," "prosocial," or "helping" behaviors, they must be careful not to assume that these behaviors are relevant to the classical philosophical question of whether humans are capable of genuine altruism. This issue involves the capacity in humans to behave in a manner that enhances the net welfare of another at some net cost to themselves. Reinforcement-based theories of human nature insist that individuals are ultimately always motivated to maximize their net gains, be they forms of pleasure, feelings of self-esteem, or genetic fitness (see Gelfand and Hartmann, 1982, for a review of research suggesting that many, and perhaps all, helping behaviors are controlled either by reinforcement or the expectation of reinforcement). Incidents of apparent altruism challenge reinforcement theories. Centuries of philosophical writings contain the arguments of those who adduce examples of apparent altruism and the counterarguments of those who adduce selfish motives to explain them. We will explore this issue in greater depth later, especially during discussions of sociobiological fitness and empathy.

A BRIEF HISTORY OF RESEARCH ON AGGRESSION AND ALTRUISM

Although the origins of human aggressiveness were speculated upon in early social psychology texts (e.g., McDougall, 1926), it was not until the publication in 1939 of the monograph, *Frustration and Aggression* (Dollard, Doob, Miller, Mowrer, and Sears, 1939) that the systematic experimental investigation of human aggression began in earnest. Indeed, the ideas in this classic work dominated research on aggression for two decades following its publication. Interestingly, the next major influence on aggression research was primarily methodological in nature. During the early 1960s, Arnold Buss (1961) and Leonard Berkowitz (1962) invented techniques for measuring aggression in the laboratory that paved the way for hundreds of subsequent studies. By the early 1970s, the first trickle of what was to become a torrent of books on aggression appeared (e.g., Bandura, 1973; Baron, 1977; Johnson, 1972). Within a few years aggression had become a "core" chapter in social psychology texts.

In the early half of the twentieth century there was significantly more research on aggression than on altruism. To consider one measure, aggression appeared in the index of the 1928 volume of *Psychological Abstracts;* whereas altruism did not achieve the status of an index item until 1968. Although philosophers and biologists have been interested in altruism for many centuries (see Rushton and Sorrentino, 1981), and although psychologists investigated phenomena such as volunteering and gift giving in the 1950s (see Blake, Rosenbaum, and Duryea, 1955), it was not until the 1960s that research on prosocial behavior really began. An influential paper by the sociologist Gouldner in 1960 laid the foundations for research on reciprocity. A research program on "social responsibility" launched by Berkowitz and Daniels in 1963 helped stimulate research on prosocial behavior. In the late 1960s, Darley and Latane (1968) published the first studies on bystander intervention; Bryan and Test (1967) published a series of catchy naturalistic studies on the modeling of prosocial behavior; Campbell (1965)

addressed altruism from a nascent sociobiological perspective; and Aronfreed (1968) published the book *Conduct and Conscience.* According to Wispe (1972), Bryan and Test (1967) and Rosenhan and White (1967) introduced the term "prosocial behavior" into the social psychological literature almost simultaneously.

Prosocial behavior and altruism properly acquired the status of a new area of social psychological investigation in the early 1970s. During this time three reviews of the literature were published (Bryan, 1972; Midlarsky, 1968; and Krebs, 1970) and the first of many edited volumes (Macauley and Berkowitz, 1970), appeared. By the mid 1970s, the empirical and theoretical advances in the area were so extensive that reviews of the literature began to appear in monograph length (e.g., Bar-Tal, 1976; Staub, 1978), and social psychology texts began to include chapters on altruism and prosocial behavior. By the end of the decade, virtually all social psychology texts featured chapters on altruism, and the quantity of research on altruism reached a level comparable to that on aggression (see Richardson, Tomarelli and Hendrick, 1978).

PARADIGMS FOR EXPERIMENTAL RESEARCH ON ALTRUISM AND AGGRESSION

Bar-Tal (1984) examined research on prosocial behavior, categorized it under nine major headings, and determined the number of studies published in each category during the 1970s in the major U.S. social and developmental journals. A condensed version of the outcome of this analysis is presented in Table 1.

As revealed in Table 1, most research on prosocial behavior has investigated the effect of situational variables, particularly research published in the social psychological journals.

Bar-Tal (1984) also classified research on prosocial behavior in terms of the methods employed. He found that 70 percent of the studies published in U.S. social and developmental journals were based in the laboratory and experimental in nature. Approximately 20 percent of the studies published in social journals were the products of field experiments. The trends documented in Bar-Tal's analysis are also evident in aggression research.

A typical social psychological study on altruism and aggression exposes subjects to various levels of one or more independent variable, and then provides them with an opportunity to help or harm another.

TABLE 1
Classification of Articles on Helping Behavior According to Subject Matter in Five Journals Between 1970–1979

SUBJECT MATTER	J. PERSONALITY AND SOCIAL PSYCHOLOGY		J. EXPERIMENTAL SOCIAL PSYCHOLOGY		J. APPLIED SOCIAL PSYCHOLOGY		DEVELOPMENTAL PSYCHOLOGY		CHILD DEVELOPMENT	
	ARTICLES		*ARTICLES*		*ARTICLES*		*ARTICLES*		*ARTICLES*	
	No.	*Percentage*	*No.*	*Percentage*	*No.*	*Percentage*	*No.*	*Percentage*	*No.*	*Percentage*
Person variables[a]	9	9.5%	3	12%	3	8.3%	2	6.7%	5	16.6%
Situational variables	53	55.8	19	76	27	75.0	5	16.7	5	16.1
Personal and situational variables	8	8.4	1	4	4	11.1	2	6.7	2	6.5
Cultural variables	5	5.3	—	—	1	2.8	—	—	1	3.2
Process of helping[b]	6	6.3	1	4	—	—	—	—	1	3.2
Mediating factors	8	8.4	—	—	—	2.8	3	10.0	—	—
Parents' socialization practices	2	2.1	—	—	—	—	3	10.0	1	3.2
Social learning conditions	4	4.2	1	4	—	—	8	26.6	11	35.5
Cognitive developmental processes	—	—	—	—	—	—	7	23.3	5	16.2
Total	95	100.0%	25	100%	36	100.0%	30	100.0%	31	100.0%

[a] Personal variables include personality and demographic variables
[b] Process of helping includes studies that focused on the general question how a person decides to perform a helping act.

SOURCE: Bar-Tal, 1984, p. 66.

As indicated by Bar-Tal, 1984, (p. 72):

The great majority of research has investigated situations in which subjects had an opportunity to help strangers with a single act. In laboratory situations, subjects often knew nothing about each other, the act of helping was isolated from a naturalistic sequence of interaction, and a very specific time constraint was imposed on the encounter. Moreover, often the episode was detached from all other events in the course of the subjects' everyday life and took place in an unfamiliar setting and context.

These observations are even more pertinent to research on aggression.

Although strong parallels exist in the types of independent variables manipulated in studies of altruism and aggression, the range of dependent measures employed in studies on altruism is much broader than that found in studies on aggression. Most measures of altruism involve either rescuing, donating, sharing, or aiding, there is considerable diversity in the ways in which each of these types of prosocial behavior have been operationalized. For example, giving aid may involve behaviors that range from helping a stranger pick up dropped pencils in an elevator (Latane and Dabbs, 1975) to making boxes for a superior in a lab (Berkowitz and Daniels, 1963). Rescuing may involve behaviors that range from reporting an apparent fire to intervening in an apparent assault (see Piliavin, Dovidio, Gaertner, and Clark, 1981). In contrast, the majority of studies on aggression have employed one of three measures.

The most popular measure of aggression was devised by Buss in 1961. In this procedure subjects are recruited to participate in a study purported to be concerned with the effects of punishment on learning. The subject is always assigned the role of the "teacher," and a confederate is assigned the role of the "learner." The teacher presents various materials to the learner who must attempt to master them. When the learner makes a correct response, the teacher is instructed to reward him or her by illuminating a light indicating that he or she has responded appropriately. When an error is made, the teacher is instructed to punish the learner by delivering an electric shock. The teacher has control over both the intensity and the duration of the shocks. The confederate is not connected to the apparatus and thus does not receive any shocks.

The second measure of aggression was devised by Berkowitz (1962, 1964). When subjects report to the lab-

oratory, they are informed that they will participate with another individual (actually a confederate) in a study concerned with the effects of stress upon problem-solving ability. They are required to supply a written solution to a problem posed by the experimenter, which they are told will be evaluated by their partner. The partner expresses his or her reaction by delivering anywhere from one to ten electric shocks to the subject. The more favorable the judge's evaluation, the fewer are the electric shocks delivered. The subject receives a predetermined number of shocks, then the subject and confederate reverse roles. The number, and sometimes the duration of the shocks delivered by the subject constitute the measure of aggression.

The third measure was devised by Taylor (1970). Subjects compete with a partner (a confederate) on a series of reaction-time trials (usually twenty to twenty-eight), with the slower reactor receiving an electric shock on each trial. The level of the electric shock is established by the opponent. The number of times that the subject loses and the intensity of the shocks that he or she receives are predetermined. The strength of the shocks subjects set for the confederate on each trial constitutes the measure of aggression.

Although questions have been raised about the ecological validity of measures of altruism (see Krebs, 1983b), measures of altruism look good on this criterion in comparison to measures of aggression. Few individuals encounter the opportunity to zap a stranger with an electric shock outside a laboratory context. The question, then, becomes: How representative of the types of aggression that individuals display in their everyday lives are lab-based measures of aggression? Berkowitz and Donnerstein (1982) review the evidence on this issue and conclude that an individual's tendency to administer electric shocks in a laboratory setting correlates positively with his or her tendency to engage in various real-life aggressive behaviors. While hopeful, this evidence should not necessarily increase our confidence that the variables that affect aggressive behavior in the laboratory affect real-life aggression in the same way.

It is important to note that the acts of aggression evoked in the laboratory are customarily justified—indeed required. Subjects are not compelled to decide *whether* to behave aggressively, but, rather, *how* aggressive to be. In contrast, in real life contexts we almost always are interested in the factors that cause people to aggress in the first place. Note also that the Berkowitz and Taylor measures are generally confined to reciprocated (versus spontaneously displayed) aggression. The principles governing the former may well be different from the principles governing the latter.

A CONCEPTUAL SCHEME

Because of the quantity of research on altruistic and aggressive behaviors, the task of organizing it in an overview is challenging indeed. The strategy adopted in this chapter is to view the determinants of altruism and aggression from three general levels of analysis: (1) biological and cultural, (2) personal and situational, and (3) affective and cognitive (see Fig. 1). The biological and cultural level of analysis is the broadest and most abstract. The issues here concern relatively distal or ultimate determinants of altruism and aggression, determinants such as genetic dispositions and cultural prescriptions. The classical philosophical issues of the role of altruism and aggression in human nature are most salient at this level of analysis.

The second level of analysis is less broad and abstract than the first. At this level, we ask how characteristics of people and characteristics of situations interact to give rise to altruistic and aggressive behavior. In general, personality research tends to be correlational; that is, it seeks to identify the types of traits that covary with altruism and aggression. In contrast, situational re-

search tends to be experimental; that is, investigators manipulate aspects of situations and observe their effect on behavior.

At the final, most microscopic, and proximal level of analysis, we consider the effect on behavior of affective mediators of altruism and aggression such as anger and empathy, and of cognitive mediators, such as moral reasoning and attributional processes. Biologically and culturally based dispositions interact with aspects of various situations and people to produce changes in the cognitive and affective states of individuals that give rise to altruistic and aggressive behaviors (see Fig. 1). Contemporary social psychologists are becoming increasingly interested in the nature of these internal changes.

It is possible to consider particular determinants of altruistic and aggressive behaviors from each of the three levels of analysis. For example, at the biological and cultural level, one might attribute prosocial behavior to the norm of reciprocity; at the personal and situational level, attribute the same behavior to the receipt of a favor; and, at the affective and cognitive level, attribute it to a feeling of gratitude. A full understanding of the causes of altruistic and aggressive behaviors will involve all three levels of analysis.

It is unusual for altruism and aggression to be discussed together: They tend to be viewed as polar opposites. However, considering these two types of behavior

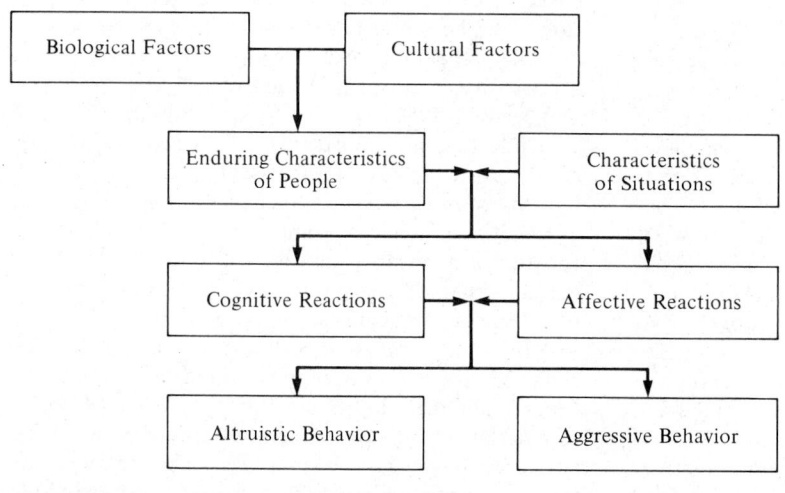

FIGURE 1
The interaction between three levels of influence on altruistic and aggressive behavior.

in the same context enables one to obtain a useful perspective on the extent to which they, as instances of social behavior, are determined by the same general processes that give rise to all social behavior and the extent to which their determinants are qualitatively distinct. As we have indicated, the types of biological and cultural variables that give rise to altruism and aggression have a great deal in common, and most of the general conclusions that we reach about them are applicable to other types of social behavior. However, as we move to more proximal levels of analysis, the processes that mediate these types of behavior (processes such as empathy and anger) tend to become more unique.

THE BIOLOGICAL BASIS OF PROSOCIAL BEHAVIOR, ALTRUISM, AND AGGRESSION

The history of controversy in philosophy and the social sciences about the genetic basis of socially desirable and socially undesirable behaviors is a long and bitter one. Traditionally, this controversy has been stated in terms of a contest between biological and cultural determinants—between "nature" and "nurture." The most popular view holds that humans inherit a primitive or "animal" nature, which, if the human race is to survive, must be moderated, displaced, stifled, or sublimated by society. It attributes incidents of human selfishness, aggression, callousness, sexuality, and other sins to the inadequate suppression of genetically based instincts or urges. This "original-sin" model of human nature underlies Judeo-Christian religious doctrine and pervades most contemporary theories of socialization.

Opponents of the original-sin assumption have turned it on its head and argued that although individuals inherit intrinsically prosocial dispositions (i.e., they are born basically good), culture corrupts them (makes them bad). Rousseauian "natural goodness" models of human nature have been espoused most ardently in contemporary psychology by those with a humanistic persuasion.

Arguments pitting original-sin against natural-goodness models of human nature have continued for centuries. In our view they are based on two sets of false polarities. First, behaviors that are good or prosocial from one point of view may be evil or antisocial from another. Second, the evidence quite unequivocally shows that both biological and cultural factors always affect both "prosocial" and "antisocial" behaviors. In fact,

biological and cultural factors are inseparable; they are, in effect "two sides of the same behavioral coin" (Van den Berghe, 1978, p. 26). In place of the old "innate" versus "learned" dichotomy, modern biologists are substituting types of interactions between hereditary and environmental factors. For example, Alcock (1979) distinguishes between four overlapping types of interaction: (1) closed instincts, (2) open instincts, (3) restricted learning, and (4) flexible learning.

While human behavior is unique in its amenability to modification through flexible learning, it is nonetheless susceptible to the other, more "primitive" types of influence. As reflected in the structure of the brain where the high learning centers have developed around—not instead of—subcortical mechanisms, the behavior of human beings may be influenced by the "old brain" forces that are part of their genetic make-up. As Van den Berghe states, "For all of the plasticity and diversity of behavior on which we pride ourselves, our behavioral repertoire, though greater than any animal known to us, is far from infinite. There *is* such a thing as human nature, just as there is a chimp nature, or an elephant nature" (1978, p. 34). Our goal in this section is to examine the biological basis of behaviors commonly called altruistic and aggressive. In the following section we will examine the cultural basis of these behaviors and conclude with a consideration of the nature of the interaction between these two distal determinants of human social behavior.

PRINCIPLES OF EVOLUTION: THE SELECTION OF AGGRESSIVE AND ALTRUISTIC BEHAVIORS

The most powerful and pervasive platform supporting biological explanations of human social behavior is Darwin's theory of evolution. Darwinian theory is popularly interpreted as implying that the direction of evolution is toward increasing competitiveness, selfishness, and aggressiveness. It is assumed that the individuals who prevail in the "struggle for existence" are those who defeat their rivals, "red in tooth and claw," in a sort of Hobbesian war of all against all. For this reason, evolutionary theory is commonly adduced in support of the original-sin model of human nature. This view of Darwinian theory, however, is spurious. Consider aggression as an example. Although there is a seductive inclination to assume that individuals must defeat or injure one another when they compete (i.e., that competition entails aggression); individuals may "compete" in the "struggle for survival" without engaging anyone else in conflict. The ability to beat a quick retreat, to hide, to climb, to "play possum," to disguise oneself, to shed a limb, to imitate another species, to exude an unpleasant odor, to find sanctuary under a protective covering, or to join forces with others may well entail more adaptive modes of competition than fighting.

The Adaptiveness of Aggression

Viewed from the perspective of Darwinian theory, aggression is one of many types of competitive strategy. The general advantage of aggression lies in its potential to mediate the acquisition of a scarce resource and to counteract a threat to it at the same time. However, aggression possesses a number of potential disadvantages. For one, it generally requires a heavy investment of energy. An exhausted victor may be vulnerable to defeat from a second antagonist. Defeating a competitor may render a benefit to another rival (who also is in competition with the individual who has been defeated). And, perhaps foremost among the costs of aggression, every individual who engages in a hostile encounter with another individual risks injury or death. The costs and benefits of aggression, of course, vary in accordance with factors such as one's own prowess, the prowess of one's antagonists, the value of the resource for which one is fighting, the availability of other ways of obtaining the resource, and so forth. The general principle that emerges from an evolutionary analysis of aggression is that dispositions to aggress should evolve when aggression enhances the fitness (or more exactly the inclusive fitness) of the individuals in a species.

A central condition governing the costs and benefits of aggression is the reactions of potential antagonists. Maynard-Smith (1975) has outlined a model to explain the evolution of aggression in groups containing individuals programmed to react to the aggressiveness of others in a variety of ways. Central to this model is the idea that the patterns of behavior that evolve in a species tend to comprise an *evolutionarily stable strategy,* that is, one that can maintain an equilibrium over time. Maynard-Smith illustrates his position by describing two opposing strategies—hawk (aggressive) and dove (pacifistic). Hawks always stand and fight; doves always turn and run. In an environment where doves outnumber hawks (and, therefore, where hawks are more likely to encounter a dove than a hawk), the hawk strategy will pay off. However, because the hawks will thrive in this circumstance, their number will tend to increase in the population relative to doves until, eventually, hawks will out-

number doves. As this occurs, the hawk strategy will become increasingly costly (hawks will encounter more hawks), and the dove strategy will reap increasingly greater benefits, causing doves to flood the population. The abundance of doves, in turn, will cause the hawk strategy to pay off once again, and so on. Thus, neither the hawk nor the dove strategy is evolutionarily stable.

Maynard-Smith (1975) and others have considered a number of strategies that are more complex than the hawk or dove strategy because they are conditional on the reactions of others. For example, in the *retaliator* strategy, an individual behaves peacefully toward doves and aggressively toward hawks. In the *prober-retaliator* strategy, an individual tentatively assumes a hawklike posture but abandons it if the opponent retaliates. Computer simulations have revealed that these complex strategies are more evolutionarily stable than their more simple counterparts, a finding that explains why complex threat, bluff, and tournament rituals have evolved in many species. An interesting example of a condition that appears to regulate aggressiveness in some species is an individual's history of wins and losses. In a rather ingenious study, Alexander (1961) found that the willingness of crickets to fight decreased lawfully with the number of fights an experimenter rigged for them to lose. From this perspective "pecking orders" reflect evolutionarily stable strategies of aggression.

A second condition governing the costs and benefits of aggression is the availability of resources. Closely related to the availability of resources is the much discussed phenomenon of territoriality, that is, the protection of resources. Popular writers such as Ardrey (1961) have attributed human aggression primarily to territoriality. Indeed, the reknown ethologist Eibl-Eibesfeld (1975) has defined aggressive behaviors as those that "serve the function of spacing" (p. 32). Although we consider Eibl-Eibesfeld's definition too narrow, it points to the significance of territory and overcrowding in the ecology of aggression. Observations of numerous species, including our own, have revealed that they may be highly territorial and aggressive at one time or in one place and highly pacifistic at another time or in another place, depending on the availability of resources.

There appears to be an inverse relationship between territoriality and hierarchical social structures in most species of primates. For example, highly territorial species such as the lemur and gibbon, display little within-group conflict, whereas nonterritorial species such as the baboon and macague form dominance hierarchies. Van den Berghe (1978) has suggested that humans are unique among primates in their disposition to display both between-group territoriality and within-group dominance.

A third condition that regulates aggression is the relationship between the aggressor and the recipient of aggression. The form assumed by aggression toward members of one's own species is typically quite different from the form assumed by aggression toward members of other species: "A cat stalking its prey displays a totally different behavior from one fighting with a con-specific" (Eibl-Eibesfeld, 1975, p. 32). In a similar but typically less dramatic sense, aggression directed toward outgroup members may differ significantly from aggression directed toward members of ingroups. In general, outgroup aggression is more similar to cross-species aggression than is ingroup aggression; it is more uninhibited and lethal. Because of the adaptive potential of ingroup cohorts, aggression against them is more constrained. Its function relates more to the maintenance of dominance and status relations, especially concerning mating priorities, than to the extermination of an enemy. The tendency to mistreat strangers is well documented in the animal kingdom: As put so dramatically by Ardrey (1961): "However the animosity for strangers is expressed, whether through attack or avoidance, xenophobia is there, and it is as if throughout the animal world invisible curtains hang between the familiar and the strange" (p. 15). According to E. O. Wilson (1975), "This xenophobic principle has been documented in virtually every group of animals displaying higher forms of social organization" (p. 249).

The dynamics of ingroup aggression are more complex than the dynamics of outgroup aggression in social animals. The task faced by an ingrouper is to maximize his or her resources within the group without jeopardizing the potential of the group to prevail in between-group competitions. Behaviors designed to achieve the gains of aggression without incurring the costs are particularly prevalent within groups: "The goal of aggressive behavior [toward ingroup members] is not physical destruction of the opponent. Quite the contrary: Those species in which individuals are equipped with dangerous weapons, and who could easily kill their rivals in a fight, have evolved special inhibitory mechanisms; in most cases, then, the partner is not seriously damaged" (Eibl-Eibesfeld, 1975, p. 34).

What implications do these general principles have for the evolution of aggression in the human species? There are clear parallels between the form of aggressive behavior in human and other primate species. The threat displays of humans and chimpanzees are remarkably

similar. Ethologists have noted that humans employ a range of appeasement gestures in face-to-face encounters that resemble those of other primates and that these gestures customarily have an inhibiting effect on aggression. In both humans and other primates, aggression is much more prominent in males than females and most aggressive exchanges are resolved without physical conflict. The availability of mates and territory and one's status in dominance hierarchies appear to influence aggression in human and other primate species.

Concerning the evolutionary stability of aggressive strategies in the human species, there are numerous possibilities for ethological observations. The behavior of children on playgrounds, in camps, and schools should supply a rich source of data for those interested in charting the undoubtedly complex strategies of probing, threatening, bluffing, and politicking for cohorts that regulate face-to-face aggression in these settings.

Human territoriality has received some attention from researchers. Hall (1966) has documented the need of individuals from various cultures to maintain their personal space. Paluck and Esser (1971) have reported cases of territoriality in mentally retarded boys. Felipe and Sommer (1966) showed that normal students reacted with notable discomfort while they were studying in the library when confederates invaded their personal space. The focus of studies such as these is on "personal space." It is surprising that there are not more ethological studies on the defense of larger territories, such as home sites, neighborhoods, and nations. Or perhaps there is no need for these studies—perhaps the disposition for humans to defend such territories is lethally obvious.

The focus of any discussion of biologically based dispositions to aggress must be on face-to-face aggression since it was the only form of aggression available to us for 99 percent of our evolutionary history. It is important, however, to acknowledge that although face-to-face aggression is one of the most significant regulators of social relations, especially among elementary and high school boys, most of the killing we humans do is from a distance. Lorenz (1966) has made much of the fact that humans are unique among the creatures of the earth in their ability to kill on a large scale without facing their enemy and, thus, without confronting the biologically based inhibitory mechanisms that regulate aggression in other species. As put by Lorenz (1966), "The invention of artificial weapons upset the equilibrium of killing potential and social inhibitions; [and] when it did, man's position was very nearly that of a dove which, by some unnatural trick of nature, has suddenly acquired the beak of a raven'' (p. 34). Culture is the villain here; not biology.

In summary, the fundamental theoretical conclusion about aggression to which Darwinian theory gives rise is deceptively simple: As one of many strategies of competition, the disposition to behave aggressively should evolve when it supplies an efficient means for enhancing the fitness of the individuals who possess it. Because of its potentially high costs, aggressive behavior should be employed mainly in circumstances where other methods of satisfying needs are not available (e.g., in overcrowded situations, when there are insufficient resources) and/or when the potential gains of aggression are great. Because of the potential costs to individuals in most social species of the injury and death of an ingroup cohort, ingroup aggression should be more constrained than outgroup aggression. Finally, it has been suggested that one of the greatest crises facing the human species results from the availability of culturally produced means for killing and maiming others, methods not amenable to control by the natural inhibitions that evolved to regulate face-to-face conflict.

The basic principles that apply to the evolution of aggressive behaviors also apply to the evolution of prosocial behaviors other than altruism. Although Darwinian theory is popularly viewed as inconsistent with the evolution of prosocial behaviors, any characteristic that is adaptive may evolve, and quite clearly there are many circumstances in which it is more adaptive to cooperate with and assist one's fellows than it is to dominate and destroy them.

The Adaptiveness of Prosocial Behavior:
The Case of Reciprocity

Although members of different species and different groups may form cooperative exchanges, cooperation is generally greatest within groups. The adaptive payoff in most cooperative exchanges is immediate and obvious. Cooperative pack-hunting by wolves, hyenae, and other animals, and the sharing of food among chimpanzees and whales supply prototypical cases in point. In addition to obvious cases of immediate cooperation, there are less direct ways of engaging in mutual assistance. Of particular interest are systems of reciprocity.

When a benefit is returned at some later time, cooperation involves reciprocity. A helping behavior that clearly involves a sacrifice and therefore seems altruistic may reap any number of rewards in the future. In an influential 1971 article, the sociobiologist Robert Trivers presented a mathematical model demonstrating how helping behaviors could evolve if they increased the probability of future reciprocal assistance. For example, Trivers demonstrated that it is in an individual's best (genetic) interest to help save a drowning person if the costs of helping are low and if the act of helping increases the probability that the beneficiary will help the ''altruist'' in the future. (Incidentally, this example demonstrates an important point about prosocial behavior: The costs and benefits of helping may be drastically disproportionate. One individual may save another individual's life by barely lifting a finger.) Trivers (1971; 1983) and others (see Barash, 1977) cite examples of reciprocal helping exchanges in many species. The exchanges among baboons documented by Packer (1977) are particularly noteworthy.

As pointed out by Trivers (1983), the conditions that favor the evolution of reciprocal altruism were particularly prevalent in the human case—conditions such as (1) a long life-span, (2) a low dispersal rate, (3) mutual dependence, (4) long parental care, and (5) absence of a rigid dominance hierarchy. Trivers speculates that certain emotions evolved to support systems of reciprocal altruism: Interpersonal attraction and friendship mediate the formation of altruistic partnerships. A sense of fairness monitors the balance between giving and taking. Moralistic aggression is evoked by cheating. Gratitude extends to those from whom one receives help. Sympathy is directed to those who need help. Guilt induces cheaters to pay their debts.

As is the case with aggression, from the perspective of evolutionary biology, it does not matter what proximal mechanisms mediate reciprocity; all that matters is that the system ''works.'' A group containing individuals who aided others unconditionally would eventually be overrun by nonreciprocating cheaters. Ubiquitous cheating would produce the demise of reciprocity and if the system of reciprocity were vital to the fitness of the individuals, it could lead to the extinction of the species. In order for reciprocity to work, it must be conditional: Cheaters must not prosper.

In an award-winning article, Axelrod and Hamilton (1981) tested a number of cooperative strategies by staging a computer tournament. Employing a Prisoner's Dilemma format, these investigators solicited strategies from scientists in a number of fields and played them off in a 200-move game. Of the fourteen strategies submitted, one was a clear winner, ''Tit for Tat,'' or concrete reciprocity, which involves making an initial cooperative response and then reciprocating with whatever response is made to it. In a second contest involving some three million choices, this strategy prevailed over sixty-two entries. Axelrod and Hamilton (1981) established that the Tit for Tat strategy will resist any "mutant" strategy, providing that the probability of two interactants meeting again is sufficiently large.

Establishing that Tit for Tat reciprocity is a stable strategy should not, of course, imply that individual selfishness (promoting one's immediate interest, regardless of whether one's partner is cooperative or not) is not also evolutionarily stable. As shown by Axelrod and Hamilton, selfish individualism is a stable strategy—no matter what the probability of future interaction. A difficult question then arises: If we assume, as Axelrod and Hamilton do, that selfish individualism was the original strategy in the human species ("the primeval state"), how could concrete reciprocity have received a start? Axelrod and Hamilton (1981) show that if a "cluster" of individuals programmed for Tit for Tat reciprocity invade a group of selfish individualists, they eventually will prevail as long as there is a "nontrivial probability of meeting another individual who will reciprocate the cooperation" (p. 1399). This demonstration shows how an existing system of concrete reciprocity could displace a system of selfish individualism, but it begs the original question: How could concrete reciprocity have evolved in the first place?

Given a system of selfish individualism, concrete reciprocity requires two *altruistic* acts to get it started. The giver must take an initial chance and the recipient, who is in a position to cheat (not reciprocate), must elect not to do so. Even though Tit for Tat yields greater net gains than selfish individualism in the long run, a selfishly disposed individual would never experience the long-term gains of reciprocity because he or she would never make the initial giving or ensuing reciprocal response. Thus, explaining how a system of concrete reciprocity could get started in any species necessitates explaining an even more difficult phenomenon—how a group of individuals could acquire the disposition to take an altruistic chance and to reciprocate in the first instance.

The Adaptiveness of Altruism

In his 1971 article, Trivers calls reciprocal helping "altruism." In our view this label is misleading. From the perspective of Darwinian theory, altruism is defined as enhancing the net fitness of another individual at some net cost to one's own fitness. Neither cooperative nor reciprocal helping meet the criteria of this definition. Indeed, the existence of reciprocity supplies a rich source of ammunition for those who would argue against the evolution of altruism. Faced with evidence that an individual assisted another without receiving any immediate compensation, cynics could suggest that the act was designed to establish credit or curry future favor.

As recognized by Darwin himself, the occurrence of apparently altruistic acts constitutes a significant problem for his theory of evolution. If dispositions toward altruism involve, by definition, a reduction in fitness, they should decrease the chances of the individuals who possess them prevailing in the process of natural selection. Altruistic individuals, and with them their altruistic dispositions, should become extinct.

In a 1975 presidential address to the American Psychological Association Donald Campbell endorsed the idea that evolutionary theory precludes the selection of biologically based dispositions for altruism in the human species. Campbell's basic position is that "genetic competition among the cooperators" has produced a core of natural selfishness in the human species. In adopting this position, Campbell recanted a position he advocated in an earlier 1965 article entitled "Ethnocentric and Other Altruistic Motives." In the 1965 article, Campbell argued that altruistic dispositions evolved in humans through group selection—through "the superior survival value of group-organized complex social interdependence as compared with individualistic modes of adaptation" (Campbell, 1978, p. 41).

Group Selection. Campbell's old position—the idea that a genetic disposition toward altruism evolved through group selection—is appealing to many. The model it projects is one of conflict between self and other, between individual and society. As put so eloquently by William James (1890), "As with all gregarious animals, 'two souls,' as Faust says, 'dwell within his breast,' the one of sociability and helpfulness, the other of jealousy and antagonism to his mates." The basic argument in favor of group selection asserts that groups that contain individuals willing to sacrifice themselves to protect their fellows will prevail over those that do not and thereby foster the evolution of altruism.

However, as Campbell came to realize, there is a lethal problem with the logic of group selection: Despite the contribution that altruists make to competition *between* groups, these individuals fare poorly in the competition that occurs *within* their groups. Within a group, individuals with altruistic genes will diminish as they sacrifice themselves for the group, whereas the more selfish individuals will not. Eventually the altruistic individuals will die out, leaving a group that is selfish by nature. Although some biologists have argued that altruism may evolve through group selection in extraordinary circumstances, most experts agree that this occurrence is exceedingly rare. Recently, D. S. Wilson (1980) argued that in conditions where individuals are not distributed randomly in breeding populations ("structured demes"), "weak altruism" may evolve. Weak altruism involves behaviors that produce an absolute gain in the fitness of the altruist but benefit the recipient even more (thus producing a *relative* decrease in the fitness of the helper). However, even in these conditions, "strong altruism" (reducing the helper's absolute as well as relative fitness) will not evolve. Relinquishing the idea of group selection on which his early position was based, Campbell (1975, 1978) abandoned the idea that strong altruism could have evolved in the human species through biological means.

Campbell was widely criticized for the position he advanced in his 1975 address. Although he refined it a little, he has not recanted the basic conclusion that biological evolution cannot produce altruism in species where there is competition among the competitors. In a recent paper, Campbell (1983) attempts to trace the route to human altruism. Appealing to three main biological concepts—structured deme theory, non-selective deterrence, and reciprocity—he concludes that they are insufficient to produce strong altruism.

In addition to presenting a case for the evolution of weak altruism in nonrandomly distributed breeding populations, D. S. Wilson explains how individuals who are dependent on groups may be forced to behave in ways that are beneficial to the group (nonselective deterrence) as a "second-choice strategy." Campbell speculates that a diminution of dominance hierarchies must have paved the way for the evolution of Tit for Tat reciprocity. He goes on to suggest that certain sensitivities ("criterion images") must have evolved in humans to permit them to monitor prosocial and antisocial behavior. For example, humans must have acquired the capacity to detect cheating in reciprocal exchanges and the detection of cheating must have come to evoke negative emotional reactions such as moralistic aggression. Campbell suggests that a self-serving bias might well have been selected

that leads individuals to develop lower thresholds for the detection of antisocial behavior in others than in the self.

The basic conclusion reached by Campbell is that the best that biological evolution can do for the human species is to mediate a weak version of altruism. According to Campbell, humans do behave altruistically, but dispositions for true self-sacrificial altruism are acquired through cultural, not biological, evolution. In reaching this conclusion, Campbell (1983) explicitly rejects the idea popular with contemporary sociobiologists that altruism may evolve through kin selection. Although he acknowledges the significance of kin selection in the evolution of other social behaviors, stating that it may well support the processes in cultural evolution that promote altruism, he nonetheless insists that kin selection is not adequately equipped to mediate the evolution of true altruism. Although we agree with Campbell that kin selection is limited, we feel that a slight extension of this process may supply a more complete route to altruism than assumed by Campbell.

Kin selection.   Although Darwin had no knowledge of genetics, we now know that it is not the survival of individuals and the propagation of their offspring that fosters the evolution of the characteristics they possess; it is the propagation of copies of their *genes*. In the majority of cases, the most efficient way for individuals to propagate copies of their genes is to insure their own survival, that is, to reproduce and to insure the survival of their offspring and their offspring's offspring. But this principle does not hold in all cases. In a situation where individuals are unlikely to reproduce, they can propagate their genes by enhancing the fitness of those who possess replicas of them, that is, their relatives. Thus, modern evolutionary or sociobiological theory assumes that it is not individual fitness that fosters the evolution of characteristics; rather, it is *inclusive fitness,* defined in terms of an individual's net genetic representation in succeeding generations. Hamilton (1963) offered the following general formula applicable to all species for the viability of altruistic behavior: altruism should occur when $K > 1/r$, where K equals the ratio of gain to loss in fitness resulting from altruism and where r equals genetic relatedness (fraction of genes identical by descent).

The implications of the evolution of altruism through inclusive fitness may well be profound in the human species. In fact, the principle of inclusive fitness may have supplied the impetus for the origin of systems of reciprocity. As recognized by Axelrod and Hamilton (1981, p. 1399):

> Not defecting in a single-move Prisoner's Dilemma... can evolve if the two interactants are sufficiently related.... Recalculation of the payoff matrix in such a way that an individual has a part interest in the partner's gain (that is, reckoning payoffs in terms of inclusive fitness) can often eliminate the inequalities... in which case cooperation [i.e., Tit for Tat reciprocity] becomes unconditionally favored... thus, it is possible to imagine that the benefits of cooperation... can begin to be harvested by groups of closely-related individuals.

The Anomaly of Altruism

Viewing individuals in terms of their genetic similarity gives rise to an interesting perspective on human nature and social relations. Although different individuals possess distinct bodies, they are, to varying degrees, identical at a genetic level. We are half the same as our sons and daughters, mothers and fathers, and sisters and brothers, and an eighth the same as our cousins, and so on. A sociobiological analysis suggests that when we help our relatives, we are, in effect, helping our (genetic) selves (or, at least, some portion of our genetic selves), and when we harm our relatives, we are harming ourselves.

The appropriateness of the principle of inclusive fitness to some types of human altruism is easy to discern. For whom are we most willing to make sacrifices? Clearly, for our children. In most societies, individuals' obligations toward relatives outweigh their obligations toward others. Anthropological studies of prosocial behavior demonstrate clearly that the preponderance of helping that occurs in preliterate societies is between kin (see Graves and Graves, 1983; Whiting, 1983). (It is interesting in this respect that one of the conditions for receiving a hero's medal from the Carnegie Commission is that the recipient of the help not be related to the helper.) The principle of inclusive fitness supplies an explanation for the generosity of grandparents toward their grandchildren, and of spinster aunts and bachelor uncles toward their nephews and nieces and for tensions between in-laws, (i.e., those who are not related by blood). The principle is consistent with the significance attached to kinship in all known societies. However, most of the people with whom we interact are not closley related to us.

As Campbell and others have pointed out, kin selection may explain the evolution of altruism toward relatives (if one accepts such behaviors as altruistic), but it does not explain the evolution of altruism toward nonrelatives. Krebs (1983) has offered a slight extension of the principle of kin selection that, he argues, may account for the evolution of dispositions to behave altruistically toward members of ingroups. Krebs suggests that even though evolutionary theory precludes the evolution of dispositions to behave altruistically toward nonrelatives, early humans may not have acquired the ability to discriminate clearly between relatives and nonrelatives. We really do not know for certain how related we are to others. Thus, our responses to others may well be influenced by dependable correlates or cues of genetic relatedness, or more specifically, by factors that were highly correlated with genetic relatedness in our evolutionary past—factors such as physical similarity, familiarity, proximity, and ingroup status.

Social psychologists have tended not to focus on degree of relatedness as a critical variable in the investigation of altruism and aggression, probably because this characteristic does not lend itself to investigation through traditional student subject based experiments. However, social psychologists have investigated characteristics of recipients that tend to evoke altruistic and aggressive responses. Many of the characteristics that have proven most powerful can be viewed as cues or correlates of genetic relatedness—characteristics such as physical similarity, racial similarity, ingroup-outgroup status, and familiarity.

In addition to physical cues, there may be behavioral bases for discriminating between relatives and nonrelatives. Indeed, the receipt of assistance in itself may be a cue to relatedness. This possibility has powerful implications for the evolution of reciprocity (Axelrod and Hamilton, 1981, p. 1394):

> When a cooperative choice has been made, one cue to relatedness is simply the fact of reciprocation of the cooperation. Thus modifiers for more selfish behavior after a negative response from the other are advantageous whenever the degree of relatedness is low or in doubt. As such, conditionality is acquired, and cooperation can spread into circumstances of less and less relatedness. Finally, when the probability of two individuals meeting each other again is sufficiently high, cooperation based on reciprocity

can thrive and be evolutionary stable in a population with no relatedness at all.

It is appropriate at this point to comment on the implications of this analysis for the definition of altruism. We have elected to label the types of helping that foster inclusive fitness "altruistic" because they involve the sacrifice of individual fitness in the service of the fitness of other individuals. However, when viewed from the perspective of genetic transmission, the behaviors are selfish (see Dawkins, 1978). Although individuals may sacrifice their lives for the sake of others, the propagation of genes is regulated by a mechanism that selects only those that give rise to behaviors that help the genes take care of themselves or, more exactly, their replicas in succeeding generations. Our reading of modern evolutionary theory suggests that "pure" altruism (that is to say, assistance that is not compensated by gains in inclusive fitness) comprises an evolutionary anomaly, fostered by an overgeneralization of the (inclusive fitness enhancing) disposition to aid relatives.

To this point, our discussions of the evolution of aggression, reciprocity, and altruism have been largely theoretical. We have outlined the principles that determine the evolution of dispositions toward these types of behavior in all species. It is now time to examine the evidence concerning the proposition that such dispositions have evolved in the human species.

THE EVOLUTION OF PROSOCIAL BEHAVIOR AND AGGRESSION IN THE HUMAN SPECIES

The most appropriate basis from which to draw conclusions about the evolution of human behavior is the history of the human species. Only there can we find the proper match between the structural clay and environmental mold. Unfortunately, however, archaeological evidence concerning early humans is scanty. Because there are no direct traces of behavior in fossil evidence, conclusions about how prosocial or aggressive our ancestors were are necessarily inferential. For this reason, the same data can, and has been, interpreted in quite opposite ways.

Most accounts of human evolution begin by tracing the differentiation of the species from about two million years ago. In a recent paper, Lovejoy (1981) points out

that although the evidence indicates that tool use and brain expansion originated about two million years ago, the human species began to differentiate from other species about twelve million years ago. According to Lovejoy (1981), popular accounts of the origin of the species err in attributing the differentiation of the species to the forces that caused the selection of physical characteristics that developed relatively late in the process. He proposes a model that focuses on the adaptiveness of particular *behavioral* traits that developed much earlier. Lovejoy observes that the environment of our earliest ancestors changed from exclusively forest to more diverse or mosaic conditions about twelve million years ago. He suggests that the critical adaptation made by early hominids in response to the increasing diversity of the environment and climatic conditions was a cooperative food-sharing arrangement in which males foraged quite broadly, while their "wives" and children remained at home. This arrangement would work for males only if it were associated with a system of pairbonding in which the paternity of the infants whom the males were supporting could be assured. According to Lovejoy, the adaptive advantages of pairbonding and cooperative division of labor mediated the selection of characteristics that distinguish the human species from other primate species—characteristics such as prominent sexual features, bipedalism (to facilitate the carrying home of food), and prolonged gestation in infants. For our purpose, the central implication of Lovejoy's analysis is the existence of strong selective pressures to cooperate with one's mate and to care for one's young.

Later archaeological evidence is quite consistent in suggesting that sometime between one-half and two million years ago humans were, in effect, forced to band together in larger groups, probably initially made up of extended families. Two main reasons have been given for this adaptation—ecological changes necessitating or facilitating the hunting of large game and ecological changes necessitating the banding together for mutual defense against predators (including other bands of humans). The archaeological evidence is clear in establishing that at least one-half million years ago, the diet of our ancestors began to change from that of eating small animals such as lizards, birds, and fish, to that of eating large animals such as mastodons, rhinoceros, and bears. These animals could not have been killed without two innovations; the invention of weapons and the formation of cooperative hunting groups. The implications of these innovations are stated well by Richard Leakey and Roger Lewin (1977, p. 45):

> Throughout our recent evolutionary history, particularly since the rise of a hunting way of life, there must have been extreme selective pressures in favor of our ability to cooperate as a group: organized food gathering and hunts are successful only if each member of the band knows his task and joins in with the activity of his fellows. The degree of selective pressure toward cooperation, group awareness and identification was so strong, and the period over which it operated was so extended, that it can hardly have failed to have become embedded to some degree in our genetic makeup.

It is plausible that the adaptive advantage of cooperation was enhanced significantly by the selection of increasingly efficient means of communication, especially the development of language. In turn, the adaptive advantages of the ability to communicate may have given rise to the development of the neocortex and human (symbolic) intelligence. Although the adaptive advantage of weapon use is commonly identified as the critical determinant of brain enlargement, evidence for large-scale, weapon-mediated game hunting is less than one-half million years old, a fact suggesting that these innovations were more an effect than a cause of brain development (although, of course, evidence for tool use is considerably older).

Humans are terrestrial, omnivorous, bipedal, physically vulnerable primates whose central form of adaptation may well have been social in nature. Without the ability to form cooperative groups, the human species could not have prevailed. In this sense, our ancestors developed a form of adaptation that was more parallel to that of the social carnivores than to that of their genetically similar cousins, other primates. They lived in groups, probably consisting mainly of extended families; the males hunted cooperatively and returned to a home base; the females foraged and took care of the young. It is not unreasonable to view the social organization of existing hunter-gatherers as a model for our early ancestors. Kalahari Bushmen live in groups of twenty to forty individuals related by blood or marriage. They maintain home bases ranging from five to twenty meters. There is a basic but flexible division of labor, the women tend to gather, and the men tend to hunt.

The central implications that archaeological evidence on early humans has for the evolution of altruism and aggression include:

1. Dispositions toward altruisim would be expected to be evoked primarily by kin and individuals who resemble kin.

2. Humans should possess quite strong dispositions to cooperate with members of their ingroups.

3. Dispositions to aggress should be evoked primarily by outgroup members who are perceived as competing for scarce resources.

Perhaps the most lethal combination of all is ingroup cooperation for the purpose of outgroup aggression—a combination whose most terrible consequences are manifest in war.

CONCLUDING PROVISOS

Whatever our biological disposition to discriminate between members of ingroups and members of outgroups, there is nothing in this analysis that negates the possibility that individuals will feel disposed to behave prosocially toward strangers and members of outgroups and aggressively toward relatives and members of ingroups *under certain conditions*. Individuals may form cooperative relations with anyone, even members of other species, when these relations enhance their inclusive fitness (or, more exactly, when they did so in their evolutionary past). An individual may behave aggressively in order to enhance his or her inclusive fitness in any circumstance. Extrapolating from the behavior of primates and social carnivores, we would expect aggressive overtures to possess a functional value in the regulation of dominance and status relations among humans in groups, and we would expect considerable ingroup conflict in conditions of scarcity (especially of food and mates).

Durham (1979) has shown that there is a high correlation between the aggressiveness of various preliterate tribes and whether (1) they are in competition with other tribes for resources, (2) the population is at or above the carrying capacity of the environment, and (3) they are able to claim an area that contains a reliable resource. For example, as Durham points out, a critical effect of the head-hunting expeditions of the Munduruci of Brazil was the elimination of competitors for their main source of protein, the peccary; moreover, the tendency of the ferocious Yanomamo of Venezuela to go to war was highly correlated with the density of their population and the availability of women. One implication of this view is that the advent of agriculture was instrumental in giving rise to large-scale warfare because farming led to the creation of bounded resources possessed by networks of cooperative groups (i.e., societies).

We also should note that although the evolutionary evidence suggests that altruistic dispositions originating from the care of offspring ought to be especially adaptive in females and although aggressive dispositions associated with hunting and defense ought to be especially adaptive in males, there is no necessary connection between gender and social role. Among lions, the males tend the young, and the females do the hunting. Among birds, females almost always tend the young, and the males forage. Among social carnivores, the division of labor is more flexible. However, among the 175 preliterate tribes of humans examined by Murdock (1949), hunting bands and armies were exclusively male in 97 percent of the tribes and primarily male in the remaining 3 percent of the tribes. The reason for this arrangement probably relates to the physical adaptations in females for childbearing, the limitations imposed on physical activity during pregnancy and child birth, and the necessity of maternal care (especially breast-feeding) for infants.

There is a rough correspondence between the degree of sexual dimorphism in a species and the degree of biologically based behavioral difference between the sexes. Human males differ from human females more than both male wolves and male chimpanzees differ from their female counterparts but less than male baboons, orangutans, and gorillas differ from their female counterparts. Thus, we would expect a moderate degree of sexual dimorphism in human behavior, with stronger dispositions in males than females to form cooperative ingroups and to behave aggressively and with stronger dispositions in females to engage in caretaking types of activity.

THE BIOLOGICAL BASIS OF ALTRUISM AND AGGRESSION: SUMMARY AND CONCLUSION

The ultimate goals of surviving, reproducing, and insuring the welfare of offspring and other relatives present essential problems for the individuals of all species. The means available for solving these problems are limited by their physical and behavioral capabilities as they interact with aspects of the environment. Individuals of various species inherit dispositions to solve the problems in ways that have worked for their progenitors. It follows, then, that the dispositions possessed by humans that have the strongest biological base are (a) those directed toward the self-satisfying personal goals of eating, drinking, copulating, protecting oneself, and obtaining territory and (b) those directed toward the other-oriented goals of fostering the welfare of relatives and ingroup members.

It is plausible to infer that biologically based dispositions toward aggression and altruism are experienced primarily as the affective reactions anger and sympathy or empathy. Note that neither type of experience is associated with a primary need such as hunger or sexual arousal. There is no spontaneous internal bodily demand to feel angry or sympathetic. Individuals need not behave in these ways regularly in order to satisfy any internal need. Rather, these reactions appear to be "called out" by situational circumstances. In view of the significance of cooperation in our early ancestral history, humans also would be expected to possess dispositions to be part of a group, to work together with others. Because cooperation is an indirect means to ends that may often be met by selfish means and, in a sense, is "derived" from or reinforced by selfish outcomes, we would not expect cooperative dispositions to manifest themselves as clearly and intensely in affective experience. Constructs such as "group spirit" and "solidarity" may refer to the affective dispositions that motivate cooperative behavior. We will examine the evidence on affective mediators of prosocial and aggressive behavior in greater detail later.

Although the focus of this discussion is on the biological basis of prosocial behavior and aggression, the influence of culturally induced cognitive factors cannot be dismissed. Whether an individual feels angry or sympathetic and, if so, what he or she does about it depends, to a great extent, on how the individual interprets the situation. Environmental inputs are filtered through cognitive processors, and the consequences of behavioral reactions are gauged mentally before their implementation. The power of cognitive interveners may be viewed from phylogenetic and ontogenetic perspectives. Phylogenetically, the connection between environmental events, internal reactions, and behavior is much more direct, stereotyped, and invariant (i.e., "instinctual") in species with simple brains. The more complex the brain of an animal, the more potentially variable is the connection between environmental events, internal responses, and behavior. (In general terms, the behaviors that follow from cognitive interventions are considered relatively "noninstinctive.") Ontogenetically, we would expect more direct, stereotyped, and invariant connections between adaptive stimuli and related responses in infants and children than in adults. Cognitive development would be expected to mediate behavioral flexibility.

CULTURAL INFLUENCES ON ALTRUISTIC AND AGGRESSIVE BEHAVIOR

Whatever emphasis one chooses to place on biological determinants of human social behavior, no representative account can ignore the influence of culture. Even the most ardent sociobiologists acknowledge the impact of culture on the human species. For example, while insisting that "we are products of biological evolution: a slow, natural process that proceeds by the differential reproduction of individuals and, hence, the gradual replacement of genes in a population," Barash (1977) acknowledges that "we also are experiencing cultural evolution, an incredibly rapid progression of events that occurs even within the lifespan of a single individual" (p. 318; see also Dawkins, 1978, p. 203; Lorenz, 1966, p. 249).

THE CONTENTS OF CULTURE

Concerning altruistic and aggressive behaviors, the most significant aspect of culture is its prescriptive standards (norms, values, laws, customs, moral traditions, commandments) or guides to "proper," culturally sanctioned conduct. The type of standard that has received most attention from social psychologists is norms. Writers have made a variety of distinctions between norms and related concepts such as conventions, laws, and values (see Rokeach, 1973; Schwartz and Howard, 1981; Vidmar and Miller, 1980); yet there is still considerable ambiguity about the definition of a norm. According to one reviewer "the concepts of value and norm are among the most vaguely distinguished concepts in sociology" (Scott, 1971, p. 81). For the present purpose we will employ Homans's (1961) definition of norm: "a statement made by members of a group, not necessarily all of them, that its members ought to behave in a certain way in certain circumstances" (p. 40).

As an aspect of culture, a norm is a prescriptive statement, a standard, or rule—something that is preached. It is important to distinguish between normative standards and normative behavior—between statements about how people should behave, and patterns of conduct. In many cases patterns of conduct correspond to normative statements; for example, people both preach that we should help those who help us and reciprocate assistance. However, this correspondence need not necessarily indicate a causal relationship. Individuals may reciprocate assistance for reasons other than that a statement in their culture says they should. Although baboons engage in prosocial reciprocity, this "normative" behavior is not guided by social norms, at least as defined by Homans (1961). It follows that the common tendency among social psychologists to infer that a particular behavior is caused by a social norm simply because it corresponds to a normative statement is misguided.

Most of the empirical work pertinent to social norms (as well as to personal values and beliefs) has centered around prosocial behavior, probably because of the assumption of original sin that underlies most formal and implicit theories of human nature. For example, Campbell (1978) argues that all complex societies develop cultural prohibitions opposing biologically based "temptations" such as cowardice, lying, stealing, behaving greedily, and giving vent to murderous rage, and cultural norms and values to promote characteristics that have not evolved biologically—characteristics such as industry, abstemiousness, doing one's unique duty, and group loyalty.

It is important to note that the cultural prohibitions and prescriptions outlined by Campbell are prosocial mainly in relation to an individual's ingroup. Exhorting an individual to behave bravely in battle, for example, typically entails encouraging the person to maim and murder the outgroup "enemy," even if this behavior generally is called by other names, such as patriotism or loyalty.

A representative account of the effect of norms and other cultural prescriptions on altruistic and aggressive behavior must supply answers to at least three questions:

1. How do norms originate in a culture—what causes some prescriptive statements to prevail and others to become extinct?

2. In what ways do norms influence behavior—from the outside, as aspects of external control, and/or from the inside, as internal standards?

3. How are norms evoked in particular situations—what causes individuals to pattern their behavior after one norm and not another?

THE ORIGIN, TRANSMISSION, AND SELECTION OF NORMS AND OTHER CULTURAL TRADITIONS: CULTURAL EVOLUTION

The process of cultural evolution, especially the ways in which norms originate, endure, and become transmitted to later generations, is at present poorly understood. Most accounts of the origin of norms are based on original-sin models of human nature and utilitarian, functionalist premises. Gouldner (1960), for example, argues that the function of the norm of reciprocity is to help stabilize social relationships and constrain the exploitation of the weak by the strong. Similarly, Walster, Walster, and Berscheid (1978) suggest that norms of equity are imposed on individuals by society to prevent them from following their natural inclination to "maximize their outcomes" at the expense of others, and to ensure that resources are distributed in a manner that benefits the collectivity.

Viewed in analogy with biological evolution, theories such as these are based on the principles of group selection. Unfortunately, however, they generally fail to specify the mechanisms through which norms are selected. Campbell's (1978) analysis of cultural evolution constitutes a provocative attempt to compensate for this omission. Campbell suggests that social evolution proceeds in accordance with the same general principles as biological evolution—"blind variation and systematic selective retention." However, instead of operating on genes, "social evolution operates on codified beliefs, moral norms, and rules of social organization." According to Campbell *variation* occurs either in a haphazard manner or more intelligently, for example, in the revisions of legal codes, and *systematic retention* occurs through various methods of socialization. In response to the critical question of "who or what decides which novelties will be perpetuated, and how this is decided" (cf. Alexander, 1979), Campbell suggests that selection occurs at the level of social systems: Particular norms and conventions are selected in terms of their ability to enhance the adaptiveness of the groups that espouse them. According to Campbell (1978), individuals need not be aware of the adaptiveness of values or norms in order to perpetrate them: "In social evolution we can contemplate a process in which adaptive belief systems

could be accumulated which none of the innovators, transmitters, or participants properly understood, a tradition wiser than any of the persons transmitting it" (p. 1107). On the basis of this assumption Campbell suggests that psychologists should be more respectful toward characteristics such as conformity and deference to authority.

Although agreeing that cultural evolution is guided by the same general principles as biological evolution, several biologically oriented theorists have differed with Campbell about the level at which cultural norms are selected. For example, Alexander (1979) and Durham (1979) argue that norms and other cultural traditions are not selected on the basis of their benefit to the group, as Campbell suggests, but on the basis of their contributions to individual inclusive genetic fitness (in the same manner that physical characteristics are selected).

In describing the process through which the selection of cultural traditions occurs, Durham suggests that a number of "selective biases" have evolved in humans that cause them to internalize or conform to cultural innovations that are to their net biological benefit. He identifies the following four selective biases:

1. A learned capacity in children to conform only to social norms and traditions that are "for their own good;"

2. A biological tendency to conform to practices that are reinforcing or satisfying;

3. Biases toward "prepared learning" caused by the physical evolution of the brain;

4. A tendency for cultural instructions conveyed by parents to children that enhance the children's biological fitness to get copied into "more little heads" (cf. Cloak, 1977).

In response to the question of whether cultural selection at the individual level could maintain traits that were detrimental to the group, Durham hypothesizes that because the well-being of individuals is dependent on the well-being of the groups of which they are members, it is in most individuals' biological best interest to accept "norms, rules, and cultural controls on excessively selfish individual behaviors" (p. 52). Similarly, Alexander (1979) believes that biological evolution should foster a well-developed tendency for individuals to conform to culture and a resistance toward cultural innovations that run contrary to the vested interests of individuals or subgroups.

It is important to note that individuals may be differentially disposed to enforce normative behavior than to conform to it themselves. The disposition to preach conformity and to detect and punish transgressions may be much stronger than the disposition to conform and to monitor one's own behavior. Campbell (1983) speculates that the "criterion images for prosocial and antisocial behavior will be more fundamentally focused on the behavior of fellow group members, only secondarily...on own behavior.... Any 'innate ethical sense'...will be motivated primarily by preferences as to other's behavior, not own.... The invoking of implicit norms...will be primarily in response to others' violations. Own self-and-progeny serving violations, if undetected by others, will tend to go unnoticed." These possibilities have important implications for theories of internalization.

The issue of cultural evolution is integral to the understanding of altruistic and aggressive behaviors because it supplies a basis for inferring which types of norms and traditions will evolve and, thus, the types of influence that will be exerted on individuals through culture. In Campbell's "original-sin" model, the function of cultural prescriptions is to counteract biologically based selfishness. Thus, cultural prescriptions are viewed as intrinsically prosocial. In contrast, because the ultimate determinant of cultural evolution in Durham and Alexander's model is biological inclusive fitness, the implications of the model for prosocial behavior, altruism, and aggression parallel those of biological evolution. Norms favoring cooperation and reciprocity (prosocial exchanges that are mutually advantageous to participating individuals), altruism toward close relatives, and aggression against outgroup members should prevail, but norms favoring self-sacrificial altruism to nonrelatives should evolve in only highly specialized circumstances. In our view, the weight of the evidence favors the inclusive fitness model suggesting that both prosocial and antisocial behaviors are influenced by both biologically and culturally based dispositions. Now, once evolved, how do norms and other cultural standards influence behavior?

SOCIALIZATION: THE SHAPING OF ALTRUISTIC AND AGGRESSIVE BEHAVIORS

In explaining the influence of norms, most theories adopt a developmental model involving the transformation of children from unsocialized animals to civilized citizens of society. Theories differ, however, in the emphasis they place on various mechanisms of socialization, and, correspondingly, on what it means to be socialized. The central difference among theories lies in the emphasis they place on external mechanisms of social control as opposed to internal mechanisms of self-control and, correspondingly, on a definition of socialization as behavioral conformity versus a definition of socialization as internal self-guidance. Original-sin theories tend to view socialization as a process through which adults attempt to curb what Hobbes termed "the recurrent barbarian invasion" from each new generation. Natural-goodness theories, on the other hand, tend to view socialization more as a process of self-actualization.

There is a common tendency to pit theories that emphasize external control against those that emphasize internal guidance; however, the evidence suggests that socialization involves behavioral conformity, the internalization of norms and values, and the development of more autonomous internal principles. Whereas developmental research has tended to focus on the internalization of standards, social psychological research has tended to focus on techniques of external control such as those involving rewards and punishments, models, and preaching.

Karen Dion (in Chapter 16) reviews research on socialization, much of which is relevant to the determination of altruistic and aggressive behaviors. The socialization of altruistic and aggressive behaviors had been discussed extensively by Bandura (1977a), Hoffman (1977a), Rushton (1980), Staub (1979b), and others. We will content ourselves here with outlining representative findings on the effects of reinforcement, modeling, preaching, and the internalization of evaluative standards, with an emphasis on distinguishing between their transitory and long-term effects.

The Effects of Reinforcement
Both operant and classical conditioning have been shown to affect the tendency of individuals to engage in altruistic and aggressive behaviors. In an early study, Fischer (1963) demonstrated that the number of marbles shared by children ages three and one-half to four and one-half years increased more when sharing was reinforced with bubble gum than when it was reinforced with praise. Gelfand and Hartmann (1982) supply a review of more recent research on the operant conditioning of prosocial behavior. They describe a series of studies in which young children play a game, win pennies that can be cashed in for prizes, and are given an opportunity to con-

tribute pennies to another child who is faring more poorly at the game. These investigators have found that praising and fining the children for donating and not donating affects the number of pennies contributed to the other child. Gelfand and Hartmann also describe naturalistic studies in which positive and negative reinforcements were found to affect prosocial behavior. These researchers make the point that because many of the reinforcers that sustain prosocial behavior are subtle and because both observers and actors tend to misattribute the motives underlying prosocial behavior, the idea of "pure" (i.e., unreinforced) altruism may be mythical. In addition, "definitions of altruistic behavior that exclude the possibility of extrinsic reinforcement are unnecessarily narrow and probably misguided" (p. 1976).

The durability of prosocial behavior sustained through reinforcement has been found to vary in accordance with a number of conditions (see Barton and Ascione, 1979). In a recent study, Rushton and Teachman (1978) found that children who were complimented for donating gave significantly more tokens to charity, immediately and after a two-week period, than children who were told that it was silly for them to donate.

Although socializing agents do not typically seek to reinforce aggressive behavior, considerable research indicates that aggressive behaviors are as sensitive to reinforcement as other types of behavior (see Bandura, 1973, 1977). In an interesting field study, Patterson, Littman, and Bricker (1967) found that passive children who succeeded in their attempts to retaliate subsequently became more aggressive than those who did not. Many studies have found that approval positively affects the incidence of aggression—both the particular aggressive behavior that is complimented and other types of aggression (e.g., Slaby, 1974).

Aronfreed (1968) has conducted a number of studies that demonstrate the power of classical conditioning in the socialization of prosocial behavior. The general design of these studies involves exposing children to a "resistance-to-temptation" situation in which they are punished for playing with a desirable toy and then, later, giving them an opportunity to play with the toy when they think no one is looking. In the initial situation, punishment exerts a quite powerful effect. Virtually all children cease playing with the desirable toy. However, unless it is delivered in particular ways, the effects of punishment are transient; the children play with the toy as soon as the punishing agent is gone. The main goal of Aronfreed's research is to determine the extent to which such parameters of conditioning as the timing of punish-

ment increase the tendency of children to resist temptation in comparable situations in the future. Aronfreed has found that the earlier in the process of handling the toy that the children get punished, the greater their subsequent resistance to temptation in a similar context. Aronfreed makes the point that behavior learned through conditioning is, in effect, internalized behavior. The better it is learned (i.e., the more resistant it is to extinction), the more internalized it is even though it is not mediated by any cognitive standards.

In an unpublished but influential study, Aronfreed and Paskal (1966) (see Aronfreed, 1968, pp. 143–147), demonstrated how empathic reactions could be acquired through classical conditioning. They showed that children who were exposed to a model who expressed sounds of joy and then hugged them after a red light came on subsequently were more likely than children in other conditions to press a lever that illuminated the light rather than a lever that delivered candies. Aronfreed and Paskal suggest that sounds of joy in others serve as conditioned stimuli that, when paired with pleasure-producing hugs, evoke empathic conditioned reactions and that these reactions mediate altruistic behavior.

In addition to demonstrating the prosocial effects of conditioning, Aronfreed (1968, 1976) shows how the statements of socializing agents can enhance the persistence of learned behavior, even when these statements are virtually meaningless. In a series of experiments Aronfreed demonstrates that verbalizations may serve as conditioned stimuli that are, in effect, carried around in children's heads; and that these stimuli may evoke anxiety and guide behavior in situations removed from the original conditioning paradigm. Aronfreed insists that it is primarily the affective reactions associated with ideas that exert control over behavior, concluding that one of the most powerful processes in socialization involves the conditioned association between anxiety and ideas—an association that involves greater internalization than the association between anxiety and external or proprioceptive stimuli.

In addition to being animals who are easily conditioned, humans also are able to interpret their experiences. They possess the capacity to reflect on their history of conditioning and to discern the principles underlying it. In addition to their affective influence, rewards and punishments have informational value. A child might, for example, discover that a common dimension underlying an array of punitive experiences is that he or she has failed to pay people back; thus, the child might develop the idea that he or she should abide by the norm of reciprocity. Once formed, this idea might acquire motivational properties quite independent from the original conditioning experiences from which it was derived.

The Effects of Modeling

Like reinforcement, modeling may constrain behavior in the immediate situation, mediate long-term learning, and supply information about social standards. In the early years of the study of prosocial behavior, modeling was the single most frequently investigated determinant (see Krebs, 1970, pp. 270–271). Similarly, research on the modeling of aggression comprises a large portion of that literature (see Bandura, 1973; Baron, 1977). As suggested by Krebs (1970), most studies on the modeling of altruistic and aggressive behaviors are parsimoniously interpreted in terms of the temporary states they induce in observers—that is, as studies on social influence. In this respect models may (1) increase the salience of behavioral alternatives or norms, (2) supply information about the appropriateness of various courses of action, and (3) supply information about the consequences of various alternatives. When the role of modeling in the inculcation of more enduring standards of behavior is considered, the emphasis changes from parameters of performance to the processes through which cognitive representations are acquired and the processes through which these representations become translated into behavior.

The modeling of altruistic behavior. Social-learning theorists such as Rushton (1980, 1982), have investigated the durability and cross-situational generality of altruistic behavior induced by modeling. In one study, for example, Rushton (1975) arranged for children ages seven to eleven years to observe a model play a bowling game, win tokens, and donate varying amounts to a "Save the Children Fund." The children then played the game, won tokens, and donated to charity. Two months later, half of the children were called out of class by the same experimenter, taken to the same room, given another chance to play the game, and reminded that they could donate to the same charity. The other half of the children were called out of class by a different experimenter, taken to a room in a different part of the school, invited to play the same game, and told that they could donate to a different charity ("The poster of Bobby was changed from a yellow background depicting one poorly dressed little English boy to a red one depicting three obviously starving Asian children"; Rushton, 1975, p. 462). Rushton found a highly significant difference on the immedi-

ate test between the number of tokens donated by children who observed generous versus selfish models (7.1 tokens vs. 1.5 tokens across conditions, compared to 4.1 tokens for children in the control group). Although the magnitude of the difference was reduced after two months (5.1 tokens versus 2.8 tokens), it was nevertheless statistically significant. There was no appreciable difference between the number of tokens donated by children who were returned to similar surroundings and those who were returned to dissimilar surroundings.

In interpreting the findings of his study, Rushton (1975) concludes, "It would seem that a model does more than induce temporary situational conformity mediated by some vaguely defined form of 'demand characteristics' or experimenter effect"; and that the children in his study had demonstrated "new learning or internalization of the prosocial behavior in question" (p. 464). To buttress this conclusion, he cites evidence that the verbalizations of models about whether people should share or not did not affect the donation behavior of the children on the immediate test.

The question raised by this and similar studies concerns the extent to which the modeled behaviors prevail at different times and in different situations, which in turn relates to the depth of their internalization. Although most studies employ only one- or two-week follow-up tests (see Rushton, 1980, for a review), two months would seem a sufficient interval to demonstrate significant durability. The degree of cross-situational generality involved in the Rushton (1975) study, however, is more questionable. Although one-half of his subjects were escorted by a different experimenter to a different room, they nonetheless undoubtedly perceived that they were part of the same experiment as the one in which they had participated previously. It seems safe to assume that most, if not all the children had never been taken from class for such a purpose, had never played a game to win tokens, and had never donated to a charity. Thus, although studies such as that of Rushton (1975) demonstrate convincingly that children will model the behavior of unfamiliar adults in novel contexts and that they will behave consistently in replications and approximations of the original contexts, these studies do not show that such modeling induces the disposition to behave generously in other, extra-experimental situations (such as, for example, donating to the Red Cross when a tin is passed around in the classroom).

The modeling of aggressive behavior. The dynamics of modeling are not, of course, confined to culturally sanctioned behaviors. As documented extensively by social-learning theorists such as Bandura (1973, 1977c), models may exert a significant influence on the acquisition, instigation, and regulation of aggressive behavior. Indeed, it is in this domain that the social-learning perspective has been the most elaborately developed.

Bandura (1977c) provides an excellent overview of research on the modeling of aggression. He points out that learning aggressive responses through modeling is particularly adaptive because the inevitable mistakes that occur in trial-and-error learning may prove so costly. Bandura cites evidence to show that children and adults acquire entire repertoires of novel aggressive behaviors through modeling, and that individuals may extract "general tactics and strategies of behavior that enable them to go beyond what they have seen or heard." He mentions three principal sources of aggressive models—the family, subculture, and mass media. Of these sources, the mass media, particularly television, has received the most attention in recent years (Liebert, Sprafkin, and Davidson, 1982; Singer and Singer, 1981).

In addition to affecting the acquisition of aggressive behavior, models may play an important role in whether or not aggressive responses are performed. Bandura (1977c) identifies four ways in which models may instigate aggressive behavior:

1. By implicitly or explicitly indicating that aggression is an appropriate, desirable, or permissable response;

2. By disinhibiting observers from constraining themselves;

3. By stimulating emotional arousal;

4. By directing the attention of observers to various objects that can be employed aggressively.

Finally, Bandura (1973, 1977c) reviews evidence showing that individuals who observe models receiving rewards for behaving aggressively are significantly more likely to engage in similar behavior than individuals who observe models receiving punishments.

The literature on the modeling of aggression is extensive. Because it has been reviewed by several writers (e.g., Bandura, 1973, 1975; Baron, 1977), we will not discuss it further here. The upshot of this research is that the disposition to behave aggressively in both children and adults is influenced by the aggressive (and nonaggressive) behaviors they observe in others and by the ensuing consequences.

The Effects of Preaching

A third, and in one sense the most obvious, way in which culture is transmitted to children is through preaching. Parents, adults, and other socializing agents possess ideas about how children ought to behave, and they frequently communicate their ideas with vigor. These ideas may (or may not) guide the reinforcement contingencies they set up, and they may (or may not) guide the behavior they display as models.

As with the effects of conditioning and modeling, it is important to distinguish between the immediate, potentially transient effect of verbal statements on the performance of altruistic and aggressive behaviors (i.e., the social influence involved) and the more long-term effects that are mediated through learning and the acquisition of standards. It seems plausible that instructions or commands to do highly specific things would have the most transient effects, and more general exhortations about, say, social norms or moral principles would have potentially more general and long-term effects. Research on prosocial behavior has shown that specific exhortations affect both altruistic and aggressive behaviors in immediate situations (see Grusec, Kuczynski, Rushton, and Simutis, 1978; Milgram, 1974; White and Burman, 1975), but preaching general principles is relatively ineffective. A number of studies have found that preaching general principles has more significant long-term effects (see Bryan, 1972, 1975; Rushton, 1975).

Parental Influences on the Socialization of Altruism and Aggression

The parameters of learning that we have been considering find close counterparts in child-rearing practices—approval, praise, physical punishment, love withdrawal, and induction. There has been a spate of research on the effect of such practices on a number of aspects of socialization, including the tendency to behave altruistically and aggressively. Reviewing this research would take us beyond the scope of the present chapter. It has been summarized and evaluated by a number of other reviewers (see Baron, 1977; Hoffman, 1977; Rushton, 1980; and Staub, 1979b).

The Social-learning Synthesis of Socialization Techniques

The main theoretical influence on research concerned with the socialization of altruistic and aggressive behaviors has been social-learning theory. This theory has been

ORIGINS OF AGGRESSION	INSTIGATORS OF AGGRESSION	REGULATORS OF AGGRESSION
Observational learning	Modeling influences	External reinforcement
Reinforced performance	Disinhibitory	Tangible rewards
Structural determinants	Facilitative	Social and status rewards
	Arousing	Expressions of injury
	Stimulus enhancing	Alleviation of aversive treatment
	Aversive treatment	
	Physical assaults	Punishment
	Verbal threats and insults	Inhibitory
	Adverse reductions in reinforcement	Informative
	Thwarting	
	Incentive inducements	Vicarious reinforcement
	Instructional control	Observed reward
	Bizarre symbolic control	Observed punishment
		Self-reinforcement
		Self-reward
		Self-punishment
		Neutralization of self-punishment
		Moral justification
		Palliative comparison
		Euphemistic labeling
		Displacement of responsibility
		Diffusion of responsibility
		Dehumanization of victims
		Attribution of blame to victims
		Misrepresentation of consequences

FIGURE 2
Social Learning Analysis of Aggression
SOURCE: Bandura, 1977c, p. 4.

elaborated most extensively in the study of altruism by Rushton (1980, 1981, 1982) and in the study of aggression by Bandura (1973, 1977c). For a presentation of Rushton's approach, see Rushton (1982). For a critique of this approach, see Krebs (1982b).

Bandura's (1977c) analysis of aggression provides the best developed application of social-learning theory (see Fig. 2).

As indicated in Fig. 2, the social-learning analysis is rooted in reinforcement theory. People behave aggressively because it pays off for them; it increases their rewards and decreases their punishments. However, in addition, Bandura emphasizes the power of observational learning both in the acquisition and in the performance of aggressive behavior. Individuals learn how to behave aggressively by watching others, and the behavior of others influences their tendency to perform the aggressive behaviors they have acquired. In place of the frustration-aggression link, Bandura substitutes an arousal-prepotent response model. In this model, aversive stimuli (e.g., physical pain, insult, threat, and noise) produce heightened arousal, which increases the probability of a prepotent response. The nature of the prepotent response depends on how the aversive stimuli are interpreted and the way in which an individual has learned to cope with stress.

Whereas Bandura stressed the informational value of reinforcement and the cognitive retention of templates for action acquired through observation of models in early presentations of social-learning theory, he has placed increasing emphasis on mechanisms of self-reinforcement in later years. In Bandura's words, "People are not simply reactors to external influences. Through self-generated inducements and self-produced consequences they can exercise some influence over their own behavior." People evaluate their own conduct in terms of internal standards and reward and punish themselves accordingly. Some individuals, such as members of youth gangs, value aggression and reward themselves when they behave aggressively. Other individuals abhor aggression and punish themselves when they display it (Perry and Bussey, 1977).

Although Bandura acknowledges that individuals may evaluate their own behavior, he also emphasizes that evaluative processes are often distorted through various cognitives devices. In some circumstances evaluative processes may not be activated, and individuals may engage in behaviors that circumvent or violate their own moral standards. Individuals may justify aggressive and immoral acts by convincing themselves that they are serv-

ing moral ends. Hence they may view these acts as appropriately vindictive, displace responsibility to others, blind themselves to the consequences of their actions, and devalue their victims. The self-regulatory mechanisms discussed by Bandura (1977c) in the analysis of aggression bear a strong similarity to the cognitive processes discussed by Schwartz (1977) in the analysis of altruistic behavior (which we discuss later).

Whereas the emphasis in Bandura's (1977c) work is on the effect of cognition on behavior, the emphasis in cognitive-developmental theory is on cognition per se—on the nature and growth of organized structures of judgment and reasoning. In Bandura's model, the standards that individuals internalize are attributed to a synthesis of external influences such as reinforcement and modeling. In cognitive-developmental theory, the standards that individuals develop are attributed to the interaction between experience and the ongoing tendency for individuals to improve their understanding of their worlds.

The Cognitive-developmental Model of Internalization

Cognitive-developmental theories of moral development contrast with traditional theories of socialization in two primary ways. First, according to cognitive-developmental approaches, children construct or discover their own norms and values through their own experiences; they do not passively accept those imposed on them from the outside. From this perspective, reinforcement, models, and preaching are grist, as it were, for the cognitive mill. Inputs such as these are processed cognitively and shaped into organized structures of ideas that govern the processing of new information and guide social behavior. Second, the cognitive-developmental position disputes that there is a single process of internalization, arguing instead that the ideas about justice developed by children and adults typically undergo qualitative transformations several times throughout their lives. As children mature, their conceptions of justice become broader, better integrated, and more differentiated. With these changes come changes in norms, values, and behavior.

Although cognitive-developmental models view socialization and moral development in terms of internalization, the construct of internalization assumes a significantly different meaning from that associated with the idea of introjecting external standards. Kohlberg's stages of moral development constitute ways of thinking that are decreasingly related to external, physical concerns. At his first stages, children define their rights and duties in terms of externally originating rewards and punishments. At his intermediate stages, children orient themselves to more "internal" factors such as social approval and disapproval, conventions, and laws. At the final stages, morality becomes defined in terms of highly internal, general, and abstract moral principles. Thus, there is a consistent tendency as one ascends Kohlberg's stages to appeal to constructs that do not contain explicit external referents.

Although cognitive-developmental approaches share the same basic assumptions about internalization, they vary in terms of whether they assume that children acquire moral standards by applying the logic of the other cognitive structures they have acquired to the moral domain, or by developing independent structures of moral reasoning.

Evidence favoring the idea that norms of justice are acquired through applications of fundamental principles of logic has been reviewed by Hook and Cook (1979). These investigators supply compelling evidence for a close association between age-related changes in "logico-mathematical" reasoning and age-related changes in endorsement of various norms of distributive justice. In their words, "Allocation behaviors seem to follow a sequence of stages similar to those of thought in general and are roughly correspondent to Piaget's sequential stages of intellectual development" (pp. 441–442).

Hook and Cook implicitly assume that when children think about justice, they employ the same cognitive structures they do when they think about nonsocial relationships. Kohlberg (1969, 1976) and other cognitive-developmental theorists (e.g., Damon, 1976; Turiel, 1978) advance a somewhat different view. According to Kohlberg, although cognitive development is a necessary condition for the development of moral reasoning, it is not sufficient. An individual may possess a highly sophisticated ability to reason about physics or chemistry but fail to develop a mature concept of justice. Although a number of studies have supplied support for Kohlberg's general position, the evidence indicates that the relationship between different types of structures is more complex than he suggests (see Damon, 1976; Haan, Weiss, and Johnson, 1981; Krebs and Gillmore, 1982; Walker, 1980).

A current shortcoming of cognitive-developmental theory lies in its failure to elucidate the expected relationship between structures of reasoning and various types of behavior. Although a relatively large number of investigators have assessed the correlation between scores on tests of moral judgment and a number of "moral" behaviors, only recently have theorists attempted to explicate the conditions under which moral standards would be expected to give rise to moral behaviors and the reasons why. There has been virtually no work on the relationship between moral judgment and aggression, although a number of studies have investigated the relationship between moral judgment and delinquency.

THE ACTIVATION OF NORMATIVE BEHAVIOR

Sociological and anthropological theories have focused on the evolution of norms in societies, and developmental research has focused on the internalization of norms in children. In contrast, social psychological research has focused on the conditions that elicit normative behavior in specific situations. Social psychologists have given special attention to three types of norms: norms of reciprocity, norms of social responsibility, and norms of justice. We will summarize briefly the research associated with each.

The Norm of Reciprocity

Gouldner (1960) proposed that there is a universal norm of reciprocity that makes two interrelated demands: (1) people should help those who have helped them, and (2) people should not injure those who have helped them (p. 171). In effect, the norm of reciprocity requires that the powerful return benefits received from the weak. Evidence from social psychological and anthropological research suggests that young children and individuals from a variety of cultures behave in accordance with the norm of reciprocity (see Staub and Sherk, 1970; Gergen, Ellsworth, Maslach, and Seipel, 1975; Walster *et al.,* 1978). Gouldner suggested that four factors affect the impact of the norm of reciprocity: (1) the need of the recipient, (2) the resources of the donor, (3) the motives of the donor, and (4) the amount of freedom the donor has to behave in a nonnormative manner. Studies have supported this suggestion (see Saxe and Greenberg, 1976; Gergen, Ellsworth, Maslach, and Seipel, 1975; Nemeth, 1970, and Tesser, Gatewood, and Driver, 1968).

Although we might expect the norm of reciprocity to prescribe revenge in situations where people are harmed by others, it would appear to serve a somewhat more prosocial function. The original intent of the "eye for an eye and tooth for a tooth" dictate of the Hammurabi code was to restrict, not encourage, revenge by demanding that people, in avenging themselves, inflict no more harm than that which was done to them.

The Norm of Social Responsibility

Although pervasive, the norm of reciprocity does not pertain to all helping behavior. As Gouldner (1960) pointed out, the norm of reciprocity does not apply in situations where a recipient is dependent—for example, too young, too sick or too old to reciprocate. According to Leonard Berkowitz (1972), in these situations, another norm—the norm of social responsibility—takes force.

The norm of social responsibility prescribes that people should help those who are dependent upon them for assistance. In an attempt to verify the existence of this norm experimentally, Berkowitz and his colleagues conducted a number of experiments using the paradigm of a worker-supervisor relationship. The general finding of these pioneering experiments was that the greater the supervisor's need for help (i.e., the more dependent he was on the worker to gain rewards), the more help the worker gave, even when the worker believed that his or her behavior was anonymous (Berkowitz and Daniels, 1963).

Berkowitz cautions that the norm of social responsibility is not always reflected in behavior. He cites factors related to the helper's psychological state, the helper-victim relationship, the context in which the helper and the victim find themselves, and the influence of others on whether or not the norm will be expressed behaviorally (Berkowitz, 1972).

The Norm of Equity and Other Norms of Justice

In recent years, the norms that have received most attention in social psychological research are norms of justice (see Greenberg and Cohen, 1982). Singled out for special attention have been norms of equity (Walster *et al.,* 1978), equality (Sampson, 1969), and humanitarianism (Schwartz, 1977). Of these three norms, equity has received the most attention (see Walster, Walster, and Berscheid, 1978). The norm of equity dictates that individuals should attempt to maintain a balance between the ratio of their outcomes to their inputs and the ratio of their outcomes to the inputs of those with whom they interact. This norm, therefore, may prescribe prosocial, generous, selfish, or aggressive behavior depending on the circumstances.

Equity theory has been explored most fully in two areas: resource allocation and compensatory behavior (see Krebs, 1982c, for a review). Investigations of resource allocation focus on the principles people employ when dividing or sharing resources. Investigations of compensatory behavior focus on people's reactions to the perpetration of an inequity—a topic we will discuss in more detail later.

The burgeoning research on resource allocation indicates that individuals, even young children, frequently distribute resources to themselves and others proportionate to each of their inputs. Most impressive in this research is evidence indicating that people will give more to another than to themselves, even under anonymous conditions, if their own inputs are less than that of the other (Leventhal, 1976). However, the evidence also indicates that individuals sometimes fail to conform to the dictates of equity when they distribute resources. As indicated by Leventhal (1976), studies have found that "instead of rewarding recipients in accordance with their inputs, an allocator may follow a rule of allocating in accordance with needs, or a rule of equal distribution" (p. 94). And, to make matters even more complicated, there is evidence indicating that although subjects tend to divide resources equitably when they have contributed less than their partners, they tend to divide resources equally when they have contributed more—a phenomenon termed "the politeness ritual" by Mikula and Schwinger (1978).

A variety of explanations have been offered to account for deviations from the norm of equity. One is that the norm of equity may not be salient in all situations. A second is that norms other than equity may apply in many situations. A third is that the material or psychological costs of behaving equitably may be greater than those incurred by not behaving equitably. A fourth is that what constitutes an "input" may differ from situation to situation, with the consequence that equitable behavior takes different forms across different situations. For example, a person's "humanity" may be the relevant input in one situation, and a person's "effort" may be the relevant input in another situation. It is difficult to adjudicate between these and other explanations of apparent deviations from the norm of equity.

In summary, there is a spate of social psychological research supporting the assumption that the behavior of individuals tends to conform to the norms of reciprocity, social responsibility, and justice *under certain conditions.* However, research on all three types of norms has revealed that people's behavior often departs from the dictates of these norms, and that a host of situational variables may affect the probability and frequency of normative behavior (see Mikula, 1980, p. 155).

The Relationship between Normative Standards and Normative Behavior

An issue that has not been adequately addressed by social psychologists concerns the relationship between normative standards and normative behavior. Most investigators in the area assume that characteristics of particular situations "activate" internal normative standards, which, in turn, mediate normative behavior. Consider the models of Berkowitz, Leventhal, and Lerner, for example. According to Berkowitz (1972) a dependent other makes the norm of social responsibility salient and thus activates it as a guide to behavior. Leventhal (1976) emphasizes the importance of the goal of an interaction in determining the activation of an appropriate norm: "An allocator may follow the equity norm to maximize productivity; follow the equality norm to reduce dissatisfaction and conflict; and follow the norm of adherence to commitments to foster harmony and reduce cognitive strain" (p. 123). In a similar vein, Lerner (Lerner, 1977; Lerner, Miller, and Holmes, 1976; Lerner and Whitehead, 1980) suggests that the norm that guides a person's behavior in a situation will depend upon the type of relationship the individual perceives himself or herself to have with the other relevant parties. In antagonistic, or what Lerner terms "non unit," relationships, self-interest will prevail; in contrast, in "unit" relationships where people view themselves as interdependent with others, the norms of fairness and equality will dominate. More particularly, according to Lerner, the norm of equity is most applicable in situations where people perceive themselves as being in a similar position or role to another (e.g., coworker), and humanitarian norms prevail in situations where people identify with others. Other investigators have suggested that social models (Harvey and Enzle, 1981) and even linguistic cues (Langer and Abelson, 1972) may influence which norm is activated and acted upon in a particular situation.

In addition to the factors that activate norms, research has endeavored to identify the factors that inhibit the activation of relevant norms. Conditions such as anonymity that lead individuals to be nonreflective or deindividuated appear especially likely to interfere with norm activation (Diener, 1980; Dipboye, 1977). According to Diener (1980) deindividuated individuals lose contact with self-standards and relinquish the capacity for self-regulation and future planning. Because a deindividuated individual is influenced primarily by external stimuli, the form of his or her behavior depends upon the circumstances. As Diener observes, "A person may be-

come destructive if deindividuated while angry, may become altruistic or physically affectionate in the presence of cues for such actions, or may become childish or silly under certain circumstances" (p. 231).

On the other side of deindividuation, research has indicated that self-aware individuals are strongly influenced by norms. Here again, heightened self-awareness may either increase or decrease pro- or anti-social behavior depending upon what is considered more normatively desirable (Carver, 1974; Rule, Nesdale and Dyck, 1977; Wegner and Schaefer, 1978).

Although the various models of norm activation offered by social psychologists seem plausible, there has been relatively little research on the assumption that relevant experimental manipulations actually activate internal normative standards in individuals and that it is these standards that guide the resulting behavior. In most cases investigators infer that a normative standard has been activated on the basis of the normative behavior that is observed. The problem with this practice was pointed out by Krebs (1970, pp. 294–295):

> A particular response can be predicted on the basis of a norm. If it occurs, the norm is said to have had an effect. If it does not occur, the situation is said to fall outside the range of the norm. The danger with normative analysis is that norms can be invented post hoc to explain almost anything.

Clearly, different norms exist, and clearly, individuals behave in ways that correspond to normative prescriptions. The question is, What is the relationship between these two phenomena? What influence do normative standards have on normative behavior? At present, social psychological models supply at best a general description of patterns of prosocial behavior and the situational variables that evoke them.

THE INTERACTION BETWEEN BIOLOGICAL AND CULTURAL INFLUENCES: A SYNTHESIS AND SUMMARY

Our review of the evidence indicates that both biological and cultural factors are involved in both altruistic and aggressive behaviors. We humans are somewhat good and somewhat evil by nature and by nurture. Biologically and culturally based dispositions may either counteract or complement one another. Original-sin and natural-goodness positions emphasize the conflict between nature and nurture, but the complementarity may be more significant for some types of behavior. Consider reciprocity as an example.

Sociobiologists have attached great importance to the evolution of dispositions to reciprocate and to the strength of reciprocal relations as evolutionarily stable strategies. Sociologists have attached great importance to the norm of reciprocity, which, they argue, is induced through enculturation. Social psychologists have shown that a substantial portion of social behavior is reciprocal in structure. Although original-sin models suggest that cultural prescriptions to reciprocate evolved to counteract biologically based dispositions to cheat, it seems as plausible that the cultural norm of reciprocity evolved to complement the biologically based disposition. Underlying models of both biological and cultural evolutions is the assumption that behaviors that pay off are selected and those that do not are not. As our species acquired the capacity to reflect on its behavior, it might have "discovered" (consciously or unconsciously) the natural value of reciprocity and then have begun to preach reciprocity as a cultural norm or prescription. In this view both prosocial and aggressive prescriptions such as "do unto others as you would have them do unto you" and "an eye for an eye and a tooth for a tooth" are explications of evolutionarily stable strategies—insights or intuitions about what "works" or is biologically adaptive in a particular social system.

Of particular significance in this model is the difference between immediate and long-range payoffs. One of the primary functions of cultural prescriptions may be to convey the wisdom (ultimate adaptiveness) of cooperative behaviors—to encourage individuals to behave "altruistically" long enough to discover its ultimate benefits and to discourage individuals from cheating. Note that in this model behaviors are selected in terms of their benefits to individuals, not to groups, even though the effect of the behaviors (and the tone of the norms that promote them) may be to enhance the adaptiveness of the group.

One of the central ways in which cultural evolution differs from biological evolution is in terms of its flexibility and amenability to rapid change. An important implication of this observation is that although the basic principles of human interaction (e.g., the principle of reciprocity) may be biologically based, the conditions that govern them may be determined much more by learning. Thus, although everyone may feel disposed to pay others back or to behave aggressively in order to obtain scarce resources, when, where, and how these dispositions are activated may vary widely from society to society. It is probably for this reason that situational factors exert such a strong influence on normative behavior.

It can be said that there are two levels in both biological and cultural analyses of behavior. First, one must discover what the basic principles are that govern human behavior. Second, one must specify the conditions that determine when the principles go into effect. The fundamental principle that governs human behavior appears to be to maximize inclusive fitness. Norms of loyalty, patriotism, reciprocity, social responsibility, and justice appear to have evolved to serve this end. The focus of social psychological research has been on the conditions that govern the behavior subsumed by various norms.

One of the characteristics that emerges from our analysis as especially significant is the degree of similarity between individuals. What appears to be a biologically based disposition to behave altruistically toward others in relation to their degree of apparent genetic similarity is reinforced by a variety of cultural prescriptions. Similarly, although the disposition to behave aggressively may be employed to regulate ingroup dominance relations, it appears to be activated in its greatest intensity against individuals who are different, particularly members of threatening outgroups. Because of the general advantages of both ingroup cooperation and outgroup hostility (Campbell, 1965), we would expect that prosocial norms and values of a culture would pertain primarily to relations among members of ingroups and that antisocial or aggressive norms and values would pertain primarily to relations with outgroup competitors. It is tempting to assume (or at least to hope) that, ultimately, the greatest individual adaptive gains will derive from the broadest possible extension of ingroup identification—to the brotherhood and sisterhood of all humans. In this context, two limitations to universal peace are suggested: the difficulty of getting nations to cooperate long enough for them to experience the long-term benefits, and the difficulty of controlling cheating.

PERSONALITY AND SITUATIONAL INFLUENCES ON ALTRUISTIC AND AGGRESSIVE BEHAVIORS

Faced with incidences of altruistic and aggressive behavior a psychologist, like the "naive observer" (cf. Heider, 1958), may attribute them to (1) "relatively stable traits, enduring dispositions, and other propensities" thought to reside "within" individuals, such as empathy or hostility, (2) "features of social situations," such as whether an individual is alone or in a group, or (3) "the interactive influence of dispositional features and situational features" (see Synder and Ickes, Chapter 28). Our goal in this discussion is to review a representative sample of research on person-specific and situation-specific determinants of altruistic behavior and to examine the nature of the interaction between these two kinds of influence.

PERSONALITY AND PROSOCIAL BEHAVIOR

Researchers have addressed four central issues in the investigation of personality and altruism. The first concerns the cross-situational consistency of helping behavior; the second concerns the relevance of evidence on the situational consistency of helping behavior to the issue of an altruistic personality; the third concerns the assessment of a "trait" of altruism; and the fourth concerns the relationship between a variety of personality traits and behavioral measures of helping. We will examine the evidence on each of these issues.

The Cross-situational Consistency of Prosocial Behavior

The first major study to investigate the situational consistency of prosocial behavior was the classic *Character Education Inquiry,* conducted by Hartshorne and May (1928, 1930). This monumental study is described in detail by Rushton (1980, 1981). The central conclusion of this study was as follows: "A child's conduct in any situation is determined more by the circumstances that attend the situation than by any mysterious entity residing within the child...cheating, lying and stealing are mainly the products of unfortunate situations..." (p. 755).

In the years following publication of the *Character Education Inquiry,* a number of investigators have re-examined the issue of cross-situational specificity. Burton (1963) took exception to the extreme situational position adopted by Hartshorne and May and re-analyzed a portion of their data. He found a factor of honesty or moral character that accounted for 35 percent to 40 percent of the variance (see also Burton, 1976). Nelson, Grinder, and Mutterer (1969) replicated Hartshorne and May's study on a smaller sample of children and reached essentially the same conclusions as Burton (1963)

and the original investigators. A number of recent investigations have examined the cross-situational consistency of small samples of helping behavior, usually in laboratory contexts. Rushton (1976) reviewed these studies and concluded that "Mischel's (1968) magic number of .3 once again emerges as the overall representative correlation" (p. 90).

Although the results of contemporary research are consistent with Hartshorne and May's conclusion that altruistic behavior is situationally specific, a number of investigators have challenged this conclusion. Epstein (1979, 1980) has supplied persuasive evidence that the low cross-situational correlations reported in the literature on altruistic behavior are largely "artifacts of unreliable measurement," associated with assessing single rather than multiple occurrences of behavior—a possibility suggested by Rushton in his 1976 review (see also Snyder and Ickes, Chapter 28). In support of this view, Rushton (1980, 1981) reviewed the evidence from studies that have employed multiple measures of altruistic behavior (e.g., Dlugokinski and Firestone, 1973, 1974; Krebs and Sturrup, 1982; Strayer, Wareing, and Rushton, 1979) and revised his earlier conclusion as follows: "On the basis of this evidence it would seem that there is a 'trait' of altruism. Some people are consistently more generous, helping, and kind than others" (p. 66). To buttress his conclusion, Rushton re-examined the early Hartshorne and May data and pointed out that in calculating estimates of the relationship between combinations of measures, the researchers obtained considerably higher correlations than they did when they assessed the relationship between single variables. For example, Hartshorne and May found that a battery of measures of altruistic behavior and honesty correlated in the .60 range with measures of altruistic reputation and reputation for honesty.

Although the evidence suggests that improvements in methods produce increases in coefficients of consistency, the correlations from multiple measures still leave from 64 percent to 84 percent of the variance unexplained. Moreover, the sample of situations that has been investigated is rather constricted. Most studies in the area are staged in a laboratory context. Few studies have investigated the types of altruism that occur so prevalently in families, role-related altruism, the altruism involved in large-scale social reform, or dramatic types of self-sacrificial altruism (see Bridgeman, 1983; Krebs, 1983). Indeed, few studies have investigated helping behavior in the situations where it customarily manifests itself in everyday life. It is plausible to expect significantly less consistency in altruistic behavior across a more diverse array of situations.

Although the amount of variance left unexplained by even multiple measures of altruistic behavior and the limitations on the range of situations that have been investigated suggest that altruistic behavior may be more situationally specific than assumed by investigators such as Rushton (1981), methodological problems in contemporary research also may have led investigators to underestimate the degree of consistency. First, relatively few studies have investigated altruistic behavior naturalistically, but in the words of Bowers (1973), "Behavioral stabilities are more apt to emerge when correlational and interactional analysis are applied to naturalistic and clinical data...[where] a person is able to engender interpersonal circumstances characteristic for him" (p. 160). And, indeed, the strongest support for the situational consistency of helping behavior has tended to come from naturalistic studies (e.g., Krebs and Sturrup, 1982; Strayer *et al.,* 1979). Almost all studies in this area have employed children as subjects, and children's behavior may be less consistent than that of adults. Finally, and probably most devastatingly, the criterion of consistency employed by most investigators is questionable.

It is useful to distinguish between what might be called phenotypic and genotypic consistency. Most investigators define consistency phenotypically—in terms of the observable effect or consequence of a behavior—in the case of altruistic behavior, to render some benefit to another. Thus, a child who shares more candy than other children in one situation but donates less money to charity in another is assumed to have behaved inconsistently. However, at a genotypic or underlying, internal level, the child may have been behaving perfectly consistently. For example, the child might believe that it is right to share with friends but wrong to give to strangers and guide his or her behavior accordingly. Although investigators may assume that behaviors such as sharing candy, donating to charity, and stopping to help a lady fix a flat tire constitute altruistic behaviors in the situations they investigate, the subjects may not share this assumption. Indeed, even at a phenotypic level of analysis, consistency might be expected only for particular types of helping behavior (for example, either bystander intervention in emergencies or donating to charity). It would not be unreasonable for an investigator to expose a sample of subjects to an array of situations, determine which ones evoke helping

behavior, and define the situation as "altruistic" on that basis. Related to the previous two points is the observation that individuals may display a consistent tendency to behave altruistically in the manner of their choice. An individual may refuse to donate to charity and prefer not to intervene in an emergency but consistently share everything he or she owns with personal acquaintances.

In conclusion, although the trend in relevant research has been to obtain increasingly strong correlations between altruistic behaviors across situations, conceptual and methodological problems preclude a definitive conclusion about the cross-situational consistency of altruistic behavior. There is reason to expect that as consistency becomes more clearly defined, and as methods for assessing it are improved, evidence for cross-situational consistency in altruistic behavior will become more compelling.

Situational Consistency and the "Altruistic Personality"

Investigators such as Rushton (1980) interpret evidence that some individuals are "consistently more generous, helping, and kind than others" as support for the assumption that there is a "trait" of altruism. Although one might adopt a behavioral perspective and define the construct of trait in terms of regularities in behavior, most investigators assume that traits are internal dispositions that give rise to behavior. It should be clear that evidence of rank-order consistency of prosocial behavior cannot, in itself, establish the existence of an independent *internal* trait of *altruism*. The reason, quite simply, is that the observed consistency in prosocial behavior could originate from a similarity in situational demands or "nonaltruistic" traits such as a need for social approval, a need for adventure, or a need for control. Because most of the data on cross-situational specificity have been collected in laboratory studies, it is not unreasonable to wonder whether at least a portion of the observed consistency across (experimental) situations originates from the disposition to conform to implicit demands of social psychological experiments. Thus, although cross-situational consistency might be a necessary condition for establishing the existence of a personality trait of altruism, it is not sufficient.

There is a certain parallel between the construct of norm and the construct of trait. Both constructs may be used to describe patterns of behavior, and both tend to be invoked to explain the regularities they describe. However, in order to draw any conclusion about the influence of a norm or trait on behavior, an investigator must assess the hypothesized internal construct independently from the behavior it is employed to explain.

It is important to note that in referring to individuals who possess an altruistic personality, we generally assume that they behave more altruistically than the average person. However, an investigator could obtain a perfect positive correlation between incidents of altruism across situations without having observed even one individual who exceeded a reasonable normative range of altruism. Similarly, an investigator could observe a strong negative correlation between the behaviors of an individual across situations but still find that this individual behaved exceptionally altruistically (e.g., was willing to risk his or her life for others) in particular circumstances. Dramatic incidents of extreme altruism in highly specific situations may supply more compelling evidence for a trait of altruism than rank-order consistency across a wider array of different situations.

In summary, the evidence on the situational consistency of altruistic behavior leads us to the conclusion that it is largely centered around a pseudo issue. Although such evidence may be useful for the practical purpose of predicting how an individual will behave in various situations, it cannot supply a basis for establishing the existence of an altruistic personality trait. Our conclusions about these matters extend with little modification to the domain of antisocial behavior and aggression.

Personality Tests of "Altruism"
If there is a trait of altruism, this trait should be accessible through conventional psychometric means. A number of investigators have attempted to develop pencil-and-paper tests of altruism. The most popular psychometric strategy for assessing the disposition to behave altruistically involves some sort of self-rating. Krebs (1970, p. 283) evaluated a number of rating scales and concluded that none met a reasonable criterion of validity. Recently, Rushton, Chrisjohn, and Fekken (1981) published a "self-report altruism scale" consisting of twenty specific statements such as "I have helped push a stranger's car out of the snow." The most representative index of the validity of the scale probably is its .21 correlation with peer ratings of global altruism, which reach a level of .33 when corrected for attenuation.

Other strategies employed to assess the personality trait of altruism have involved the adaptation of existing personality tests and the invention of new ones. For example, Ribal (1963) defined altruism in terms of a high score on nurturance and a low score on succorance on Edward's Personal Preference Schedule, and Sawyer (1966) invented a scale that pitted an individual's proclaimed willingness to obtain benefits for self at cost to others against the individual's willingness to obtain benefits to others at cost to self. Krebs (1970, pp. 283–284) evaluated tests such as these and failed to find evidence that they met acceptable criteria of validity.

Another strategy adopted in the assessment of a trait of altruism has been to give subjects a battery of pencil-and-paper tests that purport to measure a variety of prosocial traits (traits such as nurturance, social responsibility, empathy, and moral development) and to determine the extent to which they constitute a coherent factor. Staub (1974) provides a good demonstration of this strategy. He describes a factor that he calls "composite prosocial orientation," which consists of the following attributes:

Rokeach value helpful	+.58
Rokeach value comfortable life	−.58
Rokeach value equality	+.56
Rokeach value ambition	−.40
Rokeach value cleanliness	−.33
Christie—Machiavellianism	−.70
Schwartz—ascription of responsibility	+.59
Berkowitz and Lutterman— social responsibility	+.51
Kohlberg—moral development	+.46

This composite prosocial orientation factor correlated in the .40 to .50 range with a behavioral measure of helping across four experimental conditions, indicating, in Staub's (1974) words, that this orientation "probably represents, primarily, a way of looking at, of thinking about, other people's welfare, and one's own responsibility toward other people" (p. 335).

The final issue we shall consider in this discussion of personality and altruistic behavior is different from the ones we have been discussing. Rather than attempt to establish the existence of an altruistic personality or to develop a test to assess a trait of altruism, investigators have tried to determine which of a vast array of other personality traits are correlated with various altruistic behaviors.

Personality Correlates of Altruistic Behavior

Most investigations of the relationship between various personality traits and altruistic behaviors involve obtaining scores on one or more personality tests and a measure of altruistic behavior, and computing the correlation between the two. Usually, personality tests are given to ordinary subjects in conventional experiments as an adjunct to experimental manipulations.

To the average person the most salient question in this area is, What kinds of people behave altruistically? Implicit in this question is the assumption that there are people who either consistently behave more altruistically than others or occasionally engage in extremely altruistic acts. However, as we have seen, the evidence on the cross-situational consistency of altruistic behavior is equivocal. In order to assess the relationship between a personality trait and the tendency to behave altruistically, an investigator would have to obtain a representative sample of altruistic behavior. There are, at present, only a handful of studies that have obtained more than one measure of altruistic behavior; none has obtained a representative sample outside of the laboratory. Thus, this question remains unanswered. It is important to note that the conclusions drawn by an investigation of the relationship between a particular personality trait and one incident of altruistic behavior must be restricted to the specific conditions under which the behaviors were assessed. Although a study of this kind may be able to conclude, for example, that individuals who have a high sense of social responsibility tend to behave helpfully toward their "superiors" in an experimental situation (see Berkowtiz and Lutterman, 1968), it cannot conclude that social responsibility determines or is even associated with "altruistic" behavior, in general.

A number of writers have reviewed the evidence concerning the relationship between personality traits and altruistic behavior (see Gergen, Gergen, and Meter, 1972; Krebs, 1970; Piliavin, Dovidio, Gaertner, and Clark, 1981; Rushton, 1980; Staub, 1978). None of these reviewers found any consistent trends in the literature: Most studies reported weak or nonsignificant relationships. However, the weak relationships populating the literature may be artifacts of the methods employed by most investigators. To begin with, most experiments are designed to examine the effect of situational variables,

and obtain personality measures as an adjunct or afterthought. Studies of this sort employ procedures designed to maximize the situational variance and minimize the variance that results from individual differences. Thus, ironically, "personality researchers, by carefully structuring their experimental situations, may thereby eliminate much of the same individual difference variance they are in fact purporting to study!" (see Snyder and Ickes, Chapter 28 for an elaboration of this point and supporting evidence).

In addition, investigators should attend to the effect of particular personality traits in particular situations on particular altruistic behaviors. A study by Gergen, Gergen, and Meter (1972) supplies a good illustration of this point. Gergen *et al.* (1972) gave a sample of students a battery of personality tests and then exposed them to five different kinds of opportunity to help. These investigators found that there was little consistency across the five situations in the behavior of individual subjects. In fact, in some cases traits that were positively associated with one type of prosocial behavior were negatively associated with other types of prosocial behavior. For example, the trait "sensation seeking" was positively associated with volunteering to help with research on unusual states of consciousness but negatively associated with volunteering to help with research on deductive thinking. The conclusion drawn by these investigators was that prosocial behavior results from the interaction between particular personality dispositions (e.g., sensation seeking) and particular situations (e.g., situations that promise sensational experiences). Although studies that sample only one situation are not equipped to assess the type of relationships analyzed by studies such as those of Gergen *et al.,* their results should always be interpreted in terms of the interaction between the particular trait and the particular behavior they assess.

In most studies the correlation between the personality trait and the altruistic behavior in question is computed across all subjects, regardless of the particular treatment conditions of the subjects—a practice designed to increase the *n* associated with the correlation. Unfortunately, however, this practice may obscure significant interactions. A study by Staub, Erkut and Jaquette (described by Staub, 1974) demonstrates the dangers of this practice. Staub *et al.* examined the relationship between personality measures (e.g., locus of control, moral development, Machiavellianism, social responsibility, and various values and beliefs) and a sequence of stimuli for help involving a cry of distress, an indication from a confederate that he could help himself, and permission to leave a room. These investigators found that most of the variance in helping behavior was accounted for by the interaction between particular personality measures and particular conditions of the experimental situation. For example, subjects who scored at Stage 5 on Kohlberg's test of moral development helped a person in distress more than subjects who scored at lower stages, but only if previously they had been given implicit permission to enter the room containing the victim. Similarly, low-scoring Machiavellian subjects were significantly faster at getting a prescription filled for a needy other than higher scorers but, again, only if previously they had been given implicit permission to leave the room. Staub (1974) concludes that, in this study, "personality was strongly related to helping behavior—but the relationships were affected by the surrounding conditions (treatments), the exact nature of the personality characteristics, and the nature of the help needed" (p. 329).

Perhaps the sharpest distinction that has been made in the domain of prosocial behavior is between emergency and nonemergency situations. It is generally assumed that because emergencies are "more compelling than more mundane help-rendering situations...person variables [should] have less potency in determining bystander response as the situation becomes more emergency-like" (Piliavin, Dovidio, Gaertner, and Clark, 1981, pp. 184–185). In support of this intuition, many early investigations failed to find significant relationships between emergency intervention and personality traits such as social desirability, social responsibility, authoritarianism, Machiavellianism, alienation (Darley and Latane, 1976; Latane and Darley, 1970; Staub, 1971), autonomy, deference, submissiveness (Korte, 1969), trustworthiness, and independence (Yakimovich and Saltz, 1971).

Appealing to the strategy exemplified by Gergen *et al.* (1972) and Staub (1974), however, we might expect personality traits that relate more specifically to the processes involved in emergency helping to supply better predictors of the tendency to intervene; and, indeed, there is some support for this assumption. Piliavin *et al.* (1981) reviewed some of the evidence on this issue. Emergency intervention typically involves a spontaneous reaction; therefore, impulsive people might be expected to intervene more frequently than reflective people. One study found that subjects who scored high on a measure of impulsiveness stood up more quickly after hearing distress noises than subjects who were more reflective; how-

ever, the impulsive subjects were not more likely to intervene. It seems plausible to assume that individuals who are concerned with their own safety might be relatively unlikely to intervene in emergencies. Michelini, Wilson, and Messe (1975) found that subjects who scored high on Maslow's need for safety were less prone to assist someone who had dropped some objects than subjects who scored high on need for esteem (see Wilson, 1976, for a replication and extension). In another study, Liebhard (1972) found that bystanders who scored high on "sympathetic orientation" and "disposition to take instrumental action for relief of one's own distress" intervened more quickly in an emergency than bystanders who scored low on these characteristics. Bystander intervention typically involves some risk. Huston, Geis, and Wright (1976) interviewed recipients of California's Good Samaritan awards and reported that one of their distinguishing traits was risk taking. Interestingly, the other distinguishing trait was a "low boiling point."

If variations in the tendency to infer that another needs help mediate variations in altruistic behavior, then individual differences in information-processing abilities relevant to such inferences should exert a moderating influence. Several studies have investigated the effect of individual differences in styles of information processing on altruistic behaviors. In one study Denner (1968) examined the effect of perceptual decision-making style on the probability of reporting an attempted theft. Denner measured the speed with which subjects reported a change in stimuli in leveling-sharpening and autokinetic tasks and then arranged for the subjects to witness an attempted theft. He found that subjects who were slow to report changes in the stimuli on the physical tasks were less likely to report the theft than subjects who were quick to report the perceptual changes. In another study Weiner (1976) found that in a situation involving stimulus overload, subjects who scored high on cognitive complexity were more likely to assist a woman who appeared to be injured than those who scored low. Apparently, cognitively complex individuals were better able to maintain their information processing abilities in the face of stimulus overload than those who were less cognitively complex.

A noteworthy implication of the finding that intrinsically nonaltruistic (or, in the Huston, Greis, and Wright (1976) study even aggressive) traits mediate altruistic behavior relates to the definition of altruism. On the one hand, one may, as most investigators in the area do, label a behavior such as volunteering for an experiment on unusual states of consciousness "prosocial" because its *effect* is helpful. However, looked at another way, one might argue that because the motivation underlying the behavior appears to be to satisfy a need for sensation, the behavior is most adequately called "sensation-seeking." From this perspective the most appropriate basis on which to define a behavior is in terms of its internal motives or intentions. Definitional questions such as this become even more acute when raised in connection with the construct of altruism (see Krebs, 1978; 1981; 1982b; 1983).

Personality Correlates of Altruistic People

As indicated, a limitation of most studies on the relationship between personality and altruistic behavior involves the failure of investigators to obtain a representative sample of altruistic behavior. One way to counteract this limitation is to select a group of individuals who are considered altruistic by some criterion and assess their personalities. Allen and Rushton (in press) adopted this strategy in a recent study. These investigators searched *Psychological Abstracts, Social Science Citation Index* and *Current Contents* for studies on the personality correlates of community mental health volunteers. This search revealed that the following personality traits were characteristic of such "altruists": internal locus of control, social responsibility, inner directedness, achievement via independence, self-control, flexibility, superego strength, self-acceptance, capacity for intimacy, and nurturance.

Although the strategy of examining the personality characteristics of individuals who may be considered altruistic on the basis of life-style behavior helps counteract some problems with assessing the relationship between personality and less representative samples of behavior, the conclusions drawn from such investigations must be confined to the type of altruism in question (for example, in the Allen and Rushton study, volunteering to aid in community mental health projects). It seems plausible that different personality characteristics would relate to other types of altruism (such as, for example, heroism).

In summary, research on the relationship between personality and altruistic behavior lacks conceptual definement. The criteria for cross-situational consistency are unclear, and evidence on the cross-situational consistency of altruistic behavior cannot establish the existence of a trait of altruism. Attempts to assess altruism as a personality trait with various pencil-and-paper tests have produced largely inconclusive results. The strategy of employing validated tests of prosocial traits such as empathy and social responsibility and computing a composite prosocial orientation score seems more promising. Although most studies in the area are not equipped to answer general questions about the personality correlates of altruistic behavior, some have elucidated the relationship between particular personality traits and particular prosocial reactions in particular situations, and others have found that patterns of prosocial personality traits characterize "altruistic" individuals such as community mental health workers.

PERSONALITY AND AGGRESSION

In comparison to research on personality and altruistic behavior, there has been relatively little research on personality and aggression. When investigators assess personality correlates of aggression, they tend to do so in order to elucidate an independent variable. For example, an investigator who is manipulating expectations about the effectiveness of aggression might assess a personality trait such as locus of control (see Dengerink, O'Leary, and Kasner, 1975). Our goal in this section will be to supply a brief review of what evidence exists on the cross-situational consistency of aggressive behavior, to examine the relevance of this evidence to the assessment of the "aggressive personality", and to review research on the personality characteristics of both extremely violent individuals and individuals who engage in more moderate forms of aggression.

The Cross-situational Consistency of Aggressive Behavior

Experimental studies comparable to those that have assessed altruistic behavior across situations do not exist in the area of aggression, probably because of the methodological and ethical difficulties involved in repeatedly placing subjects in aggression-evoking contexts. One study, however, obtained a verbal indication of the cross-situational generality of various aggressive acts. Endler and Hunt (1969) gave subjects a "hostility instrument" consisting of descriptions of fourteen aggression-provoking situations (e.g., "You are trying to study, and there is incessant noise.") and ten responses (e.g., "lose patience," "feel irritated") and found considerable consistency across the reported reactions of individuals. The amount of variance accounted for by persons was about 20 percent for males and 15 percent for females—which was about three to four times as much as the variance accounted for by situations and considerably more than the variance accounted for by persons on a comparable scale of anxiety. Endler and Hunt concluded that "individual differences in the intensity of the trait of hostility are genuinely more prominent than individual differences in the intensity of the trait of anxiousness" (p. 296) but warned that the observed consistency may have been affected by constrictions on the selection of situations.

The possibility that aggressiveness is consistent in individuals across situations receives the strongest support from longitudinal research. Olweus (1979) reviewed the evidence on the stability of aggression in males over time spans ranging from one-half year to eighteen years and reached the strong conclusion that "the degree of longitudinal consistency in aggressive behavior patterns is much greater than has been maintained by proponents of the behavioral specificity position" [and indeed] "not much lower than the stability typically found in the domain of intelligence testing" (p. 852).

Situational Consistency and the "Aggressive Personality"

The type of longitudinal stability in aggression found in males supplies a firmer basis for inferences about personality traits than the cross-situational consistency reported for altruistic behavior. First, the sample of situations assessed in longitudinal studies is considerably more diverse than the sample assessed in cross-situational research. Second, longitudinal studies have tended to obtain naturalistic rather than laboratory measures. Finally, measures of aggression typically involve the rating or assessment of two or more judges. Thus, for example, instead of making the tenuous assumption that individuals who deliver a strong electric shock in one situation and tell a story full of violence in another are behaving consistently, investigators make the more plausible assumption that if different observers rate an individual as more aggressive than other individuals on different occasions, his or her disposition to aggress is a stable one. An important implication of these points is that longitudinal studies accommodate to the differences in the form that aggression may assume throughout a person's life.

Olweus (1979) explicitly examined the similarity in situations assessed over time in the studies he reviewed. He found considerable diversity. Observing that there are strong social sanctions against aggression and, thus, strong situational pressures for aggressive children to

change, Olweus (1979) concluded that: "In the studies surveyed, there is little evidence supporting a view that stable differences in aggression level are primarily a consequence of consistently different environmental conditions....Overall, the...results and analyses strongly suggest that the observed stability over time of aggressive reaction patterns is, to a considerable measure, determined by relatively stable, individual-differentiating reaction tendencies or motive systems within individuals" (p. 872). Because aggressive dispositions manifest themselves early in the lives of young boys, and for other reasons, it is plausible to suspect that they have a strong biological base.

In summary, a comparison of the research on the consistency of altruistic and aggressive behavior reveals an interesting divergence. Research on altruism has investigated the cross-situational consistency of a constricted array of responses over relatively short periods of time; in contrast, research on aggression has investigated the longitudinal stability of general patterns of behavior across widely differing situations over long periods of time. Investigators from both areas have interpreted the evidence as supporting the assumption that individuals possess altruistic and aggressive personality traits; however, in our view, the evidence for this inference is much stronger in the domain of aggression. Studies on the longitudinal stability of altruistic behavior would make a significant contribution to this area of research.

Personality Correlates of Aggression

Although most of the evidence on altruistic personality pertains to ordinary incidents, most of the evidence on the "aggressive personality" relates to extreme acts. The reasons for this difference in emphasis probably relate to the availability of samples of violent individuals who are incarcerated and the social value attached to controlling them.

Extremely violent individuals. Two investigators, Toch (1969, 1980) and Megargee (1966, 1967), have investigated the personalities of extremely violent individuals. Toch (1969) arranged for prisoners and recent parolees from state penal institutions to conduct extensive interviews with seventy-seven other prison inmates and parolees who had a history of violence. An analysis of these interviews gave rise to a descriptive typology. Three main types of aggressive personality were identified. The most common type, the "self-indulgent compensator," has both a very low opinion of himself and a fear that others will come to share this view. In order to ward off these feelings, he responds aggressively to even the slightest insult or provocation. A second type, the "self-indulger," holds the infantile view that others exist simply to satisfy his needs and wants. When people do not cater to his whims, he resorts to "treachery" with violence. A third type, the "self-defender," possesses an intense fear of others and attacks in order to guard against being attacked.

Megargee's research has focused both on individuals who exhibit chronic violence and on individuals whose violence is momentary but exceedingly brutal. On the basis of extensive interviews, Megargee delineated two types of violent individuals: an "undercontrolled" type and an "overcontrolled" type. Individuals of the former type lack the controls and inhibitions that prevent most people from engaging in aggression. Individuals of the latter type are constrained and inhibited but commit extremely violent acts when their frustration mounts to a point where they "explode."

Personality correlates of aggression in ordinary people. One of the important principles that emerged from our consideration of the association between personality and altruistic behavior concerned the interactive nature of the relationship. Consistent with this principle, the primary purpose of assessing individual differences in aggression has been to elucidate the effect of intervening cognitive or affective states. Consider three studies as representative examples. In the first study, Dengerink, O'Leary, and Kasner (1975) reasoned that because locus of control has been found to relate to "expectations concerning future outcomes" (Shortell, Epstein, and Taylor, 1970), externals should expect less instrumental value from aggression than internals; therefore, they should not employ aggressive behaviors as much to achieve their ends. In support of this idea, these investigators found that internals were more likely than externals to match the shock-intensity level of opponents on Taylor's competitive reaction-time task. (They gave strong shocks after receiving strong shocks and weak shocks after receiving weak shocks.)

In the second study, Taylor (1970) hypothesized that because fear of censure has been found to reduce aggression (Taylor and Epstein, 1967), individuals with a high need for social approval should evidence less aggression than those with a low need for social approval. In support of this hypothesis, Taylor found that persons with a low need for approval consistently chose higher levels of shock on a competitive reaction-time task than did those with a high need for approval.

In the third study, Knott, Lasater and Sherman (1974) tested the hypothesis that individuals who scored high on a measure of guilt would behave less aggressively than individuals who scored low. As expected, subjects who scored high on the hostility guilt subscale of the Mosher (1968) Forced Choice Guilt Inventory delivered fewer shocks in Hokanson's "minimal social situation" (see Hokanson, Willers and Koropsak, 1968) than those who scored relatively low. In addition, high-guilt subjects delivered less intense shock and were less likely to become aggressive when rewarded than their low-guilt counterparts.

Other studies have investigated the relationship between other personality variables and aggressive behavior in other situations. Because the primary goal of these studies is to explore the effect of various cognitive and affective mediating states (states such as guilt, need for approval, and expectations about outcomes), we will review the findings from these studies, when appropriate, in our discussion of the associated cognitive and affective states.

SITUATIONAL INFLUENCES ON ALTRUISTIC BEHAVIOR AND AGGRESSION

"Situational" influences are customarily contrasted with person-specific influences on various social behaviors. The general idea underlying situational attributions is that behaviors are somehow "pulled out" of, or evoked from, individuals by the external circumstances in which they find themselves: The reason why people behave altruistically and aggressively is because they encounter situations that give rise to these types of behavior.

Snyder and Ickes (see Chapter 28) distinguish between "strong" and "weak" situations. Strong situations are those that "provide salient cues to guide behavior and have a fairly high degree of structure and definition." Strong situations evoke relatively uniform responses from those who encounter them. Conversely, weak situations are more unstructured and ambiguous, and different people tend to behave differently in them.

Some of the most dramatic studies in social psychology demonstrate the power of strong situations to evoke altruistic and aggressive behaviors. The studies by Milgram (1974) on obedience to authority, by Haney, Banks, and Zimbardo (1972) on prison behavior, and by Darley and Latane (1968) on bystander intervention come quickly to mind. Interpreted broadly, the implication of studies such as these is that as individuals go about their day-to-day business of living, the "strong" situations they encounter tend to evoke predictable patterns of behavior. People who are subjected to pressure from authorities behave compliantly. People in prison behave like prisoners, or guards.

Although some investigators have advocated an extreme situationalist approach to the analysis of social behavior (see Mischel, 1968; Morgan, 1973), most social psychologists recognize, at least in principle, that it is always the interaction between aspects of people and aspects of situations that gives rise to altruistic and aggressive behaviors. There are, however, significant differences among researchers in the way they interpret the interaction between personality and situational variables.

THE INTERACTION BETWEEN PERSONS AND SITUATIONS

Among the models of interactionism, it is important to distinguish between what Overton and Reese (1973) have called *mechanistic,* or statistical, and *organic,* or dynamic models. The mechanistic model is patterned after the analysis of variance statistics. Independent variables (aspects of people and aspects of situations) are seen as exerting a joint, unidirectional causal influence on dependent variables such as altruistic and aggressive behaviors. The organic model interprets interactions more dynamically and reciprocally. People are viewed as active agents who select the situations they enter, process them for meaning, and influence their structure. Aspects of people affect aspects of situations as much as the reverse, with each factor feeding back on the other.

Mechanistic or Statistical Interactions

Most people like a contest, so it is not surprising that psychologists raised on the analysis of variance would pit the amount of variance accounted for by aspects of people against the amount of variance accounted for by aspects of situations, and determine which is greater. Bowers (1973) reviewed the evidence on this issue and concluded that the average variance attributed to people was about 13 percent, the average variance attributed to situations was about 10 percent, and the average variance attributed to an interaction between people and situations was about 21 percent. Among the studies Bower reviewed, two assessed aggression (Raush, Dittman, and Taylor, 1959; Raush, Farbman and Llewellyn, 1960) and found that the variance accounted for by the interaction of persons and situations was from three to seven times larger than the variance accounted for by either factor alone. Endler and Hunt (1969) however, found that although the interaction between persons and situations accounted for about twice as much of the variance as situational factors in the assessment of hostility, person factors accounted for even more of the variance. Nelson, Grinder, and Mutteren (1969) assessed the prosocial behavior, honesty. They found that the variance associated with persons across six temptation situations was 21 percent and the variance associated with settings was 14 percent. The interaction effect was not computed.

Earlier we reviewed studies by Gergen *et al.* (1972) and Staub (1974) that exemplified the advantages of considering the interaction between specific personality traits (such as need for sensation) and specific situations (such as those that supply excitement) in the analysis of prosocial behavior. In spite of the advantages of this sort of mechanistic interaction approach, it suffers from a number of limitations. Krebs (1978) has suggested that "The multivariate approach is essentially a quantitative extension of the situational approach" (p. 146) and as such is plagued by both its methodological and epistemological problems. Methodologically, the number of potentially interacting person and situation variables is infinite. Epistemologically, "multivariate interaction studies manipulate discrete and measurable units of analysis—dependent and independent variables— even though they employ more of them [than situational studies] and make some attempt to attend to the relationship among them. The problem is that . . . investigators ignore the more general, abstract, and significant aspects of situations and people such as the *meaning* of [various prosocial behaviors], the implicit rules of politeness that guide social behavior, and the normative structure of social expectations" (Krebs, 1978, pp. 146–147). In addition, critics of the mechanistic interaction approach have questioned the assumption that the direction of influence is always from personality or situation to behavior, and not vice versa, and that the form of the relationship is always monotonic or linear instead of, for example, curvilinear or reciprocal. Considered together, these points raise serious questions about the methods traditionally employed by social psychologists in the investigation of altruistic and aggressive behavior.

Organic or Dynamic Interactions

Endler and Magnusson name four assumptions of "modern" organic or dynamic forms of interactionism (1976, p.12):

1. Behavior is determined by a continuous process of interaction between the individual and the situation he encounters (feedback).

2. The individual is an intentional, active agent in this interaction process.

3. Cognitive factors are important in interaction.

4. The psychological meaning of the situation to the individual is an essential determinant of behavior.

In the dynamic model, individuals are viewed as active selectors of situations and processors of (situational) information. The reason why different individuals react differently in different situations is because they select the situations, interpret them, and process the information involved in them differently (affectively or cognitively). In many instances, the same physical situation is psychologically different to different people because it has a different meaning to them: "The spectacle seen depends upon the methodological and conceptual spectacles worn; what is known depends as much upon schemes inside the knower as it does upon the world outside him" (Bowers, 1973, p. 153). Of course, external events exert some effect on how the situations are perceived (or, more exactly, conceived). In Piagetian terms, individuals both assimilate information to existing schemes and accommodate to the constraints of the objects of understanding.

As elaborated by Wachtel (1973), individuals actively construct their social environments. Individuals do not wander haphazardly into this or that situation; they select and create the types of situations they experience. Kelley and Stahelski's (1970) finding that competitive individuals consistently evoke competitive exchanges in game-playing situations (by competing with otherwise cooperative partners) is a good case in point.

Snyder and Ickes (Chapter 28) discuss the advantages and disadvantages of the organic or dynamic in-

teractional approach. They elaborate on one aspect of it that they (in our view somewhat misleadingly) label the "situational strategy."

AFFECTIVE MEDIATORS OF ALTRUISM AND AGGRESSION

If you ask the average person why people behave aggressively, he or she is likely to say that the reason is because they are irritable, angry, or enraged. In a similar vein, the average person is likely to attribute incidents of altruistic behavior to affective states such as a good mood or sympathy. Thus, in the layman's implicit theories of altruism and aggression, how people feel—their affective state—plays an important role in the determination of their behavior. Our purpose in this section is to review the research on affective antecedents of helping and harming.

INSTINCT EXPLANATIONS OF AGGRESSION

The idea that emotional or affective states give rise to aggression is an old one in psychology. In the early history of the field, aggressive behavior was attributed either to an inborn instinct that assumed the form of a tension state (Freud, 1933) or to a reaction produced by the thwarting of other instincts (McDougall, 1926). The idea that aggression is instinctive captured considerable attention in the 1960s, with the popularization of the work of ethologists such as Lorenz (1966). According to Lorenz, aggression occurs when the tension caused by an aggressive instinct is released by an appropriate cue. The greater the tension state, the less powerful the releasing cue needs be. In Lorenz's hydraulic or "steam-boiler" model of aggression, if aggressive tension is not released, the threshold for aggression will become so low that aggression will, in effect, explode from the individual. Lorenz argues that the major problem with modern society is the absence of constructive outlets for pent-up aggression. Lorenz's conception of instinct is similar in many respects to that of Freud, and constructs in his theory of aggression bear some resemblance to the psychoanalytic ideas of displacement, sublimation, and catharsis.

Although we believe that dispositions toward aggression have a strong biological basis in the human species, this conclusion does not entail an endorsement of hydraulic models of instinctual affect. Aggressive behaviors regulated by ongoing physiological needs are not equivalent to "appetitive behaviors" such as eating or copulating which might be said to be energized by hunger or sex instincts (see Crook, 1968, pp. 172–173). Rather, the evidence suggests that aggression is the "expression of the effect of the interaction of a number of factors both intrinsic and extrinsic to the performers" (Crook, 1968, p. 153). In addition, as we will see, the evidence on the occurrence of displacement and catharsis is equivocal (see Montagu, 1968).

FRUSTRATION AND AGGRESSION

Following closely behind instinct theories in influence on the early study of aggression was the "frustration-aggression hypothesis" originally advanced by Dollard, Doob, Miller, Mowrer, and Sears (1939). In an attempt to bridge the psychoanalytic instinct theory of aggression and the behavioristic perspective that was gaining influence in the late 1930s, Dollard *et al.* suggested that frustration always leads to some form of aggression and that aggression always stems from frustration.

The frustration model of aggression was simple, bold, and consistent with the intuitions of the average person; it signified a clear break with the instinct theories of the past, and it captured the spirit of the regnant behaviorism of its day. However, it soon became clear that, at the very least, Dollard *et al.* had overstated their case. Two years after the publication of the original model, Miller offered a revised version. Retreating from the earlier position that frustration always leads to aggression, Miller (1941) postulated that "frustration produces instigations to a number of different types of responses, one of which is an instigation to some form of aggression" (p. 338). Miller did not demur, however, from the earlier position that all aggression originates from frustration (see Berkowitz, 1962; and Zillmann, 1979, for more elaborate accounts of the controversy associated with the frustration-aggression hypothesis).

Part of the appeal of the frustration model of aggression lay in its ability to account for the phenomenological state most saliently associated with aggression (i.e., frustration); but a careful reading of Miller's formulation reveals that this source of appeal is unfounded. Miller defined frustration behavioristically as the thwarting of a goal-directed activity, not as an affective state. The causal chain in Miller's model was S → R. Subsequent revisions of the frustration-aggression model, however, attended to the mediating role of the affective experience evoked by the thwarting of goal-directed behavior (see Berkowitz, 1962; Brown and Farber, 1951). The label most commonly given to this mediating affective state is *anger*.

FRUSTRATION, ANGER, AND AGGRESSION

The modern version of the frustration model of aggression can be portrayed as follows:

Frustrating Event → Anger → Aggression → Reduction in Anger and Aggression

Research on this model has focused on the invariance of the relationships involved. In particular, research has centered around three questions:

1. Do frustration and anger always go together—if an individual is frustrated, will he or she always become angry; and if an individual is angry, does that always mean he or she has been frustrated?

2. Do anger and aggression always go together—if an individual is angry, will he or she always behave aggressively; and if an individual behaves aggressively, does that always mean that he or she was angry?

3. Does aggression always reduce anger and subsequent aggression?

Frustration and Anger

As indicated by Miller's (1941) revision of the original frustration-aggression hypothesis, the evidence suggests that although anger is the prepotent response to frustration, frustration may produce other affective reactions. Individuals whose goals are thwarted may become depressed, resigned, or fearful instead of angry (see Baron, 1977, for a review of the evidence). Similarly, anger (and aggression) may be instigated by nonfrustrating events. For example, Menninger (1942) pointed out that although getting your toe stepped on may produce both anger and the instigation to aggress, this action does not constitute frustration; and Buss (1961) has argued that insults produce more anger and aggression than frustrating events. In addition, there is now considerable empirical evidence indicating that the experience of pain itself is sufficient to produce both anger and aggressive behavior in humans (e.g., Berkowitz, Cochran and Embree, 1981). Finally, research has established that anger can become a conditioned response, evoked by "neutral" situations originally associated with frustration (Berkowitz, 1974).

The position one adopts about the invariance of the frustration-anger association may depend on a semantic preference. It could be argued that having your toe stepped on, experiencing pain, and being insulted are frustrating experiences because they involve the thwarting of such goals as securing comfort, maintaining a sense of well-being, and preserving high self-esteem. However, stretching the definition of frustration in this way tends to rob the original hypothesis of much of its rigor.

Anger and Aggression
Research on the relationship between anger and aggression has tended to measure anger in one of two ways—either with self-reports or measures of physiological arousal. Research that has employed self-reports of anger has quite consistently found a positive relationship between anger and aggression (e.g., Baron, 1971a, 1971b, 1972; Gentry, 1970; Rule and Hewitt, 1971). In addition, Megargee and his colleagues (Megargee, 1966; Megargee and Mendelsohn, 1962; Megargee, Cook and Mendelsohn, 1967) have found that people who report that they control their anger tend to aggress less across a variety of situations than those who do not. Unfortunately, however, research that has employed physiological measures of anger has not supplied consistent support for this relationship. Although many studies have found that frustration-induced physiological arousal is positively related to aggression (Zillmann, 1979), others have found either no relationship between arousal and aggression or a curvilinear relationship, with arousal increasingly positively related to aggression up to a certain level, and then increasingly negatively related (Baron and Bell, 1976).

Many explanations have been offerred for the inconsistencies in findings on the relationship between anger and aggression. Some relate to the validity of self-report measures. When subjects rate their anger before aggressing, they may adjust their subsequent level of aggression accordingly; and when they report their anger after aggressing, they may infer their level of anger from their level of aggression. Others relate to the validity of physiological measures. It is exceedingly difficult to distinguish physiologically between emotional states (see Fehr and Stern, 1970). As a consequence, the relationship between physiologically based measures of anger and aggression may be confounded by other types of

physiological arousal, such as fear. This point raises an important question: What exactly is anger? Since investigators have failed to find patterns of physiological arousal that correspond to distinct emotional states, it is possible that anger is more appropriately defined as a subjective label that is attributed to an affective state than as a distinct physiological reaction (Mandler, 1975; Schachter and Singer, 1962; Zillmann, 1979). In this case, self-report measures of anger would supply a more valid predictor of aggression than levels of physiological arousal. We will return to this possibility later. A final explanation for the inconsistencies in findings on the relationship between anger and aggression posits that this relationship occurs only under particular conditions. For example, Berkowitz (1969, 1974) has suggested that anger leads to aggression only when aggressive cues are present in the situation. (By aggressive cues, Berkowitz means stimuli that have been associated with aggression in an individual's experience.)

Catharsis
The last link in the frustration-anger-aggression association concerns the consequences of behaving aggressively. The questions that have guided research on this issue relate to the phenomenon of catharsis. Before reviewing this research, it is important to recognize that the construct of catharsis has been used to represent a number of different relationships. Originally it was used by Aristotle (Poetics 6) to refer to the purging of "violent passions" that occurs after *witnessing* the emotional expression of these passions. Freud subsequently used the term to refer to the purging of hostile and aggressive feelings that occurs after the affective *expression* of such feelings. Dollard *et al.* used the term to refer to the reduction of aggressive *behavior* following the behavioral act of aggression.

Because of its centrality to both the hydraulic instinctual and frustration-aggression theories of aggression and its practical implications, the construct of catharsis has received a great deal of attention from social psychologists. Research in this area has tended to define catharsis either in terms of a reduction in physiological arousal or aggressive behavior following aggression (see Quanty, 1976). Although these two outcomes are conceptually linked in both hydraulic and drive theories of aggression, they are theoretically separable. Research on the physiologically based model of catharsis has failed to produce consistent results. Although some studies have found a negative relationship between aggression and arousal, as the catharsis hypothesis indicates, others have found a positive relationship or no relationship at all (see Geen and Quanty, 1977, for a review). How aggression affects physiological arousal appears to depend on a variety of factors such as the status of the target (Hokanson and Shetler, 1961; Hokanson and Burgess, 1962) and the personality characteristics of the perpetrator (e.g., Meyer, 1967; Schill, 1972).

In order to test the behavioral catharsis model, an investigator must show both that aggressive behavior diminishes after displays of aggression and that individuals experience a decrease in their motivation to aggress. Although some studies have found that individuals aggress less after behaving aggressively (e.g., Doob and Wood, 1972), others have found that behaving aggressively *facilitates* subsequent aggression (Berkowitz and Geen, 1966; Buss, 1966a; Downey, 1973; Konecni, 1975b). Geen and Quanty (1977) offer four explanations for the somewhat counterintuitive finding that aggressive behavior sometimes increases aggression. First, aggression may serve to reduce an individual's inhibitions. Second, a person's aggressive behavior may serve as an aggressive cue that, like other aggressive cues, may increase the probability of subsequent aggression (cf. Berkowitz, 1962). Third, individuals who behave aggressively may feel compelled to behave consistently across a subsequent situation. Fourth, the initial act of aggression may be reinforced through drive reduction, feelings of power, or social feedback.

Distinguishing between the physiological and behavioral dimensions of catharsis creates the possibility that an act of aggression may reduce physiological arousal but increase subsequent aggression, or increase physiological arousal but decrease subsequent aggression. Two studies have reported that aggression both reduced arousal and increased subsequent aggression (Geen, Stonner, and Shope, 1973; Kahn, 1966).

In our discussion of the biological basis of aggression, we argued that biological determinants of social behavior are best interpreted as dispositions that are shaped by experience and regulated by the cognitive construction and interpretation of environmental events. Research on catharsis exemplifies this point well. Aggression may increase or decrease tension, and it may increase or decrease the probability of subsequent aggression, depending on an individual's past experience, expectations, and interpretation of situational cues.

In summarizing the research pertinent to the frustration-anger-aggression linkage, two general points emerge. First, there is no consensus in the area about what, exactly, frustration or anger is and about how these constructs can be measured. Second, the existing empirical evidence suggests that although frustration and anger often go together, frustration may lead to other emotional states, such as depression and fear; and variables other than frustration, such as insult and pain, may produce anger. Similarly, although angry people often behave aggressively, they do not always engage in aggressive behavior, and not all aggression is preceded by anger. Finally, although aggression sometimes reduces anger and the probability of future aggression, it by no means does so in an invariant manner.

AROUSAL AND AGGRESSION

Although instinct and frustration-based theories tend to assume that the affective state that mediates aggression is a qualitatively distinct one, such as anger, more recent models have tended to focus on the diffuse, general energizing effects of emotional arousal (Zillmann, 1979, 1982). Inspired by theories such as those of Schachter and Singer (1962) and Zillmann (1979), researchers have found that frustration-induced arousal may facilitate nonaggressive activities (Bandura, 1973) and that non-frustration-induced arousal may facilitate aggression (Zillmann, 1982). For example, heightened arousal originating from participation in competitive activities (Christy, Gelfand and Hartmann, 1971), vigorous exercise (Zillmann, Katcher and Milausky, 1971), loud noise (Glass and Krantz, 1975), and injections of stimulating drugs (O'Neal and Kaufman, 1972) have been found to facilitate aggression. In addition, a number of studies have found that sexual arousal sometimes facilitates aggression (see Malamuth and Donnerstein, 1983). Let us consider this interesting line of research somewhat more closely.

A number of studies have revealed that sexual arousal, produced by the viewing of erotic films, increases aggression (Jaffe, Malamuth, Feingold, and Feshbach, 1974; Meyer, 1972; Zillmann, 1971); however, others have failed to replicate these findings. Indeed, some research has found that sexual arousal mediates a decrease in aggression (Baron, 1974; Frodi, 1977). Baron (1977) has proposed that the inconsistency in this area has arisen because different experiments have induced different levels of sexual arousal in subjects. Baron contends that low levels of sexual arousal decrease aggression, but high levels increase aggression. A study by Baron and Bell (1977) supported Baron's contention. Donnerstein, Donnerstein, and Evans (1975) account for the observed curvilinear relationship between sexual arousal and aggres sion by positing that low levels of sexual arousal serve to distract individuals from provocation and consequently inhibit aggression; whereas high arousal serves to energize people, and thus facilitates aggression.

What can we conclude about the idea that affective states give rise to aggressive behavior? First, it is important to note that a great deal of aggression is instrumental in nature (Buss, 1961); it does not stem from strong affective states. Second, as plausible as the idea that anger leads to aggression may be, the evidence supporting it is not compelling. Anger may be more appropriately viewed as a general energizer of behavior than as a specific drive toward aggression (Bandura, 1973). The link between affect and aggression is not invariant. A variety of other factors influence the relationship, especially those that are cognitive in nature.

AFFECT AND ALTRUISM

Investigators interested in the relationship between affective reactions and altruism have focused on the means through which and the extent to which affective reactions are evoked by the perception of distress in others and mediate the disposition to help. For the most part research in this area has centered around four questions:

1. Do individuals characteristically experience affect when they confront another in need?

2. What is the nature of this affect if it in fact occurs?

3. Are affective reactions related to subsequent help?

4. If they are related to subsequent help, why are they related?

The first and third questions are descriptive in nature, the second and fourth explanatory.

The first question is perhaps the one most easily answered. In both human and nonhuman species, increased physiological arousal has been found to be a frequent, although not inevitable, response to the observation of another's suffering (see Stotland, Mathews, Sherman, Hansson, and Richardson, 1978 for a review of the evidence). The more salient and pronounced the suffering of others, the more intense the physiological reaction is likely to be (Gaertner and Dovidio, 1977). Self-report and facial expression measures support the psychophysiological findings (see Hamilton, 1973; Krebs, 1975; Piliavin *et al.,* 1981; and Stotland *et al.,* 1978).

What then is the nature of this arousal? As pointed out by Piliavin *et al.* (1981) affective reactions may be mediated by two quite different arousal systems—the orienting response system and the "fight or flight" type of defensive response system. These investigators adduce evidence to show that severe emergencies tend to evoke arousal of the defensive type, while relatively innocuous types of distress tend to evoke an orienting response. Piliavin *et al.* suggest that defensive arousal reflects emotional involvement in a situation, and an orienting response reflects interest in what is happening. According to these researchers, individuals display an orienting response when they initially attend to someone in distress; then, if the distress is severe, they may experience defensive arousal.

Piliavin *et al.* (1981) persuasively demonstrate that individuals who observe others in serious distress typically experience physiological reactions similar to the reactions that they experience when they themselves are in distress. It is quite plausible to assume, as Piliavin *et al.* do, that this type of arousal indicates emotional involvement in the situation. However, in addition, these investigators suggest that arousal associated with the distress of another is vicarious in nature. Unfortunately, there is little evidence to support this assumption.

It is commonly assumed that affective responses to the plight of another are empathic; however, in order for an emotional reaction to meet the criteria of empathy, it must be vicarious, that is, it must be evoked by the emotional state of another, and in addition, it must match the type of emotion that the other is experiencing. As Berger (1962) pointed out more than two decades ago, the conditions necessary to establish that an affective reaction is vicarious are strict. The central problem is to control for the physiological effects of other sources of stimulation such as cries of distress or cues that evoke fear. Although some investigatiors have made the effort to control for pseudovicarious sources of arousal (see Batson and Coke, 1981; Krebs, 1975; Stotland *et al.,* 1978), most have not. Thus, few studies are equipped to comment on the nature of the arousal.

The third question concerns the relationship between distress-contingent arousal and the probability of help. Most studies on the issue have found that the greater the degree of arousal produced by the sight of a distressed other, the greater and faster is the subsequent help (Gaertner and Dovido, 1977; Geen and Jarmecky, 1973; Krebs, 1975; Weiss, Buchanan, Alstatt, and Lombardo, 1971). In addition, at least two factors that have been found to produce an elevation in arousal—the severity of an emergency and the clarity of a victim's need for help—also have been found to increase the probability of helping.

The final question concerns the reasons why affective reactions are related to helping. The most popular explanation of the link between distress-contingent arousal and helping behavior is based on the idea of drive reduction (Weiss *et al.,* 1973; Piliavin and Piliavin, 1972). It is assumed that since the distress of another produces distress in the observer, reduction of the victim's distress will also reduce the observer's distress. Because distress reduction is reinforcing, individuals are motivated to learn and perform helping responses in these situations. Indeed, Weiss *et al.* (1971) have found that the relief of another's distress is sufficient to reinforce a variety of nonhelping responses.

As plausible as the drive-reduction account seems, it has a number of weaknesses. First, there is only anecdotal evidence to support the key assumption that people who help others in distress experience a reduction in physiological arousal (see Latané and Darley, 1976; Murphy, 1937). Second, this account fails to explain why individuals should elect to reduce their arousal by helping another person rather than by other means such as running away. Avoidance would seem to be a more effective means of drive reduction than helping in many situations because helping brings the observer in closer proximity to the distress of the victim.

Batson, Duncan, Ackerman, Buckley, and Birch (1981) have proposed an alternative to the drive-reduction account of the relationship between arousal and helping. These investigators suggest that it is not the desire to reduce their own vicariously-experienced arousal that motivates individuals to help a distressed other but rather genuine concern for the other. According to Batson *et al.* (1981), arousal mediates help indirectly by serving as a cue to observers of their concern for the victim. In order to motivate helping behavior effectively, arousal must be labeled as sympathetic or empathic in nature.

By way of summary, in the case of both altruism and aggression we have considered the contention that an affective state (empathy or sympathy/anger) mediates between an environmental event (a distressed other/thwarting of goal-directed activity) and a behavioral response (help/aggression). There has been controversy about the nature of both empathy and anger. Do these constructs refer to physiological states or are they best de-

fined as experiences that emerge from the (cognitively based) labeling of physiological arousal? Although the evidence is clear in establishing the existence of a positive correlation between the occurence of certain types of environmental events (the thwarting of goal-directed activity, the appearance of a distressed other), certain types of affective reactions (anger, empathy), and certain types of behavior (aggression, altruism), these relationships are not invariant, and their underlying dynamics are at best only partially explained.

In addition to internal mediating processes that are primarily affective in nature (or, at least, that are considered to be affective by researchers), investigators have examined the effect of internal processes that are primarily cognitive in nature. A diverse array of studies has investigated the link between various aspects of situations, cognitive reactions, and altruistic and aggressive behaviors. The central assumption underlying these studies is that how individuals define and interpret situations determines to a great extent whether or not they will behave aggressively or altruistically.

THE COGNITIVE MEDIATION OF ALTRUISTIC BEHAVIOR

It is safe to assume that altruistic behavior is always mediated by complex interactions among multiple situational, cognitive, and affective factors. However, because researchers have tended to investigate the effect of particular processes in isolation from others, we will organize our discussion of the cognitive mediation of altruism in terms of the cognitive constructs that have received the most research attention. After this discussion, we will describe and evaluate a number of decision-making models that attempt to show how various cognitive and affective factors interact with one another in the determination of altruistic behavior.

INFERENCES ABOUT ANOTHER'S NEED FOR ASSISTANCE

Although individuals may emit altruistic responses in the absence of any apparent external inducement to do so (because, for example, they feel good or guilty), the preponderance of altruistic behavior occurs in response to the perception or inference that another needs help. In cases where another's need for help is readily apparent—when for example, he or she collapses in front of you, drops a bag of groceries, or requests assistance—the inference is easy. In cases where another's need for help is more subtle—when individuals attempt to hide their feelings, or when situational cues are ambiguous—the inference that another needs help may involve cognitive processes of a higher order.

In the vast majority of experimental studies on prosocial behavior, observers are presented with a clear indication that another needs assistance. For this reason, there has been relatively little research on factors that affect the probability that observers will perceive a need for help in situations where the cues are not readily apparent. One exception to this trend is research on the effects of environmental overload.

Environmental Overload and the Perception of Need

Most of the research on the effects of environmental overload has been guided by Milgram's (1970) hypothesis that "the ultimate adaptation to an overloaded social environment is to totally disregard the needs, interests, and demands of those whom one does not define as relevant to the satisfaction of personal needs" (p. 1462). It is important to note that there is a telling ambiguity in the term "disregard." It may imply either the failure to perceive another's need for help or the tendency to perceive it but not to respond to it.

Korte and Grant (1980) demonstrated convincingly that environmental overload may produce a constriction of attention. These investigators found that pedestrians were significantly less likely to notice unusual things such as a female holding a bright yellow teddy bear or a newspaper headline saying "Attention—Project in Progress" while walking along streets where the traffic noise was relatively loud than while walking along more quiet streets. In addition, these investigators found that subjects walked faster and looked straight ahead more when the level of noise was high than when it was low.

Other research has indicated that a constriction of attention may decrease the probability of noticing that another needs help and, therefore, also decrease the probability of helping. Korte, Ypma, and Toppen (1975) found that pedestrians were significantly less likely to help a person who appeared to be having trouble reading a map when they were walking along streets characterized by high-noise level, dense traffic, large numbers of pedestrians, and many visible establishments than when they were walking along streets with less environmental input. However, factors other than a constriction of attention may also mediate the inhibition of helping in

overload conditions. For example, Korte *et al.* (1975) found that pedestrians were disinclined to grant an interview to a confederate in a high-input condition. Because the pedestrians clearly perceived the need of the confederate in this situation, their refusal to help must have been caused by some other consequence or correlate of environmental input. This point applies to a number of other studies. In one, Weiner (1976) exposed subjects to a bombardment of sensory stimulation while they were working on a number of simultaneously presented tasks. Then, during a second exposure to this situation, he arranged for a woman entering the room in which the subjects were working to fall and to grab her ankle. Weiner (1976) found that the subjects who were exposed to a high level of sensory input were less likely to render direct assistance to the distressed woman than those who were exposed to low levels of stimulation (although they were not less likely to render more indirect help). Again, because there was no question in this situation that all subjects noticed the woman in distress, the tendency for the subjects in the high overload conditions to "disregard" the plight of the victim cannot be attributed to attentional factors.

The Salience of Need and the Severity of Distress

A number of studies have found a positive relationship between the "clarity" of others' need for help in emergencies and the probability that subjects will intervene. For example, Yakimovich and Saltz (1971) found that the number of subjects who came to the aid of a maintenance man who had "fallen" from a ladder increased significantly when he cried for help; and Clark and Word (1972) and Solomon, Solomon, and Store (1978) found that bystanders were more likely to intervene when they could both see and hear a person in distress than when they could only hear the cues to his or her distress. Other studies have found that the latency of intervention decreases systematically as the ostensible severity of another's distress increases. This effect has been found in studies involving electric shock (Geen and Jarmecky, 1973), falling bookcases (Ashton and Severy, 1976), rat bites (West and Brown, 1975), and an overdose of sleeping pills (Shotland and Huston, 1979). It is safe to assume that all subjects in these studies, including those in the low-salience and low-severity conditions, perceived that another needed help; therefore the variations in their helping behavior could not have been caused by variations in this perceptual factor. At present it is unclear which cognitive (and affective) processes are activated by variations in the clarity and severity of cues of distress and how they mediate the observed variations in subsequent helping.

In much the same way that bystanders have been found to disregard the needs of others in conditions of environmental overload even though the needs are readily apparent, they also appear to be disposed to disregard the distress of others unless it is imposed on them with considerable forcefulness. Indeed, in many situations, bystanders appear to be motivated to evade the perception that another needs help. The upshot of studies on environmental overload, clarity and severity of distress cues, and other factors is that although the average person will render assistance to others in highly compelling situations (e.g., when there are few background distractions, when the need for assistance is highly salient, and when responsibility is focused on him or her), the probability of helping diminishes rapidly as the cues that another needs help become less compelling. Part of the diminished inclination to help may be due to the failure of the needs of others to meet some threshold for evoking help (because, for example, they seem able to help themselves), and part may be due to the influence of conflicting, self-interested motives.

The Influence of Bystanders on the Attribution of Need

In situations where there is some ambiguity about another's need for assistance, the reactions of bystanders may exert a profound effect on how observers interpret the situation. One of the early explanations offerred for the finding that individuals are less likely to intervene in emergencies when other bystanders are present than when they are alone (the "bystander effect") was that passive bystanders implicitly convey the impression that the incident is not significant enough to warrant intervention (see Latané and Darley, 1970). The susceptibility of individuals under ambiguous conditions to informational influence from others is firmly established in the social psychological literature (Deutsch and Gerard, 1955; Festinger, 1954; Schachter, 1957).

If observers turn to bystanders for information that will help them decide whether another needs help, they should be sensitive to others' verbal and nonverbal reactions. Several studies have supported this idea. Smith, Vanderbilt, and Callen (1973) found that the probability of bystanders intervening was significantly increased when a confederate acted alarmed. Darley, Teger, and Lewis (1973) found that significantly more bystanders

intervened when they were facing another bystander than when they were facing in the opposite direction. In an attempt to test the effect of explicit definitional verbalizations, Bickman (1972) arranged for subjects to hear a tape recording of a bookcase falling on another subject. Following this incident, a third party made one of the following comments: (1) "it sounds like the bookcase fell on the subject," (2) "it sounds like the bookcase fell," or (3) "something must have fallen on the subject." The more explicit the definition of the situation as an emergency, the more likely was the subject to intervene. This basic finding was replicated by Staub (1974). Considered together, these studies demonstrate that at least part of the reason why passive bystanders inhibit helping is that they implicitly convey the impression that the situation in question does not demand or warrant a helping response.

INFERENCES ABOUT THE APPROPRIATENESS OF HELPING

Although perceiving that another needs help and deciding that the need for help is compelling enough to warrant intervention are necessary conditions for helping in many situations, they are not by any means sufficient. Observers also must decide that it is appropriate for them to help.

People's desire to behave in a socially appropriate manner is a powerful determinant of altruistic and aggressive behaviors. In many cases, the appropriate course of action is apparent. In others, however, individuals must search for cues that will help them define the situation in which they find themselves and determine the role that they are expected to play. Central among the cues that supply such guidance are the reactions of the other individuals present.

Inasmuch as observers assume that it is appropriate to help people who need help, any behavior that calls attention to another's need for help may evoke the inference that it is appropriate to help him or her. A number of studies have found that verbalizations from adult experimenters about expected courses of action exert clear effects on the helping behavior of children. For example, Poulos and Liebert (1972) found that children who encountered an adult who said "I think it would be good to give some tokens" were significantly more likely to donate to charity than children who were not exposed to this verbalization. In a similar vein Staub (1970, 1971) and Ashton and Severy (1976) have shown that giving children and adults permission to enter or leave a room in which they are working increases their tendency to intervene in an emergency.

In many situations, of course, bystanders don't say anything. Nevertheless, what they do or what they do not do may exert considerable influence on observers' judgments of appropriateness. A spate of studies has found that children and adults tend to model the helping behavior of others (see Rushton, 1981; Staub, 1978, for reviews). As indicated earlier, models serve a number of functions, one of which is to supply information about the appropriateness of various courses of action. Inactive bystanders (i.e., models) may implicitly convey the impression that helping is inappropriate.

INFERENCES ABOUT DESERVING

Closely associated with, and in many cases inextricably bound with, inferences about whether or not it is appropriate to help another are inferences about whether or not another deserves to be helped. A number of factors may influence attributions of deservingness—factors such as the amount of help needed by a victim, the victim's ability to help himself or herself, and the extent to which the victim is perceived to be responsible for his or her state of need.

The findings from studies investigating the effect of such variables as the severity of another's distress and the degree of another's dependency were reviewed earlier. Studies also have found that the apparent legitimacy of another's need may affect the probability that he or she will receive help. For example, Bickman and Kamzan (1973) and Field (1974) found that shoppers and sales clerks were more likely to help a customer who was ten cents or thirty cents short when the customer needed the money to buy necessary items such as milk or ointment than when he or she needed the money to buy luxury items such as cookies or beer.

The most extensive set of studies on victim deservingness has focused on the extent to which individuals who need help are responsible for their dependency. Many diverse experimental studies have found that a victim whose state of need is perceived to be caused by his or her own actions receives less help than a victim whose state of need is perceived to be caused by factors beyond his or her control (e.g., Berkowitz, 1969; Horowitz, 1968; Miller and Smith, 1977). Corroborating the findings of these laboratory studies are the results of Bryan and Davenport's investigation (cited in Berkowitz, 1980) of the donations received by the one hundred "neediest"

cases advertised in the *New York Times* during the Christmas season. These investigators found that more money was given to people whose trouble seemed externally caused, such as children who were victims of abuse, than to people who seemed to be the source of their own troubles, such as mental patients.

The fact that culpable victims evoke less assistance than inculpable victims is well established in the literature. It is not, however, entirely clear why. At least two different explanations have been proposed. The first explains the effect in terms of social norms (e.g., Walster, Walster, and Berscheid, 1978). In this view, social norms prescribing that individuals ought to help only those who deserve to be helped are viewed as functional for society. Refusing to help blameworthy victims is thought to serve an important social function, namely, increasing the likelihood that the victim and others will modify their future behavior. Perhaps the strongest evidence for this interpretation is the frequency with which irresponsible victims, whether they are helped or not, are rebuked, often publically, for causing their problems and enjoined to "mend their ways" or "shape up" in the future (Brickman, Rabinowitz, Karuza, Coates, Cohen, and Kidder, 1982).

Another explanation for why attributions of deservingness are important is found in the writings of Lerner and his colleagues (Lerner and Miller, 1978; Lerner, Miller and Holmes, 1976). According to Lerner, individuals are motivated to preserve their belief that the world is just, that is, that individuals get what they deserve. In cases where an individual is suffering undeserved misery, observers are motivated to rectify this injustice. However, in cases where a victim is perceived as deserving his or her fate, the victim's suffering is perceived as just, and the motivation to help is diminished. Perhaps the strongest evidence for the just-world interpretation of the "deservingness effect" is the finding that in addition to helping victims who are responsible for their plight less than victims who are not, observers are inclined to label as undeserving those victims who cannot for one reason or another be helped effectively (Miller, 1977a, 1977b).

SELF-ATTRIBUTIONS OF RESPONSIBILITY AND THE DIFFUSION OF RESPONSIBILITY

Individuals may perceive that another needs help; they may deem it appropriate to help; and they may decide that the other deserves to be helped; yet, they may not render any assistance because they do not feel personally responsible for helping. Several lines of research have produced results supporting the idea that situational and personal characteristics serving to focus responsibility on observers are among the most significant determinants of altruistic behavior.

Situational Characteristics That Focus Responsibility

One of the most direct and obvious ways to focus responsibility is to put individuals in a position of authority. Staub (1970) explicitly told kindergarten children that he was leaving them "in charge," and found that this verbalization increased the probability that they would investigate sounds of distress in an adjoining room. Similarly, Moriarty (1975) found that virtually everyone who had been asked to watch a confederate's belongings intervened to stop a "thief" from stealing a radio or suitcase; in contrast, approximately two-thirds of those who were not asked did not.

In many situations, especially those characteristic of experimental research on altruistic behavior, who is responsible for what is left relatively ambiguous. Certainly this is the case in much of the research on bystander intervention. One of the earliest explanations for the bystander effect was that responsibility was "diffused" among the observers (see Latané, Nida, and Wilson, 1981). Studies have found that the inhibiting effect of bystanders is minimized when they are not in a position to help (Korte, 1969; Bickman, 1971, 1972) and when they are less qualified to help others because, for example, they are children (Ross, 1971), or blind (Ross and Brabend, 1973). In addition, several studies have found that the presence of a bystander who seems especially qualified to help (e.g., because he or she has had medical training) will decrease the probability of other bystanders intervening (Schwartz and Clausen, 1970; Piliavin and Piliavin, 1972). Schwartz and Ben David (1974) found that students who were led to believe that they were poorly qualified to handle rats helped less when a woman was threatened by a rat than students who were told that they were well qualified.

Earlier, we reviewed evidence supporting the idea that the bystander effect was due to the tendency of individuals in groups to infer that helping is inappropriate (because no one else is helping). Here we have suggested that the effect is due to diffusion of responsibility. In addition, the bystander effect has been attributed a third factor, labeled "evaluation apprehension," "audience inhibition," or "normative social influence." The idea behind this explanation is that it is the capacity of bystanders to form negative judgments about one another (especially in cases where one of them misjudges an emergency) that decreases their disposition to help. Latané *et al.* (1981) review evidence supporting this explanation.

In view of the plausibility and empirical support for each of the three explanations for bystander inhibition, one might wonder which one to believe. In the words of Latané *et al.* (1981) the answer is "not one, not two, but all three." Reasoning that diffusion of responsibility is the only process that can operate when bystanders cannot see and hear one another, that audience inhibition involves being visible to others but not necessarily vice versa, and that informational influence involves being able to see other bystanders but not necessarily vice versa, Latané and Darley (1976) found that all three processes exerted independent and additive influences. Similarly, Piliavin *et al.* (1981, p. 144) concluded:

> The results of several independent investigations . . . support the notion that informational social influence, normative social influence, and diffusion of responsibility are dynamically distinct processes. . . . Informational social influence typically exerts its effect soon after the onset of the emergency. . . . Diffusion of responsibility, if it occurs, appears later in the postemergency sequence.
> . . . Normative social influence effects also occur later and are related to concern about the evaluation of others.

In summary, research on situational factors that influence attributions of responsibility indicates that individuals are significantly more likely to help others when they have been singled out in any one of many ways as being responsible for helping than when they have not. When an individual is the only one present, his or her choice is either to help the victim or to permit him or her to suffer. However, when there are other people present, the decision becomes one of determining who is most obliged to help. It is here that the type of situational factors that we have been considering become influential.

Self-Awareness and the Focus of Responsibility

Duval, Duval, and Neely (1979) have suggested that factors that increase the probability that individuals will focus awareness on themselves will also tend to increase their self-attributions of responsibility in situations involving a distressed other. These investigators manipulated self-focus by exposing subjects to their images on television or by having them complete a bibliographic questionnaire before or after viewing a videotape of victims of a venereal-disease epidemic or of poverty-striken Latin Americans. They found that subjects who were made self-aware immediately before and after viewing the scenes of distress felt more responsibility for and were more willing to help the victims than those who were less self-aware. Interestingly, increasing self-focus in these studies did not affect the attitudes of the subjects or their sense of normative obligation toward the victims.

In an extension of the general idea that factors that increase self-awareness also increase the tendency of individuals to feel responsible for the welfare of others, Wegner and Schaefer (1978) conducted a study in which they manipulated the number of bystanders relative to victims present in a situation. These investigators predicted that increasing the number of bystanders should decrease self-focus, and thus inhibit helping, and that increasing the number of victims should increase self-focus, and thus enhance helping. Although the results supported their predictions, the investigators failed to establish that their manipulations produced differences in self-focus and, therefore, that it was differences in self-focus that produced the observed differences in behavior.

SELF-PERCEPTION AND SELF-ATTRIBUTION

In addition to attributions of responsibility, there is another type of self-attribution that has been found to exert an effect on altruistic behavior, namely, attributions about the extent to which one possesses altruistic personality traits or dispositions. Several studies have found that individuals who are induced to help others with little extrinsic incentive subsequently help more than individuals who help under conditions of high extrinsic inducement (Batson and Coke, 1981; Uranowitz, 1975; Zuckerman, Lazzaro and Waldgeir, 1979). It is assumed that people who decide to help in circumstances of little external incentive infer that they are helpful people and, therefore, subsequently behave in a manner that is consistent with their self-perception; in contrast, those who help because of pressure or inducement do not make this inference. In support of this explanation, Batson and Coke (1981) found that subjects in a condition of high extrinsic justification described themselves as less altruistic than

those in a condition of low intrinsic justification. A number of manipulations have been employed to alter subjects' self-perceptions. They include (1) making attributions of subjects' motivation to help (Batson, Harris, McCaul, Davis, and Schmidt, 1979), (2) labeling subjects' dispositions directly (Miller, Brickman, and Boalen, 1975; Jenson and Moore, 1977; Grusec *et al.,* 1978) and (3) making subjects think that this helping occurred because of a model (Thomas, Batson and Coke, 1981).

The logic of self-perception theory assumes that people make inferences about the types of disposition they possess in much the same way that they make inferences about the dispositions possessed by others (Bem, 1972) and that these inferences affect their subsequent behavior. Although this line of reasoning seems plausible in its general form, it is unclear why people who are led to infer that they are altruistic feel inclined to reaffirm this attribution by helping more rather than by deciding that they had helped enough, or why people who are led to believe that they are not altruistic would not feel inclined to alter the unfavorable self-perception. In fact a body of research has shown that individuals are motivated to eradicate negative impressions. For instance, individuals who receive information that they are prejudiced subsequently behave in a less discriminatory way (Dutton, 1976; Katz, 1981); and people who have harmed others are more inclined to help than those who have not (see Krebs, 1982c, for a review). In addition to these problems, it is difficult to understand how self-perceptions can be changed by a single experience in a laboratory and what factors induce specific self-attributions (I am helpful in this situation) as opposed to global self-attributions (I am a helpful person).

INFERENCES ABOUT THE COSTS AND CONSEQUENCES OF HELPING AND NOT HELPING

As indicated in our discussion of the biological basis of altruistic and aggressive behaviors, the social sciences are dominated by utilitarian models of human nature. Central among the assumptions of these models is the idea that behavior is governed by the pursuit of desirable and avoidance of undesirable outcomes. Inasmuch as this assumption contravenes the definition of pure altruism (i.e., behavior whose purpose is to enchance the welfare of another at some cost to self), evidence of altruism creates the same kind of challenge to the principle of reinforcement as it does to the principle of natural selection (see Krebs and Holder, 1981).

Exceedingly little, or perhaps no prosocial behavior is altruistic (see Krebs, 1983, pp. 62–69). The anticipated costs and benefits of helping have been found to play a significant role in the types of nonaltruistic prosocial behavior customarily studied by social psychologists. Consider research on bystander intervention for example. Piliavin *et al.* (1981) postulate that "The bystander will choose that response to an emergency that will most rapidly reduce his or her arousal, incurring in the process as few net costs (costs minus rewards) as possible" (p. 83). Piliavin *et al.* (1981) evaluate this proposition by reviewing studies on the effects of (1) "personal costs for helping," (2) "potential rewards for helping," and (3) "costs for the victim receiving no help."

The main types of personal costs for helping examined by Piliavin *et al.* are psychological aversion, physical harm, time and effort, money, social sanctions, and loss of social rewards. They reviewed research showing that the following variables affect the probability of bystander intervention: whether or not the victim has blood trickling from his mouth (Piliavin and Piliavin, 1972), whether or not the victim possesses a physical stigma (Piliavin, Piliavin and Rodin, 1975; Ungar, 1979), the level of shock an individual must endure in order to help (Midlarsky and Midlarsky, 1973), the amount of danger involved in helping (Anderson, 1974), the amount of free time available to a potential helper (Batson, Cochran, Biederman, Blasset, Ryan, and Vogt, 1978), the amount of money necessary in order to help (Wagner and Wheeler, 1969), and the probability of social censure (McGovern, 1976).

As far as the rewards for helping are concerned, Piliavin *et al.* mention those associated with interacting with similar and attractive recipients, then go on to review studies that have found that helping is affected by monetary compensation (Wilson and Kahn, 1975), expressed appreciation from the recipient (McGovern, Ditzian, and Taylor, 1975), and variables designed to construe helping in altruistic terms.

Turning to costs associated with failing to help, Piliavin *et al.* review research suggesting that variables such as (1) the victim's deservingness and need, and the extent to which responsibility is focused on the observer, and (2) the amount of empathically experienced arousal (which, they contend, is affected by situational variables such as the severity and clarity of the emergency and the closeness of the victim) affect the probability and latency of bystander intervention. We evaluated research on these variables earlier.

In the model proposed by Piliavin *et al.* individuals who encounter others who need assistance are expected to engage in an unconscious hedonistic calculus—weighing the costs and benefits of helping and not helping and adopting the course of action that they anticipate will maximize their gains. When helping involves small costs to the benefactor and great gains to the recipient, people are most likely to help—a rather obvious relationship. However, in situations where the costs of both helping and not helping are high (i.e., the type of situation involved in most emergencies), "the most salient response for most people seems to be direct intervention" (Piliavin *et al.*, p. 113)—a finding that runs contrary to the hedonistic model (see Piliavin *et al.* pp. 110–111).

Faced with data that are inconsistent with the hedonistic model of human nature, Piliavin *et al.* attempt to rescue the model by provisionally hypothesizing that observers caught in the dilemma associated with high costs for helping and high costs for not helping will attempt to reinterpret the situation as one in which help is unnecessary, one in which they are not responsible, or one in which the victim does not deserve to be helped. If this is not possible, they will re-evaluate the costs for helping. In situations where none of the above are possible but where a bystander sees an opportunity to render indirect help, the bystander will adopt this course of action. A careful examination of the available data, however, fails to reveal consistent support for these hypotheses.

Because of the pervasiveness and plausibility of the idea that individuals select the courses of action that they anticipate will maximize their gains, it is surprising that the supporting evidence is so inconsistent. This inconsistency may be due to the impossibility of assessing subjects' expectations about costs and benefits. In the words of Piliavin *et al.* (1981), "It is a rare study in which attempts are actually made to assess the bystander's interpretations of the situation in any meaningful way" (p. 84). When tangible physical variables such as the possibility of injury and the loss of money are involved, the quantification of costs may seem plausible; however, when subtle hypothetical variables such as feeling disgust because someone has blood trickling from his mouth, feeling pleasure by being with someone who seems similar to you, and experiencing gains and losses in self-esteem, and hence "empathy costs," are involved, the quantification of costs and gains becomes unwieldy.

Evidence that individuals intervene impulsively in potentially high cost, life-threatening emergencies appears to entail an exception to the hedonistic model of human nature. Although it is not possible to establish that observers in such situations do not experience some compensating gain (such as reduction of distressful empathic arousal), it is difficult to imagine how the potential gains could exceed the potential costs.

COGNITIVE REACTIONS TO THE RECEIPT OF ASSISTANCE

In virtually all of the studies we have considered in this section so far, the benefactor and recipient had no history of interaction—they encountered one another for the first time when the measure of helping was obtained. In many situations, however, individuals encounter one another repeatedly. As indicated in our discussion of biological and cultural factors, the tendency to reciprocate assistance is universal. Receiving help evokes a powerful inducement to give help in return.

How a recipient reacts to assistance from a donor has been found to depend, to a great extent, on the kinds of motives and intentions attributed to the donor. As mentioned earlier, Gouldner (1960) drew attention to the significance of donors' motives in his original paper on the norm of reciprocity. Attribution theory suggests that dispositions are attributed to others mainly in situations involving minimal external control. Consistent with the idea, studies have found that recipients of help are significantly more likely to attribute altruistic dispositions to donors when the donors' assistance is perceived as deliberate than when it is not (Enzle and Schopflocher, 1978). Recipients also are more likely to reciprocate aid when it is seen as voluntary (Greenberg and Frisch, 1972) than when it is seen as compulsorily given. Inasmuch as social norms entail a form of external control, nonnormative and unexpected assistance should evoke more positive attributions than normative and expected assistance, and indeed, there is evidence that this is the case (Morse and Gergen, 1970). It should be mentioned, however, that assistance that violates situational norms may produce negative attributions when, for example, such assistance seems inappropriate (Morse, Gruzen, and Reis, 1976), or when recipients do not need help (Schwartz and Tessler, 1972).

Another postulate of the attributional account concerns the costs associated with actions. Studies of proso-cial behavior have found that recipients are more likely to attribute altruistic and other favorable dispositions to benefactors whose assistance is viewed as costly than to benefactors whose assistance is not viewed in this way (Fisher and Nadler, 1976). As we might expect, there is a positive correlation between favorable attributions, feelings of obligation to reciprocate, and actual reciprocity (Tesser, Gatewood, and Driver, 1968).

Considered as a whole, the evidence we have been reviewing suggests that individuals generally attribute positive qualities to those who help them and that such attributions mediate subsequent reciprocity. There also is evidence, however, that receiving assistance may give rise to the attribution of negative qualities—to both the donor and recipient—and that receiving assistance may reduce the recipient's disposition to reciprocate. The general reason why individuals resent assistance appears to relate to the implications to their self-concept, sense of freedom, and relationship to the donor.

A number of studies have found that individuals form more negative evaluations of those who help them when they, the recipients, are not in a position to reciprocate than when they are (Gross and Latane, 1974). Being offered assistance may imply that the recipient is deficient in a number of ways. Recipients appear to resent assistance offered by those with whom they compare themselves, apparently because the offer casts them in an inferior position (Fisher, Harrison, and Nadler, 1978; Nadler, Fisher, and Streufert, 1976). Consistent with reactance theory, recipients tend to resent and resist assistance that they perceive reduces their freedom (Brehm and Cole, 1966). There also is evidence that recipients resent assistance rendered in relation to tasks in which they take pride (Gergen *et al.*, 1972).

The upshot of research on the cognitive reactions of individuals to the receipt of assistance is that giving and receiving help has important implications for the balance of power and affection in relationships between people and for their conceptions of themselves. Individuals value assistance that does not implicitly put them in an undesirable position vis-à-vis the donor. In contrast, people feel little gratitude when the assistance they receive is not perceived to be voluntary, not intended to be helpful, or when it seems inappropriate. People resent those who draw attention to their inferiorities by assisting them, increase their dependency, or put them in a disadvantaged social position. Fisher, DePaulo, and Nadler, (1981) and Fisher, Nadler, and Whitcher (1982) supply a thorough review of the research on the mixed blessings of receiving help.

DECISION-MAKING MODELS OF PROSOCIAL BEHAVIOR

By now it is apparent that a vast array of cognitive (and affective) factors are linked to altruistic behavior. Ultimately, we will need to specify the ways in which these factors interact. At least three investigators have taken a step in this direction (Latané and Darley, 1970; Piliavin *et al.,* 1981; Schwartz, 1977). Despite significant differences in the models presented by these investigators they have two features in common: (1) they endeavor to show the interrelationships among various cognitive and affective factors, and (2) they interpret altruistic action as the consequence of a multistep decision-making process. Considering the central components of these models and the types of interaction they posit supplies an appropriate summary of our discussion of cognitive mediators of altruistic behavior.

Latané and Darley's Model

The first psychologists to interpret altruistic action as the consequence of a decision-making sequence were Latané and Darley (1970). The model proposed by Latané and Darley focuses on altruism in rescue or emergency situations and is concerned primarily with how the presence of other bystanders affects the probability of intervention.

Darley and Latané contend that the act of intervening in an emergency involves a sequence of five steps or decisions. Specifically, a bystander must:

1. Notice that something is happening.
2. Accurately interpret the situation as an emergency.
3. Decide if he or she has personal responsibility to act.
4. Decide what form of assistance he or she can give.
5. Decide the best means of implementing his or her course of action.

Latané and Darley have focused on steps two and three, which they contend are especially affected by the presence of other bystanders. As we have seen, the results of several studies have supported the idea that individuals' interpretation of an emergency and sense of responsibility exert a significant effect on their tendency to intervene.

Schwartz's Normative Decision-making Model

Like Latané and Darley, Schwartz believes that the decision to aid another represents the culmination of a number of steps or psychological junctures. Unlike Latané and Darley, Schwartz does not restrict his range of focus to helping in emergency situations. Whereas the bystander intervention model emerges from the group dynamic tradition, Schwartz's model owes its principal intellectual debt to the attitude tradition. Schwartz outlines a nine-step sequence to prosocial behavior:

ATTENTION

1. Awareness of a person in a state of need.
2. Perception that there are actions that could relieve the need.
3. Recognition of one's ability to provide relief.

GENERATION OF FEELINGS OF OBLIGATION

4. Apprehension of some responsibility to become involved.
5. Activation of a pre-existing or situationally constructed personal norm.

ANTICIPATORY EVALUATION

6. Assessment of costs and evaluation of probable outcomes.

DEFENSE

7. Reassessment and redefinition of the situation by denial.
8. Interactions of earlier steps in view of reassessments.

BEHAVIOR

9. Action or inaction.

According to Schwartz, the motivation to help someone in need is generated by the discrepancy between the expectation that the people one encounters will be in an acceptable state of well-being and the perception that they are not. Whether or not observers experience feelings of moral obligation will depend on the extent to which they believe that they are able to render some kind of assistance.

One of the most important steps in Schwartz's model involves the activation of internal norms and values.

According to Schwartz, if individuals decide that they are able to help, they will consider the implications of the various courses of action open to them for the values that they hold. The product of this cognitive process is the construction of a "personal norm" for each course of action, which gives rise to feelings of moral obligation to engage in the course of action that is most valued. In Schwartz's model, personal norms consist of cognitive and affective components. The more central the values associated with an action are to a person's self-concept, the more powerful is the affective arousal. "Anticipated compliance elicits feelings of self-satisfaction and anticipated inaction elicits feelings of self-deprecation" (Schwartz and Howard, 1981, p. 199). Schwartz has created a test designed to assess personal norms. This test requires individuals to indicate whether they would feel morally obliged to engage in particular behaviors, such as donating an organ, in particular circumstances, such as one in which the recipient is a friend or stranger. Schwartz and others (see Schwartz and Howard, 1981) have found that endorsement of a variety of personal norms correlates weakly but significantly (from .24 to .43) with behaviors such as donating blood and volunteering to help blind students or elderly welfare recipients.

The activation step in Schwartz's model bears a close similarity to recent models of the relationship between attitudes and behavior. Ajzen and Fishbein (1977), for example, emphasize the importance of assessing either the relationship between particular attitudes and particular behaviors or the relationship between general attitudes and general patterns of behavior.

Turning to the next step in Schwartz's model, individuals engage in a cost-benefit analysis of anticipated courses of action. We reviewed research relevant to this process and considered some of the problems with such conceptualizations earlier. In situations where anticipated consequences favor acts that individuals feel obligated to perform, the individuals are highly likely to perform them. However, Schwartz suggests that in many situations individuals experience a conflict between feelings about what they ought to do and their reluctance to suffer. In such situations, individuals may engage in a defensive type of cognitive reconstruction of the situation. Schwartz describes four types of defense—denial that the other really needs help, denial that costly courses of action will be effective, denial that one is qualified to help, and denial that one has a responsibility to help.

Helping (or not helping) marks the end of the decision-making process, but the action (or inaction) engaged in by an individual modifies the situation in such a way that the actor may return to the beginning of the sequence.

Although several processes outlined in the first three stages of the model have received empirical support, Schwartz and Howard (1981) make it clear that "no single study has tested the full causal process represented in the complete model..." (p. 195). Somewhat problematically, the results of relevant research, some by Schwartz and his colleagues, have failed to supply consistent support for the model. Some studies have found "boomerang effects," a negative relationship between factors such as personal norms, salience of need, and awareness of consequences and helping behavior (see Schwartz and Howard, 1981, pp. 207–208 for a review of these studies).

The Piliavin et al. Model

Although the model of helping first proposed by Piliavin and Piliavin (1972) and recently revised by Piliavin *et al.* (1981) shares many features with the other two models discussed, it has certain distinctive features. The following constitute some of the steps, or phases, this model identifies:

1. Awareness of another's need,

2. The experience of physiological arousal,

3. The labeling of the arousal,

4. A reward/cost analysis of the available options,

5. Decision—direct help, indirect help, non-intervention.

Like the Latané and Darley model, this model is concerned mainly with emergency situations. The four major propositions of this model are:

1. The sight of a distressed other produces a state of physiological arousal in observers.

2. This arousal may be labeled in several different ways by those who experience it.

3. Arousal labeled as sympathy will lead the individual to consider the various rewards and costs associated with direct and indirect help as well as nonintervention.

4. The outcome of the reward/cost analysis will determine the individual's actions.

Piliavin *et al.* endorse an "economic model of man," suggesting that the decision of whether or not to intervene in an emergency is similar to any decision involving rewards and costs. In emphasizing costs and benefits, Piliavin *et al.* align themselves more with the exchange-theory tradition (e.g., Homans, 1961) than with either the group or attitude tradition. A large body of research pertinent to the various steps or phases of their model is reviewed by Piliavin *et al.* (1981).

The Three Models: A Critical Comparison and Assessment

It is interesting to note that the focus of all three models is on why people do not help. The three models differ in the importance they give to arousal, with Piliavin *et al.* according it the most prominence and Darley and Latané the least; however, they are all similar in the high degree of importance they attach to cognitive processes.

The concept of a decision is central to all three models, and for this reason it is important to consider closely the status of this concept. Although it seems safe to assume that individuals who help have decided to help, a failure to act may reflect either a decision not to act or indecision. For example, Latané and Darley (1970) have observed that many subjects who had not intervened after ten minutes seemed to have been in a state of indecision the whole time.

A second problematic feature of the decision-making models concerns the form that decisions assume. All three models acknowledge that decisions need not necessarily be conscious, and none attempts to specify exactly what kind of decision making actually takes place. The occurrence of a decision is inferred from behavior. Thus, the concept of decisions seems to be used primarily in a heuristic sense, and the proposed decision-making models seem very much to be "as-if" models.

It is *as if* people go through a number of steps or decisions before they act or do not act. This approach is, of course, the rule rather than the exception in social psychology. Although this approach generally has proven useful, there always exists the risk that the hypothetical or heuristic nature of concepts will become obscured. Each of these models specifies relationships between certain observable variables and observable behaviors and assumes that these relationships are mediated by internal cognitive and affective processes. Confidence that such processes exist grows with the number of additional relationships successfully predicted by the model.

A third limitation of decision-making models is that helping sometimes occurs without deliberation and that this type of helping is largely unaffected by the variables that the various models consider. Piliavin *et al.* (1981) review research on "impulsive" helping that, as the term suggests, does not seem to involve a reward/cost analysis or rational decision-making. Similarly, Schwartz acknowledges that much help giving is routinized or scripted and is not affected by personal norms or elaborate information processing. With growing interest in behavior that is only minimally guided by cognitive activity (Abelson, 1981; Langer, 1978) more evidence of "mindless" helping behavior should emerge.

The sequential element of the various models also merits examination. Here too we are dealing mainly with an "as-if" concept for which there is no direct evidence. Support for the various proposed sequences is logical rather than empirical. Although certain steps (e.g., awareness of another) seem to be logically necessary for helping to occur, other steps involve only plausible possibilities.

We have been considering cognitive processes that mediate altruistic behavior in the typical subject. It is the case, however, that subjects may differ significantly from one another. We considered differences in personality style earlier. Another way in which individuals differ is in terms of the level to which their cognitive abilities have developed. The two cognitively based individual differences that have been investigated most thoroughly in research on altruism are perspective-taking ability and moral reasoning. We will discuss each briefly in turn.

DEVELOPMENTAL DIFFERENCES IN PERSPECTIVE-TAKING ABILITY AND PROSOCIAL BEHAVIOR

The cognitive process that is most relevant to the inference that another needs help is role taking, or perspective-taking ability. A large number of studies have assessed the relationship between perspective-taking ability and a variety of altruistic behaviors. These studies have been summarized by Kurdek (1978) and Krebs and Russell (1981). Conducting a meta-analysis of the results of existing studies, Underwood and Moore (1982) concluded that there is a significant positive relationship between perspective taking and altruism. However, as pointed out by Krebs and Russell (1981), there is considerable inconsistency in relevant findings: "Approximately half of the studies found a positive relationship; approximately half failed to find a significant relationship; and three studies found some evidence for a negative correlation between the two measures" (pp. 140–141).

Krebs and Russell (1981) examined the literature on the relationship between role-taking ability and altruistic behavior and noted problems with (1) the validity of existing measures of role taking, (2) the validity of existing measures of altruism, and (3) assumptions about the relationship between these two variables. As documented by these reviewers, investigators have tended to employ different measures of both role taking and altruism, and the correspondence between the measures employed by different experimenters is minimal. Many measures have little ecological validity, and many are insensitive to the developmental level of the subjects who take part in the experiments.

It is interesting to note that none of the existing studies on the relationship between role taking and altruism has attempted to determine whether the subjects actually engaged in perspective taking in the situation in which their altruistic behavior was assessed. Rather, all studies assessed the general ability of the subjects to take the role of another and assumed that this ability was activated when the dependent measure was assessed. Perspective taking is a cognitive tool whose function is to obtain knowledge about the subjective states of others. Thus, at best, this ability is a necessary condition for altruistic behavior in situations where it supplies the only means of inferring that another wants or needs help. In situations where another's need for help is readily apparent (e.g., when a victim asks for help), perspective-taking abilities may not even be activated. And, once engaged, perspective taking need not necessarily mediate altruistic behavior. One may take the role of others in order to anticipate their moves in a game or even to exploit them.

Krebs and Russell (1981) suggest that role taking may give rise to a cognitive state that is conducive to the motivation to behave altruistically in two ways: by producing a state of cognitive disequilibrium ("This person needs help: something must be done.") and by stimulating a sense of moral responsibility ("I have an obligation to help people who need help."). Thus, although "role taking is an information-gathering process that is not in itself intrinsically altruistic, the cognitive

states it produces and the moral reasoning it mediates may give rise to altruistic motivation" (p. 161).

Finally, even in cases where perspective taking gives rise to the motivation to help others, there are many circumstances in which the motivation will not be fulfilled. "People who want to help others may lack the courage, initiative, opportunity, and resources to help" (Krebs and Russell, 1981, p. 162). Other moderating variables such as assertiveness (Barrett and Yarrow, 1972) or empathic arousal (Stotland *et al.*, 1978) may mediate the relationship.

DEVELOPMENTAL DIFFERENCES IN MORAL REASONING

Blasi (1980) has supplied a thorough and insightful review of research on the relationship between moral judgment and moral behavior. Concerning the relationship between moral judgment and altruistic or prosocial behaviors, Blasi concludes that "of 19 studies, 11 offer a clear and unambiguous confirmation of the hypothesis that relates moral cognition and altruistic behavior, 4 present negative results, whereas the remaining 4 studies. . . . report mixed or ambiguous findings" (p. 34).

Krebs (1978, 1981, 1982a, 1982d, 1983) has attempted to define the expected relationship between moral reasoning and altruistic behavior. He points out that Kohlberg's stages of moral judgment do not define stages of altruism and suggests that the tendency to equate morality and altruism should peak at Kohlberg's third stage of moral judgment, where individuals acquire the ability to adopt the perspective of the "generalized other." This stage is usually reached in early adolescence and is characteristic of a sizable portion of the adult population. Krebs (1982d) suggests that "inasmuch as moral conceptions become motivating forces, Stage 3 altruism seeks to meet the expectations of significant others, fulfill the demands of stereotyped social roles (for example, to be a good husband or wife, father or mother), and to gain social approval" (p. 74). He points out that altruistic behavior is not necessarily moral ("inasmuch as the idea of altruism means giving more than one's share, or giving more than one 'should,' it entails a violation of the balance of reciprocity that defines justice") and, therefore, argues that a monotonic relationship between stages of moral judgment and the tendency to engage in altruistic behaviors should not be expected.

When one realizes how broadly based stages of moral development are (individuals pass through only two or three of them in all of adulthood), it seems appropriate to equate them with equally broadly based samples of behavior. The path from a stage of moral development to a particular behavioral decision in a particular situation is a tortuous one; however, individuals would be expected to display behaviors consistent with their stage of moral reasoning as a general life-style pattern. Few studies have investigated patterns of naturally occurring altruistic behavior; however, measures of reputation and delinquency appear to be more consistently related than measures of more specific behaviors to stages of moral development (see Blasi, 1980, pp. 13–19). This point is similar to the one made by Ajzen and Fishbein (1977) in their analysis of the relationship between attitudes and behavior.

Concerning the expected relationship between moral reasoning and situationally specific samples of prosocial behavior, Krebs and Rosenwald (1977) suggest that a logical first step is for investigators to examine the structures of reasoning that define each stage of moral development and to deduce the ways in which the individuals who employ them should interpret the moral obligations involved in the situations to which they are exposed. It is important to recognize that in the model advanced by Krebs and Rosenwald (1977) and elaborated by Krebs (1982a), it is entirely possible for individuals at two quite different stages of moral development to arrive at the same conclusion about whether or not to behave prosocially for quite different reasons. Indeed, individuals at all stages of moral development may argue that the character in the first dilemma on Kohlberg's test should steal a drug to save his dying wife. It also is important to recognize that there may be significant differences between the hypothetical type of moral reasoning assessed by Kohlberg's test (which involves mainly dilemmas relating to prohibitive justice about individuals other than the self) and the practical, real-life reasoning employed by individuals faced with moral decisions in their everyday lives (see Damon, 1976; Haan, 1977; Eisenberg, 1982). In addition, even if a test were able to predict reliably the moral decisions that individuals make, in a cognitive sense, we still would expect people to differ in their willingness or ability to carry out the decision behaviorally. Although knowing what is right may instill the motivation to do what is right, it is far from a guarantee.

Whatever the theoretical plausibility of the model presented previously, it runs into an interesting empirical obstacle; namely, some investigators have found that moral reasoning *is* monotonically related to *moral* behavior (see McNamee, 1978). Candee and Kohlberg (1982) suggest that when tests of moral reasoning such as those employed by Haan *et al.* (1981) are rescored in accordance with Kohlberg's revised scoring system, the scores received by subjects relate monotonically to their scores on moral behavior. Candee and Kohlberg (1982) present a model of moral judgment and moral action outlined in Fig. 3. Granting that the "deontic" choices that individuals at different stages of moral judgment make are only loosely correlated with stages of moral development, Candee and Kohlberg argue that individuals at higher stages of moral development make increasingly powerful judgments of personal responsibility. Thus, although individuals at all stages may decide that it is right to help a person in distress, individuals at high stages

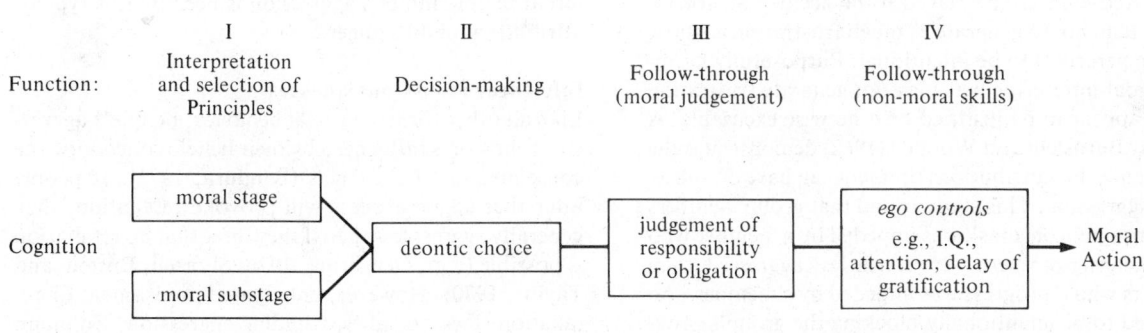

FIGURE 3
SOURCE: D. Candee, and L. Kohlberg, 1982.

will feel a greater sense of personal responsibility to carry out this action. Candee and Kohlberg (1982) review evidence that supports this model.

THE COGNITIVE MEDIATION OF AGGRESSIVE BEHAVIOR

Cognitive processes are featured much more prominently in the literature on altruism than they are in the literature on aggression. The main reason probably relates to the assumption that aggression is less cognitively based than altruism.

COGNITIONS CONCERNING THE TARGET OF AGGRESSION

The cognitive mediators that have attracted most attention in research on aggression are those pertaining to the target of aggression. Research has focused on information and inferences that inhibit the aggressive behavior. Three types of information have proven especially significant in this regard: (1) information concerning the intentions or motives behind the target's previous behavior, (2) information concerning the likelihood that the target will retaliate, and (3) information concerning the degree of distress experienced by the target.

Attributions of Motivation and Intent

When psychologists began to subject the frustration-aggression hypothesis to rigorous examination, it became clear that it is impossible to determine how much an action frustrates an individual without knowledge of how the individual perceives the action (e.g., Pastore, 1952). Acts that are perceived to be accidental, for instance, tend not to generate as much frustration as those that are perceived to be intentional. Purposefully harmful or goal-interfering acts may not generate frustration if they appear to be justified or otherwise excusable. A study by Burnstein and Worchel (1962) demonstrates the importance that attributions of intent can have on subsequent aggression. This study found that group members whose progress on a task was impeded by a member who had a hearing problem were much less aggressive than members whose progress was impeded by a member who appeared to be intentionally blocking the group's progress. Other studies have demonstrated that the intensity of retaliatory aggression is dependent upon the level of

intentionality that the retaliator attributes to the harm-doer (eg., Greenwell and Dengerink, 1973; Nickle, 1974).

An experiment conducted by Dyck and Rule (1978) demonstrates how important cognitive processes can be in determining retaliatory behavior. This study found that the same level of aggression (aversive noise) provoked less retaliation from subjects who believed their aggressor (a confederate) had beaten them at a reaction-time task than from subjects who believed that they had beaten their aggressor. The subjects appeared to assume that the victory of the confederate in the reaction-time task justified, at least partially, his aggression.

A number of other studies indicate that people whose frustrating actions can be attributed to external factors provoke less aggression than do people whose frustrating behavior seems more under their personal control (e.g., Kulik and Brown, 1979). Zillmann and Cantor (1976) attempted to determine whether this is because people who attribute the frustrating behavior of others to external factors become less angry than those who do not, or whether it is because they feel compelled to make allowances due to social norms and a sense of fairness. These investigators exposed subjects to an obnoxious experimenter and varied (1) whether or not they were given mitigating information about him ("He's really upset about a mid-term exam he has tomorrow.") and (2) whether they were given this information before or following their encounter with the experimenter. Both physiological measures (such as blood pressure and heart rate) and evaluation of the experimenter showed that the before-provocation subjects were much less aroused and less angry than were either the control or after-provocation subjects. The results of this study suggest that one reason why attributing the harmful acts of another to external factors inhibits aggression is because this type of attribution inhibits anger.

Inferences about Consequences

Like all other forms of social behavior, people's aggressive behavior is influenced by their beliefs concerning the consequences of their acts (Bandura, 1973). If people infer that aggressiveness will provoke retaliation, they generally aggress less than if they infer that no retaliation is possible (e.g., Dengerink, 1976; Shortell, Epstein and Taylor, 1970). However, anticipated punishment or retaliation does not always inhibit aggression. Zillmann (1979) suggests that when individuals are in a highly aroused state (as is often the case when aggression is involved), inferences concerning anticipated consequences, like other cognitive inhibitors, are less likely to be activated or at least are less likely to guide behavior.

Salience of the Victim's Pain Cues
Earlier we learned that visible distress cues evoke more help more quickly than do less salient cues, presumably because they generate more empathy. This finding would seem to imply that the perception of pain in the target of aggression would produce an inhibition in aggression. The experience of empathy seems incompatible with aggressive behavior (Baron, 1977; 1983). However, from a drive-theory perspective, we might predict that pain cues would, in fact, increase aggressive behavior, since they would serve to reinforce the aggressive drive of the individual (Feshbach, 1970). The evidence is generally consistent with the inhibition prediction (e.g., Geen, 1970; Rule and Leger, 1976). Geen (1970) found, for example, that males who had been angered as well as those who were treated considerately behaved less aggressively toward their antagonist when he expressed anguished cries than when he suffered in silence.

SELF-AWARENESS AND SENSITIVITY TO PERSONAL STANDARDS

Earlier we saw that self-focus and awareness of personal standards have been found to affect altruistic behavior. These cognitive states also have been found to affect aggression. Research pertinent to this issue is found most commonly in investigations of two phenomena: (1) deindividuation and (2) objective self-awareness.

Deindividuation and Aggression
In most situations an individual's attention fluctuates between the environment and the self. In some situations, however, an individual will be basically unaware of himself or herself. A person in such a state is said to be *deindividuated* (Festinger, Pepitone, and Newcomb, 1952). Diener (1980) recently defined deindividuation as a lack of self-awareness and self-regulation caused by situational factors such as anonymity, arousal, and sensory overload. The most common finding to emerge from research on deindividuation is that people aggress more when they are in a deindividuated state than when they are not (see Diener, 1980, for a review). A well-known study by Zimbardo (1969) is illustrative of this research. In this experiment college women were deindividuated by

shrowding them in hoods and placing them in groups of four in a dark room. In contrast, other women were "individuated" by wearing large prominent name tags and taking part in the experiment in a bright room. Zimbardo found that the deindividuated women delivered longer shocks than the individuated women when given an opportunity to aggress against a victim. Moreover, although individuated women administered fewer shocks to an undeserving victim than to a deserving victim, deindividuated women did not discriminate between the two types of victims. The most common explanation for the effects of deindividuation is that a deindividuated individual is less aware of personal standards and less concerned with self- and other evaluation than an individual in a non-deindividuated state. It bears pointing out, however, that a person's tendency to behave against norms when deindividuated does not always result in increased antisocial behavior; it also may lead to more prosocial and affectionate behavior (Diener, 1980).

Self-Consciousness and Aggression
Research on deindividuation is concerned with the conditions that lead individuals to lose their identities and self-standards and with the consequences of this loss of self-awareness. Research generated by Duval and Wicklund's (1972) objective self-awareness theory is concerned with just the opposite issue: What happens to people who are made more aware of themselves? We have already seen that self-awareness increases the probability of altruistic behavior. Self-focused individuals also tend to aggress less than those whose attention is focused more externally (e.g., Scheier, Fenigstein, and Buss, 1974). Self-focus appears to make individuals both more aware of their internal standards and more inclined to act in accordance with these standards. However, self-standards do not always prohibit aggressive behavior, as a study by Carver (1974) demonstrates. On the basis of a preliminary attitude assessment, Carver divided male subjects into those who favored physical punishment and those who did not. He then required subjects to deliver shocks to a student each time the student made a mistake on a learning task. Subjects were free to select the intensity of the shock. A state of high self-awareness was induced by placing a mirror in front of the subjects. As expected, increased self-awareness produced a diminution in the intensity of shocks delivered by those who were opposed to punishment; however, it produced a substantial intensification in the severity of shocks delivered by those who favored

punishment. In both groups of subjects, increased self-consciousness appeared to produce a greater adherence to personal values.

THE INTERACTION BETWEEN AFFECTIVE AND COGNITIVE MEDIATORS OF ALTRUISM AND AGGRESSION

Although we have discussed affective and cognitive determinants of altruistic and aggressive behavior separately, they usually, if not always, are interdependent. In this section we review research that has investigated the interaction between affective and cognitive processes and the effect of these interactions on altruistic and aggressive behavior.

GENERAL AROUSAL AND COGNITION

It has been known for many years that level of arousal affects behavioral (Hebb, 1966) and perceptual performance (Easterbrook, 1959). The familiar inverted U-shaped curve outlines the general form of the relationship. Research has shown that the more complex the cognitive function guiding an altruistic or aggressive act, the greater is the potential influence of arousal. In discussing aggression, Zillmann (1982) has proposed that complex functions such as anticipating consequences, making attributions, and forming moral judgments are more likely than simple functions such as recognition and identification to be disrupted under conditions of high arousal. However, as Easterbrook (1954) has suggested, high levels of arousal may also disrupt even simple perceptual attentional processes.

The interaction between cognitive and affective factors is featured prominently in the Piliavin *et al.* (1981) model of emergency helping. According to these investigators, individuals process information about potential helping situations "preattentively." This initial scanning may produce one of three outcomes: (1) the conclusion that nothing of significance has happened, (2) the conclusion that something worth attending to has occurred, and (3) the perception that an emergency is in process. In cases where individuals conclude that something interesting has happened, they experience an affectively positive orienting response that is associated with cognitive and attentional openness and the intake of information. In contrast, the perception of an emergency produces extreme levels of aversive arousal and a constriction of attention.

Piliavin *et al.* (1981) review research showing a positive relationship between (1) the severity of an emergency, (2) the clarity of a victim's distress, and (3) the degree of involvement with a victim, the magnitude of psychophysiological arousal, and the probability of helping. In the Piliavin *et al.* model, arousal that is attributed to the distress of another is expected to mediate helping, whereas arousal attributed to other factors is not. In situations involving severe emergencies, the effect of arousal is to cause attention to become focused on the dominant feature of the situation—namely the victim's plight—and to preempt the usual rational weighing of cost-benefit considerations (see Gaertner and Dovidio, 1977). In situations that do not involve severe emergencies, arousal that is construed as "empathic concern" (see Coke, Batson, and McDavis, 1978) mediates helping.

MOOD AND COGNITION

In addition to investigating the effect of extreme arousal on helping and harming behavior, investigators have explored the effects of lighter moods. Most of the research in this area has focused on altruistic behavior. Moods have been induced in a variety of ways. Investigators have found that experiences such as receiving an unexpected gift (Isen and Levin, 1972; Levin and Isen, 1975), enjoying a sunny day (Cunningham, 1979), and undergoing success (Berkowitz and Connor, 1966; Isen, 1970; Kazdin and Bryan, 1971) increase the probability of altruistic behavior; and that negative experiences such as failure diminish the disposition to help (see Rosenhan, Karylowski, Salovey, and Hargis, 1981, for a review).

A number of explanations for the influence of mood on altruistic behavior have been suggested. Events such as success have been hypothesized to produce, among other things, a "glow of good will" (Berkowitz, 1972), a generalized feeling of benevolence (Rosenhan, Underwood, and Moore, 1973), an increased attraction to others (Byrne, 1971), and a wish to prolong a positive state (Masters and Furman, 1970). The detrimental impact of failure on helping also has been attributed to a variety of factors including the tendency of failure to lead to generalized pessimism, perceived unattractiveness, and self-preoccupation (Cialdini and Kenrick, 1976; Moore, Underwood, and Rosehan, 1973; Underwood, Froming, and Moore, 1977).

Isen and her colleagues (Isen, Shalker, Clark, and Karp, 1978) suggest that changes in mood induce changes in the cognitive state of people that, in turn, mediate behavioral changes. According to Isen *et al.*, positive moods evoke positive cognitions. For example, Clark and Isen, 1981 found that when people are in a good mood, they are more likely to recall positive experiences involving help in the past, be more optimistic about their ability to help, and so forth. In a similar vein, Hornstein (1976) has shown that bad moods can adversely affect thought and behavior. In one study Hornstein arranged for subjects to overhear a bogus newscast in which a flagrant instance of inhumanity was reported. He found that subjects who heard this newscast subsequently endorsed a more pessimistic view of human nature, were more likely to find defendants in hypothetical trials guilty, were more competitive in a task situation, and displayed more social discrimination than control subjects. Hornstein explained these findings by contending that bad news induces pessimism in people that causes them to "look out for themselves" and show little compassion for others. The perceived efficacy of help or punishment may also be reduced when one is in a bad or fearful mood (Miller and Vidmar, 1981; Vidmar and Miller, 1980).

The plausibility of the positive association between moods and behavior notwithstanding, a number of studies have found that bad moods sometimes mediate good behaviors. Several investigations have induced negative states in subjects by persuading them to knock over index cards, ruin an experiment, destroy equipment, lie, or "shock" a confederate (see Carlsmith and Gross, 1969; Freedman, Wallington and Bless, 1967; Rawlings, 1968; Wallington, 1973). These studies quite consistently have found that individuals induced to transgress are more likely to comply with subsequent requests for help both from victims of the transgression and from noninvolved persons than individuals who have not been induced to transgress. Freedman (1970) explained these results by positing that the negative state intervening between transgression and compliance stems from a sense of guilt and that the request for subsequent help provides individuals with an opportunity to assuage this guilt. Other investigators have suggested that transgressing evokes a reduction of self-esteem and that the function of subsequent compliance is to raise, at least partially, the temporarily lowered self-esteem of the transgressor (see Apsler, 1975; Carlsmith and Gross, 1969; Krebs, 1970, 1982a; McMillen, 1971).

The self-esteem explanation seems somewhat more plausible than the guilt explanation because it is better able to explain why transgressors are as, or even more, disposed to help third parties than to help the victims of their transgressions (Carlsmith and Gross, 1969). It is not clear why guilt generated in one relationship should affect behavior in other relationships; however, displaying laudatory behavior in front of anybody may raise one's self-esteem. Indeed, helping a noninvolved person might even be *more* effective in repairing a damaged self-image than helping a victim.

Cialdini, Darby and Vincent (1973) have questioned the validity of both the guilt and the self-esteem accounts of the relationship between transgression and compliance, noting that these accounts do not supply a plausible explanation for the finding that individuals who witness another being mistreated are as disposed to engage in subsequent helping as individuals who are responsible for the harm (Konecni, 1972; Rawlings, 1968; Regan, 1971).

Cialdini *et al.* (1973) offer a "negative relief model" to account for the reactions of both the doer of harm and the observer. This model contains two assumptions: (1) the sight of a harmed other causes one to feel bad (regardless of whether one is responsible for the harm or not), and (2) helping is one means, among many, that people use to make themselves feel good. The most provocative prediction to which this model gives rise is that any pleasant event or experience will both dissipate the negative feeling caused by harm and nullify the need to help. Employing a tried-and-true manipulation of transgression, Cialdini *et al.* exposed subjects to a rigged accident in which a deck of computer cards was dumped on the floor. These investigators led one-half of the subjects to believe they were responsible for the accident and the other half to believe that a confederate was responsible. Some subjects were then exposed to an event (praise or an unexpected and noncontingent sum of money) designed to offer "relief" from their negative state. The dependent measure in this study was the amount of time subjects were willing to volunteer to help a fellow student with a class project. In line with the negative-relief model, subjects who underwent a positive experience did not differ from controls in their helping response, whether they were responsible for the transgression or not. Subjects who did not undergo a positive experience offered significantly more help.

The negative-relief model supplies a parsimonious explanation for the relationship between both doing harm and observing harm and offering subsequent help. However, the results would seem to imply that people who feel bad for any reason ought to be more disposed to behave altruistically than those who do not—an implication that has not been supported by relevant research (Isen, 1970; Thompson, Cowan, and Rosenhan, 1980; Underwood, Froming, and Moore, 1977). A partial resolution of the inconsistency in findings on the effects of negative moods is to posit that experiences that make people feel bad about their *lot* in the world tend to reduce subsequent helping behavior; whereas experiences that make people feel bad about *themselves* tend to increase subsequent helping behavior, provided that the act of helping elevates their self-esteem.

THE LABELING OF AFFECTIVE STATES

Various psychologists have contended that emotional experiences result from inferences that are made on the basis of (1) visceral, physiological, and motoric cues and (2) the contexts in which these cues occur (Mandler, 1975; Schachter and Singer, 1962; Zillmann, 1979). According to this model, a central determinant of how individuals behave is how they label their affective experiences. In support of this idea, research has indicated that frustrated subjects who are induced to attribute their arousal to sources other than the frustration do not aggress as much as subjects who are not so induced (Baron and Bell, 1975; Geen, Rakosky, and Pigg, 1972; Harris and Huang, 1974). Conversely, inducing subjects to label arousal produced by means other than frustration as anger has been found to mediate an increase in aggression (Zillmann, 1979). Further, showing subjects bogus physiological evidence indicating that they are angry has been found to produce an increase in their level of aggression (Berkowitz and Page, 1967; Berkowitz and Geen, 1967). Of course, simply inferring that one is angry does not ensure that one will aggress. Among the factors that determine whether anger will be translated into aggressive behavior are the individual's perceptions of the justifiability of his or her anger (Berkowitz and Turner, 1974), the individual's expectation of being punished or receiving disapproval, and the individual's own evaluation of aggression (Bandura, 1973).

Dienstbier, Hillman, Lehnhoff, Hillman, and Valkenaar (1975) have provided an impressive general demonstration of the impact of labeling on antisocial behavior. These researchers induced children to commit a transgression and then provided them with the information that they felt either "guilty" or "fearful." The children behaved differently depending on the label they were assigned. Recently a similar point about the specificity of mood states and labels was made by Cunningham, Steinberg, and Gireu (1980).

There is a close parallel between studies on the attribution of anger and studies on the attribution of empathy. When individuals are led to misattribute victim-provoked arousal to another source, they help less (Batson and Coke, 1981). Conversely, when individuals are aroused by extraneous means and induced to attribute their arousal to the distress of another, they help more (Mueller and Donnerstein, 1981). Finally, when individuals are led to infer that they are more disturbed by the suffering of another than they actually are, they have been found to increase their level of helping (Kidd and Berkowitz, 1976).

Why should labels such as anger, empathy, guilt, and shame influence behavior? One possibility is that these labels serve as cues to appropriate action. The label of anger/empathy may lead to the impulse to aggress/help in the same way the label of hunger leads to the impulse to eat. Sequences of behavior often begin with an affective state. These sequences often resemble what Abelson and his colleagues have called scripts (Abelson, 1981; Schank and Abelson, 1977). There is, for example, the jealous-rage script, and the frustrated-employee script, and the empathic-bystander script. It is possible that the labeling of an emotional state initiates scripted sequences of behavior: deciding that one is angry predisposes one to play out an aggressive script.

A phenomenon that has not received much attention in the literature is resistance to labels. For instance, most people do not like to appear angry or jealous and try to control their behavior when they infer that they are in these states. Indeed, many people may even resist the inference that they are experiencing an emotion that is discrepant with their self-image. By refusing to accept that they are in a particular affective state (by resisting the label), they may succeed in constraining the behavior associated with it.

CONCLUSION

The basic questions addressed in this chapter have been: Why do people behave altruistically? and, Why do people behave aggressively? We have organized the answers to these questions offered by social scientists in terms of three levels of generality—biological and cultural, personal and situational, and cognitive and affective. The central assumptions of this conceptual framework are that although biological and cultural, personality and situational, and affective and cognitive factors are inextricably bound, it is useful to distinguish between them on the basis of their proximity to behavior and the generality of their effects. We have suggested that altruistic and aggressive behaviors always originate from an interaction between interactions (see Fig. 1). Although scientists investigate the effect of specific variables, it is highly integrated, infinitely complex individuals who help and harm others.

Although social psychological research on both altruism and aggression initially focused on the influence of situational variables, recent research has shifted toward a consideration of cognitive and affective mediating variables. There are at least three reasons why we can expect future research to focus more exclusively on the interaction between cognitive and affective variables:

1. The trend in the field of social psychology in general to focus on the interaction between cognitive and affective variables (see Markus and Zajonc, Chapter 4),

2. The growing tendency of researchers interested in cognitive and affective processes to choose the behaviors of altruism and aggression as the testing grounds for their hypotheses,

3. The epistemological tendency for individuals to feel that the more proximal the locus of a determinant of behavior, the greater is its capacity to supply an explanation for the behavior.

Considering research on altruism and aggression in the same context casts the similarities and differences between these two areas of inquiry in an interesting perspective. We have been impressed by the parallels between research on these seemingly polar opposite behaviors—parallels in the types of factors that determine them and in the conceptual and methodological problems that have impeded their elucidation. However, we have noted differences as well. Perhaps the most striking contrast between the two areas of investigation lies in the different theoretical and empirical attention that investigators have given to cognitive as opposed to affective mediators of altruism and aggression. Investigators appear to assume that affective factors are more influential in the determination of aggressive behaviors than altruistic behaviors and that cognitive factors are more influential in the determination of altruistic behaviors than aggressive behaviors. As a result, there is much more research on the relationship between altruism and internal standards, perspective-taking ability, moral reasoning, attri-

bution, and other cognitive processes than there is on the relationship between aggression and such cognitive variables. Further, although several investigators have proposed decision-making models of altruism, none has proposed a decision-making model of aggression. On the converse side, there is considerable literature on the physiological, neurological, and hormonal basis of aggressive behavior (Baron, 1977; Geen and Donnerstein, 1983), but virtually none in the domain of altruism. And although it is common to speculate on the chromosomal, neurological, or physiological abnormalities in people who have lived violent lives or who suddenly become violent (see Marks and Ervin, 1970), rarely is there such speculation about people who have lived saintly lives or who have engaged in acts of heroism.

It is possible that the emphasis in research reflects the relative power of cognitive and affective factors in the determination of altruistic and aggressive behavior. However, the asymmetry in research may also reflect "original-sin" types of bias that exist in the naive assumptions of psychologists. Or it may stem primarily from the differences in the types of questions that have guided work in the two areas. For example, social scientists may be primarily interested in those factors that override social norms and internal standards in the study of aggression but that activate them in the study of altruism.

Despite an impressive body of empirical findings in the investigation of altruism and aggression, there is no sign of an over-arching theory emerging in either area. This is not necessarily a failing, however, since the behaviors subsumed under the rubrics of altruism and aggression are so diverse that even if a single theory could encompass them all, it would be more a theory of social behavior than a theory of altruism and aggression. The decision-making models of Piliavin *et al.* (1981) and Schwartz (1977) constitute laudable attempts to integrate determinants of altruistic behavior; however, even the most elaborate models seem destined to supply at best a limited synthesis (see Krebs, 1982e).

Over the years, investigators increasingly have focused on particular types of prosocial behavior such as resource allocation (Lerner and Lerner, 1981) and rescue behavior (Piliavin *et al.,* 1981), and particular types of determinants (e.g., personal norms, justice reasoning, anger, empathy, and reinforcement). Although the case for subareas or subtypes of aggression has been made by almost every major theorist (e.g., Bandura, 1973; Berkowitz, 1978; Buss, 1961; Feshbach, 1970), distinct areas of research have not really emerged in the study of aggression.

In addition to the focus on particular types of helping and harming behaviors, there is a tendency in current research for investigators to employ more non-laboratory-based and nonexperimental research methodologies. Bronfenbrenner (1977) has characterized developmental psychology as "the science of the strange behavior of children in strange situations with strange adults for the briefest possible periods of time" (p. 513). The same may be said of traditional social psychological investigations of altruism and aggression in adults. The heyday of the manipulation of external, situationally based variables and the assessment of their effect on unrepresentative laboratory-based measures of altruism and aggression appears to be declining. The trend is toward more naturalistic investigators of more common manifestations of the ways in which people help and harm one another. In the future we may expect investigators to attend increasingly to the give and take of helping and harming in everyday life (see Bar-Tal, 1984).

Finally, and associated with the trend away from exclusively laboratory-based research, investigators appear to be focusing increasingly on prominent social issues and problems. Consider, for example, recent research on the influence of television on pro- and anti-social behavior (Liebert, Sprafkin, and Davidson, 1982), correlates of organ and blood donations (Rushton, 1984), the influence of pornography on violent behavior (Malamuth and Donnerstein, 1983), the social psychological causes of rape (Cann, Calhoun, Selby, and King, 1981), and the interpersonal determination of domestic violence (Dutton and Painter, 1981).

In summary, we should say that although social psychologists have made considerable gains toward the identification of the psychological basis of altruistic and aggressive behaviors, the discipline is poorly equipped to answer many of the questions about these phenomena asked by the average individual. Some of the most interesting questions about altruism and aggression are biological, ethical, and philosophical in nature, not social psychological. The question of whether we humans are basically good or evil will never rest exclusively in the domain of any one discipline.

REFERENCES

Abelson, R. P. (1981). Psychological status of the script concept. *Amer. Psychologist, 36,* 715–729.

Ajzen, I., and M. Fishbein (1977). Attitude-behavior relations: a theoretical analysis and review of empirical research. *Psychol. Bull., 84,* 888–918.

Alcock, J. (1979). *Animal behavior: an evolutionary approach.* Sunderland, Mass.: Sinauer Associates, Inc.

Alexander, R. D. (1961). Aggressiveness, territoriality, and sexual behavior in field crickets (Orthoptera: Gryllidae), *Behavior, 17,* 130–223.

———— (1979). Evolution and culture. In N. A. Chagnon and W. Irons (Eds.), *Evolutionary biology and human social behavior: an anthropological perspective.* N. Scituate, Mass.: Duxbury Press.

Allen, N. J., and J. P. Rushton (In press). The personality of community volunteers: a review. *J. Voluntary Action Res.*

Anderson, J. (1974). Bystander intervention in an assault. Paper presented at the meeting of the Southeastern Psychological Association, Hollywood, Florida, May 3rd.

Apsler, R. (1975). Effects of embarrassment on behavior toward others. *J. Pers. soc. Psychol., 32,* 145–153.

Ardrey, R. (1961). *African Genesis.* New York: Antheum.

Aronfreed, J. (1968). *Conduct and conscience.* New York: Academic Press.

Aronfreed, J., and V. Paskal (1966). The development of sympathetic behavior in children: an experimental test of a two-phase hypothesis. Unpublished manuscript, University of Pennsylvania.

Aronfreed, S. (1976). Moral development from the standpoint of general psychological theory. In T. Lickman (Ed.), *Moral development and behavior.* New York: Holt, Rinehart & Winston.

Ashton, N. L., and L. J. Severy (1976). Arousal and costs in bystander intervention. *Pers. soc. Psychol. Bull., 2,* 268–272.

Axelrod, R., and W. D. Hamilton (1981). The evolution of cooperation. *Science, 211,* 1390–1396.

Bandura, A. (1973). *Aggression: a social learning analysis.* Englewood Cliffs, N.J.: Prentice-Hall.

———— (1977a). *Social learning theory.* Englewood Cliffs, N. J.: Prentice-Hall.

———— (1977b). Self-efficacy: toward a unifying theory of behavioral change. *Psychol. Rev., 84,* 191–215.

———— (1977c). Psychological mechanisms of aggression. *Conference on Human Ecology: claims and limits of a new discipline.* Bad Homburg.

Bar-Tal, D. (1976). *Pro-social behavior: theory on research.* Washington, D.C.: Hemisphere.

———— (1984). American study of helping behavior—what? why? and where? In E. Staub, D. Bar-Tal, J. Karylowski and J. Reykowski (Eds.), *Development and maintenance of prosocial behavior: international perspectives.* New York: Plenum Press.

Barash, D. P. (1977). *Sociobiology and behavior.* New York: Elsevier.

Baron, R. A. (1971a). Aggression as a function of audience presence and prior anger arousal. *J. Pers. soc. Psychol., 7,* 515–523.

———— (1971b). Aggression as a function of magnitude of victim's pain cues, level of prior anger arousal, and aggressor-victim similarity. *J. Pers. soc. Psychol., 18,* 48–54.

_____ (1972). Aggression as a function of ambient temperature and prior anger arousal. *J. Pers. soc. Psychol., 21,* 183–189.

_____ (1974). The aggression-inhibiting influence of heightened sexual arousal. *J. Pers. soc. Psychol., 29,* 117–124.

_____ (1977). *Human aggression.* New York: Plenum.

_____ (1983). The reduction of human aggression: an incompatible response strategy. In R. G. Geen and E. Donnerstein (Eds.), *Aggression: theoretical and empirical reviews.* New York: Academic Press.

Baron, R. A., and P. A. Bell (1975). Aggression and heat: mediating effects of prior provocation and exposure to an aggressive model. *J. Pers. soc. Psychol., 31,* 825–832.

_____ (1976). The influence of ambient temperature, negative affect, and a cooling drink on physical aggression. *J. Pers. soc. Psychol., 33,* 245–255.

_____ (1977). Sexual arousal and aggression by males: effects of type of erotic stimuli and prior provocation. *J. Pers. soc. Psychol., 35,* 79–87.

Barrett, D. E., and M. R. Narrow (1977). Prosocial behavior, social inferential ability and assertiveness in children. *Child Development, 48,* 475–481.

Barton, E. J., and F. R. Ascione (1979). Sharing in preschool children: facilitation, stimulus generalization, response generalization, and maintenance. *J. appl. behav. Analysis, 12,* 417–430.

Batson, C. D., P. J. Cochran, M. Biederman, J. L. Blosser, M. J. Ryan, and B. Vogt (1978). Failure to help when in a hurry: callousness or conflict? *Pers. soc. Psychol. Bull., 4,* 97–101.

Batson, C. D., and J. S. Coke (1981). Empathy: a source of altruistic motivation for helping? In J. P. Rushton and R. M. Sorrentino (Eds.), *Altruism and helping behavior.* Hillsdale, N.J.: Erlbaum.

Batson, C. D., B. D. Duncan, P. Ackerman, T. Buckley, and K. Birch (1981). Is empathic emotion a source of altruistic motivation? *J. Pers. soc. Psychol., 40,* 290–302.

Batson, C. D., A. C. Harris, K. D. McCaul, M. Davis, and T. Schmidt (1979). Compassion or compliance: alternative dispositional attributions for one's helping behavior. *Soc. Psychol. Quart., 42,* 405–409.

Bem, D. J. (1972). Self-perception theory. In L. Berkowitz (Ed.), *Advances in experimental social psychology.* Vol. 6. New York: Academic Press.

Berger, S. M. (1962). Conditioning through vicarious instigation. *Psychol. Rev., 69,* 450–466.

Berkowitz, L. (1962). *Aggression: a social psychological analysis.* New York: McGraw-Hill.

_____ (1964). Aggressive cues in aggressive behavior and hostility catharsis. *Psychol. Rev., 71,* 104–122.

_____ (1967). Stimulus qualities of the target of aggression: a further study. *J. Pers. soc. Psychol., 5,* 364–368.

_____ (1969). The frustration-aggression hypothesis revisited. In L. Berkowitz (Ed.), *Roots of aggression.* New York: Atherton Press.

_____ (1972). Social norms, feelings and other factors affecting helping behavior and altruism. In L. Berkowitz (Ed.), *Advances in experimental social psychology.* Vol. 6. New York: Academic Press.

_____ (1974). Some determinants of impulsive aggression: the role of mediated associations with reinforcements for aggression. *Psychol. Rev., 81,* 165–176.

_____ (1978). Whatever happened to the frustration-aggression hypothesis? *Amer. behav. Scientist, 21,* 691–708.

_____ (1980). *A survey of social psychology,* 2nd ed. New York: Holt, Rinehart & Winston.

Berkowitz, L., S. T. Cochran, and M. C. Embree (1981). Physical pain and the goal of aversively stimulated aggression. *J. Pers. soc. Psychol., 40,* 687–700.

Berkowitz, L., and W. H. Connor (1966). Success, failure and social responsibility. *J. Pers. soc. Psychol., 4,* 664–669.

Berkowitz, L., and L. R. Daniels (1963). Responsibility and dependency. *J. abnorm. soc. Psychol., 66,* 429–436.

Berkowitz, L., and E. Donnerstein (1982). External validity is more than skin deep: some answers to the criticisms of laboratory experiments. *Amer. Psychologist, 37,* 245–257.

Berkowitz, L., and R. G. Geen (1966). Film violence and the cue properties of available targets. *J. Pers. soc. Psychol., 3,* 525–530.

Berkowitz, L., and A. Le Page (1967). Weapons as aggression-eliciting stimuli. *J. Pers. soc. Psychol., 7,* 202–207.

Berkowitz, L., and K. G. Lutterman (1968). The traditionally social responsibility personality. *Publ. Opin. Quart., 32,* 169–187.

Berkowitz, L., and C. W. Turner (1974). Perceived anger level, instigating agent and aggression. In H. London and R. E. Nisbett (Eds.), *Cognitive alteration of feeling states.* Chicago: Aldine Press.

Bickman, L. (1971). The effect of another bystander's ability to help on bystander intervention in an emergency. *J. exp. soc. Psychol., 7,* 367–380.

_____ (1972). Social influence and diffusion of responsibility in an emergency. *J. exp. soc. Psychol., 8,* 438–445.

Bickman, L., and L. Kamzan (1973). The effect of race and need on helping behavior. *J. soc. Psychol., 89,* 73–77.

Blake, R., M. Rosenbaum, and R. Duryea (1955). Giftgiving as a function of group standards. *Hum. Relat., 8,* 61–73.

Blasi, A. (1980). Bridging moral cognition and moral action: a critical review of the literature. *Psychol. Bull., 88,* 1–45.

Bowers, K. S. (1973). Situationalism in psychology: an analysis and a critique. *Psychol. Rev., 80,* 307–336.

Brehm, J. W., and A. H. Cole (1966). Effect of a favor which reduces freedom. *J. Pers. soc. Psychol., 3,* 420–426.

Brickman, P., V. C. Rabinowitz, J. Karuza, D. Coates, E. Cohn, and L. Kidder (1982). Models of helping and coping. *Amer. Psychol., 37,* 368–384.

Bridgeman, D. L. (1983). *The nature of prosocial development: interdisciplinary theories and strategies.* New York: Academic Press.

Bronfenbrenner, U. (1977). Toward an experimental ecology of human development. *Amer. Psychol., 32,* 513–531.

Brown, J. S., and I. E. Farber (1951). Emotions conceptualized as intervening variables—with suggestions toward a theory of frustration. *Psychol. Bull., 48,* 465.

Bryan, J. H. (1972). Why children help: a review. *J. soc. Issues, 28,* 87–104.

Bryan, J. H., and M. J. Test (1967). Models and helping: naturalistic studies in aiding behavior. *J. Pers. soc. Psychol., 6,* 400–407.

Burnstein, E., and P. Worchel (1962). Arbitrariness of frustration and its consequences for aggression in a social situation. *J. Pers., 30,* 528–541.

Burton, R. V. (1963). Generality of honesty reconsidered. *Psychol. Rev., 70,* 481–499.

——— (1976). Honesty and dishonesty. In T. Lickona (Ed.), *Moral development and behavior: theory, research and social issues.* New York: Holt, Rinehart & Winston.

Buss, A. H. (1961). *The psychology of aggression.* New York: Wiley.

——— (1966). The effect of harm on subsequent aggression. *J. exp. Res. Pers., 1,* 249–255.

Byrne, D. (1971). *The attraction paradigm.* New York: Academic Press.

Campbell, D. T. (1965). Ethnocentric and other altruistic motives. In D. Levine (Ed.), *Nebraska symposium on motivation.* Lincoln: Univ. of Nebraska Press.

——— (1975). On the conflict between biological and social evolution and between psychology and moral tradition. *Amer. Psychol., 30,* 1103–1126.

——— (1978). On the genetics of altruism and the counterhedonic components in human culture. In L. Wispé (Ed.), *Altruism, sympathy, and helping.* New York: Academic Press.

——— (1983). The two distinct routes beyond kin selection to ultrasociality: implications for the humanities and social sciences. In D. L. Bridgeman (Ed.), *The nature of prosocial behavior.* New York: Academic Press.

Candee, D., and L. Kohlberg (1982). The relationship of moral judgement to moral action. Paper read at the 90th Annual Meeting of American Psychological Association.

Cann, A., L. G. Calhoun, J. W. Selby, and H. E. King (Eds.), (1981). Rape. *J. soc. Issues, 37*(4).

Carlsmith, J. M., and A. Gross (1969). Some effects of guilt on compliance. *J. Pers. soc. Psychol., 11,* 240–244.

Carver, C. S. (1974). Facilitation of physical aggression through objective self-awareness. *J. exp. soc. Psychol., 10,* 365–370.

Christy, P. R., D. M. Gelfand, and D. P. Hartmann (1971). Effects of competition-induced frustration on two classes of modeled behavior. *Develop. Psychol., 5,* 104–111.

Cialdini, R. B., B. L. Darby, and J. E. Vincent (1973). Transgression and altruism: a case for hedonism. *J. exp. soc. Psychol., 9,* 502–516.

Cialdini, R. B., and D. T. Kenrick (1976). Altruism as hedonism: a social development perspective on the relationship of negative mood state and helping. *J. Pers. soc. Psychol., 34,* 907–914.

Clark, M. S., and A. M. Isen (1981). Toward understanding the relationship between feeling states and social behavior. In A. H. Hastorf and A. M. Isen (Eds.), *Cognitive social psychology.* New York: Elsevier/North-Holland.

Clark, R. D. III, and L. E. Word (1972). Why don't bystanders help? Because of ambiguity. *J. Pers. soc. Psychol., 24,* 392–400.

Cloak, F. T. Jr. (1977). Comment on "The adaptive significance of cultural behavior." *Human Ecology, 5,* 49–52.

Coke, J. S., C. D. Batson, and K. McDavis (1978). Empathic mediation of helping: a two stage model. *J. Pers. soc. Psychol., 36,* 752–766.

Crook, J. H. (1968). The nature and function of territorial aggression. In A. Montagu (Ed.), *Man and aggression.* New York: Oxford Univ. Press. Pp. 141–178.

Cunningham, M. R. (1979). Weather, mood, and helping behavior: the sunshine samaritan. *J. Pers. soc. Psychol., 37,* 1947–1956.

Cunningham, M. R., J. Steinberg, and R. Greu (1980). Wanting to and having to help: separate motivations for positive mood and guilt-induced helping. *J. Pers. soc. Psychol., 38,* 181–192.

Damon, W. (1976). *The social world of the child.* San Francisco: Jossey-Bass.

Darley, J. H., A. E. Teger, and L. D. Lewis (1973). Do groups always inhibit individuals' responses to potential emergencies? *J. Pers. soc. Psychol., 26,* 395–399.

Darley, J. M., and B. Latane (1968). Bystander intervention in emergencies: diffusion of responsibility. *J. Pers. soc. Psychol., 8,* 377–383.

Dawkins, R. (1978). *The selfish gene.* New York: Oxford Univ. Press.

Dengerink, H. A. (1976). Personality variables as mediators of attack-instigated aggression. In R. G. Geen and E. C. O'Neal (Eds.), *Perspectives on aggression.* New York: Academic Press.

Dengerink, H. A., M. R. O'Leary, and K. H. Kasner (1975). Individual differences in aggressive responses to attack: internal-external locus of control and field dependence-independence. *J. Res. Pers., 9,* 191–199.

Denner, B. (1968). Did a crime occur? Should I inform anyone? A study of deception. *J. Pers., 36,* 454–466.

Deutsch, M., and H. B. Gerard (1955). A study of normative and informational social influences on individual judgments. *J. abnorm. soc. Psychol., 51,* 629–636.

Diener, E. (1980). Deindividuation: the absence of self-awareness and self-regulations in group members. In P. B. Paulus (Ed.), *The psychology of group influence.* Hillsdale, N.J.: Erlbaum.

Dienstbier, R. A., D. Hillman, J. Lehnhoff, J. Hillman, and M. C. Valkenaar (1975). An emotion-attribution approach to moral behavior: interfacing cognitive and avoidance theories of moral development. *Psychol. Rev., 82,* 299–315.

Dipboye, R. L. (1977). Alternative approaches to deindividuation. *Psychol. Bull., 84,* 1057–1075.

Dlugokinski, E., and I. J. Firestone (1973). Congruence among four methods of measuring other-centeredness. *Child Development, 44,* 304–308.

——— (1974). Other-centeredness and susceptibility to charitable appeals: effects of perceived discipline. *Develop. Psychol., 10,* 21–28.

Dollard, J., L. W. Doob, M. E. Miller, O. H. Mowrer, and R. R. Sears (1939). *Frustration and aggression.* New Haven: Yale Univ. Press.

Donnerstein, E., M. Donnerstein, and R. Evans (1975). Erotic stimuli and aggression: facilitation or inhibition? *J. Pers. soc. Psychol., 32,* 237–244.

Doob, A. N., and L. Wood (1972). Catharsis and aggression: the effects of annoyance and retaliation on aggressive behavior. *J. Pers. soc. Psychol., 22,* 156–162.

Downey, J. (1973). *An interference theory of the catharsis of aggression.* Unpublished Ph.D. dissertation. Univ. of Missouri.

Durham, W. H. (1979). Toward a coevolutionary theory of biology and culture. In N. A. Chagnon and W. Irons (Eds.), *Evolutionary biology and human social behavior: an anthropological perspective.* N. Scituate, Mass.: Duxbury Press.

Dutton, D. G. (1976). Tokenism, reverse discrimination and egalitarianism in intersocial behavior. *J. soc. Issues, 32,* 93–108.

Dutton, D. G., and S. Painter (1981). Traumatic bonding: the development of emotional attachments in battered women and other relationships of intermittent abuse. *Victimology 6,* 139–155.

Duval, S., V. H. Duval, and R. Neely (1979). Self-focus, felt responsibility and helping behavior. *J. Pers. soc. Psychol., 37,* 1769–1778.

Duval, S., and R. A. Wicklund (1972). *A theory of objective self-awareness.* New York: Academic Press.

Dyck, R., and B. G. Rule (1978). The effect of causal attributions concerning attack on retaliation. *J. Pers. soc. Psychol., 36,* 521–529.

Easterbrook, J. A. (1959). The effect of emotion on cue utilization and the organization of behavior. *Psychol. Rev., 66,* 183–201.

Eibl-Eibesfeld, I. (1975). *Ethology, the biology of behavior.* New York: Holt, Rinehart, & Winston.

Eisenberg, N. (1982). *The development of prosocial behavior.* New York: Academic Press.

Endler, N. S., and J. M. Hunt (1969). Generalizability of contributions from sources of variance in the S–R inventories of anxiousness. *J. Pers., 37,* 1–24.

Endler, N. S., and D. Magnusson (1976). Toward an interactional psychology of personality. *Psychol. Bull., 83,* 956–976.

Enzle, M. E., and D. Schopflocher (1978). Instigation of attribution processes by attributional questions. *Pers. soc. Psychol. Bull., 4,* 595–599.

Epstein, S. (1979). The stability of behavior: I. on predicting most of the people much of the time. *J. Pers. soc. Psychol., 37,* 1097–1126.

———— (1980). The stability of behavior: II. implications for psychological research. *Amer. Psychol., 35,* 790–806.

Fehr, R. S., and J. A. Stern (1970). Peripheral psychological variables and emotion: the James-Lange theory revisited. *Psychol. Bull., 74,* 411–424.

Felipe, N. J., and R. Sommer (1966). Invasions of personal space. *Soc. Problems, 14,* 206–214.

Feshbach, S. (1970). Aggression. In P. H. Mussen (Ed.), *Carmichael's manual of child psychology.* New York: Wiley, 159–259.

Festinger, L. (1954). A theory of social comparison processes. *Hum. Relat., 7,* 117–140.

Festinger, L., A. Pepitone, and T. Newcomb (1952). Some consequences of deindividuation in a group. *J. abnorm. soc. Psychol., 47,* 382–389.

Field, M. (1974). Power and dependency: legitimation of dependency conditions. *J. soc. Psychol., 92,* 31–37.

Fischer, W. F. (1963). Sharing in preschool children as a function of amount and type of reinforcement. *Genetic Psychol. Monogr., 68,* 215–245.

Fishbein, M., and I. Ajzen (1975). *Belief, attitude, intention, and behavior: an introduction to theory and research.* Reading, Mass.: Addison-Wesley.

Fisher, J. D., B. M. De Paulo, and A. Nadler (1981). Extending altruism beyond the altruistic act: the effects of aid on the helping recipient. In J. P. Rushton and R. M. Sorrentino (Eds.), *Altruism and helping behavior.* Hillsdale, N.J.: Erlbaum.

Fisher, J. D., C. L. Harrison, and A. Nadler (1978). Exploring the generalizability of donor-recipient similarity effects. *Pers. soc. Psychol. Bull., 4,* 627–630.

Fisher, J. D., and A. Nadler (1976). Effect of donor resources on recipient self-esteem and self-help. *J. exp. soc. Psychol., 12,* 139–150.

Fisher, J. D., A. Nadler, and S. Whitcher-Alagner (1982). Recipient reactions to aid. *Psychol. Bull., 91,* 27–54.

Freedman, J. L. (1970). Guilt, equity, justice, and reciprocation. In J. Macauley and L. Berkowitz (Eds.), *Altruism and helping behavior.* New York: Academic Press.

Freedman, J. L., S. A. Wallington, and E. Bless (1967). Compliance without pressure: the effect of guilt. *J. Pers. soc. Psychol., 7,* 117–124.

Freud, S. (1933). *New introductory lectures on psycho-analysis.* New York: Morton.

Frodi, A. (1977). Sexual arousal, situational restrictiveness and aggressive behavior. *J. Res. Pers., 11,* 48–58.

Gaertner, S. L., and J. F. Dovidio (1977). The subtlety of white racism, arousal and helping behavior. *J. Pers. soc. Psychol., 35,* 691–708.

Geen, J. H., and L. Jarmecky (1973). The effect of being responsible for reducing another's pain on subjects' response and arousal. *J. Pers. soc. Psychol., 26,* 232–237.

Geen, R. G. (1970). Perceived suffering of the victim as an inhibitor of attack-induced aggression. *J. soc. Psychol., 81,* 209–215.

Geen, R., and E. Donnerstein, Eds. (1983). *Aggression: theoretical and empirical review.* New York: Academic Press.

Geen, R. G., and M. B. Quanty (1977). The catharsis of aggression: an evaluation of a hypothesis. In L. Berkowitz (Ed.), *Advances in experimental social psychology.* Vol. 10. New York: Academic Press.

Geen, R. G., J. J. Rakosky, and R. Pigg (1972). Awareness of arousal and its relation to aggression. *Brit. J. soc. clinic. Psychol., 11,* 115–121.

Geen, R. G., D. Stonner, and G. L. Shope (1975). The facilitation of aggression by aggression: evidence against the catharsis hypothesis. *J. Pers. soc. Psychol., 31,* 721–726.

Gelfand, D. M., and D. P. Hartmann (1982). Response consequences and attributions: two contributors to prosocial behavior. In N. Eisenberg (Ed.), *The development of prosocial behavior.* New York: Academic Press.

Gentry, W. D. (1970). Effects of frustration, attack and prior aggressive training on overt aggression and vascular processes. *J. Pers. soc. Psychol., 16,* 718–725.

Gergen, K. J., D. Ellsworth, C. Maslach, and M. Seipel (1975). Obligation, donor resources, and reaction to aid in 3 cultures. *J. Pers. soc. Psychol., 31,* 390–400.

Gergen, K. J., M. M. Gergen, and K. Meter (1972). Individual orientations to prosocial behavior. *J. soc. Issues, 8,* 105–130.

Glass, D. C., and D. S. Krantz (1975). Noise and behavior. In B. B. Wolman (Ed.), *International encyclopedia of neurology, psychiatry, psychoanalysis and psychology.* New York: Springer.

Gouldner, A. W. (1960). The norm of reciprocity: a preliminary statement. *Amer. Sociol. Rev., 25,* 161–179.

Graves, N. B., and T. D. Graves (1983). The cultural context of prosocial development: an ecological model. In D. L. Bridgeman (Ed.), *The nature of prosocial behavior.* New York: Academic Press.

Greenberg, J., and R. L. Cohen (1982). *Equity and justice in social behavior.* New York: Academic Press.

Greenberg, M. S., and D. M. Frisch (1972). Effect of intentionality on willingness to reciprocate a favor. *J. exp. soc. Psychol., 8,* 99–111.

Greenwell, J., and H. A. Dengerink (1973). The role of perceived versus actual attack in human physical aggression. *J. Pers. soc. Psychol., 26,* 66–71.

Gross, A. E., and J. G. Latané (1974). Receiving help, reciprocation, and interpersonal attraction. *J. appl. soc. Psychol., 4,* 210–223.

Grusec, J. E., L. Kuczynski, J. P. Rushton, and Z. Simutis (1978). Modeling, direct instruction and attributions: effects on altruism. *Develop. Psychol., 14,* 51–57.

Haan, N. R. (1977). Two moralities in action contexts: relationships to thought, ego regulation, and development. *J. Pers. soc. Psychol., 36,* 286–305.

Haan, N., R. Weiss, and U. Johnson (1981). The role of logic in moral reasoning and development. *Develop. Psychol.*

Hall, E. T. (1966). *The hidden dimension.* New York: Doubleday.

Hamilton, M. L. (1973). Imitative behavior and expressive ability in facial expression of emotion. *Develop. Psychol., 8,* 138.

Hamilton, W. D. (1963). The evolution of altruistic behavior. *Amer. Naturalist, 97,* 354–356.

Haney, C., W. C. Banks, and P. G. Zimbardo (1973). Interpersonal dynamics in a simulated prison. *International J. Criminol. Penol., 1,* 69–97.

Harris, M. B., and L. C. Huang (1974). Aggression and the attribution process. *J. soc. Psychol., 92,* 209–216.

Hartshorne, H., and M. A. May (1928). *Studies in the nature of character.* Vol. I: *Studies in deceit.* New York: Macmillan.

Hartshorne, H., and M. A. May (1929). *Studies in the nature of character.* Vol. II: *Studies in self-control.* New York: Macmillan.

Hartshorne, H., M. A. May, and F. K. Shuttleworth (1930). *Studies in the nature of character.* Vol. III: *Studies in the organization of character.* New York: Macmillan.

Harvey, M. D., and M. E. Enzle (1981). A cognitive model of social norms for understanding the transgression-helping effect. *J. Pers. soc. Psychol., 41,* 866–875.

Hebb, D. O. (1966). *A textbook of psychology* (2nd ed.). Philadelphia: Saunders.

Heider, F. (1958). *The psychology of interpersonal relations.* New York: Wiley.

Hoffman, M. L. (1977). Personality and social development. In M. R. Rosenzweig and L. W. Porter (Eds.), *Annual review of psychology.* Vol. 28. Palo Alto, Calif.: Annual Reviews.

Hokanson, J. E., and M. Burgess (1962). The effects of status, type of frustration and aggression on vascular processes. *J. abnorm. soc. Psychol., 65,* 232–237.

Hokanson, J. E., and S. Shetler (1961). The effect of overt aggression on physiological arousal. *J. abnorm. soc. Psychol., 63,* 446–448.

Hokanson, J. E., K. R. Willers, and E. Koropsak (1968). The modification of autonomic responses during aggressive interchange. *J. Pers., 36,* 386–404.

Homans, G. C. (1961). *Social behavior: its elementary forms.* New York: Harcourt, Brace & World.

Hook, J. G., and T. D. Cook (1979). Equity theory and the cognitive ability of children. *Psychol. Bull., 86,* 429–445.

Hornstein, H. A. (1976). *Cruelty and kindness: a new look at aggression and altruism.* Englewood Cliffs, N.J.: Prentice-Hall.

Horowitz, I. A. (1968). Effect of choice and locus of dependence on helping behavior. *J. Pers. soc. Psychol., 8,* 373–376.

Huston, T. L., G. Geis, and R. Wright (1976). The angry samaritans. *Psychology Today, 85,* 61–64.

Isen, A. M. (1970). Success, failure, attention and reaction to others: the warm glow of success. *J. Pers. soc. Psychol., 15,* 294–301.

Isen, A. M., and P. F. Levin (1972). Effect of feeling good on helping: cookies and kindness. *J. Pers. soc. Psychol., 21,* 384–388.

Isen, A. M., T. E. Shalker, M. Clark, and L. Karp (1978). Affect, accessibility of material in memory and behavior: a cognitive loop? *J. Pers. soc. Psychol., 36,* 1–12.

Jaffe, Y., N. Malamuth, J. Feingold, and S. Feshbach (1974). Sexual arousal and behavioral aggression. *J. Pers. soc. Psychol., 30,* 759–764.

James, W. (1890). *The principles of psychology.* Vols. I and II. New York: Henry Holt.

Jensen, R. E., and S. G. Moore (1977). The effect of attribute statements on cooperativeness and competitiveness in school-age children. *Child Development, 48,* 305–307.

Johnson, R. N. (1972). *Aggression.* Philadelphia: Saunders.

Kahn, M. (1966). The physiology of catharsis. *J. Pers. soc. Psychol., 3,* 278–286.

Katz, I. (1981). *Stigma: a social psychological analysis.* Hillsdale, N.J.: Erlbaum.

Kazdin, A. E., and J. H. Bryan (1971). Competence and volunteering. *J. exp. soc. Psychol., 7,* 87–97.

Kelley, H. H., and A. J. Stahelski (1970). Social interaction basis of cooperators' and competitors' beliefs about others. *J. Pers. soc. Psychol., 16,* 66–91.

Kidd, R. F., and L. Berkowitz (1976). Effect of dissonance arousal on helpfulness. *J. Pers. soc. Psychol., 33,* 613–622.

Knott, P. D., L. Lasater, and R. Sherman (1974). Aggression-guilt and conditionability for aggressiveness. *J. Pers., 42,* 332–344.

Kohlberg, L. (1969). Stage and sequence: the cognitive-developmental approach to socialization. In D. Goslin (Ed.), *Handbook of socialization theory and research.* Chicago: Rand McNally.

_____ (1976). Moral stages and moralization: the cognitive-developmental approach. In T. Lickona (Ed.), *Moral development and behavior.* New York: Holt, Rinehart & Winston.

Konecni, V. J. (1972). Some effects of guilt on compliance: a field replication. *J. Pers. soc. Psychol., 23,* 30–32.

_____ (1975a). Annoyance, type and duration of post annoyance activity and aggression: the "cathartic effect." *J. exp. Psychol.: General, 104,* 76–102.

_____ (1975b). The mediation of aggressive behavior: arousal level versus anger and cognitive labeling. *J. Pers. soc. Psychol., 32,* 706–712.

Korte, C. (1969). Group effects on help-giving in an emergency. *Proceedings of the 77th annual convention of the American Psychological Association, 4,* 383–384.

Korte, C., I. Ypma, and A. Toppen (1975). Helpfulness in Dutch society as a function of urbanization and environmental input level. *J. Pers. soc. Psychol., 32,* 996–1003.

Krebs, D. L. (1970). Altruism—an examination of the concept and review of the literature. *Psychol. Bull., 73,* 258–303.

_____ (1975). Empathy and altruism. *J. Pers. soc. Psychol., 32,* 1134–1146.

_____ (1982a). Moral knowledge and moral conduct. Paper read at the 90th Annual Meeting of American Psychological Association, Washington, D.C.

_____ (1982b). Psychological approaches to altruism: an evaluation. *Ethics, 92,* 147–158.

_____ (1982c). Prosocial behavior, equity, and justice. In J. Greenberg and R. C. Cohen (Eds.), *Equity and justice in social behaviors.* New York: Academic Press.

_____ (1982d). Altruism: a rational approach. In N. Eisenberg (Ed.), *The development of prosocial behavior.* New York: Academic Press.

_____ (1982e). Helping in emergencies: the construction and disintegration of a model. *Contemporary Psychol., 27,* 775–777.

_____ (1983). Commentaries and critiques. In D. Bridgeman (Ed.), *The nature of prosocial development. Interdisciplinary theories and strategies.* New York: Academic Press.

Krebs, D., and J. Gillmore (1982). The relationship among the first stages of cognitive development, role-taking ability, and moral development. *Child Develop., 53,* 877–886.

Krebs, D. L., and M. Holder (1981). Evolution, altruism, and reinforcement. In D. Krebs (Ed.), *Readings in social psychology: contemporary perspectives* (2nd ed.). New York: Harper & Row.

Krebs, D. L., and A. Rosenwald (1977). Moral reasoning and moral behavior in conventional adults. *Merrill-Palmer Quart. Behav. Develop., 23,* 77–88.

Krebs, D. L., and C. Russell (1981). Role-taking and altruism: when you put yourself in the shoes of another, will they carry you to their owner's aid? In J. P. Rushton and R. M. Sorrentino (Eds.), *Altruism and helping behavior: social, personality and developmental perspectives.* Hillsdale, N.J.: Erlbaum.

Krebs, D. L., and B. Sturrup (1982). Role taking ability and altruistic behavior in elementary school children. *J. Moral Education, 11,* 94–100.

Krebs, D. L., and L. G. Wispé (1974). On defining altruism: a rejoinder to L. J. Severy. *J. soc. Issues, 30,* 194–199.

Kulik, J. A., and R. Brown (1979). Frustration, attribution of blame and aggression. *J. exp. soc. Psychol., 15,* 183–194.

Kurdek, L. (1978). Perspective taking as the cognitive basis of children's moral development: a review of the literature. *Merrill-Palmer Quart. Behav. Develop., 24,* 3–28.

Langer, E. J. (1978). Rethinking the role of thought in social interaction. In J. H. Harvey, W. Ickes, and R. F. Kidd, (Eds.), *New directions in attribution research.* Vol. 2. Hillsdale, N.J.: Erlbaum.

Langer, E. J., and R. Abelson (1972). The semantics of asking a favor: how to succeed in getting help without really dying. *J. Pers. soc. Psychol., 24,* 26–32.

Latané, B., and J. M. Dabbs, Jr. (1975). Sex, group size and helping in three cities. *Sociometry, 38,* 180–194.

Latané, B., and J. M. Darley (1970). *The unresponsive bystander: why doesn't he help?* New York: Appleton-Crofts.

_____ (1976). *Help in a crisis: bystander response to an emergency.* Morristown, N.J.: General Learning Press.

Latané, B., S. A. Nida, and D. W. Wilson (1981). The effects of group size on helping behavior. In J. P. Rushton and R. M. Sorrentino (Eds.), *Altruism and helping behavior: social, personality, and developmental perspectives.* Hillsdale, N.J.: Erlbaum.

Leaky, R. E., and R. Lewin (1977). *Origins.* New York: Dutton.

Lerner, M. J. (1977). The justice motive: some hypotheses as to its origins and forms. *J. Pers., 45,* 1–53.

Lerner, M. J., and S. C. Lerner (1981). *The justice motive in social behavior.* New York: Plenum.

Lerner, M. J., and D. T. Miller (1978). Just world research and the attribution process: looking back and ahead. *Psychol. Bull., 85,* 1030–1051.

Lerner, M. J., D. T. Miller, and J. G. Holmes (1976). Deserving and the emergence of forms of justice. In L. Berkowitz and E. Walster (Eds.), *Advances in experimental social psychology,* Vol. 9. New York: Academic Press.

Lerner, M. J., and L. A. Whitehead (1981). Procedural justice viewed in the context of justice motive theory. In G. Mikula (Ed.), *Justice in social interaction.* New York: Huber.

Leventhal, G. S. (1976). The distribution of rewards and resources in groups and organizations. In L. Berkowitz and E. Walster (Eds.), *Advances in experimental social psychology.* Vol. 9. New York: Academic Press.

Levin, P. F., and A. M. Isen (1975). Further studies on the effect of feeling good on helping. *Sociometry, 38,* 141–147.

Liebert, R. M., J. N. Sprafkin, and E. S. Davidson (1982). *The early window: the effects of television on children and youth* (2nd ed.) Elmsford, N.Y.: Pergamon.

Liebhart, E. (1972). Empathy and emergency helping: the effects of personality, self-concern, and acquaintance. *J. exp. soc. Psychol., 8,* 404–411.

Lorenz, K. (1966). *On aggression.* New York: Harcourt, Brace and World.

Lovejoy, C. O. (1981). The origin of man. *Science, 211,* 341–350.

Macauley, J. R., and L. Berkowitz (1970). *Altruism and helping behavior.* New York: Academic Press.

McDougall, W. (1926). *An introduction to social psychology* (Rev. ed.). Boston: Luce.

McGovern, L. P. (1976). Dispositional social anxiety and helping behavior under three conditions of threat. *J. Pers., 44,* 84–97.

McGovern, L. P., J. L. Ditzian, and S. P. Taylor (1975). Sex and perceptions of dependency in a helping situation. *Bull. psychon. Soc., 5,* 336–338.

McMillen, D. L. (1971). Transgression, self-image, and compliant behavior. *J. Pers. soc. Psychol., 20,* 176–179.

McNamee, S. (1978). Moral behavior, moral development, and motivation. *J. Moral Education, 7,* 27–31.

Malamuth, N. M., and E. Donnerstein (1983). The effects of aggressive-erotic stimuli. In L. Berkowitz (Ed.), *Advances in experimental social psychology.* Vol. 15. New York: Academic Press.

Mandler, G. (1975). *Mind and emotion.* New York: Wiley.

Mark, V., and F. Ervin (1970). *Violence and the brain.* New York: Harper & Row.

Masters, J. C., and W. Furman (1976). Effects of affective states on non-contingent outcome expectancies and beliefs in internal or external control. *Develop. Psychol., 12,* 481–482.

Maynard-Smith, J. (1974). The theory of games and the evolution of animal conflict. *J. Theoretical Biology, 47,* 209–221.

Megargee, E. I. (1966). Undercontrolled and overcontrolled personality types in extreme anti-social aggression. *Psychol. Monogr., 80* (Whole No. 611).

Megargee, E. I., P. E. Cook, and G. A. Mendelsohn (1967). Development and evaluation of an MMPI scale of assaultiveness in overcontrolled individuals. *J. abnorm. Psychol., 72,* 519–528.

Megargee, E. I., and G. A. Mendelsohn (1962). A cross validation of twelve MMPI indices of hostility and control. *J. abnorm. soc. Psychol., 65,* 431–438.

Menninger, K. (1942). *Love against hate.* New York: Harcourt, Brace & World.

Meyer, R. G. (1967). The relationship of blood pressure levels to the chronic inhibition of aggression. *Dissertation Abstracts, 28,* 2099.

Meyer, T. P. (1972). The effects of sexually arousing and violent films on aggressive behavior. *J. sex Res., 8,* 324–333.

Michelini, R. L., J. P. Wilson, and L. A. Messe (1975). The influence of psychological needs on helping behavior. *J. Psychol., 91,* 253–258.

Midlarsky, E. (1968). Aiding responses: an analysis and review. *Merrill-Palmer Quart., 14,* 229–260.

Midlarsky, E., and M. Midlarsky (1973). Some determinants of aiding under experimentally induced stress. *J. Pers., 41,* 305–327.

Mikula, G. (1980). On the role of justice in allocation decisions. In G. Mikula (Ed.), *Justice and social interaction.* New York: Springer-Verlag.

Mikula, G., and T. Schwinger (1978). Intermember relations and reward allocation. In H. Brandstatter, J. H. Davis, and H. Schuler (Eds.), *Dynamics of group decision.* Beverly Hills, Calif.: Sage.

Milgram, S. (1970). The experience of living in cities. *Science, 167,* 1461–1468.

Milgram, S. (1974). *Obedience to authority.* New York: Harper.

Miller, D. T. (1977a). Personal deserving versus justice for others: an exploration of the justice motive. *J. exp. soc. Psychol., 13,* 1–13.

———— (1977b). Altruism and threat to a belief in a just world. *J. exp. soc. Psychol., 13,* 113–125.

Miller, D. T., and J. Smith (1977). The effect of own deservingness and deservingness of others on children's helping behavior. *Child Development, 48,* 617–620.

Miller, D. T., and N. Vidmar (1981). A social psychological analysis of punishment reactions. In M. J. Lerner and S. Lerner (Eds.), *The justice motive in social behavior.* New York: Plenum.

Miller, N. E. (1941). The frustration-aggression hypothesis. *Psychol. Rev., 48,* 155–178.

Miller, R. L., P. Brickman, and D. Bolen (1975). Attribution versus persuasion as a means of modifying behavior. *J. Pers. soc. Psychol., 31,* 430–441.

Mischel, W. (1968). *Personality and assessment.* New York: John Wiley.

Montagu, M. F. A., Ed. (1968). *Man and aggression.* New York: Oxford Univ. Press.

Moore, B., B. Underwood, and D. L. Rosehan (1973). Affect and altruism. *Develop. Psychol., 8,* 99–104.

Morgan, W. G. (1973). Situational specificity in altruistic behavior. *Representative Res. soc. Psychol., 4,* 56–66.

Moriarty, T. (1975). Crime, commitment and the responsive bystander: two field experiments. *J. Pers. soc. Psychol., 31,* 370–376.

Morse, S., and J. Gergen (1970). Social comparison, self-consistency, and the concept of self. *J. Pers. soc. Psychol., 16,* 148–156.

Morse, S. J., J. Gruzen, and H. T. Reis (1976). The nature of equity restoration: some approval-seeking considerations. *J. Pers. soc. Psychol., 12,* 1–8.

Mosher, D. L. (1968). Measurement of guilt in females by self-report inventories. *J. consult. clinic. Psychol., 32,* 690–695.

Mueller, C. W., and E. Donnerstein (1981). Film-facilitated arousal and pro-social behavior. *J. exp. soc. Psychol., 17,* 31–41.

Murdock, G. (1949). *Social structure.* New York: Macmillan.

Murphy, L. B. (1937). *Social behavior and child personality: an exploratory study of some roots of sympathy.* New York: Columbia Univ. Press.

Nadler, A., J. D. Fisher, and S. Streufert (1974). The donor's dilemma: recipient's reactions to aid from friend or foe. *J. appl. soc. Psychol., 4,* 275–285.

———— (1976). When helping hurts: the effects of donor-recipient similarity and the recipient's self-esteem on the reaction to aid. *J. Pers., 44,* 392–409.

Nelson, E. A., R. E. Grinder, and M. L. Mutterer (1969). Sources of variance in behavioral measures of honesty in temptation situations: methodological analyses. *Develop. Psychol., 1,* 265–279.

Nemeth, C. (1970). Effects of free versus constrained behavior in attraction between people. *J. Pers. soc. Psychol., 15,* 302–311.

Nickel, T. W. (1974). The attribution of intention as a critical factor in the relation between frustration and aggression. *J. Pers., 42,* 482–492.

Olweus, D. (1979). Stability of aggressive reaction patterns in males: a review. *Psychol. Bull., 86,* 852–875.

O'Neal, E. C., and L. Kaufman (1972). The influence of attack, arousal and information about one's arousal upon interpersonal aggression. *Psychon. Sci., 26,* 211–214.

Overton, W. F., and H. W. Reese (1973). Models of development: methodological implications. In J. R. Nesselroade and H. W. Reese (Eds.), *Lifespan developmental psychology: methodological issues.* New York: Academic Press.

Packer, C. (1977). Reciprocal altruism in Papio anubis. *Nature, 265,* 441–443.

Paluck, R., and A. H. Esser (1971). Territorial behavior as indicator of changes in clinical behavioral condition of severely retarded boys. *Amer. J. Mental Deficiency, 76(3),* 284–290.

Pastore, N. (1952). The role of arbitrariness in the frustration-aggression hypothesis. *J. abnorm. soc. Psychol., 47,* 728–731.

Patterson, G. R., R. A. Littman, and W. Bricker (1967). Assertive behavior in children: a step toward a theory of aggression. *Monogr. Soc. Res. Child Development, 32,* No. 5 (Serial No. 113).

Perry, D. G., and K. Bussey (1977). Self-reinforcement in high-and-low aggressive boys following acts of aggression. *Child Development, 48,* 653–657.

Piliavin, I. M., J. A. Piliavin, and J. Rodin (1975). Costs, diffusion, and the stigmatized victim. *J. Pers. soc. Psychol., 13,* 289–299.

Piliavin, J. A., J. F. Dovidio, S. L. Gaertner, and R. D. Clark (1981). *Emergency intervention.* New York: Academic Press.

Piliavin, J. A., and I. Piliavin (1972). The effect of blood on reactions to a victim. *J. Pers. soc. Psychol., 23,* 353–361.

Poulos, R. W., and R. M. Liebert (1972). Influence of modeling, exhortative verbalization and surveillance on children's sharing. *Develop. Psychol., 6,* 402–408.

Quanty, M. (1976). Aggression catharsis. In R. G. Geen and E. C. O'Neal (Eds.), *Perspectives on aggression.* New York: Academic Press.

Raush, H. L., A. T. Dittman, and T. J. Taylor (1959). Person, setting, and change in social interaction. *Hum. Relat., 12,* 361–378.

Raush, H. L., I. Farbman, and L. G. Llewellyn (1960). Person, setting, and change in social interaction: II. a normal control study. *Hum. Relat., 13,* 305–332.

Rawlings, E. I. (1968). Witnessing harm to others: a reassessment of the role of guilt in altruistic behavior. *J. Pers. soc. Psychol., 10,* 377–380.

Regan, J. (1971). Guilt, perceived injustice and altruistic behavior. *J. Pers. soc. Psychol., 18,* 124–132.

Ribal, J. E. (1963). Social character and meanings of selfishness and altruism. *Sociol. soc. Res., 47,* 311–321.

Richardson, D. C., M. M. Tomarelli, and C. Hendrick (1978). Bibliography of journal articles in *Personality and Social Psychology:* 1977. *Pers. soc. Psychol. Bull., 4,* 638–652.

Rokeach, M. (1973). *The nature of human values.* New York: Macmillan.

Rosenhan, D. L., and G. M. White (1967). Observation and rehearsal as determinants of prosocial behavior. *J. Pers. soc. Psychol., 5,* 423–431.

Rosenhan, D. L., J. Karylowski, P. Salovey, and K. Hargis (1981). Emotion and altruism. In J. P. Rushton and R. M. Sorrentino (Eds.), *Altruism and helping behavior.* Hillsdale, N.J.: Erlbaum.

Rosenhan, D. L., B. Underwood, and B. Moore (1974). Affect moderates self-gratification and altruism. *J. Pers. soc. Psychol., 30,* 546–552.

Ross, A. S. (1971). Effect of increased responsibility on bystander intervention: the presence of children. *J. Pers. soc. Psychol., 19,* 306–310.

Ross, A. S., and J. Braband (1973). Effect of increased responsibility on bystander intervention II: the cue value of a blind person. *J. Pers. soc. Psychol., 25,* 254–258.

Rule, B. G., and L. S. Hewitt (1971). Effects of thwarting on cardiac response and physical aggression. *J. Pers. soc. Psychol., 19,* 181–187.

Rule, B. G., and G. J. Leger (1976). Pain cues and differing functions of aggression. *Canadian J. Behav. Sci., 8,* 213–222.

Rule, B. G., and A. R. Nesdale (1976). Emotional arousal and aggressive behavior. *Psychol. Bull., 83,* 851–863.

Rule, B. G., A. R. Nesdale, and R. Dyck (1977). Objective self-awareness and differing standards of aggression. *Representative Res. soc. Psychol., 8,* 89–96.

Rushton, J. P. (1975). Generosity in children: immediate and long-term effects of modeling, preaching, and moral judgment. *J. Pers. soc. Psychol., 31,* 459–466.

_____ (1976). Socialization and the altruistic behavior of children. *Psychol. Bull., 83,* 898–913.

_____ (1980). *Altruism, socialization and society.* Englewood Cliffs, N.J.: Prentice-Hall.

_____ (1981). The altruistic personality. In J. P. Rushton and R. M. Sorrentino (Eds.), *Altruism and helping behavior.* Hillsdale, N.J.: Erlbaum.

_____ (1984). The altruistic personality: evidence from laboratory, naturalistic, and self-report perspectives. In E. Staub, D. Bar-Tal, J. Karylowski, and J. Reykowski (Eds.), *The development and maintenance of prosocial behavior: international perspectives.* New York: Plenum Press.

Rushton, J. P., and A. C. Campbell (1977). Modelling, vicarious reinforcement and extraversion on blood donating in adults. Immediate and long term effects. *Europ. J. soc. Psychol., 7,* 297–306.

Rushton, J. P., R. D. Chrisjohn, and G. C. Fekken (1981). The altruistic personality and the self-report altruism scale. *Pers. individual Differences, 2,* 293–302.

Rushton, J. P., and R. M. Sorrentino (1981). *Altruism and helping behavior.* Hillsdale, N.J.: Erlbaum.

Rushton, J. P., and G. Teachman (1978). The effects of positive reinforcement, attributions, and punishment on model induced altruism in children. *Pers. soc. Psychol. Bull., 4,* 322–325.

Rushton, P. (1982). Altruism and society: a social learning perspective. *Ethics, 92(3),* 425–446.

Sampson, E. E. (1969). Studies of status congruence. In L. Berkowitz (Ed.), *Advances in experimental social psychology.* Vol. 4. New York: Academic Press.

Sawyer, J. (1966). The altruism scale: a measure of cooperative, individualistic, and competitive interpersonal orientation. *Amer. J. Sociol., 71,* 407–416.

Saxe, L., and M. Greenberg (1974). Reaction to a help attack: importance of locus of help initiation and nature of outcome. Paper presented at the meeting of the Eastern Psychological Association, Philadelphia.

Schachter, J. (1957). Pain, fear, and anger in hypertensives and normotensives: a psychophysiological study. *Psychosom. Med., 19,* 17–29.

Schachter, S., and J. E. Singer (1962). Cognitive, social and psychological determinants of emotional state. *Psychol. Rev., 69,* 379–399.

Schank, R., and R. Abelson (1977). *Scripts, plans and knowledge.* Hillsdale, N.J.: Erlbaum.

Scheier, M. F., A. Fenigstein, and A. H. Buss (1974). Self-awareness and physical aggression. *J. exp. soc. Psychol., 10,* 264–273.

Schill, T. R. (1972). Aggression and blood pressure responses of high and low-guilt subjects. *J. consult. clinic. Psychol., 38,* 461.

Schwartz, S. H. (1977). Normative influences on altruism. In L. Berkowitz (Ed.), *Advances in experimental social psychology.* Vol. 10. New York: Academic Press.

Schwartz, S. H., and T. Ben David (1976). Responsibility and helping in an emergency: effects of blame, ability, and denial of responsibility. *Sociometry, 39,* 406–415.

Schwartz, S. H., and G. T. Clausen (1970). Responsibility, norms, and helping in an emergency. *J. Pers. soc. Psychol., 16,* 229–310.

Schwartz, S. H., and J. A. Howard (1981). A normative decision-making model of altruism. In J. P. Rushton and R. M. Sorrentino (Eds.), *Altruism and helping behavior.* Hillsdale, N.J.: Erlbaum.

Schwartz, S. H., and R. C. Tessler (1972). A test of a model for reducing measured attitude-behavior discrepancies. *J. Pers. soc. Psychol., 24,* 225–236.

Scott, J. F. (1971). *Internalization of norms: a sociological theory of moral commitment.* Englewood Cliffs, N.J.: Prentice-Hall.

Shortell, J., S. Epstein, and S. P. Taylor (1970). Instigation to aggression as a function of degree of defeat and capacity for massive retaliation. *J. Pers., 38,* 313–328.

Shotland, R., and R. L. Huston (1979). Emergencies: what are they and do they influence bystanders to intervene? *J. Pers. soc. Psychol., 37,* 1822–1834.

Singer, J. L., and D. G. Singer (1981). *Television, imagination and aggression: a study of preschoolers.* Hillsdale, N.J.: Erlbaum.

Slaby, D. (1974). Verbal control of resistance to temptation in children. *Dissertation Abstracts International, 34(9-B),* 4641, 55:9385.

Smith, R. E., K. Vanderbilt, and M. B. Callen (1973). Social comparison and bystander intervention in emergencies. *J. appl. soc. Psychol., 3,* 186–196.

Snyder, M., and W. J. Ickes (1985). Personality and social behavior. In G. Lindzey and E. Aronson (Eds.), *The handbook of social psychology* (3rd ed.). New York: Random House.

Solomon, L. Z., H. Solomon, and R. Store (1978). Helping as a function of number of bystanders and ambiguity of emergency. *Pers. soc. Psychol. Bull., 4,* 318–321.

Staub, E. (1970). A child in distress: the influence of age and number of witnesses on childrens' attempts to help. *J. Pers. soc. Psychol., 14,* 130–140.

_____ (1971). Helping a person in distress: the influence of implicit and explicit "rules" of conduct on children and adults. *J. Pers. soc. Psychol., 17,* 137–144.

_____ (1974). Helping a distressed person: social, personality, and stimulus determinants. In L. Berkowitz (Ed.), *Advances in experimental social psychology.* Vol. 7. New York: Academic Press.

_____ (1978). *Positive social behavior and morality.* Vol. 1. New York: Academic Press.

_____ (1979a). Understanding and predicting social behavior—with emphasis on prosocial behavior. In E. Staub (Ed.), *Personality: basic issues and current research.* Englewood Cliffs, N.J.: Prentice-Hall.

_____ (1979b). *Positive social behavior and morality.* Vol. 2. New York: Academic Press.

Staub, E., and L. Sherk (1970). Need for approval, children's sharing behavior, and reciprocity in sharing. *Child Development, 41,* 243–252.

Stotland, E., K. E. Mathews, S. E. Sherman, R. O. Hanson, and B. Z. Richardson (1978). *Empathy, fantasy, and helping.* Sage Library of Social Research, *65.*

Strayer, F. F., S. Wareing, and J. P. Rushton (1979). Social constraints on naturally occurring preschool altruism. *Ethology and Sociobiology, 1,* 3–11.

Taylor, S. P. (1970). Aggressive behavior as a function of approval motivation and physical attack. *Psychon. Sci., 18,* 195–196.

Taylor, S. P., and S. Epstein (1967). Aggression as a function of the interaction of the sex of the aggressor and the sex of the victim. *J. Pers., 35,* 474–486.

Tesser, A., R. Gatewood, and M. S. Driver (1968). Some determinants of gratitude. *J. Pers. soc. Psychol., 9,* 233–236.

Thomas, G. C., C. D. Batson, and J. S. Coke (1981). Do good samaritans discourage helpfulness? Self-perceived altruism after exposure to highly helpful others. *J. Pers. soc. Psychol., 40,* 194–200.

Thompson, W. C., C. L. Cowan, and D. L. Rosenhan (1980). Focus of attention mediates the impact of negative affect on altruism. *J. Pers. soc. Psychol., 38,* 291–300.

Toch, H. (1969). *Violent men.* Chicago: Aldine.

_____ (1980). *Violent men* (Rev. ed.). Cambridge, Mass.: Schenkman.

Trivers, R. L. (1971). The evolution of reciprocal altruism. *Quart. Rev. Biology, 46,* 35–57.

_____ (1983). The evolution of cooperation. In D. L. Bridgeman (Ed.), *The nature of prosocial behavior.* New York: Academic Press.

Turiel, E. (1978). Social regulations and domains of social concepts. In W. Damon (Ed.), *New directions for child development: social cognition.* San Francisco: Jossey-Bass.

Underwood, B. J., W. J. Froming, and B. S. Moore (1977). Mood, attention, and altruism: a search for mediating variables. *Develop. Psychol., 13,* 541–542.

Underwood, B., and B. Moore (1982). Perspective-taking and altruism. *Psychol. Bull., 91,* 141–173.

Ungar, S. (1979). The effects of effort and stigma on helping. *J. soc. Psychol., 107,* 23–28.

Uranowitz, S. W. (1975). Helping and self-attributions: a field experiment. *J. Pers. soc. Psychol., 31,* 852–854.

Van den Berghe, P. (1978). *Man in society: a biosocial view* (2nd ed.). New York: Elsevier North-Holland.

Vidmar, N., and D. T. Miller (1980). Social psychological processes underlying attitudes toward legal punishment. *Law and Society Review, 14*(3), 401–409.

Wachtel, P. (1973). Psychodynamics, behavior therapy, and the implacable experimenter: an inquiry into the consistency of personality. *J. abnorm. Psychol., 82,* 324–334.

Wagner, C., and L. Wheeler (1969). Model, need and cost effects in helping behavior. *J. Pers. soc. Psychol., 12,* 111–116.

Walker, L. J. (1980). Cognitive and perspective-taking prerequisites for moral development. *Child Development, 51,* 131–139.

Wallington, S. A. (1973). Consequences of transgression: self-punishment and depression. *J. Pers. soc. Psychol., 28,* 1–7.

Walster, E., G. W. Walster, and E. Berscheid (1978). *Equity: theory and research.* Boston: Allyn and Bacon.

Wegner, D. M., and D. Schaefer (1978). The concentration of responsibility: an objective self-awareness analysis of group size effects in helping situations. *J. Pers. soc. Psychol., 36,* 147–155.

Weiner, F. (1976). Altruism, ambience and action: the effects of a rural rearing on helping behavior. *J. Pers. soc. Psychol., 34,* 112–124.

Weiss, R. F., J. L. Boyer, J. P. Lombardo, and M. H. Stitch (1973). Altruistic drive and altruistic reinforcement. *J. Pers. soc. Psychol., 25,* 390–400.

Weiss, R. F., W. Buchanan, L. Alstatt, and J. P. Lombardo (1971). Altruism is rewarding. *Science, 171,* 1262–1263.

West, S. G., and T. J. Brown (1975). Physical attractiveness, the severity of the emergency and helping: a field experiment and interpersonal simulation. *J. exp. soc. Psychol., 11,* 531–538.

White, G. M., and M. A. Burnam (1975). Socially cued altruism: effects of modeling, instructions, and age on public and private donations. *Child Development, 46,* 559–563.

Whiting, B. B. (1983). The genesis of prosocial behavior. In D. L. Bridgeman (Ed.), *The nature of prosocial behavior.* New York: Academic Press.

Wilson, D. W., and A. Kahn (1975). Rewards, costs, and sex differences in helping behavior. *Psychol. Reports, 36,* 31–34.

Wilson, E. O. (1975). *Sociobiology: the new synthesis.* Cambridge, Mass.: Belknap Press.

Wilson, J. P. (1976). Motivation, modeling and altruism: a person × situation analysis. *J. Pers. soc. Psychol., 34,* 1078–1086.

Wispé, L. G., Ed. (1972). Positive forms of social behavior. *J. soc. Issues, 28,* No. 3.

Yakimovich, D., and E. Saltz (1971). Helping behavior: the cry for help. *Psychon. Sci., 23,* 427–428.

Zillmann, D. (1971). Excitation transfer in communication-mediated aggressive behavior. *J. exp. soc. Psychol., 7,* 419–434.

_____ (1979). *Hostility and aggression.* Hillsdale, N.J.: Erlbaum.

_____ (1982). Transfer of excitation in emotional behavior. In J. T. Cacioppo and R. E. Petty (Eds.), *Social psychophysiology.* New York: Guilford Press.

Zillmann, D., and J. R. Cantor (1976). Effect of timing of information about mitigating circumstances on emotional responses to provocation and retaliatory behavior. *J. exp. soc. Psychol., 12,* 38–55.

Zillmann, D., A. H. Katcher, and B. Milavsky (1972). Excitation transfer from physical exercise to subsequent aggressive behavior. *J. exp. soc. Psychol., 8,* 247–259.

Zimbardo, P. G. (1969). The human choice: individuation, reason, and order versus deindividuation, impulse, and chaos. *Nebraska Symposium on Motivation, 17,* 237–307.

Zuckerman, M., M. M. Lazzaro, and D. Waldgeir (1979). Undermining effects of the foot-in-the-door technique with extrinsic rewards. *J. appl. soc. Psychol., 9,* 292–296.

CHAPTER 15

Attribution and Social Perception

Michael Ross
University of Waterloo

Garth J. O. Fletcher
Illinois State University

Attribution refers to the linking of an event to its causes. Attributions enable us to understand and react to our surroundings. It matters, for example, whether a person attributes his poor piano playing to inability or to a lack of effort, and whether a woman attributes her husband's inattentiveness to waning love or fatigue. The goal of attribution theorists is to describe how the average person comes to attribute events to one or more of their possible causes.

In the 1970s the field of social psychology was dominated by attribution theorists and researchers. Attribution theory came to rival cognitive dissonance as one of the most imperialistic theories in social psychology. Attribution theory was seen as relevant to the study of person perception, event perception, attitude change, the acquisition of self-knowledge, therapeutic interventions, and much more.

The focus on attribution had a dual impact on the field. First, formal theories of attribution were proposed and tested. Second, attribution implied a certain approach to the study of social behavior. Thus, research was conducted that did not explicitly test the attribution formulations, but borrowed their orientation. People were characterized as naive scientists striving to understand, predict, and control the course of events in their lives.

In the initial sections of this chapter we discuss theories of attribution and examine research that derives directly from them. Subsequently, we review research that is consonant with the attribution approach and that has served to illuminate such areas as the study of emotions, self-perception, and errors in attribution. This partition is not perfect. Some studies could be placed on either side of the divide and, at times, we made our decision on the basis of ease of presentation.

THEORIES OF ATTRIBUTION

Theories of attribution take two general forms. The first assumes that causal analyses follow a set of formal guidelines and essentially occur de novo in each situation. The theories of Kelley (1967) and Jones and Davis (1965) exemplify this approach. The second type of theory is based on the assumption that people have expectations or preconceptions about causality. This knowledge allows the individual to dispense with the formal guidelines and take shortcuts. Kelley's (1972) extension of his original theorizing and the formulations of Reeder and Brewer (1979) and of Nisbett and L. Ross (1980) are attempts to detail people's preconceptions.

There are two other significant features of attribution theory. Most attribution theorists are not concerned with the validity of the attributions that the layperson produces. Instead, theorists focus on the cognitive processes involved in forming attributions. Second, attribution theorists tend to concentrate on people's explanations of human behavior, rather than on their understanding of the nonsocial world. Of the three attribution models we present, only Kelley's was intended as a general model applicable to people's understanding of the physical as well as the social world.

The major theoretical thrust in attribution has been provided by Heider (1944, 1958), Jones and his colleagues (Jones and Davis, 1965; Jones and McGillis, 1976), and Kelley (1967, 1972, 1973). We begin by describing their respective theories and some of the research generated to test their models.

HEIDER'S "NAIVE" PSYCHOLOGY

The genesis of attribution theory in social psychology is usually traced to Fritz Heider and his attempts to provide a systematic, conceptual explication of "naive" psychology. Heider's work culminated in 1958 in the publication of *The Psychology of Interpersonal Relations*. In this book, Heider noted a similarity between the goals and activities of scientists and those of people in their everyday lives. People strive to understand, predict, and control events that concern them. On the basis of observation, they form beliefs or theories about what is occurring. New observations then serve to support, refute, or modify these theories. Heider's reasoning is similar to that of George Kelly (1955) who commented, "The aspirations of the scientist are essentially the aspirations of all men" (p. 43).

Heider argued that it is important to understand this naive psychology. People act on the basis of their beliefs. Therefore, these beliefs must be taken into account if psychologists hope to account for human behavior. Note that this is true whether or not the beliefs are valid. A person may well act on the basis of false beliefs. Again there is a parallel with G. Kelly (1955) who asserted the importance of taking seriously an individual's personal constructs or representations of the world.

Heider also suggested that psychologists can learn a great deal from commonsense psychology. He stressed the importance of taking the ordinary person's explanations and understanding of events and behavior seriously. In Heider's words, the ordinary person "has a great and profound understanding of himself and other people which, though unformulated or only vaguely conceived, enables him to interact with others in more or less adaptive ways" (Heider, 1958, p. 2).

Four ideas central to Heider's account of commonsense causal reasoning have exerted a tremendous influence over subsequent theorizing and research. First, Heider noted that people do not merely observe and mentally record events and behaviors. Rather, they subject the observed events to "psychological" analysis in an effort to understand their causes. More important, Heider suggested that certain types of causes tend to be preferred. People are inclined to attribute actions to stable or enduring causes, rather than to transitory or variable causes. Hence, they will seek to explain behaviors in terms of personal traits (attitudes, needs, beliefs, personality structures) or in terms of permanent properties or structures in the environment (e.g., social institutions). Heider (1958) called such causes dispositional (p. 79):

> It is an important principle of common-sense psychology, as it is of scientific theory in general, that man grasps reality, and can predict and control it, by referring transient and variable behavior and events to relatively unchanging underlying conditions, the so-called dispositional properties of his world.

Note how the social world would appear if perceivers did not attribute behavior to dispositional properties. People would seem to change character with their every action—likes becoming dislikes, bright people becoming dull people, and so forth. Such variability in the same person would be disturbing to say the least. The social world would seem unstable, unpredictable, and uncontrollable. Thus, one of Heider's major themes is that people engage in attributional analyses to discern the dispositional or invariant properties that underlie the variable behavior of others.

Second, Heider stressed the importance of the distinction between intentional and unintentional behavior. He suggested that personal dispositions are more readily inferred from intentional actions than from unintentional actions. How does a perceiver "know" whether a behavior is intentional? Inferences of intentionality are governed by three main criteria: equifinality, local causality, and exertion. Equifinality refers to one of the essential features of human action: it is goal directed rather than means centered. Thus, there is evidence for intentionality when people adopt a variety of strategies to surmount difficulties in working toward a goal. Local causality is established when individuals are seen as the agents or originators of the action rather than as passive recipients of environmental forces (e.g., diving into the swimming pool vs. being pushed in). Finally, Heider claimed that perceivers infer intention from exertion; people are presumed to strive to achieve intended effects or goals.

Third, Heider suggested that environmental and personal factors are two general classes of force that enter into the production of action. He further speculated that a hydraulic relation is perceived to exist between causes within the person and causes within the environment. The more the person is seen as causing an action, the less causal influence the environment will be perceived to exert and vice versa.

Fourth, Heider suggested that the covariation principle is fundamental to the attribution process. This principle states that an effect is attributed to an event (cause) that is present when the effect is present, and absent when the effect is absent.

Fritz Heider was the dominant figure in making naive psychology a legitimate area of interest in social psychology. His insights were brilliant and provocative, but he presented his ideas in a relatively discursive fashion. Jones and Davis (1965) and Kelley (1967) systematized and expanded Heider's ideas; in their hands, attribution theory became an explicit, hypothesis-generating set of principles. The result was an explosion of research as attribution theory became one of the major concerns of social psychologists in the 1970s.

CORRESPONDENT INFERENCE THEORY

Jones and Davis (1965) described how an "alert perceiver" might infer another's intentions and personal dispositions (personality traits, attitudes, etc.) from his or her behavior. Their theory derives its name from the concept of correspondent inference. Perceivers make correspondent inferences when they infer another's personal dispositions directly from behavior; for example, perceivers may infer a disposition of kindness from a kindly act. Thus, inferences are correspondent when the behavior and the disposition can be assigned similar labels (e.g., kind).

According to Jones and Davis (1965), there are two major stages in the process of inferring personal dispositions: the attribution of intention and the attribution of disposition.

Stage one: The attribution of intention. Jones and Davis proposed that observers make dispositional attri-

butions only on the basis of intentional behaviors. Consequently, an intention attribution must precede a dispositional attribution. Perceivers judge an act to be intentional when they believe that (1) the actor knew that the behavior would produce the consequences observed and, (2) the actor possessed the ability to achieve the observed consequences when he or she desired to. The attribution of intention thus presupposes knowledge, ability, and behavioral freedom.

Stage two: The attribution of disposition. If an act is judged to be intentional, then perceivers attempt to infer the personal disposition that caused the act. They can begin by comparing the consequences of chosen and nonchosen acts. For example, you might feel that you have learned something about my preferences in entertainment when you discover that I have chosen to see a slapstick movie, when I could just as easily have gone to the symphony or a Shakespearian play.

Inferring dispositions from the effects of an intentional behavior can be complicated though. Chosen and nonchosen acts may have similar consequences. A perceiver learns little about the reasons for a person's behavior from such shared consequences. For example, you learn relatively little about my preferences if I choose to go to a slapstick movie when no forms of entertainment are available other than slapstick movies. As a result, Jones and Davis proposed the principle of noncommon effects. A perceiver makes a correspondent inference (e.g., the inference that the target person prefers lowbrow entertainment) when the chosen action has a few relatively unique or noncommon consequences. It is from such unique consequences that a perceiver can determine with some confidence *why* the person chose that particular behavior.

In addition, there is a corollary to the principle of noncommon effects. A perceiver can generally make more confident inferences about personal dispositions when noncommon effects are scarce rather than plentiful. A perceiver cannot be certain which effect was intended if the chosen and nonchosen acts have many different consequences.

The attribution of dispositions involves more, however, than simply contrasting the consequences of chosen and nonchosen acts. Jones and Davis argued that an "alert perceiver" will also consider whether the target's behavior is normative. A target who helps someone in a situation in which most normal human beings would be expected to help is not seen as a helpful person. A target is seen as helpful only if his or her helpfulness extends beyond that expected of the average person. Correspondent inferences are made from nonnormative behaviors.

How is the normativeness of a behavior assessed? Jones and Davis suggest that it is inferred from the social desirability of the consequences of the behavior. The more desirable a consequence is, the more likely it is that people, in general, would want to achieve it. Hence, correspondent inferences occur primarily when the consequences of the chosen behavior are socially undesirable.

Finally, Jones and Davis incorporated two motivational concepts in their theory: hedonic relevance and personalism. Hedonic relevance refers to the degree to which the perceiver is pleased or displeased by the target's chosen actions. As hedonic relevance increases, there is an increase in the probability that inferences will be correspondent. When the action has hedonic relevance, the possible consequences of chosen and nonchosen behaviors will be grouped in terms of their affective significance for the perceiver. This grouping results in fewer noncommon effects because otherwise different effects are combined into the same affective bundle. Consequently, there is an increase in perceived correspondence.

There is a second, related way in which hedonic relevance could increase correspondence. Heider (1958) quotes Bertrand Russell's comment that "one of the odd effects of the importance which each of us attaches to himself is that we tend to imagine our own good or evil fortune to be the purpose of other people's actions..." (p. 120). Thus, if an action has multiple effects, the one hedonically relevant to self tends to be seen as the intended goal of the action and serves as the basis of a correspondent inference.

Jones and Davis introduced the concept of personalism to distinguish between actions that are conceivably affected by the presence of the perceiver and actions that are not so affected. Personalism is high if perceivers see another's behavior as an intentional effort to harm or benefit them. Personalism is low if perceivers view any harm or benefit they receive as an accidental by-product of acts directed toward other objectives.

Hedonically relevant acts that are high in personalism yield attributions that are more correspondent than acts low in personalism. If someone deliberately sets out to harm me, I am more apt to see him as a bad person than if the harm were accidental, or if the harm befell another person.

In summary, a perceiver examines the potential consequences of a target's chosen and nonchosen behaviors and infers the reasons for the choice. The less socially desirable the consequences of the chosen action are, the greater the inferred correspondence between act and underlying disposition. Finally, correspondence increases with hedonic relevance and personalism.

A MODIFICATION OF CORRESPONDENT INFERENCE THEORY

In 1976, Jones and McGillis modified the model in a number of interesting ways. First, correspondence was redefined: "Given an attribute-effect linkage which is offered to explain why an act occurred, correspondence refers to the degree of information gained regarding the probability or strength of the attribute" (p. 391). Thus correspondence reflects changes in the probability of inferring a disposition from a behavior. Second, the impact of social desirability on correspondence was replaced by a more precise formulation concerning the prior probability that the actor would want a particular consequence. If the perceiver already had good reason to expect that the actor would strive for that consequence, then the actor's doing so tells the perceiver little that is new about the actor. Only behaviors that disconfirm expectancies yield considerable information gain (correspondence).

Jones and McGillis also discussed the source of the perceiver's expectancies. *Target-based* expectancies are derived from prior information about the specific target person in question. *Category-based* expectancies reflect the perceiver's knowledge that the target person is a member of a particular category or group. For example, a perceiver may expect university students to behave differently than senior citizens.

Although these changes do not alter the basic features of the earlier model, they do produce a more elaborate and, in some ways, a conceptually cleaner version. In the previous model social desirability seemed unnecessarily confounded with expectancy. It was assumed that socially desirable behaviors would be associated with high expectancies and thus yield little information with regard to dispositions. Yet this assumption is not always valid. Many socially desirable actions occur infrequently, for example, outstanding achievements, acts of unusual courage, and so forth.

On the other hand, the new definition of correspondence introduces a certain amount of semantic confusion. Should we continue to think of correspondence in terms of its everyday meaning? Is an inference correspondent if there is an assumed congruence between the behavior and the disposition (e.g., kind act and kindly disposition)? If so, the reformulation seems to imply that a perceiver should refuse to infer a correspondence between behavior and disposition unless there is information gain. Yet surely a behavior can be perceived as highly correspondent with a previously inferred disposition (e.g., a kind behavior enacted by a person already known to be kind). Perhaps Jones and McGillis should have replaced *correspondence* with a new term that more appropriately reflects information gain.

One additional assumption of correspondence inference theory warrants discussion. Jones and Davis argued that an attribution of intention must necessarily precede a dispositional inference. This reasoning seems overly restrictive. There are dispositions that are defined in terms of unintentional behaviors, such as carelessness or forgetfulness. There are also many dispositions that may be derived from both intentional and unintentional behaviors. For instance, one may attribute coldness or aloofness, in part, on the basis of such unintentional nonverbal behaviors as body posture, eye contact, and so forth. On the other hand, it could be argued that Jones and Davis are largely correct though they overstate the case. Perhaps the majority of dispositions are inferred from intentional behaviors rather than from unintentional behaviors.

EMPIRICAL TESTS OF CORRESPONDENT INFERENCE THEORY

Two studies provide direct support for Jones and Davis's principle of noncommon effects (Ajzen and Holmes, 1976; Newtson, 1974). Subjects read descriptions of hypothetical situations in which an actor selected one of several behavioral alternatives (e.g., a tourist choosing among different cities to visit). As predicted by the theory, the more noncommon effects there were among the consequences of the various choices, the less confident subjects were in their attributions of choice-related traits. Using a similar paper and pencil approach, Chaikin and Cooper (1973) demonstrated the hypothesized impact of hedonic relevance on correspondent attributions.

The best developed line of research devised to test predictions arising from the model concerns the attribution of attitudes (Jones and Harris, 1967). In the initial experiment, subjects were presented with attitude statements allegedly made by an unknown target person. Subjects were informed either that the target made these statements of his or her own free will (high choice condition) or that he or she was required to support that

viewpoint, for example, in the context of a debate (low choice condition). Also, the opinion expressed was either normative or nonnormative. After receiving this information, subjects were asked to infer the target's attitudes. Subjects assumed a greater correspondence between the opinion expressed and the target's true attitude when the opinion was nonnormative rather than normative, and elicited under high-choice rather than low-choice conditions. Subsequent research has yielded results consistent with these findings (Jones, 1979).

The effect for the normativeness of the opinion offers support for correspondent inference theory. Recall that correspondence inferences are more likely when behavior is seen to be nonnormative. It is perhaps less evident how the effect of the choice manipulation should be derived from the model. Jones and McGillis (1976) suggest that the choice variable is a manipulation of the number of noncommon effects. They state that (p. 394)

> there are more reasons for making the statement in the non-choice than in the choice condition, since the non-choice case includes all the reasons of the choice case plus those associated with obedience to authority, avoidance of embarrassment, not appearing to misunderstand the instructions, and so on.

It is possible to argue the opposite, however. Where salient external factors provide a plausible explanation of behavior (as in the low-choice condition) the number of potential causes for the behavior should be perceived as reduced, in comparison to voluntary behavior that may reflect innumerable motives and purposes. An alternative explanation for the impact of choice centers on the inference of intention, so central to the original Jones and Davis (1965) formulation. Only the consequences of freely chosen behaviors should be seen as intended and hence yield correspondent attributions.

Jones and Harris (1967) reported another finding that has been replicated a number of times (Jones, 1979). The opinions expressed by the target person affected the attitude attributions of perceivers, even when the opinions were supposedly elicited under low-choice conditions. For example, a person who was required to state a pro-Castro opinion was seen as more favorable toward Castro than a person who was required to state an anti-Castro opinion.

In a study that illustrates this phenomenon in a more realistic social setting, subjects interacted with an individual whose friendly or unfriendly behavior was either spontaneous or explicitly forced by role requirements

(Napolitan and Goethals, 1979). The target who behaved in a friendly manner was seen as truly friendly regardless of whether the behavior was known to be spontaneous or forced. Similarly, the target who behaved in an unfriendly way was seen as truly unfriendly, regardless of constraints.

Why do attributors perceive any degree of correspondence when behavior is constrained? Perhaps this effect is not surprising (Hamilton, 1980). Even in the low-choice conditions of experiments, the target person had some degree of choice about performing the behavior; for example, he could have refused to voice an opinion favorable to Castro in the Jones and Harris study. On these grounds, it makes sense for perceivers to hold the target at least partially responsible for the behavior and to perceive a degree of correspondence. Consistent with this reasoning, subjects in the attitude attribution studies rated the target person with high-choice closer to the complete freedom end of a choice scale, than the target person with low-choice was rated to the complete constraint end of the scale (Jones, 1979).

On the other hand, some authors saw the data from the attitude attribution studies as indicating that perceivers are too ready to attribute causality to internal or personal dispositions (Jones, 1979; L. Ross, 1977). Ross (1977) labeled this propensity the "fundamental attribution error" and defined it as the "general tendency to overestimate the importance of personal...factors relative to environmental influences" (p. 184). Jones (1979) attempted to analyze the bases of this "error." He suggested that behavior may be more salient than the constraining, contextual cues and thus exert a stronger influence on attributions. Also, subjects may assume a correspondence between acts and dispositions unless persuaded otherwise. The perceiver may then insufficiently adjust this hypothesis in light of the information regarding contextual factors.

Ajzen and his colleagues have obtained data consistent with this latter interpretation (Ajzen, Dalton, and Blyth, 1979). They suggested that the direction of the opinion statements in the attitude attribution studies provided subjects with a hypothesis about the target's attitudes. The subjects then evaluated this hypothesis in the light of information they received about the writer's background (in the Jones and Harris, 1967, study, the author of the essay was described "as a student at the University of North Carolina, a resident of the state, and the son of an automobile salesman") or information they derived from the style and organization of the essay.

Ajzen and his colleagues demonstrated that subjects do indeed form such a hypothesis on the basis of the direction of opinion statements. More important, subjects' evaluation of this hypothesis is biased in favor of its confirmation. Once individuals have formed a hypothesis about the target's attitudes, they tend to interpret ambiguous, new information as consistent with the hypothesis. This finding is compatible with other evidence concerning the effect of preconceptions or hypotheses on information processing and retrieval (Darley and Fazio, 1980; Nisbett and L. Ross, 1980; Snyder and Swann, 1978; Snyder, Tanke, and Berscheid, 1977; Taylor and Crocker, 1981).

Yet this explains only part of the process. Why do observers form a hypothesis about the target's attitudes in the first place instead of simply seeing constrained behavior as irrelevant to attitudes? A number of answers to this question have been suggested. Behavior is often much more salient than context; as a result, perhaps the context in which the behavior occurs is overlooked (Heider, 1958; Jones, 1979).

Alternatively, Jellison and Green (1981) posited a norm-favoring internal attribution. They found that internal explanations are viewed more favorably than external explanations. For example, a target who provides internal responses on Rotter's I.E. scale is evaluated more positively than one who provides external responses. Also, subjects perceive themselves as more disposed to making internal attributions than is the average other person. Jellison and Green speculated that in Western societies individuals are reinforced for making internal attributions and that this response becomes normative.

Others have also concluded that internal attributions are normative, but they did so on the basis of an analysis of attributions of responsibility from a legal perspective (Fincham and Jaspars, 1980; Hamilton, 1980). In law, it is presumed that an individual has internal control over his or her behavior unless convincing evidence to the contrary is presented. Hamilton (1980, p. 770) summarized this argument as follows:

> Even if a variety of other factors ultimately caused one to act, if one could have done otherwise one is still responsible. Role requirements, situational pressures, and social conventions may mitigate responsibility but they do not eliminate it.

In summary, perceivers are more inclined to make attributions to personal factors than correspondent inference theory would imply. Attribution theorists such as Jones (1979) and L. Ross (1977) believe that perceivers err in emphasizing the internal determinants of behavior. This "fundamental attribution error" became almost an article of faith in the attribution literature (Harvey, Town, and Yarkin, 1981).

The basis of this faith is probably twofold. First, some of the best known research in social psychology, that on conformity and bystander intervention, reveals that situations exert a stronger influence over behavior than many of us would have anticipated or preferred to believe (Asch, 1956; Latané and Darley, 1970; Milgram, 1965). Second, in most social psychological experiments, context is manipulated and shifts in behavior are observed. This research does not permit the study of the impact of enduring personal dispositions on behavior. As a result, perhaps, social psychologists are often inclined to see behavior as situationally determined. When their subjects disagree with them, the subjects are deemed to be in error.

The assessment of error is a difficult and possibly fruitless exercise, however. How are we to decide who is right? In many circumstances, there are simply no clear criteria for establishing the validity of causal attributions. A more useful approach, then, may be to delineate the circumstances in which plausible situational determinants of behavior are, or are not, attended to (Ajzen *et al.*, 1979; Harvey *et al.*, 1981).

To this point, we have discussed research stimulated by correspondent inference theory. We now turn, briefly, to research questions that have not been examined. The Jones and Davis model has rarely been tested in settings in which perceivers must extract information from ongoing behavioral sequences. Instead, subjects have been supplied with written descriptions of a target's chosen and nonchosen behaviors (e.g., Ajzen and Holmes, 1976; Chaikin and Cooper, 1973; Newtson, 1974). In more naturalistic settings, it may not always be evident to a perceiver what should be included in the realm of nonchosen behaviors—there may be an infinite number of possibilities. One potentially interesting question concerns how perceivers narrow the field.

It is necessary to ask a more fundamental question, however. Do perceivers typically pay much attention to nonchosen behaviors and their consequences? There are no data that bear directly on this question, but the evidence from related research appears to contradict this basic assumption of correspondent inference theory. Perceivers seem to treat nonoccurrences as considerably less important than occurrences in making inferences. Null information often tends to be disregarded (Einhorn and Hogarth, 1978; Fazio, Sherman, and Herr, 1982; Nisbett and L. Ross, 1980; L. Ross, 1977). The implication of this evidence for correspondent inference theory is as follows. Suppose I want to know whether to attribute a disposition of kindness to someone who has engaged in a kind behavior. I am rather unlikely to consider the other (nonchosen) behaviors he or she might have engaged in. Instead, I am likely to look for further positive instances of kindness—for example, has he or she acted kindly in the past (Snyder and Swann, 1978)? In short, perceivers may seek information more along the lines proposed by Kelley's (1967) theory, which we turn to next, than the Jones and Davis theory.

KELLEY'S MODEL OF THE ATTRIBUTION PROCESS

Kelley's (1967) analysis of the attribution process is not limited to interpersonal perception. In a more general sense, his theory concerns the subjective experience of attributional validity. He addresses the following question. How do individuals establish the validity of their own or of another person's impressions of an object?

Kelley suggested that perceivers examine three different kinds of information in their efforts to establish subjective validity: consensus information (Do all or only a few people respond to the stimulus in the same way as the target person?), distinctiveness information (Does the target person respond in the same way to other stimuli as well?), and consistency information (Does the target person always respond in the same way to this stimulus?). For example, suppose I learn that a friend likes a particular restaurant. How do I decide whether I can trust his or her judgment? For Kelley, this question means I want to know whether to attribute the person's liking of the restaurant to something about the person or to something about the restaurant. I can answer this question by considering consensus, consistency, and distinctiveness information.

Three combinations of this information are particularly important. The target person's judgment of the restaurant (It is a good restaurant.) should be perceived as valid if the perceiver knows that (1) other people like the restaurant (high consensus), (2) the target person seldom likes restaurants (high distinctiveness) and, (3) the target person enjoys the restaurant every time he or she goes there (high consistency). Thus, the combination of high consensus, high distinctiveness, and high consistency is understood to imply something about the relevant stimulus.

In contrast, the combination of low consensus, low distinctiveness, and high consistency yields information about the person enacting the behavior. If a perceiver knows that (1) most people do not like the target person's restaurant (low consensus), (2) the target person likes most restaurants (low distinctiveness), and (3) the target person enjoys the restaurant each time he or she goes there (high consistency), then the perceiver attributes the target person's enjoyment of the restaurant to something about him or her (e.g., he or she likes to eat out) rather than to something unique about the restaurant.

An attribution to the particular circumstances in which the response occurred is the likely inference with the combination of low consensus, high distinctiveness, and low consistency: few other people like the restaurant, the target person seldom likes restaurant meals, and he or she has disliked this restaurant in the past. A perceiver will probably conclude that the present enjoyment is something of a fluke and is perhaps accounted for by the target person's liking for the wine and company rather than the food. A lack of consistency over contexts will generally yield circumstance attributions (Orvis, Cunningham, and Kelley, 1975).

More complex attribution patterns also occur. Kelley (1967) describes entity by person interactions. The effect reflects both something about the person and something about the stimulus. Food preferences are a familiar example of this. Peggy finds pickles particularly tasty when she is pregnant. In this instance, Peggy's enjoyment is dependent both on something about her (pregnancy) and on an external stimulus (pickles).

These are some of the combinations of the consensus, distinctiveness, and consistency dimensions and their implications for the attribution process. Other combinations are possible, but they are likely to be more ambiguous in terms of their attributional significance.

Self-perception.   The impact of Kelley's theorizing is not limited to his enunciation of formal principles of attribution. He also reoriented the field by asserting that self-perception as well as social perception was a proper domain for attribution theory. Though this was implicit in Heider's (1958) analysis, Jones and Davis (1965) restricted their discussion to social perception. Kelley (1967) expanded on Heider's discussion by incorporating Daryl Bem's (1965) theory of self-perception into the attribution framework.

Consider how social perception and self-perception differ. The basic problem we face as social perceivers is that other people's feelings, attitudes, and beliefs are not directly observable. Consequently, we are forced to infer these unobservables from people's behavior (including verbal reports) and a consideration of the situation in which the behavior occurs.

Our intuitions tell us that self-perception is an entirely different matter, that we have introspective access to our own experiences and mental events. Needless to say, attribution theorists do not completely deny the contribution of introspection to self-knowledge; however, they do stress the role of information from the external environment in helping individuals define and describe their internal feelings and beliefs.

What are the external cues that are employed when individuals are unable to label their feelings directly? According to Bem (1965, 1967), when internal feelings are weak or ambiguous, individuals rely on the same external cues that observers use when they infer another's internal states. Thus people can infer their own attitudes and other internal feelings (e.g., hunger, fear, enjoyment, etc.) from observations of their own behavior and the situation in which it occurs.

Kelley (1967) added theoretical substance to this hypothesis by incorporating Bem's idea into attribution theory. Kelley argued that the attributional processes involved in self-perception parallel those invoked for perception of others. Note that Kelley's analysis posits more extensive cognitive processing, and is more specific than Bem's with respect to the role of past behavior in the attribution process. The consistency and distinctiveness criteria suggest that individuals consider their relevant behaviors with respect to the object in question at different times and in different contexts. On the other hand, the consensus dimension requires that they consider the relevant behaviors of other people. For example, I am likely to assume that I have a favorable attitude toward restaurants if I like to go to many restaurants (low distinctiveness), I like them on each visit (high consistency), and other people seem less enthusiastic about going to restaurants than I am (low consensus). Thus, according to Kelley (1967), my attitude inference is based on the outcome of an information search involving a number of publicly observable events, rather than a single introspective event.

Causal schemata.   In his initial analysis, Kelley (1967) assumed that individuals withhold their causal judgments or at least make them with low confidence until they possess information about consensus, distinctiveness, and consistency. It seems unlikely, however, that people very often engage in these elaborate information-gathering procedures. Perceivers may lack the time and motivation, or it may not be possible for them to obtain the relevant information. In fact, Heider (1958) argued that people often make attributions on the basis of what he termed the minimum data pattern: one instance of joint absence of the object and effect, and one instance of joint presence. We judge the movie to be good or the restaurant to be superb on the basis of a single experience.

In his subsequent papers, Kelley (1972, 1973) proposed that individuals typically make attributions on the basis of limited information. They are able to do so because they have theories or preconceptions about what causes are associated with what effects. Kelley labeled these preconceptions "causal schemata." For example, individuals may suppose that there are three basic data patterns associated with stimulus, person, and circumstance attributions. These data patterns are high consensus, high distinctiveness, and high consistency for a stimulus attribution (HHH); low consensus, low distinctiveness, and high consistency for a person attribution (LLH); and low consensus, high distinctiveness, and low consistency for a circumstance attribution (LHL). Each of these patterns can be viewed as a causal schema. A perceiver can interpret information by comparing it to, and integrating it with, a schema.

Thus, a perceiver who has only high-consensus information may nonetheless presuppose the HHH schema, since it is the only one that incorporates high consensus. The consequence of assuming the HHH pattern is that it implies a stimulus attribution. Similarly, a person who has only low-distinctiveness information should assume the LLH pattern and a person attribution. From these examples it is evident that the minimum data pattern is not quite as minimal as Heider (1958) perhaps supposed. I have been to other movies and restaurants. If I judge the present one to be outstanding, then at the very least I have high-distinctiveness information. More often than not, I probably also have some consensus information—my companions also like the movie or restaurant. These two sources of information should lead me to invoke the HHH schema and confidently make a stimulus attribution.

Kelley described a number of other basic causal schemata, the most important being the multiple sufficient and multiple necessary schemata. Some effects are explained in terms of multiple sufficient causes: Any of several causes acting individually can produce the effect.

For example, people may work at a task because they like it, because they are being rewarded for it, or because they have been ordered to do it by a superior. Other phenomena are interpreted in terms of multiple necessary causes. Several causes must operate together to produce the effect. For instance, I could run a mile in under four minutes only if I trained for a long time, I ran downhill, and there was a hurricane blowing at my back. Kelley hypothesized that the multiple necessary schema will be invoked to account for unusual or extreme effects.

Kelley also postulated a number of attributional principles that accompany the causal schemata. The two that have received the most empirical attention are the discounting and augmentation principles. The discounting principle states that attributors perceive a given cause as contributing less to an effect if other plausible causes are also present. This principle is associated primarily with the multiple sufficient schema in which any of a number of causes can produce an effect. The augmentation principle concerns inhibitory causation. A perceiver should make stronger attributions to other causes if an effect occurs in the presence of an inhibitory cause. For instance, passing a difficult test (an inhibitory cause) may lead to stronger attributions of effort and ability than passing an easy test. The augmentation principle applies to both the multiple sufficient and multiple necessary causal schemata.

EMPIRICAL TESTS OF KELLEY'S FORMULATIONS

In the first comprehensive assessment of the predictions from Kelley's (1967) original model, subjects were supplied with brief descriptions of behavioral episodes and information concerning consensus, distinctiveness, and consistency (McArthur, 1972). The results supported Kelley's model. Stimulus attributions were most frequent when a response was characterized by high consensus, high distinctiveness, and high consistency. Conversely, low consensus, low distinctiveness, and high consistency information produced person attributions.

Other studies, using a format comparable to McArthur's, similarly have found that consensus, distinctiveness, and consistency information play an important role in object, person, and circumstance attribution (e.g., McArthur, 1976; Orvis, Cunningham, and Kelley, 1975; Pruitt and Insko, 1980; Zuckerman, 1978). Pruitt and Insko (1980) also examined comparison object consensus. They reasoned as follows. If I want to know, for example, whether to attribute a person's liking for a restaurant to the person or to the restaurant, the similarity of the person's judgments of other restaurants to those of other diners (comparison object consensus) would be a relevant piece of information. High-comparison object consensus increases attribution to the stimulus (the restaurant under consideration is a good restaurant); whereas, low-comparison object consensus increases attribution to the person.

Research on the later version of Kelley's theory examines the role of schemata in causal inference. If Kelley's theory of causal schemata is correct, then people who receive incomplete information should assimilate this information to the closest appropriate schema, and make attributions accordingly. For example, if a person receives high-consensus and high-distinctiveness information, the closest schema (HHH) assumes high consistency and a corresponding stimulus attribution. In a test of this hypothesis, subjects were provided with information concerning one or two of the three dimensions of consensus, distinctiveness, and consistency and required to rate the attribution target on the absent dimension (Orvis, Cunningham, and Kelley, 1975). The results were generally in accord with hypotheses derived from Kelley's (1972, 1973) theory of causal schemata.

Kelley's analysis of multiple sufficient and multiple necessary causal schemata has also received support from studies utilizing a paper-and-pencil methodology. For example, Kun and Weiner (1973) found that subjects believed that success at a difficult task (an uncommon effect) required both high ability and high effort (the multiple necessary schema). On the other hand, success at an easy task (a common effect) was seen as caused by either high ability *or* high effort (the multiple sufficient schema). Finally, people tend to associate the multiple necessary schema with occurrences of extreme magnitude across a wide range of event categories (Cunningham and Kelley, 1975).

Although most aspects of Kelley's theorizing have received empirical attention, researchers have tended to focus on three particular concerns: the covariation principle, the role of consensus in the attribution process, and the discounting principle. We consider each of these in turn.

THE COVARIATION PRINCIPLE

Kelley (1967) based his analysis of the attribution process on the covariation principle. Yet a number of studies suggest that people are not very skilled at assessing

covariation between variables (for reviews see Abramson and Alloy, 1980; Crocker, 1981; Shweder, 1977). For example, the elegant and well-known studies of Chapman and Chapman (1967, 1969) revealed that adults' perceptions of covariation between responses on psychodiagnostic tests and patient symptoms were more dependent on a priori expectations of what ought to go together with what, than on the information subjects were provided with.

In general, studies of covariation demonstrate that adults will "see" a correlation between unrelated sets of stimuli when they believe that the sets ought to be causally related. Conversely, they fail to observe unanticipated relations that do exist. This research makes an important point. Not only are attributions theory driven, in the sense that covariation information is utilized according to causal schemata, but the observations of the underlying data patterns themselves are also powerfully influenced by the attributor's a priori causal theories. On the basis of such data, Nisbett and L. Ross (1980, p. 101) concluded that

> people's views of covariation in the social world
> . . . are not formed primarily on the basis of some
> computational procedures analogous to the
> statistician's procedures. Rather, the layperson's
> views of the data are greatly influenced by theories
> and expectations.

The difficulty in detecting covariation may explain, in part, why some experiments have produced results less consistent with Kelley's theorizing than those just described. In McArthur-type questionnaire studies the covariation information is provided in an explicit and organized manner. Such experiments provide "plausibility" tests of Kelley's theory. In these relatively sterile contexts, individuals are capable of using the consensus, distinctiveness, and consistency information to make attributions more or less as Kelley's theory would predict they should. On the other hand, the data seem to be less confirmatory when subjects have to abstract consensus, distinctiveness, or consistency information from an ongoing stream of behavior or from the natural flow of events, though there are few relevant experiments (Stevens and Jones, 1976; Tillman and Carver, 1980).

Nisbett and L. Ross (1980) have suggested that causal analyses in naturalistic settings are unlikely to follow the normative strategies proposed by attribution theorists. Instead, people may select causes primarily on the basis of two characteristics: their similarity to effects (the "resemblance criterion") and their salience. The resemblance criterion may be exemplified by the conspiracy theories that follow major political assassinations. The layperson expects great events to have great causes. Surprisingly, there appear to be few empirical demonstrations of the resemblance criterion in social psychology, though Nisbett and Ross provide a host of anecdotal and anthropological evidence that is consistent with their reasoning (see also Shweder, 1977). An observational study of crapshooting provides some support for the resemblance criterion (Henslin, 1967). Crapshooters tend to believe that a hard throw of the dice will produce a high number and a soft throw a low number.

In contrast, the salience criterion has received a considerable amount of attention from social psychologists. There is considerable evidence that perceptually salient or figural stimuli are more likely to be chosen as causal agents than perceptually nonsalient stimuli (Kanouse, 1971; McArthur and Post, 1977; Pryor and Kriss, 1977; Taylor and Fiske, 1978).

The resemblance and salience criteria demonstrate the importance of bringing perceptual or figural factors into attribution theory. The theories of Jones and Davis and Kelley have perhaps overemphasized information processing variables to the detriment of perceptual factors. As Kelley (1978, p. 378) noted more recently in commenting on the resemblance criterion:

> If you hear a big bang you look for something big that banged or if you see a big "heavy" footprint you look for a big, fat elephant. It becomes clear to me that if we are going to deal with that kind of thing as part of the attribution process, then we have to distinguish between some process of simply perceiving properties like size and intensity and another process, perhaps partly related to and supported by the first, of inferring causes.

Although this emphasis on salience and resemblance seems warranted, they do not replace covariation as the sine qua non of causal inference. Salient or similar events may be selected as causes only when they seem to covary with the effect. Admittedly, people may, at times, see covariation where none exists or overlook covariations that do occur. That people may sometimes be poor detectors of "objective" covariation does not undermine the covariation principle, however. The perception of covariation underlies causal inference. The degree to which such perceptions accurately mirror objective reality is a separate issue.

In addition, it should be emphasized that resemblance and salience are not simply perceptual dimensions. Whether X appears to resemble Y often depends upon prior experiences and knowledge. For example, part of Freud's genius was to spot resemblances where others did not. More mundanely, have you noticed how grandparents always seem to think that the new grandchild resembles their side of the family?

Similarly, consider the factors that contribute to salience. Causes can be salient because they stand out perceptually—they grab our attention. However, they may also stand out because we are primed to look for certain causes and not others. We have theories about what causes should be related to what effects. For example, where the personality psychologist sees behavior as caused by personal dispositions, the social psychologist sees it as caused by situational factors. Like resemblance, salience is perhaps more conceptual than perceptual.

Finally, theory-driven expectations can affect covariation detection in another important way. Perceivers' expectations may influence both their own behavior and the behavior they elicit from others. The most convincing research evidence for this relationship comes from the literature on self-fulfilling prophecies. In one particularly elegant study, Snyder and his colleagues demonstrated that males who thought they were having a telephone conversation with an attractive female elicited more animated and sociable behavior from the female, than males who believed they were talking to an unattractive female (Snyder, Tanke, and Berscheid, 1977). The males thus elicited behavior that confirmed their theories concerning the behavior of attractive and unattractive women.

CONSENSUS INFORMATION AND ATTRIBUTIONS

One of the liveliest controversies to emerge from the empirical work testing Kelley's model has been concerned with the role of consensus information in causal attribution (see Kassin, 1979, for an extensive review of this literature). In McArthur's (1972) experiment, consensus accounted for the least amount of variance of Kelley's three dimensions. This result was replicated in a later study (McArthur, 1976).

Doubts concerning the role of consensus reached their epitome in a paper by Nisbett and Borgida (1975) who found that people make little or no use of consensus information in the formation of social judgments. Subjects were presented with descriptions of two previously conducted psychology experiments. In one of these experiments, most participants had agreed to accept a high level of electric shock (Nisbett and Schachter, 1966) and in the other, most participants had failed to help a person in need (Darley and Latané, 1968). Subjects in the Nisbett and Borgida study were either told or not told how the majority of people had responded in these two previous experiments. Knowledge of the distribution of responses did not influence subjects' attributions about the causes of the behavior of hypothetical participants in the original study, or subjects' predictions of their own behavior in those situations.

A considerable amount of subsequent research has shown that the appropriate question is not *whether* consensus has an effect on social judgment, but under what conditions it has an impact. In Nisbett and Borgida's study, subjects were supplied with information that was probably discrepant with their expectations. They would expect subjects in experiments to refuse to tolerate high levels of shock and to be willing to help a person in need. In this situation, subjects have a tendency to view the experimental sample as unrepresentative of the population in general and thus not evidence of consensus (Wells and Harvey, 1977). When it is stressed that the sample is representative of the population, consensus information does affect subjects' judgments (Wells and Harvey, 1977; Hansen and Donoghue, 1977).

In addition, judgments of stimuli that the individual has experienced directly may be less responsive to consensus information than judgments of stimuli with which the individual has no direct experience (Feldman, Higgins, Karlovac, and Ruble, 1976; Hansen and Donoghue, 1977; Tyler, 1980). When individuals experience an object directly, they tend to see their own responses as being caused by the object (Heider, 1958; Jones and Nisbett, 1972). For example, if I enjoy a movie, I normally conclude that it is a good movie (an entity attribution) rather than that I was in a good mood, or that I am inclined to like certain movies. Note that this entity attribution will affect my belief about how others will respond to the movie—they too should like it. Consequently, the actual provision of high-consensus information may have little impact on my attribution; I have already made an entity attribution.

What happens if I subsequently learn that others don't like the movie (low consensus)? Having already attributed my response to the entity, I am predisposed to attribute the discrepant responses of others to their personal characteristics: perhaps they are a nonrepresentative sample, or perhaps they are too insensitive to appreciate the film.

As usual, however, things are not quite this simple. People do not always deny the relevance of consensus information when they have direct experience with an object (Kulik and Taylor, 1980). When people lack confidence in their judgments or are uncertain of their feelings, they may welcome and utilize the inputs of others. Also, some responses are seen as relatively idiosyncratic and individuals may not attribute their own reactions to the entity. For example, I realize that my tastes in food and drink are not shared by everyone. "Tastes" are individual and consensus information will likely affect my judgment of how others respond to the subject in question.

Possibly the most intriguing factor discovered so far to influence the utilization of consensus information concerns the degree to which people can incorporate the information within their intuitive theories of causation. (Ajzen, 1977; Tversky and Kahneman, 1979). Ajzen showed that consensus information had a stronger influence on people's predictions when the information had causal implications. For example, subjects' estimates of the likelihood that a target person would pass an exam were affected by information concerning the percentage of persons who had passed or failed the exam. In this context, the consensus information has causal implications. It provides evidence of the difficulty of the test that is causally linked to the likelihood of an individual's success. On the other hand, noncausal consensus information had much less of an impact on predictions. Thus, some subjects were told that a psychologist had interviewed students who had taken an exam. Because he was most interested in reactions to success, the psychologist chose a sample in which 75 percent of the students had passed the test. Subjects were then asked how likely it was that a particular target person in this sample had passed or failed the test. This form of consensus data is noncausal in that it is uninformative with respect to the difficulty level of the test, and it is underutilized in comparison to the causally relevant consensus information.

Note that Ajzen examined the effect of the causal and noncausal base rate information on *predictions*. Presumably comparable effects could be obtained on more direct measures of causal attribution but this remains to be demonstrated.

The perception of consensus. Another aspect of consensus that has received a good deal of empirical attention concerns the degree to which people perceive their own impressions as universal. This issue was perhaps first raised in the developmental literature on role taking and egocentricism. Role taking involves the ability to see things from another person's perspective; egocentricism refers to a person's inability to shed his or her own point of view. Higgins (1981) related the development of role-taking skills to the capacity to prevent one's own characteristics and views from intruding upon and interfering with one's inferences about others.

Though this role-taking ability is thought to improve with age, there is also evidence of apparent self-intrusions in the adult literature. Adults often assume that others are more similar to them in beliefs, feelings, and behavior than they in fact are. This phenomenon has been discussed under such labels as "attributive projection" (Holmes, 1968), "looking glass perceptions" (Fields and Schuman, 1976), and the "false consensus effect" (L. Ross, Greene, and House, 1977). The effect has been shown to occur in a variety of contexts, including estimates of the popularity of one's own political and racial attitudes in the general population (Fields and Schuman, 1976; Korte, 1972), estimates of the degree of similarity between one's own and one's partner's views on the causes of conflict in a close relationship (Harvey, Wells, and Alvarez, 1978), and judgments of the typicality of one's own behavioral choices (L. Ross *et al.,* 1977).

Heider (1958) also discussed projection of affect, though this has received little empirical attention. When we are in a good mood others seem happy, the environment seems beneficent, life seems wonderful; when we are in a bad mood everything seems dark and gloomy. Yet we don't usually attribute these consequences to our mood—they seem to be "out there." The world really is different.

There are a number of possible explanations for the phenomenon of attributive projection. As noted earlier, individuals tend to perceive their attributions as characteristics of the stimulus object rather than judgments about the stimulus object. As a result, an attributor who considers blacks to be lazy should expect this perspective to be shared by others in the same way that they would share his perception that blacks are darker than whites; both are seen to be characteristics of the stimulus object.

An alternative view is that people distort the typicality of their opinions as a means of justifying their beliefs and values (Goethals and Darley, 1977; Kelley, 1967; L. Ross *et al.,* 1977). By assuming consensual validation, people can believe that their own opinions are correct (i.e., entity caused), rather than reflections of personal dispositions. Along these lines, people are inclined to see advocates of their own attitude position as being a more diverse group of individuals than supporters of the opposing position (Goethals, Allison, and Frost, 1979). The perception of diversity with respect to values and beliefs supports an entity attribution. It is not just the case that people of a certain type (e.g., racial bigots) favor the advocated position.

We thus have a chicken-egg problem. Entity attributions could foster the perception of consensus and diversity; or the assumptions of consensus and diversity could yield an entity attribution. It is entirely possible, of course, that both processes occur.

Moreover, there are a number of additional possible interpretations. The assumption of consensus may reflect our greater exposure to similar rather than dissimilar people and the greater ease with which we can imagine behavior similar to our own as opposed to dissimilar behavior (L. Ross *et al.,* 1977). The phenomenon may also reflect people's belief that even small samples are representative of the population from which they are drawn. As a demonstration of this belief, Nisbett and Borgida (1975) showed that subjects' predictions of the behavior of a sample were very much affected by information concerning the behavior of two nonrandomly selected members of that sample. Thus, perhaps there is nothing uniquely important about the self that leads to "attributive projection." People are always ready to generalize from a limited sample of behavior to population characteristics. We do so more often on the basis of our own behavior and opinions because they happen to be salient and familiar to us.

This list certainly doesn't exhaust the possibilities. However, the research does not allow us to distinguish among the various interpretations, and it is time to turn the tables and note that people also often seem to see themselves as unique.

The perception of uniqueness. Perhaps the earliest study of the false perception of uniqueness was conducted in a small, rural community in New York (Schanck, 1932). Most of the inhabitants belonged to the

Methodist Church and expressed attitudes in opposition to card playing and to the use of liquor and tobacco. Nonetheless, during the two years he stayed in the town, Schanck was invited on several occasions to participate in card games, to drink hard cider, and to smoke with individuals who had previously expressed the "proper" Methodist attitudes. Nearly all of these individuals believed themselves to be the only ones engaging in such nefarious activities.

More recently, the perception of uniqueness has been demonstrated in a number of contexts. M. Ross and his colleagues have shown that people take more responsibility for a group product than other participants allocate to them (M. Ross, 1981; M. Ross and Sicoly, 1979). This effect occurs in both ongoing social relationships and ad hoc groups formed in the laboratory. Thus individuals do not see themselves as one of the crowd. Instead they tend to see themselves as leading actors.

Individuals similarly distinguish themselves from others when it comes to predicting the future. For example, university students are unduly optimistic about their own prospects. They believe that they have an above average chance (relative to their peers) of experiencing positive life events such as living past 80 or owning their own house, and a below average chance of experiencing negative life events such as being divorced or having a heart attack before the age of 40 (Weinstein, 1980; see also, Larwood, 1978).

It is intriguing to speculate about the implications of an inflated vision of our own contributions and powers. Some of the potential consequences are certainly undesirable. We may not plan well for the future if we all expect to be the exception rather than the rule. Simone de Beauvoir (1973) has written eloquently about our failure to prepare adequately for old age, in part because we don't anticipate becoming old and feeble. Further, it comes as a shock and disappointment to realize that our colleagues do not hold us in quite as high esteem as we hold ourselves. This may be made known to us in work settings when we are passed over for raises, promotions, tenure, or awards.

For some individuals, the tendency to claim uniqueness has more serious consequences. A good deal of therapy and counseling is devoted to helping people view their reactions as normal rather than idiosyncratic (Miller and Porter, in press; Nisbett, Borgida, Crandall, and Reed, 1976; Valins and Nisbett, 1971).

Nonetheless, an inflated view of our own powers and uniqueness may, at times, be beneficial. If I see myself in charge, I am likely to engage in efforts to improve my own or my group's outcomes rather than wait for someone else to come to my aid. There is probably an element of self-fulfilling prophecy here, too. By taking appropriate actions, I may produce the desired outcome.

The self-fulfilling prophecy implications of control attributions are particularly noteworthy in regard to negative events. Lefcourt (1973) summarized a good deal of research across different species that demonstrates that the perception of control, even if illusory, increases hope and enhances an individual's ability to cope with aversive stimulation. On the other hand, a lack of perceived control and hope in the face of stressful negative events has been associated with a host of undesirable outcomes, including ulcerous lesions and death.

Summary.   The literature on perceived consensus is contradictory. On the one hand, there is attributive projection; people overestimate the representativeness of their feelings, opinions, and behaviors. On the other hand, there is the false perception of uniqueness. People sometimes view their own reactions and responses as overly idiosyncratic. Judgments of false uniqueness seem to occur principally when individuals evaluate their own control over past and future events, or when they perceive their own behavior to be surprising or inappropriate. Note, however, that even when people perceive themselves as relatively unique, they overestimate the degree to which others share this view (M. Ross, 1981). Thus, there is an assumed consensus with regard to these judgments.

Finally, the relevance of the perceived consensus research for Kelley's theorizing should be emphasized. Consensus (or a lack of consensus) is probably more often assumed than sought. Again, what seemed to be explicit information-gathering operations in Kelley's (1967) initial attribution model seem more appropriately characterized as cognitive schemata. Attribution is truly a theory-driven process.

THE DISCOUNTING PRINCIPLE

Kelley's discounting principle has probably generated more research than any other aspect of his theorizing. In particular, there has been a good deal of research with children that is directly relevant to this principle. This research has encompassed both perception of others and self-perception.

The most popular experimental technique in the study of social perception has been to present children with story pairs. In one story in the pair, a character engages in a behavior in the presence of a plausible cause X. In the contrasting story, a different character engages in the same behavior in the presence of two plausible causes, X and Y. According to the discounting principle, perceivers should be less certain about the contribution of X to the behavior of the story character in the latter story than in the former story. As a consequence, the role of X in causing the behavior should be discounted relative to the degree of causality attributed to X in the first story.

In most of the studies employing this technique, the common cause (X) has been "internal" to the story character (e.g., liking, kindness), whereas the added cause (Y) has been external (e.g., an extrinsic reward or a parental command). In one study, subjects of different ages were read stories about a child who was rewarded for playing (or commanded by a parent to play) with a toy and a child who played with the same toy of his own accord (Smith, 1975). Subjects were asked to report which story character wanted to play with the toy and why he wanted to play with it. Kindergarten children chose the unconstrained target person only about half of the time. Smith interpreted this as random responding. Older children and college students employed the discounting principle in a reliable fashion, as evidenced by their choice of the unconstrained target person as the one who wanted to play with a toy (Shultz, Butkowsky, Pearce, and Shanfield, 1975, report comparable findings).

Karniol and Ross (1976) obtained results similar to these, but argued that children in the younger age group were not responding randomly. When individual consistency in use of the discounting principle was examined across story pairs, it became evident that a substantial proportion of kindergarten children consistently chose the constrained target person as the one who wanted to play with, and liked, the toy. In short, many kindergarten children responded opposite to the predictions of the discounting principle. These children appeared to use an additive principle: extrinsic constraints (in particular, rewards) were seen as adding to the value of the activity. Use of the additive principle decreased, and use of the discounting principle increased, with age.

There is evidence from other research that at least for some young children, use of an additive principle developmentally precedes use of a discounting principle (Baldwin and Baldwin, 1970; Butzin, 1979; Costanzo, Grumet, and Brehm, 1974). For example, Constanzo and his colleagues found that grade 1 children inferred liking in line with adult sanctions. When an adult prevented a child from playing with a toy, first-graders assumed the child liked the toy less, whereas sixth-graders assumed the child liked it more, as compared to a situation in which there was no adult prohibition.

Evidence of use of an additive principle has also been found in young children's attributions for achievement behavior. Adults tend to infer an inverse relation between ability and effort. The high-ability person is assumed to exert less effort to produce success than the low-ability person. Similarly, success in the presence of low effort implies higher ability than success in the presence of high effort (Anderson and Butzin, 1974; Heider, 1958). On the other hand, young children appear to consider effort and ability to be directly rather than inversely related (Kun, 1977). When two hypothetical persons performed equally well, first-graders reported that the one who possessed more ability also exerted more effort.

An intriguing explanation that has been offered for the failure of some young children to discount concerns Piaget's concept of compensation (Kun, 1977; Surber, 1981). If a physical effect remains invariant, a change in the magnitude of one cause must be accompanied by a compensating change in the magnitude of another cause. Piagetian demonstrations of compensation include the famous conservation tasks in which, for example, the same amount of water is poured into glasses of varying diameters and children are asked which glass holds more water. Many young children are unable to compensate for changes in the height and width of the glasses and base their judgments on the water level. Research on such physical judgment tasks suggests that compensation develops during the concrete operational stage, ages 7–11 (Gelman and Weinberg, 1972).

It could be argued that discounting involves application of a compensation rule. If so, one would expect it to be largely absent prior to the age of seven. There are good reasons not to equate discounting and compensation, however. In the Piagetian tasks, the compensation rule is a necessary outcome of the law of conservation of mass. On the other hand, discounting is a socially or experientially learned phenomenon. It is not logically necessary that I discount a child's liking for an activity because he or she is getting rewarded. It is simply that I can be less *certain* of the individual's preferences than I would be if he or she engages in the same activity without a reward.

No logical principle is broken if I later learn that the rewarded individual truly enjoys the activity.

One area of social perception in which the compensation schema may appear to apply logically is that of achievement behavior. All other things being equal, I do have to work harder at tasks for which I have low rather than high ability. This does not mean, however, that there is always a negative relation between effort and ability. I may work hard at tasks that I excel at. In fact, everyday observation suggests that people often put more effort and time into activities they are good at than into activities that they are bad at. Thus, in the absence of performance information, adults expect a positive correlation between ability and effort (Kepka and Brickman, 1971).

In short, compensation in physical settings is a logical principle that is likely to be learned through commerce with the environment. In contrast, discounting is a social principle that follows from increasing knowledge and sophistication about the relation between internal and external causes, rather than a logical imperative. Children learn that strong external constraints often imply a desire to perform the prohibited or nonreinforced behavior. Prisons have bars because many prisoners would leave if they could; similarly, a prohibition against toy play, or incest, or drinking, or speeding, implies that the target persons wish to engage in the behavior—that's why the prohibition is necessary.

This inference about the relation between external constraints and internal causes can be quite wrong, however. Note that the additive heuristic employed by some young children in the Karniol and Ross (1976, 1979) studies can make at least as much logical and psychological sense as the discounting principle. Some young children may simply believe that the stimulus person will prefer activities selected for them by their parents, to activities they would select for themselves. Cynicism sets in with advancing age.

In a related discussion, Heider (1958) noted that some activities may gain in attractiveness because they become a means to an end. For example, "a hated task may become a pleasure when done for someone one loves" (p. 127). Thus, the distinction between intrinsic desire and induced motivation is really quite subtle. Discounting is by no means the only plausible response when an activity is seen to be done for some extrinsic goal.

To this point, we have focused on the application of the discounting principle to social perception. We now consider its use in self-perception. A good deal of research has examined the effects of rewards and other ex-

ternal constraints on children's interest in a task. The paradigmatic experiment on the effects of rewards on intrinsic motivation was conducted on nursery school children (Lepper, Greene, and Nisbett, 1973). The children drew pictures with felt-tip markers under one of three experimental conditions: (1) they anticipated and received a reward for doing the drawing, (2) they received the reward unexpectedly after finishing the drawing, or (3) they were neither promised nor given a reward. Intrinsic interest in drawing with the felt-tip marker was assessed one to two weeks later in a free-play situation, in which a number of other activities were available and no rewards were given. During this period, subjects who had been in the expected-reward condition were less likely to play with the markers than subjects in the remaining two conditions which did not differ from each other.

One plausible interpretation of these results is that the children who anticipated and received a reward attributed their initial performance of the activity to the reward and discounted their own intrinsic interest in drawing with felt-tip markers. As a result, they were less likely to persist in this activity during the subsequent free play when no reward was available. Presumably, unexpected rewards did not reduce intrinsic interest because the children could not logically attribute their initial performance of the activity to the reward. The finding that expected rewards reduce intrinsic interest in enjoyable activities has been obtained many times with adults (e.g., Calder and Staw, 1975; Deci, 1971; Deci and Ryan, 1980), as well as children (see Lepper and Greene, 1978, and M. Ross, 1976, for reviews).

Much subsequent research has been directed at specifying when rewards lead to a discounting of intrinsic interest. For example, an attributional analysis does not imply that intrinsic motivation will be discounted whenever external rewards are anticipated. The more salient or figural external consequences become, the more likely individuals should be to regard them as the reason for their behavior and to perceive their actions as extrinsically motivated. Consistent with this reasoning, highly salient rewards (e.g., a cue reminding subjects of the forthcoming reward was present during initial task performance) have been found to yield a greater decrease in nursery school children's intrinsic interest in an activity than less salient rewards (M. Ross, 1975).

On the other hand, Fazio (1981) examined the impact of the salience of children's initial attitudes toward the task. The adverse effects of rewards on children's intrinsic interest were eliminated when the salience of the children's initial, positive attitudes was increased. This study is one of the few that demonstrates that subjects will discount the impact of plausible external causes when internal cues are made salient. The reverse has been demonstrated repeatedly.

Note that research on intrinsic interest has been broader at both the independent and dependent variable ends than is indicated in this brief review. For example, Lepper and Greene (1975) showed that surveillance, an external constraint other than a reward, can decrease children's intrinsic interest. McGraw (1978) and Condry and Chambers (1978) provide reviews of research assessing the detrimental effects of rewards on learning and performance.

Studies of social perception indicate that children's use of the discounting principle increases with age and that some young children seem to employ an additive rule. Yet the data from studies of intrinsic motivation suggest that young children can and do apply the discounting principle in deriving self-attributions. Morgan (1981) attempted to examine the relation between social and self-perception. Eight-year-old children were identified as adders or discounters on the basis of their responses to social perception problems of the type used by Smith (1975). The children were subsequently either rewarded or not rewarded for working on a jigsaw puzzle. The rewarded children evidenced a decline in interest in the puzzle regardless of their classification on the social perception problems. Even children who appeared not to employ the discounting principle in social perception showed a decrease in their own intrinsic motivation when they were rewarded for performing an interesting activity.

A number of authors have offered intriguing speculations concerning the discrepant results in the social and self-perception literature (Guttentag and Longfellow, 1977; Lepper and Gilovich, 1981; Morgan, 1981). The discrepancy may be more apparent than real, however. Young children's attributions may differ according to social context. For example, Karniol and M. Ross's (1979) adders attributed benign intentions to the targets' mother: She was seen as attempting to please the target, rather than attempting to constrain his toy play. On the other hand, a benign attribution may be less likely if the reward agent were a peer or an adult stranger (as in the self-perception research). Moreover, even the mother's intentions may be questioned in contexts in which direct personal experience has led children to conclude that they are being bribed to engage in a nonpreferred behavior (e.g., the offer of a dessert contingent on eating a vegetable).

There are two implications of this reasoning. First, social and self-perception must be compared in similar social contexts if we are to conclude anything about the relative sophistication of young children's reasoning in these two domains. Second, young children's attributions may be more context bound than those of older children and adults (Lepper and Gilovitch, 1981). Perhaps young children have not derived general principles or theories such as discounting, which they apply across a broad range of contexts.

In conclusion, though Kelley's analysis of the attribution process is a conceptual cousin to that of Jones and Davis (1965), the sweep is far broader. As a consequence, Kelley's theorizing has sparked a tremendous amount of remarkably divergent research. As we have seen, Kelley's analysis has something to offer researchers interested in social perception, self-perception, adult attributions, and children's attributions.

ATTRIBUTION IN ACHIEVEMENT CONTEXTS

Despite the breadth of Kelley's analysis, still some aspects of Heider (1958) are not covered in Kelley's writing. Most important, neither Jones and Davis (1965) nor Kelley (1967, 1972) considered achievement attributions to any great extent in their theoretical models. Yet the commonsense analysis of achievement-related behaviors has been one of the most influential sections of Heider's book. He suggested that an individual's level of performance on a task will be attributed either to factors within the person or to factors within the environment. The two major personal factors are ability and effort ("can" and "try"). Heider also noted that temporary personal factors, such as fatigue, may be seen as contributing to performance. The two major environmental factors are luck (or opportunity) and task difficulty.

Heider described ability as a stable characteristic of the person. He did qualify this contention somewhat, however. "Certain facets of ability, for example, knowledge...are less permanently an integral part of the person than others, as for example, intelligence or strength" (p. 93). Heider depicted effort as a variable or unstable personal characteristic. The two major environmental factors were similarly distinguished on the stability dimension: task difficulty is a stable characteristic of the environment, whereas luck is a variable characteristic.

Heider also discussed the contribution of a number of other factors to the perception of a person's being able to perform an activity, including status and possessions. Perhaps the most intriguing other factor is need. A strong need may foster the belief that one is able to do something.

Finally, Heider's analysis suggests that perceivers should be biased toward selecting ability and task difficulty attributions over the remaining possibilities. People prefer to attribute performances to enduring or dispositional causes because such attributions are more likely to satisfy their desire for a stable, predictable, and controllable world.

Weiner and his colleagues have conducted the most extensive research program stemming from this analysis of achievement attributions. Typically, subjects are asked to make judgments about a hypothetical other's performance in terms of ability, effort, luck, and task difficulty. Weiner and his associates (1972) found that people tended to link rewards and punishments for a performance more to effort than to ability: High effort is rewarded, low effort punished. Effort, an internal-unstable cause, of course, is seen as under the actor's control. Also, attributions of luck and effort (unstable causes) increase as a function of the discrepancy between an outcome and the prior performance of an individual. On the other hand, attributions to the task and to ability (stable causes) increase with increasing consistency between the outcome and previous performance.

The importance of the stability and locus of causality dimensions has been substantiated in other research. Expectancies for continuing success on a task are higher among subjects making attributions to stable causal factors (ability and task ease) rather than unstable ones (effort and luck), but expectancies are unaffected by locus of causality (Weiner *et al.,* 1972). On the other hand, affective reactions to successes or failures appear to be more strongly connected to the locus of causality dimension. Feelings of pride for success and shame for failure are heightened when the performance is seen as caused by the internal factors of ability and effort rather than the external factors of luck and task difficulty (McFarland and M. Ross, 1982; Reimer, 1975; Weiner, Russell, and Lerman, 1978).

Other researchers have questioned Heider's characterization of the four basic causes (Darley and Goethals, 1980; Deaux, 1976; Feather and Simon, 1973; Valle and Frieze, 1976). Each of the causes can be interpreted in terms opposite to those presented by Heider. For example, effort can be seen as a stable, dispositional cause (a lazy or vigorous person); moreover, inferences about people's degree of motivation, inferred from effort, are at least as important for predicting and controlling their behavior as are inferences of ability. Similarly, perceivers convert chance from an external, variable cause to a personal, dispositional cause when they think of people as being lucky or unlucky. And, task difficulty need not be seen as stable. Tasks may be viewed as easier at some times than at others, as when a person claims to think better on a full stomach.

In addition, it appears that the four causes of ability, effort, luck, and task difficulty do not play as dominant a role in commonsense explanations as Heider seemed to imply. Most research has relied on Heider's analysis and employed only the four basic causes, often in a forced choice format. Yet open-ended studies of attribution have shown that people often explain performances with reference to other factors (e.g., Elig and Frieze, 1979; Frieze, 1976). In the Elig and Frieze study, subjects were asked to explain their own performance on an anagrams task. Their open-ended responses were subsequently coded into attribution categories. Consistent with Heider's analysis, the dispositional causes of ability and task difficulty were the two factors most frequently coded, with effort being the third most frequent cause. On the other hand, luck or chance was rarely mentioned. Also, at times people use explanations other than the basic four, including mood, personality, fatigue, and interest (Darley and Goethals, 1980; Elig and Frieze, 1975, 1979).

Research by Jones and his associates has taken achievement attributions in a different and interesting direction (Jones and Goethals, 1971; Jones, Rock, Shaver, Goethals, and Ward, 1968). They examined the effects of different patterns of performance on observers' attributions of ability. Observers judged a target person who experienced a descending pattern of success to be more intelligent and expected him to do better on future problems, than a target showing an ascending pattern of success.

One interpretation of these results is that estimates of ability were formed early in the sequence and were maintained in the face of discrepant information. Later performances are likely to be attributed to shifts in luck or effort rather than to changes in a stable and enduring factor such as ability.

SEX DIFFERENCES IN ACHIEVEMENT ATTRIBUTIONS

In this section, we examine whether there are systematic differences in the attributions offered for similar performances by males and females and consider the bases of such differences. Two general forms of experiments have been conducted: social perception experiments in which male and female subjects report their attributions for the performance of a hypothetical male or female target person; and self-perception studies in which male and female subjects report their attributions for their own performance. A review of the literature indicates a good deal of inconsistency across studies. Some experiments reveal sex differences in attribution, others do not. Despite this variability, however, three general conclusions seem warranted.

1. There is little effect for sex of subject in the social perception studies. That is, male and female perceivers agree on the attributions to be made for success and failure by male and female performers (Bird and Williams, 1980; Etaugh and Brown, 1975; Feldman-Summers and Kiesler, 1974).

2. When differences in attribution do occur as a function of the performer's sex, certain patterns are evident in both the self-perception and social perception studies. A male's success is more likely to be attributed to ability and less likely to be attributed to luck or effort than is a female's success (Deaux and Emswiller, 1974; Etaugh and Brown, 1975; Feather, 1969; Feather and Simon, 1975). A male's failure is more likely to be attributed to bad luck or lack of effort and less likely to be attributed to lack of ability than is a female's failure (Dweck and Reppucci, 1973; Etaugh and Brown, 1975; Deaux and Emswiller, 1974; Feather, 1969; Feather and Simon, 1975; Nicholls, 1975).

3. The most popular explanation for the effects of sex of the performers on attributions focuses on the differential expectations attributors have for male and female performers (Deaux, 1976; Deaux and Emswiller, 1974; Feather and Simon, 1975; Feldman-Summers and Kiesler, 1974). Males typically have higher expectations of success than females do, and social perceivers often report higher expectations of a male's success than of a female's success (Crandall, 1969; Deaux, 1976; Feldman-Summers and Kiesler, 1974). Research has demonstrated that expected outcomes tend to be attributed to stable factors such as ability and unexpected outcomes to variable factors such as luck (Feather and Simon, 1971; Miller and Ross, 1975). Thus, it follows that success by a male and failure by a female should tend to be attributed to ability, whereas, failure by a male and success by a female should tend to be attributed to the variable factors of luck and effort.

This expectations hypothesis seems to provide a plausible and parsimonious account of the sex differences in attribution, and it has received qualified empirical support. There are at least three social perception experiments in which the hypothesis was tested directly by a manipulation of the sex-appropriateness of a task (Deaux and Emswiller, 1974; Feather and Simon, 1975; Feldman-Summers and Kiesler, 1974). The results obtained on masculine tasks tended to be consistent with the expectations hypothesis. Success on a male task was more likely to be attributed to ability in a male than in a female; failure on a masculine task was more likely to be attributed to lack of ability in a female than in a male. The predicted reversal of this pattern was not obtained on the supposedly feminine tasks, however. One reason for this discrepancy is that it has proved difficult to find activities on which males are expected to perform poorer than females. In short, a strong and enduring sex difference in expectations has made assessment of the expectations hypothesis a difficult endeavor in social perception research.

Rosenfield and Stephan (1978) manipulated the sex-appropriateness of a task in a *self-perception* experiment. In the masculine version, subjects were told that the task was designed to yield information about the "masculine personality"; in the feminine version, the same task was allegedly designed to yield information about the "feminine personality." Males attributed success on the masculine task more internally (skill and effort) and failure more externally (luck and task difficulty) than females. On the feminine task, females made more internal attributions for success and more external attributions for failure than males did. Thus, subjects evidenced the anticipated reversal to the typical pattern when a "feminine" task was employed.

Nonetheless this study can be criticized on the grounds that the manipulation may have induced self-presentational concerns. Perhaps subjects were embarrassed when they exhibited the "wrong" personality. They may have felt compelled to deny publicly that personal factors contributed to their success at a sex-inappropriate task or to their failure at a sex-appropriate task.

The preceding review documents sex differences in attribution and relates them to expectancies. Dweck and her colleagues have extended this work by examining the impact of socialization patterns on sex differences in attribution. Their research has focussed on children's self-attributions for failure. Children who attribute their failure to factors that imply that it is insurmountable (e.g., lack of ability) tend to show impaired performance and decreased persistence at a task. These children are termed "helpless" by Dweck. Conversely, children who attribute failure to surmountable factors (e.g., lack of effort) tend to maintain or improve their performance in the face of failure feedback. Dweck describes these children as "mastery oriented" (Diener and Dweck, 1978; Dweck, 1975; Dweck and Bush, 1976; Dweck and Repucci, 1973).

Dweck's research suggests that girls are more likely than boys to display the helpless orientation and less likely than boys to be mastery oriented. The puzzle is why this difference should occur when girls tend to perform at least as well in school as boys. Observational research conducted in several fourth and fifth grade classrooms suggested a possible answer (Dweck, Davidson, Nelson, and Enna, 1978). When teachers are critical of girls, the criticism tends to relate directly to the intellectual aspects of their work whereas teachers' criticism of boys relates to different aspects of their behavior, including neatness, conduct, and so on. This pattern is reversed with praise. Boys tend to be praised for the intellectual aspects of their work; girls are praised more generally for neatness, good conduct, and so forth, as well as for the intellectual quality of their work.

This difference in teacher feedback presumably arises because girls are better behaved and better all-around citizens than boys. Yet the attributional implications of these patterns of teacher feedback are harmful to girls. According to Kelley's covariation principle, boys should not be inclined to attribute negative feedback to their intellectual ability as the feedback is associated with many different aspects of their behavior (low distinctiveness). For girls, negative feedback is almost uniquely associated with intellectual endeavors (high distinctiveness)—and therefore their failures should be attributed to their lack of ability. Conversely, positive feedback is linked uniquely to intellectual endeavors in boys, and hence should be attributed to ability. Girls experience positive feedback across different contexts and therefore it should be less strongly associated with ability.

Dweck has experimentally examined the implications of these differential feedback patterns for reactions to failure. The kind of failure feedback provided boys (negative feedback for intellectual and nonintellectual aspects of a task) caused both fifth-grade boys and girls to attribute their failure on an experimental task to lack of effort (Dweck *et al.,* 1978). In contrast, the pattern of failure feedback provided to girls (negative feedback for

intellectual aspects of the task only) caused both boys and girls to attribute failure to lack of ability.

This research is significant because it represents one of the few attempts to examine the origins of sex differences in attribution. As we have seen, by no means all studies reveal such differences. The social perception studies described earlier suggest, however, that both sexes share a theory about the causes for intellectual performance by males and females. A classroom situation is likely to be a powerful influence in the development and maintenance of this theory, partly because the feedback for performance is often public. (But see Parsons, Kaczala, and Meece, 1982, for a failure to replicate the Dweck findings.)

More recent research also points to the importance of parental influences in the development of such theories (Parsons, Adler, and Kaczala, 1982). Mothers and fathers reported sex-differentiated perceptions of their children's aptitude for mathematics despite similar performances by boys and girls. Daughters were seen as having to work harder to do well in math than sons. In addition, parents' perceptions of their children's performance were more directly related to the children's self-concepts and expectancies than were the children's past performances in math.

ATTRIBUTION THEORY RE-EXAMINED

This concludes our review of the major theories of attribution and the research that is directly pertinent to them. At this point, we adopt a more critical stance in an attempt to explicate the central theoretical issues in attribution theory. We begin by addressing considerations that have been relatively ignored by attribution theorists but may be important to the layperson's understanding of causality. We then analyze some of the major assumptions that underlie the theories of Heider, Jones and Davis, and Kelley.

THE CONCEPT OF CAUSALITY

Perhaps surprisingly, the concept of causality itself largely has remained an unanalyzed concept in attribution theory. The issues involved in such an analysis are complex and difficult, as anyone who has dabbled in the voluminous philosophical literature on the topic will attest to. (Cook and Campbell, 1979, provide an excellent overview of the basic issues from a psychological perspective.) In the simplest causal relationship, event *X* (billiard ball *A* hits billiard ball *B*) causes event *Y* (billiard ball *B* moves). In this prototypic billiard ball model, causality may be characterized as a relationship between two events where the cause temporally precedes, and is spacially and temporally contiguous to, the effect. According to this Humean model, the regular covariation between such *X*'s and *Y*'s provides the basis for any subsequent causal judgment.

Unfortunately, the concept of causality is too complex to be captured in the billiard ball model, even in the physical or inanimate world. First, causes are not confined to events. We also pick out dispositional qualities as causes (the glass breaks because it's fragile), and even nonevents as causes (the kettle boiled dry because the thermostat failed to switch it off). Second, events or dispositions can be both causes and effects at the same time, as in for example, weather systems, machinery with feedback mechanisms, and so forth. Third, causes and effects are often linked by causal chains so that some causes are considerably removed both temporally and spatially from the effect.

Even this superficial analysis suggests that the classical attribution models are overly simplistic. This is perhaps most evident with regard to the temporal dimension. Many events have both proximal and distal antecedant causes (Brickman, Ryan, and Wortman, 1975; Kelley, 1983). My rude behavior can be attributed to a personality trait (a proximal cause), which, in turn, could be attributed to my upbringing, which, in turn, could be attributed to the personality of my parents, and so on. Perceivers have to cut off their causal analysis somewhere to avoid infinite regression. The question is, where?

One answer may be that the choice of cause will depend upon the perceiver's reason for making the attribution (Jones and Thibaut, 1958; Kruglanski, Hamel, Maides, and Schwartz, 1978). It has typically been suggested that people make causal attributions when they are curious about the determinants of behavior or when they want to predict and perhaps control another's behavior.

Consider each of these reasons for making causal attributions. When is a perceiver's curiosity aroused? A likely answer is that it tends to be aroused when a behavior is unexpected—either because it is discrepant from the actor's past behavior or from the perceiver's normative expectations (Jones and McGillis, 1976; Napolitan and Goethals, 1979). But how is curiosity related to

choice of proximal or distal causes? Perhaps the more unusual or unexpected the action, the more curious the perceivers are. As a result, they delve deeper into the causes of behavior, and more distal causes are considered.

The goals of prediction and control may affect the attributor's choice of cause more directly. Perceivers are particularly sensitive to causes that satisfy their goals. For example, professional helpers are more likely than nonprofessionals to attribute their client's problems to personal dispositions. One explanation that has been proposed for this finding is that it is easier to change aspects of the client than to change aspects of his or her social situations (Batson, 1975; Carkhuff, 1968; Goffman, 1961). Thus, when they experience a need for control, attributors may assign causality to controllable rather than uncontrollable factors.

Attributors motivated by a need for control need not stop at the level of personal dispositions, however. Information about the causes of someone's personal dispositions can provide important evidence concerning the strength or centrality of those dispositions. For example, if I link Fred's lack of confidence to his unhappy childhood, then I should rate this disposition as more central and harder to change than if I explained his lack of confidence in terms of his age or inexperience. Perhaps the more motivated people are to make accurate judgments about the personal dispositions of other people, for whatever reason, the more likely they will be to consider distal as well as proximal causes for behavior.

Curiosity, prediction, and control do not exhaust the possible reasons for making attributions. Often, I make attributions about my own or another's behavior primarily because I have been asked to do so by others. The causes(s) I then select will depend in part on what I assume the questioner wants to know. Suppose I am asked why Alice is rude. I am not being very informative if I reply that she is rude because she is a rude person. Consequently, I am more likely to discuss her upbringing, other personality variables (she is insecure), situational factors, and so forth. Similarly, on an analyst's couch I am more likely to weave a connection between my current behavior and childhood experiences than I would in a conversation with a friend.

My causal explanation is thus determined by both conversational conventions and my assumptions about the questioner's expectations. In addition, I may want to influence the questioner's judgment. I can focus on one cause if I want to induce sympathy and another cause if I don't. For example, to promote a favorable image, I may attribute Alice's rudeness to situational factors rather than to personal dispositions. In other words, I can choose a cause to suit my own needs and the demands of the situation from the array of proximal and distal causes that may be seen as legitimately contributing to a behavior.

Finally, it seems likely that there are individual differences in the degree of attributional complexity people exhibit. Fletcher (1981, 1983a) examined attributions for marriage separations. He found that the better educated the subject the more likely he/she was to, (1) cite more causes for the marriage breakup, (2) use more interactive causes focussing on the relationship than single spouse attributions, (3) use more abstract dispositional causes (e.g., attitudes, beliefs) than simple behavioral traits or events, and (4) mention more attributions from the distant past.

PERSONAL VERSUS IMPERSONAL CAUSALITY

Another important issue for attribution theory concerns its scope. Can the same causal model be applied to both the inanimate physical world and the personal world of human behavior and experience? Of the three models discussed previously, only Kelley's (1967) is intended as a general causal model applicable to judgments of social and physical causality. Yet by 1972, Kelley himself was wondering whether it makes sense to treat personal and impersonal attribution in the same terms (p.173).

The personal versus impersonal attribution distinction is reminiscent of a debate about whether social and nonsocial perception require different theoretical accounts. The same basic proposition appears to lie behind the viewpoint that person perception and personal causality are special cases: people and inanimate objects are fundamentally different sorts of "things." As Tagiuri (1969, pp. 395–396) noted,

> In the sense that we perceive or infer primarily psychological properties or potentialities through various cues, persons are doubtless special objects.
> . . . The observations or inferences we make are principally about intentions, attitudes, emotions, ideas, abilities, purposes, traits, thoughts, perceptions, memories—events that are *inside* the person and strictly psychological—we attribute to a person

properties of *consciousness* and *self-determination,* and the capacity for *representation of his environment,* which in turn mediates his actions.

Many of the central concepts in Heider's (1958) and Jones and Davis's (1965) theories of attribution seem to be peculiar to persons. This includes such pivotal concepts as choice, responsibility, intentionality, and motives. Conversely, Kelley's (1967, 1972) model can explain both person and thing causality because it treats persons like things and excludes such concepts; Kelley focuses instead on the covariation between cause and effect. Thus, the answer to the question of whether one theory can embrace both classes of attribution depends on the level of abstraction one wants to achieve. Kelley's theory does not depict the richness of interpersonal perception when it fails to deal with issues as fundamental as judgments of intentionality and responsibility. Few layperson perceivers would be satisfied with this level of abstraction. On the other hand, Kelley's theory cuts a wide swath; and, as a result perhaps, it has generated more research than any of the other approaches. At a more microlevel, though, we believe that separate models are necessary to capture the important differences between persons and things, and the associated causal theories people utilize.

THE MAJOR ASSUMPTIONS UNDERLYING ATTRIBUTION THEORY

Jones and Davis and Kelley have embodied some of Heider's major assumptions about the attribution process in their models. Three of these assumptions that have been the focus of some debate are: (1) Commonsense provides the basis for attribution theory. (2) Perceivers prefer to attribute behavior to stable personal dispositions. (3) The person-environment (internal-external) distinction represents the pivotal causal attribution dimension. We discuss each of these assumptions in turn.

COMMON SENSE AND ATTRIBUTION THEORY

The tension between description and explanation, in relation to common sense, is a key issue in attribution theory and research. The contention that we should pay attention to common sense in our description of attribution processes appears tame enough to raise few hackles. In contrast, the claim that we should build common sense into our explanatory theories may appear to be an arbitrary and onerous restriction (Calder, 1977; Mandler, 1975). This issue should not be confused with whether we are obliged to retain all the beliefs, folk psychology, and generalizations inherent in common sense. Few social psychologists would invest the conventional wisdom with revelationary qualities. What is at stake here is not the sanctity of commonsense beliefs or theories, but the importance to scientific discourse of the concepts and distinctions inherent in those beliefs and theories.

Heider treated common sense as a valuable resource both for describing the attribution process, and for constructing psychological theory to explain this process. Most social psychologists have used and adapted such commonsense, psychological concepts in their theory building as need, motive, attitude, belief, drive, emotion, reward, punishment, and so forth. Moreover, those psychological systems that have attempted to eliminate our commonsense conceptual schema have not fared well when applied to human behavior. The radical behaviorism of Skinner is possibly the most illuminating example. Skinner (1953) labelled commonsense language the "language of the market-place" and rejected it as unscientific. In its place he advocated a simple model utilizing a handful of technical concepts, the main ones being "reinforcement," "stimulus," and "response."

Skinner's principal strategy is to translate commonsense expressions into "behavioral" expressions using his technical concepts, thus purging the language of mentalistic terms and supposedly producing a tight scientific discourse. One of the major criticisms levelled at Skinner's theory concerns the status of these behavioral translations. Although Skinner's technical concepts, such as reinforcement, are defined in a precise enough way in the laboratory with rats or pigeons, their meaning becomes less clear when applied to human social relations. In this context, the allegedly exact reformulations of commonsense language are often rescued from either incoherence or falsity by vague and metaphorical interpretations of his technical concepts. Yet terms such as reinforcement then simply become poor substitutes for those in ordinary usage (Chomsky, 1959). Thus, radical behaviorism smuggles commonsense surreptitiously in the back door after officially throwing it out the front door (Fletcher, 1984).

Why should commonsense concepts be so difficult to discard? The answer may be that there are a number of commonsense beliefs and associated concepts that are necessary for maintaining an intelligible view of the world. Among these we might include the belief that the world exists independently of our perception of it and the associated concept of existence; the belief that the world is a reasonably consistent place and the associated concept of causality; and the belief that human beings are capable of intentional action and the associated network of mentalistic concepts we use to explain and understand people's behavior. Many of the concepts central to attribution theory appear to fall into the last two categories.

This reasoning does not imply that social psychologists are necessarily prevented from refining concepts borrowed from common sense, proposing new concepts, or inventing entire conceptual schemes. Indeed, to cleave too closely to commonsense conceptual schemes, as a matter of course, is likely to stifle the development of dynamic, innovative theory. Moreover, Heider and other attribution theorists never intended that we sanctify common sense, but that we treat it as a valuable resource in theory building (see Fletcher, 1984, for a more extended discussion of these issues).

THE ROLE OF PERSONAL DISPOSITIONS IN ATTRIBUTION THEORY

The prime importance of personal dispositions has been an article of faith in attribution theory. Indeed, there has been a tendency at times to define the attribution process as being exclusively concerned with dispositional attributions (e.g., Kelley, 1967, p. 193). Yet internal or person attributions need not be dispositional. Internal, episodic causal attributions (emotions, images, transitory beliefs or intentions, fatigue, etc.) are common in everyday life (Darley and Goethals, 1980; Elig and Frieze, 1975). It is perhaps unfortunate that attribution theorists and researchers have occasionally slipped into the habit of equating internal with dispositional.

Although personal dispositions are given such an elevated status in attribution theory, none of the theorists attempts a comprehensive conceptual analysis of these dispositions. The different kinds of dispositions (attitudes, beliefs, feelings, abilities, habits, personality characteristics) are treated as a largely homogenous class. Nonetheless, there are important differences among them. Alston (1975) noted one general distinction that appears significant from the standpoint of attribution theory. He differentiated "pure frequency" dispositions (e.g., domineering or aggressive) from "purposive-cognitive" dispositions (e.g., abilities, needs, attitudes).

With pure frequency dispositions, the relevant behavior is one of the necessary criteria for attribution of the concept, and constitutes the meaning of the expression. For example, one necessary criterion for ascribing aggressiveness is that the person behaves in aggressive ways in some situations. On the other hand, the behaviors relevant to purposive-cognitive dispositions do not necessarily have to be exhibited. One can possess an attitude without expressing it, or have an ability without exercising it.

Reeder and Brewer (1979) have also argued that the rules of dispositional inference may vary depending on the nature of the attribute to be inferred. They discussed three general schemata, each embracing three different classes of disposition. To take one example, the hierarchically restrictive schema specifies that individuals possessing a high degree of the disposition (e.g., ability) may exhibit a wide range of performance, whereas those possessing a low degree of the disposition are incapable of reaching a high level of performance. For instance, a person who paints an outstanding work of art *must* have high artistic ability; a person who fails to produce an outstanding work of art may also have high artistic ability. He may simply have had a bad day, or perhaps he is lazy and doesn't try. Reeder and his colleagues have found that dimensions such as introversion-extroversion, intelligence-unintelligence, as well as the more obvious skill dimensions, operate according to this schema (Messick and Reeder, 1974; Reeder and Fulks, 1980; Reeder, Messick, and Van Avermaet, 1977).

The major point of this discussion is that the content of the attribution matters. Theories of attribution that ignore the distinctions among dispositions fail to deal with the richness and complexities of interpersonal perception.

THE INTERNAL-EXTERNAL DISTINCTION

The internal-external distinction occupies an important place in all three theories. This dimension has meanings that have not always been differentiated in attribution theory or research. We might mean internal-external in a spatial sense. Everything located inside the person such as personality dispositions, emotions, intentions, and illnesses is internal, and everything located outside, such as the weather or the behavior of other people, is external. Alternatively, one might construe the dimension in terms of personal control or freedom (Weiner, 1979; Weiner *et al.,* 1972). In this sense, illnesses, emotions, and some

abilities are external, and plans, beliefs, and intentions are internal. This latter formulation is more consistent with Heider's (1958, p. 100) analysis. Studies utilizing multidimensional scaling or factor analytic procedures have indicated that people's causal attributions for success and failure can be distinguished in terms of both control and spacial location (Meyer, 1980; Passer, 1977).

One of the potentially disturbing features of the internal-external distinction is the ease with which statements seeming to imply external attributions can be rephrased into statements implying internal attributions and vice versa (Monson and Snyder, 1977; L. Ross, 1977). For instance, the statement, ''Mike likes mystery stories because they are exciting'' implies an external attribution. Mike's preference for mysteries is caused by a characteristic of the stories. Conversely, ''Mike likes mystery stories because he likes to be excited'' indicates an internal attribution. This statement seems to attribute Mike's preference to something about Mike. Yet the first version of the statement makes sense only if we assume that Mike enjoys being excited. Consequently, the two statements are virtually identical in content. Is it reasonable to distinguish statements containing such comparable content in terms of causality?

The answer to this question appears to be ''yes.'' Grammatical differences do not reflect random whims of language usage: rather they are valid indicators of an underlying psychological reality (M. Ross and DiTecco, 1975; Kanouse, 1971). For example, shifts in grammatical form occur in a meaningful and predictable way in newspaper reports of baseball and football games, with the result that more internal responsibility is assigned to athletes for wins than for losses (Lau and Russell, 1980). Similarly, there are subtle differences in the way athletes from winning and losing teams describe the outcome of the game (M. Ross and Lumsden, 1982). All of the players from winning teams reported the outcome of the game as ''we won'' (rather than that their opponents had lost), whereas a significant number of the losers reported the game as ''they (i.e., the opponents) won,'' rather than ''we lost.'' These results suggest that the participants were inclined to take more responsibility for winning (''we won'' implies ''we did the winning'') than for losing (''we lost'' would imply ''we did the losing''). Finally, Fletcher (1983a, 1983b) had spouses who were separated account for the breakdown of their marriages. Internal and external attributions assessed on standard rating scales were significantly related to differences implicit in the grammatical structure of subjects' spontaneous verbal accounts of the marriage breakdown.

A second issue needs to be raised with respect to the internal-external distinction. Heider (1958) posited a hydraulic relation between personal and situational causality: the more the person is seen as causing the action, the less causal influence the environment will be perceived to exert. Many researchers have accepted the premise that personal and situational sources of causality operate in a complementary fashion. As a consequence, some have employed a single measure in which personal attributions anchor one end of the scale and situational attributions the other end. In other studies, separate measures of personal and situational attributions are combined to form a composite index. In still others, subjects' responses are expressed in terms of percentages or proportions such that increased attribution to one dimension necessarily forces decreased attribution to the other.

The results from studies in which the relation between the two attribution dimensions has been explicitly examined have been less than encouraging, however. Researchers have typically reported low and nonsignificant correlations between measures of personal and situational attribution (Lepper, 1973; McArthur and Post, 1977; Taylor and Koivumaki, 1976). McArthur and Post concluded from their results "that situational and dispositional attributions are not psychological reciprocals of one another...In view of this researchers would be well advised to employ separate measures for the two attributions" (p. 530).

In retrospect it seems obvious that in many circumstances perceivers will not consider situational and personal attributions to be inversely related. As noted earlier, events have proximal and distal causes, some of which may be internal and others of which may be external. For example, my rudeness may be attributed to an internal personality disposition that, in turn, could be attributed to my socialization, an external factor.

Moreover, both Heider (1958) and Kelley (1972) suggested that complex patterns of causality are possible in which a behavior can be seen as reflecting something about a person as well as something about an external stimulus. For instance, enjoyment of an object might depend on both a person's state and the presence or absence of the object. Earlier, we used the example of pickles and pregnancy to make this same point.

Such reasoning is considered to be quite sophisticated. The perceiver must take into account covariance patterns involving both the person and the object. Heider argued that perceivers favor simple attributions to the person or to the situation over such complex attributions, though the complex attributions may more often be correct. Interestingly, people are more likely to employ combinations of person and situation attributions when attributional accuracy is seen as important (Kassin and Hochreich, 1977).

The failures to observe a hydraulic relation between personal and situational causality suggest that complex patterns of attribution may be more common than Heider supposed. Personal and situational attributions are not always and may not even typically be inversely related.

There is a final point that needs to be raised with respect to the internality or externality of attributions. Largely as a result of Kelley's theorizing, this distinction has come to be seen as the most important distinguishing feature of causes. It is not evident that such emphasis is fully warranted (Kruglanski, 1980). As we have already seen, lay attributors may have a variety of goals in mind when formulating attributions. Dimensions other than the internality or externality of the cause may be seen as more important to these goals—dimensions such as stability, temporal contiguity, predictability, and so forth. In addition, the perceiver may be interested in the particular content of the attribution rather than in such general dimensional qualities as its degree of internality.

SUMMARY

In examining some of the central issues in attribution theory we noted differences between judgments of personal and impersonal causality. The discussion included an analysis of the temporal dimension and the perceiver's goals in the attribution process. We then evaluated some of the major assumptions of attribution theorists. Our discussion of the role of common sense led us to affirm its importance in theory building. Next we argued for the need for a careful analysis of the distinctions among personal dispositions. Finally, we considered the usefulness of the internal-external distinction and questioned whether the importance attribution theorists have accorded this dimension is warranted.

This concludes our discussion of the classical theories of attribution. We now turn to a number of specific domains in which the attribution approach has been applied. We begin with a body of research that has had a profound impact on the field—work by Schachter and his colleagues on the self-perception of an emotion. We then proceed to discuss research on self-perception, actor-observer attributions, motivation, misattribution, and introspective awareness.

THE SELF-ATTRIBUTION OF EMOTIONAL STATES

The analysis of emotional experience has been one of the most enduring and intriguing problems in psychology (see Leventhal, 1974, 1980, and Zillman, 1978, for reviews). The high points of this history are familiar. The James-Lange theory of emotion (James, 1890/1950; Lange, 1885/1922) reversed commonsense notions of the temporal relation between the cognitive experience of emotion and physiological arousal. James and Lange suggested that the perception of an emotion-provoking event yields autonomic and/or skeletal responses that are then experienced as the emotion. Cannon (1927) attacked the James-Lange theory on several grounds: (1) emotional behavior can occur without an intact autonomic nervous system, (2) artificially invoked autonomic changes do not produce emotional experiences, and (3) skeletal reactions are insufficiently differentiated and visceral reactions too slow and diffuse to account for the range and latency of emotional experience. Cannon attributed emotional states to central neural activity, specifically, thalamic processes. In a similar vein, Lindsley's (1951) activation theory of emotion related the intensity of emotional experience to the level of cortical arousal.

Social psychologists got into the act with Schachter's theory of emotion (Schachter, 1964; Schachter and Singer, 1962; Schachter and Singer, 1979; Schachter and Wheeler, 1962). Schachter postulated two necessary conditions for the experience of emotion: physiological arousal and cognitions that define the arousal as a particular emotional state. The emotion-provoking event produces physiological arousal in some rather ill-defined manner. The person notices the arousal, and in the absence of an a priori explanation for it, searches the environment for information to label and define the arousal. Mandler (1975) has termed Schachter's theory the "juke box" theory of emotion: arousal is the turntable motor and cognition is the record that defines the tune. Research by Schachter and his colleagues lent support to the cognitive-arousal model (Schachter and Singer, 1962; Schachter and Wheeler, 1962; Singer, 1963).

The model has its detractors, however. The data from the early experiments were equivocal and some of the hypotheses were rescued only by questionable internal analyses (Plutchik and Ax, 1967). Also, more recent attempts at replication have failed and have led to the suggestion that unexplained physiological arousal tends to produce negative affect (Marshall and Zimbardo, 1979; Maslach, 1979).

Further, Schachter's theory explains only a limited range of emotional experience. It does not appear to account for the emotional feelings of young infants who exhibit distinguishable affects before they acquire the linguistic abilities and social understanding that are presumably necessary to label emotion in Schachter's terms (Leventhal, 1980). Additionally, the theory may underestimate the role of memories and learning in determining emotional responses to stimuli (Harris and Katkin, 1975; Leventhal, 1980). Finally, feedback from facial muscles may play a more important role in defining emotional experience than either James or Schachter envisioned (Laird, 1974; Lanzetta, Cartwright-Smith, and Kleck, 1976), though the data are not entirely consistent (Leventhal, 1980; Tourangeau and Ellsworth, 1979).

Be that as it may, Schachter and his colleagues presented an elegant and parsimonious account of emotions. Moreover, their research and theorizing influenced the direction of social psychology in the next two decades. If emotions can be considered to be self-attributions, heavily dependent on the presence of external cues, might not other forms of self-knowledge such as feelings, beliefs, and attitudes be determined by similar attributional processes? Daryl Bem answered this question with a resounding yes.

THE SELF-PERCEPTION OF ATTITUDES AND FEELINGS

Bem (1965, 1967, 1970, 1972) argued that to the extent that internal cues are ambiguous, the individual is in the same position as an external observer: "Individuals come to 'know' their own attitudes, emotions, and other internal states partially by inferring them from observations of their own overt behavior and/or the circumstances in which this behavior occurs" (Bem, 1972, p. 2). As we have already seen, this hypothesis received some support from research on the effects of rewards on intrinsic motivation. Extrinsic factors appear to influence children's and adult's estimates of their intrinsic interest in a task. A number of other studies offer additional support with respect to the self-perception of attitudes (M. Ross, Insko, and Ross, 1971; Seligman, Fazio, and Zanna, 1980; Valins, 1966), the self-perception of physical discomfort (Bandler, Madaras, and Bem, 1968; Corah and Boffa, 1970), and self-perceptions of mathematical ability (Miller, Brickman, and Bolen, 1975).

On the other hand, there is ample evidence that people do not always make self-inferences from their behavior or external cues. Kiesler, Nisbett, and Zanna (1969) showed that a behavior affected attitudes only when its relevance to subjects' beliefs was made salient. Taylor (1975) found that subjects inferred their attitudes from false physiological feedback only when they would not have to act upon their attitudes. When their attitudes had behavioral consequences, subjects apparently used information other than the feedback to assess their feelings.

Few attempts have been made to assess the validity of Bem's own caveat that individuals infer their attitudes from their behaviors, only to the extent that internal cues are weak and ambiguous. A study conducted by Chaiken and Baldwin (1981) is an exception. Subjects with well-defined or poorly defined attitudes toward ecology were identified and asked to complete a questionnaire that made salient either their past pro-ecology or past anti-ecology behaviors. Subjects with poorly defined attitudes subsequently reported attitudes that were consistent with the pro- or anti-ecology behaviors made salient by the questionnaire manipulation. The attitudes of subjects with well-defined feelings toward ecology were not influenced by the manipulation. These results supported Bem's hypothesis. People with weak internal cues (poorly defined attitudes) inferred their beliefs from their past behavior.

Not surprisingly, then, self-attributions are multidetermined. Own behavior is only one relevant source of information pertaining to feelings and attitudes. The person will draw on other sources of information, to the extent that they are salient and available. In addition, the extent of processing that the individual engages in (the likelihood that he or she will go beyond the immediately salient and available information) depends, in part, on the importance of the judgment.

SELF-PERCEPTION THEORY VERSUS COGNITIVE DISSONANCE THEORY

Bem initially offered his theory of self-perception as an alternative, nonmotivational interpretation of cognitive dissonance phenomena. Cognitive dissonance theory portrays people as motivated to avoid and reduce discomfort caused by inconsistencies between cognitions (Aronson, 1969; Festinger, 1957). On the other hand, self-perception theory implies that people are often not aware of their own feelings, or cognitions, let alone of inconsistencies between them.

Bem (1965, 1967) attempted to show the validity of a self-perception interpretation of dissonance results, through a series of interpersonal simulations. Subjects were given a written description of one of the conditions of a dissonance experiment and asked to estimate the attitude of the person whose behavior was described. Bem (1965, 1967) found that the attitude estimates of subjects in the simulation experiments corresponded closely to the attitude reports of subjects in the original dissonance experiments. He concluded that this correspondence indicates that the subjects in the simulation experiments and those in the original dissonance experiments derived their attitude judgments from the same data—namely, the behavior of the original subjects and the context in which that behavior occurred.

Both dissonance and self-perception theorists assume that a person's attitudes may be influenced by his or her behavior when the behavior cannot be attributed solely to external circumstances. It is the explanation of how the influence occurs that differentiates the two theories. Dissonance theory posits an unpleasant arousal state that results from a clash between attitudes and behavior. The arousal is reduced by a shift in attitudes. Self-perception theory begins with a different premise: Individuals often do not know their own attitudes. As a result, they do not experience dissonance between those unknown attitudes and the behavior. Rather, individuals infer their attitudes from their behavior, taking into account the circumstances under which it occurred.

The results of the simulation experiments are consistent with Bem's reasoning. Dissonance theory cannot explain the attitude judgments of the subjects in the simulation experiments, unless it is assumed that they were aware of the dissonance experienced by the original subjects and were able to deduce its effects. It seems unlikely that they possessed this degree of psychological sophistication. On the other hand, the interpersonal simulation experiments provide only weak support for Bem's theory. Parallel results need not necessarily be explained by the same psychological processes. Conceivably, the attitude judgments of subjects in the original experiments were mediated by dissonance reduction, whereas those of subjects in the interpersonal simulations reflected attributional processes.

Attempts to resolve the issue in a more direct fashion have yielded rather mixed results. Consistent with Bem's position, there is evidence that subjects' recall of their initial attitudes is inaccurate when it is obtained after they have engaged in a counterattitudinal behavior (Bem and McConnell, 1970: Goethals and Reckman, 1973; M. Ross and Shulman, 1973; Wixon and Laird, 1976). Subjects recall their earlier attitude as being more or less equivalent to the attitude they espouse following the counterattitudinal behavior, even though a significant amount of attitude change has occurred in the interim. Introspective access to the earlier attitude is an important component of the cognitive dissonance explanation. In the absence of such awareness, the person would presumably experience no dissonance. On the other hand, there is evidence supporting the dissonance theory contention that freely choosing to perform a counterattitudinal behavior produces a state of arousal or discomfort (Higgins, Rhodewalt, and Zanna, 1979; Kiesler and Pallak, 1976; Pallak and Pittman, 1972; Waterman, 1969; Zanna and Cooper, 1976). Self-perception theory cannot readily account for the role of arousal in these studies.

We have thus come to somewhat of an impasse, with neither theory gaining ascendency. Greenwald (1975) argued that this lack of resolution is inevitable, because the two theories are not sufficiently articulated to permit critical tests. Bem (1972) has concluded that his theory of self-perception plays an important role in nondissonance related phenomena and its significance should be judged more on this basis than on its potential for reinterpreting dissonance phenomena.

Like Schachter's theory of emotion, then, the impact of Bem's self-perception theory on social psychology is somewhat different from one of its original purposes. At best, Bem's self-perception theory fares no better than dissonance theory in explaining dissonance phenomena. At best, Schachter provided an incomplete description of emotional experience. Nonetheless, the combined impact of Schachter's and Bem's theories on attribution-related work has been dramatic. Four major trends in the social psychology of the 1970s can be traced, in part, to their work:

1. An examination of actor-observer differences in attribution.

2. A shift from the motivational orientation of consistency theories such as dissonance to a cognitive, information-processing approach to the understanding of human behavior.

3. A focus on misattribution or errors in the attribution process, stemming from Schachter's evidence of the apparent lability of emotional reaction.

4. A tendency to downplay the role of introspection as a basis of self-knowledge.

We now consider the research developments related to each of these four concerns.

ACTOR-OBSERVER DIFFERENCES IN ATTRIBUTION

How do the attributions that people make for their own behavior differ from the attributions offered by observers of that behavior? Perhaps this question seems too broad to be taken seriously. One is tempted to respond that the answer depends upon such factors as whom the observers are, what their relationship is to the actor (the person engaged in the behavior), the nature of the behavior, the context in which it occurs, and so forth. Nonetheless, a number of authors have offered bold generalizations with regard to actor-observer attributions. As we have seen, Bem (1967, 1972) argued that individuals' attributions for their own behavior are often based on the same information that is available to observers. As a result, the attributions of actors and observers should be quite similar. On the other hand, Heider (1958) suggested that there may be circumstances in which intrapersonal and interpersonal attributions differ: "The person tends to attribute his own reactions to the object world, and those of another, when they differ from his own, to personal characteristics in [the other]" (p. 157).

In a highly influential paper, Jones and Nisbett (1972) developed Heider's theme further. They reasoned that individuals are disposed to locate the cause of their own behavior within the environment, whereas observers attribute the same behavior to stable traits possessed by the actors. Thus, Jones and Nisbett removed the qualifying "when they differ from his own" from Heider's statement of actor-observer differences.

Jones and Nisbett presented their argument as an "actuarial proposition" to which there "are undoubtedly many exceptions." At the same time, they described so many factors that might conspire to produce the actor-observer discrepancy, that it may seem difficult to imagine a disconfirmation of their hypothesis.

First, the actor-observer difference may reflect the actors' better knowledge of his/her past history. Actors are prevented from drawing trait inferences from a behavior when it is at variance with some of their past actions. For instance, an actor would not interpret his or her gift to charity as indicative of a benevolent disposition knowing that he or she has often refused to donate to charities in the past. Conversely, observers who lack knowledge of the actor's past actions may assume that the new behavior is representative and use it as a basis for a trait attribution.

Jones and Nisbett also offered a more subtle variation of this theme. In most of our relationships, we tend to meet with others in a fairly limited range of contexts, for example, student-teacher interactions. The professor who appears to be so verbally fluent and witty week after week in his or her lectures may be shy and withdrawn in most other social situations. The students see consistency, however, and lack the evidence of cross-situational variability in behavior that is available to the professor (actor). This perception of consistency leads the observer to infer traits from behavior where the actor would not.

Further, observers often obtain consensual validation for their trait attributions. The observer associates with similar others whose relationships with the actor parallel his or her own. Thus students validate their impressions of a professor by comparing their views with those of other students; teachers compare their impressions of a student with those of other teachers.

An alternative set of explanations centers on the different aspects of the situation that may be salient to actors and observers. The actor's visual receptors are aimed toward the environment, whereas an observer may focus directly on the actor. This differential focus can account for the actor-observer discrepancy if it is assumed that more salient or figural cues are likely to be chosen as causes of behavior.

A final set of explanations concerns the possible motivational bases of the discrepancy. Jones and Nisbett offered two motivational interpretations. First, an actor may attempt to avoid responsibility for socially undesirable behavior by attributing it to the situation. Observers who do not share the actors' concern for his or her self-image may attribute the undesirable behavior to the actor. Because the Jones and Nisbett hypothesis includes

neutral and positive as well as socially undesirable behavior, this motivational interpretation has limited explanatory power.

A more encompassing motivational view concerns the actor's need to feel in control of his or her outcomes. By attributing their behavior to the situation, actors can see themselves as maximally flexible, able to adapt their behaviors to differing situations rather than being controlled from within by a powerful disposition.

We now turn briefly to the research generated by the Jones and Nisbett hypothesis. The initial research efforts were devoted to establishing the actor-observer discrepancy. Perhaps the best known set of experiments was conducted by Nisbett and his colleagues (Nisbett, Caputo, Legant, and Maracek, 1973). In one study, these investigators elicited differing degrees of compliance from actor-subjects by offering large or small incentives. Observers were more inclined than the actors to form a trait attribution on the basis of the actors' degree of compliance. In a second study, subjects ascribed a larger number of personality traits to other people than to themselves. In addition, subjects reported that their own behavior was more affected by the situation than was the behavior of others.

The number of personality traits ascribed to other people did not differ, however, with degree of acquaintanceship—a null result replicated by Taylor and Koivumaki (1976). This seems to contradict one of the explanations for the actor-observer discrepancy. The better we know someone, the more likely it should be that we see that person in different contexts. As a result, we should perceive an increase in the variability of that person's behavior and be less likely to make trait attributions. The evidence suggests, instead, that actors ascribe more personality traits to others than to self, regardless of the actor's relationship to the other.

Although Jones and Nisbett offered a variety of explanations for the actor-observer discrepancy, the research emphasis has been on the focus-of-attention interpretation. Considerable evidence has accumulated in support of the hypothesis that observers attribute causality for behaviors to salient or figural environmental stimuli (McArthur and Post, 1977; Taylor, Crocker, Fiske, Sprinzen, and Winkler, 1979; Taylor and Fiske, 1975; Taylor and Fiske, 1978; Wicklund, 1975). Moreover, it is possible to influence the direction of the actor-observer discrepancy by shifting a subject's point of view. Storms (1973) videotaped two-person conversations using cameras positioned to record the interactions from the visual perspective of each participant. Individuals were less inclined to attribute their own behavior to characteristics of the situation when they were allowed to view the tape of the conversation from what had been the other person's (observer's) visual perspective.

There has also been research that points to the many exceptions posited by Jones and Nisbett (see Monson and Snyder, 1977, for a review). For example, participants in a prisoner's dilemma game are more likely to attribute their behavior to personality traits, and less inclined to attribute it to the situation than are uninvolved observers (Miller and Norman, 1975). The explanation offered for this result was that the actors avoided situational attributions because they wanted to perceive themselves as exercising control over their environment. Curiously, Jones and Nisbett (1972) had suggested that the opposite pattern could similarly be explained by a need for control. The actor "would lose the sense of freedom to the extent that he acknowledged powerful dispositions in himself" (Jones and Nisbett, 1972, p. 92). Jones (1978, pp. 379–380) has attempted to clarify the issue:

> In the original statement, we implied that you were much more likely to feel commanded by a disposition (and we want to resist that implication of being controlled) than you would feel you were commanded by the situation. I think that's not necessarily true. You have to make a further differentiation. If you ask people, did the situation make you do this, they'll say no. But if you ask them if they wanted to do this because of the nature of the situation, they'll say yes, because they have control then. I think that's an important distinction. Many of the discrepancies in the data that followed from working with the Jones-Nisbett hypothesis can be accounted for by making allowances for this need for control.

In short, actors will attribute their behavior to the situation as long as the attribution can be phrased in a way that does not threaten their sense of control.

In a number of the studies of actor-observer attributions, researchers examined subjects' speculations about their own and others' behavior in hypothetical situations (e.g., Miller, Gillen, Schenker, and Radlove, 1974; Snyder, 1976; Taylor and Koivumaki, 1976). For example, Taylor and Koivumaki provided subjects with statements such as "you are smiling at another person." Subjects were then asked whether qualities of the self or

situational factors were responsible for the behavior. The data from such studies have often failed to support the Jones and Nisbett hypothesis, yielding null or opposite results (Monson and Snyder, 1977). It is not evident, however, that such research constitutes a valid test of the hypothesis. Contextual cues may be much more salient to actors when they are actually engaged in a behavior, rather than speculating about it.

Along these lines, Jones and Nisbett point out that political leaders often interpret their past actions differently than the general public. The public attributes political triumphs and disasters to characteristics of the leader. Leaders note the situational constraints on their behavior and see their actions as inevitable. We would add that the candidate for political office seems to believe that he or she, if elected, would have the power to produce massive change. No doubt this is, in part, a ploy to get elected just as the previous leader's retrospective attributions are, in part, self-serving. Nonetheless, we suspect that in speculating about or predicting their behavior, people anticipate a great deal more personal control than they are likely to recall having after the event. Some experimental evidence for this view may be derived from studies indicating that observers appear to overestimate their own abilities to withstand compliance pressures in Asch- or Milgram-type conformity studies (Miller *et al.,* 1974; Wolosin, Sherman, and Mynatt, 1972).

Why would people persist in their hopes of control when their past experiences seem to argue against it? Perhaps it is a manifestation of the effectance motivation posited by so many theorists. The need for control and prediction is presumably greater for future than for past events. Also, people may be able to imagine a number of quite different scenarios with regard to how the future might unfold; whereas, the past has already revealed itself and seems, in retrospect, inevitable (Fischhoff, 1975; Fischhoff and Beyth, 1975). Alternatively, the phenomenon may be more restricted. Individuals may have limited experience with conformity experiments (or their real-life analogues) and high political office. As a consequence, they may simply underestimate the power of situational forces in such contexts.

What, then, is the current status of the Jones and Nisbett hypothesis? On the basis of an extensive review of the actor-observer literature, Monson and Snyder (1977) concluded that the attributions of actors and observers do differ but not always in the direction posited by Jones and Nisbett. What is now needed, they argued, is a "specification of the 'when', 'why', and 'where' of particular asymmetries between the causal view-points of actors and observers'' (Monson and Snyder, 1977, p. 93). Some of the research findings have contributed to this effort, especially with regard to the role of effectance motivation.

Monson and Snyder provided their own attempt at theoretical specification. They reasoned that the attributions of actors are generally more correct than those of observers, because actors possess greater knowledge of their own behavioral histories and mental processes. As a result, actors (p. 96)

> should make more situational attributions than should observers about behavioral acts that are under situational control; by contrast, actors' perceptions of behaviors that are under dispositional control ought to be more dispositional than the perceptions of observers.

Though Jones and Nisbett, too, implied that actors are more accurate than observers, they tended to avoid discussion of the accuracy issue. We would suggest that there is a good reason for this hesitancy. There are a host of potential interpretations for any behavior, and judgments of the credibility of various explanations will differ across cultures or subcultures. For instance, children who believe in immanent justice may think that an individual who is struck by lightning is being punished for some misdeed; most adults would deny this possibility. Yet even if we assume that our particular culture's theories of causality are plausible, we still don't have satisfactory criteria for unequivocally establishing the validity of our attributions for behavior (we consider this issue in greater detail in our discussion of the role of introspection in self-knowledge).

THE IMPACT OF MOTIVATION ON THE ATTRIBUTION PROCESS

Most theorists have acknowledged the role of motivation in the attribution process. Heider (1958) stated that an acceptable causal attribution depends upon two factors: ''(1) the reason has to fit the wishes of the person and (2) the datum has to be plausibly derived from the reason'' (p. 172). Thus, assuming it is plausible to do so, we explain our own and others' behaviors in terms that ''flatter us'' and ''put us in a good light.'' Note that wish fulfillment precedes rationality in this quote from Heider.

Many other forms of motivational influence have been proposed, including ''evaluative needs'' that impel individuals to seek explanations for ambiguous internal states (Schachter and Singer, 1962), hedonic relevance and personalism (Jones and Davis, 1965), and a need to understand what motivates the cognitive processes entailed in attribution (Kelley, 1967). In his 1972 paper, Kelley shifted his views somewhat. The layperson as ''pure scientist'' in 1967 became the layperson as ''applied scientist'' in 1972. The layperson not only needs to understand, but he wants to apply ''his knowledge of causal relations in order to *excercise control* of his world'' (p. 2). Orvis, Kelley, and Butler (1976) went one step further. On the basis of data from research on attributional conflict in young couples, they reasoned that attributions may often be motivated by the need to justify one's own behaviors and criticize the actions of others.

Of the major theorists, only Daryl Bem explicitly denied motivation a role in the attribution process. Nonetheless, many attribution theorists and researchers adopted a skeptical attitude toward motivational explanations. For example, they argued that just because an attribution may appear to serve an ego-protective function does not necessarily mean that the attribution was prompted by ego-protective impulses (e.g., Bem, 1972; Kelley, 1972; Miller and M. Ross, 1975; Nisbett and L. Ross, 1980; L. Ross, 1977). As Bem noted (1972, p. 262), ''Self should be innocent until proven guilty.''

An emphasis on rationality dictates a certain research strategy and logic. Only if the contribution of cognitive or information-processing factors can be ruled out is motivation ruled in. This cognitive emphasis can be seen, in part, as a reaction to an earlier tendency in social psychology to accept too readily and uncritically a multitude of motivational interpretations of behavior (Bem, 1972; Nisbett and L. Ross, 1980).

Yet the cognitive approach is often no more parsimonious than the motivational orientation that preceded it. One can invent at least as many cognitive interpretations for a result as motivational interpretations (Miller and M. Ross, 1975; Tetlock and Levi, 1982). If we must eliminate each and every cognitive interpretation before accepting a motivational explanation, we are unlikely to ever arrive at the latter. As a result, perhaps, the role of motivation in the attribution process has tended to be underplayed. Nevertheless, there are three domains in which motivational processes have been closely examined: the impact of effectance motivation on the attribution process, self-serving biases in attributions for success and failure, and moral evaluation.

EFFECTANCE MOTIVATION

The hypothesis that people make attributions, in part, to enhance their control over the environment has received empirical support. The need or desire for control can be inferred from studies that demonstrate that people exaggerate their personal powers. For example, gamblers experience an illusion of control over chance events (e.g., Henslin, 1967; Langer, 1975; Langer and Roth, 1975; Strickland, Lewicke, and Katz, 1966; Wortman, 1975, 1976). The desire for control can also be deduced from research on Lerner's just-world theory. Lerner suggests that to maintain a belief that they can control their own fates, perceivers derogate innocent victims (Lerner, 1980; Lerner, Miller, and Holmes, 1976). Also, as we have already noted, the need for control may account for some of the apparent discrepancies in the actor-observer literature.

More direct support for Kelley's contention can be derived from studies in which people's need for control is manipulated. The basic assumption of this research is that individuals' evaluations of what they can learn from stimulus information is affected by their need for prediction and control. Thus subjects believe that they have learned more from observing a target person when they expect to interact with him in the future (and, hence, there is a need for prediction and control), than when they don't expect to meet him. This effect is obtained even when the expectation of interaction is induced after the target has been observed (Berscheid, Graziano, Monson, and Dermer, 1976; Feldman and Ruble, 1981; Miller and Norman, 1975; Miller, Norman, and Wright, 1978).

SELF-SERVING BIASES IN ATTRIBUTION

One of the most extensive literatures on motivational determinants of attribution concerns the need to view oneself in a favorable way following a success or failure. This research has revealed what may be one of the best established, most often replicated, findings in social psychology. People take more personal responsibility for their successes than for their failures (see Bradley, 1978, Miller and M. Ross, 1975, and Zuckerman, 1979, for reviews of the relevant literature). A controversy has emerged over the appropriate interpretation of this result, however. Many authors view the asymmetry as reflecting a motivational bias. It can be argued that people attribute success more than failure to personal factors because they are motivated to enhance or protect their self-esteem, because they are motivated to maintain their sense of mastery over the environment, or because they are motivated to present a favourable impression to others (e.g., Bradley, 1978; Miller and M. Ross, 1975; Schlenker, 1980).

Needless to say, nonmotivational interpretations also abound. For example, it can be argued that people (or at least the college sophomores employed in most of the experiments) intend and expect their behavior to produce success. If success can be seen as flowing from one's efforts, whereas failure occurs in spite of one's desires and efforts, then it may be perfectly reasonable for the individual to accept more responsibility for success than for failure (Miller and M. Ross, 1975; L. Ross, 1977).

There is also a controversy over whether the asymmetry represents a bias in reporting or a bias in perception (Bradley, 1978; Miller, 1978; Nisbett and L. Ross, 1980; Schlenker, 1980). As Miller (1978, p. 1221) noted,

> The attributions that a person offers to account for his or her successes and failures can serve the person in two ways. First, they can serve to protect or enhance how the person perceives himself or herself. Second they can serve to protect or enhance how others perceive the person.

The experimenter is the important other in most research. It is difficult to eliminate the possibility, in spite of the usual anonymity and confidentiality of reporting, that subjects are knowingly fudging their reported attributions to present themselves in the best possible light.

One of the major motivational interpretations of the asymmetry is that individuals shift their attributions to maintain or enhance their self-esteem. Yet until recently, there was no direct evidence that the differing attribution patterns accomplished their supposed aim. There are now a number of studies relating attribution to affect and self-esteem; the results have tended to support the self-esteem assumption (McFarland and M. Ross, 1982; Reimer, 1975; Ruble, Parsons, and Ross, 1976; Weiner, Russell, and Lehrman, 1978, 1979). For example, McFarland and Ross (1982) provided subjects with false feedback concerning their degree of success at a task and induced them to attribute their performance either to task difficulty (an external cause) or to ability (an internal cause). Failure led to more negative affect and lower self-esteem than success only when the performance was attributed to ability. This study does not demonstrate that people shift their attributions *in order* to maintain self-esteem. Whatever the basis of the shift, however, it does seem to serve this end.

An enormous amount of research has been conducted on asymmetries in attribution following success and failure. From our perspective at least, the motivational versus cognitive processing controversy has not been resolved and may well be unresolvable. Part of the difficulty is that two general orientations are being compared rather than well-articulated competing theories that are open to more critical tests. With a little ingenuity one can always dredge up yet another information-processing or motivational interpretation to deal with allegedly recalcitrant data. The most reasonable conclusion is that each view is surely correct. People are both rational and rationalizers. At times we are concerned with explanation, at times with justification; at other times we are concerned with both, and at still other times with neither.

For example, in the real world, attributions are often public and performers may mainly be concerned with saving face in front of others (Bradley, 1978; Buss, 1978; Orvis *et al.,* 1976). Not surprisingly, then, there have been a number of attempts to relate theories of self-presentation to biases in attribution. The basic premise of such self-presentation theories is that a performer who does poorly at a task wishes to avoid low-ability attributions (Darley and Goethals, 1980; Snyder and Wicklund, 1981). It has been found, for example, that people who expect to fail exert less effort than people who anticipate doing well (Archibald, 1974; Diggory, 1966). One interpretation of this finding is that people try less hard so that they can legitimately attribute failure to a nonability factor (effort). Similarly, Jones and Berglas (1978) reasoned that alcoholics may overindulge, in part, so that inadequate performance can be attributed to alcohol rather than to ability factors. Darley and Goethals (1980) described a number of other often exquisitely subtle maneuvers that a performer may enact to avoid the attribution of poor performance to ability.

Melvin Snyder and his colleagues have presented an intriguing theory of attributional ambiguity that is compatible with the above proposition (Snyder, Kleck, Strenta, and Mentzer, 1979; Snyder and Wicklund, 1981). They argue that individuals sometimes attempt to obscure the causes of their actions. Three major motivations are proposed to account for this tendency: the desire to maintain self-esteem, to save face, and most important, to maximize one's sense of control over one's own behavior. According to Snyder and Wicklund (1981), people like to believe that they possess personalities and abilities that allow for a full range of behaviors.

This theory suggests that one reason people may prefer high-ability attributions is that low-ability attributions are more constraining in terms of their behavioral implications. According to Snyder and Wicklund, people adopt various strategies to prevent both self and others from drawing such constraining trait inferences from their behavior. For example, they may act inconsistently (which prompts a circumstance rather than trait explanation for their behavior), or provide a number of plausible reasons for their actions, thus making it difficult for an observer to draw correspondent inferences.

Research conducted by Trope (1979, 1980) seems to qualify some of the assertions of attribute ambiguity theory. Snyder and Wicklund (1981) assert that individuals prefer to appear to have as much ability as possible, and will avoid actions that might lead to low-ability attributions. In contrast, Trope finds that people choose to engage in tasks that will allow them to acquire information about their ability, even when they know that the news is likely to be bad. Trope argues that rather than avoid a task to the extent that it might disclose low ability, "people strive to attain a realistic assessment of their weaknesses and strengths in order to be better able to predict and effectively cope with their environment" (Trope, 1980, p. 117).

As usual, the truth probably lies somewhere between the somewhat distasteful image of man represented by the Darley-Goethals, Snyder-Wicklund theories, and the more flattering portrait presented by Trope. It could be argued that face-saving concerns were not aroused in Trope's studies because subjects' responses were anonymous and confidential. At the very least, though, Trope's research demonstrates that people do not always prefer self-deception over self-discovery.

A final question needs to be addressed. How effective are the machinations described by Darley and Goethals or Snyder and Wicklund likely to be in terms of warding off negative evaluations? These theorists assume that attributions affect evaluations, and there is ample evidence that this is so. For example, observers are more likely to help victims who are not responsible for their own fate than victims who are perceived as responsible (e.g., Braband and Lerner, 1975; Schopler and

Matthews, 1965). Moreover, people who have been attacked retaliate more when the causal basis of the attack is attributed to dispositional properties of the aggressor than when it is attributed to situational factors (Dyck and Rule, 1978; Kulik and Brown, 1979).

In short, observers' reactions are influenced by the attributions they make for the target person's behavior, and a cunning performer can project the "right" attributions for his or her behavior. On the other hand, the evidence that individuals may be held responsible for chance occurrences and that observers may underestimate the impact of situational factors suggests that attributional self-presentational strategies may not be wholly effective in deflecting blame for negative outcomes (e.g., Jones and Harris, 1967; Jones and Nisbett, 1972; Lerner, 1980; Stokols and Schopler, 1973; Wortman, 1976).

MORAL EVALUATION

The role of motivation in the attribution process has also been examined in the context of moral evaluation. Heider (1958) suggested that there are five distinct bases for attributing moral responsibility. At the most primitive level (association), individuals are held responsible for any action that is connected with them, however remote. For example, descendants may be held responsible for the alleged actions of their forefathers. At the next level (commission), people are viewed as responsible for anything they cause, even though they could not possibly have foreseen or intended the consequences of the action. At the third level (foreseeability), individuals are perceived as responsible for any result of their actions that they might have foreseen, even though they were not intended. For instance, the golfer who drives the ball over a hill without checking to see if the way is clear may be perceived as responsible for injuries that might thereby occur. At the next level (intentionality), people are seen as responsible only for the consequences of their actions that they intended to produce. At this stage the individual is no longer held responsible for the results of accidents. At the fifth and final level (justification), individuals are not seen as responsible even for consequences that they intentionally produced if the circumstances were such that anyone would have acted as they did. For example, the military law of many countries stipulates that a soldier may not be found guilty of war crimes when he is ordered to commit them by a superior who backs his commands with threats of severe punishment.

Thus, Heider proposed that judgments of responsibility can be distinguished from judgments of causality. There are a number of different ways of assigning responsibility. Individuals may or may not be seen as responsible for outcomes they have caused. Moreover, they may even be seen as responsible for outcomes they have not caused (association). Heider suggested that there is a progression from relatively primitive, undifferentiated judgments of responsibility, in which individuals are seen as responsible for any events they have caused or are associated with, to sophisticated attributions that take into account various factors in the situation.

Yet Heider provided little in the way of guidance as to what leads an observer to choose one or another interpretation of responsibility. He did seem to agree, however, with Piaget's (1948) observation that young children tend to make primitive attributions, ignoring intentions, whereas more mature individuals weigh intentions very heavily. This suggestion received support from research conducted by Shaw and Sulzer (1964) in which children (six through nine years old) and college students were presented with brief stories depicting Heider's five interpretations of responsibility. In assigning responsibility for positive and negative outcomes to agents in the stories, college students tended to differentiate more than did the children those situations in which the consequences of the actions could have been foreseen or intended, from those in which foreseeability and intentionality were clearly absent.

Shaw and Sulzer studied only two groups differing widely in age and the results may reflect differences in memory for the stories, or in understanding of the experimental instructions (Fincham and Jaspars, 1980; Harris, 1977). There have been a number of more recent efforts to examine the developmental implications of Heider's analysis. Perhaps the most comprehensive study was conducted by Fincham and Jaspars (1979). They constructed brief stories reflecting Heider's levels of responsibility and administered them to subjects ranging from grade two to college students. Subjects of all ages were sensitive to the distinctions posed by Heider. Children as young as six differentiated accidental from intentional outcomes; children as young as eight distinguished intentionality from justifiability. No age group distinguished between the lowest two levels, association and commission.

Sedlak (1979) also found that children provided attributions of responsibility (praise and blame) that were quite similar to those offered by adults in response to stories incorporating Heider's levels. More interestingly, she interviewed her eight- and eleven-year-old subjects and observed that when individual children deviated from the adult pattern in assigning praise or blame, they appeared to be interpreting the stories differently from adults. Moreover, the direction of the difference was always the same. These children attributed intentionality to the actor (and correspondingly greater praise or blame) when adults did not. Thus, some children apparently differed from adults in their inference of intentionality, rather than in their knowledge of the link between intentionality and attributions of responsibility.

This research shows that both children and adults are sensitive to the major distinctions provided in Heider's analysis of responsibility judgments. There is little evidence, though, of a developmental sequence in which children initially assign responsibility in a primitive way. Even young children seem to consider intentionality in ascribing praise or blame.

A similar conclusion can be derived from research stemming more directly from Piagetian theory. Piaget (1948) suggested that before the age of ten the child generally ignores the actor's intentions and evaluates the badness of an act in terms of the negative consequences it produces. Although early research tended to support Piaget's analysis, Karniol (1978) arrived at a different conclusion after an extensive review of the literature. Contrary to Piaget's reasoning, young children often do differentiate between ill-intentioned, well-intentioned, and accidental acts. In one of the more intriguing demonstrations along these lines, children in grade one were able to take into account circumstances that in a legal sense excuse intentional harmdoing acts (Darley, Klossman, and Zanna, 1978).

Piaget's (1948) analysis of the belief in immanent justice is also relevant to the present concerns. Piaget suggested that young children pass through a stage in which they believe in supernatural punishment for misdeeds. To assess this belief, researchers have presented subjects with brief vignettes about a child who transgresses and then suffers an apparently accidental adversity (e.g., Dennis, 1943; Johnson, 1962; Karniol, 1980; MacRae, 1954; Piaget, 1948). For example, a child who steals apples subsequently walks across a bridge that collapses and he falls into the water. After hearing about these events, subjects are asked why the bridge collapsed and whether the collapse would have occurred if the child hadn't committed the crime. Responding that the collapse wouldn't have occurred in the absence of the crime is interpreted as reflecting a belief in immanent justice. This belief would imply that children are holding the target responsible for "accidents." Piaget found that immanent justice responding declined with age; he also observed that some "simple souls" persist in this belief into adulthood.

More recently, Karniol (1980) has demonstrated that children's responses to Piaget's stories may reflect causal judgments rather than moral beliefs. Her research suggests that many of the children who attribute the adversity to the misdeed are actually contemplating a chain of events that link the adversity and the misdeed in a naturalistic way. For example, they may believe that the bridge collapsed because it was old and the stolen apples were too heavy a load. Karniol found relatively little evidence of "pure" immanent justice responding; moreover, the frequency of such responding did not change over age.

Yet attributions of blame or responsibility are not always as rational or sensible as the results from these studies would indicate. Heider (1958) suggested that, at times, even adults ignore intentions and make attributions solely on the basis of outcomes (p. 235):

> The relationship between goodness and happiness, between wickedness and punishment is so strong, that given one of these conditions, the other is frequently assumed. Misfortune, sickness, accident are often taken as signs of badness and guilt.

This argument has received empirical support from research examining people's need to believe in a just world. For example, observers derogate strangers who have been assigned punishment in an experiment, thus making outcomes consistent with deserving (Lerner and Simmons, 1966). Similarly, a worker who by chance is highly paid is perceived as working harder than a worker who by chance is not paid (Lerner, 1965). These data suggest that primitive responsibility attributions are one means by which people maintain their belief in a just or fair world.

There is also evidence that feelings of similarity to a victim of misfortune reduce blaming responses by observers (Chaikin and Darley, 1973; Shaver, 1970b). This finding has been interpreted as support for a defensive attribution hypothesis. If a person is like me, then I should be motivated to see that individual as not responsible for an accident. By denying his or her culpability, I am able to avoid possible blame for myself in the future, should I somehow "cause" a similar accident to occur.

To this point, we have considered only attributions of responsibility for another's behavior. There are a number of laboratory studies that provide evidence of primitive *self-attributions* of responsibility. For example, people often behave as though they have control over chance outcomes in gambling settings (Langer, 1975; Wortman, 1975). In one study, subjects received a prize, the value of which was determined by the color of a marble drawn blindly from a container (Wortman, 1975). Subjects felt more responsible for determining the prize if they, rather than the experimenter, drew the marble and if they knew the relation of the color of the marble to the value of the prize prior to the draw (i.e., knew what color marble they wished to draw). Thus in Heider's terms, the combination of commission and foreseeability enhanced feelings of responsibility for a chance outcome.

There is also laboratory evidence that primitive attributions of responsibility represent one way in which people make sense of unpleasantness in their lives (Comer and Laird, 1975). Subjects who were randomly chosen to engage in an unpleasant task (e.g., eating a worm) responded to their lot in one of three mutually exclusive ways. Some of the subjects decided that the task was not so bad after all. Others enhanced their self-images, giving themselves accolades for bravery. The final group engaged in self-blame and saw themselves as deserving of suffering.

In the real world there are, alas, fates even worse than eating worms and there is ample evidence of primitive self-attributions of blame. For example, parents of children with leukemia may blame themselves, in part, for the child's illness (Chodoff, Friedman, and Hamburg, 1964). Further, cancer patients, and victims of wars, natural disasters, or freak accidents may blame themselves for their fate (Bettelheim, 1943; Bulman and Wortman, 1977; Lerner and Miller, 1978; Wortman, 1976).

Wortman (1976) has offered several explanations for this tendency to exaggerate responsibility for negative events. Self-blame permits the individual to comprehend an otherwise inexplicable event—it is one answer to the "why me" question. Although this answer is distressing, it makes sense of the event in a way that allows individuals to maintain their belief in a stable, predictable, and just world (Lerner and Miller, 1978). Moreover, if an individual accepts blame, there is the implication that he or she could act to prevent future occurrences of the event. Thus, women may accept part of the responsibility for rape because it reduces the unpredictability of the event, and facilitates avoidance of it in the future (Medea and Thompson, 1974; Wortman, 1976). There is also the possibility that acceptance of blame is, at times, a self-presentational strategy (Wortman, 1976). People may feel that they can gain sympathy from others by declaring themselves to be more guilty than they feel.

A number of authors have discussed whether acceptance of blame facilitates coping with misfortune (e.g., Abrams and Finesinger, 1953; Chodoff *et al.,* 1964; Lerner and Miller, 1978; Seligman, 1975; Wortman, 1976). Although compelling empirical evidence one way or another is scarce, Bulman and Wortman (1977) did find that degree of self-blame was positively correlated with coping well with spinal injuries.

Despite an apparent wealth of research, there have been few empirical attempts to delineate when primitive self-attributions of responsibility occur. A review of the conditions in which primitive self-attributions appear to occur may provide further clues concerning the antecedents of this response. The possible contribution of the following factors is suggested by an examination of the literature: emotional arousal, the absence of a salient, culpable external agent other than chance, the unexpectedness and low prior probability of the event, the timing of the attribution assessment, and the need for future control over the outcome.

Arousal and negative affect.   Many of the primitive assessments of blame previously described occur when the attributor is in a state of emotional arousal. Grief and emotional arousal are likely to lead to a focussing inward, a self-absorption. The self may thus be a particularly salient target of attribution. Further, an inward focus combined with negative affect may increase the likelihood that individuals will retrieve unpleasant memories about themselves and engage in negative self-thoughts (Bower, 1981; Isen, Shalker, Clark, and Karp, 1978; Wicklund, 1975).

The absence of someone to blame.   Research from a variety of settings reveals that people are unlikely to attribute their outcomes spontaneously to such factors as chance or bad luck (e.g., Elig and Frieze, 1979; Kahneman and Tversky, 1973; Karniol, 1980). This avoidance of chance attributions may reflect individuals' need for control and their desire for a stable, predictable world. Nonetheless, it limits the range of possible attributions and increases the likelihood of self-attributions when salient external agents of blame are unavailable.

The unexpectedness of the event. The misfortunes that yield primitive attributions are typically unexpected in two senses: the individual has little prior warning of its onset and the probability of the event's occurrence is quite low. According to Jones and Davis's (1965) theory of correspondent inference, individuals are more likely to make correspondent inferences if an outcome is rare. Similarly, from the perspective of Kelley's (1967) theory of attribution, a lack of consensus (it happens to me and not to others) prohibits situational attributions, and increases the probability of attributions to the person.

Timing. Lerner and Miller (1978) note that there is little research on the timing sequence. They suggest that self-attributions of blame may occur only after anger has proven to be ineffective. Similarly, Kubler-Ross (1969) proposed a stage model of reactions to death in which self-blame is just one of several stages people go through.

The need for control. It has been hypothesized that victims engage in self-blame, in part, because it implies that they can act to prevent future occurrences of a negative event. Yet this is true of only some forms of self-blame (Janoff-Bulman, 1979). When individuals blame their past actions for an outcome, future occurrences of the outcome are avoidable if they modify their behavior. On the other hand, avoidance seems less possible when individuals attribute the outcome to enduring, personal dispositions. Consequently, behavioral attributions should be more common than characterological attributions if self-blame results from a need for control.

Janoff-Bulman examined this hypothesis by having workers in rape crisis centers estimate the percentage of rape victims who engage in characterological versus behavioral self-blame. The workers reported that almost three-quarters of the rape victims blamed themselves, to some extent, for the rape. However, consistent with the control hypothesis, the vast majority engaged in behavioral self-blame (e.g., "I should not have walked alone; I shouldn't have left my window open; I should have locked my car") rather than characterological self-blame (e.g., "I am too trusting; I am the kind of person who attracts trouble").

Yet it is not necessary to conclude that even behavioral self-blame is motivated by the need for control. It might simply reflect a rational inference, based on the evidence. The instances of behavioral self-blame just provided exemplify Heider's foreseeability level of responsibility. The victims were taking responsibility for an event they might have foreseen, even though it was unintended. Whether their acceptance of blame is "rational," depends in part on the a priori probability of the event —should they really have been able to foresee it? If one accepts the rape victim's premises, then one must accept her conclusions. Yes, she should have locked her window if there was reason to believe a rapist would crawl through it. Nonetheless, one suspects that if the window had been locked and the rape had still occurred the victim would find other reasons to berate herself (she should have rented an apartment on a higher floor, purchased a dog, had mace under her pillow, acquired a roommate, etc.). Though the evidence is far from conclusive, one is tempted to infer that such explanations are offered, at least in part, because they are functional. They promote feelings of control and allow the victim to make sense of an apparently random event.

The ready acceptance of a motivational component in such attributions is perhaps reflected in the fact that there have been fewer attempts to test competing motivational and nonmotivational explanations of phenomena in the moral evaluation area than in the other contexts we have discussed. Most psychologists seem to see moral evaluation as one area in which motivation clearly plays a role, wreaking havoc with the rational attribution processes posited by theorists such as Kelley and Jones and Davis.

Conclusions. The amount of speculation on the antecedents of self-blame far exceeds the amount of available data. This is unfortunate, for the study of primitive self-attributions is clearly justifiable from the standpoint of its practical implications. It is also important for a theoretical understanding of the attribution process, because its occurrence seems to challenge several of the basic assumptions of attribution theorists, namely: (1) Heider's implicit assumption that adults engage in relatively sophisticated analyses of responsibility in which the actor's intentions are pivotal; (2) the associated belief that personal attributions are made principally on the basis of freely chosen, intentional behavior; and (3) the commonly held assumption that individuals select attributions to maximize their feelings of self-esteem.

It thus appears that the attribution process may be more primitive than theorists such as Heider and Kelley have suggested. Note, however, that we have swung back and forth on this issue in previous sections of the chapter. At times we argue that the attribution process is less complex than is implied by the theoretical analyses, and at other times that it is more sophisticated. In truth, we believe both conclusions are warranted. The complexity level is presumably affected by a host of situational factors (including the person's reasons for making the attribution) as well as by individual differences in personality or cognitive style. Future research should be aimed at investigating the determinants of attribution complexity.

MISATTRIBUTION

Schachter and his colleagues suggested that individuals could be induced to misattribute internal arousal that was elicited by an injection of epinephrine to plausible and salient features of the environment (e.g., an anger-inducing questionnaire). If emotional attributions are apparently so labile, why not self-attributions of all sorts? Thus, researchers were inspired to examine misattribution effects in a variety of settings. Much of this research capitalizes on Kelley's discounting principle. Subjects are provided with a bogus but plausible explanation of their feelings with the result that they discount the true source of those feelings.

In an experiment that established the paradigm for much that followed, subjects anticipated receiving either low- or high-intensity electrical shocks (Nisbett and Schachter, 1966). In addition, subjects were provided with a placebo pill that would allegedly produce either fear-relevant symptoms (e.g., a pounding heart) or fear-irrelevant symptoms (e.g., numb feet). Nisbett and Schachter expected subjects who ingested a fear-relevant symptoms placebo to tolerate more shocks; they should attribute some of their fear symptoms to the placebo and infer that they are less afraid of the shocks than subjects receiving fear-irrelevant symptoms placebos. Fear-relevant placebo subjects did tolerate more shock than did fear-irrelevant placebo subjects, but only when low-intensity shocks were expected (low-fear condition). Nisbett and Schachter reasoned that the manipulation failed in the high-fear condition because misattribution was more difficult to induce. High-fear subjects may have attributed their symptoms to the anticipated high shock level, regardless of the presumed impact of the pill.

In a conceptual replication of this study, L. Ross, Rodin, and Zimbardo (1969) led some subjects to believe that exposure to a noise would produce fear-relevant symptoms; others received a description of fear-irrelevant symptoms. While being exposed to the noise, subjects participated in a task that allowed them to work either to avoid an electrical shock or to gain a monetary reward. Subjects who associated the noise with fear-relevant symptoms were less likely to work to avoid shock than were subjects provided with the fear-irrelevant symptoms description. Presumably, subjects who were provided with the fear-relevant description attributed some of their arousal symptoms to the noise and consequently perceived themselves to be less afraid of the shock.

The list of target symptoms apparently susceptible to misattribution is quite broad, including guilt (Dienstbier and Munter, 1971), stress produced by crowding (Worchel and Yohai, 1979), and snake phobia (Valins and Ray, 1967). The study that perhaps had the most impact, though, was conducted on insomniacs (Storms and Nisbett, 1970). Subjects took placebo pills shortly before going to bed. Some subjects were told that the pills would increase their arousal. Others were told that the pills would relax them. On the assumption that emotionality at bedtime precipitates insomnia, Storms and Nisbett reasoned that insomnia should be alleviated if insomniacs could be induced to attribute their arousal to a placebo, an emotionally neutral external agent. On the other hand, a relaxation placebo should exacerbate insomnia. Subjects who mistakenly believe themselves to be under the influence of a relaxing pill might infer (consistent with Kelley's augmentation principle), "If I feel as aroused as I do now, when the drug is operating to reduce my arousal, then I must be very aroused indeed" (Storms and Nisbett, 1970, p. 320). These subjects may then interpret their arousal in emotionally charged terms (e.g., "I must be particularly worried about something"), which further worsens their insomnia. The results supported this logic. Subjects who received the arousal placebos reported falling asleep more quickly than usual. Subjects who received the sedation placebo reported that they took longer to fall asleep than usual.

Such results fostered considerable optimism about the relevance of attribution processes to the treatment of emotional disorders (e.g., Valins and Nisbett, 1971). This state of affairs did not last long, however. Attempts to replicate the Storms and Nisbett findings proved unsuccessful (Bootzin, Herman, and Nicassio, 1976; Kellogg and Baron, 1975; Lowery, Denney, and Storms, 1979; Steinmark and Borkovec, 1974).

Efforts to modify other clinically relevant target behaviors by attributional approaches have produced inconsistent results. Misattribution techniques failed to facilitate efforts to reduce smoking (Chambliss and Murray, 1979) and failed to alter speech anxiety (Singerman, Borkovec, and Baron, 1976). On the other hand, Brodt and Zimbardo (1981) successfully induced shy subjects to be more talkative by having them attribute a portion of their arousal symptoms to a loud noise rather than to their shyness.

In sum, the misattribution effects that occur reliably on nonclinical target behaviors often fail to generalize to clinically relevant behaviors. There are probably a number of reasons for this failure (for a more extended discussion of this issue see M. Ross and Olson, 1981). First, subjects may have been so familiar with their symptoms that it was difficult to induce them to misattribute the source of their arousal. Note that many of the experiments on nonclinical target behaviors involved symptoms that were quite unfamiliar to subjects (e.g., most people probably have had little or no direct exposure to electric shock), and the potential for misattribution may have been greater. L. Ross, Rodin, and Zimbardo (1969) anticipated this difficulty but argued that it could be circumvented by the much more powerful manipulations that would be possible in therapeutic settings (p. 287).

> Individualized treatment would . . . allow more powerful manipulation of the elements involved in emotional attribution. Specific information about the pattern of a particular individual's subjective physiological symptoms and much more forceful communication of this information would, for instance, be possible in a therapeutic setting.

Of the studies cited, only that by Brodt and Zimbardo approached this ideal. Interestingly, this was also one of the few experiments to produce successful misattribution with a clinically relevant target behavior.

Second, the attribution predictions fail to take into account the possibility that the subjects' arousal levels or emotionality might be affected by administration of the placebo. For example, Storms and Nisbett's theoretical analysis rests on the assumption that subjects experienced their normal level of arousal at bedtime, despite the alleged arousing or relaxing effects of the pill. There

is no reason to believe, however, that placebos are typically perceived as ineffective (M. Ross and Olson, 1981, 1982). If the placebo has an impact on how subjects felt following its administration, then the attribution predictions may not hold.

Third, the dependent measures, particularly in the insomnia studies, were relatively indirect measures of the subjects' causal attributions. For the arousal placebo in the insomnia studies to affect latency of sleep onset, subjects must (1) misattribute some of their symptoms to the placebo, (2) infer that their insomnia is not severe this particular evening, (3) consequently, fall asleep more quickly and, (4) report to the experimenter that they fell asleep more quickly than usual. Conceivably, either or both of the first two steps could occur and not the last two.

In contrast, most of the studies of nonclinically relevant target behaviors included measures that more directly related to subjects' causal inferences. For example, subjects' perceptions of their fear of shock would be expected to influence directly their decision to work either to avoid the shock or to gain a reward (Calvert-Boyanowsky and Leventhal, 1975; L. Ross *et al.,* 1969). Consequently, the studies of clinically relevant target symptoms may have employed measures too tenuously related to subjects' causal inferences. Conceivably, such measures are particularly relevant to clinical practice. Nonetheless, it is not surprising that these measures would, at times, fail to reveal misattribution effects.

In summary, misattribution effects have been demonstrated in a variety of settings. This research provides further support for the position advocated by Schachter and Bem. At times, self-knowledge does appear to be based on a causal inference process. However, the limits of this analysis are also evident in the misattribution literature. Individuals cannot always be induced to attribute their responses to events staged by an experimenter. We discussed a number of possible reasons for the repeated failure to obtain misattribution effects on clinically relevant target behaviors.

The misattribution studies also raise the issue that we shall consider next. Even in the successful misattribution experiments, there is little direct evidence of the attribution processes that supposedly underlie the results. Although few researchers report attempts to assess the attributions that are thought to mediate the obtained effects, the data that do exist are not encouraging: subjects rarely report the "appropriate" attributions. It is exactly this sort of evidence that has lead some psychologists to argue that people have little or no introspective access to the causes of their own behavior (Nisbett and Wilson, 1977a). We turn now to a consideration of this thesis.

THE ROLE OF INTROSPECTION IN SELF-ATTRIBUTION

Schachter and Singer (1962) challenged the common-sense view that emotions are directly accessible to consciousness; instead, they argued that people's labeling of their feelings depends on an attributional analysis of the cause of their emotional arousal. Similarly, Bem (1967, 1972) argued against the naive view that attitudes are known in the sense that individuals can access them on demand. Rather, often people must deduce their attitudes from their behavior and the context in which it occurs. Nisbett and Wilson (1977a) provided an additional blow to the naive introspectionist's sense of the validity of his or her self-perceptions. They proposed that people have little or no direct introspective access to the causes of their behavior.

Nisbett and Wilson's thesis was actually even more sweeping than this. They argued that people have no direct introspective awareness of higher order cognitive processes. Nonetheless, they concentrated on only one class of cognitive processes, judgments of the causes of one's own behavior. They argued that reports of causality "are based on a priori, implicit theories, or judgments about the extent to which a particular stimulus is a plausible cause of a given response" (p. 231). Further, the accuracy of the causal judgment is not a reflection of the person's ability to observe causal processes directly— "accurate reports will occur when influential stimuli are salient and are plausible causes of the responses they produce, and will not occur when stimuli are not salient or are not plausible causes" (p. 231).

At a conceptual level, their reasoning is almost certainly valid (Bowers, 1981; Nisbett and L. Ross, 1980). It is logically impossible to observe causal processes per se, whether they be in one's head or in the outside world. As Hume noted several centuries ago, we can merely perceive that events or states are related. We observe correlations between events. All judgments of causality are just that—*judgments* based on causal theories and empirical observations such as analyses of covariation. If the "true" causal determinants conflict with our preconceptions, or are nonsalient, we may very well make an error in judgment.

Nisbett and Wilson (1977 a, b) presented a number of studies that were designed to provide direct support for their analysis. A great deal of criticism has been directed at this research. The standard procedure was to establish the accuracy of a causal proposition by an experimental manipulation of subjects' behavior. Subjects were then asked to explain their actions. Nisbett and Wilson examined whether subjects were able to identify the experimental manipulation as a cause of their behavior. Observer-subjects also were often employed, and Nisbett and Wilson tested their hypothesis by comparing the attributions of actors and observers. They claimed support for their argument if the actors failed to mention the experimental manipulation, but agreed with the causal accounts of the observers (as seemed to be the case in these studies). Nisbett and Wilson argued on the basis of such data that actors were not deriving their accounts from introspection, but were basing their judgments on the same socially shared theory as the observers.

Although this methodology seems straightforward enough, it is difficult to assess the significance of the results. The standard experimental design, utilizing comparisons of group means, is an excellent instrument for determining whether a particular factor is causal, but it is a relatively poor device for specifying *how* a cause exerts its impact through a chain of intermediary causal links (Fiske, Kenny, and Taylor, 1982). For example, in one study conducted by Nisbett and Wilson, passers-by in a shopping mall were invited to assess the quality of an array of consumer goods (stockings) that were, in fact, identical. There was a pronounced position effect, such that the right-most garments were preferred to the left-most garments. Yet subjects denied that the order of the stockings exerted any influence on their judgments and reported other, rather elaborate explanations for their choice. As Smith and Miller (1978) have pointed out, the position of the stockings may have helped produce certain intermediary cognitive processes that the subjects had perfect introspective access to and duly reported on. Though subjects failed to pick out the causal factor that the experimenter has identified (position in the array), their causal reports are not necessarily invalid; the subjects may be focussing on other equally important causes.

Additional criticisms of the Nisbett and Wilson research include the arguments that: (1) They have selected subjects who are naive and then misled them in ways that the subjects can't appreciate from their vantage point. As a consequence, the results cannot be generalized to people's understanding of naturally occurring events, for in the real world events are choreographed with less artifice. (2) The behaviors studied are trivial—individuals would be more accurate in assessing the causes of their behavior when it really mattered. (3) The between-subject designs of the studies conducted by Nisbett and his colleagues deny subjects information that is available to the experimenter and pertinent to the causal judgments, especially the data from the control condition. In the absence of such data, it is not surprising that subjects are less accurate than the experimenter. (4) The between-subjects designs employed in these studies prevent Nisbett and his colleagues from determining whether individual subjects are accurate or not. A within-subjects design might reveal that some subjects do recognize the causes of changes in their behavior. (5) Memory decays over time. Causal judgments would be more accurate if elicited while the behavior was occurring (Bowers, 1981; Ericsson and Simon, 1980; Smith and Miller, 1978; White, 1980).

We agree with some of the criticisms of Nisbett and Wilson's research. Their data that seemingly points to a lack of introspective awareness is vulnerable to too many alternative interpretations to be compelling. Moreover, we suspect that it is possible to devise experiments that would show that people can accurately assess the causes of their own behavior—and the Nisbett and Wilson paper is likely to open the floodgates to such research (e.g., Wright and Rip, 1981). Yet such research would appear to miss the central point in the Nisbett and Wilson paper. Whether people's judgments of causality are accurate or not may be irrelevant to the question of introspective access. An accurate judgment could simply indicate that the person's theory about the cause of his or her behavior is correct. Hence research on accuracy can illuminate the types of theories people adopt, but it cannot establish whether people have direct introspective access to the causal processes involved.

Nisbett and L. Ross (1980, Chapter 9) have presented a spirited defense of the original studies. More important, they revised the Nisbett and Wilson position in two ways. First, they presented Nisbett and Wilson's central argument about introspective access to causal processes as a conceptual point, rather than as an empirical generalization. We are in full agreement with this shift. The conceptual point is compelling, whatever one's judgment of the experiments.

Second, Nisbett and L. Ross (1980) acknowledge more strongly that people do have privileged access to

their own mental events, and that, at times, the individual may have an edge over an observer in forming causal inferences. This implies that the individual bases his or her inference on a different data pattern than is available to an observer. As a result, I may often be a more informed theorist with respect to the causes of my behavior than most observers could be. As Nisbett and L. Ross, also note, however, the greater abundance of information available to me does not *guarantee* that my accounts will be more accurate than an observer's. This extra information may not be causally relevant, and I may be misled by incorrect beliefs or theories about the plausible causes of my behavior.

The bottom line is this: both actors and observers can only infer the causes of the actor's behavior. When there are differences of opinion, actors are more likely to be correct, because they generally have more information. There is no reason to assume, however, that the actor's judgment will necessarily be valid.

SOME GENERAL COMMENTS AND CONCLUSIONS

By focussing on causal attributions in this chapter we may seem to imply that every social judgment is fundamentally a causal one. Clearly, this is not true. In everyday life, our interest in another's behavior is not restricted to causal issues (Jones and Thibaut, 1958; Kruglanski, 1980; Kruglanski *et al.,* 1978). For example, we may wonder whether an individual is likely to help us achieve certain goals or interfere with our efforts. We then consider the value of that person to us, rather than his or her basic nature. Alternatively, we may want to evaluate the appropriateness of another's behavior and do so by contrasting it to relevant standards or norms, rather than by assessing its causes (Jones and Thibaut, 1958). In short, there is no reason to assume that people are forever pondering or even curious about the causes of their own or other's behavior.

What, then, of the supposed isomorphism between the goals and activities of scientists and those of people in their everyday lives? The answer is that the ordinary person's attributional investigations may, at times, mirror the scientific process. But people have other goals, and other needs as well.

Nevertheless, we do not wish to diminish the significance of the attribution process. To illustrate its importance we need only consider social policy decisions. An important question in most Western societies concerns why women have lower status and lower paying jobs than men. One answer to this question identifies the woman as the root of the problem (she fears success, lacks assertiveness, etc.). Alternatively, the disparity can be attributed to external factors such as sexual prejudice in the work place, societal definitions of appropriate sex-role behavior, inadequate daycare facilities, and so forth. One's judgment of the value of equal rights legislation is likely to depend, in part, on which of these attributions one chooses.

Thus, attributions do matter. Can we say the same about attribution theory and research? Have we learned much about the ordinary person's attributional reasoning from this very extensive literature? Many of the criticisms that we have directed at the classic theories reflect our belief that they are partial, oversimplified views of complex phenomena. Of course this is not surprising; all theories simplify nature. In various sections of the chapter, we have presented attempts by others and ourselves to point to and fill in some of the obvious gaps.

More serious criticisms can be directed at the research inspired by attribution theories. Studies aimed explicitly at testing the derivations of the various theories have been conceived on a somewhat narrow basis, almost always using a paper-and-pencil methodology and often using the model itself as the conceptual base for framing the independent and dependent variables. For instance, in many studies the dependent measures assess only the internal-external dimension of causality. On the basis of this research it is often concluded that the internal-external dimension is *the* central, causal dimension. Yet we tend to find what we look for; the relative importance of the locus of causality dimension cannot be established by such procedures. Another example is that much of the research on attributions for success and failure has utilized as its dependent variables the factors first postulated by Heider: ability, effort, task difficulty, and luck. In effect, researchers have relied on the intuitions of the theorists and in so doing have failed to consider sufficiently a range of important issues. These include assessments of the different kinds of causal dimensions people use, and the nature, type, and frequency of attributions as they occur in everyday life. The failure of attribution researchers to examine causal concepts (such as the internal-external distinction) inherent in the ordinary person's thinking is termed by Kelley and Michela (1980) the "central irony" of attribution research.

A comparable concern can be voiced with respect to the second direction in which attribution research has

proceeded. As we have noted, many researchers have used attribution as a framework or way of thinking about various phenomena, including insomnia and intrinsic motivation. The general strategy of this research is to modify subjects' attributions about the bases of their behavior or feelings. The research often seems premature, however, in the absence of data concerning people's naturally occurring attributions.

Despite the cognitive emphasis of attribution theory, many researchers have adopted a "black box" approach to experimentation. Before we attempt to modify the attributions of insomniacs or speech-anxious people, wouldn't it make sense first to assess their spontaneous attributions and the theories that underlie them? An elegant study by Diener and Dweck (1978) in the area of learned helplessness demonstrates the utility of such an approach.

Finally, note that we are not denigrating the bulk of mainstream attribution research. On the contrary, we believe that attribution research represents a dynamic and innovative area of astonishing diversity and intellectual vigor, from which much can be learned. All research has its limitations and assumptive bases; these must be taken into account if the research is to be evaluated properly.

REFERENCES

Abrams, R. D., and J. E. Finesinger (1953). Guilt reactions in patients with cancer. *Cancer, 6* (3), 474–482.

Abramson, L. Y., and L. B. Alloy (1980). Judgment of contingency: errors and their implications. In A. Baum and J. E. Singer (Eds.), *Advances in environmental psychology.* Hillsdale, N.J.: Erlbaum.

Ajzen, I. (1977). Intuitive theories of events and the effects of base-rate information on prediction. *J. Pers. soc. Psychol., 35,* 303–314.

Ajzen, I., C. A. Dalton, and D. P. Blyth (1979). Consistency and bias in the attribution of attitudes. *J. Pers. soc. Psychol., 37,* 1871–1876.

Ajzen, I., and W. H. Holmes (1976). Uniqueness of behavioral effects in causal attribution. *J. Pers., 44,* 98–108.

Alston, W. P. (1972). Can psychology do without private data. *Behaviorism, 1,* 71–102.

———— (1975). Traits, consistency and conceptual alternatives for personality theory. *J. theory soc. Behav., 5,* 17–48.

Anderson, N. H., and C. A. Butzin (1974). Performance = Motivation × Ability: an integration-theoretical analysis. *J. Pers. soc. Psychol., 30,* 598–604.

Archibald, W. P. (1974). Alternative explanations for self-fulfilling prophecy. *Psychol. Bull., 81,* 74–84.

Aronson, E. (1969). The theory of cognitive dissonance: a current perspective. In L. Bertowitz, Ed., *Advan. exp. soc. Psychol., 4,* 1–34.

Asch, S. E. (1956). Studies of independence and conformity. I. A minority of one against a unanimous majority. *Psychol. Monogr., 70,* 9 (whole No. 416).

Baldwin, C. P., and A. L. Baldwin (1970). Children's judgments of kindness. *Child Development, 41,* 29–47.

Bandler, R. J., G. R. Madaras, and D. J. Bem (1968). Self-observation as a source of pain perception. *J. Pers. soc. Psychol., 9,* 205–209.

Batson, C. D. (1975). Attribution as a mediator of bias in helping. *J. Pers. soc. Psychol., 32,* 455–466.

Bem, D. J. (1965). An experimental analysis of self-persuasion. *J. exp. soc. Psychol., 1,* 199–218.

_____ (1967). Self-perception: an alternative interpretation of cognitive dissonance phenomena. *Psychol. Rev., 24,* 183–200.

_____ (1968). The epistemological status of interpersonal simulations: a reply to Jones, Linder, Kiesler, Zanna, and Brehm. *J. exp. soc. Psychol., 4,* 270–274.

_____ (1970). *Beliefs, attitudes and human affairs.* Monterey, Calif.: Brooks/Cole.

_____ (1972). Self-perception theory. In L. Berkowitz (Ed.), *Advances in experimental social psychology.* Vol. 6. New York: Academic Press.

Bem, D. J., and H. K. McConnell (1970). Testing the self-perception explanation of dissonance phenomena: on the salience of premanipulation attitudes. *J. Pers. soc. Psychol., 14,* 23–31.

Bernstein, W. M., W. G. Stephan, and M. H. Davis (1979). Explaining attributions for achievement: a path analytic approach. *J. Pers. soc. Psychol., 37,* 1810–1821.

Berscheid, E., W. Graziano, T. Monson, and M. Dermer (1976). Outcome dependency: attention, attribution, and attraction. *J. Pers. soc. Psychol., 34,* 978–989.

Bettelheim, E. (1943). Individual and mass behavior in extreme situations. *J. abnorm. soc. Psychol., 38,* 417–452.

Bird, A. M., and J. M. Williams (1980). A developmental-attributional analysis of sex role stereotypes for sport performance. *Develop. Psychol., 16,* 319–322.

Bootzin, R. R., C. P. Herman, and P. Nicassio (1976). The power of suggestion: another examination of misattribution and insomnia. *J. Pers. soc. Psychol., 34,* 673–679.

Bower, G. H. (1981). Emotional mood and memory. *Amer. Psychol., 36,* 129–148.

Bowers, K. S. (1981). Knowing more than we can say leads to saying more than we can know: on being implicitly informed. In P. Magnusson (Ed.), *Toward a psychology of situations: an interactional perspective.* Hillsdale, N.J.: Erlbaum.

Braband, J. E., and M. J. Lerner (1975). A little time and effort: who deserves what from whom? *Pers. soc. Psychol. Bull., 1,* 177–181.

Bradley, G. W. (1978). Self-serving biases in the attribution process: a reexamination of the fact or fiction question. *J. Pers. soc. Psychol., 36,* 56–71.

Brickman, P., K. Ryan, and C. B. Wortman (1975). Causal chains: attribution of responsibility as a function of immediate and prior causes. *J. Pers. soc. Psychol., 32,* 1060–1067.

Brodt, S. E., and P. G. Zimbardo (1981). Modifying shyness-related social behavior through symptom misattribution. *J. Pers. soc. Psychol., 41,* 437–449.

Bulman, R. J., and C. B. Wortman (1977). Attributions of blame and coping in the "real world": severe accident victims react to their lot. *J. Pers. soc. Psychol., 35,* 351–363.

Butzin, C. (1979). Children's moral judgments of ulterior motives. *Abstracts of individual papers. Biennial Convention of the Society for Research in Child Development, 2.*

Buss, A. R. (1978). Causes and reasons in attribution theory: a conceptual critique. *J. Pers. soc. Psychol., 36,* 1311–1321.

Calder, B. J. (1977). Endogenous-exogenous versus internal-external attributions: implications for the development of attribution theory. *Pers. soc. Psychol. Bull., 3,* 400–406.

Calder, B. J., and B. M. Staw (1975). Self-perception of intrinsic and extrinsic motivation. *J. Pers. soc. Psychol., 31,* 599–605.

Calvert-Boyanowsky, J., and H. Leventhal (1975). The role of information in attenuating behavioral responses to stress: a reinterpretation of the misattribution phenomenon. *J. Pers. soc. Psychol., 32,* 214–221.

Cannon, W. B. (1927). The James-Lange theory of emotions: a critical examination and an alternative theory. *Amer. J. Psychol., 34,* 106–124.

Carkhuff, R. R. (1968). The differential functioning of lay and professional helpers. *J. counsel. Psychol., 15,* 417–426.

Chaiken, S., and M. W. Baldwin (1981). Affective-cognitive consistency and the effect of salient behavioral information on the self-perception of attitudes. *J. Pers. soc. Psychol., 41,* 1–12.

Chaikin, A. L., and J. Cooper (1973). Evaluation as a function of correspondence and hedonic relevance. *J. exp. soc. Psychol., 9,* 257–264.

Chaikin, A. L., and J. M. Darley (1973). Victim or perpetrator: defensive attribution of responsibility and the need for order and justice. *J. Pers. soc. Psychol., 25,* 268–275.

Chambliss, C., and E. J. Murray (1979). Cognitive procedures for smoking reduction: symptom attribution versus efficacy attribution. *Cognit. Therapy Res., 3,* 91–95.

Chapman, L. J., and J. P. Chapman (1967). Genesis of popular but erroneous psychodiagnostic observations. *J. abnorm. Psychol., 72,* 193–204.

_____ (1969). Illusory correlation as an obstacle to the use of valid psychodiagnostic signs. *J. abnorm. Psychol., 74,* 271–280.

Chodoff, P., S. Friedman, and D. Hamburg (1964). Stress defenses and coping behavior: observations in parents of children with malignant disease. *Amer. J. Psychiatry, 120,* 743–749.

Chomsky, N. (1959). Review of Skinner's verbal behaviour. *Language, 35,* 26–58.

Comer, R., and J. D. Laird (1975). Choosing to suffer as a consequence of expecting to suffer: why do people do it? *J. Pers. soc. Psychol., 32,* 92–101.

Condry, J., and J. Chambers (1978). Intrinsic motivation and the process of learning. In M. R. Lepper and D. Greene (Eds.), *The hidden costs of reward.* Hillsdale, N.J.: Erlbaum.

Cook, T. D., and D. T. Campbell (1979). *Quasi-experimentation: design and analysis issues for field settings.* Chicago: Rand McNally.

Corah, N. L., and J. Boffa (1970). Perceived control, self-observation, and response to aversive stimulation. *J. Pers. soc. Psychol., 16,* 1–4.

Costanzo, P. R., J. F. Grumet, and S. S. Brehm (1974). The effects of choice and source of constraint on children's attributions of preference. *J. exp. soc. Psychol., 10,* 352–364.

Covington, M. V., and C. L. Cmelich (1979). Are causal attributions causal? A path analysis of the cognitive model of achievement motivation. *J. Pers. soc. Psychol., 37,* 1487–1504.

Crandall, C. V. (1969). Sex differences in expectancy of intellectual and academic reinforcement. In C. P. Smith (Ed.), *Achievement-related motives in children.* New York: Russell Sage.

Crocker, J. (1981). Judgment of covariation by social perceivers. *Psychol. Bull., 90,* 272–292.

Cunningham, J. D., and H. H. Kelley (1975). Causal attributions for interpersonal events of varying magnitude. *J. Pers., 43,* 74–93.

Darley, J. M., and R. H. Fazio (1980). Expectancy confirmation processes arising in the social interaction sequence. *Amer. Psychol., 35,* 867–881.

Darley, J. M., and G. R. Goethals (1980). People's analyses of the causes of ability-linked performances. In L. Berkowitz (Ed.), *Advances in experimental social psychology.* Vol. 13. New York: Academic Press.

Darley, J. M., E. C. Klosson, and M. P. Zanna (1978). Intentions and their contexts in the moral judgments of children and adults. *Child Development, 49,* 66–74.

Darley, J. M., and B. Latane (1968). Bystander intervention in emergencies: diffusion of responsibility. *J. Pers. soc. Psychol., 8,* 377–383.

Deaux, K. (1976). Sex: a perspective on the attribution process. In J. H. Harvey, W. J. Ickes, and R. F. Kidd (Eds.), *New directions in attribution research.* Hillsdale, N.J.: Erlbaum.

Deaux, K., and T. Emswiller (1974). Explanations of successful performance on sex-linked tasks: what is skill for the male is luck for the female. *J. Pers. soc. Psychol., 29,* 80–85.

de Beauvoir, S. (1973). *The coming of age.* New York: Warner.

Deci, E. L. (1971). Effects of externally mediated rewards on intrinsic motivation. *J. Pers. soc. Psychol., 18,* 105–115.

Deci, E. L., and R. M. Ryan (1980). The empirical exploration of intrinsic motivational processes. In L. Berkowitz (Ed.), *Advances in experimental social psychology.* Vol. 13. New York: Academic Press.

Dennis, W. (1943). Animism and related tendencies in Hopi children. *J. abnorm. soc. Psychol., 38,* 21–36.

Diener, C. I., and C. S. Dweck (1978). An analysis of learned helplessness: continuous changes in performance, strategy, and achievement cognitions following failure. *J. Pers. soc. Psychol., 36,* 451–462.

Dienstbier, R. A., and P. C. Munter (1971). Cheating as a function of the labeling of natural arousal. *J. Pers. soc. Psychol., 17,* 208–213.

Diggory, J. S. (1966). *Self-evaluation: concepts and studies.* New York: Wiley.

Dweck, C. S. (1975). The role of expectations and attributions in the alleviation of learned helplessness. *J. Pers. soc. Psychol., 31,* 674–685.

Dweck, C. S., and E. S. Bush (1976). Sex differences in learned helplessness: I. Differential debilitation with peer and adult evaluators. *Develop. Psychol., 12,* 147–156.

Dweck, C. S., W. Davidson, S. Nelson, and B. Enna (1978). Sex differences in learned helplessness: II. The contingencies of evaluative feedback in the classroom and III. An experimental analysis. *Develop. Psychol., 14,* 268–276.

Dweck, C. S., and N. D. Reppucci (1973). Learned helplessness and reinforcement responsibility in children. *J. Pers. soc. Psychol., 25,* 109–116.

Dyck, R. J., and B. G. Rule (1978). Effect on retaliation of causal attributions concerning attack. *J. Pers. soc. Psychol., 36,* 521–529.

Einhorn, H. J., and R. M. Hogarth (1978). Confidence in judgment: persistence of the illusion of validity. *Psychol. Rev., 85,* 395–416.

Elig, T., and I. Frieze (1975). A multidimensional scheme for coding and interpreting perceived causality for success and failure events: the CSPS. *Catalog sel. doc. Psychol., 5,* 313. (MS 1069).

———— (1979). Measuring causal attributions for success and failure. *J. Pers. soc. Psychol., 37,* 621–634.

Ericsson, K. A., and H. A. Simon (1980). Verbal reports as data. *Psychol. Rev., 87,* 215–251.

Etaugh, C., and B. Brown (1975). Perceiving the causes of success and failure of male and female performers. *Develop. Psychol., 11,* 103.

Fazio, R. H. (1981). On the self-perception explanation of the overjustification effect: the role of salience of initial attitude. *J. exp. soc. Psychol., 17,* 417–426.

Fazio, R. H., S. J. Sherman, and P. M. Herr (1982). The feature-positive effect in the self-perception process: does not doing matter as much as doing? *J. Pers. soc. Psychol., 42,* 404–411.

Feather, N. T. (1969). Attribution of responsibility and valence of success and failure in relation to initial confidence and task performance. *J. Pers. soc. Psychol., 13,* 129–144.

Feather, N. T., and J. G. Simon (1973). Fear of success and causal attributions for outcome. *J. Pers., 41,* 515–542.

———— (1971). Attribution of responsibility and valence of outcome in relation to initial confidence and success and failure of self and other. *J. Pers. soc. Psychol., 18,* 173–188.

———— (1975). Reactions to male and female success and failure in sex-linked occupations: impressions of personality, causal attributions, and perceived likelihood of different consequences. *J. Pers. soc. Psychol., 31,* 20–31.

Feldman, N. S., E. T. Higgins, M. Karlovac, and D. N. Ruble (1976). Use of consensus information in causal attributions as a function of temporal presentation and availability of direct information. *J. Pers. soc. Psychol., 34,* 694–698.

Feldman, N. S., and D. N. Ruble (1981). The development of person perception: cognitive and social factors. In S. S. Brehm, S. M. Kassin, and F. X. Gibbons (Eds.), *Developmental social psychology.* New York: Oxford Univ. Press.

Feldman-Summers, S., and S. B. Kiesler (1974). Those who are number two try harder: the effect of sex on attributions of causality. *J. Pers. soc. Psychol., 30,* 846–855.

Festinger, L. (1957). *A theory of cognitive dissonance.* Evanston, Ill.: Row, Peterson.

Fields, J. M., and M. Schuman (1976). Public beliefs and the beliefs of the public. *Publ. Opin. Quart., 40,* 427–448.

Fincham, F. D., and J. M. Jaspars (1979). Attribution of responsibility to self and other in children and adults. *J. Pers. soc. Psychol., 37,* 1589–1602.

———— (1980). Attribution of responsibility: from man the scientist to man as lawyer. *Advances in experimental social psychology.* Vol. 13. New York: Academic Press.

Fischhoff, B. (1975). Hindsight ≠ Foresight: the effect of outcome knowledge on judgment under uncertainty. *J. exp. Psychol.: Hum. Percept. Perform., 1,* 288–299.

———— (1976). Attribution theory and judgment under uncertainty. In J. H. Harvey, W. J. Ickes, and R. F. Kidd (Eds.), *New directions in attribution research.* Vol. 1. Hillsdale, N.J.: Erlbaum.

Fischhoff, B., and R. Beyth (1975). "I knew it would happen"—remembered probabilities of once-future things. *Organizat. Behav. hum. Perform., 13,* 1–16.

Fiske, S. T., D. A. Kenny, and S. E. Taylor (1982). Structural models for the mediation of salience effects on attribution. *J. exp. soc. Psychol., 18,* 105–127.

Flapan, D. (1968). *Children's understanding of social interaction.* New York: Univ. Teacher's College Press.

Fletcher, G. J. O. (1981). Causal attributions for marital separation. Unpublished doctoral dissertation. University of Waikato, New Zealand.

———— (1983a). The analysis of verbal explanations for marital separation: implications for attribution theory. *J. appl. soc. Psychol., 13,* 245–258.

———— (1983b). Sex differences in causal attributions for marital separation. *New Zealand Psychologist, 12,* 82–89.

———— (1984). Psychology and common sense. *Amer. Psychol., 39,* 203–213.

Frieze, I. (1976). Causal attributions and information seeking to explain success and failure. *J. Res. Pers., 10,* 293–305.

Gelman, R., and D. H. Weinberg (1972). The relationship between liquid conservation and compensation. *Child Development, 43,* 371–383.

Goethals, G. R., S. J. Allison, and M. Frost (1979). Perceptions of the magnitude and diversity of social support. *J. exp. soc. Psychol., 15,* 570–581.

Goethals, G. R., and J. M. Darley (1977). Social comparison theory: an attributional approach. In J. M. Suls and R. L. Miller (Eds.), *Social comparison processes: theoretical and empirical perspectives.* Washington, D.C.: Hemisphere.

Goethals, G. R., and R. F. Reckman (1973). The perception of consistency in attitudes. *J. exp. soc. Psychol., 9,* 491–501.

Goffman, E. (1961). *Asylums: essays on the social situation of mental patients and other inmates.* Garden City, N.Y.: Doubleday.

Greenwald, A. G. (1975). On the inconclusiveness of "crucial" cognitive tests of dissonance versus self-perception theories. *J. exp. soc. Psychol., 11,* 490–499.

Guttentag, M., and C. Longfellow (1977). Children's social attributions: development and change. In H. E. Howe and C. B. Keasey, *Nebraska symposium on motivation.* Vol. 25. Lincoln: Univ. of Nebraska Press.

Hamilton, V. L. (1980). Intuitive psychologist or intuitive lawyer? Alternative models of the attribution process. *J. Pers. soc. Psychol., 39,* 767–772.

Hansen, R. D., and J. M. Donoghue (1977). The power of consensus: information derived from one's own and other's behavior. *J. Pers. soc. Psychol., 35,* 294–302.

Harris, B. (1977). Developmental differences in the attribution of responsibility. *Develop. Psychol., 13,* 257–265.

Harris, V. S., and E. S. Katkin (1975). Primary and secondary emotional behavior: an analysis of the role of autonomic feedback on affect, arousal, and attribution. *Psychol. Bull., 82,* 904–916.

Harvey, J. H., J. P. Town, and K. L. Yarkin (1981). How fundamental is "the attribution error?" *J. Pers. soc. Psychol., 40,* 346–349.

Harvey, J. H., K. L. Yarkin, J. M. Lightner, and J. P. Town (1980). Unsolicited interpretation and recall of interpersonal events. *J. Pers. soc. Psychol., 38,* 551–568.

Harvey, J. H., G. L. Wells, and M. D. Alvarez (1978). Attribution in the context of conflict and separation in close relationships. In J. H. Harvey, W. Ickes, and R. F. Kidd (Eds.), *New directions in attribution research.* Vol. 2. Hillsdale, N.J.: Erlbaum.

Heider, F. (1944). Social perception and phenomenal causality. *Psychol. Rev., 51,* 358–374.

————(1958). *The psychology of interpersonal relations.* New York: Wiley.

Henslin, J. M. (1967). Craps and magic. *Amer. J. Sociol., 73,* 316–330.

Higgins, E. T. (1981). Role-taking and social judgment: alternative developmental perspectives and processes. In V. H. Flavell and L. Ross (Eds.), *New directions in the study of social-cognitive development.* Cambridge: Cambridge Univ. Press.

Higgins, E. T., F. Rodewalt, and M. P. Zanna (1979). Dissonance reduction: its nature, persistence and reinstatement. *J. exp. soc. Psychol., 5,* 16–34.

Holmes, D. S. (1968). Dimensions of projection. *Psychol. Bull., 69,* 248–268.

Isen, A. M., T. E. Shalker, M. Clark, and L. Karp (1978). Affect, accessibility of material in memory, and behavior: a cognitive loop? *J. Pers. soc. Psychol., 36,* 1–12.

James, W. (1950). *The principles of psychology.* New York: Holt.

Janoff-Bulman, R. (1979). Characterological versus behavioral self-blame: inquiries into depression and rape. *J. Pers. soc. Psychol., 37,* 1798–1809.

Jellison, J. M., and J. Green (1981). A self-presentation approach to the fundamental attribution error: the norm of internality. *J. Pers. soc. Psychol., 40,* 643–649.

Johnson, R. C. (1962). A study of children's moral judgments. *Child Development, 33,* 327–354.

Jones, E. E. (1978). A conversation with Edward E. Jones and Harold H. Kelley. In J. H. Harvey, W. J. Ickes, R.F. Kidd (Eds.), *New directions in attribution research.* Vol. 2. Hillsdale, N.J.: Erlbaum.

———— (1979). The rocky road from acts to dispositions. *Amer. Psychol., 34,* 107–117.

Jones, E. E., and S. Berglas (1978). Control of attributions about the self through self-handicapping strategies: the appeal of alcohol and the role of under-achievement. *Pers. soc. Psychol. Bull., 4,* 200–206.

Jones, E. E., and K. E. Davis (1965). From acts to dispositions: the attribution process in person perception. In L.

Berkowitz (Ed.), *Advances in experimental social psychology*. Vol. 2. New York: Academic Press.

Jones, E. E., and G. Goethals (1971). *Order effects in impression formation: attribution context and the nature of the entity*. Morristown, N.J.: General Learning Press.

Jones, E. E., and V. A. Harris (1967). The attribution of attitudes. *J. exp. soc. Psychol., 3,* 1–24.

Jones, E. E., and D. McGillis (1976). Correspondent inferences and the attribution cube: a comparative reappraisal. In J. H. Harvey, W. J. Ickes, and R. F. Kidd (Eds.), *New directions in attribution research*. Vol. 1. Hillsdale, N.J.: Erlbaum.

Jones, E. E., and R. E. Nisbett (1972). The actor and the observer: divergent perceptions of the causes of behavior. In E. E. Jones, D. E. Kanouse, H. H. Kelley, R. E. Nisbett, S. Valins, and B. Weiner (Eds.), *Attribution: perceiving the causes of behavior*. Morristown, N.J.: General Learning Press.

Jones, E. E., and J. W. Thibaut (1958). Interaction goals as bases of inference in interpersonal perception. In R. Tagiuri and L. Petrullo (Eds.), *Person perception and interpersonal behaviour*. Stanford: Stanford Univ. Press.

Jones, E. E., L. Rock, K. G. Shaver, G. R. Goethals, and L. M. Ward (1968). Pattern of performance and ability attribution: an unexpected primacy effect. *J. Pers. soc. Psychol., 10,* 317–340.

Kahneman, D., and A. Tversky (1973). On the psychology of prediction. *Psychol. Rev., 80,* 237–251.

Kanouse, D. E. (1971). *Language, labeling and attribution*. Morristown, N.J.: General Learning Press.

Karniol, R. (1978). Children's use of intention cues in evaluating behavior. *Psychol. Bull., 85,* 76–85.

_____ (1980). A conceptual analyses of immanent justice responses in children. *Child Development, 51,* 118–130.

Karniol, R., and M. Ross (1976). The development of causal attributions in social perception. *J. Pers. soc. Psychol., 34,* 455–464.

_____ (1977). The effect of performance-relevant and performance-irrelevant rewards on children's intrinsic motivation. *Child Development, 48,* 482–487.

_____ (1979). Children's use of a causal attribution schema and the inference of manipulation intentions. *Child Development, 50,* 463–468.

Kassin, S. M. (1979). Consensus information, prediction, and causal attribution: a review of the literature and issues. *J. Pers. soc. Psychol., 37,* 1966–1981.

Kassin, S. M., and D. J. Hochreich (1977). Instructional set: a neglected variable in attribution research? *Pers. soc. Psychol. Bull., 3,* 620–623.

Kelley, H. H. (1967). Attribution theory in social psychology. In D. L. Vine (Ed.), *Nebraska symposium on motivation*. Lincoln, Neb.: Univ. of Nebraska Press.

_____ (1972). *Causal schemata and the attribution process*. Morristown, N.J.: General Learning Press.

_____ (1973). The processes of causal attribution. *Amer. Psychol., 28,* 107–128.

_____ (1978). A conversation with E. Jones and H. Kelley. In J. H. Harvey, W. Ickes, and R. F. Kidd (Eds.), *New directions in attribution research*. Vol. 2. New York: Wiley.

_____ (1983). Epilogue: perceived causal structures. In J. Jaspars, F. Fincham, and M. Hewstone (Eds.), *Attribution theory: essays and experiments*. London: Academic Press.

Kelley, H. H., and J. L. Michela (1980). Attribution theory and research. *Ann. Rev. Psychol., 31,* 457–501.

Kellogg, R., and R. S. Baron (1975). Attribution theory, insomnia, and the reverse placebo effect: a reversal of Storms and Nisbett's findings. *J. Pers. soc. Psychol., 32,* 231–236.

Kelly, G. A. (1955). *The psychology of personal constructs*. Vol. 1. New York: Norton.

Kepka, E. J., and P. Brickman (1971). Consistency versus discrepancy as clues in the attribution of intelligence and motivation. *J. Pers. soc. Psychol., 20,* 223–229.

Kiesler, C. A., R. E. Nisbett, and M. P. Zanna (1969). On inferring one's beliefs from one's behavior. *J. Pers. soc. Psychol., 11,* 321–327.

Kiesler, C. A., and M. S. Pallak (1976). Arousal properties of dissonance reduction. *Psychol. Bull., 83,* 1014–1025.

Korte, C. (1972). Pluralistic ignorance about student racism. *Sociometry, 35,* 576–587.

Kruglanski, A. W. (1980). Lay epistemo-logic-process and contents: another look at attribution theory. *Psychol. Rev., 87,* 70–87.

Kruglanksi, A. W., I. Z. Hamel, S. A. Maides, and J. M. Schwartz (1978). Attribution theory as a special case of lay epistemology. In J. H. Harvey, W. Ickes, and R. F. Kidd (Eds.), *New directions in attribution research*. Vol. 2. Hillsdale, N.J.: Erlbaum.

Kubler-Ross, E. (1969). *On death and dying*. New York: Macmillan.

Kulik, J. A., and R. Brown (1979). Frustration, attribution of blame, and aggression. *J. exp. soc. Psychol., 15,* 183–194.

Kulik, J. A., and S. E. Taylor (1980). Premature consensus on consensus? Effects of sample-based versus self-based consensus information. *J. Pers. soc. Psychol., 39,* 871–879.

Kun, A. (1977). Development of the magnitude-covariation and compensation schemata in ability and effort attributions of performance. *Child Development, 48,* 862–873.

Kun, A., and B. Weiner (1973). Necessary versus sufficient causal schemata for success and failure. *J. res. Pers., 7,* 197–207.

Laird, J. D. (1974). Self-attribution of emotion: the effects of expressive behavior on the quality of emotional experience. *J. Pers. soc. Psychol., 29,* 475–486.

Lange, C. (1922). The emotions, in Istar Haupt Translation. (Originally published in Denmark, 1885.) K. Dunlop (Ed.), *The emotions*. Baltimore, Md.: Williams and Wilkins.

Langer, E. J. (1975). The illusion of control. *J. Pers. soc. Psychol., 32,* 311–328.

Langer, E. J., and J. Roth (1975). Heads I win, tails it's chance: the illusion of control as a function of the sequence of outcomes in a purely chance task. *J. Pers. soc. Psychol., 32,* 951–955.

Lanzetta, J. T., J. Cartwright-Smith, and R. E. Kleck (1976). Effects of nonverbal dissimilation on emotional experience and outcome arousal. *J. Pers. soc. Psychol., 33,* 354–370.

Larwood, L. (1978). Swine flu: a field study of self-serving biases. *J. appl. soc. Psychol., 9,* 283–289.

Latané, B., and J. M. Darley (1970). *The unresponsive bystander: why doesn't he help?* New York: Appleton-Century-Crofts.

Lau, R. R., and D. Russell (1980). Attributions in the sports pages. *J. Pers. soc. Psychol., 39,* 29–38.

Lefcourt, H. M. (1973). The functions of the illusions of control and freedom. *Amer. Psychol., 28,* 417–425.

Lepper, M. (1973). Dissonance, self-perception, and honesty in children. *J. Pers. soc. Psychol., 25,* 65–74.

Lepper, M. R., and T. J. Gilovich (1981). The multiple functions of reward: a social-developmental perspective. In S. S. Brehm, S. M. Kassin, and F. X. Gibbons (Eds.), *Developmental social psychology.* New York: Oxford Univ. Press.

Lepper, M. R., and D. Greene (1975). Turning play into work: effects of adult surveillance and extrinsic rewards on children's intrinsic motivation. *J. Pers. soc. Psychol., 31,* 479–486.

Lepper, M. R., and D. Green, Eds. (1978). *The hidden costs of reward: new perspectives on the psychology of human motivation.* Hillsdale, N.J.: Erlbaum.

Lepper, M. R., D. Greene, and R. E. Nisbett (1973). Undermining children's intrinsic interest with external rewards: a test of the overjustification hypothesis. *J. Pers. soc. Psychol., 28,* 129–137.

Lerner, M. J. (1965). Evaluation of performance as a function of performer's reward and attractiveness. *J. Pers. soc. Psychol., 1,* 355–360.

———— (1980). *The belief in a just world: a fundamental delusion.* New York: Plenum.

Lerner, M. J., and D. T. Miller (1978). Just world research and the attribution process: looking back and ahead. *Psychol. Bull., 85,* 1030–1051.

Lerner, M. J., D. T. Miller, and J. G. Holmes (1976). Deserving and the emergence of forms of justice. In L. Berkowitz (ed.), *Advances in experimental social psychology.* Vol. 9. New York: Academic Press. Pp. 133–162.

Lerner, M. J., and C. H. Simmons (1966). Observer's reactions to the "innocent victim": compassion or rejection. *J. Pers. soc. Psychol., 4,* 203–210.

Leventhal, H. (1974). Emotions: a basic problem for social psychology. In C. Nemeth (Ed.), *Social psychology: classic and contemporary integrations.* Chicago: Rand McNally.

———— (1980). Toward a comprehensive theory of emotion. In L. Berkowitz (Ed.), *Advances in experimental social psychology.* Vol. 13. New York: Academic Press.

Lindsley, D. B. (1951). Emotion. In S. Stevens (Ed.), *Handbook of experimental psychology.* London: Chapman and Hall.

Livesley, W., and D. Bromley (1973). *Person perception in childhood and adolescence.* London: Wiley.

Lowery, C. R., D. R. Denney, and M. D. Storms (1979). Insomnia: a comparison of the effects of pill attributions and nonpejorative self-attributions. *Cognit. Therapy Res., 3,* 161–164.

McArthur, L. Z. (1972). The how and what of why: some determinants and consequences of causal attribution. *J. Pers. soc. Psychol., 22,* 171–193.

———— (1976). The lesser influence of consensus than distinctiveness information on causal attributions: a test of the person-thing hypothesis. *J. Pers. soc. Psychol., 33,* 733–742.

McArthur, L. Z., and D. L. Post (1977). Figural emphasis and person perception. *J. exp. soc. Psychol., 13,* 520–535.

McFarland, C., and M. Ross (1982). The impact of causal attributions on affective reactions to success and failure. *J. Pers. soc. Psychol., 43,* 937–946.

McGraw, K. O. (1978). The detrimental effects of reward on performance: a literature review and a prediction model. In M. R. Lepper and D. Greene (Eds.), *The hidden costs of reward.* Hillsdale, N.J.: Erlbaum.

MacRae, D. (1954). A test of Piaget's theory of moral development. *J. abnorm. soc. Psychol., 49,* 14–18.

Mandler, G. (1975). *Mind and emotion.* New York: Wiley.

Marshall, G. D., and P. G. Zimbardo (1979). Affective consequences of inadequately explained arousal. *J. Pers. soc. Psychol., 37,* 970–988.

Maslach, C. (1979). Negative emotional biasing of unexplained arousal. *J. Pers. soc. Psychol., 37,* 953–969.

Medea, A., and K. Thompson (1974). *Against rape.* New York: Farrar, Straus & Giroux.

Messick, D. M., and G. Reeder (1974). Roles, occupations, behaviors, and attributions. *J. exp. soc. Psychol., 10,* 126–132.

Meyer, J. P. (1980). Causal attribution for success and failure: a multivariate investigation of dimensionality, formation, and consequences. *J. Pers. soc. Psychol., 38,* 704–718.

Milgram, S. (1965). Some conditions of obedience and disobedience to authority. *Hum. Relat., 18,* 57–76.

Miller, A. G., B. Gillen, C. Schenker, and S. Radlove (1974). The prediction and perception of obedience to authority. *J. Pers., 42,* 23–42.

Miller, D. T. (1978). What constitutes a self-serving attributional bias? A reply to Bradley. *J. Pers. soc. Psychol., 36,* 1211–1223.

Miller, D. T., and S. A. Norman (1975). Actor-observer differences in perceptions of effective control. *J. Pers. soc. Psychol., 31,* 503–515.

Miller, D. T., S. A. Norman, and E. Wright (1978). Distortion in person perception as a consequence of the need for effective control. *J. Pers. soc. Psychol., 36,* 598–607.

Miller, D. T., and C. A. Porter (in press). Errors and biases in the attribution process. In L. Abramson (Ed.), *Attribution processes and clinical psychology.* New York: Guilford Press.

Miller, D. T., and M. Ross (1975). Self-serving biases in the attribution of causality: fact or fiction? *Psychol. Bull., 82,* 213–225.

Miller, R. L., P. Brickman, and D. Bolen (1975). Attribution versus persuasion as a means for modifying behavior. *J. Pers. soc. Psychol., 31,* 430–441.

Monson, T. C., and M. Snyder (1977). Actors, observers, and the attribution process: toward a reconceptualization. *J. exp. soc. Psychol., 13,* 89–111.

Morgan, M. (1981). The overjustification effect: a developmental test of self-perception interpretations. *J. Pers. soc. Psychol., 40,* 809–821.

Napolitan, D. A., and G. R. Goethals (1979). The attribution of friendliness. *J. exp. soc. Psychol., 15,* 105–113.

Newtson, D. (1974). Dispositional inferences from effects of actions: effects chosen and effects forgone. *J. exp. soc. Psychol., 10,* 489–496.

Nicholls, J. G. (1975). Causal attributions and other achievement-related cognitions: effects of task outcome, attainment value and sex. *J. Pers. soc. Psychol., 31,* 379–389.

Nisbett, R. E., and E. Borgida (1975). Attribution and the psychology of prediction. *J. Pers. soc. Psychol., 32,* 932–943.

Nisbett, R. E., E. Borgida, R. Crandall, and H. Reed (1976). Popular induction: information is not always informative. In J. Carroll and J. Payne (Eds.), *Cognition and social behavior.* Hillsdale, N.J.: Erlbaum.

Nisbett, R. E., C. Caputo, P. Legant, and J. Marecek (1973). Behavior as seen by the actor and as seen by the observer. *J. Pers. soc. Psychol., 27,* 154–165.

Nisbett, R. E., and L. Ross (1980). *Human inference: strategies and shortcomings of social judgment.* Englewood Cliffs, N.J.: Prentice-Hall.

Nisbett, R. E., and S. Schachter (1966). Cognitive manipulation of pain. *J. exp. soc. Psychol., 2,* 227–236.

Nisbett, R. E., and T. D. Wilson (1977a). Telling more than we can know: verbal reports on mental processes. *Psychol. Rev., 84,* 231–259.

_____ (1977b). The halo effect: evidence for unconscious alteration of judgments. *J. Pers. soc. Psychol., 35,* 250–256.

Orvis, B. R., J. D. Cunningham, and H. H. Kelley (1975). A closer examination of causal inferences: the roles of consensus, distinctiveness, and consistency information. *J. Pers. soc. Psychol., 32,* 605–616.

Orvis, B. R., H. H. Kelley, and D. Butler (1976). Attributional conflict in young couples. In J.H. Harvey, W.J. Ickes, and R.F. Kidd (Eds.), *New directions in attribution research.* Vol. 1. Hillsdale, N.J.: Erlbaum.

Pallak, M., and T. S. Pittman (1972). General motivational effects of dissonance arousal. *J. Pers. soc. Psychol., 21,* 349–358.

Parsons, J. E., T. F. Adler, and C. M. Kaczala (1982). Socialization of achievement attitudes and beliefs: parental influences. *Child Development, 53,* 310–321.

Parsons, J. E., C. M. Kaczala, and J. L. Meece (1982). Socialization of achievement attitudes and beliefs: classroom influences. *Child Development, 53,* 322–339.

Passer, M. W. (1977). *Perceiving the causes of success and failure revisited: a multidimensional scaling approach.* Unpublished doctoral dissertation. Los Angeles: Univ. of California.

Piaget, J. (1948). *The moral judgment of the child.* Glencoe, Ill.: Free Press.

_____ (1954). *The construction of reality in the child.* New York: Basic Books.

Plutchik, R., and A. F. Ax (1967). A critique of determinants of emotional state by Schachter and Singer. *Psychophysiology, 4,* 79–82.

Pruitt, D. J., and C. A. Insko (1980). Extension of the Kelley attribution model: the role of comparison-object consensus, target-object consensus, distinctiveness, and consistency. *J. Pers. soc. Psychol., 39,* 39–58.

Pryor, J. B., and M. Kriss (1977). The cognitive dynamics of salience in the attribution process. *J. Pers. soc. Psychol., 35,* 49–55.

Reeder, G. D., and M. B. Brewer (1979). A schematic model of dispositional attribution in interpersonal perception. *Psychol. Rev., 86,* 61–79.

Reeder, G. D., and J. L. Fulks (1980). When actions speak louder than words: implicational schemata and the attribution of ability. *J. exp. soc. Psychol., 16,* 33–46.

Reeder, G. D., D. M. Messick, and E. Van Avermaet (1977). Dimensional asymmetry in attributional inference. *J. exp. soc. Psychol., 13,* 46–57.

Reimer, B. S. (1975). Influence of causal beliefs on affect and expectancy. *J. Pers. soc. Psychol., 31,* 1163–1167.

Rosenfield, D., and W. G. Stephan (1978). Sex differences in attribution for sex-typed tasks. *J. Pers., 46,* 244–259.

Ross, L. (1977). The intuitive psychologist and his shortcomings: distortions in the attribution process. In L. Berkowitz (Ed.), *Advances in experimental social psychology.* Vol. 10. New York: Academic Press.

Ross, L., D. Greene, and P. House (1977). The "false consensus effect": an egocentric bias in social perception and attribution processes. *J. exp. soc. Psychol., 13,* 279–301.

Ross, L., J. Rodin, and P. G. Zimbardo (1969). Toward an attribution therapy: the reduction of fear through induced cognitive–emotional misattribution. *J. Pers. soc. Psychol., 12,* 279–288.

Ross, M. (1975). Salience of reward and intrinsic motivation. *J. Pers. soc. Psychol., 32,* 245–254.

_____ (1976). The self-perception of intrinsic motivation. In J. H. Harvey, W. J. Ickes, and R. F. Kidd (Eds.), *New direction in attribution research.* Vol. 1. Hillsdale, N.J.: Erlbaum.

Ross, M. (1981). Egocentric biases in attributions of responsibility: antecedents and consequences. In E. T. Higgins, C. P. Herman, and M. P. Zanna (Eds.), *Social cognition: The Ontario Symposium* (Vol. 1). Hillsdale, N.J.: Erlbaum.

Ross, M., and D. DiTecco (1975). An attributional analysis of moral judgments. *J. soc. Issues, 31,* 91–109.

Ross, M., C. A. Insko, and H. S. Ross (1971). Self-attribution of attitude. *J. Pers. soc. Psychol., 17,* 292–297.

Ross, M., and A. Lumsden (1982). Attributions of responsibility in sport settings: its not how you play the game, but whether you win or lose. In H. Hiebsch, H. Brandstatter, and H. H. Kelley (Eds.), *Social psychology.* East Berlin: VEB Deutscher Verlag der Wissenschaften.

Ross, M., and J. M. Olson (1981). An expectancy-attribution model of the effects of placebos. *Psychol. Rev., 88,* 408–437.

_____ (1982). Placebo effects in medical research and practice. In J. R. Eiser (Ed.), *Social psychology and behavioral medicine.* London: Wiley.

Ross, M., and R. F. Shulman (1973). Increasing the salience of initial attitudes: dissonance versus self-perception theory. *J. Pers. soc. Psychol., 28,* 138–144.

Ross, M., and F. Sicoly (1979). Egocentric biases in availability and attribution. *J. Pers. soc. Psychol., 37,* 322–336.

Ruble, D. N., J. E. Parsons, and J. Ross (1976). Self-evaluative responses of children in an achievement setting. *Child Development, 47,* 990–997.

Schachter, S. (1964). The interaction of cognitive and physiological determinants of emotional state. In L. Berkowitz (Ed.), *Advances in experimental social psychology*. Vol. 1. New York: Academic Press.

Schachter, S., and J. E. Singer (1962). Cognitive, social and physiological determinants of emotional state. *Psychol. Rev., 69,* 379–399.

——— (1979). Comment on the Maslach and Marshall-Zimbardo experiments. *J. Pers. soc. Psychol., 37,* 989–995.

Schachter, S., and L. Wheeler (1962). Epinephrine, chlorpromazine and amusement. *J. abnorm. soc. Psychol., 68,* 121–128.

Schanck, R. L. (1932). A study of a community and its groups and institutions conceived of as behaviors of individuals. *Psychol. Monogr., 43,* No. 2.

Schlenker, B. R. (1980). *Impression management: the self-concept, social identity, and interpersonal relations.* Monterey, Calif.: Brooks/Cole.

Schopler, J., and M. W. Matthews (1965). The influence of the perceived causal locus of partner's dependence on the use of interpersonal power. *J. Pers. soc. Psychol., 2,* 609–612.

Sedlak, A. (1979). Developmental differences in understanding plans and evaluating actors. *Child Development, 50,* 536–560.

Seligman, C., R. H. Fazio, and M. P. Zanna (1980). Effects of salience of extrinsic rewards on liking and loving. *J. Pers. soc. Psychol., 38,* 453–460.

Seligman, M. E. P. (1975). *Helplessness.* San Francisco: Freeman.

Shaver, K. G. (1970). Defensive attribution: effects of severity and relevance on the responsibility assigned for an accident. *J. Pers. soc. Psychol., 14,* 101–113.

Shaw, M. E., and J. L. Sulzer (1964). An empirical test of Heider's levels in attribution of responsibility. *J. abnorm. soc. Psychol., 69,* 39–46.

Shultz, T. R., I. Butkowsky, J. W. Pearce, and H. Shanfield (1975). Development of schemes in the attribution of multiple psychological causes. *Develop. Psychol., 11,* 502–510.

Shweder, R. A. (1977). Likeness and likelihood in everyday thought: magical thinking in judgments about personality. *Current Anthropology, 18,* 637–648.

Siegler, R. S. (1975). Defining the locus of developmental differences in children's causal reasoning. *J. exp. child Psychol., 20,* 512–525.

Singer, J. (1963). Sympathetic activation, drugs and fear. *J. compara. physiol. Psychol., 56,* 612–615.

Singerman, K. G., T. D. Borkovec, and R. S. Baron (1976). Failure of a misattribution therapy manipulation with a clinically relevant target behavior. *Behav. Therapy, 7,* 306–313.

Skinner, B. F. (1953). *Science and human behavior.* New York: Macmillan.

Smith, E. R., and F. D. Miller (1978). Limits on perception of cognitive processes: a reply to Nisbett and Wilson. *Psychol. Rev., 85,* 355–362.

Smith, M. C. (1975). Children's use of the multiple sufficient cause schema in social perception. *J. Pers. soc. Psychol., 32,* 737–747.

Snyder, M. (1976). Attribution and behavior: social perception and social causation. In J. H. Harvey, W. J. Ickes, and R. F. Kidd (Eds.), *New directions in attribution research.* Hillsdale, N.J.: Erlbaum.

Snyder, M., and W. B. Swann (1978). Behavioral confirmation in social interaction: from social perception to social reality. *J. exp. soc. Psychol., 14,* 148–162.

Snyder, M., E. D. Tanke, and E. Berscheid (1977). Social perception and interpersonal behavior: on the self-fulfilling nature of social stereotypes. *J. Pers. soc. Psychol., 35,* 656–666.

Snyder, M. L., R. E. Kleck, A. Strenta, and S. J. Mentzer (1979). Avoidance of the handicapped: an attributional ambiguity analysis. *J. Pers. soc. Psychol., 37,* 2297–2306.

Snyder, M. L., and R. A. Wicklund (1981). Attribute ambiguity. In J. H. Harvey, W. Ickes, and R. F. Kidd (Eds.), *New directions in attribution research.* Vol. 3. Hillsdale, N.J.: Erlbaum.

Steinmark, S. W., and T. D. Borkovec (1974). Active and placebo treatment effects on moderate insomnia under counterdemand and positive demand instructions. *J. abnorm. Psychol., 83,* 157–163.

Stevens, L., and E. E. Jones (1976). Defensive attribution and the Kelley cube. *J. Pers. soc. Psychol., 34,* 809–820.

Stokols, D., and J. Schopler (1973). Reactions to victims under conditions of situational detachment: the effects of responsibility, severity and expected future interaction. *J. Pers. soc. Psychol., 25,* 199–209.

Storms, M. D. (1973). Videotape and the attribution process: reversing actors' and observers' points of view. *J. Pers. soc. Psychol., 27,* 165–175.

Storms, M. D., and R. E. Nisbett (1970). Insomnia and the attribution process. *J. Pers. soc. Psychol., 16,* 319–328.

Strickland, L. H., R. J. Lewicke, and A. M. Katz (1966). Temporal orientation and perceived control as determinants of risk-taking. *J. exp. soc. Psychol., 2,* 143–151.

Surber, C. F. (1981). *Asynchrony in development of the discounting principle for social and nonsocial events.* Paper presented at the meeting of the Society for Research in Child Development. Boston.

Tagiuri, R. (1969). Person perception. In G. Lindzey and E. Aronson (Eds.), *The handbook of social psychology.* Reading, Mass.: Addison-Wesley.

Taylor, S. E. (1975). On inferring one's attitudes from one's behavior: some delimiting conditions. *J. Pers. soc. Psychol., 31,* 126–131.

Taylor, S. E., and J. Crocker (1981). Schematic bases of social information processing. In E. T. Higgins, C. P. Herman, and M. P. Zanna (Eds.), *Social cognition: the Ontario symposium.* Hillsdale, N.J.: Erlbaum.

Taylor, S. E., J. Crocker, S. T. Fiske, M. Sprinzen, and J. D. Winkler (1979). The generalizability of salience effects. *J. Pers. soc. Psychol., 37* (3), 357–368.

Taylor, S. E., and S. T. Fiske (1975). Point of view and perceptions of causality. *J. Pers. soc. Psychol., 32,* 439–445.

——— (1978). Salience attention and attribution: top of the head phenomena. In L. Berkowitz (Ed.), *Advances in experimental social psychology.* Vol. 11. New York: Academic Press.

Taylor, S. E., and J. H. Koivumaki (1976). The perception of self and others: acquaintanceship, affect, and actor-observer differences. *J. Pers. soc. Psychol., 33,* 403–408.

Tetlock, P. E., and A. Levi (1982). Attribution bias: on the inconclusiveness of the cognition-motivation debate. *J. exp. soc. Psychol., 18,* 68–88.

Tillman, W. S., and C. S. Carver (1980). Actors' and observers' attributions for success and failure: a comparative test of predictions from Kelley's cube, self-serving bias, and positivity bias formulations. *J. exp. soc. Psychol., 16,* 18–32.

Tourangeau, R., and P. C. Ellsworth (1979). The role of facial response in the experience of emotion. *J. Pers. soc. Psychol., 37,* 1519–1531.

Trope, Y. (1979). Uncertainty-reducing properties of achievement tasks. *J. Pers. soc. Psychol., 37,* 1505–1518.

_____ (1980). Self-assessment, self-enhancement, and task preference. *J. exp. soc. Psychol., 16,* 116–129.

Tversky, A., and D. Kahneman (1971). Belief in the law of small numbers. *Psychol. Bull., 76,* 105–110.

_____ (1979). Causal schemata in judgments under uncertainty. In M. Fishbein (Ed.), *Progress in social psychology.* Hillsdale, N.J.: Erlbaum.

Tyler, T. R. (1980). Impact of directly and indirectly experienced events: the origin of crime-related judgments and behaviors. *J. Pers. soc. Psychol., 39,* 13–28.

Valins, S. (1966). Cognitive effects of false heart-rate feedback. *J. Pers. soc. Psychol., 4,* 400–408.

Valins, S., and R. E. Nisbett (1971). *Attribution processes in the development and treatment of emotional disorders.* Morristown, N.J.: General Learning Press.

Valins, S., and A. A. Ray (1967). Effects of cognitive desensitization and avoidance behavior. *J. Pers. soc. Psychol., 7,* 345–350.

Valle, V. A., and I. Frieze (1976). Stability of causal attributions as a mediator in changing expectations for success. *J. Pers. soc. Psychol., 33,* 579–587.

Walster, E. (1966). Assignment of responsibility for an accident. *J. Pers. soc. Psychol., 3,* 73–79.

Waterman, C. K. (1969). The facilitating and interfering effect of cognitive dissonance on simple and complex parent associates learning tasks. *J. exp. soc. Psychol., 5,* 31–42.

Weiner, B. (1979). A theory of motivation for some classroom experiences. *J. educat. Psychol., 71,* 3–25.

Weiner, B., H. Heckhausen, W. U. Meyer, and R. C. Cook (1972). Causal ascriptions of achievement behavior: a conceptual analysis of effort. *J. Pers. soc. Psychol., 21,* 239–248.

Weiner, B., D. Russell, and D. Lerman (1978). Affective consequences of causal ascriptions. In J. H. Harvey, W. J. Ickes, and R. F. Kidd (Eds.), *New directions in attribution research.* Vol. 2. Hillsdale, N.J.: Erlbaum.

_____ (1979). The cognition-emotion process in achievement related contexts. *J. Pers. soc. Psychol., 37,* 1211–1220.

Weinstein, N. D. (1980). Unrealistic optimism about future life events. *J. Pers. soc. Psychol., 39,* 806–820.

Wells, G. L., and J. H. Harvey (1977). Do people use consensus information in making causal attributions? *J. Pers. soc. Psychol., 35,* 270–293.

White, P. (1980). Limitations on verbal reports of internal events: a refutation of Nisbett and Wilson and of Bem. *Psychol. Rev., 87,* 105–112.

Wicklund, R. A. (1975). Discrepancy reduction or attempted distraction? A reply to Liebling, Seiler and Shaver. *J. exp. soc. Psychol., 11,* 78–81.

Wixon, D. R., and J. D. Laird (1976). Awareness and attitude change in the forced-compliance paradigm: the importance of when. *J. Pers. soc. Psychol., 34,* 376–384.

Wolosin, R., S. J. Sherman, and C. R. Mynatt (1972). Perceived social influence in a conformity situation. *J. Pers. soc. Psychol., 23,* 184–191.

Worchel, S., and S. M. L. Yohai (1979). The role of attribution in the experience of crowding. *J. exp. soc. Psychol., 15,* 91–104.

Wortman, C. B. (1975). Some determinants of perceived control. *J. Pers. soc. Psychol., 31,* 282–294.

_____ (1976). Causal attributions and personal control. In J. H. Harvey, W. J. Ickes, and R. F. Kidd (Eds.), *New directions in attribution research.* Vol. 1. Hillsdale, N. J.: Erlbaum.

Wright, P., and P. D. Rip (1981). Retrospective reports on the causes of decisions. *J. Pers. soc. Psychol., 40,* 601–614.

Zanna, M. B., and J. Cooper (1976). Dissonance and the attribution process. In J. H. Harvey, W. J. Ickes, and R. F. Kidd (Eds.), *New directions in attribution research.* Vol. 1. Hillsdale, N.J.: Erlbaum.

Zillman, D. (1978). Attribution and misattribution of excitatory reactions. In J. H. Harvey, W. Ickes, and R. F. Kidd (Eds.), *New directions in attribution research.* Vol. 2. Hillsdale, N.J.: Erlbaum.

Zuckerman, M. (1978). Use of consensus information in prediction of behavior. *J. exp. soc. Psychol., 14,* 163–171.

_____ (1979). Attribution of success and failure revisited, or: the motivational bias is alive and well in attribution theory. *J. Pers., 47,* 245–287.

CHAPTER 16

Socialization in Adulthood

Karen K. Dion
University of Toronto

INTRODUCTION

Discussions of socialization within psychology often focus on child rearing. Although the study of childhood socialization is undeniably important, the need for expanding this emphasis has become evident. Various conceptual accounts of the socialization process during childhood are not sufficient for fully understanding socialization in later life (Neugarten, 1968a; Looft, 1973). As Brim (1966) noted, adult roles necessitate additional preparation beyond that provided during childhood; furthermore, considerable change in various facets of society may occur across the life course of an individual. Hence, the process of socialization continues throughout adulthood. Accordingly, this chapter concerns adult socialization, particularly in early and middle adulthood, and attempts to foster greater interest among psychologists in the study of socialization during these phases of the life span.

In comparison with childhood socialization, adult socialization has received less attention from psychologists. (For a discussion of the history of research on so-

cialization in psychology and other disciplines see Clausen, 1968). At the most general level, the study of socialization is a central issue for social psychology. Within psychology, socialization as it occurs in the various contexts of adulthood (e.g., work, parenthood) merits more attention than it has received during the last two decades from North American social psychologists.

There is some literature within psychology pertaining to socialization in adulthood, especially in life-span developmental psychology, an area that has attracted increasing interest (Baltes, Reese and Lipsitt, 1980). Some of this interest may be attributed to the continuation of various classic longitudinal studies of development, such as the Berkeley studies, into the adulthood of participants (Charles, 1970; Baltes *et al.,* 1980). Moreover, adult development has been studied at various centers of research in particular universities (e.g., the University of Chicago) for several decades (Havighurst, 1973; Baltes *et al.,* 1980). Indeed Baltes (1979) has persuasively argued that a life-span perspective on development is most accurately characterized as the reappearance of an approach that can be traced to much earlier historical sources than is typically assumed.

Socialization during adulthood has received more attention within sociology than within psychology in part because one major feature of adult socialization, name-

The author would like to thank Orville G. Brim, Jr. and Melvin L. Kohn for their helpful comments on an earlier draft of this chapter.

ly, role-related functioning, has been an area of study within this discipline (Brim, 1966; Clausen, 1968). Interest in adult socialization is demonstrated by various essays and reviews that have appeared during the past two decades (e.g. Brim and Wheeler, 1966; Brim, 1968; Mortimer and Simmons, 1978). In addition, a major contribution to the sociological and the psychological literature on socialization, Goslin's (1969a) *Handbook of Socialization Theory and Research,* focused on socialization both within and across various phases of the life span. Frequently, however, major adult roles have been studied in the context of a particular subfield, such as family sociology; thus the empirical literature relevant to adult socialization is quite fragmented. Therefore the present chapter not only will examine research pertaining to a particular domain but also will include some discussion of the relation between different contexts.

CENTRAL CONSTRUCTS OF ADULT SOCIALIZATION

ROLES

Socialization has been defined as "the process by which persons acquire the knowledge, skills, and dispositions that make them more or less able members of their society" (Brim, 1966, p. 3). During adulthood, as noted earlier, a person's adaptation to various roles has been emphasized as a central feature of socialization. Brim (1966), for example, distinguished between early and later socialization by suggesting that childhood socialization is characterized by the acquisition of fundamental values; in contrast, adult socialization emphasizes various role-related behaviors, with effects likely for the most part to be limited to particular role contexts. Becker (1964) proposed that "situational adjustment" could account for much behavioral change in adulthood and that behavioral stability could be attributed to "commitments" such as to various roles. With an adult's involvement in multiple roles comes the possibility of strain or conflict because of the demands of different roles. One aspect of adult socialization involves societally endorsed principles referred to by Brim (1966) as "metaprescriptions" that have the function of helping the individual deal with pressures from conflicting roles.

The discussion so far has focused on the individual's adaptation to particular roles or combinations of roles. This emphasis should not, however, be taken to imply that the individual fully adheres to societal demands across all roles; indeed the value of this outcome has been questioned. For example, both Rosow (1965) and Brim (1966) have suggested that in the context of a changing social system, the extreme represented by complete socialization is probably not the optimal state for adult functioning. Moreover, in conceptual analyses of "role negotiation" and related processes, adult socialization is portrayed as bidirectional in support of the idea that the individual is not merely the passive target of societal demands (Goslin, 1969b; Albrecht and Gift, 1975; Mortimer and Simmons, 1978). Also, as Goslin (1969b) noted, many role-related contexts provide considerable opportunity for the individual to influence how a particular role will be enacted; even more highly formalized contexts do not completely restrict the person's opportunities.

DEVELOPMENTAL TASKS

The relation between society and the individual has also been conceptualized in terms of developmental tasks, a construct that has been discussed by Havighurst for several decades (Havighurst, 1948, 1952, 1953, 1972) and defined as follows (1953, p. 2):

> A developmental task . . . arises at or about a certain period in the life of the individual, successful achievement of which leads to . . . happiness and to success with later tasks, while failure leads to unhappiness . . . disapproval by the society, and difficulty with later tasks.

As Havighurst (1973) has noted, although his view of developmental tasks is influenced by Erikson's (1950, 1963) theoretical framework, it also emphasizes among other factors, explicit societal demands, as can be seen, for example, in the role-related tasks presented for adulthood. These tasks therefore represent one major class of events likely to be experienced by most individuals at a particular age-related phase of their lives (Brim and Ryff, 1980); they have been labeled "normative age-graded events" in recent life-span conceptual perspectives on development (Baltes, 1979; Baltes *et al.,* 1980). The specific developmental tasks reflect a given sociocultural context (Havighurst, 1972). Furthermore, as Riegel (1975) noted, this role-related demarcation of the life span into various phases itself reflects a particular societal structure.

During periods of relative societal stability, characterized by a normative sequence of adult roles and consensus on the nature of these roles, the developmental tasks of adjusting to role transitions and the demands of expected role-related events are central aspects of adult socialization. As discussed later in this chapter, some research concerning satisfaction with adult roles has focused on adults adhering to a normative pattern (e.g., the family life-cycle perspective on marital satisfaction). When, however, adult roles undergo periods of greater instability either in terms of role definition or in terms of the sequencing of roles, specific developmental tasks may become increasingly complex, since traditional role expectations may coexist with elements of change. If, as noted earlier, the criteria for success on developmental tasks are personal satisfaction and societal approval, achieving both of these may sometimes be difficult.

The relation between development during adulthood and major role transitions can be viewed from various perspectives. Adult development may be closely related to role transitions. Lowenthal, Thurnher and Chiriboga (1975) examined the adaptive responses made by individuals in four different "pretransitional stages" of the life span, (e.g., newly married, anticipating retirement from work). In his conceptualization of men's development during early and middle adulthood, Levinson (1978) argued that men's development is not attributable to specific events *per se* that he called "marker events." Most of the men in his sample did, however, focus their lives around two traditional role-related areas (work and family); thus some changes in early and middle adulthood occurred in the context of these roles. Brim and Ryff (1980) have suggested that personal change in adulthood is likely to be viewed as resulting from events characterized by high salience, such as changes associated with major adult roles. However, as these authors point out, change in the individual may have occurred much more gradually or be attributable to events that are not as salient.

Timing of Role-Related Tasks

It has been suggested that one aspect of adult socialization involves age norms which define the range of years in an individual's life regarded as the appropriate time for the occurrence of various events and behaviors (Neugarten, Moore and Lowe, 1965). Neugarten (1969) proposed that "socially-defined time" is an important feature of adulthood. Specifically, the impact of age norms is reflected in a person's expectation that certain events will occur at particular points in his or her life span. Hence an adult may feel "early", "late" or "on time" for any given event, and this awareness may affect his or her self-evaluation concerning that event (Neugarten, 1969).

In some cases, deviation from the normative timetable may be associated with negative circumstances. For example, in one study, women who married "early", "late" or "on time" relative to their peers were found to have quite different life outcomes, respectively (Elder and Rockwell, 1976). An early marriage for women in this cohort was associated with a series of adverse events, which the authors described as "a life course of relative deprivation" (p. 51) characterized, for example, by limited schooling and financial strain. When the women in this study were interviewed in middle age about the ideal schedule for life events, a number of the women marrying quite late for their cohort and especially those marrying early hoped for a more normative pattern for their own daughters. Although this particular example concerns marriage, the timing of various roles is also important to consider in other contexts as will be seen in subsequent sections.

Finally, age norms for various role transitions may undergo transformation as a function of societal change attributable to historical factors, whether these are particular events or more gradual processes (Neugarten and Datan, 1973). Hence, a person's definition of the timing of specific events as typical or atypical is susceptible to change.

Personal Time and the Life Span

Although chronological age may be employed as a convenient marker by various agencies and institutions, the meaning of this dimension to the individual is more complex. Thus, an adult's "subjective age" (i.e., a sense of his or her age) may show relatively little agreement with actual chronological age; moreover, subjective age itself may not be unidimensional (Kastenbaum, Derbin, Sabatini and Artt, 1972). Socioeconomic factors may be associated with different views of the ages that separate major developmental phases. Some early evidence suggested that working-class individuals perceived both middle age and old age as occurring earlier than did their middle-class counterparts (Neugarten and Peterson, 1957). Within certain groups, passage through various phases of adulthood may elicit changing perspectives on time, with "time-left" becoming increasingly more salient than "time-since-birth," that is, chronological age (Neugarten, 1968b).

In addition to subjective age, the adult's personal view of the pattern of her or his life—both actual and anticipated—must be taken into account. Neugarten (1969) suggested that a distinctive feature of adulthood is "a sense of the life-cycle," a new perspective on personal time not present in childhood. The individual's expectation about the probable course of life events partly reflects societal expectations. Hence persons from the same socioeconomic group or the same subculture may have a similar set of expectations that, in turn, are related to the degree of satisfaction with the life course at a specific point in time (Bortner and Hultsch, 1974).

OTHER SOURCES OF CHANGE IN ADULTHOOD

Although the discussion thus far has stressed role-related developmental tasks as central features of adult socialization, other factors contribute to personal change in adulthood. Brim and Ryff (1980) have proposed a framework for conceptualizing life events in which the traditional role-related transitions comprise only one of several classes of events. These authors stress the need to consider more systematically other types of events as well as to identify important life experiences that are not formally labeled by society or even by the individual. Baltes (1979) and his associates (Baltes *et al.,* 1980), have suggested that one important source of change during adulthood is the occurrence of "non-normative life events" (for example, unemployment; serious illness). Unlike the "normative age-graded events" referred to earlier, these events do not occur in any predictable pattern, nor do most individuals within a given society necessarily encounter a particular event within this group. The extent to which an individual is affected by various life events will to some degree be related to the time of their occurrence and their sequencing in her or his life (Hultsch and Plemons, 1979). In terms of the need for personal adaptation, it is the unexpected events that have been proposed as likely to elicit the greatest sense of crisis on the part of the individual (Neugarten, 1970, 1976, Albrecht and Gift, 1975).

Factors associated with cohort membership also provide a context for change in adulthood. Individuals born at a given point in time, thus comprising a particular *birth cohort,* encounter certain sociohistorical events (e.g., war, economic conditions). Each cohort thus has its own unique setting formed by these historical conditions (Neugarten, 1970, 1976; Riley, 1973), and this sociohistorical context shapes the pattern of life events (Brim and Ryff, 1980). These events have been categorized as "normative history-graded influences" (Baltes,

1979; Baltes *et al.,* 1980) in life-span conceptualizations of development. The impact of this type of event on members of a birth cohort will depend in part on other factors, such as the individual's position in the social structure (Rosow, 1978).

Both life-span developmental psychologists (e.g., Schaire, 1965; Baltes, 1968) and sociologists (e.g., Riley, 1973) have noted that in developmental research using traditional research designs, the findings may reflect cohort factors; moreover, the contribution of life-span developmental factors cannot be separated from the cohort dimension in this type of study. However, an awareness of the possible contribution of cohort-related factors can suggest an interpretation of patterns that occur across several studies, an approach which will be used in various sections of this chapter. Finally, as Rosow (1978) has noted, much like chronological age, the cohort dimension is basically a marker variable; therefore an issue of continuing importance is the meaning of cohort effects.

DOMAINS OF ADULT SOCIALIZATION

Let us now turn to a discussion of three domains of adult socialization—work, marriage, and parenthood. Within each of these areas selected issues are considered from the psychological and sociological literature, mostly from the past two decades. Almost all the research discussed in this chapter was conducted in North America.

WORK AND OCCUPATIONAL ROLES: MEN

The occupational role traditionally has been considered a salient feature of adulthood for men. Within life-span developmental frameworks, establishing and maintaining an occupational commitment have been proposed as important developmental tasks during early to middle adulthood (Havighurst, 1972). Similarly, Henry (1971) suggested that work was "the central and most binding continuity of the years between age 20 and 70" (p. 126). This emphasis on the importance of work has received some support from surveys in which a sizable proportion of male respondents indicated that they would prefer to continue working even if it were not financially necessary (e.g., Morse and Weiss, 1955; Powers and Goudy, 1971). Although occupational experience has been discussed as a significant aspect of adulthood for men, most of the research literature on vocational development has, however, focused on identifying characteristics of the individual (such as traits, interests) that may predict occupational choice or adjustment to particular occupations (Osipow, 1973). In contrast to this approach, there has been some recent interest in examining how various dimensions of work may affect the individual, an area of research of particular relevance to this discussion of adult socialization.

Work and Men's Socialization

Various indexes have been proposed to assess occupational status (e.g., Hollingshead and Redlich, 1958; Duncan, 1961; Blishen, 1967). There is considerable consensus across diverse groups concerning the relative prestige of various occupations (Hakel, Hollman and Dunnette, 1968; Braun and Bayer, 1973; Plata, 1975; Treiman, 1977). Moreover, there is evidence that rankings of occupational prestige have been quite stable for several decades (Hakel *et al.,* 1968; Plata, 1975).

Various studies have suggested that the meaning and value of work differ for working-class and middle-class men. For example, in an early descriptive study of factory workers, Chinoy (1955) contrasted the "tradition of opportunity" stressing unlimited possibilities for personal achievement in North American society with the actual limited chances for personal advancement confronted by a factory worker. Although a substantial number of Chinoy's respondents expressed interest in another type of work, typically involving more personal autonomy (e.g., owning a small business), most workers remained at the factory, redirecting their personal goals toward achievement in the context of the factory, financial security, acquisition of material possessions, and ambition for their children. Similar themes also appeared in the study by Morse and Weiss (1955) referred to earlier, in which employed men were asked whether they would continue working even if they inherited sufficient money to ensure economic well-being. Although many of the men expressed a desire to keep working, the reasons given varied, with middle-class workers stressing work-related achievement and interest in their jobs and working-class men emphasizing activity per se (that is, "keeping occupied" as opposed to being idle). Much like the factory workers in Chinoy's study, men in working-class occupations compared to either men in middle-class occupations or farmers were more likely to express an interest in another type of job, particularly that of starting their own business.

During the past two decades, the relation of work experiences to men's attitudes in a variety of domains has received more systematic attention, particularly in Kohn and Schooler's program of research. Initially, these researchers (Kohn and Schooler, 1969) examined the relation among social class and attitudes toward work, parental values, and personal values, based on interviews conducted with a representative sample of men who were in civilian occupations within the United States. Socioeconomic status was related to various values and other beliefs. For example, the higher the socioeconomic status, the greater was the emphasis on "self-direction" as both a personal value and as a parental value and on more intrinsic features of work (e.g., its interest value, use of own skills). Individuals at lower levels of socioeconomic status were more likely to endorse "conformity to externally-imposed rules" as a general value and, in addition, to emphasize more extrinsic aspects of work (e.g., salary, job-related security). Kohn and Schooler (1969) have proposed that a particular type of work experience, specifically the degree to which a job allows "occupational self-direction," namely, the chance "to use initiative, thought, and independent judgment in work" (p. 659) underlies these differences. From this perspective, observed class differences in attitudes and values are partially reflective of the work opportunities and experiences available. The work situation encountered by the individual is therefore viewed as molding and shaping important values.

In a subsequent analysis of these data, Kohn and Schooler (1973) examined in greater detail the relation between particular work experiences and various psychological dimensions, including an index of "intellectual flexibility" and attitudes toward the self. They found more occupational self-direction, especially the "substantive complexity" of a job, was associated with higher levels of functioning on both dimensions. (The index of substantive complexity was based on ratings of the complexity of a particular job on three dimensions, namely, work with "things", "data" and "people"; its general complexity, and estimates of time spent on each of these three job dimensions). These findings still held after the researchers controlled for the effects of such dimensions as income, education, occupational status, age, race, nationality, religion, and urban versus rural residence during childhood. Moreover, the index of substantive complexity derived from the job descriptions was quite highly correlated with a more objective index of job requirements for various occupations. This finding provided support for the authors' contention that the men's perceptions of their jobs' demands were reasonably accurate and therefore did not simply represent a more indirect measure of psychological functioning. The authors noted that the degree of occupational self-direction characterizing a job had more influence on the psychological dimensions studied than did a number of other job-related variables, including interpersonal factors such as team work versus working alone and competition with coworkers. Finally, they attempted to estimate the reciprocal effects of work structure and psychological functioning and concluded that "job affects man more than man affects job" (p. 114).

Subsequently, in a follow-up survey conducted in 1974 with a representative subsample of men (under age sixty-five) from the original survey done in 1964, Kohn and Schooler (1978, 1981) found further support for the impact of work-related variables, particularly substantive complexity, on intellectual flexibility. In addition, however, analysis of these longitudinal data also revealed that intellectual flexibility had a "lagged" effect on the substantive complexity of a man's job, suggesting as Kohn (1981) noted a "truly reciprocal process." Recently, Kohn and Schooler (1982) have extended their analyses of these longitudinal data to consider several social psychological dimensions, including self-evaluation, anxiety, and various interpersonal orientations. Of particular interest to the present discussion, occupational self-direction, most notably the substantive complexity component, continued to emerge as an especially important dimension contributing to aspects of men's personal belief system about self and others. Kohn and Schooler have interpreted the findings from their program of research as for the most part reflecting a "learning-generalization process" that consists of "a direct translation of the lessons of the job to outside-the-job realities" (Kohn, 1981, p. 290). From this perspective, the socializing impact of work for men thus extends considerably beyond the occupational role context and has a more pervasive influence on the individual.

Additional evidence for this view of work-related socialization has been reported by Mortimer and Lorence (1979) who examined the contribution made by perceived "work autonomy" to young men's self-ratings, in particular the "competence" component of self-concept. Using a mailed survey format, they did a follow-up survey of men from an earlier study (done when the men were undergraduates) ten years after their university graduation. Most men in this sample were then in the early years of professional and other high-status occupations. Work autonomy was assessed by respondents' ratings of three aspects of their jobs, (e.g., "decision-making latitude"). Mortimer and Lorence found that work autonomy contributed to the men's "self-competence," even after taking into account their self-rated competence assessed a decade earlier. In contrast, reported income did not have an impact on self-ratings of competence. As the authors noted, more objective measures of work autonomy would have been desirable to provide validation for the respondents' ratings of their jobs. The pattern of results is, however, consistent with Kohn and Schooler's findings discussed previously.

In summary, there is growing evidence that there are important links between specific features of work and several social psychological dimensions. The hypothesis that occupational dimensions contribute to class-related differences in various belief systems has received support, most notably in Kohn and Schooler's research. In contrast, there has been less attention given to minority-group experience and occupational socialization. In reviewing the literature pertaining to vocational development, Smith (1975), noted that since theories concerning this process are largely pertinent to white, middle-class men, relatively little is known about the occupational development of black men, including issues such as the relation between work experiences and beliefs concerning oneself. Race was included as a variable in Kohn and Schooler's research where it was found to be related to the substantive complexity of work, even in the second wave of interviews in 1974, though these researchers (Kohn and Schooler, 1978) noted that the impact of race on this dimension seemed to be lessening. Since, however, substantive complexity of earlier work was a strong predictor of the complexity of subsequent jobs, a cumulative effect might well have occurred. Because of this possibility, the process of work socialization across the life span of black men and of men belonging to other minority groups warrants more systematic attention.

Occupational Advancement

Given the assumption that the occupational role is an important aspect of adulthood for men, the impact of actual (relative to expected) occupational advancement on the individual is of central importance in a societal context where occupational mobility and advancement traditionally have been valued for men. Consistent with this view, in one investigation (Feather, 1975) university students predicted that at the early entry stages to various professions, especially those dominated by males, the experience of failure would be particularly stressful to young men. Indeed failure seemed to be a more salient dimension than success, since ratings of perceived dissatisfaction with failure were more extreme than perceived satisfaction with success.

Once past the entry stage, the individual's personal assessment of the degree of accomplishment he has achieved in a given occupation is at least partly related to his advancement. Typically, only a small number of individuals will achieve positions at the highest levels within a particular occupation. For those individuals who initially aspired to but did not reach top positions, the discrepancy between these aspirations and their actual present position presents a major coping problem in adulthood.

This issue has been addressed from various perspectives. From a life-span viewpoint, Clausen (1976) discussed the findings from follow-up interviews conducted with middle-aged men who had participated in two well-known longitudinal studies of development, the Berkeley Guidance Study (participants born in 1928 and 1929) and the Oakland Growth Study (participants born in the early 1920s). Those men taking part in these follow-up interviews were mostly middle class white individuals. In a subsample from the Oakland study, over one-half of the men interviewed at age thirty-eight still anticipated career advancement; this proportion dropped considerably when the men were interviewed ten years later. Most men in the Berkeley study interviewed at age forty continued to expect and strive for career-related progress. Interestingly, Clausen noted that in both groups, middle-class men who were currently at the same status level relative to the status of their fathers ("middle-class stables") were especially likely to strive for progress in their careers. Men in these studies who originally came from working-class backgrounds but who were now in middle-class occupations did not indicate the same desire for occupational advancement as those who originally came from middle-class backgrounds despite the fact that both groups of men had jobs of comparable status.

Neugarten (1968b) researched career development concerns in a sample of occupationally successful upper middle-class men. Neugarten commented that for these men, perceived "career-line" and "life-line" appeared related; that is, the men focused their attention on career

progress relative to chronological age. Especially salient to this group, therefore, were concerns about timing, in particular, whether they were "on-time" or "late" in personal advancement. More recently, Levinson (1978) has suggested that one aspect of a man's development during the middle years of adulthood quite frequently involves his accomodating to his growing awareness that "he will fall far short of his early Dream" (p. 220).

From a sociological tradition, Faulkner (1974) analyzed adults' expectations for occupational advancement and their responses to their current positions. He interviewed individuals from the middle levels of two very different areas of work, specifically, men in professional sports (hockey players) and men and women in the performing arts (musicians in symphony orchestras). (The latter sample was predominantly male). Faulkner proposed that the "coming to terms" with one's occupational position was associated with age-related expectations about the likelihood of advancement given the norms in particular fields and involved a change in self-conception that occurred gradually over time. His interview data suggested that the individuals used a variety of coping approaches, such as emphasizing other aspects of their lives (e.g., their families), stressing the advantages of their current status within their field, noting the hardships associated with advancement to top positions, and redirecting their own goals towards achieving an "average" degree of personal accomplishment. Although the themes emerging in these interviews are provocative, it remains to be seen how effective these coping strategies are in fostering self-esteem and reducing perceived stress, since these variables were not directly measured. In a recent study of coping strategies used by adults to deal with perceived stress, specific strategies, such as redefining the perceived importance of work to the individual, were not shown to be particularly helpful in reducing stress (Pearlin and Schooler, 1978). The specific areas of reported occupational stress involved, however, issues of work pressure, personal relations at work, financial rewards, and physical features of the work itself rather than the issue of personal achievement or advancement discussed by Faulkner. Faulkner himself also noted that the generality of the coping strategies he observed needed to be tested in other occupational contexts. Of particular interest, he argued that the structure of specific occupations made it more or less possible for an individual to hope for advancement past a normative time period. Thus in fields characterized by frequent fluctuations in personal outcomes, it may be possible to have "the illusion and pleasure of viewing oneself if not forever young, then at least forever promising" (p. 160). In contrast, the relatively more stable status structure of other work contexts (such as the symphony orchestra), may make this type of belief more difficult to maintain. Thus, features of the work situation itself may well be important predictors of the specific type of coping shown by the individual.

These findings suggest an interrelation between work-related dimensions of socialization and changes in men's self-images at particular phases in the life span. Because the samples studied to date represent a limited range of cohorts, more investigation with other recent cohorts is needed before one can attribute these responses predominantly to life-span change. Nydegger (1976), for example, in commenting on several studies of adult development during middle adulthood including Clausen's (1976) discussion of the Berkeley and Oakland data, noted that research with other cohorts is necessary and that current longitudinal studies should provide a valuable starting point. In addition, the study of work experiences and change across the life span of minority-group men has been neglected. Cohort comparison within specific minority groups should be of particular interest.

Among white, middle-class men, there is some suggestion that cohort effects relevant to the discussion in this chapter may occur. As stated earlier, one assumption is that the work role is of central psychological importance for most men as well as having a functional value for them. This assumption seems warranted for men taking part in the studies described previously. From this perspective, coping with occupational advancement is a salient life-span issue, whether considered in terms of dimensions of timing and/or the structure of the individual's occupational context. Although it seems plausible to assume that the work role continues to be of considerable psychological importance for many individuals, there may be more diversity in the meaning of work among some cohorts. For example, when responding to accounts of a hypothetical male peer's academic or early career-related success, some male university students' responses suggested disenchantment and dissatisfaction with the value of goals such as occupational achievement (Horner, 1972; Hoffman, 1974). If these individuals maintain this attitude across early to middle adulthood, they will provide an interesting comparison with peers who regard work-related achievement as important.

WORK AND OCCUPATIONAL ROLES: WOMEN

Variables related to women's achievement behavior and occupational attainment are most fully understood in the context of various demographic factors. The number of women working in the labor force in the United States has grown markedly during the previous three decades (U.S. Bureau of the Census, 1976). Despite this increase in the number of women working outside the home, the occupational distribution of women compared to men is notably different. For both white men and white women, education was the most important factor contributing to occupational status, as shown in various surveys (Treiman and Terrell, 1975; McClendon, 1976). Although the average occupational status or prestige rating has been found to be similar for white working women and men, men tend to be more concentrated in the extreme upper (Treiman and Terrell, 1975; McClendon, 1976) and the lower end of the distribution (McClendon, 1976). Also, women continued to be proportionally overrepresented in occupations such as clerical or health service work (U.S. Bureau of the Census, 1976).

In addition to these differences in distribution across occupations, differences in salary also have been found between men and women. For example, in 1974, across most occupational groups, female workers (full-time year-round) earned approximately 55 to 60 percent of the salaries earned by male workers (U.S. Bureau of the Census, 1976). As various surveys have indicated, even when one considers comparable training and work experience in various occupations, women's salaries have been found to be lower than those of men (Treiman and Terrell, 1975; Suter and Miller, 1973; Perrucci, 1970). In summary, this evidence documents differences in the relative representation of women and men in various occupations and the existence of salary differences between women and men in a number of occupations.

Gender Role and the Evaluation of Women's Achievement

In this and subsequent sections, the term *gender role* will be used in preference to *sex role* in accord with Unger's (1979) suggestion that *gender* refers to "those nonphysiological components of sex that are culturally regarded as appropriate to males or to females" (p. 1086). (The term *sex role* will appear occasionally, reflecting the earlier usage of this term.)

The relation between gender role and occupational attainment has been a central issue in the study of women's occupational achievement. For example, Stein and Bailey (1973) reviewed evidence suggesting that role-related expectations for females were associated with a pattern of beliefs and behavior that made occupational achievement in adulthood more difficult. The impact that these expectations have on women's achievement goals and accomplishments has been discussed in the social sciences literature across several decades, with an emphasis on describing the pressures reported by college and university women.

In an early study, Komarovsky (1946) discussed the dilemma confronted by women who reported being encouraged to achieve, provided their level of achievement did not conflict with parental and male-peer expectations about their adult roles as spouse and parent. These expectations were revealed in various ways, such as advising women to conceal their intellectual competence in the company of male peers or parental encouragement to pursue goals such as marriage. Comments from these interviews suggested that the intellectually competent woman was regarded with some hostility or at least ambivalence, especially in contexts involving open competition and comparison with men. Some vestiges of this type of ambivalence were still found some two decades later when college women were asked to write stories in response to a verbal cue describing a young woman's success in a traditionally male field (Horner, 1968). A theme in these stories was the assumption that the protagonist's success would be associated with rejection by her peers or social isolation.

Although university students' reactions to academic and occupational excellence in women have shown changes in the 1970s relative to findings from earlier decades, there is some evidence testifying to the persistence of various aspects of the female gender role described by women in Komarovsky's (1946) study. Some studies have assessed the influence which perceived competence has on students' evaluations of women portrayed as having more "masculine" versus "feminine" interests. Spence and Helmreich (1972) found that university women expressed greater liking for a competent than an incompetent woman and liked a woman with traditionally masculine interests better than her more feminine counterpart. Male students were most attracted to the competent woman with masculine interests and liked least the incompetent woman with masculine interests. In subsequent research, Spence, Helmreich, and Stapp (1975)

added a new condition that required participants to respond to several open-ended questions (specifically a form of TAT questions) before assessing the likeability of the stimulus person. In this condition, women expressing more liberal attitudes towards women preferred the competent woman with masculine interests to the competent woman with feminine interests. In contrast, more traditionally oriented women and men and more liberal men showed the reverse pattern by preferring the competent woman with feminine interests. Spence and her colleagues suggested that the open-ended questions helped to uncover feelings of ambivalence about changing gender roles.

The findings of two other studies are also pertinent to the present discussion. In one study, a competent woman was liked more by male and female students when she was depicted as endorsing a number of behaviors characterizing the traditional female role than when she was depicted as endorsing a number of behaviors reflecting traditional male role preferences (Shaffer and Wegley, 1974). In another study, a highly capable female Ph.D. was portrayed as planning to commit herself to either family or career (Pines, 1979). Although university women with more liberal attitudes toward women liked the career-oriented woman more than the family-oriented woman, no differences between conditions occurred for the more traditionally oriented men and women. Interestingly, the more liberal men tended to be more attracted to the woman expressing family rather than career commitment, though this difference was not significant. Thus, this last group did not favor the career-oriented woman despite their expressed attitudes toward women's roles (Pines, 1979).

The pattern of findings in this research is also consistent with the results from another study conducted with male university students (Komarovsky, 1973). Some ambivalence emerged when individuals were questioned further after responding to structured items. Although the majority of men in this sample endorsed "intellectual companionship" with female friends, relatively few men anticipated making major accomodation in their career plans to allow for the occupational goals of their future wives. Komarovsky noted that the men's modal response could be characterized as "modified traditionalist"; that is, they assumed that the woman would stop working outside the home during the years of child rearing and would possibly resume her occupational goals later on. Respondents justified this assumption by suggesting that full-time maternal care was important for children's well-being. In summary, although competence and intelligence were respected in women, most of the young men interviewed continued to assume that "the husband should be the superior achiever" (Komarovsky, 1973, p. 119).

Finally, responses to competence in women may be affected by gender-related expectations associated with various areas of achievement. For example, Deaux and Emswiller (1974) found that assessment of competent task performance (attributed to an alleged partner) was influenced both by the sex of the partner and the nature of the task itself, which was masculine or feminine as defined by gender stereotypes. The female partner's success on a masculine task was rated as reflecting less skill or ability (on an *ability-luck* scale) than the same performance by a male partner. However, no differences occurred on perceived ability or skill attributed to a male versus a female partner in the feminine task condition.

In another study (Feather, 1975), Australian university students rated the relative satisfaction and dissatisfaction of male versus female stimulus persons described as having succeeded or failed at the competitive early phase of various occupations (qualifying examinations, job interviews). Specifically, they were asked to choose whether the male or the female would be happier with success (or unhappier with failure) and to rate the degree of happiness or unhappiness. The occupations differed in terms of status and the extent to which they were typically held by males or females, though participants' ratings showed that these two dimensions were related, with high status associated with male-dominated occupations.

Across most (though not all) of the occupations, both women and men perceived the stimulus person as happier with success or unhappier about failure in occupations dominated by individuals of the same sex. Thus, for example, a woman was inferred to be more pleased with success than a man in a female-dominated job (which also tended to be lower in status), while the reverse occurred for male-dominated occupations. For the most part, therefore, individuals described as complying with sex-typed patterns for occupational choice were seen as likely to experience both greater personal benefits and costs in comparison to peers choosing atypical occupations (relative to most members of their sex.)

Several studies have found that attributes traditionally ascribed to women may differ from the personal characteristics assumed to be related to successful func-

tioning as an adult. Broverman and her colleagues suggested that women faced conflicting expectations, since many traits assumed to characterize mature and capable adults overlapped considerably with traits attributed to men (Broverman, Vogel, Broverman, Clarkson and Rosenkrantz, 1972). A similar pattern was found in two studies that examined the traits inferred to be necessary for success in one type of occupational role. In the first of these studies, men from middle management in several different organizations were asked to characterize either "men in general," "women in general," or "successful middle managers" (Schein, 1973). For the sample as a whole, the ratings of traits attributed to men showed a significant similarity to those attributed to successful managers, but this similarity did not occur between the ratings of women and of successful managers. Interestingly, additional analysis revealed that in the case of older respondents, the ratings of women and of managers did show a significant (though small) similarity. A replication of this procedure with women from middle management found that trait ratings were significantly similar for both men and managers and women and managers, but the latter degree of similarity was weaker than the former (Schein, 1975). In addition, among women who had been in middle management for a short period of time, their ratings of women and successful managers did not show a significant resemblance; however, their ratings of men and managers were significantly similar. In this study, therefore, women in the early stages of their own careers were especially likely to view an occupational role involving responsibility and decision-making as requiring traits more characteristic of males than females.

In part, these findings reflect the fact that the middle management role has been occupied predominantly by men. Schein (1973) noted that relatively few women were in middle levels of management. Thus, the traditional presence of men in this role was perhaps a particularly salient factor influencing those women in the early phases of their careers as managers. It would be interesting to examine the conditions under which a woman's successful performance in an occupational role over time is associated with a weakening of these expectations. Moreover, the relation between these expectations and assessment of one's own performance warrants attention in view of the findings from a study of women in managerial positions. Deaux (1979) found that female managers rated their own job performance, intelligence, and ability less favorably than did men in comparable managerial positions. Women were also less likely to attribute job-related success to their own ability. In contrast, the supervisors of these women and men did not differentially evaluate the managers' general performance or ability as a function of whether the manager was female or male.

Occupational Achievement and Gender Role
Research discussed in an earlier section suggests that one major challenge for the woman oriented toward occupational achievement is the set of expectations associated with marital and parental roles. Both occupational attainment and perceived role conflict, or strain, are related to these expectations. Considering occupational attainment first, findings from various studies suggest that the timing of marriage and parenthood have been important predictors of occupational achievement for women. (In their discussion of research pertaining to women's work and family roles, Huston-Stein and Higgins-Trenk (1978) have similarly concluded that the timing of these roles is an important factor in women's development.)

As noted earlier, level of education achieved is a predictor of occupational status for white women and white men. One study found that after taking into account the education of their parents in a sample of young white women, the younger the woman was at the birth of her first child, the less formal education she completed (Waite and Moore, 1978). Even among women with a high level of education, expected patterns of behavior associated with the roles of *parent* and *spouse* have often continued to influence women's career development.

One pattern for responding to these role expectations has been for the woman to withdraw from active career involvement during early to middle adulthood; this behavior is consistent with traditional assumptions that the woman should be the primary caretaker of young children. For example, Rossi (1965) cited U.S. 1960 census data showing that women who were natural scientists or engineers were likely to voluntarily withdraw from the work force during ages twenty-five to forty-five years; that is, during the child-bearing/child-rearing years. In contrast, very few men in this age group left their professions. Baruch (1967) in a study of highly-educated alumnae found that high levels of "achievement motivation" occurred less frequently among women ten years after graduation compared to women five years after graduation. The author suggested that this difference reflected increased attention to family responsibilities that were likely to occur at that time.

Another pattern of role accommodation has been to reduce or eliminate the demands of marital or parent roles. Perrucci (1970) noted in a survey of engineers and scientists that a higher percentage of females than males in the sample were likely to remain unmarried. Those women who did marry were more likely either to have no children or to have only one child, with the first birth often occurring later.

The findings from other research also suggest that the timing of marriage and parenthood is related to occupational attainment in women. Card, Steel, and Abeles (1980) conducted a study which had several follow-up surveys of a high-school sample (first tested in 1960) one, five, and eleven years after the students' expected graduation from high school. In ninth grade, the level of achievement was higher for girls than for boys. Eleven years after high school graduation, this difference was reversed; the men had achieved more education and among those working full time, had higher incomes than the women. Men had not, however, achieved higher-prestige jobs than the women. When a subgroup of highly capable adolescents was considered in the later followups, differences in occupational development were especially notable between ages twenty-three and twenty-nine years, a period of greater growth for men than women. For this subgroup, different dimensions differentiated "high-potential/high-achievement" men and women from their "high-potential" same-sex peers who had achieved less by their late twenties, with job factors and socioeconomic background significant for the men and interpersonal dimensions (age at first marriage, number of children) and self-ratings (in grade nine) on two dimensions, (specifically, "maturity" and "leadership"), significant for the women. The authors interpreted their findings in terms of the demands on women associated with family roles in early adulthood. They commented that "for women more than men the onset of marriage, and especially parenthood, is often at the expense of career-related achievement" (Card, Steel, and Abeles, 1980, p. 20). Furthermore, they speculated that the men might continue to exceed the women in occupational achievement even in later years because of greater work experience and job-related seniority.

A similar pattern emerged in a study of wives' occupational attainment (Scanzoni, 1979), in which white women (ages eighteen to twenty-nine years in 1971) were interviewed twice in their early adulthood (1971 and 1975). Women working at both points, labeled the "high involvement" group, were more educated, married later and had a smaller number of children (in 1971 and 1975) than women in the "moderate involvement" group (working at one of the two interview points). For women in the "high work involvement" group, one measure of their sex-role beliefs (in 1971), specifically, reflecting more "sex-role egalitarianism," predicted greater work continuity (number of months worked during 1971 to 1975) as did the women's perception (in 1971) of more supportiveness on the part of their husbands for the wives' employment. As the author noted, consistency of employment traditionally has been assumed to be an important feature of male occupational attainment.

Various researchers have found perceived spouse support to be related to women's occupational attainment. This dimension was a predictor of subsequent labor force participation for white married women in a longitudinal survey of working-class and middle-class women (Shea, Roderick, and Kim, 1973). In a small sample of couples (mostly upper-middle and upper class), the women's career attainment (in 1974) was negatively related to their husbands' "power motivation" and positively related to their spouses' level of "affilation motivation" measured fourteen years earlier when the men were college students (Winter, Stewart and McClelland, 1977). Winter and his colleagues suggested that one plausible interpretation of these findings was that the men who were characterized by a high need for power during early adulthood might have perceived their wives' careers as potentially threatening to their dominance; hence they might have attempted to discourage and work against their wives' occupational goals. This interpretation is consistent with a pattern appearing in several studies discussed by Winter and his colleagues that suggests that power-oriented men have trouble successfully relating to women. In contrast, highly affiliative men are presumably more supportive of their spouses' career plans.

Various studies describing the role relations existing in two-career couples have suggested that expectations concerning a woman's contribution to family-related roles are associated with a career-family dilemma for at least some women actively pursuing their own careers. Rapoport and Rapoport (1969) used the term *dual-career* to characterize couples in which both partners have "jobs which are highly salient personally, have a developmental sequence and require a high degree of commitment" (p. 3). This definition distinguishes *dual-career* from *dual-job* couples, with the latter simply describing two-worker families without any assumption of equal and sustained occupational commitment for both part-

ners. The Rapoports interviewed a small sample of British dual-career couples who had at least one child at home. Not surprisingly, these couples emphasized the necessity for a high level of physical energy. Furthermore, they described a number of stresses associated with this pattern, namely, strains resulting from holding norms for personal behavior that differed from the prevailing social norms, (e.g. being a dual-career couple) and "role-cycling dilemmas" either between family and occupational roles or between the work roles of each partner, which required some sacrifice of individual career interests. Interestingly in this sample, the women appeared to assume that the family-career pressures were problems for them to resolve as individuals rather than as part of a husband and wife team.

Similarly, Heckman, Bryson and Bryson (1977) reported that in a survey of professional couples both members of which were pursuing careers in psychology that pressures arising from role demands of spouse and parent continued to be mentioned by women; some women expressed the view that they were largely responsible for child care and domestic tasks. Various comments also suggested that at least some women relegated their own career to a position of lesser importance to that of their husbands when career and family responsibilities conflicted. Epstein (1971) studied a small group of white women (mostly forty to sixty years old) in law partnership with their husbands. Frequent themes emerging from the interviews included the view that the women were assisting their husbands and were often assigned to the less prestigious tasks in the firm. In addition, the women were seen as responsible for household work; furthermore all the women expressed concern about doing well in the maternal role. Cartwright (1978), in a follow-up study of young women who were physicians, found that although most women were very satisfied with their careers, a number of women reported some difficulty in combining different types of roles. When women who were both very satisfied with their careers and who perceived little role strain were compared to the rest of the sample, there was a near-significant tendency for the speciality of this group to be pediatrics, a field more consistent with traditional gender-role expectations for women relative to many other medical specialities.

As this section indicates, considerable empirical attention has been devoted to the potentially conflicting demands of the traditional adult female roles of spouse /parent and occupational achievement. Perceived role strain has been reported in various samples consisting of white, middle-class women—the focus of most studies. In addition, there is some evidence that across a greater range of socioeconomic levels, role-related factors such as perceived spouse support for wife's employment are predictive of dimensions such as work history.

In this context, research that examines whether these factors also predict occupational attainment in black women is particularly interesting. Although the evidence in this area is scattered, the pattern emerging from a number of studies to date is different from the findings obtained for white women. Until very recently, black women in the United States have been more active in the work force than white women (U.S. Bureau of the Census, 1976). In the 1970s, census data suggested that this difference was no longer as marked because of the increasing participation in the work force of white women. As of the mid 1970s, black women were still more frequently concentrated in occupations at the lower income level than were white women, although some changes in occupational distribution were apparent (U.S. Bureau of the Census, 1976).

For example, compared to 1965, in 1974 more black women were employed in "white collar" occupations (U.S. Bureau of the Census, 1976). One survey of occupational status attainment found that although level of education was an important predictor for black men and black women, the women appeared to gain more from more schooling (in terms of occupational status achieved) than the men. In terms of income, however, black women seemed to be at a disadvantage relative to black men (Treiman and Terrell, 1975).

In various surveys, family role-related factors predictive of level of education or employment for white women were not as predictive for black women. For example, a woman's age at birth of first child was not as strongly related to years of schooling completed by black women as by white women (Waite and Moore, 1978). Black women have not been as likely to withdraw from the work force as have white women during the early phase of child rearing (U.S. Bureau of the Census, 1976). As stated earlier, husband's attitude toward wife's employment was found to predict certain aspects of employment for white women. At least one survey, however, found that this variable did not predict wife's employment for black women (Shea *et al.*, 1973).

In view of the earlier discussion of work versus family commitments, what are the experiences reported by black, middle-class women in this domain? Preliminary research suggests that although there are various stresses, the pattern of work versus family demands for some black women in high-status occupations may differ from those for some white women in similar occupations. Epstein (1973), for example, interviewed a small sample of black women following professional careers in fields traditionally occupied for the most part by white men and identified several distinctive themes emerging from the interviews. Most notably, these women did not appear to show the same degree of ambivalence between family roles and occupational goals as reflected in their attitudes toward marriage and child-rearing. Thus if married, they did not regard their occupational careers as "supplemental" to those of their husbands. The descriptive data from Epstein's study are consistent with the findings from at least one "fear of success" study done with black female college students. As mentioned earlier, during the late 1960s and early 1970s "fear of success" concerns expressed by white women received considerable attention (Horner, 1972). During this time period, a study conducted with black women found that a lower proportion of them wrote stories expressing the type of role conflict between academic success and femininity found among some white college women (Weston and Mednick, 1970).

Evidence from other studies also suggests that gender-role expectations for black women may differ in some respects from those for white women as far as work and family are concerned. For example, when white university students were asked to indicate the role responsibilities of hypothetical two-career couples, Peterson and Peterson (1975) found that both male and female students favored the mother's being responsible for child care. However, a replication of the Peterson and Peterson procedure with black university students (Thomas and Neal, 1978) revealed that black males did not regard child care as predominantly a female role responsibility as often as did the white males in the Peterson and Peterson study, a finding that the authors interpreted as suggesting more role flexibility in the raising of children on the part of black males compared to their white counterparts.

In part, this greater role flexibility may reflect the historical and economic conditions that made employment difficult for many black men. Scanzoni (1975) suggested that because of these conditions black women have participated more in the labor force, resulting in a wife's employment being more normative. According to Scanzoni, one correlate of this situation may be the emergence of a different role pattern in marriage; black adults may be more likely than white adults to support "married female autonomy." In a survey of the role-related attitudes of black married couples and white married couples, the findings across several dimensions suggested to Scanzoni (1975) that black men and black women seemed to endorse "more fundamental and basic changes in marital role stuctures" (p. 135), and that white men and white women seemed to endorse "more moderate or neo-traditional forms of the wife role..." (p. 135). Also, black women rated themselves more favorably than did white women on a task-competence dimension (a general factor including various skills and abilities). Black women were more likely than white women to endorse items concerning "institutionalized equality," specifically, believing that husband and wife should divide domestic and child-care responsibilities equally if the wife is employed (Scanzoni, 1975).

In Epstein's (1973) study, most of the women were married to men whose occupational status was lower than their own. Also, some evidence has suggested that years of formal schooling completed resulted in greater gains (in terms of occupational status) for black women than for black men (Treiman and Terrell, 1975). Considering these points, one source of stress for some black couples may be the employment opportunities available to the wife as opposed to those available to the husband. However, it should not be assumed that the gender-role expectations found in some research with black couples are solely attributable to restricted employment opportunities and discrimination—a perspective suggesting that these expectations evolved largely as a response to adverse circumstances. Contemporary black families may have retained African cultural forms that survived in, as well as responded to, a North American context, as proposed for example in Nobles's (1978) "Afro-centric" view of the black family.

Of particular interest to this discussion, Nobles described the black family structure as "a child-centered system" (p. 687) characterized by flexibility in carrying out various family roles, such as providing child care and extensive support between different family groups. Compatible with this description, Epstein (1973) commented that the black women in her sample could frequently rely on help with child-rearing responsibilities from an extended family system. When comparing black families with white families matched on relevant dimensions (socioeconomic status, marital status, size of family, and geographic mobility), Hays and Mindel (1973) found

that members of the extended family assisted with caring for children more often in the black families than in the white families. The authors interpreted this finding as consistent with the perspective that the extended kinship system in black families functioned as a "supportive structure," emerging as a reaction to external conditions such as discrimination; however, the data are also consistent with Nobles's view of the black family.

In conclusion, findings from various studies, especially some research on the family role expectations of black adults and descriptive data from interviews with black middle-class women combining career and family roles, suggest the need for caution in discussions of role conflict for women within contemporary North America. The gender-related conflict between family responsibilities and occupational achievement, a topic that has received considerable attention in psychological and sociological literature, has been based for the most part on research with white, middle-class women; the experiences of women in minority groups have received less attention. At the very least, the pattern of findings discussed in this section suggests the need for further study of work and family roles among women in various minority groups.

Women and Job-related Socialization

Research on women's employment has focused on identifying the factors associated with levels of occupational achievement. Recently, there has been some research on how aspects of the work situation itself may affect women (Miller, Schooler, Kohn and Miller, 1980). The women interviewed were the wives of the men who participated in the follow-up survey discussed earlier concerning the relation between job conditions and men's psychological functioning (Kohn and Schooler, 1973; 1978). Specifically, the sample for this study consisted of wives employed at least ten hours a week. The women's work circumstances differed on a number of dimensions from the men's job conditions. For example, the women were more likely to be employed in jobs characterized by lower levels of complexity and more direct work supervision than the men. The women were less likely to be found in upper level jobs as supervisors of others' work or to be owners than the men. The women also reported less work-related pressure on several dimensions compared to the men (for example, anticipating major job-related change). In general, these women as a group were in jobs which could be partly characterized both as making fewer personal demands but also as providing fewer opportunities for personal growth or advancement than the men's jobs.

Of particular interest, Miller and her colleagues found an inter-relation for women between dimensions associated with work and various measures of psychological functioning, a result similar to that obtained in the earlier research with men. Again, the "occupational self-direction" dimension emerged as important. Thus, the existence of greater opportunity for self-direction in one's work was related to "more effective intellectual functioning and a generally positive, flexible, and responsible social orientation" (Miller *et al.*, p. 78). Additional analyses indicated that these findings held even after controlling for the effects of variables such as education, race, religion, and parents' education. Furthermore, the effects obtained were not contingent on other variables such as commitment to one's work or certain role-related factors (e.g., having young children). Therefore, although the women as a group were less likely than men to be doing more complex work, the evidence suggested that those who did have more demanding jobs were affected by their work conditions just as much as were the men in the sample. Miller and her associates concluded that these results indicated that "for women, as for men, work has a decided psychological impact" (Miller *et al.*, p. 91).

ADAPTATION IN MARRIAGE

In life-span accounts of development, the role of marital partner has been discussed as a significant aspect of adulthood (Havighurst, 1972), and U.S. census data from the mid-1970s suggested that marital dyads remain an important family form (Glick, 1977). Marriage, therefore, continues to be an important socializing influence. Moreover, reported marital satisfaction can be viewed as one type of societal norm for assessing a "successful marriage" (Roberts, 1979). This section will therefore examine personal adaptation to marital roles as illustrated by research on marital satisfaction during the past two decades.

A number of studies have examined the factors associated with marital satisfaction. Various writers have distinguished between the formal role requirements of the spouse relationship and the more qualitative elements of this relationship, such as personal involvement. It has been suggested that middle-class couples differ from working-class couples in the relative emphasis they attribute to these two aspects of the marital role. For example, Bernard (1964) proposed that middle-class couples were likely to adhere to an "interactional" type of spouse relationship that emphasized the affective tie between partners and the personal qualities of each individual. Although role duties were expected, they were not sufficient to maintain the relationship. In contrast, working-class couples were described by Bernard as emphasizing role obligations in their marriages, forming more personal ties within a group of same-sex peers.

Developing this distinction further, Kerckhoff and Bean (1970) proposed "role structure" and "interpersonal structure" as two different though mutually dependent components within a dyad, such that when one component was more fully developed, the other would be correspondingly less salient. Thus in relationships where sharply defined roles were not present, the "interpersonal qualities" of each partner should be more important. The authors commented that for both partners of a middle-class marriage achieving personal satisfaction was an important goal. Moreover, they noted that in an "interactional role relationship," each partner might be expected to be under some strain given the necessity of "constantly 'finding' or 'creating' the bases of a satisfying relationship" (Kerckhoff and Bean, 1970, p. 270).

Marital Satisfaction:
Family Life-Cycle Perspective

Marital satisfaction in middle-class couples frequently has been studied in the context of a developmental perspective on the family, in which the family has been described as progressing through a series of phases, each having its own tasks or challenges (e.g., Duvall, 1971). This sequence of family stages assumes the presence of children and has been defined by the various developmental phases of the children. For example, Duvall (1971) stated that "the norm is for the young married couple to be a family-in-the-making...they think of themselves as potential parents long before children actually arrive" (p. 119). From this perspective, therefore, the family-life cycle begins before the birth of the first child, passes through a series of child-bearing and child-rearing stages, culminates in a "launching" phase as the children leave home, and finally ends with the phases of the "empty nest" and the aging parents.

Various early studies suggested that levels of reported marital satisfaction decreased across phases of the family cycle, though whether this reported decline was continuous or mostly occurred in specific phases was unclear. For example, Pineo (1961) reported decreasing "marital adjustment" scores for a large sample of couples relative to their scores at an early point in their marriage. In addition, a marked reduction was observed in the extent to which men and women reported sharing common interests over time. Luckey (1966) found a negative relation between length of marriage and general marital satisfaction. Also, the greater the length of the marriage, the less positive the impressions of the spouse on a variety of personality traits, while self-perceptions for the most part were not negatively related to length of marriage. Rollins and Feldman (1970) assessed marital satisfaction in a large sample of couples in various stages of the family-life cycle, from early marriage before the arrival of the first child to the retirement of the husband. Both the men and women showed declining frequencies of reported "positive companionship," particularly comparing couples in the earliest stage of marriage to those in the early phase of child rearing (i.e., those with preschool children). After this phase, this dimension did not show much change for the rest of the sample, namely, couples who were in the later stages of the family-life cycle.

Other evidence suggested, however, that marital satisfaction, rather than consistently decreasing across the family-life cycle, might show an initial decrease followed by an increase at the later stages. Rollins and Feldman (1970) noted that although reported "positive companionship" declined, the pattern of findings on a measure of "general marital satisfaction" showed a decrease followed by an increase in the latter part of the family cycle. Roberts (1979) noted that most respondents in a sample of long-married couples (postretirement) reported high levels of satisfaction with spouse and marriage. Burr (1970) asked a small sample of middle-class couples to indicate their satisfaction with several facets of their marriage (including companionship) and found that the most pronounced reduction in satisfaction was reported in the "school-age" phase of the family cycle, followed by some improvement for several components during the later phases. As Burr noted, the pattern overall for the six domains was not one of a consistent decrease across the family cycle. Finally, Spanier, Lewis and Cole (1975) in a rigorous test of the hypothesis of a curvilinear relation between marital adjustment and family stage found "only limited support" for this hypothesis.

A more detailed analysis of specific phases of the marital role seems warranted, since a given phase may

have unique features relevant to understanding marital satisfaction. Different phases of a role have different requirements and expectations (Nydegger, 1976). As noted earlier, both formal role duties and more interpersonal qualities have been discussed as components of marital roles. In addition to the class-related differences mentioned previously, various family stages and/or family circumstances may be associated with differential emphasis on these two dimensions (Fengler, 1973; Thurnher, 1976). Thurnher, for example, found that in a cross-sectional study of adults at different transition points, the middle-aged group when asked to describe their partners, was more likely to emphasize the carrying out of various role-related obligations; in contrast, those married recently stressed the individual, more distinctive qualities of their spouses. Older men and women (preretirement phase) also included role-related features when characterizing their spouses; in addition, however, members of this group were likely to point out more individual qualities. Greater emphasis on the interpersonal aspects in contrast to the "instrumental" features of the marital role was found in another study of older individuals at the last stage of the family cycle (Roberts, 1979). It is of interest to note that these couples were characterized by relative financial and personal autonomy (i.e., living in own home rather than with their children or in institutions). In part, therefore, changes in personal satisfaction with marital roles may be associated with the increased salience of formal role demands during specific phases of family development. Less satisfaction may be reported during these phases, since as noted earlier, the norms for middle-class marriage presumably stress the desirability of interaction that focuses on more personal qualities.

Women's and Men's Reports of Marital Satisfaction

There is also evidence that a given phase of family development may not necessarily be associated with the same degree of satisfaction for women as compared to men. In fact, differences between men's and women's reports of marital satisfaction have occurred in various studies. In Rollins and Feldman's (1970) study of couples drawn from different stages of the family cycle, women more often than men reported "negative feelings" toward their spouses (such as resentment and feeling misunderstood); moreover, for women, this dissatisfaction was especially pronounced during particular phases of the family cycle, notably those of child bearing and the socialization of the children. This result is consistent with

Hall's (1975) finding that for married women "life stage" (defined by number and ages of children) was related to perceived role strain; moreover this type of role strain was negatively related to reported happiness (Hall and Gordon, 1973). However, Rollins and Feldman (1970) found that men's negative responses toward spouse were not systematically associated with a given family stage. Also, Rollins and Feldman suggested that for men, the decrease reported in "positive companionship" with spouse did not seem to be accompanied by a more general decline in the men's satisfaction with marriage. Thurnher (1976) studying women and men at various transition points in their lives found that in a sample of middle-aged women (youngest child in last year of high school) the respondents expressed more dissatisfaction with their spouses compared to recently married women or older women. Consistent with this pattern, middle-aged male respondents in this sample similarly reported an awareness of dissatisfaction on the part of their wives not with the husband's more formal role responsibilities—but with the dimensions of emotional support and intimacy.

Gender-related differences also were found in a survey designed to assess the relation between married women's employment status and various aspects of marital satisfaction (Locksley, 1980). No relation occurred between the women's employment status and either the wives' or the husbands' reports of "marital companionship" or "marital adjustment". Moreover, the wife's reason for working (e.g., monetary or the interest value of the work itself) was not related to "marital companionship" or "marital adjustment." Instead, the spouses' attitudes toward each other and ratings of their marriages revealed differences between men's and women's reactions; women reported less satisfaction and more discontent than men (on items such as felt annoyed with spouse, and wanted spouse to discuss feelings more). Women also reported feeling less capable as a parent than men and more often portrayed their marriage as "like two separate people" rather than "like a couple" when asked to choose between these options. As Locksley noted, the results of this survey were consistent with the analysis of particular aspects of marriage suggested by Bernard (1972).

One could argue that the pattern of findings discussed here reflects the responses of various cohorts in which the women followed traditional expectations that the role of wife should be their major adult role. Bernard (1972), for example, suggested that the housewife role was one source of considerable difficulty and strain for married women. Conceivably, the women's greater dissatisfaction with their spouses might have reflected their ambivalence or stresses associated with exclusive functioning in this housewife role. Some of the samples studied could be characterized as adhering to a more traditional pattern, such as the wife not being employed (Rollins and Feldman, 1970) or focusing predominantly on the family (Thurnher, 1976). On the other hand, studies of women working outside the home have shown comparable findings (Locksley, 1980). The results of several national surveys discussed by Wright (1978) do not support the assumption that employment status per se (namely, employed as opposed to a housewife status) is consistently or strongly related to white women's overall life satisfaction; moreover there do not seem to be marked or consistent differences in housewives' or employed women's assessments of marital satisfaction.

Another possibility is that women's reports of greater marital dissatisfaction during certain stages of the family cycle may be partly attributable to the demands of the role of parent (Rollins and Feldman, 1970; Bernard, 1972; Spanier, Lewis and Cole, 1975). Recall that the stages in the family-life cycle are primarily defined by the ages and the developmental phases of children. Recently it has been argued that the predictive power of the family stages may in fact be largely due to factors such as length of marriage and the presence or absence of children (Nock, 1979). In several surveys conducted during the 1970s, the presence of young children (under six years) was found to be negatively related to reported marital satisfaction for white women (Glenn and Weaver, 1978). Similarly, Ryder (1973) found that white middle-class women (but not men) reported increased marital dissatisfaction, particularly on perceived spouse companionship and attention, following the birth of the first child within two years of marriage. More generally, studies conducted in the 1960s and 1970s suggested that in some white, middle-class couples, most of the responsibility for child rearing continued to belong to the woman, regardless of her occupational commitment, as shown, for example, in the research discussed in an earlier section on dual-career couples. Some of the role-related conflict described by these women concerned the demands of occupational versus parent roles. As will be discussed in the next section, parenting itself has been studied largely as a process of adjustment and adaptation.

Finally, it must be noted that the perspective of the family-life cycle has some important limitations as a conceptual framework for understanding middle-class women's and men's satisfaction with marital roles. Essentially, the stages portrayed describe a sequence of events that assume both the durability of the first marriage and the presence of children. Although marriage itself continues to be normative for many adults, recent estimates suggest a pattern of divorce (with a high frequency of remarriage) for a sizable proportion of adults, emphasizing the need to systematically examine the family cycle of these individuals (Norton and Glick, 1976; Glick, 1977). Although the proportion of couples remaining voluntarily childless is relatively small, this group, nevertheless, cannot be studied within the family-cycle framework.

In addition, adults who have been divorced and have remarried may be able to provide some insights for research on marital satisfaction. For example, seeking more "personal fulfillment" or happiness in the context of marriage has been cited as one factor associated with a high rate of divorce; furthermore, with increasing financial self-sufficiency, more women as well as men can pursue this goal (Norton and Glick, 1976). Since one aspect of marital satisfaction discussed in the context of family phases is perceived quality of companionship with spouse, adults who divorce and remarry at particular phases of the traditional family cycle form a pertinent comparison group. These adults also make interpretation of cross-sectional studies of marital satisfaction ambiguous, since with the passage of time, the couples left in a particular family phase become increasingly less representative of their cohort (Miller, 1975; Spanier, Lewis and Cole, 1975). Furthermore, cohort-related changes in "commitment to marriage" and the likelihood of divorce add to existing interpretive problems (Spanier, Lewis and Cole, 1975). Finally, the meaning of greater reported marital satisfaction is ambiguous, especially in the later family stages (Troll, 1971). Considering the points raised so far, it seems likely that there are notable differences within and between cohorts in how individuals define marital satisfaction.

PARENTHOOD

It has been suggested that more than other adult roles, becoming a parent is often interpreted as indicating that an individual has reached adulthood and maturity (Hoffman and Manis, 1979). Parenthood has been described as one of the developmental tasks of adulthood (Havighurst, 1972). In his conceptualization of adult development, Guttman (1975) emphasized the parental role as

a central feature of adulthood, suggesting, for example, that in the lives of most women and men, "parenthood is still the ultimate source of the sense of meaning" (Guttman, 1975, p. 170).

Within developmental psychology, research pertaining to socialization conducted during the 1950s and the early 1960s for the most part focused on the parent as a socializing agent, examining how parental attitudes and behavior contributed to children's development across a number of dimensions. There has been, however, an increased emphasis on the "bidirectionality of effects" in childhood socialization (Bell, 1968), which has resulted in more systematic consideration of the child's influence on the parent's behavior towards him or her (e.g., Harper, 1975; Bell and Harper, 1977). However, less attention has been paid to the impact of the role of parent on the adult.

Parenthood As "Crisis"

Parenthood has been studied mostly at the point of transition when the individual first assumes this role. Various writers have suggested that little formal training precedes parental role responsibilities, at least in North American society (LeMasters, 1957; Rossi, 1968). Accordingly, the birth of the first child could be regarded as a "crisis," albeit a normative one. The perceived severity of this crisis, however, has been a topic of some debate. Early work in this area suggested that first-time parenthood required considerable adaptation. LeMasters (1957) in interviews with a small sample of middle-class couples found that a substantial proportion of them reported "extensive" or "severe" crisis after discussion between spouses and the interviewer, a finding that the author interpreted as partly attributable to a "romanticized" view of parenthood resulting in little awareness of the actual demands of the role. Dyer (1963) too found support for the hypothesis that first-time parenthood was associated with considerable reported stress. In contrast, Hobbs (1965) failed to replicate these findings; the predominant response in his sample was that of experiencing a "slight" crisis. Degree of crisis in this study was assessed by having the participants complete a checklist. Subsequently, Hobbs (1968) compared two procedures for assessing "crisis" and found in a new sample that although no women could be categorized as experiencing "severe" difficulty when the checklist format was used, nearly one-fifth of the women were placed in this category based on interview ratings. Once again, the modal response under the checklist format was a "slight" degree of reported adjustment. Procedural differences might therefore account for some of the discrepency between the findings of LeMasters and the research of Hobbs. In Hobbs's (1968) study, even the findings on the interview ratings suggested, however, that the difficulty or crisis might not be as great as initially believed. Hobbs (1968) argued that becoming a parent might more usefully be regarded "as a period of transition which is somewhat stressful" (p. 417) rather than "as a crisis experience"(p. 417). It is also possible that since the studies discussed spanned a decade, the differences in reported adjustment may have reflected changes in the degree of idealization of parenting. Unfortunately, none of these studies assessed the couples' attitudes toward parenthood before the birth of their first child.

Therefore, the view of parenthood (especially the birth of the first child) as a crisis event has been questioned. As noted earlier in this chapter, expected or normative life events have been hypothesized to be less stress provoking than unanticipated events. Moreover, as Neugarten (1970, 1976) has suggested, the timing of expected events such as parenthood (e.g., "on-time" versus "off-time") may be an important factor mediating reported stress. For example, Elder and Rockwell (1976) found that women marrying "late" advocated a considerably earlier age (relative to their own age at the birth of their first child) as the ideal time to become a parent. In Rossi's (1980) study of a small sample of mothers, the pattern of findings suggested that the greater the mother's age when the first child was born (with the mother's age at the first birth ranging from 16–39 years), the more the woman indicated difficulty with raising children during both the early and some of the later phases of child rearing. (The women had been asked to rate how hard it was to rear children of different ages). As Rossi pointed out, part of the reported difficulty might have been related to the experience of the mother being out of sequence with peers of the same age. If so, the impact of relatively late parenthood may be moderated somewhat by changing norms concerning the age range considered appropriate, particularly by peers, for having a first child.

A more balanced perspective that also considers the positive aspects of adaptation to the experience of parenthood can be found in research conducted by Russell (1974). Russell asked respondents to indicate degree of crisis, defined as aspects of parenthood that are "bothersome" (measured by Hobbs's checklist) as well as more rewarding aspects (measured by a checklist designed by

the author). The importance of parenthood to men relative to other roles was inversely related to perceived stress of parenthood. This relation did not occur for women. Overall, the level of reported crisis was mostly "slight" or "moderate." As far as reported gratification was concerned, level of education was negatively associated with this variable for men and women, as was occupational prestige for men. (The sample included working-class as well as middle-class couples). For both men and women, higher gratification scores were associated with higher placement of the role of parent in a list of adult identities. Overall, respondents reported more positive than stress-related items, particularly emphasizing the personal rewards of parenthood for them as individuals. As Russell noted, more stress might have been reported during later periods of parenthood.

Consistent with the emphasis on the positive features of parenthood, as part of a survey conducted in the United States, parents and nonparents were asked about the benefits of having children (Hoffman and Manis, 1979). In general, the most frequently expressed category of responses reflected "primary group ties and affection." Other categories included regarding children as a source of "stimulation and fun," as an "expansion of self," and as helping to confer "adult status and social identity." This last category is of particular interest. Although the authors expected less educated women to cite this reason more often than their more educated peers because of their fewer role options, this pattern occurred for white women but not for black women. In contrast, black women with more (rather than less) formal education were likely to mention the importance of children for adult identity. Participants were also asked to indicate which of several events contributed to their sense of being an adult. White parents and black mothers most often chose "becoming a parent"; black fathers most frequently chose "supporting yourself."

As noted earlier, research on adults' responses to parenthood has emphasized the phase when this role is first assumed. More systematic study of the continuing impact of parenthood on the adult subsequent to this initial phase is certainly needed, and there is some indication that interest in this issue is increasing, as shown for example in Rossi's (1980) study. Furthermore, the interrelation between functioning in this family role and other role contexts deserves further attention.The present era should be of particular interest for the study of women's work and family commitments, since a number of middle-class women have reversed the sequence of roles characteristic of earlier decades by postponing becoming a parent until after they have established occupational careers.

Voluntary Childlessness

Societal norms support parenthood as a major component of adulthood. Accordingly the decision to remain childless is a deviant one. The findings of a national survey (conducted in the United States in 1977) indicated that the majority of adults did not regard voluntary childlessness as a desirable status for a married couple (Blake, 1979). A substantial proportion of both men and women disagreed with an item describing childless couples as having "the best time in life" and disagreed that children disrupt marital bonds. Moreover, a sizable proportion of the women and men agreed that elderly childless couples were more likely to be lonely. In contrast, other items yielded more diversity of opinion, for example, the belief that a childless woman will see herself as unfulfilled or that a marriage without children is likely to be more susceptible to divorce than a marriage with children. The descriptive data on these items suggested that college-educated men were particularly more likely than college-educated women to view the absence of children as problematic. As Blake noted, this pattern suggested that being college-educated was associated with a less traditional view of childlessness on certain dimensions for women but not for men. In general, men were more likely than women to indicate that being childless was disadvantageous. However, neither men nor women for the most part were likely to regard childless couples as having distinct advantages, as stated earlier.

Consistent with this view, the frequency of childlessness among North American couples is quite low (U.S. Bureau of the Census, 1976; Veevers, 1972a). Preliminary evidence suggests that since the incidence of voluntary childlessness varies across different groups, either the normative pressures favoring parenthood may be weaker in some groups or dimensions of social structure (level of education, employment) may partly mitigate these pressures, with the latter alternative being more likely (Ritchey and Stokes, 1974). Because the choice to remain childless conflicts with established norms, however, the voluntarily childless may encounter various sanctions such as pressure to become parents and negative evaluations concerning, for example, their maturity or other related attributes (Veevers, 1972b).

Veevers (1973) interviewed a small sample of white women. As the author noted, the study was exploratory.

Nevertheless, the descriptive data suggested several issues for future work in this area. For example, although some of the women stated that they and their husbands planned to be childless from the beginning of their marriage, the more prevalent pattern was a series of postponements. In effect, the couple "gradually become aware that an implicit decision has been made to forego parenthood" (p. 360); the couple frequently was not able to specify a particular point of transition. This type of postponement process lends some indirect support for the argument mentioned earlier that certain structural variables are associated with the decision to remain childless. The women interviewed by Veevers reported feeling "stigmatized," different from others and isolated, though the author stated that they appeared to have a reasonable repertoire for coping with pressure from others. Interestingly, many women expressed an interest in adopting a child, an attitude that Veevers interpreted as largely symbolic, one that allowed the woman to present herself as "normal" and to avoid "irreversible decisions."

Other researchers have compared childless couples with couples who had children. Ory (1978) found that white, middle-class parents and nonparents perceived the societal reaction to childlessness as largely negative, thus supporting the recognition of strong normative pressures to have children. Older parents and nonparents did not report different expectations for family size before marriage, suggesting that the postponement process described by Veevers (1973) characterized the older childless couples. Certain dimensions differentiated the two groups; for example, childless wives were more likely to be employed than mothers, and childless couples were less likely to hold traditional religious beliefs or to participate actively in traditional religions. The two groups did not differ in self-ratings on either the warmth or competence group of traits identified as comprising the traditional female and the traditional male sex-role, respectively. In addition, Ory mentioned other factors that appeared to be important in supporting the couples' atypical decision, namely their association with other childless couples and with organizations sharing their views and their stressing the positive features of childlessness.

Another study compared the self-reports of marital adjustment of married women who were voluntarily childless with married mothers matched for level of education, labor force participation, and religious affiliation (Houseknecht, 1979). The childless women received higher scores than the matched group of women with children, specifically on one of four subscales, a "cohesion" dimension (in particular, sharing outside interests with spouse, "exchange of stimulating ideas," joint projects, and having a "calm discussion with spouse"). Although these findings might simply reflect a tendency of the childless women to idealize their relationship with their spouses, not all subscales yielded differences. For example, childless wives did not differ from mothers on a subscale assessing "affectional expression."

In view of the pattern of results discussed previously on women and occupational roles, voluntary childlessness merits further study. Considerably more work is needed in this area to examine both the social structural and the psychological variables that are predictive of the decision to remain childless and of coping successfully with this decision.

ROLES AND PERSONAL IDENTITY

In the preceding sections, the discussion focused on adult socialization as it pertains to functioning in major adult roles. Considering that much of adult behavior occurs in the context of these roles, an important issue concerns their impact on the individual's self-definition. Specifically, what factors affect the likelihood that an individual's sense of personal identity in adulthood is based on particular roles? The idea that an individual may choose her or his personal definition of self from among various alternatives has a long history within psychology. For example, William James (1890) wrote that "our thought, incessantly deciding...chooses one of many possible selves or characters..." (p. 310).

As mentioned at the start of this chapter, adult socialization has been viewed as involving a series of developmental tasks, many of which occur in the context of various roles. The outcomes for the individual in attempting to adapt to role-related tasks might plausibly be expected to be related to the likelihood that a given role will be regarded as an important personal definition of self. In their analysis of coping strategies used by adults to deal with role-related stress, Pearlin and Schooler (1978) suggested that through a "hierarchical ordering of life-priorities" individuals attempt to reduce stress by assigning less personal importance to areas of perceived stress. In addition, particular roles may become less salient for personal identity as a function of various role transitions, especially during middle adulthood. Some evidence from adults facing change associated with important roles suggests that this change

is seen as anticipated freedom (Lowenthal and Chiriboga, 1972). In part, individuals may interpret this freedom as a chance to "be themselves" (Chiriboga and Thurnher, 1975) and to permit the emergence of other aspects of the self (Nydegger, 1976). These hypothesized changes in self-definition may therefore involve less reliance on certain roles as salient sources of personal identity. This discussion thus far assumes a particular view of adult socialization; namely, that roles associated with major social institutions such as work and family comprise the core of personal identity in adulthood for most individuals.

This perspective has been questioned by several authors who have suggested that the importance of these roles to adults' self-definition is in the process of changing. Zurcher (1972, 1973) has proposed that a "mutable self" is becoming more prevalent in response to rapid social and cultural change and unstable social institutions. According to Zurcher (1973), "the sense of self becomes disengaged from social structure and linked with processes of the self...perceiving, thinking, feeling..." (p. 372). Similarly, Lifton's (1971) concept of the "protean man" stresses "self-process" rather than any fixed identity. Turner (1976) has suggested that a person's sense of the "real" self (which is being referred to as self-definition in this section) can be conceptualized as based in either social institutions or in personal "impulse"; furthermore he proposed that especially during the recent past, self-definition has been less likely to be based on institutional links such as various roles. In essence, these authors have suggested that a pronounced cohort effect in the sources of personal identity during adulthood is occurring. So far this suggestion still appears to be a provocative hypothesis that awaits more extensive and systematic empirical assessment. Preliminary efforts have been made by Zurcher (1972) using Kuhn and McPartland's (1954) Twenty Statements Test. Zurcher noted that the self-descriptions of university students contained fewer role-related referents relative to previous student samples. The prevalence of this pattern needs additional investigation to determine whether it will occur in more recent groups of students as well as whether it will persist into middle adulthood among individuals belonging to the cohort studied by Zurcher.

Also, the Twenty Statements Test itself has been critically examined by Wylie (1974) in her review of methodological issues associated with measuring self-concept. Of particular relevance to the present discussion, she noted the results of an investigation by Spitzer, Stratton, Fitzgerald and Mach (1966). These researchers found that some university students objected to the unstructured nature of the Twenty Statements Test when asked which of several measures provided an opportunity for the "most accurate" and "least accurate" self-description. Only a small proportion of the sample felt that their responses on the Twenty Statements Test reflected their most accurate self-description. Accordingly, reactions to the measure itself should be examined in more recent student samples as well as in nonstudent samples of adults.

In summary, it remains to be seen whether the hypothesis that individuals' sense of personal identity is increasingly diverging from role-linked identities receives additional support. Another possibility is that roles associated with major social institutions, such as family and occupation, may continue to be important sources of personal identity in adulthood, although the nature of these roles may undergo considerable change.

CONCLUDING REMARKS

In the research literature concerning socialization during adulthood, issues relevant to the major role-related areas usually have been examined within particular subfields in sociology and to a lesser extent, in psychology. In view of this fragmentation, this chapter has discussed research from these various subfields with the intent of fostering a more integrated perspective.

Socialization as it occurs in the diverse contexts of adulthood should be an area of interest to social psychologists in psychology and in sociology. During the past several years, the need for greater rapprochement between the various branches of social psychology has been stressed (e.g., House, 1977; Stryker, 1977; Cartwright, 1979). The study of adult socialization can certainly benefit from this recommendation, since a thorough understanding of this process must consider both psychological and sociological perspectives.

REFERENCES

Albrecht, G. L., and H. C. Gift (1975). Ambiguity and adult life crises. In N. Datan, and L. Ginsberg (Eds.), *Life-span developmental psychology: normative life crises.* New York: Academic Press. Pp. 237–251.

Baltes, P. B. (1968). Longitudinal and cross-sectional sequences in the study of age and generation effects. *Hum. develop., 11,* 145–171.

_____ (1979). Life-span developmental psychology: some converging observations on history and theory. In P. B. Baltes, and O. G. Brim, Jr. (Eds.), *Life-span development and behavior.* Vol. 2. New York: Academic Press. Pp. 255–279.

Baltes, P. B., H. W. Reese, and L. Lipsitt (1980). Life-span developmental psychology. *Ann. Rev. Psychol., 31,* 65–110.

Baruch, R. (1967). The achievement motive in women: implications for career development. *J. Pers. soc. Psychol., 5,* 260–267.

Becker, H. S. (1964). Personal change in adult life. *Sociometry, 27,* 40–53.

Bell, R. Q. (1968). A reinterpretation of the direction of effects in studies of socialization. *Psychol. Rev., 75,* 81–95.

Bell, R. Q., and L. V. Harper (1977). *Child effects on adults.* Hillsdale, N.J.: Erlbaum.

Bernard, J. (1964). The adjustments of married mates. In H. T. Christensen (Ed.), *Handbook of marriage and the family.* Chicago: Rand McNally.

_____ (1972). *The future of marriage.* New York: World Publishing Co.

Blake, J. (1979). Is zero preferred? American attitudes toward childlessness in the 1970s. *J. Marriage and Family, 41,* 245–257.

Blishen, B. R. (1967). A socio-economic index for occupations in Canada. *Canad. rev. Sociol. Anthrop., 4,* 41–53.

Bortner, R., and D. Hultsch (1974). Patterns of subjective deprivation in adulthood. *Develop. Psychol., 10,* 534–545.

Braun, J. S., and F. Bayer (1973). Social desirability of occupations: revisited. *Vocat. Guid. Quart., 21,* 202–205.

Brim, O. G., Jr. (1966). Socialization through the life cycle. In Brim, O. G., Jr., and S. Wheeler, *Socialization after childhood: two essays.* New York: Wiley. Pp. 3–49.

_____ (1968). Adult socialization. In J. A. Clausen (Ed.), *Socialization and society.* Boston: Little, Brown. Pp. 182–226.

Brim, O. G., Jr., and C. D. Ryff (1980). On the properties of life events. In P. B. Baltes, and O. G. Brim, Jr. (Eds.), *Life-span development and behavior.* Vol. 3. New York: Academic Press. Pp. 367–388.

Brim, O. G., Jr., and S. Wheeler (1966). *Socialization after childhood: two essays.* New York: Wiley.

Broverman, I. K., S. Vogel, D. M. Broverman, F. Clarkson, and P. Rosenkrantz (1972). Sex-role stereotypes: a current appraisal. *J. soc. Issues, 28,* 59–78.

Burr, W. R. (1970). Satisfaction with various aspects of marriage over the life cycle: a random middle-class sample. *J. Marriage and Family, 32,* 29–37.

Card, J. J., L. Steel, and R. P. Abeles (1980). Sex differences in realization of individual potential for achievement. *J. vocat. Behav., 17,* 1–21.

Cartwright, D. (1979). Contemporary social psychology in historical perspective. *Soc. Psychol. Quart., 42,* 82–93.

Cartwright, L. K. (1978). Career satisfaction and role harmony in a sample of young women physicians. *J. vocat. Behav., 12,* 184–196.

Charles, D. C. (1970). Historical antecedents of life-span developmental psychology. In L. R. Goulet, and P. B. Baltes (Eds.), *Life-span developmental psychology: research and theory.* New York: Academic Press. Pp. 23–52.

Chinoy, E. (1955). *Automobile workers and the American dream.* Garden City, N.Y.: Doubleday.

Chiriboga, D., and M. Thurnher (1975). Concept of self. In M. Lowenthal, M. Thurnher, and D. Chiriboga, *Four stages of life*. San Francisco: Jossey-Bass.

Clausen, J. A. (1968). A historical and comparative view of socialization theory and research. In J. A. Clausen (Ed.), *Socialization and society*. Boston: Little, Brown. Pp. 18–72.

_____ (1976). Glimpses into the social world of middle age. *Int. J. Aging hum. Develop., 7*, 99–105.

Deaux, K. (1979). Self-evaluations of male and female managers. *Sex roles, 5,* 571–580.

Deaux, K., and T. Emswiller (1974). Explanations of successful performance on sex-linked tasks: what is skill for the male is luck for the female. *J. Pers. soc. Psychol., 29,* 80–85.

Duncan, O. D. (1961). A socioeconomic index for all occupations. In A. J. Reiss, Jr., *Occupations and social status*. New York: Free Press of Glencoe. Pp. 109–138.

Duvall, E. M. (1971). *Family development* (4th ed.). Philadelphia: Lippincott.

Dyer, E. D. (1963). Parenthood as crisis: a re-study. *Marriage fam. Living, 25,* 196–201.

Elder, G. H., Jr., and R. Rockwell (1976). Marital timing in women's life patterns. *J. fam. Hist., 1,* 34–53.

Epstein, C. F. (1971). Law partners and marital partners. *Hum. Relat., 24,* 549–564.

_____ (1973). Positive effects of the multiple negative: explaining the success of black professional women. *Amer. J. Sociol., 78,* 150–173.

Erikson, E. (1950, 1963). *Childhood and society*. New York: Norton.

Faulkner, R. (1974). Coming of age in organizations: a comparative study of career contingencies and adult socialization. *Sociol. Work Occupations, 1,* 131–173.

Feather, N. T. (1975). Positive and negative reactions to male and female success and failure in relation to the perceived status and sex-typed appropriateness of occupations. *J. Pers. soc. Psychol., 31,* 536–548.

Fengler, A. P. (1973). The effects of age and education on marital ideology. *J. Marriage and Family, 35,* 264–271.

Glenn, N. D., and C. N. Weaver (1978). A mulivariate, multi-survey study of marital happiness. *J. Marriage and Family, 40,* 269–282.

Glick, P. C. (1977). Updating the life cycle of the family. *J. Marriage and Family, 39,* 5–13.

Goslin, D. A., Ed. (1969a). *Handbook of socialization theory and research*. Chicago: Rand McNally.

_____ (1969b). Introduction. In D. A. Goslin (Ed.), *Handbook of socialization theory and research*. Chicago: Rand McNally. Pp. 1–21.

Gutmann, D. (1975). Parenthood: a key to the comparative study of the life cycle. In N. Datan, and L. Ginsberg (Eds.), *Life-span developmental psychology: normative life crises*. New York: Academic Press. Pp. 167–184.

Hakel, M. D., T. D. Hollman, and M. D. Dunnette (1968). Stability and change in the social status of occupations over 21 and 42 year periods *Personnel Guid. J., 46,* 762–764.

Hall, D. T. (1975). Pressures from work, self, and home in life stages of married women. *J. vocat. Behav., 6,* 121–132.

Hall, D. T., and F. E. Gordon (1973). Career choices of married women: effects on conflict, role behavior, and satisfaction. *J. appl. Psychol., 58,* 42–48.

Harper, L. V. (1975). The scope of offspring effects: from caregiver to culture. *Psychol. Bull., 82,* 784–801.

Havighurst, R. J. (1953). *Human development and education*. New York: David McKay.

_____ (1948, 1952, 1972). *Developmental tasks and education*. New York: David Mckay.

_____ (1973). History of developmental psychology: socialization and personality development through the life-span. In P. B. Baltes, and K. W. Schaie (Eds.), *Life-span developmental psychology: personality and socialization*. New York: Academic Press. Pp. 3–24.

Hays, W. C., and C. H. Mindel (1973). Extended kinship relations in black and white families. *J. Marriage and Family, 35,* 39–49.

Heckman, N. A., R. Bryson, and J. Bryson (1977). Problems of professional couples: a content analysis. *J. Marriage and Family, 39,* 323–330.

Henry, W. E. (1971). The role of work in structuring the life cycle. *Hum. Develop., 14,* 125–131.

Hobbs, D. F., Jr. (1965). Parenthood as crisis: a third study. *J. Marriage and Family, 27,* 367–372.

_____ (1968). Transition to parenthood: a replication and an extension. *J. Marriage and Family, 30,* 413–417.

Hoffman, L. W. (1974). Fear of success in males and females: 1965 and 1971. *J. consult. clin. Psychol., 42,* 353–358.

Hoffman, L., and J. Manis (1979). The value of children in the United States: a new approach to the study of fertility. *J. Marriage and Family, 41,* 583–596.

Hollingshead, A. B., and F. C. Redlich (1958). *Social class and mental illness: a community study*. New York: Wiley.

Horner, M. (1968). Sex differences in achievement motivation and performance in competitive and noncompetitive situations. Unpublished doctoral dissertation. University of Michigan.

_____ (1972). Toward an understanding of achievement-related conflicts in women. *J. soc. Issues, 28,* 157–175.

House, J. S. (1977). The three faces of social psychology. *Sociometry, 40,* 161–177.

Houseknecht, S. K. (1979). Childlessness and marital adjustment. *J. Marriage and Family, 41,* 259–265.

Hultsch, D. F., and J. K. Plemons (1979). Life events and life-span development. In P. B. Baltes, and O. G. Brim, Jr. (Eds.), *Life-span development and behavior*. Vol. 2. New York: Academic Press. Pp. 1–36.

Huston-Stein, A., and A. Higgins-Trenk (1978). Development of females from childhood through adulthood: career and feminine role orientations. In P. B. Baltes (Ed.), *Life-span development and behavior*. Vol. 1. New York: Academic Press. Pp. 257–296.

James, W. (1890). *The principles of psychology*. New York: Henry Holt. (Reprinted 1950. New York: Dover.).

Kastenbaum, R., V. Derbin, P. Sabatini, and S. Artt (1972). "The ages of me": toward personal and interpersonal definitions of functional aging. *Aging hum. Develop., 3,* 197–211.

Kerckhoff, A., and F. D. Bean (1970). Social status and interpersonal patterns among married couples. *Social Forces, 49,* 264–271.

Kohn, M. L. (1981). Personality, occupation and social stratification: a frame of reference. In D. J. Treiman, and R. V.

Robinson (Eds.), *Research in social stratification and mobility*. Vol. 1. Greenwich, Conn.: JAI Press. Pp. 267–297.

Kohn, M., and C. Schooler (1969). Class, occupation and orientation. *Amer. Sociol. Rev., 34,* 659–678.

_____ (1973). Occupational experience and psychological functioning: an assessment of reciprocal effects. *Amer. Sociol. Rev., 38,* 97–118.

_____ (1978). The reciprocal effects of the substantive complexity of work and intellectual flexibility: a longitudinal assessment. *Amer. J. Sociol., 84,* 24–52.

_____ (1981). Job conditions and intellectual flexibility: a longitudinal assessment of their reciprocal effects. In D. J. Jackson, and E. F. Borgotta (Eds.), *Factor analysis and measurement in sociological research: a multi-dimensional perspective*. London and Beverly Hills, Calif.: Sage. Pp. 281–313.

_____ (1982). Job conditions and personality: a longitudinal assessment of their reciprocal effects. *Amer. J. Sociol., 87,* 1257–1286.

Komarovsky, M. (1946). Cultural contradictions and sex roles. *Amer. J. Sociol., 52,* 182–189.

_____ (1973). Cultural contradictions and sex roles: the masculine case. *Amer. J. Sociol., 78,* 111–122.

Kuhn, M., and T. S. McPartland (1954). An empirical investigation of self-attitudes. *Amer. Sociological Rev., 19,* 68–76.

LeMasters, E. E. (1957). Parenthood as crisis. *Marriage fam. Living, 19,* 352–355.

Levinson, D. J. (1978). *The seasons of a man's life*. New York: Knopf.

Lifton, R. J. (1971). Protean man. *Arch. gen. Psychiatry, 24,* 298–304.

Locksley, A. (1980). On the effects of wives' employment on marital adjustment and companionship. *J. Marriage and Family, 42,* 337–346.

Looft, W. R. (1973). Socialization in a life-span perspective: white elephants, worms, and will-o'-the wisps. *Gerontologist, 13,* 488–497.

Lowenthal, M. F., and D. Chiriboga (1972). Transition to the empty nest: crisis, challenge or relief. *Arch. gen. Psychiatry, 26,* 8–14.

Lowenthal, M. F., M. Thurnher, and D. Chiriboga (1975). *Four stages of life*. San Francisco: Jossey-Bass.

Luckey, E. B. (1966). Number of years married as related to personality perception and marital satisfaction. *J. Marriage and Family, 28,* 44–48.

McClendon, M. J. (1976). The occupational status attainment processes of males and females. *Amer. Sociol. Rev., 41,* 52–64.

Miller, B. C. (1975). Studying the quality of marriage cross-sectionally. *J. Marriage and Family, 37,* 11–12.

Miller, J., C. Schooler, M. Kohn, and K. A. Miller (1980). Women and work: the psychological effects of occupational conditions. *Amer. J. Sociol., 85,* 66–91.

Morse, N. C., and R. S. Weiss (1955). The function and meaning of work and the job. *Amer. Sociol. Rev., 20,* 191–198.

Mortimer, J. T., and J. Lorence (1979). Occupational experience and the self-concept: a longitudinal study. *Soc. Psychol. Quart., 42,* 307–323.

Mortimer, J. T., and R. G. Simmons (1978). Adult socialization. *Ann. Rev. Sociol., 4,* 421–454.

Neugarten, B. L. (1968a). Adult personality: toward a psychology of the life-cycle. In B. Neugarten (Ed.), *Middle age and aging*. Chicago: Univ. of Chicago Press. Pp. 137–147.

_____ (1968b). The awareness of middle age. In B. Neugarten (Ed.), *Middle age and aging*. Chicago: Univ. of Chicago Press. Pp. 93–98.

_____ (1969). Continuities and discontinuities of psychological issues into adult life. *Hum. Develop., 12,* 121–130.

_____ (1970). Dynamics of transition of middle age to old age: adaptation and the life cycle. *J. geriatric Psychiatry, 4,* 71–87.

_____ (1976). Adaptation and the life cycle. *Counsel. Psychol., 6,* 16–20.

Neugarten, B. L., and N. Datan (1973). Sociological perspectives on the life cycle. In P. B. Baltes, and K. W. Schaie (Eds.), *Life-span developmental psychology: personality and socialization*. New York: Academic Press, Pp. 53–69.

Neugarten, B. L., J. W. Moore, and J. C. Lowe (1965). Age norms, age constraints and adult socialization. *Amer. J. Sociol., 70,* 710–717.

Neugarten, B. L., and W. Peterson (1957). A study of the American age-grade system. *Proceed. fourth congress Int. Assoc. Gerontology, 3,* 497–502.

Nobles, W. (1978). Toward an empirical and theoretical framework for defining black families. *J. Marriage and Family, 40,* 679–688.

Nock, S. L. (1979). The family life cycle: empirical or conceptual tool. *J. Marriage and Family, 41,* 15–26.

Norton, A. J., and P. C. Glick (1976). Marital instability: past, present and future. *J. soc. Issues, 32,* 5–20.

Nydegger, C. N. (1976). Middle age: some early returns—a commentary. *Int. J. Aging Hum. Develop., 7,* 137–141.

Ory, M. G. (1978). The decision to parent or not: normative and structural components. *J. Marriage and Family, 40,* 531–539.

Osipow, S. H. (1973). *Theories of career development* (2nd ed.). New York: Appleton-Century-Crofts.

Pearlin, L. I., and C. Schooler (1978). The structure of coping. *J. Health soc. Behav., 19,* 2–21.

Perrucci, C. C. (1970). Minority status and the pursuit of professional careers: women in science and engineering. *Social Forces, 49,* 245–259.

Peterson, C., and J. Peterson (1975). Issues concerning collaborating careers. *J. Vocat. Behav., 7,* 173–180.

Pineo, P. C. (1961). Disenchantment in later years of marriage. *Marriage fam. Living, 23,* 3–11.

Pines, A. (1979). The influence of goals on people's perceptions of a competent woman. *Sex Roles, 5,* 71–76.

Plata, M. (1975). Stability and change in the prestige rankings of occupations over 49 years. *J. vocat. Behav., 6,* 95–99.

Powers, E. A., and W. J. Goudy (1971). Examination of the meaning of work to older workers. *Aging hum. Develop., 2,* 38–45.

Rapoport, R., and R. N. Rapoport (1969). The dual career family: a variant pattern and social change. *Hum. Relat., 22,* 3–30.

Riegel, K. F. (1975). Adult life crises: a dialectic interpretation of development. In N. Datan, and L. Ginsberg (Eds.), *Life-span developmental psychology: normative life crises*. New York: Academic Press. Pp. 99–128.

Riley, M. W. (1973). Aging and cohort succession: interpretations and misinterpretations. *Publ. Opin. Quart., 37,* 35–49.

Ritchey, P. N., and C. S. Stokes (1974). Correlates of childlessness and expectations to remain childless: U.S. 1967. *Social Forces, 52,* 349–356.

Roberts, W. L. (1979). Significant elements in the relationship of long-married couples. *Int. J. Aging Hum. Develop., 10,* 265–271.

Rollins, B. C., and H. Feldman (1970). Marital satisfaction over the family life cycle. *J. Marriage and Family, 32,* 20–28.

Rosow, I. (1965). Forms and functions of adult socialization. *Social Forces, 44,* 35–45.

_____ (1978). What is a cohort and why? *Hum. Develop., 21,* 65–75.

Rossi, A. (1965). Women in science: why so few? *Science, 148,* 1196–1202.

_____ (1968). Transition to parenthood. *J. Marriage and Family, 30,* 26–39.

_____ (1980). Aging and parenthood in the middle years. In P. B. Baltes, and O. G. Brim, Jr. (Eds.), *Life-span development and behavior.* Vol. 3. New York: Academic Press. Pp. 137–205.

Russell, C. S. (1974). Transition to parenthood: problems and gratifications. *J. Marriage and Family, 36,* 294–301.

Ryder, R. G. (1973). Longitudinal data relating marriage satisfaction and having a child. *J. Marriage and Family, 35,* 604–606.

Scanzoni, J. (1975). Sex roles, economic factors, and marital solidarity in black and white marriages. *J. Marriage and Family, 37,* 130–144.

_____ (1979). Sex-role influences on married women's status attainment. *J. Marriage and Family, 41,* 793–800.

Schaie, K. W. (1965). A general model for the study of developmental problems. *Psychol. Bull., 64,* 92–107.

Schein, V. E. (1973). The relationship between sex-role stereotypes and requisite management characteristics. *J. Appl. Psychol., 57,* 95–100.

_____ (1975). Relationships between sex-role stereotypes and requisite management characteristics among female managers. *J. appl. Psychol., 60,* 340–344.

Shaffer, D. R., and C. Wegley (1974). Success orientation and sex-role congruence as determinants of the attractiveness of competent women. *J. Pers., 42,* 586–600.

Shea, J. R., R. D. Roderick, and S. Kim (1973). Dual careers: a longitudinal study of labor market experience of women. (H. Parnes, Director). *Manpower research monograph.* No. 21, Vol. 2. Washington, D.C.: U.S. Dept. of Labor.

Smith, E. J. (1975). Profile of the black individual in vocational literature. *J. vocat. Behav., 6,* 41–59.

Spanier, G. B., R. A. Lewis, and C. L. Cole (1975). Marital adjustment over the family life cycle: the issue of curvilinearity. *J. Marriage and Family, 37,* 263–275.

Spence, J. T., and R. Helmreich (1972). Who likes competent women? Competence, sex-role congruence of interests and subjects' attitudes toward women as determinants of interpersonal attraction. *J. appl. soc. Psychol., 2,* 197–213.

Spence, J. T., R. Helmreich, and J. Stapp (1975). Likability, sex-role congruence of interest, and competence: it all depends on how you ask. *J. appl. soc. Psychol., 5,* 93–109.

Spitzer, S. P., J. R. Stratton, J. D. Fitzgerald, and B. K. Mach (1966). The self-concept: test equivalence and perceived validity. *Sociological Quart., 7,* 265–280.

Stein, A. H., and M. M. Bailey (1973). The socialization of achievement orientation in females. *Psychol. Bull., 80,* 345–366.

Stryker, S. (1977). Developments in "two social psychologies": toward an appreciation of mutual relevance. *Sociometry, 40,* 145–160.

Suter, L. E., and H. P. Miller (1973). Income differences between men and career women. *Amer. J. Sociol., 78,* 200–212.

Thomas, M. B., and P. A. Neal (1978). Collaborating careers: the differential effects of race. *J. vocat. Behav., 12,* 33–42.

Thurnher, M. (1976). Midlife marriage: sex differences in evaluation and perspectives. *Int. J. Aging hum. Develop., 7,* 129–135.

Treiman, D. J. (1977). *Occupational prestige in comparative perspective.* New York: Academic Press.

Treiman, D. J., and K. Terrell (1975). Sex and the process of status attainment: a comparison of working women and men. *Amer. Sociological Rev., 40,* 174–200.

Troll, L. E. (1971). The family of later life: a decade review. *J. Marriage and Family, 33,* 263–290.

Turner, R. H. (1976). The real self: from institution to impulse. *Amer. J. Sociol., 81,* 989–1016.

Unger, R. K. (1979). Toward a redefinition of sex and gender. *Amer. Psychol., 34,* 1085–1094.

U. S. Bureau of the Census (1976). *A statistical portrait of women in the United States.* U.S. Dept. of Commerce. Current Population Reports: Special Studies: Series P-23, No. 58. (Issued April, 1976). Washington, D.C.: U.S. Government Printing Office.

Veevers, J. E. (1972a). Factors in the incidence of childlessness in Canada: an analysis of census data. *Soc. Biol., 19,* 266–274.

_____ (1972b). The violation of fertility mores: voluntary childlessness as deviant behavior. In C. Boydell, C. Grindstaff, and P. Whitehead (Eds.), *Deviant behavior and societal reaction.* Toronto: Holt, Rinehart, and Winston. Pp. 571–592.

_____ (1973). Voluntarily childless wives: an exploratory study. *Sociol. soc. Res., 57,* 356–366.

Waite, L. J., and K. A. Moore (1978). The impact of an early first birth on young women's educational attainment. *Social Forces, 56,* 845–863.

Weston, P. J., and M. T. Mednick (1970). Race, social class, and the motive to avoid success in women. *J. cross-cultural Psychol., 1,* 283–291.

Winter, D. G., A. J. Stewart, and D. C. McClelland (1977). Husband's motives and wife's career level. *J. Pers. soc. Psychol., 35,* 159–166.

Wright, J. D. (1978). Are working women *really* more satisfied? *J. Marriage and Family, 40,* 301–313.

Wylie, R. C. (1974). *The self-concept.* Vol. I. Lincoln: Univ. of Nebraska Press.

Zurcher, L. A. (1972). The mutable self: an adaptation of accelerated sociocultural change. *J. appl. behav. Science, 3,* 3–15.

_____ (1973). Alternative institutions and the mutable self: an overview. *J. appl. behav. Science, 9,* 369–380.

CHAPTER 17

Sex Roles in Contemporary American Society

Janet T. Spence
University of Texas at Austin

Kay Deaux
Purdue University

Robert L. Helmreich
University of Texas at Austin

INTRODUCTION

One chapter in the initial (1935) edition of this handbook entitled ''Sex in Social Psychology'' written by Catherine Cox Miles surveyed what was known about sex differences and included a wide range of topics from the physiology of the reproductive process to differences between the sexes in personality and in physical and cognitive abilities to patterns of employment in men and women. The reasons for the inclusion of a chapter on sexual differentiations can only be inferred but appear to have been related less to the inherent interest value of the topic than to the demographic emphasis of the handbook as a whole. Other discussions in that original volume, for example, focused on the white man, the red man, the yellow man, insects, birds, and bacteria. More understandable is the absence of chapters devoted to gender-related phe-

nomena in subsequent editions, until the appearance, a half century later, of the present essay.

Throughout much of its history, social psychology—like most other areas within the discipline—has been relatively indifferent to questions bearing on sex differences and the relationships between the sexes. Despite an accumulation of social, political, and economic forces that in the late 1960s would converge to propel the question of women's status onto the national agenda, there was in psychology, as in the country as a whole, an unquestioning acceptance of the status quo. Beginning with the industrial revolution and the trend toward urbanization in Western societies, a model of the family developed in which income-producing work was separated from the household, with the husband generally assuming the public ''productive'' role and the wife assuming the unpaid domestic role of maintaining the household and caring for the children (Hunt and Hunt, 1977). Until quite recently, these sex-role arrangements, which resulted in women being subordinate to men in power and community influence, were regarded by social scientists as nonproblematic, if not as biologically inevitable or divinely ordained.

At the same time the attention of experimentally and behaviorally oriented psychologists was directed toward

Preparation of this chapter was facilitated by NIMH grant 32066 (Janet T. Spence and Robert L. Helmreich, principal investigators) and NASA grant NSG 2065 (Robert L. Helmreich, principal investigator). Appreciation is extended to Alice Eagly for her helpful comments on an earlier version of this chapter.

the development of theories of psychological processes that would have universal applicability. Individual differences among subjects, including their gender, typically had the status of nuisance variables rather than of factors demanding incorporation into such theories. Males, however, appeared with disproportionate frequency as subjects in social psychological research (Holmes and Jorgenson, 1971). Occasionally, the reasons for preferring males were made explicit. For example, in the initial studies of the implications of the Atkinson-McClelland theory of achievement motivation, done in the early 1950s, because results from males, but not females, were compatible with theoretical predictions, some investigators (e.g., McClelland, 1966) suggested that a different theory would have to be developed for females. The immediate outcome was that for the next decade or so males were used almost exclusively in achievement motivation research. In most instances, however, the preference for male subjects went unexplained. The conclusion seems inescapable that males tended to be regarded as the norm, and women to be regarded as members of a nonstandard population of lesser interest.

Exceptions to this general neglect of sex-related phenomena can be found. In child development, for example, empirical attention has long been paid to the processes leading to the development of "sex-role identification" and to the acquisition of normatively expected masculine and feminine attributes and behaviors. Even here, however, conventional sex-role distinctions were tacitly accepted as givens, and the consequences of failure to develop expected sex-role behaviors and attributes were usually implied to be deleterious. Similarly, clinical and personality psychologists tended to view cross-sex behaviors and preferences as indicative of emotional disturbance or sexual deviation. Indeed, one of the criteria used to select items for one well-known masculinity-femininity test was the items' capacity to distinguish between heterosexuals and homosexuals (Constantinople, 1973).

The re-emergence of the feminist movement in the late 1960s, which has focused societal attention on the position of women, has catapulted questions related to sex differences, sex roles, and sex-role attitudes into major research topics. Psychologists, together with other social and behavioral scientists, have begun to re-examine received wisdom about the nature of men and women and the functional value of our sex-role system and to study in detail the relationship between the sexes.

In the span of a few years, inquiries into these matters have grown from a trickle to a torrent. A survey of even the highlights of this now massive literature is impossible within the space limitation of this chapter. We will therefore confine our presentation to selected topics that are relevant to sex-role attitudes and behaviors in North America.

Although the term "sex roles" is often employed in psychology as a categorical label for all the psychological characteristics and behaviors that stereotypically distinguish males from females in a given society, we define the term more narrowly in this chapter to correspond to the usage of role theorists (e.g., Sarbin and Allen, 1968): Sex roles refer to normative expectations about the division of labor between the sexes and to gender-related rules about social interactions that exist within a particular cultural-historical context. At the level of the individual actor, variations occur in cognitions about these sets of societal expectations, in beliefs about the appropriateness of these expectations (sex-role attitudes and values), in personal preferences for various "masculine" and "feminine" activities, and in the desire to seek the rewards or avoid the negative consequences of role conformity or role violation. These role-related cognitions, attitudes, and preferences are distinguished from other gender-differentiating attributes, such as personality traits that refer to general response dispositions or self-images. Such attributes may contribute to effective performance of some types of role behaviors, and their nature or intensity may be influenced by role enactment. Nonetheless, they are conceptually distinct from sex-role attitudes and behaviors and may have implications for behaviors in settings with other types of role demands.

The role phenomena to be discussed are subject to social influences that have been undergoing rapid historical change. To document these shifts in attitudes and behaviors, data collected at different times with comparable instruments from similar subject populations will be described whenever possible. In the absence of such data, preference will be given to the findings of studies conducted over the past decade, thus providing an overview of sex-role phenomena as they operate in contemporary U.S. society. The initial section will set the scene, tracing women's educational and vocational progress over the past century and describing changes in sex-role attitudes that have taken place over the past two decades in conjunction with these changes in women's status. The next section will describe conceptions of personality differences between the sexes that have frequently been used to explain or to justify sex-role behaviors and the perpetuation of our traditional sex-role system. The remaining sections will be devoted to selected topics relevant to role-related behaviors and attitudes in vocational, social, and marital settings.

THE SOCIAL CONTEXT

TRENDS IN WOMEN'S EDUCATIONAL ATTAINMENTS

The complex web of technological, social, and ideological forces that have modified societal attitudes and governmental policies concerning the status of women need not be recounted here. We note only that these changes have been most conspicuous in the provision of equal opportunity for women and men in education and employment. Title VII of the Civil Rights Act of 1964 prohibited discrimination in employment on grounds of race, religion, national origin, or sex. The most immediate stimulus to the passage of this landmark legislation was the civil rights movement that sought to right the wrongs to which blacks and members of other ethnic minorities had been subject historically. Women were almost accidentally included among the protected groups specified in this act, since the feminist movement was several years in the offing and women's position was not yet a matter of self-conscious concern. Nonetheless, women were the beneficiaries of its provisions and of those of subsequent legislative and governmental actions, such as the 1972 Title IX amendment of the Civil Rights Act, which mandated equal opportunity in education and the establishment of affirmative action guidelines by the Office of Civil Rights.

The male-dominated occupations that women have been discouraged historically from entering most importantly include prestigious, well-paying positions that typically require at least a college degree. A century of educational progress placed women in a better position than members of most racial and ethnic minorities to take advantage of the opportunities opened up to them by civil rights legislation.

Throughout much of the nineteenth century, women's innate intellectual inferiority was accepted scientific dogma, and whether women even had a mind at all, in the same sense as men, was considered questionable. There were even suggestions that women would become physically masculinized and lose their reproductive capacities if they attempted to exercise their mental faculties. (See, Miles, 1935; Shields, 1975; Ehrenreich and English,

1979; and Cole, 1979, for accounts of some of these theories.) Despite these alarms, by the middle of the nineteenth century colleges for women began to be established. By the end of the century a number of all-male colleges and universities began to accept women, either by making the student body coeducational or by establishing a separate college for women. Even in women's colleges, the curriculum grew to resemble that offered to males (Stockard, Schmuck, Kempner, Williams, Edson, and Smith, 1980).

Women's educational attainments were further facilitated by the passage in 1912 of a federal law mandating universal compulsory education. The effect of this law was to give females equal access to public schools at both the primary and secondary levels and to make the same academic subjects available to them as to males. Subsequently, discrepancies in men's and women's overall educational attainments were not only reduced but until the mid 1970s, women's attainments were greater than men's largely because of women's greater rate of high school completion (Stockard *et al.,* 1980; Kreps and Leaper, 1976).

Although men are somewhat more likely to complete their baccalaureate degrees than women, an approximately equal proportion of each sex currently enters college (Social Indicators of Equality for Minorities and Women, 1978). The sexes differ markedly, however, in the fields in which they elect to major. In 1975 and 1976, women earned over 60 percent of the bachelor's degrees in education, fine arts, foreign languages, and home economics but 20 percent or less of the degrees in architecture, business, engineering, and the physical sciences (Stockard *et al.,* 1980). However, some signs of change can be detected. For example, although the absolute numbers remain small, four times as many women majored in business and seven times as many majored in engineering in 1978 as in 1966 according to the Census Bureau.

Women's progress in obtaining postbaccalaureate degrees, however, has not been even. The years 1920 to 1929 were a highwater mark in the production of women doctorates, falling off in the two subsequent decades and recovering to its earlier level only in the 1970s (Report of Committee on the Education and Employment of Women in Science and Engineering, 1979). In the last half of the 1970s, the proportion of women earning advanced degrees from graduate and professional school programs has accelerated. One-third of the doctorates awarded in 1980 were earned by women, as compared to one-sixth in 1972; similarly, women earned one-fourth of all professional degrees awarded in 1980, as compared to one-sixteenth in 1972 (National Advisory Council on Women's Educational Programs, 1981).

TRENDS IN WOMEN'S EMPLOYMENT

Since the beginning of industrialization in the nineteenth century, a fairly substantial proportion of urban women has had paid employment outside the home, even in periods of peace. For the first four decades of this century, close to 20 percent of white women and 40 percent of black women over fourteen years old had jobs. Most of these women were young, single, or (whatever their age or marital status) poor. Since 1940, the participation of married and middle-class women in the labor market has risen steadily (Kreps and Leaper, 1976). Most remarkable has been the upward surge in the number of working women with minor children. The first influx, noted in the 1950s, constituted women with children of elementary-school age, followed in the 1960s by women with children of preschool age (Chafe, 1976). Of all married women who are employed, currently 22 percent have preschool children and 55 percent have children under 18 years (U.S. Bureau of the Census, 1982). Because of the rise in divorce, especially among younger couples (Van Dusen and Sheldon, 1976), an increasing proportion of working women are without husbands. According to the Department of Commerce, in 1979 close to one fifth of families with children were headed by women.

Continuous employment is most likely for black women (Fichter, 1971) and, independent of race, for well-educated women. In 1970, for example, 31 percent of women with an eighth-grade education or less, 56 percent of those with college degrees, and 76 percent of those with postbaccalaureate training were gainfully employed (Huston-Stein and Higgins-Trenk, 1978).

The structure of the labor force has shown marked sex segregation historically, with female-dominated occupations tending to be low in both status and pay and, conversely, with prestigious well-paying positions being held almost exclusively by males. Differences in the college courses and vocational training programs that men and women have been encouraged or allowed to enter reinforce these sex-linked occupational patterns (Kreps and Leaper, 1976). Furthermore, women recruited into the same positions as men have been paid less, have received fewer promotions, or have been shunted into career paths in which the opportunities for advancement are limited (Chafe, 1976; Schrank and Riley, 1976).

The removal of some external barriers to women's advancement, the changes in women's undergraduate fields of specialization, and the increased rate of women's entry into postgraduate training programs presage some degree of breakdown in these sex-linked occupational patterns. However, at all occupational levels, the rate of women entering stereotypical masculine vocations has not been matched by the increase in males entering stereotypical feminine vocations. Furthermore, at all educational levels, women continue to earn considerably less than men of similar academic attainments (Social Indicators of Equality for Minorities and Women, 1978; Dunton and Feathermen, 1983).

Attitudes about the appropriateness of various occupations for men and women continue to mirror the observed segmentation in the labor force. Cummins and Taebel (1980) report, for example, that among high-school seniors from both blue-collar and middle-class backgrounds, only about 30 percent of the students were egalitarian in their beliefs about the relative suitability of men and women for traditionally masculine and feminine occupations. However, the students were less sexist in their beliefs about women occupying high-status positions (e.g., lawyer, college professor, bank president) than about men and women crossing the sex barrier to enter less prestigious, sex-typed occupations. Results obtained by Heilman (1979) complicate interpretation of the latter finding. In this investigation, high-school students were led to believe that fifteen years hence the proportion of women in two currently prestigious male-dominated professions would be at least equal to the proportion of men. An equal balance increased the attractiveness of these professions to the female students but decreased it for males. Although future cohorts, reared by working mothers in a more permissive social climate, may bring about more sexual homogeneity in the occupational structure, data such as these suggest that changes will be slow.

CHANGES IN SEX-ROLE ATTITUDES

A widely accepted characterization of the division of labor between the sexes in most societies is Parson's (1955) classic distinction between instrumental and expressive roles. Men are assigned primary responsibility for supporting and protecting their families and for managing their society's economic and political institutions (instrumental functions); women are assigned primary responsibility for care of the home and nurturance of children (expressive functions).

Within a given society the specific tasks and duties inside and outside the home that are designated as more appropriate for one sex than the other can also be identified. A myriad of other normative expectations also accrue to sex-role systems: type of dress and bodily adornment, codes of social etiquette, styles of self-presentation, patterns of sexual behaviors, rules for social interactions in various settings, and so forth. Although the particulars as well as the sharpness of these normative expectations vary across both historical periods and cultures or subcultures, they are all designed to emphasize the distinctiveness between males and females and to preserve men's generally dominant position over women and their greater access to economic and political resources.

As our review of employment trends has indicated, the idealized conceptions of the man as the breadwinner and family protector and of the woman as the nurturant homemaker that have characterized U.S. society have become progressively out of touch with the realities. Until the last decade or so, attitudes about the propriety of married women seeking employment outside the home lagged behind the quite dramatic increase in the participation of married, middle-class women in the labor force that began in the 1940s (Oppenheimer, 1970). In 1955, no less a figure than Adlai Stevenson announced to the graduating class at Smith College that their mission in life was to "influence man and boy" through the "humble role of housewife" (quoted in Chafe, 1976). In 1962, only a minority of women questioned in a Gallup Poll believed that their sex was treated inequitably, an opinion that was not to become the majority view until 1974 (Chafe, 1976).

Mason, Czajke, and Arber (1976) have chronicled the changes in women's sex-role attitudes during this critical period, using national survey data collected from adult women at three time intervals: 1964, 1970, and 1973 to 1974. The first of these time intervals was prior to the advent of the woman's movement, and the second coincided with a period during which that movement and the organizations it generated were beginning to raise national consciousness about women's status and to exert political influence. The impact of the 1964 Civil Rights Act and its sequelae, which women were learning to use to their advantage, was also being felt over the course of the years 1964 to 1974.

Marked declines in adherence to traditional attitudes and values occurred over the three time periods, including a decrease in the number of women who believed that children would suffer if their mothers worked. Earlier data analyzed by Mason and Bumpass (1975) indicated that women's attitudes toward equality of treatment of women workers was unrelated to the traditionalism of their attitudes about divisions of responsibility within the home. The later analyses by Mason *et al.* (1976) suggest that women's attitudes have become more homogeneous. At all three intervals, the women were most egalitarian in their beliefs about equal treatment of women in employment, but the amount of change over these time intervals was no greater than the change in their attitudes toward family roles.

Liberality in women's sex-role attitudes has typically been associated with higher levels of education, family income, and socioeconomic status (e.g., Spence and Helmreich, 1978; Beckman and Houser, 1979). Mason *et al.* (1976) also found these relationships; however, contrary to the belief that "women's liberation" is a cause dear only to educated middle-class women, they reported that the rate of change did not differ between highly educated women and those with lesser academic attainments. Women with full-time employment also have been found to have more positive attitudes about women's adopting multiple roles (e.g., Beckman and Houser, 1979; Houser and Beckman, 1980). Employment status was similarly related to sex-role attitudes in the Mason *et al.* (1976) study, but again, the amount of change exhibited by employed women over the three time periods did not differ from that exhibited by full-time housewives.

Shifts toward more egalitarian attitudes have been found in men as well as in women Helmreich, Spence, and Gibson, 1982. These investigators compared responses to a measure of sex-role attitudes given by predominantly middle-class students at the same university in 1972, 1976, and 1980 and by the parents of these students in 1972 and 1976. In each of these years and age groups, women were more liberal in their attitudes than men, and students were more liberal than their same-sex parent. Within each sex, both students and their parents were less traditional in 1976 than in 1972, the amount of change being similar in both cohorts. Particularly striking were changes in attitudes toward equal educational and vocational opportunities for men and women and toward men's sharing in household responsibilities.

The greater traditionalism in sex-role attitudes of older individuals than of college-age youths has typically been attributed to the respondents' stage in the life cycle and to cohort succession effects, older individuals having been brought up in a more traditionally oriented, less permissive environment than younger ones. However, the two parent groups described previously, tested only four years apart, grew up during a period in which there was relative stability in sex-role attitudes and behaviors. The differences between these samples thus suggest that middle-aged men and women have also been responsive to changes in the social climate that occurred in the 1970s and have become more relaxed in their sex-role attitudes.

Although substantial liberalization in attitudes took place between 1972 and 1976 in both age groups, no comparable changes occurred in the student groups between 1976 and 1980. After a decade or more in which sex-role attitudes caught up with behavioral and structural changes that were already underway, a point of resistance may have been reached. A national mood of greater political conservatism may also be slowing changes in sex-role attitudes.

Nonetheless, the acceptance of married women working and the commitment to the concept of equal opportunities for women in education and employment have become well established. These attitudes are mirrored in women's personal aspirations. For example, numerous surveys have indicated that although almost all young college women plan to marry and most intend to have at least one child, an increasing proportion also aspires to a career (e.g., Epstein and Bronzaft, 1972; Voss and Skinner, 1975; Hoffman, 1977). The belief of contemporary women that their vocational aspirations will not detract from their marriageability has a firm basis in reality: The percentage of young career women who never marry is low and similar to the percentage of women in general. This capacity of today's women to combine career and marriage is in stark contrast to their predecessors. Chafe (1976), for example, reports that as late as 1920, only 12 percent of women in the professions ever married.

In summary, sex-role attitudes have moved strongly away from traditional positions over the past fifteen to twenty years, thus both mirroring and stimulating changes in role-related behaviors. Although endorsement of egalitarian attitudes is strongest in the areas of employment and education, views about the patriarchial structure of the family and rigid divisions of household responsibilities have also been liberalized to some degree. Even at the level of publically expressed attitudes, however, we are still far from being an egalitarian society. Resistance to the further breakdown of sex-role distinctions may be observed, particularly among those with conservative political or religious values (e.g., Ellis and Bentler, 1973). There are also signs that in society as a whole, the rate of change in role attitudes is slowing, perhaps in response to a general trend toward conservatism and a turning away from concern about the welfare of segments of the population other than one's own.

CONCEPTIONS OF MALE-FEMALE DIFFERENCES IN PERSONALITY AND THEIR RELATIONSHIPS TO SEX ROLES

Explanations of the evolution and perpetuation of sex-role systems in which men have greater economic and political power than women have often included an appeal to underlying differences in the psychological makeup of the two sexes. Although early scientific theories placed heavy reliance on women's presumed inferiority in innate mental capacities, cognitive factors receive relatively little emphasis in contemporary accounts. Questions do remain about possible sex differences in specific cognitive abilities (e.g., spatial ability) and the origins of these differences. However, the weight of the evidence suggests that should biologically determined differences exist, they are not large and do not uniformly favor one sex (cf., Maccoby and Jacklin, 1974).

Experiments using relatively unobtrusive measures suggest that among the public at large, some suspicion lingers that women are not as intellectually able as men, particularly in tasks that are stereotypically masculine, and that successful women, in contrast to men, owe their achievement more to hard work and good fortune than to superior ability (e.g., Pheterson, Kiesler, and Goldberg, 1971; Deaux and Emswiller, 1974; Feldman-Summers and Kiesler, 1974). However, studies of sex stereotypes (e.g., Spence, Helmreich, and Stapp, 1974) suggest that men and women are generally perceived as being similar in overall intellectual competence, thus mirroring current scientific consensus.

There is common agreement, however, that the sexes differ in personality characteristics. A core distinction that appears throughout the theoretical literature contrasts what are often labeled *instrumental* qualities versus *expressive* qualities, thus calling attention to a purported parallel with Parson's (1955) distinctions between men's instrumental roles and women's expressive roles. Men are said to possess in greater abundance than women self-directing, goal-oriented characteristics such as independence, assertiveness, and decisiveness, qualities that allow them to discharge effectively their roles in both familial and extrafamilial settings. Women, on the other hand, are said to possess in greater abundance than men interpersonally oriented, emotive qualities such as kindness, sensitivity to others, emotional responsiveness, and need for affiliation. It is alleged that women's greater expressiveness allows them to perform their domestic roles within the family effectively; at the same time, women's lesser instrumentality presumably results in their being less achievement oriented and less temperamentally suited than men for demanding positions of leadership outside the home.

A parallel distinction between the personal qualities of men and women has been made by Bakan (1966), who postulated that whereas a sense of self or *agency* is dominant in men and constitutes the "male principle," a sense of selflessness or *communion* with others is dominant in women and constitutes the "female principle." Other theorists have proposed similar principles such as outer versus inner space (Erikson, 1964), field independence versus field dependence (Witkin, 1974), and allocentric versus autocentric orientation (Gutman, 1965).

Theorists differ in the weight that they assign to genetic and hormonal factors in determining the appearance of these hypothesized personality differences between the sexes. At one extreme are theorists of a sociobiological persuasion who, although not dismissing the contribution of experiential factors, propose that inborn temperamental differences between the sexes are great and lacking in malleability; thus these differences have not only shaped existing sex-role structures but also constrain the arrangements that would be feasible for any human society to devise (e.g., Tiger and Fox, 1971; Archer, 1976). Other investigators (including most psychologists concerned with sex-role development) either deny or play down the role of direct biological causation, proposing that the differential socialization received by boys and by girls in anticipation of their adult roles and the models of gender-appropriate behavior they are expected to emulate are critical in bringing about these differences in personal qualities. Contemporary theorists also disagree about the functional value of conventional sex-role distinctions (e.g., Bem, 1978; Baumrind, 1982) and hence about the desirability of encouraging sex differences in personality traits that purportedly contribute to effective enactment of gender roles or determine role choices. Although defenses of the status quo take various forms, those challenging the merits of sex-role distinctions tend to emphasize discrepancies in the power and status of the sexes and the destructive effects of these inequities on women (Hochschild, 1973). It is beyond the boundaries of this chapter to review and evaluate these particular disputes. Our purpose is to call attention to the importance assigned to purported sex differences in instrumental and expressive qualities by many theorists, despite their disagreements about the origins, desirability, or inevitability of these differences.

Most theories postulating sex differences in instrumental and expressive qualities imply or explicitly specify that these trait dimensions are strongly linked to sex-role behaviors and develop in the same way as do these behaviors. Instrumentality and expressiveness have also been postulated to have implications not only for observed differences in the role-related behaviors of males and females but also for individual differences in role preferences and attitudes within each sex. Thus for a number of writers, personality traits are central features of a larger theoretical system of so-called masculinity-femininity or sex-role identification (e.g., Kohlberg, 1966; Bronfenbrenner, 1960; Bem, 1974, 1981; Heilbrun, 1981). However, as we shall point out, this assumption of totality is seriously challenged by recent empirical findings.

A related assumption, pervasive in the earlier literature, is that instrumental and expressive characteristics are negatively correlated. That is, it was assumed that individuals who are relatively high in one of these trait clusters tend to be relatively low in the other so that, for all practical purposes, instrumentality and expressiveness form the endpoints of a single continuum, with men clustering at one end and women at the other. This conception, which is also part of folk psychology (Foushee, Helmreich, and Spence, 1979), has been disputed recently by a number of theorists (Carlson, 1971; Block, 1973; Constantinople, 1973; Bem, 1974; Spence, Helmreich, and Stapp, 1974). The current contention is that within each sex, these two personality dimensions are essentially independent.

TRAIT STEREOTYPES OF MALES AND FEMALES

The belief that the sexes differ in instrumental and expressive characteristics is also common outside the scientific community. In the most frequently cited study of sex-related trait stereotypes (Rosenkrantz, Vogel, Bee, Broverman, and Broverman, 1968), groups of college students rated the typical adult male and typical adult female on a group of over one hundred socially desirable bipolar traits that had themselves been generated by student nomination and that largely, though not exclusively, could be categorized as instrumental or expressive in nature. Consensus about sex differences was found for a number of these traits, with the prototypic man being rated higher on instrumental attributes and lower on expressive attributes than the prototypic woman.

These trait stereotypes have shown no signs of abating since the Rosenkrantz *et al.* (1968) study. In a study of students conducted in 1973 to 1974 using the same item pool, Spence *et al.* (1974) replicated these investigators' basic findings. In 1978, Ruble (1983) obtained data from students, using trait descriptors shown by Spence and her colleagues to exhibit consistent stereotypes in several samples of both sexes. Except for one item (''intellectual''), significant differences continued to be found in ratings of the typical male and female by both sexes.

The pervasiveness of these perceptions of sex differences is illustrated by Romer and Cherry's (1980) investigation of children in the fifth through the eleventh grades. The participants came from both middle-class and working-class backgrounds and were drawn from three ethnic or racial groups: Italians, Jews, and blacks. As in prior studies (e.g., Spence *et al.*, 1974), boys tended to perceive greater sex differences than girls. Several differences in perceptions associated with the children's ethnicity and social class were also found. However, within each combination of sex, ethnicity, and socioeconomic status, the outcome was uniform: Males were perceived as more instrumental and less expressive than females.

Several investigations (e.g., Williams and Bennett, 1975; Spence, Helmreich, and Holahan, 1979) have also demonstrated that, as implied by Bakan's (1966) theory of agency and communion, males are perceived as possessing to a greater extent than females undesirable, self-oriented traits (e.g., arrogant, self-centered, and domineering). Conversely, females are seen as being more likely to possess undesirable traits reflecting a lack of a healthy sense of self (e.g., servile, spineless) or a kind of verbal passive-aggressiveness (e.g., whiny, nagging, complaining).

Studies tracing the development of these positive and negative trait stereotypes indicate that they are established early. Glimmerings were detected by Kuhn, Nash, and Bruchen (1978) in two- and three-year olds. Stereotypes develop steadily from this tender age and are well established by the time youngsters are in the fifth or sixth grade (e.g., Best *et al.,* Koblinsky, Cruse, and Sugawara, 1978).

Whatever might have been the case historically, the trait stereotype literature indicates that the sexes are currently perceived as differing, not in kind, but in de-

gree. That is, on the average, the typical female is not regarded as being noninstrumental (e.g., as being passive as opposed to active) but as being less instrumental than the typical male; conversely, the typical male is not regarded as being unexpressive but as being less expressive than the typical female.

Individuals differ, however, in the magnitude of their stereotypes. Degree of stereotyping of desirable qualities, for example, has been found to be substantially correlated in both men and women with degree of traditionalism in sex-role attitudes (Ellis and Bentler, 1973; Spence, Helmreich, and Stapp, 1975). In view of this relationship, the resistance of trait stereotypes to change during a period in which sex role attitudes have become conspicuously more liberal is interesting to note.

STEREOTYPES AS BEHAVIORAL GUIDES

An issue of some significance is the degree to which individuals' beliefs about the prototypic male and female guide their reactions to members of each sex. Within-sex stereotypes have been found for men and women who occupy specific roles. For example, Clifton, McGrath, and Wick (1976) found that the characteristics ascribed to the incumbents of such roles as housewife, club woman, and career woman not only yielded different profiles of instrumental and expressive attributes but also involved characteristics that went beyond these particular trait dimensions. Similarly, work on stereotyping by investigators such as Ashmore (1981) and Taylor (1981) has suggested that the superordinate categories of male and female may be broken down into more articulated subordinate categories that can be applied with greater discrimination to the specific males and females that one encounters. These more numerous subordinate categories may or may not show consistent evidence of the instrumental-expressive distinction that is generally applied to the superordinate categories of male and female.

It is possible, then, that in practice global stereotypes about sex differences in instrumentality and expressiveness have little influence on one's responses to others, especially when more is known about these others than their sex. In one study relevant to this question, Rosen and Jerdee (1974) gave male business students identical background information, including work history, about a male or a female applicant for an executive position. For half of the students, the requirements of the position were described as demanding, calling for forceful interpersonal behavior and decisive managerial action; in contrast, for the other half, the same position was described as requiring accuracy and dependable performance. Although male applicants were rated as more acceptable than female applicants under both conditions, the discrepancy was dramatically greater in the case of the position demanding "masculine" instrumental qualities. From a slightly different vantage point, Locksley *et al.* (1980) have demonstrated that behavioral information about a male or female target, specifically concerning assertive or passive behavior, may account for more variance than gender in subsequent behavioral and trait predictions. These authors argue that stereotypes may have minimal impact on judgment when subjectively diagnostic characteristics of a person are known.

Yet in the absence of such diagnostic information, more global stereotypes may continue to affect judgments, and on a broader level than simply the instrumentality or expressiveness dimensions. For example, experiments have shown that the same behavior may be interpreted differently, even in infants (e.g., Condry and Condry, 1976), depending on whether the actor is perceived as male or female. Furthermore, it is evident that the various components of gender stereotypes are not completely unrelated to one another. Thus individuals given access to information about specific personality traits tend to make inferences about role behaviors, and vice versa (Deaux and Lewis, 1984). These implicit theories may in turn contribute to the development of sex differences in personality or may elicit patterns of behavior that confirm initial expectations.

SELF-CONCEPTS OF INSTRUMENTALITY AND EXPRESSIVENESS

In one significant respect, people's perceptions of their own (socially desirable) instrumental and expressive attributes differ radically from what has commonly been believed about the conjunction of these two personality dimensions. Data from self-report instruments in which ratings of instrumental and expressive attributes are scored separately indicate that far from being strongly correlated in a negative direction, scores on the two trait clusters are essentially orthogonal (e.g., Bem, 1974; Spence *et al.,* 1974, 1975). However, comparisons of males' and females' self-concepts on each dimension provide some confirmation of the stereotype: as a group, males perceive themselves as being somewhat more instrumental than do females, and females perceive themselves as being somewhat more expressive than do males. These basic findings have been reported within groups of males and females ranging from kindergarten children to mature adults (e.g., Bem, 1974; O'Connor, Mann, and Bardwick, 1978; Simms *et al.,* 1978; Hall, 1980; Feldman, Biringen, and Nash, 1981) and coming from a broad spectrum of ethnic and socioeconomic backgrounds (Spence and Helmreich, 1978; Romer and Cherry, 1980). Several cross-national studies (e.g., Block, 1973; Spence and Helmreich, 1978; Almeida, 1980; Diaz-Loving et al., 1981; Runge, Frey, Gollwitzer, Helmreich, and Spence, 1981) have reported similar results.

The combination of sex differences in instrumentality and expressiveness and the orthogonal relationship of these dimensions within each sex leads to differential frequencies of trait constellations in males and females. For example, when individuals are classified according to their position above or below the overall median on each dimension, members of each sex fall most frequently in the sex-typed category (relatively high instrumentality and relatively low expressiveness in the case of men and the obverse in the case of women) and least frequently in the cross-sex category. A substantial proportion of each sex, however, is relatively low on both dimensions or relatively high on both dimensions. The demonstration that men and women are capable of being androgynous (i.e., of exhibiting a high degree of both "masculine" instrumentality and "feminine" expressiveness) has generated much theoretical excitement and stimulated a flood of research aimed at exploring the implications of possession of both sets of characteristics.

Longitudinal data are not yet available to assess the stability of these sex-differentiating self-concepts over the life cycle. However, cross-sectional comparisons of groups tested with the same psychometric instrument suggest that self-concepts of instrumentality and expressiveness show some changes in response to changes in role responsibilities and other age-related factors (Abrahams, Feldman, and Nash, 1978; Spence and Helmreich, 1979; Feldman, Biringen, and Nash, 1981). Men, for example, tend to perceive themselves as somewhat more instrumental as they take on more and more adult responsibilities. Later in life (in the "grandparent stage") both men and women perceive themselves as more expressive than do younger individuals of their own sex, and women perceive themselves as more autonomous (Feldman *et al.,* 1981). Even these trends, however, are relatively small in magnitude and, overall, remarkably minor differences are observed in the means of each sex from adolescence to late middle age. These findings are consistent with the results of longitudinal studies (e.g., Block, 1977; Douglas and Arenberg, 1978; Costa, McCrae, and Arenberg, 1980) showing a high degree of stability over substantial periods of time in adults' self-concepts of their personality characteristics.

Descriptions or identifications of the self as instrumental and/or expressive may be represented in the cognitive structure as self-schema (Markus *et al.*, 1981). From this perspective, self-schema organized around the concepts of instrumentality and expressiveness may serve to categorize and interpret experience relevant to those schemata. In a recent study of the schema hypothesis, Markus *et al.* (1981) found that individuals who were identified as masculine, feminine, or androgynous schematics, according to their self-reports of their instrumental and expressive qualities, remembered more attributes that were relevant to their particular personality schemata, required shorter processing time to attribute relevant traits, and were able to supply more examples of behaviors directly relevant to those schemata. In contrast, individuals who in self-report were relatively low in instrumentality and expressiveness showed no evidence of using either of these trait domains as an organizing schema. Thus self-schema appear to serve an important role not only in self-definition but also in the processing and organization of external events. It should be noted that this two-dimensional conception of self-schema is consistent with the separation of instrumentality and expressiveness proposed here. It is not suggested (nor did Markus *et al.* find) that either masculine or feminine schematics are sensitive to all material that concerned gender. This position is contrary to one position (adopted by Bem, 1981) that implies not only a single, unidimensional schema encorporating both sets of gender-related traits but also a global gender schema in which instrumental and expressive traits are but one component.

PRESCRIPTIVE STEREOTYPES OF MEN AND WOMEN

In earlier as well as in later studies in which the attributes of the ideal man and woman or the ideal self have been assessed, most instrumental traits perceived as desirable in males and most expressive traits perceived as desirable in females have also been positively valued in members of the other sex (McKee and Sheriffs, 1959; Jenkins and Vroegh, 1969; Spence *et al.* 1974; Deutsch and Gilbert,

1976; Pleck, 1978). These ideal concepts show considerable similarity across age groups (Urberg and Labouvie-Vief, 1976; Urberg, 1979).

Experimental investigations (Kulik and Harackiewicz, 1979; Major, Carnevale and Deaux, 1981) of the likableness of males and females with various constellations of instrumental and expressive characteristics bear out the implications of these investigations. Both males and females described as being relatively high in both instrumentality and expressiveness were perceived as the most attractive; individuals described as high in instrumentality and low in expressiveness or the reverse were perceived as the next attractive group, and individuals low in both sets of qualities were perceived as the least attractive.

Although most instrumental and expressive traits are regarded as desirable to some degree in both men and women, some notable exceptions occur. For example, the qualities of dominance and aggressiveness are regarded as undesirable in women but not in men (Spence, Helmreich, and Stapp, 1974). In confirmation of these findings experimental data reported by Costrich, Feinstein, Kidder, Marecek, and Pascale (1975) indicate that women (but not men) who responded to provocation aggressively or who attempted to dominate a mixed-sex discussion group were rated less favorably than women whose behavior was less forceful.

In one of the few studies in which the relative values of instrumental and expressive attributes have been determined, male and female college students ranked a series of qualities, many referring to sex-stereotyped instrumental and expressive characteristics, in order of their importance as guiding principles to their own lives or to other members of their own sex (Unger and Siiter, 1974). The mean ranks produced by the two sexes were highly correlated, and instrumental and expressive qualities were interspersed evenly throughout the ranks. In adult samples, however, males ranked several instrumental attributes (independent, capable, ambitious) as the most valued; conversely, females ranked several expressive characteristics (loving, helpful) as the most valued (Siiter and Unger, cited in Unger, 1979). These sex differences in the relative values of personal qualities may reflect the major role commitments of these adult men and women, with men giving priority to their vocations and women to their families. Responsibility, a quality of importance to both sets of roles, was ranked high by both sexes.

Even among student groups, however, the intensity of instrumental and expressive attributes that are perceived as ideal varies with the sex of the target and the sex of the rater (Deutsch and Gilbert, 1976; Gilbert, Deutsch, and Strahan, 1978; Babledelis *et al.,* 1981; Gilbert, Waldroop, and Deutsch, 1981). Both men and women perceived the ideal man and the ideal woman as being higher in both instrumental traits and expressive traits than the self-ratings of each sex. Women, however, rated the ideal member of both sexes higher in expressiveness and the ideal woman higher in instrumentality than did men. Nonetheless, the male-female distinction tends to be preserved by both sexes; that is, men should be somewhat more instrumental than women and women should be somewhat more expressive than men.

In the Gilbert *et al.* (1978; 1981) studies, men and women were also asked to indicate their beliefs about what the other sex considered to be ideal in their own sex. Men were quite accurate in their descriptions of women's ideal man, including an appreciation of women's desire for a higher level of expressiveness in men than men wanted in themselves. Women, however, underestimated by a considerable margin the level of instrumentality men perceived as desirable in women. Similar findings were reported by Steinmann and Fox (1966) in a study of feminine role values; the women believed that men preferred women who were much more strongly family oriented and self-sacrificing than what men described as their ideal. Subsequent replications (Rappaport *et al.,* 1970; Voss and Skinner, 1975) showed no shifts in these perceptions across time. These discrepancies have interesting implications for the self-presentational strategies that women may use in interacting with men and thus for the perpetuation of exaggerated perceptions about sex differences in personality.

RELATIONSHIPS WITH SEX-ROLE ATTITUDES AND BEHAVIORS

Another indication of the pivotal position assigned to instrumentality and expressiveness in many theories about the nature of men and women and their interrelationships is the fact that they have been closely identified by many investigators with such global unidimensional concepts as masculinity-femininity, sex-role orientation, sex-role identification, or gender schemata. In fact, it has become popular to use self-report instruments primarily tapping instrumental and expressive attributes as measures of individual differences in the strength of sex-role orientation, gender schemata or other similar unidimensional constructs (e.g., Bem, 1979; 1981).

As ordinarily formulated, such concepts and the theories in which they are embedded are predicated on a common set of preconceptions; namely, that manifestations of all the attributes and behaviors normatively prescribed for men and women in a given society tend to covary and can be considered to be overt signs or diagnostic indicators of a single underlying continuum. Within each sex, individuals can thus be assigned a position along this hypothetical continuum, those who are highly sex typed or identified with their own sex falling at one extreme. These simple, straightforward assumptions are intuitively appealing and on the surface appear to be highly plausible, a fact which perhaps accounts for their popularity. However, inspection of the relevant empirical evidence indicates that they are highly suspect.

It should also be noted in passing that the contemporary investigators who have adopted these unidimensional concepts and have employed measures of instrumental and expressive characteristics to define these concepts operationally also claim that masculinity and femininity are independent. Thus these investigators are simultaneously advocating two incompatible theories, one predicated on the assumption that gender-related phenomena contribute to a single, bipolar factor and the other predicated on the assumption that these phenomena contribute to two independent factors (Spence, 1984; Spence and Helmreich, 1981).

In general, the literature suggests that the diverse collection of attributes, attitudes, and behaviors differentiating the sexes are multidimensional rather than unidimensional or bidimensional (e.g., Wakefield *et al.,* 1976). More particularly, men's and women's ratings of their instrumental and expressive qualities have little to do with their direct ratings of their own masculinity or femininity (e.g., Pedhazur and Tetenbaum, 1979), and mentions of these qualities infrequently appear in individuals' spontaneous descriptions of their masculinity or femininity (Spence and Sawin, 1985). Furthermore, within each sex only weak relationships obtain between individuals' perceptions of their instrumentality and expressiveness and their sex-role attitudes, their responsiveness to situationally induced sex-role demands, or their preference for several types of stereotypical masculine and feminine tasks (e.g., Bem and Lenney, 1976; Orlofsky, Aslin, and Ginsburg, 1977; Spence and Helmreich, 1978; Helmreich, Spence, and Holahan, 1979; Klein and Willerman, 1979; Spence, Helmreich, and Sawin, 1980). Other evidence (e.g., Baumrind, 1971, 1982; Spence and Helmreich, 1978) suggests that differences in instrumentality and expressiveness between and within each sex have complex developmental histories. For example, within each sex, instrumentality and expressiveness have been found to be related to such factors as parental personality and patterns of child rearing practices but not to parental emphasis on sex-role behaviors (e.g., discouraging play with nonstereotypic toys). Thus, in contrast to the implications of developmental theories implying that all gender-differentiating attributes and behaviors have a common etiology or flow from a single self-concept, such as sex-role identification, the data suggest that the origins of individual differences in these trait domains are typically quite independent of the origins of other gender-linked phenomena. Thus the fact that individuals' instrumentality and expressiveness are often untrustworthy clues to their sex-role attitudes and behaviors becomes intelligible.

At the same time, men's and women's self-perceptions of these trait dimensions have been demonstrated to have implications for behaviors that call upon instrumental or expressive qualities, or both. An example may be found in a series of laboratory studies conducted by Ickes and his colleagues (Ickes and Barnes, 1977, 1978; Ickes, Schermer, and Steeno, 1979; Ickes, 1981) on short-term dyadic interactions. Because of their potential significance for male-female relationships, these studies and the theoretical model they inspired will be described in some detail.

In common with a number of other investigators, Ickes (1981) has used the term "sex-role orientation" as a generic label for the two orthogonal trait dimensions, instrumentality and expressiveness, and has identified different constellations of instrumentality and expressiveness by gender-related labels. Although Ickes' (1981) discussion occasionally suggests that "sex role orientation" implies something more than instrumentality and expressiveness per se these implications are not clearly spelled out or incorporated into his theory.

The basic paradigm of the studies conducted by Ickes and his colleagues involved observation of the interaction between two previously unacquainted students who believed they were waiting for an experiment to begin. Earlier all subjects had been given a self-report measure of instrumentality and expressiveness and were paired on the basis of these scores. According to the Ickes (1981) model, dyads become maximally involved in an interaction (as assessed by self-report and such behavioral measures as talking, smiling, and gaze) when both instrumental and the expressive qualities are applied. In general, the results of the Ickes *et al.* studies support this

prediction. Observed interactions were most active and intense in dyads in which both members were androgynous, that is, high in both instrumental and expressive qualities. Dyads composed of two sex-typed men (i.e., men high only in instrumentality) or two sex-typed women (i.e., women high only in expressiveness) were less actively involved. Similarly, pairs composed of a sex-typed man and a sex-typed woman also showed less involvement than the androgynous dyads.

A second, and more subtle, assumption made by Ickes (1981) is that an individual's satisfaction with an interaction is dependent on the degree to which the level of dyadic involvement is matched to the individual's level of expressiveness. Thus individuals high in expressiveness should be most satisfied when the level of interaction is high; in contrast, individuals low in expressiveness should be most satisfied when the level of involvement is low. The results (Ickes *et al.,* 1979; Lamke and Bell, reported in Ickes, 1981) generally confirmed these predictions: Sex-typed male dyads were generally satisfied with their low level of involvement; in contrast, sex-typed female dyads were *dissatisfied* with their similarly low levels of involvement. Androgynous pairs of both sexes generally reported the highest level of satisfaction, an outcome of some significance. However, this outcome also suggests the incompleteness of Ickes' model: Since the level of expressiveness in the members of these pairs matched the level of their involvement in the dyadic interaction, their satisfaction should have equaled that in the other pairs in which the degrees of expressiveness and involvement were similar (such as two sex-typed males).

The basic propositions in the Ickes model yield predictions that are independent of the sex of the individuals in the dyad. Nonetheless, the model has crucial implications for the relationships between men and women, including marital relationships. Particularly interesting are the predictions for the mixed-sex dyad in which both members are sex typed in personality; that is, the woman is high in expressiveness but not instrumentality, and the man is the reverse. In contrast to hypotheses about the benefits of need or role complementarity, the Ickes model suggests that the low level of involvement in such dyads will lead to dissatisfaction, at least on the part of the woman. (Additional assumptions are required to predict the man's degree of satisfaction). Data from married couples, to be reviewed in a later section, provide some support for this speculation.

Instrumentality and expressiveness are thus not without implications for male-female relationships or role enactments. However, our assessment of the literature suggests that theorists have underrated both the complexity and the specificity of the relationships between personality dimensions and particular sex-role behaviors and preferences. Furthermore, even in instances in which these trait dimensions do contribute to, or are correlated with, role-related performances, the relationships are not always intuitively obvious *a priori.* For example, a study of married couples (Nyquist *et al.,* in press) found that the higher the wife's expressiveness (a "feminine" characteristic) the more her husband shared with her responsibility for routine "feminine" chores within the household.

SEX ROLES AND INTERPERSONAL BEHAVIORS

SELF-PRESENTATIONAL STRATEGIES

Descriptive stereotypes of males and females may be transformed into prescriptive roles—sets of expectations about what the typical male and female should do in a given situation. To the extent that these role expectations are communicated to the individual, differences between male and female behavior may result. It is important to realize, however, that these observed differences in behavior are not necessarily the result of different personality characteristics for men and women but may instead result from differing expectations that elicit different behaviors from a potentially similar repetoire of behavioral responses. Thus sex-role expectations may serve as a self-fulfilling prophecy, producing evidence of their "veridicality" through the application of differential pressures on the male and female.

The pervasive communication of sex-role expectations in our society certainly allows for the possibility of internalization of these norms, and hence sex-role behaviors may be performed in the absence of any direct role pressures. However, there is a growing body of evidence suggesting that specific situational influences are extremely powerful and may determine many of the apparent sex differences that are observed. In effect, then, we may be dealing with a set of self-presentational strategies that are selected on the basis of situational demands.

The literature on social influence can be considered one example of the possible operation of such strategies. Traditionally, it has been assumed that women are more easily influenced than men, changing their attitudes more readily than men in response to persuasive communica-

tions and conforming more frequently in the face of divergent group opinion. Claims that such sex differences exist are frequently found in many standard social psychology texts (Eagly, 1978). However, careful reviews of the literature (Eagly, 1978; Cooper, 1979; Eagly and Carli, 1981) suggest that sex differences are somewhat less pervasive than previously thought. For example, conformity experiments in which pressure to conform is manipulated by paper-and-pencil norms rather than by direct group pressure do not show reliable sex differences. In contrast, in those conformity situations that involve social interaction (i.e., where conformity pressure is manipulated by the opinions of other group members) a pattern of greater conformity by women than by men has been demonstrated (Eagly, 1978; Cooper, 1979; Eagly and Carli, 1981). Such findings suggest that in the presence of other people, women and/or men may be consciously choosing a presentational strategy that results in an apparent sex difference in how they are influenced by social conditions. Similarly, studies of reward allocation and perceived justice show no differences when men and women are acting as observers but evidence fairly consistent sex differences when males and females determine their own rewards in actual interactions (Deaux, 1976a; Major and Deaux, 1982).

Complicating the picture is the report by Eagly and Carli (1981) that sex differences bear some relationship to the sex of the author. Thus, studies that find that women are more easily influenced than men are more likely to be authored by males; similarly, studies showing that women have greater nonverbal decoding skill than men are more likely to be reported by female authors. These observed patterns certainly suggest caution in the interpretation of all sex-role findings in a period when politics and science are concerned with similar issues.

The influence of role expectations on an individual's self-presentation is shown more directly in studies in which these expectations were explicitly conveyed. Zanna and Pack (1975) led one group of female students to anticipate an interaction with an attractive male who held either traditional or nontraditional views of the ideal woman. In comparison to the self-descriptions they gave prior to the experimental session, those women who anticipated a traditional partner described themselves as more feminine and less intelligent, whereas women who anticipated interaction with an attractive male partner who had nontraditional views of women described themselves as less feminine. In contrast, women in the same experiment who anticipated interaction with an unattractive male showed little change in self-description in response to the traditional or nontraditional attitudes of the partner. In a second study by Zanna and his colleagues (vonBaeyer, Sherk, and Zanna, 1979), female subjects role played a job interview with a male interviewer whom they had previously been told was either traditional or nontraditional in his views of women. The dependent variable was "feminine" self-presentation, assessed by the woman's clothing, makeup, accessories, and her attractiveness as rated by the interviewer. Those women who expected to meet a traditional interviewer were more "feminine" in their appearance than those who expected a nontraditional interviewer. They were also rated as more physically attractive by the interviewer who was blind to the experimental conditions.

Additional evidence of the importance of sex-role expectations to the self-presentation of women is provided by Skrypnek and Snyder (1982). Male subjects were told that their partner (in reality, always a female) was either a male, described as having certain masculine characteristics, or a female, described as having certain feminine characteristics. The two subjects, who could neither see nor hear each other, were asked to negotiate a division of labor for a series of tasks that were either male associated, female associated, or neutral. In making their initial choices, male perceivers made significantly more masculine choices for themselves when they believed their partner was a female than when they thought she was a male. More significant is the behavior of the female targets, who had no information about the sex of their partners. Women whose partners believed them to be female chose more feminine tasks than did the women whose partners believed they were male, even when the women were free to initiate choices apart from the partner's initial pressures. It is important, however, to note that overall the average choices of all female subjects were more feminine than masculine.

Such tactics of self-presentation in response to expectations of others are not limited to women. Fried and Major (1980) asked both male and female students to describe themselves to an attractive opposite-sex person who expressed preference for either stereotypical masculine or feminine characteristics. In general, the results showed that both sexes moderated their self-descriptions to the same degree in response to the preferences of their partner for an individual of the other sex. Some recent findings on social influence suggest that men may be even more prone to use self-presentational tactics in some situations than are women. Comparing public and private conformity behaviors, Eagly, Wood, and Fishbaugh (1981) found that women's conformity behavior was relatively unaffected by conditions of surveillance. Men, in contrast, were significantly less likely to conform when their opinions would be known by the other group members than when they would not, suggesting that presenting oneself as independent may be an important concern for men in a public setting.

ROLE-PERSONALITY INTERACTIONS

In both the Skrypnek and Snyder (1982) and the vonBaeyer *et al.* (1979) studies, data were also obtained on a self-report measure that largely tapped instrumental and expressive personality traits. The tacit assumption was that individuals who are sex typed in these personality dimensions are similarly sex typed in their role behaviors and preferences, and thus they would be more responsive to the experimental manipulations. However, women's self-presentational strategies had little or no relationship to the personality measures. Similarly, Eagly *et al.* (1981) found no relationships in either sex between the subjects' instrumentality and expressiveness and their measures of conformity.

These findings give added weight to the distinction between gender-related personality characteristics, on the one hand, and role-related tasks and behaviors, on the other. Many tasks in our society have been labeled as either masculine or feminine, although these labels may have little to do with specific instrumental or expressive traits necessary to perform the behaviors. Such tasks, do however, exert strong messages about who should do the task (rather than how it should be done). Some occupations, for example, have become identified as either "masculine" or "feminine," and these expectations continue to affect the entrance of men and women into these occupations (e.g., Heilman, 1979).

The trait-role distinction is illustrated by Megargee's (1969) classic study of dominance leadership choices among college students. Mixed-sex and same-sex dyads were formed in which one member was high and the other member was low in assessed dominance, a "masculine" characteristic. In same-sex dyads and, even more strongly, in mixed-sex dyads in which the male was high, the dominant individual was far more likely to be chosen as the leader. However, in mixed-sex dyads in which personality and role expectations were noncongruent, the low dominant male emerged as the leader in the majority of pairs. Illustrating the complexity of the trait-role interaction was the finding that typically the high dominant female determined the choice of her less dominant male partner as "leader" and thus manipulated the situation so that sex-role expectations were upheld. A more recent study (Nyquist and Spence, 1984) has found similar results; despite shifts towards greater egalitarianism in professed sex-role attitudes among students, role-governed rules for behavior continue to exert an effect.

The role-trait interaction is further illustrated by a study (Klein and Willerman, 1979) in which the dominance behaviors of female subjects were observed during a problem-solving session with male or female confederates. In general, dominance behaviors were correlated with self-report measures of dominance and instrumentality (but not expressiveness). Situational pressures were evident above and beyond these individual difference factors, however. In the absence of specific instructions, all women were less dominant with male confederates than with female confederates. In contrast, when the women were instructed to be as dominant and assertive as possible, no difference in dominance behaviors with male and female confederates was observed, regardless of their personality traits. Thus implicit sex-role expectations appear to be pervasive, although they may be canceled out by specific instructional sets.

Although they show substantial independence from many behaviors that are directly influenced by *role* expectations, instrumentality and expressiveness are often reflected in forms of verbal and nonverbal communication that are regarded as "masculine" and "feminine." Investigators have found a relationship within each sex between a person's self-images of instrumentality or expressiveness (or a combination thereof) and the display of stereotypical masculine and feminine nonverbal behaviors (Ickes and Barnes, 1978; La France and Carmen, 1980). Thus men and women who report themselves as high in interpersonally oriented expressive traits are more likely to gaze while speaking and to smile while not speaking but are less likely to fill pauses than are individuals who score low in expressiveness (La France and Carmen, 1980). Again, however, as in the case of the Klein and Willerman (1979) study, it has been shown that specific situational factors can affect the nonverbal behavior of all persons, whatever their particular combination of instrumentality and expressiveness. Two recent studies (La France and Carmen, 1980; Putnam and McCallister, 1980) have systematically varied the demands of the interaction setting, in one case stressing expressiveness (a discussion topic concerning emotions or shared reactions to loneliness) and in the other case stressing more instrumental aspects (formal argumentation and effective presentation of a case or the planning of a military rescue mission). In both studies, the majority of subjects showed more expressive behaviors in the former situation and more instrumental behaviors in the latter situation, although the level of these behaviors varied as a function of the individual's assessed expressiveness and instrumentality.

RELATIONSHIPS BETWEEN SEX ROLES AND STATUS

A number of investigators have explored the parallels between the nonverbal behaviors differentiating the sexes during male-female interactions and the same behaviors that manifest themselves during interactions of same-sex individuals of unequal status. A number of behaviors, such as the initiation of touch, have been specifically linked with the perceptions and inferences of power and status (Major, 1981); many of these same differences are also found in male–female interactions. Henley (1977) has postulated that, as in situations in which same-sex individuals differ in status, men's behaviors represent the attempt to dominate, while women's behaviors reflect complementary submissiveness.

There is evidence that people perceive sharp differences in the extent and form of power used by males and females. Relying on Raven's (1965) analysis of power bases, Johnson (1976) asked subjects to indicate the likelihood that the user of a particular influence form was either a male or a female. Subjects were significantly more likely to assume a male as the source of coercion, legitimate power, expert power, and informational influence. Women, in turn, were more likely to be seen as using personal reward or sexuality as the basis for power. As Johnson (1978) points out, higher status people are generally more likely to have access to concrete resources, education, and money—those very factors that make viable coercive, legitimate, expert, and informational power.

Within male-female interactions, differences in the use of power are also evident. In confirmation of the hypothesis that a status difference is typically invoked with gender, Radecki and Jennings (1980) found that males report using more dominance behaviors toward their female coworkers than females do toward their male coworkers. Falbo and Peplau (1980), exploring the self-reported power strategies used by males and females in intimate heterosexual relationship, found that males were more likely to report the use of bilateral and direct approaches; in contrast women described using more unilateral and indirect techniques of influence. Assessing the sex-role attitudes of dating couples in conjunction with their reported use of power, Peplau (1979) found that couples with more traditional sex-role attitudes assigned greater power to the male partner, whereas couples with more liberal attitudes were more likely to report an equal sharing of power.

These findings underline the relationship between gender and status. More generally, we might assume that if gender typically invokes perceptions of differential status, then males and females might select strategies that would be consistent with the perceived power differential. Once again, the result would be observed sex differences that would be influenced by factors other than basic personality differences between the male and female. Such an interpretation is consistent with, and indeed explained more thoroughly by, the expectation-states theory developed by Berger and his associates (Berger, Rosenholtz, and Zelditch, 1980). According to the expectation-states theory, gender serves as a status characteristic that creates predictable expectation states. These expectations, which emerge in appropriate relational contexts, can determine the kind of interaction that takes place and in the process will confirm and maintain their own existence. In other words, beliefs about the differences between the sexes will serve as a self-fulfilling prophecy, providing both observers and participants with evidence for their beliefs.

MANAGEMENT AND LEADERSHIP

Although women now compose a large percentage of the work force, their representation in managerial and leadership roles is disproportionately low: 15 percent of male workers hold managerial positions in contrast to only 7 percent of women workers (U.S. Bureau of the Census, 1982). Historically, active discrimination has barred women from traditionally masculine leadership roles, thus relegating them to "women's jobs" that have a lower status in the work force. Even after more than a decade of equal opportunity and affirmative action legislation and programs, women's penetration of the man-

agerial strata of organizations remains slight, and those who occupy such positions are seen as uniquely qualified in contrast with males of equivalent status (Hennig and Jardim, 1977).

PERSONALITY FACTORS

Riger and Galligan (1980) have observed that the literature on women in management has concentrated on "person-centered" explanations of women's lower attainment that stress their deficits in necessary traits and socialization experiences. One of the most widely voiced explanations has been that women suffer from a "fear of success." According to this hypothesis, women's achievement behaviors are inhibited by a stable dispositional tendency to avoid success brought about by realization of the negative social sanctions that adhere to successful accomplishment, especially in traditionally masculine domains (Horner, 1968). Subsequent research has shown that "fear of success" is found in males as well as females and is more accurately conceptualized as a situationally linked expectation rather than as a personality trait (see reviews by Zuckerman and Wheeler, 1975; Tresemer, 1977). For example, Cherry and Deaux (1978) found much more evidence of fear of success among both male and female subjects in evaluations of students training for nontraditional, "gender inappropriate" vocations (e.g. males in nursing school, females in medical school). Furthermore, measures of "fear of success" have little predictive validity with regard to actual performance (e.g., Helmreich and Spence, 1978).

Although the stable-trait conception of "fear of success" has been found wanting as an explanatory mechanism for the differential attainment of women, evidence does suggest that role expectations may lead women to avoid acceptance of nontraditional roles, particularly in interactions with men, even if they are otherwise qualified. This tendency was demonstrated in the studies by Megargee (1969) and Nyquist and Spence (1984), described earlier, in which women students allowed men to assume a leadership role even when the women were high dominant in personality and the men low. In both field and laboratory situations neither women nor men generally expect women to fill leadership roles (Lockheed, 1977; Inderlied and Powell, 1979). Similarly, in a study in which leaders of experimental groups were asked to make nominations for leaders of future groups, women were less likely to name themselves (Eskilson and Wiley, 1976).

As outlined previously, a plausible explanation for the avoidance of nontraditional roles is that individuals fear social rejection and dislike violating role expectations. In view of attitudinal shifts, these fears may have less basis in reality than they once had. A number of studies in the interpersonal attraction literature provide evidence on this issue. In the usual paradigm, student subjects are given descriptions of a female (or occasionally male) stimulus person who is stereotypically masculine or feminine in interests and competent or incompetent in his or her chosen area (Spence and Helmreich, 1972b; Deaux, 1972; Spence, Helmreich and Stapp, 1975b). In these and similar studies, the respondents' sex-role attitudes have been found to influence their ratings of the likableness of stimulus persons; those with traditional sex-role attitudes are less accepting of individuals with nonstereotypic interests (Spence and Helmreich, 1972b; Seyfried and Hendrick, 1973; Spence *et al.,* 1975b; Costrich *et al.,* 1975). Overall, the likableness of both males and females is associated with *competence* and with *masculine* vocational and avocational interests. The latter finding suggests the generally higher value that is associated with male-dominated activities.

Although the evidence suggests that able women with nontraditional aspirations are not derogated, the data also indicate that they are not necessarily accepted wholeheartedly. A study of Kristal, Sanders, Spence and Helmreich (1975) demonstrated that competent, aspiring women are liked only if they exhibit other attributes and interests that are "feminine." Males are also likely to be ambivalent about their social involvement with competent women, on the one hand, enjoying the stimulation of the relationship and, on the other, feeling a threat to role expectations of male dominance (Komarovsky, 1979).

Another person-centered explanation of women's failure to achieve vocationally implicates deficiencies in achievement-related motives. Hoffman (1975), for example, has proposed that women have higher affiliative needs and, simultaneously, weaker intrinsic achievement motives than men. Thus, the sexes are assumed to differ in sources of job satisfaction and in the kind of job responsibilities they are willing or able to undertake.

Helmreich and Spence (1978) have found that instrumental characteristics are related to two components of achievement motivation, interpersonal competitiveness and mastery needs (striving for performance excellence and preference for challenging tasks). As can be anticipated from the finding that women perceive themselves as less instrumental than do men, women also report being less competitive and having somewhat weaker mastery needs than men. Helmreich and Spence (1978) also found that selected samples of women in demanding, traditionally masculine roles (e.g. businesswomen with master's degree in business, scientists with doctoral degrees, and successful athletes) are higher than unselected samples of women on instrumentality and mastery needs and tend to be similar to their male peers in these respects. Their greater instrumentality and mastery needs, however, are *not* gained at the expense of their expressivity.

In addition, women in these demanding roles continue to be less interpersonally competitive than their male counterparts. Although this sex difference would appear to give men some advantage, these investigators (Spence and Helmreich, 1983) have also found with several groups that competitiveness is a *negative* predictor of attainment, for example, salary in businesspersons, eminence in scientists as reflected by citations to published work, and academic performance by students.

These findings could be used to argue that even though achieving women do not differ from men in these several achievement-related traits, men are normatively advantaged because of their higher baseline scores in the general population. However, sex differences on these characteristics are small in comparison with the variability *within* each sex, and sex-linked personality differences do not appear to account for many of the observed discrepancies in vocational attainment, such as reaching managerial status (Brenner and Greenhaus, 1979).

SITUATIONAL CONSTRAINTS

Stereotypes about sex differences may operate as external barriers to women's advancement. Despite increasing egalitarianism in societal attitudes about women's place in the work force, stereotypes depicting men but not women as possessing the requisite characteristics for managerial and leadership roles persist (McGregor, 1967; Lockheed, 1977). Schein (1973), for example, asked male middle managers to rate the traits and behaviors of "men in general", "women in general", and "successful managers in general." The ratings of "men" and "successful managers" were highly similar. In contrast, the ratings of "women" had little in common with ratings of either "men" or "successful managers." A similar but less differentiated pattern of results was also reported by Schein (1975) in a replication using female managers as respondents. Massengill and DiMarco

(1979) found that this pattern of masculine stereotypes of managers persisted even in the late 1970s.

Also reflecting a differential stereotype of males and females are the patterns of attributions given to account for successful performance by the two sexes on nonfeminine tasks. Experimental studies indicate that successful performance by a man is attributed more to ability than is an equivalent performance by a woman. In contrast, attributions to effort, ease of task, or luck are generally made more strongly for a woman's successful performance than for a man's. These effects are found both in the evaluation of others and in self-reports (Feldman-Summers and Kiesler, 1974; Deaux and Emswiller, 1974; Deaux, 1976a; Deaux and Farris, 1977; Rosenfield and Stephan, 1978). In an important corollary to these attributional results, Heilman and Guzzo (1978) found that managers consider pay raises appropriate rewards for success achieved because of effort; however, promotion, which typically is accompanied by greater pay, is preferred only when success is seen as resulting from ability.

Stereotypes about the correlates of physical attractiveness may also lead to attributions unfavorable to women. Berscheid and Walster (1974) have demonstrated the ubiquity of attractiveness stereotypes and that attractive people are generally favored in society. However, because of connotations of sexuality and incompetence, attractive women may be penalized professionally. Heilman and Saruwatani (1979), for example, found that attractive female applicants were at a disadvantage in applying for managerial positions. Attractive male applicants and *unattractive* females were rated higher on such job-related, traditionally "masculine" attributes as ambition, decisiveness, and rationality.

Difficulties in obtaining mentors may also hamper women in male-dominated fields such as the military, higher management, and science. Zuckerman (1977) and Roche (1979) have stressed the importance of the mentor role in facilitating the scientific and managerial achievement of younger individuals. The rarity of females in management limits the possibility of same-sex mentors and role models. Furthermore, men appear hesitant in adopting the mentor role vis-a-vis young female managers (Hennig and Jardim, 1977; Roche, 1979). One reason may be that men's stereotyped views about women lead them to believe that the probability of their failure is too high. Another may be that male mentors fear that they may be subject to charges of sexual involvement and exploitation, particularly when the woman is physically attractive.

It has been suggested that women's advancement in management may be further hampered by the unwillingness of some female managers to sponsor young women in their organizations. This "queen bee syndrome" allegedly represents the resistance of successful women to sacrificing their uniqueness in a male-dominated domain (Staines, Tavris, and Jayaratne, 1974). However, Terborg, *et al.* (1977) report that highly achieving women are more favorable to the advancement of women in management than are women in less prestigious positions.

The reluctance of males, perceived or real, to work under the leadership of women may also increase resistance to the assignment of managerial roles to women. Bowman, Worthy and Greyser (1965) reported that 86 percent of male and 77 percent of female executives believe that men are uncomfortable working for women. Runge, Helmreich, and Wilhem (1981), in a survey of the personal attitudes of merchant marine officers and crew, reported less dramatic figures: 21 percent of officers and 32 percent of crew disliked working with women aboard ship. The majority of these respondents had experience in mixed-sex crews.

Kanter (1977) has argued that another barrier to women may be created by their relative scarcity in managerial positions. When the presence of a woman as a role incumbent is rare, such "tokens" may be much more carefully and critically evaluated and pressured to conform to stereotypes. In confirmation of this suggestion, Taylor and Fiske (1978) have demonstrated that salience (in terms of numerical infrequency) leads to exaggerated perceptions of prominence and to more extreme evaluations. Taylor, *et al.* (1978) also found that the fewer of either males or females who were present in a group, the more likely the minority sex members were to be perceived as playing out a sex-typed role.

SEX DIFFERENCES IN PERFORMANCE

The literature on female performance in leadership roles is a morass of conflicting results. A number of studies find no sex effects, while others show gender differences and provide support for the impact of expectancies and self-fulfilling prophecies. Osborn and Vicars (1976) have suggested that many gender effects in behavior show up in laboratory and not in field settings; they may be artifacts of the laboratory situation where greater control may yield significant sex differences even when such differences account for a very minor proportion of the observed variance. The short-term, constrained environment of the laboratory may also make salient visible markers of uniqueness, such as gender. In actual work situations, managers and subordinates have more information about individual capabilities and personal styles through their involvement in long-term, ongoing interactions (Feild and Caldwell, 1979). Brown (1979), in a review of thirty-two studies contrasting male and female leaders, concludes that studies using students as subjects are more likely to find sex differences in leadership supporting the female stereotype (e.g., women more considerate, communicative) than are studies conducted in genuine work situations. When situational and demographic factors are controlled, sex differences tend to be greatly attenuated. Controlling for type of occupation, amount of training, and level in the hierarchy eliminated sex differences in performance in several organizational studies (Bartol, 1976; Brief and Oliver, 1976). Similarly, Osborn and Vicars (1976) found no sex differences in job performance after controlling for age, education, and experience.

The contribution of familiarity is illustrated in a study by Schein and Bartol (1980) who investigated emergent leadership in fifty-two task groups formed from students in a course in management. After fifteen weeks of men and women working together, no significant differences were found in the proportion of males and females who emerged as leaders through sociometric choice. Performance of groups led by males and females was equivalent, and the behavioral correlates of the process of emergent leadership were similar for both male and female leaders.

However, self-fulfilling prophecies continue to operate and may be especially likely in fields in which women are just beginning to enter. A particularly informative demonstration is found in a study of the integration of female cadets into the U.S. Military Academy at West Point conducted by Rice, Bender and Vitters (1980). These investigators found that leaders and followers of each sex rated male leaders of work groups as more focussed on task performance than female group leaders. Because peer ratings of this sort are a standard part of the West Point training program, the obtained results have more ecological validity than studies in which individuals are aware that they are research subjects. As part of the same project, Rice *et al.* (1980) varied the composition of cadet work groups unbeknown to the participants. All groups had three male followers; one-half of the groups were led by an appointed female leader and one-half by an appointed male leader. The groups were further split so that one-half contained male group members who had liberal sex-role attitudes and one-half

contained males with more traditional attitudes. Groups composed of liberal males responded equivalently in their ratings of male and female leaders. Groups composed of traditional males, on the other hand, rated the group atmosphere as more positive when led by males and attributed the success of male leaders to hard work and follower cooperation. In contrast, traditional males attributed the female leaders' success to luck. Personal attitudes about the appropriateness of roles for the sexes thus appeared to form a special kind of expectancy that influenced evaluations of females as leaders. Both the sex of the leader and sex-role attitudes influenced the objectively measured performance of the groups on both structured and unstructured tasks. Overall, groups led by males performed better than those led by females. There was an additional significant interaction between follower sex-role attitudes and task structure. Groups with liberal sex-role attitudes performed better on unstructured tasks; in contrast, traditional groups were superior on structured tasks.

Overall, stereotypes and attributions about the lesser effectiveness of women as leaders remain relatively pervasive but have little empirical support in the work place. Nonetheless, the cumulative effects of these perceptions continue to hinder the advancement of women into managerial and leadership roles. The constraints on women may be externally imposed through conscious or unconscious discrimination by authorities or self-imposed through internalization of stereotyped beliefs, the lowering of aspirations, and the reduction of goal-oriented activities.

MARITAL INTERACTIONS

MATE SELECTION AND MARITAL SATISFACTION: THE CONTRIBUTION OF PERSONALITY AND SEX-ROLE ATTITUDES

Classic sex-role theories that emphasize the functional value of role reciprocity in husband-wife relationships and the contribution of instrumental and expressive qualities to role enactment would seem to imply that men and women who are sex typed in these aspects of their personalities would also be romantically attracted to each other. Winch (1963) has advanced this hypothesis as a specific version of his more general theory of complementarity in mate selection (Winch, Kitsanses, and Kitsanses, 1954). This theory essentially states that men and women choose as partners those whose personalities are different from their own and who can therefore complement each other's needs in the marital relationship.

The expressed preferences of single college students for their future spouses, however, are more supportive of the alternative similarity hypothesis (Orlofsky, 1979; Sawin, 1982). Within each sex, positive correlations are found between respondents' self-concepts of instrumentality and expressiveness and the degrees to which they consider both instrumentality and expressiveness desirable in their future spouse. The findings thus parallel results of studies in which respondents are given more general instructions to rate the ideal member of the opposite sex.

The resemblance of married couples to these professed ideals is faint. In confirmation of prior studies (e.g., Murstein, 1961; Banta and Hetherington, 1963) showing that partners' personalities tend to be similar rather than complementary, slight positive correlations have generally been found between husbands' and wives' perception of their own instrumentality and expressiveness (Antill, 1980, 1983; Sawin, 1982). When husbands and wives are each classified into categories determined by the median split method, there is a tendency for men and women who are high in their self-concepts of instrumentality and expressiveness or, conversely, who perceive themselves as low in both dimensions to be married to each other somewhat more frequently than would be indicated by random selection (Spence and Helmreich, 1978; Shaver, Pullis, and Olds, 1980; Sawin, 1982; Antill, 1983). The most frequent couple combination in most samples is one in which each partner is conventionally sex typed in personality (the husband is relatively high in instrumentality and relatively low in expressiveness and his wife the reverse). However, the occurrence of this traditional couple type is about at the chance level, its high frequency being attributable solely to the fact that the sex-typed constellation of degrees of instrumentality and expressiveness is most frequent within each sex. Other, more conspicuous characteristics, such as physical attractiveness and similar interests and values, appear to have a more salient influence on mate selection than these personality dimensions.

These personality variables do, however, contribute to marital happiness (Parelman, 1980; Shaver, Pullis, and Olds, 1980; Antill, 1983). Particularly striking is the role of expressiveness: Men and women who perceive their partners or whose partners perceive themselves as interpersonally oriented and responsive to others' needs are more satisfied with their marriage than those whose

mates are relatively nonexpressive. In both married and unmarried individuals, instrumentality has been found to contribute to the person's own personal adjustment and ability to cope with stress (e.g., Jones, Chernovetz, and Hansson, 1978; Spence and Helmreich, 1978; Shaver *et al.*, 1980). Thus, in effect, couples in which both husband and wife are relatively high in both instrumentality and expressiveness are most likely to be satisfied both with their marriage and with their life.

Contrary to conventional wisdom, couples in which both partners are sex typed in their personality are one of the least happy of all couple types, as indicated by both husbands' and wives' ratings of marital satisfaction (Antill, 1980; Shaver *et al.*, 1980). The Shaver *et al.* study suggests that the relationship may be especially difficult for women. Sex-typed women married to men they perceive as sex typed report the most symptoms of stress (tiring easily, being sad or depressed, feeling worthless) and the greatest dissatisfaction with their life as a whole. Marital satisfaction also tends to be low in dyads in which the husband is relatively low in both instrumentality and expressiveness or in which the wife exhibits this pattern and her husband is low in expressiveness, whatever his level of instrumentality.

These findings indicate that the joint personality characteristics of the couple are important determinants of marital and general life satisfaction. However, research to date on the contributions of instrumentality and expressiveness to marital satisfaction has been primarily descriptive. Yet to be developed and tested are theories identifying the dynamics of the marital relationship that mediate between the personality characteristics of husband and wife and the satisfaction of each. A promising beginning may be provided by an elaboration of the model, described earlier, that was developed by Ickes and his colleagues (Ickes, 1981) in their studies of short-term dyadic interactions between unacquainted individuals. The basic idea that satisfaction is generated by a match between the partner's level of expressiveness and preferred level of dyadic involvement may prove to be especially useful in advancing our understanding of marital contentment.

Studies of dating and of married couples also indicate a modest degree of congruence between partners in their sex-role attitudes (Spence and Helmreich, 1972, 1978; Peplau, Rubin, and Hill, 1974; Antill, Cotton, and Tindale, 1983). Relatively little is known, however, about the influence of marital satisfaction of the partners' sex-role attitudes or the division of domestic responsibilities the couple has worked out. Centers, Raven and Rodriques (1971) related spouses' ratings of marital satisfaction to a measure of decision making. Congruent with the respondents of other investigations, most couples reported that they were approximately equal in overall power. Households in which the wife was reported as clearly dominant occurred in only about 4 percent of their sample. Both husbands and wives in this small group in which the wife was the primary decision maker were less likely to be satisfied with their marriage than those in which decision making was shared or primarily assumed by the husband. Apparently wives are as discontented with husbands who allow or force them to take over the traditional leadership role as men who abdicate this role are with themselves or with their wives.

In a study of graduate students and their spouses, Parelman (1980) reported that although men's and women's general sex-role attitudes affected behavioral patterns of marital interaction, these attitudes were uncorrelated with overall marital satisfaction. Antill, Cotton and Tindale (1983) questioned a group of couples that was heterogeneous in age and education specifically about their own marital role expectations, primarily in the area of decision making. Husband's role attitudes were moderately correlated with their wives' marital happiness; the women were more pleased with their marriage when their husbands were egalitarian in their attitudes. Husbands with egalitarian attitudes were also somewhat more likely than husbands with traditional attitudes to assume some of the responsibility for routine "feminine" tasks within the household. One may speculate that when men are willing both to share power with their wives and to help with household chores, their wives are more likely to be content.

Husbands' satisfaction, on the other hand, was related to their wives' role attitudes only in the case of men with traditional attitudes. Traditional husbands expressed less contentment with their marriages when their wives were egalitarian than when their wives were also traditional in their attitude.

CURRENT DIVISIONS OF HOUSEHOLD LABOR AND THEIR CORRELATES

As noted earlier, sex-role attitudes have become more liberal in recent years. Both men and women are now more likely to indicate acceptance not only of the married woman having paid employment but also of the man helping with domestic tasks that have traditionally been assigned to women. In the case of women's employment, available statistics suggest that attitudinal shifts are paralleled by behavioral changes. Less readily available are statistics on the actual sharing of household responsibilities. Are household tasks that were traditionally assigned to the male, or more often, to the female now being shared in a manner indicated by the attitudinal shifts? Even more particularly, do husbands of working women participate in houshold duties to a greater extent than husbands of full-time housewives, or have employed women merely broadened their responsibilities with no greater sharing of roles?

Specific time estimates of husbands' and wives' participation in household tasks vary considerably; the variations are related to husband's occupation, wife's occupation, income, and other factors (Walker and Gauger, 1973; Oakly, 1974; Vanek, 1974). In general, however, it can be said that the employed woman spends less time on households tasks than does the unemployed woman, and the husband of the employed woman spends slightly more time on houshold tasks than does the husband of the full-time homemaker. Such time estimates, however, do not speak directly to the specific issue of role allocation, that is, what tasks are taking the time. Tasks within the household may be specifically divided according to gender, thus preserving traditional role assignment.

Recent data suggest that these traditional divisions are in fact being maintained in the face of shifting attitudes. Shaver *et al.* (1980) reported that in a nationwide sample of married, predominantly middle-class women, over one-half of whom were employed either full- or part-time, the vast majority reported having all or most of the responsibility for child care, cleaning and housework, cooking, shopping, and laundry. These same women reported that their husbands assumed all or most of the responsibility for car care, home maintenance and repair, yard work, and gardening. Only in the areas of disciplining the children, making major purchases and decisions, and deciding when to have sex did the majority of these women report that responsibility was about equally divided. Similar results have been reported by other investigators (Araji, 1977; Clark, Nye and Gecas, 1978; Ericksen, Yancy, and Ericksen, 1979). Clark *et al.* (1978) found little variation in these figures as a function of the number of hours that the husband worked, probably because of the small degree to which any of the men in their sample shared the household roles.

A more detailed specification of the allocation of household tasks is provided by Nyquist, Slivkin, Spence, and Helmreich (in press), in a survey of 164 predominantly middle-class Texas couples who were the parents of at least one child in the first or second grade. Respondents were asked to indicate the assignment of responsibility, ranging from completely the wife to completely the husband, for each of a number of household tasks and activities. Four specific factors emerged from an analysis of their Household Activities Questionnaire:

1. Household tasks, including cooking, marketing, cleaning, and caring for children when they were not in school;

2. Maintenance, including car maintenance, lawn care, gardening, and indoor and outdoor repairs;

3. Child rearing, including discipline, setting rules and limitations, and moral and behavioral instruction;

4. Decision making, including making financial and investment decisions and deciding whether the husband should accept a new position that requires relocation.

Allocation of these responsibilities was strongly linked to gender in two cases. As in the Shaver *et al.* findings, couples quite uniformly reported that maintenance tasks were almost completely or mainly the husband's responsibility, whereas household tasks were in most couples completely or mainly the wife's responsibility. Decision making was skewed toward male responsibility, although the modal response leaned toward more nearly equal sharing of responsibilities by husband and wife. Child-rearing, as it related to discipline and instruction, showed the most even sharing of responsibility, with more than 50 percent of the respondents reporting that both husband and wife assumed this task. In both these areas, however, there was more variability among couples than on routine household chores.

In the Nyquist *et al.* study, 64 percent of the women were employed outside the home (and 70 percent of these held full-time positions). A comparison between employed and unemployed women revealed that their employment status was related only to the factor tapping mundane "feminine" tasks: marketing, housecleaning, routine child care, and so forth. On this factor, the husbands of employed women were significantly more likely to help out with the household chores than the husbands of women who were full-time housewives. The magnitude of the difference was small, however, with even working women assuming most of these household responsibilities. The group of employed women were

subdivided further into those who held professional or managerial positions versus those in positions with lesser status (sales, clerical, semiskilled). No significant differences were found between these groups, except for a borderline tendency on the child-rearing factor: Higher status women shared slightly less responsibility with their husbands for disciplining and instructing the children than lower status women.

Similar results have been reported by Beckman (1979) and Beckman and Houser (1979). Using samples of women who were employed (in either professional or nonprofessional jobs) or unemployed, Beckman and her colleagues found that with greater employment experience, the wife tended to be responsible for a somewhat lower relative proportion of routine "feminine" tasks. There were no parallel results on "masculine" maintenance tasks or on the allocation of major decision-making tasks within the family, these tasks tended to be divided equally among husband and wife in all families.

Other evidence also points to a slight moderation of household-allocation patterns because of the wife's employment. Ericksen *et al.* (1979), for example, found that greater responsibility by the husband is associated with a lower income from the husband, higher education of the wife, and shared work roles. In addition, black husbands are more likely to do household tasks than are white husbands. Women whose employment histories are dissimilar to those of their husbands (women who work part-time and/or have a discontinuous work history) are also more likely to assume a greater responsibility for household tasks than are women whose employment histories are continuous and similar to those of their husbands (Weingarten, 1978).

Given that attitudes concerning the appropriate roles for men and women have become less traditional in recent years, one might question the relationship between such attitudes and actual household responsibilities. The available evidence suggests that these attitudes and behaviors are related, but the relationships are relatively weak and typically account for only a limited portion of the variance. Beckman and Houser (1979), for example, report correlations ranging from approximately .20 to .30 between measures of sex-role traditionalism and household behaviors in women. Perrucci, Potter, and Rhoads (1978) report correlations of similar magnitude between husbands' endorsement of traditional ideology (e.g., "Nature intended women to be homemakers and men to be workers.") and their reported household-task performance. Araji (1977) found that a majority of couples showed congruence between expressed attitudes toward role sharing and reported behavior, although the degree of congruence varied with the particular task (highest for the housekeeper role, lowest for the child-care role). It is worth noting that in the majority of cases in which incongruence between these two measures occurred, the attitudinal measures indicated shared responsibility; in contrast the behavior reported indicated greater female responsibility.

The association between the division of household responsibilities and the instrumentality and expressiveness of spouses has also been explored. In the previously described study of middle-class couples with families, Nyquist *et al.* (in press) found that these personality variables were essentially unrelated to allocation of responsibility for "masculine" maintenance tasks and for disciplining and instructing children. Since there was relatively little variability among the couples on these factors, this outcome is not surprising. However, in the areas of routine "feminine" tasks within the household and of decision-making, the constellations of characteristics exhibited by husband and wife, singly and in combination, accounted for a significant portion of the variability among couples. The interactions are complex and defy simple explanations, particularly in terms of general concepts such as sex-role orientation.

Relationships have also been found by Shaver *et al.,* (1980) between these personality dimensions and women's employment status. For example, women who perceive their husbands as low rather than high in instrumental qualities are more likely to work. Least likely to be employed full-time are women high in expressiveness and low in instrumentality married to men with the reverse pattern (28 percent versus 43 percent for the total sample).

DUAL-CAREER COUPLES

The dual-career couple represents a special case of sharing work and family roles. In distinguishing between the dual-career and the dual-worker family, Rapoport and Rapoport (1977) have defined a career as requiring more personal commitment and evidencing continuity of employment. Work, in contrast, may involve any form of gainful employment and is more likely to be characterized by discontinuity and less personal salience. Although current estimates suggest that only 2 percent of U.S. couples are engaging in a dual-career life style (Gilbert, 1980), considerable research has been focused on these couples. In considering allocation of role responsibilities, such couples become of particular interest

because they are generally more liberal in their sex-role attitudes (e.g., Beckman and Houser, 1979), and may have greater demands on their time because of greater work commitment.

The particular problems of dual-career couples have been widely documented (Rapoport and Rapoport, 1971, 1977; Bryson, Bryson, Licht, and Licht, 1976; Hunt and Hunt, 1977; Bryson and Bryson, 1978; Hall and Hall, 1979). Obstacles include the pressures for geographic relocation, the importance of continuous employment, and nepotism rules for people in the same field. Furthermore, the majority of such couples report significant conflict between career and marriage roles (Heckman, Bryson, and Bryson, 1977; Gilbert, Holahan, and Manning, 1981). However, the extent to which these conflicts are greater than those of women who simply work is not altogether clear. On the one hand, Beckman (1978) has reported that professional women associate higher costs with parenthood than do noncareer employed women. In contrast, Holahan and Gilbert (1979), comparing small samples of career and noncareer employed women (both with children) in terms of reported conflict, found that the job group reported more conflict than did the career group, particularly in the areas of "parent versus self" and "spouse versus self." Degree of spouse support appeared to moderate this relationship; career women generally received greater spouse support and hence experienced less conflict as a result.

There is no evidence that household-task allocation is shared more evenly among dual-career couples than among dual-worker couples. Professional women continue to take greater responsibility for household tasks than do their professional husbands. The major difference between these couples and more traditional couples is that professional couples are more likely to allocate some of the household responsibilities previously assumed by the wife to outside employed help (Bryson, Bryson, Licht, and Licht, 1976). In summary, literature on dual-career couples suggests that although work roles are more equally shared among these partners, many of the traditional household role-allocation patterns remain more or less intact.

SOME CONCLUDING THOUGHTS

"The great end of life," Thomas Huxley once wrote, "is not knowledge but action." Assuredly, the recent elevation of phenomena related to sex-roles and gender to major research topics among social and behavioral scientists has been motivated more by concern with societal action than by dispassionate scientific curiosity. Ideological denunciations of status inequities between the genders and questioning of previously accepted beliefs about the desirability of rigid sex-role divisions, which surfaced in the late 1960s, have sensitized the scholarly community to these political and sociological issues. As a consequence, changes in the status of women versus that of men that have been occurring over a number of decades are now being routinely detailed, and inquiries into the factors that contribute to the perpetuation of traditional sex-role attitudes and behaviors or facilitate their reformation are becoming commonplace. Attempts to describe and explain these temporal trends and their profound impact on societal institutions require an appeal to political, technological, economic, and sociological factors and to macrotheories of social change. Although not indifferent to the role of such factors, social psychologists have ordinarily left their investigation to members of other disciplines, preferring to focus (as is their wont) on the individual within the immediate group rather than on the group and larger sets of social forces.

In their new found interest in the contribution of gender to social behavior, psychologists have had few theoretical concepts to inform their work, and coherent theoretical statements of any degree of breadth are undoubtedly some years away. Unfortunately, the theoretical and empirical challenges have proven to be far more complex than was once thought. The long-standing assumption that sex-role behaviors and attitudes, personality characteristics, and other gender-related attributes could be rolled up into a single, powerful concept such as sex-role identity, self-images of masculinity/femininity, or gender schema, is not supported by the empirical data now available to us. Unidimensional ideas of this sort have recently been supplemented (rather than replaced) by the contradictory proposition that masculinity and femininity constitute two separate dimensions. The data suggests that these two hypothetical dimensions are also not all-encompassing. The various components of gender-related phenomena are infuriating free to vary among themselves, defying those theorists who would seek a simple and sovereign concept. They appear to have different developmental histories, predict different behaviors, and to be organized by different schemata in the cognitive structure. Our growing recognition of these complexities should hasten both empirical and theoretical advances.

Moreover, we have gained an increased appreciation of the role of situational factors, the social psychologists' eminent domain. Self-presentational strategies, expectation states, and other concepts that have been formulated to recognize the importance of interaction processes in the development and maintenance of gender-related behaviors move us considerably beyond the more static conception of gender as a psychological determinant. Gender is pervasive, but gender effects do not reside solely in either person or situation. An awareness of this complexity and interplay constitutes the contribution of the past decade, and this acknowledgement should provide a firmer basis for the research of the future.

REFERENCES

Abrahams, B., S. S. Feldman, and S. C. Nash (1978). Sex-role self-concepts and sex-role attitudes: enduring personality characteristics or adaptions to changing life situations? *Develop. Psychol., 14,* 393–400.

Almeida, E. (1980). Factors related to changing sex-roles: a cross-national study of four countries. Report to UNESCO.

Antill, J. K. (1980). *Marital happiness and perceived sex-role of spouse.* Unpublished manuscript.

―――― (1983). Sex-role complementarity versus similarity in married couples. *J. Pers. soc. Psychol., 45,* 145–155.

Antill, J. K., S. Cotton, and S. Tindale (1983). Egalitarian or traditional: correlates of the perception of an ideal marriage. *Australian J. Psychol., 35,* 245–257.

Araji, S. K. (1977). Husbands' and wives' attitude-behavior congruence on family roles. *J. Marriage and Family, 39,* 309–320.

Archer, J. (1976). Biological explanation of psychological sex differences. In B. Lloyd, and J. Archer (Eds.), *Exploring sex differences.* London: Academic Press.

Ashmore, R. D. (1981). Sex stereotypes and implicit personality theory. In D. L. Hamilton (Ed.), *Cognitive processes in stereotyping and intergroup behavior.* Hillsdale, N.J.: Erlbaum. Pp. 37–81.

Babledelis, G., K. Deaux, R. L. Helmreich, and J. T. Spence (1981). A cross-cultural comparison of men's and women's instrumentality, expressiveness, and achievement motives. Unpublished paper.

Bakan, D. (1966). *The duality of human existence.* Chicago: Rand McNally.

Banta, T. J., and M. Hetherington (1963). Relations between needs of friends and fiances. *J. abnorm. soc. Psychol., 66,* 401–404.

Baron, A. S. (1977). Selection, development, and socialization of women in management. *Bus. Quart., 28,* 61–67.

Bartol, K. M. (1976). Relationship of sex and professional training to job orientation. *J. appl. Psychol., 61,* 446–454.

Baumrind, D. (1971). Current patterns of parental authority. *Develop. psychol. monogr., 4,* No. 1, part 2.

―――― (1982). Are androgynous individuals more effective persons and parents? *Child Development, 53,* 44–75.

Beckman, L. J. (1978). The relative rewards and costs of parenthood and employment for employed women. *Psychol. Women Quart., 2,* 215–234.

_____ (1979). The relationship between sex roles, fertility, and family size preferences. *Psychol. Women Quart., 4,* 43–60.

Beckman, L. J., and B. B. Houser (1979). The more you have, the more you do: the relationship between wife's employment, sex-role attitudes, and household behavior. *Psychol. Women Quart., 4,* 160–174.

Bem, S. L. (1974). The measurement of psychological androgyny. *J. consult. clinic. Psychol., 42,* 155–162.

_____ (1978). Beyond androgyny: some presumptuous prescriptions for a liberated sexual identity. In J. Sherman, and F. Denmark (Eds.), *The future of women: issues in psychology.* New York: Psychological Dimensions.

_____ (1981). Gender schema theory. A cognitive account of sex typing. *Psychol. Rev., 88,* 354–364.

Bem, S. L., and E. Lenney (1976). Sex-typing and the avoidance of cross-sex behavior. *J. Pers. soc. Psychol., 33,* 48–54.

Bentler, P. M., and M. D. Newcomb (1978). Longitudinal study of marital success and failure. *J. consult. clinic. Psychol., 46,* 1053–1070.

Berger, J., S. J. Rosenholtz, and M. Zelditch, Jr. (1980). Status organizing processes. In A. Inkeles, N. J. Smelser, and R. H. Turner (Eds.), *Ann. Rev. Sociol., 6,* 479–508.

Berscheid, E., and E. Walster (1974). Physical attractiveness. In L. Berkowitz (Ed.), *Advances in experimental social psychology.* Vol. 7. New York: Academic Press.

Best, D. L., J. E. Williams, J. M. Cloud, S. W. Davis, L. S. Robertson, J. R. Edwards, H. Giles, and J. Fowles (1977). Development of sex-trait stereotypes among young children in the United States, England, and Ireland. *Child Development, 48,* 1375–1384.

Block, J. (1977). Advancing the psychology of personality: Paradigmatic shift or improving the quality of research. In D. Magnusson, and N. S. Endler (Eds.), *Personality at the crossroads: current issues in interactional psychology.* Hillsdale, N.J.: Erlbaum.

_____ (1973). Conceptions of sex-roles: some cross-cultural and longitudinal perspectives. *Amer. Psychol., 28,* 512–526.

Bowman, G. W., N. B. Worthy, and S. A. Greysar (1965). Are women executives people? *Harvard Bus. Rev., 43,* 52–67.

Brenner, O. C., and J. H. Greenhaus (1979). Managerial status, sex and personality characteristics. *J. Managmnt., 5,* 107–113.

Brief, A. P., and R. L. Oliver (1976). Male-female differences in work attitudes among retail sales managers. *J. appl. Psychol., 61,* 526–528.

Bronfenbrenner, U. (1960). Freudian theories of identification and their derivatives. *Child Development, 31,* 15–40.

Bronzaft, A. L. (1974). College women want a career, marriage and children. *Psychol. Reports, 35,* 1031–1034.

Broverman, I. K., S. R. Vogel, D. M. Broverman, F. E. Clarkson, and P. S. Rosenkrantz (1972). Sex-role stereotypes: a current appraisal. *J. soc. Issues, 28,* 59–78.

Brown, L. K. (1979). Women and business management. *Signs: J. women Culture Soc., 5,* 266–288.

Bryson, J. B., and R. B. Bryson, Eds. (1978). Dual-career couples. *Psychol. Women Quart., 3* (special issue).

Bryson, R. B., J. B. Bryson, M. H. Licht, and B. G. Licht (1976). The professional pair: husband and wife psychologists. *Amer. Psychol., 31,* 10–16.

Carlson, R. (1971). Sex differences in ego functioning. *J. consult. Clinic. Psychol., 37,* 267–277.

Centers, R., B. H. Raven, and A. Rodrigues (1971). Conjugal power structure: a re-examination. *Amer. Sociol. Rev., 36,* 264–278.

Chafe, W. H. (1976). Looking backward in order to look forward. Women, work and social values in America. In J. M. Kreps (Ed.), *Women and the American economy: a look to the 1980's.* Englewood Cliffs, N.J.: Prentice-Hall.

Cherry, F., and K. Deaux (1978). Fear of success versus fear of gender—inappropriate behavior. *Sex Roles, 4,* 97–101.

Clark, R. A., F. I. Nye, and V. Gecas (1978). Husband's work involvement and marital role performance. *J. Marriage and Family, 40,* 9–21.

Clifton, A. K., D. McGrath, and B. Wick (1976). Stereotypes of women: a single category? *Sex Roles, 2,* 135–148.

Climbing the academic ladder: doctoral women scientists in academe. (1979). Report of Committee on the Education and Employment of Women in Science and Engineering to Office of Science and Technology Policy, National Research Council.

Cole, J. R. (1979). *Fair science: women in the scientific community.* New York: Free Press.

Condry, J., and S. Condry (1976). Sex differences: a study of the eye of the beholder. *Child Development, 47,* 812–819.

Constantinople, A. (1973). Masculinity-femininity: an exception to the famous dictum? *Psychol. Bull., 80,* 389–407.

Cooper, H. M. (1979). Statistically combining independent studies: a meta-analysis of sex differences in conformity research. *J. Pers. soc. Psychol., 37,* 131–146.

Costa, P. T., Jr., R. R. McCrae, and D. Arenberg (1980). Enduring dispositions in adult males. *J. Pers. soc. Psychol., 38,* 793–800.

Costrich, N., J. Feinstein, L. Kidder, J. Marecek, and L. Pascale (1975). When stereotypes hurt: three studies of penalties in sex-role reversals. *J. exp. soc. Psychol., 11,* 520–530.

Cummings, S., and D. Taebel (1980). Sexual inequality and the reproduction of consciousness: an analysis of sex-role stereotyping among children. *Sex Roles, 6,* 631–644.

Deaux, K. (1972). To err is humanizing: but sex makes a difference. *Rep. res. soc. Psychol., 3,* 20–28.

_____ (1976a). *The behavior of women and men.* Monterey, Calif.: Brooks/Cole.

_____ (1976b). Sex: a perspective on the attribution process. In J. H. Harvey, et al. (Eds.), *New directions in attribution research.* Hillsdale, N.J.: Erlbaum.

_____ (1977). Sex differences. In T. Blass (Ed.), *Personality variables in social behavior.* Hillsdale, N.J.: Erlbaum.

_____ (1979). Self-evaluation of male and female managers. *Sex Roles, 5,* 571–580.

Deaux, K., and T. Emswiller (1974). Explanations of successful performance on sex-linked tasks: what is skill for the male is luck for the female. *J. Pers. soc. Psychol., 29,* 80–85.

Deaux, K., and E. Farris (1977). Attributing causes for one's own performance: the effects of sex, norms, and outcome. *J. res. Pers., 11,* 59–72.

Deaux, K., and L. L. Lewis (1984). Structure of gender stereotypes: interrelationships among components and gender label. *J. Pers. soc. Psychol., 46,* 991–1004.

Deutsch, C. J., and L. A. Gilbert (1976). Sex role stereotypes: effect on perceptions of self and others and on personal adjustment. *J. counsel. Psychol., 23,* 373–379.

Diaz-Loving, R., R. Diaz-Guerrero, R. L. Helmreich, and J. T. Spence (1981). Comparacion transcultural y analysis psicometrico de una medida de ragos masculinos (instrumentales) y femeninos (expresivo) *Revista de la Associacion Latinamericana de Psicologia Social, 1,* 3–37.

Douglas, K., and D. Arenberg (1978). Age changes, cohort differences, and cultural change on the Guilford-Zimmerman temperament survey. *J. Gerontology, 33,* 737–747.

Dunton, N. E., and D. L. Featherman (1983). Social mobility through marriage and careers: achievement over the life course. In J. T. Spence (Ed.), *Achievement and achievement related motives: psychological and sociological approaches.* San Francisco: Freeman.

Eagly, A. H. (1978). Sex differences in influenceability. *Psychol. Bull., 85,* 86–116.

Eagly, A. H., and L. Carli (1981). Sex of researchers and sex-typed communications as determinants of sex differences in influenceability: a meta-analysis of social influence studies. *Psychol. Bull., 90,* 1–20.

Eagly, A. H., W. Wood, and L. Fishbaugh (1981). Sex differences in conformity: surveillance by the group as a determinant of male nonconformity. *J. Pers. soc. Psychol., 40,* 384–394.

Ehrenreich, B., and D. English (1979). *For her own good: 150 years of the experts' advice to women.* Garden City, N.Y.: Anchor/Doubleday.

Ellis, L. J., and P. M. Bentler (1973). Traditional sex-determined role standards and sex stereotypes. *J. Pers. soc. Psychol., 25,* 28–34.

Epstein, G. F., and A. L. Bronzaft (1972). Female freshmen view their roles as women. *J. Marriage and Family, 34,* 671–672.

Ericksen, J. A., W. L. Yancy, and E. P. Ericksen (1979). The division of family roles. *J. Marriage and Family, 41,* 301–313.

Erikson, E. (1964). Inner and outer space: reflections on womanhood. *Daedalus, 93,* 1–25.

Eskilson, A., and M. C. Wiley (1976). Sex composition and leadership in small groups. *Sociometry, 39,* 183–194.

Falbo, T., and L. A. Peplau (1980). Power strategies in intimate relationships. *J. Pers. soc. Psychol., 38,* 618–628.

Farkas, G. (1976). Education, wage rates, and the division of labor between husband and wife. *J. Marriage and Family, 38,* 473–483.

Feild, H. S., and B. E. Caldwell (1979). Sex of supervisor, sex of subordinate and subordinate job satisfaction. *Psychol. Women Quart., 3,* 391–399.

Feldman, S. S., Z. C. Biringen, and S. C. Nash (1981). Fluctuations of sex-related self-attributions as a function of stage of family life cycle. *Develop. Psychol., 17,* 24–35.

Feldman-Summers, S., and S. B. Kiesler (1974). Those who are number two try harder: the effect of sex on attributions of causality. *J. Pers. soc. Psychol., 30,* 846–855.

Fichter, J. H. (1971). Career expectations of Negro women graduates. In A. Theodore (Ed.), *The professional woman.* Cambridge, Mass.: Schenkman.

Foushee, H. C., R. Helmreich, and J. T. Spence (1979). Implicit theories of masculinity and femininity: dualistic or bipolar? *Psychol. Women Quart., 3,* 259–269.

Fried, R., and B. Major (1980). *Self-presentation of sex-role attributes to attractive others.* Paper presented at meeting of Eastern Psychological Association. Hartford.

Garland, H., and K. H. Price (1977). Attitudes toward women in management and attributions for their success and failure in a managerial position. *J. appl. Psychol., 62,* 29–33.

Gilbert, L. A. (1980). *The men in dual-career families—do the benefits outweigh the costs?* Paper presented at the Symposium. Equality for women: the implications for men. Annual meeting of the American Psychological Association. Montreal.

Gilbert, L. A., C. J. Deutsch, and R. F. Strahan (1978). Feminine and masculine dimensions of the typical, desirable, and ideal woman and man. *Sex Roles, 4,* 767–777.

Gilbert, L. A., C. K. Holahan, and L. Manning (1981). Coping with conflict between professional and maternal roles. *Family Relat.: J. appl. Family Studies, 30,* 71–79.

Gilbert, L. A., J. A. Waldroop, and C. J. Deutsch (1981). Masculine and feminine stereotypes and adjustment: a reanalysis. *Psychol. Women Quart., 5,* 790–794.

Gutman, D. L. (1965). Women and the conception of ego strength. *Merrill-Palmer Quart., 11,* 229–240.

Hall, F. S., and D. T. Hall (1979). *The two-career couple.* Reading, Mass.: Addison-Wesley.

Hall, J. A., and A. G. Halberstadt (1980). Masculinity and femininity in children: development of the children's Personal Attributes Questionnaire. *Develop. Psychol., 16,* 270–280.

Heckman, N. A., R. Bryson, and J. B. Bryson (1977). Problems of professional couples: a content analysis. *J. Marriage and Family, 39,* 323–330.

Heilbrun, A. B., Jr. (1981). *Human sex-role behavior.* New York: Pergamon Press.

Heilman, M. E. (1979). High school students' occupational interest as a function of projected sex ratios in male-dominated occupations. *J. appl. Psychol. 64,* 275–279.

Heilman, M. E., and R. A. Guzzo (1978). The perceived cause of work success as a mediator of sex discrimination in organizations. *Organizat. Behav. hum. Perform., 21,* 346–357.

Heilman, M. E., and L. R. Saruwatari (1979). When beauty is beastly: the effect of appearance and sex on evaluations of job applicants for managerial and non-managerial jobs. *Organizat. Behav. hum. Perform., 23,* 360–372.

Helmreich, R. L., and J. T. Spence (1978). The Work and Family Orientation Questionnaire: an objective instrument to assess components of achievement motivation and attitudes toward family and career. *JSAS Catalog sel. doc. Psychol., 8,* 35, MS 1677.

Helmreich, R. L., J. T. Spence, W. E. Beane, G. W. Lucker, and K. A. Matthews (1980). Making it in academic psychology: demographic and personality correlates of eminence. *J. Pers. soc. Psychol., 39,* 896–908.

Helmreich, R. L., J. T. Spence, and R. H. Gibson (1982). Sex-role attitudes: 1972–1980. *Pers. soc. Psychol. Bull., 8,* 656–662.

Helmreich, R. L., J. T. Spence, and C. K. Holahan (1979). Psychological androgyny and sex-role flexibility: a test of two hypotheses. *J. Pers. soc. Psychol., 37,* 1631–1644.

Henley, N. (1977). *Body politics: power, sex, and nonverbal communication.* Englewood Cliffs, N.J.: Prentice Hall.

Hennig, M., and A. Jardim (1977). *The managerial woman.* Garden City, N.Y.: Anchor.

Hochschild, A. R. (1973). A review of sex role research. *Amer. J. Sociol., 78,* 1011–1029.

Hoffman, L. W. (1975). Early achievement motives. In M. T. S. Mednick, S. S. Tangri, and L. W. Hoffman (Eds.), *Women and achievement: social and motivational analyses.* Washington, D.C.: Hemisphere.

———— (1977). Changes in family roles, socialization, and sex differences. *Amer. Psychol., 32,* 644–657.

Holahan, C. K., and L. A. Gilbert (1979). Interrole conflict for working women: careers versus jobs. *J. appl. Psychol., 64,* 86–90.

Holmes, D. S., and B. W. Jorgenson (1971). Do personality and social psychologists study men more than women? *Rep. res. soc. Psychol., 2,* 71–76.

Horner, M. (1968). Sex differences in achievement motivation and performance in competitive and non-competitive situations. Unpublished doctoral dissertation, the University of Michigan.

Houser, B. B., and L. J. Beckman (1980). Background characteristics and women's dual-role attitudes. *Sex Roles, 6,* 355–366.

Hunt, J. G., and L. L. Hunt (1977). Dilemmas and contradictions of status: the case of the dual-career family. *Social Problems, 24,* 407–416.

Huston-Stein, A., and A. Higgins-Trenk (1978). Development of females from childhood through adulthood. Career and feminine role orientations. In P. Baltes (Ed.), *Life-span development and behavior.* Vol. 1. New York: Academic Press.

Ickes, W. (1981). Sex role influences in dyadic interaction: a theoretical model. In C. Mayo and N. Henley (Eds.), *Gender, androgyny, and nonverbal behavior.* New York: Springer-Verlag.

Ickes, W., and R. D. Barnes (1977). The role of sex and self-monitoring in unstructured dyadic interactions. *J. Pers. soc. Psychol., 35,* 315–330.

———— (1978). Boys and girls together—and alienated: on enacting stereotyped sex roles in mixed-sex dyads. *J. Pers. soc. Psychol., 36,* 669–683.

Ickes, W., B. Schermer, and J. Steeno (1979). Sex and sex-role influences in same-sex dyads. *Soc. Psychol. Quart., 42,* 373–385.

Inderlied, S. D., and G. Powell (1979). Sex-role identity and leadership style: different names for the same concept. *Sex Roles, 5,* 613–625.

Jenkins, N., and K. Vroegh (1969). Contemporary concepts of masculinity and femininity. *Psychol. Reports, 25,* 279–297.

Johnson, P. (1976). Women and power: toward a theory of effectiveness. *J. soc. Issues, 32* (3), 99–110.

———— (1978). Women and interpersonal power. In I. H. Frieze, J. E. Parsons, P. Johnson, D. Ruble, and G. Zellman (Eds.), *Women and sex roles: a social psychological perspective.* New York: Norton.

Jones, W. H., M. O. C. Chernovetz, and R. O. Hansson (1978). The enigma of androgyny: differential implications for males and females. *J. Clinic. Consult. Psychol., 46,* 298–313.

Kahn, A., R. E. Nelson, and W. P. Gaeddert (1980). Sex of subject and sex composition of the group as determinants of reward allocations. *J. Pers. soc. Psychol., 38,* 737–750.

Kaley, M. M. (1971). Attitudes toward the dual role of the married professional woman. *Amer. Psychol., 26,* 301–306.

Kanter, R. M. (1977). *Men and women of the corporation.* New York: Basic Books.

Kaplan, R. M., and R. D. Goldman (1973). Stereotypes of college students toward the average man's and woman's attitude toward women. *J. Counsel. Psychol., 20,* 459–462.

Klein, H. M., and L. Willerman (1979). Psychological masculinity and femininity and typical and maximal dominance expression in women. *J. Pers. soc. Psychol., 37,* 2059–2070.

Koblinsky, S. G., D. F. Cruse, and A. I. Sugawara (1978). Sex role stereotypes and children's memory for story content. *Child Development, 49,* 452–458.

Kolberg, L. A. (1966). Cognitive-developmental analysis of children's sex-role concepts and attitudes. In E. E. Maccoby (Ed.), *The development of sex differences.* Stanford: Stanford Univ. Press.

Komarovsky, M. (1979). Dilemmas of masculinity in a changing world. In J. E. Gullahorn (Ed.), *Psychology and women: in transition.* Washington D.C.: Winston.

Kreps, J. M., and R. J. Leaper (1976). Home work, market work, and the allocation of time. In J. M. Kreps (Ed.), *Women and the American economy: a look to the 1980's.* Englewood Cliffs, N.J.: Prentice-Hall.

Kristal, J., D. Sanders, J. T. Spence, and R. Helmreich (1975). Inferences about the femininity of competent women and their implications for likeability. *Sex Roles, 1,* 33–40.

Kuhn, D., S. C. Nash, and L. Brucken (1978). Sex role concepts of two- and three-year olds. *Child Development, 49,* 445–451.

Kulik, J. A., and J. Harackiewicz (1979). Opposite-sex interpersonal attraction as a function of the sex roles of the perceiver and the perceived. *Sex Roles, 5,* 443–452.

LaFrance, M., and B. Carmen (1980). The nonverbal display of psychological androgyny. *J. Pers. soc. Psychol., 38,* 36–49.

Lockheed, M. E. (1977). Cognitive style effects on sex status in student work groups. *J. educat. Psychol., 69,* 158–165.

Locksley, A., E. Borgida, N. Brekke, and C. Hepburn (1980). Sex stereotypes and social judgment. *J. Pers. and soc. Psychol., 39,* 821–831.

Maccoby, E. E., and C. N. Jacklin (1974). *The psychology of sex differences.* Stanford: Stanford Univ. Press.

McClelland, D. C. (1966). Longitudinal trends in the relation of thought to action. *J. consult. Psychol., 30,* 479–483.

McGregor, D. (1967). *The professional manager.* New York: McGraw-Hill.

McKee, J. P., and A. C. Sherriffs (1959). Men's and women's beliefs, ideals, and self-concepts. *Amer. J. Sociol., 64,* 356–363.

Major, B. (1981). Gender patterns in touching behavior. In C. Mayo and N. Henley (Eds.), *Gender, androgyny, and nonverbal behavior.* New York: Springer-Verlag.

Major, B., P. J. D. Carnevale, and K. Deaux (1981). A different perspective on androgyny: evaluations of masculine and feminine personality characteristics. *J. Pers. soc. Psychol., 41,* 988–1001.

Major, B., and K. Deaux (1983). Individual differences in justice behavior. In J. Greenberg, and R. L. Cohen (Eds.), *Equity and justice in social behavior.* New York: Academic Press.

Markus, H., M. Crane, S. Bernstein, and M. Siladi (1981). Self-schemas and gender. *J. Pers. soc. Psychol.*

Mason, K. O., and L. L. Bumpass (1975). U.S. women's sex-role ideology, 1970. *Amer. J. Sociol., 80,* 1212–1219.

Mason, K. O., J. L. Czajka, and S. Arber (1976). Change in U.S. women's sex-role attitudes, 1964–1974. *Amer. Sociol. Rev., 41,* 573–596.

Massengill, D., and N. DiMarco (1979). Sex-role stereotypes and requisite management characteristic: a current replication. *Sex Roles, 5,* 561–570.

Megargee, E. I. (1969). Influence of sex roles on the manifestation of leadership. *J. appl. Psychol., 53,* 377–382.

Miles, C. C. (1935). Sex in social psychology. In C. Murchison (Ed.), *Handbook of social psychology,* Worcester, Mass.: Clark Univ. Press.

Murstein, B. I. (1961). The complementary need hypothesis in newlyweds and middle-aged couples. *J. abnorm. soc. Psychol., 63,* 194–197.

Nyquist, L., and J. T. Spence (1984). Effects of personality and sex-role expectations on leadership choice and task behaviors. Paper presented at American Psychological Association Convention, Toronto, Canada.

Nyquist, L., K. Slivkin, J. T. Spence, and R. L. Helmreich (in press). Division of household tasks as related to the personality characteristics of husbands and wives. *Sex Roles.*

Oakley, A. (1974). *Women's work: the housewife past and present.* New York: Pantheon.

O'Connor, K., D. W. Mann, and J. M. Bardwick (1978). Androgyny and self-esteem in the upper-middle class: a replication of Spence. *J. Consult. Clinic. Psychol., 46,* 1168–1169.

National Advisory Council of Women's Educational Programs (1981). Washington, D.C.

Oppenheimer, V. K. (1970). The female labor force in the United States. *Population Monogr.* (5). Berkeley: University of California Institute of International Studies.

Orlofsky, J. L. (1977). Sex-role orientation, identity formation, and self-esteem in college men and women. *Sex Roles, 3,* 561–575.

——— (1979). *Psychological androgyny and male-female attraction.* Paper presented at the APA Convention, New York City.

Orlofsky, J., A. L. Aslin, and S. D. Ginsburg (1977). Differential effectiveness of two classification procedures on *The Bem sex role inventory. J. Pers. Assess., 41,* 414–416.

Osborn, R. N., and W. M. Vicars (1976). Sex-stereotypes: an artifact in leader behavioral and subordinate satisfaction analysis? *Acad. management J., 19,* 439–449.

Parelman, A. (1980). *Gender and sex-role influences on emotional intimacy in marriage.* Paper presented at American Psychological Association Convention, Montreal.

Parsons, T. (1955). Family structure and the socialization of the child. In T. Parsons, and R. F. Bales (Eds.), *Family, socialization, and interaction process.* Glencoe, Ill.: Free Press.

Pedhazur, E. J., and T. J. Tetenbaum (1979). Bem's Sex Role Inventory: a theoretical and methodological critique. *J. Pers. soc. Psychol., 37,* 996–1016.

Peplau, L. A. (1979). Power in dating relationships. In J. Freeman (Ed.), *Women: a feminist perspective* (2nd ed.). Palo Alto, Calif.: Mayfield.

Peplau, L. A., Z. Rubin, and C. T. Hill (1976). The sexual balance of power. *Psychology Today,* 142–151.

Perrucci, C. C., H. R. Potter, and D. L. Rhoads (1978). Determinants of male family-role performance. *Psychol. Women Quart., 3,* 53–66.

Peterson, M. J. (1975). The asymmetry of sex-role perceptions. *Sex Roles, 1,* 267–282.

Pheterson, G. I., S. B. Kiesler, and P. A. Goldberg (1971). Evaluation of the performance of women as a function of their sex, achievement, and personal history. *J. Pers. soc. Psychol., 19,* 114–118.

Pleck, J. H. (1978). Males' traditional attitudes toward women: conceptual issues in research. In J. A. Sherman, and F. L. Denmark (Eds.), *The psychology of women: future directions in research.* New York: Psychological Dimensions.

Putnam, L. L., and L. McCallister (1980). Situational effects of task and gender on nonverbal display. In D. Nimno (Ed.), *Communication yearbook 4,* New Brunswick, N.J.: Transaction.

Radecki, C., and J. Jennings (Walstedt) (1980). Sex as a status variable in work settings: female and male reports of dominance behavior. *J. appl. soc. Psychol., 10,* 71–85.

Rapoport, R., and R. N. Rapoport (1971). *Dual-career families.* Harmondsworth, England: Penguin.

——— (1977). *Dual-career families revisited.* New York: Academic Press.

Rappaport, A. F., D. Payne, and A. Steinmann (1970). Perceptual differences between married and single college women for the concepts of self, ideal woman, and man's ideal woman. *J. Marriage and Family, 32,* 441–442.

Raven, B. H. (1965). Social influence and power. In I. D. Steiner, and M. Fishbein (Eds.), *Current studies in social psychology.* New York: Holt.

Raymond, B., J. Damino, and N. Kandel (1974). Sex stereotyping in values: a comparison of three generations and two sexes. *Perceptual and Motor Skills, 39,* 163–166.

Rice, R. W., L. R. Bender, and A. G. Vitters (1980). Leader sex, follower attitudes toward women, and leadership effectiveness. *Organizat. Behav. hum. Perform., 25,* 46–78.

Richardson, D., S. Bernstein, and C. Hendrick (1980). Deviations from conventional sex-role behavior: effects of perceiver sex-role attitudes on attraction. *Basic appl. soc. Psychol., 1,* 351–355.

Riger, S., and P. Galligan (1980). Women in management; an exploration of competing paradigms. *Amer. Psychol., 35,* 902–910.

Robinson, J. P. (1977). *How Americans use time: a social-psychological analysis of everyday behavior.* New York: Praeger.

Roche, G. R. (1979). Much ado about mentors. *Harvard Bus. Rev., 57,* 14–18.

Romer, N., and D. Cherry (1980). Ethnic and social class differences in children's sex-role concepts. *Sex Roles, 6,* 246–263.

Rosen, B., and T. H. Jerdee (1974). Effects of applicant's sex and difficulty of job on evaluation of candidates for managerial positions. *J. appl. Psychol., 59,* 511–512.

Rosenfield, D., and W. Stephan (1978). Sex differences in attributions for sex-typed tasks. *J. Pers., 46,* 244–258.

Rosenkrantz, P. S., S. R. Vogel, H. Bee, I. K. Broverman, and D. M. Broverman (1968). Sex role stereotypes and self concepts in college students. *J. consult. clinic. Psychol., 32,* 287–295.

Ruble, T. L. (1983). Sex stereotypes: Issues of change in the 1970's. *Sex Roles. 9,* 397–402.

Runge, T. E., D. Frey, P. M. Gollwitzer, R. L. Helmreich, and J. T. Spence (1981). Masculine (instrumental) and feminine (expressive) traits: a comparison between students in the United States and West Germany. *J. cross-cultural Psychol., 12,* 142–162.

Runge, T. E., R. L. Helmreich, and J. A. Wilhelm (1981). *A profile of tanker officers and crew members: a preliminary report.* Unpublished manuscript.

Sarbin, T. R., and V. L. Allen (1968). Role theory. In G. Lindzey, and E. Aronson (Eds.), *Handbook of social psychology* (2nd ed.). Reading, Mass.: Addison-Wesley. Pp. 488–567.

Sawin, L. L. (1982). Instrumentality and expressiveness in self-concept and ideal mate. Unpublished manuscript. Univ. of Texas, Austin.

Schein, V. E. (1973). The relationship between sex-role stereotypes and requisite management characteristics. *J. appl. Psychol., 57,* 95–100.

_____ (1975). Relationships between sex-role stereotypes and requisite management characteristics among female managers. *J. Appl. Psychol., 60,* 340–344.

Schein, V. E., and K. M. Bartol (1980). Sex differences in emergent leadership. *J. appl. Psychol., 65,* 341–345.

Schrank, H. T., and J. W. Riley, Jr. (1976). Women in work organizations. In J. M. Kreps (Ed.), *Women and the American economy: a look to the 1980's.* Englewood Cliffs, N.J.: Prentice-Hall.

Seyfried, B. A., and C. Hendrick (1973). When do opposites attract? When they are opposite in sex and sex-role attitudes. *J. Pers. soc. Psychol., 25,* 15–20.

Shaver, P., C. Pullis, and D. Olds (1980). *Report of ladies home journal survey.* Unpublished paper.

Shields, S. A. (1975). Functionalism, Darwinism, and the psychology of women: a study in social myth. *Amer. Psychol., 30,* 739–754.

Siegel, A. E., and M. B. Haas (1963). The working mother: a review of research. *Child Development, 34,* 513–542.

Simms, R. E., M. H. Davis, H. C. Foushee, C. K. Holahan, J. T. Spence, and R. L. Helmreich (1978). *Psychological masculinity and femininity in children and their relationships to trait stereotypes and toy preferences.* Paper presented at the meeting of the Southwestern Psychological Association. New Orleans.

Skrypnek, B. J., and M. Snyder (1982). On the self-perpetuating nature of stereotypes about women and men. *J. exp. soc. Pers., 18,* 277–291.

Social indicators of equality for minorities and women. (1978). A report of the United States Commission on Civil Rights.

Spence, J. T. (1974). The thematic apperception test and attitudes toward achievement in women: a new look at the motive to avoid success and a new method of measurement. *J. consult. clinic. Psychol., 42,* 427–437.

_____ (1984). Masculinity, femininity, and gender-related traits: a conceptual analysis and critique of current research. *Progress in experimental personality research,* Vol. 13. B. A. Maher and W. B. Maher (Eds.) New York: Academic Press.

Spence, J. T., and R. L. Helmreich (1972a). Who likes competent women? Competence, sex-role congruence of interests and attitudes toward women as determinants of interpersonal attraction. *J. appl. soc. Psychol., 2,* 197–213.

_____ (1972b). The Attitudes toward Women Scale: an objective instrument to measure attitudes toward the rights and roles of women in contemporary society. *JSAS Catalog sel. doc. Psychol., 2,* 66.

_____ (1978). *Masculinity and femininity: their psychological dimensions, correlates, and antecedents.* Austin: Univ. of Texas Press.

_____ (1979). Comparison of masculine and feminine personality attributes and sex-role attitudes across age groups. *Develop. Psychol., 15,* 583–584.

_____ (1980). Masculine instrumentality and feminine expressiveness: their relationships with sex-role attitudes and behaviors. *Psychol. Women Quart., 5,* 147–163.

_____ (1981). Androgyny vs. gender schema: a comment on Bem's gender schema theory. *Psychol. Rev., 88,* 365–368.

_____ (1983). Achievement-related motives and behavior. In J.T. Spence (Ed.) *Achievement and achievement related motives: psychological and sociological approaches.* San Francisco: Freeman.

Spence, J. T., R. L. Helmreich, and C. K. Holahan (1979). Negative and positive components of psychological masculinity and femininity and their relationships to self-reports of neurotic and acting-out behaviors. *J. Pers. soc. Psychol., 37,* 1673–1682.

Spence, J. T., R. Helmreich, and J. Stapp (1974). The Personal Attributes Questionnaire: a measure of sex-role stereotypes and masculinity-femininity. *JSAS Catalog sel. doc. Psychol., 4,* 43.

_____ (1975a). Ratings of self and peers on sex-role attributes and their relation to self-esteem and conceptions of masculinity and femininity. *J. Pers. soc. Psychol., 32,* 29–39.

_____ (1975b). Likability, sex-role congruence of interests, and competence: it all depends on how you ask. *J. appl. soc. Psychol., 5,* 93–109.

Spence, J. T., R. L. Helmreich, and L. L. Sawin (1980). The Male-Female Relations Questionnaire: a self-report inventory of sex role behaviors and preferences and its relationships to masculine and feminine personality traits, sex role attitudes, and other measures. *JSAS Sel. doc. sel. doc. Psychol., 10,* 87.

Spence, J. T., and L. L. Sawin (1985). Images of masculinity and femininity. In V. O'Leary, R. Unger, and B. Wallston (Eds.) *Sex, gender and social psychology.* Hillsdale, N.J.: Erlbaum.

Staines, G., C. Tavris, and T. E. Jayaratne (1974). The queen bee syndrome. *Psychology Today, 1,* 55–48, 60.

Steinmann, A. (1963). A study of the concept of the feminine role of 51 middle-class American families. *Genetic Psychol. Monogr., 67,* 275–352.

Steinmann, A., and D. Fox (1966). Male-female perceptions of the female role in the United States. *J. Psychol., 64,* 265–276.

Stockard, J., P. A. Schmuck, K. Kempner, P. Williams, S. K. Edson, and M. A. Smith (1980). *Sex equity in education.* New York: Academic Press.

Storms, M. (1980). Theories of sex-role identity. *J. Pers. soc. Psychol., 38,* 783–792.

Taylor, S. E. (1981). A categorization approach to stereotyping. In D. L. Hamilton (Ed.), *Cognitive processes in stereotyping and intergroup behavior.* Hillsdale, N.J.: Erlbaum. Pp. 83–114.

Taylor, S. E., and S. T. Fiske (1978). Saliency, attention and attribution: top of the head phenomena. In L. Berkowitz (Ed.), *Advances in experimental social psychology.* Vol. 12. New York: Academic Press.

Taylor, S. E., S. Fiske, N. L. Etlott, and A. J. Ruderman (1978). Categorical and contextual bases of person memory and stereotyping. *J. Pers. soc. Psychol., 36,* 778–793.

Terborg, J. R., L. H. Peters, D. R. Ilgeon, and F. Smith (1977). Organizational and personal correlates of attitudes toward women as managers. *Acad. management J., 20,* 89–100.

Tiger, L., and R. Fox (1971). *The imperial animal.* New York: Holt, Rinehart, and Winston.

Tresemer, D. (1977). *Fear of success.* New York: Plenum.

Unger, R. K. (1979). *Female and male: psychological perspectives.* New York: Harper & Row.

Unger, R. K., and R. Siiter (1974). *Sex-role stereotypes: the weight of a "grain of truth".* Paper presented at the Eastern Psychological Association Meetings, Philadelphia, Penn.

Urberg, K. A. (1979). Sex role conceptualizations in adolescents and adults. *Develop. Psychol., 15,* 90–92.

Urberg, K. A., and G. Labouvie-Vief (1976). Conceptualizations of sex roles: a life span developmental study. *Develop. Psychol., 12,* 15–23.

Van Dusen, R. A., and E. B. Sheldon (1976). The changing status of American women: a life cycle perspective. *Amer. Psychol., 31,* 106–116.

Vanek, J. (1974). Time spent in housework. *Scientific American, 231,* 116–120.

vonBaeyer, C. L., D. L. Sherk, and M. Zanna (1979). *Impression management: female job applicant, male (chauvinist) interviewer.* Paper presented at meeting of American Psychological Association. New York.

Voss, J. H., and D. A. Skinner (1975). Concepts of self and ideal woman held by college women: a replication. *J. coll. stud. Personnel, 16,* 210–213.

Wakefield, J. A., Jr., J. Sasek, A. F. Friedman, and J. D. Bowden (1976). Androgyny and other measures of masculinity-femininity. *J. consult. clinic. Psychol., 44,* 766–770.

Walker, K., and W. Gauger (1973). Time and its dollar value in household work. *Fam. econ. Rev., 62,* 8–13.

U.S. Bureau of the Census (1982). Statistical Abstract of the United States: 1982–1983. (103rd ed.). Washington, D.C.: Government Printing Office.

Weingarten, K. (1978). The employment pattern of professional couples and their distribution of involvement in the family. *Psychol. Women Quart., 3,* 43–52.

Williams, J. E., and S. M. Bennett (1975). The definition of sex stereotypes via the adjective check list. *Sex Roles, 1,* 327–337.

Winch, R. F. (1963). *The modern family.* New York: Holt, Rinehart, and Winston.

Winch, R. F., T. Kitsanes, and V. Kitsanes (1954). The theory of complementary needs in mate selection: an analytic and descriptive study. *Amer. Sociol. Rev., 19,* 241–249.

Witkin, H. A. (1974). Social conformity and psychological differentiation. *Int. J. Psychol., 9,* 11–29.

Yorburg, B., and I. Arafat (1975). Current sex role conceptions and conflict. *Sex Roles, 1,* 135–146.

Zanna, M. P., and S. J. Pack (1975). On the self-fulfilling nature of apparent sex differences in behavior. *J. exp. soc. Psychol., 11,* 583–591.

Zuckerman, H. (1977). *Scientific elite: Nobel laureates in the United States.* New York: Free Press.

Zuckerman, M., and L. Wheeler (1975). To dispel fantasies about the fantasy-based measure of fear of success. *Psychol. Bull., 82,* 932–946.

CHAPTER 18

Language Use and Language Users

Herbert H. Clark
Stanford University

INTRODUCTION

Language is a social instrument. When we talk, we direct our words not to the air but to other people. Our aim is not to express our thoughts aloud but to affect the people we are talking to. We intend our listeners to recognize certain of our goals in saying what we say, and they listen, intent on recognizing them. Both what we say and what listeners understand us as saying are essential to the social activities we engage in—from chitchat to courtroom interrogations. It is easy to argue that the world's languages—English, Swahili, Navaho—have many of the features they do because they have evolved as instruments of social processes.

It is paradoxical, then, that modern social psychologists have paid so little attention to language use. Few have taken it up, and most texts in social psychology have ignored the topic altogether. The study of language has been left mainly to cognitive and developmental psychologists and, outside psychology, to linguists, philosophers, and computer scientists. These investigators have made great progress in understanding how language works, but because they aren't social psychologists, they have largely neglected the social bases of language—how it is instrumental in social processes and how it is shaped by those processes. Most of them have treated the speaker and listener as isolated individuals whose use and understanding of language is to be studied without regard for the social activities in which language is used. This view might be called the *individualist* view of language use. The successes these investigators have achieved, it could be argued, have come *in spite of* their lack of interest in social processes.

The social foundations of language use, however, have not been entirely ignored. Scattered throughout sociolinguistics, sociology, anthropology, psycholinguistics, developmental psychology, and even social psychology are investigators whose mission has been to demonstrate that social factors are essential to language use and are both systematic and describable. The crux of their arguments is that any theory of language use not

I wish to thank Eve V. Clark, Raymond W. Gibbs, Jr., and Deanna L. Wilkes-Gibbs for their valuable comments on earlier drafts of this chapter. Writing of this chapter was supported in part by Grant MH-20021 from the National Institute of Mental Health.

able to account for underlying social functions is inadequate to begin with. This view might be called the *interactionist* view of language use.

LANGUAGE USE

What, then, *is* language use? The short answer is that it is speaking and listening. But speaking and listening are themselves parts of other activities and change character from one activity to the next. Speaking in a conversation is not the same as speaking in a church service or speaking Desdemona's part in *Othello*. Nor is listening in a conversation the same as listening to a church service or listening to a production of *Othello*. To study language use, it would seem, we cannot help but refer to the activities of which speaking and listening are parts.

In the individualist approach to language use, the focus has been on the individual's mental activities in speaking and listening. By what processes does an individual speaker plan and execute what he or she says? And by what processes does the individual listener understand what a speaker said? The main impetus to the approach has come from the influential work of Noam Chomsky and other generative linguists. Since around 1960 they have developed a highly articulated view of the structure of language. In this view each person who speaks and understands a language like English possesses tacit knowledge of an intricate set of rules governing which strings of words are sentences of English and which aren't and governing the relations of sentences to their meanings. For the study of language use it is only natural to ask how this tacit knowledge is put to use in speaking and listening. If the individualist approach had a slogan, it would be: Look for the structure and see how it is used.

In the interactionist approach the stress has been on the activities of which speaking and listening are parts. How do speakers and listeners manage to take turns cooperatively in conversations? What kinds of dialogues and monologues occur, and how do they differ? How do what is said and what is understood depend on who the speakers and listeners are—on their roles in society and on other personal characteristics? If the interactionist approach had a slogan, it would be: Look for the functions.

Ultimately, there is no clean line between the individualist and interactionist approaches to language use. Indeed, a few investigators in the two traditions are trying to combine the best of both approaches. They seek not only to characterize the processes of speaking and listening by themselves but also to describe how these processes are influenced, changed, or disrupted by the activities in which they are embedded. Or from the opposite point of view they wish to see not merely how speech is regulated in dialogues and monologues but also how this regulation influences the very processes of speaking and listening. The slogan of the emerging approach might be: Look for the functions and see how they are served by the structure.

In this essay I will describe some of the main threads running through this emerging position, this *rapprochement* between the individualists and the interactionists. To do so, I will introduce the notion of coordination of action, the idea that speakers attempt to coordinate what they say with the interpretations their addresses impute to what they say. I will suggest that coordination is central at all levels of language, from individual words to conversations and narratives. It is coordination, I will argue, that enables us to characterize how speaking and listening are influenced by the activities of which they are a part and how these broader activities are regulated by the mental processes of speaking and listening.

FROM WORDS TO NARRATIVES

Utterances have meaning. When people utter sentences, they ask questions, make demands, offer apologies, and perform many other so-called speech acts. Their immediate purpose is to get certain listeners to do things in response. How do speakers and listeners bring this coordination about? In trying to answer this question, I will take up several topics: the nature of meaning itself, the possible types of speech acts, and the devices available for performing these speech acts.

Utterances, however, aren't indivisible pieces of behavior. They are assembled from parts, each part serving some function in relation to the whole. When Hamlet claims *The play's the thing wherein I'll catch the conscience of the king,* he is using the phrases *the play, the conscience of the king, the king,* and *the thing wherein I'll catch the conscience of the king* to refer to particular things, to pick these out for his listeners. And when he refers to a particular play with the words *the play,* he is using *the* and *play* to make clear that his referent is identifiable by the listener and that it is a play. Coordination is required as much for utterance parts as it is for whole utterances.

Utterances play their most obvious roles as parts of conversational turns. There the coordination required of the speaker and listeners is clear. The parties to a conversation must, by judicious use of their utterances, create and run an efficient system of turn taking, enabling the other participants to enter the conversation when they want to or are obligated to. They must also have a system for repairing that conversation when things go wrong. From a more global perspective they must use utterances for opening and closing conversations, changing topics, and managing routine conversational chores. There are many specialized devices for getting these chores accomplished.

Utterances are also the building blocks of narratives, descriptions, and other monologues. With these uses of language there at first appears to be no need to consider anyone but the speaker, since the speaker needn't interact directly with the listeners or the readers. This view has led many investigators to treat monologues as "texts," just as linguists would treat sentences—without regard for how speakers coordinate with listeners. I will suggest that this view is wrong. Stories, jokes, folktales, and other narratives are best viewed as specialized sections of conversations, as extended turns by a single speaker still genuinely interacting with his audience. The narrator must continue to coordinate his choice of utterances with his audience's interpretations of his utterances and, for that, must follow the same general principles as he would in dialogues. So coordination between speaker and listeners is essential from words to narratives. It is essential not just for accurate and efficient communication but for any communication to take place at all.

That, then, is the plan of the essay. But before I turn to utterances and their meaning, I need to introduce the notion of coordination itself.

COORDINATION

Coordination of action is part of many everyday activities. When two people want to pass through a narrow doorway at about the same time, they have to coordinate who goes first. When a pair of people want to meet, they have to coordinate where and when to meet. When a crew rows a scull, they have to coordinate their pulling of the oars. When members of a community want to drive their cars on the highway, they have to coordinate whether to drive on the right- or left-hand side of the road. Without coordination these activities would go awry. The two people going through the door might bump into each other. The pair of people trying to meet might not meet. The scullers might go around in circles and never reach their destination. And the drivers coming from opposite directions might crash into each other. Coordination is needed whenever two or more people do things that im-

pinge on the actions of one another, and this is inherent to almost all social activities.

Nowhere is coordination more important than in language use, where people's actions are *intended* to impinge on one another. For many aspects of language use, the coordination is obvious. In conversations, as I mentioned earlier, the parties have to coordinate turn taking—that is, who speaks when and for how long. Turn taking is constrained much as going through a door is constrained: Generally, only one person can do it at a time. Coordination is accomplished by a system that allows or obligates certain parties to talk at certain times.

In other aspects of language, coordination is less obvious. This is especially true of coordination between what a speaker means and what listeners understand her to mean. Whenever a speaker uses *bank,* she intends it to mean either "financial institution" or "steep incline" but not both; she and her addressees both take this for granted (unless the speaker is making a joke or pun). But if *bank,* on its own, can have either meaning, the speaker and her addressees must coordinate on which interpretation she intended on each particular occasion. It does no good if the speaker means "financial institution" while her addressees understand her to mean "steep incline." Although the example may seem obvious, the same coordination is needed for entire utterances and longer stretches of talk. When Helen tells Sam, *The Bakers are on their way,* she may be indirectly requesting Sam to start dinner, to put more logs on the fire, to call the police for protection, or any number of other things. How does Sam infer what Helen means indirectly? That again is a matter of coordination—specifically, of Helen uttering the right words in the right circumstances, confident that Sam will understand her as she intended him to.

The most basic type of coordination, I will argue, is between what the speaker means and what his addressees understand him to mean. All other types of coordination—as in turn taking, choice of conversational topics, and course of narration—are really in service of the more basic coordination between meaning and understanding. It will take me the rest of the essay to complete the argument.

COORDINATION PROBLEMS

Whenever two or more people have to coordinate their actions, they are faced with what Schelling (1960) and others have called a *coordination problem.* Lewis (1969) has offered an insightful analysis of how people solve these problems of strategy, and his analysis reveals a good deal about language use as well. Lewis's basic idea can be illustrated in the coordination problem of meeting.

Imagine that Ann and Bob want to meet on a particular day at noon. Where should each go? Consider the question from Ann's point of view. She should reason: "I should go to the place where I expect Bob to go." Where is that? "Well, if Bob truly wants to meet me, he should go to the place where he thinks I will go. So I should go to the place where he expects me to go." But where is that? "That, of course, is the place where I expect him to go, so I should go to the place where I expect him to expect me to expect him to go. And so on *ad infinitum*. Furthermore, if Bob is rational and sees the problem as I do, he should reason the same way." So Ann and Bob should go to the place where they *mutually expect* each other to go, where *mutual expectation* is defined as these reciprocal expectations that go on infinitely.

Ann and Bob, of course, cannot literally form the infinite set of expectations required here. Instead, Lewis argued, they need only have grounds for believing that this infinite set of expectations holds. What they need, he argued further, is a *coordination device* that would offer such a grounds. Lewis suggested four types of coordination devices.

The first of these is *explicit agreement*. Ann and Bob could explicitly agree on where to meet, say at the public library. The explicit agreement would give them each grounds for believing that the two of them mutually expect each other to go to the public library.

The second device is *salience*. Ann is visiting Bob's town and is known to know nothing about it except where Bob lives. Meeting at Bob's home, then, would offer them a salient solution to the coordination problem. Ann and Bob could each be confident that the solution is so salient that it would occur to the other such that they would mutually expect each other to be at Bob's home at noon.

The third device is *precedence* (actually a special form of salience). Ann and Bob could each realize that they met last time at the city hall and so that is the most salient place to meet this time too.

The final device is *convention*. Ann and Bob have met so regularly at the coffee shop that it has become, for them, a convention to meet at the coffee shop. So when they want to meet, they mutually expect each other to go to the coffee shop simply because that is the place where they conventionally meet.

Conventions, Lewis argued, evolve as solutions to recurrent coordination problems. When people drive on the highway, they have a recurrent problem—not just a onetime one—of where to drive. In America the convention that got established is that people drive on the right; in Britain it is that people drive on the left. A convention, therefore, is a *regularity in behavior* evolved by agents for solving a recurrent coordination problem (like driving on the highway). Such a regularity, Lewis argued, is a convention if and only if it is common knowledge in a community that (1) almost everyone adheres to the regularity, (2) almost everyone expects everyone else to adhere to the regularity, and yet (3) almost everyone would have adhered to a different regularity (like driving on the left instead of the right) if everyone else had done so and expected everyone else to do so. Thus not all regularities in behavior are conventions. In particular, there must be alternative regularities that could have evolved instead of the ones that did.

Language, Lewis argued, is largely a system of conventions that have evolved as solutions to certain coordination problems. Take the convention in English that *dog* means "dog." The recurrent coordination problem is that speakers want to denote dogs such that their addressees will take them as denoting dogs. The regularity that has evolved is that speakers use *dog* and addressees understand them thereby as denoting dogs. This solution fits Lewis's criteria for conventions. In particular, if history had been different, the regularity might have been to use *mog* instead. English speakers use *dog* simply because that is the conventional word people in the linguistic community use for denoting dogs. So the forms that words take are in part arbitrary, in what the linguist de Saussure (1916) called *l'arbitraire du sign*.

The study of language and language use—by linguists, psychologists, philosophers, anthropologists, and computer scientists—has been concerned almost exclusively with conventions. The rules of phonology, morphology, syntax, and semantics are, in effect, codifications of conventions people adhere to in using language. There has been a major effort by linguists to characterize these regularities and by psychologists and others to discover how the regularities arise in speaking and listening.

Conventions, however, are only one of the coordination devices people use in communication, a point that has been lost in most research on language and language use. The rarest of Lewis's coordination devices in language use is probably explicit agreement. It comes into play only when a person openly stipulates what he will call something, as in *This theory, which I will call the peptic theory of ingestion, is patently false.* The phrase *which I will call the peptic theory of ingestion,* like its relatives *let us call, the so-called, shall we say,* and others, brings about an explicit agreement between speaker and addressees.

The coordination devices of salience and precedence, however, are ubiquitous in language use. As I will show later, speakers rely on salience, for example, whenever they use a definite reference like *that dog, the woman we met last night,* and *my car,* since these descriptions—*dog, woman we met last night,* and *my car*—generally aren't sufficient to determine the reference uniquely on their own. Speakers also rely on salience in using sentences with indirect meanings, as when Helen tells Sam, *The Bakers are coming.* For Helen to expect Sam to see that she means him to go and greet them, she relies on him discovering the most salient solution to their coordination problem at that moment. Speakers rely on precedence in using certain types of ellipsis, as when Sam follows up Helen's assertion with *How soon?* meaning "How soon are the Bakers coming?" Examples of nonconventional devices for coordinating speaker meaning with listener understanding will come up again and again throughout this essay.

COMMON GROUND

For two agents to coordinate their actions, they must share certain common ground (see Clark and Carlson, 1981, 1982a, 1982b; Clark and Marshall, 1981). Recall that for a regularity in behavior to be a convention, it must be *common knowledge* within a community that it is such a regularity. It would do no good if a speaker were to use *bug* according to a convention among computer users to mean "error in a computer program" when she believed her addressees didn't also know this convention. Further, she would generally have to know that her addressees knew that *she* knew the convention and that they knew that she knew that *they* knew the convention, and so on *ad infinitum,* as Lewis (1969), Schiffer (1972), and others have demonstrated. The convention must be common knowledge (Lewis's term) or mutual knowledge (Schiffer's term) between the speaker and her addressees.

The concept I will be concerned with is *common ground,* which I define to include not only common or mutual knowledge but also common or mutual beliefs and common or mutual suppositions. That is, the common ground between Ann and Bob consists of what they

mutually know, believe, and suppose. In practice, Ann's conception of their common ground won't be 100 percent accurate, nor will Bob's. We must therefore talk about Ann's, and about Bob's, *beliefs* about their common ground.

Common ground is essential for coordination. For Ann and Bob to meet by explicit agreement, Ann must believe that it is mutually known to Ann and Bob that they made this agreement. She must also believe they mutually believe that they both want to meet and that there are no hindrances to their meeting. Bob must have the same beliefs. For Ann and Bob to coordinate by salience, they must mutually suppose that they are judging salience by the same criteria (see Clark, Schreuder, and Buttrick, 1983). And to coordinate by precedent, they must mutually believe that the precedent on which they are basing their current actions is mutually known or believed or supposed to have happened and to be recallable by them both.

If common ground is essential for coordination in general, then it must also be essential in language use. When Ann tells Bob, *That woman is my lawyer,* she relies on Bob consulting their common ground that there is a woman nearby, that she is pointing at the woman, that she, Ann, is speaking, that Bob knows English, and so on. The same sort of common ground is required for coordinating every other use of language.

How do people assess what is and what isn't in common ground? According to an analysis by Clark and Marshall (1981), two people, Ann and Bob, infer their common ground from three types of information:

1. *Linguistic evidence:* Ann and Bob take as common ground everything they have heard said as participants in the same conversation. I will return to the idea of conversational coparticipants later.

2. *Perceptual evidence:* Ann and Bob take as common ground all those experiences they have jointly had and are jointly having in each other's presence, such as seeing Ann point at the woman nearby.

3. *Community membership:* Ann and Bob take as common ground all those things they take to be universally—or almost universally—known, believed, or supposed in the many communities and subcommunities to which they mutually believe the two of them belong. Because Ann and Bob are both English speakers, they take their common ground to include their knowledge of the English most people know. Because they are both university-educated Americans, they take it to include be-

liefs about well-known people, things, and events in America, ones they assume every university-educated American knows. Because they are both members of the American middle class, they take it to include knowledge of scripted regularities in behavior known to this class, such as what happens in restaurants, doctors' offices, or classrooms (see Schank and Abelson, 1977), and beliefs common to this class about how cars, gravity, bombs, and the like work. They also take it to include beliefs peculiar to subcommunities to which they mutually believe they both belong. Because they are both computer users, they take it to include the convention that *bug* means "error in a computer program," the idea that computers run programs, the notion that programs are compiled, and so on. Because they are both San Franciscans, they take it to include general knowledge about North Beach, Nob Hill, and San Francisco newspapers and their contents. And so on.

Most parts of common ground are inferred from a combination of all three types of information.

When Ann tells Bob something, the only "context" she intends him to use in interpreting what she meant is their common ground (see Clark and Carlson, 1981). This common ground might be called the *intrinsic context* of her utterances, and all other aspects of the situation are *incidental context*. For many investigators *all* aspects of the situation are potentially part of the "context" by which an utterance is interpreted, but this interpretation is too broad. By the very nature of coordination the speaker and addressees both recognize that the speaker intends them to infer what she means on the basis of their common ground and nothing more. That is all that could be relevant, and including anything else may even lead to error.

CONCLUSIONS

It should be obvious by now that coordination is truly a social process. Ann cannot coordinate with Bob without taking him into account. She must attribute to him certain motives, beliefs, and properties and act accordingly. Coordination in language use is a special case of coordination in social processes of any sort—persuading people, conforming to norms, handling personal encounters, forming impressions of one another, and so on. Language use is an example par excellence of how social processes that require coordination work.

One caution: I have so far stressed, and I will continue to stress, coordination even though language use is sometimes competitive too. People can lie, deceive, manipulate turn taking to their own ends, and otherwise subvert the normal forms of coordination. These aspects of language use haven't yet been studied very much (but see Harder and Kock, 1976; Verschueren, 1978). But many—perhaps all—types of competition work only because language use is normally cooperative, because it is normally based on tacit assumptions of coordination. A person couldn't lie to us successfully if we didn't think she usually told the truth.

So coordination is essential to language use and, more generally, to all communication. Speakers say what they say intending it to be understood in a particular way by their addressees. To succeed, they have to coordinate with these addressees, relying on such devices as convention, salience, precedence, and even explicit agreement. Speakers and listeners must also coordinate such complex aspects of language use as turn taking, repairing utterances, and selecting topics of conversation. Before I take up the more complex types of coordination, however, I will discuss the most basic of them all—the coordination of utterances and their interpretations.

UTTERANCES AND MEANING

Utterances are a natural place to begin in considering language use. From the individualist point of view the sentence is the basic unit of analysis, and many utterances—though hardly all—are productions of complete sentences. Utterances are also the units whereby people ask questions, make commands, and offer thanks, and of all the functions of language these are among the best understood. From the interactionist point of view utterances are also basic building blocks of dialogues and monologues. Discourse would be hard to characterize without them.

Utterances are not ends in themselves. They are means to ends—means to affecting listeners in certain ways. What do speakers use utterances for? And how do they accomplish their objectives? Most people would answer the first question, "To convey meaning," and the second, "By virtue of the words they utter and what these words mean." These answers are too easy, but they bring out a crucial point about language use: We can't study it without asking, "What is meaning?"

SPEAKER'S MEANING

In 1957 H. Paul Grice published a terse but highly influential paper in which he dissected the notion of meaning. He first drew a fundamental distinction between the meaning of "natural" events, or what I will call *signs,* and the meaning of certain deliberate human acts (such as utterances), or what I will call *signals*. Later, he and others (see Grice, 1968; Schiffer, 1972) analyzed signal meaning further, distinguishing between what words and sentences mean and what speakers mean in using words and sentences on particular occasions. What makes Grice's analysis significant is that it shows how essential coordination is in the two most basic processes in language use: meaning and understanding.

To begin, Grice pointed out that the word *meaning* has two very different uses in English, as illustrated in these two sentences:

- Those spots mean measles.

- That remark, *I am hungry,* meant that the speaker, Elizabeth, was hungry at the moment she made the remark.

The first sentence describes an instance of *sign meaning* (or what Grice called natural meaning). The spots on the patient's body constitute natural evidence—they are a sign or a symptom—of the patient's having the measles. The second sentence describes an instance of *signal meaning* (or what Grice called nonnatural meaning.) The remark *I am hungry* wasn't a sign, or a symptom, or natural evidence of Elizabeth's hunger; there is no natural connection between hunger and the noises *I am hungry*. Elizabeth could be feigning hunger, reciting a line from Shakespeare, exercising her vocal cords, or quoting her brother from the day before. In signal meaning the speaker's intentions are crucial. To understand Elizabeth's remark, we must see not only what she was doing but why she was doing it.

Work on communication has often collapsed the distinction between signs and signals. In nonverbal communication (see, e.g., Knapp, 1972), for example, there are many varieties of signs and signals, but they are sometimes lumped together. In a single category of body movements we find both deliberate gestures or "emblems," which are clearly signals, and involuntary displays of emotion, which are just as clearly signs. We find a person's physique, height, and weight, which are surely signs, treated in the same way as touching, stroking, and hitting, which are often signals. Under the heading of "paralanguage" we find voice qualities that evince emotion and tension, which are signs of the emotion and tension, listed alongside such vocalizations as moaning and whispering, which are usually signals. Because these two categories are collapsed, there is the suggestion that signs and signals are produced through the same mechanisms and are understood by the same processes. But if Grice is correct, signals ought to differ from signs in their use and understanding. Genuine signals, his analysis implies, require coordination of the producer and understander. Signs do not.

In signal meaning three more distinctions are important, as illustrated here:

- The sentence *I am hungry* can mean that the speaker, whoever that is, is in need of food at the time the sentence is uttered.

- The word *hungry* can mean "in need of food."

- That remark, *I am hungry,* meant that the speaker, Elizabeth, was hungry at the moment she made the remark.

The first description is a case of *sentence meaning,* which specifies one way in which the sentence *I am hungry* could be used on a particular occasion. (It could be used in other ways too, of course.) The second description is an instance of *word meaning,* one way in which the word *hungry* can be used on a particular occasion. The third description is of *utterance meaning,* what Elizabeth's act of uttering the sentence meant on that particular occasion; on another occasion an utterance of the same sentence could have meant something quite different. The same three distinctions apply to nonverbal signals too.

The distinctions among word, sentence, and utterance meaning are crucial to any investigation of language use. Sentences and words, on the one hand, are linguistic units that are abstracted away from any occasion on which they might be used. They have been stripped of any relation to particular speakers, listeners, times, and places. Utterances, on the other hand, are the productions of words and sentences on particular occasions by particular speakers for particular purposes. What we hear in conversations aren't words and sentences but *utterances* of words and sentences. In the study of language structure linguists have been concerned mainly with words and sentences and have proposed models of word and sentence meaning. In the study of language use, however, this isn't enough. We have to be concerned with utterances and utterance meaning, too. It is often assumed that models of word and sentence meaning can be applied, without additions or alterations, as models of utterance meaning. As we shall see, this isn't so. Utterance meaning requires new principles altogether—specifically, ones that bring in the fundamental coordination between speakers and addressees.

Signal meaning of any kind, Grice argued, is secondary to, or derivative from, what has come to be called *speaker's meaning* (or utterer's meaning), as illustrated here:

- In uttering *I am hungry,* Elizabeth meant that she was hungry.

This is a description not of what the utterance of *I am hungry* meant but of what Elizabeth, the speaker, meant by uttering those words. Grice then claimed that sentences, words, and utterances only have meaning by virtue of some speaker being able to mean something by using them. Speaker's meaning is primary. Although there is some question about how to take this claim (see Kempson, 1975, pp. 138 on), the distinction between speaker's meaning and sentence, utterance, and word meaning is widely accepted.

But what exactly is speaker's meaning? One of Grice's most important contributions was to show that it consists of certain of the speaker's intentions toward his listeners (see also Bach and Harnish, 1979). When Elizabeth utters the words *I am hungry* to Thomas, she intends him to formulate the belief that she is expressing the attitude that she is hungry. Indeed, by expressing the attitude that she is hungry, she is giving Thomas good reason to think (in most circumstances) that she actually *is* hungry. But why should Thomas formulate the belief that Elizabeth is expressing the attitude that she is hungry? According to Grice's arguments, it must be in part by means of his recognition of her *intention* that he formulate this belief. The necessary ingredient here is a reflexive intention—an intention that is intended to be recognized. Grice called this reflexive intention an *m-intention.*

Utterances, therefore, are inherently relational. Elizabeth's utterance entails her having certain intentions toward Thomas. Those intentions involve Thomas himself, for she intends him to understand her by means of his recognition of those intentions. Her utterance toward Thomas creates a *relation* between them—indeed, a *social* relation—a function with two arguments, Elizabeth and Thomas. It is because of their relational character that utterances require coordination between speakers and addressees. Elizabeth must design what she says so that Thomas will recognize her intentions, and Thomas must take it that Elizabeth has designed what she said in just that way. It is misleading, then, to characterize an utterance without bringing in both speaker and addressees.

What distinguishes signals from signs, therefore, is that genuine signals are based on a person's m-intention —an intention that is intended to be recognized— whereas signs are not. Most communication involves both signals *and* signs. In conversations when a woman shakes her head, holds out her hand for silence, or utters *I am hungry,* we ordinarily take these as *signals* that she disagreed with the last remark, is asking for silence, and is asserting she's hungry. But when she jerks her head involuntarily, turns red, or takes a breath as another's turn ends, we ordinarily take these as *signs* that she was shocked by the news, was embarrassed by the last remark, and is preparing to speak next. A full theory of communication must account for both types of reactions.

Are signals and signs handled by the same mental processes? A priori, that seems implausible. When a speaker produces a signal (like the woman's utterance or headshake), she does it intending her addressees to recognize certain intentions, and that requires coordination. That process seems very different from displaying signs (like the woman's involuntary head jerk or red face), where the speaker has no such intentions and isn't trying to coordinate with her addressees. Likewise, when an addressee tries to understand a sign such as the red face, he interprets it as "direct" evidence of, say, embarrassment. This seems very different from trying to understand the woman's upheld hand, a signal, which he can only interpret in coordination with the woman and her intentions. It is as if signs and signals belong to two different but parallel channels of communication. The two channels are independent in that they can even provide contradictory information, as when a person denies being angry (a signal) while his face is red with anger (a sign). In this essay I will be concerned with signals or, more fundamentally, with what speakers mean. It is appropriate, then, to start with utterances, for in communication they are the prototypes of genuine signals.

ILLOCUTIONARY ACTS

What are utterances for? As I mentioned earlier, in common parlance we say they are used for asking questions, making promises, offering things, apologizing, thanking, bidding farewell, ordering people to do things, pleading, making requests, making assertions, and so on. The number of such uses seems limitless, with little hope that we could ever make sense of them. Yet in 1958, in a slim book called *How to Do Things with Words,* the Oxford philosopher John L. Austin developed a highly influential theory for the uses of utterances. He proposed at once both an analysis of what it means to ask questions, make promises, and the like, and a method for classifying these things. Since then, his proposals have been extended and refined by Searle (1969, 1975a), Bach and Harnish (1979), and others, but the essentials of his analysis have remained more or less intact.

The basic idea is that an utterance is an *act,* or rather a collection of acts. When Julia says to the butcher, *Please give me that roast,* she is *doing* things (recall Austin's title, *How to Do Things with Words*). At the most basic level she is performing the act of making certain noises. In doing so, she is also performing the act of uttering certain identifiable words. In doing this, she is also performing the act of uttering a particular sentence with a certain sense and reference. These acts will be of little concern here, and I will focus instead on two additional ones. In uttering *Please give me that roast,* Julia is also performing the act of requesting the butcher to give her that roast. This act Austin called an *illocutionary act.* And by or through making this request, Julia is also performing the act of trying to get the butcher to give her that roast. This act Austin called a *perlocutionary act.* Taken together, these acts have come to be called *speech acts.*

Speech acts are like other acts. For a hunter killing a deer with a gun, we can again talk about a collection of acts. The hunter performed the act of tensing the muscles in his right index finger. By doing so, he performed the act of shooting the gun at the deer. And by doing this, he performed the act of killing the deer. Different areas of human action are open to different analyses, and issuing utterances is just one more of those areas.

You can't perform illocutionary acts in just any circumstances. For such an act to be "felicitous," to use Austin's term, certain conditions have to be satisfied. For Julia to make her request of the butcher felicitously, she must believe that the butcher is able to give her the roast and that it isn't obvious he would otherwise do so in the normal course of events. She must be sincere in wanting to give it to her, and she must take her utterance as counting as an attempt to get him to give it to her. Other illocutionary acts, such as promising, apologizing, and asserting, have similar requirements.

These requirements have been stated more formally by Searle (1969, 1975b) as four *felicity conditions.* For requests such as Julia's the conditions are the following (where S stands for the speaker, e.g., Julia; H stands for the hearer, e.g., the butcher; and A stands for the requested act, e.g., the butcher's giving the roast to Julia):

- *Preparatory condition:* H is able to perform A.

- *Sincerity condition:* S wants H to do A.

- *Propositional content condition:* S predicates a future act A of H.

- *Essential condition:* S's utterance counts as an attempt by S to get H to do A.

For comparison, consider a promise, such as the butcher replying to Julia, *I'll get it for you.* (Now S is the butcher; H is Julia; and the act A is the same as before, the butcher giving the roast to Julia.) Promises have the following felicity conditions:

- *Preparatory condition:* H is able to perform A. H wants S to perform A.

- *Sincerity condition:* S intends to do A.

- *Propositional content condition:* S predicates a future act of S.

- *Essential condition:* S's utterance counts as an undertaking by S of an obligation to do A.

Felicity conditions like these, in effect, tell us when and why a speaker would want to perform a request or a promise. They should therefore have a good deal to do both with the planning of such illocutionary acts and with their understanding. I will say more about these processes later.

To anticipate a bit, note that Julia's request and the butcher's promise constitute a type of conversational unit, just like a question and answer, or like *thank you* and *you're welcome.* Julia's request sets up certain conditions, and the butcher's reply completes them. This is directly reflected in the felicity conditions. The preparatory conditions for the butcher's reply are set up by the preparatory and sincerity conditions of Julia's request. The propositional content conditions of his reply match those of her request. And the sincerity and essential conditions of the butcher's promise complete or satisfy the expectations set up by the essential condition of Julia's request. With felicity conditions, then, we have one way of characterizing fairly precisely how Julia and the butcher coordinate their illocutionary acts in this sequence of utterances [though see Bach and Harnish (1979) and others for qualifications on Searle's felicity conditions].

TYPES OF ILLOCUTIONARY ACTS

What kinds of illocutionary acts are there? Austin argued that illocutionary acts could be classified by the felicity conditions they were subject to, and he offered a classification with five main types. Searle (1975a), with slightly different felicity conditions, revised Austin's scheme into five new types. Bach and Harnish (1979) subdivided one of Searle's categories into two. I will describe Searle's proposal with Bach and Harnish's amendment.

The idea behind Searle's classification scheme is this: Illocutionary acts differ mainly in their immediate purpose, or "illocutionary point." For some illocutionary acts the point is to get listeners to do things; for others it is to commit the speaker to doing things; and so on. These illocutionary points, which are expressed in the essential conditions, fall fairly readily into six main classes: to express beliefs, to get listeners to do things, to commit the speaker to doing things, to express psychological states, to effect changes in institutional states of affairs, and to determine institutional states of affairs. Each of these points corresponds to one main type of illocutionary act, each with its own name.

1. *Assertives:* An assertive is an illocutionary act of expressing a belief. When Burton asserts to Connie, *Jill has gone to the opera,* he is expressing the belief that Jill has gone to the opera. He is also expressing an intention that Connie form this belief. Indeed, the prototypical as-

sertive is the assertion, but this category also includes diagnoses, predictions, notifications, confessions, denials, disputations, retorts, conjectures, suppositions, and many other such acts.

2. *Directives:* Directives are illocutionary acts in which the speaker tries to get the addressees to do things. In a request like *Please open the door,* the speaker is trying to get the addressee to open the door, or at least to commit himself to opening the door. With a question like *Is Irene in the pantry?* the speaker is trying to get the addressee to provide information as to whether or not Irene is in the pantry. Questions are requests for information. Directives vary in how forceful they are—in whether one demands, requires, suggests, or merely hints that the addressee do something—and vary in other ways as well. All directives "direct" the addressee to do something in the future, and that is what makes them all of one type.

3. *Commissives:* A commissive is an illocutionary act of committing oneself or of proposing to commit oneself to some future action. The prototypical commissive is the promise, as when George says to Jane, *I'll get the book.* In uttering these words, George commits himself to Jane to getting the book. To be sincere, he must truly intend to get the book—to honor his commitment. Another type of commissive is the offer, as in *Can I get you some coffee?* which is taken as a proposal to commit oneself to bring the addressee coffee if that is desirable.

4. *Expressives:* Expressives are illocutionary acts, like thanking, apologizing, congratulating, and greeting, in which the speaker expresses certain feelings toward the addressee. When Sam apologizes to Helen with *I'm sorry I'm late,* there is no question about his being late. That fact is common ground to the conversation. What Sam is doing is expressing his feeling about that fact—he regrets the fact that he is late—intending Helen to believe that he regrets it.

5. *Effectives:* Effectives are one of two types of illocutionary acts that rely on the conventions of an institution for their performance. When a speaker performs an effective, with his very utterance he changes a state of affairs that is recognized within that institution. He does this by virtue of some privilege the institution grants him. In industry a boss may fire, promote, or appoint someone. In court a judge may indict, pardon, or sentence someone. A police officer may arrest someone. In football a referee may start the game and call time-outs. In church a minister may baptize, marry, or bless someone.

In each case the speaker has the institutional power to change things by merely saying such things as *You're fired, You are hereby sentenced to three years in the pen,* or *Bless you* in the proper circumstances.

6. *Verdictives:* Verdictives are the second main type of illocutionary acts performed under institutional circumstances. With verdictives the speaker determines what is to be the case. Consider a baseball umpire who says, "Strike." He is trying to judge whether or not the ball that the pitcher has thrown has crossed the plate in the strike zone—between the batter's shoulders and knees—and he is trying to be accurate. Yet when he says "Strike," regardless of whether the ball actually did cross the plate in the strike zone, his verdict is then law: As far as the conduct of the game is concerned, the ball *did* pass through the strike zone, and the pitch is a strike. Similarly, verdictives occur in court when a judge finds a prisoner guilty or innocent, in meetings when the presiding officer overrules a point, and in academia when an editor accepts or rejects papers for publication. Verdictives play an important role in many institutional affairs.

There are several points to notice about this classification scheme. First, it is intended to classify *all* possible illocutionary acts. Second, the categories are intended to be mutually exclusive and collectively exhaustive. The scheme satisfies these two goals fairly well. There aren't obvious cases that fall into the cracks between categories or that belong to two categories at once (but see Wunderlich, 1977). Third, each category can be further subdivided on other dimensions. As I have already mentioned, for example, directives vary in how forcefully they oblige the addressee to do what is being requested, from commands and demands at the forceful end, to suggestions at the other, with requests in between. The subcategories are well described by Searle (1975b) and Bach and Harnish (1979).

ADDRESSEES, PARTICIPANTS, AND OVERHEARERS

The illocutionary acts described so far are directed at what are customarily called addressees. When George asks Jane, *Where are the boys?* his question is being asked of Jane, the addressee, and of no one else. When Helen offers Sam coffee with *Would you like some of this?* her offer is being made to Sam, the addressee, and to no one else. And when a boss fires an employee with *You're fired,* that act is directed at the employee, the addressee: The boss isn't firing anyone else. Austin's and Searle's theories are about illocutionary acts directed at addressees.

The mystery is how other listeners are to understand. First, consider overhearers, that is, listeners who are not part of the conversation in which an utterance occurs. When George asks Jane, *Where are the boys?* he doesn't have any m-intentions toward, say, Lance, who is overhearing without George's knowledge. He isn't asking Lance any question—that much is obvious—but he also hasn't designed his utterance so as to make sure that Lance can necessarily understand it. Since Lance may have no idea who "the boys" are, he couldn't understand the question George is asking. But George doesn't care. Speakers don't necessarily design utterances so that overhearers can understand them.

Speakers do design utterances, however, so that other *participants* in the conversation can understand them. Imagine that George asks his question of Jane in a conversation with Jane and Ken. To fulfill his social obligation to Ken, he must design his question so that Ken can understand it too. He must be sure, for example, that Ken will recognize who "the boys" are. Yet Ken recognizes that *he* isn't being asked the question; Jane is. In traditional speech act theory, this is impossible. Speakers don't direct illocutionary acts at anyone but addressees. George can't have any m-intentions toward Ken. He can ask Jane a question, but he can do nothing more.

To handle this case, we need an additional type of illocutionary act called the *informative* (Clark and Carlson, 1982a, 1982b). The idea is that when George utters *Where are the boys?* he is performing two illocutionary acts at the same time—an informative and a question. He is informing Jane and Ken jointly that he is asking Jane where the boys are. This is the informative. He is also asking Jane where the boys are, and this is his question. Notice that George must inform Jane and Ken *jointly* of his question to Jane since it is just as important for Jane to know that Ken knows George's question as it is for Ken to know it, and for Ken to know that she knows he knows it, and so on. A somewhat surprising part of this proposal is that George's question is performed by means of the informative. George informs Jane and Ken jointly of his question, and it is by that means that he actually asks her the question. This may seem roundabout, but there is good evidence for it.

Informatives are needed to keep all the participants in a conversation informed at all times of what is being said. As I will suggest later, conversations can be viewed as the accumulation of information in the parties' common ground. For conversations to accumulate properly, each participant must keep track at all times of what the others are saying, regardless of to whom each utterance is addressed. The only way this organization can be guaranteed is if each party informs all the others at all times of what she is doing. Informatives are essential to the process.

With this classification of illocutionary acts—both of acts directed at addressees and of acts directed at participants—we have come a long way. I began with speaker's meaning, what a person means in uttering something. Speaker's meaning, according to Grice, involves certain intentions by the speaker toward the addressee. These intentions get expressed and are then recognized, according to Austin and Searle, by means of the speaker's illocutionary acts. These illocutionary acts fall into a small number of basic categories, which are really a classification of the possible Gricean intentions a speaker can harbor in uttering things. This scheme is important, for it specifies both what building blocks discourse must be constructed from and what utterance parts must add up to.

PLANNING AND UNDERSTANDING UTTERANCES

How do speakers plan illocutionary acts, and how do listeners recognize them? At first, the answers seem straightforward. In English, if a speaker wants to ask a question, she plans an interrogative sentence, like *Is Mary here?* or *Where is the train station?* If she wants to make an assertion, she plans a declarative sentence, as in *Mary is at home* and *The train station is around the corner.* If she wants to make a request or command, she plans the imperative *Go home* or *Please hand me the newspaper.* As for the listener, he works in reverse, identifying interrogatives as questions, declaratives as assertions, and imperatives as requests or commands. The scheme assumes a one-to-one correspondence between types of illocutionary acts and sentence types.

This scheme, however, is hopelessly inadequate, for two reasons. First, there are many more types of illocutionary acts than sentence types. Within assertives I listed assertions, diagnoses, predictions, notifications, confessions, denials, disputations, retorts, conjectures, and

suppositions, and there are many more types. The other five major categories include just as many types. The types of illocutionary acts may actually be uncountable in number. Yet in English there are only *four* basic sentence moods: declarative, interrogative, imperative, and exclamatory. There are simply not enough sentence types to go around. Second, these few sentence types bear no direct relation to illocutionary acts. A request for the salt can be performed by means of a declarative sentence, like *I'd like you to pass the salt,* or an interrogative sentence, like *Would you please pass the salt?* or an imperative sentence, like *Please pass the salt.* The link between illocutionary acts and sentence types is not at all direct.

Despite the scheme's shortcomings, one good thing to come out of attempts to use it is the distinction between direct and indirect illocutionary acts. By this approach an illocutionary act is direct if it is performed by means of the sentence type appropriate to it, and it is indirect if it is performed by any other means. So as a request, *Please pass the salt* is direct since it uses the imperative construction appropriate to requests, but as a request, *Would you please pass the salt?* is indirect since it uses the interrogative construction appropriate to questions. Since there are so many more illocutionary types than sentence types, of course, this scheme collapses all the fine distinctions among direct illocutonary acts into just four categories, and this is ultimately not very helpful (see Levinson, 1980). Both requests and commands, for example, are performed directly by means of the imperative construction.

How, then, do speakers signal which illocutionary act they are performing? Austin took up what he called *performative utterances.* These are utterances like *I hereby request you to pass the salt* in which the speaker (I) explicitly says (with *hereby request*) what illocutionary act he is performing toward the addressee (*you*). By selecting the right performative verb (like *request*), the speaker can be as precise as he wants. But this proposal has problems too. Although Austin took performative utterances to be a species of direct illocutionary act, others (see Bach and Harnish, 1979) have argued that they are assertions directly and are only indirectly requests and other illocutionary acts. Further, the performative verb one chooses doesn't always specify accurately the illocutionary act one is performing. In *I promise you that Helen left an hour ago,* the speaker isn't making a promise but an emphatic assertion. So performative utterances don't help much in the analysis of types of illocutionary acts.

One value of performative utterances, however, is that they reveal the difference between illocutionary and perlocutionary acts. Note that one can say *I hereby tell you that I killed Cock Robin,* but not *I hereby convince you that I killed Cock Robin.* Telling is an illocutionary act; convincing is a perlocutionary act, something one can only do *through* illocutionary acts. Similarly, one can say *I warn you that the sky is falling,* but not *I scare you that the sky is falling.* Warning is an illocutionary act; scaring is perlocutionary. In general, illocutionary acts require that the addressee only recognize the speaker's intentions. Perlocutionary effects are a *consequence* of that recognition. The distinction between illocutionary and perlocutionary acts, though subtle, is important.

So even though the contrast between direct and indirect illocutionary acts makes sense, it is not well served by the scheme just described in which all direct illocutionary acts are collapsed into just four categories. We need a different approach altogether. Such an approach is offered by Grice's notion of the logic of conversation.

IMPLICATURES

In another important paper called "Logic and Conversation," Grice (1975, 1978) noted that people generally mean much more than they actually say. Imagine, he said, that A is standing by an obviously immobilized car as B comes along, and they have this exchange:

A: I am out of gasoline.

B: There is a gas station around the corner.

Now A takes B's utterance to be relevant to what he just said—to the fact that he is out of gasoline. That is, A takes B not simply as saying that there is a gas station around the corner but also as meaning that the gas station is probably open and would sell A gasoline, solving A's problem. The second part of B's meaning Grice called an *implicature.* He therefore distinguished between *saying* and *implicating* as two parts of speaker meaning.

How do implicatures work? Grice's answer was that they are a consequence of speakers and listeners cooperating in conversation. He built his argument around what he called the *cooperative principle,* which he stated as an injunction to speakers: "Make your conversational contribution such as is required, at the stage at which it occurs, by the accepted purpose or direction of the talk exchange in which you are engaged." When B says that

there is a gas station around the corner, A takes B as being cooperative, as acceding to the obvious purpose of A's remark, and therefore as implicating that the gas station is probably open and selling gasoline. That is, A is expected to take what is said (in Grice's sense) along with the accepted purpose of the talk exchange, however that is inferred, and derive what is implicated. Grice's proposal, then, was about what speakers mean in context.

The cooperative principle, Grice argued, divides into four maxims and further submaxims:

1. *The maxim of quantity:*
   a. Make your contribution as informative as is required (for the current purposes of the exchange).
   b. Do not make your contribution more informative than is required.

2. *The maxim of quality:* Try to make your contribution one that is true.
   a. Do not say what you believe to be false.
   b. Do not say that for which you lack adequate evidence.

3. *The maxim of relation:* Be relevant.

4. *The maxim of manner:* Be perspicuous.
   a. Avoid obscurity of expression.
   b. Avoid ambiguity.
   c. Be brief (avoid unnecessary prolixity).
   d. Be orderly.

Together, these constitute what it means to be cooperative.

These maxims are not inviolable. As long as the speaker is adhering to the overall cooperative principle, she can flout any of these maxims—deliberately violate a maxim, intending her addressees to see that the violation is deliberate—in order to produce certain implicatures. Grice offered some vivid examples. Consider A's letter of recommendation about a candidate for a philosophy job that goes as follows: "Dear Sir, Mr. X's command of English is excellent, and his attendance at tutorials has been regular. Yours, etc." Person A is not being as informative as required for a letter of recommendation. He is obviously flouting the maxim of quantity in order to implicate that there is a reason A isn't being informative: Mr. X isn't very good. Or consider A and B who both know that X has just betrayed A, and A says, "X is a fine friend.'' Person A is saying what he believes to be false, flouting the maxim of quality. But by doing so, he is implicating that he means just the opposite of what he says, that he is being ironic. Or consider the contrast between ''Miss X sang 'Home Sweet Home' '' and ''Miss X produced a series of sounds that corresponded closely with the score of 'Home Sweet Home.' '' In selecting the second remark over the first, a reviewer would be flouting the maxim of manner, ''be brief,'' implicating that Miss X's singing wasn't very good.

In certain respects Grice's distinction between saying and implicating is equivalent to the distinction between direct and indirect illocutionary acts. The most successful approach to indirect illocutionary acts has treated them as a type of conversational implicature. That is Searle's approach to indirect illocutionary acts.

INDIRECT ILLOCUTIONARY ACTS

Imagine that George is trying to call Julia on the telephone when Margaret answers. George says, ''Is Julia there?'' and Margaret responds, ''Yes, she is. I'll get her.'' What is George doing with his utterance? According to Searle (1975b), he is performing two illocutionary acts, which I will call meaning 1 and meaning 2:

- *Meaning 1:* ''I ask you whether or not Julia is home'' (a question).

- *Meaning 2:* ''I request of you that if Julia is home, you summon her to the telephone.''

Meaning 1 is often called the direct meaning or illocutionary force, and meaning 2 an indirect meaning or illocutionary force. Searle argued that meaning 2, George's request, is performed *by means of,* or *by virtue of,* his question. The request is logically dependent on the performance of the question, not vice versa. Others (e.g., Clark, 1979; Goffman, 1976) have noted that there may be more than one indirect illocutionary act at a time. If George had said, ''Can you tell me if Julia is home?'' he would have asked a question (''Can you tell me?''), thereby asking a second question (''Is Julia at home?'') and thereby making a request (''Please summon her''). The second and third illocutionary acts—the second question and the request—would *both* be indirect.

How does Margaret recognize that George is doing more than asking the direct question? How does she recognize that he is requesting her to summon Julia to the

telephone? The answers lie in Grice's cooperative principle. Given the accepted purpose of a telephone call like this, George wouldn't want to know merely whether or not Julia was home. For the question to be relevant, he must be interested in speaking to her and want Margaret to summon her to the telephone. In this view meaning 1 is what George says (in Grice's sense of saying), and meaning 2 is what he implicates. Indirect illocutionary acts are therefore a type of implicature (Searle, 1975a).

In planning her response, Margaret pays close attention to both of George's illocutionary acts (Clark, 1979). Her response can be divided into two moves:

- *Move 1:* '' Yes, she is'' (an assertion in answer to meaning 1).

- *Move 2:* ''I'll get her'' (a promise in reply to meaning 2).

Margaret's move 1 is a response to George's meaning 1; it answers his direct question. Move 2 is a response to his meaning 2; it is a promise to comply with his request. She also pays attention to the logical dependence between his two illocutionary acts. She replies to meaning 1 first and to meaning 2 second. She could also have replied simply, ''I'll get her,'' responding to George's meaning 2 alone, but she would still have implicitly answered his direct question. By saying, ''I'll get her,'' she implicates that Julia is home, and so the answer to George's direct question is yes. Note that if Margaret's answer to George's question had been, ''No, she isn't,'' his request would no longer have been in force and she needn't, even couldn't, have replied to it. So in planning her response, Margaret relies directly on what she believes to be George's meanings 1 and 2.

Grice's argument that implicatures come from the accepted purpose of the talk exchange has received experimental support (Clark, 1979). In one experiment 100 restaurateurs in the San Francisco area were called by a woman who asked either ''Do you accept American Express cards?'' or ''Do you accept credit cards?'' The restaurateurs, it was supposed, assumed she was calling because she wanted to eat at the restaurant, pay with a credit card, and find out if one of her credit cards was acceptable. Consider only those restaurateurs who could answer yes to her direct question. With *Do you accept American Express cards?* the restaurateurs could assume that she had an American Express card and that an answer of yes would be sufficient—that she wasn't implicating anything more. Indeed, 100 percent of the restaurateurs in this circumstance said yes (move 1) and nothing more. But with *Do you accept credit cards?* the restaurateurs could assume that she had two or more credit cards and therefore also wanted to know which credit cards were acceptable. In this case 84 percent of the restaurateurs answered yes (move 1), but fully 46 percent *also* offered her the list of the credit cards that were acceptable (move 2). So even though the two questions were identical except for the object of the verb *accept,* and even though they were asked in the identical situation, they were interpreted very differently—one with certain implicatures and the other without them—depending on the assumed purpose of the talk exchange.

One factor that complicates this picture is convention (Clark, 1979; Morgan, 1978; Searle, 1975a). Compare these two ways of requesting the time:

- *Conventional:* Do you know what time it is? Can you tell me the time? Do you have a watch? Do you have the time? May I ask you what time it is?

- *Nonconventional:* It's getting pretty late, isn't it? Did you happen to look at the clock just now? Are we late for our appointment? I'd guess it's nearly six, wouldn't you?

The sentences in the first group are highly conventional ones for asking for the time. They are the ones people are most likely to use and expect others to use. Those in the second group are less conventional and would generally be used only in special circumstances. Intuitively, when someone asks, "Can you tell me the time?" she is making a request, and the question is more or less irrelevant, merely a *pro forma* way of making that request. When someone says, "Are we late for our appointment?" on the other hand, he is asking the question seriously *and* requesting the time.

The proposal is, then, that speakers vary in how seriously they intend their *direct* illocutionary acts to be taken (Clark, 1979). For "Can you tell me the time?" they may be asking the direct question completely *pro forma* and not expecting an answer. Evidence supports this view. When bank clerks were telephoned and asked the conventional "Can you tell me what the interest rate is?" only 16 percent answered yes before saying the interest rate. But when bank clerks in the same circumstances were asked the less conventional "Are you able to tell me what the interest rate is?" fully 35 percent answered yes before going on to give the interest rate. Even though virtually all bank clerks took these two utterances as re-

quests, they interpreted the caller as seriously intending the direct question more often when it was nonconventional. A good deal of other evidence goes along with this conclusion.

For highly conventional ways of making requests, if the direct illocutionary act, meaning 1, isn't to be taken seriously, what is? Obviously. the indirect illocutionary act, meaning 2. It follows that for highly conventional ways of making indirect requests (like *Do you know the time?*), listeners should be more certain that the speaker actually *is* making a request, and indeed they are (Clark, 1979). Listeners should also be *quicker* to grasp the indirect request than they are the question by which it is being made, and they are (Gibbs, 1981; Schweller, 1978). For direct and indirect illocutionary acts conventions of use are critical.

THE CASE OF REQUESTS

In proposing the cooperative principle, Grice supposed that what a speaker means depends on "the accepted purpose or direction of the talk exchange," but it is devilishly difficult to characterize what the "accepted purpose or direction" of any talk exchange is. For requests and their responses, however, we can make some headway. The idea is that requests and their responses are parts of negotiations for exchanges of goods. In my earlier example, when Julia asked the butcher for a roast and he got it for her, she was placing herself under an obligation in return, one that the butcher would later call in by asking her for money. For many requests there is no immediate return of the favor. Rather, the negotiation relies on the good faith of the two parties in a more complicated system of social exchange. Social exchange, then, plays a central role in the planning and understanding of requests.

Social exchange has been argued to be central to the notion of politeness in requests. Lakoff (1973a, 1977) noted that the various ways in which one could make indirect requests differ in politeness. *Could you pass the salt?* is relatively polite among acquainted peers; *I want you to pass the salt* is not. From examples like these, she argued for two rules of politeness:

- *Rule 1:* Don't impose.

- *Rule 2:* Give options.

With *I want you to pass the salt,* for example, the speaker imposes on the listener by explicitly indicating that he wants the listener to do something, as if he has the authority to impose; *I would like you to pass the salt* would be a softer imposition and therefore more polite. With *Could you pass the salt?* the speaker gives the listener the option of saying no, she couldn't pass the salt, and this is still more polite.

Lakoff's two rules can be viewed as part of a more general scheme for politeness in conversational exchanges, as proposed by Brown and Levinson (1978; see also Goody, 1978). As applied to requests, the idea is this: Requests are potentially inequitable for the speaker S and addressee A. While S benefits from the favor he receives, A is put out by the cost of providing that favor. In Goffman's (1955, 1967) terms, S's request threatens A's *face*. For Goffman, face is the positive social value people claim for themselves. It consists of two wants: the want to be unimpeded or unhindered by others as one goes about one's business and the want to be approved of by others. People ordinarily act to maintain or gain face—that is, to avoid losing face. Person S's request is threatening to A's face because it imposes on A. Politeness is determined this way: Speakers are polite to the extent that they enhance, or lessen the threat to, their addressee's face. With requests S will be polite to the extent that he can reduce or eliminate the threat to A's face brought about by imposing his request. Let us call this the *cost-benefit theory* of politeness.

Evidence for the cost-benefit theory has been provided by a study of requests by Clark and Schunk (1980). People were asked to rate the politeness of eighteen different types of indirect requests for information, such as *May I ask you who is coming to the party? Can you tell me who is coming to the party? Do you want to tell me who is coming to the party?* All the utterances were indirect requests and differed only in their direct meanings (meaning 1)—the question that was asked directly. The way these utterances were judged to differ in politeness, then, must somehow reflect the differences in their direct meanings.

Compare *May I ask you who is coming?* and *Do you want to tell me who is coming?* With the first, the speaker is asking permission even to request the wanted information. Since the speaker is offering her addressee a lot of authority at little cost, this request ought to be relatively polite. With the second utterance, however, the speaker is asking the addressee whether or not he wants or intends to provide the desired information. This presupposes, in effect, that the addressee ought to comply, and so compared with the first request, it should be more threatening to his face. Indeed, in the Clark and Schunk

study, people's judgments of politeness pretty much followed the predicted order for the eighteen types of requests.

The cost-benefit theory should also hold for *responses* to requests. To answer *Can you tell me who is coming?* one can select from among a variety of responses: *Mary; Mary is; Mary is coming; Yes, Mary is; Yes, I can. Mary is;* and so on. From the cost-benefit theory Clark and Schunk proposed an *attentiveness hypothesis:* The more attentive the responder is to what the requester meant, the more polite he should seem in return. The responder should be considered more polite when the information he gives is clear than when it is unclear, as in *Mary* versus *Mary is.* He should be more polite, generally, when he attends to the direct question than when he doesn't, as in *Yes, Mary is* versus *Mary is.* And he should be more polite, generally, the clearer he is about his answer to the direct question, as in *Yes, I can. Mary is* versus *Yes, Mary is.* Each of these predications was confirmed in people's ratings of the politeness of the alternative responses.

Perceived politeness, by the cost-benefit theory, should also vary with the size of the request itself. The more costly the required response—on any of many dimensions—the less polite the request. So *Can you tell me who's coming?* should be more polite than *Can you tell me how good your sex life has been?* And *Can you loan me a quarter?* should be more polite than *Can you loan me two hundred dollars?* The onerousness of a request can be at least partially compensated for by using a form that offers more face-saving opportunities to the responder, as in the contrast between *Can you loan me two hundred dollars?* and *Would it be at all possible for you to loan me two hundred dollars?*

The statuses of the speaker and addressee are also critical. Under Brown and Levinson's notion of costs and benefits, two intimates should be able to negotiate a larger exchange of goods than should two people not acquainted; also, a superior should be able to make more sizable requests of an inferior than vice versa. A woman might ask her husband, "Pass the salt," but she would ask a stranger, "Would you mind passing the salt?" A general would command a private, "Open the door," while the private would have to ask, "Would it be possible for you to open the door?" Violating these principles leads to perceptions of rudeness, obsequiousness, or condescension, depending on the circumstances. The principles are real enough.

The direct meaning of utterances such as *Could you pass the salt?* must fit the speaker's accepted purpose in other ways as well. Compare *Would you tell me the time?* and *Do you know the time?* Both are direct questions requiring yes or no answers; they differ in what they directly say. With *Would you tell me the time?* the speaker presupposes that the addressee knows the time. The only doubt in the speaker's mind—at least for the purposes of this exchange—is whether the addressee is willing to tell him the time. With *Do you know the time?* on the other hand, the speaker doesn't presuppose that the addressee knows the time. Instead, he doubts—at least, he expresses the doubt as a pretext for the exchange—whether or not the addressee knows the time. So one might ask, "Would you tell me your middle name?" but never, "Do you know your middle name?" The idea is that speakers ordinarily assess what factors might keep an addressee from giving the requested response and then build their direct meanings around the greatest obstacle among these factors. If knowing the facts is the greatest obstacle, the speaker will ask, "Do you know the time?" If willingness to provide already known facts is the greatest obstacle, the speaker will ask, "Would you tell me the time?" If happening to see the clock in the next room is the greatest obstacle, the speaker will ask, "Did you happen to see the clock in the next room?"

With requests, therefore, there is coordination between the speaker and addressee at every turn. Most requests are conveyed indirectly, by means of direct illocutionary acts of one sort or another. These illocutionary acts themselves must be recognized in a coordinated fashion. Since requests are one step in the exchange of goods, the direct illocutionary act gets used as part of the compensation in this exchange. The more the direct meaning offers benefits to the addressee, within limits, the more polite the request is judged to be. The more attentive the responder is to this as well as the indirect request, the more polite *he* will be viewed as being. And finally, the direct meaning is the speaker's way of telling the addressee how he views the situation, as in *Did you happen to look at the clock just now?* He thereby offers the addressee means by which he, the addressee, can legitimately not comply with the request, as in *Sorry, I didn't.*

UTTERANCE PARTS

Utterances do not come as unanalyzable wholes. They each have parts, and each part in turn plays a distinctive role in the speech acts made with the whole utterance. I might make a request of a bartender with the utterance *Please get me a dry martini.* In doing so, I specify not only that I am asking him to do something but also what it is I am asking him to do—get me a dry martini. What I am asking him to do is often called the *propositional content* of the request, and it is typically expressed in several parts. In this request it consists of an agent (the bartender, the implicit subject of the sentence) and the action he is to perform (get me a dry martini), which in turn consists of the act itself (getting), the object of that act (a dry martini), and the recipient or experiencer of the act (me). With each of these parts I specify a critical piece of the request I am making, and with their combination I specify the request as a whole.

All this is so commonsensical that we rarely reflect on how these parts work. Just as the whole utterance can be treated as an act the speaker is performing, so can each part. So when I use the words *a dry martini,* I am performing an act toward the bartender, intending him to recognize that I am using these words to refer to a certain kind of alcoholic drink. I expect him to recognize which kind of drink that is. When I assert *That man is tall,* according to Searle (1969), I am performing two main subutterance acts (which Searle called *propositional acts*). I am making a reference with the expression *that man,* and I am making a predication with the words *is tall.* Just as I can perform an illocutionary act felicitously only under the right conditions, so I can perform reference acts and predication acts felicitously only under the right conditions.

The study of utterance parts should not be confused with the study of sentence parts, as related as these notions are. The study of sentences and their parts, of course, has long been the mainstay of linguistics in the analysis of syntax and semantics. In syntax, linguists have proposed a variety of formal models about what sentence constructions are and are not possible, say, in English (e.g., see Akmajian and Heny, 1975; Chomsky, 1965; Soames and Perlmutter, 1979). Why can we say *The man is tall* but not *Man the tall is?* In semantics, linguists have set up equally formal descriptions for the way the meanings of words and phrases combine to express meanings for whole sentences (e.g., see Allwood, Andersson, and Dahl, 1977; Katz, 1977; Montague, 1974; Partee, 1975).

But while the study of syntax and semantics can tell us how sentences and their parts can be used, this goes only halfway toward telling us how they are *actually* used on any occasion. *Stereo* can be used, according to syntactic and semantic models, as a noun meaning "stereophonic sound system" or "stereoscopic system" or "stereoscopic photograph." But when a friend tells me *I just bought a stereo,* I recognize that she intends *stereo* in just one of these three ways, and I must determine which one. She can even use the word innovatively, as in *I just stereo'd my car,* or arbitrarily, as when she stipulates *By stereo I shall mean "spayed dog or cat."* The study of syntax and semantics, as generally practiced, has nothing directly to say about the use and understanding of words on particular occasions—especially innovative or stipulated uses—or about what acts the speaker is performing with these uses. To account for utterance parts, we must again bring in the coordination of speakers and addressees.

Use and understanding have been studied intensively for only a few types of utterance parts (see Clark and Clark, 1977). I will concentrate on three of these: given and new information, definite reference, and nouns.

CONVERSATIONS ARE CUMULATIVE

Conversations consist, very roughly, of a series of utterances among two or more people, each utterance representing one or more illocutionary acts by the speaker towards one or more of the others in the conversation. Imagine a conversation among A, B, and C that consisted entirely of assertions:

SPEAKER	RESULT
A: Assertion 1	Common-ground(1)
B: Assertion 2	Common-ground(2)
A: Assertion 3	Common-ground(3)
C: Assertion 4	Common-ground(4)
A: Assertion 5	Common-ground(5)

And so on.

Although it may seem that in conversations anything goes, this clearly isn't true. We would be surprised if assertion 3 were identical to assertion 2: If B had said, "What Margaret did was go to the hospital," then A wouldn't also assert, "What Margaret did was go to the hospital." People try not to say things that are fully redundant with what has gone before. We would also be surprised if assertion 3 were irrelevant to the conversation, if it had no bearing on the current purposes of the parties to the conversation. It would be odd if each new assertion didn't *add* to the conversation, enabling it to progress in one direction or another.

Conversations are cumulative. When A, B, and C entered this conversation, they each assumed that the three of them shared a certain common ground. Let us call this common-ground(0). With A's assertion 1 she added a new piece of information to common-ground(0) and formed a new common ground called common-ground(1). With B's assertion 2 he added a new piece of information to the current state of knowledge and beliefs—that is, to common-ground(1)—and formed common ground(2). In what I will call a *canonical conversation,* each new contribution increments the common ground of all parties at once, and in this way the conversation progresses: It accumulates as a whole (Clark and Carlson, 1982a; Gazdar, 1979; Stalnaker, 1978).

For a conversation to accumulate, its participants need to coordinate with each other. They must pay close attention to the common ground as it builds up and design their contributions accordingly. Imagine that assertion 2 was "What Margaret did was go to the hospital." Conceptually, this assertion divides into two parts. With one part, B indicates he is taking it for granted that it is common knowledge among A, B, and C that Margaret had done something. This part is entirely redundant with common-ground(1), and B uses it to show A and C where the contribution is to be placed within common-ground(1). In a second part B tells A and C what Margaret had done: She went to the hospital. This part contains the *new* contribution B is making to the conversation. It is the piece of information that B wants added to common-ground(1). Thus B's assertion, so to speak, consists of an address to a place in common-ground(1) and a message to be delivered to that place. For coordination to be complete, B's address must be unambiguous, and his message must not already be stored in that place.

The distinction here is between what some have called *given* and *new information* and others have called *presupposition* and *focus* (Clark and Haviland, 1977). Most sentences can be divided into two parts, as in this example:

- *Sentence:* What Margaret did was go into the hospital.
- *Given information:* Margaret did X.
- *New information:* X = go into the hospital.

The phrase *what Margaret did* expresses the given information in this particular sentence, and the phrase *go into the hospital* expresses the new information. In most sentences the new information is specified by a phrase that contains the *focal stress,* the word or syllable in the sentence with highest pitch and heaviest accent. The new information in *Margaret went into the* **hospital** is different from that in **Margaret** *went into the hospital.* Many sentences can be divided into given and new information in more than one way. They are ambiguous in this distinction, just as they may be ambiguous because of words like *bank* or phrases like *the shooting of the hunters.*

Strictly speaking, given information and new information are properties of sentences, not of utterances or of speech acts. Yet when B utters the sentence *What Margaret did was go into the hospital,* he generally uses the given information to designate what *he* takes for granted, to be identifiable from common-ground(1), and he uses the new information to designate his contribution to the conversation, what is to be added to common-ground(1). In parallel with the contrast between sentence meaning and speaker meaning, then, let me call what the speaker does with the sentence's given and new information the speaker's given and new information. From now on I will be concerned with the speaker's given and new information.

What is so important about given and new information? With this distinction speakers and listeners have an efficient means for coordinating additions to common ground. They adhere to a convention that Clark and Haviland (1977) have called the *given-new contract,* which goes like this:

> In using given and new information the speaker has good reason to believe that the given information designates a referent that the addressees can identify uniquely on the basis of their common ground and that the new information designates information, to be attached to that referent, that is not already part of their common ground.

Following this convention, speakers cannot design their contribution to the conversation in just any way. They must tie it to the common ground with their given information and encapsulate the contribution itself in the new information.

The given-new contract is ordinarily exploited by the listeners. Consider what Clark and Haviland have called the *given-new strategy.* Listeners try to understand assertions in three steps. First, they try to identify the speaker's given and new information. In B's utterance they recognize the given information as being that Margaret did something and the new information as what that something is, namely, go into the hospital. Second, they

search their common ground for the intended referent of the speaker's given information. For B's utterance they look for the event about Margaret doing something that B must be referring to. And third, they add the new information to their common ground in association with the referent they found in step 2. For B's utterance they add the specification that the something Margaret did, which hadn't been further described in common ground, was go into the hospital. These steps may not always be done in this order, although, of course, listeners have to identify the referent of the given information in common ground before they can attach the new information to it.

The given-new strategy has a number of consequences for understanding. For instance, certain sequences should be more comprehensible than others. Compare these two sequences:

1. Margaret did something. What she did was go into the hospital.

2. Someone went into the hospital. What Margaret did was go into the hospital.

In sequence 1 the second utterance is readily understood. Listeners find it easy to identify in the common ground created by the first utterance the referent for the given information of the second. With the same stress pattern in sequence 2, however, the second utterance isn't so readily understood. There is no obvious referent for the given information in the common ground formed by the first utterance, and the new information seems redundant with that common ground. Sequence 2 seems to be designed incorrectly, making it difficult to understand. But put the main stress in 2 on *Margaret,* and it becomes quite comprehensible again, since the pattern of given and new information is again appropriate to the circumstances.

For many utterances listeners can't identify referents of given information without adding *bridging inferences* (Clark, 1975, 1977). Consider this sequence:

3. Margaret began having labor pains. What she did was go into the hospital.

With the common ground formed from the first utterance in 3, there is no direct referent for the given information of the second; the speaker isn't using *what she did* to refer to Margaret's having labor pains. The speaker intends his addressees to draw a bridging inference in order to add the referent he can then refer to with the phrase *what she did.* The bridge he intends is this:

3'. Margaret did something *because* she began having labor pains; this something is the referent of *what she did* in the second utterance.

People report making inferences like this one. There is also experimental evidence that people take longer to read an utterance for which they must form bridging inferences in its understanding (Carpenter and Just, 1977a, 1977b; Clark and Sengul, 1979; Haviland and Clark, 1974; Tanenhaus and Seidenberg, 1981). And there is evidence from studies of memory that people often incorrectly claim to have heard an utterance that expressed a bridging inference in a passage where there was no such explicit statement (Kintsch, 1974; Kintsch and Keenan, 1973).

In ordinary conversations, therefore, people keep close track of the common ground of all participants. Then speakers design each utterance with two important criteria in mind. First, it must be comprehensible against this common ground. The given information must refer to some readily identifiable part of that common ground. And second, it must contribute to the direction of the conversation. The new material must offer information that isn't already part of the common ground at the moment. For their part listeners exploit this design feature of utterances. They attempt to find the referents of the given information in the current common ground, and they try to add to that common ground what is new to the referent. Through this coordination the speaker's goals are simplified, for she can make her contribution efficiently and without fear of gross misunderstanding. Likewise, the listener can recognize the speaker's meaning equally efficiently and without fear of gross misunderstanding. Without the given-new contract, or something like it, conversations would be unmanageable.

DEFINITE REFERENCE

When we talk, we use special devices for referring to the objects we are talking about. We use definite descriptions like *the man you met yesterday* and *this book,* indefinite descriptions like *a dog in the bushes* and *one of my friends,* personal pronouns like *he* and *we,* and other expressions. How do we choose which devices to use? How do listeners figure out what we are referring to? Although reference seems simple, that is an illusion. These two questions, despite years of intense study, still don't have good answers.

One thing *is* clear: Coordination is essential to the use and understanding of reference. The best-known distinction in reference, between definite and indefinite reference, hangs directly on such a notion. If I were to tell you, *John bought a dog with brown and white spots,* I would assume that that particular dog wasn't uniquely identifiable from our common ground. If, instead, I were to tell you, *John bought the dog with brown and white spots,* I would assume that you could identify that dog uniquely from our common ground. Generally, we use indefinite reference for objects that are not in common ground and definite reference for objects that are (Clark and Marshall, 1981; Hawkins, 1978).

The issue may become clearer with another illustration. When I describe a scene for you, I am trying to get you to build up in your imagination a mental model of that scene (see Johnson-Laird, 1980). If I am describing a room, for example, I want you to imagine four walls, a ceiling, and a floor, along with all the other things I put into the room. At any point in my description I suppose that the objects I have described so far are already in your mental model, and other objects predictable from common ground are inferred to be there too. That is, I suppose that the mental model I have been getting you to create is itself now part of our common ground. I also suppose that the other objects in my model are not yet in yours, since nothing I have said yet implies their existence. At that point, then, I refer to objects in the first set with definite descriptions, such as *the desk chair* and *the lamp,* but to objects in the second set with indefinite descriptions, such as *an arm chair* and *a Moroccan rug.* The point is that once I have established that I am describing a room, I can use definite references for things in any reasonable mental model of a room, such as *the ceiling* or *the wall on the left,* even though I have not mentioned them explicitly (Brewer and Treyens, 1981; Linde and Labov, 1975). So *a* is used for introducing objects into a mental model and *the* for referring to objects already there, already part of the speaker's and addressee's common ground.

The best known psychological model of definite reference is Olson's (1970). He proposed that speakers view the referent as belonging to a *referent array,* which may be either explicit or implicit in the perceptual situation. A speaker designs his definite description so that it distinguishes the referent uniquely from the other objects in the array. To refer to one of five men you and I had just met, I couldn't simply use *the man,* or *the man we just met,* since these wouldn't distinguish the intended referent from the rest. I would have to use references like *the tallest of the man we just met* or *the man in the blue shirt,* which would pick him out uniquely. And you would identify him as the referent by assuming this was what I was trying to do.

Although Olson's model makes a tacit appeal to coordination between the speaker and addressees, this appeal is incomplete. The reference I use with you, whether *the man* or *the man in the blue shirt,* depends on what I take to be the array from which you must pick out my intended referent. Since there is no explicit array in most conversational settings, the speaker and addressee must settle on the array as well as the referent within it. The array, then, is something else they have to coordinate with each other, and it too must be part of their common ground. About this problem Olson's model has little to say.

For each object the speaker wants to refer to, of course, there are many possible descriptions to select among. One person I might want to refer to would fit any of these possibilities: *the man, the man in the blue suit, my neighbor, George, the idiot we saw dancing in the street last night,* and *the president of Rotary.* Which should I choose? For my reference to be sufficient, as Olson's model suggests, it should lead the addressees uniquely to the intended referent. The question is how to coordinate these two things—my choice of description and my addressee's identification of the referent. According to Clark and Marshall (1981), the speaker and addressee tacitly adhere to a convention about definite reference:

> In making a definite reference sincerely, the speaker has good reason to believe that the addressees can readily compute uniquely the referent on the basis of their common ground such that the description in the reference is true of the referent.

When there is an explicit referent array, the convention comes down to much the same thing as Olson's model. The array is common ground to the speaker and addressees, and the description is designed to pick out one object from that array uniquely. For other situations it suggests quite different strategies.

One strategy is to rely on precedence of description. In a study by Krauss and Weinheimer (1964) two people had to communicate with each other about six figures that were very difficult to describe, as can be seen in the

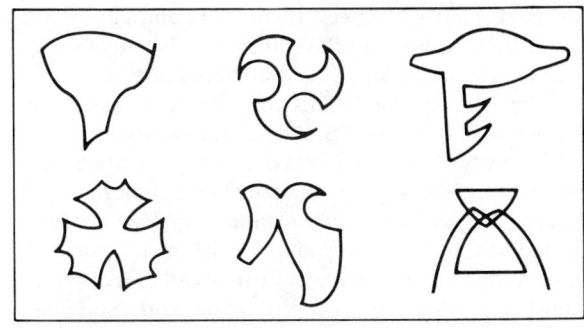

FIGURE 1
Objects Difficult to Describe
SOURCE: Krauss and Weinheimer, 1964, p. 113.

examples in Fig. 1. In the course of the task one person, the director, was required to refer repeatedly to these figures for her partner, whom she could not see. One director, for example, first described the lower rightmost figure in Fig. 1 as *the upside-down martini glass in a wire stand.* On successive references to the same figure, she shortened the phrase to *the inverted martini glass, the martini glass,* and eventually *the martini.* As later research showed, the director only shortened references with feedback from a partner. When she was asked to describe the figures into a tape recorder for some future listener, there was much less shortening with repeated references (Krauss and Weinheimer, 1966).

In the Krauss and Weinheimer studies the two partners relied on precedent. Once the director had described a particular figure as an upside-down martini glass on a wire stand, there was a precedent in her partner's and her common ground for viewing the figure this way. With that precedent she didn't need to give the full description again (as was necessary on the first trial to distinguish among the figures). She could simply allude to the precedent and be confident that if the listener could recognize the precedent, he could identify the right figure uniquely. Note that if the director had changed partners between her first and second references to a figure, there would be no such precedent, and she would have had to use some other strategy. Precedent is the basis for many varieties of definite reference.

Another strategy is to rely on another part of common ground, the broad shared cultural background of the speaker and addressees. If you and I mutually realize we are both members of the Stanford University faculty, then we can take it for granted we both know almost everything that anyone in this community would know. The name of Stanford's president, for example, is Donald Kennedy. Once our joint community membership is established, I can refer to Kennedy in the right setting as *Kennedy* (instead of *the president of Stanford University*) and be confident that you will pick him and not some other Kennedy as my referent. Virtually all uses of proper names rely on this sort of coordination, and so do many other types of definite reference.

Still another strategy is to use gestures in what is called *demonstrative reference*. When I point to a chair and say, "Please sit in that chair," you identify the chair I am referring to in part by registering my gesture, my "demonstration," which is another part of our common ground. Without the gesture you may have no way of selecting the intended referent uniquely. The demonstration, in effect, takes the place of a more complete description, such as *Please sit in the third chair from the end of the second row in the room in which you are now standing.* By pointing, I can often use a much simpler description.

With demonstrative reference, there are other complications in the coordination of reference and understanding. Imagine that I pointed to an empty chair and said, "That man is returning in five minutes." In this case I am not pointing at the referent I am describing (the man who had been sitting in the chair minutes before). I am pointing at a "demonstratum" that bears only an indirect relation to the referent. Yet once again, I am confident that with my demonstration to the chair and with my description *man,* you can identify my referent quickly and uniquely. You will see that there is an obvious function from chairs to people who have just sat in them, and so by pointing at the chair and describing a man, I must be referring to the man who just sat in that particular chair (see Clark, Schreuder, and Buttrick, 1983; Nunberg, 1979).

In Olson's model some forms of demonstrative reference should be impossible. Suppose that I point to a group of ten men jogging and tell you, "That man is my neighbor." In a traditional view such as Olson's, I shouldn't do this, since the description *man* hardly picks out one man from the referent array uniquely. But by using the demonstrative *that man,* I escape this restriction. If one of the joggers was naked, you would take me, and I would intend you to take me, as referring to the naked jogger. Here coordination is essential. You would suppose that I was confident you could pick out the man I am referring to uniquely, and the only way you thought I could have been so confident was because one of the men, the naked one, was so salient. So with demonstrative reference the listener must do more than merely register what the speaker is pointing at. He must turn to principles of coordination and reason through to the intended referent.

Coordination, therefore, is central to the use and understanding of definite reference, and common ground is essential to this coordination.

NOUNS

At the heart of most noun phrases are nouns, such as *typewriter* in *the typewriter* and *sandwich* in *this delicious sandwich*. We generally think of these nouns as descriptions of the objects being referred to in the noun phrases. So *the typewriter* refers to a typewriter, and *this delicious sandwich* refers to a sandwich. Speakers and addressees coordinate in the use of these decriptions by convention. *Typewriter* has as one of its conventional meanings "keyboard machine for printing letters and numbers on paper," and so a listener can infer that a speaker could use it in referring to such a machine.

The first complication for this view is that virtually all words have more than one conventional meaning. How does the listener know which one the speaker intended on that occasion? Often the listener can decide from the internal logic of the utterance. When the speaker says, "The bank opened its vaults at 9:00 this morning," he must have intended *bank* to mean "financial institution," since it makes no sense for a "steep natural incline" to have vaults that open at a particular time in the morning. Yet other times the listener can only select the right interpretation by consulting other parts of his and the speaker's common ground. The problem is that he cannot know in advance whether he is to select the intended sense on the basis of the local utterance or on the basis of global features of the situation they are in.

To make matters worse, the conventional senses of words may be conventional only within specialized communities. Any convention, of course, holds only for a particular group of people. The group may consist of two people (say my wife and myself) or 200 million people (say Americans over six years old). This is just as true of conventions of word meaning. As I noted earlier, *bug* has a conventional meaning for computer afficionados, "programming error," that is not conventional for English speakers at large. Computer experts realize this discrepancy when they talk, say, to their parents about such bugs, and they either avoid the term or explain what it means first. Many conventional meanings, especially technical ones, are restricted to something less than the set of people who "know English," as in the conventional meanings of *significant, reliable,* and *mode* among statisticians, and *argument, group,* and *set* among logicians and mathematicians. To use these words in their technical senses, speakers have to coordinate closely with their addressees, making certain they recognize their joint membership in the same technical subcommunity.

Slang is even more complicated because it tends to be partly conventional and partly metaphorical, where the conventions and metaphors are common ground only within selected groups of people. Consider the uses of *tea, grass,* and *dope* to refer to marijuana among marijuana users. As Nunberg (1978) has argued, you would use *grass* "to refer to marijuana just in those contexts in which it is common knowledge that everybody in the conversation knows what drugs look like, and doesn't mind if anybody else knows that he knows" (p. 305). You would use *tea* only when the speaker *does* mind if other people know. At least, this was the way *tea* was originally used, according to Nunberg, before it became dated, acquiring a cute, ironic tone, as there was less and less need to hide one's use of marijuana. And *dope,* by classifying marijuana with hard drugs, originally was used to imbue marijuana use with a certain forbidden and dangerous quality, although with changes in attitudes this meaning, too, has changed. To get these interpretations correct, speakers and addressees had to rely partly on the conventions that *grass, tea,* and *dope* denoted marijuana within a particular subcommunity and partly on coordination based on other aspects of the common ground shared by that particular subcommunity.

When the speaker makes a reference, she has a number of possible nouns she could use. In describing a dog, she could use *spaniel, dog, animal, beast, brute, mongrel, pet, thing,* or many other words. Which one should she choose? Many investigators (e.g., Brown, 1958; Cruse, 1977; Rosch, 1978) have noted that there is a default level of abstraction we tend to use. Unless there is reason to do otherwise, we prefer to use *dog* and not *spaniel* or *animal,* and to use *car* and not *vehicle* or *Chevy.* This level of abstraction, called the *basic level,* is at an intermediate degree of specificity. It is specific enough to be useful but not so specific that it provides more information than is necessary; it is general enough to be used easily but not so general that it makes too few distinctions. On a number of criteria (see Rosch, 1978), the basic level is just right.

Speakers use the basic level unless they want to implicate something extra. These implicatures have never been spelled out completely, but they are easy to recognize. For instance, the use of a term more specific than one at the basic level may be used to implicate a contrast. I would ordinarily say *My car is outside,* in which I use the basic level term *car.* If I had wanted to implicate that I have other cars that are not outside, I could have said *My Chevy is outside.* In using *car,* I implicate that I am telling you about my car as opposed to other things that I own. In using the more specific *Chevy,* I implicate that I am telling you about my Chevy as opposed to other cars that I own. The more specific the level of description, the more specific are the implicit contrasts.

Moving up from the basic level leads to other implicatures. Ordinarily, if I had parked my car (a Chevy) outside, I couldn't get away with saying *My vehicle is outside.* If I were to say this, I would generally implicate that the vehicle was not a car, truck, or other obvious vehicle (otherwise, I would have said *car, truck,* or whatever) but an unusual vehicle not easily named. Or I would implicate that I was reluctant to reveal what kind of vehicle it was. Or I could be making a joke. I could also use *vehicle* to implicate distaste, as in the contrast between *Get that car out of the way* and *Get that vehicle out of the way* (Cruse, 1977). However these examples are accounted for, they point to an important conclusion. When the speaker doesn't use the basic level, he must have chosen not to for a good reason, and listeners assume they are intended to infer what that reason is.

The basic level itself is a reflection of coordination in talk, and it can vary from community to community, depending on expertise. While for most people the basic-level terms among vehicles are *car, bus, truck,* and *pickup,* for true car buffs they may be at a more specific level, such as *Mustang, MG,* and *Volvo.* In conversation among these experts it is more often useful to talk at the more specific level. Expertise is a property not of languages but of language communities. Somali has a large number of names for camel, and Garo (a Burmese language) has a large number of names for baskets and rice (Burling, 1970), not because of something intrinsic to Somali and Garo as languages but because of the expertise of the people who use them.

There is a problem for the straightforward view of nouns and their uses, and it is innovation (see Clark, 1978, 1983; Clark and Clark, 1979; Nunberg, 1979). In conversation, newspapers, and novels, we find nothing odd about attested examples like these:

- I stopped in Perry's for a quick *crab* ["dish of crab meat"].

- Do you have one or two *radishes* ["bunches of radishes"] there?

- The *telephone* ["person on the other end of the telephone line"] managed to get a word in.

- Service for eight includes dinner plates, *salads,* cups, saucers, *soup/cereals* plus oval platter, oval *vegetable, sugar* with lid, creamer.

Yet the italicized words were all used with innovative meanings. In the china advertisement, *salad, soup/cereal, vegetable,* and *sugar* were intended to denote not what they conventionally denote, but "dish for salad," "bowl for soup or cereal," "large bowl for vegetables," and "bowl for sugar."

The problems for a model of language use are obvious. None of these innovative meanings is in the mental lexicons of the speaker or listener. How, then, can an advertiser use *sugar* to mean "bowl for sugar" and expect us readers to understand? He has to rely on our cooperation. We must collect the clues the advertisement offers about what is meant, put them together, and compute the intended meaning on the spot. To do so, the advertiser and we must adhere to a convention by which we can achieve this coordination. The convention might be stated as follows (Clark, 1983):

> In using a noun sincerely, the speaker means to denote the kind of thing that he has good reason to believe that on this occasion the addressees can readily compute uniquely on the basis of their common ground such that the kind of thing being denoted has something to do with the category denoted by the noun used.

If we readers follow this convention, we can reason through to the advertiser's innovative meanings. Without it the advertiser could mean anything or only what he literally said.

The problem of word innovations may seem minor, but it isn't. Word innovations like *salad* and *soup* occur often—in newspapers, scientific writing, novels, and everyday conversations. In each case the speaker or writer uses such a word in full confidence that we can understand. Furthermore, because we believe the speaker has provided enough information to have this assurance, we are confident we can put together the information and discover the meaning. The problem is all the more serious because we cannot know, for any noun used, whether it is being used with a conventional meaning or with an innovative one. Each time we hear a noun, we must coordinate on whether the word is intended to denote what it conventionally denotes or, instead, something connected with one of its literal denotations.

So nouns require a type of coordination analogous to the coordination needed for definite reference. Just as a definite noun phrase like *the sugar bowl* has an indefinitely large number of potential referents—my sugar bowl, your neighbor's, the one in the store window, and so on—so the noun *sugar* has an indefinitely large number of potential denotations—the sweetener proper, sugar bowl, brand of sugar, person who sells sugar, and so on. With both the speaker makes certain that the addressee's and his common ground contains the right information for the addressee to compute the intended denotation or referent uniquely.

CONCLUSIONS

When people talk, they do so to convince, request, apologize, warn, and promise. But to accomplish these things, they have to rely on the parts of the sentences they utter. Listeners are intended to put together these parts in order to see what the speaker is really doing.

Combining these parts sounds like the easiest job of all. It is a common conception that the parts of an utterance are combined according to strict grammatical rules, and what emerges is the meaning of the whole. The assumption is that there is little or no coordination required between the speaker and addressee, that everything is determined by the rules of language. What I have argued is that coordination is critical in order to use and understand each level of an utterance. With definite reference, and especially pronouns, it is easy to see that the speaker and addressees must work together to make sure they both recognize that the addressee has identified the right referent. They must work together just as closely for simple nouns. Utterance parts require the same coordination that whole utterances do (see also Clark and Murphy, 1982).

CONVERSATIONS

Utterances owe their existence to discourse, and the most basic type of discourse is conversation. In preliterate and nonliterate societies, almost everything that is said occurs in conversations, in talk among two or more people. There are ritual and other uses of language, but the forms they take appear to derive from ordinary conversations. Narratives in particular appear to have evolved from story telling in conversational settings. And children acquire language mainly by taking part in conversations and, probably less so, by listening to the conversations of others. To understand how language is used, we must understand the role utterances play in conversation. We must see how conversations work.

In conversations it is all too obvious that the speaker and listener have to coordinate. There are physical problems. The parties must be able to hear each other and must talk loudly enough to be heard. They must see each other as part of the same group in order to recognize who does and who doesn't belong to the conversation. They cannot all talk at once if they are to understand each other and expect to be understood. There are also content problems. The parties each have certain goals or purposes, and to accomplish them, they must find a way of coordinating their own goals and purposes with those of the others. They can each bring up topics, but they must coordinate who brings up what topics when. It is no mean accomplishment to have carried on a successful conversation.

The first problem I will consider is a physical one, the coordination of turn taking. The problem of allocating and timing turns, however, isn't as easy to solve as it first appears. It also has important consequences both for the form that languages have evolved into and for the uses to which language can be put.

TURN TAKING

When two or more people try to converse, only one person can talk at a time and be fully understood. It is difficult, perhaps impossible, to talk and listen at the same time, and it is equally difficult to keep track of more than two people talking at once. Perceptually, too, the speech of one person may mask that of another. On grounds of perceptual and cognitive difficulty alone, conversations should largely proceed with only one person talking at a time.

And they do. Although there are many times in conversations when more than one party talks at the same time, it has been found in careful observations that these occurrences are brief and come mainly at points of possible transition from one speaker to another. As Sacks, Schegloff, and Jefferson (1974) put it, "Overwhelmingly, one party talks at a time" (p. 700). The parties are obliged to take turns, and for that to succeed, they must adhere to a system of turn taking.

For this system to work, it must solve certain other problems too. Sacks and colleagues, in a landmark paper on turn taking, pointed out that conversations have the following properties (pp. 700–701):

1. Speaker-change recurs, or at least occurs.

2. Overwhelmingly, one party talks at a time.

3. Occurrences of more than one speaker at a time are common but brief.

4. Transitions (from one turn to a next) with no gap and no overlap are common. Together with transitions characterized by slight gaps or slight overlaps, they make up the vast majority of transitions.

5. Turn order is not fixed, but varies.

6. Turn size is not fixed, but varies.

7. Length of conversation is not specified in advance.

8. What parties say is not specified in advance.

9. Relative distribution of turns is not specified in advance.

10. Number of parties can vary.

11. Talk can be continuous or discontinuous.

12. Turn-allocation techniques are obviously used. A current speaker may select a next speaker (as when he addresses a question to another party); or parties may self-select in starting to talk.

13. Various "turn-constructional units" are employed; e.g., turns can be projectedly "one word long", or they can be sentential in length.

14. Repair mechanisms exist for dealing with turn-taking errors and violations; e.g., if two parties find themselves talking at the same time, one of them will stop prematurely, thus repairing the trouble.

Although these fourteen characteristics were put forward as observations to be accounted for, they are also just the characteristics one would like if one were creating a *rational* system of turn taking. With fairly general assumptions about why people talk to each other, it is rational for a system of turn taking to allow variation in turn order, turn size, and number of parties, and not to specify in advance what is said, the relative distribution of turns, or the length of the conversation.

For these constraints to be met, Sacks and colleagues argued, the system of turn taking must do two things. First, it must specify what it is to be a turn, and that is not easy. When a person talks, there are natural points at which she can stop, at which she completes what she has to say. We usually think of turns as consisting of complete sentences, but this view is incorrect. A turn may consist of a clause, as in B's reply to A:

A: Why did Harry buy Rosebud?

B: Because he wanted a good investment.

Or a phrase:

A: What are you doing?

B: Wondering why bats live upside down.

Or a single word, or series of moves:

A: Would you like a piece of pie?

B: Uh, yes, thank you. I'd like that very much.

The parties to a conversation, then, must listen for possible ends of turns and at each point decide whether or not the turn has really ended.

The turn-taking system must also deal with the allocation of turns. Many turns are assigned by the current speaker, who "selects" the next speaker by the illocutionary act he has directed at him. If the current speaker asks someone a question, for example, that person is obligated to take the next turn and answer the question. Other turns are allocated by a party "selecting himself" to speak next. This is done simply by speaking before anyone else begins.

So turns, Sacks, Schegloff, and Jefferson (1974) argued, are governed by the following set of rules:

1. At the first possible point of transition in a turn, if the current speaker uses a "current speaker selects next" technique, he selects the next speaker, who is thereby obligated to take the next turn at that point.

2. At the first possible point of transition in a turn, if the current speaker does *not* use a "current speaker selects next" technique, the first party to speak acquires the right to take a turn at that point.

3. At the first possible point of transition in a turn, if the current speaker does *not* use a "current speaker selects next" technique, then he may, but need not, continue unless another party speaks up first.

These rules are ordered. Rule 1 takes precedence over rule 2, which takes precedence over rule 3. They are also cyclic. If rule 3 applies, and the current speaker continues talking, then rules 1 through 3 apply again at the next possible point of transition.

These rules lead fairly directly to the fourteen characteristics of conversations listed earlier. They enable speakers to talk one at a time and to change. They allow for variation in turn order, turn size, and number of parties, and they don't specify in advance the length of the conversation, what is said, or the relative distribution of turns.

Paradoxically, the rules also predict that there should often be more than one person talking at a time. It is just that these overlaps should occur only at possible points of transition and be brief. By rule 2, when the current speaker doesn't select the next speaker, the next person to speak takes the floor. If there are two or more parties who try for the floor at the same time, they will overlap until one gives way, as in this example from Sacks, Schegloff, and Jefferson (1974, p. 705):

> *Mike:* I know who the guy is.
>
> *Vic* (simultaneously with James): He's bad.
>
> *James* (simultaneously with Vic): You know the guy?

In Beattie and Barnard's (1979) study of both face-to-face and telephone conversations, people tried to claim turns simultaneously only 5 to 10 percent of the time. If the study is representative, this source of overlap isn't very frequent.

Another reason for overlap is that it is difficult to tell when the current speaker's turn is finished, as in this example (Sacks, Schegloff, and Jefferson, 1974, p. 730) (the brackets show where Old man and Parky spoke simultaneously):

Tourist: Has the park changed much?

Parky: Oh, yes.

Old man: The Funfair changed it an ⌈awful lot, ⌈didn't it?
Parky: ⌊Th—   ⌊That—
        That changed it.

Here Parky tried starting after *The Funfair changed it,* and then after *The Funfair changed it an awful lot,* and finally succeeded after *The Funfair changed it an awful lot, didn't it?* In each case the overlap was brief, and Parky repaired his error by stopping momentarily and then starting over.

Still a third reason for overlap is the press of rule 2. If the current speaker hasn't selected the next speaker, then whoever wants to speak next must come in quickly or lose out. This leads, first of all, to short or null pauses between turns. In their study Beattie and Barnard (1979) found that 34 percent of all speaker switches—in both face-to-face and telephone conversations—were immediate, taking less than 0.2 second. It also leads to a tendency to start speaking slightly before the current speaker is finished, as in this example from Sacks, Schegloff, and Jefferson (1974, p. 706):

A: Well, it wasn't me— ⌈ee.
B: ⌊No, but you know who it
                            was.

Here the last part of *me* and the first part of *No* overlap, with B anticipating A's finish by a fraction of a second (see Jefferson, 1973). So rules 1 through 3 allow overlapping speech, but this should occur only at possible points of transition and should ordinarily be brief.

Most turns, then, have three orientations: backward to the last turn, inward to the current turn, and forward to the next turn. The orientation backward leads to *prestarts* such as *well, but, and, so,* and the so-called filled pause *uh.* When a possible next speaker wants to take the floor, he can do it with a prestart even though he isn't completely prepared with the content of his turn. Similarly, the forward orientation leads to *postcompleters,* like the tag question by the old man: *The Funfair changed it an awful lot, didn't it?* With the tag question he both makes it clear he is finished and selects Parky as the next speaker.

Switching from one speaker to the next is complicated by still another factor—the silences that occur. Sacks and colleagues argued that people "hear" silences in conversation in three different ways. *Pauses* are within-turn silences that do not indicate a possible end of turn. *Gaps* are silences at the ends of turns, and they are

ordinarily minimized. And *lapses* are generally longer silences at the ends of turns when no speaker chooses to take the floor. The problem is that a pause can sometimes be mistaken for a gap, and that is a mistake speakers want to avoid. Indeed, Maclay and Osgood (1959) suggested that speakers won't let a pause get too long for fear of forfeiting their turn, and they will therefore turn it into a filled pause, such as *uh, er,* or *um.* They should also use filled pauses as prestarts for minimizing gaps and claiming the next turn. In Beattie and Barnard's study sequences of pause-plus-filled-pause and of gap-plus-filled-pause were frequent.

Turns are not just turns of speaking but turns of action, and there are all sorts of behavior that change with turns. When a party is speaking, she tends to gaze away from her listeners during her turn and to gaze back as she finishes it. On the other hand, listeners tend to gaze at the speaker during her turn (Kendon, 1967). These patterns are especially true in conversations among strangers or about difficult topics (Beattie, 1981). And at the ends of turns speakers may also drawl on the last syllable, drop the pitch of their voice, and relax their bodies (Duncan, 1972). When they accompany their turns with gestures, they tend to complete them at the ends of their turns (Beattie, 1981). They may also use gestures to keep others from taking a turn at the end of one of their utterances (Duncan, 1972). There are other types of behavior, too.

How are we to consider these behaviors? Take gaze. It could be taken as either a *signal* (the term I have been using for an action whose intention the addressee is intended to recognize) or a *sign* (my term for a symptom or natural evidence of some internal process). As a signal, to gaze away from the speaker would be the speaker's way of telling the listener that he is still in possession of the turn; the listener must wait. As a sign, it may only indicate that the speaker cannot gaze at the listener and plan what to say next at the same time. If listeners actually rely on the speaker's gaze to determine the end of a turn, they could view it either as a signal *or* as a sign. So there are two obvious hypotheses about eye gaze in conversation (see Butterworth, 1978): the signaling hypothesis, which treats it as a signal, and the monitoring hypothesis, which treats it as a sign.

Gaze may often be only a sign, a symptom of what speakers are trying to do at the moment. Speakers tend to gaze away from their listeners when they are deep in their own planning—at the beginning of utterances and phrases and especially in hesitant speech. In Kendon's

(1967) extensive data speakers gazed at their listeners 50 percent of the time during fluent speech but only 20 percent of the time during hesitant speech. And in Beattie's (1978) data speakers made five times as many false starts when they were looking at their listeners as when they weren't. If gazes were really a signal, listeners should be able to use them to shorten the time they take in beginning their next turn. But this happens only in certain circumstances. On the telephone gazes cannot serve as either signals or signs, and yet conversations are as smooth as face-to-face conversations (Beattie and Barnard, 1979). As Beattie (1981) has argued, "gaze is not an essential cue in the regulation of turn-taking in conversation" (p. 57).

There are the same doubts about many of the other accompaniments to turn taking. It seems incorrect to assume a priori, as Duncan (1972, 1973) did, that all these behavioral cues—gaze, gestures, drawling, and the like—are signals or even that they are signs people rely on in turn taking (see Beattie, 1981; Butterworth, 1978). As Beattie has argued, turns are ordinarily ended by the content of what is said—by syntactic closure of the current utterance. The other cues are simply consequences—symptoms or signs—of the planning and execution of that content. Many behavioral cues come too late to signal a turn's end. Listeners must be projecting the turn's end at least a half a second earlier if they are to start the next turn without a pause, which they often do, or if they are to overlap slightly with the current speaker's last word, as they also often do (Jefferson, 1973). They can often project the end of a turn *only* by monitoring its content, not merely its accompanying behavioral cues.

The system of turn taking that has evolved, then, has two main properties. First, turns are managed locally. They are allocated one at a time in a system that covers all transition possibilities and does so in the order in which they come up. Turns can be organized globally, as they are in religious services where both the content and the ordering of turns are decided in advance. Likewise, in court, turns are allocated by strict rules, with the content of many turns decided on in advance. Yet in everyday conversations turns aren't determined ahead of time, and so the local structure must be governed by the rules of turn taking.

Second, turns are managed interactionally. Their content, size, and placement depend on all the parties to the conversation. They reflect the prior speaker in content and starting point, especially if the prior speaker has selected the current speaker, as with a question. They also reflect possible future speakers who will take their turns when they believe the current speaker has finished his turn and depending on who, if anyone, he selects as next speaker.

ADJACENCY PAIRS

Many turns in conversations come in pairs. When one person asks another a question, the second provides an answer to the question in the very next turn. That answer is intended to be heard not simply as a new contribution but as a contribution whose interpretation is tied to that of the question. This is what Schegloff and Sacks (1973) have called an *adjacency pair,* of which the question-answer sequence is the prototype.

Adjacency pairs, as sequences of utterances, have five basic properties. Although these properties may seem obvious, they are essential to the way adjacency pairs work (Schegloff and Sacks, 1973):

1. Adjacency pairs are two utterances in length. The two utterances are called, in the jargon of the field, "the first pair part" and "the second pair part."

2. Given the first part, the second part is relevant and expectable as the next utterance.

3. The two parts are spoken by different speakers.

4. Adjacency pairs come in types that specify which part is to come first and which second. In question-answer pairs, the question is to come first, and the answer second.

5. The form and content of the second part is dependent on the type of adjacency pair of which the first part is a part. In a question-answer pair, the answer must fit the question-answer pair of which the question is a part.

These five properties give adjacency pairs a central role in turn taking. If one speaker produces a first pair part, the next utterance should be a second pair part, and it should be uttered by the appropriate next speaker. When one party asks another a question, he selects that person as next speaker and obliges him to complete the adjacency pair with an answer. That is, the question is said to *project* an answer as the next utterance by the next speaker. Adjacency pairs are essential in the current-speaker-selects-next-speaker techniques.

What types of adjacency pairs are there? Here are examples of eight major types:

1. *Question and answer.* An example is as follows:

A: What time is it?

B: It's three o'clock.

This is the type of adjacency pair I have already considered.

2. *Request and promise:* An example is as follows:

A: Please pass the salt.

B: Okay. Just a minute.

With a request like A's, B has two options. One is to carry out the request, which completes the adjacency pair nonlinguistically. The other is to promise to carry out the request sometime in the future, as in the preceding example, where *Okay* is a promise.

3. *Summons and answer:* An example is as follows:

A: Hey, Dick.

B: Yes?

With the summons A tries to get B to agree to begin a conversation with her, and with the answer B accedes to this request.

4. *Promise and registration:* An example is as follows:

A: I'll be there in just a minute.

B: Excellent.

Here A makes a promise, and then B may register that promise. This type of adjacency pair is closely related to the next one.

5. *Offer and acceptance, or refusal:* An example is as follows:

A: Would you like a cup of tea?

B: Yes, please.

Although this is also a question-answer pair, it is indirectly an offer-acceptance pair, since A would ordinarily be seen as out of order if he didn't then bring B a cup of tea. Offers and promises, of course, belong to the same broad category of speech acts—commissives—and so they should behave very much alike.

6. *Gratitude and acknowledgment:* An example is as follows:

A: Thanks a lot, Betty.

B: Don't mention it.

Here also falls the standard *Thank you—You're welcome* of American English. There are many other analogous pairs, such as condolences and acknowledgments, congratulations and acknowledgments, and apologies and acknowledgments.

7. *Greeting and greeting:* This type includes the standard *Hello—Hello, Hi—Hi,* and *How do you do?—How do you do?* These pairs are closely related to those of gratitude and acknowledgment in that the two speakers exchange expressions of their feelings about something—namely, meeting.

8. *Terminal exchange:* Opposite the greetings are the farewells, which A and B exchange with pairs of *Goodbye—Goodbye, See you—See you,* and the like. It isn't clear, however, that the terminal exchange is always a proper adjacency pair. Two social equals trying to end a telephone conversation often say *goodbye* simultaneously. They appear to be trying to end the conversation in such a way that neither appears to cut off the other first. If so, these pairs violate the criterion that the two pair parts be adjacent, that one clearly be the first pair part and the other the second. They might be called, instead, coordinate pairs (Clark and French, 1981).

What enables one utterance to project another? It is here that illocutionary acts come in. Earlier, I noted that in Searle's theory each illocutionary act has associated with it certain felicity conditions. I considered Julia's request and the butcher's promise in the exchange:

Julia: Please give me that roast.

Butcher: I'll get it for you.

For Julia's request to be felicitous, I noted, four conditions needed to be fulfilled: The butcher had to be able to give her the roast; she had to want him to give it to her; she had to be predicating his giving her the roast; and her utterance had to count as an attempt to get the butcher to give it to her. These felicity conditions, in effect, project a certain type of response on the part of the butcher, namely, one with felicity conditions that mesh with those of Julia's request. The butcher's promise does just that. For it to be felicitous, four complementary conditions had to hold: He had to be able to give her the meat; he had to want to give it to her; he had to predicate his giving her the roast; and his utterance had to count as an undertaking by him to fulfill his obligation of giving it to her. The felicity conditions of the second pair part exactly mesh with those of the first pair part to complete the adjacency pair as a whole.

Julia's exchange with the butcher is an example of a request-promise pair, as in example 2 earlier. The other adjacency pairs just listed work the same way, with the felicity conditions of the first part projecting those of the second. The eight types work in quite a natural way. Directives, which solicit future actions, lead either to the actions themselves (as in answers to questions) or to promises of those actions (as in request-promise and summons-answer pairs). On the other hand, commissives, which oblige the speaker to future actions, lead to acceptances or rejections of those obligations. The remaining pairs exchange expressions of feelings, as dictated by the feeling that is socially appropriate in response to the speaker's expressed feelings. So these two very different approaches to the form and content of utterances—speech act theory and interaction theory—complement each other very nicely.

What is surprising is how tightly that interlocking adjacency pairs may constrain parts of a conversation. One turn can serve both as the second part of one adjacency pair and as the first part of another. Consider this brief but ordinary conversational exchange. In parentheses after each turn I have indicated the adjacency pairs to which it belongs. (So summons 1 and answer 1 are the first and second parts of adjacency pair 1, etc.)

1. *A:* Hey, Bob. (summons 1)

2. *B:* What? (answer 1 + question 2)

3. *A:* Do you know what time it is? (answer 2 + question 3 + indirect-question 4)

4. *B:* Yes, I do. It's three o'clock. (answer 3 + answer 4)

5. *A:* Already? (question 5)

6. *B:* Yes, why? (answer 5 + question 6)

7. *A:* My bus leaves in five minutes. Got to run. See you later. (answer 6 + request 7 + farewell 8)

8. *B:* Okay. See you. (accept 7 + farewell 8)

Most of these turns are parts of more than one adjacency pair: 2 is tied to 1 and projects 3; 3 is tied to 2 and projects 4 both directly and indirectly; 6 is tied to 5 and projects the first move in 7; and the last two moves in 7 project the two moves in 8. By this count there are eight interlocking adjacency pairs within eight turns. Tight organization like this is typical of routine exchanges.

PROCEDURAL MOVES

In most conversations there is a main thread running through what is said—its principal content—and yet not everything said and done is part of that thread. There are utterances I will call *procedural moves* that deal more with the procedures or workings of the conversation than with its content. I will consider two forms of procedural moves. Moves of the first type occur as parts of turns, and those of the second type come in the so-called back channel.

Imagine a door-to-door salesman saying to you, "What's your name?" His intent, let us assume, is simply to ask you for your name. Before you answer, there are two basic procedural requirements you must have satisfied (Goffman, 1974).

1. *System constraints:* You must have heard and recognized the words he said. He didn't say, "What shore name?" or "What's your aim?" If you didn't hear him well enough to satisfy you, you can request a replay, as with "Pardon me?" or "What did you say?" Hearing the speaker correctly is a usual prerequisite to understanding what he said. It is a system constraint that must ordinarily be satisfied.

You must also have understood what he meant. In asking "What's your name?" did he mean your full name, your family name, or your first name? If you aren't sure, you can question this too, as with "You mean full name?" or "Which name?" Understanding correctly is another system constraint that must ordinarily be satisfied.

2. *Ritual constraints:* Even if you heard and understood him fully, you may find his question out of order. It may be rude, inappropriate at this time, or in violation of the social ritual being played out. If so, you could respond, "None of your business," "I won't tell you," or "Go away." These, too, are procedural constraints, to be satisfied before you go on.

If you heard, understood, and accepted the salesman's question, you would ordinarily answer it directly, as with "Molly Bloom." When you do this, Goffman pointed out, you are therefore doing more than simply answering his question. You are signaling simultaneously that you heard, understood, and accepted the question too. You are implicating that the procedural constraints have been satisfied. In some cases you may make each of these signals explicit with separate moves, as in this example (cf. Goffman, 1974):

Salesman: What's your name?

Customer: What's my aim?

Salesman: No. What's your *name?*

Customer: Oh! Okay. It's Molly Bloom.

In the final turn *Oh!* signals that you have finally heard and understood the salesman; *Okay* signals that you find the question acceptable and are committing yourself to answering it; and the third move gives the answer proper. Preliminary moves like these are common.

The procedural moves just described are parts of turns—the person uttering them has the floor—but moves of the next class I will describe are not. In conversations it is common for the addressee to give feedback to the speaker without actually claiming the floor for a turn. Yngve (1970) has called this channel of communication the *back channel,* and the responses provided there he has called *back channel communications,* or *responses.*

There are a number of common back channel responses (Duncan, 1973). The addressee can give encouraging sounds like *m-hm, yeah, right, sure, of course not,* and *I see.* He can help the speaker complete sentences, as in this exchange:

A: I was having trouble finding, uh—

B: . . . George . . .

A: . . . until I saw his car outside the Wild Bill Saloon.

He can interrupt midsentence to request clarification with a word or phrase like *What? Whose car?* or *Pardon?* which the speaker honors with a midturn clarification. Or he can restate in a word or two something the speaker has just said. All these serve to affirm or deny that the basic procedural requirements are being met, that the addressee hears and understands what the speaker is currently saying.

Speakers often project certain back channel responses midsentence. For example, a speaker can try out a name on her addressees, using an upward intonational contour followed by a brief pause, as in this example:

Alice: I just got back from talking to Horace? //
who told me about the disaster at the sawmill.

Burton: Yeah (begun at slashes).

This way of pronouncing *Horace* is what Sacks and Schegloff (1979) have called a *try-marker.* Alice uses it on

the chance that Burton may not know who Horace is. If Burton knows, he is to nod or give some other affirmation of recognition without taking a separate turn. This procedure is efficient. Alice will elaborate on the name only if he doesn't recognize it. By checking midsentence, she usually doesn't have to detour into a side sequence, which would interrupt the flow of the conversation even more.

Back channel responses can, of course, be nonverbal (Dittman and Llewellyn, 1968; Krauss *et al.* 1977). The addressee can nod or shake her head, look satisfied, or look quizzical. These gestures function like the verbal signals of agreement and disagreement. She can also show in various ways that she is paying attention—or not paying attention—and that she is interested or not interested in what the speaker is saying. One way is by gazing or not gazing at the speaker, and another is by fixing her general demeanor, using subtler types of body cues.

So conversations consist not only of the turns proper, which carry the content of the topics under discussion, but also of certain procedural moves, which deal with the prerequisites for that discussion to take place at all. The parties to a conversation must make it clear that they hear, understand, and find appropriate what the speaker says before they consider responding to it.

REPAIRS

Despite people's best efforts, problems arise in conversations, and these problems often lead to repairs. When someone uses an incorrect word or makes an incorrect reference, the parties—especially the speaker—ordinarily try to correct the problem before going on. They try to satisfy the basic procedural prerequisite for communication—that all the parties understand what is being said. As Schegloff, Jefferson, and Sacks (1977) have argued, the making of repairs is highly organized. And as we might expect, it is accomplished within the system of turn taking.

Corrections may be made by the speaker or by someone else in the conversation. These are called *self-corrections* and *other-corrections,* respectively. As an example of a self-correction, consider this attested example (Schegloff, Jefferson, and Sacks, 1977, p. 364):

N: She was giving me all the people that were gone this year, I mean this quarter, you know.

J: Yeah.

Here N recognizes almost immediately after he has said *year* that he should have said *quarter,* and at the end of the sentence but before the end of the turn, he makes a self-correction. The next example is an example of an other-correction (Schegloff, Jefferson, and Sacks, 1977, p. 378):

Lori: But you know single beds are awfully thin to sleep on.

Sam: What?

Lori: Single beds. // They're

Ellen: You mean narrow? (begun at the slashes in Lori's turn)

Lori: They're awfully narrow, yeah.

Lori uses *thin* instead of *narrow,* but doesn't recognize her error, even after Sam questions her. Ellen makes her other-correction to set Lori right.

As Schegloff and colleagues have shown, self-corrections vastly outnumber other-corrections. Why, and what does it show?

Why it happens is explained by Schegloff and colleagues this way. Whereas corrections are made by either the speaker or someone else (self- and other-corrections), they are also *initiated* by either the speaker or someone else. The speaker has the greatest opportunity for initiating a correction. She can do it within her turn, before she has even finished the sentence, or at the end of her turn, as N did in the first example. The speaker, of course, is generally in a better position to recognize that she has made an error, which also puts her in a better position to initiate the correction. Furthermore, other people generally initiate corrections only after the speaker's turn is over, after she has had a chance to initiate the correction herself. And when they initiate a correction, they do it in the next turn with requests for clarification like "What?" "Which man?" "To where?" and "Met whom?"—questions that turn the floor back to the speaker, who is given the opportunity to make a self-correction. Others tend to make other-corrections only when their attempts to initiate self-corrections have failed, as in the second example I just gave. Only after Sam says *What?* and Lori still doesn't see her error does Ellen make an other-correction, and then she makes it with a hedge. Taken together, these factors lead to a preponderance of self-corrections.

This system of repairs, by accident or design, has important advantages. It gives the speaker ample opportunity to correct his own mistakes. As a consequence, each time an error occurs, there is no need for the conversation to detour into two, or even four, extra turns for a correction. The error is repaired without interrupting the sequence of turns, which could only disrupt the main direction of the conversation.

At the same time the system places a heavy burden on the speaker. He already has all the mental work he needs just planning and executing his utterances. To check for errors too, he must play the self-monitor. There are two main things he must keep track of. First, is what he actually said what he intended to say? To check, he must comprehend what he said and decide whether it was right. Second, do his addressees appear to be taking what he actually said as they were intended to take it? For this he must monitor the back channel responses for signs of understanding and misunderstanding. It is ultimately the addressees' understanding that is all-important, for without that the speaker's contribution to the conversation comes to naught.

Addressees can therefore exert a good deal of control over what the speaker says, and they do. If they want to make sure they understand completely before going on, they will elicit liberal amounts of repairs and give plenty of back channel responses. Indeed, feedback from addressees does lead to more accurate communication—at least for the addressees themselves. In an experiment by Kraut, Lewis, and Swezey (1982), people were shown an old Jimmy Stewart western and asked to summarize it to other people over a telephone hookup. For each speaker there were two listeners. One was a genuine addressee who could elicit repairs and give back channel responses. The second was an overhearer (Kraut, Lewis, and Swezey called him an eavesdropper) who thought he was giving back channel responses (just like the addressee) but couldn't be heard by the speaker since his microphone had been turned off; the speaker didn't even know he was there. It was found, first, that the more feedback the speakers got from addressees, the better summaries they created (see also Krauss and Weinheimer, 1966; Krauss *et al.,* 1977). But more surprisingly, even though the addressees and overhearers heard identical summaries, the addressees understood and later remembered the summaries better than did the overhearers. So the speakers were induced by the feedback to create more accurate summaries. But since they were reacting to the addressees and not to the overhearers, the summaries were better tailored to the addressees than to the overhearers.

Feedback like this, by which addressees tell a speaker how well they are tracking him, has other consequences too. Very generally, it reflects how *responsive* the addressees are, not just to what the speaker is saying but to him personally (see Davis, 1982). For instance, the more responsive the addressees are, the more they let the speaker know that they are interested in continuing the conversation and, in particular, the current topic of conversation. Of course, the more interest they display in what the speaker is saying, the more interest they display in the speaker himself, and this attitude comes across. Like the findings on politeness discussed earlier, findings in this area show that the more responsive the addressees are, the more they are judged by the speaker to be attractive, interested in him, and acquainted with him (Davis and Perkowitz, 1979). Because of these attributions, conversations should be facilitated insofar as they depend on cooperation oiled by personal interest. The feedback in elicitations of repairs and back channel responses is a good part of what makes interactive talk as efficient and comprehensible as it is.

With repairs, then, we see how coordination in conversation is really a consequence of the coordination inherent in speaker meaning and illocutionary acts. With illocutionary acts the speaker intends her addressees to recognize certain of her intentions by means, in part, of their recognition of her intentions—these are Grice's m-intentions. Turn taking, adjacency pairs, procedural moves, and repairs help ensure success. Turns optimize the recognition of illocutionary acts by allowing them to occur singly in everyone's full attention. Adjacency pairs generally display the two parties' correct understanding of the two or more illocutionary acts being performed. Procedural moves confirm or disconfirm the recognition of these acts. And repairs, the result of monitoring by both speaker and addressees, help ensure the correct recognition of the speaker's intentions. On the surface, coordination in conversation looks very different from the coordination in meaning and understanding I introduced earlier. Yet they are both of a piece. One cannot ordinarily exist without the other.

INTERPRETATION IN CONVERSATIONS

Turn taking, adjacency pairs, and repairs may provide some of the mechanics that enable conversations to proceed, but they don't dictate what people say and how their utterances are understood. People engage in conversations for many purposes, and it is ultimately these purposes that mold the interpretations as they emerge. Some of these purposes are to negotiate business, to exchange gossip, to make requests, to entertain each other,

or simply to pass the time, and the interpretations imposed on what is said depend on the goals that are relevant at the time. How does this process work? Where do these interpretations come from?

The key once again is coordination between the speaker's actions and the listener's interpretations of those actions. This time, however, I will consider a broader range of goals and intentions. The speaker intends his utterances to be interpreted not only against their local contexts—say, the adjacency pairs of which they are parts—but also on the basis of his apparent larger goals—making plans, gathering information, or telling stories. He intends his listeners to refer to these larger ends in inferring what he meant.

As illustration, I will consider the versatility of questions and answers. I will look first at answers, then at question-answer pairs in larger sections of conversations, and finally at questions and answers in routine requests.

QUESTIONS AND ANSWERS

As we saw earlier, the turn following a question is generally intended to be heard not simply as a new contribution to the conversation but as an answer to the question just asked. In this way its interpretation depends on the question it follows. The idea at first looks simple: When you hear a question, look in the next turn for its answer.

There are many problems with this view. The turn following a question may not look anything like an answer to the question and yet be one. Worse yet, it may look like an answer and yet *not* be. Although questions oblige or project the following turns to be answers, for procedural reasons they don't actually have to be followed by their answers. How do speakers and listeners ever keep all these possibilities straight? Let's consider some of the ways people can give genuine answers and be interpreted correctly (see Lakoff, 1973b).

1. *Full direct answer:* A simple question about the time can be answered in many different ways. One of them is shown in this example:

Ann: What time is it?

Bob: It's three o'clock.

With his utterance Bob asserts that it is three o'clock, which is something he could have done even without the preceding question. But placed as it is, Bob's utterance is interpreted as also completing the question-answer pair, as fulfilling an obligation placed on him by Ann's request for information. Ann has no need to read anything more into Bob's reply than just that, since his assertion is sufficient as an answer, and with nothing to suggest otherwise, it doesn't implicate anything more.

2. *Elliptical direct answer:* The same question can be given an elliptical answer:

Ann: What time is it?

Bob: Three.

In other contexts the word *three* wouldn't necessarily make the same assertion. In response to the question "Do you have any brothers?" it would mean "I assert that I have three brothers," and in reply to the request "How many bottles of wine can you bring?" it would mean "I offer to bring three bottles of wine." So Ann is intended to see what Bob means on *this* occasion by seeing that it is an answer to her question.

There is nothing odd about elliptical utterances. In context they sound correct, complete, and grammatical. They are standard linguistic forms that are extremely common in everyday conversations. In many contexts if Bob had answered with the full *It's three o'clock,* he would have sounded wordy or overly precise.

It is very odd, then, that elliptical utterances have been almost completely ignored in the study of grammar, speech acts, and comprehension. There has been a predilection for studying sentences, and one word utterances like *three* simply aren't considered proper sentences, at least in the traditional sense (see Morgan, 1973). Their syntactic structure is degenerate, and so is their propositional content. They can only be analyzed by reference to the contexts in which they occur.

That, however, makes them intriguing. When you say *three* to a ticket seller at a cinema, how does he know that you mean, roughly, "I request three adult tickets for the next showing of the movie currently playing at this theatre." Here there is no prior utterance, no first pair part, to serve as the parasite's host for your utterance. The ticket seller is intended to consult your common ground in order to see what you must mean by referring to the number three in that situation. Not all ellipses can be used in nonlinguistic contexts like this. Elliptical utterances like *I don't* require complete linguistic hosts for their interpretation (Hankamer and Sag, 1976; Sag, 1979; Sag and Hankamer, 1981), and these lead to quite a different pattern of use and understanding (Clark, 1979; Levelt and Kelter, 1982).

One thing is clear. Since utterances like *three* aren't traditional sentences with traditional sentence meanings,

understanding them cannot be mediated by the understanding of a *sentence,* as assumed by most models of comprehension. These models are therefore incorrect at the outset. Elliptical utterances invite us to look for quite a different model of understanding. For the utterance *three* we are forced to refer to the situation in which the speaker uttered it, which includes the addressees and their beliefs. We must assume that the speaker was trying to coordinate what he meant with what he believed the addressees would understand him to mean, and we are to work out what he meant from that.

To continue:

3. *Gestural answer:*

Ann: What time is it?

Bob: (Holds up three fingers.)

By holding up three fingers, Bob answers Ann's question just as surely as he did by uttering *three.* Many nonlinguistic acts like this are genuine illocutionary acts, which makes them fully appropriate as turns in a conversation. This example, too, shows the futility of viewing understanding as necessarily based on sentence meaning. With gestures like this, there are no words at all.

4. *Indirect answer:*

Ann: What time is it?

Bob: I just saw Mary leave for her dentist appointment.

There are many contexts in which Bob could say he just saw Mary leave, and that would be that. But placed as it is after Ann's question, Bob's utterance takes on an additional, and indirect, interpretation. If it is common ground for Ann and Bob that Mary's appointment is at three, then Bob's *indirect* assertion is that it is nearly three. The point is that Bob isn't saying something irrelevant to Ann's question or trying to change the topic of conversation. He intends her to recognize his indirect assertion in part by seeing that he is replying to her question.

5. *Direct answer to indirect question:*

Ann: What time is it?

Bob: We don't need to leave for five minutes yet.

Here Bob takes Ann's direct question to be a way of asking the indirect question "Is it time to leave yet?" If he does, it wouldn't have been appropriate simply to reply *three.* In other contexts her indirect illocutionary act could have been "Why haven't you gone yet?" or "You are late!" and then he would have responded in still other ways.

Even when the turns following questions aren't answers, they too are intended to be interpreted with reference to the instigating questions. For example, when a question is based on a false presupposition, it cannot be given an answer, as in this sequence:

Ann: When did John leave for Chicago?

Bob: Oh, he decided to stay home.

Since Ann's question projects an answer like "On Tuesday" or "Noon yesterday," Bob's utterance is clearly not an answer. But even though he couldn't provide an answer, he was expected to respond. He couldn't remain silent. The cooperative response was to correct Ann's erroneous assumption, which he did.

In cases of so-called false presumptions, there is a truthful answer that the speaker *could* give to the question, but to reply in good faith, he mustn't give it. Consider the following exchange (see Kaplan, 1981):

Ann: How many students got A's in Introductory Psychology last year?

Bob: None.

Ann: Then how many students got B's?

Bob: None.

Ann: (Incredulously.) Well, how many were taking the course?

Bob: None. It wasn't offered last year.

Bob's initial answer, while literally correct, was misleading, since it implicated that he accepted Ann's presumptions in asking the question—that the course was being offered that year, that there were students in the course, that some students got A's, and so on. To avoid misunderstanding, he should have answered from the start "It wasn't offered this year." Paradoxically, then, even when direct answers are possible, they aren't always appropriate.

QUESTION-ANSWER PAIRS

Questions and answers, by marking the negotiation of information between two participants so clearly, serve as the foundation for many types of conversational sequences. They get part of their interpretation from their placement in those longer sequences. Let us consider a few examples.

Side Sequences

As we have already seen, when listeners fail to hear or understand a speaker, they often interrupt him with procedural moves, as in this example (Schegloff, Jefferson, and Sacks, 1977, p. 367):

F: This is nice, did you make this?

K: No. Samu made that.

> *F:* Who?
> *K:* Samu.

F: (Resumes topic.)

With *Who?* F prompts K to make the clarification *Samu* in the next turn, and the conversation then resumes. With these two turns F and K have taken a short detour from the main course of the conversation in a discrete unit called a *side-sequence* (Jefferson, 1972).

Side sequences used for repairs can become quite extended. Here is a four-turn example (Garvey, 1977, p. 74):

B: This is a nice place.

> *A:* What?
> *B:* This is a nice place.
> *A:* What's a nice place? This room?
> *B:* Yup.
> *A:* Oh, yeah.

B: (Continues topic.)

This side sequence is typical in that it begins with a question, goes on until all the repair work is done, and ends with an acknowledgment of the correction. As Jefferson (1978) has argued, side sequences used for correction often consist of three turns, which can be expanded into more:

1. *A:* Correction solicitor (expanded here into the first three turns in A's and B's side sequence).

2. *B:* Correction (*Yup*).

3. *A:* Acknowledgment (*Oh, yeah*).

Other side sequences have similar organization. The point is that they have a beginning (usually a question) and an end (when all the interactional work is done). They are a clearly demarcated unit of conversation.

Insertion Sequences

A special type of side sequence may even be inserted between a question and its answer, as in this example:

A: Are you coming tonight?

    ⎡*B:* Can I bring a guest?

    ⎣*A:* Sure.

B: I'll be there.

Here A's question projects a direct answer in the next turn, but since B doesn't have enough information to form an answer, he initiates a question-answer sequence of his own. Once his question is answered, he is in a position to answer A's initial question. Schegloff (1972) has called the question-answer pair initiated by B an *insertion sequence*.

    Insertion sequences themselves can be interrupted, as in this example of three such sequences, each one embedded within the last:

A: Are you coming tonight?

    ⎡*B:* Can I bring a guest?

    ⎮ ⎡*A:* Male or female?

    ⎮ ⎮ ⎡*B:* What difference does that make?

    ⎮ ⎮ ⎣*A:* A matter of balance.

    ⎮ ⎣*B:* Female.

    ⎣*A:* Sure

B: I'll be there.

Again, each sequence has a clear beginning and end and is completed before the conversation moves on. The mental record keeping needed for such examples seems quite extraordinary.

Conversational Openings

One of the adjacency pairs brought up earlier was the summons-answer pair in which one person initiates a conversation with another person. Here is a typical summons-answer pair followed by the introduction of the first topic of conversation:

Jane: Bill?

Bill: What?

Jane: Did you happen to see Susan before you left?

Bill: Yes, she was....

As Schegloff (1968) has argued, the summons and answer are especially suitable for opening conversations, in part because they exploit the properties of questions and answers.

    Jane uses her initial summons (*Bill?*) to try to get Bill's attention and obligate him to answer her. She obligates him in the sense that if he doesn't answer, he will be taken to be insolent, angry, impolite, or whatever. One way she gets Bill's attention is by use of his name. But to obligate him to answer in the next turn, she adds a question intonation, a rise in pitch at the end of *Bill*. There are other types of summons she could have used, such as "Hey, Bill," "Excuse me," or a tapping on the shoulder. Her use of the question wasn't necessary. Yet it was effective in making the obligation clear, since questions project answers. Jane asked the question as an indirect means of making her summons.

    Bill's answer to her summons was itself a question (*What?*), which is typical of such answers (like "Yes?" "Uh huh?" or an inquiring look up at the summoner). It responds to her summons, completing the summons-answer pair, and lets her know he is available for talk. But because it is also a question, it turns the conversation back over to Jane. And because the question is so general, it allows Jane to open a topic on whatever she wants, which is just what she does.

    So questions and answers are exploited in conversational openers in a remarkable way. The summons, often a question, obligates the person summoned to answer. But the answer is itself in the form of a question, thereby requesting the summoner to raise the first topic. The design of the summons and answer is just as it should be. The person who makes the initial contact is the one who is ordinarily expected to have a reason for doing so. She is the one who is then obligated to bring up the first topic.

Topic Openers

Another device, much like the conversational opener, is the topic opener, as illustrated in this sequence (Garvey, 1977, p. 81):

A: Do you know what I want to be when I grow up?

B: What?

A: I wanna be a fireman.

B: Oh.

As Garvey has pointed out, B doesn't answer A's question with a simple *No* as he would for a simple request for information. He answers *What?* instead, showing that he has recognized A as soliciting a request for information, and he turns the floor back to A to continue the topic. Children learn this rhetorical gambit quite young and sometimes use it with taxing frequency, as with lead-ins like "You know what?" "Guess what?" and "I'll tell you what." They have learned how compelling these solicitations for contingent queries can be.

REQUEST ROUTINES

Questions and answers play an especially exacting role in routine requests. Recall the indirect request I analyzed earlier from a typical telephone opening:

George: Is Julia there?

Margaret: I'll get her.

George's direct illocutionary act is to ask whether Julia is there, but his indirect illocutionary act is to request Margaret, if Julia *is* there, to call Julia to the telephone. Margaret, in her turn, commits herself to go find Julia.

There is a good deal more to an exchange like this than first meets the eye. We can see this from a study by Merritt (1976) of a large sample of what she called service encounters—routine exchanges between servers and customers in such places as restaurants, notions counters, snack trucks, and markets. [For a related study on children, see Garvey (1975).] Let us consider three major types of routines she identified.

1. *Chaining:* In chaining there are two question-answer pairs one after the other (Merritt, 1976, p. 88):

Customer: Do you have hot chocolate?

Server: MmHmm.

Customer: Can I have hot chocolate with whipped cream?

Server: Sure. (Leaves to get.)

The customer starts by asking whether or not some necessary condition for her eventual request holds, and having been told it does, she makes the request proper. The pattern is this:

$\begin{bmatrix} C: & \text{Question 1.} \\ S: & \text{Answer 1.} \end{bmatrix}$

$\begin{bmatrix} C: & \text{Question 2 + request 3.} \\ S: & \text{Answer 2 + compliance 3.} \end{bmatrix}$

2. *Coupling:* In this type of sequence, there are again two question-answer pairs, but this time they are coupled as follows (Merritt, 1976, p. 89):

Customer: Do you have Marlboros?

Server: Yeah. Hard or soft pack?

Customer: Soft please.

Server: Okay. (Turns to get.)

The customer appears to be checking on a necessary condition for his eventual request, but by so doing, he is actually making the request too. But because the server needs more information to carry out the request, he initiates the second question-answer pair and only then complies with the indirect request. The pattern is this:

$\begin{bmatrix} \begin{bmatrix} C: & \text{Question 1 + request 2.} \\ S: & \text{Answer 1.} \end{bmatrix} \\ \begin{bmatrix} S: & \text{Question 3.} \\ C: & \text{Answer 3.} \end{bmatrix} \\ S: & \text{Promise 2 + compliance 2.} \end{bmatrix}$

3. *Elliptical coupling:* This sequence is like coupling except that the server doesn't explicitly answer question 1. Here is one example Merritt observed (p. 97):

Customer: Do you have Marlboros?

Server: Hard or soft pack?

Customer: Hard.

Server: (Turns to get.)

As Merritt argued, although the server doesn't answer the customer's first question explicitly, his follow-up question *Hard or soft pack?* implicates that the answer is yes. The pattern is like this:

```
┌ ┌ C:  Question 1 + request 2.
│ │ S:  (Answer 1.)
│ └
│       ┌ S:  Question 3.
│       └ C:  Answer 3.
└ S:  Compliance 2.
```

Chaining, coupling, and elliptical coupling form a remarkable trio of routines. They illustrate the way a highly predictable routine can get conflated, or telescoped, into a more and more efficient form (see Goffman, 1974). The telephone opener we began with could have taken any one of these forms:

1. Chaining:

   George: Is Julia there?

   Margaret: Yes, she is.

   George: Can you get her, please.

   Margaret: Okay.

2. Coupling:

   George: Is Julia there?

   Margaret: Yes, she is. Shall I get her?

   George: Yes, please.

   Margaret: Okay.

3. Elliptical coupling:

   George: Is Julia there?

   Margaret: Shall I get her?

   George: Yes, please.

   Margaret: Okay.

4. Indirect request with two-move response:

   George: Is Julia there?

   Margaret: Yes, she is. I'll get her.

5. Indirect request with elliptical response:

   George: Is Julia there?

   Margaret: I'll get her.

6. Indirect request with indirect compliance:

   George: Is Julia there?

   Margaret: Wait just a minute please.

These sequences get conflated as Margaret anticipates, as George intends her to, more and more of his ultimate request. In example 1 she anticipates none of it. In examples 2 and 3 she anticipates that he wants her to call Julia to the telephone, and so she *offers* to do that. In 4, 5, and 6 she anticipates that he wants her to call Julia to the phone, but she also takes him to be *requesting* her to do so. In 4 and 5 she directly commits herself to going to get Julia. In 6, by asking George to wait, she only indirectly commits herself to doing so. In 1, of course, she takes George's initial question seriously and answers it. She also takes it seriously in 2 and 4, where she answers it in a separate move (*Yes, she is*) even though she doesn't need to.

Which routine occurs is not a matter of accident but of coordination. It depends on the intentions signaled by the requester and on the recognition of his intentions by the respondent. These two processes depend in turn on aspects of the situation itself and how they are perceived by the two participants. In particular, the routine that occurs depends on what are perceived to be the parties' goals and plans.

GOALS AND PLANS

In arriving at what the speaker meant, addressees are generally intended to identify her goals (see Allen and Perrault, 1980; Clark, 1979; Cohen and Perrault, 1979; Hobbs and Evans, 1980; Hobbs and Robinson, 1979). How do they do that? As I argued earlier, they depend on three basic sources of information (Clark and Marshall, 1981): linguistic sources, perceptual sources, and community-wide knowledge and beliefs. Addressees assume, first, that the speaker selects what she says so that they can recognize her plans and goals easily. They assume, second, that the speaker's plans are also to be judged against what is more or less directly accessible from the perceptual world immediately around them. And they assume, third, that the speaker's plans can be inferred in part from the knowledge and beliefs common to everyone in their community. These include, among other things, general schemas or scripts about what happens in stereotypical situations such as those in the restaurants, notions counters, snack trucks, and markets that Merritt studied (see Rumelhart, 1980; Rumelhart and Ortony, 1977; Schank and Abelson, 1977). What addressees rely on, in short, is the common ground between them and the speaker.

Recall the field experiment I discussed earlier in which a woman telephoned restaurants and asked whether they accepted credit cards (Clark, 1979). In this stereotypical situation, analogous to Merritt's routine service encounters, the restaurateur who answered could attribute to the caller a hierarchy of goals. Here is a rough list of those goals, beginning with the most general:

1. The woman wants to patronize a restaurant that day or in the near future.

2. She wants to decide whether or not to patronize his, the restaurateur's, restaurant.

3. She wants to know how she or a companion can pay for their meals at the restaurant.

4. She wants to pay with something other than cash.

5. She wants to pay with a credit card.

6. She wants to know from the restaurateur whether or not she can pay with a credit card she owns—she may own more than one.

These goals could be attributed to almost anyone who called asking about credit cards. They represent beliefs most people in the community would have about such a call. The restaurateur therefore feels justified in thinking they are part of his and the caller's common ground.

The restaurateurs in this study gave clear evidence that they assumed this hierarchy of goals. Consider the restaurateurs who accepted no credit cards. When asked "Do you accept credit cards?" or "Do you accept any kinds of credit cards?" they had to answer no. Nevertheless, fully 38 percent of them added a second move about accepting personal checks or traveler's checks, as in "No, but we accept traveler's checks." Since they couldn't satisfy goals 5 and 6, they offered information pertinent to goal 4. A few merchants even added moves pertinent to goals 1 and 2, as in "Uh, yes, we accept credit cards. But tonight we are closed." These moves, it seems clear, are based on the hierarchy of goals they attributed to the caller, not merely on what she said.

What she said, however, must certainly also be critical, and it was. Compare the sequences that unfolded when the restaurateur was asked "Do you accept American Express cards?" or "Do you accept credit cards?" and he could answer yes. With the first question 100 percent of the sequences were instances of chaining:

Caller:　　　Do you accept American Express cards?

Restaurateur: Yes, we do.

Caller:　　　Do you accept any other kinds of credit cards?

Restaurateur: Master Card and Visa.

With the second question, only 44 percent of the sequences were instances of chaining:

Caller:　　　Do you accept credit cards?

Restaurateur: Yes, we do.

Caller:　　　What credit cards do you accept?

Restaurateur: We accept Master Card and Visa.

Fully 38 percent were instances of indirect requests with two-move responses:

Caller:　　　Do you accept credit cards?

Restaurateur: Yes, we accept Master Card and Visa.

Another 16 percent contained indirect requests with elliptical responses:

Caller:　　　Do you accept credit cards?

Restaurateur: We accept Master Card and Visa.

Which routine occurred, then, depended on what goals the restaurateur took the caller to be signaling by her choice of question. When she mentioned American Express cards, the restaurateurs could attribute to her a seventh subgoal, roughly as follows:

7. She wants to know whether or not she can pay with her American Express card and not with any other card.

They could then infer that she was asking only whether they accepted that type of card, and they did. But when she mentioned credit cards in general, they could attribute quite a different seventh subgoal, roughly as follows:

7'. She wants to know what credit cards the restaurant accepts in order to see if any match the two or three cards she owns.

That is, they could assume as common ground that she probably had more than one credit card but not all possible credit cards. Then she would also be asking which credit cards they accepted. Indeed, more than half the restaurateurs (54 percent) took her to be indirectly requesting a list of the credit cards they accepted. Put differently, the restaurateur assumed that the caller was quite deliberate in selecting the wording *Do you accept credit cards?* over alternative wordings (such as *Do you accept American Express cards or Visa?*) and that she chose it as a way of signaling her goals and, thereby, what she meant.

Routine service encounters can become surprisingly terse when the goal hierarchies of customer and server are constrained tightly enough. When a customer steps into a taxi, it is common ground in the community that her goal must be to hire the driver to take her from the current location to a location she must immediately specify. The only thing they need to negotiate immediately is the destination. So the following exchange would suffice:

Taxi driver: Yes?

Rider: The Mark Hopkins.

The driver's opener is a substitute for the question he assumes she takes for granted, and her reply answers that question. If she had some other goal, like asking him *where* the Mark Hopkins was, this exchange wouldn't do. She would have to make her question explicit, as in "Could you tell me where the Mark Hopkins is?" In routine encounters the parties assume the default conditions unless there is reason to assume otherwise (see also Allen and Perrault, 1980; Cohen and Perrault, 1979).

There are many ways of judging common ground and hence goal hierarchies. As Schegloff (1972) pointed out, if a New Yorker is approached by a stranger who asks, "Could you tell me how to get to the Long Island Train Terminal?" he identifies the person as a non–New Yorker—the correct name is Penn Station—and, in giving directions, assumes he has little detailed knowledge of New York. Accent and clothing can also indicate whether a speaker is native or from out of town (Krauss and Glucksberg, 1977). A common ploy in giving directions is to establish what is common ground, as in this exchange:

Stranger: Where is the Brooklyn Museum?

New Yorker: Do you know Brooklyn?

Stranger: I know Bedford-Stuyvesant.

New Yorker: Okay, then, ...

And the answer to such a question also depends on where the two people are located (Norman, 1973). In answer to "Where is the Empire State Building?" the second person would give different answers depending on whether the two of them were in China ("In the United States"), in California ("In New York City"), or in New York City ("On 34th Street"). The questioner's perceived goals change with their joint location, which is also, of course, part of their common ground.

In short, interpretations of what people say in conversations are based on many factors. There is the local context, such as the adjacency pairs of which the utterances are parts. There is also the global context, which includes the situations in which the parties are talking and the roles they play in those situations. Ultimately, interpretations by addressees are expected to be made from the speaker's mutually identifiable reasons for saying what he did—goals that are part of common ground. Making these interpretations, often a very delicate process, would be impossible without the close coordination between speaker and addressees.

CONVERSATIONAL ACTIVITIES

Insertion sequences, side sequences, and the other sequences just discussed are really local devices for creating conversational activities such as arguing, gossiping, telling jokes, and gathering information. These activities are more complex than the local devices they make use of (see Levinson, 1981). In arguments, for example, the participants have certain ostensible goals (such as trying to persuade others of their position on an issue) and usually hidden agendas as well (trying to impress, preserve dignity, pass the time, etc.). Conversations become juggling acts, with each participant keeping track of many goals as they get tossed in and out of play. Taking part requires an extra level of skill and coordination. It cannot be done one move at a time.

To interpret utterances in conversation, people have to know what kind of conversational activity the parties are engaged in. The same sequence of sentences may be interpreted one way in an argument but quite differently in a gossip session (see Levinson, 1979). Conversational activities are less conventionalized, less routinized, less tightly structured than the sequences just examined. They constrain interpretations not so much by the placement of utterances in local sequences—like adjacency pairs and routines—as by the relation of utterances to the ongoing social activities to which they belong. This feature makes conversational activities impossible to analyze without a model of the social activities, and these have not been studied very extensively.

There is one important point to be brought out about conversational activities: Narratives, stories, and other monologues are best viewed as specialized conversational activities governed by the same principles as conversations. To show this, I will introduce the notion of a section of conversation, a fairly discrete unit of talk that is associated with a coherent conversational activity. I will then move from sections of dialogue to conversational monologues to formal narratives, showing how they belong to the same extended family.

OPENING AND CLOSING CONVERSATIONS

Life isn't one long uninterrupted conversation but a series of short ones, each with a beginning and an ending. Whenever people come together and begin a conversation, they end it before parting. As Goffman (1971) has emphasized, there must be ways of marking when a conversation has begun and when it has ended, since people can be near each other but not in conversation. Most cultures have evolved certain access rituals, as Goffman called them, for making and breaking contact. We can therefore identify three major parts of a conversation between two people:

1. opening section,
2. body of conversation,
3. closing section.

It is worth considering the opening and closing sections more closely since they illustrate what conversational sections look like. I will mainly discuss two-person conversations, but the same ideas hold, with certain complications, for larger ones.

In the opening section of a conversation the potential parties must accomplish two things (Schiffrin, 1977). First, they must mutually recognize that they have identified each other, either as a member of a category (like waiters) or as a known individual (like one's father). Second, they must mutually recognize each other socially as people they are willing to enter into a conversation with; they have to display what Schiffrin called *social recognition*. This happens in what I will call the greeting, in

which, for example, two people who haven't seen each other for a while will want to reestablish their acquaintance. The two parties must then prepare each other for opening the first topic of conversation. So in the general case the opening section consists of three subsections:

1a. contact initiation,

1b. greetings,

1c. topic initiation.

When two people meet face to face, in order to initiate conversational contact, they usually have to make eye contact—that is, look at each other and mutually recognize that they are doing so. One person can initiate the eye contact with the summons described earlier, such as "Hey, Bill," "Yohoo," or "Excuse me," and the second person then confirms the contact by looking at the first and giving an answer, such as "Yes?" When it is impossible for the second to look at the first, as on the telephone, an answer such as "Hello" will suffice. When two people make eye contact 20 yards from each other, they may take each other as having made conversational contact even though they cannot yet talk. One of them would feel snubbed if the other then walked past without at least a perfunctory exchange of *hellos*. Although eye contact isn't a sufficient condition for initiating contact for a conversation—you can make eye contact with people in passing—it is often necessary, along with other ways of mutually recognizing that conversational contact has been made.

Then comes the greeting, the process of making acquaintance or reacquaintance. In urban America a typical sequence serving this function goes as follows:

Anne: Hi, Bill, how are you?

Bill: Hi. Fine. How are you?

The questions here serve as greetings. In most situations they are not expected to be answered seriously—unless Bill, say, wants to bring up his health specifically as a topic (Sacks, 1975). The greeting process can become quite extended, as is standard in certain cultures. According to Irvine (1974), a typical Wolof greeting in Senegal, where greetings are obligatory, would go like this (in a mixture of Arabic and Wolof):

Diop: Peace be with you. (Arabic)

Ndiaye: With you be peace. (Arabic)

Diop: Diop.

Ndiaye: Ndiaye.

Diop: Ndiaye.

Ndiaye: Diop.

Diop: How do you do?

Ndiaye: I am here only.

Diop: Don't you have peace?

Ndiaye: Peace only, yes.

Diop: Where are the people of the household?

Ndiaye: They are there.

Diop: Where is Lat Dior [a close relative]?

Ndiaye: He is there.

Diop: Isn't it that you aren't sick?

Ndiaye: I am praising God.

Diop: Isn't it that anyone isn't sick?

Ndiaye: They are praising God.

Diop: Thanks be to God. (Arabic)

Ndiaye: Thanks be to God. (Arabic)

Diop: Thanks be to God. (Arabic)

Ndiaye: Thanks be to God. (Arabic)

In this greeting there are even further subsections, each with a separate purpose. The Wolof use the greeting to make acquaintance and, more importantly, to establish relative status. Many of the exchanges are for jockeying into a higher or lower status, which becomes important for the next activity, like bargaining.

In the last subsection, topic initiation, it is ordinarily the initiator of the interaction who is to introduce the first topic. He can do this by various means, as with the topic opener mentioned earlier:

Anne: Do you know what happened to me yesterday?

Bill: No, what?

And with that begins the body of the conversation.

There are many occasions in which the greeting is dispensed with. Between strangers, for example, the opening section can consist of two turns:

Anne: Excuse me, sir. (making eye contact with Bill)

Bill: What is it?

Anne's turn initiates contact, leading to eye contact, and Bill's turn returns the conversation to Anne for the first topic. The greeting isn't possible for two strangers who aren't already acquainted or who aren't intending to become acquainted. If Anne, a stranger to Bill, had said instead "Hello, sir," trying to force him to return a "hello," she might be seen as trying to ingratiate herself with Bill. The greeting is also ordinarily omitted in repeated conversations with the same person on the same day. Imagine George and Jane, a married couple, at home together in the evening reading, when George starts a conversation:

George: Jane.

Jane: Yes, dear?

As with the strangers, the opening is only two turns long, as they omit the greeting subsection altogether.

The closing section of a conversation is just as complex as the opening, and it generally consists of three subsections (Clark and French, 1981; Schegloff and Sacks, 1973):

3a. topic termination,

3b. leave-taking,

3c. contact termination.

Consider a typical closing section of a telephone conversation (from Schegloff and Sacks, 1973, p. 318):

B: Well that's why I said "I'm not gonna say anything, I'm not making any comments [*C:* Hmh] about anybody."

C: Ehyeah.

B: Yeah.

C: Yeah.

B: Alrighty. Well I'll give you a call before we decide to come down. O.K.?

C: O.K.

B: Alrighty.

C: O.K.

B: We'll see you then.

C: O.K.

B: Bye bye.

C: Bye.

B: (hangs up.)

C: (hangs up.)

With the first exchange B and C terminate the final topic discussed, and with the clicks of the telephone hanging up, they terminate contact. Everything in between could be called leave-taking.

Terminating the topic, as Schegloff and Sacks (1973) have shown, has to be agreed on by both parties to the conversation. When talk about a current topic runs out, one of the parties can offer a *preclosing statement,* such as "Okay," "We-ell," or, more insistently, "Well, I gotta go now." In this way she offers the other person the chance to open another topic or, if there are no other topics, to agree to begin the closing section. If the second person responds "Okay" or "Yeah," she accepts the alternative of closing the conversation, and they move directly into leave-taking.

The overall function of the leave-taking section is to reaffirm each other's acquaintance before breaking contact (Clark and French, 1981). The two people will want to reassure each other that the break in contact is only temporary, that they are still acquainted, and that they will resume contact at some time in the future (Goffman, 1971). So in taking leave, people often summarize the content of the contact they have just had; justify ending their contact at this time; express pleasure about each other; indicate continuity in their relationship by planning, specifically or vaguely, for future contact; and wish each other well—generally in that order (Albert and Kessler, 1976, 1978; Knapp, *et al.,* 1973). The last two items—promising future contact, and wishing each other well—are often conventionalized in the terminal exchange itself, as in *see you, goodbye, good night, auf Wiedersehen, au revoir, hasta la vista, a dieu,* and *bon voyage.*

In many conversations, however, there is no need for a leave-taking subsection. One such situation is when the two parties haven't really become acquainted. For example, in telephone calls to directory assistance (or directory inquiries) at the telephone company, a typical closing section goes like this (Clark and French, 1981):

Caller: Thank you. (for the number)

Operator: You're welcome.

Caller: (Hangs up.)

Operator: (Hangs up.)

The gratitude exchange, *thank you—you're welcome,* serves as a preclosing statement and its response, and there is no leaving-taking subsection. But when a caller in these circumstances makes even minimal acquaintance with the operator by asking for more than the routine number—asking, for example, for local directions—the caller and operator are more likely to exchange *goodbyes* before hanging up. With this exchange they bring in the bare minimum of a leave-taking subsection. There is also no need for two people to take leave of each other when they are breaking contact only briefly. If they expect to resume talk minutes later, they don't need to prepare each other for a long time apart.

There are two points to note about the opening and closing sections. First, they are discrete, identifiable sections, with beginnings and endings intended to be mutually recognized by the parties to the conversation. But because creating them requires the coordination of both parties, they are still open to error and uncertainty. Second, these sections and their subsections are products of the functions they serve. The opening takes the form it does because it is used for opening up conversations, and each subsection contributes some subfunction to that goal. The same goes for the closing section. These two points are characteristic of sections of conversation. Each is relatively discrete or intended to be heard as that, and each serves a coherent function or set of functions.

SECTIONS OF CONVERSATIONS

The body of a conversation has its own identifiable sections. It may consist entirely of one brief section. In a telephone call to directory assistance all the caller does is ask for, receive, and confirm a telephone number. In most conversations the body divides into more than one major section. Traditionally, these sections have been called topics of conversation, or subjects of discussion, and this is all right as far as it goes. But it is generally more perspicuous to identify sections by the functions they serve, as we just saw for openings and closings. In each section the parties engage in a more or less distinct social process, and the talk that emerges is in part a consequence of that process. To illustrate, I will consider the process of formulating plans of action. As in openings and closings, the social process itself helps the participants coordinate.

Formulating plans, something people often do in conversations, generally takes place in a well-formed unit of discourse. To demonstrate this, Linde and Goguen (1978) analyzed a conversation, recorded on September 15, 1972, in which President Richard M. Nixon, Presidential Counsel John Dean, and Presidential Assistant H. R. Haldeman planned how to neutralize the damaging effects of an upcoming investigation by Representative Wright Patman's Banking and Currency Committee on campaign financing, hearings that could lead to a scandal about the Watergate burglaries. Their conversation broke quite naturally into three main subsections.

1. *Selection of the goal:* The session began with an announcement of the goal by John Dean (Linde and Goguen, 1978, p. 245), "But Patman's hearings, uh, his Banking and Currency Committee, and we've got to—whether we will be successful or not in turning that off, I don't know." Nixon and Haldeman, already acquainted with the problem, tacitly agreed to take part in planning a solution. In other planning sessions the goal may need to be explained, negotiated, or justified more extensively.

2. *Devising and evaluating plans:* Dean also proposed the first plan. To do so, he mentioned certain actors (p. 245), "We've got a plan whereby Rothblatt and Bittman, who are counsel for the five men who were, or actually a total of seven, that were indicted today...," and then described what they were to do: "...are going to go up and visit every member and say, 'If you commence hearings you are going to jeopardize the civil rights of these individuals in the worst way, and they'll never get a fair trial.'" This conversation is typical of plans. The planners assume or mention certain actors and props and then specify the actions the actors are to carry out with the props.

Nixon, Haldeman, and Dean negotiated five major subplans by the time they were through, each with its own actors, props, and actions. After completing each subplan, they evaluated it either explicitly or implicitly. Their approval of a plan, temporarily at least, was implicit, for example, when they moved on to the next subplan without vetoing the last one. The five subplans were all to be carried out simultaneously. For other types of planning there could instead be alternative plans for the same goal; these would eventually be compared and one of them chosen.

3. *Evaluation of the plan:* At the end of the planning session, Nixon, Haldeman, and Dean evaluated the overall plan they had come to. Nixon reiterated the need for a plan and justified the one they had devised as good "public relations." Dean and Haldeman agreed. With that the planning section ended, and the three of them turned to other matters. Here it was Nixon, the person with the highest status, who gave the final approval. In other planning sections other patterns of evaluation and approval are possible too.

As Linde and Goguen's example shows, planning is a social process in which two or more people select certain goals and then devise plans for achieving them by exchanging information, evaluating suggestions, and negotiating on the final outcome. The form the section takes, then, is not dictated by linguistic conventions about who is to say what when but by the social process it serves. What is said is determined by what the parties are trying to achieve, not vice versa.

Other sections of conversation, as associated with other social activities, have a similar character. Just as with opening, closing, and planning sections, the parties must introduce and settle on the social process they are to take part in, engage in the process itself, and end it by mutual consent, deciding the process is complete, or as complete as it will be at that time. It is through these three subsections that the parties coordinate their entrance into, carrying out of, and exit from the social process. They interpret what is said in relation to the functions each subsection serves.

The middle subsection, the body, is generally of central importance, since it is there that the parties carry out the social process itself. But conversational exchanges differ in how essential they are to that social process. A conversation among people playing basketball (see Levinson, 1979) will consist of shouts of encouragement, simple directives, and other comments interleaved with the actions of the game. The participants could probably play basketball without that talk. For processes like planning, on the other hand, the conversation is essential to the work that gets done. It is the very machinery by which the participants accomplish their goals.

DESCRIPTIONS IN MONOLOGUES

The social processes people engage in during conversations are fundamentally *joint* activities. They are processes that couldn't be carried out without close coordination, without the participants maintaining a common ground of what process they are engaged in, what they have done so far, and where they are going.

To succeed, people in conversations must ordinarily coordinate their focus of attention (see Grosz, 1981). They must each attend to the same things the other participants are attending to and at roughly the same time. The very structure of sections helps. The initial subsection brings the overall topic or problem into focus. The body, the main subsection, narrows the focus successively on each part of the overall topic; each exchange carries focus of attention from one step in the process to the next; and when there are problems, the participants initiate corrections and detour into side sequences. Finally, the concluding subsection focuses attention on the completed process, forcing everyone to stand back and survey it as a whole. In talk during basketball games the focus of attention may be coordinated more by the game than by the structure of the talk itself, but it is still coordinated; indeed, basketball players are often encouraged to talk during games as one way of coordinating their play.

Coordinating focus of attention is just as essential in monologues as in dialogues. The goal of a person describing a scene is to get his addressees to create mental models of the scene that are roughly the same as his own. He must induce them to focus attention on successive locations of the scene as he describes what they are to imagine there, and for this they all must coordinate how they mentally survey this scene. In genuine monologues—during which the addressees don't break in—the speaker cannot rely on adjacency pairs, repairs, and side sequences to coordinate focus of attention. He must achieve it entirely by the structure of his description.

The main problem is what Levelt (1982) has called the *linearization problem*. Speech is linear, a series of sentences uttered one after the other, but the scene a person wants to describe may be two- or three-dimensional or otherwise not linear. The problem is how to describe the elements of such a scene in a linear order. If the speaker describes them in random order, she can't be sure she and her addressees are coordinating their focus of attention—that they are all focusing on the part of the scene she is describing. She must devise a linearization scheme they can readily follow with her. I will consider two such options, one for events and another for static scenes.

The most obvious way to linearize an event is to describe its constituent events in chronological order, from beginning to end. One might use flashbacks or other nonchronological schemes, but they are generally more difficult to understand and remember (see Baker, 1978).

Events, or at least our mental representations of them, aren't homogeneous entities. Chafe (1979, see also 1980) has argued that they are hierarchical. At the top of the hierarchy are what he called memories; these divide into episodes, which divide into thoughts, which in turn divide into foci. From an analysis of how people described a short movie that had no dialogue, Chafe suggested that these hierarchical units correspond fairly closely to traditional units of narratives. The memory corresponds to the story as a whole, the episode to the paragraph, the thought to the sentence, and the focus to the phrase (generally a clause).

The speaker creates his description, in Chafe's view, according to a *flow model*. He orients first to the complete memory, turns to its beginning episode, and then turns to the first thought within that episode, which itself divides into several foci. He "flows" from one focus to the next within the first thought, then jumps up to the next thought, down to its first focus, and so on, until he reaches the next episode, at which point he starts from the first thought, first focus, and moves on.

The hierarchical nature of descriptions is clear in the hesitations and pauses in the speech of Chafe's respondents as they described the movie. Chafe took one respondent's transcript and asked other people to divide it into paragraphs. The points at which a new paragraph was judged to have begun were just the points at which the speaker had hesitated the longest in his description. These paragraph boundaries indeed came at points of transition between major clusters of events—that is, between episodes—and people generally took extra time to jump from one episode to the next. They took an especially long time, with long hesitations and frequent repairs, to enter the memory initially, turn to the first episode, and describe the first focus.

Sentences, which in Chafe's scheme correspond to thoughts, have natural boundaries both syntactically and intonationally. They are natural units of narratives. But in people's descriptions of the movie they were also preceded by hesitations 88 percent of the time, suggesting that they represent discrete jumps in retrieval from memory too. As for foci, they were easily identified as phrases marked by "phrase-final" intonations. Most of these were single clauses with one main verb and its arguments, like *and he walks down the ladder*. They appeared to represent the primary events of the scene, the smallest elements pertinent to the level at which the scene was being described. So Chafe's informants appeared to treat the entire event as an object segmented into episodes, thoughts, and foci. They found the event easiest to describe by moving from one segment to the next in chronological order.

Describing static scenes poses a different dilemma, since there is no straightforward way of linearizing them. Yet when faced with the problem, people nonetheless manage to come up with consistent and often ingenious solutions. Linde and Labov (1975) asked people, in the course of an interview about attitudes toward urban life, to describe their apartment layouts: "Could you tell me the layout of your apartment?" Almost all, 97 percent, of them narrated a *tour* of their apartments, as in this short example (p. 927):

You walked in the front door.

There was a narrow hallway.

To the left, the first door you came to was a tiny bedroom.

Then there was a kitchen,

and then bathroom,

and then the main room was in the back, living room, I guess.

They would begin the tour at the front door, look into each room that didn't have rooms beyond, go through each room that did, jump back to the last choice point when they reached a dead end, and, in that manner, survey every room in the apartment. By taking a tour, they turned a two-dimensional array into a one-dimensional one that they could describe chronologically as they went along. They turned a static scene into a narratable event.

There are many aspects of these tours that enable the speaker and addressee to coordinate their focus of attention. Linde and Labov's respondents always focused first on the main entrance and then directed the addressee's attention step by step through the mental apartment with such directional terms as *straight ahead, on your left,* and *directly in front of you.* They took it as common ground that apartments virtually always have a master bedroom, a kitchen, a living room, and the like, which they generally referred to with definite articles, as in *And on the left you would find the master bedroom.* They did not take it as common ground that any particular room would have closets or pantries, and they referred to these with indefinite articles, as in *with a little dressing room off that.* They didn't describe the features that every apartment must have, such as floors, walls, doors, and ceilings, but only the features that are *not* predictable from common ground (see also Brewer and Treyens, 1981).

Apartments segment conceptually into major rooms, with the minor rooms—closets, for example—as appendages. The easiest way for speakers to get addressees to build the right mental models is to take advantage of this schema, and Linde and Labov's respondents did. They would often focus on main rooms in main clauses and call attention to the minor rooms in short phrases or clauses attached to them, as in *And there's another little bathroom with a little dressing room off that.* When speakers moved from one room to the next in their descriptions, they were truly moving from one major focus of attention to the next. As Linde (1979) showed, they were highly consistent in using the pronoun *it* for objects in the current room, the current focus of attention, but the pronoun *that* for similar objects in previous rooms no longer in the focus of attention. Their intent, presumably, was indeed to distinguish things that were in their current focus of attention from things that weren't.

As the descriptions of movies and apartments show, even in monologues speakers enable their addressees to coordinate with them on what they have in focus at a given time. They assume a certain common ground—about how events cluster into episodes, for example, and about what apartments generally look like—and lead their addressees through the scene or event mentioning only those features not predictable from common ground. They first direct their addressees' attention to major benchmarks and then call attention to other objects by describing them with respect to those benchmarks.

There is little doubt that these strategies help addressees understand, but do speakers select them for that purpose? There are reasons for thinking they do. The speakers created these descriptions in settings where they cared very much whether their addressees understood them. Even if there were no interruptions from their audience, there was always the possibility of interruption. The speakers wanted to be clear. They probably selected these linearization strategies, with their segmentations into smaller units, because these had worked well before. And if it felt easy for *them,* it must also be easy for their audience. Coordinating focus of attention, then, is very likely a deliberate strategy even in monologues.

NARRATIVES

One of the most impressive types of speech performances is the telling of stories, jokes, and anecdotes—the performance of narratives. Within psychology and linguistics there is a major tradition of analysis that has focused on the internal structure of narratives, especially folktales and children's stories. The idea is that a story consists of a sequence of sentences that map onto a hierarchical scheme prescribed for folk stories, a so-called *story grammar* or *schema.* In Rumelhart's (1975) schema the story as a whole divides into a setting followed by an episode. The setting in turn divides into one or more states (which identify the time, place, and characters enabling the story to proceed). The episode in turn divides into an event followed by its reaction, and the event itself may be broken into embedded episodes, actions, changes of state, or sequences of events. And there are further divisions (see also Mandler and Johnson, 1977). In this way the sentences of a story fall into a pattern, or schema, and each sentence is interpreted by its place in that schema. In the extreme of this view the story is treated as an abstract *text,* an object with a structure and life of its own (see Halliday and Hasan, 1976; van Dijk, 1977). Its analysis doesn't depend on who told it to whom.

For psychologists, at least, the text or grammar approach to narratives has drawbacks. As Morgan and Sellner (1980) have pointed out, it fails to separate clearly three distinct levels of a story. The first is the story's *content,* the facts and events in the story's world. In Linde and Labov's apartment descriptions the analogous content would be the apartments themselves, the "worlds" those respondents were trying to describe: Each apartment had its own structure independent of the person describing it. The second level of a story is its *presentational structure,* the narrator's choice of which parts of the content to describe and what order and manner to put them in (see also Brewer, 1980). In apartment descriptions this level would be analogous to selecting which rooms and artifacts to describe and what linearization scheme to characterize them in. The third level of a story is its *linguistic form,* the actual words and phrases used for expressing it. Note that the presentational structure of a story depends on the story content but isn't identical to it. Likewise, the linguistic form of the story depends on the presentational structure but also is distinct from it. Story grammars tend not to distinguish story content from presentational structure, nor presentational structure from linguistic form.

The root of the problem is the neglect of the narrator and audience. Like descriptions and other monologues, narratives arise as parts of conversations or other social interchanges. In preliterate societies, that is

the only source. Written narratives, such as short stories and novels, are really derivatives of their spoken cousins, inheriting most of their important properties from spoken narratives. Whether talking or writing, each narrator has certain intentions in selecting content, presentational structure, and linguistic devices. He won't select a story content or rhetorical strategy he isn't confident his intended audience will understand—he wouldn't narrate Faulkner-like stories to children—just as he won't select words, phrases, or other linguistic devices they are unlikely to grasp. Narratives need as much coordinating as any other part of conversation.

In conversations, narratives are discrete sections. Like other sections, they are introduced; the narratives proper are then carried out; and they are completed, or responded to, to make way for the next section of the conversation. According to Sacks, then, narratives consist of three subsections:

1. the preface,

2. the telling,

3. response sequences.

How does this scheme work?

Many stories, according to analyses by Jefferson (1978), are "locally occasioned" in conversation. They are triggered by some event in the conversation that reminds one party of a story. They are then methodically introduced into the turn-by-turn talk with phrases like *oh by the way*, *incidentally*, and *speaking about the forties.* In the story itself the narrator generally mentions the word or event that triggered it, to show how the story is pertinent at that point in the conversation. After the story is finished, the storyteller reengages turn-by-turn conversation. She uses the story as a source for new topics of conversation or finds other ways of tying subsequent talk to the story. Storytellers have a range of devices for doing this.

Stories enter conversations for many different purposes. In an analysis of East European Jewish storytelling, Kirshenblatt-Gimblett (1974) showed that informal stories came in four basic types. Sometimes they were introduced into conversation to make a point about a topic brought up, as just illustrated. Often they were introduced to be told as ends in themselves. In this case either the stories were subordinated to other topics in the conversation, or they dominated it, being told in rounds by different parties one after the other. On some occasions an especially good storyteller would tell all the stories, but even then, according to Kirshenblatt-Gimblett, the stories were considered parts of a conversation. There were also formal settings in which stories and parables were told, as in prayers and meetings, yet these narratives had similar forms.

For different types of narratives the storyteller must therefore design different prefaces. Consider how a dirty joke is ordinarily introduced into a conversation (Sacks, 1974). At a minimum the storyteller offers to tell the others a story, and the others accept the offer. But to justify the offer, to induce the others to accept it, the storyteller also needs to assure them that they haven't heard the joke before, for it is a cardinal rule of joke telling that one shouldn't knowingly tell people a joke they have already heard. The storyteller can avoid this repetition by describing the joke briefly, as in "Have you heard the joke about the two Canadians?" or by otherwise indicating why he believes they haven't heard it before. In a joke Sacks analyzed, the narrator began, "You wanna hear, my sister told me a story last night," by which he both offered a joke and suggested that it was new. Although this was accepted by one of the parties with "I don't wanna hear it—but if you must," the narrator felt obliged to justify its quality further and to mention its topic, "To stun me she says uh there was these three girls an' they just got married?" (Note that by using a question intonation, the storyteller was still asking whether he should proceed.) After the others also agreed they hadn't heard it and wanted to hear it, the narrator went on to tell the joke itself. The preface here is a textbook example of coordination.

In American culture the telling of a story can't ordinarily be interrupted. Yet whenever a member of the audience doesn't hear or understand a word or doesn't see what is going on, he can break in and ask for a repair or repeat. Even this minimal possibility makes the telling interactive. The narrator must attend to the needs of his audience at all times, for if he doesn't, he may be stopped and questioned, interrupting the flow of his story.

In some cultures the telling of the story is explicitly interactive. Among the Ilongot of the Philippines, the storyteller narrates stories to a designated interlocutor in the audience (Rosaldo, 1980). The interlocutor has two jobs. One is to react to the storyteller's statements, to protract the narrative and intensify its drama. The other is to clarify what is going on, pinning down the referents of pronouns, for example, when characters are identified only by their actions. Interlocutors are crucial to Ilongot narratives.

If written narratives are derivative from spoken ones, they should contain vestiges of their conversational origins, and they do. Many begin with a preface to offer a story and justify its newness and interest. Consider the first lines of Herman Melville's "Bartleby the Scrivener":

> I am a rather elderly man. The nature of my avocations, for the last thirty years, has brought me into more than ordinary contact with what would seem an interesting and somewhat singular set of men, of whom, as yet, nothing, that I know of, has ever been written—I mean, the law-copyists, or scriveners.... But I waive the biographers of all other scriveners, for a few passages in the life of Bartleby, who was a scrivener, the strangest I ever saw, or heard of.

Or the first lines of M. R. James's ghost story, "The Mezzotint":

> Some time ago I believe I had the pleasure of telling you the story of an adventure which happened to a friend of mine by the name of Dennistoun, during his pursuit of objects of art for the museum at Cambridge. He did not publish his experiences very widely upon his return to England.

Or the first chapter, titled "A word of explanation," of Mark Twain's *A Connecticut Yankee in King Arthur's Court,* which begins:

> It was in Warwick Castle that I came across the curious stranger whom I am going to talk about. He attracted me by three things: his candid simplicity, his marvelous familiarity with ancient armor, and the restfulness of his company—for he did all the talking.

In each preface the author justifies the tale to induce the "listener" to read on. These devices, and many like them, are little different from the spontaneous preface of Sacks's joke teller.

In many spoken narratives, the second section, the telling of the story, is marked by a distinctive beginning. In English, fairy tales often begin "Once upon a time," a formulaic expression that sets the telling of the story off from its preface. Among East European Jews the formulas changed depending on whether the story was a parable, joke, legend, or whatever (Kirschenblatt-Gimblett, 1974). Many written stories begin with the same distinctive markings, and there have evolved, in literature, other methods of setting off story beginnings. These give the narrator and audience distinctive ways of coordinating the performance and understanding of narrative beginnings.

It is no less important in narratives than in descriptions for a speaker and audience to coordinate focus of attention. With narratives there is a cluster of methods for this chore, and among these the most important, perhaps, are designed for keeping track of the main thread of a story.

Narratives can be shown to have two kinds of structures (Grimes, 1975; Hopper, 1979; Hopper and Thompson, 1980; Labov, 1972; Polanyi-Bowditch, 1976). The first, sometimes called the *foreground,* or the *skeleton* or *backbone,* of the narrative, is the "temporal structure, which charts the progress of the narrative through time by presenting a series of events which are understood to occur sequentially" (Polanyi-Bowditch, 1976, p. 61). The second, often called the *background,* is the "durative/descriptive structure, which provides a spatial, characterological, and durational context for which the temporal structure marks time and changes of state" (Polanyi-Bowditch, 1976, p. 61). The foreground mentions *in order* the events that occurred, and the background comments on, situates, and otherwise helps characterize those events. The foreground tends to consist of events, the background of nonevents; the foreground tends to involve two or more main characters, the background one or none; the foreground tends to describe punctual kinetic actions, the background other things (Hopper and Thompson, 1980). Setting information is placed in the background, and so are incidents marginal to the main narrative line.

It would help coordinate focus of attention if narrators distinguished the foreground from the background, just as Linde and Labov's informants distinguished the main rooms from their appendages. And they do. They tend to use the simple past tense for foregrounded events, as in *I unlocked the door, went into the kitchen, and began to cook an omelette,* and to express the background in the progressive, with static verbs (like *to be*), or in subordinate positions, as in *she was standing next to the oven, singing to herself, and the radio was on.* In these and other ways the narrator helps the audience to focus on the narrative backbone as it develops and to keep that backbone distinct from the comments on it. Narrators rely on this distinction no less in written narratives than in spoken ones.

So narratives, both spoken and written, ought to be seen as conversational activities. When they are part of a conversation, they exhibit the properities of other conversational sections: They are introduced; they are used for carrying out a social process; and they are concluded and then commented on. It is just that the social process—the exchange of a narrated event and its rhetorical point—becomes largely the responsibility of the speaker. Yet as always, the speaker must gain coordination with her audience. She accomplishes this with formulaic openings, by foregrounding and backgrounding to coordinate focus of attention, by pacing herself to make sure she won't be interrupted with requests for clarification or repeats, and so on. Narratives may be the ultimate test of a speaker's ability to manage coordination, since she must ordinarily do it solo, on her own. It takes years for people to become accomplished storytellers, and most never do.

CODA

The secret to language use lies in the users—the speakers and listeners. When a person talks, he can't just utter words aloud and expect to be understood. He must consider the people he is talking to, make an encyclopedia full of assumptions about them, and design his utterances accordingly. He must design what he says so that his specific addressees can figure out what he means, and they must interpret what he says assuming that he has selected it for them. Inherent in this intricate dance is a system of coordination. Speakers and addressees must coordinate what speakers mean with what their addressees interpret them to mean.

To make language work, language users turn to coordination devices of many sorts. At the word and phrase level they typically rely on what words and syntactic constructions conventionally mean, but they also turn to salience and precedence for many descriptions and references. At the conversational level they make use of conventions and practices about turn taking, adjacency pairs, routine sequences, and the like, but they also take salience and precedence into account for indirect speech acts and other forms of indirectness. They also have available a system for repairing utterances that go wrong—utterances that are misdesigned for one reason or another. And there are typical, though not usually conventional, ways for entering, carrying out, and terminating such gross conversational processes as making plans, giving directions, and telling stories. While convention is a workhorse among coordination devices, it belongs to a team that also includes salience and precedence.

The moral of the story is that language use is really a species of social activity and, to be given a complete account, must be treated as one. So far investigators have made just a start. To go on, they need a model for handling the one characteristic that makes language use truly social, and that is coordination. Just as the uncoordinated sound of an orchestra tuning up is not music—even though in it are the same tones as in genuine music—the uncoordinated use of language isn't really language either. As with orchestral music, the social ingredient is essential. Language would sink into dissonance without it.

REFERENCES

Akmajian, A., and F. Heny (1975). *An introduction to the principles of transformational syntax.* Cambridge, Mass.: M.I.T. Press.

Albert, S., and S. Kessler (1976). Processes for ending social encounters: the conceptual archeology of a temporal place. *J. theory soc. Behav., 6,* 147–170.

_____ (1978). Ending social encounters. *J. exp. soc. Psychol., 14,* 541–553.

Allen, J. F., and C. P. Perrault (1980). Analyzing intention in utterances. *Artificial Intell. 15,* 143–178.

Allwood, J., L. G. Andersson and O. Dahl (1977). *Logic in linguistics.* Cambridge: Cambridge Univ. Press.

Austin, J. L. (1962). *How to do things with words.* Oxford: Oxford Univ. Press.

Bach, K., and R. M. Harnish (1979). *Linguistic communication and speech acts.* Cambridge, Mass.: M.I.T. Press.

Baker, L. (1978). Processing temporal relationships in simple stories: effects of input sequence. *J. verb. Learn. verb. Behav., 17,* 559–572.

Beattie, G. W. (1978). Floor apportionment and gaze in conversational dyads. *Brit. J. soc. clinic. Psychol., 17,* 7–16.

_____ (1981). The regulation of speaker turns in face-to-face conversation: some implications for conversation in sound-only communication channels. *Semiotica, 34,* 55–70.

Beattie, G. W., and P. J. Barnard (1979). The temporal structure of natural telephone conversations (directory enquiry calls). *Linguistics, 17,* 213–229.

Brewer, W. F. (1980). Literary theory, rhetoric, and stylistics: implications for psychology. In R. J. Spiro, B. C. Bruce, and W. F. Brewer (Eds.), *Theoretical issues in reading comprehension: perspectives from cognitive psychology, linguistics, artificial intelligence, and education.* Hillsdale, N.J.: Erlbaum. Pp. 221–239.

Brewer, W. F., and J. C. Treyens (1981). Role of schemata in memory for places. *Cognit. Psychol., 13,* 207–230.

Brown, P., and S. Levinson (1978). Universals in language usage: politeness phenomena. In E. Goody (Ed.), *Questions and politeness.* Cambridge: Cambridge Univ. Press. Pp. 56–310.

Brown, R. (1958). How shall a thing be called? *Psychol. Rev., 65,* 14–21.

Burling, R. (1970). *Man's many voices: language in its cultural context.* New York: Holt, Rinehart, and Winston.

Butterworth, B. (1978). Maxims for studying conversations. *Semiotica, 24,* 317–339.

Carpenter, P. A., and M. A. Just (1977a). Reading as eyes see it. In M. A. Just, and P. A. Carpenter (Eds.), *Cognitive processes in comprehension.* Hillsdale, N.J.: Erlbaum.

_____ (1977b). Integrative processes in comprehension. In D. Laberge and S. J. Samuels (Eds.), *Basic processes in reading: perception and comprehension.* Hillsdale, N.J.: Erlbaum. Pp. 217–242.

Chafe, W. L. (1979). The flow of thought and the flow of language. In T. Givon (Ed.), *Syntax and semantics 12: discourse and syntax.* New York: Academic Press. Pp. 159–181.

_____ Ed. (1980). *The pear stories: cognitive, cultural, and linguistic aspects of narrative production.* Norwood, N.J.: Ablex.

Chomsky, N. (1965). *Aspects of a theory of syntax.* Cambridge, Mass.: M.I.T. Press.

Clark, E. V., and H. H. Clark (1979). When nouns surface as verbs. *Language, 55,* 767–811.

Clark, H. H. (1975). Bridging. In R. Schank, and P. Nash-Webber (Eds.), *Theoretical issues in natural language processing.* Arlington, Va.: Center for Applied Linguistics.

_____ (1977). Inferences in comprehension. In D. Laberge, and S. J. Samuels (Eds.), *Basic processes in reading: perception and comprehension.* Hillsdale, N.J.: Erlbaum. Pp. 243–264.

_____ (1978). Inferring what is meant. In W. J. M. Levelt, and G. B. Flores d'Arcais (Eds.), *Studies in the perception of language.* London: Wiley. Pp. 295–322.

_____ (1979). Responding to indirect speech acts. *Cognit. Psychol., 11,* 430–477.

_____ (1983). Making sense of nonce sense. In G. B. Flores d'Arcais, and R. Jarvella (Eds.), *The process of language understanding.* New York: Wiley.

Clark, H. H., and Carlson, T. B. (1981). Context for comprehension. In J. Long, and A. D. Baddeley (Eds.), *Attention and performance IX.* Hillsdale, N.J.: Erlbaum. Pp. 313–330.

_____ (1982a). Hearers and speech acts. *Language, 58,* 332–373.

_____ (1982b). Speech acts and hearers' beliefs. In N. V. Smith (Ed.), *Mutual knowledge.* London: Academic Press. Pp. 1–36.

Clark, H. H., and E. V. Clark (1977). *Psychology and language: an introduction to psycholinguistics.* New York: Harcourt, Brace, Jovanovich.

Clark, H. H., and J. W. French (1981). Telephone goodbyes. *Lang. Soc., 10,* 1–19.

Clark, H. H., and S. E. Haviland (1977). Comprehension and the given-new contract. In R. O. Freedle (Ed.), *Discourse production and comprehension.* Norwood, N.J.: Ablex. Pp. 1–40.

Clark, H. H., and C. R. Marshall (1981). Definite reference and mutual knowledge. In A. K. Joshi, B. L. Webber, I. A. Sag (Eds.), *Elements of discourse understanding.* Cambridge: Cambridge Univ. Press. Pp. 10–63.

Clark, H. H., and G. L. Murphy (1982). La visée vers l'auditoire dans la signification et la référence. *Bulletin de psychologie: langage et compréhension, 35,* 767–776.

Clark, H. H., R. Schreuder, and S. Buttrick (1983). Common ground and the understanding of demonstratives. *J. verb. Learn. verb. Behav., 22,* 245–258.

Clark, H. H., and D. H. Schunk (1980). Polite responses to polite requests. *Cognition, 8,* 111–143.

Clark, H. H., and C. J. Sengul (1979). In search of referents for nouns and pronouns. *Memory and Cognition, 7,* 35–41.

Cohen, P. R., and C. R. Perrault (1979). Elements of a plan-based theory of speech acts. *Cognit. Sci., 3,* 197–212.

Cruse, D. A. (1977). The pragmatics of lexical specificity. *J. Linguistics, 13,* 153–164.

Davis, D. (1982). Determinants of responsiveness in dyadic interaction. In W. Ickes and E. Knowles (Eds.), *Personality, roles, and social behavior.* New York: Springer-Verlag. Pp. 85–139.

Davis, D., and W. T. Perkowitz (1979). Consequences of responsiveness in dyadic interaction: effects of probability of response and proportion of content-related responses on interpersonal attraction. *J. Pers. soc. Psychol., 37,* 534–551.

Dittman, A., and L. G. Llewellyn (1968). Relationship between vocalizations and head nods as listener responses. *J. Pers. soc. Psychol., 9,* 79–84.

Duncan, S. (1972). Some signals and rules for taking speaking turns in conversations. *J. Pers. soc. Psychol., 23,* 283–292.

_____ (1973). Toward a grammar for dyadic conversation. *Semiotica, 9,* 29–47.

Garvey, C. (1975). Requests and responses in children's speech. *J. child Lang., 2,* 41–64.

_____ (1977). The contingent query: a dependent act in conversation. In M. Lewis, and L. Rosenblum (Eds.), *Interaction, conversation, and the development of language: the origins of behavior, V.* New York: Wiley.

Gazdar, G. (1979). *Pragmatics: implicature, presupposition, and logical form.* New York: Academic Press.

Gibbs, R. W., Jr. (1981). Your wish is my command: convention and context in interpreting indirect requests. *J. verb. Learn. verb. Behav., 20,* 431–444.

Goffman, E. (1955). On face-work: an analysis of ritual elements in social interaction. *Psychiatry, 18,* 213–231.

_____ (1967). *Interaction ritual: essays on face-to-face behavior.* New York: Anchor.

_____ (1971). *Relations in public: microstudies of the public order.* New York: Basic Books.

_____ (1974). *Frame analysis.* New York: Harper & Row.

_____ (1976). Replies and responses. *Lang. Soc., 5,* 257–313.

Goody, E. N. (1978). Towards a theory of questions. In E. N. Goody (Ed.), *Questions and politeness: strategies in social interaction.* Cambridge: Cambridge Univ. Press. Pp. 17–43.

Grice, H. P. (1957). Meaning. *Philosoph. Rev., 66,* 377–388.

_____ (1968). Utterer's meaning, sentence-meaning, and word-meaning. *Found. Lang., 4,* 225–242.

_____ (1975). Logic and conversation. In P. Cole, and J. L. Morgan (Eds.), *Syntax and semantics 3: speech acts.* New York: Academic Press. Pp. 41–58.

_____ (1978). Some further notes on logic and conversation. In P. Cole (Ed.), *Syntax and semantics 9: pragmatics.* New York: Academic Press. Pp. 113–128.

Grimes, J. E. (1975). *The thread of discourse.* The Hague: Mouton.

Grosz, B. (1981). Focusing and description in natural language dialogues. In A. K. Joshi, B. L. Webber, I. A. Sag (Eds.), *Elements of discourse understanding.* Cambridge: Cambridge Univ. Press. Pp. 84–105.

Halliday, M., and R. Hasan (1976). *Cohesion in English.* London: Longman.

Harder, P., and C. Kock (1976). *The theory of presupposition failure.* Copenhagen: Akademisk Forlag.

Hankamer, J., and I. A. Sag (1976). Deep and surface anaphora. *Linguistic Inquiry, 7,* 391–426.

Haviland, S. E., and H. H. Clark (1974). What's new? Acquiring new information as a process in comprehension. *J. verb. learn. verb. Behav., 13,* 512–521.

Hawkins, J. A. (1978). *Definiteness and indefiniteness: a study in reference and grammaticality prediction.* London: Crom Helm.

Hobbs, J. R., and D. A. Evans (1980). Conversation as planned behavior. *Cognit. Sci., 4,* 349–477.

Hobbs, J. R., and J. Robinson (1979). Why ask? *Discourse Processes, 1,* 312–318.

Hopper, P. J. (1979). Aspect and foregrounding in discourse. In T. Givon (Ed.), *Syntax and semantics 12: discourse and syntax.* New York: Academic Press. Pp. 213–241.

Hopper, P. J., and S. A. Thompson (1980). Transitivity in grammar and discourse. *Language, 56,* 251–299.

Irvine, J. T. (1974). Strategies of status manipulation in the Wolof greeting. In R. Bauman, and J. Sherzer (Eds.), *Explorations in the ethnography of speaking.* Cambridge: Cambridge Univ. Press. Pp. 167–191.

Jefferson, G. (1972). Side sequences. In D. Sudnow (Ed.), *Studies in social interaction.* New York: Free Press. Pp. 294–338.

_____ (1973). A case of precision timing in ordinary conversation: overlapped tag-positioned address terms in closing sequences. *Semiotica, 9,* 47–96.

_____ (1978). Sequential aspects of storytelling in conversation. In J. Schenkein (Ed.), *Studies in the organization of conversational interaction.* New York: Academic Press. Pp. 219–248.

Johnson-Laird, P. N. (1980). Mental models in cognitive science. *Cognit. Sci., 4,* 71–115.

Kaplan, S. J. (1981). Appropriate responses to inappropriate questions. In A. K. Joshi, B. L. Webber, I. A. Sag (Eds.), *Elements of discourse understanding.* Cambridge: Cambridge Univ. Press. Pp. 127–144.

Katz, J. J. (1977). *Propositional structure and illocutionary force.* New York: Crowell.

Kempson, R. M. (1975). *Presupposition and the delimitation of semantics.* Cambridge: Cambridge Univ. Press.

Kendon, A. (1967). Some functions of gaze direction in social interaction. *Acta psychologica, 26,* 22–63.

Kintsch, W. (1974). *The representation of meaning in memory.* Hillsdale, N.J.: Erlbaum.

Kintsch, W., and J. Keenan (1973). Reading rate and retention as a function of the number of propositions in the base structure of sentences. *Cognit. Psychol., 5,* 57–64.

Kirshenblatt-Gimblett, B. (1974). The concept and varieties of narrative performance in east European Jewish culture. In R. Bauman, and Joel Sherzer (Eds.), *Explorations in the ethnography of speaking.* Cambridge: Cambridge Univ. Press. Pp. 283–308.

Knapp, M. L. (1972). *Nonverbal communication in human interaction*. New York: Holt, Rinehart, and Winston.

Knapp, M. L., R. P. Hart, G. W. Friedrich, and G. M. Schulman (1973). The rhetoric of goodbye: verbal and nonverbal correlates of human leave taking. *Speech Monogr., 40,* 182–198.

Krauss, R. M., C. M. Garlock, P. D. Bricker, and L. E. McMahon (1977). The role of audible and visible backchannel responses in interpersonal communication. *J. Pers. soc. Psychol., 35,* 523–529.

Krauss, R. M., and S. Glucksberg (1977). Social and nonsocial speech. *Scientific American, 236:2,* 100–105.

Krauss, R. M., and S. Weinheimer (1964). Changes in reference phrases as a function of frequency of usage in social interaction: a preliminary study. *Psychon. Sci., 1,* 113–114.

_____ (1966). Concurrent feedback, confirmation, and the encoding of referents in verbal communication. *J. Pers. soc. Psychol., 4,* 343–346.

Kraut, R. F., S. H. Lewis, and L. W. Swezey (1982). Listener responsiveness and summarization: a cowboy movie study. *J. Pers. soc. Psychol., 40,* 718–731.

Labov, W. (1972). The transformation of experience in narrative syntax. In W. Labov, *Language in the inner city.* Philadelphia: Univ. of Pennsylvania Press. Pp. 354–405.

Lakoff, R. (1973a). The logic of politeness; or, minding your p's and q's. In *Papers from the ninth annual meeting, Chicago Ling. Soc.,* Pp. 292–305.

_____ (1973b). Questionable answers and answerable questions. In B. B. Kachru, R. B. Lees, Y. Malkiel, A. Pietrangeli, and S. Saporta (Eds.), *Papers in linguistics in honor of Henry and Renee Kahane.* Edmonton, Ill.: Linguistic Research. Pp. 453–467.

_____ (1977). What you can do with words: politeness, pragmatics, and performatives. In A. Rogers, B. Wall, and J. P. Murphy (Eds.), *Proceedings of the Texas conference on performatives, presuppositions, and implicatures.* Arlington, Va.: Center for Applied Linguistics. Pp. 79–105.

Levelt, W. J. M. (1982). Linearization in describing spatial networks. In S. Peters, and E. Saarinen (Eds.), *Processes, beliefs, and questions.* Dordrecht: Reidel. Pp. 199–220.

Levelt, W. J. M., and S. Kelter (1982). Surface form and memory in question answering. *Cognit. Psychol., 14,* 78–106.

Levinson, S. C. (1979). Activity types and language. *Linguistics, 17,* 365–399.

_____ (1980). Speech act theory: the state of the art. *Lang. Ling. Teach.: Abstracts, 1,* 5–24.

_____ (1981). Some pre-observations on the modelling of dialogue. *Discourse processes, 4,* 93–116.

Lewis, D. K. (1969). *Convention.* Cambridge, Mass.: Harvard Univ. Press.

Linde, C. (1979). Focus of attention and the choice of pronouns in discourse. In T. Givon (Ed.), *Syntax and semantics 12: discourse and syntax.* New York: Academic Press. Pp. 337–354.

Linde, C., and J. A. Goguen (1978). Structure of planning discourse. *J. soc. biolog. Structures, 1,* 219–251.

Linde, C., and W. Labov (1975). Spatial networks as a site for the study of language and thought. *Language, 51,* 924–939.

Maclay, H., and C. E. Osgood (1959). Hesitation phenomena in spontaneous English speech. *Word, 15,* 19–44.

Mandler, J. M., and N. S. Johnson (1977). Remembrance of things parsed: story structure and recall. *Cognit. Psychol., 9,* 111–151.

Merritt, M. (1976). *Resources for saying in service encounters.* Ph.D. dissertation. Department of Anthropology, Univ. of Pennsylvania.

Montague, R. (1974). *Formal philosophy: selected papers of Richard Montague.* R. Thomason (Ed.). New Haven, Conn.: Yale University Press.

Morgan, J. L. (1973). Sentence fragments and the notion "sentence." In B. B. Kachru, R. B. Lees, Y. Malkiel, A. Pietrangeli, and S. Saporta (Eds.), *Papers in linguistics in honor of Henry and Renee Kahane.* Edmonton, Ill.: Linguistic Research. Pp. 719–751.

_____ (1978). Two types of convention in indirect speech acts. In P. Cole (Ed.), *Syntax and semantics 9: pragmatics.* New York: Academic Press. Pp. 261–280.

Morgan, J. L., and M. B. Sellner (1980). Discourse and linguistic theory. In R. J. Spiro, B. C. Bruce, and W. F. Brewer (Eds.), *Theoretical issues in reading comprehension: perspectives from cognitive psychology, linguistics, artificial intelligence, and education.* Hillsdale, N.J.: Erlbaum. Pp. 165–200.

Norman, D. A. (1973). Memory, knowledge, and the answering of questions. In R. L. Solso (Ed.), *Comtemporary issues in cognitive psychology: the Loyola symposium.* Washington, D.C.: Winston.

Nunberg, G. (1978). Slang, usage-conditions, and l'arbitraire du signe. In D. Farkas, W. M. Jacobsen, K. W. Todrys (Eds.), *Papers from the parasession on the lexicon.* Chicago: Chicago Linguistics Society. Pp. 301–311.

_____ (1979). The non-uniqueness of semantic solutions: polysemy. *Linguistics and Philosophy, 3,* 143–184.

Olson, D. R. (1970). Language and thought: aspects of a cognitive theory of semantics. *Psychol. Rev., 77,* 257–273.

Partee, B. (1975). Montague grammar and transformational grammar. *Linguistic Inquiry, 6,* 203–300.

Polanyi-Bowditch, L. (1976). Why the whats are when: mutually contextualizing realms of narrative. *Berkeley Ling. Soc., 2,* 59–77.

Rosaldo, R. (1980). Beyond the rules of the game. Paper read at the meetings of the American Anthropological Association, Washington, D.C.

Rosch, E. (1978). Principles of categorization. In E. Rosch, and B. B. Lloyd (Eds.), *Cognition and categorization.* Hillsdale, N.J.: Erlbaum. Pp. 27–48.

Rumelhart, D. E. (1975). Notes on a schema for stories. In D. G. Bobrow, and A. Collins (Eds.), *Representation and understanding: studies in cognitive science.* New York: Academic Press. Pp. 211–236.

_____ (1980). Schemata: the building blocks of cognition. In R. J. Spiro, B. C. Bruce, and W. F. Brewer (Eds.), *Theoretical issues in reading comprehension: perspectives from cognitive psychology, linguistics, artificial intelligence, and education.* Hillsdale, N.J.: Erlbaum. Pp. 33–58.

Rumelhart, D. E., and A. Ortony (1977). The representation of knowledge in memory. In R. C. Anderson, R. J. Spiro, and W. E. Montague (Eds.), *Schooling and the acquisition of knowledge*. Hillsdale, N.J.: Erlbaum.

Sacks, H. (1974). An analysis of the course of a joke's telling in conversation. In R. Bauman, and J. Sherzer (Eds.), *Explorations in the ethnography of speaking*. Cambridge: Cambridge Univ. Press. Pp. 337–353.

_____ (1975). Everyone has to lie. In R. Sanches, and B. Blount (Eds.), *Ritual, reality, and innovation in language use*. New York: Academic Press.

Sacks, H., and E. Schegloff (1979). Two preferences in the organization of reference to persons in conversation and their interaction. In G. Psathas (Ed.), *Everyday language: studies in ethnomethodology*. New York: Irvington Publishers. Pp. 15–21.

Sacks, H., E. Schegloff, and G. Jefferson (1974). A simplest systematics for the organization of turn-taking in conversation. *Language, 50,* 696–735.

Sag, I. A. (1979). On the nonunity of anaphora. *Linguistic Inquiry, 10,* 152–164.

Sag, I. A., and J. Hankamer (1981). Toward a theory of anaphoric processing. *Stanford working papers in cognitive science.*

Saussure, F. de. (1916). *Cours de linguistique generale*. Paris: Payot.

Schank, R., and R. P. Abelson (1977). *Scripts, plans, goals, and understanding*. Hillsdale, N.J.: Erlbaum.

Schegloff, E. (1968). Sequencing in conversational openings. *Amer. Anthropologist, 70,* (4) 1075–1095.

_____ (1972). Notes on a conversational practice: formulating place. In D. Sudnow (Ed.), *Studies in social interaction*. New York: Free Press. Pp. 75–119.

Schegloff, E., G. Jefferson, and H. Sacks (1977). The preference for self-correction in the organization of repair in conversation. *Language, 53,* 361–382.

Schegloff, E., and H. Sacks (1973). Opening up closings. *Semiotica, 8,* 289–327.

Schelling, T. C. (1960). *The strategy of conflict*. Cambridge, Mass.: Harvard Univ. Press.

Schiffer, S. (1972). *Meaning*. Oxford: Clarendon Press.

Schiffrin, D. (1977). Opening encounters. *Amer. Sociological Rev., 42,* 679–691.

Schweller, K. G. (1978). *The role of expectation in the comprehension and recall of direct and indirect requests*. Unpublished doctoral dissertation. University of Illinois at Urbana-Champaign.

Searle J. R. (1969). *Speech acts*. Cambridge: Cambridge Univ. Press.

_____ (1975a). A taxonomy of illocutionary acts. In K. Gunderson (Ed.), *Minnesota studies in the philosophy of language*. Minneapolis: Univ. of Minnesota Press.

_____ (1975b). Indirect speech acts. In P. Cole, and J. L. Morgan (Eds.), *Syntax and semantics 3: speech acts*. New York: Academic Press. Pp. 59–82.

Soames, S., and D. M. Perlmutter (1979). *Syntactic argumentation and the structure of English*. Berkeley: Univ. of California Press.

Stalnaker, R. C. (1978). Assertion. In P. Cole (Ed.), *Syntax and semantics 9: pragmatics*. New York: Academic Press. Pp. 315–332.

Tanenhaus, M. K., and M. S. Seidenberg (1981). Discourse context and sentence perception. *Discourse Processes, 4,* 197–220.

van Dijk, T. (1977). *Text and context: explorations in the semantics and pragmatics of discourse*. London: Longman.

Verschueren, J. (1978). Reflections on presupposition failure: a contribution to an integrated theory of pragmatics. *J. Pragmatics, 2,* 107–151.

Wunderlich, D. (1977). Assertions, conditional speech acts, and practical inferences. *J. Pragmatics, 1,* 13–46.

Yngve, V. H. (1970). On getting a word in edgewise. *Chicago Linguistics Society, 6,* 567–577.

CHAPTER 19

Attitudes and Attitude Change

William J. McGuire
Yale University

Our moment in history has been given many names—just to start at the top of the alphabet, the atomic age, Atlantic age, automobile age, aspirin age, age of alienation, of anxiety, of affluence, etc.—including one, the *age of advertising,* which is particularly relevant to this chapter in view of the tremendous effort currently made to influence attitudes and actions via persuasive communication. Advertisers spend over $50 billion annually in the United States and political candidates a half-billion more. Mammon and Caesar share the channels with God, 14 percent of radio stations and a whole television network being devoted exclusively to extolling evangelical Christianity (Hadden and Swann, 1981). Ubiquitous public service ads urge us to save our bodies as well as our souls by using seat belts or not using cigarettes, getting immunized against polio or diagnosed for hypertension. Appeals are made even to our altruism, urging us to preserve the environment at some personal sacrifice by saving the wolf, the whale, or the sand darter or by conserving energy, eschewing littering, desisting from burning the forests or the Bronx, or contributing to the United Fund (Rice and Paisley, 1981).

The present chapter describes how attitudes and behaviors are influenced by such communication and what this reveals about the person and society. An initial section on the history of attitude and persuasion research is followed by three sections on the nature, structure, and determinants of attitudes. Then two longer sections on attitude change describe first the directive aspects of the change process in terms of the communication/persuasion matrix and then its dynamic aspects in terms of sixteen partial views of the person underlying attitude change research.

HISTORY OF PERSUASION RESEARCH

Ever since the neolithic revolution gave rise to community and consciousness (Jaynes, 1977), persuasive skill in using words to resolve conflicts and mobilize effort has been a valued human asset (Lasswell, Lerner, and Speier, 1980). The current clamorous cacophony might suggest that human society has always been comparably argumentative, but actually open ages like ours have been rare

The writing of this chapter was greatly aided by research grant MH32588 received from the Interpersonal Processes and Problems Section, Behavioral Sciences Research Branch of the National Institute of Mental Health, and by the contributions made by Claire McGuire and Joyce Ghiroli.

in the four millennia of Western history (Popper, 1966), persuasion having been the key mode of social control and effort mobilization only in four scattered centuries: the Periclean Hellenic period, the last decades of the Roman Republic, the humanistic Renaissance, and our own mass media century. It was commonly used at other times and places (Thompson, 1977): Proselytizing has been a prevalent aspect of Christianity since the time of Christ and St. Paul (Wilder, 1964; Forman, 1979; E. Cohen, 1981), and oratory has flourished at several periods of Chinese and Indian history (Oliver, 1971; A. F. Wright, 1979) and in many preliterate societies (Bloch, 1975; Vincent, 1978). However, only in the four centuries mentioned has persuasion played so central an economic, social, and political role as to have become not just an art but an essential craft in whose rules of thumb the elite youth were trained and a recognized science with a systemized body of theory developed by savants. We shall describe these four rare eras and the social conditions giving rise to them before discussing the history of scientific attitude research in this century.

FLOURISHINGS OF ELOQUENCE

Four Eras of Persuasion

The first rhetorical century dates from 427 B.C.E. when Gorgias brought Corax's sophistry from tumultuous Syracuse to Athens, and it ended when the 338 B.C.E. victory of Philip II established a new Macedonian order that snuffed out the public contentiousness of Athens and both vindicated and terminated Demonsthenes' Philippics. Despite Plato's opposition, his Academy and Aristotle's Lyceum eventually yielded to student pressure and admitted rhetoric to the curriculum as an afternoon elective (G. A. Kennedy, 1963). Aristotle's *Synagoge Technon* reviewing other Hellenic theories of persuasion has been lost, but his *Rhetoric* and *Topics,* preserving his own persuasion theory, remain potential gold mines for social and cognitive researchers.

History's second persuasive century began with the disruptions arising when the economic and political expansion of Rome instigated unfamiliar conflicts and evoked questioning of the traditional order by the brothers Gracchi and others; it terminated with the 43 B.C.E. demise of Cicero under the knives of the Triumvirs, whom his latter-day Philippics failed to prevent from transforming the Roman Republic into an Augustinian Empire (G. A. Kennedy, 1972). Summaries of Roman persuasion theory and practice can be found in Cicero's *Orator* and *De Oratore* and most fully in the rich lode of

social and cognitive persuasion hypotheses in Quintillian's *Institutio Oratoria.*

The Italian Renaissance provided a third persuasion century that can be dated from the rediscovery and publication in 1470 of Quintillian's *Institutio Oratoria* as one of Europe's first printed books until the efforts of Peter Ramus to formalize rhetoric and textual criticism were terminated with extreme prejudice in the St. Bartholomew's Day massacre of 1572. Today we admire the Renaissance for its visual arts achievements, but the people of the period most prized their orators and humanistic rhetoricians. This apotheosis of eloquence (Gray, 1963) grew out of the new learning's conferring a faith in the word that provided a progress-generating sense of power to a revived Europe equivalent to that bestowed by love of the Blessed Virgin to thirteenth-century Europe or by hope in technology to our own age (H. Adams, 1918). The period's elaborate analyses of figurative language (Lanham, 1968; W. Taylor, 1972) and texts (W. J. Kennedy, 1978) leave rich legacies to current students of metaphor (Billow, 1977; Honeck and Hoffman, 1980) and discourse analysis (Joshi, Webber, and Sag, 1981; Kreckel, 1981; van Dijk, 1983).

Intimations of our own century's mass media persuasive ascendancy (Lears, 1983; D. Pope, 1983) were already apparent in the eighteenth century, at whose outset the *London Gazette* began to publish advertisements and by whose end Thomas Paine's pamphlets and the *Federalist Papers* were molding public opinion (McKendrick, Brewer, and Plumb, 1982). The industrial revolution's expansion of discretionary income and the spread of literacy invited mass media advertising. The first large print-age ad agency, N. W. Ayer, was founded a century ago, and the advent of the electronic media (radio in the 1920s and television in the 1950s) escalated mass media proselytizing to its current overwhelming presence, especially in the United States, where conditions from its outset, as de Tocqueville noted, called for resolving in the mass media arena such issues as slavery abolition, woman's suffrage, and alcohol prohibition (Paisley, 1981).

Social and Moral Significance

The social functions of proselytizing. Great ages of persuasion have been times of social disruption brought about by expanding economic and cultural experiences that presented new problems and challenges, sharpened cleavages among factions too numerous and too evenly matched for any to achieve hegemony, and called into question traditional verities and accustomed modes of social mobilization and control. Persuasive communication became essential for rallying one's own faction, forging alliances, and wooing the masses into temporary policy consensus. Such periods have been exciting but uncomfortable times of social mobility and instability, rich in cultural, artistic, and life-style novelties but with an accompanying vulgarization of taste, decay of liturgy, and decline of social amenities and polite conventions. The public contentiousness of these eras appalled the traditional elites, not only the political and religious Establishments but also the intelligentsia. Just as today's cultural elites find advertising and television programs distasteful, so the Platonic Academy loathed the sophists and so the Roman senatorial class despised the oratorical schools of Rhodes and Athens to which the rising commercial equites class (and not a few senators) sent their sons (G. A. Kennedy, 1980; Marrou, 1981).

Such vulgar contentiousness and hucksterism need not be long endured. The four great ages of persuasion have been nasty, brutish, and short interludes of social change that only briefly disturbed the chronic sleep of history. Agitation and propaganda were soon replaced by sterner means of social control (Lind, 1983). The tragic vanity of thinking that the word is mightier than the sword is exhibited by the fates of the rhetorical masters of each of the three previous centuries of persuasion: Demosthenes, done in by poison under the Macedonians his Philippics had failed to halt; Cicero, by the knives of the Triumvirs at whom his latter-day Philippics were aimed; and Ramus, in the St. Bartholomew's Day massacre—each dispatched by his inarticulate targets whose brutally effective responses proved that the rhetoricians had spoken against them wisely but not too well. Contentious interludes like our own soon revert to periods using structural means of social control that repress the internal contradictions of society under state authoritarianism, religious orthodoxy, or the smothering conventionality of village morality.

The ethics of persuasion The deliberate study of persuasion strikes sensitive people as distasteful and even immoral (R. K. White, 1971; Andrén, 1980; Goodin, 1980). Plato, in *Gorgias,* used his theory of knowledge to argue that since rhetoric deals with probabilities, it inevitably leads to error; Aristotle characteristically hedged by judging rhetoric a neutral means that can serve either truth or error, but he regarded it as yielding at best an inferior type of truth (G. A. Kennedy, 1963). Current elites worry that advertising hucksters are creating new and in-

satiable wants, that political candidates are selling images without ideology, and that irascible rabble-rousers are making the masses less accepting of the discomforts to which they had become fairly accustomed. Conversely, advocates of change complain that talented persuaders are co-opted to work for the dominant factions to maintain the economic, cultural, political, and religious status quo (Goodin, 1980; E. Katz and Szecsko, 1981).

Persuasion does have its defenders. There is the romantic possibility that a lost cause, an innovative idea, or an individual at risk can gain a hearing and perhaps even prevail if advocated with sufficient eloquence. While often used for oppression, persuasion more than other modes of social control can become a source of innovation. Isocrates in defending the sophists against Plato argued that rhetoric is what distinguishes humans from the beasts and has allowed the otherwise poorly endowed human species to form functioning communities within which they can endure and score their occasional triumphs. The hucksterism of our interlude is unlovable from the inside but its appeal may be more discernible in retrospect if its suppression produces a quieter society within which each knows his or her place and there are few options to be argued. At those more normal times, a few aberrant young who see visions and old who dream dreams may discern that persuasion is the worst possible mode of social mobilization and conflict resolution—except for all the others.

ATTITUDE RESEARCH SINCE 1900

Empirical psychology recently celebrated its centennial (Koch and Leary, 1984), but social psychology was born a generation later with the new century in whose first decade the earliest social psychology textbooks appeared. The field has been a mosaic of heterogeneous pieces from the start, but attitudes have always been one of the central elements in the design, early commentators as varied as sociologists W. I. Thomas and Znaniecki (1918) and behaviorist J. B. Watson (1925) regarding the topic as so central that they defined social psychology as the study of attitudes.

Three Peakings of Attitude Research
While always substantial, interest in attitudes has waxed and waned so that it has emerged as the most exciting area of social psychology in three separate periods (McGuire, 1984b). A first 1920s and 1930s peaking of interest was focused on attitude measurement, followed by a 1935–1955 interlude in which attitudes were eclipsed by

group dynamics as a research focus. A second 1950s and 1960s peaking concentrated on attitude change, after which interest subsided during the current 1965–1985 ascendancy of social perception research. A third 1980s and 1990s flourishing centered on attitude systems is now discernible. We shall describe each of the three peakings of attitude research and the interludes between them and then consider what causes such fluctuations.

Attitude measurement research in the 1920s and 1930s. The first peaking of attitude research bequeathed psychology the lasting legacy of scaling theory (Thurstone and Chave, 1929; Likert, 1932; L. Guttman, 1944) and an interest in behavioral correlates of attitudes, if only as external validations for attitude measurement procedures (LaPiere, 1934; Newcomb, 1943; Adorno *et al.*, 1950; M. B. Smith, Bruner, and White, 1956) to supplement such internal criteria as homogeneity of judges' ratings, item correlation with the total score, and unidimensionality. After the 1930s measurement issues became less central in attitude research, but advances continue to be made (S. W. Cook and Selltiz, 1964; Webb *et al.*, 1966; Dawes, 1972; Ajzen and Fishbein, 1980; Cacioppo and Petty, 1983).

The group dynamics interlude. From 1935 to 1955 group processes displaced attitudes as the most exciting focus of interest for social psychology's bright young people and their middle-aged mentors. Work on group research had picked up in the late 1930s (M. Sherif, 1936; Newcomb, 1943) and mushroomed after World War II in the work of Lewin's (1947) protégés (J. F. Brown, Festinger, Thibaut, Kelley, Deutsch, Schachter, Back, Cartwright, etc.). Topics such as cohesiveness, conformity, conflict resolution, cooperation and competition, and power became fashionable both for theory-relevant laboratory research and for group-training applications (Back, 1972).

The 1950s and 1960s as attitude change decades. When attitudes research returned to center stage in the late 1950s, its focus had shifted from static measurement and correlates topics to dynamic attitude change topics developing out of the World War II work of Hovland, Lumsdaine, and Sheffield (1949), though some good attitude change studies had been done in the earlier period (R. C. Peterson and Thurstone, 1933). In contrast to the eclectic positivism of the first period, the logical empiricism ascendancy during this second peaking assured that attitude change research was related to theory, with the

behavioristic theorizing of Hovland, D. T. Campbell, Janis, McGuire, Collins, Eagly, etc., dominating its start and the consistency theorizing of Heider, Festinger, A. R. Cohen, Brehm, Aronson, Walster, Osgood, McGuire, Wyer, etc., dominating its later phase, while smaller theoretical coteries used psychoanalytic (D. Katz, Sarnoff, Janis, M. B. Smith, etc.) and perceptual (M. Sherif, Asch, N. H. Anderson, etc.) formulations.

The social perception interlude. By the mid 1960s social psychology's fashionable focus was shifting from attitudes to social perception and by the 1970s there were debates about whether attitudes were necessary at all (Abelson, 1972; Needham, 1973; Kelman, 1974). Respectable attitude research continued in this 1965–1985 interlude (Fishbein and Ajzen, 1972; Cialdini, Petty, and Cacioppo, 1981), but social psychology focused more on perceptual topics such as causal attribution (J. H. Harvey, Ickes, and Kidd, 1981), impression formation (Schneider, Hastorf, and Ellsworth, 1979) and self-perception (Morris Rosenberg, 1979; Gara and Rosenberg, 1981; McGuire and McGuire, 1982).

An emerging attitude systems era for the 1980s and 1990s. The beginnings of a third "structuralist" surge of attitude research can be discerned for the 1980s and 1990s, focusing on the content, structure, and functioning of attitude complexes and using the systems style of research described below. It began with the more formal types of attitude consistency research of the 1960s (McGuire, 1966b; Transgaard, 1973; Eagly and Chaiken, in press) and is illustrated by current work on social judgment, inference, scripts, and cognitive responses (Hastie, 1983; Wyer and Srull, 1984) that is discussed below in the attitude structure section.

Cause of the Interest Fluctuations

Internal factors affecting fluctuations in attitude research. These waxings and wanings of attitude research derive from developments intrinsic to the research field itself and also from external forces exerted by the broader society (McGuire, 1984b). The faddish flocking of researchers to momentarily fashionable topics is not an attractive spectacle but is probably productive in concentrating a critical mass of cross-fertilizing talent on a period's Establishment enthusiasm, the early recruits typically including some of the brighter minds in the discipline. But the talent tends to be diluted as the topic's appeal spreads from the classes to the masses, camp followers flocking to the all-too-visible college while the next generation of bright young people head elsewhere to participate in the heroic age of some newer fashion, leaving to the latecomers residual issues such as the hard and plodding work of describing dispositional and situational interaction effects (Dillon and Schmeck, 1983).

Internal self-dampening derives also from the tendency for any continuing focus of research to become encrusted with conceptual overelaboration, distracting practical applications, and premature quantification, each an excess of virtue and each playing a discernible role in the decline of the first, measurement, peaking of attitude research in the 1920s and 1930s. The pages of elegant definitions and distinctions in Allport's (1935) attitudes chapter in the first English-language *Handbook of Social Psychology* illustrate excessive conceptual elaboration, useful in tidying up a well-trodden field but not the stuff to excite the revolting youth. The second type of accumulating impedimenta is the popular field's increasing application to social policy issues that result in its politicization: In the attitude measurement era even the austere techniques of Thurstone, Likert, Guttman, etc., were developed to measure attitudes on such social policy issues as capital punishment, birth control, socialism, religiosity, prejudice, fear in battle, etc. Few would have the chutzpah to advocate a mandarin "science for science's sake" concept of psychology, but it does seem a historical fact that as social science topics become more applied to servicing the needs of policymakers, there is an exodus of innovative researchers to fresh (and safer?) topics. A third encrustation is the premature quantification that progressively smothers a fashionable scientific topic, illustrated by the attitude-scaling procedures whose elegance reached the point by the 1930s where attitudes became too proudly quantitative to enter into hypothetical union with other, more grossly scaled variables.

Extrinsic factors affecting fluctuations of interest. Societal forces outside a discipline also contribute to fluctuations in topic popularity. Preoccupation with the static topic of attitude measurement during the first, 1920s, peaking was natural for the self-conscious American society that emerged from World War I wondering about its identity. Later, when the ensuing revolutions, inflations, migrations, economic depressions, total wars, and death camps discredited both authoritarian and laissez-faire social structures, social psychologists' interest understandably shifted in the 1935–1955 period to group dynamics topics like cohesiveness, peer orientation, cooperation, democratic leadership, self-determining

groups, etc. World War II constituted a pivotal point between the first and second attitude peakings, the scaling research in Volume 4 of the *American Soldier* series (Stouffer, 1950) being the final wave of the first peaking's attitude measurement work and the army indoctrination research in Volume 3 (Hovland, Lumsdaine, and Sheffield, 1949) launching the second, attitude change, peaking whose flourishing in the 1950s and 1960s was natural for a nation whose increasing consciousness of its power and ambiguous image made it desirous of being better understood and winning the hearts and minds of peoples.

Such internally and externally induced fluctuations in topic interest benefit a discipline since allowing a field like attitudes to lie fallow leaves root room for new ideas and new approaches to bloom later. The current rebirth of attitude research in the systems form, after being overshadowed by social perception work during the late 1960s and 1970s, is symptomized by the appearance of numerous attitude textbooks at the beginning of this new decade (Ajzen and Fishbein, 1980; Petty and Cacioppo, 1981; Petty, Ostrom, and Brock, 1981; Reardon, 1981; Rajecki, 1982; M. J. Smith, 1982).

Changing Styles of Attitude Research
A subtle but crucial aspect of any scientific era is its characteristic styles of research. An experiment involves dozens of steps, each of which can be taken in a variety of ways, creating hundreds of potential paths through the total research process, each path constituting a different style of research. Because choices at successive steps tend to be yoked, a few styles dominate a discipline in any period. We shall first describe the unidirectional styles that dominated the 1950s and 1960s attitude change era (with contrasting convergent and divergent variants) and then the systems style that seems likely to dominate the currently emerging attitude structure era (McGuire, 1983).

The convergent unidirectional style of attitude change research. Undirectional styles identify variables as independent, mediational, and dependent, among which causality is assumed to flow mostly in one direction via few paths. Hovland's work (Hovland, Lumsdaine, and Sheffield, 1949; Hovland, Janis, and Kelley, 1953) epitomized its convergent subtype, which dominated the first half of the attitude change period. The convergent stylist begins with an intriguing persuasion phenomenon (e.g., delayed-action or fear appeal effects), and uses a broad spectrum of theoretical orientations *convergently* to account for the maximum variance in the relationship. The convergent stylist's experimental designs usually include multiple independent variables whose main and interaction effects on attitude change are predicted. Typically, the independent variables are manipulated orthogonally to one another by rather simplistic operational procedures, while the dependent, attitude change variables are measured painstakingly by multiple finely graded response items.

This convergent pattern of choices in the early steps allows the data collection efficiency of running large groups of subjects in economical "agricultural plot" designs, each participant being placed conveniently if superficially on a predefined level for each independent variable by written passages subtly varied among the test booklets. Use of multiple issues allows each participant to serve in several conditions, the issues being rotated around the independent variable condition from participant to participant, which incidentally allows across-issue generalization or reveals interactions. The finely scaled attitude change measure allows use of sensitive within-participant differences-among-means descriptive statistics and powerful analysis-of-variance inferential statistics for testing the significance of main and interaction effects.

The divergent unidirectional style of attitude change research.   The divergent unidirectional style is typified by the dissonance theory (Festinger, 1954) research that dominated the second half of the attitude change ascendancy in the 1960s and by the attribution theory research that dominated the first half of the social perception era in the 1970s. It starts with an explanatory principle and proceeds *divergently* to show how this theoretical formulation accounts for a little of the variance in each of a wide range of phenomena. Typically, it yields hypotheses predicting the attitude change main effect of one theoretically relevant independent variable carefully manipulated over two levels to eliminate the effects of extraneous variables. By contrast, the dependent variable tends to be measured rather grossly, often by a single dichotomous response item such as whether or not the person signs a petition or chooses to wait alone or with another person.

The divergent stylist's elaborate procedures for precisely and sizably manipulating the independent variable and for holding extraneous variables constant usually require laboriously running one participant at a time, each serving in a single condition, making it impractical to use a large number of cases or to replicate across issues. The dichotomous dependent variables restrict the divergent stylist to simple descriptive statistics such as contingency coefficients and to relatively insensitive low parametric inferential statistics such as the chi-square or sign test.

The systems style of attitude structure research.   The third attitude-structure flourishing, likely to dominate social psychology in the 1980s and the 1990s, will use a "systems" style of research (McGuire, 1983). Its beginnings are discernible in current attitude research on anticipatory belief change, remote cognitive effects, information integration, cognitive responses, etc., and in some current social perception research (Anderson, 1981; McGuire, 1984a).

The systems stylist starts with a set of interacting variables among which he or she attempts to trace the multiple, often bidirectional, pathways of causality by using an inclusive research design. He or she takes a more open stance to collecting data than do either convergent or divergent unidirectional stylists, as by asking participants to report all the thoughts that come to mind regarding the attitude object rather than limiting them to reporting the object's position on an experimenter-chosen dimension (McGuire, 1964; McGuire and Padawar-Singer, 1976; Petty, Ostrom, and Brock, 1981), thus eliciting information-rich but unwieldy open-ended responses that call for content analysis.

Systems style descriptive statistics may include multidimensional analysis to reduce the number of variables, computer simulation to choose among alternative interpretations, structural-equation models like path analysis to detect the links and directions of causal flow, etc. (Bagozzi, 1982). This newer systems style is more concerned with descriptive than inferential statistics—e.g., using exploratory data analysis (Hoaglin, Mosteller, and Tukey, 1983) so that in keeping with the contextualist approach (McGuire, 1983), statistics become discovery procedures rather than being limited to the testing function they serve in the convergent and divergent unilinear styles.

NATURE OF ATTITUDES

DEFINITIONS OF ATTITUDES

Attitude researchers have been generous to a fault in clarifying attitudes by definitions and distinctions, compilations being found in Allport (1935), M. B. Smith, Bruner, and White (1956), Campbell (1963), A. G.

Greenwald (1968b), Kiesler, Collins, and Miller (1969), Lemon (1973), Himmelfarb and Eagly (1974), and Fishbein and Ajzen (1972, 1975; Ajzen and Fishbein, 1980), the latter in their 1972 review reporting that they found 500 different operational definitions of attitudes and that in 70 percent of the 200 studies in which attitude was defined in more than one way, different results were obtained depending on which definition was used. A widely shared working definition will be described before discussing basic theoretical differences that emerge when analytical conceptual definitions are attempted.

Working Definition

In most empirical studies specific attitudes are defined at least implicitly as responses that locate "objects of thought" on "dimensions of judgment" (McGuire, 1960c, 1968b). Objects of thought are foci of interest such as self, mother, equality, etc. Some are concrete (a familiar person, a specific sorrowful experience); others are more complex or abstract (humanity, evil) or are semantic compounds (the goodness of humanity, a whole's being greater than the sum of its parts). Anything that the person distinguishes from at least one other thing on at least one dimension of judgment is an object of thought for that person.

Dimensions of judgment are axes of meaning on which the person locates objects of thought when constructing meaning. Some dimensions of judgment have been phylogenetically built into the human sensory and central nervous systems as a propensity to notice certain aspects of objects, while others (at least as regards their alignment) are ontogenetically acquired, as when the child's early exposure to his or her own parents may result in distinctive attitudes on what constitutes beauty in the female (Wagatsuma and Kleinke, 1979) or the male (S. B. Beck, Ward-Hull, and McLear, 1976). Some dimensions are transcendental in that every object of thought can be meaningfully projected on them—e.g., expectancy (probability of existence), evaluation (degree of desirability), duration, complexity, etc. Other dimensions are relevant only to a subset of objects; e.g., size and weight apply only to physical objects, and deceitfulness and intelligence only to mammals, although their application can be extended metaphorically (Honeck and Hoffman, 1980), as when one speaks of a "weighty problem" or a "cruel winter."

An operational measure of attitudes typically involves asking the person to assign the object of thought to a position on some dimension of judgment. Advances in imagery measurement (Kosslyn, 1980) may yield a

"right brain" equivalent to this typical left-brain verbal operationalization. Indirect measuring procedures involve disguising the dimension by observing the person's actual or symbolic acts toward the object in storytelling, a situational test, projective technique, nonverbal behavior, life history, or autonomic physiological response (S. W. Cook and Selltiz, 1964; Cacioppo and Petty, 1983; Sechrest and Belew, 1983), etc., where these acts or responses can be interpreted as locating the object of interest on the relevant dimension of judgment.

Conceptual Definitions

We find less underlying consensus when we turn to conceptual definitions of attitudes whose assumptions and surplus meaning introduce both controversy and provocative insights. Even the fairly neutral conceptual definition that an attitude is a mediating process grouping a set of objects of thought in a conceptual category that evokes a significant pattern of responses touches on eight areas of provocative disagreement. First, this definition takes issue with positivists of the strict observance by defining attitudes as a *mediational construct* rather than as directly observable. Secondly, it assumes, in opposition to extreme situationalists, that the person *cognitively groups sets of stimuli* that share a socially significant distinctive aspect: A person's attitude toward rye bread is less interesting than his or her attitude toward Catholics or blacks—except to rye bread mavens. Thirdly, it assumes that the cognitive category is yoked to a *meaningful response pattern* of thoughts, feelings, and actions.

A fourth issue is whether the mediation involves *reception* or *response selectivity*. Darwin and Sherrington adapted the term *attitudes* to refer to an output selectivity in the form of a response readiness (Fleming, 1967), but Herbert Spencer and the Würzberg school posited an input selectivity in the form of a perceptual set to notice certain aspects of the stimulus objects. These perceptual and performance selectivities were nicely integrated by Washburn (1916) and later in Tolman's (1932) cognitive maps, Campbell's (1963) dispositions, G. A. Miller, Galanter, and Pribram's (1960) images and plans, Abelson's (1981) scripts, Tversky and Kahneman's (1981) frames, Upmeyer's (1981) internal representation and external presentation, and S. Kreitler and Kreitler's (1984) meaning, cognitive orientation, and program. However, response-readiness selectivity is still preferred by some theorists (Allport, 1935; DeFleur and Westie, 1963; N. H. Anderson, 1981; Petty, Ostrom, and Brock, 1981), while a contrasting perceptual selectivity involving assimilation of experiences to prior categories is implied by

Bartlett's (1932) schemata, M. Sherif's (1936) frame of reference, Piaget's (1936, 1963) assimilation and accommodation, Powers's (1978) templates, Cushman and Pearce's (1978) rules, Harré's (1980) ethnogenes, Moscovici's (1981) social representations, Nimmo and Combs's (1983) symbols, and Asch's (1952) notion of attitude change as involving not so much the learning of a new response to the old stimulus but rather a reconceptualization of the stimulus to which one is responding.

A fifth *directive and dynamic* issue arises because, while it is generally agreed that attitudes have a directive function in that their selectivity channels activity into certain types of responses and toward certain objects, there is disagreement on whether attitudes also have the dynamic function of energizing people to act. Hydraulic theorists like Freud conceptualize attitude change as directive only, rechanneling the person's given levels of constructive and destructive energies either toward a new target (as when hatred of a punishing father is displaced toward ethnic out-groups) or into a new response (as when self-hatred is sublimated into altruism or religious self-denial). Other theorists (L. Doob, 1947), accepting Buddha's third noble truth that desire itself can be reduced, attribute to attitudes the additional dynamic capacity so that attitude change becomes a more powerful process not merely redirecting the person's affect but also raising or reducing its level.

As regards the extent to which *attitudes are organized,* there are two perennial controversies: one, regarding the degree to which sets of attitudes are organized into coherent ideologies, will be considered later in the attitude structure section; the other, regarding the broadness of individual attitudes, is discussed here. During the first peaking of attitudes research in the 1920s, a few dispositionalists like Farris (1925) and Likert (1932) argued that attitudes such as religiosity, conservatism, honesty, etc., are broad; but the more dominant situationalists (Bogardus, 1925; Hartshorne and May, 1928) asserted that attitudes are narrowly focused so that a person is often quite conservative (or honest) in some regards and liberal (or deceitful) in others. Situationalism had also flourished earlier in the turn-of-the-century revolt of educational psychologists like Dewey and Thorndike against "faculty" psychology and, in its thirty-year cycle, peaked again in the 1960s and 1970s (Mischel, 1968; Abelson, 1972), so we can expect a 1980s reactive swing to the dispositional view of attitudes as broad (Zucker, Aronoff, and Rabin, 1983). The correlations among attitude manifestations remain clustered around $r = 0.30$; what fluctuates in these thirty-year cy-

cles is whether new generations of researchers find $r = 0.30$ surprisingly high or surprisingly low.

Attitude theorists, so contentious on most topics, are suspiciously agreed on a seventh issue, that people's attitudes are *acquired from experience* rather than genetically determined. Below, in the section "Attitude Formation," we shall argue that there is considerable genetic determination of the dynamic and some of the directive components of attitudes.

An eighth issue regarding epiphenomenal aspects of attitudes arises because conceptual definitions often add *surplus meaning* from phenomenological, physiological, or mechanistic domains of discourse, as when Allport (1935) termed attitudes "mental and neural states." Phenomenological theorists who derive creative inspiration by appeal to conscious content depict attitudes as experienced stereotypes, feeling states, or behavioral intentions, though the causal force of any such conscious content is doubtful (D. Bem, 1972; Nisbett and Wilson, 1977). Physiologizing theorists (DeFleur and Westie, 1963; Detwieler and Zanna, 1976; Cacioppo and Petty, 1983) find it provocative to conceptualize attitudes as involving sympathetic autonomic arousal patterns manifested in heart rate, sweating, respiratory changes, etc. Mechanistic theorists derive insight from assimilating attitudes to physical analogs such as computer flowcharts (G. A. Miller, Galanter, and Pribram, 1960) or guided missile homing devices (Powers, 1978). Useful insights are so needed that each theorist should be allowed any surplus meaning that provides her or him with inspiration.

LOGICAL STATUS OF ATTITUDES

Conceptually, an attitude is a unifying mediational construct that provides an economical and provocative depiction of the interrelations between a set of m antecedent conditions ($A_1, A_2, \ldots, A_m$) and a set of n consequent responses ($R_1, R_2, \ldots, R_n$). The strict positivistic approach (Bain, 1928; DeFleur and Westie, 1963) dispenses with such mediational constructs, thereby saving one variable but at the cost of having to define $m \times n$ main-effect relationships. The mediational approach suffers the added intervening attitude variable to gain a more important economy in reducing the number of main-effect relationships needing to be defined to only $m + n$ since one need only define the intervening attitude in terms of each of the m antecedents and then define each of the n responses in terms of the intervening attitude. The parsimony advantage of the mediating approach increases further (from multiplicative to exponential, $(2^m \times 2^n$ versus $2^m + 2^n)$ when interactions as well as main effects are considered. Mediating attitudinal constructs can vary in complexity from simple, unitary intervening variables to elaborate heuristically provocative hypothetical processes resembling the flowchart for a computer program (Janis and Mann, 1977; Abelson, 1981).

Mediational constructs risk impalement on the dilemma of being either unparsimoniously superfluous or meaninglessly undefined: Either the full meaning of the mediational construct variable is reducible to directly observable variables, in which case the mediator becomes unparsimoniously redundant; or else it has irreducible surplus meaning that would be scientifically meaningless. However, each horn of this dilemma is blunt. As just described, the mediational approach does introduce a new variable but gains a more valuable parsimony by reducing the number of relationships needing definition. More important, the value of a scientific formulation derives not only from its parsimonious operationalism that facilitates hypothesis testing (as regards which positivistic approaches have the advantage) but also from its creative provocativeness in stimulating hypothesis generation (in which regard mediational theories are richer).

DISTINCTIONS INVOLVING ATTITUDES

Clarification of attitudes is sometimes attempted by distinguishing them from other mediating dispositional variables such as knowledge, opinions, beliefs, values, habits, motives, traits, emotions, interests, cognitions, etc. (Allport, 1935; Campbell, 1963). The result is often confusion rather than clarification, as illustrated by attempts to distinguish between a person's *attitudes* (opinions, prejudices) and his or her more desirable *knowledge* (information, facts), the one formed by *propaganda* (or persuasion) and the other by *education* (or instruction), as in Plato's contrast between the vagueness of hazy attitudes and the clear insights of true knowledge. Others distinguish propaganda-produced attitude change from education-conveyed knowledge by whether or not the source stands to profit from the hearer's assent or whether or not the hearer already had a position on the issue. Others assert that attitudes differ from knowledge by involving more value-laden, controversial, or subjective issues, or issues having dynamic as well as directive components (L. Doob, 1947), or by changing via the agreement rather than the comprehension mediator

(McGuire, 1968a), or by stamping in rather than drawing out (Sommerville, 1983).

Attitudes and opinions likewise have been distinguished on many bases, such as that attitudes involve broader dispositions applying to more objects (Hovland, Janis, and Kelley, 1953) or are measured by more items (McNemar, 1946; Moser and Kalton, 1971). Others use *opinions* for observable beliefs and *attitudes* for more covert, latent, inferred, central, or unconscious dispositions (Bogardus, 1925; Lazarsfeld, 1959; Rokeach, 1973); or they use *opinions* for matters of fact and *attitudes* for more emotionally charged (Osgood *et al.,* 1957; M. J. Rosenberg, 1960b; Deutsch and Gerard, 1955) and less verifiable (Myrdal, 1944; Morgenbesser, 1954) matters of taste.

Attitudes and values are typically distinguished on one of two bases. They can be distinguished on a broadness continuum (Rokeach, 1973) running from beliefs (the narrowest dispositional tendencies) through progressively broader opinions, attitudes, interests, sentiments, and values, to ultimate concerns. Alternatively, they can be distinguished within an evaluation $\times$ attribution definition of an attitude in terms of the perceived conduciveness of its object to the attainment of the person's values.

Distinctions deserve to be made only insofar as they make a difference such that the distinguished variables relate differently to third variables of interest. When substantial differences do justify making a distinction, it should be communicated by labels not already in use for other distinctions and that indicate the essential difference between the concepts. Using *attitudes* as a contrast term to *opinions, beliefs,* etc., scores poorly on both these criteria. If eventually it is shown that judgments relate differently to third variables depending on whether, for example, they are made on the expectancy or the evaluation dimension (Wyer and Hartwick, 1984), then distinctive labels for the two might be "expectancy attitudes" versus "evaluative attitudes" rather than vacuous and ambiguous terms such as *opinions* versus *attitudes.*

STRUCTURE OF ATTITUDES AND ATTITUDE SYSTEMS

Three progressively broader levels of attitude structure will be considered: the structure of individual attitudes involving the placement of one object of thought on a single dimension of judgment; the structure of ideological systems of attitudes involving multiple objects of thought and/or multiple dimensions of judgment; and broader structures involving how attitudes fit within the total personality.

STRUCTURE OF INDIVIDUAL ATTITUDES

Objects on Dimensions Models

Our working definition of attitude as a response locating an object of thought on a dimension of judgment (McGuire, 1968b; Wyer, 1974a; Woelfel and Fink, 1980; Kaplowitz and Fink, 1982) is one way of analyzing the individual attitude. Each of the two components may itself be further analyzed: The object of thought may be a complicated combination of mental foci, and the dimension of judgment may be a melding of several independent dimensions.

Subject-Verb-Object Models

Several theories (Osgood and Tannenbaum, 1955; Abelson and Rosenberg, 1958; Kanouse and Abelson, 1967; H. Kreitler and Kreitler, 1976) depict attitudes and attitude change messages as the predication (the verb concept) of some property (the object concept) to some entity (the subject concept). Its most elegant development is Gollob's (1974) reduction of Heiderian (1958) balance situations to three positive main-effect components and four interaction balance components, the relative importance of which varies with conditions (Rossman and Gollob, 1976; N. H. Anderson, 1979; Wyer and Carlston, 1979).

Cognitive-Affective-Conative Models

Human experience has been analyzed into knowing, feeling, and acting components so early and often that it may reflect a deep structure in Indo-European thought, central in the thinking of Hellenic philosophers such as Plato, in the Hindu Jñāna, bhakti, and karma (knowledge, feeling, action) paths, and in the Zoroastrian three divine male radiations, asha, vohu-manō, and kshathra (thought, love, and service). It may have a basis in the brain's three evolutionary layers, the frontal cortex, limbic system, and old brain (Sagan, 1977). The trichotomization reemerged as central in modern thought since Christian von Wolff, in reprofessionalizing philosophy in the eighteenth century by systematizing it and returning it to the academy, described mind as having the three functions of thinking, feeling, and willing, properly studied by science, aesthetics, and ethics, and successively discussed by Kant in his three *Critiques,* of pure

reason, of judgment, and of practical reason. This tricomponential analysis is now used routinely (Bagozzi, 1978; Hilgard, 1980).

The three components.   The cognitive aspect of attitudes are the distinguishing properties attributed to the object of thought—e.g., the members of a given ethnic group being seen as tall, honest, inclined to alcoholism, capable soldiers, etc. It is typically measured by having the respondent indicate which characteristics on a checklist can be attributed to the object (Karlins, Coffman, and Walters, 1969; W. B. Helmreich, 1982), though occasionally it is measured (McGuire, 1984a) by the more informative approach of having the participant generate all the characteristics that come to mind about the object. The heavily studied affective component, how much the person likes the object of thought, is usually measured by self-report paper-and-pencil evaluation scales of the Likert, Thurstone, or Osgood types, though occasionally it is measured by physiological indices of autonomic sympathetic arousal (Cacioppo and Petty, 1983). The conative component involves the person's gross behavior, more often measured by his or her verbal report of intended acts toward the object on a social distance (Bogardus, 1925; Triandis, 1977) or by a behavioral intention (Ajzen and Fishbein, 1980; Saltzer, 1981) scale, than by observing actual behavior in the form of proximity, eye contact, or other nonverbal acts or by petition signing, donating money, or other situational tests.

Problems and promise of this tricomponential analysis.   Good convergent-validity homogeneity of each component is shown by high intercorrelations among alternative measures of a given component (Ostrom, 1969; but see Woodmansee and Cook, 1967). Discriminant validity is less good, measures often correlating as highly across as within components, indicating that the three components are redundant as evaluative measures. Even under hypnotic or "authoritarian personality" disturbances, discrepancies among the three are rare (Adorno *et al.,* 1950; D. Katz, 1960; M. J. Rosenberg, 1960a). However, the redundancy arises because most researchers ignore the distinctive information in each by reducing all three components to their evaluative aspect (Schegel and DiTecco, 1982), another manifestation of psychologists' peculiar evaluation monomania, reducing all information to this one dimension as if people think of themselves and other objects exclusively in terms of how good or bad they are (McGuire, 1984a).

Attribution × Evaluation Models

Another popular way of analyzing attitudes is to decompose them into the perceived probability that the object has each of several characteristics, each probability then being multiplied by the perceived desirability of the characteristic, a conceptualization variously known as the expectancy × value, instrumentality × goal, means-end, expected value, utility maximizing, etc., approach (Feather, 1982). It became popular at midcentury (Myrdal, 1944; Woodruff and DiVesta, 1948; Cartwright, 1949; M. B. Smith, 1949) and received mathematical formalization in W. Edwards (1954) and in L. J. Savage's (1954) "subjective expected utility" model. Subsequently it has been widely used by the Michigan school (Peak, 1955; M. J. Rosenberg, 1956; Atkinson, 1958; Zajonc, 1960) and its Illinois offshoot (Dulany, 1962; Fishbein and Raven, 1962; Fishbein, 1963; Triandis, 1977; Ajzen and Fishbein, 1980).

Properties and *outcome* variants of this depiction can be illustrated in terms of attitudes toward Catholic ethnics. The *properties* version (M. B. Smith, Bruner, and White, 1956; Fishbein and Hunter, 1964) presents to the person whose attitude is being measured a list of properties or traits (parochial, patriotic, anti-intellectual, superstitious, musical, hardworking, etc.) and asks the person to rate the subjective probability that the group has each trait and each probability is then multiplied by the rated desirability of the trait. The alternative *outcome* version (M. J. Rosenberg, 1956; Ajzen and Fishbein, 1980) presents a list of outcomes or values (achievement, affiliation, power, etc.) and asks the person to rate the subjective probabilities that these ethnics [or one's feelings about them (Burnett, 1977) or actions toward them (A. G. Weinstein, 1972; Ajzen and Fishbein, 1980)] lead to each outcome value; each of these probabilities is then multiplied by the rated desirability of that outcome.

Whether these attribution × evaluation cognitions combine by summation or averaging has long been debated (Gulliksen, 1956; N. H. Anderson, 1959; Willis, 1960). Applying the functional-measurement parallelism approach to unequally weighted items of information yields results indicating averaging (N. H. Anderson, 1981), as does the depolarizing of the judgment when neutral information is added to favorable (unfavorable) information (Lynch, 1979; N. H. Anderson, 1981; Hayes, 1983) at least with high-involvement beliefs (Petty and Cacioppo, 1984b), and the rareness of polarization after the person generates additional information

about the object (Simpson and Ostrom, 1976; N. H. Anderson, 1981; but see Tesser, 1978). Averaging or subadditivity is used even when adding makes more sense, as with the commodity bundles of utility theory (Shanteau, 1975), and support for the averaging rule becomes stronger the better the data (K. J. Kaplan, 1972). On the other hand, the set size effect is more simply handled by assuming the additive model (Fishbein and Ajzen, 1975; but see N. H. Anderson, 1981, pp. 135–136), though an averaging theory that includes an initial-attitude term also handles it (N. H. Anderson, 1981; Yamagishi and Hill, 1983). Probably cognitive integration will ultimately be found to incorporate an adaptively adjustable mix of additive and averaging processes (Bagozzi, 1982).

Construction-by-Aspect Models

The attribution × evaluation analysis of attitudes is superficially plausible, even embarrassingly obvious, but it implies that people form their attitudes by an implausibly tedious process, leading me to propose that attitude structure reflects rather a "construction by aspect" process analogous to Tversky's (1972) "elimination by aspect" decision-making process, which would allow the person to circumvent the onerous process of considering all the properties (or outcomes) associated with the object. Instead, the person could start with just one salient characteristic and multiply the object's perceived position on it by its perceived desirability; additional, less salient characteristics would need to be considered only until the average (or sum) of the most salient attribution × evaluation products reaches a level that justifies an attitudinal decision, a criterion probably reached more quickly with less involving issues. This easily formed construction-by-aspect attitude would usually approximate the tedious attribution × evaluation attitude, but interesting divergencies would arise when presentation frames or other factors systematically bias characteristic "availability" (Nisbett and Ross, 1980; Kahneman, Slovic, and Tversky, 1982).

Basal/Peripheral Models

An attitude can also be analyzed into basal and peripheral components (N. H. Anderson, 1959; Lazarsfeld, 1959; N. H. Anderson and Farkas, 1973; Kelman, 1980), the former firmly anchored and stable and the latter superficial and readily changed by persuasive communications. Related "slack" depictions are that there are narrow latitudes of acceptance (Sherif and Hovland, 1961) or loose linkages (McGuire, 1968b) or oscillations (Kaplowitz, Fink, and Bauer, 1983) within which attitudes can easily be changed but beyond which further changing requires intensive indoctrination procedures such as long-term psychoanalysis or brainwashing. Several recent lines of work show that laboratory and mass media communications induce only temporary elastic changes, suggesting that they involve only superficial components that quickly snap back into accord with more stable basal attitudes (Nuttin, 1975; Cialdini *et al.,* 1976; Hass and Mann, 1976).

Dimensionalizing Approaches
A seventh analysis decomposes attitudes into a list of dimensions on which attitudes vary interestingly among themselves. Some distinguish attitudes with respect to the dimensions of judgment involved, as when D. Katz (1960) distinguishes among cognitive, affective, conative, and complex attitudes. Subcomponents of the cognitive dimension have been suggested by Transgaard (1973), Funk *et al.* (1976), E. E. Davis and O'Neill (1977), J. Taylor (1980), and Bobo (1983); subcomponents of the affective by Marascuilo and Zwick (1983); and subcomponents of the conative by Triandis, Davis, and Takezawa (1965) and Triandis (1977).

Others distinguish attitudes on the basis of their objects of thought (Scott, Osgood, and Peterson, 1979). Among the object discriminations proposed are generality, differentiation, and unity (D. Katz, 1960), inclusiveness, amount of internal structure, and degree of relatedness to other thought classes (O. J. Harvey, Hunt, and Schroder, 1961), centrality and permeability (Rokeach, 1960), and differentiation, complexity, unity, and organization (Zajonc, 1960). Carrying such conceptual baggage is justified only to the extent that such characteristics appreciably affect how attitudes relate to other variables of interest.

STRUCTURE OF ATTITUDE SYSTEMS

The more complex structural issues that arise when we go from the individual attitude to systems of attitudes are becoming the main focus of the third, 1980s and 1990s flourishing of attitude research (Eagly and Chaiken, in press). Sets of attitudes operate as connected and coherent systems to the extent that there are structural relations among them, failure to maintain which results in felt discomfort, difficulty of recall, selective information seeking, drift toward optimal structure, directionally specific susceptibility to persuasion, etc. We shall consider, successively, attitude structures involving multiple objects of thought projected on a single dimension, a single object projected on several dimensions, and ideologies composed of multiple objects projected on several dimensions.

Multiple Objects/Single Dimension Structures
Simple attitudinal systems consisting of several objects of thought (such as a set of propositions) projected on a single dimension of judgment (such as truth) will first be described in terms of theoretical principles of structure and functioning, and then we shall describe empirical results on four types of implications following from the theory.

The probabilogical model. Measurement theorists derive structural rules for these single-dimension attitude systems from constraints among the subsets into which the dimension is divided—e.g., whether the subsets on the dimension constitute a nominal, ordinal, interval, or ratio scale. Cognitive social psychologists are more likely to derive structure from perceived relationships among the propositions assigning objects of thought to the dimension of judgment; e.g., the probabilogical model of cognitive functioning (McGuire, 1960c, 1968b, 1981; Wyer and Goldberg, 1970; Wyer, 1974a; Wyer and Carlston, 1979) postulates that attitude systems function in accord with the axioms of logic and probability theory. It can be illustrated by three interrelated propositions about objects of thought, such as (a) that the number of fifteen to twenty-five-year-olds in the U.S. population will decline in the 1980s and 1990s, (b) that fifteen to twenty-five-year-olds commit a disproportionate proportion of all violent crimes, and (c) that the per capita rate of violent crime in the United States will decline in the 1980s and 1990s. The probabilogical model predicts that at any given moment the person's expectancy attitudes, $p(a)$, $p(b)$, and $p(c)$, on those three propositions will be related as shown in static Eq. (1):

$$p(c) = p[c/(a \& b)] \cdot p(a \& b) \\ + p[c/ \sim (a \& b)] \cdot p \sim (a \& b) \quad (1)$$

Furthermore, if the person's $p(a)$ expectancy attitude is raised by a persuasive communication arguing that the number of 15- to 25-year-olds is declining, the model predicts that attitudes on the unmentioned conclusion about declining crime rate will also change as shown in dynamic Eq. (2):

$$\Delta p(c) = \Delta p(a) \cdot p(b) \cdot [p(c/a \& b) - p(c/ \sim (a \& b)] \quad (2)$$

Alogical functioning principles. This depiction of the person as a probabilistic logic machine hardly fits the contorted belief systems of people one observes, leading to the postulation (McGuire, 1960c, 1981) of additional alogical functioning principles such as that one's attitude on a given target issue is affected by attitudes on other related issues only to the extent that they are momentarily salient, a principle underlying the Socratic method of self-generated persuasion discussed below and the previously discussed "construction-by-aspect" theory of attitude composition. Another alogical principle is the spatial-inertia postulate of a loose linkage in belief chains that allows some give in the system so that persuasive impact on remote related issues falls progressively shorter of the amount predicted in Eq. (2) as one goes to more remote implications. A temporal-inertia postulate asserts that these remote impacts filter down only gradually over time, resulting in delayed-action effects on unmentioned related issues. A fourth, threshold, postulate implied by the loose-link notion is that the explicit target attitude must change beyond a threshold amount that takes up the slack before change is induced on remote related attitudes (McGuire, 1968b; Silverman, 1971), since without this dampening assumption any slight attitude change induced in a belief system would have a destabilizing reverberation effect. Also postulated is a hedonic consistency tendency such that the person assimilates expectancy and evaluation attitudes on a given proposition toward one another.

Additional logical "fallacies" in human belief systems were recognized by the ancients (the undistributed middle, illicit process of the major, etc.). Others such as inferential wariness and the atmosphere effect were reported in the first 1920s-to-1930s measurement flourishing of attitude research (Woodworth and Sells, 1935). Still others have been proposed at the outset of the current attitude structure flourishing (Christensen-Szalanski and Beach, 1984)—e.g., the availability and the representativeness heuristics (Tversky and Kahneman, 1974; Nisbett and Ross, 1980), the conversion operation (Revlin *et al.*, 1980), and the differential priorities given to equivalence, symmetrical, and asymmetrical relations (Sternberg and Turner, 1981). The next four sections describe findings regarding predictions implied by these logical and alogical functioning principles.

Implications regarding initial relationships among beliefs. Empirical results support the probabilogical model prediction regarding interrelations within a system of attitudes at a given time: Group correlations above +0.7 are usually found between obtained attitude levels and those predicted from static Eq. (1) (McGuire, 1960a, 1981; Wyer and Carlston, 1979), whether evaluation or expectancy attitudes are involved (Wyer, 1975) and regardless of the ordering or massing of the related propositions (Holt and Watts, 1969), of issue importance (Wyer, 1974b), or of receiver intelligence (Dillehay, Insko, and Smith, 1966). Correlation is enhanced when it is mentioned that the issues are interrelated (Rosen and Wyer, 1972), when implications and intersections rather than the union of events are used (Wyer, 1974b), and when the premises have low initial probabilities and low relevance to the conclusion (Henninger and Wyer, 1976).

Implications regarding the Socratic method of attitude change. The probabilogical and salience postulates (McGuire, 1960c, 1981) imply that attitudes can be changed not only by presenting new information from an outside source but also by enhancing the salience of information already possessed by the person. Since McGuire (1960c) initially demonstrated this Socratic effect, there have been dozens of confirmations both under the original procedure of asking questions (Watts and Holt, 1970; Henninger and Wyer, 1976) and under variant terminologies and methods (Kirfel and Denig, 1973; Salancik and Conway, 1975; Rokeach, 1975, 1979; Sherrid and Beech, 1976; Tesser, 1978; Petty and Cacioppo, 1979a; Chanowitz and Langer, 1981; C. A. Anderson, 1983), with only a few failures to confirm (Dillehay *et al.,* 1966; Holt and Watts, 1969).

The Socratic effect has been found at intervals ranging from a minute, ten minutes, two days, and a week, though it is greatest at short intervals (O'Malley and Thistlethwaite, 1980). It is most pronounced when first-session inconsistency is greatest (Henninger and Wyer, 1976) and when the issue is important (Bridge *et al.*, 1977), but it occurs whether the related beliefs are elicited contiguously or scattered, whether or not the existence of interrelationships is mentioned at the outset, whether expectancy or evaluation attitudes are involved, and regardless of how much experience the participants have had with the response scales. The effect is sizable enough to have allowed Wyer (1974b) to demonstrate that the McGuire/Wyer probabilogical model of cognitive consistency fits the obtained results better than does Osgood and Tannenbaum's (1955) congruity theory, Heider's (1958) balance theory, or Abelson and Rosenberg's (1958) psycho-logic theory. Socratic-effect clarifications are still needed as regards identifying which of the inconsistent attitudes are most likely to change and resolving whether the Socratic effect occurs as early as the later part of the first elicitation of the related beliefs.

Implications regarding inducing resistance to persuasion. The two previous implications apply to ideological material already within the believer's attitude system, while the next two concern the effects of new information communicated from outside sources. Attitudes on target issues become more resistant to persuasion if, before they are attacked, their connections to attitudes on related issues are made more salient (Holt and Watts, 1969; Watts and Holt, 1970), especially when the attacking communication argues in an inconsistency-increasing direction (McGuire, 1960b), when the person actively participates in eliciting the related beliefs (Nelson, 1968; Holt, 1970), or when the person is cognitively tuned (Zajonc, 1960) as a receiver rather than a sender of further communications on the issue (Holt and Watts, 1969; Watts and Holt, 1970).

Implications regarding remote ramifications of persuasive communications. As the theory implies, persuasive communications have sizable impacts on unmentioned but logically related beliefs, especially when these changes are in an inconsistency-reducing direction (McGuire, 1960b), when the person is cognitively tuned to transmit the information (Watts and Holt, 1970), when initial commitment is low (Holt, 1970), when texts are rigid and from a minority source (Mugny and Papastamou, 1980), and when the remote issues are made salient by recency or other factors (Götz-Marchand, Götz, and Irle, 1974; A. M. Collins and Loftus, 1975; Wyer and Srull, 1981).

Support is mixed for the spatial-inertia prediction that remote impacts on unmentioned related attitudes will fall short of the amount specified in the probabilogical dynamic Eq. (2) (McGuire, 1960c, 1981; McFarland and Thistlethwaite, 1970), but support is stronger for the temporal-inertia prediction of a gradual delayed-action seepage of impact to unmentioned related issues (McGuire, 1960a; Dillehay, Insko, and Smith, 1966; Watts and Holt, 1970); e.g., Riley and Pettigrew (1976) found that the assassination of Martin Luther King had a delayed-action ripple effect on the public's interracial attitudes. Theoretically, attitude system consistency could be maintained after a change is induced on a premise by changing either the conclusion or a parallel premise (McGuire, 1960c), but people seem to use vertical (conclusion) rather than horizontal (other premises) adjust-

ments (Holt and Watts, 1969; McFarland and Thistlethwaite, 1970).

Single Object/Multiple Dimensions Structures

Attitude systems involving a single object of thought projected on multiple dimensions of judgment have recently been heavily studied in person perception, decision making, and social judgment as well as attitude research. Particularly deserving of mention here is N. H. Anderson's (1981) functional measurement/information integration approach, Fishbein's (1980) theory of reasoned action, and McGuire/Wyer's probabilogical approach (McGuire, 1960a, 1981; Wyer and Carlston, 1979).

Across-dimensional functioning in McGuire's cognitive system approach. Positioning dimensions of judgment in meaning space may reflect a compromise between antagonistic tendencies to reduce information-inefficient redundancy by keeping dimensions orthogonal and to allow inferring an object's location on one dimension from its known locations on others by setting dimensions obliquely to one another. Across-dimensional inferences like the size-weight "illusion," while logically fallacious and leading to error in rigged laboratory tasks, actually provide heuristic insights and economic approximations in natural situations. Research has concentrated on inferences between the evaluative and expectancy dimensions, either in the wishful-thinking causal direction of inferring an object's likelihood from its desirability (Granberg and Brent, 1983) or in the rationalization causal direction of inferring its desirability from its likelihood (Sjöberg, 1978). This hedonic-consistency prediction is demonstrated by +0.70 correlations obtained between expectations and evaluations at a given point in time (McGuire, 1960c, 1981; Watts and Holt, 1970), but it is harder to show that an induced change on one dimension results in changes on the other (McGuire, 1960a; Holt, 1970).

Anderson's information integration approach to across-dimensional functioning. N. H. Anderson's (1981) judgmental research constitutes the past decade's most significant advance in the attitude field because of its elegant theory of cognitive algebra, elaborate designs and data collection procedures, ambitious range of empirical application, innovative methods of data analysis, and impressive record of empirical confirmation. Information integration theory postulates that a person judges where an object of thought falls on any dimension of judgment—typically but not necessarily evaluation (N. H. Anderson and Lopes, 1974)—by a weighted averaging of his or her perceptions of where the object falls on other dimensions and of these other dimensions' bearings on the given dimension, as shown in Eq. (3):

$$_2A_{oj} = \frac{w_{jj} \cdot {}_1A_{oj} + \Sigma w_{jk} \cdot A_{ok}}{w_{jj} + \Sigma w_{jk}} \tag{3}$$

where $_2A_{oj}$ is the person's subsequent attitude (judgment) of where object of thought o falls on a dimension of judgment j on the basis of new information. The resultant attitude is defined by the right side of the equation as the sum of the person's prior attitude $_1A_{oj}$ of where o fell on dimension j and of the new information A_{ok}, etc., about where the object falls on other k dimensions, weighted by the perceived association w_{jk} between the j and k dimensions, these weights being a function of the dimension's salience, relevance, etc., and of the information's reliability, etc. The new information about the object's locations on the k dimensions may come from inferences, memory storage, direct experiences with o, persuasive communications about o, etc.

Anderson's functional measurement strategy guides design, data collection, and analysis to yield intervally scaled values for A and w at the same time as it tests the cognitive algebra of attitude structure hypothesized in Eq. (3), freeing the researcher from having to obtain A and w estimates from doubtfully valid self-reports, regression coefficients, or arbitrary scales. Anderson makes the functional measurement assumptions that human information integration reflects the weighted-averaging cognitive algebra in Eq. (3) and that independent and interval scales have been used. The parallelism theorem then yields the prediction that in an orthogonally designed experiment, including all possible pairings of equally weighted column and row elements, two implications follow: that the $_2A_{oj}$ values yielded by the successive row (column) dimensions in combination with each of the several column (row) dimensions will produce parallel curves and that the attained column and row means will provide interval-scaled A-values. This parallelism prediction has been confirmed in a wide range of appropriately designed experiments, leading N. H. Anderson (1981) to conclude that the cognitive algebra model and the scaling assumptions are correct, it being implausible that several departures from the assumptions neatly canceled each other in study after study. There is still worry that the procedure may be too laboratory-bound (Wyer

and Carlston, 1979) or too robust to reveal some violations of its assumptions.

While Anderson usually uses the averaging cognitive algebra model and its corresponding parallelism theorem, his approach also allows testing alternatives such as the multiplicative model and its corresponding "fan" prediction. Besides its attitude change relevance, this information integration theorizing is applicable to other intra- and interpersonal processes such as psychophysical judgments, decision making, group processes, etc. (N. H. Anderson, 1981), and the functional measurement approach has even broader relevance. Related approaches are Rossi's factorial survey procedure (Rossi and Nock, 1982) and Hammond's Brunswick lens model technique (Hammond *et al.,* 1980).

Fishbein's theory of reasoned action. A popular variant of the attribution × evaluation approach is included within Fishbein's (Fishbein and Ajzen, 1975; Ajzen and Fishbein, 1980; Fishbein, 1980) theory of reasoned action whose additive cognitive algebra can be represented in the uniform terminology used in this chapter as follows:

$$A_{oe} = \Sigma A_{oj} \cdot A_{je} + \Sigma A_{on} \cdot A_{ne} \tag{4}$$

where A_{oe} is the person's attitude of where object of thought o falls on evaluation dimension e (in Fishbein, a behavioral intention toward an object), A_{oj} is the person's belief on where o falls on any salient characteristic j, and A_{je} is the person's attitude of where this j characteristic falls on the evaluative dimension e. Term A_{on} is the person's perception of his or her reference group's normative approval of o, and A_{ne} is his or her evaluation of this group approval. Miniard and Cohen (1983) suggest instead that A_{oe} determinants be given a somewhat different partitioning into personal versus normative factors.

Besides methodological differences indicated in the next section, the Fishbein and Anderson approaches differ on substantive issues. Of these the additive versus averaging controversy discussed above has been overemphasized relative to the following differences. Only Fishbein incorporates a normative-belief term, and only Anderson an initial-attitude term. Fishbein focuses even more than Anderson on evaluative attitudes but he more than Anderson goes beyond cognition and affect to behavior. Fishbein's A_{oj} weighting factor (B_i in his terminology) depends primarily on subjective probability, while Anderson's *w* is a function of various aspects of the stimulus and the information such as relevance, reliability, salience, etc. Most important, Fishbein postulates a continuing dependence of the attitude on the availability of the informational content on which it is based, while Anderson (see also Watts and McGuire, 1964; Sherman *et al.,* 1983) postulates separate memory storage of the object's location on the attitude dimension (or at least its basal component) and of the semantic content that determined this location.

Methodology of this attitude systems research.   Work in this area has been the most methodologically sophisticated in social psychology during the past decade (N. H. Anderson, 1982), but that is faint praise since the rest uses poor scaling procedures with too few response levels, neglect of anchors, and instruments like the semantic differential that fail to meet the interval-scale and common-units measurement assumptions of the models. Too often data are collected under reliability-reducing group administration conditions and are pooled across participants to estimate parameters and fit functions, even though group functions are often qualitatively different from the individual functions that they aggregate (McGuire, 1961b). Still, this area involves state-of-the-art methodology (N. H. Anderson, 1982), such as the use of the person's ratings to yield more validly scaled weight and value scores than obtainable from magnitude estimation (Stevens, 1975) or multiple regression. Occasionally, Anderson and a few others in this area even use the more valid functional measurement, goodness-of-fit criterion rather than the ubiquitous correlations between predicted and obtained values; this widely used correlational criterion is dangerous because it can, under not unlikely scaling circumstances, yield a higher predictive correlation for the less valid theory (Birnbaum, 1974). The increasing use of structural equation LISREL (Bagozzi, 1982) and other models (Catalano, Dooley, and Jackson, 1983) promises to clarify the relationship within these attitudinal systems and externally to behavior.

More Complex Ideological Systems

An end of ideology?   On the issue of whether attitude systems are organized on a broader ideological level involving multiple objects of thought projected on multiple dimensions of judgment, Establishment consensus (Converse, 1964, 1980; Nimmo and Combs, 1983) has been that people are largely nonideological, though there

are dissenters (Mosse, 1980; Himmelweit *et al.,* 1981; Judd, Krosnick, and Milburn, 1981; Apostle *et al.,* 1983). Eight kinds of evidence are used to argue against the prevalence of organized ideological systems. First, people are usually unable to give correct reasons for their attitudinal preferences (Nisbett and Wilson, 1977; P. L. Wright and Rip, 1981) and are abysmally ignorant or mistaken regarding widely publicized facts on important issues, 40 percent thinking that Israel is an Arab nation (Hechinger, 1979) and antiwar candidate Eugene McCarthy being supported in the 1968 New Hampshire Democratic primary on the misperception that he favored a more aggressive prosecution of the Vietnam War (Converse, 1975). Secondly, ideological vacuity is suggested by the frequency of "no opinion" responses on surveys on matters that seem of considerable importance and by the lack of even a word for *attitude* or *belief* in many languages (Needham, 1973). Thirdly, people's attitudes fluctuate so precipitously over time as to suggest that many adopt positions capriciously. Such political fickleness (Converse, 1964, 1970; Jennings and Niemi, 1981) accords with situationalist questioning of stability over time and issues (Brim and Kagan, 1980; Judd and Milburn, 1980; Zanna, Higgins, and Herman, 1982; Mischel, 1983).

A fourth counterindication of political ideology is the drastic effects on public opinion responses produced by trivial changes in wordings (Lipset, 1976; C. F. Turner and Krauss, 1978; Sudman and Bradburn, 1982; Schuman, Kalton, and Ludwig, 1983) or orderings of questions (Schuman and Presser, 1981b). A fifth is the low correspondence between people's cognition and affect regarding an object, as when people prefer one presidential candidate while agreeing with the other on most of the issues (Converse, 1964) or when persons' participation in demonstrations has little relation to their sympathy for the causes (Lin, 1974). A sixth is the low correlations among attitudes of similar ideological content (R. E. Lane, 1973; Veroff, Douvan, and Kulka, 1981). A seventh reason for doubt is the public's tendency to take attitudinal positions conflicting with their own self- or class interest, as when young people of draft age were more in favor of the Korean and Vietnam wars than were the safe older respondents (Erskine, 1970; Converse *et al.,* 1980) and when personal economic stakes have little effect on voting behavior (Kinder and Sears, 1981). An eighth indication of incoherence is that people's general positions often contradict their specific sentiments, as when the public loses faith in institutions in general but not in their specific members (Ladd and Lipset, 1980), or favors capital punishment in general but rejects it in most specific instances (Ellsworth, 1982), or finds groups less attractive than the individual members who compose them (D. O. Sears, 1983a), or favors civil liberties in general but not in specifics (McClosky and Brill, 1983).

Psychological mechanisms. These empirical indications of deficient ideological coherence are in accord with a half-dozen conceptual generalizations that independently gained popularity in psychology during recent years, such as the swing to situationalism (Endler and Hunt, 1968; Alker, 1972; Mischel, 1984) and D. Bem's (1972) "radical behaviorism" depiction of the person as forming attitudes only when outside demands require it. Also consonant is the notion that attitudinal differences are more style than substance, that people are differentiated more by how dogmatically they formulate their positions than by what positions they take (Rokeach, 1956) or by favoring versus opposing current orthodoxies regardless of their content (Mazlish, 1976; Billington, 1980; Feyerabend, 1978). Certain cognitive science notions such as the above-discussed salience and the loose-link postulates (McGuire, 1960c, 1981) and the separate storage of affect and information (Watts and McGuire, 1964; Nisbett and Wilson, 1977; N. H. Anderson, 1981) also accord with the apparent absence of ideology.

In defense of ideology. Absence of ideology is so counterintuitive that numerous theories have been proposed to explain away the negative findings, a dozen of which will be mentioned here, beginning with three that blame inadequate attitude measurement. First, McGuire (1960c, 1981) describes how the typical scaling practice of dichotomizing (agree versus disagree) continuous attitudes can give a spurious appearance of inconsistency. Secondly, unreliable measures of the individual attitudes, unless corrected for attenuation, can result in a spurious appearance of inconsistency. Thirdly, less educated or uninvolved participants, feeling pressured to express an opinion, might respond almost randomly; whether the resulting inconsistency can be reduced by more permissive "don't know" response options is debatable (Bishop *et al.,* 1979, 1980, 1983; Rapoport, 1979; Judd, Krosnick, and Milburn, 1981).

Seven other excuses suppose that ideological coherence may be found at least in special subdomains. For example, the organized ideologies lacking in the masses

are reported in the political elites by some researchers (Converse, 1964, 1980; Bishop *et al.,* 1980; Martin, 1981) but not others (E. H. Erikson, 1979; Milburn and Judd, 1981). The ideological coherence lacking in the U.S. public might be expected in countries like France with more ideologically oriented parties and electoral systems; however, inconsistency seems to be equally alive and well in Paris (Converse, 1975). It has also been conjectured that attitudinal orientations played little part in pre-1960 U.S. elections but that ideology has been more determining since the Johnson-Goldwater presidential campaign and other polarizing events of the 1960s (Nimmo and Savage, 1976; Nie, Verba, and Petrocik, 1979), or that the apparent inconsistency may be an artifact of recent changes of the response scales used in surveys (Bishop *et al.,* 1979; J. P. Robinson and Meadow, 1982). Others expect that organized ideologies might be found at least in certain personality types such as the maturer respondents (J. S. Meyer, DeChenne, and Albano, 1981), "analytical genius" types (Simonton, 1980), morally aware subjects (S. H. Schwartz, 1977), high-consistency groups (Chaiken and Baldwin, 1981), ideologues (Hikel, 1973), internals (Saltzer, 1981), need cognition types (Cacioppo, Petty, and Morris, 1983), self-monitors (M. Snyder, 1982), one-issue activists (Granberg, 1982a), or other extremists (Sidanius, Ekehammar, and Lukowsky, 1983). Or ideological coherence may exist at least within certain circumscribed belief domains of special personal importance, as when Tanaka (1978) finds public acceptance of nuclear power to be highly related to residing near an atomic power plant; however, even in the gripping domain of personal health, belief coherence seems primitive (Leventhal, Meyer, and Nerenz, 1980). Elite inconsistency may arise because leaders express their reference group's consensus position even when it is discrepant from their personal beliefs (E. E. Davis and Triandis, 1971).

An eleventh speculation discerns a deeper coherence beneath the apparent ideological chaos by arguing that people's attitudinal systems are organized on some basis other than the conventionally assumed left-right dimension. McGuire (1968b, 1981) has suggested that belief systems might be organized along deep structural dimensions, such as on a syntagmatic rather than paradigmatic basis (Barthes, 1967), or on the nature/culture, raw/cooked axis of thought used by Lévi-Strauss (1974; MacCormack and Strathern, 1980), or on the logocentric speech/writing, reality/appearance, male/female oppositions that Derrida and other deconstructionists (Culler, 1982) seek to undermine, or the Jungian individuating polarities (Levinson, 1978), or on a mix of means and ends (S. R. Brown, 1980). The recent "cognitive imperialism" described by Tomkins (1981) may have distracted us from noticing the role of affective dimensions in organizing ideology that may be involved in center extremism (Lipset and Raab, 1978) and middle-American radicalism (Warren, 1976) or in the organization of political attitudes around generalized predispositions such as "symbolic racism" (Kinder and Sears, 1981; but see Bobo, 1983), trust in people (Schuman and Presser, 1981a), or politicians' personalities or demographics (Kinder, 1981; Litwak, Hooyman, and Warren, 1973). Another possibility is that attitudes (such as liberalism-conservatism) analyzed as single-dimension bipolar opposites are actually two separate orthogonal attitudes (Kerlinger, 1984).

Schemata theories. In place of overall ideological organization, theorists a half century ago postulated that miniature knowledge structures guide perception and responses within circumscribed domains, as in Bartlett's (1932) schemata, Sherif's (1935) frames of reference, Michotte's (1946) and Piaget's (1930) implicit physics, etc. This idea has currently revived under such terms as implicit personality theories, scripts, modes, categories, prototypes, frames, agenda, etc. (Crothers, 1979; Hastie *et al.,* 1980; Higgins, Herman, and Zanna, 1981; Tversky and Kahneman, 1981). While the 1930s theories stressed the input, receptive, perception-organizing roles of these knowledge structures, current theories stress their central, information-organizing meaning-giving and their output, performance regulation, response-guiding functions.

Some of these miniature-structure theories postulate parallel and some series organizations. Implicit personality theorists (Schneider, 1973; Hastie *et al.,* 1980) stress the parallel clustering of traits in person perception such that perceiving the person as having a given trait leads to the inference that he or she has others in the cluster also, perhaps with a central organizing role being played by certain characteristics as in Eckblad's (1981) scheme theory, Lakoff and Johnson's (1980) experiential gestalts, and Tversky and Kahneman's (1980) causal schema. Others depict these miniature structures as being series-organized. Agenda (Plott and Levine, 1978) and script (Schank and Abelson, 1977; Tomkins, 1979; Abelson, 1981) theories describe sequential knowledge structures that lead the person through a series of inferential assumptions and behavioral steps. Perhaps parallel schemata operate mainly as templates for perception and the series schemata as flowcharts for guiding performance. Study of miniature knowledge structures, especially of the sequential type, is likely to accelerate during the third, structural, flourishing of attitude research.

ATTITUDES WITHIN THE TOTAL PERSON

The broadest structural issue, how attitudes are integrated into the total person, will be discussed in terms of two classical questions, how the person's evaluative attitude toward an object relates to her or his cognitions about the object and to her or his actions toward it. Neither link in the cognition-attitude-action chain is as strong as common sense suggests.

Attitudes and Cognitions

Close correspondence between evaluative attitudes and cognitions about the object is a basic assumption of the attitude research deriving from learning theory (Hovland, Janis, and Kelley, 1953), from attribution × evaluation theory (Cartwright, 1949; M. B. Smith, 1949; Fishbein, 1980), and from cognitive response theory (P. L. Wright, 1980; Petty, Ostrom, and Brock, 1981), though none implies the foolish "nothing but" position (Fishbein and Ajzen, 1975) that attitudes or behaviors are determined solely by information about the object. A half-dozen lines of evidence suggest that there is a small, statistically significant relationship between the favorability of cognitions about and the evaluative attitude regarding objects.

Static relationship between initial cognitions and attitudes. The simplest test of the relationship is to determine whether the person's current evaluative attitude toward an object agrees with the favorability of its currently salient characteristics. Supportive evidence has come from two lines of work, the classical attribution × evaluation approach, which uses passive responding (Ajzen and Fishbein, 1980), and the cognitive responses approach, which has the person actively generate the object's characteristics (McGuire, 1964, 1983; A. G. Greenwald, 1968a; Eagly, 1974; Petty and Cacioppo, 1981). Considering the embarrassing obviousness of the static prediction, it is surprising how low the obtained cognition-attitudes correlations are, unless the measures are especially painstaking (Fishbein and Ajzen, 1975; N. H. Anderson, 1981) or the issues especially involving (Petty and Cacioppo, 1979a).

Immediate postcommunication information acquisition and attitude change. Four dynamic approaches also yield modest positive correlations. First, postcommunication attitude change usually correlates significantly but lowly with amount of message information assimilated (McGuire, 1957; Eagly, 1974; Insko, Lind, and LaTour, 1976; Cacioppo and Petty, 1979; Baumgardner *et al.,* 1983) or own thoughts generated (Cacioppo, Harkins, and Petty, 1981; C. A. Anderson, 1983). Secondly, increasing message comprehensibility enhances persuasive impact, though the perceived pleasantness as well as greater information of the clearer message may be involved (Chaiken and Eagly, 1976; Wood and Eagly, 1981). Thirdly, attitude change is often reduced by communication variables that interfere with assimilation of message information, such as using uninvolving issues (Petty and Cacioppo, 1979a), using fewer arguments (T. D. Cook and Wadsworth, 1972), or when sources take unexpected positions (Wood and Eagly, 1981), though direct measures of the comprehension often provide no evidence of its mediating role (Borgida, 1978; Reyes, Thompson, and Bower, 1980). The effects of distraction during message presentation (Petty and Brock, 1981) and of personality variables like anxiety and self-esteem (McGuire, 1968d), though much studied, are harder to interpret in this regard since they both enhance and impede information assimilation by different mechanisms, implying overall nonmonotonic and interaction effects (McGuire, 1969a). Fourthly, the efficacy of the Socratic procedure in changing evaluations by manipulating the salience of the receiver's own thoughts about the object is further evidence for the relationship (McGuire, 1960a, 1981; Rokeach, 1975; Tesser, 1978; Sherman *et al.,* 1983).

Memory for content and the persistence of attitude change. Persistence of induced attitude change shows marginally significant correlations with memory for the inducing message contents (Watts and McGuire, 1964; T. D. Cook and Flay, 1978; Dreben, Fiske, and Hastie, 1979). Measuring recall of self-generated in addition to message-supplied cognitions increases the correlation slightly (A. G. Greenwald, 1968a; Calder, Insko, and Yandell, 1974; Higgins and Rholes, 1978; Sherman *et al.,*

1983). The lowness of the correlation may indicate that the unreliability of the change scores attenuates the correlation, or that evaluations and cognitions are separately stored with different decay rates (Watts and McGuire, 1964; Crano, 1977; N. H. Anderson, 1981), or that recall includes credulity-weakening information that impedes persistence of persuasive impact (Kelman and Hovland, 1953). Informative arguments are better recalled than uninformative ones (Schul and Bernstein, 1983).

In conclusion, the positive, statistically significant relationship between evaluative attitudes and information cognitions found in these half-dozen research approaches suggests that the two systems are connected, but the low magnitude of the relationship suggests that each system is largely determined by other variables.

Attitudes and Actions

Why study attitudes at all? Social psychology's long preoccupation with attitude change is surprising since the low correlations between attitudes and behaviors have been the scandal of the field for a half century (LaPiere, 1934). The continued interest derives in part from attitude change being interesting in its own right, aside from its impact on action. That "brainwashing" induced behavioral collaboration with their captors by over 90 percent of the U.S. Army men taken prisoner during the Korean War loses interest when subsequent studies show that this behavior is "only" overt compliance unrelated to changes in beliefs. Moreover, even if current attitudes are poor predictors of future behavior, they may be more convenient predictors than are current behaviors, since attitudes are less affected by changing situational factors, can be measured more easily and more reliably, and can be abstracted at varying levels of generality. Also, attitudes may stochastically predict behavior en masse even though the two show little within-individual correspondence (Katona, Strumpel, and Zahn, 1971).

Theoretical positions. Three causal patterns could produce a positive and the fourth a negative relationship between attitudes and actions. Most obvious is the information-processing conception (McGuire, 1972; Jaspars, 1978) that attitude change produces action change. Almost as plausible is hypothesizing the opposite causal direction, that action change leads to attitude change, as in John Wesley's contention that one preaches not because one believes but in order that one might believe, in the existentialists' tenet that one's activity precedes and leads to the creation of one's essence, and in the dissonance (Festinger, 1957; Wicklund and Brehm, 1976) and self-perception (D. Bem, 1972) theories. Thirdly, there may be a positive relationship because both attitudes and actions are coeffects of a more basic process such as a physiological mechanism (Kunst-Wilson and Zajonc, 1980; Cacioppo and Petty, 1983) or a set of generative rules (Harré and Madden, 1975). Results (M. Ross *et al.,* 1983), especially those using structural-equation modeling, suggest that all three causal paths may be involved (Reibstein, Lovelock, and Dobson, 1980; Kahle, Klingel, and Kulka, 1981; Bagozzi, 1982; Fredricks and Dossett, 1983). A fourth, hydraulic, theory predicts a negative relationship by depicting attitude change and action change as alternative outlets for a communication-induced need for change (McGuire, 1975) so that changing one's attitude may serve as a cathartic substitute for changing behavior (Burke, 1962; Patai, 1973). It receives indirect support from the finding that some communication variables have opposite effects on attitude change and on behavioral change (Leventhal, Singer, and Jones, 1965; Evans *et al.,* 1970). Dissonance, equity, and psychoanalytic theories also could predict a negative relationship between attitude change and action change, as when guilt leads to the posthumous enshrinement of a rejected leader or harassed spouse.

Empirical findings. Interest in the relationship between attitudes and actions has waxed and waned, it being a primary concern during the first, attitude measurement, peaking in the 1920s. During the second, attitude change, peaking in the 1960s a positive relationship between them was taken as self-evident and discussed mainly in the information-processing versus dissonance debate regarding its causal direction. The 1970s shift from theory relevance to practice relevance revived interest with a flurry of useful reviews (Wicker, 1969; Calder and Ross, 1973; Deutscher, 1973; McGuire, 1975; H. Kreitler and Kreitler, 1976; Schuman and Johnson, 1976; Ajzen and Fishbein, 1980; Cushman and McPhee, 1980). Since the issue came out of the closet a decade ago, reviews have been growing progressively more sanguine: Wicker's (1969) analysis of 31 studies had led him to conclude that there is little relation between the two and Abelson (1972) to wonder if attitudes are necessary at all; but then Kelman (1974) judged attitudes to be alive and well, H. Kreitler and Kreitler (1976) found that 30 percent of the

117 better studies show positive relationships, Schuman and Johnson (1976) concluded that there is a small-to-moderate positive relationship, and recently Ajzen and Fishbein (1980) reach a still more optimistic conclusion. My own dismal bottom line is that only within quite limited circumstances do attitudes account for more than 10 percent of behavioral variance except when they are correlated not with behavior per se but with self-reports of intention to behave (Albrecht and Carpenter, 1976; Fishbein and Ajzen, 1976; Songer-Nocks, 1976b).

The attitude-action correlation can be increased by both method and substance variables. It is enhanced by operations increasing the validity or reliability of the attitude or action measures such as conducting the research in the laboratory rather than the field (Hanson, 1980), using multiple items to measure the attitude (Hamersma, Paige, and Jordan, 1973; M. Snyder and Kendzierski, 1982) or to measure the behavior (Fishbein and Ajzen, 1974; Jaccard, 1979), measuring multidimensional (Schegel and DiTecco, 1982) and interpersonally shared aspects of attitudes (K. Thomas and Tuck, 1975), measuring attitudes and acts more similarly (Rokeach and Kliejunas, 1972; Ajzen and Fishbein, 1977), or within- rather than among-subjects (A. R. Davidson and Morrison, 1983), or closer in time (S. H. Schwartz, 1978; A. R. Davidson and Jaccard, 1979), or on comparable levels of situational constraint (J. A. Green, 1972). The attitude-action correlation can also be increased by substantive factors such as using more salient objects of thought (M. Snyder and Swann, 1976) or more proto-typical ones (Lord, Lepper, and Mackie, 1984), more consistent cognitive domains (Norman, 1975), more confidently held attitudes (Sample and Warland, 1973; Schuman and Johnson, 1976), more familiar action domains (Songer-Nocks, 1976a; Fazio and Zanna, 1981; Borgida and Campbell, 1982; R. E. Smith and Swinyard, 1983), more central, involving issues (Sivacek and Crano, 1982), etc. Dispositional characteristics such as a felt responsibility for one's own actions (S. H. Schwartz, 1973), self-monitoring (Zanna and Olson, 1982), self-esteem (Sjöberg, 1978), and maturity (Henschel, 1971) also enhance the size of the relationship.

Many independent variables interact to reduce the correlations between attitudes and actions by affecting one differently from the other. Conflicting attitudes within a person's belief system may have incompatible implications for a given action (Liska, 1974). Situational "hurdles" may affect the two differently, as when one's attitude is a private indulgence but one's action is scrutinized carefully because of its public consequences (Campbell, 1963; Raden, 1977). As suggested by Durkheim's grid/group theory (Douglas, 1982), the attitudes of one's significant others (Acock and DeFleur, 1975) and their expectations regarding how one should behave (Dulany, 1968; Fishbein and Ajzen, 1975) and one's sense of moral obligation (Gorsuch and Ortberg, 1983) also affect one's actions. Triandis (1977, 1980) identifies as many as seven factors to be taken into account in predicting action, and Sheth (1974) identifies four, while H. Kreitler and Kreitler (1982) distinguish the roles of four types of beliefs regarding goals, norms, self, and environment and Budd and Spencer (1984) show the advantages of taking individual differences into account. Empirical tests of these shopping list models indicate that actions are better predicted if one takes into account both the attribution × evaluation attitudes and the possibly interacting (Andrews and Kandel, 1979) perceptions of normative expectations of others regarding the act, but that little predictive power is added by taking still other factors into account (Raju, Bhagat, and Sheth, 1975; Saltzer, 1980). Behavioral intention plays a role in mediating attitude-action relations (Bagozzi, 1981), but the attitude itself is sometimes a better predictor of action, suggesting that attitudes may be related to actions by additional paths besides that of intentions (Bagozzi and Burnkrant, 1979; Bentler and Speckart, 1979; Fredricks and Dossett, 1983; Liska, 1984; Wittenbraker, Gibbs, and Kahle, 1983; but see Bagozzi, 1982).

ATTITUDE FORMATION

The remainder of the chapter will deal with attitudes in their dynamic aspects of formation and change. This first attitude formation section describes types of noncommunication forces that initially establish attitudes and then classes of situations in which communications from other people about the object produce subsequent attitude change.

ORIGINS OF ATTITUDES

Genetic endowment, transient physiological states, direct experience with the attitude object, and institutional situations are four attitude determinants that have been neglected by social psychologists but deserve mention if reality as well as research fashion is to be reflected.

Genetic Determinants of Attitudes

Attitude theorists typically abhor hypothesizing genetic influence—one of the few issues on which L. Doob (1947) and Chein (1948) agreed in their midcentury behavioristic versus humanistic debate is that attitudes are acquired through experience—but its very repugnance of the genetic hypothesis merits it special attention to compensate for likely neglect. Research on nonhuman animals provides evidence that genetic factors affect dynamic levels of both aggressive (J. P. Scott and Fuller, 1965) and altruistic (Allee, 1938; E. O. Wilson, 1975) proclivities. Some theorists (Schacter, 1982) go further and postulate a genetic influence also on the directive channeling of such proclivities into specific behaviors or toward particular targets. Without having to postulate Platonic idealism, transmigration of souls, Kantian synthetic a priori, Lamarckian evolutionism, or divine infusion, one could use natural variation and adaptive selection to account genetically for directive aspects of such attitudes as liking people with large pupillary dilation (Hess, 1975), feeling nurturant toward those with large head-to-body ratios (Alley, 1981) or disliking those ethnically different from oneself (Campbell, 1965; Holldobler and Lumsden, 1980). Even attitudes detrimental to personal reproduction such as altruistic self-sacrifice and homosexuality can be selectively bred into the race if its disadvantage to its possessor is sufficiently compensated for by its enhancing the survival of his or her own kind within a common gene pool (Campbell, 1975, 1979; E. O. Wilson, 1978; Boorman and Levitt, 1980). Quantitative models for the genetic determination of beliefs have been presented tentatively by Cavalli-Sforza and Feldman (1981) and vigorously by Lumsden and Wilson (1981).

Transient Physiological Factors

Aging and attitudes. Transitory physiological fluctuations associated with aging, illness, or body chemistry may also affect attitudes. Critical-period theorists have proposed that self-identity (E. H. Erikson, 1964) and the life-long political ideology of a generational cohort (Kertzer, 1983) are determined by the socioeconomic situations in one's adolescence or earlier (Mannheim, 1923, 1952; Bengtson and Laufer, 1974; Graubard, 1980), though empirical results are mixed on this issue (Adoni, 1979; Himmelweit *et al.,* 1981; Jennings and Niemi, 1981; Guttentag and Secord, 1983; Kertzer, 1983). Life span researchers report that men undergo dramatic midlife crises at about age forty with attitudinal changes including disillusionment with past values, preoccupation with inner concerns, and increased nurturance (Levinson, 1978). There is, however, considerable ideological continuity over the life span (Brim and Kagan, 1980; Eichorn *et al.*, 1981; Kahle, Klingel, and Kulka, 1981; D. O. Sears, 1983b), and such age-linked changes as do occur may reflect social rather than physiological changes (P. E. Murphy and Staples, 1979).

Attitudinal correlates of illness. Novelists associate certain illnesses with specific attitudes—euphoric optimism (*spes phthistica*) with tuberculosis, distrust with epilepsy, etc. Sontag (1978) has described a peculiar contrast in this metaphoric use of illness: A century ago when tuberculosis was a leading cause of death, its victims were favorably depicted in literature and popular imagination as almost too good for this world; but now that cancer has replaced tuberculosis as a leading cause of death, its victims are depicted unfavorably as constricted in capacity for love (Kaye, Appel, and Joseph, 1981). The attitudinal malaise widespread among nineteenth-century French writers (Baudelaire, Rimbaud, Maupassant, etc.), paradoxical in that it occurred at a time of more than typical social progress and economic prosperity, has been attributed by R. L. Williams (1980) to jaundiced outlooks produced by diseases prevalent among the era's authors. Life having a way of imitating art, these literary depictions deserve investigation.

Body chemistry and attitudes. Attitudes can be altered by various physiological manipulations including drugs (barbiturates, hallucinogens, caffeine), deprivations (of sleep, food, stimulation, etc.), hyperventilation, rhythmic stimulation, etc. Lobotomy and electroshock "therapies" may make the person apathetic toward previously cathected objects, remove moral inhibitions, etc. Other physiological treatments may lower susceptibility to persuasion by disrupting cognitive processing of the persuasive information or raise it by weakening the tendency to counterargue; central depressant drugs such as thiopental sodium and norepinephrine's MHPG metabolite (Maas, 1978) could reduce the impact of complex messages while enhancing susceptibility to simpler suggestions. Sensory deprivation can enhance persuadability, more by destabilizing initial attitudes than by producing a stimulus hunger that enhances attention to the attacking communication (Suedfeld and Borrie, 1978).

Direct Experience with the Object

Single significant experiences. That a streak of lightning can turn the village atheist into a saintly penitent, a traumatic childhood incident lead to a lifelong aversion (Loewenberg, 1971), and love strike at first sight are the stuff of legends, but this does not rule out their occurring also in life (Knapp, Stohl, and Reardon, 1981). Studies of war neuroses, childhood traumas, political zealotry, critical-period imprinting, religious conversion (R. F. Weiss, 1963; Rejai and Phillips, 1979; Paloutzian, 1981; Ullman, 1982) and product use (Olson and Dover, 1979) agree that a single significant experience can be critical (Read, 1983). Psychobiographical analyses report that critical childhood incidents account for the ideological appeal of Hitler's National Socialism (Merkl, 1980), at least to Protestant youth in 1932 Germany (Loewenberg, 1971), but leave unclear why the Hitler movement did not have comparative appeal to Catholic youth (Schellenberger, 1975; Broszat, 1981; R. F. Hamilton, 1982). Mass attitude shifts can be attributed to the Martin Luther King Jr. assassination (Riley and Pettigrew, 1976) and to media events (E. Katz, 1980).

Evidence for such one-trial attitude learning comes mainly from anecdotal research marred by *post-factum* rationalizations, selective recall, and lack of control groups. However, the possibility of sudden ideological shifts deserves sympathetic consideration to counterbalance the strong gradualist bias of twentieth-century science. Signs that this gradualist bias may be abating are illustrated by the paleontologists' cladist debate (Wade, 1981) and recent conjectures of evolutionary discontinuities in the rate of species' emergence (Stanley, 1981) and disappearance (Kerr, 1980; but see Archibald and Clemens, 1982). "Cataclysmic" explanations may increasingly withstand science's gradualist bias if mathematical analyses are developed (A. L. Robinson, 1982) to handle discontinuities better than has catastrophe theory (Kolata, 1977; Saunders, 1980; I. N. Stewart and Peregoy, 1983) and if scientists continue to experience the metatheoretical appeal of the Marxist-Leninist predilection for revolutionary rather than gradual change.

Effects of mere-exposure on liking. Conventional wisdom is that social movements, fads, and fashions exhibit a nonmonotonic inverted-U life cycle, a fad at first gaining popularity with increasing exposure until overexposure eventually destroys its appeal. However, Vanbeselaere (1983) reports the opposite "decrease followed by increase" relationship and the mere-exposure research (Zajonc, 1965; Schaffner, Wandersman, and Stang, 1981), with some rare exceptions (G. N. Cantor, 1968; Zajonc *et al.,* 1972), indicates that exposure results in monotonically increasing liking for the object, even when occurring to exhausting lengths, in a negative context, under low-recognition conditions (Moreland and Zajonc, 1979), and with stimuli only partially similar (Gordon and Holyoak, 1983). This clash between sophisticated expectations and experimental outcomes has been only slightly resolved by explorations of the presentation intervals (A. A. Harrison, 1977), multifactored theories of semantic satiation, arousal, and opponent-process motivation, and refined structural-equation analyses (Birnbaum and Mellers, 1979).

Interpersonal contact effects on liking.   Contact among strangers in natural living situations is generally found (Newcomb, 1961, 1981; Barrows, 1981) to increase familiarity with one another's attitudes, liking for each other, and attitudinal similarity, though the effects are small (Klineberg, 1981). Such contact-acquired attitudes may be stronger (Zohar, Cohen, and Azar, 1980) and be better predictors of behavior (Fazio, Zanna, and Cooper, 1978) than are attitudes based on third-party communication, though at some levels of cognition the indirect messages can have more impact than direct contact (P. Katz and Zalk, 1978; Olson and Dover, 1979; Tyler, 1980).

Results are less clear when the contact is forced and involves initially disliked others, a situation relevant both to theory and to social policy in the important area of integrating groups previously segregated on the basis of religion, class, ethnicity, gender, etc. (D. L. Hamilton, 1981; Bochner, 1982; N. Miller and Brewer, 1984). Experimenter bias in this research typically favors a main-effect finding that racial integration leads to intergroup liking and harmony, and yet a common finding is that interpersonal contact intensifies preexisting attitudes, making the initially positive more favorable and those initially ill-disposed more hostile (Amir, 1976). Research has suggested (Mumpower and Cook, 1978; Tajfel, 1981; Patchen, 1982) that contact conditions enhancing liking of the other race include that the integration be long sustained, felt to be voluntary, disclose ideological similarity, involve an intimate level of contact, provide mutual goal facilitation such as a favorable outcome, include intrinsically attractive others, and occur on an equal-status basis (Riordan, 1978) and with-

in a broader cultural context that is supportive of intergroup harmony. Even where such conditions have been approximated by heroic research efforts (S. W. Cook, 1978, 1979; D. L. Hamilton, Carpenter, and Bishop, 1984), the increase in liking tends to be modest.

Role of Social Institutions in Determining Attitudes
Many institutional structures have intended or unintended impact on attitudes by determining the stimulus situations to which the person is exposed, the response options available, the level and type of motivation, and the scheduling of reinforcements.

Parental introjection.   The importance of the person's early cultural experience (Zern, 1983), especially the childhood home, in establishing her or his lifelong conformity level and orientations is suggested by the abiding similarity of children's political attitudes to those of their parents and siblings (D. O. Sears, 1975; Berger, 1980; Himmelweit *et al.,* 1981; Jessop, 1982; but see Jennings and Niemi, 1974, 1981; Abramson, 1983), though such similarity could be due to cross-generational continuity of social conditions as well as to parental indoctrination. Conversely, parent-child dissimilarity could be evidence of parental influence (Kraut and Lewis, 1975), as when offspring carry out the parents' injunctions, following their preaching rather than their practice.

Peer group norms.   Nonkin institutions such as peer groups, schools, the "helping" professions (Lasch, 1977), and the mass media are probably diminishing the family's influence on ideology as modernization reduces parental control and prescriptiveness (Andrews and Kandel, 1979; Cherlin, 1981, 1983; but see Seward, 1978). Urbanization, population growth, and mass media technology that bring large numbers of homogeneously aged children into contact or expose them to common experiences have produced a distinctive centripetal youth culture as regards art forms, values, and lifestyles (Reisman, 1980; Conger, 1981; Veroff, Douvan, and Kulka, 1981; Yankelovich, 1981; Caplow *et al.,* 1982).

Ideological schooling.   School curricula include, besides knowledge and skills training, attitudinal indoctrination under such rubrics as "citizenship training" (Torney, Oppenheim, and Farnen, 1975) and "global outlook" (Barrows, 1981). School exposure has surprisingly little effect on knowledge and attitudes on specific issues (Feather, 1973; Barrows, 1981) but may affect general orientation (Rutter *et al.,* 1979; Olmsted and Smith, 1980). Length of schooling, with other demographic variables controlled, is associated with increase in ethnic tolerance (Schönbach, 1981) and respect for civil liberties but has negligible impact on other "liberal" values such as attitudes on the death penalty, abortion, and gun control (Hyman and Wright, 1979). Type of school also makes a difference: Himmelweit and Swift (1969) show that the British streaming of youths into different school systems has a long-term effect on their attitudes and behavior; Geber and Newman (1980) show comparable effects on Soweto's youth. Greeley (1977) shows that the relatively low racism of the Catholic public (Catholics being less anti-Jewish, anti-Protestant, and anti–Black than Jews, Protestants, and Blacks are anti-Catholic) declines even further with the number of years of education in Catholic schools, even when other factors are held constant (Greeley, McCready, and McCourt, 1976).

Legislating morality.   Doubt that society's laws affect the citizens' behaviors and attitudes is epitomized in Sumner's (1906) assertion that stateways cannot change folkways and Dwight D. Eisenhower's contention that one cannot legislate morality. A contrary view of internalization and "identification with the aggressor" is expressed in Lyndon B. Johnson's contention that if one grabs the enemy by his tie and pulls, his heart and mind will follow. Empirical data are equivocal regarding the effects of legalizing homosexual behavior on its judged morality (N. Walker and Argyle, 1964; Berkowitz and Walker, 1967), of civil rights legislation on southerners' attitudes on integration (Wirt, 1970; Rodgers and Bullock, 1972), and of the Schempp ruling outlawing prayer in the public schools on attitudes regarding school prayer (Muir, 1967; Birkby, 1969).

Mass media indoctrination.   In the past quarter century the mass media, primarily television, may be replacing home and school as society's primary institution for inculcating social values (Conway *et al.,* 1981), though below in the section on channel variables we shall discuss the surprising weakness of evidence regarding mass media effects on public attitudes.

Social control by art and rituals.   The efficacy of art (Frischer, 1982; Winner, 1982) and of ceremonial rites (Elliott, 1982; V. Turner, 1982) for influencing public attitudes and behaviors, as in Hitler's use of pageantry to seize public imagination (Riefenstahl, 1934), is implied by ethological, rule, and role theories (Goffman, 1959, 1976; Biddle, 1979; Harré, 1981). Ideological uses of ceremonies on the national scale have been described by Geertz (1980) in his theater state analysis of Balinese society, by Weissman (1981), Goldthwaite (1981), and Trexler (1980) in their descriptions of the communication of power through architecture and ritual in Medici Florence, by A. Guttmann (1981) on the political use of sports spectacles, by Luttwak (1977) as regards the Roman Empire's use of its army to control by ceremonial display of power rather than by actual application of military force, and by Rosen's (1982) description of the use of the U.S. armed forces in Vietnam after 1964 in accord with the limited war doctrine of sending a signal to the enemy rather than destroying enemy forces. Descriptions of current uses include Elliott (1982) on press performances as political ritual, C. Lane (1981) on the Soviet Union's use of May Day and other domestic rites to proselytize Marxism-Leninism, Guilbaut (1981) on the use of abstract expressionist art in the Cold War, E. Katz (1980) on the use of media events to manipulate public opinion, and Vélez-Ibañez (1983) on the rituals of marginality to control impoverished barrio populations. Bassiouni (1982), Schmidt and deGraaf (1982), and Weimann (1983) describe terrorists' use of violence as ritual communication, Ankerl (1981) the use of architecture to influence social relations, and Paige and Paige (1981) the use of reproductive rituals (puberty ceremonies, birth practices, etc.) in the war between the sexes.

Total institutions.   Dramatic attitudinal changes occurring in total institutions such as internment in hospitals, prisons, military camps, religious communities, cult or ethnic communes, etc., may involve thought reform procedures discussed below in "Intensive Indoctrination Situations."

TYPES OF PERSUASIVE COMMUNICATION SITUATIONS

Social psychological research on attitude change has ignored the four classes of determinants just considered in favor of social influence in the form of persuasive communications from other people about the object of thought. We shall briefly describe five types of situations—suggestion, conformity, group discussion, mass media, and intensive indoctrination—in which such communication is studied.

Suggestion Situations

Suggestion involves repetitive expression of an attitude or behavior without arguments for its adoption, as in hypnosis inductions or in advertising campaigns consisting of ubiquitous signs mentioning a product or its use. Useful reviews of the nature and correlates of suggestibility can be found in Hilgard (1965) and Barber (1969), and it is discussed with particular relevance to persuasion in Sarbin and Coe (1972), Hilgard (1977), Wagstaff (1981), and Council *et al.* (1983). Hypnotically suggested shifts in the person's liking for an object are followed within weeks by corresponding shifts in the availability of cognitions about the object (M. J. Rosenberg, 1960a). Suggestibility peaks at age ten and can be momentarily enhanced by preliminary softening-up demonstrations, by reassurance that being suggestible is not dangerous or a sign of weakness, and by reduced and monotonous stimulation, retroactive suggestions, hypnotizer prestige, prolonged repetition, etc.

Conformity Situations

Conformity situations include imitation, modeling, social facilitation (Zajonc, 1980b), etc., where the complier adopts an attitude or behavior verbally expressed or behaviorally exhibited by a source who did not argue for it or even indicate a desire for compliance, as when a person adopts the dress style of his or her age peers or work supervisor, or a research participant makes unusual responses similar to those just made by the other participants (Sherif, 1935; Luchins, 1945; Asch, 1956). Eagly (1978; Eagly, Wood, and Fishbaugh, 1981) distinguishes between conformity situations with and without group pressure. Conformity research is reviewed by Kiesler and Kiesler (1969) and Allen (1975).

Group Discussion Situations

In discussion situations sources not only express attitudes but present arguments in support of the position urged, often tailored to the motivation, capacity, and interest of receivers who can actively argue back or be asked to express agreement. Methodologically, the richness and realism of group discussion are attractive but introduce difficulties in controlling the many confounded variables unless one so thoroughly preprograms the members of the group that much of the naturalness is lost (N. H. Anderson and Graesser, 1976; J. C. Turner and Giles, 1981; P. B. Smith, 1983).

Mass Media Situations

Mass media situations discussed below under channel variables involve a one-way flow that reduces the receiver to a more passive mode than does group discussion, but typically they allow use of more skillfully produced messages from higher-status sources than can be studied in group discussion situations.

Intensive Indoctrination Situations

Inducing fundamental changes in belief systems may require the milieu control of total institutions (McEwen, 1980) that monopolize the stimuli presented, the response options available, the motivational states induced, and the reinforcements provided. Examples include one's early childhood home (G. S. Becker, 1981), brainwashing or thought-reform procedures in political prisons (Lifton, 1963), converting (Conway and Siegelman, 1978; Pavlos, 1982) or deprogramming members of religious "cult" communities (Patrick and Dulack, 1976; Shupe and Bromley, 1980; Melton and Moore, 1982), prolonged or even brief psychotherapy (Frank, 1973; Fisch, Weakland, and Segal, 1982), and living in youth gangs, asylums, military units, etc.

Effectiveness of intensive indoctrination may depend on three sets of procedures. The first set may produce an ideological vacuum in which new attitudes can emerge by weakening the person's old belief system through depersonalization, under- and over-stimulation, forced recall of details, confrontation with discrepant information that confuses and weakens confidence in one's previous frames of reference, etc. A second set of procedures, eliciting the desired new attitudes so that their occurrence can be rewarded, include monopolizing communication input, social facilitation by modeling compliance by others, putting the person in hypersuggestible dependency states by transference, regression, fatigue, etc., requiring active participation, presenting an inclusive and coherent belief system, etc. A third set of procedures, intended to heighten need states and allow reinforcement of such new attitudes as are elicited, include inducing high primary need states of hunger, fatigue, etc., arousing anxiety, raising socialization and self-esteem needs through deprivation, instigating guilt and shame, frustrating expectations, etc. Despite the tremendous effort put into such thought-reform procedures by proselytizing institutions, their success is largely confined to eliciting behavioral compliance while the person is kept within the total institution (Biderman, 1963; C. Edwards, 1979), a modest effect in keeping with the findings that psychotherapeutic impacts are limited (Prioleau, Murdock, and Brody, 1983).

Scientific research on attitude change typically involves analyzing complex situations like the five above into their component variables such as source attractiveness, message style, receiver personality, etc., that operate across most situations, and studying how each variable affects persuasive impact. The remainder of the chapter will describe the attitudinal effects of these cross-situational communication/persuasion relationships.

DIRECTIVE THEORIZING: THE COMMUNICATION/PERSUASION MATRIX

The literature on attitude change is vast: about 5 percent of the studies in a sample we drew from the 25,000 new books and articles listed each year in *Psychological Abstracts* deal with attitude change, indicating that over a thousand new studies are accumulating each year. Lipstein and McGuire (1978) list and classify over seven thousand attitude change publications that appeared in the applied literature during the past decade. If the scholar is to be carried forward rather than swamped by this vast outpouring of research, he or she needs a conceptual framework within which emerging knowledge of the communication/persuasion process can be organized. In this section a communication/persuasion, input/output matrix structure is used as a conceptual framework for describing the directive structure of the person that channels the communication input through the behavioral output steps. In a final section of this chapter the energizing motivational forces that drive this input/output processing will be described within a conceptual framework consisting of sixteen partial views of the dynamic aspects of human personality.

AN INPUT/OUTPUT ANALYSIS OF PERSUASIVE COMMUNICATION

An input/output matrix is an efficient framework for conceptualizing complex processes like communication-produced attitude change. The manipulable independent variables out of which a communication can be constructed provide the input column headings of the Table 1 matrix. The dependent variables, constituting a chain of mediating responses that lead to persuasion, provide the Table 1 matrix with its output row headings. Each cell entry describes the relationship between the independent communication variable that serves as its column input heading and the dependent persuasion-response variable that serves as its row output heading.

Components of the Model

Input communications variables. Communication has classically (Lasswell, 1948) been analyzed as a matter of who says what, via what medium, to whom, and directed at which kind of behavior, thus dividing input communication variables into five broad classes of source, message, channel, receiver, and target, each of which is subdivisible into successive orders of subclasses, as discussed in the next five sections. These communication input variables are the components out of which the practitioner constructs his or her persuasion campaign and are the attitude change hypotheses' independent variables which the researcher can manipulate to test theories.

Output steps in persuasion. The output side of the matrix, consisting of the successive response steps that the receivers must be induced to take if the communication is to have its intended persuasive impact, provides the mediating and dependent variables of attitude change hypotheses. We shall here use a twelve-step output analysis, enough to constitute a provocative checklist without becoming distractingly detailed. Longer and shorter output lists are available (McGuire, 1966a, 1978, 1980b). At this point we shall simply clarify each of the twelve output steps by mentioning some frequently used measures that tap persuasive effectiveness only through that step. First, if the communication is to have any impact, the intended recipient must be tuned in so that he or she is in a position to be exposed to it. Exposure hardly assures persuasion, but each year $10 billion worth of television ads are placed on the basis of Nielsen exposure ratings (Frank and Greenberg, 1980). Given that exposure occurs, the second needed step is that the message get the person's attention, as measured by contemporaneous eye movements or changes in EEG potentials, by subsequent ad recognition tests, etc. A third step is that the person become sufficiently engaged by the message so that subsequent steps can occur and be rewarded; it is measurable by rating scales, nonverbal indices of liking, or physio-

TABLE 1
An Input/Output Analysis of the Communication/Persuasion Process
That Underlies the Chapter's Analysis of the Directive Aspects of Attitude Change

	INPUT FACTORS (INDEPENDENT VARIABLES)				
OUTPUT STEPS (MEDIATING AND DEPENDENT VARIABLES)	SOURCE CREDIBILITY ATTRACTIVENESS POWER . . .	MESSAGE APPEALS STYLES INCLUSIVENESS . . .	CHANNEL	RECEIVER	TARGET
1. Tuning in that produces exposure to the communication					
2. Attending to it					
3. Liking, interest in it					
4. Comprehending its content (learning what)					
5. Generating related cognitions					
6. Acquiring relevant skills (learning how)					
7. Agreeing with the communication position (attitude change)					
8. Storing the change in memory					
9. Retrieving the relevant material from memory					
10. Decision making on the basis of the retrieved material					
11. Acting in accord with the decision made					
12. Postaction consolidating of the new pattern					

logical arousal traces such as heart rate, pupil dilation, voice prints, etc. (Waid and Orne, 1981; Cacioppo and Petty, 1983).

Given that interest has been aroused, a fourth step of absorbing the information in the message becomes possible, measurable by an a priori readability index (Flesch, 1948; Klare, 1963) or by an a posteriori recall or recognition test of message contents (Watts and McGuire, 1964; T. D. Cook and Flay, 1978). A fifth step of generating and retrieving related cognitive content already possessed can be measured by content-analyzing the receiver's accompanying verbalizations as regards counterarguments and additional supportive arguments (McGuire, 1960c, 1964; P. Wright, 1980). A sixth step of skill acquisition is involved when persuasive impact requires not only learning what but also learning how, as when a public health campaign against smoking must not only motivate but also convey skills for complying (Sackett and Haynes, 1976; A. J. Meyer *et al.,* 1980). A seventh acceptance step involves the receivers' agreeing with the supportive information evoked by the message, typically measured by the ubiquitous attitude change opinionnaire. The use of this attitude change step 7 as the ultimate dependent variable in most basic research is regrettably premature relative to the behavioral payoff step, but applied advertising research usually stops even earlier with measures of step 3 (ad liking) or step 4 (ad recognition), and media-use policy decisions are typically made on the basis of step 1 exposure measures.

When long-term impact is the objective, a retention step 8 is needed, and then at decision time there is need for a ninth step of search and retrieval of the convincing arguments or at least of the agreement response (Fazio *et al.,* 1982) if it is separately stored (N. H. Anderson, 1981). A tenth step is actually utilizing this retrieved material in decision making, and an eleventh step is then behaving (by voting, buying, donating blood, or whatever) in accord with this decision. Long-term adherence is enhanced by a step 12 of postbehaviorally consolidating the compliant act, either by intrapersonal cognitive reorganization that links the compliant act more securely within the person's overall belief system (McGuire, 1960c, 1981; A. G. Greenwald, 1968a; P. L. Wright, 1975) or by interpersonal proselytizing of other people that leads to self-indoctrination and supportive feedback from the new converts. This long list of output steps, while an overintellectualization of the persuasion process, serves the heuristic function of calling re-

searchers' and practitioners' attention to the large variety of mediating steps whose elicitation may enhance ultimate persuasive impact.

Evaluation of the Communication/ Persuasion Matrix

Uses of the analysis.   This Table 1 matrix, by analyzing complex persuasive communication into manageable components, provokes new insights into the process. The input side of the matrix serves the researcher as a checklist of additional independent variables that may interact with and limit the hypothesized one and it suggests to the practitioner further options for strengthening the communication. The output side alerts the researcher to a whole series of intervening processes that might mediate obtained relationships or cause artifacts or nonmonotonic and interaction effects and it provides the practitioner with a diagnostic checklist for detecting weak points in the message that need bolstering.

Nonobvious implications for avoiding common communication fallacies.   The commonsensicality of the communication/persuasion matrix may make it so obvious an analysis that it could have gone without saying, but making it explicit helps avoid a half-dozen errors commonly made in persuasion theory and practice. First, by calling attention to the long chain of effect-attenuating mediating output steps, it corrects the frequently held great-expectation fallacy that the manipulation of some independent (communication) variable will make a sizable difference in some distal output variable; e.g., how type of argument will affect behavioral compliance step 11 will be the difference between the minuscule products of two sets of ten probabilities so that the research must be designed to pick up small changes. Secondly, the matrix reveals the danger of the distal-step fallacy, e.g., predicting impact on step 11 (in terms of the desired behavior such as voting, donating blood, or buying a product) by extrapolating from the measured effect on a remote earlier step such as ad liking (step 3) or attitude change (step 7). Thirdly, the matrix also warns against the neglected-mediator fallacy of thinking in terms of just one or two momentarily salient mediators when predicting how a communication variable will affect a late step, as when the practitioner decides whether to use some message variable such as humor or metaphorical language just from a consideration of its expected facilitation of attention (step 2) or of yielding (step 7) without considering also its possible interference with comprehension (step 4) or with retrievability (step 9). The matrix provides a column of cell entries under any communication variable that expands the researcher's consciousness to other mediating steps via which the communication variable under consideration may have quite different effects on persuasion.

Fourthly, the matrix reveals that communication variables often have compensatory opposite effects on persuasion via different output steps: e.g., while receivers' intelligence protects them against persuasion by reducing gullible yielding (step 7), it increases persuadability by enhancing attention and comprehension (steps 2 and 4). A fifth, golden-mean corollary (McGuire, 1961b, 1968a), that these compensatory mediators will result in a nonmonotonic inverted-U relationship between the input communication variable and the ultimate persuasion output, helps avoid the "more is better" fallacy, as when the communicator reasons that if evoking the hearer's smile slightly enhances message impact, then producing a belly laugh will make it irresistible. A sixth, situational-weighting implication of the matrix is that since any communication variable tends to enhance persuasive impact via some mediating steps and reduce it via others, its net effect depends on situational factors that determine how much each of the steps contributes to the variance in the ultimate behavioral payoff step (McGuire, 1968b).

Shortcomings of the communication/persuasion matrix analysis. The matrix has some shortcomings on the input side in that the five classes of independent variables interact, making it hazardous to focus on just one category at a time. Also, the interesting input variables distribute unequally over the categories so that the efficiency of information equipotentiality is lost. More serious problems arise on the output side, because in actual persuasion situations some steps may be omitted or may occur in sequences other than the commonsensical one shown in the Table 1 matrix. Mass media ads and other uninvolving messages may affect attitudes or behavior with very little comprehension (Krugman, 1977; Zajonc, 1980a; Mellars, 1981; Petty and Cacioppo, 1981); a message may continue to produce attitude change after its interest value has waned (Grass and Wallace, 1969); decisions may be made without information retrieval (Nisbett and Wilson, 1977); behavioral compliance may

occur without decision, as in posthypnotic amnesia; and subliminal communications too brief or faint to reach the awareness threshold may under laboratory conditions produce attitude change (W. R. Wilson, 1979; Dixon, 1980; Bargh and Pietromonaco, 1982), though their use may be impractical or unethical in mass advertising (T. E. Moore, 1982). Still, the overly detailed Table 1 analysis of the output provides an "as if" checklist useful in calling attention to numerous mediating response steps through which a communication's impact can be predicted or enhanced (Bagozzi, 1982).

More dramatically worrisome is the occurrence of reversals of the common-sense sequence of output steps (McGuire, 1969b; Ray, 1973). In selective exposure, agreement (step 7) determines exposure (step 1) rather than the reverse; for the totalitarian personality (A. G. Greenwald, 1980) at least, agreement may act back on perception and memory; in forced compliance (Festinger, 1957; Wicklund and Brehm, 1976) behavioral change (step 11) under specifiable conditions precedes attitude change (step 7); agreement may precede comprehension as warned by Isaiah (7:9) "Unless you believe, you will not understand"; a person may know whether she or he likes or dislikes a message before she or he knows what it says (Kunst-Wilson and Zajonc, 1980; Zajonc, 1980a, 1984; but see Lazarus, 1984); and step 5 inferences may be made simultaneously with step 4 learning (Michotte, 1946; Garnham, 1982).

Another output problem is that it is difficult, though not impossible (Wegener, 1982; Cacioppo and Petty, 1983; Eagly and Chaiken, in press), to get independent measures of successive steps such as attention and comprehension. But the basic output problem—and the scandal of attitude research for the past half century, as discussed above in the attitude structure section—is that early output steps often have low correlations with later steps, as when information assimilation (step 4) poorly predicts attitudinal change (step 7) and attitude change poorly predicts behavioral change (step 11). It seems likely that the Table 1 linear information-processing depiction of output will be drastically revised during the coming "systems" era of attitude research.

Alternative and revised analyses of the process. Alternative analyses of the input communication side of the process go back to Aristotle's topics, ten categories, and four causes, to the medieval schoolmen's analysis of the knowable in terms of seven questions (*quis, quid, quibus, ubi, cur, quomodo,* and *quando*), and to the journalists' six questions (who, what, when, where, why, and how). Burke (1962) analyzes communication into scene, act, agent, agency, and purpose. L. Doob (1961) divides it into twelve components grouped into four triads in a reverberating feedback circuit. Progress is especially needed in developing more meaningful second- and third-order subdivisions to correct current hodge-podge groupings such as "vividness" (S. E. Taylor and Thompson, 1982). For example, a richer subdividing of message style and semantics may grow out of current progress analyzing verbs and other parts of natural speech (Schank, 1975; McGuire, 1984a).

As regards alternatives on the output side, slightly different analyses have been suggested by McGuire (1966a, 1976b, 1978, 1980b) and Flay, Di Tecco, and Schlegel (1981). More localized refinements are Upmeyer's (1981) division of comprehension step 4 into internal representation versus external presentation (response tendency), or the step 4 division by Folger and Woodall (1982) into comprehension and meaning, or by Ortony (1978) into integration and inference making. Other subdivisions of individual steps include Marascuilo and Zwick's (1983) division of the attitude change step 7 into separate shift and certainty processes, Sandell's (1977) distinguishing acceptance and yielding, Watts and McGuire's (1964) and Sandell's (1977) subdivisions of memory step 8, Zanna and Fazio's (1982) breakdown of retrieval step 9, and Irle and Katz's (1982) breakdown of decision step 10. More sophisticated path analyses (Bagozzi, 1982) of the output steps go beyond the simplistic unilinear ordering described here by identifying alternative pathways (as when attitude change step 7 affects behavioral step 11 by paths that circumvent behavioral intention step 10, by indentifying feedback loops that would account for "reversals" mentioned above, and by tracing different pathways for high versus low-involving issues (Krugman, 1965, 1977; Shiffrin and Schneider, 1977; Chaiken, 1980; Petty, Cacioppo, and Schumann, 1983; Petty and Cacioppo, 1984a, 1984b; Liska, 1984) or for degrees of social pressure (Tesser, Campbell, and Mickler, 1983).

SOURCE VARIABLES' EFFECTS ON PERSUASIVE IMPACT

Source research has focused on how attributed characteristics affect communication impact and so we shall describe only briefly how actual sources differ in persuasive style and impact. Wheeless, Barraclough, and Stewart (1983) describe a wide variety of compliance-gaining tactics. Variations in rhetorical techniques used by U.S. presidential candidates have been increasingly studied since the 1960 institutionalization of the "great debates" (Kraus, 1979, 1983; Bitzer and Rueter, 1980), though assessment of their differential effects remains crude. Suedfeld and Rank (1976) and Tetlock (1981) have shown that stress level and power attainment affect the complexity of political rhetoric and that this rhetorical style affects power retention. Studies of individual differences in persuasive tactics and impact (McLaughlin, Cody, and Robey, 1980) have focused on differences due to ingratiation (E. E. Jones and Wortman, 1973), Machiavellianism (Christie and Geis, 1968; F. L. Geis and Moon, 1981), self-presentation and other impression-managing tactics (Tedeschi, 1981; Schlenker and Goldman, 1982) and on ethnic and gender differences, as discussed in a later section.

The Credibility-Attractiveness-Power Analysis

Source variables are usually manipulated by attributing one or another characteristic to the purported source of a given message. The usual division of these variables into source credibility, attractiveness, and power reflects Kelman's (1961) three modes of attitude change (internalization, introjection, and compliance) and the classical cognitive-affective-conative analysis of attitudes. Internalization occurs insofar as a receiver, trying to form an objectively correct attitude and so concerned with the validity of the information, judges the source's credibility from his or her apparent competence and trustworthiness, i.e., knowledge of the truth and motivation to reveal it. Introjection- (or identification-) based persuasion occurs to the extent that receivers are trying to enhance their self-images by identifying with or being in a positive relationship to a source made attractive by his or her similarity, familiarity, likability, etc. Compliance, the third mode of persuasion, occurs when receivers are trying to obtain rewards or avoid punishments, which makes source power the critical cue, as inferred from the source's control over rewards and punishments, concern about the receiver's agreement, and ability to monitor this agreement. There is some empirical corroboration for this tricomponential analysis (Berlo, Lemert, and Mertz, 1970; Insko, Drenan, and Solomon, 1983), though the effects of the three tend to be correlated and to converge over time (B. Erickson *et al.,* 1978). Some alternative analyses overlap with these three, like Aristotle's logos-pathos-ethos distinction, while others introduce additional dimensions such as legitimacy (McCroskey and McCain, 1974).

Source Credibility Variables

Source competence determinants and effects. Perceived source credibility and therefore persuasive impact increase with general knowledgeability cues such as high level of education, intelligence, social status, professional attainment, familiarity with the issue, etc. (Hass, 1981), even when the cues are minimal (Hastie, Penrod, and Pennington, 1984), as peripheral as tallness (S. Feldman, 1971) or erect posture (Weisfeld and Beresford, 1982), and only distantly relevant to the issue (Aronson and Golden, 1962), though relevance helps (Sigall and Helmreich, 1969). Credibility cues become especially important when low involvement allows the receiver simply to accept or reject the conclusion on the basis of source competence without having to study the arguments (H. H. Johnson and Scileppi, 1969; Chaiken, 1980), when the credibility cues come early in the message before the arguments have been studied (Mills and Harvey, 1972; C. D. Ward and McGinnies, 1974), or when credulity problems arise because an extreme position is being advocated (Sternthal, Phillips, and Dholakia, 1978). Sources being incidental aspects of the communication, their effects are lessened by distractors (Sigall and Helmreich, 1969) and by time passage (Watts and McGuire, 1964; T. D. Cook *et al.*, 1979).

Still, source knowledgeability per se, when not reinforced by other characteristics like trustworthiness, contributes surprisingly little to persuasive impact (Kelman and Hovland, 1953; Bochner and Insko, 1966; McGinnies and Ward, 1980). The expected positive relationship can even be reversed by confounded variables such as the remoteness that ordinary inexpert receivers may feel from expert sources (Huston, 1973), so that a humanizing pratfall show of incidental ineptness can enhance the persuasiveness of an otherwise overly distant expert (Aronson, Willerman, and Floyd, 1966; Deaux, 1972b). A source may be most effective when he or she is slightly rather than very superior, as when children are more influenced by those just a little older than themselves than by age peers or much older children (Stukát, 1958). Expertise can also backfire when the source is made to appear personally involved in the issue and so less objective or when favorable cognitive responses are already salient (Harmon and Coney, 1982).

Cues for source trustworthiness. Besides seeming expert enough to know the truth, the source must seem trustworthy enough to want to report it. Trustworthiness derives from the source's apparent sincerity, disinterestedness in the outcome, lack of intent to persuade, etc. (Wheeless and Grotz, 1977; McGinnies and Ward, 1980). Sources appear especially sincere when arguing against their own self-interest (Walster, Aronson, and Abrahams, 1966; Eagly, Wood, and Chaiken, 1978), against the obvious preference of their audience (Mills and Jellison, 1967; Eagly, Wood, and Chaiken, 1978), or without awareness of the audience's presence (Walster and Festinger, 1962; but see L. Mann, Paleg, and Hawkins, 1978). Nonverbal cues for untrustworthiness are discussed below under channel variables.

Institutional as well as individual sources differ in trustedness: Science, medical, and academic groups tend to elicit a high degree of confidence, the military, police and judiciary somewhat less, followed by business and media leaders, with political officeholders and labor union officials trusted still less (Etzioni and Diprete, 1979; Gallup, 1981). Institutions tend to be more negatively judged than their average member (Ladd and Lipset, 1980). The ordering of various institutions in public confidence is fairly stable, but the general level of confidence has been falling since the mid 1960s (Lipset and Schneider, 1982). In July 1979 U.S. President Jimmy Carter reacted strongly to a perceived moral crisis when the Harris poll reported a general decline of public confidence in all U.S. institutions from 1973 to 1976, but the trend for that period was neither uniform nor unusually pronounced (C. F. Turner and Krauss, 1978; Converse *et al.*, 1980).

Forewarning effects on the subsequent communication's impact. The most interesting trustworthiness manipulation is forewarning of source's intent to persuade, which diminishes persuasive impact via some mediators and enhances it via others (McGuire, 1961a, 1969a). Persuasion-reducing effects of forewarning include its provoking rehearsal of belief-supporting cognitions, derogation of the attacking arguments when they arrive, dislike for the source, avoidance of the message, etc.; persuasion-enhancing effects include face-saving anticipatory belief change (McGuire and Millman, 1965), ingratiation of an attractive or powerful source (Mills and Aronson, 1965), clarification of the point of the message, etc. This complexity of mediators leads to predictable interaction effects, nonmonotonic relationships, and situational differences that depend on which mediators contribute most to the variance.

As regards interaction effects, McGuire (1964, 1969a) pointed out that forewarnings decrease attitude change to the extent that motivation or opportunity to assimilate belief-supporting arguments is enhanced, as by incubation time prior to the attack (Freedman and Sears, 1965; Hass and Grady, 1975; Petty and Cacioppo, 1977), freedom from distraction (Watts and Holt, 1979), worry about the belief's vulnerability (L. R. Anderson and McGuire, 1965), or initial commitment (Allyn and Festinger, 1961; Gaes and Tedeschi, 1978; Petty and Cacioppo, 1979b). Like other transitory discounting cues, forewarning depresses immediate attitude change impact but allows it to emerge later (Watts and Holt, 1979). Direct measures of the mediators confirm the operation of the hypothesized processes, forewarned receivers showing more thoughts on the issue (McGuire, 1964; Brock, 1967; Petty and Cacioppo, 1977) and more derogation of the attacking arguments when they come (McGuire, 1964; Papageorgis, 1967; Hass and Grady, 1975).

Anticipatory attitude change effects of forewarnings. Most interesting of the forewarning effects is "anticipatory change" such that the warning itself, before any attack arrives, produces anticipatory attitude change. It was first demonstrated by McGuire and Millman (1965), who attributed it to the forewarned receiver's expecting to be influenced and so saving face or self-esteem by an immediate attitude shift before the attack actually comes which reduces apparent gullibility by indicating that he or she agreed with the message position all along. The anticipatory change effect and various explanations of it have been studied by three strategies: varying the kind of forewarning, directly measuring the hypothesized mediators, and testing for predicted interactions. Anticipatory change is greater if one is warned not only that an attacking communication exists but also that one will be exposed to it and especially that one's own attitude will then be measured (Papageorgis, 1967; Cialdini *et al.,* 1973; Hass and Mann, 1976; Gaes and Tedeschi, 1978; Saltzstein and Sandberg, 1979). When the warning mentions the side to be advocated, the anticipatory change tends to be toward that side; when the side is not mentioned in advance, anticipatory change tends to be toward neutrality (Cialdini *et al.,* 1973; Hass, 1975; M. Snyder and Swann, 1976; Tetlock, 1983a), each an appropriate ego-defensive strategy for minimizing apparent communication-induced change.

McGuire and Millman's (1965) ego-defensive explanation of anticipatory change is also supported by intensifying interactions with social anxiety (R. G. Turner, 1977), perceived source expertise (Fitzpatrick and Eagly, 1981), issue familiarity (Dinner, Lewkowicz, and Cooper, 1972), and matters of taste rather than fact (McGuire and Millman, 1965). The strategy of directly measuring the hypothesized mediators has shown that receivers do lose esteem by appearing persuadable (Cialdini, Braver, and Lewis, 1974) and that preparatory defenses are stimulated by forewarning (McGuire, 1964; Cooper and Jones, 1970; Cialdini and Petty, 1981; McFarland, Ross, and Conway, 1984). An ego-defensive rather than argument-generation mechanism is suggested by the finding (Cialdini *et al.,* 1973) that anticipatory change is greater the more immediately the attack is expected and by the snapback finding (Cialdini and Petty, 1981) that anticipatory change on uninvolving attitudes dissipates when the person is told that the forewarned attack has been canceled, especially in public conditions (McFarland, Ross, and Conway, 1984).

Source Attractiveness Variables

Source attractiveness becomes critical to persuasive impact to the extent that the receiver is motivated to enhance sense of self, social reputation, or gratifying role relationships by identifying with admired sources and introjecting their attitudes. It receives the fullest analysis as a social influence factor in Janis's (1983) development of the "referent power" notion. The three most studied cues for source attractiveness are familiarity (whose operation is discussed above under direct experiences), likability, and similarity, which will be discussed here.

Persuasive impact of liking for source. The common-sense assumption that sources are more persuasive if they are liked is supported (Sampson and Insko, 1964), especially when the advocated position is undesirable (Eagly and Chaiken, 1975) or the arguments are weak (Brandstätter, Davis, and Stocker-Kreichgauer, 1982). Many source variables that contribute to attractiveness have been identified (Berscheid and Walster, 1978; M. Cook, 1981), with recent research emphasis on physical appearance, nonverbal behavior (see below under channel variables), and the life history of friendships and romantic attachments (Newcomb, 1981; Hendrick and Hendrick, 1982; Kelley, 1983). Physical attractiveness enhances persuasive impact regardless of gender of source or receiver (Horai, Naccari, and Fatoullah, 1974;

Dion and Stein, 1978; Chaiken, in press), perhaps due not only to beauty per se but to other factors such as self-esteem, intelligence, etc., which—life not being fair —typically do accompany physical attractiveness (Chaiken, 1979). However, negative persuasion-reducing stereotypes are also associated with beauty (Dermer and Thiel, 1975), and other cues can outweigh beauty in determining liking (LaVoie and Adams, 1978). Several researchers (Lavrakas, 1975; S. B. Beck, Ward-Hull, and McLear, 1976; Milord, 1978; Gitter *et al.*, 1983; Franzoi and Shields, 1984) have identified facial and physique cues that define physical beauty (for those who haven't noticed on their own). Comparisons can be odious, as when males find average women less attractive after watching stereotypically beautiful women (Kenrick and Gutierres, 1980).

Rather than stressing the obvious positive relationship between source attractiveness and persuasiveness, the contextualist approach (McGuire, 1983) focuses more imaginatively on the paradoxical negative relationships that obtain between liking and persuasive impact in seven special circumstances; insufficient justification, traumatic initiation, praise from a stranger, gain/loss processes, identification with the aggressor, closer scrutiny, and daring to deviate. Under insufficient-justification conditions a person induced to perform a noxious behavior (many grasshoppers have been eaten in this research) shows more internalized attitude change when complying with a disliked than a liked source, presumably because with a liked source the yielding can be justified as graciousness but with the disliked source one must change one's personal attitude to allow the compliant behavior to be attributed to personal choice in order to reduce dissonance (Zimbardo *et al.*, 1965) or to manage impressions (Schlenker, 1975). Dissonance theory also suggested the traumatic-initiation reversal such that one likes more and presumably conforms more to groups that one had to suffer to join (Aronson and Mills, 1959; Gerard and Mathewson, 1966; but see Finer, Hautaluoma, and Bloom, 1980).

In contrast to the common sense valence notion (McArthur and Zigler, 1969) that social reinforcement is more effective when the reinforcing source is a familiar liked person, there is some evidence also for the reverse "praise from a stranger" prediction that the less expected approbation from an enemy can be more influential by offering more information, hedonic satisfaction, or anxiety reduction (Gewirtz and Baer, 1958; Aronson and Linder, 1965; A. Miller *et al.*, 1980). A related "praise

from a former enemy" or gain/loss notion (Aronson, 1969a; Brothen, 1977; deCarufel and Schopler, 1979; but see Conolley, Janis, and Dowds, 1982) is that the likability and persuasiveness of a source reflects his or her rate or direction of change rather than his or her absolute level of praise or agreement (Lombardo, Weiss, and Buchanan, 1972).

The "identification with the aggressor" (A. Freud, 1946) reversal involves one's own membership group's becoming a negative reference group and one's adopting the norms of one's tormentor; e.g., German prisoners in the early 1930s National Socialist concentration camps were reported to adopt the behaviors of their brutal guards (Bettelheim, 1960), and black children were reported to identify with and prefer white over black dolls (K. B. Clark and Clark, 1947), though recent studies indicate that black children now prefer black dolls (Hraba and Grant, 1970; Winnick and Taylor, 1977) and that more care is needed in equating the dolls (H. G. Greenwald and Oppenheim, 1968; Klein, Levine, and Charry, 1979). Involved here may be a "just world" blaming-the-victim process (Ryan, 1971) or resentment against one's own kind, who are, however unintentionally, the reason for one's suffering. The "closer scrutiny" effect occurs when a more attractive or credible source elicits closer attention to the message, thus enhancing the impact of strong arguments but lessening that of weak arguments (Heersacker, Petty, and Cacioppo, 1983; Pucket *et al.*, 1983).

The "daring to deviate" reversal involves a group's more accepted leaders being able to deviate from the group's norm more than can members who feel only marginally accepted and thus not able to take the risk (Dittes and Kelley, 1956; Giordano, 1983; but see Ridgeway, 1981), though a reactance process may also be involved (J. Brehm and Mann, 1975). On the other hand, a leader representing a group may argue for the group's consensus rather than his or her own personal position (E. E. Davis and Triandis, 1971).

The contextualist approach (McGuire, 1983) can enliven banal topics such as source likability's, similarity's, etc., relationships to persuasiveness if one first explains the trite relationship by multiple theories. Then, since one can always imagine some contexts in which any relationship might obtain, one stands the banal hypothesis on its head and explains the contrary relationship also by diverse theories. Then one can test not only the original obvious relationship but also, exploiting the heuristic provocativeness of each theory, its additional predictions regarding (1) mediators of the relationship, (2) other independent variables' interactions with attractiveness in affecting the relationship, (3) aspects of attractiveness most related to persuasiveness, and (4) aspects of persuasiveness most affected by attractiveness.

Persuasive impact of source similarity.   Typically, attraction and persuasive impact increase with source-receiver similarity (Simons, Berkowitz, and Moyer, 1970; Byrne, 1971; Stoneman and Brody, 1981), both real and ideal (Wetzel and Insko, 1982) and extending to permanent assortative mating (Lesnik-Oberstein and Cohen, 1984). We shall discuss the kind of similarity that is most efficacious, the causal directions of the relationship, its theoretical interpretations, and circumstances that reverse this obvious relationship.

Considerable research has been done on the relative importance of demographic versus ideological similarity—e.g., whether a white segregationist would like better (and be more persuaded by) a black segregationist or a white integrationist (Rokeach, 1960; Triandis, 1961). Ideological similarity tends to be more important for abstract evaluation of the other person, while demographic similarity is more important for behavioral acceptance (Triandis, Davis, and Takezawa, 1965; J. E. Robinson and Insko, 1969), with the importance of ideological similarity gaining over ethnic recently in the United States (Moe, Nacoste, and Insko, 1981; Insko, Nacoste, and Moe, 1983). In more traditional and contentious societies demographic tends to catch up with ideological similarity (E. E. Davis, 1975), but even in a country as polarized as Lebanon, ideological remains more important than denominational similarity (Yabrudi and Diab, 1978). Effects of demographic similarity, such as they are, derive in part from a cognitive-polarizing effect (Osgood, 1979) such that people infer that sources demographically different from themselves also differ ideologically (Byrne and Wong, 1962; Stein, Hardyck, and Smith, 1965). In keeping with distinctiveness theory (McGuire and Padawer-Singer, 1976; McGuire, 1984a), similar others are perceived as more similar to oneself and more likable if contrasting dissimilar others are also present in the situation (Hensley and Duval, 1976).

Causality operates in both directions: Perceived similarity leads to liking and liking leads to exaggerating perceived similarity (Newcomb, 1961; Byrne and Blaylock, 1963; Moreland and Zajonc, 1982). This latter perceptual distortion is asymmetrical, the attitudes of liked others being assimilated more than the dissimilarity of disliked others is exaggerated (Granberg and Brent, 1980), perhaps because balance needs and consensus needs reinforce each other in the liked case and mutually cancel in the case of disliking.

The obvious positive relationship between source similarity and persuasive impact is derivable from numerous theories, including Burke's (1962) strategy-of-identification formulation, Heider's (1958) balance theory, Byrne's (1971) acquired reinforcement interpretation, Festinger's (1954) social comparison theory, Kelman's (1961) identification process, and Sherif and Hovland's (1961) perceptual assimilation/contrast theory. The contextualist approach (McGuire, 1983) invites focusing on circumstances producing the opposite effect, a paradoxical negative relationship such that source similarity leads to less persuasive impact. This can occur when the receiver interprets the source's acting similarly as a manipulative attempt at ingratiation (E. E. Jones and Wortman, 1973), or as frustrating the receiver's desire to be different (McGuire and Padawer-Singer, 1976; C. R. Snyder and Fromkin, 1980; Santee and Maslach, 1982), or as worrisome in an obnoxious similar other (S. E. Taylor and Mettee, 1971), or when opinions of the similar others are discounted as likely to be based on information redundant with one's own (Goethals and Nelson, 1973).

Source Power Variables

Persuasion occurs through the compliance process when the receiver wants to get a reward or avoid a punishment from a powerful source. Initially, it may involve changing only behavior that the source can observe, but internalized attitude change tends to follow if the overt compliance occurs with long duration, high volition, etc., as discussed below in the section on receiver participation. Compliance-eliciting power may derive from many cues (Wheeless, Barraclough, and Stewart, 1983), three sets of which will be discussed in turn: the source's perceived control over the receiver's rewards and punishments, concern about the receiver's complying, and ability to observe whether compliance occurs.

The source's perceived control over reinforcements.   A source's perceived power and influence grows with means and fate control (Kelley and Thibaut, 1978), with being perceived as having the will as well as the capacity to punish nonconformity (Heilman, 1976; Galbraith, 1983), with having high-power status (Kipnis, 1976; Komorita and Moore, 1976), and with the force of unanimous numbers (Fehrenbach, Miller, and Thelen, 1979; Latané and Wolf, 1981; Wolf and Latané, 1983). However, increasing the number of sources can backfire when their arguments are poor (Harkins and Petty, 1981a), when noisy hecklers evoke sympathy for the source (Sloan, Love, and Ostrom, 1974), when a single ally helps the receiver resist a multitude (Asch, 1956; W. N. Morris and Miller, 1975), and when a monolithic minority imposes its will on the majority (Moscovici, 1980; Mugny, Papastamou, and Sherrard, 1982) especially if the minority is consistent (Tanford and Penrod, 1984), has an acceptable position (Papastamou, 1983), and the compliance is private (Maass and Clark, 1984). Power to reward is often declared to be more efficacious than power to punish, but this may be confined to low-volition situations (Heilman and Garner, 1975; Axelrod and Apsche, 1982). The source can communicate power by nonverbal assertiveness cues, as discussed under channel variables. The legitimacy of the source's power adds to persuasive impact even when no additional coercive force is involved (Michener and Burt, 1975), and legitimacy is imputed with frightening ease (Milgram, 1974; Max Rosenbaum, 1982).

Dominating-through-weakness reversals of the usual relationship can occur when a disadvantaged source evokes greater compliance through sympathy (Lesk and Zippel, 1975; Levitt and Kornhaber, 1977), when a bargainer employs a "my hands are tied" ploy (Friedland, 1983), and when the greater credibility of a mild threat evokes more compliance than a severe threat (Aronson, Carlsmith, and Darley, 1963; Zanna, Lepper, and Abelson, 1973), unless the receiver's background experience makes the severe threat credible (Etzioni, 1966; Swann and Pittman, 1975; Dembroski and Pennebaker, 1977).

The source's perceived concern about compliance. Powerful sources do not always want compliance, courtiers having learned that power wielders from Henry Plantagenet to Richard Nixon occasionally prefer that their orders (and enemies) not be executed. People may prefer not being imitated by those of lower status, as when older children resent imitation by younger (Thelen and Kirkland, 1976; Thelen *et al.,* 1984). Compliance in-

creases when the powerful source does wish it, as in a common-fate situation (Deutsch, 1949) or where unanimity is necessary (Gerard, 1953) and when the desire is clearly communicated (Gaes and Tedeschi, 1978; H. H. Kelley and Thibaut, 1978).

The source's ability to scrutinize compliance. The powerful source's perceived ability to detect deviance, as when the receiver perceives the source as having a (bogus) pipeline for detecting his or her true position, usually increases compliance (E. E. Jones and Sigall, 1971; Evans *et al.,* 1978; Riess, Kalle, and Tedeschi, 1981), though surveillance can induce reactance (S. Brehm and Brehm, 1981), as with males needing to show independence (Eagly, Wood, and Fishbaugh, 1981). While power sources produce more public than private change, considerable private change occurs as well (Heilman, 1976).

Community power, diffusion of innovation, and leadership studies. Studies of community power and spread of innovations within large social systems (T. N. Clark, 1975; Kipnis, 1976; Polsby, 1980; Silk and Silk, 1980; L. A. Brown, 1981; Crano, Ludwig, and Selnow, 1981; R. L. Savage, 1981; E. M. Rogers, 1982b) have identified influentials in domains such as politics, consumer behavior, prescription of new drugs, adoption of agricultural innovations, and making use of new contraceptive procedures. Recent developments include the use of population-genetics mathematical models (Cavalli-Sforza and Feldman, 1981; Lumsden and Wilson, 1981) and the linking of micro- and macroprocesses (DeRivera, 1968; Janis, 1973; Tetlock, 1981). The disproportionate influence of elites and other single-minded minorities has been described by Moscovici (1980) and in the "spiral of silence" research (Noelle-Neumann, 1980a).

Effects of Source Demographics

Effects of the source's demographic characteristics are reducible to the credibility, attractiveness, and power dimensions just discussed. As regards source gender, males command more attention (J. Robinson and McArthur, 1982) and have slightly more influence than females (Lincoln, 1977; Dion and Stein, 1978), even on female receivers, especially those high in dogmatism (Fry, 1975). Physical beauty adds to female sources' persuasive impact on male receivers, but female sources make less use than males of physical attractiveness (Sigall, Page, and Brown, 1971; Dion and Stein, 1978) and other situational advantages (Komorita and Moore, 1976). Sex stereotypes held by both men and women attribute to males a higher rank on persuasiveness-related traits such as logicality, objectivity, ability to separate feelings and ideas, independence, aggressiveness, decisiveness, leadership, etc. (Broverman *et al.,* 1972). When the source's biological gender is varied orthogonally to assertive style variables (such as businesslike hairstyle and clothes, a loud tone of voice, strong direct gestures, etc.), the attitude change impact is determined more by the source's style than by his or her biological gender (Newcombe and Arnkoff, 1979; Mayo and Henley, 1981). Female sources may appear as less persuasive because research typically uses "male" topics (Cacioppo and Petty, 1980; Eagly and Carli, 1981) and because females' deception cues are more easily detected (Rosenthal and DePaulo, 1979). The "spiral of silence" work of Noelle-Neumann (1980a) suggests that males have more impact on public opinion because they are more willing to speak out even when their position is unpopular, giving their side an exaggerated appearance of strength, which recruits others to jump on the bandwagon.

Source ethnicity has little net effect on majority white males but may make more difference for minority and female receivers (Aronson and Golden, 1962; Banks *et al.,* 1977; Ramirez, 1977; Clore *et al.,* 1978; Stoneman and Brody, 1981), in keeping with the distinctiveness theory (McGuire *et al.,* 1978) prediction that people in low-frequency categories are more sensitive to that trait in self and others.

Output Steps That Mediate Source Effects

Content learning theories.   This first of three explanations attributes source effects to their impact on the early information-registration steps 2 and 4 of the communication/persuasion matrix. Its simplest version posits a monotonic positive relationship such that the more believable, attractive, or powerful the source, the greater is the attention to and learning of message content. This version receives little empirical support: Message content is usually learned as well with negative as with positive sources (McGuire, 1969b; T. D. Cook and Flay, 1978).

Somewhat more support is found for a "lazy receiver" variant of the usual learning theory (McGuire, 1969b) predicting a nonmonotonic relationship such that sources unknown or neutral to the receiver elicit the highest content learning, because coming from a highly positive (or highly negative) source gives the re-

ceiver a cue for economically accepting (or rejecting) the message's conclusion without bothering to study the arguments; but with an unvalenced source the receiver has to study the content to judge if the arguments warrant accepting the conclusion. Inferential support comes from the finding that for low-involved receivers source credibility is more critical than argument strength (Chaiken, 1980), while argument strength becomes more important with high receiver involvement (Petty, Cacioppo, and Schumann, 1983), issue relevance, and number of arguments (Brandstätter, Davis, and Stocker-Kreichgauer, 1982; Petty and Cacioppo, 1984b).

Content evaluation theories.   This second set of theories attributes source effects to step 3, their biasing the receiver's impression of the message's quality. Support comes from findings (McGuire, 1964; Gillig and Greenwald, 1974; Ronis *et al.,* 1977) that persuasive arguments are judged less impressive when attributed to a suspect source and that source effects are greater when source identification precedes rather than follows the message arguments (Mills and Harvey, 1972; C. D. Ward and McGinnies, 1974).

Content acceptance theories.   A third explanation of source effects is that they operate via acceptance step 7, affecting the amount of counterarguing against the message content. McGuire (1964) proposed this actively cognizing concept of the receiver as an alternative to the passive learner concept of Hovland (1954) and his followers which implies the simple content-assimilation theory of source effects. The resulting cognitive-response research (Petty, Ostrom, and Brock, 1981) shows that the amount of counterarguing is reduced by enhancing source trustworthiness and expertise (Gillig and Greenwald, 1974; Petty and Cacioppo, 1979b). Interaction implications are also confirmed: Source trustworthiness effects are enhanced if, between source mention and message presentation, an interval is introduced in which counterarguing can occur (Freedman and Sears, 1965; Petty and Cacioppo, 1977), by freeing receivers from counterarguing-interfering distractions during message presentation (Watts and Holt, 1979), and by using uninvolving issues with which there is little intrinsic motivation to counterargue.

Effects of Message Pairing on Source Valence

Numerous consistency theories (discussed in the final section of this chapter) predict that a discrepant source-message pairing affects attitude to source as well as to issue but with an assertion constant (Tannenbaum, 1956) such that receivers, particularly women (Steiner and Rogers, 1963), adjust attitudes less toward source than toward issue. Pairing a source repeatedly with undesirable positions gradually uses up clout by teaching the receiver to pay less attention to this source of painful information (McGuire, 1957; Zanna, Klosson, and Darley, 1976).

MESSAGE VARIABLES' EFFECTS ON PERSUASIVE IMPACT

Message variables have been heavily studied because of the many theoretical issues they raise and input options they offer, so we must selectively limit the present discussion to six subclasses of message variables: type of arguments and appeals, message style, inclusions and omissions, ordering of material that is included, amount and spacing of the material, and extremity of the position advocated.

Types of Arguments and Appeals

Types of arguments. For two and a half millennia rhetoricians have been analyzing types of arguments, but surprisingly little empirical work has been done on the comparative effectiveness of different argument structures (G. R. Miller *et al.,* 1977; Dion and Stein, 1978; McLaughlin, Cody, and Robey, 1980; Weber and Crocker, 1983). Aristotle in *Rhetoric* and *Topics* divides intrinsic arguments into logos, pathos, and ethos, with logos being further subdivided into inductive appeals versus deductive arguments, the latter using any of twenty-eight kinds of reasoning. Alternative argument typologies have continued to be suggested ever since: Schopenhauer describes thirty-six tactics used in debates, and Andrén (1980) and M. L. Geis (1982) give content analyses of arguments used in advertising, and Cialdini (1984) describes the arguments people actually use to influence one another. Reynolds and Burgoon (1983) present a long list of potential argument types. Danziger (1976), Fogelin (1982), Perelman (1982), and Capaldi (1979) provide contemporary informal logics of argument types, Barth and Krabbe (1982) a more formal one, and D. S. Solomon (in press) a how-to manual. P. E. Corcoran (1979), Vedung (1982), Snow (1983), Martel (1983), and B. Weinstein (1982) describe how media evolution and other cultural changes have affected

political rhetoric. Analyses of argument types shade into argument styles (O'Barr, 1982; Ghiglione and Beauvois, 1983).

Mechanisms of argument-type effects are suggested in the attitude structure section of this chapter in discussions of the McGuire/Wyer probabilogical model (McGuire, 1981), decision-making models (Janis and Mann, 1977), heuristics of thought (Tversky and Kahneman, 1981), information integration (N. H. Anderson, 1981), etc. Anecdotal examples may have more impact than general statistics (S. E. Taylor and Thompson, 1982) because of their enhancement of steps 2 and 4, attention and comprehension. Argument type interacts strongly with content, such as the verb's positivity and subjectivity (Kanouse and Abelson, 1967; Sandell, 1977).

Positive versus negative appeals. Many target issues such as urging health-preserving behavior allow use of either promise or threat appeals (Milburn and Watman, 1981; Weimann, 1982a). The complexity of predicting whether the positive or negative approach will be more effective is illustrated by their contrasting effects on the several output steps. The threatening negative appeals may produce more bureaucratic compliance (Weimann, 1982a), higher immediate intention to comply, and more reported compliance, but positive appeals may yield better recall of the recommendations and more actual compliance weeks later (Evans *et al.,* 1970; K. H. Beck, 1979). Positive appeals promote coping with the danger, while negative appeals promote coping with the affect (Monat and Lazarus, 1977; Leventhal and Nerenz, 1983), though this latter maladaptive avoidance can be reduced by announcing that the receiver's compliance can be monitored (Evans *et al.,* 1981) or by presenting vividly how the danger can be averted (R. W. Rogers and Mewborn, 1976; Leventhal, Meyer, and Nerenz, 1980).

Positive appeals have the desired effect by increasing the likelihood both of the receiver's making the desired response when he or she is in the stimulus situation and of keeping him or her in the stimulus situation. Negative, anxiety-arousing appeals have a more complex effect (Janis, 1967; Axelrod and Apsche, 1982) in that, as intended, they discourage making the punished response in the situation but also have the counterproductive effect of motivating the person to avoid the situation, as when a fear appeal to induce safer driving in teenagers backfires by causing the young person to repress thoughts of car accidents or resentfully to reject the message as coming from a hostile Establishment. These antagonistic processes would tend to produce a nonmonotonic relationship, with maximum attitude change and behavioral compliance occurring at intermediate levels of threat (McGuire, 1968a). Implied interaction effects also are found: The efficacy of threat decreases with the unavailability of coping responses (Leventhal, Singer, and Jones, 1965; R. W. Rogers and Mewborn, 1976), with chronic anxiety (Millman, 1968; Lehmann, 1970), with coping styles that involve managing affect rather than threat (M. J. Goldstein, 1966), with feelings of physical invulnerability (Niles, 1964; Leventhal and Watts, 1966), and with life-styles that lower the personal relevance of the danger (Berkowitz and Cottingham, 1960; K. H. Beck and Davis, 1978). However, implied interactions with message complexity are not confirmed (Millman, 1965; R. P. Singer, 1965), suggesting that fear appeals may disrupt short-term less than longer-term information processing. Low-fear appeals tend to catch up to high-fear messages as weeks pass (Insko, Arkoff, and Insko, 1965; Evans *et al.,* 1970; R. W. Rogers, Deckner, and Mewborn, 1978). That threat operates through this complex mediation is indicated also by direct measures of the intervening processes (Leventhal, Watts, and Pagano, 1967; Evans *et al.,* 1970; Wyer and Frey, 1983) and by causal model analysis that detects multiple pathways (R. W. Rogers and Mewborn, 1976).

When threat is analyzed in terms of the expectancy $\times$ values model, a given level of threat can be induced by varying either the likelihood or the magnitude of the danger, leading to debates on whether the certainty or severity of punishment has more crime-deterring effect (R. W. Rogers and Mewborn, 1976; Slovic, Fischoff, and Lichtenstein, 1978; R. W. Rogers, 1983). How the risky situation is framed (Tversky and Kahneman, 1981) may also affect the relative importance of likelihood and magnitude.

Message Style

Conjecturing about literary style has been a popular humanistic exercise since Aristotle and other classical rhetoricians engaged in it but is only beginning to be studied empirically (Sandell, 1977; R. L. Russell and Stiles, 1979; Kanouse and Hays-Roth, 1981; Norton, 1983) to identify its basic dimensions (Carroll, 1960; Moerk, 1973) and to ascertain the impact of stylistic variables such as the four discussed here: clarity, forcefulness, literalness, and humorousness.

Clarity of delivery.   Unclarity could affect impact in either direction through each of several mediating steps. It could diminish persuasive impact by reducing argument comprehension (output step 4), by lowering perception of source competence and thus reducing argument acceptance (output step 7), or by being aesthetically bothersome to the extent of reducing attention to and liking for the message (steps 2 and 3). On the other hand, unclarity could increase impact by putting demands on the receivers' active information processing and evoking more involvement (step 3) or by interfering with critical evaluation (step 5). The mediator mix should depend in part on whether clarity is manipulated by varying message organization and delivery fluency which affect perceived source competence or by source-irrelevant mechanical interference during transmission. In keeping with this analysis, manipulating clarity by coherence and delivery fluency affects attitude change via source credibility more than via message comprehension (McCroskey and Mehrley, 1969), while manipulating it mechanically by background noise affects attitude change via comprehension (Eagly, 1974).

Forcefulness of delivery.   Intensity of presentation (defined by speech researchers as characterized by greater vocalic amplitude, more variations in pitch, loudness, or rate, and use of flamboyant metaphors, intensifying adjectives, and aggressive *ad hominem* criticisms) could increase attitude change by attracting attention (J. Robinson and McArthur, 1982) or by enhancing clarity, or it could decrease impact by seeming too importuning. Hence it shows up as interaction effects such that with a high-trust (G. R. Miller and Basehart, 1969) or a high-prestige (Pearce and Brommel, 1972) source or a low-involved receiver (Mehrley and McCroskey, 1970), the more dynamic style has greater effect; but with a low-trust or low-prestige source or highly involved receiver, an appropriately modest, subdued style produces more persuasion.

Some "vividness" manipulations (S. E. Taylor and Thompson, 1982) involve forcefulness. Concrete information may have more impact on factual issues and abstract information may have more impact on affective issues (Kanouse and Abelson, 1967), and concrete case histories have a slight advantage over abstract statistical arguments (Ginosar and Trope, 1980; Hamill, Wilson, and Nisbett, 1980; Reyes, Thompson, and Bower, 1980). Enhancing vividness by using obscure and unusual words decreases persuasive impact, at least in frustrated receivers (Bowers, 1963; Carmichael and Cronkhite, 1965), but the use of extreme modifiers increases clarity and impact (McEwen and Greenberg, 1970; Burgoon and Miller, 1971).

Speed of delivery.   Research varying the speed of presentation up or down from the normal 150-words-per-minute speaking rate shows that speedier delivery enhances persuasive impact by making the source appear more intelligent, more knowledgeable, and (surprising in view of the fast-talking used-car salesman stereotype), more sincere (N. Miller *et al.,* 1976; Apple, Streeter, and Krauss, 1979). It has also been shown that mechanical time compression of ads by up to 40 percent increases their impact via steps 3 and 4, interestingness and comprehensibility (LaBarbera and MacLachlan, 1979), but may interfere with step 5, generating related cognitions (Schlinger *et al.,* 1983). Faster delivery of electronic ads might both enhance their impact and also save costs by reducing the amount of media time that would need to be bought.

Figurative language.   The judged intensity of prose (Bowers, 1964) and its persuasive impact are enhanced by figurative language in the form of analogies, both literal and figurative (McCroskey and Combs, 1969), and by similes and especially metaphors, particularly when sustained over several sentences (Bowers and Osborn, 1966; Reinsch, 1974). There is some support for Aristotle's and Cicero's hypothesis that metaphors add to persuasive impact by increasing the perceived competence of the source (Reinsch, 1974; J. T. Johnson and Taylor, 1981) and increasing attention (Jordan, 1972); also, aesthetic pleasingness (as suggested by Quintilian) may be involved. Study of the persuasive effects of additional figures of rhetoric (Lanham, 1968; Billow, 1977; Honeck and Hoffman, 1980), types of words (Percy, 1982), and visual images (Rossiter and Percy, 1983) used in communications should increase during the impending flourishing of attitude structure research.

Effects of humor.   Widespread use of humor in 42 percent of television ads (Markiewicz, 1974), in most political orations (Volpe, 1977), etc., demonstrates the general conviction that humor increases persuasion, perhaps via mediators such as attention (Zillman *et al.,* 1980), message liking, better comprehension and retention (R. M.

Kaplan and Pascoe, 1977), more agreement being obtained by putting the receivers in good humor (Bryant *et al.,* 1981; O'Quin and Aronoff, 1981), by increasing source attractiveness, etc. On the other hand, humor could diminsh persuasive impact by distracting attention from the message or making the source seem clownish. A recent rash of humor reviews suggest still additional mediating and interacting variables (Chapman and Foot, 1976; Gruner, 1978; McGhee, 1979; Paulos, 1980; S. Fisher and Fisher, 1981; N. H. Holland, 1982; McGhee and Goldstein, 1983).

The punch line of negative results is disappointing after this big buildup (Sternthal and Craig, 1973; Markiewicz, 1974; Gruner, 1978; Brown and Bryant, 1983). The rare significant main effects of humor on attitude change are as often negative as positive. Even more worrisome, the implied interaction effects with source credibility, initial disagreement, channel used, etc., seldom appear, nor do the implied effects on mediating variables such as message interest, retention, or source evaluation. In principle, the humor variable cries for more research attention but the past empirical yield offers little promise.

Inclusions and Omissions from the Message

The three most studied message inclusion variables will be discussed in turn: explicitly drawing the conclusion in the message versus leaving it implicit, dealing with opposition arguments (and weak points in one's position) versus ignoring them, and presenting versus omitting less strong arguments for one's own side.

Implicit versus explicit conclusions.   The probabilogical studies (McGuire, 1981) show that communications produce considerable change on unmentioned related attitudes, but the question here is whether a comparative impact would have been produced had these related issues been explicitly mentioned in the message. The purported efficacy of active participation in nondirective therapy and memory research suggests greater impact from not mentioning the related beliefs, leaving them to be drawn by the receiver. However, attitude change research has generally shown, on the contrary, that persuasive impact is lessened if the conclusion, however obvious, is left implicit so that it must be drawn by the receiver. Perhaps in attitude change situations people have less motivation and opportunity than in a therapeutic situation to do the cognitive work needed for drawing an implicit conclusion: Marrow and French (1945), Thistlethwaite and Kamenetzky (1955), and Fine (1957) provide suggestive evidence that those few receivers who are able and willing to draw the conclusion for themselves do tend to be more persuaded than those for whom the conclusion was explicitly presented in the message. Tests of predicted mediator effects and of interaction effects with source credibility, message complexity, etc., could evaluate other possible mechanisms, such as that leaving the conclusion implicit makes the source seem less organized or confident.

Ignoring versus dealing with opposition arguments. A rule of thumb in political campaigning is that one should keep on the offensive, ignoring rather than refuting opposition charges, but the current upsurge in comparison advertisements and empirical research reflects doubt about the wisdom of such stonewalling. It is better to acknowledge and refute opposition arguments, even before presenting arguments for one's own side, if they have been made salient by familiarity (Hass and Linder, 1972) or controversiality (R. A. Jones and Brehm, 1967) or by the receiver's intelligence or initial opposition. Explicitly refuting opposition arguments is especially important for conferring resistance to subsequent attacks (McGuire, 1964). Despite advertisers' worries about mass media "clutter," there is little evidence that the presence of competing messages diminishes impact (Ray and Webb, 1976; Baumgardner *et al.*, 1983).

Omitting versus including one's own weak arguments. Averaging models imply that one should use only one's strongest arguments, while additive models imply that including weak arguments also enhances impact. As discussed above under attitude structure, current evidence supports a weighted-averaging model (N. H. Anderson, 1981).

Ordering of the Message Contents
Ordering was usually discussed in classical rhetoric with regard to the sequencing among the half-dozen or so parts into which the theorist divided the total persuasive communication, as in Plato's *Phaedrus,* Aristotle's *Rhetoric,* Quintillian's *Oratoria* (G. A. Kennedy, 1980), Bali oratorical practice (Hobart, 1975), etc. Empirical research, however, has ignored this broad issue and focused instead on five more specific ordering issues, which will be discussed in turn.

Stating the message's basic position at the outset or the end. Stating one's basic position (or at least specifying the issue) at the start adds to impact by clarifying the issue and thus facilitating comprehension, by enhancing acceptance-raising credibility in making the source seem more open, trustworthy, better organized, and more expert, and by attracting the attention of those initially interested, predisposed to agree, or looking for a position on the issue. But stating one's position at the outset has disadvantages through other mediators by lowering suspenseful interest, emphasizing source partisanship and contentiousness, or alienating those initially opposed. These complexities have been only partially investigated by direct measures of the implied mediators (message liking, comprehension, acceptance, etc.) or implied interaction effects (with source expertise, message complexity, etc.).

Refuting opposition arguments before or after presenting one's own side. The conditions described above as calling for mention rather than ignoring of opposition arguments also favor dealing with them early in the message, even before presenting arguments for one's own position. Opposition arguments should be mentioned early when controversiality, receiver intelligence, or issue involvement makes them salient (Hass and Linder, 1972), when reassurance of source knowledgeability is needed, when receivers are already aware of the opposition arguments (Blakeney and MacNaughton, 1971), and when early mention is unlikely to commit the receivers to the opposition position (Freedman and Fraser, 1966; DeJong, 1979).

Ordering of own arguments with respect to their strength. Given that both strong and weak supporting arguments are to be used, the question arises as to whether attitude change is maximized by using the climax order of starting with the weak arguments and building up to the strong or by the anticlimax order of putting one's best foot forward by starting with the strong. Empirical results on the issue are mixed (Sponberg, 1946; Gulley and Berlo, 1956), as is to be expected since each ordering facilitates persuasion via some mediating output steps and impedes it via others, a situation requiring that research be designed to detect implied interactions, mediator, and monmonotonic effects.

A persuasive advantage for the climax (strong arguments last) ordering is predicted by perceptual contrast, linear-operator, and door-in-face theorizing. Perceptual contrast makes a weak argument appear even weaker when it is preceded by a strong argument (Helson, 1971; Pepitone and DiNubile, 1976; Simpson and Ostrom, 1976). The linear-operator and other proportional-change theories (N. H. Anderson, 1959) algebraically demonstrate superiority for the climax order. The door-in-face technique (Cialdini *et al.,* 1975) weakly favors the climax order in that rejection of the poor early argument would leave the receiver feeling more obliged to accept the subsequent strong argument.

On the other hand, the serial-position curve, waning-of-attention, low-ball commitment, foot-in-door, and self-redefinition theories imply that the strong arguments should be presented first. The "low-ball" commitment technique (Cialdini *et al.,* 1978) implies anticlimax superiority in that the receiver's commitment or obligation evoked by the initial strong argument (Burger and Petty, 1981) will motivate acceptance even of weak arguments to bolster the commitment. Anticlimax efficacy can also be derived tortuously from the foot-in-door theorizing (Freedman and Fraser, 1966) in that self-redefinition as a believer after receiving the strong arguments would tend to enhance acceptance of the subsequent weak arguments, especially when the initial acceptance is costly (C. Seligman, Bush, and Kirsch, 1976) and enough time elapses between strong and weak arguments to allow self-redefinition to occur (Cann, Sherman, and Elkes, 1975; Callero and Piliavin, 1983; Schwarzwald, Bizman, and Raz, 1983), though this self-redefinition mechanism is elusive (Gurwitz and Topol, 1978; Foss and Dempsey, 1979; DeJong, 1981).

Ordering of confirming arguments with respect to desirability. When a message must deal with a series of issues, a "first the good news, and then the bad" ordering enhances attitude change by reinforcing the receiver's initial attention and comprehension responses (McGuire, 1957), increasing source attractiveness, and leaving the receiver in an accepting euphoria (Hornstein *et al.,* 1975). On the other hand, it produces a perceptual contrast such that the undesirable positions may seem even worse when they come after the good news (N. H. Anderson, 1959).

The primacy-recency ordering effects. A between-message ordering issue arises when messages from different sources are presented, arguing for opposite positions on an issue. Whether there is a primacy or a recency effect—whether the first or the last message has the persuasive advantage—depends on which mediators contribute most to the variance in the given situation, since some mediators make for a primacy and others for a recency effect. Hence research should be designed to detect interaction and mediator effects rather than main effects. The earlier information-processing steps usually give the advantage to primacy, to having the first say. Attention tending to wane, manipulations that prolong attention do increase the relative impact of the second side (Crano, 1977; Tetlock, 1983b). Perception and learning also favor the first side, since the earlier information establishes a set to which the subsequent information is assimilated, attributed to a change-of-meaning mechanism by the classical perceptual theorists (Sherif, 1936; Asch, 1956) but more recently to other processes (Helson, 1971; Lingle and Ostrom, 1979; N. H. Anderson, 1981; Watkins and Peynircioğlu, 1984). N. Miller and Campbell (1959) analyze the issue in terms of proactive inhibition and forgetting, deducing that shortening the interval between the sides makes for a primacy effect and shortening the interval between the second side and the impact measure favors recency. These spacing effects are found more clearly with respect to recency and on measures of attitude change rather than on the learning mediator (N. Miller and Campbell, 1959; N. H. Anderson, 1965; W. Wilson and Miller, 1968), suggesting that there may be parallel processing.

As regards the acceptance mediator (step 7), there should be less suspicion of intent to persuade while hearing the first side; hence, any primacy advantage should be lower with controversial issues (Schultz, 1963; Lana, 1964). The linear-operator and other proportional-change models (N. H. Anderson, 1959) also predict a recency advantage, which increases as the discrepancy size widens; the door-in-face phenomenon tenuously implies recency (Cialdini *et al.,* 1975). These recency effects may be ephemeral, confined to a superficial component (N. H. Anderson and Farkas, 1973).

Amount of Message Material

For practitioners the persuasive effect of repetition is the most pressing of all research issues (Sawyer, 1974; Naples, 1979), but the topic was long neglected by basic researchers as lacking theoretical relevance. The learning theory orientation out of which the second, attitude change, peaking developed at midcentury implied that attitude change parallels content learning and would follow a similar negatively accelerated growth curve as more material is presented. Currently, appreciation that attitude change does not closely parallel content learning and renewed interest in practical issues like advertising "wearout" have stimulated research on the effects of repeated presentation of the same argument and of increasing the number of different arguments presented, topics that we shall discuss in turn.

The effects of repetition.   The amount and persistency of persuasive impact increases for the first several repetitions (R. F. Weiss, 1968; T. D. Cook and Wadsworth, 1972; Krugman, 1972; Fehrenbach, Miller, and Thelen, 1979), but further repetitions beyond the first three or so add little and may even diminish impact (L. B. Becker and Doolittle, 1975; Cacioppo and Petty, 1979; Calder and Sternthal, 1980). With regard to which mechanisms underlie this leveling off, attention and interest steps 2 and 3 decline with continued repetition (Appel, 1971; Craig, Sternthal, and Leavitt, 1976), unless the message is varied (Grass and Wallace, 1969), and negative thoughts about the target (step 5) decrease with the first few repetitions but then increase if repetition continues (Cacioppo and Petty, 1979; Belch, 1982), while positive thoughts show a slight opposite trend (but see the "mere-exposure" results discussed above). Repetition can backfire by making the weakness in poor arguments more obvious (Cacioppo and Petty, 1984).

Effects of the number of different arguments.   Adding new arguments has some obvious persuasive advantages over simply repeating old arguments with regard to retaining attention, increasing the amount of information presented, etc., but also the possible disadvantages of information overload, eliciting competing responses, distracting clutter, etc. Because this number-of-arguments variable has opposite persuasive impacts via the several mediators, it needs to be studied in designs that include interaction effects and mediator measures (Petty and Cacioppo, 1984b). Regarding attention, the agenda setting research (McCombs, 1981) implies that topic salience increases with amount of mass media discussion, at least until an asymptote is reached after a month of coverage (Winter and Eyal, 1981). Presenting more arguments increases brand salience and ad recall, though some do not find that it increases attitude change (J. L. Simon, 1969; H. H. Johnson and Watkins, 1971; Strong, 1974), while others do (Leventhal and Niles, 1965; Calder, Insko, and Yandell, 1974), especially after a delay (T. D. Cook and Insko, 1968). Increasing the num-

ber of arguments stimulates positive thoughts and first decreases and then increases negative thoughts about the conclusion and the learning of message arguments (McCullough and Ostrom, 1974; Cacioppo and Petty, 1979; Harkins and Petty, 1981a; Belch, 1982) but not linkages to own values (Rothschild and Ray, 1974). Regarding optimal spacing, Strong (1974) and H. Simon (1982) found that a pulsating bunching of ads is more effective than distributing the ads equally over the interval.

Information overload: More is less?   Government regulations that product labels must present detailed disclosure of ingredients, risks, etc., have given rise to controversy as to whether information overload might confuse rather than convince. Limitations in human information-encoding capacity allow increased absorption of one type of information only at the cost of less absorption of the other types (McGuire, 1961c; McConnell, 1970; Pool, 1983a). The main point in a message is better extracted if explanatory details are omitted and the message is kept short (Hays-Roth and Thorndyke, 1979; Reder and Anderson, 1980). Getting less from more is particularly likely with less talented (Smiley *et al.,* 1977) and more distractable (Harkins and Petty, 1981b) receivers. Reviews of cognitive science research relevant to information overload can be found in Bettman (1975), Scammon (1977), and Kanouse and Hays-Roth (1981).

Information overload decrement, elusive within the controlled laboratory conditions of basic cognitive science, is rarer still in the natural environment (Ray and Webb, 1976; Baumgardner *et al.,* 1983). Consumers in an atypically complex hypothetical shopping situation preferred getting a vast amount of brand information but actually best maximized their subjective utility with less than the highest level of information (Jacoby, Speller, and Kohn-Berning, 1974), though these interpretations are debatable (Russo, 1974; Jacoby, 1977; Malhotra, Jain, and Lagakos, 1982; Malhotra, 1984). Consumers prefer maximum disclosure of risk (L. A. Morris and Kanouse, 1980), but again the effect on amount of learning or on behavioral choice is less clear. Information-processing strain can be increased by accelerating the rate of presentation as well as increasing the amount of information, but despite some claim that time compression has decreased recall (McMahan, 1971), careful studies have found a beneficial effect of time compression (N. Miller *et al.,* 1976; LaBarbera and MacLachlan, 1979).

Extremity of the Position Urged

Message extremity or the discrepancy of message position from the receiver's initial position will be discussed in terms of its successive effects on exposure, information processing, and attitude change.

Selective exposure. That people seek out messages supporting positions they already hold and avoid discrepant messages has been claimed by such psychological notables as William James and Freud, acclaimed as the most basic process established by mass media research (Klapper, 1949, 1960), and singled out by the President's Science Advisory Committee as one of the basic principles well established by behavioral research. In view of such widespread endorsement one is not surprised to find that the selective avoidance postulate holds up poorly under empirical investigation (McGuire, 1968c; Milburn, 1979; but see Sweeney and Gruber, 1984). The postulate assumes that the person is living autistically in a fool's paradise, endeavoring to remain blissfully ignorant of belief-threatening material, even though in actual environments it is often adaptive to acquaint oneself with the opposition arguments, especially on personally relevant (Wyer and Frey, 1983) and controversial issues (Ball-Rokeach, Grube, and Rokeach, 1981) or when the receiver has high confidence (Mills and Ross, 1964; Frey, 1982; but see Behling, 1971; Ziemke, 1980), expects the arguments to be poor (Kleinhesselink and Edwards, 1975), or is in a laboratory situation where her or his competence or objectivity might be under scrutiny (E. Katz, 1968). Discrepant material may be preferred over neutral irrelevant material because it is more interesting and useful (Berlyne, 1960; Thorelli, Becker, and Engledow, 1975; Swann and Read, 1981) or because complex receivers get pleasure out of novel material somewhat discrepant from their initial preconceptions (Streufert and Streufert, 1978), especially when the issue is low in involvement (Ray, 1968) and self-esteem is not threatened (Frey and Wicklund, 1978).

Some seeming evidence for autistically motivated selective avoidance may be a sociological artifact of the community ideology's being so homogeneous that discrepant material is not available, of ingratiating sources' telling people what they want to know, or of each side's proselytizing only true believers with the goal of maintaining the loyalty of the already committed rather than making converts. This underlying complexity makes it important to design research to pick up nonmonotonic effects, the person seeking out arguments of intermediate discrepancy, with the optimal level interacting with confidence, expected refutability, etc. Two other methodological problems that must be taken into account are the poor indexing of information in the natural environment that makes avoidance difficult even if desired and the failure to distinguish between disconfirming what the receiver does believe and what he or she wants to believe (McGuire, 1957; Feather, 1969; Zanna and Olson, 1982).

Perceptual distortion. Autistic distortion of belief-discrepant material toward greater agreement with one's own position in perception, comprehension, inference drawing, recall, etc., is predicted by theories ranging from Freudian ego psychology to perceptual theories postulating assimilation-contrast, adaptation level, elastic scale, end anchor, etc., effects (Sherif and Hovland, 1961; Ostrom, 1970; Nemath and Endicott, 1976; Pepitone and DiNubile, 1976; Shaffer *et al.*, 1982). Empirical evidence for general perceptual assimilation is elusive (Greaves, 1972; S. S. Smith and Jamieson, 1972; Zanna and Olson, 1982), though it may occur when incidental learning is involved, belief concordance measures are carefully defined, and the receivers' wishes as well as beliefs are taken into account (Feather, 1969). The more complex consistency theory distortion involving assimilation of messages from liked sources and contrast distortions of disliked sources' messages has somewhat better support (Sherif, Sherif, and Nebergal, 1965; Granberg and Brent, 1974; Judd, Kenny, and Krosnick, 1983). I believe that these two autistic theories should be combined to yield a prediction of asymmetrical distortion including much assimilation distortion of material from a liked source (with whom both autistic needs, for universal consensus and for consistency, induce assimilation) but little distortion in either direction of material from a disliked source (with whom the assimilation induced by the consensus need is canceled by the consistency need for distancing). Some evidence can be found for such asymmetry (Fields and Schuman, 1976; O'Gorman, 1979; Granberg, Harris, and King, 1981).

Discrepancy and attitude change. The elegant linear-operator variant of the proportional-change models, which was transferred from mathematical learning theory to attitude change (N. H. Anderson, 1959; Boster *et al.*, 1982), predicts that attitude change is an increasing rectilinear function of message discrepancy. However, empirical research indicates an increasing but negatively accelerated function (Bochner and Insko, 1966; G. M. White, 1975).

A more complex two-factor analysis that postulates a proportional-change tendency plus a discounting tendency (such that messages tend increasingly to be rejected for incredulity as discrepancy size grows) predicts nonmonotonicity with a turndown such that extremely discrepant messages bring not just diminishing but negative returns (N. H. Anderson, 1971). However, empirical results suggest that such boomerang turndowns occur only at extreme discrepancies, indicating that incredulity manifests itself only with extravagant claims (Bochner and Insko, 1966; G. M. White, 1975), in uncommitted receivers (Shirai, 1974), and when source and receiver are on opposite sides of neutrality (Lange and Fishbein, 1983). Regarding interactions, the turndown with extreme discrepancies occurs earlier with clearer messages (Insko, Murashima, and Saiyadain, 1966) and with less credible sources (Aronson, Turner, and Carlsmith, 1963; Bochner and Insko, 1966; McGinnies, 1973). Regarding involvement's interaction with discrepancy there are both semantic and process confusions. Dissonance theorists (Festinger, 1957), using involvement in the sense of issue importance, predict that the discrepancy size producing the most attitude change increases with involvement; while commitment theorists, using involvement in the sense of attachment to one's initial position on the issue (Freedman, 1964; H. G. Greenwald, 1964), predict that involvement decreases optimal discrepancy size. Discrepancy-closing theories imply a trade-off between perceptual distortion and attitude change as alternative modes of resolution, the preferred mix depending on dispositional receiver proclivities and situational factors (Sherif and Hovland, 1961; Steiner and Johnson, 1964).

CHANNEL VARIABLES' EFFECTS ON PERSUASIVE IMPACT

Channel variables refer to the paths by which the message reaches the receiver—whether it arrives at eye or ear, is in verbal or nonverbal form, comes from a physically present source or is electronically mediated, etc. Considering the large economic stake in deciding optimal media mix for the $50 billion expended annually on U.S. advertising (e.g., $3000 per second for prime-time TV ads), it is surprising how little conclusive research on channel variables has been done, leaving controversial answers even

to such basic questions as what magnitude of impact mass media ads have on consumers' purchases or violent programs have on viewer aggression. Even less established are claims (Ong, 1977, 1982; Stevens and Garcia, 1980; Pool, 1983b) that fundamental personal and cultural transformations are produced by the introduction of dramatic new communication channels such as writing and literacy (Goody, 1977; Scribner and Cole, 1981; Pattison, 1982), the printing press (Eisenstein, 1979; Bruns, 1982), the telephone (Pool, 1977; B. D. Singer, 1982), the electronic media (Innis, 1964; McLuhan, 1964; Conrad, 1982; Czitrom, 1982), or the coming communication and information technological "revolution" (Dakin, 1979; Haigh, Gerbner, and Byrne, 1981; Dizard, 1982; Naisbitt, 1982; Schiller, 1982; Singh, 1983; Slack, 1983; F. Williams, 1982). Such technological changes may be only manifestations of or responses to more basic changes in material life rather than themselves being the source of basic changes. We shall first illustrate the high level of media exposure, then describe evidence from a half-dozen domains indicating that relative to this high exposure the effects are slight, and then mention over a dozen theories arguing that the mass media may have more impact than indicated by the evidence. Comparative media effects, nonverbal communication, and context factors will be discussed as final channel variables topics.

Levels and Correlates of Mass Media Consumption

Mass media consumption occupies 3 or 4 hours of the average European's and American's daily life, twice as much time as is spent actively socializing (Szalai, 1972; R. A. Peterson, 1981; J. P. Robinson, 1981). We shall focus on television's effects since research has concentrated on it and most exposure is to this medium: Nielsen data show that a television set is on over 6 hours per day in the average U.S. household, though seldom getting full attention (Television Audience Assessment, 1983), and that the 20,000 hours of watching television that are accumulated by the average American high school graduate (Adler *et al.*, 1980) exceeds the amount of time he or she has spent in the classroom.

The historical trends and demographic correlates of use vary for the several media (Dimmick, McCain, and Bolton, 1979; Pool, 1983a). During the past twenty years in the United States television viewing has increased (though recently it is leveling off), while newspaper reading has declined (J. P. Robinson, 1979). Television viewing is higher among women than men, blacks than whites, and by those low in education, income, frequency of church attendance, and amount of work outside the home [which underlies some of the other correlates (Hughes, 1980)], these demographic correlates usually being in the reverse direction for print exposure (Bogart, 1981). The "uses and gratifications" theorizing to explain mass media popularity has revived in the past decade (Blumler and Katz, 1974; Swanson, 1979) after lying dormant since its popularity in radio research days (Lazarsfeld and Stanton, 1949), McGuire (1974) describing sixteen classes of gratification that may account for this high mass media consumption.

So Much Watching, So Little Effect

That all this television viewing has less impact than is usually supposed is suggested by evaluation research in six effects domains, four on material deliberately constructed to be persuasive (commercial advertisements, political campaigns, public service announcements, and multimedia monolithic indoctrination) and two on the program material designed for entertainment rather than persuasion (the impact of program violence on viewers' aggression and of stereotyped portrayals on viewers' perceptions). We shall review television impact in each of these six highly studied areas while ignoring its less investigated effects on cognitive and affective development (T. D. Cook *et al.,* 1975; Dirr, 1980; Bryant and Anderson, 1983; Howe, 1983), on family relations (Brody, Stoneman, and Sanders, 1980; B. S. Greenberg *et al.,* 1980), and on health (M. Meyer, 1981; Gerbner, Morgan, and Signorielli, 1982; D. S. Solomon, 1982) and its effects through pornography (Malamuth and Check, 1981; Zillman and Bryant, 1982; Yaffe and Nelson, 1982) and "media events" (E. Katz, 1980; Ball-Rokeach, Grube, and Rokeach, 1981; deBock and vanLil, 1981). Alternative reviews of mass media effects (usually arriving at a more sanguine bottom line than we reach here) can be found in Comstock *et al.* (1978), Hapkiewicz (1979), Murray and Kippax (1979), J. P. Murray (1980), Roberts and Bachen (1981), Liebert, Sprafkin, and Davidson (1982), Pearl, Bouthilet, and Lazar (1982), McGuire (in press, a), and Chapter 23 in this *Handbook*.

Impact of commercial ads on purchases. Profit-oriented American business people spend $50 billion per year on advertising, exposing the average child to over twenty thousand television ads each year (Adler *et al.,* 1980). While this expenditure suggests that its cost-

effectiveness has been well demonstrated, it is remarkable how little impact has been found by friends and foes of the communications industries. Company-level or product-category econometric time-series analyses of the relationship between advertising budget and the brand's subsequent share of product-class sales have yielded results as inconclusive as analogous macroeconometric analyses of the dollar value of education or of research (Clarke, 1976; Metra, 1979; Albion and Farris, 1981; Aaker, Carman, and Jackson, 1982; Assmus, Farley, and Lehmann, 1984). Person-level microstudies measuring the relationship between amount of individuals' exposure to ads for an item and their level of product or brand purchase show comparably weak impact. Over-the-counter drug ads have been relatively well studied (McGuire, 1976a) because of worry about their possible effects on drug abuse as well as on legitimate sales. A dozen good studies (Weigel and Jessor, 1973; Milavsky, Pekowsky, and Stipp, 1975; Rossiter and Robertson, 1980; etc.) suggest that exposure to drug ads accounts at most for a few percent of the variance in over-the-counter drug use and has an even slighter (and perhaps negative) relationship to illegal drug use. Advertising impact on children's use of other products are reviewed by S. Ward, Wackman, and Wartella (1977) and Adler *et al.* (1980). In general, impacts of mass media advertising can be detected (Stoneman and Brody, 1981; Gorn and Goldberg, 1982; Leone, 1983; Roedder, Sternthal, and Calder, 1983) but at magnitudes remarkably small for the resources expended.

Impact of mass media political campaigning on voting. A great deal of political material is broadcast on U.S. television, including a half-billion dollars of paid political ads in a presidential year plus much unpurchased political news, interviews, debates, etc. Belief that this media coverage has a formidable impact is widespread (Meadow, 1980; Lesher, 1982; Westin, 1982) and has resulted in communications professionals taking over the design and conduct of some political campaigns (Nimmo and Combs, 1980; Chagall, 1981; Sabato, 1981), but the demonstrated effects on public attitudes and voting behavior are surprisingly slight (Chaffee and Choe, 1980; T. E. Patterson, 1980; Bybee *et al.,* 1981). Admittedly, potential effects are reduced because opposed ads may cancel each other, voluntary exposure is low except for the "great debates" between the presidential candidates (Kraus, 1983) and even they have little effect (D. O. Sears and Chaffee, 1979), and heavy consumers of television and newspaper news are typically the already-committed. Information about the candidates' stands on issues does increase progressively throughout the campaign (T. E. Patterson, 1980), and media exposure contributes marginally to children's political socialization (Conway, Stevens, and Smith, 1975) and to political knowledge (Chaffee and Tims, 1982); but while television is usually nominated by the public as its prime source of information (Nie, Verba, and Petrocik, 1979; Roper, 1979), political information is found to be more closely related to newspaper reading (T. E. Patterson, 1980; Barrows, 1981).

Paid political advertisements are found to have quite small effects on voting choice (T. E. Patterson and McClure, 1976; Kaid, 1981), mainly on late deciders, and may influence voters against as well as for the advertised candidate (Atkin *et al.,* 1973; Raj, 1982). Candidates' ad budgets are related to the percent of the vote that they obtain but the causal direction is unclear (Grush, 1980). It has been argued by some (Noelle-Neumann, 1980a, 1980b; T. E. Patterson, 1980; Glynn and McLeod, 1982) and denied by others (Key, 1977; Fiorina, 1981; Greenfield, 1982) that voters are increasingly viewing elections as sporting events in which citizens try to pick a winner rather than decide which candidate deserves one's vote; if so, the public would presumably depend on media reports to ascertain on whose bandwagon to climb, though an opposite underdog effect is as common (Roll and Cantril, 1972). However, election night television projections of the likely presidential winner based on East Coast returns have little bandwagon effect on late voters at the still-opened West Coast voting places (Lang and Lang, 1968; Tuchman and Coffin, 1971; Tannenbaum and Kostrich, 1983). With regard to the political impact of international mass media propaganda, there have been interesting hypotheses (Bogart, 1976; Chandler, 1981; P. M. Taylor, 1981) but little evaluation.

Impact of public service announcements. Short public service announcements (PSAs) are often inserted among program break television commercials to advocate public benefit practices such as getting hypertension examinations or preventing forest fires (Rice and Paisley, 1981). While confidence in their efficacy runs high (Brawley, 1983; Sprafkin, Swift, and Hess, 1983), most evaluation studies of PSAs are poor, using only peripheral dependent-variable measures such as awareness of the campaign, lacking controls to provide measures of response level without the PSAs, and embedding the PSAs in a broader advocacy program that obscures their spe-

cific effect (Hanneman, McEwen, and Coyne, 1973). The better studies show little impact (Tyler, 1984) and that more on information than attitudes (P. E. Peterson *et al.,* 1984). Schmeling and Wotring (1980) found that a carefully designed, heavily exposed campaign against drug abuse had little effect even on information level. The Louisville study (Schanie and Sundel, 1978) achieved high exposure to good material regarding the availability of mental health services but had negligible impact on the utilization or even awareness of such services. The PSAs have proven even less effective in producing behavioral changes such as use of seat belts (Robertson *et al.,* 1974) or prevention of smoking (Warner, 1977; R. D. Murphy, 1980).

Impact of monolithic campaigns on ideology and lifestyle. A fourth type of intentional mass media persuasion is community-saturating monolithic campaigns typified by ideological indoctrination in totalitarian countries with modern communications systems. Some political theorists have argued that control of the mass media conveys enduring power (Chambers, 1979; Evan, 1981; Gerbner, Gross, Morgan, and Signorielli, 1982; Rivers, 1982; Mosco and Wasco, 1983; Altschull, 1984), but mass uprisings occur against long-entrenched indoctrinating totalitarian governments (Rüstow, 1980). Frankfurt critical-school theorists (Petryszak, 1977; Habermas, 1979; Mattelart, 1980; Lanigan, 1981; E. M. Rogers, 1982a) argue that even in relatively nonideological polycentric states like the United States, media news and programming perpetuate a homogeneous elite doctrine (despite the very negative stereotyping of business people in U.S. television programs), which shapes public consciousness and behavior (Davison, 1980; Ettema and Whitney, 1982), the massive commercial advertising purportedly producing a materialistic self-indulgent America, a society of consumers preoccupied with the acquisition of material objects (Hirst and Reekie, 1977; Berman, 1981; Yankelovich, 1981; Ewen and Ewen, 1982; Gitlin, 1983; D. Pope, 1983; Fox, 1984). Commentators tend to complain that media are controlled by elites other than their own (Tracey, 1977; M. G. Cantor, 1980; Smythe, 1981; Wicklein, 1981; Gandy, 1982; Dreier, 1982; M. G. Bagdikian, 1983) who are purported to be intent on maintaining the status quo or on inducing violent change (Mattelart, 1980; Biryukov, 1981; E. Katz and Szecsko, 1981; Comstock, 1982a; Hedebro, 1982).

Testing of such broad propositions is difficult because of the operation of extraneous variables, the lack of control groups, and the need for lengthy time-series data. A distant approximation is provided by full-court press campaigns that monolithically urge adoption of more healthful life-styles. The Stanford three-cities study (Farquhar *et al.,* 1977; N. Maccoby and Alexander, 1980) and the Finnish North Karelia coronary risk project (Puska *et al.,* 1979) study found that presenting communities for several years with frequent messages to reduce cardiac risk through weight control, smoking reduction, exercise, etc., did show statistically significant risk-reducing changes in information, attitudes, and behavior and sometimes reduction in morbidity and mortality; future research should ascertain if such health campaign impacts are cost effective.

Impact of TV program violence on viewer aggressiveness. The unintended television effect on which most research attention has focused is the horrendous level of violence in television programming as possibly instigating viewers to antisocial aggression and crime (Huesmann, 1982). We shall describe first the level of televised violence, then theories that predict its impact on viewer aggression, and finally empirical evidence regarding such impact.

Violence in television programs has remained for the past ten years at the formidable level of five acts of violence per hour on prime time and eighteen per hour on the mostly cartoon Saturday morning shows directed at children, the violent acts often including willful injury or killing and perpetrated by a large percentage of the characters (Signorielli, Gross, and Morgan, 1982). An even higher level of violence is depicted in popular novels and motion pictures. The violence counts are methodologically questionable in terms of how they segment programs into units, how they count restraint, natural catastrophies, fantasy, and humor violence, how they weight and combine incidents, the use of victimization ratios, etc., but however such definitional and methodological details are resolved, the bottom line is a formidable body count that constitutes a sorry spectacle. The American child reaches adulthood having witnessed an appalling number of acts of violence on the media, far in excess of their nontrivial prevalence in actual life.

Of four television-as-cause theories, three imply a positive and the fourth a negative impact of televised violence on viewer aggressiveness; of two additional television-as-effect artifactual theories, the fifth predicts a positive and the sixth a negative relationship. The first, social learning or modeling theory (Bandura, 1977; Lefkowitz *et al.,* 1977) postulates that observing a violent model on television adds to the availability of aggressive responses in the viewer's behavioral repertoire to an extent that increases with such modeling's frequency, its being depicted as rewarding, its similarity to the life situation (Berkowitz, 1974), etc. A second, "disinhibiting," theory (Berkowitz and Rawlings, 1963) asserts that television depiction legitimizes violence by showing its pervasiveness or providing other "justifications," or it desensitizes (M. H. Thomas *et al.,* 1977) or releases the viewer from the ordinary restraints against striking out aggressively (Drabman and Thomas, 1974), especially when it is perpetrated by an attractive model, is shown purged of bad consequences, etc. A third, arousal, theory (Berkowitz and Alioto, 1973; Tannenbaum and Zillman, 1975; Tannenbaum, 1980; Zillmann, 1982) states that televised violence excites the viewer, thus multiplying ongoing response tendencies which, particularly in angry viewers, would include destructive acts. Opposite to these three theories, catharsis theory (Feshbach and Singer, 1971; Geen and Quanty, 1977) predicts that witnessing televised violence reduces viewer aggressiveness by providing a vicarious fantasy outlet that allows release of aggressive needs and so reduces the amount of pent-up aggression needing expression in actual life.

Three other theories predict artifactual relationships due to a reverse causality, including a fifth theory that aggressive persons are socially ostracized and so spend more time at home watching television; and a sixth theory that dispositional aggressiveness naturally enhances preference for violent shows (Fenigstein, 1979). A seventh theory, also postulating an artifactual reverse causality but in the negative direction, is that heavy television viewers are conventional people (Weigel and Jessor, 1973) who stay at home and watch television while more violent, drug- and person-abusing types are out on the streets perpetrating mayhem. Obtained results should be adjusted for these three artifactual self-selected viewer theories before making inferences about the causal role of television viewing.

Considering the strong independent-variable manipulation made possible by the high amount of televised violence and the sufficiency of theories predicting effects, the demonstrated impact of violence exposure on viewers' socially significant aggression is surprisingly slight. Under laboratory conditions (usually exposing children or college students to quasi-television material and measuring aggression in terms of somewhat sanitized responses that the institutional setting may legitimize), exposure to highly violent material typically produces more aggression than does exciting nonaggressive material (at least in preangered or chronically angry viewers), especially when the depicted victim resembles the viewer's potential victim, when disturbing consequences are expurgated, etc. (J. P. Murray, 1980; Comstock, 1982b; Huesmann, 1982).

Whether self-selected viewing of violent television programs in the natural environment affects the viewer's level of socially significant aggressive behavior is harder to determine. Some of the better studies find small positive correlations that reach conventionally accepted levels of statistical significance but with effect size of trivial practical significance (McLeod, Atkin, and Chaffee, 1972; Parke *et al.*, 1977; Belson, 1978; Hearold, 1979; Eron and Huesmann, 1980; J. L. Singer and Singer, 1981; Eron, 1982; Huesmann, 1982; Milavsky *et al.*, 1982b; T. D. Cook *et al.*, 1983; Freedman, 1984; Huesmann *et al.*, 1984; Kenny, 1984). Support is even smaller for the opposite prediction that exposure to televised violence reduces overt social aggression by providing a vicarious catharsis in fantasy (Feshbach and Singer, 1971; Geen and Quanty, 1977; G. W. Russell, 1983).

Aesthetic revulsion and moral unease leave me wishing for a reduction of the high level of violence in television and other popular entertainment media. However, the demonstrated effect is so small in magnitude that I am loathe to urge censorship that would restrict freedom of expression and artistic license and might deprive the public of spectacles it enjoys. Though the entertainment value of violence has not been established (Diener and DeFour, 1978), the Romans frequented Colosseum slaughters (A. Guttmann, 1983), the British attended public hangings, and we watch prizefights (J. H. Goldstein, 1983; Phillips, 1983) and consume violent novels, movies, and television shows. Perhaps we have the right to get what we want and deserve what we get.

Impact of TV program portrayals on the construction social of reality. There is considerable evidence of underrepresentation and negative stereotyping of low-power groups in television news (W. C. Adams, 1982), in prime-time entertainment programs (Gerbner *et al.*, 1980; B. S. Greenberg, 1980), and in made-for-children shows (Barcus, 1983). Women, the elderly, some ethnic minorities, and other low-power groups are underrepresented in television programs. Among prime-time television characters the elderly appear with only one-fifth their actual prevalence in the U.S. population (Kubey, 1980; R. H. Davis and Kubey, 1982) and women with only one-third (Gerbner *et al.*, 1980); blacks and especially Hispanics (B. S. Greenberg *et al.*, 1983), though not

Asian-Americans, are also underrepresented on prime time and even more so on Saturday morning children's shows (Busby, 1974; Barcus, 1983). Males receive disproportionate exposure also in the print media, outnumbering females by a ten-to-one ratio in picture-book stories for preschoolers (Weitzman *et al.*, 1972).

When they are portrayed at all, the depiction of low-power groups is often such that, as has been said of being ridden out of town on a rail, if it weren't for the honor of the thing, one might prefer to stay off altogether. The elderly are portrayed as less good at doing things, more narrow-minded, less sexually active, in poorer health, and more financially dependent than they actually are in life (Gerbner *et al.*, 1980; Kubey, 1980). Particularly sad is that while in life the elderly's involvement in criminal violence is usually as victim, television pushes the "evil old man" stereotype; i.e., elderly men are one of the few demographic categories depicted as more likely to commit than to be hurt by violence (Signorielli and Gerbner, 1977). Violence committed by the mentally ill is also exaggerated (Gerbner, Morgan, and Signorielli, 1982). Women are unfavorably depicted as passive, immature, and powerless in television entertainment programs (Sternglanz and Serbin, 1974; Downs, 1981), news programs (McNeil, 1975), advertisements (Courtney and Whipple, 1981; Bartos, 1982), and in schoolbooks (Weitzman *et al.*, 1972; J. E. Williams and Best, 1982), though the difference may be lessening (Sharits and Lammers, 1983). Some success has been reported for television series purposely designed to alter children's gender stereotypes in a less objectionable direction (E. S. Davidson, Yasuna, and Tower, 1979; Johnston and Ettema, 1982). Depictions of blacks are becoming less unfavorable (Northcott, Seggar, and Hinton, 1975; Berry and Mitchell-Kernan, 1982; MacDonald, 1983).

Cultivation analysis research (Gerbner *et al.*, 1980) suggests that this underrepresentation and unfavorable representation of low-power groups may degrade how the group members are perceived by themselves (Berry and Mitchell-Kernan, 1982) and by others. Paralleling the underrepresentation of the elderly and overrepresentation of crime on television, the public underestimates the number of elderly in society and overestimates the number of criminals and law enforcement agents, the prevalence of crime, and the dangers of the street, these misperceptions being more pronounced in heavy viewers of TV. However, Hirsch (1980, 1981) and Hughes (1980) argue (but see Hawkins and Pingree, 1982) that trends obtaining on the selected survey items reported by Gerbner *et al.* (1980, 1981) do not appear on other relevant items and disappear even on those reported items when other demographic factors associated with television viewing are partialed out simultaneously and perhaps also when personality predispositions are partialed out (Wober and Gunter, 1982). Also, A. N. Doob and Macdonald (1979) find that the relationship between TV viewing and perception of real-world dangerousness obtains more across than within residential districts, suggesting that TV exposure and perception of high crime rates are both coeffects of the real danger in one's residential neighborhood.

Post Factum Salvaging of Belief in Appreciable Mass Media Effects

Common sense and the common needs of contending factions sympathetic or hostile to the communication industry all combine to maintain the belief that television has vast effects on attitudes and behavior despite the evidence from all six areas just reviewed that television's impact is quite small. Standing on the evidence is thus a lonely position but it is in this case a secure one, since the history of social science field research teaches that the safest prediction on any topic is that sizable effects will not be found except in studies with flagrant flaws. Hence here I shall rise above the data and bend over backward to mention fourteen *post factum* salvaging conjectures that allow keeping the faith in strong television impact despite the slightness of obtained effects.

One plausible excuse is that a sizable relationship is obscured by poor measurement either of independent variables (hours of watching television, which programs were watched, what advertisements were seen, how violence is counted, etc.) or of dependent variables (amount of aggressive behavior, drug use, feeling of being menaced by crime, etc.). The obtained measures often tap farfetched analogues of the actual behavior and depend on self-reports or observers' judgment about matters that are difficult to recall, hard to judge, embarrassing to mention, or ambiguous in meaning. However, the most realistic and refined measures tend to show the least effects (Hughes, 1980; Hirsch, 1981; Milavsky *et al.,* 1982a; Phillips, 1982, 1983; Kessler and Stipp, 1984; Wasserman, 1983).

A more intricate second methodological complaint is that the usual simplistic correlational designs are insensitive or artifactually affected by the contaminating variables that operate in real-life situations or that alternative time-series models may themselves introduce unreliability or overcorrection artifacts (Eron, 1982; Milavsky *et al.,* 1982b; Kenny, 1984). However, refining the analyses

tends to reduce the size of the relationship, again suggesting that design contaminations have been producing spurious impacts rather than hiding true ones (A. N. Doob and Macdonald, 1979; Hughes, 1980; Milavsky *et al.,* 1982b).

A third, more substantive excuse is that two-sided coverage on controversial issues may result in mutual cancellation of effects. While this explanation might account for the limited impact, as measured by brand shares or which political candidate wins, it does not explain away limited effects on a whole product class such as over-the-counter drug or cigarette ads (Metra, 1979) nor the lack of "dose size" effects in econometric studies of ad budgets and market shares for brands. Fourthly, lack of media impact could be attributed to selective exposure, but media content is often poorly indexed and outweighed by counterforces such as a need to know what the opposition is saying. Also, selective exposure to high-violence shows by aggressive people would spuriously enhance rather than mask a positive relationship between media exposure and viewer aggression.

A fifth argument for justifying the sale of media time to advertisers (or for blaming the media for social ills) is the "law of mimimal effect" (Klapper, 1960) that even if media presentations do not convert anyone to new views, they keep the faith of the already committed, enhancing brand loyalty and product use by habitual buyers, firing the enthusiasm of a political candidate's supporters so that they get out and vote, (Mendelsohn and O'Keefe, 1976), or maintaining the sociopolitical status quo as argued by the Frankfurt critical school and the Pennsylvania cultivation analysis group. However, it remains to be demonstrated that ad exposure enhances brand loyalty, and ads may repel neutrals as well as rally the committed (Raj, 1982). A plausible sixth claim is that while media campaigns may have little effect on well-ingrained attitudes and actions regarding familiar objects, they may be highly effective in introducing a new brand, a new product class, or an unknown political candidate or in changing public attitudes on obscure events as in the case of the misreporting of the defeat of the 1968 Vietcong's Tet offensive (Oberdorfer, 1971; Braestrup, 1983). Election studies (T. E. Patterson, 1980) do indicate that political ads do more for the less known candidates (for minor offices, primaries, and nonincumbent parties) (but see Hofstetter and Moore, 1982). On the other hand, adoption of innovations typically depend on word-of-mouth rather than mass media communications in domains ranging from physicians' prescribing of new drugs and farmers' adoption of new seeds or implements to women's choices of new birth control procedures, new clothing styles, moviegoing, grocery purchases, and politics (E. M. Rogers and Shoemaker, 1971; Crano, Ludwig, and Selnow, 1981; W. P. Robinson, 1981). The increase of mass media exposure relative to conversational socializing (J. P. Robinson, 1979) might in the future enhance the mass media's role in diffusion of innovations.

A seventh salvaging argument is that even if the mass media have little impact on the general public, they may have sizable effects on some particularly susceptible subpopulations. For example, political materials may have more impact on uninvolved citizens (McLeod, Becker, and Burns, 1974; Atkin and Heald, 1976; Glynn and McLeod, 1982); children may be especially susceptible to advertisements because they are less critical than adults or less able to distinguish between program and advertisements (S. Ward, Wackman, and Wartella, 1977; Adler *et al.,* 1980); chronically aggressive persons may be especially susceptible to violent material (Berkowitz and Alioto, 1973); those of higher socioeconomic status may be more susceptible to the print (and even the television) media, according to the knowledge gap hypothesis (Shingi and Mody, 1976; Ettema, Brown, and Luepker, 1983; Miyo, 1983); citizens of countries like Israel and South Africa recently introduced to television may be more affected by it (R. Harrison and Ekman, 1976; van Vuuren, 1981) than the jaded publics in old-television countries who may be affected only by sensational media events (Ryback and Connell, 1978; E. Katz, 1980).

A hardy perennial (no less respectable for its age) that serves as an eighth excuse for arguing away the smallness of immediate media effects is the two-step flow hypothesis (E. Katz, 1957; J. P. Robinson, 1976) that mass media do not influence the general public directly but rather influence liaison persons (Weimann, 1982b) or elites who monitor and derive information and attitudes from the media (J. P. Robinson, 1972) and later convert the masses. Insofar as this two-step flow hypothesis is valid, elite outlets may be more influential than the mass media; e.g., news stories in prestigious periodicals may have more impact than those on television (Kadushin, 1974; Bogart, 1981; Chrisman, 1982).

A currently popular ninth argument is that even if media do not change people's attitudes on issues, they may have an agenda-setting effect (Berelson, 1942; McCombs, 1981) of making more salient or available (Tversky and Kahneman, 1974; Nisbett and Ross, 1980) the issues and products they most often mention. Public

health studies do show that people's estimates of the prevalence of various diseases correlate higher with their amount of media mention than with their actual frequency (Combs and Slovic, 1979), and voting studies show a modest positive correlation between amount of media coverage of issues during the election and their salience to the receiver (Iyengar, 1979; Erbring, Goldenberg, and Miller, 1980; T. E. Patterson, 1980), though in correlational field research the causal direction is unclear, since it may be that the media cover topics that interest the public as well as that the public becomes interested in topics stressed by the media. Laboratory manipulational studies (Iyengar, Peters, and Kinder, 1982; Iyengar, Kinder, Peters, and Krosnick, 1984) clarify causal direction, but their artificiality limits generalizability.

Three other salvaging hypotheses claim that the media affect the public indirectly and gradually. The tenth, bandwagon-theory excuse is that unequal television coverage may affect the public's perception of what is the modal consensus on the issue (Koschnick, 1982; Tannenbaum and Kostrich, 1983), causing pluralistic ignorance (O'Gorman, 1979; D. G. Taylor, 1982) or initiating a "spiral of silence" that becomes a self-fulfilling nonprophesy because supporters of the underexposed option lose heart and voice (Noelle-Neumann, 1980a; E. Katz, 1981), or the prevalence of televised violence convinces the viewer that aggressiveness is condoned as the social norm (M. H. Thomas and Drabman, 1975). However, such bandwagon effects are hard to find (Granberg and Brent, 1983), some researchers (Roll and Cantril, 1972; Ceci and Kain, 1982) even finding an antibandwagon, underdog effect. An eleventh possibility is that television's style may have impact even if its content does not, so that people are affected not on the stands they take on issues but on their attention spans and styles of thinking and deciding about issues (Seymour-Ure, 1974; J. L. Singer, 1980).

A twelfth possibility is that mass media affect the structure or functioning of social institutions and through them indirectly influence public opinion and behavior (Comstock, 1978; Lemert, 1981; Salomon, 1981); e.g., even if the media campaigns do not actually influence voters, the mistaken impression that they do may affect how candidates are selected or conduct their campaigns and spend their funds (Sabato, 1981; Greenfield, 1982; S. C. Patterson, 1982) and how incumbents behave in office (Lang and Lang, 1983). Or again, the media gatekeepers may collaborate with other elites (Gandy, 1982; F. L. Cook *et al.,* 1983).

A thirteenth excuse is that even if the media have little impact by themselves, they may have synergistic effect in conjunction with direct communication or with experience (LeJeune and Alex, 1973; Friedrich-Cofer *et al.,* 1979; Evans *et al.,* 1981; Huesmann, 1982), though the contrary finding is common, that media effects are smaller on more discussed issues (Robinson, 1976; Erbring, Goldenberg, and Miller, 1980). A fourteenth lethargic-viewer theory is that television watching is an insipid activity that disproportionately attracts passive individuals low in buying, voting, drug abuse, aggression, etc., so that there is a self-selection artifact that masks television's impact in bringing these otherwise inactive persons up to the average level.

In summary, the mass media have been shown to have some marginal effects of surprisingly small magnitudes relative to costs and to expectations. The fourteen conjectures we have proposed for arguing that there is more media impact than so far demonstrated await empirical confirmation.

Comparative Effects of Various Media and Modalities

How any channel variable (such as the written versus spoken word) affects persuasive impact can be estimated by integrating its separate effects on the dozen output steps of the communication/persuasion matrix and adding interaction effects. Media differences on exposure step 1, as measured by circulation figures, Arbitron or Nielsen ratings (Frank and Greenberg, 1980, 1982; Bogart, 1981; Austin, 1983), or more novel measures (Pool, 1983a; Television Audience Assessment, 1983), were discussed above. Steps 2 and 3, attention to and liking for the communication, are usually greater for television's vivid audiovisual presentation than radio's reduced auditory presentation or newspaper's duller still print format (Andreoli and Worchel, 1978). People report getting more information from television and regard it as more believable (Roper, 1975; Lichty, 1982),—seeing is believing—but information and attitudes are actually more closely related to print than to television exposure (T. E. Patterson, 1980; Barrows, 1981), and print evokes more thought (P. L. Wright, 1974). Physically present sources tend to be better liked than electronically mediated ones (E. Williams, 1975; Keating and Latané, 1976). Learning and recall of very difficult material is slightly superior for print over electronic media (Chaiken and Eagly, 1976; Wold, 1977) and for television over radio (E. Katz, Adoni, and Parness, 1977; Wold, 1977), and pictures added to print arguments may be more

distracting than helpful (Edell and Staelin, 1983). The effects of audiovisually mediated communication are closer to audio-only effects than to face-to-face communication effects (E. Williams, 1977).

Since even media as similar as TV and cinema may involve different processes (Ellis, 1983) and the relative advantage of different channels varies from mediator to mediator, theorizing and empirical testing should focus not on main-effect differences but on media interactions with other variables that make one or another mediating process contribute more to the variance in a given situation. For example, the attention-catching superiority of electronic media will be more important for simple material, but with very difficult material the comprehensibility advantage of the print medium will mediate more of the variance (Chaiken and Eagly, 1976); and the greater source vividness with television over print gives television the advantage when the source is highly credible but makes print relatively more persuasive when the source is suspect (Worchel, Andreoli, and Easton, 1975; Chaiken and Eagly, 1983).

Persuasiveness of Nonverbal Communication

Intentionally and unintentionally, television news professionals use nonverbal cues to benefit their preferred political candidates: In the 1976 West German election, newscasters depicted their preferred party's (SPD) candidate in ways believed to enhance attractiveness (full face, at eye level, while receiving audience approval, etc.) twice as often as the disliked parties' candidates were so favorably depicted (Noelle-Neumann, 1980a; Kepplinger, 1982); and in the 1976 U.S. presidential campaign American news reporters showed significant differences in facial expression depending on whether Carter or Ford was being discussed (Friedman, DiMatteo, and Mertz, 1980). The vast accumulation of nonverbal communication research during the past decade is reviewed by Harper, Wiens, and Matarazzo (1978), LaFrance and Mayo (1978), Key (1980), Zuckerman, DePaulo, and Rosenthal (1981), M. Davis and Skupien (1982), R. S. Feldman (1982), Heslin and Patterson (1982), Scherer and Ekman (1982a), and Bull (1983). We shall review first visual and then auditory nonverbal cues for source credibility, attractiveness, and power.

Effects of visual nonverbal source cues.　Visual cues can be categorized into facial expression, posture, body movements and gestures (kinesics), use of space (proxemics), and, by extension, dress and hair styles (Harris *et al.,* 1983). Of the three facial areas (Ekman and

Friesen, 1975) the bulk of the research has focused on the middle or eye area, especially on eye contact, with the finding that atypically low gaze by the source communicates disinterest and atypically high gaze communicates threat, so an intermediate level evokes most liking (Exline, 1972). Despite the old adage that looking the person in the eye communicates sincerity, prolonged gaze is more likely to evoke flight than agreement (Ellsworth and Langer, 1976; Kleinke, 1977). Power is communicated by the source's maintaining eye contact when speaking and looking away while listening (Dovidio and Ellyson, 1982). Pupil dilation (Goldwater, 1972; Janisse, 1977) elicits liking (Hess, 1975). Eye blinks are a cue for deceptiveness (Cutrow *et al.*, 1972), as are mouth movements such as pursing or biting the lips (R. S. Feldman, Devin-Sheehan, and Allen, 1978). Smiling and head nods enhance liking (Mackey, 1976), though continuous smiling suggests deceptiveness (Kraut, 1978).

With regard to posture, perceived power and liking is enhanced by postural asymmetry, such as leaning to one side, or bilateral differences in positioning arms or legs (Mehrabian, 1972), and an open stance (McGinley, LeFevre, and McGinley, 1975), such as leaning back in the chair with legs extended and knees and feet apart (or with one ankle over the opposite knee rather than having legs crossed) and having elbows, arms, and hands away from the body and from each other (rather than crossing arms or clasping one's hands or placing them in one's lap). Self-grooming gestures such as running one's fingers through one's hair or touching one's face suggest deceptiveness (Knapp, Hart, and Dennis, 1974; McClintock and Hunt, 1975). The source's eye contact has more effect than hand contact (Brockner *et al.*, 1982), and the impact of hand contact not surprisingly depends on place and mode of the touch and genders of touched and toucher (Nguyen, Heslin, and Nguyen, 1976).

Spatial power cues include the source's taking a face-to-face rather than oblique stance and approaching nearer (Dean, Willis, and Hewitt, 1975; Jorgenson, 1975). Proximity up to a point enhances liking, but very close approach evokes feelings of personal-space invasion, for male receivers particularly when the close approach is face-to-face and for female receivers when it is side-by-side (J. D. Fisher and Byrne, 1975). When the approach is too close for comfort, the negative impact can be mitigated by reducing eye contact to conserve an optimal level of intimacy (Argyle and Cook, 1976; Coutts and Ledden, 1977), allowing the source to maximize perceived power and attractiveness by approaching the receiver closely but lessening intrusiveness by lowering eye contact, particularly while listening.

Effects of auditory, nonverbal source cues. Source credibility can be lowered by vocalic nonverbal cues for deceptiveness (Zuckerman, DePaulo, and Rosenthal, 1981), such as high pitch (Ekman and Friesen, 1974), long latency in answering (Cutrow *et al.*, 1972; A. A. Harrison *et al.*, 1978), pauses and other nonfluencies (R. S. Feldman, Devin-Sheehan, and Allen, 1978), hedges such as "kinda," "you know," "I guess" (B. Erickson *et al.*, 1978), slowness of speech (N. Miller *et al.*, 1976), and signs of nervous tension such as speech errors. Other paralinguistic speech variables that reduce source credibility include the use of "isn't it?" tag questions at the end of sentences, the use of intensifiers (R. S. Feldman, Devin-Sheehan, and Allen, 1978), lack of synchrony between speech and kinesics (Woodall and Burgoon, 1981), and using very formal grammar, though high-status speech helps maintain upper-class power (Giles and Powesland, 1975; Pattison, 1982). Approbational verbal formulas, such as "I see," "yes," "fine," enhance liking (Rosenfeld, 1972). Source power is communicated by a variety of vocalic cues (O'Barr, 1982), such as high participation and loudness (J. Robinson and McArthur, 1982), avoidance of high pitch (Apple, Streeter, and Krauss, 1979) and of qualifiers, tag questions ("isn't it?"), interrogative intonation and syntax ("Would you close the door?"), intensifiers, hedges, and hesitations (B. Erickson *et al.*, 1978).

Complexities in interpreting nonverbal findings. A half-dozen limitations of this nonverbal research deserve mention (Scherer and Ekman, 1982b). Cues for encoding and decoding often differ, as when receivers judge deceptiveness on the basis of cues other than those that actually betray deceptiveness (Kraut, 1980; DePaulo *et al.*, 1982; Zuckerman *et al.*, 1982; Riggio and Freidmann, 1983). Also, nonverbal cues expressing a given characteristic differ from person to person (Zuckerman, Koestner, and Alton, 1984). Another complication is that many nonverbal variables relate nonmonotonically to persuasiveness: e.g., both very high and very low eye contact and proximity are perceived as unpleasant (Exline, 1972; J. D. Fisher and Byrne, 1975; Ellsworth and Langer, 1976; S. T. Fiske, 1980), and both very prolonged and very brief speech latencies and smiles suggest deceptiveness (Mehrabian, 1972; Baskett and Freedle,

1974; Kraut, 1978). Also, interaction effects are frequent, gender reversing even the direction of some relationships (Mayo and Henley, 1981; Comadena, 1982), as when duration of eye contact is negatively related to persuadability in boys and positively in girls (Mehrabian and Williams, 1969) and is positively related to perceived power during speaking and negatively during listening.

Interpreting nonverbal cues is further complicated by their varying degrees of conscious control, auditory being less controllable than visual, and body postures and gestures less than facial. Females surpass males at interpreting the source's voluntary facial cues but are poorer at interpreting unconsciously leaked posture and vocalic cues. Popularity derives from being good at interpreting consciously controllable facial cues and poor with unintentionally leaked vocalic cues, i.e., from being sensitive but not oversensitive to nonverbal cues (Rosenthal, 1979).

The most serious problem is the area's terrible nonreplication rate (Kraut, 1980), researchers having trouble replicating even their own findings (R. S. Feldman, Jenkins, and Papoola, 1979; R. S. Feldman and White, 1980), perhaps reflecting the area's atheoretical "dustbowl empiricism" fishing-expedition approach of identifying two groups of people who contrast on persuasiveness or whatever, and scoring them on a plethora of nonverbal variables to determine which discriminate the two groups (Mehrabian, 1972), a procedure that risks *post factum* capitalization on chance. Miniature theories do exist in the area, such as the Exline, Ellyson, and Long (1975) formulation regarding eye contact and power, the Rosenthal *et al.* (1979) work on sensitivity to nonverbal cues, and the B. Schwartz, Tesser, and Powell (1982) research on areal radiation of power; but nonverbal communication research lacks the deep theoretical foundation that would clarify mediating processes, provide meaningful bases for categorizing the nonverbal variables, and suggest interacting variables (Gillispie and Leffler, 1983).

Effects of Communication Context Variables

Persuadability alone versus with other people. People are more influenced if they are alone rather than with other people when they receive the persuasive message, even though the source is better liked when the message is heard in company (Keating and Latané, 1976). Lonely people are less confident of their opinions and less willing to advance their own views (Hansson and Jones, 1981),

while the presence of friends or even of strangers engenders a resistance-bolstering sense of solidarity (Tajfel, 1979) and is distracting (Knowles, 1983). Political or commercial television ads may have more impact when imbedded in programs watched alone rather than with family or friends; e.g., children may be more vulnerable to Saturday morning ads and programs they view alone than to prime-time shows viewed in a family context, when the mere presence of adults (even if they do not explicitly criticize the content) would reduce the program's impact on the children.

Effects of hedonic context during message reception. Persuasive impact is greater if the person is in a happy, benevolent mood when the message comes, noshing on peanuts and soda (Janis, Kaye, and Kirschner, 1965), watching a good program (Krugman, 1983), and with a pleasant musical background (Galizio and Hendrick, 1972), an appropriately scented other (Baron, 1983), a smile on one's face (Laird, 1974), nodding one's head (Wells and Petty, 1980), or relaxed in posture (Petty *et al.*, 1983). A positive context adds more than a negative context subtracts, and when the positive context can be attributed to human benevolence its effect is enhanced (Holloway, Tucker, and Hornstein, 1977); this finding, as well as delayed-action context effects (Leippe, Greenwald, and Baumgardner, 1982), suggests that a cognitive rather than affective mechanism is involved. Distraction is a heavily studied context variable (Haslett, 1976; Petty and Brock, 1981) whose discussion here is regretfully prohibited by lack of space.

RECEIVER VARIABLES' EFFECTS ON PERSUASIVE IMPACT

This section focuses on how persuasive impact is affected by the characteristics of the person receiving the message. The high midcentury interest in personality correlates of influenceability (Hovland and Janis, 1959) subsided during the 1960s and 1970s situationalist ascendancy but is likely to revive in the 1980s as the Establishment consensus swings back toward the dispositional pole (Mischel and Peake, 1983; Zucker, Aronoff, and Rabin, 1984). During these quarter-century dispositionalism/situationalism cycles what fluctuates are researcher expectations, making the fairly constant average obtained relationships seem either surprisingly high or surprisingly low (Brim and Kagan, 1980; Zanna, Higgins, and Herman, 1982). We shall first report the homogeneity of susceptibility within three types of social influence situations (suggestibility, conformity, and persuadability) and then analyze the theoretical principles underlying susceptibility's personality and demographic correlates.

Transsituational Generality of Influenceability
The Charcot-Liébéault controversy on the generality of suggestibility led to Binet's (1900) demonstration of predominantly low positive correlations among suggestibility tests. There seems to be a primary suggestibility factor on which motor tests like body sway and arm levitation load, a somewhat less clear secondary factor, with loadings by sensory tests like odor suggestibility and induced false recall, and probably several other special factors (Eysenck and Furneaux, 1945; Stukát, 1958; Hilgard, 1965). It seems reasonable to look for dispositional correlates of this primary common factor measured by hypnotizability, prestige-induced body sway, and other motor compliance tests but not to generalize the results to sensory task–habituated suggestibility.

A similar pattern of positive but low correlations is found among conformity tests across sources, situations, etc. (Abelson and Lesser, 1959; R. R. Sears, 1963; Harper and Tuddenham, 1964; Allen, 1975; Max Rosenbaum, 1982). There is some evidence that conformity and anticonformity (the latter manifested by doing the opposite of a conforming response) may be orthogonally independent traits rather than bipolar opposites (Willis and Hollander, 1964). Attitude change impacts of different persuasive messages also show predominantly positive correlations (Janis and Field, 1956). Across-situation correlations are even more modest (McGuire, 1968a). Stukát (1958) but not R. K. Moore (1964) found suggestibility and conformity related; and H. Linton and Graham (1959) and Abelson and Lesser (1959), but not R. K. Moore (1965), found conformity and persuadability related.

General Principles of Influenceability
Results with self-esteem (McGuire, 1968a, 1968d; Wylie, 1974, 1979), the most widely studied personality trait, illustrate the complexity of empirical findings on how personality variables relate to persuadability: In the 1950s this relationship seemed simple if ambiguous, either positive (Janis, 1954) or negative (McGuire and Ryan, 1955); by the 1960s the relationship seemed no less ambiguous but more complex, with Cox and Bauer (1964) and Silverman (1964) both finding nonmonotonic relation-

ships but in opposite directions. McGuire's (1968a) persuadability theory needs seven postulates, described below, to save these complex appearances.

The mediational postulate. The net persuasive impact of any receiver variable is mediated by its relationship to each of the dozen output steps of the comunication/persuasion matrix, a seemingly obvious point commonly overlooked because of preoccupation with the step 7 agreement mediator. For example, intelligence is assumed to be negatively related to persuadability because the greater information and critical ability of more intelligent people make them less yielding (step 7); however, this mediational postulate reminds us that the better attention, comprehension, etc., proclivities of the more intelligent raises their vulnerability to persuasion via comprehension and memory (steps 4 and 8), explaining why better educated soldiers proved more susceptible to the army indoctrination films in World War II (Hovland, Lumsdaine, and Sheffield, 1949).

The compensatory postulate. The mutually canceling operations of the mediators (just illustrated for intelligence, which is related to persuasion negatively via yielding step 7 and positively via information-encoding steps 4 and 8) is a compensatory complex that obtains, according to this second postulate, for a wide range of commonly studied receiver variables such as age, intelligence, self-esteem, anxiety, and depression. Such compensatory dynamics may be a cost-effective evolutionary adaptation for maintaining an optimal intermediate level of susceptibility, flexibly controlled by two opposing processes (McGuire, 1968a).

The nonmonotonic corollary. From the previous assumption of compensatory mediators it can be derived algebraically (McGuire, 1961b, 1968a) that personality characteristics will have nonmonotonic inverted-U relationships to influenceability. There is evidence (McGuire, 1972) that maximum persuadability occurs at intermediate levels on many dispositional variables such as age, self-esteem, anxiety, and intelligence.

Acute-chronic interaction corollary. From the above considerations it follows that manipulating a personality characteristic may either raise or lower influenceability, depending on where the person's initial chronic level fell. For example, a more anxiety-raising frightening communication increases the persuadability of a placid person with chronic anxiety well below the level that maximizes influenceability; but for a chronically anxious person already operating above this maximal anxiety level, this more frightening communication would diminish his or her persuadability. Similarly, manipulating the receiver's acute self-esteem by providing a success (failure) experience will raise or lower the person's persuadability, depending on whether his or her chronic self-esteem level is below or above the point associated with maximum influenceability.

The situational-weighting postulate. Testing the complex curves implied by the previous postulates is facilitated by the principle that an analysis of the relative importance of the mediating output steps in a given situation will yield situational/dispositional interaction predictions. For example, since intelligence enhances susceptibility via the comprehension mediator and reduces it via the yielding mediator, in typical conformity situations involving messages so simple that the comprehension mediator contributes little to the compliance variance, intelligence will be negatively related to conformity; but in persuasion situations involving complex messages, the relationship will tend to be positive (Eagly and Warren, 1976).

The confounded-variable postulate. One's theorizing tends to be in terms of pure, unidimensional variables, but a characteristic such as anxiety or self-esteem tends, in the process of living, to become embedded in a compensatory coping syndrome that complicates its relationship to influenceability. Low self-esteem in the abstract may make the person more vulnerable to persuasion through enhanced yielding, but in actuality a person of very low chronic self-esteem will have learned to protect himself or herself by diminished attention to messages (Bennis and Peabody, 1962), leaving him or her less vulnerable to subtle persuasion attempts and more vulnerable to obvious conformity pressures (Zellner, 1970). Because of this syndrome embeddedness, chronic dispositional characteristics in natural situations will relate to influenceability differently from the way their purer abstract representations do in theories or in acute laboratory manipulations where they are not embedded in compensatory-coping syndromes. Analytical studies of single personality dimensions should be supplemented by studies of complex syndromes of proclivities, activities,

interests, and styles, as in the marketing research on psychographics, life-styles and market segmentation (Sobel, 1981; J. Langer, 1983; Mitchell, 1983).

The situational interactions postulate. Multistep mediation implies ubiquitous interactions between receiver characteristics and other aspects of the communication situation (Magnusson, 1981). Intelligence can be positively or negatively related to influenceability depending on whether the message is complex or simple or whether it refutes or ignores opposition arguments (Hovland, Lumsdaine, and Sheffield, 1949). Anxiety, aggressiveness, or self-esteem enhance or reduce persuadability in predictable ways, depending on the issue involved (Leventhal and Perloe, 1962) and the type of argument used (D. Katz, 1960; Ghiglione and Beauvois, 1983).

Such intricacies in the relationships of receiver variables motivate the periodic swings toward situationalism, such as characterized the early 1970s, but it would be more productive to exploit rather than avoid the complexity by using multipostulate theories such as the above to explain known relationships and suggest new insights into higher-order interactions and nonmonotonic trends, as illustrated in the next section with respect to age, gender, and self-esteem, three of the most heavily studied receiver variables.

Influenceability Relationships of Illustrative Dispositional Characteristics

Age and influenceability. Age has a nonmonotonic inverted-U relationship to influenceability, with maximum suggestibility occurring at age nine (Stukát, 1958; Barber and Calverley, 1963; Hilgard, 1965; C. D. Ward and McGinnies, 1974; Eron *et al.*, 1983) while conformity may maximize at about twelve (Costanzo and Shaw, 1966), declining thereafter as the person grows older (Harris *et al.*, 1983). That this nonmonotonicity is the outcome of the postulated mediational processes is indicated both by direct measures of the mediators such as the young children's poor attention and comprehension (C. D. Ward and McGinnies, 1974) and by obtained interaction effects such as that age of maximum influenceability is higher for persuadability than suggestibility (Janis and Rife, 1959).

For mental age, early reviewers reported frequent failure to find significant relationships between intelligence and influenceability (G. Murphy, Murphy, and

Newcomb, 1937; Hovland, Janis, and Kelley, 1953). However, the above analysis indicates that one should look for interactions and nonmonotonic relationships rather than simple main effects (Eagly and Warren, 1976). While definitive meta-analyses are yet to be done, most correlations [and especially the significant ones (Stukát, 1958)] of mental age to suggestibility are negative and to persuadability are positive (Hovland, Lumsdaine, and Sheffield, 1949), indicating that in persuasion situations vulnerability enhancement due to the greater comprehension and inference-drawing abilities associated with intelligence (Schumacker, 1981) more than compensate for its enhancing resistance via superior critical ability.

Gender differences in influenceability. Male-female differences have always attracted attention, but politicization of the issue has accelerated research on the topic in the 1970s. At the start of that decade McGuire (1968a, 1969b) had concluded that although most studies failed to find significant gender differences in influenceability, the preponderance of results in the females-more-influenceable direction suggests that women are more susceptible. This conclusion was called into question in the mid-1970s in two careful literature reviews (E. E. Maccoby and Jacklin, 1974; Eagly, 1978) and one meta-analyses review (Sohn, 1980): For example, 84 of the 138 influenceability studies reviewed by E. E. Maccoby and Jacklin (1974) failed to show a gender difference significant at the 0.05 level. However, in keeping with McGuire's point, 44 of the 54 studies that did report significant differences showed women to be the more influenceable, an asymmetry significant well above the 0.01 level by a sign test; and in Block's (1976) identification of 154 relevant studies, 61 of the 68 reporting gender differences significant at the 0.05 level found females to be more influenceable. More recently, Eagly and Carli's (1981) meta-analyses of 148 studies on gender differences done in the past quarter century reconfirms McGuire's (1968a) conclusion that females are more influenceable (though the magnitude of the gender difference continues to be of trivial practical magnitude). Metanalysis promises to be a cost-effective methodological innovation (Glass, McGaw, and Smith, 1981; R. Rosenthal, 1983), though relationships are underestimated when researchers (Cooper, 1979) adopt the overly conservative convention of treating unascertainable male and female influenceability differences as if the means were exactly equal. A better tactic (Eagly and Carli, 1981) is to report results both with and without these underreported studies.

Mechanisms of the gender difference. McGuire (1968a, 1969b) proposed several mechanisms to account for this greater female influenceability and for a possible second tendency for dispositional variables to predict influenceability more strongly in males than females (Perry and Perry, 1975). A measurement artifact might be involved if the males' scores are more reliable because the measures are usually developed by males. The data indicate that independent personality variables are no better measured in males (McGuire, 1968a; M. Corcoran, 1981) but the dependent (influenceability) variable may be: Sistruck and McDavid (1971), Goldberg (1975), Cacioppo and Petty (1980), and Karabenick (1983) report that males are more influenceable on "women's" issues and women more on the "masculine" topics usually used in experiments, and Eagly and Carli (1981) find in addition that female influenceability is higher in studies reported by male investigators. Bartos (1982) discusses the susceptibility of women to marketing practices.

An alternative mechanism (McGuire, 1968a; Eagly, 1983) is that the greater female susceptibility and greater male predictability might both derive from socialization differences such that conforming pressures are exerted more strongly and uniformly on women, compressing them into a narrow band of high influenceability, while men's socialization, more ambiguous on this characteristic, leaves males with a lower mean and higher variability in conformity. This explanation implies two further predictions: that the gender differences would be more pronounced in conformity situations (where the yielding mediator contributes more of the variance) than in persuadability situations, as found by Eagly and Carli (1981), and that influenceability variance will be greater among males. Various other socialization interpretations are indicated by S. Bem's (1975) finding that more "feminine" participants of both sexes conform more than do men or women who score higher in "masculinity" or "adrogyny," by Eagly's (1978) finding that women have a stronger orientation toward attaining interpersonal goals when in group situations, and by Santee and Jackson's (1982) finding that females consider conformity a more positive self-defining act. Fink *et al.* (1975) find that women are more swayed by sympathy relative to reciprocity appeals, and Osman (1982) finds that men are more likely to comply with rules and women to conform to models. Women's greater influenceability might derive also (McGuire, 1968a) from their superior information-encoding ability (Wittig and Petersen, 1979; but see Eagly, 1974); if so, females will score higher on message learning as well as influenceability (J. L. Fisher and Harris, 1976), and when yielding variance is partialed out, the gender difference should be greater for persuadability than for conformity, to which the comprehension mediator contributes less, but Eagly and Carli (1981) find the reverse.

Self-esteem and influenceability. Few of the hundred-plus studies of self-esteem and influenceability survive Wylie's (1979) stringent methodological criteria, but in the course of such stern justice few studies would see publication. Here we shall season justice with mercy, risking that a hundred sinful studies survive rather than that one deserving piece of research should perish. While significant relationships are sparse, as with age and gender the directions of the small differences are often consistent when the studies are partitioned into theoretically coherent categories. Self-esteem relationships to suggestibility are negligible (Barber, 1964; Hilgard, 1965), but to conformity the small relationships are predominantly negative, especially in children and when the low self-esteem is issue-relevant (Endler, Wiesenthal, and Geller, 1972). In the more complexly mediated persuadability situations, as predicted by the seven-postulate theory described above, nonmonotonic and interaction relations tend to emerge, such as the shift of maximum influenceability to higher levels of self-esteem as message complexity increases (Gelfand, 1962; Gollob and Dittes, 1965; Nisbett and Gordon, 1967; Zellner, 1970). The importance of distinguishing chronic and acute self-esteem is illustrated by Deaux's (1972a) finding that the persuasion is lowest in the low-chronic/low-acute self-esteem condition and highest in high-chronic/low-acute self-esteem receivers who are vulnerable via both chronically good reception habits and momentarily heightened yielding state.

Effects of Receiver's Active Participation

Its conceptual relevance to learning, psychoanalytic, dissonance, and cognitive-response theories made active participation one of the most heavily investigated receiver variables since the 1950s. Memorization research showed that substituting active recitation for passive reading enhances message learning (Hovland, 1951), and

Freud urged switching from therapist-controlled procedures such as hyponotic suggestion to patient participation procedures such as free association and dream recall on the grounds that patients were more accepting of interpretations derived from their own cognitive work (Meissner, 1980). Dissonance theorists (Festinger, 1957; Wicklund and Brehm, 1976) inferred that volitional, active counterattitudinal advocacy would result in internalized attitude change, and now cognitive-response theorists (Petty, Ostrom, and Brock, 1981) stress the role of self-generated thoughts in inducing attitude change.

Low effect of active participation. Empirical support is less impressive than these multitudinous theoretical underpinnings imply. Indeed, leaving a conclusion implicit so that the receiver can participate actively by drawing it for himself or herself results in less attitude change than drawing the conclusion explicitly in the message, even when the conclusion is obvious (Hovland and Mandell, 1952). With a few exceptions (King and Janis, 1956; Janis, 1968a) researchers find that passively reading a presented speech produces more attitude change than improvising one's own speech with or without a guiding outline (McGuire, 1961a; Greenbaum, 1963). Even granting the debatable claims for the greater efficacy of nondirective therapy (Bergin and Lambert, 1978; Smith, Glass, and Miller, 1980; Prioleau, Murdock, and Brody, 1983), it should not be surprising that active participation has the reversed effect on attitude change, considering that a patient in therapy is more familiar with and more motivated to generate relevant material than are receivers in most persuasive situations. The persuasive disadvantage of requiring participation can be mitigated by providing extrinsic motivation, supplying material with which the participant can work, or allowing an incubation interval to pass (McGuire, 1964). When smokers actively role-play characters in a lung cancer tragedy, their attitudes and behaviors on smoking are more affected than when they passively observe others playing the same roles (Mann and Janis, 1968; Bandura, Blanchard, and Ritter, 1969), though the vicarious participation also has some effect (Clore and Jeffery, 1972).

Effect of size of incentive for participation. Much of the 1960s research on active participation was inspired by conflicting learning and consistency theory predictions about the effect of magnitude of motivation (incentive, justification) for the overt participation. Dissonance theory (Festinger, 1957; Wicklund and Brehm, 1976) implies an inverse relationship, since internalized attitude change becomes more necessary to justify overt compliance as the external incentives decrease; behavioristic theory, on the other hand, implies that greater external incentive for participation motivates more vigorous overt compliance and felt satisfaction and hence increases internalized attitude change.

Counterattitudinal activities used in these studies include writing an essay opposed to one's own position (J. Brehm and Cohen, 1962), telling a lie (Festinger and Carlsmith, 1959), eating a disliked food (J. Brehm, 1960; Zimbardo *et al.*, 1965), performing an embarrassing act (Aronson and Mills, 1959), and giving up a preferred toy (Aronson, Carlsmith, and Darley, 1963; Lepper, 1973). External justifications used include money inducement (Festinger and Carlsmith, 1959; Lependorf, 1964), source attractiveness (Zimbardo *et al.*, 1965), helping science (Freedman, 1963), getting a good grade (Bostrom, Vlandis, and Rosen, 1961), expending effort to overcome distraction (Zimbardo, 1965), and avoiding a threatened punishment (Aronson, Carlsmith, and Darley, 1963). The varied outcomes found among and within (Carlsmith, Collins, and Helmreich, 1966) studies illustrate Oscar Wilde's aphorism that the truth is never pure and rarely simple. Dissonance theory's "paradoxical" negative relationship between incentive size and internalized attitude change is most likely to occur when the complier perceives that she or he had a high degree of choice and that the action had foreseeable and serious consequences for which she or he is highly responsible (Collins and Hoyt, 1972; Wicklund and Brehm, 1976; Stroebe and Diehl, 1981). Besides this dissonance motivational factor, additional cognitive inference factors such as self-perception and response contagion may be involved (D. Bem, 1972; D. Green, 1974; Nuttin, 1975; Shaffer, 1975; Verhaeghe, 1976).

TARGET VARIABLES' EFFECTS ON PERSUASIVE IMPACT

Several variables in this final category have already been discussed incidentally as interacting with variables from the previous four categories. Two additional target variables, persistence of induced attitude change and techniques for conferring resistance to persuasion, deserve further discussion here because of their theoretical and applied importance.

Postcommunication Time Trends

We shall first discuss decay of induced attitude change and then the converse delayed-action attitude impacts. We shall then describe how these time trends are affected by interaction variables and by memory for the inducing message's content.

Temporal decay of induced attitude change. There is not just one single decay curve for induced attitude change, any more than there is a single situation-free forgetting curve. Decay parameters vary wildly: Some studies report most of the initially induced attitude change persisting for months (Watts, 1967; Nuttin, 1975; Rokeach, 1975; P. B. Smith, 1976); others report intermediate decay rates suggesting a half-life of about a week or two for induced attitude change (McGuire, 1957; Watts and McGuire, 1964); and still others report precipitous and complete decay in short periods (B. E. Collins and Hoyt, 1972; Ronis *et al.*, 1977) as if persuasive communications produce only superficial "elastic" changes (Cialdini *et al.*, 1976; Hass and Mann, 1976). Not only the rate but the shape and even direction of the persistence curve varies with many factors (T. D. Cook and Flay, 1978).

Delayed-action effects of persuasive communications. The vicissitudes of the discounting-cue sleeper-effect hypothesis vindicates keeping faith in a theory even in the face of contrary evidence. The reminiscence phenomena in learning (Hovland, 1939) plus the assumption that message learning mediates persuasion led Hovland, Lumsdaine, and Sheffield (1949) to discover some slight delayed-action effects in their World War II army data. Subsequent research focused on just one of the half-dozen mechanisms that they suggested, their conjecture that when a discounting cue (such as attribution to an untrustworthy source or a warning that the content is not necessarily true) accompanies a persuasive massage and diminishes its immediate impact, the incidental discounting cue is gradually dissociated from the retained persuasive arguments, resulting in an initial phase of delayed-action or at least slower decay than without a discounting cue (Watts and McGuire, 1964; T. D. Cook *et al.*, 1979). Early statements of the theory assumed that the discounting cue had to be forgotten more rapidly than the convincing arguments, but McGuire (1961b, 1968a; Bogartz, 1965) showed that the delayed-action effect can be derived algebraically without this *ad hoc* assumption.

There were several immediate post war replications, at least in some subconditions and when the researchers worked overtime to find the evidence (Hovland and Weiss, 1951; Kelman and Hovland, 1953; W. Weiss, 1953; S. J. Weber, 1972), but then the sleeper effect nodded off and was even given premature burial in the 1970s after several failures to find empirical signs of life (Capon and Hulbert, 1973; Gillig and Greenwald, 1974). More heroic resuscitation efforts in the 1980s breathed life back into the discounting-cue explanation (T. D. Cook *et al.*, 1979)—at least if the persuasive content is strong, the discounting cue is substantial enough to suppress initial impact, the ensuing delay period is of appropriate duration and one counts relative as well as absolute delayed-action trends (T. D. Cook and Flay, 1978).

Besides this first discounting cue mechanism, ten other hypothesized mechanisms for producing delayed-action effects are imaginable. A second and third involve interpersonal processes: Group members who are little influenced immediately may show delayed-action impact due to subsequent proselytizing by the more immediately affected group members; and there may be a two-step impact in that only the attentive group leaders are initially affected and they subsequently convince the passive masses. Eight other hypotheses assume intrapersonal processes. A third sensitization or agenda-setting hypothesis suggests that early communications on the topic may sensitize receivers, leaving them more susceptible to subsequent arguments. Fourthly, a lukewarm convert made by the communication may then seek out further arguments to bolster the vulnerable new belief (McGuire, 1964). A consistency reaction may be involved as a fifth possibility in that a person who has just reported "before" attitudes on a questionnaire may feel inhibited about showing a change of attitude on the immediately-after measure but might reveal change on a measure taken later when the inconsistency would not be so salient. Sixthly, reactance might be involved in that the person resists while under pressure to change and shifts later when the pressure is removed (Brehm and Mann, 1975; T. D. Cook *et al.*, 1978).

A seventh, "predispositional" explanation is that when situational factors impede the receiver's immediate acceptance of a position toward which he or she is predisposed, agreement will emerge as the situation changes with time. The eighth, temporal-inertia, hypothesis (McGuire, 1960c, 1981) predicts that a sinking-in interval is needed for a persuasive communication's implications to seep to related issues, especially if the communication is at all subtle (D. Katz, Sarnoff, and McClintock, 1956), as in Riley and Pettigrew's (1976) finding of a delayed-action impact of the Martin Luther King assassination on whites' attitudes toward blacks. The incubation-of-anxiety generalization sometimes shown in verbal conditioning studies (Mednick, 1957) may be a related ninth cognitive lag manifestation of unconscious information processing. A tenth, "Bartlett" effect prediction (Papageorgis, 1963) is that when a persuasive message argues its point moderately with qualifications and reservations, the retained content may drift subsequently to its more polarized central point as the modulating qualifications dissipate. An eleventh possibility is that in a multiple-topic communication context, initially nonchanging positions on some one issue gradually become assimilated to the large changes on the bulk of the items (Leippe, Greenwald, and Baumgardner, 1982). As compared with all these hypotheses lying in wait to explain delayed-action effects, demonstrations of their occurrence are relatively infrequent.

Interaction effects that moderate attitude change persistence. Persistence of induced attitude change being complexly mediated, interaction effects are frequent, as we shall illustrate by one example from each of the five input classes. The just-discussed discounting-cue hypothesis illustrates a source interaction such that induced attitude change decays more slowly when the message comes from a low- rather than high-credibility source (Hovland, Lumsdaine, and Sheffield, 1949; T. D. Cook *et al.*, 1979). Several interactions were mentioned in the message variables section: the slower decay of impact from subtle than from obvious messages (D. Katz, Sarnoff, and McClintock, 1956; A. R. Cohen, 1957; McGuire, 1960c), from the first than the second of two opposed messages (N. Miller and Campbell, 1959; Insko, 1964; W. Wilson and Miller, 1968), and from low- than high-fear appeals (Insko, Arkoff, and Insko, 1965). As mentioned in the channel variables section, induced change decays less rapidly when produced by more encodable preaching than by demonstration (Rushton, 1975), though modeling effects can be quite persistent (Bandura, Adams, and Beyer, 1977). Receiver variables such as need for orientation (A. R. Cohen, 1957) and ego defensiveness (Stotland, Katz, and Patchen, 1959) interact with persistence. An example of a destination variable interaction is the slower decay of impacts on remotely related issues than on the directly explicit conclusion (McGuire, 1960c, 1981). Focusing on such interaction effects is a sign of the growing sophistication of the area.

Relationships between persistence of attitude change and recall of cognitive contents. Obtained correlations between recall of message contents and persistence of induced attitude change (T. D. Cook and Flay, 1978) range from a high of +0.50 (McGuire, 1957; Papageorgis, 1963) to a negligible or even slightly negative magnitude (Haskins, 1964; Insko, 1964; Sawyer, 1973), the correlation declining as the interval lengthens (N. Miller and Campbell, 1959; Insko, 1964; Watts and McGuire, 1964). Independent variables tend to have similar effects on memory for message contents and on persistence of induced attitude change (H. H. Johnson and Watkins, 1971; Calder, Insko, and Yandell, 1974). However, the obtained correlations between the two are so small and the shape of the two decay functions so different (Watts and McGuire, 1964) as to cast doubt on simplistic versions of the information-processing model of persuasion.

The persistence of attitude change is related to memory more for some contents than others. Most important is recall of the conclusion (Watts and McGuire, 1964; T. D. Cook and Wadsworth, 1972), followed by recall of arguments, both those explicitly presented in the message (Watts and McGuire, 1964) and those that the message provoked the receiver to generate (McGuire, 1964; Watts, 1967; A. G. Greenwald, 1968a; Calder, Insko, and Yandell, 1974). Forgetting that one ever heard a persuasive message on the topic actually enhances attitude change persistence (Watts and McGuire, 1964). Attitude change tends to become functionally autonomous of the retention even of material that was initially needed to induce the change.

Procedures for Conferring Resistance to Persuasion

Resistance to persuasion appears attractive but it is probably healthier to be at an intermediate level of susceptibility such that one neither precipitously abandons old beliefs under attack nor adamantly rejects discrepant information. We shall first describe three approaches for inducing generalized resistance and then three for producing more focused resistance to certain sources or techniques or on specified issues.

Inducing resistant motivational states. Negative motivational states can be induced, such as angering people by exposure to annoying experiences, making them anxious by exposure to stress, lowering their self-esteem by contrived failure experiences, inducing depressive withdrawal by presenting sad news, or causing loneliness by isolation. Corresponding to these acute manipulations are enduring chronic personality traits (aggressiveness, anxiety, self-esteem, etc.) that have complex nonmonotonic relationships to persuasibility because of the compensatory mediating role of various output steps and embeddedness in a persisting syndrome. For example, angering the person by annoying or abusive treatments prior to the communication decreases persuadability if the message urges a benevolent position but increases susceptibility to arguments for a hostile position (W. Weiss and Fine, 1956; Berkowitz, 1974); likewise, as discussed above in the receiver variable section, manipulating the receiver's anxiety level or self-esteem level enhances or diminishes influenceability, depending on the chronic level of anxiety or self-esteem (Millman, 1968; Lehmann, 1970; Zellner, 1970).

Enhancing resistance by training in critical ability. Concern that children may be especially susceptible to advertisements (Adler *et al.,* 1980) suggests that people's resistance can be enhanced by general education that enlarges their information base, raises self-esteem, sharpens critical ability, etc. However, general education also tends to increase persuadability (Hovland, Lumsdaine, and Sheffield, 1949) by enhancing attention to and comprehension of arguments.

Training in specific critical techniques, such as recognizing, analyzing, and refuting types of arguments and being more suspicious of sources, confers some slight resistance (Tannenbaum, 1967; Huesmann *et al.,* 1983), as does encouragement to counterargue (Wellins and McGinnies, 1977). Also deserving closer study for their resistance-enhancing potential are techniques such as identity managing, negotiating, and justifying (Cialdini, 1980; McLaughlin, Cody, and Robey, 1980; Tetlock, 1983), prescriptions for resisting television ads (Primeau, 1978; Rank, 1982), or political arguments (Vedung, 1982), peer resistance techniques to help children withstand pressures to smoke (McAlister *et al.,* 1980; Evans *et al.,* 1981), procedures for inoculation to stress (Novaco, 1977), and reversal of methods used in training people to be more suggestible (Tart, 1970).

It may seem unhealthy to train people in reality-distorting message evasion tactics such as avoiding exposure to discrepant information, withholding attention, misperceiving the meaning of their experiences, and resisting therapeutic treatment (Marshall, 1982; Wachtel, 1982), but such distortion could reduce susceptibility (C. J. Patterson and Mischel, 1976; A. G. Greenwald, 1980) and may be a healthy mode of coping in environments so malevolent that it would be pathological to function sanely within them; inmates report having retained personal integrity in repulsive settings (where, in Léon Bloy's terms, the only honorable sounds are a scream of rage or a scream of pain) by adopting a schizophreniclike detachment (Bettelheim, 1960; Clifford, 1963), distancing themselves from communication as if they were watching a film.

Conferring resistance by modeling unyielding behavior. Showing models holding out against social influence pressures and being rewarded for so doing is a third, social learning, approach to resistance conferral. Participants in Milgram's (1974) obedience studies became much more resistant to an authority's pressure to inflict punishment if they observed others refusing to obey. Children resist prosocial preaching (Rushton, 1975) and temptation (Bussey and Perry, 1977) more if they witness a resisting adult or age peer.

Immunization through commitment. Lewin's (1947, 1951) World War II group decision research—second only to the contemporaneous work by Hovland, Lumsdaine, and Sheffield (1949) as an instigator of the 1950s and 1960s flourishing of attitude change research —involved "refreezing" people's attitudes by group commitment that lessened backsliding during subsequent counterpressure. Four types of commitment procedure can be distinguished. A relatively mild private-commitment procedure involves asking the person simply to think privately about her or his holding the belief prior to getting discrepant information about it, as when students who have just volunteered for an experiment are asked to think about having agreed to participate, which increases their subsequent show-up rate (Bennett, 1955), just as stating one's preference among presidential candidates on a preelection poll increases voting rate (Kraut and McConahay, 1973; Yalch, 1976; Bridge *et al.*, 1977; Traugott and Katosh, 1981). On the other hand, being asked rhetorical questions (Zillman and Cantor, 1974; Petty, Cacioppo, and Heesacker, 1981) or having to state one's opinion after each item of persuasive information seems not to confer resistance and may even interfere with resistance-conferring primacy effects (Byrne *et al.*,

1969; J. L. Farr, 1973), perhaps because the repeated responding affects the attention-dependent weights of the later items (N. H. Anderson, 1981).

A second, public-commitment procedure asking the person to state his or her initial position publicly, usually but not always (Bennett, 1955) confers more resistance than does private commitment (Hovland, Campbell, and Brock, 1957; Wicklund and Brehm, 1976). People whose commitment to conserve energy was made public resisted subsequent pressures to consume better than those in the private commitment condition (Pallak, Cook, and Sullivan, 1981). Some of the apparent superiority of public commitment may be an artifact of its directly causing an anticipatory belief change rather than enhancing resistance to a subsequent attack (S. Fisher, Rubinstein, and R. W. Freeman, 1956; Hoyt and Centers, 1972).

A third, behavioral-commitment procedure of having the person actively defend the belief or take some onerous action on the basis of it confers still more resistance (Kiesler, 1971; Janis and Mann, 1977; Halverson and Pallak, 1978), especially under conditions of felt volition, responsibility, and perception of serious consequences (Collins and Hoyt, 1972; Wicklund and Brehm, 1976). The foot-in-door (Freedman and Fraser, 1966; M. Snyder and Cunningham, 1975) and the low-ball (Cialdini *et al.*, 1978) studies show that even a trivial action commits the person to that belief, either through self-redefinition or sense of obligation (Burger and Petty, 1981). A fourth, external-commitment procedure of telling the person that one suspects that he or she holds a certain belief confers resistance (Rosenbaum and Franc, 1960), perhaps by an attribution (Munson and Keisler, 1974; R. L. Miller, Brickman, and Bolen, 1975) or labeling (Kraut, 1973) mechanism, though labeling can backfire by stimulating guilt processes (Steele, 1975).

Increasing resistance by anchoring procedures. Anchoring a person's initial belief to various types of cognitions is a fifth immunizing approach, based on the assumption that people strive to maintain connected and coherent cognitive systems and so resist changing an anchored belief because it would require onerous adjustments on the related cognitions (McGuire, 1960b, 1964; Danes, Hunter, and Woelfel, 1978). Anchoring procedures usually involve linking the belief to one of three types of cognition. Most often beliefs are anchored to values by arguing that the belief (or object or act) facilitates positive or prevents negative outcomes, as depicted in the attribution × evaluation models discussed above in the attitude structure section. Both active thinking about how one's belief is related to past behavior (Ross *et al.*, 1983) or conducive to one's values (Nelson, 1968) and passive reading about such links (Holt, 1970) confer resistance to subsequent attacks. A second anchoring technique is to link the belief to other beliefs by procedures such as McGuire's (1961d, 1981) belief-evoking Socratic questioning (Rokeach, 1975; Tesser, 1978; Wood, 1982; Loken and Wyer, 1983), by "cognitively tuning" the person as a receiver of subsequent messages (Watts and Holt, 1970), or by cognitive response approaches (Petty, Ostrom, and Brock, 1981). Thirdly, the belief may be anchored to significant others by reminding the person that his or her belief is shared by admired others (Tannenbaum, 1967), his or her peers (Bennett, 1955), or valued reference groups (Kelley, 1955; Doise and Douglas, 1978) or simply by having such significant others present (Charters and Newcomb, 1958).

Producing resistance by preexposure to belief-threatening material. A sixth approach uses a biological inoculation analogy to predict that the strength of a widely shared belief will, like the health of an animal raised in a germ-free environment, prove illusory and be vulnerable to attacking material but that resistance can be conferred by preexposure to a weakened form of the attacking material that is threatening enough to stimulate defenses but not so strong as to overwhelm them. Numerous hypotheses suggested by the inoculation analogy were confirmed by subsequent empirical work (McGuire, 1964). If prior to persuasive attack on cultural truisms or even controversial beliefs (Tannenbaum, 1967; Bither, Dolich, and Nell, 1971; Szybillo and Heslin, 1973) the person is given supportive arguments, it confers less resistance to subsequent attacks than does preexposure to belief-threatening attacking arguments (weakened by refutations or simply being stated without backing or refutation), even if the subsequent attack uses arguments different from the preexposed ones (McGuire, 1964; Tannenbaum, 1967; M. D. Miller and Burgoon, 1979). Preexposure works both by making the subsequent strong attacks seem less believable and by stimulating the person to generate more belief-supporting cognitive responses (McGuire, 1964; Tannenbaum, 1967; Frey, 1981). Cognitive complexity (Cronen and LaFleur, 1977; Suedfeld and Borrie, 1978) and information integration (Farkas and Anderson, 1976) may also be involved. The nonthreatening, supportive defenses do directly enhance beliefs prior to attacks more than do the threatening de-

fenses, but their failure to confer resistance to subsequent attacks shows that this is a "paper tiger" strength, open to several interpretations (McGuire and Papageorgis, 1961; Sawyer, 1973; Farkas and Anderson, 1976).

Supportive defenses can be given immunizing efficacy if they are accompanied by a threat such as preexposure to a weakened attacking argument (McGuire, 1961d), forewarning of an impending strong attack (McGuire and Papageorgis, 1962), or requiring difficult active participation in the defense (McGuire, 1961a); conversely, when the supportive defense is accompanied by a concurrent reassurance of peer or expert agreement, its immunizing efficacy is weakened (L. R. Anderson and McGuire, 1965). While these combinatory predictions from inoculation theory have usually been confirmed, the permutational predictions have not been supported (McGuire, 1964; Tannenbaum and Norris, 1965; Infante, 1975; Pryor and Steinfatt, 1978). Conferred resistance increases monotonically with message intensity when supportive defenses are used but has a nonmonotonic (inverted-U) relationship to intensity with intrinsically motivating threatening defenses (Burgoon and Chase, 1973). Just as biological inoculation requires the passage of an incubation period before resistance develops, threatening defenses also show delayed-action immunizing effects, conferring more resistance to attacks that come several days after the defense than to immediate attacks (McGuire, 1962; Rogers and Thistlethwaite, 1969; but see Szybillo and Heslin, 1973). This research showing the efficacy of dealing with rather than ignoring the opposition in an ideologically competitive situation has revolutionized advertising practice in the past decade. As recently as 1970, ads studiously ignored competing products but by the early 1980s one-quarter of all ads are competitive. It also has medical applications as in prior stress inoculation of patients about to undergo surgical stress (Janis, 1968b; Meichenbaum and Turk, 1983).

DYNAMIC ASPECTS OF THE ATTITUDE CHANGE PROCESS

We turn here from directive to dynamic aspects of attitude change. The preceding sections described how inputs of the communication/persuasion matrix are channeled through the dozen output steps; here we describe the dynamic, motivational forces that instigate and terminate this directive processing and reinforce its occurrence. Attitude change research has been stimulated by sixteen such psychodynamic concepts, each a partial view of human nature.

AN OVERVIEW OF THE SIXTEEN-CELL MATRIX OF DYNAMIC THEORIES

Each researcher typically draws inspiration from one currently fashionable and personally provocative partial view of human nature, depicting the person as a consistency maximizer, a meaning giver, an information processor, or whatever; but the person has numerous complex and even mutually contradictory needs, so each of these partial views yields valid predictions in some circumstances and misleads in others where the emphasized aspect is overridden by other facets of the person (McGuire, 1980a, 1983). An inclusive list of terms for human proclivities is contained in Allport and Odbert's (1936) Stakhanovite compilation of 20,000 dispositional trait names, which Cattell (1946) grouped into a (barely) manageable set of categories. Less methodically derived but more widely used compilations include Freud's three psychosexual and E. H. Erikson's (1964) eight psychosocial needs, McDougall's (1908) eleven specific propensities, H. A. Murray's (1968) twenty-eight individual needs on six levels, Maslow's (1970) seven-step hierarchy going from basic physiological to self-actualizing motives, and Rokeach's (1973) sixteen instrumental and sixteen terminal values.

Reviews of attitude research (Petty and Cacioppo, 1981; M. J. Smith, 1982) typically go beyond the single-minded preoccupation of the individual researcher by discussing the findings in terms of several partial views of the person. I have attempted a still more inclusive systematic approach (McGuire, 1974, 1983) by starting with the half-dozen most often mentioned theories and abstracting four orthogonal dimensions which, when dichotomized, yield the sixteen-cell matrix shown in Table 2, each cell including a family of attitude change theories. Two of the four dimensions concern forces that instigate action and two concern forces that terminate action. The first, being versus becoming, Apollonian/Dionysian instigating dimension, partitions theories into those that depict the person as acting to maintain the current stability (equilibrium, homeostasis) versus those that depict the person as striving to attain new levels of complexity (growth, transcendence). The second, active versus reactive, instigating dimension separates theories into those depicting behavior as actively evoked by internal needs versus those depicting behavior as a reaction to external environmental presses. These two action-initiating dimensions are shown as the column headings in Table 2.

The third and fourth dimensions, shown as the row headings of Table 2, divide dynamic theories on the basis of the goal states whose attainment are postulated to terminate action sequences. The third, cognitive versus affective, terminating dimension distinguishes between

TABLE 2
Sixteen Partial Views of Human Nature That Have Served as Guiding-Idea Theories for the Dynamic Aspects of Attitude Change

	ACTION INITIATION			
	NEED FOR STABILITY		*NEED FOR GROWTH*	
ACTION TERMINATION	*ACTIVE INSTIGATION*	*REACTIVE INSTIGATION*	*ACTIVE INSTIGATION*	*REACTIVE INSTIGATION*
Cognitive state Internal relationship	1. Consistency	2. Categorization	5. Stimulation	6. Utilitarian
External relationship	4. Hermeneutic	3. Inductional	8. Autonomy	7. Template
Affective state Internal relationship	13. Tension reduction	14. Ego defense	9. Attraction	10. Identity
External relationship	16. Expression	15. Repetition	12. Assertion	11. Contagion

theories depicting people as striving for ideational end states (such as consistency or meaning) and theories positing affective end states (such as self-esteem or tension reduction), a contrast stimulated by the "cognitive revolution" and reactions to it (Dember, 1974; Tomkins, 1981). The fourth, internal versus external, terminating dimension distinguishes between theories depicting the person as acting to achieve internal adjustments among her or his own personality components versus achieving adjustments between herself or himself and the external environment.

Alternative or additional dimensions and different cuts on the chosen dimensions could have been used here; e.g., the first instigating dimension which we have dichotomized into stability versus growth theories could instead have been trichotomized by adding a third, destructive, catabolic subset of theories that would include second law-of-thermodynamics depictions such as Freud's thanatotic death wish and oceanic depictions such as Buddhist nirvana and Hindu moksha concepts, which depict the person as striving toward self-annihilation in order to merge with a transcendental reality. All three categories are singled out in the Hindu Brahma-Vishnu-Siva (creative, sustaining, destructive) aspects of being; indeed the Siva/destructive aspect, neglected here, has received more attention within Hindu thought than the other two (O'Flaherty, 1982). These death wish theories and other alternatives have heuristic potential but so far have instigated little empirical attitude change research, and so we shall limit the present discussion to the more popular sixteen families of theories named in the cells of Table 2, taking them in blocks of four starting with the four cognitive stability theories in the upper left quadrant of the table and continuing clockwise through the other three quadrants.

COGNITIVE STABILITY THEORIES

The four families of theories named in the cells of the upper left quadrant of Table 2 agree in depicting the person as instigated to action by a need to maintain a cognitive equilibrium but differ among themselves on the other two dimensions. We shall start with cell 1 consistency theories in the upper left-hand corner and proceed clockwise around the other three cells of this quadrant.

Consistency Theories

The family of theories in this and each of the other sixteen cells will be described by mentioning first its basic insight regarding the nature of the person, then the variant forms given it by its numerous proponents, and finally some illustrative implications regarding attitude change. Cell 1 consistency theories depict the person as striving to maintain a connected and coherent cognitive system, as instigated to action in order to reduce any imbalance that occurs among his or her perceptions, memories, feelings, needs, behavior, role commitments, cultural norms, etc.

The various consistency theories, reviewed succinctly by McGuire (1966b) and in detail by Abelson *et al.* (1968) and C. J. White (1982), differ as regards the components stressed, how consistency is defined, the preferred modes of consistency restoration, etc. Heider's (1946, 1958) balance notion anticipated several variants (Weir, 1983), including interpersonal symmetry theory (Newcomb, 1953), dissonance theory (Festinger, 1957; Wicklund and Brehm, 1976), and equity theory (Adams and Freedman, 1976; J. E. Greenberg and Cohen, 1982; Messick and Cook, 1983), with social exchange theory being a sibling if not offspring (Gergen, Greenberg, and Willis, 1980; Roloff, 1981; Mills and Clark, 1982). More diverse in origin are congruity theory (Osgood and Tannenbaum, 1955), probabilogical theory (McGuire, 1960c, 1981; Wyer and Carlston, 1979), psycho-logics (Abelson and Rosenberg, 1958), and graph theory depictions of inter- and intrapersonal processes (Harary, Norman, and Cartwright, 1965; P. W. Holland and Leinhardt, 1975). Some consistency theory implications for attitude change simply repackage old notions (such as dissonance theory implications of selective exposure or internalization), but others are more innovative, such as those dealing with the Socratic method of attitude change or remote cognitive ramifications (McGuire, 1981) discussed above under attitude structure.

Categorization Theories

These categorization or perceptual theories depict the person in his or her filing clerk aspect, coping with information overload by sorting incoming impressions among phylogenetically and ontogenetically developed cognitive categories, many having affect and action tags. Not the situation in itself but how the person categorizes it determines his or her reactions to the overly complex environment. These categories are oversimplified, fuzzy, and susceptible to priming and audience-tailored messages (Higgins, Rholes, and Jones, 1977) and to distorted stereotypes (L. F. Clark and Woll, 1981; D. L. Hamilton, 1981; I. Katz, 1981; McGuire, 1983), but without them there would be paralyzing chaos. That these simplifying representations develop out of social interaction was earlier proposed by Durkheim, George Herbert Mead, and Giddings and is currently receiving renewed emphasis by symbolic interactionists (Blumer, 1969; Faules and Alexander, 1978; Manis and Meltzer, 1978), social representationalist, and others (Moscovici, 1981; Tajfel, 1981; Hewstone, Jaspars, and Lalljee, 1982; R. Farr and Moscovici, 1984; Nimmo and Combs, 1983). Other theorists stress cross-cultural differences in categorization (Lloyd and Gay, 1981; Wagner, in press). This approach is becoming so popular under such names as "rule theory," "ethogenics," and "social representations" that it threatens to become the embarrassing-in-retrospect fad of the 1980s, comparable to dissonance theory in the 1960s and attribution theory in the 1970s.

This categorizing notion is enriched by the contention of Saussure's (1916/1959) structuralist followers (particularly Lévi-Strauss and Althussen, but also Barthes in his middle phase and Foucault) that constructs are defined in synchronic relation to one another to form deep-structure polarities (nature versus culture, left versus right, etc.) which become meaning axes, assimilation to which creates and transforms beliefs (Lévi-Strauss, 1974; Osgood, 1979; Shalvey, 1979). Its psychological genesis is in Brentano's (1874) phenomenology, developed by Külpe (1922) and the Würzburg Act school and reentering psychology (through Husserl and Heidegger) via Merleau-Ponty's (1962) perceptual primacy epistemology and Derrida's (1967/1973, 1980) deconstruction strategy, if it is applied to thought rather than to the text. From the German *Einstellung* concept derive Bartlett's (1932) schema, Sherif's (1935) frame of reference, Luchins's (1942) analysis of thought process rigidity, D. Katz and Braly's (1933) stereotypes, Asch's (1952; Asch and Zukier, 1984) and Krugman's (1965) change-of-meaning depiction (but see N. H. Anderson, 1981) of attitude change as involving the perceptual rather than response processes, Rosch's (1978) fuzzy set categories, Tversky and Kahneman's (1981) frames notion, and other recent variants (Forgas, 1981; Graesser, 1981; P. L. Wright and Rip, 1981; Weber and Crocker, 1983). The perceptual nature of attitude change is also developed in Helson's (1971) adaptation level theory, Sherif and Hovland's (1961) assimilation-contrast theory (Granberg, 1982b; Pettigrew, 1982; Judd, Kenny, and Krosnick, 1983), and scaling approaches (Upshaw, 1969; Steele and Ostrom, 1974; Woelfel *et al.*, 1980; Willis, 1981; Shaffer *et al.*, 1982; Holyoak and Gordon, 1983; Eiser, 1984). The selectivity implied by these perceptual approaches is explored by Kelly's (1955) repertory grid (Shaw, 1981; M. L. Pope and Keen, 1982; J. Adams-Webber and

Mancuso, 1983) and other salience analyses of person perception (S. Rosenberg, 1977; Hastie, 1981; McGuire and McGuire, 1981; Mancuso and Adams-Webber, 1982; Wilkening and Anderson, 1982).

Induction Theories

Theories in this third cell depict the person with a meaning-generating capacity that is activated only if an externally imposed need to know requires formulating a suitable explanation, typically derived by induction from observation of past experience. This notion of thought as epiphenomenal and externally instigated is adumbrated in Marx's concept of ideology as an outgrowth of material and social conditions, in William James's (1884) theory of emotion, in Freud's theory of rationalization, and in the symbolic interactionists' (Blumer, 1969) notion that one's self-awareness is based on the same observation bases as we use to judge others. Current examples include Nisbett and Wilson's (1977) and E. J. Langer's (1978) work on the inadequacies of people's explanations and especially D. Bem's (1972) self-observational radical behaviorism theory that people lack attitudes toward objects even as important as rye bread unless outside pressures require expressing a preference, at which point they induce what their own attitude must be, just as they would induce someone else's attitude, by observing their own past behavior toward the object (S. E. Taylor, 1975). Perhaps the person operates in this passive cell 3 induction mode when in unprovocative congruent situations and in the more actively ideologizing cell 4 hermeneutic mode when in more involving or challenging incongruent situations (Fazio, Zanna, and Cooper, 1977; Schlenker, 1982). Festinger's (1957) dissonance and social comparison theories (Festinger, 1954; Suls and Miller, 1977; Goethals and Zanna, 1979) were first proposed as hermeneutic (cell 4) conceptualizations of the person as actively cogitating, but some reformulations (S. Feldman, 1966; Aronson, 1969b; Wicklund and Frey, 1981) interpret them as cell 3 induction theories by depicting the need for consonant attitudes or comparisons as arising only when instigated by extrinsic needs such as self-esteem.

Attitude change implications of induction theories include D. Bem's (1972) self-observational inferences, the foot-in-the-door (Freedman and Fraser, 1966) and other prior self-commitment procedures (McGuire, 1964; Kiesler, 1971), and self-labeling by observing one's own behavior (R. L. Miller, Brickman, and Bolen, 1975; Salancik and Conway, 1975) and being labeled by others (Kraut, 1973; M. Goldman, Seever, and Seever,

1982). These induction theories stress that when the person is forced to form an attitude, it is important to make the appropriate aspects of the object salient by procedures such as agenda-setting (McCombs, 1981), Socratic questioning (McGuire, 1960c; Salancik and Conway, 1975), or placing the person in an anchoring or contrasting reference group situation (McGuire and Padawer-Singer, 1976; Doise, Deschamps, and Meyers, 1978).

Hermeneutic Theories

The dominance of attitude change research by cell 1 consistency theories in the 1960s was matched by the 1970s hegemony of attribution theory examples of the cell 4 hermeneutic approaches that depict the person as implicit theorist spontaneously generating meanings to interpret his or her environment and experience (Csikszentmihalyi and Rochberg-Halton, 1981; Frankl, 1978; Antaki and Brewin, 1982; Jaspers, Fincham, and Hewstone, 1983; S. Kreitler and Kreitler, 1984). Helmholtz's (1866/1962; Hochberg, 1981) doctrine of unconscious inference is an early psychological use, and in the middle distance are Michotte's (1946) causality research depicting the person as an implicit physicist (Gentner and Stevens, 1983). In the past decade this approach has flourished in implicit personality (Schneider, 1973; Bromley, 1977; Powell and Juhnke, 1983) and emotional (Russell and Ridgeway, 1983) theorizing and in work on the person as implicit moralist (Siegel, 1982; Semin and Manstead, 1983), including the "just world" (Lerner and Lerner, 1981), blaming the victim (Ryan, 1971), rule attachment (Hogan, Johnson, and Emler, 1978), and responsibility attribution work (Fincham and Jaspars, 1980; V. L. Hamilton, 1980). Other current manifestations likely to receive increasing attention are the research on the person as implicit economist (Douglas and Isherwood, 1979; Hirschman, 1982; Lichtman, 1982; Maital, 1982; Stroebe and Meyer, 1982) or implicit sociologist (Ichheiser, 1949; Apostle *et al.,* 1983) and the patient as implicit biologist (Herzlich, 1969; Leventhal, Meyer, and Nerenz, 1980; Andreoli, 1981; Pennebaker, 1982; Lau and Hartman, 1983; Viney, 1983).

That a too-nice source can lose persuasiveness by appearing to be ingratiating (E. E. Jones and Wortman, 1973) is predicted by attribution theory, the 1970s most popular hermeneutic flourishing. It grew out of Heider's (1946, 1958) naive psychology, and Festinger's (1957) dissonance theory, which usually are considered to be cell 1 consistency theories but often (Stroebe and Diehl, 1981) depict the person in this cell 4 mode of striving for

explanation, for example, by generating threatening rumors after a disaster more to explain feelings than to remove inconsistencies. The early attribution research focused narrowly on causal interpretations of success and failure experiences and on the "fundamental attribution error" (J. H. Harvey and McGlynn, 1982) of overattributing causality to dispositional rather than situational factors but now is broadening (Kelley and Michela, 1980; J. H. Harvey, Ickes, and Kidd, 1981; Fiedler, 1982; Duval and Duval, 1983; Hewstone, 1983), and some of its current outgrowths such as that on the intuitive psychologist (L. Ross, 1977) and on perceived causal schema (Reeder and Brewer, 1979) promise to feed into the third, structural, flourishing of attitude research.

COGNITIVE GROWTH THEORIES

The second tetrad of theories, shown in the upper right quadrant of Table 2, like the previous four, depict the person as tending toward a cognitive (rather than affective) end state but differ from the previous four in asserting that the person strives to develop a higher level of cognitive complexity rather than to maintain the cognitive status quo. The cell 5 stimulation theories in the quadrant's upper left corner will be discussed first, and then theories in the other three cells will be taken up in clockwise order.

Stimulation Theories

These depictions of the person as a curious novelty seeker, playfully capricious, eager for fads, and avid to avoid boredom were neglected during the 1940s and 1950s behavioristic ascendancy when psychologists were conditioned to view the person as a passive reactor to outside stimulation. Only after Establishment animal-learning researchers themselves (Harlow, Kendler, Dember, etc.; but see Glow and Winefield, 1982) began to stress the motivational importance of novelty, curiosity drive, alternation behavior, need exploration, etc., even in rats and monkeys (D. W. Fiske and Maddi, 1961; Fowler, 1965), did social and personality psychologists in the early 1960s come out of the closet to make theoretical use of the human's need for varied experience and the reward value of novelty (Berlyne, 1960; Bieri *et al.,* 1966; Zuckerman, 1979, 1983).

These theories imply that the human's shortness of attention span and avidity for change require that persuasive messages be kept short and exciting by novelty in form and content, as by the use of animation, change of pace, background visual and auditory shock stimuli (J. L. Singer and Singer, 1981), reversals (Apter, 1982), etc., that avoid the dreaded wear-out (R. D. Rogers, 1979). Stimulus deprivation can cause a communication hunger that makes people vulnerable to persuasion (Suedfeld and Borrie, 1978; Moscovici and Doms, 1982). These cell 5 theories that people are attracted to surprising, belief-discrepant messages have implications dramatically opposite (McGuire, 1966b) to the cell 1 consistency theory prediction that people seek out familiar, belief-consonant messages and avoid surprisingly discrepant information. Golden-mean theorists (Berlyne, 1978; Streufert and Streufert, 1978; Veroff and Veroff, 1980; Zentall and Zentall, 1983) resolve the conflict by postulating a nonmonotonic relationship such that people are attracted to intermediate levels of novelty, unexpected enough to stretch their preexisting delusional systems a bit but not so novel as to be unassimilable.

Utilitarian Theories

Utilitarian theories stress the person's problem solving aspect, coping with challenges so as to maximize expected gain at minimum cost, getting gratification from exercising and enhancing skills, or at least perceiving the self as a competent high achiever (McClelland, 1961; A. J. Stewart, 1982; Bartz and Maehr, 1983; Fyans *et al.*, 1983; Brody, 1983). Max Weber's (1903, 1930) Protestant ethic notion (D. T. Rogers, 1978), Tolman's (1932) purposive theory, Lewin's (1951) field theory, and Adorno *et al.*'s (1950) and D. Katz's (1960) attitudinal functionalisms were earlier psychological examples, and Deci's (1980) intrinsic motivation, Toda's (1981) funguseater robot, and von Cranach *et al.*'s (1982) goal-directed action theories are current variants.

Utilitarian theories imply that persuasive messages should associate compliance with competence, self-worth, and the attainment of the receiver's goals, as epitomized in the expected-value, attribution × evaluation approaches (Fishbein, 1980; Feather, 1982) discussed above in the attitude structure section. One might construct persuasive messages by taking a checklist of values, such as Rokeach's (1973), identify which values are highly prized by the intended receivers, and argue in the message that adopting the urged attitude or behavior will facilitate attainment of these values. Such arguing is easiest when it is implicitly accepted that the attitudes or behavior is conducive to the valued goal so that the message need only enhance the goal's salience. With more

difficulty the message can establish connections to accepted values or enhance the appeal of already connected values.

Template Theories

These current purposive or teleological theories draw their imagery more from computer flowcharts or guided missile homing devices (Powers, 1978) than from the theological notions formerly associated with teleology. The person is depicted as a pattern matcher, carrying around internal representations of paths or of desired end states that serve as guiding templates to which he or she tries to establish an environmental match, either by moving through the environment to locate a matching perceptual configuration or by manipulating the environment to produce such a configuration. Max Weber's *Verstehen* concept early familiarized sociology with Dilthey's template notion, but psychologists made only rare and partial early use of this notion, as in William James's ideomotor theory of thought, Freud's secondary processes, Tolman's cognitive maps, and Hebb's cell assemblies. Psychological use proliferated with the mid-century introduction of systems theory, cybernetics, operations research, etc., first by providing models of society that legitimized a larger role for the scientific and technological elites who control the expanding professions and bureaucracies (Lilienfeld, 1978) and later by providing models for individuals' attitude and action systems when the computer became fashionable as an analogue for the human brain (Ashby, 1952; VonNeumann, 1958) and for the structuring of experience and behavior (G. A. Miller, Galanter, and Pribram, 1960). Current examples are Powers's (1973, 1978) ingenious conceptualization of behavior as the control of perception and the various versions of mental maps purportedly propelling or guiding behavior, labeled by such terms as schema (Bobrow and Norman, 1975; Eckblad, 1981; S. E. Taylor and Crocker, 1981), controls (Carver and Scheier, 1981), scenarios (Gregory, Cialdini, and Carpenter, 1982), templates (D. Bem and Lord, 1979; T. P. Hamilton, Swap, and Rubin, 1981; Swann and Read, 1981), scripts (Tomkins, 1979; Abelson, 1981), representations (R. Farr and Moscovici, 1984), prototypes (N. Cantor, Mischel, and Schwartz, 1982); agenda (Plott and Levine, 1978), paragraph structures (Crothers, 1979), frames (Minsky, 1975; Kahneman and Tversky, 1984), nodes (J. R. Anderson and Bower, 1973), categories (Rosch, 1978), and rules (Shimanoff, 1980; Harré, 1981; Kroger, 1982; Reardon, 1981; M. J. Smith, 1982).

Attitude change implications stress the importance of presenting arguments in the receiver's own idiom to allow compliance to be visualized within his or her own mental programs and pictured end states by means of available scripts, as in the "communications game" approach (Higgins, 1981). Information should be presented in a form accessible to the person's search heuristics and should allow any incipient conformity to provide feedback indicating that the receiver is homing in on a pictured end state. The concept of the person as a "rules" follower (Harré, 1981) is being increasingly applied to attitude change processes (Shimanoff, 1980; M. J. Smith, 1982). The role theory branch of template theory (Biddle, 1979; Ickes and Knowles, 1982), deriving from George Herbert Mead's Chicago school, is actively represented (but see Lewis and Smith, 1980) by symbolic interactionism (Blumer, 1969; Cardwell, 1971) and various dramaturgical approaches such as Goffman's (1959; Ditton, 1980; Wiltshire, 1982) impression management mode of inducing attitude change (Tedeschi, 1981), as well as self-monitoring (M. Snyder, 1979), ethnomethodological (Garfinkle, 1967; Leiter, 1980), and sociological phenomenology (Schütz, 1967; Thomason, 1982) and the "common sense" ethogenic approaches (Harré, 1980; Antaki, 1981), as ways of depicting people's action as guided by implicit representation of the experiences of ordinary life. However, these ethnomethodological approaches and their discourse analysis offshoots are concerned with the cell 4 hermeneutic theory function of how people account for their experiences as well as with this cell 7 function of how they select their responses.

That several of the cells so far discussed overlap in stressing mental representation is to be expected since all are cognitive theories, but it should be noted that each cell stresses a different function of these representations. Consistency theories (cell 1) stress cognitive representations as ways of enhancing the connectedness and coherence of personal organization; categorization theories (cell 2) stress their use in selectively encoding experience to simplify the environment sufficiently to allow the person to cope with information overload; induction (cell 3) and hermeneutic (cell 4) formulations stress their encoding utility in interpreting and thus giving meaning to one's experiences; while template (cell 7) theories stress representations' purposive decoding function in guiding the pattern of action. The whole person needs all these capacities, so each family of guiding-idea theories propels the researcher's creative thought in a distinct if limited direction.

Autonomy Theories

These autonomy theories stress the human's need for freedom or at least for an illusion of control over her or his own destiny and environment. They depict the person as accepting even an objectively unpleasant situation provided it allows some choice among evils and as rebelling against an imposed action or outcome that allows no options even when he or she would have chosen it had alternatives been available. During the past decade the popularity of autonomy theories has been second only to that of the cell 4 hermeneutic theories. Some students of the family (Shorter, 1975) and of industrial society (Weinstein and Platt, 1969) argue that the felt need for individual freedom is a recent development but psychologists' preoccupation with autonomy motivation has waxed and waned in twenty-year cycles, flourishing in the 1930s personological theories of Allport (1937) and H. A. Murray (1938) and again in the 1950s as a basic motive in the spectra projected by E. H. Erikson (1950) and Maslow (1970). Its 1970s resurgence (reviewed by Perlmuter and Monty, 1979) is represented by the Rotter and Phares "locus-of-control" research (Phares, 1976; Lefcourt, 1981, 1982), by Brehm's (S. S. Brehm and Brehm, 1981) reactance theory, by the health psychological work stressing that a feeling of control is important for one's physical as well as psychological well-being (Rodin and Langer, 1977; Sanders and Malkis, 1982), by the learned helplessness notion (M. E. Seligman and Garber, 1982), by Levinson's (1978) life cycle "becoming one's own man" concept, and by the illusion of control (Steiner, 1980; Paulhus, 1983; E. J. Langer, 1983) and self-determination (Deci, 1980) research.

Among the attitude change implications are the paradoxical use of people's need for autonomy to maneuver them into deserting their own attitudes and behaviors in favor of new ones that are made to seem more their own (S. S. Brehm and Brehm, 1981) and the greater conformity of externals (Spector, 1983). Perceived control can be used as a reinforcer by arguing that compliance would express one's autonomy or increase one's options. Psychoanalytic techniques for overcoming resistance offer a model for persuasion (Marshall, 1982; Wachtel, 1982). In contrast to these autonomy needs are needs for structure and standards, for the gratification obtainable from surrendering to a charismatic leader as exhibited in the persuasive appeal of totalitarian regimes (A. G. Greenwald, 1980; Zablocki, 1980) and chiliastic cult leaders (Pavlos, 1982).

AFFECTIVE GROWTH THEORIES

The remaining eight conceptualizations shown in the bottom half of Table 2 stress affective motivation in that they depict action as terminating when the person attains some desired feeling state, rather than the ideological end states posited by the eight cognitive theories just described. The four affective theories shown in the lower right-hand quadrant of Table 2 depict the person as propelled into action by a need for emotional growth (rather than to maintain current emotional equilibrium). We shall begin with cell 9 attraction theories in the upper left-hand corner of this affective growth quadrant and then take up the other three cells in clockwise order.

Attraction Theories

The most primitive manifestation of attraction is the gregarious tendency exhibited in physical congregation (Allee, 1938) and attachment (Bowlby, 1973; Harlow, 1973; Emde and Harmon, 1982; Stevenson-Hinde and Parkes, 1982). Empirical social research usually focuses on more evolved manifestations such as interpersonal liking (discussed above under source attractiveness) and altruistic helping of others. Philosophizing about altruism—earlier (Gladstein, 1984) by Kropotkin (1902), neo-Darwinians (Margolis, 1982), and Sorokin (1950) and currently by sociobiologists (E. O. Wilson, 1978) and tragedy-of-the-commons theorists (Edney, 1980; Barry and Hardin, 1982)—has been supplemented by much empirical work on dispositional and situational correlates of helping behavior (Staub, 1979; Rushton and Sorrentino, 1981; Eisenberg, 1982; Smithson, Amato, and Pearce, 1982; Willis, 1982; J. D. Fisher, Nadler, and DePaulo, 1983; Derlega and Grzelak, 1984).

These attraction theories suggest the obvious importance of attributing the persuasive message to a liked source and also that in public health campaigns against smoking or for good dental hygiene, it might be more effective to stress cosmetic benefits by appealing to the receiver's desire to be physically attractive and liked, rather than stress the life and health preservation benefits that may seem more important to the professional health communicator. Health campaigns might also make more use of altruistic appeals whose efficacy is illustrated when

people who could not give up smoking to save their own health manage to quit when they become pregnant or want to avoid giving a bad example to their children, and by persons' acting to defend others more readily than to defend themselves (Meindl and Lerner, 1983). Directed imagery and role playing can be used to evoke such altruistic behavior (Toi and Batson, 1982).

Identity Theories

That gratification can be obtained by elaborating one's sense of self via identifying with others and playing additional roles is stressed by reference group (Hyman and Singer, 1968), role (R. Linton, 1945; Biddle, 1979; Ickes and Knowles, 1982; Zurcher, 1983), self-presentation (Goffman, 1981; Tedeschi, 1981; Mummendey and Bolter, 1983), etc., theories insofar as they attribute role acquisition tendencies to need for enhancing sense of self (rather than for providing behavioral guidance, which would place them among the cell 7 template theories). More humanistic versions include Maslow's (1970) self-actualization theory and E. H. Erikson's (1964) stress on identity creation in late adolescence as a critical maturational task.

Kelman's (1958) identification process of attitude change makes general use of this notion, and it implicitly underlies specific identification-facilitating techniques such as using sources only slightly superior (Stukát, 1958), pratfalls (R. Helmreich, Aronson, and LeFan, 1970), altercasting (Goffman, 1959; Weinstein and Deutschberger, 1963), the communications game (Higgins, McCann, and Fondacardo, 1982), deindividuating (Maslach, Stapp, and Santee, in press), sensory deprivation, and adopting ethnocentric attitudes as a means of developing a positive social identity (E. H. Erikson, 1964; Reardon, 1981; Schönbach, 1981). It has been argued that current youth are becoming a narcissistic, inward-looking "me" generation (Hogan, 1975; Reisman, 1980; Conger, 1981; Veroff, Douvan, and Kulka, 1981; Yankelovich, 1981; Restak, 1982), and if so, this conceptualization will become more powerful.

Contagion Theories

Modeling, social facilitation, and social learning theories stress the gratification obtainable from imitating others, adopting their thoughts, empathizing with their feelings (J. A. Johnson, Cheek, and Smither, 1983), and matching their behaviors. Contagion theories were particularly popular among late-nineteenth-century French social and psychiatric theorists such as LeBon, Tarde, Binet, Charcot, Bernheim, Liébeault, and other students of hysteria, suggestibility, and hypnosis. These earlier proponents typically regarded the imitative tendency as phylogenetically built into the organism, while an ontogenetic acquisition is usually assumed in current social learning and modeling theorizing (Bandura, 1971b) that derives from "liberated" stimulus-response theory (N. E. Miller, 1959), though social facilitation research (Zajonc, 1980b; Glaser, 1982) may revive the assumption of a genetic basis for contagion.

That imitation of modeled behavior occurs even when compliance is not explicitly urged has aroused social concern that the pervasive modeling of violence on televised drama may increase antisocial aggression in viewers (Pearl, Bouthilet, and Lazar, 1982), but (see the channel variables section above) studies in the natural environment show a slight effect, at most.

Assertion Theories

Hard-hat dominance speculations about selfish genes and about society as a war of each against all, emphasizing the person's striving for control over others and for power-conferring status, trace back to Hobbes and Nietzsche and currently are represented in "naked ape" speculations of angry philosophers, disinhibited zoologists, failed playwrights, strayed anthropologists, and purveyors of assertiveness training (D. Morris, 1967; Lorenz, 1966; Tiger and Fox, 1971; Korda, 1975; Dawkins, 1976; Galassi and Galassi, 1977; but see S. Wright, 1980; Brain, 1981; Galbraith, 1983). More rigorous theoretical analyses of the power need are found in the individual psychology of Alfred Adler (Ansbacher, 1980) and in McClelland's work (1975; Winter, 1973; Veroff, 1982). Reviews of the empirical research on the assertion/power motive are provided by Baron (1977), Ng (1980), Henderson (1981), and Geen and Donnerstein (1983), with Dubarle (1978), Derber (1983), and Wallach and Wallach (1983) reviewing its philosophical underpinnings. Assertion theories call attention to the importance of using high-power sources and arguments that rechannel aggression (A. P. Goldstein *et al.,* 1981) and of depicting attitude change and compliance not as subservient yielding but as showing capacity to break out of one's old thought patterns to assert new viewpoints and modes of behavior. However, it is sometimes useful to distinguish aggressiveness from assertiveness (Margalit and Mauger, 1984).

AFFECTIVE STABILITY THEORIES

The remaining four theories in the bottom left quadrant of Table 2, like the four just considered, stress affective rather than cognitive goals but contrast with the preceding four by positing a need for affective stability rather than affective growth. We shall first describe cell 13 tension reduction theories in the upper left corner of this quadrant and then proceed clockwise through the other three cells.

Tension Reduction Theories

Theories in this cell depict the person as an energy system, experiencing pleasure from release and pain from increase of tension, so any stimulation or excitement is aversive. Included at one philosophical extreme are theological depictions of human destiny as reunion with an individuality-annihilating infinite unity such as the Hindu moksha and Buddhist nirvana concepts and some oceanic Judeo-Christian mysticism such as Luriantic cabalism (Scholem, 1973); while at an opposite materialistic extreme are second law of thermodynamics depictions of the person such as S. Freud's (1933/1964) thanatotic death wish theory that pleasure is tension reduction and the behavioristic formulations of drive reduction as reward (Dollard and Miller, 1950). Cathartic theories from Aristotle's *Ars Poetica* aesthetics to analytic schools of psychotherapy also stress the human's need for tension reduction (Scheff, 1980).

These formulations suggest that the persuasive message should show that compliance will reduce rather than increase tension. Health warnings have to be designed to channel the tension reduction proclivity into problem-solving coping responses rather than into problem-evading avoidance reactions (Leventhal, Meyer, and Nerenz, 1980; Lazarus, 1981). Catharsis theorists (Feshbach, 1972) have argued that viewing television violence might actually reduce aggression by allowing hostility to be vicariously expressed in fantasy and that pornographic depictions may reduce abusive sexual behavior (Zillman and Bryant, 1982; Yaffé and Nelson, 1982), but empirical results discussed in the channel variables section indicate that any cathartic effect is overridden by opposite activating tendencies (Geen and Quanty, 1977; G. W. Russell, 1983). Variant conceptualizations are that the person tends toward an optimal, intermediate level of arousal (Berlyne, 1960; R. L. Solomon, 1980) or that a difficult-to-control sequence of reactions may be involved, as when jokes within the message first raise and then reduce tensions, or that a subtle but important distinction between reducing versus avoiding tension as the basis of pleasure must be taken into account.

Ego Defense Theories

Theories in this cell emphasize the need to maintain self-esteem, if necessary by distorting unacceptable aspects of the self and the environment, as when the person uses selective perception, distorted recall, fantasy, denial, displacement, reaction formation, regression, and other defense mechanisms to repress unpleasant events and desires and to create a representation of self and world that accords with one's desires and moral principles and preserves an acceptable self-image and satisfying world despite threatening onslaughts from the superego, id, and environment.

The attitude change researchers who have made most use of the ego defense concept are the functional theorists (Adorno *et al.,* 1950; D. Katz, 1960), who depict a person's attitudes toward an object as deriving from his or her unconscious needs rather than from information about the object, suggesting that attitudes such as ethnic hostility can be changed by giving the person insight into the repressed motivations from which his or her prejudices arise. The ego defense concept also underlies McGuire's (1969a; McGuire and Millman, 1965) use of forewarning of persuasive attack to induce anticipatory attitude change, the "motivation research" advertising (Dichter, 1975) that appeals to unconscious needs far removed from the obvious function of the product, and the symbolic racism analysis (D. O. Sears *et al.,* 1980; Kinder and Sears, 1981) that traces interethnic hostility (and other political attitudes) to the individual's basic orientations rather than to specific experiences or obvious self-interest.

Repetition Theories

These repetition theories stress the person's creature-of-habit aspect such that the gratification obtained from acting in a familiar way in a situation enhances the likelihood of similar behavior in like situations in the future, especially (according to reinforcement theorists) if the action is rewarded but even (according to contiguity theorists) when the pairing is unrewarded (Locurto, Terrace, and Gibbon, 1980). Philosophical progenitors include British associationists such as Locke, Hume, and J. Mill, with a little help from Continental friends like

Condillac. Within scientific psychology it is represented by behaviorists, particularly the contiguity theorists stemming from Guthrie and Estes but also by reinforcement stimulus-response schools stemming from Skinner and Hull, the latter having analyzed hypnosis and suggestibility as a learned habit (Hull, 1933). S. Freud (1920/1922) used a repetition-compulsion concept to go beyond the pleasure principle in his postulating the thanatotic drive.

This habit notion of attitude change was heavily used in the 1940s and 1950s by the Yale group (Hovland, Lumsdaine, and Sheffield, 1949; Hovland, Janis, and Kelley, 1953; Hovland, 1957). It allows learning principles to be applied to attitude change, yielding many hypotheses (most rather banal) regarding how learning or memory mediates the persuasive impact of association (Staats, 1975, 1983a, 1983b), reinforcement (R. F. Weiss, 1968), repetition (Sawyer, 1981), etc. The notion is at the core of the cognitive behavioral therapy (Bandura, 1971a; Mahoney, 1974) and the social learning (Rotter, 1982) approaches to manipulating attitudes and behaviors.

Expression Theories

The essence of this final set of theories is that humans have an acting-out impulse, obtaining gratification from self-expression. Just as it is rewarding to exercise one's physical skills and exert oneself in strenuous sports, so pleasure is derived from forming and acting out feelings and beliefs, as when it feels lovely to be in love or to hiss the man one loves to hate. This philosophy that the journey not the arrival is what matters goes back at least to the Bhagavad Gita theme that the work is its own reward. That the exercise of a function can give delight regardless of outcome is basic to Freud's abreaction notion, to play theories (Huizinga, 1939; Cherfas and Lewin, 1980; Fagen, 1981; Schaefer and O'Connor, 1983), to the "functional pleasure" school of human development (Bühler, 1935), to many creativity theories (Lieberman, 1977), and to arousal and activation theories (Berlyne, 1968).

Stephenson (1967) has discussed the play factor in mass communications as have several arousal theorists (Tannenbaum, 1980). This approach suggests the persuasive efficacy of participatory mass political rallies and demonstrations that provide acting-out opportunities —such as the Nürnberg rally of Hitler's National Socialists (Riefenstahl, 1934), the political use of sports (Hazan, 1982) and rituals (C. Lane, 1981) in Soviet Russia, and of demonstrations by environmentalists—and so may promote as well as reflect the success of the movement, since the acting-out opportunity they provide may attract demonstrators with little initial sympathy for the cause (Lin, 1974).

RELATIONS AMONG THESE GUIDING-IDEA THEORIES

Advocates of any of these partial views of the person tend to be hostile to proponents of other viewpoints even within their own cell, as illustrated by cell 1 internecine battles between balance and dissonance theorists. Human motivation is sufficiently complex so that multiple and even contradictory needs may underlie any act. Both of the contrasting polarities on each of our four basic dimensions are reflected in a person's action, as when polar-opposite needs for stability and growth both operate in each season of human life (Levinson, 1978; Veroff and Veroff, 1980; Apter, 1982; Csikszentmihalyi, 1982). Theorists as varied as Hegel and Saussure have stressed that the simultaneous operation of opposites is the essence of thought and even being. Conceptual representations of complex realities must be oversimplifications if they are to focus the researcher's attention on one critical aspect that can provide creative impetus and direction. These partial views are complementary rather than antagonistic, and each should be used where it works well and then discarded in favor of alternative partial views when situational or dispositional changes make another theory a more useful oversimplification. The diverse directive and dynamic theories reviewed in this chapter are available to suggest answers to the many questions arising from the vast accumulation of empirical findings reviewed in preceding sections. We expect in the next two decades a renewal of substantial advances in attitude research, particularly in clarifying the content, structure, and functioning of attitudinal systems.

REFERENCES

Aaker, D. A., J. M. Carman, and R. Jacobson (1982). Modeling advertising-sales relationships involving feedback: a time series analysis of six cereal brands. *J. Market. Res., 19,* 116–125.

Abelson, R. P. (1972). Are attitudes necessary? In B. T. King and E. McGinnies (Eds.), *Attitudes, conflicts, and social change.* New York: Academic Press. Pp. 19–32.

———— (1981). The psychological status of the script concept. *Amer. Psychol., 36,* 715–729.

Abelson, R. P., E. Aronson, W. J. McGuire, T. M. Newcomb, M. J. Rosenberg, and P. H. Tannenbaum, Eds. (1968). *Theories of cognitive consistency.* Chicago: Rand McNally.

Abelson, R. P., and G. S. Lesser (1959). A developmental theory of persuasibility. In I. L. Janis and C. I. Hovland (Eds.), *Personality and persuasibility.* New Haven: Yale Univ. Press. Pp. 167–186.

Abelson, R. P., and M. J. Rosenberg (1958). Symbolic psychologic: a model of attitude cognition. *Behav. Sci., 3,* 1–13.

Abramson, P. R. (1983). *Political attitudes in America.* San Francisco: Freeman.

Acock, A. C., and M. L. DeFleur (1975). Reply to Susmilch, Elliot-Schwartz. *Amer. Sociol. Rev., 40,* 687–690.

Adams, H. (1918). *The education of Henry Adams.* Boston: Houghton Mifflin.

Adams, J. S., and S. Freedman (1976). Equity theory revisited: comments and annotated bibliography. In L. Berkowitz and E. Walster (Eds.), *Advances in experimental social psychology.* Vol. 9. New York: Academic Press. Pp. 43–90.

Adams, W. C., Ed. (1982). *Television coverage of international affairs.* Norwood, N.J.: Ablex.

Adams-Webber, J., and J. C. Mancuso, Eds. (1983). *Applications of personal construct theory.* New York: Academic Press.

Adler, R. P., G. S. Lesser, L. K. Meringoff, T. S. Robertson, and S. Ward (1980). *The effects of television advertising on children.* Lexington, Mass.: D. C. Heath.

Adoni, H. (1979). The functions of mass media in the political socialization of adolescents. *Communic. Res., 6,* 84–106.

Adorno, T. W., E. Frenkel-Brunswik, D. J. Levinson, and R. N. Sanford (1950). *The authoritarian personality.* New York: Harper.

Ajzen, I., and M. Fishbein (1977). Attitude-behavior relations: a theoretical analysis and review of empirical research. *Psychol. Bull., 84,* 888–918.

———— (1980). *Understanding attitudes and predicting social behavior.* Englewood Cliffs, N.J.: Prentice-Hall.

Albion, M. S., and P. W. Farris (1981). *The advertising controversy: evidence on the economic effects of advertising.* Boston: Auburn House.

Albrecht, S. L., and K. E. Carpenter (1976). Attitudes as predictors of behavior versus behavioral intentions: a convergence of research traditions. *Sociometry, 39,* 1–10.

Alker, H. A. (1972). Is personality situationally specific or intrapsychically consistent? *J. Pers., 40,* 1–16.

Allee, W. C. (1938). *The social life of animals.* New York: Norton.

Allen, V. L. (1975). Social support for nonconformity. In L. Berkowitz (Ed.), *Advances in experimental social psychology.* Vol. 8. New York: Academic Press. Pp. 1–43.

Alley, T. R. (1981). Head shape and the perception of cuteness. *Develop. Psychol., 17,* 650–654.

Allport, G. W. (1935). Attitudes. In C. Murchison (Ed.), *A handbook of social psychology.* Worcester, Mass.: Clark Univ. Press. Pp. 798–844.

———— (1937). *Personality: a psychological interpretation.* New York: Holt.

Allport, G. W., and H. S. Odbert (1936). Trait-names: a psycho-lexical study. *Psychol. Monogr.,* No. 211. Princeton, N.J.: Psychological Review Co.

Allyn, J., and L. Festinger (1961). The effectiveness of unanticipated persuasive communications. *J. abnorm. soc. Psychol., 62,* 35-40.

Altschull, J. H. (1984). *Agents of power: the role of the news media in public affairs.* New York: Longman.

Amir, Y. (1976). The role of intergroups contact in change of prejudice and ethnic relations. In P. A. Katz (Ed.), *Towards the elimination of racism.* New York: Pergamon Press. Pp. 245-308.

Anderson, C. A. (1983). Imagination and expectation: the effect of imagining behavioral scripts on personal intentions. *J. Pers. soc. Psychol., 45,* 293-305.

Anderson, J. R., and G. H. Bower (1973). *Human associative memory.* Hillsdale, N.J.: Erlbaum.

Anderson, L. R., and W. J. McGuire (1965). Prior reassurance of group consensus as a factor in producing resistance to persuasion. *Sociometry, 28,* 44-56.

Anderson, N. H. (1959). Test of a model of opinion change. *J. abnorm. soc. Psychol., 59,* 371-381.

_____ (1965). Primacy effects in personality impression formation using a generalized order effect paradigm. *J. abnorm. soc. Psychol., 2,* 1-9.

_____ (1971). Integration theory and attitude change. *Psychol. Rev., 78,* 171-206.

_____ (1979). Indeterminate theory: reply to Gollob. *J. Pers. soc. Psychol., 37,* 950-952.

_____ (1981). *Foundations of information integration theory.* New York: Academic Press.

_____ (1982). *Methods of information integration theory.* New York: Academic Press.

Anderson, N. H., and A. J. Farkas (1973). New light on order effects in attitude change. *J. Pers. soc. Psychol., 28,* 88-93.

Anderson, N. H., and C. C. Graesser (1976). An information integration analysis of attitude change in group discussion. *J. Pers. soc. Psychol., 34,* 210-222.

Anderson, N. H., and L. L. Lopes (1974). Some psycholinguistic aspects of person perception. *Memory and Cognition, 2,* 67-74.

Andrén, G. (1980). The rhetoric of advertising. *J. Communic., 30,* No. 4, 74-80.

Andreoli, K. G. (1981). Self-concept and health beliefs in compliant and noncompliant hypertensive patients. *Nursing Res., 30,* 323-328.

Andreoli, V., and S. Worchel (1978). Effects of media, communicator and message position on attitude change. *Publ. Opin. Quart., 42,* 59-70.

Andrews, K. H., and D. B. Kandel (1979). Attitude and behavior: a specification of the contingent consistency hypothesis. *Amer. Sociol. Rev., 44,* 298-310.

Ankerl, G. (1981). *Experimental sociology of architecture: a guide to theory, research and literature.* Berlin: Mouton.

Ansbacher, H. L. (1980). *Alfred Adler revisited.* New York: Praeger.

Antaki, C., Ed. (1981). *The psychology of ordinary explanations of social behavior.* London: Academic Press.

Antaki, C., and C. Brewin, Eds. (1982). *Attributions and psychological change: application of attributional theories to clinical and educational practice.* London: Academic Press.

Apostle, R. A., C. Y. Glock, T. Piazza, and M. Suelzle (1983). *The anatomy of racial attitudes.* Berkeley: Univ. of California Press.

Appel, V. (1971). On advertising wearout. *J. Advert. Res., 11,* 11-13.

Apple, W., L. A. Streeter, and R. M. Krauss (1979). Effects of pitch and speech rate on personal attributions. *J. Pers. soc. Psychol., 37,* 715-727.

Apter, M. J. (1982). *The experience of motivation: the theory of psychological reversals.* New York: Academic Press.

Archibald, J. D., and W. A. Clemens (1982). Late cretaceous extinctions. *Amer. Scient., 70,* 377-385.

Argyle, M., and M. Cook (1976). *Gaze and mutual gaze.* Cambridge: Cambridge Univ. Press.

Aronson, E. (1969a). Some antecedents of interpersonal attraction. In W. J. Arnold and D. Levine (Eds.), *Nebraska symposium on motivation, 1969,* Vol. 17. Lincoln: Univ. of Nebraska Press. Pp. 143-173.

_____ (1969b). The theory of cognitive dissonance: a current perspective. In L. Berkowitz (Ed.), *Advances in experimental social psychology,* Vol. 4. New York: Academic Press. Pp. 1-34.

Aronson, E., J. M. Carlsmith, and J. Darley (1963). The effect of expectancy on volunteering for an unpleasant experience. *J. abnorm. soc. Psychol., 66,* 220-224.

Aronson, E., and B. W. Golden (1962). The effect of relevant and irrelevant aspects of communicator credibility on attitude change. *J. Pers., 30,* 135-146.

Aronson, E., and D. Linder (1965). Gain and loss of esteem as determinants of interpersonal attraction. *J. exp. soc. Psychol., 1,* 156-171.

Aronson, E., and J. Mills (1959). The effects of severity of initiation on liking for a group. *J. abnorm. soc. Psychol., 59,* 177-181.

Aronson, E., J. A. Turner, and J. M. Carlsmith (1963). Communicator credibility and communication discrepancy as determinants of opinion change. *J. abnorm. soc. Psychol., 67,* 31-36.

Aronson, E., B. Willerman, and J. Floyd (1966). The effect of a pratfall on increasing interpersonal attraction. *Psychon. Sci., 4,* 227-228.

Asch, S. E. (1952). *Social psychology.* Englewood Cliffs, N.J.: Prentice-Hall.

_____ (1956). Studies of independence and conformity: a minority of one against a unanimous majority. *Psychol. Monogr., 70,* No. 9 (whole No. 416).

Asch, S. E., and H. Zukier (1984). Thinking about persons. *J. Pers. soc. Psychol., 46,* 1230-1240.

Ashby, W. R. (1952). *Design for a brain.* New York: Wiley.

Assmus, G., J. U. Farley, and D. R. Lehmann (1984). How advertising affects sales: meta-analysis of econometric results. *J. Marketing Res., 21,* 65-74.

Atkin, C. K., L. Bowen, O. B. Nayman, and K. G. Sheinkopf (1973). Quality versus quantity in televised political ads. *Publ. Opin. Quart., 37,* 209-224.

Atkin, C., and G. Heald (1976). Effects of political advertising. *Publ. Opin. Quart., 40,* 216-228.

Atkinson, J. W., Ed. (1958). *Motives in fantasy, action, and society.* Princeton, N.J.: Van Nostrand.

Austin, B. A. (1983). *The film audience: an international bibliography of research.* Metuchen, N.J.: Scarecrow Press.

Axelrod, S., and J. Apsche (1982). *The effects of punishment on human behavior.* New York: Academic Press.

Back, K. W. (1972). *Beyond words.* New York: Russell Sage.

Bagdikian, B. H. (1983). *The media monopoly.* Boston: Beacon Press.

Bagozzi, R. P. (1978). The construct validity of the affective, behavioral and cognitive components of attitude by analysis of covariance structure. *Multivariate behav. Res., 13,* 9–31.

_____ (1981). Attitudes, intentions and behavior: a test of some key hypotheses. *J. Pers. soc. Psychol., 41,* 607–627.

_____ (1982). A field investigation of causal relations among cognitions, affect, intentions, and behavior. *J. Marketng Res., 19,* 562–584.

Bagozzi, R. P., and R. E. Burnkrant (1979). Attitude organization and the attitude-behavior relationship. *J. Pers. soc. Psychol., 37,* 913–919.

Bain, R. (1928). An attitude on attitude research. *Amer. J. Sociol., 33,* 940–957.

Ball-Rokeach, S., J. W. Grube, and M. Rokeach (1981). "Roots: the next generation": who watched and with what effect? *Publ. Opin. Quart., 45,* 58–68.

Bandura, A. (1971a). Psychotherapy based on modeling principles. In A. E. Bergin and S. L. Garfield (Eds.), *Handbook of psychotherapy and behavior change: an empirical analysis.* New York: Wiley. Pp. 653–708.

_____ Ed. (1971b). *Psychological modeling: conflicting theories.* Chicago: Aldine-Atherton.

_____ (1977). *Social learning theory.* Englewood Cliffs, N.J.: Prentice-Hall.

Bandura, A., N. E. Adams, and J. Beyer (1977). Cognitive processes mediating behavioral change. *J. Pers. soc. Psychol., 35,* 125–139.

Bandura, A., E. B. Blanchard, and B. Ritter (1969). Relative efficacy of desensitization and modeling approaches for inducing behavioral, affective, and attitudinal changes. *J. Pers. soc. Psychol., 13,* 173–179.

Banks, W. C., K. R. Stitt, H. A. Curtis, and G. V. McQuater (1977). Perceived objectivity and the effects of evaluative reinforcement upon compliance and self-evaluation in blacks. *J. exp. soc. Psychol., 13,* 452–463.

Barber, T. X. (1964). Hypnotizability, suggestibility and personality: V. A critical review of research findings. *Psychol. Reports, 14,* 299–320.

_____ (1969). *Hypnosis: a scientific approach.* New York: Van Nostrand-Reinhold.

Barber, T. X, and D. S. Calverley (1963). "Hypnotic-like" suggestibility in children and adults. *J. abnorm. soc. Psychol., 66,* 589–597.

Barcus, F. E. (1983). *Images of life on children's television: sex roles, minorities, and families.* New York: Praeger.

Bargh, J. A., and P. Pietromonaco (1982). Automatic information processing and social perception: the influence of trait information presented outside of conscious awareness on impression formation. *J. Pers. soc. Psychol., 43,* 437–449.

Baron, R. A. (1977). *Human aggression.* New York: Plenum.

_____ (1983). "Sweet smell of success"? The impact of pleasant artificial scents on evaluations of job applicants. *J. appl. Psychol., 68,* 709–713.

Barrows, T. S., Ed. (1981). *College students' knowledge and beliefs: a survey of global understanding.* New Rochelle, N.Y.: Change Magazine Press.

Barry, B., and R. Hardin (1982). *Rational man and irrational society? an introduction and source book.* Beverly Hills, Calif.: Sage.

Barth, E. M., and E. C. W. Krabbe (1982). *From axiom to dialogue: a philosophical study of logics and argumentation.* Berlin: Walter de Gruyter.

Barthes, R. (1967). *Elements of semiology.* London: Cape Edint.

Bartlett, F. C. (1932). *Remembering.* Cambridge: Cambridge Univ. Press.

Bartos, R. (1982). *The moving target: what every marketer should know about women.* New York: Free Press.

Bartz, D. E., and M. L. Maehr, Eds. (1983). *Advances in motivation and achievement. Vol. 3. The development of achievement motivation.* Greenwich, Conn.: JAI Press.

Baskett, G. D., and R. O. Freedle (1974). Aspects of language pragmatics and the social perception of lying. *J. Psycholinguistic Res., 3,* 117–131.

Bassiouni, M. C. (1982). Media coverage of terrorism: the law and the public. *J. Communic., 32,* No. 2, 128–143.

Baumgardner, M. H., M. R. Leippe, D. L. Ronis, and A. G. Greenwald (1983). In search of reliable persuasion effects: II. Associative interference and persistence of persuasion in a message-dense environment. *J. Pers. soc. Psychol., 45,* 524–537.

Beck, K. H. (1979). The effects of positive and negative arousal upon attitudes, belief acceptance, behavioral intention, and behavior. *J. soc. Psychol., 107,* 239–251.

Beck, K. H., and C. M. Davis (1978). Effects of fear-arousing communications and topic importance on attitude change. *J. soc. Psychol., 104,* 81–95.

Beck, S. B., C. I. Ward-Hull, and P. M. McLear (1976). Variables related to women's somatic preferences of the male and female body. *J. Pers. soc. Psychol., 34,* 1200–1210.

Becker, G. S. (1981). *A treatise on the family.* Cambridge, Mass.: Harvard Univ. Press.

Becker, L. B., and J. C. Doolittle (1975). How repetition affects evaluation of and information seeking about candidates. *Journalism Quart., 52,* 611–617.

Behling, C. F. (1971). Effects of commitment and certainty upon exposure to supportive and nonsupportive information. *J. Pers. soc. Psychol., 19,* 152–159.

Belch, G. E. (1982). The effects of television commercial repetition on cognitive response and message acceptance. *J. Consumer Res., 9,* No. 1, 56–65.

Belson, W. (1978). *Television violence and the adolescent boy.* Farmborough, Hants.: Saxon House, Teakfield.

Bem, D. (1972). Self perception theory. In L. Berkowitz (Ed.), *Advances in experimental social psychology.* Vol. 6. New York: Academic Press. Pp. 2–63.

Bem, D., and C. G. Lord (1979). Template matching: a proposal for probing the ecological validity of experimental settings in social psychology. *J. Pers. soc. Psychol., 37,* 833–846.

Bem, S. L. (1975). Sex role adaptability: one consequence of psychological androgyny. *J. Pers. soc. Psychol., 31,* 634–643.

Bengston, J. L., and R. S. Laufer, Eds. (1974). Youth, generations and social change. *J. soc. Issues, 30* (whole No. 2 and 3).

Bennett, E. (1955). Discussion, decision, commitment and consensus in "group decisions." *Hum. Relat., 8,* 251–274.

Bennis, W. G., and D. Peabody (1962). The conceptualization of two personality orientations and sociometric choice. *J. soc. Psychol., 57,* 203–215.

Bentler, P. M., and G. Speckart (1979). Models of attitude-behavior relations. *Psychol. Rev., 86,* 452–464.

Berelson, B. (1942). The effects of print on public opinion. In D. Waples (Ed.), *Print, radio, and film in a democracy.* Chicago: Univ. of Chicago Press. Pp. 41–64.

Berger, C. R. (1980). Power and the family. In M. E. Roloff, and G. E. Miller (Eds.), *Persuasion: new directions in theory and research.* Beverly Hills, Calif.: Sage. Pp. 197–224.

Bergin, A. E., and M. J. Lambert (1978). The evaluation of therapeutic outcomes. In S. L. Garfield, and A. E. Bergin (Eds.), *Handbook of psychotherapy and behavior change: an empirical analysis* (2nd ed.). New York: Wiley. Pp. 139–190.

Berkowitz, L. (1974). Some determinants of impulsive aggression: the role of mediated associations with reinforcements for aggression. *Psychol. Rev., 81,* 165–176.

Berkowitz, L., and J. T. Alioto (1973). The meaning of an observed event as a determinant of its aggressive consequences. *J. Pers. soc. Psychol., 28,* 206–216.

Berkowitz, L., and D. R. Cottingham (1960). The interest value and relevance of fear-arousing communications. *J. abnorm. soc. Psychol., 60,* 37–43.

Berkowitz, L., and E. Rawlings (1963). Effects of film violence on inhibitions against subsequent aggression. *J. abnorm. soc. Psychol., 66,* 405–412.

Berkowitz, L., and N. Walker (1967). Laws and moral judgments. *Sociometry, 30,* 410–422.

Berlo, D. K., J. B. Lemert, and R. J. Mertz (1970). Dimensions for evaluating the acceptability of message sources. *Publ. Opin. Quart., 33,* 563–576.

Berlyne, D. E. (1960). *Conflict, arousal, and curiosity.* New York: McGraw-Hill.

――― (1968). Laughter, humor and play. In G. Lindzey and E. Aronson (Eds.), *Handbook of social psychology.* Vol. III. Reading, Mass.: Addison-Wesley. Pp. 795–852.

――― (1978). Curiosity and learning. *Motivation and emotion, 2,* 97–175.

Berman, R. (1981). *Advertising and social change.* Beverly Hills, Calif.: Sage.

Berry, G. L., and C. Mitchell-Kernan, Eds. (1982). *Television and the socialization of the minority child.* New York: Academic Press.

Berscheid, E., and E. H. Walster (1978). *Interpersonal attraction* (2nd ed.). Reading, Mass.: Addison-Wesley.

Bettelheim, B. (1960). *The informed heart.* Glencoe, Ill.: Free Press.

Bettman, J. R. (1975). Issues in designing consumer information environments. *J. Consumer Research, 2,* 169–177.

Biddle, B. J. (1979). *Role theory: expectations, identities, and behaviors.* New York: Academic Press.

Biderman, A. D. (1963). *March to calumny: the story of the American POWs in the Korean War.* New York: Macmillan.

Bieri, J., A. L. Atkins, S. Briar, R. L. Leaman, H. Miller, and T. Tripodi (1966). *Clinical and social judgment: the discrimination of behavioral information.* New York: Wiley.

Billington, J. H. (1980). *Fire in the minds of men.* New York: Basic Books.

Billow, R. M. (1977). Metaphor: a review of the psychological literature. *Psychol. Bull., 84,* 81–92.

Binet, A. (1900). *La Suggestibilité.* Paris: Scheicher Frères.

Birkby, R. H. (1969). The supreme court and the Bible belt: Tennessee reaction to the "Schempp" decision. In T. L. Becker, and M. M. Feeley (Eds.), *The impact of supreme court decisions.* New York: Oxford Univ. Press.

Birnbaum, M. H. (1974). The nonadditivity of personality impressions. *J. exp. Psychol., 102,* 543–561.

Birnbaum, M. H., and B. A. Mellers (1979). One-mediator model of exposure effects is still viable. *J. Pers. soc. Psychol., 37,* 1090–1096.

Biryukov, N. S. (1981). *Television in the west and its doctrines.* (Progress Pubs., USSR.) Chicago: Imported Publications.

Bishop, G. F., R. W. Oldendick, and A. J. Tuchfarber (1983). Effects of filter questions in public opinion surveys. *Publ. Opin. Quart., 47,* 528–546.

Bishop, G. F., R. W. Oldendick, A. J. Tuchfarber, and S. E. Bennett (1979). Effects of opinion filtering and opinion floating: evidence from a secondary analysis. *Political Methodology, 6,* 293–309.

――― (1980). Pseudo-opinions in public affairs. *Publ. Opin. Quart., 44,* 198–209.

Bither, S. W., I. J. Dolich, and E. B. Nell (1971). The application of attitude immunization techniques in marketing. *J. Marketng Res., 8,* 56–61.

Bitzer, L., and T. Rueter (1980). *Carter versus Ford: The counterfeit debates of 1976.* Madison: Univ. of Wisconsin Press.

Blakeney, R. N., and J. F. MacNaughton (1971). Effects of temporal placement of unfavorable information on decision making during the selection interview. *J. appl. Psychol., 55,* 138–142.

Bloch, M., Ed. (1975). *Political language and oratory in traditional society.* New York: Academic Press.

Block, J. H. (1976). Issues, problems and pitfalls in assessing sex differences: a critical review of "The psychology of sex differences." *Merrill-Palmer Quart., 22,* 283–308.

Blumer, H. (1969). *Symbolic interactionism: perspective and method.* Englewood Cliffs, N.J.: Prentice-Hall.

Blumler, J. G., and E. Katz, Eds. (1974). *The uses of mass communications: current perspectives on gratification research.* Beverly Hills, Calif.: Sage.

Bobo, L. (1983). Whites' opposition to busing: symbolic racism or realistic group conflict. *J. Pers. soc. Psychol., 45,* 1196–1210.

Bobrow, D. G., and D. A. Norman (1975). Some principles of memory schemata. In D. G. Bobrow and A. Collins (Eds.), *Representation and understanding.* New York: Academic Press. Pp. 131–149.

Bochner, S., Ed. (1982). *Cultures in contact: studies in cross-cultural interaction.* Elmsford, N.Y.: Pergamon Press.

Bochner, S., and C. A. Insko (1966). Communicator discrepancy, source credibility, and opinion change. *J. Pers. soc. Psychol., 4,* 614–621.

Bogardus, E. S. (1925). Measuring social distance. *J. appl. Sociol., 9,* 299–308.

Bogart, L. (1976). *Premises for propaganda: the United States information agency's operating assumptions in the cold war.* New York: Free Press.

⸺ (1981). *The press and public: who reads what, where and why in American newspapers.* Hillsdale, N.J.: Erlbaum.

Bogartz, R. S. (1965). On the assumption of a steeper avoidance gradient in Miller's conflict theory. *Psychol. Rev., 72,* 162–163.

Boorman, S. A., and P. R. Levitt (1980). *The genetics of altruism.* New York: Academic Press.

Borgida, E. (1978). Scientific deduction—evidence is not necessarily information: a reply to Wells and Harvey. *J. Pers. soc. Psychol., 36,* 477–482.

Borgida, E., and B. Campbell (1982). Belief relevance and attitude-behavior consistency: the moderating role of personal experience. *J. Pers. soc. Psychol., 42,* 239–247.

Boster, F. J., J. E. Fryrear, P. A. Mongeau, and J. E. Hunter (1982). An unequal speaking linear discrepancy model: implications for polarity shift. In M. Burgoon (Ed.), *Communication yearbook. Vol. 6.* Beverly Hills, Calif.: Sage. Pp. 395–418.

Bostrom, R. N., J. W. Vlandis, and M. E. Rosen (1961). Grades as reinforcing contingencies and attitude change. *J. educat. Psychol., 52,* 112–115.

Bowers, J. W. (1963). Language intensity, social introversion and attitude change. *Speech Monogr., 30,* 345–352.

⸺ (1964). Some correlates of language intensity. *Quart. J. Speech, 50,* 415–420.

Bowers, J. W., and M. M. Osborn (1966). Attitudinal effects of selected types of concluding metaphors in persuasive speech. *Speech Monogr., 33,* 147–155.

Bowlby, J. (1973). *Attachment and loss. Vol. 2. Separation.* New York: Basic Books.

Braestrup, P. (1983). *Big story: how the American press and television reported and interpreted the crisis of Tet 1968 in Vietnam and Washington.* New Haven: Yale Univ. Press.

Brain, C. K. (1981). *The hunters or the hunted? An introduction to African cave taphonomy.* Chicago: Univ. Chicago Press.

Brandstätter, H., J. H. Davis, and G. Stocker-Kreichgauer (1982). *Group decision making.* London: Academic Press.

Brawley, E. A. (1983). *Mass media and human services.* Beverly Hills, Calif.: Sage.

Brehm, J. W. (1960). A dissonance analysis of attitude-discrepant behavior. In C. I. Hovland, and M. J. Rosenberg (Eds.), *Attitude organization and change.* New Haven: Yale Univ. Press. Pp. 164–197.

Brehm, J. W., and A. R. Cohen (1962). *Explorations in cognitive dissonance.* New York: Wiley.

Brehm, J. W., and M. Mann (1975). Effect of the importance of freedom and attraction to group members on influence produced by group pressure. *J. Pers. soc. Psychol., 31,* 816–824.

Brehm, S. S., and J. W. Brehm (1981). *Psychological reactance: a theory of freedom and control.* New York: Academic Press.

Brentano, F. (1973). *Psychologie von empirischen Standpunkte.* Originally published 1874. [*Psychology from an empirical standpoint.*] New York: Humanities Press.

Bridge, R. G., L. G. Reeder, D. Kanouse, D. R. Kinder, V. T. Nagy, and C. M. Judd (1977). Interviewing changes attitudes—sometimes. *Publ. Opin. Quart., 41,* 56–64.

Brim, O. G., Jr., and J. Kagan, Eds. (1980). *Constancy and change in human development.* Cambridge, Mass.: Harvard Univ. Press.

Brock, T. C. (1967). Communication discrepancy and intent to persuade as determinants of counterargument production. *J. exp. soc. Psychol., 3,* 296–309.

Brockner, J., B. Pressman, J. Cabitt, and P. Moran (1982). Nonverbal intimacy, sex and compliance: a field study. *J. nonverbal Behav., 6,* 253–258.

Brody, G. H., Z. Stoneman, and A. K. Sanders (1980). Effects of television viewing on family interactions: an observational study. *Fam. Relat., 29,* 216–220.

Brody, N., Ed. (1983). *Human motivation: commentary on goal-directed action.* New York: Academic Press.

Bromley, D. B. (1977). *Personality description in ordinary language.* New York: Wiley.

Broszat, M. (1981). *The Hitler state: the foundation and development of the internal structure of the Third Reich.* (Original German edition, 1968.) New York: Longman.

Brothen, T. (1977). The gain/loss concept and the evaluator: first some good news, then some bad. *J. Pers. soc. Psychol., 35,* 430–436.

Broverman, I. K., S. R. Vogel, D. M. Broverman, F. E. Clarkson, and P. S. Rosenkrantz (1972). Sex-role stereotypes: a current appraisal. *J. soc. Issues, 28,* No. 2, 59–78.

Brown, D., and J. Bryant (1983). Humor in the mass media. In P. E. McGhee, and J. H. Goldstein (Eds.), *Handbook of humor research. Vol. 2. Applied studies.* New York: Springer-Verlag. Pp. 143–172.

Brown, L. A. (1981). *Innovation diffusion: a new perspective.* London: Methuen.

Brown, S. R. (1980). *Political subjectivity: applications of Q methodology in political science.* New Haven: Yale Univ. Press.

Bruns, G. L. (1982). *Inventions: writing, textuality and understanding in literary history.* New Haven: Yale Univ. Press.

Bryant, J., and D. R. Anderson, Eds. (1983). *Understanding TV: research in children's attention and comprehension.* New York: Academic Press.

Bryant, J., D. Brown, A. R. Silberberg, and S. M. Elliott (1981). Effects of humorous illustrations in college textbooks. *Hum. Communic. Res., 8,* 43–57.

Budd, R., and C. Spencer (1984). Latitude of rejection, centrality and certainty: variables affecting the relationship between attitudes, norms and behavioural intentions. *Brit. J. soc. Psychol., 23,* 1–8.

Bühler, C. (1935). *Kindheit und Jugend: genese des bewusstseins.* Leipzig: Hirsch. Originally published 1928. (*From birth to maturity: An outline of the psychological development of the child.*) London: Kegan Paul, French, Trubner.

Bull, P. (1983). *Body movement and interpersonal communication.* New York: Wiley.

Burger, J. M., and R. E. Petty (1981). The low-ball compliance technique: task or person commitment. *J. Pers. soc. Psychol., 40,* 492–500.

Burgoon, M., and L. J. Chase (1973). The effects of differential linguistic patterns in messages attempting to induce resistance to persuasion. *Speech Monogr., 40,* 1–7.

Burgoon, M., and G. R. Miller (1971). Prior attitude and language intensity as predictors of message style and attitude change following counterattitudinal advocacy. *J. Pers. soc. Psychol., 20,* 246–253.

Burke, K. (1962). *A grammar of motives, and a rhetoric of motives.* Cleveland: World.

Burnett, J. (1977). An integration of object and display instrumentality theories for the prediction of racial attitudes in an organizational setting. Unpublished dissertation. Univ. of Chicago, Department of Psychology.

Busby, L. J. (1974). Defining the sex role standard in network children's television programs. *Journalism Quart., 51,* 690–696.

Bussey, K., and D. G. Perry (1977). The imitation of resistance to deviation: conclusive evidence for an elusive effect. *Develop. Psychol., 13,* 438–445.

Bybee, C. R., J. M. McLeod, W. D. Luetscher, and G. Garramone (1981). Mass communication and voter volatility. *Publ. Opin. Quart., 45,* 69–90.

Byrne, D. (1971). *The attraction paradigm.* New York: Academic Press.

Byrne, D., and B. Blaylock (1963). Similarity and assumed similarity of husbands and wives. *J. abnorm. soc. Psychol., 67,* 636–640.

Byrne, D., J. Lamberth, J. Palmer, and O. London (1969). Sequential effects as a function of explicit and implicit interpolated attraction responses. *J. Pers. soc. Psychol., 13,* 70–78.

Byrne, D., and T. J. Wong (1962). Racial prejudice, interpersonal attraction and assumed dissimilarity of attitudes. *J. abnorm. soc. Psychol., 65,* 246–253.

Cacioppo, J. T., S. G. Harkins, and R. E. Petty (1981). The nature of attitudes and cognitive responses and their relationships to behavior. In R. E. Petty, T. M. Ostrom, and T. C. Brock (Eds.), *Cognitive responses in persuasion.* Hillsdale, N.J.: Erlbaum. Pp. 31–54.

Cacioppo, J. T., and R. E. Petty (1979). Effects of message repetition and position on cognitive response, recall, and persuasion. *J. Pers. soc. Psychol., 37,* 97–109.

———— (1980). Sex differences in influenceability: toward specifying the underlying processes. *Pers. soc. Psychol. Bull., 6,* 651–656.

———— Eds. (1983). *Social psychophysiology: a sourcebook.* New York: Guilford Press.

———— (1984). Central and peripheral routes to persuasion: the role of message repetition, In A. Mitchell and L. Alwitt (Eds.), *Psychological processes and advertising effects.* Hillsdale, N.J.: Erlbaum.

Cacioppo, J. T., R. E. Petty, and K. J. Morris (1983). Effects of need for cognition on message evaluation, recall, and persuasion. *J. Pers. soc. Psychol., 45,* 805–818.

Calder, B. J., C. A. Insko, and B. Yandell (1974). The relation of cognitive and memorial processes to persuasion in a simulated jury level. *J. appl. soc. Psychol., 4,* 62–93.

Calder, B. J., and M. Ross (1973). *Attitudes and behavior.* Morristown, N.J.: General Learning Press.

Calder, B. J., and B. Sternthal (1980). Television commercial wear-out: an information-processing view. *J. Marketng Res., 17,* 173–186.

Callero, P. L., and J. A. Piliavin (1983). Developing a commitment to blood donation: the impact of one's first experience. *J. appl. soc. Psychol., 13,* 1–16.

Campbell, D. T. (1963). Social attitudes and other acquired behavioral dispositions. In S. Koch (Ed.), *Psychology: a study of a science.* Vol. 6. New York: McGraw-Hill.

———— (1965). Ethnocentrism and other altruistic motives. In D. Levine (Ed.), *Nebraska symposium on motivation.* Vol. 13. Lincoln: Univ. of Nebraska Press.

———— (1975). On the conflicts between biological and social evolution and between psychology and moral tradition. *Amer. Psychol., 30,* 1103–1126.

———— (1979). Comments on the sociobiology of ethics and moralizing. *Behav. Sci., 24,* 37–45.

Cann, A., S. J. Sherman, and R. Elkes (1975). Effects of initial request size and timing of a second request on compliance: the foot in the door and the door in the face. *J. Pers. soc. Psychol., 32,* 774–782.

Cantor, G. N. (1968). Children's "like-dislike" ratings of familiarized and nonfamiliarized visual stimuli. *J. exp. Child Psychol., 6,* 651–657.

Cantor, M. G. (1980). *Prime-time television: content and control.* Beverly Hills, Calif.: Sage.

Cantor, N., W. Mischel, and J. C. Schwartz (1982). A prototype analysis of psychological situations. *Cognit. Psychol., 14,* 45–77.

Capaldi, N. (1979). *The art of deception* (2nd ed.). Buffalo, N.Y.: Prometheus.

Caplow, T., H. M. Bahr, B. A. Chadwick, R. Hill, and M. H. Williamson (1982). *Middletown families: fifty years of change and continuity.* Minneapolis: Univ. of Minnesota Press.

Capon, N., and J. Hulbert (1973). The sleeper effect—an awakening. *Publ. Opin. Quart., 37,* 333–358.

Cardwell, J. D. (1971). *Social psychology: a symbolic interaction perspective.* Philadelphia: F. A. Davis.

Carlsmith, J. M., B. E. Collins, and R. L. Helmreich (1966). Studies in forced compliance: I. The effect of pressure for compliance on attitude change produced by face-to-face role playing and anonymous essay writing. *J. Pers. soc. Psychol., 4,* 1–13.

Carmichael, C. W., and G. L. Cronkhite (1965). Frustration and language intensity. *Speech Monogr., 32,* 107–111.

Carroll, J. B. (1960). Vectors of prose style. In T. A. Sebeok (Ed.), *Style in language.* New York: Wiley. Pp. 283–292.

Cartwright, D. (1949). Some principles of mass persuasion. *Hum. Relat., 2,* 253–267.

Carver, C. S., and M. F. Scheier (1981). *Attention and self-regulation: a control theory approach to human behavior.* New York: Springer-Verlag.

Catalano, R. A., D. Dooley, and R. Jackson (1983). Selecting a time series strategy. *Psychol. Bull., 94,* 506–523.

Cattell, R. B. (1946). *The description and measurement of personality.* Yonkers, N.Y.: World Book.

Cavalli-Sforza, L. L., and M. W. Feldman (1981). *Cultural transmission and evolution: a quantitative approach.* Princeton, N.J.: Princeton Univ. Press.

Ceci, S. J., and E. L. Kain (1982). Jumping on the bandwagon with the underdog: the impact of attitude polls on polling behavior. *Publ. Opin. Quart., 46,* 228–242.

Chaffee, S. H., and S. Y. Choe (1980). Times of decision and media use during the Ford-Carter campaign. *Publ. Opin. Quart., 44,* 53–69.

Chaffee, S. H., and A. R. Tims (1982). News media use in adolescence: implications for political cognitions. In M. Burgoon (Ed.), *Communication yearbook.* Vol. 6. Beverly Hills, Calif.: Sage. Pp. 736–758.

Chagall, D. (1981). *The new kingmakers.* New York: Harcourt, Brace, Jovanovich.

Chaiken, S. (1979). Communicator's physical attractiveness and persuasion. *J. Pers. soc. Psychol., 37,* 1387–1397.

Chaiken, S. (1980). Heuristic versus systematic information processing and the use of source versus message cues in persuasion. *J. Pers. soc. Psychol., 39,* 752–766.

—— (In press). Physical appearance variables and social influence. In C. P. Herman, E. T. Higgins, and M. P. Zanna (Eds.), *Physical appearance, stigma and social behavior. The third Ontario symposium.* Hillsdale, N.J.: Erlbaum.

Chaiken, S., and M. W. Baldwin (1981). Affective-cognitive consistency and the effect of salient behavioral information on the self-perception of attitudes. *J. Pers. soc. Psychol., 41,* 1–12.

Chaiken, S., and A. H. Eagly (1976). Communication modality as a determinant of message persuasiveness and message comprehensibility. *J. Pers. soc. Psychol., 34,* 605–614.

—— (1983). Communication modality as a determinant of persuasion: the role of communicator salience. *J. Pers. soc. Psychol., 45,* 241–256.

Chambers, D. W., Ed. (1979). *Liberation and control: the uses of knowledge and power.* Wawin Ponds, Australia: Deakin Univ. Press.

Chandler, R. W. (1981). *War of ideas: the U.S. propaganda campaign in Vietnam.* Boulder, Colo.: Westview Press.

Chanowitz, B., and E. J. Langer (1981). Premature cognitive commitment. *J. Pers. soc. Psychol., 41,* 1051–1063.

Chapman, T., and H. Foot, Eds. (1976). *Humour and laughter: theory, research, and applications.* London: Wiley.

Charters, W. W., and T. M. Newcomb (1958). Some attitudinal effects of experimentally increased salience of a membership group. In E. E. Maccoby, T. M. Newcomb, and E. L. Hartley. *Readings in social psychology.* New York: Holt. Pp. 276–281.

Chein, I. (1948). Behavior theory and the behavior of attitudes. *Psychol. Rev., 55,* 175–188.

Cherfas, J., and R. Lewin (1980). *Not work alone: a cross-cultural view of activities superfluous to survival.* Beverly Hills, Calif.: Sage.

Cherlin, A. (1983). Changing family and household: contemporary lessons from historical research. *Ann. Rev. Sociol., 9,* 51–66.

Cherlin, A. J. (1981). *Marriage, divorce, remarriage.* Cambridge, Mass.: Harvard Univ. Press.

Chrisman, M. U. (1982). *Lay culture, learned culture: books and social change in Strasbourg, 1480–1599.* New Haven: Yale Univ. Press.

Christensen-Szalanski, J. J. J., and L. R. Beach (1984). The citation bias: fad and fashion in the judgment and decision literature. *Amer. Psychologist, 39,* 75–78.

Christie, R., and F. L. Geis (1968). *Studies in Machiavellianism.* New York: Academic Press.

Cialdini, R. B. (1980). Full-cycle social psychology. In L. Bickman (Ed.), *Appl. soc. psychol. ann., 1,* 21–47.

—— (1984). *Influence: how and why people agree to things.* New York: Morrow.

Cialdini, R. B., S. L. Braver, and S. K. Lewis (1974). Attribution bias and the easily persuaded other. *J. Pers. soc. Psychol., 30,* 631–637.

Cialdini, R. B., J. T. Cacioppo, R. Bassett, and J. A. Miller (1978). Low-ball procedure for producing compliance: commitment then cost. *J. Pers. soc. Psychol., 36,* 463–476.

Cialdini, R. B., A. Levy, C. P. Herman, and S. Evenbeck (1973). Attitudinal politics: the strategy of moderation. *J. Pers. soc. Psychol., 25,* 100–108.

Cialdini, R. B., A. Levy, C. P. Herman, L. T. Kozlowski, and R. E. Petty (1976). Elastic shifts of opinion: determinants of direction and durability. *J. Pers. soc. Psychol., 34,* 663–672.

Cialdini, R. B., and R. E. Petty (1981). Anticipatory opinion effects. In R. E. Petty, T. M. Ostrom, and T. C. Brock (Eds.), *Cognitive responses in persuasion.* Hillsdale, N.J.: Erlbaum. Pp. 217–235.

Cialdini, R. B., R. E. Petty, and J. T. Cacioppo (1981). Attitude and attitude change. In M. R. Rosenzweig and L. W. Porter (Eds.), *Annual review of psychology.* Vol. 32. Palo Alto, Calif.: Annual Reviews. Pp. 357–404.

Cialdini, R. B., J. E. Vincent, S. K. Lewis, J. Catalan, D. Wheeler, and B. L. Darby (1975). Reciprocal concessions procedure for inducing compliance: the door-in-the-face technique. *J. Pers. soc. Psychol., 31,* 206–215.

Clark, K. B., and M. P. Clark (1947). Racial identification and preference in Negro children. In T. M. Newcomb and E. L. Hartley (Eds.), *Readings in social psychology.* New York: Holt.

Clark, L. F., and S. B. Woll (1981). Stereotype biases: a reconstructive analysis of their role in reconstructive memory. *J. Pers. soc. Psychol., 41,* 1064–1072.

Clark, T. N. (1975). Community power. In A. Inkeles *et al.* (Eds.), *Annual review of sociology.* Vol. 1. Palo Alto, Calif.: Annual Reviews. Pp. 271–295.

Clarke, D. G. (1976). Econometric measurement of the duration of advertising effects on sales. *J. Marketng Res., 13,* 345–357.

Clifford, J. W. (1963). *In the presence of my enemies.* New York: Norton.

Clore, G. L., R. M. Bray, S. M. Itkin, and P. Murphy (1978). Interracial attitudes and behavior at a summer camp. *J. Pers. soc. Psychol., 36,* 107–116.

Clore, G. L., and K. M. Jeffery (1972). Emotional role playing, attitude change and attraction toward a disabled person. *J. Pers. soc. Psychol., 23,* 105–111.

Cohen, A. R. (1957). Need for cognition and order of communication as a determinant of opinion change. In C. I. Hovland (Ed.), *Order of presentation in persuasion.* New Haven: Yale Univ. Press. Pp. 79–97.

Cohen, E. (1981). The propaganda of saints in the middle ages. *J. Communic., 31,* No. 4, 16–26.

Collins, A. M., and E. F. Loftus (1975). A spreading-activation theory of semantic processing. *Psychol. Rev., 82,* 407–428.

Collins, B. E., and M. F. Hoyt (1972). Personal responsibility-for-consequences: an integration and extension of the "forced compliance" literature. *J. exp. soc. Psychol., 8,* 558–593.

Comadena, M. E. (1982). Accuracy in detecting deception: intimate and friendship relationships. In M. Burgoon (Ed.), *Communication yearbook.* Vol. 6. Beverly Hills, Calif.: Sage. Pp. 446–472.

Combs, B., and P. Slovic (1979). Newspaper coverage of causes of death. *Journalism Quart., 56,* 837–843, 849.

Comstock, G. (1978). The impact of television on American institutions. *J. Communic., 28,* No. 2, 12–28.

———— (1982a). Information management and the mass media: menace or myth. In J. P. Gibbs (Ed.), *Social control: views from the social sciences.* Beverly Hills, Calif.: Sage.

———— (1982b). Violence in television content: an overview. In D. Pearl, L. Bouthilet, and J. Lazar (Eds.), *Television and behavior: ten years of scientific progress and implications for the eighties.* Vol. 2. Washington, D.C.: Government Printing Office. Pp. 108–125.

Comstock, G., S. Chaffee, N. Katzman, M. McCoombs, and D. Roberts (1978). *Television and human behavior.* New York: Columbia Univ. Press.

Conger, J. J. (1981). Freedom and commitment: families, youth and social change. *Amer. Psychol., 36,* 1475–1484.

Conolley, E. S., I. L. Janis, and M. M. Dowds, Jr. (1982). Effects of variations in the type of feedback given by the counselors. In I. L. Janis (Ed.), *Counseling on personal decisions: theory and research on short-term helping relationships.* New Haven: Yale Univ. Press. Pp. 127–143.

Conrad, P. (1982). *Television: the medium and its manners.* Boston: Routledge and Kegan Paul.

Converse, P. E. (1964). The nature of belief systems in mass publics. In D. E. Apter (Ed.), *Ideology and discontent.* New York: Free Press. Pp. 206–261.

———— (1970). Attitudes and non-attitudes: continuation of a dialogue. In E. R. Tufte (Ed.), *The quantitative analysis of social problems.* Reading, Mass.: Addison-Wesley. Pp. 168–189.

———— (1975). Some mass-elite contrasts in the perception of political spaces. *Soc. sci. Info., 14,* No. 3/4, 49–83.

———— (1980). Rejoinder to Judd and Milburn. *Amer. Sociol. Rev., 45,* 644–646.

Converse, P. E., J. D. Dotson, W. J. Hoag, and W. H. McGee (1980). *American social attitudes data sourcebook 1947–1978.* Cambridge, Mass.: Harvard Univ. Press.

Conway, F., and J. Siegelman (1978). *Snapping: America's epidemic of sudden personality change.* Philadelphia: Lippincott.

Conway, M. M., A. J. Stevens, and G. R. Smith (1975). The relation between media use and children's civic awareness. *Journalism Quart., 52,* 531–538.

Conway, M. M., M. L. Wyckoff, E. Feldbaum, and D. Ahern (1981). The news media in children's political socialization. *Publ. Opin. Quart., 45,* 164–178.

Cook, F. L., T. R. Tyler, E. G. Goetz, M. T. Gordon, D. Protess, D. R. Leff, and H. L. Molotch (1983). Media and agenda setting: effects on the public, interest group leaders, policy makers, and policy. *Publ. Opin. Quart., 47,* 16–35.

Cook, M., Ed. (1981). *The bases of human sexual attraction.* New York: Academic Press.

Cook, S. W. (1978). Interpersonal and attitudinal outcomes in cooperating interracial groups. *J. Res. Develop. Education, 12,* 97–113.

———— (1979). Social science and school desegregation: did we mislead the Supreme Court? *Pers. soc. Psychol. Bull., 5,* 420–437.

Cook, S. W., and C. Selltiz (1964). A multiple-indicator approach to attitude measurement. *Psychol. Bull., 62,* 36–55.

Cook, T. D., H. Appelton, R. F. Conner, A. Shaffer, G. Tomkin, and S. J. Weber (1975). *Sesame Street revisited.* New York: Russell Sage.

Cook, T. D., and B. R. Flay (1978). The persistence of experimentally induced attitude change. In L. Berkowitz (Ed.), *Advances in experimental social psychology.* Vol. 11. New York: Academic Press. Pp. 1–57.

Cook, T. D., C. L. Gruder, K. M. Hennigan, and B. R. Flay (1979). History of the sleeper effect: some logical pitfalls in accepting the null hypothesis. *Psychol. Bull., 86,* 662–679.

Cook, T. D., and C. A. Insko (1968). Persistence of attitude change as a function of conclusion reexposure: a laboratory-field experiment. *J. Pers. soc. Psychol., 9,* 322–328.

Cook, T. D., D. A. Kendzierski, and S. V. Thomas (1983). The implicit assumptions of television research: an analysis of the 1982 NIMH report on *television and behavior. Publ. Opin. Quart., 47,* 161–201.

Cook, T. D., and A. Wadsworth (1972). Attitude change and the paired-associates learning of minimal cognitive elements. *J. Pers., 40,* 50–61.

Cooper, H. M. (1979). Statistically combining independent studies: a meta-analysis of sex differences in conformity research. *J. Pers. soc. Psychol., 37,* 131–146.

Cooper, J., and R. A. Jones (1970). Self-esteem and consistency as determinants of anticipatory opinion change. *J. Pers. soc. Psychol., 14,* 312–320.

Corcoran, M. (1981). Sex differences in measurement error in status attainment models. In G. W. Bohrnstedt and E. F. Borgatta (Eds.), *Social measurement: current issues.* Beverly Hills, Calif.: Sage. Pp. 209–227.

Corcoran, P. E. (1979). *Political language and rhetoric.* Hamel Hempstead, England: Prentice-Hall International.

Costanzo, P. R., and M. E. Shaw (1966). Conformity as a function of age level. *Child Development, 37,* 967–975.

Council, J. R., I. Kirsch, A. R. Vickery, and D. Carlson (1983). "Trance" versus "skill" hypnotic inductions: the effects of credibility, expectancy, and experimenter modeling. *J. consult. clinic. Psychol., 51,* 432–440.

Courtney, A. E., and T. W. Whipple (1981). *Sex stereotyping in advertising.* Lexington, Mass.: D.C. Heath.

Coutts, L. M., and M. Ledden (1977). Nonverbal compensatory reactions to changes in interpersonal proximity. *J. soc. Psychol., 102,* 283–290.

Cox, D. F., and R. A. Bauer (1964). Self-confidence and persuasibility in women. *Publ. Opin. Quart., 28,* 453–466.

Craig, C. S., B. Sternthal, and C. Leavitt (1976). Advertising wearout: an experimental analysis. *J. Marketng Res., 13,* 365–372.

Crano, W. D. (1977). Primacy versus recency in retention of information and opinion change. *J. soc. Psychol., 101,* 87–96.

Crano, W. D., S. Ludwig, and G. W. Selnow, Eds. (1981). *Annotated archive of diffusion references: empirical and theoretical works.* East Lansing: Center for Evaluation and Assessment, Michigan State Univ.

Cronen, V. E., and G. LaFleur (1977). Inoculation against persuasive attacks: a test of alternative explanations. *J. soc. Psychol., 102,* 255–265.

Crothers, E. J., Ed. (1979). *Paragraph structure inference.* Norwood, N.J.: Ablex.

Csikszentmihalyi, M. (1982). Toward a psychology of optimal experience. In L. Wheeler (Ed.), *Review of personality and social psychology.* Vol. 3. Beverly Hills, Calif.: Sage. Pp. 13–36.

Csikszentmihalyi, M., and E. Rochberg-Halton (1981). *The meaning of things: symbols in the development of the self.* Cambridge: Cambridge Univ. Press.

Culler, J. (1982). *On deconstruction: theory and criticism after structuralism.* Ithaca, N.Y.: Cornell Univ. Press.

Cushman, D. P., and R. D. McPhee, Eds. (1980). *Attitude-behavior relationship.* Beverly Hills, Calif.: Sage.

Cushman, D. P., and W. B. Pearce (1978). Generality and necessity in three types of human communications theory, with special attention to rule theory. *Hum. Communic. Res., 4,* 243–252.

Cutrow, R. J., A. Parks, N. Lucas, and K. Thomas (1972). The objective use of multiple physiological indices in the detection of deception. *Psychophysiology, 9,* 578–588.

Czitrom, D. J. (1982). *Media and the American mind: from Morse to McLuhan.* Chapel Hill: Univ. of North Carolina Press.

Dakin, J. (1979). *Feedback from tommorrow (Research in planning and design set).* New York: Methuen.

Danes, J. E., J. E. Hunter, and J. Woelfel (1978). Mass communication and belief change: a test of three mathematical models. *Hum. Communic. Res., 4,* 243–252.

Danziger, K. (1976). *Interpersonal communication.* New York: Pergamon Press.

Davidson, A. R., and J. J. Jaccard (1979). Variables that moderate the attitude-behavior relation: results of a longitudinal survey. *J. Pers. soc. Psychol., 37,* 1364–1376.

Davidson, A. R., and D. M. Morrison (1983). Predicting contraceptive behavior from attitudes: a comparison of within- versus across-subjects procedures. *J. Pers. soc. Psychol., 45,* 997–1009.

Davidson, E. S., A. Yasuna, and A. Tower (1979). The effects of television cartoons on sex-role stereotyping on young children. *Child Development, 50,* 597–600.

Davis, E. E. (1975). *A study of the structure and determinants of the behavioral components of social attitude in Ireland.* Dublin: Economic and Social Research Institute. No. 83.

Davis, E. E., and M. O'Neill (1977). *An Irish personality differential: a technique for measuring affective and cognitive dimensions of attitudes toward persons.* Dublin: Economic and Social Research Institute. No. 88.

Davis, E. E., and H. C. Triandis (1971). An experimental study of black-white negotiations. *J. appl. soc. Psychol., 1,* 240–262.

Davis, M., and J. Skupien (1982). *Body movement and nonverbal communication: an annotated bibliography, 1971–1980.* Bloomington: Indiana Univ. Press.

Davis, R. H., and R. W. Kubey (1982). Growing old on television and with television. In D. Pearl, L. Bouthilet, and J. Lazar (Eds.), *Television and behavior: ten years of scientific progress and implications for the eighties.* Vol. 2. *Technical reports.* Washington, D.C.: U.S. Government Printing Office. Pp. 201–208.

Davison, W. P. (1980). The media kaleidoscope: general trends in the channels. In H. D. Lasswell, D. Lerner, and H. Speier (Eds.), *Propaganda and communication in world history.* Vol. 3. Honolulu: Univ. of Hawaii Press. Pp. 191–248.

Dawes, R. M. (1972). *Fundamentals of attitude measurement.* New York: Wiley.

Dawkins, R. (1976). *The selfish gene.* New York: Oxford Univ. Press.

Dean, L. M., F. W. Willis, and J. Hewitt (1975). Initial interaction distance among individuals equal and unequal in military rank. *J. Pers. soc. Psychol., 32,* 294–299.

Deaux, K. (1972a). Anticipatory attitude change: a direct test of the self-esteem hypothesis. *J. exp. soc. Psychol., 8,* 143–155.

_____ (1972b). To err is humanizing: but sex makes a difference. *Rep. Res. soc. Psychol., 3,* 20–28.

DeBock, H., and J. van Lil (1981). "Holocaust" in the Netherlands. In G. C. Wilhoit, and H. DeBock (Eds.), *Mass communication review yearbook.* Vol. 2. Beverly Hills, Calif.: Sage. Pp. 639–647.

deCarufel, A., and J. Schopler (1979). Evaluation of outcome improvement resulting from threats and appeals. *J. Pers. soc. Psychol., 37,* 662–673.

Deci, E. L. (1980). *The psychology of self-determination.* Lexington, Mass.: D.C. Heath.

DeFleur, M. L., and F. R. Westie (1963). Attitude as a scientific concept. *Social Forces, 42,* 17–31.

DeJong, W. (1979). An examination of self-perception mediation of the foot-in-the-door effect. *J. Pers. soc. Psychol., 37,* 2221–2236.

_____ (1981). Consensus information and the foot-in-door effect. *Pers. soc. Psychol. Bull., 7,* 423–430.

Dember, W. N. (1974). Motivation and the cognitive revolution. *Amer. Psychol., 29,* 161–168.

Dembroski, T. M., and J. W. Pennebaker (1977). Social class and threat effects on compliance and attitude in black children. *J. soc. Psychol., 102,* 317–318.

DePaulo, B. M., R. Rosenthal, J. Rosenkrantz, and C. R. Green (1982). Actual and perceived cues to deception: a closer look at speech. *Basic appl. soc. Psychol., 3,* 291–312.

Derber, C. (1979). *The pursuit of attention: power and individualism in everyday life.* Cambridge, Mass.: Schenkman.

De Rivera, J. H. (1968). *The psychological dimensions of foreign policy.* Columbus, Ohio: Merrill.

Derlega, V., and J. Grzelak, Eds. (1984). *Living with other people: theories and research on cooperation and helping behavior.* New York: Academic Press.

Dermer, M., and D. L. Thiel (1975). When beauty may fail. *J. Pers. soc. Psychol., 31,* 1168–1176.

Derrida, J. (1973). *La voix et le phénomène.* Paris: Presse Universitaires du France, 1967. [*Speech and phenomena.*] Evanston, Ill.: Northwestern Univ. Press.

———— (1980). *La carte postale de Socrate à Freud et au-dela.* Paris: Flammarion.

Detweiler, R. A., and M. P. Zanna (1976). Physiological mediation of attitudinal responses. *J. Pers. soc. Psychol., 33,* 107–116.

Deutsch, M. (1949). A theory of co-operation and competition. *Hum. Relat., 2,* 129–152.

Deutsch, M., and H. Gerard (1955). A study of the normative and informational social influences upon individual judgment. *J. abnorm. soc. Psychol., 51,* 629–636.

Deutscher, I. (1973). *What we say/what we do: sentiments and acts.* Glenview, Ill.: Scott, Foresman.

Dichter, E. (1975). *Packaging: the sixth sense.* Boston: CBI.

Diener, E., and D. DeFour (1978). Does television violence enhance program popularity? *J. Pers. soc. Psychol., 36,* 333–341.

Dillehay, R. C., C. A. Insko, and M. B. Smith (1966). Logical consistency and attitude change. *J. Pers. soc. Psychol., 3,* 646–654.

Dillon, R. F., and R. R., Schmeck, Eds. (1983). *Individual differences in cognition.* Vol. 1. New York: Academic Press.

Dimmick, J. W., T. A. McCain, and W. T. Bolton (1979). Media use and the life span. *Amer. Behav. Scientist, 23,* 7–31.

Dinner, S. H., B. E. Lewkowicz, and J. Cooper (1972). Anticipatory attitude change as a function of self-esteem and issue familiarity. *J. Pers. soc. Psychol., 24,* 407–412.

Dion, K. K., and S. Stein (1978). Physical attractiveness and interpersonal influence. *J. exp. soc. Psychol., 14,* 97–108.

Dirr, P. J. (1980). The future of television's teaching face. In E. L. Palmer, and A. Dorr (Eds.), *Children and the faces of television: teaching, violence, selling.* New York: Academic Press. Pp. 99–108.

Dittes, J. E., and H. H. Kelley (1956). Effects of different conditions of acceptance upon conformity to group norms. *J. abnorm. soc. Psychol., 53,* 100–107.

Ditton, J., Ed. (1980). *The view from Goffman.* New York: St. Martins Press.

Dixon, N. F. (1980). *Preconscious processing.* London: Wiley.

Dizard, W. (1982). *The coming information age: an overview of its technology, economics, and politics.* New York: Longman/Annenberg.

Doise, W., and G. Douglas (1978). *Groups and individuals: explanations in social psychology.* Cambridge: Cambridge Univ. Press.

Doise, W., J. C. Deschamps, and G. Meyer (1978). The accentuation of intra-category similarities. In H. Tafjel (Ed.), *Differentiation between social groups: studies in the social psychology of intergroup relations.* London: Academic Press. Pp. 159–168.

Dollard, J., and N. E. Miller (1950). *Personality and psychotherapy.* New York: McGraw-Hill.

Doob, A. N., and G. E. Macdonald (1979). Television viewing and fear of victimization: is the relationship causal? *J. Pers. soc. Psychol., 37,* 170–179.

Doob, L. W. (1947). The behavior of attitudes. *Psychol. Rev., 54,* 135–156.

———— (1961). *Communication in Africa.* New Haven: Yale Univ. Press.

Douglas, M., Ed. (1982). *Essays in the sociology of perception.* London: Routledge and Kegan Paul.

Douglas, M., and B. Isherwood (1979). *The world of goods: an anthropologist's perspective.* New York: Basic Books.

Dovidio, J. F., and S. L. Ellyson (1982). Decoding visual dominance: attributions of power based on relative percentages of looking while speaking and looking while listening. *Soc. Psychol. Quart., 45,* 106–113.

Downs, A. C. (1981). Sex-role stereotyping on prime-time television. *J. Genetic Psychol., 138,* 253–258.

Drabman, R. S., and M. H. Thomas (1974). Does media violence increase children's toleration of real-life aggression? *Develop. Psychol., 10,* 418–421.

Dreben, E. K., S. T. Fiske, and R. Hastie (1979). The independence of evaluative and item information: impression and recall order effects in behavior-based impression formation. *J. Pers. soc. Psychol., 37,* 1758–1768.

Dreier, P. (1982). The position of the press in the U.S. power structure. *Soc. Problems, 29,* 298–310.

Dubarle, D., Ed. (1978). *Le pouvoir.* Paris: Editions Beauchesne.

Dulany, D. E. (1962). The place of hypothesis and intentions: an analysis of verbal control in verbal conditioning. In C. W. Eriksen (Ed.), *Behavior and awareness.* Durham, N.C.: Duke Univ. Press. Pp. 102–129.

———— (1968). Awareness, rules and propositional control: a confrontation with S-R behavior theory. In T. R. Dixon, and D. L. Horton (Eds.), *Verbal behavior and general behavior theory.* Englewood Cliffs, N.J.: Prentice-Hall. Pp. 340–387.

Duval, S., and V. H. Duval (1983). *Consistency and cognition: a theory of causal attribution.* Hillsdale, N.J.: Erlbaum.

Eagly, A. H. (1974). Comprehensibility of persuasive arguments as a determinant of opinion change. *J. Pers. soc. Psychol., 29,* 758–773.

———— (1978). Sex differences in influenceability. *Psychol. Bull., 85,* 86–116.

———— (1983). Gender and social influence: a social psychological analysis. *Amer. Psychol., 38,* 971–981.

Eagly, A. H., and L. L. Carli (1981). Sex of researchers and sex-typed communications as determinants of sex differences in influenceability: a meta-analysis of social influence studies. *Psychol. Bull., 90,* 1–20.

Eagly, A. H., and S. Chaiken (1975). An attribution analysis of the effect of communicator characteristics on opinion change: the case of communicator attractiveness. *J. Pers. soc. Psychol., 32,* 136–144.

———— (In press). Cognitive theories of persuasion. In L. Berkowitz (Ed.), *Advances in experimental social psychology.* New York: Academic Press.

Eagly, A. H., and R. Warren (1976). Intelligence, comprehension, and opinion change. *J. Pers., 44,* 226–242.

Eagly, A. H., W. Wood, and S. Chaiken (1978). Causal inferences about communicators and their effect on opinion change. *J. Pers. soc. Psychol., 36,* 424–435.

Eagly, A. H., W. Wood, and L. Fishbaugh (1981). Sex differences in conformity: surveillance by the group as a determinant of male nonconformity. *J. Pers. soc. Psychol., 40,* 384–394.

Eckblad, G. (1981). *Scheme theory: a conceptual framework for cognitive-motivational processes.* New York: Academic Press.

Edell, J. A., and R. Staelin (1983). The information processing of pictures in print advertisements. *J. Consumer Research, 10,* 45–61.

Edney, J. J. (1980). The common problems: alternative perspectives. *Amer. Psychol., 35,* 131–150.

Edwards, C. (1979). *Crazy for God: the nightmare of cult life.* Englewood Cliffs, N.J.: Prentice-Hall.

Edwards, W. (1954). The theory of decision making. *Psychol. Bull., 51,* 380–417.

Eichorn, D. H., J. A. Clausen, N. Haan, M. P. Honzik, and P. H. Musssen, Eds. (1981). *Present and past in middle life.* New York: Academic Press.

Eisenberg, N., Ed. (1982). *The development of prosocial behavior.* New York: Academic Press.

Eisenstein, E. L. (1979). *The printing press as an agent of change: communication and cultural transformations in early-modern Europe.* 2 Vols. Cambridge: Cambridge Univ. Press.

Eiser, J. R., Ed. (1984). *Attitudinal judgment.* Secaucus, N.J.: Springer-Verlag.

Ekman, P., and W. V. Friesen (1974). Detecting deception from the body or face. *J. Pers. soc. Psychol., 29,* 288–298.

——— (1975). *Unmasking the face.* Englewood Cliffs, N.J.: Prentice-Hall.

Elliott, P. (1982). Press performance as political ritual. In D. C. Whitney, E. Wartella, and S. Windahl (Eds.), *Mass communication review yearbook.* Vol. 3. Beverly Hills, Calif.: Sage. Pp. 583–619.

Ellis, J. (1983). *Visible fictions.* London: Routledge and Kegan Paul.

Ellsworth, P. C. (1982). Public attitudes to capital punishment in general and in specific cases. *Personal communication.*

Ellsworth, P. C., and E. J. Langer (1976). Staring and approach: an interpretation of the stare as a nonspecific activator. *J. Pers. soc. Psychol., 33,* 117–122.

Emde, R. N., and R. J. Harmon (1982). *The development of attachment and affiliative systems.* New York: Plenum.

Endler, N. S., and J. McV. Hunt (1968). S–R inventories of hostility and comparisons of the proportions of variance from persons, responses, and situations for hostility and anxiousness. *J. Pers. soc. Psychol., 9,* 309–315.

Endler, N. S., D. L. Wiesenthal, and S. H. Geller (1972). The generalization effects of agreement and correctness on relative competence mediating conformity. *Canad. J. Behav. Sci., 4,* 322–329.

Erbring, L., E. N. Goldenberg, and A. H. Miller (1980). Front page news and real-world cues: a new look at agenda-setting by the media. *Amer. J. politic. Sci., 24,* 16–49.

Erickson, B., E. A. Lind, B. C. Johnson, and W. M. O'Barr (1978). Speech style and impression formation in a court setting: the effects of "powerful" and "powerless" speech. *J. exp. soc. Psychol., 14,* 266–279.

Erikson, E. H. (1950). *Childhood and society.* New York: Norton (2nd edition, 1964).

——— (1979). *Dimensions of a new identity.* New York: Norton.

Eron, L. D. (1982). Parent-child interaction, television violence, and aggression of children. *Amer. Psychol., 37,* 197–211.

Eron, L. D., and L. R. Huesmann (1980). Adolescent aggression and television. *Annals N.Y. Acad. Sci., 347,* 319–331.

Eron, L. D., L. R. Huesmann, P. Brice, P. Fischer, and R. Mermelstein (1983). Age trends in the development of aggression, sex typing and related television habits. *Develop. Psychol., 19,* 71–77.

Erskine, H. (1970). The polls: is war a mistake? *Publ. Opin. Quart., 34,* 134–150.

Ettema, J. S., J. W. Brown, and R. V. Luepker (1983). Knowledge gap effects in a health information campaign. *Publ. Opin. Quart., 47,* 516–527.

Ettema, J. S., and D. C. Whitney, Eds. (1982). *Individuals in mass media organizations: creativity and constraint.* Beverly Hills, Calif.: Sage.

Etzioni, A. (1966). Threat and obedience. *Transaction, 3,* 55.

Etzioni, A., and T. A. Diprete (1979). The decline in confidence in America: the prime factor, a research note. *J. appl. Behav. Sci., 15,* 520–526.

Evan, W. M., Ed. (1981). *Knowledge and power in a global society.* Beverly Hills, Calif.: Sage.

Evans, R. I., R. M. Rozelle, T. M. Lasater, T. M. Dembroski, and B. P. Allen (1970). Fear arousal, persuasion, and actual versus implied behavioral change: new perspective utilizing a real-life dental hygiene program. *J. Pers. soc. Psychol., 16,* 220–227.

Evans, R. I., R. M. Rozelle, S. E. Maxwell, B. E. Raines, C. A. Dill, T. J. Guthrie, A. H. Henderson, and P. C. Hill (1981). Social modeling films to deter smoking in adolescents: results of a three-year field investigation. *J. appl. Psychol., 66,* 399–414.

Evans, R. I., R. M. Rozelle, M. B. Mittelmark, W. B. Hansen, A. L. Bane, and J. G. Havis (1978). Deterring the onset of smoking in children: knowledge of immediate physiological effects and coping with peer pressure, media pressure and parent modeling. *J. appl. soc. Psychol., 8,* 126–135.

Ewen, S., and E. Ewen (1982). *Channels of desire: mass images and the shaping of American consciousness.* New York: McGraw-Hill.

Exline, R. V. (1972). Visual interaction: the glances of power and preference. In J. K. Cole (Ed.), *Nebraska symposium on motivation, 1971, 19.* Lincoln: Univ. of Nebraska Press. Pp. 163–206.

Exline, R. V., S. L. Ellyson, and B. Long (1975). Visual behavior as an aspect of power role relationships. In P. Pliner, L. Krames, and T. Alloway (Eds.), *Advances in the study of communication and affect.* Vol. 2. *Nonverbal communication of aggression.* New York: Plenum. Pp. 21–52.

Eysenck, H. J., and W. D. Furneaux (1945). Primary and secondary suggestibility: an experimental and statistical study. *J. exp. Psychol., 35,* 485–503.

Fagen, R. M. (1981). *Animal play behavior.* New York: Oxford Univ. Press.

Farkas, A. J., and N. H. Anderson (1976). Integration theory and inoculation theory as explanations of the "paper tiger" effect. *J. soc. Psychol., 98,* 253–268.

Farquhar, W. J., N. Maccoby, P. D. Wood, J. K. Alexander, H. Breitrose, B. W. Brown, W. L. Haskell, A. L. McAlister, A. J. Meyer, J. D. Nash, and M. P. Stern (1977). Community education for cardiovascular health. *Lancet, 4,* 1192–1195.

Farr, J. L. (1973). Response requirements and primacy-recency effects in a simulated selection interview. *J. appl. Psychol., 57,* 228–232.

Farr, R., and S. Moscovici (1984). *Social representation.* Cambridge: Cambridge Univ. Press.

Farris, E. (1925). The concept of social attitudes. *J. appl. Sociol., 9,* 404–409.

Faules, D. F., and D. C. Alexander (1978). *Communication and social behavior: a symbolic interaction perspective.* Reading, Mass.: Addison-Wesley.

Fazio, R. H., J. Chen, E. C. McDonel, and S. J. Sherman (1982). Attitude accessibiity, attitude-behavior consistency and the strength of the object-evaluation association. *J. exp. soc. Psychol., 18,* 339–357.

Fazio, R. H., and M. P. Zanna (1981). Direct experience and attitude-behavior consistency. In L. Berkowitz (Ed.), *Advances in experimental social psychology.* Vol. 14. New York: Academic Press.

Fazio, R. H., M. P. Zanna, and J. Cooper (1977). Dissonance and self-perception: an integrative view of each theory's proper domain of application. *J. exp. soc. Psychol., 13,* 464–479.

_____ (1978). Direct experience and attitude-behavior consistency: an information processing analysis. *Pers. soc. Psychol. Bull., 4,* 48–51.

Feather, N. T. (1969). Attitude and selective recall. *J. Pers. soc. Psychol., 12,* 310–319.

_____ (1973). Value change among university students. *Australian J. Psychol., 25,* 57–70.

_____, Ed. (1982). *Expectations and actions: expectancy-value models in psychology.* Hillsdale, N.J.: Erlbaum.

Fehrenbach, P. A., D. J. Miller, and M. H. Thelen (1979). The importance of consistency of modeling behavior upon imitation: a comparison of single and multiple models. *J. Pers. soc. Psychol., 37,* 1412–1417.

Feldman, R. S., Ed. (1982). *Development of nonverbal behavior in children.* New York: Springer-Verlag.

Feldman, R. S., L. Devin-Sheehan, and V. L. Allen (1978). Nonverbal cues as indicators of verbal dissembling. *Amer. educat. Res. J., 15,* 217–231.

Feldman, R. S., L. Jenkins, and O. Popoola (1979). Detection of deception in adults and children via facial expressions. *Child Development, 50,* 350–355.

Feldman, R. S., and J. B. White (1980). Detecting deception in children. *J. Communic., 30,* No. 2, 121–128.

Feldman, S., Ed. (1966). *Cognitive consistency.* New York: Academic Press.

_____ (1971). The presentation of shortness in everyday life—height and heightism in American life. Presentation at American Sociological Association Annual Convention, Chicago.

Fenigstein, A. (1979). Does aggression cause a preference for viewing media violence? *J. Pers. soc. Psychol., 37,* 2307–2317.

Feshbach, S. (1972). Reality and fantasy in filmed violence. In J. P. Murray, E. A. Rubinstein, and G. A. Comstock (Eds.), *Television and social behavior.* Vol. 2. *Television and social learning.* Washington, D.C.: Government Printing Office. Pp. 318–345.

Feshbach, S., and R. D. Singer (1971). *Television and aggression: an experimental field study.* San Francisco: Jossey-Bass.

Festinger, L. (1954). A theory of social comparison processes. *Hum. Relat., 7,* 117–140.

_____ (1957). *A theory of cognitive dissonance.* Stanford: Stanford Univ. Press.

Festinger, L., and J. M. Carlsmith (1959). Cognitive consequences of forced compliance. *J. abnorm. soc. Psychol., 58,* 203–210.

Feyerabend, P. (1978). *Against method.* London: Verson.

Fiedler, K. (1982). Causal schemata: review and criticism of research on a popular concept. *J. Pers. soc. Psychol., 42,* 1001–1013.

Fields, J. M., and H. Schuman (1976). Public beliefs about the beliefs of the public. *Publ. Opin. Quart., 40,* 427–448.

Fincham, F. D., and J. M. Jaspars (1980). Attribution of responsibility: from man as scientist to man as lawyer. In L. Berkowitz (Ed.), *Advances in experimental social psychology.* Vol. 13. New York: Academic Press. Pp. 81–138.

Fine, B. J. (1957). Conclusion-drawing, communicator credibility, and anxiety as factors in opinion change. *J. abnorm. soc. Psychol., 54,* 369–374.

Finer, W. D., J. E. Hautaluoma, and L. J. Bloom (1980). The effects of severity and pleasantness of initiation on attraction to a group. *J. soc. Psychol., 111,* 301–302.

Fink, Edward L., L. D. Rey, K. W. Johnson, K. I. Spenner, D. R. Morton, and E. T. Flores (1975). The effects of family occupational type, sex, and appeal style on helping behavior. *J. exp. soc. Psychol., 11,* 43–52.

Fiorina, M. P. (1981). *Retrospective voting in American national elections.* New Haven: Yale Univ. Press.

Fisch, R., J. H. Weakland, and L. Segal (1982). *The tactics of change: doing therapy briefly.* San Francisco: Jossey-Bass.

Fishbein, M. (1963). An investigation of the relationship between beliefs about an object and the attitude towards that object. *Hum. Relat., 16,* 233–239.

_____ (1980). A theory of reasoned action: some applications and implications. In H. Howe and M. Page (Eds.), *Nebraska symposium on motivation, 1979.* Vol. 27. Lincoln: Univ. of Nebraska Press. Pp. 65–116.

Fishbein, M., and I. Ajzen (1972). Attitudes and opinions. In P. H. Mussen and M. R. Rosenzweig (Eds.), *Ann. Rev. Psychol., 23,* 487–544.

_____ (1974). Attitudes towards objects as predictors of single and multiple behavioral criteria. *Psychol. Rev., 81,* 59–74.

_____ (1975). *Belief, attitude, intention, and behavior.* Reading, Mass.: Addison-Wesley.

_____ (1976). Misconceptions revisited: a final comment. *J. exp. soc. Psychol., 12,* 591–593.

Fishbein, M., and R. Hunter (1964). Summation versus balance in attitude organization and change. *J. abnorm. soc. Psychol., 69,* 505–510.

Fishbein, M., and B. H. Raven (1962). The AB scales: an operational definition of beliefs and attitudes. *Hum. Relat., 15,* 35–44.

Fisher, J. D., and D. Byrne (1975). Too close for comfort: sex differences in response to invasions of personal space. *J. Pers. soc. Psychol., 32,* 15–21.

Fisher, J. D., A. Nadler, and B. M. DePaulo (1983). *New directions in helping:* Vol. 1. *recipient reactions to aid.* New York: Academic Press.

Fisher, J. L., and M. B. Harris (1976). The effect of three model characteristics on imitation and learning. *J. soc. Psychol., 98,* 183–199.

Fisher, S., and R. Fisher (1981). *Pretend the world is funny and forever: a psychological analysis of comedians, clowns, and actors.* Hillsdale, N.J.: Erlbaum.

Fisher, S., I. Rubinstein, and R. W. Freeman (1956). Intertrial effects of immediate self-committal in a continuous social influence situation. *J. abnorm. soc. Psychol., 52,* 200–207.

Fiske, D. W., and S. R. Maddi (1961). *Functions of varied experience.* Homewood, Ill.: Dorsey.

Fiske, S. T. (1980). Attention and weight in person perception: the impact of negative and extreme behavior. *J. Pers. soc. Psychol., 38,* 889–906.

Fitzpatrick, A. R., and A. H. Eagly (1981). Anticipatory belief polarization as a function of the expertise of a discussion partner. *Pers. soc. Psychol. Bull., 7,* 636–642.

Flay, B. R., D. DiTecco, and R. P. Schlegel (1981). Mass media in health promotion: an analysis using an extended information-processing model. *Health Educat. Quart., 7,* 127–147.

Fleming, D. (1967). Attitude: the history of a concept. *Perspect. Amer. Hist., 1,* 285–365.

Flesch, R. F. (1948). A new readability yardstick. *J. appl. Psychol., 32,* 221–233.

Fogelin, R. J. (1982). *Understanding arguments* (2nd ed.). New York: Harcourt, Brace, Jovanovich.

Folger, J. P., and W. G. Woodall (1982). Nonverbal cues as linguistic context: an information-processing view. In M. Burgoon (Ed.), *Communication yearbook.* Vol. 6. Beverly Hills, Calif.: Sage. Pp. 63–91.

Forgas, J. P. (1981). *Social cognition: perspectives on everyday understanding.* London: Academic Press.

Forman, C. W. (1979). Christian missions in the ancient world. In H. D. Lasswell, D. Lerner, and H. Speier (Eds.), *Propaganda and communication in world history.* Vol. 1. *The symbolic instrument in early times.* Honolulu: Univ. of Hawaii Press. Pp. 330–347.

Foss, R. D., and C. B. Dempsey (1979). Blood donation and the foot-in-the-door technique: a limiting case. *J. Pers. soc. Psychol., 37,* 580–590.

Fowler, H. (1965). *Curiosity and exploratory behavior.* New York: Macmillan.

Fox, S. (1984). *The mirror makers: a history of American advertising and its creators.* New York: Morrow.

Frank, J. D. (1973). *Persuasion and healing. A comparative study of psychotherapy* (Rev. ed.). (First edition, 1961.) Baltimore: Johns Hopkins.

Frank, R. E., and M. G. Greenberg (1980). *The public's use of television: who watches and why.* Beverly Hills, Calif.: Sage.

_____ (1982). *Audiences for public television.* Beverly Hills, Calif.: Sage.

Frankl, V. E. (1978). *The unheard cry for meaning: psychotherapy and humanism.* New York: Simon and Schuster.

Franzoi, S. L., and S. A. Shields (1984). The body esteem scale: multidimensional structure and sex differences in a college population. *J. Pers. Assessment, 48,* 173–184.

Fredricks, A. J., and D. L. Dossett (1983). Attitude-behavior relations: a comparison of the Fishbein-Ajzen and the Bentler-Speckart models. *J. Pers. soc. Psychol., 45,* 501–512.

Freedman, J. L. (1963). Attitudinal effects of inadequate justification. *J. Pers., 31,* 371–385.

_____ (1964). Involvement, discrepancy, and change. *J. abnorm. soc. Psychol., 69,* 290–295.

_____ (1984). Effect of television violence on aggressiveness. *Psychol. Bull., 96,* 227–246.

Freedman, J. L., and S. C. Fraser (1966). Compliance without pressure: the foot-in-the-door technique. *J. Pers. soc. Psychol., 4,* 195–202.

Freedman, J., and D. Sears (1965). Selective exposure. In L. Berkowitz (Ed.), *Advances in experimental social psychology.* Vol. 2. New York: Academic Press.

Freud, A. (1946). *The ego and the mechanism of defense.* New York: International Univ. Press.

Freud, S. (1922). *Beyond the pleasure principle.* Originally published 1920. London: The International Psychoanalytical Press.

_____ (1964). *New introductory lectures on psycho-analysis.* Original German Edition, 1933. London: Hogarth.

Frey, D. (1981). Postdecisional preferences for decision-relevant information as a function of the competence of its course and the degree of familiarity with this information. *J. exp. soc. Psychol., 17,* 51–67.

_____ (1982). Different levels of cognitive dissonance, information seeking and information avoidance. *J. Pers. soc. Psychol., 43,* 1175–1183.

Frey, D., and R. A. Wicklund (1978). A clarification of selective exposure: the impact of choice. *J. exp. soc. Psychol., 14,* 132–139.

Friedland, N. (1983). Weakness as strength: the use and misuse of a "My hands are tied" ploy in bargaining. *J. appl. soc. Psychol., 13,* 422–426.

Friedman, H. S., M. R. DiMatteo, and T. I. Mertz (1980). Nonverbal communication on television news: the facial expression of broadcasters during coverage of a presidential election campaign. *Pers. soc. Psychol. Bull., 6,* 427–435.

Friedrich-Cofer, L. K., A. Huston-Stein, D. M. Kipnis, E. J. Susman, and A. S. Clewett (1979). Environmental enhancement of prosocial television content: effects on interpersonal behavior, imaginative play, and self-regulation in a natural setting. *Develop. Psychol., 15,* 637–646.

Frischer, B. (1982). *The sculpted word: epicureanism and philosophical recruitment in ancient Greece.* Berkeley: Univ. of California Press.

Fry, P. S. (1975). Effects of male and female endorsement of beliefs on the problem solving choices of high and low dogmatic women. *J. soc. Psychol., 96,* 65–77.

Funk, S., A. D. Horowitz, R. Lipshitz, and F. W. Young (1976). The perceived structure of American ethnic groups: the use of multidimensional scaling in stereotype research. *Sociometry, 39,* 116–130.

Fyans, L. J., Jr., F. Salili, M. L. Maehr, and K. A. Desai (1983). A cross-cultural exploration into the meaning of achievement. *J. Pers. soc. Psychol., 44,* 1000–1013.

Gaes, G. G., and J. T. Tedeschi (1978). An evaluation of self-esteem and impression management theories of anticipatory belief change. *J. exp. soc. Psychol., 14,* 579–587.

Galassi, M. D., and J. P. Galassi (1977). *Assert yourself: how to be your own person.* New York: Human Sciences Press.

Galbraith, J. K. (1983). *The anatomy of power.* Boston: Houghton Mifflin.

Galizio, M., and C. Hendrick (1972). Effects of musical accompaniment on attitudes: the guitar as a prop for persuasion. *J. appl. soc. Psychol., 2,* 350–369.

Gallup Poll (1981). 24–27 June.

Gandy, O. H. (1982). *Beyond agenda setting: information subsidies and public policy.* Norwood, N.J.: Ablex.

Gara, M. A., and S. Rosenberg (1981). Linguistic factors in implicit personality theory. *J. Pers. soc. Psychol., 41,* 450–457.

Garfinkle, H. (1967). *Studies in ethnomethodology.* Englewood Cliffs, N.J.: Prentice-Hall.

Garnham, A. (1982). Testing psychological theories about inference making. *Memory and Cognition, 10,* 341–349.

Geber, B. A., and S. P. Newman (1980). *Soweto's children: the development of attitudes.* New York: Academic Press.

Geen, R. G., and E. Donnerstein, Eds. (1983). *Aggression: theoretical and methodological reviews.* Vol. 1: *Theoretical issues.* Vol 2: *Issues in research.* New York: Academic Press.

Geen, R. G., and M. B. Quanty (1977). The catharsis of aggression. In L. Berkowitz (Ed.), *Advances in experimental social psychology.* Vol. 10. New York: Academic Press. Pp. 1–37.

Geertz, C. (1980). *Negara: the theatre state in 19th century Bali.* Princeton, N.J.: Princeton Univ. Press.

Geis, F. L., and T. H. Moon (1981). Machiavellianism and deception. *J. Pers. soc. Psychol., 41,* 766–775.

Geis, M. L. (1982). *The language of television advertising.* New York: Academic Press.

Gelfand, D. M. (1962). The influence of self-esteem on the rate of verbal conditioning and social matching behavior. *J. abnorm. soc. Psychol., 65,* 259–265.

Gentner, D., and A. L. Stevens (1983). *Mental models.* Hillsdale, N.J.: Erlbaum.

Gerard, H. B. (1953). The effect of different dimensions of disagreement on the communication process in small groups. *Hum. Relat., 6,* 249–272.

Gerard, H. B., and G. C. Mathewson (1966). The effects of severity of initiation on liking for a group: a replication. *J. exp. soc. Psychol., 2,* 278–287.

Gerbner, G., L. Gross, M. Morgan, and N. Signorielli (1980). The "mainstreaming" of America: violence profile No. 11. *J. Communic., 30,* No. 3, 10–29.

―――― (1981). Final reply to Hirsch. *Communic. Res., 8,* 259–280.

―――― (1982). Charting the mainstream: television's contributions to political orientations. *J. Communic., 32,* No. 2, 100–127.

Gerbner, G., L. Gross, N. Signorielli, and M. Morgan (1980). Aging with television: images on television drama and conceptions of social reality. *J. Communic., 30,* No. 1, 37–47.

Gerbner, G., M. Morgan, and N. Signorielli (1982). Programming health portrayals: what viewers see, say, and do. In D. Pearl, L. Bouthilet, and J. Lazar (Eds.), *Television and behavior: ten years of scientific progress and implications for the eighties. Vol. 2. Technical reviews.* Washington, D.C.: U.S. Government Printing Office. Pp. 291–307.

Gergen, K. J., M. S. Greenberg, and R. H. Willis, Eds. (1980). *Social exchange: advances in theory and research.* New York: Plenum.

Gewirtz, J. L., and D. M. Baer (1958). Effects of brief social deprivation on behavior for a social reinforcer. *J. abnorm. soc. Psychol., 56,* 49–56.

Ghiglione, E., and J. L. Beauvois (1983). Language attitudes and social influence. *J. soc. Psychol., 121,* 97–109.

Giles, H., and P. F. Powesland (1975). *Speech style and social evaluation.* London: Academic Press.

Gillig, P. M., and A. J. Greenwald (1974). Is it time to lay the sleeper effect to rest? *J. Pers. soc. Psychol., 29,* 132–139.

Gillispie, D. L., and A. Leffler (1983). Theories of nonverbal behavior: a critical review of proxemic research. In R. Collins (Ed.), *Sociological theory 1983.* San Francisco: Jossey-Bass.

Ginosar, Z., and Y. Trope (1980). The effects of base rates and individuating information on judgments about another person. *J. exp. soc. Psychol., 16,* 228–242.

Giordano, P. C. (1983). Sanctioning the high-status deviant: an attributional analysis. *Soc. Psychol. Quart., 46,* 329–342.

Gitlin, T. (1983). *Vertical hold: inside prime time TV.* New York: Pantheon.

Gitter, A. G., J. Lomranz, L. Saxe, and Y. Bar-Tal (1983). Perceptions of female physique characteristics by American and Israeli students. *J. soc. Psychol., 121,* 7–13.

Gladstein, G. A. (1984). The historical roots of contemporary empathy research. *J. Hist. behav. Sci., 20,* 38–59.

Glaser, A. N. (1982). Drive theory of social facilitation: a critical reappraisal. *Brit. J. soc. Psychol., 21,* 265–282.

Glass, G. V., B. McGaw, and M. L. Smith (1981). *Meta-analysis in social research.* Beverly Hills, Calif.: Sage.

Glow, P. H., and A. H. Winefield (1982). Effect of regular noncontingency sensory changes on responding for sensory change. *J. gen. Psychol., 107,* 121–137.

Glynn, C. J., and J. M. McLeod (1982). Public opinion, communication processes and voting decisions. In M. Burgoon (Ed.), *Communication yearbook.* Vol. 6. Beverly Hills, Calif.: Sage. Pp. 759–774.

Goethals, G. R., and R. E. Nelson (1973). Similarity in the influence process: the belief-value distinction. *J. Pers. soc. Psychol., 25,* 117–122.

Goethals, G. R., and M. P. Zanna (1979). The role of social comparison in choice shifts. *J. Pers. soc. Psychol., 37,* 1469–1476.

Goffman, E. (1959). *Presentation of self in everyday life.* Garden City, N.Y.: Doubleday.

_____ (1976). *Gender advertisements.* New York: Harper & Row.

_____ (1981). *Forms of talk.* Philadelphia: Univ. of Pennsylvania Press.

Goldberg, C. (1975). Conformity to majority type as a function of task and acceptance of sex-related stereotypes. *J. Psychol., 89,* 25–37.

Goldman, M., M. Seever, and M. Seever (1982). Social labeling and the foot-in-the-door effect. *J. soc. Psychol., 117,* 19–23.

Goldstein, A. P., E. G. Carr, W. S. Davidson, and P. Wehr, Eds. (1981). *In response to aggression: methods of control and prosocial alternatives.* Elmsford, N.Y.: Pergamon.

Goldstein, J. H., Ed. (1983). *Sports violence.* New York: Springer-Verlag.

Goldstein, M. J. (1966). Relationship between perceptual defense and exposure duration. *J. Pers. soc. Psychol., 3,* 608–610.

Goldthwaite, R. A. (1981). *The building of renaissance Florence: a social and economic history.* Baltimore: Johns Hopkins.

Goldwater, B. C. (1972). Psychological significance of pupillary movements. *Psychol. Bull., 77,* 340–355.

Gollob, H. F. (1974). The subject-object-verb approach to social cognition. *Psychol. Rev., 81,* 286–321.

Gollob, H. F., and J. E. Dittes (1965). Effects of manipulated self-esteem on persuasibility depending on threat and complexity of communication. *J. Pers. soc. Psychol., 2,* 195–201.

Goodin, R. E. (1980). *Manipulatory politics.* New Haven: Yale Univ. Press.

Goody, J. R. (1977). *The domestication of the savage mind.* New York: Cambridge Univ. Press.

Gordon, P. C., and K. J. Holyoak (1983). Implicit learning and generalization of the "mere exposure" effect. *J. Pers. soc. Psychol., 45,* 492–500.

Gorn, G. J., and M. E. Goldberg (1982). Behavioral evidence of the effects of televised food messages on children. *J. Consumer Research, 9,* 200–205.

Gorsuch, R. L., and J. Ortberg (1983). Moral obligation and attitudes: their relation to behavioral intentions. *J. Pers. soc. Psychol., 44,* 1025–1028.

Götz-Marchand, B., J. Götz, and M. Irle (1974). Preference of dissonance reduction modes as a function of their order, familiarity, and reversibility. *Europ. J. soc. Psychol., 4,* 201–228.

Graesser, A. C. (1981). *Prose comprehension beyond the word.* New York: Springer-Verlag.

Granberg, D. (1982a). Family size preferences and sexual permissiveness as factors differentiating abortion activists. *Soc. Psychol. Quart., 45,* 15–23.

_____ (1982b). Social judgment theory. In M. Burgoon (Ed.), *Communication yearbook.* Vol. 6. Beverly Hills, Calif.: Sage. Pp. 304–329.

Granberg, D., and E. E. Brent (1974). Dove-hawk placements in the 1968 election: application of social judgment and balance theories. *J. Pers. soc. Psychol., 29,* 687–695.

_____ (1980). Perceptions of issue positions of presidential candidates. *Amer. Scient., 68,* 617–625.

_____ (1983). When prophecy bends: the preference-expectation link in U.S. presidential elections, 1952–1980. *J. Pers. soc. Psychol., 45,* 477–491.

Granberg, D., W. Harris, and M. King (1981). Assimilation but little contrast in the 1976 U.S. presidential election. *J. Psychol., 108,* 241–247.

Grass, R. C., and W. H. Wallace (1969). Satiation effects of TV commercials. *J. advertising Res., 9* (3), 3–9.

Graubard, S. R., Ed. (1980). *Generations.* New York: Norton.

Gray, H. H. (1963). Renaissance humanism: the pursuit of excellence. *J. Hist. Ideas, 24,* 497–514.

Greaves, G. (1972). Conceptual system functioning and selective recall of information. *J. Pers. soc. Psychol., 21,* 327–332.

Greeley, A. M. (1977). *The American Catholic: a social portrait.* New York: Basic Books.

Greeley, A. M., W. C. McCready, and K. McCourt (1976). *Catholic schools in a declining church.* Kansas City: Sheed & Ward.

Green, D. (1974). Dissonance and self-perception analyses of "forced compliance": when two theories make competing predictions. *J. Pers. soc. Psychol., 29,* 819–828.

Green, J. A. (1972). Attitudinal and situational determinants of intended behavior toward blacks. *J. Pers. soc. Psychol., 22,* 13–17.

Greenbaum, C. W. (1963). The effects of choice and reinforcement on attitude change in a role-playing situation. Ph.D. dissertation. New York University.

Greenberg, B. S., Ed. (1980). *Life on television: content analysis of U.S. TV drama.* Norwood, N.J.: Ablex.

Greenberg, B. S., N. Buerkel-Rothfuss, K. A. Neuendorf, and C. K. Atkin (1980). Three seasons of television family role interactions. In B. S. Greenberg (Ed.), *Life on television.* Norwood, N.J.: Ablex. Pp. 149–171.

Greenberg, B. S., M. Burgoon, J. K. Burgoon, and F. Korzenny (1983). *Mexican Americans and the mass media.* Norwood, N.J.: Ablex.

Greenberg, J. E., and R. L. Cohen, Eds. (1982). *Equity and justice in social behavior.* London: Academic Press.

Greenfield, J. (1982). *The real campaign: the media and the battle for the White House.* New York: Summit.

Greenwald, A. G. (1968a). Cognitive learning, cognitive response to persuasion, and attitude change. In A. G. Greenwald, T. S. Brock, and T. M. Ostrom (Eds.), *Psychological foundations of attitudes.* New York: Academic Press. Pp. 147–170.

_____ (1968b). On defining attitude and attitude theory. In A. G. Greenwald, T. C. Brock, and T. M. Ostrom (Eds.), *Psychological foundations of attitudes.* New York: Academic Press. Pp. 361–388.

_____ (1980). The totalitarian ego: fabrication and revision of personal history. *Amer. Psychol., 35,* 603–618.

Greenwald, H. J. (1964). The involvement-discrepancy controversy in persuasion research. Unpublished Ph.D. dissertation. Columbia University, New York.

Greenwald, H. J., and D. B. Oppenheim (1968). Reported magnitude of self-misidentification among Negro children—artifact? *J. Pers. soc. Psychol., 8,* 49–52.

Gregory, W. L., R. B. Cialdini, and K. M. Carpenter (1982). Self-relevant scenarios as mediators of likelihood estimates and compliance: does imagining make it so? *J. Pers. soc. Psychol., 43,* 89–99.

Gruner, C. R. (1978). *Understanding laughter.* Chicago: Nelson-Hall.

Grush, J. E. (1980). Impact of candidate expenditures, regionality, and prior outcomes on the 1976 Democratic presidential primaries. *J. Pers. soc. Psychol., 38,* 337–347.

Guilbaut, S. (1983). *How New York stole the idea of modern art: abstract expressionism, freedom, and the cold war.* Chicago: Univ. of Chicago Press.

Gulley, H. E., and D. K. Berlo (1956). Effect of intercellular and intracellular speech structure on attitude change and learning. *Speech Monogr., 23,* 288–297.

Gulliksen, H. (1956). Measurement of subjective values. *Psychometrika, 21,* 229–244.

Gurwitz, S. B., and B. Topol (1978). Determinants of confirming and disconfirming responses to negative social labels. *J. exp. soc. Psychol., 14,* 31–42.

Guttentag, M., and P. F. Secord (1983). *Too many women? The sex ratio question.* Beverly Hills, Calif.: Sage.

Guttman, L. A. (1944). A basis for scaling qualitative data. *Amer. Sociol. Rev., 9,* 139–150.

Guttmann, A. (1981). Sports spectators from antiquity to the renaissance. *J. sport Hist., 8* (2), 5–27.

_____ (1983). Roman sports violence. In J. H. Goldstein (Ed.), *Sports violence.* New York: Springer-Verlag. Pp. 7–19.

Habermas, J. (1979). [*Communication and the evolution of society.*] (T. McCarthy, translator.) Boston: Beacon Press.

Hadden, J. K., and C. E. Swann (1981). *Prime time preachers: the rising power of televangelism.* Reading, Mass.: Addison-Wesley.

Haigh, R. W., G. Gerbner, and R. B. Byrne, Eds. (1981). *Communications in the twenty-first century.* New York: Wiley.

Halverson, R. R., and M. S. Pallak (1978). Commitment, ego-involvement, and resistance to attack. *J. exp. soc. Psychol., 14,* 1–12.

Hamersma, R. J., J. Paige, and J. E. Jordan (1973). Construction of a Guttman facet designed cross-cultural attitude-behavior scale toward racial-ethnic interaction. *Educ. psychol. Measurmt., 33,* 565–576.

Hamill, R., T. D. Wilson, and R. E. Nisbett (1980). Insensitivity to sample bias: generalizing from atypical cases. *J. Pers. soc. Psychol., 39,* 578–589.

Hamilton, D. L., Ed. (1981). *Cognitive processes in stereotyping and intergroup behavior.* Hillsdale, N.J.: Erlbaum.

Hamilton, D. L., S. Carpenter, and G. D. Bishop (1984). Desegregation of suburban neighborhoods. In N. Miller and M. B. Brewer (Eds.), *Groups in contact: the psychology of desegregation.* New York: Academic Press.

Hamilton, R. F. (1982). *Who voted for Hitler?* Princeton, N.J.: Princeton Univ. Press.

Hamilton, T. P., W. C. Swap, and J. Z. Rubin (1981). Predicting the effects of anticipated third party intervention: a template matching approach. *J. Pers. soc. Psychol., 41,* 1141–1152.

Hamilton, V. L. (1980). Intuitive psychologist or intuitive lawyer? Alternative models of the attribution process. *J. Pers. soc. Psychol., 39,* 767–772.

Hammond, K. R., G. H. McClelland, and J. Mumpower (1980). *Human judgment and decision making: theories, methods and procedures.* New York: Praeger.

Hanneman, G. J., W. J. McEwen, and S. A. Coyne (1973). Public service advertising on television. *J. Broadcasting, 17,* 387–404.

Hanson, D. J. (1980). Relationship between methods and findings in attitude-behavior research. *Psychology, 17,* 11–13.

Hansson, R. O., and W. H. Jones (1981). Loneliness, cooperation, and conformity among American undergraduates. *J. soc. Psychol., 115,* 103–108.

Hapkiewicz, W. G. (1979, Spring). Children's reactions to cartoon violence. *J. clinic. Child Psychol.,* 30–34.

Harary, F., R. Z. Norman, and D. Cartwright (1965). *Structural models.* New York: Wiley.

Harkins, S. G., and R. E. Petty (1981a). Effects of source magnification of cognitive effort on attitudes: an information-processing view. *J. Pers. soc. Psychol., 40,* 401–413.

_____ (1981b). The multiple source effect in persuasion: the effects of distraction. *Pers. soc. Psychol. Bull., 7,* 627–633.

Harlow, H. F. (1973). *Learning to love.* San Rafael, Calif.: Albion Corp.

Harmon, R. R., and K. A. Coney (1982). The persuasive effects of source credibility in buy and lease situations. *J. Marketng. Res., 19,* 255–260.

Harper, F. B. W., and R. D. Tuddenham (1964). The sociometric composition of the group as a determinant of yielding to a distorted norm. *J. Psychol., 58,* 307–311.

Harper, R. G., A. N. Wiens, and J. D. Matarazzo (1978). *Nonverbal communication: the state of the art.* New York: Wiley.

Harré, R. (1980). *Social being.* Totowa, N.J.: Rowman & Littlefield.

_____ (1981). Rituals, rhetoric, and social cognitions. In J. P. Forgas (Ed.), *Social cognition.* London: Academic Press. Pp. 211–224.

Harré, R., and E. Madden (1975). *Causal powers.* Totowa, N.J.: Rowman & Littlefield.

Harris, M. B., J. James, J. Chavez, M. L. Fuller, S. Kent, C. Massanari, and F. Walsh (1983). Clothing: communication, compliance and choice. *J. appl. soc. Psychol., 13,* 88–97.

Harrison, A. A. (1977). Mere exposure. In L. Berkowitz (Ed.), *Advances in experimental social psychology.* Vol. 10. New York: Academic Press. Pp. 39–83.

Harrison, A. A., M. Hwalek, D. F. Raney, and J. G. Fritz (1978). Cues to deception in an interview situation. *Soc. Psychol., 41,* 156–161.

Harrison, R., and P. Ekman (1976). TV's last frontier: South Africa. *J. Communic., 26,* No. 1, 102–109.

Hartshorne, H., and M. A. May (1928). *Studies in the nature of character: V. Studies in deceit.* New York: Macmillan.

Harvey, J. H., W. Ickes, and R. Kidd, Eds. (1981). *New directions in attribution research.* Vol. 3. Hillsdale, N.J.: Erlbaum.

Harvey, J. H., and R. P. McGlynn (1982). Matching words to phenomena: the case of the fundamental attribution error. *J. Pers. soc. Psychol., 43,* 345–346.

Harvey, O. J., D. E. Hunt, and H. M. Schroder (1961). *Conceptual systems and personality organization.* New York: Wiley.

Haskins, J. B. (1964). Factual recall as a measure of advertising effectiveness. *J. Advertising Res., 4,* No. 1, 2–8.

Haslett, D. M. (1976). Distracting stimuli: do they elicit or inhibit counterargumentation and attitude shift? *Europ. J. soc. Psychol., 6,* 81–94.

Hass, R. G. (1975). Persuasion or moderation? Two experiments on anticipatory attitude change. *J. Pers. soc. Psychol., 31,* 1155–1162.

_____ (1981). Effects of source characteristics on cognitive responses and persuasion. In R. E. Petty, T. M. Ostrom, and T. C. Brock (Eds.), *Cognitive responses in persuasion.* Hillsdale, N.J.: Erlbaum. Pp. 141–172.

Hass, R. G., and K. Grady (1975). Temporal delay, type of forewarning, and resistance to influence. *J. exp. soc. Psychol., 11,* 459–469.

Hass, R. G., and D. E. Linder (1972). Counterargument availability and the effects of message structure on persuasion. *J. Pers. soc. Psychol., 23,* 219–233.

Hass, R. G., and R. W. Mann (1976). Anticipatory belief change: persuasion or impression management? *J. Pers. soc. Psychol., 34,* 105–111.

Hastie, R. (1981). Schematic principles in human memory. In E. T. Higgins, C. P. Herman, and M. P. Zanna (Eds.), *Social cognition: the Ontario symposium,* August 1978. Vol. 1. Hillsdale, N.J.: Erlbaum.

_____ (1983). Social inference. *Ann. Rev. Psychol., 34,* 511–542.

Hastie, R., T. Ostrom, E. Ebbesen, R. T. Wyer, D. Hamilton, and D. Carlston, Eds. (1980). *Person memory: the cognitive basis of social perception.* Hillsdale, N.J.: Erlbaum.

Hastie, R., S. D. Penrod, and N. Pennington (1984). *Inside the jury.* Cambridge, Mass.: Harvard Univ. Press.

Hawkins, R. P., and S. Pingree (1982). Television's influence on social reality. In D. Pearl, L. Bouthilet, and J. Lazar (Eds.), *Television and behavior: ten years of scientific progress and implications for the eighties.* Vol. 2. *Technical Reviews.* Washinton, D.C.: U.S. Government Printing Office. Pp. 224–247.

Hayes, S. C. (1983). When more is less: quantity versus quality of publications in the evaluation of academic vitae. *Amer. Psychol., 38,* 1398–1400.

Hays-Roth, B., and P. W. Thorndyke (1979). Integration of knowledge from text. *J. verb. Learn. verb. Behav., 18,* 91–108.

Hazan, B. A. (1982). *Olympic sports and propaganda games.* New Brunswick, N.J.: Transaction.

Hearold, S. L. (1979). Meta-analysis of the effects of television on social behavior. Unpublished doctoral dissertation. University of Colorado.

Hechinger, F. M. (1979). About education: Council to fight U.S. students' parochial view. *New York Times.* March 13. Pp. C–5.

Hedebro, G. (1982). *Communication and social change in developing nations: a critical view.* Ames: Iowa State Univ.

Heersacker, M., R. E. Petty, and J. T. Cacioppo (1983). Field dependence and attitude change: source credibility can alter persuasion by affecting message-relevant thinking. *J. Pers., 51,* 653–666.

Heider, F. (1946). Attitudes and cognitive organization. *J. Psychol., 21,* 107–112.

_____ (1958). *The psychology of interpersonal relations.* New York: Wiley.

Heilman, M. E. (1976). Oppositional behavior as a function of influence attempt, intensity, and retaliation threat. *J. Pers. soc. Psychol., 33,* 574–578.

Heilman, M. E., and K. A. Garner (1975). Counteracting the boomerang: the effects of choice on compliance to threats and promises. *J. Pers. soc. Psychol., 31,* 911–917.

Helmholtz, H. L. F. von (1962). *Handbuch der physiologischen Optik.* Vol. 3. 1866. (Translated: *Treatise on physiological optics.* New York: Dover.)

Helmreich, R., E. Aronson, and J. LeFan (1970). To err is humanizing—sometimes: effects of self-esteem, competence, and a pratfall on interpersonal attraction. *J. Pers. soc. Psychol., 16,* 259–264.

Helmreich, W. B. (1982). *The things they say behind your back: stereotypes and the myths behind them.* Garden City, N.Y.: Doubleday.

Helson, H. (1971). Adaptation-level theory: 1970 and after. In M. H. Appley (Ed.), *Adaptation-level theory: a symposium.* New York: Academic Press.

Henderson, A. (1981). *Social power: social-psychological models and theories.* New York: Praeger.

Hendrick, C., and S. Hendrick (1982). *Liking, loving and relating.* Monterey, Calif.: Brooks/Cole.

Henninger, M., and R. S. Wyer (1976).The recognition and elimination of inconsistencies among syllogistically related beliefs: some new light on the "Socratic effect." *J. Pers. soc. Psychol., 34,* 680–693.

Henshel, A. M. (1971). The relationship between values and behavior: a developmental hypothesis. *Child Development, 42,* 1997–2007.

Hensley, V., and S. Duval (1976). Some perceptual determinants of perceived similarity, liking and correctness. *J. Pers. soc. Psychol., 34,* 159–168.

Herzlich, C. (1969). *Santé et maladie: analyze d'une représentation sociale.* Paris: Mouton. [Translation: (1973). *Health and illness: a social psychological study.* London: Academic Press.]

Heslin, R., and M. L. Patterson (1982). *Nonverbal behavior and social psychology.* New York: Plenum.

Hess, E. H. (1975). *The tell-tale eye.* Cincinnati: Van Nostrand.

Hewstone, M., Ed. (1983). *Attribution theory: social and functional experience.* Oxford: Basil Blackwell.

Hewstone, M., J. Jaspars, and M. Lalljee (1982). Social representations, social attribution and social identity: the intergroup images of "public" and "comprehensive" schoolboys. *Europ. J. soc. Psychol., 12,* 241–269.

Higgins, E. T. (1981). The "communications game": implications for social cognition and persuasion. In E. T. Higgins, C. P. Herman, and M. P. Zanna (Eds.),

Social cognition: the Ontario symposium. Vol. 1. Hillsdale, N.J.: Erlbaum.

Higgins, E. T., C. P. Herman, and M. P. Zanna, Eds. (1981). *Social cognition: the Ontario symposium, August 1978.* Vol. 1. Hillsdale, N.J.: Erlbaum.

Higgins, E. T., C. D. McCann, and R. Fondacaro (1982). The "communications game": goal directed encoding and cognitive consequences. *Social Cognition, 1,* 21–37.

Higgins, E. T., and W. S. Rholes (1978). "Saying is believing": effects of message modification on memory and liking for the person described. *J. exp. soc. Psychol., 14,* 363–378.

Higgins, E. T., W. S. Rholes, and C. R. Jones (1977). Category accessibility and impression formation. *J. exp. soc. Psychol., 13,* 141–154.

Hikel, G. K. (1973). *Beyond the polls: political ideology and its correlates.* Lexington, Mass.: D. C. Heath.

Hilgard, E. R. (1965). *Hypnotic susceptibility.* New York: Harcourt, Brace, and World.

_____ (1977). *Divided consciousness: multiple controls in human thought and action.* New York: Wiley.

_____ (1980). The trilogy of mind: cognition, affection, and conation. *J. Hist. behav. Sci., 16,* 107–117.

Himmelfarb, S., and A. H. Eagly (1974). Orientation to the study of attitudes and their change. In S. Himmelfarb, and A. H. Eagly (Eds.), *Readings in attitude change.* New York: Wiley. Pp. 2–49.

Himmelweit, H. T., P. Humphreys, M. Jaegers, and M. Katz (1981). *How voters decide: a longitudinal study of political attitudes and voting extending over fifteen years.* London: Academic Press.

Himmelweit, H. T., and B. Swift (1969). A model for the understanding of the school as a socialization agent. In P. Mussen (Ed.), *Trends and issues in developmental psychology.* New York: Holt, Rinehart, and Winston.

Hirsch, P. M. (1980). The "scary world" of the nonviewer and other anomalies: a reanalysis of Gerbner *et al.*'s findings on cultivation analysis. *Communic. Res., 7,* 403–456.

_____ (1981). Distinguishing good speculation from bad theory: rejoinder to Gerbner *et al. Communic. Res., 8,* 73–95.

Hirschman, A. O. (1982). *Shifting involvements: private interest and public action.* Princeton, N.J.: Princeton Univ. Press.

Hirst, I. R. C., and W. D. Reekie, Eds. (1977). *The consumer society.* New York: Tavistock/Methuen.

Hoaglin, D. C., F. Mosteller, and J. W. Tukey (1983). *Understanding robust and exploratory data analysis.* New York: Wiley.

Hobart, M. (1975). Orators and patrons: two types of political leaders in Balinese village society. In M. Bloch (Ed.), *Political language and oratory in traditional society.* New York: Academic Press. Pp. 65–92.

Hochberg, J. (1981). On cognition in perception: perceptual coupling and unconscious inference. *Cognition, 10,* 127–134.

Hofstetter, C. R., and D. W. Moore (1982). Television news coverage of presidential primaries. *Journalism Quart., 59,* 651–654.

Hogan, R. (1975). Theoretical egocentrism and the problem of compliance. *Amer. Psychol., 30,* 533–540.

Hogan, R., J. A. Johnson, and N. P. Emler (1978). A socioanalytical theory of moral development. In W. Damon (Ed.),

New directions for child development. San Francisco: Jossey-Bass. Pp. 1–18.

Holland, N. H. (1982). *Laughing: a psychology of humor.* Ithaca, N.Y.: Cornell Univ. Press.

Holland, P. W., and S. Leinhardt (1975). Local structures in social networks. In D. R. Heise (Ed.), *Sociological methodology 1976.* San Francisco: Jossey-Bass. Pp. 1–45.

Holldobler, B., and C. J. Lumsden (1980). Territorial strategies in ants. *Science, 210,* 732–739.

Holloway, S., L. Tucker, and H. A. Hornstein (1977). The effects of social and nonsocial information on interpersonal behavior of males: the news makes news. *J. Pers. soc. Psychol., 35,* 514–522.

Holt, L. E. (1970). Resistance to persuasion on explicit beliefs as a function of commitment to and desirability of logically related beliefs. *J. Pers. soc. Psychol., 16,* 583–591.

Holt, L. E., and W. A. Watts (1969). Salience of logical relationships among beliefs as a factor in persuasion. *J. Pers. soc. Psychol., 11,* 193–203.

Holyoak, K. J., and P. C. Gordon (1983). Social reference points. *J. Pers. soc. Psychol., 44,* 881–887.

Honeck, R. P., and R. R. Hoffman, Eds. (1980). *Cognition and figurative language.* Hillsdale, N.J.: Erlbaum.

Horai, J., N. Naccari, and E. Fatoullah (1974). The effects of expertise and physical attractiveness upon opinion agreement and liking. *Sociometry, 37,* 601–606.

Hornstein, H. A., E. LaKind, G. Frankel, and S. Manne (1975). Effects of knowledge about remote social events on prosocial behavior, social conception, and mood. *J. Pers. soc. Psychol., 32,* 1038–1046.

Hovland, C. I. (1939). Experimental studies in rote-learning theory. IV. Comparison of reminiscence in serial and paired-associate learning. *J. exp. Psychol., 24,* 466–484.

_____ (1951). Human learning and retention. In S. S. Stevens (Ed.), *Handbook of experimental psychology.* New York: Wiley. Pp. 613–689.

_____ (1954). Effects of the mass media on communication. In G. Lindzey (Ed.), *Handbook of Social Psychology.* (2nd ed). Vol 2. Reading, Mass.: Addison-Wesley Pp. 1062–1103.

_____ Ed. (1957). *Order of presentation in persuasion.* New Haven: Yale Univ. Press.

Hovland, C. I., E. H. Campbell, and T. Brock (1957). The effect of "commitment" on opinion change following communication. In C. I. Hovland (Ed.), *Order of presentation in persuasion.* New Haven: Yale Univ. Press. Pp. 23–32.

Hovland, C. I., and I. L. Janis, Eds. (1959). *Personality and persuasibility.* New Haven: Yale Univ. Press.

Hovland, C. I., I. L. Janis, and H. H. Kelley (1953). *Communication and persuasion.* New Haven: Yale Univ. Press.

Hovland, C. I., A. A. Lumsdaine, and F. D. Sheffield (1949). *Studies in social psychology in World War II.* Vol. 3. *Experiments on mass communication.* Princeton, N.J.: Princeton Univ. Press.

Hovland, C. I., and W. Mandell (1952). An experimental comparison of conclusion-drawing by the communicator and by the audience. *J. abnorm. soc. Psychol., 47,* 581–588.

Hovland, C. I., and W. Weiss (1951). The influences of source credibility on communication effectiveness. *Publ. Opin. Quart., 15,* 635–650.

Howe, M., Ed. (1983). *Learning from television: psychological and educational research.* New York: Academic Press.

Hoyt, M. F., and R. Centers (1972). Temporal situs of the effects of anticipated publicity upon commitment and resistance to countercommunication. *J. Pers. soc. Psychol., 22,* 1–7.

Hraba, J., and G. Grant (1970). Black is beautiful: a reexamination of racial preference and identification. *J. Pers. soc. Psychol., 16,* 398–402.

Huesmann, L. P. (1982). Television violence and aggressive behavior. In D. Pearl, L. Bouthilet, and J. Lazar (Eds.), *Television and behavior: ten years of scientific progress and implications for the eighties.* Vol. 2. *Technical Reviews.* Washington, D.C.: U.S. Government Printing Office. Pp. 126–137.

Huesmann, L. P., L. D. Eron, R. Klein, P. Brice, and P. Fischer (1983). Mitigating the imitation of aggressive behaviors by changing children's attitudes about media violence. *J. Pers. soc. Psychol., 44,* 899–910.

Huesmann, L. P., K. Lagerspetz, and L. D. Eron (1984). Intervening variables in the TV violence-aggression relation: evidence from two countries. *Develop. Psychol., 20,* 746–775.

Hughes, M. (1980).The fruits of cultivation analysis: a reexamination of some effects of television watching. *Publ. Opin. Quart., 44,* 287–302.

Huizinga, J. (1939). *Homo ludens: a study of the play element in culture.* Amsterdam: Pantheon. (London: Routledge & Kegan Paul, 1949.)

Hull, C. L. (1933). *Hypnosis and suggestibility.* New York: Appleton-Century-Crofts.

Huston, T. L. (1973). Ambiguity of acceptance, social desirability and dating choice. *J. exp. soc. Psychol., 9,* 32–42.

Hyman, H. H., and E. Singer (1968). *Readings in reference group theory and research.* New York: Free Press.

Hyman, H. H., and C. R. Wright (1979). *Education's lasting influence on values.* Chicago: Univ. of Chicago Press.

Ichheiser, G. (1949). *Misunderstandings in human relations.* Chicago: Univ. of Chicago Press.

Ickes, W., and E. S. Knowles, Eds. (1982). *Personality, roles, and social behavior.* New York: Springer-Verlag.

Infante, D. A. (1975). The effects of opinionated language on communicator image and in conferring resistance to persuasion. *Western Speech, 39,* 112–119.

Innis, H. (1964). *The bias of communication.* (2nd ed.) Toronto: Univ. of Toronto Press.

Insko, C. A. (1964). Primacy versus recency in persuasion as a function of the timing of arguments and measures. *J. abnorm. soc. Psychol., 69,* 381–391.

Insko, C. A., A. Arkoff, and V. M. Insko (1965). Effects of high and low fear-arousing communications upon opinions toward smoking. *J. exp. soc. Psychol., 1,* 256–266.

Insko, C. A., S. Drenan, and M. R. Solomon (1983). Conformity as a function of the consistency of positive self-evaluation with being liked and being right. *J. exp. soc. Psychol., 19,* 341–358.

Insko, C. A., E. A. Lind, and S. LaTour (1976). Persuasion, recall and thought. *Rep. Res. soc. Psychol., 7,* 66–78.

Insko, C. A., F. Murashima, and M. Saiyadain (1966). Communicator discrepancy, stimulus ambiguity, and influence. *J. Pers., 34,* 262–274.

Insko, C. A., R. W. Nacoste, and J. L. Moe (1983). Belief congruence and racial discrimination: review of the evidence and critical evaluation. *Europ. J. soc. Psychol., 13,* 153–174.

Irle, M., and L. B. Katz, Eds. (1982). *Studies in decision making: social psychological and socio-economic analyses.* Berlin: Walter de Gruyter.

Iyengar, S. (1979). Television news and issue salience: a reexamination of the agenda-setting hypothesis. *Amer. Politics Quart., 7,* 395–416.

Iyengar, S., D. R. Kinder, M. D. Peters, and J. A. Krosnick (1984). The evening news and presidential evaluations. *J. Pers. soc. Psychol., 46,* 778–787.

Iyengar, S., M. D. Peters, and D. R. Kinder (1982). Experimental demonstrations of the "not-so-minimal" consequences of television news programs. *Amer. Political Sci. Rev., 76,* 848–858.

Jaccard, J. (1979). Personality and behavioral prediction: an analysis of behavioral criterion measures. In L. Kahle, and D. Fiske (Eds.), *Methods for studying person-situation interactions.* San Francisco: Jossey-Bass.

Jacoby, J. (1977). Information load and decision quality: some contested issues. *J. Marketng. Res., 14,* 569–573.

Jacoby, J., D. E. Speller, and C. Kohn-Berning (1974). Brand choice behavior as a function of information load: replication and extension. *J. Consumer Research, 1,* 33–42.

James, W. (1884). What is an emotion? *Mind, 9,* 188–205.

Janis, I. L. (1954). Personality correlates of susceptibility to persuasion. *J. Pers., 22,* 504–518.

———— (1967). Effects of fear arousal on attitude change: recent developments in theory and experimental research. In L. Berkowitz (Ed.), *Advances in experimental social psychology.* Vol. 3. New York: Academic Press. Pp. 166–224.

———— (1968a). Attitude change via role playing. In R. P. Abelson *et al.* (Eds.), *Theories of cognitive consistency: a sourcebook.* Chicago: Rand McNally. Pp. 810–818.

———— (1968b). *The contours of fear: psychological studies of war, disaster, illness, and experimental stress.* New York: Wiley.

———— (1973). *Victims of groupthink.* Boston: Houghton Mifflin.

———— (1983). The role of social support in adherence to stressful decisions. *Amer. Psychol., 38,* 143–160.

Janis, I. L., and P. B. Field (1956). A behavioral assessment of persuasibility: consistency of individual differences. *Sociometry, 19,* 241–259.

Janis, I. L., D. Kaye, and P. Kirschner (1965). Facilitating effects of "eating-while-reading" on responsiveness to persuasive communications. *J. Pers. soc. Psychol., 1,* 181–186.

Janis, I. L., and L. Mann (1977). *Decision making.* New York: Free Press.

Janis, I. L., and D. Rife (1959). Persuasibility and emotional disorder. In C. I. Hovland, and I. L. Janis (Eds.), *Personality and persuasibility.* New Haven: Yale Univ. Press. Pp. 121–140.

Janisse, M. P. (1977). *Pupillometry: the psychology of the pupillary response*. Washington, D.C.: Hemisphere.

Jaspars, J. M. (1978). The nature and measurement of attitudes. In H. Tajfel, and C. Fraser (Eds.), *Introducing social psychology*. London: Penguin.

Jaspars, J. M., F. D. Fincham, and M. Hewstone, Eds. (1983). *Attribution theory and research: conceptual, developmental, and social dimensions*. London: Academic Press.

Jaynes, J. (1977). *The origins of consciousness in the breakdown of the bicameral mind*. Boston: Houghton Mifflin.

Jennings, M. K., and R. G. Niemi (1974). *The political character of adolescence: the influence of families and schools*. Princeton, N.J.: Princeton Univ. Press.

_____ (1981). *Generations and politics: a panel study of young adults and their parents*. Princeton, N.J.: Princeton Univ. Press.

Jessop, D. J. (1982). Topic variation in levels of agreement between parents and adolescents. *Publ. Opin. Quart., 46,* 538–559.

Johnson, H. H., and J. A. Scileppi (1969). Effects of ego-involvement conditions on attitude change to high and low credibility communicators. *J. Pers. soc. Psychol., 13,* 31–36.

Johnson, H. H., and T. A. Watkins (1971). The effect of message repetitions on immediate and delayed attitude change. *Psychon. Sci., 22,* 101–103.

Johnson, J. A., J. M. Cheek, and R. Smither (1983). The structure of empathy. *J. Pers. soc. Psychol., 45,* 1299–1312.

Johnson, J. T., and S. E. Taylor (1981). The effect of metaphor on political attitudes. *Basic appl. soc. Psychol., 2,* 305–316.

Johnston, J., and J. S. Ettema (1982). *Positive images: breaking stereotypes with children's television*. Beverly Hills, Calif.: Sage.

Jones, E. E., and H. Sigall (1971). The bogus pipeline: a new paradigm for measuring affect and attitude. *Psychol. Bull., 76,* 349–364.

Jones, E. E., and C. Wortman (1973). *Ingratiation: an attributional approach*. Morristown, N.J.: General Learning Press.

Jones, R. A., and J. W. Brehm (1967). Attitudinal effects of communicator attractiveness when one chooses to listen. *J. Pers. soc. Psychol., 6,* 64–70.

Jordan, W. J. (1972). A reinforcement model of metaphor. *Speech Monogr., 39,* 223–226.

Jorgenson, D. O. (1975). Field study of the relationship between status discrepancy and proxemic behavior. *J. soc. Psychol., 97,* 173–179.

Joshi, A., B. Webber, and I. Sag, Eds. (1981). *Elements of discourse analysis*. New York: Cambridge Univ. Press.

Judd, C. M., D. A. Kenny, and J. A. Krosnick (1983). Judging the positions of political candidates: models of assimilation and contrast. *J. Pers. soc. Psychol., 44,* 952–963.

Judd, C. M., J. A. Krosnick, and M. A. Milburn (1981). Political involvement and attitude structure in the general public. *Amer. Sociol. Rev., 46,* 660–669.

Judd, C. M., and M. A. Milburn (1980). The structure of attitude systems in the general public: comparisons of a structural equation model. *Amer. Sociol. Rev., 45,* 627–643.

Kadushin, C. (1974). *The American intellectual elite*. Boston: Little, Brown.

Kahle, L. R., D. M. Klingel, and R. A. Kulka (1981). A longitudinal study of adolescents' attitude-behavior consistency. *Publ. Opin. Quart., 45,* 402–414.

Kahneman, D., P. Slovic, and A. Tversky, Eds. (1982). *Judgment under uncertainty: heuristics and biases*. Cambridge: Cambridge Univ. Press.

Kahneman, D., and A. Tversky (1984). Choices, values, and frames. *Amer. Psychologist, 39,* 341–350.

Kaid, L. L. (1981). Political advertising. In D. D. Nimmo, and K. R. Sanders (Eds.), *Handbook of political communication*. Beverly Hills, Calif.: Sage. Pp. 249–271.

Kanouse, D. E., and R. P. Abelson (1967). Language variables affecting the persuasiveness of simple communications. *J. Pers. soc. Psychol., 7,* 156–163.

Kanouse, D. E., and B. Hayes-Roth (1981). Cognitive considerations in the design of product warnings. In L. A. Morris, M. B. Mazis, and I. Barofsky (Eds.), *Product labeling and health risks*. New York: Banbury. Pp. 147–164.

Kaplan, K. J. (1972). From attitude formation to attitude change: acceptance and impact as cognitive mediators. *Sociometry, 35,* 448–467.

Kaplan, R. M., and G. C. Pascoe (1977). Humorous lectures and humorous examples: some effects on comprehension and retention. *J. educ. Psychol., 69,* 61–65.

Kaplowitz, S. A., and E. L. Fink (1982). Attitude change and attitudinal trajectories: a dynamic multidimensional theory. In M. Burgoon (Ed.), *Communication yearbook*. Vol. 6. Beverly Hills, Calif.: Sage. Pp. 364–394.

Kaplowitz, S. A., E. L. Fink, and C. L. Bauer (1983). A dynamic model of the effect of discrepant information on unidimensional attitude change. *Behav. Sci., 28,* 233–250.

Karabenick, S. A. (1983). Sex-relevance of content and influenceability: Sistrunk and McDavid revisited. *Pers. soc. Psychol. Bull., 9,* 243–252.

Karlins, M., T. L. Coffman, and G. Walters (1969). On the fading of social stereotypes: studies in three generations of college students. *J. Pers. soc. Psychol., 13,* 1–16.

Katona, G., B. Strumpel, and E. Zahn (1971). *Aspirations and affluence: comparative studies in the United States and Europe*. New York: McGraw-Hill.

Katz, D. (1960). The functional approach to the study of attitudes. *Publ. Opin. Quart., 24,* 163–204.

Katz, D., and K. W. Braly (1933). Racial stereotypes of 100 college students. *J. abnorm. soc. Psychol., 28,* 280–290.

Katz, D., I. Sarnoff, and C. McClintock (1956). Ego-defense and attitude change. *Hum. Relat., 9,* 27–45.

Katz, E. (1957). The two-step flow of communication: an up-to-date report on an hypothesis. *Publ. Opin. Quart., 21,* 61–78.

_____ (1968). On reopening the question of selectivity in exposure to mass communications. In R. P. Abelson *et al.* (Eds.), *Theories of cognitive consistency*. Chicago: Rand McNally. Pp. 788–796.

_____ (1980). Media events: the sense of occasion. *Studies visual Communic., 6 (3)*, 84–89.

_____ (1981). Publicity and pluralistic ignorance: notes on the "spiral of silence." In H. Baier, H. M. Kepplinger, and K. Reumann (Eds.), *Public opinion and social change: for Elisabeth Noelle-Neumann*. Wiestaden: Westdeutscher Verlag. Pp. 28–38.

Katz, E., H. Adoni, and P. Parness (1977). Remembering the news: what the picture adds to recall. *Journalism Quart., 54*, 231–239.

Katz, E., and T. Szecsko (1981). *Mass media and social change*. Beverly Hills, Calif.: Sage.

Katz, I. (1981). *Stigma: a social psychological analysis*. Hillsdale, N.J.: Erlbaum.

Katz, P. A., and S. R. Zalk (1978). Modification of children's racial attitudes. *Develop. Psychol., 14*, 447–461.

Kaye, J., M. Appel, and R. Joseph (1981). Attitude of medical students and residents toward cancer. *J. Psychol., 107*, 87–96.

Keating, J. P., and B. Latané (1976). Politicians on TV: the image is the message. *J. soc. Issues, 32*, No. 4, 116–132.

Kelley, H. H. (1955). Salience of membership and resistance to change of group-anchored attitudes. *Hum. Relat., 8*, 275–290.

_____ Ed. (1983). *Close relationships*. San Francisco: Freeman.

Kelley, H. H., and J. L. Michela (1980). Attribution theory and research. *Ann. Rev. Psychol., 31*, 457–501.

Kelley, H. H., and J. Thibaut (1978). *Interpersonal relations: a theory of interdependence*. New York: Wiley.

Kelly, E. L. (1955). Consistency of the adult personality. *Amer. Psychol., 10*, 659–681.

Kelman, H. C. (1958). Compliance, identification and internalization: three processes of attitude change. *J. conflict Resolution, 2*, 51–60.

_____ (1961). Processes of opinion change. *Publ. Opin. Quart., 25*, 57–78.

_____ (1974). Attitudes are alive and well and gainfully employed in the sphere of action. *Amer. Psychol., 29*, 310–324.

_____ (1980). The role of action in attitude change. In H. E. Howe, Jr., and M. M. Page (Eds.), *Nebraska symposium on motivation: beliefs, attitudes and values, 1979*. Vol. 27. Lincoln: Univ. of Nebraska Press. Pp. 117–194.

Kelman, H. C., and C. I. Hovland (1953). "Reinstatement" of the communicator in delayed measurement of opinion change. *J. abnorm. soc. Psychol., 48*, 327–335.

Kennedy, G. A. (1963). *The art of persuasion in Greece*. Princeton, N.J.: Princeton Univ. Press.

_____ (1972). The art of rhetoric in the Roman world: 300 B.C.–300 A.D. Princeton, N.J.: Princeton Univ. Press.

_____ (1980). *Classical rhetoric and its Christian and secular tradition from ancient to modern times*. Chapel Hill: Univ. of North Carolina Press.

Kennedy, W. J. (1978). *Rhetorical norms in renaissance literature*. New Haven: Yale Univ. Press.

Kenny, D. A. (1984). The NBC study and television violence. *J. Communications, 34 (1)*, 176–188.

Kenrick, D. T., and S. E. Gutierres (1980). Contrast effects and judgments of physical attractiveness: when beauty becomes a problem. *J. Pers. soc. Psychol., 38*, 131–140.

Kepplinger, H. M. (1982). Visual biases in television campaign coverage. *Communic. Res., 9*, 432–446.

Kerlinger, F. N. (1984). *Liberalism, conservatism, and the structure of social attitudes*. Hillsdale, N.J.: Erlbaum.

Kerr, R. A. (1980). Asteroid theory of extinctions strengthened. *Science, 210*, 514–517.

Kertzer, D. I. (1983). Generation as a sociological problem. *Ann. Rev. Sociol., 9*, 125–149.

Kessler, R. C., and H. Stipp (1984). The impact of fictional television suicide stories on U.S. suicides. *Amer. J. Sociol., 90*, 151–167.

Key, M. R. (1977). *Nonverbal communication: a research guide and bibliography*. Metuchen, N.J.: Scarecrow Press.

_____ Ed. (1980). *The relationship of verbal and nonverbal communication*. The Hague: Mouton.

Kiesler, C. A. (1971). *The psychology of commitment: experiments linking behavior to belief*. New York: Academic Press.

Kiesler, C. A., B. E. Collins, and N. Miller (1969). *Attitude change*. New York: Wiley.

Kiesler, C. A., and S. Kiesler (1969). *Conformity*. Reading, Mass.: Addison-Wesley.

Kinder, D. R. (1981). Presidents, prosperity and public opinion. *Publ. Opin. Quart., 45*, 1–21.

Kinder, D. R., and D. O. Sears (1981). Prejudice and politics: symbolic racism versus racial threats to the good life. *J. Pers. soc. Psychol., 40*, 414–431.

King, B. T., and I. L. Janis (1956). Comparison of the effectiveness of improvised versus non-improvised role-playing in producing opinion change. *Hum. Relat., 9*, 177–186.

Kipnis, D. (1976). *The powerholders*. Chicago: Univ. of Chicago Press.

Kirfel, P., and F. Denig (1973). [The significance of improvisation for a Socratic method of persuasion.] *Psychologische Beitraege, 15*, 321–331.

Klapper, J. T. (1949). *The effects of the mass media*. New York: Columbia Univ. Bureau of Applied Social Research.

_____ (1960). *Effects of mass communications*. Glencoe, Ill.: Free Press.

Klare, G. R. (1963). *The measurement of readability*. Ames: Iowa State Univ. Press.

Klein, P. S., E. Levine, and M. M. Charry (1979). Effects of skin color and hair differences on facial choices of kindergarten children. *J. soc. Psychol., 107*, 287–288.

Kleinhesselink, R. R., and R. E. Edwards (1975). Seeking and avoiding belief-discrepant information as a function of its perceived refutability. *J. Pers. soc. Psychol., 31*, 787–790.

Kleinke, C. L. (1977). Compliance to requests made by gazing and touching experimenters in field settings. *J. exp. soc. Psychol., 13*, 218–223.

Klineberg, O. (1981). International educational exchange: the problem of evaluation. *Amer. Psychol., 36*, 192–199.

Knapp, M. L., R. P. Hart, and H. S. Dennis (1974). An exploration of deception as a communication construct. *Hum. Communic. Res., 1*, 15–29.

Knapp, M. L., C. Stohl, and K. K. Reardon (1981). "Memorable" messages. *J. Communic., 31 (4)*, 27–41.

Knowles, E. S. (1983). Social physics and the effects of others: tests of the effects of audience size and distance on social judgments and behavior. *J. Pers. soc. Psychol., 45*, 1263–1279.

Koch, S., and D. E. Leary, Eds. (1984). *A century of psychology as science.* New York: McGraw-Hill.

Kolata, G. B. (1977). Catastrophe theory: the emperor has no clothes. *Science, 196,* No. 4287, *287,* 350–351.

Komorita, S. S., and D. Moore (1976). Theories and processes of coalition formation. *J. Pers. soc. Psychol., 33,* 371–381.

Korda, M. (1975). *Power: how to get it, how to use it.* New York: Random House.

Koschnick, W. J. (1982). Bandwagons and underdogs. *Society, 19 (6),* 12–14.

Kosslyn, S. M. (1980). *Image and mind.* Cambridge, Mass.: Harvard Univ. Press.

Kraus, S., Ed. (1979). *The great debates: Carter vs. Ford 1976.* Bloomington: Univ. of Indiana Press.

_____ Ed. (1983). *The great debates: background-perspective-effects.* Magnolia, Mass.: Peter Smith.

Kraut, R. E. (1973). Effect of social labeling on giving to charity. *J. exp. soc. Psychol., 9,* 551–562.

_____ (1978). Verbal and nonverbal cues in the perception of lying. *J. Pers. soc. Psychol., 36,* 380–391.

_____ (1980). Humans as lie detectors: some second thoughts. *J. Communic., 30 (4),* 209–216.

Kraut, R. E., and S. H. Lewis (1975). Alternate models of family influence on student political ideology. *J. Pers. soc. Psychol., 31,* 791–800.

Kraut, R. E., and J. McConahay (1973). How being interviewed affects voting: an experiment. *Publ. Opin. Quart., 37,* 398–406.

Kreckel, M. (1981). *Communicative acts and sacred knowledge in natural discourse.* London: Academic Press.

Kreitler, H., and S. Kreitler (1976). *Cognitive orientation and behavior.* New York: Springer.

_____ (1982). The theory of cognitive orientation: widening the scope of behavior prediction. In B. A. Maher and W. B. Maher (Eds.), *Progress in experimental personality research.* Vol. 11. New York: Academic Press. Pp. 102–169.

Kreitler, S., and H. Kreitler (1984). The cognitive foundations of personality. Unpublished manuscript, Tel Aviv University, Department of Psychology.

Kroger, R. O. (1982). Explorations in ethogeny: with special reference to the rules of address. *Amer. Psychol., 37,* 810–820.

Kropotkin, P. A. (1902). *Mutual aid, a factor of evolution.* New York: McClure, Phillips.

Krugman, H. E. (1965). The impact of television advertising: learning without involvement. *Publ. Opin. Quart., 29,* 349–356.

_____ (1972). Why three exposures may be enough. *J. Advertising Res., 12,* No. 6, 11–14.

_____ (1977). Memory without recall, exposure without perception. *J. Advertising Res., 17,* No. 4, 7–12.

_____ (1983). Television program interest and commercial interruption. *J. Advertising Res., 23 (1),* 21–23.

Kubey, R. W. (1980). Television and aging: past, present and future. *The Gerontologist, 20,* 16–35.

Külpe, O. (1922). *Vorlesungeün ueber Psychologie* (2nd ed.). Leipzig: Herausgegeber von Karl Buehler.

Kunst-Wilson, W. R., and R. B. Zajonc (1980). Affective discrimination of stimuli that cannot be recognized. *Science, 207,* 557–558.

LaBarbara, P., and J. MacLachlan (1979). Time-compressed speech in radio advertising. *J. Marketing, 43,* No. 1, 30–36.

Ladd, E. C., and S. M. Lipset (1980). Anatomy of a decade. *Publ. Opin., 3,* 2–9.

LaFrance, M., and C. Mayo (1978). *Moving bodies: nonverbal communication in social relationships.* Monterey, Calif.: Brooks/Cole.

Laird, J. D. (1974). Self-attribution of emotion: the effects of expressive behavior on the quality of emotional experience. *J. Pers. soc. Psychol., 29,* 475–486.

Lakoff, G., and M. Johnson (1980). *Metaphors we live by.* Chicago: Univ. of Chicago Press.

Lana, R. E. (1964). Existing familiarity and order of presentation of persuasive communications. *Psychol. Reports, 15,* 607–610.

Lane, C. (1981). *The rites of rulers: ritual in industrial society—the Soviet case.* Cambridge: Cambridge Univ. Press.

Lane, R. E. (1973). Patterns of political belief. In J. Knutson (Ed.), *Handbook of political psychology.* San Francisco: Jossey-Bass. Pp. 83–116.

Lang, G. E., and K. Lang (1983). *The battle for public opinion: the president, the press, and the polls during Watergate.* New York: Columbia Univ. Press.

Lang, K., and G. E. Lang (1968). *Voting and non-voting.* Waltham, Mass.: Blaisdell.

Lange, R., and M. Fishbein (1983). Effects of category differences on belief change and agreement with the source of a persuasive communication. *J. Pers. soc. Psychol., 44,* 933–941.

Langer, E. J. (1978). Rethinking the role of thought in social interaction. In J. H. Harvey, W. Ickes, and R. E. Kidd (Eds.), *New directions in attribution research.* Vol. 2. Hillsdale, N.J.: Erlbaum. Pp. 35–58.

_____ (1983). *The psychology of control.* Beverly Hills, Calif.: Sage.

Langer, J. (1983). *Consumers in transition: in-depth investigations of changing lifestyles.* New York: American Management Assoc.

Lanham, R. A. (1968). *A handlist of rhetorical terms.* Berkeley: Univ. of California Press.

Lanigan, R. L. (1981). A critical theory approach. In D. D. Nimmo and K. R. Sanders (Eds.), *Handbook of political communication.* Beverly Hills, Calif.: Sage. Pp. 141–167.

LaPiere, R. T. (1934). Attitudes versus action. *Social Forces, 13,* 230–237.

Lasch, C. (1977). *Haven in a heartless world: the family besieged.* New York: Basic Books.

Lasswell, H. D. (1948). The structure and function of communication in society. In L. Bryson (Ed.), *Communication of ideas.* New York: Harper.

Lasswell, H. D., D. Lerner, and H. Speier, Eds. (1979–1981). *Propaganda and communication in world history.* Vols. 1–3. Honolulu: Univ. Press of Hawaii.

Latané, B., and S. Wolf (1981). The social impact of majorities and minorities. *Psychol. Rev., 88,* 438–453.

Lau, R. R., and K. A. Hartman (1983). Common sense representations of common illnesses. *Health Psychol., 2,* 167–185.

LaVoie, J. C., and G. R. Adams (1978). Physical and interpersonal attractiveness of the model and imitation in adults. *J. soc. Psychol., 106,* 191–202.

Lavrakas, P. R. (1975). Female preferences for male physiques. *J. Res. Pers., 9,* 324–334.

Lazarsfeld, P. F. (1959). Latent structure analysis. In S. Koch (Ed.), *Psychology: a study of a science.* Vol. 3. New York: McGraw-Hill. Pp. 476–543.

Lazarsfeld, P. F., and F. N. Stanton, Eds. (1949). *Communications research, 1948 to 1949.* New York: Harper.

Lazarus, R. S. (1981). The stress and coping paradigm. In C. Eisdorfer, D. Cohen, A. Kleinman, and P. Maxim (Eds.), *Models for clinical psychopathology.* New York: Spectrum.

_____ (1984). On the primacy of cognition. *Amer. Psychologist, 39,* 124–129.

Lears, T. J. J. (1983). The rise of American advertising. *Wilson Quart., 7* (5), 156–167.

Lefcourt, H. M., Ed. (1981). *Research with the locus of control construct.* Vol. 1.: *Assessment methods.* New York: Academic Press.

_____ (1982). *Locus of control: current trends in theory and research* (2nd ed.). Hillsdale, N.J.: Erlbaum.

Lefkowitz, M. M., L. D. Eron, L. O. Walder, and L. R. Huesmann (1977). *Growing up to be violent: a longitudinal study of the development of aggression.* New York: Pergamon Press.

Lehmann, S. (1970). Personality and compliance: a study of anxiety and self-esteem in opinion and behavior change. *J. Pers. soc. Psychol., 15,* 76–86.

Leippe, M. R., A. G. Greenwald, and M. H. Baumgardner (1982). Delayed persuasion as a consequence of associative interference: a context confusion effect. *Pers. soc. Psychol. Bull., 8,* 644–650.

Leiter, K. (1980). *A primer on ethnomethodology.* New York: Oxford Univ. Press.

Lejeune, R., and N. Alex (1973). On being mugged: the event and its aftermath. *Urban Life and Culture, 2,* 259–287.

Lemert, J. B. (1981). *Does mass communication change public opinion, after all? A new approach to effects analysis.* Chicago: Nelson-Hall.

Lemon, N. (1973). *Attitudes and their measurement.* New York: Wiley.

Leone, R. P. (1983). Modeling sales-advertising relationships: an integrated time series-econometric approach. *J. Marketing Res., 20,* 291–295.

Lependorf, S. (1964). The effects of incentive value and expectancy on dissonance resulting from attitude-discrepant behavior and disconformation of expectancy. Unpublished doctoral dissertation. State University of New York at Buffalo.

Lepper, M. R. (1973). Dissonance, self-perception and honesty in children. *J. Pers. soc. Psychol., 25,* 65–74.

Lerner, M. J., and S. C. Lerner, Eds. (1981). *The justice motive in social behavior: adapting to times of scarcity and change.* New York: Plenum.

Lesher, S. (1982). *Media unbound: the impact of television journalism on the public.* Boston: Houghton Mifflin.

Lesk, S., and B. Zippel (1975). Dependency, threat, and helping in a large city. *J. soc. Psychol., 95,* 185–186.

Lesnik-Oberstein, M., and L. Cohen (1984). Cognitive style, sensation seeking, and assortative mating. *J. Pers. soc. Psychol., 46,* 112–117.

Leventhal, H., D. Meyer, and D. Nerenz (1980). The common sense representation of illness danger. In S. Rachman (Ed.), *Medical psychology.* Vol. 2. New York: Pergamon Press. Pp. 7–30.

Leventhal, H., and D. Nerenz (1983). Representations of threat and the control of stress. In D. Meichenbaum and M. Jaremko (Eds.), *Stress reduction and prevention: a cognitive behavioral approach.* New York: Plenum.

Leventhal, H., and P. Niles (1965). Persistence of influence for varying durations of exposure to threat stimuli. *Psychol. Reports, 16,* 223–233.

Leventhal, H., and S. I. Perloe (1962). A relationship between self-esteem and persuasibility. *J. abnorm. soc. Psychol., 64,* 385–388.

Leventhal, H., R. P. Singer, and S. H. Jones (1965). The effects of fear and specificity of recommendation. *J. Pers. soc. Psychol., 2,* 20–29.

Leventhal, H., and J. C. Watts (1966). Sources of resistance to fear-arousing communications on smoking and lung cancer. *J. Pers., 34,* 155–175.

Leventhal, H., J. Watts, and F. Pagano (1967). Effects of fear and specificity of recommendations on smoking behavior. New Haven: Yale Univ. Press. Department of Psychology. (Mimeo)

Levinson, D. J. (1978). *The seasons of a man's life.* New York: Knopf.

Lévi-Strauss, C. (1974). *Mythologiques, 1964–1972.* (Translation: *Introduction to a science of mythology, 1964–1972.*) New York: Harper & Row.

Levitt, L., and R. C. Kornhaber (1977). Stigma and compliance: a reexamination. *J. soc. Psychol., 103,* 13–18.

Lewin, K. (1947). Group decision and social change. In T. M. Newcomb and E. Hartley (Eds.), *Readings in social psychology.* New York: Holt, Rinehart & Winston.

_____ (1951). *Field theory in social change.* New York: Harper and Row.

Lewis, J. D., and R. L. Smith (1980). *American sociology and pragmatism: Mead, Chicago sociology, and symbolic interaction.* Chicago: Univ. of Chicago Press.

Lichtman, R. (1982). *The production of desire: the integration of psychoanalysis into Marxist theory.* New York: Free Press.

Lichty, L. W. (1982). Video versus print. *Wilson Quart., 6* (5), 48–57.

Lieberman, J. N. (1977). *Playfulness: its relationship to imagination and creativity.* New York: Academic Press.

Liebert, R. M., J. N. Sprafkin, and E. S. Davidson (1982). *The early window: effects of television on children and youth.* (2nd ed.). Elmsford, N.Y.: Pergamon Press.

Lifton, R. (1963). *Thought reform and the psychology of totalism.* New York: Norton.

Likert, R. (1932). A technique for the measurement of attitudes. *Arch. Psychol.,* No. 140.

Lilienfeld, R. (1978). *The rise of systems theory: an ideological analysis.* New York: Wiley.

Lin, N. (1974–75). The McIntire march: a study of recruitment and commitment. *Publ. Opin. Quart., 38,* 562–573.

Lincoln, A. J. (1977). Effects of the sex of the model and donor on donating to Amsterdam organ grinders. *J. soc. Psychol., 103, 33-37.*

Lind, J. (1983). The evolution of coercion in history. In R. Collins (Ed.), *Sociological Theory—1983.* San Francisco: Jossey-Bass.

Lingle, J. H., and T. M. Ostrom (1979). Retrieval selectivity in memory-based impression judgments. *J. Pers. soc. Psychol., 37, 180-194.*

Linton, H., and E. Graham (1959). Personality correlates of persuasibility. In I. L. Janis and C. I. Hovland (Eds.), *Personality and persuasibility.* New Haven: Yale University Press. Pp. 69-101.

Linton, R. (1945). *The cultural background of personality.* New York: Appleton-Century-Crofts.

Lipset, S. M. (1976). The wavering polls. *Publ. Interest, 43, 70-89.*

Lipset, S. M., and E. Raab (1978). *The politics of unreason.* (2nd ed.). Chicago: Univ. of Chicago Press.

Lipset, S. M., and W. Schneider (1982).*The confidence gap: business, labor and government in the public mind.* New York: Free Press.

Lipstein, B., and W. J. McGuire (1978). *Evaluating advertising.* New York: Advertising Research Foundation.

Liska, A. E. (1974). Emergent issues in the attitude-behavior consistency controversy. *Amer. Sociol. Rev., 39, 261-272.*

_____ (1984). A critical examination of the causal structure of the Fishbein/Ajzen attitude-behavior model. *Soc. Psychol. Quart., 47, 61-74.*

Litwak, E., N. Hooyman, and D. Warren (1973). Ideological complexity and middle American rationality. *Publ. Opin. Quart., 37, 317-332.*

Lloyd, B., and J. Gay, Eds. (1981). *Universals of human thought: some African evidence.* Cambridge: Cambridge Univ. Press.

Locurto, C. M., H. S. Terrace, and J. Gibbon, Eds. (1980). *Autoshaping and conditioning theory.* New York: Academic Press.

Loewenberg, P. (1971). The psychohistorical origins of the Nazi youth cohort. *Amer. Historical Rev., 76, 1457-1502.*

Loken, B., and R. S. Wyer, Jr. (1983). Effects of reporting beliefs in syllogistically related propositions on the recognition of unmentioned propositions. *J. Pers. soc. Psychol., 45, 306-322.*

Lombardo, J. P., R. F. Weiss, and W. Buchanan (1972). Reinforcing and attracting functions of yielding. *J. Pers. soc. Psychol., 21, 359-368.*

Lord, C. G., M. R. Lepper, and D. Mackie. (1984). Attitude prototypes as determinants of attitude-behavior consistency. *J. Pers. soc. Psychol., 46, 1254-1266.*

Lorenz, K. (1966). *On aggression.* New York: Harcourt, Brace, and World.

Luchins, A. S. (1942). Mechanization in problem solving: the effect of Einstellung. *Psychol. Monogr., 54, 1-95.*

_____ (1945). Social influences on perception of complex drawings. *J. soc. Psychol., 21, 257-273.*

Lumsden, C. J., and E. O. Wilson (1981). *Genes, mind, and culture: the coevolutionary process.* Cambridge: Harvard Univ. Press.

Luttwak, E. N. (1977). *The grand strategy of the Roman empire: from the first century to the third.* Baltimore: Johns Hopkins.

Lynch, J. G. Jr. (1979). Why additive utility models fail as descriptions of choice behavior. *J. exp. soc. Psychol., 15, 397-417.*

Maass, A., and R. D. Clark III (1984). Hidden impact of minorities: fifteen years of minority influence research. *Psychol. Bull., 95, 428-450.*

Maas, J. W. (1978). Clinical and biochemical heterogeneity of depressive disorders. *Annals of Internal Medicine, 88, 556-563.*

McAlister, A., C. Perry, J. Killen, L. A. Slinkard, and N. Maccoby (1980). Pilot study of smoking, alcohol and drug abuse prevention. *Amer. J. publ. Health, 70, 719-721.*

McArthur, L. A., and E. Zigler (1969). Level of satiation on social reinforcers and valence of the reinforcing agent as determinants of social reinforcer effectiveness. *Develop. Psychol., 1, 739-746.*

McClelland, D. C. (1961). *The achieving society.* Princeton, N.J.: Van Nostrand.

_____ (1975). *Power: the inner experience.* New York: Halsted Press.

McClintock, C. C., and R. G. Hunt (1975). Nonverbal indicators of affect and deception in an interview setting. *J. appl. soc. Psychol., 5, 54-67.*

McClosky, H., and A. Brill (1983). *Dimensions of tolerance: what Americans believe about civil liberties.* New York: Russell Sage/Basic Books.

Maccoby, E. E., and C. N. Jacklin (1974). *The psychology of sex differences.* Stanford: Stanford Univ. Press.

Maccoby, N., and J. Alexander (1980). Use of media in lifestyle programs. In P. O. Davidson, and S. M. Davidson (Eds.), *Behavioral medicine: changing health lifestyles.* New York: Brunner Mazel. Pp. 351-370.

McCombs, M. E. (1981). The agenda-setting approach. In D. D. Nimmo, and K. R. Sanders (Eds.), *Handbook of political communication.* Beverly Hills, Calif.: Sage. Pp. 121-140.

McConnell, J. D. (1970). Do media vary in effectiveness? *J. Advertising Res., 10, No. 5, 19-22.*

MacCormack, C., and M. Strathern (1980). *Nature, culture, and gender.* Cambridge: Cambridge Univ. Press.

McCroskey, J. C., and W. H. Combs (1969). The effects of the use of analogy on attitude change and source credibility. *J. Communic., 19, 333-339.*

McCroskey, J. C., and T. A. McCain (1974). The measurement of interpersonal attraction. *Speech Monogr., 41, 261-266.*

McCroskey, J. C., and R. S. Mehrley (1969). The effects of disorganization and nonfluency on attitude change and source credibility. *Speech Monogr., 36, 13-21.*

McCullough, J. L., and T. M. Ostrom (1974). Repetition of highly similar messages and attitude change. *J. appl. Psychol., 59, 395-397.*

MacDonald, J. F. (1983). *Blacks and white TV: Afro-Americans in television since 1948.* Chicago: Nelson-Hall.

McDougall, W. (1908). *An introduction to social psychology* London: Methuen.

McEwen, C. A. (1980). Continuities in the study of total and nontotal institutions. *Ann. Rev. Sociol., 6, 143-185.*

McEwen, W. J., and B. S. Greenberg (1970). The effects of message intensity on receiver evaluations of source, message, and topic. *J. Communic., 20,* 340–350.

McFarland, C., M. Ross, and M. Conway (1984). Self-persuasion and self- presentation as mediators of anticipatory attitude change. *J. Pers. soc. Psychol., 46,* 529–540.

McFarland, S. G., and D. L. Thistlethwaite (1970). An analysis of a logical consistency model of belief change. *J. Pers. soc. Psychol., 15,* 133–143.

McGhee, P. E. (1979). *Humor: its origin and development.* San Francisco: Freeman.

McGhee, P. E., and J. H. Goldstein, Eds. (1983). *Handbook of humor research.* Vol. 1. *Basic issues.* Vol. 2. *Applied studies.* Secaucus, N.J.: Springer-Verlag.

McGinley, H., R. LeFevre, and P. McGinley (1975). The influence of a communicator's body position on opinion change in others. *J. Pers. soc. Psychol., 31,* 686–690.

McGinnies, E. (1973). Initial attitude, source credibility and involvement as factors in persuasion. *J. exp. soc. Psychol., 9,* 285–296.

McGinnies, E., and C. D. Ward (1980). Better liked than right: trustworthiness and expertise as factors in credibility. *Pers. soc. Psychol. Bull., 6,* 467–472.

McGuire, W. J. (1957). Order of presentation as a factor in "conditioning" persuasiveness. In C. I. Hovland *et al.* (Eds.), *Order of presentation in persuasion.* New Haven: Yale Univ. Press. Pp. 98–114.

_____ (1960a). Cognitive consistency and attitude change. *J. abnorm. soc. Psychol., 60,* 345–353.

_____ (1960b). Direct and indirect persuasive effects of dissonance-producing messages. *J. abnorm. soc. Psychol., 60,* 354–358.

_____ (1960c). A syllogistic analysis of cognitive relationships. In M. J. Rosenberg and C. I. Hovland (Eds.), *Attitude organization and change.* New Haven: Yale Univ. Press. Pp. 65–111.

_____ (1961a). Resistance to persuasion conferred by active and passive prior refutation of the same and alternative counterarguments. *J. abnorm. soc. Psychol., 63,* 326–332.

_____ (1961b). A multi-process model for paired-associate learning. *J. exp. Psychol., 62,* 335–347.

_____ (1961c). Some factors influencing the effectiveness of demonstrational films. In A. A. Lumsdaine (Ed.), *Student response in programmed instruction.* Washington, D.C.: National Academy of Science. Pp. 187–207.

_____ (1961d). The effectiveness of supportive and refutational defenses in immunizing and restoring beliefs against persuasion. *Sociometry, 24,* 184–197.

_____ (1962). Persistence of the resistance to persuasion induced by various types of prior belief defenses. *J. abnorm. soc. Psychol., 64,* 241–248.

_____ (1964). Inducing resistance to persuasion. In L. Berkowitz (Ed.), *Advances in experimental social psychology.* Vol. 1. New York: Academic Press. Pp. 191–229.

_____ (1966a). Attitudes and opinions. In P. R. Farnsworth *et al.* (Eds.), *Ann. Rev. Psychol., 17,* 475–514.

_____ (1966b). The current status of cognitive consistency theories. In S. Feldman (Ed.), *Cognitive consistency.* New York: Academic Press. Pp. 1–46.

_____ (1968a). Personality and susceptibility to social influence. In E. F. Borgatta, and W. W. Lambert (Eds.), *Hand-*

book of personality theory and research. Chicago: Rand McNally. Pp. 1130–1187.

_____ (1968b). Theory of the structure of human thought. In R. P. Abelson, *et al.* (Eds.), *Theories of cognitive consistency: a sourcebook.* Chicago: Rand McNally. Pp. 140–162.

_____ (1968c). Selective perception: a summing up. In R. P. Abelson *et al.* (Eds.), *Theories of cognitive consistency: a sourcebook.* Chicago: Rand McNally. Pp. 769–770 and 797–800.

_____ (1968d). Personality and attitude change: an information-processing theory. In A. G. Greenwald *et al.* (Eds.), *Psychological foundations of attitudes.* New York: Academic Press. Pp. 171–196.

_____ (1969a). Suspiciousness of experimenter's intent as an artifact in social research. In R. Rosenthal, and R. Rosnow (Eds.), *Artifacts in behavioral research.* New York: Academic Press. Pp. 13–57.

_____ (1969b). The nature of attitudes and attitude change. In G. Lindzey and E. Aronson (Eds.), *Handbook of social psychology* (2nd ed.). Vol. 3. Reading, Mass.: Addison-Wesley. Pp. 136–314.

_____ (1972). Attitude change: an information-processing paradigm. In C. G. McClintock (Ed.), *Experimental social psychology.* New York: Holt, Rinehart, and Winston. Pp. 108–141.

_____ (1974). Psychological motives and communication gratification. In J. G. Blumler, and E. Katz (Eds.), *The uses of mass communications: current perspectives on gratifications research.* Beverly Hills, Calif.: Sage. Pp. 167–196.

_____ (1975). The concepts of attitudes and their relations to behavior. In H. W. Sinaiko, and L. A. Broedling (Eds.), *Perspectives on attitude assessment.* Champaign, Ill.: Pendleton. Pp. 16–40.

_____ (1976a). Position/summary paper on televised over-the-counter drug advertising. Testimony before the FTC/FCC OTC Drug Advertising to children panel. Washington, D.C.

_____ (1976b). Some internal psychological factors influencing consumer choice. *J. Consumer Research, 2,* 302–319.

_____ (1978). The communication/persuasion matrix. In B. Lipstein, and W. J. McGuire (Eds.), *Evaluating advertising: a bibliography of the communication process.* New York: Advertising Research Foundation. Pp. xxvii–xxxv.

_____ (1980a). The development of theory in social psychology. In R. Gilmour, and S. Duck (Eds.), *The development of social psychology.* London: Academic Press. Pp. 53–80.

_____ (1980b). The communication-persuasion model and health-risk labeling. In L. A. Morris, M. B. Mazis, and I. Barofsky (Eds.), *Product labeling and health risks.* New York: Banbury. Pp. 99–122.

_____ (1981). The probabilogical model of cognitive structure and attitude change. In R. E. Petty, T. M. Ostrom, and T. C. Brock (Eds.), *Cognitive responses in persuasion.* Hillsdale, N.J.: Erlbaum. Pp. 291–307.

_____ (1983). A contextualist theory of knowledge: its implications for innovations and reform in psychology research. In L. Berkowitz (Ed.), *Advances in experimental* social psychology. Vol. 16. New York: Academic Press. Pp. 1–47.

_____ (1984a). Search for the self: going beyond self-esteem and the reactive self. In R. A. Zucker, J. Aronoff, and A. I. Rabin (Eds.), *Personality and the prediction of behavior*. New York: Academic Press. Pp. 73–120.

_____ (1984b). Toward social psychology's second century. In S. Koch, and D. E. Leary (Eds.), *A century of psychology as science*. New York: McGraw-Hill.

_____ (In press, a). The myth of mass media effectiveness. In G. Comstock (Ed.), *Public communication and behavior*. Vol. 1. New York: Academic Press.

_____ (In press, b). The career of attitudes and other representational constructs in the fabrication of psychological theory. *Europ. J. soc. Psychol.*

McGuire, W. J., and C. V. McGuire (1981). The spontaneous self-concept as affected by personal distinctiveness. In M. D. Lynch, A. A. Norem-Hebeisen, and K. J. Gergen (Eds.), *Self-concept: advances in theory and research*. Cambridge, Mass.: Ballinger. Pp. 147–171.

_____ (1982). Significant others in self-space: sex differences and developmental trends in the social self. In J. Suls (Ed.), *Psychological perspectives on the self*. Hillsdale, N.J.: Erlbaum. Pp. 71–96.

McGuire, W. J., C. V. McGuire, P. Child, and T. Fujioka (1978). Salience of ethnicity in the spontaneous self-concept as a function of one's ethnic distinctiveness in the social environment. *J. Pers. soc. Psychol., 36,* 511–520.

McGuire, W. J., and S. Millman (1965). Anticipatory belief lowering following forewarning of a persuasive attack. *J. Pers. soc. Psychol., 2,* 471–479.

McGuire, W. J., and A. Padawer-Singer (1976). Trait salience in the spontaneous self-concept. *J. Pers. soc. Psychol., 33,* 743–754.

McGuire, W. J., and D. Papageorgis (1961). The relative efficacy of various types of prior belief-defense in producing immunity against persuasion. *J. abnorm. soc. Psychol., 62,* 327–337.

_____ (1962). Effectiveness of forewarning in developing resistance to persuasion. *Publ. Opin. Quart., 26,* 24–34.

McGuire, W. J., and J. Ryan (1955). Receptivity as a mediator of personality-persuasibility relationships. *University of Minnesota LRSR.* 20 pp.

McKendrick, N., J. Brewer, and J. H. Plumb (1982). The birth of a consumer society: the commercialization of eighteenth-century England. Bloomington: Indiana Univ. Press.

Mackey, W. C. (1976). Parameters of the smile as a social stimulus. *J. soc. Psychol., 129,* 125–130.

McLaughlin, M. L., M. J. Cody, and C. S. Robey (1980). Situational influences on the selection of strategies to resist compliance-gaining attempts. *Hum. Communic. Res., 7,* 14–36.

McLeod, J. M., C. K. Atkin, and S. H. Chaffee (1972). Adolescents, parents, and television use: adolescent self-report measures from Maryland and Wisconsin samples. In G. A. Comstock and E. A. Rubinstein (Eds.), *Television and social behavior*. Vol. 3. *Television and adolescent aggressiveness*. Washington, D.C.: U.S. Government Printing Office. Pp. 177–238.

McLeod, J. M., L. B. Becker, and J. E. Byrnes (1974). Another look at the agenda-setting function of the press. *Communic. Res., 1,* 131–166.

McLuhan, M. (1964). *Understanding media: the extensions of man*. New York: McGraw-Hill.

McMahan, H. (1971, 10 May). Brand misidentification grows with clutter of 30 spots. *Advertising Age.* Pp. 53–54.

McNeil, J. C. (1975). Feminism, femininity, and the television series: a content analysis. *J. Broadcasting, 19,* 259–271.

McNemar, Q. (1946). Opinion-attitude methodology. *Psychol. Bull., 43,* 289–374.

Magnusson, D., Ed. (1981). *Toward a psychology of situations: an interactional perspective*. Hillsdale, N.J.: Erlbaum.

Mahoney, M. J. (1974). *Cognition and behavior modification*. Cambridge, Mass.: Ballinger.

Maital, S. (1982). *Minds, markets, and money*. New York: Basic Books.

Malamuth, M. N., and J. V. P. Check (1981). The effects of mass media exposure on acceptance of violence against women: a field experiment. *J. Res. Pers., 15,* 436–446.

Malhotra, N. K. (1984). Reflections on the information overload paradigm in consumer decision making. *J. Consumer Research, 10,* 436–440.

Malhotra, N. K., A. K. Jain, and S. W. Lagakos (1982). The information overload controversy: an alternative viewpoint. *J. Marketing, 46,* No. 2, 27–37.

Mancuso, J. C., and J. R. Adams-Webber, Eds. (1982). *The construing person*. New York: Praeger.

Manis, J., and B. Meltzer, Eds. (1978). *Symbolic interaction: a reader in social psychology* (3rd ed.). Boston: Allyn and Bacon.

Mann, L., and I. L. Janis (1968). A follow-up study on the long-term effects of emotional role playing. *J. Pers. soc. Psychol., 8,* 339–342.

Mann, L., K. Paleg, and R. Hawkins (1978). Effectiveness of staged disputes in influencing bystander crowds. *J. Pers. soc. Psychol., 36,* 725–732.

Mannheim, K. (1952). The problem of generations. *Essays on the sociology of knowledge*. Oxford: Oxford Univ. Press. Pp. 276–320. (Original work published 1923.)

Marascuilo, L. A., and R. Zwick (1983). Comment on Barnard: another look at strength and direction of attitude using contrasts. *Psychol. Bull., 94,* 534–539.

Margalit, B. A., and P. A. Mauger (1984). Cross-cultural demonstration of orthogonality of assertiveness and aggressiveness: comparison between Israel and the United States. *J. Pers. soc. Psychol., 46,* 1414–1421.

Margolis, H. (1982). *Selfishness, altruism, and rationality*. New York: Cambridge Univ. Press.

Markiewicz, D. (1974). Effects of humor on persuasion. *Sociometry, 37,* 407–422.

Marrou, H. I. (1981). Education and rhetoric. In M. I. Finley (Ed.), *The legacy of Greece: a new appraisal*. New York: Oxford Univ. Press.

Marrow, A. J., and J. R. P. French (1945). Changing a stereotype in industry. *J. soc. Psychol., 1* (3), 33–37.

Marshall, R. J. (1982). *Resistant interactions: child, family and psychotherapist*. New York: Human Sciences Press.

Martel, M. (1983). *Political campaign debates: images, strategies and tactics*. New York: Longman.

Martin, S. S. (1981). New methods lead to familiar results. *Amer. Sociol. Rev., 46,* 670–675.

Maslach, C., J. Stapp, and R. T. Santee (In press). The individuation scale. *J. Pers. soc. Psychol.*

Maslow, A. H. (1970). *Motivation and personality* (2nd ed.). New York: Harper.

Mattelart, A. (1980). *Mass media, ideologies and the revolutionary movement.* Atlantic Highlands, N.J.: Humanities Press.

Mayo, C., and N. H. Henley, Eds. (1981). *Gender and nonverbal behavior.* New York: Springer-Verlag.

Mazlish, B. (1976). *The revolutionary ascetic: evolution of a political type.* New York: Basic Books.

Meadow, R. G. (1980). *Politics as communication.* Norwood, N.J.: Ablex.

Mednick, M. T. (1957). Mediated generalization and the incubation effect. *J. abnorm. soc. Psychol., 55,* 315–321.

Mehrabian, A. (1972). *Nonverbal communication.* Chicago: Aldine.

Mehrabian, A., and M. Williams (1969). Nonverbal concomitants of perceived and intended persuasiveness. *J. Pers. soc. Psychol., 13,* 37–58.

Mehrley, R. S., and J. C. McCroskey (1970). Opinionated statements and attitude intensity as predictors of attitude change and source credibility. *Speech Monogr., 37,* 47–52.

Meichenbaum, D. H., and D. C. Turk (1983). Stress, coping, and disease. In R. W. J. Newfield (Ed.), *Psychological stress and psychopathology.* New York: McGraw-Hill.

Meindl, J. R., and M. J. Lerner (1983). The heroic motive: some experimental demonstrations. *J. exp. soc. Psychol., 19,* 1–20.

Meissner, W. W. (1980). *Internalization in psychoanalysis.* New York: International Universities Press.

Mellars, B. (1981). Feeling more than thinking. *Amer. Psychol., 36,* 802–803.

Melton, J. G., and R. L. Moore (1982). *The cult experience: responding to the new religious pluralism.* New York: Pilgrim Press.

Mendelsohn, H., and G. J. O'Keefe (1976). *The people choose a president: influences on voter decision making.* New York: Praeger.

Merkl, P. H. (1980). *The making of a storm trooper.* Princeton, N.J.: Princeton Univ. Press.

Merleau-Ponty, M. (1962). *The phenomenology of perception.* Original French publication, 1945. Atlantic Highlands, N.J.: Humanities Press.

Messick, D. M., and K. S. Cook, Eds. (1983). *Equity theory: psychological and sociological perspectives.* New York: Praeger.

Metra Consulting Group Ltd. (1979). *The relationship between total cigarette advertising and total cigarette consumption in the U.K.* London: Metra.

Meyer, A. J., J. D. Nash, A. L. McAlister, N. Maccoby, and J. W. Farquhar (1980). Skills training in a cardiovascular health education campaign. *J. Consult. clinic. Psychol., 48,* 129–142.

Meyer, J. S., T. DeChenne, and L. J. Albano (1981). Cognitive consistency in the development of social attitudes. *Develop. Psychol., 17,* 494–498.

Meyer, M., Ed. (1981). *Health education by television and radio.* München: K. G. Saur.

Michener, H. A., and M. R. Burt (1975). Components of "authority" as determinants of compliance. *J. Pers. soc. Psychol., 31,* 606–614.

Michotte, A. E. (1946). *La perception de la causalité.* Louvain: Ed. de l'Institut Supérieur de Philosophie (Études de Psychologie), VIII. (Trans. T. R. and E. Miles. *The perception of causality.* New York: Basic Books, 1963.)

Milavsky, J. R., R. C. Kessler, H. H. Stipp, and W. S. Rubens (1982a). *Television and aggression: results of a panel study.* In D. Pearl, L. Bouthilet, and J. Lazar (Eds.), *Television and behavior: ten years of scientific progress and implications for the eighties.* Vol. 2. *Technical Reviews.* Washington, D.C.: Government Printing Office.

——— (1982b). *Television and aggression: results of a panel study.* New York: Academic Press.

Milavsky, J. R., B. Pekowsky, and H. Stipp (1975–76). TV drug advertising and proprietary and illicit drug use among teenage boys. *Publ. Opin. Quart., 39,* 457–481.

Milburn, M. A. (1979). A longitudinal test of the selective exposure hypothesis. *Publ. Opin. Quart., 43,* 507–517.

Milburn, M. A., and C. M. Judd (1981). Interpreting new methods in attitude structure research: reply to Martin. *Amer. Sociol. Rev., 46,* 675–677.

Milburn, T. W., and K. H. Watman (1981). *On the nature of threat: a social psychological analysis.* New York: Praeger.

Milgram, S. (1974). *Obedience to authority: an experimental view.* New York: Harper & Row.

Miller, A., M. Engeman, J. Polulach, D. Sweet, and R. Ullman (1980). Is positive or negative prior contact a determinant of the reinforcing function of approval? *J. Psychol., 106,* 265–276.

Miller, G. A., E. Galanter, and K. H. Pribram (1960). *Plans and the structures of behavior.* New York: Holt.

Miller, G. R., and J. Baseheart (1969). Source trustworthiness, opinionated statements, and the response to persuasive communication. *Speech Monogr., 36,* 1–7.

Miller, G. R., F. Boster, M. Roloff, and D. Seebold (1977). Compliance-gaining message strategies: a typology and some findings concerning effects of situational differences. *Communic. Monogr., 44,* 37–51.

Miller, M. D., and M. Burgoon (1979). The relationship between violations of expectations and the induction of resistance to persuasion. *Hum. Communic. Res., 5,* 301–313.

Miller, N. E. (1959). Liberalization of basic S–R concepts: extensions to conflict behavior, motivation, and social learning. In S. Koch (Ed.), *Psychology: a study of a science.* Vol. 2. New York: McGraw-Hill. Pp. 196–292.

Miller, N., and M. B. Brewer, Eds. (1984). *Groups in contact: the psychology of desegregation.* New York: Academic Press.

Miller, N., and D. T. Campbell (1959). Recency and primacy in persuasion as a function of the timing of speeches and measurement. *J. abnorm. soc. Psychol., 59,* 1–9.

Miller, N., G. Maruyama, R. J. Beaber, and K. Valone (1976). Speed of speech and persuasion. *J. Pers. soc. Psychol., 34,* 615–624.

Miller, R. L., P. Brickman, and D. Bolen (1975). Attribution versus persuasion as a means for modifying behavior. *J. Pers. soc. Psychol., 31,* 430–441.

Millman, S. (1965). The relationship between anxiety, learning and opinion change. Ph.D. dissertation. Columbia University, New York.

_____ (1968). Anxiety, comprehension and susceptibility to social influence. *J. Pers. soc. Psychol., 9,* 251–256.

Mills, J., and E. Aronson (1965). Opinion change as a function of communicator's attractiveness and desire to influence. *J. Pers. soc. Psychol., 1,* 173–177.

Mills, J., and M. S. Clark (1982). Exchange and communal relationships. In L. Wheeler (Ed.), *Review of personality and social psychology.* Vol. 3. Beverly Hills, Calif.: Sage. Pp. 121–144.

Mills, J., and J. Harvey (1972). Opinion change as a function of when information about the communicator is received and whether he is attractive or expert. *J. Pers. soc. Psychol., 21,* 52–55.

Mills, J., and J. M. Jellison (1967). Effect on opinion change of how desirable the communication is to the audience the communicator addressed. *J. Pers. soc. Psychol., 6,* 98–101.

Mills, J., and A. Ross (1964). Effects of commitment and certainty upon interest in supporting information. *J. abnorm. soc. Psychol., 68,* 552–555.

Milord, J. T. (1978). Aesthetic aspects of faces: a (somewhat) phenomenological analysis using multidimensional scaling methods. *J. Pers. soc. Psychol., 36,* 205–216.

Miniard, P. W., and J. B. Cohen (1983). Modeling personal and normative influences on behavior. *J. Consumer Research, 10,* 169–180.

Minsky, M. (1975). A framework for representing knowledge. In P. H. Winston (Ed.), *The psychology of computer vision.* New York: McGraw-Hill.

Mischel, W. (1968). *Personality and assessment.* New York: Wiley.

_____ (1984). On the predictability and consistency of behavior. In R. A. Zucker, J. Aronoff, and A. I. Rabin (Eds.), *Personality and the prediction of behavior.* New York: Academic Press.

Mischel, W., and P. K. Peake (1983). Some facets of consistency: replies to Epstein, Funder and Bem. *Psychol. Rev., 90,* 394–402.

Mitchell, A. (1983). *The nine American lifestyles: who we are and where we are going.* New York: Macmillan.

Miyo, Y. (1983). The knowledge-gap hypothesis and media dependency. In R. N. Bostrom (Ed.), *Communication yearbook 7.* Beverly Hills, Calif.: Sage. Pp. 626–650.

Moe, J. L., R. W. Nacoste, and C. A. Insko (1981). Belief versus race as determinants of discrimination: a study in southern adolescents in 1966 and 1979. *J. Pers. soc. Psychol., 41,* 1031–1050.

Moerk, E. (1973). An objective, statistical description of style. *Linguistics, 108,* 50–58.

Monat, A., and R. S. Lazarus, Eds. (1977). *Stress and coping.* New York: Columbia Univ. Press.

Moore, R. K. (1964). Susceptibility to hypnosis and susceptibility to social influence. *J. abnorm. soc. Psychol., 68,* 282–294.

Moore, T. E. (1982). Subliminal advertising: what you see is what you get. *J. Marketing, 46,* 27–47.

Moreland, R. L., and R. B. Zajonc (1979). Exposure effects may not depend on stimulus recognition. *J. Pers. soc. Psychol., 37,* 1085–1089.

_____ (1982). Exposure effects in person perception: familiarity, similarity, and attraction. *J. exp. soc. Psychol., 18,* 395–415.

Morgenbesser, S. (1954). On the justification of beliefs and attitudes. *J. Philos., 51,* 565–576.

Morris, D. (1967). *The naked ape.* New York: McGraw-Hill.

Morris, L. A., and D. E. Kanouse (1980). Consumer reactions to differing amounts of written drug information. *Drug. Intell. clinic. Pharm. 14,* 431ff.

Morris, W. N., and R. S. Miller (1975). The effects of consensus-breaking and consensus-preempting partners on reduction of conformity. *J. exp. soc. Psychol., 11,* 215–223.

Mosco, V., and J. Wasko, Eds. (1983). *The changing patterns of communication control.* Norwood, N.J.: Ablex.

Moscovici, S. (1980). Toward a theory of conversion behavior. In L. Berkowitz (Ed.), *Advances in experimental social psychology.* Vol. 13. New York: Academic Press. Pp. 209–239.

_____ (1981). On social representation. In J. P. Folgas (Ed.), *Social cognition.* London: Academic Press.

Moscovici, S., and M. Doms (1982). Compliance and conversion in a situation of sensory deprivation. *Basic appl. soc. Psychol., 3,* 81–94.

Moser, C. A., and G. Kalton (1971). *Survey methods in social investigation.* (2nd ed.). London: Heinemann.

Mosse, G. L. (1980, 10–12 Sept.). *Masses and men: nationalist and Fascist perceptions of society.* New York: Fertig.

Mugny, G., and S. Papastamou (1980). *L'influence du social dans l'influence sociale.* Paper presented at Symposium sur l'influence sociale, Barcelone.

Mugny, G., S. Papastamou, and C. Sherrard (1982). *The power of minorities.* London: Academic Press.

Muir, W. K., Jr. (1967). *Prayer in the public schools: law and attitude change.* Chicago: Chicago Univ. Press.

Mummendey, H. D., and H. G. Bolter (1983). Die Impression-Management-Theorie von Tedeschi ur Schlenker. In M. Irle, and D. Frey (Eds.), *Theorieperspektiven der Sozialpsychologie.* Bern: Huber.

Mumpower, J. L., and S. W. Cook (1978). The development of interpersonal attraction in cooperating interracial groups: the effects of success-failure, race and competence of groupmates, and helping a less competent groupmate. *Int. J. Group Tensions, 8* (3 & 4), 18–50.

Munson, P., and C. A. Kiesler (1974). The role of attributions by others in the acceptance of persuasive communication. *J. Pers., 42,* 453–466.

Murphy, G., L. B. Murphy, and T. N. Newcomb (1937). *Experimental social psychology* (Rev. ed.). New York: Harper.

Murphy, P. E., and W. A. Staples (1979). A modernized family life cycle. *J. Consumer Research, 6 (1),* 12–22.

Murphy, R. D. (1980). Consumer responses to cigarette health warnings. In L. A. Morris, M. B. Mazis, and I. Barofsky (Eds.), *Product labeling and health risks.* Cold Spring Harbor Laboratory, New York: Branbury Report, 6, 13–21.

Murray, H. A. (1938). *Explorations in personality.* New York: Oxford Univ. Press.

_____ (1968). Components of an evolving personological system. *International encyclopedia of the social sciences.* New York: Macmillan. Pp. 5–13.

Murray, J. P. (1980). *Television and youth.* Boys Town, Nebraska: Boys Town Center.

Murray, J. P., and S. Kippax (1979). From the early window to the late night show: international trends in the study of television's impact on children and adults. In L. Berkowitz (Ed.), *Advances in experimental social psychology.* Vol. 12. New York: Academic Press. Pp. 253-320.

Myrdal, G. (1944). *An American dilemma.* New York: Harper.

Naisbitt, J. (1982). *Megatrends: ten new directions transforming our lives.* New York: Warner.

Naples, M. J. (1979). *Effective frequency: the relation between frequency and advertising effectiveness.* New York: Association of National Advertisers.

Needham, R. (1973). *Belief, language and experience.* Chicago: Univ. of Chicago Press.

Nelson, C. E. (1968). Anchoring to accepted values as a technique for immunizing beliefs against persuasion. *J. Pers. soc. Psychol., 9,* 329-334.

Nemath, C., and J. Endicott (1976). The midpoint as anchor: another look at discrepancy of position and attitude change. *Sociometry, 39,* 11-18.

Newcomb, T. M. (1943). *Personality and social change.* New York: Dryden.

_____ (1953). An approach in the study of communicative acts. *Psychol. Rev., 60,* 393-404.

_____ (1961). *The acquaintance process.* New York: Holt, Rinehart, and Winston.

_____ (1981). Heiderian balance as a group phenomenon. *J. Pers. soc. Psychol., 40,* 862-867.

Newcombe, N., and D. B. Arnkoff (1979). Effects of speech style and sex of speaker on person perception. *J. Pers. soc. Psychol., 37,* 1293-1303.

Ng, S. H. (1980). *The social psychology of power.* London: Academic Press.

Nguyen, M. L., R. Heslin, and T. D. Nguyen (1976). The meaning of touch: sex and marital status difference. *Rep. Res. Psychol., 7,* 13-18.

Nie, N. H., S. Verba, and J. R. Petrocik (1979). *The changing American voter* (Enlarged ed.). Cambridge, Mass.: Harvard Univ. Press.

Niles, P. (1964). The relationship of susceptibility and anxiety to acceptance of fear-arousing communications. Ph.D. dissertation. Yale Univ., New Haven.

Nimmo, D., and J. Combs (1980). *Subliminal politics: myths and mythmakers in America.* Englewood Cliffs, N.J.: Prentice-Hall.

_____ (1983). *Mediated political realities.* New York: Longman.

Nimmo, D., and R. L. Savage (1976). *Candidates and their images: concepts, methods, and findings.* Glenview, Ill.: Scott, Foresman.

Nisbett, R. E., and A. Gordon (1967). Self-esteem and susceptibility to social influence. *J. Pers. soc. Psychol., 5,* 268-276.

Nisbet, R., and L. Ross (1980). *Human inference: strategies and shortcomings in social judgment.* Englewood Cliffs, N.J.: Prentice-Hall.

Nisbett, R. E., and T. D. Wilson (1977). Telling more than we can know: verbal report on mental processes. *Psychol. Rev., 84,* 231-259.

Noelle-Neumann, E. (1980a). *Die Schweigespirale: offentliche meinung—unsere soziale haut.* (Trans. 1984. *The spiral of silence: public opinion—our social skin.* Chicago: Univ. Chicago Press.) Munchen: R. Piper.

_____ (1980b). Mass media and social change in developed societies. In G. C. Wilholt, and H. deBock (Eds.), *Mass communication review yearbook.* Vol. 1. Beverly Hills, Calif.: Sage. Pp. 657-678.

Norman, R. (1975). Affective-cognitive consistency, attitudes, conformity and behavior. *J. Pers. soc. Psychol., 32,* 83-91.

Northcott, H., J. F. Seggar, and J. L. Hinton (1975). Trends in TV portrayal of blacks and women. *Journalism Quart., 52,* 741-744.

Norton, R. (1983). *Communicator style: theory, application and measures.* Beverly Hills, Calif.: Sage.

Novaco, R. W. (1977). Stress inoculation: a cognitive therapy for anger and its application to a case of depression. *J. Consult. clinic. Psychol., 45,* 600-608.

Nuttin, J. M., Jr. (1975). *The illusion of attitude change.* London: Academic Press.

O'Barr, W. (1982). *Language strategy in the courtroom.* New York: Academic Press.

Oberdorfer, D. (1971). *Tet! The turning point in the Vietnam war.* Garden City, N.Y.: Doubleday.

O'Flaherty, W. D. (1982). *Siva, the erotic ascetic.* New York: Oxford Univ. Press.

O'Gorman, H. (1979). White and black perceptions of racial values. *Publ. Opin. Quart., 43,* 48-59.

Oliver, R. T. (1971). *Communication and culture in ancient India and China.* Syracuse, N.Y.: Syracuse Univ. Press.

Olmsted, D. W., and D. L. Smith (1980). The socialization of youth into the American mental health belief system. *J. Health soc. Behav., 21,* 181-194.

Olson, J. C., and P. A. Dover (1979). Disconfirmation of consumer expectations through product trial. *J. appl. Psychol., 64,* 179-189.

O'Malley, M., and D. L. Thistlethwaite (1980). Inference in inconsistency reduction: new evidence on the "Socratic effect." *J. Pers. soc. Psychol., 39,* 1064-1071.

Ong, W. J. (1977). *Interfaces of the word: studies in the evolution of consciousness and culture.* Ithaca, N.Y.: Cornell Univ. Press.

_____ (1982). *Orality and literacy.* New York: Methuen.

O'Quin, K., and J. Aronoff (1981). Humor as a technique of social influence. *Soc. Psychol. Quart., 44,* 349-357.

Ortony, A. (1978). Remembering, understanding, and representation. *Cognit. Sci., 2,* 53-69.

Osgood, C. E. (1979). From yang and yin to *and* or *but* in cross-cultural perspective. *Int. J. Psychol., 14,* 1-35.

Osgood, C. E., G. J. Suci, and P. H. Tannenbaum (1957). *The measurement of meaning.* Urbana: Univ. of Illinois Press.

Osgood, C. E., and P. H. Tannenbaum (1955). The principle of congruity in the prediction of attitude change. *Psychol. Rev., 62,* 42-55.

Osman, L. M. (1982). Conformity or compliance? A study of sex differences in pedestrian behaviour. *Brit. J. soc. Psychol., 21,* 19-21.

Ostrom, T. M. (1969). The relationship between the affective, behavioral and cognitive components of attitude. *J. exp. soc. Psychol., 5,* 12–30.

_____ (1970). Perspective as a determinant of attitude change. *J. exp. soc. Psychol., 6,* 280–292.

Paige, K. E., and J. M. Paige (1981). *The politics of reproductive ritual.* Berkeley: Univ. of California Press.

Paisley, W. J. (1981). Public communication campaigns: the American experience. In R. E. Rice, and W. J. Paisley (Eds.), *Public communication campaigns.* Beverly Hills, Calif.: Sage. Pp. 15–40.

Pallak, M. S., D. A. Cook, and J. Sullivan (1981). Commitment and energy conservation. In L. Bickman (Ed.), *Applied social psychology annual 1.* Beverly Hills, Calif.: Sage. Pp. 235–253.

Paloutzian, R. F. (1981). Purpose in life and value changes following conversion. *J. Pers. soc. Psychol., 41,* 1153–1160.

Papageorgis, D. (1963). Bartlett effect and the persistence of induced opinion change. *J. abnorm. soc. Psychol., 67,* 61–67.

_____ (1967). Anticipation of exposure to persuasive message and belief change. *J. Pers. soc. Psychol., 5,* 490–496.

Papastamou, S. (1983). Strategies of minority and majority influence. In W. Doise and S. Moscovici (Eds.), *Current issues in European social psychology.* Vol. 1. Cambridge: Cambridge Univ. Press. Pp. 33–83.

Parke, R. D., L. Berkowitz, J. P. Leyens, S. G. West, and R. J. Sebastian (1977). Some effects of violent and nonviolent movies on the behavior of juvenile delinquents. In L. Berkowitz (Ed.), *Advances in experimental social psychology.* Vol. 10. New York: Academic Press. Pp. 135–172.

Patai, R. (1973). *The Arab mind.* New York: Scribners.

Patchen, M. (1982). *Black-white contact in schools: its social and academic effects.* West Lafayette, Ind.: Purdue Univ. Press.

Patrick, T., and T. Dulack (1976). *Let our children go.* New York: Dutton.

Patterson, C. J., and W. Mischel (1976). Effect of temptation-inhibiting and task-facilitating plans on self-control. *J. Pers. soc. Psychol., 33,* 209–217.

Patterson, M. L. (1983). Nonverbal behavior: a functional perspective. New York: Springer.

Patterson, S. C. (1982). Campaign spending in contests for governor. *Western Polit. Quart., 35,* 457–476.

Patterson, T. E. (1980). *The mass media: how Americans choose their president.* New York: Praeger.

Patterson, T. E., and R. D. McClure (1976). *Picture politics.* New York: Putnam.

Pattison, R. (1982). *On literacy: the politics of the word from Homer to the age of rock.* New York: Oxford Univ. Press.

Paulhus, D. (1983). Sphere-specific measures of perceived control. *J. Pers. soc. Psychol., 44,* 1253–1265.

Paulos, J. A. (1980). *Mathematics and humor.* Chicago: Univ. of Chicago Press.

Pavlos, A. J. (1982). *The cult experience.* Westport, Conn.: Greenwood.

Peak, H. (1955). Attitude and motivation. In M. R. Jones (Ed.), *Nebraska symposium on motivation.* Lincoln: Univ. of Nebraska Press. Pp. 149–188.

Pearce, W. B., and B. J. Brommel (1972). Vocalic communication in persuasion. *Quart. J. Speech, 58,* 298–306.

Pearl, D., L. Bouthilet, and J. Lazar, Eds. (1982). *Television and behavior: ten years of scientific progress and implications for the eighties.* Vol. 1.: *Summary report.* Vol. 2.: *Technical reviews.* Washington, D.C.: Government Printing Office.

Pennebaker, J. W. (1982). *The psychology of physical symptoms.* New York: Springer-Verlag.

Pepitone, A., and M. DiNubile (1976). Contrast effects in judgments of crime severity and the punishment of criminal violators. *J. Pers. soc. Psychol., 33,* 448–459.

Percy, L. (1982). Psycholinguistic guidelines for advertising copy. In A. A. Mitchell (Ed.), *Advances in consumer research.* Vol. 9. Ann Arbor, Mich.: Association for Consumer Research. Pp. 107–111.

Perelman, C. (1982). *The realm of rhetoric.* (W. Kluback, translator.) Notre Dame: Univ. of Notre Dame Press.

Perlmuter, L. C., and R. A. Monty, Eds. (1979). *Choice and perceived control.* Hillsdale, N.J.: Erlbaum.

Perry, D. G., and L. C. Perry (1975). Observational learning in children: effects of sex of model and subject's sex role behavior. *J. Pers. soc. Psychol., 31,* 1083–1088.

Peterson, P. E., D. B. Jeffrey, C. A. Bridgwater, and B. Dawson (1984). How pronutritional television programming affects children's dietary habits. *Develop. Psychology, 20,* 55–63.

Peterson, R. A. (1981). Measuring culture, leisure, and time use. *Annals Amer. Acad. polit. soc. Sci., 453,* 169–179.

Peterson, R. C., and L. L. Thurstone (1933). *The effect of motion pictures on the social attitudes of high school children.* Chicago: Univ. of Chicago Press.

Petryszak, N. (1977). The Frankfurt school's theory of manipulation. *J. Communic., 27 (3),* 32–40.

Pettigrew, T. F. (1982). Cognitive style and social behavior: a review of category width. In L. Wheeler (Ed.), *Review of personality and social psychology.* Vol. 3. Beverly Hills, Calif.: Sage. Pp. 199–223.

Petty, R. E., and T. C. Brock (1981). Thought disruption and persuasion: assessing the validity of attitude change experiments. In R. E. Petty, T. M. Ostrom, and T. C. Brock (Eds.), *Cognitive responses in persuasion.* Hillsdale, N.J.: Erlbaum. Pp. 55–79.

Petty, R. E., and J. T. Cacioppo (1977). Forewarning, cognitive responding, and resistance to persuasion. *J. Pers. soc. Psychol., 35,* 645–655.

_____ (1979a). Issue involvement can increase or decrease persuasion by enhancing message-relevant cognitive responses. *J. Pers. soc. Psychol., 37,* 1915–1926.

_____ (1979b). Effects of forewarning of persuasive intent and involvement on cognitive responses in persuasion. *Pers. soc. Psychol. Bull., 5,* 173–176.

_____ (1981). *Attitudes and persuasion: classic and contemporary approaches.* Dubuque, Iowa: W.C. Brown.

_____ (1984a). *Attitude change: central and peripheral routes to persuasion.* New York: Springer-Verlag.

_____ (1984b). The effect of involvement on responses to argument quantity and quality: central and peripheral routes to persuasion. *J. Pers. soc. Psychol., 46,* 69–81.

Petty, R. E., J. T. Cacioppo, and M. Heesacker (1981). Effects of rhetorical questions on persuasion: a cognitive response analysis. *J. Pers. soc. Psychol., 40,* 432–440.

Petty, R. E., J. T. Cacioppo, and D. Schumann (1983). Central and peripheral routes to advertising effectiveness: the moderating role of involvement. *J. Consumer Research, 10,* 135–146.

Petty, R. E., T. M. Ostrom, and T. C. Brock, Eds. (1981). *Cognitive responses in persuasion.* Hillsdale, N.J.: Erlbaum.

Petty, R. E., G. L. Wells, M. Heesacker, T. C. Brock, and J. T. Cacioppo (1983). The effects of recipient posture on persuasion: a cognitive response analysis. *Pers. soc. Psychol. Bull., 9,* 209–222.

Phares, E. J. (1976). *Locus of control in personality.* Morristown, N.J.: General Learning Press.

Phillips, D. P. (1982). The impact of fictional television stories on US adult fatalities: new evidence on the effect of the mass media on violence. *Amer. J. Sociol., 87,* 1340–1359.

_____ (1983). The impact of mass media violence on US homicides. *Amer. Sociol. Rev., 48,* 560–568.

Piaget, J. (1930). The child's conception of physical causality. London: Kegan, Paul.

_____ (1963). *La naissance de l'intelligence chez l'enfant.* Paris: Neuchatel, Delachaux & Niestle, 1936. (M. Cook, translator.) New York: International Universities Press.

Plott, C. R., and M. E. Levine (1978). A model of agenda influence on committee decisions. *Amer. Econ. Rev., 68,* 146–160.

Polsby, N. W. (1980). *Community power and political theory* (2nd rev. ed.). New Haven: Yale Univ. Press.

Pool, I. de Sola, Ed. (1977). *The social impact of the telephone.* Cambridge, Mass.: M.I.T. Press.

_____ (1983a). Tracking the flow of information. *Science, 221,* 609–613.

_____ (1983b). *Technologies of freedom.* Cambridge, Mass.: Harvard Univ. Press.

Pope, D. (1983). *The making of modern advertising.* New York: Basic Books.

Pope, M. L., and T. R. Keen (1982). *Personal construct psychology and education.* New York: Academic Press.

Popper, K. (1966). *The open society and its enemies* (5th rev. ed.). 2 Volumes. Princeton, N.J.: Princeton Univ. Press.

Powell, R. S., and R. G. Juhnke (1983). Statistical models of implicit personality theory: a comparison. *J. Pers. soc. Psychol., 44,* 911–922.

Powers, W. T. (1973). *Behavior: the control of perception.* Chicago: Aldine.

_____ (1978). Quantitative analysis of purposive systems: some spadework at the foundation of scientific psychology. *Psychol. Rev., 85,* 417–435.

Primeau, R. (1978). *The rhetoric of television.* New York: Longman.

Prioleau, L., M. Murdock, and N. Brody (1983). An analysis of psychotherapy versus placebo studies. *Behav. Brain Sci., 6,* 275–310.

Pryor, B., and T. Steinfatt (1978). The effects of initial belief level on inoculation theory and its proposed mechanism. *Hum. Communic. Res., 4,* 219–230.

Puckett, J., R. E. Petty, J. T. Cacioppo, and D. Fisher (1983). The relative impact of age and attractiveness stereotypes on persuasion. *J. Gerontology, 38,* 340–343.

Puska, P., J. Tuomilehto, J. Salonen, L. Neittaanmaki, J. Maki, J. Virtamo, A. Nissinen, K. Koskela, and T. Takalo (1979). Changes in coronary risk factors during a comprehensive five-year community programme to control cardiovascular diseases (North Karelia Project). *Brit. Med. J., 2,* No. 6198, 1177–1178.

Raden, D. (1977). Situational thresholds and attitude-behavior consistency. *Sociometry, 40,* 123–129.

Raj, S. P. (1982). The effects of advertising on high and low loyalty consumer segments. *J. Consumer Research, 9,* 77–89.

Rajecki, D. W. (1982). *Attitudes: themes and advances.* Sunderland, Mass.: Sinauer.

Raju, P. S., R. S. Bhagat, and J. N. Sheth (1975). Predictive validation and cross validation of the Fishbein, Rosenberg and Sheth models of attitudes. University of Illinois. (Mimeo)

Ramirez, A. (1977). Social influence and ethnicity of the communicator. *J. soc. Psychol., 102,* 209–213.

Rank, H. (1982). *The pitch.* Park Forest, Ill.: Counter-Propaganda Press.

Rapoport, R. B. (1979). What they don't know can hurt you. *Amer. J. polit. Sci., 23,* 805–815.

Ray, M. L. (1968). Biases in selection of messages designed to induce resistance to persuasion. *J. Pers. soc. Psychol., 9,* 335–339.

_____ (1973). Marketing communication and the hierarchy of effects. In P. Clarke (Ed.), *New models for communications research.* Beverly Hills, Calif.: Sage.

Ray, M. L., and P. Webb (1976). *Experimental research on the effects of TV clutter: dealing with a difficult media environment.* New York: American Association of Advertising Agencies.

Read, S. J. (1983). Once is enough: causal reasoning from a single instance. *J. Pers. soc. Psychol., 45,* 323–334.

Reardon, K. K. (1981). *Persuasion: theory and context.* Beverly Hills, Calif.: Sage.

Reder, L. M., and J. R. Anderson (1980). A comparison of texts and their summaries: memorial consequences. *J. verb. Learn. verb. Behav., 19,* 121–134.

Reeder, G. D., and M. B. Brewer (1979). A schematic model of dispositional attribution in interpersonal perception. *Psychol. Rev., 86,* 61–79.

Reibstein, D. J., C. H. Lovelock, and R. P. Dobson (1980). The direction of causality between perception, affect and behavior. *J. Consumer Research, 6,* 370–376.

Reinsch, N. L., Jr. (1974). Figurative language and source credibility: a preliminary investigation and reconceptualization. *Hum. Communic. Res., 1,* 75–80.

Reisman, D. (1980). Egocentrism: is the American character changing? *Encounter, 55* (2–3), 19–28.

Rejai, M., and K. Phillips (1979). *Leaders of revolution.* Beverly Hills, Calif.: Sage.

Restak, R. M. (1982). *The self-seekers.* New York: Doubleday.

Revlin, R., V. Leirer, H. Yopp, and R. Yopp (1980). The belief-bias effect in formal reasoning: the influence of knowledge on logic. *Memory and Cognition, 8,* 584–592.

Reyes, R. M., W. C. Thompson, and G. H. Bower (1980). Judgmental biases resulting from differing availabilities of arguments. *J. Pers. soc. Psychol., 39,* 2–12.

Reynolds, R. A., and M. Burgoon (1983). Belief processing, reasoning, and evidence. In R. N. Bostrom, *Communication Yearbook 7.* Beverly Hills, Calif.: Sage. Pp. 83–104.

Rice, R. E., and W. J. Paisley, Eds. (1981). *Public communication campaigns.* Beverly Hills, Calif.: Sage.

Ridgeway, C. L. (1981). Nonconformity, competence, and influence in groups: a test of two theories. *Amer. Sociol. Rev., 46,* 333–347.

Riefenstahl, L. (1934). *Triumph of will.* Motion picture.

Riess, M., R. J. Kalle, and J. T. Tedeschi (1981). Bogus pipeline attitude assessment, impression management, and misattribution in induced compliance setting. *J. soc. Psychol., 115,* 247–258.

Riggio, R. E., and H. S. Friedman (1983). Individual differences and cues to deception. *J. Pers. soc. Psychol., 45,* 899–915.

Riley, R. T., and T. F. Pettigrew (1976). Dramatic events and attitude change. *J. Pers. soc. Psychol., 34,* 1004–1015.

Riordan, C. (1978). Equal-status interracial contact: a review and revision of the concept. *Int. J. Intercultural Relat., 2,* 161–185.

Rivers, W. L. (1982). *The other government: power and the Washington media.* New York: Universe Books.

Roberts, D. F., and C. M. Bachen (1981). Mass communication effects. *Annual review of psychology.* Vol. 32. Palo Alto, Calif.: Annual Reviews. Pp. 307–356.

Robertson, L. S., A. B. Kelley, B. O'Neill, C. W. Wixom, R. S. Elswirth, and W. Haddon, Jr. (1974). A controlled study of the effect of television messages on safety belt use. *Amer. J. publ. Health, 64,* 1071–1081.

Robinson, A. L. (1982). Physicists try to find order in chaos. *Science, 218,* 554–556.

Robinson, J., and L. Z. McArthur (1982). Impact of salient vocal qualities on causal attribution for a speaker's behavior. *J. Pers. soc. Psychol., 43,* 236–247.

Robinson, J. E., and C. A. Insko (1969). Attributed belief similarity-dissimilarity versus race as determinants of prejudice: a further test of Rokeach's theory. *J. exp. Res. Pers., 4,* 72–77.

Robinson, J. P. (1972). Mass communication and information diffusion. In F. G. Kline, and P. J. Tichenor (Eds.), *Current perspectives in mass communication research.* Vol. 1. Beverly Hills, Calif.: Sage.

———— (1976). Interpersonal influence in election campaigns: two-step flow hypotheses. *Publ. Opin. Quart., 40,* 304–319.

———— (1979). Toward a post-industrious society. *Publ. Opin., 2,* No. 4, 41–46.

———— (1981). Television and leisure time: a new scenario. *J. Communic., 31,* No. 1, 120–130.

Robinson, J. P., and R. Meadow (1982). *Polls apart: a call for consistency in surveys of public opinion on world issues.* Cabin John, Md.: Seven Locks Press.

Robinson, W. P., Ed. (1981). *Communication in development.* London: Academic Press.

Rodgers, H. R., Jr., and C. S. Bullock, III (1972). *Law and social change: civil rights laws and their consequences.* New York: McGraw-Hill.

Rodin, J., and E. Langer (1977). Long-term effects of a control-relevant intervention with the institutionalized aged. *J. Pers. soc. Psychol., 35,* 897–902.

Roedder, D. L., B. Sternthal, and B. J. Calder (1983). Attitude-behavior consistency in children's responses to television advertising. *J. Marketng Research, 20,* 337–349.

Rogers, D. T. (1978). *The work ethic in industrial America, 1850–1920.* Chicago: Univ. of Chicago Press.

Rogers, E. M. (1982a). The empirical and the critical schools of communication research. In M. Burgoon (Ed.), *Communication yearbook 5.* New Brunswick, N.J.: Transaction. Pp. 125–144.

———— (1982b). *Diffusion of innovations* (3rd ed.). New York: Free Press.

Rogers, E. M., and F. F. Shoemaker (1971). Women's utilization of new birth control procedures. In E. M. Rogers, and F. F. Shoemaker, *Communication of innovations: a cross-cultural approach* (2nd ed.). New York: Free Press.

Rogers, R. D. (1979). Commentary on "The neglected variety drive." *J. Consumer Research, 6,* 88–91.

Rogers, R. W. (1983). Cognitive and physiological processes in fear appeals and attitude change: a revised theory of protection motivation. In J. Cacioppo, and R. Petty (Eds.), *Social psychophysiology.* New York: Guilford Press.

Rogers, R. W., C. W. Deckner, and C. R. Mewborn (1978). An expectancy-value theory approach to the long-term modification of smoking behavior. *J. clinic. Psychol., 34,* 562–566.

Rogers, R. W., and C. R. Mewborn (1976). Fear appeals and attitude change: effects of a threat's noxiousness, probability of occurrence, and efficacy of coping response. *J. Pers. soc. Psychol., 34,* 54–61.

Rogers, R. W., and D. L. Thistlethwaite (1969). An analysis of active and passive defenses in inducing resistance to persuasion. *J. Pers. soc. Psychol., 11,* 301–308.

Rokeach, M. (1956). Political and religious dogmatism: an alternative to the authoritarian personality. *Psychol. Monogr., 70,* 18 (Whole No. 425).

———— (1960). *The open and closed mind.* New York: Basic Books.

———— (1973). *The nature of human values.* New York: Free Press.

———— (1975). Long-term value change initiated by computer feedback. *J. Pers. soc. Psychol., 32,* 467–476.

———— (1979). Value theory and communication research. In D. Nimmo (Ed.), *Communication yearbook 3.* New Brunswick, N.J.: Transaction. Pp. 7–28.

Rokeach, M., and P. Kliejunas (1972). Behavior as a function of attitude-toward-object and attitude-toward-situation. *J. Pers. soc. Psychol., 22,* 194–201.

Roll, C. W., Jr., and A. H. Cantril (1972). *Polls: their use and misuse in politics.* New York: Basic Books.

Roloff, M. E. (1981). *Interpersonal communication: a social exchange approach.* Beverly Hills, Calif.: Sage.

Ronis, D. L., M. H. Baumgardner, M. R. Leppe, J. T. Cacioppo, and A. G. Greenwald (1977). In search of reliable persuasion effects: I. A computer-controlled procedure for studying persuasion. *J. Pers. soc. Psychol., 35,* 548–569.

Roper Organization. (1975). *Trends in public attitudes toward television and their mass media 1959–1974.* New York: Television Info Office.

_____ (1979). *Public perceptions of television and other mass media: a twenty-year review, 1959–1978.* New York: Roper.

Rosch, E. (1978). Principles of categorization. In E. Rosch and B. B. Lloyd (Eds.), *Cognition and categorization.* Hillsdale, N.J.: Erlbaum.

Rosen, N. A., and R. S. Wyer (1972). Some further evidence for the "socratic effect" using a subjective probability model of cognitive organization. *J. Pers. soc. Psychol., 24,* 420–425.

Rosen, S. P. (1982). Vietnam and the American theory of limited war. *Int. Security, 7 (2),* 83–113.

Rosenbaum, Max, Ed. (1982). *Compliant behavior.* Vol. 1. *Etiology and phenomenology.* Vol. 2. *Beyond obedience to authority.* New York: Human Sciences Press.

Rosenbaum, M. E., and D. E. Franc (1960). Opinion change as a function of external commitment and amount of discrepancy from the opinion of another. *J. abnorm. soc. Psychol., 61,* 15–20.

Rosenberg, M. J. (1956). Cognitive structure and attitudinal effect. *J. abnorm. soc. Psychol., 53,* 367–372.

_____ (1960a). Cognitive reorganization in response to the hypnotic reversal of attitudinal affect. *J. Pers., 28,* 39–63.

_____ (1960b). An analysis of affective-cognitive consistency. In M. J. Rosenberg (Ed.), *Attitude organization and change.* New Haven: Yale Univ. Press.

Rosenberg, Morris (1979). *Conceiving the self.* New York: Basic Books.

Rosenberg, S. (1977). New approaches to the analysis of personal constructs in person perception. In J. K. Cole, and A. W. Landfield (Eds.), *Nebraska symposium on motivation, 1976, 24.* Lincoln: Univ. of Nebraska Press. Pp. 179–242.

Rosenfeld, H. M. (1972). The experimental analysis of interpersonal influence processes. *J. Communic., 22,* 424–442.

Rosenthal, R., Ed. (1979). *Skill in nonverbal communication: individual differences.* Cambridge, Mass.: Oelgeschlager, Gunn & Hain.

_____ (1983). Meta-analyses: toward a more cumulative social science. *Appl. soc. Psychol. Ann., 4,* 65–93.

Rosenthal, R., and B. M. DePaulo (1979). Sex differences in eavesdropping on nonverbal cues. *J. Pers. soc. Psychol., 37,* 273–285.

Rosenthal, R., J. A. Hall, M. R. DiMatteo, P. L. Rogers, and D. Archer (1979). *Sensitivity to nonverbal communication: the PONS test.* Baltimore: Johns Hopkins.

Ross, L. (1977). The intuitive psychologist and his shortcomings: distortions in the attribution process. In L. Berkowitz (Ed.), *Advances in experimental social psychology.* Vol. 10. New York: Academic Press. Pp. 173–220.

Ross, M., C. McFarland, M. Conway, and M. P. Zanna (1983). Reciprocal relations between attitudes and behavior recall: committing people to newly formed attitudes. *J. Pers. soc. Psychol., 45,* 257–267.

Rossi, P. H., and S. L. Nock (1982). *Measuring social judgments: the factorial survey approach.* Beverly Hills, Calif.: Sage.

Rossiter, J. R., and L. Percy (1983). Visual communication in advertising. In R. J. Harris (Ed.), *Information processing research in advertising.* Hillsdale, N.J.: Erlbaum.

Rossiter, J. R., and T. S. Robertson (1980). Children's dispositions toward proprietary drugs and the role of television drug advertising. *Publ. Opin. Quart., 44,* 316–329.

Rossman, B. B., and H. F. Gollob (1976). Social inference and pleasantness judgments involving people and issues. *J. exp. soc. Psychol., 12,* 374–391.

Rothschild, M. L., and M. L. Ray (1974). Involvement and political advertising effect: an exploratory experiment. *Communic. Res., 1,* 264–285.

Rotter, J. B. (1982). *The development and applications of social learning theory: selected papers.* New York: Praeger.

Rushton, J. P. (1975). Generosity in children: immediate and long-term effects of modeling, preaching, and moral judgment. *J. Pers. soc. Psychol., 31,* 459–466.

Rushton, J. P., and R. M. Sorrentino, Eds. (1981). *Altruism and helping behavior: social, personality, and developmental perspectives.* Hillsdale, N.J.: Erlbaum.

Russell, G. W. (1983). Psychological issues in sports aggression. In J. H. Goldstein (Ed.), *Sports violence.* New York: Springer-Verlag. Pp. 157–181.

Russell, J. A., and D. Ridgeway (1983). Dimensions underlying children's emotional concepts. *Develop. Psychol., 19,* 795–804.

Russell, R. L., and W. B. Stiles (1979). Categories for classifying language in psychotherapy. *Psychol. Bull., 86,* 404–419.

Russo, J. E. (1974). More information is better: a reevaluation of Jaccoby, Speller, and Kohn. *J. Consumer Research, 1,* No. 3, 68–72.

Rüstow, A. (1980). *Freedom and domination: a historical critique of civilization.* (Abridged by Dandwart A. Rustow.) Princeton, N.J.: Princeton Univ. Press.

Rutter, M., B. Maughan, P. Mortimore, and J. Ouston (1979). *Fifteen thousand hours: secondary schools and their effects on children.* Somerset, England: Open Books.

Ryan, W. (1971). *Blaming the victim.* New York: Pantheon.

Ryback, D., and R. H. Connell (1978). Differential racial patterns of school discipline during the broadcasting of "Roots." *Psychol. Reports, 42,* 514–518.

Sabato, L. J. (1981). *The rise of political consultants: new ways of winning elections.* New York: Basic Books.

Sackett, D. L., and R. B. Haynes, Eds. (1976). *Compliance with therapeutic regimens.* Baltimore: Johns Hopkins.

Sagan, K. (1977). *Dragons of Eden: speculations on the evolution of human intelligence.* New York: Random House.

Salancik, G. R., and M. Conway (1975). Attitude inferences from salient and relevant cognitive content about behavior. *J. Pers. soc. Psychol., 32,* 829–840.

Salomon, G. (1981). *Communication and education: social and psychological interactions.* Beverly Hills, Calif.: Sage.

Saltzer, E. B. (1980). Social determinants of successful weight loss: an analysis of behavioral intentions and actual behavior. *Basic appl. soc. Psychol., 1,* 329–342.

——— (1981). Cognitive moderators of the relationship between behavioral intention and behavior. *J. Pers. soc. Psychol., 41,* 260–271.

Saltzstein, H. D., and L. Sandberg (1979). Indirect social influence: change in judgmental process or anticipatory change. *J. exp. soc. Psychol., 15,* 209–216.

Sample, J., and R. Warland (1973). Attitude and prediction of behavior. *Social Forces, 51,* 292–304.

Sampson, E. E., and C. A. Insko (1964). Cognitive consistency and conformity in the autokinetic situation. *J. Pers. soc. Psychol., 68,* 184–192.

Sandell, R. G. (1977). *Linguistic style and persuasion.* London: Academic Press.

Sanders, G. S., and F. S. Malkis (1982). Type A behavior, need for control, and reactions to group participation. *Organizat. Behav. hum. Perform., 30,* 71–86.

Santee, R. T., and S. E. Jackson (1982). Identity implications of conformity: sex differences in normative and attributional judgments. *Soc. Psychol. Quart., 45,* 121–125.

Santee, R. T., and C. Maslach (1982). To agree or not to agree: personal dissent amid social pressure to conform. *J. Pers. soc. Psychol., 42,* 690–700.

Sarbin, T. R., and W. Coe (1972). *Hypnosis: a social psychological analysis of influence communication.* New York: Holt, Rinehart, and Winston.

Saunders, P. T. (1980). *An introduction to catastrophe theory.* New York: Cambridge Univ. Press.

Saussure, F. de. (1959). *Cours de linguistique generale.* Originally published, Paris, 1916. [*Course in general linguistics.*] (Translator W. Baskin.) New York: Philosophical Library.

Savage, L. J. (1954). *The foundations of statistics.* New York: Wiley.

Savage, R. L. (1981). The diffusion of information approach. In D. D. Nimmo and L. R. Sanders (Eds.), *Handbook of political communication.* Beverly Hills, Calif.: Sage. Pp. 101–119.

Sawyer, A. G. (1973). The effects of repetition of refutational and supportive advertising appeals. *J. Marketng Res., 10,* 23–33.

——— (1974). The effect of repetition: conclusions and suggestions about laboratory research. In G. D. Hughes, and M. L. Ray (Eds.), *Buyer/consumer information processing.* Chapel Hill: Univ. of North Carolina Press. Pp. 190–219.

——— (1981). Repetition, cognitive responses, and persuasion. In R. E. Petty, T. M. Ostrom, and T. C. Brock (Eds.), *Cognitive responses in persuasion.* Hillsdale, N.J.: Erlbaum. Pp. 237–261.

Scammon, D. L. (1977). "Information overload" and consumers. *J. Consumer Research, 4,* 148–155.

Schacter, D. L. (1982). *Stranger behind the engram: theories of memory and the psychology of science.* Hillsdale, N.J.: Erlbaum.

Schaefer, C. E., and K. J. O'Connor (1983). *Handbook of play therapy.* New York: Wiley.

Schaffner, P. E., A. Wandersman, and D. Stang (1981). Candidate name exposure and voting: two field studies. *Basic appl. soc. Psychol., 2,* 195–203.

Schanie, C. F., and M. Sundel (1978). A community mental health innovation in mass media preventative education: the alternatives project. *Amer. J. Community Psychol., 6,* 573–581.

Schank, R. C. (1975). *Conceptual information processing.* Amsterdam: Elsevier North-Holland.

Schank, R. C., and R. P. Abelson (1977). *Scripts, plans, goals, and understanding.* New York: Wiley (Erlbaum).

Scheff, T. J. (1980). *Catharsis in healing, ritual, and drama.* Berkeley: Univ. of California.

Schegel, R. P., and D. DiTecco (1982). Attitudinal structures and the attitude-behavior relation. In M. P. Zanna, E. T. Higgins, and C. P. Herman (Eds.), *Consistency in social behavior: the Ontario symposium.* Vol. 2. Hillsdale, N.J.: Erlbaum.

Schellenberger, B. (1975). *Katholische Jugend und Dritten Reich.* Maintz: Matthias Grunewald Verlay.

Scherer, K. R., and P. Ekman, Eds. (1982a). *Handbook of methods in nonverbal behavior research.* New York: Cambridge Univ. Press.

——— (1982b). Methodological issues in studying nonverbal behavior. In K. R. Scherer, and P. Ekman (Eds.), *Handbook of methods in nonverbal behavior research.* New York: Cambridge Univ. Press.

Schiller, D. (1982). *Telematics and government.* Norwood, N.J.: Ablex.

Schlenker, B. R. (1975). Liking for a group following an initiation: impression management or dissonance reduction? *Sociometry, 38,* 99–118.

——— (1982). Translating actions with attitudes: an identity analytic approach to the explanation of social conduct. In L. Berkowitz (Ed.), *Advances in experimental social psychology.* Vol. 15. New York: Academic Press. Pp. 193–247.

Schlenker, B. R., and H. J. Goldman (1982). Attitude change as a self-presentation tactic following attitude-consistent behavior: effects of choice and role. *Soc. Psychol. Quart., 45,* 92–99.

Schlinger, M. J. R., L. F. Alwitt, K. E. McCarthy, and L. Green (1983). Effects of time compression on attitudes and information processing. *J. Marketing, 47* (1), 79–85.

Schmeling, D. G., and C. E. Wotring (1980). Making anti-drug abuse advertising work. *J. Advertising Res., 20* (3), 33–37.

Schmid, A. P., and J. deGraaf (1982). *Violence as communication: insurgent terrorism and the Western news media.* Beverly Hills, Calif.: Sage.

Schneider, D. J. (1973). Implicit personality theory: a review. *Psychol. Bull., 79,* 294–309.

Schneider, D. J., A. H. Hastorf, and P. C. Ellsworth (1979). *Person perception* (2nd ed.). Reading, Mass.: Addison-Wesley.

Scholem, G. (1973). *Sabbatai Sevi: the mystical messiah.* Princeton, N.J.: Princeton Univ. Press.

Schönbach, P. (1981). *Education and intergroup attitudes.* London: Academic Press.

Schul, Y., and E. Burnstein (1983). The informational basis of social judgments: memory for informative and uninformative arguments. *J. exp. soc. Psychol., 19,* 422–433.

Schultz, D. P. (1963). Primacy-recency with a sensory variation framework. *Psychol. Record, 13,* 129–139.

Schumacker, R. E. (1981). Differences in comprehension are important in studies of conformity, influence and persuasion. *Psychol. Reports, 48,* 583–586.

Schuman, H., and M. P. Johnson (1976). Attitudes and behavior. *Ann. Rev. Sociol., 2,* 161–207.

Schuman, H., G. Kalton, and J. Ludwig (1983). Context and contiguity in survey questionnaires. *Publ. Opin. Quart., 47,* 112–115.

Schuman, H., and S. Presser (1981a). *Questions and answers in attitude surveys: experiments on question form wording and context.* New York: Academic Press.

———— (1981b). The attitude-action connection and the issue of gun control. *Annals Amer. Acad. polit. soc. Sci., 455,* 40–47.

Schütz, A. (1967). *The phenomenology of the social world.* Evanston, Ill.: Northwestern Univ. Press.

Schwartz, B., A. Tesser, and E. Powell (1982). Dominance cues in nonverbal behavior. *Soc. Psychol. Quart., 45,* 114–120.

Schwartz, S. H. (1973). Normative explanations of helping behavior: a critique, proposal and empirical test. *J. exp. soc. Psychol., 9,* 349–364.

———— (1977). Normative influences on altruism. In L. Berkowitz (Ed.), *Advances in experimental social psychology.* Vol. 10. New York: Academic Press. Pp. 221–279.

———— (1978). Temporal instability as a moderator of the attitude-behavior relationship. *J. Pers. soc. Psychol., 36,* 715–724.

Schwarzwald, J., A. Bizman, and M. Raz (1983). The foot-in-door paradigm: effects of second request size on donation probability and donor generosity. *Pers. soc. Psychol. Bull., 9,* 443–450.

Scott, J. P., and J. J. Fuller (1965). *Genetics and social behavior of the dog.* Chicago: Univ. of Chicago Press.

Scott, W. A., D. W. Osgood, and C. Peterson (1979). *Cognitive structure: theory and measurement of individual differences.* New York: Halsted Press.

Scribner, S., and M. Cole (1981). *The psychology of literacy.* Cambridge, Mass.: Harvard Univ. Press.

Sears, D. O. (1975). Political socialization. In F. I. Greenstein and N. W. Polsby (Eds.), *Handbook of political science.* Vol. 2. Reading, Mass.: Addison-Wesley. Pp. 96–136.

———— (1983a). The person-positivity bias. *J. Pers. soc. Psychol., 44,* 233–250.

———— (1983b). The persistence of early political predispositions: the role of attitude object and life stage. *Rev. Pers. soc. Psychol., 4,* 79–116.

Sears, D. O., and S. H. Chaffee (1979). Uses and effects of the 1976 debates: an overview of empirical studies. In S. Kraus (Ed.), *The great debates: Carter vs. Ford, 1976.* Bloomington: Indiana Univ. Press. Pp. 223–261.

Sears, D. O., R. Lau, T. Tyler, and H. M. Allen, Jr. (1980). Self-interest versus symbolic politics in policy attitudes and presidential voting. *Amer. Polit. Sci. Rev., 74,* 670–684.

Sears, R. R. (1963). Dependency motivation. In M. R. Jones (Ed.), *Nebraska symposium on motivation.* Lincoln: Univ. of Nebraska Press. Pp. 25–64.

Sechrest, L., and J. Belew (1983). Nonreactive measures of social attitudes. *Appl. soc. Psychol. Ann., 4,* 23–63.

Seligman, C., M. Bush, and K. Kirsch (1976). Relationship between compliance in the foot-in-the-door paradigm and size of first request. *J. Pers. soc. Psychol., 33,* 517–520.

Seligman, M. E. P., and G. Garber, Eds. (1982). *Human helplessness.* New York: Academic Press.

Semin, G. R., and S. R. Manstead (1983). *The accountability of conduct: a social psychological analysis.* New York: Academic Press.

Seward, R. R. (1978). *The American family: a demographic history.* Beverly Hills, Calif.: Sage.

Seymour-Ure, C. (1974). *The political impact of mass media.* Beverly Hills, Calif.: Sage.

Shaffer, D. R. (1975). Some effects of consonant and dissonant attitudinal advocacy on initial attitude salience and attitude change. *J. Pers. soc. Psychol., 32,* 160–168.

Shaffer, D. R., R. Reardon, E. G. Clary, and C. Sidowski (1982). The effects of information on perspectives and attitude change. *J. soc. Psychol., 117,* 125–133.

Shalvey, T. (1979). *Claude Lévi-Strauss: social psychotherapy and the collective unconscious.* Amherst: Univ. of Massachusetts Press.

Shanteau, J. (1975). Averaging versus multiplying combination rules of inference judgment. *Acta Psychologica, 39,* 83–89.

Sharits, D., and H. B. Lammers (1983). Perceived attributes of models in prime-time and daytime television commercials: a person perception approach. *J. Marketing Res., 20,* 64–73.

Shaw, M. L., Ed. (1981). *Recent advances in personal construct technology.* New York: Academic Press.

Sherif, M. (1935). A study of some social factors in perception. *Arch. Psychol.,* New York, No. 187.

———— (1936). *The psychology of social norms.* New York: Harper & Row.

Sherif, M., and C. I. Hovland (1961). *Social judgment: assimilation and contrast effects in communication and attitude change.* New Haven: Yale Univ. Press.

Sherif, M., C. W. Sherif, and R. E. Nebergall (1965). *Attitude and attitude change.* Philadelphia: Saunders.

Sherman, S. J., K. S. Zehner, J. Johnson, and E. R. Hirt (1983). Social explanation: the role of timing, set and recall on subjective likelihood estimates. *J. Pers. soc. Psychol., 44,* 1127–1143.

Sherrid, S. D., and R. P. Beech (1976). Self-dissatisfaction as a determinant of change in police values. *J. appl. Psychol., 61,* 273–278.

Sheth, J. N. (1974). A field study of attitude-structure and attitude-behavior relationship. In J. N. Sheth (Ed.), *Models for buyer behavior: conceptual, quantitative and empirical.* New York: Harper & Row.

Shiffrin, R. M., and W. Schneider (1977). Controlled and automatic human information processing: II. Perceptual learning, automatic attending, and a general theory. *Psychol. Rev., 84,* 127–190.

Shimanoff, S. B. (1980). *Communication rules: theory and research.* Beverly Hills, Calif.: Sage.

Shingi, P. M., and B. Mody (1976). The communication effects gap: a field experiment on television and agricultural ignorance in India. *Communic. Res., 34.*

Shirai, S. (1974). What follows after failure of persuasion. *Jap. J. exp. soc. Psychol., 14,* 95–104.

Shorter, E. (1975). *The making of the modern family.* New York: Basic Books.

Shupe, A. D., and D. G. Bromley (1980). *The new vigilantes: deprogrammers, anti-cultists and the new religions.* Beverly Hills, Calif.: Sage.

Sidanius, J., B. Ekehammar, and J. Lukowsky (1983). Political interest, political information search, and socio-political theory: a tale of three theories. *Reports from the Department of Psychology*. University of Stockholm, No. 598.

Siegal, M. (1982). *Fairness in children: a social-cognitive approach to the study of moral development*. London: Academic Press.

Sigall, H., and R. Helmreich (1969). Opinion change as a function of stress and communicator credibility. *J. exp. soc. Psychol., 5,* 70–78.

Sigall, H., R. Page, and A. C. Brown (1971). Effort expenditures as a function of evaluation and evaluator attractiveness. *Rep. Res. soc. Psychol., 2,* 19–25.

Signorielli, N., and G. Gerbner (1977). *The image of the elderly in prime-time network television drama*. Report #12. Philadelphia: Annenberg School of Communications.

Signorielli, N., L. Gross, and M. Morgan (1982). Violence in television programs: ten years later. In D. Pearl, L. Bouthilet, and J. Lazar (Eds.), *Television and behavior: ten years of scientific progress and implications for the eighties*. Vol. 2. *Technical Reviews*. Washington, D.C.: U.S. Government Printing Office.

Silk, L., and M. Silk (1980). *The American establishment*. New York: Basic Books.

Silverman, I. (1964). Differential effects of ego threat upon persuasibility for high and low self-esteem subject. *J. abnorm. soc. Psychol., 69,* 567–572.

———— (1971). On the resolution and tolerance of cognitive inconsistency in a natural-occurring event: attitudes and beliefs following the Senator Edward M. Kennedy incident. *J. Pers. soc. Psychol., 17,* 171–178.

Simon, H. (1982). ADPULS: an advertising model with wearout and pulsation. *J. Marketing Res., 19,* 352–363.

Simon, J. L. (1969). New evidence for no effect of scale in advertising. *J. Advertising Res., 9,* No. 1, 38–41.

Simons, H. W., N. N. Berkowitz, and R. J. Moyer (1970). Similarity, credibility and attitude change: a review and a theory. *Psychol. Bull., 73,* 1–16.

Simonton, D. K. (1980). Intuition and analysis: a predictive and explanatory model. *Genetic Psychol. Mongr., 102,* 3–60.

Simpson, D. D., and T. M. Ostrom (1976). Contrast effects in impression formation. *J. Pers. soc. Psychol., 34,* 625–629.

Singer, B. D. (1982). *Social functions of the telephone*. Palo Alto, Calif.: R & E Research Associates.

Singer, J. L. (1980). The power and limitations of television: a cognitive affective analysis. In P. H. Tannenbaum (Ed.), *The entertainment functions of television*. Hillsdale, N.J.: Erlbaum.

Singer, J. L., and D. Singer (1981). *Television, imagination and aggression: a study of preschoolers*. Hillsdale, N.J.: Erlbaum.

Singer, R. P. (1965). The effects of fear-arousing communication on attitude change and behavior. Ph.D. dissertation, Univ. of Connecticut, Storrs.

Singh, I., Ed. (1983). *Telecommunications in the year 2000: national and international perspectives*. Norwood, N.J.: Ablex.

Sistrunk, F., and J. W. McDavid (1971). Sex variables in conforming behavior. *J. Pers. soc. Psychol., 17,* 200–207.

Sivacek, J., and W. D. Crano (1982). Vested interest as a moderator of attitude-behavior consistency. *J. Pers. soc. Psychol., 43,* 210–221.

Sjöberg, L. (1978, Oct.). Beliefs and values as attitude components. *International symposium on social psychophysics*. Mannheim.

Slack, J. D. (1983). *Communication technologies and society: conception of causality and the politics of technical intervention*. Norwood, N.J.: Ablex.

Sloan, L. R., R. E. Love, and T. M. Ostrom (1974). Political heckling: who really loses. *J. Pers. soc. Psychol., 30,* 518–525.

Slovic, P., B. Fischoff, and S. Lichtenstein (1978). Accident probabilities and seat belt usage: a psychological perspective. *Accident Analysis and Prevention, 10,* 281.

Smiley, S. S., D. D. Oakley, D. Worthen, J. C. Campione, and A. L. Brown (1977). Recall of thematically relevant material by adolescent good and poor readers as a function of written vs. oral presentation. *J. educat. Psychol., 69,* 381–387.

Smith, M. B. (1949). Personal values as determinants of a political attitude. *J. Psychol., 28,* 477–486.

Smith, M. B., J. S. Bruner, and R. W. White (1956). *Opinions and personality*. New York: Wiley.

Smith, M. J. (1982). *Persuasion and human action: a review and critique of social influence theories*. Belmont, Calif.: Wadsworth Publishing.

Smith, M. L., G. V. Glass, and T. L. Miller (1980). *The benefits of psychotherapy*. Baltimore: Johns Hopkins.

Smith, P. B. (1976). Social influence processes and the outcome of sensitivity training. *J. Pers. soc. Psychol., 34,* 1087–1094.

———— (1983). Social influence processes in groups. In J. Nicholson, and B. Foss (Eds.), *Psychology survey 4*. Herts: British Psychological Society.

Smith, R. E., and W. R. Swinyard (1983). Attitude-behavior consistency: the impact of product trial versus advertising. *J. Marketng Res., 20,* 257–267.

Smith, S. S., and B. D. Jamieson (1972). Effects of attitude and ego-involvement on the learning and retention of controversial material. *J. Pers. soc. Psychol., 22,* 303–310.

Smithson, M., P. R. Amato, and P. Pearce (1982). *Dimensions of helping behavior*. Oxford: Pergamon.

Smythe, D. W. (1981). *Dependency road: communications, capitalism, consciousness and Canada*. Norwood, N.J.: Ablex.

Snow, R. P. (1983). *Creating media culture*. Beverly Hills, Calif.: Sage.

Snyder, C. R., and H. L. Fromkin (1980). *Uniqueness: the human pursuit of difference*. New York: Plenum.

Snyder, M. (1979). Self-monitoring processes. In L. Berkowitz (Ed.), *Advances in experimental social psychology*. Vol. 12. New York: Academic Press. Pp. 85–128.

———— (1982). When believing means doing: creating links between attitudes and behavior. In M. P. Zanna, E. T. Higgins, and C. P. Herman (Eds.), *Consistency in social behavior. The Ontario symposium*. Vol. 2. Hillsdale, N.J.: Erlbaum.

Snyder, M., and M. R. Cunningham (1975). To comply or not to comply: testing the self-perception explanation of the "foot-in-the-door" phenomenon. *J. Pers. soc. Psychol., 31,* 64–67.

Snyder, M., and D. Kendzierski (1982). Acting on one's attitudes: procedures for linking attitudes and actions. *J. exp. soc. Psychol., 18,* 165–183.

Snyder, M., and W. B. Swann (1976). When actions reflect attitudes: the politics of impression management. *J. Pers. soc. Psychol., 34,* 1034–1042.

Sobel, M. C. (1981). *Lifestyle and social structure: concepts, definitions, analyses.* New York: Academic Press.

Sohn, D. (1980). Critique of Cooper's meta-analytic assessment of the findings on sex differences in conformity behavior. *J. Pers. soc. Psychol., 39,* 1215–1221.

Solomon, D. S. (1982). Health campaigns. In D. Pearl, L. Bouthilet, and J. Lazar (Eds.), *Television and behavior: ten years of scientific progress and implications for the eighties.* Vol. 2. *Technical Reviews.* Washington, D.C.: Government Printing Office.

———— (In press). *Message design: a manual on formative evaluation.* Norwood, N.J.: Ablex.

Solomon, R. L. (1980). The opponent-process theory of acquired motivation: the costs of pleasure and the benefits of pain. *Amer. Psychol., 35,* 691–712.

Sommerville, C. J. (1983). The distinction between indoctrination and education in England, 1549–1719. *J. Hist. Ideas, 44,* 387–406.

Songer-Nocks, E. (1976a). Situational factors affecting the weighting of predictor components in the Fishbein model. *J. exp. soc. Psychol., 12,* 56–69.

———— (1976b). Reply to Fishbein and Ajzen. *J. exp. soc. Psychol., 12,* 585–590.

Sontag, S. (1978). *Illness as metaphor.* New York: Farrar, Straus & Giroux.

Sorokin, P. A., Ed. (1950). *Explorations in altruistic love and behavior.* Boston: Beacon Press.

Spector, P. E. (1983). Locus of control and social influence susceptibility: are externals normative or informational conformers? *J. Psychol., 115,* 199–201.

Sponberg, H. (1946). A study of the relative effectiveness of climax and anti-climax order in an argumentative speech. *Speech Monogr., 13,* 35–44.

Sprafkin, J., C. Swift, and R. Hess, Eds. (1983). *Rx Television: enhancing the preventive impact of TV.* New York: Hawthorne.

Staats, A. W. (1975). *Social behaviorism.* Homewood, Ill.: Dorsey.

———— (1983a). *Psychology's crisis of disunity: philosophy and method for the revolution to a unified science.* New York: Praeger.

———— (1983b). Paradigmatic behaviorism: unified theory for social-personality psychology. In L. Berkowitz (Ed.), *Advances in experimental social psychology.* Vol. 16. New York: Academic Press. Pp. 125–179.

Stanley, S. M. (1981). *The new evolutionary timetable: fossils, genes, and the origin of the species.* New York: Basic Books.

Staub, E. (1979). *Positive social behavior and morality.* Vol. 2. New York: Academic Press.

Steele, C. M. (1975). Name-calling and compliance. *J. Pers. soc. Psychol., 31,* 363–369.

Steele, C. M., and T. M. Ostrom (1974). Perspective-mediated attitude change: when is indirect persuasion more effective than direct persuasion? *J. Pers. soc. Psychol., 29,* 737–741.

Stein, D. D., J. A. Hardyck, and M. B. Smith (1965). Race and belief: an open and shut case. *J. Pers. soc. Psychol., 1,* 281–289.

Steiner, I. D. (1980). Attribution of choice. In M. Fishbein (Ed.), *Progress in social psychology.* Vol. 1. Hillsdale, N.J.: Erlbaum.

Steiner, I. D., and H. H. Johnson (1964). Relationships among dissonance reducing responses. *J. abnorm. soc. Psychol., 68,* 38–44.

Steiner, I. D., and E. D. Rogers (1963). Alternative responses to dissonance. *J. abnorm. soc. Psychol., 66,* 128–136.

Stephenson, W. (1967). *The play theory of mass communication.* Chicago: Univ. of Chicago Press.

Sternberg, R. J., and M. E. Turner (1981). Components of syllogistic reasoning. *Acta Psychologica, 47,* 245–265.

Sternglanz, S. H., and L. A. Serbin (1974). Sex role stereotyping in children's television programs. *Develop. Psychol., 10,* 710–715.

Sternthal, B., and C. S. Craig (1973). Humor in advertising. *J. Marketing, 37,* No. 4, 12–18.

Sternthal, B., L. W. Phillips, and R. Dholakia (1978). The persuasive effect of source credibility: a situational analysis. *Publ. Opin. Quart., 42,* 285–314.

Stevens, S. S. (1975). *Psychophysics: introduction to its perceptual, neutral and social prospects.* New York: Wiley.

Stevens, J. D., and H. D. Garcia (1980). *Communication history.* Beverly Hills, Calif.: Sage.

Stevenson-Hinde, J., and C. M. Parkes, Eds. (1982). *The place of attachment in human behavior.* New York: Basic Books.

Stewart, A. J., Ed. (1982). *Motivation and society: a volume in honor of David C. McClelland.* San Francisco: Jossey-Bass.

Stewart, I. N., and P. L. Peregoy (1983). Catastrophe theory modeling in psychology. *Psychol. Bull., 94,* 336–362.

Stoneman, Z., and G. H. Brody (1981). Peers as mediators of television food advertisements aimed at children. *Develop. Psychol., 17,* 853–858.

Stotland, E., D. Katz, and M. Patchen (1959). The reduction of prejudice through the arousal of self-insight. *J. Pers., 27,* 507–531.

Stouffer, S. A., Ed. (1950). *Studies in social psychology in World War II.* Vol. 4: *Measurement and prediction.* Princeton, N.J.: Princeton Univ. Press.

Streufert, S., and S. C. Streufert (1978). *Behavior in the complex environment.* New York: Halsted.

Stroebe, W., and M. Diehl (1981). Conformity and counterattitudinal behavior: the effect of social support on attitude change. *J. Pers. soc. Psychol., 41,* 876–889.

Stroebe, W., and W. Meyer, Eds. (1982). Social psychology and economics. *Brit. J. soc. Psychol., 21.* Part 2, 79–183 (whole issue).

Strong, E. C. (1974). The use of field experimental observations in estimating advertising recall. *J. Marketing Res., 11,* 369–378.

Stukát, K. G. (1958). *Suggestibility: a factorial and experimental analysis.* Uppsala: Appelbergs Boktryckeri Ab.

Sudman, S., and N. M. Bradburn (1982). *Asking questions: a practical guide to questionnaire design.* San Francisco: Jossey-Bass.

Suedfeld, P., and R. A. Borrie (1978). Sensory deprivation, attitude change and defense against persuasion. *Canad. J. Behav. Sci., 10,* 16–27.

Suedfeld, P., and A. D. Rank (1976). Revolutionary leaders: long-term success as a function of changes in cognitive complexity. *J. Pers. soc. Psychol., 34,* 169–178.

Suls, J. M., and R. L. Miller, Eds. (1977). *Social comparison processes: theoretical and empirical perspectives.* New York: Wiley/Halsted.

Sumner, W. G. (1906). *Folkways.* Boston: Ginn.

Swann, W. B., Jr., and T. S. Pittman (1975). Salience of initial ratings and attitude change in the "forbidden toy" paradigm. *Pers. soc. Psychol. Bull., 1,* 493–496.

Swann, W. B., Jr., and S. J. Read (1981). Acquiring self-knowledge: the search for feedback that fits. *J. Pers. soc. Psychol., 41,* 1119–1128.

Swanson, D. L. (1979). Political communication research and the uses and gratifications model: a critique. *Communic. Res., 6,* 37–53.

Sweeney, P. D., and K. L. Gruber (1984). Selective exposure: voter information preferences and the Watergate affair. *J. Pers. soc. Psychol., 46,* 1208–1221.

Szalai, A., Ed. (1972). *The use of time.* The Hague: Mouton.

Szybillo, G. J., and R. Heslin (1973). Resistance to persuasion: inoculation theory in a marketing context. *J. Marketing Res., 10,* 369–403.

Tajfel, H. (1979). *Differentiation between social groups.* London: Academic Press.

―――― (1981). *Human groups and social categories: studies in social psychology.* Cambridge: Cambridge Univ. Press.

Tanaka, Y. (1978). A behavioral approach to public acceptance of nuclear energy in Japan. *Gakushuin Review of Law and Politics, 13,* 53–93.

Tanford, S., and S. Penrod (1984). Social influence model: a formal integration of research on majority and minority influence processes. *Psychol. Bull., 95,* 189–225.

Tannenbaum, P. H. (1956). Initial attitude toward source and concept as factors in attitude change through communication. *Publ. Opin. Quart., 20,* 413–425.

―――― (1967). The congruity principle revisited: studies in the reduction, induction and generalization of persuasion. In L. Berkowitz (Ed.), *Advances in experimental social psychology.* Vol. 3. New York: Academic Press. Pp. 271–320.

―――― (1980). Entertainment as vicarious emotional experience. In P. H. Tannenbaum (Ed.), *The entertainment functions of television.* Hillsdale, N.J.: Erlbaum.

Tannenbaum, P. H., and L. J. Kostrich (1983). *Turned-on television and turned-off voters: policy options for election projections.* Beverly Hills, Calif.: Sage.

Tannenbaum, P. H., and E. L. Norris (1965). Effect of combining congruity principles strategies for the reduction of persuasion. *Sociometry, 28,* 145–157.

Tannebaum, P. H., and D. Zillmann (1975). Emotional arousal in the facilitation of aggression through communication. In L. Berkowitz (Ed.), *Advances in experimental social psychology.* Vol. 8. New York: Academic Press. Pp. 149–192.

Tart, C. T. (1970). Increases in hypnotizibility resulting from a prolonged program for enhancing personal growth. *J. abnorm. Psychol., 75,* 260–266.

Taylor, D. G. (1982). Pluralistic ignorance and the spiral of silence: a formal analysis. *Publ. Opin. Quart., 46,* 311–335.

Taylor, J. (1980). Dimensionalizations of racialism and the black experience: the Pittsburgh project. In R. L. Jones (Ed.), *Black psychology* (2nd ed.). New York: Harper & Row. Pp. 384–397.

Taylor, P. M. (1981). *The projection of Britain: British overseas publicity and propaganda, 1919–1939.* New York: Cambridge Univ. Press.

Taylor, S. E. (1975). On inferring one's attitudes from one's behavior: some delimiting conditions. *J. Pers. soc. Psychol., 31,* 126–131.

Taylor, S. E., and J. Crocker (1981). Schematic bases of social information processing. In E. T. Higgins, C. P. Herman, and M. P. Zanna (Eds.), *Social cognition: the Ontario symposium.* Vol. 1. Hillsdale, N.J: Erlbaum. Pp. 89–134.

Taylor, S. E., and D. R. Mettee (1971). When similarity breeds contempt. *J. Pers. soc. Psychol., 20,* 75–81.

Taylor, S. E., and S. C. Thompson (1982). Stalking the elusive "vividness" effect. *Psychol. Rev., 89,* 155–181.

Taylor, W. (1972). *Tudor figures of rhetoric.* Whitewater, Wisconsin: Language Press.

Tedeschi, J. T., Ed. (1981). *Impression management theory and social psychological research.* New York: Academic Press.

Television Audience Assessment (1983). *Methodology report.* Boston: Television Audience Assessment.

Tesser, A. (1978). Self-generated attitude change. In L. Berkowitz (Ed.), *Advances in experimental social psychology.* Vol. 11. New York: Academic Press. Pp. 289–338.

Tesser, A., J. Campbell, and S. Mickler (1983). The role of social pressure, attention to the stimulus, and self-doubt in conformity. *Europ. J. soc. Psychol., 13,* 217–233.

Tetlock, P. E. (1981). Pre- to postelection shifts in presidential rhetoric: impression management or cognitive adjustment? *J. Pers. soc. Psychol., 41,* 207–212.

―――― (1983a). Accountability and complexity of thought. *J. Pers. soc. Psychol., 45,* 74–83.

―――― (1983b). Accountability and the perseverance of first impressions. *Soc. Psychol. Quart., 46,* 285–292.

Thelen, M. H., and K. D. Kirkland (1976). On status and being imitated: effects on reciprocal imitation and attraction. *J. Per. soc. Psychol., 33,* 691–697.

Thelen, M. H., J. Oatley, D. J. Miller, and K. Grace (1984). Being imitated: conditions under which positive reactions do not occur. *J. Genetic Psychol., 144,* 83–88.

Thistlethwaite, D. L., and J. Kamenetzky (1955). Attitude change through refutation and elaboration of audience counterarguments. *J. abnorm. soc. Psychol., 51,* 3–9.

Thomas, K., and M. Tuck (1975). An exploratory study of determinant and indicant beliefs in attitude measurement. *Europ. J. soc. Psychol., 5,* 167–187.

Thomas, M. H., and R. S. Drabman (1975). Toleration of real life aggression as a function of exposure to televised violence and age of subject. *Merrill-Palmer Quart., 21,* 227–232.

Thomas, M. H., R. W. Horton, E. C. Lippincott, and R. S. Drabman (1977). Desensitization to portrayals of real-life aggression as a function of exposure to television violence. *J. Pers. soc. Psychol., 35,* 450–458.

Thomas, W. I., and F. Znaniecki (1918). *The Polish peasant in Europe and America.* Chicago: Univ. of Chicago Press.

Thomason, B. C. (1982). *Making sense of reification: Alfred Schütz and constructionist theory.* Atlantic Highlands, N.J.: Humanities Press.

Thompson, O. (1977). *Mass persuasion in history.* Edinburgh: Paul Harris.

Thorelli, H., H. Becker, and J. Engledow (1975). *The information seekers.* Cambridge, Mass.: Ballinger.

Thurstone, L. L., and E. J. Chave (1929). *The measurement of attitude.* Chicago: Univ. of Chicago Press.

Tiger, L., and R. Fox (1971). *Imperial animal.* New York: Holt, Rinehart, and Winston.

Toda, M. (1981). *Man, robot and society: models and speculations.* Hingham, Mass.: Kluwer-Nijhoff.

Toi, M., and C. D. Batson (1982). More evidence that empathy is a source of altruistic motivation. *J. Pers. soc. Psychol., 43,* 281–292.

Tolman, E. C. (1932). *Purposive behavior in animals and man.* New York: Century.

Tomkins, S. (1979). Script theory: differential magnification of affects. In H. E. Howe, Jr. (Ed.), *Nebraska symposium on motivation, 1978.* Vol. 26. Lincoln: Univ. of Nebraska Press. Pp. 201–236.

——— (1981). The quest for primary motives: biography and autobiography of an idea. *J. Pers. soc. Psychol., 41,* 306–329.

Torney, J. V., A. N. Oppenheim, and R. F. Farnen (1975). *Civic education in ten countries: an empirical study.* New York: Wiley-Halsted.

Tracey, M. (1977). *The production of political television.* London: Routledge & Kegan Paul.

Transgaard, H. (1973). *The cognitive components of attitudes and beliefs: structure and empirical methods.* Kobenhavn: Teknisk Forlag.

Traugott, M. W., and J. P. Katosh (1981). Interviews may stimulate voting. *Institute for social research newsletter.* Ann Arbor: Univ. of Michigan, ISR, p. 3.

Trexler, R. C. (1980). *Public life in renaissance Florence.* New York: Academic Press.

Triandis, H. C. (1961). A note on Rokeach's theory of prejudice. *J. abnorm. soc. Psychol., 62,* 184–186.

——— (1977). *Interpersonal behavior.* Monterey, Calif.: Brooks/Cole.

——— (1980). Values, attitudes and interpersonal behavior. In H. E. Howe, Jr. (Ed.), *Nebraska symposium on motivation, 1979.* Vol. 27. Lincoln: Univ. Nebraska Press. 195–259.

Triandis, H. C., E. E. Davis, and S. I. Takezawa (1965). Some determinants of social distance among American, German and Japanese students. *J. Pers. soc. Psychol., 2,* 540–551.

Tuchman, S., and T. E. Coffin (1971).The influence of election night television broadcasts in a close election. *Publ. Opin. Quart., 35,* 315–326.

Tukey, J. W. (1977). *Exploratory data analysis.* Reading, Mass.: Addison-Wesley.

Turner, C. F., and E. Krauss (1978). Fallible indicators of the subjective state of the nation. *Amer. Psychol., 33,* 456–470.

Turner, J. C., and H. Giles, Eds. (1981). *Intergroup behavior.* Chicago: Univ. of Chicago Press.

Turner, R. G. (1977). Self-consciousness and anticipatory belief change. *Pers. soc. Psychol. Bull., 3,* 438–441.

Turner, V., Ed. (1982). *Celebration: studies in festivity and ritual.* Washington, D.C.: Smithsonian Institute.

Tversky, A. (1972). Elimination by aspects: a theory of choice. *Psychol. Rev., 79,* 281–299.

Tversky, A., and D. Kahneman (1974). Judgment under uncertainty: heuristics and biases. *Science, 185,* 1124–1131.

——— (1980). Causal schemas in judgments under uncertainty. In M. Fishbein (Ed.), *Progress in social psychology, 1.* Hillsdale, N.J.: Erlbaum. Pp. 49–72.

——— (1981). The framing of decisions and the psychology of choice. *Science, 211,* 453–458.

Tyler, T. R. (1980). Impact of directly and indirectly experienced events: the origin of crime-related judgments and behaviors. *J. Pers. soc. Psychol., 39,* 13–28.

Tyler, T. R. (1984). Assessing the risk of crime victimization: the integration of personal victimization experience and socially transmitted information. *J. soc. Issues, 40,* 27–38.

Ullman, C. (1982). Cognitive and emotional antecedents of religious conversion. *J. Pers. soc. Psychol., 43,* 183–192.

Upmeyer, A. (1981). Perceptual and judgmental processes in social contexts. In L. Berkowitz (Ed.), *Advances in experimental social psychology.* Vol. 14. New York: Academic Press. Pp. 257–308.

Upshaw, H. S. (1969). The personal reference scale: an approach to social judgment. In L. Berkowitz (Ed.), *Advances in experimental social psychology.* Vol. 4. New York: Academic Press. Pp. 315–371.

Vanbeselaere, N. (1983). Mere exposure: a search for an explanation. In W. Doise and S. Moscovici (Eds.), *Current issues in European social psychology.* Vol. 1. Cambridge: Cambridge Univ. Press. Pp. 239–278.

van Dijk, T. A. (1983). Discourse analysis: its development and application to the structure of news. *J. Communic., 33* (2), 20–43.

van Vuuren, D. P. (1981). *The impact of television on adolescents in South Africa.* Pretoria: Human Sciences Research Council.

Vedung, E. (1982). *Political reasoning.* Beverly Hills, Calif.: Sage.

Vélez-Ibañez, C. G. (1983). *Rituals of marginality: politics, process, and culture change in central urban Mexico, 1969–1974.* Berkeley: Univ. of California Press.

Verhaeghe, H. (1976). Mistreating other persons through simple discrepant role playing: dissonance arousal or response contagion. *J. Pers. soc. Psychol., 34,* 125–137.

Veroff, J. (1982). Assertive motivations: achievement versus power. In A. J. Stewart (Ed.), *Motivation and society.* San Francisco: Jossey-Bass.

Veroff, J., E. Douvan, and R. A. Kulka (1981). *The inner American: a self-portrait from 1957 to 1976.* New York: Basic Books.

Veroff, J., and J. B. Veroff (1980). *Social incentives: a life-span developmental approach.* New York: Academic Press.

Vincent, J. (1978). Political anthropology: manipulative strategies. In B. J. Siegel, A. R. Beals, and S. H. Tyler (Eds.), *Annual review of anthropology, 7.* Palo Alto, Calif.: Annual Reviews. Pp. 175–194.

Viney, L. L. (1983). *Images of illness.* Melbourne, Fla.: Krieger.

Volpe, M. (1977). The persuasive forces of humor: Cicero's defense of Caelius. *Quart. J. Speech, 63,* 311–323.

Von Cranach, M., U. Kalbermatten, K. Indermuhle, and B. Gugler (1982). *Goal-directed action.* London: Academic Press. Translated from German edition, 1980.

Von Neumann, J. (1958). *The computer and the brain.* New Haven: Yale Univ. Press.

Wachtel, P. L., Ed. (1982). *Resistance: problematic patient behavior in psychodynamic and behavioral therapies.* New York: Plenum.

Wade, N. (1981). Dinosaur battle erupts in British Museum. *Science, 211,* 35–36.

Wagatsuma, E., and C. L. Kleinke (1979). Ratings of facial beauty by Asian-American and Caucasian females. *J. soc. Psychol., 109,* 299–300.

Wagner, D. A. (In press). *The social and cultural origins of memory.* Elmsford, N.Y.: Pergamon Press.

Wagstaff, G. (1981). *Hypnosis, compliance and belief.* New York: St. Martin's Press.

Waid, W. M., and M. T. Orne (1981). Cognitive, social, and personality processes in the physiological detection of deception. In L. Berkowitz (Ed.), *Advances in experimental social psychology.* Vol. 14. New York: Academic Press.

Walker, N., and M. Argyle (1964). Does the law affect moral judgments? *Brit. J. Criminology, 4,* 570–581.

Wallach, M. A., and L. Wallach (1983). *Psychology's sanction for selfishness: the error of egotism in theory and therapy.* San Francisco: Freeman.

Walster, E., E. Aronson, and D. Abrahams (1966). On increasing the persuasiveness of a low-prestige communicator. *J. exp. soc. Psychol., 2,* 325–342.

Walster, E., and L. Festinger (1962). The effectiveness of "overhead" persuasive communications. *J. abnorm. soc. Psychol., 65,* 395–402.

Ward, C. D., and E. McGinnies (1974). Persuasive effects of early and late mention of credible and non-credible sources. *J. Psychol., 86,* 17–23.

Ward, S., D. Wackman, and E. Wartella (1977). *How children learn to buy: the development of consumer information processing skills.* Beverly Hills, Calif.: Sage.

Warner, K. E. (1977). The effects of the anti-smoking campaign on cigarette consumption. *Amer. J. Public Health, 67,* 645–650.

Warren, D. I. (1976). *The radical center: middle Americans and the politics of alienation.* Notre Dame, Ind.: Univ. of Notre Dame Press.

Washburn, M. F. (1916). *Movement and mental imagery.* Boston: Houghton Mifflin.

Wasserman, I. M. (1983). Political business cycles, presidential elections, and suicide and mortality patterns. *Amer. Sociol. Rev., 48,* 711–720.

Watkins, M. J., and Z. F. Peynrciğlu (1984). Determining perceived meaning during impression formation: another look at the meaning change hypothesis. *J. Pers. soc. Psychol., 46,* 1005–1016.

Watson, J. B. (1925). *Behaviorism.* New York: Norton.

Watts, W. A. (1967). Relative persistence of opinion change induced by active compared to passive participation. *J. Pers. soc. Psychol., 5,* 4–15.

Watts, W. A., and L. E. Holt (1970). Logical relationships among beliefs and timing as factors in persuasion. *J. Pers. soc. Psychol., 16,* 571–582.

———— (1979). Persistence of opinion change induced under conditions of forewarning and distraction. *J. Pers. soc. Psychol., 37,* 778–789.

Watts, W. A., and W. M. McGuire (1964). Persistence of induced opinion change and retention of inducing message content. *J. abnorm. soc. Psychol., 68,* 233–241.

Webb, E. J., D. T. Campbell, R. D. Schwartz, and L. Sechrest (1966). *Unobtrusive measures: nonreactive research in the social sciences.* Chicago: Rand McNally.

Weber, Max (1930). *The Protestant ethic and the spirit of capitalism.* Original German edition, 1903. New York: Scribners.

Weber, R., and J. Crocker (1983). Cognitive processes in the revision of stereotypic beliefs. *J. Pers. soc. Psychol., 45,* 961–977.

Weber, S. J. (1972). Opinion change as a function of associative learning of content and source factors. Unpublished doctoral dissertation, Northwestern Univ., Evanston, Ill.

Wegener, B., Ed. (1982). *Social attitudes and psychophysical measurement.* Hillsdale, N.J.: Erlbaum.

Weigel, R. H., and R. Jessor (1973). Television and adolescent conventionality: an exploratory study. *Publ. Opin. Quart., 37,* 76–90.

Weimann, G. (1982a). Dealing with bureaucracy: the effectiveness of different persuasive appeals. *Soc. Psychol. Quart., 45,* 136–144.

———— (1982b). On the importance of marginality: one more step into the two step flow of communication. *Amer. Sociol. Rev., 47,* 764–773.

———— (1983). The theater of terror: effects of press coverage. *J. Communic., 33,* (1), 38–45.

Weinstein, A. G. (1972). Predicting behavior from attitudes. *Publ. Opin. Quart., 36,* 355–360.

Weinstein, B. (1982). *The civic tongue: political consequences of language choices.* New York: Longman.

Weinstein, E. A., and P. Deutschberger (1963). Some dimensions of altercasting. *Sociometry, 26,* 454–466.

Weinstein, F., and C. M. Platt (1969). *The wish to be free: society, psyche and value change.* Berkeley: Univ. of California Press.

Weir, A. J. (1983). Notes for a prehistory of cognitive balance theory. *Brit. J. soc. Psychol., 22,* 351–362.

Weisfeld, G. E., and J. M. Beresford (1982). Erectness of posture as a mediator of dominance or success in humans. *Motivation and Emotion, 6,* 113–131.

Weiss, R. F. (1963). Defection from social movements and subsequent recruitment to new movements. *Sociometry, 26,* 1–20.

_____ (1968). An extension of Hullian learning theory to persuasive communication. In A. G. Greenwald, T. C. Brock, and T. M. Ostrom (Eds.), *Psychological foundations of attitudes*. New York: Academic Press. Pp. 109–145.

Weiss, W. (1953). A sleeper effect in opinion change. *J. abnorm. soc. Psychol., 48,* 173–180.

Weiss, W., and B. J. Fine (1956). The effect of induced aggressiveness on opinion change. *J. abnorm. soc. Psychol., 52,* 109–114.

Weissmann, R. F. E. (1981). *Ritual brotherhood in renaissance Florence*. New York: Academic Press.

Weitzman, L. J., D. Eifler, E. Hokada, and C. Ross (1972). Sex-role socialization in picture books for preschool children. *Amer. J. Sociol., 77,* 1125–1150.

Wells, G. L., and R. E. Petty (1980). The effects of overt head movements on persuasion: compatibility and incompatibility of responses. *Basic appl. soc. Psychol., 1,* 219–230.

Wellins, R., and E. McGinnies (1977). Counterarguing and selective exposure to persuasion. *J. soc. Psychol., 103,* 115–127.

Westin, A. (1982). *Newswatch: how TV decides the news.* New York: Simon and Schuster.

Wetzel, C. G., and C. A. Insko (1982). The similarity-atttraction relationship: is there an ideal one? *J. exp. soc. Psychol., 18,* 253–276.

Wheeless, L. R., R. Barraclough, and R. Stewart (1983). Compliance-gaining and power in persuasion. In R. N. Bostrom (Ed.), *Communication yearbook 7.* Beverly Hills, Calif.: Sage. Pp. 105–145.

Wheeless, L. R., and J. Grotz (1977). The measurement of trust and its relationship to self-disclosure. *Hum. Communic. Res., 3,* 250–257.

White, C. J. (1982). *Consistency in cognitive social behavior: an introduction to social psychology.* Boston: Routledge & Kegan Paul.

White, G. M. (1975). Contextual determinants of opinion judgments: field experimental probes of judgmental relativity boundary conditions. *J. Pers. soc. Psychol., 32,* 1047–1054.

White, R. K. (1971). Propaganda: morally questionable and morally unquestionable techniques. *Annals Amer. Acad. politic. soc. Sci., 398,* 26–35.

Wicker, A. W. (1969). Attitudes versus actions: the relationship of verbal and overt behavioral responses to attitude objects. *J. soc. Issues, 25,* No. 4, 41–78.

Wicklein, J. (1981). *Electronic nightmare: the new communications and freedom.* New York: Viking.

Wicklund, R. A., and J. W. Brehm (1976). *Perspectives on cognitive dissonance.* Hillsdale, N.J.: Erlbaum.

Wicklund, R. A., and D. Frey (1981). Cognitive consistency: motivational versus nonmotivational perspectives. In J. P. Forgas (Ed.), *Social cognition.* London: Academic Press. Pp. 141–163.

Wilder, A. N. (1964). *Early Christian rhetoric: the language of the Gospel.* Cambridge, Mass.: Harvard Univ. Press.

Wilkening, F., and N. H. Anderson (1982). Comparison of two-rule assessment methodologies for studying cognitive development and knowledge structure. *Psychol. Bull., 92,* 215–237.

Williams, E. (1975). Medium or message: communications medium as a determinant of interpersonal evaluation. *Sociometry, 38,* 119–130.

_____ (1977). Experimental comparisons of face-to-face and mediated communication: a review. *Psychol. Bull., 84,* 963–976.

Williams, F. (1982). *The communications revolution* (Rev. ed.). New York: Mentor.

Williams, J. E., and D. L. Best (1982). *Measuring sex stereotypes: a thirty-nation study.* Beverly Hills, Calif.: Sage.

Williams, R. L. (1980). *The horror of life.* Chicago: Univ. of Chicago Press.

Willis, R. H. (1960). Stimulus pooling and social perception. *J. abnorm. soc. Psychol., 60,* 365–373.

Willis, R. H., and E. P. Hollander (1964). An experimental study of three response modes in social influence situations. *J. abnorm. soc. Psychol., 69,* 150–156.

Wills, T. A. (1981). Downward comparison principles in social psychology. *Psychol. Bull., 90,* 245–271.

_____ (1982). *Basic processes in helping relationships.* New York: Academic Press.

Wilson, E. O. (1975). *Sociology: the new synthesis.* Cambridge, Mass.: Harvard Univ. Press.

_____ (1978). *On human nature.* Cambridge, Mass.: Harvard Univ. Press.

Wilson, W. R. (1979). Feeling more that we can know: exposure effects without learning. *J. Pers. soc. Psychol., 37,* 811–821.

Wilson, W., and H. Miller (1968). Repetition, order of presentation and timing of arguments and measures as determinants of opinion change. *J. Pers. soc. Psychol., 9,* 184–188.

Wiltshire, B. (1982). *Role playing and identity: the limits of theatre as metaphor.* Bloomington: Indiana Univ. Press.

Winner, E. (1982). *Invented worlds: the psychology of the arts.* Cambridge, Mass.: Harvard Univ. Press.

Winnick, R. H., and J. A. Taylor (1977). Racial preference—36 years later. *J. soc. Psychol., 102,* 157–158.

Winter, D. G. (1973). *The power motive.* New York: Free Press.

Winter, J. P., and C. H. Eyal (1981). Agenda setting for the civil rights issue. *Publ. Opin. Quart., 45,* 376–383.

Wirt, F. M. (1970). *Politics of southern equality: law and social change in a Mississippi county.* Chicago: Aldine.

Wittenbraker, J., B. L. Gibbs, and L. R. Kahle (1983). Seat belt attitudes, habits, and behaviors: an adaptive amendment to the Fishbein model. *J. appl. soc. Psychol., 13,* 406–421.

Wittig, M. A., and A. C. Peterson, Eds. (1979). *Sex-related differences in cognitive functioning.* New York: Academic Press.

Wober, M., and B. Gunter (1982). Television and personal threat: fact or artifact? A British survey. *Brit. J. soc. Psychol., 21,* 239–247.

Woelfel, J., M. J. Cody, J. Gillham, and R. A. Holmes (1980). Basic premises of multidimensional attitude change theory: an experimental analysis. *Hum. Communic. Res., 6,* 153–167.

Woelfel, J., and E. L. Fink (1980). *The measurement of communication processes: Galileo theory and method.* New York: Academic Press.

Wold, A. H. (1977). *Decoding oral languages.* London: Academic Press.

Wolf, S., and B. Latané (1983). Majority and minority influence on restaurant preferences. *J. Pers. soc. Psychol., 45,* 282–292.

Wood, W. (1982). Retrieval of attitude-relevant information from memory: effects on susceptibility to persuasion and on intrinsic motivation. *J. Pers. soc. Psychol., 42,* 798–810.

Wood, W., and A. H. Eagly (1981). Stages in the analysis of persuasive messages: the role of causal attributions and message comprehension. *J. Pers. soc. Psychol., 40,* 246–259.

Woodall, W. G., and J. K. Burgoon (1981). The effects of nonverbal synchrony on message comprehension and persuasiveness. *J. nonverbal Behav., 5,* 207–223.

Woodmansee, J. J., and S. W. Cook (1967). Dimensions of verbal and racial attitudes: their identification and measurement. *J. Pers. soc. Psychol., 7,* 240–250.

Woodruff, A. D., and F. J. DiVesta (1948). The relationship between values, concepts and attitudes. *Educ. psychol. Measmt., 8,* 645–659.

Woodworth, R. S., and S. B. Sells (1935). An atmosphere effect in formal syllogistic reasoning. *J. exp. Psychol., 18,* 451–460.

Worchel, S., V. A. Andreoli, and J. Easton (1975). Is the medium the message: a study of the effects of media, communicator and message characteristics on attitude change. *J. appl. soc. Psychol., 5,* 157–172.

Wright, A. F. (1979). Chinese civilization. In H. D. Lasswell, D. Lerner, and H. Speier (Eds.), *Propaganda and communication in world history.* Vol. 1. *The symbolic instrument in early times.* Honolulu: Univ. of Hawaii Press. Pp. 220–259.

Wright, P. L. (1974). Analyzing media effects on advertising responses. *Publ. Opin. Quart., 38,* 192–205.

_____ (1975). Factors affecting cognitive resistance to advertising. *J. Consumer Res., 2,* 1–9.

Wright, P. (1980). Message-evoked thoughts: persuasion research using thought verbalizations. *J. Consumer Research, 7,* 151–175.

Wright, P., and P. D. Rip (1981). Retrospective reports on the causes of decisions. *J. Pers. soc. Psychol., 40,* 601–614.

Wright, S. (1980). Genetic and organismal selection. *Evaluation, 34,* 825–843.

Wyer, R. S., Jr. (1974a). *Cognitive organization and change: an information-processing approach.* New York: Wiley/Erlbaum.

_____ (1974b). Some implications of the "socratic effect" for alternative models of cognitive consistency. *J. Pers., 42,* 399–419.

_____ (1975). The role of probabilistic and syllogistic reasoning in cognitive organization and social inference. In M. F. Kaplan, and S. Schwartz (Eds.), *Human judgment and decision processes.* New York: Academic Press.

Wyer, R. S., Jr., and D. E. Carlston (1979). *Social cognition, inference, and attribution.* Hillsdale, N.J.: Erlbaum.

Wyer, R. S., Jr., and D. Frey (1983). The effects of feedback about self and others on the recall and judgments of feedback-relevant information. *J. exp. soc. Psychol., 19,* 540–559.

Wyer, R. S., Jr., and L. Goldberg (1970). A probabilistic analysis of the relationships between beliefs and attitudes. *Psychol. Rev., 77,* 100–120.

Wyer, R. S., Jr., and J. Hartwick (1984). The recall and use of belief statements as bases for judgments: some determinants and implications. *J. exp. soc. Psychol., 20,* 65–85.

Wyer, R. S., Jr., and T. K. Srull (1981). Category accessibility: some theoretical and empirical issues concerning the processing of social stimulus information. In E. T. Higgins, C. A. Herman, and M. P. Zanna (Eds.), *Social cognition: the Ontario symposium.* Vol. 1. Hillsdale, N.J.: Erlbaum.

_____ Eds. (1984). *Handbook of social cognition.* Hillsdale, N.J.: Erlbaum.

Wylie, R. C. (1974, 1979). *The self-concept.* Vols. 1 and 2. Lincoln: Univ. of Nebraska Press.

Yabrudi, P. F., and L. N. Diab (1978). The effects of attitude similarity-dissimilarity, religion, and topic importance on interpersonal attraction among Lebanese university students. *J. soc. Psychol., 106,* 167–171.

Yaffé, M., and E. Nelson (1982). *The influence of pornography on behavior.* New York: Academic Press.

Yalch, R. F. (1976). Interview effects on voter turnout. *Publ. Opin. Quart., 40,* 331–336.

Yamagishi, T., and C. T. Hill (1983). Initial impression versus missing information as explanations of the set size effect. *J. Pers. soc. Psychol., 44,* 942–951.

Yankelovich, D. (1981). *New rules: searching for self-fulfillment in a world turned upside down.* New York: Random House.

Zablocki, B. (1980). *Alienation and charisma: a study of contemporary American communes.* New York: Free Press.

Zajonc, R. B. (1960). The process of cognitive tuning in communication. *J. abnorm. soc. Psychol., 61,* 159–167.

_____ (1965). Social facilitation. *Science, 149,* 269–274.

_____ (1980a). Feeling and thinking: preferences need no inferences. *Amer. Psychol., 35,* 151–175.

_____ (1980b). Compresence. In P. B. Paulus (Ed.), *Psychology of group influence.* Hillsdale, N.J.: Erlbaum. Pp. 35–60.

_____ (1984). On the primacy of affect. *Amer. Psychologist, 39,* 117–123.

Zajonc, R. B., P. Shaver, C. Tavris, and D. Van Kreveld (1972). Exposure, satiation, and stimulus discriminability. *J. Pers. soc. Psychol., 21,* 270–280.

Zanna, M. P., and R. H. Fazio (1983). The attitude-behavior relation: moving toward a third generation of research. In M. P. Zanna, E. T. Higgins, and C. P. Herman (Eds.), *Consistency in social behavior: the Ontario symposium.* Vol. 2. Hillsdale, N.J.: Erlbaum.

Zanna, M. P., E. T. Higgins, and C. P. Herman, Eds. (1983). *Consistency in social behavior: the Ontario symposium.* Hillsdale, N.J.: Erlbaum.

Zanna, M. P., E. C. Klosson, and J. M. Darley (1976). How television news viewers deal with facts that contradict their beliefs: a consistency and attribution analysis. *J. appl. soc. Psychol., 6,* 159–176.

Zanna, M. P., M. R. Lepper, and R. B. Abelson (1973). Attentional mechanisms in children's devaluation of a forbidden activity in a forced-compliance situation. *J. Pers. soc. Psychol., 28,* 355–359.

Zanna, M. P., and J. M. Olson (1983). Individual differences in attitudinal relations. In M. P. Zanna, E. T. Higgins, and C. P. Herman (Eds.), *Consistency in social behavior: the Ontario symposium.* Vol. 2. Hillsdale, N.J.: Erlbaum.

Zellner, M. (1970). Self-esteem, reception, and influenceability. *J. Pers. soc. Psychol., 15,* 87–93.

Zentall, S. S., and T. R. Zentall (1983). Optimal stimulation: a model of disordered activity and performance in normal and deviant children. *Psychol. Bull., 94,* 446–471.

Zern, D. S. (1983). The relationship of certain group-oriented and individualistically oriented child-rearing dimensions to cultural complexity in a cross-cultural sample. *Genetic Psychol. Monogr., 108,* 3–20.

Ziemke, D. A. (1980). Selective exposure in a presidential campaign contingent on certainty and salience. In D. D. Nimmo (Ed.), *Communication yearbook 4.* New Brunswick, N.J.: Transaction. Pp. 497–510.

Zillmann, D. (1982). Television viewing and arousal. In D. Pearl, L. Bouthilet, and J. Lazar (Eds.), *Television and behavior: ten years of scientific progress and implications for the eighties.* Vol. 2. *Technical Reviews.* Washington, D.C.: U.S. Government Printing Office. Pp. 53–67.

Zillmann, D., and J. Bryant (1982). Pornography, sexual callousness and the trivialization of rape. *J. Communic., 32* (4), 10–21.

Zillmann, D., and J. R. Cantor (1974). Rhetorical elicitation of concession in persuasion. *J. soc. Psychol., 94,* 223–236.

Zillmann, D., B. R. Williams, J. Bryant, K. R. Boynton, and M. A. Wolf (1980). Acquisition of information from educational television programs as a function of differentially paced humorous inserts. *Educ. Psychol., 72,* 170–181.

Zimbardo, P. G. (1965). The effect of effort and improvisation on self-persuasion produced by role-playing. *J. exp. soc. Psychol., 1,* 103–120.

Zimbardo, P. G., M. Weisenberg, I. Firestone, and B. Levy (1965). Communicator effectiveness in producing public conformity and private attitude change. *J. Pers., 33,* 233–255.

Zohar, D., A. Cohen, and N. Azar. (1980). Promoting increased use of ear protectors in noise through information feedback. *Hum. Factors, 22,* 69–79.

Zucker, R. A., J. Aronoff, and A. I. Rabin, Eds. (1984). *Personality and the prediction of behavior.* New York: Academic Press.

Zuckerman, M. (1979). *Sensation seeking: beyond the optimal level of arousal.* Hillsdale, N.J.: Erlbaum.

———— Ed. (1983). *Biological bases for sensation seeking, impulsivity, and anxiety.* Hillsdale, N.J.: Erlbaum.

Zuckerman, M., M. D. Amidon, S. E. Bishop, and S. D. Pomerantz (1982). Face and tone of voice in the communication of deception. *J. Pers. soc. Psychol., 43,* 347–357.

Zuckerman, M., B. M. DePaulo, and R. Rosenthal (1981). Verbal and nonverbal communication of deception. In L. Berkowitz (Ed.), *Advances in experimental social psychology.* Vol. 14. New York: Academic Press. Pp. 1–59.

Zuckerman, M., R. Koestner, and A. O. Alton (1984). Learning to detect deception. *J. Pers. soc. Psychol., 46,* 519–528.

Zurcher, L. A. (1983). *Social roles: conformity, conflict, and creativity.* Beverly Hills, Calif.: Sage.

CHAPTER 20

Social Influence and Conformity

Serge Moscovici
Ecole des Hautes Etudes En Sciences Sociales

THE ONE AND THE MANY

To the best of my knowledge, it was the West, and the West alone, that produced and refined the concept of humanity as autonomous, rational, self-directed individuals. By this exacting definition individuals were held fully accountable for their actions, they were assumed to evaluate reality solely on the basis of their own observations, and they were expected to be convinced only by arguments grounded on solid evidence. And yet even without the benefit of social psychology, it has long been apparent that each of us, far from conforming to this idealized image, readily complies with authority; goes along with the opinion of friends and relations or accepts the views of the newspaper; and adapts personal tastes, speech, and attire to the fashions of the day. This has always been common knowledge without raising any major practical or theoretical problems. No, the truth is that social psychology came into being as a response to the massification of society, which brought into the open the following paradox: Taken singly, all individuals are rational in their behavior, but taken collectively, they cease to be rational—as witnessed by the outbursts of violence, panic, enthusiasm, and cruelty in which crowds indulge. A sharp difference must therefore exist between

individual and collective psychology, which accounts for the radical transformation of the individual's psychic state and disposition when in a social setting. Were it not for such a transformation, it would be unthinkable that a person we know privately should not be his usual self in a public setting and that we would all do, say, or think things in a group that we would not consider doing, saying, or thinking on our own. It is precisely this change occasioned by our relations with other persons that reveals the influence phenomenon. We are unaware of this change; we do not know how or why it takes place. The solution to this enigma plays the same role in social psychology as the puzzle of heredity plays in biology or that of wealth in economics. All other questions come back to this basic enigma, and as long as science shirks the task of solving it, it is evading its prime concern.

The first scholars to attempt to explain this paradox, thereby laying the groundwork of social psychology, are unquestionably Tarde (1890) and Le Bon (1895). Both actually conceived it as a consequence of hypnotic suggestion exerted by and on individuals, in the course of which consciousness is somehow put to sleep and reason set aside. Liébeault first presented the concept of suggestion in 1866, applying it to a category of phenomena characterized by the fact that a person's behavior was entirely determined by another person's direct or indirect commands and that the recipient's field of consciousness was limited, with a loss both of critical faculties and of autonomy. Having been turned into a sort of psychic robot, the individual carries out everything that she is asked to do without being aware of it or remembering it exactly. In Tarde's view this state of hypnosis, which can be induced with the mentally ill, typifies the condition in which we are plunged each time we are in a group, no matter what the occasion. It induces, among other things, our copying of the behaviors and ideas of whatever individual we choose as a model, and it facilitates the uniformization characteristic of society. Imitation converts whatever is individual into something social, whatever is different into something similar; and suggestion is at the root of this drastic transformation. Le Bon expressed this explanation more dramatically by asserting that participation in the life of a psychological group deeply modifies the thinking, feelings, and actions of individuals by making them retrogress to a primitive level. Their behavior is entirely dictated from that point on by emotional and unconscious factors. In a collective situation a sort of emotional contagion of ideas and images might well occur and give rise to a mental group unity. But this contagion can take place because of a sort of reciprocal suggestibility accompanied by a loss of the normal sense of responsibilities and intellectual capacities. Binet, in his work *La Suggestibilité* (1900), initiates a systematic and experimental study of the conditions under which the suggestion phenomenon arises. He used the following method: For a given problem a child answers after an adult, whose answer gradually moves away from the truth; or else after the child gives an answer, the adult gives a different answer, which contradicts the child's answer. Binet thus measures the subject's resistance to repeated influences by another person and the stability of the subject's reactions to these influences. His merit lies essentially in having shown the possibility of experimenting in this social realm.

To the extent that psychology gave up the concept of suggestion, which explained nothing, it had to abandon at the same time Tarde's and Le Bon's classic explanation and admit that their solution to the fundamental paradox was not a genuine one. However, it failed to account sufficiently for one of the most general characteristics of social life, to wit, its regularity. Suggestion in any case was incapable of accounting for this regularity without a large number of arbitrary and unverifiable hypotheses.

It was Sherif's great merit to resume, in 1935, the investigation of the influence phenomenon, taking as his starting point the new data of learning and perception psychology. His argument might be simplified as follows: When individuals are deprived of a social frame of reference and are confronted with an unstable or ambiguous reality, their judgments and perceptions are uncertain and variable. They have no way of coming to grips with this situation and reducing their uncertainty except by engaging in an interaction during which they exchange the information available to them and establish a common norm. Once this norm is established, it becomes the frame of reference for all subsequent judgments and perceptions of this same object. The formation of a norm, therefore, accounts for the transformation of individuals into groups. In line with Durkheim's sociology Sherif's conception takes the existence of rules as the criterion for converting a psychic state into a social state, a physical reality into a social reality. His famous investigation, which has Gestalt psychology as its foundation, shows that when an object is ambiguous, the independent estimates of several persons converge; gradually, a norm emerges, ensuring stability to judgments in the absence of objective coordinates. Even after going their separate ways and after a considerable lapse of time, these persons judge the stimulus as though they were gathered together simultaneously. Once the norm has been established, it remains in effect.

There the matter might have rested had Asch not come up with a systematic criticism of the suggestion concept. He attempted to show that human beings do not blindly copy other people's opinions but adopt them in a deliberate and rational way. In other words, the paradox I presented initially is dismissed as fictitious; whether alone or in a group an individual remains an individual. In the experiment named after him, Asch set out to show that if objective reality was in fact ascertainable, nobody would submit to majority pressure, and all persons would judge for themselves. Norms would therefore have a rational rather than a social basis. He was eager to invalidate the prestige-suggestion theory, moreover, by demonstrating that by giving individuals access to objective truths usually concealed from them, they would become impervious to group pressure. The scientist proposes, however, and reality disposes. As it turned out, when individuals were subjected to the influence of a group giving the same unanimous response about the length of lines, even in the face of an obvious but conflicting correct response, Asch found that these individuals were more inclined to believe what others said than the evidence of their visual perception. The criticisms he had raised against the prestige-suggestion theory thus failed to be validated. So the Asch experiment exemplifies an experiment whose value lies in the fact that it falsified what it set out to verify and clearly invalidated his theory. It serves, on the contrary, as one of the most dramatic illustrations of conformity, of blindly going along with the group, even when the individual realizes that by doing so he turns his back on reality and truth.

The impact of this experiment on contemporary social psychology was compelling, as demonstrated by the thousands of replications and variants it inspired. Its prime contribution lies in having established that conformity to group pressure can be explained without appealing to complicated psychic processes or mysterious qualities. At the same time it tends to dismiss any emotional and illogical element from the empirical analysis and investigation of social influence phenomena. In short, Asch for the first time introduced a rational point of view where up to that time an irrational point of view prevailed. Nevertheless, for him, as for his predecessors in Europe and the United States, social influence in the group is identified with the individual's conformity to the group.

This group conformity was Festinger's (1950) and Schachter's (1951) main area of investigation. They postulated the existence of a pressure toward uniformity, which has the effect of making people feel and behave alike. One aspect of this pressure is the tendency of people in groups to reject and dislike those who are different from the rest of the members. When an individual expresses an opinion diverging from that of the majority or behaves in a very incongruous manner, he is bound to be rejected by most of the members. The possibility of being excluded from the group induces most people to become more like the other members of the group and to avoid becoming deviant. Most group members submit, either because they fear being excluded or because, for lack of objective criteria, they take the majority's assertions as an expression of reality. While conformity seems to be blind from the individual point of view, from the collective point of view it is not, since it is required for group cohesion and the execution of group objectives.

Science, like nature, abhors a vacuum. Scholars, quite naturally, were eager to extend this principle to Asch's paradigm, which, for the reasons just mentioned, lacked a theoretical foundation. They were equally anxious to integrate this paradigm into the framework of research on small groups. "From the popular perspective of social comparison theory and group dynamics, it was easy to view the Asch situation as a weak and unpromising source of conformity pressures—a sort of baseline against which more potent conformity paradigms could be evaluated" (Ross, Bierbrauer, and Hoffman, 1976, p. 148). It was all the more tempting to do so because this situation perfectly vindicated how pressure toward uniformity could affect one's perception or thinking even where an objective reality was involved. Deutsch and Gerard (1955) achieved this integration by differentiating between normative and informative social influence. In both cases interdependence forces each individual to change his or her political, aesthetic, physical, and other judgments about the world or other people. In the former case, however, this change and conformity is motivated by an individual's wish to meet the expectations of the majority. In the latter case it is motivated by the individual's acceptance of the judgments and opinions of the majority as information about objective reality, in keeping with the saying "Four eyes see more than two." In Asch's and Sherif's research both aspects of social influence were always recognized, but they now came to acquire a clear conceptual status and to serve as descriptive categories for phenomena. With this distinction between the two kinds of conformity in mind, one might say that Sherif's and Asch's experiment dealt more with informative than with normative social influence, while Festinger's and Schachter's experiments concentrated on normative rather than informative social influence.

Everything seemed to be clarified in this way, though in a rather simple fashion. Both the uniformity of individuals in the group and their conformity to the group were explained. Common sense was given its due, and empirical requirements were fulfilled. The claims of logic were not satisfied, however, since an underlying difficulty remained. The point of departure for all these theories and investigations is the notion that, on the one hand, individuals seek the truth—that they wish to be right and for that reason are willing to accept the judgments and opinions of others. On the other hand, the reason that groups exert an influence and try to eliminate deviants is to be able to adapt better to reality. There is the rub. If groups really succeed in eliminating deviants and in having individuals accept the majority point of view without reservation, by what mechanism could they introduce change that would keep them in touch with changing reality? Hundreds of experiments have demonstrated that people can be made to state and to think the opposite of what they see and believe to be the truth. In the extreme case they may even be made to succumb to the blind obedience that Milgram's (1974) elegant studies have exhaustively analyzed.

All these experiments seemed to confirm the theories in question, until one day it was noticed that in the long run group uniformity is secured at the expense of group success and group adaptation to the environment. The work of Deutsch and Gerard (1955) already revealed that even by rewarding individuals who give the correct response—even if they are told that an incorrect response, although it conforms to the group response, will entail collective failure—conformity remains the dominant form of behavior. Individuals under all circumstances prefer to agree with each other, as Tarde and Le Bon had predicted, rather than to reach correct but conflicting conclusions. An experiment by Kelley and Volkart (1962) shows that even if a certain deviance is encouraged to ensure group success by allowing the group to carry out its tasks more competently, social pressure still remains stronger than reality. The minority retreats in the face of the majority.

And this was not the end of the matter. In another experiment Kelley and Shapiro (1954) advanced the hypothesis that there would be less individual conformity in high-cohesion groups than in low-cohesion groups when conformity stood in the way of group achievement and was perceived as contrary to group interests. It was certainly plausible to assume that in very cohesive groups individuals would be more concerned about group welfare and would be less afraid of holding out against the pressure of a majority with which they felt closely linked. Notwithstanding its plausibility, this hypothesis was not supported by the data they gathered. A more recent experiment (Sakurai, 1975) confirms the same conclusion. It has thus been proven that conformity can be disadaptive and detrimental to group welfare.

Around the years 1955–1960 research on influence, despite its earlier abundance, almost came to a standstill. This decline should not be attributed to apathy or lack of imagination on the part of scholars but rather to the blind alley in which theories centered on conformity found themselves trapped. It had become obvious that under certain circumstances the individual must first and fore-

most be able to influence the group so as to ensure group survival and success. In other words, this individual, despite his or her role as a deviant, had to be envisaged not only as a target but also as a source of social pressure. It had become urgent to investigate how a minority or a deviant influences the majority, instead of studying, as had been done previously, how the majority—the group—influences the minority or the deviant. In short, social influence could no longer be envisaged as an adaptation mechanism; it had to be viewed as a mechanism for change. And if we wish to focus on change, we have to deal with innovation, not conformity, with the impact of the minority on the majority and not the opposite.

It is perfectly obvious that in terms of the available paradigms change and innovation were difficult to conceive. These paradigms were centered completely on stability and conformity. Of course, here and there research had dealt with the conditions under which an individual resists group pressures in order to preserve independence. The possibility of a backlash against these pressures, an anticonformity movement, had also been stressed. While all studies examining the manner in which human beings preserve their dignity in relation to groups expressed the concerns of a liberal ethics, they nevertheless failed to challenge the existing theoretical framework. Nor did they try to extricate research on social influence from the blind alley in which it was caught. Social psychology was now confronted with a new paradox in place of the old: Majority influence attracts or coerces the minority, and yet groups can transform themselves and survive only under the influence of this minority. In other words, our science was (and still remains) faced with a new paradox instead of the paradox of conformity: the paradox of change. And short of resolving it, there was no way to move ahead—just as physics could make no further advances until it had tackled the paradox of the atom's stability.

There was only one way out: to recognize as theoretically as possible what had been considered impossible until then—namely, that the minority (or the deviant) is as much an independent source of influence as the majority. The prevailing assumption that only one part of the group is an adaptive influence had to be thrown overboard and replaced with the broader assumption that all parts of the group are potential sources of influence, irrespective of their status and capacities (Moscovici, 1976). Henceforth, innovation had to be recognized as one of the fundamental forms of the impact individuals have on one another, on an equal footing with conformity. Change thereby becomes conceivable and meaningful within the dynamics of social processes.

It will certainly be objected that change of attitudes and behavior has not been a neglected field of social psychology. But the point is that it was viewed from a different angle. Previously, the only question that was raised was how a group changed a person. In the present context the issue is how a person changes a group, and that is quite a different matter. By shifting the stress from one social factor to another, from the majority to the minority, research about the social phenomenon can acquire much broader scope and uncover a set of realities that had not been taken account of hitherto. The problem has now become to understand how people conform as well as innovate, maintain as well as reverse the norms or the structure of society. If anything new has emerged since the last edition of this *Handbook* in the field of social influence, it is recognition of this problem—and, in its wake, research on innovation. The point is not that this research is more outstanding or significant than other types of research but that, taken as a whole, it indicates a turning point.

This evolution of ideas and shift in interests about social influence phenomena, of course, did not take place in a social and historical vacuum. Without giving an exhaustive account of the matter, I think that certain circumstances are significant enough to deserve to be mentioned. The emergence of the masses on the political and social level must be seen as the original impetus and broad impulse giving rise to mass psychology. Mass psychology deals with the causes and the general laws governing the behavior and administration of collective aggregates. And at its core is the study of conformity phenomena, of the way in which individuals are guided either through reciprocal influence or by the prestige of a leader. In addition, it offers "tricks" for ruling the masses, tricks that political leaders put to the test. For example, historians inform us that foremost among the users of ideas and techniques of mass psychology were the Nazi and Fascist movements. It is hardly surprising therefore that the German refugee scholars and writers in the United States reacted negatively toward these methods and ideas. This fact largely accounts for Asch's searching and determined criticism against the doctrine of prestige-suggestion and his eagerness to construct a rational theory of influence—in other words, a theory with respect for the individual and for democratic values.

Lewin's work even more explicitly supports these aims. Both attempted to get rid of the intellectual underpinnings of mass psychology—underpinnings to which Le Bon, Tarde, Freud, Reich, and many others had made their contribution (Moscovici, 1981).

At the same time the center of interest shifted from large groups to small groups and the role of these groups in industry, education, and psychotherapy. As an outgrowth of these studies, new concepts and techniques materialized and found widespread and successful applications. Thereafter until the 1960s, influence phenomena were studied in this context—until the time, that is, when psychology lost interest in the study of groups large and small and turned its attention to interpersonal relations. What accounts for this shift? No attempt has been made so far to clarify this point. In any case it is in the United States that the explanation must be sought. American social psychology came into its own after World War II and has maintained its leadership position since then. The late 1960s saw renewed interest in influence phenomena but from a new angle. The theoretical and internal rationale for this shift, which I mentioned earlier, must not be underestimated. However, the main impetus for the new research came from the veritable explosion of social minorities that characterized this period. Whatever answers research could offer were eagerly welcomed. From all corners of society movements appeared that wanted to change society and its values. Young people and students, women and ecologists, ethnic and religious minorities, homosexuals and prisoners—all consolidated into groups, exerting pressure on the majority to gain recognition and convert it to their ideas. All those, in a word, who used to be considered deviants now took a stand as active minorities, proclaiming their right to participate fully in society and culture. We have witnessed a significant change.

If masses were the focal point and object of our knowledge at the beginning of the twentieth century, it is these minority groups that occupy, with movements of ebb and tide, the center of the stage as the century draws to a close. At one time we felt the need to develop a mass psychology (or group psychology); now we feel the need for a minority psychology—at least if our science wishes to take up the challenge and find an answer to the important questions with which society and history confront it. In any case the interest in innovation and minorities, as well as their influence on the majority, reflects this emergence of new social movements. These movements are of a different nature and for the most part represent a reaction against mass society.

I shall leave the task of complementing, expanding, or correcting altogether the evolutionary sketch that I have just outlined to the historians of our science. Vague as the sketch is, such modifications should be easy to introduce. And yet I felt that it was indispensable to mention these links between our science and society, this constant interplay between the questions society presents us and the answers we offer it.

CONFLICT, CONSENSUS, AND SOCIAL INFLUENCE

From its very inception social psychology has thus been dominated by a conformity bias. Social psychologists have clung tenaciously to the idea that they must explain the undeniable fact that most people, to varying degrees, submit to the pressures of society. The obviousness of this idea was so overwhelming, it seems, that they failed to notice to what extent we each, in our own sphere of action, keep social pressures at arm's length and endeavor to modify the opinions, interests, or decisions of the collectivity to which we belong. This too is a form of social pressure, but one that aims to change people, not to control them.

To understand how influence can exist in such varied guises, we must take the following proposition as a sort of postulate: Influence is rooted in a conflict and strives for a consensus. Let us see what makes it plausible. As we can all observe, groups are heterogeneous by definition. Individuals belonging to a given group do not all share the same world. More often than not, individuals, classes, and professions are at loggerheads; they have incompatible norms, goals, behaviors, and, of course, interests. Majorities on many occasions are the result of delicate compromises, of barely controlled tensions. They are likely to break up at a moment's notice. We need only watch the vicissitudes of an election campaign to see what can happen. Conventions, laws, institutions, and hierarchies attempt to transform this virtual chaos into order, to turn diversity into unity.

These are trite observations, but they nevertheless draw attention to the many potential conflicts that are commonplaces of daily life. These potential conflicts are responsible for making us feel tense, for making us unsure of ourselves and our ideas, for making us withdraw from others in order to maintain our integrity or seek them out in order to reduce these tensions and doubts. Every area of society has its share of conflicts of status, interests, opinions, and values; more generally, there is disagreement about "right" or "wrong," "good" or "bad," "true" or "false." These pairs of opposites can be reduced to the single opposition between "agreement" and "disagreement" among the members of a group. Everything around us serves to reinforce our attitudes, strengthen our agreement with other people, and keep the consensus alive. Teaching devices, from textbooks to examinations, and communication, from newspaper to prayer, generally tend to implant in us the conviction that there is a "normal" response to each question, a response about which most people agree. When a disagreement does arise, it is experienced as undesirable, as a tension and a threat. It alerts us to something abnormal, to something that invalidates past consensus and puts it back on the carpet. It makes us aware of the conflict brewing under the surface of social uniformities.

Two complementary aspects of disagreement must be taken into account in this respect. The first is of a more general nature. Disagreement denotes a difference—the presence of something or someone different, of something unfamiliar. And in all species the introduction of a strange individual or the appearance of a difference or of a disagreement provokes a state of social stress, of psychic and organic panic or rejection reactions. This finding was confirmed in our laboratories. Even the anticipation of a divergent opinion has an analogous effect. C. E. Smith (1936) proceeded to measure physiological reactions in terms of variations of galvanic epidermic reactions. The subjects in this experiment were told that their opinions were different from those of fictitious persons. As a result, a stronger tension was recorded in the psychogalvanometer's reaction measurements. Back and Bogdonoff (1964) observed that the rate of fatty acids in the blood increased in groups consisting of strangers and declined in groups consisting of friends. It seems that these physiological modifications in the direction of greater anxiety in such encounter situations are due either to a feeling of uncertainty (Shapiro and Leiderman, 1964) or to a competitive atmosphere (Church, 1962).

But more is involved than uncertainty and competition. Burdick and Burns (1958) and Steiner (1966) carried out analogous experiments by more closely investigating internal-disagreement reactions. They noticed that present or future differences of opinion or belief were not the crucial factor. What really mattered was that these differences were felt to be symptoms of a possible conflict.

Steiner (1966), to whom we owe this insight, writes: "Even when they are anticipated, interpersonal controversies may presage impending disaster, predict future hardship, or confirm the existence of personal faults. Undoubtedly it is the *symbolic meaning* of a disagreement, rather than its inherent qualities, that is inconsistent with valued goals" (p. 223).

The second aspect concerning disagreement resides in its power to galvanize latent opinions, values, or behaviors that one has given up or forgotten for the sake of social consensus. Thus in a society everybody may come to be persuaded that technical progress or wealth deserves the sacrifice of justice and its citizens' liberty, or adults may, as they grow older, be induced to forget the socialist and liberal ideas of their youth. As long as convergence is preserved and the compromises are not aired, all is well. But once a social movement or one's own offspring brings contradictions of the individual into the open and gives greater weight to something that the individual weighs less heavily, doubt begins to take hold. People lose confidence in what they see or think—or if they keep their confidence intact, they must find new arguments and reestablish consensus on a new foundation.

This loss of confidence in oneself and in stable frames of reference is observed even in the laboratory. That is precisely what happened in the experiments on conformity. When individuals are faced with a judgment that deviates from the norm, as was true in the Asch situation, they are profoundly disturbed. Some of them do not believe their eyes or their minds. Describing reactions of this sort, when subjects are faced with an incorrect majority opinion that they are not in a position to reject, Samelson (1957, p. 182) writes:

> Since at the outset the task seemed quite simple, the initial expectation of observer agreement was presumably very high. The surprising discrepancy between the subject's perceptions and those of a number of other subjects, unanimous among themselves, created a conflict in the cognitive field which could not be resolved in a satisfactory manner by simply denying or disregarding the socially transmitted information.

In other words, it is as though an external conflict with others were in the process of turning into an internal conflict with oneself, a conflict that is more intensive and difficult to overcome. There arises a state of tension, which is analogous to the famous Zeigarnik effect. Each

person feels the need to resolve the discrepancy between the two opposing sets of information and feelings. On the one hand, each individual feels tendencies to shy away from the incompatible responses and the resulting discomfort. On the other hand, obligations and tendencies emanating from the group forbid the person to do so. The latter propel the individual toward the incompatible responses and cause the person to think that they are his or her own.

Conflict is thus at the root of influence, either because it arises from the presence of a difference or because the existence of a disagreement brings it into the open (Eagly and Chaiken, 1984). But that is not all we want to know. More accurate information is needed. What increases or diminishes this conflict? What effects does it have on our judgments and opinions? And so on. On the whole the magnitude, the nature, and the outcome of conflict are determined by four factors: (1) the discrepancy between the positions, (2) the nature of the alternatives, (3) the effect of commitment, and (4) the possibility of excluding the deviant. We shall examine these factors in turn. It is unfortunate that they have not been studied systematically and especially that they have not been investigated with equal thoroughness.

DISCREPANCY BETWEEN THE POSITIONS

When several persons come together to discuss or judge something and a majority or minority disagrees with our own position, we feel tense or threatened, because this disagreement implies that our ideas may be incorrect, inadequate, or deviant. The greater the disagreement, the greater is the conflict with others and, in all likelihood, with ourselves. How can this conflict be reduced? It can be reduced by coming to an agreement with the majority or, as the case may be, with the minority. In other words, the greater the conflict, the greater must be the change in our beliefs or judgments so that a new consensus can be established. This simplistic approach postulates a linear relationship between the discrepancy in positions each one occupies and the influence exerted: The greater the discrepancy, the greater is the influence.

Several well-known experiments have shown this statement to be true. Goldberg (1954) varied the discrepancy between the subjects' response and that of a fictitious influence source. He observed that the further the response of the influence source, the more the subjects modified their judgment in the direction of the source's response. Fisher and Lubin (1958), using a very different material, found an analogous tendency. Their results co-incide with the effects obtained by Hochbaum (1954), Fisher, Rubinstein, and Freeman (1956), Schroeder and Hunt (1958), and Brehm and Lipsher (1959), among others. It is unusual, however, for any relationship to be invariably applicable in social psychology, especially such a simple one. It was therefore not at all astonishing to find that beyond a certain discrepancy, influence should tend to decrease and eventually become nonexistent. This is a normal effect, for if someone expresses an opinion that deviates totally from ours and is, so to speak, situated outside our universe, it will hardly affect us and will fail to arouse any kind of conflict. If I have a discussion with a person who maintains that there is life after death or that the species do not evolve, what has been said does not affect me at all if I do not believe it, and thus it can have no impact. On the other hand, there exists a common ground for discussion with a person who asserts that a human can live 150 years or that evolution is due to chance rather than the survival of the fittest.

It makes sense that where discrepancies are too great, there is no change in belief or judgment, since there is no real conflict. Or to express myself differently, there is a curvilinear relation between the discrepancy and influence, whose shape we know. As a small discrepancy increases, so does the degree of influence; but if the discrepancy keeps increasing, influence begins to diminish; and finally, when the discrepancy becomes too large, the amount of influence becomes very small and even nonexistent. Hovland, Harvey, and Sherif (1957), Whittacker (1964), and Insko, Murashima, and Saiyadain (1966) found that an influence-increase phenomenon existed where discrepancies were moderate but not where discrepancies were very small or very large. Nemeth and Markowski (1972) also have shown that when discrepancies become very large, a sort of boomerang effect is obtained, with individuals assuming a position opposite to the one upheld by the source.

It would seem that no conclusion can be reached. When a large number of research results point in one direction and a comparable number of results point in the opposite direction, and no experiment is available to decide between them, it is difficult to claim that a single explanation fits them all. Hence offhand, there is no point in trying to relate opinion or belief change to the intensity of the conflict. But a more detailed analysis shows us that the conflicting results make sense once we take into account that the possibilities for resisting change increase to the same extent as the pressures for change. Individuals can reduce the tension caused by the disagreement by deprecating the source of the contrary opinions or by considering them less and less plausible, instead of modifying their own opinions. And the further removed these opinions are from their own, the more likely they are to do so. That is what we generally do when we call somebody crazy who thinks differently from us and when we say that his or her judgments lack common sense. If this argument makes sense, the linear relation should hold whenever it is difficult to reject the source or opinions. Several experiments have demonstrated that this is indeed the case.

It is difficult, for instance, to minimize or avoid disagreement with a friend or the author of a very credible communication. By varying disagreement between recommendations made by pairs of friends in a case of juvenile delinquency, Zimbardo (1960) found that the greater the apparent margin between the decision of the friends, the more they modified their conclusion in the direction they assumed to be their friend's conclusion. Similarly, Aronson, Carlsmith, and Turner (1963) showed convincingly that when the author of a communication enjoys great credibility, the larger the discrepancy between the opinion he upholds and public opinion, the greater is his influence on the public. Conversely, the more dubious or meager the credibility of the author, the greater is the opinion change if the discrepancies are moderate. Observations by Bergin (1962) and Bochner and Insko (1966) point in the same direction.

Montmollin (1977), on the other hand, shows that individuals avoid opinions that deviate considerably from their own, because they judge them to be less likely. However, by being exposed to them more frequently, individuals begin to consider these opinions as both more familiar and more plausible. The outcome is to make them slightly more influential. It may be assumed that the same thing occurs when extreme and even forbidden attitudes are presented frequently and in various guises. The individual will finally become accustomed to them, consider them as self-evident, and accept them. It seems, in conclusion, that conflict is a function of the discrepancy between positions advocated by members of the group. While this is evidently a necessary condition, it is not at all a sufficient one to determine the outcome.

NATURE OF THE ALTERNATIVES

Disagreement relating to categorical—that is, discontinuous responses—does not have the same meaning as disagreement about variable responses—that is, responses arrayed along a continuum. If two persons disagree about the color of an object, their controversy and concessions will differ if judgment is in terms of black and white, green and blue, or short and long wavelengths. In the first case a choice is involved—in the extreme case an all-or-nothing choice. And in the second case an evaluation with flexible limits is involved. In the first case disagreement can rapidly turn into opposition; in the second case such an eventuality seems excluded.

From the social or psychological point of view, influencing someone with respect to a categorical response is different from influencing the person with respect to a variable response. In one case it is a question of limiting the range of values an object can assume; in the other it is a matter of expanding this range to encompass something very different. Compliance has a different meaning in these two contexts. A small disagreement in judgment is noticeable with respect to a discontinuous response but may remain unnoticeable for a continuous response. A much more pronounced psychological change is required for compliance in a situation where deviance is obvious than in a situation where deviance is less noticeable. Anyone who states that he sees blue slides as green must really have undergone a change to have adopted the green response, a change that excludes the blue response. Conversely, if somebody who has listened to other persons' responses states that she sees sixty rather than fifty points on a piece of cardboard, she settles on an evaluation she has already considered and that is in no way absurd. It is misleading to compare the degree of compliance in these two cases, because the results one is comparing may well derive from two different ways of resolving psychological conflicts.

Of course, *mutatis mutandis,* all this applies to the very numerous cases where the influence process confronts dogmatic individuals with categorical opinions and beliefs or nondogmatic individuals with variable or even flexible opinions and beliefs. There have been few experiments investigating comparatively the impact of each of these forms of response. It is plausible that the clash of opinions will be more violent if they are discontinuous than if they are continuous, or to put it in quantitative terms, there will be fewer compromises between them. Some experiments by Luchins (1945) and Luchins and Luchins (1956, 1961) show that this assumption is correct, as can be seen even more clearly when a discontinuous judgment is transformed into a continuous one. Tuddenham, McBride, and Zahn (1957) asked subjects to evaluate eight instead of three discontinuous lines, so that they represented finer degrees of error with reference

to a standard line. Compromise responses between the objective truth and the erroneous response of the majority then became more and more numerous. In another study Tuddenham (1961), using a material of the same kind, found that a moderate disagreement affected his experimental subjects less but more uniformly. All these effects were obtained in situations where the influence source was a majority and where individuals were asked to conform with its point of view. As we shall see later on, these effects manifest themselves more indirectly where the influence source is a minority.

EFFECT OF COMMITMENT

We also have evidence that people hesitate to speak up or take a stand in a group. They fear that they will provoke a controversy and be rejected by others. "The fear of speaking before a group," Borden (1980) observes, "may be the most prevalent fear that people admit experiencing" (p. 100). A diffuse fear of conflict always exists, and few individuals are able to overcome it. One factor that allows them to surmount this fear is their commitment to a group or a belief. Notwithstanding their apprehensions and nervousness, they are impelled by an inner urge to proclaim what they believe to be true, to confront the judgment of others, and even to try to convince them.

This commitment may have several facets. It ranges from the certainty of being right to confidence in the superiority of one's cause, from defense of a position adopted by part of a group to involvement with some specific problem, such as nature conservation or educational reform (Kiesler, 1969). Whatever the conditions, commitment always has the same effect: On the one hand, resistance to other people's influence is strengthened; on the other hand, one's propensity to influence others is more pronounced. The former effect is due to the fact that the external conflict is less likely to be translated into an internal conflict as well, since the disagreement leads to a lower level of anxiety and doubt about the value of one's own responses in a group situation. It is commonly found, for instance, that people who are certain about the validity of their judgments change less (Montmollin, 1977). Besides, Sherif and Hovland (1961), Freedman (1964), Greenwald (1964), and Miller (1965) confirmed the idea that the impact of very discordant messages diminishes as commitment increases.

The second effect is attributable to a smaller fear of conflict generally, reinforced by the conviction that the others cannot fail to be convinced by one's arguments and share the same opinions. This effect was shown in polarization phenomena (Moscovici and Zavalloni, 1969). Groups had to make a common decision. The most extremist or the most committed individuals made greater efforts to persuade the group members that their response was the right one and that the group should accept it. They usually succeeded, and as a result, the consensus went in their favor. Consequently, the common decision was more extreme than the average of individual choices before the discussion. A reciprocal influence is involved here, since each person takes part in the discussion and later in the vote on the common position. But in view of the results it is obvious that the more committed, extreme individuals exert a disproportionate influence in comparison with the more moderate individuals, who are generally less involved and less able or willing to brave the impending conflict.

POSSIBILITY OF EXCLUDING THE DEVIANT

No matter what area of disagreement is at stake, all social conflict in the last analysis revolves around a disagreement between what is "normal" and what is "deviant," between opinions on our "own side" and opinions on the "other side." Under these conditions we are rarely neutral. Of course, when discrepancies are small, these divisions do not matter much; but when they increase, we can no longer ignore them. An experiment by Nemeth and Endicott (1974) tends to indicate that this result is indeed the case. They showed that for small differences of opinion individuals modify their opinion irrespective of whether the message is on their "own side" or on the "other side." However, for large differences individuals are more inclined to react with a change of opinion in the direction of an emitter who takes a very extremely deviant position on the "own side" of the subjects. No change occurs if the extremely deviant position is on the "other side," that is, beyond the median point of the scale. Hence if you are moderately liberal politically, you are inclined to be equally influenced by a moderate liberal or moderate conservative. But when it comes to extremes, you will only be influenced by an extremist liberal; you will not be influenced at all by an extremist conservative.

Festinger's (1950) stand is more sweeping. He presented the hypothesis that in a cohesive group disagreement of any kind leads the majority to exert persuasion in order to win over the deviant. When the deviant fails to fall in line, he or she is excommunicated from the group, which then redraws its boundaries. In other words, the community excludes one of its members, at least in psychological terms. It continues to operate as though that member were no longer there. At a given moment a university or a government may just stop worrying about student extremists or a revolutionary movement. But there are also instances where deviants have literally been eliminated, as church history or developments within ruling Communist parties testify. This hypothesis implies that a group can prevent conflicts from becoming more serious and from endangering group cohesiveness by eliminating deviants either psychologically or physically. It must be kept in mind, however, that this is a solution of last resort, even for the most homogeneous political systems. As Zinoviev (1981, p. 167), the exiled Soviet philosopher, writes:

> The suspect member is not immediately placed in the renegade category by the collectivity. This takes years, if not decades to happen. Besides, people do not become renegades from one day to the next, and they do not at once become aware of it when they have done so. In some instances, this awareness fails to materialize altogether. As a result, the victim is taken completely by surprise when suddenly he is overtaken by collective revenge.

But there are many occasions where such an exclusion is out of the question. Parents cannot break the bonds with their children. Except under conditions of extreme emergency, a state has no way of expelling its citizens, just as business owners have no way of dismissing unionized workers. Obviously, coercive measures such as corporal punishment, emprisonment, and antistrike laws remain as possible defensive measures for these groups and may well be applied over long periods of time. But eventually, a more legitimate way of dealing with the problem must be found and a certain consensus reached.

That being the case, the more difficult it is to bar or eliminate a deviant minority, the more explosive is the conflict. The fact that excommunication is either impossible or at best exceptional forces the majority to move somewhat closer to the minority. It may be a matter of just a few very small steps in this direction. Politics offer striking examples of such behavior. After silencing dissidents—the history of the Soviet Communist party amply illustrates this tactic—parties eagerly integrate into their programs the measures initially proposed by the dissidents. This happens most often in tense and difficult situations. It is understandable that the majority uses this approach. A deviant minority of this kind, by acting in a certain way or suggesting certain policies or ideas, creates an alternative and an attraction pole. There are people who are drawn to them, even though they may not realize it and even though they are reluctant to become dissidents themselves. By taking over the dissidents' position and by taking credit for their ideas, the majority prevents others from occupying the position vacated by the dissidents. At the same time this move satisfies people's needs without their having to adopt the path of deviancy and without their becoming opposed to the authorities or the majority. This way of legitimizing an opinion or a behavior that had for long periods been rejected often reinforces a party's hold on its members.

All these observations lead to the following conclusions: Pressures toward uniformity undoubtedly exist. But their impact is not one-sided, since it is exerted on the majority as well as on the minority and with equal strength. It is exerted on the majority because it cannot easily eliminate the minority. And it is exerted on the minority because its existence is barely tolerable to the majority. It may be assumed that the pressure on the majority is relatively stronger in the face of a sharp conflict, while the minority is under greater pressure in a subdued conflict. There are no experiments to validate these lines of thought, but they seem sufficiently plausible to be taken into account.

SOCIAL INFLUENCE AS A NEGOTIATION PROCESS

The whole question of social influence must be seen in the context of interaction. This view follows from placing conflict at the center of the stage. As long as influence was viewed as aiming to reduce uncertainty or giving correct judgments, the group played the role of factual mediator in the face of the environment. It served as a sort of artificial limb, a tool for alleviating the deficiencies of our mind and our senses in gathering the information needed to adapt to reality. Similarly, as long as influence is viewed as a form of power exerted over us, the influence source rests on the authority or competence of somebody on whom we depend but with whom we have no reciprocity relations. Thus in either case there is no interaction, nor can there be any conflict of opinions or a consensus to establish. But once conflict breaks out, if we keep in mind the factors described above, there will also be exchanges in points of view and attempts to reach an

agreement—hence reciprocity of influence. In dealing with other persons or groups, each person or subgroup presents its very own system of values and behaviors. It has some leeway in accepting or rejecting its antagonist's system of values and behaviors. The tensions arising from possible confrontations may quickly lead to a breaking off of communication, isolation of the participants, and the impossibility of reaching the objective of the social interaction in which they are participating. As a result, self-confidence is shaken, morale weakens, and tension manifests itself.

To avoid this predicament, each side is compelled to try to remodel its opinions and actions a little. As a result, a redefinition or reduction of the opposition takes place and stimulates concessions in turn. To the extent that the influence process occurs in such a conflictual context and tends to lead to a relative realignment, it bears close resemblance to the negotiation process. The connection between influence and negotiation has not been recognized up to now. But there are very strong analogies, if we take into account that the real stake of social partners is consensus. The majority always puts a great deal of energy into preserving the existing consensus. The minority, no matter how minimal its numerical strength or how great its dependency, can always refuse it. This power of refusal gives it considerable strength.

It is obvious that consensus is always established in somebody's favor. It takes all our ingenuity to try to establish it in our favor—all our rhetorical skill and all our strength of character to marshall the appropriate arguments. This applies as much in matters of opinion as in matters of objective judgment. There is always a dialogue, a controversy (Darwin used to say that an experiment is for or against a theory), and a common decision. As Churchman (1961) expresses it: "Essentially, a judgment is a group opinion.... We shall argue that judgment is a group belief which occurs when there are differences of opinion among the group members, because... such a judgment occurs when the judgment is the establishment of 'agreement' in the context of disagreements. Judgment is a type of negotiation" (p. 293).

What else do we have in mind when we try to persuade someone except putting an end to a conflict? And the conflict in question is usually internal as well as external. One might say that most experiments in social psychology dealing with decision making and influence involve *tacit* negotiations. In the course of these negotiations each participant tries to make his or her own point of view prevail and explores the consensus zone, even if consensus is beyond reach. In this case each type of negotiation corresponds to a different type of social influence. On the whole, just as conflict can be handled by a variety of methods, different influence modalities corresponding to these methods exist. I shall describe them further on.

A BEHAVIORAL GRAMMAR

How does the individual or group go about inducing others to believe something? As we have seen, influence implies a negotiation, verbal or otherwise. Its ultimate purpose is to establish a generally approved consensus. This consensus can be a compromise toward a middle ground. Even to reach such a compromise and to give up their preferences may well imply a hardship or a sacrifice for some participants. A political radical, for instance, must be heavily pressured into accepting a reform proposed by a liberal government. In general, even if the consensus is accepted and internalized, it will constitute a gain for one side and a loss for the other. We should expect as much when we are dealing with the outcome of a sort of match. Each side tries to "win" and takes the risk of "losing." In terms of influence the outcome can be expressed as follows: changing the other or being changed by the other. But what causes such a change? And in what way is one changed? What makes a change in favor of the majority or minority more likely? And under what circumstances does such a change amount to a compromise? We shall now try to answer these questions.

If expertise or resources at the disposal of each of the parties were the only determining factor, the powerful or the knowledgeable would invariably have the upper hand. However, it is not obvious why they should take the trouble to convince others when they could simply impose their point of view. Schelling's (1956) observation holds true for every interaction and negotiation, whether involving influence or not: " . . . if the terms imply that it is an advantage to be more intelligent, or more skilled in a debate, or to have more financial resources, more military resources, then the term does a disservice. These qualities are by no means universal advantages in bargaining situations; they often have a contrary value" (p. 283). And why should the consensus change in that case? If the game is always decided beforehand, if those who have a stake in changing it have only minimal means to succeed, then the status quo is assured.

It so happens that it is not always an advantage in a negotiation to be more knowledgeable or more powerful. At times it has the opposite effect; that is, people respond to it as unfair pressure, as an abuse on the part of those who hold a very privileged position in the social hierarchy. They will therefore reject any influence attempt on the part of persons holding such a position. As popular wisdom teaches us, weakness may be a negotiating strength. Consequently, it sometimes happens that a weaker group or a less affluent nation may carry greater weight than a stronger group or a richer nation. It may actually be able to mobilize opinion in its favor and compel its opponent to forego the benefit of its resources. Indeed, it is a common occurrence during an election campaign that a large part of the voters shift their support to the weaker party, the one that seems to be losing. Given all these considerations and others too complicated to discuss in this chapter, the following conviction is inescapable: In an interaction the crucial factor is the behavioral style of the minority or majority (Moscovici, 1976).

The concept of behavioral style refers to the organization of responses, the appropriateness and intensity of their expression. In short, it refers to behavioral and judgmental "rhetoric." These styles can be codified and reduced to rules in order to give them a meaning that is clear to everyone and arouses an appropriate reaction, just as each person understands and reacts to a language. Repeating the same gesture or the same judgment may mean rigidity in one context and may express certainty in another. Conversely, rigidity and certainty may be coded in many different ways: by repetition, tone of voice, movement of the head, and so on.

Each style projects an internal condition onto the environment, so that everybody can interpret it and predict something about the course of the interactions (Erickson *et al.,* 1978). Actually, behaviors or responses are generally decoded on two levels: that of the explicit content, which is indicated by a reference position (the person is for or against nuclear energy; the person considers a movie very good or mediocre), and that of the implicit content, which must be inferred (the person is very strongly committed to a pro- or antinuclear position; the person is very sure that the movie is excellent because of the eagerness with which the person defends it). Thus when a naive subject in a social psychology laboratory hears someone like himself repeat, "Line *A* is the same length as line *B*," he finds out two things. One is that possibly line *A* is equal to line *B*. The other is that the experimenter's confederate is sure of what she is saying and will never vary her response.

Behavioral styles generally convey simultaneously a piece of information and a meaning: They refer by their content to the object of the interaction, and they refer by their pattern to the state of the actor. As a result, they exert two related types of social pressure: a referential pressure tied to the responses advocated by the influence source, and an inferential pressure tied to the manner in which these responses are given or presented. It is one thing, obviously, to have an extreme opinion and another to maintain it consistently in a discussion with a group of persons. My stress on the meaning of behavior may seem futile to certain readers. I think it is necessary, because up to now only quantitative elements of behavior have been emphasized—the sequential order, the amount of reinforcement, the distribution of responses, and so forth—but not its meaning. (Ghiglione and Beauvois, 1983).

An impartial examination reveals several behavioral styles, only three of which have been the object of serious investigation: autonomy, consistency, and rigidity.

AUTONOMY

Independence in one's opinions and behavior is a quality likely to arouse positive feelings toward the person or group displaying it. Biographies of outstanding persons often highlight this quality to explain their great attraction and the fascination they exerted on their immediate or more remote environment. It is a quality that is perceived above all as a sign of strong convictions and strong character. Moreover, it implies autonomy with respect to external influences. A further assumption is that people or groups demonstrating independence are objective. They are assumed to have adopted a point of view after ripe reflection, without animosity or bias. Last but not least, they are attributed a conduct and a way of thinking that raises them above their personal interest or their subjective preferences. Our prototypes are scholars, scientific communities, and, to a certain extent, judges. That is why we are so ready to accept their advice or conclusions. We assume, most often rightly but sometimes erroneously, that they have weighed their judgments carefully, that no personal interest or concealed motive hides behind the solution that they advocate.

In their study Myers and Goldberg (1970) asked thirty-seven students to read a short review article on at-

mospheric pollution (which was, of course, written by the experimenters). In a high-ethos group condition the text was presented as the end product of a three-hour discussion by a panel of experts. In the second, high-ethos individuals condition the subjects were told that the article was based on a study made by a small group of eminent scientists. Finally, in the third, high-ethos individual condition the article was supposed to represent the opinion of an eminent American scientist. The greatest influence was observed in the high-ethos group condition, where the subjects believed that the article represented the outcome of a careful deliberation.

An experiment by Nemeth and Wachtler (1973) deals with the same problem. They assembled mock juries with five members and asked them to read a study. In one case an individual claimed damages for an occupational accident. The maximum legally allowed compensation was $25,000, but most of the subjects, when their opinion was asked privately, suggested $14,500. However, a confederate in the experimental situation consistently proposed the amount of $3000. The five members of each jury (four subjects and one confederate) spent forty-five minutes discussing the case, the confederate presenting arguments that he had memorized. But the experimenters had devised the seating arrangement in such a way that, depending on the experimental condition, the confederate was seated either at the end or at the side of the table. The decisive variation consisted in the fact that in the first condition the confederate "chose" his seat, while in the second the experimenter had assigned it to him. The difference between choosing a seat and being assigned one is that the first behavior denotes autonomy, while the second indicates that one goes along with the wishes of the authorities, irrespective of the seat assigned. The results were unambivalent. The confederate exerted an influence only when he "chose" his seat and not at all when he was assigned a seat. Nemeth and Wachtler (1973) point out that "the taking of the head seat, being a behavioral style, could be interpreted by others as a sign of confidence, the attribution of which then renders the individual effective. Occupation of the seat if not by choice would reveal no information about the actor regarding such traits" (p. 20).

Objectivity, as we have indicated, is another aspect of autonomy. It implies both that the author of the message communicated or the person who is trying to convince us of the value of an idea has gathered the necessary information and that she presents it to us without trying to persuade us, leaving us to make our own decision. And the very fact that someone is not trying to convince us makes her convincing to us. This line of argument postulates that each of us spontaneously reacts in a negative way to anything that seems like an influence attempt. If this argument is correct, we would expect a more pronounced change of opinions or judgments when the influence and communication source seems objective to us than when the source seems subjective. But here a delicate question arises. Is our suspicion aroused by the source's behavioral style, or do we just need to be informed of its intention? In other words, what diminishes or increases the chances of influencing us: the manner in which the other person addresses us or the warning we are given regarding the person's aims?

This question has not been investigated. However, from examining an impressive number of studies, we can gather that the manner of addressing others is more decisive than the warning itself. In one set of experiments the suspicions of the participants were aroused in connection with the message they were about to receive, read, or hear. The assumption was that the influence of the author would be reduced by putting his objectivity in doubt. However, up to now this expectation has always been disappointed. The results obtained by Hastorf and Piper (1951), Lana (1959), Allyn and Festinger (1961), McGuire and Papageorgis (1962), McGinnies and Donelson (1963), McGuire and Millman (1965), and Apsler and Sears (1968) are all convergent: Alerting the subjects that the source intends to convince them has an impact on the amount of influence. The subjects who are made aware of this intention tend to shut their minds to the arguments presented and produce counterarguments. In a relatively recent study Osterhouse and Brock (1970) also neatly demonstrated this result. When the subjects who are exposed to propaganda in the laboratory are "distracted," that is, when their attention is drawn elsewhere, they are more likely to adopt the opinions expressed than are subjects who have not been distracted. Another finding is that those who yield offer fewer counterarguments to the propaganda than those who do not yield.

But it must be admitted that the experiments do not all lead to identical results. Sometimes, the fact that an individual is aware of this intention does diminish the change of opinion. At other times it increases the change. A reduction was observed by Kiesler and Kiesler (1964), whose warning came at the beginning rather than at the end of the message, and by Freedman and Sears (1965),

who gave the warning ten minutes before the influence attempt. Greenberg and Miller (1966) confirmed the impact of this advance warning on the recipient of the message. However, an inverse effect was produced by an analogous advance warning. It was carried out by slightly different means designed to sensitize the individuals to the persuasive intentions of the source. Several authors (Lana and King, 1960; Hicks and Spaner, 1962; Holtz, 1965; Dillehay, Insko, and Smith, 1966) found that their warning, far from arousing suspicions as they expected, increased the impact of subsequent messages. In a similar context Dabbs and Janis (1965), Mills and Aronson (1965), and Mills (1966) had the same results.

The upshot of these experiments is that a warning about a person's or a group's lack of objectivity in no way diminishes effectiveness or even enhances it. What lies behind these results? We have no ready explanation. Possibly the warning galvanized the recipients' interest for what was about to be said or for the opinions emitted. Or might people in general be disinclined to reject someone for his intention to convince them and consider it a normal state of affairs? Is the experimenter not already suspect in their eyes of manipulating them in some unfathomable way?

Language is the best medium we have both for expressing our intentions and states of mind and for concealing them. Style was invented by the human species for that very purpose. Hence there is nothing surprising about the fact that one's manner of speaking and presenting a message most clearly reveals the existence of an influence attempt and determines its impact (Robinson and McArthur, 1982). However, there are very few studies dealing with this aspect; social psychologists have exhibited a lack of interest for linguistic, cultural, and logical phenomena. But in a work that goes back a number of years, Dietrich (1946) noted that an aggressive presentation of arguments, which might be termed "propaganda," was less effective in producing a change of opinion than a more fully developed presentation that came closer to conversation. Carmichael and Cronkhite (1965) obtained comparable results.

But the effect of autonomy can be illustrated in another way. On many occasions people suspect that a person does or says something with a hidden motive. He may do so because he belongs to a certain social class or family. Or he may be motivated by jealousy, ambition, or the like. When a person seems to speak or act against what everyone might assume to be his own interest, he will give the impression of being independent. He is thought to have overcome the constraints of his background, to have bridled his personal feelings or preferences. Thus his opinion will carry more weight and influence. In short, a relatively disinterested source should have more impact than a less disinterested source (a fact politicians are well aware of, since they never fail to emphasize that they sacrifice themselves to the public welfare and do all that they can to transcend their narrow interests in order to espouse the general interest). Scientists, priests, judges, and experts for their part base their authority on the image of impersonality and dispassionateness that they offer—that is, on their impartiality.

The effectiveness of this way of presenting oneself and of behaving has been repeatedly confirmed in laboratory studies. Walster, Aronson, and Abrahams (1966) exposed subjects to messages advocating that the courts should have either a greater or a smaller power to punish criminals. In two conditions the message was attributed to a prosecutor, and in two other conditions it was attributed to a criminal. The subjects considered the prosecutor and the criminal more influential and more honest when they upheld the point of view that went against their own interests—less power for the courts in the case of the prosecutor, more power in the case of the criminal. When the two individuals advocated points of view that went against their personal interests, they had greater influence regardless of their status. In fact, the lower-status individual even had greater influence than the higher-status individual when he advocated a position that went against his own interest. This confirms once more that when it comes to influence, the powerful do not have all the advantages. Powell and Miller (1967) and Mills and Jellison (1967) observed a comparable tendency, even though objectivity does not appear as the independent variable in their study. It is indeed unfortunate but true that so many experiments the greatest interest deal only accidentally with the grammar of behavior. And yet history and political science books offer a profusion of examples about its nature and importance.

To summarize, the person who seems most objective also exerts the greatest influence. This objectivity manifests itself in two ways. The individual gives the impression of having arrived at a conclusion by ripe deliberation and of being disinterested. The absence or presence of an intention to persuade is a more ambiguous element, whose consequences are contradictory. None of the experiments just described are conclusive. But tentative as they are, they still provide ample matter for further reflection.

CONSISTENCY

Behavioral consistency is viewed as a straightforward indication of certainty and commitment. Let us assume that an individual (or a group) is in a position to express an idea or to maintain a way of behaving under all circumstances. She thereby displays an unshakable belief in herself and in what she thinks or does. Such a singleness of purpose and such confidence never fail to impress and even to attract. Everyone believes that a consistent individual (or group) knows what she wants, is willing to suffer the consequences of her action, and will refuse every compromise. It is as though she had renounced all freedom of choice. She can no longer retract her choices and judgments. And she is no longer in a position to move, that is, to make a significant concession. Since she is no longer able to change, it is therefore up to the other person to yield in order to reach a consensus. By this firmness she turns a reciprocal relation into a nonreciprocal relation. Her way of speaking or acting clearly indicates that she expects the other party to comply with the demands she expresses and to make the necessary concessions. With respect to the meaning of nonreciprocity, to which I have just referred, it is wise to keep in mind Schelling's (1956) analysis: "In bargaining, the commitment is a device to leave the last clear chance to decide the outcome with the other party, in a manner that he fully appreciates; it is to relinquish further initiative, having rigged the incentive so that the other party chooses in one's favor" (p. 294).

The same can be said of any consistent behavior. It gives immense power to anyone who displays it for two additional reasons beyond the ones I just mentioned. On the one hand, he shows an unusual capacity to brave conflict. On the other, he places the responsibility for its resolution on others, thereby creating a strong pressure to change and to make concessions. "The power of a negotiator," Schelling (1975) writes elsewhere, "often rests on a manifest inability to make concessions and to meet demands" (p. 296). The inability that concerns us here stems from the fact that the individual (or group) thinks, and gives the impression of thinking, that he knows the truth, that he knows what is right or wrong.

Behavioral consistency may actually assume two guises. Intraindividual consistency involves the continuous repetition of the same response or of a particular system of responses by the same person. Interindividual consistency, or unanimity, refers to the adoption of a given response or particular system of responses by a certain number of individuals. In either guise the response variation is highly reduced. This reduction signals an action model through which the desired traits are revealed and the stable aspects of the material and social world—that is, the norms that determine behavior—are established. Or at least individuals feel that this effect results from the reduction of response variation and interpret it in this manner. Consistency has its limitations as well: It may take the negative connotation of a lack of open-mindedness, of stubbornness, of rigidity, and so on. But it appeals to the general desire to adopt relatively clear and simple opinions or judgments and to define unambiguously the realities with which one is commonly faced. Consistency may compel one to make more concessions to it than one should, but still its attraction persists. In the light of these considerations it becomes clear why Cato the Elder, by concluding each of his speeches regardless of his subject with the famous exhortation, "Carthage must be destroyed," finally convinced the Senate to send an expedition against this rival city of Rome.

Several experiments confirm the effectiveness of consistency as a behavioral style. Moscovici and Faucheux (1972) investigated the impact of intraindividual consistency. In a first experiment subjects were shown a set of drawings differing in four respects: size (large or small), color (red or green), form (round or angular), and line (dotted or continuous). Before the presentation the subjects were informed that the set would be lengthy and that there would always be four possible correct responses for each drawing. But they were asked to give only one response—whichever one, for any reason, seemed most appropriate for a given drawing. A confederate of the experimenters consistently gave the "color" response during the set of sixty-four responses. The control groups were made up exclusively of naive subjects, without a confederate. The results showed a significant increase in "color" responses in the experimental groups in comparison with the control groups.

In a second experiment verbal associations were used. The subjects, who were organized in groups of four, received a five-page notebook with eighty-nine associations printed in it. For each verbal stimulus (e.g., orange) there were two associations, one expressing a quality (round) and the other a category (fruit). The experimenter read the stimulus word aloud; then the subjects chose and stated aloud one of the two associated words that seemed more closely connected with the stimulus word printed on the same line. The experimental groups consisted of three naive subjects and one confederate; the control groups consisted of naive subjects exclusively. The confederate in the experimental groups always chose the categorical word. In addition, the verbal associations were arranged in two lists on the basis of the increasing or decreasing probability that the categorical word would be selected by the population at large. In the first list the probability of associating the categorical word with the stimulus word was greater in the beginning; the association chosen by the confederate for these stimuli therefore corresponded to the norm. In the second list, where the probability of associating the category with the stimulus was smaller at the start, the confederate's responses seemed deviant. Irrespective of the order in which the lists were presented, the increase in categorical responses in the experimental groups, compared with the control groups, was significant. In other words, the consistent confederate's influence on the responses of the majority is undeniable, no matter whether he acts according to verbal norms or he deviates from them.

Wahrman and Pugh (1972) provide additional evidence for the fact that the sooner and the more consistently an individual manifests her deviance, the greater the influence she exerts. In their experiments groups of subjects were asked to choose strategies for winning a game. From the very start a group member, a confederate of the experimenter, was instructed to behave in a very asocial and deviant way during all the trials. Futhermore, he was made to appear incompetent. Despite all these handicaps, results were clear: The more consistent he was from the start, the greater was his influence. Wahrman and Pugh (1972) conclude: "Clearly when deciding on a group choice, the group did not discount the nonconforming confederate's suggestions. Quite the contrary occurred. The confederate's nonconformity or obnoxious self-assertiveness apparently increased his influence" (p. 380).

Starting with Asch's experiment, the impact of interindividual consistency was studied, though inadvertently, in most of the experiments on conformity. Why did a minority give in to a majority? What sort of social pressure was exerted by the majority? Was it of a referential or of an inferential nature? Did the minority comply in the face of the majority's position or in the face of the way in which the majority presented its position? And did it comply with a unanimous majority because it was a majority (i.e., a large number) or because of its unanimity (i.e., its consistency, implying a strong consensus)?

The answer to these questions appears when Asch's experimental results are reanalyzed (Moscovici, 1976). As everybody knows, in these experiments a subject is faced with the wrong response of three to fifteen confederates about the length of three lines compared with a standard line. Overall, it seems that the individual complies with the majority in one out of three responses. Asch attributed this effect to dependency toward the majority. Such an explanation entails two main corollaries:

1. When the individual has to choose between the majority judgment and that proposed by another individual, he will choose the former.

2. The larger the majority, the greater is its influence.

Neither of these corollaries has been verified by any means. But several experiments showed that the contrary opinion of an isolated individual (Asch, 1955; Gerard and Greenbaum, 1962; Kiesler, 1969; Allen and Levine, 1971) greatly reduced conformity and strongly influenced the subject. On the other hand, it was found that irrespective of the size of the majority the conformist response invariably amounts to 32 percent. But if even one confederate has been instructed to disrupt the unanimity by giving a different response, the number of conformist responses drops precipitously and in certain cases does not exceed 5.5 percent. It certainly seems, for instance, that a unanimous majority of three individuals exerts a greater influence than a nonunanimous majority of seven or ten. These are sufficient grounds for concluding that unanimity—that is, the sequence of responses reflecting interindividual consistency—is more important than the mere number of persons adopting a common response. Other studies (Mouton, Blake, and Olmstead, 1956; Graham, 1962; Montmollin, 1977) reach similar conclusions.

A study by Whatley (1974) set out to deal more directly with this problem, to wit, whether the observed influence is due to dependence or to consistency. The subjects, in groups of four, indicated their preference for one of the two stimulus figures they were shown simultaneously, before going on to the following figures of the

set. But in each case they first received some information on what they believed the preference of the other members of their group was. These members displayed consensus (interindividual consistency) for each trial and for the entire set of trials with respect to the type of stimulus they preferred. Or they included a deviant member (interindividual inconsistency) who always disagreed with the other two. The subjects, moreover, believed that they were or were not dependent on the other members of the group with respect to a task they would have to accomplish together later on.

The results were clear. No significant dependency effect was found (Morris and Miller, 1975). The conformity rates were larger, on the whole, when the subjects were confronted with a unanimous (i.e., consistent) majority than when they faced a nonunanimous (nonconsistent) majority. The size of the consistent majority, furthermore, had no impact. And *last but not least,* conformity in the private condition remained the same as conformity in the public trials. This result contradicts the results of the experiment by Deutsch and Gerard (1955). In that experiment, as well as in a number of others, conformity is lower in private than in public trials. However, it does seem—and it is a fact confirmed by a large number of experiments (Moscovici, 1980) —that consistency produces much more sweeping changes than a purely external dependence with respect to an authority or a group.

The effectiveness of repetition in propaganda (Cacioppo and Petty, 1979) offers another instance of the impact of behavioral consistency that deserves to be studied in a more imaginative manner than has been done hitherto. For the time being we can draw on some interesting data derived from research in a different field, conflict resolution. The data deal with the concession dilemma. At any given moment an adversary or negotiator must envisage whether or not to make a concession, whether to show flexibility or commit herself to a position. Siegel and Fouraker (1960) have shown that a consistent strategy (high original demands, few and weak concessions) achieves better terms in a negotiation by lowering the aspirations of the opponent. Pruitt and Drews (1969) came up with analogous results. They found, in addition, that the perception of the opponents varied in the following manner. The opponent is seen as weak when he makes many concessions, even if feelings toward him are positive. Consistency therefore does represent a form of courage and a force. And finally,

Komorita and Barnes (1969) observed that the greater the pressure under which the negotiator operates and the shorter the time for developing resistance, the more effective a consistent strategy is. Scattered as they are, many studies confirm that consistency is one of the most powerful factors in producing a change of opinion, judgment, and perception. If ever leadership is analyzed seriously and systematically, what we know about this behavioral style will constitute a solid point of departure. Surely consistency, for example, is one of the manifest aspects of charisma.

It may be held against all the experiments that I have just presented, particularly those by Moscovici and Faucheux (1972), that they tend to leave the reciprocity of social relations out of account. They therefore fail to elucidate the negotiation phenomenon on which the theory is based. Worse yet, they have produced no results that would justify the claim that the findings can be generalized to cover situations in which there is a reciprocal social influence, notwithstanding their fundamental importance (Moscovici, 1976). This criticism is perfectly valid. It should, however, be mentioned that these authors view the negotiation phenomenon as an implicit and internal phenomenon. Their studies were focused on the explicit, not to say superficial, effect of behavioral style. But this focus does not imply that the negotiation phenomenon, and hence the reciprocal-influence phenomenon, has not been investigated. In a later section a review of research findings on group decision will make this clear. At this point I shall just mention two experiments showing that the effects attributable to a consistent behavioral style are of a generalizable nature.

In the first experiment Moscovici, Lage, and Naffrechoux (1973) used a paradigm involving a cognitive conflict (Hammond *et al.,* 1966). According to this paradigm, the task requires subjects to learn one of three cues that could help them in a matching task in order to give a correct response concerning an underlying concept (e.g., democracy in a certain country). The experimenter, of course, gives a feedback on each trial. The conflict stems from the fact that the individuals have received a different training. They therefore have a different approach to the features of the task. In this experiment the conflict is due to the discrepancy between the importance assigned to the cues by subjects who have learned to relate them in a linear way to the correct answer and those who have been taught to relate them nonlinearly (Hammond and Summers, 1965). The former could be said to have ac-

quired a more consistent cognitive system and the latter a less consistent system, since one is more rigid and the other more variable. These subjects were then arranged into groups where one or the other of these two cognitive styles was in the majority (two linear or two nonlinear subjects) or in the minority (one linear or one nonlinear subject).

In keeping with their hypotheses, Moscovici *et al.* determined that subjects trained nonlinearly yield more than do those with linear training; that is, they deviate more from their training than do the linear-trained subjects. And this holds true even where a single linear subject confronts two nonlinear subjects. In other words, whether in a majority or a minority position the influence of the more consistent members of the group outweighs that of the less consistent. At least in this experiment the conclusion is inescapable: Cognitive style has greater impact than the size of the influence source. Nevertheless—and this is the finding that is relevant here—in all the groups there was a convergence of all individuals, a shift toward the position of the opponent, a sign of reciprocal influence. One might say that there is a tendency toward consensus and that consensus is established more in favor of one side than of the other.

These findings were nicely confirmed in a more recent experiment by Spitzer and Davis (1978). Using Hammond's paradigm, these authors made up groups consisting of individuals with varying degrees of confidence in their strategy and stronger or weaker preferences for one of the cues. Their finding was that individuals with strong preferences influenced the weak and no-preference individuals in their groups. Nevertheless, to the extent that each individual, regardless of confidence of preference, deviated from his or her original leaning, some convergence must have taken place. We can therefore state that influence was exerted in both directions. Spitzer and Davis observe, moreover, that decision making is fastest in groups with *one* outstandingly confident member and slowest when members are more nearly equal in confidence.

Unquestionably, the link between more consistent and less consistent, or strong preference and weak preference, is purely analogical. Still, it does have some psychological plausibility. Here, again, we see that the greater impact on the group of subjects whose choice is more consistent does not prevent a reciprocal influence from manifesting itself. The two experiments involved a "cognitive" negotiation phenomenon between the members of a group. And both confirm that elements of behavioral style are decisive, even when the subjects influence others as well as respond to influence from others. If there are further confirmations of this point, we shall be able to assume that the effects we have listed in this part of the chapter have a general applicability.

RIGIDITY

The study of behavioral styles has raised some new problems, particularly the following (Sawyer, 1981): How is consistency expressed, by the repetition of the same response or by a pattern including several neighboring but nonidentical responses? More to the point, can rigid behavior be an influence cause, and if so, what is the meaning of the concept of rigidity? Usually, the word denotes both extremism and a total lack of flexibility. These two aspects of behavior should hamper persuasive effectiveness. And yet we shall see that this is not necessarily the case. As far as extremism is concerned, most theories consider it less acceptable and less effective than moderate behavior. "This postulated people, in general, will have a preference for moderately worded communication over strongly worded communication. It is a bias against 'extremism' " (Taylor, 1969, p. 122).

Like many of its kind, this postulate remains valid as long as we refrain from examining reality too closely and from prying into the presumed image of human nature hiding behind such conceptions. But on closer inspection it does not hold water. A fine experiment by Mulder (1960), which has not attracted much attention, involved a small group of shopkeepers, who had been warned of the impending opening of a supermarket in their neighborhood. The experiment showed that when one of the group adopted a firm stand, most of the others joined in. The merchant's intransigent position (actually, a confederate of the experimenter), far from blocking social interaction or being rejected, gave the participants a chance to establish a firm position. More recently, Eisinger and Mills (1968) tried to prove that if a person sending a message is on the same side as her listeners, she will be considered more sincere than an emitter on the other side, simply because the former is more popular. Conversely, they assumed that the emitter of an extremist message is less popular and considered less sincere than someone moderate. The results belied the authors' expectations: Extremist individuals aroused more positive reactions than

did the moderates. Moderation not only is not consistently respected but is the opposite style of response that arouses admiration and is "rated as more sincere, more competent, more likeable, and more trustworthy" (Eisinger and Mills, 1968, p. 231).

The other aspect of this behavorial style, the absence of flexibility, deserves to be examined more closely. Of course, such a behavior, which is lacking in subtlety and sensitiveness to the reactions of others, elicits some repugnance. At the same time it is an indication of conflict, of refusal to make any compromise or concession, and it characterizes the determination to impose one's point of view at all cost. And yet, as we shall see, it would be a mistake to underestimate its impact. One observation: Rigidity exists not only in the behavior of the individual or group but also in the eyes of the spectator.

In a fascinating experiment Ricateau (1971) gathered a group of three subjects to discuss the case of a young criminal, Johnny Rocco, and asked them to decide what type of punishment or treatment would be most appropriate. Generally, the majority tended toward leniency, but the minority, a confederate of the experimenter, insisted on a more severe punishment. The majority and the minority were asked to discuss the issue before reaching individual decisions. In addition, Ricateau asked his subjects to judge themselves and the other members of the group on a scale based on Osgood's semantic differential. The subjects had to characterize each person in terms of opposites such as active/passive and realistic/romantic.

In the first experimental condition the subjects received only two scales of opposites to record their judgments; in the second they received five; and in the third, eight. They filled in these scales at regular intervals (every ten minutes) during the discussion about the juvenile delinquent Johnny Rocco. By modifying the narrowness of the code used to characterize the minority, the experimenter wished to introduce a more or less flexible perception of the minority individual, although his behavior remained unaltered all along. He assumed that the person would have greater influence if he were perceived through a larger number of dimensions, and this assumption was verified. The degree of influence exerted by the minority varied proportionately to the number of categories used by the group members in their reciprocal evaluations. We can conclude that the majority is less likely to accept the minority's point of view when the minority's behavior seems rigid.

Two studies by Nemeth, Swedlung, and Kanki (1974) and a study by Allen and Wilder (1978) have shown that, aside from the way it is perceived, a genuinely flexible behavior is more effective than a more dogmatic, repetitive behavior. Kiesler and Pallak (1975) also examined the impact of a minority on a group, noting that it had an impact when it acted more subtly by converting a member of the majority in its favor. Mugny, Pierrehumbert, and Zubel (1973) studied the impact of a rigid style on interacting groups consisting of three persons. As was expected, a flexible minority changed more opinions in its favor than a rigid minority. Using a different material, Mugny (1974) found the same result in another study. However, in an experiment using perceptual material, Moscovici and Nève (1971) found no difference between these two shades of behavior. It does seem to be relatively well established that flexibility enhances a minority's influence.

The corpus of Mugny's research (Mugny, 1982), in which behavioral style is studied in depth, shows that this conclusion is only partly valid. In all his experiments, more than twenty in number, he systematically contrasted the effects obtained from a flexible message with those obtained from a rigid message. However, rather than measuring this effect simply by direct items (i.e., items nearly identical with those contained in the message), he measured them also by indirect items. The latter were related to the topic but not contained in any form in the message itself. A change obtained in the latter items would reflect more than a simple adoption of the minority position. It would imply a certain generalization of the message to neighboring areas—from ecology to politics and economics, for instance.

The Swiss psychologist offers the general hypothesis that when a radical person (or group) tries to convince an audience while remaining extreme and inflexible, he prevents the audience from changing in his favor, at least on the conscious level. At the same time he arouses such an intense conflict in each listener that the listener is compelled to modify his or her opinions toward problems that are only indirectly related to the problems discussed explicitly. That is how, in the sixties, the radical movements failed to have the desired impact on the ideas about revolution but, nevertheless, exerted an impact on other ideas, such as those concerning relations between the sexes, ethnic groups, generations, and life-style. In other words, a rigid behavioral style may have an impact, even if this impact makes itself felt elsewhere. And experiments using appeals about military service, pollution,

and so on, and advocating a minority position confirmed these conjectures.

We do not know much about the behavioral grammar represented by these styles. For the moment all we can do is describe them and explain some of their effects. It makes little difference which one is the most effective. In the realm of influence there is no absolute weapon, and each has its usefulness under certain conditions. What would one expect of a theory of behavioral styles? What questions would it try to resolve? What ideas would it help to clarify, and what areas might it help to unify? Surely, these are the only interesting questions, and they need to be answered. By concentrating on the study of dependency, hierarchy, and numerical majority, many of us, I am sorry to say, have carried out intensive work to analyze effects that to the best of my knowledge raise no problems and require no solution. Thus we have been asking questions not requiring any answer.

PARAMETERS OF PSYCHIC AND SOCIAL REALITY

The states of conflict and behavioral styles are the essential factors in the influence phenomenon, since they have a causal meaning and explain most of the effects associated with this phenomenon. Still, in social psychology, as in any other science, it is not enough to know the causes or effects to have a complete grasp of reality or to determine its practical operation. To build a machine, for instance, besides knowing the general laws of motion, one must also know the coefficients of friction, the composition of the materials, the configuration of the terrain on which it moves, the capacities of the worker who will utilize it, and many other factors. And yet none of these factors intervenes in the structure of these laws or the mechanical explanation of the movements the machine will produce.

Similarly, the only way to grasp concretely how social influence operates is to take into account the psychic and social materials that constitute the makeup of the individuals and groups interacting with each other. These materials are their social status, their personality characteristics, their relations of friendship or hate, their sex, and the size of the groups, among others. They have been the object of many thousands of studies in view of their practical importance. It is natural that these studies did not help us understand the influence phenomenon per se, since it was their objective to apply what was known rather than to explain the unknown. But within their own area they provided accurate and simple information, which we will present as succinctly as possible.

Before proceeding any further, let us make the following summary clarification: There are two categories of factors—variables and parameters—the former having to do with specific aspects of phenomena, the latter affecting their respective weight in a given population. Having examined the grammar of the former, we shall examine the distribution of the latter, whose three principal aspects are hierarchy, the size of the majority, and the need for dependence. My reason for stressing this distinction is to put an end to the confusion between what determines the influence phenomenon and what merely hampers or facilitates it.

HIERARCHY

Influence is perforce exerted in a group. However, there are many kinds of groups: groups of friends, groups of strangers, groups of enemies. It may be assumed that interdependence is greater among friends than among strangers, inasmuch as it presupposes a reciprocity of feelings and ideas. We know from our own experience that we are more strongly affected by disagreements with those close to us, and we try more actively to reestablish consensus with them, with all the concessions it implies. Many studies, among which the most frequently quoted are those by Bovard (1951, 1953), Back (1951), Kidd and Campbell (1955), Thibaut and Strickland (1956), Mausner and Bloch (1957), Kidd (1958), and Pollis (1967), have shown that ties of sympathy, a common past, group stability—everything that links us together—increase reciprocal influence.

That this reciprocity has been observed is not so astonishing. More astonishing is the fact that at times it has not been observed. This compels us to wonder whether at times other factors might not be concealed behind interdependence, factors such as hierarchy, which is its most codified and general form. This result is revealed by the experiment performed by LeMaine, Desportes, and Louarn (1969). Taking as their point of departure the hypothesis that we are influenced more by those we like than by those we dislike, the authors picked pairs of students from the same class and school who picked each other in a sociometric test and pairs of students who rejected each other. They expected to observe a greater convergence of judgments in the former than in the latter sets of pairs. This expectation was disappointed. But if

only the pairs where a hierarchic difference existed—to wit, where one of the partners was recognized as more influential than the other by the class as a whole—were considered, then the partners who chose each other were found to be more convergent than those who mutually rejected each other. Affective choices thus reinforce a subtle hierarchic effect, which manifests itself in interpersonal relations. Montmollin (1977) rightly notes that the link between friendship and similarity of responses may be largely attributed to the tendency we have to overestimate the knowledgeability of those we like and to underestimate that of the persons we do not like.

This conclusion leads us to note the relation that always prevails between the hierarchy of abilities, power, status, and the influence exerted: The higher-ranking individuals always have greater influence than their inferiors. Here are a few studies proving that the "experts" have more influence than the "uninformed."

Aronson and Golden (1962) presented young children with a text lauding the values of arithmetic and glorifying the benefits one could derive from its knowledge. In one experimental condition the message was presented as stemming from an engineer; in the other it was attributed to a dishwasher. The children's attitude toward arithmetic became more favorable in the first condition than in the second condition. Aronson, Turner, and Carlsmith (1963) made their subjects evaluate obscure poems and then gave them an evaluation of one of these poems to read. The poem was purposely presented as having been written either by another student or by a very famous poet. They found that the greater the discrepancy between the subjects' and the expert's judgment, the more the subjects changed their original estimate of the poem. This relation did not apply when the communication did not come from an expert.

Tannebaum (1967) reports two experiments analyzing the amount of resistance to the seduction of a subsequent persuasion. In the first experiment the subjects were the targets of identical communications attributed to a professor of clinical medicine and to a health magazine distributed by food stores. The message explicitly recommended certain hygienic practices. As predicted, the more expert the source, the greater was the resistance to subsequent messages of dissuasion. In the second experiment the procedure was reversed: Either the professor or the magazine directly attacked the individual's opinion by means of a persuasive message. The more expert source produced a greater change of opinion.

Other experiments (French and Snyder, 1959; Croner and Willis, 1961; Oakes, 1962; Miller and Hewgill, 1966; Johnson and Scileppi, 1969; Johnson and Stanicek, 1969; Goldberg, 1970) confirm the general idea that the knowledgeability of the source increases the likelihood as well as the degree of influence. But the consensus or the consistency of opinions among experts is decisive. Weiss and his collaborators (Weiss, Buchanan, and Pasamanick, 1964; Weiss, Weiss, and Chalupa, 1967) confronted subjects with counterbalancing speeches, asking them to derive a logical consensus from them. The persuasive arguments were presented as stemming from all the experts in one experiment, from less than half in another, and from 0, 25, 50, 75 and 100 percent in another. As expected, the experts between whom consensus prevailed were more influential than the others, and the influence increased with the consensus. It would seem that there is a direct relation between the size of opinion change and the consistency of opinions among the experts, as well as the amount of expertise. Where evidence exists, it confirms the wisdom of the ages—the respect of those who do not know for those who do know—on which the prestige of the literate has been based from ancient China down through our own times.

Social status is another form of inequality—and certainly the most visible manifestation of hierarchy. In the kinds of situations social psychology usually studies, one of the factors determining the likelihood that an individual will conform is his or her hierarchic position. Leaders give orders and subordinates must obey them—that is the rudimentary principle of any organization. The social value attributed to status is reflected in the characteristic features of those who make up the social hierarchy, notably, the features of seniority, amount of wealth, potential for rewarding and punishing, official authority, and the like. The classic authors summarize all these features under the heading of "prestige."

The hypothesis on which most studies are based is that, generally, the higher an individual's status, the better are the chances that his influence attempts will be successful. Hollander (1964) and Hollander, Julian, and Haaland (1965) seem to have confirmed this hypothesis. Torrance (1954) observed that the influence that members of an airforce team exerted on others in a projective task was in direct relation to their ranks. Strodbeck and Mann (1956) found that professional status determined the frequency of influence attempts, the frequency of success, and the choice of leaders. Many other authors noted similar tendencies.

But there are also striking exceptions. Thus Harvey and Consalvi (1960) and Berkowitz and Macauley (1961) found that the second in command, who is only one grade below the top and is the symbol of our middle class, manifests more conformity than do people with the highest or the lowest status. And this result makes sense: The former have nothing to gain by conforming; the latter have nothing to lose by not conforming. It is only the persons sitting between the two chairs of the social order who expect to benefit from conformity or who fear a loss from nonconformity.

What can we conclude from these results? We conclude that there is certainly a correlation between one's position on the social scale and the degree of influence exerted or experienced. This is not a linear correlation, however; it does not increase regularly with one's position in the hierarchy—or at least we have no evidence to that effect. Thus the impact of hierarchic position still deserves to be studied systematically. The presently available findings cannot be considered as conclusive.

SIZE OF THE MAJORITY

The people's voice is always the voice of the numerical majority, and one would normally think that the greater this number, the stronger the voice. We imagine offhand that the more compact the majority facing an individual whose opinion differs from that of the majority and the lonelier he feels with his opinion, the greater is the influence exerted on him. And yet experiments show that an individual's tendency to yield to group pressure is almost the same, irrespective of whether the majority consists of only three persons or as many as sixteen, as long as it is unanimous (Asch, 1952; Allen, 1965).

Three seems to be a magic number. Below this number influence increases proportionally to the number of individuals in the group. Above it the number makes no difference: A majority of four, five, ten, or fifteen individuals produces exactly the same amount of conformity. Why is three a magic number? Could it be that starting with this number the group norm asserts itself as both visible and unshakable? Is there a diminishing return for information provided by more than three individuals? Does three constitute the minimum number for forming a coalition? For the time being we can offer no real explanation for this fact. No attempt has been made to find one, probably because it has been hoped that sooner or later it would be belied by further findings.

People are loath to accept the idea that influence does not vary proportionally with numbers. This hope is sustained by our laboratories. As it is, these laboratories challenge us with two sets of completely contradictory results: One set confirms that social pressure is not proportional to numbers (Goldberg, 1954; Luchins, 1955; Kidd, 1958; Rosenberg, 1961), and the other set proves that it is proportional to numbers (Gerard, Wilhelmy, and Conolley, 1968; Milgram, Bickman, and Berkowitz, 1969). Sometimes, it turns out that three plus one and two still equal three, while at other times they may equal four or perhaps five. Wilder (1977) has found a way out of this dilemma by reformulating the concept of majority. He has opened up an interesting line of thought. "What is a unanimous majority?" he wondered. Just individuals taken together who happen to agree on something? No; it is the consensus of a group consisting of individuals who behave autonomously (which demonstrates once more that it presupposes a particular behavioral style). In other words, the psychological size of the group equals the sum of *independent* individuals it contains and not the sum of individuals who happen to be present simultaneously in the same place at the same moment.

In two experiments Wilder (1977) studied the relation between social influence and the number of persons attempting to exert influence. His hypothesis was that if a connection is established between the members of the majority, notably in terms of reciprocal conformity, the majority will count as a single source of influence and will have no more influence than a single individual. In contrast, if the members of the majority are perceived as independent entities, their interindividual or intergroup consistency will reinforce the credibility of their common response. The situation is defined as a mock-jury decision.

The participants in the experiment read about the case of a baby burnt as a result of a defective vaporizer. The case is presented in such an ambiguous manner that the manufacturer and the mother each appear partially responsible. Before the subjects make their decision concerning the responsibility for the accident, they are invited to listen to arguments from one or several sources, by means of videotapes, arguments that put the blame on the mother and exculpate the manufacturer. In a set of experimental conditions the subjects listen to the opinion of one, two, three, four, or six persons. The independent character of their response is emphasized by making it clear that the different persons are reading a statement that they drew up individually before presenting it before the camera. In the group conditions, two, three, four, or six persons develop their arguments together, so their responses are interdependent. Finally, in three other conditions the subjects see several videotapes, which correspond either to two groups of two persons, two groups of three persons, or three groups of two persons.

Now, what results were obtained? The influence of independent persons increases with their number, stabilizing at three persons. Just as velocities stop being additive when they approach the speed of light, so influences stop being additive when group size reaches the number three! If the manipulation induces the subjects to consider the members of the majority as forming a single group, influence does not increase proportionately to the number of members. When, conversely, the number of groups increases, even with an equivalent number of persons, influence also increases. Two groups of three persons have more influence than one group of six persons. Finally, if we compare the influence of two persons with that of two groups or of three persons with that of three groups, the influence is greater in the case of groups.

The reason for this result seems very simple to me: If several independent persons or groups converge toward a single judgment, this judgment appears much more objective and perhaps more difficult to reject as biased than if it emanates from a single individual or a single group. Thus the paradox is solved. Surely, several voices have more impact than a single voice—but only on condition that they are really *solo* voices and not a choir, that is, on condition that they are autonomous and not conformist. One can therefore assert that what counts is the number or size of the majority consisting of different individuals or groups and not the number or size of a majority consisting of similar individuals or groups.

An omission becomes noticeable when one reads through these studies. Their authors seem to have disregarded the issue of whether the number of persons on whom influence is exerted makes any difference. Are people more susceptible to influence when they happen to be in a small group or in a large one? According to Duval and Wicklund, objective self-awareness must increase conformity. Taking their hypothesis as a starting point, one is lead to conclude that the smaller the size of the minority, the stronger is its tendency to conform. Duval (1976) attempted to confirm this conclusion and was fully successful. Newton and Mann (1980) also addressed themselves to this specific question. By their observations and the analysis of documents, they made an effort in particular to isolate the impact of crowd size on persuasion. By examining several of Billy Graham's crusades, they have deduced that the preacher's impact increases with the size of the crowd that on its own initiative gathers around him. This effect may be attributable to the massive participation of women and young people. However, on the basis of observations drawn from politics, we are inclined to believe that this result is generally valid. At any rate the problem raised by this study, which has the value of being based on a real group, is still in need of an answer.

NEED FOR DEPENDENCE

From the sixteenth century on political thinkers have worried and wondered about the propensity of human beings to accept voluntary servitude, as reflected in their submitting, without revolting, to the harshest humiliations and the most unbearable tyrants. What induces them to comply with the injunctions of the multitude or of the powerful, even under relatively slight external coercion?

Starting with Le Bon's time and continuing until Freud's time, the classical thinkers of social psychology believed that the answer to these questions lay in postulating that each of us feels a need for dependence and admiration toward a real or ideal individual incarnating the collectivity, whose prototype is the father. It was Tarde, and after him Freud, who claimed that from childhood on our personalities are shaped so as to find satisfaction and security in obedience. Contemporary social psychology resurrected this idea by trying to describe the personality types most susceptible to be influenced by and to submit to the injunctions of the majority or of authority. It assumes that a kind of need for other people exists in anxious individuals, who lack self-esteem and are insecure about their worth and their opinions. This need can be designated by different labels—need for social approval, need for affiliation, need for reassurance—but all of them connote approximately the same psychic reality. The evidence presented to us by the literature is not very clear, and we shall therefore examine it in detail.

It has been assumed for a long time that a personality trait exists that consists of the predisposition to accept the suggestions of others. This assumption implies that no matter what tasks there are to accomplish or what situations may arise, very suggestible individuals should be susceptible to influence but unsuggestible individuals

should not. In a tightly reasoned discussion of studies dealing with suggestibility, Coffin (1941) notes that no very solid evidence has been obtained for the existence of such a personality trait. It would seem likely that with advances in measurement techniques and the refinement of concepts more coherent results would be obtained. Many attempts certainly were made in this direction, and certain correlations were found between the need for group approval and the degree of compliance. Let us look at some of these studies.

Moeller and Applezweig (1957) and later Crowne and Marlowe (1964) established that in different types of situations the degree of compliance parallels the test scores measuring the strength of the social approval motive. Dittes (1959) showed, in addition, that subjects who were led to believe that they were accepted by a group felt attracted to the group. The lower their self-esteem, the more likely they were to conform to group pressures. Hardy's (1957) frequently quoted study starts out from the hypothesis that individuals who have strong motives for affiliation are more likely to give in to group pressure because of their strong need for being accepted and liked. Rather surprisingly, he fails to find any relation between the need for affiliation and conformity. However, on a closer analysis of his data he observes the following: The subjects with a strong need for affiliation conformed much less when they had a partner, while those with a weak need for affiliation conformed much more in the presence of a partner. It would seem that the first category of individuals found in another person the needed support for resisting group pressures, while the second category experienced another person as additional group pressure.

What do these results imply? They imply simply that it makes no sense to speak of conformist or nonconformist personality traits. Conformity or nonconformity assumes a different guise according to the personality trait in question and for specific reasons. Leventhal (1970) had already discovered that people with a low opinion of themselves (low self-esteem) were least likely to be influenced at once by a communication that aroused a great deal of fear, while those who had a good opinion of themselves were most likely to change their behavior. However, let us take a closer look at some experiments.

Rotter (1966) distinguished between two kinds of persons according to the control they exert: inner-directed persons, who measure their effectiveness and responsibility in terms of the good or bad results they obtain, and other-directed persons, who see no connection between their own behavior and events, which are beyond their control and responsibility, determined only by external sources such as luck and the power of others. In short, there are autonomous and heteronomous personalities. Theoretically, one might think that heteronomous individuals are more easily influenced by others and manifest more conformity than autonomous individuals. Odell (1959) and Crowne and Liverant (1963) confirm this prediction. They find that heteronomous people conform more and show less confidence in their judgment than autonomous individuals. These results are perfectly logical.

Sherman (1973) used a slightly different technique to induce an opinion change. In one condition, in particular, he asked the subjects to write a passage disagreeing with the opinion they expressed earlier. In keeping with the theory of cognitive dissonance, an individual carrying out an action that goes against her belief changes in the direction of this action. So an individual who has written such a text will be self-persuaded and change in a direction opposite to her initial opinion. In another condition Sherman tried to persuade the subjects by means of messages that were obviously in conflict with their attitudes. What was the outcome? Did the autonomous subjects generally modify their point of view less than the heteronomous subjects? The answer was negative. Actually, the type of influence used determined the degree of change. The autonomous subjects were more strongly affected by having written a text that was in conflict with their attitude. The heteronomous subjects, in contrast, tended to react more strongly to persuasive messages. In other words, the former submitted to internal conflict and the latter to external conflict. This finding is not unexpected, since the two types of subjects have completely different visions of other people and of the world.

In an experiment by Cialdini and Mrels (1976) autonomous or heteronomous individuals (inner-directed or outer-directed) were under the impression that they were attempting to influence that attitude of a confederate on two topics. The confederate either yielded or resisted the influence attempts of the persuaders. Although they experienced the same success or failure in their influence attempts, the relations of the autonomous subjects with the conforming or nonconforming confederate did not correspond to those of the heteronomous subjects.

On the basis of clinical findings we have strong reasons to believe that autonomous individuals probably have a higher opinion of themselves and of the impor-

tance of their actions. Autonomous persons therefore quite naturally think of the person who yielded as more attractive and intelligent than the person who resisted. Conversely, heteronomous individuals do not have a very high opinion of themselves and do not attribute much importance to what they do. They can be expected to have the opposite reaction, that is, attributing greater intelligence to the resister. From all we know about the effects of self-esteem and all that we have learned from psychoanalysis about narcissism, these results make good sense. They may clarify, furthermore, why those belonging to the poor classes and to minorities make no attempt to exert any influence. They probably believe that those who belong to the majority, to the wealthy classes (and are thus people of greater worth than themselves), will certainly resist their influence attempts.

We are dealing here with something that may not be purely a subjective vision unrelated to experience. In many cases it may be the outcome of repeated failures met by individuals trying to influence others. Repeated failures will make occasional successes seem so exceptional that these successes will be attributed to the low standing of those who submit to them. They will be seen as even more dependent than themselves and as having an even lower opinion of themselves than they do.

An example illustrates the consequence of such failures. In an experiment by Wahrman and Pugh (1972) we cited earlier, we saw that a consistent deviant influenced the majority of the group from the start. But the deviant was a male, and the majority also consisted of males. What would happen if he were replaced by an individual whose psychological and social dependence was solidly attested—to wit, a female? In a subsequent experiment Wahrman and Pugh (1974) found the answer. The sooner the female confederate began to resist, the less influence she had. This tendency was opposite the tendency observed with male confederates, namely, that the "precocious" nonconformist had an increased influence. When male subjects were asked to what extent they wished to collaborate with a female deviant, they insisted that they wanted to have nothing to do with her. Although they expressed a preference for male deviants over male conformists as fellow workers, they manifested a pronounced aversion toward nonconformist females. Only conformist women won their approval. And these subjects were students!

In this experiment, which closely reflects reality, one can see what obstacles dominated individuals, in this case women, have to overcome. Their concrete experiences, the opinions others have of them, and the reasons for their acceptance or rejection in a group are diametrically opposed to the obstacles and experiences faced by dominant individuals. Our penalties for deviance and rewards for conformity are applied more stringently to the most dependent among us than to the most independent. For this reason anyone who has known the hardship and humiliation of servitude has greater respect for anyone who resists. He has less respect for anyone who complies and judges him in a negative fashion—as he judges himself, in fact.

In their brilliant analysis of the relation between personality and society, Marlowe and Gergen (1969) broached all facets of the relationship between people's needs for others (their need for approval, respect, affiliation with others, etc.) expressed as a personality trait and the tendency to conform. However, they found it difficult to reach general conclusions, and I must agree with them. If one still insists on drawing such conclusions, one might say that a need or character trait exists that makes certain individuals more conformist than others. But this trait or need will manifest itself purely in terms of the given situation (Steiner and Johnson, 1964; Allen, 1966), so the same individual who complies in a certain situation will not comply in a different one. Conversely, it is nonsensical to speak of an independent, nonconformist personality. In other words, no type of human being exists who is unaffected by social pressures, has no need for others, and lives in psychological autarchy. In short, no human is free from a life common to all. It is therefore absurd to say that some individuals are suggestible and others are not. This would amount to claiming that there are people who live in society and others who do not. The truth is that each type of personality resolves its divergences with others and changes opinions and beliefs in its own way. And if we delve a little further into the matter, we see that differences in character correspond to differences in concrete experience and to different images of society, in which some are always more or less equal than others.

OTHER PARAMETERS

We could have taken additional parameters into account, such as age, sex, and the physical qualities of individuals. Thus researchers have raised the question of whether women are more conformist than men (Eagly, 1978). The answer seems to be positive (Harris and Cooper, 1979),

but there are qualifications. Researchers have also raised the question of whether the physical features of certain individuals are to be credited for making them more persuasive than others. For instance, does being more physically attractive make a person more influential than somebody who is less well endowed? Chaiken (1979) attempted to settle the matter by a laboratory experiment, and the answer was definitely positive. Unfortunately, just one fleeting look at the photographs of the most influential public figures of our time must give us pause. Not by the furthest stretch of the imagination would anyone judge these persons to be outstandingly attractive physically—and people have often claimed the opposite to be the case. As far as the importance of age is concerned, the findings are too scattered to mention here.

Despite numerous gaps there is a wealth of research on the psychological and social parameters determining influence, or, to be more exact, conformity. For it is safe to assume that when we deal with innovation, these parameters do not operate in the same direction or in the same way. Surely, nobody can claim to master this vast literature. I will therefore limit myself here to a cross section. In the process of surveying this sample, I found many contradictory results. Unfortunately, it is not always possible to analyze the reason for these contradictions in view of the highly varied conditions under which researchers have operated. Nevertheless, on the whole the tendencies that emerge are in keeping with the conclusions researchers have been drawing for many years on the basis of their painstaking and painful observations of social life. Here and there studies have brought us surprising insights and compelled us to define concepts more accurately. Such is the case with respect to the importance of numbers. But, essentially, in this field social psychology has expanded and consolidated the great lessons of "naive" psychology.

THE THREE SOCIAL INFLUENCE MODALITIES: NORMALIZATION, CONFORMITY, AND INNOVATION

In previous sections I limited myself to defining the framework in which the social influence process functions. The moment has come to analyze the process itself. As I noted, the crucial fact in human relations is the existence of conflict—social conflict between individuals or groups and at the same time psychic conflict within the individual or the group. Society has invented a thousand methods for mastering it. We will concern ourselves here with only a few.

The first method is to offer proof so that we can settle which of two conflicting opinions is correct. If you say the length of a piece of material is five meters, and I say it is three meters, we can take a meter stick and measure it, thereby settling the differences between our two estimates. This method assumes a prior consensus on the unit of measurement and its use, something that is not a matter of course. The Renaissance astronomers, for instance, refused to use telescopes as instruments for observation, and their refusal was based on sound optical reasons. But once this consensus is established, one can say that the divergence is eliminated by demonstrating the answer.

The second method for eliminating conflict is the use of the police, of legitimate violence, or of money to silence dissident voices and to compel deviants to change their opinion or belief. Thus the church imposed forced baptisms or excommunicated those who failed to obey. In this case the outcome depends on the relations of strength and resources available. The power to impose a solution reduces antagonism.

The third method, finally, consists of trying to convince other people, possibly by making concessions on certain points and expecting others to do likewise. This method makes it possible to increase or diminish, as the case may be, divergences until a consensus can be reached between individuals or groups. In the main the objective is to negotiate the conflict, and influence was conceived with this objective in mind.

To be sure, none of these methods of mastering conflict is used in isolation, and generally, in real life they are used in combination and act in conjunction. We differentiate between them for analytical convenience and for highlighting each of these methods by means of contrasts between them. Influence is thus distinctive from power and from the rational demonstration of the truth or falsity of a judgment. What we do when we use our influence is to negotiate the solution of a conflict and group consensus. Influence is not, as some believe (French and Raven, 1959), manipulating or exercising power, nor is it acquiring a more accurate view of our capacities and of the world, as others suppose (Asch, 1952; Festinger, 1954; Deutsch and Gerard, 1955; Montmollin, 1977). Influence may have either of these purposes, but they are not its specific function. A power depending on persuasion would be weak. Knowledge founded on convention would at best be plausible rather than objective. I have explained elsewhere (Moscovici, 1976) why the failure to take this specific function into account leads to unfortunate confusions.

But influence is related to conflict negotiation by three modalities: normalization, conformity, and innovation. The first modality tends to avoid conflict by compromises, the second tends to resolve it in favor of the group majority, and the third tends to create and intensify the conflict in such a way that the group consensus is changed in favor of the minority. Until now, attention has been focused on an all-pervasive social influence, which was confused at one time with suggestion (Le Bon, 1895), at another time with imitation (Tarde, 1890), and more recently with conformity (Asch, 1952). We must henceforth approach and study it in terms of these autonomous modalities for facing social conflict.

NORMALIZATION

Normalization can be defined as a gradual change in behavior or opinion on a person's part. It aims to go along with the change in behavior and opinion of other persons and finally to establish a common behavioral and intellectual norm. I can think of no better analogy than the market mechanism; there prices are set by the law of supply and demand, until finally a price emerges and regulates all subsequent buying and selling transactions. But in the case at hand the norm is usually a compromise between each one's point of view. Under what conditions does it occur? What sort of influence is exerted among members of the group to induce them to formulate and accept a compromise? In other words, why do individuals try to establish a consensus and therefore a norm? Why do they desist from establishing this consensus in their favor and from imposing their particular viewpoint as the common norm?

Let us take it as an accepted fact that when an individual (or group) observes a phenomenon or a situation, no matter whether or not it is ambiguous, he is capable of having some idea about it and arrives at a norm of his own. Once he has reached that point, he begins to exchange opinions with several other individuals or groups. They will notice perforce that their points of view on the same matter do not coincide. In short, they meet disagreement where they expected agreement. And this plurality becomes problematic insofar as it gives rise to a conflict, with two negative consequences. On the one hand, disagreement with others tends to turn external op-position into an internal tension, which makes everyone uncertain of himself and his response. On the other hand, it makes reality ambiguous where it was not before or more ambiguous where it was ambiguous already. Contrary to what has often been said, what is at the origin of the judgmental disagreement is not the ambiguity of the stimulus or of reality but, rather, the inverse. In science, to choose the most extreme example, phenomena take on several meanings and become "ambiguous" only when two or more theories arise with respect to them. This was the case, for instance, during the twenty years when scientists did not know whether X rays were waves or corpuscles.

To extricate themselves from this anxiety-producing situation, individuals try to reduce their disagreement and to attenuate its effects by a consensus satisfactory to all. I must stress this essential point: What compels people to move closer toward one another is the existence of a conflict of opinions with its possible repercussions. That is the decisive factor and not, as Sherif asserted, the absence of an objective criterion for settling the correctness of different points of view. Nor do people in this predicament seek to reestablish their own certainty by resorting to the opinion of others.

In truth, why would a person who is in no position to arrive at a correct judgment, for lack of adequate means, assume that other persons in the same position would be any better off to make a correct judgment? In the absence of a clock for telling time, the individual who tries to tell time by looking at the sun will do so neither more nor less correctly than someone else using the same technique. Moreover, if individuals perceive a stimulus as ambiguous, then judgmental diversity is justified and each person judges things correctly from his or her own point of view. One really sees no reason why a common norm should be sought or how an agreement could reassure them about the validity of this norm. At best each might feel relieved not to be the only one who is mistaken. But people have absolutely no reason to think that separately they are wrong and together they are right.

Conflict as such is therefore the driving force. Thus the specific character of the situation lies in the absence of any prior consensus or norm that would indicate in what direction the conflict could be resolved. In short, there is no legitimate majority or deviant minority; each one is equally legitimate for oneself and deviant for others. That is exactly how a pluralistic society is defined.

Since there is no way of using such a consensus as a yardstick and imposing one's own point of view, each one renounces this step on condition that the others do likewise. Each one is resigned to make concessions on one's own truth and one's own rights, as long as nobody insists on imposing his or her truth and rights. Thus concessions made in a group are based on reciprocity and gradually lead to a reduction of tension. The less committed that individuals or groups are on a given matter and the less important that the object of agreement is to them, the easier it is for them to give up trying to make others give in and accept their own position. Another factor might be equality of social status, which incites them to reciprocity, so that nobody claims to dominate others and impose a solution on them. "Being in the equal power position promoted more behavioral cooperation from subjects in reciprocation to an expression of an intent to cooperate than did being in either the strong or weak position" (Tedeschi *et al.,* 1969, p. 258). The reason for avoiding conflict therefore lies both in the fact that there is no legitimate direction for its solution and in the fact that psychological and social factors militate against any of the partners imposing their views.

In his pioneering work Sherif studied this influence modality with great insight. It is true, of course, that he thought he was proving how norms generally are formed and established, while he only studied averaging norms, but what he did establish has not become outdated. In order to get accurate results, he invented a situation with a maximum of stimulus ambiguity. A stationary light source is shown in total darkness; the autokinetic phenomenon, as it is called, consists of the fact that under the circumstances the light source creates a subjective impression of motion. In a first phase the subjects are asked to estimate this displacement, until their judgment stabilizes and becomes a personal norm. But this judgment varies from one individual to the next. In a second phase two or three individuals, who diverge from each other, are brought together to proceed jointly with the same estimation. In the course of the session a growing convergence in their judgments toward a common norm or a central value is observed. What was actually studied here was not the formation of norms but the transformation of several norms into a single one.

Sherif's effect has been replicated several times, but in my opinion his interpretation and his hypotheses have rarely been challenged. Montmollin (1965) showed that as was to be expected, this normalization does not affect all individuals to the same extent. Extreme subjects change more than do moderate subjects, since their distance from the central value is greater. Coffin (1941) proved long ago that the vaguer and more unfamiliar the stimulus is for the subject, the more individuals will move toward each other. Studies of this kind (of which there are too few, as I said before) have confirmed the ideas presented by Sherif.

One criticism of Sherif's interpretation was suggested by Asch. According to him, the subjects converge because they know or believe that the movement they are judging has an objective character and implies an accurate response. The cause of the influence observed was therefore not the illusive ambiguity of the stimulus but, on the contrary, its potential nonambiguity. Had the subjects been warned that the effect was subjective, no convergence would have taken place. In support of his criticism Asch cited an experiment by Sperling (Asch, 1952, p. 487) that had presumably yielded such a result. In two unpublished experiments carried out solely to verify this claim, first G. Lemaine and then Nève and myself failed to duplicate Sperling's results. It made no difference whether the subjects were told that the stimulus was subjective or objective. For once they had more faith in what they saw than in what the experimenter told them.

The illusion of objectivity, for that matter, has nothing to do with the case. Several sets of data, as well as common sense, confirm my interpretation. It was observed, first of all, that if plurality decreases, there is no convergence. In his first experimental condition Montmollin (1977) told the subjects that four of their colleagues had given estimates about a cluster of points whose average was 110 and that were relatively far apart (80, 100, 120, 140); in another condition, the responses mentioned had the same average (110) but were much more tightly clustered (100, 107, 113, 120). In the first condition subjects tended to converge; in the second they tended to move toward extremes. We also found that when subjects are committed by their judgments, they polarize instead of converge. In a further unpublished experiment in collaboration with Nève, we replicated Sherif's situation exactly as a first condition. In a second and third experimental condition we told the subjects either that their judgment about the light source reflected something in their personality or that it measured their ability to judge things precisely. When the subjects were not involved, they converged; when they were, they polarized.

As I stated before, compromise is possible because there is no norm requiring that consensus take place in one direction rather than another and enabling individuals to use it for support in inflecting the consensus in their favor. This is what studies on group decisions show (Moscovici and Zavalloni, 1969). Actually, the results of the discussions that took place in a group always led to a group consensus that was more extreme and constituted an overstatement of existing norms; the persons favorable to the death penalty, for instance, became even more favorable to it; the feminists became more feminist; and so forth. Things turned out as though the extremist minority drew its strength from this norm to convince the others to converge toward its own opinion and not toward the average of their respective opinions. Alexander *et al.* (1970) showed in connection with the autokinetic effect that uncertainty is not unbearable and that individuals do not spontaneously tend to converge. They begin to do so only when somebody serves as a model and takes the lead in finding a compromise. Thus it is not a fluid and ambiguous environment as much as a set of relations between group members—which incite them to reach a consensus by mutual concessions and in which each one's point of view is recognized on condition that he does the same for others—that is crucial for the formation of norms. Conflict is avoided in this way, and its resumption is prevented by the adoption of a less controversial, average point of view. Riecken (1952) noted this fact: "The consensus that is reached in many cases is nothing but an agreement not to disagree" (p. 252).

But once this consensus is adopted by the group, it endures even after the individual is alone again. In several experiments Sherif (1935) observed that collective estimations of the autokinetic phenomenon had some permanence: Subsequent judgments by isolated individuals remained close to their group judgments. Bovard (1948), Rohrer *et al.* (1954), and Luchins and Luchins (1961) show that they persist for a lapse of time that varies from one day to a year.

To summarize, normalization results form reciprocal influence exerted among several social partners who are looking for a "reasonable" solution to their disagreement or, as Riecken puts it, who basically agree not to disagree. Such transactions not only lead to a positive movement toward mutual comprehension but also offer an escape hatch to choosing between conflicting points of view. Legal procedures, politics, or the settlement of international affairs are in many cases based on such psychological and social mechanisms and provide them with an institutional framework.

CONFORMITY

The Problem of Stability

In a society that is as disdainful of traditions as ours is and that is racked and burdened with conflicts, it is not surprising that people have wondered how society would be able to reach and maintain a certain level of stability. From the earliest days of social psychology its creators raised this question and tried to answer it. One might say that it was under their impetus that social psychology became a science of conflict resolution.

Sherif believed that stability could be attained by attenuating differences and establishing, thanks to mutual concessions, a common norm that would be internalized and would then uniformly determine everyone's thought and behavior. But as we observed, this solution is valid only in a strictly pluralist society in which no norms exist for distinguishing between majorities and minorities or between legitimate and illegitimate beliefs or behaviors. As soon as such an asymmetrical situation exists, as soon as a human group permits certain things and forbids others or labels certain ways of seeing things as "good" and others as "bad," as soon as the failure to think and act like everybody else is taken to be an asocial act, and as soon as individuals or groups have strong beliefs, the solution proposed by Sherif has little chance of being applied.

The problem of stability presents itself in terms of a conflict between two mutually exclusive perspectives, between a legitimate majority perspective and a deviant minority perspective. This conflict can be resolved only one way in society: by the submission of the minority to the majority, that is, by the resorption of deviance and the transformation of the autonomous individual into a heteronomous individual.

Conformist Majority and Deviant Minorities

Conformity is the process that leads to stability. It is generally described as a changing of feelings, opinions, and behavior on a person's part as a result of physical or symbolic pressures exerted by a leader or a group. It was engineered in Asch's classic battery of experiments. In these experiments a single individual is opposed by a majority composed of individuals having the same status

and giving a response that is clearly opposite to the individual's own and objectively incorrect to boot. Two flash cards are used as follows: On the first (to the left of the subject) a line is drawn with a length varying between 5 and 22 centimeters approximately; on the second flash card (to the right of the subject) are three bars of obviously very different lengths, one of which is always equal to the standard line. The experimenter asks the subject to judge which of the three variable lines has the same length as the standard line.

The experiment proceeds as follows: The "naive" individual answers second to last, after the other individuals, who are confederates of the experimenter. The latter, whose responses have been programmed by the experimenter, give an obviously wrong answer in two-thirds of the trials, choosing the noticeably shorter bar in a third of the cases, the noticeably longer bar in another third, and giving the correct response in the final third. The subject is thus in a conflict situation between what he or she sees and the unanimously opposed group response. We already know the results: in 33 percent of the trials the naive subject conforms to the unanimous group response.

Let us try to see which factors generally diminish or increase conformity. Is it the nature of the task? In other words, if the material is made more or less ambiguous or if one gives the subject a chance to measure the differences between the lines, will he or she conform more or less? Asch (1956) finds no significant change. Other studies compel us to hedge this conclusion. It does seem that the more complicated and difficult the task, the more conformity inducing it is. Crutchfield (1955), for instance, observes that if problems give rise to more incorrect responses, the subjects' conformity to the unanimously wrong solution urged on them increases. Blake, Helson, and Mouton (1957) find that when the speed of a metronome is increased, thereby making counting more difficult, the subject's response changes more if he or she is subjected to group pressure. Coleman, Blake, and Mouton (1957) have a similar result with a set of information questions (geography, politics, literature, etc.). Montmollin (1977), using the same technique, observes three times as many conformist responses to difficult problems as to easy ones.

The question may also arise whether an individual participating in a group collectively resolving several types of problems one after the other would conform uniformly or would conform more for one type of problem and less for another type. In other words, is the individual's compliance wholly blind, without reference to the object being judged? In the same year Crutchfield (1955) and Linton (1955) arrived at totally contradictory results. The former found a perfect correlation between conformist judgments with respect to several tasks; the latter found no correlation at all. Blake, Helson, and Mouton (1957) found an intermediate degree of correlation. This amounts to saying that up to the present we have not found a clear-cut solution to our problem.

Why do these findings matter to us? They matter simply because contemporary psychology postulated that social behavior was determined by "an active process for striving for validity" (Marlowe and Gergen, 1969, p. 610) and that each of us in relation with others had two objectives: to make a correct judgment and not to lose the respect of others who expect a certain behavior from us. From our findings, though, this result is far from certain. Observation does not authorize us to keep this postulate as a starting point for our thinking. Given these contradictions, we are not entitled to maintain that the influence process hinges on the degree of ambiguity of reality or the degree of difficulty of the problems in relation to which individuals or groups conform in social life. In any case these confrontations are not the way individuals satisfy their need to know the world and to validate their thinking, where they find the evidence they need for shaping their conceptions. At best these confrontations give them a chance to create a social reality that reflects their capacity for convincing others to adopt their opinions, to think or see things as they do.

Let us now turn to explicitly social conflicts between individuals and groups, between the convictions of the former and the pressures of the latter, in order to understand how and why conformity comes into being. In all these experiments this is the conflict that actually materializes: The subject always finds himself placed in a deviant, minority position, faced by a majority that seeks to impose its view on him unilaterally. This majority, as we found earlier, acts not by virtue of its numerical strength but by virtue of the unanimity of the consensus, from which the subject is excluded. This has the effect of undermining the subject's confidence in himself, in his perceptions, and in his judgment (Asch, 1955; Allen and Levine, 1968). Thus even if a single member of the majority expresses his disagreement with the majority and even if the response he gives on his own account is erroneous, the conformity rate drops drastically. Mouton,

Blake, and Olmstead (1956) also showed, on the basis of more ambiguous material, that a nonunanimous majority is much less influential than a unanimous majority.

Why is this unanimity so terribly effective? On the one hand, it is effective because, through group consistency, it displays its commitment, maintains its position, and gives the individual to understand that it expects her to make all the concessions. In a way it downgrades the content itself to stress the weight of the influence source. Concessions are what are actually at stake, and that is how individuals interpret the matter, as can be gauged from the following results: If in Asch's experiment the wrong majority response is moderate, the conforming subjects give the same moderate response as the majority; if the wrong majority response is extreme, however, the conformist subjects adopt a compromise response. The effect depends not on the content but on the source. Since Ference's (1971) experiment, which showed that subjects based their judgment on the information content when the conflict was moderate and on the choice between sources when the conflict was intensive, we can be sure that that is the way things are.

On the other hand, any unanimous consensus excludes the possibility that the response of the majority is biased as a result of a common illusion or prejudice. Even if this were the case, nobody could establish this fact and everyone has to take it at face value, as though it expressed reality. "A judgment of high consensus is generally attributable to the entity, while a judgment of low consensus is attributable to the persons" (Goethals, 1976, p. 291). In Gerard and Greenbaum's (1962) classic experiment this mechanism had already been demonstrated: The individual becomes uncertain, loses faith in her judgment, and recovers it as soon as anyone loosens the iron collar of this consensus. Unanimity thus focuses the whole social conflict on the individual, in this case the deviant, first by highlighting her opposition to the majority and second by giving her to understand that there is no alternative and there can be no alternative to its point of view, just as there is no alternative to its group, its language, or its culture. In other words, it transforms the individual's situation into a closed situation with no choice but that of the majority. Hence the "double bind." People are told: "Look around, act, open your eyes, but see what we see, act as we act." If the weight of authority is added to the weight of the majority, the only answer to this double bind is blind obedience. Binet (1900) and Luchins (1944, 1955) already showed how the approval given to group opinion, reinforced by a professor's authority, changes into obedience, the extreme form of conformity.

But Milgram's (1974) famous experiments have certainly offered the most striking illustration of obedience to authority. In each trial the experimenter brought together two partners, one playing the role of professor and the other (the confederate) playing the role of student. The professor is instructed to present a set of stimuli to the student. The student, who is wired to an electric chair in a separate room, is presumed to react appropriately to each stimulus by pressing one of four levers in front of him. This reaction in turn flashes one of the lights in front of the professor. As a contribution to the learning process, the professor is informed that he should administer a gradually increasing electric shock each time the student gives a wrong answer or fails to answer at all. Each time the student fails to give the right answer, the subject (professor) is supposed to increase the voltage and make the shock more and more painful. We know that about two-thirds of the subjects did what they were told, despite the pain they were presumably inflicting. This result shows that an unbelievably large proportion of people will inflict pain to others to obey authority. Here the experimenter represents authority, since he is acting in the name of science and within the institutional framework representing it, the university.

Exemplifying perfectly the relation between what Gramsci (1953) called mass-man and individual man, these studies prove its logical end product: obedience to personal and impersonal authority, on the one hand, and dehumanization of the deviant, who is not like everybody and who is excluded from humanity, on the other. Milgram's experiments have aroused a flood of virtuous protests and insinuations on ethical grounds, and the Pontius Pilates are well represented among us. Unfortunately, they present us with the mirror of a truth about our social nature that we are loathe to face squarely and that only those who have known the horrors of war and the horrors of peace in concentration camps find trifling.

Interdependence and Pressure Toward Uniformity
We find unanimity at work again in group dynamics in the guise of interdependence among individuals held together by common characteristics or common goals. Unanimity has three effects: (1) attraction toward the majority, (2) pressure toward uniformity, and, as always, (3) compliance with the majority. But in all three

cases whatever highlights unanimity increases conformity. Let us start with the most rudimentary aspect.

As common sense has been claiming for a long time, birds of a feather flock together. The inverse is equally valid: People who flock together become birds of a feather. Our tendency to let ourselves be influenced by those who are like us can actually be observed in various areas. The reason may be that we are attracted to them or that we are likely to imitate them by taking them as models for our thought and behavior. In several studies Stotland and Patchen (1961) and Stotland and Dunn (1962) found that people sympathize with those like themselves, adopt their feelings, and even change their opinions to move closer to them. Back (1951) showed that two persons who are told that they are similar influence each other and reach similar interpretations of photographs that are in fact different from each other, without their being aware of it. In connection with this aspect studies by Byrne and Nelson (1964) and Byrne and Griffitt (1966) showed a result that had been anticipated by Freud, to wit, that affection for others increases with the number of common attitudes a subject is told that he or she shares with these other persons. And this attraction is related to conformity, for we know that there is a propensity to be influenced by those to whom an individual feels attracted. Almost all theories, from the exchange theory to the equilibrium theory, predict this result, and those few experiments carried out to confirm them produced results in keeping with the theories (Newcomb, 1943; Lott and Lott, 1961; Hare, 1962; Kiesler and Corbin, 1965; Mills, 1966).

The correlation between similarity and conformity is easier to understand in a group context. Here it constitutes an index of group cohesion. Festinger (1950) hypothesized that in a cohesive group any disagreement gives rise to efforts to reestablish agreement. The majority attempts to persuade the deviant to change his individual opinion and to adopt the group opinion. In the absence of any possibility for confirming his opinion by looking at reality (because it offers no sure clues) or by turning to somebody else (because there is a unanimous majority), the deviant finally complies. And if he fails to comply, he is condemned to "social death," that is, exclusion. All this is quite familiar. Schachter (1951) found that the members of the majority address more messages to the deviant than they exchange among themselves. The more extreme the deviant or the greater his resistance to their pressure, the more frequent are the messages. If he persists in his opposition, the majority stops concerning itself with him and excludes him from its mind psychologically. Emerson (1954) found comparable results. One might say that a pressure toward uniformity is exerted between two friends, two similar persons. Its purpose is to avoid a break between them, conformity being the price paid for maintaining the relation that unites them.

In an extension of these studies Deutsch and Gerard (1955) provided the clearest demonstration of the connection between the pressure toward uniformity and conformity. Taking up materials similar to those used by Asch, they created a "solidarity" situation in which the subject was instructed that the five best groups would be rewarded. The response of each individual thus became a constituent element in the performance of the group, and the reward each one received hinged on collective success. In the "nonsolidarity" situation each subject was asked to respond as accurately as possible. The wrong answers given under the influence of a unanimous majority were twice as frequent for individuals in the solidarity situation as for the others.

This result surprises us by its banality. If one keeps literally to the letter of instructions, it is quite apparent that a rational interpretation of the collective interest implies that each one should say what he sees, not what he hears the others say. But saying what one sees would mean getting into the conflict with the group, disagreeing with it. In the face of this dilemma most individuals prefer agreement with each other at the risk of common failure. Compliance with the majority in the last analysis constitutes an obstacle to the execution of the assigned task. Collective unity is maintained at the expense of collective action and adaptation to the world. That is the paradox to which I was referring at the beginning of this chapter: While group conformity commonly prevents the individual from giving his or her best, the only way that people can fulfill themselves as human beings is by participating in group life.

The rather inconclusive experiment done by Kelley and Shapiro (1954) marks a turning point in the interpretation of conformity by broaching the question, How does the group react when the majority maintains a point of view that proves more and more incompatible with effective action? Will the propensity to conform persist, without meeting any resistance, even when it impedes collective success? Who, finally, will have the courage to deviate? By a method that I will not describe here, the experimenters led one individual to think that the others always gave the same response. This situation obviously

became more and more incompatible with reality and clearly led to failure. Under these conditions the individual, by changing his response, made a break with group consensus while increasing his chances of success. It was found that the persons who were led to believe that they were wholeheartedly accepted by the group conformed slightly more than the others. Who turned out to resist? The resisters, first of all, were those who attached little importance to group affiliation. Second, some resisters were those who did attach great importance to group affiliation. Finally, the rest showed massive conformity. The success of a group therefore depends on those members who do not care about the group and, to a lesser extent, on those who care sufficiently to brave a conflict with it.

Asch's and Milgram's studies had shown the negative consequences of obedience on the individual; the studies we have just mentioned show its negative consequences for the group as well. If we retrace these classical research trends, a well-defined evolution emerges. At first the focus was on the threat of deviance to stability and the implementation of group aims. In the end emphasis shifted to the risks incurred when conformity blocks change and prevents objective interests from being taken into account. At first interest lay in how to reduce or even eliminate deviancy. In the end the main concern became discovering how deviancy could be encouraged and who might become a deviant. Here the problem was not how the individual could maintain his independence against the group by resisting it but how he could show his independence, for the sake of the group, by acting on it.

Defense of Conformity and Resistance to Conformity

Social norms are constantly under a twofold threat: the attacks of their adversaries and the indifference or the lack of articulateness of their upholders. According to McGuire (1964), the indifference of the latter is attributable to the fact that one is never asked to speak up for cultural truisms. And individuals are not motivated to gain this kind of experience, since they believe, mistakenly, that these norms are invulnerable. It follows that any method to shore up the defenses of the "believers," must, among other things, motivate them to strengthen the claims of such truisms as "You must brush your teeth after every meal," or "Mental illness is not contagious," even though their validity is beyond question. This motivation can be reinforced by making the believers aware that what they consider invulnerable is, on the contrary, quite vulnerable. The only way to rally people to the defense of a truism is to give them the impression that it is under attack.

For this purpose McGuire introduces the medical analogy of immunity: Resistance to illness is reinforced in individuals by exposing them to a weaker dose of the harmful agent, strong enough to stimulate antibodies but not strong enough to neutralize them. This procedure implies subjecting individuals to a short preliminary exposure that they are capable of countering, thereby immunizing them against fully developed presentations of the same argument that they will face later. In several experiments (McGuire and Papageoris, 1961, 1962; McGuire, 1962; Tannenbaum and Norris, 1965; Tannenbaum, 1967) this analogy proved to be accurate. Preliminary propaganda, in the shape of a diluted attack against our beliefs, strengthens our motivation to defend them, and in the process we become more competent in defending them. Research also shows that this type of practice permits us to resist not only concentrated versions of the same argument but also sharp attacks on unrelated points. It is not, on the whole, from the reassuring refutation of the argument that individuals draw their strength but from their having been immunized against the threatening aspect of the material as such. Moreover, this vaccination confers not only a greater degree of resistance but also a more durable resistance, whose effect may even manifest itself with a time lag. Work in this sector offers us an abundant corpus of results that fully corroborate the analogy with inoculation to the extent that we are dealing with general social norms. It has taught us how to resist change and all sorts of counternorms successfully. We now know how these things happen, and we hope someday to know the underlying reason.

It is no less interesting to know how individuals resist *attacks on their conformity* than it is to know how they resist *conformity*. This question then arises: How can one oppose majority pressure? Asch showed in one of his experiments how this opposition is possible when individuals have the support of a single other person. Hochbaum (1954), on the other hand, found that the more certain deviant subjects are at first, the less they let themselves be influenced. In recent years the function of social support in resistance to conformity has received some attention. Social support satisfies two complementary requirements: It throws doubt on the majority's firmness of opinion by showing that there is no unanimi-

ty with respect to them, and it increases the confidence of a minority whose confidence is weak or vacillating.

Allen (1975) is the social psychologist who has devoted the largest number of studies to the discovery of the conditions in which resistance to influence occurs. In general, he created a conformity situation in which an individual who is faced with a unanimous majority is supported by one other individual. In a great variety of experiments Allen found that the tendency to conform is reduced by the physical or moral presence of this ally, especially if he responds after the subject. Nonconformity is usually generalizable from one content to another but not from a verbal to a perceptive task. Moreover, social support is effective irrespective of whether the supporting response is right or wrong, as long as it differs from the majority, whether it is a black or a white who supports a racist subjected to group pressures, and so on. On the whole, whatever opposition there is to the majority, whether its grounds are valid or invalid, it will help the deviant resist social pressures.

However, the question arises whether nonconformity based on social support is equivalent to real independence or whether it is another form of conformity, this time toward the partner. Darley, et al. (1974) examined this question by introducing an additional phase in their experiment on social support and resistance to the majority, where conformity pressure is exerted by this very partner. They found that the individual complies with the person who made it possible for him to stand up against group pressure. As we can see, one conformism is exchanged for another, and resistance is not necessarily a sign of independence. In truth, we need some social support to become and remain independent.

An experiment by Kimbal and Hollander (1974) shows that individuals can escape majority pressures thanks to the example set by a minority, which serves as a model for dissidence. Each group member is thereby incited to behave more freely. In contrast, in another set of experiments it was shown that individuals reject majority influence in order to recover independence. In these studies (Sensenig and Brehm, 1968; Heller, Pallak, and Picek, 1973; Heillman and Garner, 1975) reaction against the majority seems to be a generalized phenomenon. As pressure is exerted more explicitly, this reaction becomes more pronounced. Other factors undoubtedly intervene. Persons who feel competent in a task (Wicklund and Brehm, 1968), for instance, are resistant to all change. They polarize even against a majority that wishes to impose its views on them with respect to a subject they know better than the majority. Furthermore, a certain divergence must already have been present initially for resistance toward the group to have become full-fledged. Worchel and Brehm (1971) reveal that in a conformity situation only those subjects who are already somewhat in disagreement with the person who then threatens their autonomy will stand up against persuasion attempts.

No matter how you look at it, human nature will always be full of surprises. Some say that we are naturally inclined toward obedience; others claim that we are naturally inclined toward liberty. And there are facts that confirm both of these opposite theses. Social psychology has no better answers on this score than philosophy or political science. At any rate it has been observed (Heillman, 1976) that when people are faced with a threat of power, they make fewer efforts to recover their liberty. A further experiment by Montgomery, Hincke, and Enzie (1976) predicts a direct link between the degree of authoritarianism prevailing in society and the degree of resistance of its members. Of course, the higher the degree of authoritarianism, the less is the resistance. But while they confirm this relation, they also find that arbitrary norms have a stronger hold in groups formed by authoritarian individuals than in groups with unauthoritarian individuals. From this result the authors conclude that "low authoritarians are somehow more volatile and prone to revolution than high authoritarians" (Montgomery, Hincke, and Enzie, 1976, p. 707). This conclusion is hardly surprising, but it is reassuring to have it discovered in a laboratory, thus proving that what is observed there is not unconnected with reality.

In the final analysis autonomy does seem to be a factor involved in resistance, if not as a sort of psychic need, then at least as an internal condition of the individuals living in a certain society and wishing to be in control of their capacities or to maintain certain values, among which liberty is certainly one of the most undisputed, if not the most important. One must conclude that the two bodies of research—the one dealing with the defense of collective norms and the other concerning resistance to collective pressures—both lead to coherent and valid results. However, as long as their findings are viewed separately and are not interrelated and fitted into a more general model of social influence, their deeper significance will remain in doubt.

The Proper Application of Conformity

We soon learn to turn conformity to our own advantage, either to preserve our personal integrity or to become outwardly successful. Hypocrisy and politeness make tolerable social relations that would be unbearable if sincerity and spontaneity prevailed. All the methods invented to circumvent conformity are based on a very simple principle: winning the confidence of an individual or group and, once this confidence has been granted, exploiting it for one's own benefit so as to change existing relations in one's favor. Flattery is one of these methods that go back to time immemorial. Classical drama has portrayed it in its many variations and exploited its comic effects to the fullest. Under the new name of *ingratiation* (act of seeking somebody's good graces), Jones (1964) studied it in the laboratory. He examined how lower-status persons, by simulating compliance, influence their superiors; the methods applied are such that neither of the participants recognizes the opportunism of this ingratiation. In a few quite complex experiments Jones showed that as the subordinate individual becomes more attractive, the powerful individual moves closer to her point of view and evaluates it more favorably. Conformity makes it possible to increase the dependence of individuals who have power or wealth and to diminish the dependence of individuals wanting these goods. This promising field of research seems to have been given up prematurely, so nothing conclusive can be stated about it.

Under the heading of "innovation" Hollander (1960) investigated how we can gain the confidence of both our equals and our inferiors and how, once this confidence has been won, we can introduce changes we consider necessary and have others go along with us. In short, we conform to others to induce them to conform to us. Hollander asserts that by obeying common rules as well as, if not better than, others, the individual accumulates a capital or credit of favorable dispositions on the part of group members. The greater his credit, the more the group will put its trust in him; he will therefore be in a much better position to deviate and to impose his wishes and his opinions on the majority. The innovation tactic, like ingratiation, consists of two phases: first gaining authority over the group by seeming to adhere to its norms and aims; then once the person has reached the top, modifying the group's norms and objectives, since the others will perforce follow the innovator and accept his deviance. Had Lenin followed this approach, he should have become Czar of all of Russia and then introduced the Soviet revolution.

This hypothesis is obviously based on the idea that while groups reject any form of deviance, they do tolerate certain deviations from the norms on the part of individuals with a high social status, with a certain competence, or with an important role to play, because these members, after all, have already proven themselves. In a few experiments (Hollander, 1958; Hollander, Julian, and Haaland, 1965; Julian, Regula, and Hollander, 1968), subjects were confronted with a confederate behaving normally and showing competence in the task assigned. But after a certain point she diverged from her line of behavior and began to act deviantly. It was then found that the more conformist she seemed to be at the beginning, the greater was her influence on others.

These findings leave me unconvinced, and they could be countered by many findings pointing in the opposite direction. Jones, Jones, and Gergen (1963) found, for instance, that when an individual seems dependent and conformist, he gains no credit. However, even if he is strongly conformist, he is judged favorably as long as this conformity is not displayed in a context that makes him seem dependent. Furthermore, Wahrman and Pugh (1972) showed that an individual who deviates a great deal exerts as much influence in a group as an individual who deviates less, as long as she is consistent.

Notwithstanding its weak empirical foundation, Hollander's hypothesis is very plausible and reflects everyday experiences. It is typical of the way many small innovations are produced in stable and hierarchic groups and reflects the desire of some people to bring about changes without rocking the boat—or, as the saying goes, to make an omelet without breaking any eggs. Indeed, it would imply a surprise-free and untroubled history.

New Trends in Conformity Research

At first glance one gains the impression that there have hardly been any new studies in the past fifteen years in the area dealing with conformity. It would seem as though the rich vein discovered at the start had been exhausted. There are, certainly, occasional experiments that spell out some specific point or replicate well-known results with the help of a more sophisticated technique and in the up-to-date terminology of attribution or cognitive dissonance theory. But one becomes convinced that social psychology has almost lost interest in the influence phenomenon.

Much as one might deplore this state of affairs, since influence phenomena are at the heart of the discipline, it must be accepted as a fact. But it would be a mistake to carry this impression too far. Actually, even within the

classical framework—which may seem to some, including myself, to have become a closed chapter—research of the greatest interest continues to be done. There is no cause for surprise in that result. In his analysis of scientific revolutions Kuhn (1962) has shown how, even after anomalies have begun to pile up alarmingly and even after a new theoretical paradigm has emerged, normal science continues to advance and prosper in the traditional direction, just as nature in the fall brings to full bloom flowers that are doomed to wither in a matter of hours once the first frost appears. There is nothing contradictory from an epistemological point of view about asserting that a line of research has become a closed chapter and that under its aegis scholars are doing outstanding work or that they are looking into hitherto neglected problems.

Among these studies let us first mention those that have been devoted to a more accurate interpretation of the Asch situation—and hence conformity. In an article of great intellectual acuteness Ross, Bierbrauer, and Hoffman (1976) raised the question of why an individual facing a group majority is unable to dissent. Their answer rests on attribution theory. They found that in the Asch experiment the person who would like to dissent is trapped in a double impossibility. On the one hand, she is incapable of explaining the differences in judgment that have arisen. On the other hand, she cannot conceive how her peers would interpret her dissent. For lack of a satisfactory way out of this dilemma she yields to the majority. They try to show in several experiments that if the possibility is given to account for the difference or to anticipate a favorable interpretation on the part of their peers, conformity will decline. And the frequency of dissent and confidence in dissent will increase correspondingly. What they prove thereby is that the Asch situation represents an ideal conformity situation. For all practical purposes it blocks all deviation by an individual faced with a majority that forces her to misjudge reality. In this analysis by Ross, Bierbrauer, and Hoffman the cognitive change that may be taking place is hardly taken into account. To a certain extent the analysis disregards it.

Allen and Wilder (1980), though, focus on this very change. According to them, the modifications of opinion or judgment attributed to conformity are derived from this cognitive change. To summarize, they make the hypothesis that influence is due to the fact that the stimulus acquires a new or different meaning in the group. What really takes place on closer inspection? At first, when one's opinion diverges from that of a unanimous group, one reinterprets the stimulus object. Then this reinterpretation of the stimulus makes the position of the majority appear more acceptable. What is the consequence? The individual moves toward the majority position. In other words, the conflict in judgment and opinion leads to a change of meaning in favor of the group. This is a very plausible argument, which is verified experimentally by the authors by using opinion items. But a doubt persists. Can such an argument be generalized to the Asch situation? In the Asch situation the meaning must be unequivocal. It is difficult to see how meaning can be permanently modified by it. Despite this qualification Allen and Wilder's hypothesis is of great interest.

Somehow, certain questions keep coming up over and over again because they lack a satisfactory answer. Such is the case with the cultural variant of the question of whether conformity is a child of our culture and/or our time—in other words, the question of whether group compliance is greater or smaller in one country or another, at one historical juncture or another. Frager (1970) broaches this question by making use of the Asch situation. His research, which was carried out in Japan, seems to show that Japanese students are less conformist than their American or European counterpart. It also brought to light a fairly high level of spontaneous anticonformity, a phenomenon that had gone unnoticed hitherto and noteworthy in its own right.

But the two English authors Perrin and Spencer (1980) are the ones whose claim is the most provocative. They argue that the generally acknowledged Asch effect is not at all a rock-bottom phenomenon. It is simply a product of its time and culture. To support their argument, they conducted an exact replication of Asch's original study. Exposing British students (engineers, mathematicians, and chemists) to the influence attempts of a unanimous majority of six confederates in a face-to-face situation, they obtained a dramatic result: In only one out of 396 trials did a subject join the majority. On these grounds the authors conclude that the effect is "a useful indicator of the cultural expectations subjects bring to the experiment from their contemporary world." (Perrin and Spencer, 1980, p. 406). At once Doms and Van Avermaet (1981) set out to invalidate this assertion. The rates of conformity obtained with Belgian subjects belonging to comparable groups are on the whole close to the rates obtained by Asch. According to these authors, we are dealing with a universal and timeless phenomenon. Whatever the outcome of this controversy, here is an area of problems calling for solu-

tions. It is puzzling, in fact, that nobody has so far considered devoting the necessary talent and energy to them.

Anyone who has observed or actively participated in the political scene knows that there are two extreme forms in which conformity can manifest itself in society: by blind obedience and by apathy. Some leaders have sought to overcome these two forms either by generating a state of resistance or by mobilizing the masses. Mass psychologists have all dealt with this problem in a very general way (Moscovici, 1981). The most up-to-date and impressive investigation of obedience is presented in Milgram's famous experiments. In their research on bystanders Latané and Darley (1970) have opened up the investigation of apathy. I might illustrate the contrast between these two sets of studies by an analogy drawn from a historical event some of us have experienced personally: the holocaust. Milgram raises and tries to answer the following question: How could German soldiers and officers agree without protest to commit actions that are so contrary to morality and human rights? Conversely, Latané and Darley attempt to elucidate the following question: How can people stand by passively without reacting to a situation that is detrimental to them or to someone else? This question has puzzled many with respect to concentration camps. Among those who were their victims and those who were on hand to see what was happening, many failed to react in self-defense or to help the victims.

I am not implying that these authors were explicitly referring to these questions. Social psychologists avoid all references to history and large-scale social phenomena. They think that they can thus isolate research from political or social commentary—which implies that we know where to draw the line between the two. In beginning their exploration of such a vast area, Latané and Darley very cleverly combine studies inside and outside the laboratory. As everyone knows, emergency situations are devised in these studies: smoke, victims of an attack, and so on. An individual, either alone or in the presence of two or three others, becomes the bystander in a situation that requires a reaction on everybody's part to avoid a disaster, help a person in distress, and the like. What one wants to determine is whether the individual will react more promptly alone or in a group.

Latané and Darley assert that in a case of emergency an isolated individual will react more appropriately and faster than the same individual surrounded by others. How can this assertion be explained? There are two main reasons. On the one hand, the individual experiences the paralyzing constraint of other people's judgment and perception. Not knowing what others are thinking and what their view of him is, the person is slow to act: "Social influence, then, turns out to be a major determinant of bystander intervention in emergencies even though bystanders may not be aware that they are being influenced. Similar social influence processes, we believe, can account for many of the cases of bystander 'apathy' appearing in the newspapers" (Latané and Darley, 1970, p. 89). On the other hand, a diffusion of responsibility occurs in the group. Each group member feels less involved with what is happening. Nobody knows exactly what his role or responsibility is. On the whole, the presence of others prevents people from perceiving the emergency, deciding, and acting.

Experiments have fully confirmed these hypotheses. Latané and Darley show, for instance, that when an individual is locked up in a room where there is smoke, she will smell and report it after three or four minutes if she is alone. If she is in the same room with two passive confederates, however, she will be much less inclined to report the smoke. And if she does so, it will be with a much greater delay. They also show that if the group of bystanders is made up of friends, rather than strangers, the individual will more quickly come to the rescue of a victim. Similarly, in the course of two experiments they noted that individuals were more likely to report a crime if they witnessed it alone than if somebody else was a witness too.

All these studies show the constraining effect of conformity and its detrimental impact on society. Conformity is to blame for making members of society apathetic and irresponsive to threats against themselves and their close relations. At the same time these studies confirm a thesis that Le Bon (1895) repeatedly maintained—to wit, that when an individual is part of a group, he is incapable of seeing reality, of deciding, and of reacting. Hence he even ventures to claim that one witness is more trustworthy than a group of witnesses. In short, a single pair of eyes is more reliable than several pairs, which see nothing at all.

In keeping with this line of thought, Latané, Williams, and Harkins (1978, 1980) have shown that most individuals gathered in groups make less of an effort. Suppose male students are assigned to make as much noise as possible by shouting or clapping their hands, and they are given this task either alone, in pairs, or in groups of six. It appears that the collective performance is less than the sum of individual performances. But once the members of these groups are identifiable, there is an increase in the joint effort. So there is such a thing as social loafing. People are less energetic when they are immersed in a collectivity than when they are alone. One might say that our tendency to expend the least effort is legitimated and reinforced by the presence of our colleagues. Hence there are a lowered profit and a reduced benefit for all. This situation may be unfortunate. But one might also raise the question: What entitles us to believe that the criterion for a group performance is the sum of all individual performances? It might well be that, as I believe, the group is the precondition for every kind of performance, including individual performance. Perhaps, when the individual is on his own, he does *too much,* just to remedy the absence of others, as the famous Robinson Crusoe attests.

Latané and Nida (1980) have suggested a theory of social impact. Although it may be premature to present this theory or to pass judgment on it, it is of some value to devote a few words to it. It is offered as a justification for a mathematical law comparable to the laws that exist in psychophysics. According to this theory, the impact of a source consisting of several individuals on a target individual is a function of the strength, immediacy, and number of individuals. It specifies what happens when the target receives support from other people. A set of studies on stage fright, new interest, imitation, bystander intervention, and conformity seems to support these ideas. Despite the evidence it must be recognized that factors such as strength and immediacy are very imprecise and hard to measure in psychological terms. I very much doubt, moreover, that an exact relation between the size of the group, for instance, and its social impact will be possible to establish. Beyond these formal aspects it must be admitted that the psychosociological content of the theory is still limited and certainly very classical. Unquestionably, there is nothing to prevent this theory from reaching its goal by some as yet unpredictable routes and from making discoveries of real interest, at least in the field of social engineering. However, for the time being it raises many more questions than it answers.

Beyond Conformity

Now that studies on the influence of individuals and minorities have spotlighted their impact and their role in innovation, one has come to take a kinder view of these deviants than in the past and to look at them in a very positive way. Admittedly, they are avoided, disdained, and rejected. But at the same time they exert a very strong attraction. This paradox has awakened a renewed interest in the deviance phenomenon: How do people react to it? What are its effects? And so on. In broaching these questions, the various researchers perforce disengage themselves somewhat from conformity. And in the process they tend to lay the ground for a compromise between the classical and the more recent analyses (Levine, 1980). As history tells us, such compromises are generally precarious. They serve a useful role, however, in clarifying facts and concepts. According to Levine and others with the same outlook, reaction to opinion deviance and to the deviant is determined by the following motivations: (1) to attain opinion evaluation, (2) to obtain validation, (3) to avoid interpersonal conflict, and (4) to maintain the group as a viable and distinct entity.

Levine, Saxe, and Snyder (1976) set out to verify these ideas by observing group responses to a deviant who either agreed or disagreed consistently. Another set of observations dealt with a deviant who started out by agreeing with the group and then disagreed, or the converse. As was to be expected, an individual who first disagrees with the group and then agrees is better liked than an individual who shows consistent disagreement. A repentant deviate is better liked than a renegade. In this experiment as well as in a subsequent one (Levine, Sroka, and Snyder, 1977), the researchers showed that a deviate who breaks away from the majority is influential. Hence someone who has the courage to break away from his own group and oppose it is likely to provoke the most intense conflict and thereby instigate the greatest change. Another finding is that when a deviant enjoys low social support, he has more influence than when he has high social support. This result implies that he is more convincing because he seems autonomous. These studies, to be sure, reiterate familiar facts—for instance, that nonconformity attracts group attention but at the same time predisposes the group to evaluate negatively the opinions and motivations of the deviate (Ridgeway, 1978). It must be recognized, however, that a "neutral" person, one who wants to conciliate everybody and remains indecisive and moderate, is also disliked and rejected (Levine and Ranelli, 1978).

Another finding is that the evaluation of a deviate by the members of the majority is affected by the grounds on which the deviant justifies his or her position. Thus a person expressing lack of concern for the discussion topic is rated less favorably than one admitting ignorance or ambivalence toward the two antinomic response options. Objective conditions also affect this evaluation. Over-

manned groups are more likely to reject a deviate than undermanned ones (Arnold and Greenberg, 1980). It comes as no surprise that a tolerant majority rates deviants more favorably than an intolerant one (Ruback and Levine, 1979). The fact remains, irrespective of positive or negative reactions, that the deviant in all cases maintains his or her influence. Therein lies the explanation for the fact that a minority's impact is relatively independent of how favorable or unfavorable its impression is or how much like or dislike it generates in the majority. It would be desirable to expand the range of these studies in order to explore more fully the question of affective responses to dissenting (Moscovici, 1976). It is reasonable to hope that research in this area will continue and will broaden our knowledge and that the day will come when the following question will be raised: What is so fascinating about someone who transgresses norms, overthrows established opinions, and creates something unanticipated? Furthermore: What gives certain individuals (or groups) the strength of character, to do so?

INNOVATION

Majority and Minority Influence

The innovation process in its genuine form stands at the opposite pole from the conformity process and cannot conceivably be one of its manifestations. It follows that the minority that sets off the process benefits from no prior "credit." It is not expected to have any claim to the truth, and it can base itself neither on a norm nor on a unanimous group. On the contrary, it is discredited, its assertions are a priori wrong, and it is rejected by the norm as well as the group, thereby becoming identified as deviant. It can therefore appeal to no power or competence as a method of action. How can it then make its opinions, feelings, or behaviors prevail? This question has only recently become a subject of investigation, but we already have some answers that are significant from a theoretical and experimental point of view. The following discussion is a survey of the main ideas.

When a group of individuals must confront a set of realities or problems and when it must find a solution and reach a decision with respect to them, there are two types of situations that may arise. In the first type of situation no explicit rules, norms, or models exist to guide them in their options, and under these conditions individuals tend to hesitate and to react relatively inconsistently. As they become aware of the divergences separating them and yet have neither an incentive nor a method for taking an aggressive stand for their point of view, their first reaction is to try to avoid conflict by concluding a compromise. The normalization process is at work. However, this process of mutual concessions is blocked if one of the individuals refuses to play this compromise game and indicates his preference for a well-defined option. By taking this stand, the individual not only defies the logical norm, which would be an average, but also exploit his own worth. In addition to the negative aspect of his obstruction, his proposal plays a positive role by offering an alternative solution that is as valid as any other and has the advantage of being clear and definite. For reasons of this sort a resolute and consistent minority—which, in contrast with the other members of the group, is willing to engage in conflict—may succeed in having the consensus develop around the position it maintains and the solution it advocates. Several studies (Gurnee, 1937; Torrance, 1959; Shaw, 1963; Moscovici and Faucheux, 1972) confirm this view.

In the second type of situation the majority already has a consensus or a particular point of view that acts as a norm, and the minority consciously attempts to modify it. The presence of a norm is generally revealed by the spontaneous conformity of the individuals who share it. It induces each group member to accept unhesitatingly a certain way of speaking or living, of feeling or thinking, and to reject all other ways with equally little hesitation. When an individual (or subgroup), instead of complying or resisting purely internally, not only refuses this way of doing things but proposes something different, he or she offers an alternative solution where none existed before and none could exist. The minority's first impact is on the consistency of social pressure exerted on each group member by denying the social consensus. Then it introduces totally new dimensions of the problem or object and upsets existing values, thereby perturbing internal (intraindividual) consistency and turning fine certainties into deep uncertainties. If it keeps up a continuous pressure, a minority succeeds in making its own point of view as familiar as the commonly accepted one, and eventually, it may make its view equally persuasive.

One of the reasons why the minority appeals to such superior entities as truth, beauty, history, and God is that, at least in part, it wishes to strengthen the solution it advocates by making it seem indispensable and to increase tension so as to force everyone to take it into consideration. On the other hand, by refusing compromise as much as, if not more than, the majority does, the minority simultaneously maintains the intensity of the conflict and testifies to its unwillingness to make concessions. That is, it indicates clearly that it expects concessions from the other side. In this light one might say that the group or individual who innovates also creates conflict and that the negotiation that takes place between the majority and the minority revolves around the creation of a conflict where none existed previously. Herein lies the particular character of innovation as an influence modality. It is centered on the creation of conflicts, just as normalization is centered on their avoidance and conformity is centered on the control or resolution of conflicts.

The first studies carried out in this framework were intended to show that minority consistency acts to change majority judgments and perceptions. These studies used the following experimental procedures:

1. The response conflict was intensified by minority consistency and majority consensus.

2. All possibility of opposing social pressure to physical reality was eliminated as totally devoid of interest.

3. Instead of varying stimulus structure to produce influence, the studies used response structure (i.e., behavioral style) as an independent variable.

4. Physical properties intervened only to highlight the deviant character of the minority response and its opposition to that of the majority.

In other words, an attempt was made to simulate a real-life situation in which a minority finally wins out despite its many handicaps.

In a set of experiments Moscovici, Lage, and Naffrechoux (1969) and Moscovici and Lage (1976) studied the influence of a consistent minority on the majority's visual judgment. The following experimental paradigm was used. Groups consisting of four naive subjects and two confederates of the experimenter were asked to make a set of color perception judgments. All the slides used were blue. Each subject was asked to name aloud the simple color that he saw and to estimate its light intensity in numerical terms. The results of a control condition in which there were only naive subjects showed that the stimuli were quite unambiguous and that the slides were clearly perceived as blue. Therefore nothing facilitated the influence effect in this situation, neither stimulus ambiguity nor the presence of a consistent majority. In one of the experimental conditions the two confederates claimed that they saw green at each trial. They therefore displayed intra- and interindividual consistency in giving a judgment that was at odds with physical evidence. In a second experiment the confederates asserted that they saw green on only two-thirds of the slides. Although the confederates maintained their interindividual consistency, the intraindividual consistency of their responses was disrupted. In the third condition the two confederates gave completely inconsistent responses. The results showed that the judgment of the naive subjects was influenced in the first experiment (32 percent of the subjects gave 8–10 percent *green* responses) but not in the other two conditions. The consistent minority behavior undoubtedly influenced the majority, even under such adverse circumstances.

Nemeth, Swedlund, and Kanki (1974) have come up with the hypothesis that, generally, consistency is a response pattern associated with a person's (or group's) position, and that the repetition of the same response is not the most effective pattern. Using the same paradigm, they include a set of conditions where the confederates' responses are slightly inconsistent but follow a pattern agreeing with the stimulus property—namely, light intensity. In these conditions the minority is more flexible than the minority in the set of rigid conditions. A nonrepetitive pattern of responses, these authors conclude, may generate a perception of confidence and certainty, as long as the pattern suggests that the agent who is exerting influence maintains a consistent and identifiable position. These findings are compatible with those of Doise and Moscovici (1969–1970): When a deviant makes himself noticeable in an abrupt fashion from the very beginning of the experiment, the group members are less influenced than when his deviance becomes noticeable only gradually. But as will be shown later, what is gained on the level of public impact is lost on the level of private impact, and vice versa.

In one guise or another an obvious relation exists between the minority's behavioral style and its influence. Consistency on the part of the minority creates an impression of certainty and of confidence, and its uncompromising attitude induces everyone else to take the positions it upholds seriously and to make concessions, in the hope that it will do likewise. In the current climate of thought in social psychology, however, it will be difficult for people to recognize behavorial style as a crucial factor. If one keeps adhering to the prevalent dominant model, one might imagine that all this is completely irrel-

evant to innovation or consistency (Doms, 1978; Levine, 1980). And one would insist that all this amounts to nothing but a sort of person-to-person conformity exerted by a tiny majority. It is a snowball phenomenon: The two confederates influence the nearest subject; then all three form a small group influencing the subject in the fourth position; and so on. It is an ingenious version of Hollander's idea.

That such interpretations can be advanced demonstrates how deeply the conformity bias (Moscovici and Faucheux, 1972) is rooted in social psychology. It also shows how difficult it is to present social reality from the minority point of view. It is likely that we do not yet know how to study them appropriately in the laboratory. But current difficulties will one day be overcome. In any case we do not yet have sufficient data accumulated to confirm or invalidate existing hypotheses satisfactorily. Until we have reached that stage, no test-tube experiment can possibly invalidate what each of us observes in social reality. For the moment the main point is to investigate the field of innovation, to gain a grip on the relevant phenomena, and to test the limits of the existing model.

Adopting a compromise position, the Belgian psychologist Doms (1978) studied the way in which social support (Janis, 1983) determines minority influence. To present the matter succinctly, let us say that she has done for innovation what Allen has done for conformity. The stimulus material is a modified version of Asch's lines instead of colored slides. In a first experiment Doms set up an innovation condition (two confederates representing the minority and four naive subjects) and a control condition. There was a significant difference between the two conditions. Thus the minority did exert some influence on the majority. An analysis of the results as a function of the response order revealed the following conclusions. The closer the subjects were to the minority, the stronger was the influence on them. We might think (and this idea would be worth checking) that we are dealing here with a sort of microconformity. The two minority members induce the individual who responds immediately after them to yield more than the other subjects.

As a test of whether this distance was really a determining factor, a second experiment was conceived, where the response order was varied systematically. The minority influence remained undiminished. This time, however, the subjects closest to the minority were less influenced (5.5 percent errors) than those who were a greater distance from them (23 percent errors). In any case the subjects' response order did not affect minority influence. Despite these latter results, I do believe that the distance in relation to the minority has a certain impact.

Now here is another question: What happens when an individual is simultaneously subjected to minority and majority pressure? In a third experiment a condition was first created in which two minority confederates tried to influence four naive subjects. Then in several conditions one naive subject was in the presence of two minority and three majority confederates. The two minority confederates either maintained a correct response or randomly made 12.5 percent errors similar to those made by the minority source. In all conditions naive subjects gave their responses in the last place. The most significant influence was obtained in the pure innovation condition, where four subjects were faced with two minority confederates. Conversely, when a correct majority confronted an incorrect minority, influence was drastically reduced. Again, one notes that there was no pronounced decline in influence as a function of the subjects' response order in the pure innovation condition. On the whole, the normal and consistent majority was as effective in combating minority pressure as a consistent minority was in combating a majority pressure.

The same problem was tackled in the fourth and more complex experiment. There were four mixed innovation conditions, with two deviant confederates giving incorrect responses, three normal confederates giving, in general, correct responses, and one naive subject. This subject had to choose between the erroneous *and* deviant and the correct *and* common responses. In the first of four conditions the majority confederates randomly made 12.5 percent errors similar to those of the minority. All subjects responded in the last place. In the second condition they made the same errors, but the errors were systematic. All subjects responded in the third place. In the third condition majority confederates went along with the source when (and only when) the naive subject did so. All subjects again responded in the third place. Finally, in the fourth condition the majority confederates did the same thing as in the previous condition. However, their response was independent of that of the subject. All subjects responded in the third place. The results showed that minority impact was greatest when the majority made the same errors as the minority (second condition) or made its response after the subject, without imitating him (fourth condition). But this influence was exerted only when the subjects responded right after the minority (second condition), not when they followed the majority

(first condition). Response order thus seems to have a certain impact. Finally, in the last condition there was a tendency to observe a greater shift in favor of innovation than in the first condition.

As was to be expected, the reactions of the majority do intervene in determining how strong the impact of a deviant minority is. In thinking over this set of experiments, one is led to conclude that a consistent minority has an impact on a majority (see especially the pure innovation conditions) and that this impact is direct. Within certain limits the presence of social support does not affect either resistance to influence or compliance. Innovation is thus an independent process rather than a form of conformity; it is not even conformity in reverse (Hollander, 1958; Moscovici and Nemeth, 1974; Doms, 1978). At the same time independence must not be confused with separation and isolation. Majority and minority reactions both have a share in determining the overall effect of the latter on a group or on society as a whole.

Factors That Increase or Diminish Minority Influence

Other studies have explored the conditions under which a consistent minority has a greater or smaller degree of influence on the majority. Of course, whatever reinforces the perception of its behaviorial consistency and makes it seem more autonomous or objective increases its impact. Whatever facilitates its rejection—whatever converts deviance into an arbitrary tendency—diminishes it.

Some investigations confirm that things actually take place in this manner. In a study to which I have already referred, Nemeth and Wachtler (1974) invent a situation in which four subjects and a confederate are assigned the role of a mock jury. Their deliberation concerns a case of compensation for an injury. Once the facts are presented, the subjects are asked to make an individual suggestion about the proper amount of the compensation for the victim. They are then taken to a room where there is a rectangular table with two seats at either of the long sides of the table and one seat at the head of the table. In half the groups the subjects are asked to sit at the table. The confederate chooses either the seat at the head or the seat at the side of the table. In the other groups the experimenter determines the seating arrangement, with the confederate following instructions by sitting down either at the head or at the side of the table. The subjects are then asked to deliberate and reach a unanimous conclusion about the amount of compensation to be granted. During the discussion the confederate consistently adopts a clearly deviant position, suggesting a figure of $3,000 where the others suggest between $10,000 and $25,000.

It turns out that the confederate exerts some influence in the condition where he is both autonomous (chooses a seat that puts him in a conspicuous position) and consistent. Yet he exerts little or no influence when he appears consistent but not autonomous (his seat assigned to him by somebody else). Moreover, the confederate's influence extends to a new case that was not discussed when the confederate chose his seat. Responses to the postexperimental questionnaire indicate that when the confederate chooses the seat at the head of the table, he seems more consistent and confident than in the other conditions.

Another way to study the problem is to reinforce the minority numerically. If several deviants express the same point of view, it becomes much more difficult to reject it by attributing it to idiosyncratic factors or to a personal bias of the minority, and its objective validity must be admitted. In a first experiment Papastamou (1979) developed two conditions: In one condition the subjects received a message that expressed a minority position on pollution; in the other they read the same message in the form of a text whose two parts fit together, but the first half was attributed to minority group X and the second half to minority group Y. The order of presentation and the attribution to group X or group Y was randomly determined. Moreover, the message style was either rigid or flexible, so there were several possible conditions: a rigid source, a flexible source, two rigid sources, or two flexible sources. The author found that two messages emitted by two flexible sources did not exert more influence than a single source. Conversely, two messages emitted by two rigid sources exerted significantly more influence than a message issued from a single rigid source. The convergence of two minorities thus has an impact only when their position seems extreme and their behavior exaggerated, not otherwise: Two deviants are not more effective than a single one.

In a second experiment analogous to the first, the subjects were asked to read two messages attributed to different groups expressing minority opinions on the pollution problem. However, before familiarizing themselves with the messages, they read an introductory page describing the relations between these groups. In one condition they were told that the groups in question were combining in the antipollution campaign—which at the time in Greece was far from popular. In another condi-

tion they were told that they were groups competing for influence, each of them trying to outdo the other in its antipollution campaign. The minority thus seemed to be either cooperating or competing. In addition, they were either rigid or flexible.

Overall, the relations between the minorities apparently had no impact, since no difference was observed between the cooperative and the competitive situations. It was found, however, that the rigid minorities exerted more influence than the flexible minorities. In other words, the convergence of two minorities facilitates their influence only where they are extreme and inflexible. They are more difficult to reject in this case, despite the hostility their behavior arouses by its "arbitrary," "capricious," and "exaggerated" character. From another point of view these results show that whatever makes the position of the minority seem biased, partisan, or contrary to the norm is not an intrinsic obstacle to influence (Moscovici, 1976); the only factor that has a detrimental impact is its being given an excessive expression.

Another experiment by Nemeth and Wachtler (1973) showed that this characteristic may even play a positive role. In their study the minority—consisting of a single individual openly showing his bias, which went counter to the norm (a fictitious German consistently manifesting his preference for German paintings in a group whose norm was to like Italian painting)—was more influential than a minority of one that outdid the majority in always proclaiming its preference for Italian paintings. Furthermore, this deviant, who assumed an even more extreme position than did the majority, far from influencing them in his direction, polarized the subjects around a position opposite to his own. He did in fact bring about a change, but it was a negative change.

This effect occurs frequently enough. Thus in an experiment using color slides Biener (1971) tried to increase the subjects' resistance to minority pressure by informing them of an objective fact—namely, that the slides were blue—before exposing them to the minority's deviant responses—that the slides were green. For purposes of comparison she also set up the inverse situation: The subjects were first informed of the minority responses and then presented with the objective majority responses. What were the findings? It might have been expected that the prior objective information would shield the subjects against the impact of the biased information. And yet contrary to this expectation, the results went in the opposite direction: One was more likely to be influenced by the minority when one has been warned against it than otherwise. In addition, the subjects evaluated the minority much more positively than those who were supposed to help them resist it. In other words, the more the deviant response of the minority is highlighted, the greater is its influence and attraction by contrast.

But what might contribute to diminishing its impact significantly if neither majority support nor the support of reality makes a difference? We do know the answer in the light of research results. They show that two rigid sources are more influential than a single source, because the idiosyncratic, unmotivated character of the deviant position is thereby attenuated. If, on the contrary, it were reinforced, the opposite phenomenon would be observed. In fact, this method is one of the methods whereby social systems immunize themselves against their deviants. It is often found that one of the ways in which they are disparaged is to explain their position in terms of personality traits or even pathology (schizophrenia, paranoia, dogmatism, etc.). That is why dissidents are locked up in psychiatric hospitals instead of being put into prison—so that the subjective, arbitrary, even delirious character of their ideas can be identified. Let us call this method whereby the value of the minority's opinion is nullified *psychologization*.

Mugny and Papastamou (1976–1977) and Papastamou (1979) have investigated this phenomenon, whose purpose is to devaluate anomic content in order to prevent its appearing to reflect some sort of social reality. In the first experiment, which was conceived on the basis of the ones that we described above, the subjects received a communication about the Swiss army. So that the communication source rather than its message was emphasized, the subjects were asked to characterize the source by means of a list of adjectives to be circled corresponding to "the image suggested to them by reading the message." But some of them received a list of adjectives using political labels (liberal, anarchist), and the rest received a list with adjectives of a more psychological sort (tolerant, authoritarian). It was noted that the subjects who had to judge the source in political terms changed their opinion with respect to the army, whereas the subjects who *also* judged the source in psychological terms did not change.

In the second experiment the subjects received a rigid message about pollution attributed to a minority source. Part of the subjects were told that they should try to guess, after simply reading the text, the main personality traits of the author, recording their judgment on a

questionnaire. The other subjects were simply given the task of summarizing the same text. Once more it was found that in the second experimental condition the subjects changed their minds significantly more than in the first condition, where they were induced to interpret the message of the minority by assigning it "psychological" characteristics. In short, the very fact that someone is induced to evaluate deviant behavior in psychological terms or in terms of psychological flaws is enough to reduce the impact of deviant behavior. One thus rediscovers in the laboratory the effects of a procedure to which groups frequently resort in order to nullify the influence of protesters and dissidents—and thereby oppose innovations that might change the order of things or attack the weight of the ideas they themselves uphold.

Maass, Clark, and Haberkorn (1981) raise the question of whether influence functions the same way when it is exerted by real minorities. The authors show that if a minority displays some self-interest, as is typical of all minorities in society, it is less effective. It then seems, as we observed earlier, to be less objective. On the whole, it is not enough for it to display a consistent behavioral style. It helps if its position also appears objective. Furthermore, this study tends to show that no minority is influential when the Zeitgeist runs counter to its position—a plausible conclusion in the laboratory but a much less plausible one in real life. In any case the authors demonstrate that a bridge can be built between the fictitious creatures of theory and the flesh-and-blood creatures of society.

Groups, Minorities, and Norms

As is well known, the study of small groups has demonstrated that a pressure exists toward uniformity of opinion, which gives rise to communication and social influence processes. In response to this pressure the majority tends to change the point of view of deviant members. If the social influence process fails to reduce divergences of opinion, the members of the group are induced to redefine the psychological composition of the group by rejecting the members who refuse to conform to group norms. This model (Festinger, 1950) and subsequent studies (Schachter, 1951) are based on the implicit hypothesis that pressures toward uniformity are invariably resolved in favor of the majority position. The members who are in a deviant or minority position on a given question find themselves forced to adopt the group norm or are put on notice to leave it.

The model describes another possibility too. To be sure, the majority might change on its own as a way of reducing the pressures toward uniformity. This possibility has always remained purely theoretical. It was never invoked or studied until the model I presented stressed the importance of the minority. The theory is in any case incomplete and inadequate. The model, first of all, does not indicate why or how a minority could exert pressure on the majority. Second, this change on the part of the majority appears to be the result of the majority's failure to reduce deviance, not the successful outcome of the minority's persuasion attempt. We must certainly revise our concept of group dynamics (Moscovici and Mugny, 1983), but this is not the place for it.

As we have seen, it is obvious that when the majority of group members are faced with a consistent minority defending its position in terms that exclude all compromise—demonstrating thereby that uniformity will never be obtained by forcing it to give up its point of view—the majority will have no alternative but to change the group norm in the direction of the deviant position. It certainly has the option of rejecting the deviant as well, but this is a serious decision endangering the existence of the group. It thus remains a measure to be taken as a last resort (Zinoviev, 1981). In any case it is evident that in a conflict situation modifying the group's position seems a better way of dealing with the problem than schism or altering its boundaries and composition. Consequently, uniformity pressures may operate just as well in favor of the minority as in favor of the majority; on the whole, the minority is not only an influence target in the group but also its source.

Wolf (1977) showed this result in an experiment. The subjects were led to believe that they acted as group members and that they had a majority point of view on a particular problem. One of the group members maintained an ostensibly deviant position during the whole interaction. Three variables were manipulated: the deviant's behavioral style (strong or weak consistency), group coherence (strong or weak), and the opportunity to reject the deviant (possible or impossible). The first dependent variable was the extent to which individual judgment on the problem changes from the time prior to the interaction to the time after the interaction. It was generally observed that the more cohesive the group, the more individuals changed in the direction of the minority position. If the other variables were taken into account, it was found that the minority exerted a maximal influence

when it was very consistent in groups that have no possibility to reject it. However, and this is a surprising result, it preserved its influence even if it was less consistent and even in groups that did have a possibility to reject it. Furthermore, results showed that opinion changes were public as well as private, thereby reflecting an internalized acceptance of the minority position.

In light of this experiment, it is undeniable that pressures toward uniformity in a group can operate both in the direction of innovation and in the direction of conformity, depending on the behavior of the minority or the majority. In another experiment Nemeth (1983) compared these relative effects of conformity and innovation in a judgmental task of varying difficulty involving geometric figures. The subjects were arranged by groups of six. In the conformity condition there were four confederates and two naive subjects; in the innovation condition the proportions were reversed. The confederates agreed with each other in each of the trials. In all conditions they gave all the easy answers as well as one difficult answer. The difficult answer was either right or wrong. Nemeth found that in the conformity condition the amount of influence exerted was greater than in the innovation condition. Notwithstanding, the subjects who were confronted with a minority found more correct but difficult answers than those facing a majority.

What was the reason? On the one hand, as was observed by means of other measures, the state of mind of the subjects was quite different in the two contexts: In the conformity framework the subjects claimed to be more awkward, embarrassed, and unhappy and more in the grips of a conflict than the subjects in the innovation framework. On the other hand, the minority incited the members of the majority to think through the solutions again, without at the same time compelling them to take one direction rather than another. Consequently, certain subjects maintained their independence, while others adopted the minority position. But the most significant result was that the chance of finding new and correct solutions to the problems presented increased. In this sense the minority made a positive contribution to the group.

And finally, an experiment by Moscovici and Lage (1978) used color slides. Instead of asking the subjects exposed to deviant influence to give objective responses, they asked them to give original responses. The outcome was that there was not only an increase in deviant responses but also the invention of a whole set of unexpected new responses.

Some independent studies show how much benefit can be derived from analyzing groups from the point of view of minority influence instead of limiting oneself to majority influence. A case in point is the study by Snortum, Klein, and Wynn (1976) on juries. The authors tried to assess the influence of a jury on the decision taken in common. They trained a confederate to argue forcefully for the guilt of the accused. And this confederate was then expected to persuade *ad hoc* juries composed of five or twelve members. In both the smaller and the larger juries, jurors confronted with an assertive confederate were more likely to cast a final vote of guilty. To be sure, the confederate's influence was maximized in the five-member juries. It remained pronounced in twelve-member juries.

In a very significant departure from prevailing tendencies, Dion and his colleagues started out by raising the question: How do minority groups respond to discrimination? It is surely none too soon to pay heed in the social realm as well as in other realms to the psychological consequences of domination and to the effect of being the victim of such and such a prejudice. By devoting the same attention to these relations as do other sciences, we can finally reach the point where we can view social reality from the perspective of racial, social, or intellectual minorities and thereby open up many new lines of development for social psychology. Dion and Earn (1978) studied the consequences of facing another person's contempt because of belonging to a racial minority. They created a situation in which a member of such a group (in this case a Jew) interacted with individuals belonging to the majority and failed at a task performance. This failure was revealed to him as being due to the negative evaluation of these individuals. In this prejudice situation persons belonging to racial minorities reacted with a greater feeling of sadness, aggression, and anxiety. They also reported a greater identification with their own group, and this identification was always positive.

I believe that these reactions are quite general. And it would still be interesting to know how minorities transform these negative experiences—these affective wounds—into sources of personal strength, which allow them to survive and to act autonomously. It was Lewin (1948) who noted long ago in one of the first studies on minorities: "However, the Jew will have to realize that for him as well as for any underprivileged group the following statement holds: only the efforts of the group itself will achieve the emancipation of the group" (p. 163).

We are a long way from having tackled such phenomena systematically, but I felt the need to mention the attempts that have been made in this direction.

COMPLIANT BEHAVIOR AND CONVERSION BEHAVIOR

In view of the central position of the influence phenomenon, it is not surprising that it has been studied in connection with most psychological processes: mass communication, change of attitudes, attraction toward other persons, collective judgment, and so on. Irrespective of the intrinsic interest of these studies, the limited framework of this chapter prevents my taking them into account. I will therefore give attention to just one last question that arises quite naturally: Has the influence exerted on someone been fictitious or authentic? In other words, must we view the change observed as purely external or as reflecting an internal modification?

The reason for raising this question, of course, is that we live in societies where the public and private spheres of existence are separate. Our private response need not in the least coincide with our public response, and in certain groups it is even perfectly permissible for them to be opposite. Clearly, this question is highly important both theoretically and practically. It implicates the general process of change in human behavior. It is equally relevant in understanding the technical as well as ethical consequences of persuasion.

There is no doubt that, logically speaking, various solutions are conceivable. At one extreme we can visualize an individual's going along with an authority or group and making only surface concessions. She might keep her opinions to herself (Personnaz, 1974), refusing to believe her own statements. At the other extreme we can conceive of somebody who makes no concessions, resists pressures exerted on him, and yet, without knowing it, changes and is influenced. Moscovici and Nève (1971) and Brehm and Mann (1975) found that in a variety of circumstances direct influence on somebody may be nearly nonexistent, while indirect influence, of which he is unaware, is very great. Certain researchers have interpreted this indirect influence as a sort of anticipation of future conformity in analogous situations (Hass and Mann, 1976) without genuine modification of personal judgment. Saltzenstein and Sandberg (1979) did show that this anticipation is associated with an actual intellectual change. More precisely, they observed that direct influence was minimal and not significant, while indirect influence was both substantial and significant.

I do not believe that we have as yet found an adequate answer to this question. But the very fact of raising the question and looking for a solution has clarified the relations between influence phenomena and behaviors. Kelman (1958) sketched a taxonomy of these relations in terms of the influence target's dependence with respect to the source. The latter, according to conformity theory, is defined by its credibility, its attraction, or its power. Each of these characteristics induces a modification of opinions or behaviors by the intervention of three psychological mechanisms: internalization, identification, and compliance. The internalization of a value or opinion is the most deeply rooted effect of social influence. If we perceive the person (or group) exerting influence as trustworthy and having a sound judgment, we accept the ideas he or she advocates and integrate them into our outlook. Once they have become part of our system, they lose their dependence on the source and prove extremely durable. By identification we mean a response to influence caused by our desire to be similar to what influences us and serves us as a model. As a result, we adopt ideas or behaviors not because we believe in them or because they seem correct to us but because, by adopting them, we display our attachment to the model and become similar to it. We may thus come to believe in certain things by imitation or fashion instead of conviction. Compliance means a public acquiescence to an opinion upheld by a powerful group or individual, without private commitment to it. Such an acquiescence lasts as long as does the power to reward or punish us and to control our actions, if required.

The experiment illustrating this taxonomy confirms it within reasonable limits. But only one of these modalities has been studied in depth—namely, compliance—for it is specifically related to conformity. The other two have been viewed less as influence aspects than as general aspects of attitude changes. In fact, a number of years earlier Festinger (1953) had already distinguished between compliance (public acquiescence without private acceptance) and attitude change (public acquiescence and private acceptance). According to him, threats or coercion may make a person conform, but they will not change the person's attitudes. She will change them only if her relation with another group or person is of value to her. Festinger also suggests two ways of distinguishing between sheer compliance and an authentic modification of opinion. One is to record the public behavior that goes with the private response; the second is to observe the change in response before and after the influence source is removed, that is, during the social phase and during the individual phase. If after the group influence has been removed, for instance, the individual stops conforming, obviously his attitude was simply compliance to social pressures.

Most experiments have confirmed this line of thought. On the whole (McBride, 1954; Burdick, 1955; Deutsch and Gerard, 1955; Dittes and Kelley, 1956; Argyle, 1957; Jones, Wells, and Torrey, 1958; Raven, 1959), all agree in showing that public responses, which can be observed by other individuals in the group, are more conformist than private, usually written, responses. The decisive factor is in all likelihood the control everybody exerts over everybody else. Indeed, Mouton, Blake, and Olmstead (1956) observe that conformity is greater when the name of the subject can be determined than when it is anonymous. But a no less striking result, which proves that a change did in fact take place, is that the individual continues to conform somewhat even when he is alone and anonymous. All in all, there is never mere compliance or mere change in attitude. And as we know because of the introduction of the cognitive dissonance theory, a forced compliance may result in an authentic change in attitude. This change results because individuals try to reduce the discrepancy between their actions and their thoughts, their public and their private opinions. Pascal recognized the fact long ago: Pray, and faith will follow.

All these results are very likely and have even been verified with respect to a normative majority and a conformity situation. But as soon as one deals with a deviant minority and the innovation it attempts to introduce in a group, the previous analyses can no longer be applied unmodified. And yet here too arises the question of whether it exerts a superficial or an authentic influence. On this point we must look for an answer that is general enough to encompass both majority and minority influences.

To formulate it, let us take an experimental observation as a starting point: After the influence source has been removed, private responses show a greater change in an innovation situation than in a conformity situation, while public responses show the inverse tendency. One might say that two types of behavior are involved: compliance behavior and conversion behavior. The former amounts to acquiescence in a social situation combined with a tendency to resume one's own opinions and judgments in an individual situation. We recognize this in the fact that the number of public responses influenced is greater than the number of private responses influenced. The second behavior, conversion, is characterized by a conscious or unconscious modification (Hochberg, 1981) of one's own system of opinions, by an adoption of values or ideas one was not under compulsion to accept. It seems as though this modification is produced in the individual (or group) only after the influence has stopped being exerted—as though while the influence was being exerted, it could not take effect. Conversion is reflected in the fact that private responses change more frequently than (or at least as frequently as) public responses. In short, in the case of compliance direct influence exceeds indirect influence, and in the case of conversion the inverse holds.

The explanation for these behaviors seems to be as follows: First, as we already noted, both the majority and the minority can create a conflict of opinions or beliefs. The more consistent, objective, or rigid their behavioral style, the more intensive this conflict will be. Second, this conflict proceeds differently if it is set in motion by a majority or by a minority.

If we are dealing with a majority, the individual on whom influence is exerted wonders, like any deviant, why he fails to see or think like the other members of the group. He makes no attempt to resolve this problem by coming back to the controversial object or reality, since he is familiar with them and since, in principle, the majority's response must be correct and legitimate. All he can do is to engage in a *comparison process* between the two sets of responses in order to uncover the reasons for the disagreement, particularly when these others are unanimous. Because he has no power to exert pressure on them, he is tempted to make concessions, being impelled by the need to reach a consensus, even if consensus is actually unjustified.

When the individual is faced with a minority whose responses are from the start viewed as deviant or erroneous, an additional amount of verification is needed to deal with it and reject it. Each member of the majority wonders, "How can it see what it sees, think as it does?" If the minority persists in its judgment, the individuals belonging to the majority broach a *validation process* —that is, a confrontation between the minority responses and the reality in question—before seeking to negotiate an agreement and reestablishing a consensus. But in attempting to see what the minority sees and to think

what it thinks in the course of the social interaction, they change without realizing it. As a result, when each person finds himself alone again in front of the same object later on, he perceives and judges it in a way that is closer to the minority's view, since his own point of view has been modified (Tesser *et al.,* 1983).

It would be an overstatement, but not a misrepresentation, to say that when the individual disagrees with the majority, his entire attention is concentrated on the others in the group; when the individual disagrees with a minority, his entire attention is riveted on reality, on what it is and what are its properties. Majority influence therefore hardly extends beyond the period of interaction, and the individual finds himself relatively unchanged before the object of controversy. Minority influence, in contrast, persists much longer, because the individual has changed meanwhile, positively or negatively, and he no longer perceives the object in the same way (Maass and Clark, 1984).

Finally, negotiation or conflict resolution is always inclined to follow the more accessible path if one of the paths is blocked. Obviously, in conformity situations the public path is more accessible than the private path, since it is easier to modify one's opinion or behavior in the presence of the "normal" pole of an alternative than in the presence of the "deviant" pole. When faced with a majority, the individual can best reduce internal and external tension by modifying her public responses while leaving her private responses nearly intact. It is thus possible both to conform and to resist conformity, to give society its due and to preserve one's individuality. When dealing with a minority, the individual is in the opposite situation. The only path that is accessible for resolving the conflict is in the private domain, since it is very difficult to make direct concessions, to change behaviors or judgments publicly. Few people will bring themselves to do so unhesitatingly, since most are not inclined to become social deviants in turn, even after having accepted the deviant point of view or behavior.

These three reasons explain why compliance behavior is more common with respect to a majority and conversion behavior is more common with respect to a minority. This does not mean that majorities never convert or that minorities never produce compliance. But as I have pointed out, a privileged relationship exists perforce between each type of influence and each type of behavior (Moscovici, 1980).

Mugny (1975, 1976) and Papastamou (1979) tried to show in a set of experiments that the sharper the conflict provoked by a consistent minority, the greater was its indirect influence and the more clear-cut was the conversion effect. In these different experiments the subjects were presented a communication reflecting a flexible position and another communication reflecting a rigid position, both of them advocating, of course, a point of view opposed to the prevailing norms. Furthermore, the communications were attributed to minority groups. The effect of the messages on individual opinion was measured by means of two sets of questions: direct items related to the content they had just read and indirect items dealing with matters connected with this content but not included in the message. A change in the first category of items thus reveals a direct influence and the change in the second category an indirect influence. Here conversion is reflected in the difference between direct and indirect influence. That is, even though individuals have been persuaded by the minority, they do not give in to it, but they do modify their judgment by a sort of internal debate in a wider intellectual field.

In all these experiments, almost without exception, the following phenomenon was observed: A flexible minority produced almost as many changes of opinion on direct questions as on indirect questions (Saltzstein and Sandberg, 1979). In other words, its direct and indirect influences were about equal. Conversely, a rigid minority produced few or no response changes on the direct questions and considerably more changes on the indirect questions. Its indirect influence was thus always significantly greater than its direct influence. This result clearly shows that the less the individuals belonging to the majority can reduce divergences on the message level itself, the more they resolve them on the level of a related content. On the whole, where an immediate reaction is blocked, we witness an inference process, a more extensive cognitive effort. Compliance as such rarely manifests itself in these experiments. But as Papastamou (1979) has shown, as soon as the same message is attributed to a majority and social control is imposed on the subjects, compliance reemerges, and influence on the direct questions is more marked than influence on the indirect questions.

The same phenomenon has been studied in the realm of color perception (Moscovici, 1976). Reference has already been made to a previous study where it was shown that individuals subjected to the influence of a minority that claimed to see green in blue slides tended to show less influence in public situations than in private situations. It was as if they were continuing to call something blue that they saw as green. Moreover, the less they had given the deviant response in the presence of others, the more they

gave it when they were alone again. (This behavior is comparable to the one observed in persons who receive the message of a rigid minority.)

To check whether this result involved a genuine perceptual modification, Moscovici and Personnaz (1980) made the following experiment: In the previous studies subjects were shown a set of blue slides, which a confederate described publicly as green. By a set of appropriate instructions this confederate was made to represent the majority in one condition and the minority in another. This time, however, the negative afterimage was used to measure perceptive modification subsequent to the social interaction, instead of the usual color tests. As is well known, if one stares at a white screen after having stared at a color for several seconds, one sees the complementary color. In this case the complementary color for blue is yellow-orange, and for green it is red-purple. On the basis of our knowledge about this effect, we can make the following assumptions:

1. If the subjects have merely modified their verbal and public responses, the negative afterimage from blue slides will be in the yellow-orange spectrum range.

2. If the subjects have really modified their perception, even without changing their verbal responses, the chromatic aftereffect will be the complementary color of green, which is close to red-purple.

The negative afterimage judgment was, of course, made in private.

As predicted, we found, first of all, that the percentage of "green" responses was relatively low (5 percent) and, second, that the subjects exposed to minority pressure did see the complementary color of green significantly more often after looking at blue slides than did subjects who were confronted with a majority pressure, where such an increase was not found. This result confirms that we are dealing here with a change in perceptive responses exceeding the change in purely verbal responses.

Doms and Van Avermaet (1980) replicated this experiment and found the same effects. In addition, they showed that when the influence source is a majority, a certain percentage of negative afterimages (shifts to the complementary color of green) will occur, especially in the physical absence of the influence source. Conversion behavior thus seems to be a general phenomenon. Moreover, it can occur with majorities as well as with minorities. Subsequent studies should determine more accurately which conditions are favorable to the former and which to the latter.

Sorrentino, King, and Leo (1980) attribute these effects to judgmental rather than perceptual changes. This interpretation makes an interesting point, but the distinction between the purely judgmental and the purely perceptual may be hard to draw. Their experiment cannot claim to have decided the matter one way or the other. They do obtain an intriguing and important result that deserves further exploration. They observe that the more suspicious the subjects, the stronger is the afterimage. This result would presuppose that individuals attempt to avoid being influenced overtly by a minority. But for that very reason the latent influence is marked. If this hypothesis is accurate, then by warning people beforehand and making them suspicious toward a message, one would actually increase their vulnerability without their realizing it. There are sound reasons to assume that this mechanism is operative mainly in confrontations with minorities (Moscovici, 1980). It might be objected that the results of the preceding experiments were somewhat contaminated by the verbal character of the responses. But by using a spectrometer, Personnaz (1981) replicated the presence of the negative afterimage when the influence source was a minority and its absence when it was a majority.

This set of experiments tends to illustrate the general idea that influence processes are associated with both compliance and conversion behavior (Ullman, 1982). But here we are faced with a new set of questions. After research had established what produced compliance, research focused on the way people *internalized* (i.e., made private) what they had accepted publicly. To the extent that innovation is more likely to produce conversion, we are faced with the inverse phenomenon, that is, the *externalization* of private responses. All theories of attitude change have dealt with the phenomenon of internalization, notably by invoking cognitive dissonance theory. But when we are attempting to explain externalization, we are asking what makes an individual abandon norms in which she no longer believes and state what she really sees or thinks.

Without treating all sides of this problem, Moscovici and Doms (1981) concentrated on investigating the conditions in which it is possible to attenuate the conflict and weaken a person's resistance to a judgment he finds shocking. Under these circumstances it is plausible that overt and conscious influence will have the greatest impact. Latent and almost unconscious influence will be nonexistent. We used the same stimulus material, the same situations, and the same measures as in the previous experiment. One modification, however, was incorporated. *After* having been subjected to the influence of a confederate presented as belonging to either a minority or a majority, the subject and the confederate underwent a period of sensory deprivation, a rather short interlude of forty-five minutes. Each subject was then asked to record, during a new set of trials, the color of the slides and the complementary color he saw on the white screen. We obtained some startling results. When the confederate represented a minority, 9 percent of the responses in the public situation and 20 percent of the responses in the private situation were green. And when the confederate supposedly represented a majority, the percentages were 27 percent and 23 percent, respectively. (These are the highest percentages ever obtained with this stimulus material in an innovation situation.)

As the evidence shows, sensory deprivation facilitates the expression of perceptual judgments that are generally inhibited. Naturally, these results do not prove that giving the "green" response resolves the response conflict and thus acts as a substitute for and impedes the negative afterimage. And yet such a substitution seems to have occurred. For what do we find? The subjects who yielded and answered "green" do not show any chromatic afterimage. Those who did not yield, on the contrary, tend to show such an effect. This is confirmed especially when the confederate represents a minority, as was true in the study by Moscovici and Personnaz (1980). Although we still have a very long way to go before these phenomena are clarified, at least we are now aware of their existence and of their significance.

GROUP POLARIZATION PHENOMENA: NORMALIZATION AND INNOVATION

GROUP AVERAGING AND GROUP POLARIZATION

Social influence assumes an especially important role when groups want to communicate, on the one hand, and to act jointly, on the other. In terms of communication social influence intervenes as a persuasion factor; in terms of joint action it is a decision factor. Most of the studies to which I have referred so far view influence as a persuasion factor, as the unilateral action of a majority on a minority and the converse. And its effect is expressed by partial or total yielding. Leaving aside extreme setups, however, there is no doubt that social life offers us mainly reciprocal influences, whose outcome is a more or less explicit consensus. For this reason conformity and innovation alike are the result of negotiation (Moscovici and Faucheux, 1972). This conclusion does not invalidate the results obtained in well-known studies, but it does indicate within which limits they are applicable.

Among the phenomena studied by social psychology is one that is contingent on consensus: the phenomenon of group decision. As a preliminary to all collective action (Misumi, 1981), this type of decision presupposes a balancing between individual and social factors, between the minority and the majority faction of the group. This balancing act makes negotiation overt, since it allows influence strategies to be converted into consensus. In the past twenty years we have witnessed several discoveries about the group decision phenomenon, discoveries that deserve some attention. One glance at their origin is enough to explain how great their interest is. To anticipate what follows, let me just say that their interest lies in the fact that they involve both normalization and innovation tendencies, pressures toward uniformity and pressures toward change within a group.

It all started with Stoner's (1968) rediscovery of a phenomenon first noted by Ziller (1957), which had not received the attention it deserved—to wit, that groups are willing to take more risks than individuals are. This proposition ran counter (Marquis, 1962) to the conformity theory, which predicts the avoidance of deviant opinions (Schachter, 1951). It also contradicts the normalization theory, which predicts an averaging of group opinions and norms (Sherif and Hovland, 1961).

As is well known, the fact that several persons gathered together are more daring than a single person was identified as the risky-shift phenomenon. Under the stimulus of Kogan and Wallach, who recognized its real meaning, this fact was investigated by a very large number of scholars. Dion, Baron, and Miller (1970), Vinokur (1971), and Clark (1971) offer an exhaustive and critical survey of the literature on the subject. From their writings it becomes quickly apparent that the risky shift was viewed as an exception from the point of view of social influence theories. It was explained by its content, that is, by its dilemmas in which one option was riskier than the other. In other words, one tried to explain why, generally, groups were more daring than individuals.

But most researchers failed to notice a different aspect of the phenomenon. If one took into account the choices groups were asked to make and which concerned attitudes toward a problem—choice of a career, choice of a course of action—things appeared in a different light.

From that perspective Stoner's and Ziller's discovery —while remaining exceptional, if not anomalous, in terms of conformity and normalization theories—agreed with attitude theory. A large number of studies, above all Sherif's classic work, showed that the more individuals are socially and personally involved, the more extreme are the positions they assume. It was reasonable to imagine that here too such a mechanism was activated and that deviant and extremist individuals, who are committed to a position, are less inclined to yield. The moderates, on the contrary, are more willing to make concessions to save the group consensus. In any case it is possible to interpret these decisions not from the point of view of their content (risky or cautious) or from the point of view of social influence but from the point of view of attitude change. Such shifts of perspective and synthesizing of distinct areas of research are always fruitful in science.

With these considerations as a starting point, Moscovici and Zavalloni (1969), who had previously worked in the field of attitudes, surmised that the risky shift might best be viewed as a particular case of a more familiar and better-known phenomenon, attitude change. They therefore offered a group polarization hypothesis: The opinion of a group involved in a decision process will tend to be more extreme in the direction of the norm than the initial opinions of its members. This hypothesis contains a description of the empirical procedure: Individual opinions must be recorded before bringing the individuals together in a group; then group opinion must be collected. However, the very concept of an extreme decision implied that the realm of choice was hierarchically structured by a norm that was "for" or "against," by the notions of "good" or "bad" and "true" or "false," and so on. Furthermore, this hypothesis has three corollaries:

1. The less the decision involves the group (Petty and Cacioppo, 1984), the less it will deviate from the average of individual opinions.

2. Group consensus changes individuals' opinions and preferences.

3. Discussion structures communication and information around a normative dimension. It therefore leads to a reduction in the number of common categories of judgment or attitudes.

The hypothesis and its corollaries were verified with respect to material unrelated to risk. It dealt with political attitudes toward General de Gaulle and ethnic attitudes toward Americans. One can now see what constituted the main value of the hypothesis: making it possible to envisage group polarization as something that occurred as frequently in group decisions as group averaging. The explanation for this result was to be found in the general mechanisms of group dynamics rather than in any particular content (risky or not risky, etc.). In short, as often happens in science, it was revealed that what had been taken to be an anomaly, the risky shift, was a normal effect after all: group polarization.

Several researchers, particularly in England and Switzerland, were eager to test the soundness of these results. They were the ones who established the validity of the effect. Doise showed in several studies that polarization is enhanced by reference to an outside group (Doise, 1969), exists among children, and occurs in a large number of circumstances (Doise, 1970, 1971, 1973). Doise (1971) also made it clear that certain findings, which seemed to speak against Moscovici and Zavalloni's hypotheses, were actually in line with their predictions. Fraser and Billig (1971) established that the risky shift is a special case of group polarization. They argued, in fact, that if this were the case, it would be relatively easy to obtain a cautious shift by picking the right items—that is, items for which individual responses were already in the cautious direction. In a carefully designed experiment it was shown that this is exactly what happens. Several studies by Fraser and his colleagues validated both the soundness of the group polarization hypothesis and its general applicability (Fraser, 1971; Stroebe and Fraser, 1971; Gouge and Fraser, 1972).

Simultaneously, research was carried on in two directions. First, the hypothesis was applied in the United States and to a variety of attitudes to test whether it was applicable under these conditions. Myers and Bishop (1970, 1971) thus utilized racial attitudes. They showed that groups consisting of racist members become more racist, while groups consisting of less racist members become less racist after discussion. These same authors obtained analogous results with life dilemmas. Myers and Bach (1974) failed to obtain equally clear results with militarist and pacifist items. On the other hand, Paicheler and Bouchet (1973), using items about women, as well as Nève and Gauthier (1978), using items about abortion attitudes, all obtained systematic polarization effects. In a fine piece of work McCauley (1972) made clear that the polarization of opinions within the group does not imply the polarization of individual opinions. By now there exists a fair consensus that can be noted everywhere and with respect to any topic on the phenomenon that concerns us here.

Second, an additional set of studies set out to prove that in other areas, such as judgment of others and how people are perceived, groups are more extreme and more strongly for or against than individuals. Doise (1970) presented the photograph of a person described as relatively introverted or extroverted to several groups. As expected, after the discussion he did observe extremization of perception of introversion or extroversion. In several articles Moscovici and colleagues (Moscovici and Nève, 1972; Moscovici, Zavalloni, and Louis-Guérin, 1972; Moscovici, Zavalloni, and Weinberger, 1972) reported polarization of social judgment and impression formation about a personality. Andrews and Johnson (1971) obtained similar results with subjects having to describe a hypothetical faculty. Myers (1975) replicated these findings in a very carefully designed study. Unfortunately, Semin and Glendon (1973), studying real business committees, found that their judgments did not change during the group discussion. This finding reminds us that, notwithstanding the positive results obtained, we must remain on our guard.

These studies cannot be presented as exhaustively and in as much detail here as they should be. A fuller account of these initial studies can be found elsewhere (Moscovici and Doise, 1974). Myers and Lamm (1976) have summed up more recent findings. Complete as it is, their survey would have benefited from being more historically grounded. One might also wonder whether they were right in trying to apply to the group polarization phenomenon the very theories that had been used to explain the risky shift. It is rather strange and unusual to carry over interpretations for an "anomaly" in Kuhn's (1962) sense to a phenomenon interpreted as normal and general. Such interpretations are usually discarded, and the phenomenon is viewed from a new perspective. If this were not the common practice, science would never change. It would limit itself to pile facts upon facts, stringing them together with the help of the same old theory. Despite this qualification their review offers much useful material, as do the articles by Meertens (1976, 1978) and by Gauthier (1981).

The moment has come to focus on the factors affecting group negotiations and the outcome of the influence that its members exert reciprocally. These factors can be classified under three headings:

1. Factors affecting the quality of the group interaction (existence of a hierarchy, behavioral style of its members, physical environment, degree of group heterogeneousness).

2. Factors affecting the relations among group members and the decision (existence of a social norm with respect to the problem under consideration, conspicuousness of this norm, consequence of the decision for the group, degree of individual involvement).

3. Factors affecting the availability of information.

We will not attempt to present a theory or model encompassing these factors. All we hope to do is to indicate what kind of data and concepts should be elements of such a theory or model. I believe that it is relatively easy to discern certain regularities in this respect. However, it may be very difficult to produce strong predictions that lend themselves to analytic treatment. At this stage it seems more appropriate to raise problems in a general way and to avoid concentrating on questions of analysis and explanation.

THE WEIGHT OF NORMS

In groups, decisions are necessarily a function of norms. Indeed, the space in which human beings exchange their views and prepare their actions is always a space involving values. There is no culture in which it can remain neutral. No matter how decisions are taken, they are always a function of shared norms. For when norms are not shared, no decision can be made. Or to put it differently, the decision is reached not to come to a consensus: people agree to disagree. Changes of norms must also be taken into account, since they are themselves the outcome of decisions. "It is important that a social standard to be changed does not have the nature of a 'thing' but of a 'process' " (Lewin, 1958, p. 257).

We need only look at the data to realize how closely norms and group decisions are related. Most studies reveal a very strong correlation between the mean initial response to an item and its mean polarization (Vinokur, 1969). Cvetkovich and Baumgardner (1973) found that groups that were tolerant toward civil disobedience became even more tolerant after discussion, while more intolerant groups did not. Myers (1975) observed that groups that held a liberal view regarding the role of women became even more tolerant after the discussion of relevant items. In these studies the authors observe specifically that the general polarization trend is consistent with the prevailing norm.

The tendency for consensus to be established in the direction of the prevailing norm thus seems to be consis-

tently valid. Nevertheless, some exceptions have been observed, and we do not yet have any explanation for them. The tendency in question does not mean that polarization represents an effect of conforming to the norm—or to put it differently, a majority effect (Lambert, 1969; Lamm, Trommsdorf, and Rost-Schande, 1973). In several experiments (Moscovici and Zavalloni, 1969; Moscovici and Nève, 1972; Zaleska, 1976) it was possible to verify that this result was not the case. And there is no lack of examples, to which we will come back, where minorities won out. But they won out by "being more royalist than the king," that is, by opting for a more extreme position than the shared norm.

THE ACQUISITION AND AVAILABILITY OF INFORMATION

In group decisions norms play the same preponderant role that information plays in individual decisions. It is true, nonetheless, that as the discussion proceeds, individuals do learn something from one another. Discussion reveals positions and allows exchanges of knowledge and of opinions. Each person brings out a different aspect of the question, showing others what he sees himself.

Vinokur and Burnstein (1974) observed closely what kind of information circulates in a group. They established that the most pertinent information is one that expresses a direction (pro or con), contains some novelty, and has cogency. These authors went so far as to construct a mathematical model that they tried to verify. Other researchers have looked into the specific conditions that allow information to be effective. Kaplan (1977), for instance, presented a set of arguments to mock juries. He noted that the more recent arguments were remembered best and determined polarization. Myers, Bach, and Schreiber (1974) revealed the distribution of positions taken on some risk-taking items to the subjects prior to their making their own decision. What impact did this procedure have? Subjects who had this information took more extreme positions than those who were not aware of the positions adopted by the other members of the group. Myers and Kaplan (1976) obtained analogous results by showing some groups a complete distribution of the opinion of others (exposing them to an extreme model) and showing other groups nothing but the group average.

Clearly, polarization occurs only in conditions where individuals are informed about the opinion of others, not otherwise. It is therefore reasonable to assume that lack of information about the positions prevailing in the group leads to group averaging. Conversely, the availability of information encourages deviation in the direction of extreme points of view. Anderson and Graeser (1976), in a very ambitious analysis of the way in which information is incorporated, suggest a model for attitudes observed in the wake of group discussions.

This is not the place to discuss such a model, which could be applied in any situation, though it is remote from any social context. The authors note that information that is extremely positive or negative—that is, has an extreme valence—tends to be assigned greater weight than more neutral information. This observation corroborates the preceding experimental results. It is as though uncertainty about the position of the group members—whether from lack of information regarding it or from its inherent moderation—inclines toward normalization (averaging). Conversely, reduction of this uncertainty inclines toward innovation (polarization), that is, a change of opinions toward more extreme positions. Approaching the matter from the inverse end, we find a confirmation in Burnstein, Vinokur, and Pichevin's (1974) experiment. The authors show that presumably people who adopt extreme choices are equipped with cogent arguments. And the general tendency to perceive others as more neutral simply reflects ignorance about their choices. In other studies, such as Burnstein and Vinokur (1975), and Ebbesen and Bowers (1974), there is further confirmation of this point.

To summarize, it seems that the direction of the consensus reached by individuals in a group is determined by the availability, recency, and relatively extreme (emphatic, novel) character of the information. It goes without saying, though it bears repeating, that much remains to be done before these findings deserve to be taken as fully proven.

THE NATURE OF THE ARGUMENTS

When individuals must make a group decision, each person is eager to convince the others that his own position is well founded. Each person is therefore compelled to present the information he has convincingly as arguments for or against. At the same time arguments are more likely to be heeded and to win out if they are legitimate, that is, if they are in the direction of the dominant norm (Moscovici, 1976). Thus individuals are led to select, consciously or unconsciously, the arguments they offer and pay attention to their style of presentation. The obvious consequence is that group discussion generates pre-

dominantly legitimate arguments, favoring the initially stronger alternative. Discussion inhibits the presentation of illegitimate arguments, thereby reinforcing the movement toward the choice of an extreme alternative.

In several experiments Burnstein and Vinokur (1975, 1977) and Burnstein, Vinokur, and Trope (1973) tried to show that arguments center on utilities of outcome; that is, they have an informative content. The American researchers noted, furthermore, that legitimate arguments consistent with the dominant tendency are rated more persuasive than illegitimate ones, which go against the dominant tendency. In addition, original arguments, which by definition have a richer informative content, have more impact than trivial arguments.

Judd (1975) made clear how the direction of the norm influences the selection of arguments. He observed that while 65 percent of written arguments were already in the direction of the common norm, 79 percent of the discussed arguments favored the dominant alternative. In a very detailed study Meertens (1976) observed a similar tendency. He also found that the preponderance of risky arguments in the total number of arguments presented by a group member is related to the initial risk. Convergence at this level was shown to exist as well. In fact, in this Dutch study the riskier the arguments presented by one person, the more cautious were the arguments he received in reply from the other group members; the converse was equally true. Generally speaking, the more numerous or the more telling the arguments one has at one's disposal in either an extreme or a cautious direction, the more extreme or cautious one's decision is likely to be. This result is in keeping with observations by Kleiven, Fraser, and Gouge (1974), Vinokur and Burnstein (1974), Essen and Bowers (1974), and Semin (1975).

What happens when a member of the group presents arguments that are emphatically contrary to group norms? Paicheler (1977) organized a group discussion during which a consistent confederate upheld reactionary positions that were at odds with general social norms about women. A group split could be observed, with a number of initially moderate individuals being amenable to the confederate's arguments. The other individuals, whose initial position was firm, resisted. In the event, no group consensus was attained. Instead, there was a break on the one hand and a bipolarization of attitudes on the other.

On the whole, there is agreement between the observed facts. In group discussions legitimate arguments have more weight and help in the polarization of group decisions. For this purpose the arguments should include quite novel information and allow convergence on everybody's part toward a common position.

BEHAVIORAL STYLE AND CONSENSUS

As we know, group discussion leading to a consensus actually represents a negotiation. In the course of this negotiation the effectiveness of the arguments depends not only on their content but also on their form or style. The findings discussed in the preceding section make a compelling case for the determining role of legitimate arguments, but they leave us in the dark about the presentation of these arguments. And yet this point is not irrelevant. Meertens (1976), for instance, states in his study that there is a direct correlation between how much a person speaks and is addressed, as well as how her contribution is evaluated, and the degree of influence she is credited with in the discussion. This result does not necessarily imply that there is a close correspondence between the group decision and her initial choice. Sheer talkativeness alone does not induce change.

That behavioral style is an essential factor was established in several studies by Paicheler (1976). In her experiments she introduced a confederate who defended his positions without any concessions (i.e., showed consistency) in certain groups. In other groups the confederate maintained his positions sometimes with and sometimes without concessions (i.e., showed inconsistency). This confederate, a minority of one, assumed extreme attitudes that went in the direction of the social norm. The results showed that the consistent minority elicited strong group polarization. The polarization was weaker in the face of an inconsistent minority. In addition, the impact was durable. After the discussion the individuals were relatively faithful to the group consensus. Thus polarization is intensified when the individual's position is both consistent and in keeping with the norm.

Nemeth (1981) rightly called attention to the fact that there is an inherent incompatibility between consistent behavior in which all concessions are rejected and the act of negotiation, which implies concessions. Her point is especially applicable to real groups: political parties, juries, and committees. In one experiment in which a mock jury was asked to make a decision, she created a condition where a confederate made very early concessions. In another condition he maintained his extreme position up to the last of ten trials. In this last trial

he made a significant concession in favor of a consensus. As predicted by the theory of minority influence, she observed that consistency induced a significant private change and polarization of attitude but that it was less effective in producing a public consensus. The compromise, belated as it was, did produce such a consensus. On the whole, the most effective strategy is for an individual to be consistent and yet capable of making concessions at the critical moment. Such results indicate that behavioral styles have an impact on group polarization. Let us now examine which circumstances encourage polarization and which are more favorable to compromise.

INTERACTION AND INVOLVEMENT

The act of negotiating and exchanging arguments within a group is symptomatic of an interaction between individuals having an opinion of their own. However, just as individuals differ in the position they maintain, they also differ in their degree of involvement (or commitment) in this position. Attitude theory postulates that the commitment of more extreme individuals is stronger than that of moderate individuals, who therefore find it easier to shift. And the group polarization hypothesis (Moscovici and Zavalloni, 1969) considers this commitment to play a decisive role. On this point it converges with several other hypotheses (Arrow, 1974; Schelling, 1975; Janis and Mann, 1977) that emphasize the relevance of involvements (or commitments) in the way agreements are reached between human beings. It follows that the degree of initial involvement on the part of the group members determines the intensity of the interaction: The more committed each member is to his or her point of view, the more heated the exchange of arguments will be.

At the same time it should be remembered that the interaction intensity is likely to make people feel involved, even when they were not involved originally. This reciprocal relation is still in need of further elucidation as part of a more sweeping view of group dynamics. At any rate it is plausible to imagine that an intense interaction or opinion conflict leads to group polarization. The absence of such an interaction or conflict, in contrast, produces group averaging. In short, whatever attenuates interaction and conflict (hierarchy, formal interrelations, etc.) enhances normalization and reciprocal compromise (Kaplan and Miller, 1983).

Several experiments illustrate that things happen exactly in this way. Moscovici and Lecuyer (1972) predicted that by varying the seating arrangements in a group, group polarization or group averaging would be produced. The former was expected to occur when decisions were made face to face; the latter was expected when seating was side by side. Lecuyer (1975) asked groups of individuals seated face to face to make decisions either in a cold, very large, and formal room, or in a warm, relatively small, and more intimate one. The former discourages interaction; the latter makes it feasible. As expected, group polarization was significantly greater in the warm than in the cold setting. Moscovici, Doise, and Dulong (1972) asked a set of groups to make decisions, but only after having selected a secretary and taken cognizance of the procedure to follow. In comparison with the groups reaching decisions spontaneously, where polarization is pronounced, these formal groups established a consensus by averaging.

Using a very different material (audiovisual stimuli), Forgas (1977) studied a similar phenomenon. He found significant group polarization when spontaneous group discussion was encouraged. When spontaneous group discussion was restrained, a tendency to adopt a less polarized consensus became apparent. In a more recent experiment Forgas (1981) varied the formality of the interaction directly. He observed that groups in the informal condition were inclined to make more extreme judgments about responsibility for an action than did individuals. In the formal condition, on the contrary, there is no apparent difference in the extremeness of individual and group judgments. In other words, group averaging appears.

Finally, Rabbie and Visser (1976) noted that in a situation measuring relations between groups (involving a certain amount of competition and commitment to one's own group) there was a clear tendency toward polarization. Generally speaking, there seems to be a parallelism between the amount of interaction—and hence commitment of the group members—and the amount of polarization. These findings parallel those of Janis (1972) and make them more plausible.

DECISIONS AND RULES

Even the most spontaneous group transactions obey certain rules. There are a number of conceivable rules, the simplest and most familiar of which are majority and unanimity rules. Davis (1977) and Kerr *et al.* (1975) investigated how groups apply these rules. No clear picture about these rules (social decisions schemes) can be said to

have emerged as yet. We often opt, undoubtedly, for majority rule and for the rule that implies congruence of choice with the external reference group norm. There are undoubted conditions where we prefer a unanimous consensus. But we do not know when, how, and why one or the other of these rules prevails. Gauthier (1981) notes that there is only one rule that all groups observe—to wit, to reject from the start alternatives for which nobody shows any strong preference and to negotiate about those for which there are pronounced preferences.

Miller and Anderson (1979) studied the relation between decision rules and deviance in an interesting experiment. They discovered that whenever the deviant was unable to bring about a decision favorable to him and adverse to the other members, the decision rules used made no difference. However, when the deviant does sway these decisions, there is a difference apparently between the dictatorship rule and the rule of unanimity. With the former the deviate is more likely to be rejected than when the latter is in effect.

Admittedly there are promising beginnings in this field, but much remains to be done—all the more so inasmuch as group polarization seems to play a vital role in the area of legal practice. A whole set of studies has revealed that juries act like all other groups (Kalven and Zeisel, 1966; Walker and Mavis, 1973; Louche, 1975). Among their findings is the fact that the verdicts handed down are more extreme than the jury members' initial individual judgments, but they are always in the same direction as the initial judgments. Myers and Kaplan (1976), Vidmar (1972), Laughlin and Izett (1973), and Bray and Noble (1978) all found that in a mock-jury experiment high-authoritarian jurors and juries reached guilty verdicts more frequently and imposed more severe punishments than low-authoritarians. Davis *et al.* (1981) detected an asymmetry, namely, that "not-guilty" majorities are more influential than "guilty" majorities; and the most likely reason is that the "not-guilty" verdict is in keeping with the social norm. However, a few lines or even a few pages cannot begin to do justice to as vast and serious a topic as the analysis of jury decisions. And yet it could well hold the clue to the secret of how decision rules operate in society.

SOME OBSERVATIONS

Not surprisingly, group polarization and group-averaging phenomena have stimulated a large number of studies. And the data we have presented are on solid ground. I am certain that they will not be called into question again in the foreseeable future. One should, however, expect to see them reexamined in the light of analyses that could reveal unknown connections between already known facts.

But such analyses should do more than provide a new language or reinterpret the data in order to give illustrations for this language. As Festinger (1980) commented, "Too often the notion of originality lay in finding an alternative interpretation to someone's work" (p. 248). This comment is particularly applicable here, where one sees researchers present and discuss experiments without looking into the original hypotheses that served as the underpinnings for predicting such or such an effect. In addition, it is hoped that these analyses will be structured around the group and not, as is presently the case, around interpersonal relations.

We are dealing here with complex phenomena of social life. Their complexity stems from the fact that they involve both innovation pressure, which arises from a conflict of opinions or interests, and normalization pressure, a propensity toward compromise, which is a prerequisite for reaching a consensus. The inherent tension between these two aspirations dominates human relations. For that reason it is at the very heart of their social psychology.

CONCLUSION

I have attempted in this chapter to give an overview of the reasons why influence became the central problem to be solved by social psychology. I stressed the fact that it was first identified with conformity. We attempt now to include the new field of innovation but not without difficulty and resistance. It is natural in such a chapter to stress continuity of ideas and methods. However, this focus does not exclude the existence of sharp breaks and discontinuities. And these discontinuities obviously have a polemical side. A large part of Asch's work arose out of opposition to the findings of Sherif and classical collective psychology, just as our own arose from opposition to research based on the functionalist model of social relations in which conformity played a central role. As a result of this discontinuous evolution, we are faced with three distinct paradigms for the study of social influence: normalization, conformity, and innovation paradigms. By reinterpreting all three carefully, however, we obtain a comprehensive theoretical model from which established facts acquire new meaning and new facts can be predicted. Nonetheless, in terms of the importance of this field of research, surprisingly few scholars are working in this area and, in comparison with the past, studies are relatively few.

My other purpose was to draw attention to certain extensions of social influence theory in which it does not have obvious applications, to wit, in the field of group decision. But I am fully aware of my failure to cover all the aspects deserving to be mentioned and all the studies deserving to become better known. I hope that the readers will not hold the omissions against me and will make the effort to look them up themselves. Europe has been particularly prolific in the field of social influence and related areas. Since many of these studies appeared in French and Flemish as well as English, I felt that they warranted being summarized at greater length, so readers could evaluate their interest and implications.

To avoid overburdening this chapter, I decided against presenting certain findings on interpersonal and intergroup relations or on the way that minorities and majorities change these relations. If these phenomena are viewed from the standpoint of a general influence theory, including innovation, they will appear to us in a different perspective and present new aspects that deserve to be investigated.

The main conclusion to be drawn from the preceding findings is that what amounts to a paradigmatic reversal has taken place. We now look at social relations not exclusively from the vantage point of majorities but from the minority perspective as well. Social change, including social control, is a focal point in these relations. Thanks to this reversal, it now becomes possible to reach out to new layers of reality and to see them with an unjaundiced eye.

REFERENCES

Alexander, C., Jr. Norman, L. G. Zucker, and C. L. Brody (1970). Experimental expectations and autokinetic experiences: consistency theories and judgmental convergence. *Sociometry, 33,* 108–122.

Allen, V. L. (1965). Situational factors in conformity. In L. Berkowitz (Ed.), *Advances in experimental social psychology.* Vol. 2. New York: Academic Press. Pp. 133–175.

———— (1966). Personality correlates of conformity pressure at different degrees of extremeness of the group norm. Unpublished manuscript.

———— (1975). Social support for nonconformity. In L. Berkowitz (Ed.), *Advances in experimental social psychology.* Vol. 8. New York: Academic Press. Pp. 1–43.

Allen, V. L., and J. M. Levine (1968). Social support, dissent and conformity. *Sociometry, 31,* 138–149.

———(1971). Social pressure and personal preference. *J. exp. soc. Psychol., 7,* 122–124.

Allen, V. L., and D. A. Wilder (1978). Perceived persuasiveness as a function of response style: multi-issue consistency over time. *Europ. J. soc. Psychol., 8,* 289–296.

———(1980). Impact of group consensus and social support on stimulus meaning: mediation of conformity by cognitive restructuring. *J. Pers. soc. Psychol., 38,* 1116–1174.

Allyn, J., and L. Festinger (1961). The effectiveness of unanticipated persuasive communications. *J. abnorm. soc. Psychol., 62,* 35–40.

Anderson, N. H., and C. Graesser (1976). An information integration analysis of attitude change in group discussion. *J. Pers. soc. Psychol., 34,* 210–222.

Andrews, I. R., and D. L. Johnson (1971). Small group polarization of judgments. *Psychon. Sci., 24,* 191–192.

Apsler, R., and D. O. Sears (1968). Warning, personal involvement and attitude change. *J. Pers. soc. Psychol., 9,* 162–166.

Argyle, M. (1957). Social pressure in public and private situations. *J. abnorm. soc. Psychol., 54,* 172–175.

Arnold D. W., and C. I. Greenberg (1980). Deviate rejection within differentially manned groups. *Soc. Psychol. Quart., 41,* 419–424.

Aronson, E., and B. W. Golden (1962). The effect of relevant and irrelevant aspects of communicator credibility on attitude change. *J. Pers., 30,* 135–146.

Aronson, E., J. A. Turner, and J. M. Carlsmith (1963). Communicator credibility and communication discrepancy as determinants of opinion change. *J. abnorm. soc. Psychol., 67,* 31–36.

Arrow, K. J. (1974). *The limits of organization.* New York: W. W. Norton.

Asch, S. E. (1952). *Social psychology.* New York: Prentice-Hall.

———(1955). Opinions and social pressure. *Sci. Amer., 193,* 31–35.

———(1956). Studies on independence and conformity: a minority of one against a unanimous majority. *Psychol. Monogr., 70,* No. 9 (whole No. 416).

Back, K. W. (1951). Influence through social communication. *J. abnorm. soc. Psychol., 46,* 9–23.

Back, K. W., and M. D. Bogdonoff (1964). Plasma lipid responses to leadership, conformity and deviation. In P. H. Leiderman and D. Shapiro (Eds.), *Psychobiological approaches to social behavior.* Stanford: Stanford Univ. Press. Pp. 24–42.

Bergin, A. E. (1962). The effect of dissonant persuasive communications on changes in a self-referring attitude. *J. Pers., 30,* 423–438.

Berkowitz, L., and J. R. Macauley (1961). Some effects of differences in status level and status stability. *Hum. Rel., 14,* 135–148.

Biener, L. (1971). The effect of message repetition on attitude change: a model of informational social influence. Doctoral dissertation, Columbia University.

Binet, A. (1900). *La suggestibilité.* Paris: Schleicher.

Bishop, G. D., and D. G. Myers (1974). Information influence in group discussion, *Organizational behavior and human performance, 12,* 92–104.

Blacke, R. R., H. Helson, and J. S. Mouton (1957). The generality of conformity behavior as a function of factual anchorage, difficulty of task and amount of social pressure. *J. Pers., 25,* 294–305.

Bochner, S., and C. A. Insko (1966). Communicator discrepancy, source credibility and opinion change. *J. Pers. soc. Psychol., 4,* 614–621.

Borden, R. I. (1980). Audience influence. In P. B. Paulus (Ed.), *Psychology of group influence.* Hillsdale, N.J.: Erlbaum. Pp. 99–132.

Bovard, E. W., Jr. (1948). Social norms and the individual. *J. abnorm. soc. Psychol., 42,* 62–69.

———(1951). Group structure and perception. *J. abnorm. soc. Psychol., 46,* 398–405.

———(1953). Conformity to social norms in stable and temporary groups. *Science, 117,* 361–363.

Bray, R. M., and A. M. Noble (1978). Authoritarianism and decision of mock juries: evidence of jury bias and group polarization. *J. Pers. soc. Psychol. 36,* 1424–1430.

Brehm, J. W., and D. Lipsher (1959). Communicator-communicatee discrepancy and perceived communicator trustworthiness. *J. Pers., 27,* 352–361.

Brehm, J. W., and M. Mann (1975). Effect of importance of freedom and attraction to group members on influence produced by group pressure. *J. Pers. soc. Psychol., 31,* 816–824.

Burdick, H. A. (1955). The compliant behavior of deviates under conditions of threat. Doctoral dissertation, University of Minnesota.

Burdick, H. A., and A. Y. Burns (1958). A test of "strain toward symmetry" theories. *J. abnorm. soc. Psychol., 57,* 367–370.

Burnstein, E., and A. Vinokur (1975). What a person thinks upon learning he has chosen differently from others. *J. exp. soc. Psychol., 11,* 412–426.

———(1977). Persuasive argumentation and social comparison as determinants of attitude polarization. *J. exp. soc. Psychol., 4,* 66–94.

Burnstein, E., A. Vinokur, and M. F. Pichevin (1974). What do differences between own, admired and attributed choices have to do with group induced shifts in choices? *J. exp. soc. Psychol., 10,* 428–443.

Burnstein, E., A. Vinokur, and V. Trope (1973). Interpersonal comparison versus persuasive argumentation. *J. exp. soc. Psychol., 9,* 236–245.

Byrne, D., and W. Griffitt (1966). A developmental investigation of the law of attraction. *J. Pers. soc. Psychol., 4,* 699–702.

Byrne, D., and D. Nelson (1964). Attraction as a function of attitude similarity-dissimilarity: the effect of topic importance. *Psychon. Sci., 1,* 93–94.

Cacioppo, J. T., and R. E. Petty (1979). Effects of message repetition and position on cognitive response, recall, and persuasion. *J. Pers. soc. Psychol., 37,* 97–109.

Carmichael, C. W., and G. L. Cronkhite (1965). Frustration and language intensity. *Speech Monogr., 32,* 107–111.

Chaiken, S. (1979). Communicator physical attractiveness and persuasion. *J. Pers. soc. Psychol., 37,* 1387–1397.

Church, R. M. (1962). The effect of competition on reaction time and palmar skin conductance. *J. abnorm. soc. Psychol., 65,* 32–40.

Churchman, C. W. (1961). *Predictions and optimal decisions.* Englewood Cliffs, N.J.: Prentice-Hall.

Cialdini, R. B., and H. L. Mrels (1976). Sense of personal control and attributions about yielding and resisting persuasion targets. *J. Pers. soc. Psychol., 33,* 395–402.

Clark, R. D. III (1971). Group-induced shift toward risk: a critical appraisal. *Psychol. Bull., 76,* 251–270.

Coffin, T. E. (1941). Some conditions of suggestion and suggestibility: a study of certain attitudinal and situational factors influencing the process of suggestion. *Psychol. Monogr., 53,* 1–125.

Cohen, B. P., and H. Lee (1975). *Conflict, conformity and social status.* Amsterdam, Oxford, New York: Elsevier.

Coleman, J. F., R. R. Blacke, and J. S. Mouton (1958). Task difficulty and conformity pressures. *J. abnorm. soc. Psychol., 57,* 120–122.

Croner, M. D., and R. H. Willis (1961). Perceived differences in task competence and asymmetry of dyadic influence. *J. abnorm. soc. Psychol., 62,* 705–708.

Crowne, D. P., and S. Liverant (1963). Conformity under varying conditions of personal commitment. *J. abnorm. soc. Psychol., 61,* 547–555.

Crowne, D. P., and D. Marlowe (1964). *The approval motive: studies in evaluative dependence.* New York: Wiley.

Crutchfield, R. S. (1955). Conformity and character. *Amer. Psychologist, 10,* 195–198.

Cvetkovich, G., and S. R. Baumgardner (1973). Attitude polarization: the relative influence of group structure and reference group norms. *J. Pers. soc. Psychol., 26,* 159–165.

Dabbs, J. M., Jr., and I. L. Janis (1965). Why does eating while reading facilitate opinion change. An experimental inquiry. *J. exp. soc. Psychol., 1,* 133–144.

Darley, J. M., T. Moriarity, S. Darley, and E. Berscheid (1974). Increased conformity to a fellow deviant as a function of prior deviation. *J. exp. soc. Psychol., 10,* 211–223.

Davis, J. H. (1973). Group decision and social interaction: a theory of social decisions schema. *Psychol. Rev., 80,* 97–125.

Davis, J. H., R. W. Holt, C. E. Spitzer, and G. Stasser (1981). The effect of consensus requirements and multiple decisions on mock juror verdict preferences. *J. exp. soc. Psychol., 71,* 1–15.

Deconchy, J. P. (1980). *Orthodoxie religieuse et sciences humaines.* Paris: Mouton La Haye.

Deutsch, M., and H. B. Gerard (1955). A study of normative and informational social influence upon individual judgment. *J. abnorm. soc. Psychol., 51,* 629–636.

Dietrich, J. E. (1946). The relative effectiveness of two models of radio delivery in influencing attitudes. *Speech Monogr., 13,* 58–65.

Dillehay, R. C., C. A. Insko, and M. B. Smith (1966). Logical consistency and attitude change. *J. Pers. soc. Psychol., 3,* 646–654.

Dion, K. L., R. S. Baron, and N. Miller (1970). Why do groups make riskier decisions than individuals? In L. Berkowitz (Ed.), *Advances in experimental social psychology.* Vol. 5. New York: Academic Press.

Dion, K. L., and B. M. Earn (1978). The phenomenology of being a target of prejudice. *J. Pers. soc. Psychol., 32,* 944–950.

Dion, K. L., B. M. Earn, and P. H. N. Yee (1978). The experience of being a victim of prejudice: an experimental approach. *Int. J. Psychol., 13,* 197–214.

Dittes, J. E. (1959). Effect of changes in self-esteem upon impulsiveness and deliberation in making judgments. *J. abnorm. soc. Psychol., 58,* 348–356.

Dittes, J. E., and H. H. Kelley (1956). Effect of different conditions of acceptance upon conformity to group norms. *J. abnorm. soc. Psychol., 53,* 100–107.

Doise, W. (1969). Intergroup relations and polarization of individual and collective judgments. *J. Pers. soc. Psychol., 12,* 136–143.

_____ (1970). L'importance d'une dimension principale dans les jugements collectifs. *Année psychol., 70,* 151–159.

_____ (1971). An apparent exception to the extremization of collective judgments. *Europ. J. soc. Psychol., 1,* 511–518.

_____ (1973). La structuration des décisions individuelles et collectives d'adultes et d'enfants. *Revue de Psychol. et sc. de l'éducation, 8,* 133–146.

Doise, W., and S. Moscovici (1969–1970). Approche et évitement du déviant dans des groupes de cohésion différente. *Bulletin de Psychologie, 23,* 522–525.

Doms, M. (1978). Moscovici's innovatie-effekt: poging tot integratie met het conformisme-effekt. Doctoral dissertation, Katholieke Universiteit te Leuven.

Doms, M., and Van Avermaet (1980). Majority influence, minority influence and conversion behavior: a replication. *J. exp. soc. Psychol., 16,* 283–292.

_____ (1981). The conformity effect: a timeless phenomenon? Louvain, 7 pp. (Mimeo)

Duval, S. (1976). Conformity on a visual task as a function of personal novelty on attitudinal dimensions and being reminded of the object status of self. *J. exp. soc. Psychol., 12,* 87–98.

Eagly, A. H. (1978). Sex differences in influenceability. *Psychol. Bull., 85,* 86–116.

Eagly, A. H., and S. Chaiken (1984). Cognitive theories of persuasion. In L. Berkowitz (Ed.), *Advances in experimental social psychology.* New York: Academic Press.

Ebbesen, E. B., and R. L. Bowers (1974). Proportion of risky to conservative arguments in group discussion and choice. *J. Pers. soc. Psychol., 29,* 316–327.

Eisinger R., and J. Mills (1968). Perception of the sincerity and competence of a communicator as a function of the extremity of his position. *J. exp. soc. Psychol., 4,* 224–232.

Emerson, R. (1954). Deviation and rejection: an experimental replication. *Amer. sociol. Rev., 19,* 688–693.

Erickson, B., E. A. Lind, B. C. Johnson, and W. M. O'Barr (1978). Speech style and impression formation in a court setting: the effects of "powerful" and "powerless" speech. *J. exp. soc. Psychol., 14,* 266–279.

Ference, T. P. (1971). Feedback and conflict as determinants of influence. *J. exp. soc. Psychol., 7,* 1-16.

Festinger, L. (1950). Informal social communication. *Psychol. Rev., 57,* 217-282.

———— (1953). An analysis of compliant behavior. In M. Sherif, and M. O. Wilson (Eds.), *Group relations at the crossroads.* New York: Harper. Pp. 232-256.

———— (1954). A theory of social comparison processes. *Hum. Rel., 7,* 117-140.

Festinger, L. (Ed.) (1980). *Retrospections on social psychology.* New York: Oxford University Press.

Fine, B. J. (1957). Conclusion-drawing, communicator credibility and anxiety as factors in opinion change. *J. abnorm. soc. Psychol., 54,* 369-374.

Fisher, S., and A. Lubin (1958). Distance as a determinant of influence in a two-person serial interaction situation. *J. abnorm. soc. Psychol., 56,* 230-238.

Fisher, S., I. Rubinstein, and R. W. Freeman (1956). Intertrial effects of immediate self-committal in a continuous social influence situation. *J. abnorm. soc. Psychol., 52,* 200-207.

Forgas, J. P. (1977). Group effects on person perception judgments as a function of group interaction style. *Europ. J. soc. Psychol., 7,* 175-187.

———— (1981). Responsibility attributions for life dilemmas: group polarization and moderation effects. University of New South Wales. (Mimeo)

Frager, R. (1970). Conformity and anticonformity in Japan. *J. Pers. soc. Psychol., 15,* 203-210.

Fraser, C. (1971). Group risk taking and group polarization. *Europ. J. soc. Psychol., 1,* 493-510.

Fraser, C., and M. Billig (1971). Risky shifts, caution shifts and group polarization, *Europ. J. soc. Psychol., 1,* 7-29.

Freedman, J. L. (1964). Involvement, discrepancy, and change. *J. abnorm. soc. Psychol., 69,* 290-295.

Freedman, J., and D. Sears (1965). Warning, distraction and resistance to influence. *J. Pers. soc. Psychol., 1,* 262-266.

French, J. R. P., Jr., and B. H. Raven (1959). The bases of social power. In D. Cartwright (Ed.), *Studies in social power.* Ann Arbor: Univ. of Michigan Press.

French, J. R. P., Jr., and R. Synder (1959). Leadership and interpersonal power. In D. Cartwright (Ed.), *Studies in social power.* Ann Arbor: Univ. of Michigan Press. Pp. 118-149.

Freud, S. (1962). *Psychologie collective et analyse du moi.* Paris: Payot.

Gauthier, J. M. (1981). Etude sur la polarisation des décisions en groupe. Unpublished thesis, Paris.

Gerard, H. B., and C. W. Greenbaum (1962). Attitudes toward an agent of uncertainty reduction. *J. Pers., 30,* 485-495.

Gerard, H. B., R. A. Wilhelmy, and R. S. Conolley (1968). Conformity and group size. *J. Pers. soc. Psychol., 8,* 79-82.

Ghiglione, E., and J. L. Beauvois (1983). Language attitudes and social influence. *J. soc. Psychol., 121,* 97-109.

Goethals, G. R. (1976). An attributional analysis of some social influence phenomena in *New directions in attribution research,* Vol. 1. New York: Wiley.

Goldberg, S. C. (1954). Three situational determinants of conformity to social norms. *J. abnorm. soc. Psychol., 49,* 325-329.

———— (1970). Attitude change as a function of source credibility, authoritarianism, and message ambiguity. *Proceedings of the 78th annual convention of the A.P.A.,* Miami Beach.

Gouge, C., and C. A. Fraser (1972). A further demonstration of group polarization. *Europ. J. soc. Psychol., 2,* 95-97.

Graham, D. (1962). Experimental studies of social influence in simple judgment situations. *J. soc. Psychol., 56,* 245-269.

Gramsci, A. (1953). *Note sul Machiavelli, sulla politica etsullo Stato moderno.* Torino: Einaudi, 1966.

Greenberg, B. S., and G. R. Miller (1966). The effect of low credibility sources on message acceptance. *Speech Monogr., 33,* 127-136.

Greenwald, H., (1964). The involvement-discrepancy controversy in persuasion research. Doctoral dissertation, Columbia University.

Grove, M. G. (1975). Attitude convergence in small groups. *J. Communication, 15,* 226-238.

Gurnee, E. (1937). A comparison of collective and individual judgment of fact. *J. exp. Psychol., 21,* 106-112.

Hammond, K. R., and D. A. Summers (1965). Cognitive dependence and non-linear cues. *Psychol. Rev., 72,* 215-224.

Hammond, K. R., F. Todd, M. Wilkins, and T. Mitchell (1966). Cognitive conflict between persons: application of the "lens model paradigm." *J. exp. soc. Psychol., 2,* 88-97.

Hardy, K. R. (1957). Determinants of conformity and attitude change. *J. abnorm. soc. Psychol., 54,* 289-294.

Hare, A. P. (1962). *Handbook of small group research.* New York: Free Press.

Harris M., and J. Cooper (1979). A meta-analysis of sex differences in community research. *J. Pers. soc. Psychol., 37,* 141-146.

Harvey, J. H., and C. Consalvi (1960). Status and conformity to pressure in informal groups. *J. abnorm. soc. Psychol., 60,* 182-187.

Harvey, J. H., W. J. Ickes, and R. F. Kidd, Eds. (1976). *New directions in attribution research.* Hillsdale, N.J.: Erlbaum.

Hass, R.G., and R. Mann (1976). Anticipatory belief change: persuasion in impression management. *J. Pers. soc. Psychol., 34,* 105-111.

Hastdorf, A. H., and G. W. Piper (1951). A note on the effect of explicit instructions on prestige suggestion. *J. soc. Psychol., 33,* 289-293.

Heillman, M. E. (1976). Oppositional behavior as a function of influence attempt intensity and retaliation threat. *J. Pers. soc. Psychol., 33,* 574-578.

Heillman, M. E., and K. A. Garner (1975). Counteracting the boomerang: the effects of choice on compliance to threats and promises. *J. Pers. soc. Psychol., 31,* 911-917.

Heller, J. F., M. S. Pallak, and J. M. Picek (1973). The interactive effects of intent and threat on boomerang attitude change. *J. Pers. soc. Psychol., 26,* 273-279.

Hicks, J. M., and F. F. Spaner (1962). Attitude change and mental hospital experience. *J. abnorm. soc. Psychol., 65,* 112-120.

Hochbaum, G. H. (1954). The relation between the group member's self-confidence and their reaction to group pressure to uniformity. *Amer. soc. Rev., 19,* 678-687.

Hochberg, J. (1981). On cognition in perception: perceptual coupling and unconscious inference. *Cognition, 10,* 127-134.

Hollander, E. P. (1958). Conformity, status and idiosyncrasy credit. *Psychol. Rev., 65,* 117-127.

_____ (1960). Competence and conformity in the acceptance of influence. *J. abnorm. soc. Psychol., 61,* 361–365.

_____ (1964). *Leaders, groups and influence.* New York: Oxford Univ. Press.

Hollander, E. P., J. W. Julian, and G. A. Haaland (1965). Conformity process and prior group support. Paper presented at the A.P.A. annual convention, Atlantic City.

Holtz, R. F. (1965). An experimental investigation of the influence of awareness of manipulatory intent on reactions to persuasive communications. Master's thesis. Boston University, School of Public Communication.

Hovland, C. I., O. J. Harvey, and M. Sherif (1957). Assimilation and contrast effects in communication and attitude change. *J. abnorm. soc. Psychol., 55,* 242–252.

Hovland, C. I., and W. Mandell (1952). An experimental comparison of conclusion-drawing by the communicator and by the audience. *J. abnorm. soc. Psychol., 47,* 581–588.

Insko, C. A., F. Murashima, and M. Saiyadani (1966). Communicator discrepancy, stimulus ambiguity and influence. *J. Pers., 34,* 262–274.

Janis, I. L. (1972). *Victims of group think.* Boston: Houghton Mifflin.

_____ (1983). The role of social support in adherence to stressful decisions. *Amer. Psychol., 38,* 143–160.

Janis, I. L., and L. Mann (1977). *Decision-making: a psychological analysis of conflict, choice and commitment.* New York: Free Press.

Johnson, H. H., and J. A. Scileppi (1969). Effects of ego-involvement conditions on attitude change in high and low credibility communicators. *J. Pers. soc. Psychol., 19,* 31–36.

Johnson, H. H., and F. F. Stanicek (1969). Relationship between authoritarianism and attitude change as a function of implicit and explicit communications. *Proceedings of the 77th Annual Convention of the A.P.A.* Pp. 415–416.

Jones, E. E. (1964). *Ingratiation: a social psychological analysis.* New York: Appleton-Century-Crofts.

Jones, E. E., R. G. Jones, and K. J. Gergen (1963). Some conditions affecting the evaluation of a conformist. *J. Pers., 31,* 270–278.

Jones, E. E., H. H. Wells, and R. Torrey (1958). Some effects of feedback from the experimenter on conforming behavior. *J. abnorm. soc. Psychol., 57,* 207–213.

Judd, B. (1975). Information effects in group shifts. Unpublished master thesis, Texas.

Julian, J. W., C. R. Regula, and E. P. Hollander (1968). Effects of prior agreement by others on task confidence and conformity. *J. Pers. soc. Psychol., 9,* 171–178.

Kalven, H., and H. Zeisel (1966). *The American jury.* Chicago: Univ. of Chicago Press.

Kaplan, M. F. (1977). Discussion polarization effects in a modified jury decision paradigm, informational influences. *Sociometry, 40,* 262–271.

Kaplan, R. M., and C. E. Miller (1983). Group Discussion and Judgment, In P. B. Paulus (Ed.) *Basic group processes.* New York: Springer Verlag.

Kelley, H. H., and M. M. Shapiro (1954). An experiment of conformity to group norms where conformity is detrimental to group achievement. *Amer. Sociol. Rev., 19,* 667–677.

Kelley, H. H., and E. H. Volkart (1962). The resistance to change of group anchored attitudes. *Amer. sociol. Rev. 17,* 453–465.

Kelman, H. C. (1958). Compliance, identification and internalization: three processes of attitude change. *J. conflict Resolution, 2,* 51–60.

Kerr, N. L., J. H. Davis, D. Meck, and A. K. Riesman (1975). Group position as a function of member attitudes: choice shift effects from the perspective of social decision scheme theory. *J. Pers. soc. Psychol., 31,* 574–593.

Kidd, J. S. (1958). Social influence phenomena in a task-oriented group situation. *J. abnorm. soc. Psychol., 56,* 13–17.

Kidd, J. S., and D. T. Campbell (1955). Conformity to group as a function of group success. *J. abnorm. soc. Psychol., 51,* 390–393.

Kiesler, C. A. (1969). Group pressure and conformity. In J. Mills (Ed.), *Experimental social psychology.* New York: Macmillan. Pp. 235–306.

Kiesler, C. A. (1971). *The psychology of commitment.* New York: Academic Press.

Kiesler, C. A., and L. H. Corbin (1965). Commitment, attraction and conformity. *J. Pers. soc. Psychol., 2,* 890–895.

Kiesler, C. A., and S. B. Kiesler (1964). Role of forewarning in persuasive communications. *J. abnorm. soc. Psychol., 68,* 547–549.

Kiesler, C. A., and M. S. Pallak (1975). Minority influence: the effect of majority reactionaries and defectors, and minority and majority compromisers, upon majority opinion and attractions. *Europ. J. soc. Psychol., 5,* 237–256.

Kimbal, R. K., and E. P. Hollander (1974). Independence in the presence of an experienced but deviate group member. *J. soc. Psychol., 93,* 281–292.

Kleiven, J., C. Fraser, and C. Gouge (1974). Are individual and group decisions dependent on the available information? *Scandin. J. Psychol., 15,* 178–184.

Kogan, N., and M. A. Wallach (1964). *Risk-taking: a study in cognition and personality.* New York: Holt.

Komorita, S. S., and M. Barnes (1969). Effects of pressures to reach agreement in bargaining. *J. Pers. soc. Psychol., 13,* 245–252.

Kuhn, T. (1962). *The structure of scientific revolutions.* Chicago: University of Chicago Press.

Lambert, R. (1969). Extrémisation du comportement de prise de risque en groupe et modèle majoritaire. *Psychol. francaise, 14,* 113–125.

Lamm, H., G. Trommsdorf, and E. Rost-Schande (1973). Group-induced extremization: review of evidence and a minority-change explanation. *Psychol. Reports, 33,* 471–484.

Lana, R. E. (1959). A further test of the pretest-treatment interaction effect. *J. appl. Psychol., 43,* 421–422.

Lana, R. E., and D. J. King (1960). Learning factors as determiners of pretest sensitization. *J. appl. Psychol., 44,* 189–191.

Latané, B., and I. M. Darley (1970). *The unresponsive bystander: why doesn't he help?* Englewood Cliffs, N.J.: Prentice Hall.

Latané, B., S. Harkins, K. Williams (1980). *Many hands make light the work: social loafing as a social disease.* American Association for the Advancement of Science.

Latané, B., and S. Nida (1980). Social impact theory and group influence. A social engineering perspective. In P. B. Paulus (Ed.), *Psychology of group influence*. Hillsdale, N.J.: Erlbaum. Pp. 3–35.

_____ (1981). Ten years of research on group size and helping. *Psychol. Bull.*,

Latané, B., K. Williams, and S. Harkins (1978). Many hands make light the work: causes and consequences of social loafing. *J. Pers. soc. Psychol., 37,* 822–832.

Laughlin, P. (1975). Group size, member ability and social decision schemes on an intellective task. *J. Pers. soc. Psychol., 31,* 522–535.

Le Bon, G. (1895). *Psychologie des foules*. Paris: Félix Alcan.

Lecuyer, R. (1975). Space dimensions: the climate of discussion and group decisions. *Europ. J. soc. Psychol., 5,* 509–514.

Lemaine, G. (1974). Social differentiation and social originality. *Europ. J. soc. Psychol., 4,* 17–52.

Lemaine, G., J. P. Desportes, and J. P. Louarn (1969). Rôle de la cohésion et de la différenciation hiérarchique dans le processus d'influence sociale. *Bull. CERP, 18,* 237–253.

Leventhal, H. (1970). Findings and theory in the study of fear communications. In L. Berkowitz (Ed.), *Advances in experimental social psychology*. Vol. 5. New York: Academic Press. Pp. 119–186.

Levine, J. M., K. R. Saxe, and H. N. Snyder (1976). Reaction to attitudinal deviance: impact of deviate's direction and distance of movement. *Sociometry, 39,* 97–107.

Levine, J. M. (1980). Reaction to opinion deviance in small groups. In P. B. Paulus (Ed.), *Psychology of group influence*. Hillsdale, N.J.: Erlbaum. Pp. 375–429.

Levine, J. M., and C. J. Ranelli (1978). Majority reaction to shifting and stable attitudinal deviates. *Europ. J. soc. Psychol., 8,* 55–70.

Levine, J. M., K. R. Sroka, and H. N. Snyder (1977). Group support and reaction to stable and shifting agreement/disagreement. *Sociometry, 40,* 214–224.

Lewin, K. (1948). *Resolving social conflicts*. New York: Harper and Row.

_____ (1958). Group decision and social change. In E. Maccoby, T. Newcombe, and E. Hartley (Eds.), *Readings in social psychology*. 3rd ed. New York: Holt, Rinehart and Winston. Pp. 197–211.

Liébault, A. A. (1866). *Du sommeil et des états analogues, considérés surtout du point de vue de l'action de la morale sur la physique*. Paris: Masson.

Linton, H. B. (1955). Dépendence on external influence: correlates in perception, attitudes and judgment. *J. abnorm. soc. Psychol., 51,* 502–507.

Lott, A. J., and B. E. Lott (1961). Group cohesiveness, communication level and conformity. *J. abnorm. soc. Psychol., 62,* 408–412.

Louche, C. (1975). La préparation d'une négociation en groupe et ses effets sur les comportements des négociateurs et leurs représentations. *Bulletin de Psychologie, 28,* 113–117.

Luchins, A. S. (1944). On agreement with another's judgment. *J. abnorm. soc. Psychol., 39,* 97–111.

_____ (1945). Social influences on perception of complex drawings. *J. soc. Psychol., 21,* 257–273.

_____ (1955). A variational approach to social influences on perception. *J. soc. Psychol., 42,* 113–119.

Luchins, A. S., and E. H. Luchins (1955). On conformity with true and false communications. *J. soc. Psychol., 42,* 283–303.

_____ (1956). Discovering the source of contradictory communications. *J. soc. Psychol., 44,* 49–64.

_____ (1961). On conformity with judgments of a majority or an authority. *J. soc. Psychol., 53,* 303–316.

McBride, D. (1954). The effects of public and private changes of opinion on intragroup communication. Doctoral dissertation, University of Minnesota.

McCauley, C. R. (1972). Extremity shifts, risky shifts and attitude shifts after group discussion. *Europ. J. soc. Psychol., 2,* 417–436.

McGinnies, E., and E. Donelson (1963). Knowledge of experimenter's intent and attitude change under induced compliance. College Park: Department of Psychology, University of Maryland. (Mimeo)

McGuire, W. J. (1962). Persistence of the resistance to persuasion induced by various types of prior belief defenses. *J. abnorm. soc. Psychol., 64,* 241–248.

_____ (1964). Inducing resistance to persuasion. In L. Berkowitz (Ed.), *Advances in experimental social psychology*. Vol. 1. New York: Academic Press. Pp. 191–229.

McGuire, W. J., and S. Millman (1965). Anticipatory belief lowering following forewarning of a persuasive attack. *J. Pers. soc. Psychol., 2,* 471–479.

McGuire, W. J., and D. Papageorgis (1961). The relative efficacy of various types of prior belief-defense in producing immunity against persuasion. *J. abnorm. soc. Psychol., 62,* 327–337.

_____ (1962). Effectiveness of forewarning in developing resistance to persuasion. *Publ. Opin. Quart., 26,* 24–34.

Maier, N. R. F., and R. A. Maier (1957). An experimental test of the effects of "developmental" versus "free" discussion in the quality of group decisions. *J. appl. Psychol., 41,* 320–323.

Main, E. G., and T. G. Walker (1973). Choice shifts and extreme behavior: judicial review of the federal courts. *J. soc. Psychol., 91,* 215–222.

Marlowe, D., and K. Gergen (1969). Personality and social interaction. In G. Lindzey, and E. Aronson (Eds.), *The handbook of social psychology*. Vol. 3. Reading, Mass.: Addison-Wesley. Pp. 590–665.

Marquis, D. G. (1962). Individual responsibility and group decisions involving risk. *Industrial Management Rev., 3,* 8–23.

Maass, A. and R. D. Clark III (1984). Hidden Impact of Minorities: fifteen years of minority influence research. *Psychol. Bull., 95,* 428–450.

Maass, A., R. D. Clark III, and G. Haberkorn (1981). *Moscovici's theory of minority influence: is it applicable to actual minorities?* Tallahassee. (Mimeo)

Mausner, B., and B. L. Bloch (1957). A study of the additivity of variables affecting social interaction. *J. abnorm. soc. Psychol., 54,* 250–256.

Meertens, R. W. (1976). Aspecten van groepspolarisat. Doctoral dissertation, Groningen.

_____ (1978). *Groepspolarisatie*. Deventier.

Milgram, S., (1974). *Soumission à l'autorité*. Paris: Calmann-Levy.

Milgram, S., L. Bickman, and L. Berkowitz (1969). Note on the drawing power of crowds of different size. *J. Pers. soc. Psychol., 13,* 79–82.

Miller, G. R., and M. A. Hewgill (1966). Some recent research on fear arousing message appeals. *Speech Monogr., 33,* 377–391.

Miller, N. (1965). Involvement and dogmatism as inhibitors of attitude change. *J. exp. soc. Psychol., 1,* 121–132.

Mills, J. (1966). Opinion change as a function of the communicator's desire to influence and liking for the audience. *J. exp. soc. Psychol., 2,* 152–159.

Mills, J., and E. Aronson (1965). Opinion change as a function of communicator's attractiveness and desire to influence. *J. Pers. soc. Psychol., 1,* 173–177.

Mills, J., and J. M. Jellison (1967). Effect of opinion change of how desirable the communication is to the audience the communicator addressed. *J. Pers. soc. Psychol., 6,* 98–101.

Misumi, J. (1981). Action research on group decision making and organisational development. International Congress of Psychology, Leipzig. (Mimeo)

Moeller, G., and M. M. Applezweig (1957). A motivational factor in conformity. *J. abnorm. soc. Psychol., 55,* 114–120.

Montgomery, R. L., S. W. Hinkle, and R. F. Enzie (1976). Arbitrary norms and social change in high- and low-authoritarian societies. *J. Pers. soc. Psychol., 33,* 698–708.

Montmollin, G. de (1965). Influence des réponses d'autrui sur les jugements perceptifs. *Année psychol., 65,* 377–395.

————— (1977). *L'influence sociale. Phénomènes, facteurs et théories.* Paris: Presses Universitaires de France.

Morris, W. N., and R. S. Miller (1975). The effects of consensus-breaking and consensus-preemting partners on reduction of conformity. *J. exp. soc. Psychol., 11,* 215–223.

Moscovici, S. (1976). *Social influence and social change.* London: Academic Press.

————— (1980). Toward a theory of conversion Behavior. *Advances exp. soc. Psychol., 13,* 209–239.

————— (1981). *L'âge des foules.* Paris: Fayard.

Moscovici, S., and W. Doise (1974). Decision making in groups. In C. Nemeth (Ed.), *Social psychology: classic and contemporary integrations.* Chicago: Rand McNally. Pp. 250–287.

Moscovici, S., W. Doise, and R. Dulong (1972). Studies in group decision. II. Differences of positions, differences of opinion, and group polarization. *Europ. J. soc. Psychol., 2,* 385–399.

Moscovici, S., and M. Doms (1981). Minority influence, majority influence and compliance behaviour after a sensory deprivation experience. Louvain and Paris. (Mimeo)

Moscovici, S., and C. Faucheux (1972). Social influence, conformity bias, and the study of active minorities. In L. Berkowitz (Ed.), *Advances in experimental social psychology.* Vol. 6. New York: Academic Press. Pp. 149–202.

Moscovici, S., and E. Lage (1976). Studies in social influence. III. Majority versus minority influence in a group. *Europ. J. soc. Psychol., 6,* 149–174.

————— (1978). Studies in social influence. IV. Minority influence in a context of original judgments. *Europ. J. soc. Psychol., 8,* 349–365.

Moscovici, S., E. Lage, and M. Naffrechoux (1969). Influence of a consistent minority on the responses of a majority in a color perception task. *Sociometry, 32,* 365–379.

————— (1973). Conflict in three-person groups: the relationship between social influence and cognitive style. In L. Rappoport and D. A. Summers (Eds.), *Human judgment and social interaction.* New York, Chicago, San Francisco: Holt, Rinehart and Winston. Pp. 304–314.

Moscovici, S., and R. Lecuyer (1972). Studies in group decision. I. Social space, patterns of communication and group consensus. *Europ. J. soc. Psychol., 2,* 221–244.

Moscovici, S., and G. Mugny (1983). Minority influence. In P. B. Paulus (Ed.) *Basic group processes.* New York: Springer Verlag. Pp. 41–65.

Moscovici, S., and C. Nemeth (1974). Minority influence. In C. Nemeth (Ed.), *Social psychology: classic and contemporary integrations.* Chicago: Rand McNally. Pp. 217–249.

Moscovici, S., and P. Nève (1971). Studies in social influence. I: Those absent are in the right: convergence and polarization of answers in the course of a social interaction. *Europ. J. soc. Psychol., 1,* 201–213.

————— (1972). Studies on group polarization of judgments. III. Majorities, minorities and social judgments. *Europ. J. soc. Psychol., 2,* 221–244.

Moscovici, S., and B. Personnaz. (1980). Studies in social influence V: Minority influence and conversion behavior in a perceptual task. *J. soc. exp. Psychol., 10,* 270–282.

Moscovici, S., and M. Zavalloni (1969). The group as a polarizer of attitudes. *J. Pers. soc. Psychol., 12,* 125–135.

Moscovici, S., M. Zavalloni, and C. Louis-Guérin (1972). Studies on polarization of judgments. I. Group effects on person perception. *Europ. J. soc. Psychol., 2,* 87–91.

Moscovici, S., M. Zavalloni, and M. Weinberger (1972). Studies on polarization of judgments. II. Person perception, ego involvement and group interaction. *Europ. J. soc. Psychol., 2,* 92–94.

Mouton, J. S., R. R. Blake, and J. A. Olmstead (1956). The relationship between frequency of yielding and the disclosure of personal identity. *J. Pers., 24,* 339–347.

Mugny, G. (1974). Négociations et influence minoritaire. Doctoral dissertation, University of Geneva.

————— (1975). Bedeutung der Konsistenz bei der Beeinflussung durch eine konkordante oder diskordante minderheitliche Kommunikation bei sozialen Beurteilungsobjekten. *Zeitschrift für Sozialpsychologie, 6,* 324–332.

————— (1976). Quelle influence majoritaire? Quelle influence minoritaire? *Revue suisse de Psychologie, 35,* 255–268.

Mugny, G., and S. Papastamou (1976–77). Pour une nouvelle approache de l'influence minoritaire: les déterminants psychosociaux des stratégies d'influence minoritaires. *Bulletin Psychologie, 30,* 573–579.

Mugny, G., S. Papastamou, and C. Sherrard (1982). *The power of minorities.* London: Academic Press.

Mugny, G., B. Pierrehumbert, and R. Zubel (1973). Le style d'interaction comme facteur de l'influence sociale. *Bulletin de Psychologie, 26,* 789–793.

Mulder, M. (1960). The power variable in communication experiments. *Hum. Relat., 13,* 241–257.

Myers, D. G. (1975). Discussion-induced attitude polarization. *Human relations, 28,* 699–714.

_____ (1978). Polarizing effects of social comparison. *J. exp. soc. Psychol., 14,* 554–563.

Myers, D. G., and P. J. Bach (1974). Discussion effects on militarism-pacifism: a test of group polarization hypothesis. *J. Pers. soc. Psychol., 30,* 741–747.

Myers, D. G., P. J. Bach, and F. B. Schreiber (1974). Normative and informational effects of group interaction. *Sociometry, 37,* 275–285.

Myers, D. G., and G. D. Bishop (1971). Enhancement of dominant attitudes in group discussion. *J. Pers. soc. Psychol., 20,* 386–391.

Myers, D. G., and M. F. Kaplan (1976). Group-induced polarization in simulated juries. *Pers. soc. psychol. Bull., 2,* 63–66.

Myers, D. G., and H. Lamm (1976). The group polarization phenomenon. *Psychol. Bull., 83,* 602–627.

Myers, M. T., and A. A. Goldberg (1970). Group credibility and opinion change. *J. Communication, 20,* 174–179.

Nemeth, C. (1975). Understanding minority influence: a reply and a digression. *Europ. J. soc. Psychol., 5,* 265–267.

_____ (1979). The role of an active minority in intergroup relations. In W. G. Austins and S. Worchel (Eds.), *The social psychology of intergroup relations.* Monterey, Calif.: Brooks/Cole. Pp. 225–236.

_____ (1981). Negociations vs influence. Conference on Minority Influence, Barcelona. (Mimeo)

Nemeth, C., and J. Endicott (1974). The midpoint as an anchor: another look at discrepancy of position and attitude change. (Mimeo)

Nemeth, C., and J. Markowski (1972). Conformity and discrepancy of position. *Sociometry, 35,* 562–575.

Nemeth, C., M. Swedlund, and B. Kanki (1974). Patterning of the minority's responses and their influence on the majority. *Europ. J. soc. Psychol., 4,* 53–64.

Nemeth, C., and J. Wachtler (1973). Consistency and modification of judgment. *J. exp. soc. Psychol., 9,* 65–79.

_____ (1974). Creating the perceptions of consistency and confidence: a necessary condition for minority influence. *Sociometry, 37,* 529–540.

_____ (1983). Creative problem solving as a result of majority versus minority influence. *Europ. J. soc. Psychol., 13,* 45–55.

Nève, P., and J. M. Gauthier (1978). Effets de l'implication. *Bulletin de Psychologie, 2,* 334–360.

Newcomb, T. M. (1943). *Personality and social change.* New York: Dryden.

Newton, J. W., and L. Mann (1980). Crowd size as a factor in the persuasion process: a study of religious crusade meetings. *J. Pers. soc. Psychol., 39,* 874–883.

Oakes, W. E. (1962). Effectiveness of signal light reinforces given various meanings on participation in group dicussion. *Psychol. Reports, 11,* 469–470.

Odell, M. (1959). Personality correlates of independence and conformity. Unpublished master's thesis. Ohio State University.

Osgood, C. E., G. Suci, and P. H. Tannenbaum (1957). *The measurement of meaning.* Urbana, Ill.: Univ. of Illinois Press.

Osterhouse, R. A., and T. C. Brock (1970). Distraction increases yielding to propaganda by inhibiting counter-arguing. *J. Pers. soc. Psychol., 15,* 344–358.

Paicheler, G. (1976). Norms and attitude change. I. Polarization and styles of behaviour. *Europ. J. soc. Psychol., 6,* 405–427.

_____ (1977). Norms and attitude change. II. The phenomenon of bipolarization. *Europ. J. soc. Psychol., 7,* 5–14.

Paicheler, G., and J. Bouchet (1973). Attitude polarization, familiarization and group process. *Europ. J. soc. Psychol., 3,* 83–90.

Papastamou, S. (1979). Stratégies d'influence minoritaires et majoritaires. Doctoral disssertation. Paris: Ecole des Hautes Etudes en Sciences Sociales.

Personnaz, B. (1974). La conformité minoritaire: Perte d'identité sociale ou clandestinité des référents? Unpublished manuscript. Paris.

_____ (1981). Researches in social influence; conversion in a perceptual task. Study with the spectrometer method. *Europ. J. soc. Psychol., 11,* 431–438.

Perrin, S., and C. Spencer (1980). The Asch-effect: a child of its time? *Bull. Brit. psychol. Soc., 32,* 405–406.

Petty, R. E., and J. T. Cacioppo (1984). The effect of involvement on responses to argument quantity and quality: central and peripheral routes to persuasion. *J. Pers. soc. Psychol., 46,* 69–81.

Pollis, N. P. (1967). Relative stability of scales formed in individual togetherness and group situations. *Brit. J. soc. clin. Psychol., 6,* 249–255.

Powell, F. A., and G. R. Miller (1967). Social approval and disapproval cues in anxiety-arousing communications. *Speech Monogr., 34,* 152–159.

Pruitt, D. G., and J. L. Drews (1969). The effect of time pressure, time elapsed, and the opponent's concession rate on behavior in negotiation. *J. exp. Psychol., 5,* 43–60.

Rabbie, J. M., and L. Visser (1976). Bargaining strength and group polarization in inter-group polarization. *Europ. J. soc. Psychol., 2,* 401–416.

Raven, B. H. (1959). Social influence on opinions and the communication of related content. *J. abnorm. soc. Psychol., 58,* 119–128.

Ricateau, P. (1971). Processus de catégorisation d'autrui et les mécanismes d'influence. *Bulletin de Psychologie, 24,* 909–919.

Ridgeway, C. L. (1978). Conformity, group-oriented motivation, and status attainment in small groups. *Soc. Psychol., 41,* 175–188.

Riecken, H. W. (1952). Some problems of consensus and development. *Rural Sociol., 17,* 245–252.

Robinson, J., and L. Z. McArthur (1982). Impact of salient vocal qualities on causal attribution for a speaker's behavior. *J. Pers. soc. Psychol., 43,* 236–247.

Rohrer, J. H., S. H. Blaron, E. L. Hoffman, and D. V. Swander (1954). The stability of autokinetic judgment. *J. abnorm. soc. Psychol., 49,* 595–597.

Rosenberg, L. A. (1961). Group size, prior experience and conformity. *J. abnorm. soc. Psychol., 63,* 436–437.

Ross, L., G. Bierbrauer, and S. Hoffman (1976). The role of attribution processes in conformity and dissent: revisiting the Asch situation. *Amer. Psychologist, 31,* 148–157.

Rotter, J. B. (1966). Generalized expectancies for internal versus external control of reinforcement. *Psychol. Monogr., 180,* No. 1 (whole No. 609).

Ruback, R. B., and J. M. Levine (1979). Reaction to opinion deviance: impact of others' tolerance of deviate and deviate's expressed confidence. *Eastern Psychol. Assoc.*

Sakurai, M. (1975). Small group cohesiveness and detrimental conformity. *Sociometry, 38,* 340–357.

Saltzenstein, H. D., and L. Sandberg (1979). Indirect social influence: change in judgmental process or anticipatory conformity. *J. exp. soc. Psychol., 15,* 209–216.

Samelson, F. (1957). Conforming behavior under two conditions of conflict in the cognitive field. *J. abnorm. soc. Psychol., 55,* 181–187.

Sawyer, A. G. (1981). Repetition, cognitive responses, and persuasion. In R. E. Petty, T. M. Ostrom, and T. C. Brock (Eds.), *Cognitive responses in persuasion.* Hillsdale, N.J.: Erlbaum. Pp. 237–261.

Schachter, S. (1951). Deviation, rejection and communication. *J. abnorm. soc. Psychol., 46,* 190–207.

Schelling, Th. C. (1956). An essay on bargaining. *Amer. Econ. Rev., 46,* 281–306.

——— (1975). *The strategy of conflict.* London: Oxford Univ. Press.

Schroeder, H. M., and D. E. Hunt (1958). Dispositional effects upon conformity at different levels of discrepancy. *J. Pers., 26,* 243–258.

Schwilk, G. L. (1956). An experimental study of the effectiveness of direct and indirect methods of character education. *Union Coll. Stud. Char. Educ., 1,* 199–299.

Semin, G. R. (1975). Two studies in polarization. *Europ. J. soc. Psychol., 5,* 121–132.

Semin, G. R., and A. I. Glendon (1973). Polarization and the established group. *Brit. J. soc. clin. Psychol., 12,* 113–121.

Sensenig, J., and J. W. Brehm (1968). Attitude change from an implied threat to attitudinal freedom. *J. Pers. soc. Psychol., 8,* 324–330.

Shapiro, D., and P. H. Leiderman (1964). Acts and activation: a psychophysiological study of social interaction. In P. H. Leiderman and D. Shapiro (Eds.), *Psychobiological approaches to social behavior.* Stanford: Stanford Univ. Press. Pp. 110–126.

Shaw, M. E. (1963). Some effects of varying amounts of information exclusively possessed by a group member upon his behavior to the group. *J. gen. Psychol., 68,* 71–79.

Sherif, M. (1935). A study of some social factors in perception. *Arch. Psychol., 27,* No. 187.

Sherif, M., and C. I. Hovland (1961). *Social judgment.* New Haven: Yale Univ. Press.

Sherif, C., and C. W. Sherif (1967). *Attitudes, ego involvement and attitude change.* New York: Wiley.

Sherman, S. J. (1973). Internal-external control and its relationship to attitude change under different social influence techniques. *J. Pers. soc. Psychol., 26,* 23–29.

Siegel, S., and L. E. Fouraker (1960). *Bargaining and group decision making.* New York: McGraw-Hill.

Smith, C. E. (1936). A study of the automatic excitation resulting from the interaction of individual opinions and group opinion. *J. abnorm. soc. Psychol., 30,* 138–164.

Snortum, J. R., S. J. Klein, and A. Sherman Wynn (1976). The impact of an aggressive juror in six- and twelve-member juries. *Criminal Justice and Behavior, 3,* 255–262.

Snyder, M. L., and R. A. Wicklund (1976). Prior exercise of freedom and reactance. *J. exp. soc. Psychol., 12,* 120–130.

Sorrentino, R. M., G. King, and G. Leo (1980). The influence of the minority on perception: a note in a possible alternative explanation. *J. exp. soc. Psychol., 16,* 293–301.

Spitzer, C. E., and J. H. Davis (1978). Mutual social influence in dynamic groups. *Soc. Psychol., 41,* 24–33.

Steiner, I. D. (1966). Personality and the resolution of interpersonal disagreements. In B. A. Mahler (Ed.), *Progress in experimental personality research.* Vol. 3. New York: Academic Press. Pp. 195–239.

Steiner, I. D., and H. H. Johnson (1964). Relationships among dissonance reducing responses. *J. abnorm. soc. Psychol., 68,* 38–44.

Stephenson, G. M., and C. J. Brotherton (1975). Social progression anapolarization: a study of discussion and negotiation in groups of mining supervisors. *Brit. J. soc. clin. Psychol., 14,* 241–252.

Stotland, E., and R. Dunn (1962). Identification, "oppositeness", authoritarianism, self-esteem and birth order. *Psychol. Monogr., 76,* No. 9 (whole No. 528).

Stotland, E., and M. Patchen (1961). Identification and changes in prejudice and in authoritarianism. *J. abnorm. soc. Psychol., 62,* 265–274.

Strodtbeck, F. L., and R. D. Mann (1956). Sex role differenciation in jury deliberations. *Sociometry, 19,* 3–11.

Stroebe, W., and C. Fraser (1971). The relationship between riskiness and confidence in choice dilemma decisions. *Europ. J. soc. Psychol., 1,* 519–526.

Tannenbaum, P. H. (1967). The congruity principle revisited: studies in the reduction, induction and generalization of persuasion. In L. Berkowitz (Ed.), *Advances in experimental social psychology.* Vol. 3. New York: Academic Press. Pp. 271–320.

Tannenbaum, P. H., and E. L. Norris (1965). Effects of combining congruity principle strategies for the reduction of persuasion. *Sociometry, 28,* 145–157.

Tarde, G. (1890). *Les lois de l'imitation. Etude sociologique.* Paris: Alcan.

——— (1901). *L'opinion et la foule.* Paris: Alcan.

Taylor, H. F. (1969). *Balance in small groups.* New York: Van Nostrand-Reinhold.

Tedeschi, J. T., S. Lindskold, J. Horai, and J. P. Gahagan (1969). Social power and the credibility of promises. *J. Pers. soc. Psychol., 13,* 253–261.

Tesser, A., J. Campbell, and S. Mickler (1983). The role of social pressure, attention to the stimulus, and self-doubt in conformity. *Europ. J. soc. Psychol., 13,* 217–233.

Thibaut, J., and L. M. Strickland (1956). Psychological set and social conformity. *J. Pers., 25,* 115–129.

Torrance, E. P. (1954). Some sequences of power differences on decision making in permanent and temporary three-man groups. *Research Studies, State College of Washington, 22,* 130–140.

——— (1959). The influence of experienced members of small groups on the behavior of the inexperienced. *J. soc. Psychol., 49,* 249–257.

Tuddenham, R. D. (1961). The influence upon judgment of the apparent discrepancy between self and others. *J. soc. Psychol., 53,* 59–79.

Tuddenham, R. D., P. McBride, and V. Zahn (1957). Studies in conformity and yielding. I: Development of standard experimental series. II: The influence upon judgment of a grossly distorted norm. Office of Naval Research, Group Psychology Branch, Study performed under contract. N.R. 180.159. *Technical Report.* No. 1 and 2.

Ullman, C. (1982). Cognitive and emotional antecedents of religious conversion. *J. Pers. soc. Psychol., 43,* 183–192.

Vidmar, N. (1970). Group composition and the risky shift. *J. exp. soc. Psychol., 6,* 153–166.

———— (1972). Group-induced shifts in simulated jury decisions. (Mimeo)

Vinokur, A. (1969). Distribution of initial risk level and group decisions involving risk. *J. Pers. soc. Psychol., 13,* 207–214.

———— (1971). A review and theoretical analysis of the effect of group processes upon individual and group decisions involving risk. *Psychol. Bull.,* 231–250.

Vinokur, A., and E. Burnstein (1974). The effect of partially shared persuasive arguments on group-induced shifts: a group problem solving approach. *J. Pers. soc. Psychol., 29,* 305–315.

Wahrman, R., and M. D. Pugh (1972). Competence and conformity. Another look at Hollander's study. *Sociometry, 35,* 376–386.

———— (1974). Sex, nonconformity and influence. *Sociometry, 37,* 137–147.

Walker, T. G., and E. C. Main (1973). Choice-shifts in political decision making: federal judges and civil liberties cases. *J. appl. soc. Psychol., 2,* 39–48.

Wallach, M., N. Kogan, and R. Burt (1968). Are risk takers more persuasive than conservatives in group decisions? *J. exp. soc. Psychol., 4,* 76–89.

Walster, E., E. Aronson, and D. Abrahams (1966). On increasing the persuasiveness of a low prestige communicator. *J. exp. soc. Psychol., 2,* 325–342.

Weiss, R. F., W. Buchanan, and B. Pasamanick (1964). Social consensus in persuasive communication. *Psychol. Reports, 14,* 95–98.

Weiss, R. F., J. J. Weiss, and L. M. Chalupa (1967). Classical conditioning of attitudes as a function of source consensus. *Psychon. Sci., 9,* 465–466.

Whatley, J. L. (1974). Consistency and dependence as sources of conformity influence and the relation to psychological reactance. Doctoral dissertation, Duke University.

Whittacker, J. O. (1964). Parameters of social influence in the autokinetic situation. *Sociometry, 27,* 88–95.

Wicklund, R. A., and J. W. Brehm (1968). Attitude change as a function of felt competence and threat to attitudinal freedom. *J. exp. soc. Psychol., 4,* 64–75.

Wilder, D. A. (1977). Perception of groups, size of opposition and social influence. *J. exp. soc. Psychol., 13,* 253–268.

Wolf, S. (1977). The effectiveness of dependence and consistency as sources of minority influence. Doctoral dissertation, Duke University.

Worchel, S., and J. W. Brehm (1971). Direct and implied social restoration of freedom. *J. Pers. soc. Psychol., 18,* 294–304.

Zaleska, M. (1976). Majority influence on group choices among bets. *J. Pers. soc. Psychol., 33,* 8–17.

———— (1974). The effects of discussion on group and individual choices among bets. *Europ. J. soc. Psychol., 4,* 229–250.

Ziller, R. C. (1957). Four techniques of group decision-making under uncertainty. *J. appl. Psychol., 41,* 384–388.

Zimbardo, P. G. (1960). Involvement and communication discrepancy as determinants of opinion conformity. *J. abnorm. soc. Psychol., 60,* 86–94.

Zinoviev, A. (1981). *Le communisme comme réalité.* Paris: Julliard.

CHAPTER 21

Interpersonal Attraction

Ellen Berscheid
University of Minnesota

THE ROLE OF INTERPERSONAL ATTRACTION IN HUMAN LIFE

Who is attracted to whom, and when and where and how, plays a special and exceedingly important role in human life. From the perspective of the individual, the importance of attraction cannot be exaggerated. Each of us owes our very existence to the attraction that once existed between a man and a woman, and because we are dependent upon others from our entry into life to its end, the duration and quality of each of our lives is continuously affected by the answers to the question of who likes and loves us and who is indifferent, dislikes, or even hates us.

Important as the matter of interpersonal attraction is to the individual, its significance is raised to the highest power when the role it plays in the welfare and survival of the species is considered. For a species to survive, its members need to find food, to avoid injury, to reproduce, and, for higher animals, to rear the young. These

The author wishes to express her deep appreciation to Elliot Aronson, University of California, Santa Cruz; Ted Huston, Pennsylvania State University; George Levinger, University of Massachusetts, Amherst; James Olson, University of Western Ontario; and Robert Sternberg, Yale University for their extraordinarily valuable comments on an earlier version.

adaptive behaviors not only engage issues of interpersonal attraction for the individual but also present vital concerns and problems for all of human society (see Mellen, 1981; Plutchik, 1980).

Because our feelings of attraction and repulsion for other people are rooted in our most basic and fundamental biological needs, it is not surprising that sentiment for others is often regarded as the theme of interpersonal relations (e.g., Heider, 1958). Indeed, positive or negative sentiment appears to be the thread running through all of our transactions with the environment, the physical environment as well as the social. This fact has been documented in many ways, but it is perhaps best exemplified by the results of studies that have examined the dimensions that underly our symbolic representations of objects and our interactions with them. Osgood and his associates (e.g., Osgood, Suci, and Tannenbaum, 1957) have repeatedly found that the evaluative (good-bad) factor is the primary theme of human language, and they have given an evolutionary interpretation to the ubiquity of this finding (Osgood, May, and Miron, 1975, p. 395):

> We humans are still animals at base. What is important to us now, as it was back in the age of Neanderthal man, about the sign of a thing, is, first, does it

refer to something *good* for me or *bad* for me (is it an antelope or a saber-toothed tiger)?...Survival, then and now, depends upon the answers.

Matters of interpersonal attraction, then, carry a significance that goes far beyond what might be imagined from examining the contents of Gothic romance novels and corporate training programs in effective salesmanship. They are, quite literally, of life and death importance, not just to the individual but to all of humankind.

As a consequence, humans are among the most social creatures in the animal kingdom, and our evolutionary development has led to a hair-trigger disposition for making discriminative judgments along the attraction dimension. Those early humans who were either indifferent to or incapable of making evaluative judgments of other humans—who could not differentiate between friend and foe—did not survive. The result over evolutionary time is an animal who can and will make such judgments, even in circumstances in which the exposure to the stimulus is so brief that the individual cannot even tell precisely what the stimulus was, only whether he or she likes it (Zajonc, 1980). The fact that people can often say whether they like or dislike another person even when they can say little else about them was demonstrated in another way by Hartley (1946), who asked people to describe their impressions of "Danerians," "Pirenians," and "Wallonians," as well as Americans, Englishmen, and several other national groups. Undoubtedly because they had neither read nor heard anything about Danerians, Pirenians, and Wallonians nor had had any social contact with them (since these groups were figments of Hartley's imagination), there was no consensus about the characteristics of these peoples. Nevertheless, Hartley's respondents were in confident agreement with each other about one thing: They didn't *like* them!

THE STUDY OF
INTERPERSONAL ATTRACTION

Because issues of interpersonal attraction permeate human life, it is not surprising that people have been especially interested in discovering the laws that govern attraction. Testimony to the magnitude of this interest is provided by the fact that a small book entitled *How to Win Friends and Influence People* (Carnegie, 1937) made publishing history by remaining on the best-seller list for a record-breaking ten years and remains today, along with the Bible and other classics, enormously popular. A perusal of the contents of Carnegie's engaging treatise also testifies, however, that the public demand for information about attraction has often exceeded the supply, a state of affairs that has reflected the difficulty of the problem more than it has a lack of attention to it by all disciplined endeavors to understand human nature.

To the discipline of psychology, an understanding of attraction processes has been vital because human life is conceived, lived, and terminated within social relationships, and thus most human behavior takes place within a social context. The ultimate understanding of human behavior requires, therefore, recognition and understanding of the role of this context, which, in turn, is saturated with the causes and consequences of interpersonal attraction. Accordingly, attempts to identify the laws of attraction are as old as psychology itself. From the early philosopher-psychologists (e.g., Aristotle), to those who marked the emergence of psychology into a behavioral science (e.g., William James), to present-day psychologists, problems of attraction have consistently received attention.

Nevertheless, as is true of many other psychological problems, the use of systematic observation to investigate questions of attraction is a relatively recent development. Indeed, the major historical marker for this event occurred only half a century ago when J. L. Moreno published a book called *Who Shall Survive?* (1934, 1953) in which he presented his technique designed to measure and describe the attractions and repulsions between pairs of individuals within a group. Although Theodore Newcomb had developed a similar technique earlier and had already published a study using it (see Newcomb, 1978), it was Moreno's book and subsequent efforts to promote "sociometry," as he called it, that changed the face of social psychology. As Lindzey and Byrne (1968) observe in their comprehensive review of sociometric theory and research, "There are few instances where a single individual has exerted so pervasive an influence on the evolution of a social-science area" (p. 454).

With the advent of sociometry, sociometric measures became an integral part of the emerging discipline of social psychology, and systematic observation within what became known as the interpersonal attraction area burgeoned. It did so despite a lack of theoretical guidance. Even after two decades of systematic empirical effort, in fact, Newcomb (1956) was forced to observe in his presidential address to the American Psychological Association that "I think it not much of an exaggeration to say that there exists no very adequate theory of interpersonal attraction'' (p. 575). Newcomb then proceeded to present his own theoretical approach to the subject, and this approach, along with the publication of his classic study of friendship development, *The Acquaintance Process* (1961), marked the beginning of the phenomenal growth of research on attraction that occurred in the 1960s. Much of this research was the result of an intrinsic interest in attraction phenomena, but (and perhaps in larger part) it was also stimulated by a recognition that questions of attraction are central to an understanding of many social psychological phenomena—group dynamics, social perception, antisocial behavior, and socialization, to name just a few.

OVERVIEW OF CHAPTER

Social psychological interest in the antecedents, consequences, and correlates of interpersonal attraction has continued to surge so that today social psychology can offer the student of attraction a host of theories and a legion of investigations on the subject (for reviews, see Berscheid and Walster, 1969, 1978; Byrne and Griffitt, 1973; Huston, 1974; Huston and Levinger, 1978; Rubin, 1973), much of which will be reviewed in this chapter. For example, the conceptualization and measurement of interpersonal attraction will be discussed in the next major section, and the many theoretical approaches to the study of interpersonal attraction that have guided past research will be outlined after that. The subject of affiliation with others, which is of great importance in its own right and one to which the dynamics of interpersonal attraction are integrally related, will be addressed in the section ''Affiliation and Attraction.'' Then the great deal that is known about the role of attraction in initial encounters will be presented, although it should be noted that this chapter will not consider in detail the impression formation processes (e.g., information integration processes), since these topics are treated elsewhere in this *Handbook*. Finally, emerging theory and evidence relevant to attraction and relationship development, maintenance, and dissolution will be discussed.

Although this topical organization reflects the field of interpersonal attraction as it currently exists, it does not adequately telegraph the degree to which the attraction area is in the process of transition and change. Many of the anomalies and problems that have emerged over the years to plague the investigation of attraction phenomena are now under concerted discussion and attack. Since space will not permit some of the more regrettable of these problems to be discussed in each of their myriad manifestations in existing theory and research, and since the outcomes of the current remedial efforts are only beginning to appear, a bird's-eye view of the field, with special attention to its peculiarities, is provided next to alert the reader to their general nature.

AN OVERVIEW OF THE SOCIAL PSYCHOLOGY OF INTERPERSONAL ATTRACTION

A disinterested critic would undoubtedly find the most notable characteristic of the current portrait of interpersonal attraction to be unevenness. Entire portions of the canvas remain virtually blank, and it cannot be said that these undeveloped areas of inquiry are peripheral to the subject. The role of attraction over time within close relationships, for example, is only now beginning to receive attention. Other areas, such as that concerning the varieties of attraction, have been given only impressionistic treatment, with sweeping brushstrokes and colorful dialogue presently sketching their dimensions. In contrast, certain other portions of the attraction area have been drawn in painstaking detail. The role of attraction in initial encounters between strangers, for example, encompasses a robust literature of theory and investigation, and many researchers continue to refine knowledge of this subject, as testified to by the fact that more than two-thirds of the studies in the attraction area published from 1972 to 1976 focused upon an individual's impression of another after he or she was given information about that other or after a brief encounter with the other (see Huston and Levinger, 1978).

There are good reasons for this unevenness. For example—and with respect to the most glaring omission, that of enduring relationships and all the vital questions of attraction they encompass—the obstacles to systematic study have been both numerous and formidable. They have included social taboo against their empirical investigation (see Burgess and Wallin, 1953) as well as severe ethical problems. Ethically, for example, it is one thing to experimentally examine the influence of a variable upon attraction within the context of a relationship newly formed between two strangers in a laboratory setting, and it is quite another to experimentally evaluate that variable within an ongoing relationship. Thus the experimental method, so vital a tool in the psychologist's methodological armory, is often rendered impotent by the ethical problems involved in its use outside the laboratory.

In fact, so ethically sensitive are issues of attraction in daily life and within naturally occurring relationships, reflecting their importance in the human scheme of things, that even simple observational studies of attraction in naturalistic settings do not escape acute ethical dilemmas (e.g., Rubin and Mitchell, 1976).

Rivaling social and ethical obstacles to the study of attraction in its natural social settings have been methodological difficulties. Largely denied the use of experimentation in these settings, social psychologists have not been equipped to systematically untangle the complex causal skeins in which attraction is enmeshed in social life. On this front, however, the situation is rapidly changing. Spurred primarily by increasing public demand for marital and family therapy (see Olson, Russell, and Sprenkle, 1980, for reviews of that emerging discipline) as well as by traditional sociological interest in marriage and the family (see Broderick, 1971, for a review), investigators are rapidly developing new methods for examining questions of attraction within *in vivo* relationships (e.g., Gottman, 1979; Weiss, Hops, and Patterson, 1973). Furthermore, and within social psychology itself, techniques have been developed for drawing causal inferences through quasi-experimental designs suited for investigations in naturalistic situations (e.g., Cook and Campbell, 1979), and new analytical tools have been created to help discern causal relationships from nonexperimental data (e.g., Campbell and Fiske, 1959). Most of these advances are too recent to have yet made visible inroads on the attraction landscape, and thus they represent promissory notes for the future.

Many other factors contribute to the present uneven state of the attraction area. Perhaps the most important of these factors are confounds that seriously limit extrapolation from current findings to other, even closely associated questions of attraction and that, further, restrict the range of applicability of a single set of empirical findings on one question to precisely the same question but as it might be posed for a different social context. There is, for example, a ubiquitous confound between the questions that have been investigated and the nature of the persons for whom they have been asked, namely, persons who are white, who are also middle class, and who in addition happen to be college students in the United States and, thus, who are of above-average intelligence, are within a restricted age range, and are representative of a single subculture within a single general culture. Each of these demographic characteristics subsumes numerous other variables, some known but most unknown,

that act and interact to produce the lion's share of current answers to attraction questions.

The availability of college sophomores for study has also directed researchers' attention to some questions of attraction, those relevant to persons in this age group (e.g., questions of courtship), and away from others (e.g., questions of long-term attraction to another). Even more seriously, the comparative ease with which questions of attraction may be studied with college students in laboratory settings is partially, although not wholly, responsible for the fact that attraction generally has been studied outside the context of ongoing relationships (see Huston, 1974). This factor, in turn, is undoubtedly both cause and consequence of one of the most problematical, if not patently specious, assumptions underlying the interpersonal attraction literature to date: that the laws that govern interpersonal attraction transcend the nature of the relationship in which they are displayed in such a clear manner that the investigator may ignore the social context in which the variables were examined when drawing inferences about the dynamics of attraction.

This central problem is compounded by the fact that even when attraction in ongoing relationships has been examined, very few social contexts have been represented. As Huston and Levinger note (1978, pp. 117–118):

> Only three relationships have been given extensive attention: same-sex *friendships,* primarily among college students, though a few studies have examined friendships among elderly; cross-sex *romantic* relationships, again chiefly among college students; and *marriage.* Other sorts of relationships, such as between young and old or between people generally tied by kinship or occupation, are hardly ever studied by attraction researchers; nor are cross-sex friendships, homosexual partnerships, or extramarital relationships.

Current answers to questions of attraction, then, are often confounded not only with the type of person studied but also with the type of relationship. It is not the case, of course, that all possible forms of social interaction occur, that all possible types of social relationship exist (see Leinhardt, 1977), or that all questions of attraction are equally relevant or cogent to all persons or all relationships. Nevertheless, the current range of person and relationship contexts within which attraction has been investigated is unduly restrictive. Fortunately, attraction theorists and researchers are increasingly recognizing that the antecedents and consequences of attraction vary as a function of social context (e.g., see Huston, 1974).

Other confounds contributing to the unevenness of the interpersonal attraction literature are not untypical of any discipline, but they are limiting nonetheless. There is, for example, often a confound between the nature of the question that is asked and the method by which the answer is sought. The role of similarity between two persons and their attraction for one another, to take just one instance, has been studied primarily through use of the Bryne (1971) bogus stranger technique (see the next section). There is, in addition, not infrequently a confound between the type of question asked and the theoretical perspective that led to the query and guided the investigation.

In this respect the nature and progress of attraction research has been deeply influenced by the major theoretical approaches that have swept through its host discipline of social psychology, these approaches being, in the late 1950s and 1960s, the cognitive consistency theories and, in the late 1960s and 1970s, the cognitive attribution theories. Attraction inquiry also shows the deep imprint of learning theory formulations within psychology, especially as these theories have been translated for applicability to social behavior. Each of these major theoretical approaches has also spawned minitheories that are used to predict and account for limited sets of attraction phenomena, for no theoretical perspective encompassing all questions of interpersonal attraction has yet emerged. Other theoretical formulations popular within other areas of psychology and sociology (e.g., psychoanalytic theory, role theory, and symbolic interactionism) have not been well represented in the investigation of interpersonal attraction.

Two other characteristics of the attraction literature are worthy of note, although they have been implied in the foregoing: First, since attraction has largely been studied outside the context of ongoing relationships, little information on the developmental course of attraction exists, and longitudinal studies of attraction (e.g., Hill, Rubin, and Peplau, 1976; Newcomb, 1961) are notable in their rarity. As Huston (1974) observes, well over 80 percent of the research findings about attraction between people have been derived from persons who had never met each other prior to the study and, presumably, never saw each other again. Second, the interpersonal attraction literature focuses almost exclusively upon West-

ern culture, especially as it is manifested in the United States (see Rosenblatt, 1974). Attraction researchers have shown a distinct disinterest in directly investigating whether the principles of attraction thus far formulated have the quality of being panhuman, and even when available cross-cultural materials are used, they are often employed in dubious ways (see Rosenblatt and Anderson, 1981). Little on the horizon suggests that this particular aspect of the attraction literature will change in the foreseeable future.

A thumbnail characterization of the social psychology of interpersonal attraction, with special attention to its uneven nature, has been drawn to emphasize that like any other line of scientific inquiry, the area of interpersonal attraction "just grew," proceeding without the advantage of a master plan provided by God or Omniscient Jones or, more importantly, without the advantage of the hindsight a reviewer, critic, or student of attraction theory and research now enjoys. The result is a relatively young area of inquiry that is marked by not a few irregularities and peculiarities, many of which are neither intrinsically logical nor reflective of an optimal development of knowledge of the antecedents, consequences, and correlates of interpersonal attraction. It is important to recognize this fact for at least two reasons: First, historical practice not infrequently becomes tradition and unjustifiably acquires a status of its own. Second, the perception of an investigative area as it currently is often exerts a tyrannical influence over the vision of what it could be.

Or, in this case, as it surely will be. As previously noted, the study of interpersonal attraction is in transition. Investigators are turning from a focus upon attraction phenomena as they occur in initial encounters between strangers to a study of attraction in the context of ongoing relationships; from a view of attraction as a monolithic global construct to a recognition that it is fruitful to differentiate varieties of attraction; from an exclusive study of the mild forms of attraction (e.g., liking) to studies that include the more intense forms (e.g., love); from investigations of a single stimulus at a single point in time and its influence upon attraction to an interest in how a variety of causal conditions may contribute to an attraction phenomenon and how they all may evolve and change over time; from an exclusive focus upon how the characteristics of the individual (or of the other, or of their combination) influence attraction to a consideration of how these characteristics may interact with environmental variables, both physical and social, to affect attraction and how attraction itself may subsequently influence all of these variables. In part these changes are taking place in recognition of the limitations and problems previously outlined. But they are also taking place because social taboos against investigation of many important attraction phenomena have weakened or dissipated and because, in fact, public demand for information about attraction phenomena has never been more acute. In executing the transition, attraction investigators within social psychology are, more than ever before, turning outward to their colleagues in other branches of psychology and in other behavioral sciences for theory, data, and methodological approaches that may prove useful to an understanding of interpersonal attraction.

Because the social psychology of attraction is in transition, it is particularly important that the past not cast an unduly long shadow over new students of the subject or even old students renewing their acquaintance with it. For this reason, the remainder of this chapter represents an attempt not only to present the field of interpersonal attraction as it exists but also to do so in a way that anticipates the concerns of attraction theorists and researchers in the foreseeable future.

THE CONCEPTUALIZATION
AND MEASUREMENT OF
INTERPERSONAL ATTRACTION

How one conceives of a thing necessarily determines how one measures it. Unfortunately, the conceptualization of interpersonal attraction has been plagued by two antipodal views. The first is "It can't be done"; the second is "Not only can it be done, but it's so simple and obvious a task that it is beneath actual performance." The former view maintains that attraction to others is so nebulous and ephemeral that its outlines can only be suggested and mused upon. The latter view assumes that attraction is such a ubiquitous and important element in human relations that virtually everyone knows what is meant by such words as *like, dislike, love,* and *hate* and that, therefore, to carefully describe their conceptual meanings and presumed empirical referents would be a superfluous academic exercise.

Both views have led to a conspicuous disregard of explicitly defining and refining the construct of attraction (see Huston, 1974). This result has been unfortunate because attraction is a hypothetical construct; it is not a real entity whose measurement is unequivocally dictated by its obvious properties and the tools available to measure those properties. As a psychological construct, attraction thus deserves conceptual respect as an inferred state that cannot be straightforwardly identified with any one or two measuring devices, including those that rely upon verbal self-report. Further, since attraction is an inferred internal state without clearly implied and easily measurable external referents, it follows that there will be a good deal of variance among individual conceptions of its nature. When these conceptions are left unspecified, all manner of problems can be expected to ensue, as indeed they have for interpersonal attraction researchers.

ATTRACTION AS ATTITUDE

It is not, oddly enough, that attraction has not been regarded as a hypothetical construct. To the contrary, it has been almost universally identified with another hypothetical construct, that of attitude. The statements that "almost all theorists agree that interpersonal attraction is a positive or negative attitude toward another person" (Berscheid and Walster, 1978, p. 1) and "interpersonal attraction, as defined by social psychologists, refers to...attitudinal positivity" (Huston and Levinger, 1978, p. 1) are typical of virtually all surveys of the ways in which attraction has been conceived. The problem, then, is not that the status of attraction as a hypothetical construct has been overlooked; rather, it is that after saying attraction is an attitude, few have felt obliged to say anything more.

The primary reason few have found it necessary to say more undoubtedly has been that the term *attitude* is as familiar to social psychologists as the term *attraction* is. The construct of attitude has reigned supreme throughout the history of the discipline, with attitude theory and research counting for the lion's share of social psychological effort (see Chapters 10 and 20 of this *Handbook*). Given the regnancy of the construct of attitude within the parent discipline, it was perhaps predictable that social psychologists would define attraction as an attitude toward another person.

The identification of the attraction construct with the attitude construct has afforded the investigation of attraction a number of advantages. Among these advantages is that the concept of attitude as a "disposition to respond in a favorable or unfavorable manner to given objects" (Oskamp, 1977) is broad enough to encompass most concerns an investigator might have within the attraction area. More importantly, the close alliance of the attraction construct with the attitude construct has permitted attraction researchers to capitalize upon attitude theory, measurement, and research. This advantage derives particularly from the fact that the affective or evaluative aspect of attitudes—the predisposition to respond in a favorable or unfavorable way toward the object of the attitude—has been increasingly stressed in attitude theory and research in recent years (see Oskamp, 1977). As a result, liking or disliking for another has been one of the most popular dependent measures in attitude research, with obvious benefits for those interested in uncovering the principles of attraction.

As real and as important as the advantages are that have accrued from the identification of the construct of attraction with the construct of attitude, the association between the two has also resulted in a number of disadvantages for attraction research that are often overlooked. The first disadvantage, that it has led to little independent conceptual work directly addressed to the attraction construct, has been mentioned. This disadvantage, however, pales in comparison to those that stem directly from the traditional conceptualization of attitude and the several assumptions it carries.

Traditionally, an attitude has been conceived as having three components:

1. The cognitive component, which has referred to the ideas and beliefs held about the object of the attitude.

2. The affective or evaluative component, which has referred to the positivity or negativity of the emotions and feelings precipitated by the attitude object.

3. The behavioral component, which has referred to the actions (or action tendencies) that are directed toward the object.

Until recently, little had been done to theoretically or empirically explicate the relationship, if any, between these components (e.g., see Fishbein and Ajzen, 1975, for one possible theoretical solution). In fact, whether the distinction is worthwhile has been increasingly questioned (e.g., McGuire, 1969), and many have resolved the issue by simply focusing upon the affective or evaluative aspect of attitudes, as previously noted. In doing so, however, and in conceiving of an attitude primarily as a positive or negative predisposition to respond to the object of the attitude (e.g., person X), researchers generally have assumed that the favorability of the beliefs held about X,

the positivity of the emotions and feelings experienced in association with X, and the favorability of the actions directed toward X are predominantly of one affective quality—favorable or unfavorable. Thus affective harmony within the "attitude toward X" kingdom has been implicitly assumed.

The assumption of affective homogeneity rests upon other assumptions—that the determinants of the affective quality of beliefs about another's properties are either identical to or overlap importantly with the determinants of the affective quality of the emotions and feelings the other precipitates and that these determinants, in turn, overlap importantly with the determinants of the affective quality of the actions directed toward the other (e.g., whether they are approached or avoided). And so the inevitable conclusion has been that when one determines the nature of the affective component of an attitude, or determines attraction to X, it matters little which of the three components—beliefs, emotions, or actions toward X—are assessed; it tends to be assumed that whichever is chosen for measurement purposes, the other behaviors that have X as their principle referent will possess the same affective tone. This cluster of assumptions has created serious difficulties within the attitude area (see Schuman and Johnson, 1976, for a review of one empirical controversy that stems from them), and their effect upon attraction research has been grave and far reaching (as, for example, the history of research on the determinants of affiliation outlined in the section "Affiliation and Attraction" illustrates).

The impact of the alliance between the attitude and the attraction constructs in general, and of the assumption of affective homogeneity in particular, can be most clearly seen in the traditional means of measuring attraction. Attraction toward another typically has been measured just as attitudes have been measured; since it is the so-called affective component of the attitude toward person X that has been of interest, attraction customarily has been measured on a simple bipolar scale, where the respondent has been asked, "How much do you like X?" and instructed to respond on a dimension ranging from, say, +3, or "like very much," to −3, "dislike very much." This measure is commonly called an affective appraisal. Another measure that sometimes has been used as a substitute for this measure, or used in conjunction with it, asks the respondent to indicate his or her beliefs concerning person X's properties [e.g., the respondent is asked, "How kind (or industrious, or other adjective) is X?"], and then the known or presumed affective loadings of the properties ascribed to X [many of which have been suggested by Anderson (1968)] are totaled or combined in some manner to arrive at the affective value of X to the respondent. These measures are also called affective appraisals, or, sometimes, cognitive appraisals. These two measures, used singly or in combination, reflect the assumption that the respondent's attraction toward X is best characterized by a disposition to respond to X in a favorable *or* an unfavorable manner.

Unfortunately, many of the most interesting questions and critical problems presented by attraction phenomena currently lie buried under this approach to measuring attraction and the assumptions carried by the construct of attitude that support it. One of the most important is the question of the varieties of attraction, an issue that was raised early by Newcomb (1956) but was subsequently submerged by reliance on bipolar, unidimensional attraction scales and the nominal definition of attraction as an attitude. The problem that has resulted, and which continues to be relevant (see Huston, 1974), was described by Marlowe and Gergen (1969) in their criticism of interpersonal attraction research (p. 622):

> Social attraction seems to have been relegated to that felicitous state made up of "common understanding" and generalized inexplicitness. Few psychologists would accept such a definition across the wide and unmanageable range of human experience implied. The differences among such phenomena as the comradeship felt by members of a team, the respect held for a powerful leader, sexual attraction for a person of the opposite sex, a mother's devotion for a child, and the gratitude of a person relieved of distress far outweigh the similarities.

Whether the differences among the many varieties of attraction actually outweigh the similarities is not currently known, since few have investigated the matter. Part of the reason for this neglect is popular acceptance of the assumption that all of these instances of attraction have a large common denominator consisting of a positive or negative attitude toward the other, with the residuals of each constituting insignificant effluvium. Another reason the matter has not been explored is that each of the instances of attraction cited by Marlowe and Gergen refer to attraction as it occurs in different types of ongoing relationships and that attraction typically has been studied outside its relationship context.

Another set of important questions that currently lie submerged under traditional measurement practice are all those concerning the affective heterogeneity of the responses another prompts, including the favorability of the beliefs held about the other's properties, the positivity of the emotions and feelings precipitated by the other, and the favorability of the actions taken with respect to the other. These questions become critical as investigators turn toward the investigation of attraction phenomena as they occur in the context of ongoing relationships, because the affective harmony in "attitude toward X," so frequently assumed and observed in the laboratory, is often not seen in naturalistic contexts. To the contrary, as Berscheid (1982, p. 42) states:

> What we see is people who love each other (or at least they say so, on their bi-polar affective appraisals) literally beating each other about the head and shoulders, as those who investigate family violence are documenting (e.g., Straus and Hotaling, 1980). We see people experiencing the most intense positive emotion in association with persons whom they indicate, on the ubiquitous "kind" and "industrious" adjective check-list, to be neither "kind" nor "industrious," but rather thoroughly unreliable scoundrels, and, conversely, we see persons giving the most glowing appraisals to a person they have just decided to dump in the divorce court—"a prince of a fellow," she says, "but I no longer wish to associate with him." We see people approaching and maintaining contact with others whom they *say* they despise and with whom, we observe, they experience emotions that are predominantly negative in quality.

In other words, in ongoing relationships the diverse and voluminous domain of an individual's behavior that has person X as its principal referent is often not characterized by one homogeneous affective tone, favorable or unfavorable, but by many, even at a single point in time and certainly across time. A bipolar measurement approach that assumes person X to have one single affective value to the respondent cannot begin to address the questions such heterogeneity raises. Furthermore, even the most obvious of these questions, such as those that concern ambivalence toward another, which have historically assumed a good deal of clinical and anecdotal importance among the affective phenomena, remain unasked and unexplored, because the traditional means of assessing attraction do not allow them to be discovered (see Berscheid and Walster, 1978).

There is, however, yet another reason why questions concerning affective heterogeneity in responses toward another have been neglected. As previously noted, attraction most often has been investigated between strangers who have never encountered each other before and who expect to never encounter each other again and who have been, therefore, largely irrelevant to the respondent's welfare. Unfortunately, virtually all theorists who have sought to understand affective reactions to people and objects, particularly theorists of emotion (see Plutchik, 1980, for a review), have consistently emphasized that one's affective reaction to another depends importantly, if not exclusively, upon the implications that the other is perceived to have for "*my* personal survival and *my* welfare," that is, whether the other is perceived to be "good for me" or "bad for me" in terms of "*my* needs, *my* goals, and *my* plans." In ongoing relationships, where the other often impinges on many different needs, plans, and goals, the reactions the other prompts are likely to be affectively heterogeneous because the answer to the question "Good for me or bad for me?" is likely to be that X is good for some things and bad for others. Even a single trait of X's (e.g., industrious) may be good for some things and bad for others, and thus it may not carry a single, stable affective loading. When the other is personally irrelevant, however, a single, simple bipolar scale may be adequate to capture the total of the limited and mild affective reaction he or she evokes.

Because the attitude construct carries an assumption of stability (e.g., see Katz and Stotland, 1959), it also has been at least partially responsible for the fact that little attention has been devoted to the question of stability of affective responses toward another across substantial time frames. But again, the practice of focusing upon affective reactions to personally irrelevant stimulus persons also may be partially responsible for the neglect of questions of stability (see Berscheid, 1982). For example, if the affective quality of an individual's responses toward another is rooted in the way in which the other's properties interlock with the individual's needs, plans, and goals, then the stability or instability of an individual's affective reaction to the other depends on whether the other's relevance to these needs, goals, and plans changes. Thus changes in affective reaction to another may occur because the properties of the other have changed (e.g., new information has been received about the other that revises or adds to the old, thereby changing the way in which the other interlocks with current needs and plans) or because the information about the other has stayed the same but the needs and plans have changed, and thus the way in which the other interlocks

with them has changed. If so, the favorability of attitude toward another is likely to stay stable only if the other stays the same and the individual's needs and plans stay the same, or if both change in tandem, thereby preserving the interlock.

However, an individual's affective reaction to another may stay stable for yet another reason: The other may be irrelevant to the individual and remain irrelevant. For example, the respondent's attraction to a stranger may stay stable even over long periods of time as long as the stranger remains irrelevant, as is likely to be the case in laboratory settings. But since the other is rarely irrelevant to the individual's needs and plans in ongoing relationships, and since people's needs and plans change over time and the properties of the other person also often change, more attention to questions of affective instability in behavior toward another over time in relationships in naturalistic settings will be required, along with conceptualizations of attraction and the construction of measurement techniques that do not presume stability.

The current reliance upon unidimensional, bipolar affective appraisals, even for the measurement of attraction in ongoing close relationships, has, however, produced an interesting set of questions. All of these questions may be subsumed under the general question of how people manage to respond to such scales. How, for example, does a person who has been married for twenty years manage to review and sum over an extraordinarily voluminous and affectively complex set of information, received over a long period of time, in order to respond to the most frequently used marital statisfaction scale, the Locke-Wallace scale (Locke and Williamson, 1958)? There, respondents are told that an endorsement of +35 should be reserved for "those few who experience extreme joy or felicity in marriage" and a rating of 0 should be endorsed by "those few who are very unhappy in marriage." Do the respondents have some theory that all marriages are supposed to be happy and does this theory determine their response? Do they review their history of emotional events in the marriage, and if so, what do they remember?

Recent research suggests that negative events are better remembered when the respondent is in a negative mood and positive events are better remembered in a positive mood (e.g., Bower, 1981; Isen, Shalker, Clark, and Karp, 1978). So how much does the content of such reviews depend upon positivity of mood at the moment of response? Furthermore, is it true that, other things being equal, affectively positive events are better remembered over time than negative events and that both positive and negative events are better remembered than affectively neutral events, as some have suggested (e.g., Matlin and Stang, 1978)? Or rather, as still others have argued, is it true that the personally aversive behaviors of another, such as a spouse, are selectively tracked and remembered better than affectively pleasant behaviors (e.g., Weiss, Hops, and Patterson, 1973)? And if respondents do review their emotional history, what affective mathematics do people commonly use to arrive at their, say, +21 response?

Little is currently known about the origin of global affective appraisals in relationships in which the respondent possesses a great deal of information about another and in relationships in which the ways the other is relevant to the respondent are complex and have changed over time. Although it is clear that such appraisals within ongoing relationships traditionally have had distressingly unimpressive predictive validity (for information on the Locke-Wallace scale, see Spanier, 1976), they do present questions that are interesting in themselves and deserve systematic examination.

It is unfair to blame all of the inadequacies of attraction measurement, or even just those outlined above, on the conceptual identification of attraction with the construct of attitude. For example, the neglect of motivational factors, so important to an understanding of attraction, has pervaded much of psychology in recent years and is not limited to the attitude area. It should be recognized more than it has been, however, that to conceptualize attraction as an attitude not only does not adequately solve the problem of conceptualizing attraction but also carries assumptions that act as blinders to the discovery and investigation of many important attraction phenomena.

ATTRACTION AS EMOTION AND FEELING

Interpersonal attraction theorists and researchers rarely have drawn upon the theoretical and empirical fruits of psychological investigations of emotion for inspiration and aid. They have not done so despite the following facts:

- It has been the affective component of attitude that has been of major interest within attraction research.

- Intense emotional states are commonly regarded as intense affective states, and many would agree with

Bowlby (1973) that "affectional bonds and subjective states of emotion go together" (p. 40).

- Several presumed varieties of attraction (e.g., passionate love) appear to fall within the realm of emotion.

- Attraction is popularly thought of as "feeling" toward another, and since feelings are tacitly assumed to be "little emotions" (see Candland, 1977), knowledge of the emotions should illuminate the antecedents and consequences of feelings.

Historically, there were good reasons for bypassing the emotion area. Not only has attitude been the construct of choice within social psychology, thus providing a strong incentive for attraction researchers to identify themselves with that investigative area, but also the area of emotion and feeling traditionally has been one of the most confused, contradictory, and tortuous lines of inquiry within psychology. For example, at the same time that attraction research was burgeoning in the late 1950s and early 1960s, work on the problem of emotion had been frustrated once again and was lying abandoned (see Arnold, 1960).

This situation was to change dramatically in the late 1960s, however, when an explosion of interest within psychology in the problem of emotion was sparked by the work of Schachter (1964). That interest was subsequently fueled by theorists and researchers in many other subdisciplines of psychology (see Strongman, 1978, for a review) so that by the late 1970s work on the problem had increased to the extent that an entire volume of the *Nebraska Symposium on Motivation* (1978) was devoted to emotion, and the foundations of a general theory of emotion were emerging in comprehensive theoretical syntheses (e.g., Izard, 1977; Mandler, 1975; Plutchik, 1980). As a consequence, emotion theory and research now has a good deal to offer to attraction researchers.

Contemporary views of emotion carry a different flavor and different assumptions from views traditionally associated with the construct of attitude, as Plutchik's (1980) definition of emotion illustrates (p. 361):

An emotion is an inferred complex sequence of reactions to a stimulus, and includes cognitive evaluations, subjective changes, autonomic and neural arousal, impulses to action and behavior designed to have an effect upon the stimulus that initiated the complex sequence. These complex reaction sequences may suffer various vicissitudes, which affect the probability of appearance of each link in the chain. These complex reactions are adaptive in the struggle in which all organisms engage for survival.

Thus in addition to the explicit recognition that the phenomenon of interest is composed of cognitive, physiological, and behavioral processes intertwined and integral to each other, virtually all contemporary views of emotion emphasize its adaptive service in fulfilling the biological needs of the individual. As one result, attention to the motivations that underlie all affective phenomena is virtually dictated, as is attention to the social context in which these phenomena are displayed.

There are at least four other differences in assumption between the attitude and emotion constructs. First, while the attitude construct carries an assumption of affective stability and constancy, the emotion construct does not. The question of the stability or instability of emotion precipitated by a given stimulus or across stimuli within a given person is, in fact, a central one in emotion research.

Second, although emotion, like attitude, is a hypothetical construct that refers to an internal state inferred on the basis of various kinds of observable evidence, emotion researchers generally do not regard emotion as a state always reportable by the individual experiencing it and thus usually do not accept self-reports at face value, as is typical in attitude research. Emotion has not been closely identified with the subjective and reportable experience of it for the following reasons (Plutchik, 1980):

- Self-reports may depend upon an individual's particular conditioning history as well as on his or her facility with words. Furthermore, since many emotional phenomena of interest take place in animals, infants, young children, and other persons who are unable to provide any direct verbal reports of their feeling states, dependence upon verbal report would preclude investigation in these instances.

- Self-reports may be ambiguous, and so knowledge of the context in which they are made is particularly important in determining their referent and meaning. When context is known, the investigator's label may be more accurate than the respondent's: "For example, an outside impartial observer is more likely to correctly describe the pattern of jealousy than the person experiencing it, since to the latter it

may appear as indignation or annoyance" (Plutchik, 1980, p. 89).

- Self-reports may be, and usually are, retrospective reports and thus are dependent upon memory, which is subject to numerous distortions.

- Self-reports are subject to the problem that observing a thing may change it, particularly in the case of the report of a person's immediate emotional state.

- Self-reports of emotion, like self-reports of attitude, may be deliberate attempts to deceive another or may be distortions or partial truths for conscious or unconscious reasons.

As a consequence, verbal self-report generally constitutes only one bit of evidence in the measurement of emotion—and a particularly suspect bit of evidence at that.

Third, although the two dimensions of hedonic sign (positive versus negative) and intensity (intense versus mild) found to underlie emotion (e.g., Block, 1957) are the same two dimensions presumed to underlie attraction when it is viewed as an attitude, they have been treated differently in the two cases. Rather than conceive of affectional space as defined by one bipolar dimension (e.g., -10 to $+10$), recent studies have suggested that it may be useful to conceive of two relatively independent dimensions, one positive and one negative (e.g., 0 to $+10$ and 0 to -10), as underlying the description of emotional experiences (e.g., Zevon and Tellegen, 1982; but see Russell, 1980). These investigations suggest that people may feel both positively and negatively toward a person at the same time and experience one of these affective states intensely and the other weakly, also at the same time.

Recent views that depression may be accounted for better by the absence of positively valued experiences than by the presence of negatively valued experiences (e.g., Lewinsohn, 1974; but see Sweeney, Shaeffer, and Golin, 1982) are compatible with this position, as are studies of marital interaction that have found it profitable to distinguish pleasurable events from displeasurable events rather than to simply rely upon a summative evaluation of the overall positivity of spouse behaviors (e.g., Weiss, Hops, and Patterson, 1972). Further support for this position is provided by Rodin (1978), who cites a number of attraction data inconsistent with the assumption that liking-disliking is a unidimensional judgment and suggests that they be viewed as independent judgments. It is also supported by a study conducted by Braiker and Kelley (1979) in which no relationship was found between level of love-interdependence and level of conflict in any stage of courtship among "successful" couples (who eventually married); the fact that conflict can and does coexist with positive satisfactions, at least in the early stages of a relationship, indicates that "these appear to be two independent dimensions of close relationships" (p. 156).

Fourth, it perhaps goes without saying that emotion theorists and researchers have been painfully aware of the many varieties of emotion that eventually need to be accounted for under one theoretical umbrella. However, it is not assumed that the similarities among the emotions outweigh their differences; rather the identification of such similarities and differences constitutes a central empirical issue.

It remains to be seen, of course, how useful current theory and research on emotion and feeling will be to attraction researchers. At the present time, however, several potentially valuable lines of theory and research are emerging. One approach has been developed by Isen and her associates, who have demonstrated that the positivity or negativity of an individual's relatively long-lasting feeling state, induced by pleasant or unpleasant experiences, is an important determinant of the positivity of an individual's impressions of and behavior toward another (e.g., Isen and Levin, 1972), and attention has now turned to the processes by which these effects occur (see Clark and Isen, 1984, for a review). Another concerns the investigation of the impact of certain physiological effects associated with autonomic nervous system arousal, often conceived to be necessary for emotional experience, upon affective appraisals of another (e.g., Clark, 1981). And yet another approach is represented by Berscheid's (1983) theoretical analysis of intense emotional events within ongoing close relationships, which takes it as a given that the prediction of the occurrence of emotional events within a relationship does not necessarily depend upon such things as the individual's global appraisal that the other possesses good or bad properties.

Thus recent advances in theory and research on emotion may provide both an alternative for and a potential complement to attitude theory and research for future attempts to explicate and refine the construct of attraction, as well as for the investigation of many attrac-

tion phenomena that heretofore either have been overlooked or have appeared to be mysterious and inexplicable.

ATTRACTION AS BEHAVIOR

Another approach to the problem of conceptualizing interpersonal attraction is exemplified in the work of Byrne and his colleagues (e.g., G. L. Clore, C. R. Ervin, W. Griffitt, J. Lamberth, and D. Nelson; and see Byrne, *The Attraction Paradigm,* 1971). Believing that the relationship between attitude similarity and attraction provided an opportunity for paradigmatic research on interpersonal attraction, Byrne developed a methodology in which identical or equivalent operations of a single stimulus (attitudinal similarity/dissimilarity) and of a single attraction response served as consistent connecting links across experiments.

The measure of attraction consisted of responses to two 7-point rating scales. On the first, respondents were asked to indicate how much they liked the other, who was always a "bogus stranger" whose responses to an attitude questionnaire (previously read by the respondents) were constructed so as to represent various degrees of attitudinal similarity to themselves. On the second, respondents were asked to indicate how much they would enjoy working with the stranger. These items were embedded as the last two items in a six-item Interpersonal Judgment Scale (IJS), and the responses to them were summed to yield the measure of attraction. Byrne's approach, then, was essentially to establish a stimulus-response relationship that seemed intuitively relevant to attraction and then to cautiously introduce new variations upon the basic stimulus and response operations to determine their generality and dynamics.

Unfortunately, Byrne's intuitive choice of a stimulus and of a response, particularly the latter, did not always meet with the approval of other attraction researchers whose personal, if sometimes unspecified, conceptions of attraction were often far broader and richer than two check marks on two 7-point scales in the bogus stranger context suggested to them (e.g., Levinger, 1972; Wright, 1971). Much of the controversy that subsequently surrounded Byrne's approach was also a philosophical one on how progress in understanding attraction phenomena might best be made. In this regard Byrne selected a measure that possessed some face validity, and he and his associates proceeded to develop a large body of evidence demonstrating its antecedents, correlates, and consequences. Byrne and his associates were also among the few to show concern for systematic exploration of questions of attraction, for reliability of measures, for cross-cultural generality, for variety of subject populations including children, and for individual-difference variables. That this approach, now largely abandoned by Byrne and many of his colleagues (see the section on theoretical approaches), has been considered unnecessarily circumscribed and restrictive says a good deal about the magnitude of the problem of interpersonal attraction, for there are obvious benefits to be had from focusing upon a behavior of interest and from jettisoning ill-conceived and unexplicated constructs. Some of these benefits are illustrated by Dermer's (1982) radical behaviorist analysis of some putative attraction behaviors (e.g., the verbal operant, "I like Joe"), which emphasizes the contemporaneous environmental variables controlling a behavior and effectively uncovers many of the unexamined assumptions that have formed the foundation of much attraction research.

OTHER CONCEPTUALIZATIONS AND MEASURES OF ATTRACTION

The ways in which interpersonal attraction has been conceived and assessed are far more diverse than has been suggested so far. One of these measures, that of approach and avoidance behavior with respect to another, will be extensively discussed in the section on affiliation. Other measures have been devised to assess certain varieties of attraction, and these measures will be discussed in the section on theoretical approaches in the context of theoretical frameworks that differentiate between forms of attraction.

All of the above measures, however, still do not exhaust the ways in which attraction has been assessed. Most of the remaining measures have been devised independent of an explicit conceptualization of attraction; they have tended to simply possess whatever face validity they could muster in the specific context in which they were used. These measures have included doing favors for another or conferring benefits upon the other in various ways (e.g., Bramel, 1969), eye contact (Argyle, 1967; Exline, 1971; Rubin, 1970), and other forms of nonverbal behavior (e.g., Hess, 1975; Mehrabian, 1972).

The principal problem with using such behaviors to assess attraction is that they are known to be responsive to a variety of factors, some not commonly associated with attraction. Thus unless extraneous influencing factors are controlled in the social context in which the behavior is assessed, and unless the measure's presumed correspondence to the investigator's concept of attraction is spelled out, its validity as a measure of attraction remains ambiguous at best and misleading at worst. To take just one example, visual attention to another (or the amount of eye gaze directed at another) is known to be a function of both the novelty of the other and the importance of the other. Although importance is positively related to attraction (Berscheid *et al.*, 1976), unless the degree of familiarity/novelty to the other is controlled, amount of attention, including visual gaze, cannot be expected to be a reliable and valid indicant of attraction, even in circumstances where the social mores governing eye gaze behavior in face-to-face interaction (e.g., Ellsworth, Carlsmith, and Henson, 1972) do not apply. When they do apply, the validity of eye gaze as a measure of attraction is even more suspect.

SUMMARY

Although how one measures attraction depends upon how one conceptualizes it, little effort has been devoted to the conceptualization of interpersonal attraction. Rather, either attraction has been nominally identified with the construct of attitude, or, as in the case of Byrne and his colleagues, its conceptualizaton has been developed in an inductive manner in a single context of known stimulus qualities. The limitations of the latter approach have been frequently voiced, but the limitations of the former have not. As interpersonal attraction theorists and researchers have turned to more sophisticated questions of attraction, especially as they arise in actual social relationships in naturalistic settings, the need for careful conceptual work has become evident. The renaissance of interest within psychology in the area of emotion and feeling—as well as growing concern in the attitude area with the traditional compotential view of attitude and with other attitudinal issues (e.g., Abelson, 1981; Ajzen and Fishbein, 1980; Triandis, 1980)—present potentially valuable avenues for furthering the conceptualization of attraction.

It also has become apparent that the aim of future conceptual efforts ought to be a far more comprehensive and yet more detailed view of attraction than has yet been offered. For example, in outlining the problems involved in the conceptual analysis of *love,* Kelley (1983) has observed that the word has been used with reference to such different things as actions, processes, states, and dispositions. The same is true, of course, for the term *attraction* itself.

Unfortunately, attraction theorists and investigators are rarely explicit about which of these things, or which cluster of these, they are addressing and, if the latter, rarely make explicit the presumed interrelationships between the components of the cluster. It is not necessary, as Kelley points out, to choose among actions, processes, states, and dispositions. On the contrary, he notes, any comprehensive conceptual analysis will include all these things, but it will do so explicitly and with specific attention to the observable phenomena, including actions and events, that are deemed important and of interest; the contemporaneous causes hypothesized to be responsible for the observed phenomena; the historical causes of the current causes and phenomena, including circular causal processes by which current events and states act to change the initiating causal conditions or allow them to remain stable in their influence; and the hypotheses about the future course of the phenomena, given the causes and processes currently underway. Until such work is addressed to the concept of attraction, the answer to the question "How should attraction be measured?" necessarily remains uncertain.

THEORETICAL APPROACHES TO THE STUDY OF INTERPERSONAL ATTRACTION

The many theoretical statements that have guided investigations of interpersonal attraction fall into three overlapping categories:

1. General social psychological theories that have predictive implications for a number of social phenomena, including attraction.

2. Theories focused exclusively upon interpersonal attraction.

3. Theoretical statements principally addressed to particular varieties of attraction (e.g., romantic love) and/or to phenomena commonly believed to be closely associated with attraction (e.g., relationship development).

Of these categories, the first still accounts for most theory-derived research in the attraction area.

GENERAL SOCIAL PSYCHOLOGICAL THEORIES RELEVANT TO ATTRACTION

The general social psychological theories influential in attraction research themselves fall into two major categories—the cognitive consistency theories and the reinforcement theories. Both, of course, have dominated research within social psychology, and it is thus understandable that they have played an important role in the investigation of attraction. The third major theoretical force within social psychology, the attribution theories (e.g., Jones and Davis, 1965; Kelley, 1967), have been less directly influential, although the processes by which attributions are made of another's dispositional properties are understood, of course, to be critical to an understanding of attraction.

The Cognitive Consistency Approach

All of the cognitive consistency theories assume that people try to keep their cognitions—their thoughts about people and objects—in some kind of psychologically consistent relationship with one another. They assume that inconsistency is uncomfortable and that, as a consequence, people strive either to attain consistency between their cognitions and/or to reduce inconsistencies. Insofar as some of our most important cognitions include our feelings of attraction or disaffection for others, all of the cognitive consistency theories have implications for attraction phenomena. Most influential within the attraction area, however, have been Heider's balance theory, Newcomb's strain-toward-symmetry theory, and Festinger's theory of cognitive dissonance.

Heider's balance theory. Heider's balance theory (1958) addresses both the antecedents and the consequences of interpersonal attraction. It focuses upon two kinds of relationships that may exist between three entities: a person (P), another (O), and a third person or other entity (X). The two relationships are sentiment relationships (e.g., liking and disliking) and unit relationships (e.g., the perception that any two of these persons or entities do or do not belong together). Heider proposed that sentiment relationships and unit relationships tend toward a harmonious *balanced* state, where positive sentiments are felt for those with whom individuals perceive they are in a unit relationship and negative sentiments are felt for those with whom they are not. Heider's theory assumes that imbalance is uncomfortable, and therefore attempts will be made to restore balance, either by coming to like or to dislike the other or to form or break a unit relationship. It also assumes that people strive toward balance and thus predicts that the appropriate sentiment relationship may be induced by the existence of a unit relationship with another.

Balance theory has not stimulated a great deal of experimental research, but at least two exceptions exist within the attraction area. One exception is a line of research derived from Heider's hypothesis that the formation of a unit relationship between two people will induce liking. Darley and Berscheid (1967), for example, found that the anticipation that time would be spent in interaction with another (presumably generating perception of a unit relationship with the other) produced liking for the other. This effect of the prospect of future interaction upon attraction has since been corroborated by numerous studies (e.g., Aderman, 1969; Berscheid, Boye, and Darley, 1968; Tyler and Sears, 1977).

Another line of research generated by balance theory was stimulated by an hypothesis advanced by Deutsch and Solomon (1959), who reasoned that people who like themselves should like people who like them, but people who do not like themselves should not because another's esteem creates cognitive imbalance. These investigators found that persons who had performed poorly on a task and received praise (an inconsistent evaluation) did not like the evaluator as much as did those individuals who also received praise but had performed well. The preferred interpretation of this finding—that the cognitive inconsistency aroused by a favorable evaluation of a poor performance decreased liking for the other—proved to be controversial, principally because differential liking may have been created by differential credibility of the consistent and inconsistent evaluators. As a result, the more general question of how individuals' attraction to another is affected by that other's positive or negative appraisals of them subsequently received a good deal of attention (see the section "Attraction and Initial Encounters").

A number of modifications to Heider's balance theory were proposed by Newcomb (1968). Perhaps the most important of these stemmed from Newcomb's finding that the P–O relationship is far more important than (and thus is not directly comparable to) any other relationship within the P–O–X triad. If the P–O relationship is characterized by positive sentiment, Heider's predictions appear to be confirmed. If the P–O sentiment relationship is negative, however, Heider's predictions are not supported as frequently; when we do not like others,

we appear to be indifferent about what they may or may not think or feel about a third object or person. Such situations, characterized by indifference, Newcomb termed "nonbalanced."

Another of Newcomb's findings was that even situations that are balanced in Heider's terms tend to be regarded as unpleasant if the sentiment relationship between P and O is negative; only those triadic configurations characterized by Heider as balanced and also characterized by a positive P–O relationship are consistently rated as pleasant. A strong preference for positive P–O relationships was also suggested by people's unwillingness to change the sign of a P–O relationship from positive to negative to achieve balance and by a high willingness to change the negative sign of a P–O relationship to a positive one in nonbalanced relationships. Other things being equal, then, people appear to prefer to like other people rather than to dislike them, even when disliking them may present, in Heider's terms, a more balanced situation than does liking them. Newcomb's "attraction effect," as it has come to be called, has since been replicated (e.g., Cacioppo and Petty, 1981), and its dynamics have been of some interest (e.g., Insko and Adewole, 1979).

Newcomb's strain-toward-symmetry theory. Newcomb's cognitive consistency theory (1953, 1961) adopted Heider's general position. But Heider's theory was principally addressed to the P–O–X triad, while Newcomb was interested in cognitive consistency within a larger group of persons. Newcomb hypothesized that if a collective system is in fact imbalanced, then one or more of the members of the collectivity will discover the fact; that the individual member will, following the discovery, attempt to reduce the imbalance; and, finally, that these strain-instigated changes, which may include changes in attitude as well as changes in attraction, will tend to reduce collective imbalance.

To examine the hypothesis that balance in a collective system increases with the persons' length of acquaintance, Newcomb offered free room and board to male incoming transfer college students (all initially strangers to one another) in return for participation in his project. Each man's attitudes and values were assessed before he met the others, and these, as well as his attraction to the other men, were reassessed periodically over the course of the school term. The results, reported in *The Acquaintance Process* (1961), generally supported the hypothesis. Although initially there was little relationship between actual attitude similarity and attraction, for example, there was a significant and positive relationship between the degree to which the men actually shared similar attitudes and their attraction for each other in the final weeks of the study.

Like Heider, and as Festinger (1957; 1954) emphasizes in his own cognitive consistency theory as well as in his theory of social comparison processes, Newcomb (1968) stresses the fact that knowledge of other people's attitudes is of critical adaptive importance to humans (p. 28):

> We ignore properties of the "real" world at our peril. Stones will bruise, and fire will burn—these things we learn by direct, sensory experience, aided by the teachings of others. . . . As we find that our own experience and the testimony of persons whom we trust are mutually supportive, we tend to rely on the latter—it short-circuits trial and error, enables us to avoid painful experiences, often leads to direct satisfaction. And so their testimony, too, is ignored at our peril. But the time comes when the two sources of evidence do not support each other, but yield conflicting evidence: our senses, or our own inferences therefrom, tell us one thing and our associates another. . . . The world is at odds if one's own sources of belief are contravened by those whom one is accustomed to trust—or, indeed, must trust, *faute de mieux*.

It could not help but be the case, then, that the correspondence between others' attitudes and our own should have strong implications for our attraction to them (see the section "Attraction and Initial Encounters"). Newcomb's empirical demonstration of this fact still stands today as one of the most ambitious investigations of attraction ever undertaken, as well as one of the few field studies conducted.

Festinger's cognitive dissonance theory. Festinger's (1957) theory of cognitive dissonance holds that cognitions about any person or object are dissonant when they are psychologically illogical or incompatible, and that dissonance is uncomfortable and produces attempts to reduce or eliminate it. Dissonance theory has furthered an understanding of attraction in a number of ways, but perhaps its principal contribution has been to demonstrate that although an individual's attraction to another is commonly thought of as being caused by the other's

characteristics and behavior, attraction is also importantly influenced by the individual's own behavior toward the other, which may be under the control of forces quite independent of the other.

The first experiment to illustrate dissonance theory's implications for attraction phenomena was conducted by Aronson and Mills (1959). Women who had undergone a severe initiation experience to be admitted to what they later discovered to be a dull discussion group reduced the dissonance thereby generated by rating the discussion as more interesting, and the other group members more positively, than did women who experienced either a mild initiation or no initiation at all. This experiment demonstrated, then, that increases and decreases in feelings of attraction for others can be the result not of changes in the other's behavior but rather of personal attempts to achieve cognitive consistency.

Another experiment to demonstrate that changes in attraction for another can be brought about through dissonance reduction processes, and one of the most important within the dissonance tradition in stimulating subsequent attraction research, was performed by Davis and Jones (1960). These investigators reasoned that since most people think of themselves as kind, actions injurious to another often generate dissonance that may be reduced through coming to believe that the victim deserved to suffer. To test the hypothesis that an individual who is led to harm another will come to dislike him or her, people were induced to give another a harsh personality evaluation. Some were coerced into delivering the negative evaluation, while others were given some choice in the matter. Half of each of these groups expected to later have an opportunity to explain that they didn't really mean the harsh evaluation, while the other half were led to believe that a subsequent meeting with the other was impossible. Davis and Jones found that those who had some choice about whether to deliver the negative evaluation, and who also knew that they could not subsequently undo the harm they had done, did come to derogate and dislike their victim, presumably as a result of dissonance reduction processes.

The Davis and Jones findings stimulated further investigation of the circumstances under which harming another unjustly will affect our feelings of attraction for them, work largely carried out under the aegis of equity theory (see the section "The Equity Theories"). It also stimulated research, much of it conducted by Lerner and his associates (see Lerner, 1980), on the effects of people's beliefs in a "just world"; one finding of this research was that the simple observation that another has been unjustly treated by fate or by people other than oneself also may lead to decreases in attraction to him or her.

The Reinforcement Approach

Although the cognitive consistency theories have made important contributions, reinforcement theories have dominated research in interpersonal attraction from the very beginning. In the first theoretical statement directly addressed to attraction, Newcomb (1956) proposed that an individual's attraction to another is a function of the frequency with which the other rewards the individual and, further, that the likelihood of an individual's receiving rewards from another varies with the frequency with which the individual rewards the other. It was, in fact, consideration of reciprocal reward processes that led Newcomb to hypothesize that attraction should vary with degree of perceived attitude similarity, because attitude similarity (and the cognitive consistency it often represents) was hypothesized to be rewarding.

As Newcomb's theorizing illustrates, it is often difficult to distinguish between the reinforcement approach and the cognitive consistency approach to understanding attraction phenomena. Since the cognitive consistency theories stress that consistency is desirable and inconsistency is punishing (and those who are a source of inconsistency presumably are punishing also), they specify one class of rewards and punishments that individuals mete out to others. Furthermore, of course, many of the reinforcement theories are highly cognitive (e.g., they emphasize subjective perceptions of what constitutes a reward, as well as various cognitive processes presumed to be involved in such perceptions). In addition, and at their motivational base, both the cognitive consistency theories and the reinforcement theories implicitly assume that the individual is engaged in a struggle for survival and well-being.

The reinforcement theories directly emphasize the role that rewards and punishments, administered by another or by the physical environment, play in that process. The cognitive consistency theories, on the other hand, stress the role that an individual's cognitive representation of the environment plays in his or her ability to control and manipulate the environment so as to obtain rewards and avoid punishments (e.g., see Singer, 1966). The two types of theories, then, are not fundamentally antithetical to each other, and in fact, virtually all recent theories relevant to attraction represent syntheses of these two approaches to understanding behavior (e.g., Kelley, 1979; Tedeschi, 1974). In the past, however, the cognitive consistency and reinforcement theories have differed enough in orientation and emphasis that their theoretical implications for attraction phenomena sometimes have appeared to conflict, and they have had differential heuristic value for different attraction problems. For example, the findings that suggest that we sometimes show increases in attraction for people for whom we have suffered can be explained by the reward model as well as the cognitive consistency model, but the explanation becomes so lengthy and convoluted that it becomes distinctly uninteresting; more importantly, it is unlikely that such findings would have been generated by a reward model.

Most of the reinforcement theories influential in attraction research have been derived from theories generated within experimental psychology to understand and predict learning behavior, often the learning behavior of infrahumans. Many of these theories, and all of those discussed below, have been popularly termed the *social exchange theories* (although only Homans explicitly uses the term) because each assumes that to understand social interaction in general, and attraction phenomena in particular, one must understand the principles that underlie the exchange of rewards and punishments that takes place when people interact.

Homans's social exchange theory. In *Social Behavior: Its Elementary Forms* (1961, 1974), Homans adapted Skinner's theory of operant behavior for use in the prediction of social behavior. Using the assumptions and findings of behavioral psychology as well as those of elementary economics, Homans conceives of social interactions as similar to economic transactions. People are viewed as reward-seeking and punishment-avoiding creatures who try to maximize their rewards and minimize their punishments (or "costs") to obtain the most "profit" they can from their social interactions. The learning principle of satiation (analogous to the economic principle of diminishing marginal utility) is invoked to account for the fact that the more a person has of a commodity, the less valuable are further units of it (e.g., for someone who has received a great deal of social approbation, affection from still another person is not worth as much as it is to an individual who is starved for it). Similarly, the more of a given kind of cost an individual has incurred, the more unpleasant additional such costs are. Homans further proposed a principle of scarcity in which the scarcer a valued commodity is, the higher is the price a person can exact for giving it.

The esteem one individual may give another plays a central role in Homans's social exchange theory because, he believes, it comes as close to being a "generalized reinforcer" for humans as any other commodity people exchange in interaction: "Men give social approval, as a generalized reinforcer, to others that have given them the activity they value, and so make it more likely that the others will go on giving the activity" (1961, p. 129). Thus Homans hypothesizes that those persons who can give rare and highly rewarding services can command, in return, a great deal of esteem from other people. Homans hypothesizes, too, that independently caused increases in frequency of interaction between two people leads more often than not to attraction, because each probably will find some of the other's activities valuable, if only because they can be obtained at less cost than from a third party at a greater distance away.

For attraction researchers, however, it was Homans's distributive justice hypothesis that subsequently captured the most interest (1961, p. 75):

> A man in an exchange relation with another will expect that the rewards of each man be proportional to his costs—the greater the rewards, the greater the costs—and that the net rewards, or profits, of each man be proportional to his investments—the greater the investments, the greater the profit.

Homans theorizes that the more to an individual's disadvantage the rule of distributive justice fails to be realized, the more likely he or she is to become angry, which, of course, has implications for the individual's attraction to the other.

The equity theories.   Adams (1963a, 1965) integrated Homans's concept of distributive justice, the concept of relative deprivation developed by Stouffer and his associates (1949) in *The American Soldier,* as well as some propositions derived from Festinger's cognitive dissonance theory, into a theory of inequity in social exchange. Adams proposed that inequity exists for individuals when they perceive that the ratio of their outcomes to inputs in a relationship with another and the ratio of the other's outcomes to inputs are unequal. Since inequity is presumed to create tension, the individual is

motivated to eliminate or reduce it. One way in which people may eliminate or reduce inequity is to alter their own inputs into the relationship, either by increasing them or decreasing them, depending upon whether the equity is personally advantageous or disadvantageous. Subsequent experiments conducted by Adams and his colleagues in industrial work situations demonstrated that people will indeed alter their inputs in such a way as to achieve equity when they perceive that injustice exists.

Although the principle of equity in social exchange was initially applied primarily to industrial and work situations to predict such phenomena as worker productivity and personnel turnover, equity theory was subsequently formalized, refined, and extended to many other social exchange situations (e.g., see Berkowitz and Walster, 1976; Walster, Walster, and Berscheid, 1978), and its implications for attraction were directly explored. Equity theory has been more recently extended to intimate social relationships (see Hatfield, Utne, and Traupmann, 1979), and it is now clear (see McClintock and Keil, 1982) that equity theory, as a general theory of social interaction, has strong and specific implications for attraction in a wide range of social relationships and contexts. The continuing interest in equity phenomena, particularly recent attempts to incorporate equity theory and its associated empirical findings into a broader theoretical framework addressed to the general problem of the antecedents and effects of perceived justice in social relationships (see Leventhal, 1980), can be expected to further benefit an understanding of attraction.

Thibaut and Kelley's theory of social interdependence. Thibaut and Kelley's theory attempts to predict and explain many social phenomena, including the emergence of norms governing the relationship between two or more people and power and dependence within a relationship, as well as attraction phenomena. It focuses upon the behavior outcome matrix characteristic of a relationship, which describes the ways in which two (or more) individuals are dependent upon the behavior of each other in achieving favorable outcomes for themselves. It accepts as a basic premise, just as Homans's theory does, that social behavior will not be repeated unless it is reinforced in some way, and it stresses that an individual's behavior in a relationship is a function of the behavioral payoff matrix characteristic of the relationship (or the configuration presented by *both* persons' behavior outcome matrices) rather than a function of the individual's payoff matrix alone. It recognizes that the goodness of an individual's outcomes for the performance of a certain behavior is affected by another's response to that behavior and, thus, that the other can often influence the kinds of behavior the individual exhibits by varying his or her own behavior in response to the individual's behavior.

Perhaps the most important concepts introduced by Thibaut and Kelley relevant to attraction are the concepts of comparison level (CL) and comparison level for alternatives (CL$_{alt}$). Comparison level is conceived to be the standard by which people evaluate the rewards and costs of a given relationship in terms of what they feel they deserve, and it is defined as the average value of all of the outcomes known to the individual (either through direct experience or through their symbolic representation, each weighted by its salience) to be characteristic of relationships of that type (e.g., marital; employer-employee). It is hypothesized that relationships whose outcomes are above the CL will be relatively satisfying and attractive to the individual, and relationships whose outcomes fall below the CL will be considered relatively unattractive. Comparison level for alternatives, on the other hand, is conceived to be the standard an individual uses to decide whether to maintain or terminate a relationship; CL$_{alt}$ is defined as the lowest level of outcomes people will accept in light of the outcomes they believe are available to them in an alternative relationship.

The two standards, CL and CL$_{alt}$, are differentiated in recognition of the fact that people often must remain in circumstances they regard as unsatisfactory, and they must continue to interact with others whom they regard as unattractive, simply because they have no better alternative. Thibaut and Kelley's analysis thus directly implies that a relationship (and presumably the person with whom a relationship is shared) may be highly attractive to the individual without his or her necessarily being dependent upon the relationship's continuance for good outcomes since other good alternatives may exist. Similarly, this analysis suggests that an individual may be extremely dependent upon a relationship with another without that relationship being attractive to any great degree.

In distinguishing between an individual's degree of attraction to a relationship and dependence upon that relationship, these theorists departed from previous writers (e.g., Waller and Hill, 1951) who suggested that dependence and attraction are closely associated. This supposition may be true in practice, of course (i.e., it often may

be the case that when outcomes are above CL, they tend also to be above CL$_{alt}$), but it is conceptually clear that the two need not covary. It is worthwhile, therefore, to preserve the distinction between the two. Further, since these concepts have been found to be extremely useful, especially in various theoretical frameworks relevant to the prediction of divorce (e.g., Levinger, 1976) and to the longevity of other close heterosexual relationships (e.g., Berscheid and Campbell, 1981), the determinants of CL and CL$_{alt}$ as they are perceived by the individual, the relationship of each to various behaviors of interest, and the relationship between the two standards deserve far more empirical attention than they have yet received.

Kelley and Thibaut (1978) have recently elaborated upon and extended their theory with an analysis of the numerous patterns of interdependence that may be characteristic of relationships. In doing so, they have distinguished between the given outcome matrix of the relationship, as it is determined by environmental and personal factors, and the effective outcome matrix, which often results from the participants' reactions to and transformation of the given matrix. Individuals in some relationships may, for example, transform the given matrix by invoking a rule that they will maximize joint outcomes, even though one person could enjoy better outcomes if the rule were not adopted. The effective outcome matrix is considered to be more closely linked to behavior than the given outcome matrix. Kelley (1979) has further addressed the transformation of given outcome matrices in close heterosexual relationships, with special attention to how the attribution of dispositions to the other in the relationship both affects and is affected by the transformations that take place upon the given outcome matrix.

Because given matrices are especially likely to undergo transformation in relationships of any duration, recognition that it is the transformed outcome matrix that guides behavior, rather than the given matrix (especially as it is viewed by an outside observer), is especially likely to prove beneficial to researchers as they investigate the role of attraction in enduring social relationships. Clark and Mills (1979) argue, in fact, that in most marital relationships the given matrix has been transformed such that the relationship has become what they term a communal relationship, one in which the giving of a benefit in response to a need is appropriate, rather than an exchange relationship, one "in which the giving of a benefit in response to the receipt of a benefit is appropriate" (p.

2). These investigators have found experimental support for their view that the request for rewards from another in a communal relationship will result in a different attraction response from the other than will a similar request made within an exchange relationship.

THEORIES SPECIFIC TO INTERPERSONAL ATTRACTION

In addition to general theories of social behavior that have stimulated many investigations of attraction, several more circumscribed theories have been influential. These theories, constructed especially for application to questions of attraction, often have been derived and adapted to social behavior from more general theories of behavior.

Lott and Lott's Theory of the Role of Reward in the Acquisition of Positive Interpersonal Attitudes

Lott and Lott (e.g., 1960, 1974) have used the learning principles associated with Hull, Spence, and Mowrer to facilitate understanding of the development and the consequences of attraction to another. They conceive of attraction as a positive attitude toward another, liking as an anticipatory goal response, and a liked person as a secondary reinforcer (e.g., Lott and Lott, 1968, 1972).

The basic hypothesis underlying Lott and Lott's (1974) theoretical approach to the antecedents of attraction is that "liking for a person will result under those conditions in which an individual experiences *reward in the presence of that person,* regardless of the relationship between the other person and the rewarding event or state of affairs" (p. 172). An individual may receive rewards in the presence of another because the other possesses personal characteristics that reward those in close proximity (e.g., the other's appearance is aesthetically pleasing), because the other directly provides rewards to the individual (e.g., money), or because the other is instrumental, by virtue of expertise or competence, in mediating certain rewards for the individual (e.g., assures the success of a group project). Another type of situation hypothesized to increase attraction to another is one in which the other is consistently associated with independent reinforcing states. Thus both instrumental and classical conditioning processes are conceived to be integral to the acquisition of positive interpersonal attitudes.

The Lotts and their associates have generated a good deal of research designed to demonstrate that reward is effective in increasing the attractiveness of others who have been associated with a reward but not instrumental in the individual's receipt of it. Lott and Lott (1968) demonstrated, for example, that children who were systematically rewarded by their classroom teacher increased their liking for their classmates significantly more than did children who either had been ignored or who had received unfavorable treatment. Other evidence that classical conditioning processes can account for increases or decreases in attraction to others comes from a variety of sources. Griffitt and Veitch (1971), for example, found that negative attitudes toward a stranger tended to be expressed by individuals who were in an uncomfortably hot room that was also crowded. And as previously mentioned, there is evidence that when individuals bring to their interaction with another a good mood generated by events prior to the interaction, they tend to feel and behave more positively toward the other (e.g., Isen, 1970).

In addition to specifying the antecedents of attraction, Lott and Lott (1974) outline its consequences: "As positive secondary reinforcing stimuli, people we like should have consequences for perception and memory, stemming from their heightened salience and distinctiveness; consequences for performance, stemming from their incentive or drive-arousing quality; and consequences for learning, because they can function as rewards" (p. 173). Lott and Lott (1972) present a good deal of evidence that attractive others do indeed function as secondary reinforcers and are capable, therefore, of modifying a wide variety of behaviors.

Aronson's Gain-Loss Theory of Attraction

Aronson (1969) observed that although virtually all of the known antecedents of interpersonal attraction can be loosely summarized under a general reward-cost theory, the usefulness of such a theory is diminished because many social rewards do not seem to be transituational; they may function as a reward in some situations, even in most situations, but they may have no effect or even the opposite effect in other situations. Aronson, Willerman, and Floyd (1966) subsequently demonstrated that even such a well-established finding that able and competent others are liked more than incompetent people has exceptions. In what has become known as the pratfall experiment, it was found that although a person of average competence who committed a blunder was liked less than when he did not blunder, and although a person of superior ability was always liked more than one of average ability, a person of superior ability who committed a social blunder was considered *more* attractive than an exceptionally competent person who did not.

Aronson argued that the limitations of a general reward theory might be defined by the development and test of various minitheories of attraction that would not be intended to account for a large body of attraction findings but that would further the understanding of a small set of attraction data. Gain-loss theory was proposed as just such a theory. Its central hypothesis is that increases in rewarding behavior from another have more impact on an individual than consistent, invariant reward; similarly, losses in rewarding behavior from another have more impact than invariant punitive behavior.

To test this hypothesis, Aronson and Linder (1965) constructed a situation in which individuals conversed with another on several occasions, and after each conversation they overheard the other evaluate them to a third party. Some overheard the other say exclusively positive things about them; others received exclusively negative evaluations; still others (those in the "gain" condition) overheard their evaluator say negative things initially but gradually develop a positive view of them; and finally, other individuals (those in the "loss" condition) heard positive evaluations at first, with the evaluator growing negative over time. The gain evaluator, as predicted, was generally liked best, and the loss evaluator was liked least. These investigators observe that a theory that simply summed the rewards and punishments the other dealt to the individual would have led to a different prediction—that the person who was consistently positive would be liked best and the individual who was consistently negative would be liked least.

Gain-loss theory drew attention to some of the corollaries of more general reward theories that were, and are, often overlooked in their application to attraction phenomena. As Lott and Lott (1974) remarked upon the Aronson and Linder findings: "It has long been recognized, although often lost sight of, that effective reinforcement must be relevant to the motivational state and/or preceding experiences of the organism being reinforced" (pp. 173–174). Learning the nature of the previous experiences of any animal is difficult (unless, of course, the animal resides in a cage in the laboratory), but

knowledge of these experiences is vital, as gain-loss theory emphasizes. Among such experiences, the extent to which the person recently has been deprived of social approval is important in predicting attraction to another who delivers the reward of esteem or the punishment of disapproval, as Aronson and Linder demonstrated. Other experiments, performed within other theoretical contexts, also illustrate the importance of knowing the extent to which the individual has received a particular reward in the past for gauging attraction to another who offers that same reward. For example, a number of investigators (e.g., Stapert and Clore, 1969) have found that although attitudinal similarity is generally rewarding, it is far more likely to generate attraction after the individual has disagreed with others in the immediate past than when it follows many previous instances of agreement.

In addition to calling attention to events in the individual's past that help form the context in which rewards and punishments are received in the present, gain-loss experimentation has also illustrated that the nature of events occurring concurrently with the specific rewards and punishments also form their context and thus help determine their effect. For example, Berscheid, Brothen, and Graziano (1976) demonstrated that changes in the concurrent contextual factors that surround the provision of gains in reward may produce attraction effects quite different from those found by Aronson and Linder. Although the original gain finding was replicated under the original conditions of a single evaluator overheard over several occasions, when the individual had an opportunity to overhear two evaluators, one of whom gave consistently positive evaluations and the other who provided a gain in positivity of evaluations, individuals liked the consistently positive other better. And this was found even though they preferred to listen to the gain evaluator and to tune out the consistently positive evaluator.

Gain-loss theory and experimentation, then, have helped to underscore that contextual effects are vital to the prediction of interpersonal attraction. To predict attraction, not only must one take into consideration the nature of the events occurring in the relationship between the individual and the other, but one must also consider the social context of these events. The context in which a reward is provided can change its meaning and its value to the individual and, consequently, greatly affect whether or not it increases attraction to the person providing it.

Byrne's Attraction Paradigm

Initially, and as previously discussed, Byrne was principally guided by what he himself termed a "rather vague" (1971, p. 268) reinforcement approach, and he concentrated his efforts on the question of whether, when, and how attitude similarity with another modified attraction responses. After a good deal of experimentation that demonstrated, at least within the bogus stranger experimental paradigm, that attraction was associated with the proportion (rather than sheer number) of similar attitudes shared with the other, Byrne stated: "A tentative law of attraction is proposed as $A_x = mPR_x + k$, or attraction toward X is a positive linear function of the proportion of positive reinforcements received from X" (Byrne and Nelson, 1965, p. 662).

Later, however, in association with Clore (e.g., Byrne and Clore, 1970; Clore and Byrne, 1974), and influenced both by their own empirical findings and those of Lott and Lott (e.g., 1960), Byrne became more interested in theoretical matters and the original law of attraction was revised so as to de-emphasize its rewards received aspect and to state that rewards need only be associated with X: "attraction toward X is a positive linear function of the sum of the weighted positive reinforcements (Number × Magnitude) associated with X divided by the total number of weighted positive and negative reinforcements associated with X" (1971, p. 279). He also noted, however, that a formula that reduces all stimuli to positive and negative elements of varying weights is "deceptively simple" (1971, p. 271).

Clore and Byrne (1974) later proposed an associational affect model of attraction that elaborates the manner in which reinforcement and attraction are linked. Its principal elements are a stimulus with reinforcement properties that serves as the independent variable, an implicit affective response that is conceived to be an intervening variable, and any evaluative response, such as attraction, as the dependent variable of interest. The implicit affective response, an unobservable, is assumed to fall along a subjective pleasant-unpleasant continuum and to be produced by an unconditioned stimulus possessing reinforcement properties (as determined through prior examination of its capacity to alter response probability). Byrne and Clore (1970) have provided a number of experimental demonstrations that similar and dissimilar attitude statements do appear to evoke differential affective responses, and that when these stimuli are associated with neutral stimuli, the latter also come to evoke differential affective responses.

Even more recently, Clore and Kerber (1981) and Tedeschi (1974) have emphasized the importance, in predicting attraction, not only of the role of rewards that have been received from or associated with the other in the past and in the immediate present but also the role of rewards the individual anticipates he or she will receive from the other in the future. Investigation of the role of expected rewards may prove especially useful in understanding strong increases in attraction to another based on extremely brief interaction with the other and very limited information about them.

THEORETICAL STATEMENTS ADDRESSED TO CERTAIN VARIETIES OF ATTRACTION

The foregoing theories assume that the general principles they outline are relevant to all varieties of attraction and across all social relationships and contexts in which attraction may be experienced. In practice, however, most of the research derived from these theories has focused upon discovering the antecedents of liking, or of mild positive sentiment for others. In part, this focus has been due to the fact that until recently it was largely assumed that the determinants of both mild and strong forms of attraction were similar if not identical, with those determinants simply being more potently in force in the case of the strong forms of attraction. In other part, the emphasis upon the mild forms of attraction has been brought about by the typical setting in which attraction has been investigated—between strangers in laboratory settings. Recently, however, some investigators have attempted to distinguish, both theoretically and empirically, between certain varieties of attraction, particularly between liking and more intense positive sentiment.

Liking Versus Love

Investigators have increasingly questioned whether liking and love represent different quantitative expressions of attraction along essentially the same dimension or whether they are qualitatively different phenomena altogether, with the antecedents of the one differing importantly from the antecedents of the other. This concern has been prompted by anecdotal observation that greater and greater increases in liking do not seem to culminate in love as frequently as one would expect if their antecedents differed only in magnitude. Further, liking and at least one variety of love, romantic love, appear to differ in ways that suggest that their determinants may differ in kind. For example, as Berscheid and Walster (1974a) outline:

- Romantic love often seems to have a swift onset, while liking often appears to grow gradually.

- Romantic love seems to differ from liking in its fragility; mild forms of attraction seem to be relatively stable (although this is often more of an assumption than an empirically documented fact), and more intense forms of attraction appear to be more volatile and short-lived.

- Attraction researchers generally assume that it is the actual rewards that are exchanged in interaction that are of primary importance in creating liking, but it appears that it is the anticipation of rewards to be received in future association with another that are of particular importance in generating the intensity of attraction typical of romantic love.

- The nature of the rewards that have been shown to be important in generating liking seem sensible, but events more associated with punishment—such as suffering, agony, frustration, and fear—often appear not to diminish romantic love but to even increase its intensity.

Whatever the degree of overlap in their antecedents proves to be, it is now clear that liking and romantic love are measurably different. Rubin (e.g., 1974) succeeded in developing a Love Scale and a Liking Scale by collecting a pool of items and examining those endorsed by persons asked to describe their relationship with their opposite-sex lover as opposed to the items endorsed when they were asked to describe their relationship with a platonic friend of the opposite sex. Rubin subsequently found that scores on the Love Scale, but not on the Liking Scale, highly correlated with self-reports of being in love with that other and also that Love Scale scores more strongly differentiated between heterosexual dating partners and same-sex friends than did Liking Scale scores.

Other investigators have examined the reliability and validity of Rubin's scales with favorable results (e.g., Dion and Dion, 1976). One particularly interesting examination of the validity of these scales, which highlights the association between romantic love and sexual desire, was conducted by Dermer and Pyszczynski (1978). Men were asked to complete the Love and Liking Scales with respect to the person of the opposite sex they were most attracted to after they had been exposed either to sexually arousing materials or to control materials. It was found that Love scores significantly increased from the non-arousal to the arousal conditions but Liking scores did not, thus providing evidence of the discriminant validity of these two scales.

Love

Rubin (1973) speculates that the dimensions underlying the Love Scale are attachment, caring for the welfare of the other, and intimacy (e.g., a willingness to self-disclose to the other), while the primary dimensions underlying liking seem to be affection and respect, which are often evidenced in favorable evaluations of the other's personal traits and properties. Several investigators agree on the basis of their own evidence that affection and respect appear to underlie liking (e.g., Kiesler and Goldberg, 1968; Mettee and Aronson, 1974).

With respect to the dimensions underlying love, Swensen (1972) has found evidence that certain behaviors seem to differentiate between loved persons and acquaintances. Factor analysis of the responses of people who were asked to endorse items that described the behaviors and feelings characteristic of their relationship with certain loved ones revealed that behavior toward a loved person of the opposite sex included self-disclosure, giving both material (e.g., gifts) and nonmaterial benefits (e.g., emotional and moral support) to the other, as well as verbal and physical (e.g., hugging) expressions of affection. In addition, respondents had more positive feelings (e.g., were happier) in the presence of the other and were more willing to tolerate unpleasant aspects of loved ones. Since all of these were found to be separate factors, it is clear that behavior toward a particular loved opposite-sex person may differ markedly along these dimensions. Rubin, of course, found only one general factor (or Love items that correlated highly with one another), but this may be due to the fact that he focused upon discriminating between relationships that were characterized by the respondents' self-reports that they were in love with the opposite-sex partner (as opposed to being friends) and Swensen asked his respondents to select their "closest friend of the opposite sex" (defined as the spouse if the person was married) who was also "loved."

As the above discussion implies, there are undoubtedly many varieties of love, which may help account for the apparent mysteries and paradoxes surrounding the phenomenon, and one potentially important distinction is between a person's being in love with another and loving them (e.g., "I love him, but I'm not 'in love' with him"). A point for future investigation is whether some of the current confusion in findings is traceable to the fact that some investigators ask respondents to describe a relationship with a person of the opposite sex whom they love and other investigators ask them to describe their relationship with a person with whom they are "in love", with both groups assuming that the two terms describe the same population of others from which the respondent is to select an instance and also that the two terms refer to the same variety of love in laypersons' lexicon.

What varieties of love, or of strong positive affective responses to another, may be useful to attempt to distinguish among is, at present, an open question. Several candidates, however, immediately suggest themselves from an examination of the anecdotal and clinical literature, from an examination of the major scientific conceptions of love, and from consideration of what is now known of the differing antecedents and consequences of certain attraction phenomena. These candidates are proposed and briefly discussed in the following paragraph.

Altruistic love.   As Kelley (1983) observes, many conceptions of love emphasize the element of the individual's caring about the other person's welfare as well as the individual's acting in ways that promote the other's well-being, sometimes even at the expense of the individual's own. This is the variety of love the Greeks called agapé and Fromm discusses in his classic book *The Art of Loving* (1956). It is also sometimes called brotherly, charitable, or communal love, emphasizing its quality of responding to another's need rather than giving with expectation of return. This variety of love also appears to correspond to what Maslow (1954) termed "B-love," or love for another's being, as opposed to "D-love," or deficiency love, that grows out of the individual's needs and what the other is perceived to be able to do to satisfy those needs.

The determinants of altruistic behavior toward another are multitudinous and have been explored at length by social psychologists (see Chapter 14 of this *Handbook*). What is significant about these determinants for present purposes is that they include many more factors than attraction, affection, or liking for the other. That is, people not infrequently care about and act to promote the welfare of persons they personally neither like nor respect, would not want to associate with for any period of time, and whom they may, in fact, not know very well, if at all. Thus although altruistic love may well accompany other forms of attraction, as the caring items on Rubin's Love Scale suggest, it may be hypothesized that it need not and that the determinants of altruistic love may differ importantly from determinants of other forms of love. At the least, this conception of love clearly focuses on behavior that promotes the welfare of the other and not upon positive appraisals of the other's properties, nor upon positive feelings and emotions experienced in association with the other, nor upon behavior that promotes proximity to the other.

Attachment.   Rubin suggests that attachment is one component of the Love Scale. The determinants of attachment behavior, or behavior that promotes close physical proximity to another, have been of great interest (see the section "Affiliation and Attraction"), particularly in infants (e.g., see Bowlby, 1969), in infrahuman animals (e.g., Harlow, 1958; Lorenz, 1952), and recently, although tangentially, in human adults (e.g., Weiss, 1975). Again, what is significant about these determinants is that they appear to revolve around the sheer familiarity of the other and do not importantly include how much the other is liked (e.g., in terms of favorable evaluations of the other's qualities or perceptions that the other can directly provide need satisfaction). Thus, although it probably is more frequently the case than not that familiar persons are evaluated favorably and that interaction with them is rewarding, proximity-promoting behavior and separation distress apparently may be exhibited toward persons who have become familiar but who are not particularly well regarded and with whom interaction is not especially rewarding (and may, in fact, be punishing).

Philias, or friendship.   Although *liking* usually implies a milder sentiment than *love*, it is clear that liking sometimes develops into a Damon-and-Pythias depth and intensity where it might be more properly termed *love*, at least in popular parlance. The determinants of liking have been explored at length, both theoretically (as previously discussed) and empirically (see the section "Attraction and Initial Encounters"), and appear to importantly revolve around the rewards two people receive or anticipate receiving from their interaction with each other. They are often evidenced, also as previously discussed, in favorable evaluations of the other's qualities. This conception of love also has been termed "pragmatic love" (see Kelley, 1983).

Eros, or romantic love. This variety of love has received the most interest and attention, undoubtedly because it is one of the most dramatic forms of attraction and also because it has assumed special importance in our culture as the sine qua non of marriage (see Campbell and Berscheid, 1976; Kephart, 1967). Although the determinants of romantic love are still the subject of conjecture, as will be discussed later, it seems probable that they differ importantly from the determinants of liking or friendship (e.g., as Rubin's successful development of the Love and Liking Scales suggests), of attachment [e.g., romantic love tends to appear in the first stages of a relationship when the other is relatively unfamiliar and appears to dissipate over time and with familiarity (e.g., Blood, 1967)], and of altruistic love (e.g., tales of the atrocities romantic lovers sometimes perpetrate upon each other are legion).

It seems reasonable that although all forms of love may be experienced in different blends at one time in the same relationship, certain varieties may be more characteristic of some stages of a relationship than others, partially because their determinants are more likely to be in force at some stages than at others. Investigation of this hypothesis requires that attention be directed toward length of relationship, which implies finding samples that exhibit a wider range on this dimension than the range that may be presumed to be typical of unmarried college sophomores. Furthermore, some varieties may occur differentially in different types of relationships and social contexts (e.g., Pam, Plutchik, and Conte, 1975), perhaps as a reflection of popular beliefs that some varieties are more appropriate to certain relationships than to others. Some varieties also may be more characteristic of individuals at some developmental and life cycle stages than others, and investigation of this hypothesis additionally requires a wider subject population than that represented by young adults. The investigation of all of these and other hypotheses, however, depends importantly upon a careful conceptual explication of the components implicitly incorporated in the various conceptions of love, as Kelley (1983) has emphasized.

Confusion surrounding the topic of love stems not only from the fact that the word *love* has a wide and bewildering variety of referents but also from the fact

that even the addition of such qualifiers as *romantic* does not always add precision of meaning. For example, the term *romantic love* is sometimes used synonymously with the term *heterosexual love* to refer to any positive feeling, no matter how mild, toward any person of the opposite sex (as opposed to a person of the same sex). More frequently, however, it is used interchangeably with the phrase *passionate love* to refer to more intense feelings toward opposite-sex others. In addition to presumptions of intensity and of the experience of strong emotion associated with, precipitated by, or directed toward the romantically loved one, most conceptions of romantic love presume strong sexual desire for the other. Some current conceptions of romantic love also contain one or more of the elements previously mentioned but, more frequently, altruistic love, attachment, and friendship are combined under such rubrics as "companionate love" (see Berscheid and Walster, 1978; Walster and Walster, 1979)—which may be felt for same-sex as well as opposite-sex persons—to differentiate it from love spurred or accompanied by sexual desire, which is usually felt for persons of the opposite-sex.

Many discourses on the subject of romantic love are available today; indeed, they abound. Most have been formulated by clinical psychologists (e.g., Peele, 1975; Reik, 1944; Tennov, 1979), and many of these theories invoke the concept of perceived psychological dependency (see Berscheid and Fei, 1977), positing a crucial relationship between perceived dependence upon another for comfort, well-being, and happiness and love for him or her. These theories of romantic love differ from more general social psychological reward theories of attraction in their special emphasis on the role that deprivation plays in making a social stimulus event a reward, as well as in their emphasis upon the importance of fantasy, idealization of the other, and the role of anticipated rewards in the production of this intense form of attraction.

Following a somewhat different tack from the clinicians, Walster and Berscheid (1971; Berscheid and Walster, 1974a) have argued that since romantic love is often experienced as an emotion (or as a series of emotional events experienced in association with another), it must follow the known rules of all the emotions. Thus, and in accord with Schachter's (1964) two-component theory of emotion, they theorized that individuals will experience romantic love whenever two conditions coexist: (1) They are strongly aroused physiologically, and (2) situational cues indicate that romantic love is the appropriate interpretation of their feelings. Tangential experimental support relevant to that hypothesis was provided in experiments conducted by Brehm, Gatz, Goethals, McCrimmon, and Ward (1967) and by Dutton and Aron (1974), who, advancing a similar hypothesis, found direct experimental evidence to support the proposal that the arousal generated by fear-producing stimulus may be, in conducive circumstances, misattributed and interpreted as attraction to another.

Subsequent support for the misattribution implications of this formulation have been mixed. Kendrick, Cialdini, and Linder (1979), for example, conducted four experiments to attempt to demonstrate that the arousal produced by a fear stimulus could be misattributed as attraction to another and failed to do so, and Kendrick and Cialdini (1977) have preferred to reinterpret such supporting evidence as exists within a negative reinforcement model. White, Fishbein, and Rutstein (1981), on the other hand, found clear evidence that physiological changes often associated with peripheral arousal derived from one source may be misattributed and result in increased attraction to another. The work of Zillman and his associates (1978) on the transfer-of-excitation hypothesis also supports the notion that physiological changes generated by factors extraneous to a particular relationship and stimulus situation may be misattributed and result in increased attraction to another.

In most naturalistic situations, of course, increases in arousal may be correctly (rather than incorrectly) attributed to the presence or actions of the other, and such increases may facilitate the romantic love interpretation by persons who believe love to be associated with the experience of physiological arousal. If so, the prediction of the experience and temporal course of romantic love depends in part but importantly upon knowledge of the kinds of situations and persons that are likely to generate arousal in a given individual and upon the subjective beliefs of the individual concerning the phenomenon of romantic love, particularly the conditions (such as arousal) believed to be associated with its occurrence.

Information regarding the kinds of events likely to precipitate arousal has been facilitated by the renaissance of interest in emotion and general theories such as Mandler's (1975, 1984), which has been extended to apply to emotion as it may or may not occur in close personal relationships (Berscheid, 1983). However, not a great deal is known about the beliefs people hold about romantic love, even though beliefs about this form of attraction heavily influence the behavioral phenomena associated with it. Whether the popular beliefs about romantic love are true or false (and no systematic study has yet identified precisely what they are), they undoubtedly influence the determinants, dynamics, and consequences of romantic love as it is experienced.

To illustrate, Dion and Dion (1973) speculated that since romantic love is popularly believed to be an external force that strikes with the capriciousness of a bolt of lightning, the romantic experiences of individuals possessing an internal locus-of-control orientation would differ from those who possessed an external locus-of-control orientation. Indeed, fewer internals than externals reported having been romantically attached; internals experienced romantic attraction as being less mysterious and volatile than externals; and internals more strongly opposed an idealistic view of romantic love than externals did. This finding demonstrates that conceptions of heterosexual love are not monolithic, as does recent work on the development of a typology of love styles (Lee, 1976). With respect to the oft-presumed association between the experience of arousal and romantic love, it seems apparent that not all persons make the association (e.g., see Dion and Dion, 1973), although it is not clear what the relative frequencies are and for what populations.

It should be emphasized that despite sustained theoretical interest in romantic love, as well as a recent surge of interest in the topic within social psychology, within sociology (see Berardo, 1980), and within sociobiology (e.g., Mellen, 1981; Symons, 1979), empirical evidence relevant to the subject is still scant. A number of factors have been responsible for the current lack of empirical evidence, and at least one of these continues to exert its influence today. That is, although the severe taboo imposed upon social scientists for investigating romantic love has lifted, this form of attraction remains very much a highly revered cultural value in our society (see Ellis, 1954), which adds controversy and complexity to its study.

SUMMARY

The discussion in this section by no means exhausts the many theoretical statements that are relevant to interpersonal attraction (many of which will be discussed in the following sections). Some of the remainder have been formulated by investigators who have found general theories of attraction too loosely fitted to the predictive problems they address and who have thus developed theoretical frameworks more narrowly focused on the particular attraction phenomena of special interest to them. Other theorists have been especially interested in attraction phenomena as they occur in certain types of relationships (e.g., marital relationships), yet others in attraction phenomena as they occur in certain social contexts (e.g., courtship), and still others in attraction phenomena as they engage certain problems (e.g., loneliness).

In addition, several theorists recently have changed their focus from attraction per se to identifying its role in relationship development. (These theories will be discussed in the final section of this chapter.) This change in focus reflects recent recognition that social attraction processes are essentially interactive ones, as well as a new willingness to contemplate the long and complex causal and consequential chains within which many attraction phenomena are embedded. It also, however, reflects dissatisfaction with the general reinforcement approach that underlies most models directly addressed to attraction phenomena.

The nature of the dissatisfaction is that, as Levinger (1974) put it, "the strength of reinforcement theory is simultaneously its weakness; that which explains everything explains nothing. The 'laws' of reinforcement and of exchange must be moved toward greater specificity and their elements differentiated" (p. 117). However, and ironically, at the same time that many critics have been dissatisfied with the generality of the reinforcement approach, they have been equally dissatisfied with the narrowness with which its constructs have been operationalized in many empirical investigations. In fact, it is the way in which theories devised to account for the learning behavior of rats and other infrahumans have been applied to problems of human attraction that has most often met with dissatisfaction. The complex interactive nature of human social behavior is easily overlooked when bald extrapolations to humans are made from the behavior of rats in Skinner boxes. There, the animal's responses to the receipt of a food pellet have no subsequent influence whatsoever upon the machinery that delivered the pellet nor upon the experimenter who devised the reinforcement schedule. For example, the angry rat who thinks that his pellets are neither large enough nor delivered fast enough cannot threaten to deprive the experimenter of *his* dinner if the matter is not soon rectified.

The social exchange theories, of course, represented an advance over early demonstrations that the principles that hold in the infrahuman experimental world generally apply to human social behavior as well, demonstra-

tions that often took the form of showing that a single stimulus (e.g., a reward) influenced a single putative attraction response. The social exchange theories directly addressed the interactive nature of social behavior and emphasized that a person's behavior is influenced not only by his or her own behavioral reward matrix in a relationship with another but also by the other's reward matrix, or, specifically, the configuration presented by the two together.

Nevertheless, there also is a good deal of dissatisfaction with the social exchange theories. This dissatisfaction principally stems from the serious problems involved in their actual use (see Gergen, 1980). Among these problems is the difficulty, if not the impossibility, of calculating the rewards and costs present in any specific situation, as well as reducing these to a common standard for predictive purposes. Another issue concerns predicting the kinds of rewards people are likely to exchange, which, like other problems, sometimes has been addressed through the development of auxiliary theories [e.g., Foa and Foa's (1980) resource theory].

The major problem with the general reinforcement approach, however, and one that continues to plague the exchange theories, is the determination of what constitutes a reward or a cost to whom and when. A pellet is likely to be reward to a rat who has not eaten for several days, but what is a reward or a cost is not so easily determined for humans in social situations. As a consequence, not only has recent theorizing moved toward taking an interactive approach, but it also has moved toward careful consideration of the meaning and value of stimulus events to the individual.

It should be emphasized, however, that dissatisfaction with the general reinforcement models of attraction stems largely from their major virtue—their generality and apparent applicability to virtually any social encounter. As a consequence, and despite the fact that there is now a trend away from attempts to discover context-free principles of global and undifferentiated attraction responses, it is likely that the exchange theories will continue to constitute a major theoretical orientation for understanding social behavior in general and attraction in particular. It also should be noted that it was the formalization of these theories that allowed their inadequacies to appear and dissatisfaction with their level of abstraction to develop, and it is this dissatisfaction, in turn, that stimulated current theoretical efforts to place attraction in its natural context and to move the laws of social reinforcement toward greater specificity. In addition, in testing hypotheses derived from a reinforcement view, investigators have learned a great deal about the nature of the stimuli that do appear to act as rewards in social interaction for most people most of the time and that, consequently, often produce attraction.

AFFILIATION AND ATTRACTION

Matters of affiliation, of who associates with whom, form the framework within which each individual lives his or her life as well as the fabric of human society. They thus furnish, as Schachter (1959) observed, "the substance of the social sciences which in good part are devoted to the study of the process and products of human association" (p. 1).

Historically, the subject of affiliation has carried special import for attraction research for several reasons. First, and most importantly, the question of who interacts with whom and why is obviously related to the question of who likes whom and why. Not only has attraction often been assumed to be both necessary and sufficient for affiliation to occur, but increased attraction frequently has been considered to be a consequence of association with another. Furthermore, and given the long assumed isomorphism between affiliation and attraction (see Levinger and Snoek, 1972), measures of association often have been used as measures of attraction, a practice that continues to the present day. For example, the popular Interpersonal Judgment Scale (Byrne, 1971) combines a liking rating with a rating of desire to work with the other. Finally, of course, and as previously noted, it was the assumed relationship between affiliation and attraction that marked the emergence of systematic empirical research in interpersonal attraction.

SOCIOMETRY: MEASUREMENT OF THE DESIRE TO AFFILIATE

Sociometry was originally devised by Moreno (1934) to measure attraction and repulsion within a group. As Lindzey and Byrne (1968) describe in their review of sociometric research, a sociometric measure "usually involves each member of the group privately specifying a number of other persons in the group with whom he would like to engage in some particular activity and, further, a number of persons with whom he would not like to participate in the activity" (p. 455). The sociometric technique initially was used in a wide variety of settings, especially educational and institutional settings. Gradu-

ally, it was modified in many ways, and by the time of Lindzey and Bryne's review, it had undergone so many permutations that it had lost its distinctiveness: "It seems evident that there has been a progressive merging of the various methods of assessing social choice, with the end result that most investigators treat various types of rating scales and sociometric measures more or less interchangeably" (1968, p. 510). The "rating scales" to which Lindzey and Byrne referred often were scales upon which individuals were asked to rate the degree to which they liked another and/or to rate the degree to which the other possessed favorable or unfavorable personality traits.

The merging of social choice and attraction measures was undoubtedly due to many factors, among them the failure to explicate the attraction construct and the fact that sociometric research was conducted in a theoretical void. The result was that the terms *sociometric literature* and *interpersonal attraction literature* were considered to be synonymous. It has become clear in recent years, however, that the discussion and interpretation of many sociometric data often confused three conceptually distinct factors: (1) an expressed desire to affiliate with another, (2) the actual fact of affiliation with another, and (3) attraction to the other. The melding of these three factors reflected not only a lack of appreciation of the limitations of the standard sociometric technique but also the assumption that the desire to affiliate with another was an outgrowth of attraction to the other and that both led to actual affiliation.

Concern with the proper conceptual referents of responses on standard sociometric measures first emerged within the sociometric literature itself. For example, Darley, Gross, and Martin (1951) asked women students in a housing project to name their roommate preferences, their choices of another woman to be with when among strangers, their choices of confidantes "in time of personal trouble," and their choices for intimate friendship. These four items appeared to the investigators "to be in the same general domain of interpersonal relations" (p. 573), and thus they expected consistency of response within individuals. From the actual correlational data, however, the investigators concluded that "these sociometric questions appear to tap nonequivalent or differential responses on the part of the students in each house. Although the questions seem similar on *a priori* grounds, they are not so perceived by the respondents" (Darley, Gross, and Martin, 1951, p. 573).

Not only did sociometric researchers find that who the individual was attracted to depended upon the activity to be shared, but they also found that it depended upon the nature and size of the group. Since the number of persons in a specified group usually was smaller than the number of persons actually available to the respondent for interaction in daily life, and since only a rank order of choice was often obtained, it was quite possible for the person named as "most preferred" within a specified group to be disliked (although disliked less than anyone else in the group) and for actual interaction with that person to be shunned, perhaps in preference for interaction with people outside the group.

Subsequent affiliation research uncovered three distinct issues: (1) the role of attraction in generating actual attempts to affiliate with another, (2) the identification of other determinants of affiliation, and (3) the effect affiliation has upon attraction. The substance of this research, as will be discussed below, suggests that the assumption of isomorphism between attraction and affiliation is not warranted.

THE ROLE OF ATTRACTION IN AFFILIATION

If attraction is defined as liking for another, many factors other than attraction prompt people to interact with another; attraction is not a necessary condition for affiliation to occur. One obvious example of affiliation without attraction is an involuntary relationship (see Thibaut and Kelley, 1959) where the individual has no alternative but to associate with the other (e.g., as in the relationship between a prisoner and a guard). For this reason, it is useful to recognize that most social situations may be placed somewhere along a continuum of voluntariness of interaction with others in that setting.

Murstein (1970), for example, has designated a closed-field situation as one in which the persons "are forced to interact by reason of the environmental setting in which they find themselves. Examples of such situations might be that of students in a small seminar in a college, members in a law firm, and workers in complementary professions such as doctor-nurse and boss-secretary" (p. 466). In contrast to attraction in an open-field situation, such as a cocktail party where each person is relatively free to interact with another or not, attraction in a closed field is less likely to be a determinant of interaction. Recent theories of relationship termination (e.g., Levinger, 1976) also emphasize that associations with others may be maintained not because of positive sentiment for the other but because dissolution of the association would be too costly for the individual.

Just as there is often a lack of correspondence between attraction and de facto affiliation, there is also an imperfect correspondence between attraction and an individual's expressed desire to interact with another. Mills and Aronson (1965), for example, varied both the physical attractiveness and the positivity of evaluation a woman gave male experimental participants and found that although the beautiful-positive evaluator was liked most and the beautiful-negative evaluator was liked least, the men frequently expressed a desire to return and be in another experiment with the latter. That attraction can be assumed neither from an expressed desire to affiliate nor from the fact of affiliation is also implicit in the development of ingratiation theory and research (see the next major section), which represents, at least in part, a recognition that the desire to interact with another, along with actual affiliation, is not infrequently prompted by motives other than attraction to the other and that expressions of attraction may serve as camouflage for these motives.

Attraction is not only not a necessary condition for affiliation but it also is not a sufficient condition; attraction to another does not always, or perhaps even usually, lead to attempts to interact with another. Attraction researchers have documented that choices to affiliate with another, even in open-field situations, are often made within a set of constraints that modify the association between attraction and social choice. Among these constraints is the individual's anticipation that the other will reject his or her approach attempts.

Anticipation of Acceptance or Rejection

Several investigators have demonstrated that people may not always approach others they find highly attractive. For example, men who were assured that each woman in an array of possible dating choices would welcome an opportunity to interact with them chose a more physically attractive woman than did men who did not receive such assurance, suggesting that the latter perceived their chances to be less with attractive women (e.g., Huston, 1973; Shanteau and Nagy, 1976).

The anticipation of acceptance or rejection is also presumed to mediate the finding that persons of approximately equal, as opposed to disparate, social desirabilities more often choose to affiliate with one another. The matching hypothesis of social choice was first experimentally tested by Walster, Aronson, Abrahams, and Rottman (1966), who derived their predictions from level-of-aspiration theory (Lewin, Dembo, Festinger, and Sears, 1944), which emphasizes that a decision to attempt to reach a goal is influenced not only by the desirability of the goal but also by the subjective probability of success if an attempt should be made. It was predicted that among the young men and women paired for a college computer dance, those of approximately equal social desirability (as assessed by their physical attractiveness, personality, intelligence, and social skills) would like each other more and make more attempts to interact with each other later than would those of disparate levels of social desirability.

The matching hypothesis was not supported by the results of this experiment (physical attractiveness was overwhelmingly the most important determinant of liking for the date and the men's later attempts to interact with their partners). But subsequent studies, in which probability of acceptance was more uncertain than in the computer dance situation, did support it (e.g., Berscheid, Dion, Walster, and Walster, 1971; and see Berscheid and Walster, 1974b, for a review), as do White's (1980) findings that similarity in physical attractiveness level is predictive of courtship progress for dating couples.

Other evidence that subjective probability of rejection influences affiliation choice comes from studies in which an individual's self-esteem has been experimentally raised or lowered. Kiesler and Baral (1970), for example, found that men whose self-esteem had been lowered displayed more romantic approach behaviors toward a moderately physically attractive woman than toward a very attractive one, while men whose self-esteem had been raised showed the reverse pattern. The self-esteem manipulation presumably altered the men's subjective probabilities of rejection. Anticipation of rejection may also partially underlie shyness (see Zimbardo, 1977), an individual-difference factor that may also inhibit an individual's attempts to interact with others.

On the basis of these and other data, Huston and Levinger (1978) have proposed a two-factor model of social choice, where (pp. 126–127):

> the person contemplating initiating an encounter must consider at least two factors: (a) the degree to which he finds the attributes of the potential partners attractive, and (b) the degree to which he anticipates they would find his attributes attractive and hence respond favorably to his initiative.

They note, however, that specific situations may carry additional constraints for some individuals. For example: "Within dating situations, many females, holding traditional views regarding sex-roles, would not take the initiative even if they believed a male to be both attractive and receptive" (Huston and Levinger, 1978, p. 128).

This particular example is of interest because it illustrates that even where attraction exists, there are undoubtedly social norms governing the appropriateness of attempts to affiliate with certain others in particular situations and that, as Huston (1974) has noted, attempts to interact with another may be seen to be an appropriate manifestation of one variety of attraction but not of another (e.g., respect). Although the identity of these norms remains unexplored, they undoubtedly act to further limit the instances in which attraction will lead to actual affiliation attempts and to further underscore that attraction is neither necessary nor sufficient for affiliation to occur.

OTHER DETERMINANTS OF AFFILIATION

As the concept of closed field implies, people are often involuntarily thrown together in time and place by fate and chance. Apart from these external forces, and also apart from reasons of felt attraction to another, people undoubtedly have as many reasons for voluntarily interacting with others as they have needs and goals that others can help them satisfy. Although there no doubt exists an infinite variety of social motivations underlying the attempts of certain individuals to interact with specific others under certain circumstances, investigators have identified some of the more general conditions under which people are especially likely to approach others. These conditions are discussed in the following paragraphs.

Social Comparison and Affiliation

Perhaps the first theory to outline the circumstances under which individuals will especially want to interact with others was Festinger's (1950) theory of informal social communication. Three major forces were theorized to prompt individuals to communicate with others in their social group: (1) the existence of an emotional state in the individual, (2) the desire of individuals to change their social position within the group or to move to another group, and (3) pressures toward uniformity of opinion and/or behavior within the group.

Of these forces Festinger primarily focused his theoretical attention upon pressures toward uniformity of opinion, which were theorized to spring from two sources: group locomotion, or the desirability (and sometimes the necessity) of group uniformity of opinion and/or behavior in order for the group to move toward a goal, and social reality, or individuals' desire to discover the opinions of others in order to assess the correctness of their own. Consideration of these sources led Festinger to hypothesize that pressure upon an individual to communicate with others in a group increases with increases in perceived discrepancy of opinion between the individual and others, increases as the relevance of the opinion to the functioning of the group increases, and increases as the cohesiveness of the group increases. Support for these hypotheses was found in a number of studies (e.g., Festinger, Schachter, and Back, 1950), including Schachter's (1951) classic experiment in which communication patterns were observed in groups that varied in cohesiveness as well as in the extent to which the issue on which an opinion discrepancy emerged was relevant to group function.

In his theory of social comparison processes (1954) Festinger extended and elaborated social communication theory to focus more directly upon individual behavior and to specifically address the circumstances under which individuals seek interaction with others in order to assess the validity of their opinions and beliefs or in order to assess their standing along some personal dimension (e.g., an ability dimension). Social comparison theory assumes that when individuals have no objective, nonsocial means of evaluating the correctness of their opinions and/or of assessing their ability, they will turn to others for comparison information, especially to others whom they perceive to be similar to themselves.

Social comparison theory captured the imagination of many investigators and stimulated a great deal of research that outlines the relationship between social comparison needs and selective affiliation (see Wheeler, 1974, for a review). This large body of findings documents that individuals' uncertainty about the correctness of their opinions does lead to a desire to affiliate with others for comparison purposes and, further, that people who doubt their opinion often choose to affiliate with others whom they suspect will be in agreement with them and/or others whom they believe possess expertise on the subject. In addition, uncertainty about the extent of one's ability also appears to lead to affiliation attempts, especially with others of apparently similar ability. Individuals who are uncertain about the degree to which they possess a specific personality trait also appear to seek out others for comparison purposes, but they frequently choose those they believe to be at the extremes of the dimension in question, presumably in order to place themselves between these two defining anchors.

Social comparison theory has been extended and modified over the years (e.g., Darley and Goethals, 1980; Rofé, 1984; Suls and Miller, 1977) and continues to stimulate further explorations of this source of the tendency to affiliate with others. The body of supportive research associated with it testifies to the fact that a vitally important source of people's desire to interact with others stems from a need to hold correct beliefs about themselves and their environment.

Emotional Arousal and Affiliation

Apart from Festinger's work, which had indicated that the drive for self-evaluation is a force acting on people to associate with others, Stanley Schachter (1959) observed that "we have no precise idea of the circumstances that drive men either to seek one another out or to crave privacy'' (p. 1). To better understand the nature of these circumstances, Schachter began by examining the autobiographical reports of persons who had experienced severe social deprivation (e.g., religious hermits, prisoners of war). These accounts illustrated that absolute social isolation can be devastatingly painful and produce such varied and dramatic effects as hallucinations, extreme apathy, and, frequently, severe anxiety. Schachter reasoned on an intuitive basis that if isolation produces anxiety, then perhaps anxiety leads to affiliation.

In *The Psychology of Affiliation* (1959), Schachter reported the results of his classic experiments designed to explore the relationship between fear and affiliation. In the first experiment, for example, some women anticipated that they would receive a series of mild-electric shocks while other women expected strong shocks. Since there was a ten-minute delay before the shocks could be administered, the women could choose to wait alone or they could wait with some of the other participants. A strong positive relationship between fear and the desire to associate with others was found. Subsequent experimentation by Schachter and others (e.g., Zimbardo and Formica, 1963) revealed that, as Schachter put it, "misery doesn't love just any kind of company, it loves only miserable company" (p. 24). People generally prefer to affiliate with others who are in much the same situation and who are responding with approximately the same emotional intensity as well (e.g., Darley and Aronson, 1966).

Further experimentation has suggested that under certain conditions, however, emotionality may lead to a heightened desire to avoid the company of others. Sarnoff and Zimbardo (1961), for example, replicated Schachter's results under fear of shock conditions but not when oral anxiety was induced by instructing the participants that the experimental procedure required them to suck on objects associated with infantile oral behavior. The latter manipulation reduced rather than increased affiliative tendencies, presumably because the participants felt embarrassed by their anxiety and/or the anticipated task. The fact that heightened emotion may not always lead to increased affiliation tendency is also clear in evidence presented by Latané and Wheeler (1966). Men who participated in a body search following an airplane crash and who were also highly emotional about it indicated little desire to talk to others, while nonemotional men wrote more letters home and also wanted to talk to others more. In a review of these and other studies, Wheeler (1974) concludes that the choice between affiliation or solitude under conditions of emotional arousal "may be mediated by (a) the desire to avoid embarrassment or a depressive reaction; (b) the absence of any need to reduce uncertainty; or (c) a desire to avoid having the emotional response further stimulated" (p. 318).

Interest in the mediators of the emotional arousal-affiliation relationship has continued (e.g., Friedman, 1981), and the need to reduce uncertainty has been clearly identified as one of these. Emotional arousal may be associated with uncertainty along a number of dimensions, including the appropriateness of one's own emotional response to the situation (e.g., Gerard, 1963; Gerard and Rabbie, 1961). Appropriateness of response often may be best assessed through comparison with the responses of others in a similar situation. Another mediating factor appears to be the individual's birth order. Schachter (1959) and others (e.g., Helmreich and Collins, 1967) have found evidence that firstborn children have stronger affiliative needs under conditions of emotional arousal than do later-borns. Firstborns also appear to like those with whom they share stress more than later-borns do, and they appear to be more likely to avoid affiliation when it might stimulate or intensify negative emotions (e.g., Darley and Aronson, 1966).

Under conditions of emotional arousal people may seek out others not only to obtain social comparison information but also, as Schachter (1959) observed, to learn ways of escape from the situation, for more general reasons of cognitive clarity about the nature of the situation and its meaning, for indirect anxiety reduction through distraction and diversion, and for direct anxiety reduction through reassurance and through other processes. With respect to this last condition evidence indicates that both people and animals in stressful stiuations sometimes show less severe physiological disturbance if another animal of the same species is present, particularly a familiar animal who remains calm (see Epley, 1974, 1975, for reviews). Latané and Glass (1968), for example, found that rats who were placed in a fear-arousing situation accompanied by a fellow rat showed less fear than did those who confronted the frightening situation with only a red toy car for companionship. Even those rats whose companion rat was anesthetized, and therefore immobile and oblivious to the world, showed less fear than those who met their fate alone.

Loneliness

A number of theorists and investigators have recently examined the experience of loneliness (e.g., see Peplau and Perlman, 1982; Weiss, 1973) and have found it to be strongly linked to feelings of sadness, desperation, boredom, restlessness, and other forms of unhappiness. Although few people ever experience the absolute social deprivation of a religious hermit or shipwrecked castaway, loneliness is not an uncommon human experience, if a national survey cited by Weiss (1973) is any indication. When people were asked, "During the past few weeks, did you ever feel very lonely or remote from other people?" 26 percent responded that they had.

A remoteness from other people suggests a physical remoteness, but investigators currently take a far more sophisticated approach to the problem of loneliness, an approach that allows for the fact that an individual may feel lonely in a crowd. Weiss (1973), for example, has observed that "loneliness appears always to be a response to the absence of some particular type of relationship or, more accurately, a response to the absence of some particular relational provision" (p. 17). He has hypothesized that two types of relational deficits are common and lead to two major types of loneliness (Weiss, 1973, pp. 18–19):

> We have repeatedly found in our studies that a form of loneliness that appears in the absence of a close emotional attachment, which we characterize as "the loneliness of emotional isolation," can only be remedied by the integration of another emotional attachment or the reintegration of the one that had been lost.

Conversely, we have found that the form of loneliness associated with the absence of an engaging social network—the "loneliness of social isolation"—can be remedied only by access to such a network.

Apart from identifying the state of loneliness and devising scales to measure it (e.g., Rubenstein and Shaver, 1980; Russell, Peplau, and Ferguson, 1978), investigators have also been interested in the attributions people make for the cause of their loneliness (e.g., self-blaming attributions versus external environmental attributions) and the influence these perceptions are likely to have upon the perpetuation of loneliness. Childhood antecedents of adult loneliness are also beginning to be explored (Shaver and Rubenstein, 1980), as are such contemporaneous factors as physical isolation from others. The identification and investigation of factors that play a role in loneliness and in many other attraction phenomena have been complemented by a growing interest in social networks.

Social Networks

The term *social network* refers to those persons with whom an individual is in *actual* contact (see Holland and Leinhardt, 1979; Leinhardt, 1977). As contrasted to a sociometric network, derived from measures of the extent to which a restricted number of individuals desire to interact with each other, social network analysis attempts to determine with whom and how frequently individuals actually do interact with each other.

Although questions of attraction only occasionally have been addressed through the use of social network theory (e.g., Ridley and Avery, 1979), interest in social networks has increased as attraction researchers have recognized that attraction to another always takes place within a relationship and that the social context surrounding the relationship imposes constraints upon it. The number and the nature of the other persons with whom the individual and the other in a relationship frequently interact, as well as the number and the nature of the persons potentially available to each for interaction, form a significant portion of that social context, and it, in turn, undoubtedly affects attraction. For example, the existence of other persons within the individual's social network who can and may provide the same social rewards the other can (or the lack of such persons) is bound to affect the generation and maintenance of an individual's attraction to that other. Further, the size and nature of a person's social network is likely to affect the

individual's Cl_{alt}, which may affect the stability of the relationship between the individual and the other.

Social network data are usually obtained by the researcher asking people to recall with whom they have interacted and how frequently. A technique superior to those that rely upon the individual's long-term memory, however, has been devised by Wheeler and Nezlek (1977). Their interaction record (IR) requires the individual to complete a short fixed-format diary for every social interaction that occurs during a specified interval (e.g., two weeks) and that is ten minutes or longer. A social interaction is defined as any encounter with another person(s) in which the individual attends to the other and adjusts his or her behavior in response to the other. Wheeler and Nezlek report acceptable levels of reliability for the IR despite the fact that it is demanding for the respondent. The IR technique is currently being used to construct an individual's social network as well as to examine various hypotheses relevant to attraction. For example, Reis, Nezlek, and Wheeler (1980) found that physical attractiveness was strongly related to the quantity of social interaction for men, with attractive men showing more interactions with the opposite sex and fewer interactions with persons of the same sex.

ATTRACTION AS A CONSEQUENCE OF AFFILIATION

Not only has attraction often been assumed to be a necessary and sufficient condition for affiliation, but the fact of affiliation itself has also been assumed to frequently lead to attraction. Indeed, the association between close physical proximity and attraction is one of the best documented within the attraction literature.

Physical Proximity and Attraction

Numerous studies have found an association between the sheer physical distance between one individual and another and the extent to which they find each other attractive. For example, Nahemow and Lawton (1975) found that among the elderly residents of a city housing project, 88 percent of all first-chosen friends lived in the same building as the individual and almost half lived on the same floor. Friendships with others more distant tended to occur primarily when certain factors known to be associated with attraction (e.g., similarity) were present; when they were not present, friendship was found to occur almost exclusively when the individuals lived in close proximity.

The positive correlation between physical proximity and attraction in part may be due to the fact that people who like each other tend to move into close proximity to each other; the achievement of physical proximity, then, often may be a consequence of attraction. It also has been demonstrated, however, that proximity often facilitates the development of attraction. Segal (1974), for example, found that among police trainees who were assigned to rooms and to classroom seats in the alphabetical order of their surnames, the closer together in the alphabet the surnames of any two trainees were, the more likely it was that they would name each other as being one of their closest friends in the group. Similarly, Newcomb (1961) found that proximity frequently overcomes dissimilarity in friendship formation, for even dissimilar roommates were likely to become friends.

The degree of physical distance between two people usually approximates the degree to which they are available and accessible to each other for interaction. That this is not always true, however, and that it is availability rather than physical distance that is important for friendship formation, was demonstrated by Festinger, Schachter, and Back (1950) in their investigation of the development of friendships in a new housing project for married students. For example, persons who lived physically close to others but whose house faced in a direction opposite to the others (and who thus were less accessible) had many fewer friendships than those who were an equal distance away but whose houses faced each other.

Physical proximity also has been shown to be an important factor in mate selection, where, as in other types of social choice, selection must be made within a field of availables (see Kerckhoff, 1974). Physical proximity helps define the field of availables, but other factors that affect interaction availability undoubtedly contribute as well. Persons who by virtue of their occupation or ill health, or who for other reasons have neither the time, the energy, nor the inclination for social interaction, tend not to be in an individual's field of availables even though they may be within close physical proximity.

Social norms also influence another's availability. Such norms clearly operate in mate selection, and Winch (1958) introduced the phrase *field of eligibles* to refer to those categories of persons that society deems to be appropriate candidates for marriage. Kerckhoff (1974) observes that "these categories are, for the most part, defined in terms of endogenous marriage patterns—the tendency to prefer to marry someone in one's own racial group, religious denomination, social class, general age category and so on" (pp. 61–62). Social norms undoubt-edly affect availability in a number of ways. For example, third persons are more likely to actively prevent interaction opportunities with those who fail to fall into the field of eligibles for an activity; at the least, they may fail to facilitate interaction with them.

Mediators of the Relationship Between Accessibility and Attraction

Although people are more likely to interact with those who are easily accessible for interaction than those who are not, whether that interaction will result in attraction or dislike obviously depends upon the content of the interaction (e.g., the rewards received or anticipated and the information conveyed and impressions formed). Documentation of that fundamental truth and evidence that the fact of interaction itself does not inevitably produce attraction have been amply supplied by efforts to reduce prejudice between hostile groups by simply bringing them together in close proximity (e.g., see Sherif, Harvey, White, Hood, and Sherif, 1954; Stephan, 1978; and Chapter 24 of this *Handbook*). It is also supported by evidence that proximity to a disliked other increases dislike, whereas proximity to a liked person appears to enhance attraction to them (Schiffenbauer and Schiavo, 1976).

Apart from the precise content of the interaction and the previous feelings and attitudes people bring to it, evidence suggests that, other things being equal, interaction with another may more frequently lead to attraction than not. The hypothesis that interaction should often lead to attraction can be derived from a number of theoretical frameworks. Heider's (1958) balance theory, for example, predicts that the appropriate sentiment relationship may be induced from the existence of a unit relationship created by frequent interaction. Most exchange theories, too, would predict that interaction may frequently lead to attraction, since the proximity usually implied by interaction reduces the costs involved in relationship transactions.

In addition to the facts that proximity and interaction with another may initiate cognitive consistency processes that facilitate attraction and that proximity may also reduce the price of social exchange, a number of factors intrinsic to most social interactions may lead to attraction as well. One of these factors is that the very meaning of the word *interaction* implies a responsivity of two entities to each other.

Responsiveness.   To act and to have another respond to one's action may be in itself—and apart from the content of the action or the response—one rewarding by-product of social interaction. Some suggestive evidence that it is has been gathered by Latané and his colleagues (see Latané and Hothersall, 1972), who have examined some of the determinants of affiliation among rats. Although rats have been thought to be unsociable creatures for a number of reasons, including the fact that they show little interest in peering at another caged rat with whom they cannot interact, rats placed together in an open field approach each other and maintain greater-than-chance proximity. Since rats are not interested in each other in the one situation but are in the other, Latané and Glass (1968) reasoned that an important factor in interrodent attraction is the rats' responsiveness to each other in interaction.

To test this hypothesis, Latané and Glass placed rats in an open field either alone, with another normal rat, with an anesthetized rat, with a stationary toy car, or with a moving car that was preprogrammed and so was not responsive to the rat. As measured by approach and distance-maintaining behavior, the rats overwhelmingly preferred the normal rat over the anesthetized rat and over either of the two toys. In subsequent studies, in fact, Latané and his associates found that rats placed together in a large enclosure and allowed to run freely spent from 50 to 70 percent of their time interacting with each other—chasing and sniffing each other, climbing over and under each other, and so on. Latané and Hothersall (1972) conclude that what accounts for most of the attraction rats have for each other in this open-field situation is the mutual responsiveness of the interaction; even a human hand projecting into the open field through a slot was attractive to the rats as long as it was active and responsive (Werner and Latané, 1974).

Responsiveness also seems to be an important quality of human interaction and one that may produce or increase attraction to another (e.g., Werner and Latané, 1974). Davis (1982) and her associates define interpersonal responsiveness in terms of three sequential response contingencies:

1. The probability with which each person in the interaction responds to the communicative behaviors of the other.

2. The proportion of responses that are related in content to the preceding behaviors of the other.

3. The proportion of responses that are of the appropriate (or demanded by the other) degree of elabora-

tion (e.g., a monosyllabic response versus an extensive comment).

Davis and Perkowitz (1979) found some evidence to support their contention that both the other's probability of response and his or her proportion of content-related responses influence attraction. Responsiveness (in terms of acknowledgment or acceptance of the other's influence attempts) has also been recently found to differentiate distressed and nondistressed marital couples (Koren, Carlton, and Shaw, 1980), as has reciprocity (Gottman, 1979), defined as occurring when the conditional probability of the other's response to the individual's previous behavior is significantly greater than the unconditional probability of that same response.

Responsiveness in interaction is important for a number of reasons. Davis (1982) observes that since repeated failure to respond will ultimately result in a termination of the interaction, responsiveness to another is usually necessary to maintain interaction. Furthermore, the responsiveness of the other generally enhances the individual's degree of predictability and control over the relationship, and this control, in turn, may facilitate the individual's interaction goals. In addition, a lack of responsiveness on the part of the other probably communicates that "the other is interested neither in oneself nor in what one has to say" (Davis and Perkowitz, 1979, p. 536) and, thus, that the other is neither attracted to oneself nor to the relationship.

But beyond the secondary rewards that may be obtained in social interaction only if the other is responsive, there may be something fundamentally rewarding about the responsiveness of one's environment, whether that environment be physical or social. To have one's person or behavior make a difference in the world would seem to be rewarding in itself. Just how much the factor of making a difference may be valued by the human under some conditions can be seen in almost any grammar school classroom where misbehavior, guaranteed to bring the punishment of authority and the derision of peers, is often engaged in only for the sake of the response it elicits from teachers and fellow students. When it is ignored, it often extinguishes, as Patterson and his colleagues have shown (e.g., Patterson, Cobb, and Ray, 1972); its primary value sometimes is simply obtaining a response from others, and even negative responses may be preferable to indifference. The responsiveness of others, then, may partially satisfy what has been termed "effectance motivation" (White, 1959), or the motivation to discover the effects of one's behavior on the environment. To discover that one does have an effect has implications for the control of one's rewards and punishments in the future (see Seligman, 1975) and may eventually acquire value in itself.

The implications of the responsiveness concept for attraction is far reaching, for it intuitively seems possible that people might prefer to occasionally interact with those whose behavior is responsive although punishing to those whose behavior is noncontingent but always rewarding. Needless to say, this hypothesis is in need of test. At the least, the interaction responsivity of another would seem to be especially deserving of additional investigation since it would seem to have both direct and indirect effects upon attraction.

Familiarity.   Close physical proximity with another almost always results in increases in familiarity with that other, whether interaction occurs or not and despite the content of that interaction if it does occur. At least two lines of investigation suggest that, other things being equal, familiarity should lead to attraction. The first stems from Bowlby's (e.g., 1969, 1973) theory of attachment; the second derives from the mere exposure hypothesis.

Attachment.   Bowlby, along with other psychologists and ethologists who take an evolutionary point of view, maintains that the primary purpose of affectional bonds is to promote the individual's physical proximity to other members of the species who can and will act to protect the individual from survival threats. Particularly for the infant or child some instinctive proximity-promoting mechanism that leads the individual to stay physically close to persons who can supply food and shelter and protection from disease and injury is essential.

That most animals are born with such a mechanism was first dramatically demonstrated by Lorenz (e.g., 1952) in his classic imprinting experiments. Its importance was later demonstrated in Harlow's work with monkeys (e.g., 1958, 1971), which showed that the failure of the affectional system to develop normally, especially in the infant-mother relationship, may impair the individual's later socioemotional adjustments. Human infants, too, quickly develop a strong preference for a person who meets certain minimum visual, auditory, or tactile requirements and who also is the first they've become familiar with—most usually the infant's caretaker, typically the infant's mother—and they exhibit attachment behavior toward that person.

Attachment behavior has been conceived as behavior that has two distinctive features: First, it results in the achievement or maintenance of proximity between one individual and another; for example, "whether the behavior is crying, calling, following, clinging, or any other, if it results in proximity it counts as attachment behavior" (Bowlby, 1973, pp. 42–43). Second, it is usually exhibited by a younger, or subordinate, or weaker animal toward an older, or more dominant, or stronger one. Although attachment behavior is especially evident between the child's first and third years, Bowlby argues that attachment behavior characterizes people of all ages, and "so far from its being regressive, as is sometimes suggested, attachment behavior is a normal and healthy part of human nature from the cradle to the grave" (1973, p. 46). This conclusion is based on evidence that attachment behavior is elicited particularly easily and intensely in animals that are especially vulnerable to predators because of size or condition (e.g., illness or injury) and evidence that attachment behavior is always elicited at high intensity in situations of alarm. These events may occur at any age, and thus attachment behavior in adults is likely to be evident when the individual is distressed, ill, or afraid, as Festinger's supposition that the experience of emotion leads to a desire to communicate with others suggests and as Schachter's work on fear and affiliation supports.

Attachment theory and research has a number of unexplored implications for the study of interpersonal attraction. Among these implications is the hypothesis, first advanced by Freud and endorsed by attachment theory, that the nature of a person's affectional bonds in adult life is significantly determined by the nature of the affectional events, or lack of them, that have taken place during childhood, particularly within the child-mother relationship. It was, in fact, the observation of the association between the disruption of child-mother bonds and later psychopathology that led Bowlby to examine the function and development of affectional bonds.

Interest in the hypothesis that disruption of childhood attachments affects adult affectional behavior has escalated in recent years as the divorce rate and fragmentation of the traditional family unit has increased. Pertinent evidence largely remains restricted, however, to studies of the effect of parental divorce on the mental health and adjustment of children (e.g., Hetherington, Cox, and Cox, 1979). How children from homes disrupted by death, divorce, or marital separation fare in their adult attachments, particularly in heterosexual bonding (which is, along with infant-caretaker bonding, the most frequent form of bonding in most species), seldom has been systematically examined (but see Shaver and Rubenstein, 1980, for an exception), although it remains the object of much clinical observation and gloomy speculation (e.g., Klimek, 1979). The view that an individual's childhood emotional pattern significantly determines the emotional pattern with the spouse, and identification of the causal pathways between the two, also receives only clinical anecdotal support (e.g., Saul, 1979).

Perhaps the most interesting feature of attachment theory for students of attraction, however, is that it attempts to account for evidence that strong affectional preferences and bonds do not always, nor perhaps even usually in the first stages of life, follow reward-punishment principles. Thus attachment theory takes a very different view from that which has dominated the attraction literature. As Bowlby observes (1973, pp. 40–41):

> Until the mid-1950s only one view of the nature and origin of affectional bonds was prevalent, and on this matter, if on few others, psychoanalysts and learning theorists were at one. Bonds between individuals develop, it was held, because an individual discovers that, in order to reduce certain drives, e.g., for food in infancy and for sex in adult life, another human being is necessary. . . . As Anna Freud puts it, it is a cupboard love theory of human relations.

Attachment theory, then, was designed to help account for the fact that strong bonds can develop between infant and caretaker even in instances where punishment has been predominant. The proximity-seeking behaviors of a battered child, puppy, or kitten toward the punishing adult caretaker are particularly poignant examples that attachments can develop and persevere despite repeated punishments from the attachment figure. So, too, is the continuing devotion of some parents to their children in the face of the chronic grief their offspring inspire. And the persistence of some adult marital and other relationships that outside observers can only believe to contain little reward and a great deal of punishment provides yet another example. To term the approach and proximity-maintaining behavior of such individuals toward the source of their pain as *masochistic* describes, but does not explain, the behavior. At the least, the frequency of such behavior constitutes an important exception to the "We like those who reward us and dis-

like those who punish us" rule, and it deserves more consideration than it has yet received.

Attachment theory and research also underscore the necessity for more careful conceptualization of the attraction construct. Proximity-seeking and -maintaining behavior has frequently been assumed to be a good behavioral index of attraction to another when attraction has been defined as the positivity of feeling and appraisal of the other. That attachment behavior and attraction responses on various paper-and-pencil measures frequently diverge is becoming apparent in examination of reactions to marital separation (see Weiss, 1975). People often attempt to regain proximity with disliked spouses after the physical separation for which they fervently wished and may have initiated has actually occurred. Such phenomena, confusing to the individuals involved as well as to investigators who take a strong reinforcement view of attraction, require careful consideration of the meaning of the term *attraction* as well as attention to its varieties.

And finally, attachment theory and research suggests that some theories of interpersonal attraction may be more useful at some developmental stages of individuals and of relationships than at others. Examination of developmental attraction phenomena has been neglected, but as interest in these phenomena increases, the work of ethologists and developmental and clinical psychologists may prove to be especially helpful.

Mere exposure.   Other evidence also suggests that frequent interaction between two individuals should lead to attraction, other things being equal. It has been hypothesized that simple repeated exposure to a stimulus is a sufficient condition for the enhancement of attraction toward that stimulus. The mere exposure hypothesis was introduced by Zajonc (1968), who found support for it in the results of studies that showed an association between familiarity and positive reactions to words, music, art, and other aesthetic stimuli. Zajonc also presented evidence that when individuals were exposed in varying frequencies to graduation portraits of men, their ratings of their liking for each man as a person increased with increases in their familiarity with the portrait.

The exposure-attraction hypothesis has been the focus of a great many investigations (for reviews, see Harrison, 1977; Hill, 1978). In general, and as Harrison (1977) summarizes, this research documents that repeated exposure to a stimulus leads to liking for it under a wide range of conditions, including conditions in which the exposures have been reduced to a fraction of a second. Furthermore, the effect seems to hold whether the initial affective reaction to the stimulus is positive or negative (although the negative reactions investigated can only be said to have been mild; e.g., Zajonc, Markus, and Wilson, 1974) and despite the degree of positivity of the context in which the stimulus is encountered. It should be noted, however, that most of the experiments using social stimuli have represented other persons only by name or by photograph (but see Saegert, Swap, and Zajonc, 1973).

One possible limitation to the generality of the mere exposure hypothesis has been uncovered. Attraction often does not seem to increase indefinitely with successive exposures to the stimulus, and in some cases, repeated exposure appears to lead to decreases in attraction. One factor that appears to be important in determining the individual's response to a highly familiar stimulus is the period of time that has elapsed between exposure to the stimulus and the rating of its attractiveness. Studies conducted both with humans and with lower animals have suggested to Hill (1978) that repeated exposure to a stimulus tends to produce a long-term increase in preference for it but a short-term decrease (or reduced preference immediately following exposure). How attractive familiar persons are, then, may depend on how long one has been away from them, other things being equal.

Even aside from the time at which the attraction measure is taken, other factors may not be equal, even in highly controlled, noninteractive laboratory situations, and when one considers the effect of repeated exposure through actual interaction in naturalistic situations, the likelihood that other things will be equal diminishes markedly. Most social interactions, in addition to increasing exposure to the other, also monumentally increase the amount of information the individual has about the other, and this information, in turn, may overwhelm any attraction effects that might otherwise have been obtained as function of mere exposure. However, the degree of exposure to another's name, photo, or other products prior to interaction may lead the individual to initiate actual interaction with the other. Brockner and Swap (1976), for example, found that the more frequently individuals had seen another, the more they chose to interact with and to disclose intimate items of personal information to that other. Increased exposure prior to interaction, then, may be one determinant of voluntary affiliation.

Consideration of the probable effect of repeated exposure upon attraction in naturalistic settings also may require some attention to the variety of attraction that may or may not result from increased familiarity with the other. For example, a good deal of research suggests that increased familiarity diminishes rather than increases sexual attraction [see Dewsbury (1981) for a review of evidence gathered from infrahuman animals relevant to the Coolidge effect hypothesis]. Much of the evidence with respect to humans comes from cross-cultural studies (see Rosenblatt and Anderson, 1981, for a review). The most frequently cited study was conducted by Talmon (1964), who found that marriage rarely, if ever, takes place between male and female children raised together from infancy in Israeli kibbutzim. Although this finding has a number of alternative explanations, other cross-cultural work (e.g., Wolf, 1966) also suggests that when familiarity between opposite-sex persons is high, sexual attraction is unlikely to occur.

Whatever the extent to which simple repeated exposure to another accounts for variance in attraction to others in naturalistic settings, the large volume of evidence that supports the general familiarity-attraction relationship testifies that attraction may be generated by a factor that does not easily fit into a reward-punishment attraction framework (at least without stretching the meaning of *reward* beyond popular recognition and usefulness). In this regard, the mere exposure hypothesis and evidence bear marked similarity to attachment theory and evidence: Both assume and demonstrate that simple exposure to another may lead to attraction, despite the fact that the other may be punishing or negatively regarded. Both also draw, at least in part, upon an evolutionary interpretation of their predictions and findings, specifically, the survival value of remaining in proximity to the familiar (and safe) and of avoiding the unfamiliar (and therefore potentially dangerous). Attachment theory, tested largely with children and lower animals, has almost exclusively used approach behavior as an index of attraction. The mere exposure research has demonstrated that the general shape of the familiarity-attraction effect may be obtained in noncritical periods of development (e.g., with adults) with both social and nonsocial stimuli and can be exhibited as well upon traditional attraction-rating scales requiring, one may presume, some conscious cognitive mediation. As attraction researchers become more interested in identifying the determinants of attraction in long-term relationships and in understanding the effects of separation from familiar (although sometimes punishing) partners, the findings produced by attachment theory and the mere exposure hypothesis may be useful.

SUMMARY

Although attraction to another is undoubtedly one of the most important determinants of attempts to affiliate with that other, people approach and maintain interaction with others for a variety of reasons, some of which have little to do with feelings of liking for the other or with positive regard for the other's qualities. Thus attraction researchers have increasingly recognized that attraction is not a necessary condition for affiliation, at least when attraction is viewed as anything other than approach behavior toward another person. Investigators have also documented that attraction is not sufficient for approach attempts to be made, for a variety of factors may intervene to inhibit such attempts. Just as attraction is neither necessary nor sufficient for affiliation, affiliation itself is neither necessary nor sufficient for attraction to occur. Nevertheless, a good deal of theory and evidence suggests that, other things being equal, physical proximity to and frequent interaction with another may be more likely than not to lead to attraction.

Despite the conceptual ease and empirical usefulness of distinguishing between such factors as liking for another, desire to affiliate with another, and actual attempts to approach or maintain an association with another, the interpersonal attraction literature is still rife with confusions among these factors and with assumptions about their presumed correspondence to one another. In large part this confusion has been the result of a failure to explicate the attraction construct. It also, however, has been the result of studying attraction outside its natural social context, where factors external to the individual and his or her desires often act to inhibit or prevent association with some people and to virtually dictate association with certain others.

ATTRACTION AND INITIAL ENCOUNTERS

As we have discussed, attraction to another frequently has been presumed to be the primary motivation underlying attempts to initiate, develop, and maintain a relation-

ship with that other. The investigation of the role that attraction actually plays in the initiation and subsequent developmental course of a relationship has required consideration of the concept of relationship and of what, therefore, constitutes the beginning of a relationship.

THE INITIATION OF RELATIONSHIPS IN OPEN-FIELD SETTINGS

The term *relationship* has been defined in myriad ways. Nevertheless, as Kelley, Berscheid, Christensen, Harvey, Huston, Levinger, McClintock, Peplau, and Peterson (1983) observe, virtually all conceptualizations of the relationship construct refer to the fact that persons who are in a relationship with one another have some sort of causal impact on each other's behavior. That is, some events associated with the other cause a change in the state of the individual (e.g., a change in internal physiological state, a change in cognitive state, and/or a change in overt actions)—a change from what that state otherwise would have been had the event associated with the other not occurred.

The *beginning* of a relationship, then, can be conceptually traced to the first time that the other has caused some change in the individual, and frequently, that first change is a change in the individual's attention. Levinger and Snoek (1972), for example, suggest that "the beginnings of a relationship appear when one person becomes aware of another. In defining this level, it is unimportant whether O in turn notices P. The only pertinent event is that P has information that forms the basis for his unilateral evaluation of O" (p. 6). Thus the problem of predicting the initiation of relationships in open-field situations has been viewed as a problem of selective attention: "Given a potential initiator, in a social environment consisting of relatively unfamiliar others A, B, C, . . . , N, to whom, if to any of these, will P spontaneously attend?" (Berscheid and Graziano, 1979, p. 36).

Social Attention

The prototypical problem in relationship initiation, then, is viewed as analogous to that of predicting to whom a person standing at the threshold of a cocktail party will award his or her attention, and all theories of selective attention and related data become directly relevant to the problem (see Berscheid and Graziano, 1979). Unfortunately, these theories, as well as most investigations of attention phenomena, focus almost exclusively upon the perception of physical stimuli, for only recently have social psychologists (e.g., Taylor and Fiske, 1978) become interested in the question of attention in social contexts.

Two principles, novelty and importance, appear to govern attentional processes in general (e.g., see Berlyne, 1960). Stimuli that are novel (that are unfamiliar, for example, or that disconfirm the individual's expectations about them) have been demonstrated to capture attention in competition with less novel stimuli. Furthermore, stimuli that are important to the individual are more likely to capture attention than stimuli of lesser importance. What is important to any given person is a motivational question, and thus the problem of selective attention to social stimuli in an open field is partially a motivational one, which complicates it considerably. The number of needs that individuals may experience at any given point in their lives—and the extent to which another may be perceived as possessing the potential to satisfy each of these needs—is infinite, and yet knowledge of these factors is critical to assessing the importance of a stimulus to an individual.

One general principle underlying the importance of another has been suggested, however. Berscheid and Graziano (1979) have hypothesized that there is a direct relationship between another's importance and the individual's outcome dependence upon that other. Extrapolating from Thibaut and Kelley's (1959) social exchange theory, they theorize that an individual is outcome-dependent upon another to the extent that the individual has some need, the individual perceives that the other possesses resources that would satisfy that need, and the individual's subjective probability that the other may deliver or withhold those resources is less than certainty. Thus they argue (Berscheid and Graziano, 1979, p. 41):

> Persons who possess no power to affect our welfare and persons who do possess such power but are unlikely to use it are unlikely targets for our attention and for relationship initiation. These are also the people for whom, according to attraction theorists who take a social-exchange approach, we are unlikely to develop affection or dislike, for they are irrelevant to us and indifference is our probable response to them.

To test the hypothesis that there is a correspondence between the importance principle, attention, and attraction, Berscheid, Graziano, Monson, and Dermer (1976) devised an experimental situation in which an individual's outcome dependence upon each of three equally unfamiliar others differed. It was found that when novelty was controlled, the amount of attention spontaneously awarded to another in an open field increased monotonically with increases in the degree to which individuals believed they were dependent upon the other for their outcomes. Moreover, those who were highly outcome-dependent upon the other generally tended to remember more about the other, to evaluate the other more confidently and with more extreme ratings on a variety of traits, and to regard the other as more attractive.

Attention and Attraction

The notion that attention and attraction are directly associated has a good deal of precedent in folklore [e.g., "You never pay any attention to me; (therefore) you don't love me anymore!"], and it receives experimental support as well. For example, people placed in open fields that include both physically attractive and unattractive people award the attractive more visual attention (e.g., Dion, 1977; Fugita, Agle, Newman, and Walfish, 1977). Furthermore, Kleck and Rubenstein (1975) found that in a conversational interview setting, a physically attractive woman elicited more smiling and visual attention from her male partner, and later, the men reported having thought more about the attractive woman, remembered more about her appearance, and indicated more liking for her than did men who interacted with an unattractive woman. Exline (1971) has concluded from his studies, in fact, that there is "rather good evidence that persons are more prone to engage in mutual glances when they find the relationship with another attractive rather than aversive" (p. 181), and other researchers (e.g., Mehrabian, 1972; Rubin, 1974) have also argued that the more a person likes or loves another, the more he or she looks at him or her.

However, other investigators (e.g., Berscheid and Graziano, 1979; Harrison, 1977) have concluded that attention to another is probably a poor indicant of attraction in most settings for a number of reasons. Perhaps the most important reason is that social stimuli in naturalistic situations differ not only in importance to the individual but also in novelty. People may pay little or no attention to attractive others simply because these individuals have become familiar and predictable, and in the fierce competition for attention more novel and unpredictable stimuli tend to win out (Berscheid, Brothen, and Graziano, 1976). Thus the relationship between attention to others and attraction for others is complex. The importance of social stimuli is a central consideration in attraction, and it is also, other things being equal, a central factor in attention. The critical element that is often not equal, however, but that is of import in determining attention, is the extent to which the other constitutes a novel, unfamiliar, or incongruous stimulus; although such stimuli invite attention, they are not necessarily regarded as attractive.

Whether a relationship with another is spontaneously initiated in an open-field situation, then, probably depends both upon the kinds of people the individual regards as unfamiliar and unpredictable and upon the degree to which those persons are regarded by the individual as important. Since the latter factor engages the question of the motivational state of the individual, which will influence degree of attention to another in the first place, it also influences how the information gained about the other as a result of that attention is cognitively processed. [Unfortunately, most current information-processing models of impression formation neglect the role of motivation (see Schneider, Hastorf, and Ellsworth, 1979, for a review).] How the information is processed will undoubtedly affect whether attraction develops in the initial stage of the relationship. For example, Stephan, Berscheid, and Walster (1971) found that men who evaluated a woman while sexually aroused perceived her to be a very different kind of person and more attractive than did men who formed an impression of her from the same information but who were not aroused.

Despite the great variety of specific motivational and experiential factors that may determine whether an individual attends to another and subsequently attempts to further their relationship with them, a good deal is known about the general factors that are associated with attraction to another once an initial encounter has occurred—whether due to the individual's spontaneous initiation of that encounter or to their finding themselves in a closed field with the other.

DETERMINANTS OF ATTRACTION IN INITIAL ENCOUNTERS

To investigate the determinants of attraction in initial encounters, investigators typically have brought two persons, strangers to one another, into the laboratory where, at the instigation of the experimenter (and to earn $2 or two experimental points), they are often directed to consider certain information about the other (e.g., the

other's responses to an attitude questionnaire, a photo of the other, or a list of personality traits the other presumably possesses) and then to report their degree of liking or disliking for the other. For the participants such experimental situations represent a closed field; that is, the individual's attention is directed by the experimenter toward a particular other (or toward artifacts produced by the other), and participants usually comply for reasons apart from an intrinsic desire to know and interact with the other to the exclusion of available alternative activities. Three factors have been demonstrated to be especially potent precursors of attraction in such encounters: the physical attractiveness of the other, the similarity of the other to the individual, and the degree to which the individual presumes the other likes or dislikes him or her.

Physical Attractiveness and Attraction

Interest in the role that another's physical appearance plays in generating attraction to him or her is relatively recent. It was not so long ago that Lindzey (1965) noted the neglect of morphological factors within psychology and called for their investigation in his presidential address to APA's Division 8. A few years later Aronson (1969) commented specifically upon the strange neglect within the attraction area of one morphological factor, physical attractiveness, and suggested that social psychologists may have been reluctant to investigate this "undemocratic" variable for fear of discovering it to be a potent determinant of attraction.

If social psychologists were initially reluctant to confront the possibility that physical attractiveness plays a role in social interaction, they have overcome that reluctance with a vengeance. The impact of physical attractiveness upon attraction was first demonstrated by Walster, Aronson, Abrahams, and Rottman (1966), who, as previously described, found that among students who attended a college computer dance, physical attractiveness alone was associated with attraction. And today the physical attractiveness literature is one of the largest within the attraction area (for reviews, see Adams and Crossman, 1978; Berscheid and Walster, 1974b; Huston and Levinger, 1978). For example, in just the years 1972 through 1976 more than 40 studies were conducted pertaining to physical appearance and attraction (see Huston and Levinger, 1978). The bulk of these investigations reveal that the effects of an individual's physical attractiveness are pervasive in frequency, considerable in strength, and generally monolithic in nature. They are such that the physically attractive—across age, sex, race, and all socioeconomic stations—receive numerous preferential social treatments.

For example, the influence of physical attractiveness appears to begin virtually from the moment infants draw their first breath (Corter, Trehub, Boudydis, Ford, Celhoffer, and Minde, 1978; Hildebrandt and Fitzgerald, 1976; Langlois, 1981). The correspondence between a child's physical attractiveness in nursery and elementary school and his or her peer popularity has been demonstrated by a number of investigators (e.g., Dion and Berscheid, 1974; Kleck, Richardson, and Ronald, 1974), and evidence suggests, too, that teachers give attractive children more information, better evaluations, more opportunity to perform, and more support to their educational endeavors (e.g., Adams and LaVoie, 1974; Clifford and Walster, 1973).

A person's physical attractiveness also affects the kind of treatment he or she receives from other authorities. For example, physically attractive children who have committed a transgression seem to be dealt with less severely by adults than are unattractive children who have committed the identical transgression (e.g., Dion, 1972), and mock jury research suggests that unattractive individuals are often treated more harshly (e.g., receive longer jail sentences) than attractive defendants (e.g., Efran, 1974; Stewart, 1980), although this effect may depend on the nature of the crime (e.g., Sigall and Ostrove, 1975). Attractive people also receive more assistance in general from others (e.g., Benson, Karabenick, and Lerner, 1976); people are more likely to cooperate with them in conflict situations (e.g., Sigall, Page, and Brown, 1971); and the job recommendations of experienced personnel consultants have been found to be influenced by the candidate's attractiveness, even when personal appearance could have no conceivable relationship to actual job performance (e.g., Cash, Gillen, and Burns, 1977). Furthermore, the physically attractive tend to be the recipients of more self-disclosure from others (e.g., Brundage, Derlega, and Cash, 1977). In general, then, physically attractive persons appear to receive virtually all of the benefits commonly associated with interpersonal attraction.

One important mediating factor of the preferential treatment accorded the physically attractive has been shown to be a physical attractiveness stereotype such that people infer a number of other desirable, but less visible, qualities from an individual's physical attractiveness level. Dion, Berscheid, and Walster (1972), for example, demonstrated that both males and females who viewed pictures of men and women of varying attractiveness lev-

els believed the physically attractive to possess numerous desirable personality traits, and they were also believed to be more likely to capture better jobs, to have more successful marriages, and to experience happier and more fulfilling lives than less attractive persons. Although a few discordant notes in the stereotype have been found (e.g., Dermer and Thiel, 1975; Wilson, Cash, and West, 1978), some of which do not always replicate (e.g., Marks, Miller, and Maruyama, 1981), the existence of a robust and strongly favorable physical attractiveness stereotype has been well documented with young children (e.g., Adams and Crane, 1980) and with various populations of adults (e.g., Adams and Huston, 1975). The inferences drawn from a person's physical attractiveness level to other personal characteristics undoubtedly account for much of the attraction generated by physically attractive persons.

Two other factors may help account for the popularity of the physically attractive. First, the physical attractiveness stereotype may contain a kernel of truth. Physical attractiveness has been shown to be associated with a positive self-concept (e.g., Lerner and Karabeneck, 1974) and with good mental health (e.g., Adams, 1981), and both attractive children and adults appear to be more assertive and self-confident than their unattractive peers (e.g., Dion and Stein, 1978; Jackson and Huston, 1975). Second, people may prefer to interact with the physically attractive not only because they are perceived to have better personalities and more opportunities than the unattractive, which indeed they may have (not the least because of the existence of a physical attractiveness stereotype that favors them), but also because association with a physically attractive person may bring an individual increased status and esteem from others. Sigall and Landy (1973), for example, asked some people to evaluate a man who was seated (and associated) with an attractive woman and others to evaluate the same man when he was with an unattractive woman. Not only did the man receive more favorable ratings when he was with the attractive woman, but his association with the unattractive woman actually detracted from the positivity of the evaluation he otherwise would have enjoyed.

The impact of a woman's physical attractiveness upon attraction and other variables has been more fully documented than the impact of a man's (see Allen, 1978), no doubt reflecting the popular belief that a woman's physical attractiveness is more important to others than is a man's. The fact that female stimuli have been largely chosen for investigation is regrettable for several reasons, one of which is that male physical attractiveness may be becoming a more important factor in opposite-sex attraction than ever before (see Berscheid, 1981). With the increased economic and legal independence of women has come unprecendented social independence, including the freedom to interact socially with and to date and to marry men for reasons other than financial security and social status.

The tendency for mate selection to be made on the basis of beauty when practical grounds are unimportant has been documented for other cultures (Rosenblatt, 1974), and the relationship between physical attractiveness and heterosexual love and marriage has been well documented for this culture (e.g., Ellis, 1954). The recent shift from practical to other grounds in women's marital choices may be evidenced in a recent replication of Kephart's (1967) study in which men and women of prime marital age were asked: "If a man (or woman) had all the other qualities you desired, would you marry this person if you were not in love with him (her)?" Whereas only 24.3 percent of Kephart's women said no, Campbell and Berscheid (1976) found that 80 percent of their women now said being in love was a necessary condition for marriage. Men, too, showed an increase, although a less dramatic one—from 65 percent in the original study saying no to 86 percent in the replication—suggesting that the importance of physical attractiveness in heterosexual dating and mating choice for both men and women is unlikely to diminish in the foreseeable future.

Another area that has not been explored as much as warranted is the impact of physical attractiveness beyond initial encounters, although many have speculated that as a relationship unfolds and additional information is received about a person, physical attractiveness effects diminish. In one of the few tests of this hypothesis Mathes (1975) asked college men and women to sign a contract to complete five dates during the course of an experiment. Mathes's hypothesis that on the first date, and possibly the second, attractiveness would strongly determine liking for the date, but on later dates, after the men and women had become more acquainted with each other, physical attractiveness would dissipate as a factor in attraction, was not confirmed. Rather, physical attractiveness increased in importance from the first date to subsequent dates.

Finally, the effects of other morphological factors upon attraction have been infrequently investigated. One obvious omission has been the relative height of the male and the female and its influence upon date and mate selection. Until very recently, only anecdotal evidence that this factor influenced heterosexual social choice existed

(see Berscheid and Walster, 1974b), but Gillis and Avis in 1980 provided documentation of its importance. These investigators collected height data (unfortunately, self-report information) from the bank account application forms of a large sample of couples and found that although chance expectation for the occurrence of couples in which the woman was taller was 2 in 100, the actual occurrence was only 1 in 720 (the number of couples in the sample). The influence of other morphological variables, such as physique, upon attraction principally has been explored with children (e.g., Lerner and Gellert, 1969), although its influence in adult attraction has captured some attention (e.g., Roberts and Herman, 1980; Wiggins, Wiggins, and Conger, 1968).

Similarity and Attraction

In his historical review of evidence pertaining to the similarity-attraction relationship, Byrne (1971) notes that even before the turn of the century Galton had found evidence of homogamy in mate selection and Pearson had hypothesized that the observed similarity between spouses was due to the selection of "like by like." Others subsequently added evidence that assortative mating occurs along the similarity dimension. Burgess and Wallin (1943), for example, found engaged couples to be similar on almost every characteristic examined. Although such correlational data frequently have been taken to indicate that people actively chose their mates and their friends on the basis of similarity, just as Pearson supposed, they do not by themselves justify such a conclusion. At least part of the association between similarity and social choice undoubtedly is due not to personal preference but to the fact that people tend to be thrown together in time and space with others similar to themselves (see Kerckhoff, 1974).

The first evidence that similarity is a causal determinant of attraction was obtained in Newcomb's (1961) classic study of friendship formation, where (as previously described) degree of preacquaintance attitudinal value similarity was found to be associated with attraction after actual association. A great deal of additional evidence that similarity, at least attitude similarity, is a determinant of attraction has been provided by Byrne and his associates (see Byrne, 1971, for a review) within the bogus stranger experimental paradigm (also previously described). Today it is accepted that similarity is a general determinant of attraction, and rather than further document this fact, investigators have attempted to identify the factors that mediate and define the boundaries of the similarity-attraction association.

Some investigators, including Byrne, believe that the discovery that another holds similar attitudes is directly reinforcing. Supporting this view are data demonstrating that positive affect is elicited by the receipt of similar attitude statements and negative affective responses are elicited by dissimilar attitude statements (e.g., Byrne and Clore, 1970), as well as data suggesting that similar and dissimilar attitude statements can act as positive and negative reinforcers, respectively, of other responses (e.g., Golightly and Byrne, 1964). In answer to the question of why similar and dissimilar attitudinal statements have reinforcing properties, a number of theorists (e.g., Byrne, 1969; Festinger, 1954; Newcomb, 1961) argue that, as Byrne (1971) puts it, "the expression of similar attitudes by a stranger serves as a positive reinforcement because consensual validation for an individual's attitudes and opinions and beliefs is a major source of reward for the drive to be logical, consistent, and accurate in interpreting the stimulus world" (p. 338).

A number of other factors help account for some similarity-attraction effects. The information that another holds similar attitudes may suggest that the other will like the individual, and it is known that the anticipation of being liked often generates attraction in return. Jones, Bell, and Aronson (1972), for example, found that when individuals were provided direct information that the other disliked (or liked) them, they disliked a similar but disliking other more than a dissimilar but liking other. Even in the face of direct information concerning the other's degree of attraction, however, similarity information probably has some effect on the amount of attraction the other generates (Byrne and Griffitt, 1966). Furthermore, people rarely have direct information concerning how much the other likes or dislikes them in naturalistic settings; they may more frequently know of some shared or dissimilar attitudes, and these, in turn, undoubtedly lead to attraction inferences. For example, Walster and Walster (1963) found that people preferred to associate with dissimilar others when they were assured that the dissimilar others would like them but chose to interact with similar people when they were cautioned to choose others who would like them and were given no additional information. Attitude similarity may often produce attraction, then, because it is anticipated that the similar other will like the individual and attraction often breeds attraction in return. [Attraction also, it should be noted, breeds perceptions of similarity (Granberg and King, 1980; Levinger and Breedlove, 1966), which may feed back upon and further enhance attraction.]

There are still other interpretations of the similarity-attraction effect. Ajzen (1974) has suggested that attraction effects found within the bogus stranger experimental paradigm may be accounted for by the fact that the favorability of an individual's attitude toward another person (or object) is determined by his or her beliefs that the other possesses certain attributes, multiplied by his or her affective evaluations of each of those attributes (Ajzen and Fishbein, 1980). Thus Ajzen contends that similarity is usually found to be related to attraction because there is an association between the affective value of a trait to the individual and the likelihood that the individual himself or herself also possesses that trait (Stalling, 1970). If individuals discover another possesses traits similar to their own, they are likely to regard the other favorably simply because the other possesses favorably regarded traits, not because of similarity per se.

To test his hypothesis, Ajzen used the bogus stranger technique to give people personality feedback about themselves and another. He predicted, and found, that attraction toward the other increased with the desirability of the personality traits used to describe the other, irrespective of the degree to which those traits were similar to those characteristic of the individual; attraction was not significantly influenced by similarity in itself. In a second study this effect was replicated when information about the other person's opinions, rather than personality traits, was provided.

Ajzen's approach may prove helpful in interpreting and predicting instances where another's similarity does *not* generate attraction (see Huston and Levinger, 1978), and it is now clear that a number of such instances must be reconciled. Despite considerable effort to find a relationship between friendship choice and personality (as opposed to attitude) similarity, for example, the evidence for this hypothesis remains unconvincing (e.g., Hoffman and Maier, 1966.) However, efforts to find evidence against it and in support of Winch's (e.g., 1958) need complementarity hypothesis of social choice also have been unsuccessful (e.g., Meyer and Pepper, 1977; and see Murstein, 1976). Thus the role of personality similarity/dissimilarity in friendship and mate selection, if any exists, is undoubtedly more complex than is often assumed (see Levinger, 1983).

A further problem is that even attitude similarity fails to produce attraction under certain conditions. Some of these conditions have been explored by Snyder and Fromkin (1980), who have found support for their hypothesis that persons who perceive they share a moderate amount of similarity with another often react positively, but when the degree of an individual's similarity to another is very high, a negative reaction occurs. In addition, even moderate similarity with another may be distressing under some circumstances. Heider (1958) observed that "similarity can evoke disliking when the similarity carries with it disagreeable implications" (p. 186), and researchers have found this observation to be true. Novak and Lerner (1968), for example, found that people are less willing to interact with an attitudinally similar other than with a dissimilar person if the former is believed to have had a history of emotional disturbance. Further, Cooper and Jones (1969), as well as Taylor and Mettee (1971), found that the more similar individuals perceive themselves to be to others who are obnoxious and undesirable, the more they will change their attitudes so as to publicly disagree and socially disassociate themselves from them.

More often, however, attitude similarity has agreeable implications. Not only does it often provide the individual with consensual validation and imply that the other finds the individual attractive, but also, since dissimilar others are often unknown and unpredictable, it probably permits the individual greater prediction, and thus greater control, of the other's behavior in social interaction. Further, to the extent that a similar other is more familiar than a dissimilar other, the similar person ought to generate more attraction on this basis alone, according to the mere exposure hypothesis. And finally, similarity often implies that the individual will enjoy interacting with the other in mutually pleasurable activities, many of which require a partner similarly disposed in attitudes and ability to oneself.

Probably, then, it is not so much similarity itself that is rewarding or dissimilarity alone that is punishing; rather, it is the implications, presumed or anticipated, of those facts that are responsible for similarity-attraction effects and for their limitations and exceptions. Or as Huston and Levinger (1978) conclude in their recent review, there are probably a multiplicity of similarity-attraction effects, each of which depends both upon the nature of the similarity and upon the context in which it is experienced.

With respect to context they note that the experimental literature is limited almost entirely to data gathered from college students via the bogus stranger technique; in well-established relationships between individuals the meaning of a similarity or dissimilarity is likely to be somewhat different, with possibly different effects. Furthermore, the importance of a particular kind of similarity may differ in different contexts. For example, the attitude similarity-attraction relationship, so well documented in the laboratory, has not emerged as a determinant of courtship progress for dating couples. Hill, Rubin, and Peplau (1976) found that couples who remained together over a two-year period were more similar than couples who broke up, with respect to age, intelligence, and physical attractiveness but not to attitudes, and others also have failed to find a relationship between attitude similarity and dating progress (e.g., Levinger, 1972). An understanding of attraction as it occurs in naturalistic settings will require, therefore, a more careful delineation of what kinds of similarity are important to whom and in what social contexts.

Evaluative Appraisals and Attraction

The essence of Dale Carnegie's advice on how to win friends and influence people was to be hearty in one's approbation and lavish in one's praise of another. Carnegie's instruction makes good sense, at least on the surface. For example, it will be recalled that Homans (1961) considers social approval to be a transitional reinforcer, something that people find pleasing in almost all circumstances and from all sources.

Although it was recognized long ago that friends often constitute mutual admiration societies, Backman and Secord (1959) were the first to experimentally demonstrate that attraction breeds attraction. Other experimenters have since replicated their general finding that the discovery that another likes us, or regards us positively along one or more dimensions, tends to generate attraction to them—at least more attraction than is produced by those who fail to give a positive appraisal or who have actually given a negative evaluative appraisal (e.g., Aronson and Worchel, 1966; Jones and Panitch, 1971; Pepitone and Wilpinksi, 1960).

Most experimental demonstrations of reciprocity of liking imply that positive evaluations are accepted in a straightforward manner and, just as straightforwardly, elicit liking in return. Mettee and Aronson (1974) suggest, however, that even when it appears that another's appraisal has been accepted at face value, the process by which the individual arrived at acceptance of the appraisal may have been a careful one in which stringent standards of authenticity and validity were applied. They also observe that in almost all studies that have demonstrated liking reciprocity, the appraisals were given in the context of other events that have helped place the evaluation above suspicion of invalidity or unauthenticity (e.g., the evaluation was communicated not directly by the evaluator but through the medium of a third person).

Since positive appraisals given in naturalistic settings may not meet these standards, Mettee and Aronson argue that clear-cut instances of reciprocity of liking may be not so frequent in daily life where the fact that positive appraisals are carefully screened becomes more apparent.

Ingratiation. Indeed, investigations of ingratiation phenomena have documented that most people are attuned to detecting any insincerity, invalidity, or ulterior motive behind a positive appraisal. As viewed by Jones and his associates (Jones, 1964; Jones and Pittman, 1982; Jones and Wortman, 1973), ingratiation is a strategic self-presentational strategy individuals employ to augment or maintain power in a relationship by inducing the other to like or to attribute favorable characteristics to the individual. The determinants of ingratiation are theorized to be as follows:

1. Incentive value, or the importance to the individual that the other be attracted to them.

2. Subjective probability of success, or the individual's perceived likelihood that the other's attraction can be secured should certain actions be taken.

3. Perceived legitimacy, or the individual's view of the moral considerations involved in performing in behaviors designed primarily to elicit the other's attraction.

The twin facts that, first, the incentive value of ingratiation increases to the degree to which the individual is dependent upon the other for good outcomes and that, second, the subject probability of success decreases with increases in the degree of dependence combine to create what Jones has called the "ingratiator's dilemma." The more important it is for the individual to capture the attraction of the other, the less likely it is that a simple attraction-inducing strategy will be successful. It is less likely to be successful because dependence defines at least one condition under which positive appraisals are likely to be carefully scrutinized for authenticity.

Dickoff (1961), for example, varied the extent to which an evaluator could profit from the recipient's becoming attracted to her. Dickoff found that when no possibility of ulterior motive was present, attraction increased as the favorability of the evaluation increased; when there was the possibility of an ulterior motive for the positive evaluation, however, the recipient's attraction failed to increase when the favorability of the

evaluator's comments exceeded the recipient's opinion of himself or herself. What is seen as flattery, then, may depend not only upon the perception of ulterior motive but also upon the extent to which an evaluation is congruent with the recipient's self-concept.

Consistency of other's appraisal with self-appraisal. Deutsch and Solomon (1959), as previously discussed, were the first to test the hypothesis that favorable evaluations inconsistent with the recipient's self-appraisal elicit less attraction than favorable, consistent evaluations. They concluded from their data that although consistency may modify the attraction an appraisal would otherwise generate, as they predicted, there is also a positivity effect such that positive appraisals tend to produce some attraction even when they are inconsistent. Subsequent research on the issue produced mixed results, with the consistency of an appraisal sometimes being shown to be an important factor in producing attraction and positivity less so (e.g., Dutton, 1972) and with positivity other times being shown to be the predominant determinant (e.g., Skolnick, 1971).

In his review of the research relevant to the positive versus consistent appraisals issue, Shrauger (1975) concludes that people generally do think favorably of themselves, or at least have a desire to do so, and for this reason they tend to like positive appraisers more than negative appraisers. People also, however, seem to have more respect for cognitively consistent evaluations than they do for inconsistent ones, and thus the inconsistency of a positive evaluation may attenuate the degree to which it generates attraction. Shrauger points out that when another's positive appraisal is inconsistent, three factors may reduce attraction:

1. The inconsistency itself may arouse discomfort, as the cognitive consistency theories assume, and thereby reduce attraction.

2. The inconsistent appraisal may be perceived as inaccurate and thus lead the individual to attribute certain unfavorable characteristics—such as stupidity, insensitivity, or lack of discernment—to the appraiser and thereby diminish attraction.

3. The inconsistent appraisal may immediately raise the specter of ingratiation.

With respect to the ingratiation possibility Mettee and Aronson (1974) cite suspicion of the appraiser as the theme running through most studies in which positive but inconsistent evaluations do not produce attraction. They also maintain, however, that the original hypothesis that inconsistent positive evaluations should fail to produce attraction is flawed: "What the person does himself may indeed have to be congruent with his self-evaluation to be deemed desirable and appropriate, but there is no compelling reason why the reactions of others should conform to these same strictures" (p. 244). They go on to argue that if there is no objective standard present, if the objective quality of a performance or attribute is ambiguous, or if there is no social consensus with respect to that particular performance or attribute, then another's evaluation should not necessarily be regarded as invalid even when it does not agree with the individual's own. Indeed, Dutton (1972) and others (e.g., Jones and Schneider, 1968) have found that when people are uncertain about the quality of their task performance (and even when they have made some good guesses about how well they have done), they prefer positive appraisers to negative appraisers.

Since people rarely have concrete authoritative information on the extent to which they do or do not possess a particular attribute, it seems reasonable to conclude that in daily life most evaluative appraisals fall within the uncertain category. If so, positive appraisals generally can be expected to produce attraction. And they may do so for yet other reasons. As Jones, Gergen, and Davis (1962) discovered, one response to a discrepant positive evaluation may be to quickly revise one's own appraisal so as to make it consistent with the other's appraisal. In addition, of course, if liking and respect are indeed two independent dimensions that often underlie attraction responses, then positive but inconsistent evaluators may be seen as fools undeserving of respect, but rather endearing fools all the same.

Negative evaluations, as Mettee and Aronson (1974) observe in their review of available data, do not seem to be as susceptible as positive evaluations are to the influence of screening standards. Rather, they are often taken at face value. Sometimes, however, reactions to negative evaluations are complex; for example, a negative evaluation may produce an increase in approach tendencies toward the evaluator or may produce conciliatory behaviors designed to win the other over (e.g., Jones and Schneider, 1968). It also should be mentioned that an evaluation need not be very negative to be perceived as such by the recipient, for even evaluations regarded by outside observers as neutral may be regarded as negative (see Berscheid and Walster, 1978). This sensitivity to neg-

ative overtones in an evaluation, as well as a tendency for positive evaluations to elicit at least some attraction even when they fail to fully satisfy screening criteria of authenticity, underscores how highly people value the positive regard of others and how willing they are to confer, in turn, their own regard upon them.

The state of the person appraised. Somewhat related to the question of the effect of inconsistent appraisals upon attraction is the association between self-esteem and responses to favorable or unfavorable evaluators (see Jones, 1973, for a review). Dittes's (1959) original finding, since replicated by a host of other investigators (e.g., Jacobs, Berscheid, and Walster, 1971; Jones and Pines, 1968; Walster, 1965), was that people who suffer from chronically low self-esteem appear to be more affected by other's appraisals of them. That is, they react more positively to favorable evaluators than do persons with high self-esteem and more negatively to negative evaluators. Similarly, those who have a high need for social approval (see Chapter 30 of this *Handbook*) may react more strongly to its being given or withheld than those who do not (e.g., Holstein, Goldstein, and Bem, 1971). Furthermore, the extent to which a person has in the past received a great deal of social approval or disapproval may affect reactions to another's evaluative appraisal (e.g., Aronson and Linder, 1965; Stevenson and Odom, 1962).

Finally, and as previously noted, virtually all clinical theories of attraction, particularly those addressed to heterosexual attraction and to romantic love, emphasize the importance of need states for the generation of strong attraction. Thus reactions to another's evaluative appraisals depend not only upon the perceived authenticity and validity of the appraisal but also upon its relationship to the individual's needs at the moment. These factors, in turn, are heavily determined by the social context in which the appraisal is received.

THE CONTINUING INFLUENCE OF INITIAL ENCOUNTERS UPON ATTRACTION IN A DEVELOPING RELATIONSHIP

Social psychologists often have been faulted for focusing so intensely upon the determinants of attraction between strangers in their initial encounter with one another. This criticism, however, is not as justified as it may seem at first glance. It has been logical for investigators to begin at the beginning by examining attraction as it may or may not occur in the initial stages of a relationship between two people, as well as to examine attraction in the setting that has been most vulnerable to causal dissection. Furthermore, a growing body of research findings suggests that the determinants and outcomes of an initial social encounter may cast their influence over the entire relationship—influencing not just whether it dies aborning but also, if it lives, both its nature and its course.

The initial encounter is obviously a critical point in a relationship, because if the initial interaction is not rewarding, and if the initial information the individual has gained from the encounter is such that future interactions are anticipated to be unrewarding also, the individual is likely to terminate the relationship. Such an outcome is most probable in open-field situations that present alternative relationship possibilities and is least probable in closed-field situations. Since most social contexts in which initial encounters occur are neither wholly open nor wholly closed, but rather lie somewhere between these points on a continuum of greater or lesser alternative relationship opportunities, whether the relationship is continued or terminated probably represents an interaction between the degree of attraction generated in the initial encounter and the nature of the alternative relationship context.

But whether the initial encounter leads to voluntary attempts to continue the relationship or whether it is continued for reasons extrinsic to the relationship, the impact of the conditions surrounding the initial encounter upon the perception of the other and the feelings of attraction that result are likely to continue to influence the relationship as it develops. There are a number of reasons for their enduring influence, and most stem from the fact that in the initial encounter the individual forms expectancies about the other person and that person's behavior in the future, about himself or herself and his or her own future behavior, and about the relationship and the nature of the interaction that is likely to be characteristic of it. These expectancies are often confirmed in the ensuing interactions between the individual and the other—even if they are in error.

Expectancy Confirmation and Attraction

The notion that an individual's expectancies about another often serve as self-fulfilling prophecies was introduced by the sociologist Robert Merton (1948, 1957), who observed (1957, p. 423):

The self-fulfilling prophecy is, in the beginning, a *false* definition of the situation evoking a new behavior which makes the originally false conception come *true*. The specious validity of the self-fulfilling prophecy perpetuates a reign of error. For the prophet will cite the actual course of events as proof that he was right from the very beginning.

There is no doubt that self-fulfilling prophecy effects do occur in social interaction (see Darley and Fazio, 1980, for a recent review), and just how expectancy confirmation occurs has been of much interest.

Some expectancy confirmation processes have been well documented. For example, it is well known that what an individual expects to see helps determine what will be seen (see Chapter 16 of this *Handbook*). The halo effect—in which initially favorable information about another casts a rosy glow over the meaning and interpretation of ensuing information about the other—is, as Asch (1946) was the first to demonstrate, one example.

Initial expectancies, then, may color the meaning and interpretation of later-received information about an individual, particularly in cases where that information is ambiguous and vulnerable to a wide latitude of interpretive possibilities. Moreover, expectancies direct attentional processes and thus may ensure that information incongruent with the initial expectancy is not perceived. Zadny and Gerard (1974), for example, demonstrated that individuals who were asked to observe another's behavior, some of which was consistent with their expectancies about the other and some of which wasn't, later tended to recall primarily those behaviors that confirmed their expectancies. And in a second experiment these investigators found evidence to suggest that the reason the observers had not reported the behaviors inconsistent with their expectancies was not because their memories had failed them in this instance [although such selective forgetting may be responsible for some expectancy confirmation effects (see Snyder and Swann, 1978)] but because they hadn't seen the behavior in the first place. Their expectancies had led them to direct their attention to certain aspects of the other's behavior and away from others.

There is yet another reason why an individual's expectancies about another may come to be confirmed in interaction. An individual's behavior toward another, prompted by his or her initial expectancies, may elicit from the other the very behaviors the individual expected the other to demonstrate. Just such a process was demonstrated by Snyder, Tanke, and Berscheid (1977), who asked men and women to converse with a stranger of the opposite sex over the telephone in order to become acquainted with him or her. Unknown to the women, some men were led to believe (via a photograph) that the woman with whom they were to speak was physically attractive, while others were led to believe she was unattractive. Outside observers, who knew nothing of the circumstances of the conversation, were asked to listen to each woman's portion of the conversation, which had been recorded separately from the man's, and form an impression of her. Their judgments of the woman's actual behavior were in agreement with the men's expectancies (as assessed on a preinteraction, first-impression questionnaire) about her. The women who had been talking to a man who believed them to be physically attractive were perceived by the observers to be more poised, sociable, animated, and confident than the women who had been talking to a man who believed them to be physically unattractive. Thus the men had elicited the very behaviors they expected the women to exhibit. When observers listened to the men's contributions to the conversation, they evaluated the men who believed they were talking to an attractive woman as more sociable, sexually warm, interesting, outgoing, and humorous than the men who believed they were talking to an unattractive woman. The men's differential expectancies apparently led to different behaviors on their part, which elicited from the women differential behaviors that supported the men's initial expectancies.

In social interaction the other person is also forming or revising an impression of the individual, and these impression-related expectancies are guiding the other's behavior in such a way that the subsequent behavior of the two persons often confirms both of their sets of expectancies. Jones and Panitch (1971), for example, found that men who were led to believe that their partner disliked them behaved more competitively in a game than did those who believed their partner liked them, and the partners (who knew nothing of the other's beliefs), in turn, came to like those who behaved cooperatively and to dislike those who had behaved competitively. Their degree of attraction presumably would have directed their behavior toward the other in continuing interaction, with the effect that the relationship would have become even more entrenched in pleasant or hostile channels. And it is unlikely, as Darley and Fazio (1980)

discuss, that either one would have been able to pinpoint the source of his affection or enmity for the other in anything but the other's favorable or unfavorable personal characteristics—so obviously displayed for even objective outside observers to see.

Whatever the precise routes by which an individual may come to confirm his or her initial expectancies about another in interaction with that other (and there are many), clearly the original evidence upon which an initial impression is formed often may be no longer needed to sustain belief in it (e.g., Regan, Straus, and Fazio, 1974). An initial impression of a situation often gains a form of functional autonomy that allows it to persevere even in the face of subsequent disconfirming evidence (e.g., Ross, Lepper, and Hubbard, 1975). For this reason alone the initial encounter assumes a particularly important status in the development of a relationship.

Implications for Attraction Phenomena

Among the many implications expectancy confirmation processes have for the understanding and prediction of attraction phenomena, only two will be mentioned here. First, all that is known of the perceptual factors that affect initial impressions of another [such as order effects and information integration processes (e.g., Kaplan and Anderson, 1973)] is relevant to an understanding of attraction as it may or may not develop from the initial stage of a relationship. Second, given that the initial encounter is particularly important to the form and manner in which the relationship develops, the causal conditions that are relevant to attraction and that surround the initial encounter are probably of special importance to the relationship and thus deserve special attention; for even if the initial conditions subsequently dissipate and new ones emerge, the effects produced by the original conditions may be self-sustaining. Thus the social context surrounding the initial encounter, within which many of these causal conditions of attraction are embedded, deserves more attention than it has yet received.

For example, each of the previously discussed major determinants of attraction in initial encounters is heavily dependent upon social context. With respect to similarity, whether two individuals perceive they are similar to one another depends not only upon the objective degree of similarity they exhibit in interaction but also upon the nature of the context in which that interaction takes place. As Heider (1958) illustrates: "If two Americans meet among people of other nationalities, they readily stand out as a pair, whereas if they are surrounded by other Americans, this grouping does not occur'' (p. 178). Perceptions of physical attractiveness also depend upon social context. Kendrick and Gutierres (1980) found that men who rated the physical attractiveness of a woman immediately after watching a popular television program featuring three highly physically attractive women judged her to be significantly less attractive than did men who had not recently viewed such a program. And finally, the social context in which an evaluative appraisal is received, particularly whether others in the social environment have recently deprived (or satiated) the individual of social approbation, will affect, as previously discussed, reactions to it.

SUMMARY

Although recently some effort has been devoted to the factors that prompt people to spontaneously pay attention to and initiate an encounter with another in an open-field setting, most attraction research has been directed toward understanding the determinants of attraction within initial encounters that take place in closed-field settings. Three such determinants have been shown to be the physical attractiveness of the other, the perceived similarity of the other, and the extent to which the other is perceived (or anticipated) to genuinely like the individual. Each of these factors is likely, other things being equal, to prompt the initiation of relationships in open-field settings.

Each of the determinants of attraction in initial encounters upon which social psychologists have especially focused are dependent not only upon the absolute properties of the individual and the other (e.g., their physical attractiveness) and their behavior (e.g., the degree of similarity they display to each other in interaction) but also upon the interaction between these factors and the social context in which the initial encounter is embedded. For this reason, consideration of all aspects of the initial encounter, including context, is especially important. What is known of expectancy confirmation processes suggests that even when the properties of the individual have changed (e.g., the acute need state for social approval induced by a rejection from others has dissipated), when the properties of the other have changed (e.g., the political opinion he or she initially expressed has been reversed), and/or when the original social and physical context has changed (e.g., the two Americans have arrived home from their European summer

vacation), the attraction effects generated by the conditions of the initial encounter may live on, having acquired a life of their own.

Thus although attraction researchers often have been faulted for focusing upon initial encounters to the neglect of attraction at subsequent stages of a relationship, some investigators have argued that ''the *raison d'etre* of any social relationship, as well as the relationship's complexity of character at any stage of its growth or deterioration, cannot be fully understood unless one also understands the conditions under which it was initiated'' (Berscheid and Graziano, 1979, p. 32), since those conditions exert their influence long after they have disappeared. Accordingly, since a large portion of the answer to the oft-heard query ''What *does* she see in him? is often ''What she *once* saw in him a long time ago,'' the considerable effort devoted to the identification of the causal determinants of attraction between strangers in their first encounter with one another has not been misplaced.

ATTRACTION AND RELATIONSHIP DEVELOPMENT, MAINTENANCE, AND DISSOLUTION

Since relationships are the context within which all attraction phenomena occur, interest in attraction leads inevitably to an interest in relationships. Conversely, attraction has implications for all aspects of relationships. Attraction may play a central role in the initiation of a relationship, as we have discussed, and it also plays a role in the further development of the relationship, its maintenance, and its dissolution.

THE ANALYSIS OF ATTRACTION WITHIN RELATIONSHIPS

Although attraction has most frequently been viewed as a property of a person (e.g., as an attitude), attraction also can be viewed as a property of a relationship. If a relationship between two people is conceived as the pattern of interdependence that exists between them (see Kelley *et al.,* 1983), and since interdependence is defined by the quantity and kind of influence each person has upon the other's behavior, then all properties of a relationship, including attraction, are evidenced in the amount and kind of influence each person has on the other. It follows that to assess the property of attraction of a relationship, one must examine certain aspects of the causal impact each person in the relationship has on the other's behavior. For example, and depending upon the investigator's conception of attraction, an examination might be made of the number of times each individual aids the other when he or she perceives the other to be in distress, the number and vigor of attempts to regain proximity to the other when separated, and so on. Thus it is within interaction that attraction, as well as other relationship properties, are evidenced.

To move from a descriptive analysis of attraction within a relationship to a causal analysis requires an understanding of the relatively stable causal conditions (see Kelley *et al.,* 1983) that affect the interaction pattern between the individual and the other. These conditions may be classified into two general categories, personal and environmental causal conditions. Thus Kelley and his colleagues have proposed that an understanding of attraction, for example, as it may be displayed in an individual's initial interaction with another requires knowledge of the following personal causal conditions:

- The P factors, or the relatively stable properties of the individual that are brought to the interaction (e.g., the individual's attitude toward strangers).

- The O factors, or the relatively stable properties the other also brings to the interaction.

- The $P \times O$ factors, or how the P factors and O factors interact with one another.

Lay causal analyses of interpersonal attraction often focus upon P factors and O factors alone. For example, when people are asked why they like another, they often respond by naming such O factors as the other's honesty, sense of humor, and so on. Attraction researchers, too, have identified certain P and O factors that are important in predicting attraction, as we have discussed (e.g., physical attractiveness), but they have especially recognized the importance of $P \times O$ factors, which produce effects upon the interaction that are not predictable from knowledge of either the P factor alone or the O factor alone. For example, from knowledge that P generally dislikes strangers and dislikes to participate in psychology experiments and that O feels likewise, one might predict that the initial encounter between the two in the context of a psychology experiment is likely to be unpleasant and unlikely to produce attraction. However, a relevant $P \times O$ factor that needs to be taken into consideration in this case is the attitude similarity these people share, which, if the similarity is perceived by the individual and the other, ought to generate attraction. Attitude similarity, then, is a $P \times O$ causal factor in that the causal factor is located in neither person but, rather, "is defined by the conjunction of properties of the two persons" (Kelley *et al.,* 1983).

Environmental causal conditions also affect how individuals respond to one another, since the interaction between the individual and the other always takes place within a physical environment (E_p) and within a social environment (E_s). These factors form the context of the relationship itself and often place the constraints upon the interaction. With respect to an initial encounter, for example, such E_p causal conditions as are represented by an unbearably hot day and the fact that the two available chairs in the cafeteria are placed side by side rather than face to face undoubtedly affect the interaction that ensues between the individual and the other, as do such E_s factors as the availability of an old friend only a few feet away who presents a more appealing conversation alternative to the individual than the other does. Thus as Brenner has observed (1980, p. 2):

> An adequate understanding of human action necessitates, first of all, a consideration of the *natural social context* in which it occurs. Just as we cannot conceive of the flow of a river without paying attention to, among other factors, its bed, it would be wrong to treat human action as if it were context-free, unconstrained by particular natural "social forms."

Unfortunately, and in contrast to personal causal conditions, environmental causal conditions have been relatively ignored in causal analyses of attraction phenomena. As we have discussed, the physical and social contexts of most relationships examined by attraction researchers have been those as are defined, physically, by a laboratory within an academic building and, socially, by a psychology experiment. Furthermore, it is often tacitly assumed that these particular E_p and E_s factors surrounding the initial encounter do not impinge upon the relationship directly or even indirectly. The validity of this assumption is highly doubtful, of course, and the validity of the more general assumption that behavior of any kind can be understood without reference to the context within which it takes place has come under increasingly severe attack within social psychology in recent years (e.g., Harré and Secord, 1972) and within other areas of psychology as well (e.g., Jenkins, 1981).

Apart from their direct effects [e.g., Griffitt and Veitch (1971) who found a relationship between room temperature and attraction responses], environmental causal conditions undoubtedly interact with personal causal conditions and thus also may have an indirect influence upon attraction. For example, a stroll in the moonlight through a meadow of wildflowers (E_p causal conditions) may be conducive to one kind of interaction for some people, but for individuals who suffer night blindness and hay fever (P causal conditions), another kind of result may be expected. Or to take an example closer to home, most initial encounters in the laboratory take place under the aegis of an authority figure, the experimenter. An authoritarian personality (a P causal factor) may interact with this E_s condition such that while the individual would ordinarily greet a stranger with cold hostility, warm friendliness toward the other may be exhibited in this context as part of an effort to please the authority.

Increased recognition of the role contextual factors play in attraction is at least partially responsible for the recent and dramatic rise in interest in studying attraction phenomena as they occur in the context of naturally formed relationships and naturalistic settings. Although increasing numbers of attraction researchers are beginning to examine attraction *in vivo* and *in situ,* the task they have set for themselves is an imposing one for at least two reasons. First, the task is made difficult because past efforts devoted to the identification of personal causal conditions that affect attraction have been matched neither by comparable efforts to identify relevant environmental causal conditions nor by efforts to learn of the manner in which these factors interact with each other and with the personal factors that influence attraction. Second, the task escalates from difficult to formidable when one considers that relationships are indeed like rivers; they flow through time and space, never static, always changing, as the values of the causal parameters that impinge upon them change and as the identity of the parameters themselves undoubtedly change as the relationship develops.

Given the magnitude of the problem of investigating attraction in its natural context, it perhaps is not surprising that heretofore attraction researchers have not strayed far from the wellspring of the river—that they have focused their causal analyses upon attraction phenomena as they may occur immediately after the relationship has sprung into existence. It also is not surprising that the environmental factors surrounding the beginnings of the relationship have, in effect, been standardized and that investigations have focused primarily upon personal causal conditions. And it is clear, too, why the stream of the relationship has not been allowed to flow in time but, rather, has been frozen in its course immediately after birth to facilitate its causal dissection, since it is the time element in relationships that makes their causal analysis so difficult. As the relationship moves from one time frame to the next, all the contemporaneous causal conditions impinging upon the relationship at the latter point must be identified, and some of these will have emerged from the previous point in time. Norms, agreements, understandings, and even attraction itself, for example, may emerge from an initial encounter and now constitute relatively stable causal conditions that interact with a new set of causal conditions that may have come into effect at this later point in time, and all together may act to affect various properties of the relationship, including its present property of attraction.

Difficult though it may be, it is a causal analysis of extended interactional time-series data that must be performed if many important attraction questions are to be answered. Consider, for example, a common attraction question that practitioners of marital therapy are called upon to answer: "What happened to the love we once had for each other?" The marital therapist here is in much the same position as a freshwater marine biologist in St. Louis who has been asked by the local fishermen why the fish are now dying in the Mississippi. A causal analysis of the situation may quickly reveal that the proximal cause of death is a lack of oxygen in the water. The distal causes of death are more complex and difficult to identify, however, because the several factors that emerged and interacted to reduce the oxygen may have occurred weeks ago in time and miles upstream in space. Yet these causal factors, and their manner of interaction with each other over time, frequently must be identified if intelligent action is to be taken or if accurate prognostications about the future are to be made.

The full causal analysis of why attraction has died— or grown—in a specific relationship over time cannot be expected to be any less complex. It is, however, answers to just such questions that people currently seek (see Berscheid and Peplau, 1983). As social psychologists now move toward finding the answers, they join not only those in the young field of marital and family therapy (see Olson, Russell, and Sprenkle, 1980) but also sociologists of marriage and the family, ethologists and anthropologists, and clinical psychologists and psychiatrists, who have long struggled to gain an understanding of behavioral phenomena that are deeply embedded in social relationships characterized by past histories and anticipated futures. From these combined efforts a science of relationships is beginning to emerge (e.g., see Hinde, 1980), with a more complete understanding of interpersonal attraction being a potential benefit. Currently, however, attraction investigators are just beginning their theoretical and empirical expeditionary movements away from the base they have established with initial encounters. The question that has so far captured the most attention is, perhaps, the logical next step in a long series for the future: "What causes a tiny spring to grow into a mighty river?"

RELATIONSHIP DEVELOPMENT

Social psychologists have become increasingly interested in devising conceptual frameworks within which the development of a relationship may be characterized and within which the reasons for its growth and maintenance, or lack of it, may be explored (e.g., see Burgess and Huston, 1979; Duck and Gilmour, 1981a, 1981b). Since, as previously noted, virtually all conceptions of relationship refer to the fact that the two people involved influence each other, the growth of a relationship may be viewed as an increase in the impact two people have on each other's behavior. Some relationships grow to be close or deep relationships in that the degree of interdependence between the two persons becomes very high—or the relationship is characterized by a high frequency of causal impact between the individuals, by diversity of the impact to many different kinds of behavioral events, and by a high strength of causal impact per each occurrence (see Kelley *et al.,* 1983). Usually, such growth must take place over time, and thus fully developed relationships are usually relationships of some duration.

Not all relationships that are born grow over time, of course. As Levinger (1980) has observed, we pursue relationships with only a small fraction of the people whom we meet, and this is true even if the initial encounter has been favorable and has produced attraction. Furthermore, and as discussed previously, attraction need not always be a characteristic of a developing relationship nor even a characteristic of an established relationship. For this reason recent conceptual frameworks of relationship make no reference to the degree of attraction that may or

may not exist between individuals in classifying two persons as in a relationship with each other (see Berscheid, 1983). Rather, an individual is conceived to be in a relationship with another to the extent that the other has causal impact upon the individual, whether that impact is considered to constitute attraction for the other, hatred for the other, or points in between on the attraction dimension.

Theories of Relationship Development

Despite the fact that we seem to pursue relationships with only a small number of people to whom we are attracted, attraction—at least under open-field conditions where the individual enjoys some choice in the matter—is almost universally seen to be an important condition facilitating the growth of a relationship. At the least, the same conditions believed to promote an individual's attraction to another (e.g., the individual's evaluations of the rewards he or she is currently receiving in the relationship and his or her forecasts of future rewards) are believed to be the conditions that promote relationship growth and development. Altman, for example, states (1974, p. 128):

> Following initial contact, persons *evaluate immediate rewards and costs* from the exchange and make forecasts, or projections, to potential rewards from future exchange. If evaluations and forecasts are favorable, the relationship should continue to grow; if they are negative, the bond should terminate or proceed slowly.

Other theorists of relationship development share this view. Huesmann and Levinger (1976), for example, theorize that "a progressing relationship is one in which expected rewards become increasingly probable relative to expected costs; in contrast, a deteriorating relationship is one in which expected rewards become less and less probable, and the costs more and more probable" (Levinger, 1980, p. 525).

While theorists of relationship development agree that mutually rewarding relationships tend to develop further and unrewarding relationships tend to be terminated, they differ with respect to their conceptualization of the stages relationships may pass through, as well as in the nature of the causal factors and processes they presume to be crucial to further relationship development at each stage. It should be noted that all of the theories discussed here are addressed, sometimes explicitly but more often implicitly, to adult relationship development (although the type of adult relationship focused upon sometimes differs) and that interest in the development of friendship relationships between children has also increased in recent years (see Dickens and Perlman, 1983, and Hartup, 1983, for reviews).

Relationship stages.   Most theories of relationship development view relationships as proceeding from a superficial stage (such as that typical of an initial encounter between strangers) to a deep, intimate, or close stage (such as that perhaps enjoyed by a couple married many years). For example, Levinger and his associates (e.g., Levinger and Snoek, 1972) theorize that relationships may progress through three levels:

- Level 1, where the individual is aware of the other without the other necessarily reciprocating the awareness.

- Level 2, characterized by brief interaction governed primarily by the participants' social roles.

- Level 3, characterized by mutual relationship, where the partners possess shared knowledge of each other, assume responsibility for furthering each other's outcomes, and share private norms for regulating their association.

Furthermore, two processes are hypothesized to be critical to relationship development: the process of interpersonal discovery and disclosure, where each person discloses increasingly more about his or her unique self to the other and shares emotionally significant attitudes and feelings, and the process of mutual investment, where the individual and the other increasingly coordinate their behavior and activities with one another and care emotionally about each other.

Altman and Taylor's social penetration theory (Altman, 1974; Altman and Taylor, 1973) also assumes that as a relationship develops, the individual and the other gradually and systematically move toward more intimate areas of social exchange, so that in close relationships the personality of each is penetrated (or made known to the other in its most complete sense, including knowledge of the individual's needs, values, and feelings). In such relationships both persons are conceived to engage in a great deal of behavioral exchange at all levels of intimacy and in all areas of personality.

Murstein's (1970) stimulus-value-role theory, addressed principally to adult heterosexual courtship development, views this type of relationship as moving through three chronological stages:

1. A stimulus stage, where the individual perceives the other's physical, social, mental, or reputational attributes, evaluates the potential profitability of association with the other, and also evaluates his or her own qualities that might prove attractive to the other.

2. A value stage, where actual interaction occurs and the persons appraise their value compatibility (e.g., their attitudes toward life, politics, etc.), which, in turn, helps them assess the potential rewards of continued association.

3. A role stage, where the two persons evaluate themselves and each other concerning their suitability for the role of spouse (or, presumably, any other role perceived to be relevant to the developing relationship).

Secord and Backman (1974; see also Backman, 1981) have postulated four stages of relationship development, each stage distinguished from the others by the predominant processes presumed to be characteristic of it:

1. An early stage, where the principals explore the rewards that may be available in a potential relationship.

2. A bargaining stage, where both try to negotiate the terms of the relationship.

3. A commitment stage, where there is progressive reduction in the sampling and estimation of rewards available in the present relationship relative to alternative relationships, as well as increasing dependence on the relationship.

4. An institutionalization stage, where "shared expectations emerge, recognizing the rightness and legitimacy of the exclusiveness of the relationship and the patterns of exchange that have developed, these expectations being shared not only by members of the pair but by others in general" (Backman, 1981, p. 6).

Scanzoni (1979), too, posits an exploration stage, where the individual and the other attempt to discover whether it would be profitable to maintain or develop the relationship further, and where the processes of communication and negotiation of rules of exchange, as well as the development of trust, are deemed especially important. This stage is conceived to be followed by an expansion of interlocking-interest spheres, where the two persons increasingly intermesh their goals and objectives. Finally, a third developmental stage is theorized to be marked by commitment, or by feelings of solidarity with the relationship; the process of conflict resolution is believed to be especially important to the evolution of a relationship to the commitment stage.

Implications for attraction.   These theories of relationship development, and the relatively sparse supporting data associated with each, have a number of implications for understanding attraction phenomena. One implication is that the causal determinants of attraction may differ at different stages of a relationship and/or the potency of the various causal factors may differ at different stages. This implication is most obvious in filter theories of relationship development, such as Murstein's, where relatively external stimulus factors are believed to play a crucial role initially, but then value factors are hypothesized to later assume importance in courtship relationship development. Another type of filter hypothesis regarding courtship development was advanced by Kerckhoff and Davis (1962), who assessed, over a seven-month period, need complementarity and consensus on family values in couples who were seriously considering marriage. These investigators found that for couples whose relationship was eighteen months or more of age, need complementarity, but not value consensus, was associated with the couples' estimations of the relationship's progress toward permanence. For couples whose relationship was younger than eighteen months, the reverse was true—value consensus only was related to perceived progress. Interesting as these findings are, they have not survived replication attempts (e.g., Levinger, Senn, and Jorgensen, 1970), and indeed, not a great deal is known about how the force of commonly accepted determinants of attraction may wax or wane during the development of a relationship.

Nevertheless, it seems reasonable to expect that some variables will be more important for attraction and for relationship growth at some stages of a relationship than at others, and the matter continues to receive some theoretical thought (e.g., Duck, 1977) and empirical attention (e.g., Duck and Craig, 1978). However, even the few filter hypotheses that have been offered so far have a number of weaknesses. As Levinger (1983) points out, current filter models and their empirical tests tend to assume that the personal and environmental causal conditions relevant to a relationship remain stable over time; that all relationships develop at approximately the same rate; and that the filters operate in simple linear fashion. All these assumptions are patently dubious.

Among the changing causal conditions that impinge upon a relationship as it moves through time are all those associated with the developmental changes individuals undergo as they themselves move through time [see Huston (1974) for a discussion of this point]. As individuals grow older, so do their long-term relationships, and separating those relationship changes that have emerged primarily from the internal dynamics of the relationship as it has progressed from those that are simply due to the fact that the principals are now older (and perhaps wiser) is difficult. Such separation is especially difficult since little is known of how the nature and function of adult relationships vary with the individual's place in the life cycle (but see Shulman, 1975). Even information concerning the sheer number of relationships typical of adults at various ages is sparse and plagued by methodological problems, but Dickens and Perlman (1981) tentatively conclude from their review that the number of friendships appears to peak in late adolescence and early adulthood, that marriage and parenthood reduces the number of nonkin relationships, that friendships decline in old age, and that across the life cycle same-sex friendships predominate. Since number of relationships appears to vary with place in the life cycle, it seems likely that their nature and function will be found to vary also.

Other important causal conditions that undoubtedly change as a relationship moves through time concern changes in the social context of the relationship. For example, the number and nature of possible alternative relationships will change over time for one or both of the relationship participants, and the reactions of persons currently in the social network to the relationship itself may also change. It should be emphasized, then, that while contextual factors have been relatively ignored in attraction research to date, it will be especially disastrous to continue to do so when the role that attraction plays in relationship development, maintenance, and dissolution is examined.

The second, if indirect, implication that theories of relationship development have for attraction is that the causal factors associated with attraction may differ not only with the stage of the relationship but also with the type of relationship. Currently, however, most theories of relationship development are either presumed to apply to all types of relationships or focus upon adult heterosexual courtship relationships. The potential advantage of investigating questions of attraction and relationship development in the context of specific relationship types has not been explored, partially because such investigation is dependent upon information concerning useful taxonomies of social relationships.

Although little effort has been devoted to discovering the dimensions that actually underlie social relationships, some recent effort has been directed toward uncovering the dimensions that seem to underlie people's perceptions of them. Wish, Deutsch, and Kaplan (1976), for example, asked men and women to rate twenty of their own personal relationships on numerous bipolar scales, as well as twenty-five common role relationships (e.g., husband-wife). They found four dimensions to underlie the ratings: (1) cooperative/friendly versus competitive/hostile; (2) equal versus unequal; (3) intense versus superficial; (4) socioemotional/informal versus task-oriented/formal. Interestingly, the relative importance of these dimensions varied systematically across various subgroups (e.g., the socioemotional/informal versus task-oriented/formal dimension appeared to be more salient to younger, single persons than to the older, married persons). Further, some dimensions (e.g., intense versus superficial) appeared to be more important in people's evaluations of their own relationships than in evaluations of common abstract role relationships.

The dimensions underlying the perception of typical role relationships have been examined by a few investigators. Marwell and Hage (1970), for example, identified three factors:

1. Intimacy, characterized by relationships that have, in part, a large number of different activities and/or different locations of interaction.

2. Visibility, or the extent to which the interactions are public rather than private.

3. Regulation, or the amount of specification of activities, times, and locations of interaction.

More recently, Rands and Levinger (1979) asked respondents to estimate the probabilities of various behaviors (e.g., self-disclosure) in male same-sex, female same-sex, and cross-sex relationships at four levels of closeness (e.g., casual acquaintance). All types of behavior examined were perceived to increase in probability as the relationship grew closer, but this was especially true for praise, criticism, and affectionate-touching behaviors. Furthermore these increases were higher for cross-sex than for same-sex relationships.

Another recent effort to uncover relationship dimensions is represented by Forgas and Dobosz's (1980) attempt to construct a taxonomy of romantic relationship prototypes. College students were asked to sort items describing heterosexual relationships (e.g., a short, mutual first love) into homogeneous categories, to identify the most salient feature of the relationships in each category, and to rate each on a number of bipolar scales. Forgas and Dobosz found that three dimensions adequately represented the relationship space:

1. Desirability, characterized by the desirable/ undesirable, one-sided/mutual, and frustrating/satisfying scales.

2. Love and commitment, marked by the loving/ unloving, committed/uncommitted, and transient/permanent scales.

3. Sexuality, or physical and sexual kinds of relationships, such as one-time sexual encounters, versus platonic and emotional kinds of relationships.

Although it is not known whether the determinants of attraction differ importantly with type of relationship, it seems likely that some will be more potent in some types of relationships than others. Pam, Plutchik, and Conte (1975), for example, found suggestive evidence that physical attractiveness was more important for heterosexual love relationships than for dating relationships and more important for dating relationships than for friendship relationships. This P factor, then, may interact with relationship type to affect both the degree and the variety of attraction experienced in the relationship. For example, if two people define their relationship as a friendship and not as a potential romantic love relationship (possibly because of a number of factors, including commitments elsewhere), physical attractiveness may play a relatively minor role in generating attraction, whereas in a potential love relationship it may assume greater causal importance.

And to take this example of the problem of predicting the role of attraction in relationship development a step further, if romantic love does emerge within the relationship, it may at this point interact with certain other P causal factors to determine further relationship development. For instance, Rubin (1973) found that Love Scale scores predicted relationship progress primarily for those who also scored high on a romanticism scale. Thus certain personal causal conditions (e.g., physical attractiveness) may interact with relationship type (e.g., potential romantic love relationship) to affect attraction (e.g., romantic love), and attraction may then, in turn, interact with certain other existing personal causal conditions (e.g., the trait of romanticism) to affect subsequent relationship development.

As this example suggests, a third implication that questions of relationship development have for attraction is that the variety of attraction experienced also may differ systematically with type of relationship. Perhaps the most obvious example of a variety of attraction that tends to be peculiar to a certain type of relationship is romantic love. In fact, the existence of romantic love is itself often used to distinguish relationship type. Presumably, however, some types of relationship are more conducive to the development of this variety of attraction than are other types of relationship, and this could be ascertained before the fact of its occurrence.

Finally, and relatedly, another implication that issues of relationship development have for attraction is that the variety of attraction experienced within a relationship may differ systematically with the stage of a relationship. Again, an obvious example is romantic love. Both theoretical analyses of this intense variety of attraction (e.g., Berscheid, 1983) and such empirical data as are available suggest that romantic love occurs largely in the early stages of a relationship and that it dissipates over time (e.g., Blood, 1967; Cimbalo, Faling, and Mousaw, 1976). On the other hand, deep friendship may be possible only in relationships that have endured for some time, as may be true also for companionate love (Walster and Walster, 1979).

Presumed Critical Processes in Relationship Development

Theorists appear to agree about the nature of the changes people display in relationships that are growing closer. Burgess and Huston (1979) summarize the prevailing opinions (p. 8):

1. They interact more often, for longer periods of time, and in a widening array of settings.

2. They attempt to restore proximity when separated, and feel comforted when proximity is regained.

3. They "open up" to each other, in the sense that they disclose secrets and share physical intimacies.

4. They become less inhibited, more willing to share positive and negative feelings, and to praise and criticize each other.

5. They develop their own communication system, and become ever more efficient in using it.

6. They increase their ability to map and anticipate each other's views of social reality.

7. They begin to synchronize their goals and behavior, and develop stable interaction patterns.

8. They increase their investment in the relationship, thus enhancing its importance in their life space.

9. They begin increasingly to feel that their separate interests are inextricably tied to the well-being of their relationship.

10. They increase their liking, trust, and love for each other.

11. They see the relationship as irreplaceable, or at least as unique.

12. They more and more relate to others as a couple rather than as individuals.

Despite this measure of agreement, little systematic study has been done of the changes that actually do take place in relationships over time. As the above summary implies, however, certain processes, particularly self-disclosure, and certain transition points, especially commitment to continuing the relationship, have been frequently mentioned as important. Each is also often believed to be both a cause and a consequence of attraction.

Self-disclosure. Self-disclosure plays a central role in Altman and Taylor's (1973) social penetration theory, and it appears in virtually all other discussions of relationship development as well. Indeed, knowledge of the most personal and intimate aspects of the other, presumed to be obtained primarily through self-disclosure, is often considered to be a hallmark of a fully developed close relationship (e.g., Levinger, 1977). Unfortunately, although the topic of self-disclosure has had a long history within social psychology and is of much current interest (for reviews, see Archer, 1980; Chaikin and Derlega, 1974; Cozby, 1973), next to nothing is known of its role in ongoing relationships of some duration and little is known of its role in developing relationships in naturalistic, nonlaboratory contexts.

Laboratory studies have well documented that, in this setting at least, there are stong disclosure reciprocity effects; that is, an individual's disclosure of personal information at a specific level of intimacy is likely to elicit a disclosure from the other at approximately the same level of intimacy. Apparently, as Archer (1980) observes, "disclosure from another is a thing of value that must be paid back" (p. 201). Laboratory studies have also documented that apart from certain limiting conditions, a person who discloses intimate information is often found to be more attractive than one who doesn't (e.g., Archer, Berg, and Runge, 1980) and certainly more attractive than one who fails to reciprocate an intimate disclosure. Further, various causal factors associated with attraction seem also to be causally associated with intimate self-disclosure. For example, people appear to disclose more to physically attractive persons (e.g., Brundage, Derlega, and Cash, 1977) and to disclose more in physically comfortable circumstances (e.g., Chaikin, Derlega, and Miller, 1976). Thus self-disclosure and attraction may be mutually facilitative of each other and, together, of further relationship development.

It should be noted, however, that virtually all laboratory settings in which the antecedents and consequences of self-disclosure have been examined bear an unsettling similarity to a stranger-on-a-train setting. That is, the relationship, taking place as it does in the context of a psychological experiment, constitutes no more than a minuscule, encapsulated bubble on the globe of an individual's actual life space—and perhaps an irrelevant bubble at that. A stranger's disclosures, even his or her most intimate disclosures, may be neither here nor there with respect to the individual's own life and outcomes. In contrast, persons in ongoing relationships are to some extent, and often to a great extent, dependent upon one another, and thus the content of the other's disclosures often have important implications for the individual's welfare. These implications may act to overturn even well-established self-disclosure principles. It is not obvious, for example, that a husband's intimate disclosure that he was recently overcome with an irresistible impulse to gift his female colleague with a black negligee will elevate his wife's attraction to him, nor is it clear that his affection for her will always be enhanced by her reciprocation of an equally intimate disclosure if that disclo-

sure is that it was she, not a stray meteorite, who just wrecked his new car.

Thus although self-disclosure has often been presumed to enhance liking and trust within a relationship and to promote further relationship development, this presumption is in severe need of examination in ongoing relationships of some duration. At the least the implications of the content of the disclosure for the welfare of the recipient surely has to be taken into consideration more than it has in predicting the impact of a self-disclosure upon another's attraction; knowledge of the intimacy level of the disclosure alone is unlikely to suffice for predicting attraction in ongoing relationships. Furthermore, the mode of self-disclosure in ongoing relationships warrants examination. In most studies of self-disclosure the information is transmitted orally, face to face. Individuals in ongoing relationships have many more alternatives (e.g., the one-way ticket to Australia casually left on the hall table), and it seems likely that these alternatives are taken advantage of in certain circumstances and in certain types of relationships and with different effects upon attraction and upon the relationship.

The role of self-disclosure in newly established and developing relationships is not a great deal more clear. Rubin, Hill, Peplau, and Dunkel-Schatter (1980) examined self-disclosure in couples who had been going together (the modal duration of the relationship was eight months and most were dating exclusively) and report the following (p. 313):

> The most striking aspect of our results is the extent to which the student couples in our sample engaged in—or believed that they had engaged in—full and equal self-disclosure, even in highly intimate areas. For example, as many as 73 percent of the men and 74 percent of the women reported that they had disclosed "fully" their feelings about their sexual relationship, 57 percent of each sex had provided full information about their sexual experiences, and 48 percent of the men and 46 percent of the women had disclosed fully their thoughts about the future of the relationship.

Rubin and his colleagues found only small correlations between self-disclosure and duration of relationship, and even in those couples who had been dating less than six months, 46 percent of the women and 45 percent of the men reported that they had fully disclosed to their partners. These findings are especially interesting since many theorists conceive of self-disclosure as taking place only gradually within a relationship and because they also suggest that self-disclosure may play a different role in different stages of a relationship. For example, if the couples' self-reports are veridical, after a relatively short time they have little left to disclose to each other, and thus this factor may cease to play a role in attraction or in further relationship development.

Self-disclosure may play a diminishing role in attraction and relationship development for yet another reason. As a relationship develops, voluntary self-disclosure by the other is less likely to be the sole source of information about the other. The other's friends, acquaintances, and family with whom the individual may have become acquainted may later constitute even better sources of information, and the amount of personal observational data concerning the other's behavior is also likely to increase with time, decreasing the necessity to rely on the other's self-report.

Commitment. The term *commitment* has been used in a variety of ways, but it often is conceived to be "an avowed or inferred intent of a person to maintain a relationship" (Rosenblatt, 1977, pp. 73–74; and see Kiesler, 1971; Levinger, 1980; Rubin, 1973). Despite the fact that commitment intuitively seems to constitute an important aspect of a relationship—and indeed is sometimes singled out as a relationship stage (e.g., Secord and Backman, 1974)—little is known about its role in attraction and relationship development.

Little is known despite the fact that attraction to a person and/or to the relationship is often presumed to be an antecedent of commitment to a relationship, at least voluntary commitment. There are other presumed determinants (e.g., normative pressures), however, and as Rosenblatt (1977) observes, "commitment is different from and perhaps even independent of love, attraction, intimacy, the quality of communication in a relationship, and marital satisfaction" (p. 75). Suffice it to say that the role of attraction in producing commitment is not clear, nor are consequences of commitment for attraction or for other aspects of the relationship.

The role attraction plays in commitment and vice versa is not clear partially because how commitment may be most usefully conceptualized is itself not clear. It may be viewed as a state of mind, as the most common defini-

tion above suggests. But even when viewed as a state of a person, it may be considered to be a discrete variable (e.g., the person is committed or not) or a continuous one. Relatedly, it may be seen as a chronic state (once committed, always committed, other things being equal) or as fluctuating in strength and subject to continuous reconsideration. Commitment may also be viewed as a property of a relationship, and, if it is, the quality of asymmetry of the individual's and the other's commitment to the relationship automatically becomes important in examining the associations between attraction and commitment. Commitment may also be viewed as a process (see Backman, 1981) or as a set of causal conditions and processes that contribute to relationship stability (see Kelley, 1983). In addition, it may be viewed as being reflected by a certain set of behaviors; for example, commitment is often hypothesized to be associated with a decreased tendency to consider and sample the goodness of outcomes available in alternative relationships (e.g., Scanzoni, 1979).

Each of these conceptualizations of commitment have various and differing implications for attraction. For example, if committed persons do not compare the goodness of the outcomes they receive from their partner with those available elsewhere, a number of exchange theory predictions for attraction are likely to become less applicable to committed relationships.

RELATIONSHIP MAINTENANCE

The notion of relationship maintenance implies that the relationship has reached some plateau in its degree of interdependency. Different relationships, of course, will reach different levels of interdependence. Some, perhaps most, social relationships will be maintained at a relatively low degree of interdependence (often characterized as superficial relationships), while others will have reached very high degrees of interdependence (often described as close relationships). Furthermore, the nature of the interdependency between the individual and the other may differ within different levels of closeness.

The beginning of the maintenance stage of close relationships is often thought to be particularly marked by conflict and negotiation (e.g., Scanzoni, 1979). Conflict has also sometimes been considered an important relationship stage in itself. For example, on the basis of their experience with couple therapy, Goldstine, Larner, Zuckerman, and Goldstine (1977) have proposed a three-stage developmental model of marital relationships. In this model the harmony and mutual delight they term Stage I is succeeded, "with the relentlessness of death and taxes," by Stage II, where "to a couple's distress, real life gradually impinges on their relationship. Conflict surfaces, failure intrudes, and boredom casts its pall. The bright illusion *We are one* fades into the bleak conviction *We are hopelessly different*" (Goldstine *et al.*, 1977, p. 9). If the relationship survives these storms, the couple is presumed to graduate to a third stage where their major conflicts have been resolved through compromise, through mutual adaptation, through "agreeing to disagree," or, perhaps not infrequently, through eliminating from their relationship those spheres of interaction that were sources of friction and dispute.

Although the role of conflict in relationship development and maintenance is ambiguous, much of the marital and family therapy literature testifies that the road to closeness in relationships does not run smooth and that conflict is indeed inevitable for many couples (e.g., Christensen, 1983; Peterson, 1983). However, the meaning and forms of conflict may change as relationships develop, as Braiker and Kelley (1979) found in their examination of couples' retrospective accounts of their relationship from initial acquaintance through the first six months of their marriage. They concluded from their data that, first, with increased interdependence came the circumstances for conflict; second, although some conflict was common to all relationships, the types and intensity of conflict in the developmental process differed for different couples; third, and as discussed previously, conflict was not necessarily disruptive of relationship growth and continuation. Not only was the degree of love the couples reported and their accounts of conflict unrelated at all stages of the relationship, but maintenance activities, such as problem-solving behavior and attempts by the partners to change each other or themselves, were associated with love early in the relationship (later in the relationship, however, these activities were associated with conflict and negativity).

Conflict, then, may not be disruptive of a young relationship; indeed, it may be constructive in its development. It is also clear, however, that unresolved conflict is often associated with dissatisfaction, especially in older relationships, and is probably partly responsible for the decline in satisfaction many marital relationships seem to undergo over time (e.g., Blood and Wolfe, 1960; Rands, Levinger, and Mellinger, 1981). Unfortunately, longitu-dinal studies of marital satisfaction and of its correlates are still rare (see Spanier and Lewis, 1980), and the more usual cross-sectional studies present numerous interpretative problems. A recent exception to the rule of cross-sectional studies, however, is a longitudinal study of the role of conflict in friendship development conducted by Eidelson (1980), who proposed that intrapersonal conflict between an individual's affiliative need and need for autonomy results in rises in satisfaction with friendship relationships at low levels of involvement, declines in satisfaction at intermediate levels, and rises in satisfaction once again as involvement further intensifies. His data supported his affiliation-independence model, which also supposes that a decline in satisfaction prompts the individual to carefully evaluate the current and anticipated rewards and costs in the relationship.

Clearly, whether, and how, two people resolve their differences has many important implications for their attraction to one another and for the fate of the relationship. It is also clear that the occurrence of conflict and the likelihood of its satisfactory resolution engage many of the issues we have previously discussed. For example, the degree to which partners disclose to each other their thoughts, feelings, and desires is frequently deemed to be important both to the occurrence of conflict and the probability of its resolution (e.g., Knudson, Sommers, and Golding, 1980), and the degree to which the partners feel committed to the relationship is likely to affect the probability that they will work to resolve their differences. Thus many of the recent investigations of conflict in marital interaction and of the efficacy of various marital treatment methods (e.g., Gottman, 1979; Raush, Barry, Hertel, and Swain, 1974; Weiss, Hops, and Patterson, 1972) can be expected to contribute importantly to knowledge of the role of conflict in relationships in general and to knowledge of whether, and when, it has beneficial or destructive effects upon the partners' attraction to each other and to the relationship.

Especially significant for the future is recent interest in the direct examination of interaction processes in ongoing relationships (see McClintock, 1983, for a review) and in the development of analytical (e.g., Gottman, 1979) and statistical techniques (e.g., Porges, Bohrer, Cheung, Drasgow, McCabe, and Keren, 1980) applicable to the time-series data that a study of relationships necessarily entails. Useful, too, is the increased interest within social psychology in social episodes (e.g., Forgas, 1979), or recurring interaction routines in social life, and in the cognitive scripts and schemas (e.g., Schank and Abelson, 1977; Tesser and Reardon, 1981) that are often associated with them.

RELATIONSHIP DISSOLUTION

The extent to which two people feel attraction or disaffection for one another has obvious implications for the likelihood that they will dissolve their relationship. It is popularly assumed, in fact, that when people no longer like each other, they will terminate their relationship and that, conversely, when two people terminate their relationship, they must have felt little attraction for one another. The truth of the matter is not so simple, however. Sociologist Willard Waller (1930, 1969) observed a long time ago that the stability of a relationship is not necessarily related to the sweetness of its contents. And recent investigations of the emotional aftermath of the termination of marital relationships suggest that even when the dissolution of the relationship is voluntarily initiated, a wide range of feelings for the partner subsequently may be experienced (see Weiss, 1975).

Thus whether a relationship will continue or dissolve probably depends only partially upon the attraction the principals feel for one another. For example, Levinger (1976) has proposed that the continuance of a relationship is a function of its cohesiveness, where three categories of forces determine cohesiveness:

1. The attractiveness of the relationship itself, which is assumed to vary directly with the rewards the individual receives in the relationship and to vary inversely with perceived costs.

2. The attractiveness of actual or potential alternatives to the relationship, where the greater the outcomes available in alternative relationships, the less the cohesiveness.

3. The barriers that act to contain the persons in the relationship, where barriers are the anticipated costs of relationship termination that act to increase cohesiveness.

In Levinger's framework, then, barriers contribute to the continuance of even extremely unsatisfying relationships in which neither partner feels attraction for the other.

Extending Levinger's analysis, Berscheid and Campbell (1981) have argued that in addition to a direct effect on relationship stability, a lack of barriers to marital relationship termination may indirectly affect the other two factors that contribute to the pair's cohesiveness—attraction for the partner and the attractiveness of alternatives. With respect to the latter they argue that as barriers to termination decrease, more marriages dissolve, and as more marriages dissolve, more alternatives are added to the pool of alternative partners for persons in existing marriages, thereby increasing the probability that some of these alternatives will prove to be more attractive than the current partner. Furthermore, it is argued that because barriers to marital termination have diminished rapidly in number and force in recent years, the individual's *raison d'être* for remaining in the relationship has increasingly fallen upon the "sweetness of its contents." When the burden of purpose and justification for maintaining the relationship is placed upon the presence of rewards within the relationship (including the presence of positive emotions and feelings toward the partner), the contents themselves may be more likely to sour than they otherwise would have, because the costs of maintaining the relationship necessarily increase. As Berscheid and Campbell (1981) discuss (pp. 23–24):

> The freedom to stay or go has a price. To have a perpetual choice means that one must choose—not once, but over and over again. And to do so, one must continually expend time and energy in evaluating and re-evaluating the wisdom of the choice.

The cost is increased further when the partner also is perceived to have few barriers to termination, for it then becomes necessary for the individual to continually take the internal pulse of the relationship to divine the partner's satisfaction with it and to also assess the partner's alternatives.

These theoretical analyses of the paths to relationship dissolution, the number of relevant variables, and the complexity of their causal feedback loops suggest that attraction to the partner is both cause and consequence of many other variables that are likely to be found to contribute to relationship maintenance or dissolution. However, longitudinal studies on divorce and remarriage are virtually nonexistent, and single-factor approaches abound (see Berardo, 1980). Even studies of the dissolution of courtship are scarce. With respect to longtitudinal data, a study reported by Hill, Rubin, and Peplau (1976) remains the outstanding exception [apart from Burgess and Wallin's (1953) classic study of engagement and marriage]. These investigators examined the breakups before marriage of over a hundred student couples whose relationships had ended after they began participation in the two-year study. Those whose relationships dissolved tended to be less intimate or less attached to each other when the study began, their degree of involvement in the relationship tended to be unequal, and they tended to be less similar in age than couples who did not part. A significant minority of breakups tended to occur during the school year, and these breakups were initiated by the more involved partner. Finally, very few breakups were mutually desired.

Interest in emotional reaction to separation and divorce in marital relationships has increased in recent years, but these data, too, remain anecdotal and sketchy. The richest descriptive account is provided by Weiss (1975), who derived his observations from interviews with persons in Parents Without Partners groups and seminars conducted for separated persons. Weiss's discussion of various aspects of the failing marriage, emotional reactions to separation, and the continuing relationship of husbands and wives after divorce joins Waller's classic account of the social and emotional consequences of marital separation and divorce, *The Old Love and the New* (1930, 1967), as a fertile source of hypotheses for systematic study. Death, too, dissolves relationships, and current studies of grief and readjustment processes (e.g., Kubler-Ross, 1969) will also provide additional insight into the meaning and dynamics of the deep bonds humans often form with each other.

SUMMARY

Much of the ferment and change that the study of interpersonal attraction is now undergoing has been occasioned by an interest in examining attraction phenomena as they occur in ongoing relationships within naturalistic settings. This change in investigative focus has followed a natural evolutionary course. With evidence that individual characteristics (P and O causal factors) alone did not predict attraction to another, attention shifted to an examination of $P \times O$ factors, and these factors now play a central role in the understanding of attraction phenomena.

From recognition of the importance of $P \times O$ causal factors in the prediction of attraction, researchers have now proceeded to the next logical step, which is to recognize that attraction is also strongly influenced by the physical and social environments that form the context of the individual's relationship with the other. In addition, interest has grown in the concept of relationship itself and in the role that attraction plays in the initiation, maintenance, and dissolution of relationships. As concern with attraction phenomena within naturalistic settings has increased, so also has interest in certain issues that are especially relevant to ongoing relationships. The problem of loneliness, the problem of separation and divorce—especially emotional reactions to these events and the prediction of the occurrence of voluntary relationship termination—questions of self-disclosure and of the occurrence of strong emotion within relationships, including jealousy (see Pines and Aronson, 1983; White, 1977), are all gathering more interest and attention.

Thus social psychological research on interpersonal attraction is moving from the simple to the complex. Beginning with reward and punishment principles, with the conceptualization of attraction as an attitude, and with an interest in the milder forms of attraction as they may or may not take place in initial encounters, investigators have gradually moved toward grappling with the enormous complexities of attraction phenomena as they occur in ongoing relationships in naturalistic situations. One important consequence of this shift in focus is that the necessity for more careful conceptualization of the attraction construct has become apparent. So, too, has become the need for social psychologists interested in attraction to avail themselves of the theoretical, empirical, and methodological fruits of a variety of other disciplines.

The challenge for the future is enormous. What is remarkable, however, is that attraction researchers have moved as quickly as they have to addressing highly complex issues. However difficult and frustrating these issues prove to be, there can be no doubt that the problem is worth the effort. No understanding of human behavior can hope to be complete without an intimate knowledge of the dynamics of interpersonal attraction.

REFERENCES

Abelson, R. (1981). Psychological status of the script concept. *Amer. Psychol., 36,* 715–729.

Adams, G. R. (1981). The effects of physical attractiveness on the socialization process. In G. W. Lucker, K. A. Ribbens, and J. A. McNamara, Jr., (Eds.), *Psychological aspects of facial form.* (Monograph #11, Craniofacial Growth Series), Ann Arbor, Mich.: Center for Human Growth and Development.

Adams, G. R., and P. Crane (1980). An assessment of parents' and teachers' expectations of preschool children's social preference for attractive or unattractive children and adults. *Child Development, 51,* 224–231.

Adams, G. R., and S. M. Crossman (1978). *Physical attractiveness: a cultural imperative.* Roslyn Heights, N.Y.: Libra Publishing.

Adams, G. R., and T. L. Huston (1975). Social perception of middle-aged persons varying in physical attractiveness. *Develop. Psychol., 11* (5), 657–658.

Adams, G. R., and J. C. Lavoie (1974). The effect of sex of child, conduct, and facial attractiveness of teacher expectancy. *Education, 95,* 76–83.

Adams, J. S. (1963). Toward an understanding of inequity. *J. abnorm. soc. Psychol., 67,* 422–436.

———— (1965). Inequity in social exchange. In L. Berkowitz (Ed.), *Advances in experimental social psychology.* Vol. 2. New York: Academic Press. Pp. 266–300.

Aderman, D. (1969). Effects of anticipating future interaction on the preference for balanced states. *J. Pers. soc. Psychol., 11,* 214–219.

Ajzen, I. (1974). Effects of information on interpersonal attraction: similarity versus affective value. *J. Pers. soc. Psychol., 29,* 374–380.

Ajzen, I., and M. Fishbein (1980). *Understanding attitudes and predicting social behavior.* Englewood Cliffs, N.J.: Prentice-Hall.

Allen, B. P. (1978). *Social behavior: fact and falsehood.* Chicago: Nelson-Hall.

Altman, I. (1974). The communication of interpersonal attitudes: an ecological approach. In T. L. Huston (Ed.), *Foundations of interpersonal attraction.* New York: Academic Press.

Altman, I., and D. A. Taylor (1973). *Social penetration: the development of interpersonal relationships.* New York: Holt, Rinehart, and Winston.

Anderson, N. H. (1968). Likableness ratings of 555 personality-trait words. *J. Pers. soc. Psychol., 9,* 272–279.

Archer, R. L. (1980). Self-disclosure. In D. M. Wegner and R. R. Vallacher (Eds.), *The self in social psychology.* New York: Oxford Univ. Press.

Archer, R. L., J. H. Berg, and T. E. Runge (1980). Active and passive observer's attraction to a self-disclosing other. *J. exp. soc. Psychol., 16,* 130–145.

Argyle, M. (1967). *The psychology of interpersonal behavior.* Baltimore, Md.: Penguin Books.

Arnold, M. B. (1960). *Emotion and personality.* (2 Vols.). New York: Columbia Univ. Press.

Aronson, E. (1969). Some antecedents of interpersonal attraction. In W. J. Arnold and D. Levine (Eds.), *Nebraska symposium on motivation.* Vol. 17. Lincoln: Univ. of Nebraska Press.

Aronson, E., and D. Linder (1965). Gain and loss of esteem as determinants of interpersonal attractiveness. *J. exp. soc. Psychol., 1,* 156–172.

Aronson, E., and J. Mills (1959). The effect of severity of initiation on liking for a group. *J. abnorm. soc. Psychol., 67,* 31–36.

Aronson, E., B. Willerman, and J. Floyd (1966). The effect of a pratfall on increasing interpersonal attractiveness. *Psychon. Sci., 4,* 227–228.

Aronson, E., and P. Worchel (1966). Similarity vs. liking as determinants of interpersonal attractiveness. *Psychon. Sci., 5,* 157–158.

Asch, S. E. (1946). Forming impressions of personality. *J. abnorm. soc. Psychol., 41,* 258–290.

Backman, C. W. (1981). Attraction in interpersonal relationships. In R. Turner and M. Rosenberg (Eds.), *Sociological perspectives on social psychology.* New York: Basic Books. Pp. 235–268.

Backman, C. W., and P. F. Secord (1959). The effect of perceived liking on interpersonal attraction. *Hum. Relat., 12,* 379–384.

Benson, P. L., S. A. Karabenick, and R. M. Lerner (1976). Pretty pleases: the effects of physical attractiveness, race, and sex on receiving help. *J. exp. soc. Psychol., 12,* 409–415.

Berardo, F. M. (1980). Decade preview: some trends and directions for family research and theory in the 1980's. *J. Marriage and Family, 42,* 723–728.

Berkowitz, L., and E. Walster (1976). Equity theory: toward a general theory of social interaction. In L. Berkowitz (Ed.), *Advances in experimental social psychology.* Vol. 9. New York: Academic Press.

Berlyne, D. E. (1968). *Conflict, arousal and curiosity.* New York: McGraw-Hill.

Berscheid, E. (1981). An overview of the psychological effects of physical attractiveness and some comments upon the psychological effects of knowledge of the effects of physical attractiveness. In G. W. Lucker, K. Ribbens, and J. A. McNamara (Eds.), *Psychological aspects of facial form.* (Monograph #11, Craniofacial Growth Series), Ann Arbor, Mich.: Center for Human Growth and Development.

———— (1982). Attraction and emotion in interpersonal relationships. In M. S. Clark and S. T. Fiske (Eds.), *Affect and cognition.* Hillsdale, N.J.: Erlbaum.

———— (1983). Emotion. In H. H. Kelley, E. Berscheid, A. Christensen, J. Harvey, T. L. Huston, G. Levinger, E. McClintock, A. Peplau, and D. R. Peterson, *Close relationships.* San Francisco: Freeman.

Berscheid, E., D. Boye, and J. M. Darley (1968). Effect of forced association upon voluntary choice to associate. *J. Pers. soc. Psychol., 8,* 13–19.

Berscheid, E., T. Brothen, and W. Graziano (1976). Gain/loss theory and the "law of infidelity": Mr. Doting vs. the admiring stranger. *J. Pers. soc. Psychol., 33,* 709–718.

Berscheid, E., and B. Campbell (1981). The changing longevity of heterosexual close relationships: a commentary and forecast. In M. Lerner (Ed.), *The justice motive in times of scarcity and change.* New York: Plenum.

Berscheid, E., K. Dion, E. Walster, and G. W. Walster (1971). Physical attractiveness and dating choice: a test of the matching hypothesis. *J. exp. soc. Psychol., 7* (2), 173–189.

Berscheid, E., and J. Fei (1977). Sexual jealousy and romantic love. In G. Clanton and G. Smith (Eds.), *Sexual jealousy: an anthology of research and reflection*. Englewood Cliffs, N.J.: Prentice-Hall. Pp. 101–109.

Berscheid, E., and W. Graziano (1979). The initiation of social relationships and social attraction. In R. L. Burgess and T. L. Huston (Eds.), *Social exchange in developing relationships*. New York: Academic Press. Pp. 31–60.

Berscheid, E., W. Graziano, T. Monson, and M. Dermer (1976). Outcome dependency: attention, attribution, and attraction. *J. Pers. soc. Psychol., 34,* 978–989.

Berscheid, E., and L. A. Peplau (1983). The emerging science of relationships. In H. H. Kelley, E. Berscheid, A. Christensen, J. Harvey, T. L. Huston, G. Levinger, E. McClintock, A. Peplau, and D. R. Peterson, *Close relationships.* San Francisco: Freeman.

Berscheid, E., and E. Walster (1969). *Interpersonal attraction* (1st ed.). Reading, Mass.: Addison-Wesley. [2nd ed., 1978.]

_____ (1974a). A little bit about love. In T. L. Huston (Ed.), *Foundations of interpersonal attraction.* New York: Academic Press.

_____ (1974b). Physical attractiveness. In L. Berkowitz (Ed.), *Advances in experimental social psychology.* Vol. 7. New York: Academic Press.

Block, J. (1957). Studies in the phenomenology of emotions. *J. abnorm. soc. Psychol., 54,* 358–363.

Blood, R. O., Jr., (1967). *Love match and arranged marriage.* New York: Free Press.

Blood, R. O., and D. M. Wolfe (1960). *Husbands and wives: the dynamics of married living.* Glencoe, Ill.: Free Press.

Bower, G. H. (1981). Mood and memory. *Amer. Psychol., 36,* 129–148.

Bowlby, J. (1969, 1973). *Attachment and loss.* Vol. I. *Attachment.* Vol. II. *Separation: anxiety and anger.* New York: Basic Books.

_____ (1973). Affectional bonds: their nature and origin. In R. S. Weiss (Ed.), *Loneliness: the experience of emotional and social isolation.* Cambridge, Mass.: M.I.T. Press.

Braiker, H. B., and H. H. Kelley (1979). Conflict in the development of close relationships. In R. L. Burgess and T. L. Huston (Eds.), *Social exchange in developing relationships.* New York: Academic Press.

Bramel, D. (1969). Interpersonal attraction, hostility, and perception. In J. Mills (Ed.), *Experimental social psychology.* New York: Macmillan.

Brehm, J. W., M. Gatz, G. Goethals, J. McCrimmon, and L. Ward (1967). *Psychological arousal and interpersonal attraction.* Unpublished manuscript, Duke University.

Brenner, M. (1980). The structure of action: introduction. In M. Brenner (Ed.), *The structure of action.* New York: St. Martin's Press.

Brockner, J., and W. C. Swap (1976). Effects of repeated exposure and attitudinal similarity on self-disclosure and interpersonal attraction. *J. Pers. soc. Psychol., 33,* 531–540.

Broderick, C. B. (1971). Beyond the five conceptual frameworks: a decade of development in family theory. In C. B. Broderick (Ed.), *A decade of family research and action 1960–1969.* Minneapolis, Minn.: National Council on Family Relations.

Brundage, L. E., V. J. Derlega, and T. F. Cash (1977). The effects of physical attractiveness and need for approval on self-disclosure. *Pers. soc. Psychol. Bull., 3,* 63–66.

Burgess, E. W., and P. W. Wallin (1943). Homogamy in social characteristics. *Amer. J. Sociol., 49,* (2), 109–124.

_____ (1953). *Engagement and marriage.* Philadelphia: Lippincott.

Burgess, R. L., and T. L. Huston, Eds. (1979). *Social exchange in developing relationships.* New York: Academic Press.

Byrne, D. (1969). Attitudes and attraction. In L. Berkowitz (Ed.), *Advances in experimental social psychology.* Vol. 4. New York: Academic Press.

_____ (1971). *The attraction paradigm.* New York: Academic Press.

Byrne, D., and G. L. Clore (1970). A reinforcement model of evaluative responses. *Pers. int. J., 1,* 103–128.

Byrne, D., and W. Griffitt (1966). A developmental investigation of the law of attraction. *J. Pers. soc. Psychol., 4,* 699–702.

_____ (1973). Interpersonal attraction. *Ann. Rev. Psychol., 24,* 317–336.

Byrne, D., and D. Nelson (1965). Attraction as a linear function of proportion of positive reinforcements. *J. Pers. soc. Psychol., 1,* 659–663.

Cacioppo, J. T., and R. E. Petty (1981). Effects of extent of thought on the pleasantness ratings of P–O–X triads: Evidence for three judgmental tendencies in evaluating social situations. *J. Pers. soc. Psychol., 40,* 1000–1009.

Campbell, B., and E. Berscheid (1976). *The perceived importance of romantic love as a determinant of marital choice: Kephart revisited ten years later.* Unpublished manuscript.

Campell, D. T., and D. W. Fiske (1959). Convergent and discriminant validation by the multitrait-multimethod matrix. *Psychol. Bull., 56,* 81–105.

Candland, D. K. (1977). The persistent problems of emotion. In D. K. Candland, J. P. Fell, E. Keen, A. I. Leshner, R. Plutchik, and R. M. Tarpy, *Emotion.* Monterey, Calif.: Brooks/Cole.

Carnegie, D. (1937). *How to win friends and influence people.* New York: Simon and Schuster.

Cash, T. F., B. Gillen, and D. S. Burns (1977). Sexism and "beautyism" in personnel consultant decision making. *J. appl. Psychol., 62* (3), 301–310.

Chaikin, A. L., and V. J. Derlega (1974). *Self-disclosure.* Morristown, N.J.: General Learning Press.

Chaikin, A. L., V. J. Derlega, and S. J. Miller (1976). Effects of room environment on self-disclosure in a counseling analogue. *J. counsel. Psychol., 23,* 479–481.

Christensen, A. (1983). Intervention. In H. H. Kelley, E. Berscheid, A. Christensen, J. Harvey, T. L. Huston, G. Levinger, E. McClintock, A. Peplau, and D. R. Peterson *Close relationships.* San Francisco: Freeman.

Cimbalo, R. S., V. Faling, and P. Mousaw (1976). The course of love: a cross-sectional design. *Psychol. Reports, 38,* 1292–1294.

Clark, M. S. (1981). Enhancing the link between positive feeling states and positive judgments through arousal. Talk delivered to 17th Annual Carnegie-Mellon Symposium on Cognition ("Affect and Cognition").

Clark, M. S., and A. M. Isen (1984). Toward understanding the relationship between feeling states and social behavior. In A. Hastorf and A. M. Isen (Eds.), *Cognitive social psychology.* New York: Elsevier North-Holland.

Clark, M. S., and J. Mills (1979). Interpersonal attraction in exchange and communal relationships. *J. Pers. soc. Psychol., 37,* 12–24.

Clifford, M. M., and E. Walster (1973). The effect of physical attractiveness on teacher expectations. *Sociol. Educat., 46,* 248–258.

Clore, G. L., and D. A. Byrne (1974). A reinforcement-affect model of attraction. In T. L. Huston (Ed.), *Foundations of interpersonal attraction.* New York: Academic Press.

Clore, G. L., and K. W. Kerber (1981). *Toward an affective theory of attraction and trait attribution.* Manuscript available from senior author.

Cook, T. D., and D. T. Campbell (1979). *Quasi-experimentation: design and analysis for field settings.* Chicago: Rand McNally.

Cooper, J., and E. E. Jones (1969). Opinion divergence as a strategy to avoid being miscast. *J. Pers. soc. Psychol., 13,* 23–40.

Corter, C., S. Trehub, C. Boukydis, L. Ford, L. Clehoffer, and K. Minde (1978). Nurses' judgments of the attractiveness of premature infants. *Infant behav. Develop., 1,* 373–380.

Cozby, P. C. (1973). Self-disclosure: a literature review. *Psychol. Bull., 79,* 73–91.

Darley, J. M., and E. Aronson (1966). Self-evaluation vs. anxiety reduction as determinants of the fear-affiliation relationship. *J. exp. soc. Psychol., 1,* 66–79.

Darley, J. M., and E. Berscheid (1967). Increased liking as a result of the anticipation of personal contact. *Hum. Relat., 20,* 29–40.

Darley, J. M., and R. H. Fazio (1980). Expectancy confirmation processes arising in the social interaction sequence. *Amer. Psychol., 35,* 867–881.

Darley, J. M., and G. R. Goethals (1980). A naive psychological analysis of the causes of ability-linked performances. In L. Berkowitz (Ed.), *Advances in experimental social psychology.* Vol. 13. New York: Academic Press.

Darley, J. G., N. Gross, and W. E. Martin (1951). Studies of group behavior: stability, change, and interrelations of psychometric and sociometric variables. *J. abnorm. soc. Psychol., 46,* 565–576.

Davis, D. (1982). Determinants of responsiveness in dyadic interaction. In W. Ickes and E. S. Knowles (Eds.), *Personality, roles and social behavior.* New York: Springer-Verlag.

Davis, D., and W. T. Perkowitz (1979). Consequences of responsiveness in dyadic interaction: effects of probability of response and proportion of content-related responses on interpersonal attraction. *J. Pers. soc. Psychol., 37,* 534–550.

Davis, K. E., and E. E. Jones (1960). Changes in interpersonal perception as a means of reducing cognitive dissonance. *J. abnorm. soc. Psychol., 61,* 402–410.

Dermer, M. (1982). *Interpersonal attraction—a behavioristic interpretation.* Unpublished manuscript. (Available from Univ. of Wisconsin—Milwaukee.)

Dermer, M., and T. Pyszczynski (1978). Effects of erotica upon men's loving and liking responses for women they love. *J. Pers. soc. Psychol., 36,* 1302–1309.

Dermer, M., and D. L. Thiel (1975). When beauty may fail. *J. Pers. soc. Psychol., 31* (6), 1168–1176.

Deutsch, M., and L. Solomon (1959). Reactions to evaluations by others as influenced by self-evaluations. *Sociometry, 22,* 93–112.

Dewsbury, D. A. (1981). Effects of novelty on copulatory behavior: the Coolidge effect and related phenomena. *Psychol. Bull., 89* (3), 464–482.

Dickens, W. J., and D. Perlman (1981). Friendship across the life cycle. In S. Duck and R. Gilmour (Eds.), *Personal relationships 2: developing personal relationships.* London: Academic Press.

Dickhoff, H. (1961). *Reactions to evaluations by another person as a function of self-evaluation and the interaction context.* Unpublished doctoral dissertation, Duke Univ. Press.

Dion, K. K. (1972). Physical attractiveness and evaluations of children's transgressions. *J. Pers. soc. Psychol., 24,* 207–213.

——— (1977). The incentive value of physical attractiveness. *J. Pers. soc. Psychol., 3,* 67–70.

Dion, K., and E. Berscheid (1974). Physical attractiveness and peer perception among children. *Sociometry, 37,* 1–12.

Dion, K., E. Berscheid, and E. Walster (1972). What is beautiful is good. *J. Pers. soc. Psychol., 24,* 285–290.

Dion, K. K., and S. Stein (1978). Physical attractiveness and interpersonal influence. *J. exp. soc. Psychol., 14,* 97–108.

Dion, K. L., and K. K. Dion (1973). Correlates of romantic love. *J. consult. clinic. Psychol., 41,* 51–56.

——— (1976). Love, liking, and trust in heterosexual relationships. *Pers. soc. Psychol. Bull., 2* (2), 187–190.

Dittes, J. E. (1959). Attractiveness of group as function of self-esteem and acceptance by group. *J. abnorm. soc. Psychol., 59,* 77–82.

Duck, S. W. (1977). *The study of acquaintance.* London: Saxon House.

Duck, S. W., and R. G. Craig (1978). Personality similarity and the development of friendship: a longitudinal study. *Brit. J. soc. clinic. Psychol., 17,* 237–242.

Duck, S., and R. Gilmour, Eds. (1981a). *Personal relationships 1: studying personal relationships.* London: Academic Press.

——— Eds. (1981b). *Personal relationships 2: developing personal relationships.* London: Academic Press.

Dutton, D. G. (1972). Effect of feedback parameters on congruency versus positivity effects in reactions to personal evaluations. *J. Pers. soc. Psychol., 24,* 366–371.

Dutton, D. G., and A. P. Aron (1974). Some evidence for heightened sexual attraction under conditions of high anxiety. *J. Pers. soc. Psychol., 30* (4), 510–517.

Efran, M. G. (1974). The effect of physical appearance on the judgment of guilt, interpersonal attraction, and severity of recommended punishment in a simulated jury task. *J. Res. Pers., 8* (1), 45–54.

Eidelson, R. J. (1980). Interpersonal satisfaction and level of involvement: a curvilinear relationship. *J. Pers. soc. Psychol., 39,* 460–470.

Ellis, A. (1954). *The American sexual tragedy*. New York: Twayne.

Ellsworth, P. C., J. Carlsmith, and A. Henson (1972). The stare as a stimulus to flight in human subjects: a series of field experiments. *J. Pers. soc. Psychol., 21*, 302–311.

Epley, S. W. (1974). Reduction of the behavioral effects of aversive stimulation by the presence of companions. *Psychol. Bull., 81*, 271–283.

———— (1975). The presence of others may reduce anxiety: the evidence is not conclusive. *Psychol. Bull., 82*, 886.

Exline, R. (1971). Visual interaction: the glances of power and preference. In J. Cole (Ed.), *Nebraska symposium on motivation*. Lincoln: Univ. of Nebraska Press.

Festinger, L. (1950). Informal social communication. *Psychol. Rev, 57*, 271–282.

———— (1954). A theory of social comparison processes. *Hum. Rel., 7*, 117–140.

———— (1957). *A theory of cognitive dissonance*. Evanston, Ill.: Row, Peterson.

Festinger, L., S. Schachter, and K. Back (1950). *Social pressures in informal groups: a study of human factors in housing*. Stanford: Stanford Univ. Press.

Fishbein, M., and I. Ajzen (1975). *Belief, attitude, intention, and behavior: an introduction to theory and research*. Reading, Mass.: Addison-Wesley.

Foa, E. B., and V. G. Foa (1980). Resource theory: interpersonal behavior as exchange. In K. J. Gergen, M. S. Greenberg, and R. H. Willis (Eds.), *Social exchange: advances in theory and research*. New York: Plenum.

Forgas, J. (1979). Social episodes: the study of interaction routines. *European monograph in social psychology 17*. London: Academic Press in cooperation with the European Association of Experimental Social Psychology.

Forgas, J. P., and B. Dobosz (1980). Dimensions of romantic involvement: towards a taxonomy of heterosexual relationships. *Soc. Psychol. Quart., 43*, 290–300.

Friedman, L. (1981). How affiliation affects stress in fear and anxiety situations. *J. Pers. soc. Psychol., 40*, 1102–1117.

Fromm, E. (1956). *The art of loving*. New York: Harper & Row.

Fugita, S. S., T. A. Agle, I. Newman, and N. Walfish (1977). Attractiveness, self-concept, and a methodological note about gaze behavior. *Pers. soc. Psychol. Bull., 3*, 240–243.

Gerard, H. B. (1963). Emotional uncertainty and social comparison. *J. abnorm. soc. Psychol., 66*, 568–573.

Gerard, H. B., and J. M. Rabbie (1961). Fear and social comparison. *J. abnorm. soc. Psychol., 62*, 586–592.

Gergen, K. J. (1980). Exchange theory: the transient and the enduring. In K. J. Gergen, M. S. Greenberg, and R. H. Willis (Eds.), *Social exchange: advances in theory and research*. New York: Plenum.

Gillis, J. S., and W. E. Avis (1980). The male-taller norm in mate selection. *Pers. soc. Psychol. Bull., 6*, 396–401.

Goldstine, O., K. Larner, S. Zuckerman, and H. Goldstine (1977). *The dance-away lover*. New York: Ballantine.

Golightly, C., and D. Byrne (1964). Attitude statements as positive and negative reinforcements. *Science, 146*, 798–799.

Gottman, J. M. (1979). *Marital interaction: experimental investigations*. New York: Academic Press.

Granberg, D., and M. King (1980). Cross-lagged panel analysis of the relation between attraction and perceived similarity. *J. exp. soc. Psychol., 16*, 573–581.

Griffitt, W., and R. Veitch (1971). Hot and crowded: influences of population density and temperature on interpersonal affective behavior. *J. Pers. soc. Psychol., 17*, 92–98.

Harlow, H. F. (1958). The nature of love. *Amer. Psychol., 13*, 673–685.

———— (1971). *Learning to love*. San Francisco: Albion Pub. Co.

Harre, R., and P. F. Secord (1972). *The explanation of social behavior*. Oxford: Blackwell.

Harrison, A. A. (1977). Mere exposure. In L. Berkowitz (Ed.), *Advances in experimental social psychology*. Vol. 10. New York: Academic Press.

Hartley, E. L. (1946). *Problems in prejudice*. New York: King's Crown Press.

Hartup, W. (1983). Peer relations. In P. H. Mussen (Ed.), *Handbook of child psychology* (4th ed.). Vol. 4. New York: Wiley.

Hatfield, E., M. K. Utne, and J. Traupman (1979). Equity theory and intimate relationships. In R. L. Burgess and T. L. Huston (Eds.), *Social exchange in developing relationships*. New York: Academic Press.

Heider, F. (1958). *The psychology of interpersonal relations*. New York: Wiley.

Helmreich, R. L., and B. E. Collins (1967). Situational determinants of affiliative preference under stress. *J. Pers. soc. Psychol., 6*, 79–85.

Hess, E. H. (1975). *The tell-tale eye*. New York: Van Nostrand Reinhold.

Hetherington, E. M., M. Cox, and R. Cox (1979). Play and social interaction in children following divorce. *J. soc. Issues, 35*, 26–49.

Hildebrandt, K. A., and H. E. Fitzgerald (1976). *Adult responses to infant cuteness*. Unpublished master's thesis. East Lansing: Michigan State Univ.

Hill, C. T., Z. Rubin, and L. A. Peplau (1976). Breakups before marriage: the end of 103 affairs. *J. soc. Issues, 32* (1), 147–168.

Hill, W. F. (1978). Effects of mere exposure on preferences in nonhuman mammals. *Psychol. Bull., 85* (6), 1177–1198.

Hinde, R. A. (1980). *Towards understanding relationships*. New York: Academic Press.

Hoffman, L. R., and N. R. F. Maier (1966). An experimental reexamination of the similarity-attraction hypothesis. *J. Pers. soc. Psychol., 3*, 145–152.

Holland, P. W., and S. Leinhardt, Eds. (1979). *Perspectives on social network research*. New York: Academic Press.

Holstein, C. M., J. W. Goldstein, and D. J. Bem (1971). The importance of expressive behavior, involvement, sex and need approval in inducing liking. *J. exp. soc. Psychol., 7*, 534–544.

Homans, G. C. (1961). *Social behavior: its elementary forms*. New York: Harcourt, Brace, and World.

———— (1974). *Social behavior: its elementary forms*. (Rev. ed.). New York: Harcourt, Brace, Jovanovich.

Howe, H. E., Jr., and R. A. Dienstbier, Eds. (1979). *Nebraska symposium on motivation 1978*. Vol. 26. Lincoln: Univ. of Nebraska Press.

Huesmann, L. R., and G. Levinger (1976). Incremental exchange theory: a formal model for progression in dyadic interaction. In L. Berkowitz and E. Walster (Eds.), *Advances in experimental social psychology*. Vol. 9. New

York: Academic Press.

Huston, T. L. (1973). Ambiguity of acceptance, social desirability, and dating choice. *J. exp. soc. Psychol., 9,* 32–42.

_____ (1974). A perspective on interpersonal attraction. In T. L. Huston (Ed.), *Foundations of interpersonal attraction.* New York: Academic Press.

Huston, T. L., and G. Levinger (1978). Interpersonal attraction and relationships. *Ann. Rev. Psychol., 29,* 115–156.

Insko, C. A., and A. Adewole (1979). The role of assumed reciprocation of sentiment and assumed similarity in the production of attraction and agreements effects in P–O–X triads. *J. Pers. soc. Psychol., 37,* 790–808.

Isen, A. M. (1970). Success, failure, attention, and reaction to others: the warm glow of success. *J. Pers. soc. Psychol., 15,* 294–301.

Isen, A. M., and P. F. Levin (1972).The effect of feeling good on helping: cookies and kindness. *J. Pers. soc. Psychol., 21,* 384–388.

Isen, A. M., T. Shalker, M. Clark, and L. Karp (1978). Affect accessibility of material in memory and behavior: a cognitive loop? *J. Pers. soc. Psychol., 36,* 1–12.

Izard, C. E. (1977). *Human emotions.* New York: Plenum.

Jackson, D. J., and T. L. Huston (1975). Physical attractiveness and assertiveness. *J. soc. Psychol., 96,* 79–84.

Jacobs, L., E. Berscheid, and E. Walster (1971). Self-esteem and attraction. *J. Pers. soc. Psychol., 17,* 84–91.

Jenkins, J. J. (1981). Can we have a fruitful cognitive psychology? In H. E. Howe, Jr., and J. H. Flowers (Eds.), *Cognitive processes: Nebraska symposium on motivation, 1980.* Lincoln: Univ. of Nebraska Press.

Jones, E. E. (1964). *Ingratiation: a social psychological analysis.* New York: Appleton-Century-Crofts.

Jones, E. E., L. Bell, and E. Aronson (1972). The reciprocation of attraction from similar and dissimilar others. In C. G. McClintock (Ed.), *Experimental social psychology.* New York: Holt, Rinehart, and Winston.

Jones, E. E., and K. E. Davis (1965). From acts to dispositions: the attribution process in person perception. In L. Berkowitz (Ed.), *Advances in experimental social psychology.* Vol. 2. New York: Academic Press.

Jones, E. E., K. J. Gergen, and K. E. Davis (1962). Some determinants of reactions to being approved or disapproved as a person. *Psychol. Monogr., 76,* (whole No. 521).

Jones, E. E., and T. S. Pittman (1982). Toward a general theory of strategic self-presentation. In J. Suls (Ed.), *Psychological perspectives on the self.* Hillsdale, N.J.: Erlbaum.

Jones, E. E., and C. Wortman (1973). *Ingratiation: an attributional approach.* Morristown, N.J.: General Learning Press.

Jones, S. C. (1973). Self- and interpersonal evaluations: esteem theories versus consistency theories. *Psychol. Bull., 79* (3), 185–199.

Jones, S. C., and D. Panitch (1971). The self-fulfilling prophecy and interpersonal attraction. *J. exp. soc. Psychol., 7,* 356–366.

Jones, S. C., and H. A. Pines (1968). Self-revealing events and interpersonal evaluations. *J. Pers. soc. Psychol., 8,* 277–281.

Jones, S. C., and D. J. Schneider (1968). Certainty of self-appraisal and reactions to evaluations from others. *Sociometry, 31,* 395–403.

Kaplan, M. F., and N. H. Anderson (1973). Information integration theory and reinforcement theory as approaches to interpersonal attraction. *J. Pers. soc. Psychol., 28* (3), 301–312.

Katz, D., and E. Stotland (1959). A preliminary statement to a theory of attitude structure and change. In S. Koch (Ed.), *Psychology: a study of a science 3.* New York: McGraw-Hill.

Kelley, H. H. (1967). Attribution theory in social psychology. In D. Levine (Ed.), *Nebraska symposium on motivation.* Vol. XV. Lincoln: Univ. of Nebraska Press.

_____ (1979). *Personal relationships: their structures and processes.* Hillsdale, N.J.: Erlbaum.

_____ (1983). Love and commitment. In H. H. Kelley, E. Berscheid, A. Christensen, J. Harvey, T. L. Huston, G. Levinger, E. McClintock, A. Peplau, and D. R. Peterson, *Close relationships.* San Francisco: Freeman.

Kelley, H. H., E. Berscheid, A. Christensen, J. Harvey, T. L. Huston, G. Levinger, E. McClintock, A. Peplau, and D. R. Peterson (1983). The analysis of close relationships. In H. H. Kelley, E. Berscheid, A. Christensen, J. Harvey, T. L. Huston, G. Levinger, E. McClintock, A. Peplau, and D. R. Peterson, *Close relationships.* San Francisco: Freeman.

Kelley, H. H., and J. W. Thibaut (1978). *Interpersonal relations: a theory of interdependence.* New York: Wiley-Interscience.

Kendrick, D. T., and R. B. Cialdini (1977). Romantic attraction: misattribution vs. reinforcement explanations. *J. Pers. soc. Psychol., 35,* 381–391.

Kendrick, D. T., R. B. Cialdini, and D. E. Linder (1979). Misattribution under fear-producing circumstances: four failures to replicate. *Pers. soc. Psychol. Bull., 5,* 329–334.

Kendrick, D. T., and S. E. Gutierres (1980). Contrast effects and judgments of physical attractiveness: when beauty becomes a social problem. *J. Pers. soc. Psychol., 38,* 131–140.

Kephart, W. M. (1967). Some correlates of romantic love. *J. Marriage and Family,* August, 470–474.

Kerckhoff, A. C. (1974). The social context of interpersonal attraction. In T. L. Huston (Ed.), *Foundations of interpersonal attraction.* New York: Academic Press.

Kerckhoff, A. C., and K. E. Davis (1962). Value consensus and need complementarity in mate selection. *Amer. Sociol. Rev., 27* (3), 295–303.

Kiesler, C. A. (1971). *The psychology of commitment.* New York: Academic Press.

Kiesler, C. A., and G. N. Goldberg (1968). Multidimensional approach to the experimental study of interpersonal attraction: effect of a blunder on the attractiveness of a competent other. *Psychol. Reports, 22,* 693–705.

Kiesler, S. B., and R. L. Baral (1970). The search for a romantic partner: the effects of self-esteem and physical attractiveness on romantic behavior. In K. L. Gergen and D. Marlowe (Eds.), *Personality and social behavior.* Reading, Mass.: Addison-Wesley.

Kleck, R. E., and C. Rubenstein (1975). Physical attractiveness, perceived attitude similarity and interpersonal attraction in an opposite-sex encounter. *J. Pers. soc. Psychol., 31,* 107–114.

Kleck, R. E., S. A. Richardson, and L. Ronald (1974). Physical appearance cues and interpersonal attraction in children. *Child Development, 45,* 305–310.

Klimek, D. (1979). *Beneath mate selection and marriage: the unconscious motives in human pairing.* New York: Van Nostrand-Reinhold.

Knudson, R. M., A. A. Sommers, and S. L. Golding (1980). Interpersonal perception and mode of resolution in marital conflict. *J. Pers. soc. Psychol., 38,* 751–763.

Koren, P., K. Carlton, and D. Shaw (1980). Marital conflict: relations among behaviors, outcomes, and distress. *J. consult. clinic. Psychol., 48,* 460–468.

Kubler-Ross, E. (1969). *On death and dying.* New York: Macmillan.

Langlois, J. (1981). *From the eye of the beholder to behavioral reality: the development of social behaviors and social relations as a function of physical attractiveness.* Talk delivered at the Third Ontario Symposium. "Physical Appearance, Stigma, & Social Behavior." Toronto, Ontario.

Latané, B., and D. C. Glass (1968). Social and non-social attraction in rats. *J. Pers. soc. Psychol., 9,* 142–146.

Latané, B., and D. Hothersall (1972). Social attraction in animals. In P. C. Dodwell (Ed.), *New horizons in psychology 2.* New York: Penguin Books. Pp. 259–275.

Latané, B., and L. Wheeler (1966). Emotionality and reactions to disaster. *J. exp. soc. Psychol., 1,* 95–102.

Lee, J. A. (1976). *The colors of love.* New York: Bantam.

Leinhardt, S., Ed. (1977). *Social networks: a developing paradigm.* New York: Academic Press.

Lerner, M. J. (1980). *The belief in a just world: a fundamental delusion.* New York: Plenum.

Lerner, R. M., and E. Gellert (1969). Body build identification, preference and aversion in children. *Develop. Psychol., 1,* 456–462.

Lerner, R. M., and S. A. Karabenick (1974). Physical attractiveness, body attitudes, and self-concept in late adolescents. *J. Youth Adolescence, 3,* 307–316.

Leventhal, G. S. (1980). What should be done with equity theory? New approaches to the study of fairness in social relationships. In K. J. Gergen, M. S. Greenberg, R. H. Willis (Eds.), *Social exchange: advances in theory and research.* New York: Plenum.

Levinger, G. (1972). Little sandbox and big quarry: comment on Byrne's paradigmatic spade for research on interpersonal attraction. *Rep. Res. soc. Psychol., 3,* 3–19.

——— (1974). A three-level view on attraction: toward an understanding of pair relatedness. In T. L. Huston (Ed.), *Foundations of interpersonal attraction.* New York: Academic Press.

——— (1976). A social psychological perspective on marital dissolution. *J. soc. Issues, 32,* 21–47.

——— (1977). The embrace of lives: changing and unchanging. In G. Levinger and H. L. Raush (Eds.), *Close relationships: perspectives on the meaning of intimacy.* Amherst: Univ. of Massachusetts Press.

——— (1980). Toward the analysis of close relationships. *J. exp. soc. Psychol., 16,* 510–544.

——— (1983). Development and change. In H. H. Kelley, E. Berscheid, A. Christensen, J. Harvey, T. L. Huston, G. Levinger, E. McClintock, A. Peplau, and D. R. Peterson, *Close relationships.* San Francisco: Freeman.

Levinger, G., and J. Breedlove (1966). Interpersonal attraction and agreement: a study of marriage partners. *J. Pers. soc. Psychol., 3,* 367–372.

Levinger, G., D. J. Senn, and B. W. Jorgensen (1970). Progress toward permanence in courtship: a test of the Kerckhoff-Davis hypotheses. *Sociometry, 33* (4), 427–443.

Levinger, G., and J. D. Snoek (1972). *Attraction in relationship: a new look at interpersonal attraction.* New York: General Learning Press.

Lewin, K., T. Dembo, L. Festinger, and P. Sears (1944). Level of aspiration. In J. McV. Hunt (Ed.), *Personality and the behavior disorders.* New York: Ronald.

Lewinsohn, P. M. (1974). A behavioral approach to depression. In R. Friedman and M. Katz (Eds.), *The psychology of depression: contemporary theory and research.* Washington, D.C.: V. H. Winston.

Lindzey, G. (1965). Morphology and behavior. In G. Lindzey and C. S. Hall (Eds.), *Theories of personality: primary sources and research.* New York: Wiley.

Lindzey G., and D. Byrne (1968). Measurement of social choice and interpersonal attractiveness. In G. Lindzey and E. Aronson (Eds.), *The handbook of social psychology.* (2nd ed.) Vol. 2. Reading, Mass.: Addison-Wesley.

Locke, H. J., and R. C. Williamson (1958). Marital adjustment: a factor analysis study. *Amer. Sociol. Rev., 23,* 562–569.

Lorenz, K. (1952). *King Solomon's ring.* London: Methuen.

Lott, A., and B. Lott (1968). A learning theory approach to interpersonal attitudes. In A. G. Greenwald, T. C. Brock, and T. M. Ostrom (Eds.), *Psychological foundations of attitudes.* New York: Academic Press.

——— (1972). The power of liking: consequences of interpersonal attitudes derived from a liberalized view of secondary reinforcement. In L. Berkowitz (Ed.), *Advances in experimental social psychology.* Vol. 6. New York: Academic Press.

——— (1974). The role of reward in the formation of positive interpersonal attitudes. In T. L. Huston (Ed.), *Foundations of interpersonal attraction.* New York: Academic Press.

Lott, B. E., and A. J. Lott (1960). The formation of positive attitudes toward group members. *J. abnorm. soc. Psychol., 61,* 297–300.

McClintock, C. G., and L. J. Keil (1982). Equity and social exchange. In J. Greenberg and L. Cohen (Eds.), *Equity and justice in social behavior.* New York: Academic Press.

McClintock, E. (1983). Interaction processes. In H. H. Kelley, E. Berscheid, A. Christensen, J. Harvey, T. L. Huston, G. Levinger, E. McClintock, A. Peplau, and D. R. Peterson, *Close relationships.* San Francisco: Freeman.

McGuire, W. J. (1969). The nature of attitudes and attitude change. In G. Lindzey and E. Aronson (Eds.), *The handbook of social psychology.* (2nd ed.) Vol. 3. Reading, Mass.: Addison-Wesley.

Mandler, G. (1975). *Mind and emotion.* New York: Wiley.

——— (1984). *Mind and body: psychology of emotion and stress.* New York: Norton.

Marks, G., N. Miller, and G. Maruyama (1981). Effect of targets' physical attractiveness on assumptions of similarity. *J. Pers. soc. Psychol., 41* (1), 198–206.

Marlowe, D., and K. Gergen (1969). Personality and social interaction. In G. Lindzey and E. Aronson (Eds.), *The handbook of social psychology.* (2nd ed.) Vol. 3. Reading, Mass.: Addison-Wesley.

Marwell, G., and J. Hage (1970). The organization of role relationships: a systematic description. *Amer. Sociol. Rev., 35,* 884–900.

Maslow, A. H. (1954). *Motivation and personality.* New York: Harper & Row.

Mathes, E. W. (1975). The effects of physical attractiveness and anxiety on heterosexual attraction over a series of five encounters. *J. Marriage and Family,* November, 769–773.

Matlin, M. W., and D. J. Stang (1978). *The Pollyanna principle: selectivity in language, memory, and thought.* Cambridge, Mass.: Schenkman.

Mehrabian, A. (1972). *Nonverbal communication.* Chicago: Aldine-Atherton.

Mellen, S. L. W. (1981). *The evolution of love.* Oxford: Freeman.

Merton, R. K. (1948). The self-fulfilling prophecy. *Antioch Rev., 8,* 193–210.

———— (1957). *Social theory and social structure.* New York: Free Press of Glencoe.

Mettee, D. R., and E. Aronson (1974). Affective reactions to appraisal from others. In T. L. Huston (Ed.), *Foundations of interpersonal attraction.* New York: Academic Press.

Meyer, J. P., and S. Pepper (1977). Need compatibility and marital adjustment in young married couples. *J. Pers. soc. Psychol., 35* (5), 331–342.

Mills, J., and E. Aronson (1965). Opinion change as a function of the communicator's attractiveness and desire to influence. *J. Pers. soc. Psychol., 1,* 173–177.

Moreno, J. L. (1953). *Who shall survive?* (2nd ed.) Beacon, N.Y.: Beacon House. [1st ed. published 1934.]

Murstein, B. I. (1970). Stimulus-value-role: a theory of marital choice. *J. Marriage and Family, 32,* 465–481.

———— (1976). *Who will marry whom? Theories and research in marital choice.* New York: Springer Publishing Co.

Nahemow, L., and M. P. Lawton (1975). Similarity and propinquity in friendship formation. *J. Pers. soc. Psychol., 32* (2), 205–213.

Newcomb, T. M. (1953). An approach to the study of communicative acts. *Psychol. Rev., 60,* 393–404.

———— (1956). The prediction of interpersonal attraction. *Amer. Psychol., 11,* 575–586.

———— (1961). *The acquaintance process.* New York: Holt, Rinehart, and Winston.

———— (1968). Interpersonal balance. In R. P. Abelson, E. Aronson, W. J. McGuire, T. M. Newcomb, M. J. Rosenberg, and P. H. Tannenbaum (Eds.), *Theories of cognitive consistency: a sourcebook.* Chicago: Rand McNally.

———— (1978). The acquaintance process: looking mainly backward. *J. Pers. soc. Psychol., 36* (10), 1075–1083.

Novak, D. W., and M. J. Lerner (1968). Rejection as a function of perceived similarity. *J. Pers. soc. Psychol., 9,* 147–152.

Olson, D. H., C. S. Russell, and D. H. Sprenkle (1980). Marital and family therapy: a decade review. *J. Marriage and Family, 42,* 973–993.

Osgood, C. E., W. H. May, and M. S. Miron (1975). *Cross-cultural universals of affective meaning.* Urbana: Univ. of Illinois Press.

Osgood, C. E., G. J. Suci, and P. H. Tannenbaum (1957). *The measurement of meaning.* Urbana: Univ. of Illinois Press.

Oskamp, S. (1977). *Attitudes and opinions.* Englewood Cliffs, N.J.: Prentice-Hall.

Pam, A., R. Plutchik, and R. Conte (1975). Love, a psychometric approach. *Psychol. Reports, 37,* 83–88.

Patterson, G. R., J. A. Cobb, and R. S. Ray (1972). Direct intervention in the classroom: a set of procedures for the aggressive child. In F. Clark, D. Evans, and L. Hamerlynck (Eds.), *Implementing behavioral programs for schools and clinics.* Champaign, Ill.: Research Press.

Peele, S. (1975). *Love and addiction.* New York: Taplinger.

Pepitone, A., and C. Wilpinski (1960). Some consequences of experimental rejection. *J. abnorm. soc. Psychol., 60,* 359–364.

Peplau, L. A., and D. Perlman, Eds. (1982). *Loneliness: a sourcebook of current theory, research and therapy.* New York: Wiley-Interscience.

Peterson, D. (1983). Conflict. In H. H. Kelley, E. Berscheid, A. Christensen, J. Harvey, T. L. Huston, G. Levinger, E. McClintock, A. Peplau, and D. R. Peterson, *Close relationships.* San Francisco: Freeman.

Pines, A., and E. Aronson (1983). Antecedents, correlates, and consequences of sexual jealousy. *J. Pers., 51,* 108–136.

Plutchik, R. (1980). *Emotion: a psychoevolutionary synthesis.* New York: Harper & Row.

Porges, S. W., R. E. Bohrer, M. N. Cheung, F. Drasgow, P. M. McCabe, and G. Keren (1980). New time-series statistic for detecting rhythmic co-occurrence in the frequency domain: the weighted coherence and its application to psychophysiological research. *Psychol. Bull., 88* (3), 580–587.

Rands, M., and G. Levinger (1979). Implicit theories of relationship: an intergenerational study. *J. Pers. soc. Psychol., 37,* 649–661.

Rands, M., G. Levinger, and G. Mellinger (1981). Patterns of conflict resolution and marital satisfaction. *J. Fam. Issues, 2,* 297–321.

Raush, H. L., W. A. Barry, R. K. Hertel, and M. A. Swain (1974). *Communication, conflict, and marriage.* San Francisco: Jossey-Bass.

Regan, D. T., E. Straus, and R. Fazio (1974). Liking and the attribution process. *J. exp. soc. Psychol., 10,* 385–397.

Reik, T. (1944). *A psychologist looks at love.* New York: Lancer Books.

Reis, H. T., J. Nezlek, and L. Wheeler (1980). Physical attractiveness in social interaction. *J. Pers. soc. Psychol., 38,* 604–617.

Ridley, C. A., and A. W. Avery (1979). Social network influence on the dyadic relationship. In R. L. Burgess and T. L. Huston (Eds.), *Social exchange in developing relationships.* New York: Academic Press.

Roberts, J. V., and C. P. Herman (1980). *Physique stereotyping: an integrated analysis.* Paper presented to the Canadian Psychological Association Convention.

Rodin, M. J. (1978). Liking and disliking: sketch of an alternative view. *Pers. soc. Psychol. Bull., 4,* 473–478.

Rofé, Y. (1984). Stress and affiliation: activity theory. *Psych. Review, 91,* 235–250.

Rosenblatt, P. C. (1974). Cross-cultural perspective on attraction. In T. L. Huston (Ed.), *Foundations of interpersonal attraction*. New York: Academic Press.

_____ (1977). Needed research on commitment in marriage. In G. Levinger and H. L. Rausch (Eds.), *Close relationships: perspectives on the meaning of intimacy*. Amherst: Univ. of Massachusetts Press.

Rosenblatt, P. C., and R. M. Anderson (1981). Human sexuality in cross-cultural perspective. In M. Cook (Ed.), *The bases of human sexual attraction*. London and New York: Academic Press. Pp. 215–250.

Ross, L., M. Lepper, and M. Hubbard (1975). Perseverance in self-perception and social perception: biased attributional processes in the debriefing paradigm. *J. Pers. soc. Psychol., 32,* 880–892.

Rubenstein, C. M., and P. Shaver (1980). Loneliness in two northeastern cities. In J. Hartog and R. Audy (Eds.), *The anatomy of loneliness*. New York: International Universities Press.

Rubin, Z. (1970). Measurement of romantic love. *J. Pers. soc. Psychol., 16* (2), 265–273.

_____ (1973). *Liking and loving: an invitation to social psychology*. New York: Holt, Rinehart, and Winston.

_____ (1974). From liking to loving: patterns of attraction in dating relationships. In T. L. Huston (Ed.), *Foundations of interpersonal attraction*. New York: Academic Press.

Rubin, Z., C. T. Hill, L. A. Peplau, and C. Dunkel-Schetter (1980). Self-disclosure in dating couples: sex roles and the ethic of openness. *J. Marriage and Family, 42,* 305–317.

Rubin, Z., and C. Mitchell (1976). Couples research as couples counseling: some unintended effects of studying close relationships. *Amer. Psychol., 31,* 17–25.

Russell, D., L. A. Peplau, and M. L. Ferguson (1978). Developing a measure of loneliness. *J. Pers. Assess., 42,* 290–294.

Russell, J. A. (1980). A circumplex model of affect. *J. Pers. soc. Psychol., 39,* 1161–1178.

Saegert, S. C., W. C. Swap, and R. B. Zajonc (1973). Exposure, context, and interpersonal attraction. *J. Pers. soc. Psychol., 25,* 234–242.

Sarnoff, I., and P. G. Zimbardo (1961). Anxiety, fear, and social affiliation. *J. abnorm. soc. Psychol., 62,* 356–363.

Saul, L. J. (1979). *The childhood emotional pattern in marriage*. New York: Van Nostrand-Reinhold.

Scanzoni, J. (1979). Social exchange and behavioral interdependence. In R. Burgess and T. Huston (Eds.), *Social exchange in developing relationships*. New York: Academic Press.

Schachter, S. (1951). Deviation, rejection, and communication. *J. abnorm. soc. Psychol., 46,* 190–207.

_____ (1959). *The psychology of affiliation*. Stanford: Stanford Univ. Press.

_____ (1964). The interaction of cognitive and physiological determinants of emotional state. In L. Berkowitz (Ed.), *Advances in experimental social psychology*. Vol. 1. New York: Academic Press.

Schank, R., and R. Abelson (1977). *Scripts, plans, goals and understanding*. Hillsdale, N.J.: Erlbaum.

Schiffenbauer, A., and R. S. Schiavo (1976). Physical distance and attraction: an intensification effect. *J. exp. soc. Psychol., 12,* 274–282.

Schneider, D. J., A. H. Hastorf, and P.C. Ellsworth (1979). *Person perception*. (2nd ed.) Reading, Mass.: Addison-Wesley.

Schuman, H., and M. P. Johnson (1976). Attitudes and behavior. *Ann. Rev. Sociol., 2,* 161–207.

Secord, P. F., and C. W. Backman (1974). *Social psychology*. (2nd ed.) New York: McGraw-Hill.

Segal, M. W. (1974). Alphabet and attraction: an unobtrusive measure of the effect of propinquity in a field setting. *J. Pers. soc. Psychol., 30,* 654–657.

Seligman, M. E. P. (1975). *Helplessness: on depression, development, and death*. San Francisco: Freeman.

Shanteau, J., and G. Nagy (1976). Decisions made about other people: a human judgment analysis of dating choice. In J. Carroll and J. Payne (Eds.), *Cognition and social judgment*. Hillsdale, N.J.: Erlbaum.

Shaver, P., and C. Rubenstein (1980). Childhood attachment experience and adult loneliness. In L. Wheeler (Ed.), *Review of personality and social psychology*. Vol. 1. Beverly Hills Calif.: Sage.

Sherif, M., O. J. Harvey, B. J. White, W. R. Hood, and C. W. Sherif (1954). *Experimental study of positive and negative intergroup attitudes between experimentally produced groups*. Robbers' Cave Study. Norman: Univ. of Oklahoma. (Multilithed)

Shrauger, J. S. (1975). Responses to evaluation as a function of initial self-perception. *Psychol. Bull., 82* (4), 581–596.

Shulman, W. (1975). Life-cycle variations in patterns of close relationships. *J. Marriage and Family* (November), 813–821.

Sigall, H., and N. Ostrove (1975). Beautiful but dangerous: effects of offender attractiveness and nature of the crime on juridic judgment. *J. Pers. soc. Psychol., 31* (3), 410–414.

Sigall, H., R. Page, and A. C. Brown (1971). Effort expenditure as a function of evaluation and evaluator attractiveness. *Rep. Research soc. Psychol., 2* (2), 19–25.

Sigall, J., and D. Landy (1973). Radiating beauty: effects of having a physically attractive partner on person perception. *J. Pers. soc. Psychol., 28,* 218–224.

Singer, J. E. (1966). Motivation for consistency. In S. Feldman (Ed.), *Cognitive consistency: motivational antecedents and behavioral consequents*. New York: Academic Press.

Skolnick, P. (1971). Reactions to personal evaluations: a failure to replicate. *J. Pers. soc. Psychol., 18,* 62–67.

Snyder, C. R., and H. L. Fromkin (1980). *Uniqueness: the human pursuit of difference*. New York: Plenum.

Snyder, M., and W. B. Swann (1978). Behavioral confirmation in social interaction: from social perception to social reality. *J. exp. soc. Psychol., 14,* 148–162.

Snyder, M., E. D. Tanke, and E. Berscheid (1977). Social perception and interpersonal behavior: on the self-fulfilling nature of social stereotypes. *J. Pers. soc. Psychol., 35,* 656–666.

Spanier, G. B. (1976). Measuring dyadic adjustment: new scales for assessing the quality of marriage and similar dyads. *J. Marriage and Family, 38,* 15–28.

Spanier, G. B., and R. A. Lewis (1980). Marital quality: a review of the seventies. *J. Marriage and Family, 42* (4), 825–839.

Stalling, R. S. (1970). Personality similarity and evaluative meaning as conditioners of attraction. *J. Pers. soc. Psychol., 14,* 77–82.

Stapert, J. C., and G. L. Clore (1969). Attraction and disagreement-produced arousal. *J. Pers. soc. Psychol., 13,* 64–69.

Stephan, W. G. (1978). School desegregation: an evaluation of predictions made in Brown vs. Board of Education. *Psychol. Bull., 85,* 217–238.

Stephan, W., E. Berscheid, and E. Walster (1971). Sexual arousal and heterosexual perception. *J. Pers. soc. Psychol., 20,* 93–101.

Stevenson, H. W., and R. D. Odom (1962). The effectiveness of social reinforcement following two conditions of social deprivation. *J. abnorm. soc. Psychol., 65* (6), 429–431.

Stewart, J. E. (1980). Defendant's attractiveness as a factor in the outcome of criminal trials: an observational study. *J. appl. soc. Psychol., 10,* 348–361.

Stouffer, S. A., E. A. Suchman, L. C. DeVinney, S. A. Starr, and R. M. Williams (1949). *The American soldier: adjustment during army life.* Vol. 1. Princeton, N.J.: Princeton Univ. Press.

Straus, M. A., and G. T. Hotaling, Eds. (1980). *The social causes of husband-wife violence.* Minneapolis, Minn.: Univ. of Minnesota Press.

Strongman, K. T. (1978). *The psychology of emotion* (2nd ed.). New York: Wiley.

Suls, J. M., and R. L. Miller, Eds. (1977). *Social comparison processes: theoretical and empirical perspectives.* Washington, D.C.: Hemisphere.

Sweeney, P. D., D. E. Shaeffer, and S. Golin (1982). Pleasant events, unpleasant events, and depression. *J. Pers. soc. Psychol., 43,* 136–144.

Swensen, C. H. (1972). The behavior of love. In H. A. Otto (Ed.), *Love today: a new exploration.* New York: Association Press.

Symons, D. (1979). *The evolution of human sexuality.* New York: Oxford Univ. Press.

Talmon, Y. (1964). Mate selection in collective settlements. *Amer. Sociol. Rev., 29,* 491–508.

Taylor, S. E., and S. T. Fiske (1978). Salience, attention, and attribution: top of the head phenomena. In L. Berkowitz (Ed.), *Advances in experimental social psychology.* Vol. 11. New York: Academic Press.

Taylor, S. E., and D. Mettee (1971). When similarity breeds contempt. *J. Pers. soc. Psychol., 20,* 75–81.

Tedeschi, J. T. (1974). Attributions, liking, and power. In T. L. Huston (Ed.), *Foundations of interpersonal attraction.* New York: Academic Press.

Tennov, D. (1979). *Love and limerence: the experience of being in love.* New York: Stein & Day.

Tesser, A., and R. Reardon (1981). Perceptual and cognitive mechanisms in human sexual attraction. In M. Cook (Ed.), *The bases of human sexual attraction.* New York: Academic Press.

Thibaut, J. W., and H. Kelley (1959). *The social psychology of groups.* New York: Wiley.

Triandis, H. C. (1980). Values, attitudes, and interpersonal behavior. In H. E. Howe, Jr. and M. M. Page (Eds.), *Nebraska symposium on motivation.* Vol. 27. Lincoln: Univ. of Nebraska Press.

Tyler, T. R., and D. O. Sears (1977). Coming to like obnoxious people when we must live with them. *J. Pers. soc. Psychol., 35,* 200–211.

Waller, W. (1930, 1967). *The old love and the new: divorce and readjustment.* Carbondale: Southern Illinois Univ. Press.

Waller, W. W., and R. Hill (1951). *The family: a dynamic interpretation.* New York: Dryden.

Walster, E. (1965). The effect of self-esteem on romantic liking. *J. exp. soc. Psychol., 1,* 184–197.

Walster, E., V. Aronson, D. Abrahams, and L. Rottmann (1966). Importance of physical attractiveness in dating behavior. *J. Pers. soc. Psychol., 4* (5), 508–516.

Walster, E., and E. Berscheid (1971). Adrenaline makes the heart grow fonder. *Psychology Today, 5,* 46–50; 62.

Walster, E., and G. W. Walster (1963). Effect of expecting to be liked on choice of associates. *J. abnorm. soc. Psychol., 67,* 402–404.

Walster, E., G. W. Walster, and E. Berscheid (1978). *Equity: theory and research.* Rockleigh, N.J.: Allyn and Bacon.

Walster, E. H., and W. Walster (1979). *A new look at love.* Reading, Mass.: Addison-Wesley.

Weiss, R. L., H. Hops, and G. R. Patterson (1972). A framework for conceptualizing marital conflict, a technology for altering it, some data for evaluating it. *Banff International Conference on Behavior Modification* (4th).

————— (1973). A framework for conceptualizing marital conflict. In L. A. Hamerlynck, L. C. Handy, and E. S. Mash (Eds.), *Behavior change.* Champaign, Ill.: Research Press.

Weiss, R. S. (1973). *Loneliness: the experience of emotional and social isolation.* Cambridge, Mass.: M.I.T. Press.

————— (1975). *Marital separation.* New York: Basic Books.

Werner, G., and B. Latané (1974). Interaction motivates attraction: rats are fond of fondling. *J. Pers. soc. Psychol., 29,* 328–334.

Wheeler, L. (1974). Social comparison and selective affiliation. In T. L. Huston (Ed.), *Foundations of interpersonal attraction.* New York: Academic Press.

Wheeler, L., and J. Nezlek (1977). Sex differences in social participation. *J. Pers. soc. Psychol., 35,* 742–754.

White, G. (1977). Jealousy model. In G. Clanton and L. G. Smith (Eds.), *Jealousy.* Englewood Cliffs, N.J.: Prentice-Hall.

————— (1980). Physical attractiveness and courtship progress. *J. Pers. soc. Psychol., 39,* 660–668.

White, G. L., S. Fishbein, and J. Rutstein (1981). Romantic attraction: Misattribution of arousal on secondary reinforcement. *J. Pers. soc. Psychol.*

White, R. W. (1959). Motivation reconsidered: the concept of competence. *Psychol. Rev., 66,* 297–334.

Wiggins, J. S., N. Wiggins, and J. C. Conger (1968). Correlates of heterosexual somatic preference. *J. Pers. soc. Psychol., 10,* 82–90.

Wilson, M., T. F. Cash, and S. G. West (1978). *Divergent effects of physical attractiveness as a function of the situational context.* Paper presented at the Eastern Psychological Association Convention, Washington, D.C.

Winch, R. F. (1958). *Mate-selection: a study of complementary needs.* New York: Harper.

Wish, M., M. Deutsch, and S. J. Kaplan (1976). Perceived dimensions of interpersonal relations. *J. Pers. soc. Psychol., 33,* 409–420.

Wolf, A. P. (1966). Childhood association, sexual attraction, and the incest taboo: a Chinese case. *Amer. Anthrop., 68,* 883–898.

Wright, P. H. (1971). Byrne's paradigmatic approach to the study of attraction: misgivings and alternatives. *Rep. research soc. Psychol., 2,* 66–70.

Zadny, J., and H. B. Gerard (1974). Attributed intentions of informational selectivity. *J. exp. soc. Psychol., 10,* 34–52.

Zajonc, R. B. (1968). The attitudinal effects of mere exposure. *J. Pers. soc. Psychol.* (Monograph Supplement 2) *9,* part 2, 1–27.

_____ (1980). Feeling and thinking: preferences need no inferences. *Amer. Psychol., 35,* 151–175.

Zajonc, R. B., H. Markus, and W. R. Wilson (1974). Exposure effects and associative learning. *J. exp. soc. Psychol., 10,* 248–263.

Zevon, M. A., and A. Tellegen (1982). *The structure of mood change: an idiographic/nomothetic analysis. J. Pers. soc. Psychol., 43,* 111–122.

Zillman, D. (1978). Attribution and misattribution of excitatory reactions. In J. H. Harvey, W. Ickes, and R. F. Kidd (Eds.), *New directions in attribution research.* Vol. 2. Hillsdale, N.J.: Erlbaum.

Zimbardo, P. G. (1977). *Shyness: what it is, what to do about it.* Reading, Mass.: Addison-Wesley.

Zimbardo, P., and R. Formica (1963). Emotional comparison and self-esteem as determinants of affiliation. *J. Pers., 31,* 141–162.

CHAPTER 22

Leadership and Power

Edwin P. Hollander
State University of New York at Buffalo

Leadership is essential to the organized functioning of society, and its scope is very wide. Almost anything related to joint activity involves leadership, or at least is associated with it. As a process by which individuals are directed toward collective action, leadership shows the vital element of interdependence in social relationships. The *quality* of leadership also is significant in determining the health and progress of a group, an organization, or a society.

Whenever people become involved in a joint activity, a leadership structure develops. Whether it comes from tradition or from the demands of new circumstances, the leadership structure is the framework within which the process of leader-follower relations occurs. Its main purpose is to organize and direct the activity toward achieving the goal set by the particular task. There are many daily person-to-person relationships that involve influence between parent and child, for example, or teacher and student, husband and wife. These dyads show features of leadership. However, they lack the special character of leadership in groups, large organizations, and nations, where more attention is needed to a whole set of relationships for joint activity to go on.

Some form of leadership is universal in human groups, although it is not uniquely human. It exists as authority in the formal case of nations and organizations, and as dominance among animals. Indeed, whether among apes, wolves, tigers, or gulls, the existence of some kind of leadership structure is widespread. That structure is determined by dominance or programmed patterns of behavior rather than by such external factors as opportunities for appointment and promotion in organizations. Often the largest male is dominant in ape colonies, although age is also a factor among gorillas, where the "gray-back" male usually dominates the group (Emlen and Schaller, 1960). In prides of lions, females lead the hunt and largely dominate the group's life to the exclusion of males (Schaller, 1972).

In preparing this chapter, I benefited greatly from the very capable assistance of Susan J. Grelick with library research and Linda J. Hereth with manuscript preparation. I am very glad to express my appreciation to both of them for their immensely helpful and dedicated efforts. It is also a pleasure to acknowledge my particular indebtedness to James W. Julian, with whom I enjoyed a fruitful collaboration in this field in years past. He, as well as Martin G. Evans, Raymond G. Hunt, and James T. Lester, read an earlier version of this chapter; each gave me astute criticisms and suggested revisions, for which I am extremely grateful. As usual, I take full responsibility for what appears here.

An analogue to such dominance in human groups is the exercise of power. Essentially power demands compliance through coercion rather than persuasion. At its high pole, power takes the form of control in which one or more persons are forced to do the bidding of one or more others, or suffer consequences. Although leadership does not require the *use* of power in its day-to-day practice, the actual or perceived *threat* of power is sufficient in many situations to arouse feelings analogous to those generated by strong likes and dislikes in interpersonal relations. Indeed for some researchers leadership and power are virtually the same. As Fiedler (1970), for one, has put it: "Leadership, essentially, means power over other people, and power over others enables a man to do things, to get things, to accomplish feats that, by himself, are unattainable" (p. 1). This is not a widely shared view; more probably at times and places leadership *may* be infused with power ranging from implied coercion, masquerading as persuasion, to clear control.

Whether boldly or more subtly, leaders in various settings certainly can wield considerable power from a position of legitimacy conferred by an orgnization. How much they do so is likely to be a matter of personal predilection or style. At the extreme, one corporate head is quoted in a recent *Fortune* magazine article (Menzies, 1980) as saying that leadership is demonstrated when the ability to inflict pain is confirmed. This extremity of power is not the norm in the usual leadership situations of a nonautocratic, noncontrolling form.

SCOPE AND DEFINITIONS

If it is not first evident, the study of leadership and power covers an immense terrain that is not easily comprehended in any single, systematic treatment. That is one of the reasons why this chapter makes no pretense at being encyclopaedic. Also there is no single way to organize and study the phenomena encompassed by these terms, though attempts in this direction have been made (e.g., regarding leadership, see Jago, 1982). Leadership and power are pervasive and take many forms throughout society, including corporate, social service, governmental, political, production, and military settings, among many others. That being so, this chapter is aimed primarily at identifying some relevant *social psychological* variables in various kinds of leadership events, with special emphasis on more salient topics in current work, particularly since the publication of Stogdill's *Handbook of Leadership* (1974), now revised by Bass (1981).

Furthermore, since a chapter appears here on organizations, a balance has been struck that is less weighted toward organizational leadership. There also are several relatively current chapters on organizational leadership (Vroom, 1976b; Barrow, 1977; Evans, 1979), one by Katz (1973) on political leadership, a book by Ng (1980) on the social psychology of power, and two new multidisciplinary anthologies on leadership (Rosenbach and Taylor, 1984; Kellerman, 1984a). There is also the useful series of books emanating from the Southern Illinois University Leadership Symposia (Fleishman and Hunt, 1973; Hunt and Larson, 1974, 1975, 1977, 1979; Hunt, *et al.,* 1981).

The plan of this chapter is to deal first with some definitional matters, highlight pertinent historical developments and approaches to the study of leadership, then survey a variety of topic areas that help to cluster research (e.g., leader authority and emergence, personality and style, follower effects on leaders, gender effects), and conclude with some comments on the current field. Since leadership implicates many processes studied in social psychology, including socialization, role behavior, attitude change, and conformity, its study has wide applicability.

LEADERSHIP, THE LEADER, AND FOLLOWERS

Leadership has been defined in a great many ways. The most consistent element noted is that leadership involves a process of *influence* between a leader and followers to attain group, organizational, or societal goals. In informal groups, for example, the leader is commonly considered to be that person who shows the most influence.

The term *power* is used as a substitute for influence in some definitions of leadership. But as noted, power implies features of coercion and control, whereas influence indicates greater persuasion. Therefore the distinction between these terms is meaningful and will be maintained here. The intricate relationship of leadership and power will be given special consideration as well.

Other approaches to leadership define the leader's status by *relative rank*. Such a position may be assigned, as in the case of an *office* in organizations, or it may be an individual's acquired *identity,* based on the traditional social criteria of economic, political, and personal prestige (Davis, 1966). The last of these comes closest to valued "leadership qualities" that give a person higher status in the eyes of others.

A more utilitarian approach to defining the leader in most formal situations is to identify the person or persons with a directive role. This encompasses all of those supervisory, managerial, administrative, and executive functions that are identified foremost with organizational leadership. A role of this kind usually involves authority and responsibility and may ensure compliance through the use of power vested in one's role. However, routine *role performance* may be insufficient for group productivity and satisfaction. In that respect Katz and Kahn (1978) define organizational leadership as "the influential increment over and above mechanical compliance with the routine directives of the organization." They say that such an influential increment derives from "the fact that human beings rather than computers are in positions of authority and power" (p. 528). Of course, the *symbolic value of authority* may translate into great influence, as revealed in the story of the Old West where the question, "How come you sent us *only one* Ranger for the riot?" was answered by, "Well, there was *only one* riot, wasn't there?"

Although the leader role ordinarily is central in a leadership process, leadership is not the leader's task alone. The process involves others, usually called followers, and sometimes subordinates; they also may have an active role in concerted activities, which can include prodding the leader. While these activities may therefore seem to be centered on the particular individual who is the leader, they require distributed group efforts. Difficulties arise, however, from the categorical quality of the words *leader* and *follower,* suggesting that they must be sharply differentiated on an activity dimension. The facts are quite different.

All leaders to some degree are followers at times; and followers are not cast forever in a "passive" nonleader role. They may and do at times become leaders. Granting that only a few people can occupy the status of leader in a particular setting, the qualities needed to be a leader are not possessed just by those individuals. Furthermore the leader cannot do everything, though he or she might try. In any group or organization there are different leadership functions to be fulfilled, which include the roles of director of activity, problem-solver and planner, communicator, adjudicator of conflict, advocate, and liaison with the external environment. Being a leader is therefore a complex of roles, and the functions these encompass require assistance through astute delegation.

In sum, leadership is a process and not a person (McGregor, 1944), though the leader is the one most often seen as the focal point of activity. His or her actions are most likely to command attention, as history illustrates with predictable regularity. The reasons are not hard to identify. Leaders typically show more activity than those around them. And generally leaders are more influential than others, in the sense of "getting things done." However, their accomplishments require responsive followers who contribute to the outcome, even if credited to the leader. Therefore acts of "leadership" may be achieved by the efforts of those labeled "followers."

The fact that organizations require "followership" from leaders arrayed at all levels of the hierarchy means that the quality of being an active and responsive subordinate will call attention to the evident leadership potential of someone being considered for a higher position. Therefore, the kinds of behavior seen as representing effective leadership include attributes of good followership. These are not sharply separated, except in language, because leadership frequently depends upon people being mutually responsive, whoever bears the designation of "leader."

A leader also may play a significant psychological part in group functioning, for example, by providing a definition of reality to followers and by showing concern for them through the quality of fairness. In that vein Freud proposed an affective conception of leadership in his *Group Psychology and the Analysis of the Ego* (1921). He construed the leader as an ego-ideal with whom the members of a group were bound together in a mutual identification, that is, a shared allegiance. He saw this as an element that distinguishes leadership from excessive dominance in the coercive-power sense.

At the other extreme from the high-intensity, power-infused leadership, there is the aimlessness and drift that may cause followers to complain about a "lack of leadership" and to yearn for "strong leadership." There may be so little sense of decisive direction that chaos reigns, with resulting ambiguities and uncertainties for followers. Such a crisis can occur in association with political and economic instabilities in society, as Fromm (1941) has noted in his analysis of the rise of nazism in Germany.

In a broader perspective there are many contextual elements, beyond the leader and followers, that affect the leadership process. Among these are such factors as the nature of the activity, its history and actors, the availability of human and material resources, and the quality of leader-follower relations. The latter relations are of course affected by the leader's attributes, among which are his or her perceived competence, motivation, and personality characteristics, and those of the followers. To some extent any of them may play a part in shaping follower perceptions of the leader and responses to the leader.

Clearly then, the study of leadership presents a level of complexity that may explain why even its staunchest adherents express some awe and even pessimism. In the preface to his *Handbook of Leadership,* Stogdill (1974) says, "The endless accumulation of empirical data has not produced an integrated understanding of leadership" (p. vii). He was nonetheless a passionate proponent of doing empirical work as a means of gaining sound generalizations (see Stogdill, 1977). Another researcher, Sims (1977), has said, "Leadership is perhaps the most researched and least understood area of organizational behavior" (p. 133).

Some other critics are frankly dubious about the fruits to be harvested from studying the interpersonal features of leadership. McCall (1976) has expressed strong skepticism about the limitations of research on leadership in organizations. Kerr (1977) has argued for recognizing "substitutes for leadership," particularly the organizational rules and customs that keep the enterprise going (cf. Kerr and Jermier, 1978; Howell and Dorfman, 1981). And Calder (1977) has contended that leadership depends more on attribution made by followers than on leader actions.

Despite the critiques and outright skepticism represented by these observations, leadership is a social process whose effectiveness involves the activities of leaders and those they lead. "Leadership effectiveness" is usually measured by productivity, cohesiveness, and satisfaction. In these outcomes leaders are inescapably seen as significant factors, even granting the effects of situational factors, including social structure, past events, and the crust of custom.

The position of leadership is sought for a variety of motives. McClelland (1975) contends that explanations of this process may emphasize the motive of *personal* power, to dominate others, rather than recognize *socialized* power, oriented toward organizing activities and helping followers gain goals through their efforts. Furthermore, there are non-power motives, such as achievement, which he says may be involved in seeking the leader role. Obviously leaders gain the potential for "having an effect" and greater attention. In organizations leaders are among the best paid and generally are able to exercise greater control over their use of time

(Jaques, 1961). Leaders also are likely to get "special handling" with respect to deferential behavior by others, not only by subordinates.

On the potentially negative side, leaders typically are perceived to be more responsible for outcomes in groups and organizations, as well as in society, precisely because of the element of greater authority vested in the role (e.g., Jacobs, 1970; Homans, 1974). With authority comes responsibility. Since leaders are more visible, their failings as well as successes are apparent, especially to detractors who covet their role. The leader role often involves contention with others who are would-be successors or peers involved in "battles" for resources and territory. In this respect the availability of power and counterpower is vital in contending successfully for such benefits and in being able to fend off adversaries.

Leadership and the leader are embedded in a set of circumstances. For example, the historic political context plays an important part in the relationship of the royal leader and followers, especially regarding expectations of a fair exchange. During the pageantry associated with the wedding in 1981 of Britain's Prince Charles, an American television interviewer asked passersby on a London street whether they thought the price of royalty was too high. Few said it was, with the comments shown distinctly favoring the monarchy. One woman put it succinctly, saying: "Yes, they do cost a lot, but a dictator would cost us a great deal more, and the people would get far less for it."

POWER AND INFLUENCE

In common usage, power is the ability to exert a degree of control over persons, things, and events. Influence is used more to suggest the exercise of persuasion rather than control. As Pruitt (1976) observes, "influence and power are omnipresent in human affairs. Indeed, groups cannot possibly function unless their members can influence one another. Power can of course be used for the wrong purposes. But if so, it must be understood in order to protect oneself and others" (p. 343).

A classic statement of the distinction between influence and power is by Bierstedt (1950), who said, "Influence does not require power, and power may dispense with influence. Influence may convert a friend, but power coerces friend and foe alike" (p. 731). Practically speaking, power relations have two features: the ability to *exert* power, in the sense of controlling others and events, and the capacity to *defend* against power. Cartwright (1959) has called the latter "counter-power."

Both elements are involved in studying the effects of power. As Weber (1947) wrote: "Power is the probability that one actor within a social relationship will be in a position to carry out his own will despite resistance" (p. 152). Quite simply, having enough power means you can get your own way. A yearning for personal power will generate great efforts toward that end. Indeed the psychoanalytic thinker Alfred Adler (1925) considered the individual striving for personal power to be as central to psychodynamic functioning as the sexual drive is to Freud's psychoanalytic theory.

The power construct is used in at least three major ways in social psychology (Ng, 1980). First, power is *motivational,* in the sense of striving for mastery or control (Winter, 1973; McClelland, 1975). Second, power is used in *cognitive* terms, as in perceived locus of control (Rotter, 1966) and the concepts of personal causation and self-efficacy (deCharms, 1968; Bandura, 1977). Third, power is *behavioral,* as in Heider's (1958) "can" factor in the analysis of actions of individuals and the distinction made between "behavior control" and "fate control" by Thibaut and Kelley (1959).

Most analyses of leadership and power begin with the basis on which one person, usually a leader, is able to exert power over others. In organizations the most fundamental sources of power are structural and personal (Wood, 1973). These refer to position or place and to individual qualities, respectively, including "resource dependency" on persons (see Pondy, 1977; Pfeffer, 1981). A well-known formulation (French and Raven, 1959) elaborates several "bases of power," including legitimate power, reward power, coercive power, referent power, and expert power. The first of these is akin to the concept of the leader's legitimacy of authority, insofar as the leader's position is seen as validated by some acceptable mechanism, such as appointment or election. Reward and coercive power represent gains or losses for compliance or noncompliance with a person in authority. Referent power represents an extension of reward power through a process of identification with that person. Once such an identification has occurred, it is no longer necessary for the person in authority to monitor the behavior of the less powerful person continuously. As the term suggests, expert power arises from specialized knowledge or distinctive competence that is valued.

While power and influence constitute different processes, they are intertwined insofar as leaders may use both depending upon the circumstances and the particular followers involved. Even appointed leaders, "put in charge" within an organization, must rely on influence, in the sense of persuasion, as much as or more than on power. The unfettered use of power can be highly dysfunctional in creating numerous points of resistance and lingering negative feelings. Therefore both elected and appointed leaders are called upon to use persuasion in many instances, instead of the full power supposedly at their disposal.

The exercise of power has costs, both to the power-wielder and the person to whom it is directed. Among other things, there may be resentment when one person can exercise power over another, and the imbalance in their relative strength is thereby made explicit. Also the greater dependence of the less powerful person on the more powerful one stands out as a feature of their relationship. Emerson (1962) says that such unequal dependence can promote the use of power, whereas a greater balance in dependence can discourage its use. In this regard Mulder (1981) has recently pointed up the effect of "power distance," which he sees as heightening the disparity between leader and followers, especially due to differences in information.

Since the possession of information makes for power (Pondy, 1977), persuasion may phase into power when the leader provides a definition of what is real or true for followers, even if not firmly based on facts. This purely observational comment from Kurt Vonnegut (1981, p. 10) is pertinent—or impertinent—as you choose:

> Persuasive guessing has been at the core of leadership for so long . . . that it is wholly unsurprising that most of the leaders on this planet, in spite of all the solid information that is suddenly ours, want the guessing to go on . . . It is intolerable to politicians, so melodious with their guesses, that ordinary citizens, having been to a public library, can say, with absolute authority, "You're wrong."

These points of definition take on particular significance when seen against the historical backdrop of thought and study regarding leadership. A mystique has so long permeated the concepts of leader and leadership that it is essential to understand the developments producing more contemporary viewpoints. We turn now to some highlights of those developments.

HISTORICAL DEVELOPMENTS

Trends in the study of leadership parallel those in psychology regarding the sources of behavior, which range from the biological to the social ends of the spectrum, with individual cognitive processes in between. Hereditary and instinct conceptions emphasized biological determinants. Trait approaches grew out of these notions but moved more toward a recognition of personality adapted to the circumstances of leadership events. Situational approaches moved further along the scale toward social determinants, almost to the exclusion of individual differences in personality. Today's interest in perceptual-attributional conceptions reflect a fundamental point that permeates psychology: The effect of all events, and other so-called situational factors, depends upon perceptions—and at times relatively transient ones. Therefore it is not so novel to assert that leadership is an "attribution" or "inferred state." So are being in love and acting bravely, using a parallel psychological analysis originating with the earliest philosophers.

EARLY CONCEPTIONS OF LEADERSHIP

Ideas about leadership date back to antiquity, as exemplified in the writings of Confucius, Plato, and Plutarch. Plutarch said in his biographies that leadership resides not in histories but in lives: "The most glorious exploits do not always furnish us with the clearest discoveries of virtue or vice . . . [S]ometimes a matter of less moment, an expression or a jest, informs us better of their characters and inclinations" (quoted in Eliot, 1909, p. 4).

An emphasis on such special qualities of leaders long held sway in the study of leadership. Clearly much of history is written about the attainments of leaders and their personal qualities. The idea that "leaders are born, not made" still has wide appeal, even though it has been largely discredited. "Leadership" behavior is not limited to just an innately endowed few. Instead it may be that there are personality characteristics, including motivation, that combine to increase the probability that certain individuals will respond to situational demands that "make" them leaders. As Gibb (1947) proposed: "Leadership is a concept applied to the personality-environment relation. . ." (p. 267).

TRAIT APPROACHES

In the first half of this century a great deal of attention in psychology was directed to the study of "traits" of leaders, but without considering these situational factors. Cowley (1928) was one of the investigators who put the case simply: "The approach to the study of leadership has usually been and must always be through the study of traits" (p. 144). However, he recognized even then that there also were "situational traits" that required attention in understanding the context of leadership. At about the same time, in sociology, Thrasher (1927, pp. 245, 248) described leaders of Chicago youth gangs he had studied, thereby giving expression to a "trait-in-situation" model:

> Lacking the traits of a natural leader, a boy often manages to exert control in the gang through the possession of some special qualifications . . . The leader of the gang is what he is because in one way or another he is what the boys want . . . the natural leader comes nearest fitting the requirements of his function: he "fills the bill."

In its pure form the trait approach grew out of the "great-man" theory, which is probably the oldest conception about the basis for leadership. Whenever events are explained by recourse to the distinctive characteristics of prominent individuals, this theory is to some degree invoked. An extreme expression of it comes from the philosopher Sidney Hook (1955), who wrote that "all factors in history, save great men, are inconsequential" (p. 14). Alternatively an evaluation of the validity of the great-man theory led the sociologist Gustav Spiller (1929, p. 218) to write as follows:

> It is widely held that the man of genius is born, not made: that to him epoch-making ideas come in a flash and that he unfailingly imposes those on his social environment. If this view is correct, the secret of greatness lies just in being born great, but it is only fair to inquire how far particular individual, social, and historical circumstances possibly account for the phenomenon of greatness.

His more pointed conclusion was that "greatness, like littleness, is apparently determined by a combination of individual, social, and historical circumstances" (p. 231).

Juxtaposed to the great-man theory was the theory that came under the broad heading of "the times." It emphasized the situation and context of events. Such events were considered to set the groundwork for some people to take on the role of leader and exert influence in line with the force of these events. Therefore, while certain individuals do appear to matter in shaping events, the broader framework of events sets the conditions for their actions and results. In Tolstoy's historical novel *War and Peace,* for example, the Russian general says that Napoleon was doomed by events once he chose to invade Russia.

Looking at the question of "the man or the times," the historian Frederick Woods (1913) studied monarchs and concluded that the flourishing of a nation depended upon a strong monarch. However, he was unable to establish definitely whether the monarch was the creator of that happy state or whether the strength of the monarch was created by the good times.

The so-called trait approach stressed the personal qualities of those in leader roles. It was favored by psychologically oriented investigators who studied the personalities and other attributes of leaders (see Gibb, 1968, pp. 214–228). These studies, conducted mainly during the first half of this century, dealt both with who becomes a leader and with what qualities make a leader effective, sometimes disregarding the difference between the two. The assumption of a hereditary basis for leader qualities was also a feature of the classic trait approach, as in the work of Sir Francis Galton with the success of members of eminent families.

Galton saw these as genetic characteristics of a family. In his book *Hereditary Genius* (1869) he reported evidence of families where for generations male members followed a particular career line, such as the law, with evident distinction. However, this could be as much a sign of the "right" family ties as of genetic qualities. In a later time there was more possibility of getting ahead without such family ties. The prospect of greater social mobility meant that becoming a leader was seen to be related more to individual capabilities, to *what one could do,* rather than to conditions of birth. The leader's own character and other personal qualities were then viewed as of greater importance.

Early in this century trait research placed considerable stress on such factors as height, weight, appearance, intelligence, self-confidence, and any other variables that might be correlated positively with leadership. The broad aim was to determine what factor or factors *made* a person a leader. The results were summarized in an influential review by Stogdill (1948), which revealed a very mixed picture. The major finding was that, on the average, leaders tended to be slightly more intelligent than nonleaders. More will be said about this shortly.

Mann (1959) later reviewed 125 studies of leadership and personality characteristics representing over seven hundred findings. Once again intelligence stood out as the factor with the highest percentage of positive relationships with leader status. With lower percentages general adjustment, extroversion, and dominance were found to be positively related to being a leader. However, Mann pointed out that the bulk of these studies involved a group organized around an *assigned discussion task*. Therefore the "superiority" of the leader has to be viewed as likely to be affected by that kind of situation.

More recently Stogdill (1974) concluded in his *Handbook of Leadership* that the typical leader is only slightly more intelligent than the group average. He said that there is nothing like a perfect relationship between intelligence and leader status. The most intelligent person in the group is not the one most likely to become the leader. Furthermore measures of association between being the leader and level of intelligence indicate that other variables may intervene, especially when looking at the effective leader. For instance, a study of infantry squad leaders by Fiedler and Leister (1977) found that leader intelligence and group task performance were variously related as a function of situational "screens" allowing "openness" to the leader's intellectual output. In short, a leader's ability to use intelligence may be limited by the working circumstances, not the least by who is his or her superior.

An additional point about the relationship between intelligence and leading was made by Gibb (1968), who indicated that studies showed that nonleaders do not like to be led by those who are very much higher in intelligence than themselves. Although "the evidence suggests that every increment of intelligence means wiser government . . . the crowd prefers to be ill-governed by people it can understand" (p. 218). Earlier he said, "Followers subordinate themselves, not to an individual whom they perceive as utterly different, but to a member of their group who has superiority at this time and whom they perceive to be fundamentally the same as they are, and who may, at other times, be prepared to follow" (Gibb, 1954, p. 915).

With respect to adjustment, as conventionally understood, it need not necessarily mean that being "well adjusted" is requisite to the leader role. Schrag (1954) long ago reported that leaders among prison inmates tended to be *more* psychologically disturbed than their followers. Kelley, Condry, Dahlke, and Hill (1965) have observed that the most anxious individuals tend to gain visibility and disproportionate influence in high-stress situations, such as a panic, thus creating contagion effects by their influence.

Various earlier investigations (e.g., Gibb, 1947; Jenkins, 1947; Bass *et al.,* 1953; Hollander, 1954) have suggested or implied that a leader's perceptiveness is important as a factor in followers' acceptance of that leader. The more evident quality may be seen in social facility and responsiveness to salient follower needs. Recent work considers that such a quality or social trait may be mediated by various situational factors. For example, Argyle and Little (1972) specify these as rules, role-relationships, others' behavior, motives aroused, and relevance of different personal attributes.

As a general failing the study of leader traits left out a number of important factors. Among these are the features of the situation, including the followers and the conditions in which they are involved that shape the leader's actions. One of the major conditions is the leader's source of authority, through *appointment* or *emergence* with the support of followers, as in the particular case of election. A comparison of these sources will be presented later.

Although situational factors now are recognized more than before in leadership, there is persisting interest in two questions about the qualities of leaders. The first concerns the characteristics that *distinguish* leaders from followers. This effort has not been very productive, thereby raising skepticism about Gibb's (1954) assertion that when situations are delimited leaders do exhibit various "outstanding qualifications."

The second question concerns the qualities that make leaders *effective* with respect to specifiable criteria, such as the outcomes of productivity, satisfaction, and morale. This pragmatic matter can be studied within certain situational contexts, such as organizations where managerial and executive ability are evaluated. The demands of situations clearly are important in determining effectiveness, especially when personal qualities are associated with positive evaluations. For instance, verbal fluency is a basic feature of executive performance found to be related to a good deal of activity required of organizational leaders (Mintzberg, 1973). This aspect of effectiveness, which deals with communications, is actually a complex of qualities involving task competence and interpersonal-relations skills.

Furthermore any assessment of a leader's qualities must take account of task-specific conditions, among which are resources that he or she has at hand. Detaching the leader from situational factors is unrealistic, especially because followers see the leader as part of the situation and as someone who also helps to shape and define it for them (Hollander and Julian, 1969). From this perspective the leader is an authority who gives something and

gets something. Followers expect that the leader will perform competently in the main task, show fairness in dealing with others, and provide a realistic outlook for them. In return the leader receives the greater influence that goes with status, recognition, and esteem (Homans, 1974). These are the elements of a leader's legitimacy in exercising authority, as will be considered more fully below.

Beyond legitimacy, leaders have personal qualities that followers perceive and that affect their responsiveness to the leader. Today there is a resurgence of interest in the qualities of those who fill the leader role, whether in the organizational or the political realms. This feature is seen in various contemporary approaches to leadership, to be discussed shortly, in which it is possible to relate qualities to task demands and other aspects of the situation such as the level of organizational leadership (e.g., Boyatzis, 1982).

A leader's perceived competence is an especially significant factor in leadership effectiveness. However subjective, judgments about "getting results," "showing ability," and other such qualities carry weight in followers' perceptions of the leader. This factor also is a source of the leader's latitude to exert influence and to take innovative initiatives. Though there is usually a greater sense of investment in a person that followers have put in the leader's position, the elected leader is more vulnerable to being replaced. For continued support from followers, a leader needs to be perceived as competent and motivated. In his "functional theory of leadership behavior," Lord (1977) proposes that an understanding of another feature of the leadership-perception link may be of direct value to leaders. This theory indicates that while a leader has a greater potential for exerting influence, making it easier to implement policies or programs, the failure to perform well lowers the leader's standing with followers, thereby undermining his or her ability to take remedial action.

A larger aspect of the issue of competence and motivation has to do with whether the presence or absence of a given person as a leader would make a major difference, for example, in social movements. Would American independence have been achieved without George Washington? In contemporary times, would the civil rights movement have achieved major goals without Martin Luther King, Jr.? One answer is that others would probably have filled these roles, though very likely in a different manner (see Hook, 1955). Another view holds that no one person makes a difference once the basic groundwork is present in the climate of the times (Elkind, 1971). Therefore the conclusion seems to be that a leader's qualities or traits need to be viewed in the situation in which they are applied.

At an ealier time it was thought to be enough to point to desirable personality traits of leaders to explain leadership. Qualities such as courage, wisdom, and character are examples of those traits said to *make* a person a leader. Today someone with these traits might be admired but not necessarily assumed effective in implementing a particular set of leader functions. Yet through the first half of this century the role of leader was still seen as relatively homogeneous. In short, the emphasis remained on traits that *made* a person a leader, independent of the situation.

Rather than being static, traits are dynamic. They are important in an interpersonal context (see J. McV. Hunt, 1965; Mischel, 1969; Bem and Allen, 1974). Followers have expectations about what it is that the leader ought to be doing here and now, rather than absolutely. For example, a sense of humor might be a desirable characteristic absolutely, but in some situations it could make a leader appear to treat too lightly what seriously concerns others.

Returning to the two kinds of trait research, the original one was to identify the traits that might distinguish leaders from followers, and the second and newer one was to distinguish effective leaders from ineffective ones. Clearly there is virtue in maintaining the second comparison (see, e.g., Fiedler, 1961; Hollander, 1971). On the other hand the problem of assessing leader effectiveness in different situations is more complicated than identifying who is the leader. As a result there are considerable variations in the descriptions of effective leaders, so that "any list of qualities that meant anything at all would be bound to exclude someone who had succeeded in leadership and include many who had failed" (Jay, 1971, p. 63). We turn now to the descriptive approach.

THE DESCRIPTION OF LEADER BEHAVIOR

A major departure in leadership research occurred with the study of leader behavior. Previous work on traits too easily *assumed* that a measured trait, such as dominance, was a good indicator of action across a range of situations, when in actuality there was no measure of such consistency of behavior. Accordingly the deficiencies of the original trait approach led to two interrelated devel-

opments. One was the study of the behavior of organizational leaders, initially through descriptive ratings by subordinates. The other was the emergence of a distinctive "situational approach," emphasizing the characteristics of the particular situation and task in which the leader and followers were mutually involved. The primary stress was on the demands made for particular leader characteristics there.

The landmark development was the program of research on leader behavior begun in 1947 by the Personnel Research Board at Ohio State University (see Stogdill and Shartle, 1948; Shartle, Stogdill, and Campbell, 1949). Much of the early work was conducted in military commands. The main interest was in providing information on leaders in higher-level positions in such organizations. Studies were done looking at patterns of the leader behavior in those positions as well as patterns that cut across various positions.

As one example of the studies' findings, eight identifiable roles were found in senior naval officers based on various responsibilities in their positions. In actuality any one officer might fill several roles. Stogdill and his colleagues found that the behavior of officers in each of these positions was set by certain organizational constants. These were primarily responsibilities and others' expectations. However, some features of behavior varied among officers within a given position, such as how much they delegated authority. In short, the particulars of leader roles were defined by responsibilities and others' expectations about them. Across situations the most consistent leader differences in these studies were in interpersonal relations, that is, patterns of interacting with subordinates.

The Ohio State researchers created a questionnaire that required subordinates to rate leaders on each of nine behaviors (see Fleishman, 1953; Stogdill and Coons, 1957). These were initiation, membership, representation, integration, organization, domination, communication, recognition, and production. Called the Leader Behavior Description Questionnaire (LBDQ), it was administered to people in many different organizations, in each case with respondents describing their supervisors by the frequency with which they showed these behaviors from "always" to "never" (Hemphill and Coons, 1957; Halpin, 1957; Stogdill, 1963).

When these ratings were analyzed, they fell into four main factors (Halpin and Winer, 1957). The ones that accounted for the bulk of leader behavior were "consideration" and "initiation of structure." The other two were "production emphasis" and "sensitivity." Remembering that all of these are based on follower perceptions of leader-member relations internal to the group, the first pair, which is best known, may be described as follows:

- *Consideration*—including such leader behavior as helping subordinates, doing favors for them, looking out for their welfare, explaining things, and being friendly and available.

- *Initiating structure*—including such leader behavior as getting subordinates to follow rules and procedures, maintaining performance standards, and making the leader and subordinate roles explicit.

Although consideration (C) and initiating structure (IS) are usually associated with a "human relations" and a "task" emphasis, respectively, these factors are not opposites. A variety of studies have shown that different combinations of consideration and initiating structure may be required, depending upon situational conditions (see, e.g., Korman, 1966; Fleishman, 1973; Stogdill, 1974, pp. 393–397). In a major one of these studies Halpin (1955a) compared supervisors in two roles, school administrators and air force command pilots. He found they differed on these dimensions, with school administrators more likely to show consideration, and command pilots more initiation of structure. Other research by Halpin (1954, 1955b) indicated that air crews were satisfied more when their commanders showed more consideration, but the commanders' superiors approved of them more for initiating structure. Halpin also found that air crews scoring highest on overall effectiveness were led mainly by commanders who were *high on both* consideration and initiating structure. By contrast, for crews scoring lowest on overall effectiveness, most of their commanders were *low* on both factors.

An industrial study by Fleishman and Harris (1962) examined the rate of grievances as a function of these two factors in foremen's behavior. The findings indicated that lack of consideration took precedence as a contributor to grievances. Where a foreman was low in consideration, initiation of structure had little effect on rate of grievances. But a foreman who was high in consideration could initiate greater structure with only a small increase in employee grievances (cf. Weissenberg and Kavanagh, 1972).

Broadly speaking, the research done on the relationship of these factors to group productivity, satisfaction, and cohesiveness has been mainly positive. Stogdill's (1974) summary of these results indicates 54 positive relationships, 18 zero relationships, and only 5 negative ones. He concludes that "consideration and structure interact to influence productivity and satisfaction. The most effective leaders tend to be described as high on both scales" (pp. 396–397).

Kerr, Schriesheim, Murphy, and Stogdill (1974) have identified a set of situational factors that affect the relationship of C and IS in producing effective leadership, especially subordinate satisfaction. It may not be true that if both are high, the group's productivity and satisfaction will be high as well. The factors they specify are:

- *Job pressure*—when it is high, the relationship between C and IS will be more positive.

- *Intrinsic interest in the task*—when it is high, C is less necessary; when it is low, C is more necessary, with some degree of IS.

- *Need for information*—when it is high for subordinates, then IS will be better accepted to reduce ambiguity.

- *Upper-management C tendencies*—when it is low, the relationship of the manager's C and the satisfaction of direct subordinates will be lower.

- *Superior's upward influence in the organization*—when it is high, the relationship of C to subordinate satisfaction will be more positive.

In general, high-morale work groups more often describe their supervisor as being more interested in the well-being of the employees. Such supervisors tend to keep workers informed about what is happening in the company, keep them posted on how well they are doing, and pay attention to complaints and grievances.

Badin (1974) has pointed out the moderator influences on the relationships between C, IS, and various organizational criteria. His primarily focus was on group size, tenure, position power, and task structure. C was found to be positively related to satisfaction across all of these variables, as well as to group effectiveness in high position power and high task-structure conditions. On the other hand IS was negatively related to group effectiveness for small groups, experienced employees, low position power, and high task structure. IS did not show significant relationships with satisfaction and group effectiveness for large groups, new employees, high position power, and low task structure. The conclusion drawn is that IS is more affected by situational variables, while C shows greater consistency across situations. For predicting satisfaction, Larson, Hunt, and Osborn (1976) have raised questions about what they call the "myth" that the combination of high C and high IS necessarily produces superior leadership. They find that simpler single-variable leadership models often are parsimonious in making predictions about C only or IS only. However, there may be moderator variables that intervene in what seem to be only single-variable effects.

Some additional comment is necessary on critiques of the psychometric properties of the Ohio State scales, which include the Leader Behavior Description Questionnaire (LBDQ), the Leader Opinion Questionnaire (LOQ), and the LBDQ-XII (Stogdill, 1963). Schriesheim and Kerr (1974) reviewed the evidence regarding the validity, reliability, and scaling adequacy of the four versions of the OSU scales and noted a number of shortcomings that they attributed to either a lack of relevant data or inadequacies in the scales themselves. They find sufficient evidence to suggest that the four versions are substantially different psychometrically.

Regarding descriptions of a leader's consideration behavior, Schriesheim, Kinicki, and Schriesheim (1979) report that leniency—a tendency to describe others in favorable but probably untrue terms—accounts for a substantial proportion of the variation in correlations between C and dependent variables. Further confirmation of this effect has been reported by Drory and Ben-Porat (1980).

In a strict sense the description of leader behavior is a measure of followers' perceptions of, or attitudes about, their leader. It is not a "direct" measure of behavior. As Calder (1977) has indicated, a large element of attribution is involved. In fact, few direct measures of social behavior exist without the intervention of person perception. This point will be considered further later in connection with implicit-leadership theory.

THE SITUATIONAL APPROACH

In the broad stream of development, the situational approach to leadership grew out of the restlessness created by the obvious limitations of the trait approach. This new wave took hold in the 1950s, although it was presaged by much previous thinking, as seen in the statements by Cowley (1928) and Thrasher (1927) already noted. In the 1500s, anticipating the situational approach, Machiavelli (1950, p. 21) said that *opportunity* was essential to the exercise of a leader's "powers":

> It was thus necessary that Moses should find the people of Israel slaves in Egypt and oppressed by the Egyptians, so that they were disposed to follow him in order to escape from their servitude. It was necessary that Romulus should be unable to remain in Alba, and should have been exposed at his birth, in order that he might become King of Rome and founder of that nation. It was necessary that Cyrus should find the Persians discontented with the empire of the Medes . . . Theseus could not have shown his abilities if he had not found the Athenians dispersed. These opportunities, therefore, gave these men their chance, and their own great qualities enabled them to profit by them, so as to ennoble their country and augment its fortunes.

More recently Mazlish (1981) has echoed this point in saying that in politics "there is no 'leader' for all peoples and all seasons. A potential leader must find the right circumstances and the right group to lead . . . In discovering, or creating his own political identity, the great leader also creates a political identity for his followers" (pp. 218–219). This view meshes with modern conceptions of "charismatic leaders" (see House, 1977), to be discussed later.

The full-fledged emergence of the situational approach came most notably through the writings of Hemphill (1949b), Fillmore Sanford (1950), and Gouldner (1950), among others. Essentially the situational approach was an effort to define what was demanded of leaders in their situations. This provided a needed contrast to the trait approach, which looked for stable qualities of leaders *across* situations. In the attempt, it had largely overlooked the set of relationships and expectations in a given group engaged in a particular activity. As Gouldner (1950, p. 26) put it:

> There is a certain degree of persistence or patterning in the activities which a group undertakes, be it bowling, playing bridge, engaging in warfare, or shoplifting. These persisting or habitual group activities, among other things, set limits on the kind of individuals who become group members and, no less so, upon the kind of individuals who come to lead the group.

Indeed, as noted earlier, Cowley had made a parallel point in 1928: "The significant thing now is to make a distinction between the traits that an individual possesses and the traits that a situation demands" (p. 147). He stressed that various traits were required for being a leader in a particular situation. However, by "trait" he meant any of an individual's attributes, including age and religion. As examples, he indicated that a person must be a natural-born citizen and at least thirty-five years of age to be president of the United States, and a Catholic to become a cardinal in the Roman Catholic Church. Therefore Cowley was not defining traits as features of personality or intelligence. They could be anything about a person, whether observed behaviors or ascribed qualities. A failure to make a distinction between the two can present confusion because it confounds active and passive situational requirements (see Hollander, 1964, pp. 229–230).

A significant element in the more modern situational approach was that leaders were seen as needing to fulfill different *functions* in situations with different tasks. The chair of a civic committee making recommendations to a city council about urban problems needs to show characteristics different from those needed by the coach of a football team or the supervisor of assembly-line workers. These functions all require the leader to exercise influence, but the content and context of the activity make for different demands for behavior (Argyle and Little, 1972, pp. 26–28).

Because the task to be done is the most central element in most leadership activity, early research on the situational approach focused primarily on similarities and differences between tasks as a basis for determining who emerged as a leader (e.g., Carter and Nixon, 1949; Bell and French, 1950). To the extent that the recurring task was similar, such as problem solving in a group, it was found that the same person tended to emerge as the leader. This is hardly surprising considering that the task serves to define the complex pattern that is the group structure. Another element in that structure is the set of organizational rules and traditions within which it operates. One more element is the nature of the human, material, and temporal resources, or "inputs," available to handle the task.

Some other less noted but important elements in the situation include the past history of the group and its feeling tone. These "sentiments," as Homans (1974) calls them, affect the group's interpersonal relationships and also the outlook of group members. Their states of expectation, hope, or despair need to be taken into account for an adequate inventory of the situation. Such attitudes are basic to the "definition of the situation," which plays a vital role psychologically in human activity.

The kinds of relationship the group or organization has with similar units are also important. A highly competitive atmosphere, for example, is bound to have effects dissimilar from a cooperative one. This applies as well to essential differences between a turbulent or a stable environment, a period of expansion or consolidation, or a time of economic growth or depression. The group's size is still another example of a situational element that can affect leadership. Greater size can depersonalize leader-follower relations and may thereby affect prospects for successful performance and group satisfaction.

Such features of a situation, beginning with the task, help to create demands on a leader. Indeed the situational approach emphasized the leader's qualities that were appropriate relative to a group functioning in a particular situation. Hemphill (1949a) expressed this point in asserting that "there are no absolute leaders, since successful leadership must always take into account the specific requirements imposed by the nature of the group which is to be led" (p. 225). For example, the leader should have acceptable competence on a task of importance to the group's functioning, but several group members, not just one, may have such competence and might serve as a leader if given the opportunity.

In the world of everyday activity the tasks of leadership situations are often similar enough that an individual may be able to function effectively as a leader in many of them. Where tasks are similar, the same kinds of qualities are likely to be demanded of the leader. Executives, as noted earlier, are typically required to have certain communication skills that may well be a dominant factor for effectiveness across a variety of situations (see Mintzberg, 1975).

In putting to rest the trait-based conceptions of the past, the situational approach did achieve a considerable gain. However, it at times neglected the characteristics of people who were in leadership roles. To some, "situational" was taken too literally to mean "not individual," when in fact individual qualities of leaders did matter.

Since so much of the research using the situational approach was centered on task differences as the source of situational variability, other situational factors received less attention. At the heart of the matter, the catch-all quality of the term *situation* itself created a problem. As already noted, it failed to distinguish adequately between task demands, which received the major play, and the structure, history, size, and resources of the group, as well as its setting. Furthermore the leader and the situation are not as sharply differentiated as it appeared. From the followers' standpoint the leader is an element in the situation and one who also helps to shape and define it for them (see Hollander and Julian, 1969, pp. 388–389).

As occurred with the trait approach, the situational approach became exaggerated. It failed to provide a view of processes of leader-follower relations over time. These processes include sources of rising or falling status and the problems of leaders maintaining as well as attaining their status. Much of the time the leader was traditionally viewed as someone who "held" a position. The leader's success was usually measured by the ability to exert influence, which has been a highly favored dependent variable for most leadership research.

In sum, pure "situationism" had distinct failings. More recent developments in the study of leadership have gone beyond these limitations to a greater interest in several matters: the characteristics of people who occupy leader roles in a particular situation; the effect of a leader's legitimacy on the perceptions of followers and the self-perceptions of leaders; and the system of relationships in leader-follower relations, including power, authority, and social exchange. What began as a counterbalance to the trait approach therefore became much more. The situational approach prevailed and led the way to these other developments. Among the most important of these are the contingency models of leadership and the development of transactional approaches to leader-follower interaction.

CONTINGENCY MODELS

As an outgrowth of the situational approach, contingency models attempt to specify the factors that make various leader qualities effective given certain contingencies. In short, they emphasize conditions that call forth different leader attributes for effectiveness.

The most prominent work of this kind is Fiedler's (1967, 1971a, 1971b, 1974) LPC contingency model. It is built around the leader's style, distinguishing between leaders who are task-oriented and those who are relationship-oriented. Fiedler measures these by a "least-preferred coworker" (LPC) score, obtained by asking people to think of the one person with whom they were

least able to work well among all those with whom they had worked. Respondents then rate this person on a set of eight-point rating scales, such as friendly-unfriendly and cooperative-uncooperative. The LPC score is the sum of these ratings over a range of scales from 16 to 22. Those *low* on LPC describe their least-preferred coworker in relatively unfavorable terms, and those high in LPC in favorable ones. *Lows* are considered to be primarily task-oriented, and *highs* as primarily relationship-oriented.

In the LPC model these leader orientations can produce greater or lesser effectiveness depending upon three main factors in the situation: the quality of leader-member liking, the degree of task structure, and the extent of power the position gives the leader. The early research by Fiedler (1964, 1967, 1974) and his colleagues on groups from boards of directors to basketball teams tended to support the model's predictions. The basic findings are to the effect that the high-LPC, relationship-oriented leaders perform best in relatively *uncertain* conditions where these three factors are mixed or intermediate, while the low-LPC, task-oriented leaders perform best in the most *certain* conditions of high favorability or unfavorability. For instance, the most successful combinations for the task-oriented leaders are good leader-member relations, a highly structured task, and strong position power, *or* poor leader-member relations, an unstructured task, and weak position power. From this work Fiedler concludes that both the relationship- and task-oriented leaders perform well under some conditions but not under others.

Proponents of Fiedler's contingency model point to strong confirming support from experiments by Chemers and Skrzypek (1972), Csoka (1975) with military groups, and a comprehensive review by Strube and Garcia (1981) of 125 empirical tests of the model. Furthermore, as Chemers (1983) contends, the Fiedler model has successfully predicted group productivity as an output. Rice (1981) reports similarly that low-LPC leaders have subordinates who are more satisfied in high-control conditions, while those of high-LPC leaders are more satisfied in moderate-to-low-control conditions. According to Chemers (1983), satisfaction as well as performance are therefore predictable from the interaction of leader LPC and situational control.

Using a technique called the "psychological isotope," Chemers, Goza, and Plumer (1979) first generated conflict in three-person groups by giving members different and sometimes contradictory information about the best solution to a problem. Then they traced the use of the information provided and found that high-LPC leaders, as predicted, were more likely to use participation in decision making to resolve conflicts than were low-LPC leaders. They also found that groups performing best had leaders and followers with complementary LPC scores.

Granting its significant place as a contribution to thought and study about leadership, issues continue to surround the LPC model. Prominent among these is a basic criticism that it is a theory build on *post hoc* analyses, with many of the early correlational findings fitted into categories, even though some of the coefficients barely attained significance (Graen, Alvares, Orris, and Martella, 1970; cf. Fiedler, 1971a and Rice, 1978b). In addition to this concern with the model's validity, there also are questions of what the LPC measures (Rice, 1978a) and how reliably it does so (McMahon, 1972). As Kerr (1977), among others, has commented, the LPC score is unstable and shows changes over time. Indeed,

LPC has been found to be situationally variable. Offermann (1984) presents results from an experiment with mixed-sex groups indicating that the leader's LPC score varied considerably *after* group interactions, depending upon whether leaders were of the same or opposite sex than followers. For example, women who led groups of men had *lower* LPC scores afterward than women who led a group of women. This finding raises a serious question about the presumed stability of the LPC score as a measure of a leader's persisting style independent of such situational factors as group composition.

An extensive review by Rice (1978a) of twenty-five years of research with the LPC concludes that Fiedler's essential distinction is upheld insofar as low scorers on the LPC are primarily task-oriented and high scorers relationship-oriented. However, Rice contends that the LPC classification of task and interpersonal realms deals basically with a value-attitude dimension rather than with a leader's behavioral style (see also Ashour, 1973a), and further that this typology fails to consider individu-

TABLE 1
Comparison of Major Elements in Three Contingency Models

MODEL	LEADER BEHAVIOR	CONTINGENCY FACTORS	OUTCOME CRITERIA
Fiedler's LPC	Task-Oriented (Low LPC) Relationship-Oriented (High LPC)	Leader-Member Relations Task Structure Leader Position Power	Leader Effectiveness
Vroom and Yetton's Decision-Making	Autocratic, Consultative, or Group Style	Importance of Decision Quality Degree Needed Information Is Available to Leader and Followers Problem Structure Followers' Probable Acceptance and Motivation Regarding Decision Disagreement among Followers about Preferred Solutions	Quality of Decision Acceptance of Decision by Followers Time Required to Reach Decision
House's Path-Goal	Directive, Supportive, Achievement-Oriented, or Participative Style	Subordinate Characteristics and Personal Perceptions Environmental Factors: Task, Authority System, Primary Work Group	Follower Satisfaction, Acceptance of Leader, and Effort to Gain Rewards

SOURCE: Reprinted with permission of the Macmillan Company from p. 35 of *Leadership Dynamics,* by Edwin P. Hollander. Copyright © 1978 by The Free Press, a Division of the Macmillan Publishing Company, Inc.

als who value success in *both* realms. Nevertheless Rice (1981) reports that there is evidence of an orderly relationship between the leader's LPC and followers' satisfaction.

Another criticism is that the model is static and heavily one-sided in that it deals with a leader whose position is fixed (Ashour, 1973b) and gives followers little attention except incidental to the situational favorableness for the leader. Although Fiedler considers that group performance does not depend upon situational favorableness, Shiflett (1973) asserts that it evidently does so. Moreover, the reliance on just three factors to define favorableness has been challenged because moderator variables have been shown to be involved (McMahon, 1972; Kerr, 1974; Filley, House, and Kerr, 1976).

Finally, there is the matter of the mixed conditions, which Fiedler says favor the relationship-oriented leader. Such *uncertain* conditions are likely to be more probable than those at the extremes of certainty, which he says favor the task-oriented leader. Therefore the interpersonal awareness that characterizes the relationship-oriented leader might actually be a necessary quality in many real-life situations. Furthermore the LPC model elaborates and sharply differentiates consideration and initiation of structure and treats them as types of leader personality. This presents a static and limited emphasis, which can omit follower characteristics. However, as noted above, Rice (1981) finds from a review of leader LPC and follower satisfaction that there is evidence of an orderly relationship between them.

The extension of the LPC approach into a training program for leadership effectiveness (Fiedler, Chemers, and Mahar, 1976) heightens the typology issue and begs some questions: Is it possible to make a personality difference the basis for a theory to guide leadership training in which the leader's personality or "orientation" is considered to be fixed? Are leaders to be "trained" essentially in the awareness of their inevitable responses to various combinations of situational favorability? Such questions point up some issues that have provoked serious reservations about the suitability of the LPC model for training (see e.g., Hosking and Schreisheim, 1978; Kabanoff, 1981; Shiflett, 1981).

As the oldest and best-known contingency model, Fiedler's LPC clearly has generated much research and no little amount of debate. Schreisheim and Kerr (1977b) have presented an especially strong critique of it, to which Fiedler (1977) offers a rebuttal, with a rejoinder by them in the same symposium volume (1977a). Research findings of a disconfirming character also have been

forthcoming (e.g., Utecht and Heier, 1976; Vecchio, 1977). Many of the issues posed are unlikely to be reconciled to the satisfaction of the divergent viewpoints. As Rice and Kastenbaum (1983) have recently concluded from their review of these issues, "Factors other than leader orientation and situational favorableness must enter into a thorough understanding of leadership effectiveness" (p. 389). Nonetheless, to its credit the LPC model provided a large step in helping to bridge the trait and situational approaches and opened the way for other useful contingency concepts.

In a newer contingency model Vroom and Yetton (1973) are specifically concerned with leader styles in the process of decision making in organizations. Their primary point of interest is to specify particular styles of decision making required by various situational factors. A related issue then becomes the relationship of these styles to standards of organizational effectiveness. They call this a *normative model of decision making,* which means that it emphasizes what is appropriate.

Many complex matters are included within this model. In the first place, three main styles are distinguished for arriving at the solution to group problems. These are the *autocratic, consultative,* and *group* styles, representing increasing degrees of participation or input allowed from subordinates. The styles may vary in effectiveness on three standards or criteria, following on the work of Maier (1963): quality or rationality of the decision, time required to arrive at it, and acceptance of it by subordinates.

While the leader may have to make some decisions, certain conditions favor greater participation by the group. Vroom and Yetton list eight kinds of issues that the leader is asked to consider in deciding on an appropriate process of decision making. These can be summarized briefly as follows:

- The importance of decision quality.

- The amount of information the leader possesses to arrive at a high-quality decision alone.

- The amount of information followers possess to arrive at a high-quality decision.

- The clarity with which the problem is structured.

- The degree to which the followers' acceptance is necessary to the implementation of the decision.

- The probability that the leader's decision made alone will be accepted by the followers.

- The degree to which the followers are motivated to attain the objectives of the problem to be solved.

- The level of disagreement among followers about preferred solutions.

The Vroom and Yetton model relies on the leader's judgment about what the situation requires rather than on a persisting personality style. The Fiedler LPC model, though predicated on a leader style, also includes the leader's orientation to the situation. Both models are leader-centered, but Vroom and Yetton are more attentive to follower acceptance of decisions and the relevant information available to followers as well as to the leader.

A virtue of the normative model is supposed to rest on the encouragement it provides the leader to look at the conditions and criteria for group decision making. In this regard Vroom and Yetton have developed a training program designed to have managers learn to differentiate these decision processes and then apply that knowledge in working through standardized cases. As part of the training, films depicting different leaders handling identical situations were presented at preselected points. The original studies developing this program turned up the unexpected finding that the use of the model's decision rules yielded a more autocratic than participative style of leadership. Accordingly the cases were modified to limit the inaccurate perception of the situation that was considered to be at the root of the unexpected outcome. Continuing work on these refinements has been reported by Jago and Vroom (1978).

In a critique of the training program Eilon (1978) has questioned the validity of the assumptions on which the crucial element of the model's situational variables, or issues, is based. He also is dubious about the evaluation of the decision quality by trainees: "Only trivial and unimportant decisions can be summarily evaluated soon after the event; for significant decisions...long periods of time must elapse before a proper analysis and evaluation can take place" (p. 477). To balance the ledger, Eilon (1978) affirms the view that the main contribution of the Vroom and Yetton model is in showing that managerial styles need not be polarized between a task and human-relations orientation and that no one style is consistently demanded of organizational leaders. Even more affirmatively Baker (1980, p.10) has said:

The manner in which the authors set out the normative model as a decision tree is perhaps the clue to its proper description as a technique. In effect, it pre-

sents problem solving behaviour in sequential steps emphasising that a successful solution is linked to acceptance by subordinates which in turn is associated with leadership styles... The usefulness of this technique is not in codifying the method of decision making for given situations but as a starting point from which to discuss with managers how they make decisions.

Vroom and Jago (1978) tested the comparative validity of the model and have concluded that it is more powerful than other models in predicting decision quality and acceptance by subordinates. At its core, the model does extend the contingency concept in a useful manner, despite the limitations noted, including the problems associated with having managers use the decision rules in practice (see Filley, House, and Kerr, 1976).

Another contingency model is the *path-goal theory* based on individual motivations in groups (Georgopoulos, Mahoney, and Jones, 1957; Vroom, 1964; House, 1971). The fundamental extension of the theory to leadership was developed initially by Evans (1970), who said that the way a manager influences subordinates' performance and satisfaction is through their motivation, and subsequently extended by House (1971). Managers will be effective to the extent that they make rewards available to subordinates contingent on their accomplishment of specific goals. In concrete terms Evans (1970) contended that leader behavior, represented by consideration and initiation of structure, influences follower perceptions of "path-goal instrumentality," which is the degree to which a given path is seen to help or hinder the individual in achieving his or her goals. In a sense the theory is related to the idea of the definition of the situation. The leader's function is to define a path along which the followers expend effort to attain a group goal. Essentially, then, path-goal theory is built on the concept that followers can be guided to do things they believe will produce satisfying outcomes.

The current statement of the theory is identified most with House (1971) and House and Mitchell (1974). It provides an analysis of the leader's behavior as a basis for increased follower motivation. Three contingencies of required leader behavior are also incorporated in the theory: the task, the nature of the subordinates, and the nature of the group in which the subordinates work.

Two propositions are central to the path-goal theory: first, that the leader's behavior is acceptable to subordinates if they see such behavior as either immediately satisfying to them or as likely to determine their being satisfied in the future; second, that the leader's behavior increases subordinates' effort if such behavior makes the satisfaction of subordinate needs contingent on effective performance. In the latter respect, the leader's behavior complements the environment of subordinates by providing support and guidance for effective performance (House and Mitchell, 1974). The leader's motivational function is to increase the number and kinds of personal payoffs to followers for attaining work goals. The leader also makes the paths to these payoffs easier to travel by pointing them out clearly, reducing roadblocks and pitfalls, and increasing the opportunities for the followers' satisfactions along the way. On balance, Schriesheim and Von Glinow (1977) report mixed results from studies testing the two central propositions of this theory (cf. Schriesheim and DeNisi, 1981). Such inconsistencies may be accounted for by the difficulties of measurement and the different instruments employed in path-goal studies (see Schriesheim and Kerr, 1977b).

As regards the task situation, path-goal theory predicts that consideration (*C*) by the leader will be more effective in situations with low role ambiguity for followers, and initiating structure (*IS*) more effective in situations with high role ambiguity and high job complexity. To the extent that the leader's behavior is congruent with the followers' behavioral preferences, followers will be more satisfied. These relationships have been studied in seven organizations (Dessler, 1973), with generally confirming results. However, Dessler found stronger support for path-goal predictions with regard to the satisfaction of subordinates rather than their performance. In updating the theory, House and Dessler (1974) have substituted the terms *supportive* and *instrumental leadership* for *consideration* and *initiating structure*.

With respect to the personal characteristics of followers, those scoring high on authoritarianism, which means an uncritical acceptance of authority and an orientation to power as a value, were found in Dessler's cross-organizational study to be *less* favorable to a leader using a participative style. The characteristic of internal versus external control—referring to where the individual sees his or her sources of reward originating—also shows a relationship with this style. The more *internally oriented* individual is *more* satisfied with the participative leader style, sees himself or herself as the origin of rewards, and feels more confident in participating (Runyon, 1973).

As regards the task, a major contingency is its degree of structure, as noted above. In brief, the path-goal theory indicates that followers are more likely to respond well to the leader's directive behavior when the task is unstructured, and less well when it is structured. In the structured case the leader does not need to be as directive. Therefore followers respond better and are more satisfied with less directive behavior. These relationships have been found to hold up in similar studies repeated in seven organizations. Wofford and Srinivasan (1983) have recently proposed a Leader-Environment-Follower-Interaction (LEFI) theory built on the basic House (1971) view that leader effectiveness is seen in follower performance. They report some initial evidence for the hypothesized interactions regarding that performance.

If these three contingency theories seem to come out differently, the reason is attributable to their emphases. Each stakes out its own terrain and the variables of note there. To some extent they are addressing different concerns. A comparison of their features is shown in Table 1.

TRANSACTIONAL MODELS

Paralleling and even preceding the development of contingency models are new paradigms of leadership that stress the two-way interaction of leaders and followers. These models take account of the perceptions and counterperceptions involved in the relationship, even at a distance in macroleadership where leaders have large numbers of followers.

At the microlevel, for instance, there is the phenomenon of "interpersonal accommodation" studied by Crowe, Bochner, and Clark (1972). They considered that in a given situation managers accommodate their supervisory style to adapt to the expectations and requirements of subordinates, as well as the reverse. In an experiment in which subjects played the role of a leader, and well-coached confederates played subordinates displaying democratic or autocratic tendencies, these investigators found that the subjects' managerial behavior varied with that of the confederate-subordinates on the democratic-autocratic dimension. This work tends to support the existence of reciprocal influence in leadership, though there are limits to accommodation beyond which the parties may break off the relationship.

More consideration of the effect of followers on leaders will be provided later. For the moment it is useful to note the significance attached to the followers' perceptions of the leader's actions and motives in a transactional approach. Three decades ago Fillmore Sanford (1950, p. 4) made the basic point in this way:

> There is some justification for regarding the follower as the most crucial factor in any leadership event

and for arguing that research directed at the follower will eventually yield a handsome pay-off. Not only is it the follower who accepts or rejects leadership, but it is the follower who perceives both the leader and the situation and who reacts in terms of what he perceives.

Sanford was striving to break out of the then dominant situational approach by arguing that followers were vital to the leadership process, as well as the leader and the situation within which task demands are defined. As a related point the leader also may be viewed as a resource for the followers. Many of these elements of the transaction between the leader and followers come together in recognizing that in leadership there is a *dynamic* relationship with followers who *perceive* and *evaluate* the leader in the context of situational demands. In this vein Evans (1979) has discussed what managers *can do* to achieve desired effects. Yukl's (1981) practitioner-oriented book also is useful for understanding these relationships.

Viewing the leader as a group resource implicates two kinds of transactional considerations. As noted, one is that followers have expectations about leaders and their contributions. A second is that functional groups operate as a system, with inputs from members to produce desired outputs. Between leaders and followers there also is a process of social exchange, to be considered more completely shortly. A key to the transactional view is that leadership is maintained by a two-way influence process, as seen in a social exchange. The potential therefore exists for the leader to be influenced by followers as well as to influence them. The traditional view of the leader as the sole influence source has left out this essential matter of counterinfluence.

As Homans (1961) has succinctly put it, "influence over others is purchased at the price of allowing one's self to be influenced by others" (p. 286). In this sense the willingness of group members to accept the influence of a leader depends upon a process of exchange in which the leader gives something and gets something in return. Hollander (1978) has proposed that the leader provides *system progress* and *equity* in return for esteem and responsiveness.

The term *transaction* signifies a more active role by followers in an exchange relationship with the leader, including two-way influence. Speaking to this feature of the leader-follower relationship, Hollander and Julian (1969, p. 390) have said:

> the person in the role of leader who fulfills expectations and achieves group goals provides rewards for

others which are reciprocated in the form of status, esteem, and heightened influence. Because leadership embodies a two-way influence relationship, recipients of influence assertions may respond by asserting influence in return, that is, by making demands on the leader. The very sustenance of the relationship depends upon some yielding to influence on both sides.

This more active view of the follower role is evident, for instance, in Jones's (1964, 1965) conceptual treatment of ingratiation. Here, the lower status and therefore less powerful person in an interaction seeks ways to gain from the one with greater status and power who has desirable benefits to bestow. Among these tactics are both flattery and a favorable self-presentation, to enhance one's value in the exchange relationship with the more powerful person.

Another concept involving an exchange relationship is the "idiosyncrasy credit" model, which emphasizes sources of earned status among followers and the leader's related latitude for innovation (Hollander, 1958, 1964). This model begins from the apparent paradox that leaders may appear to conform to the *group's norms* and yet are likely to be influential in bringing about innovations. Such conformity, with evident contributions to the group through competence, earns credit with followers. Verba (1961) offered a similar concept dubbed "acceptance capital," built up by the leader via conformity to the group's expectations (p. 201). However, the idiosyncrasy credit model includes perceived competence among the time-linked features of interaction between the leader, or would-be leader, and followers. In their initial contact credits are gained by signs of a *contribution to the group's primary task* and *loyalty to the group's norms*. These are the two factors referred to by the summary terms *competence* and *conformity*. With sufficient signs of both of these, the individual gains enough status to exercise influence directed toward change. Even more, there is the expectation that accumulated credits will be used to take actions that are in the direction of needed innovation. A failure to do so may result in the loss of credits, because of the unfulfilled expectations of followers. The leader who "sits" on his or her credits may be seen as lacking the "will" to take action in line with role obligations.

Credits exist in the shared perceptions that group members gain of the others over time. But credits have operational significance in allowing later deviations that would otherwise be viewed negatively if a person did not have a sufficient balance to draw upon. For instance, a newcomer to a group is usually poorly positioned to assert influence or to take innovative action, unless he or she has a special or unique qualification, such as the apparent solution to a pressing problem. Furthermore a person may bring derivative credit from another group, based on his or her reputation. Therefore the credit concept can apply to appointed leaders as well as to elected ones, even though followers are not the major source of legitimacy for appointed leaders.

The credit model assumes that a process of interpersonal evaluation occurs in leadership. Whether appointed or elected, a leader usually is judged with respect to competence, at the very least, and probably conformity to group norms as well. Research with problem-solving groups supports this and other points in the credit model (Hollander, 1960). It was found that early nonconformity by an otherwise competent group member blocked the acceptance of that person's influence, while later nonconformity produced changes in the group's norms. Indeed, nonconformity to group norms was accepted more readily from someone already granted high accorded status than from someone who was low. Recently Ridgeway (1981) has argued that nonconformity may be a greater initial source of influence and has presented experimental evidence that appears to be contrary to the idiosyncrasy credit model. Certainly within a short time-frame an individual may call attention to himself or herself by nonconforming behavior, as in a figure-ground contrast effect. But this will also be judged in due course by signs of competence in making a task contribution. As Hollander (1964, p. 228) put it:

> Conformity depends upon the perception held of the actor, and what therefore may be perceived as nonconforming for one member of the group may not be perceived as nonconforming for another. The implication of this having specific regard to the effective functioning of leadership is this: the person who breaches a common expectancy of a group and in the process succeeds in helping the group to achieve its goal will be judged differently from the one who fails to do so in deviating. Thus, the outcome of any given act of nonconformity in terms of the group's function is an obvious point of reference for judging the actor.

Accordingly, an experiment by Alvarez (1968) indicated that in "successful" organizations the *higher*-status person lost credits at a *slower* rate than the *lower*-status person for the *same* infractions of work rules. In "unsuccessful" organizations the opposite was true. There the higher-status person evidently lost credits faster as a result of getting greater blame for the unfavorable outcome.

Wahrman and Pugh (1972) found that subjects in all-male groups disliked and resented procedural norm violations from a member who had *not* first contributed competent behaviors and conformity. But in contrast to the earlier finding (Hollander, 1960), this pattern did *not* yield an apparent loss of influence. Early nonconformity was associated with greater influence. This result is not necessarily at odds with the model, since nonconformity can readily serve to call attention to a group member, as just noted. This is an obvious parallel to the influence evidently generated by the quantity of talking in discussion groups. However, both effects are no doubt limited, and a point will be reached where a person is rejected.

In another experiment Wahrman and Pugh (1974) found that if the deviating member was not of the same sex as the other group members, credits were not earned for competence as in the all-male groups studied earlier, and early nonconformity did not yield influence. These results with a female nonconformer among males suggest that a member may not as readily deviate if the individual has been set apart, which fits a basic feature of labeling theory (see Lemert, 1972). This quality of being seen as different in an organization has been well-captured in an unusually clever light work by Kanter and Stein (1980).

A leader is given latitude to deviate from general norms in exchange for sticking more closely to the expectancies others have about the leader role. The idiosyncrasy-credit model makes a distinction between norms to which group members are expected to conform, from which leaders may deviate, and particular expectancies associated with the leader's role. In practice this means that a leader may be late to meetings or be able to take independent stands with relatively less disfavor. But followers are likely to reject a leader who seems to be acting largely in behalf of his or her own *self-interest* or in an unfair way (Hollander, 1961b). Also important, an experiment by Lawler and Thompson (1978) showed the effects on followers of a leader's perceived *responsibility* for an inequity. They found that the subordinates' attitudes and behavior were more positive toward a leader if he or she was *not* seen as responsible. In highly stratified groups the attribution of responsibility to the leader for inequity was far greater, and revolt by subordinates more likely.

Former British prime minister Harold Macmillan was asked in a 1980 television interview about General

Eisenhower's ability as supreme allied commander in Europe in World War II. He said from his association then that Eisenhower was "absolutely first-rate," adding that he had an indispensable quality of leadership, that is, *fairness*.

Jacobs (1970) has put this point within the more general framework of a "fair exchange" in organizational leadership. A justification for having an exchange perspective, according to Gouldner (1960), is that it encourages awareness of the needs of others and thereby serves as a check on egoism. Jacobs says in this vein, "The leader, who holds a position of 'high place,' should be the one in the group who can function best for the common good" (p.80). A fair exchange in these terms occurs when the leader performs well and deserves the benefits of leader status. If the leader does not do well, particularly because of lack of effort rather than lack of ability, followers are likely to have a sense of inequity in the relationship.

More will be said about these points in connection with the effects of power. For the moment we return to a more basic consideration of legitimacy and its associated processes of leader emergence and source of authority.

LEGITIMACY, LEADER EMERGENCE, AND SOURCE OF AUTHORITY

From the perspective of a cultural anthropologist, "All societies have authority structures and values concerning the allocation of authority" (LeVine, 1960, p. 58). In social psychology two main sources of authority can be differentiated. Each is diverse, yet not exclusive, with respect to implications for the other. The first includes a range of appointed leaders within a variety of organizational frameworks. The second covers emergent leaders who achieve their role by the willing support of followers, up to and including election in the political realm, as well as in freely functioning "informal groups." Both rely on legitimacy in achieving authority.

LEGITIMACY

The point of legitimacy is that it involves a process conferring the perceived right to have authority. How the leader receives authority may be as important as the source of that authority because of the requirement for legitimacy. Indeed Read (1974) found in an experiment with teenagers that leaders who usurped authority, and so were not "properly" legitimated, had less influence than appointed or elected leaders; also they were perceived less favorably than those leaders on such ratings as competence and likability.

In traditional organizations leaders are "put in charge," which is to say they are imposed on those in the internal structure by "higher-ups" in the external structure. Who those external legitimators are, and their perceived competence, will affect judgments of the leader's ability by subordinates and others (Knight and Weiss, 1980). To exercise authority requires dealing effectively with peers and subordinates, not only with the person or group conferring legitimacy as the source of authority in an organizational context.

A historical instance of the significant role played by this broadened conception of legitimacy occurred in 1943 (Hough, 1980). Admiral Lord Louis Mountbatten was attending a World War II meeting of Allied leaders in Quebec City when Winston Churchill asked him to come with him for a stroll. A cousin of the king, Mountbatten already had considerable legitimacy from family ties, but also had distinguished himself as a naval hero showing inspirational leadership of the crew of the ship *Kelly* he commanded when in 1941 it was sunk by German divebombers off Crete. This event provided the basis for the Noel Coward film, *In Which We Serve,* popular during World War II. Subsequently he was made chief of combined operations, a commando force that conducted raids in occupied Europe.

As British prime minister, Churchill came quickly to the point by asking Mountbatten whether he felt "up to anything," to which he replied yes. Then, in a rapid-fire way, Churchill said he needed to have Mountbatten put the situation in Southeast Asia in order. Mountbatten thought he was being sent on a trip there to prepare a report, and said so. "A trip! . . . I'm offering you the job of Supreme Allied Commander of Southeast Asia. What do you think of that?" After pausing to digest this surprise proposal, Mountbatten said that he would like twenty-four hours to think it over, to which Churchill countered by asking if he was afraid he could not do the job. "Not at all," said Mountbatten. "I have a congenital weakness for feeling certain I can do anything, but I do want to ask the British and U.S. Chiefs of Staff to satisfy myself that they agree with your choice wholeheartedly and will back me to the full." Churchill assured him of President Roosevelt's support and said, "He's as keen as I am, but you can talk to the Chiefs." Mountbatten did, receiving the commitments he felt he needed to carry out his role, and took the assignment

(Hough, 1980, pp. 163–167). After successfully fulfilling it until the conclusion of the war, he was appointed the last Viceroy of India, to lead it to independence from Britain.

A further consideration about legitimacy is that a leader's office, however high, does not necessarily ensure follower responsiveness. The leader's actions and other qualities still matter. As Katz and Kahn (1978, p. 527) observe, for instance, the president of a company has a *position* of leadership, which carries the legitimacy of high office. It is greater than that of a supervisor. Yet the president might be less successful in achieving the desired response from subordinates. The supervisor might show a greater *exercise* of leadership by a more affirmative subordinate response. Fulfilling legitimacy through the use of authority therefore depends to a great extent on how followers respond to the leader's characteristics.

Authority also can be viewed as a resource that the leader is expected to use in meeting responsibilities in a social exchange with followers (Hollander, 1978a,b). However, having authority is essentially a potential for action within a system of relationships. It may not be used for a variety of personal and situational reasons that constrain its exercise in a particular circumstance (see Coleman, 1980).

LEADER EMERGENCE

Even in formal structures there are emergent leaders who gain influence from a following among peers. They are legitimated by an informal process of acceptance of their influence through the impact of their personal qualities. In the military service this may be realized in the form of "battlefield promotions." In political campaigns emergent leadership involves seeking office through a process of securing a party's nomination to candidacy and then gaining enough votes from a constituency, as will be discussed further in connection with the U.S. presidency.

As a prototype of emergent leadership, political leaders offer an illustration of the capacity to produce positive identifications, often highly charged ones, among followers. When political leaders are popular and successful, it is not usually because they are autocratic—at least not at first. Under the appropriate circumstances they may have an enormous following that identifies with them to the point of subscribing to unexamined ideologies and revolutionary programs. Often they become leaders by saying and doing things that followers yearn to hear, and so *emerge* with a dedicated constitu-

ency. However, the notion that leaders "emerge" from popular consent can be overblown, insofar as the desire for status and influence is contrastingly underplayed. People wishing to be leaders are typically far more active in developing a following by encouraging supporters, even if at first in quiet, relatively unobtrusive ways (see Erikson, 1969).

Hemphill (1961) offered this summary of the motivational factors that encourage individuals to attempt to lead: rewards associated with accomplishing the group task; expectations that the group task can be accomplished; task characteristics that may not be clearly understood but that create the need for someone to lead; personal acceptance by other group members shown in an affirmative response to an individual's attempts to lead. Hemphill finds from his research two other sources of encouragement: possession of task-relevant information, not easily transmitted to others, and previous leader status in the group.

Who becomes an emergent leader has been the object of a good deal of study. The research literature primarily reveals that rate of interaction is a major determinant (Hare, 1962). Talking, more with regard to *quantity* than quality of output, appears to put a person in a leader role (e.g., Bales, 1953; Riecken, 1958; Regula and Julian, 1973; and Gintner and Linskold, 1975). Sorrentino and Boutillier (1975) conclude from their research that the amount a group member talks takes precedence at first because it is considered an indicator of his or her motivation. The *quality* of what is said is more an indicator of ability and appears to come after quantity in making an impression. In these studies the usual definition of the "leader" is determined by perceived and/or actual influence. However, the amount of participation may be related back to individual characteristics, such as age or social status.

Schneier and Bartol (1980) and Bartol (1974) investigated sex differences among emergent leaders of fifty-two task groups. While O'Leary (1974), and Fallon and Hollander (1976), among others, found results indicating less emergence of women than men as leaders of mixed-sex groups, this investigation showed no significant differences in the proportion of men and women emerging as leaders by sociometric choice. Moreover, rated behaviors in the process of emergence were *similar* for leaders of *both sexes,* as was the performance of groups led by men or by women. Irrespective of sex, emergent leader behavior was perceived more *positively* than nonleader behavior. In another study Schneier (1978) found that, regardless of sex, emergent leaders had significantly lower LPC scores, that is, were more task-oriented, than nonleaders.

In groups where discussion is central to the task, people who *speak first* also have a greater likelihood of becoming leaders, or at least of being perceived as such (Hemphill, 1961; Hollander, 1974). They have the attention of others and what they say provides a firmer basis for their assertion of influence. The research by Bass and his colleagues (1953) with the leaderless group discussion (LGD) technique showed such regularities. Their findings suggest that ascendant behavior, very probably growing out of greater self-assurance from a past history of successful influence, gave some members a "head start" in becoming leader.

A series of studies by Strodtbeck and his associates (Strodtbeck, James and Hawkins, 1958; Strodtbeck and Hook, 1961) on simulated jury deliberations has shed some light on these relationships. In the choice of a foreman, those jurors who initially sat at the ends of the jury table were found to have a significantly higher probability of being selected by the others as foremen. There was a clear positional effect, but further analyses revealed that those people who became foremen were higher up the socioeconomic scale with respect to education, occupation, and income. A reasonable inference, therefore, is that sitting in the "leader's place" was a result of self-selection associated with these characteristics.

On the other side of the leader-activity and emergent-leadership equation, Morris and Hackman (1969) studied participation in groups, using Bales-type interaction categories. They found that a third of the *high* participators were rated *below average* in leadership; furthermore only about 25 percent of the variance for leadership ratings was accounted for by participation rates. These authors concluded that participation may be important but is not a necessary or sufficient condition for the achievement of a leader role. Stein (1975, 1977) has suggested that the disparity between this finding and the other literature on leader emergence may well be in the absence of attention to nonverbal cues throughout much of the research on emergent leadership. He proposes that such leadership be studied as a process of followers choosing leaders, or allowing emergence, rather than leaders emitting leader activity. An extension in this direction is seen in the work of Stein, Hoffman, Cooley, and Pearse (1979), who have developed a valence model of leadership emergence. The basic concept is that valences are generated for particular solutions in problem-solving groups, and these valences are a key to identifying the person who becomes a leader (see Hoffman, 1979).

Various experiments have indicated that leader behavior can be encouraged or otherwise modified. An early example is the work of Pepinsky, Hemphill, and Shevitz (1958) in which male students who were *low* in speaking out and initiating structure in groups were identified and then exposed to a contrived discussion where others in the group indicated support for their assertions. This process elicited much more leader behavior from them in a later discussion. The reverse procedure was also tried with similar students who were initially found to be *high* on leader activity. When exposed to disagreement by other group members, they subsequently dropped markedly in leader activity.

Other research has shown that even the use of signal lights as reinforcers can have a significant effect on a person's proportion of talking time as well as perceived leadership status (Bavelas, Hastorf, Gross, and Kite, 1965; Zdep and Oakes, 1967). The lights not only produced an increase in leader acts but also created the impression of greater influence. As in the Pepinsky *et al.* procedure, individuals were identified who had a low or a high level of speaking out in a group discussion session. Then in a second session for each group someone who had been low was given "approval" by the experimenter through flashing a green light on a signal panel in front of that person. In some groups a red light showing "disapproval" was simultaneously flashed to the other group members. In short, the green light was to indicate that the individual was saying things that contributed to the group discussion, and the red light things that hindered the discussion.

Individuals who had previously said little were found to increase their talking significantly by the flashing of the green light. They also showed an increase in the activity ratings given by other group members. A comparison with other low-level participants, who received no lights, showed that the increase in participation depended upon the green lights. When red lights were flashed to other, active members, the effect was even greater; therefore when the more active members were inhibited in this way, the usually less active ones receiving green lights were found to be the most talkative members.

The inference drawn from such research is that speaking out is made easiest for low-level participants by having positive reinforcement when others are receiving negative reinforcement. In a similar way Rudraswamy (1964) made some groups' members believe that they had higher status. They showed more attempts at leader activity than others in their group and even out-distanced those members who were given more task-relevant information beforehand.

Strickland, Guild, Barefoot, and Paterson (1978) studied leader emergence with groups of college students meeting face-to-face or via video conferencing on five occasions to solve human relations problems. Face-to-face conditions produced the usual form of leadership development, with status measures systematically related to behaviors including verbal output. These relationships were much diminished in the condition of mediated communication.

In a related vein, Stein (1977) found no significant difference in the judgment of leadership hierarchies by thirteen process consultants and forty-one untrained undergraduates who viewed videotaped group discussions. Both categories of subjects were in relatively high agreement with the group members' rankings of one another, thus leading to the conclusion that the information about leader behavior from the videotapes was picked up with relative accuracy by both trained and untrained observers.

Even with encouragement and favorable conditions, there are still individual differences in the disposition to lead. In a field study with army squads, Gordon and Medland (1965) found that a measure of "aspiration to lead" was significantly related to positive peer evaluations on "leadership ability." Although the causal direction of this relationship cannot be determined, it seems reasonable to consider that acting as an emergent leader, or the potential to do so, depends upon self-evaluations that are consistent with the expectations of others. Such expectations differentially affect appointed or elected leaders, especially regarding their sense of follower support.

EFFECTS OF APPOINTED OR ELECTED LEADERSHIP

Whether a leader's authority comes from appointment or election has been found to have distinct consequences for leader-follower relations, implicating several psychological states. Appointing or electing a leader not only creates different expectations but even different environments for the leader and followers. Elected leaders generally tend to have followers who have a greater investment in them than do appointed leaders. On the obverse side, research also indicates that elected leaders may be more vulnerable to being rejected when things go wrong (Hollander and Julian, 1970, 1978). Appointment or election therefore affects a leader's actions, the perception of the actions by the leader and the followers, and their reactions. This process is seen in a recent experiment by Ben-Yoav, Hollander, and Carnevale (1983).

In a classic experiment varying source of authority, Goldman and Fraas (1965) had leaders in male groups selected by three methods: election by a vote, appointment by competence, or appointment by random selection. There also was a control condition without a leader. The task was the game of "Twenty Questions," and the main measures of performance were time required and number of questions needed to reach a solution. The groups with leaders appointed for their competence performed best, with those having elected leaders a close second. Both randomly-appointed-leader and no-leader groups showed poorer performance, which was attributed to a weak basis of legitimacy.

Another experiment with problem-solving groups found that members were more willing to accept the "self-oriented" action of an elected leader than that of an appointed one (Hollander, Julian, and Perry, 1966). The action involved the division of the group's "winnings" based on points earned. Under the rules the leader had the authority to make a decision about that division. In the self-oriented condition he assigned the greatest share to himself, and in the equalitarian condition he assigned everyone an equal share, including himself. This experiment also provided a measure of leader influence and a report by members afterward on how much they had been influenced by the leader. With an elected leader, members were more willing to acknowledge the extent to which they had been influenced than with an appointed one.

In a related experiment, appointed and elected leaders were studied in the role of group spokesman (Julian, Hollander, and Regula, 1969). This role had previously been found to be especially sensitive to followers' perceptions of the leader's competence and motivation (see Sherif, 1962). Serving as a spokesman puts an individual's standing to a test because contention and negotiation "at the boundary" pose a threat to the group's integrity (Miller and Rice, 1967). The spokesman role in this experiment was achieved either through appointment or through election. Two other variables were involved as well: the leader's initially perceived competence for the task of being the group spokesman, and his evident success or failure in presenting the group's position effectively to an external authority. The task involved four-man discussion groups developing an effective defense for a fellow student accused of cheating. It was hypothesized that the elected spokesman would generally be more frequently chosen to remain in this role than the appointed one, other things remaining equal. To the contrary, however, the most striking finding was that the elected spokesman was more likely to be rejected than the appointed one if he either was initially perceived to lack competence or failed to produce a favorable outcome.

The significance of the "boundary function" of leadership in dealing with the external world has been given special attention by Miller and Rice (1967) and Adams (1976). In another study Lamm (1973) reviewed findings on the performance of negotiators relative to their source of authority. In intergroup relations the leaders elected by the group showed greater toughness than nonleaders, that is, those not confirmed through election. Imposed leaders were found to be tough only when they had to consult their group members during negotiations. Lamm indicates that the accountability of a leader to the group is a major variable determining status effects on negotiation. This process had been studied further in a line of research on negotiation and integrative bargaining by Carnevale, Pruitt, and Britton (1979) and Carnevale, Pruitt, and Seilheimer (1981).

Boyd (1972) looked at three factors that might affect a negotiator's behavior, one of which was source of authority. He predicted that elected representatives would feel freer to yield in negotiation than appointed ones. With a discussion task involving human relations problems, Boyd found support for this hypothesis and concluded that election created greater perceived status, thereby allowing more latitude without concern for compromising group loyalty.

A case can be made therefore for the proposition that election creates in followers a greater sense of responsibility and higher expectations for the leader's success. One interpretation is to see this as a form of social exchange in which the group gives the leader a "reward" in advance by electing him or her, and then group members feel a claim on the leader to "pay back" by producing favorable outcomes (Jacobs, 1970). Indeed one thrust of the research noted is that follower support makes higher demands on the leader. Even managers who may derive justifiable support from subordinates are vulnerable to these demands, with higher expectations and costs.

Another experiment on source of authority was done by Hollander, Julian, and Sorrentino (1969) to study the effects on appointed or elected leaders of disagreements with their followers. The primary purpose was to examine the leader's willingness to deviate from group decisions, with a "strong" or "not strong" treatment cutting across the leader's election or appointment. The elected leaders told they had strong group endorsement were found to be significantly more likely to show total reversals of their group's decision—in fact on about half the critical trials—than in the other conditions. Based on a content analysis of their messages to the group, such leaders showed lower indications of conciliation with respect to group judgments. Evidently the elected leaders in this condition felt freer to expend their credits by breaking with the group judgment.

An experiment by Read (1974), with male high school juniors serving in groups of four as mock jurors, used four sources of authority for the "foreman": election by the group, appointment by an external authority who was expert in the group's task, appointment by an external authority who was not an expert, and self-appointment. This was the same order that Read expected and also found to hold as a basis for legitimacy. His results indicated that the leader's source of authority had immediate and lasting effects upon his task influence and the evaluation of him by others. However, the actual behavior of the leader did contribute to his ability to exert influence and to have continued legitimacy. Read found that the most negative responses to the foreman stating deviant opinions occurred when he was appointed by a nonexpert or was self-appointed.

The relationship between appointment and election and various dependent measures can be quite complex. In a study by Klein (1976), as an example, elected leaders were found to be given more responsibility and were seen as more competent than appointed leaders in a simulated panic situation of comparatively low threat; otherwise the differences narrowed and were reversed for the two kinds of leaders.

Firestone, Lichtman, and Colamosca (1975) conducted an experiment in which male college students elected their group's leader, after being rated by observers in a leaderless group discussion (LGD). Where the person with the highest LGD rating was elected leader, the groups performed *most* promptly when faced with an emergency. The worst performance was found in groups where the election had been contrived so that the member with the *lowest* LGD rating was elected leader. The main conclusion was that the leader who is legitimated by the group through election, after a process of emergence, is in a strong position to achieve prompt action.

Pursuing the broader line of research on appointment or election, two related experiments (Hollander, Fallon, and Edwards, 1977) were done with leaders who were elected or appointed and whose groups were told that they had done well ("success") or not well ("failure"). In the first experiment twelve groups composed of four male students each were presented with the typical urban problems from a fictional city called Colossus. They were to arrive at rankings of programs to alleviate these problems.

The first of the experiments found the influence of elected leaders to be greater than that of appointed leaders. Furthermore the influence of elected leaders increased after failure feedback and decreased after success feedback. This effect was interpreted in line with Hamblin's (1958) concept that a "crisis," created by the apparent failure, produces a "rallying around" the elected leader, at least initially. In the success condition, however, there was no crisis and accordingly group members acted out of a greater security in their own judgments.

The second experiment also used the Colossus problems, with a third phase added to study the results of having a change in leaders by appointment or election, and with the identical success or failure feedback as before. The main hypothesis was that the newly elected leader would be more influential initially than the newly appointed leader. The longer-range interest was to look more closely at the followers' tolerance of the leader and their willingness to have him continue. The findings of this experiment showed that the heightened influence of the elected leader in the second phase was indeed brief. If the group saw no signs of greater success, then the leader was deposed despite his rise to greater influence following the crisis. After a point, then, the perpetuation of the crisis did not serve to sustain the leader's position.

A leader may have personal authority, sometimes called "presence," which is attached distinctively to the leader's person, because of reputation. The film *Kagamusha,* directed by the acclaimed Akada Kurasawa, provides an interesting illustration of the personal feature of a leader's position. An undefeated Japanese warlord in the Middle Ages is severely wounded in battle. Before he dies, a convicted thief is substituted as his double so that his troops, and especially the enemy warlords, will think he is still alive. The uncanny resemblance of the double makes it possible for him to carry on the surface features of the public role successfully for several years. Howev-

er, the leader functions are actually being handled by others, particularly the warlord's brother, grown son, and generals. In a crucial battle led by the son, the double is brought to a knoll and seated in plain view to the rear of his forces to intimidate the enemy soldiers, who soon scatter. The son too readily claims the victory as his own, and initiates a second battle despite the strong objections of the others. They fear a loss, now that the double has been dismissed and a funeral for the warlord held. This time, because the enemy no longer is threatened by the warlord, the battle ends in a disastrous loss for the son and his forces.

THE CASE OF THE PRESIDENCY

A prime instance of the force of election is seen in the American presidency. It combines the fixed-term elective office of "head of government" with the office of "head of state," the traditional role of a monarch, as in Great Britain, for example. Though George Washington disliked a majestic construction of the office, there are still major concerns that a president may behave like monarchs of old. This is evident in expressions about the "imperial presidency" (Schlesinger, 1973), and the "arrogance of power" (Fulbright, 1966) when a president takes foreign initiatives without consulting Congress or allies.

Presidents benefit initially from the widespread belief that once legitimated by even a slim victory, each then holds the highest place in the nation. George Reedy (1973), a former press secretary to Lyndon Johnson, contends that, "There are all sorts of reasons why a man might have only 51 percent of the votes, or even less, and still be able to make some rather sweeping changes.... Many presidents have found their following has increased enormously the day after election" (p. 26). To a major extent, this may be an instance of respect for the process and living with its results. However, it also shows that legitimacy is not only vested in the office but very much depends on appropriate responsiveness by followers in practice.

A systematic behavioral science conception or approach to the presidency has not clearly emerged, despite the volume of writings on the topic by political scientists, journalists, historians, and not least presidents past and present. Political scientists have understandably dominated the field (see e.g., Neustadt, 1960; Burns, 1965, 1984; Barber, 1972; Kernell, 1978; Cronin, 1980; Kinder, 1981). It is evident that a president is seen as both the embodiment of the nation and as the most personal officer in government. Two common statements reflect these bases for supporting a president: "We only have one president at a time," and "The president is president of all the people." Also a past-president, even one who has "fallen" or "failed," is usually accorded a place of virtual reverence as well as opportunities for substantial income if desired. Psychologically, identification with a president can dramatically shape the perceptions and voting of their party loyalists. Even where their own economic well-being has declined, those who identify with a president of their own party show highly similar attitudes about the favorability of the nation's economic picture (Hollander, 1983). This phenomenon fits Freud's (1921) conception noted earlier of the leader as a commonly shared "ego ideal" from whom followers gain a picture of social reality. It also is readily explainable in cognitive balance terms.

From his political history perspective, Burns (1978, 1984) says that presidents who are "transformational leaders" are interested in more than garnering votes; they want to bring about change (1984, p. 103):

The dynamic of such leadership is recognizing expressed and unexpressed wants among potential followers, bringing them to fuller consciousness of their needs, and converting consciousness of needs into hopes and expectations, and ultimately into feelings of entitlement that can be transmuted into demands on the political system, including the original leadership. The secret of transforming leadership is the capacity of leaders to have their goals clearly and firmly in mind, to fashion new institutions relevant to those goals, to stand back from immediate events and day-to-day routines and understand the potential and consequences of change.

Burns considers President Reagan to be this kind of leader, ideologically very different but in this aspect comparable to President Franklin Roosevelt. Years before, the psychologist Cowley (1928) pointed out that office holding is not the same as leading. A major difference lies in whether there is persuasion in pursuit of a program.

In his book on *Politics as Leadership,* Tucker (1981) has delineated three phases of the process of engaging people in pursuing a political program: *diagnosing* the problem facing the constituency; *prescribing* a course of action, which is "policy formulation"; and *mobilizing* action, which is "policy implementation." But a president's version of social reality and a needed pro-

gram can be a shared definition of the situation only as long as the President retains credibility, which often equates with popularity. While that is the case, a president is relatively assured of continued support. This also means that at least for a time a disastrous program could be sustained by the popularity of a president.

Generally, shifts in a president's popularity may be predictably linked with certain events and responses to them. As instances, Kernell (1978) reports that opinion polls show increased support when there is a dramatic crisis abroad, but that prolonged conflicts such as the Korean and Vietnam Wars drain support from a president. Also, there are sequence effects, such as the usual finding that a new president benefits from a "honeymoon period," which then dissipates when expectations are unfulfilled. The initial "era of good feelings" may be a function of hope and respect for the integrity of the electoral process, if not for the person. Sometimes, popularity is stated as "favorableness" or "approval," which politicians and pollsters believe equates with support on issues, though not necessarily liking.

Great efforts are expended by the White House staff to improve a president's favorableness ratings by actions, and by statements which can serve as action when reported in the mass media. This image building is familiar as the social psychological phenomenon of "impression management." Stage setting and news managing are built into the everyday White House scene because the president both makes news and is news and has an enormous press entourage following him whenever it can (Burns, 1965, p. 185).

The stakes are high in maintaining popularity. While Mueller (1970) concludes that its influence at election time is exaggerated, a retrospective analysis done by Lewis-Beck and Rice (1982) indicates that for presidents running for reelection from 1956 to 1980, presidential popularity in the June Gallup Poll would successfully predict the outcome if the Gallup approval rating was 50 percent. This indicator is reported to predict election results better than the Gallup preelection poll, which asks respondents for whom they intend to vote just a few days before election day in November.

In gaining the nomination, incumbency is a powerful ally. Neither major party in recent times has denied the nomination to an incumbent who desired it. Presidents Ford and Carter, in 1976 and 1980 respectively, tenaciously held out for the nomination—and then each lost in the general election. These cases illustrate the operation of the traditional two-stage electoral process in which a candidate must win nomination by the party and then win election nationally. The party is therefore virtually indispensable as a vehicle for attaining the presidency.

Though presidential partisanship may be an annoyance, particularly to those of the "other" party, it gives an edge to the incumbent for renomination. But it does not mean victory in the November election, as shown by the Ford and Carter instances just cited. In the process of gaining the party's nomination and holding the allegiance of party loyalists who dominate primaries and nominating conventions, a narrow array of partisan positions on issues is established, even if there is a later move toward the middle ground.

Once a candidate is nominated, there is then a need for a "joining of hands" across party factions with differing positions to heal intraparty wounds. Especially in a first presidential candidacy, compromises need to be struck to be able to achieve victory in the national election. Party adversaries may be then forced into alliances for the general campaign, such as Kennedy with Johnson and Reagan with Bush. Finally, and not least, what appealed to partisans in gaining the nomination may not appeal to the electorate at large. All of these circumstances present challenges to political skill, which Kellerman (1984b) points out is basic to an effective presidency. From a social exchange perspective, she says that the president and constituents evolve into an ongoing relationship over time, and presidential leadership must be accomplished from within the "world of other people," their needs and aspirations. In this function, a president who is a more extroverted, sociable person is more likely to be attentive to others, and show this political skill. As recent examples of more introverted presidents who did not have such skill she cites Nixon and Carter.

McClelland (1975) postulates that political leadership generally has been discredited in America because of the tendency for social scientists and others to explain it in the *personal* power, self-aggrandizing motives sense. There is however an alternative basis which he says is *socialized* power, as noted earlier. It is more oriented toward strengthening and inspiring followers by making goals clear and creating confidence that they can achieve those goals. This is more a matter of influence, rather than an attempt to dominate one or more others, as it is in the personal power form. Indeed, McClelland also disavows the idea that political leadership necessarily requires power motivation, although the socialized form clearly is better fit to a social exchange.

Essentially, presidents and other elected leaders have a social contract with constituents. They have a

grant of status with more influence over others, and the prospect of exerting control over expectations and events. This comes at a price, a vital part of which is represented in greater responsibility and accountability for failures, unfulfilled expectations, or inaction in the face of problems or threats to the well-being of constituents. Avoiding this responsibility can produce cynicism with perceived inequities in "the system." Not least, clarity of purpose is repeatedly mentioned as vital if the leader-follower transaction is to be soundly based.

FOLLOWER EFFECTS ON LEADER BEHAVIOR

Most of the literature on leadership in social psychology treats it at the microlevel, usually regarding interpersonal relations and influence. A repeated finding in studies of leadership is that leader behavior affects followers' behavior (e.g., Vroom, 1964; Korman, 1966). Until the late 1960s, however, leadership research was distinctly unidirectional, insofar as studies mainly considered this linkage but did not recognize that its obverse might also occur. Indeed a central issue in the leadership field today is the challenge posed to the traditional link between the leader's behavior and the performance of followers (e.g., Barrow, 1976; Pfeffer, 1977).

Two early studies by Lowin and Craig (1968) and Farris and Lim (1969) represented a departure in indicating the influence of subordinate performance on leader behavior. While these studies both showed the strong possibility of an effect of subordinates on leaders' style, the results did not necessarily rule out the existence of the more orthodox reverse relationship. Specifically Farris and Lim (1969) tested the prediction that various aspects of leadership behavior may be a function of subordinate performance. They employed role-playing and problem-solving tasks in which past group performance was manipulated by giving the leaders different information about the quality of the group's performance.

Some leaders were told that their groups were among the ten best-performing groups in the company, and others that their groups were among the ten worst performers. When the subordinates were asked after the problem-solving session to report their perceptions of the leader's behavior, their descriptions of leader behavior were significantly different between the two feedback conditions for eleven out of eighteen items describing leader behavior. For instance, superiors were seen as being more considerate toward the "high-performance" group and less considerate toward the "low-performance" group.

Among the problems with this study, which Farris and Lim themselves point out, is the possibility that subordinates may have learned from their leader that they were low or high performing, attributed this past performance to his leadership capabilities, and then perceived the quality of his leadership behavior with respect to a negative or positive "halo." A second problem is that the design of the study did not allow a determination of the processes by which past performance affects leadership. Care is obviously needed in interpreting single-point-in-time correlations in determining causality between leader behavior and performance. However, in one respect at least this study did demonstrate the well-known effect of expectations.

The study by Lowin and Craig (1968) was also intended to counter the commonly held assumption of unidirectional leader to subordinate behavior effects by demonstrating "the extent to which managerial style can be affected by subordinate productivity" (p. 441). Subjects who believed that they had been hired for a supervisory position in an office were observed to react to subordinates who were directed to behave either as the conscientious-competent worker or the unconscientious-incompetent one. The results clearly showed that when the subordinates performed competently, the supervisor displayed more consideration, initiated less structure, and allowed the subordinate more participation in decision making. On the other hand managers of "incompetent" subordinates supervised more closely, gave more detailed instructions, and displayed less consideration.

Herold (1974) has indicated that one of the major flaws of the Lowin and Craig study was that the *experimenter's direction* of the "subordinates" precluded the operation of an influence process that might affect their behavior. In short, if the leader could not actually affect the follower, one would more likely expect to find that the follower affected the leader. Similarly in the Farris and Lim study, starting with the leaders' perceptions, their expectations were manipulated and then the perceptions of the subordinates were sought. Here again the manipulation of one member of the dyad, the leader, did not allow the operation of influence processes flowing from subordinate to leader. Herold argues that these researchers had done the same thing they were criticizing in earlier studies, that is, creating unidirectionality.

All in all, Herold (1977) contends that the designs employed in both studies precluded the possibility of testing a mutual-influence process. Dependency of members on the relationship and power to control rewards and costs varied from absent to moderate. A main difficulty in studying mutual effects on behavior is the achievement of an experimental setting where both individuals behave spontaneously, without programming or manipulation. If such were the case, then behavior as well as responses to that behavior could be studied for both parties, and variations in the behavior of each could be introduced to observe their consequences reciprocally.

The experiment by Crowe, Bochner, and Clark (1972) noted earlier presents another case of difficulties with imposing causal interpretations upon correlational evidence. In their experiment they found that subordinates' expectations and preferences may be strong enough to bring about a change in leader style from managers who have other preferences. That is, a democratically oriented manager exposed to autocratically oriented subordinates was found to behave more autocratically than his preferred style would have suggested. Alternatively an autocratic manager exposed to democratic subordinates was found to behave more democratically. When a manager's preferred leadership style and his subordinates' preferences were congruent, no accommodation was required of the manager, and he behaved according to his initial intentions. In fact the Crowe, Bochner, and Clark (1972) study recalls the much earlier work of Haythorn, Couch, Haefner, Langham, and Carter (1956) in which a leader working with highly authoritarian group members was found to behave in a more authoritarian manner regardless of his own personality characteristics; similarly the leader of a low-authoritarian group tended to behave in a more democratic fashion.

Barrow (1976) used a simulated leadership situation to study consideration and task orientation of supervisors. He found that the complexity of the task, not performance by workers, affected the latter significantly. Consideration, as well as punitive-performance emphasis and autocratic leader behaviors, was affected most by how well workers performed. Increased performance by them was associated directly with greater leader consideration, and the obverse was true in generating more leader punitiveness and autocratic behavior.

Generally the current literature presents evidence that leaders do exhibit behavioral flexibility. For instance, Fiedler and Chemers (1974) indicate that leaders tend to adjust their behaviors to changes in the favorableness of the situation for them. Other writers, such as Heller (1971), Rubin and Goldman (1968), and

Tannenbaum and Schmidt (1958), have proposed that leaders may change their leadership style when confronted with varying environments, a topic to which we now turn.

PERSONALITY AND LEADER STYLE

In the traditional trait approach to leader personality, a major failing was to impute too much to persisting traits alone, thereby slighting situational variations (Hollander and Julian, 1968, p. 892). By contrast, the term *style* is less ponderous in that it suggests greater flexibility, as in the training of "management styles."

Although a characteristic style may be shown by a leader, it cannot be entirely separated from the situation in which the leader and followers are involved and its requirements. Leaders may therefore reveal a range of behaviors depending upon the circumstances and the others present, including the particular followers with whom they interact. Even relatively consistent dispositions have been found to be controlled by external factors, such as a crisis. Accordingly a style may be a modal tendency, but it usually is still "relational" insofar as particular followers and circumstances may draw forth more or less of certain qualities from the leader.

For example, Hill (1973) observed 124 supervisors and found that only 14 percent of them used a single style over four distinct situations. Bass, Farrow, Valenzi, and Solomon (1975) measured five management styles with a "profile questionnaire" made up of thirty-one scales. These styles were direction, negotiation, consultation, participation, and delegation. In this research, 78 managers and 407 of their subordinates completed the questionnaire on the behavior of the managers. The five styles were found to be differently related to various organizational, task, and interpersonal factors. For instance, direction was associated most with situations of structure and clarity, and negotiation with short-term objectives and group harmony. Participation and delegation were both related to greater interpersonal warmth. Clarity was another situational determinant of participation, and a lack of routine tasks a determinant of delegation. Therefore these characteristics were found to combine in several ways as the framework for the leader's behavior, so that most of the managers showed two or three of the management styles in their profiles.

A characteristic style may stamp a leader's relationship with followers but may vary depending upon *which* followers are involved. Graen (1975) has formalized this in his vertical dyadic linkage (VDL) model of "role mak-

ing," which deals with the development of norms about how the leader and particular followers distinctively will behave in a given situation. Graen considers that each leader has close and more distant circles of followers. While the first share a closer relationship with the leader, they do not necessarily have it easier as a result. In fact higher demands may be made on them to perform to the leader's standard. Therefore an added cost is associated with such closeness. That cost often is a stricter code of loyalty and obedience. Usually a follower who is close to a leader becomes more capable of making the leader appear effective or ineffective, especially because a leader generally is considered responsible for the acts of a subordinate given authority by the leader. Therefore if the member fails, the leader may be perceived to have failed unless mitigating factors prevail.

Other costs occur to the follower because the leader can give only a limited part of his or her resources to do even critical tasks (Graen and Cashman, 1975, p. 154). The follower must do enough with these resources to avoid the high risks of failure that would hurt the leader. By contrast, success is more likely to be seen as the leader's. For those in the outer circle the leader makes fewer personal demands. These followers are usually group members of relatively lower status or newcomers who are treated more as a bloc. However, they are still required to show the performance helpful to attaining the group's goals. Additional refinements from this model have been reported by Dansereau and Dumas (1977) and Dansereau, Alutto, Markham, and Dumas (1981).

In line with the VDL model, Liden and Graen (1980) found that subordinates reporting high-quality relationships with their supervisors assumed greater job responsibility, contributed more, and were rated as higher performers than were subordinates reporting low-quality relationships with their supervisors. Applying this model, Graen, Cashman, Ginsburg, and Schiemann (1977) studied 103 managerial dyads in service organizations and found that the quality of the perceived effectiveness of the leader-member exchange was directly related to the members' satisfaction with the quality of the "linking pin" with their managers (see Likert, 1961).

Another example of style is seen in the extent to which a leader consults followers and in general allows participation. Vroom and Yetton (1973), whose contingency model of decision making in leadership was taken up earlier, find that consultation varies considerably as a function of many factors. Even an otherwise "nonautocratic'' person may adopt an autocratic leadership style because of circumstances, such as the pressure of a deadline and the unique possession of information not readily shared with followers.

A further complexity associated with style is the consideration that leader may favor a particular mode of action but not be observed to behave that way consistently. Accordingly a leader who likes to think that he or she encourages participation may be unaware of the poor basis for participation provided. In general, leader self-descriptions do not match subordinate ratings of them (e.g., Bass, 1981, p. 603). As a case in point, Argyris (1968) studied effectiveness in research and development organizations and reported that "over 85% of the research superiors whom we interviewed described their leadership style as facilitative of autonomy, openness, risk-taking, innovation, and self-responsibility, and yet when we observed them, we noted they facilitated the opposite condition" (p. 349).

One of the most important favorable conditions is sufficient sharing of information. Participants are inevitably unequal in access to information about the task and the decisions to be made (Mulder, 1971). Expertise is more likely to be held by those who have information and who already are influential. They therefore dominate the situation and also are most probably the ones responsible for setting the agenda and carrying through afterward. Among other things, this again suggests the importance of the situational context for participation and other leadership activities to become appropriate and then to be manifested.

Theories about a leader's effectiveness in obtaining good performance often stress a particular leader quality or variable in the situation (cf. Halal, 1974). In the so-called human relations approach, interpersonal relations are the key, as exemplified in the works of McGregor (1967), Likert (1961, 1979), and Argyris (1962, 1976), among numerous others. An extension of this approach is seen in the Blake and Mouton (1964) "managerial grid," which combines leader concern for followers' needs and task efforts, thus paralleling the variables of consideration and initiation of structure.

Richer conceptions of the leader-and-group-performance linkage are found in Stogdill and Coons's (1957) recognition that leader behavior is interwoven with the history, structure, and composition of the group, and that these variables affect outcomes. Even further, Tannenbaum and Schmidt (1958) have indicated that a manager's style depends in some important ways on that person's values, confidence in subordinates, and other

personal inclinations. Their applicability is conditioned by organizational factors, such as traditions, size, and the dispersion of units and personnel.

To this catalogue might be added ambiguity, which has been identified as a stressor in organizational life by several observers of leadership from a psychodynamic perspective (e.g., Zaleznik, 1965). In a recent examination of this scene, Kets de Vries (1980) has reported some of the "Kafkaesque" features of organizations that can be a giant maze of paradoxes, contradictions, and irrationalities (cf. Cohen and March, 1974). Such a setting is particularly hard on managers who have a need to be loved and are unable to make difficult decisions in the face of ambiguity. However, they may in turn hide themselves in ambiguous statements and thereby avoid confrontations.

On the other hand, says Kets de Vries, these organizations can have great attractiveness for individuals who find it much easier to operate in a power mode with cold, hostile interpersonal relations than with warm ones. Such managers, according to his work, often are fast-track upward strivers who want nothing to impede the pursuit of their goals and therefore are remarkably adaptive to an interpersonally cold working environment. At either extreme, subordinates of these managers become confused about the standards of performance expected and the means of evaluation being applied.

Clearly, personality traits are important relative to the situation in which they are displayed (Argyle and Little, 1972). Personality measures had been previously applied to leaders independent of leadership roles or their functions in different situations. No wonder that Mann (1959) found such measures yield highly inconsistent relationships with being the leader. To take one example, "dominance" and "extroversion" are related positively to the status of leader in some studies, but in others are related neither positively nor negatively to such status. There were accordingly differential findings concerning qualities required to be a leader and to be a successful one. Mainly the source for this variability appears to be the different expectations about the functions the leader is to perform. That is why it is necessary to consider the characteristics of the leader as they are perceived to be *relevant* by other group members, within the demands of a given situation.

In studying the personality characteristics of political leaders, another kind of problem is presented, namely, getting close enough to the subjects. Hermann (1977, 1979) and Winter (1980) are two researchers who have analyzed the personality dynamics of political lead ers from a distance. To do otherwise presents severe hurdles, since these leaders are rarely accessible for penetrating interviews by social scientists. Instead their words, in the form of public statements, are utilized as a basis for analysis. One procedure is to content analyze such statements and speeches. Winter and Stewart (1977) used this procedure with twentieth-century U.S. presidents' inaugural addresses and found that the needs for power and affiliation together correlated significantly with the kind of foreign policy they advocated. Distrust versus trust has also been closely identified with the power-seeking "warfare personality" described by Tucker (1965) and with ethnocentrism (LeVine and Campbell, 1972). Regarding political leadership, Fromm (1941) gave his basic formulation of personality factors in saying that "the psychology of the leader and that of the followers are, of course, closely linked with each other. If the same ideas appeal to them their character structure must be similar in important aspects" (p. 65).

Two personality characteristics that have been given special attention in leadership research are Machiavellianism and locus of control, that is, internality versus externality (I-E) (Rotter, 1966). Past research has shown that high scorers on the Machiavellianism scale (Christie and Geis, 1970) tend to take control in small groups and exploit others for self-gain (Geis, 1968). Okanes and Stinson (1974) administered the Machiavellianism scale (Mach V) to 120 college seniors participating in a management simulation organized into twenty-four groups and run for ten weeks. Initially group members selected high Machs significantly more as the informal group leader after five hours of participation, but *not* at the end of the simulation. The dramatic shift was attributable in part to the notion that there was more latitude for improvisation, that is, less structure at the beginning than at the end.

This particular point is in accord with the Geis (1968) notion that the Machiavellian leader will move into unstructured situations more readily than into structured ones. This hypothesis was investigated by Gleason, Seaman, and Hollander (1978) in an experiment with sixteen groups of four male students each. The groups were composed of one high, two medium, and one low Mach, based on scores on the Mach V scale. The specific hypothesis investigated was that high Machs would show more leadership-related behaviors and would be perceived to be leaders more than would low Machs when there was a task of low rather than high structure. In both structure conditions subjects were given instructions for a model-building task, allowing a

ten-minute session for planning, followed by a fifteen-minute period for model construction. During both periods the groups were observed with respect to members' interactions showing "ascendant" or "accepting" behaviors. After the interaction periods, they completed a questionnaire dealing with their group experiences and rated one another. Another observation measure was the "time of possession" of the plan sheet, that is, control of a key resource.

The results of these measures indicated that "accepting" statements were made significantly more often with high structure than with low structure. The plan sheet was held significantly longer in the low-structure than in the high-structure conditions. With regard to the expected interaction between Machiavellianism and structure, the postinteraction questionnaire item on how well members thought their group did relative to other groups showed the greatest mean for high Mach and low structure. Perhaps most interesting, and not predicted, was the postinteraction measure of the kind of person whom members would be most willing to have as the leader in a similar group in the future. Medium Machs were chosen as leaders significantly more often than either the high or low Machs in conditions of both high and low structure. Machiavellianism therefore did make a difference in leader choice. It also showed that the low-structure situation evidently did provide more maneuverability for emergent leadership. This finding is consistent with the Durand and Nord (1976) research indicating that subordinate perceptions of leader initiation, structure, and consideration were associated with the leader's locus of control and Machiavellianism scores.

Drory and Gluskinos (1980) did an experiment with eighty-four male task groups led by fourteen high Machs and fourteen low Machs under either a favorable or an unfavorable situation. In the former instance the leader was presented as technically qualified and his authority was emphasized, while in the latter case the leader's qualities and special status were not emphasized. Also differential criteria were applied: a single-criterion (structured task) or a multiple-criteria (unstructured task) evaluation. Although no performance differences were found between high-Mach- and low-Mach-led groups, significant differences were observed regarding group interactions. High-Mach leaders were found to give more orders and to be less involved in reducing tension, but not so much when the situation was unfavorable. On the other hand the behavior of low-Mach leaders remained consistent across situations. One implication of this work is to suggest that Machiavellians are more inclined to adapt to changing circumstances in order to maintain control, whereas this is less observed, and perhaps unnecessary, among the low Machiavellians.

In a study by Hiers and Heckel (1977) the relationship of seating choice and locus of control was studied to test the hypothesis that subjects choosing positions associated with the leader role would be more likely to be internals than those who chose more distant seating. Each of sixty-five subjects completed a brief questionnaire and the Rotter I-E and then were asked to select a preferred seat in five group situations. Significant correlations were found between internality and the choice of a "leader" seat. Parallel findings were obtained by Anderson and Schneier (1978), who examined the relationship between I-E and leader group performance. Their results indicated that leaders were more likely to be internals than externals, with "superior performance" being achieved more often by internal leaders and by groups led by internals. The observation was made that internals exhibited behaviors more consistent with an instrumental, task-oriented style, and that externals exhibited behaviors more in keeping with a socioemotional style.

Finally, on the matter of leader personality there do not appear to be broad and invariant characteristics that generally distinguish leaders from nonleaders, or "effective" from "ineffective" ones, as Vroom (1976b) has noted. However, in connection with the performance of organizational leaders, he says, "it may be possible to identify classes or families of situations, each characterized by relatively invariant relations between leader personality and criteria of effectiveness....Effective and ineffective leaders may not be distinguishable by a battery of psychological tests but may be distinguished by their characteristic behavior patterns in their work roles" (p. 1530). An essential point he makes is that there is need to search for behavioral correlates of *effective leadership* in such settings instead of studying the personality of an effective leader.

EFFECTS OF POWER

In a traditional form of leadership like autocracy the leader holds power as the all-knowing, even godlike, provider of guidance to the flock. Moreover, in line with the comment earlier from Vonnegut (1981), the leader is to be obeyed as the unquestioned authority. Their obedience gives followers assurance that these benefits are not withdrawn and that their complete dependence is dis-

played. Power of this autocratic form still exists in various places and in groups such as religious cults (see Conway and Siegelman, 1979), even if it is mainly true as Maccoby (1981) contends that "the old models of leadership no longer work" (p. 23).

Whatever the leader's *qualitative source* of power, as in the French and Raven (1959) scheme noted earlier, the quantitative variable of *how much* power is of fundamental importance, as Mulder (1959) long has noted. For example, he points out that power differences may still act as an impediment to authentic worker participation in organizations (Mulder, 1971). A good part of this effect may be due to variations in available information and expertise related to status in organizations. Accordingly low status participants may feel even more frustration when exposed to a supposed participation situation where they are not equipped with these resources. Mulder asserts that no participation is therefore preferable to sham participation.

Also noteworthy, Mechanic (1962) has indicated that there may be informal as well as formal power in organizations. Tannenbaum's (1968) model of power and control in organizations proposes that these can be highly dispersed in an organization, with people of both lower and higher status having access to power. Informal power may be exercised by people who are relatively low on the status ladder—such as secretaries, bookkeepers, and hospital attendants—but who are structurally well placed. Such positions provide for opportunities for control of others, not because of a grant of authority or personal qualities, but by their *location* in the organization. An updated integration of this concept is provided in Blackburn (1981).

Dahl (1957) has proposed the following "intuitive" definition of power: "A has power over B to the extent that he can get B to do something that B would not otherwise do" (pp. 202–203). This parallels Weber's definition, discussed earlier, involving the exercise of will, but with more emphasis on overcoming resistance. Therefore, while Weber conceives of power positively as an enactment of one's own will, Dahl's definition points up the thwarting of another's will. Since power is not exerted only in conflict situations but perhaps more paternalistically, this "negating" form of definition is *not* the same as one stressing action from one's own will.

Furthermore power is neither a fixed state nor an all-or-none quality, but a potential with gradations. Hence Dahl defines one person's amount of power over another with specific regard to the change in probability of getting compliance from the other person. The amount of power means the degree of potential for change toward greater compliance. For instance, in their study of the voting patterns of the thirty-four U.S. senators holding office from 1946 to 1954, Dahl and his colleagues (Dahl, March, and Nastair, 1957) were able to analyze the *relative* power positions of these senators by their roll-call votes in relation to the final Senate votes, showing that power in practice operates by degrees.

In a related vein, discussing the process of negotiation Pruitt (1981, p. 88) points out that it is the *perception of power* rather than power itself which is useful in understanding what transpires in the process. He says that bargainers who perceive themselves as more powerful will delay concessions, while those who perceive themselves as less powerful may be encouraged to try to build power as they define it, or make unilateral concessions. The self-definition of relative power can be crucial to the outcome.

From a sociological view Wrong (1979) has offered a threefold division of power: *force, manipulation*, and *persuasion*. In this view power is intentional, *whether or not* its intended effects are realized. Also, with others (e.g., Willis and Levine, 1976; Hersey and Blanchard, 1982), he defines power essentially as the ability or potential to exert influence, thereby mixing the concepts.

Michener and Burt (1975a, 1975b) have indicated that two components are involved in being able to exercise "legitimate power": the "normativity" of the role and the "endorsement" of the role encumbent by followers. In research with groups of college students, they found that holding office more readily produced compliance with the leader. However, endorsement had less impact on followers but more on the leader, especially in determining whether the leader acquiesced to group pressure or resisted it. Michener and Lawler (1975) measured six conditions in groups to see which of these had the greatest effect on members' endorsement of the leader. Their findings indicated that members more often endorsed the leader when the group was successful, when more rewards were available to members than to the leader, or when the leader was removable by members.

Another intriguing linkage, as Gamson (1968) has observed in *Power and Discontent,* is that a leader experiencing low endorsement from followers may feel it necessary to use coercive power on them. In short, coercion may be a response to weakness and a sense of threat from indulging in a reciprocal influence process. Regarding social exchange relationships, for instance, Baldwin (1978) says that power does play a part, even though such theorists as Blau (1964) have accentuated the distinction between social exchange and power. Blau disputes the assumption that an unbalanced power relation is unstable and tends toward balance, because he says the more powerful person has an interest in maintaining the imbalance.

Another issue in the use of power is centered in negative versus positive sanctions, or coercive versus noncoercive exchange, as Homans (1974) puts it. An example of a coercive exchange would be "Your money or your life." Reducing this to simple exchange terms—"You give me your money and I will let you keep your life"—is not satisfactory with respect to the element of choice supposed to exist in the usual, noncoercive exchange. The argument is made, however, that coercive power can operate in more subtle ways so that the idea of voluntary choice is illusory, for instance, in retaining one's position in an organization. Menzies (1980) cites the cases of a high-level executive, verbally abused before others by his chief executive in a meeting, who is reminded near its end of the huge sums he has at stake in stock options and other benefits, which he would lose if he quit. On the other hand if the chief chooses not to make punishing statements, this can be taken as a reward. Similarly the occasional use of "negative power," to say no to a request or turn down a proposal or program, can make approvals seem more gratifying (see Emerson, 1962).

A more subtle form of negative power is for the power-holder to raise questions so phrased as to exaggerate possible pitfalls in a course of action. Although these can be quite legitimate points of concern, they may actually be legalistic ways of preventing action. Kets de Vries (1980) says that this is a way by which older executives keep down younger, threatening ones. For instance, a proponent of a new idea may be confronted with questions posed in the form *"Isn't it possible that* this course of action could lead to...?"* Or, alternatively, there is the still stronger form *"Can we be absolutely sure that* this course of action will...?"* The effect of such questions in a relationship of power imbalance is to negate the proponent's arguments.

Within a social exchange perspective, according to Jacobs (1970, pp. 286–287), true leadership involves more persuasion and less power. He sums up a main feature of this process in saying (p. 340):

> Where mutual expectations for what is necessary or desired can be developed, one member of a relationship can then initiate action in conformity with the expectations of the other, without causing the other to incur a "cost." Thus, authority relationships in formal organizations serve to protect participants

from exposure to power, and to increase the efficiency with which formal organizations conduct their business.

Bold assertions of coercive power usually have costs to the power-holder as well as to the individual toward whom it is directed and the others involved, even as observers. This is made abundantly clear by Kipnis (1976) in *The Powerholders*. He is particularly interested in the effects of holding a position of power and wielding it. He presents a set of concepts about the "metamorphic effect of power," going beyond Lord Acton's (1887) famous adage that "Power tends to corrupt; absolute power corrupts absolutely," and analyzing its redounding effects.

Kipnis (1976) identifies four corrupting influences of power, which are seen to operate in sequence: (1) the desire to have power becomes an end in itself, with all that is implied by means-end relationships; (2) access to power tempts the individual to use institutional resources for self-benefit illegally; (3) holding a power position creates the basis for false feedback from others and an exalted sense of self-worth; and (4) power over others leads to a devaluation of their worth and a desire to avoid having close social contacts with them. It is not so much the fate of the power-holder that concerns Kipnis as it is the destructive effects of excessive power wielding in relationships.

One limit to the generalizability of laboratory research is that the "reality" of power cannot be easily simulated, except in merely trivial ways—for example, by awarding or withholding extra credit for taking part in an experiment. When leadership is being studied, there is the added problem of creating an analogue to an ongoing institutional structure, where power holding has longer-range consequences (see Wood, 1973). The nearest approximation to this, relatively, would be the Stanford prison study (Haney and Zimbardo, 1977) in which students filling the role of guards wielded considerable power over students filling the role of prisoners and displayed some of Kipnis's "metamorphoses," even over a reasonably brief time span.

CHARISMATIC LEADERS

The term *charismatic leader* was coined in a 1921 paper by Max Weber, using the Greek word *charisma* for divine gift. It describes a leader who attracts loyal followers and who therefore has considerable power over them. Weber said that charismatic leaders are most likely to emerge when there is a crisis and great enthusiasm to have something done about it. Charismatic leaders often head highly cohesive political and social movements, although they may take on positions of formal authority after creating social change.

Several explanations have been offered for the supposedly magical powers of charismatic leaders. House (1977) says that such a leader becomes the active agent of a cause, not because of a personality characteristic so much as because of the leader's unique appeal to followers who perceive a way to achieve a significant goal through the leader. Katz and Kahn (1978, pp. 545–546) put it this way:

> Charisma derives from people's emotional needs and from the dramatic events associated with the exercise of leadership. The critical period of a war and the dependence of people upon their military leaders is productive of charisma. In less strenuous times bold and imaginative acts of leadership help to create a charismatic image of the leader.
>
> Charisma is not the objective assessment by followers of the leader's ability to meet their specific needs. It is a means by which people abdicate responsibility for any consistent, tough-minded evaluation of the outcome of specific policies. They put their trust in their leader, who will somehow manage to take care of things.

In the organizational realm, close contact between leader and subordinate may undercut the perception of a leader's magical powers by making human failings more evident. According to Katz and Kahn, distance enhances the perception of charisma. Handy (1976) contends that organizations may have leaders who have a devoted following ("commando leaders") and who come into play when there are challenging and exhilarating tasks to be done. They show charismatic qualities, particularly if the task can sustain interest. But, says Handy, these commando leaders can turn into a "glamorous nuisance" because they have become indispensable to their group's effective performance (p. 131).

Several psychodynamic conceptions help to explain supposedly charismatic powers. As noted before, Freud (1921) spoke of the group leader as a common "ego-ideal," with whom followers share identification. Such an identification may provide a shared outlook or ideology. In fact the charismatic leader can say things publicly that others feel privately but cannot or do not express. Then these things become slogans for the movement, as with "We shall overcome," used by Martin Luther King, Jr. Even more deeply, Fromm (1941, p. 65) has asserted that the leader's personality structure

> will usually exhibit in a more extreme and clear-cut way the particular personality structure of those to whom his doctrines appeal; he can arrive at a clearer and more outspoken formulation of certain ideas for which his followers are already prepared psychologically.

In a psychoanalytic treatment of leadership and power, Zaleznick and Kets de Vries (1975) have differentiated *consensus leadership* from *charismatic leadership*. They use these terms to describe ideal types, that is, flexible-conciliatory versus self-centered and allegiance demanding. Going further, they distinguish positive and negative charisma, with the former providing "loving relations" and the latter "destructive capabilities from an unforgiving superego," which defines good and bad. In an analysis of corporate behavior, Chatov (1981) has used this distinction and points up the impact of the charismatic leader in upsetting an organization's acceptance of the status quo, which is more placidly accepted with a consensus leader.

On the other hand a limitation of this theory is that it makes little allowance, if any, for mixed types, such as the consensus leader who is charismatic in the loving or punitive—or both—form. Consider a simple fact. The president of the Supreme Soviet addresses a proposal to its approximately fifteen hundred members assembled in conclave, and the proposal is passed unanimously. Is the president showing he is a consensus leader or charismatic leader? If the latter, is he demanding allegiance or gaining it through wide respect, admiration, or even love? The answer is not at all evident from these categorical terms. Indeed the demarcations involved seem reminiscent of the distinction being made lately between "authoritarian" and "totalitarian" regimes. Both involve a high degree of coercive power, arbitrariness in variously punishing people without necessarily following legal processes, and centralized authority vested in a supreme leader or group. This sounds quite familiar under the heading of *dictatorship,* an older term that still seems to fill the bill for a coercive political system that denies individual freedom and rights (cf. Fromm, 1941; Tucker, 1965).

Finally, a major political figure may lose supposed charisma once out of office because the luster of the position itself carried a great deal of the weight. Also, much depends upon the perception of how well the leader did, and what occasioned the loss of office—failure to win reelection, displacement by a revolution, the end of a normal period of service, and so forth. Essentially, then, charisma depends upon a continued following, and without it the leader's charisma may have little appeal.

GENDER EFFECTS IN MIXED-SEX GROUPS

Leadership traditionally has been a male domain, despite inroads made recently by women in leader roles. The evidence indicates that women and men are more inclined to expect a man rather than a woman to occupy a leader role (Lockheed, 1979; Inderlied and Powell, 1979). In a parallel way the study of leadership in groups has been done mainly with men, as the literature amply reveals. Hare's revised *Handbook of Small Group Processes* (1976) indicates generally that the situation has changed only a little since his earlier edition. Evidently our knowledge about leadership in groups has largely been founded on studies with men and far less on studies with women, or with men and women in groups of mixed composition. Only recently has there been concerted interest in women actually leading such groups (e.g., Bartol, 1974; O'Leary, 1974).

The conventional wisdom continues to be that women and men differ in certain aspects of their social behavior. While there is some support for that view, as Deaux (1976) and O'Leary (1977) have noted, such data have to be interpreted cautiously because of a good deal of confusion about the biological and social bases of femininity and masculinity. One serious consequence of entrenched stereotypes is that women as leaders of mixed-sex groups may need to be occupied as much with overcoming negative attitudes as with performing their jobs well. Therefore women may face an extra handicap, which also may be faced by minority group members: They must prove themselves against higher odds and very likely, as the adage has it, "be like gold to be seen as silver."

Furthermore, with respect to leadership, the traditional sex-role "stereotype" of men as more task-oriented and women as more relationship-oriented in groups has to be viewed in this light. Experiments such as those by Bond and Vinacke (1961) and Strodtbeck and Mann (1956), which have found male performance to be exploitative and competitive, and female performance to be more accommodative and tension reducing, are hardly conclusive in what they imply, other than that women are socialized differently (see Eagly, 1978). However, such results do conform to Bales and Slater's (1955) longstanding distinction between the task role, associated with the father, and the socioemotional role, associated with the mother, and thereby create a basis for too-ready generalizations. Plainly much social learning and a tradition of societal expectations exist, even though they are not applicable any longer to a situation in which over half the married women in the United States are working (*Statistical Abstract of the United States,* 1983). The Bales and Slater (1955) dichotomy also obscures the reality that married women perform tasks in the home, even if they are not working at a job, and their husbands can provide socioemotional support in addition to being wage-earners. The growing interest in psychological androgyny is pertinent to recognizing this overlap (see S. L. Bem, 1974, 1975).

A large part of the issue of women as leaders is contained in outmoded ideas about activity and dominance. Although differences in these qualities have been observed between women and men in groups, the nature of the activity and its context are important. For instance, women show less physical aggression, bearing in mind that there is considerable cultural encouragement for boys to engage in physically aggressive contact sports, as Mead (1949) has long since noted. Girls may be "aggressive," but not as much in physical ways. Deaux (1976) contends that women are as active as men, but that the areas in which they may strive to achieve are different. With respect to being dominant, assertive, or competitive, women in mixed-sex company are often constrained to be less obviously so than men. In fact, women in leader roles may not be able to use power as directly as men (Johnson, 1976). However, as Bunker and Bender (1980) indicate, while men and women managers compete differently, they nonetheless compete.

Leadership research with groups of mixed-sex composition is only relatively recent. One element that has emerged from experiments in such groups is that women show less inclination to see themselves as leaders or to seek that role, as Megargee (1969) found in dyads made up of men and women in combinations of high and low dominance. Even women high in dominance gave way to a man, though low in dominance, as leader. However, this widely cited finding is suspect not only for being dated but also for its basis in dyads, which are not directly comparable to groups of larger number. Furthermore the experimenter was a male, a fact that is now known to elicit different behaviors from female subjects than if the experimenter is female.

When women believe that they have task-relevant skills, they *do* show initiative as leaders. Eskilson and Wiley (1976) created such a self-perception by giving women the belief that they had become the leader because they exhibited task-relevant skills, and found that they showed greater performance output and more leaderlike activity than women who had been randomly appointed. On the other hand men who were leaders in this study were not found to be similarly affected by the process by which they attained that role. As Hollander and Yoder (1980) have concluded from their review of this literature, observed differences in the leader behavior of women and men can be attributed to the interrelationship of role expectations, style, and task demands in the particular setting. Indeed Maccoby and Jacklin (1974) have indicated that the choice of a task itself can create a biased condition for women or for men. Clement and Schiereck (1973) have encouraged the use of non-sex-specific tasks in group research, such as signal detection.

There also is the consideration of social expectations. Much of the literature on leadership indicates or implies that the writers (who routinely refer to the leader as "he"), and people generally, expect the leader role to be filled by a man. For instance, in a study by Schein (1973) male middle managers rated women in general, men in general, or successful middle managers on their overall characteristics, attitudes, and temperaments. On sixty of the eighty-six items, men and successful managers were rated similarly, while on only eight items were women and successful managers rated similarly. Parallel results were obtained in a replication by Massengill and DiMarco (1979).

Yerby (1975) studied women as leaders and found that groups of two men and two women were most satisfied, and those that were all men were least satisfied. Furthermore men may harbor a sense that another man would be uncomfortable working as the subordinate of a woman (Cohen, Bunker, Burton, and McManus, 1978). Indeed a national sample of male managers and executives, presented with various scenarios about either a male or a female employee, indicated negative expectations about married women executives, for example, that these women could not balance the responsibilities of home and career (Rosen, Jerdee, and Prestwich, 1975). Another survey found that both men and women preferred men as bosses and professionals (Ferber, Huber, and Spitze, 1979). Such attitudes may readily serve to rationalize male intolerance of women in executive roles. For the woman involved, this may necessitate the resolution of a role conflict between the traditional feminine role and the organizational leader role (Yerby, 1975). Among the situational influences affecting the resolution of this conflict are the gender composition of the group, subordinates' attitudes, task demands, success or failure of the group, and the leader's source of status (Hollander and Yoder, 1980, p. 273).

Accordingly O'Leary (1974) points out that a basic concern exists among women and men about whether the leader role is appropriate for a woman in a mixed-sex setting. The success of women therefore may be inhibited not only by external expectations but also by attitudes held by the woman herself. An ineffectual male leader may need to cope with a greater sense of failure for mismanaging his role, but a successful female leader might need to face the fact that societal attitudes do not readily acknowledge or applaud her success in the leader role (Pheterson, Kiesler, and Goldberg, 1971; Jacobson and Effertz, 1974; Gold, 1978).

There have been comparatively few studies of women who serve as leaders of mixed-sex groups, whether through appointment, election, or some informal process of emergence (cf. Aries, 1976). In one attempt in this direction, Fallon and Hollander (1976) studied thirty-two groups, each composed of two men and two women undergraduate students who were able to elect a leader in a discussion task concerned with urban problems, set in the city called Colossus. Each group talked about the first two problems for about ten to fifteen minutes and made a group ranking of the alternative action programs for each. A secret ballot was then distributed. Of the thirty-two groups, fourteen elected men and ten elected women as leaders; two men tied, and a coin toss yielded the choice; in six groups a woman and a man tied, and the woman was made the winner to offset what was an overall tilt to elect men. However, by the process used, the leader was *always* the most or equal to the most chosen person in the group. Following the first two phases, half the groups were given success feedback and half failure feedback on performance. Regardless of the type of feedback, men leaders were found to be significantly more influential than women leaders in the last phases. There was, however, no difference by leader gender in the *satisfaction* item of the postinteraction questionnaire, although men leaders were seen by both men and women as

having significantly *more task-leadership ability*. Pretesting did not reveal any gender-bias in the task. Therefore in this case men evidently fared better as leaders than did the women, and women generally joined men in seeing women leaders as less able on the task.

In a related experiment at the U.S. Military Academy at West Point, Rice, Bender, and Vitters (1980) compared men and women cadets as leaders of three-man cadet groups. They had previously measured the men's attitudes toward women, using the Spence-Helmreich attitudes-toward-women scale (1972). While leader gender did not appear to affect performance and morale, these attitudes proved to be quite decisive in determining the attributions made about the women as compared to the men leaders. A comparable finding has been reported recently by Forsyth and Forsyth (1984) using female confederates as leaders behaving in a task or interpersonal way with mixed-sex groups. At West Point, when the group was "successful" with a woman leader, both the leader and the men followers attributed it more to "luck." With a man leader they attributed success more to the leader's ability. This finding parallels and confirms others regarding attributions made differentially about the results of efforts by men or women leaders.

In two recent field studies with women and men cadets at West Point, Rice, Instone, and Adams (1984) analyzed ratings subordinate cadets gave to more senior cadets who were unit leaders in summer training. No main leader-sex effects were found across the two settings. Unlike the previous results, the female leader with male subordinates did not receive such negative descriptions. But female subordinates with female leaders stood out for their generally less favorable attitudinal judgments of the leader. Moreover, two attributional judgments regarding the leader's skill and the leader's hard work as contributors to unit performance were found to be more highly correlated for male than for female leaders in both settings.

Earlier results by Hollander and Neider (1978), indicated a comparable gender-linked finding. Critical incidents about good or bad leadership were obtained in an open-ended fashion from male and female respondents. Males rarely mentioned female leaders in either the good or bad categories, which no doubt reflects the base rate of women as leaders. On the other hand female respondents cited many more incidents with female leaders showing bad leadership than with male leaders doing so. For good leadership the female respondents mentioned male and female leaders about equally. The interpretation offered for these results was that females may have had more experience than males with female leaders, and they also may be more critical of females who are leaders. Clearly the factors that affect the leadership behavior of women and men are quite often complex and interactive. There may also be subtle differences in the situation that may go unnoticed. There also are differential effects of gender composition. For instance, groups of women show more disclosure of feelings about self and others than groups of mixed composition (Kraft and Vraa, 1975). On the other hand groups of women take fewer risks than groups of men, with mixed groups being intermediate (Bauer and Turner, 1974).

As stated earlier, when a woman is put in charge of a group or an organization as an executive or a manager, she is likely to be at an initial disadvantage. However, Kanter (1977) concludes in her book *Men and Women of the Corporation* that individual differences matter more than a woman's gender in managerial roles. She asserts this despite the contentions elsewhere that women will often face the extra burden of overcoming negative attitudes in managing mixed-sex groups (e.g., O'Leary, 1974). On this point Denmark (1977, pp. 110–111) supports a middle-ground view:

> Many of the assumptions that women managers are basically different from men are just not supported by data. The one difference investigators generally agree upon is women's greater concern for relationships among people; this should be considered a plus in terms of leadership effectiveness. Alleged sex differences in ability, attitudes, and personality have been based on sex-role stereotypes, rather than empirical observations of women leaders.

The leader's style, as a personal quality, may therefore be more a function of individual differences than of gender differences (Day and Stogdill, 1972; Bartol and Wortman, 1979).

Bartol and Butterfield (1976) investigated the extent to which sex-role stereotypes affected evaluations of leader behavior. Women and men business students were given one of two versions of their questionnaire containing four stories, each one depicting a leadership style based on initiating structure, consideration, production emphasis, or tolerance for freedom. Two versions were prepared, with the manager's name given, indicating whether it was a woman or a man. Responses to evaluations for the leadership styles confirmed the hypothesis that the leader's gender did affect the evaluations of

managerial behavior, although the effect varied for the different styles, with initiating structure varying more highly for males, and consideration for females. No significant influence on the evaluation of production emphasis and tolerance for freedom was found by leader gender.

A field study with supervisory employees in a large psychiatric hospital (Bartol and Wortman, 1976) did not find that self-perceptions for women and men in such roles fit sex-role stereotypes. Though there were differences, the results generally supported indications from research on subordinate ratings that there may be few job-related performance differences between women and men supervisors. This conclusion is offered despite the fact that the women leaders tended to describe themselves as performing with more consideration and tolerance of uncertainty, and as being more satisfied with co-workers, than did the male supervisors. Schneier and Bartol (1980) investigated fifty-two task groups working in conjunction with a fifteen-week course in personnel administration and found no significant differences in the proportion of men and women emerging as leaders through sociometric choice. Furthermore member ratings on the Bales interaction categories showed the behavioral correlates of the emergence process to be similar for men and women leaders. For example, irrespective of gender, emergent leaders were more likely than nonleaders to be perceived typically to exhibit positive behaviors. Group performance was not found to be differentiated by whether the leader was a woman or a man.

In a study of ratings among a class of British medical students (Frank and Katcher, 1977), each was asked to characterize himself or herself and other group members at the start of the term and again at its end. Women were ranked relatively low on dominance by the men students at both points. With respect to task orientation, group composition mediated ratings such that in groups with one woman, women were ranked relatively low on this variable, while in groups with more than one woman, women were equally distributed along the ranks in task orientation. The results support the tendency to stereotype women's behavior, with some moderation by the experience of their presence in greater numbers.

In this vein it is noteworthy that Chapman (1975) has reported that in a sample of college students, men and women did not score differently on Fiedler's LPC scale. Further, as noted earlier, Schneier (1978) found that emergent leaders of both sexes scored significantly lower on LPC than did nonleaders. Since this scale is supposed to measure a tendency to be either task-oriented (low) or relationship-oriented (high), the absence of a sex difference challenges the usual expectations regarding the behavior of women and men.

Two characteristic designs are used in studying differences between women and men as leaders: (1) assign women or men to the role of leader, keeping other factors constant, or (2) examine the leader's and group's reactions to women or men who are already in place as leaders, for example, those who are managers. The first procedure addresses the general question of whether women *assigned* to be leaders can be as effective as men. The second asks whether women who choose to be leaders are as effective as men who choose the leader role. Given these differences and the problem of clearly specifying "effectiveness," it is not surprising that these two approaches produce conflicting research findings (Brown, 1979; Hollander and Yoder, 1980). Studies reporting gender differences in leadership behavior usually take a sample from the general population of women and thrust them into the leader role; studies finding few differences between women and men leaders tend to sample the population of actual leaders (Darley, 1976; Osborn and Vicars, 1976; Foster and Kolinko, 1979). The factor that appears to be critical is *whether the individual has the initiative* in taking on the leader role in the particular setting.

On balance, the evidence indicates that women in leader roles are likely to be treated differently by the men with whom they work (cf. Larwood and Lockheed, 1979). This pattern of differential conduct may include sexual harrassment, which presents a social problem that has received heightened attention recently. There is also a tendency for women's comments to be interrupted, overlooked, ignored, or "unheard" by men not used to paying attention to what women say in mixed-sex groups; and unfortunately women may themselves ignore other women (Bunker and Seashore, 1975). In the world of real-life leadership, serving as a manager of a group made up of men and women may present extra impediments for a woman or a member of a minority group. However, the need not be so. Welsh (1979) presents results indicating a positive change in the trend of undergraduate women's views of women as leaders. But undergraduate men remained more traditional in those views. Osborn and Vicars (1976) report evidence from two organizations that suggests the leader's gender was not related either to leader behavior or to subordinates' satisfaction.

In addition to the growing interest in gender effects on leadership, recent work has focused attention on race,

notably differential responses to black and white leaders. Bartol, Evans, and Stith (1978) have called attention to three major areas of importance in studying such differential responses: leader behavior, leader potential on job performance, and job attitudes and job satisfaction. Although black and white leaders appear similar in many respects, ethnic factors are seen to affect all three areas, a finding that requires considerable additional study. A rare comparative work by Allen and Ruhe (1976) investigated verbal behaviors of black and white leaders of biracial groups in two different samples, 96 college students and 288 naval recruits. They worked on two laboratory tasks in three-person groups of mixed racial composition and were rated with the Bales interaction-process categories by two trained observers. The broad conclusion was that the leaders in the two settings did not employ significantly different patterns of leader behavior, and no significant effects by race were reported. Such results represent an opening to a more adequate picture of race composition as a factor in leadership.

As with gender differences, the point needs to be made again that the two distinct approaches to such research must be viewed with special attention to their consequences: Using gender or race as an independent variable, the design in laboratory studies assigns women and men, or blacks and whites, to the leader role and then measures certain of the outcomes regarding such dependent variables as leader influence and group performance. Alternatively, in the field it is common to look at the leader's and group's reactions to women and men or blacks and whites who already are in place as leaders, for example, as supervisors or managers.

The overall picture regarding gender effects is not entirely disheartening, since many of the studies that show women at a disadvantage may become increasingly less applicable to changing conditions. Futhermore task-confidence and evidence of competence do carry weight. As more women and minority group members move into leader roles and perform capably, their numbers may well reduce the disadvantages they have encountered (Hollander, 1983b).

IMPLICIT LEADERSHIP THEORY: THE ATTRIBUTION PERSPECTIVE

The preconceptions followers may hold about leaders have gained considerable recent attention. Such preconceptions, in the nature of an "implicit leadership theory," could account for the factors that have been found in questionnaire ratings of leaders by followers (Rush, Thomas, and Lord, 1977). Calder (1977) asserts that a good deal of leadership exists mainly in follower attributions. At a more general level this view fits the concept of an "implicit-personality theory" that Schneider (1973) contends raters bring to situations, apart from the others they rate there.

Earlier Cronbach (1955) had suggested the importance of subjective elements in trait ratings and in their associations. Mulaik (1964) demonstrated that it is not necessary to rate actual people to obtain personality ratings associated with trait words, that is, the characteristics they evoke. Julian and Hollander (1966) found that simple descriptions of leader characteristics, or their absence, in various combinations produced quite consistent responses. For example, poor performance was more likely to be excused if the supposed leader was said to be "highly motivated" rather than unspecified.

Weiss and Adler (1981) argue that in such instances the implicit-leadership theories held by individuals may fairly accurately reflect regularities in the covariation among the behaviors itemized in leader behavior scales, though still serving as organizing schema for respondents. The data presented from their research indicate that the cognitive complexity of respondents is unrelated to their ratings of leaders, which raises a question about the plausibility of implicit theories of leadership. To see if they do correspond to reality requires yet unavailable, independent measures of reality (Eden and Levitan, 1975).

The evident interest in applications of attribution theory to leadership is identified with Calder (1977), Pfeffer (1977), and Green and Mitchell (1979). Calder contends that Heider's (1958) attribution theory provides a framework for looking at leadership as a function of "naive psychology," that is, the everyday thoughts of individuals. In these terms leadership is a label that can be applied to behavior so as to account for its causes. In this everyday sense, leadership locates the reasons for behavior squarely in the personal dispositions of the actors. Both behavior and its results are taken as evidence of leadership if they distinguish an actor from others who are not leaders. In short, observers believe that the quality of leadership produces certain behavior and results. As Calder puts it, "leadership is an inference. An individual may be more or less competent about this inference. The central problem for the individual inferring leadership is the adequacy of the behavioral evidence available" (1977, p. 188).

Pfeffer (1977) contends that the leadership concept is used inferentially by observers to make sense out of past events. This personification of social causality is important, whether or not leader behavior actually influences performance or effectiveness because people believe it does. Furthermore, says Pfeffer, the attribution of causality to leaders and leadership makes leaders come to be *symbols*. If something has gone wrong, one cannot fire the entire staff, but the firing of a manager may convey a sense of removing the cause. Such a process may be reinforced by organizational forms including inauguration, a choice process, and providing the leader with symbols and ceremonies. Alternatively, Pfeffer says that if for instance leaders are chosen by drawing random numbers others are less likely to believe in their effect as causal agents.

This attributional perspective has several implications for the field of leadership study. Perhaps of greatest importance, Calder (1977) suggests, is to move leadership from a scientific concept that is "out there" to the study of observers' perceptions. As Mitchell (1979, p. 269) has assessed it:

> The meaning of the term leadership becomes a study in how the label is used, when it is used, and how one develops assumptions about the nature of leadership. This social reality will undoubtedly be related to how the observers (e.g., subordinates) behave and perform, but the level of analysis and the research process are very different (p. 269).

He goes on to note that if an attributional approach has validity, then all the studies using subordinates or observers as raters of leader behavior has questionable validity, since these ratings are likely to be biased by the observers' social reality and are therefore poor indicators of how a leader "actually" behaved (cf. Green and Mitchell, 1979; Rush and Beauvais, 1981; Rush, Phillips, and Lord, 1981; Larson, 1982).

Further research suggests that perceptions of leadership and leader behavior are significantly affected by performance information (cf. Mitchell, Larson, and Green, 1977; Lord, Benning, Rush, and Thomas, 1978). It is also noteworthy that a factor consistently associated with leadership perceptions, broadly labeled as "social prominence" (Stein and Heller, 1979), may be equated with salience with respect to "standing out" in a figure-ground fashion (Hollander, 1964, pp. 227–231). However, experiments in which subjects have been exposed to the same behaviors still reveal differences in ratings of the "leader" observed (e.g., Rush, Thomas, and Lord, 1977). More recently Phillips and Lord (1981) have found experimental evidence supporting a cognitive categorization process, based on contextual and behavioral information, as the basis for classifying a person as a leader. However, these investigators indicate that this does not mean that a process of causal analysis does not occur or is unimportant, since causal ascription can flow from the categorization. It is also noteworthy that the characteristics of raters, gender, and similarity to the leader may affect ratings assigned (Durand and Nord, 1976; Butterfield and Bartol, 1977; Weiss, 1977).

Regarding attribution processes, Hogan and Schroeder (1981) have criticized contemporary laboratory research on leadership for its superficiality. They say this accounts for the not surprising finding that the "problem" of leadership is largely an "illusion," insofar as "there are no leaders and followers, but only situations that determine roles" (p. 12). These critics go on to address studies of "personality characteristics associated with effective leadership," which they see as inconsistent with the first line of work insofar as these studies acknowledge that there are leaders and that clearly "some personalities make better leaders than others" (p. 12). In fairness, however, it should be said that these two lines of research are not usually pursued by the same investigators.

Furthermore a gap exists once again between studying *who* is a leader in a given situation and determining whether that leader is *effective*. Apart from begging the question of what constitutes effectiveness, the point of this evident disparity lies in the basic issues of *identifying a person as a leader*, and then *identifying those factors making for a successful leader*. In trait terms this refers to the differential qualities for *becoming* and *performing*. The "becoming" issue was the one that for so long dominated trait-based research on leadership, and not nearly so much "success in performing."

OBSERVATIONS AND CONCLUSIONS

Given the wide range and diversity of current work, general comments about the study of leadership are admittedly risky. However, several points stand out in covering what can seem a boundless terrain, where conflicting ideas seem to occur with high frequency.

One overarching observation is that the study of leadership not only involves numerous definitions but also embodies an underlying distinction between micro-

and macroleadership that needs to be made more explicit. Most of the research literature in social psychology treats leader-follower relationships at the microlevel, usually regarding interpersonal relations. Microleadership ordinarily is centered in small groups (see Steiner, 1964).

Alternatively, as noted in connection with the presidency, macroleadership operates on a larger scale. It is seen more in the goal-setting, planning, and other strategic functions of leadership. The leader is not indifferent to followers in this mode, but the interpersonal realm is not central, even if consideration for followers is clearly present. Indeed the leader may serve them well by providing a better picture of social reality. The leader gives needed direction for change. This process is central to what Burns (1978, 1984) speaks about when he suggests that some leaders are capable of achieving "transforming leadership," thereby creating a decided shift in the way followers perceive and act. More than a transaction, this phenomenon operates as a social movement. Macroleadership processes need more attention in social psychology to balance the microleadership emphasis in studying the face-to-face relationship of the leader and followers in groups.

Macroleadership most clearly requires defining reality in the political arena and in organizations. As discussed here, the Presidency offers ready examples of the need for this larger concept, seen for instance in the cliche of calling for "strong leadership" (cf. Burns, 1984). Mainly the issue involved is *change,* which is not as readily translatable from the usual focus of microleadership processes within laboratory groups.

No wonder then that voices have been raised critically in recent years regarding the overconcern with leadership in interpersonal terms, as microlevel influence, without recognizing the broader system of controls operating in organizations (Miner, 1975). The task and organizational qualities called "substitutes for leadership" (Woodward, 1973; Kerr, 1977) now have gained more and clearly justified attention. Kerr (1977, p. 139) says that if these situational controls are ignored,

> then efforts at leadership training, organizational development, and task design may well result in ineffectiveness for the organization and frustration for its members, as they come to realize that inflexible policies, invariant work methodologies, or other barriers. . . are interfering with intended changes and preventing desired benefits.

A second observation is that there appears to be considerable variability in the way leadership is approached scientifically and in lay terms as an everyday phenomenon. Among participants in political and organizational life there is little doubt that leaders and leadership are real; indeed they occupy a place of considerable interest. In everyday life people have no hesitation in seeing a change of leader as a causal factor in subsequent events. Calder (1977) has extended this point in saying that positive or negative outcomes are attributed to the leader, and if things go wrong, someone has to be blamed—an executive, the coach, or the manager.

By contrast, while usually acknowledging that leaders and leadership have a role, it is as if now social scientists interested in leadership were obliged to draw back, expressing skepticism about their authenticity or definition. Davis and Luthans (1979) are among those who have stressed the absence of behavioral evidence that leadership affects organizational effectiveness. Alternatively, Campbell (1977) has observed with some exaggeration that most workers in the leadership field act as if the ability of the individual leader "plays no part in the proceeding" (p. 232).

Whatever the source or sources of the ability, the lay person will probably reject the sophisticated notion that it did not matter for performance. The reason for rejection clearly would be the perceptions of everyday experience. Organizations would not support executive and management training programs without the expectation that leader ability mattered and that it could be developed or improved in some degree. Fiedler (1970) earlier put the point in traditional terms by saying that "an organization's success or failure, indeed its very survival, depends in large part on the leadership it is able to attract" (p. 1). The larger issue involved may be to secure adequate or better performance indicators. This is the outcome question that asks a sequence of actions, presumed to be initiated by the leader, produced by way of consequences. Too often in past research this has left off at asking whether the leader was influential, and to what degree, without asking *toward what ends.*

A prior question, still largely omitted in research, is the leader's impetus for action, and the limits on it. One essential point is how much freedom does the leader actually have? For example, in *Choices for Managers* Stewart (1981) presents a scheme that goes further in articulating the range of discretion available to those who are leaders. She identifies *demands* with respect to "required" leader activity, *constraints* on what is suit-

able leader activity, and *choices*—that is, the opportunities for leaders in similar posts to do different things in different ways. In a parallel fashion, we need to know more about leader self-perceptions and self-expectations, as Lundberg (1978) has noted, including relative power.

An enlarged perspective on the foundations of leader action must necessarily consider the constraints that followers create by their expectations about leader activity and the intentions perceived to be behind it. If leaders are to be able to do different things in different ways, then followers must respond positively, which depends upon how they perceive the leader's course and motives. Conversely the leader needs to preserve the basis for discretionary choice.

So much of leadership research has been directed to the effects of leaders on followers that such bases for leader actions have received relatively scant attention. The prior question of *origins,* rather than *effects,* has been largely unexamined (see Green and Mitchell, 1979). One result of this major omission is a poorly developed picture of the motivational factors that underlie the behavior of individual leaders, including their so-called style.

A contemporary attempt in this direction, derived from Fromm's (1941) work on social character, is Maccoby's (1976) psychological analysis of four managerial types: the craftsman, the company man, the jungle fighter, and the gamesman. Maccoby says that the gamesman now dominates the top echelon of innovative organizations because of problem-solving acuity, a willingness to take calculated risks, a fascination with technique, and coolness under stress. The gamesman furthermore lacks firm convictions, thrives best on competition, and energizes winning teams by a combination of seductive and supportive appeals. On the negative side the gamesman shows tendencies toward rashness, fantasy, manipulation, and lying, which create a detachment from reality, emotional and otherwise. As with most, this typology is intended to describe major tendencies, with relatively few individuals being pure exemplars of one type. Also each type has positive and negative aspects that may make for effectiveness in one situation and ineffectiveness in another.

In a later book Maccoby (1981) presents a set of case histories of "new-style" leaders "who are trying to make business and government more humane and effective." They go beyond the recently prevalent management style of the gamesman to greater concern with people functioning "in interdependent teams at different levels" (p. 21). More such studies in depth, extended over time, are needed to establish the links between leader motives, aspirations, and actions. In fact, using a retrospective view, there is a tradition of work on "psychohistory," which studies the motivation of leaders within a historical framework (see, e.g., Erikson, 1969; Mazlish, 1972; deMause, 1982).

Leadership research has generally dealt *more* with its *static* than its *dynamic* features, such as succession. Even in simple systems, and certainly in large-scale mergers, a change in the cast of leaders can be a threatening-to-shattering experience. Indeed leadership succession in any setting is among the more significant leadership processes, not only because it is unsettling to participants but also because it destabilizes the system's equilibrium and thereby affects its outputs (Miller and Rice, 1967). Stability and predictability may be two variables that can themselves be significant outputs, beyond the usual and more obvious ones of performance and satisfaction. In short, we need to know more about the openness to change arising from a leadership process. Certainly it is difficult enough to disentangle the many factors that ordinarily are treated as dependent and independent variables in leadership, but we need to give more consideration to the time differential.

A good deal of the disenchantment, even nihilism, observed in the current criticism of leadership is probably due to the truly multiplex features it presents, especially as one tries earnestly to comprehend them. Yet the focus on positional leaders assigned to direct the activities of others, about whom the basic question is whether they succeed in being influential, trivializes the process. Followers are given relatively less attention, when they should be getting more, and the richness of the interchange of leader and followers is fitted into a static, unidirectional model of influence. The essential question of "Toward what ends?" also continues to be obscured and very much needs attention in value terms.

One last observation concerns the persisting problem of generalizability. The difficulty with any coverage of leadership research is that laboratory experiments may be faulted for dealing only minimally at best with the realities of larger systems, such as the elements of power, change, and career striving, but many such experiments are nevertheless generalized. On the other hand field research, often of a "case study" form, also has a slim base for generalization with respect to the particular locale, personalities, and task involved. The nature of the technology may also dictate other relationships (see, e.g., Woodward, 1965; Miller and Rice, 1967; R. G. Hunt, 1970). Despite these constraints, the findings of such work may be generalized even more than laboratory research because of a "real-world" connection.

Issues of generalizability are endemic to the narrow-band work that almost inevitably is frustrated in accomplishing a comprehensive view, even if the "pieces" can be aggregated. Unfortunately the mosaic produced may still have a fragmentary, chaotic quality. The basic difficulty is not just the narrowness of the band but seeing it as wider and therefore more generalizable than is warranted. While there is abundant research dealing with one or another "leader-style" construct, for instance, most of it slights contextual and comparative effects from other sources, thus showing the "attributional error" (Jones, 1979). Nonetheless its adherents lay claim to a larger territory. Leader styles evidently can have a significant effect on system outcomes but do not account for nearly so much variance as do contextual factors, such as the relative size of competing organizations and the degree of concentration in an industry (Lieberson and O'Connor, 1972). Therefore not enough information is provided by the often limited focus represented by "style," thereby producing a sense of disenchantment when data do not reveal very much across studies, after all. A major challenge to the study of leader style is to arrive at a firmer understanding of those relational qualities, such as trust, which bind leader-follower relationships and help to produce exceptional performance (see e.g., Peters and Waterman, 1983).

Finally, several salient problems are evident in the study of leadership and they deserve to be addressed. The leader role is not of one piece but rather is multifaceted and variegated. Still it is narrowly conceived predominantly as the direction of activity through the exercise of influence or power. More attention is needed to the wider range of behaviors the leader role represents and the meanings these have for leaders and followers in context. Greater specification also is required of the distinctive elements of situations in which diverse features of leadership are variously called forth, such as planning and conflict reduction. Not least, a fuller appreciation of change processes in leadership is needed, along with additional attention to assessing outcomes.

Despite the tone conveyed by cataloguing these problems, the overriding impression nonetheless is that the study of leadership in social psychology has come a long way from its origins early in the century. By now, conceptual and methodological sophistication have been greatly extended, as well as related empirical knowledge. Therefore the "insiders' " inclination to be critical of shortcomings in the area can be seen as a sign of vitality, ferment and growth. The leadership area clearly demands and deserves even more astute attention.

REFERENCES

Acton, Lord (John Emerich Dalberg) (1887). *Letter to Bishop Mandell Creighton.*

Adams, J. S. (1976). The structure and dynamics of behavior in organizational boundary roles. In M. D. Dunnette (Ed.), *Handbook of industrial and organizational psychology.* Chicago: Rand McNally.

Adler, A. (1925). *The practice and theory of individual psychology* (rev. ed.). London: Routledge and Kegan Paul.

Allen, W. R., and J. A. Ruhe (1976). Verbal behavior by black and white leaders of biracial groups in two different environments. *J. appl. Psychol., 61,* 441–445.

Alvarez, R. (1968). Informal reactions to deviance in simulated work organizations: a laboratory experiment. *Amer. Sociol. Rev., 33,* 895–912.

Anderson, C. R., and C. E. Schneier (1978). Locus of control, leader behavior and leader performance among management students. *Acad. management J., 21,* 690–698.

Argyle, M., and B. R. Little (1972). Do personality traits apply to social behaviour? *J. Theory soc. Behav., 2* (1), 1–35.

Argyris, C. (1962). *Interpersonal competence and organizational effectiveness.* Homewood, Ill.: Dorsey.

_____ (1968). On the effectiveness of research and development organizations. *Amer. Scient., 56,* 344–355.

_____ (1976). Leadership, learning, and changing the status quo. *Organizat. Dynamics, 4,* 29–43.

Aries, E. (1976). Interaction patterns and themes of male, female, and mixed groups. *Small Group Behavior, 7,* 7–18.

Ashour, A. S. (1973a). The contingency model of leadership effectiveness: an evaluation. *Organizat. Behav. hum. Perform., 9,* 339–355.

_____ (1973b). Further discussion of Fiedler's contingency model of leadership effectiveness. *Organizat. Behav. hum. Perform., 9,* 369–376.

Badin, I. J. (1974). Some moderator influences on relationships between consideration, initiating structure, and organizational criteria. *J. appl. Psychol., 59,* 380–382.

Baker, C. (1980). The Vroom-Yetton model of leadership—model, theory or technique. *Omega, 8,* 9–10.

Baldwin, D. A. (1978). Power and social exchange. *Amer. polit. Sci. Rev., 72,* 1229–1242.

Bales, R. F. (1953). The equilibrium problem in small groups. In T. Parsons, R. F. Bales, and E. A. Shils (Eds.), *Working papers in the theory of action.* New York: Free Press. Pp. 111–161. Reprinted in A. P. Hare, E. F. Borgatta, and R. F. Bales (Eds.), *Small groups: studies in social interaction.* New York: Knopf. Pp. 424–463.

Bales, R. F., and P. E. Slater (1955). Role differentiation in small decision-making groups. In T. Parsons et al. (Eds.), *Family, socialization, and interaction process.* Glencoe, Ill.: Free Press.

Bandura, A. (1977). *Social learning theory.* Englewood Cliffs, N.J.: Prentice-Hall.

Barber, J. D. (1972). *The presidential character: predicting performance in the White House.* Englewood Cliffs, N.J.: Prentice-Hall.

Barrow, J. C. (1976). Worker performance and task complexity as causal determinants of leader behavior, style, and flexibility. *J. appl. Psychol., 61,* 433–440.

_____ (1977). The variables of leadership: a review and conceptual framework. *Acad. management Rev., 2,* 231–251.

Bartol, K. M. (1974). Male versus female leaders: the effect of leader need for dominance and follower satisfaction. *Acad. management J., 17,* 225–233.

Bartol, K. M., and D. A. Butterfield (1976). Sex effects in evaluating leaders. *J. appl. Psychol., 61,* 446–454.

Bartol, K. M., C. L. Evans, and M. T. Stith (1978). Black versus white leaders: a comparative review of the literature. *Acad. management Rev., 3,* 293–304.

Bartol, K. M., and M. S. Wortman (1976). Sex effects in leader behavior self-descriptions and job satisfaction. *J. Psychol., 94,* 177–183.

_____ (1979). Sex of leader and subordinate role stress: a field study. *Sex Roles, 5,* 513–518.

Bass, B. M. (1981). *Stogdill's handbook of leadership: a survey of theory and research* (rev. ed.). New York: Free Press.

Bass, B. M., D. L. Farrow, E. R. Valenzi, and R. J. Solomon (1975). Management styles associated with organizational, task, personal, and interpersonal contingencies. *J. appl. Psychol., 60,* 720–729.

Bass, B. M., C. R. McGehee, W. C. Hawkins, P. C. Young, and A. S. Gebel (1953). Personality variables related to leaderless group discussion behavior. *J. abnorm. soc. Psychol., 48,* 120–128.

Bauer, R. H., and J. H. Turner (1974). Betting behavior in sexually homogeneous and heterogeneous groups. *Psychol. Reports, 34,* 251–258.

Bavelas, A., A. H. Hastorf, A. E. Gross, and W. R. Kite (1965). Experiments on the alteration of group structure. *J. exp. soc. Psychol., 1,* 55–70.

Bell, G., and R. French (1950). Consistency of individual leadership position in small groups of varying membership. *J. abnorm. soc. Psychol., 45,* 764–767.

Bem, D. J., and A. Allen (1974). On predicting some of the people some of the time: the search for cross-situational consistencies in behavior. *Psychol. Rev., 81,* 506–520.

Bem, S. L. (1974). The measurement of psychological androgyny. *J. consult. clinic. Psychol., 42,* 155–162.

_____ (1975). Sex role adaptability: one consequence of psychological androgyny. *J. Pers. soc. Psychol., 31,* 634–643.

Ben-Yoav, O., E. P. Hollander, and P. J. D. Carnevale (1983). Leader legitimacy, leader-follower interaction, and followers' ratings of the leader. *J. soc. Psychol., 121,* 111–115.

Bierstedt, R. (1950). An analysis of social power. *Amer. Sociol. Rev., 15,* 730–738.

Blackburn, R. S. (1981). Lower participant power: toward a conceptual integration. *Acad. management Rev., 6,* 127–131.

Blake, R. R., and J. S. Mouton (1964). *The managerial grid.* Houston: Gulf.

Blau, P. M. (1964). *Exchange and power in social life.* New York: Wiley.

Bond, J. R., and W. E. Vinacke (1961). Coalitions in mixed-sex triads. *Sociometry, 24,* 61–75.

Boyatzis, R. E. (1982). *The competent manager.* New York: Wiley-Interscience.

Boyd, N. K. (1972). Negotiation behavior by elected and appointed representatives serving as group leaders or as spokesmen under different cooperative group expectations. Doctoral dissertation. University of Maryland, Department of Psychology.

Brown, S. M. (1979). Male versus female leaders: a comparison of empirical studies. *Sex Roles, 5,* 595–611.

Bunker, B. B., and L. R. Bender (1980). How women compete: a guide for managers. *Management Rev., 69,* 55–62.

Bunker, B. B., and E. W. Seashore (1975). Breaking the sex role stereotypes. *Publ. Management, 57,* 5–11.

Burns, J. M. (1965). *Presidential government: the crucible of leadership.* Boston: Houghton Mifflin.

――― (1978). *Leadership.* New York: Harper & Row.

――― (1984). *The power to lead: the crisis of the American Presidency.* New York: Simon and Schuster.

Butterfield, D. A., and K. M. Bartol (1977). Evaluation of leader behavior: a missing element in leadership theory. In J. G. Hunt, and L. L. Larson (Eds.), *Leadership: the cutting edge.* Carbondale: Southern Illinois Univ. Press.

Calder, B. J. (1977). An attribution theory of leadership. In B. M. Staw, and G. R. Salancik (Eds.), *New directions in organizational behavior.* Chicago: St. Clair Press.

Campbell, J. (1977). The cutting edge of leadership: an overview. In J. G. Hunt, and L. L. Larson (Eds.), *Leadership: the cutting edge.* Carbondale: Southern Illinois Univ. Press.

Carnevale, P. J. D., D. G. Pruitt, and S. D. Britton (1979). Looking tough: the negotiator under constituent surveillance. *Pers. soc. Psychol. Bull., 5,* 118–121.

Carnevale, P. J. D., D. G. Pruitt, and S. D. Seilheimer (1981). Looking and competing: accountability and visual access in integrative bargaining. *J. Pers. soc. Psychol., 40,* 111–120.

Carter, L., and M. Nixon (1949). Ability, perceptual, personality and interest factors associated with different criteria of leadership. *J. Psychol., 27,* 377–388.

Cartwright, D. (Ed.) (1959). *Studies in social power.* Ann Arbor: Research Center for Group Dynamics, Univ. of Michigan.

Chapman, J. B. (1975). Comparisons of male and female leadership styles. *Acad. management J., 18,* 645–650.

Chatov, R. (1981). Cooperation between government and business. In P. C. Nystrom, and W. H. Starbuck (Eds.), *Handbook of organizational design.* Vol. I. New York: Oxford Univ. Press.

Chemers, M. (1983). Leadership theory and research: a systems-process integration. In P. B. Paulus (Ed.), *Basic group processes.* New York: Springer-Verlag.

Chemers, M. M., B. K. Goza, and S. I. Plumer (1979). Leadership style and communication process: an experiment using the psychological isotope technique. *Resources in education.*

Chemers, M. M., and G. J. Skrzypek (1972). An experimental test of the contingency model of leadership effectiveness. *J. Pers. soc. Psychol., 24,* 172–177.

Christie, R., and F. Geis (1970). *Studies in Machiavellianism.* New York: Academic Press.

Clement, D. E., and J. J. Schiereck (1973). Sex composition and group performance in a visual signal detection task. *Memory and Cognition, 1,* 251–255.

Cohen, M. D., and J. G. March (1974). *Leadership and ambiguity.* New York: McGraw-Hill.

Cohen, S. L., K. A. Bunker, A. L. Burton, and P. D. McManus (1978). Reactions of male subordinates to the sex-role congruency of immediate supervision. *Sex Roles, 4,* 297–311.

Coleman, J. S. (1980). Authority systems. *Publ. Opin. Quart. 44,* 143–162.

Conway, F., and J. Siegelman (1979). *Snapping: America's epidemic of sudden personality change.* New York: Delta.

Cowley, W. H. (1928). Three distinctions in the study of leaders. *J. Abnorm. soc. Psychol., 23,* 144–157.

Cronbach, L. J. (1955). Processes affecting scores on understanding of others and assuming "similarity." *Psychol. Bull., 52,* 177–193.

Cronin, T. E. (1980). *The state of the presidency.* (2nd Ed.) Boston: Little, Brown.

Crowe, B. J., S. Bochner, and A. W. Clark (1972). The effects of subordinates' behavior on managerial style. *Hum. Relat., 25,* 215–237.

Csoka, L. S. (1975). Relationship between organizational climate and the situational favorableness dimension of Fiedler's contingency model. *J. appl. Psychol., 60,* 273–277.

Dahl, R. A. (1957). The concept of power. *Behav. Sci., 2,* 201–215.

Dahl, R. A., J. March, and D. Nastair (1957). Influence ranking in the United States Senate. Cited in R. A. Dahl. The concept of power. *Behav. Sci., 2,* 201–215.

Dansereau, F., J. Alutto, S. Markham, and M. Dumas (1981). Multiplexed supervision and leadership: an application of within and between analysis. In J. G. Hunt, and C. Schreisheim (Eds.), *Leadership beyond establishment views.* Carbondale: Southern Illinois Univ. Press.

Dansereau, F., and M. Dumas (1977). Pratfalls and pitfalls in drawing inferences about leader behavior in organizations. In J. Hunt, and L. Larson (Eds.), *Leadership: the cutting edge.* Carbondale: Southern Illinois Univ. Press.

Darley, S. (1976). Big-time careers for the little woman: a dual-role dilemma. *J. soc. Issues, 32,* 85–98.

Davis, K. (1966). Status and related concepts. In B. J. Biddle, and E. J. Thomas (Eds.), *Role theory: concepts and research.* New York: Wiley.

Davis, T. R. V., and F. Luthans (1979). Leadership reexamined: a behavioral approach. *Acad. management Rev., 4,* 237–248.

Day, D. R., and R. M. Stogdill (1972). Leader behavior of male and female supervisors: a comparative study. *Personnel Psychol., 25,* 353–360.

Deaux, K. (1976). *The behavior of women and men.* Monterey, Calif.: Brooks/Cole.

deCharms, R. (1968). *Personal causation.* New York: Academic Press.

deMause, L. (1982). *Foundations of psychohistory.* New York: Creative Roots.

Denmark, F. L. (1977). Styles of leadership. *Psychol. Women Quart., 2* (2), 99–113.

Dessler, G. (1973). An investigation of the path-goal theory of leadership. Doctoral dissertation. Bernard M. Baruch College, City University of New York.

Drory, A., and A. Ben-Porat (1980). Leadership style and leniency bias in evaluation of employees' performance. *Psychol. Reports, 46,* 735–739.

Drory, A., and U. M. Gluskinos (1980). Machiavellianism and leadership. *J. appl. Psychol., 65,* 81–86.

Durand, D. E., and W. R. Nord (1976). Perceived leader behavior as a function of personality characteristics of supervisors and subordinates. *Acad. management J., 19,* 427–438.

Eagly, A. H. (1978). Sex differences in influenceability. *Psychol. Bull., 85,* 86–116.

Eden, D., and U. Leviatan (1975). Implicit leadership theory as a determinant of the factor structure underlying supervisory behavior scales. *J. appl. Psychol., 60,* 736–741.

Eilon, S. (1978). Editorial: the Vroom-Yettom Leadership model. *Omega, 6,* 469–478.

Eliot, C. W., Ed. (1909). *Plutarch's Lives.* (Translated, corrected and revised by A. H. Clough.) *The Harvard Classics.* Vol. 12. New York: Collier.

Elkind, D. (1971). Praise and imitation. *Sat. Rev.,* January 16. P. 51ff.

Emerson, R. M. (1962). Power-dependence relations. *Amer. Sociol. Rev. 27,* 31–41.

Emlen, J. T., and G. B. Schaller (1960). In the home of the mountain gorilla. *Animal kingdom, the bulletin of the New York zoological society, 63* (3), 98–108.

Erikson, E. H. (1969). *Gandhi's Truth: on the origins of militant non-violence.* New York: Norton.

Eskilson, A., and M. G. Wiley (1976). Sex composition and leadership in small groups. *Sociometry, 39,* 183–194.

Evans, M. G. (1970). The effects of supervisory behavior on the path-goal relationships. *Organizat. Behav. hum. Perform., 5,* 277–298.

———(1979). Leadership. In S. Kerr (Ed.), *Organizational behavior.* Columbus, Ohio: Grid Publishing.

Fallon, B. J., and E. P. Hollander (1976). Sex-role stereotyping in leadership: a study of undergraduate discussion groups. Paper presented at the Annual Convention of the American Psychological Association, Washington, D.C.

Farris, G. F., and F. G. Lim (1969). Effects of performance on leadership, cohesiveness, influence, satisfaction, and subsequent performance. *J. appl. Psychol., 53,* 490–497.

Ferber, M., J. Huber, and G. Spitze (1979). Preference for men as bosses and professionals. *Soc. Forces, 58,* 466–476.

Fiedler, F. E. (1961). Leadership and leadership effectiveness traits. In L. Petrullo, and B. M. Bass (Eds.), *Leadership and interpersonal behavior.* New York: Holt. Pp. 179–186.

———(1964). A contingency model of leadership effectiveness. In L. Berkowitz (Ed.), *Advances in experimental social psychology.* Vol. 1. New York: Academic Press.

———(1967). *A theory of leadership effectiveness.* New York: McGraw-Hill.

———(1970a). *Leadership.* Morristown, N. J.: General Learning Press.

———(1970b). Leadership experience and leader performance—another hypothesis shot to hell. *Organizat. Behav. hum. Perform., 5,* 1–14.

———(1971a). Notes on the methodology of the Graen, Orris, and Alvares studies testing the contingency model. *J. appl. Psychol., 55,* 202–204.

———(1971b). Validation and extension of the contingency model of leadership effectiveness: a review of empirical findings. *Psychol. Bull., 76,* 128–148.

———(1974). The contingency model—new directions for leadership utilization. *J. contemp. Bus., 3* (4), 65–79.

———(1977). A rejoinder to Schriesheim and Kerr's premature obituary of the contingency model. In J. G. Hunt, and L. L. Larson (Eds.), *Leadership: the cutting edge.* Carbondale, Ill.: Southern Illinois Univ. Press.

———(1978). Recent developments in research on the contingency model. In L. Berkowitz (Ed.), *Group processes.* New York: Academic Press. Pp. 209–225.

Fiedler, F. E., and M. M. Chemers (1974). *Leadership and effective management.* Glenview, Ill.: Scott, Foresman.

Fiedler, F. E., M. M. Chemers, and L. Mahar (1976). *Improving leadership effectiveness: the leader match concept.* New York: Wiley.

Fiedler, F. E., and A. F. Leister (1977). Leader intelligence and task performance: a test of a multiple screen model. *Organizat. Behav. hum. Perform., 20,* 1–14.

Filley, A. C., R. J. House, and S. Kerr (1976). *Managerial process and organizational behavior* (2nd ed.). Glenview, Ill.: Scott, Foresman.

Firestone, I. J., C. M. Lichtman, and J. V. Colamosca (1975). Leader effectiveness and leadership conferral as determinants of helping in a medical emergency. *J. Pers. soc. Psychol., 31,* 243–248.

Fleishman, E. A. (1953). The description of supervisory behavior. *J. appl. Psychol., 37,* 1–6.

———(1973). Twenty years of consideration and structure. In E. A. Fleishman, and J. G. Hunt (Eds.), *Current developments in the study of leadership.* Carbondale: Southern Illinois Univ. Press. Pp. 1–37.

Fleishman, E. A., and E. F. Harris (1962). Patterns of leadership related to employee grievances and turnover. *Personnel Psychol., 15,* 43–56.

Fleishman, E. A., and J. G. Hunt, Eds. (1973). *Current developments in the study of leadership.* Carbondale: Southern Illinois Univ. Press.

Forsyth, D. R., and N. M. Forsyth (1984). Subordinates' reactions to female leaders. Paper presented at the Eastern Psychological Association Convention, Baltimore.

Foster, L. W., and T. Kolinko (1979). Choosing to be a managerial woman: an examination of individual variables and career choice. *Sex Roles, 5,* 627–634.

Frank, H. H., and A. H. Katcher (1977). The qualities of leadership: how male medical students evaluate their female peers. *Hum. Relat., 30,* 403–416.

French, J. R. P., Jr., and B. H. Raven (1959). The bases of social power. In D. Cartwright (Ed.), *Studies in social power.* Ann Arbor: Univ. Michigan Press. Pp. 118–149.

Freud, S. (1960). *Group psychology and the analysis of the ego.* New York: Bantam. (Originally published in German in 1921.)

Fromm, E. (1941). *Escape from freedom.* New York: Rinehart.

Fulbright, J. W. (1966). *The arrogance of power.* New York: Random House.

Galton, F. (1869). *Hereditary genius: an inquiry into its laws and consequences.* London: Macmillan. (Paperback edition by Meredian Books, New York, 1962.)

Gamson, W. A. (1968). *Power and discontent.* Homewood, Ill.: Dorsey.

Geis, F. (1968). Machiavellianism in a semireal world. *Proceedings of the 76th annual convention of the American psychological association, 3,* 407–408.

Georgopoulos, B. S., G. M. Mahoney, and N. W. Jones (1957). A path-goal approach to productivity. *J. appl. Psychol., 41,* 345–353.

Gibb, C. A. (1947). The principles and traits of leadership. *J. abnorm. soc. Psychol., 42,* 267–284.

———— (1954). Leadership. In G. Lindzey (Ed.), *Handbook of social psychology.* Vol. 2. Cambridge, Mass.: Addison-Wesley. Pp. 877–920.

———— (1968). Leadership. In G. Lindzey, and E. Aronson (Eds.), *The handbook of social psychology* (2nd ed.). Vol. 4. Reading, Mass.: Addison-Wesley. Pp. 205–282.

Gintner, G., and S. Lindskold (1975). Rate of participation and expertise as factors influencing leader choice. *J. Pers. soc. Psychol., 32,* 1085–1089.

Gleason, J. M., F. J. Seaman, and E. P. Hollander (1978). Emergent leadership processes as a function of task structure and Machiavellianism. *Soc. Behav. Pers., 6,* 33–36.

Gold, A. R. (1978). Reexamining barriers to women's career development. *Amer. J. Orthopsychiatry, 48,* 690–702.

Goldman, M., and L. A. Fraas (1965). The effects of leader selection on group performance. *Sociometry, 28,* 82–88.

Gordon, L. V., and F. F. Medland (1965). The cross-group stability of peer ratings of leadership potential. *Personnel Psychol., 18,* 173–177.

Gouldner, A. W., Ed. (1950). *Studies in leadership.* New York: Harper.

———— (1960). The norm of reciprocity: a preliminary statement. *Amer. Sociol. Rev., 25,* 161–179.

Graen, G. (1975). Role-making processes within complex organizations. In M. D. Dunnette (Ed.), *Handbook of industrial and organizational psychology.* Chicago: Rand McNally. Pp. 1201–1245.

Graen, G., K. M. Alvares, J. B. Orris, and J. A. Martella (1970). Contingency model of leadership effectiveness: antecedent and evidential results. *Psychol. Bull., 74,* 285–296.

Graen, G., and J. F. Cashman (1975). A role-making model of leadership in formal organizations: a developmental approach. In J. G. Hunt, and L. L. Larson (Eds.), *Leadership frontiers.* Kent, Ohio: Kent State Univ. Press. Pp. 143–165.

Graen, G., J. F. Cashman, S. Ginsburg, and W. Schiemann (1977). Effects of linking-pin quality on the quality of working life of lower participants. *Admin. Sci. Quart., 22,* 491–504.

Green, S. G., and T. R. Mitchell (1979). Attributional processes of leaders in leader-member interactions. *Organizat. Behav. hum. Perform., 23,* 429–458.

Halal, W. E. (1974). Toward a general theory of leadership. *Hum. Relat., 27,* 401–416.

Halpin, A. W. (1954). The leadership behavior and combat performance of airplane commanders. *J. abnorm. soc. Psychol., 49,* 19–22.

———— (1955a). The leader behavior and leadership ideology of educational administrators and aircraft commanders. *Harvard Educ. Rev., 25* (1), 18–32.

———— (1955b). The leadership ideology of aircraft commanders. *J. Appl. Psychol., 39,* 82–84.

———— (1957). *Manual for the leader behavior description questionnaire.* Columbus: Ohio State Univ., Bureau of Business Research.

Halpin, A. W., and B. J. Winer (1957). A factorial study of the leader behavior descriptions. In R. M. Stogdill, and A. E. Coons (Eds.), *Leader behavior: its description and measurement.* Columbus: Ohio State Univ., Bureau of Business Research.

Hamblin, R. L. (1958). Leadership and crises. *Sociometry, 21,* 322–335.

Handy, C. B. (1976). *Understanding organizations.* Harmondsworth and Baltimore: Penguin Books.

Haney, C., and P. G. Zimbardo (1977). The socialization into criminality: on becoming a prisoner and a guard. In J. L. Tapp, and F. L. Levine (Eds.), *Law, justice and the individual in society: psychological and legal issues.* New York: Holt, Rinehart, and Winston. Pp. 198–223.

Hare, A. P. (1962). *Handbook of small group research.* New York: Free Press.

———— (1976). *Handbook of small group research* (2nd ed.). New York: Free Press.

Haythorn, W. W., A. Couch, D. Haefner, P. Langham, and L. F. Carter (1956). The effects of varying combinations of authoritarian and equalitarian leaders and followers. *J. abnorm. soc. Psychol., 53,* 210–219.

Heider, F. (1958). *The psychology of interpersonal relations.* New York: Wiley.

Heller, F. A. (1971). *Managerial decision-making: a study of leadership styles and powersharing among senior managers.* London: Tavistock.

Hemphill, J. K. (1949a). The leader and his group. *Educ. res. Bull., 28,* 225–229, 245–246.

———— (1949b). *Situational factors in leadership.* Columbus: Ohio State Univ., Personnel Research Board.

_____ (1961). Why people attempt to lead. In L. Petrullo, and B. M. Bass (Eds.), *Leadership and interpersonal behavior.* New York: Holt. Pp. 201–215.

Hemphill, J. K., and A. E. Coons (1957). Development of the leader behavior description questionnaire. In R. M. Stogdill, and A. E. Coons (Eds.), *Leader behavior: its description and measurement.* Columbus: Ohio State Univ., Bureau of Business Research.

Hermann, M. G. (1979). Indicators of stress in policy-makers during foreign policy crises. *Political Psychol., 1,* 27–46.

Hermann, M. G., with T. W. Milburn (1977). *A psychological examination of political leaders.* New York: Free Press/Macmillan.

Herold, D. M. (1974). Interaction of subordinate and leader characteristics in moderating the consideration satisfaction relationship, *J. appl. Psychol., 59,* 649–651.

_____ (1977). Two-way influence processes in leader-follower dyads. *Acad. Management J., 20,* 224–237.

Hersey, P., and K. H. Blanchard (1982). *Management of organizational behavior* (4th ed.). Englewood Cliffs, N.J.: Prentice-Hall.

Hiers, J. M., and R. V. Heckel (1977). Seating choice, leadership, and locus of control. *J. soc. Psychol., 103,* 313–314.

Hill, W. A. (1973). Leadership style: rigid or flexible? *Organizat. Behav. hum. Perform., 9,* 35–47.

Hoffman, L. R. (1979). *Group problem-solving.* New York: Praeger.

Hogan, R., and D. Schroeder (1981). Seven biases in psychology. *Psychology Today, 15* (7), July. P. 8ff.

Hollander, E. P. (1954). Authoritarianism and leadership choice in a military setting. *J. abnorm. soc. Psychol., 49,* 365–370.

_____ (1958). Conformity, status, and idiosyncrasy credit. *Psychol. Rev., 65,* 117–127.

_____ (1960). Competence and conformity in the acceptance of influence. *J. abnorm. soc. Psychol., 61,* 361–365.

_____ (1961a). Emergent leadership and social influence. In L. Petrullo, and B. M. Bass (Eds.), *Leadership and interpersonal behavior.* New York: Holt. Pp. 30–47.

_____ (1961b). Some effects of perceived status on responses to innovative behavior. *J. abnorm. soc. Psychol., 63,* 247–250.

_____ (1964). *Leaders, groups, and influence.* New York: Oxford Univ. Press.

_____ (1971). Style, structure, and setting in organizational leadership. *Admin. Sci. Quart., 16,* 1–9.

_____ (1974). Processes of leadership emergence. *J. contemp. Bus., 3* (4), 19–33.

_____ (1978a). *Leadership dynamics: a practical guide to effective relationships.* New York: Free Press/Macmillan.

_____ (1978b). What is the crisis of leadership? *Humanitas, 14* (3), 285–296.

_____ (1983a). Paradoxes of presidential leadership: party, popularity, promise, performance...and more. Invited address, Division of Personality and Social Psychology, American Psychological Association Convention, Anaheim, Calif.

_____ (1983b). Women and leadership. In H. H. Blumberg, A. P. Hare, V. Kent, and M. Davies (Eds.), *Small groups and social interaction,* Vol. 1. London and New York: Wiley.

Hollander, E. P., B. J. Fallon, and M. T. Edwards (1977). Some aspects of influence and acceptability for appointed and elected group leaders. *J. Psychol., 95,* 289–296.

Hollander, E. P., and J. W. Julian (1968). Leadership. In E. F. Borgatta, and W. W. Lambert (Eds.), *Handbook of personality theory and research.* Chicago: Rand McNally. Pp. 890–899.

_____ (1969). Contemporary trends in the analysis of leadership processes. *Psychol. Bull., 71,* 387–397.

_____ (1970). Studies in leader legitimacy, influence, and innovation. In L. Berkowitz (Ed.), *Advances in experimental social psychology.* Vol. 5. New York: Academic Press. Pp. 33–69.

_____ (1978). A further look at leader legitimacy, influence, and innovation. In L. Berkowitz (Ed.), *Group processes.* New York: Academic Press. Pp. 153–165.

Hollander, E. P., J. W. Julian, and F. A. Perry (1966). Leader style, competence, and source of authority as determinants of actual and perceived influence. *ONR Technical Report No. 5.* Reported in E. P. Hollander, and J. W. Julian (1970) *Supra,* Pp. 44–50. Reprinted in L. Berkowitz, Ed. (1978) *Group processes.* New York: Academic Press. Pp. 126–132.

Hollander, E. P., J. W. Julian, and R. M. Sorrentino (1969). The leader's sense of legitimacy as a source of constructive deviation. *ONR Technical Report No. 12.* Reported in E. P. Hollander, and J. W. Julian, *supra,* Pp. 55–65. Reprinted in L. Berkowitz (Ed.), *Group processes.* New York: Academic Press. Pp. 137–147.

Hollander, E. P., and L. L. Neider (1978). Critical incidents and rating scales in comparing "good"-"bad" leadership. Paper presented at the American Psychological Association Convention; Toronto.

Hollander, E. P., and J. Yoder (1980). Some issues in comparing women and men as leaders. *Basic appl. soc. Psychol., 1,* 267–280.

Homans, G. C. (1961). *Social behavior: its elementary forms.* New York: Harcourt, Brace, and World.

_____ (1974). *Social behavior: its elementary forms* (rev. ed.). New York: Harcourt, Brace, Jovanovich.

Hook, S. (1955). *The hero in history.* Boston: Beacon Press.

Hosking, D. M., and C. A. Schriesheim (1978). Review of Fiedler, Chemers and Mahar's *Improving leadership effectiveness: the leader match concept. Admin. Sci. Quart., 23,* 496–505.

Hough, R. (1980). *Mountbatten.* New York: Random House.

House, R. J. (1971). A path-goal theory of leader effectiveness. *Admin. Sci. Quart., 16,* 321–338.

_____ (1977). A 1976 theory of charismatic leadership. In J. G. Hunt, and L. L. Larson (Eds.), *Leadership: the cutting edge.* Carbondale: Southern Illinois Univ. Press.

House, R. J., and G. Dessler (1974). The path goal theory of leadership: some post hoc and a priori tests. In J. G. Hunt and L. L. Larson (Eds.), *Contingency approaches to leadership.* Carbondale: Southern Illinois Univ. Press.

House, R. J., and T. R. Mitchell (1974). Path-goal theory of leadership. *J. contemp. Bus., 3* (4), 81–97.

Howell, J. P., and P. W. Dorfman (1981). Substitutes for leadership: test of a construct. *Acad. management J., 24,* 714–728.

Hunt, J. G., and L. L. Larson, Eds. (1974). *Contingency approaches to leadership*. Carbondale: Southern Illinois Univ. Press.

———— Eds. (1975). *Leadership frontiers*. Kent, Ohio: Comparative Administration Research Institute, Kent State University.

———— (1977). Some additional facets of the cutting edge: an epilog. In J. G. Hunt, and L. L. Larson (Eds.), *Leadership: the cutting edge*. Carbondale: Southern Illinois Univ. Press.

———— (1979). *Crosscurrents in leadership*. Carbondale: Southern Illinois Univ. Press.

Hunt, J. G., R. N. Osborn, and L. L. Larson (1975). Upper level technical orientation and first level leadership within a noncontingency and contingency framework. *Acad. Management J., 18,* 476–488.

Hunt, J. G., U. Sekran, and C. Schriesheim, Eds. (1981). *Leadership: beyond establishment views*. Carbondale: Southern Illinois Univ. Press.

Hunt, J. McV. (1965). Traditional personality theory in the light of recent evidence. *Amer. Scient., 53,* 80–96.

Hunt, R. G. (1970). Technology and organization. *Acad. management J., 13,* 235–252.

Inderlied, S. D., and G. Powell (1979). Sex-role identity and leadership style: different labels for the same concept? *Sex Roles, 5,* 613–625.

Jacobs, T. O. (1970). *Leadership and exchange in formal organizations*. Alexandria, Va.: Human Resources Research Organization.

Jacobson, M. B., and J. Effertz (1974). Sex roles and leadership perceptions of the leaders and the led. *Organizat. Behav. hum. Perform., 12,* 383–396.

Jago, A. G. (1982). Leadership: perspectives in theory and research. *Management Sci., 28,* 315–336.

Jago, A. G., and V. H. Vroom (1978). Predicting leader behavior from a measure of behavioral intent. *Acad. management J., 21,* 715–721.

Jaques, E. (1961). *Equitable payment*. London: Wiley.

Jay, A. (1971). *Corporation man*. New York: Random House. (Paperback edition by Pocketbooks, New York, 1973.)

Jenkins, W. O. (1947). A review of leadership studies with particular reference to military problems. *Psychol. Bull., 44,* 54–79.

Johnson, P. (1976). Women and power: toward a theory of effectiveness. *J. soc. Issues, 32,* 99–110.

Jones, E. E. (1964). *Ingratiation*. New York: Appleton-Century-Crofts.

———— (1965). Conformity as a tactic of ingratiation. *Science, 149,* 144–150.

———— (1979). The rocky road from acts to dispositions. *Amer. Psychol., 34,* 107–117.

Julian, J. W., and E. P. Hollander (1966). A study of some role dimensions of leader-follower relations. *ONR Technical Report No. 3*. Reported in E. P. Hollander, and J. W. Julian, 1970, *supra,* Pp. 39–43. Reprinted in L. Berkowitz (Ed.), *Group processes*. New York: Academic Press, 1978. Pp. 121–125.

Julian, J. W., E. P. Hollander, and C. R. Regula (1969). Endorsement of the group spokesman as a function of his source of authority, competence, and success. *J. Pers. soc. Psychol., 11,* 42–49.

Kabanoff, B. (1981). A critique of leader match and its implications for leadership research. *Personnel Psychol., 34,* 749–764.

Kanter, R. M. (1977). *Men and women of the corporation*. New York: Basic Books.

Kanter, R. M., with B. A. Stein (1980). *A tale of "O": on being different in an organization*. New York: Harper Colophon Books.

Katz, D. (1973). Patterns of leadership. In J. Knutson (Ed.), *Handbook of political psychology*. San Francisco: Jossey-Bass.

Katz, D., and R. L. Kahn (1978). *The social psychology of organizations* (2nd ed.). New York: Wiley.

Kellerman, B. Ed. (1984a). *Leadership: multidisciplinary perspectives*. Englewood Cliffs, N.J.: Prentice-Hall, 1984.

———— (1984b). *The political presidency: practice of leadership*. New York: Oxford Univ. Press.

Kelley, H. H., J. C. Condry, A. E. Dahlke, and A. H. Hill (1965). Collective behavior in a simulated panic situation. *J. exp. soc. Psychol., 1,* 20–54.

Kernell, S. (1978). Explaining presidential popularity. *Amer. polit. Sci. Rev., 72,* 506–522.

Kerr, S. (1974). Discussant comments. In J. G. Hunt, and L. L. Larson (Eds.), *Contingency approaches to leadership*. Carbondale: Southern Illinois Univ. Press. Pp. 124–129.

———— (1977). Substitutes for leadership: some implications for organizational design. *Organizat. admin. Sci., 8,* 135–146.

Kerr, S., and J. Jermier (1978). Substitutes for leadership: their meaning and measurement. *Organizat. Behav. hum. Perform., 22,* (4), 375–403.

Kerr, S., C. A. Schriesheim, C. J. Murphy, and R. M. Stogdill (1974). Toward a contingency theory of leadership based upon the consideration and initiating structure literature. *Organizat. Behav. hum. Perform., 12,* 62–82.

Kets de Vries, M. F. R. (1980). *Clinical approaches to management*. London: Tavistock.

Kinder, D. R. (1981). Presidents, prosperity, and public opinion. *Publ. Opin. Quart., 45,* 1–21.

Kipnis, D. (1976). *The powerholders*. Chicago: Univ. of Chicago Press.

Klein, A. L. (1976). Changes in leadership appraisal as a function of the stress of a simulated panic situation. *J. Pers. soc. Psychol., 34,* 1143–1154.

Knight, P. A., and H. M. Weiss (1980). Effect of selection agent and leader origin on leader influence and group member perceptions. *Organizat. Behav. hum. Perform. 26,* 7–21.

Konar-Goldband, E., R. W. Rice, and W. Monkarsh (1979). The time phased inter-relationships of group atmosphere, group performance, and leader LPC. *J. appl. Psychol., 64,* 401–409.

Korman, A. K. (1966). "Consideration," "initiating structure," and organizational criteria: a review. *Personnel Psychol., 19,* 349–361.

Kraft, L. W., and C. W. Vraa (1975). Sex composition of groups and pattern of self-disclosure by high school females. *Psychol. Reports, 37,* 733–734.

Lamm, H. (1973). Intragroup effects on intergroup negotiation. *Europ. J. soc. Psychol., 3,* 179–192.

Larson, J. R., Jr. (1982). Cognitive mechanisms mediating the impact of implicit theories of leader behavior on leader behavior ratings. *Organizat. Behav. hum. Perform., 29,* 129–140.

Larson, L. L., J. G. Hunt, and R. N. Osborn (1976). The great hi-hi leader behavior myth: a lesson from Occam's razor. *Acad. management J., 19,* 628–641.

Larwood, L., and M. Lockheed (1979). Women as managers: toward second generation research. *Sex Roles, 5,* 659–666.

Lawler, E. J., and M. E. Thompson (1978). Impact of leader responsibility for inequity on subordinate revolts. *Soc. Psychol., 41,* 264–268.

Lemert, E. M. (1972). *Human deviance, social problems, and social control.* (2nd ed.). Englewood Cliffs, N.J.: Prentice-Hall.

LeVine, R. A. (1960). The internalization of political values in stateless societies. *Hum. Organizat., 19,* 51–58.

LeVine, R. A., and D. T. Campbell (1972). *Ethnocentrism: theories of conflict, ethnic attitudes, and group behavior.* New York: Wiley.

Lewis-Beck, M. S., and T. W. Rice (1982). Presidential popularity and presidential vote. *Publ. Opin. Quart. 46,* 534–537.

Liden, R. C., and G. Graen (1980). Generalizability of the vertical dyad linkage model of leadership. *Acad. management J., 23,* 451–465.

Lieberson, S., and J. F. O'Connor (1972). Leadership and organizational performance: a study of large corporations. *Amer. Sociol. Rev., 37,* 117–130.

Likert, R. (1961). *New patterns of management.* New York: McGraw-Hill.

——— (1979). From production- and employee-centeredness to system 1–4. *J. Management, 5,* 147–156.

Lockheed, M. E. (1977). Cognitive style effects on sex status in student work groups. *J. Educat. Psychol., 69,* 158–165.

Lord, R. G. (1977). Functional leadership behavior: measurement and relation to social power and leadership perceptions. *Admin. Sci. Quart., 22,* 114–133.

Lord, R. G., J. F. Binning, M. C. Rush, and J. C. Thomas, (1978). The effect of performance cues and leader behavior on questionnaire ratings of leadership behavior. *Organizat. Behav. hum. Perform., 21,* 27–39.

Lowin, A., and J. R. Craig (1968). The influence of level of performance on managerial style: an experimental object-lesson in the ambiguity of correlational data. *Organizat. Behav. hum. Perform., 3,* 440–458.

Lundberg, C. (1978). The effect of self-expectations on perceived leadership: an experimental inquiry. Paper presented to the Annual Meeting of the Academy of Management, San Francisco.

McCall, M. W., Jr. (1976). Leadership research: choosing gods and devils on the run. *J. Occupat. Psychol., 49,* 139–153.

Maccoby, M. (1976). *The gamesman, the new corporate leaders.* New York: Simon and Schuster.

——— (1981). *The leader.* New York: Simon and Schuster.

Maccoby, E. E., and C. N. Jacklin (1974). *The psychology of sex differences.* Stanford: Stanford Univ. Press.

McClelland, D. (1975). *Power: the inner experience.* New York: Irvington.

McGregor, D. (1944). Conditions of effective leadership in the industrial organization. *J. Consult. Psychol., 8* (2), 55–63.

——— (1967). The professional manager. New York: McGraw-Hill.

Machiavelli, N. (1950). *The prince and the discourses* (2nd ed.). New York: Random House.

McMahon, J. T. (1972). The contingency theory: logic and method revisited. *Personnel Psychol. 25,* 397–410.

Maier, N. R. F. (1963). *Leadership methods and skills.* New York: McGraw-Hill.

Mann, R. D. (1959). A review of the relationships between personality and performance in small groups. *Psychol. Bull., 56,* 241–270.

Massengill, D., and N. DiMarco (1979). Sex-role stereotypes and requisite management characteristics: a current replication. *Sex Roles, 5,* 561–570.

Mazlish, B. (1972). *In search of Nixon.* New York: Basic Books.

——— (1981). Leader and led, individual and group. *Psychohistory Rev., 9,* 214–237.

Mead, M. (1949). *Male and female.* New York: Morrow.

Mechanic, D. (1962). Sources of power of lower participants in complex organizations. *Admin. Sci. Quart., 7,* 349–364.

Megargee, E. I. (1969). Influence of sex roles on the manifestation of leadership. *J. appl. Psychol., 53,* 377–382.

Menzies, H. D. (1980). The ten toughest bosses. *Fortune, 101,* 62–69.

Michener, H. A., and M. R. Burt (1975a). Components of ''authority'' as determinants of compliance. *J. Pers. soc. Psychol., 31,* 606–614.

——— (1975b). Use of social influence under varying conditions of legitimacy. *J. Pers. soc. Psychol., 32,* 398–407.

Michener, H. A., and E. J. Lawler (1975). Endorsement of formal leaders: an integrative model. *J. Pers. soc. Psychol., 31,* 216–223.

Miller, E. J., and A. K. Rice (1967). *Systems of organization.* London: Tavistock.

Miner, J. B. (1975). The uncertain future of the leadership concept: an overview. In J. G. Hunt, and L. L. Larson (Eds.), *Leadership frontiers.* Kent, Ohio: Comparative Administration Research Institute.

Mintzberg, H. (1973). *The nature of managerial work.* New York: Harper & Row.

——— (1975). The manager's job: folklore and fact. *Harvard Bus. Rev. 53* (4), 49–61.

Mischel, W. (1969). Continuity and change in personality. *Amer. Psychol., 24,* 1012–1018.

Mitchell, T. R. (1979). Organizational behavior. In M. R. Rosenzweig, and L. W. Porter (Eds.), *Ann. Rev. Psychol., 30,* 243–281.

Mitchell, T. R., J. R. Larson, and S. G. Green (1977). Leader behavior, situational moderators and group performance: an attributional analysis. *Organizat. Behav. hum. Perform., 18,* 254–268.

Morris, C. G., and J. R. Hackman (1969). Behavioral correlates of perceived leadership. *J. Pers. soc. Psychol., 13,* 350–361.

Mueller, J. E. (1970). Presidential popularity from Truman to Johnson. *Amer. Polit. Sci. Rev., 64,* 18–34.

Mulder, M. (1959). Power and satisfaction in task oriented groups. *Acta Psychologica, 16,* 178–275.

——— (1971). Power equalization through participation? *Admin. Sci. Quart., 16,* 31–38.

_____ (1981). On the quantity and quality of power and the Q.W.L. Paper presented at the International Conference on the Quality of Work Life, Toronto.

Mulaik, S. A. (1964). Are personality factors raters' conceptual factors? *J. consult. clinic. Psychol., 28,* 506–511.

Neustadt, R. E. (1960). *Presidential power: the politics of leadership.* New York: Wiley.

Ng, S. H. (1980). *The social psychology of power.* New York: Academic Press.

Offermann, L. R. (1984). Short-term supervisory experience and LPC score: effects of leader sex and group sex composition. *J. soc. Psychol., 123,* 115–121.

Okanes, M., and J. E. Stinson (1974). Machiavellianism and emergent leadership in a management simulation. *Psychol. Reports, 35,* 255–259.

O'Leary, V. E. (1974). Some attitudinal barriers to occupational aspirations in women. *Psychol. Bull., 81,* 809–826.

_____ (1977). *Toward understanding women.* Monterey, Calif.: Brooks/Cole.

Osborn, R. N., and W. M. Vicars (1976). Sex stereotypes: an artifact in leader behavior and subordinate satisfaction analysis? *Acad. management J., 19,* 439–449.

Pepinsky, P. N., J. K. Hemphill, and R. N. Shevitz (1958). Attempts to lead, group productivity, and morale under conditions of acceptance and rejection. *J. abnorm. soc. Psychol., 57,* 47–54.

Peters, T. J., and R. H. Waterman (1983). *In search of excellence.* New York: Harper & Row.

Pfeffer, J. (1977). The ambiguity of leadership. In M. W. McCall, Jr., and M. M. Lombardo (Eds.), *Leadership: where else can we go?* Durham, N.C.: Duke Univ. Press.

_____ (1981). *Power in organizations.* Marshfield, Mass.: Pitman.

Pheterson, G. I., S. B. Kiesler, and P. A. Goldberg (1971). Evaluation of the performance of women as a function of their sex, achievement, and personal history. *J. Pers. soc. Psychol., 19,* 114–118.

Phillips, J. S., and R. G. Lord (1981). Causal attributions and perceptions of leadership. *Organizat. Behav. hum. Perform., 28,* 143–163.

Pondy, L. R. (1977). The other hand clapping: an information processing approach to organizational power. In T. H. Hammer, and S. B. Bacharach (Eds.), *Reward systems and power distributions.* Ithaca, N.Y.: Cornell Univ. Press.

Pruitt, D. G. (1976). Power and bargaining. In. B. Seidenberg and A. Snadowsky (Eds.), *Social psychology: an introduction.* New York: Free Press.

_____ (1981). *Negotiation behavior.* New York: Academic Press.

Read, P. B. (1974). Source of authority and the legitimation of leadership in small groups. *Sociometry, 37,* 189–204.

Reedy, G. E. (1973). *The presidency in flux.* New York: Columbia Univ. Press.

Regula, C. R., and J. W. Julian (1973). The impact of quality and frequency of task contributions on perceived ability. *J. soc. Psychol., 89,* 115–122.

Rice, R. W. (1978a). Construct validity of the least preferred coworker score. *Psychol. Bull., 85,* 1199–1237.

_____ (1978b). Psychometric properties of the esteem for least preferred coworker (LPC) scale. *Acad. management Rev., 3,* 106–118.

_____ (1981). Leader LPC and follower satisfaction: a review. *Organizat. Behav. hum. Perform., 28,* 1–25.

Rice, R. W., L. R. Bender, and A. G. Vitters (1980). Leader sex, follower attitudes toward women, and leadership effectiveness: a laboratory study. *Organizat. Behav. hum. Perform., 25,* 46–78.

Rice, R. W., and M. M. Chemers (1975). Personality and situational determinants of leader behavior. *J. appl. Psychol., 60,* 20–27.

Rice, R. W., D. Instone, and J. Adams (1984). Leader sex, leader success, and leadership process: two field studies. *J. Appl. Psychol., 69,* 12–31.

Rice, R. W., and D. R. Kastenbaum (1983). The contingency model of leadership: some current issues. *Basic appl. soc. Psychol., 4,* 373–392.

Ridgeway, C. L. (1981). Nonconformity, competence, and influence in groups: a test of two theories. *Amer. Sociol. Rev., 46,* 333–347.

Riecken, H. W. (1958). The effect of talkativeness on ability to influence group solutions to problems. *Sociometry, 21,* 309–321.

Rosen, B., T. H. Jerdee, and T. L. Prestwich (1975). Dual-career marital adjustment: potential effects of discriminatory managerial attitudes. *J. Marriage and Family, 37,* 565–572.

Rosenbach, W. E., and R. L. Taylor Eds. (1984). *Contemporary issues in leadership.* Boulder, Colo.: Westview.

Rotter, J. B. (1966). Generalized expectancies for internal versus external control of reinforcement. *Psychol. Monogr., 80* (1), (whole No. 609).

Rubin, I. M., and M. Goldman (1968). An open system model of leadership performance. *Organizat. Behav. hum. Perform., 3,* 143–156.

Rudraswamy, V. (1964). An investigation of the relationship between perception of status and leadership attempts. *J. Indian Acad. appl. Psychol., 1,* 12–19.

Runyon, K. E. (1973). Some interactions between personality variables and management styles. *J. appl. Psychol., 57,* 288–294.

Rush, M. C., and L. L. Beauvais (1981). A critical analysis of format-induced versus subject-imposed bias in leadership ratings. *J. appl. Psychol., 66,* 722–727.

Rush, M. C., J. S. Phillips, and R. G. Lord (1981). Effects of a temporal delay in rating on leader behavior descriptions: a laboratory investigation. *J. appl. Psychol., 66,* 442–450.

Rush, M. C., J. C. Thomas, and R. G. Lord (1977). Implicit leadership theory: a potential threat to the internal validity of leader behavior questionnaires. *Organizat. Behav. hum. Perform., 20,* 93–110.

Sanford, F. (1950). *Authoritarianism and leadership.* Philadelphia: Institute for Research in Human Relations.

Schaller, G. B. (1972). The sociable kingdom. In National Geographic Society, *The marvels of animal behavior.* Washington, D.C.

Schein, V. E. (1973). Relationship betwen sex role stereotypes and requisite management characteristics. *J. appl. Psychol., 57,* 95–100.

Schlesinger, A. M. (1973). *The imperial presidency.* Boston: Houghton Mifflin.

Schneider, D. J. (1973). Implicit personality theory: a review. *Psychol. Bull., 79,* 294–309.

Schneier, C. E. (1978). The contingency model of leadership: an extension to emergent leadership and leader's sex. *Organizat. Behav. hum. Perform., 21,* 220–239.

Schneier, C. E., and K. M. Bartol (1980). Sex effects in emergent leadership. *J. appl. Psychol., 65,* 341–345.

Schrag, C. (1954). Leadership among prison inmates. *Amer. Sociol. Rev., 19,* 37–42.

Schriesheim, C. A., and A. S. DeNisi (1981). Task dimensions as moderators of the effects of instrumental leadership: a two-sample replicated test of path-goal leadership theory. *J. appl. Psychol., 66,* 589–597.

Schriesheim, C. A., and S. Kerr (1974). Psychometric properties of the Ohio State leadership scales. *Psychol. Bull., 81,* 756–765.

_____ (1977a). R.I.P. LPC: a response to Fiedler. In J. G. Hunt, and L. L. Larson (Eds.), *Leadership: the cutting edge.* Carbondale: Southern Illinois Univ. Press. Pp. 51–56.

_____ (1977b). Theories and measures of leadership: a critical appraisal of current and future directions. In J. G. Hunt, and L. L. Larson (Eds.), *Leadership: the cutting edge.* Carbondale: Southern Illinois Univ. Press. Pp. 9–45.

Schriesheim, C. A., A. J. Kinicki, and J. F. Schriesheim (1979). The effect of leniency on leader behavior descriptions. *Organizat. Behav. hum. Perform., 23,* 1–29.

Schriesheim, C. A., and M. A. Von Glinow (1977). Tests of the path-goal theory of leadership: a theoretical and empirical analysis. *Acad. management J., 20,* 398–405.

Shartle, C. L., R. M. Stogdill, and D. T. Campbell (1949). *Studies in naval leadership.* Columbus: Ohio State University, Personnel Research Board.

Sherif, M. Ed. (1962). *Intergroup relations and leadership.* New York: Wiley.

Shiflett, S. C. (1973). The contingency model of leadership effectiveness: some implications of its statistical and methodological properties. *Behav. Sci., 18,* 429–440.

_____ (1981). Is there a problem with the LPC score in leader match? *Personnel Psychol., 34,* 765–769.

Shiflett, S. C., and S. M. Nealey (1972). The effects of changing leader power: a test of "situational engineering." *Organizat. Behav. hum. Perform., 7,* 371–382.

Sims, H. P., Jr. (1977). The leader as a manager of reinforcement contingencies: an empirical example and a model. In J. G. Hunt, and L. L. Larson (Eds.), *Leadership: the cutting edge.* Carbondale: Southern Illinois Univ. Press. Pp. 121–137.

Sorrentino, R. M., and R. G. Boutillier (1975). The effect of quantity and quality of verbal interaction on ratings of leadership ability. *J. exp. soc. Psychol., 11,* 403–411.

Spence, J. T., and R. Helmreich (1972). The attitudes toward women scale: an objective instrument to measure attitudes toward the rights and roles of women in contemporary society. *J. Suppl. Abstract Service, 2,* 66.

Spiller, G. (1929). The dynamics of greatness. *Sociol. Rev., 21,* 218–232.

Statistical Abstract of the United States (1983). Washington, D.C.: U.S. Bureau of the Census.

Staw, B. M. (1975). Attribution of the "causes" of performance: a general alternative interpretation of cross-sectional research on organizations. *Organizat. Behav. hum. Perform., 13,* 414–432.

Staw, B. M., and G. R. Salancik, Eds. (1977). *New directions in organizational behavior.* Chicago: St. Clair Press.

Stein, R. T. (1975). Identifying emergent leaders from verbal and nonverbal communications. *J. Pers. soc. Psychol., 32,* 125–135.

_____ (1977). Accuracy of process consultants and untrained observers in perceiving emergent leadership. *J. appl. Psychol., 62,* 755–759.

Stein, R. T., and T. Heller (1979). An empirical analysis of the correlations between leadership status and participation rates reported in the literature. *J. Pers. soc. Psychol., 37,* 1993–2002.

Stein, R. T., L. R. Hoffman, S. J. Cooley, and R. W. Pearse (1979). Leadership valence: modeling and measuring the process of emergent leadership. In J. G. Hunt, and L. L. Larson (Eds.), *Crosscurrents in leadership.* Carbondale: Southern Illinois Univ. Press.

Steiner, I. (1964). Group dynamics. In P. Farnsworth et al. (Eds.), *Annual review of psychology.* Vol. 15. Palo Alto, Calif: Annual Reviews.

Stewart, R. (1982). *Choices for the manager.* Englewood Cliffs, N.J.: Prentice-Hall.

Stogdill, R. M. (1948). Personal factors associated with leadership. *J. Psychol., 25,* 35–71.

_____ (1963). *Manual for the leader behavior description questionnaire—form XII.* Columbus: Ohio State University, Bureau of Business Research.

_____ (1974). *Handbook of leadership.* New York: Free Press.

_____ (1977). *Leadership abstracts and bibliography 1904 to 1974.* Columbus: College of Administrative Science, Ohio State University.

Stogdill, R. M., and A. E. Coons (1957). *Leader behavior: its description and measurement.* Columbus: Ohio State University, Bureau of Business Research.

Stogdill, R. M., and C. L. Shartle (1948). Methods for determining patterns of leadership behavior in relation to organization structure and objectives. *J. appl. Psychol., 32,* 286–291.

Strickland, L. H., P. D. Guild, J. C. Barefoot, and S. A. Paterson (1978). Teleconferencing and leadership emergence. *Hum. Relat., 31,* 583–596.

Strodtbeck, F. L., and L. H. Hook (1961). The social dimensions of a twelve-man jury table. *Sociometry, 24,* 397–415.

Strodtbeck, F. L., R. M. James, and C. Hawkins (1958). Social status in jury deliberations. In E. E. Maccoby, T. M. Newcomb, and E. L. Hartley (Eds.), *Readings in social psychology.* (3rd ed.). New York: Holt. Pp. 379–388.

Strodtbeck, F. L., and R. D. Mann (1956). Sex role differentiation in jury deliberations. *Sociometry, 19,* 3–11.

Strube, M. J., and J. E. Garcia (1981). A meta-analytic investigation of Fiedler's contingency model of leadership effectiveness. *Psychol. Bull., 90,* 307–321.

Tannenbaum, R. (1968). *Control in organizations.* New York: McGraw-Hill.

Tannenbaum, R., and W. H. Schmidt (1958). How to choose a leadership pattern. *Harvard Bus. Rev., 36* (2), 95–102.

Thibaut, J. W., and H. H. Kelley (1959). *The social psychology of groups.* New York: Wiley.

Thrasher, F. M. (1927). *The gang.* Chicago: Univ. of Chicago Press.

Tucker, R. C. (1965). The dictator and totalitarianism. *World Politics, 17,* 55–83.

_____ (1981). *Politics as leadership.* Columbia: Univ. of Missouri Press.

Utecht, R. E., and W. D. Heier (1976). The contingency model and successful military leadership. *Acad. management J., 19,* 606–618.

Van Fleet, D. D. (1974). Toward identifying critical elements in a behavioral description of leadership. *Pub. personnel Management, 3* (1), 70–82.

Vecchio, R. P. (1977). An empirical examination of the validity of Fiedler's model of leadership effectiveness. *Organizat. Behav. hum. Perform., 19,* 180–206.

Verba, S. (1961). *Small groups and political behavior: a study of leadership.* Princeton, N.J.: Princeton Univ. Press.

Vonnegut, K. (1981). A truly modern hero. *Psychology Today, 15,* 9–10.

Vroom, V. H. (1964). *Work and motivation.* New York: Wiley.

_____ (1976a). Can leaders learn to lead? *Organizat. Dynamics, 4,* 17–28.

_____ (1976b). Leadership. In M. D. Dunnette (Ed.), *Handbook of industrial and organizational psychology.* Chicago: Rand McNally.

Vroom, V. H., and A. G. Jago (1978). On the validity of the Vroom-Yetton model. *J. appl. Psychol., 63,* 151–162.

Vroom, V. H., and P. W. Yetton (1973). *Leadership and decision-making.* Pittsburgh: Univ. of Pittsburgh Press.

Wahrman, R., and M. D. Pugh (1972). Competence and conformity: another look at Hollander's study. *Sociometry, 35,* 376–386.

_____ (1974). Sex, nonconformity and influence. *Sociometry, 37,* 137–147.

Weber, M. (1946). The sociology of charismatic authority (originally published in 1921). Reprinted in H. H. Gerth, and C. W. Mills (Translators and Eds.), *From Max Weber: essays in sociology.* New York: Oxford Univ. Press. Pp. 245–252.

_____ (1947). *The theory of social and economic organization.* (Translated and edited by T. Parsons, and A. M. Henderson.) New York: Oxford Univ. Press.

Weiss, H. M. (1977). Subordinate imitation of supervisor behavior: the role of modeling in organizational socialization. *Organizat. Behav. hum. Perform., 19,* 89–105.

Weiss, H. W., and S. Adler (1981). Cognitive complexity and the structure of implicit leadership theories. *J. appl. Psychol., 66,* 69–78.

Weissenberg, P., and M. J. Kavanagh (1972). The independence of initiating structure and consideration: a review of the evidence. *Personnel Psychol., 25,* 119–130.

Welsh, M. C. (1979). Attitudinal measures and evaluation of males and females in leadership roles. *Psychol. Reports, 45,* 19–22.

Willis, R. H., and J. M. Levine (1976). Interpersonal influence and conformity. In B. Seidenberg, and A. Snadowsky (Eds.), *Social psychology: an introduction.* New York: Free Press.

Winter, D. G. (1973). *The power motive.* New York: Free Press.

_____ (1980). An exploratory study of the motives of southern African political leaders measured at a distance. *Political Psychol., 2,* 75–85.

Winter, D. G., and A. J. Stewart (1977). Content analysis as a technique for assessing political leaders. In M. G. Hermann (Ed.), *A psychological examination of political leaders.* New York: Free Press.

Wofford, J. C., and T. N. Srinivasan (1983). Experimental tests of the leader-environment-follower interaction theory of leadership. *Organizational Behav. hum. Perform., 32,* 35–54.

Wood, M. T. (1973). Power relationships and group decision making in organizations. *Psychol. Bull., 79,* 280–293.

Woods, F. A. (1913). *The influence of monarchs.* New York: Macmillan.

Woodward, J. (1965). *Industrial organization: theory and practice.* London: Oxford Univ. Press.

_____ (1973). Technology, material control, and organizational behavior. In A. R. Negandhi (Ed.), *Modern organizational theory.* Kent, Ohio: Kent State Univ. Press.

Wrong, D. H. (1979). *Power.* New York: Harper & Row.

Yerby, J. (1975). Attitude, task, and sex composition as variables affecting female leadership in small problem-solving groups. *Speech Monogr., 42,* 160–168.

Yukl, G. (1981). *Leadership in organizations.* Englewood Cliffs, N.J.: Prentice-Hall.

Zaleznik, A. (1965). The dynamics of subordinacy. *Harvard Bus. Rev., 52,* 119–131.

Zaleznick, A., and M. F. R. Kets de Vries (1975). *Power and the corporate mind.* Boston: Houghton Mifflin.

Zander, A. (1979). The psychology of group processes. In M. R. Rosenzweig, and L. W. Porter (Eds.), *Ann. Rev. Psychol., 30,* 417–451.

Zdep, S. M., and W. I. Oakes (1967). Reinforcement of leadership behavior in group discussion. *J. exp. soc. Psychol., 3,* 310–320.

CHAPTER 23

Effects of Mass Communication

Donald F. Roberts
Stanford University

Nathan Maccoby
Stanford University

MASS COMMUNICATION RESEARCH

AN EMERGING DISCIPLINE

Two decades ago, Wilbur Schramm characterized communication research as "an extraordinarily lively area of theory and research" but one that had "not become an academic discipline" (1963, p. 1). Rather, he described the field as a "crossroad where many have passed but few have tarried," noting that it was only natural that communication, as the fundamental social process, should have drawn the occasional attention of psychologists, sociologists, and political scientists, but that it had remained an "auxiliary study," the function of which was to contribute to theory in the established disciplines.

Many of Schramm's observations have withstood the test of time. Certainly symbolic communication is generally recognized as the fundamental human process—that which most sharply differentiates human functioning from that of other living organisms and

which makes human institutions unique (DeFleur and Ball-Rokeach, 1982; Roberts, 1971). Indeed, it has become *de rigueur* for texts in mass communication to echo at least implicitly Cooley (1909) or Sapir (1931), acknowledging that the study of communication is coterminous with the study of society and noting that contemporary industrial society could not exist without mass media as we know them (e.g., Davison, Boylan and Yu, 1976; Dennis, 1978; Pool and Schramm, 1973; Sandman, Rubin and Sachsman, 1976; Schramm, 1973; Severin and Tankard, 1979). Similarly, Schramm's "lively area of theory and research" continues to manifest the interdisciplinary flavor captured in his crossroad metaphor. If anything, the diversity of disciplines meeting at that crossroad has increased over the years. Today, communication scholars must search not only the psychology, sociology, and political science journals but also to publications in anthropology, linguistics, education, history, health and medicine, economics, law, public policy, information sciences, and more as well as numerous communication journals.

The intervening decades have also seen dramatic changes, however. The "small number of scholars" who devoted entire careers to the study of communication have spawned several generations of followers. The

Preparation of this chapter was partly supported by a grant from the John and Mary R. Markle Foundation. We are grateful to W. Andrew Collins for his comments on an earlier draft of this chapter.

"impressive shelf" of books and articles has become a major, rapidly expanding library. One recent bibliography, *limited* to scientific studies of television and human behavior published in English through the early 1970s, contains over 2300 citations of books and articles (Comstock and Fisher, 1975). Similarly, there are now a number of journals and annuals devoted to communication research that simply did not exist a decade ago. And finally, a growing number of academic departments and research centers are now devoted predominantly to the scientific study of the process and effects of mass communication (DeFleur and Ball-Rokeach, 1982; Schramm, 1980).

In short, today's mass communication research operates as at least a subdiscipline in its own right. Fortunately, its interdisciplinary and applied heritage has thus far kept communication programs from erecting some of the conventional disciplinary walls against which Donald Campbell (1969) warned some years ago. Nevertheless, a contemporary reviewer encounters a relatively well-marked area of research presented in a well-defined set of publications devoted exclusively to the study of communication. Returning to Schramm's metaphor, then, the crossroad has grown into a metropolis, to and from which many roads travel, but large and sophisticated enough in and of itself to attract a permanent community of scholars.

THE EFFECTS PERSPECTIVE

Context

Mass communication research in the United States has been dominated by a concern with "effects," with the empirical demonstration of whether and how mass communications influence human behavior (DeFleur and Ball-Rokeach, 1982; Gans, 1980; McLeod and Reeves, 1980). The field's emphasis on empiricism reflects its roots in the logical positivist traditions of most social science in the United States. Its concentration on effects is largely attributable to its applied beginnings, a heritage which has given the field a "problem orientation" (Roberts and Bachen, 1981). That is, much of the impetus behind mass communication research came from the kinds of concrete questions posed by media practitioners and policy makers (cf. Weaver and Gray, 1979). Such a problem orientation is understandable given the ubiquity of the media in U.S. society. It is difficult to conceive of a dimension of social life not at least potentially influenced by mass communication. Educa-

tion, economics, politics, health, consumer behavior, prosocial and antisocial behavior, attitudes toward almost every identifiable group in society, all these and more are designated by parents, policy makers, educators, and media practitioners as being influenced, for better or worse, by mass communication (Chaffee, 1979; Comstock *et al.,* 1978; Pearl, Bouthilet and Lazar, 1982; Withey and Abeles, 1980).

Most research on the effects of mass communication asks one of two types of question, each representing a different concern with how the mass media influence human behavior. One is concerned with the intent of the source of the message, asking how the media can be used best to influence people intentionally (e.g., How do we design programs to attract the largest audience? How do we convince the public to conserve energy? How do we teach preschool children the alphabet?) The other is more concerned with the audience. Although it recognizes the presumed intent of a given message, it is more interested in the "unintended" effects of media content, asking about the consequences presumed to follow from media exposure regardless of the source's intent (e.g., Do television portrayals of violence increase antisocial behavior among viewers? Does editorial selection of news stories shape public perceptions of what is important? What are the gratifications that people obtain from each of the media?).

The Direct-Effects Model

Stated in this way, both kinds of effects questions appear to assume a simple stimulus-response model of human behavior. They presume that relatively direct and immediate responses will follow from exposure to a mass-communicated message. Although most researchers have long since moved away from such "hypodermic theories" of communication effects toward more complex models of the relationship between symbolic communications and human response (e.g., Berlo, 1977; Rogers and Kincaid, 1981; Schramm, 1973), the public still tends to view the power of the mass media in relatively straightforward cause and effect terms.

Popular attributions of direct and powerful media influences are not surprising given the "obvious" manner in which mass communications intrude on people's consciousness. At an individual level, for example, it is "clear" to most parents whose three-year-olds have begun to count with the ascending volume characteristic of a *Sesame Street* lesson that television affects children. Similarly, the losing candidate in a local election "knows" that the local newspaper's editorial supporting her opponent was instrumental in her defeat. More dramatically, it would be difficult to convince a relative of one of the many people who have died imitating the Russian roulette scene from *The Deer Hunter* that the film was not directly responsible for the person's death (National Coalition on Television Violence, 1983). At a more sociological level, the panic purported to have swept the United States the night Orson Welles in a radio broadcast brought the Martians to earth has become part of the folklore of the power of mass communications (Koch, 1970), despite evidence that a relatively small proportion of listeners "panicked" (Cantril, 1940). And when the press of several countries reify a television personna by fueling popular interest in "who shot J.R.?" (a prime-time television, soap-opera villain whose near assassination at the end of the 1979-1980 season led to a summer of speculation about the culprit's identity) to the point that the victim's photograph adorned the cover of this nation's largest circulation news magazine (*Time,* 1980), it is difficult not to believe that the media have powerful effects.

The Limited-Effects Model

Until recently, however, much the opposite view dominated the thinking of communication researchers, many of whom contended that the mass media had only minimal effects on public beliefs and behavior. The prototypical "limited-effects" position was articulated in Joseph Klapper's *The Effects of Mass Communication* (1960), which summarized the existing research as demonstrating that "mass communication *ordinarily* does not serve as a necessary and sufficient cause of audience effects" and that its major function was to reinforce existing values and attitudes.

Given the advantage of hindsight, it is easy to ask why so many scholars overlooked or ignored the various qualifying statements that Klapper included in his book, many of which indicated that under some conditions at least some groups within society might be greatly affected by mass communications. Similarly, we can ask why reinforcement of the status quo should have been accepted as a not very interesting, not very important effect of the media. From today's perspective, such an outcome is seen as terribly important. However, hindsight should also remind us of the historical context that nourished the limited-effects model. It has been characterized as one of reaction to early assumptions that the mass audience was at the mercy of the mass media (Bauer

and Bauer, 1960; DeFleur and Ball-Rokeach, 1982). Mass communication research was largely spawned by a fear that the mass media offered an unequaled mechanism to insure exposure to the kind of blatant propaganda used in World War I and a fear that exposure to what ultimately turned out to be gross misrepresentations of the truth was sufficient to persuade people. Such fear, of course, was not unreasonable given the conception of individuals and society that characterized early twentieth-century social science. On the one hand, the image of a mass society that dominated sociological thought gave rise to a conception of a mass audience, one that could be treated as a monolith. This, in turn, led to a concern with how the public (as opposed to various publics) was affected by media (Friedson, 1953). On the other hand, the emergence in psychology of mechanistic, stimulus-response theories of behavior led to an image of individuals at the mercy of external stimuli and hence to expectations of rather direct and immediate effects given well-crafted, persuasive messages.

Small wonder that the resulting picture of the individual and the public gave rise to excessive claims of the powerful and dangerous impact of the mass media (DeFleur and Ball-Rokeach, 1975). Small wonder, too, that subsequent failures to demonstrate large changes in people's attitudes or behavior as a result of mass communication campaigns led to over-reaction in the opposite direction—toward attributing little or no influence to the mass media.

With the development of more sophisticated survey and analysis techniques than had previously been available, several early voting studies found no effect of the mass media on voting decisions (Berelson, Lazarsfeld, and McPhee, 1954; Lazarsfeld, Berelson, and Gaudet, 1948). Similarly, attempts to use media to increase public levels of information met with little success (Hyman and Sheatsley, 1947; Star and Hughes, 1950). Moreover, these "failures" occurred at a time when psychology was moving away from simplistic S–R conceptions of humankind toward models that paid attention to the activities and characteristics of the individual intervening between perception of a stimulus and performance or lack of performance of a response. Thus, a growing recognition that individuals were not simply at the mercy of any message they happened to encounter but that they actively engaged in interpreting and "deciding" whether and how to respond, in concert with the failure of large-scale surveys to demonstrate significant changes attributable to mass communications, spawned a number of new, quite reasonable explanations of why mass media were limited to relatively minor effects and why audiences would remain fundamentally obstinate (Bauer, 1964; Hyman and Sheatsley, 1947; Lazarsfeld and Merton, 1948), at least when studied outside of the laboratory (Hovland, 1959).

Models of Powerful Effects under
Limiting Conditions

Currently, however, it appears that the limited-effects model is also being abandoned. Although few, if any, contemporary researchers accept the earlier conception of a mass audience generally at the mercy of all-powerful media, many do subscribe to the view that the mass media have important, often very powerful, effects on the way in which various *publics* think and behave.

The return to a view of significant media influences largely derives from developments in three areas: psychology, political science, and communication research. First, models developed by psychologists in the early 1960s to explain conditions under which children learn and perform aggressive behaviors (Bandura, Ross and Ross, 1963; Bandura and Walters, 1963; Berkowitz, 1962) were applied extensively to television under the auspices of the Surgeon General's Scientific Advisory Committee on Television and Social Behavior (1972). In particular, Bandura's elaboration of social-learning theory (1969, 1977) gave communication researchers a theoretical framework ideally suited to examining television's impact on behavior. Although much of the resulting experimental work was (and is) questioned on the grounds of its inability to be generalized to nonlaboratory settings, the consistent finding of increases in aggressive responses subsequent to viewing televised portrayals of violence across a variety of samples and operationalizations of both independent and dependent variables convinced many researchers that television has important effects on people (Comstock *et al.,* 1978; M. Paisley, 1972). Second, by the 1970s, journalists and political scientists began to note dramatic changes in the nature and role of political parties in the United States (Barber, 1980; Broder, 1972; Graber, 1980), as well as to report declines in the ability to predict voting behavior by using such traditional variables as socioeconomic status and party affiliation (Nie, Verba and Petrocik, 1976). One result of these observations was renewed attention to the role of mass media in the political process at a time when a number of relationships between media use and various criterion variables related to politics were reported (Chaffee, 1975). Finally, the past decade witnessed a change in the characteristics of scholars engaged in communication research. Rather than being a collection of "wayfarers" from other disciplines (Schramm, 1963), many people who now study the process and effects of mass communication have earned their degrees from *communication* programs. Moreover, a good many of these brought with them significant experience as media practitioners; hence they approached the field with what can be called a "clinical sense" that the media do have important effects.

The upshot of these developments has been a resurgence of activity in the field and a revival of models of powerful effects (Roberts and Bachen, 1981). Current thinking, however, also views the power of the media as highly conditional, depending on a variety of contingent and/or contributory third variables. Chaffee (1977) discusses a trend away from research concerned with demonstrating effects on only 10 percent of a full population toward studies suggesting a 100 percent effect on a *specifiable* group that may comprise only 10 percent of the population. In other words, recent models posit powerful media effects limited by specifiable (and empirically demonstrable) conditions.

EXAMINING THE EFFECTS
OF MASS MEDIA

Testing any effect in the social sciences requires knowledge of the stimulus, control of its application, assessment of effect, and elaboration of the underlying mechanism(s) or process(es) (McLeod and Reeves, 1980). Thus, concern with the effects of mass media on human behavior demands:

1. Control and/or assessment of media and/or media content,

2. Control and/or assessment of exposure to the media and their content,

3. Definition and assessment of the consequences of exposure,

4. Assessment, elaboration, and interpretation of the conditions and processes that explain the relationship between exposure and its outcomes.

To a large extent, the resurgence in mass communication studies recognizes that each of these requirements necessitates more complex conceptualizations than were characteristic of earlier days. The terms "media" and "media content" are no longer approached as unidimensional constructs. The audience is no longer conceived as an undifferentiated mass with exposure taken almost for granted. Recognition of the multidimensionality of media effects has led to more complex conceptualizations of effects, including not only consideration of their nature (e.g., cognitions, attitudes, behaviors), but also such dimensions as time, unit of analysis, degree of content specificity (e.g., a specific behavior versus a class of behaviors), and type of impact (e.g., establishing, changing, or stabilizing a response). Finally, there is a growing theoretical attention to identification and elaboration of the role of third variables in the media-effects relationship.

ASSESSMENT OF MEDIA CONTENT

One reason for a lack of uniformity in results across many studies of media effects stems from the fact that there are wide variations in how the media stimulus is conceptualized. An awareness of such variations is particularly critical to media researchers because of the "conglomerate" nature of media content that makes it amenable to different levels of analysis (Weiss, 1969). Because each successively more global content unit contains within it more refined units, an effect attributed to the larger unit may derive from one or more of its components but be totally unrelated to others.

Size of the unit of analysis, then, is one of the more important dimensions along which media content can vary. At one extreme, media content can be defined as broadly as a medium or even "the media," the impetus for effects deriving from the sheer fact of their presence or absence (e.g., Chaffee and Wilson, 1977; Cramond, 1976; Eisenstein, 1968; Lerner and Schramm, 1967; Schramm and Lerner, 1976; Williams, 1979). At the other extreme, media content can be conceived in relatively miscroscopic terms, ranging downward from the presence of such elements as background music or number of scene changes, to sentences and headlines, and even to single words (e.g., Anderson *et al.,* 1979; Huston *et al.,* 1981; Krull and Husson, 1979; Liebert, Sprafkin, Liebert and Rubinstein, 1977; Tannenbaum, 1955).

Typically, however, media-content units lie somewhere between the extremes, the stimulus being conceived in terms of types of content (e.g., violence, political information). Here too, of course, the problem of stimulus size remains. For example, content used to investigate the effects of television portrayals of violence experimentally have ranged from single scenes or brief, specially prepared sequences that allow one to focus on a specific contingency associated with the violent act (e.g., Bandura, 1965; Berkowitz and Rawlings, 1963), to highly edited television programs (Leifer and Roberts, 1972), to controlled diets of programs or films that continue for several days or weeks (Feshbach and Singer, 1971; Parke *et al.,* 1977). And within surveys, "violent" content has been operationalized as the number of "favorite" programs containing violence (McIntyre and Teevan, 1972), the actual number of "violent" programs viewed per week (McLeod, Atkin and Chaffee, 1972a, 1972b), and by implication at least, as prime-time dramatic television (Gerbner and Gross, 1976a, 1976b).

Clearly, as the content moves from a single scene to an extended television diet, the questions posed and inferences that can be drawn change dramatically, for as size varies, so too do a number of interrelated stimulus dimensions that influence the nature of any effect. These include stimulus duration, frequency, and strength; the degree to which content is a natural, self-contained unit; whether the content is created for and by the media or whether the media simply provide a conduit for a "natural" event; and so forth (Chaffee, 1977; McLeod and Reeves, 1980; Weiss, 1969).

Overriding each of the preceding dimensions, however, is a more basic issue of the substance of the content. Regardless of the frequency, strength, duration, naturalness, or discriminating aspects of a content unit, researchers of media effects have been fundamentally concerned with *what* the media say. The basic assumption is that responses (effects) are shaped by the content of the stimulus. Indeed, one of the more common ways of organizing discussions of the literature in this field is in terms of the effects of various content categories, ranging from the generic (westerns, news, soap operas) to the specific (politics, violence, sex).

The assumption of a correlation between stimulus content and response content makes valid and reliable knowledge of media content imperative. Unfortunately such "knowledge" is frequently based on subjective assessments of media content. One reason for this is that mass communication research often originates from public concern over various social issues, and most "publics" tend to perceive trends in media content that hone the edges of their own axes. Impressionistic assessments of "obvious" content trends are also fueled by the simple fact that systematic content analysis can be expensive, difficult, and time consuming (Gerbner, 1969;

Holsti, 1969; Rosengren, 1981). And finally, much research on media effects is experimental, and it is possible
to study experimentally potential effects of any stimulus
totally independent of whether the stimulus is *representative* of media content. For instance, it is easy to obtain an
example of prosocial behavior (sharing, helping, altruism) from current television fare to use in an experiment
concerned with whether children can learn prosocial behavior from television (e.g., Rubinstein *et al.,* 1974).
Nevertheless, although a systematic content analysis is
lacking, it is reasonable to question whether prosocial
portrayals are representative of television content. As we
move from laboratory to field studies, questions regarding the representativeness of the content become critical.

Fortunately, the same public concerns that lead to
subjective statements about media content also may engender more systematic content analyses, as exemplified
by analyses of media portrayals of violence that followed
from expressions of concern over crime and violence. For
example, the Warren Commission's investigation of the
causes and prevention of violence sparked a number of
such analyses (e.g., Baker and Ball, 1969; Clark and
Blankenberg, 1972; Gerbner, 1972). Indeed, concern
with violence in our society has made examinations of
media violence something of a mainstay for content analysts (e.g., Gerbner *et al.,* 1978, 1979, 1980, 1981; National Coalition on Television Violence, 1983). Similarly,
public debate about equal rights for minorities and for
women has engendered studies of how members of these
groups are portrayed in the media (Butler and Paisley,
1980; U.S. Commission on Civil Rights, 1977, 1980).
Other social issues have led to such analyses of media
content as sex on television (E. Roberts, 1982; Silverman,
Sprafkin and Rubinstein, 1979; Sprafkin and Silverman,
1981), portrayals of older people and aging on television
(Arnoff, 1974; Cassata *et al.,* 1980; Gerbner *et al.,* 1980),
and television commercials directed at children (Barcus,
1980; Meringoff, 1980).

Analyses of media content are not limited to current
issues or to television. Lasswell's (1927; Lasswell, Leites
et al., 1949) pioneering examinations of propaganda
began a continuing tradition of analysis of such dimensions of mass-mediated political information as international relations (Hedman, 1981), civil rights coverage
(Carter, 1957), and political images versus political issues
(Patterson and McClure, 1976). Other analyses deal with
topics as diverse as television portrayals of alcohol abuse
(Greenberg, 1981) and values articulated in children's

school readers (deCharms and Moeller, 1962). Recently,
there has been a move toward assessing overall trends in
news coverage in order to describe the media agenda
(e.g., Funkhouser, 1973; McCombs and Shaw, 1972;
Noelle-Neumann, 1977), as well as examining total message systems in order to characterize the structure and assumptions underlying the message-producing culture
(Gerbner, 1969; Gerbner and Gross, 1976a; Gerbner *et
al.,* 1978, 1979, 1980).

Systematic mapping of media content is a necessary
precondition for valid studies of effects. However, a
major challenge confronting effects research, particularly nonexperimental studies, is that what content analysis
reveals need not correspond to what some people see
when confronted with the same stimulus. For example,
what a content analysis characterizes as a highly violent
television scene may to some viewers be simply playful
competition. Indeed, one of the bases on which the
"Violence Index" of Gerbner and his associates is sometimes criticized is that it classes as aggressive content acts
that many television viewers refuse to place in that category (e.g., the "humorous" pushing and shoving that occurs in some situation comedies). This problem, of
course, is endemic to all behavioral research. Nevertheless, it is worth emphasizing in discussing the effects of
mass-mediated messages, if only because the ubiquity
and *assumed* homogeneity of media content can make
one forget that meanings are not in messages, but in people.

ASSESSMENT OF MEDIA EXPOSURE

Carl Hovland's (1959) now classic reconciliation of experimental and survey results argued that as communication research moves from the laboratory to the field, fundamental changes occur in the kind of "exposure"
achieved, changes that mediate large differences in possible inferences about the impact of mass communication.
The captive nature of the audience in an experiment
makes application of the stimulus synonymous with exposure—exposure distributed across all members of the
audience, regardless of differences in predispositions, biases, interests, and abilities that operate on these people
outside the experimental context. In surveys, on the other
hand, the audience is anything but captive. Exposure
here is largely a result of self-selection, guided by the very
predispositions rendered inoperable in an experiment,
and the variables underlying audience self-selection tend

to be just those that mediate against attitude change. Small wonder that experimental effects tend to be larger and more clear-cut than those obtained in "naturalistic" settings.

Recent research has broadened the kinds of outcomes we consider to be legitimate effects of mass communications (Chaffee, 1977; Roberts and Bachen, 1981) and has attempted to bring the laboratory and the field closer together either by locating "natural experiments" (Cook and Campbell, 1979; Murray and Kippax, 1978; Williams, 1979) or by transferring laboratory-like control of exposure to field settings (Farquhar *et al.,* 1977; Feshbach and Singer, 1971; Parke *et al.,* 1977; Stein and Freidrich, 1972). Nevertheless, communication research still confronts conflicting results derived from very different conceptualizations of exposure. We continue to conduct experiments that operationalize exposure as participation in one or another treatment condition. Much of the research on children's responses to various television presentations falls into this mold (Comstock *et al.,* 1978; Williams, 1981). We also continue to conduct surveys in which exposure varies, since it is controlled largely by the survey participants, thus making the researcher's task one of assessing such variations. Studies of the political effects of mass communication (Kraus and Davis, 1976), evaluations of communication campaigns (Rice and Paisley, 1981), and recent examinations of the cultivation hypothesis (Gerbner, Gross, Morgan and Signorielli, 1981a, 1981b; Hawkins and Pingree, 1982; Hirsch, 1980, 1981a, 1981b) and of the impact of television violence (Milavsky, Kessler, Stipp and Rubens, 1982) exemplify this research. And of course, we continue to face the task of reconciling the different results of these two methodologies. Fortunately, extensive work on audience self-selection (Sears and Freedman, 1967) and a good deal of communication policy debate in which media defenders have confronted advocates of change with gross differences in the results of the two methodologies, attacking experimental findings for the very reason that the exposed audience does not generalize (e.g., Surgeon General's Advisory Committee, 1972) have helped keep the discipline sensitive to these kinds of differences.

Less fortunately, the kind of attention paid to differences in exposure inherent in experimental and survey designs has not been devoted to the concept of exposure as it occurs in natural settings. Indeed, given that some assessment of exposure is necessary for any valid inference about effects, there has been remarkably little conceptual development to buttress the many operationalizations of exposure populating the literature.

Measures range from the very global, the presence of a medium in a community being a suffient reason to assume exposure (e.g., Lerner, 1958; Himmelweit, *et al.,* 1958), to the microscopic, little or no distinction being drawn between exposure and attention (e.g., Bechtel, Achepol and Akers, 1972; Clarke and Kline, 1974). More common are operationalizations of exposure lying somewhere between, based on respondents' self-reports of the frequency or amount of time devoted to each medium (Gerbner *et al.,* 1981; Greenberg and Dervin, 1970; Palmgreen, 1979).

Usually, however, a measure of time spent with a medium is a poor assessment of exposure to a specific kind of content. If one wishes to draw conclusions about effects of exposure to television, regardless of content, then a measure of time spent viewing is appropriate. However, if one is concerned with the effect of a specific type of content, a more fine-grained assessment of exposure to that particular content is required. For example, to the extent that a "daily newspaper reader" limits herself to the sports page, reliance on an overall measure of frequency of "newspaper" reading would attenuate any relationship between "exposure" and an outcome concerned with political information.

An examination of ten surveys that correlated exposure to television violence with children's aggressive behavior illustrates the point (Comstock *et al.,* 1978). Some of the studies found no relationship between television viewing and aggression-related outcomes; some found small, positive relationships that held only for particular subgroups of children; some found consistent, moderate relationships that held up across various subgroups. Although there are a number of possible explanations for such varied results, the reason proved to be differences in exposure measures that distinguished between surveys which did and did not find a relationship. Two studies used global measures (availability of television in the home; total hours of viewing) and found no relationship between "exposure" and aggressive behavior (Himmelweit *et al.,* 1958; Schramm *et al.,* 1961). Six others used measures that classified children as high or low viewers of violence on the basis of what they nominated as their three or four favorite shows. Three found a weak positive relationship between viewing violence and aggressiveness that held only for particular subgroups of males (Eron,

1963; McIntyre and Teevan, 1972; Robinson and Bachman, 1972); two found no relationship (Lefkowitz, Eron, Walder and Heusmann, 1972; McLeod, Atkin and Chaffee, 1972a), and one found a moderate, negative relationship for aggressive feelings (Friedman and Johnson, 1972). Finally, two surveys used more direct measures of violence viewing. Dominick and Greenberg (1972) had children indicate which programs from a list of the twenty most violent they viewed each week; McLeod, Atkin and Chaffee (1972a, 1972b) obtained students' self-reports of how many violent programs they actually viewed per week. Both studies report consistent, positive relationships between the viewing of violent programs and a variety of aggression measures. Moreover, the relationships remained even when a variety of other varibles were controlled. The trend is clear; as measures of exposure to violent programming become more direct, a positive relationship between viewing of violence and aggressiveness becomes more likely.

A measure of total viewing as a proxy for the viewing of violence ignores the many hours of programming available that contain little violence. Similarly, a few favorite programs represent a very small part of a child's total television diet, and may not be at all representative of what the child views. That is, a violent favorite may be the very program parents prohibit the child from watching *because* it is violent and is a favorite. Or a violent program may be listed as a favorite because it is one of very few action-packed programs viewed in a given household, for whatever reason. The point is that neither total viewing nor expressed preferences for violent programs adequately estimate the viewing of violence. Demonstrations of only modest relationships between such measures and more direct assessments of exposure to televised violence support the point (Chaffee, 1972; McLeod, Atkin and Chaffee, 1972a, 1972b).

Finally, Clarke and Kline (1974) argue that we should abandon media use as an index of communication experience altogether, at least as far as exposure to information is concerned. They propose to substitute a measure of "message discrimination" as the independent or predictor variable in mass communication studies. Message discrimination—the degree to which a respondent perceives some symbols about an issue, event, or person—is assessed by asking respondents, first, to suggest problems faced by the community about which they have read, heard, or seen anything in the media, and then to describe them in terms of how they were presented (i.e., the content) and the channel of communication. Of course, it can be argued that such questions are as much measures of attention and/or recall as of exposure, both of which should relate more strongly to information levels than less focused exposure indexes. Thus, it is not surprising that several studies using message discrimination measures report strong positive correlations with information levels (Becker *et al.,* 1979b; Clarke and Fredin, 1978; Clarke and Kline, 1974; Edelstein, 1974; Palmgreen *et al.,* 1974). One study reporting a comparison found message discrimination to be more strongly related to information level than are more general measures of media use (Palmgreen, 1979).

The conclusion seems quite straightforward. Exposure measures should parallel the particular kind of content being studied as closely as possible. The point seems almost too obvious to mention were it not for the fact that it is often ignored. For example, the issue of the specificity of exposure measures has recently surfaced in discussions of mass communication campaigns and of the cultivation hypothesis (Gerbner and Gross, 1976a, 1976b; Gerbner *et al.,* 1980); indeed, the latter has sparked a good deal of debate over the degree to which measures of daily viewing of television can be presumed to identify exposure to "typical" television content.

ASSESSMENT OF MEDIA EFFECTS

Domains of Effects

The effects of mass communication can be conceptualized in a number of ways. One of the more striking developments in the field has been an increase in both the number and the nature of consequences considered to be important media effects. In a sense, a deemphasis on immediate attitude change as the major effect of mass media (Chaffee, 1977; Katz, 1980; Kline, 1972; Rogers and Kincaid, 1981) has legitimated consideration of a wide variety of effects that were previously noted, but seldom deemed important. The result has been not only a proliferation of problem areas receiving attention (Roberts and Bachen, 1981), but also many "reconsiderations" and "reconceptualizations" of the various domains and dimensions of effects (Chaffee, 1975, 1977; Clark and Kline, 1974; Katz, 1977, 1980; McLeod and Reeves, 1980; Roberts, 1971; Rogers, 1981). Nevertheless the impact of mass communication on attitudes and values is still being studied. The field continues to develop messages specifically designed to influence attitudes and values (e.g., Children's TV Workshop, 1977; Johnstone, Ettema and Davidson, 1980) and to assess the attitudinal impact of entertainment productions (Christenson and Roberts, 1983; Elliott and Schenck-Hamlin, 1979; Graves, 1980; Vidmar and Rokeach, 1974). And attitude and value considerations remain at the heart of what Katz (1978, 1980) labels theories of "ideological effects" (e.g., Gerbner *et al.,* 1978, 1979; Glasgow Group, 1976; Hall, 1977; Tuchman, 1977).

The change in orientation, then, has not been to abandon research on attitudinal effects but to put it in its proper conceptual place (Chaffee, 1977). It is now recognized that although some campaigns and programs may primarily influence attitudes and values, others have little to do with them. Moreover, with few exceptions, it appears that even when the impact of mass communication is primarily affective, attitude change usually is characterized by a slow process of erosion and accretion rather than by one of sudden upheaval and conversion. Finally, the realization is mounting that what influence occurs takes place through changes in cognitions that, in turn, influence peoples' attitudes and behavior. It is argued that even when concern focuses primarily on attitudinal or behavioral effects, any influence of mass media content depends on how people interpret messages relative to previously established conceptualizations of the world—fundamentally a cognitive effect (Roberts, 1971). In short, the historical tendency to overemphasize the attitudinal dimension of the familiar attitudinal-cognitive-behavioral effects trichotomy (McGuire, 1969; Rosenberg and Hovland, 1960) has given way to a recognition that often

1. Attitudinal effects are neither necessary nor sufficient to influence corresponding behaviors,

2. Cognitive effects are necessary and sufficient to influence corresponding behaviors,

3. Cognitive effects are important consequences in and of themselves (Chaffee, 1977).

Attention to cognitive effects has sparked new approaches to the kinds of outcomes included under this trichotomy. The media's cognitive impact has been measured typically in terms of information acquisition assessed via knowledge tests comprised of specific questions about the content under study (e.g., Alper and Leidy, 1970; Becker and Whitney, 1980; Chaffee, Ward and Tipton, 1970; Douglas, Westley and Chaffee, 1970; Drew and Reeves, 1980; Hovland, Lumsdaine and Sheffield, 1949; Patterson and McClure, 1976; Wade and Schramm, 1969). Clarke and Kline (1974), however, ar-

gue that although knowledge based on this kind of "textbook" approach to learning is salient to educators and researchers, it may not be relevant to the public. They advocate more audience-centered indicators of "information holding" based on the number of "problems" that people identify and on the number of solutions and actors they relate to those problems. Several studies employ this approach to measuring information acquired from the mass media (Becker, Sobowale and Casey, 1979; Clarke and Fredin, 1978; Edelstein, 1974; Palmgreen, 1979; Palmgreen, Kline and Clarke, 1974).

Agenda-setting research also deals with cognitive effects. This approach focuses on how the media influence people's levels of awareness about issues as opposed to how the media influence their knowledge about those issues (McCombs and Shaw, 1972; Shaw and McCombs, 1977). Still other cognitions influenced by the media concern people's beliefs about the nature of social reality. Noelle-Neumann (1973, 1974, 1977) investigated how the media affect perceptions of what constitutes "popular" as opposed to "minority" opinion at any given time. Similarly, Gerbner and his colleagues (Gerbner and Gross, 1976a, 1976b, 1980; Gerbner *et al.,* 1979) have examined television's ability to "cultivate" perceptions of the nature of the social order by influencing people's images of the standardized roles and behaviors acceptable in a given cultural context.

Of course, the most convincing demonstrations of the effects of mass media remain behavioral. Theoretical models that posit attitudes and/or cognitions as intervening variables notwithstanding, specific behaviors following exposure to logically related media content quite reasonably carry more weight than any verbal measure of attitudinal or informational impact yet devised. We remain inclined to believe what people do as opposed to what they say.

Historical concern with the manipulative ability of the mass media in the political and commercial arenas continues to be reflected in studies relating exposure to election and sales campaigns to such behaviors as voting and product selection (cf., Chaffee, 1975; Comstock *et al.,* 1978; Nimmo and Sanders, 1981). However, the variety of behaviors toward which mass media campaigns have been directed has grown. Recent studies examine the effectiveness of media attempts to influence a variety of health-related behaviors (Maccoby and Solomon, 1981; Solomon, 1983), family planning practices (Taplin, 1981), use of automobile seat belts (Robertson *et al.,* 1974), energy conservation acts (Farhar-Pilgrim and

Shoemaker, 1981; Leonard-Barton, 1979), forest fire prevention (McNamara, Kurth and Hansen, 1981), and environmental protection (Stamm, 1972). Indeed, it is an unusual campaign that does not attempt to influence some sort of behavior, and such campaigns have become so common that the term "social marketing" has been coined to denote an entire subarea of study (Solomon, 1981).

Longstanding concern with the behavioral impact of noncampaign content also remains. Although early questions about the influence of media portrayals of crime and violence on antisocial behavior continue to be addressed (e.g., Surgeon General's Advisory Committee and Television and Social Behavior, 1972; Palmer and Dorr, 1980), they have been joined by studies of behaviors as varied as helping, sharing, delay of gratification, social interactions, friendship choices, and overcoming of various phobias. Recent work has even examined the relationship between television content and rates of automobile and airplane accidents, murder, and suicide (Phillips, 1979, 1980, 1982).

The potential for mass communications to engender, enhance, or depress emotional responses also deserves mention as a domain of effect. Questions about the emotional impact of films were raised at least as early as the Payne Fund studies (Dysinger and Ruckmick, 1933) and the radio dramatization of *The War of the Worlds* (Cantril, 1940). The consideration of emotional reactions to television content (Himmelweit *et al.*, 1958; Schramm *et al.*, 1961) and of mood changes following exposure to violent films (Handlon, 1962; Tannenbaum and Gaer, 1965) maintained this tradition through the 1950s and 1960s. Recent studies examine how violent television content affects physiological arousal among children and how that arousal is related to subsequent behavior (Cline, Croft and Courier, 1972; Osborn and Endsley, 1971; Tannenbaum, 1972). Zillman (Zillman 1971; Zillma, Hoyt and Day, 1974) has extended this work to adults and to erotic and other potentially arousing types of content. Other work in this tradition has found that children who view a great deal of television violence are less aroused by and less responsive to portrayals of aggressive behavior (Cline, *et al.*, 1972; Stein and Friedrich, 1972) and that exposure to televised violence decreased children's subsequent sensitivity to the possible consequences of violence in what they perceived to be a real-life situation (Drabman and Thomas, 1974; Thomas and Drabman, 1974).

Types of Effect

Regardless of the response domain, the effects of mass communication vary on many dimensions. Effects can be conceived in terms of the formation of totally new attitudes, cognitions, behaviors or emotions; in terms of the straightforward reinforcement of existing responses; in terms of the crystallization of existing but not clearly articulated responses; and in terms of a change in existing attitudes, cognitions, behaviors or emotions, with this change ranging from relatively minor modifications of existing responses to dramatic conversions. We noted previously how the field's early concentration on attitude change led some to minimize the degree to which media engender significant effects. We also noted a recent trend toward recognizing the theoretical and practical significance of less dramatic, less visible, consequences of mass communication. Indeed, some argue that the failure to achieve important social change is, to a greater or lesser extent, attributable to the media's tendency to reinforce the status quo and that this maintenance of the status quo is perhaps the most important consequence of mass communication, although less dramatic and less easy to measure than is change (e.g., Gerbner *et al.*, 1980; Hall, 1977; Noelle-Neuman, 1977; Tuchman, 1977). In addition, some work on the impact of media on youngsters notes that attitudes, cognitions, and behaviors cannot be changed until they are formed, adopted, or otherwise established in children's response repertoires (Chaffee, Ward and Tipton, 1970; Roberts, Hawkins and Pingree, 1975), an argument that is also sound for adults. From this perspective, the ability of the mass media to form or crystalize responses in any domain is at least as important as their ability to change existing responses.

Dimensions of Effect

Time is critical to the assessment of media effects. Cartwright (1949) noted the critical linkage between an advocated behavior and locating the path of action in time. Studies of innovation diffusion have long recognized the importance of time in the communication-decision-action process (Katz, 1962; Rogers, 1983). Until recently, however, few studies outside the diffusion tradition have attended to such factors as the amount of time between exposure and consequence, duration of consequence, differential processes mediating ephemeral as opposed to enduring effects, different rates of change for different kinds of outcomes, and so forth. Fortunately, a growing number of questions about the role of the media in areas that are clearly time dependent (e.g., socialization, agenda setting, health maintenance), about the long-term, cumulative effects of exposure, and about various time-related processes that mediate the effects of mass communication (e.g., attention, story comprehension) have increased attention to time as a factor in the assessment of effects. Several papers concerned with time in communication research have facilitated this trend (Arundale, 1977; Davis and Lee, 1980; Kline, 1977; Krull and Paulson, 1977; Watt and van den Berg, 1978).

Concern with media effects also requires that a distinction be made between acquisition and performance. Acquisition refers to the processing and storing of information that may be translated into subsequent behavior. Performance is simply the display of the acquired information in the form of some behavior. It is important to be sensitive to the separateness of the two processes because acquisition is not directly observable. That is, the only way to determine whether a behavior has been acquired, or how the manipulation of some third variable affects acquisition, is to observe behavior (Kuhn, 1973). For example, we typically measure such acquisition processes as comprehension or retention by means of a written test, by eliciting the performance of a particular kind of behavior in order to make inferences about a nonobservable process. The problem is that failure to perform does not necessarily imply failure to acquire. Quite the contrary, it is relatively easy to manipulate elements in a performance situation in order to inhibit or facilitate the display of a given behavior (Bandura, 1965, 1977). The ambiguity arises because many of the same variables that affect acquisition also affect performance, and the former is a necessary condition for the latter. Thus, for example, changing the source of a message, or the promised reward, or even the medium by which it is transmitted may influence acquisition, or performance, or both. However, it is almost impossible to separate the role of the variables that operate on both processes. When studying the literature of mass communication effects, then, one must remember that most discussions of acquisition processes, by definition, implicate performance processes, simply because acquisition is measurable only through performance.

Another dimension that differentiates media effects is the degree to which they directly relate to specific content (Chaffee, 1977). The typical research paradigm attempts to relate particular classes of outcomes to similar classes of content; however, there is a wide range in how broadly the class is defined. There can be extensive variance in the degree to which a particular "effect" replicates the stimulus (e.g., does viewing a televised shoving match result in subsequent shoving? punching? shooting?). Similarly, there can be variance in the degree to which a particular outcome can be tied to a *specific bit* of content (e.g., is a child's increased preference for toy guns to be related to his or her watching a model shoot a dart gun at a bobo doll? a war movie? a season of police-crime drama?).

At another level, effects research can take a more "content-diffuse" approach (McLeod and Reeves, 1980) by examining outcomes that do not obviously follow from the manifest content of the stimulus, although they are logically related to it. Watt and Krull (1977), for example, predicted aggressive behavior from such structural factors as the unpredictability of audio and visual elements, which were totally independent of the content of a program. Zillman *et al.* (1974) find that under some conditions aggressive behavior can be enhanced by erotic content, an effect more attributable to the arousal potential of the portrayal than to the content eliciting the arousal. Content-diffuse effects are implicated in McLuhan's contention that the form in which a medium provides symbols is the source of the important consequences of various communication technologies and in Salomon's (1979a, 1979b) work on how the nature of each medium's symbols has consequences independent of the content transmitted by those symbols.

At an even more "diffuse" level, there is research concerned with the impact of media on how people distribute their time; Schramm, Lyle and Parker (1961), for example, examine the influence of the introduction of television on the time children gave to play, sleep, films, reading, homework, and so on. Williams and Handford (1977) look at how television changed patterns of behavior within Canadian towns in terms of what community activities gained or lost participation. Medrich, Roizen, Rubin and Buckley (1982) consider the consequences for children's use of time of their living in a "continuous" television environment. Indeed, almost any study concerned with patterns of media use at least implicitly examines some noncontent related outcomes. Perhaps most distant from specific content are the potential effects of the mass media attributable to their very existence; the economic implications of producing them (trees needed to produce paper pulp); their function as status objects (the presence or absence of a television set);

the redistribution of advertising budgets; the reformulation of political campaign strategies; the demise of general interest, entertainment magazines; and the growth of specialized publications (probably influenced by the functions taken over by television).

The unit of analysis locates still another dimension in the assessment of the effects of mass communication. The field is dominated by "microlevel" studies. Emphasis on the individual is due partly to the historical design of experimental research that tends to limit attention to individuals. It is also partly traceable to a tradition of public-opinion polling that often aggregates responses from many individuals in order to describe a presumably higher level concept—public opinion, a procedure that has been called a "grand reification" of individually measured responses that may have little connection to the way the society is organized (McLeod and Reeves, 1980). Of course, many important consequences of reading, viewing, or listening tend to occur at the level of the individual audience member. However, it is also critical to note that there are other levels of effect beyond the individual, levels that from some perspectives have even greater social significance.

To the extent that we believe that mass communication plays an integral role in the operation of modern societies, we should investigate media influences on the groups, communities, social structures and organizations that form them. For example, the list of studies that indicate the use of mass media is strongly related to interpersonal interactions (Chaffee, 1979; Bostian and Ross, 1965; Kent and Rush, 1976; Kline, 1971; Westley and Severin, 1964), suggests that a move toward analyses that consider the influence of media on dyads and groups is in order. At an even more "macro" level of analysis, we can look at the distribution across different communities and social strata of various mass-mediated "resources" (i.e., knowledge, beliefs, values, awareness). Studies have examined how "advantaged" segments of a community gain relatively more knowledge from the media than do less advantaged segments (Donohue *et al.,* 1975; Tichenor *et al.,* 1970, 1973), and have reanalyzed data from the *Sesame Street* evaluations (Ball and Bogatz, 1970; Bogatz and Ball, 1971) with an emphasis on differentiating gains in knowledge as a function of the viewer's socioeconomic status (Cook *et al.,* 1975). Similarly, any test of the "gap" hypothesis, the idea that different segments of a population acquire information from the media at different rates, requires analyses

of population segments, not individuals. Indeed, many of the more interesting hypotheses about the impact of mass communication on the shaping, maintenance, and alteration of social institutions require more attention to macrolevel effects assessed at more macroscopic levels of analysis than generally has been done.

ELABORATION OF CONDITIONS AND PROCESSES

One of the more significant trends in communication research has been a move away from questions posed in terms of main effects (e.g., Does exposure to television violence cause aggressive behavior?). Current work tends to be more interested in identifying and elaborating the various conditions that lead some audience members to be affected in one way, others in another, and still others not at all. It confronts the fact that messages causing some people to respond in one direction and others in the opposite way are not accurately characterized in terms of net change.

However, the move toward conditional analyses is not simply one of including various third variables in traditional correlational procedures or of ensuring that multiple-regression equations include third-variable interaction terms. Rather, it follows, or should follow, a theory-based approach. Understanding the nature of the relationship, not simply its statistical demonstration, is what is critical. McLeod and Reeves (1980) point out that although traditional statistical procedures are adequate for demonstrating that different amounts of media exposure may interact with differing levels on some conditioning variable to mediate a number of contingent and/or contributory effects (e.g., high and low television exposure by high and low levels of perceived reality may lead to differential effects on aggressive behavior), the nature of all possible conditional relationships would not be revealed by such traditional correlational analyses. For example, unless specified and looked for, a perfect crossover interaction between perceived reality and amount of exposure would be missed by traditional procedures (large amounts of change averaging to zero). Hence, any analysis of conditional variables is potentially misleading unless the operating relationship of that variable to exposure and effect is explicitly specified and studied (McLeod and Reeves, 1980). The power of the conditioning approach, then, lies neither in the recognition that exposure/effects relationships often depend on third variables nor in the statistical procedures available to test the influence of third variables. Rather, its strength depends on the theoretical underpinnings leading to the hypothesis that a particular conditioning variable operates in a specified way. In other words, conditional analyses *should* be conceived in terms of theoretical development, not simply as one more methodology in the service of brute empiricism.

So many third variables "condition" the relationship between media exposure and effects that some type of classification scheme is needed to facilitate the cross-study comparisons necessary for theoretical development. Three current approaches offer such help.

The first is the approach of McLeod and Reeves (1980). They differentiate between contingent and contributory conditions and classify conditioning variables on the basis of whether they operate before, during, or after media exposure. Contingent variables locate the presence or absence of effects within different subgroups or situations; contributory variables influence the likelihood that effects will occur or the rate of their occurrence. To illustrate, the "gap" hypothesis posits that any gains in knowledge depend on the preexposure educational characteristics of audience members (e.g., Tichenor *et al.,* 1970), viewing education as a condition on which the effect is contingent. Similarly, viewers who are provoked to anger before viewing a violent television program are more likely to exhibit aggressive responses after seeing the program than are viewers who are not provoked (Berkowitz, 1962; Hartmann, 1969); anger functions as a contributory condition.

Similar contingent and/or contributory third variables operate during exposure. For example, it appears that *Sesame Street's* initial effectiveness as a teacher was conditioned by parents' comments during their children's exposure to the program, although there remains some question about whether such "encouragement" served to contribute to the amount of learning (Ball and Bogatz, 1970), or whether gains in knowledge were contingent on the parental encouragement (Cook *et al.,* 1975).

Postexposure conditions also influence the exposure/effect relationship. For example, exposure to the Carter-Ford television debates mediated interpersonal political discussion that subsequently contributed to such other political effects as candidate choice and decision to vote (McLeod, Durall, Ziemke and Bybee, 1979). Similarly, decisions regarding the "winner" of each debate were contingent on the viewers reading post-debate newspaper evaluations of the encounters (Lang and Lang, 1979). Both findings are notable for their reasonableness and for the rarity of their approach. Indeed, the relative lack of attention to postexposure conditions and delayed consequences in studies of the effects of mass communication is surprising given diffusion research's history of concern with third variables intervening between communication of knowledge about an innovation and peoples' decisions to adopt or reject it (Rogers, 1983).

A second way of organizing conditioning variables is to classify them in terms of where they occur: (1) in the person processing the stimulus, (2) in the stimulus itself, or (3) in the environment (Comstock *et al.,* 1978). Person-related factors include an individual's level of cognitive development, intelligence, life-cycle position, personality, sex, race, and mood. Stimulus-related factors include media and channels; message structure, content, and elements; source characteristics; and so on. Environmental factors include conditions external to the stimulus and the individual that operate either during exposure (e.g., distractions that impede attention) or after exposure (e.g., the degree to which a subsequent behavioral setting reflects conditions presented in the message). Of course, these "locations" are not totally independent. Environmental variables certainly influence person-related variables, and conditions in the media influence both the environment and the people who inhabit it.

A third scheme for elaborating variations in people's responses to mass communication(s) can be generalized from McGuire's (1969, 1973) information-processing approach to persuasion. He posited six processing behaviors between message input and behavioral output: exposure, attention, comprehension, yielding, retention, and behavior. When yielding is changed to a term such as "acceptance" to avoid the implication of giving up an established position, this sequence is as relevant to informational, educational, and entertainment messages as it is to persuasion. The model has served to sensitize researchers to various possible interactions that changes in message elements or receiver characteristics or environmental conditions might engender (e.g., a change in message format designed to facilitate comprehension might at the same time inhibit attention). Later versions of this sequence include additional steps (McGuire, 1981), and there is some question about whether the order is invariant. Nevertheless, for present purposes, the sequence is useful in that it serves to focus attention on the many operations and transformations to which messages are subjected if and when exposure is achieved.

The preceding three approaches can be seen as concerned with *when* a condition operates (before, during, or after exposure), with *where* it is located (within the person, the communication stimulus, or the environment), and with *what* it affects (any or all information-processing stages). To the extent that these represent generally independent dimensions, they can be combined into a larger organizational framework.

McGuire (1969, 1973) presented his information-processing sequence as column headings in a "persuasive communication matrix," the rows of which consisted of five "components" of the communication process: source, message, channel, receiver, destination. His purpose was both to organize a large, diffuse literature and to provide a framework for considering how the components might interact with the processing steps to influence outcomes. For our purposes, McGuire's communication components can be subsumed under the classification scheme that categorizes conditioning variables on the basis of their location as person-, stimulus-, or

environment-related. When these locations are crossed with the information-processing steps, a table of possible condition by process relationships that could influence mass communication effects is obtained. In addition, since McLeod and Reeves' (1980) temporal approach to third-variable conditions is generally independent of the "location" classification (Comstock *et al.,* 1978) an important third dimension can be added, resulting in the matrix presented in Fig. 1. In this view, a "condition" contributing to or controlling the relationship between message input and behavioral output inhabits one of the three general locations (the person, the stimulus, the environment), functions in a temporal relationship with exposure (before, during, or after), and operates on one or more of the "activities" in the information-processing sequence.

If, for example, we were interested in the effect of exposure to television violence on subsequent behavior, the outcome might well be a condition of whether and when the viewer is angered. That is, the level of anger (a person-related condition) might influence exposure (and possibly attention) if the person experienced this emotion prior to entering the communication situation. However, if anger was experienced during exposure, the level of

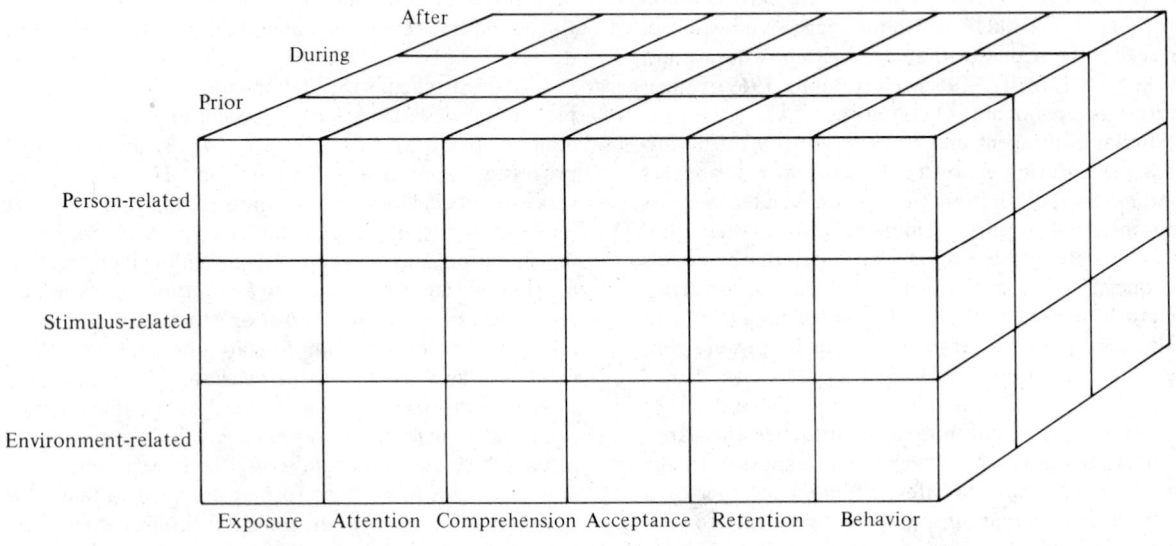

FIGURE 1
Dimensions of Variables Conditioning the Effects of Mass Communication

anger is likely to operate on attention and/or comprehension; if anger was experienced subsequent to exposure, it could affect recall and behavior. Failure to think in terms of at least these dimensions could result in failure either to note some conditional effects or to understand the nature of the effects that are obtained.

PATTERNS OF MEDIA USE

In 1977, U.S. consumers spent over 38 billion dollars on mass communications (McCombs and Eyal, 1980). Although the categories used to define mass media are rather unclear, Bureau of the Census (1981) data indicate that since 1960, Americans have spent between 43 percent and 45 percent of all leisure dollars on mass media of one type or another (Peterson, 1981).

Similar aggregate statistics reveal large expenditures of time on media. In 1971, average per household radio use approached three hours; in 1975, over 45 percent of adults reported reading a newspaper every day, and in 1976, the average television set was operating 6.8 hours per day (Comstock *et al.,* 1978).

It is important to note that this last figure is an average; many households report having the television operating for even longer periods of time. Medrich *et al.,* (1982) classified over 35 percent of a sample of California families as "constant television" households, in which the set was operating "most of the afternoon, during dinner, and most of the evening"; and over 25 percent of a national sample of mothers reported that their television set was operating at least nine hours per day (Newspaper Advertising Bureau, 1978). Of course, the time the television set is operating is not synonymous with individual amounts of viewing; however, when an operating television set is a constant feature of the environment, individuals tend to watch it (Medrich, 1979). Estimates of average hours of television viewing by adults vary between two and three hours per day, depending on how and when the question is asked (Newspaper Advertising Bureau, 1980c; Bower, 1973; Sahin and Robinson, 1981).

Although such aggregate statistics are interesting, they do not begin to characterize the important dimensions that will help us to understand media use. More interesting are the variations subsumed by those summaries, variations both within the population and across time. Most work on predictors of exposure to mass media, then, tends to focus on various environmental, social, and psychological conditions that operate to influence the availability and the accessibility of types of media and types of content and the skills, interests, and needs that shape people's use of media.

TELEVISION

Television is the dominant medium in the United States. Its use has increased steadily since the 1960s. Between 1963 and 1976, the time the television set was operating in all U.S. households increased from 5.8 to 6.8 hours per day (Comstock *et al.,* 1978), a trend strongly correlated with a concomitant increase in the amount of available leisure time, almost all of which appears to have been devoted to viewing television (Peterson, 1981; Robinson, 1977; Sahin and Robinson, 1981). The trend over the past four or five years is less clear (Peterson, 1981), although the increase in viewing appears to be diminishing.

Of course, different segments of the audience differ greatly in amount of television use. Recent surveys and summaries tend to agree that most of the same demographic patterns that existed a decade or two ago continued to hold both in the United States (Bower, 1973; Chaffee and Wilson, 1975; Comstock *et al.,* 1978; Greenberg and Dervin, 1970; LoScuito, 1972; Lyle, 1972; Lyle and Hoffman, 1972a; Medrich *et al.,* 1982; Newspaper Advertising Bureau, 1978, 1980a, 1980c; Robinson, 1969, 1979; Schramm, 1971a; Steiner, 1963) and internationally (Murray and Kippax, 1979; Robinson, 1972). For example, women continue to view more television than do men; children and retirees view more television than do adolescents and working adults; viewing is negatively related to education, income, and occupational status.

However, more important than the persistence of the same general television-use patterns is the fact that differences between demographic groups are no longer as distinct as they once were. Neilsen data reveal that between 1970 and 1976, there was an overall increase of 18 minutes in the time the set was operating in U.S. households, from 6.5 to 6.8 hours per day. However, within homes in which the head of the household had less than one year of college education, the increase was only 12 minutes (from 6.8 to 7.0 hours), while in homes with the head of household reporting more than one year of college, the increase was almost 48 minutes (from 5.6 to just under 6.4 hours [Comstock *et al.,* 1978]). These results continue a trend reported for the 1960s by Bower (1973). Similarly, Robinson's analysis (1977, 1979) of two time-use studies from 1965 to 1966 and 1975 to 1976 finds a reduction in the differences between groups in viewing time not only on such indexes as educational level but also income, occupational status, and gender. Indeed, in a reversal of the typical finding that women watch more television than men, Sahin and Robinson (1981) found that when only those men and women in the paid labor force are compared, men watch much more television than do women (131 minutes versus 99 minutes per day). These authors characterize the trend in television use over the 1970s as moving "in the direction of levelling of past differences and convergence towards truly *mass* viewing" (p. 91).

Age, because it is one of the better predictors of differential abilities, needs, interests, and particularly available time, is strongly related to television use. Unfortunately, national samples that represent children in narrow enough age categories to be helpful are rare. Although the Neilsen sample includes children, it reports results for just two groups: those children ages two through eleven years and teenagers ages twelve through seventeen years (it is possible, however, to break out figures for children ages two to five years and six to eleven years). One recent survey reports a national probability sample of television viewing for children ranging in age from six to seventeen years in three-year categories (Newspaper Advertising Bureau, 1978; 1980a, 1980b, 1980c). More common, however, are scattered, small-scale studies conducted for different purposes, using different sampling, measurement, and reporting procedures. Not surprisingly, there is a good deal of variance in the findings.

From one point of view, variations across studies are frustrating because they produce confusion about precisely how much television the average child watches. However, such variations can also be a strength. Taken together, the studies include children manifesting almost all the demographic and psychological characteristics one might want to employ to describe patterns of media use, and they offer an opportunity to examine where different studies converge. To the extent that at any given age, the "average" viewer is an elusive creature at best, it is possible to synthesize results from many small studies to construct a composite picture of television use through the first twenty years of life (Comstock *et al.,* 1978). The result, shown in Fig. 2, reveals that purposive television viewing begins between ages two and three years (Anderson *et al.,* 1979; von Feilitzen, 1976), rises sharply to about the time children begin school (ages five to six

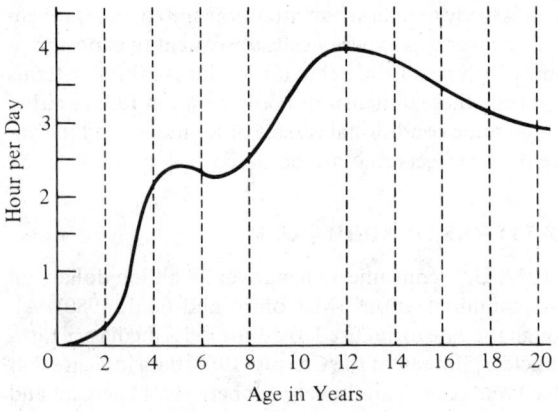

FIGURE 2
Constructed Curve of Average Hours of Daily Television Viewing during the First Twenty Years of Life
SOURCE: G. Comstock, S. Chaffee, N. Katzman, M. McCombs and Donald Roberts, *Television and Human Behavior* (New York: Columbia University Press, 1978). Copyright © 1978 by The Rand Corporation. Used by permission.

years) and then drops off somewhat. Viewing then continues to grow again at a rapid rate until about the time children change from elementary to junior high school (approximately twelve years of age), after which it decreases steadily to a low point near the end of adolescence. Studies of adults indicate that time spent viewing television increases slightly but remains relatively low during the early adult years, begins to climb gradually during later adulthood, and then moves rapidly toward its high point among men and women ages sixty years and older, the age group that views the most television (Atkin, 1976; Bower, 1973; Chaffee and Wilson, 1975; Comstock, 1978; Schramm, 1971a).

The relationships between age and amount of television viewing are tied to time demands from competing activities characteristic of different life-cycle stages. The decrease in viewing at the beginning of both elementary school and junior high school occurs when the demands of school and related social activities begin to compete for the child's time. The increase in viewing across the elementary-school years coincides with the steady erosion of bed times typical of late childhood. Reduced viewing among adolescents and young adults parallels increases in social activities, work, and family demands. And clearly, the dramatic increase in all media use at the oldest end of the age distribution marks a period when household demands subside and when retirement provides time to view television, listen to the radio, and read. Available time also explains some of the demographic differences noted earlier (Bower, 1973). For example, lower levels of television viewing among well-educated people and/or those of higher socioeconomic status (SES) tend to be a result of greater competing demands on the time of these particular demographic groups (Samuelson, Carter and Ruggels, 1963), and available time explains sex differences in television viewing by adults (Comstock *et al.,* 1978). Indeed, Sahin and Robinson's (1981) finding that employed women view less television than employed men confirms this explanation in that a women's entry into the paid labor force does not appear to relieve her of more traditional, time-consuming household activities.

Variations within age groups (or, for that matter, within any category used to describe viewing patterns) are also instructive. For example, in one sample of kindergarten and first-grade black boys, television viewing ranged from five to forty-two hours per week (Murray, 1972). Over 25 percent of a sample of sixth graders reported no television viewing on a given weekday, while another 25 percent reported over 5.5 hours of viewing on that same day (Lyle and Hoffman, 1972); nineteen-year-olds varied in their estimates of daily viewing from zero to over three hours per day (Robinson and Bachman, 1972). These are not random variations. Comstock and his colleagues' (1978) review finds that television viewing among children is negatively related to such factors as IQ, school grades, creativity, and family socioeconomic status. However, they also point out that these relationships interact with age. Many of them do not begin to appear until the child is old enough for a particular variable to make a difference. That is, although studies of adolescents consistently find a negative relationship between IQ scores or grades and the amount of television viewing, (Himmelweit, Oppenheim and Vince, 1958; Himmelweit and Swift, 1976; Lyle and Hoffman, 1972a; McLeod, Atkin and Chaffee, 1972a; Schramm, Lyle and Parker, 1961), these studies and others (Childers and Ross, 1973) find little or no relationship among younger children. Some of the brightest younger children are among the heaviest viewers of television (and among the heavier readers and radio listeners, etc.; Schramm, Lyle and Parker, 1961). The effect of parental socioeconomic status depends on age, probably because the competing activities and resources that increased socioeconomic status makes available are not really relevant to younger children. Children must be old enough to attend summer camp or take dancing lessons before the availability of these resources to provide competing experiences to television viewing makes a difference.

There is also evidence that, across age levels, both blacks and Spanish surname groups view more television than do whites, even when socioeconomic-status controls are applied (Greenberg and Dervin, 1970; Lyle and Hoffman, 1972a; McIntyre and Teevan, 1972). There is, however, reason to approach these results with caution. Allen and Bielby (1979) demonstrate wide variations in media behavior among blacks and warn against conceiving of them as a homogenous subpopulation or of expecting their media behavior to parallel that of whites. Indeed, patterns of media use within the black population depart rather sharply from expectations based on white samples. For example, younger black adults view more television than do older blacks, and better educated blacks spend more time viewing television than do their lesser educated counterparts (Comstock *et al.,* 1978). Moreover, studies attempting to equate the socioeconomic status black and white children's families on the basis of occupational status have encountered difficulty establishing the same criterion for the two groups, particularly at higher levels. Failure to find enough black families at the higher levels has necessitated lowering the criterion for the black sample (e.g., Greenberg and Dervin, 1970), thus calling comparisons into question. Moreover, occupational classifications are established on the basis of the "main wage earner." To the extent that the likelihood of this person being a father, mother, or someone else differs across racial or ethnic groups, even identical occupational criteria do not ensure comparable socioeconomic-status groupings. Finally, at an even more fundamental level, we can ask whether a college education or the attainment of middle-income status identifies the same environments, opportunities, and experiences for blacks as for whites. If our suspicion that they may not is correct, then to the extent that socioeconomic-status measures are simply a way of describing environments, any single socioeconomic-status index is inappropriate for equating blacks and whites in the United States.

PRINT MEDIA

Many of the same variables that predict television use also predict print use, although often the direction of the relationships is reversed. Print use is directly related to age, appearing early in the elementary-school years and continuing to increase across the life span (Newspaper Advertising Bureau, 1978; Robinson and Jeffres, 1979). Daily newspaper reading is positively and strongly related to income and education; whites tend to use more print media than do blacks; there is less availability of newspapers in households with younger children and in single-parent households (Newspaper Advertising Bureau, 1978; Robinson and Jeffres, 1979).

However, recent evidence also suggests that although many of the same patterns that described newspaper-reading habits some years ago still hold, overall there is a very large, very real decline in newspaper readership. Robinson and Jeffres (1979; Robinson, 1980) report that the proportion of adults claiming to read a newspaper daily dropped from 73 percent in 1967, to 66 percent in 1975, and to 57 percent in 1978. They also found that over 85 percent of respondents over sixty years old report "using a newspaper yesterday" as compared to just 51 percent of adults under twenty-nine years old. Particularly disturbing is that these findings reveal an increase in the age differences found a decade earlier. That is, there is a strong trend toward decreasing newspaper readership across age cohorts. Hence, younger adults who do not have the newspaper-reading habit are less likely than they formerly were to develop it as they grow older (Jennings and Niemi, 1973; Robinson and Jeffres, 1979). Moreover, there is a parallel trend for each succeeding generation to be more likely than its predecessor to express a preference for television over the newspaper as its primary news source (Roper Organization, 1977).

Various factors have been offered to explain this trend. Such sociological phenomena as a decline in home ownership, an increase in single-person households, an increase of women in the labor force, the fractionation of the city, and changes in amounts of available time, all of which are negatively related to newspaper reading, have been cited (Bogart, 1975b; Denbow, 1975; Robinson and Jeffres, 1979). Similarly, Stamm and Fortini-Campbell (1977) note strong, positive correlations between people's sense of belonging to a community and newspaper relationship, a finding that leads to speculation about the role of geographic mobility. On the psychological side, various civic attitudes, "traditional" values, and "satisfaction with life" have also been implicated (Bryant, *et al.,* 1976; McCombs and Poindexter, 1978). And finally, Bogart (1975a) points out that the increase in viewing of television news has moved hand in hand with an increase in the amount of television news programming available. Whatever the source of the move away from print news

and toward television, the findings take on a somewhat ominous import in light of evidence, to be discussed later, that knowledge about government and current affairs tends to be much more strongly related to newspaper reading than to television news viewing.

The future of print may not be as bleak as the decline in newspaper readership makes it seem, however. Although the introduction of television displaced some kinds of print, it had little effect on others (Parker, 1963a, 1963b); in view of the burgeoning circulation figures of nonfiction, special interest books and magazines, television appears to have benefited some kinds of reading. Indeed, consumer expenditures for all print materials have remained relatively constant, and "the long range trend in public support for print media has continued undisturbed" (McCombs and Eyal, 1980; p. 158). Robinson (1980) reports a moderate increase in the reading of magazines and books over the past decade or so. And for those of us who, for whatever reason, cling to a faith in the importance of print, it is encouraging to note that younger generations report larger gains in exposure to books and magazines (Robinson, 1980), a finding that parallels the increase in the proportion of younger respondents saying that they prefer magazines over television as a source of political information (Jennings and Niemi, 1975). The emerging cable-television and home-computer technologies will undoubtedly continue to influence both the video/print mix and the within-print mix of materials (newspapers, magazines, books, computer display copy). However, we suspect that the use of print media and reading activities are likely to continue at a relatively constant level.

USES AND GRATIFICATIONS OF MASS MEDIA

Uses and gratifications research, because of its concern with how people use media and the gratifications they expect to gain from such use, is often viewed as centered on the audience. Studies in this tradition are typically characterized as asking what people do with the media as opposed to what the media do to people. However, a more complete description (Katz, Blumer and Gurevitch, 1974, p. 20) of the uses and gratifications tradition summarizes it as

> concerned with (1) the social and psychological origins of (2) needs, which generate (3) expectations of (4) the mass media or other sources, which lead to (5)

differential patterns of media exposure (or engagement in other activities), resulting in (6) need gratifications and (7) other consequences, perhaps mostly unintended ones.

The uses and gratifications approach has recently engendered a remarkable amount of theoretical debate and empirical research. Although claims that uses and gratifications research has become the most important and popular approach to studies of mass communication are a bit strong (Swanson, 1979a, 1979b), it is clear that this approach "is well and truly launched on a third major phase of its development..." (Blumler and Katz, 1974). Blumler and Katz characterize the first phase, through the 1940s and 1950s, as devoted mainly to describing the orientations to the different forms of the content of various subgroups of the audience (e.g., Herzog, 1944; Wolfe and Fiske, 1949). The second phase, through the 1960s, shifted emphasis to operationalizing the psychosocial needs presumed to lead to different patterns of media use (e.g., Katz and Foulkes, 1972; Katz, Gurevitch and Haas, 1973; McQuail, Blumler and Brown, 1972). Finally, the current (third) phase is primarily explanatory. It attempts to link gratifications data to other variables in the communication process with which audience expectations and motivations might be connected (e.g., Becker, 1976; Blumler and McQuail, 1969; Kline, Miller and Morrison, 1974; McLeod and Becker, 1974, 1981). Although descriptive and operational studies continue (Frank and Greenberg, 1980), work concerned with relating media-use patterns to social and psychosocial needs, and hence to elaborating the relationship between patterns of gratifications sought and obtained and other, "unintended" media effects, is beginning to emerge. Nevertheless, empirical demonstrations of the source of the basic needs presumed to engender media consumption, or of how gratifications constructs condition more "traditional" effects, or even of the manner in which the "active" audience acts (is it at the level of exposure? attention? interpretation?) are more the exception than the rule.

Adults report that they attempt to gratify an extensive list of needs through the mass media, including: affective guidance, alienation, anticipated communication, behavioral guidance, entertainment, escape, excitement, information acquisition, interpretation, knowledge, learning, reassurance, relaxation, self- and personal identity, social contact, social integration, and social parasocial interactions (Becker, 1979; Canadian Broadcasting Corporation, 1975; Frank and Greenberg,

1980; Katz, Gurevitch and Haas, 1973; Kippax and Murray, 1977; Levy, 1977; McLeod and Becker, 1974; Nordlund, 1978; Peled and Katz, 1974; Wenner, 1977). Studies of children's and adolescents' reasons for using different media (Bachen *et al.*, 1982; Brown *et al.*, 1974; Greenberg, 1974; Johnstone, 1974; Lometti, Reeves and Bybee, 1977; Rubin, 1979; von Feilitzen, 1976) as well as those of elderly respondents (Danowski, 1975; Werner, 1976) report similar lists of needs.

Such a profusion of needs is probably more the result of the looseness of the needs definition that Swanson (1977) criticizes than the result of any real proliferation of needs. Murray and Kippax (1979), for example, surveyed cross-national studies and found that four basic clusters of needs emerged: self and personal identity, social contact, diversion and entertainment, and information and knowledge about the world. Similarly, Blumler (1979) argues for a reduction to three need categories: cognitive, diversion, and personal. In either case, almost all of the needs listed previously easily fit into the reduced categories. And, regardless of whether one settles on three, four, or even more clusters of orientations, there is a high degree of similarity across various lists, a convergence that Katz (1979) finds convincing for the very reason that it emerges from such diversity.

Looseness of terminology is also apparent at a slightly higher conceptual level, since the majority of studies tend to support Swanson's (1977, 1979a) contention that such central constructs as "use," "gratification," "function," "need," and "motive" are infrequently defined, let alone fully explicated. Similarly, there appears to be a good deal of variance in the idea of the "active" audience (Blumler, 1979; Elliot, 1974). Usually activity has referred to selective exposure or attention (Katz, 1979). Swanson (1979b), however, argues that activity should be defined as an interpretational act, occurring during the assignment of meaning rendering the typical strategy of relating exposure or attentional patterns to gratifications inappropriate to the demonstration of an active audience. There is also a tendency to ignore the possibility that activity, at whatever level it occurs, may vary across time and media; thus it may be better conceptualized as a continuum than as an either/or matter (Blumler, 1979). Problems in the approach's concentration on the individual as system as opposed to the individual within system are also emphasized. Messaris (1977) describes the uses and gratifications approach as a strategy that "seems to have blinded researchers to many aspects of the intricate chain of interrelations by which an individual's interaction with the mass media is linked to the imperatives of a social system'' (p. 317). Uses and gratifications research is also taken to task for failing to provide systematic linkages between media gratifications and their social and psychological origins (Katz *et al.,* 1974; Levy, 1977). The reasons are twofold: Its ''atheoretical'' nature makes it more a research strategy than a theory (Becker, 1979; Elliott, 1974; Swanson, 1977; Weiss, 1976) and as a functional theory, it is fraught with tautological shortcomings (Anderson and Meyer, 1975; Carey and Kreiling, 1974; Elliot, 1974).

Finally, various writers (Becker, 1979, Elliott, 1974; Messaris, 1977) question the approach because of its reliance on self-report data. They argue that the strategy of asking people to state why they select the media and content they do and of taking those responses at face value assumes a high degree of individual self-awareness. Such a procedure not only risks eliciting stereotyped beliefs and conventional responses in its implicit expectation of a level of awareness and an analytical ability that respondents simply may not have but also forces people to treat all media exposure as a result of deliberate choice. Thus such other factors as habit, social expectations, and causal encounters are ignored. The self-report method also is subject to distortion because of its retrospective nature. Finally, it provides no independent method for validating either the existence or the importance of respondent-identified needs.

Although much of this criticism is deserved, many of the issues raised by these critiques have begun to be addressed, some by the critics themselves (Katz, 1979). For example, Becker (1979; McLeod and Becker 1981), reports on three distinct strategies to measure audience motives—inference, self-report, and manipulation—thus making a significant step toward validation of gratifications measures. Other studies concerned with the validation issue as well as with examining the idea of motives for avoiding mass communications (i.e., reasons for not viewing, not reading, not listening) also have begun to appear (Blumler, 1979; Levy, 1977; McLeod and Becker, 1974). Evidence of the validity of the uses and gratifications approach is also implicit in work testing the assumption that people do differentiate among channels and content on the basis of expected gratifications and that different needs or motives are indeed satisfied by different media (Adoni, 1979; Lometti, Reeves and Bybee, 1977; Stroman and Becker, 1978). Work concerning gratifications sought versus gratifications received as independent dimensions also addresses validity and methodological questions. To the extent that people's re-

ports of motives for selecting various media are simply reflections of what they get, independent measures of gratifications sought and received should be highly correlated and manifest almost identical factor structures. However, several studies that have obtained independent measures of these dimensions report that these dimensions are by no means synonymous, findings that argue against the teleological criticism that any gratification sought must be obtained (McLeod and Becker, 1981; Palmgreen and Rayburn, 1979; Palmgreen, Wenner and Rayburn, 1980). Finally studies attempting to support the active-audience assumption by examining evidence for linkages between gratifications sought (or avoidances) and various traditional ''effects'' are beginning to appear. Although most of this research tends to focus on ''political effects'' (e.g., political information and attitudes, perceptions of issue salience) (Becker, 1976; McLeod and Becker, 1974; McLeod, Becker and Byrnes, 1974; McLeod *et al.,* 1977), at least one study has examined reading achievement as a function of children's motives for viewing television and for reading (Bachen *et al.,* 1982).

A concern with political issues dominates the current literature on the uses and gratifications of mass media. That is, contrary to early studies that examined people's uses of entertainment content (Herzog, 1944; Suchman, 1942; Warner and Henry, 1948; Wolf and Fiske, 1949), the focus of current studies is decidedly cognitive and instrumental. Current uses and gratifications researchers tend to concentrate on the utilitarian, informational aspects of media consumption. Studies are conducted in the context of political campaigns (Blumler and McQuail, 1969; Becker, 1979), news (Levy, 1977, 1978), political scandals (Becker, 1976), and wars (Dotan and Cohen, 1976). Adolescents are asked about political values (Adoni, 1979) or about such obviously instrumental issues as family planning (Kline *et al.,* 1974). Examination of the match between gratifications sought and received occurs in the context of public television, a decidedly informational medium (Palmgreen and Rayburn, 1979). This tendency is worth noting because most media time is devoted to television, and most television viewing is in the service of entertainment and/or escape (Comstock *et al.,* 1978; Gans, 1980; Tannenbaum, 1980). Of course, even studies of news programs generate mention of such motives as diversion, entertainment, and escape. Nevertheless, it is remarkable that such central functions of contemporary mass communications as these currently receive so little attention from uses and gratifications researchers. It is ironical that a strategy developed to examine what people do with media has almost closed its eyes, or at least its questionnaires, to the kinds of entertainment content that most people use most of the time.

COGNITIVE EFFECTS

THE ACQUISITION OF INFORMATION AND KNOWLEDGE

A common theme of theories concerned with eliciting or influencing behavior is that a necessary precursor to behavior is the acquisition of cognitions about how to act and about the conditions under which given behaviors are or are not appropriate (Bandura, 1977; Rogers, 1983; Schank and Abelson, 1977). Thus, regardless of whether the interest is in how the media effect emotions, attitudes, or behavior, basically any influence of mass communication on people originates with the questions of whether and how they interpret and incorporate mass-mediated information into their existing conceptualizations of the world (Roberts, 1971). This incorporation of such cognitions we consider to be learning, the basic effect.

Given that in Western societies the primary role of the news media is to inform the public (Becker, McCombs and McLeod, 1975; Halberstam, 1979; Rivers *et al.,* 1980; Siebert, Peterson and Schramm, 1956), it is not surprising that most research on the media's ability to transmit information is conducted in the context of news and public-affairs content. However, with the appearance of such "educational" television programs as *Sesame Street* (Ball and Bogatz, 1970) and *Feeling Good* (Mielke and Swinehart, 1976) and of programs that concern neither current events nor totally educational matters but that certainly transmit information (e.g., the *CBS National Citizenship Quiz,* Alper and Leidy, 1970), evidence about information acquisition from nonnews content is also beginning to appear.

People perceive themselves as acquiring information from the mass media. When asked where they received most of their information about "what's going on in the world," over 95 percent of a national sample of adults responded in terms of the mass media (Roper Organization, 1977). Early reports that children seldom attend to news and public affairs (Lyle and Hoffman, 1972; Schramm *et al.,* 1961) have given way to evidence

that even relatively young children are exposed to news media in growing numbers, whether or not they actually pay attention to them (Atkin, 1978; Egan, 1978; Hawkins, Pingree and Roberts, 1975; Prisuta, 1979; Rubin, 1978; Tolley, 1973). And when asked where they received their information about current events, children ranging from age seven years upward gave the lion's share of the nominations to mass media (Atkins and Elwood, 1978; Chaffee, Jackson-Beeck, Durall and Wilson, 1977; Egan, 1978; Hollander, 1971; Newspaper Advertising Bureau 1982a; Tolley, 1973), although at least one study found that they at the same time voiced skepticism about the wisdom of such a choice (Rubin, 1976).

The typical procedure for testing people's reports that they learn from exposure to news and public-affairs media is to relate news exposure to scores on knowledge tests, usually composed of questions about current political events or figures (e.g., Who is governor of our state?) and/or slightly more general kinds of knowledge (e.g., What is the legal voting age in this state?). Recent work continues to replicate the findings of earlier studies (reviewed in Becker *et al.,* 1975; Kraus and Davis, 1976) in which moderately positive relationships between the use of public-affairs media and scores on knowledge tests consistently emerged. Such results have been obtained with various U.S. samples (Atkin *et al.,* 1976; Atkin and Heald, 1976; Becker and Whitney, 1980; Chaffee and Tims, 1982; Patterson and McClure, 1976; Palmgreen, 1979; Quarles, 1979) and with adults in other countries (Chaffee and Izcaray, 1975; Feigert, 1976). Positive correlations between exposure to the content of public-affairs media and knowledge scores have also been found with children (Atkin, 1977; Atkin and Gantz, 1978; Comstock *et al.,* 1978; Conway, Stevens and Smith, 1975; Tolley, 1973) and adolescents (Chaffee and Tims, 1982; Chaffee, Ward and Tipton, 1970; Rubin, 1978; Tan and Vaughn, 1976), although several studies report negative relationships (Chaffee *et al.,* 1977; Jackson-Beeck, 1979). Usually the exposure/knowledge relationship has withstood controls for education, although such controls generally reduce the relationship. Indeed, in many cases education alone is a stronger predictor of knowledge than is media use (Tichenor, Donahue and Olien, 1970; Wade and Schramm, 1969).

Clarke and Kline (1974) call for new approaches to the measurement of both media exposure and knowledge of public affairs, arguing that it is premature to accept the conventional wisdom that education is more important to the acquisition of knowledge about current affairs than is exposure to the news media. They contend that the typical knowledge test is normative, intrusive, and based on the kinds of "textbook" information that fascinates educators and researchers but that is probably not at all relevant to the public. Although researchers may be interested in the identity of office holders or of sanctioned viewpoints, members of various publics are probably more attuned to information about such things as contamination of a local drinking water supply or layoffs in a local industry. Clarke and Kline deal with this discrepancy by developing measures of "information holding" that they view as more audience centered because the important "issues" are audience generated. An "information-holding" score is obtained simply by asking respondents to identify what they perceive to be the major problems facing a particular political jurisdiction (city, state, country) and then probing whether respondents are aware of any solutions that have been advanced to deal with the issue and whether they know of groups or persons trying to influence the adoption of the solution(s). They also urge changes in the measurement of exposure (Clarke and Kline, 1974), arguing that typical measures of frequency of exposure are several steps removed from perception of relevant symbols—relevant, that is, to particular current-events issues. As an antidote to this gap, they propose a measure of "message discrimination" based on asking people whether they have recently read, heard, or seen anything about the self-nominated problems and then on obtaining descriptions of the channel and content of these "discriminated" messages.

Several studies using these more audience-centered measures of information holding and message discrimination have begun to appear in the literature. Generally, their results replicate those obtained by studies relating conventional measures of exposure to knowledge indexes, revealing positive relationships between discrimination and information as indicated by information-holding scores (Becker, Sobowale, and Casey, 1979a; Clarke and Fredin, 1978; Clarke and Kline, 1974; Edelstein, 1974; Palmgreen, Kline, and Clarke, 1974). Under some conditions, message discrimination has been found to be more strongly related to information holding than is either the amount of use of public-affairs media (Palmgreen, 1979) or education (Clarke and Kline, 1974).

One of the strongest impressions derived from the literature on information acquisition from the media is

that the term "media" is far too general. Indeed, common use of "media" as a singular noun (e.g., The media is biased!) reveals not only poor grammar but also poor thinking because it places radio, television, newspapers, magazines, and books together into some kind of monolith, all parts of which operate in the same way. If all media were the same, it would not matter whether people used television, print, or radio to acquire information. However, the data indicate that it matters very much which medium is used.

Contrary to popular conceptions that television has become the dominant information source, research comparing public-affairs print use versus television use as predictors of public-affairs knowledge find a stronger relationship between print use and information level than between television use and information. Although modest positive relationships between television news or exposure to public-affairs programs and knowledge levels are not unknown (Atkin, Galloway and Nayman, 1976; Atkin and Heald, 1976), most studies give the nod to print, with the television relationship often hovering near zero (Becker *et al.,* 1979b; Becker and Whitney, 1980; Clarke and Fredin, 1978; Quarles, 1979; Patterson and McClure, 1976; Tan and Vaughn, 1976; Wade and Schramm, 1969). It is often stated that most people receive most of their information from television news (Roper Organization, 1977), and this may well be true. However it appears to be more a statement about low levels of public information than about either the power of television to inform or the characteristics of that part of the public most dependent on television. And it is also worth noting that additional studies find television dependency to be related to political cynicism, feelings of inefficacy, misperceptions of candidate strength, and negative attitudes toward the government (Becker and Whitney, 1980; Robinson, 1974, 1975, 1976). Although these are, of course, correlational findings, they are nevertheless disturbing because of the evidence reviewed earlier showing a decline in regular newspaper use with each succeeding generation and a parallel increase in reported dependence on television for public-affairs information.

This is not to say that television is powerless to provide people with current-events information. Several studies of television documentaries have demonstrated that people who view television learn a good deal. Fitzsimmons and Osburn (1968) showed college students one of five network documentaries dealing with various public-affairs topics (e.g., birth control, migrant workers, automation), and found significant gains in information. Alper and Leidy (1970) measured teenagers' knowledge of the U.S. constitution a month before and a week after the initial broadcast of the *CBS National Citizenship Quiz* and then compared scores of viewers and nonviewers. They controlled for differences due to audience self-selection by including items dealing with information not contained in the program. There were no prebroadcast differences in the scores produced by the two samples, and there were no postbroadcast differences on the control items. On questions about information covered in the program, however, viewers did substantially better than nonviewers. Although this design does not rule out the possibility that those most likely to learn deliberately chose the program, it clearly shows that those who did view the program did learn from it. A number of other studies that have tailored knowledge measures to parallel television content report similar findings. For example, exposure to televised political commercials is related to increased information about candidates and their stands on particular issues (Atkin and Heald, 1976; Patterson and McClure, 1976). Similarly, studies of televised political debates demonstrate that when viewers and nonviewers are compared in terms of their information about candidates, differences between them, and their stands on various issues, viewers score higher than do nonviewers (Bishop, Oldendick and Tuchfarber, 1978; Dennis, Chaffee and Choe, 1979; Miller and McKuen, 1979; Wald and Lupfer, 1978). Several extensive reviews of the effects of the presidential debates are available (Chaffee, 1978; Chaffee and Dennis, 1979; Kraus, 1962, 1979; Sears and Chaffee, 1979).

The finding that learning from the public-affairs content of television is demonstrable with instruments tailored to that medium points to the most common explanation of the "superior" power of the use of print to predict knowledge levels, namely, that differences in learning derive from differences between the media in format and content. It is argued that television's search for exciting visuals leads to a focus on action, events, and peripheral aspects of the news rather than on issues and policies (Carey, 1976; Hofstetter and Zukin, 1979; Robinson, 1975). Patterson and McClure (1976) write: "Network news may be fascinating. It may be highly entertaining. But it is simply not informative" (p. 54). It is difficult not to agree that television emphasizes action over issues. However, it is also important to note that simple differences in time and space dictate that less material can be covered in a single news program than in an issue of a daily paper. A related explanation argues that our educational system still reflects norms and expectations developed prior to the advent of broadcasting and thus still trains people to deal with print when seeking information. This statement implies that differences in the predictive power of the two media simply reflect differences in training (Becker and Whitney, 1980). However, the results of at least one experiment indicate that literate adults acquire more information from television news than do nonreaders, a finding suggesting that the skills necessary for reading may also enhance ones ability to decode audiovisual information (Stauffer, Frost and Rybolt, 1978). An equally plausible explanation is that the readers' superior previous knowledge enables them to obtain more from the newscasts.

It appears, then, that people who depend on television news obtain a fragmented view of the world that mediates against their acquisition of substantive current-events information. There is, of course, a clear-cut value judgment in such a position—one arguing that the information the print media present is somehow more substantive, more important, than that which television presents. We suspect that most academicians (who, after all, construct most of the knowledge tests) tend to place a high value on print media and the kinds of information they provide. Evaluation of this literature should be tempered with this fact in mind. Nevertheless, we also point out that as eminent a representative of television news as Walter Cronkite has often stated that one cannot understand the issues of the day by relying on television alone, if for no other reason than the amount of content in a television-news program cannot match that in a daily paper.

The relationship between the medium used and the information level generated is influenced by a number of conditioning variables, most of which operate independently of whether attention focuses on print or television and many of which also interact with the type of medium. Not only do more obvious demographic variables such as age and education affect the relationship between the use of public-affairs media and information levels but also so too do such social-psychological factors as interest in politics, motivations for using the news media, degree of black nationalism, group membership, and the number of similarly oriented peers and discussion partners (Atkin *et al.,* 1976; Chaffee and Iscaray, 1975; Genova and

Greenberg, 1979; Quarles, 1979; Palmgreen, 1979; Tan and Vaughn, 1976). The relationships are not simple, as recent work on the knowledge-gap hypothesis illustrates.

THE KNOWLEDGE-GAP HYPOTHESIS

The knowledge-gap hypothesis was originally formulated in terms of how people of differing socioeconomic status acquire mass-mediated information. It states that people of higher socioeconomic status acquire information from the media at a faster rate than do those of lower socioeconomic status, thus increasing the difference between the two groups in the amount of information held on any issue (Tichenor *et al.,* 1970). Stated thus, the hypothesis does not specify the factors mediating socioeconomic-status differences in the rate of acquisition of knowledge, and it implies that any attempt to use the media to equalize knowledge levels across groups not only will fail but also will increase inequities. However, under certain conditions the media have been shown to reduce information gaps in the undereducated, or at least to benefit them (e.g., Donohue *et al.,* 1975; Maccoby *et al.,* 1977; McLeod *et al.,* 1979; Shingi and Mody, 1976; Tichenor *et al.,* 1973). This evidence points to the need for a careful examination of factors that might mediate variations in the knowledge gap. Moreover, socioeconomic status is only one of several variables that locate differential rates of information acquisition.

Although many factors have been offered to account for the gap phenomenon, they can be reduced to three categories of explanatory mechanisms (Ettema and Kline, 1977):

1. Ceiling effects imposed by the amount or nature of the information of concern (that operate to narrow gaps between groups),

2. Communication deficits within one of the groups under consideration (e.g., lack of communication skills among respondents of lower socioeconomic status),

3. Between-group differences in perceived relevance of, or motivation to acquire, the specific information under study (e.g., socioeconomic status locates different perceptions of the utility of a given kind of information).

Although no direct tests of the three explanations have been published, there is some evidence for each. If we assume that one population subgroup begins with substantially more of the knowledge available on a given topic, then to the extent that the less knowledgeable group continues to acquire information after the more knowledgeable group has obtained it and to the extent that the knowledge criterion does not change, continued presentation of the information will close the gap between the groups (Shingi and Mody, 1976). More often than not, however, criteria do change. Hence, new information is presented, and the lagging group falls even further behind (Katzman, 1974).

Initial differences between groups also underlie one of several deficit explanations of the gap in knowledge. It has been argued that the rate of information acquisition is a function of initial information levels; people who begin with less information must work harder and/or must deal with a more difficult part of the "test" assessing their knowledge. Thus, if no ceiling is encountered, the rich get richer. This explanation is particularly powerful in terms of gaps in resources other than knowledge (e.g., farmers who are economically better off are more able to take advantage of new agricultural technologies that make them even more economically advantaged; Rogers and Adhikarya, 1979). Another deficit explanation looks at differences in information-processing skills located by whatever criterion is used to divide the population. For example, Cook and his colleagues (1975) attribute the more rapid rate of learning from *Sesame Street* displayed by children of higher socioeconomic status to the differences between them and children of lower socioeconomic status in exposure and retentional skills. Similarly, if we divide population groups on the basis of such factors related to socioeconomic status as reading skill or English as a first language, they would exhibit differential rates of knowledge acquisition from the print media or from an English language campaign. These differences are legitimately attributed to "deficits," although not the transituational deficits discussed by Ettama and Kline (1977). Indeed, it seems to us that the debate over transituational deficits somewhat misses the point. Recent changes in conceptualizations of the audience (e.g., Dervin, 1981) argue that to the extent that the mass media attempt to inform the population, the onus of responsibility for failure lies with the source, not with the audience. It appears, then, that many deficits in communication skills can be overcome by the producers and transmitters of information, a point implicit in Sears and Freedman's (1967) discussion of selective exposure, and to which we will return in our consideration of campaigns.

Ettema and Kline (1977) favor a difference explanation for the gap in knowledge. They argue that most studies demonstrating a widening of the knowledge gap were conducted under conditions that can reasonably be expected to reduce the motivation of lower socioeconomic-status groups to seek and retain information. Their findings show that on issues about which there is little controversy, the gap widens (Tichenor *et al.,* 1970) and that on local issues about which community conflict exists the gap narrows (Donohue *et al., 1975*), supporting this explanation. Motivational differences should be overcome when conflict about an issue increases the salience of mass-mediated information and the likelihood of interpersonal discussion among different groups in the community. This interpretation is also supported by evidence that interest is a better predictor of the knowledge gap than is socioeconomic status (Genova and Greenberg, 1979), which leads us to speculate that any condition designed to increase motivation to acquire information will tend to negate an information "gap" effect. A study of "equivalences" in the use of and the responses to the Carter-Ford debates and in communication about the debates adds support to such a difference interpretation (McLeod *et al., 1979*). This study compared groups in terms of "equivalence of exposure" and "equivalence of effects." The results indicate that although less educated, younger, and less interested respondents were less exposed to the debates than were their better educated, older, and more interested counterparts, *per unit of exposure* there was no difference in the amount of information gained by either group. The additional finding that gaps are more likely to occur on measures other than knowledge (involvement, participation in the campaign) points to an important area for further study.

AGENDA SETTING

Although the term "agenda setting" is a relatively new one in mass communication research (McCombs & Shaw, 1972), the idea that the media are especially suited to direct public attention toward particular issues is at least a half-century old (McCombs, 1981). Lippmann's (1922) discussion of the role of the media in the formation of public opinion foreshadows the agenda-setting approach, as does Lazarsfeld and Merton's (1948) "sta-

tus conferral function" of the media. Recent articulation of the agenda-setting idea—that the media are particularly powerful in their ability to influence what the public thinks about as opposed to what to think—has created a lively area of investigation. The popularity of agenda-setting research is partly due to its emergence just as the field was becoming disenchanted with models of direct effects on attitudes and opinions (McCombs, 1981). In addition, any approach that affirms both the power of the media and the independence of the individual seems destined to meet with approval from the research community.

The hypothesis was formulated in terms of aggregate phenomena. It states that the distribution of attention given to issues by the mass media determines the degree to which the public ascribes importance to those issues (McCombs and Shaw, 1972). The causal hypothesis varies from predicting an overlap between media and public agendas with no regard for ordering, to positing similar rankings of issues, to predicting similar weightings of issues across media and public agendas (McCombs, 1977). Regardless of which hypothesis is tested, however, designs that permit causal inferences and that are based on careful measurement of both media and public agendas are necessary. Unfortunately, agenda-setting research has not been very consistent on either count.

Conceptually, "media agenda" refers to those issues that the mass media portray as most important at any time. Issue importance is generally conceived in terms of the amount and the quality of coverage. Operationally, however, a number of decisions that affect the nature of the measured agenda must be made. For example, media agendas have been examined in terms of single or short-term events such as the visit of a national candidate to a local city or the presidential debates (Becker *et al.,* 1979b; Kaid *et al.,* 1977), in terms of single, ongoing events or issues such as Watergate (Weaver *et al.,* 1975b), or in terms of many issues that capture media attention over some period of time, even that of several decades (MacKuen, 1981). Measurement has consisted of straightforward counts of articles devoted to various issues by various news media (Funkhouser, 1973; MacKuen, 1981; McCombs and Shaw, 1972), sometimes with the addition of weighting factors such as the amount of air time in the case of radio or television, column inches in the case of newspapers, or location in the newspaper or television or radio program (Gormley, 1975; Williams and Semlak, 1978). There are also variations in the time interval over which the measures are taken, in the use of local versus national issues, and in other issue-related dimensions (Eyal, 1979; Eyal *et al.,* 1979; Palmgreen and Clarke, 1977).

Not surprisingly, as the ease with which the agenda-setting effect is demonstrated increases, the more broadly "issue" is defined (Gormley, 1975). We suspect for example, that an issue category as general as "economic conditions" would usually receive high attention from the media and frequent nominations from the public as being important. But we question whether such a finding would advance our understanding of the agenda-setting process. It would be an unusual person who failed to mention some aspect of "economic conditions" as salient, media coverage or not. Use of narrower categories (e.g., social security, inflation, interest rates), on the other hand, might well locate enough differential emphasis to enable examination of an agenda-setting effect in the economic arena. Becker (1982) notes that the ways researchers, the media, and the audience define "issues" may all be quite different.

Similar problems are encountered with measurement of the audience agenda that, at a conceptual level, refers to what the public perceives to be the salient or important issues of the day. The assumption is made that people can at least classify issues in terms of some kind of high-low "importance" ranking. This seems a reasonable expectation as long as "importance" or "salience" means the same thing across respondents. However, at least three different ways in which audience members classify issues as important have been identified (McLeod, Becker and Byrnes, 1974). First, there is an interpersonal criterion that defines importance in terms of people's nominations of problems having personal relevance (McCombs and Shaw, 1972). Second, people can be asked to think about importance in terms of the larger social group—the community or the country (Ebring *et al.,* 1980; MacKuen, 1981)—a kind of "perceived issue salience" (McLeod *et al.,* 1974). Finally, people can be asked to use a somewhat more behavioral criterion—how often they talk about various issues with other people (Becker *et al.,* 1975; Becker *et al.,* 1979b; Williams and Semlak, 1978); this approach assumes that more salient issues are more likely to be discussed. Each of these approaches can be operationalized in terms of either closed-ended scales or open-ended questions.

The agenda-setting hypothesis assumes that the direction of influence is from media to public. Yet to the extent that the news media are charged with reporting about what concerns the public, it is possible that public concerns influence the media agenda. Even more plausible is the possibility that, at least on some issues, both the public and the media agendas simply reflect events in the environment. Indeed, there is evidence that for certain economic issues the public responds to the environment independent of media treatment (MacKuen, 1981), and we suspect that major events that are directly experienced by the public influence both agendas independently. Fortunately, some work has introduced some necessary controls to support causal inferences. The results of several studies based on time-lagged correlational designs agree that the media influence the public agenda rather than the reverse (McCombs, 1977; Sohn, 1978; Tipton *et al.,* 1975). Other work reports that media emphasis on some issues fluctuates from "objective" indicators of those issues (e.g., crime coverage and crime statistics do not always concur), and that public perceptions of importance follow media concern (Funkhouser, 1973; MacKuen, 1981). Overall, evidence is beginning to accumulate to support the causal influence of the media on the public agenda—for at least some issues under some conditions.

There are attempts to go beyond the main-effect prediction to locate factors that condition agenda-setting outcomes. Some of the attention to contingent and intervening factors probably stems from the number of studies that have failed to demonstrate a straightforward agenda-setting main effect (Becker, 1982). Still another source is what Winter (1981) calls a drive for "innovative" approaches that has "overwhelmed the scientific prerequisite of at least partial replication," a contention supported by the growing profusion of "suggested" variables upon which the effect may (or may not) depend. To date, two potential conditioning factors have received sufficient attention to permit some tentative generalizations to be made.

First, the strength of the agenda-setting effect, when it occurs, seems directly related to the amount of news exposure. The more people read, view, or listen, the more likely their perceptions of salient issues reflect media emphasis (McClure and Patterson, 1976; Weaver *et al.,* 1975a, 1975b). Chaffee and Wilson's (1977) examination of public agendas as a function of the available media diet provides further support for this tendency. They found that the greater the number of newspapers available in a given community, the more diversity there was in the public agendas, a macrolevel analysis that provides convergent validation for the exposure/strength generalization.

Second, there has been a good deal of work on the nature of the medium as a factor in agenda setting. McCombs and Shaw's (1972) seminal study found an agenda-setting effect for both television and print but no difference between the two media. Agenda setting has also been demonstrated in several studies of the impact of broadcast news (Siune and Borre, 1975; Zucker, 1978), and Patterson and McClure (1976) report that exposure to televised political commercials raises issue salience. On the other hand, at least one study found no evidence for an agenda-setting effect of television exposure to the Carter-Ford debates (Becker *et al.,* 1979b). Moreover, studies that compare the influence on public agendas of newspapers and television tend to agree that print exposure has a greater effect (Benton and Frazer, 1976; Eyal, 1979; Patterson and McClure, 1976; McCombs, 1977; Mullins, 1977; Tipton *et al.,* 1975; Weaver, 1977; Williams and Larsen, 1977). There is evidence that the two media vary in their agenda-setting potential as a function of the kind of issue being considered. Patterson and McClure (1976) argue that television is particularly adept at making salient uncomplicated, dramatic, and highly pictorial events that sustain intense, extended coverage. Palmgreen and Clarke (1977) report that print is more powerful for local issues. McCombs (1977) finds that the effect varies over time, the influence of television coverage increasing over the course of an election campaign (although never surpassing the power of local newspapers).

Several studies have attempted to relate the agenda-setting effect to a measure of "need for orientation," an index of curiosity about the environment containing items ranging from interest in a political campaign, to degree of certainty about candidates or issues, to political participation. Although some studies report that people who score higher in "need for orientation" tend to be more responsive to the media agenda (Weaver, 1977; Weaver, Auh, Stehla, and Wilhoit, 1975; Weaver, McCombs, and Spellman, 1975), the operating mechanism remains unclear. For example, interest would appear to be a critical item in such a need-for-orientation index, yet studies employing a measure of interest alone have found it to be both positively and negatively related to the agenda-setting effect (MacKuen, 1981; McLeod *et al.,* 1974). Similarly, Williams and Semlak (1978) considered eight variables that might be included in such an index and obtained different results as a function of

whether the agenda was based on print or television exposure. Other audience-related factors examined as possible conditioning variables include age, education, amount of political information, and preference for one medium over another (MacKuen, 1981; McLeod *et al.,* 1974; Mullins, 1977; Williams and Larsen, 1977; Williams and Semlak, 1978). Finally, studies have begun to examine the influence of interpersonal discussion on the phenomenon; some work indicates that interpersonal discussion increases the agenda-setting influence of the media (Atwood *et al.,* 1976), and other work indicates that it reduces the impact (Weaver, Auh, Stehla, and Wilhoit, 1975). Here, too, the need for replication is obvious. However, given Chaffee's (1982) argument about the futility of thinking in terms of a competition between mass media and interpersonal channels, we suspect that this may be one of more fruitful lines of research on the agenda-setting effect.

CAMPAIGN EFFECTS

THE NATURE OF CAMPAIGNS

The term communication "campaign" often elicits images of combat in which self-interested sources attack the public with an armory of propaganda and persuasion techniques uniquely suited to manipulate beliefs and behaviors, and the public ranges from utterly defenseless to almost totally impregnable.

Whether application of what was originally a military term to electioneering was a cause or consequence of making warfare one of the more common metaphors for politics is unclear. Nevertheless, today political campaigns are often characterized as battles in which votes are the spoils of victory. From this linkage of combat and politics, it seems to have been a short step to noting similarities in techniques used to seek votes and those used to seek consumer dollars. Indeed, to some extent the military and commercial connotations of "campaign" have become almost indistinguishable; the aim of a political campaign is the "selling" of a president (McGinnis, 1969), and product advertising campaigns are "battles" for a larger share of the market.

The combative connotations of campaign are unfortunate, particularly in societies that opt to persue social change via communication rather than coercion. Paisley (1981) remarks that in the United States, a remarkable amount of resources has been devoted to using communication media in the service of reform and social change.

And while it is difficult to deny that this approach often relies on persuasion (he argues that the "American experience" provided an ideal environment in which to refine the art of persuasion), it is also important to note that information and education are not only important elements in most public communication campaigns but also often the primary elements. And they are elements somewhat at odds with battlefield metaphors. Of course, the distinction between education and persuasion has long posed problems for communication researchers. One person's educational message is often another person's propaganda (McGuire, 1969), just as one person's social reform is often another's social repression. However, since our concern is with campaigns rather than with persuasion or education *per se,* we have side-stepped this issue by conceiving of campaigns more generally.

Communication campaigns attempt to influence someone else's beliefs (both cognitions and attitudes) and/or behavior through a series of planned, organized activities, at the heart of which are mass-communicated messages. This definition, which borrows heavily from Paisley (1981), is broad enough to encompass political campaigns, product campaigns, and public (social reform) campaigns. It recognizes that regardless of important differences among them, many of the same behavioral principles mediating change apply to each (Comstock *et al.,* 1978; O'Keefe, 1975; Ray, 1973; Solomon, 1981). That is, whatever the ultimate goal, all three types of communication campaigns engage the same processing behaviors (e.g., exposure, comprehension, etc.) and must be concerned with most of the same communication elements (e.g., source, message, channel, receiver, and destination variables).

On the other hand, it is important to note fundamental differences among the campaign types. Even the most casual observer can see that campaigns to sell cigarettes differ from those to encourage people to stop smoking. Fundamentally those differences stem from assumptions about how audiences will respond to different kinds of campaigns, assumptions that different audience expectations mediate different responses. Of course, the idea of such audience "power" is nothing new. It was implicit in Cartwright's (1949) examination of World War II war bond campaigns, Bauer's (1964) conception of the obstinate audience, and the large literature on selective exposure (Sears and Freedman, 1967). Recently, however, there has been an explicit move away from considering differences in how audiences approach and interpret messages as fundamentally attitude determined (as, to a large extent, the preceding studies did) to more cognitively oriented assumptions. Thus, much of the current work on campaigns reflects the field's growing attention to information-processing approaches to mass communication. Interpretation of meaning is viewed less as a process of discovery of what is inherent in a message than as a function of the interaction of message elements with pre-existing cognitions and attitudes, previous and current expectations, the nature of the perceived social and physical environment, and so forth. (Boulding, 1966; Dervin, 1981; Roberts, 1971; Swanson, 1981).

This more cognitive, audience-centered approach to campaigns is exemplified in comparisons of product and political advertising (Comstock *et al.,* 1978) and in treatments of social marketing (Lovelock and Wineberg, 1978; Solomon, 1981). These point to similarities and differences among product, political, and public campaigns in the differential roles in influencing audience responses assigned to such factors as prior involvement, opportunity for selective exposure, perceived bias, norms of rationality, quality of information, relevance of other stimuli, nature of the social structure, and so on. For example, information from political campaigns coexists with the extensive news coverage common to election races. Such relevant external stimuli generally influence the quality of the information that must be presented by the political campaign, although they are usually irrelevant to a product campaign and operate in a public campaign as a function of its goal (e.g., energy may or may not be a news topic over the course of an energy conservation campaign). Similarly, norms of rationality are more likely to operate when people are interpreting political and public campaigns than during product campaigns; perceived bias is higher in product and political campaigns than in public campaigns; campaigns advocating social reforms run a higher risk of being impeded by social-structure barriers than do those advocating purchases or seeking votes. Still another crucial element in some social campaigns (e.g., the case of smoking cessation) is the goal of long-term changes in habits, which require not just knowledge and attitude change but also the learning and practice of the skills needed to adopt and maintain new habits.

We will not extend this comparison or review the extensive literature on the different types of communication campaigns. Extended discussions of research on campaigns are available elsewhere (Comstock *et al.,* 1978; Kotler, 1972; Lovelock and Wineberg, 1978;

Nimmo and Sanders, 1981; O'Keefe, 1975; Ray, 1973; Rice and Paisley, 1981). Our purpose here is simply to note a change in the direction that research on campaigns has taken since the preceding edition of this volume (Weiss, 1969) and then to examine more closely two campaign-related issues that have received increasing attention over the past decade: the role of communication campaigns in social change and the impact of commercial advertising campaigns on children.

CAMPAIGNS FOR SOCIAL CHANGE

Much of the early skepticism about the impact of mass communication campaigns derived from studies that found little net change following from campaigns conducted in the United States (Weiss, 1969). At the same time that this "limited effects" view of mass media campaigns took hold in the United States, however, a growing literature on the role of communication in economic and social development, particularly in third-world countries, was optimistic about the changes mass media could help bring about (Lerner and Schramm, 1967; Rogers, 1983; Schramm, 1964). Ironically, the past decade has witnessed a reversal in these positions. Development scholars have become less sanguine about the potential for mass communications to engender meaningful change, especially in the third world (Rogers, 1976a, 1976b). Conversely, findings from a number of campaigns dealing with such public issues as smoking cessation (McAlister, 1981), heart disease prevention (Farquhar et al., 1977); forest fire prevention (McNamara, Kurth and Hanse, 1981), and energy conservation (Farhar-Pilgrim and Shoemaker, 1981) have generated optimism among U.S. researchers.

Of course, part of the current U.S. interest in public communication campaigns may simply be an "only wheel in town" response following the failure of engineering and enforcement strategies to achieve social change in the 1960s and 1970s (Paisley, 1981). Nevertheless, evidence mounts that the introduction of new media, and of "show business" and marketing techniques to campaigns for social change, together with the development and coordination of a planned sequence of precampaign, campaign, and postcampaign activities, have made public communication campaigns more effective than in the past.

A number of health-related campaigns report significant effects. For example, although the televised health program *Feeling Good* drew a relatively small audience

(and hence enjoyed a relatively short life), several behavior changes were reported among those who saw it (Mielke and Swinehart, 1976). Exposure to the television program *VD Blues* is reported to have increased knowledge about, and the perceived seriousness of, venereal disease and to have increased substantially the number of people visiting venereal disease clinics in the days immediately after the broadcast (Greenberg and Gantz, 1976). Rogers (1976b) describes several radio-based public-health and nutrition projects that were successful in Tanzania. And a number of campaigns for social change have used television successfully to encourage and train smokers in cessation procedures (Dubren, 1977; McAlister, 1981; McAlister et al., 1980).

The work of the Stanford Heart Disease Prevention Program (SHDPP) illustrates how the application of contemporary campaign-design strategies helps to facilitate significant social change (Farquhar et al., 1977; Maccoby et al., 1977; Maccoby and Solomon, 1981). The SHDPP used a community-based, quasi-experimental design (Farquhar, 1978) to examine the ability of mass media to influence peoples' smoking, dietary, and exercise habits in order to reduce the risk of heart disease. Two communities underwent a three-year campaign involving persuasive, informational, and educational messages via radio, television, newspapers, billboards, posters, and direct mail. In one of these communities, media were augmented with intensive, face-to-face instruction of a subsample of "high-risk" individuals (inserted as a standard against which to compare the effectiveness of the more economically feasible "mass media only" treatment). No campaign intervention was applied in a third control community. By the end of one year, individuals in both campaign communities manifested large increases in their knowledge of the risk factors of heart disease, and significant decreases in such risk factors as the number of cigarettes smoked, saturated fat intake, plasma-cholesterol levels, and systolic blood pressure. There was a somewhat greater impact in the "augmented treatment" community, but overall the risk of heart disease was reduced in both treatment community samples, although it actually increased in the control community. By the end of the second year of the campaign, risk reduction was dramatically greater, and the community subjected to only the media campaign revealed as much change as did the one augmented by the face-to-face instruction. Finally, by the end of the third year of the campaign, most of the achieved risk reduction was maintained, although the maintenance campaign was significantly more effective in the augmented-treatment community (Farquhar *et al.*, 1984; Maccoby, 1980). The investigators speculate that these final results may derive from a "diffusion effect" initiated by the high-risk individuals who participated in face-to-face instruction in the augmented treatment, or that the true risk reduction is the mean of the two mass media towns (one with the intensive instructees omitted and the remaining sample reconstituted to be a representative one).

The SHDPP project included many features that have operated in other successful public communication campaigns (Maccoby and Alexander, 1979, 1980; Maccoby and Solomon, 1981). Some of these, such as the use of formative evaluation in message design and an emphasis on creative selection and utilization of media and media scheduling, pertain directly to the program's communication components. For example, the SHDPP approach reflects Cartwright's (1949) contention that over the course of a campaign, messages must serve different functions for different receivers and for the same receivers at different times. Thus the study used different messages and message mixes to serve each of five separate functions:

1. Creating awareness of the heart-disease problem,

2. Providing information,

3. Providing motivation to change,

4. Providing training (e.g., many people would stop smoking if only they knew how),

5. Providing cues necessary for continued self-maintenance of achieved changes (Maccoby and Solomon, 1981).

These elements were conceived as neither definitive nor exclusive. For example, occasional persuasive messages were employed (although remarkably few people need to be persuaded that smoking is unhealthy; Roberts, 1975). Similarly, some messages were made to serve several functions (e.g., a training message can also teach maintenance cues and create awareness), and most communication components were designed to interact with others so that various elements of the campaign reinforced each other.

The use of thirty-second television spots provides a good example of the latter point. Televised public service announcements were used to reach large audiences, although with relatively low information messages. The primary goal of those messages was simply to make people aware of the problem and the program. They encouraged viewers to write or call for more detailed information, but even more important, they were intended to sensitize people to the issue of reducing the risk of heart disease on the premise that heightened awareness would increase the likelihood of attention to more information-packed messages provided by print media. In a sense, this use of television spots (and to some extent, billboards) attempted to use agenda-setting principles in the service of directed social change.

Equally as important as the project's communication components, however, were program elements that recognized that change projects must consider more than mass communications. Indeed, perhaps the most striking feature of the SHDPP campaign is its recognition that communication is not a sufficient condition for meaningful social change. The "community-based" nature of the interventions reflects the belief that change occurs within a social structure and that characteristics of that structure facilitate or impede change both independent of and in interaction with the campaign's mass communication components. Thus, precampaign activities included obtaining information about the people inhabiting the communities and about the social structures of the communities and establishing contacts within those social structures. Local medical and public health personnel were alerted to what the campaign was designed to do; various community organizations that might help or hinder the campaign were contacted; and levels of public knowledge were assessed. Program subgoals and communication components were then designed with pre-existing social conditions in mind (e.g., English/Spanish message mix; need for persuasion versus information versus training). In short, the entire campaign attempted to fit the inherent structural requirements of the communities (rather than ignoring or even conflicting with those structures, as many campaigns appear to do).

SHDPP is conducting a replication and extension of this work using five larger communities, stressing organized community self-help as a primary means of long-term maintenance of change, and adding cardiovascular morbidity and mortality measures as indexes of a reduction in the risk of heart disease (Farquhar *et al.*, 1984). The campaign is scheduled to last at least six years with input from Stanford University and then to continue in the communities themselves with minimal participation from the university. Similar projects are being conducted in Minnesota, Rhode Island, Pennsylvania,

South Africa, Australia, Switzerland (Maccoby and Solomon, 1981), and Finland (Tumilehto *et al.,* 1980).

The issue of adapting campaigns for social change to fit the realities of social structure is central to the current pessimism regarding the role of communication in economic and social development in third-world countries. Recent criticism of the role of mass communication in general and diffusion models in particular, when applied to the third-world development attempts, point to the failure of "Western" communication paradigms to account for the realities of non-Western social structures (Beltran S., 1975; Diaz Bordenave, 1976; Roling, Ashcroft and Chege, 1976). Certainly there are numerous examples concerning how third-world development campaigns have widened the gap between segments of the population, the benefits accruing at a higher rate to the already more advantaged social groups (Rogers, 1976b; Roling *et al.,* 1976). Such results point to a failure of many planned change efforts to adapt campaign strategies to the realities of particular social structures. It makes little sense, for example, to advocate the use of a new kind of fertilizer in a country where credit conditions preclude poor farmers from ever being able to obtain it. However, evidence that various U.S. campaigns (presumably using the same "Western" paradigms) also sometimes create gaps in knowledge and resources indicates that the "failures" of some development campaigns may lie more in the way in which the models are operationalized than with the models per se. Recent examinations of the history of development efforts and suggestions for new directions offered by critics of past development campaigns (Diaz Bordenave, 1976) obviate neither the diffusion model nor the fact that mass communication has an important role to play in planned social change. Rather they serve to help sensitize campaign planners and evaluators to the need to operationalize fundamentally sound theoretical concepts in ways that recognize the social structure and conditions in which they are being employed.

Some researchers and planners are beginning to respond to the complexities of development in various third-world countries with appropriately more complex strategies. Just as U.S.-based public communication campaigns are emphasizing formative evaluation in their planning (Palmer, 1981), campaigns in at least some third-world countries have begun to use findings from earlier diffusion studies for both formative and predictive purposes (Roling *et al.,* 1976; Shingi and Mody, 1976). Rogers's (1976c, 1977) merging of the diffusion model with network analysis procedures represents another imaginative response to structural constraints. Other analyses of mass communication both as it facilitates and impedes change (Whiting, 1976), the development of native conceptions of the role of communication in different kinds of change programs and/or in different social structures (Chu, 1976; Rogers, 1976b), and recent attempts to design a completely new paradigm for national development research (Nordenstreng and Schiller, 1979) are all precursors of a lively future for research on the role of communication campaigns in national development.

COMMERCIALS AND CHILDREN

Research concerned with the impact of commercials on *children* has accumulated quite rapidly over the past decade. Recognition of the potential profitability of the youth market and of the ensuing development of child-oriented television commercials did not occur until the mid 1960s (Helitzer and Heyel, 1970; Melody, 1973). However, once advertising directed primarily toward children appeared, our longstanding tradition of viewing children as a "special" audience led to questions about the propriety of deliberately attempting to persuade them to seek, purchase, consume, and/or want various products. Television researchers have long viewed children as particularly vulnerable because they lack the cognitive skills and life experiences to evaluate entertainment or informational messages as adequately as adults do (Comstock *et al.,* 1978; Roberts, 1973; Roberts and Bachen, 1981). Hence, messages *intentionally* produced to influence children for someone else's profit almost automatically created yet another communication research "problem area" (Roberts, 1982), several federal investigations (Federal Communications Commission, 1974; Federal Trade Commission, 1978), and a rapidly growing literature on children's responses to television advertising (Adler *et al.,* 1977; Comstock *et al.,* 1978; Esserman, 1981; Palmer and Dorr, 1980; Roberts, 1982).

The average child sees over 20,000 commercials per year (Adler *et al.,* 1977). Several recent reviews report that both parents and children state that commercials are one of the most important sources of information about child-relevant products. These reviews describe a range of studies citing positive relationships between exposure to television commercials and attitudes toward advertised products, increased requests for products, acceptance of commercial claims, and belief in the truthfulness of ads in general (Comstock *et al.,* 1978; Roberts, 1982). One longitudinal study demonstrated that multitudinous toy commercials appearing in the weeks immediately preceding Christmas are sufficient to overcome the defenses of children who were relatively resistant to commercial appeals several months earlier (Rossiter and Robertson, 1974).

To a large extent such findings simply demonstrate that commercials do what they are designed to do—create an awareness of and a desire for advertised products. The critical question in the debate over commercials and children, then, is not whether children are influenced nor even whether they are more easily persuaded than are adults. Rather, the question is whether, given children's abilities and limitations in processing and evaluating any symbolic message (Roberts, 1982; Roberts *et al.,* 1980), they process ads in such a way that they comprehend, evaluate, and (should they choose) discount them as adults are presumed to do (Federal Trade Commission, 1978).

Young children clearly respond to commercials differently from their older counterparts. Attention decreases with age. Younger children are attracted by the perceptual attributes of commercials. As they grow old enough to process ads conceptually, the attraction of perceptual changes diminishes, along with the amount of attention they pay both at the outset and across commercial breaks (Comstock *et al.,* 1978; Roberts, 1982). There are also age-related increments in children's ability to recognize and recall commercials and their content, the major increase in memory occurring between kindergarten and third grade (Wartella, 1980). This is the same period during which children begin systematically to encode information into meaningful units, to organize it, and to develop systematic retrieval strategies when faced with recall tasks (Flavell, 1977). Related work demonstrates a negative relationship between age and trust in commercials, with a majority of children under seven years old tending to be positively disposed, a negative orientation emerging between the second and third grade, and as much as 80 percent of children in late elementary and junior high school expressing intense skepticism toward television advertising (Christenson, 1982; Roberts *et al.,* 1980; Robertson and Rossiter, 1977; Rossiter 1977, 1981; Ward, Wackman and Wartella, 1977). Wartella (1980) notes a general trend of skepticism among children moving from distrust based on personal experience with specific products to a more general skepticism toward all advertising, a progression that parallels the development

of a more sophisticated understanding of the nature of advertising.

Such age-related differences in attention, memory, and trust imply differences in comprehension of advertising, although fundamental questions about whether young children differ from older children or adults in their conception of what advertising is and does, how it works, and how it should be evaluated remain. Perceptual differentiation of commercials from programs occurs quite early. Estimates of the ability to make such distinctions *nonverbally* range from 50 percent of four-year-olds (Zuckerman and Giannino, 1981) to 90 percent of four- and five-year-olds (Gaines and Esserman, 1981). Most studies agree that a majority of children begin to verbalize the selling intent of commercials sometime between kindergarten and third grade, with variations occurring as a function of children's backgrounds, the design and context of the studies, and the wording of the questions (for reviews see Comstock *et al.,* 1978; Roberts, 1982; Wartella, 1980). The less verbally based the questions are, the higher is the proportion of young children who "understand" the selling intent of commercials. Ward, Wackman and Wartella (1977), for example, found dramatic increases (from 10 percent to 62 percent) in the proportion of four- and five-year-olds indicating that a commercial is designed "to sell a product" as a question format moved from general and abstract ("What is a commercial? What do commercials try to do?") to specific and concrete ("What does this commercial [child views] for *X* want you to do?").

If we accept that the understanding that "commercials are intended to sell products" adequately indicates comprehension of the nature of advertising, then most children appear to understand them quite early. However, this criterion fails to recognize the *persuasive* nature of commercials and certainly does not characterize what persuasion researchers would view as full, "adult" understanding of commercials. Use of "intent to sell" as the criterion denoting understanding equates commercials with classified ads and totally ignores their emphasis on factors influencing yielding and the inherent bias (characteristic of all persuasive messages) following from that emphasis. "Adult" comprehension of a commercial implies recognition of at least four attributes (Roberts, 1982, p. 27):

1. That the source has other perspectives, hence other interests, than those of the receiver;

2. That the source intends to persuade;

3. That persuasive messages are, by definition, biased;

4. That biased messages demand different interpretation strategies than do primarily informational (or educational or entertainment) messages. Finally, 'adult processing' of a commercial requires development of the skills and experience necessary to engage in such interpretational strategies.

Few studies have directly addressed the distinction between the informational and the persuasive functions of the selling intent of commercials (e.g., "A commercial shows what you can buy" versus "Commercials try to get you to buy things"). However, the literature on the development of social cognition suggests "adult" processing of commercials requires relatively sophisticated role-taking and meta-cognitive skills that may not appear until age seven years or later (Flavell, 1977; Selmon and Damon, 1975; Shantz, 1975). Two studies are directly relevant. Gaines and Esserman (1981) report that over 60 percent of four- and five-year-olds understood the "selling intent" of commercials but that only 10 percent of this age group defined commercials with reference to persuasion. Work currently under way at Stanford University finds that fewer than 20 percent of children under age seven define commercials in terms of persuasion, that from 20 percent to 40 percent of seven- and eight-year-olds use this attribute, and that over 90 percent of nine-year-olds recognize the persuasive aspect of commercials.

Empirical research, then, offers relatively convincing evidence that commercial campaigns influence children to want and request (and sometimes buy) advertised products and that children do not interpret commercial messages in the same way that adults do. Such results can not resolve the debate over the fairness or unfairness of commercials directed at children, however, and/or of whether and how to regulate child-oriented advertising. Those questions depend on value judgments. Although empirical research can show that commericals persuade children, it "cannot decide whether it is a good or bad thing for children to be persuaded to want various advertised products" (Rossiter, 1980, p. 269). That depends on the judgments of those engaged in the debate. And given the values of the various parties arguing the issue, people will probably continue to differ over its solution, at least insofar as regulation is concerned. There are, however, several nonregulatory strategies receiving attention. These include the development of school curricula designed to help children to better understand tele-

vision in general (Dorr, 1978; Singer, Singer and Zuckerman, 1981) and commercials in particular (Roberts *et al.*, 1980) and some preliminary work on developing public service announcements that use something like the commercial format to teach children about commercials and "consumer information processing" (Christenson, 1982; Goldberg, Gorn and Gibson, 1978).

A final dimension of the influence of commercials on children that warrants more attention has to do less with their creation of desires for particular products than with their possible role in the development of a kind of materialistic mentality. Goldberg and Gorn (1978), for example, report that exposure to toy commercials in an experimental context influenced preschool children to make more "materialistic" as opposed to "social" choices in a postviewing test situation. Work like this, although relatively rare, raises questions about the long-term social implications of exposing generations of children to tens of thousands of messages, the basic theme of which is that "to consume is to be happy" (Roberts *et al.*, 1980). Such questions point to just one of a number of possible socialization effects of mass communication.

SOCIALIZATION EFFECTS

MASS MEDIA AND SOCIALIZATION

Concern with whether and how the content of mass media influences the way people, particularly young people, view and behave in their social world is nothing new. The question, in one form or another, is implicit in Plato's advocacy of censorship of storytellers, in the bowdlerization of *Grimm's Fairy Tales* and of similar children's literature, in the Payne Fund studies of motion pictures and youth (Charters, 1933), in early government investigations of comic books (U.S. Senate, 1955) and in more recent examinations of television (Pearl *et al.*, 1982; Surgeon General's Scientific Advisory Committee, 1972; United States Commision on Civil Rights, 1977).

Christenson and Roberts (1983) attribute such concern to several underlying assumptions about both children and the content of mass communication. One is that children are particularly vulnerable to symbolic messages because of their less developed cognitive capabilities, their lack of life experiences, and the fact that childhood is a period dominated by information acquisition. Another is that the fictional content of most media, but especially of television, is particularly forceful both because of its ubiquity and because it frequently combines symbolic structure and representational realism and thus enhances learning by focusing attention and providing closure in ways that real life cannot do (cf. Gerbner and Gross, 1976a). The influence of fictional content may be further heightened because, since it is fictional, the "truth standards" usually applied to informational, educational, or persuasive messages seldom apply. Thus, the suspension of disbelief characteristic of the entertainment relationship (Schramm, 1971b) possibly increases the socializing potential of the content of mass-media entertainment. Finally, much of the concern reflects a fear of any content that fails to coordinate with the value and belief structures of parents (or of certain interest groups) and that, because of its availability in the mass media, threatens the relative information monopoly parents enjoy (Roberts, 1973). This fear is evidenced by the preponderance of attention paid to "harmful" as opposed to "prosocial" effects of the media (Christenson and Roberts, 1983; Comstock *et al.*, 1978; Palmer and Dorr, 1980).

"Socialization" refers to the process by which people learn the fundamental parameters of their culture; they acquire an understanding of the nature of the society in which they must relate and function adequately and of the rules and norms that guide such functioning. Although some discussions of socialization tend to accent people's acquisition of rules by focusing on the proscribed and prescribed behaviors characteristic of given social groups, they must also learn the definitions and expectations underlying those rules. We follow Roger Brown's (1965) lead in conceiving of socialization not only in terms of specific norms or behaviors that come to be associated with some part of the social world but also in terms of how that world is defined. Thus, for example, socialization consists of learning not only the norms associated with a category of actions like "aggressive behavior" but also what constitutes aggressive behavior, basically a task of category definition.

People learn from many different kinds of media content, only some of which are intended to inform or teach. Indeed, the majority of recent research on mass communication, particularly that focusing on television, is concerned with incidental learning, the acquisition of information that is neither sought nor expected by the audience and that is either unintended or highly incidental to the aim of the producer of the message (Maccoby, E., 1954; Schramm, Lyle and Parker, 1961). For example, questions about the impact of media violence, about mass communication's role in establishing or maintain-

ing any of the numerous "isms" that command the attention of public consciousness at any given time, and about the degree to which the media cultivate an image of the world that shapes expectations (hence, social behavior) are all articulated in terms of incidental learning, particularly from the prime-time television content that so dominates public attention.

The mass media, particularly television, operate as important socialization agents for children (Berry, 1980a; Comstock *et al.*, 1978; Liebert, Sprafkin and Davidson, 1982; Leifer, 1975; Leifer, Gordon and Graves, 1974; Roberts, 1973) and for adults (Gerbner and Gross, 1976a, 1976b; Gerbner *et al.*, 1980; Schramm, 1971a). This is not to say that the media dominate, but simply to recognize that they have become major socialization agents, which, depending on conditions, contend sometimes more and sometimes less equally with such traditional agents as parents, peers, schools, and churches. For example, although parents exert a dominant influence on most behaviors and norms, in a rapidly changing technological society there

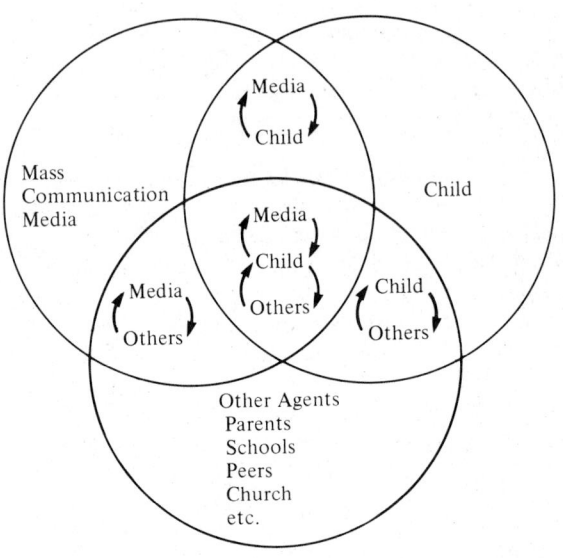

FIGURE 3
Possible Interrelationships among Mass Media, Other Socialization Agents, and Children

Adapted from A. D. Leifer, N. J. Gordon and S. B. Graves, *Children and Television: Recommended Directions for Future Efforts.* Report to the Office of Child Development, May, 1973, p. 19.

are many issues with which they cannot, will not, or do not deal (Roberts, 1973). The definitions and norms appropriate to these dimensions of the world are often transmitted at the social-system level (Bandura, 1969), by the mass media. As Fig. 3 illustrates, neither the person being socialized nor the various socialization agents operate in a vacuum. Rather, the socialization process and the role of the media within it are best characterized in terms of multiple, mutual interactions with influence moving between person and socialization agent and among the agents themselves. Finally, the fact that the mass media interact with other socialization agents does not diminish their importance in the socialization process. Any socialization agent interacts with others. The important point is that the media must be considered as significant contending forces among the full array of socialization influences the shape the way people come to view their world.

ANTISOCIAL EFFECTS

Questions concerning the impact of film and television portrayals of violence have dominated studies of the socialization effects of mass media over the past twenty years. Comstock *et al.* (1978) estimate that studies of violence on television outnumber work in other problem areas by at least four to one, and the list of reviews and interpretations of the influence of violence on television published since *1970* approaches several dozen (e.g., Comstock *et al.*, 1978; Goranson, 1970; Murray, 1980; Murray and Kippax, 1979; Palmer and Dorr, 1980; Stein and Friedrich, 1975).

As noted earlier, at first glance the results of correlational studies of the relationship between exposure to television violence and aggressive attitudes and/or behavior appear to be mixed. However, when those studies are examined in terms of how the direct viewing of violence (as opposed to merely viewing television or stating a preference for violent shows) inpacts viewers, there is consistent evidence that children and adolescents who view televised portrayals of violence obtain higher scores on various indices of aggression than those who do not. These findings survive controls for an array of relevant third variables (Dominick and Greenberg, 1972; McLeod *et al.*, 1972a, 1972b). There is also evidence that viewing violence on television is negatively related to various indicators of socioeconomic status and positively related to measures of delinquent behavior, frequency of fighting, and parent-child conflict (McCarthy *et al.*, 1975). Moreover, aggressive attitudes predict subsequent viewing of violence, although parental restrictions on such exposure can moderate the likelihood of additional viewing of violence (Atkin *et al.*, 1979). The number of studies and variety of procedures and measures that indicate some form of relationship between viewing violence and aggressive behavior is impressive. The relationships have been obtained with children ranging in age from eight years (Eron, 1963) through late adolescence (McLeod *et al.*, 1972a, 1972b) and early adulthood (Robinson and Bachman, 1972); the studies have employed aggression measures ranging from self-reports of aggressive attitudes (Dominick and Greenberg, 1972) and behaviors (Belson, 1978) to ratings of aggressive behavior made by peers (Lefkowitz *et al.*, 1972) and school officials (Friedman and Johnson, 1972), and the results have been replicated internationally (Murray, 1980). Belson (1978), for example, reports a large-scale study in London conducted over a twelve-year period with boys ages twelve to seventeen years. He found that when low- and high-violence viewers (who were carefully matched on an extensive array of other relevant variables) were compared, high-violence viewers were much more likely to report involvement in "serious" violent acts (e.g., "I bashed a boy's head against the wall"; "I tried to force a girl to have sexual intercourse with me"). Of course, although extensive procedures can rule out a variety of third-variable explanations for the relationship between viewing violence and aggression, Belson notes that they cannot address the possibility that the direction of causality is from behavior to stimulus rather than the reverse. It remains quite reasonable that more aggressive youngsters prefer to watch more violent television.

One correlational attempt to address this possibility used a cross-lagged panel design to compare viewing violence and aggression scores obtained from a sample of children when they were eight years old and again when they were eighteen years old (Lefkowitz *et al.*, 1972, 1977). Results revealed a moderate positive correlation between early viewing of violence and later aggressiveness ($r = .31$), a positive but somewhat weaker correlation between early viewing of violence and early aggressiveness (.21), and no relationship between either later viewing of violence and later aggressiveness ($-.05$) or between later and early aggressiveness (.01). The authors' conclusion that early viewing of television violence *causally* contributed to subsequent aggressive behavior sparked a good deal of debate about the general issue of basing causal inferences on correlational data and about various methodological problems associated with this particular study (e.g., Howitt, 1972; Huessman *et al.,* 1973; Kaplan, 1972). Nevertheless, after an extensive examination of the statistical and methodological arguments in that debate, Comstock *et al.* (1978) conclude that in the context of the findings of numerous synchronous correlations reported in other studies as well as in the experimental literature to be discussed, the causal interpretation survives relatively intact.

Causality, of course, is less easily disputed under experimental conditions. Although moving into the laboratory brings with it many disadvantages of artificiality that threaten the capability of results to be generalized to the "real" world, it provides the only undisputed opportunity to examine what exposure to a given stimulus *can* do when all other things are equal. In the typical violence-viewing experiment, youngsters are randomly assigned to two or more treatment conditions that vary in terms of the quantity and/or nature of portrayed violence. They are then placed in some kind of measurement situation in which "aggressive responses" may vary. Inferences about the effect of viewing are based on the differences in responses among the various treatment groups.

A number of stimulus-related, person-related, and environment-related factors have been varied within and across this general design. The age of participants has ranged from preschool children (Bandura, Ross and Ross, 1961, 1963), through grade schoolers (Drabman and Thomas, 1974; Feshbach, 1972; Savitsky *et al.,* 1971) and adolescents (Hartman, 1969; Walters and Thomas, 1963) to college students and adults (Berkowitz and Geen, 1966, 1967; Hoyt, 1970), and a few studies have included a range of ages within the same experiment (Collins, 1973; Collins *et al.,* Collins and Zimmerman, 1975; Leifer and Roberts, 1972). Stimuli have varied from brief, specially prepared films (Bandura, 1965) to excerpts from feature films (Berkowitz and Rawlings, 1963), to edited television programs (Collins and Zimmerman, 1975), to full, unedited programs (Leifer and Roberts, 1972) or films (Worchel *et al.,* 1976). Content variations have also been extensive: the amount of violence; a focus on consequences, on motives, and on pain cues; reality versus fantasy; characteristics of the aggressor and the victim; justification for the aggression; context of the portrayal; cartoons versus realistic films; and so forth (Comstock *et al.,* 1978). In many of the studies conducted with older subjects, participants were angered or frustrated before viewing violence (Berko-

witz, 1965; Hartmann, 1969; Hoyt, 1970), a treatment that consistently increased aggressive responses.

As illustrated in Table 1, there has been a similar variation in the dependent variables used as indicators of aggressiveness. These have ranged from paper and pencil measures on which subjects indicate how aggressive they

TABLE 1

Examples of "Measures of Aggression" Used in Various Experimental Studies of the Impact of Television Violence on Young Persons

TYPE OF MEASURE	STUDY[a]
Observation of imitative and nonimitative aggressive behavior toward inanimate objects in controlled settings	Bandura, Ross, and Ross, 1963
Observation of imitative and nonimitative aggressive behavior toward a human in controlled settings	Hanratty et al., 1969
Observation of aggressive behavior in uncontrolled free-play situations	A. H. Stein and Friedrich, 1972
Shocks ostensibly administered to others	Hartmann, 1965
Noxious noise ostensibly administered to others	Feshbach, 1972
Noxious heat ostensibly administered to others	Liebert and Baron, 1972
Willingness to punish a live rat	Stoessel, 1972
Preference for "aggressive" vs. "nonaggressive toys	Lovaas, 1961
Expressed desire to pop a balloon	Mussen and Rutherford, 1961
Paper and pencil responses to hypothetical situations	Leifer and Roberts, 1972
Paper and pencil measures of "hostility"	Berkowitz, Corwin, and Heironimus, 1963
Toleration of aggressive behavior in others	Drabman and Thomas, 1974

[a]Many of the measures have been employed in a number of studies. The studies listed are illustrative.

SOURCE: G. Comstock, S. Chaffee, N. Katzman, M. McCombs and Donald Roberts, *Television and Human Behavior* (New York: Columbia University Press, 1978). Copyright, The Rand Corporation, 1978.

might be in various hypothetical situations, to opportunities to apply noxious stimuli (e.g., shocks to others), to direct observations of aggressive play behavior in controlled and free-play situations. Such person-related conditioning variables as age, sex, previous aggressiveness, cognitive abilities, and social class have also been examined (Comstock *et al.*, 1978; Dorr and Kovaric, 1980). In addition, such viewing-environmental contingencies as the presence or the absence of a commenting adult (Hicks, 1968) and such post-viewing environmental contingencies as the presence or the absence of another child in the performance situation (Thomas and Drabman, 1974) and the degree of similarity between the context of portrayed violence and the performance environment (Berkowitz and Geen, 1967; Geen and Berkowitz, 1966, 1967) have been examined.

Not surprisingly, this range of differences among experimental procedures has produced a complex array of findings, some of which conflict, some of which stand alone, but a remarkable number of which show convergence. Indeed, several extensive examinations of this literature (Andison, 1977; Comstock, 1980; Comstock *et al.*, 1978; Dorr and Kovaric, 1980; Goranson, 1970; Stein and Friedrich, 1975) reach similar conclusions about what exposure to television violence can do, all other things being equal. For example, there is little disagreement that even very young children can learn novel, relatively complex behaviors from a single viewing of film-mediated violent behavior. More important, the evidence that portrayals of violence can disinhibit previously acquired aggressive responses is quite solid. It also seems safe to say that the more violence viewed, the greater is the likelihood of aggressive responses. Moreover, the way in which the violence is portrayed is a particularly important mediator of subsequent violent responses. When aggression is shown as rewarded, useful, justified, and/or appropriate, observers are more likely to respond aggressively than when the reverse obtains. Furthermore, there appears to be an "expectation effect" in that when violence is not punished, children behave as if it were rewarded (i.e., failure to see expected negative consequences operates as a positive consequence). The evidence is also fairly consistent that initially more aggressive children are more affected by portrayals of violence, that boys are more affected than girls, and that the more similar the performance environment is to the observed context in which the symbolic violence takes place, the higher is the probability that the viewer will respond aggressively. In short, the evidence from labora-

tory experiments points to a strong causal linkage between exposure to mediated portrayals of violence and subsequent aggressive behavior. Nevertheless, there are dangers in generalizing such results to day-to-day life. Laboratory experiments insure focused attention, frequently use highly edited or atypical stimuli, remove the many distractions inherent in at-home viewing settings, and perhaps most important, place participants in performance situations in which the normal and expected sanctions against aggressive behavior are removed. Thus, no matter how impressive is the experimental evidence, a question always remains about the degree to which the causal relationship can be generalized beyond the laboratory.

One response to such criticism has been to conduct naturalistic field experiments. These give up some of the control and neatness available in the laboratory in order to overcome as many of the laboratory's "artificialites" as possible and still maintain the causal power of the experimental design.

We have identified ten such experiments, one of which took advantage of the introduction of television into a Canadian town to make comparisons of aggressive behavior both before and after exposure to television violence and between communities (Joy *et al.*, 1977). The remaining nine attempted "naturalistic" manipulations of violence exposure to participants of different ages in different settings. Among younger children, control of exposure was achieved through parental manipulation of television viewing at home (Cameron and Janky, 1971) or by making the viewing of prosocial, neutral, or antisocial programs part of the "normal" preschool experience (Stein and Friedrich, 1972; Steuer *et al.*, 1971). Such a "part of the program" technique was also used with children ages six through twenty years attending a summer sports camp in Canada (McCabe and Moriarity, 1977). The other studies were conducted in residential homes, schools, or institutions in which the television diet was manipulated via controls over what programs could/would be viewed by boys (ranging from ages eight to eighteen years) in different living units (Feshbach and Singer, 1971; Wells, 1973) or by controlling the availability of free tickets to violent or nonviolent films at nearby theaters (Parke *et al.*, 1977). The periods of exposure to violent television programs ranged from one or two days, to seven weeks, to, in the case of the natural experiment in Canada, several years. For the most part, aggression measures were based on observations of participants' behavior in normal play, school, and living situations, although some also included various self-reports, teacher ratings, peer ratings, or parent ratings of aggressiveness. Most studies conducted observations over various time intervals before, during, and after the exposure period.

Although these ten "naturalistic experiments" vary in strength and in many details and although all are open to at least minor (and sometimes major) methodological criticisms, the general agreement in the results is remarkable: eight report increases in aggressive behavior as a function of viewing violence; one reports no between-group differences, and one reports a decrease in aggressive behavior. Moreover, the five that strike us as least open to criticism (because neither the exposure situations, the stimuli, nor the measurement situations were artificial) are all consistent with each other and with most of the experimental literature in pointing to a causal relationship in which viewing violence leads to increases in aggressive behavior.

These are but a few of the bewildering array of studies examining the effects of viewing violence on subsequent aggressive behavior. The violence issue was one of the earliest raised following the introduction of television, and it has been a continuing one. Thus it is no surprise that there is so much empirical work in the area—a good deal of it, we admit, of questionable import. To trace the chronological sequence of studies of television violence is to watch researchers from several different disciplines work out how best to conduct studies that have both the theoretical relevance and the sophistication to advance our understanding of the effects of mass communication, as well as the kind of external validity necessary to convince skeptics in the public sector and the mass communication industry that the findings of their work should be taken seriously beyond the laboratory. Research in more recent problem areas (e.g., prosocial effects; political socialization; effects of commercials) has gained greatly from hard-won knowledge obtained from the early studies of viewing violence on television. Finally, to reiterate a point made several times in this section, our confidence in the general trend of the results increases with the ever-increasing number of studies. Most are open to criticism on various grounds, but few are vulnerable on all the same grounds. And given the differences in samples, measures, stimuli, conditions and contingencies, it is difficult to ignore the fact that the overwhelming proportion of results point to a causal relationship between exposure to mass communication portrayals of violence and an increased probability that viewers will behave violently at some subsequent time.

PROSOCIAL EFFECTS

Research on prosocial effects covers a number of relatively recent studies concerned with what are generally thought to be positive social consequences of viewing: helping behavior, cooperation, kindness, altruism, sharing, friendliness, empathy, creativity, and so on. Although there is a good deal of overlap in some of these outcomes, there is also a good deal of difference among them. In a sense, the variety reveals the relative newness of work focusing on the positive consequences of broadcast television—"positive" including almost anything that can be defined as socially valued (Rushton, 1979, 1982).

Research in this area has been stimulated by two factors:

1. The recognition that the same principles underlying learning and performance of television-mediated antisocial behavior should operate equally well for more positive behavior;

2. The recognition that since the daily television schedule is finite, one way to reduce portrayals of violence is to replace them with portrayals of prosocial behaviors, whatever they might be.

Evidence of positive social outcomes might influence policy makers and the mass communication industry to listen more carefully when programming changes are demanded. The result has been a scattering of studies based primarily on models of social-learning theory and benefiting greatly from earlier work. That is, the research on television and antisocial behavior showed what to do and what to avoid to the degree that research on prosocial effects has moved rapidly away from laboratory studies conducted with specially prepared stimuli (Comstock *et al.*, 1978) toward experiments that are often conducted in the field and that use naturally occurring television programs as stimuli.

Interviews with children ranging from ages seven to eleven years found that regardless of whether they were part of a captive audience or were interviewed some hours after viewing television at home, over 90 percent recalled at least one prosocial message from an episode of *Fat Albert and the Cosby Kids,* and that similar results apply to a number of other Saturday morning shows, one goal of which was to present positively valued social ideas and behaviors (Columbia Broadcasting System, 1974, 1977). Other work on thirty-second public service announcements designed to teach children about health and safety found that, depending on the issue presented and various presentation factors, children as young as four years may comprehend and recall a good deal of the relevant information (Roberts and Gibson, 1979; Roberts, Bachen, Christenson, and Gibson, 1979; Roberts, Gibson, and Bachen, 1979).

Stein and Friedrich's (1972) naturalistic experiment on the impact of a month's viewing of violent television also included a prosocial treatment in which a group of preschool children watched episodes of *Mr. Rogers' Neighborhood,* a program for young children that stresses such themes as kindness, cooperation, and sharing. Children who viewed this program showed increased self-control in the day-to-day nursery school environment: children from lower socioeconomic status families who viewed the prosocial programs also manifested increases in such prosocial interpersonal behavior as nurturance of others and cooperation. Further studies conducted with the same program over varying time intervals (Friedrich and Stein, 1975; Stein *et al.,* 1973) have replicated and extended these results, revealing increases in helping behavior. Another study found that a week's exposure to *Mr. Roger's Neighborhood* in a nursery school setting resulted in increases in the number of social contacts the children had and in their giving of positive reinforcement to other children. Among children in the same study who viewed *Sesame Street,* there was also an increase in their giving of both positive reinforcement and punishment and in social contacts, but only among children who had seldom viewed *Sesame Street* prior to the study (Coates *et al.,* 1976). Increases in young children's imaginative play, creativity, and productive fantasy subsequent to extended viewing of *Mr. Rogers' Neighborhood* have also been reported (Fox *et al.,* 1977; Singer and Singer, 1976).

Research focusing on programs designed more to entertain than to teach found similar results. In one study second- and third-grade children increased in cooperative behavior on both verbal problem-solving and behavioral-helping measures subsequent to viewing an episode of *The Waltons* that emphasized cooperative problem solving (Baran *et al.,* 1979). Another study showed that an action-adventure program edited to show the protagonist "cooperatively coping" with an interpersonal conflict engendered more subsequent helping behavior among fourth- through tenth-grade children than did either an aggressive or a neutral program (Collins and Getz, 1976). Poulos *et al.* (1975) describe an experiment in which first-grade children were exposed to one of three unedited programs, an episode of *Lassie* in which a small boy risked his life to save an endangered puppy, an epi-

sode of *Lassie* that featured dogs but gave no example of helping behavior, and an episode of a family situation comedy in which neither dogs nor helping behavior was featured. After viewing, children were placed in a situation engineered to make them think that they were playing an unrelated, highly attractive and rewarding game. The "helping" measure consisted of the length of time the child would turn away from the game to push a button calling for assistance when confronted with the illusion that one of the puppies was in trouble. The results are striking in that children who saw the helping version of the *Lassie* episode spent almost twice as much time seeking help as did viewers of the neutral version of *Lassie* and well over twice the amount of time spent by viewers of the situation comedy. Finally, Ahammer and Murray (1979) offered a diet of either neutral or prosocial programs to children for one-half hour each day for four weeks in a preschool setting. Stimuli consisted of such commercial programs as *Lassie, I Love Lucy,* and the *Brady Bunch,* and the prosocial episodes were selected on the basis of an extensive content analysis (Rubinstein *et al.,* 1974). Children who viewed the prosocial television diet performed significantly greater levels of helping behavior in the preschool setting than did children who viewed the neutral diet.

Of course, a number of factors condition such main effects. Many are the same conditions that influence the impact of viewing violence on television—age, initial levels of prosocial behavior, the specific type of behavior being examined, how it is portrayed, and so forth (Coates *et al.,* 1976; Collins and Getz, 1976; Friedrich and Stein, 1975; Silverman, 1977). In addition, there is evidence that combining prosocial television programs with various supplementary activities that can be carried out in school settings (e.g., role playing, verbal labeling) can boost the impact of prosocial portrayals (Ahammer and Murray, 1979; Friedrich and Stein, 1975).

Finally, several studies that have reported only minimal effects of exposure to prosocial programs (Silverman, 1977; Sprafkin and Rubinstein, 1979) as well as differences among children in response to prosocial content point to problems that remain to be addressed. Some of the obtained differences are probably due to variations in presentation factors, some to differences in what the children bring to the exposure situation, and some to the particular prosocial behavior being portrayed (Baran *et al.,* 1979; Coates *et al.,* 1976; Sprafkin and Rubinstein, 1979). Although all these need to be investigated, a major need is for precision in the definition(s) of "prosocial content." Almost any behavior with positive value seems to be tossed into this pot, since little attention has been paid to conceptual differences among behaviors. Yet it is quite reasonable to expect differences in what children expect regarding each of the various behaviors, and it is just as reasonable to expect qualitative differences in the way television portrays helping behavior versus task persistence versus altruism, and so on. Given what we know about comprehension as a function of differences in both the child viewer and the presentation factors, it seems reasonable to expect differences in response across these different prosocial behaviors.

ATTITUDES AND VALUES

Early Research

The influence of mass media on a number of social attitudes and values, in addition to those included under the headings of antisocial and prosocial behavior, have been examined in many studies. One of the earliest and most ambitious projects, the Payne Fund Studies of Motion Pictures and Youth (Charters, 1933), reports surveys, experiments, and quasi-experiments concerned with a wide variety of potential effects, many of which concern social attitudes. For example, Peterson and Thurston (1933) examined the impact of viewing one or more of thirteen different feature films that were expected to influence different attitudes. *All Quiet on the Western Front* was examined for its effect on attitudes toward Germans; racial attitudes were expected to be influenced by *Birth of a Nation,* and so on. Other attitude domains included crime, prohibition, war, capital punishment, Chinese people, and prison reform. Results quite clearly indicated that even a single exposure to the films resulted in significant attitude change (e.g., viewing *Birth of a Nation* resulted in less favorable attitudes toward blacks). The effects were cumulative, in that seeing several films presenting a consistent position on a given topic (e.g., war) resulted in more attitude change than a single viewing. Many of the changes endured for as long as eight months.

Christenson and Roberts (1982) note that these findings have been criticized on a number of methodological grounds, although experience in conducting similar studies in recent years has led many researchers to learn to live with the weakness of such designs in order to gain from their strengths. Indeed, there is a tendency to repeat many of the same designs (Reeves and Wartella, 1982) in current studies of the effects of media on attitudes and values related to politics and government, consumer behavior, racial and ethnic groups, sex roles, occupations, and so forth.

Sex-Role Attitudes

Recent concern with the status of women in society, in combination with the pervasive sex-role stereotypes in the content of mass media (Butler and Paisley, 1980; U.S. Commission on Civil Rights, 1977), has directed much attention to the influence of the media on sex-role attitudes. Empirical studies have begun to appear in spite of difficulties locating unexposed control groups and nontraditional, nonsex-stereotyped media portrayals of males and females (Pingree and Hawkins, 1980).

Attempts to document the effects of current television fare have tried to show that heavy viewing is associated with more sex-role stereotyping. For example, interviews with groups of three- through six-year-olds about career aspirations revealed that those who viewed the most television were those most likely to prefer occupations that matched common sex stereotypes (Beuf, 1974). Similarly, in a sample of children ranging from ages six through eleven years, those who viewed more than twenty-five hours per week of television manifested more traditional sex-role adoption than did those who viewed ten hours or less of television. The relationship survived controls for age and sex, although boys and older children tended to give more stereotyped responses (Freuh and McGhee, 1975). Finally, a longitudinal study conducted with adolescents over a two-year period found that, among girls, television viewing in the first year significantly mediated third-year sex-role attitudes, such that heavy viewers were more likely to agree that women are happiest raising children, men have more ambition than women, and so on (Morgan, 1980). Morgan also predicted and found that heavier viewers at the beginning of the study set their occupational and educational sights higher two years later, a result he explains in terms of television's over-representation of professional women but which is somewhat contradictory in view of the more traditional influence reported in other studies (Christenson and Roberts, 1982). Overall, Morgan concludes that his results support the general hypothesis that television "cultivates" a traditional view of women.

Another approach to the issue of sex-role stereotypes is to examine the degree to which nonstereotypic portrayals can reduce the degree of acceptance of traditional attitudes. One correlational study (Miller and Reeves, 1976) measured the frequency with which grammer-school children viewed each of five nontypical programs, nontypical because they featured women in traditionally male occupations (police officer, television producer, park ranger). The results showed a strong positive relationship between frequency of viewing such counter-stereotypical shows and children's indications that it was acceptable for girls to aspire to such occupations. The relationship held equally for boys and girls.

Several experiments have exposed children and adolescents to counter-stereotypical portrayals of women, then compared their responses on questions about sex-role attitudes and expectations to those from unexposed children. High school girls exposed to a series of fifteen commercials emphasizing the importance of physical beauty increased their perceptions of the importance and desirability of physical beauty, although expectations concerning success as a wife or in a career were unaffected by these stimuli (Tan, 1979). Pingree (1978) showed eight- to thirteen-year-olds commercials portraying women in nontraditional occupational roles (athletes, doctors, engineers, etc.) and found that although such nontraditional stimuli can alter sex-role perceptions, the results depend on the mental set with which the children viewed the commercials.

When similar nontraditional commercials were embedded in a children's program and shown to seven-through ten-year olds, the children who saw the commercials were more likely to believe that women could attain similar jobs (judge, computer programmer and television technician) (Atkin and Miller, 1975). Even younger children were exposed to one of three cartoon shows, one portraying a girl performing well at traditional male activities (e.g., sports, building a clubhouse); one showing a woman engaging in stereotyped activities; one paying no particular attention to sex roles (Davidson *et al.,* 1979). The five- and six-year-old girls who viewed the nonstereotyped cartoon produced significantly lower sex-role stereotype scores, although the authors are uncertain about which of the several variations among the program contributed to the observed differences in responses.

Finally, an extensive evaluation of *Freestyle,* a television series explicitly designed to reduce sex-role stereotyping among grade-school children and to expand girls' career awareness, provides encouraging results (Johnston and Davidson, 1980; Johnston *et al.,* 1980).

Viewers were more accepting of such portrayals as men helping with housework or child care, girls performing mechanical tasks, girls in leadership roles, and more men being in "female" jobs, although some of these outcomes obtained only for girls and others only for boys. There were, however, a number of targeted attitudes and expectations that were not changed (e.g., girls in athletics, girls taking more physical risks, wives providing financial support for the family, etc.). Positive effects were enhanced when the program was viewed in a school setting and accompanied by classroom discussion. Under these conditions, over 60 percent of the obtained effects persisted up to nine months after exposure.

In general, then, there is solid evidence that the way sex roles are portrayed in the mass media can affect children's and adolescents' attitudes and perceptions of what is and is not appropriate for the two sexes.

Ethnic and Racial Attitudes

Media impact on racial and ethnic attitudes has also received some empirical scrutiny, although much more speculation and condemnation (Berry, 1980b; Pierce, 1980). There is evidence that programs designed to influence racial attitudes can have such an effect. For example, Bogatz and Ball (1971) found that after two years of viewing *Sesame Street,* both black and white children manifested more positive attitudes towards blacks and Hispanics. A Canadian study inserted content designed to create favorable attitudes toward Orientals, Indians, and French-Canadians into *Sesame Street* programs, and then exposed three-, four-, and five-year-olds to either treated or control programs (Gorn *et al.,* 1976). Children who viewed the special programs were more willing to pick nonwhite children as potential playmates from a group of photographs. Mays *et al.* (1975) also found that children ages six through ten years who viewed sixteen, one-half hour episodes of a television series designed to portray minorities positively increased their acceptance of and friendliness toward minority group members.

Of the few studies that have examined the effects of commercial entertainment programs on the racial attitudes of children, Graves (1975) found that positive portrayals produced positive changes and negative portrayals produced negative changes. She reports that a single exposure to relevant children's cartoons significantly influenced attitudes, that the reactions of white children were stronger than those of black children, and that "integrated" portrayals produced more change in both black and white children than did black or nearly all-black portrayals. Similiar findings have been reported with prime-time programs (Leifer, Graves and Phelps, 1976), although black children were more likely than white children to change in a negative direction in this study. Graves's (1980) extensive review of the literature on television's impact on racial and ethnic attitudes concludes that purposive programming can positively alter children's racial attitudes, especially with prolonged exposure. The conclusions to be drawn from the few studies with commercial programs, however, remain much less clear.

Other Attitudes

Other work that belongs in the attitudes and values category includes examination of the impact of the media on perceptions and knowledge of various occupational roles (DeFleur and DeFleur, 1967), a concern that is also reflected in studies of sex-role stereotyping. The general conclusion here is that the media do influence expectations concerning various occupational roles, particularly in the absence of alternative sources of information. There has also been interest in whether exposure to over-the-counter drug advertisements influence children's attitudes about, or their use of, either illicit or licit drugs. There is no clear evidence for such a relationship; if anything, exposure to drug advertising is negatively related to use of illicit drugs (Milavsky *et al.*, 1975). On the other hand, attitudes related to health anxiety, the taking of medicine, belief in the efficacy of medicine and use of proprietary drugs are related to exposure to drug ads (Milavsky *et al.*, 1975; Robertson *et al.*, 1979).

Finally, a few studies examine the relationship between children's exposure to news and public affairs programming and their attitudes toward various aspects of government and politics. Alper and Leidy's (1970) examination of the *National Citizenship Test* found strong and enduring changes in teenagers' acceptance of the principles of the Bill of Rights. Several correlational studies report relationships between exposure and increased interest in government and political affairs and more favorable attitudes toward government among younger children, although the results are quite mixed with samples of teenagers (Roberts *et al.*, 1975; Rubin, 1978; Atkin and Gantz, 1978). Indeed, Tolley's (1973) large-scale examination of children's sources of information and attitudes about the Vietnam war found very few instances of the media influencing the attitudes of even the younger children in his sample. Thus, although the evidence discussed earlier quite convincingly indicates that the mass media play an important role in contributing to children's knowledge about the world of politics and government, questions concerning media influences on political attitudes and values remain just that—questions.

CULTIVATION OF BELIEFS

Closely related to studies of the effects of mass communication on specific attitudes and values are several approaches, for the most part articulated in terms of adult audiences, that view the media as a major source of social and political definitions of the world. They are seen as cultivating entire belief systems. Ironically, such "powerful effects" theories return to the idea that the dominant effect of the media is reinforcement, once seen as evidence for limited effects but now viewed as reason for alarm.

Basically, theories of "ideological" effects (Katz, 1980) hold that the latent structure of media messages distorts reality in ways that perpetuate the interests of the existing power structure. They assume, all too often implicitly, that most people lack alternative sources of information necessary to serve as a corrective to such distortion, at least for more than a few, specific issues. For example, an active union member might have independent information she can use to evaluate media presentations about trade union activities, although she is unlikely to have first-hand or conflicting information about many other dimensions of the sociopolitical world. Most proponents of this view focus attention on the latent messages in news and public-affairs media. They contend that the economic and organizational structure of the mass media industry creates routine news practices that perpetuate existing social and political norms and relationships (Tuchman, 1977), legitimize the investiture of power in the managerial class (Glasgow Group, 1976), advocate parliamentarianism (Hall, 1977) and ratify popular, establishment opinion while muting minority voices (Noelle-Neumann, 1973, 1974). Another approach is more concerned with the message of television drama, arguing that in the United States the fundamental message pertains to the definition of power in society—power that resides in white, middle-class males who embody established norms and conventions (Gerbner and Gross, 1976a, 1980; Gerbner *et al.*, 1978, 1979).

Of course, the critical test of such theories is whether people do, indeed, perceive such latent messages and, if they do, whether the way they define (and presumably act in) their world is influenced by them. To date there has been a good deal more attention paid to content analyses and comparisons of media reality to independent measures of reality than to studies of effects on overall belief systems. Nevertheless, several recent attempts to operationalize measures of "consciousness" in order to examine the degree to which the media cultivate entire belief systems and the debate these attempts have ignited promise a good many empirical tests of some of the more interesting recent hypotheses concerning the effects of mass communication.

Noelle-Neumann's (1973, 1974) "spiral of silence" theory, for example, assumes that in order to avoid social isolation, people voice opinions they perceive to be popular with others and suppress those they view as unpopular. This tendency leads to perceptions of increased dominance of the majority opinion, which, in turn, leads to further suppression of minority opinion, creating a spiral of silence. She contends that this process is greatly compounded by the news media that cannot help but create an opinion environment that facilitates and magnifies the spiral of silence effect for all but establishment opinion. News media are ubiquitous; their messages are highly repetitive; there tends to be a unanimity among journalists in their view of the world, and it tends to reflect the establishment view. Thus, news media are viewed as limiting individual selective perception, hence limiting independent judgment, hence ensuring that the dominant opinion environment supports the establishment. Comparisons over time between measures of public opinion and results of rigorous content analyses of news and public-affairs media in Germany, indicate that the media may, indeed, operate to restrict individual selective perception and that the more they do so, the more salient minority voices become (Noelle-Neumann, 1977). There needs to be a good deal more replication of this work, particularly in countries with different mass media systems. Nevertheless, this line of research manifests the beginning of an empirical basis for one approach to a "powerful effects" view of the media.

An even stronger view of the reinforcing impact of the mass media, particularly television, is articulated by Gerbner and his colleagues (Gerbner and Gross, 1976a, 1976b, 1980; Gerbner *et al.*, 1978, 1979, 1980, 1981a, 1981b). They assert that "television is the central cultural arm of American society" and that it serves to reinforce rather than to subvert conventional beliefs and values. They view television as having a unique ability to "cultivate" basic assumptions about the nature of social reality. This ability derives from the following:

1. The uniformity of its message system, that reflects the conventional values, beliefs, and behaviors underlying and perpetuating the status quo,

2. The realism with which this uniform view of the nature of society is presented, a realism that hides the synthetic selective nature of television drama, and

3. The almost universal, ritualistic, and nonselective use people make of the medium.

Given these assumptions, it is hypothesized that the more one uses television, the more one's view of social reality will reflect television's view, an influence that may be manifested as a straightforward positive relationship between amount of television exposure and acceptance of television's reality or in one of two subprocesses. The first is called "mainstreaming" and refers to the diminishing influence of competing social forces among heavy viewers of television in a particular subgroup. For example, the impact of many information sources providing definitions of reality that diverge from the television view, that more educated higher income groups are documented to use, appears to be neutralized, if not overpowered, among members of that particular social group who are also heavy television viewers. The second is called "resonance" and refers to the amplification of the cultivation effect when television's view of reality converges with everyday reality (Gerbner *et al.*, 1980).

Tests of the cultivation hypothesis require several kinds of data. First, there must be periodic analyses of large aggregates of television programming in order to obtain comprehensive descriptions of television's world and to demonstrate that the view it perpetuates is fundamentally one that reinforces the status quo. In addition, if adequate tests of the effect of viewing are to be made, these analyses need to identify those dimensions on which television's world differs from everyday social reality. Much of this work has been carried out as part of Gerbner and his colleagues' cultural indicators project (Gerbner, 1972; Gerbner and Gross, 1976a; Gerbner *et al.*, 1978; 1979; 1980), which characterizes television's world as a rather frightening place, ruled by violence. Second, there is a need to examine whether viewing is, indeed, nonselective and universal and whether simply a measure of the amount of television watched is an adequate index of exposure to television's scary world. As indicated in our earlier discussion of the assessment of exposure, there is good reason to question this assumption. Finally, it must be demonstrated that the view of reality held by heavy and light television viewers differs on those dimensions where the television view diverges from everyday reality such that those who view the most television reflect the television view. Gerbner has reported a number of studies in which both children and adults characterized as "heavy viewers" express greater fear of victimization, less trust in people, and higher estimates of the number of people engaged in law enforcement occupations and of their own chances of being involved in violence, all dimensions that reflect the television view of the world (Gerbner and Gross, 1976a; 1980; Gerbner *et al.*, 1978; 1979). A more recent analysis also reports various "mainstreaming" and "resonance" effects, although admittedly as post-hoc explanations of obtained subgroup differences rather than as theoretically predicted outcomes, as well as data from a longitudinal study indicating that adolescents' amount of viewing during one year predicted greater acceptance of television definitions of the social reality the subsequent year, even when a variety of relevant third variables were controlled (Gerbner *et al.*, 1980).

The cultivation hypothesis has engendered a good deal of attention and debate (e.g., Doob and MacDonald, 1979; Gerbner *et al.*, 1981a, 1981b; Hawkins and Pingree, 1982; Hirsch, 1980, 1981a, 1981b; Hughes, 1980; Newcomb, 1978; Wober, 1978). Some derives from fundamental questions about assumptions basic to the theoretical model. Some centers on methodological issues concerning the nature of the data used to test the hypothesis, the frequent reliance on correlational analyses, the appropriateness or inappropriateness of various statistical procedures, and the post-hoc nature of some explanations offered to explain the data.

There have been several unsuccessful attempts to replicate some of the Gerbner group's "mean world" findings (Doob and MacDonald, 1979; Wober, 1978) as well as some partially successful ones (Hawkins and Pingree, 1980). Newcomb (1978) questions whether what is described as television's view of the world is really the image of social reality that viewers perceive. Others question the assumption that the amount of viewing is an adequate measure of the amount of exposure to any specific dimension of television's view of social reality (Christenson and Roberts, 1983; Hawkins and Pingree, 1982). They argue, for example, that it is difficult to believe that viewers who watch mostly situation comedies would obtain a view of a "mean" or "scary" world. One study indicates that narrower measures of exposure are

needed to demonstrate a cultivation effect but argues that with more careful specification of exposure, there is a higher probability of demonstrating such an effect (Hawkins and Pingree, 1980). Finally, a number of even more fundamental questions are raised by an extensive re-analysis of the National Opinion Research Center data sets on which Gerbner and his colleagues base many of their conclusions (Hirsch, 1980, 1981a, 1981b). Hirsch reports "remarkably little support" for a cultivation effect, arguing that acceptance of the hypothesis is premature. Although, as Whitney and Wartella (1982) note, there has been a bit more acrimony in Hirsch's critique and the Gerbner group's reply (Gerbner *et al.*, 1981a, 1981b) than one might wish, we concur with their conclusion that the importance of the exchange cannot be underestimated. It has led to a wide-ranging consideration of theoretical and methodological issues important to anyone interested in understanding the effects of mass communication and the way in which they need to be assessed. Hawkins and Pingree's (1982) examination of the literature relevant to television's impact on conceptions of social reality, both in terms of tests of the cultivation hypothesis and in terms of other approaches to media effects, illustrates some of the benefits likely to flow from exchanges over this and other theories of "powerful" effects.

CODA AS PROLOGUE

The preceding examination of various dimensions of the effects of mass communication makes no claim to be comprehensive. A number of problem areas, both past and present, are either omitted or touched on only lightly. Some of the topics that received attention several decades ago are mentioned here primarily to aid understanding of the major trends in research today. For example, we noted the earlier concern with direct attitudinal effects in order to provide a context within which to evaluate the current emphasis on indirect, more cognitive consequences of exposure to the media. We have only briefly mentioned some emerging areas of research such as the interaction between interpersonal and mass communication and the ways in which children process information from television. In the former case, although several recent papers point to the inadequacy of examining interpersonal and mass communication independent of each other (e.g., Chaffee, 1979; 1981; Rogers, 1977; Sears and Chaffee, 1979), their conclusions are primarily based on the results of past research that did not directly address this issue. We expect the next decade to witness many direct examinations of how the processes and effects of mass and interpersonal communication continually interact. Similarly, we have only alluded to recent work on the processing of mass communications, a decision we would willingly change were it not for space constraints. On the one hand, studies of children's attention to (e.g. Alwitt *et al.,* 1980; Anderson, *et al.,* 1979, 1981;) Krull and Husson, 1979) and comprehension of (Collins, 1979, 1983a, 1983b) television content rank as some of the most exciting and promising work we have reviewed. On the other hand, since the work is thus far limited almost exclusively to children's information processing and emphasizes process over effect, we made the hard choice simply to note this body of work and point to several recent considerations of how children (and to some extent adults) process mass-mediated messages (e.g., Bryant and Anderson, 1983; Christenson and Roberts, 1983; Collins, 1979; Comstock *et al.,* 1978; Dorr, 1980; Worth and Gross, 1974). Finally, again because of space constraints, we have omitted coverage of studies of media organizations and the factors that shape production of mass communication stimuli in the first place. Again it is a decision we made regretfully. However, given the sociological and economic orientation of much of this work, we opted simply to point readers to a recent collection of papers devoted exclusively to such organizational studies (Ettema and Whitney, 1982).

Our impression at the end of this review is that current research on the effects of mass communication reflects two broad, complementary trends. On the one hand, since the publication of the second edition of this handbook, there has been a tremendous outpouring of empirical research on a wide array of effects. This outpouring continues unabated. Moreover, much of the recent work manifests new perspectives concerning what constitute the effects of mass communication and new ideas about how to study them. Such testing of new ideas and new directions is paralleled by an almost self-concious effort of the field to assert independence from the parent disciplines of the past—psychology and sociology. On the other hand, this testing and exploration strikes us as proceeding hand in hand with a kind of consolidation of what has gone before. Early visions of all-powerful media, and mid-century minimal-effects models are merging into the recognition that the influence of mass communication need not be approached in terms of all-or-nothing propositions. Rather, current work conceptualizes the mass media as one of several elements operating within a larger social system, exerting neither more nor less important influences on social behavior

than such institutions as schools, governments, and families. Consolidation is also inherent in recent moves away from the kind of brute empiricism endemic to any "problem-oriented" field toward higher level generalizations, as exemplified in the various recent syntheses and reconceptualizations noted earlier. Still another encouraging sign of consolidation is that many of these higher level conceptual statements are grounded in empirical data because they are emerging from meta-analyses. That is, the field has accumulated enough empirical results to support the kinds of cross-study comparisons and analyses that facilitate development of theories of the middle range (Merton, 1968; Rogers, 1981).

The heading of this final section, then, reflects a view of a field that is entering its adolescence. It is testing and attempting to break free from many of its early roots and at the same time also integrating much of the empirical work of its childhood into more general principles about the process and effects of mass communication, principles that may guide it toward maturity. It is our sense that the field is likely to have a healthy adolescence, sometimes rewarding, sometimes frustrating, often difficult, occasionally comic, but almost always interesting.

REFERENCES

Adler, R. P., B. Z. Friedlander, G. S. Lesser, L. Meringoff, T. S. Robertson, J. R. Rossiter, and S. Ward (1977). *Research on the effects of television advertising on children.* Washington, D.C.: Government Printing Office.

Adoni, H. (1979). The functions of mass media in the political socialization of adolescents. *Communic. Res., 6,* 84–106.

Ahammer, I. M., and J. P. Murray (1979). Kindness in the kindergarten: the relative influence of role playing and prosocial television in facilitating a truism. *Int. J. behav. Develop., 2,* 133–157.

Allen, R. L., and W. T. Bielby (1979). Blacks' attitudes and behaviors toward television. *Communic. Res., 6,* 437–462.

Alper, W. S., T. R. Leidy (1970). The impact of information transmission through television. *Publ. Opin. Quart., 33,* 556–562.

Alwitt, L. F., D. R. Anderson, E. P. Lorch, and S. R. Levin, (1980). Preschool children's visual attention to attributes of television. *Hum. Communic. Res., 7,* 53–67.

Anderson, D. R., L. F. Alwitt, E. P. Lorch, and S. R. Levin (1979). Watching children watch television. In G. A. Hale, and M. Lewis (Eds.), *Attention and cognitive development.* New York: Plenum. Pp. 331–361.

Anderson, D. R., and S. R. Levin (1976). Young children's attention to "Sesame Street." *Child Development, 47,* 806–811.

Anderson, D. R., E. P. Lorch, D. E. Field, and J. Sanders (1981). The effects of TV program comprehensibility on preschool children's visual attention to television. *Child Development, 52,* 151–157.

Anderson, J. A., and T. P. Meyer (1975). Functionalism and the mass media. *J. Broadcasting, 19,* 11–22.

Andison, F. S. (1977). TV violence and viewer aggression: a cumulation of study results, 1956–1976. *Publ. Opin. Quart., 41,* 314–331.

Arnoff, C. (1974). Old age in prime time. *J. Communic., 24,* 86–87.

Arundale, R. A. (1977). Sampling across time for communication research. In P. M. Hirsch, P. V. Miller, and F. G. Kline (Eds.), *Strategies for communication research.* Beverly Hills, Calif.: Sage. Pp. 257–285.

Atkin, C. K. (1976). Mass media and the aging. In H. J. Oyer, and G. H. Oyer (Eds.), *Aging and communication.* Baltimore, Md.: Univ. Park Press. Pp. 99–118.

———— (1977). Effects of campaign advertising and newscasts on children. *Journalism Quart., 54,* 503–508.

———— (1978). Broadcast news programming and the child audience. *J. Broadcasting, 22,* 47–61.

Atkin, D., J. Galloway, and O. Nayman (1976). News media exposure, political knowledge, and campaign interest. *Journalism Quart., 53,* 231–237.

Atkin, C. K., and W. Gantz (1978). Television news and political socialization. *Publ. Opin. Quart., 42,* 183–198.

Atkin, C., B. Greenberg, F. Korzenny, and S. McDermott (1979). Selective exposure to televised violence. *J. Broadcasting, 23,* 5–13.

Atkin, C., and G. Heald (1976). Effects of political advertising. *Publ. Opin. Quart., 40,* 216–228.

Atkin, C., and M. Miller (1975). The effects of television advertising on children: experimental evidence. Presented at the annual meetings of the International Communication Association, Chicago.

Atkins, P. A., and H. Elwood (1978). TV news is first choice in survey of high schools. *Journalism Quart., 55,* 596–599.

Atwood, L. E., A. Sohn, and H. Sohn (1976). Community discussion and newspaper content. Presented at the annual meetings of the Association for Education in Journalism. College Park, Md.

Bachen, C. M., M. C. Hornby, D. F. Roberts, and P. Hernandez-Ramos (1982). Television viewing behavior and the development of reading skills. Presented at the annual meeting of the American Educational Research Association, New York City.

Baker, R. K., and S. J. Ball Eds. (1969). Violence and the media. *A staff report to the National Commission on the Causes and Prevention of Violence.* Washington, D.C.: Government Printing Office.

Ball, S. J., and G. A. Bogatz (1970). *The first year of Sesame Street: an evaluation.* Princeton, N.J.: Educational Testing Service.

Bandura, A. (1965). Influence of models' reinforcement contingencies on the acquisition of imitative responses. *J. Pers. soc. Psychol., 1,* 589–595.

———— (1969). *Principles of behavior modification.* New York: Holt, Rinehart, and Winston.

———— (1977). *Social learning theory.* Englewood Cliffs, N.J.: Prentice-Hall.

Bandura, A., D. Ross, and S. A. Ross (1961). Transmission of aggression through imitation of aggressive models. *J. abnorm. soc. Psychol., 63,* 575–582.

———— (1963). Imitation of film-mediated aggressive models. *J. abnorm. soc. Psychol., 66,* 3–11.

Bandura, A., and R. H. Walters (1963). *Social learning and personality development.* New York: Holt, Rinehart, and Winston.

Baran, S. J., L. J. Chase, and J. A. Courtright (1979). Television drama as a facilitator of prosocial behavior: "The Waltons." *J. Broadcasting, 23,* 277–285.

Barber, J. D. (1980). *The pulse of politics: electing presidents in the media age.* New York: Norton.

Barcus, F. E. (1980). The nature of television advertising to children. In E. L. Palmer, and A. Dorr (Eds.), *Children and the faces of television: teaching, violence, selling.* New York: Academic Press. Pp. 273–285.

Bauer, R. A. (1964). The obstinate audience: the influence process from the point of view of social communication. *Amer. Psychol., 19,* 319–328.

Bauer, R. A., and A. H. Bauer (1960). America, mass society and mass media. *J. soc. Issues, 16* (3), 3–66.

Bechtel, R. B., C. Achelpohl, and R. Akers (1972). Correlates between observed behavior and questionnaire responses on television viewing. In E. A. Rubinstein, G. A. Comstock, and J. P. Murray (Eds.), *Television and social behavior.* Vol. 4. *Television in day-to-day life: patterns of use.* Washington, D.C.: Government Printing Office. Pp. 274–344.

Becker, L. B. (1976). Two tests of media gratifications: Watergate and the 1974 election. *Journalism Quart., 53,* 29–33, 87.

———— (1979). Measurement of gratifications. *Communic. Res., 6,* 54–73.

———— (1982). The mass media and citizen assessment of issue importance: a reflection on agenda-setting research. In D. C. Whitney, and E. Wartella (Eds.), *Mass communication review yearbook.* Vol. 3. Beverly Hills, Calif., Sage. Pp. 521–536.

Becker, L. B., M. E. McCombs, and J. M. McLeod (1975). The development of political cognitions. In S. H. Chaffee (Ed.), *Political communication: issues and strategies for research.* Beverly Hills, Calif.: Sage. Pp. 21–63.

Becker, L. B., I. A. Sobowale, and W. E. Casey (1979a). Newspaper and television dependencies: effects on evaluations of public officials. *J. Broadcasting, 23,* 465–475.

Becker, L. B., D. H. Weaver, D. A. Graber, and M. E. McCombs (1979b). Influence on public agendas. In S. Kraus (Ed.), *The great debates: Carter vs. Ford, 1976.* Bloomington, Ind.: Indiana Univ. Press. Pp. 418–428.

Becker, L. B., and D. C. Whitney (1980). Effects of media dependencies: audience assessment of government. *Communic. Res., 7,* 95–120.

Belson, W. (1978). *Television violence and the adolescent boy.* London: Saxon House.

Beltran, L. R. (1975). Research ideologies in conflict. *J. Communic., 25* (2), 187–193.

Benton, M., and P. J. Frazier (1976). The agenda-setting function of mass media at three levels of information holding. *Communic. Res., 3,* 261–274.

Berelson, B., P. F. Lazarsfeld, and W. N. McPhee (1954). *Voting.* Chicago: Univ. of Chicago Press.

Berkowitz, L. (1962). *Aggression: a social psychological analysis.* New York: McGraw-Hill.

——— (1965). Some aspects of observed aggression. *J. Pers. soc. Psychol., 2,* 359–369.

Berkowitz, L., and R. G. Geen (1966). Film violence and the cue properties of available targets. *J. Pers. soc. Psychol., 3,* 525–530.

——— (1967). Stimulus qualities of the target of aggression: a further study. *J. Pers. soc. Psychol., 5,* 364–368.

Berkowitz, L., and E. Rawlings (1963). Effects of film violence on inhibitions against subsequent aggression. *J. abnorm. soc. Psychol., 66,* 405–412.

Berlo, D. (1977). Communication as process: review and commentary. In B. D. Rubin (Ed.), *Communication year-book* I. New Brunswick, N.J.: Transaction Books. Pp. 11–27.

Berry, G. L. (1980a). Children, television, and social class roles: the medium as an unplanned educational curriculum. In E. L. Palmer, and A. Dorr (Eds.), *Children and the faces of television: teaching, violence, selling.* New York: Academic Press. Pp. 71–82.

——— (1980b). Television and Afro-Americans: past legacy and present portrayals. In S. B. Withey, and R. P. Abeles (Eds.), *Television and social behavior: beyond violence and children.* Hillsdale, N.J.: Erlbaum. Pp. 231–248.

Beuf, A. (1974). Doctor, lawyer, household drudge. *J. Communic., 24* (2), 142–145.

Bishop, G. F., R. W. Oldendick, and A. J. Tuchfarber (1978). Debate watching and the acquisition of political knowledge. *J. Communic., 28* (4), 99–113.

Blumler, J. G. (1979). The role of theory in uses and gratifications studies. *Communic. Res., 6,* 9–36.

Blumler, J. G., and E. Katz (1974). Forward. In J. G. Blumler, and E. Katz (Eds.), *The uses of mass communications: current perspectives on gratifications research.* Beverly Hills, Calif.: Sage. Pp. 13–16.

Blumler, J. G., and D. McQuail (1969). *Television in politics: its uses and influences.* Chicago: Univ. of Chicago Press.

Bogart, L. (1975a). How the challenge of television news affects the prosperity of daily newspapers. *Journalism Quart., 52,* 403–410.

——— (1975b). The future of the metropolitan daily. *J. Communic., 25* (2), 30–43.

Bogatz, G. A., and S. J. Ball (1971). *The second year of Sesame Street: a continuing evaluation.* 2 Vols. Princeton, N.J.: Educational Testing Service.

Bostian, L. R., and J. E. Ross (1965). Functions and meanings of mass media for Wisconsin farm women. *Journalism Quart., 42,* 69–76.

Boulding, K. E. (1966). *The image: knowledge in life and society.* Ann Arbor: Univ. of Michigan Press.

Bower, R. T. (1973). *Television and the public.* New York: Holt, Rinehart, and Winston.

Broder, D. S. (1972). *The party's over: the failure of politics in America.* New York: Harper & Row.

Brown, J. R., J. K. Cramond, and R. J. Wilde (1974). Displacement effects of television and the child's functional orientation to media. In J. G. Blumler, and E. Katz (Eds.), *The uses of mass communications current perspectives on gratifications research.* Beverly Hills, Calif.: Sage. Pp. 93–112.

Brown, R. (1965). *Social Psychology.* New York: Free Press.

Bryant, B., F. Currier, and A. Morrison (1976). Relating life style factors of a person to his choice of newspaper. *Journalism Quart., 53,* 74–79.

Bryant, J., and D. A. Anderson Eds., (1983). *Children's understanding of television: research on attention and comprehension.* New York: Academic Press.

Bureau of the Census (1981). *Statistical abstract of the United States: 1980.* Washington, D.C.: Government Printing Office.

Butler, M., and W. Paisley (1980). *Women and the mass media: source book for research and action.* New York: Human Sciences Press.

Cameron, P., and C. Janky (1971). The effects of TV violence upon children: a naturalistic experiment. *Proceedings of the 79th annual convention of the American Psychological Association.* Washington, D.C.: American Psychological Association. Pp. 233–234.

Campbell, D. T. (1969). Ethnocentrism of disciplines and the fish-scale model of omniscience. In M. Sherif, and C. W. Sherif (Eds.), *Interdisciplinary relationships in the social sciences.* Chicago: Aldine. Pp. 328–348.

Canadian Broadcasting Corporation (1975). *Dimensions of audience response to television programs in Canada.* Toronto: CBC.

Cantril, H. (1940). *The invasion from Mars.* Princeton: Princeton Univ. Press.

Carey, J. W. (1976). How media shape campaigns. *J. Communic., 26* (2), 50–57.

Carey, J. W., and A. L. Kreiling (1974). Popular culture and uses and gratifications: notes toward an accomodation. In J. G. Blumler, and E. Katz (Eds.), *The uses of mass communication: current perspectives on gratifications research.* Beverly Hills, Calif.: Sage. Pp. 225–248.

Carter, R. E., Jr. (1957). Segregation and the news: a regional content study. *Journalism Quart., 34,* 3–18.

Cartwright, D. (1949). Some principles of mass persuasion: selected findings of research on the sale of U.S. war bonds. *Hum. Relat., 2,* 253–267.

Cassata, M. B., P. A. Anderson, and T. D. Skill (1980). The older adult in daytime serial drama. *J. Communic., 30* (1), 48–49.

Chaffee, S. H. (1972). Television and adolescent aggressiveness. In G. A. Comstock, and E. A. Rubinstein (Eds.), *Television and social behavior.* Vol. 3. *Television and adolescent aggressiveness.* Washington, D.C.: Government Printing Office. Pp. 1–34.

——— Ed. (1975). *Political communication: issues and strategies for research.* Beverly Hills, Calif.: Sage.

——— (1977). Mass media effects: new research perspectives. In D. Lerner, and L. Nelson (Eds.), *Communication research—a half century appraisal.* Honolulu: East-West Center Press. Pp. 210–241.

——— (1978). Presidential debates—are they helpful to voters? *Communic. Monogr., 45,* 330–353.

——— (1982). Mass media and interpersonal channels: competitive, convergent or complementary? In G. Gumpert and R. Cathcart (Eds.), *Inter/Media: interpersonal communication in a media world*. New York: Oxford Univ. Press. Pp. 57–77.

———— (1981). Mass media in political campaigns: an expanding role. In R. E. Rice, and W. J. Paisley (Eds.), *Public communication campaigns*. Beverly Hills, Calif.: Sage. Pp. 181–198.

Chaffee, S. H., and J. Dennis (1979). Presidential debates: an empirical assessment. In A. Ranney (Ed.), *The past and future of presidential debates*. Washington, D.C.: American Enterprise Institute. Pp. 75–106.

Chaffee, S. H., and F. Izcaray (1975). Mass communication functions in a media rich developing society. *Communic. Res., 2,* 367–395.

Chaffee, S. H., M. Jackson-Beeck, J. Durall, and D. Wilson (1977). Mass communication in political communication. In S. A. Renshon (Ed.), *Handbook of political socialization: theory and research*. New York: Free Press. Pp. 223–258.

Chaffee, S. H., and A. R. Tims (1982). News media and use in adolescence: implications for political cognitions. In M. Burgoon (Ed.), *Communication yearbook 6*. Beverly Hills, Calif.: Sage. Pp. 736–758.

Chaffee, S. H., L. S. Ward, and L. P. Tipton (1970). Mass communication and political socialization. *Journalism Quart., 47,* 657–659; 666.

Chaffee, S. H., and D. Wilson (1975). Adult life cycle changes in mass media use. Paper presented at the meeting of the Association for Education in Journalism, Ottawa, Ontario.

———— (1977). Media rich, media poor: two studies of diversity in agenda-holding. *Journalism Quart., 54,* 466–476.

Charters, W. W. (1933). *Motion pictures and youth: a summary*. New York: Macmillan.

Childers, P. R., and J. Ross (1973). The relationship between viewing television and student achievement. *J. educat. Res., 66,* 317–319.

Children's Television Workshop (1977). A children's television series about science and technology. A proposal by the Children's Television Workshop.

Christenson, P. G. (1982). Children's perceptions of TV commercials and products: the effect of PSAs. *Communic. Res., 9,* 491–524.

Christenson, P. G., and D. F. Roberts (1983). The role of television in the formation of children's social attitudes. In M. J. A. Howe (Ed.), *Learning from television: psychological and educational research*. London: Academic Press. Pp. 79–99.

Chu, G. C. (1976). Group communication and development in mainland China—the functions of social pressure. In W. Schramm, and D. Lerner (Eds.), *Communication and change: the last ten years—and the next*. Honolulu: Univ. of Hawaii Press. Pp. 119–133.

Clark, D. G., and W. B. Blankenburg (1972). Trends in violent content in selected mass media. In G. A. Comstock, and E. A. Rubinstein (Eds.), *Television and social behavior*. Vol. 1. *Mass content and control*. Washington, D.C.: Government Printing Office. Pp. 188–243.

Clarke, P., and E. Fredin (1978). Newspapers, television and political reasoning. *Publ. Opin. Quart., 42,* 143–160.

Clarke, P., and F. G. Kline (1974). Media effects reconsidered: some new strategies for communication research. *Communic. Res., 1,* 224–240.

Cline, V. B., R. G. Croft, and S. Courrier (1972). Desensitization of children to television violence. *J. Pers. soc. Psychol., 27,* 360–365.

Coates, B., H. E. Pusser, and I. Goodman (1976). The influence of "Sesame Street" and "Mister Rogers' Neighborhood" on children's social behavior in the preschool. *Child Development, 47,* 138–144.

Collins, W. A. (1973). Effects of temporal separation between motivation, aggression, and consequences: a developmental study. *Develop. Psychol., 8,* 215–221.

———— (1979). Children's comprehension of television content. In E. Wartella (Ed.), *Children communicating: media and development of thought, speech, understanding*. Beverly Hills, Calif.: Sage. Pp. 21–52.

———— (1983a). Interpretation and inference in children's television viewing. In J. Bryant and D. R. Anderson (Eds.) *Children's understanding of television: research on attention and comprehension*. New York: Academic Press. Pp. 125–150.

———— (1983b). Social antecedents, cognitive processing, and comprehension of social portrayals on television. In E. T. Higgins, D. Ruble and W. Hartup (Eds.) *Social cognition and social development*. New York: Cambridge Univ. Press. Pp. 110–133.

Collins, W. A., T. Berndt, V. Hess (1974). Observational learning of motives and consequences for television aggression: a development study. *Child Development, 45,* 799–802.

Collins, W. A., and S. K. Getz (1976). Children's social responses following modeled reactions to provocation: prosocial effects of a television drama. *J. Pers., 44,* 488–500.

Collins, W. A., and S. A. Zimmerman (1975). Convergent and divergent social cues: effects of televised aggression on children. *Communic. Res., 2,* 231–246.

Columbia Broadcasting System, Office of Social Research (1974). *A study of messages received by children who viewed an episode of Fat Albert and the Cosby Kids*. New York: Columbia Broadcasting System, Inc.

Columbia Broadcasting System (1977). *Communicating with children through television: studies of messages and other impressions conveyed by five childrens programs*. New York: CBS Economics and Research.

Comstock, G. (1980). New emphases in research on the effects of television and film violence. In E. L. Palmer, and A. Dorr (Eds.), *Children and the faces of television: teaching, violence, selling*. New York: Academic Press. Pp. 129–148.

Comstock, G., S. Chaffee, N. Katzman, M. McCombs, and D. Roberts (1978). *Television and human behavior*. New York: Columbia Univ. Press.

Comstock, G., and M. Fisher (1975). *Television and human behavior: a guide to the pertinent scientific literature*. Santa Monica, Calif.: Rand Corp.

Conway, M. M., A. J. Stevens, and R. G. Smith (1975). The relation between media and children's civic awareness. *Journalism Quart., 52,* 531–538.

Cook, T. D., and D. T. Campbell (1979). *Quasi-experimentation: design and analysis issues for field settings*. Boston: Houghton Mifflin.

Cook, T. D., H. Appleton, R. F. Conner, A. Shaffer, G. Tamkin, and S. J. Weber (1975). *"Sesame Street" revisited*. New York: Russell Sage.

Cooley, H. C. (1909). *Social organization.* New York: Scribners.

Cramond, J. (1976). Introduction of TV and effects upon children's daily lives. In R. Brown (Ed.), *Children and television.* Beverly Hills, Calif.: Sage. Pp. 267–283.

Danowski, J. (1975). Informational aging: interpersonal and mass communication patterns in a retirement community. Presented at Gerontological Society Convention, Louisville, Kentucky.

Davis, D. K., and J. Lee (1980). Time-series analysis models for communication research. In P. R. Monge, and J. N. Cappella (Eds.), *Multivariate techniques in human communication research.* New York: Academic Press. Pp. 429–454.

Davidson, E. S., A. Yasuna, and A. Tower (1979). The effects of television cartoons on sex-role stereotyping in young girls. *Child Development, 50,* 597–600.

Davison, W. P., J. Boylan, and F. T. C. Yu (1976). *Mass media: systems and effects.* New York: Praeger.

DeCharms, R., and G. H. Moeller (1962). Values expressed in American children's readers: 1900–1950. *J. abnorm. soc. Psychol., 64,* 136–142.

DeFleur, M. L., and S. Ball-Rokeach (1982). *Theories of mass communication* (4th ed.). New York: David McKay.

DeFleur, M. L., and L. B. DeFleur (1967). The relative contribution of television as a learning source for children's occupational knowledge. *Amer. Sociol. Rev., 32,* 777–789.

Denbow, C. (1975). A test of predictors of newspaper subscribing. *Journalism Quart., 52,* 744–748.

Dennis, E. E. (1978). *The media society: evidence about mass communication in America.* Dubuque, Iowa: Wm. C. Brown.

Dennis, J., S. H. Chaffee, and S. Y. Choe (1979). Impact on partisan image and issue voting. In S. Kraus (Ed.), *The great debates: 1976, Ford vs. Carter.* Bloomington: Indiana Univ. Press. Pp. 314–330.

Dervin, B. (1981). Mass communicating: changing conceptions of the audience. In R. E. Rice, and W. J. Paisley (Eds.), *Public communication campaigns.* Beverly Hills, Calif.: Sage. Pp. 71–87.

Diaz Bordenave, J. (1976). Communication of agricultural innovations in Latin America: the need for new models. *Communic. Res., 3,* 135–154.

Dominick, J. R., and B. S. Greenberg (1972). Attitudes toward violence: the interaction of television, exposure, family attitudes, and social class. In G. A. Comstock and E. A. Rubinstein (Eds.), *Television and social behavior.* Vol. 3. *Television and adolescent aggressiveness.* Washington, D.C.: Government Printing Office. Pp. 314–335.

Donohue, G. A., P. J. Tichenor, and C. N. Olien (1975). Mass media and the knowledge gap: a hypothesis reconsidered. *Communic. Res., 2,* 3–23.

Doob, A. N., and G. E. MacDonald (1979). Television viewing and fear of victimization: is the relationship causal? *J. Pers. soc. Psychol., 37,* 170–179.

Dorr, A. (1978). Children's advertising rulemaking comment. Testimony to the Federal Trade Commission's Rulemaking Hearings on Television Advertising and Children, San Francisco, California.

——— (1980). When I was a child I thought as a child. In S. B. Withey, and R. P. Abeles (Eds.), *Television and social be-havior: beyond violence and children.* Hillsdale, N.J.: Erlbaum. Pp. 191–230.

Dorr, A., and P. Kovarick (1980). Televised violence and its effects. In E. L. Palmer, and A. Dorr (Eds.), *Children and the faces of television: teaching, violence, selling.* New York: Academic Press. Pp. 183–199.

Dotan, J., and A. A. Cohen (1976). Mass media use in the family during war and peace. *Communic. Res., 3,* 393–402.

Douglas, D. F., B. H. Westley, and S. H. Chaffee (1970). An information campaign that changed community attitudes. *Journalism Quart., 47,* 479–487.

Drabman, R. S., and M. H. Thomas (1974). Does media violence increase children's toleration of real-life aggression? *Develop. Psychol., 10,* 418–421.

Drew, D., and B. Reeves (1980). Learning from a television news story. *Communic. Res., 7,* 121–135.

Dubren, R. (1977). Evaluation of a televised stop-smoking clinic. *Publ. Health Reports, 92,* 81–84.

Dysinger, W. S. and C. A. Ruckmick (1933). *The emotional responses of children to the motion picture situation.* New York: MacMillan.

Ebring, L., E. N. Goldenberg, and A. H. Miller (1980). Front-page news and real-world cues: a new look at agenda-setting by the media. *Amer. J. politic. Sci., 24,* 16–49.

Edelstein, A. S. (1974). *The uses of communication in decision-making: a comparative study of Yugoslavia and the United States.* New York: Praeger.

Egan, L. M. (1978). Children's viewing patterns for television news. *Journalism Quart., 55,* 337–342.

Eisenstein, E. (1968). Some conjectures about the impact of printing on Western society and thought: a preliminary report. *J. mod. Hist., 40,* 1–53.

Elliott, P. (1974). Uses and gratifications research: a critique and a sociological alternative. In J. G. Blumler and E. Katz (Eds.), *The uses of mass communications: current perspectives on gratifications research.* Beverly Hills, Calif.: Sage. Pp. 249–268.

Elliott, W. R., and W. J. Schenck-Hamlin (1979). Film, politics, and the press: the influence of "All the President's Men." *Journalism Quart., 56,* 546–553.

Eron, L. (1963). Relationship with TV viewing habits and aggressive behavior in children. *J. abnorm. soc. Psychol., 67,* 193–196.

Esserman, J. F. (1981). New research vs. old assumptions. In J. F. Esserman (Ed.), *Television advertising and children: issues, research and findings.* New York: Child Research Service. Pp. 5–15.

Ettema, J. S., and F. G. Kline (1977). Deficits, differences, and ceilings: contingent conditions for understanding the knowledge gap. *Communic. Res., 4,* 179–202.

Ettema, J. S., and D. C. Whitney, Eds. (1982). *Individuals in mass media organizations: creativity and constraint.* Beverly Hills, Calif.: Sage.

Eyal, C. H. (1979). *The roles of newspapers and television in agenda-setting.* Annual meetings of the American Association of Public Opinion Research, Buck Hills Falls, Penn.

Eyal, C. H., J. P. Winter, and W. F. DeGeorge (1979). Time frame for agenda-setting. Presented at annual meeting of the American Association for Public Opinion Research. Buck Hills Falls, Penn.

Farhar-Pilgrim, B., and F. F. Shoemaker (1981). Campaigns to affect energy behavior. In R. E. Rice, and W. J. Paisley (Eds.), *Public communication campaigns*. Beverly Hills, Calif.: Sage. Pp. 161–180.

Farquhar, J. W. (1978). The community-based model of life style intervention trials. *Amer. J. Epidem., 108,* 103–111.

Farquhar, J. W., N. Maccoby, and D. S. Solomon (1984). Community applications of behavioral medicine. In W. D. Gentry (Ed.), *Handbook of behavioral medicine*. New York: Guilford Press.

Farquhar, J. W., N. Maccoby, P. Wood, J. Alexander, H. Breitrose, B. Brown, W. Haskell, A. McAlister, J. Nash, and M. Stern (1977). Community education for cardiovascular health. *Lancet,* 1192–1195.

Federal Communications Commission (1974). Children's television programs: report and policy statement, 39, *Federal Register, 39,* 25505–25510.

Federal Trade Commission (1978). *FTC staff report on television advertising to children*. Washington, D.C. Federal Trade Commission.

Feigert, F. B. (1976). Political competence and mass media use. *Publ. Opin. Quart., 40,* 234–238.

Feshbach, S. (1972). Reality and fantasy in filmed violence. In J. P. Murray, E. A., Rubinstein, and G. A. Comstock (Eds.), *Television and social behavior*. Vol. 2. *Television and social learning*. Washington, D.C.: Government Printing Office. Pp. 318–345.

Feshbach, S., and R. D. Singer (1971). *Television and aggression: an experimental field study*. San Francisco: Jossey-Bass.

Fitzsimmons, S. J., and H. G. Osburn (1968). The impact of social issues and public affairs television documentaries. *Publ. Opin. Quart., 32,* 379–397.

Flavell, J. H. (1977). *Cognitive development*. Englewood Cliffs, N.J.: Prentice-Hall.

Fox, S., A. H. Stein, L. C. Friedrich, and D. M. Kipnis (1977). Prosocial television and children's fantasy. Paper presented at the biennial meeting of the Society for Research in Child Development, New Orleans.

Frank, R. E., and M. G. Greenberg (1980). *The public's use of television: who watches and why*. Beverly Hills, Calif.: Sage.

Freidson, E. (1953). Communications research and the concept of the mass. *Amer. Sociol. Res., 18,* 313–317.

Freuh, T., and P. E. McGhee (1975). Traditional sex role development and amount of time spent watching television. *Child Development, 11,* 109.

Friedman, H. L., and R. I. Johnson (1972). Mass media use and aggression: a pilot study. In G. A. Comstock, and E. A. Rubinstein (Eds.), *Television and social behavior*. Vol. 3. *Television and adolescent aggressiveness*. Washington, D.C.: Government Printing Office. Pp. 336–360.

Friedrich, L. K., and A. H. Stein (1975). Prosocial television and young children: the effects of verbal labeling and role playing on learning and behavior. *Child Development, 46,* 27–38.

Funkhouser, G. R. (1973). Trends in media coverage of the issues of the 60's. *Journalism Quart., 50,* 533–538.

Gaines, L., and J. F. Esserman (1981). A quantitative study of young children's comprehension of television programs and commericals. In J. F. Esserman (Ed.), *Television advertising and children: issues, research and findings*. New York: Child Research Service. Pp. 95–105.

Gans, H. J. (1980). The audience for television—and in television research. In S. B. Withey, and R. P. Abeles (Eds.), *Television and social behavior: beyond violence and children*. Hillsdale, N.J.: Erlbaum. Pp. 55–81.

Geen, R. G., and L. Berkowitz (1966). Name-mediated aggressive cue properties. *J. Pers., 34,* 456–465.

_____ (1967). Some conditions facilitating the occurrence of aggression after the observation of violence. *J. Pers., 35,* 666–676.

Genova, B. K. L., and B. S. Greenberg (1979). Interests in news and the knowledge gap. *Publ. Opin. Quart., 43,* 79–91.

Gerbner, G. (1969). The case for cultural indicators, with violence in the mass media as a case in point. Paper presented at the annual meetings of the American Political Science Association, New York City.

_____ (1972). Violence in television drama: trends and symbolic functions. In G. A. Comstock, and E. A. Rubinstein (Eds.), *Television and social behavior*. Vol. 1. *Media content and control*. Washington, D.C.: Government Printing Office. Pp. 28–187.

Gerbner, G., and L. Gross (1976a). Living with television: the violence profile. *J. Communic., 26,* (2) 173–199.

_____ (1976b). The scary world of television. *Psychol. Today,* 41–45, 89.

_____ (1980). The violent faces of television and its lessons. In E. L. Palmer, and A. Dorr (Eds.), *Children and the faces of television: teaching, violence, selling*. New York: Academic Press. Pp. 149–162.

Gerbner, G., L. Gross, M. Jackson-Beeck, S. Jeffries-Fox, and N. Signorielli (1978). Cultural indicators: violence profile No. 9. *J. Communic., 28* (3), 176–207.

Gerbner, G., L. Gross, M. Morgan, and N. Signorielli (1980). The "mainstreaming" of America: violence profile No. 11. *J. Communic., 30* (3), 10–29.

Gerbner, G., L. Gross, M. Morgan, and N. Signorielli (1981a). A curious journey into the scary world of Paul Hirsch. *Communic. Res., 8,* 39–72.

_____ (1981b). Final reply to Hirsch. *Communic. Res., 8,* 259–280.

Gerbner, G., L. Gross, N. Signorielli, M. Morgan, and M. Jackson-Beeck (1979). The demonstration of power: violence profile No. 10. *J. Communic., 29* (3), 177–196.

Glasgow University Media Group (1976). *Bad news*. London: Routledge.

Goldberg, M. E., and G. Gorn (1978). Some unintended consequences of TV advertising to children. *J. consum. Res., 5,* 22–29.

Goldberg, M. E., G. Gorn, and W. Gibson (1978). TV messages for snack and breakfast foods: do they influence children's preferences? *J. consum. Res., 5,* 73–81.

Gormley, W. T. Jr. (1975). Newspaper agendas and political elites. *Journalism Quart., 52,* 304–308.

Gorn, G. J., M. E. Goldberg, and R. N. Kanungo (1976). The role of educational television in changing the intergroup attitudes of children. *Child Development, 47,* 277–280.

Graber, D. A. (1980). *Mass media and American politics*. Washington, D.C.: Congressional Quarterly Press.

Goranson, R. E. (1970). Media violence and aggressive behavior: a review of experimental research. In L. Berkowitz (Ed.), *Advances in experimental social psychology*. Vol. 5. New York: Academic Press. Pp. 1–31.

Graves, S. B. (1975). Racial diversity in children's television: its impact on racial attitudes and stated program preferences in young children. *Dissertation Abstracts International, 36,* 4665B. (University Microfilms No. 76-06595).

_____ (1980). Psychological effects of black portrayals on television. In S. B. Withey, and R. P. Abeles (Eds.), *Television and social behavior: beyond violence and television*. Hillsdale, N.J.: Erlbaum. Pp. 259–289.

Greenberg, B. S. (1974). Gratifications of television viewing and their correlates for British children. In J. G. Blumler, and E. Katz (Eds.), *The uses of mass communications: current perspectives on gratifications research*. Beverly Hills, Calif.: Sage. Pp. 71–92.

_____ (1981). Smoking, drinking and drugging in top rated TV series. *J. Drug Educat., 11* (3), 227–233.

Greenberg, B. S., and B. Dervin (1970). *Use of mass media by the urban poor*. New York: Praeger.

Greenberg, B. S., and W. Gantz (1976). Public television and taboo topics: the impact of VD blues. *Publ. Telecommunications Rev. 4:* 59–64.

Halberstam, D. (1979). *The powers that be*. New York: Knopf.

Hall, S. (1977). Culture, the media, and the "ideological effect." In J. Curran, M. Gurevitch, and J. Woollacott (Eds.), *Mass communication and society*. London: Arnold. Pp. 315–348.

Handlon, J. H. (1962). Hormonal activity and individual responses to stresses and easements in everyday living. In R. Roessler, and N. S. Greenfield (Eds.), *Physiological correlates of psychological disorder*. Madison: Univ. of Wisconsin Press. Pp. 157–170.

Hartmann, D. P. (1969). Influence of symbolically modeled instrumental aggression and pain cues on aggressive behavior. *J. Pers. soc. Psychol., 11,* 280–288.

Hawkins, R. P., and S. Pingree (1980). Some processes in the cultivation effect. *Communic. Res., 7,* 193–226.

_____ (1982). TV influence on social reality and conceptions of the world. In D. Pearl, L. Bouthilet and J. Lazar (Eds.), *Television and behavior: ten years of scientific and implications for the 80's*, Vol. 2. National Institute of Mental Health, Washington, D.C. Pp. 224–247.

Hawkins, R. P., S. H. Pingree, and D. F. Roberts (1975). Watergate and political socialization: the inescapable event. *Amer. Polit. Quart., 3,* 406–422.

Hedman, L. (1981). International information in daily newspapers. In K. E. Rosengren (Ed.), *Advances in content analysis*. Beverly Hills, Calif.: Sage. Pp. 197–214.

Helitzer, M. L., and C. Heyel (1970). *The youth market: its dimensions, influence and opportunities for you*. New York: Media Books.

Herzog, H. (1944). What do we really know about daytime serial listeners? In P. F. Lazarsfeld, and F. N. Stanton (Eds.), *Radio research 1942–1943*. New York: Duell, Sloan, and Pearce. Pp. 3–33.

Hicks, D. J. (1968). Effects of co-observer's sanctions and adult presence on imitative aggression. *Child Development, 38,* 303–309.

Himmelweit, H. T., A. N. Oppenheim, and P. Vince (1958). *Television and the child*: New York: Oxford Univ. Press.

Himmelweit, H. T., and B. Swift (1976). Continuities and discontinuities in media usage and taste: a longitudinal study. *J. soc. Issues, 32,* (4) 133–156.

Hirsch, P. M. (1980). The "scary world" of the nonviewer and other anomalies: a reanalysis of Gerbner et al. findings on cultivation analysis, Part I. *Communic. Res., 7,* 403–456.

_____ (1981a). Distinguishing good speculation from bad theory: rejoinder to Gerbner et al. *Communic. Res., 8,* 73–96.

_____ (1981b). On not learning from one's own mistakes: a renanalysis of Gerbner et al. findings on cultivation analysis, Part II. *Communic. Res., 8,* 3–38.

Hofstetter, C. R., and C. Zukin (1979). TV network political news and advertising in the Nixon and McGovern campaigns. *Journalism Quart., 56;* 106–115, 152.

Hollander, N. (1971). Adolescents and the war: the sources of socialization. *Journalism Quart., 58,* 472–479.

Holsti, O. R. (1969). Content analysis. In G. Lindzey, and E. Aronson (Eds.), *The handbook of social psychology*. Vol. 2. *Research methods*. Reading, Mass.: Addison-Wesley. Pp. 596–692.

Hovland, C. I. (1959). Reconciling conflicting results derived from experimental and survey studies of attitude change. *Amer. Psychol., 14,* 8–17.

Hovland, C. I., A. A. Lumsdaine, and F. D. Sheffield (1949). *Experiments in mass communication.* Princeton, N.J.: Princeton Univ. Press.

Howitt, D. (1972). Television and aggression: a counterargument. *Amer. Psychol., 27,* 969–970.

Hoyt, J. L. (1970). Effect of media violence "justification" on aggression. *J. Broadcasting, 14,* 455–464.

Huesmann, L. R., L. D. Eron, M. M. Lefkowitz, and L. O. Walder (1973). Television violence and aggression: the causal effect remains. *Amer. Psychol., 28,* 617–620.

Hughes, M. (1980). The fruits of cultivation analysis: a reexamination of the effects of television watching on fear, victimization, alienation, and the approval of violence. *Publ. Opin. Quart., 44,* 287–302.

Huston, A. C., J. C. Wright, E. Wartella, M. L. Rice, B. A. Watkins, T. Campbell, and R. Potts (1981). Communicating more than content: formal features of children's television programs. *J. Communic. 31* (3), 32–48.

Hyman, H. H., and P. B. Sheatsley (1947). Some reasons why information campaigns fail. *Publ. Opin. Quart., 11,* 413–423.

Jackson-Beeck, M. (1979). Interpersonal and mass communication in children's political socialization. *Journalism Quart., 56,* 48–53.

Jackson-Beeck, M., and S. H. Chaffee (1975). Family communication, mass communication, and differential political socialization. Presented at annual meeting of the International Communication Association, Chicago.

Jennings, M. K., and R. G. Niemi (1973). The transmission of political values from parent to child. In J. Dennis (Ed.), *Socialization to politics: a reader*. New York: Wiley. Pp. 323–348.

Johnston, J., and T. Davidson (1980). *The persistence of effects—a supplement to "An evaluation of 'Freestyle': a* television series to reduce sex role stereotypes.'' Ann Arbor, Mich.: Institute for Social Research, Univ. of Michigan.

Johnston, J., J. Ettema, and T. Davidson (1980). *An evaluation of "Freestyle": a television series to reduce sex role stereotypes.* Ann Arbor, Michigan: Institute for Social Research, University of Michigan.

Johnstone, J. W. C. (1974). Social integration and mass media use among adolescents: a case study. In J. G. Blumler, and E. Katz (Eds.), *The uses of mass communications: current perspectives on gratifications research.* Beverly Hills, Calif.: Sage. Pp. 35–47.

Joy, L. A., M. Kimball, and M. L. Zabrack (1977). Television exposure and children's aggressive behavior. Symposium paper presented at the annual meetings of the Canadian Psychological Association, Vancouver, B.C.

Kaid, L. L., K. Hale, and J. A. Williams (1977). Media agenda setting of a specific political event. *Journalism Quart., 54,* 584–587.

Kaplan, R. M. (1972). On television as a cause of aggression. *Amer. Psychol., 27,* 968–969.

Katz, E. (1962). The social itinerary of technical change: two studies on the diffusion of innovation. *Hum. Organ., 20,* 70–82.

_____ (1977). *Social research on broadcasting: proposals for further development.* London: British Broadcasting Corp.

_____ (1978). Looking for trouble. *J. Communic.* 28 (2): 90–95.

_____ (1979). The uses of Becker, Blumler, and Swanson. *Communic. Res., 6,* 74–83.

_____ (1980). On conceptualizing media effects. In T. MacCormak (Ed.), *Communications studies: decade of dissent.* Greenwich, Conn.: JAI Press. Pp. 119–141.

Katz, E., J. G. Blumler, and M. Gurevitch (1974). Utilization of mass communication by the individual. In J. G. Blumler and E. Katz (Eds.) *The uses of mass communication: current perspectives on gratifications research.* Beverly Hills, Calif.: Sage. Pp. 19–32.

Katz, E., and D. Foulkes (1972). On the use of media for "escape": clarification of a concept. *Publ. Opin. Quart., 26,* 377–388.

Katz, E., M. Gurevitch, and H. Haas (1973). On the use of mass media for important things. *Amer. Sociol. Rev., 38,* 164–181.

Katzman, N. (1974). The impact of communication technology: some theoretical premises and their implications. *Ekistics, 225,* 125–130.

Kent, K. E., and R. R. Rush (1976). How communication behavior of older persons affects their public affairs knowledge. *Journalism Quart., 53,* 40–46.

Kippax, S., and J. P. Murray (1977). Using television: programme content and need gratification. *Politics, 12,* 56–69.

Klapper, J. T. (1960). *The effects of mass communications.* Glencoe, Ill.: Free Press.

Kline, F. G. (1971). Media time budgeting as a function of demographics and life style. *Journalism Quart., 48,* 211–221.

_____ (1972). Theory in mass communication research. In F. G. Kline, and P. J. Tichenor (Eds.), *Current perspectives in mass communication research.* Beverly Hills, Calif.: Sage. Pp. 17–40.

Kline, F. G. (1977). Time in communication research. In P. M. Hirsch, P. V. Miller, and F. G. Kline (Eds.), *Strategies for communication research.* Beverly Hills, Calif.: Sage. Pp. 187–204.

Kline, F. G., P. V. Miller, and A. J. Morrison (1974). Adolescents and family planning information: an exploration of audience needs and media effects. In J. G. Blumler, and E. Katz (Eds.), *The uses of mass communications: current perspectives on gratifications research.* Beverly Hills, Calif.: Sage. Pp. 113–136.

Koch, H. (1970). *The panic broadcast.* New York: Avon.

Kotler, P. (1972). A generic concept of marketing. *J. Marketing, 36,* 46–54.

Kraus, S., Ed. (1962). *The great debates.* Bloomington: Indiana Univ. Press.

_____ Ed. (1979). *The great debates: 1976, Ford vs. Carter.* Bloomington: Indiana Univ. Press.

Kraus, S., and D. Davis (1976). *The effects of mass communication on political behavior.* University Park, Penn.: Pennsylvania State Univ. Press.

Krech, D., and R. S. Crutchfield (1948). *Theory and problems of social psychology.* New York: McGraw-Hill.

Krull, R., and W. Husson (1979). Children's attention: the case of TV viewing. In E. Wartella (Ed.), *Children communicating: media and development of thought, speech, understanding.* Beverly Hills, Calif.: Sage. Pp. 83–114.

Krull, R., and A. S. Paulson (1977). Time series analysis communication research. In P. M. Hirsch, P. V. Miller, and F. G. Kline (Eds.), *Strategies for communication research.* Beverly Hills, Calif.: Sage. Pp. 231–256.

Kuhn, D. Z. (1973). Imitation theory and research from a cognitive perspective. *Hum. Develop., 16,* 157–180.

Lang, G. E., and K. Lang (1979). Immediate and mediated responses: first debate. In S. Kraus (Ed.), *The great debates: Carter vs. Ford, 1976.* Bloomington: Indiana Univ. Press. Pp. 298–313.

Lasswell, H. D. (1927). *Propaganda techniques in the world war.* New York: Knopf.

_____ (1948). The structure and function of communication in society. In L. Bryson (Ed.), *The communication of ideas.* New York: Harper. Pp. 37–51.

Lasswell, H. D., N. Leites and associates (1949). *The language of politics: studies in quantitative semantics.* New York: George Stewart.

Lazarsfeld, P. F., B. Berelson, and H. Gaudet (1948). *The people's choice.* New York: Columbia Univ. Press.

Lazarsfeld, P. F., and R. K. Merton (1948). Mass communication, popular taste, and organized social action. In L. Bryson (Ed.), *The communication of ideas.* New York: Harper. Pp. 95–118.

Lefkowitz, M. M., L. D. Eron, L. O. Walder, and L. R. Huesmann (1972). Television violence and child aggression: a followup study. In G. A. Comstock, and E. A. Rubinstein (Eds.), *Television and social behavior.* Vol. 3. *Television and adolescent aggressiveness.* Washington, D.C.: Government Printing Office. Pp. 35–135.

_____ (1977). *Growing up to be violent.* New York: Pergamon Press.

Leifer, A. D. (1975). Research on the socialization influence of television in the United States. *Fernsehen und Bildung, 9,* 26–53.

Leifer, A. D., N. J. Gordon, and S. B. Graves (1974). Children's television: more than mere entertainment. *Harvard Educat. Rev. 44,* 213–245.

Leifer, A. D., S. B. Graves, and E. Phelps (1976). Monthly report of critical evaluation of television project. Unpublished manuscript. Center for Research in Children and Television, Harvard University.

Leifer, A. D., and D. F. Roberts (1972). Children's responses to television violence. In J. P. Murray, E. A. Rubinstein, and G. A. Comstock (Eds.), *Television and social behavior.* Vol. 2. *Television and social learning.* Washington, D.C.: Government Printing Office. Pp. 43–180.

Leonard-Barton, D. (1979). Diffusion of energy conserving practices among California homeowners. Unpublished Ph.D. dissertation. Stanford: Stanford University Press.

Lerner, D. (1958). *The passing of traditional society.* Glencoe, Ill.: Free Press.

Lerner, D., W. Schramm, Eds. (1967). *Communication and change in the developing countries.* Honolulu: East-West Center Press.

Levy, M. R. (1977). Experiencing television news. *J. Communic., 27* (4), 112–117.

––––––– (1978). Opinion leadership and television news uses. *Publ. Opin. Quart., 42,* 402–406.

Liebert, D. E., J. N. Sprafkin, R. M. Liebert, and E. A. Rubinstein (1977). Effects of television disclaimers on the product expectations of children. *J. Communic. 27* (1), 118–124.

Liebert, R. M., and R. A. Baron (1972). Some immediate effects of televised violence on children's behavior. *Develop. Psychol., 6,* 469–475.

Liebert, R. M., J. N. Sprafkin, and E. S. Davidson (1982). *The early window: effects of television on children and youth* (2nd ed.). New York: Pergamon Press.

Lippmann, W. (1922) *Public opinion.* New York: MacMillan.

Lometti, G. E., B. Reeves, C. R. Bybee (1977). Investigating the assumptions of uses and gratifications research. *Communic. Res., 4,* 321–338.

LoSciuto, L. A. (1972). A national inventory of television viewing behavior. In E. A. Rubinstein, G. A. Comstock, and J. P. Murray (Eds.), *Television and social behavior.* Vol. 4. *Television in day-to-day life: patterns of use.* Washington, D.C.: Government Printing Office. Pp. 33–86.

Lovelock, C. H., and C. B. Weinberg (1978). *Readings* in *public and nonprofit marketing.* Palo Alto, Calif.: Scientific Press.

Lyle, J. (1972). Television in daily life: patterns of use. In E. A. Rubinstein, G. A. Comstock, and J. P. Murray (Eds.), *Television and social behavior.* Vol. 4. *Television in day-to-day life: patterns of use.* Washington, D.C.: Government Printing Office. Pp. 1–32.

Lyle, J., and H. R. Hoffman (1972). Children's use of television and other media. In E. A. Rubinstein, G. A. Comstock, and J. P. Murray (Eds.), *Television and social behavior.* Vol. 4. *Television in day-to-day life: patterns of use.* Washington, D.C.: Government Printing Office. Pp. 129–256.

McAlister, A. (1981). Antismoking campaigns: progress in developing effective communications. In R. E. Rice, and

W. J. Paisley (Eds.), *Public communication campaigns.* Beverly Hills, Calif.: Sage. Pp. 91–103.

McAlister, A., P. Puska, K. Koskele, U. Pallonen, and N. Maccoby (1980). Mass communication and community organization for public health education. *Amer. Psychol., 35:* 375–379.

McCabe, A. E., and R. O. Moriarity (1977). A laboratory field study of television violence and aggression on children's sport. Paper presented at the biennial meeting of the Society for Research in Child Development, New Orleans.

McCarthy, E. D., T. S. Langner, J. C. Gersten, J. G. Eisenberg, and L. Orzeck (1975). Violence and behavior disorders. *J. Communic., 25* (4), 71–85.

Maccoby, E. E. (1954). Why do children watch television? *Publ. Opin. Quart., 18,* 239–244.

Maccoby, N. (1980). Promoting positive health behavior in adults. In L. A. Bond, and J. C. Rosen (Eds.), *Competence and coping during adulthood.* Hanover, N.H.: Univ. Press of New England. Pp. 195–218.

Maccoby, N., and J. Alexander (1979). Field experimentation in community intervention. In R. F. Munoz, L. R. Snowden, and J. G. Kelley (Eds.), *Research in social contexts: bringing about change.* San Francisco: Jossey-Bass. Pp. 69–100.

––––––– (1980). Use of media in lifestyle programs. In P. O. Davidson, and S. M. Davidson (Eds.), *Behavioral medicine: changing health lifestyles.* New York: Brunner/ Mazel. Pp. 351–370.

Maccoby, N., J. W. Farquhar, P. D. Wood, and J. Alexander (1977). Reducing the risk of cardiovascular disease: effects of a community-based campaign on knowledge and behavior. *J. Community Health, 3,* 100–114.

Maccoby, N., and D. S. Solomon (1981). Heart disease prevention: community studies. In R. E. Rice, and W. J. Paisley (Eds.), *Public communication campaigns.* Beverly Hills, Calif.: Sage. Pp. 105–125.

McCombs, M. E. (1977). Newspapers versus television: mass communication effects across time. In D. L. Shaw, and M. E. McCombs (Eds.), *The emergence of American political issues: the agenda-setting function of the press.* St. Paul, Minn.: West Publishing. Pp. 89–105.

––––––– (1981). The agenda-setting approach. In D. D. Nimmo, and K. R. Sanders (Eds.), *Handbook of political communication.* Beverly Hills, Calif.: Sage. Pp. 121–140.

McCombs, M. E., and C. H. Eyal (1980). Spending on mass media. *J. Communic., 30* (1), 153–158.

McCombs, M., and P. Poindexter (1978). Civic attitudes and newspaper readership. Presented at annual meeting of Midwest Association Public Opinion Research, Chicago.

McCombs, M. E., and D. L. Shaw (1972). The agenda-setting function of mass media. *Publ. Opin. Quart., 36,* 176–187.

McGinnis, J. (1969). *The selling of the president 1968.* New York: Trident Press.

McGuire, W. J. (1969). The nature of attitudes and attitude change. In G. Lindzey, and E. Aronson (Eds.), *The handbook of social psychology.* Vol. 3. *The individual in a social context.* Reading, Mass.: Addison-Wesley. Pp. 136–314.

––––––– (1973). Persuasion, resistance and attitude change. In I. de Sola Pool, W. Schramm et al. (Eds.), *Hand-*

book of communication. Chicago: Rand McNally. Pp. 216–252.

_____ (1981). Theoretical foundations of campaigns. In R. E. Rice, and W. J. Paisley (Eds.), *Public communication campaigns.* Beverly Hills, Calif.: Sage. Pp. 41–70.

McIntyre, J. J., and J. J. Teevan, Jr. (1972). Television violence and deviant behavior. In G. A. Comstock, and E. A. Rubinstein (Eds.), *Television and social behavior.* Vol. 3. *Television and adolescent aggressiveness.* Washington, D.C.: Government Printing Office. Pp. 383–435.

MacKuen, M. B. (1981). Social communication and the mass policy agenda. In M. B. MacKuen, and S. L. Coombs, *More than news: media power in public affairs.* Beverly Hills, Calif.: Sage. Pp. 19–144.

McLeod, J. M., C. K. Atkin, and S. Chaffee (1972a). Adolescents, parents, and television use; adolescent self-report measures from Maryland and Wisconsin samples. In G. A. Comstock, and E. A. Rubinstein (Eds.), *Television and social behavior.* Vol. 3. *Television and adolescent aggressiveness.* Washington, D.C.: Government Printing Office. Pp. 173–123.

_____ (1972b). Adolescents, parents and television use: self report and other report measures from the Wisconsin sample. In G. A. Comstock, and E. A. Rubinstein (Eds.), *Television and social behavior.* Vol. 3. *Television and adolescent aggressiveness.* Washington, D.C.: Government Printing Office. Pp. 230–313.

McLeod, J. M., and L. B. Becker (1974). Testing the validity of gratification measures through political effects analysis. In J. G. Blumler, and E. Katz (Eds.), *The uses of mass communications: current perspectives on gratifications research.* Beverly Hills, Calif.: Sage. Pp. 137–164.

_____ (1981). The uses and gratifications approach. In D. D. Nimmo, and K. R. Sanders (Eds.), *Handbook of political communication.* Beverly Hills, Calif.: Sage. Pp. 67–99.

McLeod, J. M., L. B. Becker, and J. E. Byrnes (1974). Another look at the agenda-setting function of the press. *Communic. Res., 1,* 131–166.

McLeod, J. M., J. D. Brown, L. B. Becker, and D. A. Ziemke (1977). Decline and fall at the Whitehouse: a longitudinal analysis of communication effects. *Communic. Res., 4,* 3–22.

McLeod, J. M., C. R. Bybee, and J. A. Durall (1979). Equivalence of informed political participation: the 1976 presidential debates as a source of influence. *Communic. Res., 6,* 463–487.

McLeod, J., J. A. Dorall, D. A. Ziemke, and C. R. Bybee (1979). Reactions of young and older voters: expanding the context. In S. Kraus (Ed.), *The great debates: Carter vs. Ford, 1976.* Bloomington: Indiana Univ. Press. Pp. 348–367.

McLeod, J. M., and B. Reeves (1980). On the nature of mass media effects. In S. B. Withey, and R. P. Abeles (Eds.), *Television and social behavior: beyond violence and children.* Hillsdale, N.J.: Erlbaum. Pp. 17–54.

McLuhan, M. (1964). *Understanding media: the extensions of man.* New York: McGraw-Hill.

McNamara, E. F., T. Kurth, and D. Hansen (1981). Communication efforts to prevent wildfires. In R. E. Rice, and W. J. Paisley (Eds.), *Public communication campaigns.* Beverly Hills, Calif.: Sage. Pp. 143–160.

McQuail, D., J. G. Blumler, and J. R. Brown (1972). The television audience: a revised perspective. In D. McQuail (Ed.), *Sociology of mass communications.* Hammondsworth: Penguin. Pp. 135–165.

Mays, L., E. H. Henderson, S. K. Seidman, and V. S. Steiner (1975). *An evaluation report on Vegetable Soup: the effects of a multi-ethnic children's television series on intergroup attitudes of children.* Unpublished manuscript. New York State Department of Education.

Medrich, E. A. (1979). Constant television: a background to daily life. *J. Communic., 29* (3), 171–176.

Medrich, E. A., J. A. Roizen, V. Rubin, and S. Buckley (1982). *The serious business of growing up: a study of children's lives outside school.* Berkeley: Univ. California Press.

Melody, W. (1973). *Children's TV: the economics of exploitation.* New Haven: Yale Univ. Press.

Meringoff, L., Ed. (1980). *Children and advertising: an annotated bibliography.* New York: Children's Advertising Review Unit, Council of Better Business Bureaus, Inc.

Merton, R. K. (1968). *Social theory and social structure.* New York: Free Press.

Messaris, P. (1977). Biases of self-reported functions and gratifications of mass media use. *Et cetera: a review of general semantics, 34,* 316–329.

Mielke, K. W., and J. W. Swinehart (1976). *Evaluation of the "Feeling Good" television series.* New York: Children's Television Workshop.

Milavsky, J. R., R. C. Kessler, H. H. Stipp, and W. S. Rubens (1982). *Television and aggression: a panel study.* New York: Academic Press.

Milavsky, J., B. Pekowsky, and H. Stipp (1975). Television drug advertising and proprietary and illicit drug use among teenage boys. *Publ. Opin. Quart., 39,* 457–481.

Miller, A. H., and M. MacKuen (1979). Informing the electorate: a national study. In S. Kraus (Ed.), *The great debates: Carter vs. Ford 1976.* Bloomington: Indiana Univ. Press. Pp. 269–297.

Miller, M. M., and B. Reeves (1976). Linking dramatic TV content to children's occupational sex-role stereotypes. *J. Broadcasting, 20,* 35–50.

Morgan, M. (1980). Television and adolescent role socialization. Paper presented at the annual meeting of the International Communication Association, Acapulco.

Mullins, M. E. (1977). Agenda-setting and the young voter. In D. L. Shaw, and M. E. McCombs (Eds.), *The emergence of American political issues: the agenda-setting function of the press.* St. Paul, Minn.: West. Pp. 133–148.

Murray, J. P. (1972). Television in inner-city homes: viewing behavior of young boys. In E. A. Rubinstein, G. A. Comstock, and J. P. Murray (Eds.), *Television and social behavior.* Vol. 4. *Television in day-to-day life: patterns of use.* Washington, D.C.: Government Printing Office. Pp. 345–394.

_____ (1980). *Television and youth: 25 years of research and controversy.* Boys Town, Neb.: Boys Town Press.

Murray, J. P., and S. Kippax (1978). Children's social behavior in three towns with differing television experience. *J. Communic., 28* (1), 19–29.

_____ (1979). From the early window to the late night show: international trends in the study of television's impact on children and adults. In L. Berkowitz (Ed.), *Advances in ex-*

perimental social psychology. Vol. 12. New York: Academic Press. Pp. 253–320.

National Coalition on Television Violence (1983). *NCTV News, 4* (1), January.

Newcomb, H. (1978). Assessing the violence profiles of Gerbner and Gross: a humanistic critique and suggestion. *Communic. Res., 5,* 262–282.

Newspaper Advertising Bureau (1978). *Children, mothers, and newspapers.* New York: Newspaper Advertising Bureau.

_____ (1980a). *Children and newspapers: changing patterns of readership and their effects.* New York: Newspaper Advertising Bureau.

_____ (1980b). *Daily newspapers in American classrooms: a national study of their impacts on student attitudes, readership and political awareness.* New York: Newspaper Advertising Bureau.

_____ (1980c). *Mass media in the family setting: social patterns in media availability and use by parents.* New York. Newspaper Advertising Bureau.

Nie, N. H., S. Verba, and J. R. Petrocik (1976). *The changing American voter.* Cambridge, Mass.: Harvard Univ. Press.

Nimmo, D. D., and K. R. Sanders, Eds. (1981). *Handbook of political communication.* Beverly Hills, Calif.: Sage.

Noelle-Neumann, E. (1973). Return to the concept of powerful mass media. In H. Eguchi, and K. Sata, (Eds.), *Studies of broadcasting, 9,* 67–112. Tokyo: Nippon Hoso Kyokai.

_____ (1974). The spiral of silence: a theory of public opinion. *J. Communic., 24* (2), 43–51.

_____ (1977). Turbulences in the climate of opinion: methodological applications of the spiral of silence theory. *Publ. Opin. Quart., 41,* 143–158.

Nordenstreng, K., and H. I. Schiller, Eds. (1979). *National sovereignty and international communication.* Norwood, N.J.: Ablex.

Nordlund, J. (1978). Media interaction. *Communic. Res., 5,* 150–175.

Osborn, D. K., and R. C. Endsley (1971). Emotional reactions of young children to TV violence. *Child Development, 42,* 321–331.

O'Keefe, G. H. (1975). Political campaigns and mass communication research. In S. H. Chaffee (Ed.), *Political communication: issues and strategies for research.* Beverly Hills, Calif.: Sage. Pp. 129–164.

Paisley, M. B. (1972). Television and social behavior: violence done to policy research. Paper presented at the annual meeting of the Pacific Chapter of the American Association of Public Opinion Research, Asilomar, Calif.

Paisley, W. (1981). Public communication campaigns: The American experience. In R. E. Rice, and W. J. Paisley (Eds.), *Public communication campaigns.* Beverly Hills, Calif.: Sage. Pp. 15–40.

Palmer, E. (1981). Shaping persuasive messages with formative research. In R. E. Rice, and W. J. Paisley (Eds.), *Public communication campaigns.* Beverly Hills, Calif.: Sage. Pp. 227–238.

Palmer, E. L., and A. Dorr, Eds. (1980). *Children and the faces of television: teaching, violence, selling.* New York: Academic Press.

Palmgreen, P. (1979). Mass media use and political knowledge. *J. Monogr., 61.*

Palmgreen, P., and P. Clarke (1977). Agenda-setting with local and national issues. *Communic. Res., 4,* 435–452.

Palmgreen, P. C., F. G. Kline, and P. Clarke (1974). Message discrimination and information-holding about political affairs. Presented at annual meeting of International Communication Association, New Orleans.

Palmgreen, P., and J. D. Rayburn (1979). Uses and gratifications and exposure to public television: a discrepancy approach. *Communic. Res., 6,* 155–179.

Palmgreen, P., L. A. Wenner, and J. D. Rayburn (1980). Relations between gratifications sought and gratifications obtained: a study of television news. *Communic. Res., 7,* 161–192.

Parke, R. D., L. Berkowitz, J. P. Leyens, S. West, and R. J. Sebastian (1977). Some effects of violent and nonviolent movies on the behavior of juvenile delinquents. In L. Berkowitz (Ed.), *Advances in experimental social psychology.* Vol. 10. New York: Academic Press. Pp. 135–172.

Parker, E. B. (1963a). The effects of television on magazine and newspaper reading: a problem in methodology. *Publ. Opin. Quart., 27,* 315–320.

_____ (1963b). The effects of television on public library circulation. *Publ. Opin. Quart., 27,* 578–589.

Patterson, T. E., and R. D. McClure (1976). *The unseeing eye: the myth of television power in national elections.* New York: Putnam.

Pearl, D., L. Bouthilet, and J. Lazar Eds. (1982). *Television and behavior: ten years of scientific progress and implications for the eighties.* 2 Vols. U.S. Dept. of Health and Human Services: National Institute of Mental Health. Rockville, Md.

Peled, T., and E. Katz (1974). Media functions in wartime: the Israel home front in October 1973. In J. G. Blumler, and E. Katz (Eds.), *The uses of mass communications: current perspectives on gratifications research.* Beverly Hills, Calif.: Sage. Pp. 49–69.

Peterson, R. A. (1981). Measuring culture, leisure, and time use. *Annals Amer. Acad. politic. soc. Sci., 453,* 1969–1979.

Peterson, R. C., and L. L. Thurstone (1933). *Motion pictures and the social attitudes of children.* New York: Macmillan.

Phillips, D. P. (1979). Suicide, motor fatalities, and the mass media: evidence toward a theory of suggestion. *Amer. J. Sociol., 84,* 1150–1174.

_____ (1980). Airplane accidents, murder, and the mass media: towards a theory of imitation and suggestion. *Soc. Forces, 58,* 1001–1024.

_____ (1982). The impact of fictional television stories on U.S. adult fatalities: new evidence on the effect of the mass media on violence. *Amer. J. Sociol., 87,* 1340–1359.

Pierce, C. M. (1980). Social trace contaminants: subtle indicators of racism in TV. In S. B. Withey, and R. P. Abeles (Eds.), *Television and social behavior: beyond violence and children.* Hillsdale, N.J.: Erlbaum. Pp. 249–257.

Pingree, S. (1978). The effects of nonsexist television commercials and perceptions of reality on children's attitudes about women. *Psychol. Women Quart., 2,* 262–277.

Pingree, S., R. P. Hawkins (1980). Children and media. In M. Butler, and W. Paisley, *Women and the mass media: sourcebook for research and action.* New York: Human Sciences Press. Pp. 279–299.

Pool, I. de Sola, and W. Schramm, Eds. (1973). *Handbook of communication.* Chicago: Rand McNally.

Poulos, R. W., E. A. Rubinstein, and R. M. Liebert (1975). Positive social learning. *J. Communic., 25* (4), 90–97.

Prisuta, R. H. (1979). The adolescent and television news: a viewer profile. *Journalism Quart., 56,* 277–282.

Quarles, R. C. (1979). Mass media use and voting behavior: the accuracy of political perceptions among first-time and experienced voters. *Communic. Res., 6,* 407–436.

Ray, M. (1973). Marketing communication and the hierarchy of effects. In P. Clarke (Ed.), *New models for communication research.* Beverly Hills, Calif.: Sage. Pp. 147–176.

Reeves, B., and E. Wartella (1982). For some children under some conditions: a history of research on children and media. Paper presented at the annual meetings of the International Communication Association, Boston, Mass.

Rice, R. E., and W. J. Paisley, Eds. (1981). *Public communication campaigns.* Beverly Hills, Calif.: Sage.

Rivers, W. L., W. Schramm, and C. G. Christians (1980). *Responsibility in mass communication* (3rd ed.). New York: Harper & Row.

Roberts, D. F. (1971). The nature of human communication effects. In W. Schramm, and D. F. Roberts (Eds.), *The process and effects of mass communication.* Urbana, Ill.: Univ. Illinois Press. Pp. 347–387.

_____ (1973). Communication and children: a developmental approach. In I. deSola Pool, W. Schramm et al. (Eds.), *Handbook of communication.* Chicago: Rand McNally. Pp. 174–215.

_____ (1975). Attitude change research and the motivation of health practices. In A. J. Enelow, and J. B. Henderson (Eds.), *Applying behavioral science to cardiovascular risk.* American Heart Association. Pp. 42–57.

_____ (1982). Children and commercials: issues, evidence, interventions. *Prevention in Human Services, 2,* 19–36.

Roberts, D. F., and C. M. Bachen (1981). Mass communication effects. *Ann. Rev. Psychol., 32,* 307–356.

Roberts, D. F., C. M. Bachen, P. G. Christenson, and W. Gibson (1979). Children's responses to consumer information and nutrition information television spots. Paper presented at the annual meetings of the American Psychological Association, New York City.

Roberts, D. F., P. Christenson, W. A. Gibson, L. Mooser, and M. E. Goldberg (1980). Developing discriminating consumers. *J. Communic., 30* (3), 94–105.

Roberts, D. F., and W. Gibson (1979). Children's comprehension of animated health and safety public service announcements: an evaluation. Technical report to ABC Television, Inc. Stanford University, Institute for Communication Research. (Mimeo)

Roberts, D. F., W. Gibson, and C. M. Bachen (1975). The impact of animated public service announcements on children's responses to questions about health and safety. Technical report to ABC Television, Inc. Stanford University, Institute for Communication Research. (Mimeo)

Roberts, D. F., R. P. Hawkins, and S. P. Pingree (1975). Do the mass media play a role in political socialization? *Australian and New Zealand J. Sociol., 11,* 37–43.

Roberts, E. J. (1982). Television and sexual learning in childhood. In D. Pearl, L. Bouthilet, and J. Lazar (Eds.), *Television and behavior: ten years of scientific progress and implications for the eighties.* Vol. 2. U.S. Dept. of Health and Human Services: National Institute of Mental Health. Rockville, Md. Pp. 209–223.

Robertson, L. S., A. B. Kelley, B. O'Neill, C. M. Wixom, R. S. Eisworth, and W. Haddon, Jr. (1974). A controlled study of the effect of television messages on safety belt use. *Amer. J. Publ. Health, 64,* 1071–1080.

Robertson, T. S., and J. R. Rossiter (1977). Children's responsiveness to commercials. *J. Communic. 27* (1), 101–105.

Robertson, T. S., J. R. Rossiter, and T. C. Gleason (1979). Televised medicine advertising and children. *J. Consumer Res., 6* (3), 247–255.

Robinson, J. P. (1969). Television and leisure time: yesterday, today, and (maybe) tomorrow. *Publ. Opin. Quart., 33,* 210–223.

_____ (1972). Television's impact on everyday life: some cross-national evidence. In E. A. Rubinstein, G. A. Comstock, and J. P. Murray (Eds.), *Television and social behavior.* Vol. 4. *Television in day-to-day life: patterns of use.* Washington, D.C.: Government Printing Office. Pp. 410–431.

_____ (1977). *How Americans use time.* New York: Praeger.

_____ (1979). Toward a post-industrious society. *Publ. Opin.,* 4 (August/September).

_____ (1980). The changing reading habits of the American public. *J. Communic., 30* (1), 141–152.

Robinson, J. P., and J. G. Bachman (1972). Television viewing habits and aggression. In G. A. Comstock, and E. A. Rubinstein (Eds.), *Television and social behavior.* Vol. 3. *Television and adolescent aggressiveness.* Washington, D.C.: Government Printing Office. Pp. 372–382.

Robinson, J. P., and L. W. Jeffres (1979). The changing role of newspapers in the age of television. *Journalism Monogr., 63.*

Robinson, M. J. (1974). The impact of the televised Watergate hearings. *J. Communic., 24* (2), 17–30.

_____ (1975). American political legitimacy in an era of electronic journalism: reflections on the evening news. In D. Cater, and R. Adler (Eds.), *Television as a social force: new approaches to TV criticism:* New York: Praeger. Pp. 97–139.

_____ (1976). Public affairs television and the growth of political malaise: the case of "The Selling of the Pentagon". *Amer. Political Sci. Rev., 70,* 409–432.

Rogers, E. M. (1976a). Communication and development: the passing of the dominant paradigm. *Communic. Res., 3,* 213–240.

_____ (1976b). New perspectives on communication and development: overview. *Communic. Res., 3,* 99–106.

_____ (1976c). Where are we in understanding the diffusion of innovations? In W. Schramm, and D. Lerner (Eds.), *Communication and change: the last ten years—and the next.* Honolulu: Univ. of Hawaii Press. Pp. 204–222.

_____ (1977). Network analysis of the diffusion of innovations: family planning in Korean villages. In D. Lerner, and L. M. Nelson (Eds.), *Communication research—a half century appraisal.* Honolulu: East-West Center Press. Pp. 117–147.

_____ (1981). Methodology for meta-research. Presidential Address to the annual meetings of the International Communication Association, Minneapolis, Minn.

——— (1983). *Diffusion of innovations* (3rd ed.). New York: Free Press.

Rogers, E., and R. Adhikarya (1979). Diffusion of innovations: an up-to-date review and commentary. In D. Nimmo (Ed.), *Communication Yearbook III*. New Brunswick, N.J.: Transaction. Pp. 67–81.

Rogers, E. M., and D. L. Kincaid (1981). *Communication networks: toward a new paradigm for research*. New York: Free Press.

Roling, N. G., J. Ashcroft, and F. W. Chege (1976). The diffusion of innovations and the issue of equity in rural development. *Communic. Res., 3*, 155–170.

Roper Organization (1977). *Changing public attitudes toward television and other media*. New York: Television Information Office.

Rosenberg, M. J., and C. I. Hovland (1960). Cognitive, affective and behavorial components of attitudes. In C. I. Hovland, and M. J. Rosenberg (Eds.), *Attitude organization and change*. New Haven: Yale Univ. Press. Pp. 1–14.

Rosengren, K. E., Ed. (1981). *Advances in content analysis*. Beverly Hills, Calif.: Sage.

Rossiter, J. R. (1977). Reliability of a short test measuring children's attitudes toward TV commercials. *J. Consumer Res. 3*, 179–184.

——— (1980). Children and television advertising: policy issues, perspectives, and the status of research. In E. L. Palmer, and A. Dorr (Eds.), *Children and the faces of television: teaching, violence, selling*. New York: Academic Press. Pp. 251–272.

——— (1981). Research on television advertising's general impact on children: American and Australian findings. In J. F. Esserman (Ed.), *Television advertising and children: issues, research and findings*. New York: Child Research Service. Pp. 223–237.

Rossiter, J. R., and T. S. Robertson (1974). Children's TV commercials: testing the defenses. *J. Communic., 24* (4), 137–144.

Rubin, A. M. (1976). Television in children's political socialization. *J. Broadcasting, 20*, 51–60.

——— (1978). Child and adolescent television use and political socialization. *Journalism Quart., 55*, 125–129.

——— (1979). Television use by children and adolescents. *Hum. Communic. Res., 5*, 109–120.

Rubinstein, E. A., R. M. Liebert, J. M. Neale, and W. Poulos (1974). *Assessing television's influence on children's prosocial behavior*. Stony Brook, N.Y.: Brookdale International Institute. (Occasional paper 74–11.)

Rushton, J. P. (1979). Effects of prosocial television and film material on the behavior of viewers. In L. Berkowitz (Ed.), *Advances in experimental social psychology*. Vol. 12. New York: Academic Press. Pp. 321–351.

——— (1982). Television and prosocial behavior. In D. Pearl, L. Bouthilet and J. Lazar (Eds.), *Television and behavior: ten years of scientific progress and implications for the eighties*. Vol. 2. U.S. Dept. of Health and Human Services: National Institute of Mental Health. Rockville, Md. Pp. 248–257.

Sahin, H., and J. P. Robinson (1981). Beyond the realm of necessity: television and the colonization of leisure. *Media, culture, and society, 3* (1), 85–95.

Salomon, G. (1979a). *Interaction of media, cognition, and learning*. San Francisco: Jossey-Bass.

——— (1979b). Shape, not only content: how media symbols partake in the development of abilities. In E. Wartella (Ed.), *Children communicating: media and development of thought, speech, understanding*. Beverly Hills, Calif.: Sage. Pp. 58–82.

Samuelson, M., R. F. Carter, and L. Ruggels (1963). Education, available time and use of mass media. *Journalism Quart., 40*, 491–496.

Sandman, P. M., D. M. Rubin, and D. B. Sachsman (1976). *Media: an introductory analysis of American mass communications* (2nd ed.). Englewood Cliffs, N.J.: Prentice-Hall.

Sapir, E. (1931). Communication. In E. R. A. Seligman (Ed.), *Encyclopedia of the social sciences*. Vol. 4. New York: Macmillan. Pp. 78–80.

Savitsky, J. R., R. W. Rogers, C. E. Izard, and R. M. Liebert (1971). Role of frustration and anger in the imitation of filmed aggression against a human victim. *Psychol. Reports, 29*, 807–810.

Schank, R., and R. Abelson (1977). *Scripts, plans, goals, and understanding: an inquiry into human knowledge structures*. Hillsdale, N.J.: Erlbaum.

Schramm, W. (1963). Communication research in the United States. In W. Schramm (Ed.), *The science of human communication*. New York: Basic Books. Pp. 1–16.

——— (1964). *Mass media and national development: the role of information in the developing countries*. Stanford: Stanford Univ. Press.

——— (1971a). The mass media in the North American life cycle. *Publics et techniques de la diffusion collective*. Brussels: Editions de l'Institute de Sociologie, University Libre de Bruxelles.

——— (1971b). The nature of communication between humans. In W. Schramm, and D. F. Roberts (Eds.), *The process and effects of mass communication*. Urbana, Ill.: Univ. Illinois Press. Pp. 1–53.

——— (1973). *Men, messages and media: a look at human communication*. New York: Harper & Row.

——— (1980). The beginnings of communication study in the United States. In D. Nimmo (Ed.), *Communication Yearbook 4*. New Brunswick, N.J.: Transaction. Pp. 73–82.

Schramm, W., and D. Lerner, Eds. (1976). *Communication and change: the last ten years—and the next*. Honolulu: Univ. Press of Hawaii.

Schramm, W., J. Lyle, and E. B. Parker (1961). *Television in the lives of our children*. Stanford: Stanford Univ. Press.

Sears, D. O., and S. H. Chaffee (1979). Uses and effects of the 1976 debates: an overview of empirical studies. In S. Kraus (Ed.), *The great debates: Carter vs. Ford, 1976*. Bloomington: Indiana Univ. Press. Pp. 223–261.

Sears, D. O., and J. L. Freedman (1967). Selective exposure to information: a critical review. *Publ. Opin. Quart., 31*, 194–213.

Selman, R., and W. Damon (1975). The necessity (but insufficiency) of social perspective taking for conceptions of justice at three levels. In D. DePalma, and J. Foley (Eds.), *Moral development: current theory and research*. Hillsdale, N.J.: Erlbaum. Pp. 57–74.

Severin, W. J., and J. W. Tankard, Jr. (1979). *Communication theories: origins, methods, uses.* New York: Hastings House.

Shantz, C. V. (1975). The development of social cognition. In E. M. Hetherington (Ed.), *Review of child development research.* Vol. 5. Chicago: Univ. of Chicago Press. Pp. 257–323.

Shaw, D. L., and M. E. McCombs (1977). *The emergence of American political issues.* St. Paul, Minn.: West Publishing.

Shingi, P. M., and B. Mody (1976). The communication effects gap: a field experiment on television and agricultural ignorance in India. *Communic. Res., 3,* 171–190.

Siebert, F., T. Peterson, and W. Schramm (1956). *Four theories of the press.* Urbana: Univ. of Illinois Press.

Silverman, L. T. (1977). Effects of Sesame Street programming on the cooperative behavior of preschoolers. *Dissertation Abstracts International, 38,* 3124A. (University Mictofilms No. 77-25727)

Silverman, L. T., J. N. Sprafkin, and E. A. Rubinstein (1979). Physical contact and sexual behavior on prime time TV. *J. Communic., 29* (1), 33–43.

Singer, D. G., and J. L. Singer (1976). Family television viewing habits and the spontaneous play of preschool children. *Amer. J. Orthopsychiatry, 46* (3), 496–502.

Singer, D. G., J. L. Singer, and D. M. Zuckerman (1981). *Teaching television: how to use TV to your child's advantage.* New York: Dial Press.

Siune, K., and O. Borre (1975). Setting the agenda for a Danish election. *J. Communic., 25* (1), 65–73.

Sohn, A. B. (1978). A longitudinal analysis of local nonpolitical agenda-setting effects. *Journalism Quart., 55,* 325–333.

Solomon, D. S. (1981). A social marketing perspective on campaigns. In R. E. Rice, and W. J. Paisley (Eds.), *Public communication campaigns.* Beverly Hills, Calif.: Sage. Pp. 281–292.

——— (1982). Mass media campaigns for health promotion. *Prevention in human services, 2,* 115–123.

Sprafkin, J. N., and E. A. Rubinstein (1979). Children's television viewing habits and prosocial behavior: a field correlational study. *J. Broadcasting, 23,* 265–276.

Sprafkin, J. N., and L. T. Silverman (1981). Update: physically intimate and sexual behavior on prime-time television, 1978-79. *J. Communic., 31* (1), 34–40.

Stamm, K. R. (1972). Environment and communication. In F. G. Kline, and P. J. Tichenor (Eds.), *Current perspectives in mass communication research.* Beverly Hills, Calif.: Sage. Pp. 265–294.

Stamm, K. R., and L. Fortini-Campbell (1977). Readership and community identification. Presented at the annual meeting of the Association for Education in Journalism, Houston.

Star, S. A., and H. M. Hughes (1950). Report on an educational campaign: the Cincinnati plan for the United Nations. *Amer. J. Sociol., 55,* 389–400.

Stauffer, J., R. Frost, and W. Rybolt (1978). Literacy, illiteracy, and learning from television news. *Communic. Res., 5,* 221–232.

Stein, A. H., and L. K. Friedrich (1972). Television content and young children's behavior. In J. P. Murray, E. A. Rubinstein, and G. A. Comstock (Eds.), *Television and social behavior.* Vol. 2. *Television and social learning.* Washington, D.C.: Government Printing Office. Pp. 202–317.

——— (1975). The impact of television on children and youth. In E. M. Hetherington (Ed.), *Review of child development research.* Chicago: Univ. of Chicago Press. Pp. 183–256.

Stein, A. H., L. K. Friedrich, F. Deutsch, and C. Nydegger (1973). The effects of aggressive and prosocial television programs on the social interaction of preschool children. Paper presented at the meeting of the Midwestern Psychological Association, Chicago.

Steiner, G. A. (1963). *The people look at television.* New York: Knopf.

Stever, F. B., J. M. Applefield, and R. Smith (1971). Televised aggression and the interpersonal aggression of preschool children. *J. expt. Child Psych., 11,* 442–447.

Stroman, C. A., and L. B. Becker (1978). Racial differences in gratifications. *Journalism Quart., 55,* 767–771.

Suchman, E. (1942). An invitation to music. In P. F. Lazarsfeld, and F. N. Stanton (Eds.), *Radio research, 1941.* New York: Duell, Sloan, and Pearce. Pp. 140–188.

Surgeon General's Scientific Advisory Committee on Television and Social Behavior (1972). *Television and growing up: the impact of televised violence.* Report to the Surgeon General, United States Public Health Service. Washington, D.C.: Government Printing Office.

Swanson, D. L. (1977). The uses and misuses of uses and gratifications. *Hum. Communic. Res., 3,* 214–221.

——— (1979a). The continuing evolution of the uses and gratifications approach. *Communic. Res., 6,* 3–7.

——— (1979b). Political communication research and the uses and gratifications model: a critique. *Communic. Res., 6,* 37–53.

——— (1981). A constructivist approach. In D. D. Nimmo, and K. R. Sanders (Eds.), *Handbook of political communication.* Beverly Hills, Calif.: Sage. Pp. 169–191.

Tan, A. S. (1979). TV beauty ads and role expectations of adolescent female viewers. *Journalism Quart., 56,* 283–288.

Tan, A. S., and P. Vaughn (1976). Mass media exposure, public affairs knowledge, and black militancy. *Journalism Quart., 53,* 271–279.

Tannenbaum, P. H. (1955). The indexing process in communication. *Publ. Opin. Quart., 19,* 292–302.

——— (1972). Studies in film- and television-mediated arousal and aggression: a progress report. In G. A. Comstock, E. A. Rubinstein, and J. P. Murray (Eds.), *Television and social behavior.* Vol. 5. *Television's effects: further exploitations.* Washington, D.C.: Government Printing Office. Pp. 309–350.

——— (1980). An unstructured introduction to an amorphous area. In P. H. Tannenbaum (Ed.), *The entertainment functions of television.* Hillsdale, N.J.: Erlbaum. Pp. 1–12.

Tannenbaum, P. H., and E. P. Gaer (1965). Mood change as a function of stress of protagonist and degree of identification in a film viewing situation. *J. Pers. soc. Psychol., 2,* 612–616.

Taplin, S. (1981). Family planning communication campaigns. In R. E. Rice, and W. J. Paisley (Eds.), *Public communication campaigns.* Beverly Hills, Calif.: Sage. Pp. 127–142.

Thomas, M. H., and R. S. Drabman (1974). Some new faces of the one-eyed monster. Paper presented at the meeting of the Society for Research in Child Development, Denver.

Tichenor, P. J., G. A. Donahue, and C. N. Olien (1970). Mass media and differential growth in knowledge. *Publ. Opin. Quart., 34,* 158-170.

Tichenor, P. J., J. M. Rodenkirchen, C. N. Olien, and G. A. Donohue (1973). Community issues, conflicts and public affairs knowledge. In P. Clarke (Ed.), *New models for communication research.* Beverly Hills, Calif.: Sage. Pp. 45-79.

Time (1980). TV's *Dallas:* Whodunit? August 11, *116,* 6, 60-66.

Tipton, L. P., R. D. Haney, and J. R. Baseheart (1975). Media agenda-setting in city and state election campaigns. *Journalism Quart., 52,* 15-22.

Tolley, H. (1973). *Children and war: political socialization to political conflict.* New York: Univ. Teachers College Press.

Tuchman, G. (1977). The exception proves the rule: the study of routine news practice. In P. M. Hirsch, P. V. Miller, and F. G. Kline (Eds.), *Strategies for communication research.* Beverly Hills, Calif.: Sage. Pp. 43-62.

Tuomilehto, J., A. Nissinen, J. T. Salonen, T. E. Kottke, and P. Puska (1980). Community programme for control of hypertension in North Karelia, Finland. *The Lancet, 2,* 900-903.

United States Commission on Civil Rights (1977). *Window dressing on the set: women and minorities on television.* Washington, D.C.: Government Printing Office.

United States Commission on Civil Rights (1980). *Window dressing on the set: women and minorities in television, an update.* Washington, D.C.: Government Printing Office.

United States Senate, Committee on Judiciary (1955). *Comic books and juvenile delinquency.* Interim Senate Report No. 62, 84th Congress. Washington, D.C.: U.S. Government Printing Office.

Vidmar, N., and M. Rokeach (1974). Archie Bunker's bigotry: a study in selective perception and exposure. *J. Communic., 24* (1), 36-47.

von Feilitzen, C. (1976). The functions served by the media. In R. Brown (Ed.), *Children and television.* Beverly Hills, Calif.: Sage. Pp. 90-115.

Wade, S. E., and W. Schramm (1969). The mass media as sources of public affairs, science and health knowledge. *Publ. Opin. Quart., 33,* 197-209.

Wald, K. D., and M. B. Lupfer (1978). The presidential debate as a civics lesson. *Publ. Opin. Quart. 42,* 342-353.

Walters, R. H., and E. L. Thomas (1963). Enhancement of punitiveness by visual and audiovisual displays. *Canadian J. Psychol., 17,* 244-255.

Ward, S., D. Wackman, and E. Wartella (1977). *How children learn to buy: the development of consumer information-processing skills.* Beverly Hills, Calif.: Sage.

Warner, W. L., and W. E. Henry (1948). The radio day time serial: a symbolic analysis. *Genetic Psychol. Monogr., 37,* 3-71.

Wartella, E. (1980). Individual differences in children's responses to television advertising. In E.L. Palmer, and A. Dorr (Eds.), *Children and the faces of television: teaching, violence, selling.* New York: Academic Press. Pp. 307-322.

Watt, J. H., and R. Krull (1977). An examination of three models of television viewing and aggression. *Hum. Communic. Res., 3,* 99-112.

Watt, J. H., Jr., and S. A. Van Den Berg (1978). Time series analysis of alternative media effects theories. In B. D. Ruben (Ed.), *Communication yearbook 2.* New Brunswick, N.J.: Transaction. Pp. 215-240.

Weaver, D. H. (1977). Political issues and voter need for orientation. In D. L. Shaw, and M. E. McCombs (Eds.), *The emergence of American political issues: the agenda-setting function of the press.* St. Paul: West Publishing. Pp. 107-119.

Weaver, D. H., T. S. Auh, T. Stehla, and C. Wilhoit (1975). A path analysis of individual agenda-setting during the 1974 Indiana senatorial campaign. Presented at annual meetings of the Association for Education in Journalism, Ottawa, Canada.

Weaver, D.H., and R. H. Gray (1979). *Journalism and mass communication research in the United States: past, present and future.* Bloomington: Indiana Univ. Press, School of Journalism.

Weaver, D. H., M. E. McCombs, and C. Spellman (1975). Watergate and the media: a case study of agenda-setting. *Amer. Politics Quart., 3,* 458-472.

Weiss, W. (1969). Effects of mass media of communication. In G. Lindzey, and E. Aronson (Eds.), *The handbook of social psychology* (2nd Ed.) Vol. 5. *Applied social psychology.* Reading, Mass.: Addison-Wesley. Pp. 77-195.

_____ (1976). Review of J. G. Blumler, and E. Katz (Eds.), The uses of mass communications: current perspectives on gratifications research. *Publ. Opin. Quart., 40,* 132-133.

Wells, W. D. (1973). Television and aggression: replication of an experimental field study. Unpublished manuscript. Graduate School of Business, Univ. of Chicago.

Wenner, L. A. (1977). Political news on television: a uses and gratifications study. *Dissertation Abstracts International, 39,* 12A. (University Microfilms No. 78-10395)

Werner, L. (1976). Functional analysis of TV viewing for older adults. *J. Broadcasting, 20,* 77-88.

Westley, B. H., and W. J. Severin (1964). A profile of the daily newspaper non-reader. *Journalism Quart., 41,* 45-50.

Whiting, G. C. (1976). How does communication interface with change? *Communic. Res., 3,* 191-212.

Whitney, D. C., and E. Wartella, Eds. (1982). *Mass communication review yearbook.* Vol. 3. Beverly Hills, Calif.: Sage.

Williams, T. (1979). The impact of television: a study of three Canadian communities. Presented at the biannual meetings of the Society for Research in Child Development, San Francisco, Calif.

_____ (1981). How and what do children learn from television? *Human Communic. Res., 7,* 189-192.

Williams, T. M., and G. Handford (1977). Television and community life. Symposium paper presented at the annual meetings of the Canadian Psychological Association, Vancouver, B.C., Canada.

Williams, W., Jr., and D. C. Larsen (1977). Agenda-setting in an off-election year. *Journalism Quart., 54,* 744-749.

Williams, W., Jr., and W. Semlak (1978). Campaigns 76: agenda-setting during the New Hampshire primary. *J. Broadcasting, 22,* 531-540.

Winter, J. P. (1981). Contingent conditions in the agenda-setting process. In G. C. Wilhoit, and H. de Bock (Eds.), *Mass communication review yearbook.* Vol. 2. Beverly Hills, Calif.: Sage. Pp. 235–243.

Withey, S. B., and R. P. Abeles, Eds. (1980). *Television and social behavior: beyond violence and children.* Hillsdale, N.J.: Erlbaum.

Wober, J. M. (1978). Televised violence and paranoid perception: the view from Great Britain. *Publ. Opin. Quart., 42,* 315–321.

Wolfe, K. M., and M. Fiske (1949). The children talk about comics. In P. F. Lazarsfeld, and F. N. Stanton (Eds.), *Communication research 1948–1949.* New York: Harper. Pp. 3–50.

Worchel, S., T. W. Hardy, and R. Hurley (1976). The effects of commercial interruption of violent and nonviolent films on viewers' subsequent aggression. *J. exp. Psychol., 2,* 220–232.

Worth, S., and L. Gross (1974). Symbolic strategies. *J. Communic., 24* (4), 27–39.

Zillman, D. (1971). Excitation transfer in communication-mediated aggressive behavior. *J. exp. soc. Psychol., 7,* 419–434.

Zillman, D., J. L. Hoyt, and K. D. Day (1974). Strength and duration of the effect of aggressive, violent, and erotic communications on subsequent aggressive behavior. *Communic. Res., 1,* 286–306.

Zucker, H. G. (1978). The variable nature of news media influence. In B. D. Rubin (Ed.), *Communication yearbook 2.* New Brunswick, N.J.: Transaction. Pp. 225–240.

Zuckerman, P., and L. Gianinno (1981). Measuring children's responses to television advertising. In J. F. Esserman (Ed.), *Television advertising and children: issues, research and findings.* New York: Child Research Service. Pp. 83–93.

CHAPTER 24

Intergroup Relations

Walter G. Stephan
New Mexico State University

INTRODUCTION

When I agreed to write this chapter, I reviewed the chapters written in previous volumes by Harding, Kutner, Proshansky, and Chein (1954, 1969). These chapters covered psychoanalytic-, sociological-, developmental-, and personality-oriented explanations of prejudice and discrimination. The evolution of a specific level of analysis and methodological paradigm in the social psychology of intergroup relations since the publication of these chapters makes it unreasonable to attempt such a comprehensive analysis in this volume. The explosion of knowledge in social psychology and in other areas that contribute to an understanding of intergroup relations makes such an analysis impossible. Having no desire to be unreasonable or to accomplish the impossible, I have limited my goals to a social psychological analysis of intergroup relations.

The author wishes to thank the following people who read and commented on portions of the manuscript: Elliot Aronson, David Hamilton, Leslie McArthur, Thomas Pettigrew, Cookie Stephan, and David Wilder. He also wishes to thank Yvonne Boudreau, Joyce Dean, Karen Preuss, Peggy Smits, Debbie Stefan, Maria Telles-McGeagh, and Debbie Valverde for their assistance in preparing this chapter.

Intergroup relations from the social psychological perspective consist of the systematic study of relations between individuals as they are affected by group membership. Several aspects of this definition merit elaboration.

First, the level of analysis of a social psychological inquiry into intergroup relations is the individual and his or her relationships with social groups. The primary justification for focusing on the individual level of analysis is that it is the individual's perception of social reality and the processing of this information that influence individual behavior. It is the individual's interpretations of social reality that are crucial rather than the "real" nature of the situation. For example, even if there are clear social norms against favorable intergroup behavior in a given situation, people who are unaware of them or choose to ignore them will not be influenced by them. The intergroup cognitions that individuals bring into social situations and the way these cognitions influence information processing and resultant behavior will be of particular interest in this chapter. Relations between groups *qua* groups (nations, social classes, ethnic groups, etc.) will not be of prime interest, not because they are unimportant to an understanding of intergroup cognitions and behavior, but because they belong to a different level of analysis. For instance, the role of social norms and roles as determinants of discrimination will be examined only when their effects are mediated by individuals' perceptions. Thus institutional racism will not be emphasized, but individual racism will be.

Second, this chapter heavily emphasizes empirical studies of intergroup relations, especially laboratory and field experiments. Scant attention will be paid to descriptive studies or surveys. While descriptive studies and surveys have much to offer to an understanding of intergroup cognitions and behavior, they are generally more useful for generating theories and hypotheses than for testing them.

Third, an attempt will be made to generate hypotheses and conclusions that are not tied to specific situations or groups. Thus I will be less concerned with intergroup relations in schools or housing projects or between blacks and whites or men and women than in hypotheses and conclusions dealing with in-groups and out-groups in situations characterized by general qualities such as cooperation or equal status among the participants. However, in an examination of intergroup relations it is impossible to avoid a heavy concentration on race because it has been *the* major problem in intergroup relations in this country for as long as these issues have been studied.

Unavoidably, my own biases as well as those of social psychology are reflected in what I have written. The one that I am most aware of was intentional. I have emphasized the cognitive approach to intergroup relations. I have done so because I believe that in the interval since the publication of the last *Handbook,* this area is the one in which the greatest advances in our knowledge have occurred. The cognitive approach also makes it possible to broaden the focus beyond the traditional topics of prejudice and stereotyping to include a wider range of cognitions and their role in information processing and overt behavior. This approach encompasses the organization of knowledge about groups into higher-level cognitive structures such as schemata, scripts, and prototypes, as well as providing new insights into the operation of expectancies and biased perceptions of intergroup behavior. It is also useful in understanding the affective complexity of intergroup cognitions as reflected in theories stressing ambivalence toward out-groups.

Despite this general emphasis on cognitive processes in intergroup relations, it is inevitable that much attention will be devoted to prejudice and stereotyping. Thus definitions of prejudice and stereotyping will be offered.

Definitions of these concepts have been the topic of considerable discussion in the literature (e.g., Allport, 1954; Ashmore, 1970; Harding *et al.,* 1969). I have tried to distill from these discussions two simple definitions that capture the essence of the previous discussions of these concepts.

Prejudice consists of negative attitudes toward social groups. If there is a controversial aspect of this definition, it is in the omission of a moral rejection of prejudice as unjustified and wrong. I have chosen to exclude this idea, not because I believe that prejudices are not harmful, but because it is difficult to establish criteria by which to judge whether a given attitude is unjustified. Also, the idea that a prejudice must be unjustified eliminates consideration of instances in which negative attitudes can be justified. For instance, a misogynist male may dislike women because they are physically weaker than men. For the most part such a negative attitude has the same consequences as an attitude that is less justifiable on a statistical basis.

Stereotypes are sets of traits attributed to social groups. Stereotypes have defining features and characteristic features (cf., Smith, Shoben, and Rips, 1974). The defining features of stereotypes are used to categorize people into social groups, while characteristic features (traits) are used to predict and explain behavior (Stephan and Rosenfield, 1982). Stereotypes are often unjustified overgeneralizations, but even when they are not, they have the same implications for information processing and behavior. For this reason these common aspects of the definition of stereotypes have been excluded here.

The organization of the chapter is relatively simple. In the first section the cognitive information-processing approach to intergroup relations is examined. This discussion follows the general flow of information through the system, starting with attentional processes and continuing on to encoding and then retrieval. In each case particular emphasis is devoted to biases in the processing of social information that affect intergroup relations. In the second section the relationship between intergroup cognitions and behavior is explored. The two major emphases in this section are the relationship between intergroup attitudes and discriminatory behavior and the role of expectancies in intergroup interactions. The final section considers techniques that have been employed to improve intergroup relations. In this section techniques that have practical utility, particularly those that can be used in school settings, are highlighted.

THE COGNITIVE INFORMATION-PROCESSING APPROACH TO INTERGROUP RELATIONS

In organizing this discussion of the application of cognitive models to prejudice and stereotyping, I have adopted a highly simplified model of information processing. Literature will be reviewed in three general areas: attention, encoding, and retrieval. While complex models are available (e.g., Hastie, 1980; Wyer and Srull, 1980), they are more detailed than is required for a basic understanding of the literature on intergroup cognitions. The distinctions among attention, encoding, and retrieval are somewhat artificial since these three aspects of information processing do not operate independently nor do they operate in a strictly linear fashion. Thus while it is generally the case that attention determines to a considerable degree what information is encoded, and what is encoded determines to some extent what can be retrieved, it is also the case that experiences that have been previously encoded—and the recency with which particular categories have been retrieved from memory—also determine what will be attended to. An attempt will be made in the separate discussion of each process to include relevant aspects of the interactions among them.

ATTENTION

It is the function of attention to aid us in managing the environment, to bring our prior knowledge to bear on the current context in an effort to predict and control the events occurring within it. The allocation of attention depends on contextual variables, such as salience, and factors internal to the organism, including needs, level of arousal, expectations, and previously learned schemata, scripts, and prototypes. In the area of intergroup relations attentional processes are germane to the processing of information in intergroup interactions, particularly who is attended to, the inferences that will be made about the behavior of others, what prior knowledge is considered pertinent (especially whether expectations based on stereotypes are elicited), what types of processing are performed on the information that is attended to, what will be encoded and stored in long-term memory, and what behavioral responses are likely to be made.

Automatic Attentional Processes

Attention may be consciously allocated or it may be relatively automatic. Active allocation of attention occurs when people formulate hypotheses or hold expectancies concerning the behavior of others. Before these active processes are considered, more passive types of selective attention will be discussed. Automatic allocation of attention may be due to the properties of the stimulus situation or the perceiver.

Stimulus variables. In social situations selective attention is likely to be determined by the behavior of the stimulus persons, especially deviant, unexpected, negative, or colorful behavior. Support for this general proposition is provided in a study by Langer and colleagues (1976). They found that people spend more time processing information about others who are unusual or novel, such as the physically handicapped, than about others who are not novel. Another study found that when a group was presented as possessing a list of traits, the negative traits were more likely to be used to describe the group than the positive traits, suggesting that the negative traits were salient (Fulero and Rothbart, cited in Rothbart, 1981). Consistent with these results, Graziano, Brothen, and Berscheid (1980) found that subjects spent more time attending to a negative evaluator than to a positive one.

Two consequences of situationally induced salience of social stimuli that have been empirically studied are its effects on causal attributions and evaluations of others. In general, it appears that the causes of an observed behavior are attributed to aspects of the situation that are the focus of attention. This hypothesis has been offered by Jones and Nisbett (1972) to explain actor-observer differences in attribution and by Ickes, Wicklund, and Ferris (1973) to account for the self-attributions of people who are objectively self-aware. Several studies have manipulated the salience of different aspects of situations and then examined subsequent attributions. For instance, McArthur and Post (1977) found that when aspects of a videotape of a getting-acquainted conversation were made salient by bright lighting or by having a person move or wear an unusual shirt, they were more likely to be used to explain an actor's behavior than nonsalient stimuli. In one study in this series the behavior of an actor who was in the minority in a mixed-sex group was attributed more to the situation than the behavior of an actor who was in a group where the sex composition was balanced. McArthur and Post attribute this finding to the fact that the majority forms a unit in this situation and therefore becomes the focus of attention. In a subsequent study (McArthur and Soloman, 1978) causality for a hostile interaction was attributed to a person who was salient because she was physically handicapped.

Salience also polarizes evaluations of people who are the focus of attention (McArthur, 1981; McArthur and Soloman, 1978). In a study that examined this hypothesis in a setting involving stereotypes, Taylor and colleagues (1978) found that more extreme evaluations occurred for males or females to the degree that they were in the numerical minority in a group. In three studies McArthur and Friedman (1980) found that when in-group members appeared infrequently in a set of case histories, they were evaluated more favorably than when they appeared frequently; whereas when out-group members appeared infrequently, they were evaluated more negatively than when they appeared frequently. This effect was obtained for age, race, and gender. Thus the effects of salience on evaluations appear to hold for members of stereotyped groups as well as for nonstereotyped individuals.

It is important to note that these polarized responses can occur for both positive and negative evaluations, depending on the nature of the interaction and attitudes toward the group being evaluated. For instance, in the McArthur and Soloman study when the victim of the videotaped hostile encounter was rated favorably on a trait (e.g., friendliness) in the control condition, she was rated more favorably on this trait in the experimental condition (i.e., when she was more salient because she was wearing a leg brace). For traits where the control confederate was somewhat unfavorably rated (e.g., passivity), she was rated more unfavorably when she was salient. The polarization of evaluative responses may occur at various stages in the social cognition process (cf. Eiser and Stroebe, 1972). In the McArthur and Soloman study it appears to have been caused solely by attentional processes, since an additional condition using a red-haired woman in a full-color or black-and-white videotape produced similar polarization effects only in the color edition.

Perceiver variables. Among the perceiver characteristics that influence attention are the perceiver's arousal level, motivational factors such as needs, and the groups with which the perceiver is most familiar or of which she or he is a member. The primary effect of arousal on attention is to narrow the range of cues to which an individual attends (Easterbrook, 1959; Kahneman, 1973). A study demonstrating that arousal can affect the salience of social categories has been done by Wilder, Cooper, and Thompson (cited in Wilder, 1981). They found that aroused subjects were more likely to perceive several people who were interacting together as a group than were

unaroused subjects. Wilder (1980) argues that this increased tendency to categorize was due to limitations on cognitive processing caused by the arousal.

Specific rather than general arousal states, particularly those due to needs, may also influence attentional processes. The thrust of the new look in perception (Bruner and Goodman, 1947) was that need states such as poverty and hunger influence perception. Tests of this hypothesis have been notoriously inconsistent (for reviews, see Secord and Backman, 1974; Tajfel, 1968), but most have not been concerned with the processing of social information.

One need that appears to influence the processing of social information is the need to maintain a positive self-image. Eiser and Stroebe (1972) argue that people most frequently use those categories that enable them to maintain a positive view of themselves. Evidence supporting this phenomena has been obtained by Brewer (1979a). From extensive cross-cultural data she concludes that ingroup members tend to define in-group –out-group differences in terms of dimensions on which favorable social comparisons can be made. Dimensions on which the in-group perceives itself to be inferior to the out-group or on which there are minimal differences are unlikely to be employed to distinguish between groups. This line of reasoning implies that distinctions favorable to the in-group are more likely to be salient than unfavorable ones. Also, the more important the category distinctions are within the individual's value system, the more salient they are likely to be (cf. Eiser and Stroebe, 1972; Tajfel, 1972).

Prejudicial attitudes may also heighten the salience of some categories. A study by Allport and Kramer (1946) demonstrates the relationship between prejudice and salience. They found that students who were anti-Semitic were more accurate in identifying Jewish faces than were students who were low in anti-Semitism. Subsequent studies of this finding indicate that the reason for the higher accuracy of anti-Semitic subjects is that they "are more willing to label a face Jewish on the basis of limited information than are unprejudiced subjects" (Quanty, Keats, and Harkins, 1975, p. 454). These studies suggest that the social category of Jews is more salient for the anti-Semitic students than for unprejudiced students. Secord (1959) found that high- and low-prejudice persons differed in the degree to which they attributed aspects of the black stereotype to pictures of people. When the depicted people possessed more negroid features, the prejudiced people stereotyped them more than the nonprejudiced group did, but for more Caucasian faces there was little difference between the two groups. Thus it appears that for prejudiced people members of the group toward which they are prejudiced may be more salient than for nonprejudiced people. It seems likely that very intense positive as well as intense negative attitudes toward particular groups would make those group categories salient.

Familiarity with particular social categories may also increase category salience. A certain minimal level of familiarity is probably necessary before categorical distinctions can be made easily. As familiarity increases, the categorical distinctions should become clearer and easier to make and thus should be more salient. This idea is supported by a study in which it was found that familiarity increased the clarity of the stereotypes of Greeks and Americans (Triandis and Vassilou, 1972). However, at extremely high levels of familiarity categorical distinctions may be only superficially encoded if they are encoded at all. For instance, when no out-group members are present, people are unlikely to attend to the fact that they are interacting with ingroup members.

Situational factors may also interact with perceiver characteristics in determining the effects of salience. When people find themselves in social situations, some of their own characteristics will become figural against the background of the characteristics of other people in the situation. In a series of studies McGuire and his colleagues have shown that the self-concepts of children reflect the qualities that set them apart from their social milieu (McGuire and Padawer-Singer, 1976). Ethnic identity is more likely to be mentioned as a self-descriptor by students to the degree that they are in the ethnic minority in their schools (McGuire *et al.,* 1978). Likewise, sex is more likely to be mentioned to the extent that the opposite sex predominates in the child's household (McGuire, McGuire, and Winton, 1979). Thus distinctive stimulus properties become salient.

The individual's immediate prior experience may also make some categories more salient than others. A study by Wilder (1978) illustrates this suggestion. Subjects interacted with others who were categorized into groups or others who were not categorized into groups. The subjects who had participated in the groups were more likely to categorize a set of people they subsequently observed into a single group than were subjects who had initially interacted with others as individuals. The prior categorization made group distinctions salient and affected the encoding of subsequent social information. A study by Higgins and Petty (reported in Higgins and King, 1981) indicates that situationally induced sa-

lience of group membership may also influence the processing of information about other people on stereotypical trait dimensions. This study found that being a lone male or female in a group affected recall of sex stereotype information about stimulus persons. For male stimulus persons, more feminine and fewer masculine behaviors were recalled by lone males or females than by subjects whose sex was in the majority in the experimental context. For female stimulus persons a parallel effect was obtained, namely, less recall of feminine behaviors and more recall of masculine behaviors. It is possible that minority status made sex role stereotypes salient and subjects selectively attended to and recalled behaviors that were inconsistent with their stereotyped expectancies. Minority status may prime associated stereotypes and make them more available for use in encoding and retrieving information.

Explicit manipulations of priming support this suggestion. For instance, Thompson, Stephan, and Schvaneveldt (1980) tachistoscopically presented sex labels (male, female) as primes in a word-nonword decision task. Subsequent reaction times were faster for stereotype-related trait words than for unrelated words. The sex prime apparently passively activated the associated stereotype, which then facilitated the processing of category-relevant information. In another priming study Gaertner and McLaughlin (1983) found that using ethnic labels (black, white) as visual primes facilitated lexical decisions for affectively toned words among their white subjects. Reaction times were faster for positive words when preceded by the word white than when primed by the word black.

Most of the factors affecting the salience of categorical distinctions that have their origins primarily within the individual may be thought of in terms of the availability heuristic (Tversky and Kahneman, 1973). Prior experience causes people to strongly associate specific categories with specific situations, and these categories become more available than others in that situation. The strength of association varies as a function of such factors as the frequency of pairing situations and relevant categories, the vividness or uniqueness of such pairings, their utility and importance, and their fit with previously learned associations.

Controlled Attentional Processes

When we process information from the environment, we are not simply passive receivers who respond to the salience, intensity, duration, and frequency of stimuli, nor are we entirely dominated by internal states of arousal or need. Much of the time we actively select what information to attend to. A variety of different cognitive factors influence selective attention to social information, including schemata, scripts, and expectancies.

Schemata are cognitive structures consisting of the representation of knowledge concerning a stimulus domain (Neisser, 1976; Taylor and Crocker, 1980). In the social domain they provide perceivers with hypotheses about what will happen in specific situations and what to expect from people occupying specific roles or from members of socially defined groups. This knowledge serves to focus the perceiver's attention. It also structures what is perceived and provides interpretations for behavior. Scripts are schemata for episodic sequences of behavior in particular types of social situations (Schank and Abelson, 1977).

Expectancies tend to be highly specific. For instance, the relations between events in a script set up expectancies. Expectancies related to social categories may also be derived from sources other than scripts or schemata. Information provided by others about a social group or social situation may set up expectancies concerning what is going to happen or how members of a given group are going to behave.

Generally speaking, schemata, scripts, and expectancies influence the processing of information by guiding attention, by structuring encoding, and by determining what information is most likely to be retained, how it will be stored, and the degree to which it will subsequently be available.

Expectancies.

"Confident expectation of a certain intensity or quality of impression will often make us sensibly see or hear it in an object which really falls far short of it" (James, 1890, p. 424).

There appear to be three principal origins of expectancies: our direct experience with social situations and with other people, our observations of our own behavior, and information we acquire indirectly through socialization and from such sources as the mass media and our peers. Expectancies affect the focus of attention, the inferences that are made in social situations, and the retention of expectancy-confirming information.

The initial effect of expectancies is that they bias the selection of information to be processed. In a series of four studies Snyder and Swann (1978a) found that subjects proposed to test hypotheses about the traits of another person by selecting questions that would tend to

provide confirming evidence. For example, if the subjects were asked to determine whether another person was an extravert, they acted as if they expected the other person to be extraverted and proposed to gather evidence that would confirm their expectancies. A conceptual replication using roles instead of traits was also consistent with this analysis (Snyder and Cantor, 1979). A study reported by Rodin and Langer (1980) found that middle-aged people proposed to use less difficult questions in interviewing the elderly than in interviewing young people, presumably because they expected elderly people to be less intellectually competent.

This bias toward collecting expectancy-confirming evidence is followed by a bias toward selectively attending to expectancy-confirming information during social interactions. Evidence supporting this idea has been obtained in studies by Snyder and Frankl (1976) and Eisen and McArthur (1979). In a study by Langer and Abelson (1974) traditional therapists and behavioral therapists viewed a videotape of a social interaction that was described as a job interview or an interview with a mental patient. The traditional therapists perceived the patient to be significantly more disturbed than the job applicant, but the behavioral therapists evaluated them similarly. The authors suggest that the behavior therapists may have attended more to manifest behavior and were less influenced by expectancies associated with the background information than the traditional therapists because their training discouraged labeling people as patients. This result is important because it is one of the few reported in the literature that suggests that an active attempt to overcome expectancies can be successful.

Additional studies have shown that stereotyped trait inferences are influenced by expectancies. In one study an interaction among school teachers was taped in such a way that every participant's role in the initial interaction was played by both males and females (Taylor *et al.,* 1978, study 3). Subjects who listened to these tapes while viewing slides of the speakers reported that the males were more influential, confident, analytic, and negative and less warm and sensitive than the females, regardless of which roles the males portrayed in the interaction. The most likely interpretation of these results is that sex role stereotypes established expectancies in the subjects' minds, and the subjects then selectively perceived confirming evidence. Parallel results for an interracial interaction have been reported by Duncan (1976). In Duncan's study an ambiguous aggressive encounter was staged. White subjects perceived the encounter and the perpetrator as being more aggressive when the perpetrator was black than when he was white. In a conceptual replication of this study the results indicated that blacks as well as whites viewed minor incidents of hostility as being more aggressive when performed by a black than when performed by a white (Sagar and Schofield, 1980). Again, it appears that stereotypes established expectancies that were perceived as being confirmed.

Category-based expectancies not only may affect the perception of social information that is presented, they may also lead to the belief that nonpresented related information has been perceived. For instance, Cantor and Mischel (1977) informed half their subjects that they would be reading about an extravert or an introvert. All subjects read ten statements about extraverted or introverted stimulus persons, and their recognition memory was assessed for traits that were included or not included among the descriptors. Subjects who expected to be learning about extraverts were more confident that they had seen nonincluded related descriptors of extraverts than subjects who expected to learn about introverts. These effects did not appear when no category information was provided. Rothbart, Evans, and Fulero (1979) found that prior expectancies that a group would consist of either intelligent or friendly people led subjects to perceive a higher frequency of intelligent or friendly behavior, although the actual frequencies of these behaviors were equal in the descriptions they read. In a related study Hamilton and Rose (1980) found that subjects overestimated the occurrence of traits presented with occupational roles when the traits were part of the stereotype for these roles but not when the traits were unrelated to the roles. These studies indicate that social category information often leads people to expect and then perceive behavior that is associated with the category even if it has not been observed.

Subsequent retention of expectancy-relevant information may also be biased toward expectancy-confirming information. For instance, Zadny and Gerard (1974, study 2) led subjects to believe that they were viewing a videotape of two people committing a burglary or of two people trying to find a friend's drugs before his room was raided. These expectancies led to greater recall of theft-related and drug-related information, respectively. This effect occurred only when the subjects were given the instructions before rather than after viewing the videotapes, indicating that the effect was caused by attentional

processes and not by a retroactive organization of the stored information (cf. Snyder and Frankl, 1976). Retention may sometimes be biased toward expectancy-disconfirming information (Hastie and Kumar, 1979). The salience literature and studies such as Hastie and Kumar's indicate that we attend more to novel, deviant, negative, or otherwise unusual behavior, whereas the majority of the expectancy studies suggest that we attend more to confirming events. This issue will be dealt with in some detail at the end of this section.

The evidence that expectancies influence attention is comparatively strong. Situation-based expectancies and category-based expectancies have both been shown to affect what is attended to, some of the inferences that are made about observed behavior, and what is likely to be available for subsequent recall. The type of information that is selectively attended to is primarily information that would confirm the expectancies. Material that is associatively linked to category-based expectancies may also influence perception. The data suggest that stereotype categories and their associated traits set up expectancies that are likely to lead to selective perceptions that confirm the existence of the stereotyped traits, even in some cases when no supporting information is actually presented.

While these studies clearly indicate that expectancies play a significant role in determining attention, they provide only limited insight into some important related issues. One issue that is unclear is when expectancies are elicited. The triggering of expectancies may depend in part on the salience of social category information in particular situations, but it is also likely to depend on the individual's prior experiences and the strength of the expectancy. Since many of the characteristic features of stereotypes are only loosely associated with them, it is an issue of considerable importance to know when such expectancies will affect attention. Category-based expectancies are obviously more important than situation-based expectancies for stereotyping, but important interactions may occur between them. Most stereotype-based expectancies, such as the expectation that men will be independent, only apply to given types of situations.

While many stereotype-based expectancies will be negative, some, particularly those associated with the ingroup, will be positive. It would be valuable to know whether expectancies for positive and negative behaviors have the same effects on attention and perception. The studies discussed above report on some positive expectancies (e.g., a group of friendly people) and some negative expectancies (e.g., blacks are aggressive), but mostly they are neutral (e.g., introverts are quiet). In addition, it would be valuable to know when our pervasive desire to be correct and to perceive the world consistently, and even as just, would conflict with a desire to maximize our rewards. For instance, a woman may expect men to try to dominate her, but she may not want to be dominated and may resent it when a man tries to do so. Is this expectancy as likely to lead to selectively perceiving confirming evidence as the case of a male who expects women to be submissive and prefers it when they are?

Perhaps the most perplexing issue associated with expectancies is when they bias attention in the direction of perceiving confirming evidence and when attention is dominated by unexpected or novel information. At present we can frame some of the dimensions relevant to answering this question, but little evidence bears directly on the answer. McArthur (1981), from research on illusory correlation (McArthur and Friedman, 1980), has argued that impressions of minority group members will be determined more by behaviors that confirm stereotypes than by novel behaviors. The generalizability of this hypothesis probably depends on the clarity and strength of the expectancies. The more explicit an expectancy is and the stronger its association with a particular social group, the more likely it is to determine attention.

Another factor of importance is the degree of discrepancy between the expected behavior and the actual behavior, with the probability of attending to unexpected behavior increasing as the discrepancy increases. The importance of the expected behavior may also influence attention. The costs and rewards to the perceiver of expected or unexpected behaviors may increase the chances of perceiving confirming evidence or carefully discriminating unexpected from expected behaviors. Costly unexpected behavior (e.g., treachery) may be especially closely attended to. The number and consistency of expectations that the perceiver has are also likely to affect attention. Inconsistent expectancies (e.g., kind and stingy) may reduce the chances that unexpected behavior will be attended to. Large amounts or highly complex information may favor novel events over expectancy-confirming events, since novelty may be required to attract attention. On the other hand, highly explicit expectancies could provide essential guides to attention in such situations. Finally, the frequency of unexpected behaviors as well as their extremity may be important. While it would seem that highly frequent unexpected behaviors would be more likely to command attention, re-

search on illusory correlation suggests that infrequent behaviors often influence impressions when paired with minority groups (e.g., Hamilton and Gifford, 1976).

Schemata. Social schemata may be situation-based, person-based, or category-based. They can be built up gradually over time through direct and vicarious experience, or they can be learned quickly. The schemata that appear to be most relevant to intergroup relations are self-schemata, out-group schemata, and causal schemata. These schemata are likely to influence a variety of aspects of attention, including the speed with which information is processed and how social information is organized and retained.

A number of studies indicate that self-schemata affect the speed with which schema-relevant information is processed. When people are asked to make judgments regarding another person that are relevant to their own self-schemata, they are slower than when making judgments for nonrelevant stimuli. Markus and Smith (1980) found that males who were schematic for masculinity had longer response latencies when judging whether others had masculine traits than when judging feminine traits. It is not clear why these differences exist. Taylor and Crocker (1980) have suggested that schema-relevant information is processed faster than nonschematic information when the processing is automatic but more slowly when schemata are used in the course of controlled processing.

Self-schemata appear to influence not only the speed with which schema-relevant information is encoded but also what information will be encoded and subsequently recalled. For instance, Taylor (1980) found that individuals who were highly masculine or feminine used sex as a category system to organize information more than individuals who were androgynous. Similarly, Markus and Smith (1980) found that males who had self-schemata for masculinity more frequently described another male by using masculine traits than males who were aschematic with regard to masculinity. Tunnell (1981) found that women who were schematic with respect to femininity described females with more feminine traits than did women who were aschematic. Not surprisingly, several studies indicate that self-schemata facilitate the subsequent recognition and recall of schema-relevant traits contained in descriptions of others (Higgins and King, 1981; Higgins, Mavin, and King, 1980, cited in Higgins and King, 1981; Mueller, Bailis, and Goldstein, 1979), although not all studies on this topic have obtained differential recall effects (Markus and Smith, 1980).

Self-schemata also influence the perception of the traits that others possess (Hastorf, Richardson, and Dornbusch, 1958). This influence may take one of two forms. First, we may perceive that others possess the same traits as we do, and we may expect them to behave in the same ways that we do (projection) (cf. McCauley, Stitt, and Segal, 1980; Ross, 1977). Alternatively, we may perceive others as differing from us along trait dimensions on which we can locate our own standing. That is, we use ourselves as an anchor and differentiate others from us as being more or less extreme on a given dimension than we are (a contrast effect) (Berkowitz, 1960).

In-group and out-group schemata may also affect evaluations of group members. A set of studies by Linville and Jones (1980) provides an example. In one study white subjects read about a law school applicant who was either white or black and well or poorly qualified. The well-qualified black applicant was rated more favorably than the well-qualified white, but the poorly qualified black was rated less favorably than the comparable white. The authors interpret these findings in terms of the complexity of in-group and out-group schemata. They argue that owing to the extensive experience people have with members of their own group, they have a more complex view of the in-group than of the out-group. These complex schemata for in-group members lead to moderate judgments, because any new information is averaged with the positive and negative evaluations that already exist on the wide variety of dimensions that make up the in-group schemata. Out-group schemata, being less complex, lead to extreme judgments, because new information can exert a greater impact on evaluations than it would when placed in the context of in-group schemata.

An alternative to the schema complexity interpretation of these results can be derived from a motivational explanation offered by Katz and Glass (1979) to explain what they have labeled response amplification effects. Katz and Glass (1979) suggest that their findings that members of stigmatized groups are often judged more positively or more negatively than members of nonstigmatized groups are attributable to the arousal of ambivalent attitudes toward members of stigmatized groups. The conflict between these feelings of sympathy and aversion is resolved by emphasizing the positive or negative affective response, depending on the nature of the situation. This motivational explanation has received support from studies showing that response amplification is enhanced by the importance of the implications (hedonic relevance) of the out-group member's behavior for the in-group member (Gergen and Jones, 1963; Gibbons *et al.,* 1981) and studies indicating that negative response amplification rarely occurs in low-hedonic-relevance situations (Carver *et al.,* 1977). These studies suggest that when salience leads to the use of out-group schemata to process information, bidirectional, evaluative response polarization is likely to result. When these schemata are not activated, as in the studies where hedonic relevance is low, then only positive amplification will occur (cf. Carver, *et al.,* 1979).

Thus the response amplification hypothesis suggests that out-group schemata are affectively ambivalent, and evaluations of out-group members depend on whether the current situation is positive or negative. The explanation proposed by Linville and Jones (1980) is that out-group schemata are inherently simple and that current evaluations are biased in favor of the evaluative information available in the situation. In neither set of studies is the complexity or evaluative content of out-group schemata measured. It appears that a resolution of these conflicting explanations will await the manipulation of these two variables.

Among the most common and important schemata in social situations are causal schemata (Jones and Davis, 1965; Kelley, 1967; Reeder and Brewer, 1979). Causal schemata provide rules that enable us to infer the causes of behavior. When social categories and causal schemata are both activated in a given situation, the stereotypes associated with the social group furnish a ready set of potential causes. This effect can lead to the "ultimate attribution error" (Pettigrew, 1979). This term refers to a pattern of attributions in which positive behaviors performed by in-group members and negative behaviors performed by out-group members are attributed to internal factors, whereas negative in-group behaviors and positive out-group behaviors are attributed to external factors. According to Pettigrew, four patterns of explanation may be used to explain away the positive behavior of out-group members:

1. They may be perceived as exceptions to the rule.

2. Their positive behavior may be attributed to some special advantage such as affirmative action.

3. They may be perceived as having overcome the limitations of members of their group through hard work.

4. Situational factors such as role demands may be used to explain their positive behavior.

Explanations 2 and 4 are more external than 1 and 3, but in all cases different and more positive internal explanations would be expected for in-group members. Pettigrew further suggests that these attribution tendencies will be greatest among groups with a history of conflict, for people who are highly prejudiced, and for racial and ethnic differences that covary with national and socioeconomic differences.

Evidence for the ultimate attribution error was obtained in a study by Taylor and Jaggi (1974). In their study Hindu office clerks attributed each of four positive behaviors more to internal factors when they were engaged in by Hindu than by Moslem actors. For four negative behaviors internal attributions were greater for Moslem than for Hindu actors. Since all four sets of behaviors could be seen as being related to the stereotypes held by the Hindu subjects, expectancy confirmation effects can account for these results. If the positive behaviors were expected of in-group members on the basis of traits associated with the in-group stereotype, then it would have been reasonable for the in-group members to attribute them to internal factors. Correspondingly, internal factors could be discounted as causes of negative in-group behaviors because they would not have been expected on the basis of the in-group stereotype. Likewise, for the out-group, stereotype-consistent negative behaviors would be attributed internally, but unexpected positive behaviors would not be attributed to internal factors. Additional evidence for the ultimate attribution error may be found in several other studies (Duncan, 1976; Feldman-Summers and Kiesler, 1974; Mann and Taylor, 1974; Sagar and Schofield, 1980; Stephan, 1977; Stephan and Beane, 1978; Stephan and Woolridge, 1977). Stereotype-based expectancies can account for all these results but not those of a study by Greenberg and Rosenfield (1979).

The Greenberg and Rosenfield study indicates that attributional bias may sometimes extend beyond the specific content of in-group and out-group stereotypes. After pretesting white subjects to determine that extrasensory-perception abilities were believed to be equivalent in blacks and whites, they asked their subjects to make attributions for the positive or negative performance of blacks and whites on an ESP task. For the ethnocentric subjects, but not for those who were not ethnocentric, the positive performance of the whites and the negative performance of the blacks were attributed to internal factors. A mediating mechanism other than stereotype expectancy confirmation must have been operating in this study, since expectancies were equal for the two

groups. These investigators and others have suggested that this mediator may be attitudes toward the in-group and the out-group. In support of this suggestion Wang and McKillip (1978) found that ethnocentric Chinese and Americans made attributions for a car accident that were consistent with the ultimate attribution error. Each group blamed the driver more if he was an out-group member than if he was an in-group member. American college students who were not ethnocentric did not make differential attributions to the driver on the basis of nationality.

These studies suggest that stereotyping and prejudicial attitudes may both play a role in the ultimate attribution error. Where the stereotype provides clear expectancies and in-group–out-group distinctions are salient, the expectancy-confirmation pattern may be activated (i.e., expectancy confirming behaviors will be attributed to internal factors). When in-group attitudes are highly ethnocentric, in-group–out-group attributional bias may be activated, even in the absence of stereotype-based expectancies. When the ultimate attribution error is evoked, the consequence is that stereotype-consistent or attitude-consistent causal inferences will be made. The results in most cases will sustain negative perceptions of out-group members and positive perceptions of in-group members. The causal nature of these inferences may have the effect of justifying discrimination against out-group members in situations such as employment or academic settings, where evaluations of motives are a determinant of advancement. Biased causal interpretations of out-group behavior can also have a negative influence on the course of intergroup social interactions by creating misunderstandings and leading to inappropriate responses to out-group members based on the inferred causes of their behavior.

Scripts.   A particularly important subclass of schemata consists of scripts or plans. A script is a "conceptual structure which explains for the believer why a specific social action or sequence of actions has occurred or might occur" (Abelson, 1975, p. 275). Scripts can be used to anticipate and interpret behavior. Scripts are important in intergroup interaction because they provide the participants with behavioral expectations. Scripts can result in misunderstandings and conflict when they differ between groups. They may set up inappropriate expectancies and lead to erroneous inferences. A study by Schofield (1980) provides an example. In the desegregated school where she did her study, the black students viewed the whites as prejudiced and conceited. In contrast, the whites viewed themselves as unprejudiced, and they occasionally extended offers of help to the blacks. According to Schofield (1981), the "Black students often see such offers of help as yet another indication of white feelings of superiority and conceit. White students who do not perceive themselves as conceited feel mystified and angry when what to them seem to be friendly and helpful overtures are rejected" (p. 79). The script for the whites consists of plans to help blacks, but blacks' scripts for this interaction substitute patronization as the intention. Similar types of script-based conflicts are at the heart of the cultural-assimilator technique of modifying intergroup interactions (Triandis, 1976).

The priming of scripts has been shown to affect behavior in a study by Wilson and Capitman (1982). They found that males who read a boy-meets-girl script subsequently treated a female confederate in a friendlier manner then males who had not read the script. It appears that scripts can also increase recall of nonpresented information and decrease the recall of information that is presented but does not fit the script (Bransford and Johnson, 1973).

Scripts would seem to offer great potential as tools for the study of intergroup relations. Unfortunately, this potential has yet to be realized. The principal reasons appear to be that the concept is relatively new, it is often difficult to determine what scripts apply to social situations because they are usually implicit rather than explicit, and it is difficult to stage interactions in which subtle sequencing of behaviors is altered.

ENCODING

The control of attention by expectancies, schemata, and scripts has its basis in prior-knowledge structures stored in memory. Each of these cognitive structures affect not only attention but also what is encoded and available for subsequent processing and retrieval. The set of factors that we will consider next has its effects on information processing primarily at the encoding stage. They influence how information is organized to a greater extent than they influence what is attended to.

Categorization

"If perceptual experience is ever . . . free of categorical identity, it is doomed to be a gem, serene, locked in the silence of private experience" (Bruner, 1973, p. 9).

The organization of social and other stimuli into categories constitutes the basis for imputing meaning to stimuli. Objects are placed into categories on the basis of their similiarity along one or more defining dimensions. When objects are perceived to belong to a given category, the differences among them along the dimensions defining category membership are considered to be less important than their similarity along these dimensions. For example, the category of elderly people is comprised of people within a given age range. The age differences of people within this range are considered to be less important than the similarity of their ages. Likewise, the nature of an individual's handicap is less important than the fact that the individual has one when we speak of handicapped people.

The boundaries between categories may be highly distinctive so that there is little confusion about what category a given object falls in. However, with social categories the boundaries are often imprecise (Cantor and Mischel, 1979; LeVine and Campbell, 1972). Age is a good example. The boundaries between infancy, childhood, adolescence, adulthood, and old age are all imprecise. Other social categories have similarly fuzzy boundaries, such as membership in religious and ethnic groups. The looseness of category boundaries and the inevitable variety of people within a category can lead to the development of subcategories. For instance, Brewer, Dull, and Lui (1981) have demonstrated that the category "older persons" can be broken down into the subcategories of "grandmothers," "elder statesmen," and "senior citizens." It is often the case that extended experience with a given set of categories leads to the development of subcategories (Feldman, Crino, and Velez, 1980). The result is that many classification schemata are basically hierarchical in structure.

While categories range in magnitude from the finite to the infinite, there appears to be an optimal level of categorization (Rosch *et al.,* 1976). It is clear that categories such as race and sex are often used as basic categories in processing information about others (Pliske and Smith, 1979; Taylor *et al.,* 1978). In the study by Taylor and colleagues (1978) students were asked to indicate which person in a discussion group had made specific suggestions. When the groups contained both blacks and whites, the students made more intraclass identification errors than interclass identification errors. Parallel results were obtained for mixed-sex groups. This latter result indicates that the students categorized the stimulus persons by sex, enabling them to more easily recall whether a male or a female had made a given suggestion than which individual had made the suggestion. Feldman, Crino, and Velez (1980) have recently shown that subcategories including race, present social class, and social class background may be basic enough so that information concerning these categories is processed automatically.

Prototypes. Work by Rosch (1978) and others on the use of prototypes in the categorization of objects has been extended to individuals by Cantor and Mischel (1977, 1979). When an individual is classified into a social category, a featural comparison is performed. An exemplar is compared with the most typical member of a category, the prototype, and a decision is made about the degree of similarity between the two. For person categories this judgment depends on the breadth of resemblance between an exemplar and the prototype (i.e., the number of traits that are similar), the dominance of category-consistent traits in the information that is used to make the judgments, and the frequency of prototype-incompatible behaviors (Cantor and Mischel, 1979). Attributes that are consistent with the prototype appear to have a greater impact than prototype-incompatible attributes (Tversky, 1977). When information is limited, people tend to rely most on the presence of behavior consistent with traits that are central to the prototype (Cantor, 1978, cited in Cantor and Mischel, 1979). Exemplars that are high in prototypicality for a given object category can be categorized faster, can be learned more easily, are subsequently more available, and have a greater facilitation effect on information processing when used to create a set than exemplars that are low in prototypicality (Rosch, 1978). When a person is judged to be high on prototypicality for a given category, it is likely that this judgment structures the organization of subsequent information processing. It may set up expectancies, lead to a search for other prototype-consistent behaviors, cause prototype-consistent information to be "filled in" in memory (Cantor and Mischel, 1977), and lead to behaviors that take the presumed nature of the other person into account.

For social groups, classification is probably based primarily on a comparison of the features of an individual with the defining features of prototypical members of the group. The more readily apparent the defining features are, the more likely it is that people will be categorized into groups on the basis of the features. Thus age, sex, skin color, attractiveness, styles of dress, and handicapped condition are all easily perceived in face-to-face interactions and may account for their widespread use as defining features in social categories (Fiske and Cox, 1979; McArthur, 1981). Many social stimuli are multiply categorized, and a question of considerable importance is the degree to which some categories or combinations of categories are more salient than others.

For stereotyped social categories the defining features of group membership are supplemented by varying numbers of characteristic features that are probabilistically associated with category membership (cf. Smith, Shoben, and Rips, 1974). Experimental studies demonstrating the link between defining and characteristic features of categories have been done by Gurwitz and Dodge (1977), Secord (1959), and Razran (1950). In the Gurwitz and Dodge study women who were categorized as sorority members were perceived as possessing the characteristic traits associated with the stereotype of sorority women, even though the other members of the sorority were not described as being stereotypical. In Secord's study when subjects categorized a photo as being of a black or a white person, they then attributed traits associated with the respective stereotypes to the stimulus persons. Razran (1950) found that people were judged differently along a variety of traits when they had been categorized into ethnic groups than when judged in the absence of group identifications. In all of these studies, evoking the category activated the associated characteristic features.

A recent study of Locksley and colleagues (1980) provides additional information on the operation of this effect of categorization. In one of their experiments subjects attributed assertiveness or passivity to a male or female stimulus person in a manner consistent with sex role stereotypes when irrelevant social information was provided. These conditions are conceptually parallel to those of the Gurwitz and Dodge and the Razran studies. However, when behavioral information on assertiveness was explicitly provided, evaluations of the stimulus persons' assertiveness reflected this information, even when it was inconsistent with expectancies based on the sex of the stimulus person. A second study found that when stimulus persons were described as repeatedly engaging in assertive (or passive) behaviors, masculine (or feminine) traits were attributed to them regardless of their sex. These behavioral descriptions of assertive people probably elicited implicit personality theories of traits associated with assertiveness (or passivity) that were more powerful than the sex stereotypes because the behavioral descriptions were more vivid (cf. Nisbett, *et al.,* 1976). This result suggests that the types of categories that will be used to encode social information may depend on what categories are most salient in a given situation.

The defining features of social groups that cause an

individual to be categorized may also elicit the affective responses associated with the groups. This result is suggested in a set of studies by Fiske (1982). In one study she found that stereotyped campus groups (e.g., ROTC members) were reacted to more negatively if they engaged in neutral stereotype-consistent behaviors (dating, playing football) than if they engaged in neutral stereotype-inconsistent behaviors (cooking, arranging flowers). The authors argue that when the appearance (e.g., wearing green fatigues) and behavioral cues were consistent, the negative affect associated with the category was elicited. When the appearance and behavioral cues were inconsistent, the individual was not defined as a prototypical group member and the affective response associated with the group was not elicited.

The study of prototypes provides some insights into why stereotypes are so difficult to modify. For instance, a wide range of prototype-inconsistent behaviors may be needed to change a stereotype, since low frequencies of prototype-incompatible behavior tend to be discounted. Also, if central prototype-confirming behaviors are present, it may be difficult to modify judgments of prototypicality even when considerable discrepant behavior occurs.

Assimilation and contrast. The categorization of objects is based on similarity within categories and differences between categories. Assimilation and contrast effects refer to the amplification of these basic processes involved in categorization. Assimilation occurs when within-category similarity is perceived to be greater than it actually is, and contrast effects occur when the differences between categories are perceived to be greater than they actually are. The implications of assimilation and contrast for stereotyping are as important as they are obvious. Assimilation and contrast lead to distortions in the processing of information about social groups that facilitate the formation of stereotypes, promote negative attitudes between groups, facilitate the generation of inappropriate expectations, lead to the dehumanization of out-group members, and hinder attempts to change stereotypes. In the case of social groups the placement of individuals into categories on the basis of the defining features of group membership will lead to assimilation and contrast effects with regard to the characteristic traits associated with the group stereotypes. A study that illustrates assimilation effects found that students who were asked to rate two Indian students and two Canadian students perceived the students from each group to be more similar to one another on characteristic features of the respective group stereotypes than on traits that were irrelevant to the stereotypes (Tajfel, Sheikh, and Gardner, 1964).

Even in the absence of prior stereotypes, categorizing people into groups will promote the perception of within-group similarity. In a study by Wilder (1978, study 1) the subjects evaluated the similarity of stimulus persons whom they were told were part of one discussion group, were members of two discussion groups, or were simply an aggregate of unrelated individuals. After hearing the initial, prediscussion opinion of one person regarding a civil suit, the subjects were asked to predict the initial opinion of a second person. The predicted similarity was greater when the second person was presented as being a member of the same discussion group than when the second person was presented as being a member of a different discussion group or as one person among an aggregate of unrelated individuals.

One of the major effects of assimilation on intergroup relations is to increase the tendency to interact with others in terms of group memberships rather than as individuals. The perception of within-group homogeneity produced by assimilation makes it easier to regard all out-group members similarly. Studies by Malpass and Kravitz (1969) and Chance, Goldstein, and McBride (1975) suggest that assimilation effects may operate differently for in-groups and out-groups. Subjects in these studies were better able to recall faces of strangers who were in-group members than faces of out-group members. Apparently, subjects could differentiate in-group faces because of the greater depth at which they were processed (Chance and Goldstein, 1981), but assimilation effects made recognition of out-group faces more difficult. Brigham and Barkowitz (1978) in a similar study found that blacks and whites more easily recognized faces of in-group members than out-group members. In addition, they found that women recognized faces of females better than faces of males, but there were no differences for men. In contrast to these studies, Taylor and colleagues (1978), using a task in which subjects tried to recall which person had offered a given opinion in a group discussion, found assimilation effects (intragroup errors) for both in-group and out-group members. These studies suggest that in most cases assimilation effects are greater for out-group members than for in-group members.

The conflicting results of these studies on assimilation are mirrored in the literature concerning the cognitive differentiation of in-groups and out-groups. There are two opposing positions on this issue. One of them, outlined by Wilder (1981) and Linville and Jones (1980), proposes that in-groups are perceived as being more differentiated than out-groups. In Wilder's study subjects were randomly divided into groups on the basis of their ''preferences'' for paintings by Klee or Kandinsky. The subjects then estimated the range of opinions to be found among members of one of the two groups. In-group members (people who shared the subjects' ''preferences'') were believed to have a wider range of political beliefs, opinons on a legal case, and artistic preferences than out-group members. Thus this study indicates that in-groups are perceived as being more complex than out-groups.

In contrast, Stephan (1978) has argued, on the basis of studies of the perception of liked and disliked others (Irwin, Tripodi, and Bieri, 1967; Soucar, 1970, 1971), that out-groups are perceived as being more differentiated than in-groups. In Stephan's study students in integrated or segregated schools evaluated two out-groups and their in-group on ten trait dimensions. The out-groups were perceived as being more differentiated than the in-groups. Similarly, Schonbach and colleagues (1981) found that German students had more differentiated views of Italians than of Germans. However, in this study no differences occurred in in-group and out-group perceptions of another nationality group (Turks). Bruner and Perlmutter (1957) found that people used more traits to describe out-group members than in-group members, thus providing additional evidence that out-groups are perceived more complexly than in-groups.

We can reconcile these conflicting sets of results by examining the meaning of differentiation in these studies. Wilder studied differentiation within traits, whereas Bruner and Perlmutter, Schonbach and colleagues, and Stephan examined differentiation across traits. Possibly, for most traits the in-group is perceived as being highly differentiated, but with a preponderance of people falling toward the positive pole of the trait dimensions. Across a set of traits prototypical in-group members would appear to be relatively undifferentiated because they would be rated at the positive end of most traits. Out-group members may be perceived as varying more across traits owing to the mixture of negative and positive traits attributed to them, but they may also be seen as more uniform than in-group members within traits owing to ignorance and assimilation effects.

The tendency for assimilation effects to occur is promoted by comparing the in-group with out-groups. Doise, Deschamps, and Meyer (1978) have shown that Swiss children perceive Swiss ethnic groups as being more similar when they were judged along with non-Swiss groups than when judged by themselves. Thus the introduction of an out-group reduced the differences perceived between subcategories of in-group members. Wilder, Thompson, and Cooper (1979, cited in Wilder, 1981) have shown that the presence of a more extreme group led to reduced discrimination against a group differing only moderately from the subjects. The presence of comparison out-groups may cause increased assimilation among similar groups.

A study by Allen and Wilder (1979) serves to illustrate how assimilation effects and contrast effects can be combined. Subjects were randomly assigned to one of two groups and asked to predict the beliefs of members of the two groups. The results revealed that the subjects perceived members of their own group to be more similar to them than out-group members were. One consequence of the perceived dissimilarity between groups that results from contrast effects is likely to be negative attitudes toward out-groups. Hensley and Duval (1976) extended the findings by Byrne (1961) and others, which showed that dissimilarity leads to disliking, to include groups as well as individuals. Their results indicated that as the opinions of the subject and a cluster of others became increasingly different from another cluster of individuals, attitudes toward the dissimilar others became more negative. These increases in negative attitudes toward the dissimilar others were accompanied by assimilation effects leading to increased liking for similar others.

The generality of this finding for established stereotypes may depend on the nature of the traits on which the groups are perceived to differ. In cases where the out-group differs from the in-group in a negatively evaluated direction (e.g., less intelligent), contrast effects should lead to disliking. However, when the out-group differs in a positively evaluated direction (e.g., more intelligent), contrast effects may not promote negative attitudes. Since negatively evaluated group differences usually predominate over positive ones (Brewer, 1979a), however, the most likely result of contrast effects is heightened prejudice.

The processes set in motion by assimilation and contrast can hinder changes in stereotypes. Assimilation effects inhibit category modification because they operate to reduce differentiation rather than to increase it. Assimilation effects foster a narrow view of out-group behavior by limiting attention to individual out-group members. Consistent with this proposition, Wilder (1979a, cited in Wilder, 1981) found that the behavior of an individual interacting with four people was segmented into finer units when the four people were labeled as an aggregate of individuals than when they were labeled as a group. This suggests that less attention was paid to individuals when they were members of a group.

The principle of least effort also hinders attempts to modify distortions created by assimilation. "The principle of least effort inclines us to hold coarse and early formed generalizations as long as they can possibly be made to serve our purposes" (Allport, 1954, p. 172). Categories are resistant to change because their absence requires us to treat others as individuals and seems to make the world more complex and less predictable. As Allport put it, "Our point is merely that life becomes easier when the category is not differentiated. To consider every member of a group as endowed with the same traits saves us the pains of dealing with them as individuals" (Allport, 1954, p. 169).

The tendency toward greater assimilation in the perception of out-group members may lead to the perception that out-groups are more homogeneous than in-groups. One consequence of this perceived homogeneity of out-groups is that it is easier to generalize from the behavior of an individual group member to the group as a whole in the case of out-groups than in the case of in-groups (Quattrone and Jones, 1980). Thus assimilation and contrast promote stereotyping of out-groups to a greater extent than they promote stereotyping of in-groups.

By definition, contrast effects magnify perceived differences between groups. Several processes combine to maintain these distorted perceptions. To the extent that perceived dissimilarity leads to negative attitudes toward out-groups, contact with out-group members is likely to be avoided. In addition, people are likely to seek out information that confirms or maintains their perceptions of group differences and the negative attitudes based on them. The operation of this process has been explored by Wilder and Allen (1978). After an arbitrary division into groups, subjects were given an opportunity to review information about the similarity or dissimilarity of in-group and out-group members. The subjects chose to see information indicating that the in-group was similar to them and that the out-group was dissimilar to them. Thus as in the Snyder and Swann (1978) studies, the subjects chose information that would confirm categorical distinctions between people. Recall of information about in-groups and out-groups is similarly biased. People are better able to recall information indicating that the in-group members are similar and out-group members are dissimilar to them (Wilder, 1979a, cited in

Wilder, 1981). These biases operate in the service of maintaining contrast effects.

When categorization activates stereotypes, expectations are created that will often bias information processing and behavior in the direction of expectancy confirmation. Thus inappropriate trait attributions based on contrast effects will tend to be perceived as being confirmed. Contrast effects may also lead people to regard in-group attitudes as being correct. Evidence for this idea comes from the study by Hensley and Duval (1976), who found that increasing the actual differences between two clusters of people led to increases in the perceived correctness of the subjects' own opinions (and presumably of people similar to the subject).

In-group–Out-group Bias

One of the most intriguing consequences of categorization is that the mere division of people into groups leads to biased evaluations of the groups and their products and to discrimination in favor of in-group members and against out-group members. The research in this area indicates that virtually any categorization process can lead to in-group–out-group bias. While in some studies arbitrarily dividing individuals into groups has not led to bias, in others assigning people to groups on the basis of a coin flip has led to bias (Billig, 1973; Billig and Tajfel, 1973; Rabbie and Horwitz, 1969). Providing a minimally meaningful basis for categorization such as picture preferences, even in the absence of anticipated interaction, generally causes bias (Doise *et al.,* 1972; Tajfel, 1970). The mere existence of other groups, even without explicit competition, also causes in-group–out-group bias (Ferguson and Kelley, 1964), as does the anticipation of interaction (Doise, 1969; Rabbie and Wilkins, 1971). It is important to note that these are *ad hoc* groups that bear no relationship to the social categories that play a direct role in self-identity processes. The in-group–out-group bias in these situations serves no function in maintaining established group distinctions. Also, no possibility of direct self-gain is involved in most of these studies. The out-group members are often strangers and they are usually anonymous.

Studies of this bias indicate that it can be enhanced or reduced under some circumstances. Factors that have been shown to be important include the salience and magnitude of in-group–out-group differences, levels of in-group cohesiveness, and cooperation or competition between groups. Some of the evidence for the idea that the salience of intergroup distinctions promotes bias comes from studies that have varied the number of in-group and out-group members who interact with one another in the experimental context. Studies using both real distinctions and laboratory-created distinctions have found greater in-group–out-group bias when multiple members of the groups are present than when one-on-one interactions occur (Dustin and Davis, 1970; McKillip, DiMiceli, and Luebke, 1977). It can be argued that the salience of group membership is greater when the number of out-group members increases beyond one (Gerard and Hoyt, 1974). Studies of real social groups indicate that minority group members display greater in-group–out-group bias than majority group members (Branthwaite and Jones, 1975; Brewer and Campbell, 1976; Dutton, 1976). In-group–out-group distinctions may be more salient for minority members than for majority group members.

A second line of evidence indicating that salience plays a role in in-group–out-group bias comes from a study by Doise (1976). He found that when members of two groups (Swiss students and apprentices) were told that they would only be evaluating one group, but then were asked to evaluate both groups, no differences occurred between in-group and out-group evaluations. However, when the subjects were informed beforehand that they would be evaluating both groups, they rated the in-group more favorably than the out-group. Thus in this study, making in-group–out-group distinctions salient led to in-group–out-group bias (cf. Turner, 1975). Additional evidence that the salience of in-group–out-group differences is a significant determinant of bias comes from studies of similarity within groups and dissimilarity between groups. If the magnitude of in-group–out-group differences contributes to the salience of these differences, greater similarity within groups and greater dissimilarity between groups should increase bias. Factors that create the perception of in-group similarity and between-group dissimilarity, such as assimilation and contrast, should also lead to in-group–out-group bias. A number of studies have obtained results that are compatible with this suggestion. Billig and Tajfel (1973) found that providing subjects with information on the similarity of in-group and out-group members with respect to a single trait enhanced in-group–out-group bias in comparison with a completely arbitrary division of subjects into groups. In this case both increased in-group similarity or increased dissimilarity to the out-group contributed to greater bias. A study by Allen and Wilder (1975) used the categorization manipulation employed by Tajfel (1970) and added manipulations of belief similarity for in-group and out-group members. Here in-group–out-group bias was enhanced as the similarity of in-group members increased, but out-group dissimilarity did not significantly increase in-group–out-group bias. In general, when similarity information is salient and when it indicates that in-group members are highly similar or out-group members are highly dissimilar to the in-group, heightened in-group–out-group bias is the result.

Multiple-group categorization could be expected to decrease bias to the extent that it decreases the salience of categorization on any one dimension. For instance, Doise (1969) crossed ethnic groups with a laboratory manipulation of group membership and found less intergroup bias when memberships along these two dimensions were crossed than when they coincided. This result was replicated with children, using sex and a color label as dimensions (Doise, 1976). Similarly, Commins and Lockwood (1978) found that crossing religion with categorization based on a dot estimation task reduced intergroup bias below the level that existed for categorization based only on the dot task.

A second factor that can enhance in-group–out-group bias is in-group cohesiveness. Cohesiveness among in-group members can be related to the previous discussion of similarity among in-group members in the sense that one of the common by-products of increased similarity is greater liking for in-group members. A number of studies have attempted to measure or manipulate cohesiveness directly (see Dion, 1979, for a review). In the Sherifs' camp studies (Sherif and Sherif, 1969) a strong "we group" feeling was accompanied by feelings of superiority to out-groups even before contact with the out-group was initiated. Ferguson and Kelley (1964) found that attraction to the in-group covaried with overevaluations of the in-group's products. Consistent with this set of findings, Druckman (1968) reported that in-group and out-group attitudes were negatively correlated. Dion (1973) created high- and low-cohesiveness groups and found that evaluations of in-group members were highest in the high-cohesiveness groups. Evaluations of out-group members were unaffected by cohesiveness, however. Reward allocations paralleled these results.

Taken together, these studies demonstrate that in-group cohesiveness is associated with positive treatment and evaluations of the in-group, as indeed it would have to be for the term to have any meaning. The evidence that in-group cohesiveness causes bias toward the out-group is less compelling. In fact, some studies have found that attitudes toward the in-group and out-groups are positively correlated (Stephan and Rosenfield, 1978b; Wilson and Kayatani, 1968). Holmes (1975, cited in Dion, 1979) has proposed that the relationship between in-group and out-group attitudes is mediated by the nature of the relationship between the groups. When the groups are in conflict, high in-group cohesiveness would be expected to be related to increased rejection of the out-group, but when the groups' goals do not conflict, a positive relationship or no relationship would be expected between attraction to the in-group and the out-group.

The results of studies examining anticipated competition generally support the proposition that incompatibility of goals leads to in-group–out-group bias. Kahn and Ryen (1972) found that in-group–out-group evaluative bias was greater for subjects anticipating intergroup competition than for subjects anticipating cooperation. Likewise, Rabbie and colleagues (1974) found that anticipated competition caused in-group members to feel more hostility toward the out-group than did anticipated cooperation. A study of Doise and colleagues (1972) showed that when the stakes were high, anticipated competition led to higher evaluative bias than cooperation did. This finding provides one interpretation for the failure to find these effects in other studies. Possibly, the manipulations of competition did not lead to the perception that the outcomes were important in studies by Rabbie and Wilkins (1971) and Brewer and Silver (1978).

Two general classes of explanations have been offered for the in-group–out-group bias that occurs in minimal social situations. The first class of explanations focuses on cognitive factors. Doise (1976) proposed that differentiation at the representational (cognitive), evaluative, or behavioral level leads to differentiation along the other dimensions. To account for the effects of competition on in-group–out-group evaluations, Doise suggested that categorization into competitive groups activates an anticipatory-justification process that results in devaluing one's antagonists (cf. Sumner, 1906). In a similar vein, Dion (1973) argued that assimilation and contrast lead to a cognitive differentiation between the in-group and the out-group. In a subsequent discussion of this issue Dion (1979) added that unit relationships, such as an individual being a member of a group, and sentiment relationships (e.g., liking for the group) tend toward consistency (Darley and Berscheid, 1967; Heider, 1958). This consistency can account for positive

attitudes toward the in-group and negative attitudes toward the out-group provided one has a positive attitude toward the self. Dion also suggested that factors that promote unit-forming tendencies, such as cohesion and competition, should heighten in-group–out-group bias by leading to greater differentiation between the groups (also see Brewer, 1979b).

In contrast to the theories that emphasize cognitive explanations for in-group–out-group bias, other theories incorporate motivational factors in their explanations. Principal among these theories is the social identification explanation offered by Billig (1976), Tajfel (1972, 1978), and Turner (1975, 1978). The motivational crux of this approach is the proposition that people with an insecure sense of social identity—virtually everyone, according to Tajfel (1978)—will desire to make favorable social comparisons between the in-group and the out-group. This social comparison process is instigated by categorization into groups, where the individual identifies with one of the groups. This type of categorization into groups makes the individual's social identity salient and leads to evaluations and behavior couched in terms of relations between groups rather than individuals.

The desire to achieve a positively valued differentiation from others can account for bias in the absence of competition and cohesiveness. The motivational explanation also appears to be particularly well suited to account for the fact that in the majority of the studies of bias the in-group is evaluated and treated more positively as a result of categorization, instead of the out-group being treated more negatively (Brewer, 1979b). The motive typically is to create positive social comparisons, a result that can be achieved by evaluating the in-group positively without negatively evaluating the out-group.

The idea that bias is due to an anticipatory justification of hostility toward the out-group (Doise, 1976) cannot account for the finding that bias primarily favors the in-group. Another explanation that has difficulty with the unidirectional aspect of bias is the "generic norm of in-group–out-group bias" proposed by Tajfel (1970). According to this theory, a norm leads people to favor in-group members and discriminate against out-group members. This norm is learned through socialization and is considered to be so basic to social existence that people are generally unaware of it. The normative explanation also does not provide a full account of the effects of cohesiveness and competition on in-group bias. For instance, cohesiveness would be expected to increase conformity to the norm of discrimination against out-groups and therefore lead to more negative attitudes and behavior, but it does not (Dion, 1973).

Illusory Correlation

Illusory correlation is an encoding bias that frequently, but not always, involves categorization. It is due to misjudgments of the co-occurrence or covariation of two sets of events. Most studies of this bias have been concerned with the overestimation of sets of events that people expect to be associated (Jenkins and Ward, 1965; Ward and Jenkins, 1965). In one early study Chapman and Chapman (1969) explored judgments of the relationship between male homosexuality and certain types of responses on the Rorschach test. In one experiment they found that clinicians reported observing invalid signs that clinical lore suggests are related to homosexuality, such as anal references, feminine clothing, and genitalia, and failed to report more valid signs, such as seeing animalized humans or contorted humans and animals on certain cards. On the basis of this finding the investigators presented undergraduates with Rorschach protocols in which there was no relationship between homosexuality and the invalid signs. Nonetheless, the subjects, like the clinicians, overestimated the frequency of co-occurrence of these two events.

The results of these studies have been interpreted in terms of the availability heuristic by Tversky and Kahneman (1973). According to these investigators, people use the ease with which events can be recalled in making subsequent judgments. In explaining illusory correlation, they say, "When a person finds the association between items is strong, he is likely to conclude that they have been frequently paired" (p. 224). They suggest that strength of association depends on such factors as prior association between the items, the relatedness of the items, and how distinctive they are. The research by Jenkins and Ward and by the Chapmans can be interpreted in terms of the perceived relatedness of the items.

In an application of relatedness to personality traits, Tversky and Kahneman (1973) found that related traits were judged to have co-occurred more frequently than unrelated traits, although they were equally frequent in the stimulus materials presented to the subjects. In a study concerned with relatedness effects derived from implicit personality theory, Berman and Kenny (1976) found that people believed they had observed correlations between traits that did not exist in the materials they had read (cf. Dewhirst and Burman, 1978; Shweder, 1977). Hamilton and Rose (1980) conducted one of the

only studies relating illusory correlation directly to stereotypes. They found that pairings of occupations and related traits were overestimated compared with pairings of occupations with unrelated traits, although all pairings occurred with equal frequencies.

The relatedness explanation of illusory correlation can account for the results of all of the preceding studies, but it has been most clearly tested by Rothbart, Evans, and Fulero (1979), who manipulated relatedness. They led subjects to believe that a group of people was more likely than average to possess a given trait. After reading about the traits of members of the group, subjects estimated the frequency of occurrence of the trait thought to be related to group membership and of an unrelated trait. Although the actual frequency of the two types of traits was equal, the subjects estimated that the related traits occurred more frequently than the unrelated traits. This study also indicated that the illusory correlations occurred during encoding rather than retrieval. The high frequency estimates for related traits only occurred when the relatedness information was provided before reading of the materials. When this information was provided afterward, related and unrelated traits were judged to have occurred with equal frequencies.

Some evidence also shows that the distinctiveness of the association between two sets of events can lead to overestimates of the frequency of co-occurrence. Deviant, low-frequency, unexpected, or negative behavior, when paired with unusual groups or groups with few members, may form distinctive pairs that will be readily available in memory. To test this hypothesis, Hamilton and Gifford (1976) presented subjects with materials in which positive behaviors were either more or less frequent than negative ones. One group whose members engaged in these behaviors was large, while a second group was small. Both groups were presented as having engaged in positive and negative behaviors with the same relative frequencies. Nonetheless, the subjects overestimated the frequency with which low-frequency behaviors were paired with the minority group. The minority group was also evaluated less favorably than the majority group if negative behaviors were overestimated and more positively if positive behaviors were overestimated. The results of this study have been replicated by Jones and colleagues (1977). In a more recent study McArthur and Friedman (1980) examined the effects of shared infrequency on attributions to real social groups. In one study subjects read eight case histories in which old people outnumbered young ones three to one or vice versa. For all of the patients positive behaviors outnumbered negative behaviors two to one. The subjects subsequently attributed more negative traits than positive traits to old people when old people appeared infrequently in the case histories. More negative than positive traits were also attributed to the young people when they appeared infrequently, but not to the same degree as for older people. Thus there was evidence of a distinctiveness effect; negative traits were overattributed to the infrequently appearing group. If one assumes that the young subjects associate negative traits with old people, evidence of a relatedness effect also occurred in this study; negative traits tended to be attributed to the infrequently appearing group more for old people than for young people. Similar results were obtained for male subjects' ratings of males and females, but not for female subjects' ratings or for white subjects' ratings of blacks and whites. This result suggests that for real social groups shared infrequency does not always bias judgments of co-occurrence.

Two studies by Rothbart and colleagues (1978) also demonstrate the role of distinctiveness in biasing estimates of frequency. In these studies the frequency of group members who displayed extreme behaviors was overestimated. In one study subjects overestimated the frequency with which extremely serious crimes (e.g., murder, rape) had been paired with stimulus persons. When less serious crimes (e.g., shoplifting) were paired with the stimulus persons, estimated frequencies were more accurate. Rothbart (1981) has offered the following summary of his results: "Our perceptions of groups may be disproportionately influenced by the characteristics of the group's most memorable constituents" (p. 36.)

These studies suggest that people may be prone to overestimate the occurrence of low-frequency negative behaviors committed by disliked or threatening out-groups because such pairings are likely to be readily available in memory owing to their distinctiveness (cf. Kanouse and Hanson, 1971). This bias may contribute to the generally negative stereotypes that are formed about out-groups. The increased availability of distinctive pairings should also mean that stereotype-inconsistent behaviors will be overestimated (Rothbart, Evans, and Fulero, 1979), setting the stage for changes in stereotypes. However, other biases, such as the failure to perceive unexpected, valid correlations, may often supercede this bias (cf. Hamilton, 1982). For instance, in a study by Dewhirst and Berman (1978), when two variables were correlated with each other but only one was correlated with a criterion, subjects were less confident

that the variable related to the criterion was a valid predictor than when the two variables were uncorrelated. Similarly, in the Chapman and Chapman (1969) study, when the more valid predictors of homosexuality were actually correlated with homosexuality in the Rorschach protocols, their subjects failed to perceive these relationships. It seems that the existence of illusory correlations can obscure the perception of actual correlations. Thus availability biases contribute to stereotype maintenance by augmenting beliefs in expected associations between groups and traits and hinder changes in stereotypes by making stereotype-inconsistent information more difficult to perceive.

Base-Rate, Categorical, and Individuating Information

According to Kahneman and Tversky (1973), people tend to predict outcomes that are representative of the evidence currently available to them, and they underutilize other relevant information, such as prior probabilities derivable from base rates. In one study demonstrating this phenomenon, Kahneman and Tversky (1973) asked their subjects to assess the probability that a personality sketch belonged to a lawyer or an engineer. Although the subjects had been given information on the base rates of lawyers and engineers in the population, the individuating personality information had a greater impact on the probability estimates than the base rates did (the effect for base rates was significant, however).

This set of studies sparked a considerable number of experiments investigating the representativeness bias. These studies have varied enormously in method, content, and results. One of the primary reasons for the apparent diversity of results is that the information with which subjects have been provided and the judgments they have been asked to make differ across studies. The information that has been provided to subjects consisted of base rates and individuating trait or category membership information. The judgments that they have been asked to make have concerned the category membership of individuals, the traits of individuals, and even the base rate of traits in a population. These judgments were probability assessments in some cases, while in others they were discrete choices between alternatives.

Four combinations of information and judgments are particularly relevant to stereotyping. The first concerns judging category membership from information on base rates and personality traits (or similar individuating information). This combination is important because the processes that underlie categorical judgments provide insights into when people will be categorized into groups with all the consequences that categorization entails. The second combination of relevance to stereotyping is judging traits from base rates and category membership. Here the issue is whether the traits associated with the category will be imputed to an individual in disregard of base-rate information. The third combination concerns judging traits from categorical information and individuating information. In this situation the category furnishes information about base rates if the category is associated with a stereotype. The issue is whether this base-rate information is ignored when individuating information is also present. A fourth combination of relevance to stereotyping is judging base rates from individuating trait information and category information. In this case the issue is whether individuating information affects the impressions one forms of groups in disregard of the base-rate information implicit in categorical stereotypes. Each of these four combinations will be considered in turn.

Judging category membership from base rates and personality trait information. Individuating information appears to overwhelm base-rate information in making categorical judgments to the extent that the individuating information is useful in diagnosing category membership. In a study supporting this proposition, Ginosar and Trope (1980) found that when they reduced the diagnosticity of individuating information by providing inconsistent or irrelevant trait information or by making the judgment categories similar, base rates were employed in making the category judgments. When diagnosticity was high, base rates were ignored. In interpreting their results, they suggest that when diagnostic individuating information is available, the information is processed schematically, if schemata relevant to the judgment exist. When applied to stereotypes, this interpretation suggests that people will be assigned to categories if individuating information about them is consistent with the stereotype for a category, regardless of the frequency of category members in the population.

A second condition under which base rates tend to be underutilized is when the individuating information can be viewed as causal. Ajzen (1977) has suggested that causal schemata provide mechanisms that can be used to relate individuating information to subsequent judgments. When individuating information can be seen as potentially causing the event to be judged, noncausal information, such as base rates, tends to be underutilized.

However, even base-rate information can be viewed as causal under some conditions, and then it too is likely to be used in judgments (Ajzen, 1977, experiment 2). Kahneman and Tversky (1980) have compared the use of diagnostic and causal information in making judgments. They consistently found that causal information was more influential. They conclude that "inferences from causes to consequences are made with greater confidence than inferences from consequences to causes" (p. 57). If this line of reasoning is applied to prejudice, it suggests that people would be more likely to predict that a prejudiced person would commit an act of racial discrimination than that a person who committed a discriminatory act would be prejudiced. The reason is that in the former case the information is causal, but in the latter it is only diagnostic.

The use of causal base-rate information appears to depend on whether the base rate indicates that the majority of people behave in socially desirable or socially undesirable ways. Zuckerman (1978) has suggested that one explanation for the failure to find that base rates influenced judgments in studies by Nisbett and Borgida (1975) is that the base-rate information indicated that the majority of people behave in socially undesirable ways (e.g., do not help in emergencies). The results of Zuckerman's study indicated that causal base rates were ignored if they indicated that people typically behave in undesirable ways. However, base rates that were high in social desirability were used to make judgments about the probability of helping a specific individual. There appear to be no studies contrasting the influence of base rates for positive and negative behaviors with the influence of positive and negative individuating information. The possibilities here are intriguing. A variety of studies indicate that negative individuating information is more impactful than positive information (cf. Kanouse and Hanson, 1971). Perhaps negative individuating information is only influential when underlying base rates for behavior lead one to expect socially desirable behaviors. If socially undesirable behavior is expected, then positive individuating information should have a greater impact on judgments. One could test these ideas by using stereotypes with contrasting positive and negative traits.

Judging personality traits from base-rate and category membership information. The individuating information that was provided in the majority of the studies just reviewed concerned personality traits and behavior. A different type of individuating information that is particularly relevant to stereotyping is information concerning the category membership of the individual. The impact of this type of information can be compared with the influence of base rates in judging the probability that an individual possesses traits associated with category membership. Two types of base rates are relevant to this situation: The first consists of the base rate of the trait in the population, and the second concerns the base rate of the trait among members of the category.

McCauley and Stitt (1978) have argued that stereotypes can be defined in terms of the contrast between the judged base rate of a trait in a population and the probability of the trait given the category. Stereotypes consist of traits for which the probability of their presence in a given category of people is perceived to be substantially higher than their probability in the population at large. McCauley and Stitt refer to the difference between the population base rate and the base rate given the category as the diagnostic ratio. For traits with diagnostic ratios close to one, the individuating information provided by category membership adds little to the base-rate information. For traits relevant to a stereotype where the diagnostic ratio is greater than one, population base-rate information may be combined with base-rate information generated from categorical membership in making judgments.

A study that tested the relative influence of population base rate and categorical individuating information was done by Manis and colleagues (1980). In one of their experiments subjects predicted the attitudes of individuals whose appearance was associated with particular stereotypes. For instance, after being given information on the population base rates concerning attitudes toward the legalization of marijuana use, subjects were shown pictures of people who had been independently judged to be likely to favor legalizing marijuana or to be opposed to it. Both types of information were used to make predictions concerning this person's attitudes toward marijuana use. Follow-up experiments using other attitudes confirmed that population base rates and categorical information may be used additively in making judgments.

A consideration of the relationship between McCauley and Stitt's (1978) diagnostic ratio and an analogous one proposed by Ajzen and Fishbein (1975) provides an explanation for how the ultimate attribution error occurs. According to Ajzen and Fishbein (1975), the probability that a given explanation (H_1) out of a set of explanations (H_1, H_2, H_3) will be used to explain a behavior (B) depends on the implicit calculation of a set of diagnostic ratios. These ratios consist of the perceived probability of an explanation being used to explain a given behavior divided by the probability of that explanation being employed to explain any behavior, $(H_1/B)/p(H_1)$. The largest diagnostic ratio among a set of plausible explanations, $p(H_1/B)/p(H_1)$, compared with $p(H_2/B)p(H_2)$, and so on, will be selected. These explanations may be internal or external and thus may include stereotyped traits.

The ultimate attribution error may consist of a combination of McCauley and Stitt's stereotype diagnostic ratio and Ajzen and Fishbein's attributional diagnostic ratio. In studies of this phenomena—and often in real life—people are confronted by information on group membership as well as by individuating information concerning particular behaviors. In an attempt to explain the behavior, a set of hypotheses may be generated, each with its respective diagnostic ratio. The selection among these hypotheses, however, may be influenced by the second bit of available information, that is, group membership. Any one of a number of selection rules may then be applied; the simplest, perhaps, would be to look for a conjunction between the two sets of ratios. Thus in analyzing why a male student did well on a math test, one would compare the sets of explanations available (ability, ease of the test, luck, etc.) with the characteristic traits of the group (aggressive, independent, skilled in math and science, etc.) and select overlapping items (ability, math skill) as explanations. More complex rules involving mathematical operations applied to the matrix generated by these two diagnostic ratios are also possible.

Judging personality traits from categorical and individuating information. Since stereotypes embody base-rate information, one could also compare the use of base rates in situations where categorical membership is presented in conjunction with more specific individuating information. Under these circumstances base rates may be underutilized in comparison with the individuating information. This pattern of results was obtained by Locksley and colleagues (1980) in a study where sex and sex-stereotyped behaviors of a stimulus person were varied. Diagnostic individual information on assertiveness had a greater effect on judgments of sex-stereotyped traits than did the stimulus person's sex. The explanation for the greater power of individuating information in this study may be that while assertiveness is merely diagnostic of sex, it is causal for traits related to assertiveness by an implicit personality theory. Thus assertiveness may lead to greater competitiveness, decisiveness, insensitivity to others, and so on. If this interpretation is correct, this study again illustrates the primacy of causal over diagnostic information in making personal judgments. In a subsequent study Locksley, Hepburn, and Ortiz (1982) found that individuating information on past assertiveness was relied on more heavily in judgments of future assertiveness than was information on the stimulus person's sex. In a second experiment both irrelevant and relevant individuating information was sufficient to offset the effects of the base-rate information implied by a group stereotype. Judgments of the traits of "day people" and "night people" differed significantly when no individuating information was provided, but they did not differ when relevant or irrelevant individuating information was provided.

A contrasting set of results was obtained in a study by Grant and Holmes (1981). They found that categorical information on ethnicity had a greater impact on judgments of stereotype-relevant personality traits than individuating information that was stereotype-consistent or -irrelevant. Since no stereotype-inconsistent individuating information was presented, this study did not address the issue of whether contradictory information can reverse stereotyped judgments, as suggested by the Locksley (1980) study. However, even if stereotype-inconsistent information does reverse the attribution of stereotyped traits to an individual by replacing them with traits from an implicit personality theory, the individual may gain little advantage unless the implicit personality traits are more accurate than the stereotype.

Judging base rates from individuating and categorical information.   The final combination of pieces of information relevant to stereotyping is when individuating information is presented with categorical information, and the judgments concern the traits of people in the category (rather than the traits of the individual). Here the base rate is embodied in stereotypes associated with categorical judgments, and the issue is whether information about specific category members will modify perceptions of the group. In two studies Hamill, Wilson, and Nisbett (1980) have shown that individuating information dominates categorical information even when the individual is presented as being atypical of the population. For instance, when the case of a humane prison guard is presented to subjects along with the information that this person is atypical of prison guards, prison guards are thought to be more humane than when subjects are presented with no case history. Knowing whether these changes persist over time would be valuable, because if they do, stereotypes may be more easily modified than is generally believed. It seems more likely that in this study the availability and salience of individuating information leads to momentary modifications in preexisting schemata but that these modifications are lost over time.

In social interactions some types of categorical information are invariably present. In addition, individuating information may exist owing to prior experience, or the interaction itself may furnish individuating information. For many of the traits associated with stereotypes, population base-rate information may be vague or unavailable (e.g., the frequency with which people are materialistic, competitive, passive, or lazy). Thus in social situations the most relevant combination of information consists of categorical and individuating information. The types of judgments that would appear to be of greatest import in social interactions where there is categorical and individuating information are deciding whether the individuating information is diagnostic of category memberships other than those on which information exists, making predictions about the person's behavior on the basis of category and individuating information, and revising stereotypes on the basis of stereotype-inconsistent individuating information. The research that has been reviewed indicates that these judgments will depend upon the diagnosticity of the available information, the degree to which it is consistent with causal and stereotype schemata, and its evaluative significance.

RETRIEVAL

The operation of selective attention, the loss of material that does not get beyond short-term memory, and a wide variety of encoding biases limit the information that is retained in memory. Typically, the meaning of incoming information and inferences based on it are retained rather than the exact details of the information (Anderson, 1980; Smith and Miller, 1979). This meaningful information is then structured or organized in memory, but the exact nature of these organizational processes is a topic of considerable debate. One of the models of these organizational processes that is particularly relevant to the study of stereotyping is the configurational network approach (Anderson and Bower, 1973; Kintsch, 1974; Norman and Rumelhart, 1975). This theory proposes that meaningful bits of information come to be related to one another through experience. Each bit of knowledge, called a node, may be related to a small or a large number of other bits of knowledge. The meaning of any bit of information is defined by the configuration of its relations to other bits of knowledge and to sensory and motor information.

When configurational network theory is applied to stereotypes, it suggests that categorical group labels are nodes in a network of related concepts consisting of defining and characteristic features. The defining features are strongly associated with the category label node, but the characteristic features are less strongly associated with it.

The use of social categories to organize information has been examined in a series of studies by Ostrom and colleagues (1980). In these studies information that was relevant or irrelevant to an occupational stereotype was presented to subjects who were then asked to make one or more occupational judgments. The dependent variables consisted of various measures tapping the organization of the presented information in the subjects' memories. As was the case with the schema research, the results consistently revealed that category-relevant information was more likely to be retained than irrelevant information. These studies provide evidence for the idea that category judgments lead people to organize incoming information into theme nodes. Subsequent access to this information depends on its association with the theme node. Theme-relevant information is more accessible than theme-irrelevant information because it is more closely associated with the theme node. These studies would appear to be especially relevant to contexts in which people use social categories to classify unfamiliar others as they acquire information about them.

The effect of categorical encoding on subsequent recall has been demonstrated in a study in which the amount of particularizing information to be encoded was systematically varied (Lingle and Ostrom, 1979). In this study subjects judged the suitability of a stimulus person for a given occupation (e.g., dentist). Later, they judged the stimulus person's suitability for an occupation that was either related (doctor) or unrelated (comedian) to the first occupation. The subjects took longer to make the second judgments for unrelated than for the related occupations. This result suggests that the original information was organized around occupations, and thus when the second judgment was similar to the first, the relevant information was readily accessible in memory. More important, the amount of information relevant to the first judgment did not affect the speed of second judgments when they were related to the first judgments. This result implies that in making the second judgment, the subjects were accessing the original occupational category and its associated characteristic traits rather than the particular sets of traits that were provided to them by the investigators. If they had been accessing the specific traits provided to them, then the decision times for the second judgment task would have reflected the amount of information they had been given about the particular individual.

In another study Lingle and colleagues (1979) found that the evaluative content of information about a stimulus person had less impact on subsequent trait evaluations than the occupational judgments that were made on the basis of the information. For instance, a person described only in negative terms was judged to make a poor physicist but subsequently was presumed to be more intelligent than a person who was judged to be a good waiter on the basis of the positive information provided about this person. Apparently, the availability of information associated with the social category was greater than the availability of the information that the subjects were given concerning the particular person they had judged. Thus when people are making memory-based judgments of others, particularizing information or category-irrelevant information is less likely to be accessible than the characteristic traits of a category or information that is consistent with a categorical judgment. This process may occur as a consequence of biased encoding or of biased retrieval.

The latter bias has been demonstrated in a study by Snyder and Uranowitz (1978). This study found that when subjects received categorical information after they had acquired more detailed individuating information, the retrieval of the individuating information was influenced by the category. The subjects in this study received detailed information about a fictitious person who was later described as a lesbian or a heterosexual. Subsequent recognition tests revealed that subjects selectively remembered information that was consistent with the sexual preference stereotype. Specifically, if the stimulus person was labeled as heterosexual, the subjects more accurately remembered information consistent with a heterosexual life-style than when the stimulus person was labeled as a homosexual. The subjects also erred in remembering information about the stimulus person, incorrectly believing that the information they had read contained facts consistent with the sexual preferences. Two recent studies have failed to replicate these results (Belleza and Bower, 1981; Clark and Woll, 1981). One of these studies did find that when subjects were unsure of their memories, they tended to guess in ways that were consistent with the stereotype labels they had been given (Belleza and Bower, 1981).

Rose and Hamilton (1979) found that the stereotypes of males and females affected immediate recognition memory of stereotype-consistent information. Subjects were better able to remember whether a given descriptor was used to describe a male or a female when the descriptor was stereotype-consistent than when it was not. They were also faster in responding to the stereotype-consistent descriptors. Confusing this situation still further, Brewer, Dull, and Lui (1981) found that both stereotype-consistent information and information that is extremely inconsistent with the stereotype are better recalled than information that comes from a related subcategory of stereotypes. In this study subjects viewed slides of prototypical "elderly women," "grandmothers," and "young women," and they were given descriptive information about each person. After five minutes a free-recall test indicated that subjects remembered more stereotype-consistent information (e.g., the grandmother likes to cook) and stereotype-inconsistent information (e.g., the grandmother keeps up with fashions in dress) than information from a related subcategory of stereotype (e.g., the grandmother relies on food stamps, a statement associated with the stereotype of the elderly). These results can be reconciled with those of Rose and Hamilton and Snyder and Uranowitz if the stereotypes in those studies (male and female, heterosexual and homosexual) are viewed as being semantically related (sex role stereotypes and sexual-preference stereotypes) in the same sense that grandmother and elderly people are (stereotypes of older people). In all three studies stereotype-consistent information could be said to better recalled than information that was consistent with a semantically related stereotype. There remains only the issue of the nonreplication of Snyder and Uranowitz's results, a puzzle that awaits further investigation.

A set of studies by Dutta, Kanungo, and Freibergs (1972) indicate that affective relatedness can also facilitate retrieval. In one study in this series English Canadian students who were prejudiced toward French Canadians read lists of traits that were attributed to the two groups. On a recall task the subjects remembered more of the positive traits attributed to the in-group than to the out-group and more of the negative traits attributed to the out-group than to the in-group. To demonstrate that this bias was a retrieval rather than an encoding bias, the experimenters told subjects in one condition that they had mixed up the lists of traits possessed by the two groups. This information was provided after the subjects had read the lists but before they were asked to recall them. In this condition the results indicated that the subjects reorganized the information they had been given and again recalled more positive traits for the in-group and more negative traits for the out-group. In this and other studies in this series (Dutta and Kanungo, 1967; Kanungo and Dutta, 1966) information that was affectively consistent with attitudes toward a social group was more likely to be recalled than affectively inconsistent information (cf. Alper and Korchin, 1951).

Several studies have shown that the effects of affective relatedness on recall increase over time (Higgins and Rholes, 1978; Higgins, Rholes, and Jones, 1977). In a study by Higgins and Rholes (1978) subjects made inferences about the character of a stimulus person immediately after reading about the person. Subsequent measures of recall for the stimulus information indicated that subjects tended to recall information consistent with the evaluative nature (positive or negative) of their inferences, and this effect increased over a two-week time period. Two additional studies indicate that when the inference concerns ethnic group membership, a similar bias toward greater evaluative consistency over time exists. In one study black and white teenagers heard a passage about a black baseball player, and then they were asked to repeat the passage immediately and after a delay of three days (Taft, 1954). For immediate recall no differences appeared between blacks and whites in the proportions of favorable and unfavorable events that were recalled. However, for delayed recall the blacks recalled more favorable events and the whites recalled more unfavorable events. If one assumes that both groups were ethnocentric, then the results show that their evaluation of the group the stimulus person belongs to and the evaluative dimension of their recall of the event record became more consistent over time. In a second study white high school students displayed their ethnocentrism directly, and no assumptions need be made about their evaluations of whites and blacks (Higgins and Ross, cited in Higgins and King, 1981). Subjects in this study read about a white or black stimulus person and then recalled this information immediately or after a delay of one week. The recall of traits possessed by the black stimulus person revealed that more negative than positive distortions occurred and that this effect increased over time. Again, the evaluation of the group and the evaluative dimension of the event record became more consistent over time.

Considered in the aggregate, these studies indicate that evaluative inferences about ethnic group members increasingly override factual information across time. While the event record is readily accessible in memory, it is likely to be accurately and completely recalled, and if there are inconsistencies with prior inferences about the group, these inconsistencies may appear. As the event record decays, the evaluative nature of the attitudes toward the group and the inferences made about the group begin to exert a greater influence over what material will be retained. Information that is evaluatively consistent with the attitudes or inferences is more likely to be retained than inconsistent information, and distortions that are consistent with the evaluative dimension of the inference are more likely to be introduced than inconsistent distortions.

In summary, when social categories are used, the preexisting conceptions of these categories will influence how incoming information is organized and how it will be retrieved from memory. Previously acquired information in the form of stereotypes may be closely associated with particular category labels. These stereotypes will be used as a template against which incoming information about particular members of a social group can be compared. Information that is consistent with the stereotype will be more likely to be retained than inconsistent information, which will tend to be lost over time. Even when social categories are not used during encoding, they can influence retrieval. When information becomes available about a social category of which an individual is a member or when a categorical judgment is called for, the retrieval processes that are set in motion are likely to provide information that is semantically related and affectively consistent with the social category.

INTERGROUP COGNITIONS AND OVERT BEHAVIOR

The preceding sections provide clear evidence that cognitive processing of social information is influenced by social categories. The cognitions associated with social category information also affect overt behavior. The traditional approach to the cognition-behavior relationship has been to focus on the relationship between attitudes

and behavior. This narrow focus has led to an unduly pessimistic view of the correspondence between what people think and what they do. For instance, Deutscher (1966) has suggested that "no matter what one's theoretical orientation may be, he has no right to expect to find congruence between attitudes and actions and every reason to expect to find discrepancies between them" (p. 247).

In the intergroup relations area investigators have been concerned primarily with the relationship between prejudice and discrimination. A major problem in this research is that prejudice is only one type of intergroup cognition. Intergroup cognitions are actually much more complex, as documented in the preceding sections of this chapter. Not only do they include prejudice and stereotypes, but they also include schemata, scripts, prototypes, and expectancies. The prediction of intergroup behavior requires that cognitions besides prejudice be taken into consideration. Another important problem associated with studying the relationship between intergroup cognitions and overt behavior is that much more attention has been paid to measuring cognitions (especially prejudice) than to measuring behavior. The vast majority of the studies in this area have examined a single behavior in one setting, directed toward one out-group member at a particular point in time. The limitations of this approach are that such measures are invariably of uncertain reliability and limited generalizability. Fishbein and Ajzen (1975) have advocated the collection of repeated measures of multiple, conceptually related behaviors, but this approach has rarely been employed. In addition to this limitation, most studies have examined intergroup behaviors that occur in nonnaturalistic settings or have employed very pallid measures of intergroup discrimination. Also, the behaviors that have been examined in empirical studies represent only a small subset of behaviors that might conceivably demonstrate intergroup discrimination. Another general criticism of studies of prejudice and discrimination is that they rarely capture the full interactive nature of intergroup behavior. With few exceptions the situations that have been investigated explore one unidirectional causal hypothesis: the effect of individuals' attitudes on their behavior. The reciprocal interplay that characterizes ongoing interactions is absent from most studies (e.g., the effects of discrimination on the subsequent attitudes and behavior of people who have been discriminated against).

Before reviewing the studies dealing explicitly with the intergroup cognition–intergroup behavior relation-

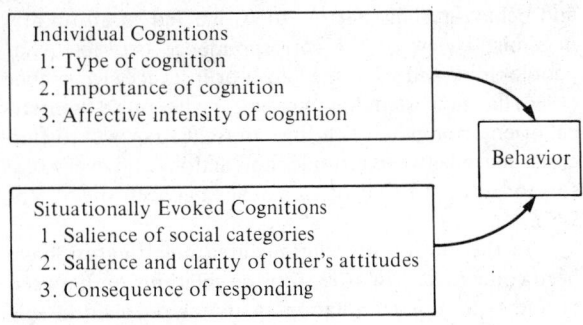

FIGURE 1
Cognition—Behavior Model

ship, it may be useful to frame the central question clearly. In every human interaction a variety of group differences exist among the people who are interacting. Obviously, most of these differences have little or no effect on behavior. The issue, then, is, When do group differences give rise to cognitions that affect behavior? The answer to this question may be conceptualized in terms of a general model. This model consists of two classes of cognitions that may influence behavior: characteristics of the individual's cognitions regarding social groups and cognitions evoked by situational factors. The aspects of the cognitions that the individual brings to the situation that would appear to be most relevant are the type of cognitions (stereotypes, scripts, beliefs or traits imputed to group members, etc.), the importance of the cognitions for the individual, and the affective intensity of the cognitions (cf. Ehrlich, 1973; Katz and Gurin, 1969). The role of three situational factors seems to be most important. Group differences are most likely to affect behavior under the following circumstances:

1. When social category information is highly salient in a particular situation.

2. When cognitions concerning the attitudes of others toward intergroup relations are salient and unambiguous.

3. When important consequences result from responding to others in terms of their group membership (see Fig. 1).

The proposed model has much in common with those of Cook and Selltiz (1964) and Brigham (1971). They proposed that behavior is determined by attitudes toward members of a given group, other characteristics of the actor (including values, motives, and other attitudes relevant to the situation), and characteristics of the situation (including norms, expectations of others, and the consequences of behavior). The proposed model is also similar to one developed by Fishbein and Ajzen (1975; Ajzen and Fishbein, 1980). In their model behavior is regarded as being a direct product of intentions. These intentions, in turn, are caused by behavioral beliefs, especially those concerning the perceived rewards and costs of engaging in a given behavior, and normative beliefs, including the individuals' beliefs about whether or not others think he or she should engage in the behavior and how motivated the individual is to engage in the behavior. The proposed model of the cognition-behavior relationship differs from others in emphasizing a broader range of cognitions, in emphasizing the relative salience and affective intensity of these cognitions, and in placing somewhat less emphasis on behavioral intentions. The discussion of the proposed model begins with a consideration of studies that focus on cognitions that individuals bring to intergroup interaction settings.

COGNITIONS AND BEHAVIORS

There is a fairly substantial literature devoted to the relationship between intergroup cognitions and behavior. A wide range of attitudes has been measured in these studies, including authoritarianism, ethnocentrism, political attitudes, intentions, attitudes toward civil rights, prejudice, stereotyping, and symbolic racism. Most studies measure clusters of attitudes of a rather broad and nonspecific nature. The behaviors that these measures are expected to predict are usually highly specific (e.g., helping, voting, renting an apartment, signing a petition, committing oneself to pose for interracial pictures). As Fishbein and Ajzen (1975) point out, the disparity in the level of specificity with which attitude and behavioral data are collected may account for the failure to obtain stronger relationships in some studies (cf. Brigham, 1971).

Nearly all of the studies of the intergroup cognition-behavior relationship deal with race. A substantial number measure intergroup behavior in situations where no members of the other race are present. I will review these studies first and then consider those involving direct contact between groups.

A series of studies has examined white subjects' willingness to pose for interracial photographs. In the first of these studies DeFluer and Westie (1958) found a strong association between attitudes and behavior. It should be noted that the attitude and behavior measures in this study were at a comparable level of specificity. The attitude measure consisted of a social distance scale concerning willingness to have blacks or whites engage in a variety of activities. The behavioral measure consisted of agreeing to pose for heterosexual interracial photos. Most subsequent studies have replicated these findings (Cook, cited in Hyman, 1969; Darroch, 1971, cited in Fishbein and Ajzen, 1975; Green, 1972). However, a study using a highly specific measure of attitude found no relationship between attitudes and behavior (Linn, 1965). In this study the attitudes consisted of stated willingness to pose for interracial pictures, and the behavior consisted of signing release forms to actually pose for such pictures. One of the important differences among these studies is that the experimenters were black in the Linn study but not in the others. The presence of a black experimenter may have led some students who expressed prejudiced attitudes to be reluctant to act on their prejudices for fear of disapproval. In general, the results of studies within this paradigm support the idea that attitudes and behavior tend to be consistent when few costs are associated with behaving in either discriminatory or nondiscriminatory ways. This suggestion is also supported in several other studies where the attitude and behavior measures were more varied.

Two of three studies using general measures of prejudice toward blacks found that prejudice was correlated with behavior. In one study prejudice was correlated with signing documents favoring or opposing integrated housing (DeFriese and Ford, 1969). In another prejudice was related to commitments to engage in a variety of interracial activities (Warner and DeFluer, 1969). The third study found that prejudice was unrelated to modeling black or white petition signers (Himelstein and Moore, 1963).

Four studies have examined voting in political elections, specifically, mayoral contests in Los Angeles pitting a black candidate against a white candidate (Jeffries and Ransford, 1972; Kinder and Sears, 1981; McConahay and Hough, 1976; Sears and Kinder, 1971). Sears and Kinder found that general prejudice toward blacks did not predict voting for the white candidate, but a more symbolic measure of attitudes toward blacks (e.g., blacks have gotten more than they deserve, Negroes who receive welfare could get along without it) was related to voting. Jeffries and Ransford, however, did find that a general measure of prejudice toward blacks was significantly related to voting for whites. In the McConahay and Hough

study voter preferences rather than reported votes were obtained. As in the Sears and Kinder study, a measure of symbolic racism (e.g., Negroes are getting too demanding in their push for equal rights) was related to preferences for the white candidate among white suburbanites. In the most recently published study Kinder and Sears found that evaluations of the candidates were significantly related to symbolic racism. Another study of voting found that prejudice was related to preference for a black or a white candidate in a Massachusetts senatorial race (Becker and Heaton, 1967). With the exception of the general prejudice measure in the Sears and Kinder study, these studies were consistent in finding that measures of interracial attitude were related to behavior. These relationships occurred in situations where they might not have been anticipated, given that the measures were all very broad and that the situation was a highly specific one in which race may not have been the most salient feature for many respondents. The authors of the symbolic-racism scales argue that interracial cognitions among white-Americans are less openly racist than in the past (cf. Crosby, Bromley, and Saxe, 1980). They believe that general cognitions concerning moral evaluations of intergroup relations may now occupy a central place in schemata of racial groups. To the extent that they are correct, it is reasonable to expect that such cognitions would exert a considerable influence on behavior.

The studies of the cognition-behavior relationship that involve no direct contact between groups are remarkably consistent in finding substantial relationships between attitudes and discrimination. Perhaps these findings occur because so few other factors enter into behavioral decisions in these situations. The behavior is often anonymous, thus eliminating concerns about others' evaluations of one's behavior. Also, the reactions of out-group members to the behavior do not have to be dealt with. In addition, the costs of engaging in attitude-consistent behaviors are usually not very great, while the benefits include being able to view oneself as consistent.

When behaviors involving direct contact are considered, the situations are considerably more complex. Correspondingly, the findings of these studies are more complex, and we cannot interpret them without taking into consideration factors other than prejudicial attitudes. Among these factors the most important is the individual's appraisals of the costs and benefits of different behavioral options in a given context. The most extensively studied behavior involving direct intergroup contact is helping. I will review studies of this topic first and then discuss a series of more diverse studies.

In one sudy of helping no relationship between a general measure of attitudes toward blacks and helping in an emergency was observed (Gaertner, 1975). In a second, attitudes toward minorities and assisting in a survey conducted by a "Negro" interviewer were found to be negatively related (Katz, Cohen, and Glass, 1975, experiment I). Subjects who refused to participate in the survey had more favorable attitudes toward minorities than those who participated. This study raises questions about the validity of expressions of low levels of prejudice. This issue has been addressed directly in two studies by Dutton.

In the first study (Dutton and Lake, 1973) subjects who rated themselves as being low in prejudice were given false physiological feedback indicating that they were prejudiced. These subjects subsequently donated more money to a black panhandler than subjects whose feedback did not indicate that they were prejudiced. Thus a threat to the subjects' self-presentations as nonprejudiced people produced high levels of immediate interracial helping. The second study suggests that this elevated helping response may be transitory (Dutton and Lennox, 1974). In this study nonprejudiced students were again given feedback indicating that they were prejudiced, and again the experimental group was panhandled by a black. Two days later a request for assistance in running an interracial "brotherhood week" was made of all subjects. The responses to the initial request for help showed higher donations to a black than to a white panhandler. However, in response to the second request for help, those subjects who had been panhandled by a black helped less than those who had been panhandled by a white. The results of the study by Dutton and Lennox have been replicated with an American sample (Dutton used Canadian students) by Rosenfield and colleagues (1982). In addition, these investigators found that when a black seeking signatures for a campaign against sickle-cell anemia was substituted for the black panhandler, the subjects subsequently offered to help more with interracial activities.

Another study demonstrating the instability of interracial helping behavior among people who express liberal attitudes found that whites who were politically liberal terminated a request for help from a black stranger more quickly than requests from a white stranger (Gaertner, 1973). When the caller actually succeeded in making the complete request for assistance, both conservative and liberal whites assisted whites more than blacks, but the conservatives assisted to a greater degree than the lib-

erals. In two later studies Gaertner and Dovidio (1977) found no relationship between prejudice toward blacks and helping a black or white victim in an emergency. Similarly, Dovidio and Gaertner (1981) found no relationship between prejudice and helping. Overall, blacks were helped more frequently than whites by the white subjects in this study, but blacks in higher-status positions were helped less than those in lower-status positions, suggesting that whites responded most favorably to blacks occupying positions consistent with cultural stereotypes of blacks' social status. In one of their studies Gaertner and Dovidio (1977) found that black victims were helped more slowly than white victims in unambiguous emergency situations where the subjects were provided with a placebo to which they could misattribute the arousal elicited by the emergency. Thus while attitudes had no direct effects on helping, discrimination against blacks occurred in a situation where the subjects' motivation to intervene was reduced by attributing their arousal to a non-race-related source.

The primary source of inconsistent findings in these studies of helping comes from subjects who were low in expressed levels of prejudice. Numerous investigators have suggested that whites' attitudes toward blacks are often a mixture of sympathy for the underdog and feelings of aversion (Dutton and Lake, 1973; Dutton and Lennox, 1974; Gaertner, 1976; Gaertner and Dovidio, 1977; Katz, Cohen, and Glass, 1975; Katz and Glass, 1979; Kovel, 1970; Myrdal, 1944; Poskocil, 1977). One sentiment or the other may be translated into behavior, depending upon the situation. Subjects who express low levels of prejudice are apparently displaying their sympathy for out-groups on measures of attitude, but their behavior is frequently dominated by feelings of aversion. Nonprejudiced attitudes may be expressed by these people because they find such attitudes more acceptable within their own value systems and would prefer to have others regard them as unprejudiced. In most attitude measurement situations no costs are involved in expressing nonprejudiced attitudes. However, in interracial interaction situations costs may be attached to responding sympathetically. One of the consequences of offering help to an out-group member is to bring oneself into a more personal relationship with this person, with all the anxiety, uncertainty, and potential disapproval from others associated with this proximity. Where little cost is associated with not helping, this response is more likely than a helpful response. However, in some situations the costs of not helping will be great. These costs may be related to the individual's self-image as a nonprejudiced person, or they may be related to sanctions from others, including the victim or in-group and out-group members who may be observing the behavior. When the costs for not helping are greater than those for helping, then helping is the most likely response.

Most of the studies of interracial helping can be interpreted within this cost-benefit framework (cf. Piliavin, Piliavin, and Rodin, 1975; Piliavin, Rodin, and Piliavin, 1969). In the first study by Dutton black panhandlers were helped most by nonprejudiced white subjects whose self-perceptions as nonprejudiced people were threatened. The cost of not helping under these conditions would have been to substantiate a threat to the person's self-image. The costs of helping were minimal—brief contact with an out-group member. This interpretation is supported in two studies by Katz and colleagues (cited in Katz and Glass, 1979), who found that whites engaged in more low-cost helping toward blacks than toward whites when the negative aspects of their attitudes were made salient. In these studies whites were led to criticize a black or a white, and later they had an opportunity to assist this person in a study by writing sentences. Apparently, the threat posed to their self-images as nonprejudiced people led the whites who had criticized blacks to engage in high levels of low-cost helping. In the second study by Dutton whites whose nonprejudiced attitudes were threatened helped blacks more than they helped whites in response to direct requests, but in response to indirect requests for help these subjects gave less help to blacks than whites. In the case of the indirect request for help the costs of not helping were minimal, and the cost of helping would have been sustained contact with out-group members. The results of the Rosenfield study, which found that helping a black petitioner for sickle-cell anemia increased subsequent helping of blacks, may have been due to a positive experience with a "good" person overcoming the subjects' reluctance to interact with blacks, making it seem less costly to commit themselves to subsequent interactions.

In the Gaertner (1973) and Katz and colleagues (1975) studies phone requests for assistance were more frequently turned down by liberal whites if they were made by blacks than by whites. Here the costs of helping were small, but the costs of not helping were even smaller, since the requests were made by strangers in situations involving no face-to-face interaction. In the Gaertner and Dovidio (1977) study the opportunity to attribute the arousal elicited by the emergency to a non-race-related source probably served to reduce the costs of not helping, because the emergency could be defined as relatively unimportant.

The remaining studies on the cognition-behavior issue that involve intergroup interaction have focused on a variety of different behaviors. To give some organization to these diverse studies, I will present them in terms of when in the interaction sequence the intergroup behaviors were measured. Ten studies examined whether or not attitudes were related to the occurrence of discriminatory behavior before or during the initial phases of interracial interactions.

In two early studies no relationship between attitudes and behavior was found. La Pierre (1936) examined the responses of hotel and restaurant personnel to a Chinese-American couple touring the United States. In 95 percent of these encounters the couple was served with no noticeable negative reactions. However, in response to a questionnaire asking the owners or managers of these establishments if they would accept the couple, only 1 percent said yes. Similar results were obtained by Kutner, Wilkins, and Yarrow (1952), who found that a black woman in the company of three whites was served without incident in restaurants that refused to respond to letters asking them whether they would serve blacks. Twenty years later, Dutton (1971) found that restaurants that had a policy of serving only people who wore ties allowed more blacks than whites to violate this rule. Consistent with the discrepancies between policies and behavior found in these three studies, McGrew (1967) found that the attitudes of apartment managers who were unwilling to rent to black couples were often discrepant from their behavior. Similarly, Johnson (1980) found that attitudes toward the act of renting an apartment to a black person were not significantly correlated with renting the apartment in a sample of white managers. However, in this study behavioral intentions were significantly correlated with renting to a black person.

In the first of two studies by Fendrich (1967a, 1967b) attitudes toward blacks were found to be unrelated to participation in NAACP discussion groups when this measure was presented before a more specific measure of behavioral intentions. However, when the attitudes were measured after the behavioral intentions, a strong relationship between attitudes and behavior was found. In the latter case the attitudes and intentions were more closely related than in the former, suggesting that a consideration of interracial behavioral intentions led to attitude statements that were consistent with the intentions, but the reverse did not occur. The second study found that agreeing to attend or actually attending an NAACP meeting was related to racial attitudes and that this behavior and the racial attitudes were both related to perceived reference group support.

Stephan and Rosenfield (1978a) found that a measure of whites' attitudes toward minorities that was obtained prior to desegregation was not significantly related to amounts of interracial contact after desegregation, although prior contact was significantly correlated with postdesegregation attitudes. This result suggests that in this situation contact determined attitudes, but attitudes did not determine contact.

Two studies created ''interaction'' situations where there was no actual contact between blacks and whites. One of these studies found that attitudes toward blacks were positively correlated with the rated friendliness of setting up chairs for the interracial interaction (Weitz, 1972). A more specific attitude measure (attitudes toward the particular black person with whom the subjects were to interact) was negatively correlated with ratings of the whites' voice tones as they read experimental materials to this black person. This attitude measure was also negatively correlated with the intimacy of the tasks the subjects selected, their willingness to wait with the black person, and their willingness to continue working with this person. In the second study the responses of whites during a simulated interaction were observed (Sappington, 1974). Whites who were pro–civil rights addressed more remarks to a black ''participant,'' and these remarks expressed higher degrees of immediacy (positive affect). In addition, pro–civil rights whites choose to work with the black ''participant'' more often than anti–civil rights whites did. Thus in both studies general measures of attitude and behavior were found to be related. However, in the former study attitudes toward a particular out-group member were negatively correlated with behavior, suggesting that subjects were attempting to compensate for their dislike of the other person by treating him positively (cf. Katz, Cohen, and Glass, 1975; Katz *et al.,* cited in Katz and Glass, 1979).

In the next set of studies the interactions actually took place, and behavior during these interactions was examined. Katz and Benjamin (1960) found a positive relationship between whites' authoritarianism and the amount of deferential behavior that occurred toward blacks in interracial work groups. Blacks who were in the group with highly authoritarian whites were more assertive toward whites than were blacks who were working with whites who were low in authoritarianism. Consistent with this finding, the authoritarian whites rated the blacks in their groups as being more dominating, mature, and bright. The authoritarian whites may have feared the blacks and perceived that little support for antiblack behavior would be found in this setting. In a study of interracial aggression Genthner, Shuntich, and Bunting (1975) found that white subjects who were prejudiced, as measured by a scale of attitudes toward desegregation, delivered more electric shock to a black opponent than did white subjects who were low in prejudice. In this situation, unlike the situation in the Katz and Benjamin study, no possibility for retaliation existed, thereby making it easier for the prejudiced whites to behave in a discriminatory fashion.

Two studies of whites' conformity to blacks' judgments of the autokinetic effect have been done (Berg, 1966; Bray, 1950). Bray found that high-prejudice subjects conformed more to whites' autokinetic judgments than to blacks' judgments. However, a measure of anti-Semitism revealed a negative relationship between prejudice and conformity. Anti-Semitic Gentiles conformed more to the judgments of Jews than of Gentiles. In Berg's study the correlation between a social distance scale and conformity to blacks' autokinetic judgments was not significant.

Three other studies have dealt with more explicit attempts at persuasion during interracial interactions. Davis and Triandis (1971) found that for their white subjects the amount of attitude change toward the position adopted by a black ''negotiation team'' was significantly correlated with two measures of attitudes toward blacks. Similarly, Aronson and Golden (1962) found that white students who endorsed negative stereotypes of blacks were less persuaded by a black communicator than white students who did not endorse the negative stereotypes. A third study finding a parallel effect was conducted by Smith and Dixon (1968). They found that white subjects who were highly prejudiced toward blacks were less easily conditioned by a black experimenter than by a white experimenter on a verbal-conditioning task. The general conclusion to be drawn from these studies is that prejudiced whites are less easily influenced by blacks than are less prejudiced whites.

Three studies have examined behavior after intergroup interactions. In two studies Rokeach and Mezei (1966) found that prejudice toward blacks was unrelated to whites' choices of coffee partners after a fifteen-minute discussion of current topics. Berkowitz (1959) found that anti-Semitism was unrelated to liking for a Jewish or a Gentile codiscussant after a fifteen-minute discussion of how a management dispute should be handled. In contrast, Mann (1959) found, after much more extensive discussions (twelve sessions), that white subjects' sociometric choices of in-group over out-group members were negatively correlated with their prejudice as rated by other members of their discussion groups. For blacks the opposite effect was obtained; those who showed the most in-group favoritism were rated as most prejudiced by other members of their discussion groups. One interpretation of these results is that the prejudiced whites attempted to behave in nonprejudiced ways in interracial settings. This interpretation is consistent with Weitz's (1972) finding that negative attitudes toward a particular black were related to positive affect and behavior as expressed in voice tone and intimacy of task selections.

The majority of these studies can be explained in terms of the general cost-reward model presented for the helping studies. In the studies by La Pierre and by Kutner and colleagues few costs were associated with expressing prejudiced attitudes over the telephone or through the mail. In addition, expressing negative attitudes could have the benefit of preventing a potentially difficult interaction from occurring. In the actual interaction situations the hotel and restaurant managers probably behaved in nonprejudiced ways because to do otherwise could have involved the costs of coping with the negative reactions of the out-group members as well as calling attention to their own behavior. In the McGrew study, expressing nonprejudiced attitudes over the phone was obviously easier than having to live with the potential costs of renting an apartment to a black couple (e.g., disapproval from white tenants). In the La Pierre and the Kutner and colleagues studies little evidence of actual discrimination was shown, but in the McGrew study blacks were discriminated against. The reason would appear to be that the potential costs of renting an apartment are greater than having out-group patrons on a temporary basis.

In the Fendrich studies, where the general attitude measure and the commitment to attend the NAACP meeting occurred in the same setting, the positive correlations between attitudes and behavior may arise because any discrepancies between them would be readily apparent to the subjects and others (the experimenters). In the Stephan and Rosenfield study the attitude measure was unrelated to subsequent contact. In desegregated schools interracial interaction may be disapproved of by peer group members, which could attenuate any relationship between predesegregation attitudes and postdesegregation behavior (measured more than a year later). The finding that predesegregation intergroup contact was correlated with subsequent attitudes may be due to the fact that those students who did have higher levels of intergroup contact had already dealt with whatever costs were associated with those behaviors.

In the study by Johnson, as in two out of three comparisons in Fendrich's studies, specific behavioral intentions were found to be related to behavior. However, beliefs about the consequences of renting to blacks were not related to behavior in Johnson's study. This finding is puzzling, both because it is a key concept in Fishbein and Ajzen's (1975) model and because it is an invitation to the subjects to think about precisely the issues (costs and rewards of renting to blacks) that should be relevant within the cost-reward model. The problem may be that the particular consequences Johnson chose to ask the white managers about were more relevant to their perceptions of an apartment building being largely occupied by blacks than to renting one apartment to blacks (e.g., increases in petty crime, noise, use of illegal drugs, dirty apartments). Also, little variability may have existed for this measure, since most consequences were clearly negative.

Among the studies of behaviors occurring during interactions, most found that general measures of prejudice were related to discrimination against blacks (Aronson and Golden, 1962; Bray, 1950; Davis and Triandis, 1971; Genthner *et al.*, 1975; Sappington, 1974; Weitz, 1972). Among those that did not find a positive relationship between attitudes and behavior, the Katz and Benjamin results suggest that authoritarian whites are submissive to blacks because they fear disapproval or retaliation by the blacks. The findings by Bray that anti-Semites conform more to the judgments of Jews may have been due to a stereotyped belief that Jews are intelligent and therefore will make correct judgments. The finding of no correlation between attitudes and autokinetic judgments by Berg may have been due to the method employed in this study. Unlike Bray, he did not contrast conformity to a black with conformity to a white but instead had both black and white confederates making autokinetic judgments prior to the subjects. If a subject wished to adopt the low-cost strategy of appearing nonprejudiced in this context, the best approach would be to make intermediate choices. This alternative was not available in the Bray study.

In the Rokeach and the Mezei and the Berkowitz studies the behaviors the subjects engaged in, the choice of coffee partners or willingness to work with a discussion partner, are ones for which discrimination would have been fairly obvious if it had occurred. Thus nondiscriminatory behavior may have been elicited because the subjects could avoid disapproval by engaging in it. The results of the Mann study, in which whites who made ethnocentric sociometric choices were rated as low in prejudice, suggests that these whites were sensitive to the disapproval of others and may therefore have obscured their real feelings by behaving in nondiscriminatory ways. Likewise, in Weitz's study the whites who expressed negative evaluations toward the black with whom they were to work may have attempted to avoid letting their attitudes show in direct negative behaviors toward their partners.

COGNITIONS EVOKED
IN THE SITUATION

One of the most important situational determinants of behavior consists of social norms—the rules for appropriate behavior in a given group. Norms influence the individual's perception of the rewards and costs that will result from given behaviors. The costs or rewards of conformity or deviance may be mediated by others (i.e., perceived or actual approval or disapproval), or they may be internally mediated (i.e., pride, shame). For any given behavior one or more reference groups may furnish the individual with norms. These normative prescriptions may be consistent or they may be inconsistent. Thus predicting behavior on the basis of normative injunctions involves a consideration of the costs-rewards associated with compliance or deviance from each relevant norm.

In addition to norms provided by reference groups, another source of social influence consists of the attitudes and beliefs of significant others. These attitudes and beliefs about the appropriateness of behavior may be consistent with those of an individual's reference groups, but where they are not, considerable conflict is likely to be generated. The significant others, like reference-group members, need not be present in the interaction setting to influence behavior.

The people who are present in the situation are likely to influence the behavior that occurs in that setting. The presumed and actual costs and rewards controlled and administered by others in the situation may also be consistent with those of reference groups or significant others. When they are not, the relative costs of complying with or deviating from each set of prescriptions for behavior are likely to determine what the individual does.

In intergroup interaction situations the reference group whose norms are apt to be most important is the in-group that is salient *vis-à-vis* a particular out-group. Among the most important significant others are likely to be family members, peers, and authority figures. Other individuals who are likely to be important are the members of the out-group with whom the individual is interacting.

Unfortunately, empirical studies of the influence of others on intergroup behavior typically have not separated the influence of reference groups and significant others. Eight studies have examined the influence of reference groups and/or significant others on interracial behavior. Fendrich (1967b) found a strong relationship between whites' participation in NAACP discussion groups and perceived support from friends, parents, and additional significant others. DeFriese and Ford (1969) found a strong relationship between whites' willingness to sign a petition favoring integrated housing and perceived support from relatives, friends, neighbors, and work associates. In accord with these findings, Johnson (1980) found that perceived attitudes of family, owners of apartments, and tenants were correlated with apartment managers' discrimination against blacks. Also, Darroch (1971, cited in Fishbein and Ajzen, 1975) found that the correlation between intentions to pose for interracial photos and signing release forms for the photos after they had been taken was raised substantially by including various measures of the attitudes of others (e.g., parents).

In a study of interracial discussions on civil rights Davis and Triandis (1971) found that the positions adopted by whites after the discussion were more highly correlated with the positions of their reference group than with their own prior positions. The reference-group positions in this study were generated through a caucus with in-group members prior to the intergroup discussions. Mezei (1971) found that behavioral intentions toward out-group members were significantly related to perceived approval from parents and friends for a variety of intimate social interactions (e.g., accept as a friend or a date). The correlations were not significant for most nonintimate interactions (e.g., fish with or eat with). Silverman (1974) found that choice of a black or white roommate by white college students was strongly correlated with the perceived approval of parents, best friends, and other students. Ewens and Ehrlich (reported in Ehrlich, 1973) found that the attitudes of reference others were better predictors of willingness to engage in race-related activities (e.g., interviewing about racial attitudes) than were racial attitudes. Thus all eight of these studies found a clear relationship between the perceived attitudes of others and interracial behavior.

The next set of studies examined whether or not the fact that others would know about the behavior or would be observing it influenced the behavior. Warner and DeFluer (1969) found that when whites' commitments to engage in interracial behavior would be publicized in the student newspaper, they were less likely to agree to engage in these behaviors than they were when the commitments would be private. Green (1972) found that agreements to pose for interracial photographs varied as a function of the intimacy of the poses and the degree of exposure the photos were to be given. When the intimacy of the pose was great (a close heterosexual relationship), the subjects were more reluctant to pose as the exposure of the photo became more widespread (from publication in a Peace Corps textbook to publication in a national magazine). When the intimacy would be minimal, the exposure of the photo was unrelated to willingness to pose.

A study by Gaertner (1975), found that black victims were helped less by whites when there were white bystanders than when there were no bystanders (white victims were helped equally in both conditions). A later study replicated these findings (Gaertner and Dovidio, 1977). In each of these studies behavior toward blacks was less positive when others would know about this behavior than when the behavior occurred under more private circumstances (although this was only true for intimate behaviors in the Green study). The direction of this influence suggests that the subjects anticipated that others would disapprove of their engaging in prosocial or intimate interracial behavior (for an exception see Donnerstein and Donnerstein, 1973).

Interestingly, a parallel pattern of results emerges from studies of antisocial interracial behavior. Two studies by the Donnerstein's have examined public and private aggression toward blacks by whites. In their studies whites were provided with opportunities to punish a black person in the context of an experiment on learning. The intensity (direct aggression) and duration (indirect aggression) of shock for incorrect answers and the

magnitude of rewards for correct answers constituted the dependent measures. When the subjects' behaviors were recorded on videotape for subsequent viewing by the white experimenters, they displayed less direct aggression toward the black learners than when their behavior was anonymous (Donnerstein and Donnerstein, 1973, 1978). Aggression toward whites was not affected by videotaping (Donnerstein and Donnerstein, 1973). These studies suggest that the subjects were responding as if the experimenters would disapprove of overtly hostile behavior toward blacks. A final study varied the behavior of a white model and examined the interracial aggression of white subjects (Donnerstein and Donnerstein, 1976). When the model delivered low aggression, the subjects gave less shock to a black person than when the model's behavior was highly aggressive or unspecified. This result suggests that aggressive behavior will occur when a model's behavior indicates that aggression has no negative consequences (cf. Bandura, Ross, and Ross, 1963).

On the basis of these studies we might be tempted to conclude that there are norms that proscribe prosocial and overt antisocial behavior toward out-group members. The intriguing aspect of this conclusion is its consistency with the idea of aversive racism (Gaertner, 1976; Jones, 1972). Apparently, in-group members believe that others will generally disapprove of both prosocial and antisocial behavior toward out-group members. The implicit injunction would appear to be to simply avoid interacting with out-group members. This basic orientation toward intergroup interaction may prevail in situations having no countervailing forces, such as strong personal prejudices, unambiguous norms favoring overt pro- or antisocial behavior, or substantial rewards or costs for pro- or antisocial behavior.

A series of studies by the Donnersteins illustrates the role that the perceived attitudes or expected reactions of out-group members in the interaction setting play in determining the behavior of in-group members. Several of their studies have shown that when whites believe that black "learners" will have an opportunity to retaliate against them, they express less *direct* aggression toward blacks than when no opportunities for retaliation exist (Donnerstein and Donnerstein, 1975, 1977; Donnerstein *et al.,* 1972). Aggression toward whites is unaffected by opportunities for retaliation (Donnerstein and Donnerstein, 1973). However, an opportunity for retaliation increases *indirect* aggression (shock duration) toward blacks (Donnerstein and Donnerstein, 1972), but perhaps only if the blacks are perceived as being dissimilar to the whites (Donnerstein and Donnerstein, 1975). The increased indirect aggression suggests that an underlying hostility toward blacks is being suppressed by fear of retaliation. One of the Donnersteins' studies also found that when the white subjects were introduced to the blacks there was less direct aggression than when the subjects were anonymous (Donnerstein *et al.,* 1972). However, indirect aggression increased in the nonanonymous condition. An opportunity for retaliation led to increases in rewards to blacks, while anonymity led to decreases in rewards (Donnerstein and Donnerstein, 1972, 1975, 1977). Greater fear of retaliation from blacks than from whites combined with an underlying antipathy would appear to explain all of these results (Donnerstein *et al.,* 1972).

Not only do whites fear retaliation by blacks, apparently blacks do as well. A study by Wilson and Rogers (1975) found that black subjects in a situation similar to the Donnersteins' experiments also gave more intense shocks to blacks who could not retaliate than to those who could. Again, aggression toward whites was unaffected by opportunities for retaliation, although they did receive more aggression than the black targets. These studies indicate that the perceived attitudes of others, particularly fear of retaliation, can play an important role in determining intergroup behavior.

One issue that remains to be resolved is how conflicts between the perceived attitudes of various others are reconciled. Ajzen and Fishbein (1980) employ a weighted combination of perceived attitudes of others and motivation to comply with these attitudes. One problem with this approach is that a situation in which there are two reference others holding weak conflicting attitudes with which the individual is not motivated to comply is equivalent to a situation in which there are two reference others, strong conflicting attitudes, and strong motivations to comply. The second situation involves considerable ambivalence, which would seem to make it very different from the first. As Katz and Glass (1979) have argued, ambivalence frequently does not lead to moderate behaviors; rather it tends to lead to amplified positive or negative behaviors.

Generally, the studies of the relationship between situational cognitions (norms, cost-reward appraisals) and intergroup behavior have yielded evidence that is considerably stronger and more consistent than results of studies of the relationship between individual cognitions

(prejudice, stereotypes) and intergroup behavior. One reason may be that in this particular behavioral domain (i.e., race relations) the perceived attitudes of others are more likely to be salient and unambiguous than they are in many other domains. In the past, relations between the races have been subject to regulation by law in the United States (in some countries they still are), and normative regulation of relations between ethnic groups has a long history in the United States (Blalock, 1967; Van den Berghe, 1967). Thus costs are associated with violating these norms and rewards are associated with compliance. These rewards and costs appear to be greater than those associated with behaving in terms of one's attitudes. In most situations norms and attitudes are likely to be closely correlated (e.g., Foley, 1976; Johnson, 1980). In cases where there are conflicts, the normative injunctions and rewards-costs mediated by others who will know about the behavior are likely to be the more powerful determinants of behavior.

EXPECTANCIES AND BEHAVIOR

In addition to attitudes, the only other type of intergroup cognition that has been extensively investigated in relation to behavior is expectancies. Intergroup expectancies concerning behavior may be generated from a wide variety of sources. In intergroup relations the most important source is probably stereotypes. In this case the characterisic traits associated with stereotypes lead people to expect certain types of behavior from others and to plan their own interaction strategies accordingly. Expectancies may also be generated from scripts, the assumed dissimilarity of out-groups' beliefs, values, and cultural practices, and the prejudices of in-group members (Brigham, 1971; Byrne and Andres, 1964). In addition, expectancies may be evoked by aspects of the situation such as roles and norms that are relevant to the situation or a consideration of what behaviors will be rewarded or punished in a given context. Thus expectancies may be derived from the individual's cognitions concerning out-groups or they may be evoked by the situation.

Unlike the relationship between prejudice and discrimination, the relationship between expectancies and intergroup behavior has been investigated in interaction contexts where the reciprocal interplay between in-group and out-group behavior has been explored. The research to be reviewed below indicates that expectancies influence the behavior of in-group members, the responses of out-group members, and the subsequent reactions of in-group members to the behavior of the out-group. Although many of these relationships have been extensively discussed by sociologists (e.g., Becker, 1963; Goffman, 1963; Merton, 1949; Rist, 1970; Schur, 1971; Tannen-baum, 1938), their approach has been largely descriptive. In the review that follows, I will focus primarily on empirical studies of these processes.

Expectancies and In-group Behavior

Research by Rosenthal and his associates (e.g., Rosenthal, 1966; Rosenthal and Jacobson, 1968) has amply demonstrated that expectancies affect the behavior of the individuals who hold them. The nature of this effect is that people often act in ways that will bring about results that are consistent with their expectancies.

Two studies have varied race and teacher expectancies. In a study in which race and expected levels of ability were varied, Rubovits and Maehr (1973) found that black students were treated less positively than white students by white "teachers." This finding suggests that black students were not expected to do well (cf. Coates, 1972; Harvey and Slatin, 1975; Mercer, Iadicola, and Moore, 1980; also see Datta, Schaeffer, and Davis, 1968; Jensen and Rosenfeld, 1974; Mazer, 1971, for evidence that lower-class blacks are especially negatively evaluated) and were treated in a manner that would fulfill this expectancy. This study replicated the finding by Rosenthal and others (reviewed by Rosenthal, 1973) that gifted white students are treated more positively than non-gifted white students. However, the gifted black students received the least positive treatment from the teachers. One interpretation of this effect rests on the implications of such treatment. If the negative treatment of the gifted black students resulted in poor performance, this result would fulfill low expectancies for black students based on stereotypes. Apparently, the teachers in this study acted in ways that would fulfill their own prior low expectancies for blacks.

A contrasting set of results was obtained by Taylor (1979). She found that gifted black students were treated more favorably than nongifted blacks. The student teachers in Taylor's study indicated that they expected the blacks to perform better than the whites. The results of this study also suggest that the teachers acted in ways that would fulfill the ability-level expectations created by the experimenter rather than their own expectancies.

If they had been attempting to fulfill their own prior expectancies, they would have treated the nongifted blacks most positively in order to bring about a high level of performance. Because these two studies differ in a number of respects, it is difficult to determine why they obtained discrepant results. One possibility is that the teachers' prior expectancies were stronger than the experimentally induced expectancies in the Rubovits and Maehr study, while the opposite was true in the Taylor study.

A study by Snyder and Swann (1978a) found that subjects' expectancies concerning the traits of another person influenced their behavior. Subjects whose partners were described as hostile directed more aggression toward them than subjects whose partners were described as nonhostile. Similarly, subjects who expected others to be competitive behaved in more competitive ways on a prisoner's dilemma game than subjects who expected people to be cooperative (Kelley and Stahelski, 1970; Kuhlman and Wimberly, 1976; Miller and Holmes, 1975). A study by Yarkin, Harvey, and Bloxom (1981) provides additional evidence on this process. They created positive and negative attitudes toward a stimulus person by presenting a videotape and biographical information to their subjects. The subjects were then interviewed by the stimulus person. The subjects had more positive conversations, maintained eye contact longer, and spoke longer to the positive than to the negative interviewer. These effects were greatest when the subject made attributions about the interviewer before the interview. Probably the set to expect positive and negative behaviors from the interviewer that was created by the background information was made salient by the attribution questionnaire and, as a consequence, had a greater impact on the subjects' behavior. This study indicates that the more salient an expectancy is, the greater the probability is that it will affect behavior.

Expectancies and the Behavior of Others

When peoples' expectancies influence their behavior, we would expect this behavior to affect the recipients. These effects may take several forms. The main thrust of research on this topic has been to demonstrate that in-group behavior based on expectancies leads out-group members to act in ways that confirm the expectancies. This behavior can occur as a direct response to the behavior of the in-group member. An example would be when in-group members expect out-group members to be aggressive and hostile and their own preemptively aggressive behavior elicits hostility in return. Alternatively, the out-group member may perceive what is expected by the in-group member and respond accordingly. For example, a woman who perceives that her chauvinist employer expects her to be submissive may elect to comply. In this case the response to the expectancy is indirect; it is mediated by the out-group member's perception of the expectancy. The perception of what is expected by others may be based on verbal expressions of expectancies, it may be a logical inference from their behavior, or it may be the result of an out-group member imputing expectancies to an in-group member where none exist. In any case, when out-group members perceive expectancies, they can determine their own responses, which raises the possibility of noncompliance as an option. This type of reaction to expectancies has received less attention in the literature than expectancy confirmation.

Again, one of the primary sources of evidence that expectancies can influence the behavior of others comes from the work of Rosenthal (1973). In his best-known study (Rosenthal and Jacobson, 1968) he found that when teachers were led to expect that some students would "bloom" intellectually in their classes, the academic performance of these students increased. Internal analyses of these data revealed that the Mexican-American students who were judged to look most Mexican benefited the most from being in the high-expectancy condition. The authors account for this increase by suggesting that the teachers probably had the lowest expectations for these students who therefore had the most to gain from the expectancy manipulation. The majority of the early studies of teacher expectancies did not examine the teachers' behavior, and for this reason the process by which the expectancies were confirmed is unclear. Considerable recent research has been directed toward examining the processes by which expectancies affect the behavior of others.

A substantial amount of evidence suggests that expectancies can be directly confirmed by the behavior of others. In a study by Farina, Allen, and Saul (1968) subjects were asked to communicate in writing to another subject the fact that they had been hospitalized with mental problems. Although this information was not actually communicated to their partners, the students who thought their partners believed that they were mentally ill were spoken to less and liked less than were students in the control condition. Apparently, the students who

thought that others believed they were stigmatized acted in ways that led them to be rejected. Thus this study suggests that when an expectancy is erroneously attributed to another individual (e.g., he will reject me because I am mentally ill), the person who holds the false expectancy may behave in ways that result in the fulfillment of the expectancy. Another study found that white interviewers behaved differently toward black and white interviewees (Word, Zanna, and Cooper, 1974). Specifically, the interviewers sat at a greater distance from the blacks, made more speech errors, and terminated the interview sooner. When a confederate in a second study adopted these behaviors of the interviewer, interviewees were judged less favorably on demeanor and overall performance by neutral observers, and the interviewees disliked the interviewer. Thus when the behavior of the confederate matched the original white interviewer's behavior from study I, this discriminatory behavior elicited behavior that would have confirmed negative expectancies of blacks held by the interviewers.

In a parallel set of studies Feldman and Prohaska (1979) led students to expect that their teachers were competent or incompetent. Students who believed their teachers were incompetent performed more poorly and displayed less immediate nonverbal behaviors than students with competent teachers (the teachers were confederates). When confederates imitated the nonverbal behavior of students in the first study, the teachers' behavior was effected. Their nonverbal behavior mirrored that of the "students." Also, observers rated their teaching as less adequate if the students behaved like those in the first study who believed their teachers were incompetent than if the students behaved like those who believed their teachers were competent. In a conceptually similar study Snyder, Tanke, and Berscheid (1977) found that males behaved differently toward attractive and unattractive females. Independent judges of the females' responses to this treatment showed that the females' behavior fulfilled the males' stereotypes of attractive or unattractive women. This study is a particularly forceful demonstration of the self-fulfilling prophecy, because the expectancies, the behavior of the people holding the expectancies, and the responses to the expectancies were all independently measured within a single context.

All four of these studies indicate that peoples' expectancies influenced their behavior, and these behaviors led to behavior from others that confirmed the expectancies. However, a study by Kleck and Strenta (1980) failed to find that expectancies affected the behavior of others. In this study the subject believed that another person thought she had a stigmatizing facial scar. The subject was told that the experimenters were studying the effects of this scar on the other's behavior. Although subjects in this condition perceived that this stigma affected the behavior of their interaction partners, observers detected no effects. Thus it appears that the subjects' expectations that they would be treated differently were not fulfilled. However, the interaction partners were confederates, and it is possible that their responses became routinized during the course of the study so that they were insensitive to the subjects' expectancies and behavior.

In several subsequent studies Snyder has sought to support and supplement these findings. In one study subjects were asked to test hypotheses about the traits of their interaction partners (Snyder and Swann, 1978b). These hypotheses apparently functioned as a kind of expectancy in the sense that the perceivers sought to test them by asking questions that would confirm the hypotheses. The consequence of framing questions in this way was that the respondents ultimately provided information that confirmed the hypotheses. For instance, when the subjects were asked to determine whether their partner was an extravert, they asked questions such as "In what situations are you most talkative?" and received responses that independent judges regarded as more energetic, poised, and extraverted. In another study subjects who expected to interact with hostile people treated them more aggressively and were in turn treated more aggressively than subjects who expected to interact with nonhostile people (Snyder and Swann, 1978a).

Evidence that the effect of expectancies can be mediated by their perception is found in studies that have examined the responses of people who are led to believe that others expect them to behave in specific ways. In the majority of these studies no differential treatment is associated with these expectancies on the part of those who are said to hold the expectancies.

A study by Zanna and Pack (1975) found that college women who were led to believe that desirable male interaction partners held traditional stereotypes of women presented themselves differently than women who were told that the males' attitudes were nontraditional. These women presented their attitudes as being more traditional and did worse on an achievement task if they thought their partners preferred traditional over nontraditional women. These differences were only obtained when the interaction partner was described in a desirable way (a tall Princeton senior with no girlfriend). This finding suggests that people will fulfill others' expectancies when they perceive rewards for doing so. This suggestion is supported in a second study by Zanna (Von Baeyer, Sherk, and Zanna, 1981). In this study women interviewing for a job were informed that the male interviewers held traditional stereotypes of women or held nontraditional attitudes. The women who believed the interviewers held traditional stereotypes wore more makeup and accessories, gazed at the interviewer less, and talked to him less during the interview than subjects confronting nontraditional interviewers.

A similar interpretation in terms of costs and rewards can be used to explain the results of a study by Katz, Roberts, and Robinson (1965). In this study black students performing in the presence of a white tester performed better on a task when it was described as a hand-eye coordination task that when it was described as an intellectual task. The opposite pattern of results was obtained in the presence of a black experimenter. Apparently, the subjects were behaving in accordance with their perceptions of the whites' expectancies concerning intellectual ability in an attempt to avoid the disapproval of the white experimenter.

Another set of studies has dealt with the effects of labeling. It is not difficult to understand why people behave in ways that confirm positive labels that have been imputed to them by others, as several studies have shown. Here behavior that confirms the label allows individuals to attribute the positive traits associated with the label to themselves. The case of negative labels is more complex, as we shall see. A study illustrating the effects of positive labeling has been done by Miller, Brickman, and Bolen (1975). In one of their experiments (II) they found that when high math ability (you are intelligent) or motivation (you are a hard worker) was attributed to second-grade students, the math achievement of the students improved more than if the experimenters simply reinforced them for doing math or attempted to persuade them to do better. Kraut (1973) found that labeling people as charitable or uncharitable on the basis of their prior helping affected donations to a second charity. Subjects who were given these labels contributed more or less than subjects whose behavior had not been labeled after the first request for help. Thus, in this study there is evidence that people confirm both positive and negative labels. Confirmation of another somewhat negative label was found by Langer and Benevento (1978). Subjects were labeled as assistants or bosses on a cooperative task. The subjects who were in the less prestigious role performed a set of simple math problems worse than those in the more prestigious role or those given no label.

People do not always act to confirm the positive and negative labels imputed to them. For instance, Baumeister, Cooper, and Skib (1979) found that women to whom a positive trait was publicly attributed did not perform as well on an anagram task as women to whom a negative trait was attributed when it was said that poor performance would confirm the presence of the trait. No differences in the performances of women resulted when the attributions were made in private. Thus the trait attributed to them was confirmed only when it would confirm others' beliefs that they possessed a positive trait. Steele (1975) also found that people react to having negative traits attributed to them by behaving in positive ways. He found that both relevant and irrelevant negative attributions (unhelpful, unconcerned with driving safely) increased subsequent helping more than no prior attributions.

One answer to the question of when people will react to negative labels by disconfirming them and when they will confirm them comes from a study by Gurwitz and Topol (1978). In two experiments they found that people would confirm negative traits imputed to them if they were presented with evidence that they and many members of their group possessed these traits. In one experiment subjects in one condition were asked to review situations in which they lacked self-confidence and were told that most other students at their university also lacked self-confidence. These students rated themselves as less self-confident than students who did not review these situations or who were not told that other students commonly had this problem. Apparently, students found it easier to admit possessing a negative trait if similar others also possessed it. Additional evidence from this study indicated that when the subjects did not accept the negative traits imputed to them and were led to believe that many members of their group did possess the negative traits, they acted to disconfirm them. Under these circumstances acting to disconfirm a negative trait label served as a way of positively differentiating oneself from a group.

The majority of the preceding studies did not explicitly consider the degree to which the expectancy or label was consistent with the person's self-image. A study by Swann and Hill (1982) indicates that this factor may influence reactions to labeling. Subjects who labeled themselves as dominant or nondominant were given feedback by another "subject" that was consistent or inconsistent with these self-images. If the subjects were given an opportunity to interact with the confederate who gave them the feedback, they attempted to counteract the inconsistent labels (e.g., dominant people who were labeled submissive acted more dominant than those labeled dominant). When they had no opportunity to interact with the confederate, subjects given inconsistent feedback changed their self-perceptions in the direction of the feedback. This study suggests that people may attempt to disconfirm the expectancies of others that are clearly discrepant with their self-images if they have the opportunity.

Taken together, these studies provide evidence that three factors are important in determining whether people will act to confirm or disconfirm expectancies: the positive or negative nature of the expectancy or label, whether the individuals accept or reject the trait implied by the expectancy or label, and whether or not the trait or label characterizes salient groups of which they are members. Label-confirming behavior is most likely when a positive or negative label is self-accepted and characterizes the in-group. Label-disconfirming behavior is most likely when a positive or negative label is rejected by the self and characterizes the out-group. However, rewards or punishments may counteract these tendencies.

Effects of Confirmation and Disconfirmation

After a behavior confirms or disconfirms an expectancy held or perceived to be held by another person, this confirmation or disconfirmation affects both the person holding the expectancy and the behaver. For the person who holds the expectancy, some of the cognitive consequences of expectancy confirmation and disconfirmation have already been reviewed. Because of selective attention, encoding, and retention, perceivers are likely to believe that their expectancies have been fulfilled even when they have not been. Thus traits associated with expectancies often will be attributed to the other person regardless of that person's behavior. In addition to these cognitive consequences, expectancy fulfillment also has affective and behavioral consequences. Several studies indicate that people who confirm perceivers' expectancies will be liked more than those who disconfirm expectancies. An illustrative experiment has been done by Taylor and Gardner (1969), who found that when a French Canadian presented himself as disconfirming the stereotypes held by English Canadians, he was liked less than when he confirmed the stereotype. Likewise, Gergen and Jones (1963) found that when another person's unexpected behaviors had negative consequences for their subjects, the subjects disliked a "mental patient" more than a "normal" person, but they liked the "mental patient" more than the "normal" person if his behavior confirmed their expectancies. In three studies Costrich and associates (1975) found that men and women who behaved in nonstereotyped ways were liked less or seen as more in need of therapy than men and women who behaved normatively. And Rosenthal and Jacobson (1968) found that students who were not expected to "bloom" intellectually, but who did register academic gains, were evaluated less favorably than students who confirmed their teachers' expectations.

The behavioral consequences of confirmation/disconfirmation are hinted at in studies of the prisoner's dilemma game. In a study by Kelley and Stahelski (1970) people with competitive orientations expected their opponents to be competitive. When these expectations were disconfirmed, the competitors did not modify their behavior. In contrast, cooperative people who expected others to be either competitive or cooperative became competitive when confronted with a competitive partner. Subsequent research by Kuhlman and Wimberley (1976) indicated that when cooperative subjects were given a noncompetitive option, they too did not modify their behavior in response to a competitive partner. These studies are interesting because the subjects' behavioral intransigence costs them money. They suggest that at least initially people will not modify their behavior in response to disconfirmatory behavior from others. This response would seem especially likely to the degree that the perceivers do not change their expectancies.

Confirmation and disconfirmation of expectancies also have cognitive, affective, and behavioral effects on the people engaging in the confirming or disconfirming behaviors. Behaving in accordance with others' expectancies can lead the individual to adopt the traits implied by the expectancies. This behavior is likely to occur when the traits are positive ones such as academic ability. In the case of conformity to negative expectancies the fact that others have the expectancy provides a convenient attribution for engaging in the behavior and may enable the individual to avoid making internal attributions to explain the behavior [this is similar to the argument made by dissonance theorists that forced compliance leads to little attitude change (Wicklund and Brehm, 1976)]. A more damaging possibility is that confirmed negative expec-

tancies will lead to acceptance of the implied traits. This possibility appears to have been what the social scientists who wrote a brief for the *Brown* (1954) case had in mind when they said of school segregation (Allport *et al.*, 1953, p. 429)

> Minority group children learn the inferior status to which they are assigned. . . . They often react with feelings of inferiority and a sense of personal humiliation. . . . Under these conditions, the minority group child is thrown into a conflict with regard to his feelings about himself and group. He wonders whether his group and he himself are worthy of no more respect than they receive. This conflict and confusion leads to self-hatred.

This effect would seem particularly likely to the degree that there is a consensus concerning the expectancy and the people holding the expectancy have high credibility.

The affective consequences of confirmation or disconfirmation depend to a great degree on whether the expectancy is positive or negative. Confirmation of positive expectancies and disconfirmation of negative expectancies would be expected to elicit favorable affective reactions in the behaver, such as pride and happiness. Disconfirmation of positive expectancies and confirmation of negative expectancies may lead to negative affect, such as sadness and low self-esteem or resentment and hostility directed toward the self or the holder of the expectancy. An interesting pair of studies bearing on these issues has been done by Dion. In one study Jewish students engaged in a communication task with several opponents (Dion and Earn, 1975). After doing poorly on this task, the Jewish students attributed their failure to prejudice more if their partners were described as Christians than when no description was provided. They also felt more sad, anxious, and aggressive when their opponents were Christians. In addition, students in this condition rated themselves more favorably on positive traits underlying the Jewish stereotype (e.g., love of tradition, industrious, clever). The second study found that females who lost badly to male opponents were lower in self-esteem than females who lost badly to female opponents (Dion, 1975). When they attributed their failures to prejudice, they evaluated themselves more favorably on positive traits underlying the female stereotype (e.g., fair, considerate, trusting) than when they did not attribute their failures to prejudice. The females also retaliated more against male opponents than against female opponents when they lost badly. While the expectancies of the Jewish and female subjects in these studies were not obtained, their belief that their out-group opponents were prejudiced suggests that they believed that their opponents expected or wanted them to do poorly and acted in a way that caused their failure. This undesired confirmation of negative expectancies had affective consequences (sadness, anxiety, low self-esteem), cognitive consequences (self-affirmation of positive stereotyped traits), and behavioral consequences (retaliation).

The study by Snyder and Swann (1978b) cited earlier provides additional evidence that confirmation of negative expectancies has behavioral consequences. In that study subjects who were expected to be hostile confirmed this expectancy by behaving aggressively. If they were led to attribute their aggression to internal factors, they were more aggressive toward a different opponent than if they were led to make external attributions for their behavior. In this case self-acceptance of the negative trait implied by the expectancy (a cognitive consequence of expectancies) led to later behavior that was consistent with the expectancy. The importance of this finding is that it suggests that when the self-fulfilling prophecy leads others to believe they possess the traits imputed to them, they may engage in the associated behaviors in later interactions. A follow-up on Snyder and Swann (1978a) by Fazio, Effrein, and Falender (1981) also supports this notion. In this study subjects were led to behave in introverted or extraverted ways by having an interviewer ask them the questions that Snyder and Swann had previously found were proposed by subjects seeking to confirm that their partners were introverts or extraverts. Subjects who behaved in a more extraverted manner in response to this interview subsequently rated themselves as more extraverted and, in an unrelated situation, behaved in a more extraverted manner than subjects who responded to the introvert interview. Outside the microcosm of the laboratory this process may induce members of stereotyped groups to adopt behaviors and self-concepts consistent with the stereotypes.

CHANGING INTERGROUP COGNITIONS AND BEHAVIOR

Thus far I have reviewed one type of contribution that social psychology has made to the study of intergroup relations, namely, providing empirically based theoretical models of how individuals process and act upon information about social groups. A second major contribution that social psychology has made is to examine techniques of improving intergroup relations. A sizable literature has been devoted to this topic. In reviewing this literature, I will start with a discussion of the most prominent approach to modifying intergroup relations, the contact hypothesis. This discussion will be followed by reviews of approaches based on therapeutic techniques, learning theories, and educational and propoganda programs.

THE CONTACT HYPOTHESIS

Lessened hostility will result from arranging intergroup collaboration, on the basis of personal association of individuals as functional equals on a common task jointly accepted as worthwhile. (Williams, 1947, p. 69).

Prejudice. . . may be reduced by equal status contact between majority and minority groups in the pursuit of common goals. The effect is greatly enhanced if this contact is sanctioned by institutional supports (i.e., by law, custom, or local atmosphere), and provided it is of a sort that leads to the perception of common interests and common humanity between members of the two groups (Allport, 1954, p. 281).

Attitude change favorable to a disliked group will result from equal status contact with stereotype-disconfirming persons from that group, provided that the contact is cooperative and of such a nature as to reveal the individual characteristics of the person contacted and that it takes place in a situation characterized by social norms favoring equality and equalitarian association among the participating groups (Cook, 1978, pp. 97–98).

An extensive literature details the effects of intergroup contact on intergroup cognitions and behavior. A substantial number of investigations in this area have examined naturally occurring contact situations that were expected to improve intergroup relations. While the majority of these studies have supported this hypothesis, a not-inconsiderable minority have found no differences or negative effects (Amir, 1969, 1976). As indicated in the quotations at the beginning of this section, many attempts have been made to catalogue the relevant dimensions of these studies (Allport, 1954; Amir, 1969, 1976; Ashmore, 1970; Cook, 1969, 1970, 1978; Pettigrew, 1969, 1973, 1975; Rose, 1981; Williams, 1947, 1977). Two principal categories of variables emerge as important in these discussions. One category concerns aspects of the situation, particularly the nature of the interactions that occur and the outcomes of the interactions. The second category concerns the characteristics of the participants, including their relative statuses and skills.

The dimension of interaction that has received the most attention is the type of interdependence that exists among the interactants. Numerous studies have examined cooperation as a technique of improving intergroup relations. In many studies cooperative interdependence is compared with competition. Cooperation and competition within groups is often accompanied by cooperation or competition between groups. These combinations of cooperation and competition can affect both intragroup relations and intergroup relations. The bulk of these studies have been conducted in laboratory settings using white subjects. Of particular relevance to intergroup relations are those studies that have examined the effects of cooperation in groups with heterogeneous compositions.

In general, the laboratory studies indicate that cooperation leads to increased attraction to members of the group regardless of whether relations between groups are cooperative or competitive (Deutsch, 1949; Doise *et al.*, 1972; Dunn and Goldman, 1966; Goldman, Stockbauer, and McAuliffe, 1977; Grossack, 1954; Julian, Bishop, and Fiedler, 1966; Kahn and Ryen, 1972; Myers, 1962; Ryen and Kahn, 1975; Sherif and Sherif, 1956; Stephenson, Skinner, and Brotherton, 1976; Worchel, Andreoli, and Folger, 1977). When intragroup cooperation is associated with intergroup competition, relations between groups usually suffer (Blake and Mouton, 1961; Campbell, 1965; Dunn and Goldman, 1966; Kahn and Ryen, 1972; Dion, 1973; Rabbie *et al.*, 1974; Sherif and Sherif, 1956; Worchel and Norvell, 1980; Worchel, Lind, and Kaufman, 1975; Worchel *et al.*, 1977), although no negative effects were found in several studies (Doise *et al.*, 1972; Goldman *et al.*, 1977; Ryen and Kahn, 1975; Stephenson *et al.*, 1976). Intergroup cooperation has typically been found to improve relations between groups (Burnstein and McRae, 1962; Dunn and Goldman, 1966; Rabbie *et al.*, 1974; Sherif and Sherif, 1956; Worchel *et al.*, 1977).

Additional research suggests that these general findings can be influenced by three factors: the outcomes of cooperation, the similarity of the group members, and their relative competence. Cooperation within and between groups leads to more favorable evaluations of ingroup and out-group members primarily when it is successful (Kennedy and Stephan, 1977; Myers, 1962; Ryen and Kahn, 1975; Sherif and Sherif, 1969; Wilson and Miller, 1961; Worchel and Norvell, 1980; Worchel *et al.*, 1977). In-group members who are dissimilar tend to show less in-group preference than those who are similar (Allen and Wilder, 1975; Blanchard and Cook, 1976; Blanchard, Adelman, and Cook, 1975; Dion, 1973; Stephenson *et al.*, 1976). Also, incompetent group members are liked less than competent group members in cooperative groups (Rosenfield, Stephan, and Lucker, 1981).

Recently, several studies have examined cooperation among members of preexisting social groups as a technique of improving intergroup relations. The majority of these studies have been done in field settings, usually schools, and most involve cooperation between blacks and whites. Thus these studies provide information on the external validity of the laboratory studies. They also reveal the importance of a variety of other factors that have not been investigated in laboratory settings.

In a series of studies Aronson and his colleagues have examined the effects of the ''jigsaw classroom'' (Aronson and Osherow, 1980; Aronson *et al.*, 1978). In this technique students work together in multiethnic groups on standard academic materials. The technique creates means interdependence by employing peer teaching, but the students are graded independently. Typically, the material to be studied is divided into as many sections as there are students in each group. Each student is then responsible for teaching the other students in the group the material he or she has learned. The teachers serve as facilitators but do not directly teach any of the material. No competition occurs between the groups, which usually last for about six to eight weeks.

In the first of a series of studies fifth-grade teachers were trained in the use of the jigsaw technique (Blaney *et al.*, 1977). Anglo, Mexican-American, and black students were evenly distributed into six-person groups. The groups met for one class period three times a week for six weeks. The results indicated that compared with a control group that studied the same materials in a more traditional competitive manner, the students in the cooperative groups liked their group members more, liked school more, and increased in self-esteem and in their beliefs that other students could serve as learning resources. The results were not analyzed by ethnic group of rater or ethnic group being rated, but they do suggest that intragroup cooperation produces favorable attitudes toward group mates. A second study employed tenth-grade

Anglo and Mexican-American students as subjects (Geffner, 1978). The students in the jigsaw classrooms increased in self-esteem and had more favorable attitudes toward school than students in less structured cooperative groups or those in traditional classes. Overall liking for classmates, including interethnic liking, became more favorable in the cooperative classes but not in the traditional classes. The attitudes of Mexican-Americans toward the academic abilities of Anglos became more favorable in the cooperative classes. The attitudes of Anglos toward the Mexican-American's academic abilities apparently did not change, although the Anglos did believe that the Mexican-Americans viewed themselves more favorably at the end of the study.

In a third study the ratio of Anglos and Mexican-Americans within the groups was systematically varied (Gonzales, 1979). Taken together, the jigsaw groups did not increase in self-esteem or liking for school more than the control groups. The participants in the jigsaw groups did evaluate Mexican-Americans more favorably than those in the control groups did, but there were no changes in attitudes toward Anglos. The favorable changes in attitudes toward Mexican-Americans were greater in the ethnically balanced groups than in unbalanced groups.

These studies suggest that the jigsaw technique can improve intergroup attitudes, particularly when the groups are ethnically balanced. This technique often produces other desirable effects as well. It generally leads to increases in self-esteem and more positive attitudes toward school. Increases in internal locus of control (Gonzales, 1979) and enhanced role-taking skills (Bridgeman, 1977) have also been noted. These beneficial effects of participating in jigsaw groups do not occur at the expense of academic achievement. In fact, the jigsaw groups, particularly the minority group members of these groups, have been found to outperform students in traditional classes who were studying the same materials (Gonzales, 1979; Lucker *et al.*, 1977).

A second series of studies on multiethnic groups has been conducted by Cook and his colleagues (Cook, 1978). In a study by Weigel, Wiser, and Cook (1975) students from desegregated schools worked together part time for seven months in small multiethnic groups. They discussed academic materials and films and gathered information to make reports to the class. The groups competed for extra points that were allotted to the most effective groups. Thus a degree of goals interdependence as well as means interdependence was employed in this technique. Anglo students increased their liking for Mexican-American classmates and their choices of Mexican-Americans as friends, but Mexican-Americans and blacks did not change. No changes in general ethnic attitudes were found for any of these groups. Another study in this series examined the attitudes of mothers who worked together in interracial groups to improve their abilities to stimulate the intellectual growth of their children. At the end of seven months of weekly training sessions no racial discrimination in attraction ratings was displayed, and cross-race interactions predominated. However, there were no changes in general racial attitudes and no differences in attitudes between groups that differed in the amount of structured cooperative interaction they had experienced (Cook, Gray, and Vietze, cited in Cook, 1978).

A third study was done in a laboratory setting (Cook, 1969). Students were hired to work together for twenty days. The interactions involved making decisions on a railroad management game. The participants consisted of prejudiced whites interacting with black confederates. The whites and blacks occupied equal-status roles. They were led to believe that they were competing against another team, and in the end they were told that they had won. The white subjects were less prejudiced at the end of the game than a control group. They also had highly favorable opinions of their black co-workers. Three subsequent studies employed the same game and varied the outcomes of the game and the competence of the participants. The subjects were white military servicemen each of whom worked with a white and a black confederate for about an hour and a half. One study found no race differences in attraction to group mates (Blanchard, Adelman, and Cook, 1975). A second study found that an incompetent black was liked less than a competent black, especially when the group failed. No differences were found in the evaluations of competent and incompetent whites (Blanchard, Weigel, and Cook, 1975). A related study done by a different set of investigators found that whites cooperating with a black confederate liked him less when the group failed than when it succeeded (Burnstein and McRaie, 1962). The black confederate was also perceived as being less competent when the group failed than when it succeeded. This finding suggests that failure amplifies negative evaluations of out-group members in cooperative groups (see also Gibbons *et al.*, 1981). The last study in the series by Cook found that when the white subjects were induced to help an incompetent member of the group, they liked this person more than when this person was helped by another member of the group. No race differences in liking were found in this study (Blanchard and Cook, 1976). In all three studies liking for group mates was greater after success than after failure.

A group of investigators at Johns Hopkins has developed and tested two cooperative-learning techniques (e.g., DeVries and Slavin, 1978; DeVries, Edwards, and Slavin, 1978). In one of these techniques, student-teams-achievement-divisions (STAD), students engage in peer teaching in small multiracial groups for four to ten weeks. They are tested in weekly quizzes, and their scores are compared with their own prior performances or with those of students at comparable achievement levels. Team scores are made available to all teams. In the second technique, teams-games-tournaments (TGT), the scoring system is based on academic tournaments between students of comparable achievement levels. An early study in this series found that when the scores were totaled within teams, there was greater cross-ethnic helping and more cross-ethnic friendships than when the students were scored individually. The students' outcomes (success or failure) were correlated with cross-racial behavior (DeVries and Edwards, 1974). In a review of three later studies using TGT, DeVries, Edwards, and Slavin (1978) reported that cross-racial friendship choices increased. Similar increases were also found in studies using STAD (Slavin, 1977, 1979). These positive effects occurred for both high- and low-achievement students and they endured into the next year in one study (Slavin, 1979). Another study found increases in cross-ethnic choices for whites but not for blacks (Slavin and Oickle, 1980). In a final study cross-racial interactions during free time in school were found to increase after participation in STAD (Slavin, 1977). As in the Aronson technique, there were no losses and some gains in academic achievement as a consequence of participating in the cooperative groups (DeVries and Slavin, 1978).

Another study that combined cooperation within groups with competition between groups has been done within the framework of the Johnsons program of research on cooperation (Johnson and Johnson, 1975). This study compared interethnic cooperation to a treatment involving competition within groups and to individualized instruction. It was done in a desegregated school (Cooper *et al.,* 1980). The students studied curricula in English, science, and geography for three hours a day for three weeks. The students in the cooperative groups developed one set of answers to material provided for each class hour, whereas other students developed their own answers. More cross-ethnic helping was displayed among the students in the cooperative groups than among competitive or individually graded students. Both cooperative and competitive groups had higher cross-ethnic friendship choices than the students in the individualistic condition. In another study in this research program fifth- and sixth-grade white students worked cooperatively or individually for ten weeks on a math curriculum (Johnson, Johnson, and Scott, 1978). At the end of this period students in the cooperative condition had more favorable attitudes toward working with students who were different, students who had different skin colors, or were from a foreign country than students in the individualized-instruction group. This effect was obtained in the absence of any ethnic heterogeneity in the cooperative groups, suggesting that cooperation rather than intergroup contact was responsible for the effect. Alternatively, the individualized instruction may have been alienating and may have reduced students' willingness to work with others.

A fourth program of research involving interracial small groups has been directed by Cohen (e.g., Cohen, 1980). The origin of this research effort lies in studies showing that white students dominate black students in interracial work groups (Cohen, 1972; Katz, Goldston, and Benjamin, 1958). In an initial attempt to offset these differences, Cohen and Roper (1972) trained black students to be competent at building a transistor radio. Two of these trained black students then worked together with two untrained whites, teaching them how to build the radio. This treatment produced equal initiation rates by blacks and whites on a subsequent decision-making game when the blacks were explicitly told that they would be competent team members when working with whites and the whites saw videotapes of the blacks successfully building the radio (cf. Lohman, 1970). The results of this study have been replicated using Canadian Indians and whites as subjects (Cook, 1974) and using Eastern and Western Jews in Israel (Cohen and Sharan, 1977).

These results have been interpreted within the framework of expectation states theory (Berger, Cohen, and Zelditch, 1972, Humphreys and Berger, 1981). According to this theory, people possess diffuse status characteristics (such as race, sex, and ethnicity) that are associated with generalized expectancies such as the belief that whites are more intellectually competent than blacks. In addition, people possess specific status characteristics such as skill at a specific task. Cohen's approach has been to counteract the expectancies created by diffuse characteristics (whites dominate blacks because they are expected to) with conflicting, specific status characteristics (blacks are pretrained to be superior to whites on a specific task). In a study designed explicitly to test this theory, white subjects made joint decisions with a partner about whom they knew the diffuse characteristic of race and the specific characteristic of competence (Webster and Driskell, 1978). Subjects agreed more with a competent black partner than with a partner of undefined competence, who they assumed was white. The specific status reduced but did not eliminate the effect of the diffuse status.

In another study by Cohen the expectation-training technique was compared with a cooperative-learning program (Cohen, Lockheed, and Lohman, 1976). The setting for this study was an interracial summer school. Pretrained competent black students taught whites to do four different tasks, and again the white students saw videotapes showing that the blacks were competent. Both treatments led to equal rates of speech initiation by blacks and whites in a subsequent group decision game. This equal-status behavior endured for the five additional weeks of the summer school.

An earlier study by Katz and Cohen (1962) suggests that increases in the social influence of blacks in cooperative decision-making groups may occur at the cost of decreased liking. They found that blacks who were given assertiveness training became more influential in interracial cooperative decision groups than those who hadn't received this training. However, white students liked the blacks who had received assertiveness training less than the blacks who had not. Possibly, when blacks violate whites' expectancies by behaving in competent ways, they are disliked, at least in the short term.

The general findings of these studies are quite clear: Cooperation in multiethnic groups improves intergroup relations. No reports of negative results have appeared, while many studies report a mixture of no results and positive results, and a few report almost entirely positive results. These positive results include favorable changes in attitudes toward team members and out-groups, increased interethnic helping, decreased interethnic conflict, and increased participation and influence by minority group members. The aspects of the situation that these techniques share are strong normative and institutional support for intergroup contact, positive contact experiences, interdependence of team members, an individualizing of out-group members, longer durations than

laboratory studies, settings with high ecological validity, and, with the exception of expectancy training, equal status within the groups. The differences in the techniques raise a number of interesting questions about the optimal conditions for improving intergroup relations by using cooperative groups.

Early theorists of the effects of cooperation stressed the importance of interdependence with respect to ends as well as means. One of the techniques reviewed, the jigsaw classroom, produced favorable effects without interdependence of ends. One advantage of eliminating interdependence of ends is that it may circumvent the negative effects of differences in competence within the group. These negative effects include resentment of low-competence students for lowering team outcomes and the confirmation of negative stereotypes when negative expectancies for minority student performance are confirmed. The jigsaw classroom was not successful in eliminating negative evaluations of low-competence group members, however (Rosenfield, Stephan, and Lucker, 1981). The reason was probably that the less competent students were perceived as having hindered the more competent students in their attempts to learn the assigned materials. This negative effect apparently was not counteracted by the opportunity to help less competent students, which should have increased liking (Blanchard and Cook, 1976).

Two of the other techniques attempted to overcome the negative effects of competence differences in other ways. In STAD and TGT the students' contributions to their team's scores depend on the students' scores relative to others of comparable ability or to their own prior scores. In the expectancy-training technique the students who are expected to be less competent are trained to be more competent than the other team members. However, as the Webster and Driskell (1978) study indicated, this training may not completely compensate for the negative effects of low perceived competence. Clearly differential competence is a greater problem when the team does poorly than when it does well. This conclusion is consistent with the finding from the laboratory studies indicating that favorable outcomes are important in creating positive intragroup and intergroup attitudes. The majority of the multiethnic cooperative techniques do not try to ensure positive outcomes. One of the few studies that did ensure success produced favorable changes toward the out-group in general, a rare result in this literature (Cook, 1970). In one study where the participants' outcomes ranged along the continuum from failure to success, no changes in general prejudice toward out-group members were obtained (Weigel, Wiser, and Cook, 1975). In other studies it is difficult to determine if improved intergroup relations extended beyond teammates in the cooperative groups to include other members of the out-group.

This observation raises the question of how to promote the generalization of favorable changes beyond the out-group members on the cooperative team. Cohen (1979) changed the composition of the teams from session to session but did not measure attitudes toward out-group members, so the success of this promising technique cannot be determined. A lack of competition between teams would also seem more likely to promote generalization than team competition, although most of the techniques reviewed have obtained positive results by using team competition.

The complexity of this literature makes it difficult to draw firm conclusions about what aspects of cooperative intergroup contact promote favorable relations. However, we can still attempt to formulate a tentative list of variables that has considerable theoretical and empirical support:

1. Cooperation within groups should be maximized and competition between groups should be minimized.

2. Members of the in-group and the out-group should be of equal status both within and outside the contact situation.

3. Similarity of group members on nonstatus dimensions (beliefs, values, etc.) appears to be desirable.

4. Differences in competence should be avoided.

5. The outcomes should be positive.

6. Strong normative and institutional support for the contact should be provided.

7. The intergroup contact should have the potential to extend beyond the immediate situation.

8. Individuation of group members should be promoted.

9. Nonsuperficial contact (e.g., mutual disclosure of information) should be encouraged.

10. The contact should be voluntary.

11. Positive effects are likely to correlate with the duration of the contact.

12. The contact should occur in a variety of contexts with a variety of in-group and out-group members.

13. Equal numbers of in-group and out-group members should be used.

As Williams (1977) noted of a similar list, "This is a very long list, but long as it is, it is surely incomplete" (p. 267).

APPROACHES BASED ON THERAPEUTIC AND GROUP INTERACTION TECHNIQUES

A variety of other attempts have been made to reduce prejudice in group interaction settings. Some studies have employed techniques adapted from group therapy; others have employed group discussion and other types of structured interactions. Most of these techniques have been successful. In contrast to the subject populations used in the study of cooperative groups, the majority of these studies have been done with adults. An early study examined the effects of training in client-centered counseling on prejudice (Haimowitz and Haimowitz, 1950). The training lasted for six weeks and produced more acceptance of racial and national groups on a social distance measure. A study that examined the effects of group therapy on hospitalized mental patients also found reductions in prejudice (Pearl, 1955). These reductions may have been mediated by improvements in the subjects' self-concepts (Pearl, 1954). In a later study by Carkhuff and Banks (1970) white teachers and black parents received communcations training in which they role-played helper and helpee roles. Improvements in crossracial communication skills were found for both groups. Biracial groups of teachers were given ninety-six hours of training in promoting school desegregation in a study conducted by Robinson and Preston (1976). Sensitivity training, films, seminars, and group discussions of topics related to prejudice and discrimination comprised the curriculum. The interracial behaviors and racial attitudes of the white teachers improved as a result of the training, and these changes were sustained over a period of sixteen months. The behavior and attitudes of the black teachers did not change as a result of the program, although sixteen months after the training blacks who had participated did have less negative stereotypes than blacks who had not participated.

Sensitivity training was also examined in a study by Rubin (1967). The multiracial sensitivity-training groups met for two weeks and were successful in reducing prejudice. The data also indicated that increases in self-acceptance were associated with reductions in prejudice. A study using a group process treatment with biracial groups of children increased cross-racial sociometric choices after two and a half months (Williams *et al.,* 1971). However, this increase was not significantly greater than one that occurred for the control group. Small sample sizes could account for the lack of significance. A somewhat similar nontherapy-oriented group process treatment reduced prejudice in groups of adults (Mann, 1959). The subjects were black and white students in a graduate seminar where standard course material was discussed four times a week for three weeks. A six-week intergroup relations workshop was also successful in reducing prejudice among adults (Levinson, 1954; Levinson and Shermerhorn, 1951). The workshop consisted of lectures and discussions of prejudice and discrimination plus intergroup interaction and recreational activities. The participants represented a variety of racial and religious groups.

The possibility that discussion groups can have adverse effects on prejudice has been explored in a study by Myers and Bishop (1970). In this study group discussion among low-prejudice subjects led to reductions in prejudice compared with prediscussion measures, but discussions among high-prejudice subjects led to increases in prejudice. Since most attempts to change prejudice are presumably directed at prejudiced people, these findings raise an important issue concerning the content of discussion. If the group members are allowed to focus on each other's relatively high levels of prejudice, this focus may support and amplify the prejudices of the individual group members. The probability of such negative effects occurring is likely to be reduced when the group leader disapproves of prejudice or when the content of the discussions is focused on providing positive information about other groups.

A number of promising group techniques have been developed by social scientists concerned with the resolution of ongoing conflicts between contending groups (see Hill, 1982, for a review). These techniques bring representatives of contending groups into face-to-face contact to discuss the nature of the conflict. Social scientists typically serve as group leaders. The participants are enjoined to take an analytical perspective toward the conflict and to learn how the conflict is perceived by the other group. These groups have been used among parties to the Cyprus conflict (Burton, 1969), the Somali conflict (Doob, 1970), the conflict in Northern Ireland (Doob and Foltz, 1973), the Middle East conflict (Kelman

and Cohen, 1979), and the Pakistani conflict (Cohen *et al.,* 1977). Unfortunately, no empirical data were gathered from these workshops that can be used to measure their success. Other human relations–oriented workshops have been developed for use with whites in the United States, but they also do not appear to have been empirically tested (Baptiste and Baptiste, 1979; Fromkin and Sherwood, 1976; Gabelko and Michealis, 1981). An exception is a workshop developed by Katz (1978). This two-week workshop, which focuses on confronting whites with the discrepancies between the myths and reality of American racial ideologies, has been found to reduce prejudice (Katz and Ivey, 1977).

Several studies have examined therapeutic techniques designed for use with individuals rather than groups. In one study white subjects read materials designed to give them insight into the operation of scapegoating, projection, and compensation as sources of prejudice (Katz, Sarnoff, and McClintock, 1956). This treatment was compared with a condition in which subjects were given information designed to overcome misinformation as a cause of prejudice. Although no immediate changes in prejudice resulted in response to either treatment, a significant decrease in prejudice for subjects in the insight condition was obtained on a six-week follow-up test. Subjects who were moderate or low in ego defensiveness were most likely to have changed (see also Katz, McClintock, and Sarnoff, 1957; Stotland, Katz, and Patchen, 1959).

Another study employing an individually oriented change technique was done by Sappington (1976). In this study systematic desensitization was used to reduce the anxiety of prejudiced white subjects concerning interracial interaction. Subjects undergoing this three-week treatment rated Negroes more positively after treatment than before; a control group did not change.

APPROACHES BASED ON LEARNING THEORIES

Although the idea that intergroup cognitions and behavior can be modified by reinforcing positive cognitions and behavior and punishing negative ones seems obvious and compelling, empirical research on this idea has been limited. The majority of this work has been done by Williams and his colleagues (e.g., Williams and Morland, 1976). The procedure that they have used most frequently consists of presenting young white children with biracial photographs and asking them which person has specific positive qualities (e.g., smart, kind, nice) or negative qualities (e.g., mean, stupid, dirty). The children are reinforced for attributing positive qualities to blacks or negative qualities to whites and punished for attributing negative qualities to blacks or positive qualities to whites. Under these conditions children rapidly modify their typical pattern of attributing positive qualities to whites and negative qualities to blacks (Edwards and Williams, 1970; McMurtry and Williams, 1972). These modified responses generalize to new sets of materials. A subsequent study indicated that these modifications appear to gradually shift back toward the typical prejudiced pattern so that one year after treatment they are midway between the pretest scores and the scores immediately after they have been treated (Williams, *et al.,* 1975). The racial bias of blacks, who also tend to attribute positive qualities to whites and negative qualities to blacks on the biracial photograph test, has also been successfully modified in one study (Spencer and Horowitz, 1973). Modifying children's preferences for the color white has effects similar to those of modifying race preferences (McAdoo, 1970; Shanahan, 1972; Spencer and Horowitz, 1973; Traynham, 1974; Williams and Edwards, 1969; for an exception, see Katz and Zalk, 1978). In two studies Katz (1973; Katz and Zalk, 1978) has found that a learning task in which children learn to label faces of blacks and whites by name reduces prejudice.

A study using white adult subjects found that verbal conditioning of positive adjectives in response to pictures of blacks increased the use of positive adjectives and decreased the use of negative adjectives (Primac, 1980). However, when these subjects were given a posttest in which no conditioning took place, the frequency of negative adjectives was as high as during the pretest. The experimental and control groups all displayed less prejudice at the posttest period, indicating that the treatment had no effect on attitudes.

A study by Parish and Fleetwood (1975) used classical conditioning of responses to the colors black and white to modify prejudice. Positive words were associated with the color black. This procedure led to unbiased attributions of positive qualities to blacks and whites on a biracial photograph test when the conditioning technique was used repeatedly (eight sessions). Two other studies using less extensive classical conditioning training procedures have been unsuccessful in modifying behavior (Collins, 1972; Parish, 1972).

While these studies suggest that classical and instrumental conditioning can modify racial preferences, the techniques that have been employed are not very practical for common use. In addition, these studies give no information on the relationship of the observed changes in attitudes to changes in behavior. Apparently, only one study attempted to modify behavior rather than attitudes (Hauserman, Walen, and Behling, 1973). In this study black children in a desegregated school were reinforced for sitting with "new friends" at lunch. This behavior resulted in increased interracial interaction in the cafeteria and for the free period following lunch. However, the interracial behaviors dropped to baseline levels soon after reinforcements ceased. A number of studies have investigated other techniques of modifying prejudice and discrimination in natural settings, but most have not relied explicitly on learning theory.

EDUCATIONAL TECHNIQUES, ROLE TAKING, AND PROPAGANDA

One of the most widely advocated techniques of modifying intergroup relations is the use of courses or segments of courses on intergroup relations in school settings. While studies examining the effects of such courses have a long history, the total number of studies appears to be quite small. These studies suffer from a number of limitations. Most do not have adequate control groups, and alternative explanations for positive results, especially the effects of demand characteristics, often exist. The majority of these studies concern courses that are of short duration, and only rarely do they include follow-up data that could be used to determine their long-term effects. Few of the studies compare alternative techniques, so we have little information on what types of courses and course materials are most effective. Even fewer studies include measures of behavior. Finally, almost all of the studies have examined prejudice toward blacks among whites, which limits the generalizability of the results (cf. Stephan and Stephan, 1984).

Williams (1947), in a review of the early work involving educational techniques, found that six of eleven studies had obtained evidence of positive changes in intergroup attitudes. None of the studies found evidence of negative changes. Subsequent studies reveal a similar pattern. Positive changes have been observed in seven studies. Litcher and Johnson (1969) found that the use of a multiethnic second-grade reader decreased social distance between whites and blacks in a sample of white students. Leslie, Leslie, and Penfield (1972) found that prejudice toward blacks decreased among sixth-grade white students exposed to a multimedia classroom curriculum and intergroup contacts. However, this group did not improve significantly more than their classmates who were exposed to presentations on intergroup relations by students in the experimental condition. The positive changes in attitudes for this "control" condition were probably due to a combination of the effects of the presentations and interacting with their peers in the experimental group. The use of multiethnic school curricula led to reductions in the prejudices of four-year-old black students in a study by Yawkey and Blackwell (1974). Also, Yawkey (1973) found that a four-week multiethnic curricula reduced the prejudices of seven-year-old white students.

Slavin and Madden (1979), in a study of fifty-one desegregated high schools, found that the use of multiethnic readers was unrelated to white and black prejudice. Classroom discussions of race were related to lower levels of prejudice for whites but not for blacks. In this study the factor that was most closely related to positive race relations was working together with members of the other ethnic group. A study applying the cultural assimilator technique (Fiedler, Mitchell, and Triandis, 1971) to relations between groups within a culture has been conducted by Weldon and colleagues (1975). In this study white subjects studied a self-paced learning module designed to acquaint them with the values, norms, and perceptions of disadvantaged blacks. These subjects stereotyped blacks less after completing the training than subjects in an untrained control group. Glass and Trent (1982) found that a two-week, one-hour-a-day learning unit devoted to providing information about aging was successful in bringing about positive changes in attitudes toward older people.

Findings of no differences due to educational interventions have been found in three studies. Greenberg, Pierson, and Sherman (1957) found that a single lecture, debate, or discussion designed to reduce prejudice did not. Best and associates (1975) designed a twelve-hour race-related curriculum for white kindergarten students. This curriculum had no effect on racial attitudes. An eight-week curriculum in which white junior high school students read and prepared reports about different ethnic groups and received supplementary materials in a variety of media did not have any effect on prejudice (Lessing and Clarke, 1976).

Comparing the treatments that were effective with those that were not produces few generalizations about what techniques are effective in changing attitudes. The result is a large and unfortunate gap in our knowledge of techniques of changing intergroup cognitions and behavior. The use of ethnic-oriented curricula, presentations of historical information, and other classroom educational techniques designed to reduce prejudice is widespread. As the studies reviewed above indicate, we have little information concerning how effective these techniques are. Adding to this problem is the fact that the studies that have been done have employed such limited and unimaginative treatments. A vast literature on attitude change exists, but it has rarely been applied to empirical studies of prejudice, although excellent discussions of such applications do exist (e.g., Williams, 1977). Perhaps in no other area of intergroup relations could such valuable information be obtained with so little effort as would result from a systematic evaluation of techniques that are currently being employed in classrooms around the country.

In a simulation game involving role playing of blacks by white high school students, De Kock (1969) found that whites became more tolerant in racial attitudes. A study with white kindergarten children also found reductions in prejudice when the children were given training in role taking (Hohn, 1973). In this study the role taking was not directly related to race, although the children were asked to take the role of a poor person. This study suggests that at a very young age perspective taking can help children see the world in a less egocentric and apparently ethnocentric manner.

In another study employing a role-playing procedure Culbertson (1957) found that having white college students role-play an advocate of integrated housing led to more favorable attitudes toward integration and toward blacks. Observers of these psychodramas also changed their attitudes in a favorable direction but not as much as the role players. If we assume that these subjects were initially opposed to integration, then this technique may be drawing on the powers of counterattitudinal arguments to create attitude change. A study that demonstrates this effect more clearly has been done by Carlson (1956). The topic was also integrated housing, and Carlson found that formulating arguments supporting integration led to positive attitude changes in a sample of presumably white college students. These results were replicated by Peak and Morrison (1958).

One reason that counterattitudinal advocacy is effective is that it creates a discrepancy between the individuals' prior attitudes and their current expressions of opposing attitudes. This conflict can be resolved by modifying the prior attitudes. A similar process may be operating in the prejudice reduction procedure developed by Rokeach (1971). In this technique white students rank the values of freedom and equality among sixteen other values. The discrepancy between their rankings of these two concepts is pointed out to them, and the relationship between these values and support for civil rights is discussed. Most students are confronted with the fact that they rank equality lower than freedom and that doing so is related to not actively participating in civil rights issues. One and a half years later students in this condition of the study were more likely to have participated in the NAACP than subjects in a control group who only filled out the value and attitude scales. The students in the experimental condition also ranked freedom and equality higher in their value systems after the treatment.

Williams's (1947) review of the early literature on the effects of propaganda on intergroup relations indicates that in the short run most types of propaganda do produce changes in prejudice. He cites nine studies, seven of which found reductions in prejudice as a result of exposure to oral presentations, written materials, or movies. This knowledge base does not appear to have been greatly expanded by subsequent studies of intergroup relations. Most studies of movies, television, and written communications designed to reduce prejudice indicate that these techniques can be successful (Davis and Fine, 1975; Goldberg, 1956; Kraus, 1960; Mitnick and McGinnies, 1958; Rosen, 1948), although some studies have obtained mixed results or no differences from the use of propaganda techniques (Cooper and Dinerman, 1951; Gardiner, 1972; Rath and Trager, 1948).

As was the case with the curriculum studies, most of the favorable results in these studies could be attributed to demand characteristics. These studies also suffer from most of the other limitations of the curriculum studies, a failure to exploit the vast literature in related areas, lack of long-term follow-up data, little behavioral data, and a concentration on the prejudices of whites toward blacks.

The most remarkable aspect of these studies of changes in intergroup cognitions and behavior is the relative ease with which changes can be brought about. A variety of approaches to reducing prejudice, stereotyping, and discrimination have been reviewed, and most have been shown to be effective. As methodologically flawed and theoretically weak as these studies are, they clearly indicate that it is not necessarily difficult or expensive to change intergroup cognitions and behavior. Techniques

employing intergroup interaction and discussions, vicarious exposure to out-groups, propaganda concerning outgroups, and exposure of value inconsistencies that promote prejudice can all be implemented under conditions that would improve intergroup relations in situations such as schools, recreational settings, and some work settings.

CONCLUDING NOTE

This chapter has been concerned with what social psychologists have learned about intergroup relations. Our knowledge has increased greatly in the past 17 years. But large gaps still exist in our understanding of how information about social groups is processed. In particular, little work has been done on the pivotal role of organizational structures such as schemata, scripts, and prototypes. The ecological validity of much of the work in this area is low, and it remains to be determined when phenomena such as illusory correlation, the dominance of individuating information, in-group–out-group bias, and the ultimate attribution error operate in everyday social interactions. The study of the relationship between intergroup cognitions—other than prejudice and stereotypes—and overt behavior has hardly begun. Theoretical models that integrate the information-processing approach with the study of intergroup behavior are much needed. We also have too little information on what techniques are the most effective in modifying intergroup relations and the processes underlying these changes.

Much has been accomplished. Much remains to be done.

REFERENCES

Abelson, R. P. (1975). Concepts for representing mundane reality in plans. In D. G. Bobrow, and A. Collins (Eds.), *Representation and understanding. Studies in cognitive science.* New York: Academic Press. Pp. 273–309.

Ajzen, I. (1977). Intuitive theories of events and the effects of base-rate information on prediction. *J. Pers. soc. Psychol., 35,* 303–314.

Ajzen, I., and M. Fishbein (1975). A Bayesian analysis of attribution processes. *Psychol. Bull., 82,* 261–277.

–––––– (1980). *Understanding attitudes and predicting behavior.* Englewood Cliffs, N.J.: Prentice-Hall.

Allen, V. L., and D. A. Wilder (1975). Categorization, belief similarity, and intergroup discrimination. *J. Pers. soc. Psychol., 32,* 971–977.

–––––– (1979). Group categorization and attribution of belief similarity. *Small group Behav., 10,* 73–80.

Allport, F. H. et al. (1953). The effects of segregation and the consequences of desegregation: a social science statement. *Minn. Law Rev., 37,* 429–440.

Allport, G. W. (1954). *The nature of prejudice.* Cambridge, Mass.: Addison-Wesley.

Allport, G. W., and B. M. Kramer (1946). *Some roots of prejudice. J. Psych., 22,* 9–39.

Alper, T. G., and S. J. Korchen (1951). Memory for socially relevant material. *J. abnorm. soc. Psychol. 47,* 25–37.

Amir, Y. (1969). Contact hypothesis in ethnic relations. *Psychol. Bull., 71,* 319–342.

_____ (1976). The role of intergroup contact in changes of prejudice and ethnic relations. In P. A. Katz (Ed.), *Towards the elimination of racism.* New York: Pergamon Press.

Anderson, J., and R. Hastie (1974). Individuation and reference in memory: proper names and definite descriptions. *Cognit. Psychol., 6,* 495–514.

Anderson, J. R. (1980). *Cognitive psychology and its implications.* San Francisco: Freeman.

Anderson, J. R., and G. H. Bower (1973). *Human associative memory.* Washington, D.C.: Winston and Sons.

Aronson, E., and J. M. Carlsmith (1962). Performance expectancy as a determinant of actual performance. *J. abnorm. soc. Psychol., 65,* 178–182.

Aronson, E., and B. W. Golden (1962). The effect of relevant and irrelevant aspects of communicator credibility on opinion change. *J. Pers., 30,* 135–146.

Aronson, E., and N. Osherow (1980). Cooperation, prosocial behavior, and academic performance: Experiments in the desegregated classroom. In L. Bickman (Ed.), *Applied social psychology annual.* Beverly Hills, Calif.: Sage.

Aronson, E., C. Stephan, J. Sikes, N. Blaney, and M. Snapp (1978). *The jigsaw classroom.* Beverly Hills, Calif.: Sage.

Ashmore, R. D. (1970). In B. Collins, *Social psychology.* Reading, Mass.: Addison-Wesley.

Bandura, A., D. Ross, and S. A. Ross (1963). Imitation of film-mediated aggressive models. *J. abnorm. soc. Psychol., 66,* 3–11.

Baptiste, H. P., Jr., and M. L. Baptiste (1979). *Developing the multicultural process in classroom instruction.* Washington, D.C.: University Press.

Baumeister, R. F., J. Cooper, and B. A. Skib (1979). Inferior performance as a selective response to expectancy: taking a dive to make a point. *J. Pers. soc. Psychol., 37,* 424–432.

Becker, H. S. (1963). *Outsiders.* New York: Free Press.

Becker, J. F., and E. E. Heaton, Jr. (1967). The election of Senator Edward A. Brooke. *Pub. Opin. Quart., 31,* 346–358.

Belleza, F. S., and G. H. Bower (1981). Person stereotypes and memory for people. *J. Pers. soc. Psychol., 41,* 856–865.

Berg, K. R. (1966). Ethnic attitudes and agreement with a Negro person. *J. Pers. soc. Psychol., 4* (2), 215–220.

Berger, J., B. P. Cohen, M. J. Zelditch (1972). Status conceptions and social interactions. *Amer. soc. Rev., 37,* 241–255.

Berkowitz, L. (1959). Anti-semitism and the displacement of aggression. *J. appl. soc. Psychol., 59,* 182–187.

_____ (1960). The judgmental process in personality functioning. *Psychol. Rev. 67,* 142–150.

Berman, J. S., and D. A. Kenny (1976). Correlational bias in observer ratings. *J. Pers. soc. Psychol., 34,* 263–273.

Best, D. L., S. C. Smith, D. J. Graves, and J. E. Williams (1975). The modification of racial bias in preschool children. *J. exp. Child Psychol., 20,* 193–205.

Billig, M. (1973). Normative communication in a minimal intergroup situation. *Europ. J. soc. Psychol., 3,* 339–343.

_____ (1976). *Social psychology and intergroup relations.* London: Academic Press.

Billig, M., and H. Tajfel (1973). Social categorization and similarity of intergroup behavior. *Europ. J. soc. Psychol., 3,* 27–52.

Blake, R. R., and J. S. Mouton (1961). Reactions to the intergroup competition under win-lose conditions. *Management Sci., 7,* 420–435.

Blalock, H. M., Jr. (1967). *Toward a theory of minority-group relations.* New York: Wiley.

Blanchard, F., L. Adelman, and S. Cook (1975). The effect of group success and failure upon interpersonal attraction in cooperating interracial groups. *J. Pers. soc. Psychol., 31,* 1020–1030.

Blanchard, F., and S. Cook (1976). Effect of helping a less competent member of a cooperating interracial group on the development of interpersonal attraction. *J. Pers. soc. Psychol., 34,* 1245–1255.

Blanchard, F. A., R. H. Weigel, and S. W. Cook (1975). The effect of relative competence of group members upon interpersonal attraction in cooperating interracial groups. *J. Pers. soc. Psychol., 32,* 519–530.

Blaney, N., C. Stephan, D. Rosenfield, E. Aronson, and J. Sikes (1977). Interdependence in the classroom: A field study. *J. educ. Psychol., 69,* 121–128.

Bransford, J. D., and M. K. Johnson (1973). Considerations of some problems of comprehension. In W. G. Chase (Ed.), *Visual information processing.* New York. Academic Press.

Branthwaite, A., and J. E. Jones (1975). Fairness and discrimination: English versus Welsh. *Europ. J. soc. Psychol., 5,* 323–338.

Bray, D. W. (1950). The prediction of behavior from two attitude scales. *J. appl. soc. Psychol., 45,* 64–84.

_____ (1979a).The role of ethnocentrism in intergroup conflict. In W. G. Austin, and S. Worchel (Eds.), *The social psychology of intergroup relations.* Monterey, Calif.: Brooks/Cole.

Brewer, M. B. (1979b).In-group bias in the minimal intergroup situation: a cognitive-motivational analysis. *Psychol. Bull., 86,* 307–324.

Brewer, M. B., and D. T. Campbell (1976). *Ethnocentrism and intergroup attitudes: East African evidence.* New York: Halsted.

Brewer, M. B., V. Dull, and L. Lui (1981). Perceptions of the elderly: Stereotypes as prototypes. *J. Pers. soc. Psychol., 41,* 656–670.

Brewer, M. B., and M. Silver (1978). Ingroup bias as a function of task characteristics. *Europ. J. soc. Psychol., 8,* 393–400.

Bridgeman, D. (1977). *The influence of cooperative, interdependent learning on role taking and moral reasoning: a theoretical and empirical field study with fifth grade students.* Unpublished Ph.D. dissertation. Santa Cruz: University of California.

Brigham, J. C. (1971). Ethnic stereotypes. *Psychol. Bull., 76*, 15–38.

Brigham, J. C., and P. Barkowitz (1978). Do "they all look alike?" The effect of race, sex, experience, and attitudes on the ability to recognize faces. *J. appl. soc. Psychol., 8*, 306–318.

Brown, R. U. (1954). Mass phenomena. In G. Lindzey (Ed.), *Handbook of social psychology*. Vol. 2. Reading, Mass.: Addison-Wesley.

Bruner, J. S. (1973). *Beyond the information given*. New York: Norton.

Bruner, J. S., and C. C. Goodman (1947). Value and need as organizing factors in perception. *J. abnorm. soc. Psychol., 42*, 33–44.

Bruner, J. S., and H. V. Perlmutter (1957). Compatriot and foreigner: a study of impression formation in three countries. *J. abnorm. soc. Psychol., 55*, 253–260.

Burnstein, E., and A. V. McRae (1962). Some effects of shared threat and prejudice in racially mixed groups. *J. abnorm. soc. Psychol., 64*, 257–263.

Burton, J. W. (1969). *Conflict and communication*. New York: Free Press.

Byrne, D. (1961). Interpersonal attraction and attitude similarity. *J. abnorm. soc. Psychol., 62*, 713–715.

Byrne, D., and D. Andres (1964). Prejudice and interpersonal expectancies. *J. Negro Educ., 33*, 441–445.

Campbell, D. T. (1965). Ethnocentrism and other altruistic motives. In D. Levine (Ed.), *Nebraska symposium on motivation*. Lincoln: University of Nebraska Press.

Cantor, G. N. (1972). Effects of familiarization on children's ratings of pictures of whites and blacks. *Child Development, 43*, 1219–1229.

Cantor, N., and W. Mischel (1977). Traits as prototypes: effects on recognition memory. *J. Pers. soc. Psychol., 35*, 38–48.

——— (1979). Prototypicality and personality: effects on free recall and personality impressions. *J. Res. Pers., 13*, 187–205.

Carkhuff, R. R., and G. Banks (1970). Training as a preferred mode of facilitating relations between races and generations. *J. counsel. Psychol., 17*, 413–418.

Carlson, E. R. (1956). Attitude change through modification of attitude structure. *J. abnorm. soc. Psychol., 52*, 256–261.

Carver, C. S., F. X. Gibbons, W. G. Stephan, D. C. Glass, and I. Katz (1979). Ambivalence and evaluative response amplification. *Bull. Psychon. Soc., 13*, 50–52.

Carver, C. S., D. C. Glass, M. C. Snyder, and I. Katz (1977). Favorable evaluations of stigmatized others. *Pers. soc. Psychol. Bull., 3*, 232–235.

Chance, J. E., A. G. Goldstein, (1981). Depth of processing in response to own- and other-race faces. *Pers. soc. Psychol. Bull., 7*, 475–480.

Chance, J. E., A. G. Goldstein, and L. McBride (1975). Differential experience and recognition memory of faces. *J. soc. Psychol., 97*, 243–253.

Chapman, L. J., and J. P. Chapman (1969). Illusory correlation as an obstacle to the use of valid psychodiagnostic signs. *J. abnorm. Psychol., 74*, 271–280.

Clark, L. F., and S. B. Woll (1981). Stereotype biases: a reconstructive analysis of their role in reconstructive memory. *J. Pers. soc. Psychol.: Attitudes soc. Cognit., 41*, 1064–1072.

Coates, B. (1972). White adult behavior toward black and white children. *Child Development, 43*, 143–154.

Cohen, E. G. (1972). Interracial interaction disability. *Hum. Relat., 25*, 9–24.

——— (1979). *Design and redesign of the desegregated school: problems of status, power and conflict*. Unpublished manuscript. School of Education, Stanford University.

——— (1980). *A multi-ability approach to the integrated classroom*. Paper presented at the American Psychological Association, Montreal, Canada.

Cohen, E. G., M. E. Lockheed, and M. R. Lohman (1976). The center for interracial cooperation: a field experiment. *Sociol. Educ., 49*, 47–58.

Cohen, E. G., and S. Roper (1972). Modification of interracial interaction disability: an application of status characteristic theory. *Amer. Sociological Rev., 37*, 643–657.

Cohen, E. G., and S. Sharan (1977). *Modifying status relations in Israeli youth: an application of expectation states theory*. Paper presented at the annual meeting of the American Education Research Association, San Francisco.

Cohen, S. P., H. C. Kelman, F. D. Miller, and B. L. Smith (1977). Evolving intergroup techniques for conflict resolution: an Israeli-Palestinian pilot workshop. *J. soc. Issues, 33*, 165–189.

Collins, J. L. (1972). The effect of differential frequency of color adjective pairings on the subsequent retaining of color meaning and racial attitude in preschool children. Master's thesis. East Tennessee State University.

Commins, B., and J. Lockwood (1978). The effects on intergroup relations of mixing Roman Catholics and Protestants: An experimental investigation. *Europ. J. soc. Psychol., 8*, 383–386.

Cook, S. W. (1969). Motives in a conceptual analysis of attitude-related behavior. In W. J. Arnold, and D. Levine (Eds.), *Nebraska symposium on motivation*. Lincoln: Univ. of Nebraska Press.

——— (1970). Motives in a conceptual analysis of attitude-related behavior. In W. J. Arnold, and D. Levine (Eds.), *Nebraska symposium on motivation*. Vol. 18. Lincoln: Univ. of Nebraska Press.

——— (1978). Interpersonal and attitudinal outcomes in cooperating interracial groups. *J. Res. Develop. Educ., 12*, 97–113.

Cook, S. W., and C. Selltiz (1964). A multiple-indicator approach to attitude measurement. *Psychol. Bull., 62*, 36–55.

Cook, T. (1974). Producing equal status interaction between Indian and White boys in British Columbia. Unpublished doctoral dissertation. Stanford University.

Cooper, E., and H. Dinerman (1951). Analysis of the film, "Don't be a Sucker": a study in communication. *Publ. Opin. Quart. 15*, 243–264.

Cooper, L., D. Johnson, R. Johnson, and F. Wilderson (1980). The effects of cooperative, competitive and individualistic experiences on interpersonal attraction among heterogeneous peers. *J. soc. Psychol., 111*, 243–252.

Costrich, N., J. Feinstein, L. Kidder, J. Maracek, and L. Pascale (1975). When stereotypes hurt: three studies of penalties for sex-role reversals. *J. exp. soc. Psychol., 11,* 520–530.

Crosby, F., S. Bromley, and L. Saxe (1980). Recent unobtrusive studies of black and white discrimination and prejudice: a literature review. *Psychol. Bull., 87,* 546–563.

Culbertson, F. M. (1957). Modification of an emotionally held attitude through role playing. *J. abnorm. soc. Psychol., 54,* 230–233.

Darley, J. M., and E. Berscheid (1967). Increased liking caused by the anticipation of personal contact. *Hum. Relat., 20,* 29–40.

Darroch, R. K. (1971). Attitudinal variables and perceived group norms as predictors of behavioral intentions and behavior in the signing of photographic releases. Doctoral Dissertation, University of Illinois.

Datta, L., E. Schaefer, and M. Davis (1968). Sex and scholastic aptitude as variables in teachers' ratings of the adjustment and classroom behavior of Negro and other seventh-grade students. *J. educ. Psychol., 59,* 94–101.

Davis, E. E., and M. Fine (1975). The effects of the findings of the U.S. National Advisory Commission on Civil Disorders: an experimental study of attitude change. *Hum. Relat., 28,* 209–227.

Davis, E. E., and H. C. Triandis (1971). An experimental study of black-white negotiations. *J. appl. soc. Psychol., 1* (3), 240–262.

DeFleur, M. L., and F. R. Westie (1958). Verbal attitudes and overt acts: an experiment on the salience of attitudes. *Amer. Sociological Rev., 23,* 667–673.

DeFriese, G. H., and W. S. Ford (1969). Verbal attitudes, overt acts, and the influence of social constraint in interracial behavior. *Soc. Prob., 16,* 493–505.

DeKock, D. (1969). Simulations and change in racial attitudes. *Soc. Educ.,* 181–183.

Deschamps, J. C., and W. Doise (1978). Crossed category memberships in intergroup relations. In H. Tajfel (Ed.), *Differentiation between social groups.* New York: Academic Press.

Deutsch, M. (1949). The directions of behavior: a field-theoretical approach to the understanding of inconsistencies. *J. soc. Issues, V,* 43–49.

Deutscher, I. (1966). Words and deeds: social science and social policy. *Soc. Prob., 13,* 235–254.

DeVries, D. L., and K. J. Edwards (1974). Student teams and learning games: their effects on cross-race and cross-sex interaction. *J. educ. Psychol., 66,* 741–749.

DeVries, D. L., K. J. Edwards, and R. E. Slavin (1978). Biracial learning teams and race relations in the classroom: four field experiments using teams-games-tournaments. *J. educ. Psychol., 70,* 356–362.

DeVries, D. L., and R. E. Slavin (1978). Teams-games-tournament (TGT): review of ten classroom experiments. *J. Res. Develop. Educ., 12,* 28–38.

Dewhirst, J. R., and J. S. Berman (1978). Social judgments of spurious and causal relations between attributes and outcomes. *J. exp. soc. Psychol., 14,* 313–325.

Dion, K. L. (1973). Cohesiveness as a determinant of ingroup-outgroup bias. *J. Pers. soc. Psychol., 28,* 163–171.

––––––– (1975). Women's reactions to discrimination from members of the same or opposite sex. *J. Res. Pers., 9,* 294–306.

––––––– (1979). Intergroup conflict and intragroup cohesiveness. In W. Austin, and S. Worchel, *The social psychology of intergroup relations.* Monterey, Calif.: Brooks/Cole.

Dion, K. L., and B. M. Earn (1975). The phenomenology of being a target of prejudice. *J. Pers. soc. Psychol., 32,* 944–950.

Doise, W. (1969). Intergroup relations and polarization of individual and collective judgments. *J. Pers. soc. Psychol., 12,* 136–143.

––––––– (1976). L'articulation psychosociologique et les relations entre groupes. Brussels: De Baeck.

Doise, W., G. Csepeli, H. D. Cann, C. Gouge, K. Larson, and A. Ostell (1972). An experimental investigation into the formation of intergroup representations. *Europ. J. soc. Psychol., 2,* 202–204.

Doise, W., J. C. Deschamps, and G. Meyer (1978). The accentuation of intracategory similarities. In H. Tajfel (Ed.), *Differentiation between social groups.* New York: Academic Press.

Donnerstein, E., and M. Donnerstein (1972). White rewarding behavior as a function of the potential for black retaliation. *J. Pers. soc. Psychol., 24* (3), 327–333.

––––––– (1973). Variables in interracial aggression: potential ingroup censure. *J. Pers. soc. Psychol., 27* (1), 143–150.

––––––– (1975). The effect of attitudinal similarity on interracial aggression. *J. Pers., 43,* 485–502.

Donnerstein, E., M. Donnerstein, S. Simon, and R. Ditrichs (1972). Variables in interracial aggression: anonymity, expected retaliation, and a riot. *J. Pers. soc. Psychol., 22* (2), 236–245.

Donnerstein, M., and E. Donnerstein (1976). Variables in interracial aggression: exposure to aggressive interracial interactions. *J. soc. Psychol., 100,* 111–121.

––––––– (1977). Modeling in the control of interracial aggression: the problem of generality. *J. Pers., 45,* 100–116.

––––––– (1978). Direct and vicarious censure in the control of interracial aggression. *J. Pers., 48,* 162–175.

Doob, L. W., ed. (1970). *Resolving conflict in Africa: the Fermeda workshop.* New Haven: Yale Univ. Press.

Doob, L. W., and W. J. Foltz (1973). The Belfast workshop: an application of group techniques to a destructive conflict. *J. conflict Resolution, 17,* 489–512.

Dovidio, J. F., and S. I. Gaertner (1978). The subtlety of white racism: differences in accepting and soliciting help from a black or a white partner. Washington, D.C.: *Eastern Psychological Association.*

Dovidio, J. F., and S. I. Gaertner (1981). The effects of race, status, and ability on helping behavior. *Soc. Psychol. Quart., 44,* 192–203.

Druckman, D. (1968). Ethnocentrism in the inter-nation simulation. *J. conflict Resolution, 12,* 45–68.

Duncan, B. L. (1976). Differential social perception and attribution of intergroup violence: testing the lower limits of stereotyping of blacks. *J. Pers. soc. Psychol., 34,* 590–598.

Dunn, R., and M. Goldman (1966). Competition and noncompetition in relationship to satisfaction and feelings toward own-group and nongroup members. *J. soc. Psychol., 68,* 299–311.

Dustin, D. W., and H. P. Davis (1970). Evaluative bias in group and individual competition. *J. soc. Psychol., 80,* 103–108.

Dutta, S., and R. N. Kanungo (1967). Retention of affective material: a further verification of the intensity hypothesis. *J. Pers. soc. Psychol., 5,* 476–481.

Dutta, S., R. N. Kanungo, and V. Freibergs (1972). Retention of affective material: effects of intensity of affect on retrieval. *J. Pers. soc. Psychol., 23,* 64–80.

Dutton, D. G. (1971). Reactions of restaurateurs to blacks and whites violating restaurant dress regulations. *Canad. J. behav. Sci., 3,* 298–302.

_____ (1976). Tokenism, reverse discrimination and egalitarianism in interracial behavior. *J. soc. Issues, 32,* 93–107.

Dutton, D. G., and R. Lake (1973). Threat of own prejudice and reverse discrimination in interracial situations. *J. Pers. soc. Psychol., 28,* 94–100.

Dutton, D. G., and V. L. Lennox (1974). Effect of prior "token" compliance on subsequent interracial behavior. *J. Pers. soc. Psychol., 29* (1), 65–71.

Easterbrook, J. A. (1959). The effect of emotion on cue utilization and the organization of behavior. *Psychol. Rev., 66,* 183–201.

Edwards, C. D., and J. E. Williams (1970). Generalization between evaluative words associated with racial figures in preschool children. *J. exp. Res. Pers., 4,* 144–155.

Ehrlich, H. J. (1973). *The social psychology of prejudice.* New York: Wiley.

Eisen, S. V., and L. Z. McArthur (1979). Evaluating and sentencing a defendant as a function of his salience and the perceiver's sex. *Pers. soc. Psychol. Bull., 5,* 48–52.

Eiser, J. R., and W. Stroebe (1972). *Categorization and social judgment.* London: Academic Press.

Farina, A., J. G. Allen, and B. B. Saul (1968). The role of the stigmatized person in affecting social relationships. *J. Pers., 36,* 169–182.

Fazio, R. H., E. A. Effrein, and V. J. Falender (1981). Self perceptions following social interaction. *J. Pers. soc. Psychol., 41,* 232–242.

Feldman, J. M., M. D. Crino, and J. I. Velez (1980). *Categorical inference and information-processing approaches to the stereotyping process.* Unpublished manuscript. University of Florida.

Feldman, R. S., and T. Prohaska (1979). The student as Pygmalion: effect of student expectation on the teacher. *J. educ. Psychol., 71,* 485–493.

Feldman-Summers, S. A., and S. B. Kiesler (1974). Those who are number two try harder: the effects of sex on attributions of causality. *J. Pers. soc. Psychol., 30,* 846–855.

Fendrich, J. M. (1967a). A study of the association among verbal attitudes, commitment and overt behavior in different experimental situations. *Social Forces, 45,* 347–355.

_____ (1967b). Perceived reference group support: racial attitudes and overt behavior. *Amer. Sociological Rev., 32,* 960–970.

Ferguson, C. K., and H. H. Kelley (1964). Significant factors in overevaluation of own-group's product. *J. abnorm. soc. Psychol., 69,* 223–228.

Fiedler, F. E., T. Mitchell, and H. C. Triandis (1971). The culture assimilator: an approach to cross-cultural training. *J. appl. Psychol., 55,* 95–102.

Fishbein, M., and I. Ajzen (1975). *Belief, attitude, intention and behavior: an introduction to theory and research.* Reading, Mass: Addison-Wesley.

Fiske, S. T. (1982). Schema triggered affect: applications to social perception. In M. S. Clark, and S. T. Fiske (Eds.), *Affect and cognition: the 17th annual Carnegie symposium on cognition.* Hillsdale, N.J.: Erlbaum.

Fiske, S. T., and M. G. Cox (1979). Person concepts: the effect of target familiarity and descriptive purpose on the process of describing others. *J. Pers., 47,* 136–161.

Foley, L. A. (1976). Personality and situational influences on changes in prejudice: a replication of Cook's railroad game in a prison setting. *J. Pers. soc. Psychol., 34,* 846–856.

Fromkin, H. L., and J. J. Sherwood (1976). *Intergroup and minority relations: an experimental handbook.* La Jolla, Calif.: University Associates.

Gabelko, N. H., and J. U. Michaelis (1981). *Reducing adolescent prejudice.* New York: Univ. Teacher's College Press.

Gaertner, S. L. (1973). Helping behavior and racial discrimination among liberals and conservatives. *J. Pers. soc. Psychol., 25,* 335–341.

_____ (1975). The role of racial attitudes in helping behavior. *J. soc. Psychol., 97,* 95–101.

Gaertner, S. L., and J. F. Dovidio (1977). The subtlety of white racism, arousal, and helping behavior. *J. Pers. soc. Psychol., 35* (10), 691–707.

Gaertner, S. L., and J. P. McLaughlin, (1983). Changing not fading: racial stereotypes revealed by a non-reactive, reaction time measure. *Soc. Psych. Quart., 46,* 23–30.

Gardiner, G. S. (1972). Complexity training and prejudice reduction. *J. soc. Psychol., 2,* 326–342.

Geffner, R. (1978). *The effects of cooperation and interdependent interactions on the self-esteem, attitudes, interethnic relations, and intraethnic perceptions of elementary school children: a field experiment.* Unpublished doctoral dissertation. Santa Cruz: University of California.

Genthner, R., R. Shuntich, and K. Bunting (1975). Racial prejudice, belief similarity, and human aggression. *J. Psychol., 91,* 229–234.

Gerard, H. B., and M. F. Hoyt (1974). Distinctiveness of social categorization and attitude toward ingroup members. *J. Pers. soc. Psychol., 29,* 836–842.

Gergen, K. J., and E. E. Jones (1963). Mental illness, predictability, and affective consequences as stimulus factors in person perception. *J. abnorm. soc. Psychol., 6,* 95–104.

Gibbons, F. X., W. G. Stephan, B. Stephenson, and C. R. Petty (1981). Contact relevance and reactions to stigmatized others: response and amplification vs. sympathy. *J. exp. soc. Psychol., 16,* 591–605.

Ginosar, Z., and Y. Trope (1980). The effects of base rates and individuating information on judgments about another person. *J. exp. soc. Psychol., 16,* 228–242.

Glass, J. C., and C. Trent (1982). Change students' attitudes toward older persons. In J. Keating (Ed.), *Annual editions: social psychology 82/83.* Guilford, Conn.: Dushkin.

Goffman, E. (1963). *Stigma: notes on the management of spoiled identity.* Englewood Cliffs, N.J.: Prentice-Hall.

Goldberg, A. L. (1956). The effects of two types of sound motion pictures on the attitudes of adults toward minorities. *J. educ. Sociol., 29,* 386–391.

Goldman, M., J. Stockbauer, and T. McAuliffe (1977). Intergroup and intragroup competition and cooperation. *J. exp. soc. Psychol., 13* (1), 81–88.

Gonzales, A. (1979). *Classroom cooperation and ethnic balance.* Paper presented at the Annual Convention of the American Psychological Association, New York.

Grant, P. R., and J. G. Holmes (1981). The integration of implicit personality theory, schemas and stereotype images. *Soc. Psychol. Quart., 44,* 107–115.

Graziano, W. G., T. Brothen and E. Berscheid (1980). Attention, attraction, and individual differences in reaction to criticism. *J. Pers. soc. Psychol., 38,* 193–202.

Green, J. A. (1972). Attitudinal and situational determinants of intended behavior toward blacks. *J. Pers. soc. Psychol., 22* (1), 13–17.

Greenberg, H., J. Pierson, and S. Sherman (1957). The effects of single-session education techniques on prejudice attitudes. *J. educ. Sociol., 31,* 82–86.

Greenberg, J., and D. Rosenfield (1979). Whites' ethnocentrism and their attributions for the behavior of blacks: A motivational bias. *J. Pers., 47,* 643–657.

Grossack, M. (1954). Some effects of cooperation and competition upon small group behavior. *J. abnorm. soc. Psychol., 49,* 341–347.

Gurwitz, S. B., and K. A. Dodge (1977). Effects of confirmations and disconfirmations on stereotype-based attributions. *J. Pers. soc. Psychol., 35,* 495–500.

Gurwitz, S. B., and B. Topol (1978). Determinants of confirming and disconfirming responses to negative social labels. *J. exp. soc. Psychol., 14,* 31–42.

Haimowitz, M. L., and N. R. Haimowitz (1950). Reducing ethnic hostility through psychotherapy. *J. soc. Psychol., 31,* 231–241.

Hamill, R., T. D. Wilson, and R. E. Nisbett (1980). Insensitivity to sample bias: generalizing from atypical cases. *J. Pers. soc. Psychol., 39,* 578–589.

Hamilton, D. L. (1982). Stereotyping and intergroup behavior: some thoughts on the cognitive approach. In D. L. Hamilton (Ed.), *Cognitive process in stereotyping and intergroup behavior.* Hillsdale, N.J.: Erlbaum.

Hamilton, D. L., and R. K. Gifford (1976). Illusory correlation in interpersonal perception: A cognitive basis of stereotypic judgments. *J. exp. soc. Psychol. 12,* 392–407.

Hamilton, D. L., and T. L. Rose (1980). Illusory correlation and the maintenance of stereotypic beliefs. *J. Pers. soc. Psychol., 39,* 832–845.

Harding, J., B. Kutner, N. Proshansky, and I. Chein (1954). Prejudice and ethnic relations. In G. Lindzey (Ed.), *The handbook of social psychology.* Vol. II. Cambridge, Mass.: Addison-Wesley.

Harding, J., H. Proshansky, B. Kutner, and I. Chein (1969). Prejudice and ethnic relations. In G. Lindzey, and E. Aronson (Eds.), *The handbook of social psychology* (2nd ed.). Vol. V. Reading, Mass.: Addison-Wesley.

Harvey, D. G., and G. T. Slatin (1975). The relationship between child's SES and teacher expectations: a test of the middle-class bias hypothesis. *Social Forces, 54,* 140–159.

Hastie, R. (1980). Memory for behavioral information that confirms or contradicts a personality impression. In R. Hastie, T. M. Ostrom, E. B. Ebbesen, R. S. Wyer, Jr., D. L. Hamilton, and D. E. Carlston (Eds.), *Person memory: the cognitive basis of social perception.* Hillsdale, N.J.: Erlbaum. P. 155.

Hastie, R., and P. A. Kumar (1979). Personal memory: personality traits as organizing principles in memory for behaviors. *J. Pers. soc. Psychol., 37,* 25–38.

Hastorf, A. H., S. A. Richardson, and S. M. Dornbusch (1958). The problem of relevance in the study of person perception. In R. Tagiuri, and L. Petrullo (Eds.), *Person perception and interpersonal behavior.* Stanford: Stanford Univ. Press. Pp. 54–62.

Hauserman, N., S. R. Walen, and M. Behling (1973). Reinforced racial integration in the first grade: a study in generalization. *J. appl. behav. Anal., 6,* 193–200.

Heider, F. (1958). *The psychology of interpersonal relations.* New York: Wiley.

Hensley, V., and S. Duval (1976). Some perceptual determinants of perceived similarity, liking, and correctness. *J. Pers. soc. Psychol., 34,* 159–168.

Higgins, E. T., W. S. Rholes, and C. R. Jones (1977). Category accessibility and impression formation. *J. exp. soc. Psychol., 13,* 141–154.

Higgins, E. T., and W. S. Rholes (1978). "Saying is believing": effects of message modification on memory and liking for the person described. *J. exp. soc. Psychol., 14,* 363–378.

Higgins, E. T., and G. King (1981). Accessibility of social constructs: information processing consequences of individual and contextual variability. In N. Cantor, and J. F. Kihlstrom (Eds.), *Personality, cognition, and social interaction.* Hillsdale, N.J.: Erlbaum.

Himelstein, P., and J. C. Moore (1963). Racial attitudes and the action of negro- and white-background figures as factors in petition-signing. *J. soc. Psychol., 61,* 267–272.

Hohn, R. L. (1973). Perceptual training and its effect on racial preferences of kindergarten children. *Psychol. Reports, 32,* 435–441.

Humphreys, P., and J. Berger (1981). Theoretical consequences of the status characteristics formulation. *Amer. J. Sociol., 86,* 953–983.

Hyman, H. H. (1969). Social psychology and race relations. In I. Katz, and P. Gurin (Eds.), *Race and the social sciences.* New York: Basic Books. Pp. 3–48.

Ickes, W. J., R. A. Wicklund, and C. B. Ferris (1973). Objective self-awareness and self-esteem. *J. exp. soc. Psychol., 9,* 202–219.

Irwin, M., T. Tripodi, and J. Bieri (1967). Affective stimulus value and cognitive complexity. *J. Pers. soc. Psychol., 5,* 444–448.

James, W. (1890). *Principles of psychology.* New York: Holt.

Jeffries, V., and H. E. Ransford (1972). Idealogy, social structure, and the Yorty-Bradley mayoral election. *Soc. Prob., 19,* 358–372.

Jenkins, H. M., and W. C. Ward (1965). The judgment of contingency between responses and outcomes. *Psychol. Monogr., 79,* No. 1 (whole No. 594).

Jensen, M., and L. B. Rosenfeld (1974). Influence of mode of presentation, ethnicity, and social class on teachers' evaluations of students. *J. educ. Psychol., 66,* 540–547.

Johnson, D. A. (1980). *Racial discrimination and attitude-behavior consistency.* Unpublished manuscript.

Johnson, D. W., and R. Johnson (1975). *Learning together and alone: cooperation, competition, and individualization.* Englewood Cliffs, N.J.: Prentice-Hall.

Johnson, D. W., R. Johnson, and L. Scott (1978). The effects of cooperative and individualistic instruction on student attitudes and achievement. *J. soc. Psychol., 104,* 207–216.

Jones, E. E., and K. E. Davis (1965). From acts to dispositions: the attribution process in person perception. In L. Berkowitz (Ed.), *Advances in experimental social psychology.* Vol. 2. New York: Academic Press.

Jones, E. E., and R. E. Nisbett (1972). The actor and the observer: divergent perceptions of the causes of behavior. In E. E. Jones, D. E. Kanouse, H. H. Kelley, R. E. Nisbett, S. Valins, and B. Weiner (Eds.). *Attribution: perceiving the causes of behavior.* Morristown, N.J.: General Learning Press. Pp. 79–94.

Jones, J. M. (1972). *Prejudice and racism.* Reading Mass.: Addison-Wesley.

Jones, R. A., J. Scott, J. Solernou, A. Noble, J. Fiala, and K. Miller (1977). Availability and formation of stereotypes. *Percept. motor Skills, 44,* 631–638.

Julian, J. W., D. W. Bishop, and F. E. Fiedler (1966). Quasi-therapeutic effects of intergroup competition. *J. Pers. soc. Psychol., 3,* 321–327.

Kahn, A., and A. Ryen (1972). Factors influencing the bias toward one's own group. *Int. J. group Tensions, 2,* 33–50.

Kahneman, D. (1973). *Attention and effort.* Englewood Cliffs, N.J.: Prentice-Hall.

Kahneman, D. and A. Tversky (1973). On the psychology of prediction. *Psychol. Rev., 80,* 237–251.

———— (1980). Causal schemata in judgments under uncertainty. In M. Fishbein (Ed.), *Progress in social psychology.* Hillsdale, N.J.: Erlbaum.

Kanouse, D. E., and L. R. Hanson (1971). Negativity in evaluations in C. E. Jones, D. E. Kanouse, H. H. Kelley, R. E. Nisbett, S. Valins, and B. Weiner, *Attribution: perceiving the causes of behavior.* Morristown, N.J.: General Learning Press.

Kanungo, R. N., and S. Dutta (1966). Retention of affective material: frame of reference or intensity? *J. Pers. and soc. Psychol., 4,* 27–35.

Katz, D., C. McClintock, and D. Sarnoff (1957). The measurement of ego-defense as related to attitude change. *J. Pers., 25,* 465–474.

Katz, D., D. Sarnoff, and C. McClintock (1956). Ego-defense and attitude change. *Hum. Relat., 9,* 27–45.

Katz, I., and L. Benjamin (1960). Effects of white authoritarianism in biracial work groups. *J. abnorm. soc. Psychol., 61,* 448–456.

Katz, I., and M. Cohen (1962). The effects of training negroes upon cooperative problem solving in biracial teams. *J. abnorm. soc. Psychol., 64,* 319–325.

Katz, I., S. Cohen, D. L. Glass (1975). Some determinants of cross-racial helping behavior. *J. Pers. soc. Psychol., 32* (6), 964–970.

Katz, I., and D. C. Glass (1979). An ambivalence-amplification theory of behavior toward the stigmatized. In W. Austin, and S. Worchel (Eds.), *The social psychology of intergroup relations.* Monterey, Calif.: Brooks/Cole.

Katz, I., and P. Gurin (1969). *Race and the social sciences.* New York: Basic Books.

Katz, I., J. Goldston, and L. Benjamin (1958). Behavior and productivity in biracial work groups. *Hum. Relat., 11,* 123–141.

Katz, I., S. O. Roberts, and J. M. Robinson (1965). Effects of task difficulty, race of administrator, and instructions on digit-symbol performance of negroes. *J. Pers. soc. Psychol., 2,* 53–59.

Katz, J. (1978). *White awareness: handbook for anti-racism training.* Norman: Univ. of Oklahoma Press.

Katz, J. H., and A. Ivey (1977). White awareness: the frontier of racism awareness training. *Personnel Guid. J., 55,* 485–489.

Katz, P. A. (1973). Stimulus predifferentiation and modification of children's racial attitudes. *Child Develop., 44,* 232–237.

Katz, P. A., and S. R. Zalk (1978). Modification of children's racial attitudes. *Develop. Psychol., 14,* 447–461.

Kelley, H. H. (1967). Attribution theory in social psychology. In D. Levine (Ed.), *Nebraska symposium on motivation.* Vol. 15. Lincoln: Univ. of Nebraska Press.

Kelley, H. H., and A. J. Stahelksi (1970). The inference of intentions from moves in the prisoner's dilemma game. *J. exp. soc. Psychol., 6,* 401–419.

Kelman, H. C., and S. P. Cohen (1979). Reduction of international conflict. In W. G. Austin, and S. Worchel (Eds.), *The social psychology of intergroup relations.* Monterey, Calif.: Brooks/Cole.

Kennedy, J., and W. G. Stephan (1977). The effects of cooperation and competition on ingroup-outgroup bias. *J. appl. soc. Psychol., 2,* 115–130.

Kinder, D. R., and D. O. Sears (1981). Prejudice and politics: symbolic racism versus racial threats to the good life. *J. Pers. soc. Psychol., 40* (3), 414–431.

Kintsch, W. (1974). *The representation of meaning in memory.* Hillsdale, N.J.: Erlbaum.

Kleck, R. E., and A. Strenta (1980). Perceptions of the impact of negatively valued physical characteristics on social interaction. *J. Pers. soc. Psychol., 39,* 861–873.

Kovel, J. (1970). *White racism: a psychohistory.* New York: Pantheon.

Kraus, S. (1960). Modifying prejudice: attitude change as a function of the race of the communicator. *AV communic. Rev., 10,* 14–22.

Kraut, R. E. (1973). Effects of social labeling on giving to charity. *J. exp. soc. Psychol.,* 551–562.

Kuhlman, D. M., and D. L. Wimberley (1976). Expectations of choice behavior held by cooperators, competitors, and individualists across four classes of experimental game. *J. Pers. soc. Psychol., 34,* 69–81.

Kutner, B., C. Wilkins, and P. R. Yarrow (1952). Verbal attitudes and overt behavior involving racial prejudice. *J. abnorm. soc. Psychol., 47,* 649–652.

Langer, E. J., and R. P. Abelson (1974). A patient by any other name...clinician group difference in labeling bias. *J. consult. clinic. Psychol., 42,* 4–9.

Langer, E.J., and A. Benevento (1978). Self-induced dependence. *J. Pers. soc. Psychol., 36,* 886–893.

Langer, E. J., S. T. Fiske, S. E. Taylor, and B. Chanowitz (1976). Stigma, staring and discomfort: a novel stimulus hypothesis. *J. exp. soc. Psychol., 12,* 451–463.

LaPierre, R. T. (1936). Type-rationalizations of group antiplay. *Social Faces, 15,* 232-237.

Leslie, L. L., J. W. Leslie, and D. A. Penfield (1972). The effects of a student centered special curriculum upon the racial attitudes of sixth graders. *J. exp. Educ., 41,* 63-67.

Lessing, E. E., and C. C. Clarke (1976). An attempt to reduce ethnic prejudice and assess its correlates in a junior high school sample. *Educ. Res. Quart., 1,* 3-16.

LeVine, R. A., and D. T. Campbell (1972). *Ethnocentrism: theories of conflict, ethnic attitudes and group behavior.* New York: Wiley.

Levinson, D. J. (1954). The intergroup relations workshop: its psychological aims and effects. *J. Psychol., 38,* 103-126.

Levinson, D. J., and R. A. Schermerhorn (1951). Emotional-attitudinal effects of an intergroup relations workshop on its members. *J. Psychol., 31,* 243-256.

Lingle, J. H., N. Geva, T. M. Ostrom, M. R. Leippe, and M. H. Baumgardner (1979). Thematic effects of person judgments on impression organization. *J. Pers. soc. Psychol., 37,* 674-687.

Lingle, J. H., and T. M. Ostrom (1979). Retrieval selectivity in memory-based impression judgments. *J. Pers. soc. Psychol., 37,* 180-194.

Linn, L. S. (1965). Verbal attitudes and overt behavior: a study of racial discrimination. *Social Forces, 44,* 353-364.

Linville, P. W., and E. E. Jones (1980). Polarized appraisals of out-group members. *J. Pers. soc. Psychol., 38,* 689-703.

Litcher, J. H., and D. W. Johnson (1969). Changes in attitudes toward Negroes of white elementary school students after use of multiethnic readers. *J. educ. Psychol., 60,* 148-152.

Locksley, A., E. Borgida, N. Brekke, and C. Hepburn (1980). Sex stereotypes and social judgment. *J. Pers. soc. Psychol., 39,* 821-831.

Locksley, A., C. Hepburn, and V. Ortiz (1982). Social stereotypes and judgments of individuals: an instance of the base rate fallacy. *J. exp. soc. Psychol., 18,* 23-42.

Lohman, M. (1970). Changing a racial status ordering by means of role modeling. Technical Report No. 2. Stanford: Stanford Univ. School of Education.

Lucker, G. W., D. Rosenfield, J. Sikes, and E. Aronson (1977). Performance in the interdependent classroom: a field study. *Amer. Educ. Res. J., 13,* 115-123.

McAdoo, J. L. (1970). *An exploratory study of racial attitude change in black preschool children using differential treatments.* Doctoral dissertation. Univ. of Michigan.

McArthur, L. Z. (1981). Judging a book by its cover: a cognitive analysis of the relationship between physical appearance and stereotyping. In A. Hastorf, and A. Isen (Eds.), *Cognitive social psychology.* New York: Elsevier North-Holland.

McArthur, L. Z., and S. Friedman (1980). Illusory correlation in impression formation: variations in the shared distinctiveness effect as a function of the distinctive person's age, race, and sex. *J. Pers. soc. Psychol., 39,* 615-624

McArthur, L. Z., and D. L. Post (1977). Figural emphasis and person perception. *J. exp. soc. Psychol., 13,* 520-535.

McArthur, L. Z., and L. K. Solomon (1978). Perceptions of an aggressive encounter as a function of the victim's salience and the perceiver's arousal. *J. Pers. soc. Psychol., 36,* 1278-1290.

McCauley, C., and C. L. Stitt (1978). An individual and quantitative measure of stereotypes. *J. Pers. soc. Psychol., 36,* 929-940.

McCauley, C., C. L. Stitt, and M. Segal (1980). Stereotyping: from prejudice to prediction. *Psychol. Bull., 87,* 195-208.

McConahay, J. B., and J. C. Hough, Jr. (1976). Symbolic racism. *J. soc. Issues, 32,* 23-45.

McGrew, J. M. (1967). How "open" are multiple-dwelling units? *J. soc. Psychol., 72,* 223-226.

McGuire, W. J., and A. Padawer-Singer (1976). Trait salience in the spontaneous self-concept. *J. Pers. soc. Psychol., 33,* 743-754.

McGuire, W. J., C. V. McGuire, P. Child, and T. Fujioka (1978). Salience of ethnicity in the spontaneous self-concept as a function of one's ethnic distinctiveness in the social environment. *J. Pers. soc. Psychol., 36,* 511-520.

McGuire, W. J., C. V. McGuire, and W. Winton (1979). Effects of household sex composition on the salience of one's gender in the spontaneous self-concept. *J. exp. soc. Psychol., 15,* 77-90.

McKillip, J., A. J. DiMiceli, and J. Luebke (1977). Group salience and stereotyping. *Soc. Behav. Pers., 5,* 81-85.

McMurthy, C. A., and J. E. Williams (1972). The evaluation dimension of the affective meaning system of the preschool child. *Develop. Psychol., 6,* 238-246.

Malpass, R. S., and J. Kravitz (1969). Recognition for faces of own and other race. *J. Pers. soc. Psychol., 13,* 330-334.

Manis, M., I. Dovalina, N. E. Avis, and S. Cardoze (1980). Base rates can affect individual predictions. *J. Pers. soc. Psychol., 38,* 231-248.

Mann, J. F. (1959). The relationship between cognitive, affective, and behavioral aspects of racial prejudice. *J. soc. Psychol., 49,* 223-228.

Mann, J. F., and D. M. Taylor (1974). Attribution of causality: role of ethnicity and social class. *J. soc. Psychol., 94,* 3-13.

Markus, H., and J. Smith (1980). The influence of self-schemas on the perception of others. In N. Cantor, and J. Kihlstrom (Eds.), *Personality, cognition and social interaction.* Erlbaum.

Mazer, G. E. (1971) Effects of social-class stereotyping on teacher expectation. *Psychol. Schools, 8,* 373-378.

Mercer, J. R., P. Iadicola, and H. Moore (1980). Building effective multiethnic schools. In W. G. Stephan, and J. R. Feagin (Eds.), *School desegregation.* New York: Plenum.

Merton, R. K. (1949). Discrimination and the American creed. In R. M. MacIver (Ed.), *Discrimination and national welfare.* New York: Institute for Religious and Social Studies. Pp. 99-126.

Mezei, L. (1971). Preceived social pressure as an explanation of shifts in the relative influence of face and belief on prejudice across social interactions. *J. Pers. soc. Psychol., 19* (1), 69-81.

Miller, D. T., and J. G. Holmes (1975). The role of situational restrictiveness on self-fulfilling prophecies: a theoretical and empirical extension of Kelley and Stahelski's triangle hypothesis. *J. Pers. soc. Psychol., 31,* 661-673.

Miller, R. L., P. Brickman, and D. Bolen (1975). Attribution versus persuasion as a means for modifying behavior. *J. Pers. soc. Psychol., 31,* 430-441.

Mitnick, L. L., and E. McGinnies (1958). Influencing ethnocentrism in small discussion groups through a film communication. *J. abnorm. soc. Psychol., 56,* 82-90.

Mueller, J. H., K. L. Bailis, and A. G. Goldstein (1979). Depth of processing and anxiety in facial recognition. *Brit. J. Psychol., 70,* 511-515.

Myers, A. (1962). Team competition, success, and the adjustment of group members. *J. abnorm. soc. Psychol. 65,* 325-332.

Myers, D. G., and G. D. Bishop (1970). Discussion effects on racial attitudes. *Science, 169,* 778-789.

Myrdal, G. (1944). *An American dilemma.* New York: Harper & Row.

Neisser, U. (1976). *Cognition and reality: principles and implications of cognitive psychology.* San Francisco: Freeman.

Nisbett, R. E., and E. Borgida (1975). Attribution and the psychology of prediction. *J. Pers. soc. Psychol., 32,* 932-943.

Nisbett, R. E., E. Borgida, R. Crandall, and H. Reed (1976). Popular induction: information is not necessarily informative. In J. S. Carroll, and J. W. Payne (Eds.), *Cognition and social behavior.* Hillsdale, N.J.: Erlbaum. P. 113.

Norman, D. A., and D. E. Rumelhart, (1975). *Exploration in cognition.* San Francisco: Freeman.

Ostrom, T. M., J. H. Lingle, J. B. Pryor, and N. Geva (1980). Cognitive organization of person impressions. In R. Hastie, T. Ostrom, E. Ebbesen, R. Wyer, D. Hamilton, and D. Carlston (Eds.), *Person memory: the cognitive basis of social perception.* Hillsdale, N.J.: Erlbaum.

Parish, T. S. (1972). *Changing anti-negro attitudes in caucasian children through mediated stimulus generalization.* Unpublished doctoral dissertation. Univ. of Illinois.

Parish, T. S., and R. S. Fleetwood (1975). Amount of conditioning and subsequent change in racial attitudes of children. *Percept. motor Skills, 40,* 79-86.

Peak, H., and H. W. Morrison (1958). The acceptance of information into attitude structure. *J. abnorm. soc. Psychol., 57,* 127-135.

Pearce, D. M. (1976). *Black, white and many shades of gray: real estate brokers and their racial practices.* Ph.D. thesis. Univ. of Michigan.

Pearl, D. (1954). Ethnocentrism and the self concept. *J. soc. Psychol., 40,* 137-147.

———— (1955). Psychotherapy and ethnocentrism. *J. abnorm. soc. Psychol., 50,* 227-230.

Perlman, D., and S. Oskamp (1971). The effects of picture content and exposure frequency on evaluations of negroes and whites. *J. exp. soc. Psychol., 7,* 503-514.

Pettigrew, T. F. (1969). Racially separate or together? *J. soc. Issues, 25,* 43-69.

———— (1973). Busing: a review of the evidence. *Publ. Int., 30,* 88-118.

———— (1975). Preface. In T. F. Pettigrew (Ed.), *Racial discrimination in the United States.* New York: Harper & Row.

———— (1979). The ultimate attribution error: extending Allport's cognitive analysis of prejudice. *Pers. soc. Psychol. Bull., 5,* 461-476.

Piliavin, I. M., J. A. Piliavin, and J. Rodin (1975). Costs, diffusion, and the stigmatized victim. *J. Pers. soc. Psychol., 32* (3), 429-439.

Piliavin, I. M., J. Rodin, and J. A. Piliavin (1969). Good samaritanism: an underground phenomenon? *J. Pers. soc. Psychol., 13* (4), 289-299.

Pliske, R., and K. Smith (1979). Semantic categorization in a linear order problem. *Memory and Cognition, 4,* 297-302.

Poskocil, A. (1977). Encounters between blacks and white liberals: the collision of stereotypes. *Social Forces, 55,* 715-727.

Primac, D. W. (1980). Reducing racial prejudice by verbal operant conditioning. *Psychol. Reports, 46,* 655-669.

Quattrone, G. A., and E. E. Jones (1980). The perception of variability within in-groups and out-groups: implications for the law of small numbers. *J. Pers. soc. Psychol. 38,* 141-152.

Quanty, M. B., J. A. Keats, and S. G. Harkins (1975). Prejudice and criteria for identification of ethnic photographs. *J. Pers. soc. Psychol., 32,* 449-454.

Rabbie, J. M., F. Benoist, H. Oosterbaan, and L. Visser (1974). Differential power and effects of expected competitive and cooperative intergroup interaction on intragroup and outgroup attitudes. *J. Pers. soc. Psychol., 30,* 46-56.

Rabbie, J. M., and M. Horwitz (1969). Arousal of ingroup-outgroup bias by a chance win or loss. *J. Pers. soc. Psychol., 13,* 269-277.

Rabbie, J. M., and G. Wilkens (1971). Inter-group competition and its effect on intragroup and intergroup relations. *Europ. J. soc. Psychol., 1,* 215-234.

Rath, L. E., and F. N. Trager (1948). Public opinion and crossfire. *J. educ. Sociol., 21,* 345-349.

Razran, G. (1950). Ethnic dislikes and stereotypes: a laboratory study. *J. abnorm. soc. Psychol., 45,* 7-27.

Reeder, G. D., and M. B. Brewer (1979). A schematic model of dispositional attribution in interpersonal perception. *Psychol. Rev., 86,* 61-79.

Rist, R. (1970). Student social class and teacher expectations: the self-fulfilling prophecy in ghetto education. *Harvard Educ. Rev., 40,* 411-412.

Robinson, J. W., and J. D. Preston (1976). Equal-status contact and modification of racial prejudice: a reexamination of the contact hypothesis. *Social Forces, 54,* 911-924.

Rodin, J., and E. Langer (1980). Aging labels: the decline of control and the fall of self-esteem. *J. soc. Issues, 36,* 12-29.

Rokeach, M. (1971). Long range experimental modification of values, attitudes and behavior. *Amer. Psychol., 26,* 453-459.

Rokeach, M., and L. Mezei (1966). Race and shared belief as factors in social choice. *Science, 151,* 167-172.

Rosch, E. (1978). Principles of categorization. In E. Rosch, and B. B. Lloyd (Eds.), *Cognition and categorization.* Hillsdale, N.J.: Erlbaum.

Rosch, E., C. Mervis, W. Gray, D. Johnson, and P. Boyes-Braem (1976). Basic objects in natural categories. *Cognit. Psychol., 8,* 382-439.

Rose, T. L. (1981). Cognitive and dyadic processes in intergroup contact. In D. Hamilton (Ed.), *Cognitive processes in stereotyping and intergroup behavior.* Hillsdale, N.J.: Erlbaum.

Rose, T. L., D. L. Hamilton (1979). *Stereotypes as schemata.* Paper presented at Western Psychological Association meeting, San Diego, Calif.

Rosen, I. C. (1948). The effect of the motion picture "Gentleman's Agreement" on attitudes toward Jews. *J. Psychol., 26,* 525-536.

Rosenfield, D., J. Greenberg, R. Folger, and R. Borys (1982). Effect of an encounter with a black panhandler on subsequent helping for blacks: tokenism or negative stereotyping. *Pers. soc. Psychol. Bull., 8,* 664–671.

Rosenfield, D., W. G. Stephan, and G. W. Lucker (1981). Attraction to competent and incompetent members of cooperative and competitive groups, *J. appl. soc. Psychol., 11,* 416–433.

Rosenthal, R. (1966). *Experimenter effects in behavioral research.* New York: Appleton-Century-Crofts.

_____ (1973). On the social psychology of the self-fulfilling prophecy: further evidence for Pygmalion effects and their mediating mechanisms. *MSS Modular Pub.,* 1973 Module 53, 1–28.

Rosenthal, R., and L. Jacobson (1968). *Pygmalion in the classroom.* New York: Holt, Rinehart, and Winston.

Ross, L. (1977). The intuitive psychologist and his shortcomings: distortions in the attribution process. In L. Berkowitz (Ed.), *Advances in experimental social psychology.* Vol. 10. New York: Academic Press.

Rothbart, M. (1981). Memory processes and social beliefs. In D. Hamilton (Ed.), *Cognitive processes in stereotyping and intergroup perception.* Hillsdale, N.J.: Erlbaum.

Rothbart, M., M. Evans, and S. Fulero (1979). Recall for confirming events: Memory processes and the maintenance of social stereotypes. *J. exp. soc. Psychol., 15,* 343–356.

Rothbart, M., S. Fulero, C. Jenson, J. Howard, and P. Birrell (1978). From individual to group impressions: availability heuristics in stereotype formation. *J. exp. soc. Psychol., 14,* 237–255.

Rubin, I. (1967). The reduction of prejudice through laboratory training. *J. appl. behav. Sci., 3,* 29–50.

Rubovits, P. C., and M. L. Maehr (1973). Pygmalion black and white. *J. Pers. soc. Psychol., 25,* 210–218.

Ryen, A. H., and A. Kahn (1975). Effects of intergroup orientation on group attitudes and proxemic behavior. *J. Pers. soc. Psychol., 31,* 302–310.

Sagar, H. A., and J. W. Schofield (1980). Racial and behavioral cues in black and white children's perceptions of ambiguously aggressive acts. *J. Pers. soc. Psychol., 39,* 590–598.

Sappington, A. A. (1974). Behavior of biased and non-biased whites towards blacks in a simulated interaction. *Psychol. Reports, 35,* 487–493.

_____ (1976). Effects of desensitization of prejudiced whites to blacks upon subjects' stereotypes of blacks. *Percept. motor Skills, 43,* 938.

Schank, R., and R. Abelson (1977). *Scripts, plans, goals and understanding: an inquiry into human knowledge structures.* Hillsdale, N.J.: Erlbaum.

Schofield, J. W. (1980). Complementary and conflicting identities: images and interaction in an interracial school. In S. Asher, and J. Gottman (Eds.), *The development of children's friendships.* Cambridge: Cambridge Univ. Press.

Schonbach, P., P. Gollwitzer, G. Stiepel, and U. Wagner (1981). *Education and intergroup attitudes.* New York: Academic Press.

Schur, E. M. (1971). *Labeling deviant behavior: its sociological implications.* New York: Harper & Row.

Sears, D. O., and D. R. Kinder (1971). Racial tensions and voting in Los Angeles. In W. Z. Hirsch (Ed.), *Los Angeles:*

viability and prospects for metropolitan leadership. New York: Praeger.

Secord, P. F. (1959). Stereotyping and favorableness in the perception of Negro faces. *J. abnorm. soc. Psychol., 59,* 309–315.

Secord, P. F., and C. W. Backman (1974). *Social psychology.* New York: McGraw-Hill.

Shanahan, J. K. (1972). *The effects of modifying black-white concept attitudes of black and white first grade subjects upon two measures of racial attitudes.* Doctoral dissertation. Univ. of Washington.

Sherif, M., and C. W. Sherif (1956). *An outline of social psychology.* Rev. ed. New York: Harper & Row.

_____ (1969). *Social psychology.* New York: Harper & Row.

Shweder, R. A. (1977). Comments on illusory correlation and the MMPI controversy. *J. consult. clinic. Psychol., 45,* 917–924.

Silverman, B. I. (1974). Consequences, racial discrimination, and the principle of belief congruence. *J. Pers. soc. Psychol., 29,* 497–508.

Slavin, R. (1977). How student learning teams can integrate the desegregated classroom. *Integrated Educ., 15,* 56–58.

_____ (1979). Student team learning as a total instructional program: effects on achievement and attitudes. Center for Social Organization of Schools, Johns Hopkins University.

Slavin, R., and N. A. Madden (1979). School practices that improve race relations. *Amer. educ. Res. J., 16,* 169–180.

Slavin, R., and E. Oickle (1980). Effects of student teams and individual expectations on race relations and achievement in a rural school. Center for Social Organization of Schools, Johns Hopkins University.

Smith, E. E., E. J. Shoben, and L. J. Rips (1974). Structure and process in semantic memory: a featural model for semantic decisions. *Psychol. Rev., 81,* 214–241.

Smith, E. R., and F. D. Miller (1979). Salience and the cognitive mediation of attribution. *J. Pers. soc. Psychol., 37,* 2240–2252.

Smith, E. W. L., and T. R. Dixon (1968). Verbal conditioning as a function of race of the experimenter and prejudice of the subject. *J. exp. soc. Psychol., 4,* 285–301.

Snyder, M., and N. Cantor (1979). Testing hypotheses about other people: the use of historical knowledge. *J. exp. soc. Psychol., 15,* 330–342.

Snyder, M., E. D. Tanke, and E. Berscheid (1977). Social perception and interpersonal behavior: on the self-fulfilling nature of social stereotypes. *J. Pers. soc. Psychol., 35,* 656–666.

Snyder, M., and W. B. Swann, Jr. (1978a). Hypothesis testing processes in social interaction. *J. Pers. soc. Psychol., 36,* 1202–1212.

_____ (1978b). Behavioral confirmation in social interaction: from social perception to social reality. *J. exp. soc. Psychol., 14,* 148–162.

Snyder, M., and S. W. Uranowitz (1978). Reconstructing the past: some cognitive consequences of person perception. *J. Pers. soc. Psychol., 36,* 941–950.

Snyder, M. L., and A. Frankel (1976). Observer bias: a stringent test of behavior engulfing the field. *J. Pers. soc. Psychol., 34,* 857–864.

Soucar, E. (1970). Students' perceptions of liked and disliked teachers. *Percept. motor Skills, 31,* 19–24.

_____ (1971). Vigilance and the perceptions of teachers and students. *Percept. motor Skills, 32,* 83–86.

Spencer, M., and F. Horowitz (1973). Effects of systematic social and token reinforcement on the modification of racial and color concept attitudes in black and white pre-school children. *Develop. Psychol., 9,* 246–254.

Steele, C. M. (1975). Name calling and compliance. *J. Pers. soc. Psychol., 31,* 361–369.

Stephan, W. G. (1977). Stereotyping: the role of ingroup-outgroup differences in causal attribution for behavior. *J. soc. Psychol., 101,* 255–266.

_____ (1978). School desegregation: an evaluation of predictions made in *Brown vs. the Board of Education. Psychol. Bull., 85,* 217–238.

Stephan, W. G., and W. E. Beane (1978). The effects of belief similarity and ethnicity on liking and attributions for performance. *Int. Amer. J. Psychol., 12,* 153–159.

Stephan, W. G., and D. Rosenfield (1978a). Effects of desegregation on racial attitudes. *J. Pers. soc. Psychol., 36,* 795–804.

_____ (1978b). The effects of desegregation on race relations and self-esteem. *J. educ. Psychol., 70,* 670–679.

_____ (1982). Racial and ethnic stereotypes. In A. G. Miller (Ed.), *In the eye of the beholder.* New York: Praeger.

Stephan, W. G., and C. W. Stephan (1983). The role of ignorance in intergroup relations. In N. Miller, and M. B. Brewer, *Groups in contact.* New York: Academic Press.

Stephan, W. G., and D. W. Woolridge (1977). Sex differences in attributions for the performance of women on a masculine task. *Sex Roles, 3,* 321–328.

Stephenson, G. M., M. Skinner, and C. J. Brotherton (1976). Group participation and intergroup relations: an experimental study of negotiation groups. *Europ. J. soc. Psychol., 6,* 51–70.

Stotland, E., D. Katz, and M. Patchen (1959). The reduction of prejudice through the arousal of self-insight. *J. Pers., 27,* 507–531.

Sumner, W. G. (1906). *Folkways.* Boston: Ginn.

Swann, W. B., and C. A. Hill (1982). When our identities are mistaken: reaffirming self conceptions through social interaction. *J. Pers. soc. Psychol., 42,* 59–65.

Taft, R. (1954). Selective recall and memory distortion of favorable and unfavorable material. *J. abnorm. soc. Psychol., 49,* 23–28.

Tajfel, H. (1968). Social and cultural factors in perception. In G. Lindzey, and E. Aronson (Eds.), *Handbook of social psychology.* Vol. 3. Reading, Mass.: Addison-Wesley.

_____ (1970). Experiments in intergroup discrimination. *Scientific Amer., 223,* 96–102.

_____ (1972). Experiments in a vacuum. In J. Israel, and H. Tajfel (Eds.), *The context of social psychology: a critical assessment.* London: Academic Press.

_____ (1978). La categorisation sociale. Cited in H. Tajfel, *Differentiation between social groups.* London: Academic Press.

Tajfel, H., A. A. Sheikh, and R. C. Gardner (1964). Content of stereotypes and the inference of similarity between members of stereotyped groups. *Acta Psychologica, 22,* 191–201.

Tannenbaum, F. (1938). *Crime and the community.* Boston: Ginn.

Taylor, D. M., and R. C. Gardner (1969). Ethnic stereotypes: their effects on the perception of communications of varying credibility. *Canad. J. Psychol., 23,* 161–173.

Taylor, D. M., and V. Jaggi (1974). Ethnocentrism and causal attribution in a south Indian context. *J. Cross-Cultural Psychol., 5,* 162–171.

Taylor, M. C. (1979). Race, sex, and the expression of self-fulfilling prophecies in a laboratory teaching situation. *J. Pers. soc. Psychol., 37,* 987–912.

Taylor, S. E. (1982). A categorization approach to stereotyping. In D. L. Hamilton (Ed.), *Cognitive processes in stereotyping and intergroup behavior.* Hillsdale, N.J.: Erlbaum.

Taylor, S. E., and J. Crocker (1980). Schematic bases of social information processing. In E. T. Higgins, C. P. Herman, and M. P. Zanna (Eds.), *Social cognition: the Ontario symposium on personality and social psychology.* Hillsdale, N.J.: Erlbaum.

Taylor, S. E., and S. T. Fiske (1978). Salience, attention and attribution: top of the head phenomena. In L. Berkowitz (Ed.), *Advances in experimental social psychology.* Vol. 11. New York: Academic Press.

Taylor, S. E., S. T. Fiske, N. L. Etcoff, and A. J. Ruderman (1978). Categorical and contextual bases of person memory and stereotyping. *J. Pers. soc. Psychol., 36,* 778–793.

Thompson, J. S., W. G. Stephan, and R. W. Schvaneveldt (1980). *The organization of social stereotypes in semantic memory.* Rocky Mountain Psychological Association.

Traynham, R. N. (1974). *The effects of modifying color meaning concepts on racial concept attitudes in five- and eight-year old children.* Master's thesis. Univ. of Arkansas.

Triandis, H. C. Ed., (1976). *Variations in black and white perceptions of the social environment.* Urbana, Ill.: Univ. of Illinois Press.

Triandis, H. C., and V. Vassiliou (1967). Frequency of contact and stereotyping. *J. Pers. soc. Psychol., 7,* 316–328.

_____ (1972). Interpersonal influence and employee selection in two cultures. *J. appl. Psychol., 56,* 140–145.

Tunnell, G. (1981). Sex role and cognitive schemata: person perception in feminine and androgynous women. *J. Pers. soc. Psychol., 40,* 1126–1136.

Turner, J. C. (1973). *Competition and category-conflict: self versus group for social value versus economic gain.* Unpublished manuscript. Univ. of Bristol.

_____ (1975). Social comparison and social identity: some prospects for intergroup behaviour. *Europ. J. soc. Psychol., 5,* 5–34.

_____ (1978). Social categorization and social discrimination in the minimal group paradigm. In H. Tajfel, *Differentiation between social groups.* New York: Academic Press.

Tversky, A. (1977). Features of similarity. *Psychol. Rev., 84,* 327–352.

Tversky, A., and D. Kahneman (1973). Availability: a heuristic for judging frequency and probability. *Cognit. Psychol., 5,* 207–232.

Van den Berghe, P. L. (1967). *Race and racism*. New York: Wiley.

Von Baeyer, C. L., D. L. Sherk, and M. P. Zanna (1981). Impression management in the job interview: when the female applicant meets the male (chauvinist) interviewer. *Pers. soc. Psychol. Bull., 7,* 45–51.

Wang, G., and J. McKillip (1978). Ethnic identification and judgments of an accident. *Pers. soc. Psychol. Bull., 4,* 296–299.

Ward, W. C., and H. M. Jenkins (1965). The display of information and the judgment of contingency. *Canad. J. Psychol., 19,* 231–241.

Warner, L. G., and M. L. DeFleur (1969). Attitude as an interactional concept: social constraint and social distance as intervening variables between attitudes and action. *Amer. Sociol. Rev., 34* (2), 153–169.

Webster, M. Jr., and J. E. Driskell, Jr. (1978). Status generalization: a review and some new data. *Amer. Sociol. Rev., 43,* 220–236.

Weigel, R. H., P. L. Wiser, and S. W. Cook (1975). The impact of cooperative learning experience on cross-ethnic relations and attitudes. *J. soc. Issues, 31,* 219–244.

Weitz, S. (1972). Attitude, voice, and behavior: a repressed affect model of interracial interaction. *J. Pers. soc. Psychol., 24* (1), 14–21.

Weldon, D. E., D. E. Carlston, A. K. Rissman, L. Sloboden, and H. C. Triandis (1975). A laboratory test of effects of culture assimilator training. *J. Pers. soc. Psychol., 32,* 300–310.

Wicklund, R. A., and J. Brehm (1976). *Perspectives on cognitive dissonance*. Hillsdale, N.J.: Erlbaum.

Wilder, D. A. (1978). Perceiving persons as a group: effects on attributions of causality and beliefs. *Soc. Psychol., 41,* 13–23.

———— (1981). Perceiving persons as a group: categorization and intergroup relations. In D. Hamilton (Ed.), *Cognitive processes in stereotyping and intergroup behavior.* Hillsdale, N.J.: Erlbaum.

Wilder, D. A., and V. L. Allen (1978). Group membership and preference for information about others. *Pers. soc. Psychol. Bull., 4,* 106–110.

Williams, J. E., D. L. Best, D. A. Boswell, L. A. Mattson, and D. J. Graves (1975). Preschool racial attitude measure II. *Educ. psychol. Meas., 55,* 3–18.

Williams, J. E., and C. D. Edwards (1969). An exploratory study of the modification of color concepts and racial attitudes in preschool children. *Child Development, 40,* 737–750.

Williams, J. E., and J. K. Morland (1976). *Race, color, and the young child*. Chapel Hill: Univ. North Carolina Press.

Williams, R. M., Jr. (1947). The reduction of intergroup tensions: a survey of research on problems of ethnic, racial, and religious group relations. New York: Social Science Research Council, Bulletin 57.

———— (1977). *Mutual accommodation: ethnic conflict and cooperation*. Minneapolis: Univ. of Minnesota Press.

Williams, R. L., W. H. Cormier, G. L. Sapp, and H. B. Andrews (1971). The utility of behavior management techniques in changing interracial behaviors. *J. Psychol., 77,* 127–138.

Wilson, L., and R. W. Rogers (1975). The fire this time: effects of race of target, insult, and potential retaliation on black aggression. *J. Pers. soc. Psychol., 32* (5), 857–864.

Wilson, T. D., and J. A. Capitman (1982). Effects of script availability on social behavior. *Pers. soc. Psychol. Bull., 8,* 11–19.

Wilson, W., and M. Kayatani (1968). Intergroup attitudes and strategies in games between opponents of the same or of a different race. *J. Pers. soc. Psychol., 9,* 24–30.

Wilson, W., and N. Miller (1961). Shifts in evaluation of participants following intergroup competition. *J. abnorm. soc. Psychol., 63,* 428–431.

Worchel, S., A. Lind, and K. Kaufman (1975). Evaluations of group products as a function of expectations of group longevity, outcome of competition, and publicity of evaluations. *J. Pers. soc. Psychol., 31,* 1089–1097.

Worchel, S., V. A. Andreoli, and R. Folger (1977). Intergroup cooperation and intergroup attraction: the effect of previous interaction and outcome of combined effort. *J. exp. soc. Psychol., 13,* 131–140.

Worchel, S., and N. Norvell (1980). Effect of perceived environmental conditions during cooperation on intergroup attraction. *J. Pers. soc. Psychol., 38,* 764–772.

Word, C. O., M. P. Zanna, and J. Cooper (1974). The nonverbal mediation of self-fulfilling prophecies in interracial interaction. *J. exp. soc. Psychol., 10,* 109–120.

Wyer, R. S., Jr., and T. K. Srull (1980). The processing of social stimulus information: a conceptual integration. In R. Hastie, T. M. Ostrom, E. B. Ebbesen, R. S. Wyer, Jr., D. L. Hamilton, and D. E. Carlston (Eds.), *Person memory: The cognitive basis of social perception*. Erlbaum.

Yarkin, K. L., J. H. Harvey, and B. M. Bloxom (1981). Cognitive sets, attribution and social interaction. *J. Pers. soc. Psychol., 41,* 243–252.

Yawkey, T. D. (1973). Attitudes toward black Americans held by rural and urban white early childhood subjects based upon multi-ethnic social studies materials. *J. Negro Educ., 42,* 164–169.

Yawkey, T. D., and J. Blackwell (1974). Attitudes of 4-year-old urban black children toward themselves and whites based upon multi-ethnic social studies materials and experiences. *J. Educ. Res., 67,* 373–377.

Zadny, J., and H. B. Gerard (1974). Attributed intentions and informational selectivity. *J. exp. soc. Psychol., 10,* 34–52.

Zanna, M., and S. Pack (1975). On the self-fulfilling nature of apparent sex differences in behavior. *J. exp. soc. Psychol., 11,* 583–591.

Zuckerman, M. (1978). Use of consensus information in prediction of behavior. *J. exp. soc. Psychol., 14,* 163–171.

CHAPTER 25

Public Opinion and Political Action

Donald R. Kinder
University of Michigan

David O. Sears
University of California at Los Angeles

INTRODUCTION

This chapter provides an account of public opinion and political action congenial to social psychological tastes. It is both an advanced introduction to various topics—public opinion, voters and elections, political action, media and politics, political socialization—and a general exhortation on behalf of a livelier and more intimate exchange between research on political behavior, on the one hand, and social psychological analysis, on the other.

The chapter opens with a discussion of public opinion—"a task," V. O. Key (1961) once wrote, "not unlike

Many people commented on preliminary aspects of the chapter. We thank them all, especially Robert Abelson, Paul Abramson, Samuel Barnes, Philip Converse, Jerry Clubb, Faye Crosby, Heinz Eulau, Morris Fiorina, Susan Fiske, Charles Franklin, Maureen Graves, John Jackson, M. Kent Jennings, D. Roderick Kiewiet, Jon Krosnick, Richard Lau, Gregory Markus, David Mayhew, Walter Mebane, Warren Miller, Mark Peters, and Randolph Wagner. The manuscript was prepared, again and again, with great competence and good cheer by Mary Marsh at Yale University and by Nancy Brennan, Kathryn Jones, Maureen Kozumplik, Barbara Lohr, and Joyce Meyer at the Institute for Social Research at the University of Michigan. As usual, Steven Rosenstone and Janet Weiss helped enormously (not the least by eventually convincing Kinder that it was time to quit).

coming to grips with the Holy Ghost" (p. 8). First we describe the informational underpinnings of opinion and then consider the antecedents of opinion: in ideological principles, in self-interest, in group identification, in core values, in personal needs, and in the lessons of history. We then move on to voters and elections, distinguishing between the determinants of individual choice, about which we have much to say, and the determinants of collective choice, about which we are more modest. The chapter next considers why it is that some people are moved to political action while others stay home. By political action we mean participation of all varieties, from turning out to vote to taking part in revolution. We particularly emphasize social psychological accounts of action, those that stress the interplay between internal predispositions and external circumstances. We then take up the role of media in mass politics. Over the last forty years, the influence of the media has been judged in turn as pernicious and as benign. As we will see, there is evidence enough to support both views. Finally, we take up processes of socialization: the formation of political dispositions in childhood and adolescence and their development through later life.

Research on each of these topics has grown explosively in the fifteen years that have elapsed since the publication of the preceding handbook (Sears, 1969), and so has controversy. Much of what we thought we knew about public participation in political life is now regarded by many as false or, at least, as hopelessly anachronistic. Rewriting the "laws" of political behavior has been motivated in part by the development of new ideas and by advances in statistical analysis, but perhaps most of all by change transpiring outside the academy—by the striking changes in U.S. politics in the last two decades. It has been a tumultuous time, marked by assassinations, race riots, a deeply unpopular war, public disorder, flagrant violations of public trust, soaring inflations and deep recessions. These events shook up U.S. society and with it, much conventional wisdom regarding the politics of everyday life. Our major task here is to decide how much of that conventional wisdom actually needs to be rewritten and how much of it has been sustained.

Before getting underway we should mention the chapter's general limitations. First and foremost, the chapter addresses only a portion of the broad field described as "political behavior." Lane's (1963) typology of the field distinguished among six political processes. In addition to public opinion and elections, these included legislative, administrative, judicial and legal, international, and integrative processes. Only the first is dealt with here.

Furthermore, our discussion pays little or no attention to the *consequences* of opinion and action. That is, we ignore whether popular participation in politics makes a political difference. From the perspective of a science of politics, this omission is, of course, glaring. As Key put it, the study of public opinion and political action is "bootless unless the findings about the preferences, aspirations, and prejudices of the public can be connected with the workings of the governmental system" (1961, p. 535). But because our interests here are less political than they are psychological, we shall put aside that body of work dedicated to identifying the ways in which mass publics influence, and fail to influence, their governments. (For an introduction to a variety of perspectives on this ancient and formidable question, consult: Achen, 1978; Brody, 1978; Burstein, 1979; Converse, 1975a; Dahl, 1961; Gamson, 1975; Key, 1961; Lipsky, 1968; Miller and Stokes, 1966b; Page and Shapiro, 1981; Pateman, 1970; Piven and Cloward, 1977; Schattschneider, 1960; Verba and Nie, 1972.)

Another limitation concerns generalizing across political systems. Enthusiasm for empirical social science has been primarily, though not exclusively, a U.S. phenomenon. Hence most evidence has been collected in the United States. With occasional but important exceptions, other nations get no attention here. Limiting our aspirations to the understanding of U.S. mass politics scarcely reduces the size of the task, of course. But if we occasionally imply greater generality ahead, it is usually not intended.

A final and unavoidable limitation is that set by history. Most of the available evidence comes not only from the United States but also from the United States during the post-war period. These are rich and interesting years but of indeterminate historical generality. How radically what we say here will require revision in the future only time—and the next edition of the handbook—will tell.

THE NATURE OF PUBLIC OPINION

Romantic renditions of democracy presume the "omnicompetent citizen": attentive to and informed about the persons and problems that animate public life, familiar with the policies and philosophies that divide contending candidates and parties, and possessed of a coherent vision of government and society. Needless to say, such presumptions have proven presumptuous. In the first section of this chapter we describe just how drastically everyday thinking about politics departs from omnicompetence. We also suggest how people *do* reason about public life, quite apart from how they "ought" to reason.

PRIVATISM

More than one-half century ago, Walter Lippmann (1922) advanced the argument that the trials and tribulations of daily life are compelling in a way that politics can never be. To expect ordinary people to become absorbed in the affairs of state, wrote Lippmann, would be to demand of them an appetite for political knowledge quite peculiar, if not pathological. Over the years, Lippmann's thesis has aged with uncommon grace, collecting a cast of distinguished supporters (e.g., Campbell, Converse, Miller, and Stokes, 1960; Dahl, 1961; Downs, 1957; Lane, 1973), and more important, a mountain of corroborating evidence.

Consider these examples. When asked to describe their fondest hopes and worst fears, Americans named family considerations—economic well-being, health, and aspirations for children in particular—much more often than political ones (Cantril, 1965, p. 36; also see Watts and Free, 1978). Similarly, whether Americans are happy depends principally on matters close to home: on good family relations, a sound marriage, financial security, suitable housing, an interesting job, and good friends. In studies by Campbell and his colleagues, satisfaction with national government ranked tenth out of twelve domains in its contribution to personal satisfaction (Campbell, Converse, and Rodgers, 1976; Campbell, 1981). Lane (1962) put it this way, in summarizing his exploration of the common man's ideology: "The lives of men of Eastport, like most Americans' lives, are much more concerned with the business of buying and selling, earning and disposing of things, than they are with the 'idle' talk of politics" (p. 25). Indeed, about one quarter of the U.S. public conceded (in 1960) that they *never* discussed public affairs (Almond and Verba, 1963). These examples, which could be multiplied easily, testify to the preeminence of privatism. The vicissitudes of personal life are central preoccupations, while the events of political life are, for most of us, most of the time, peripheral curiosities.

"DARK AREAS OF IGNORANCE"

If politics is a side show, subordinate to the demands and activities of private life, then people may see little point to becoming politically informed. If political information promises few benefits, then "...voters are no fools to remain ignorant" (Converse, 1975a, p. 96). The extent of ignorance is nevertheless striking. Table 1 offers some miscellaneous though representative examples of this ignorance.

As indicated in Table 1, events and personalities do occasionally command the attention of the entire public, at least momentarily. Nearly everyone (99.8 percent) had heard about President Kennedy's assassination within five hours after its occurrence (Sheatsley and Feldman, 1965). Ninety-six percent of the public claimed to have read or heard about the breakdown of the nuclear power plant at Three Mile Island near Harrisburg, Pennsylvania, shortly after it occurred. And as the 1980 presidential contest kicked off, virtually everyone both recognized incumbent President Carter and claimed to know something about him. Thus people and events that dominate the headlines and the evening news for extended periods reach everybody. However, these are exceptions: Once analysis goes beyond the biggest stories, public knowledge thins out rapidly.

For instance, legislative proposals that cause commotion in Washington seldom disturb anyone's sleep in Peoria. In the spring of 1979, only a narrow majority of the U.S. public (58 percent) claimed to know anything

TABLE 1
Familiarity with Public Affairs

	POLL DATE (MONTH/YEAR)	PERCENT
JFK assassination	11/63	100%
President Gerald Ford	2/76	99
Three-Mile Island nuclear accident	4/79	96
U-2 plane downed	6/60	96
Chappaquiddick	6/71	95
John Glenn, astronaut	8/63	89
McCarthy's charges about subversives in the State Dept.	7/50	78
Henry Kissinger	2/73	78
House Ethics Committee— "Koreagate"	8/77	71
John Birch Society	8/64	68
Federal budget unbalanced	7/77	67
John Glenn, Senator	11/74	65
House Committee on Un-American Activities	1/49	64
Democrats control House	11/78	59
Senator William Proxmire	11/74	57
Senator Barry Goldwater	3/63	51
Democrats control House	11/58	47
Governor Jerry Brown	11/74	42
Senator Lyndon Johnson	6/56	32
Americans for Democratic Action	2/48	23
Jimmy Carter	2/76	20
U.N. Ambassador Warren Austin	9/47	11

SOURCE: Principally Gallup Polls.

about Salt II, the proposed nuclear-arms agreement between the United States and the Soviet Union. Nor is awareness automatically translated into preference. Nearly one-third of those who declared they knew something about Salt II went on to admit that they held no opinion one way or the other about it. Policies that deeply divide political elites thus provoke only "miniature conflicts" in the general public (Key, 1961, p. 82).

Opinions that are expressed, moreover, may not always be authentic. Many people volunteer ideas about matters they know little or nothing about. How many Americans could have been familiar with the utterly obscure Agricultural Trade Act of 1978? Yet when asked about it, 31 percent of respondents in a national survey offered an opinion. (They favored it 2:1, Schuman and Presser, 1980.) Taking this design to its logical conclusion, Bishop and his colleagues (1980) found that 33 percent of their Cincinnati area respondents expressed an opinion on the 1975 Public Affairs Act, a fictitious proposal invented expressly for the survey.

In the same vein, explorations of the factual underpinnings of public opinion can uncover quite remarkable misapprehensions. In late summer of 1977 Panama and the United States announced a widely publicized agreement regarding ownership of the Panama Canal. The following January, 81 percent of the U.S. public claimed to have "heard or read about the debate over the Panama Canal Treaty." But of those, fully one-third believed—quite erroneously—that the canal frequently served U.S. aircraft carriers and supertankers. Converse (1975a) provided a more unsettling example, drawn from a survey taken in the United States in 1961 just after the erection of the Berlin Wall. Almost one-half the sample "did not happen to know that Berlin was encircled in depth by hostile military troops" (p. 80). Such knowledge presumably would have tempered the public's considerable enthusiasm for military countermeasures. In both examples, aspects of a political problem that devoted readers of *The New York Times* would think obvious became seriously garbled in the minds of the general public.

Presented in Table 2 is evidence concerning the U.S. public's recognition of presidential candidates. Incumbents aside, most presidential hopefuls begin the campaign not exactly as household words. In February of 1976, for example, just 20 percent of the public claimed to know anything about the ex-governor of Georgia, Jimmy Carter. Of course, two months later, after a series of stunning primary victories, Mr. Carter's recognition level rose dramatically, to 77 percent (Patterson, 1980).

TABLE 2
Recognition of Presidential Contenders

	FEBRUARY, 1976	FEBRUARY, 1980
Gerald Ford	93%	92%
Ronald Reagan	85	87
Jimmy Carter	20	99
Edward Kennedy	—	95
Walter Mondale	—	73
Jerry Brown	—	67
George Wallace	76	—
Fred Harris	12	—
Henry Jackson	27	—
Frank Church	20	—
Birch Bayh	21	—
Morris Udall	23	—
John Connally	—	64
Howard Baker	—	44
George Bush	—	38
Robert Dole	—	32
Philip Crane	—	6

SOURCE: Patterson, 1980, Table 10.1, p. 109 (1976 data); CPS National Elections Study (1980 data).

Sustained coverage *can* convert a nobody into a somebody, but not often and not easily.

Consider the ordeal of Fred Harris. After more than a full term as a U.S. Senator from Oklahoma, several prominent positions in the national Democratic Party, a run for the presidency in 1972 and a full year's campaigning prior to the 1976 New Hampshire primary, Harris entered the 1976 campaign a stranger to all but 12 percent of the public. That is also how he departed; by June, Mr. Harris had improved his recognition level by a scant 4 points (Patterson, 1980).

Idealized renderings of democracy usually demand more of citizens than merely the capacity to recognize candidates for high public office. In representative governments, free and open elections constitute an instrument, if a blunt one, for conveying the public's preferences regarding government policy. Often thought essential to this process is an electorate capable of distinguishing the package of policies promoted by one candidate from the package promoted by competitors. In this respect (as in others), the public often seems confused and ill-informed.

Some substantial part of this, we should hasten to add, is due to the candidates themselves. Take the nondebate over Vietnam policy that in a curious way was the centerpiece of the 1968 presidential campaign. Neither Hubert Humphrey nor Richard Nixon was at all clear, publicly at least, about his position on the war. By their silence, imprecision, and vacillation, Humphrey and Nixon invited citizens to become confused, an invitation that evidently few could resist (Page and Brody, 1972).

Public ignorance and confusion are diminished when candidates stake out distinctive positions on central policy questions. In recent history, the candidacy of Goldwater in 1964 represents perhaps the purest case. In the South and elsewhere, Goldwater spoke forcefully on behalf of states' rights, citing his vote against the Civil Rights Act as proof of his conviction. Partly as a consequence, more than three quarters (77 percent) of the public in the fall of 1964 claimed familiarity with the Civil Rights Act, and of those, most everyone (84 percent) knew that Goldwater opposed it (RePass, 1971).

In this respect Goldwater seems to be the exception; Humphrey and Nixon the rule. Policy declarations play a modest part in the modern presidential campaign. They are typically planted in special-interest periodicals (such as *Education News* or *Missiles and Rockets*) or tucked away in speeches to sympathetic local audiences. Even there, candidates' proposals tend to express general values more than they do ideas about specific actions (Page, 1978; candidates for the U.S. Senate do the same: Poole, 1981; Elling, 1982). In short, presidential candidates cultivate ambiguity. When they do not, when they offer clear and distinctive proposals, public confusion diminishes.

Spotty enough regarding would-be presidents, public knowledge becomes sparser still regarding candidates for Congress. Following the 1958 off-year election, just 23 percent of Americans could recall the name, identify the party, and claim some minimal familiarity of the Democratic candidate running for the House of Representatives in their district; just 21 percent could clear all three hurdles for the Repulican candidate. These figures edged upwards in 1964 and then receded to 1958 levels in the 1978 mid-term election, when the same questions were repeated (Pierce and Converse, 1980, p. 11 and Table 6).

In part this reflects the peripheral place of politics—particularly congressional election politics—in people's lives. No doubt it also reflects the limited opportunities people are offered to learn about congressional candidates: An analysis of newspaper coverage of candidates for the House during the 1958 elections was abandoned, since references to the candidates were so few and far between (Converse, 1975a). As in presidential contests, too, some portion of public ignorance and confusion on these matters should be ascribed to the candidates themselves. Congressional campaigns are rarely vehicles for the presentation of strong policy initiatives (Fenno, 1978; Kingdon, 1973).

Every now and then, of course, events conspire to center public attention upon congressional contests. A widely cited example is the 1958 campaign in Arkansas's Fifth District. There the incumbent representative had become entangled in the federal government's efforts to resolve the Little Rock school integration crisis. Hardly an integrationist, the incumbent was nevertheless portrayed as soft on civil rights and was defeated by a write-in campaign on behalf of a staunch defender of segregation. In the Fifth District in Arkansas in 1958, *every* voter interviewed claimed to have heard something about both candidates (Miller and Stokes, 1966a, pp. 369–370). This exception proves the general rule, however: In-depth knowledge of candidates for the U.S. House of Representatives is uncommon.

Though the evidence is much less complete, familiarity with the candidates for the many obscure state and local offices for which the public is asked to cast ballots is generally rarer still. In principle, because the local offices are closer to home, the issues and candidates should be more familiar. In practice, this seems most unlikely. Voting in these races must be based on something other than detailed analysis of the alternatives.

In summary, four decades of research on public opinion have replaced the omnicompetent citizen with a less perfect creature. Americans are indifferent to much that transpires in the political world, hazy about many of the principal players, lackadaisical regarding debates on policies that preoccupy Washington, ignorant of facts that experts take for granted, and unsure about the policies advanced by candidates for the highest public offices. Although it may seem otherwise, this rather dreary recitation is no indictment—not, at least, of the ordinary citizen. Some of the indifference, ignorance, and confusion documented in the preceding pages is due to candidates and officials who, in an effort to assemble fragile majorities in a contentious world, often steer clear of distinctive and controversial positions. Some of it must also be traced to the subordinate place of politics in the lives of Americans. Who are we to quarrel with such priorities? Furthermore, when the political process does intrude upon cherished values—as in the Fifth District in Arkansas in 1958—the public seems quite capable of paying attention. It should also be said that the distribution of ignorance and confusion is scarcely evenhanded: Among the U.S. public there is enormous variation in political interest and knowledge (e.g., Converse, 1976; Francis and Busch, 1975). Some are dedicated spectators, while others almost literally "know nothing" of politics (Hyman and Sheatsley, 1947). Finally, we should not glibly generalize this sketch of public opinion to other places or to the United States in other times. In emerging nations, where government's monopoly over the distribution of benefits and services may mean survival itself or at special moments in U.S. history when the regime seemed threatened, our sketch may be quite misleading (Hayward, 1976; Iyengar, 1979a).

So the case for privatism and ignorance is not a simple one. Nor should it be read as an invitation to deplore the public's errant ways. Privatism and dark areas of ignorance are this chapter's first facts, however. In what follows we will be deeply suspicious of claims that presume on the public's part a voracious appetite for political information or even much taste for complex and extended reasoning about public life.

IDEOLOGICAL INNOCENCE?

We are left with the mystery of how people arrive at those political opinions they do hold. What are the sources of U.S. public opinion? How do Americans put their political ideas together?

One thoroughly researched possibility is that Americans deduce their opinions on events, policies, and candidates from general ideological principles—sweeping ideas about how government and society should be organized. But the earliest systematic national surveys, conducted a quarter century ago, turned up few full-fledged liberals or conservatives, much less more exotic political types. According to these early explorations, the vast majority of Americans appeared in fact to be thoroughly innocent of ideology (Campbell *et al.,* 1960; McClosky *et al.,* 1960; McClosky, 1964; Prothro and Grigg, 1960).

In the past decade, however, consensus on this point has come undone. The field is now in "crisis" (Bennett, 1977). In place of the cozy consensus of the past are often unfriendly arguments: some arcanely technical, some broadly methodological, some interpretational, and some plainly political. To be faithful to this complex and treacherous literature, we review it in five parts. First we quickly sketch the original claim—that the U.S. public is largely innocent of ideology, particularly as realized in the writings of Converse (1963, 1964, 1975a, 1975b). We concentrate on Converse because his rendering of the ideological innocence argument is the most powerful and because it effectively set the terms for most subsequent work—indeed, for too much subsequent work. Though accepting his terms, researchers who followed Converse have often been critical of his conclusions; that revisionist literature is reviewed next. Then we take up two proposals regarding ideology that lie largely outside the principal tussle between Converse and his critics but bear obviously on it: First, that ideological labels (like "liberal" and "conservative") organize political thinking; and second, that ideology in ideographic form is pervasive. In the final section we draw the various pieces together and deliver a general verdict on the claim of ideological innocence.

The Original Claim

Converse approached the problem of ideology by trying to describe the public's belief systems more generally. These he defined as configurations "of ideas and attitudes in which the elements are bound together by some form of constraint or functional interdependence" (1964, p. 207). Guided by this definition and making use of national surveys conducted by the Michigan Survey Research Center in 1956, 1958, and 1960, Converse concluded that dramatic, perhaps unbridgeable, differences divided elites from masses. Turning from the political belief systems of activists to those of ordinary citizens, "constraint declines across the universe of idea-elements,...the range of relevant belief systems becomes narrower and narrower. Instead of a few wide-range belief systems that organize large amounts of specific information, one [discovers] a proliferation of clusters of ideas among which little constraint is felt..." (Converse, 1964, p. 213). At the same time, "the character of the objects that are central in a belief system undergoes systematic change. These objects shift from the remote, generic, and abstract to the increasingly simple, concrete, or 'close to home' " (p. 213).

Converse was led to these conclusions in part because of Americans' unfamiliarity with ideological concepts. Those questioned in the 1956 survey were asked to discuss the good and bad points of the two major political parties and, in a parallel series of questions, to comment on the major presidential candidates. According to Converse's coding, active use of ideological terms was confined to just 2.5 percent of the public. Near ideologues, those who made some use of abstract concepts but appeared neither to rely upon them heavily nor to understand them very well, comprised another one-tenth of the national sample. This left fully 88 percent of the general public ideologically innocent.

Mere recognition of standard ideological terms was not widespread, either. The 1960 interview included a series of questions designed to ascertain citizens' understanding of liberalism and conservatism. Those interviewed were asked to assign these labels to the two parties (if they first indicated that meaningful party differences existed) and then to explain what they meant. Just one-sixth of the public both assigned the labels properly and explained party differences in terms of broad ideological themes.

Of course, ideology might still flourish among the public, if it turned out that many people simply could not articulate or recognize the principles that in fact determined their beliefs. If many Americans really used ideological principles but could not express them easily or quickly, their opinions on various issues should still exhibit consistency, tied together by the underlying ideological principles. To test for such "constraint," Converse computed correlations between opinions on topical issues within two groups, both interviewed in 1958: a national cross-section of the general public and a smaller group made up of candidates for the U.S. House of Representatives. Respondents in each group were asked their opinions on a series of domestic and foreign issues: for example, aid to education, government guarantee of employment, military support for countries menaced by Communist aggression, and the like. Substantial constraint betweeen opinions on such issues was apparent only for the candidates. Indeed, among the public, there was little consistency at all. Converse concluded that opinions expressed by ordinary citizens on particular issues do not derive from widely shared, general principles. Measly correlations across different topics reflected citizens' failure to master and employ the abstract ideological concepts that might have tied the topics together (Aberbach *et al.,* 1981, Chapter 5; Butler and Stokes, 1974; Converse and Pierce, 1985; Klingemann, 1979; Miller and Miller, 1976).

Policy opinions not only appeared largely insulated from one another but also seemed to wobble capriciously back and forth over time. The policy questions included in the 1958 national survey were also posed to the same respondents two years earlier, in the 1956 survey, as well as two years later, in the 1960 survey. Although there were virtually no aggregate shifts in opinion on any of these issues across this period and despite the precautions taken to discourage superficial replies, at the individual level change was the rule. Stability coefficients (Tau-Beta's) ranged from .28, in the case of the issue that perhaps best reflected the enduring philosophical dispute between liberals and conservatives—whether the federal government should have any role in the construction of housing and the production of electricity—to .43 and .47 in the case of policies that impinged upon blacks—establishing a commission on fair employment practice and school desegregation, respectively. On average, less than two thirds of the public came down on the same side of a policy controversy over a two-year period; one-half would be expected to do so by chance alone.

Oddly enough, opinions on public policy expressed by survey respondents in 1960 could be predicted just as well by their opinions in 1956 as by their opinions in 1958. This pattern led Converse to develop his "black and white" model of opinion change, which partitioned the public on any particular issue into two groups: one composed of citizens who are quite indifferent to it and when pressed either admit ignorance or invent a "non-attitude" (Converse, 1963) and the other consisting of those who possess genuine opinions and hold onto them tenaciously. The heart of Converse's message here is that the real opinion holders are usually outnumbered.

In summary, most Americans approach the political world innocent of ideology: indifferent to standard ideological concepts, lacking a consistent perspective on public policy, and holding authentic opinions on only a handful of policy questions. All this, of course, is according to the conventional wisdom of two decades ago.

Counterclaims

The most elaborate challenge to the conventional wisdom came in the form of Nie, Verba, and Petrocik's *The Changing American Voter* (1979). Nie and associates argued that one way the U.S. voter had changed since the 1950s was by becoming more ideological. Like Converse, Nie, Verba, and Petrocik also looked at citizens' replies to the open-ended candidate and party questions, but this time they examined the replies to surveys conducted from 1952 to 1976. They reported that ideological reactions to candidates, virtually invisible in 1952, increased dramatically in 1964 and then declined sharply in 1976. Nie, Verba, and Petrocik concluded that given proper circumstances—like the ideologically polarized contest between Johnson and Goldwater—a substantial fraction of the U.S. public is capable of thinking ideologically, a conclusion that quickly became the new conventional wisdom (also see Field and Anderson, 1969; Pierce, 1970; note that chapters 7, 20, and Appendix 2C of the "enlarged edition" of *The Changing American Voter* should be read in conjunction with the corrections furnished by Nie, Verba, and Petrocik, 1981).

There are serious deficiencies in the new wisdom, however. Nie and his associates worked not from verbatim readings of the original protocols, as had Converse, but from replies precoded into general categories. As a consequence, in their measurement of ideological reasoning, Nie and his colleagues merely tallied up the incidence of ideological terms rather than qualitatively coding the actual use of abstract concepts, as Converse did. Replications of the latter indicate that the U.S. public's use of ideological concepts has increased since the 1950s but that the increase has been glacial: from roughly 2.5 percent in Converse's analysis to about 7 percent in several analyses from the late 1960s and early 1970s (Klingemann, 1979; Klingemann and Wright, 1973; Miller and Miller, 1976; Pierce and Hagner, 1982). Moreover, these replications do not support the revisionist claim that ideological reasoning responds to fluctuations in the ideological character of political debate.

How, then, should the quite sensational changes reported by Nie, Verba, and Petrocik be interpreted? Presumably they reflect a facility on the public's part to pick up the labels that ideologically charged campaigns make prominent. Of course, the use of an ideological vocabu-

lary in no way guarantees that the underlying ideas are deeply understood or even that the terms are correctly used. It appears that revisionists have demonstrated increases only in what might be called the nonideological use of ideological terminology (Levitin and Miller, 1979; Smith, 1980; Nie, Verba, and Petrocik, 1981 now say this is what they meant all along). Such demonstrations do little damage to the original claim of innocence.

This brings us to the empirical centerpiece of the revisionist argument: the compelling demonstration of greater cohesion in the U.S. public's beliefs on public policy beginning in the 1960s (Nie and Andersen, 1974; Nie, Verba, and Petrocik, 1979). Nie and his associates replicated Converse's original analysis of constraint in seven national surveys running from 1956 to 1972. Through the late 1950s and early 1960s, Nie *et al.* found (as had Converse) little constraint between opinions on issues of social welfare, equality of opportunity, foreign relations, and the like. This changed in 1964. Suddenly opinions on school integration became aligned with feelings about big government, views on foreign policy became linked to beliefs regarding the federal government's responsibility to subsidize medical care, and so on. Detected first in 1964, this new-found structure in public opinion persisted at about the same level through 1968 and has since slightly declined (e.g., Miller and Miller, 1977; Nie, Verba, and Petrocik, 1979, p. 369). Nie and his colleagues interpreted these results to indicate a monumental change in public thinking, provoked by the tumultuous events of the 1960s.

Not so. In 1964, coincident with the increase in cohesion in public thinking on policy matters, the formats of the questions on public policy were altered. The changes seem innocuous enough: from a conventional Likert format to an arrangement in which respondents were asked to choose between a pair of opposing alternatives and from a gentle to a somewhat more insistent invitation to admit to no opinion at all. Could such subtle changes explain what Nie and Andersen took to be "dramatic shifts in both the breadth and depth of liberal/conservative attitude structure..." (p. 571)? They could and probably did. (The most lethal weapon in this debate has been the experiment; see especially Sullivan, Piereson, and Marcus, 1978; Sullivan, Piereson, Marcus, and Feldman, 1979.) It is now clear that most of the apparent change in opinion structure is artificial, produced not by political metamorphosis but by mundane alterations in question wording. This radically inverts the revisionists' message. *Despite* profound changes in U.S. politics through the 1960s, the structure of public opinion hardly changed at all.

This conclusion has nothing to say about whether structure is estimated better by the old-style questions or by the new. With Sullivan and his colleagues (1978), we favor the latter, both because they encourage acquiescence less (Jackson, 1979) and because they capture better the essence of classical liberal-conservative debate. Hence Converse's original anaysis somewhat understated the public's capacity to develop consistent positions on issues.

Surely the most devastating element of the original claim of ideological innocence was how few people seemed to possess real preferences regarding public policy. Converse understood the public's prodigious wandering from one side of a policy question to the other over time to be symptomatic of the shallowness of opinion. Reluctant to own up to their own ignorance, people invented evanescent opinions—liberal on one occasion, conservative on the next.

Well, maybe not. Converse's critics interpret this instability to be a reflection instead of unclear questions. Responses may not be stable, but the underlying opinions are. Instability reflects vague questions, not vague citizens (Achen, 1975, 1983; Converse, 1974, 1980; Erikson, 1978; Jackson, 1982; Judd and Milburn, 1980; Judd, Krosnick, and Milburn, 1981; Pierce and Rose, 1974).

If revisionists are correct, the original claim comes undone, at two points. Threatened first is the nonattitude thesis itself—that on many matters of public policy, most people possess no genuine preference at all. Also threatened is the analysis of attitude constraint. Once purged of measurement error, the public's opinions on questions of public policy no longer seem quite so feebly structured (see Achen 1975, Table 3).

In adjudicating this conflict, much hinges on how instability is understood. According to Converse's interpretation, instability on any particular issue should vary from one person to the next. Stability should be comparatively high among people engaged by the issue and comparatively low among people whose political interests lie elsewhere. Testing this prediction was Achen's (1975) way of resolving the debate. Achen regressed his estimate of the measurement error associated with each policy question for each survey respondent against demographic characteristics (e.g., education, income, occupation) and measures of general political interest (e.g., concern over election outcome, interest in campaign, etc.), with feeble returns. Variation in education or in political en-

gagement proved to be weak predictors of error. Achen concluded that since unreliability was spread so evenly across the public, it should properly be ascribed not to citizen confusion but to questionnaire imperfection. (For comparable tests, see Erikson, 1978, and Judd *et al.,* 1981.)

However, Achen's results are in fact compatible with a strict reading of Converse's argument. Converse emphasized the fragmentation of the public into narrow factions, each preoccupied with different policy matters. Demonstrating that *general* interest in politics fails to predict opinion stability does no damage to this view. A persuasive disconfirmation of Converse's claim requires showing, for example, that those citizens intrigued by matters of foreign policy do not differ from the rest of the population in the stability of their opinion on aid to foreign countries.

Although comparisons of this sort are scarce, those that have been reported favor Converse's original claim: Policy-specific interest *does* seem to be associated with the durability of opinion over time (Converse, 1964, pp. 244-245; Schuman and Presser, 1981, Chapter 9). Moreover, collateral evidence of various kinds would seem to constitute serious anomalies for the critics of the nonattitude thesis. First, political elites appear to cling tenaciously to *their* political beliefs. The best evidence of this kind available now is provided by Putnam and his associates (1979) in a panel study of Italian regional councillors. Interviewed first in 1970 and again in 1976, the councillors remained remarkably steadfast in their political opinions. On the question of government workers' right to strike, for example, councillors' opinions were substantially more stable across a *six*-year period (Pearson r = .75) than were the U.S. public's beliefs across *two* years, on *any* of the policy questions included in the 1956–1960 panel study. Does this radical contrast mean that Putnam and his associates have made historic breakthroughs in the formulation of questions, or does it reflect the greater attention and thought given to politics by Italian councillors than by average Americans? (For equally striking contrasts involving French deputies and the French public, see Converse and Pierce, 1985.) Or consider that by simple correlations, identification with a political party is vastly more stable over time than are preferences on policy questions (Converse, 1964; Converse and Markus, 1979). Revisionists are forced to interpret this to mean that writers of questions have stumbled upon comparatively precise ways of asking respondents about their party affiliations, but haven't yet discovered how to ask questions about policy. This seems tortured, especially in light of recent agitation over the need to improve the measurement of party identification (e.g., Weisberg, 1980).

In short, instability in political opinion cannot be reduced entirely to technical problems of measurement. Instability reflects both fuzzy measures *and* fuzzy citizens. This conclusion is supported as well by the observation that public opinion is sensitive to the context of opinion elicitation. Opinion varies as a function of question wording (Bennett, 1976, Chapter 4; Mueller, 1973, p. 44; Schuman and Presser, 1981; Tversky and Kahneman, 1981) and question order (Bishop *et al.*, 1982; Sears and Lau, 1983; Schuman and Kalton, 1985; Turner and Kraus, 1978). The occasionally striking susceptibility of public opinion to context implies that Americans often fail to supply their own. Thus confronted with policy debates of great and abiding interest to political elites, many Americans do little more than shrug. Instability largely reflects the fleeting attention commonly paid to politics and the preeminence of private desires over public ones.

The durability of public opinion on policy matters also depends, finally, on the character of the policy itself. One of the clearest and least controversial lessons of recent research is that Americans are decisively more stable on some policy matters than on others. In particular, when policies become entangled with moral, racial, and religious values, indifference and nonattitudes may vanish altogether. In the mid 1970s, for example, nearly every American knew what the government should do about abortion, racial busing, and equal rights for women (Converse and Markus, 1979; Kinder and Rhodebeck, 1982). Whether Americans shrug or become impassioned when confronted with policy alternatives has therefore much to do with the nature of the policy itself.

Ideological Self-identification

Most recently, a somewhat different view of ideology has begun to emerge, stimulated in part by the observation that many Americans are quite willing to describe themselves in ideological terms. Since 1972, those interviewed in the Michigan Survey Research Center national election studies have been asked whether they think of themselves as liberals or conservatives and, if so, to locate themselves on a seven-point scale, ranging from extreme liberal (on the far left of the scale, naturally) to extreme conservative (on the far right). Roughly two-thirds of the public claim identifications, and these seem quite mean-

ingful: Liberals tend to favor redistributive welfare policies and social change while conservatives tend to oppose racial integration and government interference in the marketplace. Of course, Americans may not understand the implications of these labels in the same terms that elites do, and indeed there may be only a modest public consensus about their meaning. Yet for some Americans, ideological identifications do seem to summarize a general political stance (Conover and Feldman, 1981; Levitan and Miller, 1979; Sears, Lau, Tyler, and Allen, 1980).

Such identifications are *not* based strongly in issue preferences: Correlations with opinions on issues of public policy seldom exceed .3 and are apparent really only among the most politically engaged (Converse and Pierce, 1985; Levitan and Miller, 1979; Stimson, 1975). Indeed, many Americans find it difficult to determine which policy preference "liberals" and "conservatives" generally hold or what their differences over policy might be (Levitan and Miller, 1979). Instead, ideological self-identifications appear to be grounded in group attachments (or antagonisms) and moral preferences. Liberals tend to support the political causes of blacks and women, while conservatives support business, the police, and the military (Cobb and Elder, 1976; Conover and Feldman, 1981; Sears *et al.*, 1979).

In short this "new look" at ideology is somewhat orthogonal to the old debate. It assumes that people have strong evaluative commitments to symbols associated with ideological labels and that these shape political thinking. The content of these self-identifications may not be rich in policy preferences, and indeed many citizens may have strong self-identifications whose content is quite different than that conventionally perceived as "correct" by elites (Levitan and Miller, 1979), a point that supports Converse's original (1964) claim. Nevertheless, ideological labels are widely recognized and can trigger strong evaluative reactions.

Ideographic Ideology

Although referring to the diverse critics of innocence as though they belonged to the same club represents crude stereotyping on our part, there is at least one kernel of truth to it. The promoters of the original claim and their critics partake of a common paradigm. However much revisionists tinker with method, however much their conclusions depart from ideological innocence, they nevertheless accept the basic terms established by Converse two decades ago. Others do not. Converse's most persistent and able critic over the years has been Robert Lane (1962, 1969, 1973). Lane not only puts forward a powerful, layered attack on Converse's approach, but also argues for and illustrates in his own work an alternative approach, here called *ideographic*.

Lane complains first of all that Converse (and nearly everyone else) examines only the products of political reasoning, not the *process* of reasoning. To learn how people think about politics requires, according to Lane, radical departures from the conventional survey interview. Lane's *Political Ideology* (1962) was based upon a set of intensive, intimate, individually tailored interviews. Through what Lane calls a "contextual analysis" of these conversations, the process of political reasoning is supposedly revealed (1962, pp. 9–10):

> An opinion, belief, or attitude is best understood in the context of other opinions, beliefs, and attitudes, for they illuminate its meaning, marks its boundaries, modify and qualify its force. Even more important, by grouping opinions the observer can often discover latent ideological themes; he can see the structure of thought: premise, inference, application. There is no other satisfactory way to map a political ideology.

Lane criticizes Converse also for holding up his own ideas about how beliefs should be patterned as the uniquely appropriate standard for the public, a complaint made by many others in the ideographic camp (e.g., Bennett, 1976, 1977; Brown, 1970, 1980; Conover and Feldman, 1980; Marcus, Tabb, and Sullivan, 1974). According to Lane, Converse's "confusion" on this point—imposing his understanding of what political beliefs should belong with what other beliefs—slants his results. Lane avoids this problem in his work by providing his subjects with ample opportunity to express their own perhaps unique patterning of ideas and in their own terms.

The confusion Lane ascribes on these matters to Converse in fact properly belongs mainly to Lane (a point that is itself usually confused). First of all, Lane's criticism ignores Converse's analysis of the persistence of opinion over time. Such an analysis requires no assumptions regarding the particular ways in which beliefs should be patterned, only that they show reasonable stability. Indeed, this is a major reason why Converse undertook the analysis in the first place.

Secondly, although Converse does indeed impose his own standards elsewhere in his analysis, he does so deliberately. He may be wrong in his choice, but he is not at all confused. His choice is of course the standards imputed to characterize the thinking of political elites: reliance upon abstract, general principles. Lane is perfectly correct to insist that we should not conclude from the public's apparent failure to organize its policy preferences in these terms that the public therefore has no capacity to organize its political ideas at all. Converse did not; nor should we.

Thirdly, Lane's cure for Converse's alleged confusion has problems of its own. Objectivity and replicability are hardly the hallmarks of contextual analysis. Although not without real virtues, Lane's approach is vulnerable to the charge that he has not so much discovered the ordinary persons's ideology as he has contributed to its momentary creation.

Of course, the ideographic approach need not—and has not—relied exclusively on in-depth interviewing. More objective data collection and analysis procedures that still permit a measure of idiosyncrasy in belief organization have also been used, such as individual difference multidimensional scaling (Marcus *et al.,* 1974) and Q-methodology and factor analysis (Bennett, 1976; Brown, 1970, 1980; Conover and Feldman, 1984). These approaches center attention on *personalized* systems of beliefs, trying with some success to demonstrate, as Bennett (1976) put it, that "all people don't make sense of politics in the same way, but most people make sense of politics in some way" (pp. 18–19).

Lane's most valuable contribution to the investigation of ideology has been to broaden its meaning. In Converse's analysis, and in most that followed, opinions on public policy were paid great attention—to Lane's way of thinking and to ours, inordinate attention. Although political belief systems surely include policy preferences they also incorporate "the fundamental views which form the ideational counterpart to a constitution: ideas on fair play and due process, rights of others, sharing of power, the proper distribution of goods in society (equality), uses and abuses of authority . . ." (Lane, 1962, p. 15).

Consider Lane's discerning examination of the ordinary citizen's beliefs regarding equality. The uniquely egalitarian style of U.S. social relations has struck observers from de Tocqueville to the present. Lane argues, however, that members of the working class generally do not want equality; that they are, in fact, afraid of it; and that inequality provides to them important gratifications. According to this view, economic equality would deprive citizens of the goals of life. For the common man, an egalitarian society would bring bewilderment and alienation, for "their life goals are structured around achievement and success in monetary terms. If these were taken away, life would be a desert" (1962, p. 78). Lane concluded from these and other results that citizens do entertain genuine, occasionally deeply felt, political beliefs, not only about equality but about other fundamental political matters as well (Hochschild, 1981; Lamb, 1974; Sennett and Cobb, 1972; Ward, 1982).

Contrary to popular opinion, this conclusion in no way undermines Converse's original claim. Because Lane and Converse (and hence, Lane and most everyone else) mean quite different things by ideology—Lane explores everyday notions of freedom, equality, and democracy, while Converse worries about the public's appraisal of parties, candidates, and especially public policy—their conclusions barely touch.

Rather than as a disconfirmation, Lane's findings may be regarded as contributing another piece to the puzzle of political reasoning. If the ingredients of political ideology are broadened beyond conventional practice in the manner urged by Lane, then the ordinary American may properly be characterized as ideological. People make sense of equality, freedom, and democracy, though the sense is often personalized and idiosyncratic. It is an ideology not to be confused with that of the articulate, self-reflective, political sophisticate. But it is an ideology nevertheless.

Although the in relationship is predominantly complementary, Lane's and Converse's arguments *do* directly intersect at one point. To aid his description of the working-class man's political ruminations, Lane distinguished between two opposite modes of thought: "contextualizing," or thinking that places political events in topical, temporal, and historical perspective and "morselizing," or thinking that considers events in isolation. Lane concluded that, with an occasional exception, morselizing was the dominant tendency (1962, p. 353):

> This treatment of an instance in isolation happens time and again and on matters close to home: a union demand is a single incident, not part of a more general labor-management conflict; a purchase on the installment plan is a specific debt, not part of a budgetary pattern—either one's own or society's. The items and fragments of life remain itemized and fragmented....

Constraint must therefore be provided other than by deduction from abstract, general principles. In this way, but moving from a different conception of ideology and a radically different method, Lane reinforces the conclusion of ideological innocence.

Innocence Reappraised

"Belief systems have never surrendered easily to empirical study" (Converse, 1964, p. 206). So Converse began his seminal essay nearly two decades ago; so it is today. Indeed, it would be difficult to imagine a more fitting tribute to Converse's assertion than the tangle of arguments and evidence spilled across the preceding pages. The recalcitrance of the subject is not all that we have learned, however.

We have learned in the first place that ideological innocence is a fully appropriate verdict *if* by innocence we mean that few Americans make sophisticated use of sweeping ideological ideas. Few do. Innocence of ideology is revealed also in the political connections Americans never make. Few Americans express consistently liberal, conservative, or centrist positions on policy—no less so during the turbulent, ideological 1960s as during the serene Eisenhower years. In Lane's felicitous phrase, Americans "morselize" their political beliefs (1962, p. 353). However, the nonattitude thesis, certainly the most controversial allegation in the original claim of ideological innocence, now seems less powerful. Opinion instability is partly the product of hazy questions. It is also clearer than before that issue publics need not be limited to narrow splinters of the general public: Some issues engage the attention of nearly everybody. This leaves us somewhat more confident in the public's capacity to develop genuine political preferences than where Converse left things in 1964.

That the original claim of ideological innocence is largely sustained does not mean that the American mind is empty of politics. Innocent though Americans may typically be of ideological principles, they are hardly innocent of political ideas. Such ideas defy parsimonious description, however. Some beliefs are classically liberal, some classically conservative. There are some authentic opinions, tenaciously held and some nonattitudes, casually expressed. There are patches of knowledge and expanses of ignorance. "A realistic picture of political belief systems in the mass public, then" wrote Converse (1964, p. 247), "is not one that omits issues and policy demands completely nor one that presumes widespread ideological coherence; it is rather one that captures with some fidelity the fragmentation, narrowness, and diversity of these demands.''

PLURALISTIC ROOTS OF POLITICAL BELIEFS

Where do the fragmented, narrow, and diverse political ideas that lurk in the American mind come from? On this point, the last twenty years of research have been more destructive than constructive. One prominent possibility—that political ideas are deduced from sweeping ideological principles—has been emphatically dispatched. This is an important lesson, but because of the field's fixation on the ideology question, we now know rather more about how Americans do *not* think about politics than about how they do. In this section of the chapter, we will take up six alternative ways for thinking about the roots of political belief. If not by a wide-ranging, coherent ideology, perhaps the ordinary person's political thinking is shaped by:

1. The single-minded pursuit of self-interest;

2. Identification with salient social groups, whose fortunes and prospects are seen to be affected by political decisions;

3. The influence of opinion leaders, especially presidents;

4. The affirmation of core values;

5. The expression of private needs and motives; and

6. Inferences drawn from the unfolding of political history.

Self-Interest

Surely there is no more familiar a presumption than self-interest. Of course people support policies that promote their own material interests and oppose policies that threaten them. Beliefs on public policy are determined not by a coherent ideological stance but by ''primitive self-interest,'' as *The American Voter* (Campbell *et al.,* 1960) put it (p. 205).

Although the presumption of self-interest is strong, the evidence is weak. For example, the economic predicaments of private life generally have weak influences on which policies citizens endorse. Neither losing a job, nor deteriorating family financial conditions, nor pessimism

about the family's economic future has much to do with support for policies designed to alleviate personal economic distress (Denney, Hendricks, and Kinder, 1980; Kinder, 1981; Kinder and Kiewiet, 1981; Lowery and Sigelman, 1981; Schlozman and Verba, 1979; Sears and Citrin, 1982; Sears, Lau, Tyler, and Allen, 1980). Economic self-interest influences policy beliefs only when the stakes are especially clear and large (e.g., Sears and Citrin, 1982), and even then the effects tend to be highly circumscribed. For instance, the unemployed, more than working people, believe that the national government should provide jobs, although they do not support unconventional or drastic solutions to unemployment, or favor schemes to redistribute income (Schlozman and Verba, 1979). Consider another anomaly for self-interest: Disruptions to private life occasioned by the sudden onset of energy shortages in 1974 seemed to have had no ramifications for opinion on energy policy. People whose lives were most disrupted were no more likely to support greater energy conservation or the development of alternative energy sources than were their more fortunate counterparts whose personal lives went on unaffected by the crisis (Sears, Tyler, Citrin, and Kinder, 1978). Similarly, although war would seem to engage self-interest in an ultimate way, those people with close relatives or friends in Korea or Vietnam did not seem to have negative opinions about the conflict (Mueller, 1973; Lau, Brown, and Sears, 1978). A final case, equally problematic for the self-interest presumption, comes from research on public opinion on school busing for racial desegregation. Opposition to busing, it turns out, has little to do with its personal consequences. Parents of children enrolled in public schools in neighborhoods affected by busing for desegregation are generally no more opposed to busing than any other segment of the public (Gatlin, Giles, and Cataldo, 1978; Kinder and Rhodebeck, 1982; Kinder and Sears, 1981; McConahay, 1982; Sears and Allen, 1984; Sears, Hensler, and Speer, 1979; Sears and Kinder, 1971).

Laid end to end, these studies do much to undermine the faith widely invested in material self-interest. As a basis for political belief, primitive self-interest seems to have been drastically overpromoted. Why this is so —why the links between self-interest and belief are so tenuous—is not yet clear. One possibility is that self-interest is typically overwhelmed by long-held, emotionally powerful predispositions. According to this account, people acquire predispositions (like racial prejudice or nationalism) rather early in life that shape their political views in adulthood. Interpretation and evaluation of political events are essentially affective responses to salient symbols that resemble the attitude objects to which similar emotional responses were conditioned in earlier life. Whether or not the event has some tangible consequence for the citizen's personal life is irrelevant; the pertinent personal stake is a symbolic one, which triggers long-held, affect-laden, habitual responses (Sears, Hensler, and Speer, 1979; Sears, Lau, Tyler, and Allen, 1980; Kinder and Sears, 1981).

Another general possibility directs attention to how people understand their own predicaments—particularly the causes they see for their problems and how they think such problems could and should be solved. In the economic domain, Americans seldom blame themselves for their own predicaments, but neither do they blame government. Nor do they look to government for assistance in solving their economic difficulties. Instead, Americans see their predicaments as the result of proximal, particularistic causes and rely on their own resources in seeking remedies. Thus people typically understand (economic) problems in ways that muffle their political ramifications. In so doing, the power of self-interest is eroded (Brody and Sniderman, 1977; Kinder and Kiewiet, 1979; Kinder and Mebane, 1983).

Group Identification

Can groups succeed where self fails? Perhaps the development of political ideas reflects the web of allegiances and antipathies that individuals develop toward groups. From this perspective, political opinions are "badges of social membership": They are declarations, to others and to ourselves, of social identity (Smith, Bruner, and White, 1956). Support for affirmative action reflects sympathy for the plight of blacks (Kinder and Sears, 1981); opposition to social welfare programs derives from hostility toward the poor (Feldman, 1983); support for war in Asia reflects fear of Communism (Mueller, 1973); enthusiasm for political repression hinges on whose phones are to be tapped (Sullivan *et al.,* 1981); and so forth.

Perhaps the most effective general demonstration of the important role played by social identity in political reasoning is the persistent prominence of social groups in Americans' appraisals of political parties and presidential candidates. In Converse's original coding of open-ended replies in the 1956 survey, citizens who made use of social groups comprised by far the largest single category—42 percent of the entire public. Such citizens typical-

ly named benefits and deprivations that parties and candidates had visited upon social groups in the past or might deliver in the future. According to Campbell and his colleagues (1960, p. 234), this is not a genuine abstract ideology at work, but:

> ideology by proxy, [since there] . . . is little comprehension of "long-range plans for social betterment," or of basic philosophies rooted in postures toward change or abstract conceptions of social and economic structure of causation. The party or candidate is simply endorsed as being "for" a group with which the subject is identified or as being above the selfish demands of groups within the population. Exactly *how* the candidate or party might see fit to implement or void group interests is a moot point, left unrelated to broader ideological concerns.

These findings seem quite representative of other times and places. References to groups continue to occupy a central place in citizens' appraisals of parties and candidates—and not only in the United States (Kagay and Caldeira, 1980; Klingemann, 1979). But *which* group identifications are important?

One natural possibility is social class. According to Lipset (1960, p. 234):

> The most impressive single fact about political party support is that in virtually every economically developed country the lower-income groups vote mainly for the parties of the left, while the higher-income groups vote mainly for parties of the right.

Indeed, middle- and upper-class Americans differ from their working- and lower-class compatriots in the candidates they choose, the parties they support, and the social welfare policies they advocate (e.g., Alford, 1963; Centers, 1949; Converse, 1958; Hamilton, 1972; Ladd and Hadley, 1975; Vanneman and Pampel, 1977).

At least as impressive as the regularity of the association between class and political preference in the United States, however, is its modesty. "Class struggle" is much too strong a phrase to impose on the rather anemic correlations typically reported; even "class conflict" may be too strong. Among Western democracies, the United States finishes close to last on measures linking class and political choice (Alford, 1963). Although from a comparative perspective it is never very imposing, the link between class and political belief in the United States has in the past three decades eroded still further (Abramson, 1974; Inglehart, 1983; Ladd and Hadley, 1975; Schlozman and Verba, 1979). Declining economic conditions or class-polarizing government policies may resurrect this weakening association, but in the meantime, we need to look at lines of conflict other than those defined by class.

Race is one obvious choice. Over the past four decades, whenever surveys have been taken, black and white Americans have differed systematically and often enormously in their support for open housing, federal assistance to "minorities," school integration, welfare, and other matters of policy touching race. In a 1976 survey, for example, while blacks favored school integration by more than five to one, most whites declared that school integration was none of the federal government's business (this comparison and those that follow are taken from Converse *et al.,* 1980, and Miller *et al.,* 1980). Blacks and whites also divide deeply over the progress U.S. society has made in ridding itself of racial discrimination. Substantial differences emerge as well on questions that, although manifestly unrelated to race, nevertheless evoke the recent political experience of black Americans. Over the last several decades, for instance, far fewer blacks than whites worried that the federal government was too powerful, and far fewer blacks than whites supported tax-limitation movements (e.g., Sears and Citrin, 1982). And in surveys conducted in the late 1960s and early 1970s, blacks were much more likely than whites to approve of protest as a legitimate means to political change.

The differences cited here seem primarily to reflect racial-group membership and identification and not education, income, or other correlated characteristics: Multivariate analysis sustains race as the preeminent predictor (Knoke, 1979). Moreover, political differences between blacks and whites rapidly diminish on questions that bear only obliquely on race. Although more blacks than whites support an activist federal government in the realms of employment, medical care, and housing, the differences are much less dramatic than on policies dealing directly with race.

Thus, the power of racial-group identifications is most pronounced on questions that bear directly and unambiguously on the fortunes of racial groups. This is no small thing, in a political system so deeply divided over race.

A group identification with special relevance for partisan choice is of course the personal attachments Americans develop to one of the major political parties (Campbell, Gurin, and Miller, 1954). Once established, such attachments appear to exercise considerable influence over partisan beliefs, especially evaluations of public figures. For example, after General Eisenhower, previously uncommitted as to party preference and even seriously considered as a candidate for the 1948 *Democratic* presidential nomination, declared himself to be a Republican, the U.S. public suddenly divided along party lines: Republicans loved Ike; Democrats were not so sure (Converse and Dupeux, 1966; Hyman and Sheatsley, 1953). Essentially the same point is made by innumerable scaling exercises, in which evaluations of leaders (or occasionally pairwise judgments of their similarity) are subjected to factor analysis (or to multidimensional scaling). However the analysis is done, a strong party dimension *always* emerges (e.g., Nygren and Jones, 1977; Rusk and Weisberg, 1972; Weisberg and Rusk, 1970). Finally, party identification has been and continues to be the single most powerful predictor of voting in partisan contests (e.g., Campbell *et al.,* 1960; Mann and Wolfinger, 1980; Markus and Converse, 1979; Nie, Verba, and Petrocik, 1979. More on this later).

Party identification predicts citizens' opinions on public policy much less successfully. Over the past thirty years, Democrats and Republicans have disagreed sharply over social-welfare policies. Democrats have long favored government-subsidized health care in greater numbers than have Republicans; proportionately more Democrats than Republicans have insisted that it is government's responsibility to provide employment if the private sector cannot. Once beyond such proposals, however, Democrats and Republicans in the general public are difficult to distinguish (Bishop and Frankovic, 1981; Campbell *et al.,* 1960; Key, 1961; Miller *et al.,* 1980).

Party activists are another story entirely. In comparison to their rank and file, Democratic and Republican officials are deeply divided over policy. Delegates to the national nominating conventions typically are (Farah, Jennings, and Miller, 1981; Jackson *et al.,* 1982; Kirkpatrick, 1976; McClosky *et al.,* 1960); so, too, are candidates for the U.S. Congress (Bishop and Frankovic, 1981). In 1978, for example, 97 percent of Republican congressional candidates favored large cuts in federal income taxes, while just 23 percent of the Democratic candidates did. Meanwhile, and quite characteristically, Democratic and Republican identifiers in the general public hugged the center: In 1978 42 percent of Democratic voters and 43 percent of Republican voters supported tax cuts (Bishop and Frankovic, 1981). So the potency of party identification for policy preference diminishes drastically as we move from professional politicians to ordinary citizens.

Leadership

Just as identification with groups may influence political belief, so, too, may identification with political leaders. Presidents in particular seem able to mobilize support for bold initiatives. Consider, as one example, the case of the U.S. invasion of Cambodia in the spring of 1970. Prior to the invasion, just 7 percent of the U.S. public favored committing U.S. ground troops to Cambodia. Shortly after U.S. soldiers moved across the border, the public continued to express considerable skepticism. By a two-to-one margin, Americans believed the invasion would lengthen the war, not shorten it; by nearly as great a margin, the public thought the invasion would widen the war, not contain it. *Despite* such skepticism, the public supported President Nixon's policy: By 50 to 43 percent, Americans agreed that Nixon was right to send U.S. troops into Cambodia (Rosenberg, Verba, and Converse, 1970). Another such case was uncovered serendipitously by Barton (1974–75) in a study of U.S. political elites in the summer of 1971. As it happened, Barton's interviewing was in progress when President Nixon suddenly announced wage and price controls. Among Republicans in Barton's elite sample, less than one-quarter of those interviewed prior to Nixon's announcement supported the imposition of controls; among Republicans interviewed afterwards, supporters of wage and price controls outnumbered opponents by better than two to one. (For similar findings, from different periods, see Kernell, 1976; Mueller, 1973, p. 70; Rosi, 1965; and Sears *et al.,* 1978.)

A president's influence can of course be undercut, and at several points. Presidents are not always popular; they tend to shy away from bold proposals; and the media's attention—and the public's—are often elsewhere. On those occasions when these hurdles to influence are cleared, however, a president's effect on public opinion can be considerable.

Mobilizing support for particular actions is one thing; shaping the public's broader understanding of politics may be something else again. Whether *packages* of ideas can be effectively communicated from leaders to publics has never really been seriously examined. Because all presidents attempt to instruct the public in this broader way, it would be interesting to know how well, and under what circumstances, they succeed.

Values

Values may also organize ordinary political thinking. By values we mean general and enduring standards. In theoretical reconstructions of belief systems, values are usually accorded a more central position than attitudes. According to Allport (1961), attitudes in fact depend on pre-existing social values. And according to Rokeach (1973), values "lead us to take particular positions on social issues"; "predispose us to favor one particular political or religious ideology over another"; help us ". . .to evaluate and judge, to heap praise and fix blame on ourselves and others" (p. 13). The psychological machinery here is apparently quite simple. Policies, actions, and candidates are supported to the degree they are understood to further cherished values and to impede pernicious ones (Dawson, 1979; Rosenberg, 1968). Three values have been regarded as particularly relevant to contemporary U.S. politics and so are examined in turn here: individualism, egalitarianism, and postmaterialism (Hofstadter, 1948; Huntington, 1981; Inglehart, 1977; Lipset, 1963a; Merton, 1957; Myrdal, 1944; Pole, 1978).

American individualism is something of an omnibus symbol, incorporating under one label equal individual rights, limited government, *laissez-faire,* equal opportunity, and individual freedom (Lukes, 1973). The most investigated and politically consequential strain of individualism pertains to economic life. Economic individualism includes a presumption against government regulation of economic conduct. It celebrates the virtues of hard work and sacrifice. It equates idleness with sin. Its most central element is the conviction that in the United States, hard-working and talented people, regardless of origin, will eventually find success.

Defined in these ways, economic individualism is widely endorsed by Americans—even by poor Americans whose own experiences are evidently insufficient to shake support for the individualistic creed. "All men can better themselves: the circumstances of American life do not imprison men in their class or station—if there is such a prison, the iron bars are within each man." So argue the working-class men of Eastport (Lane, 1962, p. 61); the middle class and the rich, naturally enough, concur (Feldman, 1983; Goodban, 1981; Huber and Form, 1973; Hyman, 1953; Schlozman and Verba, 1979).

Americans are also inclined to believe that the poor are responsible for their own poverty. Explanations of poverty that emphasize class exploitation, racial prejudice, or deficiencies in the educational system attract faint support. The primary causes of poverty are located within the poor themselves, in their lassitude and their malfeasance (Feagin, 1975; Feldman, 1983; Gurin, Gurin, and Morrison, 1978; Ryan, 1971; Strumpel, 1976). Popular *cures* for poverty also reflect the imprint of individualism. Economic hardships can (and should) be surmounted through individual diligence and discipline. Collective efforts to overcome poverty are regarded as much less desirable even by the poor or unemployed themselves (Feldman, 1983; Gurin *et al.,* 1969; Schlozman and Verba, 1979; Sniderman and Brody, 1977).

Each of these components of economic individualism has its parallel in Americans' racial beliefs. While acknowledging the existence of some racial discrimination, many, if not most, white Americans believe that opportunities are plentiful for blacks; that blacks are themselves largely to blame for their disadvantaged economic position; and that blacks—like everyone else—can and should overcome poverty, discrimination, and other obstacles through individual effort, not through collective efforts, and especially not through "government handouts" (Feldman, 1983; Kinder and Sears, 1981).

Direct evidence on the consequences of individualism for political belief is unfortunately mainly circumstantial, as in the discovery of a form of racial prejudice—called "symbolic racism"—that seems to fuse conventional antiblack sentiments with traditional American values, economic individualism most of all. Symbolic racism appears to partially underly whites' opposition to welfare, "reverse discrimination," "forced" busing, and other government programs that violate individualism (Kinder and Sears, 1981; McConahay and Hough, 1976; Sears and Kinder, 1971). Although white Americans support compensatory programs that foster equal *opportunity* for blacks, they strongly oppose preferential treatment that guarantees racially equal *results,* presumably because to do so would amount to a desecration of individualism (Lipset and Schneider, 1978). Such programs betray and ridicule the effort and sacrifice of those who do work, according to the comfortable middle class of Orange County (Lamb, 1974) and working-class men of New England (Lane, 1962; Sennett and Cobb, 1972).

These investigations unfortunately do not assess economic individualism and political belief separately; thus we are left uncertain about the connection that supposedly joins them. More recent efforts correct this limitation: For example, Feldman's (1983) analysis of a 1972 national survey reveals consistent associations between economic individualism on the one hand and resis-

tance to welfare-state policies on the other. Embracing the vision of the United States as the land of opportunity appears to dull enthusiasm for government-subsidized health care and employment. We say "appears to" because Feldman's analysis presumes that values cause beliefs but not the reverse. Perhaps Feldman is right: Certainly consistent with this point is the panel evidence he presents indicating that Americans' ideas about economic opportunity, a central element of individualism, hardly changed between 1972 and 1976. However, the priorities people assign to values may also be influenced by their opinions on policy questions. Conclusive evidence on the power of individualism therefore awaits a more sophisticated analysis, one that allows for more complex causal possibilities.

According to Lipset (1963a; Ladd and Lipset, 1981), much of U.S. political history can be seen as a competition between individualism and egalitarianism. If so, it is a competition that egalitarianism often loses. As Pole (1978) put it: "Only at comparatively rare—and then generally stormy—intervals has the idea of equality dominated American debates on major questions of policy. Equality is normally the language of the underdog..."(p. ix). The consequences of the American commitment to egalitarianism are nevertheless apparent: in the comparatively early institution of universal suffrage, in Americans' widespread support for public education, and in the now nearly unanimous opposition among the white majority to racial discrimination.

The consequences of egalitarianism for individual political beliefs have been treated most thoroughly by Rokeach (1969, 1973). For example, whites' reactions to the assassination of Martin Luther King were associated with the importance they attached to equality (egalitarians more often reported anger and shame). Egalitarianism was also associated with support for racial desegregation, sympathy for the poor, enthusiasm for social-welfare policies, support for anti–Vietnam War student protests, and opposition to the war itself. Rokeach also found that equality was prized much more by blacks than by whites: In a list of eighteen values, blacks ranked equality second, while whites placed it eleventh. All this evidence certainly sustains Pole's argument—equality does indeed seem to be the language of the underdog—but it cannot solve the causal question. Does egalitarianism lead to support for racial integration, or is it the other way round?

Another approach to the political consequences of values begins with Maslow's (1954) theory that human action is motivated by five general sets of needs, ordered hierarchically by their urgency: physiological needs; safety and security; affection and belongingness; esteem; and finally, self-actualizations, encompassing mental health, "peak experiences," creativity, a highly refined aesthetic sense, and so on. Though the general implications of Maslow's scheme for political belief have been recognized for some time (for general discussions, see Davies, 1963; Knutson, 1972; Lane, 1969), they were given special life by Inglehart (1977, 1979) who joined Maslow's psychological theory to a sociologically grounded analysis of "postindustrial society" (Bell, 1973). According to Inglehart, the unprecedented prosperity and comparative security that have characterized Western societies since World War II have produced fundamental shifts in the character of political demands. Older generations, who experienced crippling economic circumstances and devastating war in their formative years, are naturally preoccupied by sustenance and safety. They are "materialists." The immediate post-war generations, fortunate enough to have avoided economic catastrophe and the devastation of war, are oriented more to the higher needs: affection, esteem, and even self-actualization. They are "postmaterialists."

The materialist/postmaterialist distinction is measured by inviting people to choose among various *political* goals. Maintaining order, ensuring economic growth, and providing a strong defense all presumably reflect materialistic priorities. Postmaterialism is at work, according to Inglehart, in those who express interest in a friendlier and less impersonal society, one that honors ideas more than money, that protects freedom of speech, and that encourages widespread participation in decision making.

In the United States as in other Western countries, people tend to endorse either materialistic or postmaterialistic goals, but not both. Furthermore, postmaterialism in the United States as elsewhere is more common (though not widespread) among the younger generations and is predicted well in cross-national aggregate analyses by the level of affluence a populace enjoyed a generation before (Dalton, 1977; Inglehart, 1979). And in line with the customary insistence that values should be *enduring* standards, panel evidence indicates that people hold on to their materialist/postmaterialist priorities tenaciously (Inglehart *et al.*, 1982). Finally, postmaterialists are inclined to embrace the left and oppose establishment institutions and groups, while materialists tend to endorse the right and defend tradition (Barnes and Kaase, 1979,

Chapters 11 and 12; Inglehart, 1977, Chapter 9; 1981). Whether materialist/postmaterialist values *cause* such beliefs, however, is once again ambiguous. Moreover, these results do not establish a connection between *personal* needs and *political* beliefs. Because personal needs for safety, affection, and the like are never assessed directly, Inglehart can enlist Maslow's theory of personality development only by analogy. The findings on materialism/postmaterialism bear obviously and directly on the shift in political values in the West, of course, but they are quite irrelevant to how political thinking might be shaped by personal needs.

The evidence is tantalizing. According to the most perceptive observers, individualism and egalitarianism are central to the U.S. political tradition. They seem clearly implicated in our public policy and social practice, and they are somehow bound up with the public's political beliefs. A convincing case can also be made for the recent emergence of postmaterialism. In principle, core values such as these stand in an intermediate position between broad, encompassing ideological frames of reference, which have proven to be of little use in understanding the U.S. public's political thinking, and specific opinions on particular topics and candidates, which come and go as the political seasons change. Core values would therefore seem to offer the prospect of greater understanding of public opinion and of fundamental political change. But do values in fact occupy the center of the web of opinions Americans develop toward politics? We do not know yet.

Personality

Moving a layer "deeper" than values, we next suppose that political beliefs may be rooted in personality. As Smith, Bruner, and White put it (1956, p. 1):

> A pattern of opinions may be for one man a basis of personal serenity in the face of a changing world, for another a goad to revolutionary activity. Opinions, in short, are part of a man's attempt to meet and master his world. They are an integral part of personality.

How to interpret the often complex pathways that connect personality and belief—indeed, how to discover them—depends upon one's theoretical tastes. Because such tastes range widely, it would be foolish to attempt to summarize here the vast and uneven work that falls under the heading of personality and politics (for a more comprehensive effort, see Greenstein, 1974). Instead, we will draw attention only to one general tradition, that which treats political opinions as externalized versions of the mind's inner conflicts.

Smith, Bruner, and White (1956) refer to the general process by which political beliefs come to stand for or express internal troubles as "externalization," occurring when "an individual, often responding unconsciously, senses an analogy between a perceived environmental event and some unresolved inner problem. He adopts an attitude toward the event in question which is a transformed version of his way of dealing with his inner difficulty. By doing so, he may succeed in reducing some of the anxiety which his own difficulty has been producing" (p. 43). In their analysis of the opinions regarding the Soviet Union held by ten young men, Smith, Bruner, and White often discerned externalization at work. Thus (according to them, p. 271) one man's

> defeated hopes caused him to emphasize the optimism and youthful vigor of the Russian Communists while another's problem with aggression and inferiority disposed him to perceive the Russians as unfortunate underdogs who might nevertheless become dangerously savage.

The externalization hypothesis was given the grandest expression, of course, in *The Authoritarian Personality* (Adorno *et al.*, 1950). There is no need to recount in detail here the study itself or the methodological fusilade it set off. Hyman and Sheatsley's (1954) essay still stands as the most comprehensive and most damaging critique of the original work. But in effectively discrediting the evidence marshaled by Adorno and his colleagues, Hyman and Sheatsley did no necessary damage to the externalization hypothesis itself. In fact, evidence reported in the three decades following publication of *The Authoritarian Personality,* though it has come in a trickle, generally sustains the insistence of Adorno and his colleagues that political belief and personality are intimately entwined (Brown, 1965; Kirscht and Dillehay, 1967; Wilson, 1973; also in this regard, see the series of papers on personality and political belief by Chong, McClosky, and Zaller, 1980; McClosky, 1958, 1967; Sniderman and Citrin, 1971).

Lane (1962) also enlisted externalization in his discussion of working-class men coping with the burdens of freedom. Lane suggested that those men who felt most troubled by freedom—who could not fully enjoy it themselves, who thought freedom dangerous, who worried extravagantly about its extension—were also those most uneasy about their own impulses. Apprehensions over sexual and aggressive appetites, over impulsive purchasing habits, and over eating and drinking sprees seemed to lead to hesitation and ambivalence about political freedom. Lane wrote in 1962 (p. 55):

> The burden of freedom for modern (and ancient) man comes from relying on an inadequate system of personal controls. For him, therefore, the solution is the reinforcement of convention, the specification of behavioral codes, the demand for sanctions against behavior, the encroachment of the criminal code upon the area of individual choice.

Recent work on political intolerance reinforces Lane's point. Sullivan and his colleagues (Sullivan, Marcus, Feldman, and Piereson, 1981) defined political intolerance as a willingness to impose restrictions upon the activities of unpopular groups. They found that intolerance was especially common among those Americans who were "psychologically insecure"—who, on an omnibus measure of personality, were revealed to be dogmatic (Rokeach, 1960), misanthropic and authoritarian (Rosenberg, 1956), low in self-esteem (Sniderman, 1975), and preoccupied with safety and sustenance (Maslow, 1954). Thus personal inadequacies, which the psychologically insecure presumably possess in abundance, are projected onto disreputable political groups. Such groups must be carefully monitored and controlled, lest they somehow spoil the American way.

The externalization thesis is decidedly out of fashion in an era that looks more to economics than to depth psychology for insights into mass political behavior. Yet ethnocentrism, conservative values, the burdens of freedom, political intolerance—all may have a partial basis in "inner troubles."

History

A final alternative we consider here is history, which entails a switch in perspective. So far we have tried to suggest the ways in which particular opinions might be derived from general dispositions, like group identification or core values. Now we want to introduce an explicitly dynamic perspective, to demonstrate how public opinion may be influenced by the unfolding of events.

The last ten years have seen an explosion of this kind of work: on continuity and change in the public's attachment to the political parties (Abramson, 1979; Converse, 1976); on the public's support for racial equality (Greeley and Sheatsley, 1971; Taylor, Sheatsley, and Greeley,

1978); on the trust Americans place in their national government (Citrin, 1974; Miller, 1974); on opposition to war (Mueller, 1971, 1973); and on what problems the American public regards as important (Behr and Iyengar, 1985; Hibbs, 1979; MacKuen, 1981). Here, for illustrative purposes, we will concentrate on three: change in the short term, represented by the dynamics of public opinion over presidential campaigns; change in the medium term, as illustrated by the dynamics of presidential support between campaigns; and change in the long term, as indicated by the dynamics of the American public's tolerance for political dissent across two decades.

Although not as effectively as many commentators would like, presidential campaigns do inform the public, by providing a stream of details about the candidates. As the campaign unfolds, citizens develop clearer and more elaborate impressions of the principal candidates. Between February and October of 1980, for example, the proportion of the public claiming to know something about Mr. Reagan rose from 86 percent to 95 percent; the proportion of the public willing to assess his personal qualities, from about 70 percent to about 85 percent; the proportion ready to attribute positions to him on the major issues, from roughly 60 percent to roughly 80 percent. Furthermore, over the course of the campaign, Mr. Reagan's conservative orientation became more widely appreciated. To take the most dramatic example, in February, just 23 percent of the public thought Mr. Reagan favored increasing funds for defense; by October, 43 percent thought so (Markus, 1982; Miller and Shanks, 1982). The general point here, which seems to apply comfortably to other times, is that as the campaign rolls along, citizens develop richer impressions of the candidates (Berelson *et al.,* 1954; Lazarsfeld *et al.,* 1948; Patterson, 1980).

This process of impression elaboration is generally *not* accompanied by drastic changes in evaluation, however. Those evaluative changes that do occur are modest and seem traceable to changes in circumstances. In 1980, for instance, the public's assessment of Mr. Carter's competence deteriorated a bit between February and April—presumably a reflection of deteriorating conditions at home and abroad. Between April and October, moreover, citizens became somewhat less convinced of Carter's integrity, and fewer acknowledged that they felt sympathy for him, changes that may have been associated with an increasingly bitter and partisan campaign.

On the other side, toward the end of the 1980 campaign, citizens were much more likely to report that Mr. Reagan made them feel afraid and uneasy—presumably a reflection of Democratic efforts to portray the Republican candidate as reckless and likely to catapult the United States into war. In short, the evaluative side of the impressions the public develops of the major candidates changes modestly over the course of the campaign and in ways that seem responsive to campaign and larger events (Kinder and Abelson, 1981).

This same contrast—substantial cognitive elaboration versus modest evaluative alteration—also surfaces in the many studies of presidential debates. Since 1960, whenever they have been held, televised debates between the principal presidential candidates have been the campaign's best attended event. For all the attention they draw, however, debates produce limited effects, confined primarily to elaboration and clarification of impressions (for reviews of this evidence, see Katz and Feldman, 1962; Sears and Chaffee, 1979). For instance, the first Carter-Ford debate in 1976 did lead to greater clarity about where each candidate stood on policy questions—but only under special circumstances: (1) when the problem introduced in the debate was already at the very top of the public's agenda, (2) when it was given great attention in the debate itself, and (3) when the two principals sharply disagreed about what should be done. Although unemployment fulfilled these requirements well in 1976, many consequential national problems did not (Sears and Chaffee, 1979).

The major effect of debates is the reinforcement of predebate attitudes. This point was established first in studies of the "great debates" between Kennedy and Nixon in 1960. Although journalists wrote that the debates turned the electoral tide decisively to Kennedy, surveys done immediately before and immediately afterwards told a less dramatic story. The dominant effect was reinforcement. Kennedy supporters going into the debates agreed overwhelmingly that Kennedy had won; Nixon enthusiasts believed Nixon had (Katz and Feldman, 1962). The consequences for shifts in preference were accordingly minimal. Studies of the 1976 Carter-Ford debates reached essentially the same conclusion: a dominant effect of reinforcement and no real advantage accruing to either candidate (Sears and Chaffee, 1979).

More generally, campaigns seem primarily to *harmonize* voters' opinions. This was a major conclusion of

The People's Choice, Lazarsfeld, Berelson, and Gaudet's (1948) classic panel study of the 1940 presidential contest between Roosevelt and Willkie. They found that as the campaign progressed, citizens' opinions became more internally consistent. Vote intentions, overall evaluations of the candidates, opinions on the desirability of a third term, judgments regarding the relative importance of government versus business experience for a president—all these highly partisan evaluations lined up more and more consistently as the campaign unfolded. Markus (1982) reported essentially the same result for the 1980 campaign: Overall evaluations of Mr. Carter and Mr. Reagan and ratings of their competence and integrity all became more tightly interdependent from the primary season to the closing days of the general election campaign. As election day neared, a change in any single attitude tended to have large and increasing consequences for the others. (For additional examples of the harmonizing effect of campaigns, see Becker and Heaton, 1967; Sears and Chaffee, 1979; Sullivan, 1966; Wolfinger and Greenstein, 1968.)

Such changes that do occur in citizens' impressions of the candidates' personal qualities and policy positions seem to be channeled by longstanding political predispositions, the most notable of which is party identification. The decline in the public's assessment of Mr. Carter's competence through the 1980 campaign, for example, was steep among Republicans and negligible among Democrats. Similarly, the overall stability in judgments of Mr. Reagan's competence concealed two divergent tendencies: Over the campaign, Democrats became more convinced that Mr. Reagan could not handle the job, while Republicans moved in the opposite direction (and more decisively). One effect of the campaign, therefore, was to bring candidate appraisals into alignment with party identification. As the campaign developed, Democrats and Republicans developed increasingly polarized appraisals of the two major contenders (Miller and Shanks, 1982).

In sum, campaigns clarify, elaborate, and harmonize the public's impressions of the rival candidates. Ordinarily these processes serve to align impressions with standing predispositions. We say "ordinarily" because dramatic events or glaring revelations may sometimes intrude upon a campaign, substantially altering how the candidates are understood as well as the standards by which they are evaluated. McGovern's dismissal of Senator Eagleton as his running mate in 1972 and the takeover

of the U.S. embassy in Teheran during the preprimary phase of the 1980 campaign may be two such instances. Under such dramatic circumstances, as we will see later, even the voters' "standing predispositions"—like party identification—may change. And of course, a shift of a few percentage points, although by some absolute standards small, is nevertheless very great in close contests. But as an actuarial proposition, the typical effect of a campaign is to elaborate impressions of the candidates without altering them in evaluatively consequential ways.

If stability is the hallmark of election campaign dynamics, change is the outstanding feature of public support *between* elections. Between elections, the incumbent president's popularity in the general public occasionally soars. Much more often, it declines. With the exception of Eisenhower, every president since Franklin Roosevelt has departed the office less popular than when he entered it. This singular fact led Mueller (1973), who was the first to examine the dynamics of presidential support systematically, to include time in his regression equation. According to Mueller's estimates, a president's popularity suffered a bit during deep recessions and unpopular wars and was boosted temporarily during international crises. But the overriding determinant of a president's support was simply time. Mueller concluded that time erodes a president's support because more time means more opportunities to "create intense, unforgiving opponents of former supporters" (1973, p. 205).

However, time may merely mask the events that are, in fact, responsible for fluctuations in presidential support. When more adequate measures of events are substituted for time and more appropriate estimation techniques are followed, changes in presidential support turn out to be closely tied to performance. A president's support depends in the first place on the vitality of the nation's economy: High unemployment, rising prices, and slow growth in real disposable income all eat away at a president's support. So does U.S. involvement in unpopular wars: As the number of Americans killed in action in Vietnam grew, public support for Presidents Johnson and Nixon deteriorated. Presidents also suffer when they flagrantly violate—or at least appear to—the public's trust. During the Watergate period, with each additional incriminating revelation, President Nixon's support dwindled still further. Finally, dramatic, sharply focused international crises involving the president typically boost his support. No doubt President Carter has been the greatest recent beneficiary of this phenomenon. The seizure of the U.S. embassy in Teheran followed in short order by the Soviet invasion of Afghanistan produced an extraordinary surge in popular support for the president—enough of a boost, perhaps, for Carter to repel Kennedy's challenge in the primary season (Hibbs, Rivers, and Vasilatos, 1982a, 1982b; Kernell, 1978; Kernell and Hibbs, 1981).

Considered together, economic conditions, war, scandal, and international crises explain virtually all of the post-war variation in aggregate presidential support ratings. This implies a sharp responsiveness of aggregate public opinion to conspicuous national and international events.

Of course, history does not simply and neatly announce its lessons. Events must be interpreted. According to our earlier analysis, the meaning of events should be revealed in part as they are filtered through the citizen's own needs, group identifications, core values, and the like. Hints that this is so can be found in the recent investigation by Hibbs and his colleagues (1982b) into the dynamics of presidential support within occupational groups. Blue- and white-collar workers responded in highly similar fashion to international crises and to Watergate revelations. But the drop in presidential support because of mounting U.S. casualties in Vietnam was greater among the working class than among the middle class. And the damage done by increasing unemployment was more pronounced among the working class, while the damage done by increasing inflation was greater among the middle class.

These class differences may be understood in terms of self-interest. Thus the Vietnam findings "square with data indicating that the children of lower-status workers suffered a disproportionate share of the casualties" (Hibbs *et al.,* 1982b, p. 324). And the unemployment/inflation results are broadly consistent with the distribution of "the burdens and rewards conferred by fluctuations in aggregate economic conditions"(p. 326).

Both sets of results are compatible with other interpretations, however. Regarding the first, Schuman (1973) identified two forms of opposition to the Vietnam War: moral opposition based on criticism of the war's goals and how it was conducted and pragmatic opposition, based on disillusionment over failing to win it. The moral calculus was more prevalent among middle-class opponents; the pragmatic calculus motivated working class opposition to the war. So the presidential approval results may reflect not class bias in the distribution of casualties (and therefore, self-interest) but class differences in the logic by which the war was evaluated.

In addition, the findings that working-class Americans seem especially sensitive to changes in the unemployment rate in their presidential evaluations and that the middle class are influenced especially by changes in inflation need not be seen in self-interest terms, either. For one thing, Americans whose personal lives have been plagued by serious economic difficulties are generally no more likely to disparage the president's performance than the economically untroubled (Kinder, 1981). For another, although the Democratic party draws its supporters disproportionately from the working class, the Republican party does better among the middle class. And in the postwar period at least, the Democratic party has championed the maintenance of full employment, while the Republican party has worried more about restraining inflation. Hence the class difference may conceal what is really a partisan difference. Indeed, Hibbs *et al.* found party differences greater than those associated with social class. That is, changes in unemployment affected Democrats' support for the president more than Republicans' support, while changes in prices affected Republicans' support more than Democrats' support, and these party differences were more pronounced than the corresponding class differences (Hibbs *et al.,* 1982b).

In short, although the particular processes that underlie the dynamics of presidential support are not yet clear, there can be no doubting the general point: That the lessons of history are filtered through the citizen's own individual dispositions. Furthermore, the basic relationship at the aggregate level seems well established. Changes in presidential support are driven by salient and consequential changes in national and international life.

According to political theorists of various persuasions, democracy cannot survive without widespread support for the extension of constitutional rights to all citizens, however unsavory or unpopular their views might be (Sullivan, Piereson, and Marcus, 1979, p. 781):

> Although a democratic regime may be divided by fierce conflicts, it can remain stable if citizens remain attached to democratic or constitutional procedure and maintain a willingness to apply such procedures—the right to speak, to publish, to run for office—on an equal basis to all, even to those who challenge its way of life.

In studies carried out in the 1950s, most Americans failed this test. Stouffer's (1955) *Communism, Conformity, and Civil Liberties* documented in great detail Americans' unwillingness to grant constitutional rights to communists and to other dissidents and nonconformists. Two of every three Americans declared that communists should not be permitted to speak publicly, that books written by them should be removed from public libraries, and that government should be permitted to tap communists' telephone conversations. Three of four endorsed the idea that communists should have their U.S. citizenship revoked. Nine of ten stood against communists teaching in the public schools. And fully one-half the U.S. public believed it a good idea to throw avowed communists into jail. Stouffer's results, along with those provided by Prothro and Grigg (1960) and McClosky (1964), shattered the idea that Americans would extend democratic procedures and rights to unpopular groups.

However, remember that these surveys were carried out at the height of the Cold War, with, as Stouffer (1955, p. 14) put it, the free world living under the "menacing shadow" of communist imperialism. A natural question to raise here, and the motivating question of this section, is whether the U.S. public has grown more tolerant of dissent. Stouffer found that the well-educated, younger generation was much more tolerant than the poorly educated, older generation (as have many others: Davis, 1975; Jackman, 1972; McClosky, 1964; Nunn, Crockett, and Williams, 1978; Prothro and Grigg, 1960) and so foresaw increased tolerance as well-educated younger generations gradually replaced older ones.

To be sure, the U.S. public has become dramatically more educated over the last two decades. And in an analysis of a 1972–1973 NORC national survey that carried some of the same questions that had appeared in Stouffer's original study, Davis (1975) found evidence of massive increases in support for civil liberties. Roughly twice as many Americans were prepared to grant communists, socialists, and atheists constitutional rights as had been true two decades before. A substantial share of this remarkable change was compositional, as Stouffer had forecast. The gradual replacement of the older, comparatively poorly educated cohorts with better educated citizens accounted for about one-third of the increase in tolerance. Davis also found, however, that regardless of cohort or education, Americans became more tolerant as they traveled from the 1950s into

the 1970s. Nunn, Crockett, and Williams (1978) reported similar results from their 1973 national survey, concluding that "citizens who are most supportive of civil liberties have emerged as the majority in our society" (p. 12). What a drastic change from the gloomy results of two decades before!

The celebration may be premature, however. Sullivan and his colleagues (1979, 1981) argue that tolerance is at issue only under conditions of strong disagreement. That is, political tolerance "implies a willingness to permit the expression of those ideas or interests that one opposes. A tolerant regime, then, like a tolerant individual, is one that allows a wide berth to those ideas that challenge its way of life" (p. 784). Thus the magnificent change in the U.S. public's willingness to grant procedural rights to communists and to others on the left does *not* signal a surge in political tolerance in any general sense and perhaps no real change at all. Instead, the recorded change may mean only that the public no longer regards communists, socialists, and atheists as the sinister threats they once were during the Cold War. Perhaps political intolerance has not so much declined but spread to more diverse targets: to the Black Panthers, the Ku Klux Klan, and the antiabortionists, to name but a few.

To test this claim, Sullivan *et al.* developed a new set of measures in which each respondent was asked to identify the group he or she liked least. Each was then taken through a Stouffer-like battery of questions dealing with the granting of constitutional rights to members of this least-liked group. Although comparisons with the original Stouffer items are unfortunately inexact, the responses to the new questions severely challenge the conclusion that the U.S. public is dramatically more tolerant. Only one-half the national sample was prepared to grant members of their least-liked group the right to make a public speech; 40 percent endorsed the tapping of their telephones; and 70 percent thought that the group should be outlawed altogether. Such results do not inspire celebration.

In studying change, especially change over several decades, care must be taken to distinguish change in attitude from change in the attitude *object*. Exact replication of original items, usually desirable, may lead to technically correct results but erroneous conclusions. In the Cold War years of the early 1950s, Stouffer perhaps really was studying political tolerance in some general sense. Communists, socialists, and atheists may well have been regarded by the U.S. public as the most prominent and sinister threats to political order. Certainly tolerance for *these* groups has increased dramatically in two decades, and this is no mean feat. But has *tolerance* increased? It is impossible to say.

SUMMARY

The sources of Americans' political beliefs are pluralistic. Political beliefs are, in the first place, badges of social membership. Here we have stressed the allegiances people develop to class, race, and party. Political beliefs also reflect other social characteristics that at certain moments, on certain public questions, become politically relevant: ethnicity (e.g., Greeley, 1975), religion (e.g., Converse, 1966a; Lipset, 1963b), gender (e.g., Klein, 1984), union membership (e.g., Converse and Campbell, 1968), and more.

   Political beliefs also seem to reflect the values citizens embrace. Underneath Americans' continuing ambivalence toward race, welfare, affirmative action, and income redistribution, is a more fundamental struggle between egalitarianism and individualism—a contest that individualism customarily wins. Political beliefs sometimes have still deeper, more personal roots: They may occasionally be resolutions of needs or the symptoms of inner distress. Political ideas are also shaped by the "lessons of history": War, recession, and other lesser events leave their imprint on U.S. public opinion. Finally, for a small portion of the U.S. public, political beliefs are governed by ideology; they are deductions from elaborate and abstract ideas about the nature of government and society.

   The earlier verdict of ideological innocence is therefore sustained but only in a narrow sense. Americans are not creatures of coherent, wide-ranging ideologies. But their ideas do reflect, in complex ways, numerous preferences of more modest scope. In this sense, Americans' political beliefs *are* ideological. It is an ideology of many and diverse pieces, a mosaic of partisan attachments, social relations, values, personality, and history.

VOTERS AND ELECTIONS

Our discussion of voters and elections is organized by several distinctions. First, we divide voting into two components: candidate preference is treated first; the decision whether to vote at all is analyzed later, as part of a broader discussion of how people take part in politics. Second, we consider mainly *presidential* voters and elec-

tions. Until very recently, research on voting has been preoccupied with presidential contests; for better or worse, our discussion reflects this practice. Finally, we devote more space to individual choice than to collective choice. Understanding voters and understanding elections are related enterprises, of course, but they are not identical, and the former is the more obviously psychological problem of the two.

DETERMINANTS OF INDIVIDUAL VOTE CHOICE

Psychological Imperialism

Our story begins with *The People's Choice,* Lazarsfeld, Berelson, and Gaudet's (1948) historic attempt "to discover how and why people decided to vote as they did" (p. 1). The people in this case were residents of Erie County, Ohio; the election was the 1940 presidential contest between Roosevelt and Willkie. Based on panel interviews spanning the entire election season, from May to November, Lazarsfeld's team concluded that the campaign had two basic effects: It *reinforced* the choices made by early deciders, and it *activated* the latent predispositions of those who were initially uncommitted. In either instance, the campaign played upon predispositions that were principally sociological. At the core of Lazarsfeld, Berelson, and Gaudet's account were the voter's social characteristics: " a person thinks, politically, as he is, socially. Social characteristics determine political preferences" (p. 27).

   In operational terms, the voter's social characteristics were represented by the Index of Political Predisposition (IPP), reflecting the voter's standing on three demographic variables: social class, religion, and place of residence (urban versus rural). So constructed, the IPP correlated quite strongly with the vote. Rural, middle-class, Protestants tended to vote for the Republican Willkie (74 percent did so), while urban, working-class Catholics favored Roosevelt (83 percent did so). Voters with politically contradictory predispositions—middle-class Catholics, for example—were "cross-pressured." Being in conflict, they vacillated, decided late, and often failed to vote at all.

   The People's Choice (and *Voting,* its worthy successor: Berelson, Lazarsfeld, and McPhee, 1954) provided an important initial explanation of voting, but it was one that never quite took hold. Its most serious shortcoming was an inability to account for the radical (and seemingly systematic) swings attending presidential elections. With the sociological composition of the electorate remaining more or less constant, how could Truman's "miraculous" victory for the Democrats in 1948 be followed in short order by Eisenhower's Republican landslide in 1952?

Such anomalies quickened interest in a new view, one that shifted explanatory emphasis from voters' demography to their attitudes. This new (and now dominant) view was developed by a psychologically oriented research group located at the Survey Research Center (SRC) of the University of Michigan, headed by Campbell, Converse, Gurin, Miller, and Stokes. The SRC approach was psychological not because it borrowed specific hypotheses from psychology, because it did not. Apart from a nod to Lewinian field theory, and intermittent acknowledgements of reference group theory, the Michigan group has been largely indifferent to theoretical developments in psychology. Nor was the approach psychological in the sense of identifying the needs, motives, or personality characteristics that might underlie participation in political life (some contemporaries did take this route: Lane, 1962; McClosky, 1958; Smith, Bruner, and White, 1956). The approach was psychological, however, in that it centered attention on the individual's attitudes. Campbell and associates put it this way (1960, p. 9):

> Our hypothesis is that the partisan choice the individual voter makes depends in an immediate sense on the strength and direction of the elements comprising a field of psychological forces, where these elements are interpreted as attitudes toward the perceived objects of national politics.

Within this field of psychological forces, the central and causally decisive element was taken to be party identification. In *The Voter Decides,* a nationwide study of the 1952 presidential contest, Campbell, Gurin, and Miller (1954) found that party identification correlated powerfully with the vote. Stevenson received most of the votes cast by Democrats, and Eisenhower was an even greater success among Republicans. Moreover, strong party identifiers declared that they would readily support disagreeable candidates of their own party and reported more frequent straight party-line voting than those with weaker identifications. From this evidence party identification seemed to be an essential component of the voter's decision.

The implications of these results for a theory of individual choice were developed in grand style in *The American Voter* (Campbell *et al.,* 1960). There, in a most consequential move, party identification was treated as a prior cause of the voter's partisan evaluations. In 1956, the typical Republican liked Ike, expressed reservations about Stevenson, thought Republican management of the government sound, and endorsed Republican policy positions regarding domestic and international problems. The typical Democrat, meanwhile, took an opposite view on each of these points. Such differences were interpreted as testimony to the potency of party identification to color evaluation. Partisan attitudes were substantially, though certainly not entirely, creatures of party identification. According to *The American Voter,* party identification was a standing commitment, a "persistent adherence" (p. 146) that profoundly influenced how voters looked at the political world (Stokes, 1966a, pp. 126–127):

> To the average person the affairs of government are remote and complex, and yet the average citizen is asked periodically to formulate opinions about these affairs. At the very least he has to decide how he will vote, what choice he will make between candidates offering different programs and very different versions of contemporary political events. In this dilemma, having the party symbol stamped on certain candidates, certain issue positions, certain interpretations of political reality is of great psychological convenience.

The privileged position of party identification was strengthened further in Converse's (1966b) development of the normal vote. He noted that sharp fluctuations in the vote from one presidential election to the next coexisted with virtually no change in the aggregate distribution of party identification. This suggested to Converse that the vote could profitably be partitioned into two components: the "normal vote," reflecting voters' durable commitments to party and short-term deviations from the normal vote, reflecting "response to transient election circumstances which do not materially affect the abiding division of party loyalties" (Converse, 1966b, p. 101). Converse estimated that in the absence of short-term forces, strong Democrats should present 95.7 percent of their votes to the Democratic candidate; weak Democrats, 81.8 percent; independents, 49.2 percent; weak Republicans, 16.2 percent; and strong Republicans, 3.7 percent (1966a, p. 27; these estimates demand the strong assumption that party identification is itself unmoved by short-term forces, an assumption that later we will have reason to doubt). For the electorate as a whole in the 1950s and early 1960s, Converse's calculations work out to a modest Democratic advantage. With short-term forces equal, the Democratic presidential candidate should then have received 54 percent of the two-party vote.

As in life, so, too in politics, things are rarely equal. The Democrats' normal vote did not guarantee them control of the White House; the Republicans' task was difficult but not impossible. Stokes (1966a) concluded that under the eight-point normal vote advantage enjoyed by the Democrats, the likelihood that the minority Republican party could capture the presidency was about one in four. Stokes demonstrated also that modest shifts in the underlying distribution of party identification, and hence in the normal vote, would materially alter the Republicans' presidential chances. If the Democratic normal vote advantage were halved, for instance, the Republican candidate's odds would improve sharply, to about 4 in 10. Stokes drew from such calculations further confirmation of the overriding importance of party identification.

The account of voting expressed in *The American Voter* and in Converse's normal vote concept was richly illustrated in the SRC team's reports on the presidential elections of 1960, 1964, and 1968 (Converse, Campbell, Miller, and Stokes, 1961; Converse, Clausen, and Miller, 1965; Converse, Miller, Rusk, and Wolfe, 1969). Each report continued to insist on the preeminence of party identification. Each also identified short-term forces that tipped the balance to one side or to the other and gave to each election its unique character.

The 1960 contest was notable in this respect for the mobilization of religious conflict. Using normal vote analysis, Converse and his colleagues demonstrated that Kennedy's Catholicism cost him votes among Protestants (particularly among Protestants who attended church regularly) and won him votes among Catholics. In 1964 the most significant short-term force operating was the widespread concern that Goldwater might plunge the country into war. Since the New Deal the Republicans had been the party of peace in the public mind. The Goldwater candidacy changed that, converting a 2:1 Republican advantage on peace and war in 1960 to a 3:1 Democratic advantage in 1964, with obvious and calamitous consequences. And in 1968, Converse and his colleagues ascribed Nixon's victory to the electorate's deep displeasure with the Johnson-Humphrey Democratic administration: to exasperation over the bleeding war in Vietnam, to worries provoked by increasingly violent

confrontations between blacks and whites, and to escalating fears about crime in the streets. In each of these three elections, then, a unique configuration of short-term forces seemed to play against a stable background provided by the voters' enduring commitment to party.

Party Identification Reassessed

If party identification provides the foundation for the SRC position on voting, then tampering with its conceptualization and measurement threatens the entire edifice. As we will see, there has been no shortage of it, summarized here under two broad headings.

The decline (but not demise) of party identification. Between 1945 (when measurements were first taken) and 1964, the distribution of party identification in the U.S. public remained virtually constant. In mid 1965, however, the distribution began to shift. More Americans began to call themselves Independents, and fewer claimed to be strong partisans of either party. Both tendencies continued through 1974 and seem now to have plateaued (see Fig. 1). In relative terms neither party has lost: The *balance* of partisanship over roughly the last forty years has remained essentially stationary. Nevertheless, the change is one of massive proportions. Once a distinct minority, Independents outnumbered Republicans in 1974 by 5:3 and approached within sampling error the number of Democrats (Converse, 1976; Norpoth and Rusk, 1982).

The trend away from the parties seems an obvious menace to the voting doctrine set out in *The American Voter.* Citizens who make no explicit claim on party can hardly be counted as party voters. In a period of advanced party decline, a theory whose center is the voter's commitment to party obviously requires rehabilitation, or perhaps it should be discarded altogether.

The surge of Independents also raises questions about the quality of electoral choice. In popular mythology, political independents are thoughtful, absorbed in the great issues of the day, and unmoved by nakedly partisan appeals. In reality, compared to partisans, independents (Campbell *et al.,* 1960, p. 143; see also Agger, 1959; Berelson *et al.,* 1954):

> have somewhat poorer knowledge of the issues, their image of the candidates is fainter, their interest in the campaign is less, their concern over the outcome is relatively slight, and their choice between competing candidates, although it is indeed made

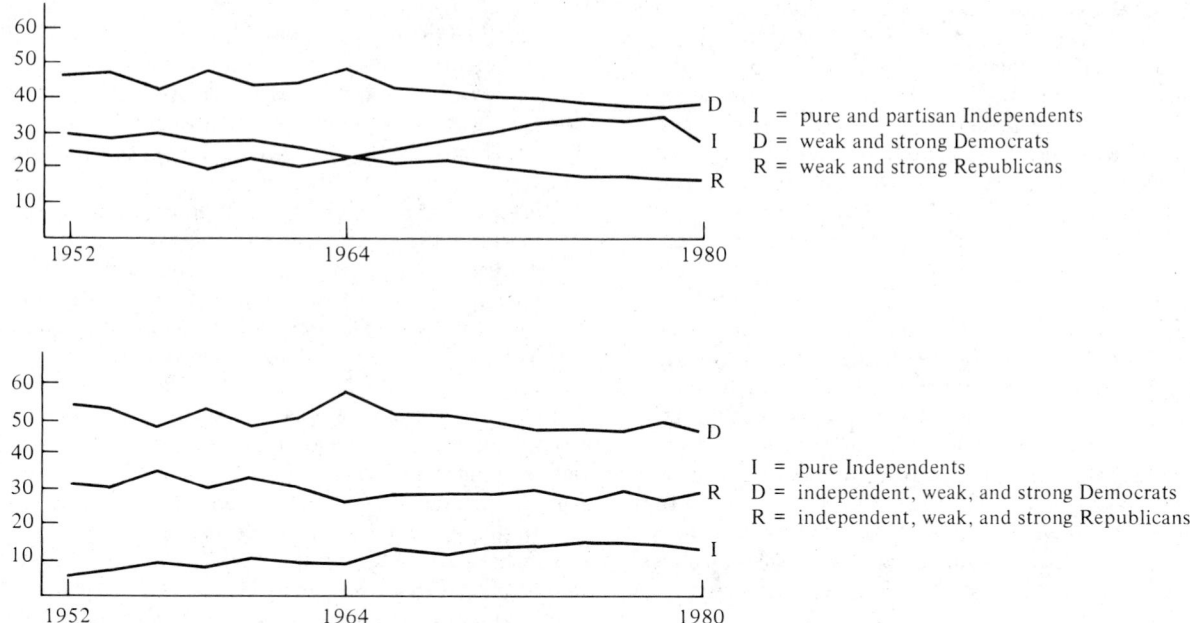

I = pure and partisan Independents
D = weak and strong Democrats
R = weak and strong Republicans

I = pure Independents
D = independent, weak, and strong Democrats
R = independent, weak, and strong Republicans

FIGURE 1
The Decline of Party Identification
SOURCE: CPS National Election Studies, 1952–1980.

later in the campaign, seems much less to spring from discoverable evaluations of the elements of national politics.

A public swollen with Independents not only would threaten the SRC position on voting, but also, rather more seriously, would imply an electorate less able to make intelligent political decisions.

Neither implication stands up very well to inspection. Those who have relied upon SRC data to chart trends in party loyalty, as in *The Changing American Voter* (Nie, Verba, and Petrocik, 1979), have usually attended only to the first round of the standard series of questions concerning party identification. They typically ignore replies to a follow-up question asking those who claimed to be Independents on the first round whether they lean towards the Republican party, the Democratic party, or neither. This turns out to be a mistake. Partisan Independents—those who first claim to be Independents and then indicate a party preference—differ substantially from pure Independents—those who claim no party preference whatsoever. Partisan Independents express a

keener interest in politics and public affairs, know more, vote more frequently, and participate more avidly in campaigns than do pure Independents. Furthermore, partisan Independents vote even more consistently for the nominee of their party than do weak partisans. Between 1952 and 1976, Independents inclined toward the Democratic party voted 70 percen t, on the average, for the Democratic candidate (compared to 64 percent for weak Democrats), while Independents inclined toward the Republican party gave an average of 88 percent of their votes to the Republican nominee (compared to 85 percent for weak Republicans). In contrast, pure Independents swing widely with short-term forces: Lyndon Johnson, a Democrat, received 75 percent of their votes in 1964; Richard Nixon, a Republican, received 75 percent of their votes in 1972 (Keith *et al.,* 1977; Petrocik, 1974). As a consequence, the accusation of civic sloth and weak partisanship taken from *The American Voter* applies only to pure Independents and not to partisan Independents—not now and not in the 1950s.

To understand the increasing numbers of Independents over the past fifteen years requires knowing precisely what types have contributed to this category. In 1952, the 22 percent of the public that declared themselves to be Independents included 6 percent pure Independents and about 17 percent partisan Independents. By 1980, when 35 percent of the public considered themselves to be Independents, pure Independents amounted to 13 percent and partisan Independents to 21 percent. Thus a little more than one-half the gain in the Independent category since 1952 can be ascribed to pure Independents.

In view of this more finely drawn portrait of the political Independent (or Independent*s*), the erosion of partisanship now seems less revolutionary (Wattenberg, 1981). Declines in the capacity of the electorate to reach intelligent electoral choices now appear less precipitous, particularly since pure Independents rarely vote, a disinclination that has increased sharply over the past two decades. And if partisan Independents are in fact loyal (if covert) supporters of the parties, then the consequences of the much heralded erosion of party identification have been exaggerated, a point made powerfully in Fig. 1.

Party identification *has* declined, of course. The proportion of the public *strongly* identified with one of the major parties has diminished by better than one-third since 1952, making for a more volatile electorate. Moreover, those Americans who have held on to a party identification are now more likely than before to defect, to support opposition candidates. Nie, Verba, and Petrocik (1979, Figure 4.2, p. 51) showed that defection from party in presidential elections increased from about 15 percent in 1952, 1956, and 1960 to about 25 percent in 1968 and 1972. The same point is made in Miller's (1979) updating of the normal vote parameters first calculated by Converse (1966b). Using election studies from 1962 to 1972, Miller found that the expected defection from each party category increased over Converse's estimates from an earlier period. As it happened, the partisan implications of these changes canceled so that the Democratic presidential candidate still enjoyed a 54–46 normal vote advantage. It was of course an advantage that the Democrats could count on less. Miller's new estimates expanded the confidence interval bracketing the normal vote, another symptom of the weakening of party.

Do these results reflect a secular and irreversible erosion of party? Only time will tell. But evidence from the 1976 and 1980 elections suggests that the onward march of party decomposition may have halted. Defection from party occurred no more often in 1976 or 1980 (though John Anderson's presence complicates comparisons) than in the supposedly "party-line" contests of 1952, 1956, or 1960 (Abramson, 1983).

Another indication of the decline of party, however, is the increase in recent decades of ticket splitting. Voters who divided their support between a Republican presidential candidate and a Democratic House candidate, or vice versa, nearly doubled from about 15 percent of the electorate during the 1950s to over 25 percent in the 1970s (Miller *et al.,* 1980; for aggregate evidence of increased ticket splitting, see Burnham, 1983). Split-ticket voting increased steeply in 1964 among Republicans and in 1972 among Democrats—presumably a reflection of displeasure with presidential candidates Goldwater and McGovern. So increases in ticket splitting, like increases in defection, seem to reflect in part the erosion of party and also the intermittent appearance of unpopular presidential candidates who drive huge numbers of their own party momentarily to the opposition.

In summary, reports of the demise of party identification have been exaggerated. Fewer Americans now than in the 1950s define themselves in party terms, but many remain covert party supporters. Though voters honored party less in selecting a president in 1968 and 1972 than in previous elections, the power of party rebounded in 1976 and 1980. Ticket splitting has also increased, but again, this seems to reflect at least as much the occasional appearance of unattractive presidential candidates as it does the irreversible decline of party. Party identification remains the single most important determinant of individual voting decisions. We see nothing in the evidence to suggest that theories of voting should abandon it.

Party identification as cause and effect.   Not abandon, but perhaps modify. *The American Voter* defined party identification as a "durable attachment, not readily disturbed by passing events and personalities." Indeed, "only an event of extraordinary intensity can arouse any significant part of the electorate to the point that its established party loyalties are shaken" (p. 151). Critics have since disagreed, arguing that party identification should be regarded *not* as a standing decision but as a "running balance sheet on the two parties" (Fiorina, 1977, p. 618). Is party identification responsive to new events or is it not?

Several aggregate observations favor the critics' view. There is first of all the fact of party decline. Although it has been exaggerated, the decline of party is real enough, and it has taken place during a period of trouble for U.S. government. It is *as if* citizens responded to conspicuous political failures at home and abroad by withdrawing their support from the parties, just as the metaphor of the running balance sheet would have them do. A similar point is made by the changes that have gradually taken place in the social-group composition of the two parties over the last forty years. The most striking changes have involved race, class, and region: Beginning with the 1936 election, blacks began to move decisively away from the party of Lincoln, eventually becoming the staunchest participants in the Democratic coalition; class differences in party support—with the working class identifying with the Democratic party and the middle class claiming the Republican party—declined by the mid 1970s almost to the vanishing point; and the solid South is solidly Democratic no longer (Ladd and Hadley, 1975; Petrocik, 1981). Such transformations seem discordant with the old view of party identification and consistent with the new.

Party decline and changes in the demographic bases of party coalitions need not imply the frailty of *individual* attachments, however. Much of the decline of party was accomplished not by individual change but by generational replacement: older, partisan cohorts being replaced by younger, Independent-minded cohorts (Converse, 1976; Nie, Verba, and Petrocik, 1979; Norpoth and Rusk, 1982). Furthermore, longitudinal observations of the same individuals suggest that Americans do not abandon their party lightly. Although two-year panel correlations for policy opinions hover around .35, the corresponding correlation for party identification is about .85—and in an era of party decline as well as in the supposedly strong party years of the Eisenhower presidency. What movement there is consists primarily of people traveling in and out of the Independent categories rather than from one party to the other (Converse, 1964; Converse and Markus, 1979).

Not all the long-term aggregate change can be accounted for by generational replacement, however. Nor does the panel analysis of individuals fully support the old view of party identification as essentially fixed. Because party identification falls short of perfect stability, it leaves room for the revisionist position, namely, that voters withdraw or invest support in the parties as their appraisal of events dictate. There is now good evidence that this happens. In the first place, change in party identification does reflect a kind of running balance sheet on the performance of government—most notably, on matters of peace and war, unemployment and inflation,

and civil rights (Brody, 1977; Dobson and St. Angelo, 1975; Fiorina, 1981a; Kinder and Kiewiet, 1981; Rivers, 1980). For example, changes in the *intensity* of Americans' party identification between 1972 and 1976 followed changes in their assessments of the parties' proficiencies on economic matters. Across the four years, Democrats became more strongly identified with their party to the extent they took a dim view of the current (Republican) administration's economic performance; Republicans showed a complementary pattern, though not as consistently or as strongly (Kinder and Kiewiet, 1981). These results support the revisionist position in principle, though without doing much violence to the traditional conception of party identification as a standing decision. Although statistically significant and theoretically important, the effects cited here are confined to alterations in the intensity rather than in the direction of party identification, and in any case they are not large.

Policy disagreements may also motivate change in party identification. Markus (1979) found modest movement toward the Democratic party among high school seniors in 1965, provoked by their support for racial integration and opposition to the Vietnam War. However, these two most important political events of the 1960s —the civil rights movement and the Vietnam War— did not shake their parents' party identifications at all. (For additional evidence of the impact of policy positions on party identification, see Franklin and Jackson, 1983; Jackson, 1975a, 1975b.)

Finally, voting for the opposition party's candidate also leads to shifts in party support. Both Knoke (using the 1956–1960 SRC panel; 1977, Chapter 6) and Markus and Converse (using the 1972–1976 panel; 1979) concluded that voting against one's party diminishes identification with the party in subsequent elections. Again, however, the effects were modest. Conversion from one party to the other would require, by these estimates, an uninterrupted and extended *series* of contrary votes—a path few voters follow.

Thus party identification is not completely immovable: It is influenced by the performance of government, by policy disagreements, and by the emergence of new candidates. Over the long haul, a party's performance, the policies it espouses, and the candidates it nominates can materially affect the support it receives from established and novice voters alike. This new view of party identification as sensitive to events constitutes an important theoretical change. Party identification moves to the center of the political process. The loyalty Americans feel toward parties reflects what parties do and what they fail to do. At a more practical level, this new view of party identification makes trouble for empirical procedures, like normal vote analysis and much of standard regression analysis, which presume the unilateral causal primacy of party identification (Achen, 1979; Brody and Page, 1972; Jackson, 1975a).

We should not press this too far, however. Although party identification does respond to political events, it does so sluggishly. It is one thing for Republicans to feel less loyalty toward their party after a period of sustained national difficulty presided over by a Republican administration and quite another to embrace the opposition. The latter seldom happens. In this respect, the metaphor of the running balance sheet is quite misleading. The strongest message of the evidence reviewed here is party identification's durability, how difficult it is to budge Americans from their attachments to party.

Public Policy and the Responsible Voter

U.S. presidential elections are not just contests between parties. To some degree they are also struggles over policy. In the voting literature and in the popular press, voters who weigh public policy in their electoral decisions are commended for their rationality and their civic responsibility. By supporting candidates whose views on public policy most resemble their own, citizens supposedly contribute to the formation of policy itself. Responsive, democratic governments are often imagined to work that way.

But according to *The American Voter,* the typical voter seems ill-prepared to make such a contribution. Many citizens interviewed confessed to having no opinion on policy questions; some substantial fraction of those who did seemed to do so capriciously; few claimed to know current government policy; many thought the parties did not differ appreciably in the policies they advocated. Campbell and his associates (1960) concluded that opinions on specific matters of policy ordinarily play a modest role in presidential elections.

This conclusion provoked a strong reaction. Beginning with V. O. Key's posthumously published volume, *The Responsible Electorate* (1966), a major preoccupation of research on voting over the past fifteen years has been to rehabilitate the ordinary citizen by demonstrating that policy voting is in fact more widespread than originally alleged in *The American Voter.* Succinctly put, Key's argument was that "voters are not fools" (p. 7) or

at least no more foolish than the political systems they inhabit. If provided clear alternatives, voters will be "moved by concern about central and relevant questions of public policy..." (pp. 7–8).

Although Key's empirical findings should not be taken too seriously (Converse, 1975a; Margolis, 1977; Sears, 1969), his argument caught on and was influential in sparking a revival of interest in the possibilities of policy voting. One of many inspired by *The Responsible Electorate* was Pomper (1972) who argued that it was parties and candidates that were confused (or at least confusing), not the voters. *The American Voter* discovered little policy voting because the parties failed to offer distinct programs in the 1950s and not because voters were incapable of fulfilling their civic obligations. Pomper showed that between 1956 and 1968 the proportion of the public who thought that the two parties differed on specific policy questions edged upwards from about one-half to about two-thirds, and that greater consensus developed regarding the positions taken by the parties. The perceived differences of the two major parties on questions of racial policy between 1960 and 1964 were particularly striking. In 1960, the Democratic party was identified as sympathetic to integration no more often than was the Republican party, but by 1964, the Democratic party was judged as more integrationist by a margin of nine to one! Such radical shifts presumably reflected Goldwater's conspicuously conservative position on race in the 1964 campaign and thereby help to establish Pomper's general point: Clarity about policy in the voter's mind does indeed depend on the clarity of the choices available.

Another question is whether voters respond when the parties do stake out clear alternatives. Nie, Verba, and Petrocik, in *The Changing American Voter* (1979), claimed they do. To make this point, they constructed a policy index based upon voters' replies to questions on social welfare, race, and foreign affairs. Based on a regression analysis, Nie and his associates reported that this global policy index augmented the prediction of presidential voting over that accounted for by party identification alone by 1 percent in 1956, 2 percent in 1960, 9 percent in 1964, 6 percent in 1968, 11 percent in 1972, and 2 percent in 1976. This pattern conforms well to the character of these campaigns themselves, since the 1964 and 1972 contests much more than others featured candidates with clear policy differences (Page, 1978). Thus policy voting appears to wax and wane according to the clarity and aggressiveness with which rival candidates promote alternative programs (also see Hartwig, Jenkins, and Temchin, 1980; Nie, Verba, and Petrocik, 1979, p. 380; Rosenstone, 1983).

A clinching demonstration of this point is provided by Page and Brody's (1972) staging of mock elections. Page and Brody first showed that late in the 1968 campaign, opinions on Vietnam policy correlated trivially with voters' preferences between Humphrey and Nixon. The frailty of this connection Page and Brody ascribed *not* to voters' inability or unwillingness to develop ideas about what the United States should do in Vietnam but rather to Humphrey and Nixon's failure to articulate alternative policies for voters to choose between. In contrast, rival candidates who differ on important matters and say so clearly and conspicuously should encourage policy voting. In the debate over Vietnam in 1968, Eugene McCarthy and George Wallace fulfilled these requirements well. In fact, Page and Brody showed that voting in an hypothetical election pitting McCarthy against Wallace reflected voters' opinions on Vietnam policy much more fully than did the 1968 election itself (*cf*. Abramowitz, 1981; Converse *et al.,* 1969; Petrocik, 1979).

Page and Brody's demonstration also provided an essential reminder of the limits of the connection between policy positions and voting choice. Despite the clarity and extremity of the positions on Vietnam staked out by McCarthy and Wallace, confusion on these matters in the general public was widespread. In mid August, only about two-thirds of the public were able to assign a position to McCarthy and to Wallace, of whom less than one-half correctly believed McCarthy to be advocating a more dovish position than Wallace. By foregoing the safety of ambiguity and by dwelling on policy differences, then, candidates can induce more policy-based voting; however, many voters will never notice.

Assessments of Government Performance

Compared to policy voting, the informational demands of what we call here performance voting are quite modest. Are economic conditions improving? Is the government corrupt? Is the nation's defense sound? In answering such questions, voters are not required to master the policies that rival candidates promote but only to take stock of how things are generally going and then to credit or blame the incumbent party candidate accordingly. The intricacies of policy debates may often surpass ordinary citizens' expertise and exhaust their curiosity, but evidence on government performance is readily available, in newspapers, television programs, and the mundane experiences of everyday life. And while presidential hopefuls cultivate ambiguity in their policy proposals (if they cannot avoid them altogether), they are eager to talk about performance—their own many accomplishments and their opponents' many failures (Page, 1978). Thus, "the pre-eminent means by which the public simplifies the complexity of government action is by shifting its attention from policies to performance—from government action to the values that government may achieve" (Butler and Stokes, 1974; p. 285).

Is performance voting as irresistible as Butler and Stokes portray it to be? Downs (1957), Fiorina (1981a), and Key (1966) argued that it is, that governments and particularly presidents are judged more by results than by proposals. Examining national surveys from 1952 to 1976, Fiorina (1981a) discovered strong support for performance voting. Assessments of government performance—especially concerning peace, prosperity, and civil rights—correlated consistently and occasionally powerfully with evaluations of the incumbent president, which in turn were strongly associated with vote. From Fiorina's presentation and from evidence reported by others (Kinder, 1981; Kinder and Kiewiet, 1979, 1981; Kinder and Mebane, 1983; Page, 1978, Chapter 7; Popkin *et al.,* 1976), it seems safe to conclude that presidential elections are, in part, referenda on the administration's performance.

This conclusion implies that assessments of performance should affect incumbent candidates and their challengers in different ways (Downs, 1957). Although voters' assessments of government performance should impinge powerfully upon their evaluations of the incumbent, appraisals of challengers, with no comparably conspicuous records, should depend more on general impressions of party competence. These predictions were borne out nicely for economic performance in the 1972, 1976, and 1980 elections (Kinder and Abelson, 1981; Kinder and Kiewiet, 1981).

But how do voters know whether an incumbent has succeeded or failed? With respect to economic performance, voters may simply examine their own circumstances, supporting candidates and parties that best advance their own economic interests. Yet such "pocketbook" voters are difficult to find. Although the economic predicaments of personal life do occasionally influence political choice, the effects are never very strong and usually they are utterly trivial. Declining financial condition, job loss, preoccupation with personal economic problems—none of these seems generally to motivate presidential voting (Fiorina, 1981a; Kiewiet, 1981; Kinder and Abelson, 1981; Kinder and Kiewiet, 1981; Sigelman and Tsai, 1981), and results are generally less friendly to "pocketbook" assumptions in House elections (e.g. Fiorina, 1981a; Hibbing and Alford, 1981; Kinder and Kiewiet, 1979, 1981).

Whereas pocketbook voters might ask the political system and its officials, "What have you done for *me* lately?" (Popkin *et al.,* 1976), "sociotropic" voters would ask, "What have you done for the *country* lately?" (Kinder and Kiewiet, 1981). The political preferences of "sociotropic" voters are shaped by the country's economic predicament, not their own; they support candidates and parties that appear to best advance the nation's well-being. And indeed, presidential voting seems to reflect more the assessment of national economic conditions than the economic circumstances of private life (Fiorina, 1981a; Kiewiet, 1981; Kinder and Abelson, 1981; Kinder and Kiewiet, 1979, 1981; Kinder and Mebane, 1983; Schlozman and Verba, 1979; Sniderman and Brody, 1977; but see Kramer, 1983). Moreover, people clearly distinguish between their own economic circumstances and those of the nation. Personal economic predicaments are largely autonomous from judgments Americans reach about economic problems in society (Kinder and Kiewiet, 1981; Mebane, 1982; the same holds true in Britain; Alt, 1979).

The familial (or pocketbook) and the national (or sociotropic) frames of reference do not exhaust the possibilities for performance voting, of course. Between the family and the nation is the group. Presidential choice may well reflect assessments of how well one's group has been doing, in terms of prosperity, power, and prestige. As the relevant group narrows, group interest becomes difficult to distinguish from self-interest; as it widens, it becomes difficult to distinguish from the national interest. In between the two extremes are many intermediate possibilities, where group interest stands independently from the other two (Kinder, Rosenstone, and Hansen, 1983).

Appraisals of Candidates

In *The Voter Decides* (Campbell *et al.,* 1954), the vote was partitioned into three elements: parties, policies, and candidates. In the ensuing debate over the quality of voting decisions, however, parties and policies drew most of the attention; candidates receded into the back-

ground. There were, of course, occasional exceptions. Despite wide variation in purpose and method, all the research made the same, perhaps unremarkable, point: Citizens vote in overwhelming numbers for the presidential candidate they like most (Brody and Page, 1968; Kelley and Mirer, 1974; Kinder and Abelson, 1981; Markus, 1982; Markus and Converse, 1979; Page and Jones, 1979).

But what is candidate-centered voting? Are candidates anything more than the party they represent, the policies they promote, and the results they have appeared to generate? They seem to be, in at least two ways: in the *traits* they convey and in the *feelings* they elicit.

On the first point, presidential candidates may succeed or fail partly because of the people they seem to be. Certainly voters often describe candidates in personal terms. Every four years since 1952, Americans have been asked what they like and dislike about the presidential candidates of the major parties. Roughly one quarter mention personal qualities—intelligence, warmth, dishonesty, or some such trait (Kagay and Caldeira, 1975).

From the citizen's perspective, it is easy to appreciate the appeal of trait-based voting. Rather than keeping in mind details of policy and performance and personal biography, voters may instead develop a few global impressions about a candidate's "real" dispositional qualities. This psychological inclination, strong by itself (Jones and Nisbett, 1971), is no doubt encouraged in politics by the heavy emphasis placed upon the personal qualities of candidates by campaigns and journalists alike (e.g., Graber, 1976; Patterson and McClure, 1976). Trait-based voting would seem to be a useful and efficient simplification and therefore one device by which ordinary people might manage the complexities of political choice (Popkin *et al.,* 1976).

Naturally not just any trait judgment will do. Central traits for presidents and presidential hopefuls include at least *competence* and *integrity*. Each shows up frequently in voters' open-ended candidate commentaries (Miller and Miller, 1976; Page, 1978), and in factor analysis of trait batteries (Kinder and Abelson, 1981; Kinder, 1984). Competence and integrity also surface more generally in person-perception studies: in investigations of task and socioemotional leadership in small groups (Cartwright and Zander, 1968), in attitude-change research on expertise and trust as components of source credibility (McGuire, 1969), in the distinction between respect and affection in studies of interpersonal attraction (Rubin, 1973), and in the emergence of the dimensions of intellectual and social competence in the structural analysis of person impressions (Rosenberg, 1977). Assuming that citizens possess implicit theories regarding the personalities of presidential candidates, as they apparently do about each other (Schneider, 1973), then central to such theories are competence and integrity. Finally, and most important, voters' assessments of the candidates' competence and integrity substantially affect the choices they eventually make (Dennis, 1982; Kinder, 1984; Kinder and Abelson, 1981; Markus, 1982).

The relative importance voters attach to competence and integrity in particular cases may vary enormously, in part because of the special qualities of candidates. McGovern's celebrated campaign fiascoes in 1972, for example, seemed to direct voters' attention to competence. His downfall may have had less to do with his leftist policy proposals than with his apparent inability to manage a campaign, much less a government (Popkin and associates, 1976). More generally, assessments of competence seem to carry greater weight in political evaluation than considerations of integrity; however, there are occasional and revealing exceptions. In the 1980 primary season, Edward Kennedy and John Connally, apparently by virtue of their special histories, managed to reverse the public's customary priorities. For Kennedy and Connally alone among a set of 1980 presidential hopefuls, judgments of integrity—preponderantly pejorative—were more consequential in shaping preference than were considerations of competence (Kinder and Abelson, 1981). The general point here is that the distinctive and conspicuous qualities of candidates may alter the relative importance the public assigns to competence and integrity.

Variation in the relative power of competence and integrity may also derive from individual differences among voters. For example, when citizens were asked to define their conceptions of an *ideal president,* those whose ideal president embodied competence more than integrity also weighed considerations of competence more heavily than integrity in their evaluations and their votes (and conversely; Kinder, Peters, Abelson, and Fiske, 1980).

The tenor of the times may also contribute to the mix of competence and integrity at work in political evaluation (Barber, 1980; Page, 1978). The "long national nightmare" of Watergate enhanced the importance of integrity in the 1976 campaign and may have contributed to the success of Carter's candidacy, with its unrelenting emphasis upon decency and trust. Conversely, the experience of the Carter White House no doubt made competence the central characterological question in 1980.

The second element of candidate-centered voting, which has drawn much less attention, concerns the particular emotions a candidate elicits. This neglect is peculiar, since one thing presidential campaigns surely try to do is mobilize the electorate's emotions. Success at the polls would seem to depend in no small measure on the candidate's ability both to evoke various positive emotions from potential voters and perhaps especially to avoid stirring up negative ones. In a very general way, this claim is supported by current thinking in social psychology (e.g., Leventhal, 1980; Zajonc, 1980). Particularly provocative is Zajonc's assertion that there are two largely independent systems of evaluation: a crude and fast affective system and a slower, more detailed cognitive one. In short, candidate-centered voting should be based not only on the voter's analysis of the candidate's personal traits but also on the affective reactions the candidate evokes.

To test this idea, Kinder, Abelson, and Fiske developed an affect checklist to represent the basic possibilities in Roseman's (1979) structural theory of emotions and then included it in several recent national surveys. (Those interviewed were asked whether, say, President Carter had ever made them feel angry, proud, and so forth, the emotions drawn from a list of either seven or sixteen affect terms, depending on the survey.) Such affective reports turned out to be widespread, with particular politicians eliciting distinctive profiles. For example, Edward Kennedy especially elicited anger and sadness; Jimmy Carter, frustration and unease. In general, the inclination to report positive feelings for a particular politician was only faintly related to the failure to report negative feelings. That is, *mixed* feelings were the norm. Most important, affective reports were not at all redundant with trait judgments: They contributed independently and powerfully to individual choice (Abelson, Kinder, Peters, and Fiske, 1982; Kinder and Abelson, 1981; on the last point, for parallel results in a different domain, see Tyler, 1980).

Voting in Other Contexts

One natural question is whether the account of voting set out here would hold at other times and in other places. Because of the voting specialists' preoccupations with presidential elections, it is difficult to say how well theories of voting developed in the last two decades apply to other contexts. However, some hints regarding their generalizability can be obtained by examining U.S. House elections. By presidential standards, the votes citizens cast in House elections seemed to early researchers (Stokes and Miller, 1962) ill-informed, lightly considered, and party based. Voters appeared to know little about incumbent representatives and even less about the challengers. Over the years, the Miller-Stokes characterization of House voters—living preponderantly in darkness and following the party line—was seldom challenged. In 1978, however, the CPS National Election Study for the first time mapped in detail relations between citizens and their representatives. The ensuing explosion of publications has made plain the need to rethink the Miller-Stokes view.

In the first place, the predominance of party identification in the Miller-Stokes account now appears somewhat inflated, an accident of history. In House elections between 1956 and 1978, party voting was strongest in 1958, the year Miller and Stokes undertook their study. Since then, party voting has gradually declined. Roughly 80 percent of the votes cast in House contests fell along party lines during the 1950s (counting independent partisans as partisans); about 70 percent did so during the 1970s (Abramson, 1983, p. 79). Consistent with the evidence on party decomposition reviewed earlier, this trend indicates a definite decline but certainly no demise of party identification. Party remains extremely important in House voting, but somewhat less important now than a quarter-century ago.

Coincident with a decline in party has been an increase in the importance of incumbency. Defections from party identification in House voting increasingly favor the incumbent (Cover and Mayhew, 1977). In the 1978 elections, for example, nearly 90 percent of the voters who deviated from their party supported the incumbent (Mann and Wolfinger, 1980). Partly as a consequence, incumbent representatives almost always win, often by overwhelming margins. In the past thirty years, of House incumbents seeking re-election, fewer than 2 percent were defeated in primary challenges and only 6 percent lost general elections. House elections have also become more and more one-sided; fully three-quarters of House incumbents running for re-election in recent years secured more than 60 percent of the votes in their districts (Cover and Mayhew, 1977; Mann and Wolfinger, 1980).

The electoral advantages of incumbency in part can be attributed to the invisibility of the opposition. Incumbents are vastly better known than their challengers. Incumbents win so easily partly because their opponents fail to mobilize the resources required to mount a serious campaign (Mann and Wolfinger, 1980). Incumbents also dominate their opponents because they are popular. Voters may deplore the Congress, but they love their representatives (Fenno, 1975; Fiorina, 1981b).

If the advantages of incumbency are to be found partly in incumbent popularity, then House voting may be importantly candidate-centered. Indeed, when asked what they like and dislike about House candidates, voters refer most often to leadership qualities (or more commonly to their absence), to competence and experience, and to other personal qualities (Fiorina, 1981b; Jacobson, 1981; Mann and Wolfinger, 1980; Parker, 1981). Because even incumbents leave shallow impressions on constituents, candidate-centered voting in House elections is no doubt greatly assisted when the candidates display their personal qualities in some especially conspicuous way. Flagrant acts of moral turpitude is one method (Mann, 1978; Peters and Welch, 1980). Another is for the candidate to take decisive action on those occasions when the folks back home are watching, as in the opportunity presented to members of the House Judiciary Committee during its deliberations over President Nixon's impeachment. According to Wright's (1977) analysis, Republican committee members who supported impeachment were subsequently rewarded by voters in the 1974 mid-term elections, while Nixon loyalists received a smaller share of the vote than they otherwise would have won. Voters evidently interpreted the well-publicized impeachment decisions of their representatives as diagnostic of more general personal qualities—excellence of judgment, independence of mind, and so forth—and voted accordingly. Thus incumbency can be overridden by those occasional dramatic events that seem to disclose deep flaws (or distinctive strengths) of character.

Incumbents may also lose when they take positions that stray too far from the opinions held by their constituents, though this probably happens rather infrequently. Few voters have solid impressions of their incumbents' policy preferences, much less what rival candidates might be proposing (Fiorina, 1981b; Hurley and Hill, 1980; Mann and Wolfinger, 1980; Stokes and Miller, 1962). Thus it is not surprising that efforts to demonstrate the role of policy in House elections have met with spotty success (e.g., Abramowitz, 1980; Erikson, 1971; Jacobson, 1981; Mann, 1978; Parker, 1981; Schoenberger, 1969). Exceptional circumstances aside, the votes citizens cast for congressional candidates seldom are influenced by questions of policy.

They may, however, be influenced by the state of the nation. Time-series analysis consistently discloses substantial effects of national conditions on House races. Mid-term elections seem especially vulnerable to national tides. When the president's popularity slips or the economy declines, House candidates of the president's party suffer (Hibbing and Alford, 1981; Kramer, 1971; Tufte, 1978). Studies of individual voters show similar if somewhat diminished effects (Kernell, 1977; Kiewiet, 1981; Kinder and Kiewiet, 1979, 1981; Nelson, 1978; Piereson, 1975; Ragsdale, 1980). Thus voters appear to choose between rival House candidates partly on the basis of national circumstances. Moreover, national conditions may also effect congressional elections *indirectly,* since unfavorable national tides produce attractive, well-financed challengers, and favorable national conditions yield weaker challengers (Jacobson and Kernell, 1981).

In sum, voting for congressional representatives is not the same as voting for president. House elections have their own special properties, which are reflected in the determinants of choice. Party and incumbency typically dominate House voting decisions, leaving little room for other considerations—some for conspicuous displays of character (perhaps especially failures of character), a little for national conditions, a bit for policy.

PROSPECTS FOR A GENERAL THEORY OF INDIVIDUAL CHOICE

Our understanding of voting has come a long way since *The People's Choice.* Demographic explanations of the vote have given way to accounts that assign first priority to the voter's attitudes. Voting is now understood to be a complex act; it is no longer regarded as the inexorable working out of social class or, for that matter, as the habitual and single-minded affirmation of loyalty to party. Recent developments emphasize instead the multiplicity of the determinants that shape the vote. To be sure, the new view includes party identification (though its meaning has changed) but also character, emotion, the nation's predicaments, and pressing policy questions.

Identifying the major determinants of individual choice solves one problem but produces two others, and these are both formidable obstacles to a general theory of individual choice. First, although party identification, candidate appraisals, government performance, and policy opinions are conceptually independent, they are empirically entangled. For example, if a presidential can-

didate seems to take essentially the same position on policy matters across an entire campaign, voters may be encouraged to see him or her as trustworthy. At the same time, a candidate who begins a campaign with a reputation for integrity may be forgiven an inconsistency or two. Similarly, just as evidence that the economy is falling apart will lead voters to wonder about the president's competence, so, too, will prior reservations about him or her based on other evidence color voters' interpretations of economic conditions. That the determinants of choice affect each other in complicated ways is something that is just beginning to be fully appreciated and unraveled. For a discussion of the statistical problems of identification and efficient estimation, see Bentler, 1980; Kenny, 1985; for applications to the vote, see Brody and Page, 1972; Jackson, 1975a; Markus, 1982; Markus and Converse, 1979; Page and Jones, 1979.

A second problem, intimately bound up with the first, concerns assigning importance to the various determinants. Is party identification more or less important than government performance? Do policy opinions carry more or less weight in individual vote choice than do trait assessments? Simply entering a set of variables into a multiple regression program and equating importance with the size of the resulting partial coefficients, which is the customary way such questions are answered, will not do. The procedure ignores relations among the explanatory variables themselves and therefore the very real possibility that variables with minimal direct effects on voting may nevertheless materially affect voting indirectly through their influence on more proximal determinants. Assertions about the relative importance of party identification, candidate appraisals, and other determinants of the vote require attention to the structure of the causal relations among them.

Complicating matters further, such assertions must always be conditional. The relative importance of the various determinants will depend in part on the voters themselves: according to the characteristic way they understand public problems (Kinder and Mebane, 1983; Lau and Sears, 1981), the particular policy questions they take to be important (Rabinowitz, Prothro, and Jacoby, 1982), the normative standards they apply (Kinder *et al.,* 1980), and so on. It will depend also on variation in the political context. What candidates and media choose to emphasize may profoundly affect which determinants predominate. To take just one example, the importance of policy for individual choice hinges decisively on strategic decisions made by candidates: Evasion and ambiguity will curtail the role of policy, while sharp and repeated disagreements will enhance it (Page and Brody, 1972; Petrocik, 1980). Political choice depends partly on the criteria of party, performance, and so on that voters bring to politics and partly on the clarity and distinctiveness of the information the political environment provides relevant to those criteria.

In the face of all this complexity, it is certainly unrealistic and perhaps even undesirable to hope for a single, coherent theory of political choice (though Fishbein and Ajzen, 1981, believe they have already delivered one). The act of voting is a complex activity that takes place over an extended period of time in response to many different informational and affective bombardments. How could a single theory explain such a complicated phenomenon? There is no Newton on the voting literature horizon.

DETERMINANTS OF COLLECTIVE CHOICE

In this final section our attention turns from voters to elections, from the mysteries of the individual voter to the mysteries of the collective vote. This amounts to a move away from the psychological, towards the political. "If the specialist in electoral behavior is to be a student of politics," wrote Key (1960, p. 55), "his major concern must be the population of elections, not the population of individual voters" (*cf.* Kramer, 1983; Rosenstone, 1983).

Short-term Electoral Change

The narrow presidential victory for the Democratic party in 1948 was followed in short order by two Republican landslides. John Kennedy squeaked by for the Democrats in 1960; four years later, Lyndon Johnson demolished the Republicans and Barry Goldwater. These were dramatic instances of electoral change, yet none was accompanied by major shifts in the underlying distribution of voters' party identifications. They were *temporary* defections, not permanent conversions (Campbell *et al.*, 1960; Converse *et al.*, 1965; Converse *et al.*, 1969). The key to understanding short-term change thus rests with the identification of forces that deflect the electorate from its normal decision.

Stokes's (1966b) ingenious analysis of electoral change identified candidates as a major force in this alteration of aggregate votes. (Others have since brought Stokes's analysis up to 1976; Kagay and Caldeira, 1980; Popkin *et al.,* 1976.) Stokes first estimated the impact of six factors on electoral choice for each presidential election taken separately and then calculated the partisan advantage provided by each. He found that most factors gave a steady advantage to one party's candidate or to the other's across elections. The Republican candidate generally won votes on foreign policy and administrative competence, but lost votes on domestic policy and especially on group benefits. In contrast, the relative attractiveness of the candidates themselves moved sharply from one election to the next. According to this method, Eisenhower's personal magnetism was decisive in 1952 and 1956, just as Goldwater's image in 1964 was decisive in the opposite direction. Stokes concluded that the dynamics of presidential elections are "particularly tied to the emergence of new candidates. . . ."(p. 28).

Electoral outcomes are also responsive to changes in national conditions—particularly to changes in national *economic* conditions. In House elections between 1896 and 1964, Kramer (1971) found that prosperity advantaged candidates of the incumbent president's party, while economic decline enhanced the chances of the opposition. A torrent of work followed Kramer's example, mainly fortifying this point. The link between economic conditions and short-term electoral change holds for presidential as well as for House elections. It affects both Democratic and Republican administrations. It survives whether or not the dependent variable includes the share of the national vote captured by splinter parties, regardless of how or whether the model explicitly represents the electorate's long-term partisanship, in cross-sectional and time-series analyses where individual states furnish the critical comparisons, and where estimates are provided by simultaneous equations that permit election outcomes to feedback upon economic conditions. (e.g., Bloom and Price, 1975; Monroe, 1979; Rosenstone, 1983; and Tufte, 1978, provide a useful guide to this rapidly expanding literature.)

Fluctuations in national conditions that power electoral change need not be exclusively economic, of course. Governments may also be held accountable for preserving peace, avoiding corruption, maintaining order at home, upholding prestige abroad, and so on. Time-series measures of such conditions are not as readily available as are the various economic indicators, although there is no particular reason to doubt that they will eventually become part of a more fully developed theory of electoral change.

Thus, deviations from the electorate's normal vote seem provoked primarily by the emergence of new candidates and by changes in national circumstances. Commanding personalities and national crises can tilt the electorate's preferences in one direction or the other. If these short-term forces accentuate the electorate's "normal vote," then the majority party candidate wins, in a "maintaining" election. If the short-term forces run powerfully against the majority party, then the minority party candidate captures the White House, in a "deviating" election. "Maintaining" and "deviating" elections (Campbell, 1966) represent temporary alterations. When the candidates pass from the scene or when the national crisis eases, the electorate tends to return to the normal division of the vote.

Critical Elections and Party Realignment

Electoral change is not always a short-lived deviation from a stationary equilibrium point, however. At special junctures in U.S. history, the equilibrium point itself has shifted. The hallmark of such turning points is the critical election, characterized by "a sharp and durable electoral realignment between parties" (Key, 1955, p. 16). Critical elections and the realignments of party strength that accompany them have occurred three times since the origins of the modern two-party system: in the 1850s, in the 1890s, and most recently in the 1930s, in the depths of the Great Depression (Burnham, 1970; Campbell, 1966; Clubb, Flanigan, and Zingale, 1980; Sundquist, 1973).

Although theorizing about realignments with just three cases may seem hazardous, there has been, nevertheless, quite a bit of it. According to various accounts, past realignments and presumably any future ones are instigated by the emergence of a grave national crisis (Burnham, 1970; Campbell, 1966; Clubb *et al.,* 1980; Sundquist, 1973). In response to the crisis, the rival political parties travel in opposite directions, offering sharply alternative solutions (Ginsberg, 1982, Chapter 4; Sundquist, 1973). These policy differences often then become moralistic ones. The injection of moral fervor into political debate, against a backdrop of extreme crisis, may account for the intensity of public engagement that typically accompanies critical elections (Burnham, 1970; Key, 1955).

Sundquist's account of the realignment process especially emphasizes its ideological character. Although calamitous national circumstances provide a congenial context for realignment and although imposing personalities may hasten or retard it, party realignments are essentially driven by broad disagreements between the parties (Burnham, 1970; Campbell, 1966; Sundquist, 1973). This is an important point, since it restores some polish to the otherwise tarnished reputation of the policy-

motivated voter. Our conclusions regarding the proximal determinants of the individual vote, remember, emphasized loyalty to party, appraisals of the contending candidates, and assessments of government performance. The influence of policy opinions appeared by comparison quite modest, attentuated by ambiguous proposals on the candidates' part and by private preoccupations on the voters' part. Similarly, electoral change in the short run seems traceable primarily to candidates and national circumstances, not to policy. But according to Sundquist, lasting rearrangements of party support are driven by policy—by ideas about what the government should and should not do. Fifty years ago, Roosevelt voters became Democratic identifiers because they believed, as the Democratic party did and as the Republican party did not, that it was primarily the federal government's responsibility to help those who could not help themselves.

Not everyone accepts this policy-oriented interpretation, however. In dissent, Clubb, Flanigan, and Zingale (1980) argue that realignment begins with dissatisfaction with the *performance* of government, and not with enthusiasm for new policy proposals. If the dissatisfaction is profound, the incumbent party will be swept out of office. This gives the newly empowered party effective control over government policy. Perhaps more important, the new party is now widely seen as responsible for whatever follows. If what follows is good—if the national crisis subsides—then realignment is set in motion. What matters here is not how the new government manages to generate such results, or even that it has a role in this process, but that the public *believes* it is so. It is performance (really, the appearance of performance) that counts, not policy.

Regardless of the mix of policy and performance at work in realignments, there remains a further question: Do realignments take place through the *conversion* of the opposition or through the *mobilization* of the unaffiliated? Most writing on realignment presumes conversion (Burnham, 1970; Key, 1955; Sundquist, 1973). The case for mobilization has been made most forcefully by Andersen for the realignment of the 1930s (1979; also see Beck, 1975). She showed that as 1930 approached, the U.S. party system was at least ripe for mobilization. The number of potential voters without firm commitments to either of the parties was then very great, because of the recent extension of the franchise to women, because of the unusually large number of potential voters who abstained in 1920 and 1924, and especially because of rapid, massive European immigration. According to

Andersen, the Democrats became the majority party by successfully mobilizing these groups.

A persistent frustration for those interested in realignment is that reputable survey evidence does not extend back even to the most recent of the three great party upheavals. Andersen tried to finesse this problem partly by inventive use of voting statistics. She showed that the enormous expansion of the electorate between 1920 and 1936 was almost entirely a Democratic expansion. Across the sixteen-year period, the total vote for the Republican presidential candidate remained essentially constant, while the Democratic vote shot up dramatically, especially in the industrial cities of the Midwest and Northeast, which were home to most of the immigrants and which became the epicenters of the New Deal realignment. Registration figures revealed the same trends, as did more detailed and disaggregated analysis (Andersen, 1979, especially Chapter 6; Wanat, 1979).

To push her claim further, Andersen set about to reconstruct the New Deal realignment by taking seriously the recollections about the past offered by respondents interviewed in national election studies between 1952 and 1972. Those interviewed were asked not only about their current party identification but also about whether they had ever changed parties and if so, when. With such testimony, Andersen suggested that the realignment period was dominated by a single, sweeping change: a massive expansion of the active electorate, attributable entirely to voters who eventually came to call themselves Democrats. Andersen concluded that the driving force behind the New Deal realignment was mobilization, not conversion.

There are problems with Andersen's reconstruction, however (see, for example, Erikson and Tedin, 1981). The most serious is that recollections of the past are distorted by views of the present (*cf.* Bem and McConnell, 1970). Because people under-report change in their own partisanship (Markins, 1984; Niemi, Katz, and Newman, 1980), Andersen's reconstruction of the New Deal realignment almost certainly underestimated the actual amount of conversion.

Mobilization is, however, also favored by evidence that avoids the problems inherent in recollections of the distant past. Campbell, Converse, Miller, and Stokes (1960) examined respondents' reports about their *current* party identification, taken from pooling the 1952, 1954, 1956, and 1958 national election studies, and arranged by the respondents' date of birth. This comparison revealed that older cohorts, born before 1905, were predomi-

nantly Republican in the 1950s, while younger cohorts born after 1916 were predominantly Democratic. The steep transition between the two was centered among the Depression generation, those born between 1905 and 1912, who came of political age in the 1930s. This evidence implies that the New Deal realignment was accomplished at least in part by the Democratic party's mobilization and eventual capture of the politically uninitiated.

Although at the present time, the evidence favors the mobilization more than the conversion thesis, the creation of a Democratic majority in the 1930s probably resulted from some of each. And the implication that conversion means radical transformation may be overstated. To the degree that conversion went on in the 1930s, it was probably limited to change of a more modest kind: tentative attachments to one party evolving gradually into tentative attachments to another.

In either instance, the account of realignment offered here fits comfortably with the role we earlier ascribed to party identification in individual choice. As for American individuals so, too, for the American electorate, attachment to party is a durable commitment. Large-scale rearrangements have intruded rarely in the past and have seemed to require an "intricate conjunction of events" (Converse, 1975a): the emergence of a grave national crisis, massive numbers of potential voters susceptible to mobilization, rival parties deeply divided over how the crisis should be solved (perhaps), and the eventual appearance of government success. Party attachments are not easily rearranged.

POLITICAL ACTION

Voting in presidential elections is of course but one way —and even in a realigning election, a rather innocuous way—to take part in politics. Our next task is to enumerate the full range of possible forms of political participation and then to summarize the extensive literature on why people participate as they do (or do not participate at all). We then address the steady (and to some, alarming) decline in voter turnout over the last five U.S. presidential elections.

FORMS OF PARTICIPATION

Some people are moved to political action, but most stay home. In a national survey, Verba and Nie (1972) found that only about 11 percent of U.S. citizens were real activists, distinguished by their commitment to campaigns, their presence in organizations dedicated to the resolution of local grievances, their willingness to pressure government officials, and their inveterate voting. Almost one-quarter of the public took no part in any of these political activities. This contrast holds up in other countries. In Austria, India, Japan, Netherlands, Nigeria, and Yugoslavia (Verba, Nie, and Kim, 1978), as in the United States, intense political participation is confined to a thin layer of activists. "Politics is a sideshow in the great circus of life" (Dahl, 1961, p. 305).

Participation in unconventional political action is even less common. Boycotters, strikers, demonstrators, and rioters are practically invisible in representative national surveys. Of 1500 Americans surveyed near the height of protest against the Vietnam War, for example, just eight lonely souls said they had taken part in an antiwar demonstration (Verba and Brody, 1970).

The *potential* for unruly political activity may be considerable, however. Barnes and Kaase (1979; also Marsh, 1977) presumed that one effect of the waves of protest that swept over advanced industrial Western nations in the 1960s was the widespread diffusion of the potential for unconventional political participation. To measure such potential, Barnes and Kaase developed a scale based on citizens' approval of, and readiness to perform, such unconventional political acts as signing petitions, attending lawful demonstrations, participating in boycotts, and so on. In these terms, and compared to their counterparts in Austria, Britain, Germany, or the Netherlands, Americans were less likely to embrace an exclusively confrontational style of participation but also much less likely to be politically inactive altogether.

Just how large is the U.S. appetite for unruly political action is impossible to say in the abstract. The *realization* of unconventional participatory potential depends on external factors—on provocations and opportunities as well as on citizens' predispositions. We will have more to say about provocations and opportunities later. In the meantime, Barnes and Kaase's analysis serves as a valuable reminder of the diversity of political action. In developing accounts for why some people participate and others do not, we will try to keep such diversity in mind.

ECONOMIC EXPLANATIONS

The economic approach to political action begins with the presumption of rationality. Citizens arrive at their political choices through careful calculation of benefits and costs. They try to do their very best, approaching "every situation with one eye to the gains to be had, the other eye on costs, a delicate ability to balance them, and a strong desire to follow wherever rationality leads" (Downs, 1957, pp. 7–8; see also Frohlich and Oppenheimer, 1978; Riker and Ordeshook, 1973; for an incisive critique, see Barry, 1970). With these strong assumptions in place, the economic approach then proceeds to descriptions of how people *do* behave politically as well as to prescriptions about how they *ought* to behave. Such claims bear on the dynamics of competition among rival political parties (with parties assumed to be in the business of maximizing votes; Downs, 1957; Ordeshook, 1976); the strategic decisions faced by candidates—when to run, how to allocate scarce campaign resources, which qualities to stress and which to conceal, and so on (Aldrich, 1980; Jacobson and Kernell, 1981); the formation, development, and demise of voluntary political organizations (Fainstain and Fainstain, 1974; Olson, 1965); and finally, our principal concern here, a decision faced by ordinary citizens on election day—whether to vote or to abstain (Downs, 1957; Ferejohn and Fiorina, 1975; Frohlich *et al.*, 1978; Riker and Ordeshook, 1968; Tullock, 1968).

In Downs's (1957) enormously influential *An Economic Theory of Democracy* (a book that is to the economic analysis of political action what *The American Voter* is to the behavioral tradition), voter turnout is analyzed in simple cost-benefit terms. The major *costs* of voting in Downs's scheme are time, money, and foregone opportunities. The *benefits* of voting are compounded of two elements. First is the "expected party differential": the difference between the "stream of utility" from government activity expected if the incumbent party were to continue in office and that expected if the opposition party were to take office. Naturally, voters prefer the party that is expected to deliver to them a steadier, richer stream of utility. In deciding whether to register such preferences at the polls, however, voters must also consider whether their vote will make a difference. Rational voters must discount their expected party differential by the probability that their own vote will be decisive. Multiplying the expected party differential by the probability that a single vote will prove decisive amounts, of course, to a gigantic discount. In U.S. presidential elections, the likelihood that one vote will sway the election is rather smaller than being run over by a bus on the way to the polls. This is somewhat embarrassing, since it implies that, because the costs of voting are nontrivial, no rational voter should show up on election day. That millions do suggests that voting is irrational.

Downs's solution to the apparent irrationality of voting was to suppose another, or second, source of voting benefits. Potential voters consider not only the (tiny) discounted party differential but also the value of the act of voting itself, derived from the citizen's allegiance to democratic forms of government (Downs, 1957, pp. 261–262):

> The citizens of a democracy subscribe to its principles and therefore derive benefits from its continuance; hence they do not want it to collapse [as it would if an election were held and no one showed up]. For this reason they attach value to the act of voting *per se* and receive a benefit from it.

Just enough benefit, evidently, to propel many of them to the polls.

This is no solution. The supposition that some voters absorb the short-term costs of voting in order to contribute to the long-term maintenance of democracy violates economic rationality, since the benefits of democracy will fall upon voters and nonvoters alike (Barry, 1970).

In a famous paper that sets out "a theory of the rational calculus of voting," Riker and Ordeshook (1968) ignored Downs's solution altogether and concentrated instead on the original puzzle. They began by scolding Downs for concluding that "voting, the fundamental political act, is typically irrational" (p. 25). (This was Downs's *interim* conclusion, of course, not his final word.) Riker and Ordeshook then proceeded to offer their own solution to the apparent irrationality of voting that differed from Downs's only in its nomenclature. As did Downs, Riker and Ordeshook emphasized the benefits of voting accruing from the act itself. Their contribution, rather, was to operationalize the elements of rational-choice theory and to test it with national surveys conducted by the Survey Research Center in 1952, 1956, and 1960. They measured the benefits of the voting act itself by potential voters' scores on a "citizen duty" index, comprised of replies to four questions concerning the importance of voting. Potential voters' declarations of how much they cared about which candidate would win the upcoming presidential election stood in for the expected party differential—the differential benefits they expected to reap if their preferred candidate won. Finally, potential voters' judgments that their own vote would swing

the election to their candidate and therefore bring about a realization of these benefits were operationalized by predictions about the closeness of the impending election. Riker and Ordeshook found, perhaps unremarkably, that turnout was systematically related to each of the three elements independently and took this evidence as ratification for their theory of "the rational calculus that does in fact occur in the act of deciding whether or not to vote" (p. 38).

Neither Barry (1970) nor Ferejohn and Fiorina (1974) were much impressed with this conclusion. First of all, it is no tribute to the rationality of voting to demand, as Riker and Ordeshook did, that voters grossly inflate the likelihood that their own vote might make a difference. Second, according to Riker and Ordeshook's own analysis, the satisfactions of the act of voting itself dominated the other two ingredients of choice. Turnout depends much more on the importance voters place on the principle of voting than on the benefits they expect to receive should their candidate win or on how close they predict the election to be. That is, "people vote because they derive satisfaction from voting for reasons entirely divorced from the hope that it will bring about desired results" (Barry, 1970, p. 16). This reason contradicts instrumental rationality.

These difficulties with the economic approach have done nothing to discourage the widespread presumption that political action springs from calculations of tangible benefits and costs. The presumption is commonly enlisted, for example, to explain why it is that most citizens take part so sporadically and so superficially in their own governance. Widespread indifference reflects the remoteness of politics from citizens' material interests. When government policies intrude—when they become "doorstep issues"—interest, attention, and participation all supposedly escalate (Converse, 1975a; Downs, 1957; Lippman, 1922; Popkin *et al.*, 1976).

For all its eminent plausibility, this familiar argument turns out to have remarkably thin empirical support. Once beyond Jennings's (1979) effective demonstration that becoming a parent enhances interest in local school politics, the case largely evaporates. If anything, personal economic adversity generally inhibits participation (Barnes and Kaase, 1979; Brody and Sniderman, 1977; Rosenstone, 1982; Schlozman and Verba, 1979, Scott and Acock, 1979): The poor and the unemployed do not seek solutions for their problems at the polls. Nor does affluence lead to greater turnout, despite wealthy people's apparently greater stake in election outcomes

(Wolfinger and Rosenstone, 1980). Nor, most directly, does turning out to vote on tax-relief propositions have anything to do with the benefits to be gained by their successful passage (Sears and Citrin, 1982). Perhaps participation should be regarded as an ethical act, transcendent of immediate self-interest (Meehl, 1977). Political action may indeed be provoked when politics impinges upon cherished values, but these values may be largely independent of the material interests of private life.

SOCIOLOGICAL EXPLANATIONS

Sociological accounts of participation leave aside the theme of rationality and seek the causes of political action in social location, indexed by demographic variables such as education, income, occupation, gender, race, ethnicity, age, and the like. We now know a great deal in this respect about participation—about turning out to vote in particular. People of high status vote much more frequently than do people of low status (Lane, 1959; Milbrath and Goel, 1977; Nie and Verba, 1975), and of the various indicators of status, education is by far the most important (Wolfinger and Rosenstone, 1980). According to Wolfinger and Rosenstone's calculations, with other demographic characteristics held constant, the turnout rate in the 1972 U.S. presidential election among those with a college degree was 38 percentage points higher than among those who had less than five years of formal schooling. The impact of education on participation is strongest in the United States, though it shows up in other Western countries and for a variety of conventional campaign and community political activities in addition to voting (Barnes and Kaase, 1979; Nie and Verba, 1975).

The better educated also approve most of boycotts, demonstrations, strikes, and the like. Here again, education is a more powerful determinant than income, occupation, or class (Barnes and Kaase, 1979). In parallel fashion, militancy was more common among well-educated American blacks than among, as the McCone Commission so quaintly put it, the "riffraff" (e.g., Fogelson, 1968; Sears and McConahay, 1973).

Although the differences in conventional participation between men and women in the United States were once very great, now they are negligible. In the 1920 presidential contest, the first in which women were permitted to vote throughout the nation, Merriam and Gosnell (1924) found that 75 percent of the men but only 46 percent of the women voted in Chicago. By 1972, however, men outvoted women nationwide by just 2 percent (Wolfinger and Rosenstone, 1980), and sex differences on various other conventional political activities and on protest potential were also minimal (and smaller in the United States than elsewhere: Abeles, 1976; Barnes and Kaase, 1979; Welch, 1977). The sole exception was participation in the great urban eruptions of the 1960s, which was undertaken more often by men than by women, according both to police arrest records and the self-reports of survey respondents (e.g., Fogelson, 1968; Sears and McConahay, 1973).

Participation differences between blacks and whites in the United States have also narrowed appreciably over the last thirty years (Danigelis, 1978; Verba and Nie, 1972). Some of this narrowing was of course the result of the Voting Rights Acts of 1965 and 1970 coupled with concerted efforts to register Southern blacks (e.g., Converse, 1972). However, the historical trend is clear for other activities as well. Blacks no longer take part less than whites in a wide variety of conventional forms of political participation, nor do they protest less than whites (Barnes and Kaase, 1979; Eisenger, 1974). Moreover, when researchers control for correlated demographic characteristics, blacks may actually surpass the participation of whites in voting and other conventional political activities (Olson, 1970; Verba and Nie, 1972; but see Wolfinger and Rosenstone, 1980).

For social psychological tastes, these demographic patterns are tantalizing. *Why* do the well-educated march to the polls while the poorly educated stay home? Perhaps schooling teaches skills that make politics less formidable or inculcates reverence for the political process. Perhaps the various bureaucratic encounters entailed in schooling prepare students to make their way successfully through the tangle of procedures required to become a registered voter in the first place. These conjectures, which we have taken from Wolfinger and Rosenstone (1980), seem plausible and that is something of a problem. Education and the other consequential demographic characteristics need to be linked up with attitudinal predispositions and environmental opportunities—in short, with a social-psychological analysis of participation—which is our next topic.

SOCIAL PSYCHOLOGICAL EXPLANATIONS

Our review of the social psychological approach assembles evidence both on actor dispositions and on external circumstances. The review is spottier and more schematic than we would like; we offer it partly as an invitation to future work.

Disaffection

It is clear that Americans are strikingly less trusting of their national government now than they were two decades ago; they place less confidence in institutions and less faith in politicians (Citrin, 1977, and Miller, 1980). However, the behavioral implications of these trends are not as clear. The common assumption that disaffection causes people to withdraw from conventional political activities has so far found little empirical support. The disaffected do *not* vote less, participate less in campaigns, give less of their time and money to mainstream political organizations, and so forth. However it is measured (and there is a stormy argument over this: Citrin *et al.,* 1975; Lodge and Tursky, 1979; Muller, 1979), disaffection is feebly related to conventional forms of political action in the United States and in western Europe (Aberbach and Walker, 1973; Citrin, 1974, 1977; Farah, Barnes, and Heunks, 1979; Miller, 1980; Katosh and Traugott, 1981). Nor is there much evidence that voters avoid the polls when they admire none of the candidates (Brody, 1978; Weisberg and Grofman, 1981). Thus displeasure with presidential candidates, like disaffection from government more generally, does not appear to lead people to give up on conventional forms of political action.

Disaffection *does* seem to motivate unconventional participation, however. In a survey of San Francisco area residents conducted in the summer of 1972, for example, Citrin (1977) found quite strong relationships between disaffection and participation in sit-ins, boycotts, and peaceful and even violent protests (also see Sniderman, 1981). Muller (1979) reported similar results from surveys of Waterloo Iowans in the spring of 1970 and of the West German public in the fall of 1974. In each location, endorsement of confrontational political activities was associated with feelings of disaffection—that the legal system was unfair, that basic rights were routinely violated, and that political leaders were corrupt.

A milder strain of disaffection—unhappiness with government performance on important public problems—has also predicted protest, in each of five nations including the United States (Farah, Barnes, and Heunks, 1979). Similarly, Sears and McConahay (1973) found that participation in the Watts riot in Los Angeles was motivated by blacks' disaffection with local institutions and local authorities, especially discrimination by local government agencies and merchants, police brutality, and an indifferent if not actively hostile local political structure (also see Aberbach and Walker, 1973).

Hence disaffection does appear to be a powerful motivator of confrontational politics. If there is an ideology of protest, a web of ideas and feelings that sustains activism, then disaffection would seem to be part of it.

Relative Deprivation

Another element of protest would seem to be relative deprivation. In *The American Soldier,* Stouffer *et al.* (1949) employed the concept of relative deprivation to explain, among other curiosities, how it could be that soldiers who on objective grounds were the best off had the worst morale. According to the concept of relative deprivation, resentments stem not from appraisals of objective reality but from invidious social comparisons.

This idea has since developed into a family of theories (Crosby and Gonzalez-Intal, 1982; Davis, 1959; Gurr, 1970; Pettigrew, 1967; Runciman, 1966). Relative deprivation occurs when people:

1. *Desire* something they do not possess;

2. Feel *entitled* to possess it;

3. Do *not blame* themselves for failing to possess it.

It is widely assumed that protest and political violence are among the consequences of relative deprivation. According to Gurr (1969), relative deprivation "is as fundamental to understanding civil strife as the law of gravity is to atmospheric physics: relative deprivation...is a necessary precondition for civil strife of any kind" (p. 596).

In keeping with this bold assertion, Gurr's *Why Men Rebel* (1970) is dotted with examples from history: social banditry in medieval Europe, the French and Bolshevik revolutions, the rise of Fascism, and the civil rights movement in the United States; all these are treated as manifestations of relative deprivation. The central idea here is that sudden increases in the gap between expectation and outcome lead to feelings of relative deprivation and thus to political unrest. More audacious was Davies (1962, 1969) who promoted relative deprivation as *the* driving force behind the French Revolution, the American Civil War, Doar's Rebellion in Rhode Island in 1842, and more. The interpretation of famous and not so famous revolutions in terms of relative deprivation suggests the power and reach of the theory. But sketchy historical case studies constitute weak tests.

Quantitative empirical tests of relative deprivation are in fact plentiful and come in two varieties. The first attempts to explain protest and violence at the *aggregate* level, generally yielding weak support for the relative-deprivation hypothesis. In a study of collective violence in France between 1830 and 1960, for example, Snyder and Tilly (1972) found that relative deprivation, measured by increases in food prices and decreases in industrial activity, was unrelated to the incidence of industrial violence. Similarly, short-run economic deprivation proves to be a rather minor cause of strike activity, according to quantitative historical studies of several nations (Hibbs, 1976; Shorter and Tilly, 1974; Snyder, 1975; Tilly, 1978). Nor does relative deprivation theory seem capable of accounting for the epidemic of violence that spread through U.S. cities in the 1960s: city-based measures of relative deprivation do not distinguish those cities that experienced serious racial disorders from those that did not (e.g., Spilerman, 1976). Nor, finally, do cross-national studies find relative deprivation to be of much use in explaining patterns of political violence (e.g., Gurr, 1968; Gurr and Duvall, 1973; Hibbs, 1973).

Individual-level studies of relative deprivation attempt to explain not where or when protest breaks out but rather *who* are the protestors, usually by examining special populations in the immediate aftermath of a disturbance (as in the study carried out in Watts in the months following the major riot there; Sears and McConahay, 1973). Do the relatively deprived participate most? Apparently not. Feelings of relative deprivation seem to contribute weakly if at all to participation in demonstrations and riots, across numerous studies (e.g., Barnes, Farah, and Heunks, 1979; Caplan and Paige, 1968; Muller, 1979; Sears and McConahay, 1973; Useem, 1980).

However, this bleak record may reflect imperfections mainly in the tests. Relative deprivation is typically indexed as the discrepancy between what people have and what they aspire to possess. But this procedure fails to take into account two other essential preconditions of relative deprivation: entitlement and blame. When entitlement and blame are taken into account, the evidence improves, according to Muller's (1979) analysis of a 1974 West German survey. West Germans whose

personal lives fell short of what they felt entitled to *and* who blamed the government for their predicament were substantially more enthusiastic about rent strikes, factory takeovers, brawling with police, and toppling the government by force. Muller concluded that the major influence of relative deprivation on protest and political violence is indirect, mediated through feelings of political disaffection. The relatively deprived grow disenchanted with political institutions and authorities, and it is this disenchantment that is the proximal determinant of action.

Thus the many apparent failures of relative deprivation theory may be just another reminder of the rocky road from concepts to operations; they do no damage to the theory itself (e.g., Crosby, 1979). Abandoning relative deprivation for organizational, structural, or political explanations seems therefore misguided (e.g., Gurr and Duvall, 1973; Hibbs, 1973; Skocpol, 1978; Tilly, 1978). Concepts like organizational strength and balance of power are indispensable for understanding protest and revolution. But a place remains for psychological factors in general and for relative deprivation in particular.

In fact, the place of relative deprivation in such accounts might well be enlarged. Most tests of relative deprivation have assessed individuals' views of their *own* predicaments. Deprivation is thus *egoistical* (Runciman, 1966). But political action may be motivated more by feelings of *fraternal* deprivation—comparisons regarding groups—than by feelings of egoistical deprivation—comparisons regarding self (Runciman, 1966). Thus participation of black college students in the civil rights movement in the South in the 1960s was predicted better by their discontent over how well blacks were doing in comparison to whites than by their discontent with their own lives (Geschwender and Geschwender, 1973; Orbell, 1967). Militancy among Cleveland blacks in 1969 was unrelated to their feelings of egoistical deprivation but was associated with their feelings about the position of blacks relative to other groups (Abeles, 1976). White working-class participants in the Boston antibusing movement were motivated especially by their resentments about the gains of blacks and professionals and less by their own personal troubles (Useem, 1980; in a related vein, see Guimond and Dube-Sinard, 1983 and Vannemann and Pettigrew, 1972).

Why do fraternal deprivations loom large in the motivation of protest and violence? Perhaps because group deprivations are likely to be understood as a violation of what the group deserves, and because group deprivations invite explanations that locate responsibility not in isolated individuals but in institutions. If so, then tests of fraternal deprivation—which consistently turn out positively—are more faithful to relative deprivation theory than are the many tests of egoistical deprivation that ignore entitlement and blame.

There is one final lesson to be extracted from the many tests of relative deprivation theory. Such tests may be regarded as genuine disconfirmations of the theory or as failures to test the theory properly. Under either view, the results indicate the difficulty of mobilizing the discontents of personal life. In many respects, the deepest puzzle here is not occasional protest but pervasive tranquility—why, in Moore's (1978) words "people so often put up with being the victims of their societies" (xiii).

Powerlessness

Political action may also flow from feelings of competence and mastery. Political efficacy is the most common such concept, defined by Campbell, Gurin, and Miller (1954) as "the feeling that individual political action does have, or can have, an impact upon the political process" (p. 187). The politically efficacious believe that public officials are responsive, that government listens to the ordinary person, that voting is not the only way the public can influence government, and that politics can be understood. Campbell *et al.* found that such people were much more likely to vote and to otherwise take part in the 1952 campaign than those who expressed opposite views. Since then, the efficacy-participation connection has shown up repeatedly not only in the United States but also in Austria, Britain, West Germany, Italy, Mexico, and the Netherlands (e.g., Almond and Verba, 1963; Barnes and Kaase, 1979; Campbell *et al.,* 1960; Katosh and Traugott, 1981, 1982; Nie *et al.,* 1969a, 1969b).

But according to Lane (1959), a sense of political effectiveness combines both *personal political efficacy*—the image of the self as politically effective—and *system responsiveness*—the image of government as responsive to popular will—and these turn out in fact to be quite separate. People often reach very different conclusions about their own political effectiveness, on the one hand, and the openness of the political system in general, on the other (Finifter, 1970; Gamson, 1968; Muller, 1970). Moreover, the two components of efficacy have followed different trends in the United States over the past two decades. Americans are typically just as confident about their own ability to understand and influence

government now as they were twenty years ago, but are much less confident about the responsiveness of their political institutions (House and Mason, 1975; Miller *et al.,* 1980). And protest seems to be most common among people whose image of political self and government clash, who regard themselves as politically efficacious but their government as unresponsive (e.g., see Balch, 1974; Caplan, 1970; Farah, Barnes, and Heunks, 1979; Gamson, 1968; but see Sigelman and Feldman, 1982).

There is another useful distinction to be made here. *"Group* efficacy," the sense that one's group is shut out of the political process, also appears to motivate participation, at least when it is supported by certain other beliefs. Turnout and other forms of conventional participation increase among members of subordinate groups (the poor, blacks, women, and young) who identify with their group, believe their group to possess less power than the dominant group, *and* explain their group's disadvantaged position in society by citing "systemic obstacles and institutional arrangements" (Gurin *et al.,* 1980, p. 32; Aberbach, 1977; Miller, Gurin, and Gurin, 1978; Miller, Gurin, Gurin, and Malanchuck, 1981).

Contextual Determinants of Participation

Political action depends both on internal predispositions and on external environments. However, empirical research has much more often sought the antecedents of political action among the subjective dispositions of potential actors than in the characteristics of situations. Here we must be content to summarize the smattering of evidence regarding environmental sources of political action, under the broad headings of provocations and opportunities.

Provocations to political action.   One obvious example is the regular rhythm of "surge and decline" in U.S. national elections. Presidential elections draw one-half as many voters as do the adjacent mid-term elections. Campbell (1960) asserted that "high-stimulus elections" (like presidential contests) enlist peripheral voters not drawn out by "low-stimulus elections" (such as the mid-term congressional contest) because of the more intense party activity and the greater mass media coverage associated with them. Since presidential and mid-term elections differ sharply in these ways, their alternation produces a saw-toothed pattern of voter turnout.

More generally, intense party effort materially increases turnout. Evidence supporting this point, virtually all of it from the United States, comes from experiments such as Gosnell's (1927) studies of party contact and turnout in the 1924 presidential contest in Chicago (Adams and Smith, 1980; Bachel and Denver, 1971; Eldersveld, 1956); from aggregate statistical inquiries that find that districts with relatively elaborate, well-financed, and active party organizations also have high turnout rates (with controls on social and demographic characteristics; e.g., Crotty, 1971; Cutright and Rossi, 1958; Katz and Eldersveld, 1961); and from surveys showing that people who report that they have been contacted during the campaign by a party representative are also more likely to vote (Kramer, 1970).

Friends and neighbors may also induce turnout. In *The American Voter,* Campbell and associates (1960) found that many people voted who seemed to have no psychological tie to the campaign at all. Even those who were quite indifferent to the candidates, who expressed no interest in the campaign, who did not care who won, who regarded themselves as politically impotent, and who showed no signs of civic obligation nevertheless still voted—in 1956, some 20 percent did (also see Miller, 1980). Perhaps, as Campbell *et al.* suggested, unengaged voters were driven to the polls, both figuratively and literally, by their more involved friends and neighbors.

Even interviewers can turn out the vote. Clausen (1968) found that survey respondents voted 2 percent to 8 percent more often in the 1964 election than did the populace as a whole (after careful adjustments for sample bias and inflated claims of voting). The perpetrator of this turnout gap Clausen took to be the pre-election interview. An hour or more of conversation dedicated to politics, Clausen guessed, just might have been sufficient to move some people to the polls who otherwise would have sat out the election. Later experimental work provided support for Clausen's hunch. In fact, Kraut and McConahay (1973) found that a standard interview conducted two weeks prior to a local primary election *doubled* turnout (also see Yalch, 1976).

In various ways, then, turning out to vote depends importantly on external circumstances: on the character of the campaign, the intensity of party efforts, the interests of friends and neighbors, and even on the rare intrusions of interviewers. This all testifies to the importance of external provocations. Although we have extensive evidence only about voting, Lieberson and Silverman's (1965) catalogue of events that precipitated major race riots in the United States in this century, or Hibbs's (1973) cross-national finding that collective protest tends to elicit repressive acts from those in power, which in turn transforms protest into internal war, are further if lonely illustrations of richer possibilities.

Opportunities for political action. Opportunities defined in legal and organizational terms also affect participation. To become eligible to vote, Americans must first register, an act that lacks the immediate gratification of voting and that often involves more obscure information and a longer journey at a less convenient time (Wolfinger and Rosenstone, 1980, p. 61). Particularly in the United States, registration procedures entail costs that many potential voters refuse to pay. The cumbersome, unexciting nature of registration is one major reason why turnout in the United States lags behind turnout in nations where the government, not the individual citizen, assumes responsibility for registration (Powell, 1980).

Within the United States, variation in registration procedures accounts for a substantial share of city-by-city and state-by-state differences in turnout (Kelley *et al.,* 1967; Kim, Petrocik, and Enokson, 1975; Wolfinger and Rosenstone, 1980). The registration provision with the greatest impact appears to be the closing date: the last day citizens can register before the election. In 1972, if all states had adopted the most lenient closing date (North Dakota's is election day itself), then turnout would have increased by about 6.1 percentage points—an addition of eight million voters nationwide.

The consequences of contemporary registration practices nevertheless pale in comparison to those of the literacy test and poll tax widely administered throughout the American South in days gone by. Through these procedural devices, blacks were for generations effectively disenfranchised (Stanley, 1981). Contemporary effects also pale in comparison to those associated with more general historical developments in election practice. Turnout declined steeply around the turn of the twentieth century after the adoption of stringent registration procedures discouraged not only various corrupt practices, as intended, but also, perhaps, many marginally involved citizens. A lively argument persists about the details and meaning of this sudden decline in turnout eighty years ago, although there is no disagreement about its proximate antecedents in stiffer registration procedures (Burnham, 1974; Converse, 1974; Cox and Kousser, 1981).

Opportunities to participate are defined also in organizational terms by the presence and vitality of mobilizing groups, as illustrated by Muller's (1979) analysis of political action among West Germans. As noted earlier, Muller found that the single best predictor of confrontational participation was disaffection from political institutions and authorities. Of interest here is that this relationship was sharply accentuated among Germans residing in university communities. In the spring of 1974, West German universities no doubt provided many convenient outlets for the expression of disaffection. In the same way, the link between alienation and protest discovered among residents of the San Francisco Bay area was stronger for people who lived near centers of protest. Proximity to such centers would seem to reflect susceptibility to group mobilization (Citrin, 1977; also see Schuman and Presser, 1981).

These results suggest the argument, presented most forcefully by Tilly (1978) and by Gamson (1975), that political action—especially unruly political action—should be understood as a competition among mobilizing groups. The essential problem from this perspective is not the origins of grievance but rather the translation of grievance into an open struggle for power. Organizations may determine not only the form political action takes but also whether political action occurs at all.

Organizations need not be explicitly political to have political effects, of course. In *The Civic Culture,* Almond and Verba (1963) initiated a line of inquiry into the political consequences of participation in ostensibly nonpolitical groups. They discovered that in the United States, Great Britain, Germany, Italy, and Mexico alike, members of voluntary organizations (and especially *active* members) felt more confident in their ability to influence political decisions, participated more, and knew and cared more about politics than did nonmembers. Almond and Verba concluded that: "Pluralism, even if not explicitly political pluralism, may indeed be one of the most important foundations of political democracy" (p. 265).

This claim now seems too sweeping. Voluntary everyday organizations do appear to enhance conventional political participation (though even here there are causal ambiguities); however, they do so without instilling in their members any special knowledge of or reverence for the process (Nie *et al.,* 1969a, 1969b; Schlozman and Verba, 1979; Verba and Nie, 1972).

When organizations are more central, however, their political effects may be pervasive. Denney's (1979) study of California farm laborers compared those favorably disposed to Cesar Chavez's UFW (United Farm Workers) but who had not (yet) joined the organization (and with statistical controls on social background) with

UFW members. The UFW members were more involved and active in conventional political activities, expressed deeper civic obligations, believed more ardently in democratic institutions, and expressed stronger dissatisfaction with the performance of the political system than nonmembers. Thus although casual involvement in voluntary associations may furnish no bridge to political activity, membership in organizations that touch the center of life may have profound consequences for political participation and for the network of attitudes that sustain participation.

So, at least, argued Pateman, in *Participation and Democratic Theory* (1970). Inspired by Rousseau's vision of a participatory society, Patemen directed attention to the political potential of organizational arrangements at work, arguing that hierarchical patterns of authority on the job instill apathy and passivity, while democratic patterns promote political efficacy and (therefore) participation. For evidence, Pateman could only cite Almond and Verba's (1963) finding that workers who reported that they were consulted about decisions affecting their jobs or who claimed to feel free to protest such decisions also expressed a stronger sense of competence regarding their dealings with the political system than workers who did not inhabit such a work place. This evidence constitutes faint support for Pateman's thesis on two grounds: The correlation is causally ambiguous, and consulting the workers is not exactly what Pateman had in mind by democracy in the work place. There is now a considerable literature on democratic arrangements at work, but one crippled by self-inflicted methodological wounds (e.g., Elden, 1981). Perhaps a radical restructuring of the organization of work would produce a more active citizenry, perhaps not. Our ignorance here is an embarrassment.

THE PUZZLE OF DECLINING TURNOUT

If one puzzle has commanded the attention of students of participation, it is the decline of voter turnout in U.S. presidential elections. Since 1960, without interruption, turnout in U.S. presidential elections has declined from 63 percent to 54 percent. While Ronald Reagan was receiving nearly forty-four million votes in 1980, seventy-four million potential voters stayed home. Compared to other representative governments, such figures make the United States decisively undemocratic (Burnham, 1981; Dahl, 1971; Powell, 1980).

The steady decline in presidential voting across two decades is curious in part because it runs counter to other indications of public engagement: For example, there has been *no* decline at all in the importance Americans place on voting, in their sense of political effectiveness, in their claiming to follow government and public affairs closely, or most curious of all, in their active participation in campaigns (Miller *et al.,* 1980, pp. 288, 307). Declining turnout is peculiar also because both higher levels of education and liberalized registration laws should have substantially *increased* participation. Over the last twenty-five years, the proportion of Americans successfully pursuing a postsecondary education more than doubled (Cavanaugh, 1979), while the Twenty-fourth Amendment eliminated the poll tax and the Voting Rights Act of 1965 suspended literacy tests (Rosenstone and Wolfinger, 1978). Why have these changes not *increased* turnout?

For one thing, the current electorate is substantially younger than its 1960 counterpart, thanks to the postwar baby boom and the nationwide enfranchisement of eighteen-year-olds in 1972. Because the young vote less faithfully than their elders, this compositional change alone can explain perhaps two or three points of the decline (Rosenstone and Wolfinger, 1978; Shaffer, 1981). For another, the economic troubles of recent years—deep recessions, slow economic growth, and soaring inflation—have also cut the likelihood of potential voters making it to the polls (Rosenstone, 1982).

Perhaps not all of the decline in turnout can be explained by compositional age changes or deteriorating economic conditions, however. Declining turnout may be the product of political disenchantment as well, the growing belief that the electoral outcome does not matter very much (Ferejohn and Fiorina, 1979). That fewer and fewer Americans care who moves into the White House may reflect in turn the erosion of party ties and the increasing sense that government does not listen (Abramson and Aldrich, 1982; Shaffer, 1981). And these may be traced, finally, to government's conspicuous failures of the last two decades: race riots, campus disorders, defeat in southeast Asia, scandal at home, economic decline, and all the rest.

Burnham (1980, 1981) takes a darker view. For Burnham, declining turnout since 1960 is simply the latest installment of a century-long demobilization—a "gradual euthanasia of the American electorate" (1981, p. 40). Two facts about this historic decline in participation are especially revealing to Burnham. One is the unusually strong association between class and turnout in U.S. elections. The other is that the recent sharp decline in turnout is most pronounced among the lower classes. Both these facts reflect, according to Burnham, the failure of the Democratic Party to organize and mobilize potential voters, a failure that is uniquely American. Thus Burnham locates the causes of declining participation in politics itself. Burnham asks: "How relevant is electoral politics in the United States to the latent or manifest needs of the lower class" (1981, p. 39)? Not very, is his answer.

MEDIA AND POLITICS

The growth of the electronic media during the twentieth century has led to a previously unimagined level of mass communication. Television in particular has been singled out by many commentators as the most potent influence over citizen politics, in democratic and authoritarian societies alike. But there is a yin and yang in scholarly judgment of media influence, as we shall see.

THE GREAT SCARE

The modern era begins, in a sense, in 1920 when regularly scheduled radio broadcasts began. By the 1930s, radio broadcasts were widely available in homes and public places throughout the Western world. Talking movies, with accompanying newsreels, had become a source of mass entertainment. For the first time, propagandists could reach huge masses of people, not merely through the printed word but also through audio and visual channels. It was a cultural change as revolutionary as that instigated by the invention of the printing press, but one vastly more widespread, since it reached to the masses. And the heat and apparent verisimilitude of the audio and visual presence were far cries from even the yellowist printed journalism.

As communication technology developed, the Western world saw the rise of charismatic political leaders who were extremely effective mass communicators. Hitler, Goebbels, and Mussolini were the European and more successful counterparts of the American Father Charles Coughlin, the rightwing Catholic priest with a popular weekly radio program, and Huey Long, the Louisiana populist. Franklin Roosevelt's Fireside Chats and Winston Churchill's radio broadcasts rallying the British people from near defeat early in World War II seemed to give additional evidence of radio's great power. Hadley Cantril's celebrated study of the effects of Orson Welles's 1938 radio broadcast, *War of the Worlds,* added to the case. He described "thousands of Americans" becoming "panic-stricken by a broadcast purported to describe an invasion of Martians which threatened our whole civilization. Probably never before have so many people in all walks of life and in all parts of the country become so suddenly and so intensely disturbed...'' (1952, p. 198).

Social scientists greeted such behavior with horror. The mob psychologies made popular among intellectuals by LeBon (1896) and Freud (1922) immediately seemed prophetic. In response, some social scientists attempted to formalize a comprehensive list of ''the principles of propaganda'' (e.g., Doob, 1935). The Institute for Propaganda Analysis, formed by a legion of the era's most prominent liberal academic social scientists, published regular newsletters as well as detailed exposés of the propagandistic devices employed by such speakers as Father Coughlin (e.g., Institute for Propaganda Analysis, 1939). The work of these social scientists was explicitly motivated by their political and social values, especially by their effort to combat fascism and the evils of commercialism as manifested in radio advertising. And it was guided by the belief that such analysis would help the ordinary citizen to withstand such influence.

Most important for our purposes here are the assumptions social scientists of the time shared about the effectiveness of propaganda. They were convinced first of all that political propaganda was extremely persuasive. The mass audience was captive, attentive, and wholly gullible. The days of skeptical folks sitting around the cracker barrel in the crossroads store were over. Now they sat glued to the radio, helpless victims. And what made propaganda persuasive were rhetorical tricks— what Hovland and Janis and their colleagues (e.g., 1959) later called, less dramatically, ''message factors.'' Though these assumptions were asserted quite confidently and their social implications were quite frightening, none was tested empirically.

MINIMAL EFFECTS

During the 1930s Paul Lazarsfeld and Frank Stanton organized the Office of Radio Research at Columbia University. Their goal was to conduct systematic empirical research on the impact of the mass media, using the newly discovered methods of public opinion polling. Their initial intention was to do a detailed study of how advertising affected consumer preferences; however, unable to obtain the necessary funding, they turned instead to an in-depth study of the 1940 presidential election, reasoning that the psychological and social processes would be similar in the two cases (Rossi, 1959). The ultimate

product was *The People's Choice* (Lazarsfeld, Berelson, and Gaudet, 1948), described earlier. Its major conclusion was that media simply strengthen predispositions already in place. Voters were primarily exposed to propaganda favoring their own candidate and selectively interpreted communications on both sides as supporting their predispositions. Hence mass communications either reinforced prior preferences or activated latent ones, a conclusion that was soon corroborated by other investigations in different settings (e.g., Trenamen and McQuail, 1961).

Experimental psychologists added further to this impression of limited impact. An extensive and well-controlled series of studies undertaken during World War II as part of an army attempt to indoctrinate new draftees found that films were highly effective in passing along information about the war effort. However, they were generally ineffective in changing opinions (except on points covered very explicitly) or in changing behavioral intentions (Hovland, Lumsdaine, and Sheffield, 1949). Minimal effects occurred despite the advantages conferred by forced exposure to the communication, a situation quite unlike the sporadic and selective exposure that is typically the case in political communications.

Meanwhile, both social psychologists and sociologists began to emphasize the great influence of primary groups relative to authoritative leaders' communications. From experiments in a variety of different realms, Kurt Lewin and his colleagues concluded that authoritarian leadership was considerably less effective than democratic decision making in producing lasting behavioral or attitudinal changes (Cartwright and Zander, 1968; also see Shils and Janowitz, 1948).

These several strands of research were ably drawn together by Klapper (1960) in *The Effects of Mass Communications*. There he developed and made explicit an influential viewpoint that came to be known as ''the law of minimal consequences.'' Instead of a gullible, captive people led easily astray by clever political appeals, Klapper sketched a U.S. public that seemed, under ordinary circumstances, to be quite immune to political persuasion.

MINIMAL EFFECTS REASSESSED

The late 1960s and 1970s ushered in a new phase of respect for the media's powers. This was due in part to the ubiquity of television and the apparent devotion of the U.S. public to watching it. It was also due in part to broader political and institutional changes. Increasingly presidents attempted to reach massive audiences by command performances on prime-time television. Media consultants became ever more prominent in political campaigns, spending fantastic sums to merchandise their candidates. The Vietnam War became the first television war, shown nightly in the living rooms across the country. Movies and television became increasingly violent. Sexually provocative material became much more freely available in movies, books, and magazines. And after many years in which a highly partisan press had been pressured to become more evenhanded, investigative journalism suddenly became fashionable. These developments revived concern about the powerful and perhaps pernicious effects of the mass media.

Current research in this vein can be conveniently organized around four general claims. Each represents a challenge—some more direct than others—to the verdict of minimal media consequences:

1. The media present a view of political reality that is systematically misleading.

2. Exposure to the media, particularly to political television, is so vast and widespread that it represents a total and therefore sinister environment.

3. Media set the public's agenda: What problems are important, which candidates are serious, and how events are to be understood are all determined by those who work in the mass communication industry.

4. The conclusion of minimal consequences is itself outdated: Under certain conditions, the media in fact have a major persuasive impact upon the public's attitudes.

MEDIA BIAS?

A common complaint, lodged usually by people in and out of government with real interests at stake, is that media fail to reflect political reality faithfully. Events are not only simplified (by necessity) but also distorted. This is an important claim, but one difficult to assess, since political reality seldom surrenders easily to quantification. Still, some rough-and-ready evidence can be brought to bear on the general question of bias. Several empirical comparisons suggest that the correspondence between what is happening of consequence in the world

and what appears on the evening news or in the morning newspaper is very far from perfect (Behr and Iyengar, 1985; Mellman, 1981). Mellman found, for example, no relationship at all between fluctuations in international conflict involving the United States between 1968 and 1978 and corresponding fluctuations in coverage of conflict by the network evening news.

One especially familiar version of the allegation of bias is that the media are too critical of U.S. institutions (Robinson, 1976). A careful content analysis of a national sample of newspapers during the 1974 congressional campaign suggests that newspapers, at least, are not. In the aftermath of Watergate, Miller, Goldenberg, and Erbring (1979) found that only 31 percent of front-page political stories carried *any* criticism of specific persons, policies, or actions. Not surprisingly, most criticism emerged in stories about public confidence in government, misuse of power in government, and specifically the Watergate scandal. (Among the most critical newspapers, however, were the *New York Times* and *Washington Post*, which are at the forefront of the attention of political influentials.) Similar findings were obtained in Graber's (1976) content analysis of press and television coverage of the 1968 and 1972 campaigns and in Schultz and Petrocik's (1982) analysis of major media in the 1980 presidential campaign: Although unfavorable stories slightly outnumbered favorable ones, most were neutral.

How news organizations (and for that matter, campaign organizations) decide what is newsworthy and what is not and how they present those stories deemed suitable for public consumption are just beginning to receive attention. Epstein (1973), for network news, and Sigal (1973) for newspapers, have argued that decisions about news coverage are shaped by a variety of organizational constraints: economic imperatives, routine bureaucratic procedures, and external political pressures. They may be shaped as well by journalists' definition of political news.

In particular, in covering presidents and presidential campaigns, members of the press seem to assume that the public will naturally be intrigued by news (and pictures) about the campaign itself, with who is ahead and why—that is, by the strategic side to politics. One consequence of this assumption is that news organizations pay special attention to events during a campaign that seem to bear on the eventual outcome. Witness during the 1976 presidential campaign the extensive coverage given to Ford's gaffe about eastern Europe and to Carter's *Playboy* interview. These "events" were deemed important not because of their substantive implications but because of their potential electoral consequences—for Ford's possible loss of support among Americans of eastern European origins and for Carter's expected loss of support among the straightlaced. Consider also the extraordinary attention conferred upon the New Hampshire primary as well as other early tests of strength. Patterson (1980) has argued that the media employ a "winner-take-all" principle in covering primaries. A candidate fortunate enough to win the New Hampshire primary may be instantly transformed into the "frontrunner"; his face appears on the cover of *Time* and *Newsweek,* and money and support pour in (Arterton, 1984; Patterson, 1980).

Another consequence is that coverage of issues gets subordinated to coverage of tactics and outcomes. Policy statements are accorded attention only as they bear on the dynamics of the campaign. Consider the sustained coverage of McGovern's ill-fated income-redistribution proposal in 1972 or of Reagan's opposition to the Panama Canal Treaty in 1976. Such proposals were treated not as an opportunity to explore the candidate's programs but as potential mistakes or miscalculations that might diminish the candidate's support (see Arterton, 1984, for additional examples; Mathews, 1978, makes a similar point). This preoccupation with the strategic side to campaigns at the expense of the substantive side was nowhere more evident than in the coverage of the 1976 presidential debates. Although the debates themselves were crammed with facts, statistics, and policies, the postdebate coverage concentrated on who had won and how each candidate had prepared for the competition (Sears and Chaffee, 1979).

That presidential campaigns are seldom portrayed as a clash of ideologies and alternative policies is much lamented. Inevitably, the media are chastised for their role in subverting the democratic process. Patterson and McClure (1976) pick on television news in particular, claiming that network journalism degrades presidential elections by presenting campaigns as sporting events on a grand scale, with much attention paid to the superficial and the dramatic (p. 22):

> The nightly network newscasts of ABC, CBS, and NBC present a distorted picture of a presidential election campaign. These newscasts pay only limited attention to major election issues. These newscasts almost entirely avoid discussion of the candidates'

qualifications for the presidency. Instead of these serious matters, ABC, CBS, and NBC devote most of their election coverage to the trivia of political campaigning that make for flashy pictures. Hecklers, crowds, motorcades, balloons, rallies and gossip—these are the regular subjects of network campaign stories.

It is hard to disagree with Patterson and McClure's accusation. Media certainly do become infatuated with the campaign. This is hardly a uniquely contemporary phenomenon, however. Lazarsfeld, Berelson, and Gaudet made precisely the same point in their analysis of the 1940 campaign in Erie County (1948, p. 115). More important, if *candidates* pay scant attention to "major election issues," then it is hardly fair to scold only the media (Page, 1978).

A TOTAL ENVIRONMENT?

Television is widely assumed to command a vast and attentive audience. In the United States, 97 percent of the households possess at least one television receiver; the average set operates about seven hours per day; the average male viewer watches television for the equivalent of 3000 days (nine full years) by the age of 65; the average child has spent 20,000 hours in front of the set by the age of 18 (or more time than in classrooms, churches, and all other educational and cultural activities combined), and on and on (e.g., Comstock *et al.,* 1978; Minow *et al.,* 1973).

But the claim of vast attentive audiences is based more on the wide distribution of television sets and on rating services' reports about how much of the time they are operating than it is on careful measurement of actual viewing. Some studies have video-recorded the area in front of the family's television set and have found that the set is fulfilling its side of the bargain considerably more conscientiously than are the family members. As much as 40 percent of the time the set is operating, no person is in the room, and/or no one is watching it (Allen, 1965). Even when someone is watching, television viewing is often a secondary activity—28 percent of the time, according to one careful study (Szalai, 1972)—providing a colorful and noisy background to an astonishing variety of other activities, of which eating and conversation are the most common but also including dancing, sorting wash, playing Monopoly, scolding children, and reading, to mention only some of the mentionable ones (see Comstock *et al.,* 1978, p. 144).

Ratings for television *news,* furthermore, run well behind ratings for entertainment television. Among eighteen to forty-nine year olds, audiences generally run one-half to two-third those for prime-time entertainment programs (Comstock *et al.,* 1978, p. 113). Similarly, Bechtel *et al.* (1972) found that Americans were more likely *not* to watch an operating television set when the news was on than when any of nine other kinds of programming were being shown. Only commercials drove as many viewers away.

Finally, even the watchers seem not to watch very carefully. In a telephone survey in the San Francisco Bay area of people who had watched one of the network news shows earlier in the evening, Neuman (1976) found that people could recall, on the average, only 1.2 of the 19.8 stories covered in the average program. Memory improved when the interviewer ran down the list of headlines. Then another 4.4 stories were remembered with supporting details, and 4.3 without. Still, one-half the stories were completely forgotten. Thus attention to everyday political news is sporadic and superficial even among those sufficiently motivated to tune in.

Although about one quarter of the adult public tunes into the evening news each night (Robinson, 1971), estimates for daily newspaper reading run higher—by a factor of two or three (Combs, 1981; Robinson, 1972; Schneider, 1982; Sharon, 1973). At the same time, Americans believe, quite decisively, that they learn more about national happenings from television than from newspapers. Americans rate television among several sources as the fairest, most objective, and most complete (Comstock *et al.,* 1978). This paradox—that more Americans read a newspaper each day than tune into the evening news, yet claim to learn about national events mainly from television, not newspapers—may simply reflect the diverse offerings that draw people to newspapers: sports, want ads, housekeeping hints, schedules of local events, astrological advice, business news, and comics in addition to coverage of national events.

Special political events—like the national nominating conventions—occasionally capture much larger audiences than would be implied by these estimates of exposure to the regular flow of political news. The 1960 Democratic convention was particularly arresting, apparently because of its wide-open, suspenseful character,

and several attractive candidates. As a consequence, 92 percent of homes with televisions turned in to some portion of the proceedings, for an average of 15.5 hours (Katz and Feldman, 1962). Election-night coverage also typically draws huge audiences: Fuchs (1966) estimated that over 90 percent of people with televisions heard the 1964 presidential election returns, and Jackson (1984) estimated that 77 percent at least heard of President Carter's early concession speech in 1980.

Among the largest draws of the occasional political programs on television are the debates held during presidential campaigns. In 1960, Senator John Kennedy and Vice-President Richard Nixon met in this way on four occasions. The first drew the attention of over 60 percent of U.S. adults; 80 percent watched at least one; across the four debates, the average viewer put in more than two hours (Katz and Feldman, 1962). Exposure was just as massive to the 1976 and 1980 debates (Sears and Chaffee, 1979; 1980 figures come from a CBS News/NY Times Poll of "probable voters").

Presidential addresses also often reach large audiences, particularly those made during "prime time." Franklin Roosevelt's fireside chats are thought to have attracted large audiences; the first one apparently reached nearly two-thirds of the available radio receivers. Similarly, huge audiences were reached by President Nixon's prime-time, three-network addresses to the nation. Using statistics garnered from the television ratings services (which, as indicated above, considerably overestimate audience presence and attention), Minow *et al.* (1973) estimated that Nixon's prime-time audience for news conferences, State of the Union addresses, and speeches announcing new initiatives in the Vietnam War or new Watergate defenses ranged from forty to eighty million people (pp. 55–63).

On occasion, the public's attention is drawn momentarily to an unusual political event. The most intense such instance in the postwar era has been the assassination of President Kennedy. Network television dealt with little else for the remainder of that day and the three following. Much of the nation's normal activities closed down. A survey done soon after found that on each of these days, 95 percent of the public watched some part of the postassassination programming, and that overall, the median adult spent no less than thirty-four hours with these events (Sheatsley and Feldman, 1965). Of course, ordinary political programs do not attract nearly this kind of attention.

Cases of *sustained* attention to political content in the media, moreover, are quite uncommon. To be sure, the televised encounters between Carter and Ford in 1976 attracted, at one time or another, well over 80 percent of the public. But the massiveness of the cumulative audience is deceptive. A much smaller audience was present throughout the series of debates. Nielson estimated that 42 percent of the households tuned in to *any* part of *all* three presidential debates, and one survey of persons found only 28 percent tuned in to some part of all four debates. And only about 25 percent of the public, at most, seemed to have watched *all* of *any* given debate. Moreover, pursuit of information and analysis following the debates tended to be superficial (Sears and Chaffee, 1979).

The major point here is that political stories ordinarily draw comparatively small and often inattentive audiences. Although programs of political happenings sometimes capture huge audiences, they usually cannot hold them: Interest dissipates quickly; attention turns elsewhere. Exposure to political news is thus rather infrequent and quite casual.

Exposure is often thought to be highly selective as well. The "principle" of selective exposure—the supposedly strong tendency for people to find themselves encountering communications with which they already agree—was in fact commonly enlisted to explain the minimal effects reported in the communications research of the 1940s and 1950s, cited earlier (e.g., Klapper, 1960). Selective exposure presumably reflected a general psychological preference for supportive information, a view that fit nicely with the later contention in cognitive dissonance theory that nonsupportive information created unpleasant psychological tensions and would therefore be avoided (Abelson *et al.*, 1968; Festinger, 1957).

A look at the evidence led eventually to a distinction between two forms of selective exposure: "de facto selectivity," which was defined as a bias in audience composition, such that people initially agreeing with the message were overrepresented, and "motivated selectivity," which was a psychological preference for exposure to supportive rather than nonsupportive information (Sears and Freedman, 1967). De facto selectivity turns out to be a reasonably general phenomenon, though not as strong a bias as usually represented. However, there is little support at all for motivated selectivity (Sears, 1968a; Janis and Mann, 1977). Moreover, many of the media innovations in recent years—such as less explicit partisanship in

newspaper, radio, and television coverage or brief prime-time political ads that are hard to avoid—have served to bypass whatever obstacle selective exposure used to pose. Hence, the main impediment to persuasion at the exposure level would seem to be low absolute levels of interest and attention, not selectivity: "The problem for most political propagandists is not that they fail to reach their enemies but that they fail to reach anyone at all" (Sears and Whitney, 1973, p. 7).

AGENDA SETTING

The idea of agenda setting originates with Lippmann's (1922) eloquent warning, set out many years ago in *Public Opinion*. There he emphasized the heavy responsibility borne by the press in a free society, since the press alone describes and interprets the events of public life that few citizens experience directly. Eloquence was not enough. Lippmann's warning that news organizations might profoundly shape what the public regards as important had little immediate impact on empirical research. Social scientists of the time, remember, were preoccupied with the more sinister possibility of mass persuasion. The steady stream of limited effects that followed through the 1940s and 1950s eventually led researchers to other hypotheses, however, and to agenda setting in particular. Bernard Cohen's (1963) analysis of the role of the press in forming foreign policy was especially influential. Quite in keeping with the spirit of Lippmann's original argument, Cohen claimed that "the mass media may not be successful much of the time in telling people what to think, but the media are stunningly successful in telling their audience what to think about" (p. 16).

This proposition could be tested two ways: cross sectionally and longitudinally. That the media are in fact "stunningly successful" in determining what Americans think about was the conclusion reached by McCombs and Shaw (1972), using a cross-sectional design. They found that the political problems uncommitted voters in one community thought most important were also the problems paid most attention by their media. This demonstration inspired a torrent of replications and, unhappily, considerable confusion (Becker, McCombs, and McLeod, 1975; Erbring, Goldenberg, and Miller, 1980; Iyengar, 1979b). The most sophisticated cross-sectional test of agenda setting found only modest and mysteriously context-dependent effects (Erbring, Goldenberg, and Miller, 1980). "Stunningly successful" overstates this evidence considerably.

Tests of agenda setting over time yield more positive results, however. In an important early study, Funkhouser (1973) discovered substantial concurrence between the amount and timing of attention paid to various problems in the national press between 1960 and 1970 and the importance accorded problems by the U.S. public. Across the decade, public opinion seemed to follow, not lead, the agenda set by the press. These results were fortified by MacKuen's (1981) more sophisticated and more genuinely dynamic analysis. MacKuen found that over the past two decades public concern for political problems (such as civil rights, Vietnam, and inflation) closely reflected changes over time in the attention paid them by national media. He also discovered that dramatic events have consequences for public opinion above and beyond the volume of coverage devoted to them. Thus upsurges in public concern over crime stemmed particularly from the riots and assassinations of the late 1960s; concern about inflation, from conspicuous flurries of presidential activity (also see Behr and Iyengar, 1985; Mellman, 1981).

These time-series results are neatly complemented by the findings from a recent series of experiments on agenda setting (Iyengar and Kinder, 1985; Iyengar, Kinder, Peters, and Krosnick, 1984; Iyengar, Peters, and Kinder, 1982). By unobtrusively inserting into television newscasts stories from previous broadcasts (compiled by the Vanderbilt Television News Archive), the researchers brought the evening news under experimental control. Despite the rather subtle manipulations, each of the several experiments found strong support for agenda setting. In one study, for example, exposure to just four stories that emphasized deficiencies in U.S. defense preparedness, sprinkled over a week's work of daily newscasts, sharply increased the importance the viewers in the experiment ascribed to defense as a national problem compared to that attributed by the viewers in a control condition. These experiments also suggest that in paying attention to some problems while ignoring others, network news programs alter the criteria by which viewers evaluate government performance. Thus when viewers were asked to evaluate President Carter after their exposure to a steady stream of stories exposing the nation's energy problems, ratings of presidential performance on energy became more powerful in determining evaluations of Carter's overall performance. Hence simply by narrating the specific events of the day, news programs shape the standards by which presidents, and perhaps government more generally, are evaluated.

PERSUASION REEXAMINED

The most direct challenge to the minimal effects verdict is the claim that the media, and television in particular, do in fact have pervasive and powerful persuasive effects. As presented in greatest detail by Kraus and Davis (1976), this claim takes two paths. It emphasizes situations that seem to overcome the obstacle of low public interest in, and hence, little media exposure to, the ongoing political world, such as prime-time political programming that attracts the viewing public for other reasons (e.g., brief political commercials). Or it directs attention to circumstances in which powerful political predispositions are neutralized (e.g., primary elections). In either case, however, the evidence for substantial media impact is not very compelling. According to Kraus and Davis's review, either little evidence exists one way or another, or in fact the evidence points to minimal impact. Moreover, political events that attract large audiences also usually evoke powerful predispositions. As a practical matter, then, the combination of heavy exposure and weak predispositions is relatively rare. Hence the effects are minimal as in keeping with Klapper's original verdict.

The many studies of presidential debates have contributed substantially to the minimal effects conclusion. Table 3, which summarizes results from the presidential debates of 1960, 1976, and 1980, shows how sharply evaluations of debate performance polarize along partisan lines. Because of this, debates typically have minimal impact on evaluations of the candidates. Although there was evidence that each debate created some movement toward the "winning" candidate, both in terms of evaluations and vote intentions, this effect appeared to dissipate within a few days. Instead, the dominant effect of the debates was to reinforce viewers' prior preferences and to increase the consistency of their partisan attitudes (all these data are summarized in Katz and Feldman, 1962, and in Sears and Chaffee, 1979).

Reinforcement of standing predispositions is also the rule in entertainment television. The series *Roots* drew a massive audience. Nevertheless, the best predictor of whites' sympathy for the hardships of slavery proved to be their attitudes toward current racial policies. Indeed, in multivariate analyses, exposure to the series had

TABLE 3
Who Did the Better Job?

The first Nixon-Kennedy debate in 1960:

		KENNEDY	NO CHOICE	NIXON	TOTAL PERCENT
	Kennedy	71	26	3	100
Pre-debate	**Undecided**	26	62	12	100
Preference	**Nixon**	17	38	45	100

SOURCE: Adapted from Sears and Whitney (1973).

The First Ford-Carter Debate in 1976:

		CARTER	NO CHOICE	FORD	TOTAL PERCENT
	Carter	62	32	6	100
Pre-debate	**Undecided**	25	47	28	100
Preference	**Ford**	5	25	70	100

SOURCE: Adapted from *The Ann Arbor News,* September 24, 1976, p. 1.

The Carter-Reagan debate in 1980:

		CARTER	NO CHOICE	REAGAN	TOTAL PERCENT
	Carter	69	21	10	100
Pre-debate	**Undecided**	27	43	30	100
Preference	**Reagan**	5	13	82	100

SOURCE: Adapted from CBS News release, October 29, 1980.

no significant effect at all, although the demographics usually associated with racial attitudes (age and education) retained their effects (Hur and Robinson, 1978; for similar results, see Ball-Rokeach *et al.,* 1981; Brigham and Giesbrecht, 1976).

That predispositions may sometimes work in the service of attitude change has one of its most powerful, and frightening, applications in cases of aroused patriotism. The "rally 'round the flag effect" describes the frequent tendency for the public to rally behind a national leader's controversial actions in foreign affairs. President Roosevelt's popularity rose following Pearl Harbor, Eisenhower's after the embarrassing U-2 affair, and Kennedy's after the Bay of Pigs invasion (Katz and Piret, 1964; Mueller, 1973).

All these findings of momentary change, small enduring effects, and the predominantly reinforcing quality of communications, finally, parallel those in other areas of mass communications. Violent television and movie programs tend to have little lasting effect upon viewers' aggressive behavior (Freedman, Sears,

and Carlsmith, 1981; Kaplan and Singer, 1976; though see Comstock, 1980, and Rubinstein, 1980). Pornographic communications tend to increase habits of sexual behavior rather than provoke unusual or novel or antisocial ones (Commission on Obscenity and Pornography, 1970).

Yet we should not push the minimal effects conclusion too far. That new information is interpreted and evaluated in terms of standing predispositions still leaves open the possibility of marginal change. And a series of marginal effects in the short run may nevertheless cumulate to substantial effects in the longer haul. One striking case is Mueller's (1973) finding that U.S. opposition to the wars in Korea and Vietnam grew as casualties mounted. Mass media presumably were the carriers of this grim news. Another comes from the analysis by Hibbs and his colleagues (1982b) of changes in public support for the president, noted earlier, which effectively tied Nixon's precipitous decline in the polls to media coverage of Watergate revelations. The greater the number of stories and the more they incriminated the president, the deeper Nixon slid. More generally, support for the president fluctuates with changes in economic conditions, deteriorates as U.S. casualties in foreign wars grow, and surges with dramatic, sharply focused international crises. All this adds to a strong presumptive case for cumulative media effects (e.g., Brody and Page, 1975; Haight and Brody, 1977; Hibbs *et al.*, 1982a, 1982b; Kernell, 1978; Smith, 1978). Miller, Goldenberg, and Erbring's (1979) analysis of the effects of critical political coverage in newspapers upon readers' feelings of cynicism toward government provides one final example. They found that newspapers in the fall phase of the 1974 campaign varied a good deal in how critical their political stories were. Contrary to the fears expressed by Robinson (1976) and others, institutions were not bearing the brunt of the attack; malfunctioning incumbents were. And critical newspapers in this sense did apparently contribute to their readers' feelings of cynicism. Thus sources of news that develop and maintain a particular slant may eventually nudge their audience in the same direction.

We should also say, as a second amendment to the minimal effects verdict, that what seem in absolute terms to be small effects may nevertheless have large political consequences. Endorsements of candidates by newspapers fit into this category (Combs, 1981; Mason, 1973; Mueller, 1970; Robinson, 1974). Erikson (1976) found, for example, that between 1960 and 1964, the Democratic share of the presidential vote increased most sharply in areas served by newspapers that changed their endorsement from Nixon in 1960 to Johnson in 1964. According to Erikson's estimates, a switch in endorsement by itself produced a corresponding shift in the vote of about 5 percent. Modest effects of this size are typical in this literature; in close contests they may determine who wins and who loses.

A similar point is made by research on the influence exerted by election-night broadcasts: exit polls, computer projections, concession speeches, and the other premature communications of election outcomes. The concern here is partly practical, since all the polls are generally not closed (especially on the West Coast) when such results are announced; thus the fears that the vote will be influenced and especially that turnout will be reduced if it appears that the outcome has already been settled. With increasingly sophisticated use of exit polls, results can actually be projected long before the polls are closed in *any* part of the country, thus broadening the concern. Indeed, an analysis of enormous Census Bureau

samples concluded that network projections cut turnout in the Pacific states in the 1972 presidential election by about 2.7 percent (Wolfinger and Linquiti, 1981). A stronger case can be made for 1980. On Election Day, network projections began appearing even before the polls closed in many eastern states, and President Carter publicly conceded over an hour before balloting concluded in California. In the days that followed, several prominent Democratic senators and congressmen attributed their narrow defeats to reduced Democratic turnout brought on by these media events. Perhaps with good reason. According to a careful analysis of a postelection national survey by Jackson (1984), turnout was cut by more than 20 percent among those potential voters who heard the projections or concession speech and had not voted by six o'clock in the evening, eastern standard time. This amounted to a reduction in turnout of 6 percent in the East and 12 percent in the West.

Finally, we should not forget television's unique power, even if it is seldom fully realized. Who can forget the four days following the assassination of John F. Kennedy? Beginning with his shooting at about 12:30 P.M. central standard time, Friday, November 22, 1963, the networks covered the various related events virtually nonstop through his funeral, held the next Monday. Some seventy hours were given to the Oswald murder, to processionals, to the requiem service, to the cortege to the gravesite, and to innumerable interviews with prominent people (Rubin, 1967). Exposure was massive, with the median U.S. adult watching almost one-half of the assassination-related programming. Although it is impossible to separate the effects of the media coverage from those of the event itself, their combined emotional and attitudinal effects were extraordinary. According to a NORC survey completed within the following week (Sheatsley and Feldman, 1965), only 19 percent of the public said they had carried on "pretty much as usual"; 30 percent said they felt more upset than most people (and only 8 percent, less); 53 percent said they cried, and 48 percent said they had had trouble sleeping, compared to the roughly 20 percent who did under more normal circumstances. Wolfenstein and Kliman (1965) document equally profound effects among preadults on the basis of clinical data. The attitudinal effects were no less impressive: One-half the population called Kennedy one of the best two or three presidents in history, and only 2 percent called him "somewhat below average." In fact, Kennedy ran behind his party and barely won election; his approval ratings were unexceptional (see Mueller, 1973); and historians have subsequently judged him to be somewhere in the middle of the pack. Television was a full partner in this remarkable transformation.

POLITICAL SOCIALIZATION

The research discussed previously treats people cross sectionally, or at least across brief segments of their lives, without much regard to age or life stage. The area of political socialization, on the other hand, treats people developmentally. It both emphasizes early experience and analyzes later experience in terms of specific developmental stages. As such it represents a distinctive slice of the political behavior pie.

Interest in political socialization originally stemmed from two rather different questions, and thus has led to two rather separate and self-contained literatures. The first was concerned with the ancient question of how nations do (and/or can) train children to become good citizens. Charles Merriam's pioneering work, *The Making of Citizens* (1931), was followed much later by a host of survey studies of children's budding *attachments* to symbols of political authority and the political regime (most notably by Greenstein 1965, Hess and Torney 1967, and by Easton and Dennis 1969). The second question originated in the observation that *partisanship* was a longstanding predisposition, with its origins apparently in preadult family influence. This was the conclusion of Hyman's (1959) influential review, a product of the same Columbia sociological tradition that had emphasized the primacy of predispositions in voting choices (Berelson *et al.,* 1954; Lazarsfeld *et al.,* 1948) and mass-communication effects (Klapper, 1960), and of *The American Voter's* analysis of voting behavior (Campbell *et al.,* 1960). If party identification was such a potent force in voting behavior, its origins needed to be investigated directly. Later research drew the parallel to other psychologically similar predispositions such as racial prejudice and ethnic or class identification (see Sears, 1975), to tolerance for the civil liberties of others (Zellman and Sears, 1971), to a wide variety of values (Inglehart, 1971; Simpson, 1977), and ultimately to preadults' responses to partisan issues such as the Vietnam War and Watergate (Tolley, 1977). As this aspect of the socialization literature developed, it took on its own momentum and began to investigate the origins and development of any political (or politically consequential) orientation

through an individual's entire life-span and, in that way, began to resemble life-span developmental psychology.

Concern for political dispositions, occasionally controversial ones, inevitably brought passionate ideological convictions into the research arena. Most of the earliest research was conducted by conventionally liberal researchers with a pluralistic view of society, describing a loyal, law-obeying, tax-paying citizenry committed to one or the other of the two centrist political parties. Where such conditions did not hold, as in some war-torn Western nations or in postcolonial regions, the task of political socialization was presumably to produce them (Almond and Verba, 1963). This focus was later criticized as simply helping to perpetuate power and economic inequalities and/or a "false consciousness." This led to an interest in the origins of black protest (Sears and McConahay, 1973), class consciousness (Stacey, 1977), and antiwar activism in the Vietnam era (Flacks, 1969), and other cases of political radicalism.

This contrast highlights a central dispute about the nature of political socialization. The most common definition implies *society's molding of the child* to some a priori model, usually one perpetuating the status quo. Such terms as "training," "indoctrination," "inculcation," "acculturation," "civilizing," "cultural transmission," and "adopting cultural norms" are common synonyms for this usage. The concern is with promoting the stability of the status quo and maintaining the control over the citizenry by conventional authorities (whether liberal democrats, right-wing dictators, or Marxists). Often overlooked is an alternative definition emphasizing *the child's idiosyncratic personal growth,* in which the developing human being gradually attains her own personal identity, which allows her to express herself and to seek to meet her own idiosyncratic needs and values in her own way. Viewed in this latter vein, the study of political socialization is not necessarily the study of conformity to the status quo and indeed can on occasion treat radical or revolutionary action as normative.

The boundaries of political socialization can be either narrow or broad (Greenstein, 1968, p. 551):

Narrowly conceived, political socialization is the deliberate inculcation of political information, values and practices by instructional agents who have been formally charged with this responsibility. A broader conception would encompass all political learning, formal and informal, deliberate and unplanned, at every stage of the life cycle, including not only explicitly political learning but also nominal non-political learning that affects political behavior, such as the learning of politically relevant social atti-tudes and the acquisition of politically relevant per-sonality characteristics.

In part, this issue devolves into how far back into distal causes of behavior the causal chain should be carried. In part, it rests on the empirical question of how much the "political self" is influenced by ostensibly nonpolitical factors.

A related distinction is made between *general* and *specific* dispositions, for example, between general con-servatism and support for a specific conservative policy like "law and order." It is often assumed that youthful socialization is very general whereas dispositions ac-quired in adulthood are highly specific, within the gener-al boundaries set by earlier predispositions (e.g., Weissberg, 1974). It may be, however, that earlier social-ization is more specific than that implies, which would account for the limited constraint among youthful pre-dispositions that is commonly found. Thus change from early to later life could occur fairly readily when attitude objects change in meaning (see Sears, 1975, pp. 132–135 for this argument).

Finally, the universal underlying variable in political socialization work is age or life stage. As we will see later, various models of susceptibility to change as a function of life stages have been proposed. The central question here, and one that will occupy much of our attention later, regards the *persistence* of early learning. The re-mainder of the chapter is organized by life stage and by this worry over persistence. First we take up political learning during childhood and adolescence and then con-front the question of persistence directly by tracing the later life history of consequential political dispositions.

CHILDHOOD AND ADOLESCENCE

Our discussion of preadult learning distinguishes be-tween "attachment to the system" and "partisanship," since they have been investigated quite separately. The distinction has its problems, but we will defer their con-sideration until the main outlines of the research findings themselves are clear. The most influential conceptualiza-tion is that proposed by Easton (1965), distinguishing three sets of attitude objects:

1. The political community—the group of persons bound together politically;

2. The regime—the constitutional order, including political roles and institutions and the rules or norms for handling matters politically, especially with re-spect to who wields power, how they are permitted to wield it, who is to comply, and conditions of their obligation;

3. The authorities—occupants of authority roles.

The "regime level" includes most of the objects nor-mally investigated under the rubric of "attachment" and relates to what Easton calls *legitimating ideologies*. These concern support for, or challenges to, the ongoing regime and the right of the authorities to rule, that is, be-liefs in the legitimacy of authority roles and other regime structures. Much of the research on early attachment is intended to investigate the origins of *diffuse system sup-port,* that is, a generalized belief in the legitimacy of the regime and the authorities: "the conviction on the part of the member that it is right and proper for him to accept and obey the authorities and to abide by the requirements of the regime" (Easton, 1965, p. 278).

On the other hand, *partisan ideologies* are con-cerned with day-to-day policy opinions and partisan preferences among specific incumbents or candidates (Easton, 1965, pp. 286–287, 336–338). These are princi-pally focused at "the authorities" level, though not exclusively concerned with evaluations of incumbent po-litical officials.

Early Attachment

The principal contents normally categorized under at-tachment include evaluations of regime symbols (flag, public buildings, historical documents, slogans, glorious national heroes and events), generalized political trust, support for institutions, support for government policy (especially foreign policy) and behavioral compliance with it, and endorsement of the reigning rules of the po-litical game. The attention accorded to the child's early attachment to symbols of the political system comes be-cause forming this relationship has been thought crucial for the development of an adult sense of political legiti-macy and because it is one of the earliest evaluative re-sponses children seem to make to the political arena.

Easton and Dennis (1969) developed the most influ-ential theory relating childhood political socialization to variations in the persistence of political systems. To maximize system persistence, in their theory, early political socialization should proceed as follows. Children first become aware of the political system (politicization), chiefly through the proximal figure with whom they have personal contact (the policeman) and the most salient personal symbol of remote government (the president). They thus view government as symbolized by these two persons (personalization), whom they regard as powerful and benevolent (idealization). As children mature, this early personalized and idealized view of government gradually evolves into a view in which government is symbolized by institutions, which children generally approve (diffuse system support). Diffuse system support among the citizenry is seen as critical to system persistence in the long run. Hence early idealization of the authority structure, viewed in personal terms, generates lasting diffuse support for the political system.

The experience of newly created nations (and, indeed, the instability of much older ones) has made it clear just how important a stable basic framework of rules and conventions can be. The institution or maintenance of any political system is partly contingent, in the long run, upon "consent of the governed," even if only passive consent. Of course, in one way or another, the child's attachment to the political system is enhanced by almost any experience that furthers his or her internalization of conforming, normative patterns of thinking and action. Here, however, we are concerned exclusively with identifying those attitudes that are explicitly political and that are acquired in childhood. What is the early course of development of support for the system?

Personalizing and Idealizing

Data collected in the late 1950s and early 1960s by Easton and Dennis (1969), Greenstein (1965), and by Hess and Torney (1967) provided a set of benchmarks against which all subsequent work has been assessed. Their conclusions emphasized the young child's personalized and idealized view of government, which was thought to result from the young child's special cognitive limitations and psychodynamic needs. The child initially came into contact with government through familiarity with its most salient leaders. For example, Greenstein (1960, 1965) found that although 96 percent of a fourth-grade sample could name the president, familiarity with other aspects of government was much less. Similarly, second graders, when asked to pick the "two best pictures of government," tended to select George Washington and

President Kennedy (86 percent), and picked the president as "running the country" (also 86 percent) and as making the laws (76 percent; Easton and Dennis, 1965). The child therefore *personalized* government, thinking it consists simply of its great leaders rather than of institutions, roles, laws, or buildings.

Young children also tended to *idealize* the president. Second graders rated him, along with their fathers, as close to "my favorite of all"; the president "cares a lot what you think if you write to him," according to 75 percent of the sample; and he was rated as highly on "would always help me if I needed it" (Hess and Torney, 1967). Evaluations of President Eisenhower among fourth to eighth graders were so positive in the late 1950s that Greenstein (1960) described him as "the benevolent leader" in their eyes.

Early research also found young U.S. children expressing strong positive feelings toward their nation. For example, Hess and Torney (1967, p. 26) reported that nearly 95 percent of their large sample of white school children, at every level from grade two through grade eight, agreed that the "American flag is the best flag in the world" and that "America is the best country in the world." These opinions were characterized by superlative positive affect and by association of the concept "America" with such conventional symbols as the flag or the Statue of Liberty.

Conventional rationalizations for patriotic feelings were apparent only among the older children, represented by such answers as "freedom" and "the right to vote" to the question, "What makes you proud to be an American?" Similarly, the United States and Russia were seen only as "good" and "bad," respectively, by the second graders, but eighth graders differentiated them in terms of "freedom" and "democracy" (Lambert and Klineberg, 1967, p. 30). Children's highly favorable evaluations of the president also developed without much initial supporting cognitive content. Greenstein says of his fourth-graders: "using the most generous coding standards, less than a fourth of them could describe the President's duties. Substantial amounts of information about the Presidency become evident only from sixth grade on" (1965, pp. 33, 58–59).

Among older children, this personalized view of government was replaced by more realistic perceptions of the roles of institutions, laws, and other authorities. In the Easton and Hess study, only 58 percent of the eighth graders thought the president ran the country, and only 5 percent thought he made the laws (Hess and Torney,

1967). Instead they increasingly viewed institutions, such as Congress, as central in the system. Moreover, approval of other authorities in the system also increased, and their idealization of the president declined.

These early data had serious potential limitations in generality, since they had been collected primarily from white, middle-class, urban and suburban U.S. children at only one historical point in time. Scores of studies have been conducted subsequently, encompassing a much wider range of children and of political systems. They have discovered quite a different picture of children's attitudes. Children do not invariably personalize government, nor do they necessarily idealize political authority.

The Unknown Mover?
In the United States, the president is ordinarily the best-known public figure, to be sure, among children and adults alike. So it was with de Gaulle in France as well (Roig and Billon-Grand, 1968), and Queen Elizabeth of England (Greenstein, 1975). However, in other nations the political leader is not so well known. In both Australia (Connell, 1971) and Canada (Pammett, 1971), children's familiarity with the U.S. president well outstripped their knowledge of their own prime minister. In Canada, children knew less about their prime minister than about Parliament (Pammett, 1971), and in Colombia the youngest children ascribed more centrality in government to Congress and more power to the Supreme Court than to the president (Reading, 1968). In all these cases, the visibility of a national leader to children seems to depend more on his actual role in the system and on his particular reputation than on children's needs to personalize government.

The Malevolent and/or Fallible Leader?
The original "benevolent leader" was discovered among mainly white, middle-class children at the end of Eisenhower's term and at the beginning of John F. Kennedy's presidency (Greenstein, 1960, 1965; Hess and Easton, 1960). Now we have available data from a broader historical period (including other, less popular presidents), from a broader range of the population, and from other political systems, and they yield a different picture.

Later U.S. presidents simply have not elicited such idealized views. Jaros, Hirsch, and Fleron (1968) found that white children in a strongly Republican area of Appalachia did not evaluate President Johnson very positively at all in 1967. Samples of children tested in 1968

through 1971 evaluated both Presidents Johnson and Nixon at best lukewarmly (Sears, 1975; Tolley, 1973; Vaillancourt, 1972). These investigators introduced the terms "the malevolent leader" and "the fallible leader" to describe this youthful cynicism. Nor did overwhelming idealization emerge in studies of children in France, England, or the Netherlands (see Sears, 1975).

The events surrounding Watergate were much more negative for the image of the president than were those even surrounding the ultimately beleaguered Lyndon Johnson. Watergate severely damaged the reputation of President Nixon, even in the eyes of young children. Some studies compared children's attitudes in the midst of Watergate with those in comparable samples in the early 1960s (Arterton, 1974; Dennis and Webster, 1975; Greenstein, 1975). They found:

1. Much less favorable attitudes toward President Nixon than toward then-President Kennedy;

2. Considerable idealization of the president still in evidence among very young children (grade four and under);

3. Much more negative attitudes toward "Nixon" in any form than toward such abstractions as "the President";

4. Much more negative attitudes on dimensions such as benevolence and trustworthiness than on power and competence.

In all these cases, young children prove, in the aggregate, to have mimicked the ebbs and flows of adult support for our various recent presidents. The same parallel between adults and children emerges in various social-group comparisons. Preadolescent black and Mexican-American children were highly negative toward President Nixon but strongly positive toward Kennedy and Johnson, just as were their adult counterparts (see Sears, 1975). In Tolley's (1973) study of attitudes about Vietnam, middle-income white children and children from military families expressed vastly more positive attitudes toward President Nixon than did those from upper-income and/or civilian families. Similarly, the youthful idealizing of the policeman dropped off generally in the late 1960s especially among black children. In each of these cases, children's opinions seem to reflect variations in adult opinion.

In retrospect, the early findings of idealization now seem partly an accident of history. The Easton and Hess and the Greenstein projects focused on Presidents Eisenhower and Kennedy—the first, an extremely popular president surrounded by relatively little partisan controversy and the second, a president evidently unusually appealing to children (Sears, 1975). Thus personalizing and idealizing alike seem to have been most common in one historical period (the late 1950s and early 1960s) and one political system (the United States). Later presidents, the police, and chiefs of state in other nations have not consistently drawn such responses from young children. And within the United States itself, certain groups of children have shown very definite disapproval of both president and police, especially when adults' evaluations of them have been antagonistic or conflicted.

EARLY PARTISANSHIP

Partisan predispositions exist in wide variety, focusing on individual political leaders, on various political, social, nationality, and religious groups, on various issue positions, and toward historical events. It is now well established that partisan predispositions have their origins in childhood. Just how early, strong, and persistent these childhood predispositions are is less clear.

Nations, Races, and Social Classes

Children reveal primitive partisan attitudes to a number of political and social objects in the early and middle grade-school years. As already indicated, children soon feel good about their own nationality, and indeed, they can readily express simple feelings toward various countries in the earliest grade-school years. Tajfel (1969, p. 87) says, "At the age of six and seven children in Britain agree more about which countries they like and dislike than about practically anything else concerning these countries." Usually only by age ten or so do sizable numbers of children develop comparable levels of dislike for rival or enemy nationalities—Israeli children for Arabs, U.S. and West German children for Russians, etc. (cf. Lambert and Klineberg, 1967; Lawson, 1963; Middleton, Tajfel, and Johnson, 1970). This "we-they" pattern represents a somewhat different set of attitudes than the system-support attitudes emphasized by Easton and Dennis, since it involves antagonism toward enemies or rivals as well as support for one's own nation.

Systematic racial attitudes also originate in the preschool and early grade-school years. Harding *et al.* (1969) suggest that U.S. children normally pass through three distinctive stages: "racial awareness" by ages three

to four, "racial orientation" with primitive categories and affects by ages four to eight, and clear "racial attitudes" by the early grade-school years. Katz (1976) argues that these early racial attitudes have two components: They are integrally related to the child's development of a sense of his or her own identity, and they are associated with the learning of positive or negative evaluations of abstract social groupings. By ages seven or eight, children will often have learned the cognitive content of the conventional racial and ethnic stereotypes.

As far as race is concerned, especially, conventional norms are reinforced by the obvious differences in skin color and other anatomical characteristics. These color and other physical differences themselves also become associated with good and bad affects early in childhood. White children even before kindergarten evaluate white stimuli positively and black negatively, and they associate white with good human qualities and black with bad ones (e.g., Williams and Stabler, 1973).

Differential evaluations of social classes already appear to be present in the beginning grades (Tudor, 1971) as does clear awareness of occupational prestige differences (Simmons and Rosenberg, 1971). By the time children are ten-years old, they are clearly aware of social inequalities and status symbols. Children in Western democracies also seem to learn to accept such inequalities as being the natural order of things (Leahy, 1983). Working-class children often appear to be less class conscious than higher status children and to feel that the status system is more malleable, presumably contributing to a more stable system, one that is accepting of existing inequalities (Stacey, 1977).

Party Identification

Party identification also generally originates prior to adolescence. Early studies in the United States, done in the 1958–1962 period, found a rapid increase in the proportion of children with a party preference until about the fifth grade (age eleven or so) and then a more gradual increase during the rest of life. In the Easton-Hess study, 55 percent of the fifth graders had a preference (Hess and Torney, 1967), and Greenstein (1965) found that 61 percent did. Subsequent studies have verified that the proportion of children with a party identification increases much more slowly after this age. By the twelfth grade, 64 percent had a party preference in the 1965 study by Jennings and Niemi (1974).

These early commitments are cognitively more barren than those of adults (Greenstein, 1965; Hess and

Torney, 1967). Children are much more vague than are adults regarding what the parties are or about the differences that might distinguish them (see Sears, 1969, for a summary of the adult data). Many children have difficulty associating even the most visible political leaders with their parties: In a study of children in Fresno, California, for example, the correct party was given by only a minority for Governor Reagan (46 percent), President Nixon (48 percent), Kennedy (37 percent), Humphrey (40 percent), and Vice President Agnew (36 percent), with an average of 14 percent of the children actually assigning the opposite party (Sears, 1975).

By mid-adolescence, party identifications of U.S. children are approaching the affective stability and consistency of those of adults (see Sears, 1975). However, there is a more gradual development than is usually assumed, both in the *number* of children with commitments and in the *strength* of the commitments. And the evidence is still somewhat ambiguous on the actual strength of these early attitudes. Their apparent stability over time could arise not from strong commitment but from lack of an effective challenge in the attitudinally homogeneous, rather unpolitical environments in which much early political socialization takes place. So it is quite possible that these adolescent attitudes are potentially highly vulnerable to change. But the main point is that the "early political socialization" of partisan predispositions is a gradual matter, cresting in mid-adolescence, rather than something finished and done by the end of childhood.

Finally, young U.S. children nowadays do not seem to acquire a party identification as often as in times past. An increasing number have been designating themselves as "Independents" when they reach adolescence and voting age (Glenn, 1972; Jennings and Niemi, 1974). These findings seem to arise from some decrease in recent years in the proportion of U.S. children acquiring a firm partisan preference rather than from anything intrinsically related to age (i.e., they are "generational" rather than "life cycle" effects; see Abramson, 1974; Glenn and Hefner, 1972).

Early Positivity, Later Partisanship
Despite the foregoing, young children ages eight to ten, just becoming aware of the world of politics, seem almost invariably much more positive toward its various symbols than are comparable older children as they move into adolescence (i.e., ages twelve to fifteen). Such age differences show up almost universally, across admini-

strations, time, nations, ethnic groups, and wherever political socialization research has been done (Sears, 1975). The growing number of negative evaluations occurs principally as children move toward more partisan evaluations of standard political symbols. Age produced the greatest drop in respect for the police among black children (Greenberg, 1970) and for President Kennedy among Republican children (Easton and Dennis, 1969). It is not yet clear whether there is also a drop in positive affect among children who, when grown, would normally be expected to like the object in question (e.g., Democratic children in adulthood liking a Democratic president). There is some indication that the drop occurs later with less politically sophisticated children (Sears, 1975).

THE LATER LIFE HISTORY OF POLITICAL PREDISPOSITIONS

In the 1970s developmental psychology transcended its traditional preoccupation with infancy and early childhood by expanding into "life-span developmental psychology" to acknowledge that development continues throughout life. So too did the study of political socialization move to a concern with development over the entire life span. This shift raises the general question of how much, and in what ways, political behavior varies systematically by life stage. The most important question concerns persistence. To what extent do the residues of preadult socialization persist into adult life and continue to influence the adult's political behavior?

A life cycle approach to political behavior dates from the early 1950s, at least in the systematic application of survey evidence to it. Lipset and his colleagues (1954, pp. 1143–1150) started by identifying five life stages they thought might have distinctive political characteristics. Hyman (1959) followed with a more detailed review on the idea of political generations. These then triggered the avalanche of work on preadult political socialization reviewed previously (see Sears, 1975) and the more recent investigations of life cycle and generational effects among adults that form the core of the remainder of this chapter. (For other reviews of this latter literature, see Abramson, 1975; Converse, 1975a, 1976; Cutler, 1977; Jennings and Niemi, 1981; Sears, 1969, 1975; Sigel and Hoskin, 1977.)

The Question of Persistence
The importance of preadult political socialization lies primarily in the impact its residues have on adult atti-

tudes and behavior. To have such an impact they must of course persist into and through adulthood in some form or another. But do they in fact persist? Some early writers regarded persistence as at least partially demonstrated by available data, such as adults' retrospective accounts of their own attitudes (Butler and Stokes, 1974, Chapter 3; Campbell *et al.*, 1960, pp. 161–164; Converse, 1966b), or by longitudinal studies (Bloom, 1964, p. 173; Feldman and Newcomb, 1969, pp. 320–322). Others simply assumed persistence (Davies, 1965; Dawson and Prewitt, 1969), were willing to accept it provisionally in the absence of hard research (Easton and Dennis, 1969), or raised it as a research question (Jennings and Niemi, 1968; Langton, 1969).

These early statements for the persistence viewpoint have been succeeded by an equally impressive backlash against it. Searing *et al.* (1973, 1976) put forward the argument that "the primacy principle" had been overstated. Long-term longitudinal studies appeared, implying that partisan tendencies change more after the preadult years than the persistence view conceded (Himmelweit *et al.*, 1981; Jennings and Niemi, 1981). Empirical demonstrations were published to the effect that voters' recall underestimates the extent to which they had changed their minds over the years (Niemi *et al.*, 1980). And some resoundingly critical reviews appeared (see especially Marsh, 1971; and Peterson and Somit, 1982). Even some of the pioneers in political socialization have come to see a more limited role for the effects of preadult experiences in dictating adult behavior (e.g., Greenstein, 1974). These doubts about the persistence of early socialization residues have been swept up in a more general, nearly ideological, drive to alter psychologists' traditional belief in the power of early experiences: "The view that emerges from this work [a 754-page handbook titled *Constancy and Change in Human Development*] is that humans have the capacity for change *across the entire life span*" (Brim and Kagan, 1980, p. 1; emphasis added). Nevertheless, other researchers have continued to emphasize the striking stability of certain attitudes through the life cycle, particularly party identification and racial prejudice (Converse, 1975a, 1976; Kinder and Rhodebeck, 1982; Miller and Sears, 1983). So the last word is not yet in on this difficult problem.

Attitudes certainly vary in their stability over time and presumably as well in their intrinsic resistance to change. People are highly ego-involved in some attitudes but not at all in others (e.g., Sherif and Cantril, 1947). Following a substantial amount of earlier research, we have suggested that individual attitudes can be conceived as falling somewhere on a dimension of affective strength running from *enduring predisposition* to *nonattitude* (Sears, 1975; Sears *et al.*, 1980). The question of persistence is largely moot for attitudes at the "nonattitude" or low ego-involvement end of this dimension, since they are plainly extremely malleable. It becomes interesting only for attitudes that are relatively more resistant to change.

If we limit our discussion to enduring predispositions what attitudes will we be dealing with? As we have seen, the attitudes of U.S. adults, considered as a whole public, do not meet even minimum standards of stability regarding many political objects. The clearest examples are party identification and racial attitudes, at least as regularly measured in contemporary surveys. One can make a good case also (though on the basis of much less definitive data) for widespread commitments to some versions of ethnic and class attitudes, chauvinism and nationalism, sloganized versions of democratic ideology, moral values, and attitudes toward a few central public figures.

Models of Change Through the Life Cycle

Many hypotheses have been posed about how the potential for change in dispositions varies with age or life stage. Oversimplifying a little, they can be grouped into four basic ideas (Sears, 1975, 1981a; also see Dawson *et al.*, 1977; Jennings and Niemi, 1981; Sigel and Hoskin, 1977). The *lifelong openness* idea suggests that dispositions have an approximately uniform potential for change at all ages; it essentially asserts age is irrelevant for attitude change. The *life cycle* view suggests that people are particularly susceptible to adopting certain dispositions at certain life stages; it essentially asserts that age and attitudinal content interact in producing attitude change. Familiar examples would be the alleged radicalism of youth and conservatism of the aged. A third view could be termed the *impressionable years* viewpoint, which suggests that any dispositions are unusually vulnerable in late adolescence and early adulthood, given sufficient pressure to change. In other stages of life, people resist change, and of course, even in the vulnerable stage, they do not change in the absence of substantial pressures. A special, and particularly interesting, instance of the impressionable years hypothesis is the generational effect. This occurs when those in the supposedly impressionable life stage (late adolescence and early adulthood) are subjected to a common massive pressure to change, for example, when the nation is engaged in an unpopular war. The final viewpoint is *persistence,* which suggests that the residues of early (preadult) socialization are relatively immune from any change in later years.

We should note that "age" and "life stage" are used somewhat interchangeably in this literature, even though some life stages plainly cross a number of ages. For example, full-time mothering of small children appears to diminish political involvement (Jennings and Niemi, 1981), although mothering may occur in late adolescence or in early middle age. Age is a crude measuring instrument for life stage, and it should be recognized that truly sensitive research on the political effects of life stage will index it more finely.

All four of these models of change presumably describe a two-step process, in which the effects of life stage upon receptivity to change are mediated by other characteristics of that stage. If late adolescents are highly susceptible to the *Zeitgeist,* for instance, it is presumably because the inexperience that accompanies that life stage has produced weak attachment to traditional values, because some streak of rebelliousness and independence that often accompanies that life stage produces a special attraction for innovative and contemporary ideas, or because the unique social location of adolescents (e.g., universities) especially exposes them to the *Zeitgeist.* Thus the effects of life stage on vulnerability to change would operate through these mediators. Ideally, then, a life stage analysis of political behavior would begin by describing the characteristics of each life stage that ought to foster political behavior specific to that stage. Very little attention has been paid to such mediating variables. Several taxonomies exist (Glenn, 1980; Sears, 1983; Sigel and Hoskin, 1977), but the empirical work remains to be done.

Methods of Assessing Persistence

The earliest studies of persistence relied heavily upon the citizen's own retrospective judgment of his or her earlier attitudes (e.g., Campbell *et al.,* 1960). It will come as no surprise to learn that these retrospections overestimate stability. Systematic evidence on this point is now accumulating (e.g., Himmelweit *et al.,* 1978; Niemi *et al.,* 1980).

A more attractive alternative is longitudinal evidence, in which the child is tested and then interviewed again as an adult. Such evidence is hard to come by. The best data on political attitudes are furnished by some rel-

atively recent studies, especially Jennings and Niemi's (1981) eight-year follow-up of the high school students and parents initially interviewed in 1965, several reinterviews by Himmelweit and her colleagues (1981) of adolescent boys originally contacted in 1951, and the Newcomb *et al.* (1967) twenty-year follow-up of Bennington College graduates. A related technique is the use of shorter panels, such as the four-year studies of the general public initiated by SRC/CPS in 1956 and 1972 (Converse, 1964; Converse and Markus, 1979; Kinder and Rhodebeck, 1982; Niemi *et al.,* 1980; Sears and Gahart, 1980). Despite their obvious attractions, longitudinal studies have their limitations. First of all, the effects of aging are confounded with cohort and period effects in any longitudinal study. The cohort that is tracked was born at one historical time and experiences just one unique historical period. Hence those interviewed by Jennings and Niemi were members of the famed postwar "baby boom" and spent their late adolescence and early adulthood in the midst of the Vietnam and Watergate eras. One cannot isolate the effects of life stage from these external influences. There are minor irritants with any longitudinal study as well. Sample attrition may produce important biases (e.g., Jennings and Niemi successfully reinterviewed 83 percent of the whites but only 59 percent of the nonwhites). And inevitably some questions that later turn out to be important were not anticipated in early waves (e.g., Vietnam was skipped in Jennings and Niemi's first interview, conducted in 1965).

Another method of assessing persistence is cohort analysis. This involves the comparison of a given birth cohort's attitudes across two different measurement points, for example, persons born in the 1924–1931 period are sampled in 1956 and then again in 1960. If the attitudes of these two samples, taken from a common birth cohort, are roughly comparable at the two measurement points, the inference is that the individuals' attitudes have not changed very much or at least not in a uniform direction. Since the cohort analysis tracks the aggregated attitudes of an entire birth cohort, inferences about the stability or change of *individuals'* attitudes are, of course, chancy. And cohort analyses by their nature are unable to unconfound period, aging, and cohort effects (Glenn, 1977; Mason *et al.,* 1973), since only two independent variables (birthdate and time of interview) are available to assess those three effects.

A final method of assessing persistence is to compare people who have been exposed to some estimable potential influence with people who have not. Grand political events, changes in the immediate environment because of geographical or status mobility, and personal experiences have been examined in this respect. Ideally, one would like to randomly assign respondents of different life stages to varying degrees of pressure to change; however in practice that has rarely been done even in laboratory experiments. Hence one must rely on natural experiments and post hoc controls.

In the study of persistence and the life cycle, then, there is no free lunch.

EVIDENCE ON PERSISTENCE

Longitudinal Studies

The best longitudinal data on attitude stability come from the Jennings-Niemi panel study (1974, 1981), based on a national sample of high school seniors and their parents, interviewed in 1965 and again in 1973. Their report gives substantial evidence of the incompleteness of political socialization at age seventeen. Over the many attitudes they considered, stability coefficients ranged from the negligible to the imposing. Estimates of the persistence of a wide variety of attitudinal dispositions—on civil liberties, school policy, social groups, and political efficacy and trust—yielded tau-b's averaging somewhat over .20, for the youth generation, and for the parental generation, the average was somewhat higher but rarely exceeded .40. For political trust, the figures were .18 and .27; for internal political efficacy, .28 and .39. As Jennings and Niemi (1981) concluded "rather than being unusual, change is a characteristic pattern of the adult years" (p. 384).

Equally impressive, however, are those attitudes that show a high level of stability. Party identification is a clear example. Only 9 percent of all 1965 Democrats and Republicans in the Jennings-Niemi youth sample had switched to the opposite party by 1973. Similarly, using the SRC panels of the late 1950s and early 1970s, Converse and Markus (1979) reported two-year stabilities for party identification that exceeded .80. When corrected for unreliability, these two-year coefficients rose to about .95. Sears and Gahart (1980) and Kinder and Rhodebeck (1982) found equally high estimates for the stability of racial prejudice over the 1972–1976 panel. Finally, the Newcomb *et al.* (1967) twenty-year follow-up of Bennington College alumnae discovered impressive stability: Their senior-year conservatism during the 1930s correlated +.47 with their 1960 conservatism and +.48 with the number of Republican presidential candidates supported in the interim.

As Jennings and Niemi put it, "Both change and stability abound" (1981, p. 300).

Cohort Analysis

Cohort analysis has been the primary analytic technique used to test the "life cycle" hypothesis that stage-specific needs result in the adoption of particular political attitudes. Cohort analyses have found no diminution in the number of self-professed Independents nor any rush to the Republicans or to conservatism more generally as cohorts age (Glenn, 1980). Likewise, Abramson (1974) found no marked change in the rate of class-based voting as any given birth cohort has aged to (and through) the supposedly self- and family-preoccupied middle years. For other analyses yielding similar results, see the reviews by Cutler (1977) and Glenn (1980). One exception is party identification. Commitment to party appears to strengthen somewhat over the life cycle (Abramson, 1979; Converse, 1976, 1979). This implies that party identification should be less susceptible to change among older people, which does appear to be the case. Indeed, Jennings and Niemi (1981) found their youthful cohorts to be less stable than their parents in virtually every instance.

Cohort analyses have also generally shown greater shift by younger than older cohorts in response to such "period" forces as increasing liberalism on civil liberties issues, the decline in partisanship in the late 1960s and 1970s (see Converse, 1976; Crewe *et al.*, 1977; Cutler, 1977; Glenn, 1980; Nunn *et al.*, 1978), and usually negligible shifts among the older groups. So the evidence leans toward an "impressionable years" viewpoint. Although in any given case other explanations are possible, of course, the overall burden of evidence is surprisingly uniform.

"Natural Experiments"

Another approach to the persistence problem is to test whether older people change their attitudes less than do younger ones in response to systematic pressure to change. One such literature examines the effects of distal political events upon basic predispositions and particularly considers their possible greater impact upon those in "the impressionable years." An excellent example is Markus's (1979) analysis of the impact of Vietnam and racial conflict upon party identification and cynicism. Using the Jennings-Niemi panel data, he found:

1. A substantial level of persistence, especially for the older (parental) cohort;

2. A clear impact of reactions to those political events, such that pro-black and anti-Vietnam reactions moved people in pro-Democratic and/or cynical directions (though the race issue did not influence cynicism in this period);

3. A generally stronger impact of these events upon the younger than the older cohort.

Similarly, Jackson (1975b; Franklin and Jackson, 1983) has found that the party attachments of younger citizens are much more influenced by policy preference than are the attachments of their elders. These results fit neatly with the mounting revisionist argument that party identification is in part an ongoing political choice, especially for those in the "impressionable years" (see among others, Fiorina, 1981a; Jackson, 1975b).

Whenever people are placed in an environment with social and political norms contrary to those of their original political socializations, there is pressure to change. The classic case study is Newcomb's (1943) analysis of Bennington women's adaptation to the college environment. As nearly everyone must know by now, these undergraduates, mainly initially conservative and attending a small, new, progressive college during the 1930s, moved toward political progressivism substantially more than did students at other small eastern colleges during the same period. Newcomb presented evidence that the greatest resocialization occurred in women who were most identified with the Bennington subculture. When these women were reinterviewed some twenty years later, Newcomb *et al.* (1967) found substantial continuity; moreover, the supportiveness or discrepancy of their postcollege social environments had a powerful effect upon the persistence (or "regression") of their college-originated attitude changes. Hence a local political *Zeitgeist* can powerfully and durably change the attitudes of young, already socialized people. And the key mechanism both for initiating and for maintaining attitude change seems to be, as Mannheim (1952) emphasized, the individual's affective ties to a concrete social group. Even such a powerful experience does not completely override the effects of initial political socialization, however; adulthood attitudes were highly correlated with *both* pre-Bennington (freshman-year) and post-Bennington (senior-year) attitudes. The higher correlations in the latter case indicate substantial, but far from complete, resocialization.

More general treatments of the same point consider geographical mobility and status mobility, which have the effect of exposing people to new environments whose social and political norms may differ from those dominating their original socialization. The most systematic quantitative analysis of the effects of geographical mobility (Brown, 1981) found that:

1. Migration is much more common for relatively young people (under 30);

2. Young and old people alike shade their party identifications toward the dominant norms of their new environments;

3. The amount of adaptation, as well as its frequency, is greater among the young;

4. Adaptation is greater for those who have spent relatively more time in the new environment.

An analogous hypothesis is that status mobility might induce resocialization to the prevailing norms of the class of destination. There is an extensive literature on this problem that can only be alluded to here. Mobile young adults do seem to adapt partially (though not completely) to the political norms of their destination social class (e.g., Abramson, 1972). Although the extent to which such mobility effects continue to occur through the rest of the life span is unclear, the best current guess is that the lion's share of mobility-instigated resocialization is accomplished in late adolescence and early adulthood (see Barber, 1970, and Knoke, 1973, on party identification and Hodge and Treiman, 1966, on the racial prejudice of U.S. adults; Abramson, 1973, Himmelweit *et al.*, 1981, and Lopreato, 1967, on European voters). A parallel account of how occupation and the work place influence individuals' political attitudes is provided by Sigel and Hoskin (1977). Since the type of work people do tends to be set, within some limits, by their initial entry into the work force, this research primarily describes the resocialization of young workers by the dominant norms of their work place. Miller and Sears (1983) then generalized these various findings by considering the relative impact of preadult and adulthood indicators of social location upon whites' racial attitudes in particular. They concluded that the dominant pattern is for adulthood social environments to perpetuate the norms of racial prejudice or tolerance common in the individual's early life, for the earlier environment to have stronger effects, and for the adulthood environment to have a significant influence too (as well as more general period effects). All these data point to the persistence and "impressionable years" models and suggest that it may be the lack of pressure to change as well as intrinsic resistance to change that stabilizes older people's attitudes.

Direct personal experiences with political matters, according to most psychological theories, ought to have a special potential for eroding the residues of preadult socialization. Unfortunately, all too few studies have been conducted on this question. One exception is the Jennings and Markus (1977) report on the 1965 high school seniors who subsequently served in the armed services in and out of Vietnam. Indices of initial political socialization, such as pre-Vietnam levels of political cynicism, faith in the government, civic tolerance, and measures of social background such as race and educational level, all had powerful residual effects upon post-Vietnam attitudes, independent of the effects of Vietnam experiences (e.g., measures of military service and attitudes about the war itself). However powerful the Vietnam experience upon these late adolescents and young adults was, therefore, their prior attitudes had strong residual effects. And in fact the Vietnam experience itself had only "modest" (in the authors' words) effects upon these youths' political attitudes.

Another potential personal source of pressure to change is self-interest. People's selfish political interests change over time (e.g., their taxes go up, their children enter and then leave school, etc.), and this could conceivably induce self-serving changes in political attitudes. This seems not to happen very often, however. In an extensive series of studies pitting private self-interest against longstanding predispositions as determinants of policy attitudes and voting preferences, self-interest turns out to have remarkably little effect, as indicated in an earlier section (and see Kinder and Sears, 1981; Kinder and Rhodebeck, 1982; Sears *et al.,* 1980; among others). The most notable exception is some fairly strong self-interest effects in the recent California tax revolt (Sears and Citrin, 1982). However, even here, standing predispositions accounted for large shares of the variance; many types of self-interest had no effect (e.g., being service recipients); and at most self-interest generally had narrow attitudinal effects. These studies suggest that adults' longstanding predispositions are difficult to alter even through changes in self-interest.

In summary, at a simple descriptive level, four main findings represent the burden of the evidence on persistence:

1. Adults steadily resist any systematic pressure to change their longstanding predispositions;

2. Nevertheless, longitudinal studies indicate some change back and forth with time (though few people move from one extreme to the other);

3. Any major resocialization, even in early adulthood, apparently demands an exacting and unusually powerful social situation;

4. However, the major systematic defections from initial childhood socialization appear to occur during and immediately following adolescence.

In its simplest form, then, the persistence view overstates the case. More plausible is a view of stability and change that takes into account continuing socialization and occasional resocialization through adolescence and into adulthood and diminishing but still noticeable levels of change thereafter.

Distinguishing Attachment and Partisanship

Finally let us return briefly to an early theme—the origins of diffuse system support. As indicated earlier, Easton and Dennis (1969) argued that children's idealization of political authority was a prerequisite to their later developing, and implementing as adults, diffuse support for the political system and a belief in its legitimacy. What can we say about this particular version of the persistence hypothesis?

We can say a good deal but settle rather little. To start with, there is the familiar and obvious distinction between "attachment to the system" and "partisan predispositions." It is clearly sensible enough in theory. Its problems in practice derive from the difficulty in identifying indicators of system support. These problems are both conceptual and empirical. The manifest content of measures of attachment do not seem at first glance to present major conceptual problems; most seem clearly to focus on the "regime" rather than on the "authorities." Let us review the main categories:

1. Generalized measures of political trust, cynicism, disaffection;

2. Support for institutions, the political parties, "the government," the police, and the president or monarchy;

3. Support for regime symbols, such as "democracy" and flag, glorious past revolutions, infamous past national misdeeds, the monarchy, and glorious or infamous past national leaders;

4. Support for regime norms, such as freedom of dissent or other specific democratic norms, and compliance with law;

5. Behavior consistent with regime norms or in support of the regime in time of crisis, such as voting and

partisanship, lack of interest in emigration, support of national foreign policy, especially in time of crisis, support of the president after assassination or election, and refusal to become involved in protest demonstrations, acts of civil disobedience, or riots.

For references to all these, see Sears (1975).

Not everyone would agree that these are really measures of system support. The problem is that regime norms tend to be fuzzy and at times conflicting. Is it system supportive for children to model themselves on past national heroes, such as Churchill and Washington, or to reject past leaders like Hitler? Should a patriotic child oppose national enemies, such as Communists, or grant them freedom of speech? Should a child rush to the president's support in time of war or oppose the nation's demeaning itself in immoral war crimes? These are analytic and conceptual quandaries, not empirical matters. Philosophers as well as politicians will always debate the content and application of regime norms—especially how far the norm of obedience to authorities should take the citizen in violation of other regime norms. No amount of industry or ingenuity will solve these problems for the empirical researcher. They render research on system support inherently ambiguous; it is never crystal clear just what constitutes support.

A second major problem is empirical. In practice, it is almost impossible to distinguish "legitimacy" of the regime from "partisanship" about incumbent authorities and their policies. Virtually all the indexes of system support just listed turn out to be correlated empirically with partisanship. This can be seen in the party, racial, or class cleavages that exist in support for the British monarchy, presidents, the police, the Supreme Court, and other aspects of the judicial process; Congress and other legislative institutions, free elections, freedom of speech, U.S. foreign policy; going to war; and even reactions to presidential assassinations (for references, see Sears, 1975). There seems to be no governmental role, incumbent, institution, or norm that does not elicit some partisan cleavage. That is, items ostensibly measuring "legitimacy" invariably also draw "partisan" reactions originating in agreement with specific policies or in association with affect-laden partisan symbols. As policies change or new incumbents take over, the locus and often the degree of public support change as well.

It might seem appealing to fall back on behavioral measures of system support as more valid and unambiguous than these attitudinal measures. But they turn out to be even more impure. The level of coercive restraint or simple opportunity strongly determines such disparate behaviors as registration and voting, engaging in demonstrations or riots, and obeying traffic laws. And even when they do not, the "meaning" of the act is open to much debate. For example, participation in ghetto riots has been interpreted variously as a harmless and meaningless spree, as a justifiable protest against injustice, or as a dangerous revolutionary act against the regime.

Two points need to be made about this intrusion of partisanship into measures of system support. The methodological point is that none of the ostensible measures of system support cited above is in fact pure. More sophisticated statistical methods must be employed to distinguish the two sources of variance (diffuse system support and partisanship) in each measure. It cannot be assumed that any one item is a pure measure of either.

The second point raises a more interesting substantive question. Although Easton's regime-versus-authorities distinction may seem intuitively plausible at first glance, it may not correspond to the way people actually think. Possibly system support is constantly varying with various groups' changing and differential satisfaction with outcomes. Hence legitimacy may be in question and in flux at all times. The search for two distinct sources of variance may be misguided.

This mixture is particularly graphic in the case of black children. Many observers have written that blacks grow up with more cynical, disaffected, distrustful attitudes than do whites because of the ill treatment they have been subjected to in the United States. On the other hand, there is Myrdal's (1944) well-known observation that blacks are "exaggerated Americans who believe in the American creed more passionately than whites." Certainly black children have been quite partisan. They have been clearly more negative than white children toward their own partisan adversaries, as they have come to be defined. They have been dramatically more negative to the police, "law and order," the Vietnam War, President Nixon and other conservative Republicans, and they have felt less efficacious and powerful in political life. On the other hand, they have consistently been more favorable than white children to their political allies, such as the Kennedys and President Johnson, and have consistently rejected racial stereotypes and favored racial protest more than have white children. So there is broad evidence of highly partisan socialization of black children since the late 1960s (see Abramson, 1975; Sears, 1975).

But what of black children's attachment to the system? Measures of attachment focusing on compliance to the law and generalized political trust have generally shown only small differences between black and white children, though they increased somewhat after 1967 (Abramson, 1975; Sears, 1975). Where black children seem to be more disaffected is on measures whose manifest content concerns attachment, but which seem clearly to be eliciting mostly racial or political partisanship. Their greater antagonism toward the president and police in recent years probably reflects their partisan reactions against the authorities rather than against the regime (or the system itself). Blacks felt positive toward the Democrats, Ted Kennedy, and the black leader Angela Davis but negative toward the Republicans and Republican leaders Nixon and Reagan. They were not much more negative than whites toward ''the president'' and ''our government'' when one considers them in a more institutional and less partisan context. Finally, blacks were generally even more supportive than white children with respect to criticism of government and U.S. relations with other countries.

The distinction between legitimacy and partisanship is certainly an important one to research, not the least because it is so great a part of normal political debate. But at present it is difficult to determine that regime attitudes are in fact independent of partisan attitudes and to separate the two sources of variance in traditional measures.

REFERENCES

Abeles, R. P. (1976). Relative deprivation, rising expectations, and black militancy. *J. soc. Issues, 32,* 119–137.

Abelson, R. P. (1975). Social clusters and opinion clusters. In P. W. Holland and S. Leinhardt (Eds.), *Perspectives on social network research.* New York: Academic Press.

Abelson, R. P., E. Aronson, W. J. McGuire, T. M. Newcomb, M. J. Rosenberg, and P. H. Tannenbaum (1968). *Theories of cognitive consistency: a sourcebook.* Chicago: Rand McNally.

Abelson, R. P., D. R. Kinder, M. D. Peters, and S. T. Fiske (1982). Affective and semantic components in political person perception. *J. Pers. soc. Psychol., 42,* 619–630.

Aberbach, J. D. (1977). Power consciousness: a comparative analysis. *Amer. polit. Sci. Rev., 71,* 1544–1560.

Aberbach, J. D., R. D. Putnam, and B. A. Rockman (1981). *Bureaucrats and politicians in western democracies.* Cambridge, Mass.: Harvard Univ. Press.

Aberbach, J. D., and J. L. Walker (1973). *Race in the city.* Boston: Little, Brown.

Abramowitz, A. I. (1980). A comparison of voting for U.S. senator and representative in 1978. *Amer. polit. Sci. Rev., 74,* 633–640.

_____ (1981). Choices and echoes in the 1978 U.S. senate elections: a research note. *Amer. J. polit. Sci., 25,* 112–118.

Abramson, P. R. (1971). Social class and political change in Western Europe: a cross-national longitudinal analysis. *Comp. polit. Stud., 4,* 131–155.

_____ (1972). Intergenerational social mobility and partisan choice. *Amer. polit. Sci. Rev., 66,* 1291–1294.

_____ (1973). Intergenerational social mobility and partisan preference in Britain and Italy: a cross-national comparison. *Comp. polit. Stud., 6,* 221–234.

_____ (1974). Generational change in the American electorate. *Amer. polit. Sci. Rev., 68,* 93–105.

_____ (1975). *Generational change in American politics.* Lexington, Mass.: D.C. Heath.

_____ (1979). Developing party identification: a further examination of life-cycle, generational, and period effects. *Amer. J. polit. Sci., 23,* 78–96.

_____ (1983). *Political attitudes in America.* San Francisco: Freeman.

Abramson, P. R., and J. H. Aldrich (1982). The decline of electoral participation in America. *Amer. polit. Sci. Rev., 76,* 502–521.

Achen, C. H. (1975). Mass political attitudes and the survey response. *Amer. polit. Sci. Rev., 69,* 1218–1231.

_____ (1977). Measuring representation: perils of the correlation coefficient. *Amer. J. polit. Sci., 21,* 805–815.

_____ (1978). Measuring representation. *Amer. J. polit. Sci., 22,* 475–510.

_____ (1979). The bias in ''normal vote'' estimates. *Polit. Meth., 6,* 343–356.

_____ (1983). Toward theories of data: the state of political methodology. In A. W. Finifter (Ed.), *Political science: the state of the discipline.* Washington, D.C.: American Political Science Association.

Adams, W. C., and D. J. Smith (1980). Effects of telephone canvassing on turnout and preferences: a field experiment. *Publ. Opin. Quart., 44,* 389–395.

Adorno, T. W., E. Frenkel-Brunswick, D. J. Levinson, and R. N. Sanford (1950). *The authoritarian personality.* New York: Harper & Row.

Agger, R. E. (1959). Independents and party identifiers: characteristics and behavior in 1952. In E. Burdick and A. J. Brodbeck (Eds.), *American voting behavior.* Glencoe, Ill.: Free Press. Pp. 308–329.

Aldrich, J. H. (1980). *Before the convention strategies and choices in presidential nomination campaigns.* Chicago: Univ. of Chicago Press.

Alford, R. R. (1963). *Party and society: the Anglo-American democracies.* Chicago: Rand McNally.

Allen, C. L. (1965). Photographing the TV audience. *J. adver. Res., 5,* 2–8.

Allport, G. W. (1961). *Pattern and growth in personality.* New York: Holt, Rinehart, and Winston.

Almond, G. A., and J. S. Coleman (1960). *The politics of the developing areas.* Princeton, N.J.: Princeton Univ. Press.

Almond, G. A., and S. Verba (1963). *The civic culture.* Princeton, N.J.: Princeton Univ. Press.

Alt, J. E. (1979). *The politics of economic decline.* London: Cambridge Univ. Press.

Andersen, K. (1975). Working women and political participation, 1952–1972. *Amer. J. polit. Sci., 19,* 439–453.

_____ (1979). *The creation of a democratic majority 1928-1936.* Chicago: Univ. of Chicago Press.

Arterton, F. C. (1974). The impact of Watergate on children's attitudes toward political authority. *Polit. Sci. Quart., 89,* 269-288.

_____ (1984). *Media politics. The news strategies of presidential campaigns.* Lexington, Mass.: D.C. Heath.

Bachel, J. M., and D. T. Denver (1971). Canvassing, turnout, and party support. *Brit. J. polit. Sci., 1,* 257-269.

Balch, G. I. (1974). Multiple indicators in survey research: the concept "sense of political efficacy." *Pol. Meth., 1,* 1-43.

Ball-Rokeach, S. J., J. W. Grube, and M. Rokeach (1981). "Roots: The next generation"—Who watched and with what effect? *Publ. Opin. Quart., 45,* 58-68.

Barber, J. A., Jr. (1970). *Social mobility and voting behavior.* Chicago: Rand McNally.

Barber, J. D. (1980). *The pulse of politics.* New York: Norton.

Barnes, S. H., B. G. Farah, and F. Heunks (1979). Personal dissatisfaction. In S. H. Barnes and M. Kaase, *et al., Political action: mass participation in five western democracies.* Beverly Hills, Calif.: Sage. Pp. 381-408.

Barnes, S. H., and M. Kaase, *et al.* (1979). *Political action: mass participation in five western democracies.* Beverly Hills, Calif.: Sage.

Barry, B. (1970). *Sociologists, economists and democracy.* Chicago: Univ. of Chicago Press.

Barton, A. H. (1974-75). Consensus and conflict among American leaders. *Publ. Opin. Quart., 38,* 507-530.

Barton, A. H., and R. W. Parsons (1977). Measuring belief system structure. *Publ. Opin. Quart., 41,* 159-180.

Bechtel, R. B., C. Achelpohl, and R. Akers (1972). Correlates between observed behavior and questionnaire responses on television viewing. In E. A. Rubinstein, G. A. Comstock, and J. P. Murray (Eds.), *Television and social behavior.* Vol. 4. *Television in day-to-day life: patterns of use.* Washington, D.C.: U.S. Government Printing Office.

Beck, P. A. (1975). A socialization theory of partisan realignments. In R. Niemi (Ed.), *The politics of future citizens.* San Francisco: Jossey-Bass. Pp. 199-219.

Becker, J. F., and E. E. Heaton (1967). The election of Senator Edward W. Brooke. *Publ. Opin. Quart., 31,* 346-358.

Becker, L., M. McCombs, and J. McLeod (1975). The development of political cognitions. In S. Chaffee (Ed.), *Political communication.* Beverly Hills, Calif. and London: Sage.

Behr, R. L., and S. Iyengar (1985). Television news, real-world cues, and changes in the public agenda. *Publ. Opin. Quart., 49,* in press.

Bell, D. (1973). *The coming of post-industrial society.* New York: Basic Books.

Bem, D. J., and H. K. McConnell (1970). Testing the self-perception explanation of dissonance phenomena. *J. Pers. soc. Psychol., 14,* 23-31.

Bennett, W. L. (1976). *The political mind and the political environment.* Lexington, Mass.: Lexington Books.

_____ (1977). The growth of knowledge in mass belief studies: an epistemological critique. *Amer. J. polit. Sci., 21,* 465-500.

Bentler, P. M. (1980). Multivariate analysis with latent variables: causal modeling. *Ann. Rev. Psychol., 31,* 419-456.

Berelson, B. R., P. F. Lazarsfeld, and W. N. McPhee (1954). *Voting: a study of opinion formation in a presidential campaign.* Chicago: Univ. of Chicago Press.

Bishop, G. F., and K. A. Frankovic (1981). Ideological consensus and constraint among party leaders and followers in the 1978 election. *Micropol., 1,* 87-111.

Bishop, G. F., R. W. Oldendick, and A. J. Tuchfarber (1982). Political information processing: question order and context effects. *Polit. Behav., 4,* 177-200.

Bishop, G. F., R. W. Oldendick, A. J. Tuchfarber, and S. E. Bennett (1980). Pseudo-opinions on public affairs. *Publ. Opin. Quart., 44,* 198-209.

Bloom, B. S. (1964). *Stability and change in human characteristics.* New York: Wiley.

Bloom, H. S., and H. D. Price (1975). Voter response to short-run economic conditions: the asymmetric effect of prosperity and recession. *Amer. polit. Sci. Rev., 69,* 1240-1254.

Brigham, J. C., and L. W. Giesbrecht (1976). All in the family: racial attitudes. *J. Communic., 26,* 75-84.

Brim, O. G., Jr., and J. Kagan (1980). *Constancy and change in human development.* Cambridge, Mass.: Harvard Univ. Press.

Brody, R. A. (1977). Stability and change in party identification: presidential to off-years. Paper delivered at the 1977 annual meeting of the American Political Science Association, Washington, D.C.

_____ (1978). The puzzle of political participation in America. In A. King (Ed.), *The new American political system.* Washington, D.C.: American Enterprise Institute for Public Policy Research.

Brody, R. A., and B. I. Page (1968). Indifference, alienation and rational decisions. *Publ. Choice, 15,* 1-17.

_____ (1972). Comment: the assessment of issue voting. *Amer. polit. Sci. Rev., 66,* 450-458.

_____ (1975). The impact of events on presidential popularity: the Johnson and Nixon administrations. In A. Wildavsky (Ed.), *Perspectives on the presidency.* Boston: Little, Brown. Pp. 136-148.

Brody, R. A., and P. M. Sniderman (1977). From life space to polling place: the relevance of personal concerns for voting behavior. *Brit. J. polit. Sci., 7,* 337-360.

Brown, R. (1965). *Social psychology.* New York: Free Press.

Brown, S. R. (1970). Consistency and the persistence of ideology: some experimental results. *Publ. Opin. Quart., 34,* 60-80.

_____ (1980). *Political subjectivity.* New Haven: Yale Univ. Press.

Brown, T. A. (1981). On contextual change in partisan attributes. *Brit. J. polit. Sci., 2,* 427-447.

Burnham, W. D. (1970). *Critical elections and the mainsprings of American politics.* New York: Norton.

_____ (1974a). Theory and voting research: some reflections on Converse's "change in the American electorate." *Amer. polit. Sci. Rev., 68,* 1002-1023.

_____ (1974b). The United States: the politics of heterogeneity. In R. Rose (Ed.), *Electoral behavior.* New York: Free Press. Pp. 653-725.

_____ (1975a). American politics in the 1970's: beyond parties? In W. N. Chambers and W. D. Burnham (Eds.), *The*

American party systems: stages of political development. New York: Oxford Univ. Press.

_____ (1975b). Party systems and the political process. In W. N. Chambers and W. D. Burnham (Eds.), *The American party systems: stages of political development.* New York: Oxford Univ. Press.

Burnham, W. D. (1980). The appearance and disappearance of the American voter. In R. Rose (Ed.), *Electoral participation: a comparative analysis.* Beverly Hills, Calif.: Sage.

_____ (1981). Shifting patterns of congressional voting participation in the United States. Paper presented at annual meeting of the American Political Science Association, New York.

_____ (1983). *The current crisis in American politics.* New York: Oxford Univ. Press.

Burstein, P. (1979). Public opinion, demonstrations, and the passage of antidiscrimination legislation. *Publ. Opin. Quart., 43,* 157–172.

Butler, D., and D. Stokes (1974). *Political change in Britain* (2nd ed.). New York: St. Martin's Press.

Campbell, A. (1960). Surge and decline: a study of electoral change. *Publ. Opin. Quart., 24,* 397–418.

_____ (1966). A classification of presidential elections. In A. Campbell, P. E. Converse, W. E. Miller, and D. E. Stokes (Eds.), *Elections and the political order.* New York: Wiley.

_____ (1981). *The sense of well-being in America.* New York: McGraw-Hill.

Campbell, A., P. E. Converse, W. E. Miller, and D. E. Stokes (1960). *The American voter.* New York: Wiley.

Campbell, A., P. E. Converse, and W. L. Rodgers (1976). *The quality of American life.* New York: Russell Sage.

Campbell, A., G. Gurin, and W. E. Miller (1954). *The voter decides.* Evanston, Ill.: Row, Peterson.

Cantril, H. (1952). The invasion from Mars. In G. E. Swanson, T. M. Newcomb, and E. L. Hartley (Eds.), *Readings in social psychology* (Rev. ed.). New York: Hold & Co. Pp. 198–207.

_____ (1965). *The pattern of human concerns.* New Brunswick, N.J.: Rutgers Univ. Press.

Caplan, N. (1970). The new ghetto man: a review of recent empirical studies. *J. soc. Issues, 26,* 59–73.

Caplan, N., and J. M. Paige (1968). A study of ghetto rioters. *Scientific Amer., 219,* 15–21.

Cartwright, D., and A. Zander (1968). *Group dynamics: research and theory* (3rd ed.). New York: Harper & Row.

Cavanagh, T. E. (1979). Changes in American electoral turnout, 1964–1976. Paper presented at the annual meeting of the Midwest Political Science Association, Chicago.

Centers, R. (1949). *The psychology of social classes.* Princeton, N.J.: Princeton Univ. Press.

Chong, D., H. McClosky, and J. Zaller (1980). Patterns of support for democratic and capitalist values. Paper delivered at the annual meeting of the American Political Science Association, Washington, D.C.

Citrin, J. (1974). Comment: the political relevance of trust in government. *Amer. polit. Sci. Rev., 68,* 973–988.

_____ (1977). Political alienation as a social indicator: attitudes and action. *Soc. Ind. Res., 4,* 381–419.

Citrin, J., H. McClosky, J. M. Shanks, and P. M. Sniderman (1975). Personal and political sources of political alienation. *Brit. J. polit. Sci., 5,* 1–31.

Clausen, A. R. (1968). Response validity in surveys. *Publ. Opin. Quart., 32,* 588–606.

Clubb, J. M., W. H. Flanigan, and N. H. Zingale (1980). *Partisan realignment.* Beverly Hills, Calif.: Sage.

Cobb, R., and C. Elder (1976). Symbolic identification and political behavior. *Amer. polit. Quart., 4,* 305–332.

Cohen, B. (1963). *The press and foreign policy.* Princeton, N.J.: Princeton Univ. Press.

Collins, B. (1974). Four separate components of the Rotter I–E scale: belief in a difficult world, a just world, a predictable world, and a politically responsive world. *J. Pers. soc. Psychol., 29,* 381–391.

Combs, S. L. (1981). Editorial endorsements and electoral outcomes. In M. B. MacKuen and S. L. Combs, *More than news.* Beverly Hills, Calif. and London: Sage.

Commission on Obscenity and Pornography. (1970). *The report of the commission on obscenity and pornography.* New York: Bantam.

Comstock, G. (1980). New emphases in research on the effects of television and film violence. In E. L. Palmer and A. Dorr (Eds.), *Children and the faces of television: teaching, violence, selling.* New York: Academic Press. Pp. 129–148.

Comstock, G., S. Chaffee, N. Katzman, M. McCombs, and D. Roberts (1978). *Television and human behavior.* New York: Columbia Univ. Press.

Connell, R. W. (1971). *The child's construction of politics.* Melbourne: Melbourne Univ. Press.

Conover, P. J., and S. Feldman (1980). Belief system organization in the American electorate: an alternative approach. In J. C. Pierce and J. L. Sullivan (Eds.), *The electorate reconsidered.* Beverly Hills, Calif.: Sage.

_____ (1981). The origins and meanings of liberal/conservative self-identifications. *Amer. J. polit. Sci., 25,* 617–645.

_____ (1984). How people organize the political world. *Amer. J. polit. Sci., 28,* 95–126.

Converse, J. M. (1976–77). Predicting no opinion in the polls. *Publ. Opin. Quart., 40,* 515–530.

Converse, P. E. (1958). The shifting role of class in political attitudes and behavior. In E. E. Maccoby, T. M. Newcomb, and E. L. Hartley (Eds.), *Readings in social psychology* (3rd ed.). New York: Holt, Rinehart, and Winston.

_____ (1963). Attitudes and non-attitudes: continuation of a dialogue. Paper presented at meeting of the International Congress of Psychology, Washington, D.C. Published in 1970 in E. R. Tufte (Ed.), *The quantitative analysis of social problems.* Reading, Mass.: Addison-Wesley. Pp. 168–189.

_____ (1964). The nature of belief systems in mass publics. In D. E. Apter (Ed.), *Ideology and discontent.* New York: Free Press. Pp. 206–261.

_____ (1966a). Religion and politics: the 1960 election. In A. Campbell, P. E. Converse, W. E. Miller, and D. E. Stokes (Eds.), *Elections and the political order.* New York: Wiley.

_____ (1966b). The concept of a normal vote. In A. Campbell, P. E. Converse, W. E. Miller, and D. E. Stokes, *Elections and the political order*. New York: Wiley.

_____ (1972). Change in the American electorate. In A. Campbell and P. E. Converse, *The human meaning of social change*. New York: Russell Sage. Pp. 307–317.

_____ (1974). Comment: the status of nonattitudes. *Amer. polit. Sci. Rev., 68,* 650–660.

_____ (1975a). Public opinion and voting behavior. In F. Greenstein and N. Polsby (Eds.), *Handbook of political science*. Vol. 4. Reading, Mass.: Addison-Wesley. Pp. 75–169.

_____ (1975b). Some mass elite contrasts in the perception of political spaces. *Soc. Sci. Inf., 14,* 49–83.

_____ (1976). *The dynamics of party support. Cohort-analyzing party identification*. Beverly Hills, Calif.: Sage.

_____ (1979). Rejoinder to Abramson. *Amer. J. polit. Sci., 23,* 97–100.

_____ (1980). Comment: rejoinder to Judd and Milburn. *Amer. Sociol. Rev., 45,* 644–646.

Converse, P. E., and A. Campbell (1968). Political standards in secondary groups. In D. Cartwright and A. Zander (Eds.), *Group dynamics* (3rd ed.). New York: Harper & Row.

Converse, P. E., A. Campbell, W. E. Miller, and D. E. Stokes (1961). Stability and change in 1960: a reinstating election. *Amer. polit. Sci. Rev., 55,* 269–280.

Converse, P. E., A. R. Clausen, and W. E. Miller (1965). Electoral myth and reality: the 1964 election. *Amer. polit. Sci. Rev., 49,* 321–336.

Converse, P. E., J. Dotson, W. J. Hoag, and W. H. McGee (1980). *American social attitudes data sourcebook, 1947–1978*. Cambridge, Mass.: Harvard Univ. Press.

Converse, P. E., and G. Dupeux (1966). DeGaulle and Eisenhower: the public image of the victorious general. In A. Campbell, P. E. Converse, W. E. Miller, and D. E. Stokes, *Elections and the political order*. New York: Wiley. Pp. 292–345.

Converse, P. E., and G. B. Markus (1979). Plus ca change. . . . The new CPS election study panel. *Amer. polit. Sci. Rev., 73,* 32–49.

Converse, P. E., W. E. Miller, J. G. Rusk, and A. C. Wolfe (1969). Continuity and change in American politics: parties and issues in the 1968 election. *Amer. polit. Sci. Rev., 63,* 1083–1105.

Converse, P. E., and R. Niemi (1971). Non-voting among young adults in the United States. In W. J. Crotty *et al.* (Ed.), *Political parties and political behavior* (2nd ed.). Boston: Allyn and Bacon.

Converse, P. E., and R. Pierce (1985). *Political representation in France*. Cambridge, Mass.: Harvard Univ. Press.

Coombs, S. L. (1981). Editorial endorsements and electoral outcomes. In M. B. MacKuen and S. L. Coombs (Eds.), *More than news: media power in public affairs*. Beverly Hills, Calif.: Sage. Pp. 147–230.

Cover, A. D., and D. R. Mayhew (1977). Congressional dynamics and the decline of competitive congressional elections. In L. C. Dodd and B. I. Oppenheimer (Eds.), *Congress reconsidered*. New York: Praeger.

Cox, G. W., and J. M. Kousser (1981). Turnout and rural corruption: New York as a test case. *Amer. J. polit. Sci., 25,* 646–663.

Crewe, I., B. Sarlvik, and J. Alt (1977). Partisan dealignment in Britain 1964–1974. *Brit. J. polit. Sci., 7,* 129–190.

Crittenden, J. (1962). Aging and party affiliation. *Publ. Opin. Quart., 26,* 648–657.

Crosby, F. (1976). A model of egoistical relative deprivation. *Psychol. Rev., 83,* 85–113.

_____ (1979). Relative deprivation revisited: a response to Miller, Bolce, and Halligan. *Amer. polit. Sci. Rev., 73,* 103–112.

Crosby, F., and A. M. Gonzalez-Intal (1982). Relative deprivation and equity theories: a comparative analysis of approaches to felt injustice. In R. Folger (Ed.), *The sense of injustice: social psychological perspectives*. New York: Plenum.

Crotty, W. J. (1971). Party effort and its impact on the vote. *Amer. polit. Sci. Rev., 65,* 439–450.

Cutler, N. E. (1977). Demographic, social-psychological, and political factors in the politics of aging: a foundation for research in "political gerontology." *Amer. polit. Sci. Rev., 71,* 1011–1026.

Cutright, P., and P. Rossi (1958). Party organization in primary elections. *Amer. J. Sociol., 64,* 262–269.

Dahl, R. A. (1961). *Who governs? Democracy and power in an American City*. New Haven, Conn.: Yale Univ. Press.

_____ (1971). *Polyarchy participation and opposition*. New Haven, Conn.: Yale Univ. Press.

Dalton, R. J. (1977). Was there a revolution? A note on generational versus life-cycle explanations of value differences. *Comp. polit. Stud., 9,* 459–475.

Danigelis, N. L. (1978). Black political participation in the United States. *Amer. Sociol. Rev., 43,* 756–771.

Davies, J. C. (1962). Toward a theory of revolution. *Amer. Sociol. Rev., 27,* 5–19.

_____ (1963). *Human nature in politics*. New York: Wiley.

_____ (1965). The family's role in political socialization. *Annals Amer. Acad. polit. soc. Sci., 361,* 10–19.

_____ (1969). The J-curve of rising and declining satisfaction as a cause of some great revolutions and a contained rebellion. In H. D. Graham and T. R. Gurr (Eds.), *Violence in America: historical and comparative perspectives*. New York: Signet Books.

Davis, J. (1959). A formal interpretation of the theory of relative deprivation. *Sociom., 22,* 280–296.

_____ (1975). Communism, conformity, cohorts, and categories: American tolerance in 1954 and 1972–73. *Amer. J. Sociol., 81,* 491–513.

Dawson, P. A. (1979). The formation and structure of political belief systems. *Polit. Behav., 1,* 99–122.

Dawson, R. E., and K. Prewitt (1969). *Political socialization*. Boston: Little, Brown.

Dawson, R. E., K. Prewitt, and K. S. Dawson (1977). *Political socialization* (2nd ed.). Boston: Little, Brown.

Denney, W. M. (1979). Participant citizenship in a marginal group: Union mobilization of California farm workers. *Amer. J. polit. Sci., 23,* 330–337.

Denney, W. M., J. S. Hendricks, and D. R. Kinder (1980). Personal stakes versus symbolic politics. Paper delivered to the 35th annual meeting of the American Association for Public Opinion Research, Cincinnati, Ohio.

Dennis, J. (1982). New measures of partisanship in models of voting. Paper delivered at the annual meeting of the Midwest Political Science Association, Milwaukee, Wisconsin.

Dennis, J., and C. Webster (1975). Children's images of the president and of government in 1962 and 1974. *Amer. polit. Quart., 3,* 386–405.

Dobson, D., and D. St. Angelo (1975). Party identification and the floating vote. *Amer. polit. Sci. Rev., 69,* 481–490.

Doob, L. W. (1935). *Propaganda, its psychology and technique.* New York: Holt.

Downs, A. (1957). *An economic theory of democracy.* New York: Harper.

Easton, D. (1965). *A systems analysis of political life.* New York: Wiley.

Easton, D., and J. Dennis (1965). The child's image of government. *Annals Amer. Acad. polit. soc. Sci., 361,* 40–57.

_____ (1969). *Children in the political system: origins of political legitimacy.* New York: McGraw-Hill.

Eisinger, P. K. (1974). Racial differences in protest participation. *Amer. polit. Sci. Rev., 68,* 592–606.

Elden, J. M. (1981). Political efficacy at work: the connection between more autonomous forms of workplace organization and a more participatory politics. *Amer. polit. Sci. Rev., 75,* 43–58.

Eldersveld, S. J. (1956). Experimental propaganda techniques and voting behavior. *Amer. polit. Sci. Rev., 50,* 154–165.

Elling, R. C. (1982). Ideological change in the U.S. Senate: time and electoral responsiveness. *Legis. Stud. Quart., 7,* 75–92.

Epstein, E. J. (1973). *News from nowhere.* New York: Vintage Books.

Erbring, L., E. M. Goldenberg, and A. H. Miller (1980). Front page news and real world cues: a new look at agenda-setting. *Amer. J. polit. Sci., 24,* 16–49.

Erikson, R. S. (1971). The electoral impact of congressional roll-call voting. *Amer. polit. Sci. Rev., 65,* 1018–1032.

_____ (1976). The influence of newspaper endorsements in presidential elections: The case of 1964. *Amer. J. polit. Sci., 20,* 207–233.

_____ (1978). Constituency opinion and congressional behavior: a re-examination of the Miller-Stokes representation data. *Amer. J. polit. Sci., 22,* 511–535.

_____ (1979). The SRC panel data and mass political attitudes. *Brit. J. polit. Sci., 9,* 89–114.

Erikson, R. S., and K. L. Tedin (1981). The 1928–1936 partisan realignment: the case for the conversion hypothesis. *Amer. polit. Sci. Rev., 75,* 951–962.

Eulau, H. (1962). *Class and party in the Eisenhower years.* Glencoe, Ill.: Free Press.

Fainstain, N. I., and S. S. Fainstain (1974). *The urban political movements.* Englewood Cliffs, N.J.: Prentice-Hall.

Farah, B. G., S. H. Barnes, and F. Heunks (1979). Political dissatisfaction. In S. H. Barnes and M. Kaase *et al., Political*

action: mass participation in five western democracies. Beverly Hills, Calif.: Sage. Pp. 409–448.

Farah, B. G., M. K. Jennings, and W. E. Miller (1981). Convention delegates: reform and the representation of party elites, 1972–1980. Paper presented at meetings of American Political Science Association, New York.

Feagin, J. R. (1975). *Subordinating the poor.* New York: Prentice-Hall.

Feldman, K. A., and T. M. Newcomb (1969). *The impact of college on students.* Vol. 1. *An analysis of four decades of research.* San Francisco: Jossey-Bass.

Feldman, S. (1982). Economic self-interest and political behavior. *Amer. J. polit. Sci., 26,* 446–466.

_____ (1983). Economic individualism and American public opinion. *Amer. polit. Quart., 11,* 3–29.

Fenno, R. F., Jr. (1975). If, as Ralph Nader says, congress is "the broken branch," how come we love our congressmen so much? In N. J. Ornstein (Ed.), *Congress in change.* New York: Praeger.

_____ (1978). *Home style: house members in their districts.* Boston: Little, Brown.

Ferejohn, J. A., and M. P. Fiorina (1974). The paradox of not voting: a decision theoretic analysis. *Amer. polit. Sci. Rev., 67,* 525–536.

_____ (1975). Closeness counts only in horseshoes and dancing. *Amer. polit. Sci. Rev., 69,* 920–925.

_____ (1979). The decline in turnout in presidential elections. Unpublished manuscript, California Institute of Technology.

Festinger, L. (1957). *A theory of cognitive dissonance.* Stanford: Stanford Univ. Press.

Field, J. O., and R. E. Anderson (1969). Ideology in the public's conceptualization of the 1964 election. *Publ. Opin. Quart., 33,* 380–398.

Finifter, A. W. (1970). Dimensions of political alienation. *Amer. polit. Sci. Rev., 64,* 389–410.

Fiorina, M. P. (1977). An outline for a model of party choice. *Amer. J. polit. Sci., 21,* 601–626.

_____ (1981a). *Retrospective voting in American national elections.* New Haven: Yale Univ. Press.

_____ (1981b). Congressmen and their constituents: 1958 and 1978. Unpublished manuscript. Pasadena, Calif.: California Institute of Technology.

Fishbein, M., and I. Ajzen (1981). Attitudes and voting behavior: an application of the theory of reasoned action. *Progress appl. soc. Psychol., 1,* 253–313.

Fitzgerald, G. (1979). *America revised.* Boston: Atlantic-Little, Brown.

Flacks, R. (1969). The liberated generation: an exploration of the roots of student protest. *J. soc. Issues, 23,* 52–75.

Fogelson, R. M. (1968). Who riots? A study of participation in the 1967 riots. Supplemental studies for the National Advisory Commission on Civil Disorders. Washington, D.C.: U.S. Government Printing Office.

Forward, J. R., and J. R. Williams (1970). Internal-external control and black militancy. *J. soc. Issues, 26,* 75–92.

Franklin, C. H. (1982). Policy preferences and party identification. Paper delivered at the annual meeting of the Western Political Science Association, San Diego, Calif.

_____ (1983). The dynamics of party identification. *Amer. polit. Sci. Rev., 77,* 957–973.

Freedman, J. L., D. O. Sears, and J. M. Carlsmith (1981). *Social Psychology* (4th ed.). Englewood Cliffs, N.J.: Prentice-Hall.

Freud, S. (1922). *Group psychology and the analysis of the ego.* London: Hogarth Press.

Frohlich, N., and J. A. Oppenheimer (1978). *Modern political economy.* Englewood Cliffs, N.J.: Prentice-Hall.

Frohlich, N., J. A. Oppenheimer, J. Smith, and O. R. Young (1978). A test of Downsian voter rationality: 1964 presidential voting. *Amer. polit. Sci. Rev., 72,* 178–197.

Francis, J. D., and L. Busch (1975). What we now know about "I don't know." *Publ. Opin. Quart., 39,* 207–218.

Fuchs, D. A. (1966). Election-day radio-television and western voting. *Publ. Opin. Quart., 30,* 226–236.

Funkhouser, G. R. (1973). The issues of the sixties: an exploratory study in the dynamics of public opinion. *Publ. Opin. Quart., 37,* 62–75.

Gamson, W. A. (1968). *Power and discontent.* Homewood, Ill.: Dorsey.

_____ (1975). *The strategy of social protest.* Homewood, Ill.: Dorsey.

Gatlin, D. S., M. W. Giles, and E. F. Cataldo (1978). Policy support within a target group: the case of school desegregation. *Amer. polit. Sci. Rev., 72,* 985–995.

Geschwender, B. N., and J. A. Geschwender (1973). Relative deprivation and participation in the civil rights movement. *Soc. Sci. Quart., 54,* 403–411.

Ginsberg, B. (1982). *The consequences of consent: elections, citizen control and popular acquiescence.* Reading, Mass.: Addison-Wesley.

Glenn, N. D. (1972). Sources of the shift to political independence: some evidence from a cohort analysis. *Soc. Sci. Quart., 53,* 494–519.

_____ (1974). Aging and conservatism. *Annals Acad. polit. soc. Sci., 33,* 176–186.

_____ (1977). *Cohort analysis.* Beverly Hills, Calif.: Sage.

_____ (1980). Values, attitudes, and beliefs. In O. G. Brim, Jr. and J. Kagan (Eds.), *Constancy and change in human development.* Cambridge, Mass.: Harvard Univ. Press. Pp. 596–640.

Glenn, N. D., and T. Hefner (1972). Further evidence on aging and party identification. *Publ. Opin. Quart., 36,* 31–47.

Goldberg, A. S. (1966). Discerning a causal pattern among data on voting behavior. *Amer. polit. Sci. Rev., 60,* 913–922.

Goodban, N. A. (1981). *Attributions about poverty.* Unpublished thesis. Department of Psychology and Social Relations, Harvard University, Cambridge, Mass.

Gosnell, H. F. (1927). *Machine politics: Chicago model.* Chicago: Univ. of Chicago Press.

Graber, D. (1976). Press and TV as opinion resources in presidential campaigns. *Publ. Opin. Quart., 40,* 285–303.

Greeley, A. M. (1975). A model for ethnic political socialization. *Amer. J. polit. Sci., 19,* 187–206.

Greeley, A. M., and P. B. Sheatsley (1971). Attitudes toward racial integration. *Scientific Amer.,* 13–19.

Greenberg, E. S. (1970). Orientations of black and white children to political authority figures. *Soc. Sci. Quart., 51,* 561–571.

Greenstein, F. I. (1960). The benevolent leader: children's images of political authority. *Amer. polit. Sci. Rev., 54,* 934–943.

_____ (1965). *Children and politics.* New Haven: Yale Univ. Press.

_____ (1968). Political socialization. In *International encyclopedia of the social sciences.* New York: Macmillan and Free Press.

_____ (1974). Personality and politics. In F. I. Greenstein and N. W. Polsby (Eds.), *Handbook of political science.* Vol. 2. *Theoretical aspects of micropolitics.* Reading, Mass.: Addison-Wesley.

_____ (1975). The benevolent leader revisited: children's images of political leaders in three democracies. *Amer. polit. Sci. Rev., 69,* 1371–1398.

Guimond, S., and L. Dube-Simard (1983). Relative deprivation theory and the Quebec nationalist movement. *J. Pers. soc. Psychol., 44,* 526–535.

Gurin, P., G. Gurin, R. Lao, M. Beattie (1969). Internal-external control in the motivational dynamics of Negro youth. *J. soc. Issues, 25,* 29–53.

Gurin, P., G. Gurin, and B. M. Morrison (1978). Personal and ideological aspects of internal and external control. *Soc. Psychol., 41,* 275–296.

Gurin, P., A. H. Miller, and G. Gurin (1980). Stratum identification and consciousness. *Soc. Psych. Quart., 43,* 30–47.

Gurr, T. R. (1968). A causal model of civil strife: a comparative analysis using new indices. *Amer. polit. Sci. Rev., 62,* 1104–1124.

_____ (1969). A comparative study of civil strife. In H. D. Graham and T. R. Gurr (Eds.), *The history of violence in America.* New York: Bantam.

_____ (1970). *Why men rebel.* Princeton, N.J.: Princeton Univ. Press.

Gurr, T. R., and R. Duvall (1973). Civil conflict in the 1960s: a reciprocal theoretical system with parameter estimates. *Comp. polit. Stud., 6,* 135–169.

Haight, T. R., and R. A. Brody (1977). The mass media and presidential popularity: presidential broadcasting and news in the Nixon administration. *Communic. Res., 4,* 41–60.

Hamilton, R. F. (1972). *Class and politics in the United States.* New York: Wiley.

Harding, J., H. Proshansky, B. Kutner, and I. Chein (1969). Prejudice and ethnic relations. In G. Lindzey and E. Aronson (Eds.), *The handbook of social psychology.* Vol. 5. Reading, Mass.: Addison-Wesley. Pp. 1–76.

Hartwig, F., W. R. Jenkins, and E. M. Temchin (1980). Variability in electoral behavior: the 1960, 1968, and 1976 elections. *Amer. J. polit. Sci., 24,* 553–558.

Hayward, F. M. (1976). A reassessment of conventional wisdom about the informed public. *Amer. polit. Sci. Rev., 70,* 433–451.

Hess, R. D., and D. Easton (1960). The child's changing image of the president. *Publ. Opin. Quart., 24,* 632–644.

Hess, R. D., and J. V. Torney (1967). *The development of political attitudes in children.* Chicago: Aldine.

Hibbing, J. R., and J. R. Alford (1981). The electoral impact of economic conditions: who is held responsible? *Amer. J. polit. Sci., 25,* 423–439.

Hibbs, D. A., Jr. (1973). *Mass political violence.* New York: Wiley.

—— (1976). Industrial conflict in advanced industrial societies. *Amer. polit. Sci. Rev., 70,* 1033–1058.

—— (1979). The mass public and macro-economic performance: the dynamics of public opinion toward unemployment and inflation. *Amer. J. polit. Sci., 23,* 705–731.

Hibbs, D. A., Jr., R. D. Rivers, and N. Vasilotos (1982a). On the demand for economic outcomes: macroeconomic performance and mass political support in the United States, Great Britain, and Europe. *J. Polit., 44,* 426–462.

—— (1982b). The dynamics of political support for American presidents among occupational and partisan groups. *Amer. J. polit. Sci., 26,* 312–332.

Himmelweit, H. T., P. Humphreys, M. Jaeger, and M. Katz (1981). *How voters decide: a longitudinal study of political attitudes and voting extending over fifteen years.* London: Academic Press.

Himmelweit, H. T., M. Jaeger, and J. Stockdale (1978). Memory for past vote: implications of a study of bias in recall. *Brit. J. polit. Sci., 8,* 365–376.

Hinckley, B. (1980). The American voter in congressional elections. *Amer. polit. Sci. Rev., 74,* 641–650.

Hochschild, J. L. (1981). *What's fair? American beliefs about distributive justice.* Cambridge, Mass.: Harvard Univ. Press.

Hodge, R. W., and D. J. Treiman (1966). Occupational mobility and attitudes toward Negroes. *Amer. Sociol. Rev., 31,* 93–102.

Hofstadter, R. (1948). *The American political tradition.* New York: Vintage Books.

House, J. S., and W. M. Mason (1975). Political alienation in America, 1952–1968. *Amer. Sociol. Rev., 40,* 123–147.

Hovland, C. I., A. A. Lumsdaine, and F. D. Sheffield (1949). *Experiments on mass communication.* Princeton, N.J.: Princeton Univ. Press.

Huber, J., and W. H. Form (1973). *Income and ideology.* New York: Free Press.

Huntington, S. P. (1981). *American politics: the promise of disharmony.* Cambridge: The Belknap Press.

Hur, K. K., and J. P. Robinson (1978). The social impact of "Roots." *J. Quart., 55,* 19–24.

Hurley, P. A., and K. Q. Hill (1980). The prospects for issue-voting in contemporary congressional elections. *Amer. polit. Quart., 8,* 425–448.

Hyman, H. H. (1953). The value systems of different classes. In R. Bendix and S. M. Lipset (Eds.), *Class, status, and power.* Glencoe, Ill.: Free Press.

—— (1959). *Political socialization.* Glencoe, Ill.: Free Press.

Hyman, H. H., and P. B. Sheatsley (1947). Some reasons why information campaigns fail. *Publ. Opin. Quart., 11,* 413–423.

—— (1953). The political appeal of President Eisenhower. *Publ. Opin. Quart., 17,* 443–460.

—— (1954). The current status of American public opinion. In D. Katz, D. Cartwright, S. Eldersveld, and A. M. Lee (Eds.), *Public opinion and propaganda.* New York: Holt, Rinehart, and Winston. Pp. 33–48.

Inglehart, R. (1971). The silent revolution in Europe: intergenerational change in post-industrial societies. *Amer. polit. Sci. Rev., 65,* 991–1017.

—— (1977). *The silent revolution.* Princeton, N.J.: Princeton Univ. Press.

—— (1979). Value priorities and socioeconomic change. In S. H. Barnes and M. Kaase *et al., Political action: mass participation in five western democracies.* Beverly Hills, Calif.: Sage. Pp. 305–342.

—— (1981). Post-materialism in an environment of insecurity. *Amer. polit. Sci. Rev., 75,* 880–900.

—— (1982). Changing paradigms in comparative political behavior. In A. W. Finifter (Ed.), *Political Science: the state of the discipline.* Washington, D.C.: American Political Science Association.

Inglehart, R., S. H. Barnes, B. G. Farah, and M. K. Jennings (1982). The persistence of materialist and post-materialist value orientations. Unpublished manuscript. ISR, The University of Michigan.

The Institute for Propaganda Analysis (1939). *The fine art of propaganda: a study of Father Coughlin's speeches.* New York: Harcourt Brace.

Iyengar, S. (1979a). Political knowledge among Indian children and adolescents. *Soc. Sci. Quart., 60,* 328–335.

—— (1979b). Television news and issue salience. *Amer. polit. Quart., 7,* 395–416.

Iyengar, S. I., and D. R. Kinder (1984). *Media and mind: television news and public opinion.* Unpublished monograph, Dept. of Political Science, Yale University.

—— (1984). The evening news and presidential evaluations. *J. Pers. soc. Psychol., 46,* 778–787.

Iyengar, S., M. D. Peters, and D. R. Kinder (1982). Experimental demonstrations of the "not-so-minimal" consequences of television news programs. *Amer. polit. Sci. Rev., 76,* 848–858.

Jackman, R. (1972). Political elites, mass publics, and support for democratic principles. *J. polit., 34,* 753–773.

Jackson, J. E. (1975a). Issues and party alignment. In L. Maisel and P. M. Sacks (Eds.), *The future of political parties.* Beverly Hills, Calif.: Sage. Pp. 101–123.

—— (1975b). Issues, party choices, and presidential votes. *Amer. J. polit. Sci., 19,* 161–185.

—— (1979). Statistical estimation of possible response bias in close-ended issue questions. *Polit. Meth., 6,* 393–423.

—— (1982). The systematic beliefs of the mass public: estimating policy preferences with survey data. Unpublished manuscript. Center for Political Studies, Institute for Social Research, Univ. of Michigan.

—— (1984). Election night reporting and voter turnout. *Amer. J. polit. Sci., 27,* 615–635.

Jackson, J. S., III, B. L. Brown, and D. Bositis (1982). Herbert McClosky and friends revisited. 1980 Democratic and Republican party elites compared to the mass public. *Amer. Polit. Quart., 10,* 158–180.

Jacobson, G. C. (1980). *Money in congressional elections.* New Haven: Yale Univ. Press.

—— (1981). Incumbents' advantages in the 1978 U.S. Congressional elections. *Leg. Stud. Quart., VI,* 183–200.

Jacobson, G. C., and S. Kernell (1981). *Strategy and choice in congressional elections.* New Haven: Yale Univ. Press.

Janis, I. L., C. I. Hovland, P. B. Field, H. Linton, E. Graham, A. R. Cohen, D. Rife, R. P. Abelson, G. S. Lesser, and B. T. King (1959). *Personality and persuasibility.* New Haven: Yale Univ. Press.

Janis, I. L., and L. Mann (1977). *Decision making.* New York: Free Press.

Jaros, D. (1967). Children's orientations toward the president: some additional theoretical considerations and data. *J. Polit., 29,* 368–387.

Jaros, D., H. Hirsch, and F. J. Fleron, Jr. (1968). The malevolent leader: political socialization in an American subculture. *Amer. polit. Sci. Rev., 62,* 564–575.

Jennings, M. K. (1979). Another look at the life cycle and political participation. *Amer. J. polit. Sci., 23,* 755–771.

Jennings, M. K., and G. B. Markus (1977). The effect of military service on political attitudes: a panel study. *Amer. polit. Sci. Rev., 71,* 131–147.

Jennings, M. K., and R. G. Niemi (1968). The transmission of political values from parent to child. *Amer. polit. Sci. Rev., 62,* 169–184.

—— (1974). *The political character of adolescence.* Princeton, N.J.: Princeton Univ. Press.

—— (1978). The persistence of political orientations: an over-time analysis of two generations. *Brit. J. polit. Sci., 8,* 333–363.

—— (1981). *Generations and politics.* Princeton, N.J.: Princeton Univ. Press.

Jervis, R. (1976). *Perception and misperception in international politics.* Princeton, N.J.: Princeton Univ. Press.

Jones, E. E., and R. Nisbett (1971). The actor and the observer: divergent perceptions of the causes of behavior. In E. E. Jones *et al.,* (Eds.), *Attribution: perceiving the causes of behavior.* Morristown, N.J.: General Learning Press.

Judd, C. M., J. A. Krosnick, and M. A. Milburn (1981). Political involvement and attitude structure in the general public. *Amer. Sociol. Rev., 46,* 660–669.

Judd, C. M., and M. A. Milburn (1980). The structure of attitude systems in the general public: comparisons of a structural equation model. *Amer. Sociol. Rev., 45,* 627–643.

Kagay, M. R., and G. A. Caldeira (1975). I like the looks of his face: elements of electoral choice, 1952–1972. Paper delivered at the 1975 annual meeting of the American Political Science Association, San Francisco, California.

—— (1980). A "reformed" electorate? Well, at least a changed electorate, 1952–1976. In W. J. Crotty (Ed.), *Paths to political reform.* Lexington, Mass.: D.C. Heath.

Kaplan, R. M., and R. D. Singer (1976). Television violence and viewer aggression: a reexamination of the evidence. *J. soc. Issues, 32,* 35–70.

Katosh, J. P., and M. W. Traugott (1981). The consequences of validated and self-reported voting measures. *Publ. Opin. Quart., 45,* 519–535.

—— (1982). Costs and values in the calculus of voting. *Amer. J. polit. Sci., 26,* 361–376.

Katz, D., and S. J. Eldersveld (1961). The impact of local party activity on the electorate. *Publ. Opin. Quart., 25,* 1–24.

Katz, E., and J. J. Feldman (1962). The debates in the light of research: a survey of surveys. In S. Kraus (Ed.), *The great debates.* Bloomington: Indiana Univ. Press. Pp. 173–223.

Katz, F. E., and F. V. Piret (1964). Circuitous participation in politics. *Amer. J. Sociol., 69,* 367–373.

Katz, P. A. (1976). The acquisition of racial attitudes in children. In P. A. Katz (Ed.), *Towards the elimination of racism.* New York: Pergamon Press.

Katz, R. S. (1979). The dimensionality of party identification: cross-national perspectives. *Comp. polit., 11,* 147–164.

Keith, B. E. *et al.* (1977). The myth of the independent voter. Paper presented at the 1977 annual meeting of the American Political Science Association, Washington, D.C.

Kelley, S., Jr., R. E. Ayres, and W. G. Bowen (1967). Registration and voting: putting first things first. *Amer. polit. Sci. Rev., 61,* 359–379.

Kelley, S., Jr., and T. Mirer (1974). The simple act of voting. *Amer. polit. Sci. Rev., 68,* 572–591.

Kenny, D. A. (1985). Quantitative methods of special interest to social psychologists. In G. Lindzey and E. Aronson (Eds.), *The handbook of social psychology* (3rd ed.). New York: Random House.

Kernell, S. (1976). The Truman doctrine speech: a case study of the dynamics of presidential opinion leadership. *Soc. Sci. Hist., 1,* 20–44.

—— (1977). Presidential popularity and negative voting: an alternative explanation of the midterm congressional decline of the president's party. *Amer. polit. Sci. Rev., 71,* 44–66.

—— (1978). Explaining presidential popularity. *Amer. polit. Sci. Rev., 72,* 506–522.

Kernell, S., and D. A. Hibbs, Jr. (1981). A critical threshold model of presidential popularity. In D. A. Hibbs, Jr. and H. Fassbender (Eds.), *Contemporary political economy.* Amsterdam: North-Holland Publishing.

Key, V. O., Jr. (1955). A theory of critical elections. *J. Politics, 17,* 3–18.

—— (1960). The politically relevant in surveys. *Publ. Opin. Quart., 24,* 54–61.

—— (1961). *Public opinion and American democracy.* New York: Knopf.

—— (1966). *The responsible electorate.* Cambridge, Mass.: Harvard Univ. Press.

Kiewiet, D. R. (1981). Policy-oriented voting in response to economic issues. *Amer. polit. Sci. Rev., 75,* 448–459.

Kim, J., J. R. Petrocik, and S. N. Enokson (1975). Voter turnout among the American states: systematic and individual components. *Amer. polit. Sci. Rev., 69,* 107–123.

Kinder, D. R. (1981). Presidents, prosperity, and public opinion. *Publ. Opin. Quart., 45,* 1–21.

_____ (1984). Presidential character revisited. Paper prepared for the 19th Annual Carnegie Symposium on Cognition. Carnegie-Mellon Univ., Pittsburgh, Pennsylvania.

Kinder, D. R., and R. P. Abelson (1981). Appraising presidential candidates: personality and affect in the 1980 campaign. Paper delivered at the annual meeting of the American Political Science Association, New York City.

_____ (1984). Candidate-centered voting. Unpublished manuscript, ISR, The Univ. of Michigan.

Kinder, D. R., R. P. Abelson, and S. T. Fiske (1979). Developmental research on candidate instrumentation: results and recommendations. Report available from Center for Political Studies, ISR, University of Michigan.

Kinder, D. R., and D. R. Kiewiet (1979). Economic discontent and political behavior: the role of personal grievances and collective economic judgments in congressional voting. *Amer. J. polit. Sci., 23,* 495–527.

_____ (1981). Sociotropic politics. *Brit. J. polit. Sci., 11,* 129–161.

Kinder, D. R., and W. R. Mebane, Jr. (1983). Politics and economics in everyday life. In K. Monroe (Ed.), *The political process and economic change.* New York: Agathon.

Kinder, D. R., M. D. Peters, R. P. Abelson, and S. T. Fiske (1980). Presidential prototypes. *Polit. Behav., 2,* 315–337.

Kinder, D. R., and L. A. Rhodebeck (1982). Continuities in support for racial equality, 1972 to 1976. *Publ. Opin. Quart., 46,* 195–215.

Kinder, D. R., S. J. Rosenstone, and J. M. Hansen (1983). Group economic well-being and political choice. Report available from Center for Political Studies, ISR, The Univ. of Michigan.

Kinder, D. R., and D. O. Sears (1981). Prejudice and politics: symbolic racism versus racial threats to the good life. *J. Pers. soc. Psychol., 40,* 414–431.

Kingdon, J. W. (1973). *Congressmen's voting decisions.* New York: Harper & Row.

Kirby, D. (1971). A counter-culture explanation of student activism. *Soc. Prob., 19,* 203–216.

Kirkpatrick, J. (1976). *The new presidential elite.* New York: Russell Sage and Twentieth Century Fund.

Kirscht, J. P., and R. C. Dillehay (1967). *Dimensions of authoritarianism.* Lexington: Univ. of Kentucky Press.

Klapper, J. T. (1960). *The effects of mass communications.* Glencoe, Ill.: Free Press.

Klecka, W. R. (1971). Applying political generations to the study of political behavior: A cohort analysis. *Publ. Opin. Quart., 35,* 358–373.

Klein, E. D. (1984). *Gender politics: the rise of the contemporary feminist movement.* Cambridge, Mass.: Harvard Univ. Press.

Klingemann, H. D. (1979). Measuring ideological conceptualizations. In S. H. Barnes and Max Kaase *et al., Political action: mass participation in five western democracies.* Beverly Hills, Calif.: Sage. Pp. 215–254.

Klingemann, H. D., and W. E. Wright (1973). Modes of conceptualization and the organization of issue beliefs in mass

publics. Paper presented at the World Congress of the International Political Science Association, Montreal, Canada.

Knoke, D. (1973). Intergenerational occupational mobility and the political party preferences of American man. *Amer. J. Sociol., 78,* 1448–1468.

_____ (1977). *Change and continuity in American politics. The social bases of political parties.* Baltimore: Johns Hopkins.

_____ (1979). Stratification and the dimensions of American political orientations. *Amer. J. polit. Sci., 23,* 772–791.

Knutson, J. N. (1972). *The human basis of the polity.* Chicago: Aldine.

Kramer, G. H. (1970). The effects of precinct-level canvassing on voter behavior. *Publ. Opin. Quart., 34,* 560–572.

_____ (1971). Short-term fluctuations in U.S. voting behavior, 1896–1964. *Amer. polit. Sci. Rev., 65,* 131–143.

_____ (1983). The ecological fallacy revisited: aggregate versus individual level findings on economics and elections and sociotropic voting. *Amer. polit. Sci. Rev. 77,* 92–111.

Kraus, S., and D. Davis (1976). *The effects of mass communication on political behavior.* University Park: Pennsylvania State Univ. Press.

Kraut, R. E., and J. B. McConahay (1973). How being interviewed affects voting: an experiment. *Publ. Opin. Quart., 37,* 393–406.

Ladd, E. C., Jr., and C. D. Hadley (1975). *Transformations of the American party system.* New York: Norton.

Ladd, E. C., Jr., and S. M. Lipset (1981). Public opinion and public policy. In. P. Duignan and A. Rabushka (Eds.), *The United States in the 1980's.* Stanford: Hoover Institution.

Lamb, K. A. (1974). *As orange goes.* New York: Norton.

Lambert, W. E., and O. Klineberg (1967). *Children's views of foreign peoples.* New York: Appleton-Century-Crofts.

Lane, R. E. (1959). *Political life: why and how people get involved in politics.* New York: Free Press.

_____ (1962). *Political ideology.* New York: Free Press.

_____ (1963). Political science and psychology. In S. Koch (Ed.), *Psychology: a study of a science.* Vol. 6. *Investigations of Man as Socius.* New York: McGraw-Hill.

_____ (1969). *Political thinking and consciousness: the private life of the political mind.* Chicago: Markham Publishing.

_____ (1973). Patterns of political belief. In J. Knutson (Ed.), *Handbook of political psychology.* San Francisco: Jossey-Bass.

Langton, K. P. (1969). *Political socialization.* Boston: Little, Brown.

Lao, R. C. (1970). Internal-external control and competent innovative behavior among Negro college students. *J. Pers. soc. Psychol., 14,* 263–270.

Lau, R. R., T. A. Brown, and D. D. Sears (1978). Self-interest and civilians' attitudes toward the Vietnam War. *Publ. Opin. Quart., 42,* 464–483.

Lau, R. R., and D. O. Sears (1981). Cognitive links between economic grievances and political responses. *Polit. Behav., 3,* 279–302.

Lawson, E. D. (1963). Development of patriotism in children: a second look. *J. Psychol., 55,* 279–286.

Lazarsfeld, P. F., B. Berelson, and H. Gaudet (1948). *The people's choice* (2nd ed.). New York: Columbia Univ. Press.

Leahy, R. L. (1983). *The child's construction of social inequality.* New York: Academic Press.

LeBon, G. (1896). *The crowd: a study of the popular mind.* London: Ernest Benn.

Leventhal, H. (1980). Toward a comprehensive theory of emotion. In L. Berkowitz (Ed.), *Advances in experimental social psychology, 13.* New York: Academic Press.

Levitin, T. E., and W. E. Miller (1979). Ideological interpretations of presidential elections. *Amer. polit. Sci. Rev., 73,* 751–771.

Lieberson, S., and A. R. Silverman (1965). The precipitants and underlying conditions of race riots. *Amer. Sociol. Rev., 30,* 887–898.

Lippmann, W. (1922). *Public opinion.* New York: Macmillan.

Lipset, S. M. (1960). *Political man.* New York: Doubleday.

_____ (1963a). *The first new nation.* New York: Basic Books.

_____ (1963b). Three decades of the radical right: Coughlinites, McCarthyites, and Birchers. In D. Bell (Ed.), *The radical right.* New York: Anchor.

Lipset, S. M., P. F. Lazarsfeld, A. H. Barton, and J. Linz (1954). The psychology of voting: an analysis of political behavior. In G. Lindzey (Ed.), *Handbook of social psychology.* Vol. 2. Reading, Mass.: Addison-Wesley. Pp. 1124–1175.

Lipset, S. M., and W. Schneider (1978). The Bakke case: how would it be decided at the bar of public opinion? *Publ. Opin., 1,* 38–44.

_____ (1981). From discrimination to affirmative action: public attitudes 1935–1980. Washington, D.C.: American Enterprise Institute.

Lodge, M., and B. Tursky (1979). Comparisons between category and magnitude scaling of political opinion employing SRC/CPS items. *Amer. polit. Sci. Rev., 73,* 50–66.

Lopreato, J. (1967). Upward social mobility and political orientation. *Amer. Sociol. Rev., 32,* 586–592.

Lowery, D., and L. Sigelman (1981). Understanding the tax revolt: eight explanations. *Amer. polit. Sci. Rev., 75,* 963–974.

Lukes, S. (1973). *Individualism.* Oxford: Blackwell.

McClosky, H. (1958). Conservatism and personality. *Amer. polit. Sci. Rev., 52,* 27–45.

_____ (1964). Consensus and ideology in American politics. *Amer. polit. Sci. Rev., 58,* 361–382.

_____ (1967). Personality and attitude correlates of foreign policy orientations. In J. Rosenau (Ed.), *Domestic sources of foreign policy.* New York: Free Press. Pp. 51–109.

McClosky, H., P. J. Hoffman, and R. O'Hara (1960). Issue conflict and consensus among party leaders and followers. *Amer. polit. Sci. Rev., 54,* 406–427.

McCombs, M. E., and D. L. Shaw (1972). The agenda-setting function of the media. *Publ. Opin. Quart., 36,* 176–187.

McConahay, J. B. (1982). Self-interest versus racial attitudes as correlates of anti-busing attitudes in Louisville. *J. Pol., 44,* 692–720.

McConahay, J. B., and J. C. Hough, Jr. (1976). Symbolic racism. *J. soc. Issues, 32,* 23–46.

McGuire, W. J. (1969). The nature of attitudes and attitude change. In G. Lindzey and E. Aronson (Eds.), *The handbook of social psychology.* Vol. 3. (2nd ed.). Reading, Mass.: Addison-Wesley. Pp. 136–314.

MacKuen, M. B. (1981). Social communication and the mass policy agenda. In M. B. MacKuen and S. L. Coombs (Eds.), *More than news: media power in public affairs.* Beverly Hills, Calif.: Sage. Pp. 19–144.

Mann, T. E. (1978). *Unsafe at any margin: interpreting congressional elections.* Washington, D.C.: American Enterprise Institute.

Mann, T. E., and R. E. Wolfinger (1980). Candidates and parties in congressional elections. *Amer. polit. Sci. Rev., 74,* 617–632.

Mannheim, K. (1952). The problem of generations. In P. Kecskemet (Ed.), *Essays on the sociology of knowledge.* London: Routledge and Kegan Paul.

Marcus, G. E., D. Tabb, and J. L. Sullivan (1974). The application of individual differences scaling to the measurement of political ideologies. *Amer. J. polit. Sci., 18,* 405–420.

Margolis, M. (1977). From confusion to confusion: issues and the American voter, 1956–1972. *Amer. polit. Sci. Rev., 71,* 31–43.

Markus, G. B. (1979). The political environment and the dynamics of public attitudes: a panel study. *Amer. J. polit. Sci., 23,* 338–359.

_____ (1982). Political attitudes during an election year: a report of the 1980 NES Panel Study. *Amer. polit. Sci. Rev., 76,* 538–560.

_____ (1984). Recollections and rationalizations of political attitude change. Paper prepared for the 19th Annual Carnegie Symposium on Cognition. Carnegie-Mellon University, Pittsburgh, Pennsylvania.

Markus, G. B., and P. E. Converse (1979). A dynamic simultaneous equation model of electoral choice. *Amer. polit. Sci. Rev., 73,* 1055–1070.

Marsh, A. (1977). *Protest and political consciousness.* Beverly Hills, Calif. and London: Sage.

Marsh, D. (1971). Political socialization: the implicit assumptions questioned. *Brit. J. polit. Sci., 1,* 453–465.

Maslow, A. H. (1954). *Motivation and personality.* New York: Harper.

Mason, K. O., W. M. Mason, H. H. Winsborough, and W. K. Poole (1973). Some methodological issues in cohort analysis of archival data. *Amer. Sociol. Rev., 38,* 242–258.

Mason, W. M. (1973). The impact of endorsements on voting. *Sociol. Meth. Res., 1,* 463–495.

Matthews, D. R. (1978). Winnowing. In J. D. Barker (Ed.), *Race for the presidency.* Englewood Cliffs, N.J.: Prentice-Hall.

Matthews, D. R., and J. W. Prothro (1966). The concept of party image and its importance for the southern electorate. In M. K. Jennings and L. H. Zeigler (Eds.), *The electoral process.* Englewood Cliffs, N.J.: Prentice-Hall. Pp. 139–174.

Mebane, W. R. (1982). The warp of sociotropic thinking. Paper delivered at the annual meeting of the Midwest Political Science Association, Milwaukee, Wisconsin.

Meehl, P. E. (1977). The selfish voter paradox and the thrown-away vote argument. *Amer. polit. Sci. Rev., 71,* 11–30.

Meier, K. J., and J. E. Campbell (1979). Issue voting. An empirical examination of individually necessary and jointly sufficient conditions. *Amer. Polit. Quart., 7,* 21–50.

Mellman, M. S. (1981). Mass media and public opinion toward defense spending. Unpublished manuscript. Department of Political Science, Yale University.

Merriam, C. E. (1931). *The making of citizens.* Chicago: Univ. of Chicago Press.

Merriam, C. E., and H. F. Gosnell (1924). *Non-voting, causes and methods of control.* Chicago: Univ. of Chicago Press.

Merton, R. K. (1957). *Social theory and social structure.* New York: Free Press.

Middleton, M. R., H. Tajfel, and N. B. Johnson (1970). Cognitive and affective aspects of children's national attitudes. *Brit. J. soc. clinic. Psychol., 9,* 122–134.

Milbrath, L. W., and M. L. Goel (1977). *Political participation* (2nd ed.). Chicago: Rand McNally.

Miller, A. H. (1974). Political issues and trust in government: 1964–1970. *Amer. polit. Sci. Rev., 68,* 951–972.

———— (1979). Normal vote analysis: sensitivity to change over time. *Amer. J. polit. Sci., 23,* 406–420.

Miller, A. H., E. N. Goldenberg, and L. Erbring (1979). Typeset politics: impact of newspapers on public confidence. *Amer. polit. Sci. Rev., 73,* 67–84.

Miller, A. H., P. Gurin, and G. Gurin (1978). Electoral implications of group identification and consciousness: the reintroduction of a concept. Paper prepared for delivery at the annual meeting of the American Political Science Association, New York.

Miller, A. H., P. Gurin, G. Gurin, and O. Malanchuk (1981). Group consciousness and political participation. *Amer. J. polit. Sci., 25,* 494–511.

Miller, A. H., and W. E. Miller (1976). Ideology in the 1972 election: myth or reality. *Amer. polit. Sci. Rev., 70,* 832–849.

———— (1977). Partisanship and performance: "rational" choice in the 1976 presidential election. Paper presented at annual meeting of the American Political Science Association.

Miller, S., and D. O. Sears (1982). Social background, adulthood change, and tolerance. Unpublished manuscript. University of California, Los Angeles.

———— (1983). Stability and change in social tolerance: a test of the persistence hypothesis. Unpublished manuscript. University of California, Los Angeles.

Miller, W. E. (1980). Disinterest, disaffection, and participation in presidential elections. *Polit. Behav., 2,* 7–32.

Miller, W. E., A. H. Miller, and E. J. Schneider (1980). *American national election studies data sourcebook, 1952–1978.* Cambridge, Mass.: Harvard Univ. Press.

Miller, W. E., and J. M. Shanks (1982). Policy directions and presidential leadership: alternative interpretations of the 1980 presidential election. *Brit. J. polit. Sci., 12,* 299–356.

Miller, W. E., and D. E. Stokes (1966a). Constituency influence in Congress. In A. Campbell, P. E. Converse, W. E. Miller, and D. E. Stokes, *Elections and the political order.* New York: Wiley.

———— (1966b). Party government and the saliency of government. In A. Campbell *et al.* (Eds.), *Elections and the political order.* New York: Wiley.

Minow, N. N., J. B. Martin, and L. M. Mitchell (1973). *Presidential television.* New York: Basic Books.

Monroe, K. R. (1979). Econometric analyses of electoral behavior: a critical review. *Polit. Behav., 1,* 137–174.

Moore, Barrington, Jr. (1978). *Injustice: the social bases of obedience and revolt.* White Plains, N.Y.: M.E. Sharpe.

Mueller, J. E. (1970). Choosing among 133 candidates. *Publ. Opin. Quart., 34,* 395–402.

———— (1973). *War, presidents, and public opinion.* New York: Wiley.

Muller, E. (1970). Cross-national dimensions of political competence. *Amer. polit. Sci. Rev., 64,* 792–809.

———— (1972). A test of a partial theory of potential for political violence. *Amer. polit. Sci. Rev., 66,* 928–959.

———— (1979). *Aggressive political participation.* Princeton, N.J.: Princeton Univ. Press.

Myrdal, G. (1944). *An American dilemma.* New York: Harper & Row.

Nelson, C. J. (1978). The effect of incumbency on voting in congressional elections, 1964–1974. *Polit. Sci. Quart., 93,* 665–678.

Neuman, W. R. (1976). Patterns of recall among television news viewers. *Publ. Opin. Quart., 40,* 115–123.

Newcomb, T. M. (1943). *Personality and social change.* New York: Dryden Press.

Newcomb, T. M., K. E. Koenig, R. Flacks, and D. P. Warwick (1967). *Persistence and change: Bennington college and its students after 25 years.* New York: Wiley.

Nie, N. H., and K. Andersen (1974). Mass belief systems revisited: political change and attitude structure. *J. Polit., 36,* 540–591.

Nie, N. H., G. Powell, G. B. Bingham, Jr., and K. Prewitt (1969a). Social structure and political participation. *Amer. polit. Sci. Rev., 62,* 361–378.

———— (1969b). Social structure and political participation. *Amer. polit. Sci. Rev., 63,* 808–832.

Nie, N. H., and S. Verba (1975). Political participation. In F. I. Greenstein and N. W. Polsby (Eds.), *Handbook of political science.* Vol. 4. Reading, Mass.: Addison-Wesley.

Nie, N. H., S. Verba, and J. R. Petrocik (1979). *The changing American voter* (Enlarged ed.). Cambridge, Mass.: Harvard Univ. Press.

———— (1981). Reply. *Amer. polit. Sci. Rev., 75,* 149–152.

Niemi, R. G., R. S. Katz, and D. Newman (1980). Reconstructing past partisanship: the failure of the party identification recall questions. *Amer. J. polit. Sci., 24,* 633–651.

Norpoth, H., and J. Rusk (1982). Partisan dealignment in the American electorate: itemizing the deductions since 1964. *Amer. polit. Sci. Rev., 76,* 522–537.

Nunn, C. Z., H. J. Crockett, Jr., and J. A. Williams, Jr. (1978). *Tolerance for nonconformity.* San Francisco: Jossey-Bass.

Nygren, T. E., and L. E. Jones (1977). Individual differences in perceptions and preferences for political candidates. *J. exp. soc. Psychol., 13,* 182–197.

Olson, M. (1965). *The logic of collective action: public goods and the theory of groups.* Cambridge, Mass.: Harvard Univ. Press.

Olson, M. (1970). Social and political participation of blacks. *Amer. Sociol. Rev., 35,* 682–697.

Orbell, J. M. (1967). Protest participation among southern Negro college students. *Amer. polit. Sci. Rev., 61,* 446–456.

Ordershook, P. C. (1976). The spatial theory of elections: a review and a critique. In I. Budge, I. Crewe, and D. Farlie (Eds.), *Party identification and beyond.* London: Wiley.

Page, B. I. (1978). *Choices and echoes in presidential elections.* Chicago: Univ. of Chicago Press.

Page, B. I., and R. A. Brody (1972). Policy voting and the electoral process: the Vietnam war issue. *Amer. polit. Sci. Rev., 66,* 979–995.

Page, B. I., and C. C. Jones (1979). Reciprocal effects of policy preference, party loyalties, and the vote. *Amer. polit. Sci. Rev., 73,* 1071–1089.

Paige, J. M. (1971). Political orientation and riot participation. *Amer. Sociol. Rev., 36,* 810–820.

Pammett, J. H. (1971). The development of political orientations in Canadian school children. *Canad. J. polit. Sci., 4,* 132–141.

Parker, G. (1981). Incumbent popularity and electoral success. In L. S. Maisel and J. Cooper (Eds.), *Congressional elections.* Beverly Hills, Calif.: Sage.

Pateman, C. (1970). *Participation and democratic theory.* London: Cambridge Univ. Press.

Patterson, T. E. (1980). *The mass media election: how Americans choose their president.* New York: Praeger.

Patterson, T. E., and R. D. McClure (1976). *The unseeing eye: the myth of television power in national elections.* New York: Putnam.

Peters, J. G., and S. Welch (1980). The effects of charges of corruption on voting behavior in congressional elections. *Amer. polit. Sci. Rev., 74,* 697–708.

Peterson, S. A., and A. Somit (1982). Cognitive development and childhood political socialization: questions about the primacy principle. *Amer. Behav. Sci., 25,* 313–334.

Petrocik, J. R. (1974). An analysis of intransitivities in the index of party identification. *Polit. Meth., 1,* 31–48.

——— (1979). Levels of issue voting: the effect of candidate-pairs in presidential elections. *Amer. Polit. Quart., 7,* 303–327.

——— (1980). Contextual sources of voting behavior. In J. C. Pierce and J. L. Sullivan (Eds.), *The electorate reconsidered.* Beverly Hills, Calif.: Sage. Pp. 257–278.

——— (1981). *Party coalitions, realignments, and the decline of the new deal party system.* Chicago: Univ. of Chicago Press.

Pettigrew, T. F. (1967). Social evaluation theory: convergence and application. In D. Levine (Ed.), *Nebraska symposium on motivation,* 241–318. Lincoln: Univ. of Nebraska Press.

Pierce, J. C. (1970). Party identification and the changing role of ideology in American politics. *Midwest J. polit. Sci., 14,* 25–42.

Pierce, J. C., and P. R. Hagner (1982). Conceptualization and party identification: 1956–1976. *Amer. J. polit. Sci., 26,* 377–387.

Pierce, J. C., and D. D. Rose (1974). Nonattitudes and American public opinion. *Amer. polit. Sci. Rev., 68,* 626–649.

Pierce, R., and P. E. Converse (1980). Candidate visibility in France and the United States. Paper delivered to the 1980 annual meeting of the American Political Science Association, Washington, D.C.

Piereson, J. E. (1975). Presidential popularity and mid-term voting at different electoral levels. *Amer. J. polit. Sci., 19,* 683–694.

Piven, F. F., and R. A. Cloward (1977). *Poor people's movements: why they succeed, how they fail.* New York: Vintage Books.

Pole, J. R. (1978). *The pursuit of equality in American history.* Berkeley: Univ. of California.

Pomper, G. M. (1972). From confusion to clarity: issues and American voters, 1956–1968. *Amer. polit. Sci. Rev., 66,* 415–428.

——— (1975). *Voters' choice: varieties of American electoral behavior.* New York: Dodd, Mead.

Poole, K. T. (1981). Dimensions of interest group evaluation of the U.S. *Amer. J. polit. Sci., 25,* 49–67.

Popkin, S., J. W. Gorman, C. Phillips, and J. A. Smith (1976). Comment: what have you done for me lately? toward an investment theory of voting. *Amer. polit. Sci. Rev., 70,* 779–805.

Powell, G. B., Jr. (1980). Voting turnout in thirty democracies: partisan, legal, and socio-economic influences. In R. Rose (Ed.), *Electoral participation: a comparative analysis.* Beverly Hills, Calif.: Sage.

Prothro, J. W., and C. M. Grigg (1960). Fundamental principles of democracy: bases of agreement and disagreement. *J. Polit., 22,* 276–294.

Putnam, R. D., R. Leonardi, and R. Y. Nanetti (1979). Attitude stability among Italian elites. *Amer. J. polit. Sci., 23,* 463–494.

Rabinowitz, G., J. W. Prothro, and W. Jacoby (1982). Salience as a factor in the impact of issues on candidate evaluation. *J. Polit., 42,* 41–63.

Ragsdale, L. (1980). The fiction of congressional elections as presidential events. *Amer. Polit. Quart., 8,* 375–398.

Reading, R. R. (1968). Political socialization in Colombia and the United States: an exploratory study. *Mid. J. polit. Sci., 12,* 352–381.

Renshon, S. A., Ed. (1977). *Handbook of political socialization: theory and research.* New York: Free Press.

RePass, D. E. (1971). Issue salience and party choice. *Amer. polit. Sci. Rev., 65,* 389–400.

Riker, W. H., and P. C. Ordershook (1968). A theory of the calculus of voting. *Amer. polit. Sci. Rev., 62,* 25–42.

——— (1973). *An introduction to positive political theory.* Englewood Cliffs, N.J.: Prentice-Hall.

Rivers, D. (1980). The dynamics of party support in the American electorate, 1952–1976. Prepared for the 1980 annual meeting of the American Political Science Association.

Robinson, J. P. (1971). The audience for national TV news programs. *Publ. Opin. Quart., 35,* 403–405.

―――― (1972). Mass communication and information diffusion. In F. G. Kline and P. J. Tichenor (Eds.), *Current perspectives in mass communication research.* Beverly Hills, Calif.: Sage.

―――― (1974). The press as king-maker. *J. Quart., 51,* 587–594.

Robinson, M. J. (1976). Public affairs television and the growth of political malaise: the case of "the selling of the Pentagon." *Amer. polit. Sci. Rev., 70,* 409–432.

Roig, C., and F. Billon-Grand (1968). La socialisation politique des enfants. *Cahiers de la fondation nationale des sciences politique,* Paris, No. 163.

Rokeach, M. (1960). *The open and closed mind: investigations into the nature of belief systems and personality systems.* New York: Basic Books.

―――― (1969). *Beliefs, attitudes, and values: a theory of organization and change.* San Francisco: Jossey-Bass.

―――― (1973). *The nature of human values.* New York: Free Press.

Rose, R., Ed. (1974). *Electoral behavior: a comparative handbook.* New York: Free Press.

Roseman, I. (1979). Cognitive aspects of emotion and emotional behavior. Paper delivered at the 87th annual meeting of the American Psychological Association, New York.

Rosenberg, M. (1956). Misanthropy and political ideology. *Amer. Sociol. Rev., 21,* 690–695.

Rosenberg, M. J. (1968). Hedonism, inauthenticity, and other goads toward expansion of consistency theory. In R. P. Abelson *et al.* (Eds.), *Theories of cognitive consistency: a sourcebook.* Chicago: Rand McNally.

Rosenberg, M. J., S. Verba, and P. E. Converse (1970). *Vietnam and the silent majority: the dove's guide.* New York: Harper & Row.

Rosenberg, S. (1977). New approaches to the analysis of personal constructs in person perception. In D. Levine (Ed.), *Nebraska symposium on motivation.* Vol. 24. Lincoln: Nebraska Univ. Press.

Rosenstone, S. J. (1982). Economic adversity and voter turnout. *Amer. J. polit. Sci., 26,* 25–46.

―――― (1983). *Forecasting presidential elections.* New Haven: Yale Univ. Press.

Rosenstone, S. J., and R. E. Wolfinger (1978). The effect of registration laws on voter turnout. *Amer. polit. Sci. Rev., 72,* 22–45.

Rosi, E. J. (1965). Mass and attentive opinion on nuclear weapons tests and fallout, 1954–1963. *Publ. Opin. Quart, 29,* 280–297.

Rossi, P. H. (1959). Four landmarks in voting research. In E. Burdick and A. J. Brodbeck (Eds.), *American voting behavior.* Glencoe, Ill.: Free Press. Pp. 5–54.

Rubin, B. (1967). *Political television.* Belmont, Calif.: Wadsworth Publishing.

Rubin, Z. (1973). *Liking and loving.* New York: Holt, Rinehart, and Winston.

Rubinstein, E. A. (1980). Television violence: a historical perspective. In E. L. Palmer and A. Dorr (Eds.), *Children and the faces of television: teaching, violence, selling.* New York: Academic Press. Pp. 113–128.

Runciman, W. G. (1966). *Relative deprivation and social justice: a study of attitudes to social inequality in twentieth-century England.* London: Routledge and Kegan Paul.

Rusk, J. G. (1974). Comment. *Amer. polit. Sci. Rev., 68,* 1028–1049.

Rusk, J. G., and H. G. Weisberg (1972). Perceptions of presidential candidates: implications for electoral change. *Mid. J. polit. Sci., 16,* 338–410.

Ryan, W. (1971). *Blaming the victim.* New York: Random House.

Schattschneider, E. E. (1960). *The semi-sovereign people.* Hinsdale, Ill.: The Dryden Press.

Schlozman, K. L., and S. Verba (1979). *Injury to insult.* Cambridge, Mass.: Harvard Univ. Press.

Schneider, D. J. (1973). Implicit personality theory: a review. *Psychol. Bull., 79,* 294–309.

Schneider, W. J. (1982). Bang-bang television: the new superpower. *Publ. Opin., 5,* 13–15.

Schoenberger, R. A. (1969). Campaign strategy and party loyalty: the electoral relevance of candidate decision-making in the 1964 congressional elections. *Amer. polit. Sci. Rev., 63,* 515–520.

Schultz, C., and J. R. Petrocik (1982). Belligerent neutrality: how the press helps the voter decide. Paper prepared for delivery at the annual meeting of the Midwest Political Science Association, Milwaukee, Wisconsin.

Schuman, H. (1973). Two sources of antiwar sentiment in America. *Amer. J. Sociol., 78,* 513–536.

Schuman, H., and G. Kalton (1985). Survey methods and interviewing. In G. Lindzey and E. Aronson (Eds.), *The handbook of social psychology* (3rd ed.). New York: Random House.

Schuman, H., and S. Presser (1980). Public opinion and public ignorance: the fine line between attitude and non-attitude. *Amer. J. Sociol., 85,* 1214–1225.

―――― (1981). *Questions and answers in attitude surveys: experiments on question form, wording, and context.* New York: Academic Press.

Scott, W. J., and A. C. Acock (1979). Socioeconomic status, unemployment experience, and political participation. *Polit. Behav., 1,* 361–381.

Searing, D. D., J. J. Schwartz, and A. E. Lind (1973). The structuring principle: political socialization and belief systems. *Amer. polit. Sci. Rev., 67,* 415–432.

Searing, D. D., G. Wright, and G. Rabinowitz (1976). The primacy principle: attitude change and political socialization. *Brit. J. polit. Sci., 6,* 83–113.

Sears, D. O. (1968). The paradox of de facto selective exposure without preferences for supportive information. In R. P. Abelson, E. Aronson, W. J. McGuire, T. M. Newcomb, M. J. Rosenberg, and P. H. Tannenbaum (Eds.), *Theories of cognitive consistency: a sourcebook.* Chicago: Rand McNally. Pp. 777–787.

―――― (1969). Political behavior. In G. Lindzey and E. Aronson (Eds.), *Handbook of social psychology* (2nd ed.). Vol. 5. Reading, Mass.: Addison-Wesley.

―――― (1975). Political socialization. In F. I. Greenstein and N. W. Polsby (Eds.), *Handbook of political science.* Vol. 2. Reading, Mass.: Addison-Wesley. Pp. 96–136.

_____ (1981a). Life stage effects upon attitude change, especially among the elderly. In S. B. Kiesler, J. N. Morgan, and V. K. Oppenheimer (Eds.), *Aging: social change.* New York: Academic Press.

_____ (1981b). Aging and political behavior. Unpublished manuscript. University of California, Los Angeles.

_____ (1983). The person-positivity bias. *J. Pers. soc. Psychol., 44,* 233–250.

_____ (1983). On the persistence of early political dispositions: attitude objects and life stages. In L. Wheeler (Ed.), *Review of personality and social psychology.* Vol. 4.

Sears, D. O., H. M. Allen, Jr. (1984). The trajectory of local desegregation controversies and whites' opposition to busing. In M. Brewer and N. Miller (Eds.), *Groups in contact: the psychology of desegregation.* New York: Academic Press.

Sears, D. O., and S. H. Chaffee (1979). Uses and effects of the 1976 debates: an overview of empirical studies. In S. Kraus (Ed.), *The great debates, 1976: Ford vs. Carter.* Bloomington: Indiana Univ. Press. Pp. 223–261.

Sears, D. O., and J. Citrin (1982). *Tax revolt: something for nothing in California.* Cambridge, Mass.: Harvard Univ. Press.

Sears, D. O., and J. L. Freedman (1967). Selective exposure to information: a critical review. *Publ. Opin. Quart. 31,* 194–213.

Sears, D. O., and M. T. Gahart (1980). The stability of racial prejudice and other symbolic attitudes. Paper presented at the annual meeting of the American Psychological Association, Montreal.

Sears, D. O., C. P. Hensler, and L. K. Speer (1979). Whites' opposition to "busing": self-interest or symbolic racism? *Amer. polit. Sci. Rev., 73,* 369–384.

Sears, D. O., and D. R. Kinder (1971). Racial tensions and voting in Los Angeles. In W. Z. Hirsch (Ed.), *Los Angeles: viability and prospects for metropolitan leadership.* New York: Praeger. Pp. 51–88.

Sears. D. O., and R. R. Lau (1983). Inducing apparently self-interested political preferences. *Amer. J. polit. Sci., 27,* 223–252.

Sears, D. O., R. R. Lau, T. Tyler, and A. M. Allen, Jr. (1980). Self-interest versus symbolic politics in policy attitudes and presidential voting. *Amer. polit. Sci. Rev., 74,* 670–684.

Sears, D. O., and J. S. McConahay (1973). *The politics of violence: the new urban blacks and the Watts riot.* Boston: Houghton Mifflin.

Sears, D. O., T. R. Tyler, T. Citrin, and D. R. Kinder (1978). Political system support and public response to the energy crisis. *Amer. J. polit. Sci., 22,* 56–82.

Sears, D. O., and R. E. Whitney (1973). *Political persuasion.* Morristown, N.J.: General Learning Press.

Sennett, R., and J. Cobb (1972). *The hidden injuries of class.* New York: Vintage Books. P. 275.

Shaffer, S. D. (1981). A multivariate explanation of decreasing turnout in presidential elections, 1960–1976. *Amer. J. polit. Sci., 25,* 68–95.

Sharon, A. T. (1973). Racial differences in newspaper readership. *Publ. Opin. Quart., 37,* 611–617.

Sheatsley, P. B., and J. J. Feldman (1965). A national survey of public reactions and behavior. In B. S. Greenberg and E. B. Parker (Eds.), *The Kennedy assassination and the American public.* Stanford: Standford Univ. Press. Pp. 149–177.

Sherif, M., and H. Cantril (1947). *The psychology of ego-involvements.* New York: Wiley.

Shils, E. A., and M. Janowitz (1948). Cohesion and disintegration in the Wehrmacht in World War II. *Publ. Opin. Quart., 12,* 280–315.

Shively, W. P. (1980). The nature of party identification: a review of recent developments. In J. C. Pierce and J. L. Sullivan (Eds.), *The electorate reconsidered.* Beverly Hills, Calif.: Sage.

Shorter, E., and C. Tilly (1974). *Strikes in France, 1830–1968.* Cambridge: Cambridge Univ. Press.

Sigal, L. V. (1973). *Reporters and officials: the organization and politics of newsmaking.* Lexington, Mass.: D.C. Heath.

Sigel, R. S., and M. B. Hoskin (1977). Perspectives on adult political socialization—areas of research. In S. A. Renshon (Ed.), *Handbook of political socialization: theory and research.* New York: Free Press. Pp. 259–293.

Sigelman, L., and S. Feldman (1982). Efficacy, mistrust, and political mobilization: a cross-national analysis. Unpublished manuscript. Department of Political Science, University of Kentucky.

Sigelman, L., and T. Tsai (1981). Personal finances and voting behavior. *Amer. Polit. Quart., 9,* 371–400.

Silvern, L. E., C. Y. Nakamura (1971). Powerlessness, social-political action, social-political views: their interrelation among college students. *J. soc. Issues, 27,* 137–157.

Simmons, R. G., and M. Rosenberg (1971). Functions of children's perceptions of the stratification system. *Amer. Sociol. Rev., 36,* 235–249.

Simpson, E. L. (1977). Preference and politics: values in political psychology and political learning. In S. A. Renshon (Ed.), *Handbook of political socialization: theory and research.* New York: Free Press. Pp. 362–388.

Skocpol, T. (1978). *States and social revolutions: a comparative analysis of France, Russia, and China.* Cambridge: Cambridge Univ. Press.

Smith, E. R. A. N. (1980). The levels of conceptualization: false measures of ideological sophistication. *Amer. polit. Sci. Rev., 74,* 685–696.

Smith, G. D. (1978). The pulse of presidential popularity: Kennedy in crisis. Unpublished doctoral dissertation. University of California, Los Angeles.

Smith, M. B., J. S. Bruner, and R. W. White (1956). *Opinions and personality.* New York: Wiley.

Smith, S. S. (1981). The consistency and ideological structure of U.S. Senate voting alignments, 1957–1976. *Amer. J. polit. Sci., 25,* 780–795.

Sniderman, P. M. (1975). Personality and democratic politics. Berkeley: Univ. of California Press.

_____ (1981). *A question of loyalty.* Berkeley: Univ. of California Press.

Sniderman, P. M., and R. A. Brody (1977). Coping: the ethic of self-reliance. *Amer. J. polit. Sci., 21,* 501–522.

Sniderman, P. M., and J. Citrin (1971). Psychological sources of political belief: self-esteem and isolationist attitudes. *Amer. polit. Sci. Rev., 65,* 401–417.

Snyder, D. (1975). Institutional setting and industrial conflict: comparative analyses of France, Italy, and the United States. *Amer. Sociol. Rev., 40,* 259–278.

Snyder, D., and C. Tilly (1972). Hardship and collective violence in France, 1830 to 1960. *Amer. Sociol. Rev., 37,* 520–532.

Spilerman, S. (1970). The causes of racial disturbances: a comparison of alternative explanations. *Amer. Sociol. Rev., 35,* 627–649.

_____ (1971). The causes of racial disturbances: tests of an explanation. *Amer. Sociol. Rev., 36,* 427–442.

_____ (1976). Structural characteristics of cities and the severity of racial disorders. *Amer. Sociol. Rev., 41,* 771–792.

Stanley, H. (1981). The political impact of electoral mobilization: the south and universal suffrage, 1952–1980. Unpublished doctoral dissertation. Department of Political Science, Yale University.

Stimson, J. A. (1975). Belief systems: constraint, complexity, and the 1972 election. *Amer. J. polit. Sci., 19,* 393–418.

Stacey, B. (1977). *Political socialization in western society.* New York: St. Martin's Press.

Star, S. A., and H. M. Hughes (1950). Report on an educational campaign: the Cincinnati plan for the United Nations. *Amer. J. Sociol., 55,* 389–400.

Stokes, D. E. (1962). Popular evaluations of government: an empirical assessment. In H. Cleveland and H. D. Lasswell (Eds.), *Ethics and bigness: scientific, academic, religious, political, and military.* New York: Harper.

_____ (1966a). Party loyalty and the likelihood of deviating elections. In A. Campbell, P. E. Converse, W. E. Miller, and D. E. Stokes, *Elections and the political order.* New York: Wiley. Pp. 125–135.

_____ (1966b). Some dynamic elements of contests for the presidency. *Amer. polit. Sci. Rev., 60,* 19–28.

Stokes, D. E., and W. E. Miller (1962). Party government and the saliency of Congress. *Publ. Opin. Quart., 26,* 531–546.

Stouffer, S. A. (1955). *Communism, conformity, and civil liberties.* New York: Doubleday.

Stouffer, S. A., E. A. Suchman, L. C. DeVinney, S. A. Star, and R. M. Williams, Jr. (1949). *The American soldier.* Princeton, N.J.: Princeton Univ. Press.

Strumpel, B. (1976). Economic life styles, values, and subjective welfare. In B. Strumpel (Ed.), *Economic means for human needs.* Ann Arbor, Mich.: Institute for Sociological Research.

Sullivan, D. G. (1966). Psychological balance and reactions to the presidential nominations in 1960. In M. K. Jennings and L. H. Zeigler (Eds.), *The electoral process.* Englewood Cliffs, N.J.: Prentice-Hall.

Sullivan, J. L., G. E. Marcus, S. Feldman, and J. E. Piereson (1981). The sources of political tolerance: a multivariate analysis. *Amer. polit. Sci. Rev., 75,* 92–106.

Sullivan, J. L., J. E. Piereson, and G. E. Marcus (1978). Ideological constraint in the mass public: a methodological critique and some new findings. *Amer. J. polit. Sci., 22,* 233–249.

_____ (1979). An alternative conceptualization of political tolerance: illusory increases 1950s–1970s. *Amer. polit. Sci. Rev., 73,* 781–794.

Sullivan, J. L., J. E Piereson, G. E. Marcus, and S. Feldman (1979). The more things change, the more they stay the same: the stability of mass belief systems. *Amer. J. polit. Sci., 23,* 176–186.

Sundquist, J. L. (1973). *Dynamics of the party system.* Washington, D.C.: Brookings Institution.

Szalai, A., Ed. (1972). *The use of time: daily activities of urban and suburban populations in twelve countries.* The Hague: Mouton.

Tajfel, H. (1969). Cognitive aspects of prejudice. *J. soc. Issues, 25,* 79–98.

Taylor, D. G., P. B. Sheatsley, and A. M. Greeley (1978). Attitudes toward racial integration. *Scientific Amer., 238,* 42–49.

Tilly, C. (1969). Collective violence in European perspective. In H. D. Graham and T. R. Gurr (Eds.), *The history of violence in America.* New York: Praeger. Pp. 4–45.

_____ (1975). Revolutions and collective violence. In F. Greenstein and N. Polsby (Eds.), *Handbook of political science.* Reading, Mass.: Addison-Wesley. Pp. 483–555.

_____ (1978). *From mobilization to revolution.* Reading, Mass.: Addison-Wesley.

Tolley, H., Jr. (1973). *Children and war: political socialization to international conflict.* New York: Univ. Teachers College Press.

_____ (1977). Childhood learning about war and peace: coming of age in the nuclear era. In S. A. Renshon (Ed.), *Handbook of political socialization: theory and research.* New York: Free Press. Pp. 389–410.

Trenaman, J., and D. McQuail (1961). *Television and the political image.* London: Methuen.

Tudor, J. F. (1971). The development of class awareness in children. *Social Forces, 49,* 470–476.

Tufte, E. R. (1978). *Political control of the economy.* Princeton, N.J.: Princeton Univ. Press.

Tullock, G. (1968). *Toward a mathematics of politics.* Ann Arbor: Univ. of Michigan Press.

Turner, C. F., and E. Kraus (1978). Fallible indicators of the subjective state of the nation. *Amer. Psychol., 33,* 456–470.

Tversky, A., and D. Kahneman (1981). The framing of decisions and the psychology of choice. *Science, 211,* 453–458.

Tyler, T. (1980). Impact of directly and indirectly experienced events. *J. Pers. soc. Psychol., 39,* 13–28.

Useem, B. (1980). Solidarity model, breakdown model, and the Boston anti-busing movement. *Amer. Sociol. Rev., 45,* 357–369.

Vaillancourt, P. M. (1972). The political socialization of young people: a panel survey of youngsters in the San Francisco Bay Area. Unpublished doctoral dissertation, University of California, Berkely.

Vanneman, R., and F. C. Pampel (1977). The American perception of class and status. *Amer. Sociol. Rev., 42,* 422–437.

Vanneman, R. D., and T. T. Pettigrew (1972). Race and relative deprivation in the urban United States. *Race, 13,* 461–486.

Verba, S., and R. A. Brody (1970). Participation, policy preferences, and the war in Vietnam. *Publ. Opin. Quart., 34,* 325–332.

Verba, S., and N. H. Nie (1972). *Participation in America: political democracy and social equality.* New York: Harper.

Verba, S., N. H. Nie., and J. Kim (1971). *The modes of democratic participation.* Beverly Hills, Calif.: Sage.

—— (1978). *Participation and political equality.* New York: Cambridge Univ. Press.

Wanat, J. (1979). The application of a non-analytic, most possible estimation technique: the relative impact of mobilization and conversion of votes in the New Deal. *Polit. Meth., 6,* 357–374.

Ward, D. (1982). Genetic epistemology and the structure of belief systems. Paper delivered at the annual meeting of the American Political Science Association, Denver, Colorado.

Wattenberg, M. P. (1981). The decline of political partisanship in the United States: negativity or neutrality? *Amer. polit. Sci. Rev., 75,* 941–950.

Watts, W., and L. A. Free (1978). *State of the nation III.* Lexington, Mass.: Lexington Books.

Weisberg, H. F. (1980). A multidimensional conceptualization of party identification. *Polit. Behav., 2,* 33–60.

Weisberg, H. F., and B. Grofman (1981). Candidate evaluations and turnout. *Amer. Polit. Quart., 9,* 197–219.

Weisberg, H. F., and J. G. Rusk (1970). Dimensions of candidate evaluation. *Amer. polit. Sci. Rev., 64,* 1167–1185.

—— (1974). *Political learning, political choice and democratic citizenship.* Englewood Cliffs, N.J.: Prentice-Hall.

Welch, S. (1977). Women as political animals? A test of some explanations for male-female political participation differences. *Amer. J. polit. Sci., 21,* 711–730.

Williams, J. E., and J. R. Stabler (1973). If white means good, then black . . . *Psychol. Today, 7,* 50–54.

Wilson, G. D. (1973). *The psychology of conservatism.* London and New York: Academic Press.

Wolfenstein, M., and G. Kliman, Eds. (1965). *Children and the death of a president.* Garden City, N.J.: Doubleday.

Wolfinger, R. E., and R. B. Arseneau (1978). Partisan change in the south, 1952–1976. In L. Maisel and J. Cooper (Eds.). *Political parties: development and decay.* Beverly Hills and London: Sage. Pp. 179–210.

Wolfinger, R. E., and F. I. Greenstein (1968). The repeal of fair housing in California. *Amer. polit. Sci. Rev., 62,* 753–769.

Wolfinger, R., and P. Linquiti (1981). Tuning in and turning out. *Publ. Opin., 4,* 56–60.

Wolfinger, R. E., and S. J. Rosenstone (1980). *Who votes?* New Haven: Yale Univ. Press.

Wright, G. C. (1977). Constituency response to congressional behavior: the impact of the house judiciary committee impeachment vote. *West. Polit. Quart., 30,* 401–410.

Wright, J. D. (1976). *The dissent of the governed: alienation and democracy in America.* New York: Academic Press.

Yalch, R. F. (1976). Pre-election interview effects on voter turnout. *Publ. Opin. Quart., 40,* 331–336.

Zajonc, R. B. (1980). Feeling and thinking: preferences need no inferences. *Amer. Psychologist, 39,* 151–175.

Zellman, G. L., and D. O. Sears (1971). Childhood origins of tolerance for dissent. *J. Soc. Issues, 27,* 109–136.

CHAPTER 26

Social Deviance

Dane Archer
University of California

INTRODUCTION

Although the term is overutilized, it does seem to be the case that a major "paradigm shift" (Kuhn, 1962) has occurred in the study of deviance. Conceptions that once seemed adequate have been supplemented (although not entirely supplanted) by a new set of questions, a new perspective, and a new intellectual stance. While the issues that once dominated the field continue to be of interest, particularly for some investigators and certain disciplines, a new agenda has been added to this research domain in the last two decades.

While this perspectival change defies simple summary, it seems fair to say that recent research and thought have produced a more complicated, more interactive, and more *social* psychological conception of deviance. Traditional approaches to deviance tended to focus on the pathology of the individual deviant. The scientific questions dominant in this approach were either *etiological* (What variables are predictive of individual deviance?) or *therapeutic* (What factors or treatments lead to remediation?).

Although these questions continue to be important, the field is no longer focused exclusively or even primarily on the individual deviant. This change reflects an increasing emphasis on the ways in which deviance is socially consequential and (at least in part) socially constructed. In terms of this new conception an exclusive focus on the deviant individual is seen as unnecessarily confining and scientifically inadequate. The theoretical changes of the past two decades have shifted the intellectual focus away from the actor per se and toward the nature of the *act* (the behavior or condition of the deviant) and the *reaction* (the definitions and responses of institutions and nondeviant individuals).

This paradigmatic shift has produced a large number of terms, ideas, and hypotheses, and these are collectively referred to by a number of descriptive terms: social construction theory, societal reaction theory, the new

A number of people have had an influence on the direction and content of this chapter. My friend and colleague John I. Kitsuse has tried to inform my understanding of the nature and history of major ideas in the field. Mary Frances Archer and Bonita Iritani have contributed extensive reading and editorial suggestions. I am grateful to the following scholars for suggestions in their areas of special expertise: Thomas F. Pettigrew, Buchanan Sharp, Mark Traugott, and Candace West. Three former students and current colleagues, Robin Akert, Lynn Erlich, and Rosemary Gartner, have contributed valuable assistance and suggestions. The period covered by this review extends to June 1982.

criminology, secondary deviance, and, perhaps the best-known term, labeling theory. Each of these theories and models contains unique elements, but as discussed later, these conceptions share a number of overlapping concerns that constitute the core of the paradigm shift occurring in the study of deviance.

The shift toward an interactive, social conception of deviance emerged as a result of a number of contributions. In particular, the work of five scholars is associated with the redirection of attention from the pathology of individual deviants to the nature and effects of societal reactions. The content and significance of each of these contributions will be described later in this chapter, and they are merely listed here. The first of the five scholars to contribute to this intellectual redirection was Edwin Lemert (1951) in his concept of secondary deviance. In the early 1960s four works appeared nearly simultaneously and together occasioned the new conception of deviance. These works included Kai Erikson's (1962, 1966) notions of social boundaries and the creation of deviance, John Kitsuse's (1962) concept of societal reaction to deviance, and Erving Goffman's (1963) treatment of the stigma that deviants experience in interactions with nondeviants. The fifth and best-known concept in this new approach to deviance, however, dates from a discussion on page 9 of Howard Becker's 1963 book *Outsiders,* where for the first time the term *label* is used to describe the quality and consequences of societal reactions to deviance:

> *Social groups create deviance by making the rules whose infraction constitutes deviance,* and by applying those rules to particular people and labeling them as outsiders. From this point of view, deviance is *not* a quality of the act the person commits, but rather a consequence of the application by others of rules and sanctions to an "offender." The deviant is one to whom that label has successfully been applied; deviant behavior is behavior that people so label.

The works of these five scholars drew attention to the central ideas that deviance was socially constructed and that the reactions of nondeviants were a major force in the emergence of deviance and the qualities it assumes. This new conception clearly differs from the field's traditional interest in the etiology of individual deviants. While etiological research continues to be of great impor-

tance, the emphasis on societal reaction clearly represents a new direction. This new conception has met with both widespread support and pointed criticism. Although the interactionist perspective continues to be debated, this perspective has perhaps special import for *social* psychologists, since it conceives deviance in terms of several actors, normal and deviant, rather than in terms of idiographic psychopathy.

Some of the intellectual disputes in the field reflect the extraordinary substantive diversity included within the scope of deviance. The adjective *deviant* has been applied to a bewildering range of acts and conditions: physical disability, homosexuality, mental retardation, alcoholism, obesity, psychosis, violence, criminality, cannibalism, and uncounted others. Since deviance occurs in these concrete forms, Becker's dictum that "deviant behavior is behavior that people so label" cannot serve (and presumably was not intended) as an operational definition.

In practice, individuals and institutions react to *instances* of deviance rather than the generic category. While we have no "institutions for the deviant" or "professionals to treat the deviant," we do have prisons, hospitals, courtrooms, special schools, white canes, psychiatrists, doctors, and criminologists. Deviance is therefore not a folk category but a scientific category—an abstract theoretical construct that is absent from most lay conceptions and from many professional discussions as well. While theoretical and generic aspects of deviance are obviously of great interest to social scientists, colloquial attention tends to focus much more concretely on specific instances of deviance and specific deviants.

The substantive diversity included under the general rubric of deviance has a number of consequences. The heterogeneity of deviant behaviors and conditions has made sweeping, comprehensive theories problematic, particularly in the area of etiology. Differences across specific types of deviance are obvious and important: Although alcoholics and psychotics are both seen as deviant, the *qualities* and *effects* of their deviance are remarkably different. This variety has meant that limited or middle-range theories (Merton, 1967) may be particularly useful for specific instances of deviance. Limited, focused theories of this kind may be needed to understand the origin or nature of particular types of deviance. The topical diversity of the field is also responsible for the fact that textbooks frequently compartmentalize the field into nominal categories like mental illness, crime, physical disability, etc. (e.g., Clinard and Meier, 1979).

At the same time a number of theoretical issues and methodological problems run throughout and across all types of deviance. This is particularly true of newer interactionalist issues that tend to impact most or even all forms of deviance: stigma, deviantization, societal reaction, passing, institutionalization, etc. In this sense the study of deviance is characterized both by middle-range theories of specific types of deviance and by concepts that are generic to the field.

One of the earliest and most common approaches to deviance has involved, explicitly or implicitly, an etiological perspective. Within this perspective has been a concern with the causes of deviance, and the problematic nature of the behavior under study has generally been assumed. In much etiological research the unit of analysis has been the individual. For example, what kind of person becomes a rapist? Do child abusers come from homes in which they themselves were abused? What personality variables characterize alcoholics? And so on. In this research the etiology of the individual *deviant* or *deviant act* is the central question.

Even when the unit of analysis is larger, the individual deviant may still be the focus. Many studies using aggregate data are also, implicitly at least, etiological. An example of this use of aggregate data is epidemiological research in which regional or ecological incident rates are examined to identify the correlates (and, implicitly, the causes) of a given form of deviance. Illustrations of this epidemiological approach include studies of mental illness (Brenner, 1973), homicide and violent crime (Archer and Gartner, 1976, 1984; Archer *et al.,* 1978), alcoholism (Keller, 1975), and suicide (Gibbs, 1971; Schneidman, 1976).

The etiological tradition in deviance emphasizes and largely presupposes the objective qualities of deviance. The prevalence of deviance in these studies is treated as the central empirical question, and the intent is to illuminate our understanding of the factors that produce the deviance under study. An analogue for etiological research is the natural science or medical model, in which deviance is analogous to a problematic medical condition like lung cancer. This approach has been extremely valuable, although a number of formidable methodological obstacles are involved.

One of the best-known problems involves the validity of the dependent variable. Researchers are often forced to rely on official statistics (crime rates, coroner's determinations of suicide, hospitalization rates as indices of mental illness, etc.). Depending on the *specific* indica-

tor, evidence shows that some official statistics are themselves the product of complicated social interactions (Kitsuse and Cicourel, 1963; Piliavin and Briar, 1964; Skogan, 1977, 1981). This problem is sometimes called the problem of underenumeration, and it reflects the certainty that many official statistics report only a systematically biased sample of the true incidence of a form of deviance.

A principal source of evidence for the hidden or "dark" figure of deviance rests on population surveys that contrast self-reported incident rates with official rates. Even with this method, of course, the possibility of doubly hidden deviance remains, e.g., offenses reported neither to the police nor to an interviewer. Some forms of deviance, like homicide, are apparently unaffected by underenumeration, while other indicators are greatly complicated by this problem. Rape is an example. Despite systematic efforts to increase the willingness of rape victims to report this offense, official statistics on rape apparently contain only *half* the rapes committed (*Sourcebook of Criminal Justice Statistics,* 1982, p. 233). This conclusion also rests on estimates, of course, since the real number of rapes is, by definition, indeterminate.

In addition, we have strong evidence that this reported half is not a random half. Rapes by strangers tend to be reported, while those committed by intimates and acquaintances are not. When women are asked about their reasons for *not* reporting rapes, the most common response appears to be the victim's belief that it was a private matter (*Sourcebook of Criminal Justice Statistics,* 1982, p. 243). This differential enumeration may explain how it is possible for the stranger rape rate to be decreasing while the nonstranger rape rate is increasing (*Criminal Victimization in the U.S.,* 1981, p. 17).

This example has been described at length because it illustrates some of the serious methodological obstacles faced by etiological researchers. Imagine, for example, a study of the personality of rapists or of the social class characteristics of rapists, which samples from prison populations or from arrest records. In view of systematic underenumeration and bias in official records (and, as a result, the population available for prosecution and possible incarceration), etiological studies of this kind would not be of rapists but only of those rapists who happened to be proceeded against. As this example makes clear, research on deviant populations may inadvertently study only those who are *successfully labeled* rather than (the presumably much larger group of) all those whose behavior could conceivably be actionable under the legal definitions of a given criminal act.

These methodological problems are recognized by many etiological researchers, and depending on the problem studied and the research design used, the threats to valid inference can be minimized in many cases (Archer and Gartner, 1984). In terms of the new conception of deviance, however, etiological issues are not the only important questions in the study of deviance. In terms of this new conception some of the most compelling approaches involve the following investigations:

1. In-depth studies of the lives, social organization, and deviant careers of labeled individuals.

2. Studies of the ways in which societal reaction, definition, social control, and treatment affect deviants and may (although not always intentionally) act to reduce their life chances.

3. Research on the ways in which attitudes, self-conceptions, and interactional behaviors of deviants are affected by labeling and other societal reactions.

4. Studies of the effect of deviant labeling on the intimates, friends, and acquaintances of the labeled person.

5. Studies of normal individuals and norm-enforcing institutions in order to understand the nature of individual, collective, and political responses to deviance.

While aspects of these new approaches remain controversial (Gove, 1980) and in some cases misunderstood (Kitsuse, 1980; Schur, 1980), the concerns and emphases of this new conception seem to include the following tenets:

1. Some arbitrariness exists in the behaviors and conditions that come to be "deviantized." The application of sanctions cannot always be explained in terms of the objective danger of a given form of deviance to individuals or society generally.

2. This arbitrariness may conceal moral righteousness and political interests, and one of the functions of deviantization is social control of the less powerful by the more powerful.

3. Deviant labels are attached to individuals in ways that can be incomplete, arbitrary, or systematically biased. These labels are attached to only some of those who could be labeled on the basis of objective behavior and belief. Conversely, false positives (unjustified labeling) also occur.

4. The concept of deviance is impossible without an *interaction* between deviants and nondeviants. The attitudes and behaviors of the nondeviants are indispensable to understanding deviance. Nondeviants can have a direct effect on deviants, or their effect can occur by implication and anticipation. The effects of nondeviants on deviants can be strong and are often adverse.

5. Objectively, problematic conditions certainly exist in some forms of deviance (like retardation), may exist in others (like neurosis), and definitely do not exist in still others (like witchcraft). For these reasons probably not all labeling occurs in a purely random fashion; i.e., objective behavior may in some cases precede labeling. In all three cases, however, deviance acquires additional qualities and importance as a result of socially constructed meaning. In each and every case the deviant individual is affected by societal reaction. The effects of these forces include powerful elements of stigmatization, stabilization of the deviant role, and social and psychological discrediting.

6. While the intent of societies regarding the deviant may be nominally therapeutic, treatment and institutionalization often produce ironic, disabling, incapacitating disadvantages for the treated.

7. Deviant labels create an attributional heuristic that unfairly and inaccurately subsumes individual variation and treats a wide range of behaviors as merely symptomatic of the deviant condition. The deviant label assumes a master status that is the most salient interpersonal feature of a deviant individual and in terms of which everything about the individual tends to be explained.

8. Far from being disorganized, as public stereotypes and some theorists have implied, the lives of deviants often reflect high levels of organization. This organization is in some cases social (i.e., jointly with others) but is in almost all cases at least systematic in the sense that deviant individuals develop mechanisms for coping with stigma and the sanctions they experience at the hands of nondeviants.

9. The social processes by means of which an individual is singled out, defined, labeled, and reacted to as deviant will have consequences. These effects may be at the level of self-conception: they may be interpersonal in the sense of tainting or coloring face-to-face interactions between deviants and nondeviants; and they may increase the probability that the individual's deviant behavior will be stabilized, perpetuated, or amplified.

10. The lives of the deviantized have much in common. Specific forms of deviance produce specific types of organization—e.g., homosexuality produces a lifestyle organized around different priorities and hazards than does paraplegia. At the same time deviants of all labels may experience similar patterns of stigma, similar attributional responses, and similarly problematic mixed contacts when interacting with nondeviants.

11. Since the detection, reporting, labeling, and institutionalization of deviants are all social processes, individuals may differ (in race, class, gender, demeanor, etc.) in terms of their ability to resist these phases and effects of deviantization. These differences have consequences for official statistics and for scientific research on deviant populations.

12. The changing, shifting, and emerging nature of deviance categories suggests that instances of deviance have their origins in specific historical periods and cultural values as much as in (or more than in) the objective behavior of individual deviants.

13. Deviance generally involves efforts at social control, and the emergence and the organization of social control institutions need to be examined to understand deviance and deviant careers.

While discussions of the new conception of deviance have tended to be theoretical rather than propositional, these tenets appear to be the major substantive tenets of this new approach. The acceptance of the new agenda does not mean that etiological and epidemiological questions must be discarded. The new agenda does, however, do two things. It brings with it a host of new questions and a perspective within which the behaviors of nondeviants, officials, and institutions are seen as problematic and empirically interesting. In this sense it expands the domain of important and compelling questions. In addition, the new perspective can serve a sensitizing function. The emphasis on the social nature of deviance indicates that some etiological research designs may mislead investigators who are unwary of the sometimes selective, discretionary, and consequential nature of labeling, deviantization, treatment, and institutionalization.

While some of the tenets and propositions of the new conception continue to be debated, it seems safe to say that the past two decades of research have greatly expanded the study of deviance. This change has been away from narrowly etiological and therapeutic assumptions and toward an interactionist perspective in which nondeviants, professionals, officials, institutions, definitions, and attributions have achieved an intellectual focus comparable to that of the deviants themselves.

The diversity of deviant behaviors and conditions complicates definitions as well as theories. Early definitions of deviance stressed the idea that deviance was statistically infrequent behavior. Contemporary definitions, however, emphasize that deviance is not merely difference. Variation is not, by itself, enough to produce an instance of deviance. In terms of current conceptions deviance refers to behaviors or conditions that are the subject of negative imputations. Deviance is therefore a form of "undesired differentness" (Goffman, 1963), and the undesired quality of deviance is reflected in definitions that stress the reactions with which institutions and nondeviants respond to the deviant. While the objective conditions of different forms of deviance vary greatly, much greater regularity seems to characterize the *processes* of societal reaction to deviants.

Beyond this area of agreement definitions of deviance differ in the qualities they choose to stress. A traditional definition has centered on deviance as norm violation, but the concept of a norm is itself more problematic than commonly has been assumed (Kitsuse, 1980). Many contemporary definitions of deviance have diminished the relative prominence of objectively deviant behavior in favor of the centrality of social reactions and imputations. Schur (1971, p. 24), for instance, says:

> Human behavior is deviant to *the extent that* it comes to be viewed as involving a *personally* discreditable departure from a group's normative expectations, *and* it *elicits* interpersonal or collective reactions that serve to "isolate," "treat," "correct," or "punish" *individuals* engaged in such behavior.

Erikson (1962, p. 308) states:

Deviance is not a property *inherent* in certain forms of behavior; it is a property *conferred upon* these forms by the audiences which directly or indirectly witness them. Sociologically, then, the critical variable is the social *audience*...since it is the audience which eventually decides whether or not any given action or actions will become a visible case of deviation.

Clinard and Meier (1979, p. 14) define deviance this way:

Deviance constitutes only those deviations from norms which are in a disapproved direction and of sufficient degree to exceed the tolerance limits of a social group such that the deviation elicits, or is likely to elicit if detected, a negative sanction.

Finally, Kituse (1962, p. 248) offers this definition:

Clearly, the forms of behavior *per se* do not activate the processes of societal reaction which sociologically differentiate deviants from non-deviants... Accordingly, deviance may be conceived as a process by which the members of a group, community, or society (1) interpret behavior as deviant, (2) define persons who so behave as a certain kind of deviant, and (3) accord them the treatment considered appropriate to such deviants.

As these examples indicate, some theoretical and definitional differences persist, particularly in terms of the relative emphasis placed on *objective* conditions (actual characteristics and behaviors of the person who comes to be defined as deviant) or, alternately, on *subjective* factors (*socially constructed* meanings as a result of labeling, societal reaction, stigma, and institutionalization). In addition, definitions differ on a number of technical matters like whether secret deviance is a logical possibility. Theorists who emphasize the objective qualities of deviance tend to believe that undetected acts and conditions can still be deviant; theorists who emphasize societal reaction argue that secret deviance is a contradiction in terms.

As discussed in a later section, we may be able to reconcile some of these differences. Most definitions of deviance contain a number of common elements:

1. The importance of conceptions (concrete or imagined, implicit or explicit) of normalcy against which an instance of deviance is contrasted.

2. The stigma and other negative imputations that are directed at the incumbents of deviant roles.

3. The degree to which forms of deviance are seen as *problematic* (regrettable, deserving of sympathy), *actionable* (morally intolerable, deserving of social control or therapeutic intervention), or both.

A deviance definition that includes these common elements might be the following:

Deviance is a perceived behavior or condition that is thought to involve an undesirable departure in a compelling way from a putative standard. These behaviors and conditions are seen either as merely regrettable or as actionable in the sense that they produce the belief that something ought to be done about them.

Having indicated that concrete definitions are somewhat elusive, we note that they may be dispensable for some purposes. Virtually all discussions and studies of deviance address specific instances of this unwieldy, global concept. Indeed, we have reason to think that the generic term has at best imprecise meaning outside the confines of social science theory. Using survey research, Simmons and Chambers (1965) asked respondents to list "those things or types of persons whom you regard as deviant." The general conclusion was that definitional variation overshadows objective conditions. In all, 252 different acts of persons were listed (with a mean of 6.4 responses per subject). An interesting corollary of this finding is that many or most individuals merit the deviant label, at least in the eyes of some labelers.

A number of deviance instances do recur in this list, and the most frequently cited categories were (in order) homosexuals, drug addicts, alcoholics, prostitutes, murderers, criminals, lesbians, juvenile delinquents, beatniks (presumably a contemporary social issue), the mentally ill, perverts, communists, and atheists. Lay conceptions of deviance are therefore so inclusive as to preclude use of the generic term. Clearly, from this inventory, however, all the cited instances have imputed qualities in common—e.g., they are seen as undesirable and problematic. A similar pattern of arbitrary definition is found for some instances of deviance, like "violence" (Blumenthal *et al.,* 1972; Archer and Gartner, 1978). Perhaps for this reason treatments of deviance tend to focus on specific instances of deviance rather than the general concept.

A few words are in order about the structure of this chapter. In the interests of readability the terms *normal* and *deviant* will be used without quotation marks throughout this chapter. Although absent, quotation marks are intended. These terms are used with the understanding that they necessarily involve definitions, reactions, and imputations. The terms *normal* and *deviant* are only significant in the context of an interaction in which these labels are socially constructed. While we do not imply that objective conditions are absent or unimportant, we do indicate that the *meaning* attached to these conditions is central to the study of deviance.

A second convention worth noting is that deviance is specific: One is deviant only with respect to the behavior or condition at hand. An individual may be seen as deviant for being undesirably different from any one of the following putative standards: heterosexuality, thinness, sightedness, honesty, God-fearingness, etc. This operational specificity is probably consistent with lay conceptions of deviance, in which generic deviance appears to be relatively uncommon. At the same time global (and generally negative) attributions are clearly made on the basis of a single instance of deviance. This attributional spillover, or "putative deviance," may cause the obese to be seen as weak personalities, the deaf to be treated as retarded, and the mentally ill to be seen as dangerous.

Finally, we mention that normalcy is probably a latent condition. One is normal only with respect to a specific deviance, and one's normalcy becomes salient only in the presence of a contradictory deviance. The presence of a dwarf creates normal height in the rest of us: a homosexual makes his heterosexual acquaintances normal; and a paraplegic crystallizes the normalcy of the ablebodied. No other qualities or global states are implied by use of the term *normal*. In particular, note that this operational specificity means that individuals can be normal in some contexts and not in others. The person who is normal (i.e., of average weight) in the presence of the obese may be deviant in terms of any number of other definitions: an ex-convict, a polygamist, a substance abuser, etc.

The study of deviance has involved the participation of many disciplines. In the case of a single form of deviance such as child abuse, for example, important contributions have been made by psychologists, sociologists, anthropologists, pediatricians, and historians. While this chapter will be sensitive to contributions from these different fields, the emphases will be on psychology and sociology. These two fields have both addressed many aspects of deviance, although the approaches have differed in qualitative ways perhaps characteristic of the two fields.

Some of these differences are methodological. For example, consistent with long-standing epistemological differences, psychologists have tended to prefer the internal validity possible through controlled laboratory comparisons, while sociologists have preferred the external validity possible through naturalistic observation and field research. Other differences occur in the substantive emphases of the two disciplines. Psychologists have been more interested in cognitive, attributional, and interpersonal aspects of deviance; sociologists have been more concerned with theory, deviant behavior, labeling and societal reaction, and institutions.

The disciplines also differ in the relative prominence of the subject. Deviance is a course in virtually all sociology departments, along with additional courses on instances of deviance like criminology. In psychology departments the subject tends to be included (if taught at all) as a topic in social psychology or abnormal psychology. Perhaps for these reasons a computer search of the literature in psychology and sociology shows some interesting differences, as indicated in Table 1. Searching for the global term *deviance* and the more specific term *stigma,* one finds that the concepts occur and are increasing in both fields. At the same time the relative prominence of the concepts appears to be greater (in terms of cita-

TABLE 1
Publications Related to Deviance or Stigma, 1966–1980

YEARS	PSYCHOLOGY		SOCIOLOGY	
	DEVIANCE	*STIGMA*	*DEVIANCE*	*STIGMA*
1966–1970	356 (4.1)*	27 (0.3)	181 (6.3)	11 (0.4)
1971–1975	683 (5.4)	67 (0.5)	391 (13.0)	58 (1.9)
1976–1980	630 (5.1)	105 (0.8)	789 (28.0)	81 (2.9)

*Absolute number of publications (and publications per 1000 bibliographic items). The source is a DIALOG computer search of the Psychological Information Data Base and the Sociological Abstracts Data Base.

tions per 1000 bibliographic items) in sociology. The rapid growth of interest in the field within sociology almost certainly reflects the paradigmatic shift toward a new conception of deviance during the past two decades.

Given the substantive range and sheer volume of publications on deviance, a fully comprehensive review of the field is not possible in a chapter, even a lengthy one. Instead, this chapter seeks to provide a review of theoretical concepts and perspectives central to all forms of deviance. In addition to this consideration of generic issues and theories, one substantive field of deviance—physical handicaps, physical characteristics, and medical conditions—will be examined in detail. For this one area of deviance, experimental, nonexperimental, and field researches are reviewed. Mental, sexual, moral, ideological, and criminal deviances are referred to in various parts of this chapter. The chapter is organized into the following sections: ''Historic and Cultural Variation in Deviance,'' ''Major Ideas, Concepts, and Theories of Deviance,'' ''Physical Handicaps, Physical Characteristics, and Medical Conditions,'' and ''A Summary of Current Issues and New Research Directions.''

HISTORIC AND CULTURAL VARIATION IN DEVIANCE

Deviance is socially constructed. This fact is somewhat counterintuitive and easily overlooked. At any one moment in time, standards may seem to be consensual concerning the unacceptability of certain deviant behaviors: child abuse, spousal violence, pederasty and other forms of sexual ''perversion,'' etc. In many ways, however, this consensus is illusory. As indicated in this section, while some continuities exist, more change than persistence is shown in terms of what acts, practices, beliefs, and lifestyles are regarded as deviant. The very same behaviors can be regarded as deviant or not, depending on time and place.

Variations across these two dimensions can assist an understanding of deviance in several ways. A comparative analysis of deviance can indicate the following:

1. Whether some forms of behavior have *always* been regarded as deviant and negatively sanctioned.

2. Whether some behaviors that were *initially* sanctioned as deviant no longer are.

3. Whether some behaviors that are *currently* regarded as deviant are not so regarded in other places or periods in time.

4. Whether changes have occurred in *both* directions or only one (e.g., toward progressive decriminalization).

5. Whether these types of variation can illuminate the *processes* whereby events and behaviors become seen as problematic, labeled as deviant, and sanctioned.

The principal sources of variation for a comparative perspective on deviance are changes in place, the evidence for which exists in the *ethnographic* record, and changes in time, the evidence for which exists in the *historical* record. The value of cross-cultural comparisons is widely recognized in social psychology (Whiting, 1968; Triandis, 1980). The social psychological use of cross-cultural comparisons is somewhat different from the goals pursued by classic ethnography. While most classical anthropologists sought to provide an intensive account of a single culture, social psychologists have been more interested in looking for hypotheses and patterns that account in some lawful way for variations in beliefs and behaviors across a sample of societies. When social psychologists do use evidence from other societies, they are likely to use multinational data sets like the Human Relations Area Files (HRAF) and other holocultural data archives (Naroll, Michik, and Naroll, 1980).

The historical record has been used less frequently by social psychologists. This omission has been criticized by a number of scholars. McGuire (1976) has argued that cross-era comparisons provide a rich data set that can make possible elegant tests of the generality of social psychological hypotheses. The literature contains a number of intriguing efforts to use samples of historical records to test general propositions.

One of these studies uses data on a sample of nineteenth-century Utopian societies to test hypotheses about group cohesion, solidarity, and community survival (Kanter, 1972). A second example uses longitudinal data from a large number of societies to test several hypotheses about the effect of wars on the rate of violent crime (Archer and Gartner, 1976, 1984). A third is a test of the military deterrence hypothesis by using historical data (Naroll, Bullough, and Naroll, 1974). A final example is a study that compares the visual images of men and women in several centuries of art works (Archer *et al.,* 1983). In general, however, for reasons that are unclear, cross-era comparisons continue to be underutilized in psychological social psychology. Social psychologists with a more sociological orientation have shown more interest in using the historical record to illuminate current issues by the light of past experience and long-term social change.

CULTURAL AND HISTORICAL VARIATION: CURIOUS FACTS ABOUT SEX, CHILDREN, EATING, AND SMOKING

From the perspective of deviance the historical and cross-cultural records can be both fascinating and theoretically useful. These two sources of comparison can provide information about the form and extent of individual and societal variety. This variation can be used to examine the complex and often changing nature of the relationship between a given society and the beliefs, behaviors, and beings it treats as deviant. If great variation occurs in the *content* of societal deviance, then a perspective on deviance that includes elements of historical and cultural relativism may be needed.

   While the notion of relativism is anything but new (Campbell, 1972), this intellectual stance is particularly indicated in the case of deviance since lay, political, and even scientific conceptions of deviance are so often laden with moralistic imputations. The moralizing with which deviant acts are regarded suggests a widespread tendency to regard these acts, and the deviants who commit them, as inherently pathological. This unstated assumption has characterized both lay conceptions of deviance and, until recently, the scientific paradigms within which deviance has been studied. While such piety is itself an important object of study, comparative evidence on deviance suggests that deviance does not inhere in acts or actors. Instead, deviance appears to be socially situated, the outcome of an interactive process of definition and societal reaction. While no attempt at comprehensiveness is possible, the usefulness and variety of historical and cultural data on deviance will be indicated by a very brief discussion of some curious facts about sex, children, smoking, and eating.

Sex

The year 1870 fell in the middle of Queen Victoria's long reign. This period is remembered for its rigid attitudes toward sexuality, so much so that we continue to use the queen's name to refer to a particular orientation toward sex. For the Victorians sexuality was the subject of strict conceptions of appropriate and inappropriate behavior (Rugoff, 1971). Victorian attitudes and practices might be summarized as fiercely monogamist, narrowly procreative rather than sensual, and staunchly opposed to a long list of sexual behaviors that were seen as deviant: nudity, nonmarital sexual relations, prostitution, adolescent sexuality, and (of course) homosexuality, masturbation, and incest.

   In view of the strict norms concerning sexual behavior, one might expect that in 1870 Anglo-American culture was one in which monogamy and marital sexuality prospered to the exclusion of other, deviant alternatives. And while many families on both sides of the Atlantic may have fit the Victorian pattern in 1870, more deviant forms of sexuality flourished alongside and in competition with the prescribed forms. In England, although historical statistics on the subject are elusive, prostitution and nonmarital sexual relations were commonplace (Marcus, 1966). In the United States in 1870 it may be true that monogamy was the preferred sexual arrangement, but rival types of sexual organization also existed. Despite the strength and prevalence of Victorian sexual ethics, the United States in 1870 witnessed widespread sexual experimentation.

   In 1870, along with the mainstream of late nineteenth-century life, American society included a very large number of alternative communities, religions, and social movements (Kephart, 1982). Three of these communities, selected here because they illustrate very different normative prescriptions for sexual life, were the Shakers, the Mormons, and the Oneidans. All three of these social movements renounced monogamy, and for large portions of the nineteenth century all three practiced alternatives that appeared to be equally viable arrangements. These collective sexual practices were all highly *normative* (i.e., conforming) within their own communities, although all three deviated radically, and in very different ways, from the sexual prescriptions of Victorian America.

The Shakers. The Shakers are remembered for many things, including their lyric poems and an astonishing number of innovations and art forms: fine carpentry, impressive architecture, and mechanical inventions like the circular saw, the propeller, flat brooms and paint brushes, the threshing machine, and the revolving oven (Noyes, 1870; Nordhoff, 1875). In addition to their material contributions, the Shakers also pioneered the "architecture" of social and family life. A cornerstone of Shaker life was the complete renunciation of sex and marriage. Men and women lived in separate dormitory-like rooms and met for work and worship—and for few other reasons. Gender segregation was practiced from infancy forward, and the physical separation of the "brothers" and "sisters" in Shaker villages was so extensive that it was possible for a member of the community to live his or her entire life without actually touching a member of the opposite sex (Kephart, 1982, p. 217).

Although they practiced complete celibacy, the Shakers were not without ecstatic physical activity of a different sort. The Shakers believed in "shaking out the evil," and they participated in exuberant, explosive Sabbath-day "marches." These marches came to be called "dances" by the outside (non-Shaker) world, and like celibacy, they became one of the best-known Shaker practices. These dances had no close parallel in secular or religious America. Even in these ecstatic activities separation of the sexes was maintained, with men and women lined up in ranks on opposite sides of a large room (Noyes, 1870, p. 603). In the height of the Shaker dance some members of the community would show signs of a spiritual "gift"—shouting, glossolalia (speaking in tongues), visions of spirits and angels, and prophesies. An indication of the nature of these activities is given in the following description by an ex-Shaker (from Kephart, 1982, p. 221):

> In the height of their ecstacy, Shakers were constrained to worship God in the dance. . . . Still more mortifying were the *jerks*. The exercise began in the head, which would fly backward and forward and from side to side, with a quick jolt . . . limbs and trunk twitching in every direction. And how such could escape injury was no small wonder to spectators. The last grade of mortification was the *barks*. These frequently accompanied the jerks . . . and one would take the position of a canine, move about on all fours, growl, snap the teeth and bark.

While the Shakers forswore sex, marriage, and (therefore) biological procreation, these practices did not present insurmountable obstacles to community survival. Tens of thousands of Shakers lived in two dozen thriving communities scattered across the eastern half of the United States for well over a century. To produce new generations of recruits, the Shakers relied on applicants from the outside world and also accepted orphans and other unfortunates. In fact, a watershed event in the Shakers' decline was the development of state (as opposed to private) care of the orphaned and indigent (Kephart, 1982, p. 228). In numbers, size, and stability, however, celibacy did not by itself prevent this highly viable community from enduring in the midst of a wider society whose sexual and marital practices it rejected.

The Mormons. Another social movement active in 1870 was the Church of Latter-day Saints, the Mormons. This movement was sparked by a heavenly visitation to Joseph Smith in 1823. The early Mormons differed from non-Mormons in terms of their theology and a large number of religious and social activities. Like several other nascent social movements, the Mormons were the victims of vicious and nearly relentless persecution, including violent mob attacks like the one in Carthage, Illinois, in 1844 in which Mormon leader Joseph Smith was murdered (Kephart, 1982, p. 240). Although Mormon life had many unique features, by far the most deviant and controversial in the eyes of non-Mormon America was the Mormons' rejection of sexual and marital monogamy. The type of nonmonogamy practiced by the Mormons was called polygamy but was, in fact, polygyny (plural wives). For the Mormons polygyny was ordained by God. In a divine revelation to Joseph Smith, recorded on July 12, 1843, the Mormon leader was informed (from Kephart, 1982, p. 244):

> If any man espouse a virgin, and desire to espouse another, and the first give her consent, . . . then he is justified; for he cannot commit adultery with that that belongeth unto him and to no one else.

In the beginning polygyny was restricted to high-ranking members of the church, and, perhaps significantly, the practice was kept secret. In 1852, five years after the Mormons had left the East for the relative safety of the Great Salt Lake Valley, polygyny was the subject of a public announcement by leader Brigham Young. Despite the divine authorization for polygyny, the majority of Mormons practiced monogamy. Estimates of the frequency of polygyny among Mormon men center around 10 percent and rarely exceed 30 percent. Even among polygynous males the pattern was usually no more than two wives. Mormon leaders, however, tended to have larger families—e.g., Brigham Young had 27 wives and 56 children; Heber Kimball had 45 wives and 68 children (Kephart, 1982, p. 246).

The growth and durability of the Mormon church suggests that polygyny, like the celibacy of the Shakers, can be both viable and normative. Indeed, the practice of polygyny would very likely have persisted as a tenet of Mormon social organization had it not been for the fearful and hostile response of non-Mormon society. The Gentile (non-Mormon) press was filled with moral outrage over the Mormon's "polygamy," and public passions over the issue ignited political attacks on the

Mormons. President Lincoln signed a bill outlawing polygamy in the territories of the United States, and following the Civil War federal agents swarmed all over Utah in search of miscreant polygynists (Kephart, 1982, p. 250).

This attempt at *criminalization* succeeded in creating secrecy concerning polygyny, with many Saints building secret passageways, hidden rooms, and underground tunnels between their homes. But criminalization did not stop polygyny. The practice continued to enjoy the normative auspices of the church and its leaders, and in 1871 the persistence of polygyny led President Grant to state in a message to Congress, "In Utah there still remains a remnant of barbarism, repugnant to civilization, and decency, and to the law of the United States."

In the end the Mormons abandoned polygyny. This decision, however, had nothing to do with the internal viability of the practice. The Mormons abandoned polygyny under the combined weight of persecution and prosecution. In 1882 a new federal law provided for punishment for individuals living in "lewd cohabitation." In all 573 Mormons had criminal convictions, hundreds of polygamists were imprisoned, and the church leadership was forced to govern from hiding. Perhaps the final straw came with the passage in 1887 of the Edmunds-Tucker Bill, which dissolved the Mormon church as a corporation and provided for the confiscation of church property, including more than $1 million in cash.

Finally, in 1890 Mormon President Wilford Woodruff had a revelation ("I went before the Lord, and I wrote what the Lord told me to write") which led to the following historic Mormon Manifesto: "I now publicly declare that my advice to the Latter-day Saints is to refrain from contracting any marriage forbidden by the law of the land" (Kephart, 1982, p. 252). Although secretive polygyny persisted on a smaller scale, with this manifesto the practice lost the normative support of the church. Again, as in the case of the Shakers, the elimination of polygyny did not reflect on its merits as a form of sexual and marital allocation. The abolition of polygyny resulted purely from the political action and criminalization practiced by the wider society.

The Oneidans.   Along with the Shakers and Mormons, another interesting community was prospering in 1870 in the middle of Victorian society: the Oneida community in rural upstate New York. Like the Shakers and Mormons, the Oneidans also rejected sexual monogamy. As we have seen, the sexual arrangements of the Shakers and Mormons made them deviant curiosities in the eyes of

monogamous outsiders. The solution developed by the Oneidans, however, marks a genuine milestone in the history of collective sexual experimentation. If the Shakers and Mormons were seen as nonconforming sexual deviants in 1870, the Oneidans were seen as greatly more radical.

The Oneidans developed a system called complex marriages. The complex-marriage system was as simple as it was revolutionary. Monogamous love (which they called special love) was forbidden. If a man desired sexual intercourse with any woman in the Oneida community, he simply asked her. If she consented, he would go to her room at bedtime and stay overnight. The principle of complex marriage was formally elaborated in *Bible Communism,* one of the community's founding documents (from Noyes, 1870, pp. 626–628):

> The new commandment is, that we love one another . . . not by pairs, as in the world, but *en masse.* We are required to love one another fervently. . . . Men and women find universally (however the fact may be concealed), that their susceptibility to love is not burnt out by one honeymoon, or satisfied by one lover. On the contrary, the secret history of the human heart will bear out the assertion that it is capable of loving any number of times and any number of persons, and that the more it loves the more it can love. This is the law of nature, thrust out of sight and condemned by common consent, and yet secretly known to all.

With the doctrine of complex marriage the Oneidans embarked on an extraordinary and apparently successful search for an alternative to monogamy. The somewhat unlikely founder and charismatic leader of the Oneidans was John Humphrey Noyes. Son of a Vermont congressman, Noyes was a Dartmouth graduate and attended theological seminars at Andover and Yale. In 1848, after an earlier effort in Putney, Vermont, Noyes and his followers created the Oneida community in New York State. While the Oneidans produced a number of distinctive spiritual and social practices, it was their sexual beliefs and behaviors that were, to say the least, distinctive in 1870 American life. Complex marriage had several key features. In addition to a prohibition on exclusive, dyadic sexual relations, the Oneidans embraced the radical idea that sex was to be entirely voluntary and unrestricted for both men and women. Noyes had a dim view of monogamy: "It is the theory that love *after* marriage should be what it is *before* marriage—a glowing attraction on both sides, and not the odious obligation of one party, and the sensual recklessness of the other" (quoted in Kephart, 1982, p. 122).

By "sensual recklessness" Noyes meant unprotected intercourse. The Oneidans distinguished between the *amative* (sexual attraction and gratification) and the *propagative* (reproductive) aspects of sexual intercourse. Briefly, he was in favor of the former but had great reservations about the latter. Noyes developed a system of what he called "Male Continence" and made it binding on the entire Oneida community. This practice is known generally by the term *coitus reservatus* (intercourse without male ejaculation). Men in the community were trained by Noyes in this form of intercourse as a condition for the privilege of "free love"—a term Noyes himself coined but later regretted. The community chose *coitus reservatus* over *coitus interruptus* because of biblical injunctions against "spilled seed." Under the male-continence system Oneidan men were permitted to ejaculate only when their partners were postmenopausal.

The system of male continence was invented by Noyes to control the propagative aspects of sexual relations, and indeed, the Oneida community had a policy (called stirpiculture) under which a man and woman could only conceive a child with the permission of a governing committee run by Noyes himself. Stirpiculture was designed as a eugenic form of human breeding. Noyes's control of this committee apparently did not prevent eugenic self-selection, and Noyes himself fathered at least ten children in the Oneida community. In addition to their eugenic concerns, Noyes and the Oneida community held a dim view of the costs of the uncontrolled propagative practices of the wider society. Among these costs they included the following criticisms (Noyes, 1870, p. 632):

> The infirmities and vital expenses of woman during the long period of pregnancy, waste her constitution. . . . The awful agonies of child-birth heavily tax the life of woman . . . the cares of the nursing period bear heavily on woman. . . . The cares of both parents, through the period of the childhood of their offspring are many and burdensome.

Despite a system of sexual allocation that was clearly deviant in the eyes of 1870 America, the Oneida community grew and prospered for four decades. The community had a vigorous economic base, and it became famous (and wealthy) for its manufacturing of traps and silverware. The community pioneered a number of progressive policies, including egalitarian treatment of women and respect for the aged. In the eyes of the outside world these worthwhile ideas were eclipsed by the salience of the Oneidans' sexual arrangements. Opposition to the system of complex marriage centered principally on the community's rejection of monogamy and the sexual participation of young members of the community.

Although Oneidan sexual norms obviously ran counter to those to which their neighbors subscribed, no evidence indicates that the Oneidan sexual arrangements were intrinsically unworkable. For all their sexual radicalism the Oneidans appeared to have developed sexual and reproductive norms that were *internally* viable. Noyes and the Oneidans felt that their sexual arrangements were "in advance of marriage and common civilization" in that they had eliminated unwanted pregnancy, bastardy, broken families, and prostitution. The community is described as having few sexual problems, few or no unplanned children, and little or no jealousy. Noyes believed that jealousy was a pathological symptom of monogamy (from Kephart, 1982, p. 128):

> No matter what his other qualifications may be, if a man cannot love a woman and be happy seeing her loved by others, he is a selfish man, and his place is with the potsherds of the earth.

The sexual radicalism of the Oneidans was eventually done in by the puritanism of the wider society. Specific features of the community became notorious. One was the practice of having young people sexually initiated by the community's older and more senior figures. Although this practice was true for both sexes, the fact that Noyes himself served as "first husband" for the young women came to be regarded as particularly scandalous by non-Oneidans. John Mears, a professor at nearby Hamilton College, published newspaper accounts attacking the "corrupt concubinage" of the Oneida community. Finally, fearing that he would be charged with statutory rape, Noyes left secretly in the middle of the night for Canada. In 1879 Noyes sent word recommending that the Oneidans abandon the practice of complex marriage. Shortly after, a large number of monogamous marriages occurred in the community, and where possible, women married the fathers of their children. The Oneidans' radical sexual experiment was ended.

Even though they existed simultaneously in 1870 —in the same year within a single society—these three social movements indicate that sexual norms can be highly variable and that sexual deviation exists in the context of social definition and societal reaction. Like the Shakers and the Mormons, the Oneidans developed norms and institutions that came to be deviantized by the wider society. Even though the sexual practices of these three communities in 1870 America were regarded as deviant, one finds it difficult to argue that these competing systems of sexual organization were not functional and, in some ways, equal or even superior to the monogamy they sought to supplant. When these sexual arrangements finally crumbled, it was not from their own weight but from the political reaction of outsiders.

Finally, these historical examples indicate that behaviors can be labeled deviant even if they reflect a high degree of coherent social organization. In all three of these communities the sexual behavior of the participants involved planning, premeditation, and institutionalization. These instances of deviance clearly were *not* the result of social disorganization or the acts of pathological individuals. In this sense the members of these social movements were conforming and not just deviant. They were governed by norms that were unlike those of neighboring communities but that were norms nonetheless.

In this sense the sexual practices of individuals in these three groups were *normative for the subcultures in which they lived.* The wider culture, by virtue of greater numbers and political power, succeeded in condemning these rival subcultural practices as deviant. Despite this outcome, which was more political than moral, the sexual deviance of these communities did not involve "pathological" behavior by marginal individuals. In other words, the sexual deviance of the Shakers, Mormons, and Oneidans resulted not from social disorganization but from rival forms of social organization.

Historic variation in sexual deviance. The historical record is a rich source of other evidence of the shifting, relative nature of sexual norms and sexual deviance. This evidence suggests that changes in deviantization and criminalization have operated in *both* directions rather than one alone. Some acts that were formerly sanctioned heavily are now regarded as less serious, while other acts that were not regarded as serious forms of deviance have acquired this status in modern times.

An example of the first type of offense (one that has been progressively decriminalized in recent centuries) is homosexuality—and, indeed, other forms of nonheterosexual activity. In premodern Europe, homosexuality and other sexual deviance carried grievous criminal sanctions. A person convicted of this offense could be

sentenced to death or to the pillory, and even the pillory could be a death penalty by means of stoning at the hands of enraged mobs. As late as 1772, a Captain Robert James was executed for the crime of sodomy in England (Stone, 1979, p. 337). At least in Western societies nonheterosexual activity appears to have been progressively *decriminalized* and *delabeled* as deviance during the last two centuries.

This trend toward decriminalization and reduced sanctions applies also to bestiality and other forms of sexual "perversion." These behaviors originally carried extreme sanctions. The celebrated Cotton Mather records a 1662 case of a citizen in New Haven who was sentenced to death for having engaged in sexual relations with animals. Prior to his own execution the convicted man was forced to witness the slaying of a cow, two heifers, three sheep, and two sows with which he had been convicted of having had sex (Ford and Beach, 1951, p. 145). The death penalty for bestiality persisted until the end of the eighteenth century, with an execution occurring in York, England, as late as 1793 (Knipe, 1867). In one of the most interesting instances from a deviance perspective, a Frenchman named Jacques Ferron was hung at Vanvres in 1750 for copulating with an ass. As in most bestiality cases, the animal's complicity was determined by legal means (Ford and Beach, 1951, p. 145):

> The animal was acquitted on the grounds that she was a victim of violence and had not participated of her own free will. The prior of the local convent and several citizens of the town signed a certificate stating that they had known said she-ass for four years, and that she had always shown herself to be virtuous both at home and abroad and had never given occasion of scandal to anyone. This document was produced at the trial and is said to have exerted a decisive influence upon the judgment of the court.

While homosexuality and perversions like bestiality appear to have been the subjects of decriminalization and decreased stigmatization over the last two centuries, heterosexual activity appears to have been regarded and regulated *more* strictly over the same period. In Elizabethan England, while sodomy and bestiality carried the death penalty, the punishment for fornication and adultery was relatively minor: Miscreants had to stand, holding a white wand, in a white sheet in the market or in church. Similarly, even within the strict sexual mores of Puritan New England, Hawthorne's heroine Hester

Prinn received for adultery a punishment no more severe than wearing the infamous scarlet letter.

In general, the 1700s appeared to be a time of a new erotic sensibility in which heterosexuality was public and unproblematic (Stone, 1979, p. 336). During this period, for example, England saw published directories and literal catalogues of available prostitutes. One of these directories, *Harris's List of Covent Garden Ladies,* published a list of call girls, complete with prices, specialties, and anatomical descriptions—e.g., despite seven years in the trade, one woman is favorably described because "the propelling labia still make the close fissure" (Stone, 1979, p. 336).

The permissiveness of this period extended to premarital sexual relations. For example, historians have used parish records to create indices of the frequency of prenuptial pregnancies—the proportion of first children who are born less than eight and a half months after the marriage. According to Stone (1979), "The index of premarital conceptions is as good a guide to the realities of premarital sexual behavior as the historian is likely to find" (p. 385). In the case of both England and New England during the latter part of the seventeenth century, this index hovered between 10 and 20 percent. In the eighteenth century, however, a startling change took place. The rate of prenuptial pregnancies increased to over 40 percent in many places on both sides of the Atlantic (Stone, 1979, p. 387).

This statistic suggests that a privatization or destigmatization of nonmarital sexuality occurred in the 1700s. This permissiveness seems to have included other aspects of family life such as divorce. For example, divorce was a legal possibility even among the Puritans. Modern opposition to divorce in the United States dates from an 1889 Bureau of Labor report that documented how common divorce had become. The report created great moral controversy and also a conservative opposition to all divorce (O'Neill, 1967). In the century since that report was issued, the trend appears to have been reversed, and family life became the subject of piety, public scrutiny, and potential stigma. At least in the first half of the twentieth century, prenuptial pregnancy and divorce became heavily stigmatized once again.

The historical record indicates that perhaps the most general statement one could make about sexual deviance is that this *category* of moral discourse has always existed. The *content* of this category has, however, proved highly variable. The specific sexual behaviors that have been deviantized have varied from period to period. The very same acts appear to carry a stigma label in some periods and not others. Also, in some cases categories of problematic sexual behavior have been created *de novo*. For example, the first antimasturbation publication was produced by an anonymous clergyman. Published in England in 1710, it was called *Onania or the heinous Sin of Self-pollution, and all its frightful Consequences in both Sexes Considered.* This English publication went through nineteen editions and was followed by similar material on the Continent. These works alleged that onanism led to serious maladies like lassitude, epilepsy, nervousness, or even death (Stone, 1979, p. 321).

While the reasons for these dramatic changes in deviantization remain unknown, it is evident that they occur. Many of these changes become more visible with greater historical distance (e.g., attitudes toward homosexuality in the nineteenth century versus ancient Greece), but it would be a mistake to assume that these transformations are not occurring at the present time. In the late twentieth century, for example, homosexuality is being decriminalized and clinically delabeled in many Western societies. Some signs also indicate that definitional changes are affecting other forms of sexual deviance, including bondage and sadomasochism, transsexualism and transvestism, and perhaps even incest. In 1981 a British royal commission charged with changing English law proposed that incest should be legalized. The change was not made, at least not in 1981, but the fact that it was contemplated suggests that definitions and sanctions for virtually all forms of sexual deviance are historically negotiable.

Cultural variation and sexual deviance.   Just as the historical record provides evidence of sweeping changes in the deviantization of specific sexual behaviors, the cross-cultural record provides a different but equally valuable comparative perspective. The theoretical significance of what anthropologists call the ethnographic record is that these accounts have described the nature of sexual arrangements (and, of course, many other facets of culture) for a very large number of societies. These records make it possible for us to discern consistencies and differences in terms of what societies have regarded as acceptable behavior or, alternatively, as deviance. In a sense the practices of these societies have been frozen by the ethnographer's effort to produce a narrative "photograph" of the depicted society at the time of contact with the outside world.

The ethnographer's account is priceless because it allows us to gauge the extent of human and cultural variation by indicating the range of possible permutations for a very large number of normative and deviant behaviors and by allowing us to see whether the solutions adopted in our own society are similar to those chosen by other cultures or whether they differ in interesting but arbitrary ways. Ethnographic accounts can capture this diversity in a historical present before it becomes transformed by contact with outside societies. Cross-national communication and contact have become increasingly pervasive, and perhaps some aspects of original cultural diversity are converging around a small number of dominant patterns. The incomparable value of the ethnographer's account, therefore, is that it informs us not merely about what did exist but also about what might exist.

Historical accounts of early cultural contacts provide vivid evidence of the degree to which many sexual values and practices are culture-specific. Explorers, travelers, traders, colonials, and missionaries from Europe found in non-Western societies many practices different from their own. With few exceptions these sojourners tended to assume that their own European forms were better than those they encountered elsewhere in the world. Researchers of this period have attributed this arrogance to general ethnocentrism and a tendency to confuse technological superiority (which the Europeans in general possessed) with moral superiority (Binney, 1968). The cultural ethnocentrism characteristic of early explorers and colonials is notable because the values and behavior of these sojourning Europeans in many cases left little room for admiration (e.g., Sinclair, 1959).

The shock of early cultural contacts appears to have been particularly great in the area of sexual behavior. Captain James Cook, perhaps the most accomplished explorer in European history, navigated throughout the Pacific at a time when this large region was first opened to outside contact. His journals indicate frank astonishment at the differences between the sexual practices he observed and those of his native England. In one Polynesian society, for example, he approached a crowd of people, only to find that the villagers had gathered to watch a couple have intercourse and shout encouragement and helpful suggestions.

The Europeans tended to make these cultural differences significant in moral terms, and in most colonial societies traditional native practices were both deviantized and purposefully undermined. In virtually all of these cultural contacts the Europeans regarded native sexual practices as unconscionable promiscuity. Nudity, which was widely practiced outside Europe, was also seen as offensive and somehow symptomatic of immorality.

As an early English colonial in New Zealand said in 1820 concerning that country's native Maori, "I hope the time is not far distant when they will all be clothed, and in their right mind, sitting at the feet of Jesus" (Binney, 1968).

As a curious footnote to this period of early cultural contact, in some cases the premise of moral superiority failed those who carried it. A number of cases of "fallen" missionaries are recorded, particularly in Polynesian societies. These individuals came to these societies to convert the natives but were themselves converted. One of these fallen missionaries, a Thomas Kendall working in New Zealand in 1822, explained his conversion as follows, "I have been almost completely turned from a Christian to a Heathen, poisoned by the apparent sublimity of their ideas" (Binney, 1968, p. 99). Kendall's superior, an important figure in Pacific history named Samuel Marsden, saw Kendall's fall somewhat differently: "By prying into the obscure mysteries of the Maoris in order to ascertain their notions of the Supreme Being, etc., his own mind was polluted, his natural passions inflamed, by which means he fell into their vices" (Sinclair, 1959).

In general, though, Europeans succeeded in deviantizing non-European sexual attitudes and practices. Fortunately for scientific and theoretical purposes, however, a record of some of this cultural diversity survives. In terms of sexual behavior and sexual deviance this record includes remarkable variation and, as well, some interesting consistencies. The classic work in this area is Ford and Beach's *Patterns of Sexual Behavior* (1951). These authors examined sexual behavior and sexual deviance as they existed in the nearly 200 cultures included in the Human Relations Area Files. The book identifies a very large number of differences across this comparative spectrum but a number of similarities as well. These differences and consistencies will be indicated briefly below, along with their implications for the study of deviance.

Differences. In general, the cross-cultural record on sexuality is one of impressive variation. The independent evolution of social arrangements in different societies produced a rich mixture of normative patterns for all sorts of conduct, including sexual behavior. Even *within* the same normative category (like heterosexual behavior) the precise forms of behavior vary enormously. From surveys with Americans, for example, Kinsey and other researchers concluded that the most common coital position was the so-called missionary position, with the woman lying on her back and the man lying above, facing her. These researchers concluded that 70 percent of

American couples had never experimented with any other coital position. While this position is the usual one in many societies other than our own, the cultural record shows that many other positions can become equally normative (Ford and Beach, 1951, p. 24):

> Lying side by side, face to face, is the preferred position among the Goajiro, Kwakiutl, and Masai. Intercourse in the sitting position, the woman squatting over the man, is the dominant pattern only on Palau and Yap.

Aside from the mechanics of heterosexual behavior, the cultural record indicates that considerable variety exists in terms of normative prescriptions for heterosexuality and mating. American society and most other Western cultures are what Ford and Beach classify as "single-mateship" societies. In these societies formal recognition is limited to one form of sexual partnership, that of one man legally married to one woman (Ford and Beach, 1951, p. 107). This norm is binding except when the union is dissolved by annulment, divorce, or the death of one spouse.

In terms of the cross-cultural record, however, how common is single-mateship? The evidence from Ford and Beach shows that monogamy is the exception and not the rule. In 84 percent of the 185 societies in their sample, men are permitted by custom to have more than one mate at the same time if they are able to do so (Ford and Beach, 1951, p. 108). In practice, this norm protecting polygyny is restricted by practical matters like the man's ability to afford more than a single wife, and many potential wives are excluded on the grounds of complex incest prohibitions. The important aspect of this comparison, however, is that polygyny is a deviant sexual arrangement in *only* 16 percent of the societies examined by Ford and Beach. This conclusion has clear implications for the likelihood that given behavior patterns will be labeled as deviant. In particular, this finding indicates that the fierce deviantization of the Mormon and Oneida communities that occurred in nineteenth-century American society would not have occurred had these societies emerged in a majority of the world's cultures instead of in the United States.

A second area of great cross-cultural variation concerns homosexuality. In our society all forms of homosexual behavior have been stigmatized and, frequently, heavily sanctioned as well. These sanctions have been applied more heavily to men than women. For example, while many states have had severe penalties for men convicted of homosexual relations, the law has in general ignored similar relations among women. In a number of other cultures as well homosexual behavior is deviantized. Among the Rwala Bedouins, for example, offenders convicted of homosexuality are sentenced to death.

In general, however, the cross-cultural record shows that the "homophobia" present in American society is the exception rather than the rule. In 64 percent of the societies for which information could be identified, Ford and Beach (1951) found that homosexual activities of one sort or another are considered normal and socially acceptable for all or at least certain members of the community. In a number of societies the homosexual role is institutionalized within the culture in the role of a *berdache,* a male who dresses like a woman, performs a woman's tasks, and takes the role of a woman in sexual relations. In many societies, however, the homosexual norm is generalized. Among the African Siwans and the Australian Aranda, homosexual behavior appears to be widespread or even universal, and males are singled out as peculiar if they do not indulge in homosexual activities (Ford and Beach, 1951, p. 132). The patterns show that the stigmatization of homosexuality is culture-specific and that the deviantization of this and other forms of sexual activity is culturally negotiable.

Similarities. While nonmonogamous and homosexual activities are deviantized only in a minority of cultures, not all forms of sexual deviance show this pattern of arbitrary variation. For example, virtually all societies distinguish between sexual relations that involve *mateship* and those that consist merely of *liaisons.* In virtually all cultures mateship relationships are distinguished by the fact that individuals enter them by means of a ceremony. When liaisons exist within a society, on the other hand, they are begun without ceremony. Liaisons are, in many cultures, not heavily sanctioned; e.g., the Toda of India have no word in their language for adultery. Similarly, even though the specific content of the rules regarding acceptable sexual practice varies dramatically across cultures, the *existence* of the rules themselves appears to be universal (Ford and Beach, 1951, p. 106):

> No human society condones promiscuous or indiscriminate mating. Every culture contains regulations that direct and restrict the individual's selection of a sexual partner or partners. Every society has its own concepts as to the number and nature of permissible partnerships that may be formed.

Other consistencies also underlie the diversity in acceptable sexual behavior. For example, even though polygyny and polyandry are considered nondeviant in a majority of cultures, the choice of spouses seems to follow certain regularities even in nonmonogamous societies. Thus in most polygynous societies the plural wives do not enjoy equal status. The first woman a man marries is in general the principal wife, and the secondary wives hold a status inferior to hers (Ford and Beach, 1951, p. 108).

In addition, even in polygamous societies two other patterns appear to hold. First, in polygynous societies the dominant form is frequently *sororal polygyny,* the marriage of a man to a woman and her sisters. This pattern is more common than polygynous marriage to unrelated women. Second, polygyny is much more common than polyandry, with the Toda of India and the Marquesans of Polynesia being two of the few cases of polyandry (Ford and Beach, 1951, p. 109). This asymmetry between the frequency of polygyny and polyandry is also reflected in a double standard concerning sanctions for extra-mateship liaisons (Ford and Beach, 1951, p. 115):

> Sixty-one percent of the 139 societies in our sample for whom evidence is available forbid a mated woman to engage in extra-mateship liaisons. In some societies the mated man is similarly restricted, although the great majority of these peoples are much more concerned with the behavior of the mated woman than with that of the mated man.

Finally, by far the best-known universal concerns incest. Incestuous sexual relationships can be classified into two types: parent-offspring relations and sibling relations. Incest between parents and their offspring is one of the very few sexual behaviors that is universally deviantized. A number of very special exceptions exist—e.g., the Azande of Africa insist that the highest chiefs enter into sexual partnership with their own daughters. In general, however, sexual liaisons with offspring is forbidden to both men and women, and this prohibition is found in every human culture (Ford and Beach, 1951, p. 112).

Brother-sister incest is nearly, but not quite, as prohibited as parent-offspring incest. In the very few cases where brother-sister incest is permitted, it is allowed only in the form of mateship and not as casual liaisons. Historic examples of brother-sister incest include the Incas and the ancient Egyptians. In both societies the royal families were for a time perpetuated by means of brother-sister incest—i.e., the powerful succeeded in defining their own incest as nondeviant. Even these exceptional cases serve to underline the universal nature of incest taboos, and in no society are incestuous matings permitted in the general population.

In all societies the deviant status attached to incest is not limited to the nuclear family. Beyond this consistency the content of nonnuclear-incest prohibitions varies widely from culture to culture. In some cases the prohibition extends only to secondary relatives like the father's sister, sister's daughter, etc. In American society the incest taboo includes relatives like first cousins. In a majority of cases, however, cultures have constructed more elaborate and extended incest prohibitions. In a number of societies the incest definition is so broad that it excludes from possible partnership half the society's population. While nuclear-family incest is a universal instance of sexual deviance, therefore, the nature of nonnuclear incest varies from society to society.

Children

Just as sexual behavior has been subject to major transformations in the boundary between acceptable and deviant forms, perceptions and treatment of children have shown great variation over time and across cultures. These changes have had important consequences for deviance and deviantization. In Western societies at the present time a number of particularly serious forms of deviance concern behaviors that impact children: sexual abuse, violence against children, child neglect, pederasty, and child pornography.

In addition to the seriousness with which these instances of deviance are regarded, Western societies have developed a series of codes and conventions designed to insulate children from what are perceived as exploitative arrangements. Child labor laws and prescriptions for universal childhood education are two examples, but a very large number of reforms and programs of legislation have had as their goal the protection of children. The protectionist quality of these efforts reflects a profoundly entrenched view that children require and deserve a unique, protected status.

The child-centered values these laws and customs reflect are laden with sentiment, and it seems inconceivable that these values have not always been a cornerstone of society. The historic record, however, indicates otherwise. The notion of childhood as a sheltered population category is relatively recent, and current attitudes about the welfare, rights, and requirements of children are for the most part new inventions (Aries, 1962). Until the very last part of the Middle Ages children were seen as little different than small adults. They were expected to participate in virtually all phases of community life alongside adults, and conceptions of the child as deserving special treatment and protection simply did not exist. While children were perceived as essential to inheritance and procreation, they appear to have been regarded without the sentiment and endearment that attaches to children in contemporary life. In part, the unsentimental treatment of children in the Middle Ages reflected their poor prospects. As a result of prevalent disease and primitive medicine, children were not expected to live (Aries, 1962, p. 39):

> The general feeling was, and for a long time remained, that one had several children in order to keep just a few. As late as the seventeenth century, in *Le Caquet de l'accouchee,* we have a neighbour, standing at the bedside of a woman who has just given birth, the mother of five "little brats," and calming her fears with these words: "Before they are old enough to bother you, you will have lost half of them, or perhaps all of them." A strange consolation! People could not allow themselves to become too attached to something that was regarded as a probable loss. This is the reason for certain remarks which shock our present-day sensibility, such as Montaigne's observation: "I have lost two or three children in their infancy, not without regret, but without great sorrow."

Infant and child mortality were commonplace and unsurprising. The precariousness of children was reflected in medieval artwork. In medieval paintings likenesses of children tend to be entirely absent, or if shown at all, they are represented crudely and unsentimentally as small, morphological adults. It is not until the thirteenth, fourteenth, and fifteenth centuries that children appear in artwork in a form recognizably childlike to the modern eye. In this period, for the first time, one sees parents playing with children and depictions of parental affection (Aries, 1962, p. 36). Portraits and images of dead children did not appear until the sixteenth century, suggesting that it was in this period that the idea emerged for the first time that child mortality was not inevitable (Aries, 1962, p. 41):

> On the walls and pillars of German churches one can still see a great many pictures of this kind which are in fact family portraits. In St. Sebastian's in Nurnberg, in a portrait from the second half of the sixteenth century, the father is shown in the foreground with two full-grown sons behind him and then a

scarcely distinguishable bunch of six boys crowded together, hiding behind each other so that some of them are barely visible. Surely these must be dead children.

In many contemporary societies childhood is conceived as a period of innocence. With the advent of psychoanalytic conceptions of child sexuality, the innocence and presumed asexuality of children received a serious challenge. What is not generally recognized, however, is that this presumed asexuality is itself a recent invention. In this sense the psychoanalytic revolution was less a revolution than a return to earlier, long-standing conceptions of childhood. While innocence became a mainstay of nineteenth- and twentieth-century conceptions of childhood, it was preceded for many centuries by a very different view.

Some of the evidence for this view obtains from chronicles like the one kept concerning the childhood of Louis XIII of France (1601–1643). These accounts indicate that society found it perfectly natural for adults to play sexually with children, to encourage childhood sexuality, and to include children in sexual games and humor that appear coarse or even vulgar to the modern eye (Aries, 1962, p. 100). Far from being suppressed beneath an illusion of innocence, sexuality was a conspicuous feature of childhood. In general, children were seen as sexually incapable, although King Louis XIII was married in every sense of the word at the age of fourteen. The important thing about this premodern conception is that children were not seen as deserving special *protection* from sexuality and sexual topics. Adults commonly played with or fondled children's genitalia, and the image of the urinating child was one of the most popular themes for paintings, fountains, and other artwork. In the eyes of succeeding generations this permissive view of child sexuality was scandalous (quoted in Aries, 1962, p. 103):

> The respect due to children was then (in the sixteenth century) completely unknown. Everything was permitted in their presence: coarse language, scabrous actions and situations: they had heard everything and seen everything.

This view of the sexual child gradually gave way to protectionism and the theme of innocence. Writers and moralists began urging parents not to allow children to sleep in the same beds with their brothers and sisters, to forbid and punish masturbation, and to discourage child nudity. At the end of the sixteenth century the emerging conception of childhood innocence led to the novel idea that children should be protected from sexual matters, sexual discussion, and reading. For the first time censored and expurgated editions of books were developed for the use of children. The notion of age grading for sexual materials dates from this period, and children began to be insulated from publications or topics seen as offensive and indecent.

In this period, then, the stage was set for emerging conceptions of propriety and paternalistic norms concerning the protection of children. While including children in sexual play and discussion was commonplace in earlier times, these same behaviors were deviantized by the discovery, in roughly the seventeenth century, of the innocence of childhood (quoted in Aries, 1962, p. 110):

> This is the age of innocence . . . the age when one can forgive anything . . . the age to which the heavens are open. Let tender and gentle respect be shown to these young plants of the Church. Heaven is full of anger for whosoever scandalizes them.

Just as an idea emerged that the child should be kept innocent of sexuality, children gradually came to be seen as deserving of protection in other ways as well. Discipline constitutes a useful illustration of this transformation, since history has seen a great many changes in definitions concerning the difference between appropriate and inappropriate punishments. Contrary to popular conceptions, the Middle Ages were not characterized by brutal corporal punishment of children. In medieval schools and colleges, for example, punishment for student misbehavior involved fines or, for extremely serious infractions, expulsion. Corporal punishment emerged later and by the sixteenth century had become the dominant form of punishment for children. During this period children were seen as weak individuals in need of the most severe forms of correction.

Whipping became widespread, and children were often flogged until they bled. This punishment was as dreaded as it was common, so much so that a seventeenth-century moral theologian used this punishment to describe for children the nature of hell ("worse a thousand times than whipping") and heaven (where children "would never be beat any more"). This punishment was also normal for young adults, and students in the colleges of Balliol and Lincoln felt the rod throughout their college careers in the 1600s (Stone, 1979, p. 118). By the late 1700s, however, this same form of corporal punishment was regarded as unjustifiable and unnecessarily bru-

tal. In the words of a leading opponent of flogging, "The birch is used only out of bad temper or weakness" (Aries, 1962, p. 263). In its place the methods of punishment changed from pain and humiliation toward sanctions based more on reason.

A number of other areas give additional evidence that children have not always been defined as deserving protection. Before the advent of laws regulating child labor in the early nineteenth century, children worked as long and as hard as adults, with little compensation. In many ways their lot was worse than that of adults. Because of their size, for example, children were given dangerous tasks like cleaning the insides of industrial chimneys. The hardships of illegitimate or abandoned children were particularly cruel. Some of these children were trained by others for use in robbery and prostitution; others had their teeth torn out to serve as artificial teeth for the rich; and still others were deliberately maimed to arouse compassion and increase charity. While we have no evidence that this cruelty toward children met with widespread approval, we have no indication that it was abhorred, either (Stone, 1979, p. 298):

> In 1761 a beggar woman, convicted of deliberately "putting out the eyes of children with whom she went about the country" in order to attract pity and alms, was sentenced to no more than two years imprisonment.

The nineteenth century saw the discovery of paternalism. This development marked a sharp departure from centuries of noninterference. Under the English common law tradition, legal guardians had held an almost unlimited right to beat their own children if necessary for their proper upbringing. This parental right was seen as inviolate, and intervention in a family's internal affairs by the state or private agencies was unknown and unthinkable. This conception began to change in the late 1800s as a number of child mistreatment cases received widespread public attention. One of the most famous occurred in 1875 and involved a nine-year-old girl named Mary Ellen who was said to have been treated viciously by her foster parents. After several mistreatment cases were publicized, the first societies for the prevention of cruelty to children were established in the 1870s (Brace, 1880; Pfohl, 1977).

During this period new formulations emerged concerning acceptable and deviant forms of parenting. While this interest was in part directed at the patent cruelties suffered by some children, this new concern was also prompted by moralistic conceptions about the inadequacies of family life among the poor. Nineteenth-century America was inundated by large numbers of immigrants from Ireland and Germany who became the nation's urban poor. Many Americans regarded these new arrivals as the dangerous classes and perceived their child-rearing practices as immoral or deviant. The passage of neglect statutes and the creation of houses of refuge were a direct response to this clash of parenting styles (Pfohl, 1977).

The interest in child mistreatment has resurfaced again in the late twentieth century, and this form of deviance is now regarded as a major social problem (Smith, Berkman, and Fraser, 1980). In this area a distinction is sometimes made between *child neglect* (failure to meet the physical and psychological needs of the child) and *child abuse* (nonaccidental emotional or physical injury to a child). The former may be thought of as an act of omission: the latter as one of commission. In the modern era, interest in child abuse can be traced in large part to a journal article published in 1946 by a pediatric radiologist named John Caffey. In his paper Caffey reported that subdural hematoma and fractures of the long bones often occur together in infants, and he speculated that the common origin of both injuries might be accidental or willful trauma inflicted by the child's parents (Caffey, 1946).

In the decades since Caffey's article child abuse has become a matter of intensive research and political activity. Because lay and legal definitions of child abuse vary, and because of the inherent sensitivity of the topic, we have very different estimates of the prevalence of this form of deviance. Recent projections range from 40,000 children to as many as 2 million (Smith, Berkman, and Fraser, 1980, p. 13). Although the magnitude of the problem has remained murky, its public and political importance has not. Spurred by scientific and medical discussions of the problem and subsequent public sentiment, legislators quickly passed statutes outlawing the abuse of children by their caretakers. The speed with which this form of deviance emerged is indicated by the fact that all fifty states acted within a four-year period beginning in 1962 (Pfohl, 1977). In addition, a number of nationwide laws were enacted (e.g., the Federal Child Abuse and Neglect Act of 1974) that require professionals like physicians and teachers to report instances in which child abuse is suspected.

In view of new, paternalistic conceptions of the innocence of children, it is not surprising that this particular form of deviance has assumed the status of a major social problem. Interestingly, though, despite the child-centered orientation of many Western societies, history indicates that child abuse (in the sense that this term is now used) is a modern invention. In the past, certainly, infanticide flourished. This practice is very different, however, from child abuse in which a parent singles out a child for physical punishment. Infanticide was generic and unrelated to the actions or alleged misdeeds of individual children.

Infanticide also appears to result in lawful ways from social conditions and social structure. In many societies, for example, cultural pressure for a family to provide a dowry (a monetary gift, a division of the family land, etc.) led in many cases to exclusively female infanticide (Malcolmson, 1977). India provides an instance of this. In cases of this kind the gender of the child was the determining factor in whether the child was allowed to survive.

Infanticide in many other societies has been influenced not by the child's gender but by the mother's social position. In England in the seventeenth and eighteenth centuries most infanticides involved unmarried women. Servants who became pregnant with illegitimate babies were dismissed without character references by their employers. Within the occupational structure of England at the time, a young woman stigmatized in this way could hope for nothing better than the most grinding menial labor, begging, or prostitution. In this historical situation, in which unwed motherhood was so heavily penalized, infanticide flourished without respect to the gender of the child. In addition, illegitimate births tended to be concealed, and if the infant's death was discovered, the mother could claim (reasonably, given prevalent mortality rates) that the child had died in birth. Although enumeration is impossible, infanticide is thought to have been common, and even *MacBeth's* witches included in their cauldron's a "Finger of birth-strangled babe/ Ditch-delivered by a drab." Finally, public outcry led to the act of 1624, which criminalized not infanticide (an offense difficult to prove) but rather concealment. A woman convicted of concealing the death of a child faced the death penalty unless she could produce at least one witness who could swear that the child was born dead.

These examples indicate that infanticide differs in important ways from contemporary child abuse. In child abuse parents presumably single out a child for injury on the basis of some behavior (ceaseless crying, disobedience, etc.). Infanticide, on the other hand, has nothing to do with the child other than the fact of his or her existence. In dowry-oriented societies the female infant is at risk; in societies that punish the parents of illegitimate children, all infants are at risk.

Interestingly, the cross-cultural record shows little evidence of the behavior of child abuse. Of course, children in many societies experience hardships, particularly if poverty is widespread. Also, some societies practice harsh initiation rites and other form of ritualized pain or injury. These practices are, however, unrelated to the familistic nature of Western child abuse. In rites of passage the practices are universal and committed in public. In addition, these cultural practices are performed at a given age and, again, are unrelated to the child's behavior. Deliberate, individual harm at the hands of a child's caretakers is rare or unknown in most non-Western societies (Ritchie and Ritchie, 1981).

As with sexuality, wide variation exists in the treatment of children. These differences appear to be both *substantive* and *definitional*. This variation is substantive in that historical periods and cultures have differed strikingly in their attitudes toward and treatment of children. These differences have produced divergent conceptions of normative and deviant child-rearing patterns. This variation is also definitional, however, in that the very *same* behaviors have been conceived as problematic in some circumstances and unproblematic in others. An example of a substantive change in child rearing might be the acceptability of physical punishment. Definitional changes, on the other hand, include the repression of childhood sexuality and the social discovery of child abuse. These changes may be influenced by sweeping changes in civilizations and consciousness. One such change may be the relatively modern conception of children as innocents deserving protection from society and, occasionally, from family as well.

Eating and Smoking

A final illustration of the power of historic and cultural variation on conceptions of deviance involves eating and smoking. These behaviors show great variation, and again, this variation has been the occasion for intriguing patterns of selective deviantization. Gustatory differences are in some cases only differences, but in many instances morality and stigma can be involved, often in surprisingly strong forms. In these cases diet can be the occasion for deviant imputations. Individuals who violate our own conceptions concerning eligible food items can inspire in us both contempt and disgust.

Normative strictures for acceptable diet include both prescribed food items and proscribed food items. In some cases, such as kosher food, the restrictions are detailed and explicit. More commonly, restrictions are unstated, although equally limiting. In addition, normative aspects of diet involve not only choices of food items but also a large number of subtle, qualitative dimensions: temperature (Americans like cold beer, the English do not), texture (the English cook green vegetables until very soft), blandness (Szechwan Chinese food versus the New England boiled dinner), and acceptable combinations (Chinese food is served on rice in the United States but is served with French fries in England). These dietary restrictions are generally unstated and become recognized only when our expectations and preferences are violated.

Deviantization is more commonly attached to variations in eligible food items. These variations sometimes reflect rational conceptions: avoidance of high-fat foods for health reasons, avoidance of meat because of political conceptions about ecology (i.e., a belief that we should eat items lower in the food chain), etc. More commonly, however, moral conceptions and arbitrary patterns of disgust are involved. For example, at least seven different levels of food chain restrictions have been identified. Individuals (or entire cultures) at each level will consume foods from all lower levels but regard diet practices at all higher levels as disgusting. The eligible-food rules and illustrative dietary items at each level are as follows:

1. No animal products—only fruits and vegetables.

2. No dead animal products—milk and cheese.

3. No mammal products—fish and chicken.

4. Some parts of some mammals—cows (beef) and pigs (pork).

5. All parts of some mammals—tripe, head cheese, tongue, pig's feet.

6. All nonbiped mammals—horses, whales, dolphins, dogs, and cats.

7. All mammals—human beings.

These eligible-food rules are crudely scalable. One's position on this scale usually includes an acceptance of items lower on the scale but revulsion and disgust toward items higher on the scale. Some of the deviantizing connected with this food chain scale is merely interesting—e.g., the vegetarian star of a professional basketball team scandalized his teammates by referring to them as "dead-flesh eaters." Similarly, visitors at Harvard University are often surprised to learn that horse meat is served at the Harvard Faculty Club. Other consequences of deviation on this food chain scale are more serious. For example, the meat-eating Eta of Japan were ostracized and made outcasts for generations.

Eligible-food rules have even affected the course of history. For example, the 1857 Sepoy Rebellion, the first armed manifestation of Indian nationalism under English colonial rule, was catalyzed by a food rule violation. Although the underlying political causes of the so-called Indian Mutiny were many and complex, the Sepoy Rebellion was sparked by word (at least partly true) that the British had furnished native soldiers with bullet cartridges greased with the fat of cows (sacred to Hindus) and pigs (anathema to Muslims). The outraged soldiers refused to use the cartridges, and the resulting mutiny led to open warfare characterized by extraordinary atrocities and great loss of life.

The final stage of the food item scale, in which human beings are regarded as an eligible food item, has been the subject of extensive moralizing and deviantizing. This practice is regarded with exceptional disgust in many Western societies, although under certain extreme situations (ship and plane wrecks, the California Donner party, etc.), it has occurred without criminal blame attaching to those who consumed human flesh. All Western societies have deviantized this food chain item fiercely, although this view was not shared, originally, in a large number of non-Western cultures. A number of these societies practiced what the anthropologists have delicately termed *selective anthropophagy* but that remains better known by the lay term of cannibalism.

In many cases humans were consumed in these societies only on ceremonial occasions or only in part. In cultures where cannibalism occurred, it was frequently connected with warfare. The victor of an intertribal war might consume a portion of a killed foe—e.g., the heart, in order to gain some of the enemy's courage. Although this practice was seen as perhaps an ultimately deviant act by Westerners, it was in fact the arrival of Europeans (or, more specifically, their guns) that in many cases made cannibalism flourish on an unprecedented scale. For example, the New Zealand chief Hongi Hika obtained muskets from the English, and in 1821 more than a thousand of his enemies were killed in the North Island; as a result, anthropophagy occurred on a wide scale (Sinclair, 1959). Even though the higher levels of the food chain are the

basis for widespread moralizing, even here cultures can legitimately vary in terms of the specific practices they label as deviant (Lips, 1937):

> Cannibalism shocks us terribly. Yet I remember talking to an old cannibal who from missionary and administrator had heard news of the Great War (World War I) raging then in Europe. What he was most curious to know was how we Europeans managed to eat such enormous quantities of human flesh, as the casualties of a battle seemed to imply. When I told him indignantly that Europeans do not eat their slain foes, he looked at me with real horror and asked me what sort of barbarians we were to kill without any real object.

The food chain thus becomes a source of potential deviantization, particularly when conflicts arise concerning eligible and deviant food items. In the course of early cultural contacts cannibalism was "successfully" deviantized by missionaries and other Westerners, and the practice has largely disappeared. In general, the resolution of food chain disputes seems to reflect relative political power more than disgust over specific diet. In India, for example, the Hindus were unable to deviantize beef consumption by convincing British colonials to abstain from beef.

The most recent case of food chain deviance again reflects cultural differences. In California in several incidents dogs and cats were trapped and eaten by recently arrived refugees from Southeast Asia. These incidents were reported in the press, and public outcry over this food chain deviance generated legislation in Sacramento that provided a six-month jail term and a $500 fine for anyone killing a dog or cat for its pelt or for food. In introducing this legislation directed at the food chain preferences of the Southeast Asians, State Senator Marz Garcia said (*San Francisco Chronicle,* 1980):

> While I respect their right to continue their former lifestyle insofar as it blends with our ways, the people of the United States have historically considered dogs and cats to be pets, in many ways members of the family, and most Americans find the idea of using them for food repugnant.

Like elements of the food chain, other dietary habits and substances can acquire selective deviantization. In some cases political and legal struggles are waged as part of efforts to criminalize certain substances. The American experience with the prohibition of alcohol is perhaps the most famous example. In the case of substance abuse, again, the dominant pattern is one of highly *selective* deviantization. Jaffe (1977) points out that while a long range of problems and conditions (including automobile exhaust, nightshade, glue sniffing, bhang, and marijuana) have long been included in the *International Classification of Diseases* and the American Psychiatric Association's *Diagnostic and Statistical Manual of Mental Disorders,* no mention of health problems associated with tobacco was made until 1975. This omission is impossible to justify in terms of the *objective* pathology of smoking, since tobacco is the largest preventable cause of premature death, illness, and disability in American society (Jarvik *et al.,* 1977).

The fact that tobacco has been omitted from medical discussions of addiction and is also invisible in criminal law indicates that the deviantization of illegal substances cannot be understood merely in terms of objective health consequences. This pattern of arbitrary and highly *selective deviantization* is also reflected in language. While heroin users are invariably termed *addicts,* the word *addiction* almost never occurs in connection with tobacco, except in jest. For most of the twentieth century the medical and psychiatric communities have been characterized by a similar reluctance to classify tobacco dependence as analogous to other substance addictions (Jaffe, 1970). Even when tobacco finally appeared in diagnostic manuals in the late 1970s, it was listed under the heading "tobacco use disorder" rather than "tobacco dependency."

This definitional reticence is particularly impressive since the clinical and epidemiological evidence on the question has been clear for some time. In addition, the historical record indicates that concerns about the pharmacological effects of tobacco dates back at least four hundred years. One of the first Europeans to comment on tobacco addiction was Bishop Bartolome de las Casas, a missionary who accompanied the Spanish to the Americas. In 1527 de las Casas described the way in which the Indians sucked in the smoke from a smoldering bundle of dried leaves, or "tobacos." The Spaniards in the region had adopted the practice, and when Bishop de las Casas reproached them for "such a disgusting habit," the soldiers "replied that they found it impossible to give it up" (de las Casas, quoted in Jaffe, 1977, p. 205). One of the most famous critics of tobacco addiction was King James I of England, who was appalled that the habit had spread from the New World to the Old (King James I, *A Counterblaste to Tobacco,* 1604, quoted in Jaffe, 1977, p. 205):

> Many in this kingdome have had such a continuall use of taking this onsavorie smoke, as now they are not able to forbeare the same, no more than an olde drunkard can abide to be long sober, without falling into an uncurable weakness and evill constitution.

Although smoking is not yet criminalized, it is increasingly deviantized in American society (Markle and Troyer, 1979). In this sense it provides an excellent illustration of the definitional and socially constructed nature of deviance. The deviantization of smoking is reflected in several changes. Twenty-six states have passed laws that prohibit smoking in various places; cigarette packages are required by law to carry increasingly grim health warnings; and surveys show growing support (even among smokers) for greater restrictions on smoking in public places. A number of political groups have been formed to increase sanctions against smoking: ASH (Action on Smoking and Health), GASP (Group Against Smokers' Pollution), and NIC (National Interagency Council on Smoking). Cigarette advertising has been removed from American television and radio, and a number of magazines like *The Reader's Digest* voluntarily refuse cigarette advertising. In the legal sphere, in addition to efforts to outlaw smoking in public, the suggestion has been made that all cigarette advertising, print and media, should be made illegal (Foote, 1977).

DEVIANCE AND THE FLUID NATURE OF THE UNACCEPTABLE

As the evidence on sex, children, eating, and smoking makes clear, deviance is not a fixed attribute of specific behaviors or specific individuals. While the *categories* of deviance and deviants may exist in all historical periods and in all societies, the *content* of these categories has proved to be remarkably fluid. The changes in definition and social construction flow in both directions. New forms of deviance (and new deviants) are created when previously unsanctioned behaviors are criminalized or stigmatized. Alternatively, decriminalization can remove sanctions and stigma by delabeling individuals and their behavior.

The recognition that deviance is situated within (and is only meaningful in the context of) specific eras and cultures does not require the abandonment of values and judgment. Instead, this perspective implies precisely the opposite: that judgment and similar definitional processes are problematic and deserve to be included in the study of deviance. Indeed, the omission of these definitional processes entails some scientific risks. Since the boundary between acceptable and unacceptable behaviors is often contested and commonly redrawn, it may be intellectually unwitting to take as given the specific definitions of deviance prevalent in a society at one historical moment.

In the past two decades many researchers have recognized that some of the most interesting questions in the study of deviance have often gone unasked:

1. How has this behavior come to be problematic?

2. What effect has this definitional process had on the incumbents of the deviant role and on the institutions who process them?

3. What groups or interests benefit from the successful deviantization of this behavior?

4. Can the sanctioning of this behavior and not other behaviors be explained on the basis of the greater harmfulness of the sanctioned behavior?

5. How much of the deviantization of this behavior reflects an aversive moral judgment applied by a defining group?

The fluid nature of deviance and deviantization has been indicated here by the examples of sexual behavior, children, and food. In each case different cultures and new eras discovered new forms of deviance and deviants. In many cases the actors and practices so discovered were seen as unproblematic in other places and at other times. The social, negotiated nature of deviance is reflected in the often arbitrary definitions by means of which behavioral variation becomes shaded into normalcy and deviance.

Other case studies could have been used in place of sex, children, and food. For example, the deviantization of cruelty to animals dates from the adoption in 1641 of the *Liberties of the Massachusetts Colony,* which provided that "no man shall exercise any tyranny or cruelty towards any brute creatures which are usually to be kept for man's use." Perhaps significantly, these *Liberties* also forbade husbands to beat their wives (Stone, 1979, p. 162). Coffee provides another example. This beverage was suppressed in Europe as an infidel drink until coffee was formally Christianized by Pope Clement VIII in the sixteenth century. While no longer outlawed, coffee continued to be sanctioned for its perceived narcotic and addictive properties, and the moral outrage over this deviant drink was the subject of J. S. Bach's famous Coffee Cantata.

Because of the fluid, emerging, and continuous nature of deviance, the list of examples could also include *current* definitional controversies: the movement to legalize and facilitate suicide for the terminally ill, the legal status of rape within marriage, conscientious objection to war and conscription, nonmarital cohabitation and nonmarital parenting, custody rights of homosexual parents in divorce cases, euthanasia of newborns with severe defects, and a large number of other areas of potential stigmatization or, alternatively, decriminalization.

Deviantization and delabeling appear to be pervasive and ceaseless. While certain continuities may exist, clearly we do not live in a fixed moral universe. The boundaries separating normalcy and deviance are many, permeable, and shifting. With very few exceptions we have no permanent moral landmarks to which the label of deviance always attaches. Instead, deviance is produced from the interaction of the defined and the individuals and institutions who perform the defining. Deviance is both socially constructed and socially dissolved, and this fluid, creative, interactive process is now recognized as one of the most important and subtle facets in the study of deviance and deviants.

MAJOR IDEAS, CONCEPTS, AND THEORIES OF DEVIANCE

As indicated in the first part of this chapter, the field of deviance has witnessed major changes in emphasis. A recurring dimension in this change has been the difference between *objectivist* and *subjectivist* approaches. Objective research on deviance has stressed concrete behaviors and conditions, and objective research has tended to be etiological, epidemiological, clinical, or therapeutic in orientation. Research on the subjective aspects of deviance, however, has emphasized definitional processes, societal reaction, stigma, and the behavior of institutions and others. While the subjective aspects are the center of newer conceptions of deviance, clearly the subjective *and* objective approaches will continue to coexist (easily or not) in the study of deviance.

This objective-subjective dimension affects not only one's overall conception of deviance but also the theories and specific methods with which deviance research is undertaken. In this section of the chapter the nature of major ideas, concepts, and theories will be indicated briefly. In many cases these issues reflect the pervasive differences between the objectivist and subjectivist traditions in the field. The use and implications of each idea, concept, or theory will be described briefly.

DISORGANIZATION AND ANOMIE

Some of the earliest recorded conceptions of deviance occur in the Bible. For example, in Ezekiel (7:23) one of the explanations God is said to have given for his wrath is that "the land is full of bloody crimes and the city is full of violence." Biblical treatments of deviance and much ensuing discussion over the following two millennia have been *absolutist*—moralistic, proscriptive prohibitions with no interest in either description or explanation. In these analyses the inherent pathology of deviance is assumed to be self-evident.

While early sociological treatments of deviance often treated the forms of deviance as givens, they were more interested in explanation. Early theoretical work suggested that deviance emerged from social change, particularly rapid changes and the social disorganization they produced. This perspective flourished in the United States in the first half of the twentieth century. During this period a rural, agrarian, traditional society was transformed into an urban, industrial, pluralist nation. In the eyes of many observers these rapid and complex changes produced a diminution of the social bonds of traditional values and stable communities.

The social disorganization thesis was pioneered by W. I. Thomas and Florian Znaniecki in their work *The Polish Peasant in Europe and America* (1920, 1958). This work argued that traditional societies have low levels of crime and deviance generally because of the personal, familial, and communal social controls that an intimate and unchanging social order makes possible. This theory drew negative attention to the city, which in these terms is more disorganized than the traditional societies from which many American immigrants derived. This social disorganization perspective established a research tradition that has come to be called the Chicago school of sociology (Carey, 1975).

While this school produced important ethnographic accounts of deviance, it has been criticized for a number of problematic assumptions. These include the implications that urban communities were inherently pathological (Clinard and Meier, 1979, p. 66) and an exclusive focus on lower-class deviance (Mills, 1943). In general, cities do have higher rates of some forms of deviantized behavior, including violent crime, and this urban-

nonurban difference occurs in most other societies as well as the United States (Wolfgang, 1968; Archer *et al.,* 1978). At the same time the reasons for the higher incidence of urban crime are not understood, although at least seven competing theoretical explanations have been offered (Archer *et al.,* 1978, p. 74). The simplistic concept of social disorganization provides an unsatisfactory explanation of deviance, however, since studies of crime and deviance suggest that they are frequently highly organized affairs.

Finally, the lower-class bias present in the social disorganization approach is now recognized and widely disputed. In part, this tendency seems to reflect long-standing conceptions about the dangerous classes (Sarbin, 1979). This bias pervades the field of deviance, so that *crime* conjures up the image for most people of street crime rather than price-fixing, dumping poisons in the environment, selling products known to be dangerous, etc. In current research this historic bias has prompted new attention to elite deviance, the behavior of the rich and powerful (Ermann and Lundman, 1978; Johnson and Douglas, 1978; Clinard and Yeager, 1980; Geis and Stotland, 1980; Katz, 1980; Schur, 1980; Simon and Eitzen, 1982). The seriousness of white-collar, corporate, and government crime has been obscured by a number of factors but is now increasingly recognized (Monahan, Novaco, and Geis, 1979, p. 118):

> People are quite as dead if they are killed by smog, defective automobiles, negligence in the factory, or other forms of industrial and corporate malevolence as they are if murdered by an armed robber.

One of the best-known conceptions of deviance dates from Robert Merton's formulation of *anomie* (1949). Although the concept originated with Durkheim and was defined as "normlessness," Merton linked the anomie to social structure. Merton was interested in whether certain types of societies would be more or less likely to generate deviant behavior. In particular, Merton speculated that the societies most prone to deviant behavior would be those in which great emphasis was placed on achieving specific goals (e.g., monetary success) but in which legitimate means for reaching these goals were unavailable to some sectors of the society's population. According to Merton, it was the *disjunction* between a society's goals and unavailable means that produced deviant or criminal alternatives.

Although it provided a somewhat more sympathetic and rational perspective, the anomie thesis still reflects a view of the poor as particularly crime-prone. In addition, this conception seems more appropriate to monetary crimes than to deviance generally. Merton's anomie theory has been both influential and widely criticized. The principal criticisms have been that official statistics and institutions greatly overstate offense rates among the poor, and that deviance tends to involve collective, concerted organization rather than the isolated acts of anomic individuals—e.g., prostitution, drug use, corporate crime (Lemert, 1967, p. 14).

FUNCTIONALIST THEORIES OF DEVIANCE

The functionalist view of deviance dates from Durkheim's views on the normal and the pathological, originally published in 1895 (Durkheim, 1950). According to Durkheim, crime and deviance serve important, latent functions for society. In the case of crime, for example, the deviant provides other members of a society with a target for moral outrage, thereby increasing the solidarity of the society. In addition, Durkheim argued that the sanctions applied to deviants (e.g., trials and punishments) serve the important instructional function of emphasizing the rules of the society and the consequences of their violation.

For these reasons the functionalist view of deviance was a radical departure from simplistic conceptions of deviance as immoral, disorganizing, or heinous. For Durkheim, crime was ubiquitous and inevitable, and the relationship between a society and its criminals was highly interdependent. A functionalist analysis has been made of several instances of deviance, and an example is the argument that prostitution is functional for society in that it complements (and therefore serves to strengthen) the sexual arrangements possible through marriage (Davis, 1937).

Contemporary versions of functionalist theory sometimes incorporate elements of the constructionist or societal reaction perspective. For example, Erikson (1966) used historical materials to study deviance in Puritan New England. Erikson found that the incidence of deviance appeared to be a function of the level of concern about deviance in a given society and, consequently, its deployment of resources of social control. As a result, Erikson argues, crime waves can be generated by fluctuations in societal concern rather than by changes in actual criminal behavior. Just as the level of concern about deviance may fluctuate, societies may differ in the *instances* of deviance about which they are most alarmed.

In this sense one guide to the form of deviance that will emerge in a given society is implicit in the society's most prevalent fears (Erikson, 1966, p. 22):

> [It] is not surprising that deviant behavior should seem to appear in a community at exactly those points where it is most feared. Men who fear witches soon find themselves surrounded by them; men who become jealous of private property soon encounter eager thieves. And if it is not always easy to know whether fear creates the deviance or deviance the fear, the affinity of the two has been a continuing course of wonder in human affairs.

Viewed in this light, deviants are not necessarily evidence of social pathology or the failure of socialization. In terms of this functionalist scheme deviants are an important part of a community's overall division of labor. Societal reactions to deviance and confrontations with individual deviants provide other members of a society with important information about normative prescriptions and proscriptions in the society. Deviants are therefore major sources of moral instruction in a society. This function appears to be one of the most important latent functions of deviance and, in particular, of societal reactions to deviance (Erikson, 1966, p. 11):

> [Members] of a community inform one another about the placement of their boundaries by participating in the confrontations which occur when persons who venture out to the edges of the group are met by policing agents whose special business it is to guard the cultural integrity of the community. Whether these confrontations take the form of criminal trials, excommunication hearings, courts-martial, or even psychiatric case conferences, they act as boundary-maintaining devices in the sense that they demonstrate to whatever audience is concerned where the line is drawn between behavior that belongs in the special universe of the group and behavior that does not.

CULTURAL, SUBCULTURAL, AND SOCIALIZATION THEORIES

A number of theories have stressed the groups within which deviance occurs and the socialization processes by means of which deviant lifestyles are created. Some of these theories have been developed in the context of crime and criminology, but some are more general in scope. Since many theorists have tried to account for the acquisition of deviance, these theories are often more appropriate for forms of deviance that are *achieved* (Mankoff, 1971) (e.g., crime, prostitution, drug use, etc.) than for those that are *ascribed* (e.g., physical handicaps, mental retardation, etc.). The goal of many theories has been to explain why some people enter a given deviant life-style while others do not.

Cultural and subcultural theorists have stressed the conditions that made deviance probable. These theorists have argued that the deviance is more likely in communities in which it is widely practiced and therefore available for adoption as a lifestyle. This argument is essentially the one behind Albert Cohen's (1955) conception of the *delinquent subculture*—a pattern of values (e.g., "short run hedonism") that run counter to middle-class values. In extreme form values favorable to crime and deviance can form a "subculture of violence" (Wolfgang and Ferracuti, 1982).

One of the most influential socialization theories has been Edwin H. Sutherland's (1978) theory (revised by Donald R. Cressey) concerning *differential association*. This theory holds that deviance is *learned* in much the same way that lawful or conforming behaviors are learned, that deviance is learned through interaction with others, and that specific techniques are learned as well as motives, attitudes, and rationalizations. One of the key tenets of differential association theory is that each individual is surrounded by people, definitions, norms, and behavior patterns that *differ* in that some are favorable to law violation while others are not. According to the theory, whether or not a person becomes deviant (delinquent, drug using, etc.) will be a function of the relative mixture of these procriminal and anticriminal experiences. The principle of differential association is that a person becomes deviant *because of an excess of definitions favorable to violation of law over definitions unfavorable to violation of law.*

Many cultural and socialization theories have been criticized as overly deterministic. These theories provide explanations for entrance into deviant life-styles, but they seem to some critics to minimize the role of individual actions and choice. In addition, these theories do not seem to provide an explanation of the *cessation* of deviance. For example, most juvenile offenders do not go on to lives of adult crime. Cultural and socialization theories seem to imply that once acquired, deviance is (like one's native language) difficult to shed. These concerns were reflected in Matza's (1964) concept of

drift—the idea that individuals could acquire deviant lifestyles but also "mature out" of them. An additional variation is represented by *control theory* (Hirschi, 1969), which focuses on the socialization forces that must be present for deviance *not* to result—i.e., for conforming, lawful, or nondeviant behavior to occur.

SOCIETAL REACTION AND LABELING THEORIES

Many deviance theories are etiological in that they are concerned with the *causes* of deviance—e.g., entry into crime, family patterns of children who become homosexuals, drinking histories of alcoholics, etc. A very different approach is reflected in societal reaction and labeling theories. As indicated at the beginning of this chapter, this new direction has been very influential in deviance both as a critique of traditional research and as a new perspective that greatly expands the domain of important research questions.

Unlike etiological theories, which emphasize events and variables prior to a person's entry into deviant behavior, societal reaction and labeling theory is concerned primarily with what happens to people *after* they have been singled out, identified, and defined as deviants (Traub and Little, 1980, p. 241). In addition, these theories are particularly concerned with the social processes by means of which individuals are labeled as deviant and with the effects of these labels on the deviant and nondeviant alike. The societal reaction and labeling perspectives have their intellectual origins in the work of Tannenbaum (1938), who was one of the first to suggest that societal reactions could consolidate, stabilize, or even create deviance. This conception argued that contrary to the usual supposition that deviance created social control, social control could also create deviance (Tannenbaum, 1938, p. 19):

> The process of making the criminal, therefore, is a process of tagging, defining, identifying, segregating, describing, emphasizing, making conscious and self-conscious.... The person becomes the thing he is described as being.

This formulation clearly has dynamic elements in common with the self-fulfilling prophecy, as developed first by Robert Merton (1949) in sociology and later by Robert Rosenthal in psychology (1966; in press). In terms of its application to deviance the societal reaction perspective and the labeling perspective have been analogous in that they have drawn attention to the effects of labeling. As indicated early in this chapter, labeling theory takes its name from Becker's (1963) statement, "The deviant is one to whom that label has successfully been applied; deviant behavior is behavior that people so label" (p. 9).

Theorists interested in the possibly self-fulfilling *effects* of labeling have stressed the consequences of definition for the defined—i.e., that labeling can perpetuate or stabilize deviance. One of the best-known theoretical formulations is Lemert's (1951) distinction between *primary deviance* and *secondary deviance*. According to Lemert, a variety of definitional and reactive processes (penalties, stigma, etc.) can act to produce *secondary deviation* —self-conceptions, behavior, lifestyle, attitudes, and conditions different from whatever led to the original labeling of the individual (Lemert, 1951, p. 76):

> When a person begins to employ his deviant behavior or a role based upon it as a means of defense, attack, or adjustment to the overt and covert problems created by the consequent societal reaction to him, his deviation is secondary.

Apart from the possibly self-fulfilling effects of labeling, societal reaction theorists have also been interested in the process of definition itself and in the effects of definitions on both the labelee and the labeler. For example, Becker (1963) argues that deviant labels create a "master status." According to Becker, deviance labels have a unique and powerful effect on interpersonal perceptions. Deviant labels constitute a master status in that the deviant label tends to override all other aspects of the individual in terms of salience and perceived importance. This master status fundamentally changes the way a person is perceived, even if the (alleged) behavior or condition was brief, fleeting, and unrepresentative of the person's overall life (e.g., rapist, murderer, mental patient).

As a result, one effect of labeling may be to reorient the cognitive dynamics of interpersonal perceptions and behavior. These changes include *retrospective interpretation,* a process by which individuals reinterpret and reconstruct the past behavior of a *labelee* in terms of new information about his or her deviance (Schur, 1979). In one of the best-known studies of retrospective interpretation, Kitsuse (1962) examined imputations that individuals made about acquaintances who were subsequently identified as homosexuals. Kitsuse found that when an individual was labeled as homosexual, his or her friends tended to reconstrue their past experiences with this person looking for subtle cues or nuances that tended to support the alleged deviance. In this sense one effect of deviant labeling may be to recast or taint perceptions and personal impressions that without the label would be very different.

While other theorists have stressed the effect of labeling on the labelee, work by Kitsuse and others on retrospective interpretation indicates that labeling can have powerful effects on the perceptions, memories, and cognitions of the *labelers* as well. In some cases retrospective interpretation may lend itself to formal diagnosis. In a famous case study Rosenhan (1973) arranged for eight "pseudopatients" to present themselves at the admitting offices of twelve psychiatric hospitals. When examined, the pseudopatients said they had been "hearing voices." With the exception of changes in names and occupations, the pseudopatients provided entirely accurate biographic information during the intake interview. After admission the pseudopatients ceased all pretense of symptoms and acted normally. The study is well known because it was extremely easy for the pseudopatients to be diagnosed as ill but extremely difficult for them to be seen as sane, even when they acted normally. The pseudopatients were hospitalized for periods ranging from seven to fifty-two days, and when they were released, it was not because they were sane but merely because they were in remission.

From the labeling perspective the most interesting aspect of the Rosenhan study was that the behavior and biographies of the pseudopatients were *interpreted in terms of the deviant label.* Once the pseudopatients had been diagnosed as psychotic, things that were otherwise entirely unremarkable were retrospectively interpreted as consistent with the deviant condition. In the context of the clinical label aspects of the pseudopatient's biographies became symptoms. For example, one pseudopatient's description of commonplace changes in personal relationships was recorded as "considerable ambivalence in close relationships." Rosenhan concluded that psychiatrists unintentionally reconceived or even distorted the pseudopatient's behavior or biography to fit (and also, of course, justify) the psychiatric label (Rosenhan, 1973, p. 256):

> Once a person is designated abnormal, all of his other behaviors and characteristics are colored by

that label. Indeed, the label is so powerful that many of the pseudopatients' normal behaviors were overlooked entirely or profoundly misinterpreted.

The imputations made about deviants constitute a potentially rich agenda for social psychologists, and the cognitive aspects of labeling are only imperfectly understood. Some elements of labeling and retrospective interpretation may be analogous to theories of cognitive consistency. For example, Lofland (1966) argues that labeling an individual as deviant produces a tendency toward "biographical reconstruction," which Lofland (1966) explains as "the social need of Others to render Actors as consistent objects. . . . Relative to deviance, the *present evil* of current character must be related to *past evil* that can be discovered in biography" (p. 150).

Viewed in this light, psychiatrists and clinicians may be seen as "specialists in biographical reconstruction" since these individuals examine the biography of the deviant person to identify those biographic elements that "explain" (i.e., are consistent with) the current deviant label. Similarly, once a death has been determined to be a suicide, the individual's biography tends to be reconstructed in a more tragic light to explain the suicide (Douglas, 1967). In these cases, apparently, the label (e.g., that a person is a murderer or that a death is a suicide) *precedes* the cognitive work required to reconstruct the biography in such a way as to yield imputational consistency with the deviant condition or act.

In addition to its effects on the cognitions and perceptions of labelers, labeling is thought to have important effects on the labelee. Most theories have argued that labels would in some ways compound, stabilize, or exacerbate whatever behaviors or conditions may have prompted the label in the first place. Theorists have spoken of "amplification" (Wilkins, 1964) or "role engulfment" (Schur, 1979). These concepts refer to the effects of the master-status quality of the deviance label. The woman convicted of prostitution *becomes* a prostitute, in her own mind as well as in the minds of others, and all of her respectable qualities and nondeviant biography recede into insignificance. Similarly, the murderer's homicide becomes a focus of self-definition, even if this violent event took only a few seconds and was completely atypical of the rest of the person's life. In this way deviant labels are thought to have profound effects upon self-definition. Unlike other kinds of attributions, deviant labels are particularly efficacious and indelible, perhaps

because they are seen as revealing the *essential* character of the labelee. For this reason, once the deviant has been labeled, his or her eligibility for an extraordinary range of social roles (employment, marriage, parenthood, etc.) may be fatally impaired (Schwartz and Skolnick, 1962).

In addition to the ideas and formulations already discussed, theorists have introduced a number of other concepts to refer to specific aspects of deviance and deviantization—the process through which deviantness is attached to behavior and individuals (Schur, 1979). One concept is the idea of status degradation ceremonies (courtroom sentencing, banishment, etc.) by means of which individuals can be moved—conspicuously and for public observation—from nondeviant to deviant status (Garfinkel, 1956). Other concepts have been suggested as well, including self-labeling, i.e., the deviant's self-conception (Schur, 1979), and relabeling and delabeling, i.e., efforts to change or repair deviantized identity (Trice and Roman, 1970). From the limited empirical evidence (e.g., Schwartz and Skolnick, 1962; Rosenhan, 1973) delabeling apparently is much more difficult and problematic than labeling.

The labeling and societal reaction perspectives have had a profound influence on the field of deviance, although a number of issues and questions remain disputed. One such issue has to do with what Lemert (1951) called primary deviation. In Lemert's formulation primary deviation consisted of the behaviors or conditions that led to labeling in the first place. In the more extreme versions of labeling theory the importance (or even the existence) of primary deviation is challenged. A second area of controversy surrounds the idea of secret deviance (e.g., Becker, 1963). Some theorists have used this concept to refer to behaviors or conditions that would be labeled as deviant if they became known, while other theorists argue that secret deviance is a contradiction in terms.

Some of this debate is definitional since some theorists (e.g., Kitsuse, 1962) argue that no deviance exists without some kind of societal reaction. A more substantial disagreement, however, centers on the relative importance of what the individual deviant brings to the labeling process, on the one hand, and what is conferred by the label and subsequent deviantization, on the other (e.g., Clinard and Meier, 1979, p. 77). Finally, a number of theorists (Kitsuse, 1980) have argued that the simple formulation of labeling theory has overstated the degree to which the labelee is a passive participant in the interaction. In a number of cases those labeled deviant can participate in a definitional struggle to change the meaning of the terms with which they have been labeled. This issue has given rise to a new interest in the degree to which deviance is embedded in broader issues of political change and, in some cases, social movements.

SOCIETAL REACTION, DEVIANCE, AND SOCIAL PROBLEMS

Labeling theory is generally conceived as a theory of *individual* deviantization. As indicated in the previous section, this theory is focused on the process (and effects) of labeling individuals and their behavior. Labeling theory is therefore concerned with relatively *micro,* or interpersonal, aspects of societal reaction. An individual who drinks may come to be defined or mapped by others into the category of alcoholic; another individual may be mapped into the category of mentally ill; and a third may be mapped into the category of homosexual. These labeling processes involve societal reaction on a microlevel since an individual person comes to be perceived by others as a member of a larger deviant category. Labeling theory is concerned with the nature and consequences of these mapping and defining processes.

Societal reaction also has a *macro* component, one that focuses on the processes by which *entire categories* of deviant behavior are created, interpreted, established, or dissolved. Just as labeling theory focuses on the mapping of individuals into categories of deviance, the more macro versions of societal reaction theory focus on the ways in which categories (of behavior, lifestyles, or conditions) are deviantized—i.e., mapped into the generic domain of deviance. A number of case studies suggests that lifestyles, behaviors, or attitudes can come to be labeled (or delabeled) as deviant—e.g., the temperance movement and drinking, the decriminalization of homosexuality, etc. This sort of collective or categorical labeling has become increasingly central to social scientists interested in deviantization, politics, and social change.

A number of concepts have been developed to refer to the social changes by means of which new forms of deviance are created or old forms of deviance are delabeled. One of the first of these was Gusfield's (1967) conception of moral passage, which he described as changes in public opinion that produced "a transition of the behavior from one moral status to another." Examples of such moral passages are the criminalization of alcohol consumption during Prohibition and the growing

tendency in the late twentieth century to perceive drug users as sick rather than criminal. Case studies of the deviantization of categories of behavior have shown that these changes involve and often result from political conflict (Lauderdale, 1980; Schur, 1980). Many of these political conflicts illustrate a definitional difference over the moral acceptability of the disputed behavior. A definitional dispute of this kind has been termed a *stigma contest* (Schur, 1980), and whether or not a given behavior, lifestyle, or condition is criminalized (or otherwise deviantized) often hinges on the outcomes of political stigma contests.

Viewed from this vantage point, societal reaction influences not only individual deviants (through stigma, the master status of the deviance, secondary deviation, etc.) but also the content of what come to be viewed as social problems in any given era. In some cases changes in definition and deviantization occur through the mobilization of large social movements (e.g., the Temperance movement). Here the initiative comes from labelers—i.e., individuals who wish to deviantize a previously nondeviant activity. In these cases the initiative comes from the social control perspective. In other cases the labelees confront and challenge the labelers in an effort to liberate themselves from the deviant label. Political movements to decriminalize marijuana use—or prostitution or, as in Britain, heroin use (Trebach, 1982)—are examples of the initiatives from the delabeling perspective.

Sometimes, these stigma contests and efforts at delabeling provide a fascinating definitional confrontation between the labelers and the labeled. A case study of such a definitional struggle is provided by Spector and Kitsuse (1977) concerning the listing of homosexuality as a "sexual deviation" (category 302.0 of the American Psychiatric Association's *Diagnostic and Statistical Manual of Mental Disorders* (*DSM*), Volume II. As a result of political lobbying, confrontation, and persuasion by a group of gay activists, the American Psychiatric Association was influenced to hold a press conference on December 15, 1973, at which a new diagnostic category ("sexual orientation disturbance") was announced. This new category referred to those who were disturbed by or wished to change their sexual orientation, and the press release added (Spector and Kitsuse, 1977, p. 20):

This diagnostic category is distinguished from homosexuality, which by itself does not necessarily constitute a psychiatric disorder. Homosexuality *per se* is one form of sexual behavior, and like other forms of sexual behavior which are not by themselves psychiatric disorders, is not listed in this nomenclature of mental disorders.

On the basis of this and other case studies, Spector and Kitsuse (1977) attempt to develop a model to describe the creation of a social problem—i.e., the effort to label some behavior or condition as deviant, problematic, unacceptable, urgent, and actionable. This model contains four stages in a sort of natural history of a social problem (Spector and Kitsuse, 1977, p. 142):

1. Group(s) attempt to assert the undesirability of some condition and create a public and political issue around it.

2. The legitimacy of the group(s) is recognized by some official organization, perhaps resulting in an investigation or creation of a problem-solving agency.

3. New claims emerge from the original group(s) and others about what is seen as the inadequacy of the response to the original claims.

4. As a result of dissatisfaction with the performance of the agency responsible for the claimed social problem, efforts are made to create counter, parallel, or alternative problem-solving institutions.

In terms of this perspective instances of deviance and other social problems are *socially constructed* by a process of claims making and political activity. In some cases these political efforts are directed at activities that are already deviant, but the argument is made that other (more or less severe) sanctions need to be instituted—e.g., debates over the death penalty, movements to increase the punishment for drunk driving, etc. This perspective shares with labeling theory *an emphasis on the crucial importance of societal reaction and social construction in defining and acting upon deviance and social problems*. In addition, like labeling theory, this view of social problems regards problematic qualities as *conferred* rather than as *inherent* in specific behaviors and conditions.

This view of deviance and social problems as socially constructed emphasizes the degree to which definitional and political activities play a fundamental role. In many instances of deviance definitional and imputational processes may determine whether something is problematic in the first place and whether something should be done about it in the second place. Many times the definitions and claims are negotiated, not in the context of rationale discourse but in the midst of passion and moral fervor. This result is particularly true for those forms of deviance thought to reflect poor character, dangerous habits, or distasteful lifestyles. For this reason deviantization often takes on some qualities of a crusade, and Becker (1963) coined the term *moral entrepreneur* to refer to a person self-righteously dedicated to deviantizing other people and their behavior.

Even in the absence of moral fervor or reformist sentiment, discussions of specific forms of deviance can involve self-interest, sometimes on a large scale. This result is particularly true in a complex society, where the deviantization of a group or condition may create increased demand for the services of one or more professional groups. Many areas of deviance, for example, have witnessed a secular trend away from purely moral judgments of deviants toward conceptions of deviance as symptoms of physical or emotional illness. As just a single example, a drug addict may come to be regarded as sick rather than merely criminal. This reconception has meant that medical interventions have replaced, nominally at least, punishment for many forms of deviance.

This trend has been described as the "medicalization" of deviance (Conrad and Schneider, 1980). Examples of this transition from a "badness" to a "sickness" explanation for deviance include hyperactivity, alcoholism, substance abuse, homosexuality, and mental illness. At the turn of the century, to the degree that they were seen as problematic at all, these behaviors and conditions were seen as morally reprehensible and punishable. In each of these instances the behavior or condition has come to be defined as reflecting medical conditions, and as a result, these instances of deviance gradually have been captured as an appropriate focus of medical treatment. As Conrad and Schneider (1980) indicate, definitional changes in deviance often involve powerful interest groups. In these instances physicians, psychiatrists, therapists, and the entire pharmaceutical industry profit to the degree that each of these forms of deviance is medicalized.

CONFLICT, SOCIAL CONTROL, AND MARXIST THEORIES

Labeling and societal reaction theories have emphasized the importance of definition and social construction. These theories argue that imputations about a behavior, rather than its inherent qualities, determine whether the behavior is deviantized. A somewhat parallel line of thought, and one that has emerged at roughly the same time, argues that deviance is often embedded within political conflict and, in many cases, in class interests as well. Like the labeling and societal reaction perspectives, the conflict perspective challenges colloquial assumptions about many forms of deviance; in addition, this perspective emphasizes the relative advantages enjoyed by powerful elements of a society in terms of defining deviance.

Conflict theories of deviance are rooted in the economic inequality that is embedded within many societies but that seems particularly pronounced in capitalist societies. A number of theorists have argued that economic and class interests affect deviance in two distinct ways: in the generation of the laws and legislation that determine which acts and behaviors are criminalized and how heavily they are sanctioned, and in the economic pressures that lead to offenses (particularly property crimes) among the poor. While labeling and societal reaction theories have emphasized the fact that deviantization is often arbitrary—i.e., unrelated to the actual harmfulness or dangerousness of a behavior—conflict theorists conceive of deviantization as a tool of the most powerful groups in a society. In terms of the conflict perspective illegal acts will be those that threaten the "ruling class" interests—or at least threaten the social stability required for these interests to prosper.

While differences among conflict theorists exist, they share a conception of criminal law and crime rates as the result of political power and social conflict—e.g., "Criminal definitions describe behaviors that conflict with the interests of the segments of society that have the power to shape public policy" (Quinney, 1970). For this reason most conflict theorists regard the law (and the deviance-defining codes it contains) as the coercive weapon of the state's dominant class. In addition, most conflict theorists agree that crime rates appear to be high among the poor both because the criminal laws were written by the rich and because "crime becomes a rational response of some social classes to the realities of their lives" (Chambliss, 1975). Contrary to many lay conceptions of crime as impulsive or pathological, conflict theorists tend to regard many crimes (particularly property and economic offenses) as highly rational given the inequitable distribution of wealth (Taylor, Walton, and Young, 1974). The specific *type* of economic offense is

also determined by class in terms of conflict theory, because the poor have no opportunities to commit corporate crime or embezzlement (Clinard and Meier, 1979).

Perhaps the most vivid support for conflict theory lies in the difference between street crime and corporate or white-collar crime. One of the first theorists to draw attention to this difference was Edwin Sutherland (1949, 1961). Sutherland examined court cases involving antitrust violations, false and misleading advertising, unfair labor practices, embezzlement, and fraud. Sutherland concluded that these offenses were generally more costly and more injurious to public safety and well-being than street crime, but curiously, these offenses seldom received heavy criminal sanctions—or often any criminal sanctions at all. Sutherland's conclusion was that virtually all participants (the offenders, regulatory agencies, the judiciary) treated these offenses as if they were not real crimes.

This double standard of deviance remains a central feature of conflict theory and is used to argue that deviantization is more a function of vested political and economic interests than of the objective harmfulness of the deviantized behavior. Interest in corporate and white-collar crime has escalated in recent years (Geis and Stotland, 1980; Simon and Eitzen, 1982). In part, this interest reflects a desire to redress the previous overemphasis on lower-class crimes. In addition, it has become increasingly clear that corporate and white-collar crime can cause serious bodily harm (dumping carcinogens, manufacturing dangerous drugs or cars, etc.) or even homicide (allowing workers to be exposed to asbestos, failing to observe standards for coal mine safety, etc.).

Although the conflict perspective emphasizes the effects of economic interests, the policies and actions of government also play a role in deviantization. For example, some of the most serious forms of deviance are those involving violence. Surveys that ask respondents to rate the seriousness of different offenses tend to find (with some exceptions) that the street crimes regarded as the most serious are those involving personal injury or death (e.g., Rossi *et al.*, 1974). At the same time recent research shows that the concept of violence is itself the subject of great definitional variation and that the acts of governments are rarely seen as violent even when injurious or fatal. This perceptual double standard has led to the theoretical concept of legal violence—acts of violence that tend not to be regarded as deviant, criminal, or problematic because they are committed with the official auspices of the government (Archer and Gartner, 1976, 1978, 1984).

Acts of legal violence include efforts at social control (e.g., beating protesters, shooting looters during a riot), punishment (e.g., homicides committed as capital punishment), and perhaps the most spectacular form of official violence, war. Studies indicate that these forms of legal violence are rarely defined as "violent" by members of the public (Blumenthal *et al.,* 1972) and also that acts of legal violence are rarely included even in scholarly treatments of violence, aggression, crime, and similar topics (Archer and Gartner, 1978). Legal violence therefore provides a fascinating case study of the importance of language and definition in the study of deviance.

The history of the most prestigious study of violence ever undertaken in the United States, the 1968 President's National Commission on the Causes and Prevention of Violence, indicates how political factors can affect scientific agenda and the definition of a social problem. The codirector of this presidential commission, James F. Short, reported that the topic of war was removed from the commission's agenda at the direct request of the White House—even though the nation was at that moment at the very height of the divisive war in Vietnam (Short, 1975). War was removed from the commission's agenda because the president and the federal government wanted the commission to focus on *illegal* violence—street crime, urban riots, and other types of "violence from below." In this instance, because the government determined the content of the commission's work, its own acts of violence were not included in the forms of deviance investigated by the commission.

In addition to its role in generating laws and shaping public and scientific definitions, government may also play a concrete role in the emergence of violence and deviance. For example, the 1967 National Advisory Commission on Civil Disorders (the Kerner Commission) concluded that although the ghetto riots of the 1960s were made possible by underlying forces of poverty and racism, the immediate cause of virtually every riot was an act of the local police (Lieberson and Silverman, 1965; Marx, 1970). In other cases government has been found to foster or produce deviance that would otherwise not have occurred. For instance, government officials may seek to discredit some political faction or social movement, and one method of producing secretive but official deviance involves use of *agents provocateur*—individuals paid by governments to encourage or cause

third parties to commit acts of violence or otherwise violate laws (Marx, 1974). Some theorists even argue that police and other agents of social control sometimes produce crimes and other deviance that would not have occurred in the absence of these agents. This issue surfaces, for example, in controversies about the effect of entrapment on crime and deviance (Marx, 1981).

EPIDEMIOLOGICAL AND ECOLOGICAL THEORIES

In addition to the theoretical traditions already discussed, the literature has included a great deal of research that does not easily fit within any single theoretical tradition. For example, a great deal of work has attempted to describe or explain distributions of deviant behavior across time and space. Deviance research of this type is perhaps best described as *epidemiological* or *ecological* since the intent is often to provide an account of the distribution of a given behavior or condition. This tradition dates from Emile Durkheim's classic *Suicide* (1897, 1951), which addressed national differences in suicide rates. Epidemiological and ecological studies on deviance are often causal in an inductive sense. Researchers in this tradition generally attempt to identify theories (largely middle range in scope) to account for the observed distributions of a given deviant behavior or condition.

In the area of crime, major ecological variables include nationality and urbanism. For the offense of criminal homicide, for example, national differences in offense rates are extremely large, as indicated by a comparison of offense rates for 110 nations between 1900 and the present (Archer and Gartner, 1980, 1984). As a single illustration, the homicide rate in the United States, while not as high as that found in Colombia and a handful of other societies, is much higher than the rate in all other industrial democracies. At the opposite end of this international violence continuum, homicide is almost unknown in New Zealand (Archer and Gartner, 1984).

Within a single society ecological variations in deviance are common. In the United States, for example, crime (and particularly violent street crime) is dramatically associated with urbanism (Wolfgang, 1968); serious crime rates and categories of city size are strongly and positively related. These differences, like national differences, are large. The effect of urbanism also appears in other societies. Even with an aggregate homicide rate much lower than that found in the United States, most other industrial societies show *relatively* higher homicide rates in larger cities; e.g., the homicide rate in Paris is higher than the French average, even though both are far lower than the American rates (Archer *et al.,* 1978). Curiously, while urbanism and serious crime are strongly related at any one moment in time, the effects of urbanization over time are less clear. As individual cities grow in population size over time, they show no consistent pattern in crime rates. This "paradox of urban crime" may indicate that it is the city's *relative urbanism* (population, etc.) rather than its absolute size that determines its crime rate (Archer *et al.,* 1978).

In addition to this ecological research on deviance, studies have been done on fluctuations over time. These studies have reflected an epidemiological approach to deviance since the general premise has been to identify patterns of causal influence. In the area of mental illness Brenner has shown that aggregate hospitalization rates are linked to economic cycles (Brenner, 1973), and other epidemiological research indicates that conspicuous suicides are at least somewhat "contagious" (Phillips, 1974). This latter finding has been called "the Werther effect" because of a 1774 novel by Goethe. In the novel a hero named Werther commits suicide, and the novel is alleged to have produced imitative suicides all over eighteenth-century Europe.

Other epidemiological research on deviance has attempted to link fluctuations in offense rates to specific events or antecedents. In a study of the effect of capital punishment, for example, Bowers and Pierce (1980) examined homicides in New York State and found (contrary to at least some versions of the deterrence hypothesis) a slight *increase* in the homicide rate in the month following an execution. Other research has examined offense rate fluctuations in an effort to evaluate the effect of specific laws—e.g., the effect of gun control laws on homicide rates (e.g., Cook, 1981).

Finally, other research in this tradition has attempted to assess the effect of broad historical forces and political events. For example, a study of the effect of wars on national homicide rates examined homicide data for fifty "nation wars" (one nation in one war). Despite the fact that wars often produce massive losses of young men—and therefore should result, *ceteris paribus,* in decreases in violent crime—this study found that wars tended to produce *increases* in national homicide rates (Archer and Gartner, 1976, 1981, 1984). These postwar increases could not be explained by a variety of alternative hypotheses, and they suggest that the wartime violence of governments can legitimate acts of violence by individual citizens.

PARALLEL AND COMPETING THEORETICAL ORIENTATIONS

Each of the theoretical perspectives described here has had an important and continuing effect on the field of deviance. Each perspective has adherents and practitioners, and each theory seems to lend itself to somewhat distinctive methods. Labeling and societal reaction theorists, for example, seem to favor case studies, interviews, or field methods like participant observation. Conflict theorists may use case studies, but they are more likely to investigate archives or other documentary evidence. Ecologically and epidemiologically oriented researchers, on the other hand, prefer working with aggregate data on incidence and offense rates.

In some areas the perspectives generated by these theories do collide. For example, societal reaction theorists have been very critical of potential bias (both in sampling and in terms of the categories that happen to be deviantized) in official crime statistics, and these data are, of course, widely used in epidemiological and ecological research (Kitsuse and Cicourel, 1963; Nettler, 1974). Critics of labeling and societal reaction, on the other hand, argue that this perspective understates the importance of primary deviation and individual differences (Gove, 1980). Conflict theories of deviance have been criticized for treating all crimes (even violent crimes in which both offender and victims are likely to be poor) as due to inequality and class interests (Clinard and Meier, 1979). Critics of the social constructionist approach to social problems argue that cultural relativist interpretations of deviance can be overstated, and they cite as evidence cross-national consistencies in the perceived seriousness of different deviant acts (Newman, 1976).

Theoretical debate has centered on these and other issues. Since each theory tends to focus on a unique aspect of deviance, however, different theories have tended to partition the field. This intellectual division has caused several different theoretical traditions to progress in parallel rather than contradictory directions. In certain substantive areas of deviance, as in the case of physical deviance, the next topic in this chapter, these different perspectives and methods have provided complementary discoveries.

PHYSICAL HANDICAPS, PHYSICAL CHARACTERISTICS, AND MEDICAL CONDITIONS

STIGMA AND THE PATHOLOGY OF MIXED CONTACTS

Although a number of important studies appeared earlier (e.g., Lemert, 1951; Macgregor, 1951; Wright, 1960; Davis, 1961; Richardson *et al.,* 1961), the catalyst for the current explosion of research on the social and psychological significance of physical handicaps was the publication in 1963 of Erving Goffman's *Stigma.* Perhaps more than any other writer, Goffman has permanently changed scholarly conceptions about the lives of the disabled and the handicapped. This work has been influential on a number of different levels, and its implications for general theories of deviance have already been indicated. *Stigma* has also provided a rich store of investigable hypotheses for later researchers, and work on some of these questions will be indicated in this section. Although Goffman's work deals with many forms of stigma, it is perhaps closest in its subject matter to the unique nature of physical handicaps.

Along with the general theoretical framework developed in *Stigma,* Goffman uses case studies and autobiographical materials from the lame, the blind, the deaf, and the disfigured to illuminate the two central concerns of this work: the strained nature of interaction between the stigmatized and the unstigmatized, and the burdens borne by the stigmatized in terms of the management of these interactions and the selective disclosure about the nature of their stigma. In its economically written 150 pages, *Stigma* creates a brilliant portrait of the social awkwardness and discomfort the handicapped experience in everyday social life. Goffman uses first-person accounts by the handicapped to capture the problematic nature of interactions between those with handicaps and those without them. These accounts indicate that handicapped-nonhandicapped interactions cause for both participants an unease and self-consciousness they would not experience when dealing "with their own kind." This problem has been of interest to other scholars as well, including Davis (1961, p. 123):

Whether the handicap is overtly and tactlessly responded to as such or, as is more commonly the case, no explicit reference is made to it, the underlying condition of heightened, narrowed, awareness causes the interaction to be articulated too exclusively in terms of it. [This] is usually accompanied by one or more of the familiar signs of discomfort and stickiness: the guarded references, the common everyday words suddenly made taboo, the fixed stare elsewhere, the artificial levity, the compulsive loquaciousness, the awkward solemnity.

Although *Stigma* is not the only (or even the first) work on the problematic nature of interaction with the handicapped, it has become a modern classic for several reasons. In addition to his compelling use of first-person materials about the lives of the handicapped, Goffman uses language effectively to dramatize the nature and importance of his subject. Although his analysis is presented entirely in qualitative form, Goffman develops both general conceptions about stigma and deviance (some of which were indicated earlier in this chapter) and also researchable hypotheses. Goffman includes in his scope a wide variety of stigma, but all have in common the fact that the stigmatized individual possesses "an undesired differentness" (p. 5) and is therefore "disqualified from full social acceptance" (Preface). Goffman discusses the significance of variation across different types of stigma. One of the most important dimensions, according to Goffman (1963, p. 4), distinguishes the *discredited* from the *discreditable:*

> The term stigma and its synonyms conceal a double perspective: does the stigmatized individual assume his differentness is known about already or is evident on the spot, or does he assume it is neither known about by those present nor immediately perceivable by them? In the first case one deals with the plight of the *discredited,* in the second with that of the *discreditable.*

Discredited stigma include deformities, gross physical handicaps, and other manifest disabilities; discreditable stigma include criminal history, sexual deviance, epilepsy, and other invisible conditions. This difference between these two types of stigma has generic consequences for social interaction. Individuals who are discredited are forced to deal with their stigma in virtually all interactions, including initial contacts. Discredited individuals do not have the option of interacting as if they were not stigmatized. For individuals with discreditable forms of stigma the interaction management strategies are more complex. These individuals need to manage information about their stigmatized condition. They may decide to inform no one about their stigma; they may decide to reveal it to selected individuals or only late in a relationship; or they may decide to make this nonobvious stigma a matter of public knowledge. While the *management of tainted social interaction* is an inescapable problem for the discredited, the *management of information* is the preoccupation of the discreditable.

In addition to the key variable of the discredited-discreditable difference, Goffman (1963, p. 4) distinguishes among three different categories of stigma. The first he refers to as "abominations of the body": physical deformities, scars, extreme ugliness, and conspicuous disabilities. The second category consists of "blemishes of individual character": alcoholism, homosexuality, unemployment, addiction, or a record of imprisonment, mental illness, or attempted suicide. The third type Goffman refers to as the "tribal stigma" of race, nation, and religion, "these being stigma that can be transmitted through lineages and equally contaminate all members of a family."

This typology obviously interacts with the discredited-discreditable distinction. Most physical deformities make their possessor discredited, although certain types (like an amputation or bodily scar) can be concealed with clothing or prosthetic devices. Characterological blemishes tend to be discreditable in that the individual can make a decision about whether to disclose a criminal history, psychiatric treatment, or similar matter. Other blemishes, like alcoholism, may be conspicuous at some times and not at others. In Goffman's third type, tribal stigma, race is generally (but not always) conspicuous, while religion is generally (but not always) invisible. The ethnicity of an individual is not always apparent (e.g., some people can be mistaken for members of another ethnic group), and religion is not always invisible (e.g., the garments and appearance of groups like the American Amish and the Chassidic Jews).

As a result of these differences, the effects of stigma on the lives of their possessors is highly variable. Ex-prisoners, homosexuals, some amputees, and other discreditable individuals may be able to "pass"—i.e., to interact as if they did not possess these forms of stigma. Except under situations of greatly reduced information (like telephone conversations or photographs), paraple-gics, the grossly retarded, and members of disvalued ethnic groups are unable to pass. While Goffman's analysis does not show that the unconcealable stigmas of the discredited are more burdensome (e.g., the discreditable may become obsessed with restricting information about their condition), the manifestly stigmatized cannot escape even for a moment the interactional consequences of their conditions.

The consequences of stigma for interaction constitute the central focus of Goffman's work. A reading of the autobiographical materials excerpted in *Stigma* demonstrates that the handicapped carry weighty interpersonal burdens in addition to whatever constraints are imposed by their physical limitations. Mixed contacts, interactions between the stigmatized and unstigmatized, constitute one of what Goffman (1963) calls the "primal scenes of sociology" since "these moments will be ones when the causes and effects of stigma must be directly confronted by both sides" (p. 13). These mixed contacts create stress for both participants, although the specific nature of the stress each one experiences is quite different.

The unstigmatized person is uncertain about how to deal with someone who violates expectations or unwritten rules about how interaction should be conducted. When interacting with a blind person, even if we are able to disattend the markers or signals of this handicap (white canes, dogs, etc.), we are likely to have an awkward interaction because the blind person cannot follow the nonverbal rules for eye contact without which orderly turn-taking and normal conversation are impossible. In this sense the effect of blindness is to disable the normal mechanisms by which facile conversation is accomplished. Similarly, when trying to communicate with the deaf, hearing individuals may exaggerate their mouth movements in the mistaken belief that most deaf people can lip-read successfully. The net effect of this well-intentioned (if strained) effort is, ironically, to reduce or eliminate the chance that any communication will succeed (Higgins, 1980). Sometimes, invisible stigma can create an interactional crisis when an unsuspected form of deviance surfaces (quoted in Goffman, 1963, p. 84):

> We who stutter speak only when we must. We hide our defect, often so successfully that our intimates are surprised when in an unguarded moment, a word suddenly runs away with our tongues and we blurt and blat and grimace and choke until finally the

spasm is over and we open our eyes to view the wreckage.

Apart from the ways in which some types of stigma can disrupt the conversational mechanics of interaction, most unstigmatized individuals respond to stigma with strong affects: aversion, anxiety, fear, loathing, pity, or even panic and flight. Most of the emotional reactions that stigma produces in unstigmatized individuals are negative. Even nominally positive reactions like sympathy or charity may be experienced by the stigmatized as negative, condescending, and patronizing since they imply that the individual merits pity or requires assistance. The premise for reactions to the stigmatized, according to Goffman, is a stated or unspoken belief that these individuals are inferior, contaminated, damaged, or spoiled in some way. This belief causes the unstigmatized to "impute unhumanness" to the handicapped (Goffman, 1963, p. 5):

> By definition, of course, we believe the person with a stigma is not quite human. On this assumption we exercise varieties of discrimination, through which we effectively, if often unthinkingly, reduce his life chances . . . . We use specific stigma terms such as cripple, bastard, moron in our daily discourse as a source of metaphor and imagery, typically without giving thought to the original meaning.

The interactional consequences of stigma are not lost on the stigmatized. These individuals learn, sometimes early in life, that their stigmatized condition produces reactions—sometimes dramatic but almost always negative—in the unstigmatized. For conditions that exist from childhood (e.g., epilepsy, blindness, etc.), sometimes the domestic circle and a range of special institutions can protect the stigmatized individual from perceiving fully the consequences of this stigma. Eventually, however, virtually all stigmatized individuals must leave this psychologically sheltered existence. According to Goffman, the experiences of entering school, dating, or seeking employment precipitate the greatest challenge to the illusions of the stigmatized person (quoted in Goffman, 1963, p. 33):

> I think the first realization of my situation, and the first intense grief resulting from this realization, came one day, very casually, when a group of us in our early teens had gone to the beach for the day. I was lying on the sand, and I guess the fellows and

girls thought I was asleep. One of the fellows said, "I like Domenica very much, but I would never go out with a blind girl." I cannot think of any prejudice which so completely rejects you.

The largely negative reactions the stigmatized experience at the hands of the unstigmatized can lead to a number of strategies. For the discredited, who cannot conceal their stigma, mixed contacts are invariably sensitive. These individuals not only face visible signs of rejection but also must think about what the unstigmatized person *really* thinks no matter what he or she says (Goffman, 1963, p. 14). Partly for this reason discredited individuals may prefer to avoid mixed contacts entirely by constructing friendships with other stigmatized individuals or even by working or living in voluntarily segregated settings. This same interactional tension can be experienced by discreditable individuals when their stigma becomes known. The anticipation of the reactions by the unstigmatized becomes a major variable in whether the discreditable person decides to confide in others the nature of his or her stigma. If the stigma is obvious, slips out, or is intentionally confided, the result is an apparently unavoidable episode of mutual scrutiny (Goffman, 1963, p. 18):

> We [the unstigmatized] may feel that if we show direct sympathetic concern for [the stigmatized person's] condition, we may be overstepping ourselves; and yet if we actually forget that he has a failing we are likely to make impossible demands of him or unthinkingly slight his fellow-sufferers. Each potential source of discomfort for him when we are with him can become something we sense he is aware of, aware that we are aware of, and even aware of our state of awareness about his awareness; the stage is then set for the infinite regress of mutual consideration that Meadian social psychology tells us how to begin but not how to terminate.

One strategic response to this pathology of interaction is for the stigmatized person to try to pass as unstigmatized. While this behavior may conceal (or at least defer disclosure of) one's stigma, it does so only at some cost. At the very least the discreditable individual must go to great lengths to keep submerged the nature of his or her stigma. In some cases, in addition to the effort required by passing, the discreditable individual may pay a steep price in terms of identity and self-esteem. These

two costs of passing can be illustrated by first-person reports of the discreditable (quoted in Goffman, 1963, pp.
87, 88):

> I managed to keep Mary from knowing my eyes were
> bad through two dozen sodas and three movies. I
> used every trick I had ever learned. I paid special at-
> tention to the color of her dress each morning, and
> then I would keep my eyes and ears and my sixth
> sense alert for anyone that might be Mary. I didn't
> take any chances. If I wasn't sure, I would greet
> whoever it was with familiarity. They probably
> thought I was nuts, but I didn't care. I always held
> her hand on the way to and from the movies at night,
> and she led me, without knowing it, so I didn't have
> to feel for curbs and steps.

> When jokes were made about "queers" I had to
> laugh with the rest, and when talk was about women
> I had to invent conquests of my own. I hated myself
> at such moments, but there seemed to be nothing
> else that I could do. My whole life became a lie.

While mixed contacts may be inherently problematic, certain conditions exist under which these problems
can be negotiated or managed. For certain types of stigma, for example, an intimate circle of unstigmatized individuals may work with a discreditable individual to
manage information about his or her condition. A family
with a diabetic child may help the child conceal the condition from friends. Alcoholism, at least in some cases, is
another example. Sexual conditions like sterility, impo-
tence, or frigidity are also discreditable conditions that
unstigmatized intimates may assist the stigmatized person to conceal. In these cases the discrediting information about an individual is managed by domestication—i.e., is kept among family members and other
intimates.

Other forms of management may be possible, at
least in some instances. Some stigmatized individuals
may be able to move beyond the awkwardness and strain
that inevitably taint mixed contacts, at least early in a relationship. Individuals with a physical handicap sometimes report that with prolonged contact some unstigmatized individuals are less put off by the disability, making
normalization a possibility (Goffman, 1963, p. 52). The
strategies the stigmatized develop to try to achieve normalization have been called "breaking through" (Davis,

1961, p. 127). Experimental research on the normalization of stigma is indicated later in this section.

In *Stigma* Goffman's approach is theoretical and his
evidence is qualitative. At the same time passages in the
book provide a rich resource of researchable hypotheses
that the attentive reader can infer from Goffman's analysis. These implicit hypotheses refer to the stigmatized,
the unstigmatized, and their interaction.

1. *Any stigma can become a master status and provide
the basis for a number of irrationally global attributions.*
According to Goffman (1963), "We tend to impute a
wide range of imperfections on the basis of the original
one" (p. 5). In cases of physical deviance, sometimes
people assume that a single disability is pervasive—as
when people shout at the blind as if they were deaf or
speak slowly to stutterers as if they had trouble
comprehending. As indicated later in this chapter, some
stigmas (like obesity) are also used to make attributions
about the personality, character, and general competence of the stigmatized individual.

2. *The unstigmatized discriminate against the stigmatized.* Even though the unstigmatized may regard the
stigmatized with sympathy, they commonly act in ways
that reduce the life chances of the handicapped (Goffman, 1963, p. 5). As indicated later, evidence supports
this hypothesis.

3. *People make a supposition that a stigma is compensated by a gain in some other quality.* Unstigmatized individuals may believe that physical handicaps produce sensory compensation (e.g., increased auditory sensitivity in
the blind) or even special understanding due to a "sixth
sense" (Goffman, 1963, p. 5). This compensatory hypothesis may be shared by the stigmatized person, who
may feel that his or her suffering teaches one about life
and people (Goffman, 1963, p. 11).

4. *When one's stigma is known, a wide range of behaviors are regarded as symptomatic and attributed to it.*
According to Goffman, ex-mental patients are afraid to
engage in vigorous arguments with intimates, coworkers, or employers for fear that any strong affect will
be seen as a symptom. Similarly, when the mentally
retarded experience any problem, this problem is likely to
be "explained" in terms of their intellectual competence—even if this problem occurs commonly among the
unstigmatized (Goffman, 1963, p. 15). This pattern of
global attribution is sometimes referred to as putative
deviance.

5. *The stigmatized person has less privacy and can be approached, touched, interrogated, or invaded at will.* The physically handicapped are routinely stared at—and not merely by children. They are often offered assistance when such assistance is unwanted or embarrassing. Perhaps more important, the stigmatized experience an invasion of privacy not known by the unstigmatized (Goffman, 1963, p. 16). They may be asked about their lives by complete strangers (e.g., "Do you have a gland problem?" "How did you lose your fingers?").

6. *Because they themselves have extensive practice at concealment, the stigmatized are better than normals at detecting the discreditable.* The deaf, or people who live with them, may be better than the hearing at identifying other deaf people (Goffman, 1963, p. 85). Some stigmas may be recognizable to insiders because they produce consistent coping strategies—e.g., the illiterate may ask others to read things for them by explaining that they forgot their glasses.

7. *Discreditable individuals may use an unwritten code to recognize one another.* Since discreditable stigma is, by definition, closeted, it may pose for its possessor the problem of how to meet similar others. Unidentified male homosexuals, for example, may identify and communicate by means of nonverbal communication —e.g., mutual eye contact, which is different from the momentary glances permissible between heterosexual men (Goffman, 1963, p. 98).

FIELD RESEARCH ON PHYSICAL DEVIANCE AND REACTIONS TO IT

Goffman's *Stigma* has had a strong effect on both experimental and nonexperimental research. More than perhaps any other theorist, he has helped to transfer research attention from naive descriptive accounts of deviant lives to the ways in which these lives are affected, often adversely, by the attitudes and actions of the unstigmatized. At the present time we have a growing literature on the reactions the stigmatized experience at the hands of both individuals and institutions. The first of these concerns a micro issue of interest in the study of interpersonal behavior. The second of these is a macro problem embedded in the study of official, organizational reactions to deviance. While there are many exceptions, these two areas tend to be pursued by, respectively, psychologists and sociologists. Experimental research, much of it conducted by psychologists, will be reviewed

in the next section of this chapter. In this section the nature of field research on physical deviance will be indicated briefly.

A number of field studies has examined the dynamics of mixed contacts. This research lends support to the theoretical importance of Goffman's distinction between the discredited and the discreditable. In a camp setting, for example, Richardson, Ronald, and Kleck (1974) studied sociometric preferences among boys between the ages of eight and thirteen. The children were in the camp for three weeks. Roughly half the children in the camp were unhandicapped. Some of the handicapped children had visible handicaps like amputations and cosmetic deformities. The other handicapped children had less obvious disabilities, such as hearing impairment. Richardson, Ronald, and Kleck constructed sociometric measures (choices for bunk mates, etc.) to reflect the patterns of interpersonal preference in the camp. In general, boys without handicaps were preferred to those with disabilities.

The visibility of the stigma seemed to be an important determinant of sociometric ranking. Boys with visible handicaps were chosen less frequently than boys with less visible handicaps. Interestingly, this visible-invisible difference was greatest in rankings made by boys who were not in the same subgroup. This result suggests that the boys with invisible handicaps may have passed as unhandicapped in the eyes of the boys who knew them less well. In the clinical judgment of the researchers the *behavior* of the visibly handicapped boys may have contributed to their low standing in the camp's sociometry. Several of these boys were judged to behave in ways that were socially incompetent, and the poor ratings they received might be due in part to behavior rather than disability per se. If interpersonal incompetence and disability severity are correlated, of course, the interesting question arises of whether the former is a cumulative symptom of the latter. Richardson, Ronald, and Kleck (1974) concluded, "The present study suggests that the evaluation of how well a handicapped child gets along with peers must take into account the degree of visibility and type of handicap and his level of skill in interpersonal relations" (p. 151).

Visibility varies along a continuum, and this continuum determines the relative discreditability of a given physical stigma. Some are relatively invisible in public life, like an amputation successfully concealed by a prosthetic device. Some semivisible markings have historical significance, like the numbers tattooed on the wrists of survivors of World War II concentration camps. Other physical stigmas are invisible until the bearer moves, like a major hip injury. Still others cannot be concealed in any interaction, like severe facial scarring (Macgregor, 1951), and their effects upon interaction are therefore pervasive. Highly visible stigmas also include cases of deviant physical stature, and some evidence indicates that anomalous size has significant social and psychological consequences.

In one of the few studies of dwarfs and midgets, Truzzi (1968) described the effects of unusually small stature. These individuals prefer the neutral term *small people* to other historic labels for their condition. For small people a recurrent problem is being taken for (and treated as) children. These individuals are subject to a variety of public indignities. They may be given pats on the head, helped to cross a street, and offered children's portions in restaurants. As a result, small people may devise a number of strategies to disambiguate the meaning of their small size: conspicuous cigars, facial hair, and formal attire. Dwarfism is rarely apparent from birth; instead, it becomes visible as development occurs without growth. In this sense deviant stature acquires visibility gradually and requires recognition and diagnosis. As this physical stigma is revealed, the child's parents must decide how to communicate to the child the nature of this deviant fate (Truzzi, 1968, p. 203):

> The greatest shock, however, is that experienced by the child upon his learning of his affliction. Many midgets never fully recover from this experience. Since the child is quite young (usually about nine or ten) when he experiences this fateful revelation, its full implications are usually not immediate; and there is often a hopeful disbelief and an expectancy that growth may still come.

Other field research has examined the decision-making and information control strategies of individuals with invisible, discreditable forms of stigma. This research supports the idea that while the dominant issue in the lives of the discredited concerns tensions generated in interpersonal behavior, the dominant issue in the lives of the discreditable is tension generated by the management of information. Epileptics are an example of discreditable individuals. For most epileptics medication now allows them to control the seizures that previously made it impossible for them to conceal their condition.

Kleck (1968a) conducted interviews with a sample of eighteen epileptics (with a median age of approximately thirty) who were identified for Kleck by the neurologists who had diagnosed their condition. In keeping with Goffman's conceptions of the discreditable, the epileptics in Kleck's sample had all decided to keep their condition secret from most intimates, friends, and co-workers. When asked how many persons they had voluntarily confided in, the median answer was a mean of only 2.4 individuals. One individual in the study had never revealed her condition to another person. Parents were the most likely targets for disclosure, and among friends and acquaintances epileptics tended to be more willing to confide in women than in men. The epileptics appeared to have been influenced strongly by parental reactions to their conditions. Virtually all the parents were described by the epileptics as extremely secretive in regard to their children's epilepsy. In this case, at least, these discreditable individuals were encouraged to try to pass by their parents' reactions to their stigma.

From eighty interviews with epileptics Schneider and Conrad (1980) focus on the strategies used by epileptics to keep their condition in the closet. The epileptics in Schneider and Conrad's study did not make their decisions about passing in isolation; instead they were influenced in their decision by "stigma coaches"—individuals who advised the person to conceal this condition and offered advice about how to do it. Some stigma coaches were encountered in employment settings. Disclosure in the job setting takes on particular significance for epileptics since significant job discrimination against epileptics persists in a wide range of occupations (Schneider and Conrad, 1980, p. 34). The most important stigma coaches, as Kleck's research had suggested, were parents. Parents communicated the strength and undesirability of the epilepsy stigma to their children in a variety of ways ("We have never had anything *like that* in the family," etc.). The influence of parental stigma coaching was something profound, as in the case of an epileptic woman who was trying to decide whether to reveal her condition to the man she was planning to marry (Schneider and Conrad, 1980, p. 36):

> I talked to Mom about it. She said, "Don't tell him because some people don't understand. He may not understand. That's not something you talk about." I asked her, "Should I talk to him about passing out?" She said, "Never say 'epilepsy.' It's not something we talk about."

The consequences of widespread concealment are, by definition, a sense of private stigma and great social isolation. If virtually everyone with a given stigma is closeted, then solidarity, shared experiences, and collective political action are difficult, if not impossible. As a result of widespread passing, the vast majority of the individuals in the Schneider and Conrad study did not know a *single* other epileptic. Many of these individuals followed a strategy of selective concealment. They chose carefully among individuals in terms of disclosure, and the reactions of the first confidant was extremely important. If early disclosures met with positive responses, the individual tended to choose a more disclosing pattern. The reverse sequence also occurred. Some individuals were driven *into* the closet by negative responses. For example, being denied a driver's license or a job because of revealed epilepsy prompted, not surprisingly, a decision to conceal the condition on subsequent applications. Quite apart from the psychological consequences of stigma, passing is in this instance highly instrumental (Schneider and Conrad, 1980, p. 39):

> [Being] out of or in the closet of *epilepsy* may often have much less to do with one's "identity" than with the more practical matter of preventing others from applying limiting and restrictive rules that disqualify one from normal social roles.

For most epileptics the strategy of selective concealment is pursued in preference to total secrecy. One function of disclosure, clearly, is therapeutic. The individual can overcome some of the isolation of being in the closet by sharing information and by allowing the veil of passing to drop. Telling others about one's epilepsy also can serve important instrumental functions, referred to by Schneider and Conrad as "preventive telling." Particularly with friends and intimates, who may be likely to witness a seizure, preventive telling makes it possible for these acquaintances to recognize a seizure and not be shocked by it. As part of preventive telling, an epileptic may tell friends what to do in case of a seizure and also what not to do (e.g., not to send for an ambulance, etc.).

Preventive telling can also provide the epileptic with a test of the strength of a developing relationship. By introducing disclosure into a relationship at a fairly early stage, an epileptic can prevent potentially much greater pain if the disclosure occurs at a later stage of the relationship. As one epileptic in the Schneider and Conrad (1980) study said, "If they're going to leave, better it be

sooner than later." Preventive telling also occurs in romantic relationships. As one epileptic said, "Why go through all the trauma of falling in love with someone if they are going to hate your guts once they find out you're an epileptic?" (p. 41). In general, research on this group of individuals with discreditable forms of stigma supports the general proposition that information management and selective disclosure are pivotal features of their experience.

Field studies of discredited individuals have focused on problematic aspects of their interactions with the unstigmatized, and on the organized treatment of these individuals by various institutions. One study of an interesting group of the discredited, the obese, is described later in this chapter (Millman, 1980). Even though it is generally impossible (by definition) for the discredited to pretend to be unstigmatized, some limited, situation-specific passing is sometimes possible. Examples of situation-specific passing include telephone conversations and partial photographs involving amputees, the blind, and the obese. Other examples in which reduced information makes the perception of many forms of discredited stigma impossible include pen pal relationships and the newsreel footage that concealed from the public the extent of President Franklin Roosevelt's paralysis.

Even in face-to-face situations, sometimes information can be managed about major forms of discredited stigma. On a research trip in Europe, for example, I arranged to get together with a scholar with whom I had corresponded but had never met. I was greeted at the train station by the scholar's wife, who explained that her husband was illegally parked in a car in front of the station. I carried my luggage outside and climbed in the rear seat of the car. I was introduced to the scholar, and as he drove us to their house, we had a very interesting hour-long conversation about mutual research interests, life in their city, and other topics. When we arrived at the house, he let his wife and me off at the front door and went to park the car.

She and I entered the house and I was then surprised to see her propelling a wheelchair out toward the garage. She explained that her husband had been a childhood victim of polio. In retrospect, I think this incident involved a premeditated (and highly successful) attempt to manage information about stigma. As a result of the way our meeting was arranged, I was given the opportunity of an hour of undiscredited interaction. Thus I could form an impression of this man uncontaminated by the master status of his disability. This strategy allowed this man to normalize impression formation by subordinating or deferring the attributional consequences of his disability. Even in cases of serious physical stigma some circumstances like this one may allow the individual to achieve at least some control over information and disclosure.

Some forms of discredited stigma are so encompassing that the individual has few or no interactions in which the disability is not conspicuous. Gross retardation is one such case. Other physical disabilities, particularly sensory deprivations like blindness and deafness, affect most if not all interactions. In an interesting study Scott (1969) describes the ways in which the competence and identity of sightless individuals can be affected by the institutions that are designed to ameliorate the negative effects of their condition. The focus of this work, unlike that of most studies in physical stigma, is on *institutional reactions* to deviance rather than on the lot of stigmatized individuals. Called *The Making of Blind Men,* this study draws attention to the ironies of institutional care and the unwitting ways in which the providers of care can contribute to the perpetuation of dependence.

In many cases social agencies are approached by the blind in an effort to secure a specific, limited service (finding a housekeeper, locating a reader, etc.). The agencies studied by Scott, however, interpreted the problems of the blind more globally. From the perspective of workers in these agencies, blindness was regarded as more fundamentally incapacitating and as a condition requiring extensive services or nearly custodial care. According to Scott, workers with the blind employ two strategies or goals. The first is the *restorative approach,* which seeks to restore the blind to a high level of independence. The second is the *accommodative approach;* in this approach independence is unlikely, and a variety of services are provided for the blind person who is seen as relatively helpless.

For a variety of reasons workers in the agencies studied by Scott pressured their blind clients to accept an accommodative interpretation of their condition. In part, this behavior reflected the view that many blind people were unrealistically optimistic about the degree to which they could function in the seeing world. Scott argues that the transactions within these agencies compel the client to abandon restoration as a goal. This tendency may be inherent in the nature of treatment organizations. The accommodative approach, after all, perpetuates the blind person's dependence on the agency, while the restorative approach would simply thin the ranks of the agency's pool of clients. As a result, Scott argues, depen-

dence is produced rather than minimized—and it is in this sense that he speaks of the "making" of blind men. The blind are encouraged by the agency to use services unavailable in the outside world, such as cut-up food served in agency-run cafeterias. Even if the blind arrive at a service agency with independent functioning as a goal, "the unstated assumption of accommodative agencies is that most of their clients will end up organizing their lives around the agency" (Scott, 1969, p. 180).

Interest in studying the individuals and agencies who affect the functioning and self-conceptions of the physically disabled is increasing. Higgins (1980) provides a study of the deaf and institutions for them, and Preston (1979) focuses on social and psychological aspects of the training given individuals who work in institutions providing care for the disabled. Furthermore, social and political changes clearly can have a dramatic effect on the conditions and treatment of the physically deviant. In American society, for example, involuntary segregation of handicapped children in special programs or even special schools has been succeeded by the theory of mainstreaming—placing the physically disabled alongside the unhandicapped. This model is intended to reduce ghettoization of the handicapped, to prepare them for entry into society, and (incidentally) to reduce the anxiety and aversion with which the able-bodied respond to the disabled.

At the same time we have many indications that voluntary self-segregation is emerging along with mainstreaming as an alternate strategy for dealing with the consequences of stigma. For the discredited, self-segregation offers the prospect of escape from the tense social interactions that their conditions invariably create in the presence of the unhandicapped. Examples of self-segregation are urban collectives like the Center for Independent Living in Berkeley, California. In addition, Zola (1982) describes the community of Het Dorp in the Netherlands. Het Dorp is a 65-acre village housing hundreds of severely disabled Dutch adults. Self-segregation of this kind represents one strategy for avoiding the stresses of mixed contacts between the handicapped and those who are not.

EXPERIMENTAL RESEARCH ON STIGMA AND REACTIONS TO PHYSICAL DEVIANCE

While sociological research on physical deviance has emphasized observation, field work, and interviews with stigmatized individuals, a number of laboratory-oriented researchers have investigated this area experimentally. Perhaps the simplest method used involves recording the behavior of unstigmatized subjects in the presence of either stigmatized individuals or unstigmatized controls.

For example, Kleck, Ono, and Hastorf (1966) used a specially constructed wheelchair that permitted a confederate of the experimenter to appear as either a physically intact person or a left-leg amputee. In interactions with subjects Kleck, Ono, and Hastorf found evidence of greater emotional arousal and discomfort in the presence of the amputee. This greater emotional response was reflected in subject self-ratings and, interestingly, also in a physiological measure. When the "handicapped" confederate entered the room with the subject, Kleck and associates found a decreased skin response (GSR). This physiological measure corroborates the self-ratings these researchers had obtained: Exposure to a handicapped individual creates in the unhandicapped a detectable, aversive emotional response.

The anxiety produced by mixed contacts is also reflected in other ways. In one of their studies Kleck and colleagues report that subjects interacting with a handicapped person tended to terminate an interaction more rapidly. In addition, subjects in this condition tended to use more restricted, invariant content as indicated by much lower variance in responses to a variety of rating scales. This study provides evidence, both self-reported and physiological, of the unique discomfort produced by mixed contacts.

In addition to pronounced discomfort, interaction with the physically handicapped also produces specific behavioral and *nonverbal* responses. For example, in an experiment with a simulated disabled person Kleck (1969) found that nonhandicapped subjects chose greater speaking distances when interacting with the handicapped. In addition, experiments that compare subject behavior in the presence of a "handicapped" confederate or an unhandicapped control find that subjects show greatly reduced motor activity in the presence of the handicapped (Kleck, 1968b). In short, the unhandicapped tend to freeze their nonverbal behavior in the presence of the disabled, perhaps because "uncertainty and emotional arousal may well serve to reduce the spontaneity of behavior" (Kleck, 1968b, p. 19).

Presumably, the significance of these nonverbal changes is not lost on the disabled. Research has shown that nonverbal clues are powerful sources of information and, in many cases, are more informative than words and language (Archer and Akert, 1977; Rosenthal *et al.,* 1979). Whatever the able-bodied may say to the handi-

capped, therefore, their nonverbal behavior can provide eloquent information about the stress produced by the handicapped person's presence. One suspects that a universal experience of the disabled involves observing dramatic transformations in the nonverbal behavior (levity, casual quality, warmth, etc.) of an individual or group with the arrival of the stigmatized person.

This research suggests that interaction behaviors may be strongly affected by the presence of a handicapped person even if the underlying attitudes are never made explicit. In this sense anxiety or discomfort regarding the handicapped may be different from many forms of prejudice. For example, Snyder *et al.* (1979) found that subjects were willing to sit with a handicapped person (a confederate whose handicap was simulated by means of a metal leg brace and the presence of Canadian crutches) when a decision *not* to do so would involve an obvious expression of their preference. In this condition 58 percent of the subjects sat next to the handicapped person. When given the opportunity to make the same decision under the guise of a choice between two different movies, however, only 17 percent chose to sit with the handicapped confederate.

This research suggests that unease concerning the physically handicapped prompts a desire to avoid them. At the same time these studies indicate that this desire is not readily expressed. The conflict indicates that this form of prejudice is socially unacceptable and that there is a norm calling for positive attitudes and behavior toward the handicapped. Attitudes toward the physically handicapped, therefore, may involve a concealed motive: "People are motivated to avoid the handicapped but are unwilling to acknowledge that motive" (Snyder *et al.,* 1979, p. 2298).

The actual reasons for avoiding the handicapped remain a matter of some speculation. Perhaps the handicapped remind the nonhandicapped of their own mortality; or the handicapped may inspire irrational fears that disability may be communicable; or interaction with the handicapped may simply impose a high degree of self-consciousness on the able-bodied. Since physical stigmas are often extremely salient, they may produce in the nonhandicapped discomfort and indecision concerning appropriate conversation topics, appropriate attitudes, and appropriate nonverbal behavior.

The nonhandicapped person may experience uncertainty about whether and how to look at the handicapped person, problems of eye contact, and confusion over whether to offer assistance or whether such offers would be perceived as offensive. At the same time strong normative pressures appear to operate toward helping the handicapped and treating them with kindness. These contradictory forces may combine to make interactions with the handicapped awkward, strained, and somewhat aversive. The complex nature of interaction with the handicapped reflects Goffman's (1963) conclusion that the physically handicapped prompt "pathological" interactions when in the presence of the nonhandicapped.

Most research on mixed contacts has been focused on the behavior of the unstigmatized person. We have reason to think, however, that at least some of the tension in these interactions is produced by the handicapped person. In *Stigma* Goffman (1963) indicated this possibility by suggesting that both the unstigmatized and the handicapped experienced interactional strains, and that "during mixed contacts, the stigmatized individual is likely to feel...self-conscious and calculating about the impression he is making" (p. 14). In an intriguing experiment, which is the mirror image of most research on the handicapped, Comer and Piliavin (1972) studied the reactions of thirty disabled individuals (amputees, paraplegics, etc.) to being interviewed by another subject in a group dynamics study of initial interactions between two strangers. The second subject was a confederate of the researcher, and he appeared either able-bodied or in a wheelchair with a brace on his left leg.

The results of this experiment suggest that, like the able-bodied, the handicapped person also experiences tension and uneasiness in mixed contacts. The interaction consisted of a flexible interview schedule, and the handicapped person was able to control the duration of the interaction by the length of his answers to the interview questions. The handicapped person prolonged the interview when the interviewer was handicapped and terminated it earlier when the interviewer was able-bodied. The mean length of these interviews was 9.56 minutes when the confederate interviewer appeared to be disabled and 6.55 minutes when he was not. Additional evidence showed that the mixed-contact interview was aversive for the handicapped subjects. When the interviewer appeared as disabled, the handicapped subjects used more eye contact and more active motor behavior (head and hand movements), smiled more often, gave greater "comfort" self-ratings, and rated the interviewer as more likable and more likely to be a possible friend.

Referring to these results as a study of "the other side," Comer and Piliavin (1972) conclude that there is a "significant contribution of the handicapped individual to the 'pathology' of the interaction between the handi-

capped and the physically normal" (p. 39). While the causal sequence is not clear, this finding suggests that mixed contacts may be uncomfortable because of an escalating pattern of discomforting feedback. The handicapped person may perceive (or merely anticipate) the negative responses of the able-bodied person and, as a result, manifest his or her own signs of discomfort, anxiety, and stress. In turn, these behaviors of the handicapped person may compound the stress by making the interaction even more aversive for the able-bodied person. This experiment indicates that the stigmatized person measurably contributes to the discomfort of mixed contacts.

We should note, in passing, that the discomfort of the handicapped person is presumably grounded in cumulative experience. From studies of the behavior of unstigmatized individuals, it seems safe to assume that the stigmatized person approaches mixed contacts with a realistic expectation that his or her presence may be aversive for the able-bodied. At the same time the Comer and Piliavin study raises the intriguing possibility that mixed contacts may be influenced by the handicapped person's *expectations* concerning the rejecting or aversive behaviors of the unstigmatized. The nature and effects of these expectations are discussed later in this chapter.

Although mixed contacts clearly produce stress, discomfort, and aversion in both participants, evidence suggests that these interactions also contain a number of *positive* elements. Most of the observed negative responses to the handicapped occur in various nonverbal channels of behavior—distance, eye contact, motor restriction, smiling, etc. The *verbal* channel of mixed interactions seems to be characterized by more positive content. A number of experiments find evidence that *explicit* attitudes and evaluations of the handicapped tend to be more positive than those measured for nonhandicapped confederates. In other words, at least at the levels of overt measurement, the handicapped person tends to receive evaluations that are *more* favorable as a result of the disability.

This finding appears in several experimental studies that compare subject reactions to the same confederate who appears in either a normal or a handicapped condition. These studies indicate that the handicapped confederate tends to receive more favorable outcomes when subjects are asked to use adjective scales to rate the confederate's personal characteristics (Kleck, 1968b), provide an evaluation concerning the performance of the confederate in some task (Kleck, 1969; Gibbons *et al.,*

1980), and even punish a confederate for errors in a learning task (Farina, Sherman, and Allen, 1968). These more favorable outcomes are found in the same studies and in companion with evidence of considerable subject discomfort and unease.

Several possible explanations may account for this positive bias toward the handicapped. Subjects may be operating with a general norm calling for kindness toward the disadvantaged, or alternately, subjects may approach an interaction with lower expectations for the qualities and abilities of the disabled (Kleck, 1968b, p. 27). In the latter case interaction with the handicapped may be unexpectedly positive—or at least not as aversive as had been feared. An additional explanation, one suspects, has to do with the nature of overtly measured attitudes and impressions. Subjects in these experiments knew that their judgments would be seen (by the researchers at least) and may have wanted to appear unprejudiced.

Verbal measures of prejudice often report manifest levels that are inconsistent with (and more positive than) involuntary measures of a person's attitudes (Weitz, 1972). In experimental studies of mixed interactions the verbal and nonverbal channels of subject behavior appear to be in direct conflict. Subjects report impressions and verbal evaluations that are *favorable* to the handicapped, while their nonverbal behaviors (GSR, proxemic distance, motoric behavior, and length of interaction) are *unfavorable* to the handicapped. In this instance one is tempted to conclude in favor of nonverbal primacy; i.e., that in comparison with verbal statements and ratings, the nonverbal channels of behavior provide more accurate information about the person's reaction (Archer and Akert, 1977). If this situation is indeed one of nonverbal primacy, the negative qualities of a mixed interaction may be more salient to the stigmatized person than are the elements of positive content.

Mixed contacts, then, produce in the unstigmatized person a blend of discomfort and aversion (as seen in self-ratings and, particularly, in the person's nonverbal behavior) and also some elements of positive bias (as seen in explicit judgments about the stigmatized person and his or her performance). This blend of negative and positive elements may reflect a genuine emotional ambivalence about the disabled, and existence of this ambivalence has been suggested by Katz and Glass (1979). According to this ambivalence theory, unstigmatized individuals regard the handicapped with a mixture of aversion and compassion. The ambivalence may be compounded, of course, if the unstigmatized person feels guilty over his or her aversive reactions to the stigmatized.

The mixture of reactions to the handicapped may be less than true ambivalence, however, in the sense that an individual may experience a negative *emotional* reaction to the stigmatized person but also be *intellectually* aware of norms calling for compassion and help toward the disadvantaged. In this instance the individual is in conflict but perhaps not in true affective ambivalence, since only a single emotion (aversion) is present. Indirect evidence for the existence of an emotion-norm conflict of this kind is contained in a study by Langer *et al.* (1976). In a study of subject reactions to photographs of handicapped and unhandicapped individuals, these researchers found that subjects stared *longer* at the photographs of the handicapped when no observer was present but stared *less* at photographs of the handicapped in the presence of the observer. Presumably, the curiosity responsible for the first finding is spontaneous, while the discreet avoidance in the second finding reflects social norms ("don't stare at handicapped people").

If this blend of emotional aversion and intellectual (or normative) sympathy is present in an individual, it may influence the form of his or her response to the disabled. In particular, in interactions with the handicapped this conflict might be expected to produce higher levels of assistance but lower levels of behaviors that would prolong the interaction. In essence, this finding was precisely the one found in a well-known field experiment by Doob and Ecker (1970). In this study researchers went door to door to Palo Alto, California, and asked 121 women if they would either fill out a four-page questionnaire and return it by mail or grant a 15–20-minute interview. The request was made by a young woman who either appeared in an unstigmatized role or wore a black eye patch. Doob and Ecker found a strong effect in the mail questionnaire condition *in favor* of the stigmatized researcher: 40 percent of the subjects exposed to the unstigmatized condition accepted, completed, and returned the questionnaire, while nearly 70 percent of those exposed to the eye patch condition did so. In the interview condition, in which the person was asked to spend an additional 15-20 minutes with the researcher, the eye patch appeared to have no effect. This result suggests that the unstigmatized are, in fact, more willing to help the physically stigmatized *unless* this assistance will prolong aversive, mixed contact with the handicapped person.

The normative expectation that the handicapped should be regarded sympathetically and helped has a number of nonobvious implications. For one thing, it appears that the physically disabled will receive performance evaluations that are inappropriately positive. In an interesting experiment by Hastorf, Northcraft, and Picciotto (1979) forty-eight male undergraduates were asked to evaluate the task performance of another subject (actually a confederate). This evaluation was given in the form of direct feedback to the confederate. After each task trial the subject chose, from a six-point scale, one evaluation that ranged from "you did poorly" to "you did very well."

The task consisted of a labyrinth game in which the person tries to manipulate a ball through a maze that can be tilted in both directions. The task was performed by a confederate who appeared either as himself or in a disabled condition wearing leg braces and using Canadian crutches. Hastorf and associates used two handicapped conditions. In one the confederate did not mention his handicap; in the other, as he was being seated for the task, the handicapped person voiced some concern that his leg braces might make it difficult for him to do well at the task. In all conditions, subjects had been told that the confederate's performance (which was of equal quality in all three conditions) was worse than "people generally do." Despite the fact that the confederate showed equal proficiency in all three conditions, he received more favorable feedback in the handicapped condition and the most favorable feedback in the condition in which he had expressed concern that his leg braces might interfere with task performance. Hastorf, Northcraft, and Picciotto (1979, p. 375) conclude:

> That handicapped individuals may receive inaccurate and, in general, less critical feedback has far reaching implications. For instance, if an individual continually receives unrealistically favorable feedback regardless of performance, the quality of the feedback may be attributed to the favorable attitude of the feedback dispenser, or simply ignored.

LABELING AND THE EFFECTS OF IMAGINED PHYSICAL STIGMA

A somewhat different experimental approach consists of research on the effects of deviance labeling on face-to-face interaction. In research on labeling no observable physical deviance is involved. In some cases individuals in an experiment are informed that the person with whom they will interact is stigmatized in some way (e.g., is an epileptic, a paraplegic, a homosexual, an ex-convict, etc.). Consequent behaviors are examined for any verbal or nonverbal evidence that the existence of the label has affected an interaction. The focus of labeling experiments of this kind can be either the *subject* of the labeling (the unstigmatized individual) or the *object* of the labeling (the stigmatized individual).

Research on the effects of labeling on the *object* of the label indicates that the mere expectation of stigma has a strong, putative effect on how interaction is perceived, even if no labeling exists in fact. In an experiment by Kleck and Strenta (1980) subjects were led to believe that they were perceived by the other person in an interaction as stigmatized in some way. The focus in this study was the behavior and experience of the person who *believes* that another person perceives them as stigmatized. In this study the three stigma conditions were as follows:

1. A fictitious allergy.

2. A fictitious, treatable form of epilepsy.

3. A simulated facial scar that was applied to the subject and then covertly removed just prior to the interaction.

In actuality, the person with whom the subject interacted was a confederate who was kept blind to the purposes of the study and to the stigma label the subject believed herself to be bearing. In other words, even though the subject believed that the other person perceived her as allergic, epileptic, or scarred, no such perceptions existed. At the conclusion of a six-minute interaction, the subject was asked to rate the behavior of the confederate, using a series of verbal descriptions and bipolar scales. In general, even though no labeling had in fact occurred, the label the subjects thought they carried made a significant difference in how the behavior of the confederate was perceived.

Compared with subjects who thought they had been labeled as having an allergy, subjects who thought that they had been labeled as epileptic or who thought that they wore a facial scar rated the confederate's behavior as significantly more negative. Subjects in these conditions reported that the confederate used less eye contact, was more tense, and found the subject less attractive. As a control for the possibility of real differences, independent judges rated videotapes of the confederate in all conditions, and no significant differences were found. In this instance the *presumption* that a stigma label exists appeared to color the ways in which the apparently neutral behavior of the confederate was perceived. Kleck and Strenta (1980) interpret this finding in terms of the effect of deviant labeling on the expectations of the labeled person (p. 864):

> Subjects presumably entered the experiment anticipating how others might respond to various forms of physical deviance and, when placed in interaction with a peer, readily found evidence consistent with these expectations.

Additional evidence suggests that stigma is *presumed* to contaminate a social interaction. In the same paper, for example, Kleck and Strenta (1980) report a study in which thirty-two judges rated videotapes of the behavior of the confederates in the earlier stigma study *after* the judges were informed (incorrectly) that these confederates were knowingly interacting with a person who had either scars or an allergy. Even in this condition judges who believed that the confederate they saw was interacting with a scarred person rated the confederate's behavior as more negative. These studies indicate that while labeling may indeed have a strong effect on the unstigmatized individuals, apparently the labeling is widely *presumed* to have such an effect, too. This presumption seems to be held by individuals who believe they are the objects of the labeling and also by uninvolved third parties.

The implications of this research for an understanding of stigma are provocative. While earlier work indicates that unstigmatized individuals do behave differently in the presence of the stigmatized, this research on the effects of pseudolabels suggests that this difference would be anticipated and *imagined* even if it did not exist. The presumption that deviant labels may have negative consequences may, of course, be firmly rooted in experience and accurate perception.

This research indicates that the labeler and the labelee subscribe to similar assumptions about the negative, disruptive effects of stigma. As a result, even if the labelee is the recipient of neutral treatment, this research suggests that the labelee will perceive the labeler as responding negatively, and that this response will be attributed to the effects of the label (i.e., the labelee will *assume* that the stigma has master status). Clearly, therefore, the interpersonal weight of stigma is not merely due to the negative response of the labeler. This research indicates that the labelee's experience of stigma may lead him

or her to see the label as even more consequential than it is. The negative, disruptive effects of stigma are, therefore, *both* real and imagined.

MITIGATION STRATEGIES

The picture so far presented paints a dismal view of mixed contacts. The unstigmatized regard the handicapped with (at best) ambivalence. On the positive side the handicapped may benefit from a positive bias, particularly in terms of feedback and overtly measured impressions and attitudes. Under some conditions the handicapped may also receive help as a result of a norm in support of sympathy and assistance for the disabled.

On the negative side, however, the disabled are also unfavorably regarded. They have a chilling effect on the spontaneity of the unstigmatized, and this effect is particularly pronounced in terms of nonverbal behavior. The able-bodied stand further from the handicapped, and their behaviors are more constricted, less accepting, and even physiologically stressed. The mirror image appears to be true as well: The handicapped are themselves conspicuously less at ease around the able-bodied than when around one of their own kind. These differences are so vivid that their existence is imagined by participants who believe, wrongly, that one member of an interaction has been given a stigmatic label.

The problematic nature of mixed contacts, while incontestable, is also disquieting. Given egalitarian values concerning the importance of opportunity and the undesirability of prejudice, it seems important to ask whether the pathology of mixed interaction can be remedied. Are there, in other words, interactional strategies or structural conditions under which some of the undesirable features of mixed contacts are mitigated? Even within the research already reviewed we have some grounds for optimism on this point. Some of this research suggests that the salience and consequences of physical stigma may diminish over the life of an interaction.

In the origami (paper-folding) study by Kleck (1969) unhandicapped subjects gave inappropriately positive evaluations of handicapped confederates and also stood further from them. In this study, however, subjects participated in two sessions held forty-eight hours apart. Interestingly, the results indicate that the magnitude of the pathological behaviors (positive and negative) diminished or subsided somewhat by the time of the second session. While subjects still stood further from the handicapped confederate, this distance was less pronounced than in the first session. Similarly, other impressions and evaluations appeared to be less affected by the confederate's handicap in the second session.

This intriguing finding clearly requires additional research, but it does suggest that some normalization of mixed contacts occurs over time. Early in a mixed contact the interaction may be overwhelmed by the master status of the disabled person's handicap. With more exposure, however, the *attributional importance of the stigma may recede as it is replaced with a perception of the person's idiographic characteristics, which are unrelated to his or her stigma.* If a mixed contact becomes a mixed relationship (i.e., endures), one might expect less aversion, less condescension and positive bias, higher expectations for performance, and reduced stigma-related helping. In summary, the attributional significance of a stigma may have diminishing effects as a relationship proceeds. Since most experimental research on mixed contacts has been limited to initial meetings between strangers, an investigation of the effect (and significance) of stigma on enduring relationships seems warranted.

In addition to this normalization hypothesis, a number of researchers have been interested in short-term strategies that may have a positive impact on initial meetings between those who are handicapped and those who are not. One study suggests that having a stigmatized individual concede, explain, or acknowledge a handicap can mitigate the aversive qualities of mixed interaction. According to this conception, acknowledgment of a handicap can reduce the symbolic power of an undiscussed stigma in the minds of the unstigmatized. In this study, Hastorf, Wildfogel, and Cassman (1979) showed videotapes of two handicapped individuals to unhandicapped individuals. The confederates in the videotapes were shown in a wheelchair. Both confederates discussed a number of topics.

In an acknowledgment condition the confederate spoke of the problems of being in a wheelchair; said that he had learned to accept the inconveniences; indicated that he realized that people were afraid to talk about his handicap; and added that he encouraged people to ask questions about it anyway in order to get his handicap "out of the way" so that people could really get to know him. In the control condition the individual did not provide this acknowledgment of his handicap, but the videotapes were otherwise the same.

After being shown these two videotapes, forty-eight undergraduates were asked to complete ratings of the two confederates. They were also asked to indicate which

of the two confederates they would prefer to work with in the second session of the study. The acknowledging confederate was rated more favorably on several dimensions and, significantly, was the one chosen as the preferred person for the second session by 71 percent of the subjects. The ratings indicated that the acknowledging confederate was seen as more likable, better adjusted, and more likely to be a comfortable participant in a discussion.

In the same paper Hastorf and associates report two other studies that found that the acknowledging confederate was preferred (by roughly the same margin) to handicapped confederates who made disclosures unrelated to their handicap. The tendency to prefer the acknowledging confederate, therefore, cannot be explained by the disclosure of personal information per se. Indicating the potential relevance of the acknowledgment strategy for helping the handicapped to reduce the "psychosocial barriers confronting them [that] may prevent their entry into the mainstream of society," Hastorf, Wildfogel, and Cassman (1979) conclude (p. 1794):

> [This research suggests that] the acknowledgement tactic is effective because it helps the handicapped individual appear less sensitive about his handicap, thereby making those who interact with him more comfortable.

Some evidence also suggests that if an able-bodied person is allowed some preliminary exposure to a handicapped person, the aversive qualities of mixed contacts can be reduced. Langer *et al.* (1976) observed laboratory interactions between subjects and a confederate who appeared as either able-bodied or handicapped. Half the subjects in this study were allowed to observe their interaction partner (the confederate) in advance through a one-way mirror. Subjects given a chance to preview the handicapped person showed less aversive behaviors during the subsequent interaction. These studies on the mitigation of physical stigma have in common the implicit conclusion that *the interpersonal effects of physical stigma can be mitigated, and that the shock value of such stigma can subside in an interaction, allowing a normalization of mixed contacts.*

Although the idea is counterintuitive, perhaps *increasing* the initial, explicit salience of a physical handicap facilitates (for both interaction partners) the management of this otherwise disruptive stigma. Increasing the initial salience or explicitness of a physical stigma may help in the management of interaction by placing the stigma in context and in public view. Open acknowledgment of a disability may assist both interactants in reaching unspoken agreement about how (or even whether) the disability will figure in an interaction. Even without premeditated strategies for drawing attention to a physical stigma, the salience and attributional significance of these stigmas subside as an interaction or relationship develops. The interpersonal significance of a person's physical stigma may recede in an interaction as other information, unrelated to the stigma, becomes available.

WEIGHT AS A VOLUNTARY FORM OF PHYSICAL DEVIANCE

Most of the research literature on the physically handicapped has been focused on involuntary disabilities—the effects of genetic and birth accidents, disease, trauma, or age-related infirmities. In these instances interaction with the handicapped appears to produce in normals a confusing blend of sympathy and aversion. Even though the handicapped in these cases may in fact have had a hand in their disability (e.g., drunken driving and subsequent spinal injuries), these forms of physical disability are not generally regarded as the fault of the disabled person. Instead, the disability tends to be attributed to unpreventable misfortune.

Certain other forms of physical deviance are regarded as at least semivoluntary. In these cases the person's physical stigma is treated as the symptom of a moral flaw. Unlike trauma-related disabilities, the handicap is seen as *chosen* rather than *inflicted*. Perhaps the most conspicuous of these chosen physical disabilities is weight. While fat people have been the object of medical and commercial activity for some time, they have only recently become a center of social psychological investigation. Much of this work has emphasized etiological factors, and a review of roughly a decade of research on obesity is contained in Leon and Roth (1977). In most research on obesity, fat is assumed to be an undesirable or deviant state, and the focus of inquiry concerns causal and ontogenetic aspects of this condition.

For example, Schacter (1971a, 1971b) and several colleagues have conducted a program of research on social psychological differences between normals and the fat. Perhaps the central hypothesis to emerge from this work concerns the idea of "external-cue sensitivity." This hypothesis holds that obese individuals, unlike normals, show little or no relationship between the internal,

physical state of hunger and eating behavior. According to this hypothesis, eating in the obese is under the control of external, environmental cues rather than somatic clues about actual hunger levels; i.e., the obese may respond to the mere presence of food rather than to the body's need for it. The empirical literature on the externality hypothesis, as it has come to be called, has consisted primarily of laboratory experiments comparing the behavior of normals and the obese. In these studies the dependent variable has generally been a covert index of the amount of food consumed—the number of crackers eaten, the number of peanuts shelled, the number of sandwiches consumed.

Part of the externality hypothesis has stressed the influence of "food-cue prominence," the simple degree to which food is available and accessible. For example, Nisbett and Kanouse (1969) observed the shopping behavior of normal and fat individuals. In this study normals who had not eaten recently bought more food than those who had. For the obese, however, having eaten recently appeared to have no effect on the amount of food purchased. This finding is cited in support of the externality hypothesis and is interpreted to mean that the obese respond to the prominence or availability of food rather than to internal, physical demands for it.

Perhaps the best-known study of food prominence was done by Schacter and Friedman (cited in Schacter, 1971b). In this experiment normal and obese male college students were given a casual opportunity to eat some almonds. The almonds were available in two conditions: in their shells and with the shells removed. Unlike normals, the obese men in this study were more likely to consume the almonds when they had their shells removed. Schacter interprets this result to mean that the nuts had greater food-cue prominence when the shells were removed. The food prominence hypothesis remains controversial, with some studies finding support for it (Costanzo and Woody, 1979) and others reporting disconfirming evidence (McArthur, Solomon, and Jaffe, 1980).

Other comparisons of normals and the obese have posited a differential willingness to expend effort in obtaining food. For example, Schacter (1971b) makes an entirely casual observation that the obese are more likely than normals to choose a fork rather than the more difficult chopsticks when dining in a Chinese restaurant. This hypothesis seems to reflect lay conceptions of the obese as lazy, indolent, etc. The effort hypothesis has also been used to interpret the study in which the obese were found to consume nuts when they had been removed from their shells but not when they were in the shell. Similarly, Nisbett (1968) reported a study in which normal and obese men were given a chance to consume sandwiches. Nisbett found that the obese consumed *more* sandwiches than did normals when the sandwiches were made directly available but consumed *fewer* than normals when the subject had to obtain additional sandwiches from a nearby refrigerator. This difference was interpreted in terms of differential food prominence and the greater effort required to walk to the refrigerator for additional sandwiches.

The externality and effort hypotheses stress psychological variables and individual traits. While these interpretations may well be correct, a different and much more *interpersonal* and *social* interpretation of these results is also plausible. In the experiment on almond consumption, for instance, the obese may have been deterred from eating the nuts in their shells for fear that the discarded shells would provide embarrassing evidence of how many they had consumed. Similarly, in the sandwich study the obese may have been too embarrassed to obtain additional sandwiches by means of more conspicuous expeditions to the refrigerator. Embarrassment, which may well play a leading role in the lives of stigmatized individuals, could deter obese individuals from obtaining food through more visible means. As indicated later in this section, every aspect of food and eating becomes sensitized for the obese individual. This embarrassment explanation is rooted in the conception of stigma as inherently problematic for interaction.

Other studies of the obese have been characterized by a search for unique intellectual, perceptual, and personality factors and for variables that predict successful response to weight loss programs. While studies show very few, if any, unique personality characteristics among the obese (Leon and Roth, 1977), they do indicate some unique perceptual and intellectual patterns. For example, Rodin (1973) found that while the obese outperformed normals at tasks like proofreading under control conditions, they were more distracted than normals when exposed to irrelevant external stimulation. This research has been cited in support of a greater externality among the obese in *noneating* situations as well as in food consumption.

The search for predictors of success or failure in weight loss programs has in general failed to yield consistent findings. Some evidence, however, indicates that the age of obesity onset may be related to a number of outcomes, with mature obesity onset associated with a more favorable prognosis than juvenile onset.

Some treatment programs reflect a treatment orientation common among various substance abuse interventions. For example, a program called Overeaters Anonymous is modeled on Alcoholics Anonymous (Millman, 1980). In this program the solution to obesity is defined as abstinence from carbohydrates. The program teaches participants that they are in constant danger of an eating binge ("falling off the wagon") and uncontrolled weight gain. This group also stresses the importance of recognizing one's food addiction, and meetings often begin with the participant's statement, "Hi, my name is (first name only) and I'm a compulsive overeater." In general, actual weight reduction and long-term weight maintenance appear to be extremely difficult, and a review of weight loss programs concluded that most were of limited effectiveness (Leon, 1976). This conclusion has prompted interest in other approaches, from behavior modification to aggressive surgical procedures.

Apart from the clinical and etiological aspects of weight gain or weight loss, there is abundant research that the obese are the victims of both prejudice and discrimination. In the study already cited on children's perceptions of various physical handicaps, for example, a picture of an obese child was actually the *least preferred* of all the physical conditions shown (Richardson *et al.,* 1961; Richardson, 1971). In these studies of children's preferences more prejudice was shown against obesity than against a wide range of more serious physical disabilities including lost appendages, facial disfigurement, and paraplegia.

Although the procedures used in this research have some extensive methodological criticisms (Altman, 1981), the results indicate clearly that obese children are the objects of extensive stereotyping and prejudice. Obese individuals are surrounded by ideals of physical appearance that exclude them, and the communications media have been increasingly unfavorable in their depictions of the obese (Leonhard-Spark, 1978). Perhaps as a consequence of pervasive and unfavorable attitudes toward obesity, surveys and correlational studies of self-perceptions find that weight is associated with negative self-ratings and conceptions (Adams, 1980).

Unlike other types of physical handicaps, obesity is frequently seen as self-inflicted. While all physical disabilities may make the nondisabled nervous, only for obesity is this discomfort expressed by blaming the obese for their condition. Obesity is seen as requiring an explanation or apology.

In an experimental study of impression formation DeJong (1980) asked 226 women to rate either an obese or a normal woman from a photograph and some biographic information. The photograph of the obese woman was paired with one of three biographic statements. In the first condition the woman referred to a minor thyroid problem that created her obesity; in the second she referred to a new diet she was on that had reduced her by 25 pounds; in the third the woman mentioned neither the gland condition nor the diet. The explanation appeared to make a difference. The obese woman was rated most unfavorably when no explanation of her obesity was given. When she mentioned her diet or glandular condition, the obese woman received more favorable ratings. In either case, apparently, the explanations appeared to counteract conventional, unfavorable attributions about the character and blameworthiness of the obese. Thus the obese may experience strong social pressures to construct explanations of their stigmatized condition. This pressure was identified in interviews with the obese (Millman, 1980, p. 80):

> Sometimes the fat person feels an obligation to break the ice by being the first to mention her weight. She may make a point of saying that she is dieting, that she would like to lose the weight. These are ways of bridging the gap, of showing others that she sees things the way they do, that she is trying to observe the rules.

Nonlaboratory studies of the obese are relatively rare, but those that have been done have taken a very different direction. While laboratory research has been etiological or treatment-oriented, a number of researchers have examined obesity as an interesting case study in deviance. These studies have been concerned with the nature of interactions between normals and the obese and with the experience, self-image, and lives of these physical deviants. This approach has differed from the clinical and etiological approaches in that it examines the *consequences* of obesity for obese-normal interactions and for the social psychological experiences of the obese. In this sense some of this work has been analogous to studies of prejudice: The focus is upon both the object and the subject of aversion to obesity.

Clearly, prejudice against obesity is widespread and begins early in childhood. Given a chance to express preferences and dislikes, adults and children show a clear dislike of obese body shapes (Dibiase and Hjelle, 1968; Lerner and Gellert, 1969). A number of sociologists have been interested in the consequences and origins of this interesting form of physical prejudice. In one of the most evocative studies of the obese, Millman (1980) provides detailed accounts of the lives, experiences, and feelings of the obese. In the best tradition of field work and ethnography, Millman uses interviews and first-person materials to provide a window on this unique form of physical deviance. Millman focuses on the nature of mixed interactions and also on the ways in which the lives of the obese are impacted by organizations and programs that have developed to serve their needs.

For some time several organizations devoted to promoting weight loss and shared experiences among the obese, such as Weight Watchers, have existed. Many of these organizations have developed along clinical and therapeutic lines and have as a goal the elimination of obesity through self-help and group support. These organizations regard obesity as a medical condition involving dependence or addiction to food. In their emphasis on group support and therapy, however, these self-help groups differ from traditional medical interventions that have included shots, pills, intestinal bypass operations, or even wiring the obese person's jaws shut. Despite these radical differences in approach, the self-help organizations share with medical approaches (and the wider society) the view of obesity as socially undesirable, medically hazardous, and remediable. In this sense these organizations subscribe to the perception of obesity as a deviant condition that requires rehabilitation.

More recently, however, a number of social movements oriented toward political action have also emerged to further the collective interests of the obese. One is the National Association to Aid Fat Americans (NAAFA). This organization has emerged in an effort to defend the interests of the obese and to counter the negative effects of prejudice and discrimination.

It is not this specific organization that is important, of course, but rather the approach it has taken to defining the situation of the obese. Unlike most self-help organizations for the obese, NAAFA argues that fat can be beautiful and that dieting is in many cases of limited success. More important, NAAFA believes that human rights and privileges should not hinge on a person's weight any more than on the person's skin color. NAAFA argues that the most important problems of the obese are the prejudice, stigma, and consequent self-hatred that are produced by antiobese beliefs and attitudes. The list of hardships experienced by the obese is both long and impressive: job discrimination, social exclusion, inability to purchase health and life insurance, unsympathetic treatment by doctors, difficulty buying nice clothes, and public ridicule and shaming (Millman, 1980).

In terms of this perspective the obese have in common a career of being fat. They share a physical condition that is both highly stigmatized and highly visible. Despite great individual variation in intellect, personality, interests, and life-styles, the fat are treated by normals as essentially the same: as physically deficient and perhaps defective in character as well. Although physiological and etiological evidence on the question is far from clear, lay and medical beliefs about obesity tend to regard this condition as intentional or at least semivoluntary. As a result, obesity becomes a "master status," a fundamental basis for a wide range of attributions about the intellectual, emotional, and clinical qualities of obese individuals (Millman, 1980, Preface):

> Clearly, obesity has become mythologized in our culture into something much more than a physical condition or a potential health hazard. Being overweight is now imbued with powerful symbolic and psychological meanings that deeply affect the person's identity in the world. In other words, the state of being fat is felt to express something basic about a person's character and personality.

This tendency to make fundamental attributions to this deviant physical condition also affects the obese themselves. Obese individuals commonly regard a wide range of outcomes as due to the master status of their weight—e.g., "When I lose weight, I'll do better in school and I'll be more extroverted" (Millman, 1980, p. 61). The consistency with which the obese are regarded and treated produces intensive and extensive shared experiences. Because of societal prejudice against the obese, these individuals end up leading similar lives. Being fat becomes a pivotal, central, and governing fact in their existence, and it is in this sense that obesity becomes a career. We should emphasize that this prejudice also infects its victims, the obese themselves. In summer

camps for overweight juveniles (widely referred to as fat farms), Millman found a hierarchy organized around relative obesity even among the overweight. For example, in the company of much heavier girls, mildly overweight girls would frequently admire themselves in the mirror while complaining, "Oh, I'm so fat." This observation suggests that the obese have internalized the general social opprobrium concerning obesity, even though this stigma is one that condemns them.

This result may be a function of extensive socialization and the early onset of prejudice against the obese. For many obese individuals the defining experiences of their stigmatized condition occurred early in life: "Since she was a child, (an obese woman) has known what it is like to live in the world as a freak, and to be treated as a curiosity in the streets, in stores and in her own family" (Millman, 1980, p. 9).

As in other deviant careers, the lives of the obese are characterized by events, concerns, experiences, and feelings that are difficult for the nonobese outsider to imagine or understand. For example, while obesity is widely regarded as unattractive, fat women are sought out by men with a sexual attraction for very large bodies, even (or perhaps particularly) women weighing 300, 400, or more pounds. The men are frequently called "fat admirers," and they meet obese women by attending social functions organized by groups like NAAFA or indicate their interest by means of personal ads in newspapers (Millman, 1980).

With the exception of this special group, however, the obese are not admired. Each day and every activity is dominated by a fear of being seen, labeled, or rejected. This anxiety can become a dominant force in the obese person's life, and the obese may begin to organize their entire lives around obesity, its consequences, its elimination, and its concealment. Out of a fear of ridicule or stares and unspoken censure, obese people may eat secretively or only at home. Every aspect of food may become sensitized. The obese may make small grocery purchases in five separate stores rather than risk buying conspicuously large amounts of food in a single store.

Millman's (1980) work indicates that, in general, normal-obese interactions are strained and, for the obese at least, tainted with embarrassment, anxiety, and pain: "I've had a lot of bad experiences with diet doctors and doctors in general. A fat person hates to go to the doctor. Even if you go to the doctor because of a cold, the doctor will say, 'Lose fifty pounds,' as if that will take care of the cold'' (p. 18).

Millman (1980, p. 30) also reports:

> My daughter was going to spend Christmas with her grandmother and she baked some cookies to bring along.... While she was at school I ate all the cookies she baked for her grandmother. There was no way I could replace them for her. They were love. She and my husband couldn't believe that I ate those cookies. My husband asked me how I could do it.

Or (Millman, 1980, p. 45):

> When I was twelve or thirteen my parents had a 25th anniversary party and I brought home half of a huge cake from the party. I was supposed to be on a diet, but I played sick and stayed home from school. At first I was cutting the cake from an angle to disguise that I was eating it. But then I kept eating. When there was only a little left I purposely dropped it on the floor.... Then I gave one crumb to the dog. Then I called up my mother at work and told her that while I was trying to get a glass of milk from the refrigerator I knocked the cake on the floor and so I gave it to the dog.

The obese are aware of others' attitudes: "[Other kids] weren't being friendly when they offered you cookies. They don't look at you the way we see ourselves. Thin people look at us differently.... When they offered you food it was like offering food to the animals at the zoo" (Millman, 1980, p. 60). Another subject reports (Millman, 1980, p. 79):

> If I went to the baker, that was very problematic: you have to carry the box in the street. If it's just food in a brown bag, no one knows, but everyone knows what's inside the cake box. Sometimes I would tell them to put it in a bag, risking getting the eclairs crushed rather than having someone see me carry the box. Or I would take a taxi so I wouldn't have to walk in the street with the box.... I would make up questions: do you think this is enough for four people, so they wouldn't think it was just for me.

And another subject says (Millman, 1980, p. 10):

> I went to a physics department party that was part of my interview for my job, so the party was in my honor, but a very humiliating thing happened. This was in early March and I had had the baby three months before, during Christmas of that school year. At the party two different faculty members asked me when the baby was due.... How do you answer the question, when is the baby due, when you've already had it?

> A client came into the office to discuss some business with me, and when we were finished she said, "So what's the matter with you? Do you have gland trouble?" It's amazing how insensitive people can be to fat people. You wouldn't walk up to a cripple in the street and say, "How did you lose the use of your legs?" So I don't know why people think it's all right to say these things to us.

In terms of Goffman's (1963) dichotomy the obese are clearly discredited rather than discreditable. Their weight is a highly visible physical stigma. Except in special circumstances (telephone calls with strangers, interactions with the blind, etc.), their obesity is painfully manifest. In this sense obesity is more ubiquitous than discreditable forms of stigma, like being an ex-convict, a heretic, or a homosexual. Even compared with many forms of physical deviance (like deafness, replacement of a limb with a prosthesis, etc.), obesity is more conspicuous and a troublesome element of all social interactions. Perhaps because it cannot be concealed, obesity has become the focus of large and lucrative enterprises organized around its eradication. In this sense, and unlike other forms of physical deviance, obesity has become the economic occasion for a proliferation of entrepreneurial activity in pharmacy, recreation, medicine, and surgery.

A SUMMARY OF CURRENT ISSUES AND NEW RESEARCH DIRECTIONS

The study of deviance has changed in important ways in the last two decades, and these changes are reflected in the paradigmatic shift described at the beginning of this chapter. The subject matter of the field has expanded from a narrow focus on the individual deviant to an interactive emphasis that includes nondeviants, institutions, deviantization, the labeling and definitional processes, and political and societal reactions to deviance.

These new interests have greatly enlarged the intellectual domain of the field.

In addition, these changes are an important development for social psychologists in both psychology and sociology since the new conception of deviance is, by definition and design, eminently *social* psychological. The questions that are now of particular interest are ones for which the concepts and methods of social psychology are well suited. A number of emerging topics are indicated in this final section of the chapter, along with promising directions for new research and also some unresolved issues.

NEW DEVIANCE

New forms of deviance are continually created. In addition, old forms that have fallen into disuse are sometimes resurrected. The processes of deviantization, labeling, and societal reaction are dynamic and ongoing. Although the generic category of deviance endures, its specific elements are subject to negotiation, with some forms added over time and others deleted. Even as new instances of deviance are added, however, a number of recurrent elements of the deviantization process can be recognized: stigmatization, claims-making activities designed to show that the behavior or condition is indeed problematic, professional intervention, treatment, and, in some cases, institutionalization.

The discovery of deviance and the often arbitrary nature of deviantization are most easily discerned with the passage of time. Thus the plausibility of many imputations about a specific form of deviance fades as the contextual values and ideas of an era become historically remote. Witchcraft is an example. To the modern eye the allegations made concerning this form of deviance are exotic and implausible. For example, one of the last people hanged for witchcraft in the United States was a minister named George Burroughs. His witch trial in 1692 was attended by Harvard University President Increase Mather, and President Mather was persuaded that testimony at the trial showed Reverend Burroughs had done "such things as no man that has not a Devil to be his familiar could perform" (Hansen, 1982). While this attribution must have been compelling in 1692 (Reverend Burroughs was hanged), it is unfathomable from a distance of three centuries. In addition, the fact that this instance of deviance was plausible to President Mather (and to the judges and other leading citizens of Salem)

suggests that intelligence and position provide no immunity from the moral fervor of societal reactions to deviance.

The implausibility of the deviantization of witches extends to its smallest details. For example, Reverend Burroughs nearly escaped death at the last possible minute. Standing on the gallows, he nearly halted the execution with a recitation of the Lord's Prayer. In terms of the deviance theories of the time, this feat was supposedly impossible for witches. Unfortunately for Reverend Burroughs, the famous and zealous Cotton Mather (son of the Harvard president) was present. From horseback he shouted to the gathered crowd that this prayer was merely a new trick of the Devil and should therefore not exonerate the accused. Even though this new attribution contradicted a key tenet of witch theory, it was somehow persuasive. Cotton Mather had his way, and Reverend Burroughs swung into eternity.

The arbitrariness, victimization, haphazard labeling, and meritless attributions that characterized witch trials are readily apparent to the modern eye. At the same time one wonders whether the irrationality of this particular deviantization is obvious because witchcraft has nothing in common with modern forms of deviance or merely because centuries have passed, along with the assumptions, fears, and ideas that may be needed to make an instance of deviance credible. Probably, members of *any* historical period regard as primitive and unenlightened the deviance theories and treatment of deviants practiced in preceding eras. If this tendency is general, it raises the interesting question of what instances of recent or current deviance will be seen as exotic, inexplicable creations of our century. Will homosexuals, psychotics, polygamists, or other contemporary deviants be regarded as the unjustly victimized witches of the twentieth century?

Given the nearly imperceptible pace of historical transformations, then, additions and subtractions from the category of deviance are not often salient. They occur, however, and have made major changes in the subject matter of deviance. In this sense new deviance is constantly "discovered" (Schur, 1979, p. 416). Ideas of madness developed in the Middle Ages and continued to evolve through radical permutations (Foucault, 1967). Institutions can also be invented, as in the case of the discovery of the asylum as an appropriate disposition for the insane in the United States in the 1820s (Rothman, 1971). Changing conceptions also disestablish deviance institutions, as indicated by efforts to find alternatives to the asylum as sympathy for the insane increased during the progressive era (Rothman, 1980).

The discovery of deviance has been responsible for the invention of many categories that today may seem self-evidently deviant. The idea of delinquency, so familiar to the modern eye, dates only from the turn of the century (Platt, 1969), and the discovery of child abuse occurred in the past two decades, as described in an earlier section of this chapter (Pfohl, 1977). Specific disorders that have no precedent can also be discovered; hyperkinesis is a recent example (Conrad and Schneider, 1980). This childhood condition, thought to involve excess motor activity and short attention span, was essentially unknown until the 1950s but has since become the most common disorder treated in child psychiatry (Conrad and Schneider, 1980, p. 157).

Discoveries also involve explanations for deviance, and an interesting example was the claim that a specific genotype with an extra male chromosome (47, XYY) might be responsible for violent crime. This theory of violence attracted considerable attention and was even introduced in criminal trials as an explanation for the defendant's offenses. Despite its attractiveness as a simple explanation for deviance, the genotype theory fell into disuse when studies of inmate populations found that individuals with this genotype were *less* violent than those without it (Taylor, Walton, and Young, 1974, p. 45).

Another way in which deviance is discovered involves the realization that membership in some groups tends to be deviantized. In terms of Goffman's (1963) typology of deviance, social changes can add to the list of a society's *tribal* stigma. In some cases the extent of stigmatization of a group of new deviants is discovered by means of the careful, ethnographic accounts of researchers—e.g., Millman's (1980) analysis of the obese and Higgins's (1980) work on the deaf. In these cases it may become clear that our *understanding* of the experiences of a group can be increased by analyzing their experiences as an instance of deviantization.

An interesting case involves the poor (Pettigrew, 1980). When analyzed from a deviance perspective, the poor have much in common with other deviant groups: *degradation ceremonies* (welfare lines, conspicuous food stamps, home inspections), *stigmas* (food stamps, blaming the poor for their economic failure), and even *passing* (conspicuous consumption, the purchase of costly clothes or flashy cars in an effort to appear prosperous). An analogous argument can be made about interactions between working-class and middle-class individuals. This observation has led to an interest in the hidden injuries of class that may lead working-class people to be ashamed of their lack of autonomy and prestige, anxious for their children to enter more honored occupations, and diffident in their interactions with those of higher status (Sennett and Cobb, 1972). The stigma of poor and working-class individuals may be compounded, ironically, by the rhetoric of opportunity and meritocracy. These societal values may lead these people to attribute their failures to personal shortcomings rather than structural aspects of the society (Domhoff, 1978, p. 195).

Additions to and deletions from the generic category of deviance are continuous. As new forms of deviance are discovered, opportunities for original research are increased. In particular, the emerging deviance paradigm is particularly attractive for social psychologists. The focus is inherently interactive (e.g., in terms of deviant-nondeviant contact) and also focused on attitudes, beliefs, attributional schemata, and preferential patterns. Finally, the intellectual usefulness of many conceptions of deviance has been little tapped. Studies of attitudes toward and treatment of many stigmatized groups (the poor, obese, psychotic, elderly, terminally ill, etc.) may be enriched by drawing upon the concepts, models, and general paradigms used in deviance research.

CAUSAL EXPLANATIONS AND SOCIAL CONSEQUENCES: THE EFFECTS OF THEORY

Causal theories seek to provide explanations of the etiology of deviant conditions. The principal test of the scientific plausibility of any causal theory is, of course, whether it is supported by empirical evidence. In addition to their relative scientific merits, however, causal theories of deviance can also have specifiable *effects* of their own. Theories of deviance differ in their conceptions of the origins, mutability, and moral blameworthiness of deviance. For this reason the type of causal theory that becomes dominant in an era may strongly affect the degree to which a given behavior, condition, or lifestyle is seen as stigmatizing.

The differentially problematic effects of causal theories can be indicated by using a single substantive area of deviance. In mental illness a long-standing intellectual debate rages over the relative etiological importance of biological and social factors. On the biological side a number of scholars have argued that evidence exists for a genetic component. This argument rests on claims that mental illness is characterized by relatively consistent incidence rates in different societies, consistent incident rates over time, and also a concordant incidence within families and between separated monozygotic twins (Gove, 1980, p. 67). The case for the etiological importance of social factors in mental illness rests on a number of research traditions, including the following:

1. The persistent finding of a strong relationship between the individual's social class and the type of psychiatric diagnosis (Hollingshead and Redlich, 1958).

2. The finding that the incidence of diagnosed illness varies with the health of the economy (Brenner, 1973).

3. The finding that labeling of psychiatric disorders is easily attached and has important attributional consequences but that delabeling is difficult or impossible (Rosenhan, 1973; Langer and Abelson, 1974; Scheff, 1974).

4. The finding that treatment and institutionalization can produce destructive effects that may be mistaken for symptoms of the original condition (Goffman, 1961; Wing and Brown, 1970).

At this point the etiological question remains open. While genetic variables may turn out to be important in the onset of disturbed behavior, social and psychological factors are of incontestable importance in producing, defining, and stabilizing this form of deviance. For one thing, even the simple identification of this condition remains imprecise, and psychiatric diagnoses continue to be of dubious reliability. In addition, ample evidence suggests that labeling produces a consequential stigma for the mentally ill and also provides a generic basis for attributions about the competence of the individuals so labeled.

Possibly biological *and* social theories will prove to have some merit. That is, the onset of certain affective and behavior patterns may turn out to be at least quasi heritable. Even if some forms of mental illness are found

to reflect genetic factors, the consequences and qualities of these conditions will continue to be mediated by social factors. In addition, the effect of diagnosis and labeling may create strong patterns of secondary deviance that further disadvantage and stigmatize the individual. In summary, these two theoretical models may be less mutually exclusive than they at first appear. The advent of new evidence about the biology of mental illness, therefore, would not diminish the role of stigma, attribution, and societal reaction.

These two theoretical models differ in more than just the degree to which they provide satisfactory etiological explanations. They also differ in their probable *deviantizing effects*. The degree to which a stigma attaches to mental illness may be strongly affected by the etiological theory with which this condition is explained. If one adopts a social or psychological theory, the problem may be seen as interpersonal, situational, dispositional, or even medical. In each of these theoretical conceptions the condition will be regarded as tractable and finite in time. With appropriate treatment, insight, or medication, the afflicted individual is regarded as able to recover from this condition.

In terms of social and psychological causal theories, the condition will also be finite in terms of the number of deviantized individuals. The mentally ill individual will be seen as the person most affected, although the individual's parents and other family members will also be seen as sharing in the responsibility for the condition and its remediation. The scope of this deviant condition, however, will be seen as contained. The affected individual (and others) will regard the pathology as potentially curable, and although some stigma may diffuse throughout a family, *there will be no expectations that the deviance itself will spread* to other family members and generations.

The consequences of accepting a biological or genetic theory are likely to be quite different. In terms of these theoretical models the perceived moral responsibility of some family members may be reduced. If a biological theory is accepted, the concept of the "schizophrenogenic" parent is eliminated, presumably alleviating much parental guilt and self-blame. Because biological theories have the connotation that the explained behavior is predetermined and involuntary, these theories may be attractive to the occupants of some deviant roles, particularly where the alternative is moral culpability. In some forms of deviant sexual orientation, for example, biological and hormonal theories may be seen as excusing the individual from accountability for his or her condition (Schur, 1979, p. 303).

In some cases, therefore, deterministic theories may be a source of comfort. At the same time the acceptance of a genetic causal theory necessarily produces a *spreading stigma*. A genetic model spreads the stigma across the life course of the mentally ill individual by conceiving of him or her as genetically disabled for life, rather than affected for the course of an episode or given illness. In addition, acceptance of a genetic theory is likely to taint or stain all those who share a gene pool with the ill individual. The patient's parents may worry about their other offspring, and they may become sensitive or expectant concerning the behavior of these other children. The same sensitivity may exist in succeeding generations. If they accept a genetic theory, the ill individual and his or her siblings may become apprehensive about their own children. Alternatively, they may decide to remain childless rather than risk a repetition of the disorder in the next generation. For the same reasons those who descend from an ill individual may experience lifelong anxiety about the condition, and they may interpret some of their own behaviors as symptomatic of an emerging mental illness.

For these reasons the stigma of the original condition will be greatly *multiplied* if a genetic theory of the disorder is accepted. In addition to the stigma that attaches to the ill individual, the condition will be seen as potentially present in the person's entire kinship system. In this sense we may speak of *latent stigma*. A latent stigma would exist in cases where the *potential for deviance is seen to exist in an otherwise undeviantized individual*. A latent stigma could have important effects on the individual who is latently stigmatized. He or she may perceive (accurately or not) behaviors and affects as symptomatic of the latent condition. In this sense a latent stigma would have important effects on one's self-conception and attributions about one's own behavior.

Latent stigma would also affect major life decisions, including a person's willingness to have children. In addition, the effect of credited genetic theories would ripple throughout the deviant person's social relationships. If the presence of a disorder in a person's genealogy became known, the acceptance of a genetic theory would taint the person and reduce his or her eligibility for a wide range of activities. If an individual is seen as a carrier of genes for potential deviance, his or her life chances for marriage, employment, and parenthood would be affected. In this sense the acceptance of genetic theories of a disorder would greatly magnify the degree to which a given condition becomes potentially discreditable.

Something like this latent stigma existed for survivors of the nuclear holocausts in Hiroshima and Nagasaki. Many families who had been in these cities at the time of the bombings concealed this fact from others, fearing that suspected genetic damage from the bombs would taint their families and render their children unmarriageable. As a result, these families spent decades in a nuclear closet, with their victimization well concealed. To the degree that genetic theories of the etiology of deviance are credited, the lives of deviant individuals and their families will be colored by a similar latent stigma.

So theories of deviance have major consequences. The traditional conception of rival theories of deviance has been that they differ primarily in the degree to which each is immune to disconfirmation by the available empirical evidence. While unimpeachable from a simple hypothesis-testing perspective, this epistemological conception needs to be supplemented by an awareness that theories of the causes of deviant behavior have extremely significant consequences. These theories are likely to have strong effects on deviant individuals and on their treatment at the hands of intimates and society generally. The social consequences of theory apply to other instances of deviance as well. Although mental illness is used as the example here, other illustrations of latent stigma could be drawn in the areas of opiate addiction, alcoholism, sexual orientation, and crime.

Unlike many theories in the behavioral sciences, causal theories of deviance are strongly linked to the self-conceptions and life chances of affected individuals. Rival theories differ in the perceived origin and mutability of a deviant condition. This differential will affect the permanence of the stigma borne by the deviant and, perhaps as well, the degree to which the individual is accorded treatment, support, and perceived eligibility from nondeviant society. Because genetic paradigms involve a label that can infect entire generations, the degree to which biological theories of deviance are accepted will have major effects on the magnitude and persistence of stigma. While this argument does not imply that theories of deviance are untestable, it does indicate that these theories must be seen as operating within a social context that contains profound and enduring consequences for the individuals about whom the theories are constructed.

REFERENCES

Adams, G. R. (1980). Social psychology of beauty: effects of age, height, and weight on self-reported personality traits and social behavior. *J. soc. Psychol., 112,* 287–293.

Allen, V. L. (1975). Social support for nonconformity. In L. Berkowitz (Ed.), *Advances in experimental social psychology.* Vol. 8. New York: Academic Press. Pp. 1–43.

Altman, B. (1981). Studies of attitudes toward the handicapped: the need for a new direction. *Soc. Prob., 28,* 321–337.

Archer, D., and R. M. Akert (1977). Words and everything else: verbal and nonverbal cues in social interpretation. *J. Pers. soc. Psychol., 35,* 443–449.

Archer, D., and L. Erlich (n.d.). Traces of fear: the response to extraordinary violence. Unpublished manuscript.

Archer, D., and R. Gartner (1976). Violent acts and violent times: a comparative approach to postwar homicide rates. *Amer. Sociological Rev., 41,* 937–962.

_____ (1978). Legal homicide and its consequences. In I. L. Kutash, S. B. Kutash, and L. B. Schlesinger (Eds.), *Violence: perspectives on murder and aggression.* San Francisco: Jossey-Bass. Pp. 219–232.

_____ (1980). Homicide in 110 nations: the development of the Comparative Crime Data File (CCDF). In. E. Bittner, and S. L. Messinger (Eds.), *Criminology review yearbook.* Vol. 2. Beverly Hills, Calif.: Sage. Pp. 433–464.

Archer, D., and R. Gartner (1981). Peacetime casualties: the effects of war on the violent behavior of noncombatants. In E. Aronson (Ed.), *Readings about the social animal.* San Francisco: Freeman. Pp. 236–248.

_____ (1983). War and violent crime. In S. H. Kadish (Ed.), *The encyclopedia of crime and justice.* New York: Free Press.

_____ (1984). *Violence and crime in cross-national perspective.* New Haven: Yale Univ. Press.

Archer, D., R. Gartner, R. Akert, and T. Lockwood (1978). Cities and homicide: a new look at an old paradox. In R. F. Tomasson (Ed.), *Compara. stud. sociol.* (now *Compara. soc. Res., 1,* 73–95.

Archer, D., B. Iritani, D. D. Kimes, and M. Barrios (1983). Face-ism: five studies of sex differences in facial prominence. *J. Pers. soc. Psychol., 45,* 725–735.

Aries, P. (1962). *Centuries of childhood: a social history of family life.* New York: Vintage Books.

Becker, H. S. (1963). *Outsiders.* New York: Free Press.

Berkowitz, L., and J. Macaulay (1971). The contagion of criminal violence. *Sociometry, 34,* 239–260.

Binney, J. (1968). *The legacy of guilt: a life of Thomas Kendall.* Oxford: Oxford Univ. Press.

Blumenthal, M. D., R. L. Kahn, F. M. Andrews, and K. B. Head (1972). *Justifying violence.* Ann Arbor: Univ. of Michigan.

Bowers, W. J., and G. L. Pierce (1980). Deterrence or brutalization: what is the effect of executions? *Crime and Delinquency,* 453–484.

Brace, C. L. (1880). *The dangerous classes of New York and twenty years' work among them.* New York: Wynkoop and Hallenbeck.

Brenner, M. H. (1973). *Mental illness and the economy.* Cambridge, Mass.: Harvard Univ. Press.

Caffey, J. (1946). Multiple fractures in the long bones of infants suffering from chronic subdural hematoma. *Amer. J. Roentgenology, 56,* 163–173.

Campbell, D. T. (1972). Herskovits, cultural relativism, and metascience. In F. Herskovits (Ed.), *Cultural relativism: perspectives in cultural pluralism.* New York: Random House. Pp. v–xxiii.

Carey, J. T. (1975). *Sociology and public affairs: the Chicago school.* Beverly Hills, Calif.: Sage.

Chambliss, W. J. (1975). Toward a political economy of crime. *Theory and Society, 2,* 149–170.

Clinard, M. B., and R. F. Meier (1979). *The sociology of deviant behavior* (5th ed.). New York: Holt, Rinehart, and Winston.

Clinard, M. B., and P. C. Yeager (1980). *Corporate crime.* New York: Free Press.

Cohen, A. K. (1955). *Delinquent boys: the culture of the gang.* Glencoe, Ill.: Free Press.

Comer, R. J., and J. A. Piliavin (1972). The effects of physical deviance upon face-to-face interaction: the other side. *J. Pers. soc. Psychol., 23,* 33–39.

Conrad, P., and J. W. Schneider (1980). *Deviance and medicalization: from badness to sickness.* St. Louis: C. V. Mosby.

Cook, P. J., Ed. (1981). *Gun control.* A special issue of *The Annals of the American Academy of Political and Social Science, 455.* Beverly Hills, Calif.: Sage.

Cook, T. D., and D. Campbell (1979). *Quasi-experimentation: design and analysis issues for field settings.* Chicago: Rand McNally.

Costanzo, P. R., and E. Z. Woody (1979). Externality as a function of obesity in children: pervasive style or eating-specific attribute? *J. Pers. soc. Psychol., 37,* 2286–2296.

Davis, F. (1961). Deviance disavowal: the management of strained interaction by the visibly handicapped. *Soc. Prob., 9,* 120–132.

Davis, K. (1937). The sociology of prostitution. *Amer. Sociological Rev., 2,* 744–755.

DeJong, W. (1980). The stigma of obesity: the consequences of naive assumptions concerning the causes of physical deviance. *J. Health soc. Behav., 21,* 75–87.

Dibiase, W. J., and L. A. Hjelle (1968). Body-image stereotypes and body-type preferences among male college students. *Perceptual motor Skills, 27,* 1143–1146.

Domhoff, G. W. (1978). *The powers that be: processes of ruling class domination in America.* New York: Vintage Books.

Doob, A. N., and B. P. Ecker (1970). Stigma and compliance. *J. Pers. soc. Psychol., 14,* 302–304.

Douglas, J. (1967). *The social meanings of suicide.* Princeton, N.J.: Princeton Univ. Press.

Durkheim, E. (1950). *The rules of sociological method.* Glencoe, Ill.: Free Press. (originally published in 1895.)

_____ (1951). *Suicide.* Glencoe, Ill.: Free Press. (originally published in 1897.)

Erikson, K. T. (1962). Notes on the sociology of deviance. *Soc. Prob., 9,* 307–314.

_____ (1966). *Wayward puritans.* New York: Wiley.

Ermann, M. D., and R. J. Lundman, Eds. (1978). *Corporate and governmental deviance.* New York: Oxford Univ. Press.

Farina, A., J. G. Allen, and B. B. Saul (1968). The role of the stigmatized person in affecting social relationships. *J. Pers., 36,* 169–182.

Farina, A., M. Sherman, and J. G. Allen (1968). Role of physical abnormalities in interpersonal perception and behavior. *J. abnorm. Psychol., 73,* 590–593.

Farrington, D. P. (1979). Experiments on deviance with special reference to dishonesty. In L. Berkowitz (Ed.), *Advances in experimental social psychology.* Vol. 12. New York: Academic Press. Pp. 207–252.

Fischer, C. S. (1976). *The urban experience.* New York: Harcourt, Brace, Jovanovich.

Foote, E. (1977). The time has come: cigarette advertising must be banned. In M. E. Jarvik *et al.* (Eds.), *Research on smoking behavior.* NIDA Research Monograph 17. Washington, D.C.: U.S. Government Printing Office. Pp. 339–346.

Ford, C. S., and F. A. Beach (1951). *Patterns of sexual behavior.* New York: Harper & Row.

Foucault, M. (1967). *Madness and civilization.* New York: Mentor Books.

Garfinkel, H. (1956). Conditions of successful degradation ceremonies. *Amer. J. Sociol., 61,* 420–424.

Geis, G., and E. Stotland, Eds. (1980). *White-collar crime: theory and research.* Beverly Hills, Calif.: Sage.

Gibbons, F. X., W. G. Stephan, B. Stephenson, and C. R. Petty (1980). Reactions to stigmatized others: response amplification vs. sympathy. *J. exp. soc. Psychol., 16,* 591–605.

Gibbs, J. P. (1971). Suicide. In R. K. Merton, and R. Nisbet (Eds.), *Contemporary social problems* (3rd ed.). New York: Harcourt, Brace, Jovanovich.

Goffman, E. (1961). *Asylums.* Garden City, N.J.: Doubleday.

_____ (1963). *Stigma: notes on the management of spoiled identity.* Englewood Cliffs, N.J.: Prentice-Hall.

Gove, W. R., Ed. (1980). *The labelling of deviance: evaluating a perspective* (2nd ed.). Beverly Hills, Calif.: Sage.

Gusfield, J. R. (1967). Moral passage: the symbolic process in public designations of deviance. *Soc. Prob., 15,* 175–188.

Hansen, A. J. (1982). Vita: George Burroughs. *Harvard magazine.* P. 45.

Hastorf, A. H., G. B. Northcraft, and S. R. Picciotto (1979). Helping the handicapped: how realistic is the performance feedback received by the physically handicapped. *Pers. soc. Psychol. Bull., 5,* 373–376.

Hastorf, A. H., J. Wildfogel, and T. Cassman (1979). Acknowledgment of handicap as a tactic in social interaction. *J. Pers. soc. Psychol., 37,* 1790–1797.

Higgins, P. C. (1980). *Outsiders in a hearing world: a sociology of deafness.* Beverly Hills, Calif.: Sage.

Hirschi, T. (1969). *Causes of delinquency.* Berkeley: Univ. of California Press.

Hollingshead, A., and F. Redlich (1958). *Social class and mental illness.* New York: Wiley.

Jaffe, J. H. (1970). Drug addiction and drug abuse. In L. S. Goodman, and A. Gilman (Eds.), *The pharmacological basis of therapeutics* (4th ed.). New York: Macmillan.

Jaffe, J. H. (1977). Tobacco use as a mental disorder: the rediscovery of a medical problem. In M. E. Jarvik *et al.*

(Eds.), *Research on smoking behavior.* NIDA Research Monograph 17. Washington, D.C.: U.S. Government Printing Office. Pp. 202–217.

Jarvik, M. E., J. W. Cullen, E. R. Grit, T. M. Vogt, and L. J. West, Eds. (1977). *Research on smoking behavior.* NIDA Research Monograph 17. Washington, D.C.: U.S. Government Printing Office.

Johnson, J. M., and J. D. Douglas, Eds. (1978). *Crime at the top: deviance in business and the professions.* Philadelphia: Lippincott.

Kanter, R. (1972). *Commitment and community: communes and utopias in sociological perspective.* Cambridge, Mass.: Harvard Univ. Press.

Katz, I., and D. C. Glass (1979). An ambivalence theory of behavior toward the stigmatized. In W. Austin, and S. Worchel (Eds.), *The social psychology of intergroup relations.* Monterey, Calif.: Brooks/Cole.

Katz, J. (1980). The social movement against white-collar crime. In E. Bittner, and S. L. Messinger (Eds.), *Criminology review yearbook.* Vol. 2. Pp. 161–184.

Keller, M. (1975). Problems of epidemiology in alcohol studies. *J. Stud. Alcohol, 36,* 1442–1451.

Kephart, W. M. (1982). *Extraordinary groups: the sociology of unconventional life-styles* (2nd ed.). New York: St. Martin's Press.

Kitsuse, J. I. (1962). Societal reaction to deviant behavior: problems of theory and method. *Soc. Prob., 9,* 247–256.

_____ (1980a). The "new conception of deviance" and its critics. In W. R. Gove (Ed.), *The labelling of deviance.* Beverly Hills, Calif.: Sage. Pp. 381–392.

_____ (1980b). Coming out all over: deviants and the politics of social problems. *Soc. Prob., 28,* 1–13.

Kitsuse, J. I., and A. V. Cicourel (1963). A note on the use of official statistics. *Soc. Prob., 11,* 131–139.

Kleck, R. E. (1968a). Physical stigma and nonverbal cues emitted in face-to-face interaction. *Hum. Relat., 21,* 19–28.

_____ (1968b). Self-disclosure patterns of the nonobviously stigmatized. *Psychol. Reports, 23,* 1239–1248.

_____ (1969). Physical stigma and task-oriented interaction. *Hum. Relat., 22,* 53–60.

Kleck, R. E., H. Ono, and A. H. Hastorf (1966). The effect of physical deviance upon face-to-face interaction. *Hum. Relat., 19,* 425–436.

Kleck, R. E., and A. Strenta (1980). Perceptions of the impact of negatively valued physical characteristics on social interaction. *J. Pers. soc. Psychol., 39,* 861–873.

Knipe, W. (1867). *Criminal chronology of York Castle.* York, England.

Kuhn, T. S. (1962). *The structure of scientific revolutions.* Chicago: Univ. of Chicago Press.

Langer, E., S. E. Taylor, S. Fiske, and B. Chanowitz (1976). Stigma, staring, and discomfort: a novel-stimulus hypothesis. *J. exp. soc. Psychol., 12,* 451–463.

Langer, E. J., and R. P. Abelson (1974). A patient by any other name: clinician group difference in labeling bias. *J. consult. clinic. Psychol., 42,* 4–9.

Lauderdale, P., Ed. (1980). *A political analysis of deviance.* Minneapolis: Univ. of Minnesota Press.

Lemert, E. M. (1967). *Human deviance, social problems, and social control.* Englewood Cliffs, N.J.: Prentice-Hall.

Lemert, E. M. (1951). *Social pathology*. New York: McGraw-Hill.

Leon, G. R. (1976). Current directions in the treatment of obesity. *Psychol. Bull., 83,* 557–578.

Leon, G. R., and L. Roth (1977). Obesity: psychological causes, correlations, and speculations. *Psychol. Bull., 84,* 117–139.

Leonhard-Spark, P. J. (1978). Obesity and the popular arts. In C. Winick (Ed.), *Deviance and mass media. Sage annual review of studies in deviance.* Vol. II.

Lerner, R. M., and E. Gellert (1969). Body build identification, preference, and aversion in children. *Develop. Psychol., 1,* 456–462.

Lieberson, S., and A. R. Silverman (1965). The precipitants and underlying conditions of race riots. *Amer. Sociological Rev.,* 887–898.

Lips, J. E. (1937). *The savage hits back.* London: Lovat Dickson.

Lofland, J. (1966). *Deviance and identity.* Englewood Cliffs, N.J.: Prentice-Hall.

McArthur, L. Z., M. R. Solomon, and R. H. Jaffe (1980). Weight differences in emotional responsiveness to proprioceptive and pictorial stimuli. *J. Pers. soc. Psychol., 39,* 308–319.

Macgregor, F. C. (1951). Some psycho-social problems associated with facial deformities. *Amer. Sociological Rev., 16,* 633.

McGuire, W. J. (1976). Historical comparisons: testing psychological hypotheses with cross-era data. *Int. J. Psychol., 11,* 161–183.

Malcolmson, R. W. (1977). Infanticide in the eighteenth century. In J. S. Cockburn (Ed.), *Crime in England 1550–1800.* Princeton, N.J.: Princeton Univ. Press.

Mankoff, M. (1971). Societal reaction and career deviance: a critical analysis. *Sociological Quart., 12,* 204–218.

Marcus, S. (1966). *The other Victorians.* New York: Basic Books.

Markle, G. E., and R. J. Troyer (1979). Smoke gets in your eyes: cigarette smoking as deviant behavior. *Soc. Prob., 26,* 611–625.

Marx, G. T. (1970). Civil disorder and the agents of social control. *J. soc. Issues, 26,* 19–57.

———— (1974). Thoughts on a neglected category of social movement participant: agents, provocateurs and informants. *Amer. J. Sociol., 80,* 402–442.

———— (1981). Ironies of social control: authorities as contributors to deviance through escalation, nonenforcement and covert facilitation. *Soc. Prob., 28,* 221–246.

Matza, D. (1964). *Delinquency and drift.* New York: Wiley.

Merton, R. K. (1949). *Social theory and social structure.* Glencoe, Ill.: Free Press.

———— (1967). *On theoretical sociology.* New York: Free Press.

Millman, M. (1980). *Such a pretty face: being fat in America.* New York: Norton.

Mills, C. W. (1943). The professional ideology of social pathologists. *Amer. J. Sociol., 49,* 165–180.

Monahan, J., R. W. Novaco, and G. Geis (1979). Corporate violence: research strategies for community psychology. In T. R. Sarbin (Ed.), *Challenges to the criminal justice system: the perspectives of community psychology.* New York: Human Sciences Press. Pp. 117–141.

Naroll, R., V. R. Bullough, and F. Naroll (1974). *Military deterrence in history.* Albany: State Univ. of New York Press.

Naroll, R., G. L. Michik, and F. Naroll (1980). Holocultural research methods. In H. C. Triandis (Ed.), *Handbook of cross-cultural psychology.* Vol. 2. Boston: Allyn and Bacon. Pp. 479–521.

Nettler, G. (1974). *Explaining crime.* New York: McGraw-Hill.

Newman, G. (1976). *Comparative deviance: perception and law in six cultures.* New York: Elsevier.

Nisbett, R. E. (1968). Determinants of food intake in obesity. *Science, 159,* 1254–1255.

Nisbett, R. E., and D. E. Kanouse (1969). Obesity, food deprivation and supermarket shopping behavior. *J. Pers. soc. Psychol., 12,* 289–294.

Nordhoff, C. (1966). *The communistic societies of the United States: from personal visit and observation.* New York: Dover. Published originally under the same title. New York: Harper and Brothers, 1875.

Noyes, J. H. (1966). *Strange cults and utopias of 19th century America.* New York: Dover. Published originally under the title *History of American socialisms.* Philadelphia: Lippincott, 1870.

O'Neill, W. L. (1967). *Divorce in the progressive era.* New Haven: Yale Univ. Press.

Pettigrew, T. F. (1980). Social psychology's potential contributions to an understanding of poverty. In V. T. Covello (Ed.), *Poverty and public policy: an evaluation of social science research.* Boston and Cambridge: G.K. Hall and Schenkman.

Pfohl, S. J. (1977). The "discovery" of child abuse. *Soc. Prob., 24,* 310–323.

Phillips, D. P. (1974). The influence of suggestion on suicide: substantive and theoretical implications of the Werther effect. *Amer. Sociological Rev., 39,* 340–354.

Piliavin, I., and S. Briar (1964). Police encounters with juveniles. *Amer. J. Sociol., 70,* 206–214.

Platt, A. M. (1969). *The child savers: the invention of delinquency.* Chicago: Univ. of Chicago Press.

Preston, R. P. (1979). *The dilemmas of care: social and nursing adaptations to the deformed, the disabled, and the aged.* New York: Elsevier.

Quinney, R. (1970). *The social reality of crime.* Boston: Little, Brown.

Richardson, S. A. (1971). Children's values and friendships: a study of physical disability. *J. Health soc. Behav., 12,* 253–258.

Richardson, S. A., N. Goodman, A. Hasdorf, and S. Dornbusch (1961). Cultural uniformity in reaction to physical disabilities. *Amer. Sociological Rev., 26,* 241–247.

Richardson, S. A., L. Ronald, and R. E. Kleck (1974). The social status of handicapped and nonhandicapped boys in a camp setting. *J. special Educ., 8,* 143–152.

Ritchie, J., and J. Ritchie (1981). Child rearing and child abuse: the Polynesian context. In J. E. Korbin (Ed.), *Child abuse and neglect: cross-cultural perspectives.* Berkeley: Univ. of California Press.

Rodin, J. (1973). Effects of distraction on performance of obese and normal subjects. *J. compara. physiol. Psychol., 83,* 68–75.

Rosenhan, D. L. (1973). On being sane in insane places. *Science, 179,* 250–258.

Rosenthal, R. (1966). *Experimenter effects in behavioral research.* New York: Appleton-Century-Crofts.

_____ (In press). From unconscious experimenter bias to teacher expectancy effects. In J. B. Dusek (Ed.), *Teacher expectancies.* Hillsdale, N.J.: Erlbaum.

Rosenthal, R., J. A. Hall, M. R. DiMatteo, P. L. Rogers, and D. Archer (1979). *Sensitivity to nonverbal communication: the PONS test.* Baltimore: Johns Hopkins.

Rossi, P. H., E. Waite, C. E. Bose, and R. E. Berk (1974). The seriousness of crimes: normative structure and individual differences. *Amer. Sociological Rev., 39,* 224–237.

Rothman, D. J. (1971). *The discovery of the asylum.* Boston: Little, Brown.

Rothman, D. J. (1980). *Conscience and convenience.* Boston: Little, Brown.

Rugoff, M. (1971). *Prudery and passion: sexuality in Victorian America.* New York: Putnam.

Sarbin, T. R. (1979). The myth of the criminal type. In T. R. Sarbin (Ed.), *Challenges to the criminal justice system: the perspectives of community psychology.* New York: Human Sciences Press. Pp. 1–27.

Schacter, S. (1971a). *Emotion, obesity, and crime.* New York: Academic Press.

_____ (1971b). Some extraordinary facts about obese humans and rats. *Amer. Psychologist, 26,* 129–144.

Scheff, T. J. (1974). The labeling theory of mental illness. *Amer. Sociological Rev., 39,* 444–452.

Schneider, J. W., and P. Conrad (1980). In the closet with illness: epilepsy, stigma potential and information control. *Soc. Prob., 28,* 32–44.

Schneidman, E. S., Ed. (1976). *Suicidology: contemporary developments.* New York: Grune and Stratton.

Schur, E. M. (1971). *Labeling deviant behavior: its sociological implications.* New York: Harper & Row.

_____ (1979). *Interpreting deviance.* New York: Harper & Row.

_____ (1980a). Comments. In W. R. Gove (Ed.), *The labelling of deviance.* Beverly Hills, Calif.: Sage. Pp. 393–404.

_____ (1980b). *The politics of deviance.* Englewood Cliffs, N.J.: Prentice-Hall.

Schwartz, R. D., and J. Skolnick (1962). Two studies of legal stigma. *Soc. Prob., 10,* 133–142.

Scott, R. A. (1969). *The making of blind men: a study of adult socialization.* New York: Russell Sage.

Sellin, T., and M. E. Wolfgang (1964). *The measurement of delinquency.* New York: Wiley.

Sennett, R., and J. Cobb (1972). *The hidden injuries of class.* New York: Vintage Books.

Short, J. R. (1975). The national commission on the causes and prevention of violence: reflections on the contributions of sociology and sociologists. In M. Komarovsky (Ed.), *Sociology and public policy: the case of presidential commissions.* New York: Elsevier.

Simmons, J. L., and H. Chambers (1965). Public stereotypes of deviants. *Soc. Prob., 13,* 223–232.

Simon, D. R., and D. S. Eitzen (1982). *Elite deviance.* Boston: Allyn and Bacon.

Sinclair, K. (1959). *A history of New Zealand.* London: Oxford Univ. Press.

Skogan, W. G. (1977). Dimensions of the dark figure of unreported crime. *Crime and Delinquency, 23,* 41–50.

_____ (1981). *Issues in the measurement of victimization.* Washington, D.C.: U.S. Department of Justice.

Smith, C. P., D. J. Berkman, and W. M. Fraser (1980). *Reports of the national juvenile justice assessment centers: a preliminary assessment of child abuse and neglect and the juvenile justice system.* Washington, D.C.: U.S. Department of Justice.

Snyder, M. L., R. E. Kleck, A. Strenta, and S. J. Mentzer (1979). *J. Pers. soc. Psychol., 37,* 2297–2306.

Spector, M., and J. I. Kitsuse (1977). *Constructing social problems.* Menlo Park, Calif.: Benjamin/Cummings.

Stone, L. (1979). *The family, sex, and marriage in England, 1500–1800.* New York: Harper & Row.

Sutherland, E. H. (1961). *Whie collar crime.* New York: Holt, Rinehart, and Winston.

Sutherland, E. H., and D. R. Cressey (1978). *Criminology* (10th ed.). Philadelphia: Lippincott.

Tannenbaum, F. (1938). *Crime and the community.* New York: Columbia Univ. Press.

Taylor, I., P. Walton, and J. Young (1974). *The new criminology: for a social theory of deviance.* New York: Harper & Row.

Thomas, W. I., and F. Znaniecki (1958). *The Polish peasant in Europe and America.* Boston: Gorham Press, 1920. New York: Dover Press.

Traub, S. H., and C. B. Little, Eds. (1980). *Theories of deviance.* Itasca, Ill.: F. E. Peacock.

Trebach, A. S. (1982). *The heroin solution.* New Haven: Yale Univ. Press.

Triandis, H. C., Ed. (1980). *Handbook of cross-cultural psychology.* Boston: Allyn and Bacon.

Trice, H. M., and P. M. Roman (1970). Delabeling, relabeling, and alcoholics anonymous. *Soc. Prob., 17,* 538–546.

Truzzi, M. (1968). Lilliputians in Gulliver's land: the social role of the dwarf. In M. Truzzi (Ed.), *Sociology and everyday life.* Englewood Cliffs, N.J.: Prentice-Hall. Pp. 197–211.

U.S. Department of Justice, Bureau of Justice Statistics (1982). *Sourcebook of criminal justice statistics.* Washington, D.C.: U.S. Government Printing Office.

U.S. Department of Justice, Bureau of Justice Statistics (1981). *Criminal victimization in the United States, 1973–79 trends.* Washington, D.C.: U.S. Government Printing Office.

Webb, E. J., D. T. Campbell, R. D. Schwartz, L. Sechrest, and J. R. Grove (1981). *Nonreactive measures in the social sciences.* Boston: Houghton Mifflin.

Weitz, S. (1972). Attitude, voice and behavior: a repressed affect model of interracial interaction. *J. Pers. soc. Psychol., 24,* 14–21.

Whiting, J. W. M. (1968). Methods and problems in cross-cultural research. In G. Lindzey and E. Aronson (Eds.),

Handbook of social psychology. Vol. 2. Reading, Mass.: Addison-Wesley. Pp. 693–728.

Wilkins, L. (1964). *Social deviance.* Englewood Cliffs, N.J.: Prentice-Hall.

Wing, J. K., and G. W. Brown (1970). *Institutionalism and schizophrenia: a comparative study of three mental hospitals, 1960–1968.* Cambridge: Cambridge Univ. Press.

Wolfgang, M. E. (1968). Urban crime. In J. Q. Wilson (Ed.), *The metropolitan enigma.* New York: Doubleday Anchor. Pp. 270–311.

Wolfgang, M. E., and F. Ferracuti (1982). *The subculture of violence: towards an integrated theory in criminology.* Beverly Hills, Calif.: Sage.

Wright, B. (1960). *Physical disability: a psychological approach.* New York: Harper & Row.

Zola, I. (1982). *Missing pieces: a chronicle of living with a disability.* Philadelphia: Temple Univ. Press.

CHAPTER 27

The Application of Social Psychology

Judith Rodin
Yale University

HISTORY AND CHAPTER GOALS

The 1970s witnessed a virtual explosion of interest in studying important social problems using social psychological theories, methods, and techniques. The emergence of this field and its rapid growth were the result of several converging forces. First, there was growing dissatisfaction with the methods of traditional laboratory studies. As Smith (1973) commented: "Near the end of the 60's, doubt and self-criticism became increasingly evident among American social psychologists about the lack of cumulative gains commensurate with effort expended,...about the artificiality and human irrelevance of some of the problems...pursued with great sophistication, about the instability of laboratory findings" (pp. 610–611). McGuire (1973), in a comparable critique, noted that the most dominant paradigm in social psychology, in which investigators selected hypotheses for relevance to broad theoretical formulations and tested them by laboratory manipulational experiments, had failed. The results merely showed "whether the ex-perimenter is a sufficiently ingenious stage manager to produce in the laboratory conditions which demonstrate that an obviously true hypothesis is correct" (p. 449).

Second, there was concern about the generality of many of the social psychological theories derived from the laboratory research of the 1960s. Some critiques questioned whether laboratory experiments could ever serve as a trustworthy basis for building a science of human behavior. For example, Gergen (1973) challenged the data base of social psychology, noting that history will change the meaning of all experiments. In fact people's attitudes might be changed simply by knowledge of the experiments that discovered them in the first place. Others, notably Moscovici (1972), pointed out how strongly the laboratory-based data of experimental social psychology were influenced by Western capitalist views, such as exchange and the essential quality of altruistic behavior, and noted that such principles might have absolutely no relevance in other parts of the world.

Certainly implicit in all these criticisms was the notion that social psychology had not fulfilled its early promise. A reaction to such views led some investigators back to the roots of social psychology—displaying a renewed interest, for example, in the pioneering work of Kurt Lewin. As critics within and outside the field

The author is grateful to Philip Brickman, Faye Crosby and Irving L. Janis for the numerous helpful comments they made on an earlier version of this chapter.

disparaged its seemingly esoteric and abstract body of knowledge and its inability to help solve the social ills of the 1960s, efforts grew to learn whether social psychological principles could be applied to the understanding and solution of important social problems. Thus began a search for greater relevance in an attempt to escape from the self-criticism of performing contentless and often trivial laboratory research that, at best, had little external validity.

As efforts to conduct applied research grew, new self-criticisms emerged. It was argued that it was insufficient to select hypotheses for their social relevance and test them by field experiments or correlational analysis of naturalistic data without reexamining our research methods and strategies. Simon (1974) called for greater breadth in experimental designs, noting that the orthodox approach to experimentation, with its insistence on testing a single effect of a single "cause," produced at most a "one-bit yield of information"—that there is a relationship between an independent and a dependent variable. Most critical, if the effect in question was due to a combination of causes simultaneously, it would never be identified by this approach. Simon proposed that experiments should go beyond merely demonstrating that the presence of an experimental variable makes or fails to make a "significant" difference.

Similarly McGuire (1973, p. 448) noted that:

socially relevant hypotheses no less than theoretically relevant hypotheses tend to be based on a simple linear model, a sequential chain of cause and effect which is inadequate to simulate the true complexities of the individual's cognitive system or the social system which we are typically trying to describe. Such simple "a" affects "b" hypotheses fail to catch the complexities of parallel processing by directional causality and reverberating feedback that characterize both cognitive and social organizations.

Kahn (1981) has labeled such traditional experimental procedures, when imposed on applied settings where men and women are "playing for keeps," designs for failure. McGuire also expressed the concern that there was as much stage managing in natural-world research as there had been in laboratory experiments, and that when the field test of the hypothesis did not come out correctly, we failed to assume the hypothesis was wrong, but rather assumed that we had chosen the wrong natural setting in which to test it.

From these discussions new principles and methods for the study of the social psychology of socially relevant topics emerged, stimulated by the social activism and at the same time restrained by the continued self-examination of social psychology during the 1970s. Some of the earliest applications of social psychology to social problems of the period represented direct extrapolations of extant laboratory findings (e.g., Abelson and Zimbardo, 1970; Varela, 1969). These efforts suggested that there were real findings from the laboratory that could be directly applied to the real-world situation, but they typically did not present data from controlled studies directly testing these assertions.

Later work moved away from attempts at direct application of laboratory findings to applied domains. Research in health and medicine represents this newer approach. Social psychological variables affecting the etiology of disease were studied, suggesting strongly that many of the major causes of chronic illness were related to lifestyle. Social psychological analyses were applied to understanding reactions to illness, for example, how people attribute the causes of their illness and how they learn to recognize and interpret changes in their condition. Social psychological variables were used to explain patient-management problems, including the bases of compliance and satisfaction and the development of coping mechanisms. An understanding of the detrimental effects of the health care delivery system was also greatly advanced by the application of social psychological principles. Most significantly, prevention efforts began to utilize social psychological knowledge of decision making and mass media effects to teach necessary new behaviors and help people maintain their commitment to behavior change. The promise of these inquiries and applications led Taylor (1978) to suggest the prospect of a preventive psychology, similar in concept to preventive medicine, which would use psychological research to reduce the psychological and behavioral risk factors that are linked to the development of illness.

Social psychology began to be applied to understanding the legal process as well, particularly to studying how evidence is used and understood, jury selection and jury functioning, social influence as it occurs in the courtroom, and the deterrence value of capital punishment. Educational reform has also been a recent domain for social psychological inquiry, particularly with the failure of school desegregation per se to change racial attitudes and improve the educational system. Studies of the workplace and of consumer behavior also grew among applied social psychologists.

There have been many fine reviews of the above areas, and this discussion is not intended to duplicate them by exhaustively describing each conventionally defined domain (e.g., social psychology and law, or social psychology and medicine). Rather, this chapter considers several conceptual and theoretical categories of social psychological variables or processes in which advances have been made from substantive empirical considerations of real-world problems. In following this plan I hope to show where our knowledge base and theoretical concerns are not domain specific, where there are general principles in social psychology that have breadth and applicability beyond a particular experiment or specific setting. If applications are seen as true derivations from theory, this type of analysis can determine whether the field of social psychology has indeed made substantial achievements in the last decade.

Because of the approach described above, the present chapter does not provide a detailed review of the area of applied social psychology. Rather, studies have been selected as examples to show how social psychological theories, constructs, and findings are supported by multiple developments in different content domains, each representing what Lewin called "action research," that is, research done in an actual problem context that is socially useful as well as theoretically meaningful. It is also true that surveys are probably not represented as fully as experiments in the present review. Throughout the chapter I will attempt to describe how reflection on applied problems has frequently been capable of illuminating significant gaps in basic social psychological knowledge. I will also discuss methodological issues involved in the application of social psychology, again using examples from studies in the various areas of current research interest.

Two major issues arise when considering applied social research. The first involves the extent to which the studies should be evaluated on the degree to which they fulfill specific criteria for applied research. For example, Helmreich (1975) has identified the goals of applicability (the potential for application) and utilization (the implementation of social change). Or Hornstein (1975) has suggested evaluating applied studies on the basis of the extent to which they have "tractable variance," that is, uncovering variables that are both critical in terms of their causal role and amenable to change. But these decisions are often difficult to make. Certain problems have been studied for years, whereas others are relatively new, both in theoretical analyses of the central variables and in systematic application. Often the more apparently applicable work represents more mature rather than better research. Further, applied research may increase our understanding of a social problem, suggest new approaches, and enable prediction of events without improving our control over them (Carroll and Frieze, 1979). Thus applicability and utilization per se may not be sufficient criteria on which to evaluate research in this area.

A second debated issue is whether research in the applied arena should be done to test theory or to predict behavior. Theory testing focuses primarily on internally valid tests of hypotheses, whereas behavior prediction focuses on maximizing predictive efficiency regardless of the theoretical import of the relevant factors. Monahan and Loftus (1982), commenting on this schism in research in psychology and law, conclude as I do that ultimately science must embrace both objectives, citing Lewin's (1951) dictum that there is nothing so practical (in predicting and changing behavior) as a good theory. Likewise unexplained predictions are the principal impetus to theoretical developments and ultimately to paradigm shifts.

Even the integration of theory with the study of social problems has not been seen in only one way. There are some who view applied research primarily as an opportunity for testing specific hypotheses and thereby evaluating the external validity of existing social psychological theory (e.g., Ellsworth, 1977; Jacoby, 1975). This perspective has merit, as it is important to check the ecological validity of findings as well as to examine hypotheses in special populations and to be able to vary factors that are impossible to vary in laboratory situations. But if applied research were to proceed solely on these grounds, it could lose much of its merit. The bulk of applied research would surely become yet more atheoretical, and laboratory-based research and theory would probably continue to turn in on itself and lose contact with the real world of human behavior. Field experiments would be relegated to testing empirical generalizations of questionable importance.

An alternative view articulated by Leventhal (1980a), Rodin (1977), and Collins, Whalen, and Henker (1980) is that field research in real-life settings may become a primary domain for the *development* of social psychological theory. This view of applied research could profoundly alter our perspective on laboratory investigation. We would look to the laboratory to test the specific hypotheses that were extracted from the network of theory developed in applied settings rather than vice versa. The methods used in laboratory studies would require increased attention to the definition of the level of conceptual variables, fixing the level of contextual variables within which independent variables would vary in the laboratory. This view holds that theory can and should develop and be tested in applied settings, to be retested and elaborated in the laboratory for greater advances in social psychological knowledge. This strategy views applied research as a central arena for theory development.

As Sanford (1970) noted, for Lewin involvement with practical problems was a never-failing source of theoretical ideas and knowledge of fundamental social psychological relationships. In terms of the strategies employed to deal with its problems, and with respect to the forms of the inquiry, applied research can be and often is responsive to theory. The outcome of this form of inquiry is perhaps even more likely than laboratory research to result in more than a raw empirical finding. Research that attempts to provide answers to questions posed by the real world can lead to the formulation of general principles, in other words, the theory. As Lewin argued years ago, the promise of social psychology can best be achieved through closer cooperation between theory-oriented and problem-oriented inquiry. The present chapter takes this principle as its starting point.

Each of the sections that follows represents areas of concern to social psychological theory. These include: the role of environmental variables, person-situation interaction, social influence, social support, attribution, information processing and decision making, control, self-esteem, and physiological consequences of social psychological processes. Of course, some of these areas have clearer theoretical formulations than others; some have competing formulations and others do not. In addition, some of these areas of theoretical concern have relevance to a greater number of applied problems and issues than others. For these reasons the subheadings in some sections will represent areas of institutional relevance, for example, medicine, law, and education, or the more specific social problems, such as substance abuse and jury behavior. Then the subsection will describe and compare differing theories as they have been developed and/or tested in one or more of these substantive domains. In other sections the subheadings will represent a

particular theoretical formulation or issue, and a variety of applied topics all dealing with it will be discussed together within that subsection. This organization is intended to promote integration where possible, while still representing fairly the variability in developments across these several domains.

FOCUS ON ENVIRONMENTAL VARIABLES

The study of applied social problems has benefited greatly from the orientation of social psychology toward the social environment, that is, toward understanding the situational variables that elicit, maintain, and control behavior. One of the major achievements of social psychology, in fact, has been the demonstration of the subtlety of the operation of these situational variables. A common theme through much of this research has been that it is not bad people but rather bad situations that create social problems. Milgram's (1965) compliance research and Zimbardo's (1969) analysis of deindividuation represent earlier, noteworthy examples of this perspective that have led to a better understanding of important social problems. In each case the investigators showed how situational variables, such as the presence of an authority or a group, anonymity, a high degree of arousal, or loss of time perspective, led to aggressive and in some instances gravely antisocial behavior that potentially threatened physical and psychological well-being.

INSTITUTIONS

In a well-known and somewhat controversial study Zimbardo and his colleagues applied an analysis of situational variables to explain the current state of the prison system (Haney, Banks, and Zimbardo, 1973; Haney and Zimbardo, 1977). Stanford University undergraduates were recruited for the study and randomly assigned to the role of prisoner or guard. In these roles, the guards often became brutal and abusive and the prisoners became passive. The study was interpreted as support for the assertion that situational rather than dispositional factors explain more of the variance in predicting behavior in prisons. Despite criticisms of the study that the data were largely impressionistic rather than quantitative, and that it is hard to separate the effects of the roles shaping behavior from the actors' role playing in a way that was consistent with the roles to which they were assigned, the sheer intensity of the behaviors that emerged suggests that the social context of the experiment created a reality that permitted, if not dictated, antisocial behavior to occur.

Kelman (1973), in discussing sanctioned massacres throughout history, also asserts that the major instigators for this class of violence derive from the policy process rather than from human impulses toward violence as such. This analysis suggests three interrelated processes that lead to the weakening of moral restraints against violence: authorization (occurring in the context of an authority situation), routinization (transforming the action into mechanical, highly programmed operations, thus reducing the necessity of making decisions), and dehumanization. His ideas are consistent with those of Milgram (1964) and Zimbardo (1969) in emphasizing the importance of situational factors in brutal, violent, or aggressive actions. In all these arguments, areas where the system and social environment must or can be changed are identified.

Understanding that institutional settings and the behaviors that occur there are mandated by the norms and rules of the social process rather than by individuals' personalities provides an important focus for intervention and for social change. This was the perspective taken by Wack and Rodin (1978) when they considered the situational factors that forced nursing homes to promote dependence and passive behavior. Rules promulgated to raise the standards of nursing care and to regulate the administration of nursing homes supported by Medicare and Medicaid created environments that have had the unintended consequences of encouraging dependency and helplessness in patients, making work in nursing homes unrewarding for staff, and discouraging residents from improving enough to lead independent lives again. This dependency, created and supported by contextual variables, in turn leads to further debilitation and ill health (Langer and Rodin, 1976; Rodin and Langer, 1977; Schulz, 1976). Again the assertion is that it is situational factors and not specific characteristics of the relevant actors that determine the behavior that results.

SUBSTANCE ABUSE

Many social problems appear more amenable to change when subjected to a social psychological analysis of the situational variables that elicit and maintain behavior. Studies of substance abuse, for example, were largely influenced by pharmacological models of addiction until work such as Robins's landmark study on the returning Vietnam veterans suggested strongly that social context was of primary importance in the maintenance of drug-using habits, even for addicted heroin users (Robins, 1973). She showed that when addicts returned from Vietnam to their families and nonusing environments, many were able to give up heroin and maintain abstinence with relative ease. Subsequently Evans and his coworkers tried to prevent the onset of addictive behavior, such as cigarette smoking, by direct manipulation of the social environment (Evans, 1982; Evans, Hill, Dill, Henderson, Bray, and Gilden, 1980; Evans, Rozelle, *et. al.,* 1981).

Despite mounting evidence regarding the serious health consequences of cigarette smoking, more than 50 million Americans, or about one-third of the adult population, continue to smoke. Surveys reveal that in the past ten years, although the percentage of adult smokers in the United States has significantly declined, the percentage of teenage smokers has slightly increased, especially among females. Responses from teenagers themselves suggest that peer pressure to smoke may be one of the major influences to do so. Becoming a smoker may have the immediate value to some teenagers of being accepted by their peers or feeling more mature, because smoking is an adult behavior forbidden to the child and might even serve the function of an act of defiance to authority figures. Fear arousal appears to have limited effects on health behavior in general (see Janis and Rodin [1979] for review), and on children in particular, since the dangers of smoking may appear too diffuse and distant. Even if they were convinced that something might happen to them when they were much older, this does not appear to be an effective way to persuade many of them to resist the pressure to begin smoking. Instead, affecting their response to peer pressure may be a more direct and successful strategy. Taking this as their starting point Evans and his coworkers selected thirteen junior high schools in a single school district and divided them into treatment and control schools.

Evans and his coworkers developed a series of films that described ways to avoid peer pressure to smoke by familiarizing students with the nature of the pressures and actually recreating social situations and modeling behaviors to resist such pressures. The films, either alone or in combination, were provided several times during the seventh-, eighth-, and ninth-grade years to students in the experimental condition. This procedure precluded a components analysis of the films, since they were presented in various combinations over the course of the three-year study. Students in the control conditions simply received measurements during the relevant periods but did not receive any of the filmed communications.

The data suggested that treatment subjects, especially those receiving all the films, expressed significantly fewer intentions to smoke than control subjects and engaged in less actual smoking behavior. However, the study used a quasi-experimental design with successively cross-sectional rather than longitudinal data analysis, because the number of respondents, and indeed the specific subjects themselves, varied from year to year due to attrition, transfers, enrollment possibilities, and historical events occurring in various schools. Since students in the same classroom were not randomly assigned to experimental and treatment conditions and saw the films together, it is possible that what changed was the nature of the social environment, which made smoking less permissible in the treatment than in the control schools as a result of group participation in the study. Of course classrooms and schools also differed in a variety of ways, including racial and ethnic composition, which may also have contributed to the differences obtained. But it does seem that the procedures may have changed social norms, which permitted individual attitudes and non-smoking behavior to be maintained in a milieu in which smoking was viewed as inappropriate. By contrast, in an environment in which smoking is permissible and even valued, it is far more difficult to change individual behavior. Indeed most results suggest that change efforts focused at the individual per se are inadequate to influence substance-use behaviors.

In a theoretically similar study the Stanford three-community program compared changes in cardiovascular-risk measures in subjects from a community exposed to mass media and intensive face-to-face intervention, with subjects in a community exposed to the mass media program alone, and subjects in a community unexposed to any program. As in the Evans *et al.* study, the quasi-experimental design used a single community for each of the experimental conditions (Farquhar, 1978; Meyer, Maccoby, and Farquhar, 1980). The data showed that a complex set of risk measures, including smoking, blood pressure, and serum lipids, was significantly decreased in the community exposed to both the mass media and intensive face-to-face intervention programs. Again these data suggest that individual predisposition to change behavior is expressed most readily in a social environment that permits, and indeed supports, the predisposition to behave.

Unfortunately some procedures followed in the study make it difficult to determine fully the impact of the macrosocial variables being considered (Leventhal, Safer, Cleary, and Gutmann, 1980). For example, the intensive physiological measurement required considerable repeated individual contacts that would not be present in a typical community-based media program. Because of this emphasis on individual risk reduction, virtually no data were obtained on community processes that presumably changed as a result of the intervention in the experimental community. In addition, while there were claims for changes in lifestyle, the dependent variables did not appraise lifestyle but rather examined changes only in risk factors. A major opportunity to evaluate the impact of changing situational factors appears, unfortunately, to have been lost in this research.

EDUCATIONAL SETTINGS

School Desegregation

As in the health area, large-scale intervention studies of school integration have often lacked important design or measurement considerations. As McConahay (1978) notes, until 1978 there was not even one true experiment, and only four of the quasi-experimental studies had any real methodological rigor (Gerard and Miller, 1975; Schofield and Sagar, 1977; Shaw, 1973; Silverman and Shaw, 1973). The studies that do reveal some reliable information, however, tend to suggest a strong effect of social context on changes in racial attitudes and behaviors. For example, the racial composition of the school and the classroom appears quite important. Approximately equal proportions are best for maximizing contact and friendship formation between in-group and out-group members, since if one or another of the groups has a large percentage, it has the power to determine the signs and behaviors by which in-school status is ascribed or achieved (Koslin, Koslin, Pargament, and Waxman, 1972; St. John and Lewis, 1975).

The most successful efforts to change interracial attitudes and behaviors have been based on the creation of interracial work groups in a series of field experiments conducted by social psychologists in a wide range of school settings, grades, and regions of the country. These research programs used different techniques, but they all had in common an attempt to create interracial work groups in which status and participation inside the groups were equal, and intragroup and interethnic competition was minimized or eliminated. Furthermore, because most of these studies were true experiments with the appropriate randomly assigned control groups, we can have a great deal more confidence in their results.

In one series of studies Cook and his colleagues set up a field experiment in the seventh and tenth grades of the newly desegregated Denver public schools (Weigel, Wiser, and Cook, 1975). Ten English teachers, who did not know the hypotheses, taught one class using an approach in which the class was divided into interracial groups with four to six members in each group. The modal group was composed of three Anglos, one black, and one Mexican-American. As a control, the same teacher taught another class using a lecture-oriented whole-class method. For each teacher the experimental and control classes were decided by chance. The experiment lasted four and a half months in the tenth grade and seven months in the seventh grade. At the end of the study it was found that in the interracial-group classes all ethnic groups showed substantially more cross-ethnic helping behavior, and Anglos showed greater respect, liking, and friendship for Mexican-Americans, than was the case in the control group classes. However, none of the other racial groups showed any significant change in respect or liking for one another. Moreover, racial attitudes, as measured by at-home interviews three months after the experiment, did not differ between the experimental and control conditions. These data suggest that the social environment may begin to create the context for a change in norms with regard to overt behavior, while leaving attitudes, which are more individual dispositions, unchanged or at best changed too little to be detected by the measures used in this study.

DeVries, Edwards, and Slavin (1978) reported stronger results on the basis of four field experiments using a technique they developed known as the team games (TGT) approach. In the TGT approach the class was divided into interracial groups of four or five members from all achievement levels and both sexes. The teammates sat together at all times and engaged in peer tutoring of one another in all academic disciplines. Then at the end of the week a class tournament was held in which students from the same team competed individually in skill contests with students of comparable ability from other teams in the class. The team scores were the sum of the scores achieved by individuals in the skill contests. In studies using seventh- to twelfth-grade classes in

Maryland and Florida, the TGT approach was compared with randomly assigned control classes using traditional methods. Relative to the control group, the TGT technique produced more cross-racial sociometric friendship choices in each of the four experiments.

Perhaps the most impressive results for interracial work groups have been reported by Aronson and his associates (Aronson and Bridgeman, 1979; Aronson, Blaney, Stephan, Sikes, and Snapp). In a series of field experiments in southwestern Texas and northern California, they used a method known as the jigsaw technique to improve not only racial attitudes but also academic performance. In the jigsaw technique the students in the classroom were divided into six-person interracial and interethnic groups. The material to be learned was divided into six parts or paragraphs, and each group member given only one part of the material. Then each student was expected to master his or her own part of the material and teach it to the other students in the group. Students had to rely on one another to learn the complete material or they would do less well on the exams. The jigsaw technique incorporates Cohen's (1972) findings that blacks must be expert in a central aspect of the group task in order to overcome the "interracial interaction disability" that typically fails to make them true equals.

The results of the experiments with the jigsaw technique showed that relative to control group classrooms, this technique produced significantly more cross-racial and cross-ethnic sociometric choices, fewer ethnic stereotypes, higher self-esteem, and better academic performance. The goal of the procedure to change the basic classroom structure so that children could learn to like and trust each other apparently had been met. Thus one way for desegrated schools to get students of different races together is to make structural changes in the classroom itself, requiring participants to work together and to treat each other as resources. This in turn changes the classroom to one where students are reinforced for helping one another. The concept of interracial work groups as a means of reducing prejudice and improving race relations in schools thus has a great deal of empirical support. It is clear that this is certainly the most effective practice for improving race relations in desegregated schools that we know of to date.

Hyperactive Children

Situational factors, including the classroom structure itself, have been shown to be of major importance in understanding the behavior of hyperactive children

(Collins, Whalen, and Henker, 1980), again forcing a shift away from purely dispositional explanations. Challenging all of the earlier research which suggested that hyperactivity is a property of the child, Collins *et al.* (1980) suggested that there may be specific ecological contexts that evoke the problematic behaviors of hyperactivity. They speculated that at school there are both "provocation ecologies" that maximize the probability of the behaviors associated with hyperactivity and others that minimize the same behaviors. They also speculated that an important component of hyperactivity is located in the reaction of the ecological system to the child's behavior. Indeed their most extreme and most interesting speculation was that there may be task and context changes possible in this system that could function as equivalent to Ritalin, a psychostimulant intervention for controlling hyperactivity. If these environmental variables could be uncovered, ecological engineering could be used to supplement and/or replace the biological engineering of psychostimulant medication.

In an ambitious experiment Collins and his coworkers developed a summer school that included a school program with a naturalistic classroom setting and a series of experiments that measured attentional patterns and interpersonal skills. They held two consecutive five-week sessions, with sixteen boys in each of two classrooms or cohorts, half of them hyperactive and half normal-comparison children. The children spent two mornings a week in a classroom setting, two mornings a week participating in various structured assessment modules, and one day a week on a field trip. Video cameras were placed in most classrooms and laboratory settings. During the third week of the project a randomly assigned half of the hyperactive boys received a placebo and half received medication. During the fourth week these conditions were reversed. The classroom teacher and teaching aides had no information about the experimental design. Theoretically interesting parameters of classroom settings were also varied across the four academic periods each day. Variables manipulated within the classroom setting included self-paced versus other-paced tasks, maximum teacher availability or full supervision versus minimum teacher availability, task appropriate versus task difficult, crowded classroom versus uncrowded conditions, peer interdependence versus independent work, and noisy versus quiet conditions. A minimum of four observers continuously sampled classroom behavior on every classroom day.

The data strongly showed the situation-specific nature of hyperactivity. For example, many differences between hyperactive and comparison boys emerged in certain roles but not in others, and in certain classroom contexts but not in others. Moreover, the effects of medication interacted with the specific effects of these situations. For example, some components of the hyperactivity behavioral system, particularly social information processing, were not remedied by Ritalin.

BURNOUT

According to Maslach (1978), situational factors are most important in explaining the process and behaviors of burnout. Burnout involves a loss of concern for the people with whom one is working. In addition to physical exhaustion and sometimes even illness, burnout is characterized by emotional exhaustion in which the individual, usually a helping professional, no longer has any positive feelings, sympathy, or respect for clients or patients. As a result of this process the help recipients are viewed as somehow deserving of their problem and are blamed for their own victimization (Ryan, 1971), which results in a deterioration in the quality of care or service that they receive. Furthermore burnout is correlated with various indices of personal stress, such as increased substance abuse, tension, marital and family conflict, and other problematic life experiences among health care professionals.

Maslach (1978) has identified several situational factors associated with high rates of professional burnout. For example, the number of people for whom the professional is providing care is extremely important. Longer work hours are correlated with more stress and negative staff attitudes only when they involve continuous direct contact with patients or clients. Chronic problems also appear to cause more emotional stress for staff than do acute problems, although they may often be less severe, because acute problems are frequently more clearly linked to an identifiable cause and are therefore more amenable to some sort of staff intervention. It is also the case that in many human service institutions the nature of the staff-client interaction is such that negative feedback from clients is far more prevalent than positive feedback. Despite the impact of these powerful situational variables, when the quality of care provided by helping professionals deteriorates, all too often people are blamed rather than the work environment, according to

Maslach. It is either staff or clients who are held to be at fault for spoiling the idealistic relationship between the concerned caregiver and the appreciative recipient. Refocusing attention to factors in the environment may provide an important mechanism for reducing burnout, as will be discussed later.

SUMMARY AND CONCLUSIONS

The data suggest that analyses of situational variables contribute significantly to the understanding of social problems. Indeed an emphasis on understanding the situational determinants of behavior has enabled the study of social problems to make real progress. Yet extreme behavior, whether defined as hyperactive, altruistic, or antisocial, is often viewed by both society and the individual in question as stemming largely if not entirely from within the person. Perhaps this is due, as Nisbett and Wilson (1977) suggest, to the fact that people simply do not have conscious awareness of the situational forces that influence their behavior. Or it may be caused by a greater tendency to attend to animate than inanimate objects based simply on information-processing variables. Or it may be due to moralistic views about blame, which reflect Western views of responsibility and causation.

Whatever the reason for underestimation of the role of situational variables, it remains an important challenge for applied social research to demonstrate convincingly that variations of environmental factors can strongly change behavior specifically attributed to the disposition of the individual. Further, studies are needed to determine the circumstances in which people are likely to recognize the extent of the effects of situational factors when the stakes are high and their problems are real. Laboratory investigations of this question do not appear to be highly fruitful. Understanding the interesting paradox of the major role of situational factors in determining behavior, and people's great underestimation of it, represents a special challenge in the area of important social problems and concerns, since explicitly changing these views may lead to more adaptive behavior (Rodin and Langer, 1980).

PERSON-SITUATION INTERACTION

Thus far I have considered the effects of social context per se without viewing the person in the social setting, and it is striking how much of the variance can simply be accounted for by situational factors. Nonetheless a significant additional increment in explaining behavior can be accounted for by examining person-situation interaction variables. An impressive body of research, conceptual and theoretical development, and debates have taken place in this area (see, e.g., Bem and Allen, 1974; Bowers, 1973; Ekehammar, 1974; Endler and Magnusson, 1976; Mischel, 1973). Just as individuals vary with respect to the range and types of behavior they are likely to show in particular situations and across certain situations, similarly complex settings also vary in the degree to which they prescribe and limit the range of expected and acceptable behavior for persons in particular roles and situations. Current views of personality hold that personality expresses both stability and change, and that it is the pattern of stability and change in relation to specific situations that is worthy of inquiry (e.g., Pervin, 1976). While this complex interaction has received some direct attention in the study of social problems, it is usually taken as a given that person-related and situational variables interact, and thus, unfortunately, there are relatively few empirical tests of such interactions in applied settings.

BURNOUT

In analyzing the burnout process, person factors may interact with the situational variables described above. Probably individuals who choose helping professions are the kinds of people who would be somewhat resistant to burnout to start with but then most hard hit when burnout is experienced, because it is such a long way from the idealized views that they held when entering the helping professions. Given the tendency to make dispositional attributions, they are most likely to blame themselves as well as the recipients. It is likely that some helping professionals will be more affected by the situational factors associated with burnout than others, but an emphasis on the person-situation interaction allows a greater understanding of potential strategies for change. Maslach's (1978) formulation has pointed out the importance of this interaction.

STRESSFUL LIFE EVENTS

Suls and his colleagues (Mullen and Suls, 1982) and Kobasa (1979) have taken a person-situation interaction approach to their study of the health consequences of stressful life events. Despite the early work of Holmes and Masuda (1974) and Holmes and Rahe (1967) linking the number of life changes and individual experiences to increased likelihood of illness, more recent research has suggested that not all life changes are necessarily illness inducing (Hinkel, 1977; Kobasa, 1979). Indeed the correlations between life change and illness are around 0.12 in most studies, leaving 99 percent of the variance unaccounted for. Thus a search for individual differences in response to stress seemed warranted.

Mullen and Suls (1982) followed individuals for three weeks in order to determine the relationship between desirable and undesirable, controllable and uncontrollable, life changes and the personality dimension of high or low private self-consciousness. High private self-consciousness involves a focus on covert and internal aspects of the self (Fenigstein, Scheier, and Buss, 1975; Gibbons, Carver, Scheier, and Hormuth, 1979). Mullen and Suls (1982) reasoned that high private self-consciousness may enable the individual to avoid the illness-inducing effects of life stressors because such persons should be more likely to attend to their psychological and somatic reactions to life stressors and to take some action to cope with them. They found that only undesirable, uncontrollable life changes predisposed persons to illness and that this was true only for individuals low in private self-consciousness. Similarly Kobasa (1979) found that among executives experiencing high stress, those who had a stronger commitment to the self, its activities and internal feelings, reported less illness than individuals low in these personality traits.

WORK

While researchers studying person-situation interaction agree that understanding how a person will react in a situation requires a combination of facts about the situation and the person, they do not always agree about how this combination should be achieved (cf. Bem and Allen, 1974). In research on work, major attention has been given to one type of combination in particular—the person-environment fit model (French, Rodgers, and Cobb, 1974). The basic idea of this model is that individual adjustment consists of goodness of fit between the characteristics of a person and the properties of that person's environment. Two types of properties—objective and subjective—are defined for both person and environment characteristics, implying two measures of adjustment: objective and subjective P-E fit. Actions to

improve objective goodness of fit are called coping, and those to improve subjective P-E fit are called defense. Kahn (1981) has applied this model to postulate a U-shaped relationship between job responsibility and strain. Strain is at its minimum when the amount of responsibility corresponds to the needs of the individual and increases when responsibility is either too much or too little for the individual. For other characteristics of the work environment, the relationship of goodness of fit to strain may be monotonic rather than U-shaped.

In one study (Caplan *et al.,* 1975) more than two thousand workers in twenty-three occupations were asked about their needs and preferences and the content of their jobs. Measures of psychological strain (dissatisfaction, depression, anxiety) were obtained. Feelings of depression were most common among workers doing jobs of low complexity and least common among workers doing highly complex jobs. In this study workers had been asked about their preferences for simple and complex tasks, so it was possible to develop a goodness-of-fit score for each worker by subtracting the amount of complexity preferred by the individual from the amount provided by the job. This analysis showed an even stronger relationship between P-E fit of job complexity and depression, suggesting that feelings of depression are better understood in terms of goodness of fit than in terms of job complexity alone. This is true for many dependent variables, not only depression (Kahn, 1981). The actual shape of the curve also depends on type of occupation (Harrison, 1978).

An implication of the goodness-of-fit approach is that strains are especially likely to be reduced by organizational changes that permit individuals to modify the characteristics of their own job. This derivation may be especially important for personnel selection and placement (Hackman and Shuttle, 1977).

SUMMARY AND CONCLUSIONS

When person-relevant factors have been tested explicitly in various applied areas, they have been shown to interact with situational factors in explaining behavior. However, for the most part they have not been tested directly and have merely been presumed to be importantly interacting with situational variables. Undoubtedly some of this is due to the fact that it is often difficult to assess dispositional variables in applied experiments without destroying some of the naturalistic context of these studies. While some may conclude that the person-situation interaction may be an area of social psychological knowledge where applied research will not make a great contribution, there are many studies where assessment of person-relevant factors is possible. More empirical work is needed using both experimental and survey approaches to consider person-situation interaction questions.

SOCIAL INFLUENCE

Of all the important situational determinants of behavior, probably none is more important than the direct or indirect influence of other people. Pervasive social influence effects are evident in all human interaction, and in recent years their impact on medical and legal outcomes has been of special interest. Most of the work in the health area has focused on dyadic relationships, especially where there are differences in social power, such as those between doctors and patients. Social influence studies in the legal domain have centered primarily on group influence processes, especially those related to how juries deliberate and reach a verdict.

HEALTH CARE

Social Power

Raven and his colleagues investigated the extent to which social influence variables might contribute to an increase or decrease in nosocomial, that is, hospital-acquired or hospital-associated infection—defined as one that develops during hospitalization and that is not present or incubating at the time the patient is admitted to the hospital (Raven and Haley, 1980). It is estimated, probably conservatively, that 5 percent of the 32 million patients admitted to U.S. hospitals yearly acquire such an infection in the hospital. These patients will average seven extra days in the hospital at $100 per day, and fifteen thousand of them will die, according to Raven and Haley (1980).

The traditional approach to controlling this problem is essentially characterized by an emphasis on environmental surveillance and changes in the physical underlying bases of hospital-acquired infections. This approach emphasizes continual and intensive microbiological surveillance of likely sources of conveyance of infection (e.g., the air, the equipment, the floor). It determines where the pathogens are located in the hospital and how they spread; appropriate steps are then taken to eliminate them and thereby reduce infection. However, the environmental-surveillance-and-control approach

has been shown to have a number of drawbacks (Raven and Haley, 1980). For one, there is no clear agreement as to where the permissible limits of microbiological contamination might be. There is also a serious question as to whether sufficient personnel and equipment time can be expended so as to ensure real control over environmental spread of pathogens. Indeed the use of a broad spectrum of antibiotics destroying some sources of infection has apparently led to the development of more resilient strains of microorganisms and may have led to an increase of infection (Williams, 1971).

Raven and Haley (1980) have argued that more effective infection control might derive from controlling the behavior of hospital staff, patients, and visitors, rather than the environment per se. Thus they propose a social control or social influence approach. It begins with the assumption that quite a bit is already known about the probable location of pathogens that are likely to lead to the spread of nosocomial infection in a hospital. It proposes that a significant reduction of infection may be obtained by influencing hospital-care personnel to follow appropriate infection control procedures.

In a correlational study Raven and Haley (1980) developed a structured set of personal interviews and questionnaires, which were administered to hospital staff members who played important roles in infection control. The authors found that issues of social power and social influence were the primary determinants of the ability of the setting to maintain good infection control. While the willingness of relevant personnel to speak to violators increased with the severity of the infraction, the effect of the target was even more significant. For example, infection-control practitioners were reliably less likely to speak up to physicians, as compared with nurses or laboratory technicians. Readiness to deal directly with the violator of infection-control policy, rather than asking someone else to take action, was also significantly determined by the status of the influencing agent and the target. The greater the status differential, the less likely the individual was to speak to the target directly. While action with regard to a violation often cannot be delayed until the matter is referred to some authority, social-power differentials and the unwillingness to try to influence those targets who are seen as significantly greater in power (e.g., the physicians) made delay inevitable in many instances.

Raven and Haley (1980), after identifying differences in social power as one cause of poor infection control, tried to identify the methods used by infection-control personnel to get hospital staff members to comply with subscribed policy. As in other studies of social influence processes (French and Raven, 1959; Raven, 1974, 1978), social power was defined in terms of potential methods of influence that might be utilized by the different influencing agents. Essentially six different bases of social power have been explicated (Raven, 1974):

1. Coercive power, which stems from the ability of the influencing agent to mediate punishment for the target;

2. Reward power stemming from his or her ability to mediate rewards;

3. Legitimate power, which grows out of the target's acceptance of a role relation with the agent that obligates the target to comply with the request of the agent;

4. Referent power, which occurs when the target uses the other as a frame of reference, as a positive standard for evaluating his or her behavior, and is motivated to live up to the norms set by the other;

5. Expert power, which stems from the target's attributing superior knowledge or ability to the agent;

6. Informational power, which is the result of the persuasiveness of the information communicated by the agent to the target.

The hospital personnel were asked to rate these six bases of power in terms of how likely it would be that they would use the basis of power for each mentioned target. It is theoretically interesting that all bases of power were significantly positively correlated with one another, with the exception of informational power. Overall, informational power was the first choice for all respondents and was seen as operating on a different basis—one that was logically inconsistent with the use of other influence strategies. Interestingly respondents felt, however, that regardless of the source of power used, their expectancy of success was least with respect to physicians. Even more interesting, a sizable minority of nurses was willing to indicate on the self-report questionnaire that if a physician asked them to comply with procedures that increased risk of infection control, they would be willing to do so. We might, of course, expect nurses to underestimate on such questionnaires the extent to which they would actually comply. A sizable minority of nurses also felt that physicians do in fact sometimes make such requests.

Based on these findings, interventions to affect social influence and the use of social power are possible as a means of potential infection control. Raven and Haley (1980) note that the ideal experiment would be to choose a variety of hospitals, randomly assign them to experimental and control conditions, and manipulate several of these social influence variables. One hopes, in the future, for such an experimental design, while recognizing the difficulty of its implementation. Nonetheless such manipulation studies are requisite if one is to understand the components of social power and social influence that are most important for the spread or control of nosocomial infection.

Also concerned with the various sources of social power that are present in the health care setting, Rodin and Janis (1979) considered how they affect the relationship between physicians and patients and thus impact on significant medical outcomes. They argued that on the basis of social psychological research bearing on the differential effects of these various sources of social power, one might expect that when patients comply because of the expert, coercive, or reward power of the health care professional, they will attribute their compliance to the external incentives provided by him or her and will be less likely to perceive themselves as having personal responsibility for, or control over, their own actions (Deci, 1975; Kelman, 1958). They reviewed data suggesting that one is most likely to promote internalization of recommendations and adherence under conditions where salient external inducements for decision making are absent. Circumstances that promote internalization also serve to increase patients' feelings of choice and control, because they perceive themselves to be acting on the basis of internal self-motivated norms and goals. Research has shown that greater feelings of control increase behavioral commitment and play an important role in facilitating adherence (Collins and Hoyt, 1972; Klemp and Rodin, 1976; Pranulis, Dabbs, and Johnson, 1975). Rodin and Janis (1979) suggest that all these conditions are most likely to be met when the source of influence is referent power.

Controlled field experiments by Janis and his coworkers (Janis, 1983a, 1983b), who conducted antismoking and weight reduction clinics, support the utility of using referent power for inducing and maintaining important behavior changes. In many of these experiments noncontingent positive feedback from a counselor (as compared with neutral feedback) given during an interview that encouraged self-disclosure had the effect of fostering more positive ratings of the counselor and more adherence to the recommended low-calorie diet or smoking regimen, as measured by weight loss and smoking cessation.

Additional evidence from controlled field experiments by Rodin and her colleagues (Rodin, Clancy, Elias, Silberstein, and Wagner, 1984), also conducted in weight reduction groups, supports the hypothesis that assessing and modifying patients' attributions leading to cognitive reappraisals that facilitate adherence to medical recommendations can best be accomplished by practitioners using referent power. They have found that the practitioners can use the trust and motivating power of the relationship to build up self-control attributions that foster a sense of personal responsibility and promote internalization of recommended courses of action.

Thus far there has been little systematic comparative analysis of the bases of social power that are best suited for different types of patients, for different settings, and for different types of changes in behavior. It is possible, for example, that referent power is most effective when behavioral options are seen as available and controllable by the patient, and when long-term adherence to medical regimens is desirable. Referent power may also be most effective when patients are upset and need to have their anxiety reduced by an open and reassuring person before they can attempt to follow health-relevant measures. On the other hand when patients are extremely anxious or depressed, their dependency needs may increase, making other sources of social power more effective. In fact there is evidence (Janis, 1983a) that authorities who use expert and reward power can also be effective, even though they do not enhance self-esteem and feelings of control. This occurs especially under conditions where the health care professional is in a position to monitor the patient's behavior continuously. Where monitoring is not constant or practical, however, the use of referent power to promote internalization of recommended actions appears to be most successful. Our understanding of health-seeking and illness behavior, including stress reduction, effective coping, adherence to treatment, and recovery, is advanced by viewing the health care professional-patient relationship as a social influence process in which there are significant issues regarding the uses of power. Defining the optimal parameters for the various types of social power (as a function of type of patient, physician, and context) remains a challenge for future research.

Nonverbal Cues and Skills

The studies of DiMatteo (1979) and Friedman (1979) and their coworkers consider other important bases of social influence besides differential social power. These investigators have been especially interested in the extent to which nonverbal expressiveness and nonverbal receptivity are important determinants of the social influence that exists between patient and health care professional. The results of their studies indicate that a physician's ability to communicate emotions through nonverbal channels of facial expression and voice tone is related to his or her patient's satisfaction with health care. These findings are consistent with social psychological theories of social influence. For example, the patient may look to the physician for cues as to how he or she should respond to the medical situation and to what the patient should attribute emotional arousal. If the patient's anxiety is high regarding aspects of the treatment or details of the diagnosis, the physician's nonverbal behavior can do much to communicate that the appropriate response should be one of calmness and hopefulness rather than of panic, fear, or hopelessness. The physician's nonverbal sensitivity and expressiveness therefore appear to be linked theoretically and empirically to patient satisfaction with medical treatment.

DiMatteo, Friedman, and their coworkers have gone further, suggesting that training programs for nonverbal behavior skills for physicians and other health care professionals could be important in improving health care. There is some direct evidence already for the possibility of increasing the nonverbal sensitivity of health care professionals, that is, increasing the ability to decode accurately another's nonverbal cues (DiMatteo and Hall, in press; Rosenthal *et al.,* in press). It remains for further research to see how and when the physician's nonverbal behavior is linked to adherence to medical recommendations.

In general the studies to date strongly suggest that social influence processes are among the important specific characteristics of patient-physician interaction that contribute to patient satisfaction and dissatisfaction with medical care. The losses related to poor infection control may also be lessened with greater attention to methods of overcoming the ways that differential social power impedes needed influence attempts.

JURY BEHAVIOR

In the study of legal outcomes there has been considerable research on jury behavior in an attempt to understand how members of a jury come to influence one another and what variables determine these social influence processes. Whether one is considering jury deliberation or any group interaction, the product of most group processes typically depends on four classes of variables: the composition of the group, its structure, the nature of the group process, and the task with which the group is confronted.

According to the law, the composition of a pool of jurors must not differ substantially from that of the community, or it is considered unrepresentative. *Ballew* vs. *Georgia* (1978) relied on data from group influence studies to conclude that a particularly important reason for guaranteeing jury representativeness is that the "counterbalancing of various biases is critical to the accurate application of the common sense of the community to the facts of any given case" (p. 234). While nonrepresentativeness can occur even with a random method of drawing the venire (Ellsworth and Getman, in press), some practices explicitly violate representativeness, thus excluding important potential sources of influence while biasing the jury heavily toward others. For example, in states where the death penalty is legal, scrupled jurors (those who are against the death sentence and therefore presumably would not vote guilty) are not permitted on juries in capital cases. Thus the likelihood of conviction may be greater when this death qualification procedure is followed.

Haney (1980) has shown that the process of death qualification in jury selection affects not only the composition of the jury panel that results but also the thinking of those jurors who pass through it. In his study a group of people eligible for jury service in California were randomly assigned to view one of two videotapes that depicted jury selection in a first-degree murder case. The tapes were similar in all respects except that one depicted death qualification in the case and the other did not. Exposure to the death-qualification procedure increased the subjects' belief in the guilt of the defendant, their estimates that he would be convicted, and their estimates of the attorneys' and judge's belief in his guilt. It also increased the subjects' belief that the law disapproves of people who oppose the death penalty. If the effects of videotapes are so strong, it may be expected that going through the actual process of death qualification, which requires that jurors must publicly express their willingness to consider imposing the death penalty before they can be seated on a capital jury, further intensifies their level of commitment to it. Lewin's (1951) work on group decision and social change strongly suggests such a process. Social psychologists have been actively involved in making lawyers and judges aware of these potentially negative outcomes.

Interestingly social scientists have also been involved in producing uneven jury composition. For example, in procedures now being used by other social psychologists, Kairys, Schulman, and Harring (1975) interviewed a sample of respondents from the population from which the jury for the "Harrisburg Seven" case would be drawn. By correlating background and personality variables with attitude measures, the investigators developed prediction equations regarding the type of person who might be expected to be most and least favorable to the defendants, and the defense used these predictions in actual jury selection. Although the defendants were acquitted, Saks and Hastie (1978), reviewing all the research evidence to date, have concluded that individual characteristics of jury members account for only a small portion of the variance in the final verdict unless the evidence is highly ambiguous. The importance of this issue demands that it receive further empirical investigation, however, especially since to date, in all cases where scientific jury selection methods have been used, acquittal has been the outcome. Of course a controlled study using the same trial with different selection procedures has never been conducted.

The size of the jury is another variable that may determine the nature of the social influence processes. While small groups allow for greater participation, larger groups provide a greater and wider range of opinion and human resources. Larger groups provide more allies for the minority, and the allies afford social supports with which to resist the majority (Saks, 1977). Padawar-Singer, Singer, and Singer (1977) suggest that the effects of group size interact with whether the group is required to make a nonunanimous or unanimous decision. Only a six-member nonunanimous jury never ended in hung decisions in their experiments. Jury size research could benefit from a better analysis of the *processes* of social influence involved, rather than simply focusing on the outcomes of the deliberations. It also suffers from relying almost exclusively on simulation studies.

Risky shift or conservative shift from group polarization, another social influence process, is present in all risk-taking situations, including jury decision making. The process involved in such shifts suggests that if the jury members lean initially in one direction, group interaction and social influence processes will draw them further in that same direction (Myers and Kaplan, 1976; Myers and Lamm, 1976). This effect is due both to social comparison processes where group members compare themselves to one another and modify their self-presentations to elicit more favorable reactions from other group members, and to informational influence processes where cognitive learning takes place in the direction of the dominant role, because that is where most of the argumentation and discussion centers. The operation of these social influence processes leads to the prediction that the final outcome of a jury's deliberation will be an exaggerated version of the distribution of judgments the individuals held when they entered the jury deliberation. Mathematical models of jury decision processes, based on these social influence variables using initial-preference distributions that have been largely determined by the arguments and evidence presented at trial, can predict verdicts with a fairly high degree of accuracy (Davis, Bray, and Holt, 1977).

The processes of social influence may change when groups are cohesive, rather than being composed of strangers, which of course juries usually are at the outset of their deliberations. In all groups conformity pressures have frequently been observed. Whenever a member says something that appears out of line with group norms —longstanding or newly emergent norms—other members first increase their communication with the deviant in an effort to change his or her mind. But when groups are cohesive, the group begins to exercise substantial power over its individual members, and conformity pressures increase.

POLICY DECISIONS

Janis (1972) has examined sources of error in major American foreign policy decisions, such as the Bay of Pigs invasion and the Korean war, using the term *groupthink* to describe a mode of thinking that people engage in when they are deeply involved in a cohesive in-group, when the members' strivings for unanimity override their motivation to appraise realistically alternative sources of action. A set of eight symptoms or indices of groupthink processes was developed, such as an illusion of invulnerability shared by most group members and self-censorship of deviation from apparent group consensus because of strong pressures toward concurrence seeking. Janis's analyses suggested that when a policy-making group displays most or all of these symptoms, the members perform their task ineffectively and are likely to fail to attain their collective objectives because they fall prey to poor-quality decision making. The central explanatory concept involves "viewing concurrence-seeking as a form of

striving for mutual support based on a powerful motivation in all group members to cope with the stresses of decision making that cannot be alleviated by standard operating procedures'' (p. 202). Viewed in the context of this explanatory hypothesis, the symptoms of groupthink are understood as the result of a mutual effort on the part of group members to cope with stress and to maintain self-esteem, especially when they share responsibility for making vital decisions that pose threats of social and self-disapproval. Interestingly, if this explanatory hypothesis is correct, groupthink should be found most often when a decision poses a moral dilemma, especially if what seems to be the most advantageous course of action would require the decision makers to violate some of their own personal standards. Work is needed to investigate systematically many of the principles developed by Janis's descriptive analysis of historical data.

SUMMARY AND CONCLUSIONS

Social influence processes appear to be powerful determinants of important outcomes, such as compliance with medical recommendations and jury deliberations. By identifying the differential types of social power that operate within health care settings, targets of intervention and change can be more readily prescribed. Further, it may be that verbal and nonverbal communication skills can be taught, in order to develop more effective interpersonal influence. Finally, ensuring fairer and more just jury trials may derive in part from understanding how social influence processes change by variations in the number or composition of juries. The effectiveness of social influence interventions relative to those focusing on variables that are not interpersonal in nature remains to be determined by comparative outcome studies, but it is clear already that interpersonal influence plays a major role in behavior relevant to important social problems.

Theories regarding various bases of social influence have been extended by some of the applied studies reviewed above. For example, when all types of social power are potentially available, which has not been true in laboratory studies, the use of informational power appears inconsistent with other potential methods of influence (Raven and Haley, 1980). It appears that the others are all based on a common process—the characteristics of the persons involved or the roles they fill—whereas informational power is not owned or conferred by role or status. It would be expected, therefore, that the other sources of social power would be more resistant to change, while variations in informational power might be more easily manipulated. This question remains to be addressed by future research.

There have been efforts to apply social psychological knowledge about social influence to learning how to resist such influence, especially when it involves violating humanitarian standards of conduct, but almost all of these applications have been laboratory studies. Perhaps most relevant to applied concerns are Zimbardo's (1969) studies on deindividuation, since they specify the conditions under which individuation should occur as well. Individuation is a sense of personal identity and uniqueness, which tends to be reduced by anonymity, diffusion of responsibility, altered states of consciousness or time perspective, emotional or sexual arousal, sensory overload, and physical involvement in an aggressive act (Zimbardo, 1969). Presumably resistance to social influence should be higher under individuated than under deindividuated conditions.

Andersen and Zimbardo (1980) argue that deliberate attempts to manipulate someone else's behaviors may look very exploitative because it is assumed that the victim might have resisted had his or her informed consent been requested. Actually, however, social influence is most effective when someone is subtly or covertly led to believe that he or she has freely chosen to act (e.g., Milgram, 1965). Once having made a commitment, people appear to generate their own justification even when truly informed of the important details.

Andersen and Zimbardo (1980) suggest that what ensures the success of social influence, whether it involves buying new products or engaging in antisocial behavior, is people's blindness to the potency that situations possess. Situations with normal appearances may be the most problematic, since they do not seem to require skepticism, resistance, or even conscious attention. We often move through them automatically, without thinking, and thus are prone to being influenced without our slightest knowledge (cf. Langer, Blank, and Chanowitz, 1978).

SOCIAL SUPPORT

While serving as sources of social influence and agents of change, people also affect one another as sources of support. In the last several years there has been considerable research on the effects of help that people receive from informal supports, such as family, friends, or neighbors. Social support has been defined as having access to significant others who can provide information indicating love, esteem, and mutual obligation (Cobb, 1976; Kaplan, Cassel, and Gore, 1979). According to Silver and Wortman (1980), studies suggest that social support has several major components, including the expression of positive affect; the expression of agreement with or acknowledgment of the appropriateness of a person's beliefs, interpretations, or feelings; the provision of material aid; and the provision of information that the distressed person belongs to a network of mutual help and obligation.

Other investigations have suggested additional functions of support systems. In those circumstances where individuals feel fear and uncertainties, and when their sense of self may be threatened as a result, many people experience greater need both to clarify what is happening to them and to be supported and reassured by others. One way to learn more about the meaning and appropriateness of various behaviors is through exposure to others who are in a similar situation. As Festinger (1954) and Schachter (1959) have pointed out, social confusion and ambiguity can often be resolved through social comparison. One function of other people in such circumstances is that they provide a way to clarify and interpret feelings for the individual and may also serve a direct anxiety reduction function (Wrightsman, 1960). Other people may also set good examples or serve as models, thus showing us how to engage in a similar course of action (Bandura, 1977), or in other ways may encourage the maintenance of beneficial behaviors (Cobb, 1976).

Kahn and Antonucci (1981) have proposed the notion of a convoy of social support within which most individuals maintain relative stability in their support network across their entire lifetime. Thus they visualize a support network that is relatively stable within the framework of the normal life course, suggesting that the benefit of social support must be evaluated in the context of the individual's life experience. For example, if the person has always been a loner and an isolate by choice, interventions to provide that individual with a support network might be counterproductive. On the other hand people who have been involved in extensive support networks and suddenly find themselves ill, confined, or institutionalized and therefore isolated from these networks may experience such negative reactions as depression, loss of appetite, and other health-related problems.

Social support research clearly suggests the continuity of emotional and psychological relationships across the life cycle, but consideration of the role of social support and its continuity must be viewed within a framework that includes both positive and negative effects.

In general one tends to think only in terms of the positive effects of supportive relationships. Below I will review much work that has focused on how informal supportive relationships help individuals cope with stress and strain. However, it is important to recognize that these same informal supportive relationships can also have a negative impact on mental and physical health and quality of life (Kahn and Antonucci, 1981; Suls, 1982). Network members can act "supportively" in ways that reinforce maladaptive behaviors, such as overeating, overdrinking, chronic depression, and drug abuse. Other people can create and reinforce worry and anxiety rather than reduce it. There are other forms of maladaptive support systems as well. Some involve overprotection and others involve demeaning and debilitating forms of support. The giving of needed support sometimes includes gratuitous lessons in helplessness and loss of self. One common, though perhaps overlooked, cause of mental health problems among the elderly, for example, is the ineptitude of the family and friends who are caring for them. Our research has shown that many family members deny their elderly relatives the normal privileges of adulthood, such as choosing their own clothes, food, and entertainment and caring for themselves. Social supports such as these can have profoundly debilitating effects. An extreme case involves support and active abuse from the same source.

HEALTH: EFFECTS OF GAINS IN SOCIAL SUPPORT

Despite the possibility of negative effects of social support, there is strong consensus that, in general, support systems have both preventive and ameliorative effects, especially in the area of health. There are now many studies suggesting that people who are part of social networks are less likely to be negatively affected by stressful life events and are less likely to become ill. Moreover, there is some evidence that support systems facilitate coping and recovery if people do become ill.

To cite a few examples of this work, a favorable social environment has been linked to fewer complications during pregnancy (Nucholls, Cassel, and Kaplan, 1972), faster recovery from illness (Egbert *et al.*, 1964), and fewer health problems during stressful periods of life (Cobb, 1976; Gore, 1978). Virtually all health surveys indicate that married people report being healthier and happier than unmarried people (Comstock and Slome, 1973; Greenley and Mechanic, 1976; Wan, 1976). Lynch (1977) used mortality figures to argue that the unmarried and socially isolated die prematurely because of loneliness. Among college students, social environments characterized as low in community and cohesion, student participation, and social activities resulted in increased health problems (Moos and Van Dort, 1976). Further, Moos and Houts (1968), in examining various therapeutic institutions, found that treatments were most successful if they took place in an institution that promoted a positive social climate; and a recent review (Baekeland and Lundwall, 1975) found nineteen out of nineteen studies showing that social isolation or lack of affiliation was a major cause of dropping out of treatment. Kahn (1981) suggests that interpersonal relationships are major determinants of how the objective work environment affects an individual's subjective state, physiological responses, and ultimate health and disease. For example, French (1974) found in a study of a government agency that quantitative work load was related to diastolic blood pressure, but not among those employees who had supportive relationships with their supervisors.

These studies have suggested to some (e.g., Cassel, 1976) that it may be more feasible to attempt to improve and strengthen social supports in order to improve or retain good health than to reduce exposure to stressors or pathogens. This is similar to Raven and Haley's (1980) suggestion that reducing nosocomial infection may be more fruitful if attention is given to processes of social influence rather than to controlling the pathogens in the environment. In order to accomplish this goal, Kahn and Antonucci (1981) have suggested developing a system that anticipates the support requirements of individuals and either reinforces or creates the support reserves that will be necessary. Thus far, research specifically considering this suggestion has not been done.

There are also studies that have failed to show strong health-promoting effects of social support. The most persuasive of these are experiments by Caplan and his co-workers, who studied the effects of social support on the adherence of hypertensive patients to their treatment regimens (Caplan, Harrison, Wellons, and French, 1980; Caplan, Robinson, French, Caldwell, and Shinn, 1976). In both studies subjects were randomly assigned to groups that received various levels of social support. In both studies perceived support increased in the experimental groups, but evidence for tangible gain was sparse or inconsistent. One study (Caplan *et al.,* 1976) showed higher motivation to adhere and some increased adherence as measured by self-report in the group with increased social support; the other did not (Caplan *et al.,* 1980). Most disappointing, neither study showed differences among groups in blood pressure levels from pre- to postintervention measures.

While there are many possible explanations for the weakness of these data, they also point to a general concern for all studies looking at the relationship between health and social support, namely, how to interpret whatever gains do appear. A fundamental difficulty in understanding social support is that it is inextricably tied to several other factors that may also be health related, even when the data show positive effects. For example, persons who have a great deal of social support may be more active and more attuned to the social environment rather than to internal physical cues. Thus they may actually label their health problems differently or fail to experience negative health-related symptoms at all as a result of a focus of attention outward (cf. Leventhal and Everhart, 1979). Information processing itself therefore may be affected by the individual's level of social support. Similarly once the individual interacts with the health care system, there are multiple points at which adherence to medical recommendations may be influenced by the attitudes and opinions of other people. Thus someone with a high degree of social support may follow medical prescriptions differently as a result.

The same problems arise in interpreting studies showing that social support can ameliorate life stress. In a review of several studies Cobb (1976) noted that social support may protect people in crises by facilitating coping and adaptation. As just indicated, however, it could also be argued that an individual confronted with a major life event would perceive that event differently as a function of having or lacking social support. We must then ask whether social support would still be a predictor of health if perceptions of life events were held constant. Such studies have not been done. A similar problem in evaluating the role of social support on health concerns one's general activity and involvement with the world. A highly active person may have greater access to others and more ability to develop a social support system. If such were the case, it could be argued that activity rather than social support is the underlying factor that promotes health, especially since activity levels per se correlate positively with health variables (Gordon and Gaitz,

1977). Two studies in the aging area have specifically investigated these questions but obtained different results.

Pennebaker and Funkhauser (1979) examined the relative contribution of life change, activity, and social support to health problems, with the use of prescription drugs among a relatively healthy group of elderly living in a community housing unit as the dependent variable. During the course of a series of interviews, measures of recent life changes, general activity patterns, and social involvement were taken. One year after the interview, general changes in health were assessed. The multiple regression analysis indicated that each of the variables of life change, activity, and social support was a significant predictor of medication use. In the one-year follow-up health measure, all three conceptual variables continued to make significant independent contributions to health outcomes. These data suggest that both activity and social support independently contribute to more favorable health outcomes.

In the second study Bohm and Rodin (1983) tested randomly selected subjects living in community housing units for the elderly. The relationship between activity, social supports, and other conceptual variables such as perceived control were examined as they related to a variety of health outcomes at the time of the measurement and at a one-year follow-up. Bohm and Rodin's analysis showed a negative relationship between family relationships and activity levels and a strong positive correlation between peer relations and activity. Further, using path analytic techniques, they found that better social relationships with peers contributed to greater participation in activities rather than the reverse, and neither activity nor peer relations affected health outcome. These data suggest that a better-developed peer support system leads to greater participation in activities, but that neither affects health.

When all the possible confounding variables enumerated above are controlled, how might the social support variable be related to health? Certainly, on the broadest level, having access to others allows for a mutual transmission of health information. Peers can relay which physical symptoms are threatening and which are not. Failure to assess dangerous situations as worthy of a visit to a physician would allow time for a degenerative disease to worsen. Persons who are part of a social network may share health problems in common and serve as models for one another, or at least bolster each other's health-promoting behaviors. A friend or relative who has referent power may be especially important, since adherence increases if the helper endorses prohealth norms by providing increased incentive to maintain approval (Janis, 1983a, 1983b; Rodin and Janis, 1979). In addition, having a friendship network undoubtedly promotes a sense of responsibility to one's friends. Being responsible for another person may promote well-being in patients, since research has shown that greater responsibility for oneself is related to better health outcomes (Rodin and Langer, 1977).

On a more molecular level, a support system may mitigate physiological stress. The presence of others may directly reduce anxiety in addition to serving a social comparison function. Individuals who cannot readily compare their experiences, thoughts, and feelings may actually become even more tense or aroused (Festinger, 1954). Although such arousal or increased autonomic activity may be slight, it could have the effect of exaggerating physical problems or increasing one's attention to physical symptoms (Pennebaker, 1982).

HEALTH: EFFECTS OF LOSSES OF SOCIAL SUPPORT

The most profound health outcome, mortality, has recently been linked to changes in social support. Specifically this work considers whether and how the loss of a mate can affect the longevity of the survivor. On the basis of longitudinal and cross-sectional data, it appears that increases in mortality risk are greater following bereavement (e.g., Kraus and Lilienfeld, 1959; Rees and Lutkins, 1967). During the first six months of bereavement the relationship seems to be more pronounced for widowers than for widows, although some studies have concluded that widows are most susceptible after a longer time lapse (Cox and Ford, 1964; Ekblom, 1963; Young, Benjamin, and Wallis, 1963). The most dramatic increases in risk come from suicide, accidents, liver cirrhosis, and tuberculosis—suggesting that the widowed seem to die from those causes in which psychological factors can be presumed to play a crucial role (Gove, 1973). Also, among the recently bereaved, heart diseases represent a major cause of death. This seems highly consistent with the research that has linked diseases of the heart with stress (e.g., Glass, 1977), for loss of a partner places great stress on the remaining spouse, especially in the first few months (e.g., Lynch, 1977).

Stroebe, Stroebe, Gergen, and Gergen (1982) consider a variety of possible nonpsychological reasons for the relationship between bereavement and death, for example, shared unfavorable environments, joint accidents, or infectious diseases. However, they emphasize the importance of psychological factors, since the evidence for nonpsychological causes is very weak. Recognizing that the loss of a loved person may lead to a great deal of disruption and may foster a sense of helplessness, Stroebe *et al.* (1982) look for important mediating variables, for example, the kinds of response sequences that are disrupted and the outcomes that are lost through the death of a partner. Such questions, they argue, require a social psychological analysis of the marriage relationship. In this analysis, which features social support as a central tenet, a marital couple is viewed as a small social group in which the members, as in any social group, perform certain functions for each other and in which each has certain tasks to perform. The loss of a partner should lead to a deficit in a number of areas, which can broadly be characterized as social validation, social support, task performance, and social protection.

Loss of validation is essentially the loss of consensus information. With the death of the partner, an important source of information is lost, and consequently confident judgments and assessments of one's own achievements and capability are far more difficult. Social comparison processes also play an important part in judging the appropriateness of one's own emotional responses (Schachter, 1959). When a spouse is lost, one may face a myriad of questions about what one should be feeling emotionally, what plans are appropriate, how one is to live life alone, and so on. As Glick, Weiss, and Parkes (1974) have shown, about 40 percent of those bereaved are fearful at one time or another that they are going crazy. This may be due to the loss of a major social comparison person.

Further, the loss of one's major source of social support often brings about losses in a major source of personal esteem. With love and unconditional positive regard, partners in a happy marriage can repair many of the damages that the other's self-esteem may have suffered in the course of the day. But with the loss of his or her partner, the individual may face a significant lowering of self-regard. This decrement may be accompanied by an increased reliance on drugs or other substances and a lowered motivation to engage in health-sustaining activities for reducing suffering and furnishing a transient sense of security. All such outcomes should lend themselves to a decline in health.

The surviving spouse frequently confronts a substantial loss of material and task supports as well. The higher the specialization of roles in a marriage, the more drastic are the effects of the loss of the partner. It is also possible that the subsequent loss of socially mediated stress reduction may be one of the factors contributing to greater mortality. Having another person to share decisions lessens the load of responsibility for the decision making. Decision making is likely to be experienced as more stressful if one of the partners should suddenly be faced with the necessity of arriving at decisions or facing responsibilities without being able to consult the other.

According to the Stroebe *et al.* (1982) analysis, the consequences of losing a marital partner should be more severe the closer the relationship between the partners, the greater the role differentiation within the marital group, and the fewer alternative persons available who could serve part of the functions formerly fulfilled by the partner. This suggests, as findings support (Parkes, 1975; Weiss, 1976), that the loss of a partner, whether caused by death or by divorce, should lead to some of the same problems. The authors' basic proposition is that owing to loss of social support, psychological status changes, which in turn may lead to behavioral changes that are life threatening. This intriguing theoretical analysis merits further empirical research to test directly some of the major assumptions.

Unlike bereavement, where the individual may have help in confronting his or her loss of social support and where a clear explanation exists for the loss, ill individuals often lose social support for reasons they cannot understand and that may therefore have an even greater debilitating effect. Wortman and Dunkel-Schetter (1979) analyzed the causes of loss of social support for cancer victims in particular in a discussion that may relate to all serious illness.

According to Wortman and Dunkel-Schetter (1979), cancer patients generally receive ambivalent responses from those in their major social support network. For a variety of reasons, feelings about cancer patients are likely to be negative. Some of these feelings are specific to cancer or other forms of illness; others may occur whenever individuals are exposed to victims of undesirable life events. Cancer appears to arouse great fear and feelings of vulnerability (Knopf, 1976). The disease also seems to evoke physical aversion and disgust in others, particularly when it is associated with mutilating surgery or physical deterioration. Aversion may also stem from individuals' fears that they may catch the disease (Kleiman *et al.,* 1977).

The social psychological literature suggests that additional motivational and cognitive factors may lead individuals to react negatively to people who have experienced negative life events, including, but not exclusively, cancer victims. Theoretically these principles should apply to any situation in which people are confronted with others who have suffered in some way (Lerner, 1970, 1971). Since having cancer is regarded as an extremely undesirable fate, individuals may be strongly motivated to protect themselves by attributing the disease to others' undesirable characteristics or their past behavior. This creates ambivalence, however, because people in the cancer patients' support network also hold prior assumptions about how they should behave toward the patient. Some of these notions come from their acceptance of social norms and dictates for behavior toward those who are sick or dying. Others come from their conceptions about what types of comments and interactions are most likely to be helpful to the patient. Still others come from commitments and obligations based on their relationship with the patient. Kalish (1977) has argued that many family members believe that discussion about cancer or death will make the patient uncomfortable. Thus people appear to harbor negative feelings about cancer and cancer victims but believe that these feelings should not be expressed to the patient. Instead they assume that they must act cheerful and encouraging in their dealings with the person who has cancer. This conflict affects the frequency and quality of time that members of the support network spend with cancer patients, and the interactions that do take place are likely to evoke a certain amount of anxiety.

The Wortman and Dunkel-Schetter (1979) analysis suggests that ambivalence, confusion, and discomfort often lead the individual's major social supports to behave in ways that are unintentionally damaging to the patient's welfare, leading to avoidance, reluctance to engage in open communication about the disease, and vast discrepancies in behavior toward the cancer patient. Discrepancies in behavior may be especially likely to come from primary social supports, that is, family members, since it is the family members who generally have the most sustained contact with the patient. Clearly these outcomes are maladaptive for most patients.

Brickman and his coworkers (1982) have also considered why it is that potential supports often do turn against recipients of help. They review considerable data suggesting, in fact, that the greater the help that is needed and given, the more likely this is to occur. Even if recipients deserve help, people may be upset if they feel the recipients receive more help than they deserve. Indeed the very act of providing help may lessen someone's regard for the recipient. While part of this may be due to blaming the victim (Lerner, 1971) and ambivalence (Wortman and Dunkel-Schetter, 1979), Brickman *et al.*'s analysis suggests that the reaction of members of a person's support network to his or her need for help also depends on their attributions regarding responsibility for the causes of as well as the solutions to the person's problems. Help is most grudgingly given when people are seen as responsible for both the cause and the solution of their problems and least grudgingly given when they are seen as responsible for neither.

HEALTH: INTERVENTIONS

Given the phenomena described above, there are clear implications for potential treatment interventions in subsequent research. One treatment is suggested by the model of a family therapy program, which makes help recipients and members of their formal and informal support networks more aware of the complicated social environment in which they may be trapped and which encourages more open communication. They could be taught communication skills and strategies to combat specific problems. It might be useful to increase a person's access to others who have experienced the same problems. Wortman and her coworkers are currently performing systematic studies to evaluate their effectiveness in helping victims cope with misfortune (Wortman *et al.,* 1980). Janis and his colleagues (Janis and Hoffman, 1983) have studied another type of peer support, the buddy system, for fostering adherence to a smoking-cessation program. In their intervention, no-smoking buddies were strongly related to greater success with smoking cessation, even after a ten-year follow-up.

Maslach (1978) has also suggested that formal or informal programs where helping professionals can get together to discuss problems and receive advice and support help them to cope with job stress more successfully and thus may alleviate burnout. Burnout rates seem to be lower for those helping professionals who have access to such systems, especially if they are well developed and supported by the larger institutions. While social supports provide a valuable resource for the person experiencing strong distress by giving comfort and emotional support, serving as a social comparison reference, and providing positive feedback, they may also serve to shift people's attributional bias away from exclusively dispo-

sitional judgments toward a more situational orientation. The most positive features of social support may predominate where help is not one-sided, as is the case in these mutual-support, self-help groups. It is not surprising that in recent years we have witnessed a virtual explosion of such groups for all sorts of problems, illnesses, and human concerns. These merit systematic study.

Many specific questions about the value of interacting with social supports are worthy of attention, and it will be instructive in future research to know how the quality, rather than simply the availability, of social supports affects health outcomes. For example, Bohm and Rodin (1983) found that the scope and type of roles that family members and friends fulfilled for older persons were far more important correlates of depression and life satisfaction than was the number of relationships they reported. There is also evidence for the protective function of multiple roles. The Bohm and Rodin data also suggest the predictive utility of separating different types of social supports, showing, for example, how differently peer and family relationships function in their effects on health. Further, the quality of family and of peer relationships were not related to one another.

It is also possible to speculate about when a social support system is more likely to have adverse effects. The more serious the problem, the more likely family and friends will feel they should help but feel relatively powerless, leading to ambivalent behavior (Suls, 1982). If the problem is a rare occurrence, there is greater likelihood that family and friends will offer inappropriate or incorrect advice and information. Further, the more one-sided the support needed, the more likely it will be that adverse effects will increase.

SUMMARY AND CONCLUSIONS

Applied studies have shown clearly that social support does not always have beneficial effects. More significant than studies showing no effect, for which there are always multiple explanations, are those suggesting strongly negative effects. Such effects were not apparent until research focused on real-life problems outside the laboratory. Further, these studies suggested a lack of theoretical clarity regarding the mechanisms by which social support led to positive outcomes when it did. Studies showed that social support provides the ability for social comparison, a means for interpretation of situations and feelings, models for behavior, help, and access to significant others. Systematic analyses are now necessary to determine the separate and combined influence of each of these on a variety of outcomes in order to understand how social support has its effects.

While this review has focused primarily on health, where most research has been done, it is certainly possible to speculate that understanding the effects of social support will be important for analyzing a variety of social concerns, for example, school and work performance and achievement, or population control. Also needed, however, before the introduction of large-scale interventions is a better understanding of how and when the provision of social support may turn help givers against the recipients of their help. Not only is this issue of great practical importance, but it also clearly can elucidate an intriguing set of psychological processes, thus enriching our theories as well.

ATTRIBUTION

The early work of Heider (1958) suggested that people operate very much like quasi-scientists in their attributional activities by attempting to discover the connections between various effects and possible causes. Based on this notion, Jones and his coworkers presented a conception of the perceiver as a rational person who evaluates information and makes logical inferences about others (Jones and Davis, 1965). Kelley (1967) applied the same concepts to self-perception as well. According to Kelley, the attributor is assumed to attribute effects to those causal factors with which they covary rather than to those from which they are relatively independent. Kelley contended that past experience may provide individuals with a backlog of understanding relative to causal relations, and that individuals can call on this store of knowledge when an inference has to be made quickly, so that most attributional work is not based on a complete causal analysis. This store of knowledge of causal relations represents what Kelley refers to as causal schemata.

Study of the relevance of attributional processes for understanding consequential behavior in real-world settings has enabled both qualification and confirmation of theories based only on laboratory research. When even the most basic tenet of attribution theory—that people do make causal attributions—was challenged (Bem, 1972; Hanusa and Schulz, 1977), applied studies suggested that when the outcome in question was a major life concern, such as rape or serious injury and disease, peo-

ple certainly do ask themselves why it happened, and the answers they provide have predictable, systematic effects on their psychological state and behavior (e.g., Bulman and Wortman, 1977; Coates, Wortman, and Abbey, 1979).

LOCUS AND STABILITY OF CAUSE

Depression

The attributions most frequently made first regard locus of causation and stability—who or what is responsible for the event(s) of concern and how permanent are the causes. To understand the outcome of depression, Abramson, Seligman, and Teasdale (1978) expanded earlier attribution conceptualizations and posited three dimensions along which attributions of causality are made. These dimensions are internal-external, stable-unstable, and global-specific. They suggested that depression results from overattributing negative outcomes to uncontrollable internal, stable, and global causes. Their hypothesis is partially supported by studies of Rizley (1978) and Teasdale (1978).

Recently a somewhat different model of depression has been proposed that also incorporates an attributional component (Rehm, 1977). This work uses Kanfer's (1970, 1971) model of self-control (involving self-observation, self-evaluation, and self-reinforcement) as a basic heuristic device, adding to the self-evaluation phase the importance of self-attributed performance (internal attribution of causality). The development of an internal standard or criterion in turn influences how individuals regulate their own behavior through administration of reward and punishment. This model assumes that negative expectancies, and not the attributions themselves, are the causes of depression on the basis of the following line of reasoning (Rehm and O'Hara, 1978).

First, it is assumed that prior expectancies influence attribution (Weiner, Frieze, Kukla, Reed, Rest, and Rosenbaum, 1972). If the assumption is then made that depressed persons have a generalized negative expectancy regarding outcomes in their lives, then failure experiences will be consistent with this expectancy and will therefore be attributed to internal, stable, and global factors. Similarly success experiences, which would be inconsistent with a negative expectancy, would be attributed to external, unstable, and specific factors. This reformulation of Abramson *et al.* (1978) appears to explain better much of the recent depression data (e.g., Abramson and Sackheim, 1977). A therapy program described in Rehm and O'Hara (1979) has incorporated explicit exercises to make depressed patients aware of the nature of their attributions and to modify the manner in which they attribute causes of events to themselves, with some therapeutic success. Further work is needed, however, to determine whether it is attributional modification per se that is having the desired effect on behavior.

Loneliness

Peplau, Russell, and Heim (1978) suggest that loneliness occurs when a person's network of social relationships is smaller or less satisfying than the person desires. They further assume that people are motivated to understand the causes of their loneliness. Discovering the reasons for one's loneliness helps make sense of a distressing situation and is a first step toward reestablishing control over one's social relations. It follows from this line of reasoning that the desire to understand causes should be greater among individuals whose loneliness is most severe and long-lasting. This hypothesis is confirmed by divorce research of Harvey, Wells, and Alvarez (1978), who found that the more lonely and depressed the individuals, the more concern they had with rehashing the issues and reasons for the breakup.

The research of Peplau and her associates shows that people make attributions regarding internality and stability of both precipitating events and maintaining causes of their loneliness (Berke and Peplau, 1976; Michela, Peplau, and Weeks, 1979). These findings are theoretically important because laboratory research, focusing only on a single event isolated in time, directed attention solely to consideration of the precipitating causes of the event. In the real world of important problems, attributions regarding the maintaining causes may have substantially more impact since they are more often viewed as chronic factors.

Finally the work suggests the potential importance of attributions for interventions, including counseling and self-help. Peplau *et al.* (1978) assert that an important intervention strategy would be to identify accurately the major causes of an individual's loneliness and to assess correctly the potential changeability of these causes. This leads them to elaborate on the Abramson *et al.* (1978) and Dweck and Goetz (1978) suggestion that increased control and coping are seen when people attribute failure to low effort (unstable cause). In the case of loneliness, Peplau *et al.* show that the crucial issue is not the degree of effort a person exerts, but rather where the person's efforts are directed. Best results accrue when the

efforts are focused at the most important and potentially changeable causes. Again, laboratory studies, where the range of possible causes is greatly restricted, may not have provided this important corollary.

Limitations to the role of attributional analyses of causes have also been found. For example, Carroll (1978) and Carroll and Payne (1977a, 1977b) found that in real cases, parole board members' perceptions of risk of subsequent crime were influenced by causal attributions regarding stability and that these judgments tended to be associated with less favorable recommendations, but the theoretically more important attributional dimension of internality had no effect on subsequent decisions. College students, making the same types of decisions in a laboratory context, showed the usual attribution study results, distinguishing internal-external from stable-unstable dimensions. Either the nonlaboratory setting or the experience of real parole board members must have contributed to these differences.

Education

Working in the domain of school achievement, Dweck and her coworkers have tried explicitly to manipulate attributions. For example, Dweck (1975) trained children who were unsuccessful at school to attribute their failure to a lack of effort, thus giving direct instruction in how to interpret the causes of their failures. This procedure enabled her to determine the differential effects of attributions to stable versus unstable internal causes on behavior. Compared with children who were simply given success experiences, the attributional retraining group, when taken back to the original situation and retested, showed a significantly greater likelihood of emphasizing effort to overcome failure when it occurred and substantially improved performance.

Dweck and her associates also investigated the educational determinants of sex differences in attribution. On the basis of empirical findings, Dweck and Goetz (1978) concluded that different causal perceptions of boys and girls are a result of teachers' differential behavior toward them. Teachers more often provide boys than girls with negative feedback regarding nonintellectual aspects of their work, with feedback emphasizing effort in achievement situations, and with positive feedback contingent on the intellectual quality of their work. This differential feedback of teachers relates to differences between boys and girls in causal perceptions of success and failure. For example, boys more than girls learn to attribute failure to lack of motivation and therefore do not see failure as related to their abilities. Thus they try harder. Manipulating teachers' use of feedback has direct impact on children's attributions and subsequent performance (Dweck *et al.,* 1978).

Dweck and Goetz (1978) also suggested that attribution processes may be viewed as coping attempts. If so, attribution training, as a form of motivational training, may be a promising component of educational activity. The extent to which attributions are malleable in educational contexts, and with what effects, has not been sufficiently investigated, although it is clear that issues of motivation are central to a consideration of the ways in which schools might better achieve their academic goals.

Lepper and his colleagues have suggested that differences in the extent to which individuals view their actions as either voluntary or constrained have an important influence on their subsequent interest in, and performance of, activities previously undertaken in the presence or absence of explicit instrumental contingencies. Lepper, Greene, and Nisbett (1973) showed that extrinsic rewards decreased subsequent intrinsic interest only when the reward was presented in a manner that led children to consider their engagement in the activity as a *means to the attainment of that reward.* Further replications confirm that the detrimental effects on subsequent interest typically depend on the prior designation of the activity as a means of obtaining the proffered reward (Greene and Lepper, 1974; Lepper and Greene, 1975). This hypothesis has been further tested in two real and extended classroom settings (Colvin, 1972; Greene, Sternberg, and Lepper, 1976). Both studies show detrimental effects of relatively long-term reward programs in typical classroom settings.

The theoretical model underlying these studies is not specifically concerned with the effects of rewards but deals more generally with any form of highly visible external control that may lead students to view their behavior as extrinsically motivated. Salient adult surveillance (Lepper and Greene, 1975), grades (Harter, 1978), or superfluous temporal deadlines (Amabile, DeJong, and Lepper, 1976) have the same effects. To develop the operation of intrinsic contingencies, deCharms (1972, 1976) provided elementary school teachers with training designed to aid them in enhancing their student's perceptions of themselves as origins rather than as pawns. This led to enhanced academic motivation and achievement.

Rewards play many roles in the classroom, but the attributional approach asserts that the impact of rewards on performance and subsequent motivation is mediated by the ways in which students construe their meaning. Classroom incentives function both as a source of performance feedback and as a means of social control, but they also do serve an incentive function. Therefore it is sometimes hard to make specific recommendations regarding the use of reward versus no reward. Performance-contingent reward procedures may result in decrements, increments, or no change in subsequent intrinsic interest because of the competing effects they have on perceptions of competence and constraint (Boggiano and Ruble, 1978; Condry, 1977; Deci and Porac, 1978; Karniol and Ross, 1977; Lepper and Greene, 1978). Another caveat is that behavior change, caused by incentives leading to behavior change that itself is positive, enhances self-attributions regarding mastery (Lepper and Greene, 1978). What we can conclude from the work of Lepper, deCharms, Deci, and their colleagues is that self-regulation rather than extrinsic control is better when the goal is to maintain behavior, and that internal attributions contribute to the operation of self-regulation. Intrinsically motivated behaviors are presumed to be a manifestation of one's own interests; they flourish under conditions of competence feedback and choice (Deci and Ryan, 1980).

SITUATIONAL VERSUS DISPOSITIONAL ATTRIBUTION

A different series of studies has questioned the determinants of people making situational versus dispositional attributions for their outcomes. Jones and Nisbett (1971) suggested that actors attribute causality or responsibility for their behavior to situational causes, whereas observers attribute causality for the same behavior to stable dispositions possessed by the actor. They contend that this occurs because different aspects of available information are salient for actors and observers, and that it is this differential salience that affects the course and outcome of the attribution process. A recent review of the considerable amount of research on this hypothesis (Zuckerman, 1979) indicates that quite different results are expected for the same variables in very different research settings. One major criticism is the lack of involvement of subjects in many experiments where they are asked to imagine being actors or observers in a hypothetical situation. It may be that actors tend to make situational attributions only when the behavior performed in the situation has not been chosen by the actor. When it has, the actor is likely to make dispositional attributions (Monson and Snyder, 1977). Gould and Sigall (1977) suggest that the nature of the valence of the event is another important determinant in affecting whether actors and observers will diverge or converge in their causal attributions. Such data argue for the importance of testing and evolving attribution theory further in settings that have significant and heavily loaded outcomes.

In one such study Maslach (1978) found that helping professionals experiencing burnout typically interpreted their responses as reflections of some basic personality variable; in other words, they felt that the problem was dispositional and intrinsic to them, thus disconfirming the Jones and Nisbett (1971) hypothesis that people tend to see their own behavior as a product of situational forces and constraints. Even when they recognized the special situational stresses of their work, they were still prone to put the blame on some flaw within themselves. Consequently they experienced a sense of failure and a loss of self-esteem, and a state of depression would often follow. These data suggest that for real problems, people often are unable to use self-serving biases in perception, even when the salience of the situational factors, which would make self-serving biases tenable, is very great.

These data are especially important because a lively debate among attribution theorists has focused on whether attributional inferences are determined simply by information-processing variables or whether motivational forces also account for attributions of causality. For example, the operation of self-esteem or ego-defensive biases has been used to explain the result that individuals tend to make greater dispositional attributions for their own positive behaviors than for their negative behaviors. Maslach's (1978) analyses suggest instead an overwhelming tendency toward dispositional inference even when the outcomes and behaviors are profoundly negative.

The bias of helping professionals toward dispositional rather than situational attributions extends to their judgments about recipients as well. They often view recipients as having been the causes of their own problems rather than as suffering from situational circumstances. Maslach notes that blaming the recipient becomes more frequent when the true causes are distal and complex and the operational paradigm is a medical model, and when the requirements of record keeping exclude contextual information while highlighting personal problems.

Blaming the victim may also be the result of defensive attribution, as studies of Lerner (1970) and Walster (1966) have suggested. Coates, Wortman, and Abbey (1978) found that increased feelings of vulnerability among observers leads them to more negative evaluations of a rape victim, especially when the victim's outcomes are severe.

Much of Maslach's work has been correlational, and whether retraining people to make situational attributions would lessen the effects of burnout remains an important untested question. It has been shown, however, in a different context, that such situational reattribution can have profoundly beneficial effects. Using nursing home patients, Rodin and Langer (1980) found that over 80 percent of the people they tested made dispositional attributions regarding the sources of their problems. For example, most of them saw their illness and increasing dependence as being a function of old age. The problem with dispositional attributions in this and other contexts is that one sees the problems as unchangeable. Rodin and Langer argued that if this were true, changing patients' views and focusing their attention on situational factors in the environment that are more easily changed could have beneficial effects.

Subjects were randomly divided at the time of entry to a nursing home into three groups: a no-treatment control group; a group given factual information, which stressed that aging did not inevitably cause health and dependency problems; and a group given attributional retraining. This last group was given situational explanations for a variety of the problems that they were encountering in the nursing homes. Only subjects in the third group showed beneficial outcomes, including increased activity and sociability and better coping behavior.

Bulman and Wortman (1977) also considered the relationship between situational versus dispositional attributions and coping behavior. They interviewed young people who had been involved in sudden traumatic accidents that resulted in paraplegia or quadraplegia. Subjects were asked how much blame they attributed to themselves, to others, to the environment, or to chance, and whether they perceived the accident to have been avoidable. A measure of how well each participant was coping with his or her disability was obtained by eliciting a rating from a social worker and a nurse. Respondents were identified as coping well if they had accepted the reality of their injury and were attempting to deal positively with their paralysis (e.g., working toward improvement of their physical abilities, attending physical therapy, and the like). Patients were considered to be coping poorly if they denied the extent of their injuries despite clear medical evidence to the contrary, if they expected to get better by a miracle, or if they showed little or no interest in ameliorative physical therapy or other activities that might improve their physical condition.

The authors found that the more victims blamed someone else or the more they felt the accident might have been avoided, the worse they coped with their paralysis. The more they blamed themselves, however, the better they coped with their paralysis. Deciding whether they were to blame for the accident, many respondents seemed to be influenced by whether or not they were alone at the time of the accident and whether they voluntarily chose the activity that they were participating in because it was something they enjoyed. If so, they tended to blame themselves more, as Monson and Snyder (1977) have hypothesized.

While these data suggest that dispositional attributions for negative consequences may sometimes have adaptive rather than self-defeating consequences, the study is limited because it lacks distinctions among attributions of causality, judgments for foreseeability, and assignments of fault or blame. In fact further research has indicated that different types of self-blaming responses may have different implications for adjustment.

Janoff-Buman (1979) has suggested that there are two types of self-blame. One involves attributions to one's behaviors that are unstable (e.g., if I had not been walking alone late at night, I would not have been raped). Another concerns attributions to one's character or personality, which are stable, internal causes (e.g., if I weren't such a gullible or stupid person, I would not have been raped). Janoff-Bulman studied the adjustment of rape victims and found that behavioral self-blame of the former kind leads to better coping, presumably because it provides the woman with feelings of control over her future outcomes. In these studies, unlike the Maslach (1978) and Rodin and Langer (1978) studies, dispositional attributions appear to lead to better coping.

Whether or not an outcome is seen as avoidable the next time seems to be the pivotal determinant of whether self-blaming attributions lead to positive, adaptive behavior or negative, maladaptive outcomes. Kelley (1967), Wortman (1976), and Pittman and Pittman (1980) have argued, in fact, that the primary reason for making attributions is to obtain, or at least to maintain, control.

Pittman and Pittman's (1980) study showed that variations in experience of lack of control do affect subsequent attributional tendencies. Intervention with rape victims to teach more adaptive attributions has been shown to enhance subsequent feelings of control, thus supporting the relationship between these two variables.

It is also true that attributions alone are insufficient to explain fully people's reactions to uncontrollable outcomes. Wortman and Dintzer (1978) have suggested several other important factors—for example, whether the outcome was expected. Parkes (1975) found that the unexpected death of a spouse creates far greater problems in coping and adjustment than the expected death of a spouse. Other factors are whether the individual expects that the outcome might change independently of his behavior and how the individual judges the cost of trying to influence an outcome. If the cost is too great, coping behavior may be greatly restricted. Thus we must avoid simplistic accounts of the effects of attributions on coping, acknowledging that several other variables interact to determine final coping outcomes.

The studies just reviewed suggest a greater tendency for people to make dispositional attributions (cf. Ross, 1977) even for negative outcomes. In making dispositional attributions for certain behaviors, they appear to infer personal causality and thus assume some personal responsibility. Frequently a dispositional label carries with it assumptions that the intensity and perseverance of the reaction are motivationally based rather than stimulus bound. Attributions to disposition may be especially likely when people attempt to make sense of their own anomalous reactions or when discontinuities in their feelings affect cognitive functioning. Applied studies such as those described above suggest that in making these attributions, people ask at least two questions: Is there a rational explanation for why this is happening? This directs a search process that seeks responsible antecedents and discreet causal stimuli. And then: Why is this happening to me? This kind of question directs a different search, one where they try to discover whether other people are responding similarly, even if there is not an adequate explanatory account available.

The studies just reviewed suggest that sometimes better personal outcomes accrue when people make dispositional attributions for their negative circumstances, and at other times situational attributions appear to lead to better outcomes. One crucial determinant is whether the attribution increases expectations for control of subsequent related events. The importance of the differential salience of various causes and possible explanations appears to be another major determinant.

Collins *et al.* (1980) showed that salience was extremely important in determining which behaviors served as primary cues in the formation of internal or external, situational or dispositional, attributions regarding children's behavior in the classroom. Their data showed that the behavior of unmedicated, hyperactive boys was more conspicuous, perceptually intrusive, and distracting. In other words, their styles of behavior were particularly salient and noticeable. Collins *et al.* evaluated their observational data for behaviors that were high in energy, stood out, were sudden, and were disruptive. All four of these variables depicted unmedicated, hyperactive boys as highly salient, as figures against the ground of peers and teachers. It appears that global teacher impressions of hyperactivity were not based on a simple frequency count of all the possible relevant behaviors, but rather that rare and salient behaviors such as these contributed heavily to their global impressions. In fact the reality of the behavior in and of itself appears to make a behavioral act salient and thus more important to the process of impression formation. These data support the Taylor and Fiske (1978) assertion that salient stimuli are more likely to be used in making attributional inferences.

Labels represent another form of very salient information that affects how causal attributions are made. The power of labels can be seen in the way they control the perceptions of observers, even when the actor's behavior is independent of the label (e.g., Rosenthal and Jacobson, 1968). Not only do labels influence the way others behave toward the labeled person, but they may come to affect the way the person acts and distort self-perceptions as well (Dunn, 1979). Once a person is labeled and treated accordingly, his or her behavior may be modified by the treatment so as to validate the initial, perhaps erroneous, labeling.

Snyder, Tanke, and Berscheid (1977) have shown that stereotypes are labels that create their own social reality by directing an interaction so as to generate the behavioral evidence needed to confirm the perceiver's stereotype. In their study they measured impressions of the personality of people attributed to be either hetero- or homosexual. Rodin and Langer (1980) suggest that aging labels also function as stereotypes, leading to an information-processing search for behavioral evidence needed to confirm the stereotype. They further show that this

affects the actor as strongly as the observer, at least in the case of aged individuals. Their work shows that much of the phenomenology of aging and the behavior of aged people can be understood by considering how this dynamic process leads to a self-fulfilling prophecy.

LABELING OF AROUSAL STATES

A final aspect of the attribution process that has been greatly extended by applied research is the question of how one's own internal arousal states come to be perceived and labeled. Despite controversy over experimental procedures (Marshall and Zimbardo, 1979; Maslach, 1979), it is generally accepted that arousal is often labeled on the basis of salient external explanations (Schachter and Singer, 1962). Demonstrations of the malleability of this labeling process have generally involved inducing arousal by one means, providing a neutral alternative explanation for the arousal, and then measuring responses presumed to reflect reduction of arousal by means of this reattribution process (Nisbett and Schachter, 1966; Ross, Rodin, and Zimbardo, 1969). These procedures seemed to have important therapeutic applications. For example, several investigators asked whether the naturally occurring arousal of insomnia could be reduced by misattribution techniques, using a pill that was presumed to produce arousal comparable to the symptoms of insomnia.

One study has shown that the arousal-pill manipulation can reduce self-reported insomnia (Storms and Nisbett, 1970); one study has shown that this procedure can increase insomnia (Kellogg and Baron, 1975); and one study has shown no effect (Bootzin, Herman, and Nicassio, 1976). It may be that the placebo pill procedure is a poor way to manipulate the attributional variables specified in the model. Indeed the important question is not whether the pill works but whether the attributional model is valid. That is, is insomnia sustained by perjorative self-attributions, and can reliable treatments be developed to change these negative self-attributions and thus alleviate insomnia?

Abandoning the pill procedure, Lowery, Denney, and Storms (1979) tried to persuade insomniacs that their sleeping problem was not caused by any emotional or psychological disorder but instead was due to higher baseline levels of autonomic activity. This led to fewer negative self-attributions about insomnia and significantly less time to fall asleep. The arousal-pill procedure had no effect. Thus it appears that treating prejorative attributions regarding *causes* of sleep problems is effective.

Brodt and Zimbardo (1981) argued that shyness could also be reduced by weakening the link between arousal and its usual determinants through misattribution procedures. Individuals who normally report arousal symptoms in a social setting in response to feelings of shyness were informed that the source of their arousal symptoms was the presence of high-intensity noise. If they relabel their arousal with this nonphysiological explanation, they should show more socially responsive behavior and less maladaptive, emotional behavior. The data supported this hypothesis.

In a conceptual replication of the Storms and Nisbett design (1970), Singerman, Borkovec, and Baron (1976) examined the effects of misattribution of arousal on another clinically relevant problem, speech anxiety. The investigators asked highly and moderately anxious speech-phobic subjects to present two speeches. During the presentation of the speech, subjects were exposed to meaningless noise in a manner similar to the procedures employed by Brodt and Zimbardo (1981) and Ross *et al.* (1969). When noise was present, arousal subjects exhibited slightly and nonsignificantly more anxiety than did sedation subjects, unlike earlier findings. In this study the salience of anxiety caused by speech presentation may have been exaggerated by the experimenter's emphasis on taping subjects' speeches for later evaluation, and by the fact that observers were present and rating subjects' performance. It is not surprising then that the subjects labeled their arousal as caused by the speech situation rather than by the relevant noise.

Certainly it seems clear that it would be difficult to manipulate attributions about the source of arousal in certain clinical problems such as phobias, where the emotional response is strongly associated with a salient causal explanation. With such clinical cases the more extreme and chronic the emotional response, the more difficult it would probably be to manipulate the client's belief about the sources of arousal. Misattribution may be effective only where the source of a client's distress is not readily apparent or becomes more ambiguous during the course of treatment. The clinical utility of misattribution procedures remains to be fully tested.

Perhaps a more significant clinical application of attributional processes emerges from their effects on judgments of the self and its capabilities. Certainly generalization decrements are more likely to occur in behav-

ior if bold performances are attributed to special situational arrangements rather than to regained personal competence. A study by Davison and Valins (1969) examined the possibility that behavior change attributed to one's self would persist or be maintained to a greater degree than behavior change attributed to an external agent, such as a drug. Although their study was a laboratory investigation using shock, the model has been extended to the clinical domain.

Davison and Valins (1969) gave subjects a pill that was presumed to reduce sensitivity to pain, and after they witnessed the fact that they had stood considerably more pain than they had prior to taking the pill, half of the subjects were told that they had been given a placebo. The other half was told that the effects of the pain-dulling pill were wearing off. In the third shock series, subjects who attributed their behavior change to themselves, that is, those who believed they had taken a placebo, tolerated more shock and perceived the shocks as less painful than subjects who attributed their behavior change to the drug.

Based on Davison and Valins's (1969) results, Davison, Tsujimoto, and Glaros (1973) gave insomniacs a treatment package of a hypnotic drug, a self-induced relaxation procedure, and the scheduling and regularization of the bedtime routine. Eighty percent of the subjects improved, and then half were told the drug had been at the optimal dose for aiding sleep and half were told it was at the minimal dose and was unlikely to have been effective. The drug was then discontinued. The minimal-dosage group began to feel more responsible for their improvement and maintained their shortened period for sleep onset. Subjects in the "optimal-dosage" group returned to, and even exceeded, their original sleep onset latencies.

If these results are generalizable, they might also suggest that if individuals attribute positive behavior change to medications and consequently do not feel responsible for behavioral improvement, they are unlikely to maintain the change once medication is stopped. However, if individuals attribute positive behavioral changes to themselves, such changes are more likely to persevere. This line of reasoning was supported very strongly, although unintentionally, in a recent obesity study (Stunkard, Craighead, and Brownell, 1981). The investigators were interested in determining whether weight control would benefit from a combined therapy that involved pharmacological and behavioral interventions. Subjects were divided into those receiving fenfluramine, an anorectic agent that suppresses appetite by working on the central nervous system; those who received behavior therapy alone; and subjects in a combined-treatment group receiving both fenfluramine and behavioral treatment.

Stunkard and his coworkers found that the combined-treatment group lost significantly more weight by the end of the treatment program. However, at the six-month follow-up they had gained back significantly more weight than subjects in either of the other two groups. Rodin (1981) has interpreted these data as consistent with the Davison and Valins (1969) experiment, arguing that subjects receiving fenfluramine attributed their success to the drug and not to any behavioral changes that they were making. In the case of subjects receiving the combined treatment, this undermined attributions to real changes that they had made in their own behaviors, and they failed to continue to engage in these behaviors, leaving them vulnerable to regaining more than fenfluramine-alone subjects, since they had lost more initially. Current research by Rodin and her colleagues to test this question provides support for this hypothesis (Rodin *et al.,* 1984).

In the study by Rodin and her colleagues (1984), specific attributional manipulations were given to undermine attributions to a pharmacological appetite suppressant and to increase the salience of attributions made to behavioral changes during the course of the program. Subjects receiving such treatment lost significantly more weight than subjects in any other condition. The differences between the groups were even stronger after the six-month and one-year follow-up. Another study (Colletti and Kopel, 1979) also considered the association between self-attribution for behavioral change and long-term maintenance, in this case long-term reduction of cigarette smoking. The investigators reported that superior maintenance of treatment gain was associated with a greater degree of self-attribution at a one-year follow-up, regardless of the specific maintenance strategy employed.

In an explicit attributional manipulation of self-efficacy (Chambliss and Murray, 1979), smokers were given self-control instructions and pills that they were told would help them stop smoking, and all achieved a reduction in smoking. Half the group then was told correctly that the pills were placebos and that any reduction in smoking resulted from their own efforts; the other half thought that their success came from the pill. At one month all of the latter group had returned to their earlier levels of smoking; those who had received the attribution of self-efficacy sustained a reduction in smoking.

All these studies appear to provide support for the role of self-attributions as predictors of the maintenance of behavior change. Also several authors have noted that the induction of desired attributions for treatment gains need not involve deceptive manipulations. For example, internal attributions for behavioral improvements may be induced by gradually reducing and eliminating external aids once a client is performing the desired behaviors. This was accomplished in the Rodin *et al.* (1984) study by introducing behavioral strategies showing participants that they were able to accomplish weight loss before the drug was introduced. Similarly the drug part of the program was concluded substantially before the behavioral part of the program, and subjects continued to lose weight while making additional behavior changes. Thus therapies based on attributional techniques appear to be useful in the modification of maladaptive behavior patterns and in the maintenance of treatment gains. It is also clear, however, that under certain conditions misattribution regarding the source and level of physiological arousal may be difficult to achieve, especially where the response is clearly associated with a very salient explanation.

Attributional explanations for feelings may also help us to understand better the drug use process. Morris and Kanouse (1979) suggest that in drug use, both decisions and outcomes depend heavily on the attributions made by drug users concerning their own bodily states. Questions of interest to attribution theorists regarding this drug use process include the following: (1) what attributions lead to decisions to initiate, modify, or discontinue drug therapy, and (2) what explanations about one's state of health are used to judge a drug's success or failure.

According to Morris and Kanouse, the drug use process can be divided into four stages. The first is noticing symptoms. The initiation of drug therapy usually follows the onset of symptoms that the indvidual or the physician assumes can be modified by drugs. Identifying symptoms, however, requires attention to relevant cues and the use of labels suggestive of illness. It may be that the very experience of symptoms depends on the availability and salience of labels in the individual's active repertoire. The second stage involves the decision that drugs are appropriate forms of therapy. After a potential symptom has been attended to and labeled as a condition for which medication may be appropriate, a variety of factors influence whether the individual will begin a medication regimen, including the severity of the symptoms, their expected duration, and the availability and cost of medication. The third stage involves the drug treatment itself. Once a drug is taken, physical states are monitored for signs of change, including improvement or worsening of symptoms and the occurrence of new symptoms or side effects. Morris and Kanouse argue that this process is a very active one in which intense search and attributional processes are likely to occur. When one has a large number of physical cues to monitor in particular, one may be forced to interpret, integrate, and extrapolate a great deal of information in order to arrive at an assessment of how one is doing. These complexities offer rich material for attributional analysis. Finally, as a result of the monitoring process, drug therapy may be modified or discontinued. This represents the fourth stage.

At each stage of the drug use process just described, action is either accompanied by, or predicated upon, the formation of attributions that assign meaning to the individual's experience. Other things being equal, one is less likely to perceive cues that are unexpected unless they are of sufficient magnitude or duration to force attention—in other words, unless they are extremely salient. The choice between providing a medical or nonmedical label for a symptom may often have a strong motivational component. Often attributional errors occur because of the difficulty of distinguishing symptoms of a medical condition from the impact of temporary environmental factors (Rodin, 1978).

Lack of patient adherence to prescribed regimens is a major cause of therapeutic failure, and an attribution theory perspective on why patients modify or discontinue drug therapy can offer important cues for improving patient adherence, according to Morris and Kanouse (1979). Consider the taking of antibiotics for certain types of infections. If the infection is widespread and progressive, large numbers of microorganisms are killed, and the patient feels better. Although the physician may have prescribed ten days of treatment, the patient may discontinue drug therapy after three or four days. Unknown to the patient, the more virulent bacteria, which survive the first several days of treatment, may start to multiply and eventually cause a full relapse. Thus the initial relief of symptoms may be incorrectly interpreted as a signal that drug treatment has been successful in eliminating the infection, thus leading the patient to discontinue drug use. The attribution pitfall posed in the use of antibiotics for infection arises because patients are likely to assume that the degree of improvement in symptoms strongly covaries with the degree of recovery. If patients are warned that this is not the case, they may be more likely to complete the prescribed regimen (Sharpe and Mikeal, 1974).

With an asymptomatic condition, the individual has no clear bodily signals on which to base drug use decisions. A case in point is hypertension, which can be measured only by instruments. Many people discontinue the drug treatment regimen because they feel that the medication is not needed. Leventhal, Meyer, and Nerenz (1980) have argued that the use and discontinuation of use of hypertension medication are strongly correlated with the perception of symptoms. This line of reasoning has much to say about the kind of information that people should be given regarding the drugs they take for symptoms and their illnesses in general. If people can make proper causal assignments to drug, disease, or environmental factors, they can better understand both their illness and the course of therapy. And if they can properly interpret drug and disease effects, it is expected that they will be able to gain more control over their own health.

SUMMARY AND CONCLUSIONS

Applied studies have strongly suggested that people do make causal attributions when the outcomes in question are major life concerns, and the answers they provide have predictable, systematic effects on their psychological state and behavior. The ability for self-regulation appears especially enhanced by the nature of causal attributions, and applied studies have shown the importance of self-regulation as opposed to external control for the maintenance of adaptive behavior.

The issue of whether attributional processes reflect cold, cognitive information processing or hot, motivational variables has not been resolved by work in applied settings. In many instances it appears that people do not only choose esteem-enhancing attributions; indeed they sometimes choose those that are most damaging for their self-esteem. These applied studies have further weakened the theoretical assumptions of the actor-observer model (Jones and Nisbett, 1972) and provide stronger support for the view that attributions about one's own actions are likely to be made on the basis of the most salient attributional information

(Nisbett and Ross, 1979; Ross, 1977) and often it is dispositional. While not yet directly tested in applied research, an anchor-adjustment inferential process (Quattrone, 1982) may also be involved in the results described above. This process pushes for more dispositional attributions simply because there are more trait terms than situational terms in the English language. Stronger support for the information-processing type of variable, however, comes from other lines of investigation not specifically focusing on attributional processes per se. These will be considered next.

INFORMATION PROCESSING AND DECISION MAKING

The way people process various kinds of information and make decisions on the basis of this processing has significant consequences for their behavior. In the applied area, investigators working on questions of health behavior, population control, and judicial outcomes have been most concerned with elaborating information-processing variables.

SCHEMATIC PROCESSING OF INFORMATION: PAIN AND DISTRESS

Instructional sets have been shown to determine which information, from a full array of stimuli, is attended to. Leventhal and his coworkers assessed whether variations in stimuli attended to would affect the experience of pain and distress in a medical context (e.g., Johnson and Leventhal, 1974; Johnson, Morrissey, and Leventhal, 1973). They showed that turning subjects' attention to the objective features of potentially threatening stimuli rather than to the emotion-related features reduced stress. Presumably sensory, objective features of stimuli are not coded as threats and therefore do not provoke an emotional reaction. Focusing subjects on sensation information prior to noxious, frightening, or painful medical procedures has substantially reduced physical sensations and reactions to these procedures and has been used to reduce stress during an endoscopic examination (Johnson and Leventhal, 1974; Johnson *et al.,* 1973), removal of casts (Johnson, Kirchoff, and Endress, 1975), labor and childbirth (Leventhal, Booth, Shachman, and Leventhal, 1977), and cholecystectomy surgery (Johnson, Rice, Fuller, and Endress, 1977; Wilson, 1977).

Further work supports the information-processing explanation of these data by suggesting that *accuracy* of the sensation information does not constitute the key factor in stress reduction. In a cold pressor task, Brown, Engquist, and Leventhal (1977) gave one group of subjects accurate sensation information and also a pain warning, and another group of subjects was given only sensation information. The authors argued that while sensation information might be expected to reduce distress by integrating the noxious input with the schemata of the stimulus features of the input, the pain warning would strengthen another set of schemata, the emotionally relevant pain and distress schemata, which would also be integrated with the noxious input. Consistent with this hypothesis, subjects given the pain warning showed no distress reduction due to preparation with accurate sensory information. The Brown *et al.* (1977) study strongly suggests that distress reduction depends on the way input is processed and not merely on the accuracy of the subject's expectations.

Cohen and Lazarus (1973) studied surgical patients who were found to differ greatly in their date of postoperative recovery despite the fact that they had similar medical problems. Measuring five recovery variables —days in hospital, number of pain medications, minor medical complications that followed surgery, and negative psychological reactions—they attempted to correlate these dependent variables with different types of coping strategies. They reported that subjects who were the most vigilant, that is, who attended most to all sorts of information, were those who had the most complicated postoperative recovery. Although they speculated that the vigilant group had the most information and therefore was also most aware of possible negative complications that could have presented a problem, the correlation they observed might be attributable to preoperative hypervigilance in some of their subjects, which according to Janis and Mann (1977) is correlated with low tolerance for postoperative stress. This distinction between vigilance and hypervigilance suggests strongly that more information is not always related to better outcomes.

The work of Leventhal and his coworkers suggests, in agreement with Lazarus (1966), that an interpretation based on schematic processing of information is the major determinant of the stress. Threatening interpretations increase stress, while nonthreatening interpretations decrease stress, with the nature of the objective stressor held constant. Interestingly their studies suggest that strategies calling for stimulus monitoring with appropriate interpretation lead to habituation of stress, that is, to relatively durable stress reduction, whereas blocking strategies (nonattention or distraction) do not result in habituation of stress, although they may impose temporary control of stress.

From these studies it has been possible to develop a more general information-processing model of pain perception (Leventhal and Everhart, 1979). The assumption is that once an individual is no longer naive regarding pain, a noxious stimulus will retrieve and be integrated with the schematic memory of earlier pain experiences unless sensation information and attention lead to an alternative way of processing the stimuli. Specifically the argument is that the individual forms a schema or categorical structure that represents the informational and pain-emotion aspects of these experiences. The schema includes the representation of the visual, auditory, and kinesthetic events associated with the stimuli and also includes the representation both of pain and of the various emotional reactions that accompany the painful episode.

Although schemas are viewed as relatively concrete in nature, they are not simply photographic representations of physical pain episodes. In fact emotional schemata, unlike other kinds, can form and change by internal feedback pressures, for example, by fantasies feeding on emotion and being enriched by emotion without direct external support or experience (Leventhal and Everhart, 1979). It is this internal process that seems to be involved in the formation of such emotional schemata as the acquisition of phobias in the absence of direct injury or external conditioning (e.g., Bandura and Menlove, 1968). In this sense the treatment or removal of the phobic symptoms entails an altering of the underlying schematic system.

Field experiments by Leventhal and his colleagues provide evidence for the value of sensation information and important data on the interaction of this information with behavioral instruction for controlling noxious stimulation. In general, sensation information appears to facilitate some form of habituation or inhibition of stress to continuous stimulation. Additional gains in stress reduction occur when sensation information is combined with action instruction, detailed information, and practice in the steps needed for behavioral adaptation to the stressor setting. Sensation information and attention provide an alternative way of schematizing the stressor, which facilitates stress reduction, and the decline in stress

allows the individual to perform additional responses to control the stressful experience. The multilevel processing model of Leventhal and his coworkers (Leventhal, 1980b) has become a robust heuristic because it has helped to define more clearly the components of schematas and their interdependencies.

BEHAVIORAL CONSEQUENCES OF SCHEMATIC PROCESSING

Legal Judgments

Doob and Kirshenbaum (1973) considered how schema formation may influence jury behavior. They were specifically interested in a jury's later use of information after a judge's instruction to disregard a portion of the testimony. In their simulation experiment, subjects read a summary of a burglary case, and half of them received information in that summary about the defendant's past record, indicating five prior burglary convictions. Subjects receiving this information were consistently more likely to judge the defendant as guilty, even when subsequently instructed by the judge that this information was not relevant to decisions about his guilt or innocence in this particular instance. Social psychological studies of debriefing (e.g., Ross, Lepper, and Hubbard, 1975) suggest that people interpret subsequent information in the context of schemas developed on the basis of information they have already received, generating plausible scripts and viewpoints from new information to support the earlier evidence. Even when they are told the information was incorrect, or in the present case to ignore it, the interpretation of subsequent material to support and instantiate the first is not similarly undone because it has already been integrated in line with developed schemas.

Conceptually the Doob and Kirschenbaum (1973) and Ross et al. (1975) studies are related to studies showing that information to which a witness is exposed after an event becomes integrated into the witness's memory of the event (Lipton, 1977; Marshall, Marquis, and Oskamp, 1971). Brown, Deffenbacher, and Sturgill (1977) and Loftus, Miller, and Burns (1978) have also shown the integration of visual and verbal information into visual memory. For example, in the Loftus et al. (1978) study, subjects saw slides of a traffic accident taking place at a corner with a stop sign. Subjects who were asked questions that mentioned a yield sign remembered actually having seen a yield sign more often than control groups who were not asked misleading questions. These information-processing effects are enhanced if the witness makes a clear commitment to his or her choice (Gorenstein and Ellsworth, 1980). The implication of these studies for the manipulability of eyewitness testimony is striking.

Medical Compliance

How a patient processes and comes to understand his or her symptoms and physical sensations appears to affect compliance with medical recommendations. Noncompliance has traditionally been viewed simply as a motivational problem (Haynes, Taylor, and Sackett, 1979); however, it may also be due to information-processing variables that make noncompliance the natural outcome. Generally patients' compliance depends on their understanding of the disorder, which in turn depends on three things: information provided by the health care system, sensations and symptoms arising from the body that are highly salient, and the patients' past experience with illness. Noncompliance can occur because people generate their own representations of danger and their own coping reactions to help them deal with present and potential health threats.

Symptoms and the patients' beliefs about their determinants form the patients' implicit theory of illness. It is argued that these perceptions and beliefs around an experience of symptoms become a schema of the illness experience, which guides the search for, and interpretation of, further information and determines subsequent behavior (Leventhal, 1980b). Leventhal argues that representing the illness as highly palpable symptoms often allows for the selection of specific coping efforts, and he has suggested that because symptoms are felt, they may exert very potent control over behavior. The assumption that schemas can have a sensory component and a cognitive component is similar to Zajonc's (1980) distinction between affective and cognitive schemas. Current research efforts attempt to describe their different effects on information processing and retrieval.

Meyer, Leventhal, and Gutman (1981) used both cross-sectional and longitudinal data to provide a picture of symptom evaluation processes underlying compliance or noncompliance with hypertension treatment. Six groups of patients who varied in the length of time that they had been hypertensive, in their degree of compliance with recommendations, and in their degree of control

were interviewed regarding their beliefs about high blood pressure and its treatment. They were also asked what they had been told by medical authorities.

There were three major findings in the Meyer *et al.* (1981) study: (1) Although medical authority denies that bodily sensations are reliably associated with blood pressure elevations, the great majority of respondents thought otherwise and believed that they could identify clear symptoms. (2) The belief and use of sensation monitoring developed over time and experience with hypertension, so that it was greater with more experienced hypertensives. The symptoms that were monitored changed over time as well. (3) Because patients believed that they could monitor the symptoms of high blood pressure, they expected their treatment to modify those symptoms, and so their compliance depended on the extent to which they perceived beneficial effects as a result of the treatment. Patients who dropped out and then reentered did so because of the experience or emergence of a new symptom.

The existence of an interpretive process suggests that patients are motivated to protect themselves against health threats and that they do so in terms of their own construction of the threat and their own simplistic theories of their illness and treatment. The Meyer *et al.* (1981) data suggest that the interpretations developed by patients are organized around specific themes. For example, some patients see hypertension as a stress disease, others as an ingestive disease. These schematic beliefs or structures are different from person to person because they are based on different concrete experiences and so they have different effects on compliance behavior and the nature of the coping responses people employ.

Pennebaker's (1979) work is based on the same conceptual framework as the Leventhal studies, suggesting that the perception of internal sensations represents processes of perception similar to those that are implicated in our learning about external events. Both assume it is more likely that individuals become aware of these internal physical sensations at some times and not others. For example, when external demands are low or when people are feeling ill, especially helpless, or out of control, the probability of attending to internal sensations increases. Schemas guide their search for particular sensations, and just as schemas restrict the information that people glean from the environment, so they also restrict and shape information that people experience from internal sensations.

Hysterical Contagion

Pennebaker (1979) has applied the line of reasoning described above to understand hysterical contagion, arguing that factors that promote monitoring of internal states should increase the probability of perceived health problems. A job that is undemanding because of its repetitiveness, lack of intrinsic interest and slow pace may discourage external attentional focus. Lack of social interaction might also promote this process (cf. Cobb, 1976). Attention to internal sensations and resultant contagion may be more likely under such circumstances. Virtually every episode of hysterical contagion has occurred among workers or students who are tense, anxious, overworked, or in a state of increased autonomic activity. This arousal is sometimes the result of poor worker-management relations (cf. Colligan, 1978), poor lighting or temperature (Colligan and Urtes, 1978), crowding (Freedman, 1979), loud noise (Shepard and Kroes, 1975), role or status incongruities (Kerckhoff and Back, 1968), or daily and financial pressures (Colligan and Murphy, 1979).

No matter what the true cause of arousal, the important fact is that affected individuals are constantly experiencing a number of diverse and ambiguous internal sensations. Based on the theoretical model of schemas, it would be predicted that the more physical sensations present, the easier it would be to confirm any number of illness hypotheses. This line of reasoning suggests that the best way to circumvent the selective search process that leads to hysterical contagion and illness would be to reduce the causes of anxiety and arousal. Another, perhaps easier, way would be to train individuals to associate specific groups of sensations to the autonomic changes associated with their jobs, thus making them less likely later to attribute them to illness. This application merits further investigation.

It is clear that the illness reported after a much publicized nuclear reactor accident at Three Mile Island, Pennsylvania, was a function of the acute stress response to the accident rather than a direct effect of radiation itself. In other words, rather than any direct radiation-producing illness effects, the heightened stress caused greater attention to internal sensations and symptoms, leading to an attribution of illness. For example, the closer residents showed higher symptom reporting than the more distant residents, and the difference was greatest *before* the venting of the nuclear waste began. Clearly proximity would greatly increase stress differen-

tially in these respondents. All of the health data reported by Baum and his coworkers are consistent with this interpretation (Baum, Fleming, and Singer, 1982).

DECISION MAKING

Population Decisions

One major application of the information-processing approach has been in the area of decision making about birth control and child bearing. Testing and extension of a variety of different decision theories has emerged from this work. While these models make somewhat different assumptions about the variables influencing behavior and differ in the behavior they aim to explain, all models share the general assumption that individuals' choices are at least partly determined by their beliefs about the consequences that could result from making any given choice.

The Fishbein (1972) decision model has been tested widely in population psychology and has received empirical support (Fishbein and Jaccard, 1973; Jaccard and Davidson, 1975). The model holds that behavioral intention, which predicts actual behavior, is a function of attitude toward performing the act in question and of a normative component. Because this model includes both a normative and an attitudinal component, it allows examination of both social- and individual-level variables (Ajzen and Fishbein, 1973). It is this aspect of the theory that has made it particularly interesting for researchers in the population area, where demographic as well as psychological variables are powerful in predicting fertility-related behaviors.

In addition, and more important for present concerns, clues for intervention can be gained from analysis of the variables within the model that differentiate individuals who hold different attitudes or who have different fertility intentions. For example, Werner *et al.* (1975) identified a number of beliefs that were significantly correlated with the intention to have a third child. Insofar as these beliefs are amenable to change, modifications in intention could potentially be achieved by altering beliefs about the consequences of the behavior. Another strength of applied research using decision models is that the actual content of cognitions contributing to decisions can be examined. Areas where there is a great disparity between objective and subjective probabilities, for example, will provide particularly promising possibilities for intervention (Adler, 1979).

Application to the area of population research, however, has also shown weakness in these decision models. For example, the Fishbein (1972) model does not account for consideration of alternatives. Intention is seen as a function of attitudes and normative expectations regarding a specific behavior, and the focus is on absolute rather than relative values. The higher the level, the greater the possibility of the behavior. Most applications of the Fishbein model in the laboratory have not included a range of possible choices and have looked only at how well the attitudinal and normative components regarding a particular behavior predict intention to engage in that behavior. Thus they have not provided a real test of the Ajzen and Fishbein (1969) assertion that consideration of an individual's attitude toward each alternative in a choice situation would yield better prediction of behavioral intention than consideration of the attitude toward only one of the choices. In the area of population research, the model has been expanded and reformulated to include the consequences of individuals' having a spectrum of preferences (Terhune and Kaufman, 1973).

Adler (1979), in a study investigating women's perceptions regarding the advantages and disadvantages of different contraceptives, found that the dimensions on which any given form of contraception or, more generally, any choice is evaluated depend on the alternatives that are salient to the individual. The more salient the alternatives and the greater the number of different alternatives introduced, the more the individual's evaluation and thus behavior will change. In addition she suggests that in terms of a population-related question, variables such as the person's fertility, the accessibility of contraception or abortion, the cooperation of one's partner, and the unconscious symbolic meaning of pregnancy also affect behavior directly and could mediate the effects of an intention not to have any more children on actual behavior. Thus variables beyond the person's intention to engage in that behavior must be considered. Over time, classes of variables that interact with or mediate the effects of intention on behavior, or the relative weighting of components, should be identified and incorporated into an expanded model. Such a model would certainly be more successful in predicting a wider range of situations than are our current models.

Health Decisions

A different model from those used in population research has recently been applied with some success to health problems (Janis and Mann, 1977). This model was formulated to deal especially with decisional conflicts, since Janis and Mann (1977) assert that whenever a decision involves a vital affect-laden issue, one is dealing with hot cognitions in contrast to the cold cognitions of routine problem solving (Abelson, 1963). According to Janis and Mann (1977), conflict is elevated when hot cognitions are involved.

In the health care area many medical decisions do entail a high degree of decisional conflict. The more severe the anticipated losses for each of the available alternatives, the greater the stress engendered by decisional conflict. Janis and Mann (1977) describe five basic patterns of coping with such conflict, each of which is assumed to be associated with a specific set of antecedent conditions and a characteristic level of stress. These patterns were derived from an analysis of the research literature on how people react to emergency warnings and public health messages that urge protective action. The five coping patterns are: (1) unconflicted persistence, (2) unconflicted change, (3) defensive avoidance, (4) hypervigilance, and (5) vigilance. While the first two patterns are occasionally adaptive in saving time and emotional wear and tear, they often lead to defective decision making if the person must make a vital choice. Similarly, defensive avoidance or hypervigilance may occasionally be adaptive, but they generally reduce one's chances of averting serious losses. According to Janis and Mann's empirical analysis, all four are regarded as defective patterns of decision making. The fifth pattern, vigilance, generally leads to decisions of the best quality when the person is in conflict.

According to Janis and Mann's analysis, the vigilance pattern occurs only when the following three conditions are present:

1. Awareness of serious risks for whatever alternative is chosen;

2. Hope of finding a better alternative;

3. Belief that there is adequate time to search and deliberate before the decision is reached.

These three conditions appear to be essential for the psychological preparation needed to deal with postdecisional stress as well, especially in cases where adherence to a decision entails some degree of suffering.

Processes that are important in preparation for stress include correcting faulty beliefs; reconceptualizing the threat as a problem that can be solved; engaging in realistic self-persuasion about the value of protective action; and developing concepts and self-instruction that enable the person to cope more effectively with setbacks (Janis, 1971; Meichenbaum, 1977; Meichenbaum, Turk, and Burnstein, 1975). All of these processes are more likely when the vigilant kind of cognitive activity required for a well-conceived decision occurs.

Janis and his coworkers have been particularly interested in decision making and behavior where the incentives are somewhat weak because they involve rather remote long-term gains (Janis, 1983a, 1983b). For example, when relatively healthy people are urged by a physician to go on a diet or give up smoking or to take some other preventive course of action in order to avoid disease in the future, the incentives are obviously rather weak. Janis proposes that one way to compensate for the relatively weak incentive value of long-term goals in the face of present deprivation is to introduce some additional incentives to adhere to stressful decisions, which reduces decisional conflict. Janis and his coworkers set up community clinics in which they offered free counseling services for solving personal problems, such as excessive eating or smoking, in exchange for the opportunity to collect research data. Their studies have used stratified random assignment to contrasting counseling treatments, highlighting the possibility for controlled experiments in an applied setting.

Adherence to difficult decisions, once they are made on the basis of vigilant cognitive activity, also seems to depend on other important psychological factors. Preparation has already been discussed in the Johnson and Leventhal series of studies (Johnson and Leventhal, 1974; Johnson *et al.*, 1973); other forms of preparation, such as stress inoculation, have been successfully applied in studies of childbirth (Green and Furman, 1975; Levy and McGee, 1975) and with children on pediatric surgery wards (Wolfer and Visintainer, 1975). Studies such as these are especially important because they indicate that psychological factors affect a person's tolerance of pain, frustration, and unpleasant experiences, and these latter factors are important determinants of whether or not people are able to adhere to difficult decisions.

Additional factors that influence adherence once decisions have been made are suggested by social psychological research on commitment. Research on commitment, for example, indicates that if the person is induced to announce his or her intention to an esteemed other,

such as a physician, the person is anchored to the decision not just by anticipated social disapproval but also by anticipated self-disapproval. A study by McFall and Hammen (1971) indicates that commitment followed by reminders of the commitment and self-monitoring is sufficient to enable many heavy smokers to cut down and is as effective as several therapeutic procedures commonly used in antismoking clinics. Another pertinent finding is that forewarnings designed to prevent backsliding are likely to be effective if the person has already committed himself or herself, and ineffective or even detrimental if the person has not. These findings are now being applied by health care personnel in many different kinds of clinics where people can be asked to sign a pledge card to carry out a recommended health practice, such as to cut down on alcohol or to diet, and then can be given a mild dose of stress inoculation that calls attention to the unpleasant consequences to be expected.

Rationalistic cognitive models of personal decision making have also been applied to health decisions. The most well known is "subjective expected utility," which postulates that whenever people select a course of action, they do so in a fairly rational way by comparing the values and probabilities of the consequences that are expected to follow from each of the available alternatives (Edwards, 1954; Raiffa, 1968). As applied to making a vital, health-relevant decision, this model suggests that people first make the best possible estimate of the probability that each of the expected consequences will occur. Next they evaluate the relative importance of each of the anticipated favorable and unfavorable consequences, which represent their expected utility value from the point of view of the decisionmaker. The health belief model (Hochbaum, 1958) is essentially a subjective expected utility model, and correlational evidence from several studies provides partial support for its ability to describe how people decide whether or not to adhere to medical recommendations (Becker, 1976; Becker *et al.*, 1977). However, the model does not account for lengthy maladaptive delays in decisions to seek medical assistance among patients who have symptoms of a heart attack or cancer (Blackwell, 1973; Hackett and Cassem, 1974). Ignorance does not account for the majority of instances of procrastination. Rather, these behaviors seem like efforts to ward off anxiety by avoiding thinking about threatening cues. Conflict models seem better able to handle maladaptive patterns of coping with threat than do rational decision-making models.

Legal Decisions

Decision theory models have also been applied to understanding the legal decision-making process. Many of these current models, however, are based on evidence obtained only from laboratory experiments in which a relatively limited set of simulated decision problems have been used. As noted by Ebbesen and Konecni (1976), the majority of what are considered to be important results in the decision-making area has been obtained with procedures in which the decision task was to some extent already decomposed into the dimensions that were of primary interest to the researcher (cf. Slovic and Lichtenstein, 1971; Slovic, Fischhoff, and Lichtenstein, 1977). Even some of the applications of decision theory to real-world problems have used this procedure. For example, Keeny (1973) decomposed a decision problem, in this case the problem of distribution of fire engines in a city, such that the choice of alternatives made available to the client were presented as a list of attributes, each with an associated value and probability. This was done even though the original decision problem was described in a completely different manner and had to be decomposed by the investigator prior to presentation to the subject.

In order to determine the utility of these laboratory-based decision models, Ebbesen and Konecni have done a series of studies comparing laboratory simulations with real-world tasks. In a study of bail setting, Ebbesen and Konecni (1975) presented judges who had firsthand experience with bail setting with simulated cases and asked them to set bail in dollars exactly as they would if the case were a real one. The cues that the judges were to use in reaching their decisons were presented in decomposed form on a sheet of paper. Following a brief description of background information, which included the same charge for all cases, the following information was presented: (1) prior record; (2) the extent to which the accused was tied to the local area; (3) a dollar amount recommended by the district attorney; and (4) a recommendation by the defense attorney, also in dollars. A prior observation of actual bail hearings had showed the investigators that these cues were those that were typically presented to the judge prior to his decision, and that little other information was presented or otherwise available to the judge. The levels of the various cues were organized so that they formed a complete factorial design. An analysis of variance of the bail amount indicated that all but the defense attorney's recommendations had significant effects and that there were no interactions.

The local-ties variable accounted for significantly more variance than prior record or the district attorney's recommendation.

In the next experiment observers were trained to code unobtrusively the levels of the same variables operating in actual bail hearings presided over by the same judges used in the simulations. These judges were completely unaware that the observations were being made. Multiple regression analyses of the naturalistic data indicated that it was possible to account for almost all of the variance in the bail decisions with the same four factors manipulated in the simulation. However, quite a different pattern of results emerged: (1) The district attorney's recommendation accounted for the most variance; (2) local ties accounted for a nonsignificant portion of the variance; and (3) several interactions emerged. Even controlling for the range and interval spacing of the cues used in the simulation and the real studies, the district attorney's recommendation accounted for the most substantial portion of the predictable variance. The decision theory of Anderson (1971, 1974) provided a reasonable model for how the various pieces of information were weighed and averaged in both cases; however, different averaging models with different weights were required to explain the naturalistic and the simulation data.

In another study looking at parole decisions, Ebbesen and Konecni (1978) again found major differences as a function of procedure. The most important was the fact that in the real world the judges seemed to decide simply on the basis of the probation officer's recommendation. Case factors had their effects on the final outcome only indirectly by affecting the probation officer's recommendation. On the other hand, in simulation studies judges seemed to combine linearly crime, prior record, methods of guilt determination, and the probation officer's recommendation. A further study in a different context, this time looking at automobile-driver behavior, indicated that in driver decision making as well, experimental simulations appear to yield different results from those obtained from unobtrusive observation in decision situations actually involving risk (Ebbesen, Parker, and Konecni, 1977).

Carroll and coworkers, in a comparable series of studies (Carroll, 1978; Carroll and Payne, 1977a, 1977b), found that parole decision making differed from decision making in the context of sentencing, in addition to finding differences between variables important in lab simulations and real parole setting. The differences between sentencing and parole appear to arise from the fact that parole decisions are primarily predictive in nature, whereas sentencing decisions deal with punishment for past behavior.

Whether or not one believes that there can ultimately be better simulations that would lead to results more similar to the real-world context, it is certainly clear from these data that the specific decision strategies people use are very sensitive to a wide range of task and experience variables. According to Ebbesen and Konecni (1978), it is possible to argue from this evidence that simulation decision tasks do not reveal a few simple and basic processes, but that the really important processes "are to be found in the real world rather than in laboratory simulations, no matter how high the face validity of the latter might be" (p. 22). They argue that based only on laboratory research, rules of decision making that are highly generalizable are going to be very hard to discover, and that it will be impossible to utilize such basic rules to predict decisions in real-world tasks unless a great deal is known about the task and the decisionmaker prior to application of the rules, that is, unless real-world data have already been collected. This suggests that when one is given a real-world decision task with all of its naturally occurring complexity, the theory must be made to fit the task rather than vice versa.

Application of laboratory-based decision theories such as the Fishbein (1972) model to real-world data and applied problems has often challenged these theories and the bases on which they were developed, thus expanding and elaborating our conception of the decision-making process. Importantly these applied studies have also shown significant possibilities for major intervention. For example, Gottfredson, Wilkins, and Hoffman (1978) fed the results of their parole decision-making studies back to the decisionmakers in the form of a matrix that made explicit the factors and weights that had previously been the implicit bases of their judgments. Decisions made with the use of this information device were substantially more uniform than those made without it. The "guidelines" approach to structuring discretion has now become a major research-based approach to parole and sentencing reform (Monahan and Loftus, 1972).

SUMMARY AND CONCLUSIONS

Theories of schematic information processing have been expanded and changed as a result of their application to

questions regarding health behavior, population control, and judicial outcomes. For example, the experience of pain and stress depends in great part on how incoming sensory information is processed and interacts with extant relevant schema, and schemas that include affective experience and sensations may operate more strongly than or differently from those based only on cognitions. The applied data support the view that schemas are both malleable and resistant to change on the basis of new information. Which of these is more likely depends in part on how salient and/or affect-laden the new material is, but further research is greatly needed to specify other relevant parameters.

Some behaviors previously resistant to full understanding and intervention may be more completely analyzed by the adoption of an information-processing view. Noncompliance with medical recommendations and hysterical contagion are two such examples. Viewed in this way, not all instances of noncompliance are seen solely as poor motivation or malingering, but rather some are seen as the result of an active effort on the part of patients to engage in behavior that is most consistent with their own representations of danger.

One of the more fruitful outcomes of the application of various decision models to real-world problems has been the strong suggestion that these domains do not simply add a greater number of and/or more complex variables to decision equations. Rather they often challenge the fundamental principles on which these models are based. New decision theories, such as that of Janis and Mann (1977), emerging from and being tested by studies in applied settings are now beginning to be developed.

CONTROL

It has been argued that the desire to make decisions and affect outcomes, that is, to exercise control, is a basic feature of human behavior (Adler, 1930; White, 1959). Elaboration of the situational determinants of the motivation for control and the behavioral consequences of its presence or absence has been the subject of vigorous investigation in recent years. Distinctions among various types of control have been made. One of the most fruitful has been Averill's (1973) suggestion that control can be exercised behaviorally, decisionally, or cognitively. This trichotomy highlights the fact that outcomes can be modified by cognitive strategies as well as by behavior that directly influences or obtains a given outcome. This links the theoretical construct of control to other processes where appraisal plays an important role, as in stress and coping.

Closely tied to the concept of control is the notion of predictability. For example, if someone has control because she can bring about an outcome as a result of her own action, she is usually able to predict that outcome. Although control and predictability typically occur together, studies to disentangle the two have shown that variations in control have strong effects even when predictability is explicitly held constant (e.g., Geer, Davison, and Gatchel, 1970; Glass, Singer, Leonard, Krantz, Cohen, and Cummings, 1973).

At the moment there are at least two theories that attempt to explain the processes that lead to a perception of loss of control. According to Mandler (1975), the interruption of an integrated responses sequence, whether it is behavioral or cognitive, produces a state of arousal that develops into an emotional expression if alternative responses enabling completion or substitution are not present. Thus whenever an individual feels unable to complete an interrupted sequence and no alternative completion sequences are available, interruption causes stress and anxiety. Helplessness is an immediate response to this situation. If this builds up over a number of situations to a generalized feeling of not knowing what to do in any situation, it leads to hopelessness.

In contrast, Seligman (1975) views the frequent experience of noncontingency between one's actions and one's outcomes as a major cause of helplessness. Seligman proposes that learning that outcomes are uncontrollable is a major precursor to deleterious emotional and physical effects, both in animal and in human populations. The belief that one's outcomes are independent of one's actions, according to Seligman, generates a state of learned helplessness, which is accompanied by a loss of motivation to act, a reduction in learning ability, and emotional lability. Refinements of this formulation, (Abramson *et al.,* 1978) suggest that the occurrence of learned helplessness depends further on the manner in which one interprets the impending situation. In effect this line of argument suggests that there would be considerable variation in the degree to which one responds to loss of control with feelings of helplessness as a result of situational variables and attributional processes.

Not only do attributional processes affect the consequences of the loss of control, but according to some theoreticians (e.g., Kelley, 1967, 1971), attributional processes occur *because* the individual is motivated to attain cognitive control. This view proposes that attribution

processes are to be understood not only as a means of providing individuals with a physical view of their world but also as a means of encouraging and maintaining their effective exercise of control in the world. The purpose of causal analysis, the function that it serves, is effective control. The tendency for individuals to overestimate their degree of personal control over events that are objectively random (e.g., Langer, 1975; Wortman, 1975) is consistent with the assumption that they are motivated to believe that they are able to control their environment.

Much research has examined the effects of feeling in control on many domains of psychological and physiological functioning. This literature indicates that in general greater feelings of control have a positive impact on psychological well-being and physical health, and a diminished sense of control has undesirable consequences.

HEALTH

The relationship between loss of control and the onset of poor health has been the focus of substantial research in the recent decade. Stimulated by the early, intriguing work of Schmale and Iker (1966), many studies have pursued the question of how feelings of loss of control might be related to negative health outcomes and indeed might stand as a central mechanism in the etiology of disease. In the Schmale and Iker studies, psychiatrists examined a group of patients, all of whom had had suspicious cancerlike symptoms found in routine pap smear tests. At this point in time the cancer was only suspect. On the basis of psychiatric evaluation, patients were rated in regard to their feelings of control, helplessness, and hopelessness. Those who were high scorers were more likely actually to develop cancer. Of course from these data one could not tell whether hopelessness led to cancer or whether cancer, even before it was diagnosed, led to helplessness. But the data were suggestive and striking; when the theoretical construct of control became more firmly rooted in social psychological inquiry, these investigations gained more momentum with better-controlled designs and experimental procedures.

Type A Personality
Based on a study showing that pattern A men had more than twice the rate of heart disease during eight and a half years of follow-up than men originally judged to be pattern B (Roseman, Brand, Jenkins, Friedman, Straus, and Wurm, 1975), Glass and his coworkers (Glass, 1977) tried to explain this finding on the basis of control-

relevant processes. The Type A behavior pattern consists of such predispositions as competitive achievement striving and sense of time urgency and hostility—all of which can be elicited and observed primarily in the presence of appropriate environmental circumstances. Thus the Type A pattern is not a trait but rather a set of overt behaviors that is elicited from susceptible individuals by an appropriately challenging environment (Matthews, 1982).

In a variety of experimental tasks used by Glass and his associates, Type A's appeared to work hard to succeed, suppressed subjective states (e.g., fatigue) that might interfere with task performance, exhibited rapid pacing of their activities, and expressed hostility after being harrassed in their efforts at task completion. All of these, Glass (1977) asserts, are in the interest of exerting control over environmental demands and requirements—demands and requirements that must be at least minimally stressful for such effects to occur. A coronary-prone behavior pattern may thus be described as a characteristic style of responding to environmental stressors that threaten an individual's sense of control. Type A's are engaged in a struggle for control, whereas Type B's are relatively free of such concerns and hence free of characteristic pattern A traits.

If pattern A behavior is a strategy for coping with uncontrollable stress, enhanced performance reflects an attempt to assert and maintain control after its loss has been threatened. This interpretation receives support from experiments using a variety of techniques for inducing lack of control, including various partial-reinforcement procedures that were perceived as differentially uncontrollable. It may be that noncontingency has to be extremely salient, however, to produce these effects (Matthews, 1982). A series of reactance studies also presents evidence supporting the control interpretation of Type A behavior. If Type A's are more easily threatened by a loss of control than are Type B's, they should show more resistance to a coercive communication. Several studies have shown these hypothesized effects (Carver, 1980; Rhodewalt and Comer, 1982; Rhodewalt and Davison, 1983). The specific biological mechanisms by which these behavioral factors may lead to disease states will be reviewed later.

Life Change

Investigators have considered how control mediates the effects of major life changes on health. Glass (1977) compared hospitalized patients with nonhospitalized people in order to assess whether individuals who experience a series of uncontrollable, undesirable life events exhibit greater illness. He found that hospitalized patients reported more uncontrollable losses during the one-year period prior to hospitalization. Using both retrospective and prospective designs, Suls and his colleagues further considered how life events perceived as beyond one's personal control would be related to psychological and physiological distress and symptomatology (Mullen and Suls, 1982). In both domains uncontrollable events were related to future distress, but only if they were also undesirable. Uncontrollable positive events had no negative effects, suggesting an important modification of the view (Seligman, 1975) that exposure to all uncontrollable events, either positive or negative in nature, leads to stress and helplessness.

Medical Procedures

Illness itself may threaten a patient's sense of control. Since people generally see a health care professional only when they are ill, the difficulties and symptoms that lead them to seek professional help may diminish their feelings of control. The sensations and experiences they encounter may be unfamiliar and frightening, and they may be confused about how to make sense out of them or cope with them (Janis and Rodin, 1979). When people are confronted with physical illnesses, their ability to regulate their physiological processes may be threatened (Brody, 1980). When they are faced with psychological or psychiatric concerns, they may feel a lowered sense of efficacy in their ability to deal with their environment (e.g., Bandura, Adams, Hardy, and Howells, 1980). In both cases they may be having difficulties meeting the normal demands of daily living, such as holding a regular job and maintaining satisfactory interpersonal relationships. When people are well and not experiencing difficulties, they are less likely to be attuned to judging their degree of control in these domains. However, when they are ill and confronted with problems, vulnerable feelings centered around their personal efficacy and autonomy are likely to become more salient.

In addition to being threatened by the difficulties and symptoms that problems pose, individuals' feelings of control are likely to be threatened by the relationship with a practitioner. When they seek professional help, people are conveying the message that they do not have the competence to deal with their difficulties on their own. Furthermore health care practitioners have many sources of power over patients (Rodin and Janis, 1979);

for example, they possess information, skills, and expertise in health care that patients do not have, and they can and do exercise power on that basis. Thus patients and clients are likely to feel in a "one-down" position in relation to the professional (Barofsky, 1978; Brody, 1980).

In their relationships with health care practitioners, patients and clients typically see few areas in which they have control (Barofsky, 1978; Tagliacozzo and Mauksch, 1972). Parsons's (1951) classic conception of the doctor-patient relationship presents a model of patient behavior in which the patient assumes a passive, dependent role in regard to the doctor, who has most of the control over the interaction. In this model, patients are expected to seek and trust professional help and to cooperate fully with the prescriptions the professional makes. This type of relationship characterizes the traditional way in which health care practitioner–patient interactions are viewed (e.g., Brody, 1980; Hayes-Bautista, 1976; Stimson, 1974).

There is now a fair amount of empirical work testing the effects of control enhancement in medical settings. Some control interventions in the health domain give patients a great deal of preparatory information, including precise descriptions of expected reactions, medical procedures, and the like, as in Johnson's (1973) work in gastroendoscopy patients. These interventions enable patients to make plans for coping with the predicted stress, which can enhance feelings of control. The consequences of such preparation are to reduce significantly the degree of pain experienced, the need for medication following surgery, and the time needed for postoperative recovery (Johnson, 1973). Focusing attention on the task at hand may also increase control in other ways. For example, Pranulis, Dabbs, and Johnson (1975) found that patients had better reactions to anesthesia and surgery when their focus of attention was directed away from their own emotional reactions as passive recipients of treatment to specific tasks that made them feel more in control as active collaborators with the staff.

The value of directing the patient's attentional focus was directly tested in a study of the effectiveness of a cognitive reappraisal technique with surgical patients by Langer, Janis, and Wolfer (1975). Without encouraging the denial of realistic threats, their technique encouraged each patient to feel confident about being able to deal effectively with whatever pains, discomforts, and setbacks were subsequently encountered. The increased predictability and greater feelings of self-efficacy led to less distress, according to nurses' blind ratings, and to a decreased use of postoperative medication.

Other studies have shown similar beneficial outcomes by actually providing patients with the opportunity to have some degree of control. Work with breast cancer patients has shown that patients do better, as measured by rate of recovery from surgery, when they have had a two-stage surgical procedure as compared with those who have undergone a one-stage procedure (Taylor and Levin, 1976). The two-stage procedure allows time for orderly planning and evaluation prior to surgery or therapy and often includes active participation of the patient in the decision to resort to surgery. The patient's knowledge that she has a malignancy and her psychological preparation in advance for the removal of the breast, as well as her actual participation in the relevant planning and decision making, are likely to enhance her feelings of personal control.

In a field experiment Langer and Rodin (1976) assessed the effects of an intervention designed to encourage elderly nursing home residents to make a greater number of choices and to feel more in control of their day-to-day lives. The study was intended to determine whether the decline in health, alertness, and activity that generally occurs among the aged in nursing home settings could be slowed or reversed by giving them more responsibility for making daily decisions. The results indicated that residents in the group given more responsibility became more active and reported feeling less unhappy than a comparison group of residents that was encouraged to feel that the staff would care for them and try to satisfy their needs. In an eighteen-month follow-up (Rodin and Langer, 1977) it was found that during the period following the intervention the responsible patients showed a significantly greater improvement in health than patients in the comparison group. Even death rate was marginally different between the two groups, suggesting possible life-promoting effects of enhanced feelings of control.

Schulz (1976) also studied the consequences of variations in control and predictability in nursing home patients. Subjects in the control-enhanced condition were able to determine both the frequency and the duration of a series of visits that they received from college undergraduates. Two additional groups were given different forms of predictability over the visits, although they did not have control over frequency and duration, and the fourth group was a baseline-comparison group. The results of this study, in the short run, were comparable to those of Langer and Rodin (1976), showing significant improvements in activity, happiness, and alertness. However, in their follow-up Schulz and Hanusa (1978) found that persons who had previously improved in psychological and physical health status when an important positive event was made predictable and controllable for them exhibited significant decline after the study was terminated.

Schulz and Hanusa (1978) suggested that the interventions used by Rodin and Langer altered subjects' self-attributions regarding their ability to control outcomes in the institutional environment. The communication delivered to the experimental group, which emphasized their responsibility for themselves and their outcomes, probably encouraged subjects to make internal, stable, and global attributions. And as predicted by attribution theory, the gains evidenced by the experimental group persisted over time. On the other hand, in the Schulz (1976) study increased control could be attributed by subjects only to unstable factors, thus predicting why the impact of the intervention would be merely temporary. In addition subjects' expectations for controlling or predicting important events in their lives may have been raised by the interventions and then abruptly violated when the study terminated and the experimenters and visitors disappeared. Perhaps the decline might have been avoided if subjects were provided with substitute predictable or controllable events.

In another study (Rodin, 1983) elderly nursing home residents were specifically taught coping skills that enhanced their sense of personal control and increased dramatically the number of control-relevant behaviors that they were able to exercise. It was found that these subjects showed a significant reduction in feelings of stress, significant increases in problem-solving ability, and most strikingly, significant long-term reductions in corticosteroid level, an indicator of physiological stress. The reduction in corticosteroid level correlated significantly with increased feelings of control. Six months following this intervention, the coping-skills group showed substantial improvements in health.

Although it has been generally assumed that more information and self-reliance are better, questions still remain as to how much patients should be told (e.g., McIntosh, 1974) and how much self-care and responsibility are optimal (Linn and Lewis, 1979). Further complicating this issue is the likelihood that some individuals may benefit more than others from being highly informed about, or involved in, their own treatment.

Personality-based expectancies and beliefs about health and illness may determine the efficacy of patient-oriented approaches to health care.

In studies that made the patient a more active participant in treatment (Cromwell, Butterfield, Brayfield, and Curry, 1977), that heightened the patient's sense of choice (Mills and Krantz, 1979), or that provided for self-monitoring or self-care (Berg and LoGerfo, 1979), there appear to be substantial individual differences in reaction to these kinds of treatment interventions. Cromwell *et al.* (1977) found that heart patients given treatments congruent with their own control beliefs showed the best outcomes on several rehabilitation outcome measures. Several studies using health-specific locus-of-control measures (Lewis, Morisky, and Flynn, 1978; Wallston *et al.*, 1976) found that subjects in treatment conditions congruent with their control beliefs expressed more satisfaction and reported higher compliance with the medical regimen.

Krantz, Baum, and Wideman (1980) showed that two different attitudes toward treatment approaches can be measured reliably. The first, behavioral involvement, is concerned with attitudes toward self-care and an active role in medical care; and the second, information, is concerned with the desire to ask questions and be informed of and involved in medical decisions. These two components, which are relatively independent of one another, display a degree of specificity in their ability to predict behavior. For example, the information scale was associated with greater inquisitiveness in a medical setting, whereas the behavior involvement scale was not. On the other hand requests for specific medications and electing to choose medication were more highly correlated with scores on the behavioral involvement scale. It may be that individuals fare best when given treatments that are congruent with their usual coping styles.

ENVIRONMENTAL STRESSORS

Another important consideration of the possible stress-mediating effects of control has occurred in studies of environmental density and noise. While these stressors sometimes appear themselves to affect physical and mental health directly, there has been increasing evidence that many adverse effects are mediated by beliefs about the controllability of a stressful environment. In other words, the degree to which subjects believe they can control or escape from an environmental stressor may be a more important determinant of a stress response than the magnitude of the stressful stimulus itself. Studies by Glass and Singer (1972) and Sherrod (1974) suggest that noise and density have minimal impact upon behavior during the exposure. Rather, adverse effects are observed more typically after stressful stimulation is terminated. More important, the magnitude of the negative aftereffects varies as a function of controllability of the stressor during its presentation.

Several findings in the epidemiological literature concerning the effects of noise on health are amenable to the interpretation that a loss of control and/or a sense of helplessness affects this relationship. For example, to explain data indicating that those living in noisy slums were more likely to be admitted to a mental hospital than those not living in noisy areas, Herridge (1974) suggests that the mental stress of those exposed to prolonged noise was due more to feelings of helplessness than to the noise per se. This assertion is supported by data indicating that residents of noisy areas are less likely to complain about aircraft noise than residents of control areas. In other words, they may feel out of control with regard to their ability to escape or modify the noise. Of course it must be recognized that helplessness and feelings of loss of control may be aggravated by existing stresses associated with the social class and living conditions of areas in which noise and high density occur. It is for this reason that experimental studies of density and noise have been so important.

Experimental data on annoyance responses to noise suggest the importance of perceived lack of control and helplessness as mediating variables. Noise appears less annoying when the individual feels that those at the source of the noise are attempting to minimize its effects (Borsky, 1969). This result is similar to Glass and Singer's (1972) finding that those with access to a person with control are as unaffected by noise as those subjects who had control themselves. Annoyance is also minimized when there is less reason to be concerned about control, such as when people perceive that noise is important and feel that it is unlikely to harm their health (Borsky, 1969).

A similar analysis has been applied to the effects of density. Rodin (1976), for example, argued that high household density limits any single individual's opportunity for control and leads to decreased expectancies of a contingency between responses and outcomes. Subjects from high-density homes should therefore show less initiative and more dependence, compared with subjects from lower-density environments. Support for this no-

tion comes from studies showing that after controlling for race and socioeconomic status, and selecting only subjects all living in the same low-income housing unit, children living in crowded conditions were less likely to exercise their own choices when given an opportunity to do so. Children from high-density apartments were also more susceptible than their lower-density counterparts to experimental inductions of helplessness (Rodin, 1976).

The dormitory studies of Baum and his coworkers (Baum, Aiello, and Calasnick, 1978) provide further support for the hypothesis that control is a relevant dynamic of the experience of social density. People living in dormitories experienced as crowded (long-corridor dormitories) felt greater threats to their personal control than those living in dormitories not experienced as crowded (short-corridor dormitories). When these perceived threats to personal control occurred repeatedly and were apparently unsolvable, sequential phases of reactance and then helplessness were evident. Baum *et al.* argue, however, that in some instances the helplessness appeared to be adaptive, serving to make the individuals less stressed. Clearly context and task demands will determine whether helplessness (i.e., failure to respond) is adaptive or maladaptive.

In two experimental studies Rodin, Solomon, and Metcalf (1978) explicitly considered the hypothesis that variations in density may be especially likely to influence feelings of control and thus lead to the experience of crowding. In other words, people may label a dense situation as crowded because it affects their feelings of control. In the first study, with density held constant, subjects were randomly manipulated into positions where they had more or less control in a library elevator, determined by who had access to pushing the button. Subjects without control reported feelings more crowded than those with control. In the second study subjects randomly given greater control over a group's activities felt less crowded than those who could not exercise control, especially in a high-density setting. The results of both studies suggest that feelings of control, independent of density, influence feelings of crowding, although high density enhances the effect.

Stokols and Novaco (1980) considered whether control processes mediate commuters' well-being and the effects of different kinds of transportation systems on behavior and health, using a longitudinal field study. They proposed that the relationship between routine exposure to travel impedance, defined as distance and duration of travel, and personal well-being would be mediated by the perceived controllability of those domains. They found that conditions of travel impedance were associated with greater stress responses (e.g., physiological arousal, negative mood, and performance deficits), but the extent of these stress reactions was determined by personality variables and feelings of personal control. The subjective experience of commuting as negatively toned led to efforts actively to alter or otherwise cope with commuting demands, and successful efforts to cope with commuting demands enhanced perceptions of personal well-being.

Moos's (1980) research is interesting in light of the Stokols and Novaco (1980) analysis of environmental options for controllability, which suggests that perceived environmental quality depends on controllability of outcomes and the subjective importance of those goals on activities within the setting. Moos and his colleagues constructed a multiphasic environmental assessment procedure to assess institutional settings (Moos and Lemke, 1980). With this instrument they measure the environment and then examine the impact of environmental dimensions on individual and group outcomes. This approach makes it possible to specify the environmental factors that are related to particular outcome criteria. One of the dimensions measured was the opportunity for residents to determine their daily routine and to influence programs and policies.

In studies of housing units for the elderly, their analyses showed great variability in the opportunities for choice and control that were available to residents of ninety-three different settings. To explore the potential effects of variations in choice and control, they tried to predict the quality of the social environment and of resident functioning. Residents with better social and functioning resources and women residents were more likely to reside in settings high in choice and control. It may be, as other studies have shown, that people with more personal resources are better able to take advantage of environmental opportunities (Lawton and Nahemow, 1973; Schulz and Hanusa, 1980). Further, the relative lack of such choices as when to get up, go to bed, bathe, and eat, and whether to do their own personal laundry affected women more than men. This is probably because most of the elderly women living in group settings did not spend many of their hours outside their homes and were used to organizing their own pattern of daily activities (Bennett and Eisdorfer, 1975). Thus the impact of any one set of environmental resources on control needs to be studied in relation to the types of people for which it is provided,

as well as the general environmental context in which these people function.

Schulz and Brenner (1977) suggest that a sense of personal control may also be an important variable in mediating relocation outcomes. They argue that one's response to the stress of relocation is largely determined by the perceived controllability and predictability of the events surrounding the move, and differences in environmental controllability between pre- and postrelocation environments. Support for this model is found in numerous relocation studies, where mortality rates are typically used as dependent variables. Available findings, reviewed by Schulz and Brenner, indicate that the greater the perceived choice the individual has in being relocated, and the more predictable the environment is, the less negative the effects of relocation.

In an experimental study Krantz and Schulz (1980) found that enhancing the predictability of an institutional environment for new admissions to a long-term care center for the aged facilitated adaptation and decreased some of the physical and psychological deficits typically associated with relocation. Schulz and Hanusa (1980) note that in all of these studies, the impact on well-being is attributable to increases in control and not to absolute levels of control. In other words, individuals have expectations for controlling outcomes that are largely determined by their reference group. It is likely that just as absolute levels of control decline with age, so do expectations for control. Thus control effects, that is, positive or negative outcomes, should be expected on the basis of whether actual levels of control are discrepant from expected levels or, alternatively, when individuals undergo a change in level of control as they might as a result of experimental intervention. This analysis has important methodological implications. For example, it predicts that survey approaches investigating the relationship between environmental control and well-being may give little evidence of a relationship between these variables unless the survey is administered during or after some acute event that altered the individual's level of control.

A differentiated treatment of the concept of control provides a starting point for deriving the conditions under which environmental stressors will or will not have a range of adverse effects. Issues of personal control are also involved at many points in the process of coping with environmental stressors, since control determines whether and how one prepares for a stressor, how one responds when actually confronted with a stressor, and the delayed or cumulative costs of coping. Indeed these applied studies suggest an intimate relationship between control, self-efficacy, and coping. Control attempts are made in response to environmental challenges, and exercising control is a way of coping with them. Successful coping, in turn, enhances feelings of control.

INSTITUTIONS

Often institutions deprive adults of control over both their social and their physical environments by dictating where and with whom they interact. Such individuals are constrained not only by the absence of space and privacy but also by the feeling that they cannot control what happens to them. An analysis of prisons by Paulus and his coworkers (Paulus, Cox, McCain, and Chandler, 1975) holds that adverse effects of institutional density might be due as much to feelings of helplessness as to the direct impact of the crowded living conditions in prisons.

In another analysis of institutions Taylor (1979) focused on the hospital as a place where individuals forfeit control over virtually every task they customarily perform. She suggests that loss of control helps depersonalize the patient and that people react to such depersonalization by assuming either good-patient or bad-patient behavior (cf. Lorber, 1975)—the former associated with depression and helplessness and the latter with anger and reactance. She argues that both helplessness and reactance produce physiological, cognitive, behavioral, and affective consequences that can directly interfere with the course of recovery, and that helplessness and reactance in patients evoke reactions in hospital staff that also have undesirable consequences for patients and thus indirectly affect their health as well. Thus far there is little research that has addressed the issue of predicting who will show which reaction to hospitalization. These compelling analyses merit direct empirical testing.

LEGAL PROCEDURES

Assuming that individuals desire control because it enables them to obtain predictable and satisfactory outcomes, Thibaut and his coworkers have considered how people view legal procedures that vary the types of control available in methods of dispute resolution (Houlden, LaTour, Walker, and Thibaut, 1978; LaTour, Houlden, Walker, and Thibaut, 1976; Thibaut, Walker, and Lind, 1972). They first demonstrated that various methods of dispute resolution could be classified along the dimension of either amount of third party or amount of disputant control over the settlement of the conflict (LaTour *et al.*, 1976). The results showed an ordering from most to least third party control of autocratic, arbitration, moot, mediation, and bargaining types of conflict resolution procedures. All of these are processes of procedural justice, that is, processes by which distribution of outcome are determined. Thibaut and Walker (1975) suggest that the most important determinant of procedural justice, in fact, is the manner in which personal control is distributed among the parties in a dispute resolution procedure.

In an experimental study (LaTour, 1978) subjects participated in one of four conflict resolution procedures. In all procedures the final decision rested with a third party and was to be binding. Three of the four procedures, however, varied systematically with respect to the amount of third party control over the process of evidence presentation. The results showed that both satisfaction and perceived fairness increased monotonically as third party process control decreased. Given that perceived fairness is highly correlated with preference (Thibaut, Walker, LaTour, and Houlden, 1974), the results of this study provide support for a negative relationship between disputant preference and third party control over the presentation of evidence. A study by LaTour *et al.* (1976b) in fact suggested that disputants generally preferred procedures that placed control over the presentation of evidence in their own hands but left the decision to a third party.

Houlden *et al.* (1978) suggest that litigants demand shared control over the process of evidence presentation because it enables each of them to present his or her case in as favorable a light as possible. However, in the presence of conflict, litigants will not attempt to maximize outcomes by sharing decision control. In all probability, if litigants were to do this they would be unable to resolve their conflict but would instead endlessly veto each other's recommendations. The resulting lack of settlement might easily be as unsatisfactory as an unfavorable solution. When a third party possesses decision control, litigants can gain indirect control of the final outcome if they control the process of evidence presentation. In order to affect the third party decision, however, litigants must be free to present their case and, as they hope, to persuade the third party that they have the more legitimate claim.

On the other hand third parties might prefer procedures that give them both high process and high decision control. To a litigant a good outcome would be winning a dispute, but it seems reasonable that to a third party a good outcome would be a fair and just settlement. In the Houlden *et al.* (1978) study, subjects were asked to role play either litigants or third party to a dispute involving high conflict of interest. Both litigants and third parties most preferred the procedure that provided low third party presentation control and high third party decision control. This procedure corresponds to arbitration. Arbitration is particularly attractive to third parties because it enables them to make a binding decision. It is more strongly preferred than the procedure with high decision control and high process control because third parties apparently recognize, as do litigants, the necessity for providing a full presentation of the evidence relative to a particular dispute. However, the choice must depend on the type of case. In this experiment the case was a civil dispute between two brothers over the disposition of property provided by their father's will. Clearly other types of cases might lead to different kinds of choices. Further, the studies conducted by Thibaut and his colleagues need replication and expansion in applied settings. Their distinction between process control and decision control appears to be potentially quite fruitful.

SUMMARY AND CONCLUSIONS

There has been considerable enthusiasm among social psychologists for the notion that gains and losses in perceived control mediate the effects of a variety of possible stressors, including ill health, noise, density, and institutional demands. Within a surprisingly broad range greater control does increase positive effects in these domains, and decrements in control relate to negative effects.

In working with variations in control over major life concerns, it has become clear that the impact on well-being is attributable to perceptible increases and decreases in control and not to absolute levels of control. People's expectations for control form a baseline from which to predict the effects of changes in control. Since subjects' expectations for control are often quite low in laboratory settings, studies have had to contrive quite strenuous and often artificial restrictions in control in order to obtain effects. Interestingly, more subtle and smaller threats to control have often been shown to have large effects in applied settings.

In general, environmental controllability appears to be important not only in determining individual responses to stressors but also in specifying population groups most likely to show health-related reactions to stressful events. By this line of reasoning, environmental stressors are most likely to affect subpopulations already unable to control their outcomes (Cohen, Glass, and Phillips, 1978). Thus those in institutions, those with low income and low levels of education, and the young and very old are especially likely to show adverse reactions to a particular stressor. An important implication of this analysis is that the health of those living in stressful environments (e.g., living in high density or with excessive noise) can be improved not only by changing their environment but also by changing their attitudes toward their environment or their feelings of control. This was the basis for the procedures used by Langer and Rodin (1976) and Schulz (1976) in their nursing home studies. Cohen *et al.* (1978) suggest another technique—providing people with opportunities to terminate, periodically escape from, or at least modify unwanted stimulation, which may ameliorate the negative consequences of physical stressors. Indeed increased control over other areas of people's lives, as their review shows, results in less pronounced responses to stressors such as noise.

Aspects of the interaction between the environment and the individual may also affect the desirability of control in yet another way. Lawton (1975) has described the relationship between individual competence and environmental press, with *press* defined as the demand quality of an environment. Positive behavior or affect occurs, according to Lawton, when the individual's level of competence is adequate to deal with the press level of a given environment. This theory suggests that environmental context should be a limiting factor on the effectiveness of control-relevant interventions aimed at the individual. In a very constrained environment such as an institution, person-oriented interventions may have to be supplemented with changes in the environment for maximal benefit to the individual. Rodin and Langer (1977) noted that in their study the setting had provided the opportunity for control, and they worked on changing the individual's predisposition to exercise that control. If the setting had been antagonistic or suppressive, raising the individual's desire for control might have had negative rather than positive effects.

Even though most studies have indicated that perceived control has positive effects, some studies have found that having control can be stress inducing and that people do not always find control desirable (cf. Averill, 1973; Thompson, 1981). Indeed there are compelling data suggesting that some of the effects of stress on health may be mediated by the negative costly consequences of attempts to cope with or control that stress. For example, smoking and drinking are coping strategies that themselves may be damaging to health. Moreover, the clear poststimulation effects of environmental stressors that occur following prolonged exposure in naturalistic settings are most likely, either directly or indirectly, caused by the process of coping with stress (cf. Cohen, 1980). As a result it is necessary to specify the conditions under which perceived control is desirable and has a beneficial impact, and the circumstances under which it might not be positive. These issues are especially important before control-relevant manipulations are applied to consequential life situations. Averill (1973) concluded that the meaning of the control response for the individual, influenced largely by the context in which it is embedded, determines whether or not personal control will be stress reducing. Miller (1979) and Thompson (1981) propose that the beneficial effects of control arise because control may change the meaning of an event from one that is potentially unendurable to one that is within the limits of one's endurance. From this hypothesis it can be predicted that if a controllable event is still seen as unendurable, stress will not be lowered.

Conditions such as felt responsibility, information, and individual dispositional traits may also influence the desirability of control. Having control over a situation is likely to raise a person's perception of responsibility for the outcome. If the amount of felt responsibility is raised too high, having control may be seen as undesirable (Rodin, Rennert, and Solomon, 1980). In medical settings, for example, it is sometimes reported that patients do not want to participate in major decisions affecting them. It is possible that these individuals may feel that the responsibility placed upon them is too great.

Most important, in operationalizing the construct of control in the real world, it is necessary to distinguish whether people believe that they have the opportunity to exercise control in a given situation and whether they perceive that they have the skills necessary to exercise the control effectively. On the one hand the opportunity may exist to exercise control in a given situation, but the person may feel that she or he does not have the ability to take advantage of that opportunity. On the other hand a person may feel that she or he has the skills to exercise control in a given situation, but the situation does not allow for anyone to exercise control. Thus feeling of self-efficacy may be one of the factors that determine whether or not greater control is desirable (Schorr and Rodin, 1982).

COMPETENCE

The concept of social competence has special importance for the study of adaptive functioning in all people. This concept refers to the effective participation of the person in the activities of his or her society, which is intimately related to the construct of control. The notion of social competence views people as active and self-regulating rather than as passive and merely reactive. Social competence is not a trait but a response to specific situational demands (Wrubel, Benner, and Lazarus, 1978). Increasing feelings of competence may enhance people's feelings of efficacy (Bandura, 1977).

In some cases people may engage in behaviors that appear surprising at first blush in order to maintain their feelings of efficacy and competence. Berglas and Jones (1978) consider the use of self-handicapping tendencies as a reflection of a basic uncertainty concerning how competent one is. They define such strategies as any action or choice of performance setting that enhances the opportunity to externalize or excuse failure and to internalize and reasonably accept credit for success. As an example, they suggest that alcohol use may be viewed as a self-handicapping strategy. They hypothesize that alcoholics generally have problems with feelings of competence and are willing even to forego success to protect their feelings of competence. Use of alcohol imposes a performance barrier, and this leads to partial avoidance of personal responsibility for failure. Success, if it occurs despite the drinking problem, can readily be attributed to the self and thus enhances positive feelings. The inference that ability is the most likely potential cause of successful performance is augmented by the presence of alcohol. On the other hand the individual is able to discount the role of the self as a cause of failure if there is another salient plausible cause—the alcohol. Therefore drinking may be protective, serving the maintenance of a threatened sense of competence. Regardless then of what the performance outcome is, the self-handicapper cannot lose.

Some other examples of self-handicapping are getting too little sleep or underpreparing for an examination, exaggerating the effects of illness or injury, or in general embracing impediments and plausible performance handicaps. Self-handicapping appears to protect feelings of competence by maintaining the precarious illusion of control. Berglas and Jones (1978) suggest that individuals who use self-handicapping may paradoxically deliberately run the risk of being out of control through alcohol or drug use or inadequate preparation. The basic purpose behind such strategic choices is the control of the actor's self-attribution of competence.

Two laboratory experiments were designed to test the proposition that self-handicapping strategies (in this case, the choice of a performance-inhibiting drug) are linked to a recent history of noncontingent success. Noncontingent success was created by giving subjects successful feedback following their attempts to offer solutions to insoluble problems. Then drugs were provided that were expected either to facilitate intellectual performance or to inhibit or disrupt actual performance, and subjects were instructed to choose which drug and which dosage level they wished to take in anticipation of another round of problems. It was found that male subjects chose a performance-inhibiting drug in a condition in which they had just experienced noncontingent success, which was apparently based substantially on luck. While the data remain to be tested in a field setting, the results make more tenable the proposition that alcohol and certain forms of drug use may be facilitated by prior experiences of success unaccompanied by subjective feelings of mastery and control. Such experiences promote strategies designed to protect ill-gotten performance gains and a fragile but positive competence image.

Intervention studies of individuals with substance abuse problems, such as smoking or heavy alcohol use, as well as problems of anxiety, depression, or sexual dysfunction, are able to show great improvement in self-management when feelings of competence and control are dealt with explicitly as part of the intervention procedure (Marlatt and Gordon, 1980; Rehm, 1982; Rodin, 1978, 1983). Clinical treatments based on teaching self-regulation skills have shown strongly that competence can be viewed as a response to specific situational demands, which also makes generalization possible (Karoly and Kanfer, 1982).

SUMMARY AND CONCLUSIONS

More empirical work is needed in field settings to determine the validity of self-handicapping as a competence-maintaining strategy. Clinical studies designed to develop skills of self-regulation suggest that maintaining feelings of competence is an essential component of self-management. Thus it is likely that when future control is important, a variety of strategies, including self-handicapping, will be used.

SELF-ESTEEM

Consideration of the variables that influence the development and maintenance of self-esteem was one of the earliest applications of social psychology to real-world issues. Social psychologists argued that interethnic prejudice, minority self-esteem, and minority academic performance were interrelated in a vicious cycle. In a widely cited study (e.g., Clark and Clark, 1947) projective tests given to children had led to the conclusion that discrimination, prejudice and segregation were important factors in harming black children's self-esteem. They found that black children as young as three years old were already convinced that being black was not a good thing, as seen in their rejection of black dolls in favor of white ones, which they thought to be prettier and generally superior. Desegregation was expected to break this cycle, since being separated and deemed inferior was shown to lower blacks' self-esteem (Stephan, 1978). As a result black students' expectations for success were reduced, hurting their academic achievement. This increased blacks' prejudice, as they turned out their frustrations onto whites. It also reinforced whites' prejudice, as they attributed blacks' poor performance to their abilities, and felt and feared blacks' hostility.

SCHOOL DESEGREGATION

With the advent of desegregation in the late 1950s, minority children, no longer separated and branded as second rate, were expected to show improvements in their self-esteem and thus in their motivation and achievement. Longitudinal studies such as the work of Gerard and Miller (1975) showed, however, that long after schools were desegregated, children tended not to integrate but to stay together in their own ethnic groups. Moreover, anxiety increased and self-esteem remained low long after desegregation occurred. These trends were echoed in the majority of the studies, and the most careful scholarly reviews of research showed few, if any, benefits of desegregation on self-esteem (cf. McConahay, 1978, 1981; St. John, 1975; Stephan, 1978). Even more distressing, there was some evidence of harm.

According to Stephan's (1978) review of ten studies that measured the self-esteem of minority children following desegregation, none found a significant increase. On the contrary, in 25 percent of them desegregation was followed by a significant decrease in the self-esteem of young minority children. The Gerard and Miller (1975) study also showed that the minority students continued to have less favorable self-concepts and greater self-ideal discrepancies. Further, the minority child was more likely to derogate his or her ability in the face of failure. Gerard and Miller (1975) had assumed that following desegregation, social influence would occur such that the norms of conduct, beliefs, and values of the majority would influence the minority. Therefore they expected desegregation to increase the minority child's self-esteem. In retrospect their initial hypothesis seems incorrect, since there is little reason to assume from the social psychological literature that changes in self-esteem would occur on the basis of normative influences. Self-esteem seems a process variable rather than a norm, and therefore not something that is transmitted by association with individuals of higher self-worth.

These studies and many others like them show that while contact per se was the first step, it was clearly not enough as far as changing self-esteem was concerned. Rather, certain preconditions needed to be satisfied before there were advantageous effects of desegregation on self-esteem, performance, and prejudice. One precondition appeared to be an alteration in the interaction structure of the desegregated classroom (Aronson and Bridgeman, 1979; Aronson *et al.,* 1978).

According to the analyses of Aronson and his co-workers, interdependent groups should have a more beneficial effect on participants' feelings of self-esteem in a newly desegregated classroom than groups where the children's outcomes remained more independent. They reasoned that self-esteem is the evaluative component of the self-concept and can be defined as the amount of "worthiness" that the person perceives him- or herself to possess. Evidence about one's worthiness is provided by two main sources: the individual's interpersonal attraction and the person's experiences, accomplishments, and abilities. Thus self-esteem could be viewed as having an outer component resulting from social comparison processes and the appraisals of relevant others, and an inner component developing from objective data pertaining to successes or failures in one's interactions with the environment (Franks and Marolla, 1976). These two dimensions of self-esteem were hypothesized to develop from children's interpretations of feedback from teachers and classmates, as well as from their own learning experiences.

Aronson and Osherow (1980) argued that in the traditional, competitive classroom there are some students who succeed, attribute their success to their own abilities, and expect to do well in the future. For these students, who develop high self-esteem, there is better performance and achievement, which reciprocally elevates their self-esteem further. But most children do not have as many success experiences in the competitive classroom, especially if they are minority children. In the cooperative classroom the children have more opportunity to experience positive outcomes and to receive support from their group mates. As hypothesized, the students in the cooperative, experimental classroom increased in self-esteem to a significantly greater extent than those in the competitive classes. Indeed there is some evidence that the control students actually decreased in self-esteem.

In a subsequent study Geffner (1978) showed that relative to the traditional classroom, cooperative conditions enhanced the students' self-image regarding their social interactions and their scholastic abilities, and in fact even generalized to increase their confidence in their athletic ability and family interactions. It seems likely that having more success experiences and getting more feedback and support led to the generalized improvement in self-esteem and greater feelings of competence. While the students also significantly improved in achievement, the analyses did not allow causal inferences to be made about the relationship between changes in self-esteem and changes in actual performance.

AGING

In a different line of investigation Rodin and Langer (1980) attempted to describe how negative labeling and stigmatization of the elderly might contribute to behavior that actually confirmed prevalent stereotypes of old age and led to lowered self-esteem. They hypothesized that if stereotypes and social labels are simply summaries of cultural expectations, such expectations might be assumed to affect all members of the culture, including those about whom the labels are held. If one's self-image comes to portray these negative stereotypes (cf. Kelley, 1967; Snyder and Swann, 1978), self-esteem should decline. Several studies showed this to be the case and suggested how a change in negative stereotypes and self-labeling might reduce the negative effects on self-esteem (Rodin and Langer, 1980).

Rodin and Langer's (1980) aging studies show that as self-esteem decreases, belief in one's ability to exercise control over the environment also declines. They suggest that the ultimate consequences of these processes may have profound physiological implications. Thus there is the possibility that feelings of self-esteem and/or resultant behaviors may impact on physical processes influencing health and well-being. To date, however, no empirical data have shown a direct relationship between changes in self-esteem and changes in health or achievement performance.

PERSONAL RELATIONSHIPS

Self-esteem may also be lowered by the impact of ambiguous feedback from other people (Wortman and Dunkel-Schetter, 1979). With time, people may come to internalize the views that they perceive others hold and begin to feel shame, guilt, self-blame, self-derogation, and even self-hatred. Wortman and Dunkel-Schetter (1979) suggest how this may occur when people have serious, debilitating illnesses or experiences such as rape that may increase the likelihood of receiving ambiguous or negative feedback from their social supports. Ultimately the self-doubt and loss of self-esteem that result from disruption of one's social relationships can greatly contribute to the person's distress.

Providing negative or ambiguous feedback is not the only way that social supports may have negative effects on self-esteem. People who receive aid and support may experience it as evidence of failure, inferiority, and dependency, which threatens their self-esteem, especially when the aid giver is a similar rather than a dissimilar other (Fisher and Nadler, 1974). People who have high self-esteem therefore appear more disturbed by the receipt of assistance than low self-esteem persons (Suls, 1982). Given that friends and peers are most likely to be one's comparison others, assistance from members of one's social network may engender threat and lowered self-esteem (Suls, 1982). People who are ill or otherwise in need are quite likely to be fluctuating in self-regard. To the extent that the patient is feeling good about him- or herself, the receipt of aid may be threatening, whereas to the extent that he or she feels negative self-regard, the aid may not be perceived as a threat. These circumstances place the individual in a virtually no-win situation (Suls, 1982).

It could be seen as somewhat surprising that the above analyses show how vulnerable people are to large decrements in self-esteem, given that there also appear to be strong forces operating for self-esteem maintenance. The significant variable, perhaps, is the extent and duration of the events and circumstances that threaten one's self-esteem. One could conjecture a process in which small threats of small duration to self-esteem lead to increased and vigorous efforts at self-esteem maintenance, but with greater challenges and more time, decline becomes more evident. It is for this reason that work in applied settings on people with problems of substantial consequence and duration has been so important.

Recent studies of the role of self-esteem maintenance in personal relationships have been done by Cialdini *et al.* (1976), Tesser and Smith (1980) and Salovey and Rodin (in press). Cialdini *et al.* showed that there is the tendency to bask in reflected glory in order to promote self-esteem maintenance. They found that people whose self-esteem has temporarily been lowered are more likely to bask in the reflected glory of other people by identifying themselves as similar than are those who have not had their self-esteem lowered. Tesser argued that this should only be true when the performance of the other is not relevant to the individual. Relevance refers to the extent to which the other's performance is on a dimension that is self-defining for the person, that is, critical for his or her own definition of self-worth and self-esteem. The relevance of the other's performance increases the importance of comparison processes relative to reflection processes in self-esteem maintenance. Salovey and Rodin (in press) found that self-relevant information that was in the form of negative feedback led to jealous affect and behavior if the other person received positive feedback in the domain that was relevant to the actor. All three conditions—self-relevant feedback, constituting negative information, and a successful other person perceived as similar to the actor—were necessary for the experience of jealousy.

Tesser (1980) considered how this line of reasoning relates to interactions in families where in many cases the performance of one sibling is relevant to the other's self-definition. Although the work is preliminary at this point, it suggests that where relevance and closeness are high, differential performance effects may be very important, and one strategy used to enhance self-esteem by the sibling who comes out lower is to reduce his identification with his sibling, in that way changing the relevance. In addition the sibling may attempt to diminish the other's performance in the interest of his or her own self-esteem. The important prediction, confirmed by the Tesser (1980) and Salovey and Rodin (in press) studies, is that this should be the case only on high-relevance tasks and not on low-relevance tasks. Tesser also investigated the relationships between famous sons and their brothers and fathers, again examining the situational variables of relevance, closeness, and performance. Although these are only correlational data based on historical analyses, they support Tesser's line of reasoning and allow us some insight into family interaction patterns that go beyond Freudian sibling rivalry notions by examining situational variables that promote or reduce such rivalry, and the process—self-esteem maintenance—that it serves.

SUMMARY AND CONCLUSIONS

The study of self-esteem enhancement and reduction when a person is facing serious life concerns has shown several social and psychological processes that threaten and maintain self-esteem. First, it is clear that self-esteem does not change simply on the basis of normative influence and therefore is not something transmitted by association with individuals of higher self-worth. Instead the person must actively engage in favorable social comparison processes and receive feedback regarding the bases for his or her successes and failures in interacting with the environment. If the person receives continuously negative or ambiguous feedback, favorable comparison processes are unlikely to occur, and lower self-esteem might be expected. Groups that are stigmatized or about whom negative stereotypes are prevalent, such as blacks, old people, and the handicapped, appear lower in self-esteem because of these processes. Despite possible efforts at self-esteem maintenance, people who are exposed to large threats to self-esteem of long duration appear especially vulnerable. Applied studies describing the important causal variables have led to fruitful intervention strategies as well as greater conceptual clarity regarding the process of self-esteem change.

PHYSIOLOGICAL CONSEQUENCES OF SOCIAL PSYCHOLOGICAL PROCESSES

Research in the last decade has shown strikingly that psychosocial factors influence somatic health and illness. Certainly we have recognized recently that many medical problems, including some of the most common in modern society (e.g., heart disease and cancer) appear to be influenced by psychosocially determined variables, such as habits of living, smoking, diet, exercise, and what has been termed "psychosocial stress." Krantz, Glass, Contrada, and Miller (1981) have indicated three broad categories of variables linking psychosocial processes to physical illness.

1. *Direct psychophysiological effects.* These effects involve alterations in tissue function directly via neuro-endocrine and other physiological responses to psychosocial stimuli (Levi, 1979; Rose, 1980). This mechanism encompasses bodily changes without the intervention of external agents such as cigarette smoking or dietary risk factors, although the two sets of variables may produce interactive effects. Stress is a prime example of such a psychosocial variable.

Physiological responses to stress include neuroendocrine activity, which can in turn influence a wide range of bodily processes, including metabolic rate, cardiovascular and autonomic nervous system functioning, and altered immune reactions. Short-term stress responses include hormonal and cardiovascular reactions (e.g., increased heart rate and blood pressure), which may precipitate clinical disorders (e.g., stroke, cardiac instabilities, and pain syndromes) in predisposed individuals. If stimulation becomes pronounced, prolonged, or repetitive, the result may be dysfunction of one or more systems (e.g., the gastrointestinal tract or the cardiovascular system). The link between stress and disease is not simple, however. It depends on the context in which the stressful agent occurs, how individuals appraise it, and the social and personal resources available to them. As discussed earlier, research has shown that a variety of social and psychological factors (e.g., styles of coping, social supports provided by others) act to modify or buffer the impact of stress on illness (Cobb, 1976; Cohen, 1979; Cohen and Lazarus, 1979).

2. *Effects of habits and lifestyle on health.* A second category includes health-impairing habits and lifestyle, which play a critical role in the development of many serious diseases, as documented by the recent Surgeon General's (1979a, 1979b) report on cigarette smoking and health promotion and disease prevention. Cigarette smoking is probably the most salient behavior in this category, having been implicated as a risk factor for three leading causes of death in the United States—heart disease, cancer, and stroke. However type of diet, lack of exercise, and poor health practices (such as hygiene) have also been linked to disease outcomes. These habits may be initiated and influenced by social processes (e.g., smoking to attain peer approval) and maintained as part of an achievement-oriented lifestyle.

3. *Effects of specific health-care behavior.* Still another process through which psychosocially determined behavior leads to physical illness occurs when individuals minimize the significance of symptoms, delay in seeking medical care, or fail to comply with treatment or rehabilitation regimens. An example of this is provided by the sizable number of heart attack patients who procrasti-

nate in seeking help, or the numerous hypertension patients who fail to take the necessary medication. Some aspects of all medical therapies require that patients follow physicians' advice, and an extensive literature reports disturbingly low rates of compliance with health and medical care regimens (Haynes *et al.,* 1979). Accordingly there has been considerable research on the social and psychological processes involved in patients' reactions to pain and illness, their decision to seek medical care, and their medical compliance. This work has led to the development of interventions that have been applied to treatment and rehabilitation settings.

Each of these three broad categories of variables has led to active research efforts linking psychosocial processes to physical illness and health. Some studies have looked at disease states as outcome variables, and phases of disease as organizing points. Such studies focus on factors related to disease etiology, prevention, detection, diagnosis, treatment, and rehabilitation and specify the social psychological processes that affect these outcomes. I have reviewed several of these studies here, for example, those dealing with social supports, attributional processes, control, and self-efficacy. Other research projects have focused on one of these mediators in order to describe how it might potentially influence several different diseases. A second approach has been to focus on a single health condition and identify the multitude of interactive variables and processes that may account for the condition, for example, our own work in obesity.

STRESS

Let us consider first the role of the most widely investigated social psychological factors in the etiology and pathogenesis of a variety of diseases—stress. The problem with the concept of stress is that it is not yet clearly defined, despite the fact that it has been used so widely (Elliott and Eisdorfer, 1982). Selye (1950, 1976) first popularized the notion of stress, which he defined as the body's nonspecific physiological response to noxious agents or stressors. However, more recent use (Lazarus, 1971; Mason, 1971) has taken exception with this theory and argued that the body's response varies with the particular type of stressor and the context in which the stressor occurs. Certainly this provides a more specific and refined notion of stress, but the concept is still often used too loosely. It is probably most appropriate at this time to define psychological stress as the perception

of threat, or psychic or physical harm. And closely associated with that idea is the process of coping, which refers to the cognitive and behavioral activity through which individuals mobilize their resources in an effort to eliminate or reduce threat.

Gastrointestinal Disorders

Most studies of stress and gastrointestinal disease relate to peptic ulcers. Cobb and Rose (1973), for example, found that peptic ulcers occurred nearly twice as often among air traffic controllers as among civilian copilots, and more frequently among air controllers working at high-stress control centers than among those at low-stress centers. Such studies of course cannot prove a causal relationship between stressors and disease, but they point out the need for further study of the factors that mediate ulcer formation in such settings. Animal work suggests that uncontrollable stress, in particular, leads to increased acid secretion. If this secretion occurs over a sufficiently long time, peptic ulcers develop (Weiss, 1968, 1971). A comparable mechanism is hypothesized for humans.

Cardiovascular Disease

Studies of the effects of stress on cardiovascular disease have been particularly productive. This research falls into three broad, somewhat overlapping areas: atherosclerosis and its sequelae, arrythmogenesis and sudden cardiac death, and hypertension. Most stress-related studies of predisposing factors for atherosclerosis relate to the Type A behavior pattern. Studies have shown repeatedly that people with Type A characteristics have a much higher incidence of heart attacks than do Type B people (Rosenman, 1978).

Certain biochemical, physiological, and anatomical phenomena may be associated with fully developed Type A behavior, although different measures of Type A appear to be related to different biological responses (Matthews, 1982). Associations include elevated blood concentrations of cholesterol, triglycerides, and glucocorticoids; a greater insulin response to glucose; increased severity of coronary artery lesions; and greater lability and magnitude of blood pressure and catecholamine responses to time demand tasks (Glass, 1977). Catecholamine (epinephrine and norepinephrine) discharge is believed to induce many of the pathogenic states associated with psychological stress, including increased blood pressure and heart rate, elevation of blood lipids, acceleration of the rate of damage to the inner areas of coronary arteries over time, and induction of myocardial lesions, as well as provocation of ventricular arrhythmias believed to lead to sudden death.

Research has shown greater urinary norepinephrine secretion during the work day (Rahe, Rubin, and Arthur, 1974) and greater plasma norepinephrine responses to competition and stress (Friedman, Byers, Diamant, and Roseman, 1975) among Type A's as compared with Type B's. Other studies (Glass *et al.,* 1980a, 1980b) indicate higher elevation in plasma epinephrine among Type A individuals when both A and B subjects were exposed to a hostile competitor or to the stress of working simultaneously at two demanding tasks.

Sudden cardiac death encompasses a wide variety of phenomena that have in common the production of rapid, unexpected cardiac death (Buell and Eliot, 1982). Some research suggests that acute stress is associated with sudden cardiac death. For example, Rahe *et al.* (1974) interviewed relatives of sudden cardiac death victims, using survivors of myocardial infarctions as controls. Those who died had experienced more major life changes than those who lived, especially in the areas of work and relationships with family and friends. The few prospective studies available support these conclusions, but with very small sample sizes (e.g., Theorell, Lind, and Floderus, 1975).

Epidemiological studies have repeatedly shown correlations between hypertension and psychosocial variables that seem to have stressful quality in common (Henry and Stephens, 1972). However, experimental studies showing a link between stress and hypertension are surprisingly weak.

Immune Disorders

Studying the effects of stress on immunity represents a new area of research (Ader, 1981). Currently, immune-related disorders are thought to be affected by psychological stressors (e.g., rheumatoid arthritis and infectious diseases [Solomon and Amkraut, 1981]). In one study (Kasl, Evans, and Niederman, 1979), for example, a class of military cadets was studied retrospectively. About one-fifth of these cadets per year became infected with infectious mononucleosis, and when a quarter of this group went on to develop the clinical disease, psychosocial factors that increased the risk of clinical disease among those infected included having a high level of motivation but doing poor academic work and having overachieving fathers.

Research is beginning to uncover mechanisms through which psychosocial stressors might alter immune function in humans. Bartrop, Lazarus, and Luckhurst (1977) found that bereavement depressed lymphocyte function independently of other hormonal responses. Schleifer, Keller, McKegney, and Stein (1980) have shown that a reduction in T and B cell function can be clearly demonstrated two months following bereavement in otherwise healthy men. This study was a prospective design in which the spouses of metastatic breast cancer patients were studied prior and subsequent to their bereavement. In addition to these demonstrations that bereavement is associated with decreased lymphocyte function, a similar decrement in immunocompetence was observed in astronauts in the Skylab program for the first three days of the postflight period (Rimzey, Ritzman, Mangel, *et al.,* 1975). Some recent research suggests that the relationship between psychosocial stress and cancer may also be mediated by the effects of the central nervous system on the immune system (Ader, 1981).

Diabetes

Unlike the diseases considered thus far, it appears that the onset of diabetes is not especially influenced by stress-related factors (Johnson, 1980). But these factors appear to have a profound effect on the course of diabetes. A higher incidence of disturbance in families with poor diabetes control has been reported (Delbridge, 1975; Koski and Kumento, 1977). Minuchin and his colleagues have attempted to develop a model describing the interrelationship of stressful family interaction and chronic illness, suggesting that psychosocial factors may influence diabetes in two ways. First, emotional disturbance may result in behavior problems, such as refusing to take insulin and eating inappropriately, which can have metabolic consequences; or second, emotional disturbance may cause metabolic derangements directly through psychophysiological mechanisms.

The empirical work of Minuchin and his colleagues suggests that when family conflict occurs, leading to emotional and physiological arousal, the turnoff phase that follows, that is, the return to normal levels of physiological responding, is different in "psychosomatic" families and is exemplified by the families' attempt to avoid conflict, with a subsequent lack of conflict resolution (Baker *et al.,* 1975; Minuchin *et al.,* 1975, 1978). Of course specific family patterns (e.g., conflict avoidance) might develop in response to this heightened reactivity rather than being a unique cause of it. In either case the reason that the pattern of interaction affects diabetes control is that stress, which results in production of pituitary hormones and catecholamines, leads in turn to a decrease in insulin production and an increase in free fatty acids in the blood. The lack of insulin production in patients with diabetes makes them unable to counteract the effects of the stress hormones. As a group, the studies in this area strongly suggest that stress has direct metabolic effects that could influence diabetes stability (Meyer, Bollmeier, and Alexander, 1945; cf. Johnson, 1980). Thus stress has a particularly debilitating effect on the course of the diabetes.

Obesity

The stress concept seems not to have been as helpful for understanding either the onset or the maintenance of obesity as for other disorders. Laboratory studies of obese people suggest that eating does not significantly lower anxiety levels and that high levels of anxiety do not produce any consistent increase in eating (Abramson and Wunderlich, 1972; McKenna, 1972; Schachter, Gross, *et al.,* 1968; Spitzer and Rodin, 1981), although field studies continue to show some correlation between stress and eating among overweight people (Slochower, Kaplan, and Mann, 1981). It may be that stress is related to other eating disorders—for example, bulimia—since studies have reported more frequent episodes of binge eating during situations that are perceived as stressful (Stunkard, 1976). The current view is that all forms of arousal, rather than stress per se, may lead to overeating on a single occasion (Robbins and Fray, 1980; Spitzer and Rodin, 1981). Whether or not this leads to chronic overeating and/or obesity remains an unanswered question (Spitzer, Marcus, and Rodin, 1980).

CONTROL

Despite the apparently strong effects of stress on biological responses just reviewed, it may be that the direct effects of stress are less significant in terms of the toll they take on the body when compared with the effects of stress that are mediated by a loss of perceived control and poor coping. There is an increasing body of research, for example, suggesting that excessive workload and job responsibility may enhance coronary risk, but only when they approach the limits of the individuals' capacity to control their work (House, 1975; Jenkins, 1971; Jenkins, 1976).

In an excellent longitudinal study, Cobb and Kasl (1977) studied workers prior to, and at several points after, plant closings. They included control groups where no shutdown was anticipated and one plant in which a shutdown had been anticipated but had not occurred during the two-year period of the study. The men who were unemployed longer were more likely to be depressed, to have low self-esteem, and to be anxious, tense, irritable, easily angered, and suspicious. Their blood pressures were elevated in anticipation of, and during, their unemployment. Cholesterol levels and pulse rates, norepinephrine output, and levels of protein-bound iodine showed similar patterns. Blood sugar levels (a precursor of diabetes), pepsinogen levels (related to the formation of peptic ulcers), and serum uric acid levels (the immediate cause of gout) were all significantly elevated among the unemployed. Incidence of the development of peptic ulcers, arthritis, and hypertension increased. These effects were strongest in those people who felt least in control both over their unemployment and their possibilities for new employment. Other life dissatisfactions, including problems and conflicts in areas of finance and family, have been correlated with the presence (Orth-Gomer and Ahlbom, 1980) and future development (Haynes and Fineleib, 1980) of coronary disease. Similarly it is thought that hyperresponsiveness to a lack of control is at the behavioral root of the characteristics that place Type A's at so much risk for coronary heart disease (Glass, 1977).

While the notion of a single traumatic life event has been suspected as a cause of coronary heart disease (e.g., Engel, 1971) and cancer (Schmale and Iker, 1971), more recently investigators have suggested that the cumulative effect of repeated adjustments required by traumatic as well as less traumatic life events is more stressful because it is believed to drain the adaptive resources of the individual and increase his or her susceptibility to a variety of diseases (Dohrenwend and Dohrenwend, 1974). This appears to be especially true when these events are repeatedly seen as uncontrollable. (Rodin, Bohm, and Wack, 1982). Research suggests that an accumulation of helplessness-inducing events may be especially potent in the precipitation of coronary disease (Engel, 1978; Greene, Moos, and Goldstein, 1974).

The pathophysiological concomitants of uncontrollability are believed to result from activation of the sympathetic adrenal medullary system and the pituitary adrenal cortical axis. The pituitary adrenal system secretes a number of hormones that influence bodily systems of relevance to the development of coronary disease and suppression of the immune system. For example, corticosteroids regulate the metabolism of cholesterol and other lipids involved in the atherosclerotic process and also have strong immunosuppressive effects. It is interesting in this regard that Rodin and her coworkers (Rodin, 1980, 1981) were able to demonstrate that control-relevant interventions directly lowered levels of urinary free cortisol, which was associated with significantly reduced disease and lower mortality. Furthermore, with older people (ages 62–91), feelings of uncontrollability regarding a stressful life event may be an important determinant of whether suppressions in immune function occurs in response to stress (Rodin, unpublished data). A great number of changes that accompany aging have loss of control at their basis.

SOCIAL SUPPORT

Social support appears to buffer people from potentially negative effects of crisis and change and to facilitate coping and adaptation in many instances. There is evidence that individuals who have social supports may live longer, have a lower incidence of somatic illness, and possess higher morale and more positive mental health. In a study specifically relevant to coronary disease, it was found that among men who lost their jobs, those with high levels of emotional support from their wives had lower serum cholesterol values than those who did not (Gore, 1978). Similarly, social support processes may impact on several other physiological responses related to cardiovascular disease, such as catecholamine responses and severity of coronary artery lesions.

Less well worked out, but equally provocative, is the assumption of an association between social support variables and cancer. Unfortunately, psychosocial information is usually obtained retrospectively from the patient after the illness is diagnosed. Causal inferences from such data are tenuous of course. In a study that is unique in this area, however, psychosocial data were obtained from 913 medical students long before the clinical appearance of disease (Thomas, Duszynski, and Schaffer, 1979). The follow-up study showed that twenty men developed cancer within the next ten to fifteen years. These men reported a lack of closeness to parents in a questionnaire taken at the inception of the study. Scores on this measure best distinguished future cancer victims

from subjects who were to remain healthy. The pathophysiological mechanisms mediating this relationship are as yet unspecified.

DECISION MAKING

Data have suggested that certain patterns of decision making may be desirable not only because they lead to better decisions but also because they have differential pathophysiological consequences. In an earlier section I considered the Janis and Mann (1977) description of a hypervigilant response pattern of decision making. In its most extreme form this consists of an extremely agitated state of panic or near panic characterized by indiscriminate attention to all sorts of minor and major threat cues as the person frantically searches for a means of escaping from the anticipated danger. Other salient characteristics of hypervigilance are temporary impairment of cognitive functioning and defective decision making in which excessive vacillation is followed by impulsive choice.

An alarm or emergency reaction to a powerful threat includes a variety of physiological changes, many of which are mediated by the activity of the adrenal glands. Typically they begin with changes in breathing, which Grossman and Defares (1981) suggest may be a crucial first step leading to other major physiological and psychological changes evoked when people are exposed to powerful threat stimuli. In response to oncoming danger or imminent threat, practically everyone will start breathing hard. This in effect changes the rate and depth of respiration in the direction of hyperventilation, which is characterized by respiratory activity in excess of immediate metabolic requirements. Hyperventilation appears to have profound physiological, behavioral, and psychological consequences. As a result of the reduction of CO_2 in the bloodstream and a concomitant lowering of blood acid level, numerous systemic alterations occur in the body. These include increase in sympathetic activity, changes in renal function, increased risk of cardiac dysrhythmias, elevation of heart rate, decreased oxygen supplied to brain tissue, and heightened cerebral vasoconstriction.

Perhaps the most prominent and dramatic consequence of hyperventilation at the psychological level is a feeling of acute anxiety. According to Janis, Defares, and Grossman (in press), people who suffer a hyperventilation attack usually do not identify their symptoms as arising from their increased breathing but rather focus on the threatening situation or their somatic complaints as the source of the disturbance. This is quite understandable, because the environmental situation that brings about a hyperventilation episode is usually extremely alarming. Thus the external and internal characteristics of the situation may work synergistically to create a heightened sense of fear in the hyperventilater. The altered patterns of cerebral, electrical, and vascular activity are probably most responsible for the psychomotoric and cognitive impairments that hyperventilation induces. What is significant about this analysis is that many of the characteristic symptoms of hypervigilance appear traceable to hyperventilation. These data suggest a possible mechanism by which anxiety leads to disease onset.

ENVIRONMENTAL VARIABLES

The importance of external, situational cues has been suggested as a primary factor in the cause and maintenance of the obese condition. Interested in the labeling of bodily states, Schachter and his colleagues questioned how individuals come to identify appropriately the experience of hunger and eat in response to it (Schachter, 1968). This line of analysis challenged the heretofore conventional wisdom that hunger was a biological innate state. Conjecturing that overweight people may be those who have learned to identify the wrong cues as hunger, Schachter and his colleagues performed an ingenious series of experiments suggesting that overweight individuals were highly responsive to environmental manipulations, such as the presence of food, the time of day, the smell of food, and the sight of other people eating (Nisbett, 1968; Schachter and Gross, 1968).

Our own work and recent reviews of the literature suggest that hyperresponsiveness to external cues could lead to overeating, given a permissive environment, but that physiological factors appear to exert a more important influence on the final levels of body weight people maintain (Rodin and Slochower, 1976; Rodin, 1981; Spitzer and Rodin, 1981). In other words, not all externally responsive people become fat, and even if they do gain weight, the degree of obesity they attain is not determined by external responsiveness alone. To expect this to be true is to fail to recognize that obesity also depends on genetic factors, on fat cell number, and on individual differences in endocrine function and metabolic efficiency. These factors make it likely that, up to some limit, even with equal externality-induced overeating, some people will simply get fatter than others. For example, Rose and

Williams (1961) matched pairs of individuals who were maintaining the identical weights, which hardly varied at all over several weeks, who had comparable levels of activity, and who were approximately the same age and height. Yet one of them was often eating twice as many calories as the other. Extraordinary as this may seem, these findings suggest that in different individuals the identical type and quantity of food eaten will not necessarily or even very likely be stored or expended in the same way, even given equal activity levels. Studies such as these help to explain the lack of a strong correlation between the final degree of obesity attained and degree of responsiveness to external food cues.

Recent work has considered the mechanism by which environmental cues may contribute to overeating and weight gain. In some individuals a rise in insulin levels can be observed by simply presenting them with the sight and smell of palatable food. The greater the palatability, the larger the insulin secretion (Rodin, 1978). Insulin is involved in promoting increased ingestion and in promoting the storage of what has been eaten as fat rather than as immediately utilizable energy. Manipulating insulin directly affects hunger and makes sweet taste more pleasurable (Rodin, Wack, Ferannini, and DeFronzo, 1983). These data suggest a mechanism that may explain why newly diagnosed diabetics placed on insulin therapy appear to feel hungrier and to gain weight, despite their doctors' admonitions to the contrary.

SUMMARY AND CONCLUSIONS

In the past few years there has emerged a heightened awareness of the importance of behavioral factors in general, and perhaps social psychological factors in particular, in health and disease. Certainly the heaviest burdens of illness in the United States today are related to lifestyle (Lalonde, 1974; USDHEW, 1979b). Known behavioral risk factors include cigarette smoking, excessive consumption of alcoholic beverages, use of illicit drugs, certain dietary habits, insufficient exercise, reckless driving, noncompliance with medical regimens, and maladaptive responses to social pressure. Further, many disorders are precipitated by environmental stressors, such as moving, unemployment, or bereavement.

This section has considered how social psychological processes relate to various disease outcomes and, where possible, has specified the pathophysiological mechanisms linking these two sets of variables. Work in this area has changed our understanding of disease and has produced excellent theoretical work on the relationship between mind and body. Its practical effects on medical practice and on actual rates of morbidity and mortality are striking and represent a major achievement in the application of social psychology to important social concerns.

METHODOLOGICAL ISSUES IN APPLIED RESEARCH

It has often been assumed that experiments conducted in applied settings rather than in the laboratory compromise experimental control and rigor for greater external validity. This view, however, does not seem unequivocally correct. Many of the experiments described above show high internal validity with a clear demonstration that a relationship exists between two or more variables. On the other hand some aspects of external validity are often as problematic in an applied experiment as in laboratory experiments. For example, a social program that works in one area of the country may not give us any indication of how it would work in other areas with different populations (Saxe and Fine, 1980). In the final analysis, research in applied areas must be concerned with issues of both internal and external validity to an especially high degree. The criteria for what constitutes a good experiment and what results are to be trusted must of necessity be stringent when changes in medical or legal practice, school reform, and public policy depend on inferences from the research results.

CORRELATIONAL VERSUS EXPERIMENTAL ANALYSES

Discussions of the best research methodology for the study of applied issues have been considerable, especially as the field has expanded. Naturalistic studies of subjects exposed to significant life experiences provide the opportunity to study ecologically real processes and to generalize findings to a greater range of persons and settings. However, naturalistic studies are frequently correlational, and subjects or settings often vary on dimensions other than the variables under study. Many of these difficulties can be reduced substantially by careful matching of control groups, but the possibility of unknown confounding variables is inevitable in studies of free-living populations.

Another approach has been to attempt quasi-experiments or "true experiments" (Cook and Campbell,

1979) using randomized control groups to test hypotheses. Often this takes the form of social experimentation, which is a methodology that involves systematic application of the manipulation of social variables in natural settings, where the manipulation refers to making a social program available to randomly selected groups. Here social interventions are treated as independent variables that are manipulated in much the same way as in a laboratory experiment. While the social experiment research approach may be useful in some instances, it would be naive to assume that simple random assignment to an experimental condition solves a variety of other potential problems. For example, construct validity may be compromised by an intervention involving multiple procedures where there is a problem of knowing that the labeling of the independent variable is appropriate.

Studies that have made an explicit choice between experimental or correlational analysis in applied work provide us with some insights regarding the special issues that field researchers have thought to consider. For example, Raven and Haley (1980) intentionally used correlational analyses where experimental manipulations were possible. They considered and rejected a prospective experimental study to investigate problems of infection control in hospitals. In such a design, hospitals would be randomly assigned to experimental and control groups, and those in the experimental group would implement active infection control procedures, whereas the controls would continue without programs. Infection rates could then be monitored over several years to see if there were differences in the two sets of hospitals.

Raven and Haley (1980) noted that the plan for the experimental approach was discarded for several reasons: First, they believed that the design could be discovered and hospitals would soon become aware of whether they were in the experimental or the control group. While this is a potential problem in any experimental study where subjects in different groups could be in contact or where an intervention is salient, there are procedures that may decrease the likelihood of contamination of effects. For example, one strategy is to use control groups that are "no-treatment" with regard to the specific experimental variable of interest, but in which some sort of salient intervention is also introduced in order to make groups equivalent on this dimension.

Their second concern was that the dependent variable, infection rate, would require measurements that would introduce surveillance over the control group as well as the experimental group. Again this seems to be an issue that much psychological research confronts, and so long as both groups are under equal surveillance, it does not by itself constitute a problem. On the other hand there is the potential for interpretive difficulties in large-scale applied experiments if the measurement procedures interact with the treatment condition to produce effects that are different for the experimental and the control groups. For example, Leventhal *et al.* (1980) have criticized the Stanford three-community study (Farquhar, 1978) for not being sensitive to the fact that the very extensive medical surveillance used to determine changes in risk factors could have interacted with the face-to-face contact that was present in only one of the three conditions of the experiment. This interaction might have produced differences that remained uncontrolled for, and untested, in the original study.

By and large, it is probably the case that methodological problems are not substantially greater when working in applied settings than when working in the laboratory. It is much more likely that we simply are more comfortable and have more experience working with the methodological concerns that arise from laboratory research. Considerable attention must therefore be given to developing and evaluating methodologies that build in all the elements of rigor without compromising theoretical integrity in the area of applied social psychology. This challenge is substantial since some investigators believe that one must inevitably be sacrificed for the other. For example, Saxe and Fine (1980) suggest that because social experimentation is motivated by concern about social problems, it has low theoretical yield. With this I strongly disagree. The work of Schulz and his colleagues and our own studies of nursing homes, to take merely one familiar example, were social experiments in the full Cook and Campbell (1979) sense. Subjects were randomly assigned to conditions in a series of experiments whose goal was to improve the health and morale of nursing home residents. These studies were motivated in part by a great concern for the conditions of nursing homes (Wack and Rodin, 1978). But the specific manipulations were determined by the desire to test and extend the theoretical construct of control.

It is the contention of this chapter that theory and social relevance need not be traded for one another. Nor is it necessarily the case, as Monahan and Loftus (1982) have proposed, that the laboratory is better used for theory testing, and the field for making predictions about actual behavior. While this is sometimes true, it has been the challenge of the best of applied research both to develop and test theory and to predict behavior in naturalis-

tic settings. This work in turn has led to socially important interventions. Once a model of complex social and psychological processes develops, the investigator, as he or she wishes, may find some way to intervene in the system to bring about an observable change in a socially significant behavior. The more complete and varied the theoretical model, obviously, the more it will tell us about where, when, and how to intervene successfully.

Janis (1975b) has suggested that both theory and applied goals are best served when research projects are designed to meet the following criteria: First, the specific procedures and measures should represent plausible instances of variables that are of theoretical interest at the outset but could potentially have high generality, embracing a wide variety of specific psychological phenomena. Second, even if some or all of the assumptions that enter into judgments made about the first criterion should prove to be questionable or at fault, the empirically observed relationships that emerge from the investigation should nevertheless be of inherent interest for psychological phenomena, in that they help to specify determinants of socially important behavior as assessed in the investigation itself.

In Janis's (1982, 1983a, 1983b) own work this view has meant first selecting a dependent variable such as weight loss, which he regarded as a direct indicator of adherence to the decision to go on a low-calorie diet. He made the assumption that whatever interpersonal factors were found to have a significant influence on weight loss would have broad generality for many other, if not all, types of personal decisions. However, he also assumed that the foregoing view might prove wrong, perhaps because adherence to the decision to lose weight would be influenced to a much greater degree by unique variables such as intensity of hunger during food deprivation. Thus the findings might not apply to any other type of decision or judgment. In this case the research would still satisfy the second criterion, since it would pertain to the conditions under which people succeed in or fail to carry out their decision to lose weight, and this is a sufficiently important behavior in its own right to represent a worthwhile contribution.

SIMULATION STUDIES

Certainly, working in the field is not the only way to understand applied social problems, and there is a considerable amount of very good research that has used the laboratory to model a social process of interest. For example,

Glass and Singer (1972) in their work on urban stress and Latane and Darley (1969) in their work on bystander intervention each tried to create a laboratory simulation of the problem of interest. At the beginning point, their working hypotheses could be sufficiently flexible to defer the requirements of making the simulation totally faithful to the original problem, and studies and replication in the laboratory context were necessary. Indeed Singer and Glass (1975) note that somewhat more replication is necessary because parameters as well as relationships are under investigation. Only after completing these initial procedures was the scope of the work expanded to generalizations to other similar studies on related problems and to explicit tests of the theoretical position. Finally, field studies were undertaken (Cohen, Glass, and Singer, 1973; Piliavin, Rodin, and Piliavin, 1969), which led to elaborations and reformulations of the theories. This research strategy follows Lewin's (1947) suggestion of an important interplay between lab and field.

Another situation where use of laboratory studies is especially appropriate for considering important social problems is the case where an event already exists but is contaminated in the real world. For example, in some studies of deviance or aging, field experiments simply permit investigators to study people who are already old or occupying a deviant status. Better yet, if they are fortunate they can try to identify people who may become deviant or to follow people as they grow old. However, these experiments are costly and involve a great deal of time before fruitful results are available. An alternative, which should serve as a complement to rather than a substitute for such longitudinal prospective designs, is to create circumstances in the laboratory that produce these conditions temporarily. In this way one can show that the variables being manipulated are the crucial ones in producing feelings of deviance or aging, for example, since they alone are shown to produce the outcome of interest. Zimbardo, Andersen, and Kabat (1981) followed this approach by inducing temporary deafness through hypnosis to show that losses in hearing may produce paranoidlike behavior.

Another interesting example of this genre of research design is the work of Insko, Thibaut, *et al.* (1980), who attempted to test the redistribution theory of social evolution. Clearly unable to study several generations over time, they developed a procedure that allowed for the development of, in Insko *et al.*'s (1980) terms, a generation. They continued the procedure for nine generations and created an experimental situation where each group was required to manage the problems of redistri-

bution of goods or services. A major aspect of their methodology involved the systematic replacement of individuals in the laboratory groups so as to produce an analogue of generational succession. Their interest was in investigating the selection or emergence of a tradition specifically involving institutionalized leadership. Using this procedure they described the conditions for the establishment of institutionalized power that derives from a leadership role and how it gets transmitted over generations by rules of succession to that role.

The apparent value of such laboratory simulation, however, should not seduce us away from designing the more difficult, yet eventually more important, prospective studies in field settings. It is certainly clear, however, why simulation studies are popular. Simulation allows for randomization of experimental variables and replication of procedures, which increase internal validity, access to processes that may be inaccessible in the natural environment, and research that is usually less costly in time and money than studies conducted in the field. However, there has been considerable discussion and criticism of laboratory simulations, especially in the area of social psychology and law (Bray and Kerr, 1979; Ebbesen and Konecni, 1980; Vidmar and Miller, 1980).

Ebbesen and Konecni (1980) highlight several important problems in simulation research in the legal area that pertain, for the most part, to any substantive domain we have considered. First, the large majority of laboratory simulations use college students as subjects. These people are not always representative of participants in the real-world situation. Further, unlike decisions made by real-world participants in the legal system, laboratory subjects' behavior and decisions have no real consequences. Third, the information given to laboratory subjects in a simulation typically represents a vast oversimplification of the type and quantity of information to which participants in the real-world judicial system are exposed. Moreover, the stimuli and stimulus dimensions are typically presented in a decomposed, rather than a more holistic, form. Fourth, the treatment conditions usually represent only a few of the temporal aspects and number of events to which real jurors are exposed. For example, subjects' decisions in jury simulation studies are often made in the absence of key procedural features, such as the discussion and deliberation stages in which actual jurors engage, and the selection of a foreman. Finally, laboratory juries frequently judge the extent of guilt of the defendant on a scale, whereas their real-world counterparts have to make a dichotomous decision. Laboratory jurors are frequently asked to determine the defendant's prison term, even though the nature of his or her crime would almost never result in a prison sentence in the real world.

Ebbesen, Parker, and Konecni (1977) compared simulated and natural legal decisions on a variety of issues and procedures. They found, not surprisingly, that different factors emerged as important in predicting outcome, depending on the experimental strategy employed. But it is not always that field research is better than simulation or other kinds of research. Indeed data obtained from direct field observation in the Ebbesen, Parker, and Konecni (1977) studies, for example, were the least rich and the least accurate of all, presumably because the sentencing and hearing procedure is window dressing for a decision that has already been made. Simulation studies may continue to be useful so long as further attention is given to the appropriate subject for such studies and the consequences of providing reduced information. Indeed simulation research may actually be quite desirable in some cases because it allows for the ability to combine variables in novel ways. This permits the description of relationships that do not always exist in the natural environment.

SUMMARY AND CONCLUSIONS

The foregoing analyses suggest that applied research is important to the theoretical development of the field because social pyschological processes need to be studied in ongoing, meaningful situations, but there is disagreement in specifying the appropriate methodologies for accomplishing this goal. The task is yet more complicated since ultimately we need to study the ongoing *process* and not simply the outcome of some intervention or experimental manipulation. Indeed we often derive an erroneous assumption that the follow-up data somehow reflect the impact of the manipulation per se rather than the impact of the process set in motion by the manipulation (cf. Rodin and Langer, 1977). One way to accomplish an analysis of process is to collect data at more than two points in time and to test actual temporal causal models. Statistical procedures such as path analysis, which can be used to test such data, require specification of theoretical variables related to the process of interest and enable control of potential contaminating factors in order to make better causal inferences. Once again theory development and testing emerge as important components to applied research.

In many instances applied social psychology has veered away from the simple, or "input-output," model

of causation (Altman, 1976) to acknowledge the possibility of multidirectional causation between variables (if *a* affects *b*, it may also be the case that b affects *a*). Thus it methodologically enriches social psychological inquiry. Further, the richness of the field setting has often led to entirely different perspectives and new paradigms for ordering variables. Our methodological advances must keep pace with these conceptual developments.

CONCLUSIONS

Much research beginning in the 1970s countered earlier criticism that social psychology was becoming both theoretically bare and lacking in applicability to important social problems and real-life concerns. Instead our theories have been challenged, enriched, and changed by empirical considerations of real-world problems, leading to the view that applied research can become an arena for the development and testing of social psychological theory as well as a tool for solving social problems. Indeed many questions have been studied first in the field and then later in the laboratory, suggesting that we may begin to look to the laboratory as the context for further testing specific hypotheses extracted from a theory developed in the applied setting, rather than vice versa. One goal of this review has been to consider more fully the integration of social psychological theory and applied research. In essence we can now ask which applied areas have proved well suited for theory utilization and development and which theories have fared well, been challenged, or been extended by applied research. Let us consider each of these in turn, although they are clearly related.

The domain of health and medical practice appears to be especially rich for theory testing and development. In considering, for example, people with serious health problems such as cancer, the negative as well as positive consequences of social support have been well demonstrated. This has allowed better specification of the intervening mechanisms by which social supports may affect outcomes, including felt responsibility, stress and arousal, modeling and information processing. Social psychological theories of social support have now emerged based on process variables (e.g., Kahn and Antonucci, 1980; Wortman and Dunkel-Schetter, 1979). To take just one other health example, social psychological studies of patient compliance or adherence have shown that these behaviors do not simply represent motivational problems. Rather they vary in relation to the types of social power used by health care professionals, the degree of control felt by patients, the nature of decision making, and the processing of relevant health information. Theories of power, control, decision making, and information processing have been developed or extended by this demonstration, as in the case of Leventhal's (1980b) theory regarding schemas representing danger and other emotion-producing experiences.

Education has been another rich arena for theory utilization and testing. Atheoretical studies of the effects of desegregation yielded few results, while those based on theories of self-esteem and small-group behavior (e.g., Aronson and Bridgeman, 1979; Weigel, Wiser, and Cook, 1975) produced far stronger findings and further theoretical development. For example, it has been suggested that there exist both an outer component of self-esteem, resulting from social comparison processes and the appraisals of relevant others, and an inner component developing from data pertaining to successes or failures in one's interaction with the environment. This concept was extended by the demonstration that cooperative settings, by promoting greater social comparison and increased likelihood of success, are more likely to impact positively on self-esteem than competitive settings (Aronson and Osherow, 1980). Competition may also increase social comparison processes, however, in self-esteem-relevant areas, at least among white middle-class students (Bers and Rodin, in press) and further empirical work will be needed, based on competing theoretical perspectives, to understand more fully the processes involved in self-esteem enhancement and maintenance among school peers. Theories of attribution have also been successfully tested and extended by work in educational settings (e.g., Dweck, 1975; Lepper and Greene, 1975).

Studies of people undergoing serious life events —rape, divorce, bereavement, loneliness—expanded and challenged extant theories. For example, it is clear from the studies reviewed above that self-blaming attributions may lead to either positive adaptive behavior (Janoff-Bulman, 1979) or maladaptive behavior (Maslach, 1978; Rodin and Langer, 1980). The pivotal determinant seems to be whether or not the relevant problem is seen as avoidable the next time, that is, as under the person's own control. But of course this could only be determined in the real world, where there is a "next time." Similarly, because laboratory research focuses only on a single event isolated in time, attribution theories focused solely on consideration of the precipitating causes of the event. In the real world of important problems, for example loneliness, attributions regarding the maintaining causes may be substantially more important because they are more often viewed as chronic factors (Berke and Peplau, 1976; Michela *et al.*, 1979).

Thus far most studies of legal issues and procedures have not been intended for theory development, with the exception of the research program of Thibaut and his associates on control (Houlden *et al.*, 1978; LaTour *et al.*, 1976; Thibaut *et al.*, 1972). Theories of small-group behavior have, however, been the basis for some studies of juries (Myers and Kaplan, 1976; Saks, 1972), and theories of decision making have been tested in studies of legal decisions (Ebbesen and Konecni, 1975).

There appears to be strong evidence for theory testing and development in several studies of important social problems. Most significant, many of these contributions to theory could not have been made by laboratory research. Again, as discussed in the introduction to this review, the point is not that one or the other mode of research is better for theory development and testing, but rather that both are good. And now we can ask the reciprocal question: How have our theories fared when tested in the domain of significant personal and social problems? Considering first attribution theory, it seems clear that when the outcome is a major life concern, people do indeed make causal attributions, and these in turn affect both their psychological state and their behavior. But laboratory-based specification of the variables that lead to different types of attributions has not withstood testing in applied settings (e.g., Carroll and Payne, 1977a, 1977b). There has, however, been greater confirmation of the notion that different types of attributions lead to different predictable behaviors (e.g., Berke and Peplau, 1976; Dweck, 1975; Rodin and Langer, 1978).

Applied studies have also provided strong support for the notion of a "fundamental attribution error" (Ross, 1977), since in explaining serious and important outcomes, even negative ones, people appear to infer personal causality and assume some personal responsibility (e.g., Janoff-Bulman, 1979; Rodin and Langer, 1980). Strikingly, even when situational factors are extremely salient, people tend more often to make dispositional attributions, as Nisbett and Ross (1980) have suggested. Attributions to disposition appear especially likely when people attempt to make sense of their own anomalous reactions or when discontinuities in their feelings affect cognitive functioning.

The theoretical assumption that attributions are important for feelings of control, and indeed may be made in order to gain control (Kelley, 1967, 1971), receives support from demonstrations in areas such as substance abuse that self-regulatory behaviors require supporting attributions of self-efficacy.

Social learning theory has also fared well in applied studies. Several large-scale quasi-experiments in field settings attempting to change health behavior (e.g., Evans *et al.,* 1980; Evans, 1982; Farquhar, 1978) have tested aspects of the theory with relatively good success. Variables such as type of model, type of communication, and other social influence factors have been manipulated, and learning has been demonstrated, leading to more healthful behavior.

Theories regarding the bases of social power and their differential effects have been extended and clarified as a result of work in settings where differences in power are strong (e.g., institutions such as hospitals, Raven and Haley, 1980), or can be manipulated with important consequences (patient–health care practitioner dyads, Rodin and Janis, 1979). For example, informational power was shown to operate on a different basis, and one that was logically inconsistent with the use of other influence strategies, leading to a sharpening of theories regarding the bases of social power.

To take one final example, theories of rational decision making appear to be less valid when attempting to understand decisions regarding significant life problems with substantial costs and benefits, whereas conflict theories of decision making seem well supported. For example, in the health area the health belief model (Becker *et al.,* 1977), like other models of rational choice, fails to specify under what conditions people will give priority to avoiding subjective discomfort at the cost of endangering their lives and under what conditions they will make a more adaptive decision by seeking and taking into account the available medical information about the real consequences of alternative courses of action so as to maximize their chances of survival. Subjective expected utility models of personal decision making have also failed to predict behavior regarding fertility and birth control decision (Adler, 1979) and legal sentencing (Ebbesen and Konecni, 1975, 1978). As Janis (1982) notes, the rationalistic, cognitive type of model may be good for prescriptive or normative purposes, but it has serious shortcomings as a descriptive model.

In summary then, it is possible to show how several theories have been tested, further developed, or challenged by applied social research. Such a demonstration clearly points to the potential for a truly successful integration of theory and application.

Based on the studies reviewed in this chapter, there is little doubt that consideration of social psychological

variables has promoted major advances in our understanding of health-relevant behavior, judicial processes, education, population control, and the workplace, to name just a few examples. But these successes can be falsely seductive, for there is danger in an uncritical emphasis on the power of these applicaions without a renewed look at how much of the variance is accounted for by our manipulations. While many of the effects have been statistically reliable, there is still some doubt as to whether these are significant enough to form the basis for large-scale social interventions. Many smaller analogue studies, using statistical tests that question percentage of variance accounted for, still remain to be done. Experimental field studies will be especially important for the next stage of development. We will also need to use more comfortably new statistical tools developed in the neighboring disciplines of sociology and economics in order to better interpret and apply data gathered in the field. The causal modeling techniques of Jöreskog and his colleagues (Jöreskog and Sorbom, 1979) represent a prime example.

Quite likely, the next decade will see even more vigorous efforts to apply, test, and develop social psychological knowledge through the study of important human concerns, and the emergence of more creative ways to use both laboratory and field settings. In so doing, investigators must remain aware of the importance of systematic research rather than "one-shot" studies. Moreover, these investigations should either be theoretically based or look to develop theory as one of their goals. Our ability to predict behavior as well as the vitality of the discipline, in my view, depend on this approach.

REFERENCES

Abelson, R. P., and P. G. Zimbardo (1970). *Canvassing for peace: a manual for volunteers.* Ann Arbor, Mich.: SPSSI.

Abelson, R. P. (1963). Computer simulation of "hot cognition." In S. Tomkins and S. Messick (Eds.), *Computer simulation of personality.* New York: Coiley.

Abramson, L. Y., and H. A. Sackheim (1977). A paradox in depression: uncontrollability and self-blame. *Psychol. Bull., 84,* 838–851.

Abramson, L. Y., M. E. P. Seligman, and J. D. Teasdale (1978). Learned helplessness in humans: critique and reformulation. *J. abnorm. Psychol., 87,* 49–74.

Abramson, E. E., and R. A. Wunderlich (1972). Anxiety, fear and eating: a test of the psychosomatic concept of obesity. *J. abnorm. Psychol., 79,* 317–321.

Ader, R., Ed. (1981). *Psychoneuroimmunology.* New York: Academic Press.

Adler, A. (1930). Individual psychology. In C. Murchinson (Ed.), *Psychologies of 1930.* Worcester, Mass.: Clark Univ. Press.

Adler, N. E. (1979). Decision models in population research. *J. Population, 2,* 187–202.

Ajzen, I., and M. Fishbein (1969). The prediction of behavioral intentions in a choice situation. *J. exp. soc. Psychol., 5,* 400–416.

—— (1973). Attitudinal and normative variables as predictors of specific behaviors. *J. Pers. soc. Psychol., 27,* 41–57.

Altman, I. (1976). Environmental psychology and social psychology. *Pers. soc. Psychol. Bull., 2,* 96–113.

Amabile, T. M., W. DeJong, and M. R. Lepper (1976). Effects of externally-imposed deadlines on subsequent intrinsic motivation. *J. Pers. soc. Psychol., 34,* 92–98.

Amkraut, A., and G. F. Solomon (1977). From the symbolic stimulus to the pathophysiologic response: immune mechanisms. In S. J. Lipowski, D. R. Lipsitt, and P. C. Whybrow (Eds.), *Psychosomatic medicine: current trends and clinical applications.* New York: Oxford Univ. Press.

Anderson, N. H. (1974). Information integration theory. A brief survey. In D. H. Krantz, R. C. Atkinson, R. D. Luce, and P. Suppes (Eds.), *Contemporary developments in mathematical psychology.* Vol. 2. San Francisco: Freeman.

Anderson, N. H., and G. R. Alexander (1971). Choice test of averaging hypothesis for information integration. *Cognit. Psychol. 2 (3),* 313.

Anderson, S. M., and P. G. Zimbardo (1980). Resisting mind control. *USA Today.*

Aronson, E., and D. Bridgeman (1979). Jigsaw groups and the desegregated classroom: in pursuit of common goals. *Pers. soc. Psychol. Bull., 5,* 438–446.

Aronson, E., D. L. Bridgeman, J. Sikes, N. Blaney, and M. Snapp (1978). *The jigsaw classroom.* Beverly Hills, Calif.: Sage.

Aronson, E., and N. Osherow (1980). Experiments in the desegregated classroom: the effects of cooperation on prosocial behavior and academic performance. *Appl. soc. Psychol. Ann., 1,* 163–196.

Averill, J. R. (1973). Personal control over aversive stimuli and its relationship to stress. *Psychol. Bull., 80,* 286–303.

Baekeland, F., and L. Lundwall (1975). Dropping out of treatment: a critical review. *Psychol. Bull., 82,* 738–783.

Baker, L., S. Minuchin, L. Milman, R. Leibman, and T. Todd (1975). Psychosomatic aspects of juvenile diabetes mellitus: a progress report. In Z. Laron (Ed.), Diabetes in juveniles: medical and rehabilitation aspects. *Modern problems in pediatrics.* Vol. 12. New York: Karger.

Bandura, A. (1977). Self-efficacy: toward a unifying theory of behavioral change. *Psychol. Rev., 84,* 191–215.

—— (1980). The self and mechanism of agency. In J. Suls (Ed.), *Social psychological perspectives on the self.* Hillsdale, N.J.: Erlbaum.

Bandura, A., N. Adams, A. B. Hardy, and G. Howells (1980). Tests of the generality of self-efficacy theory. *Cognit. Therapy Res.,* 39–66.

Bandura, A., and F. Menlove (1968). Factors determining vicarious extinction of avoidance behavior through symbolic modeling. *J. Pers. soc. Psychol., 8,* 99–108.

Barofsky, I. (1978). Compliance, adherence, and the therapeutic alliance: steps in the development of self-care. *Soc. Sci. Medicine, 12,* 369–376.

Bartrop, R. W., L. Lazarus, and E. Luckhurst (1977). Depressed lymphocyte function after bereavement. *Lancet, 1,* 834–836.

Baum, A., J. Aiello, and L. E. Calesnic (1978). Crowding and personal control—social density and development of learned helplessness. *J. Pers. soc. Psychol., 39,* 1000–1011.

Baum, A., R. Fleming, and S. Singer (1982). Stress at Three Mile Island: applying psychological impact analysis. In L. Bickman (Ed.), *Applied social psychology annual.* Beverly Hills, Calif.: Sage.

Becker, M. H. (1976). Sociobehavioral determinants of compliance. In D. L. Sackett and R. B. Haynes (Eds.), *Compliance with therapeutic regimens.* Baltimore, Johns Hopkins.

Becker, M. H., D. P. Haefner, S. V. Kasl, J. P. Kirscht, L. A. Maiman, and I. M. Rosenstock (1977). Selected psychosocial models and correlates of individual health-related behaviors. *Medical Care, 156,* 27–48.

Bem, D. J. (1972). Self-perception theory: In L. Berkowitz (Ed.), *Advances in experimental social psychology.* Vol. 6. New York: Academic Press.

Bem, J., and A. Allen (1974). On predicting some of the people some of the time: the search for cross-situational consistencies in behavior. *Psychol. Rev., 81,* 506–520.

Bennett, R., and C. Eisdorfer (1975). The institutional environment and behavior change. In S. Sherwood (Ed.), *Longterm core: a handbook for researchers, planners, and providers.* New York: Spectrum.

Berg, A. O., and J. P. LoGerfo (1979). Potential effect of selfcare algorithms on the number of physician visits. *N. E. J. Med., 300,* 535–537.

Berglas, S., and E. E. Jones (1978). Drug choice as a selfhandicapping strategy in response to noncontingent success. *J. Pers. soc. Psychol., 36,* 405–417.

Berke, B., and L. A. Peplau (1976). Loneliness in the university. Paper presented at the annual meeting of the Western Psychological Association, Los Angeles.

Bers, S., and J. Rodin (In press). Social comparison jealousy: a developmental study. *J. Pers. soc. Psychol.*

Bickman, L. (1976). Fulfilling the promise: a response to Helmrich. *Pers. soc. Psychol. Bull., 2,* 131–133.

—— (1979). Program evaluation and social psychology. Toward the achievement of relevancy. *Pers. soc. Psychol. Bull., 5,* 483–490.

Blackwell, B. C. (1973). Drug therapy: patient compliance. *N. E. J. Med.,* 249–253, 289.

Boggiano, A. K., and D. N. Ruble (1978). Perception of competence and the over-justification effect: a developmental study. Unpublished manuscript. Princeton University.

Bohm, L. C., and J. Rodin (1983). Predictors of life satisfaction and depression among residents of specialized housing for older persons. Unpublished manuscript. Yale University.

Bootzin, R. R., P. H. Herman, and P. Nicassio (1976). The power of suggestion: another examination of misattribution and insomnia. *J. Pers. soc. Psychol., 34,* 673–679.

Borsky, P. N. (1969). Effects of noise on community behavior. In W. D. Ward, and J. E. Fricke (Eds.), *Noise as a public health hazard.* Washington, D.C.: The American Speech and Hearing Association.

Bowers, K. (1968). Pain, anxiety, and perceived control. *J. Consult. clinic. Psychol., 32,* 596–602.

Bowers, K. S. (1973). Situationism in psychology: an analysis and a critique. *Psychol. Rev., 80,* 307–336.

Bray, R. M., and N. L. Kerr (1979). Use of the simulation method in the study of jury behavior: some methodological considerations. *Law hum. Behav., 3,* 107–120.

Brehm, J. W. (1966). *A theory of psychological reactance.* New York: Academic Press.

Brehm, S. S., and D. A. McAllister (1980). A social psychological perspective on the maintenance of therapeutic change. In P. Karoly, and J. J. Steffen (Eds.), *Improving the long-term effects of psychotherapy.* New York: Gardner Press.

Brickman, P. (1980). A social psychology of human concerns. In R. Gilmour, and S. Duck (Eds.), *The development of social psychology.* London: Academic Press.

Brickman, P., V. C. Rabinowitz, J. Karuza, D. Coates, E. Cohn, and L. Kidder (1982). Models of helping and coping. *Amer. Psychol., 37,* 368–384.

Brodt, S. E., and P. G. Zimbardo (1981). Modifying shyness-related social behavior through symptom misattribution. *J. Pers. soc. Psychol., 41* (3), 447–449.

Brody, D. S. (1980). The patient's role in clinical decision-making. *Annals internal Med., 93,* 718–722.

_____ (1980). Psychological distress and hypertension control. *J. Hum. Stress, 6,* 2–6.

Bronfenbrenner, U. (1977). Lewinian space and ecological substance. *J. soc. Issues, 4,* 199–212.

Brown, E., K. Deffenbacher, and W. Sturgill (1977). Memory for faces and the circumstances of encounter. *J. appl. Psychol., 62,* 311–318.

Brown, D., G. Engquist, and M. Leventhal (1977). The effects of information on sensations, arousal, procedure, and painfulness on cold pressor distress. Unpublished manuscript. University of Wisconsin, Madison.

Buckhout, R. (1973). *A jury without peers.* New York: Center for Responsive Psychology.

Buell, J., and R. Eliot (1981). The clinical and pathological syndromes of sudden cardiac death. In F. Solomon, D. L. Parron, and P. B. Dews (Eds.), *Biobehavioral factors in sudden cardiac death.* Washington, D.C.: National Academy Press.

Bulman, R. J., and C. B. Wortman (1977). Attributions of blame and coping in the "real world." Severe accident victims react to their lot. *J. Pers. soc. Psychol., 35,* 351–363.

Busfield, B., P. Schneller, and D. Capra (1962). Depressive symptom or side effect? A comparative study of symptoms during pre-treatment and treatment of patients on three antidepressant medications. *J. Nervous Mental Disease, 134,* 339–345.

Caplan, R. D., S. Cobb, J. R. P. French, Jr., R. D. Harrison, and S. R. Pinneau, Jr. (1975). *Job demands and worker health: main effects and occupational differences.* Washington, D.C.: Government Printing Office.

Caplan, R. D., R. V. Harrison, R. V. Wellons, and J. R. P. French (1980). *Social support and patient adherence.* Ann Arbor, Mich.: Institute for Social Research.

Caplan, R. D., E. A. R. Robinson, J. R. P. French, J. R. Caldwell, and M. Shinn (1976). *Adhering to medical regimens: pilot experiments in patient education and social support.* Ann Arbor, Mich.: Institute for Social Research.

Carroll, J. S. (1978). Causal attributions in expert parole decisions. *J. Pers. soc. Psychol., 12,* 1501–1511.

_____ (1978). Causal attributions in expert parole decisions. *J. Pers. soc. Psychol., 12,* 1501–1511.

Carroll, J. S., and I. H. Frieze (1979). Conclusion: assessing the application of attribution theory to social problems. In I. H. Frieze, D. Bar-Tal, and J. S. Carroll (Eds.), *New approaches to social problems.* San Francisco: Jossey-Bass.

Carroll, J. S., and J. W. Payne (1976). The psychology of the parole decision process: a joint application of attribution theory and information processing psychology. In J. S. Carroll and J. W. Payne (Eds.), *Cognition and social behavior.* Hillsdale, N.J.: Erlbaum.

_____ (1977a). Crime seriousness, recidivism risk, and causal attributions in judgments of prison term by students and experts. *J. appl. Psychol., 62,* 595–602.

_____ (1977b). Judgments about crime and the criminal: a model and a method for investigating parole decisions. In B. Sales (Ed.), *Perspectives in law and psychology.* Vol. 1. *Criminal justice system.* New York: Plenum.

Carver, C. S. (1980). Perceived coercion, resistance to persuasion, and the type A behavior pattern. *J. Res. Pers., 19,* 467–481.

Cassell, J. (1976). The contribution of the social environment to host resistance. *Amer. J. Epidemiology, 104,* 107–123.

Chambliss, C., and E. J. Murray (1979). Cognitive procedures for smoking reduction: symptom attribution versus efficacy attribution. *Cognit. Therapeutic Res., 3,* 91–95.

Chanowitz, B., and E. Langer (1980). Knowing more (or less) than you can show: understanding control through the mindlessness/mindfulness distinction. In M. E. P. Seligman, and J. Garber (Eds.), *Human helplessness.* New York: Academic Press.

Cialdini, R. B., R. J. Borden, A. Thorne, M. R. Walker, S. Freeman, and L. R. Sloan (1976). Basking in reflected glory: three (football) field studies. *J. Pers. soc. Psychol., 3,* 366–375.

Clark, K. B., and M. P. Clark (1947). Racial identification and preference in Negro children. In T. M. Newcomb, and E. L. Hartley (Eds.), *Readings in social psychology.* New York: Holt.

Coates, D., C. B. Wortman, and A. Abbey (1979). Reactions to victims. In I. H. Frieze, D. Bar-Tal, and J. S. Carroll (Eds.), *New approaches to social problems.* San Francisco: Jossey-Bass.

Cobb, S. (1976). Social support as a moderator of life stress. *Psychosom. Med., 38,* 300–314.

Cobb, S., and R. M. Rose (1973). Hypertension, peptic ulcer, and diabetes in air traffic controllers. *J. Amer. Medical Assoc., 224,* 489–492.

Cohen, E. (1972). Interracial interaction disability. *Hum. Relat., 25,* (1), 9–24.

Cohen, F. (1979). Personality, stress and the development of physical illness. In G. Stone, F. Cohen, and N. Adler (Eds.), *Health psychology.* San Francisco: Jossey-Bass.

Cohen, F., and R. S. Lazarus (1973). Active coping processes, coping dispositions, and recovery from surgery. *Psychosom. Med., 35,* 375–389.

——— (1979). Coping with the stresses of illness. In G. Stone, F. Cohen, and N. Adler (Eds.), *Health psychology.* San Francisco: Jossey-Bass.

Cohen, S. (1980). Aftereffects of stress on human performance and social behavior: a review of research and theory. *Psychol. Bull., 88,* 82–108.

Cohen, S., D. Glass, and S. Phillips (1978). Environment and health. In H. E. Freeman, S. Levine, and L. G. Reeder (Eds.), *Handbook of medical sociology.* Englewood Cliffs, N.J.: Prentice-Hall.

Cohen, S., D. C. Glass, and J. E. Singer (1973). Apartment noise, auditory discrimination, and reading ability in children. *J. exp. soc. Psychol., 9,* 407–422.

Colletti, G., and S. A. Kopel (1979). Maintaining behavior change: an investigation of three maintenance strategies and the relationship of self-attribution to the long term reduction of cigarette smoking. *J. Consult. clinic. Psychol., 47,* 614–617.

Colligan, M. (1978). An investigation of apparent mass psychogenic illness in a furniture plant. Unpublished NIOSH evaluation report.

Colligan, M., and L. Murphy (1979). Mass psychogenic illness in organizations: an overview. *J. occupational Psychol., 52,* 77–90.

Colligan, M., and M. Urtes (1978). An investigation of apparent mass psychogenic illness in an electronics plant. Unpublished NIOSH evaluation report.

Collins, B. E., and M. F. Hoyt (1972). Personal responsibility for consequences: an integration and extension of the forced compliance literature. *J. exp. soc. Psychol., 8,* 558–593.

Collins, B. A., C. K. Whalen, and B. Henker (1980). Ecological and pharmacological influences of behaviors in the classroom: the hyperkinetic syndrome. In S. Salziner, J. Antrobus, and J. Glick (Eds.), *The eco-system of the "sick child."* New York: Academic Press.

Colvin, R. H. (1972). Imposed entrinsic reward in an elementary school setting: effects on free-operant rates and choices. *Dissertation abstracts Int., 32,* 5034–A.

Comstock, L., and C. Slome (1973). *A health survey of students 1: Prevalence of problems. J. Amer. Coll. Health Assoc., 22,* 150–155.

Cook, S. W. (1979). Social science and school desegregation: did we mislead the Supreme Court? *Pers. soc. Psychol. Bull., 5,* 420–437.

Cook, T. D., and D. T. Campbell (1979). *Quasi-experimentation design and analysis issues for field settings.* Chicago: Rand McNally.

Cox, P. R., and J. R. Ford (1964). The mortality of widows shortly after widowhood. *Lancet, 1,* 163–164.

Cromwell, R. L., E. C . Butterfield, F. M. Brayfield, and J. J. Curry (1977). *Acute myocardial infarction: reaction and recovery.* St. Louis: C. V. Mosby.

Davis, J. H., R. M. Bray, and R. W. Holt (1977). The empirical study of social decision processes in juries. In J. Topp, and F. Levine (Eds.), *Law, justice and the individual in society: psychological and legal issues.* New York: Holt, Rinehart, and Winston.

Davis, J. H., R. W. Holt, C. E. Spitzer, and G. Stosser (1981). The effects of consensus requirements and multiple decisions on mock juror verdict preferences. *J. exp. soc. Psychol., 17,* 1–15.

Davison, G. C., R. M. Tsujimoto, and A. G. Glaros (1973). Attribution and the maintenance of behavior change in falling asleep. *J. abnorm. Psychol., 82,* 124–133.

Davison, G. C., and S. Valins (1969). Maintenance of self-attributed and drug-attributed behavior change. *J. Pers. soc. Psychol., 11,* 25–33.

DeCharms, R. (1972). Personal causation training in the schools. *J. appl. soc. Psychol., 2,* 95–113.

——— (1976). *Enhancing motivation in the classroom.* New York: Irvington Publishers.

Deci, E. (1975). *Intrinsic motivation.* New York: Plenum.

Deci, E. L., and J. Povac (1978). Cognitive evaluation theory and the study of human motivation. In M. R. Lepper, and D. Greene (Eds.), *The hidden costs of reward.* Hillsdale, N.J.: Erlbaum.

Deci, E. L., and R. Ryan (1980). The empirical exploration of intrinsically motivated processes. In L. Berkowitz (Ed.), *Advances in experimental social psychology.* Vol. 13. New York: Academic Press.

Delbridge, L. (1975). Educational and psychological factors in the management of diabetes in childhood. *Med. J. Australia, 2,* 737–739.

DeVries, D. L., K. J. Edwards, and R. E. Slavin. (1978). Biracial learning teams and race relations in the classoom: four field experiments on teams-games-tournament. *J. educ. Psychol., 70,* 356–362.

DiMatteo, M. R. (1979). A social-psychological analysis of physician-patient rapport: toward a science of the art of medicine. *J. soc. Issues, 35,* 12–33.

DiMatteo, M. R., and J. A. Hall (1979). Nonverbal decoding skill and attention to nonverbal cues: a research note. *Environmental psychology and nonverbal behavior 3* (3), 188–192.

DiMatteo, M. R., L. M. Prince, and A. Taranta (1979). Patients' perceptions of physicians' behavior: determinants of patient commitment to the therapeutic relationship. *J. Community Health, 4,* 280–290.

DiMatteo, M. R., A. Taranto, H. S. Friedman, and L. M. Prince (1980). Predicting patient satisfaction from physicians' nonverbal communication skills. *Medical Care 18,* 376–387.

Doob, A. N., and H. M. Kirshenbaum (1973). Bias in police lineups—partial remembering. *J. police Sci. Admin., 1,* 287–293.

Dohrenwend, B. S., and B. P. Dohrenwend, Eds. (1974). *Stressful life events: their nature and effect.* New York: Wiley.

Dunn, S. R. (1979). Labelling: creating behavioral expectancies in interactive situations. Doctoral dissertation. Stanford University.

Dweck, C. S. (1975). The role of expectations and attributions in the alleviation of learned helplessness. *J. Pers. soc. Psychol., 31,* 674–685.

Dweck, C. S., and T. E. Goetz (1978). Attributions and learned helplessness. In J. H. Harvey, W. J. Ickes, and R. F. Kidd (Eds.), *New directions in attribution research.* Vol. 2. Hillsdale, N.J.: Erlbaum.

Ebbesen, E. B., and V. J. Konecni (1975). Decision making and information integration in the courts: the setting of bail. *J. Pers. soc. Psychol., 32,* 805–821.

Ebbesen, E. B., and B. H. Konecni (1980). On the external validity of decision-making research—what do we know about decision in the real world? In T. S. Wallsten (Ed.), *Cognitive processes in choice and decision behavior.* Hillsdale, N.J.: Erlbaum.

Ebbesen, E. B., S. Parker, and V. J. Konecni (1977). Laboratory and field analyses of decisions involving risk. *J. exp. Psychol.: hum. Perception Perform., 3,* 576–589.

Egbert, L. D., G. E. Battit, C. E. Welch, and M. K. Bartlett (1964). Reduction of post-operative pain for encouragement and instruction of patients. *N.E. J. Med., 270,* 825–827.

Edwards, W. (1954). The theory of decision making. *Psych. Bull., 51,* 380–417.

Ekblom, B. (1963). Significance of psychological factors with regard to risk of death among elderly persons. *Acta Psychiatrica Scandinavica, 39,* 627–633.

Ekehammar, B. O. (1974). Interactionism in personality from a historical perspective. *Psychol. Bull., 81,* 1026–1048.

Eliot, R. S., and J. C. Buell (1982). Bio-behavioral perspectives on coronary heart-disease, hypertension and sudden cardiac death. *Acta Medica Scandanavica* (5660), 203–213.

Elliott, G. R., and C. Eisdorfer (1982). *Stress and human health.* New York: Springer/Verlag.

Ellsworth, P. C. (1977). From abstract ideas to concrete instances: some guidelines for choosing natural research settings. *Amer. Psychol., 32,* 604–615.

Ellsworth, P. C., and J. G. Getman (In press). Social science in legal decision making. In L. Lipson, and S. Wheeler (Eds.), *Handbook of law and social science.* New York: Russell Sage.

Endler, N. S., and D. Magnusson (1976). Toward an interactional psychology of personality. *Psychol. Bull., 83,* 956–974.

Engel, G. L. (1971). Sudden and rapid death during psychological stress, folklore or folkwisdom. *Annals internal Med., 74,* 771–782.

——— (1978). Psychological stress vasodepressor, (vasobagal) syncope, and sudden death. *Annals internal Med., 89,* 403–412.

Evans, R. I. (1982). Deterring smoking in adolescents: a case study from a social psychological research program. In A. W. Johnson, O. Grusky, and B. H. Raven (Eds.), *Contemporary health services: social science perspectives.* Boston: Auburn House.

Evans, R. I., A. H. Henderson, P. C. Hill, and B. E. Raines (1979). Current psychological, social, and educational programs in control and prevention of smoking: a critical methodological review. In A. M. Gotto and R. Paoletti (Eds.), *Atherosclerosis Reviews.* Vol. 6. New York: Raven Press.

Evans, R. I., P. C. Hill, C. A. Dill, A. H. Henderson, J. H. Bray, and E. R. Gilden. Methodological considerations in longitudinal field research: an examination of the Houston adolescent smoking project. Paper presented at American Educational Research Association annual meeting, Boston.

Evans, R. I., R. M. Rozelle, S. E. Maxwell, B. E. Raines, C. A. Dill, T. J. Guthrie, A. H. Henderson, and P. C. Hill (1981). Social modeling films to defer smoking in adolescents: results of a three year field investigation. *J. appl. Psychol., 66* (4), 399–414.

Farquahar, J. W. (1978). The community-based model of life style intervention trials. *Amer. J. Epidemiology, 108,* 103–111.

Fenigstein, A., M. Scheier, and A. H. Buss (1975). Public and private self-consciousness: assessment and theory. *J. Consult. clinic. Psychol., 43,* 522–527.

Festinger, L. (1954). A theory of social comparison processes. *Hum. Relat., 7,* 117–140.

Fishbein, M. (1972). Toward an understanding of family planning behaviors. *J. app. soc. Psychol., 2,* 214–227.

Fishbein, M., and J. Jaccard (1973). Theoretical and methodological considerations in the prediction of family planning intentions and behavior. *Rep. Res. soc. Psychol., 4,* 37–52.

Franks, D., and J. Marolla (1976). Efficacious and social approval as interacting dimensions of self-esteem: a tentative formulation through construct validation. *Sociometry, 39,* 324–341.

Freedman, J. (1979). Theories of contagion. Paper presented at American Industrial Hygiene Conference, Chicago.

Freeman, B., V. F. Negrete, M. Davis, and B. M. Korsch (1971). Gaps in doctor-patient communication: doctor-patient interaction analysis. *Pediatric Res., 5,* 298–311.

French, J. R. P. (1974). Person-role fit. In A. McLean, *Occupational Stress.* Springfield, Ill.: Charles C. Thomas.

French, J. R. P., Jr., and B. H. Raven (1959). The bases of social power. In D. Cartwright (Ed.), *Studies in social power.* Ann Arbor: Univ. of Michigan.

French, J. R. P., W. L., Rodgers, and S. Cobb (1974). Adjustment as person-environment fit. In G. Coelho, D. Hamburg, and J. Adams (Eds.), *Coping and adaptation.* New York: Basic Books.

Friedman, H. S. (1979). Nonverbal communication between patients and medical practitioners. *J. soc. Issues, 35,* 82–99.

Friedman, M., S. O. Byers, J. Diamant, and H. Rosenman (1975). Plasma catecholamine response of coronary-prone subjects (Type A) to a specific challenge. *Metabolism, 24,* 205–210.

Frieze, I. H., D. Bar-Tal, and J. S. Carroll (1979). *New approaches to social problems.* London: Jossey-Bass.

Frieze, I. H. (1978). Self-perceptions of battered women. Paper presented at the annual meeting of the Association for Women in Psychology, Pittsburgh.

Fisher, J. D., and A. Nadler (1974). Effect on similarity between donor and recipient on recipients reactions to aid. *J. appl. soc. Psychol., 4,* 230–243.

Gatchel, R. J., and J. D. Practor (1976). Physiological correlates of learned helplessness in man. *J. abnorm. Psychol., 85,* 27–34.

Geer, J. H., G. C. Davison, and R. I. Gatchel (1970). Reduction of stress in humans through non-vertical perceived control of aversive stimulation. *J. Pers. soc. Psychol., 16,* 731–738.

Geffner, R. (1978). The effects of interdependent learning on self-esteem, inter-ethnic relations, and intra-ethnic attitudes of elementary school children: a field experiment. Unpublished doctoral dissertation. University of California, Santa Cruz.

Gerard, H. B., and H. Miller (1975). *School desegregation: a long term study*. New York: Plenum.

Gergen, K. J. (1973). Social psychology as history. *J. Pers. soc. Psychol., 26,* 309–320.

Gibbons, F. K., C. S. Carver, M. Scheier, and S. E. Hormuth (1979). Self-focused attention and the placebo effect: fooling some of the people some of the time. *J. exp. soc. Psychol., 15,* 263–274.

Glass, D. C. (1977). Stress, behavior patterns, and coronary disease. *Amer. Scient., 65,* 177–187.

Glass, D. C., L. R. Krakoff, R. Contrada, W. C. Hilton, K. Kehoe, E. G. Mannucci, C. Collins, B. Snow, and E. Elting (1980a). Effect of harassment and competition upon cardiovascular and plasma catecholamine response in type A and type B individuals. *Psychophysiology, 17,* 453–463.

Glass, D. C., L. R. Krakoff, J. Finkelman, B. Snow, R. Contrada, K. Kehoe, E. G. Mannucci, W. Isecke, C. Collins, W. F. Hilton, and E. Elting (1980b). Effect of task overload upon cardiovascular and plasma catecholamine responses in type A and type B individuals. *Basic appl. soc. Psychol., 17,* 199–218.

Glass, D. C., and J. E. Singer (1972). *Urban stress*. New York: Academic Press.

Glass, D. C., J. E. Singer, H. S. Leonard, D. Krantz, S. Cohen, and H. Cummings (1973). Perceived control of aversive stimulation and the reduction of stress responses. *J. Pers., 41,* 577–595.

Glick, I., R. S. Weiss, and C. M. Parkes (1974). *The first year of bereavement*. New York: Wiley-Interscience.

Gordon, C., and C. M. Gaitz (1977). Leisure and lives: personal expressivity across the life span. In R. H. Binstock, and E. Shanas (Eds.), *Handbook of aging and the social sciences*. New York: Van Nostrand-Reinhold.

Gore, S. (1978). The effect of social support in moderating the health consequences of unemployment. *J. Health soc. Behav., 19,* 157–165.

Gorenstein, G. W., and P. C. Ellsworth (1980). Effect of choosing an incorrect photograph on a later identification by an eyewitness. *J. appl. Psychol., 65,* 616–622.

Gottfredson, D. M., L. T. Wilkins, and P. B. Hoffman (1978). *Guidelines for parole and sentencing*. Lexington, Mass.: Lexington Books.

Gould, R., and H. Sigall (1977). The effects of empathy and outcome on attribution: an examination of the divergent-perspectives hypothesis. *J. exp. soc. Psychol., 13,* 480–491.

Gove, W. R. (1973). Sex, marital status and mortality. *Amer. J. Sociol., 79,* 45–67.

Green, J. M., and E. Furman (1975). Child's parent dies—studies in childhood bereavement. *Amer. J. Psychol., 132,* 680–681.

Greene, D., and M. R. Lepper (1974). Effects of extrinsic rewards on children's subsequent intrinsic interest. *Child Development, 45,* 1141–1145.

Greene, D., B. Sternberg, and M. R. Lepper (1976). Overjustification in a token economy. *J. Pers. soc. Psychol., 34,* 1219–1234.

Greene, W. H., A. J. Moss, and S. Goldstein (1974). Delay, denial, and death in coronary heart disease. In R. S. Eliot (Ed.), *Stress and the heart*. Mount Kisco, N.Y.: Futura.

Greenley, J., and D. Mechanic (1976). Social selection in seeking help for psychological problems. *J. Health soc. Behav., 17,* 249–262.

Griffitt, W., and T. Jackson (1973). Simulated jury decisions: the influence of jury-defendant attitude similarity-dissimilarity. *Soc. Behav. Pers., 1,* 1–7.

Grossman, P., and P. B. Defares (1981). Breathing to the heart of the matter: respiratory influences upon cardiovascular psychophysiological phenomena. In C. D. Spielberger, J. G. Sarason, and P. B. Defares (Eds.), *Stress and anxiety*. Vol. 9. New York: Wiley.

Hackett, T. P., and N. H. Cassem (1974). Development of a quantitative rating scale to assess denial. *J. Psychosom. Res., 18* (2), 93–100.

Hackett, T. P., and N. H. Cassen (1976). White collar response and blue collar response to heart attack. *J. Psychosom., 20,* 85–95.

Hackman, J. R., and J. L. Shuttle (1977). *Improving life at work*. Santa Monica: Goodyear.

Haney, C. (1980). Juries and the death penalty: *readdressing the witherspoon question. Crime and delinquency,* 512–527.

Haney, C., W. C. Banks, and P. G. Zimbardo (1973). Interpersonal dynamics in a simulated prison. *Int. J. Criminology Penology, 1,* 69–79.

Haney, C., and P. G. Zimbardo (1977). The socialization into criminality: on becoming a prisoner and a guard. In J. L. Tapp and F. J. Levine (Eds.), *Law, justice and the individual in society: psychological and legal issues*. New York: Holt, Rinehart, and Winston.

Hanusa, B. A., and R. Schulz (1977). Attributional mediators of learned helplessness. *J. Pers. soc. Psychol., 35,* 602–611.

Harrison, V. R. (1978). Person-environment fit and job stress. In C. L. Cooper and R. Payne (Eds.), *Stress at work*. New York: Wiley.

Harter, S. (1978). Pleasure derived from optimal challenge and the effects of extrinsic rewards on children's difficulty level choices. *Child Development, 49,* 788–799.

Harvey, J. H., and G. Weary (1981). *Perspectives on attributional processes*. Dubuque, Iowa: Wm. C. Brown.

Harvey, J. H., G. L. Wells, and M. D. Alvarez (1978). Attribution in the context of conflict and separation in close relationships. In J. H. Harvey, W. Ickes, and R. R. Kidd (Eds.), *New directions in attribution research*. Vol. 2. Hillsdale, N. J.: Erlbaum.

Haynes, R. B., D. W. Taylor, and D. L. Sackett, Eds. (1979). *Compliance in health care*. Baltimore: Johns Hopkins.

Haynes, S. G., and M. Feinleib (1980). Women, work, and coronary heart disease: prospective findings from the Framingham heart study. *Amer. J. publ. Health, 70,* 133–141.

Hayes-Bautista, D. E. (1976). Modifying the treatment: patient compliance, patient control and medical care. *Soc. Sci. Med., 10,* 233–238.

Heider, F. (1958). *The psychology of interpersonal relations*. New York: Wiley.

Helmreich, R. L. (1975). Applied social psychology: the unfulfilled promise. *Pers. soc. Psychol. Bull., 1,* 548–560.

Henry, J. P., L. Ely, and M. Stephens (1972). Mental factors and cardiovascular disease: psychosocial factors facilitating and inhibiting the influence of the neuroendocrine alarm responses upon the course of cardiovascular disease. *Psychiatric Annals, 2,* 25–71.

Herridge, C. F. (1974). Aircraft noise and mental health. *J. Psychosom., 18,* 239.

Himmelweit, H. T. (1975). Studies of societal influences: problems and implications. In M. Deutsch, and H. A. Hornstein (Eds.), *Applying social psychology implication for research, practice, and training.* Hillsdale, N.J.: Erlbaum.

Hinkel, L. E. (1977). The effect of exposure to culture change, social change, and changes in interpersonal relationships on health. In B. S. Dohrenwend, and B. P. Dohrenwend (Eds.), *Stressful life events: their nature and effects.* New York: Wiley.

Hiroto, D. S., and M. E. P. Seligman (1975). Generality of learned helplessness in man. *J. Pers. soc. Psychol., 31,* 311–327.

Hochbaum, G. (1958). Public participation in medical screening program: a sociopsychological study. PHS Publication #572. Washington, D.C.

Hoffman, I., and E. H. Futterman (1971). Coping with waiting: psychiatric intervention and study in the waiting room of a pediatric oncology unit. *Comprehensive Psychiatry, 12,* 67–81.

Holmes, T. H., and M. Masuda (1974). Life change and illness susceptibility. In B. S. Dohrenwend, and B. P. Dohrenwend (Eds.), *Stressful life events: their nature and effects.* New York: Wiley.

Holmes, T. H., and R. H. Rahe (1967). The social readjustment rating scale. *J. Psychosom. Res., 11,* 213–218.

Hornstein, H. A. (1975). Social psychology as social intervention. In M. Deutsch, and H. A. Hornstein (Eds.), *Applying social psychology implication for research, practice, and training.* Hillsdale, N.J.: Erlbaum.

Houlden, P., S. LaTour, L. Walker, and J. Thibaut (1978). Preference for modes of dispute resolution as a function of process and decision control. *J. exp. soc. Psychol., 14,* 13–30.

House, J. S. (1974). Occupational stress and coronary heart disease: a review and theoretical integration. *J. Health soc. Behav., 15,* 12–27.

——— (1975). Occupational stress as a precursor to coronary disease. In W. D. Gentry, and R. B. Williams, Jr. (Eds.), *Psychological aspects of myocardial infarction and coronary care.* St. Louis: C.V. Mosby.

Insko, C. A., J. W. Thibaut, D. Moehle, M. Wilson, W. D. Diamond, R. Gilmore, M. R. Solomon, and A. Lipsitz (1980). The social evolution of institutionalized power. *J. Pers. soc. Psychol., 39,* 431–448.

Jaccard, J., and A. R. Davidson (1975). A comparison of the models of social behavior: results of a survey sample. *Sociometry, 38,* 497–517.

Jacoby, J. (1975). Consumer psychology as a social psychological sphere of action. *Amer. Psychol., 30,* 977–987.

Janis, I. L. (1971). *Stress and frustration.* New York: Harcourt, Brace, Jovanovich.

——— (1972). *Victims of groupthink.* Boston: Houghton Mifflin.

——— (1975). "Reaction" to section titled "Public opinion, attitude research and health problems." In A. J. Enelow and J. B. Henderson (Eds.), *Applying behavioral science to cardiovascular risk.* New York: American Heart Association.

——— (1982). *Stress, attitudes, and decisions: selected papers.* New York: Praeger.

———, Ed. (1983a). *Changing behavior through counseling: theory and field research on dyadic helping relationships.* New Haven: Yale Univ. Press.

——— (1983b). Social support for stressful decisions. *Amer. Psychol., 38* (2), 143–161.

Janis, I. L., P. Defares, and P. Grossman (1982). Hypervigilant reactions to threat. In A. Baum and J. E. Singer (Eds.), *Advances in environmental psychology.* Vol. 4. Hillsdale, N.J.: Erlbaum.

Janis, I. L., and X. Hoffman (1983). In I. L. Janis (Ed.), Counseling on personal decisions: theory and research on short-term helping relationships. New Haven: Yale Univ. Press.

Janis, I. L., and L. Mann (1977). Decision making: a psychological analysis of conflict, choice, and commitment. New York: Free Press.

Janis, I. L., and J. Rodin (1979). Attribution, control and decision making: social psychology and health care. In G. C. Stone, F. Cohen, and N. E. Adler (Eds.), *Health psychology.* San Francisco: Jossey-Bass.

Janoff-Bulman, R. (1979). Characterological versus behavioral self-blame: inquiries into depression and rape. *J. Pers. soc. Psychol., 37,* 1798–1809.

Jenkins, C. D. (1971). Psychologic and social precursors of coronary disease. *N. E. J. Med., 284,* 244–255, 307–317.

——— (1976). Recent evidence supporting psychologic and social risk factors for coronary disease. *N. E. J. Med., 294,* 987–994, 1033–1038.

Johnson, J. E. (1973). Effects of accurate expectations about sensations on the sensory and distress components of pain. *J. Pers. soc. Psychol., 27,* 261–275.

Johnson, J. E., K. T. Kirchoff, and M. P. Endress (1975). Deferring children's distress behavior during orthopedic cast removal. *Nursing Res., 75,* 404–410.

Johnson, J. E., and H. Leventhal (1974). Effects of accurate expectations and behavioral instructions on reactions during a noxious medical examination. *J. Pers. soc. Psychol., 29,* 710–718.

Johnson, J. E., J. F. Morrissey, and H. Leventhal (1973). Psychological preparation for an endoscopic examination. *Gastrointestinal Endoscopy, 19,* 180–182.

Johnson, J. E., V. H. Rice, S. S. Fuller, and M. P. Endress (1977). Sensory information, behavioral instruction, and recovery from surgery. Paper presented at the American Psychological Association, San Francisco.

Johnson, S. B. (1980). Psychosocial factors in juvenile diabetes: a review. *J. behav. Med., 3,* 95–116.

Jones, C., and E. Aronson (1973). Attribution of fault to a rape victim as a function of respectability of the victim. *J. Pers. soc. Psychol., 26,* 415–419.

Jones, E. E., and K. E. Davis (1965). From acts to dispositions: the attribution process in person perception. In L. Berkowitz (Ed.), *Advances in experimental social psychology.* Vol. 2. New York: Academic Press.

Jones, E. E., and R. E. Nisbett (1972). The actor and the observer: divergent perceptions of the causes of behavior. In E. E. Jones, D. E. Kanouse, H. H. Kelley, R. E. Nisbett, S. Valins, and B. Weiner (Eds.), *Attribution: perceiving the causes of behavior*. Morristown, N.J.: General Learning Press.

Joreskog, K. G., and D. Sarbom (1979). Advances in factor analyses and structural equation models. Cambridge, Mass.: Abbott Books.

Kahn, R. (1981). *Work and health*. New York: Wiley.

Kahn, R. L., and T. C. Antonucci (1981). Convoys of social support: a life course approach. In S. Kiesler, J. Morgan, and V. Oppenheimer (Eds.), *Aging: social change*. New York: Academic Press.

Kairys, D., J. Schulman, and S. Harring, Eds. (1975). *The jury system: new methods for reducing prejudice*. Philadelphia: National Lawyers Guild.

Kalish, R. A. (1977). Dying and preparing for death: a view of families. In H. Feifel (Ed.), *New meanings of death*. New York: McGraw-Hill.

Kanfer, F. H. (1970). Self-regulation: research, issues, and speculations. In C. Neuringer, and J. L. Michael (Eds.), *Behavior modification in clinical psychology*. New York: Appleton-Century-Crofts.

———— (1971). The maintenance of behavior by self-generated stimuli and reinforcement. In A. Jacobs, and L. B. Sachs (Eds.), *The psychology of private events: perspectives on covert response systems*. New York: Academic Press.

Kanfer, F. H., and M. L. Seider (1973). Self-control: factors enhancing tolerance of noxious stimulation. *J. Pers. soc. Psychol., 25,* 381–389.

Kaplan, M. F., and G. D. Kemmerick (1974). Juror judgment as information integration: combining evidential and nonevidential information. *J. Pers. soc. Psychol., 30,* 493–499.

Kaplan, B. H., J. C. Cassel, and S. Gore (1979). Social support and health. In E. G. Jaco (Ed.), *Patients, physicians, and illness: a sourcebook in behavioral science and health*. New York: Free Press.

Karniol, R., and M. Ross (1977). The effects of performance-relevant and performance-irrelevant rewards on children's intrinsic motivation. *Child Development, 48,* 282–287.

Karoly, P., and F. H. Kanfer (1982). *Self-management and behavior change: from theory to practice*. New York: Pergamon Press.

Kasl, S. O., and S. Cobb (1977). Can one extrapolate chronic changes from reactivity to acute stress? *Psychosomatic Med., 39* (1), 55–56.

Kasl, S. V., A. S. Evans, and J. C. Neiderman (1979). Psychosocial risk factors in the development of infectious mononucleosis. *Psychosom. Med., 41,* 445–467.

Keeny, R. L. (1973). A utility function for the response times of engines and ladders to fires. *Urban Analysis, 1,* 209–222.

Kelley, H. H. (1967). Attribution theory in social psychology. In D. Levine (Ed.), *Nebraska symposium on motivation*. Vol. 15. Lincoln: Univ. of Nebraska Press, Pp. 192–240.

———— (1971). Attribution theory in social interaction. In E. E. Jones *et al.* (Eds.), *Attribution: perceiving the causes of behavior*. New York: General Learning Press.

Kelley, H. H., and J. W. Thibaut (1978). *Interpersonal relations: a theory of interdependence*. New York: Wiley.

Kellogg, R., and R. S. Baron (1975). Attribution theory, insomnia and the reverse placebo effect: a reversal of Storm's and Nisbett's findings. *J. Pers. soc. Psychol., 32,* 231–236.

Kelman, H. (1958). Compliance, identification and internalization: three processes of attitude change. *J. conflict Resolution, 2,* 51–60.

———— (1973). Violence without moral restraint: reflections on the dehumanization of victims and victimizers. *J. soc. Issues, 29,* 25–61.

Kerckhoff, A., and K. Back (1968). *The June bug: a study of hysterical contagion*. New York: Appleton.

Kleiman, M. A., J. E. Mantell, and E. S. Alexander (1977). Collaboration and its discontents: the perils of partnership. *J. appl. behav. Sci., 13,* 403–410.

Klemp, G. O., and J. Rodin (1976). Effects of uncertainty, delay, and focus of attention on reactions to an aversive situation. *J. exp. soc. Psychol., 12,* 416–421.

Knopf, A. (1976). Changes in women's opinions about cancer. *Soc. Sci. Medicine, 10,* 191–195.

Kobasa, S. C. (1979). Stressful life events, personality, and health: an inquiry into hardiness. *J. Pers. soc. Psychol., 37,* 1–11.

Konecni, V. J., and E. B. Ebbesen (1976). Disinhibition versus the cathartic effect: artifact and substance. *J. Pers. soc. Psychol., 34,* 352–365.

Korsch, B. M., E. K. Gozzi, and V. Francis (1968). Gaps in doctor-patient communication. I: Doctor-patient interaction and patient satisfaction. *Pediatrics, 42,* 855–871.

Koski, M., and A. Kumento (1977). The interrelationship between diabetic control and family life. In Z. Laron (Ed.), *Psychological aspects of balance of diabetes in juveniles. Pediatric adolescent endocrinology*. Vol. 3. New York: S. Karger.

Koslin, S., B. Koslin, R. Pargament, and H. Wasman (1972). Classroom racial balance and students' interracial attitudes. *Sociol. Educ., 45,* 386–407.

Krantz, D. S., A. Baum, and M. V. Wideman (1980). Assessment of preferences for self-treatment and information in medical care. *J. Pers. soc. Psychol., 39,* 977–990.

Krantz, D. S., D. C. Glass, R. Contrada, and N. E. Miller (1981). Behavior and health. In *The five-year outlook on science and technology*. Vol. 2. National Science Foundation. Washington, D.C.: Government Printing Office.

Krantz, D., and R. Schulz (1980). Personal control and health: some applications to crisis of middle and old age. In A. Baum and J. Singer (Eds.), *Advances in environmental psychology*. Vol. 2. New York: Academic Press.

Kraus, A. S., and A. M. Lilienfeld (1959). Some epidemiological aspects of the high mortality rate in the young widowed group. *J. chronic Dis., 10,* 207–217.

Lalonde, M. (1974). *A new perspective on the health of Canadians: a working document*. Ottawa: Government of Canada.

Langer, E. (1975). The illusion of control. *J. exp. soc. Psychol., 32,* 311–328.

Langer, E., A. Blank, and B. Chanowitz (1978). The mindlessness of ostensibly thoughtful action: the role of "placebic" information in interpersonal interaction. *J. Pers. soc. Psychol., 36,* 635–642.

Langer, E., I. Janis, and J. Wolfer (1975). Reduction of psychological stress in surgical patients. *J. exp. soc. Psychol., 11,* 155–165.

Langer, E. J., and J. Rodin (1976). The effects of choice and enhanced personal responsibility for the aged: a field experiment in an institutional setting. *J. Pers. soc. Psychol., 34,* 191–198.

Latane, B., and J. M. Darley (1969). *The unresponsive bystander: why doesn't he help?* New York: Appleton-Century-Crofts.

LaTour, S. (1978). Determinants of participant and observer satisfaction with adversary and inquisitional modes of adjudication. *J. Pers. soc. Psychol., 36,* 1531–1545.

LaTour, S., P. Houlden, L. Walker, and J. Thibaut (1976a). Some determinants of preference for modes of conflict resolution. *J. conflict Resolution, 20,* 319–356.

_____ (1976b). Procedure: transnational perspectives and preferences. *Yale Law J., 86,* 258–290.

Lawton, M. P. (1975). Competence, environmental press, and the adaptation of older people. In P. G. Windley, T. O. Byertst, and F. G. Ernst (Eds.), *Theory development in environment and aging.* Manhattan, Kan.: Gerontological Society.

Lawton, M. P., and L. Nahemow (1973). Ecology and the aging process. In C. Eisdorfer, and M. P. Lawton (Eds.), *The psychology of adult development and aging.* Washington, D.C.: American Psychological Association.

Lazarus, R. S. (1966). Psychological stress and the coping process. New York: McGraw-Hill.

_____ (1971). The concepts of stress and disease. In L. Levi (Ed.), *Society, stress and disease.* Vol. 1. London: Oxford Univ. Press.

Lazarus, R. S., and J. B. Cohen (1977). Environmental stress. *Hum. Behav. Environment, 1,* 89–127.

Lepper, M. R., and D. Greene (1975). Turning play into work: effects of adult surveillance and extrinsic rewards on children's intrinsic motivation. *J. Pers. soc. Psychol., 31,* 479–486.

Lepper, M. R., and D. Greene (1978). *Hidden costs of reward.* Stanford: Stanford Univ. Press.

Lepper, M. R., D. Greene, and R. E. Nisbett (1973). Undermining children's intrinsic interest with extrinsic rewards: a test of the "overjustification" hypothesis. *J. Pers. soc. Psychol., 28,* 129–137.

Lerner, M. J. (1970). The desire for justice and reactions to victims. In J. Macaulay, and L. Berkowitz (Eds.), *Altruism and helping behavior.* New York: Academic Press.

_____ (1971). Observer's evaluation of a victim: justice, guilt and veridical perception. *J. Pers. soc. Psychol., 20,* 127–130.

Leventhal, H. (1975). The consequences of depersonalization during illness and treatment. An information processing model. In J. Howard and A. Strauss (Eds.), *Humanizing health care.* New York: Wiley.

_____ (1980a). Applied social psychological research: the salvation of substantive social psychological theory. In R. Kidd and M. Saks (Eds.), *Advances in applied social psychology.* Hillsdale, N.J.: Erlbaum.

_____ (1980b). Toward a comprehensive theory of emotion. In L. Berkowitz (Ed.) *Advanced in experimental social psychology.* New York: Academic Press.

Leventhal, H., M. A. Safer, P. D. Cleary, and M. Gutman (1980). Cardiovascular risk modification by community based programs for life style change: comments on the Stanford study. *J. Consult. clinic. Psychol., 48* (2), 150–158.

Leventhal, H., C. A. Booth, S. Shacham, and E. A. Leventhal (1977). Attention, coping, and the control of distress in childbirth. Unpublished manuscript. Univ. of Wisconsin, Madison.

Leventhal, H., and P. D. Cleary (1971). Behavioral modification of risk factors: technology or science? In M. L. Pollock *et al.* (Eds.), *Heart disease and rehabilitation: state of the art.* New York: Houghton Mifflin. Pp. 297–313.

Leventhal, H., and D. Everhart (1979). Emotion, pain and physical illness. In C. E. Izard (Ed.), *Emotion and psychopathology.* New York: Plenum.

Leventhal, H., D. Meyer, and D. Nerenz (1980). The common sense representation of illness danger. In S. Rachman (Ed.), *Medical psychology.* Vol. 2. London: Pergamon Press.

Levi, L. (1979). Psychosocial factors in preventive medicine. In surgeon general's *Background papers for healthy people* report. Washington, D.C.: U.S. Government Printing Office. DHEW, Publication #79–55011A.

Levy, J. M., and R. K. McGee (1975). Childbirth as crisis—test of Janis's theory of communication and stress resolution. *J. Pers. soc. Psychol., 3,* 171–179.

Lewin, K. C. (1947). Frontiers in group dynamics: concept, method, and reality in social science: social equilibration and social change. *Hum. Rel., 1,* 5–41.

Lewin, K. (1951). *Field theory in social science.* New York: Harper.

Lewis, F. M., D. E. Morisky, and B. S. Flynn (1978). A test of the construct validity of health locus of control: effects on self-reported compliance for hypertensive patients. *Health educ. Monogr., 6,* 138–148.

Liem, G. R. (1975). Performance and satisfaction as affected by personal control over salient decisions. *J. Pers. soc. Psychol., 31,* 232–240.

Lind, E. A. (1975). The exercise of information influence in legal advocacy. *J. appl. soc. Psychol., 5,* 127–143.

Lind, E. A., S. Kurtz, L. Musante, L. Walker, and J. W. Thibaut (1980). Procedure and outcome effects on reactions to adjudicated resolution of conflicts of interest. *J. Pers. soc. Psychol., 39,* 643–653.

Lind, A., J. Thibaut, and L. Walker (1976). A cross-cultural comparison of the effect of adversary and inquisitorial processes on bias in legal decision making. *Virginia Law Rev., 62,* 271–283.

Linn, L. S., and C. D. Lewis (1979). Attitudes towards self-care among practicing physicians. *Medical Care, 17,* 183–190.

Lipton, J. P. (1977). On the psychology of eyewitness testimony. *J. appl. Psychol., 62,* 90–95.

Loftus, E. R., D. G. Miller, and H. J. Burns (1978). Semantic integration of verbal information into a visual memory. *J. exp. Psychol.: hum. Learn. Memory, 4,* 19–31.

Lorber, J. (1975). Good patients and problem patients: conformity and deviance in a general hospital. *J. Health soc. Behav., 16,* 213–225.

Lowery, C. R., D. R. Denney, and M. D. Storms (1979). The treatment of insomnia: pill attributions and nonpejorative self-attributions. *Cognit. Therapy Res., 3,* 161–164.

Lynch, J. J. (1977). *The broken heart: the medical consequences of loneliness.* New York: Basic Books.

McCain, G., V. C. Cox, and P. B. Paulus (1976). The relationship between illness complaints and degree of crowding in a prison environment. *Environment Behav., 8,* 283–290.

McConahay, J. B. (1978). The effects of school desegregation upon students' racial attitudes and behavior: a critical review of the literature and a prolegomenon to future research. *Law contemporary Prob., 42,* 77–107.

_____ (1981). Reducing racial prejudice in desegregated schools. In W. D. Hawley (Ed.), *Effective school desegregation.* Beverly Hills, Calif.: Sage.

McFall, R. M., and C. L. Hammen (1971). Motivation, structure and self-monitoring role of nonspecific factors in smoking reduction. *J. Consult. Clinic. Psychol., 37,* 80.

McGrath, J. E., and I. Altman (1966). *Small group research: a synthesis and critique of the field.* New York: Holt, Rinehart, and Winston.

McGuire, W. (1973). The yin and yang of progress in social psychology. *J. Pers. soc. Psychol., 26,* 446–456.

McIntosh, J. (1974). Processes of communication, information seeking and control associated with cancer: a selected review of the literature. *Soc. Sci. Med., 8,* 167–187.

McKenna, R. J. (1972). Some effects of anxiety level and food cues on the eating behavior of obese and normal subjects: a comparison of the Schachterian and psychosomatic conceptions. *J. Pers. soc. Psychol., 22,* 311–319.

Mandler, G. (1975). *Mind and emotion.* New York: Wiley.

Marlatt, G. A., and J. R. Gordon (1980). Determinants of relapse-implications for the maintenance of behavior-change. In D. O. Davidson, and S. M. Davidson (Eds.), *Behavioral medicine: changing health life styles.* New York: Brunner Mazel.

Marshall, J., K. H. Marquis, and S. E. Oskamp (1971). Effects of kind of question and atmosphere of interrogation on accuracy and completeness of testimony. *Harvard Law Rev., 84,* 1620–1644.

Marshall, G., and P. G. Zimbardo (1979). The effective consequences of inadequately explained physiological arousal. *J. Pers. soc. Psychol., 37,* 970–988.

Marston, M. V. (1970). Compliance with medical regimens: a review of the literature. *Nursing Res., 19,* 312–323.

Maslach, C. (1982). *Burn-out: the cost of caring.* Englewood Cliffs, N.J.: Prentice-Hall.

_____ (1978). The client role in staff burn-out. *J. soc. Issues, 34,* 111–124.

_____ (1979). Negative emotional biasing of unexplained arousal. *J. Pers. soc. Psychol., 37,* 953–969.

Mason, J. W. (1971). A re-evaluation of the concept of "non-specificity" in stress theory. *J. Psychiat. Res., 8,* 323–328.

_____ (1974). Specificity in the organization of neuroendocrine profiles. In P. Seeman and G. M. Brown (Eds.), *Frontiers in neurology and neuroscience research.* Toronto: Univ. of Toronto.

Matthews, K. A. (1982). Psychological perspectives on the type A behavior pattern. *Psychol. Bull., 91,* 293–323.

Meichenbaum, D. (1977). *Cognitive-behavior modification.* New York: Plenum.

Meichenbaum, D., and D. Turk (1976).The cognitive-behavioral management of anxiety, anger and pain. In P. O. Davidson (Ed.), *The behavioral management of anxiety, depression, and pain.* New York: Brunner Mazel.

Meichenbaum, D., D. Turk, and S. Burstein (1975). The nature of coping with stress. In I. Sarason, and C. Spielberger (Eds.), *Stress and anxiety.* Vol. 2. New York: Wiley.

Melzack, R. (1971). Phantom limb pain: implications for treatment of pathological pain. *Anesthesiology, 35,* 401–419.

Meyer, A. J. (1980). Skills training in a cardiovascular health education campaign. *J. Consult. clinic. Psychol., 48,* 129–142.

Meyer, A. J., N. Macoby, and J. W. Farquhuar (1980). Cardiovascular risk modification by community-based programs for life-style. *J. cons. Psychol., 48* (2), 159–163.

Meyer, A., L. Bollmeier, and F. Alexander (1945). Correlation between emotions and carbohydrate metabolism in two cases of diabetes mellitus. *Psychosom. Med., 7,* 335–341.

Meyer, D., H. Leventhal, and M. Gutman (In press). Common-sense models of illness: the example of hypertension. *Health Psychology.*

Meyers, D. G., and M. F. Kaplan (1976). Group-induced polarization in simulated juries. *J. Pers. soc. Psychol., 2,* 63–66.

Michela, J., L. A. Peplau, and D. Week (1979). Perceived dimensions and consequences of attribution for loneliness. Unpublished paper. California, Los Angeles.

Milgram, S. (1965). Some conditions of obedience and disobedience to authority. *Hum. Relat., 18,* 57–76.

Miller, S. M. (1979). Controllability and human stress: method, evidence and theory. *Behav. Res. Therapy, 17,* 287–304.

Mills, R. T., and D. S. Krantz (1979). Information, choice, and reactions to stress: a field experiment in a blood bank with laboratory analogue. *J. Pers. soc. Psychol., 37,* 608–620.

Minuchin, S., L. Baker, B. Rosman, R. Liebman, L. Milman, and T. Todd (1975). A conceptual model of psychosomatic illness in children. *Psychiatry, 32,* 1031–1038.

Minuchin, S., B. Rosman, and L. Baker (1978). *Psychosomatic families.* Cambridge, Mass.: Harvard Univ. Press.

Mischel, W. (1973). Toward a cognitive social learning reconceptualization of personality. *Psychol. Rev., 80,* 252–283.

Mitchell, G. W., and A. S. Glicksman (1977). Cancer patients: knowledge and attitudes. *Cancer, 40,* 61–66.

Monahan, J., and E. F. Loftus (1982). Psychology of law. *Ann. Rev. Psychol., 33,* 441–476.

Monson, T. C., and M. Snyder (1977). Actors, observers, and the attribution process: toward a reconceptualization. *J. exp. soc. Psychol., 13,* 89–111.

Moos, R. H. (1980). Specialized living environments for older people: a conceptual framework for evaluation. *J. soc. Issues, 36,* 75–94.

Moos, R., and P. Houts (1968). The assessment of the social atmosphere of psychiatric wards. *J. abnorm. Psychol., 73,* 595–604.

Moos, R., and S. Lemke (1980). Assessing the physical and architectural features of sheltered care settings. *J. Gerontology, 21,* 88–98.

Moos, R., and B. VanDort (1976). Student physical symptoms and the social climate of college living groups. Unpublished manuscript. Social Ecology Laboratory, Department of Psychiatry and Behavioral Sciences, Stanford University.

Morris, L. A., and D. E. Kanouse (1979). Attribution and the drug use process. In I. Frieze, D. Bar-Tal, and J. Carroll (Eds.), *Attribution theory: applications to social problems.* San Francisco: Jossey-Bass.

Moscovici, S. (1972). Society and theory in social psychology. In J. Isrval, and H. Tajfel (Eds.), *The context of social psychology: a critical assessment.* London: Academic Press.

Mullen, B., and J. Suls (1982). Know thyself: stressful life changes and the ameliorative effect of private self-consciousness. *J. exp. soc. Psychol., 18,* 43–55.

Myers, D. G., and M. F. Kaplan (1976). Group-induced polarization in simulated juries. *Pers. soc. Psychol. Bull., 2,* 63–66.

Myers, D. G., and H. Lamm (1976). The group polarization phenomenon. *Psychol. Bull., 83,* 602–627.

Nemeth, C., and R. H. Sosis (1973). A simulated jury study: characteristics of the defendent and the jurors. *J. soc. Psychol., 90,* 221–229.

Nisbett, R. E. (1968). Determinants of food intake in human obesity. *Science, 159,* 1254–1255.

Nisbett, R. E., and L. Ross (1979). *Human inference: strategies and shortcomings of social judgment.* Englewood Cliffs, N.J.: Prentice-Hall.

Nisbett, R. E., and S. Schachter (1966). The cognitive manipulation of pain. *J. exp. soc. Psychol., 2,* 227–236.

Nisbett, R. E., and T. D. Wilson (1977). Telling more than we can know: verbal reports on mental processes. *Psychol. Rev., 84,* 231–259.

Novaco, R. W. (1979). The cognitive regulation of anger and stress. In P. Kendall, and S. Hollon (Eds.), *Cognitive-behavioral interventions: theory, research, and procedures.* New York: Academic Press.

Nucholls, K. B., J. Cassel, and B. H. Kaplan (1972). Psychosocial assets, life crisis and the prognosis of pregnancy. *Amer. J. Epidemiology, 95,* 431–441.

Orth-Gomer, K., and A. Ahlbom (1980). Impact of psychological stress on ischemic heart disease when controlling for conventional risk indicators. *J. hum. Stress, 6,* 7–15.

Padawer-Singer, M., A. N. Singer, and L. Singer (1977). Legal and social-psychological research in the effects of pre-trial publicity on juries, numerical makeup of juries, non-unanimous verdict requirements. *Law Psychol. Rev., 3,* 71–79.

Parkes, C. M. (1972). *Bereavement: studies of grief in adult life.* London: Tavistock.

———— (1973). Factors determining the persistence of phantom pain in the amputee. *J. Psychosom. Res., 17,* 97–108.

———— (1975a). Determinants of outcome following bereavement. Omega: *J. Death Dying, 6,* 303–323.

———— (1975b). Unexpected and untimely bereavement: a statistical study of young Boston widows and widowers. In B. Schoenberg, I. Gerber, A. Weiner *et al.* (Eds.), *Bereavement: its psychosocial aspects.* New York: Columbia Univ. Press.

Parsons, T. (1951). *The social system.* New York: Free Press.

Paulus, P., V. Cox, G. McCain, and J. Chandler (1975). Some effects of crowding in a prison environment. *J. appl. soc. Psychol., 5,* 86–91.

Peck, A., and J. Boland (1977). Emotional reactions to radiation treatment. *Cancer, 40,* 180–184.

Pennebaker, J. W. (1979). Social and perceptual factors affecting symptom reporting and hysterical contagion. In M. J. Colligan and J. W. Pennebaker (Eds.), *Occupational health and social behavior.* Hillsdale, N.J.: Erlbaum. (In preparation.) Presented at symposium on detection and amelioration of mass psychogenic disorder. Sponsored by National Institute on Occupational Safety and Health, Chicago.

Pennebaker, J. W., and J. E. Funkhouser (1979). Influences of social support, activity, and life change on medication use and health deterioration among the elderly. Unpublished manuscript. Univ. of Virginia. (Mimeo)

Pennebaker, J. W., and D. Y. Sanders (1976). American graffiti: effects of authority and reactance arousal. *Pers. soc. Psychol. Bull., 2,* 264–267.

Peplau, L. A., D. Russel, and M. Heim (1978). Loneliness: a bibliography of research and theory. *JASAS catalog of selected documents in psychology, 8,* 38.

Perlmutter, L., and R. Monty (1977). The importance of perceived control: fact or fantasy. *Amer. Scientist, 65,* 759–765.

Pervin, L. A. (1976). A free-response description approach to the analysis of person-situation interaction. *J. Pers. soc. Psychol., 34,* 465–474.

Piliavin, I. M., J. Rodin, and J. A. Piliavin. (1969). Good Samaritanism: an underground phenomenon. *J. Pers. soc. Psychol., 13,* 289–299.

Pilkonis, P. A. (1977). The behavioral consequences of shyness. *J. Pers., 45,* 596–611.

Pittman, T. S., and N. L. Pittman (1980). Deprivation of control and the attribution process. *J. Pers. soc. Psychol., 39,* 377–389.

Pranulis, M., J. Dabbs, and J. Johnson (1975). General anesthesia and the patients attempts at control. *Soc. Behav. Pers., 3,* 49–54.

Quattrone, G. A. (1982). Overattribution and unit formation: when behavior engulfs the person. *J. Pers. soc. Psychol., 42,* 593–607.

Rahe, R. H., R. T. Rubin, and R. J. Arthur (1974). The three investigators study: serum uric acid, cholesterol, and cortisol variability during stresses of everyday life. *Psychos. Medicine, 36,* 258–268.

Raiffa, H. (1968). *Decision analysis: introductory lectures on choices under uncertainty.* Reading, Mass.: Addison-Wesley.

Raven, B. H. (1974). The comparative analysis of power and power preference. In J. T. Tedeschi (Ed.), *Perspectives on social power.* Chicago: Aldine-Atherton.

———— (1978). Social power, social influence, and nosocomial infection control. SENIC Technical Report S–A9–1, Institute for Social Science Research, UCLA, Los Angeles.

Raven, B. H., and R. W. Haley (1980). Social influence in a medical context. In L. Bickman (Ed.), *Applied social psychology annual.* Vol. 1. Beverly Hills, Calif.: Sage.

Rees, W., and S. Lutkins (1967). Mortality of bereavement. *British Medical J., 4,* 13–16.

Rehm, L. P. (1977). A self-control model of depression. *Behav. Therapy, 8,* 787–804.

—————— (1982). Self-management in depression. In P. Karoly and F. H. Kanfer (Eds.), *Self-management and behavior change.* New York: Pergamon Press.

Rehm, L. P., and M. W. O'Hara (1979). Understanding depression. In I. H. Frieze, D. Bar-Tal and J. S. Carroll (Eds.), *New approaches to social problems.* San Francisco, Calif.: Jossey-Bass.

Rhodewalt, F., and R. Comer (1982). Coronary-prone behavior and the experience of reactance in the choice elimination paradigm. *Pers. soc. Psychol. Bull., 8,* 152–158.

Rhodewalt, F., and J. Davison (1983). Reactance and the coronary-prone behavior pattern: the role of self-attribution in responses to reduced behavioral freedom. *J. Pers. soc. Psychol., 44,* 220–228.

Rimzey, S. L., S. E. Ritzman, C. E. Mangel *et al.* (1975). Skylab experiment results: hematology studies. *Acta Astronautica, 2,* 141–154.

Rizley, R. (1978). Depression and distortion in the attribution of causality. *J. abnorm. Psychol., 87,* 32–48.

Robins, L. (1973). *The Vietnam drug user returns.* Special action office for drug abuse prevention. Washington, D.C.: U.S. Government Printing Office.

Robbins, T., and P. Fray (1980). Stress-induced eating: fact, fiction or misunderstanding. *Appetite, 1,* 103–133.

Rodin, J. (1976). Density, perceived choice and response to controllable and uncontrollable outcomes. *J. exp. soc. Psychol., 12,* 564–578.

—————— (1977). Research on eating behavior and obesity: where does it fit in personality and social psychology? *Pers. soc. Psychol. Bull., 3,* 333–355.

—————— (1978). Somatopsychics and attribution. *Pers. soc. Psychol. Bull., 4,* 531–540.

—————— (1980). Managing the stress of aging: the role of control and coping. In H. Ursin and S. Levine (Eds.), *Coping and health.* New York: Academic Press.

—————— (1981). Psychological factors in obesity. In P. Bjorntorp (Ed.), *Recent advances in obesity research.* Vol. III. London: Libbey.

—————— (1981). Current status of the inter-external hypothesis for obesity: what went wrong? *Amer. Psychol., 36,* 361–372.

—————— (1983). Behavioral medicine: beneficial effects of self control training in aging. *International Rev. appl. Psychol., 32,* 153–181.

Rodin, J., L. C. Bohm, and J. T. Wack (1982). Control, coping and aging: models for research and intervention. In L. Bickman (Ed.), *Applied social psychology annual.* Vol. 3. London: Sage.

Rodin, J., and I. L. Janis (1979). The social power of health-care practitioners as agents of change. *J. soc. Issues, 35,* 60–81.

Rodin, J., and E. J. Langer (1977). Long term effects of a control-relevant intervention with the institutionalized aged. *J. Pers. soc. Psychol., 35,* 897–902.

—————— (1980). Aging labels: the decline of control and the fall of self-esteem. *J. soc. Issues, 36,* 12–29.

Rodin, J., K. Rennert, and S. K. Solomon (1980). Intrinsic motivation for control: fact or fiction? In A. Baum, J. E. Singer, and S. Valins (Eds.), *Advances in environmental psychology.* Hillsdale, N.J.: Erlbaum.

Rodin, J., L. Silberstein, A. Wagner, and M. Ellias (1984). Determinants of successful weight loss maintenance. Unpublished manuscript. Yale University.

Rodin, J., and J. Slochower (1976). Externality in the nonobese: the effects of environmental responsiveness on weight. *J. Pers. soc. Psychol., 33,* 338–344.

Rodin, J., S. Solomon, and J. Metcalf (1978). Role of control in mediating perceptions of density. *J. Pers. soc. Psychol., 36,* 988–999.

Rodin, J., J. Wack, E. Ferannini, and R. DeFronzo (1983). Effects of insulin and glucose on feeding behavior. Unpublished manuscript. Yale University.

Rose, G. A., and R. T. Williams (1961). Metabolic studies on large and small eaters. *British J. of Nutr., 15,* 1–9.

Rose, R. M. (1980). Endocrine responses to stressful psychological events. *Psychiat. Clinics No. Amer., 3* (2).

Rosenman, R. H. (1978). The interview method of assessment of the coronary-prone behavior pattern. In T. D. Dembroski, S. M. Weiss, J. H. Shields, S. G. Haynes, and M. Feinleib (Eds.), *Coronary-prone behavior.* New York: Springer-Verlag.

Rosenman, R. H., R. J. Brand, C. D. Jenkins, M. Friedman, R. Straus, and M. Wurm (1975). Coronary heart disease in the western collaborative group study: final follow-up experience of 8½ years. *J. Amer. Medical Assoc., 233,* 872–877.

Rosenman, R. H., and M. Friedman (1974). Neurogenic factors in pathogenesis of coronary heart disease. *Medical Clinics No. Amer., 58,* 269–279.

Rosenthal, R., J. A. Hall, M. R. DiMatteo, P. L. Rogers, and D. Archer (1979). *Sensitivity to nonverbal communication: the PONS test.* Baltimore: Johns Hopkins.

Rosenthal, R., and L. Jacobson (1968). *Pygmalion in the classroom: teacher expectation and pupils' intellectual development.* New York: Holt, Rinehart, and Winston.

Ross, L. (1977). The intuitive psychologist and his shortcomings: distortions in the attribution process. In L. Berkowitz (Ed.), *Advances in experimental social psychology.* Vol. 10. New York: Academic Press.

Ross, L., M. R. Lepper, and M. Hubbard (1975). Perseverance in self-perception and social perception: biased attributional processes in the debriefing paradigm. *J. Pers. soc. Psychol., 32,* 880–887.

Ross, L., J. Rodin, and P. G. Zimbardo (1969). Toward an attribution therapy: the reduction of fear through induced cognitive-emotional misattribution. *J. Pers. soc. Psychol., 12,* 279–288.

Rotter, J. B. (1966). Generalized expectancies for internal versus external control of reinforcement. *Psychol. Monogr., 80,* 1 (whole no. 609).

Ryan, W. (1971). *Blaming the victim.* New York: Pantheon.

Safer, M. A., Q. J. Tharps, T. C. Jackson, and H. Leventhal (1977). Determinants of three stages of delay in seeking care at a medical clinic. *Medical Care, 17,* 11–29.

St. John, N. H. (1975). *School desegregation: outcomes for children*. New York: Wiley.

St. John, N. H., and R. G. Lewis (1975). Race and the social structure of the elementary classroom. *Sociol. Educ., 48,* 346–368.

Saks, M. J. (1972). *Jury verdicts.* Lexington, Mass.: D.C. Heath.

_____ (1976).The limits of scientific jury selection: ethical and empirical. *Jurimetrics J., 17,* 3–22.

_____ (1978). Social psychological contributions to a legislative subcommittee on organ and tissue transplants. *Amer. Psychol., 33,* 680–690.

Saks, M. J., and R. Hastie (1978). *Social psychology in court.* New York: Van Nostrand-Reinhold.

Saks, M. J., C. M. Werner, and T. M. Ostrom (1975). The presumption of innocence and the American juror. *J. contemp. Law, 2,* 46–54.

Sales, S. M., and J. House (1971). Job dissatisfaction as a possible risk factor in coronary heart disease. *J. chronic Diseases, 23,* 861.

Salovey, P., and J. Rodin (In press). Some antecedents and consequences of social comparison jealousy. *J. Pers. soc. Psychol.*

Sanford, N. (1970). Whatever happened to action research? *J. soc. Issues, 26,* 3–23.

Saxe, L., and M. Fine (1980). Reorienting social psychology toward application: a methodological analysis. In L. Bickman (Ed.), *Applied social psychology annual 1.* Beverly Hills, Calif.: Sage.

Schachter, S. (1959). *The psychology of affiliation.* Stanford: Stanford Univ. Press.

_____ (1968). Obesity and eating. *Science, 161,* 751–756.

Schachter, S., and L. Gross (1968). Manipulated time and eating behavior. *J. Pers. soc. Psychol., 10,* 98–106.

Schachter, S., and J. E. Singer (1962). Cognitive, social and physiological determinants of emotional state. *Psychol. Rev., 69,* 379–399.

Scherwitz, L., H. Leventhal, P. Cleary, and C. Laman (1978). Type A behavior: consideration for risk modification. *Health values: achieving high level wellness, 2,* 291–296.

Schmale, A., and H. Iker (1966). The psychological setting of uterine cervical cancer. *Annals N.Y. Acad. Sci., 125,* 807–813.

_____ (1971). Hopelessness as a prediction of cervical cancer. *Soc. Sci. Med., 5,* 95–100.

Schleifer, S. J., S. E. Keller, F. P. McKegney, and M. Stein (1980). *Bereavement and lymphocyte function.* New Research, American Psychiatric Association, San Francisco.

Schofield, J. W., and H. A. Sagar (1977). Peer interaction patterns in an integrated middle school. *Sociometry, 40,* 130–138.

Schorr, D., and J. Rodin (1982). The role of perceived control in practitioner-patient relationships. In T. A. Wills, Jr. (Ed.), *Basic process in helping relationships.* New York: Academic Press.

Schulman, J., P. Shaver, R. Colman, B. Emrich, and R. Christie (1973). Recipe for a jury. *Psychology Today, 6* (12), 37–44, 77–119.

Schulz, R. (1976). The effects of control and predictability on the psychological and physical well-being of the institutionalized aged. *J. Pers. soc. Psychol., 33,* 563–573.

_____ (1978). *The psychology of death, dying, and bereavement.* Reading, Mass.: Addison-Wesley.

Schulz, R., and D. Aderman (1973). Effect of residential change on the temporal distance to death of terminal cancer patients. *Omega, J. Death Dying, 4,* 157–162.

Schulz, R., and G. Brenner (1977). Relocation of the aged: a review and theoretical analysis. *J. Gerontology, 32,* 323–333.

Schulz, R., and B. H. Hanusa (1978). Long-term effects of control and predictability-enhancing interventions: findings and ethical issues. *J. Pers. soc. Psychol., 36,* 1194–1201.

_____ (1979). Environmental influences on the effectiveness of control and competence-enhancing interventions. In L. Perlmutter and R. Monty (Eds.), *Choice and perceived Control.* New York: Erlbaum.

_____ (1980). Experimental social gerontology: a social psychological perspective. *J. soc. Issues, 36,* 30–46.

Seligman, M. E. P. (1975). Helplessness: on depression, development and death. San Francisco: Freeman.

Selye, H. (1950). Adaptive reactions to stress. In H. G. Wolff, J. G. Wolff, and C. C. Hare (Eds.), *Life stress and bodily disease.* Baltimore, Md.: Williams and Wilkins.

_____ (1976). *The stress of life.* New York: McGraw-Hill.

Shacham, S., and H. Leventhal (1978). Attention and the control of distress during cold pressor impact. Unpublished manuscript. Univ. of Wisconsin, Madison.

Sharpe, T., and R. L. Mikeal (1974). Patient compliance with antibiotic regimens. *Amer. J. hosp. Pharm., 31,* 479–484.

Shaw, M. E. (1973). Changes in sociometric choices following forced integration of an elementary school. *J. soc. Issues, 29* (4), 143–157.

Shepard, R. D., and W. H. Kroes (1975). Report of an investigation at the James plant. Internal report prepared for the National Institute for Occupational Safety and Health. Cincinnati, Ohio.

Sherrod, D. R. (1974). Crowding, perceived control, and behavioral after affects. *J. appl. soc. Psychol., 4,* 171–186.

Sigall, H., and D. Landy (1972). Effects of the defendent's character and suffering on juridic judgment: a replication and clarification. *J. soc. Psychol., 88,* 149–150.

Sigall, H., and N. Ostrove (1975). Beautiful but dangerous: effects of offender attractiveness and nature of the crime on juridic judgment. *J. Pers. soc. Psychol., 31,* 410–414.

Silver, R. L., and C. B. Wortman (1980). Coping with undesirable life events. In J. Garber, and M. E. P. Seligman (Eds.), *Human helplessness.* New York: Academic Press.

Silverman, I., and M. E. Shaw (1973). Effects of sudden mass school desegregation on interracial interactions and attitudes in one southern city. *J. soc. Issues, 29,* 133–142.

Simon, H. A. (1957). Administrative behavior: a study of decision-making processes in administrative organization. New York: Macmillan.

_____ (1974). How big is a chunk? *Science, 183,* 482–488.

Singer, J. E., and D. C. Glass (1975). Some reflections upon losing our social psychological purity. In M. Deutsch, and H. A. Hornstein (Eds.), *Applying social psychology implications for research, practice and training.* Hillsdale, N.J.: Erlbaum.

Singerman, K. G., T. D. Borkovec, and R. S. Baron (1976). Failure of a misattribution therapy manipulation with a clinically relevant target behavior. *Behav. Therapy, 1,* 306-313.

Slochower, J., S. Kaplan, and L. Mann (1981). The effects of life stresses and weight on mood and eating. *Appetite, 2,* 115-126.

Slovic, P., B. Fischhoff, and S. Lichtenstein (1977). Behavioral decision theory. *Ann. Rev. Psychol., 28,* 1-39.

Slovic, P., and S. Lichtenstein (1971). Comparison of Bayesian and regression approaches to the study of information processing in judgment. *Organizat. Behav. hum. Perform., 6,* 649-744.

Smith, M. B. (1973). Criticism of a social science: review of *The context of social psychology.* In J. Israel and H. Tajfel (Eds.), *Science, 180,* 610-612.

Smith, J., and A. Tesser (1980). Some effects of task relevance and friendship on helping: you don't always help the one you like. *J. exp. soc. Psychol., 16,* 582-590.

Snyder, M., and W. Swann (1978). Behavorial confirmation in social interaction: from social perception to social psychology. *J. exp. soc. Psychol., 14,* 148-162.

Snyder, M., E. D. Tanke, and E. Berscheid (1977). Social perception and interpersonal behavior: on the self-fulfilling nature of social stereotypes. *J. Pers. soc. Psychol., 35,* 656-666.

Solomon, G. F., and A. A. Amkraut (1981). Psychoneuroendocrinological effects on the immune response. *Ann. Rev. Microbiology, 35,* 155-184.

Spitzer, L., J. Marcus, and J. Rodin (1980). Arousal induced eating: a response to Robbins and Fray. *Appetite, 1,* 343-348.

Spitzer, L., and J. Rodin (1981). Human eating behavior: a critical review of studies in normal weight and overweight individuals. *Appetite, 2,* 293-329.

Staub, E., B. Tursky, and G. Schwartz (1971). Self-control and predictability: their effect on reactions to aversive stimulation. *J. Pers. soc. Psychol., 18,* 157-162.

Stephan, W. G. (1978). School desegregation: an evaluation of predictions made in *Brown* v. *Board of Education. Psychol. Bull., 85,* 217-238.

Stimson, G. V. (1974). Obeying doctor's orders: a view from the other side. *Soc. Sci. Med., 8,* 97-104.

Stokols, D. (1979). A congruence analysis of human stress. In I. G. Sarason, and C. D. Spielberger (Eds.), *Stress and anxiety.* Vol. 6. Washington, D.C.: Hemisphere.

Stokols, D., and R. W. Novaco (1980). Transportation and well-being: an ecological perspective. In I. Altman, J. Wohlwill, and P. Everett (Eds.), *Human behavior and environment: advances in theory and research.* Vol. 5. Transportation environments. New York: Plenum.

Stone, G. C. (1979). Patient compliance and the role of the expert. *J. soc. Issues, 35,* 34-59.

Storms, M. D., and R. E. Nisbett (1970). Insomnia and the attribution process. *J. Pers. soc. Psychol., 16,* 319-328.

Strodtbeck, F. L., and L. H. Hook (1961). The social dimensions of a twelve-man jury table. *Sociometry, 24,* 397-415.

Stotland, E. and A. L. Blumenthol (1964). The reduction of anxiety as a result of the expectation of making a choice. *Canad. J. Psychol., 18,* 139-145.

Stroebe, W., M. S. Stroebe, K. Gergen, and M. Gergen (1982). The effects of bereavement on mortality: a social psychological analysis. In J. R. Eisner (Ed.), *Social psychology and behavioral medicine.* London: Wiley.

Stunkard, A. J. (1976). Anorexia nervosa. In J. P. Sanford (Ed.), *The science and practice of clinical medicine.* New York: Grune and Stratton.

Stunkard, A., L. Wilcoxon, and K. Brownwell (1981). Behavior therapy of obesity: comparison with pharmacotherapy and combined treatment. In P. Bjorntorp, M. Cairella, and A. N. Howard (Eds.), *Recent advances in obesity research: III.* London: John Libbey.

Suls, J. (1982). Social support, interpersonal relations and health: benefits and liabilities. In G. Sanders, and J. Suls (Eds.), *The social psychology of health and illness.* Hillsdale, N.J.: Erlbaum.

Tagliacozzo, D. L., and H. O. Mauksch (1972). The patient's view of the patient's role. In E. G. Jaco (Ed.), *Patients, physicians and illness: a sourcebook in behavioral science and health* (2nd ed.). New York: Free Press.

Tanke, E. D., and T. J. Tanke (1979). Getting off a slippery slope: social science in judicial process. *Amer. Psychol., 34,* 1130-1138.

Taylor, S. E. (1978). A developing role for social psychology in medicine and medical practice. *Pers. soc. Psychol. Bull., 4,* 515-523.

——— (1979). Hospital patient behavior: reactance, helplessness, or control? *J. soc. Issues, 35,* 156-184.

Taylor, S. E., and S. T. Fiske (1978). Salience, attention, and attribution: top of the head phenomena. In L. Berkowitz (Ed.), *Advances in experimental social psychology.* New York: Academic Press.

Taylor, S. E., and S. Levin (1976). *The psychological impact of breast cancer: theory and research.* San Francisco: West Coast Cancer Foundation.

Teasdale, J. D. (1978). Effects of real and recalled success on learned helplessness and depression. *J. abnorm. Psychol., 87,* 155-164.

Tedeschi, J. T. (1974). Attributions, liking and power. In T. Huston (Ed.), *Foundations of interpersonal attraction.* New York: Academic Press.

Terhune, K. W., and S. Kaufman (1973). The family size utility function. *Demography, 10,* 599-618.

Tesser, A. (1980). Self-esteem maintenance in family dynamics. *J. Pers. soc. Psychol., 39,* 77-91.

Tesser, A., and J. Smith (1980). Some effects of task relevance and friendship on helping: you don't always help the one you like. *J. exp. soc. Psychol., 16,* 582-590.

Theorell, T., E. Lind, and B. Floderus (1975). The relationship of disturbing life changes and emotions to the early development of myocardial infarction and other serious illnesses. *Int. J. Epidemiology, 4,* 281-293.

Thibaut, J., L. Walker, and E. A. Lind (1972). Adversary presentation and bias in legal decisionmaking. *Harvard Law Rev., 86,* 386.

Thibaut, J., and H. H. Kelley (1959). *The social psychology of groups.* New York: Wiley.

Thibaut, J., and L. Walker (1975). *Procedural justice: a psychological analysis.* Hillsdale, N.J.: Erlbaum.

_____ (1978). A theory of procedure. *California Law Rev., 66,* 541–566.

Thibaut, J., L. Walker, S. LaTour, and P. Houlden (1974). Procedural justice as fairness. *Stanford Law Rev., 26,* 1271–1289.

Thibaut, J., L. Walker, and E. A. Lind (1972). Adversary presentation and bias in legal decision-making. *Harvard Law Rev., 86,* 386–401.

Thomas, C. B., K. R. Duszynski, and J. W. Shaffer (1979). Family attitudes reported in youth as potential predictors of cancer. *Psychosom. Med., 41,* 287–302.

Thompson, S. C. (1981). Will it hurt less if I can control it? A complex answer to a simple question. *Psychol. Bull., 90,* 89–101.

U.S. Department of Health, Education and Welfare (1979a). *Smoking and health: a report of the surgeon general.* U.S. Public Health Service Publication No. 79–50066. Washington, D.C.: U.S. Government Printing Office.

_____ (1979b). *Healthy people: a report of the surgeon general on health promotion and disease prevention.* U.S. Public Health Service Publication No. 79-55071. Washington, D.C.: Government Printing Office.

Varela, J. A. (1969). *Psychological solutions to social problems: an introduction to social technology.* New York: Academic Press.

Vickery, D. M., and J. F. Fries (1976). *Take care of yourself: a consumer's guide to medical care.* Reading, Mass.: Addison-Wesley.

Vidmar, N., and D. T. Miller (1980). Social psychological processes underlying attitudes toward legal punishment. *Law and Society Rev., 14,* 565–602.

Wack, J., and J. Rodin (1978). Nursing homes for the aged: the human consequences of legislation-shaped environments. *J. Soc. Issues, 34,* 6–21.

Walker, L., J. Thibaut, and V. Andreoli (1972). Order of presentation at trial. *Yale Law J., 82,* 216–226.

Wallston, B. S., K. A. Wallston, G. D. Kaplan, and S. A. Maides (1976). Development and validation of the Health Locus of Control (HLC) scale. *J. Consult. clinic. Psychol., 44,* 580–585.

Walster, E. (1966). Assignment of responsibility for an accident. *J. Pers. soc. Psychol., 3,* 73–79.

Wan, T. (1976). Predicting self-assessed health status: a multivariate approach. *Health Services Res., 11,* 464–477.

Weigel, R. H., P. L. Wiser, and S. W. Cook (1975). The impact of cooperative learning experiences on cross-ethnic relations and attitudes. *J. soc. Issues, 31,* 219–244.

Weiner, B. (1982). The emotional consequences of causal ascriptions. In M. S. Clark, and S. T. Fiske (Eds.), *Affect and cognition: the seventeenth annual Carnegie symposium on cognition.* Hillsdale, N.J.: Erlbaum. Pp. 185–210.

Weiner, B., I. Frieze, A. Kukla, L. Reed, S. Rest, and R. M. Rosenbaum (1972). Perceiving the causes of success and failure. In E. E. Jones, D. E. Kanouse, H. H. Kelley, R. E. Nisbett, S. Valins, and B. Weiner (Eds.), *Attribution: perceiving the causes of behavior.* Morristown, N.J.: General Learning Press.

Weiss, J. M. (1968). Effects of coping responses on stress. *J. compara. physiol. Psychol., 65,* 251–260.

_____ (1971). Effects of coping behavior in different warning signal conditions on stress pathology in rats. *J. compara. physiol. Psychol., 77,* 1–13.

Weiss, R. S. (1976). The emotional impact of marital separation. *J. soc. Issues, 32,* 135–145.

Werner, P. D., S. E. Middlestadt-Carter, and T. J. Crawford (1975). Having a third child: predicting behavioral intentions. *J. Marriage Family, 37,* 348–358.

Wheeler, D. D., and I. L. Janis (1980). *A practical guide for making decisions.* New York: Macmillan.

White, R. W. (1959). Motivation reconsidered: the concept of competence. *Psychol. Rev., 66,* 297–323.

Williams, R. E. O. (1971). Changing perspectives in hospital infection. *Proceedings of the International Conference on Nosocomial Infections.* Chicago: American Hospital Association.

Wilson, J. F. (1965). *Determinants of recovery from surgery: preoperative instruction, relaxative training and defensive structures.* Unpublished doctoral dissertation. Univ. of Connecticut.

_____ (1977). Determinants of recovery from surgery: preoperative instruction, relaxation training and defensive structure. Unpublished doctoral dissertation. University of Michigan.

Wolfer, J. A., and M. A. Visintainer (1975). Pediatric surgical patients and parents. Stress responses and adjustment as a function of psychologic preparation and stress-point nursing care. *Nurse Res., 24,* 244–255.

Wrightsman, L. S. (1960). Effects of waiting with others on changes in level of felt anxiety. *J. abnorm. soc. Psychol., 61,* 216–220.

Wrubel, J., P. Benner, and R. S. Lazarus (1978). Social competence from the perspective of stress and coping. University of California, San Francisco, University of California, Berkeley. Unpublished paper. Presented at Conference. Identification and enhancement of social competence. Ontario Institute for Studies in Education, Toronto.

Wortman, C. B. (1975). Some determinants of perceived control. *J. Pers. soc. Psychol., 31,* 282–294.

_____ (1976). Causal attributions and personal control. In J. H. Harvey, W. I. Ickes, and R. F. Kidd (Eds.), *New directions in attribution research.* Vol. 1. Hillsdale, N.J.: Erlbaum.

Wortman, C. B., and J. Brehm (1975). Responses to uncontrollable outcomes. In L. Berkowitz (Ed.), *Advances exp. soc. Psychol., 8,* 278–336.

Wortman, C. B., and L. Dintzer (1978). Is an attributional analysis of the learned helplessness phenomenon viable? A critique of the Abramson-Seligman-Teasdale reformulation. *J. abnorm. Psychol., 87,* 75–90.

Wortman, C. B., and C. Dunkel-Schetter (1979). Interpersonal relationships and cancer: a theoretical analysis. *J. soc. Issues, 35,* 120–155.

Wortman, C. B., R. L. Silver, A. Abbey, A. E. Holland, and R. Janoff-Bulman (1980). Transitions from the laboratory to the field: problems and progress. In L. Bickman (Ed.), *Applied social psychology annual.* Beverly Hills, Calif.: Sage.

Young, M., B. Benjamin, and C. Wallis (1963). Mortality of widowers. *Lancet, 2,* 454–456.

Zajonc, R. B. (1968). Cognitive theories in social psychology. In G. Lindzey, and E. Aronson (Eds.), *The handbook of social psychology.* Vol. I. Reading, Mass.: Addison-Wesley.

——— (1980). Feeling and thinking: preferences need no inferences. *Amer. Psychol., 35,* 151–175.

Zimbardo, P. G. (1969). The human choice: individuation, reason, and order versus deindividuation, impulse, and chaos. In W. J. Arnold, and D. Levine (Eds.), *Nebraska symposium on motivation, 1969.* Lincoln: Univ. of Nebraska Press.

Zimbardo, P. G. (1977). *Shyness: what it is, what to do about it.* Reading, Mass.: Addison-Wesley.

Zimbardo, P. G., S. M. Andersen, and L. G. Kabat (1981). Induced hearing deficit generates experimental paranoia. *Science, 212,* 1529–1531.

Zuckerman, M. (1979). Attribution of success and failure revisited: or the motivational bias is alive and well in attribution theory. *J. Pers., 47,* 245–287.

CHAPTER 28

Personality and Social Behavior

Mark Snyder
University of Minnesota

William Ickes
University of Texas at Arlington

INTRODUCTION

When the people of ancient Rome attended the theater, they watched actors who performed behind masks. Theatergoers knew that a performer who wore a particular mask, or persona, would be playing a character who displayed a consistent pattern of behavior and attitudes. Originally, the term *persona* designated only the theatrical mask. But as time went by, the term *persona* came to refer also to the character played by the wearer of the mask and eventually to the actor who played that character. The term *persona* is also the Latin root of the psychological term *personality*. And just as the term *persona* referred to regularities and consistencies in the characters created by actors on the stage, so too does the term *per-*sonality refer to regularities and consistencies in the behavior of individuals in their lives. To the extent that such behavioral consistencies do exist, they are thought to distinguish individuals from other individuals, to render their actions predictable, and to determine their adjustment to their environments (cf. Allport, 1937).

In what ways might the regularities and consistencies that constitute personality be reflected and manifested in the behavioral phenomena and processes of concern to social psychologists? If, indeed, meaningful regularities do exist in the behavior of individuals in social contexts, what are their social and psychological origins? And what are their implications for social psychology's theoretical understanding of the nature of social behavior? It is to questions of this form that students of personality and social behavior have sought answers. And it is the answers to such questions that are the central concerns of this chapter on personality and social behavior.

A historically convenient point of departure for any consideration of personality and social behavior is Kurt Lewin's (1936) seminal proposition: "Every psychological event depends upon the state of the person and at the same time on the environment, although their relative importance is different in different cases" (p. 12). The

The preparation of this chapter was supported in part by National Science Foundation Grant BNS 77–11346 to Mark Snyder and in part by National Science Foundation Grant BNS 79–21443 to William Ickes. Portions of this chapter were written while Mark Snyder was a fellow at the Center for Advanced Study in the Behavioral Sciences, supported in part by the Spencer Foundation. For their comments and suggestions, we thank D. C. Funder, W. G. Graziano, E. E. Jones, A. Locksley, N. S. Lutsky, T. E. Malloy, D. T. Miller, M. F. Scheier, G. Tunnell, and M. P. Zanna.

883

proposition that an individual's behavior in a social situation is determined both by characteristics of that individual (i.e., dispositional determinants of social behavior) and by characteristics of that situation (i.e., situational determinants of social behavior) is a fundamental tenet of most, if not all, strategies for conceptualizing and investigating personality and social behavior. Nevertheless, strategies for the study of personality and social behavior differ among themselves in the extent to which they attempt to identify, both theoretically and empirically, dispositional and situational sources of regularities and consistencies in the behavior of individuals in social contexts. Indeed, we have been able to define three major strategies that social psychologists may adopt for the study of personality and social behavior:

1. *The dispositional strategy:* The dispositional strategy for the study of personality and social behavior seeks to understand consistencies in social behavior in terms of relatively stable traits, enduring dispositions, and other propensities that are thought to reside "within" individuals. In particular, the dispositional strategy seeks to define those domains of social behavior within which it is possible to identify individuals who characteristically manifest the regularities and consistencies in social behavior that might reflect the influence of underlying dispositional features.

2. *The interactional strategy:* The interactional strategy for the study of personality and social behavior seeks to understand regularities and consistencies in social behavior in terms of the interactive influence of dispositional features and situational features. In particular, the interactional strategy seeks to identify those categories of traits, of behaviors, of individuals, and of situations within which such regularities and consistencies typically are to be found.

3. *The situational strategy:* The newly emerging situational strategy for the study of personality and social behavior seeks to understand consistencies in social behavior in terms of the features of social situations. In particular, the situational strategy seeks to identify the personal antecedents and the social consequences of regularities and consistencies in the settings and contexts within which individuals live their lives.

Our intent in this chapter is to examine critically the strategies that we have defined for the study of personali-

ty and social behavior, to probe the conceptual and methodological underpinnings of each strategy, to present representative illustrations of each strategy in action, and to assess the strengths and weaknesses of each strategy. It also is our intent to place the discussion of strategies for the study of personality and social behavior within the larger theoretical framework of the social psychology of personality and, in doing so, to provide some guidelines for conceptualizing and investigating the individual in social psychology.

THE DISPOSITIONAL STRATEGY FOR THE STUDY OF PERSONALITY AND SOCIAL BEHAVIOR

When social psychologists employ the dispositional strategy for the study of personality and social behavior, they are guided by a theoretical perspective that assumes that some meaningful amount of the regularities and consistencies in social behavior can be understood in terms of relatively stable and enduring propensities (e.g., dispositions, traits, needs, motives) that reside "within" individuals. The theoretical perspective of the dispositional strategy is accompanied by an empirical orientation that seeks to define domains of social behavior within which it is possible to observe the regularities over time and the consistencies across situations that are thought to constitute evidence of personality.

For example, were the dispositional strategy to be applied to the social psychological phenomenon of conformity, the user of this strategy would seek to determine whether or not there exists a conforming personality who reliably displays manifestations of conformity. If individuals who characteristically behave in a conforming fashion did exist, and if one could readily identify such individuals, then these characteristically conforming individuals would become the targets of intensive investigations of the phenomenon of conformity. In particular, by investigating the cognitive, affective, and behavioral processes by which characteristically conforming individuals cope with social situations, the practitioner of the dispositional strategy would hope to acquire an understanding of the nature of conformity. That is, by understanding the social psychology of conforming individuals, one could thereby come to understand the social psychology of conformity itself.

More generally, the logic of the dispositional strategy for the study of personality and social behavior dictates that the phenomena and processes of concern to social psychologists can be understood by focusing one's investigative efforts on the individuals who characteristically manifest those phenomena and processes. After all, the logic of the dispositional strategy continues, one could hardly study any particular social psychological phenomenon or process in individuals who rarely or never manifest that particular phenomenon or process. Accordingly, by identifying those individuals who typically manifest the social psychological phenomenon or process of concern, one gains access to the ideal candidates for investigating the social psychology of that phenomenon or process in action. That is, the identification of those individuals who characteristically manifest the phenomenon or process of concern is undertaken not as an end in itself but rather as a means toward achieving the end of understanding an important social psychological phenomenon or process.

The dispositional strategy for the study of personality and social behavior has been applied to the identification and investigation of regularities and consistencies in a wide variety of social psychological phenomena and processes. These include authoritarianism (Adorno, *et al.*, 1950; Dillehay, 1978), need for approval (Crowne and Marlowe, 1964; Milham and Jacobson, 1978), Machiavellianism (Christie and Geis, 1970; Geis, 1978), achievement motivation (McClelland *et al.*, 1953; Weiner, 1974), extraversion (Eysenck and Eysenck, 1968; Wilson, 1978), repression-sensitization (Byrne, 1964), need for cognition (Cacioppo and Petty, 1982), self-motivation (Dishman, Ickes, and Morgan, 1980), dogmatism (Rokeach, 1960), locus of control (Lefcourt, 1972; Phares, 1973; Rotter, 1966), charisma (Friedman *et al.*, 1980), cognitive complexity (Bieri, 1955; Crockett, 1965), empathy (Mehrabian and Epstein, 1972), hypnotic susceptibility (Hilgard, 1973), field dependence (Goodenough, 1978; Witkin *et al.*, 1962), attributional styles (Funder, 1980; Ickes and Layden, 1978), sex roles (Bem, 1974; Spence and Helmreich, 1978), sensation seeking (Zuckerman, 1978), power motivation (McClelland, 1975; Winter, 1973; Winter and Stewart, 1978), and self-esteem (Wylie, 1974). In addition, a variety of attempts have been made to use the dispositional strategy for the study of personality and social behavior in order to link various phenomena of concern to social psychologists to biological and morphological characteristics of individuals (e.g., Buss and Plomin, 1975; Kretschmer, 1926; Schachter and Rodin, 1974; Sheldon, 1942) and to differences in individuals' birth order (e.g., Schachter, 1959).

Needless to say, it would be impossible to provide an exhaustive review of theory and research on all of the entries in even this admittedly selected list [for a more comprehensive catalogue, see Blass (1977), London and Exner (1978), and Robinson and Shaver (1973)]. For this reason, we have chosen to focus on a small number of representative examples of the dispositional strategy in action: (1) theory and research on the authoritarian personality, (2) theory and research on the need for social approval, and (3) theory and research on Machiavellianism.

THE AUTHORITARIAN PERSONALITY

Few phenomena have captured the attention of social psychologists to the same extent as has the phenomenon of prejudice. The dispositional strategy for the study of prejudice has sought to answer three key questions. Do there exist individuals who regularly and consistently display prejudice? Do the backgrounds of prejudiced individuals provide clues to the origins of prejudice? Do the lives of prejudiced individuals reveal information about the consequences of prejudice? Foremost among the efforts to answer these questions is the attempt of Adorno *et al.* (1950) to identify and to understand *The Authoritarian Personality*. We consider now their answers to the key questions posed by the dispositional strategy for the study of prejudice and the methods by which they generated their answers.

Identifying Prejudiced Individuals

If characteristically prejudiced individuals exist, then they ought to be consistently and regularly accepting of those who are similar to them and rejecting of those who are different from them. Moreover, if there exists such a prejudiced personality, it ought to be possible to demonstrate that the individuals who harbor prejudicial attitudes toward one group (e.g., toward Jews) tend to be the same individuals who harbor prejudicial attitudes toward other groups (e.g., blacks, Puerto Ricans, Mormons, socialists, artists, foreigners). That is, from this perspective the empirical criterion for identifying the prejudiced personality is that within individuals prejudicial attitudes ought to be consistent across diverse potential targets of prejudice.

In accord with this strategy, Adorno *et al.* (1950) first identified a group of individuals who possessed anti-Semitic attitudes, and then they assessed the extent to which the possessors of anti-Semitic attitudes also possessed generally ethnocentric aversions for all people who diverge from white, middle-class American norms and values. Adorno *et al.* (1950) identified the anti-Semites among a sample of over 2000 white, non-Jewish, native-born, middle-class American residents of California. To do so, they developed and used a highly reliable (both in terms of temporal stability and internal consistency), fifty-two-item, Likert-format measure of the extent to which individuals characterize Jews as offensive, threatening, immoral, clannish, intrusive, and deserving of exclusion, restriction, and discrimination. Among the items of this Anti-Semitism Scale are "No matter how Americanized a Jew may seem to be, there is always something different and strange, something basically Jewish underneath"; "I can hardly imagine myself marrying a Jew"; and "One trouble with Jewish businessmen is that they stick together and connive, so that a Gentile doesn't have a fair chance in competition."

To determine whether or not antagonistic attitudes toward Jews were part of the consistent pattern of prejudicial attitudes toward diverse potential targets of prejudice that would constitute empirical evidence for the existence of a prejudiced personality, Adorno *et al.* (1950) examined the relationship between scores on the Anti-Semitism Scale and scores on the Ethnocentrism Scale. The Ethnocentrism Scale is a highly reliable, thirty-four-item, Likert-format measure of antagonistic attitudes toward members of various cultural, ethnic, racial, national, political, or religious out-groups (e.g., "America may not be perfect, but the American Way has brought us about as close as human beings can get to a perfect society"; "Negroes have their rights, but it is best to keep them in their own districts and schools and to prevent too much contact with whites"; "Certain religious sects who refuse to salute the flag should be forced to conform to such a patriotic action, or else be abolished"). The substantial relationship between individuals' scores on the Anti-Semitism Scale and their scores on the Ethnocentrism Scale ($r = 0.80$) suggested to Adorno *et al.* (1950) that hostility toward outsiders exists as a generalized attitudinal orientation, directed regularly and consistently toward diverse potential targets of prejudice. Apparently, according to the criterion of consistency across targets, a prejudiced personality does indeed exist.

The Origins of Prejudice

Having identified the existence of a syndrome of prejudice and ethnocentrism, Adorno *et al.* (1950) turned to intensive investigations of the lives of prejudiced and unprejudiced individuals to determine the social origins and the psychological functions of prejudice. Intensive, open-ended, unstructured interviews with relatively prejudiced individuals (upper quartile of the Ethnocentrism Scale) and with relatively unprejudiced individuals (lower quartile of the Ethnocentrism Scale) yielded a composite characterization of the developmental roots of prejudice.

Prejudiced individuals, according to Adorno *et al.* (1950), were the children of domineering fathers and punitive mothers who engaged in austere and punitive child-rearing practices. These practices involved a combination of threats, coercion, and the deliberate use of parental love and its withdrawal to promote obedience. The products of such socialization practices are children who are decidedly insecure and extremely dependent on their parents. Moreover, such children fear their parents and experience unconscious hostility toward them. Arguing from interview data and a psychoanalytic view of personality processes, Adorno *et al.* (1950) claimed that the insecurity and dependence that these individuals experienced during their childhood is translated in adulthood into submission and obedience to those in positions of power and authority. By the same token, the fear and hostility of their childhood years is translated in their adult years into hostility and antagonism toward members of minority groups and other people perceived to be less powerful than themselves.

These interviews also suggested to Adorno *et al.* (1950) that, as adults, highly prejudiced individuals should display the behavioral elements of a syndrome that has come to be known as authoritarianism. These elements include a rigid adherence to conventional values, a submissive attitude toward moral authorities, a tendency to condemn those who violate conventional values, an opposition to subjective or tender-minded phenomena, a tendency to think in stereotyped categories, a preoccupation with power and toughness, a vilification of human nature, a projection outward of emotional impulses, and an exaggerated concern with sexual happenings. To assess this possibility, Adorno *et al.* (1950) constructed a highly reliable, thirty-eight-item, Likert-format measure of the authoritarian syndrome (e.g., "Obedience and respect for authority are the most important virtues children should learn"; "If people would talk less and work more, everybody would be better off"; "People can be divided into two distinct classes: the weak and the strong"; "Human nature being what it is, there will always be war and conflict"). They named this measure the Implicit Antidemocratic Trends or Potentiality for Fascism Scale because they believed that the authoritarian syndrome made individuals susceptible to antidemocratic or fascist propaganda. This measure revealed that, as predicted, prejudice and authoritarianism go hand in hand: The correlation between the Ethnocentrism Scale and the Potentiality for Fascism Scale was a substantial +0.65 (Adorno *et al.*, 1950).

The Manifestations of Prejudice

How are the ethnocentric attitudes and authoritarian ideology of prejudiced individuals reflected and manifested in their beliefs, attitudes, and actions? The work of Adorno *et al.* (1950) and of subsequent investigators [for reviews, see, for example, Christie and Cook (1958); Christie and Jahoda (1954); Kirscht and Dillehay (1967); Titus and Hollander (1957)] has yielded considerable information about the lives of prejudiced individuals.

Within the cognitive domain authoritarians display considerable cognitive rigidity and intolerance for ambiguity (e.g., Block and Block, 1951; Frenkel-Brunswik, 1949; Jones, 1954; Rokeach, 1948; Steiner and Johnson, 1963), as well as the firm belief that other people tend to think and feel as they do (e.g., Granberg, 1972; Scodel and Mussen, 1953; Simons, 1966). Within the attitudinal domain authoritarians are rejecting of minorities and foreigners (e.g., Adorno *et al.*, 1950; Campbell and McCandless, 1951; Martin and Westie, 1959), espouse conservative political and economic attitudes (e.g., Adorno *et al.*, 1950; Leventhal, Jacobs, and Kurdirka, 1964), accept the attitudes of those in power (Izzett, 1971), and identify with authoritarian characters in television situation comedies (e.g., Chapko and Lewis, 1975). Within the behavioral domain authoritarians are more obedient to authority (e.g., Elms and Milgram, 1966), report that they vote for conservative and authoritarian candidates for public office (e.g., Higgins, 1965; Milton, 1952; Poley, 1974; Wrightsman, 1965), and raise their own children in a traditional manner, i.e., with strong parental control over the children, traditional sex roles and division of labor for the parents, and limited opportunities for the children to dissent from the opinions and dictates of their parents (e.g., Levinson and Huffman, 1955). Evidently, prejudiced individuals do live their lives in accord with their ethnocentric attitudes and authoritarian ideology.

The Prejudiced Personality in Perspective

As graphic a portrait of the prejudiced personality that Adorno *et al.* (1950) were able to present, their investigation of the dynamics of prejudice has drawn its share of criticism (e.g., Hyman and Sheatsley, 1954). Their work has been faulted for, among other potential problems, a limitation of their sample to white middle-class Californians, the development of questionnaires susceptible to acquiescence response sets, the examination of the data of the interviews in advance of developing a coding system, the coding of multiple variables from the same interview content, and the consistent negative correlations between authoritarianism and measures of education, intelligence, and socioeconomic class.

In response to these potentially troublesome criticisms, subsequent researchers have attempted to compensate for the shortcomings of the original investigations. They have, for example, been able to unconfound authoritarianism and acquiescence response sets (e.g., Christie, Havel, and Seidenberg, 1958; Couch and Keniston, 1960). In addition, they have confirmed much of the portrait of the developmental origins of prejudice in subsequent investigations using different methodologies (e.g., Frenkel-Brunswik, 1949, 1954; Frenkel-Brunswik and Havel, 1953; Martin and Westie, 1959). The combined weight of these investigations [of which there easily have been many hundreds; for reviews, see, for example, Christie and Cook (1958), Christie and Jahoda (1954), Kirscht and Dillehay (1967), Titus and Hollander (1957)] seem to support the conclusion that "the overall picture shows consistency of findings in many of the most intensively studied areas" (Christie and Cook, 1958, p. 189; see also Christie, 1978).

THE NEED FOR SOCIAL APPROVAL

Implicit, if not explicit, in most social psychological perspectives on the nature of social interaction and interpersonal relationships are the propositions that individuals value and seek the social approval of other people and that, consequently, they will engage in activities designed to achieve favorable evaluations from the people with whom they interact. When the dispositional strategy for the study of personality and social behavior is applied to the study of the need for social approval, it sets for itself these goals:

1. To identify that category of individuals who possess particularly intense needs for social approval.

2. To document that these individuals regularly and consistently engage in a wide variety of behaviors by which one might seek social approval in a wide variety of relevant situations.

3. To discover the social and psychological processes that underlie the approval-seeking orientation of these individuals to interpersonal relationships.

Prototypic of the dispositional strategy for the study of the dynamics of the quest for social approval are the programmatic investigations of Crowne and Marlowe (1964).

Assessing the Need for Social Approval

To differentiate individuals having a relatively strong need for social approval from those having a relatively weak need for social approval, Crowne and Marlowe (1960) developed the Marlowe-Crowne Social Desirability Scale, a set of thirty-three true-false, self-report items designed to measure the tendency to describe oneself in favorable, socially desirable terms. Individuals with high scores on this measure tend to agree with statements that (in the normative climate that prevailed when the measure was constructed) are socially desirable but probably untrue of most people; e.g., "I never hesitate to go out of my way to help someone in trouble"; "I have never intensely disliked anyone"; "I always try to practice what I preach"; and "I am always courteous to people who are disagreeable." At the same time individuals with high scores on this measure tend to disagree with statements that (again, according to the normative standards of the times) were socially undesirable but probably true of most people; e.g., "I can remember playing sick to get out of something"; "I like to gossip at times"; "On occasion I have had doubts about my ability to succeed in life"; and "I sometimes try to get even, rather than forgive and forget."

The guiding logic of the construction of the Marlowe-Crowne Social Desirability Scale was straightforward: The tendency of some individuals to describe themselves in socially desirable terms may reflect a more general propensity to seek the social approval that these individuals believe is accorded to people who behave in a socially desirable and a culturally acceptable fashion. The Marlowe-Crowne Social Desirability Scale is internally consistent and temporally stable (Crowne and Marlowe, 1964), and it is only modestly correlated with other measures of the tendency to endorse socially desirable statements (e.g., that of Edwards, 1957).

Behavioral Manifestations of the Need for Social Approval

Do the individuals identified by the Marlowe-Crowne Social Desirability Scale as having a high need for social approval characteristically seek the approval of other people by displaying socially desirable behaviors? In a wide variety of social situations individuals who have a high need for social approval do give socially desirable responses. They conform to social and interpersonal pressures more readily than do individuals with a low need for social approval (e.g., Marlowe and Crowne, 1961; Strickland and Crowne, 1962), particularly when these pressures emanate from other individuals of prestige and expertise (e.g., Miller *et al.,* 1965). Moreover, they are particularly persuasible, suggestible, and responsive to social and evaluative feedback (e.g., Marlowe, Stifler, and Davis, 1962; Milburn, Bell, and Koeske, 1970; Salman, 1962; Strickland, 1965; Strickland and Jenkins, 1964). Individuals with a high need for social approval are highly responsive to social reinforcement in the verbal conditioning procedural paradigm (e.g., Buckhout, 1965; Crowne and Strickland, 1961; Dixon, 1970; Marlowe, 1962; Marlowe *et al.,* 1964; Strickland, 1962, 1970; Strickland and Crowne, 1962). Furthermore, in word association tasks they limit their responses to relatively common, popular, and conventional word associations (e.g., Horton, Marlowe, and Crowne, 1963). Those with a high need for social approval tend to be cautious about setting goals in risk-taking situations (e.g., Barthel, 1963; Thaw and Efran, 1967). In perceptual defense tasks individuals with a high need for social approval are less likely to report the dirty words to which they have been exposed than are those with a low need for social approval (e.g., Barthel and Crowne, 1962). Finally, individuals with a high need for social approval are particularly likely to perform altruistic and generous actions, especially when they know that their good deeds will be witnessed by other people (e.g., Satow, 1973).

The Dynamics of Seeking Social Approval

What are the psychological processes that underlie and generate the approval-seeking activities of individuals with a high need for social approval? Crowne and Marlowe (1964) have suggested that the dynamics of approval-seeking may involve attempts to defend and to protect a vulnerable self-esteem: "Approval-motivated persons are more dependent than others on the positive evaluations of others as a means of protecting a defensively enhanced picture of themselves" (p. 133). If this interpretation of the motivational underpinnings of approval seeking is correct, then individuals with a high need for social approval ought to have particular difficulty with the recognition and expression of hostility, which typically involves the combined threats of unfavorable evaluations from others and of social rejection by others, both of which constitute threats to self-esteem. In accord with this derivation, individuals with a high need for social approval display no overt hostility to one who has double-crossed, insulted, and provoked them; in fact, in the face of this abusive treatment individuals with a high need for social approval somehow manage to remain friendly and sociable (Conn and Crowne, 1964; see also Fishman, 1965).

In further support of this interpretation of approval seeking as the defensive protection of a vulnerable self-esteem, Strickland and Crowne (1963) have reported that high need for social approval is associated with early termination of psychotherapy, an interpersonal situation that ought to produce considerable conflict between the desire to preserve vulnerable self-conceptions and the need to discuss personal problems. Individuals high in need for social approval [who typically are judged by their therapists to be particularly defensive, perhaps partially because of their highly guarded responses to projective tests; e.g., see Tutko (1962)] apparently resolve this conflict by early flight from the psychotherapeutic situation. Finally, and also in accord with the proposed self-esteem protective origins of approval seeking, individuals with a high need for social approval are seen by their peers as rather defensive in their interpersonal relationships (Barthel, 1963). Perhaps the combination of this defensive appearance and their chronic dependence on others for reassurance and esteem makes individuals with a high need for social approval relatively unpopular in sociometric choices (Crowne and Marlowe, 1964).

Evidently, the regular and consistent approval-seeking behaviors of individuals with a high need for social approval are the product of attempts to defend and preserve a vulnerable self-esteem. Perhaps individuals with a high need for social approval believe that conformity and submissiveness to the norms of socially approved conduct may involve few risks of the social rejection that would threaten their self-esteem. Perhaps, too, the same approval-seeking activities typically seen in individuals with chronically high needs for social approval may be elicited in all individuals, whatever their chronic levels of need for social approval, by those social situations and interpersonal relationships that provide significant threats to self-esteem. That is, the same processes of the defensive protection of self-esteem that seem to underlie and generate the approval-seeking behavior of individuals with a high need for social approval may also underlie and generate all approval-seeking activities in social interaction and interpersonal relationships.

THE MACHIAVELLIAN PERSONALITY

For centuries theorists have been fascinated by the question of how some individuals are able to successfully manipulate and take advantage of others (Christie and Geis, 1970, Chap. 1). Two books written circa 300 B.C.—one in China (*The Book of Lord Shang*), the other in India (the *Arthasāstra* of Kautilya)—gave practical and often chillingly ruthless advice to rulers about the most effective ways to manipulate and control their subjects. In a more modern treatment of this theme (written in the early 1500s), Niccolò Machiavelli presented a collection of essays in *The Prince* and *The Discourses* that contained a philosophy of interpersonal manipulation as well as a practical guide to manipulative tactics. These essays were used by Christie, Geis, and their associates over four hundred years later as the basis for applying the dispositional strategy to the study of interpersonal manipulation. In their 1970 book *Studies of Machiavellianism* these authors sought to answer some basic questions about personality and manipulative interpersonal behavior. First, is there a class of individuals who regularly and successfully manipulate others? Second, what are the specific behavioral tactics whereby such manipulations are effected? And third, what are the psychological orientations and processes that differentiate manipulative and nonmanipulative individuals?

Assessing Machiavellianism

Starting with the assumption that individuals who endorse Machiavelli's philosophy of interpersonal manipulation might also behave in a similar fashion, Christie and his associates developed a Machiavellianism scale comprised of items that paraphrased statements found in *The Prince* and *The Discourses*. Through various psychometric refinements of an initial pool of seventy-one items, an internally consistent, twenty-item, Likert-format scale was created. This scale (Mach IV) measured the degree of subjects' endorsement of a wide range of Machiavellian statements. Individuals with high scores on this measure tend to agree with statements such as "The best way to handle people is to tell them what they want to hear"; "Never tell anyone the real reason you did something unless it is useful to do so''; and ''The biggest difference between most criminals and other people is that criminals are stupid enough to get caught.'' At the same time individuals with high scores on this measure tend to disagree with statements such as ''Honesty is the best policy in all cases''; ''Most people are basically good and kind''; and ''Most people who get ahead in the world lead clean, moral lives.''

Significant correlations (in the -0.30 to -0.50 range) between Mach IV and Edwards's (1957) Social Desirability Scale suggested the need to develop a measure of Machiavellianism that was relatively free from a social desirability/undesirability bias. The development of the Mach V, a forced-choice version of the Mach IV that pitted the endorsement of each Machiavellian statement against that of a buffer statement having a comparable level of social desirability, appeared to answer this need. Because scores on the Mach IV and Mach V proved to be highly correlated (r's fell in the 0.60 to 0.70 range), Christie and his co-workers used scores on both of these measures to classify the individuals selected for most of their own validation research. Correlations of the Mach IV and Mach V scales with other measures indicate that Machiavellianism is unrelated to intellectual ability, psychopathology, or political preference and ideology. On the other hand, the data clearly indicate that Machiavellianism is related to a negative or cynical view of human nature.

Behavioral Manifestations of Machiavellianism

Are individuals who endorse Machiavelli's philosophy of interpersonal manipulation more manipulative in their own interpersonal behavior than individuals who do not endorse such attitudes and beliefs? Research conducted by Christie, Geis, and other investigators has revealed that high-Mach individuals have a greater capacity for interpersonal manipulation and exploitation than have low-Mach individuals. This research has also shed light on some of the specific tactics high Machs use to advance their own interests at others' expense.

One major difference between high and low Machs concerns their susceptibility to social pressure and influence. In comparison with low Machs, high Machs exhibit less opinion change in counterattitudinal advocacy situations (e.g., Epstein, 1969; Feiler, 1967), are more resistant to confessing complicity in a confederate's cheating (Exline *et al.,* 1970), and are more suspicious of others' motives and definitions of the situation (e.g., Bogart *et al.,* 1970). On the other hand, high Machs seem to be more adept than low Machs at influencing others by im-

posing their own definition and structure on interpersonal activities. They are more likely than low Machs to take over leadership functions and to mobilize resources in relatively unstructured groups (Geis, 1968; Geis, Krupat, and Berger, 1965), to persuade others to form coalitions with them (Geis, 1964, 1970) or to engage in unpleasant activities (Braginski, 1966), and to win debates when instructed to defend their own private beliefs (Novielli, 1968). High Machs also appear to differ from low Machs in their capacity for improvisational behavior. They can generate more innovative ways to disrupt another person's performance (Geis, Christie, and Nelson, 1970), can bluff or lie more successfully in ambiguous situations (e.g., Exline *et al.,* 1970; Geis and Moon, 1981, Nachamie, 1969), and appear to have a better sense of timing when they make exploitive moves in a competitive game situation (Geis, 1964, 1970).

The Psychology of Interpersonal Manipulation

Differences in the psychological orientations of high- versus low-Mach individuals contribute directly to our understanding of the psychology of interpersonal manipulation. From a psychological standpoint high Machs are characterized as being cool and detached. They are less likely than low Machs to become emotionally involved with other people (Durkin, 1970), with value-laden issues (Geis, Weinheimer, and Berger, 1970), or with attempts to save their own face in embarrassing situations (Exline *et al.,* 1970). Although high Machs are apparently as emotionally sensitive as low Machs at the physiological level (Oksenberg, 1964), they exert more control over the public expression of their emotional states (Exline *et al.,* 1970; Nachamie, 1969) and are better able to keep their covert feelings from affecting their overt behavior (Geis, 1964, 1970; Geis, Weinheimer, and Berger, 1970). The manipulative success of high Machs appears to be greatly facilitated by their cool, detached attitude. This psychological detachment not only reduces their susceptibility to the kind of social pressure that has an emotional (as opposed to a strictly rational) basis but also frees them ''to focus on explicit, cognitive definitions of the situation and concentrate on strategies for winning'' (Christie and Geis, 1970, p. 312). Indeed, the psychological detachment of high Machs appears to be so extreme that they are able to disregard even their own feelings, behaviors, beliefs, and self-images if the awareness of these elements might hinder them in the attainment of their goals.

The psychological orientation of low Machs is essentially the reverse of that characteristic of high Machs. Instead of being cool and detached, low Machs are "soft touches" (Christie and Geis, 1970, pp. 194–313). They are highly influenceable and are frequently willing to do what another person wants simply because he or she wants it. Unlike high Machs, who can treat others as objects by disregarding their personal characteristics, feelings, and other dispositions when they deem them to be antithetical or irrelevant to achieving their goals, low Machs tend to see other people as unique individuals and respond to each of them in a unique and personal way (Durkin, 1970). Because low Machs tend to become highly involved with others, they feel more obliged than high Machs do to reciprocate commitments that others have made and to avoid taking advantage of others when it is possible to do so (Geis, 1964, 1970). Low Machs also appear to be more concerned than high Machs about considerations of fairness and conventional morality, but because of their susceptibility to social pressure, they still may be induced to behave immorally or in a manner contrary to their own or others' interest (Exline *et al.,* 1970; Geis, 1970).

In summary, if the high-Mach individual is the prototypic con man, the low-Mach individual appears to be the prototypic mark. The value implications of these two contrasting personality types may not be clear-cut, however, as Christie and Geis (1970) have pointed out. The high Machs' socially undesirable propensity for exploiting and manipulating others may be countered by their resistance to the more nonrational forms of social pressure and by their seemingly "greater insight into and honesty about themselves" (Christie and Geis, 1970, p. 339). By the same token, the low Machs' socially desirable capacity for empathic involvement with others may be qualified by their apparent gullibility and inability to avoid being exploited. Christie and Geis have speculated that people in our culture may be becoming more Machiavellian over time, as evidenced by an increase in the mean scores on the Mach IV and Mach V scales in the years since these measures were constructed. The advantages and disadvantages to individuals and to society of this change in interpersonal orientation have yet to be determined, however.

ANALYSIS AND CRITIQUE OF THE DISPOSITIONAL STRATEGY

The representative examples just reviewed indicate that there do indeed exist domains of social behavior within which it is possible to identify individuals who characteristically manifest the regularities and consistencies in social behavior that are thought to reflect the operation of underlying dispositional influences. When used effectively, the application of the dispositional strategy in these behavioral domains may constitute a two-stage bootstrapping process. In the first stage of this process contrasting personality types are identified, types who presumably differ in the regularity and consistency with which they display behaviors characteristic of the domain in question. Work conducted during this stage concerns the development of an assessment instrument or procedure, the refinement of such a measure, and subsequent attempts to establish its reliability and validity through appropriate empirical tests. If the work conducted during this assessment and validation stage is successful, a second, bootstrapping stage begins in which the newly validated measure is now used to expand the researchers' conception of the particular social psychological phenomenon that the measure was designed to address.

In the bootstrapping stage, researchers are not content with merely validating their personality measure in terms of criterion behaviors that have been specified a priori (demonstrating, for example, that high Machs manipulate others more often than low Machs in competitive game situations). Instead, they explore a range of previously unexamined behaviors to determine the boundary conditions for the social psychological phenomenon of interest or to examine the processes underlying the phenomenon at a level of detail not permitted by the relatively simplistic conception that guided the researchers' earlier validation work. Thus Machiavellianism researchers—once having established that their personality measures could reliably and validly identify classes of individuals who were or were not predisposed to manipulate others—subsequently began to study other, previously noncriterial behaviors displayed by these two classes of individuals to determine exactly *how* such interpersonal manipulation was effected. In so doing, they discovered previously unrecognized differences between high Machs and low Machs in their improvisational skills, sense of timing, and degree of detachment from emotional involvements, and thereby expanded their conception of the process of interpersonal manipulation as well as their understanding of the manipulative personality.

As the example of Machiavellianism suggests, the results of the bootstrapping process can be quite impressive when the process is successfully realized. However, a number of potential problems with and limitations of the dispositional strategy may combine to make the realization of this process more difficult in practice than in principle. These possible problems and limitations provide the basis for most of the criticisms that may be directed at the dispositional strategy—criticisms that may implicate both the theory underlying the strategy and the methods used to implement it.

Conceptual and Theoretical Critique

The approach as relatively atheoretical and tautological. The major theoretical criticism that may be applied to the dispositional strategy is that it is not theoretical enough. The implicit logic underlying this strategy, as we already have seen, is that one way to study the phenomena and processes of concern to social psychologists is to first identify individuals who regularly and consistently manifest those phenomena and processes in their behavior. Once these individuals have been identified, their behavior can be studied in a controlled, detailed manner. Their behavior also can be contrasted with the behavior of individuals who have been identified as rarely or never manifesting the phenomena or processes in question. Through such investigations the researcher may gain important insights regarding the natural occurrence of the phenomenon of interest, the processes that underlie it, and the respective psychologies of the contrasting personality types who very frequently or who only rarely manifest it.

This dispositional strategy tends, however, to be rather atheoretical almost by definition. The researcher who adopts this strategy need not start with a theory of the phenomenon of interest and then proceed to test it directly. Instead, often in a virtual admission of ignorance, the researcher may begin by simply trying to identify individuals who, by their own self-reports or the reports of others, frequently manifest the phenomenon in their own behavior. Although the researcher's successful identification and subsequent study of such individuals (and their contrasting counterparts) may indeed lead to the inductive development of a well-articulated theory regarding the phenomenon of interest, it is important to note that such theory typically is the endpoint of the application of the dispositional strategy and *not* its starting point.

Moreover, to the extent that the investigator initially is ignorant regarding the behavioral manifestations of the phenomenon in question, he or she may establish an overly narrow or even quasi-tautological relationship between the personality dimension of interest and the be-

havioral phenomenon to which it is intended to correspond. For example, a researcher who desires to study the phenomenon of conversational dominance may know little or nothing about the behavioral manifestations of this phenomenon except for one relevant behavior—the vocal intensity or "loudness" of the participants' verbalizations. If the researcher therefore developed a personality measure of conversational dominance comprised of items tapping this and only this aspect of the phenomenon, the researcher's subsequent validation work might reveal that individuals who score at the extremes of this measure differ only in how loud they talk when conversing with others and do not differ in any other respects. The researcher might then conclude that conversational dominance is based only on who talks loudest during a conversation, a conclusion that may be not only overly narrow but also virtually tautological from a conceptual standpoint.

But, one might argue, if the loudness variable is highly correlated with other behavioral indices of conversational dominance, such as talking more often and/or longer than others, interrupting more frequently, giving rather than receiving advice, directions, opinions, the researcher might discover differences in these other behaviors during the bootstrapping phase of the research. Although the researcher's conception of conversational dominance probably would be broadened in such a case, in other cases this outcome might fail to occur. For example, if the researcher does not have the insight to test for differences in these other variables (a distinct possibility given the researcher's initial ignorance of them), *or* if these variables indeed are all manifestations of conversational dominance but are uncorrelated or only weakly intercorrelated (also a distinct possibility whenever behaviors are functionally equivalent such that one can be substituted for another), the researcher still may reach the premature and overly narrow conclusion that conversational dominance is nothing more or less than one person talking louder than another person in conversation. As this example indicates, although bootstrapping often may broaden the investigator's conceptualization of the phenomenon of interest, there is no guarantee that it always will do so.

We suggest that the dispositional strategy will be applied most successfully when researchers begin their endeavors with some fairly sound and well-articulated theorizing about the various behavioral manifestations of the phenomenon of interest, construct and validate behaviorally an instrument or procedure of personality assessment that taps the full range of these behaviors, and use their insight, intuition, and observational skills to test for differences on other, previously noncriterial behaviors during the bootstrapping phase of the research. By resisting an overly narrow conceptualization during the first (assessment and validation) stage, and by further broadening this conceptualization through creative extensions during the second (bootstrapping) stage, investigators can reduce the possibility that the dispositional strategy will frustrate their quest for understanding by leading them—in a circular, near-tautological manner—right back to their starting point.

The approach as overemphasizing dispositional factors and underemphasizing situational ones.

The theoretical criticism that most readily may be made of the dispositional strategy is that it gives too much emphasis to dispositional factors and not enough explicit emphasis to situational ones. This criticism implies that the dispositional strategy is relatively atheoretical not only with regard to the processes underlying the social psychological phenomenon of interest but also with regard to the types of situations in which the phenomenon is or is not likely to occur. This criticism is an important and many-faceted one, with numerous implications for the study of personality and social behavior. We consider some of these implications now, but we will reserve our consideration of others until we have developed an appropriate theoretical framework in which to discuss them.

There are two ways to respond to the criticism that the dispositional approach neglects the impact of situational influences on social behavior. One way to respond is to adopt alternative strategies to the study of personality and social behavior that give explicit attention to situational factors. And, indeed, we shortly will turn to discussions of the two major alternatives to the dispositional strategy. The other way to respond to this criticism, however, is to attempt to modify the dispositional strategy so that it can accommodate (at least implicitly) these concerns without requiring the researcher to forsake the logic and essential character of the dispositional strategy. In essence, this modification requires the identification, measurement, and validation of personality dispositions that are assumed to be specific to a particular situation or to a class of situations.

For example, the general disposition of anxiety could be subdivided into more situation-specific categories such as test anxiety, anxiety in social situations, or anxiety about future events. By focusing on dispositions that are restricted a priori to a specific class of situations, the researcher can presumably develop personality measures having a higher degree of predictive validity than measures that are not tied to particular sets of situations. Moreover, by developing and validating a number of different measures of the disposition—each specific to a different class of situations—the research can employ the full battery of these measures in research designed to identify the person × situation interactions that may typify most human social behavior.

Note, however, that this modification of the dispositional strategy requires that a large number of specific dispositions be identified, assessed, and validated (i.e., as many as the number of situational variants into which the more general disposition may be subdivided). This proliferation of dispositions often may frustrate the theorist's desire for theoretical parsimony and even may introduce an *unwarranted* degree of specificity in those cases in which a more general dispositional measure would yield an equivalent or superior level of predictive validity. The other side of this problem is experienced by the researcher who pursues the modified dispositional strategy only to discover that a situation-specific personality measure is still not specific enough or that it is not feasible to develop an assessment instrument of the desired level of specificity. Given these concerns, the researcher's decision to employ the situation-specific dispositional strategy should reflect a careful weighing of its potential gains in terms of predictive validity and person × situation specificity against its potential costs in terms of the loss of theoretical parsimony and the difficulty of conducting the necessary empirical work.

Methodological and Empirical Critique

The major methodological criticisms that potentially concern the dispositional strategy also reflect the relatively atheoretical nature of this approach. The first of these possible criticisms concerns the inadequate operational definition of *consistency* in the study of dispositionally based behavior. The second possible criticism concerns the apparent failure of the dispositional strategy to account for much of the variability in the behaviors that have been studied.

The approach as failing to provide an adequate operational definition of consistency.

The dispositional strategy is based on the assumption that some meaningful amount of the regularity and consistency in social behavior is due to relatively stable and enduring propensities that reside within individuals. However, some confusion and disagreement long has been apparent regarding the appropriate criteria by which such regularity and consistency in social behavior should be defined [e.g., see Block's (1968) analysis of the differences between phenotypic and genotypic consistency]. Unfortunately, the rudimentary logic underlying the dispositional strategy offers no clear basis for resolving this issue, but some resolution has begun to emerge from critical appraisals of the empirical literature. For example, Magnusson and Endler (1977) have reviewed the disagreements surrounding the operational definition of consistency and have summarized a number of important distinctions that have emerged from this controversy.

First, Magnusson and Endler have proposed that personality theorists and researchers need to distinguish between two categories of consistency, each associated with a different level of analysis. At the level of the process(es) that presumably precede and give rise to overt behavior (the mediating level), the investigator may be concerned with consistency in terms of the mediating variables that determine which behavioral reactions are displayed. At the level of overt behavior (the reaction level) the investigator may be concerned with consistency in terms of the behavioral variables that are measured and recorded.

Second, with regard to consistency at the behavioral reaction level, Magnusson and Endler (1977) have noted that the concept of consistency has been used in at least three different ways:

1. *Absolute consistency,* which is in evidence when "an individual displays a certain type of behavior to the same extent across situations. . . . Its counterpart is individual variability, and it can be studied directly for one individual at a time" (Magnusson and Endler, 1977, p. 7). Operationally, it is defined for a specified behavioral variable by a distribution of ipsative data for that variable, collected from the responses of a single individual across situations (e.g., Bem and Allen, 1974; Zanna, Olson, and Fazio, 1980).

2. *Relative consistency,* which is in evidence when "the rank order of a set of individuals with respect to a certain behavior is stable across situations" (Magnusson and Endler, 1977, p. 7). It can be studied only by examining the behaviors of groups of individuals who are tested across different situations,

and it is the type of consistency that typically has been examined in empirical studies of trait-behavior consistency.

3. *Coherence,* "which refers to behavior that is inherently lawful and predictable without necessarily being stable in either absolute or relative terms as discussed above" (Magnusson and Endler, 1977, p. 7). The emphasis here is on distinctive *patterns* of behavior that are both meaningful and predictable on an individual basis, despite their lack of stability in absolute (variability) or relative (rank-order) terms.

Although the dispositional strategy itself makes no clear-cut operational assumptions about consistency at the behavioral reaction level, most specific applications of the strategy appear to have been based on the operational assumptions of what Magnusson and Endler (1977) refer to as the *trait measurement model.* This measurement model specifically corresponds to trait psychology, a theoretical model of personality to which the dispositional strategy most typically has been applied. The assumptions of the trait measurement model, which are tied logically to trait psychology but *not* to the dispositional strategy per se, are that (1) a true trait score exists for each individual on a given personality dimension and (2) that a monotonic, linear relationship exists between individuals' positions on personality dimensions and their positions on behavioral measures. From the combination of these two assumptions the prediction is derived that "there are stable rank orders of individuals across situations with respect to particular behaviors" (Magnusson and Endler, 1977, p. 13), i.e., that evidence will be found for *relative consistency,* as Magnusson and Endler have defind it.

We have noted that the dispositional strategy itself is relatively atheoretical but that its use traditionally has been associated with the trait model of personality. Unfortunately, this association seems to have led many investigators to assume that the dispositional strategy is somehow equivalent to the trait model and, consequently, that it shares the assumptions of the corresponding trait measurement model as well as this model's prediction of relative consistency. In fact, however, the dispositional strategy does not depend on the assumptions of any specific model of personality. Therefore it may be applied to the study of all types of dispositions, including those that cannot be conceptualized in terms of the trait model. Because the dispositional strategy can be applied to dispositions compatible with other personality theories (e.g., cognitive, psychoanalytic), whose own measurement models may or may not coincide with the trait measurement model in their underlying assumptions or definitions of consistency, a relative consistency prediction will not always be appropriate when the dispositional strategy is employed. Thus the failure of this strategy to yield significant evidence of relative consistency need not always be seen as damning, since some dispositions will be interpretable only in terms of theories for which either absolute consistency or coherence results are implied, a point that has been made by, among others, Bem and Allen (1974), and Zanna, Olson, and Fazio (1980). For a more detailed discussion of this and related issues, the reader is referred to Magnusson and Endler's (1977) insightful analysis (see also Endler, 1982).

The approach as failing to account for much of the variance in social behavior.

A number of influential critics have reviewed much of the personality literature that has employed the dispositional strategy and have concluded that dispositions account for only a small portion of the variance in human social behavior (e.g., Argyle and Little, 1972; Bem, 1972; Bowers, 1973; Fiske, 1974; Mischel, 1968, 1973; Peterson, 1965, 1968; Sarason, Smith, and Diener, 1975). Thus Mischel (1968), for example, has reviewed diverse sources of evidence that seemed to suggest that measures of consistency in personality (whether they are measures of consistency between test and nontest manifestations of traits or measures of behavioral consistency across situations) seldom yield correlations higher than 0.30. The implications of this state of affairs for the dispositional strategy seemed rather devastating: Dispositions would, in general, be expected to exhibit only weak predictive validity and only weak consistency across situations.

These conclusions recently have come under considerable scrutiny. One of the most intense responses has come from Epstein (1977, 1979), who has argued (and claimed to have demonstrated) that Mischel's "personality coefficients" of 0.30 are largely artifacts of unreliable measurement. According to this argument, because most of the studies on which these "low-consistency" conclusions were based employed single-occurrence measures of behavior for which the error of measurement is extreme, the indices of predictive validity and stability obtained in these studies were necessarily of low magnitude. In a series of four studies Epstein (1979) demonstrated that when the error of measurement was reduced by averaging over a large sample of behaviors, measures of stability yielded very high values, frequently in the 0.80 to 0.90 range. Moreover, these measures yielded some evidence of enhanced predictive validity (but see also Mischel and Peake, 1982). A theoretical extension of this reasoning proposed by Jaccard (1977) supported the earlier observation by Hartshorne and May (1928, 1930) that prediction can be also be substantially improved by averaging across several *different* behavioral manifestations of the disposition being studied. For another demonstration of the effects of aggregation, see Cheek (1982).

After citing numerous other research examples in which improving the measures' reliability dramatically enhanced prediction (e.g., Block, 1971, 1977; Block and Block, 1980; Fishbein and Azjen, 1974; Hartshorne and May, 1928, 1930; Jaccard, 1974; Olweus, 1977; Tryon, 1973), Epstein (1979) concluded that "error of measurement appears to be the crucial consideration in demonstrating stability in personality and in relating self-ratings and ratings by others to objective data" (p. 1121). In other words, "given an adequate sample of behavior to begin with, it should be possible to 'predict most of the people much of the time' " (Epstein, 1979, p. 1124). These conclusions, if valid, would appear to refute the criticism that the dispositional strategy cannot be used to account for a substantial portion of the variance in human social behavior.

However, before we assume that the dispositional strategy can be used to "predict most of the people much of the time," we should first consider the arguments proposed by adherents of the *interactional strategy* for the study of personality and social behavior. Many of these writers also have taken issue with claims about the lack of utility of the dispositional strategy; however, they have proposed that the stability and predictive validity of dispositions can be defended only some of the time—i.e., for some people in some situations, and then only for some dispositions and for some criteria behaviors.

THE INTERACTIONAL STRATEGY FOR THE STUDY OF PERSONALITY AND SOCIAL BEHAVIOR

The interactional strategy for the study of personality and social behavior is guided by a theoretical perspective that assumes that a considerable portion of the variance in social behavior is due to the interaction of personal dispositions with situational factors. An additional assumption of this strategy is that certain moderating variables can be identified that distinguish those instances in which dispositions will predict social behavior from those instances in which they will not. The theoretical perspective of the interactional strategy is accompanied by an empirical orientation that seeks to discover which moderating variables interact with which dispositional and situational variables to determine social behavior within particular domains.

Historically, the interactional approach to the study of personality and social behavior emerged as the attempted synthesis of a dialectical tension between the dispositional approach (the original thesis) and the situationist movement that developed in reaction to it (the antithesis). In a recent review of these and other developments in personality, Cantor and Kihlstrom (1980) have traced the historical emergence of interactionism (see also Endler, 1982). Beginning with Lewin's (1935) dictum that behavior is a function of both the person and the environment, and continuing through the formulations of Murray (1938), Kelly (1955), and Neisser (1967), theorists have argued for a view of personality that assigns a central importance to the individual's interpretation of the events that he or she experiences. The individual's interpretation of these events is assumed, in all these theories, to reflect the combined influence of both dispositional and situational factors.

Although different meanings have been attributed to the term *interactionism*, the meaning on which we will focus is the meaning that has been called *mechanistic interactionism* (Magnusson and Endler, 1977) or *statistical interactionism* (Cantor and Kihlstrom, 1980). According to the definitions that have been offered, "the mechanistic [or statistical] meaning of interaction is connected with a mechanistic measurement model for interactional behavior." The mechanistic model "implies a distinction between independent and dependent variables" (Magnusson and Endler, 1977, p. 18; brackets ours), and is "modelled on the multidimensional analysis of variance or multivariate correlation" (Cantor and Kihlstrom, 1980). In addition, the interactions "are construed as unidirectional: persons and environments are considered to jointly influence behavior, but the possibility of reciprocal, feedback relations among persons, settings, and behaviors—with each influencing the others—is not addressed openly" (Cantor and Kihlstrom, 1980). Magnusson and Endler (1977) have proposed further that when the mechanistic model is applied at the behavioral reaction level, it may be used to identify four different categories of statistical interactions:

1. Interactions between *individuals* and *modes of response* (behavioral reactions);

2. Interactions between *individuals* and *situations;*

3. Interactions between *situations* and *modes of response;*

4. Three-way interactions of *individuals, modes of response,* and *situations.*

We have chosen to focus on what has been termed mechanistic or statistical interactionism, and the body of research associated with it, for two reasons. The first reason is that most of the research that has been guided by an interactionist perspective has been based upon the mechanistic or statistical measurement model. This preference is probably due to the second reason for giving careful consideration to this approach: the conceptual parsimony and psychometric economy promised by its assumption of linearity and undirectionality of the hypothesized causal relationships.

To provide a general theoretical framework for our review and discussion of relevant data, we must present our own conception of the mechanistic or statistical version of the interactional approach. Our conception is, in many respects, similar to that of Magnusson and Endler (1977), particularly in its incorporation of the four categories of statistical interaction that they have described. Our conception is somewhat broader than their conception, however, in that it incorporates additional categories of statistical interaction not included in their analysis. Any discussion of these categories depends directly on the concept of *moderating variables,* a concept that provides the starting point for our analysis.

The concept of moderating variables has emerged in the work of a number of personality theorists (e.g., Alker, 1972; Bowers, 1973; Cronbach, 1957; Endler, 1973, 1976; Endler and Magnusson, 1976). There are various ways to define this term, but we believe that a functional definition has the greatest theoretical utility. Functionally, moderating variables in personality research are variables that shift the cause of behavior from a situational locus to a dispositional one or vice versa. In most cases this shift in the causal locus of behavior will be accompanied by a corresponding shift in the focus of the individual's (i.e., actor's) attention. However, because the degree to which such attentional shifts are fully conscious is problematic (cf. Langer, 1978; Nisbett and Wilson, 1977; Schank and Abelson, 1977), our conception makes no definite assumption about their causal necessity versus epiphenomenality with regard to the processes mediating overt behavior.

What are essential to our definition of moderating variables are the notions that cues for behavior are available from both dispositional and situational loci and that moderating variables shift the cause of behavior from one locus to the other. Although the precise mechanism by which such shifts are effected frequently may be attentional in nature (cf. Carver, 1979), we do not assume that it need always be. Thus we are arguing for a general conception of moderating variables whose functional definition does not require the specification of a single, universal mechanism by which the defining function is effected.

We believe that three major classes of moderating variables are relevant to the mechanistic or statistical interactional strategy. The variables within each of our three classes all fit the functional definition of moderating variables, since they all operate to shift the cause of behavior from a situational locus to a dispositional one or vice versa. Our three classes of moderating variables are as follows:

1. Those relating to the *predictor* (i.e., to the particular trait or disposition being studied).

2. Those relating to the *criterion* (i.e., to the particular overt behaviors to which the predictor is being applied).

3. Those relating to the *link between the predictor and the criterion* (i.e., categories of situations for whom and categories of individuals for which such links typically are present or absent).

We believe that moderating variables in the first of these classes answer the question "Which traits?" by specifying the types of traits or dispositions that will or will not be good predictors of behavior. We believe that moderating variables in the second class answer the question "Which behaviors?" by specifying the types of behaviors that traits and dispositions are or are not likely to predict. And we believe that moderating variables in the third class answer the questions "Which people?" and "Which situations?" by specifying for which types of people and in which types of situations a given trait or disposition will or will not predict its criterion behaviors (see Table 1).

Let us now examine separately the four questions that moderating variables may be used to answer: Which

TABLE 1
Four Categories of Moderating Variables

CATEGORY	FUNCTION	REPRESENTATIVE EXAMPLES	REFERENCES
Predictor moderating variables	Specify the types of traits and dispositions that will or will not be good predictors of behavior	Self-reported consistency of the predictor	Bem and Allen (1974)
		Self-reported observability of the predictor	Kenrick and Stringfield (1980)
Criterion moderating variables	Specify the types of behaviors that traits and dispositions will or will not predict	Multiple-act measures of the behavioral criterion	Jaccard (1977)
		Prototypicality of the behavioral criterion	Buss and Craik (1980)
Personal moderating variables	Specify for which types of people traits and dispositions will or will not predict their criterial behaviors	Self-monitoring	Snyder (1979b)
		Self-consciousness	Carver and Scheier (1981)
Situational moderating variables	Specify in which types of situations traits and dispositions will or will not predict their criterial behaviors	Weak versus strong situations	Ickes (1982)
		Precipitating versus nonprecipitating situations	This chapter

traits? Which behaviors? Which people? Which situations? Let us also consider some representative examples of attempts to provide answers, both theoretical and empirical, to these questions.

FEATURES OF THE PREDICTOR: THE QUESTION OF "WHICH TRAITS?"

Do there exist types of traits or dispositions that typically are good predictors of an individual's social behavior? Do there exist other types of traits or dispositions that typically are poor predictors of an individual's social behavior? If these contrasting types of predictors indeed do exist, by means of what procedures can they be identified? Two of the *predictor moderating variables* that have been proposed and whose empirical utility has been documented are the self-reported consistency of the predictor (e.g., Bem and Allen, 1974) and the self-reported observability of the predictor (e.g., Kenrick and Stringfield, 1980). We consider each of these predictor moderating variables in turn.

Self-Reported Consistency

In an empirical investigation of the disposition of friendliness, Bem and Allen (1974) asked individuals the question "How much do you vary from one situation to another in how friendly and outgoing you are?" They then used the answers to this question as a moderating variable to separate respondents into those who reported high consistency and those who reported low consistency in their characteristic levels of friendliness. This simple procedure proved to be quite successful in differentiating those individuals whose actual behavior in the domain of friendliness was predictable from their scores on personality measures of the trait of friendliness [e.g., the extraversion-introversion scale of the Eysenck Personality Inventory; Eysenck and Eysenck (1968)] from those individuals whose friendliness was not predictable from the same trait measures. For those individuals who had reported high consistency in the friendliness domain, the correlation between assessed extraversion and actual friendliness behavior ($r = 0.51$) was substantially larger than was the same correlation for those individuals who had reported low consistency in the friendliness domain ($r = 0.31$). Moreover, those individuals who had reported high consistency in the friendliness domain also manifested substantial cross-situational stability in their behavior in the friendliness domain; by contrast, those

individuals who had reported low consistency in the friendliness domain manifested minimal cross-situational stability in their behavior in the friendliness domain.

Although Bem and Allen (1974) were not nearly so successful in their attempt to use self-reported consistency as a moderating variable in the domain of conscientiousness [others have experienced similar difficulties in applying the Bem-Allen approach to searching for cross-situational consistency in conscientiousness; e.g., Mischel and Peake (1981)], other investigators have documented the utility of self-reported consistency as a predictor moderating variable in a variety of trait domains (e.g., Cheek, 1982; Kenrick and Stringfield, 1980; Turner and Gilliland, 1979; Underwood and Moore, 1981).

Self-Reported Observability

In an empirical investigation of the origins of behavioral consistency in diverse trait domains, Kenrick and Stringfield (1980) had individuals rate the extent to which their behavior in each of sixteen trait domains was publicly observable or available to verification by outside observers. For example, in the trait domain of emotional/easily upset–calm/stable, these individuals answered the question "How publicly observable is your behavior on the emotional/stable dimension? (If it is easy for others to tell how emotional you are all or almost all of the time, mark a high number; if others can never or rarely tell how emotional you are, mark a low number, and so on)" on a seven-point scale.

These ratings of public observability proved to be effective in identifying those trait domains within which behavior is readily predicted from self-ratings on trait measures. For those trait domains in which individuals assigned themselves high ratings on public observability, behavioral consistency (e.g., $r = 0.68$ for self-elected trait domains) was reliably greater than it was for those trait domains in which individuals assigned themselves low ratings on public observability (e.g., $r = 0.49$ for self-elected trait domains). For another demonstration, see Cheek (1982).

On the Nature of Predictor Moderating Variables

Self-reported consistency and self-reported observability appear to be two effective procedures for identifying, on an individual-by-individual basis, those domains within which measures of traits and dispositions will serve as reliable predictors of actual behavior and within which substantial cross-situational stabilities in social behavior will occur. Although some aspects of these procedures have been called into question (e.g., Lutsky, Peake, and Wray, 1978; Mischell and Peake, 1981; Rushton, Jackson, and Paunonen, 1981; Tellegen, Kamp, and Watson, 1982), these procedures do hold out the promise of identifying, for a given individual, those trait domains in which that individual will display the behavioral regularities of personality.

Why should self-reported consistency and self-reported observability function as predictor moderating variables? We suggest that their success derives, in part or in whole, from the fact that each procedure directly solicits evidence of requirements that of necessity must be fulfilled before behavior can and will be predictable from measures of traits and dispositions. Behavior must be stable from situation to situation before measures of traits and dispositions collected in one situation will predict behavioral measures of those traits and dispositions collected in other situations. And public actions must be meaningful reflections of private traits and dispositions before measures of traits and dispositions will predict behavioral manifestations of those traits and dispositions.

From this perspective what is impressive to us is that individuals are sufficiently knowledgeable about their consistency and observability in diverse trait domains and are sufficiently willing to accurately report this knowledge to permit the simple procedures of asking individuals about consistency and observability to reveal the domains within which behavioral consistencies are to be found. We suspect that the success of other attempts to identify predictor-moderating variables may very well depend on their ability to tap knowledge of other prerequisites for and manifestations of correspondence between actions and underlying traits, dispositions, and other personal characteristics.

FEATURES OF THE CRITERION: THE QUESTION OF "WHICH BEHAVIORS?"

Do there exist types of behaviors that are maximally predictable from measures of potentially relevant underlying traits and dispositions of the individual? Do there exist other types of behaviors that are only minimally predictable from measure of traits and dispositions? If these contrasting types of behavioral categories exist, by means of what procedures can they be identified? Two of the criterion moderating variables that have been suggested and whose empirical performance has been

assessed are multiple-act (versus single-act) measures of the behavioral criterion (e.g., Fishbein and Ajzen, 1974) and the prototypicality of the behavioral criterion (e.g., Buss and Craik, 1980). We consider each of these criterion moderating variables in its turn.

Multiple-Act Measures of the Behavioral Criterion

The logic of the procedure of constructing multiple-act measures of the behavioral criterion may be illustrated by the work of Fishbein and Ajzen (1974) on the prediction of behavior from measures of attitudes. In one study, these investigators provided college students with lists of 100 behaviors, each of which dealt with religious activities (e.g., praying before meals, taking religious courses for credit) and asked them to indicate which of the behaviors they had performed. Each of the 100 responses provided by each individual constitutes a single-act criterion. The sum of the entire collection of 100 responses constitutes a multiple-act criterion.

The researchers then attempted to predict specific religious behaviors from measures of religious attitudes. Here the correlations between attitudes toward religion and each single-act criterion were minimal (about 0.10). In contrast, the correlation between attitudes toward religion and the multiple-act measure of the criterion of religious behavior was substantial (over 0.60). Other demonstrations of the greater predictability of multiple-act criteria over single-act criteria have been provided by Epstein (1979, 1980), Werner (1978), and Wiegel and Newman (1975).

The utility of multiple-act measures of the behavioral criterion has been demonstrated not only in investigations of the relationship between attitudinal predictors and behavioral criteria but also in investigations of the predictive relationship between measures of personality traits and behavioral manifestations of those traits (e.g., Epstein, 1979; Jaccard, 1974; McGowan and Gormly, 1976). In one such investigation Jaccard (1974) examined the relationship between measures of individual differences in the trait of dominance and self-reports of forty dominant behaviors (e.g., winning arguments, controlling conversations, etc.). On the average, the correlation between assessed dominance and each of the forty single-act criterion behaviors was in the neighborhood of 0.20. However, the correlation between measured individual differences in the trait of dominance and the multiple-act criterion of dominant behaviors (formed by summing across the forty individual self-reported behaviors) was in the neighborhood of .60. Clearly, the multiple-act measure of the behavioral criterion outperformed the single-act measures (see Ajzen, 1982).

Prototypicality of the Behavioral Criterion

Although multiple-act measures of the behavioral criterion seem, in general, to outperform single-act measures, we nevertheless can identify certain single-act measures of the behavioral criterion that are better predicted from measures of stable traits and enduring dispositions than are other single-act measures of the behavioral criterion. Consider the empirical demonstration conducted by Buss and Craik (1980), who sought to predict behavioral dominance (i.e., the performance of behaviors thought to reflect and manifest dominance, such as issuing orders and controlling meetings) from dispositional dominance (i.e., psychometric measures of the personality disposition of dominance, such as those from the California Psychological Inventory and the Personality Research Form).

In their demonstration Buss and Craik (1980) found that specific self-reported behavioral acts of dominance were predictable from dispositional measures of dominance to the extent that those behavioral acts were prototypic of (i.e., best examples of, clearest cases of, central members of) the category of dominance. Behavioral acts that were high in their prototypicality of the category of dominance (e.g., monopolizing the conversation, taking command of the situation) were well predicted from psychometric measures of the disposition of dominance. For example, for males the correlation between scores on the dominance scale of the Jackson Personality Research Form and acts in the top quartile of prototypicality of self-reported dominant acts was 0.67. In contrast, behavioral acts that were low in their prototypicality of the category of dominance (e.g., flattering someone in order to get one's way, asking someone out on a date) were poorly predicted from the psychometric measures of the disposition of dominance. For example, for females the correlation between scores on the dominance scale of the California Psychological Inventory and acts in the bottom quartile of prototypicality of self-reported dominant acts was 0.05. In subsequent research Buss and Craik (1981) have replicated their findings for dominance and extended their approach to the successful prediction of self-reported prototypic acts of aloofness and of gregariousness (but not of submissiveness) from measures of relevant dispositions. In addition, Mischel and Peake

(1981) have assessed the contribution of behavioral prototypicality to the temporal stability of behavioral indices of conscientiousness.

On the Nature of Criterion Moderating Variables

As criterion moderating variables, both multiple-act measures of the behavioral criterion and the prototypicality of the behavioral criterion may be used to identify those behaviors that are well predicted from measures of relevant traits and dispositions. True, most of the empirical evidence that has been offered in support of the utility of each of these criterion-moderating variables has involved only self-reports of the behavioral criteria under examination. Moreover, the prediction of self-reports of behavior may be more easily accomplished than the prediction of actual behavioral activities. Nevertheless, the potential of each criterion moderating variable seems to have been demonstrated.

Why should multiple-act measures of the behavioral criterion and the prototypicality of the behavioral criterion each perform well as criterion moderating variables? At the very least, multiple-act criteria may succeed because they provide more reliable samples of the behavioral domain than do single-act criteria. Also, prototypic measures of the behavioral criterion may succeed because they provide more valid measures of the behavioral domain than do nonprototypic measures. From this perspective any and all procedures that augment the reliability and validity of the assessment of behavioral criteria also should enhance the extent to which those behavioral criteria can be predicted from measures of relevant traits, dispositions, attitudes, and other characteristics of the individual. Although this conclusion may seem to go almost without saying, only recently have the implications of this conclusion begun to be systematically explored.

FEATURES OF THE INDIVIDUAL: THE QUESTION OF "WHICH PEOPLE?"

Do there exist categories of individuals who typically manifest the regularities and consistencies of personality in their social behavior, individuals whose social behavior is predictable from measures of their traits, dispositions, attitudes, and other personal attributes? Do there exist other categories of individuals whose social behavior is not predictable from such measures but instead is particularly sensitive to situational and interpersonal influences? If these contrasting categories of relatively dispositional individuals and relatively situational individuals exist, by means of what *personal moderating variables* can they be identified?

There have been many theoretical and empirical attempts to identify contrasting categories of relatively dispositional individuals and relatively situational individuals. Among the personal moderating variables that have been investigated are action control (Kuhl, 1981), anxiety (Grooms and Endler, 1960), ascription of responsibility (Schwartz, 1973), defensiveness (Kogan and Wallach, 1964), empathy (Hogan, 1969; Mills and Hogan, 1978), locus of control (Phares, 1976; Rotter, 1966), neuroticism (Endler, 1973), personal identity (Cheek, 1982; Hogan and Cheek, in press), psychological androgyny (Bem, 1975), repression-sensitization (Byrne, 1964), self-consciousness (Fenigstein, Scheier, and Buss, 1975), and self-monitoring (Snyder, 1974). Representative of programmatic attempts to identify such individuals are theory and research on self-monitoring (for a review, see Snyder, 1979b) and theory and research on self-consciousness (for reviews, see Buss, 1980; Carver and Scheier, 1981).

Self-Monitoring
According to the theoretical formulation of self-monitoring (Snyder, 1979b), an individual in a social setting actively attempts to construct a pattern of social behavior appropriate to that particular context. Diverse sources of information are available to guide this choice, including cues to situational or interpersonal specifications of appropriateness and information about inner states, personal dispositions, and social attitudes. Furthermore, according to the self-monitoring formulation, individuals differ in the extent to which they rely on either source of information in regulating their behavior in social contexts.

For those individuals who monitor and regulate their behavioral choices on the basis of situational information (high self-monitoring individuals), the impact of situational and interpersonal cues to social appropriateness ought to be considerable. These individuals ought to demonstrate considerable situation-to-situation specificity in their social behavior. Moreover, for these high self-monitoring individuals the correspondence between social behavior and underlying traits, dispositions, attitudes, and other personal attributes ought to be minimal.

By contrast, and of particular relevance to the search for categories of individuals who characteristical-ly manifest the regularities and consistencies of personality in their social behavior, individuals who monitor or guide their behavioral choices on the basis of information from relevant inner states (low self-monitoring individuals) ought to be less responsive to situational and interpersonal specifications of behavioral appropriateness. Their social behavior ought to manifest substantial cross-situational consistency and temporal stability. Furthermore, for these low self-monitoring individuals the covariation between social behavior and underlying traits, dispositions, attitudes, and other personal attributes ought to be substantial.

Empirical evidence has provided documentation for these theoretical propositions (for reviews, see Snyder, 1979a, 1979b). Individual differences in self-monitoring are measured by the Self-Monitoring Scale, an internally consistent and temporally stable set of twenty-five true-false, self-descriptive statements [for details of the psychometric construction of the Self-Monitoring Scale, as well as demonstrations of its convergent and discriminant validity, see Snyder (1974)]. High self-monitoring individuals (who endorse such Self-Monitoring Scale items as "When I am uncertain how to act in social situations, I look to the behavior of others for cues"; "In different situations and with different people, I often act like very different persons"; and "In order to get along and be liked, I tend to be what other people expect me to be rather than anything else") are both attentive and responsive to situational specifications of behavioral appropriateness. Accordingly, their self-presentational social behaviors manifest considerable situation-to-situation specificity (e.g., Caldwell and O'Reilly, 1982; Danheiser and Graziano, 1982; Lippa, 1976, 1978a; Rarick, Soldow, and Geizer, 1976; Shaffer, Smith, and Tomarelli, 1982; Snyder and Monson, 1975). Moreover, these individuals typically manifest minimal consistency between their social behavior and potentially relevant underlying personal attributes (e.g., Snyder and Swann, 1976; Snyder and Tanke, 1976).

By contrast, the social behavior of low self-monitoring individuals [who endorse such Self-Monitoring Scale items as "My behavior is usually an expression of my true inner feelings, attitudes, and beliefs"; "I can only argue for ideas which I already believe"; and "I would not change my opinions (or the way I do things) to please someone else or to win their favor"] characteristically manifest the consistencies and regularities in social behavior that constitute personality. In contrast to the social behavior of high self-monitoring individuals, that of low self-monitoring individuals is rarely molded and tailored to fit their situational surroundings (e.g., Snyder and Monson, 1975). Moreover, we have good reason to believe that low self-monitoring individuals manifest marked situation-to-situation stability and consistency in their social behavior in such behavioral domains as altruism, honesty, and self-restraint (e.g., Snyder and Monson, 1975), as well as within the domain of nonverbal behaviors expressive of, for example, sociability, anxiety, and sex role identity (e.g., Lippa, 1976, 1978a, 1978b; Lippa and Mash, 1979).

Additional evidence suggests that low self-monitoring individuals display considerable temporal stability in their behavior (e.g., Lutsky, Woodworth, and Clayton, 1980). Furthermore, low self-monitoring individuals typically manifest substantial correspondence between their private attitudes and intentions and their public behaviors and actions (e.g., Ajzen, Timko, and White, 1981; Becherer and Richard, 1978; Lutsky, Woodworth, and Clayton, 1980; Snyder, 1982; Snyder and Kendzierski, 1982a; Snyder and Swann, 1976; Snyder and Tanke, 1976; Zanna and Olson, 1982; Zanna, Olson, and Fazio, 1980; Zuckerman and Reis, 1978), between mood states and self-presentation (e.g., Ickes, Layden, and Barnes, 1978), between various personality attributes and corresponding expressive behaviors (e.g., Lippa, 1978a, 1978b; Lippa, Valdez, and Jolly, 1979), and between self-ratings on diverse personality dimensions and ratings by their acquaintances (Tunnell, 1980). This correspondence between personal attributes and social behavior is accompanied by (and may be a reflection of) low self-monitoring individuals' particularly well-articulated knowledge of their characteristic selves within a wide variety of domains of self-conception (e.g., Snyder and Cantor, 1980). Evidently, when it comes to correspondence between private dispositions and public actions, low self-monitoring individuals seem to constitute one category of individuals who characteristically manifest the regularities and consistencies that constitute personality.

Of what consequence are the differing behavioral orientations of high self-monitoring individuals and low self-monitoring individuals? In regulating their social behavior, high self-monitoring individuals are relatively situationally guided individuals. They are particularly sensitive to social and interpersonal cues to situational appropriateness; however, their attitudes and behaviors are virtually uncorrelated with each other. To predict and understand their actions, one would seek information about characteristics of their situations. It is as if the psychology of high self-monitoring individuals is the psychology of their social situations and interpersonal surroundings.

By contrast, in regulating their social behavior, low self-monitoring individuals are relatively dispositionally guided individuals. Their social behavior typically is a reflection of corresponding social attitudes, affective states, and personal dispositions. At the same time they are relatively unresponsive to situational specifications of behavioral appropriateness. Accordingly, one would adopt a rather different strategy for understanding the social behavior of low self-monitoring individuals. One should be able to predict their future behavior from measures of relevant present attitudes, traits, and dispositions. It is as if the psychology of low self-monitoring individuals is the psychology of their attitudes, dispositions, and other salient and relevant inner states.

Self-Consciousness

Another category of individuals whose social behavior often reflects corresponding personal characteristics are those who are high in private self-consciousness, as identified by their relatively high scores on the private–self-consciousness factor of the Self-Consciousness Scale developed by Fenigstein, Scheier, and Buss (1975). According to Fenigstein, Scheier, and Buss, "the consistent tendency of persons to direct attention inward or outward is the trait of self-consciousness" (1975, p. 522). To measure this trait, they constructed a twenty-three-item inventory that elicites self-reports of behaviors and experiences within three domains: private self-consciousness (ten items that assess attention to one's inner thoughts and feelings; e.g., "I reflect about myself a lot"), public self-consciousness (seven items that assess awareness of the self as a social object; e.g., "I'm self-conscious about the way I look"), and social anxiety (six items that assess discomfort in the presence of others; e.g., "It takes me time to overcome my shyness in new situations"). Scores on the private–self-consciousness, public–self-consciousness, and social anxiety factors of the inventory have been shown to be relatively independent of each other (Fenigstein, Scheier, and Buss, 1975; Turner, Scheier, Carver, and Ickes, 1978).

For our present purpose the private–self-consciousness factor of the inventory is of particular importance. High scorers on the private–self-consciousness factor assert that "I'm always trying to figure myself out" and "I'm constantly examining my motives." At the same time they deny that "generally, I'm not very aware of myself" and "I never scrutinize myself." The private–self–consciousness factor possesses considerable temporal stability (Fenigstein, Scheier, and Buss, 1975) and internal consistency (Turner, 1978). For evidence of the validity of the private–self–consciousness factor as a measure of the propensity to direct one's attention inward toward and to reflect upon one's own inner thoughts, feelings, and other personal attributes, see Buss (1980), Carver and Scheier (1978) and Hull and Levy (1979). For evidence of its discriminant validity, see Carver and Glass (1976) and Turner *et al.* (1978).

The outcomes of diverse empirical investigations suggest that high scorers on the private–self–consciousness factor of the Self-Consciousness Scale are individuals whose social behavior is particularly responsive to their enduring dispositional properties and to their transient affective states. Within the domain of enduring dispositional properties, Scheier, Buss, and Buss (1978) have reported that the correlation between measured aggressive dispositions and observed aggressive behaviors is substantially larger for individuals high in private self-consciousness than for individuals low in private self-consciousness. Similarly, Turner (1978) has reported that measures of the dispositions of dominance are substantially better predictors of the behavioral expression of dominance for individuals high in private self-consciousness than for individuals low in private self-consciousness (although in this investigation individuals low in public self-consciousness also manifested substantial covariation between dispositional dominance and behavioral dominance).

Within the domain of transient affective states, Scheier (1976) has demonstrated that, following provocation, angry individuals who are high in private self-consciousness display more behavioral manifestations of their anger than individuals who are low in private self-consciousness. Similarly, Scheier and Carver (1977) have shown that individuals high in private self-consciousness are more responsive to a variety of transient affective states (e.g., the mildly positive and the mildly negative affects produced by observing pleasant and unpleasant slides) than are individuals low in private self-consciousness.

Evidently, individuals who are chronically attentive to their dispositional properties and affective states also are individuals whose social behavior characteristically reflects their dispositional properties and their affective states. Clearly, these individuals who are high in private self-consciousness constitute another category of individuals whose social behavior typically reflects corresponding personal characteristics. To the extent, then, that one examines the social behavior of these individuals, one should witness the regularities and consistencies that are thought to constitute personality. In particular, one ought to be able to predict their behavior from knowledge of their attitudes, affective states, traits, and dispositions.

On the Nature of Personal Moderating Variables

With the aid of personal moderating variables such as self-monitoring and private self-conciousness, one can identify categories of individuals whose social behavior characteristically reflects relevant underlying dispositions, attitudes, and other personal attributes (i.e., relatively dispositional individuals) and other categories of individuals whose social behavior is particularly sensitive to situational influences (i.e., relatively situational individuals). The successful identification of such categories of individuals permits the specification of when predictions of the dispositional determination of social behavior will be confirmed and when predictions of the situational determination of social behavior will be confirmed. But from the perspective of theory and research on personal-moderating variables, if one does not distinguish between the categories of relatively dispositional individuals and relatively situational individuals, the ability of either dispositional or situational variables to predict social behavior will be considerably diminished.

In investigations of the moderating influences of self-monitoring, for example, the relationships between dispositional predictors and social behavior typically have been of, at best, modest magnitude. So too have been the relationships between situational predictors and social behavior. Only by considering the moderating influences of self-monitoring has it been possible to identify that category of individuals for whom dispositional predictors of social behavior perform well (i.e., low self-monitoring individuals) and that category of individuals for whom situational predictors of social behavior perform well (i.e., high self-monitoring individuals). In statistical terms, the moderating effects of self-monitoring appeared as interactions between self-monitoring and appropriate dispositional or situational predictor variables. More generally, the moderating influences of personal moderating variables appear as interactions with appropriate dispositional or situational independent variables.

What are some of the criteria that seem to characterize successful attempts to identify personal moderating variables? To the extent that we can generalize from the case of self-monitoring and from the case of private self-consciousness (two of the more extensively researched personal moderating variables), it would appear that a psychological construct will perform successfully as a personal moderating variable to the extent that it reliably and validly taps those processes by which information about the self and information about social situations are attended to and utilized in guiding social behavior. From this perspective, self-monitoring and private self-consciousness may succeed because their associated measuring instruments reliably and validly identify those individuals who believe, respectively, that "My behavior is usually an expression of my true inner feelings, attitudes, and beliefs" and "I'm generally attentive to my inner feelings," and because these individuals live their lives according to the dictates of these critical aspects of their conceptions of self.

This is not to suggest that the measure of self-monitoring and the measure of private self-consciousness are identifying the same individuals. In fact, the correlation between the two measures is a very modest +0.15 (Turner *et al.*, 1978), and the precise conceptual relations between the two constructs await a full and detailed specification (see Schneiderman, Webb, and Davis, 1981). Rather, we suggest only that self-monitoring and private self-consciousness both may have succeeded for the same reasons that we believe that *any* personal moderating variable will succeed. We believe that any personal moderating variable will succeed to the extent that it focuses on the person's preferential attentiveness and responsiveness to dispositional or situational information as guides to action in particular behavioral domains. A precise demarcation of the behavioral domains appropriate to particular personal moderating variables (including self-monitoring and private self-consciousness) must await the availability of a more extensive catalogue of successful attempts to identify personal moderating variables.

FEATURES OF THE SITUATION: THE QUESTION OF "WHICH SITUATIONS?"

Do there exist types of situations in which measures of traits and dispositions will serve as particularly good predictors of individuals' social behavior? Do there exist other types of situations in which such measures will fail to serve as good predictors of social behavior? If these contrasting types of situations indeed do exist, by means of what *situational moderating variables* can they be identified?

Strong Versus Weak Situations

Situational moderating variables, like the other types of moderating variables that we have reviewed, operate to shift the cause of behavior from a situational locus to a dispositional one or vice versa. Viewed in these terms, the most important situational moderating variable can be conceptualized as the "strength" versus "weakness" of situations as they are experienced by the individual. In general, psychologically "strong" situations tend to be those that provide salient cues to guide behavior and have a fairly high degree of structure and definition. In contrast, psychologically "weak" situations tend to be those that do not offer salient cues to guide behavior and are relatively unstructured and ambiguous. The distinction between strong and weak situations has been elaborated by Mischel (1977, p. 347):

> Psychological "situations" (stimuli, treatment) are powerful to the degree that they lead everyone to construe the particular events in the same way, induce *uniform* expectancies regarding the most appropriate response pattern, provide adequate incentives for the performance of that response pattern and require skills that everyone has to the same extent. . . . Conversely, situations are weak to the degree that they are not uniformly encoded, do not generate uniform expectancies concerning the desired behavior, do not offer sufficient incentives for its performance, or fail to provide the learning conditions required for successful genesis of the behavior.

Because strong situations should shift the cause of behavior from a dispositional locus to a situational one, measures of traits and dispositions should typically predict behavior better in weak situations than in strong ones. The distinction between strong and weak situations has clear and important implications for the empirical study of personality and social behavior. As Mischel (1977) and Monson and Snyder (1977) have indicated, most clinical and experimental treatments are intended to be strong situations in which the influences of personality variables on behavior will be minimized, if not eliminated completely. The logic underlying this intent should be fairly obvious, at least in the case of experimental treatments. Because the experiment historically evolved as a procedure for "isolating and measuring the effects" of situational variables, its application in psychology typically has been one in which "the independent variable (a situational manipulation) is designed and programmed to occur in a fixed and constant fashion, independently of the behavior of the subject" (Monson and Snyder, 1977, p. 97).

A somewhat different perspective on the experiment as a strong situation is provided by writers who have analyzed social psychological experiments from a role theory perspective provided by sociology (e.g., Alexander and Knight, 1971; Alexander and Lauderdale, 1977; Touhey, 1974). These authors have proposed that many, if not most, social psychological experiments present the subject with a well-defined, highly structured situation containing salient cues that indicate the most socially desirable and situationally appropriate mode of responding. The experiment is seen as very much like a theatrical production having its own scenario, plot line, stage props, and actors. Of these actors (whose numbers at each session or "performance" may include one or more experimenters, confederates, and subjects), only the subjects' lines and actions are not scripted in advance; all other parts are pre-scripted and relatively inflexible.

According to this view, the task of the subject in the experiment is to infer what role he or she is expected to play and then play it in the most appropriate and socially desirable manner possible. This task can be viewed either as one of selecting the most appropriate "situated identity" (Alexander and Knight, 1971; Alexander and Lauderdale, 1977) or "self-image" (Turner, 1968) to display in the situation, or as one of deciding which of many possible scripts should be enacted (Abelson, 1976; Langer, 1978; Schank and Abelson, 1977). In any case, the experiment is no longer regarded as a scientific context in which independent variables are manipulated and dependent variables measured. Instead, it is seen as a quasi-dramaturgical context in which one of the actors (the subject) is obliged to improvise his or her lines and actions in response to the pre-scripted lines and actions of the remaining actors and the settings in which these actions take place. Clearly, to the degree that such quasi-dramaturgical contexts constitute what we have called strong situations (i.e., are highly structured and un-

ambiguously scripted), all subjects should tend to respond to them in a fairly uniform manner. The influence of dispositional factors on behavior thus should be quite attenuated, if not eliminated completely, since the behavior is determined by the situation and not by the subjects' own dispositions (cf. Ickes, 1978b, 1982, 1983a, in press a).

This type of strong-situation procedure makes sense when the researcher is attempting to study the impact of situational factors on behavior, since it ideally maximizes the variance in behavior due to the particular situational factor(s) under investigation while minimizing the "error" variance due to individual differences in personality. On the other hand, when the researcher is attempting to study the influences on behavior due to individual differences in personality, the strong-situation procedure of the experiment may often be highly inappropriate (Ickes, 1978a, 1978b, 1982, 1983a, in press a). Because the personality researcher presumably is interested in identifying the variance in behavior that is due to individual-difference factors, he or she generally should be very reluctant to employ strong-situation paradigms that treat such variance as experimental error and seek to minimize, if not eliminate, it.

Ironically, however, the most cursory examination of the published literature in personality suggests that the overwhelming majority of personality studies are conducted in highly structured, psychologically strong laboratory situations in which salient and relatively unambiguous cues are provided to guide behavior. Conversely, only a small minority of personality studies are conducted in psychologically weak, unstructured situations in which individuals are forced to rely primarily on their own internal traits and dispositions to guide their behavior. "The irony is that personality researchers, by carefully structuring their experimental situations, may thereby eliminate much of the same individual difference variance they are in fact purporting to study!" (Ickes, 1982, p. 333).

That the ostensible failure of personality factors to predict behavior might be due in part to the use of highly structured, strong situations is illustrated by a set of studies designed to identify the influence of personality and role-related variables on behavior occurring in an ambiguous and relatively unstructured interaction situation (Ickes, 1982, 1983a, in press a). In these studies two individuals with no past history of interaction are left alone together in a waiting room where they are free to interact or not, as they choose. Because the individuals have not been instructed to interact, and because other external cues to guide their behavior are lacking, they essentially are forced to depend on internalized dispositions to guide their spontaneous interaction behavior.

The effectiveness of this paradigm in eliciting strong dispositional influences on social behavior has been demonstrated repeatedly in studies concerned with dispositional variables such as self-monitoring (Barnes and Ickes, 1979; Ickes and Barnes, 1977), gender and sex role orientation (Ickes, 1981, in press b; Ickes and Barnes, 1978; Ickes, Schermer, and Steeno, 1979; La-France and Ickes, 1981; Lamke and Bell, 1981), locus of control (Rajecki, Ickes, and Tanford, 1981), birth order (Ickes 1983b, Ickes and Turner, 1983), and the disposition of whites to approach or avoid interaction with blacks (Ickes, in press c). The dispositional influences found in these studies are quite clearcut and powerful. They generally yield larger mean differences and F-ratios than those obtained in studies using more structured interaction paradigms (cf. Duncan and Fiske, 1977), and such differences are typically evident across a wide range of behavioral and self-report measures. Moreover, their generalizability to real-world social interaction is likely to be enhanced by the spontaneous, unconstrained nature of the behavior that is observed. For an overview of the research conducted with Ickes's unstructured interaction paradigm, and for a detailed discussion comparing the features of this paradigm with those of more traditional ones, see Ickes (1982, 1983a).

In addition to the findings of Ickes and his colleagues, the results of an independent line of research conducted by Monson and his colleagues (Monson, Hesley, and Chernick, 1982) have provided even more direct evidence that the relationship between trait and behavioral measures depends on the strength of situational pressures. In a questionnaire investigation, Monson, Hesley, and Chernick found that individual differences on the introversion-extraversion dimension correlated more highly with predicted behaviors when situational pressures were weak ($r = +0.42$) than when they were moderate ($r = +0.32$) or strong ($r = +0.13$). In a follow-up study examining actual behaviors, introversion-extraversion scores were found to predict behavior more effectively in a getting-acquainted conversation when situational pressures were weak ($r = +0.63$) than when there were either strong situational pressures encouraging introversion ($r = +0.36$) or strong situational pressures encouraging extraversion ($r = +0.25$).

In a more recent paper (Monson *et al.,* 1983) Monson and his colleagues have proposed another reason (apart from the relative salience of the disposition) why the correlations between traits and their criterial behaviors should be attenuated in highly structured situations. This reason, which appears blindingly obvious in retrospect, is the simple statistical fact that the magnitude of any correlation is attenuated to the degree that the range of either or both of the correlated variables is restricted. In typical studies of personality conducted in the field, trait-behavior correlations are obtained in naturalistic situations to which subjects have often self-selected because of the congruence between the structure of these situations and their personalities. To the degree that these naturalistic situations are structured to promote such self-selection, the ranges of *both* the dispositional predictor variable and the behavioral criterion variable will be restricted, and any resulting correlation will necessarily be relatively low. Similarly, in typical studies of personality conducted in structured laboratory settings, the structure of the task will generally impose normative constraints on behavior that restrict the range of appropriate behavior on the criterion variable and also limit the magnitude of the trait-behavior correlation. Thus in *both* of the traditional settings for personality research, the statistical artifact of restricted range operates to virtually guarantee that trait-behavior correlations will be attenuated. The optimal research setting for avoiding this artifactual attenuation is epitomized by Ickes's paradigm—a paradigm in which the experimenter can ensure that the entire range of personality scores is represented on the predictor variable and that the unstructured nature of the test situation permits a wide range of responses on the behavioral criterion variable to be displayed.

Taken collectively, the studies by Ickes and his colleagues and those by Monson and his colleagues offer converging evidence that individual differences may have their strongest impact on behavior in relatively unstructured, psychologically weak situations. By implication, these studies also suggest that researchers should consider the alternative of the unstructured situation before committing themselves to those psychologically strong test situations that may actually eliminate the very individual differences in behavior that the researchers are attempting to study.

If it is true that traditional strong-situation paradigms are generally less well suited than weak-situation paradigms to the study of personality and social behavior, why have researchers persisted for decades in using them? Clearly, the orthodoxy of training graduate students in the experimental approach and the historical lack of alternative operational models account for some of this persistence. It is probably also true, however, that at least some strong-situation paradigms really do work; otherwise, their use would have been subject to extinction long ago. Even if we acknowledge that most of the past research in personality has yielded only tenuous and inconsistent evidence of its impact on social behavior [see Argyle (1969), Mehrabian (1972), Mischel (1968), and Shaw (1971, 1977) for some rather discouraging reviews], it still seems likely that some of the strong-situation paradigms employed in this research were better than others. If this assumption is correct, we should be able to pursue our discussion of situational moderating variables a bit further. To be specific, we should be able to identify some other situational moderating variable(s) that will enable us to distinguish between strong situations in which dispositional measures *can* be used to accurately predict social behavior and strong situations in which dispositional measures *cannot* be used for this purpose.

Precipitating Versus Nonprecipitating Situations
Of the strong-situation paradigms used in personality research, the most effective appear to be those that establish situations in which behavioral manifestations of the relevant dispositional differences are maximized. These situations may be termed *precipitating situations* because they not only shift the cause of behavior to a dispositional locus but also precipitate or polarize differences in the behavioral manifestations of the particular disposition being studied. The criteria that appear to define a precipitating situation are as follows:

1. It is relevant to the particular disposition being studied.

2. It makes the disposition salient as a guide to behavior.

3. It permits (as situationally appropriate) specific, alternative modes of responding that individuals should select differentially as a function of their location on the dispositional dimension.

As the third criterion suggests, the precipitating situation is, in essence, a kind of behavioral forced choice that ideally can be resolved only by appeal to the particular disposition to which it is relevant.

A useful example of research employing the precipitating situation is Bem and Lenney's (1976) study of sex typing and the avoidance of cross-sex behavior. In this study stereotypically sex-typed individuals (i.e., "masculine" males and "feminine" females) were instructed to make a series of forced choices regarding which of two behaviors (one masculine sex-typed, one feminine sex-typed) they were willing to perform. So that the cause of a sex-role correspondent choice could be attributed to their own sex-typing disposition, these individuals were offered slightly more money to choose the cross-sex behaviors than they were offered to choose the paired, sex-role correspondent ones. This situation evoked clearcut behavioral manifestations of the individuals' assessed dispositions, even though it was highly structured and it severely constrained the range of appropriate responses. The situation effectively precipitated disposition-based differences in behavior because the behavioral forced choices it required were relevant to the sex-typing disposition being studied, made this disposition salient as a guide to behavior, and permitted specific alternative modes of responding that individuals could select differentially as a function of their sex typing.

Many of the strong-situation paradigms commonly used in personality research may share some, but not all, of the criteria that define the precipitating situation. To the degree that all of these criteria are met, these paradigms will probably provide relatively good evidence for dispositional influences in social behavior. However, to the degree that none of these criteria are met, the resulting test situations should be nonprecipitating and should provide relatively poor evidence for dispositional influences in social behavior.

Of the three criteria we have used to define the precipitating situation, perhaps the best-investigated criterion has been the second one, the criterion that the situation should make the appropriate disposition salient as a guide to behavior. The research relevant to this criterion suggests that situations can be characterized as *self-focusing* or *non-self-focusing* according to the degree that they direct the individual's attention "inward" (toward the self) or "outward" (toward the environment).

Most of the studies contrasting self-focusing and non-self-focusing situations were designed to test derivations from Duval and Wicklund's (1972) theory of objective self-awareness. The theory is complex and many-faceted, but one of its simplest and most pervasive themes is that self-awareness enhances the impact on behavior of "internal" sources of information by increasing their *salience* relative to "external" sources of information (Shaver, 1976). In other words, the more attention an individual gives to a particular stimulus (e.g., source of information), the more likely it is that his or her subsequent behavior will be infuenced by that stimulus. In situations that have been structured to direct the individual's attention inward, onto the self, such internal sources of information as attitudes, traits, and values will tend to become salient and exert a primary influence on the individual's behavior. However, in situations that have been structured to direct the individual's attention outward, onto aspects of the environment, the relative salience of these external stimuli will cause *them* to be used as the primary guides to the individual's behavior. This reasoning suggests that a given disposition may predict overt behavior quite strongly in conditions in which it is salient, but it may predict the same behavior only weakly or not at all in conditions in which it is not salient.

From an operational standpoint, a self-focusing situation can be established in a variety of ways. In explicitly social contexts, the presence of other people may be sufficient to direct an individual's attention toward himself or herself, particularly to the degree that these other people are perceived as being different from the individual (e.g., Duval, 1976; Morse and Gergen, 1970; Taylor and Fiske, 1975, 1978) or as having the capacity and/or motivation to evaluate the individual's behavior (e.g., Scheier, Fenigstein, and Buss, 1974). In implicitly social contexts, a heightened self-focus can be created by recording some aspects of the individual's behavior in a manner that serves as an obvious reminder that other people potentially can evaluate these behaviors in the future. Procedures of this type frequently have relied on video-recording or audio-recording equipment to create a strong self-focus in conditions in which such elements are present and a weak self-focus in conditions in which they are not present. Even in contexts that are neither explicitly social nor implicitly social, one can alter the degree of self-focus by means of such stimulus elements as a large mirror (e.g., Ickes, Wicklund, and Ferris, 1973), a spotlight (e.g., Taylor and Fiske, 1975, 1978), or any other stimulus that increases the salience of the self relative to the environment.

Studies in which self-focusing and non-self-focusing situations are contrasted consistently have revealed that internal sources of information exert a stronger influence on behavior in the first type of situation than in the sec-ond type. In studies in which causality for a given event or outcome is ambiguous, the self is ascribed a relatively greater causality role in self-focusing situations than in non-self-focusing ones (e.g., Arkin and Duval, 1975; Buss and Scheier, 1976; Duval and Wicklund, 1973; Federoff and Harvey, 1976; Taylor and Fiske, 1975; Wegner and Finstuen, 1977). Similarly, in studies in which internalized standards are relevant to the display of particular behaviors, the impact of these standards on behavior is generally greatest in situations of high self-focus (e.g., Beaman *et al.,* 1980; Carver, 1975; Diener, 1980; Diener and Srull, 1979; Diener and Wallbom, 1976; Gibbons, 1978; Rule, Nesdale, and Dyck, 1975; Scheier, 1976; Scheier, Fenigstein, and Buss, 1974; Vallacher and Solodky, 1979; Wicklund, 1982; Wicklund and Duval, 1971; Wicklund and Ickes, 1972).

Of particular relevance to students of personality and social behavior are the demonstrations that relatively stable and enduring personal attributes such as self-esteem (e.g., Brockner, 1979; Brockner and Hulton, 1978; and sociability (e.g., Pryor *et al.,* 1977) exert powerful influences on behavior in self-focusing situations but exert little or no influence in non-self-focusing ones. And even when internal sources of information take the form of relatively transient and unstable dispositions such as expectancies, arousal, and/or mood states, the impact of these dispositions is also most evident in situations of heightened self-focus (e.g., Carver, Blaney, and Scheier, 1979a, 1979b; Gibbons *et al.,* 1979; Scheier and Carver, 1977; Scheier, Carver, and Gibbons, 1981). Finally, evidence suggests that the individual's self-concept may itself undergo a transformation in self-focusing situations, becoming more unique, concrete, and highly individuated, and displaying a greater degree of differentiation as well (Ickes, Layden, and Barnes, 1978; Turner, 1978). A transformation of this sort may help to account for the enhanced salience of those particular aspects of self having greatest relevance to the situation at hand.

As impressive as this evidence may be, it would be premature to conclude that meeting the salience criterion is, by itself, sufficient to establish a precipitating situation. In most, if not all, of the studies just cited, the test situation also met the two remaining criteria, since they had been designed to be relevant to the particular disposition being studied and to permit alternative modes of responding that would reflect differences on the dispositional dimension. It seems unlikely that simply making a disposition salient would substantially increase its influence on behavior in test situations that are completely irrelevant to the disposition in question and that do not permit such alternative modes of response. Although the salience criterion may be a necessary condition for establishing a precipitating situation, it probably is not a sufficient one.

Contrasts Between the Two Types of Situational Moderating Variables

Interestingly, the strengths of the strong–precipitating situation paradigm correspond to the weaknesses of the weak-situation paradigm and vice versa. The precipitating situation typically lends itself to a high degree of experimental control. It permits the experimenter to establish a definitive behavioral forced choice in which the dispositional influence can be manifested most clearly. And it permits relatively powerful and sensitive tests of specific theoretical propositions. On the other hand, because of its high degree of structure, it is generally not well suited to the study of spontaneous, face-to-face interaction behavior. It permits only a limited number of behaviors to be studied at once. And its results may not have much generalizability outside the precipitating situation itself.

A contrasting picture may be drawn of the weaknesses and strengths of the weak-situation paradigm. The weak situation permits relatively little experimental control. Its unstructured nature allows individuals to engage in a wide variety of possible behaviors that the experimenter cannot easily constrain. And it limits the experimenter's ability to force a test of specific theoretical propositions to the degree that such a test requires the imposition of additional structure on the situation. On the other hand, it generally is well suited to the study of spontaneous, face-to-face interaction behavior. It permits a wide range of behaviors to be studied at once. And its results may be broadly generalizable.

In summary, our analysis of situational moderating variables suggests that researchers concerned with personality and social behavior would be well advised to conduct more of their studies in the context of psychologically weak situations. When psychologically strong situations are employed, they should satisfy insofar as possible the criteria for precipitating situations. By becoming aware of the role that the strong/weak and precipitating/nonprecipitating moderators play in defining the types of situations in which dispositional influences are manifested behaviorally, researchers can maximize

(rather than minimize) the links between personality and social behavior that they seek to identify and understand in their empirical investigations.

PERSONAL AND SITUATIONAL MODERATING VARIABLES: SOME COMPARISONS

As we have indicated, the classes of personal and situational moderating variables are similar because they both define the presence or absence of a link between the predictor (i.e., a dispositional measure) and the criterion (i.e., a behavioral measure). The presence or absence of this link presumably determines whether or not the predictor will be found to be related to the criterion.

It is at this point, however, that the major difference emerges between personal and situational moderating variables. In the case of personal moderating variables, the link between the predictor and the criterion takes the form of relatively stable and enduring *attributes* of individuals. These attributes (e.g., self-monitoring, private self-consciousness) are ones that differentiate individuals on the basis of their preferential attention and/or responsiveness to dispositional or situational information as guides to action in particular behavioral domains. By contrast, in the case of situational moderating variables, the link between the predictor and the criterion takes the form of more transient *states*. These states are ones in which attention and/or responsiveness is differentially accorded to dispositional or situational information as a function of the structure of the situation in which behavior is observed.

A provocative implication of this distinction is that a personal moderating variable defined by the "Which people?" question may have as its counterpart a corresponding situational moderating variable defined by the "Which situations?" question. For example, the personal moderating variable of private self-consciousness may have as its counterpart the situational moderating variable of objective self-awareness. Evidence for this correspondence has been found repeatedly in studies designed to demonstrate the functional equivalence of dispositionally measured self-consciousness and situationally manipulated self-awareness as moderating variables. Behaviorally, the responses of individuals who are dispositionally high in private self-consciousness resemble those of individuals in whom a state of self-awareness has been induced by means of a mirror. Conversely, the responses of individuals who are dispositionally low in private self-consciousness resemble those of individuals in whom a state of self-awareness has not been situationally induced (e.g., Buss and Scheier, 1976; Carver and Scheier, 1978; Scheier, 1976; Scheier and Carver, 1977; Scheier, Carver, and Gibbons, 1981).

Researchers have further speculated that the personal moderator of measured public self-consciousness is analogous in function to the situational moderator of situationally induced public self-consciousness (Buss, 1980; Carver and Scheier, 1981). However, with regard to this public mode of self-consciousness, the appropriate state must be evoked not by the presence or absence of a mirror but by the presence or absence of such situational variables as an evaluative audience or a television camera. Presumably, the stimulus elements needed to evoke public self-consciousness are those that imply an externally evaluative view of the self.

In a similar vein, theoretical analyses of self-monitoring processes have proposed that social situations and interpersonal contexts may vary in the extent to which they promote the interpersonal orientation of the high self-monitoring individual or that of the low–self-monitoring individual (Snyder, 1979a). Thus researchers have suggested that individuals may be particularly likely to regulate their behavioral choices on the basis of information about their attitudes, dispositions, and other relevant personal attributes in environments that encourage a reflective, contemplative orientation to action (cf. Snyder and Swann, 1976), that enhance either one's sense of commitment or one's personal responsibility for one's actions (cf. Kiesler, 1971; Schwartz, 1973), that heighten one's awareness of self as a potential cause of behavior, as in studies of objective self-awareness (cf. Carver, 1975; Pryor *et al.,* 1977; Wicklund, 1975), that cut short the processes of avoiding and reinterpreting commitment (cf. Kiesler, Roth, and Pallak, 1974) and therefore make it impossible to define one's beliefs and attitudes as irrelevant to one's actions, or that provide normative support for congruence between behavior and belief (cf. Kiesler, Nisbett, and Zanna, 1969). In such low self-monitoring environments, social behavior should manifest the substantial correspondence with attitudes and dispositions that is chronically displayed by low self-monitoring individuals.

By contrast, individuals may be particularly likely to monitor their behavioral choices on the basis of available situational cues in environments that are novel, are unfamiliar, and contain relevant sources of social comparison (cf. Festinger, 1954; Sherif, 1937), that make individuals uncertain of or confused about their inner states (cf. Schachter and Singer, 1962), that suggest that one's attitudes are socially undesirable (cf. Dutton and Lake, 1973) or deviant (cf. Freedman and Doob, 1968), that sensitize one to the perspective of others and motivate concern with social evaluation and conformity with reference group norms (cf. Charters and Newcomb, 1958; Zimbardo, 1969), or that motivate individuals to adopt a strategic impression management or ingratiation orientation to self-presentation (cf. Jones, 1964; Snyder, 1977, 1981). In such high self-monitoring environments social behavior should manifest the substantial sensitivity to social and interpersonal specifications of behavioral appropriateness that is chronically displayed by high self-monitoring individuals.

Other cases of correspondence between personal and situational moderating variables should also exist. For any given personal moderating variable that differentiates individuals on the basis of their preferential attention and/or responsiveness to dispositional or situational cues (e.g., internal control versus external control, field independence versus field dependence), one should be able to identify corresponding situational moderators of psychological states in which an analogous differentiation occurs. A complicating factor in this analysis is that the particular stimulus elements needed to create manipulations of the situational moderators may vary according to the particular behavioral domain being studied. For example, although the presence or absence of a mirror may be used successfully to manipulate private self-consciousness, it cannot be used to manipulate public self-consciousness. Similarly, although the presence or absence of an evaluative audience may be required to manipulate public self-consciousness, the assignment of tasks determined either by skill or by chance may be required to induce feelings of either internal control or external control.

This complicating factor may be less troublesome than it first appears to be. When viewed in the context of our earlier discussion, the different stimulus elements needed to evoke different moderating states can be seen as defining psychologically strong precipitating situations for the particular behavioral domains being studied. Specifically, they serve to evoke states that are uniquely relevant to the particular disposition being studied and/or that make that disposition salient as guides to behavior. In some cases such stimulus elements may also serve to establish the third criterion of the precipitating situation—the delineation of specific, alternative modes of responding that individuals should select differentially as a function of their location on the dispositional dimension.

In contrast to the situational variation of stimulus elements that are relevant only to specific behavioral domains, the situational variation of the strong versus weak moderator may be expected to generalize *across* domains of social behavior. As the series of studies by Ickes and his colleagues suggests, the influence of a wide range of dispositions (e.g., locus of control, self-monitoring, sex role orientation) may be greater in psychologically weak situations than in psychologically strong ones, regardless of the particular domains of social behavior to which each disposition relates. For this reason, the strong versus weak variation should be the situational moderator of choice whenever the stimulus elements needed to establish the criteria for a precipitating situation cannot be specified a priori (Ickes, 1982; Ickes and Robertson, in press).

ANALYSIS AND CRITIQUE OF THE INTERACTIONAL STRATEGY

The representative examples that we have presented provide strong evidence that social behavior is determined by interactions involving both dispositional and situational factors. They also suggest that such interactions result from the operation of three major classes of moderating variables, all of which share the same defining function: that of shifting the cause of behavior from a situational locus to a dispositional one or vice versa. These three classes of moderating variables (which are summarized in Table 1) are those relating to the *predictor* (i.e., to the particular trait or disposition being studied), those relating to the *criterion* (i.e., to the particular overt behaviors to which the predictor is being applied), and those relating to the presence or absence of a *link between the predictor and the criterion*. Moderating variables in this third class can be further subdivided into *personal moderating variables* (i.e., those distinguishing individuals whose behavior is typically disposition-based from individuals whose behavior is typically situation-based), and *situational moderating variables* (i.e., those distinguishing situations in which a given disposition will de-

termine an individual's behavior from the situations in which it will not).

By acknowledging that social behavior is determined by both dispositional and situational factors, the interactional strategy defines what at first may appear to be a more modest goal for the student of personality than that defined by the dispositional strategy. Instead of attempting to predict the social behavior of "all of the people all of the time" on the basis of their assessed dispositions, the interactional strategy attempts such prediction only for some of the people some of the time (i.e., in some situations, and then only with regard to some dispositions and behaviors). We should note, however, that the apparently modest goal of the interactional strategy is somewhat deceptive and that the application of this strategy actually *enhances* the *overall* prediction of behavior. It does so by specifying a priori which type of independent-variable predictors (disposition-based versus situation-based) should be used in any given case. Thus the researcher who employs this strategy not only can make better *disposition-based* predictions in conditions in which dispositional factors determine behavior but also can make better *situation-based* predictions in conditions in which situational factors determine behavior. In pursuing the interactional approach, the researcher must alternate between acting as a personality psychologist and as an experimental social psychologist, but he or she benefits greatly by acquiring the predictive and explanatory insights associated with each of these roles.

When used effectively, the interactional strategy may also facilitate the bootstrapping process. In fact, the first goal of bootstrapping (to determine the boundary conditions for the social psychological phenomenon of interest) is guided explicitly by the logic of the interactional strategy and by the various types of moderating variables that it subsumes. As the researcher proceeds to establish the boundary conditions for the phenomenon in terms of these moderating variables, he or she is able to determine what types of dispositions can or cannot be used to predict the phenomenon, what types of overt behaviors (criteria) will or will not be indicative of it, what types of individuals will or will not manifest it, and in what types of situations it will or will not occur.

Moreover, it is not unreasonable to assume that in the course of establishing the boundary conditions for a given phenomena in terms of these classes of moderating variables, the researcher will gain considerable insight into the processes underlying the phenomenon. This specification of underlying processes (which is the second goal of boostrapping) is therefore also likely to be facilitated by the interactional strategy, although in a somewhat indirect way. In summary, then, the interactional strategy should provide a more structured and logical approach to bootstrapping than that provided by the dispositional strategy.

Having said all of these things in praise of the interactional strategy, we must now consider its possible problems and potential limitations. As in the case of the dispositional strategy, our critical analyses encompass both theoretical and methodological concerns.

Conceptual and Theoretical Critique
Unlike the dispositional strategy, the interactional strategy cannot be readily criticized as being relatively atheoretical and tautological. Nor can it be criticized as overemphasizing dispositional factors and underemphasizing situational ones, since it assumes that both sets of factors are important. If the interactional strategy manages to avoid the two major conceptual weaknesses of the dispositional strategy, on what grounds might it be viewed as conceptually deficient?

One possible conceptual weakness is revealed by comparing and contrasting the interactional strategy with situationist modifications of the dispositional strategy. Just as situational specificity can be introduced into the dispositional strategy by identifying, measuring, and validating situation-specific dispositions, so can situational specificity be introduced into the interactional strategy by delimiting precisely the set of situations in which a dispositional measure either will or will not predict its criterial behaviors. In fact, the situationalist modification of the dispositional strategy is logically complemented by the interactional strategy in that the former attempts to define situation-specific dispositions, whereas the latter attempts to define disposition-specific situations.

Given this complementarity, we should not be surprised to discover that the interactional approach, like the situationist modification of the dispositional approach, may be plagued by an apparent lack of theoretical parsimony. Clearly, the interactional strategy requires much of the researcher who seeks to apply it to the study of personality and social behavior. In addition to possessing the required skills in test construction, measurement, and validation, the researcher employing this strategy also has to contend with four conceptually distinct types of moderating variables in order to specify a

priori the conditions of greatest disposition-behavior correspondence. From an empirical standpoint the prospects of validating this strategy by testing the effects of all four types of moderating variables in a single factorial design are probably formidable enough to deter all but the most obsessive-compulsive of Ph.D candidates in personality/social psychology!

On the other hand, we acknowledge that the complexity of the interactional strategy may be warranted by the even more complex reality that it seeks to mirror. Complicated problems seldom yield to simple solutions, and this premise may be especially true of the study of personality and social behavior, as Carson (1969) has suggested. A further defense of this approach is that its apparent complexity may be mitigated by its potential to provide a general theoretical framework for specifying the domains of applicability for virtually all personality factors and individual-difference variables. No matter what disposition one chooses to study, one should be able (in theory, at least) to delimit that disposition's domain of applicability by specifying, first, which trait measures best predict the particular disposition-behavior correspondence; second, which criterial behaviors best reveal or manifest it; third, which people are most likely to demonstrate it; and fourth, which situations are most conducive to its display.

To the degree that the interactional strategy permits such theoretical generality in the treatment of all classes of dispositional variables, it represents an important theoretical advance over the dispositional strategy. It also is conceptually superior to the situationist modifcation of the dispositional strategy. The reason for this conceptual superiority is that the interactional strategy, as we have characterized it, provides a *general model* that can be applied broadly to identify the conditions of maximum disposition-behavior correspondence for virtually any disposition. In contrast, the situationist modification of the dispositional strategy provides only the simple *heuristic assumption* that many general dispositions can be further subdivided into a number of situation-specific ones if the researcher applies his or her intuitions to this task on an individual, case-by-case basis.

Although the conceptual adequacy of the interactional strategy compares favorably with that of the dispositional strategy, it has its points of theoretical vulnerability. In particular, one may direct criticism at its assumption that the causal link between personality and social behavior is always unidirectional, with personality influencing behavior but not vice versa. Also, one may reject the assumption that dispositions and situations have the status of true independent variables, both of which influence behavior but neither of which are influenced by behavior or by each other. Finally, one may question the assumption that whatever functional relationships occur in personality research are necessarily linear, or at least monotonic in form.

One possible solution to the limitations of these admittedly simplifying assumptions is provided by a more dynamic version of the interactional strategy that "stresses an interaction *process* in which persons and situations form an inextricably interwoven structure" (Magnusson and Endler, 1977, p. 18). In this dynamic version of the interactional strategy, the causal links connecting dispositions, situations, and behavior are thought to be complex and reciprocally cyclical over time. Although some proponents of dynamic interactionism have assumed these relationships to be linear or at least monotonic in form, many have not, arguing instead for the occurrence of processes that are multidetermined and multidetermining, sometimes linear in form and sometimes not. And as if this view of things weren't complicated enough, some writers further assume that this interwoven structure of dispositions, situations, and social behaviors is complicated by the various mutual influences that interacting individuals exert upon each other. The problems of correctly "punctuating" (Watzlawick, Beavin, and Jackson, 1967) social interaction sequences (i.e., correctly segmenting and structuring them in causal terms) present tremendous practical and theoretical challenges to the proponents of a dynamic version of the interactional strategy for the study of social behavior. In other words, it is already apparent that this dynamic "solution" to the limitations of statistical interactionism is fraught with its own set of problems, many of which have only begun to be addressed.

Methodological and Empirical Critique
Methodological criticisms of the interactional strategy also reveal its superiority to the dispositional strategy while suggesting its own deficiencies and limitations. Like the dispositional strategy, the interactional strategy may fail to provide an adequate operational definition of disposition-based consistency in behavior. Unlike the dispositional strategy, however, the interactional strategy should not be faulted for failing to account for much of the variance in social behavior. In fact, the efforts of various investigators to improve the predictive power of

the dispositional strategy have succeeded only insofar as they have simultaneously advanced the development of the interactional strategy. Thus, as the different classes of moderating variables were identified by Bem and Allen (1974), Epstein (1979), Ickes (1982), Snyder (1976), and others, it became possible to demonstrate that dispositions could account for over 80 percent of the variance in their criterial behaviors when the optimal conditions for disposition-behavior correspondence were established (for an informative empirical example, see Kenrick and Stringfield, 1980).

Despite the enhanced predictive power of the interactional strategy, it may have its methodological limitations. Its mechanistic, statistical assumptions generally may lead investigators to adopt research designs based on the same type of assumptions—i.e., linear, fixed-effect designs in which the dispositional and situational factors of interest are always treated as the independent variables and in which the behaviors of interest are always treated as the dependent variables. Operationally, such designs are typically implemented as experiments or quasi experiments in which the relevant dispositional and situational independent variables are systematically varied, if not manipulated directly, by the experimenter. The typical result of such attempts at experimental control using a fixed-effects design is generally a highly constrained procedure bearing only a faint resemblance to the type of social interaction that individuals normally experience in their lives. In a manner rather contrary to real life the participants in such investigations have virtually no choice regarding the settings in which they find themselves or the people with whom they are expected to interact. Moreover, they typically are able to exert only a weak influence on the situation as it is operationally defined, and then only within a narrow range of behavioral options that have been prescribed and pre-scripted by the researcher.

These considerations may leave students of personality and social behavior on the horns of a very real dilemma. On the one hand, they may be quite reluctant to relinquish the type of experimental control that for many investigators is the hallmark of rigorous scientific inquiry. On the other hand, the use of such control frequently imposes artificial constraints that may distort or even eliminate the very behaviors that they are attempting to study. We now turn to a consideration of a strategy —which we have chosen to label the *situational strategy* for the study of personality and social behavior—that is emerging from attempts to escape this dilemma.

THE SITUATIONAL STRATEGY
FOR THE STUDY OF PERSONALITY
AND SOCIAL BEHAVIOR

Clearly, the preceding development of ideas suggests that we are about to turn to a discussion of the dynamic version of the interactional strategy for the study of personality and social behavior. Yet as we contemplated this approach, we realized that its complex, many-faceted nature made it difficult to describe in a thematically unified way. The dynamic version of the interactional strategy is, in terms of its assumed causal relationships, something of a Gordian knot that is likely to frustrate even the most patient of would-be unravelers. Although we might have been able to pick up the various threads of these causal relationships and attempt to trace their interweavings, we decided that such an exercise might frustrate the readers' patience even more than our own.

Accordingly, our solution to this problem has been to choose only one of these causal strands and, insofar as possible, to trace its intertwinings with other causal strands. The one that we have chosen—the reciprocal causal relationship between situations and personality—is particularly useful for revealing many of the phenomena of personality that are uniquely implicated by the dynamic interactional approach. By tracing this one strand throughout this section, we hope to provide a thematically unified perspective on dynamic interactionism that gradually will reveal the scope and complexity of this approach. We therefore begin by considering how a *situational strategy* for the study of personality and social behavior, focusing on the influence of individuals on their situations, leads us to examine a set of phenomena that essentially are precluded by the assumptions and methodologies of other strategies for the study of personality and social behavior.

THE ORIGINS OF THE
SITUATIONAL STRATEGY

If, as suggested by theory and research generated by the interactional strategy, the regularities and consistencies in social behavior that constitute personality are questions of "Which traits?" "Which behaviors?" "Which individuals?" and "Which situations?", students of social behavior who seek evidence of such behavioral consistencies ought to direct their efforts toward discovering "those traits," "those behaviors," "those individuals," and "those situations." As promising as

the interactional strategy may be for providing precise specifications of the conditions in which behavioral consistencies are to be found, we suspect that it is also quite limiting in an important and often unrecognized way. Specifically, it may cause investigators of social psychological phenomena and processes to overlook or fail to recognize other important manifestations of consistency in personality that lie outside its theoretical bounds.

These additional phenomena of personality are quite clearly implicated by the dynamic version of the interactional approach to the study of personality and social behavior. However, because most researchers, regardless of their theoretical orientations, are still committed to the mechanistic assumptions and methodological conventions of statistical interactionism, the inherent constraints of this methodology have correspondingly limited the scope of their awareness as well as their inquiry. The prototypic model of this methodology is, of course, the experiment.

We have suggested that the social psychological experiment, with its defining characteristics of the creation of differing social situations by means of experimental manipulations and the random assignment of participants to these differing social situations, may be a methodology that provides minimal opportunities for investigators to witness manifestations of personality while providing maximal opportunities for investigators to witness manifestations of the impact of social situations on individuals' behavior (e.g., Ickes, 1982; Ickes and Robertson, in press; Snyder, 1979b, 1981b; Wachtel, 1973). By definition, investigators conduct experiments to determine the impact of manipulated independent variables on measured dependent variables. In practice, if not in principle, it is easier to control and manipulate characteristics of situations than it is to manipulate and control attributes of individuals. Accordingly, the independent variables in social psychological experiments typically are manipulations of social situations. Moreover, investigators typically exercise great care to make sure that the different levels of the independent variable (i.e., the different social situations that they create by means of their experimental manipulations) are sufficiently distinct from each other to guarantee noticeably different effects on the different groups of participants assigned to each condition of the experiment. Typically, to reduce variability in their participants' interpretations of the experimental manipulations, investigators also tailor their manipulations to fit personal, social, and demographic attributes shared by their participant populations. Moreover, investigators tend to recruit their participants from fairly homogeneous participant populations (in particular, college students, who are much less variable in personal, intellectual, social, and demographic attributes than are members of the population at large).

All of these procedures tend to increase the extent to which the social behavior of participants in social psychological experiments will be particularly sensitive to situationally manipulated independent variables (cf. Cook and Campbell, 1976). Effectively, the stage has been set to maximize the extent to which social behavior in these experimentally created situations will be a reflection of the manipulated independent variables and to minimize the extent to which social behavior in these experimentally created situations will be a reflection of the personal attributes (e.g., attitudes, traits, dispositions, self-conceptions) of the individual participants.

Of even greater importance, however, experiments (as they typically are conducted) virtually eliminate one major vehicle by which personal attributes of the participants might manifest themselves. Experiments, by definition, are designed to document the impact of the independent variable. Investigators therefore manipulate and control that independent variable to occur in fixed and preprogrammed fashion and subject their participants to one or another level of the independent variable. This procedure effectively prevents participants from doing at least two things. First, they cannot choose whether or not to be exposed to the treatment or experimental situation to which they have been randomly assigned. And second, they can exert only minimal influence on the experimentally created interpersonal situation in which they find themselves. Participants can do very little to alter those events that define the manipulated independent variable. Typically, they can only react, respond, and attempt to cope with the surrounding situation into which they have been thrust.

This, of course, is precisely how it must be if investigators are to be able to make confident statements about the impact of situational independent variables on the behavior of individuals. Yet life situations often do not involve predetermined stimulus events about which individuals have no choice and over which individuals have no influence. In the natural course of their lives, individuals typically have considerable freedom to choose where to be, when to be there, and with whom to be there. Accordingly, unlike the situations to which an individual

is assigned in a social psychological experiment, the real-world situations in which an individual finds himself or herself may be partially, if not entirely, of his or her own choosing. Moreover, once in a social situation—whether or not of the individual's own choosing—much of what transpires in that situation is determined by that individual's own actions. In particular, in the social situations of one's life, unlike the situations of social psychological experiments, how other people treat the individual is often determined to considerable extent by the individual's own actions. Quite understandably, these processes of choosing and influencing social situations are eliminated in traditional experimental procedural paradigms. The elimination of these processes helps ensure the internal validity of experimental investigations of the effects of experimentally manipulated features of social situations on the behavior of individuals assigned to those situations (cf. Aronson and Carlsmith, 1968; Campbell and Stanley, 1963).

Of what import might be the processes of choosing and influencing social situations? Some have argued that one's choices of the settings in which to live one's life and one's influences on the interpersonal situations of one's life may reflect features of one's conceptions of self, one's characteristic dispositions, one's attitudes and values, and other attributes of personality (e.g., Snyder, 1981b). For example, individuals may choose whenever possible to enter and to spend time in situations that elicit competitive behaviors precisely because they are by disposition competitive individuals. Moreover, whenever such individuals find themselves in situations that typically do not foster competitive behaviors, they may attempt to transform those situations into competitive situations precisely because they are competitive individuals. From this perspective, competitive individuals are defined as those who choose whenever possible to enter competitive situations and who act whenever possible to maximize the competitive character of their situations. In so doing, competitive individuals construct for themselves social worlds particularly conducive to the expression and manifestation of their competitive dispositions.

Not incidentally, as a direct consequence of choosing and influencing their social situations in ways that create competitive worlds within which to live, competitive individuals would provide themselves with opportunities to display competitive behaviors with high frequency and great regularity across situations and over time. In other words, these individuals would come to display the cross-situational consistency and temporal stability that traditionally are regarded as the defining features of a personality trait of competitiveness. From this perspective, the regularities and consistencies in these individuals' competitive behavior are to be regarded as the product of regularities and consistencies in the competitive social situations within which they live their lives.

Closely associated with the theoretical orientation that individuals and their personalities are to be understood in terms of their social settings is what we have chosen to call *the situational strategy for the study of personality and social behavior*. Guided by this theoretical orientation, practitioners of the situational strategy for the study of personality and social behavior have sought not only to identify regularities and consistencies in social situations but also to understand their origins and their consequences.

Consider, as an illustrative example, the application of the situational strategy to the study of the social psychological phenomenon of competition. The user of the situational strategy would seek first to determine whether a category of social situations exists that, more so than other social situations, typically elicits competitive behaviors. The user of the situational strategy would seek next to determine whether there exists a category of individuals who typically are to be found in these situations that elicit competition. Having identified those situations and those individuals, the user of the situational strategy then would seek to determine whether those individuals who are to be found in those situations that typically elicit competition are individuals who characteristically behave in a competitive fashion.

That is, the user of the situational strategy for the study of competition would pose, as his or her fundamental question, "Are competitively disposed individuals those individuals who typically are to be found in competitively oriented situations?" By so framing the fundamental question, the user of the situational strategy for the study of competition seeks a fundamentally social psychological interpretation of the origins of competitive dispositions. From this perspective, individuals with competitive personalities are those individuals who live their lives in competitive social settings and interpersonal situations.

Moreover, the user of the situational strategy for the study of competition would seek to understand why it is that some individuals characteristically find themselves in precisely those social situations that lead them to behave in competitive ways. Thus the user of the situational strategy would seek to determine the extent to which competitively disposed individuals actively *choose* to enter and to spend time in situations that foster a competitive orientation but to avoid those situations that foster a cooperative orientation. For example, do these individuals seek out situations with competitive reward structures? Moreover, the user of the situational strategy would seek to determine the extent to which competitively disposed individuals *influence* the social situations in which they find themselves in ways that increase the likelihood that those situations will become settings for the display of competition. For example, do these individuals attempt to inject competitive reward structures into situations that initially lack them? In so doing, the user of the situational strategy for the study of competition would seek to understand the processes by which competitively disposed individuals find themselves in the situations that foster the characteristic display of competitive actions.

Central to the theoretical perspective associated with the situational strategy for the study of personality and social behavior is the proposition that characteristic dispositions of individuals are reflected in the processes by which individuals choose to enter and to spend time in social situations and in the processes by which individuals influence the character of the social situations in which they find themselves. Research paradigms for the investigation of these processes require, of necessity, casting features of the *individual* (e.g., self-conceptions, values, attitudes, traits, motives, dispositions, etc.) in the role of *independent variable* and features of the *situation* (e.g., choice of social situation, influence on social situation) in the role of *dependent variable*. Within such paradigms, researchers have been able to document the manner in which characteristics of individuals are reflected and manifested in the social settings within which they live their lives. We consider, first, investigations of the choice by individuals of their social situations; then, investigations of the influence of individuals on their social situations; and finally, investigations of the impact of personality processes on the dynamics of ongoing social interaction and interpersonal relationships.

CHOOSING THE SITUATIONS OF ONE'S LIFE

Do individuals systematically choose to enter and to spend time in social situations that provide them with opportunities to act upon their characteristic traits, dispositions, attitudes, and self-conceptions? Do individuals systematically choose to enter and to spend time in social situations that will dispose them to engage in behaviors that will reflect features of their personalities? That individuals can and do engage in such processes of choosing the situations of their lives presupposes that they know or can assess what behavioral opportunities are provided by what social situations. Thus, for example, if socially extraverted individuals are to choose systematically to enter situations that foster and encourage the expression of their socially extraverted dispositions, they must be able to identify those socially extraverted situations. Accordingly, we first examine individuals' knowledge of social situations.

Several lines of research, taken together, suggest that individuals can assess the extent to which particular social situations are conducive to the behavioral expression of their personal attributes. Considerable evidence indicates that individuals can reliably assess both the appropriateness of particular behaviors for particular situations and the constraints that particular situations place on the behaviors that may be expressed in those situations (e.g., Price, 1974; Price and Bouffard, 1974; Smith-Lovin, 1979). With this knowledge of social situations, individuals ought to be able to determine which social situations will promote the expression of their own characteristic traits, dispositions, attitudes, and self-conceptions. In fact, individuals seem to be well able to assess the personal identities that can be expressed readily and appropriately in particular social situations (e.g., Alexander and Knight, 1971; Alexander and Lauderdale, 1977). Researchers have also been able to identify some of the dimensions of social situations that contribute to inferences about the personal attributes and social behaviors that can be expressed readily in particular social situations (e.g., Forgas, 1979; Wish, 1975; Wish and Kaplan, 1977; Wish, Deutsch, and Kaplan, 1976). Finally, some empirical procedures have been developed for assessing the personalities of social situations (e.g., Bem, 1982; Bem and Funder, 1978; Bem and Lord, 1979; Funder, 1982; but see also Mischel and Peake, 1982, 1981).

Evidently, individuals do possess the knowledge of social situations that would permit them to gravitate toward those situations that foster and encourage the behavioral expression of their traits, dispositions, attitudes, and other personal attributes. But do individuals actually choose preferentially to enter and to spend time in such social situations? Empirical investigations have examined the choices of situations of individuals who differ in, among others, arousal seeking (Mehrabian, 1978; Mehrabian and Russell, 1974), authoritarianism

(Stern, Stein, and Bloom, 1956), birth order (Hoyt and Raven, 1973; Schachter, 1959; Wrightsman, 1960), extraversion (Furnham, 1981), gender (Deaux, 1978; Deaux, White, and Farris, 1975; Eddy and Sinnett, 1973; Lippa and Beauvais, 1980; Reis, Nezlek, and Wheeler, 1980; Wheeler and Nezlek, 1977), locus of control (Kahle, 1980), need for achievement (Atkinson, 1957), neuroticism (Furnham, 1981), repression-sensitization (Mischel, Ebbesen, and Zeiss, 1973; Olson and Zanna, 1979), sensation seeking (Segal, 1973; Zuckerman, 1974), self-monitoring (Snyder and Gangestad, 1982; Snyder and Kendzierski, 1982b), sex-role orientation (Deaux, 1978; Lippa and Beauvais, 1980; Spence and Helmreich, 1978), social skills (Bryant and Trower, 1974), and success/failure orientation (Nisan, 1972).

In addition, several studies have demonstrated the links between various social attitudes and choices of situations (Barlett, *et al.,* 1974; Brock and Balloun, 1967; Kahle and Berman, 1979; Snyder and Kendzierski, 1982b) and the links between various features of self-conception and choices of social situations (Berglas and Jones, 1978; Jones and Berglas, 1978; Snyder *et al.,* 1979); and at least one has demonstrated the links between morphological characteristics and choices of social situations (Reis, Nezlek, and Wheeler, 1980). Furthermore, attempts have been made to investigate the settings within which individuals choose to conduct particular types of relationships (e.g., Argyle and Furnham, 1980; Jellison and Ickes, 1974). Finally, various attempts have been made to identify the personal origins of choices of leisure situations (e.g., Bishop and Witt, 1970; Furnham, 1981; Tinsley, Barrett, and Kass, 1977; Zuckerman, 1974), of choices of educational situations (e.g., Pervin, 1967a, 1967b, 1968; Pervin and Rubin, 1967; Stern, 1969; Stern, Stein, and Bloom, 1956), and of choices of occupational situations (Davis, 1965; Holland, 1976; Mortimer and Lorence, 1979; Rosenberg, 1957; Vroom, 1964). In the following section, we consider some representative examples of empirical investigations of the links between personal attributes and choices of social situations.

Characteristic Dispositions and Choices of Situations

Representative of the empirical attempts to document relationships between characteristic dispositions and the choice to enter and to spend time in particular social situations is that of Furnham (1981) on extraversion. Participants for whom the measures of dispositional extraversion provided by the Eysenck Personality Questionnaire

(Eysenck, 1975) were available reported the amount of time that they previously had spent in a wide variety of actual social situations and their preferences for spending time in a wide variety of hypothetical social situations. From these reports, Furnham concluded that extraverts, more so than introverts, seek out stimulating social situations that involve assertiveness, competitiveness, and intimacy. That is, extraverted individuals appear to choose extraverted situations that provide opportunities to engage in extraverted behaviors.

Similarly, sensation seekers appear to choose sensation-providing leisure situations (Zuckerman, 1974). And authoritarians appear to choose authoritarian educational settings (Stern, Stein, and Bloom, 1956). Moreover, individuals with an internal locus of control [who believe that their own actions can influence their outcomes (Rotter, 1966)] appear to choose situations in which their outcomes are determined by their own skills (Kahle, 1980). At the same time individuals with an external locus of control [who believe that their own actions cannot influence their outcomes (Rotter, 1966)] appear to choose situations in which their outcomes are determined by chance (Kahle, 1980). Finally, high self-monitoring individuals [who strive to mold and tailor their self-presentational behavior to social and interpersonal cues to situational appropriateness (Snyder, 1979b)] appear to actively choose social situations that permit them to adopt their characteristic interpersonal orientation. At the same time low self-monitoring individuals (who strive to enforce consistency and correspondence between their social behavior and underlying attitudes, dispositions, and other personal attributes) appear to actively choose social situations that permit them to adopt their characteristic behavioral orientation (Snyder and Gangestad, 1982).

The same general conclusion emerges from each representative example of research on the processes by which individuals choose the situations of their lives. In each case individuals appear to gravitate actively toward social situations that will foster and encourage the behavioral expression of their own characteristic dispositions and interpersonal orientations. To the extent that they succeed in regularly and consistently spending time in these situations, and to the extent that these situations promote the regular and consistent display of behavioral manifestations of their characteristic dispositions, these individuals will come to display the cross-situational consistency and temporal stability that we regard as personality.

Conceptions of Self and Choices of Situations
Within the domain of conceptions of self, empirical investigations suggest that individuals actively may seek out social situations that preserve and sustain existing and cherished conceptions of self. In particular, Jones and Berglas (1978; Berglas and Jones, 1978) have focused on conceptions of self-competence. They have proposed that individuals who regard themselves as competent, intelligent people strive to protect, preserve, and sustain their images of self-competence by actions that make it easier for them to externalize (i.e., explain away) their failures and to internalize (i.e., take credit for) their successes. In an empirical demonstration of such "self-handicapping strategies" in action, Berglas and Jones (1978) found that males who had reason to anticipate that they might not perform well on a problem-solving task chose to take drugs that would interfere with their subsequent performance, presumably in an effort to provide themselves with a readily available explanation (one that would in no way threaten their images of self-competence) for any possible failure. In addition to this evidence that individuals may choose performance settings that prevent failure from threatening their images of self-competence, some evidence also suggests that individuals may leave performance settings that become threatening to their self-competence images (e.g., Conolley, Gerard, and Kline, 1978).

More generally, Jones and Berglas (1978) have proposed that, to the extent that individuals are concerned with maintaining images of self-competence, they will try to choose settings and circumstances for their performances that maximize the implications of success for enhancing their self-competence images at the same time that they minimize the implications of failure for threatening their self-competence images. To the extent that individuals' choices of life settings meet these criteria, they will manage to live their lives in social worlds that protect and enhance both their private self-conceptions and their public images of competence.

Social Attitudes and Choices of Situations
Within the domain of social attitudes, some evidence indicates that individuals preferentially choose to enter and to spend time in social situations that provide opportunities to act upon these attitudes. Thus, for example, individuals with favorable attitudes toward particular candidates for elected political office actively seek out situations in which they will be exposed to messages favorable to their preferred candidate (Kahle and Berman,

1979). Similarly, individuals with favorable attitudes toward affirmative action are particularly eager to enter and to spend time in social situations that provide strong normative supports for the behavioral expression of their attitudes, although this finding seems to be characteristic only of individuals with low scores on Snyder's (1974) Self-Monitoring Scale (Snyder and Kendzierski, 1982b). Finally, if one is willing to regard the choice to expose oneself to particular sets of information as a form of choice of situation, then those empirical investigations that have succeeded in demonstrating that individuals will selectively expose themselves to information congruent with and supportive of their existing attitudes (e.g., Barlett, *et al.,* 1974; Brock and Balloun, 1967) constitute further evidence of the links between social attitudes and choices of social situations, although there is some suggestion that selective exposure phenomena may be limited to individuals classified as repressors by Byrne's (1964) Repression-Sensitization measure (Olson and Zanna, 1979).

Of what consequence are such links between individuals' attitudes and their choices of the social settings within which to live their lives? To the extent that individuals actively gravitate toward social situations and interpersonal settings that provide opportunities and supports for acting in ways that would reflect their attitudes, they may enhance and enforce correspondence between their private attitudes and their public actions. That is, the consistency between attitude and behavior that is one defining feature of personality may be generated by the choice of social situations that dispose individuals to perform the actions implied by their attitudes. Indeed, the active choice of the situations of one's life may constitute one major source of consistency between attitudes and behavior.

Some Exceptional Cases: Choosing
Dispositionally Incongruent Situations

We have marshalled many hypothetical and empirical examples to illustrate the proposition that individuals are particularly likely to enter and to spend time in situations that support their current conceptions of self and allow them to act upon their characteristic attitudes, traits, and dispositions. Are there, however, other hypothetical or empirical examples that do not conform to the pattern just described? A little reflection suggests that there may, in fact, be two major categories of exceptions to our rule governing individuals' choice of situations. Both of these categories represent cases in which individuals choose to

enter situations that appear to be inconsistent with their current conceptions of self or with the display of their characteristic attitudes, traits, and dispositions. It can be seen, however, that despite their essential phenotypic similarity, the categories differ genotypically according to the individuals' apparent motives for entering such situations. These underlying motives appear to be either to use the personality-shaping properties of such situations in order to change oneself or to exert one's influence in and on such situations in order to change the situation itself or to change other people.

Choosing incongruent situations to change oneself.   If individuals typically choose to enter only those situations that facilitate the expression of their characteristic dispositions, why do we observe shy people in swinging singles' bars, snake phobics in the reptile house, paunchy sybarites in a wilderness survival course, and sinners in the front row of church? Of course, individuals of these types might be more often *not* found in the situations just described than found in them, but because these exceptional cases do occur, they warrant some accounting. The most likely motive for the behavior of these individuals is that they all desire to change themselves through direct exposure to those situations most likely to effect the type of changes that they want to occur. Thus shy people might expect to gain social confidence and poise by involving themselves in situations particularly likely to elicit, shape, and reinforce the skills that underlie these attributes. Similarly, snake phobics might seek a situation in which they can safely confront and overcome their fears; paunchy sybarites might seek an ideal environment in which to become lean ascetics; and sinners might seek an environment supportive of repentance and spiritual change.

In all of these cases, the situations that our hypothetical characters enter are incongruent with their current dispositions and attributes, i.e., with "who they really are" at the time they enter these situations. Probably, however, these situations are not incongruent with the dispositions and attributes these individuals would like to possess, i.e., with "who they *ideally* would like to be" at some time in the future. Indeed, the ease with which one can generate examples of this type suggests the prevalence in our society of the belief that involving oneself in certain situations incompatible with one's current dispositions can cause, or at least facilitate, relatively dramatic and enduring changes in one's character or personality. Many, if not most, of the clinical, service, and educational institutions in our culture, including the entire clinical-applied arm of the field of psychology, seem to be founded directly on this premise.

When seen as instances in which situations are sought out and entered because of their congruence with a future, "ideal" self instead of a current, "real" one, these examples do not discredit our earlier argument that individuals tend to enter only dispositionally congruent, self-confirming situations. These examples do, however, suggest some of the complexity inherent in a dynamic interactional approach to the study of personality and social behavior by revealing that situations are sometimes chosen not to suit oneself but to change oneself instead. They also suggest that the individual's conception of his or her personality is sufficiently complex and differentiated to permit situations to be incongruent with a current, "real" self-concept and yet be quite congruent with a potential, "ideal" self-concept. Finally, they suggest that the interdependence and mutual determination of personality and situation is a phenomenon well-appreciated by laypersons, even if it is largely ignored by psychologists. Because individuals can recognize that their personalities both determine and are determined by the situations they select, they are able to apply this insight by deliberately choosing to enter the situations most likely to help shape their personalities in desired ways.

Other cases in which individuals choose incongruent situations in order to change themselves have been characterized by such value-differentiated terms as "slumming" and "broadening one's perspective." Although both of these terms refer to cases in which the changes desired by the individual generally take the form of increased knowledge, novel experience, or an altered level of sensory stimulation, it is possible that more fundamental changes in personality might also be the goal of these situational choices.

Choosing incongruent situations to change the situation or to change other people.   A second category of cases in which people voluntarily enter situations that seem at odds with their own dispositions is exemplified by the preacher in the house of ill repute, the temperance lady in the local tavern, and the Yippie in the Pentagon. The most likely motive for these individuals' behavior is their desire to exert influence in and on the situation in order to change the situation itself or to change other people. People whose choice of incongruent situations is determined by this motive tend to cast themselves in the role of social reformer on a scale that may vary greatly in ambition and

in degree of influence. Missionaries, proselytizers, social workers, reformers, revolutionaries, and radical activists provide relatively dramatic examples, but more mundane examples (e.g., the slum-reared gate-crasher of a high-society social affair) can also be identified. At times the incongruence of these individuals' personalities and the situations they enter may be so striking that their mere presence on the scene is sufficient to produce the changes they desire (e.g., the naked streaker at commencement exercises). At other times, however, such individuals may have to commit themselves to months or even years of patient work in a situation they abhor in order to effect the intended changes (e.g., health and hygiene specialists working in a filthy, rat-infested ghetto area).

A comparison of these examples with those provided for the first category of incongruent situational choices suggests an intriguing theoretical similarity in the desired ends, despite a characteristic difference in the means to those ends. In both cases people choose to enter and to tolerate situations that are currently incongruent with their own dispositions, and in both cases they do so for the sake of realizing *a potential or future congruency that does not currently exist.* However, in the first case the individuals seek to realize this congruency by choosing situations that will change *them,* so that their personalities will eventually come to suit the situations; whereas in the second case the individuals seek to realize this congruency by choosing situations that they can change so that the situations will eventually come to suit their personalities.

When seen as instances in which situations are sought out and entered because of their potential, rather than their current, congruence with the self, these examples also fail to discredit our argument that individuals tend to enter only dispositionally congruent, self-confirming situations. Instead, they suggest a further complexity of the dynamic interactional approach by revealing that some situations that initially are not suited to one's personality may be changed to be that way. Because individuals can recognize that their personalities both determine and are determined by the situations they select, they are able to apply this insight by deliberately changing situations to create the desired congruence with their own dispositions. This particular aspect of the reciprocal causal relationship between personality and situation is important enough to discuss at some length, so we will conclude this section on choosing situations and give further consideration to the question of influencing them. Before doing so, however, we should note that other theorists have been interested in the problems of the congruency or incongruency between self and situation that have been our concern in this section. In particular, Secord and Backman's (1961, 1965) congruency theory provides an excellent theoretical framework for addressing these and related issues. This theory will be discussed in considerable detail in the following two sections.

INFLUENCING THE SITUATIONS OF ONE'S LIFE

A striking example of the influence that individuals' personalities can exert on situations is provided by John Updike's (1975) description of his encounters with other writers (pp. 23–24):

> All of the writers I have met . . . carry around with them a field force that compels objects in the vicinity to conform to their literary style. Standing next to E. B. White, one is imbued with something of the man's fierce modesty, and one's sentences haltingly seek to approximate the wonderful way his own never say more than he means. . . . A room containing Philip Roth, I have noticed, begins hilariously to whirl and pulse with a mix of rebelliousness and constriction that I take to be Oedipal. And I have seen John Cheever, for ten days we shared in Russia, turn the dour world of Soviet literary officials into a bright scuttle of somehow suburban characters, invented with marvellous speed and arranged in sudden tableaux expressive, amid wistful neo-Tsarist trappings, of the lyric desperation associated with affluence. . . . My most traumatic experience of gravitational attraction came with John O'Hara. . . . Within the few seconds of this encounter I had been plunged into a cruel complex of stoic pain and social irony. . . . These not entirely fanciful reminiscences . . . mean to suggest that writers, like everyone else, see a world their personalities to some extent create.

If personality can influence situations in as forceful a manner as these examples suggest, how does such influence occur and what forms is it likely to take? In other words, what are the processes mediating personality's influence on situations, and what are the possible outcomes of these processes? Our attempt to answer these questions first considers how the influence of personality on situations is mediated by its impact on the individual's

orientation toward situations in *general* and its impact on the individual's cognitive and affective reactions to *specific* situations. We then consider the various ways in which the resulting mediated personality influences can be expressed in the individual's behavior to alter the situation in objective, as well as subjective, terms.

General Orientation Toward Situations

Considerable evidence suggests that differences in personality are associated with corresponding differences in individuals' general orientations toward situations. These differences in situational orientation mediate differences in the individuals' subsequent behavior that can directly alter the situation in which they are involved. One of the best-known and most extensively studied personality measures—locus of control (Rotter, 1966)—could easily be described as providing a fairly direct assessment of differences in situational orientation. Specifically, individuals with an internal locus of control are those whose behavior should be relatively expressive of their attitudes, traits, and other dispositions but should be relatively unconstrained by situational influences. In contrast, individuals with an external locus of control are those whose behavior should be relatively insensitive to their own dispositions but highly sensitive to situational factors.

Recent reviews of the locus-of-control literature (Lefcourt, 1976; Phares, 1976) reveal considerable evidence supporting these hypothesized differences in situational orientation—differences that appear to generalize across a range of situations, subject populations, and dependent-variable measures. Although much of this research is validational and simply reveals the expected differences on various criterial measures of locus of control, many studies in this literature further indicate that individuals whose locus of control is internal typically exert more disposition-based influence in and on their situations than do individuals whose locus of control is external (e.g., Bialer, 1961; Brown and Strickland, 1972; Felton, 1971; Gurin *et al.*, 1969; Kahle, 1980; Lao, 1970; Lefcourt, 1967; MacDonald, 1970; Midlarsky, 1971; Phares, 1976; Strickland, 1965, 1973; Tseng, 1970; Williams and Nickels, 1969). These and other studies suggest that individuals differ in their general predisposition to either influence or be influenced by the situations that they encounter.

Personality measures such as private/public self-consciousness (Fenigstein *et al.*, 1975), self-monitoring (Snyder, 1974), or inner-other directedness (Kassarjian,

1962) should also influence individuals' orientations toward situations in a manner roughly comparable to locus of control. And, in general, individuals high in private and low in public self-consciousness seem to exert more disposition-based influence in and on situations than do individuals low in private and high in public self-consciousness (Buss, 1980; Carver and Scheier, 1981). Similarly, low self-monitoring individuals appear to exert more disposition-based influence on situations than do high self-monitoring individuals (e.g., Snyder and Campbell, 1982; Snyder and Gangestad, 1982). The data for other, conceptually similar variables are expected to reveal a similar pattern, although sufficient data may not be available now to support such a claim.

What are the origins of these individual differences in situational orientation? Although the origins of the orientations associated with the self-consciousness and self-monitoring variables have not been explored, we have some relevant data for locus of control. Phares's (1976) discussion of the familial and social antecedents of the two locus-of-control orientations has associated internal control with having parents who were warm, involved, and accepting (e.g., Davis and Phares, 1969; Shore, 1967) and who were consistent in their use of reinforcement and punishment as well as in the standards they set for their children's behavior (e.g., Levenson, 1973; MacDonald, 1971; Reimanis, 1971). Internality-externality also has been associated with social class and ethnicity, such that minority status and low social class both contribute to feelings of external control (e.g., Battle and Rotter, 1963; Gruen and Ottinger, 1969; Lessing, 1969; Pedhazur and Wheeler, 1971).

Cognitive and Affective Reactions to Specific Situations

How does personality affect the individual's cognitive and affective reactions to the specific situations that he or she encounters? Perhaps the best approach to use in answering this question is provided by Secord and Backman's (1961, 1965) congruency theory. According to this theory, individuals are motivated to maintain an equilibrium state of *congruency* among the following elements: (1) an aspect of the individual's self-concept, (2) the individual's interpretation of his or her behavior relevant to that aspect, and (3) the individual's perception of how another person behaves toward and feels about him or her with respect to that aspect. Congruency is said to exist "when the behaviors of the subject (S) and the other person involved...(O) imply definitions of self congru-

ent with relevant aspects of S's self-concept. For example, if S regards himself as intelligent, if his problem-solving ability is quick and efficient, and if O asks him for help in solving a difficult problem, these three components are congruent" (Secord and Backman, 1965, pp. 91–92).

Because the other person can be viewed as an aspect of the individual's current situation, we suggest that Secord and Backman's theory can be extended to deal with both the animate and the inanimate features of the situations that the individual confronts. Accordingly, the three elements of theoretical interest can be redefined as (1) an aspect of the individual's self-concept (a self-ascribed attitude, trait, value, etc.), (2) the individual's interpretation of his or her behavior relevant to that aspect, and (3) the individual's perception of whether or not the features of the current situation imply a definition of self congruent with that aspect. This slightly revised version of the theory would retain Secord and Backman's (1965) other assumptions with little or no change. It would assume that the tendency to seek and to maintain congruency is motivated by a need for predictability in the individual's relationship to himself or herself, to other people, and to the situations he or she encounters. More importantly, it would also assume that (Secord and Backman, 1965, p. 92)

> when the features of the situation are incongruent with an individual's self concept or his own behavior, he is likely to feel uncomfortable, and various affective, perceptual, and cognitive processes may come into play to restore congruency. Under some circumstances, however, congruency may only be restored if he changes his self concept, behavior, or both. Thus the congruency or incongruency...has consequences both for stability and change.

According to Secord and Backman, a variety of factors contribute to the stability or instability of self and behavior. These include factors pertaining to the structure and organization of the self-concept, constitutional factors such as energy level and body type, and institutional and subinstitutional factors such as norms, role relationships, and cultural and subcultural stereotypes. Of particular interest for our purposes, however, are the stabilizing influences of processes that operate to maintain the type of congruency described above. We assume that the individual strives to achieve congruency by a variety of processes, five of which have been specified by Secord and Backman (1965). We have revised the description of each of these processes slightly, in line with our proposed extension of the theory (Secord and Backman, 1965, p. 97; brackets ours):

1. *Cognitive restructuring:* S may misperceive features of the situation so as to achieve congruency with aspects of his behavior and self concept. He may also misinterpret his own behavior so as to achieve maximum congruency with an aspect of his self concept and his perception of the situation.

2. *Selective evaluation:* S maximizes congruency by evaluating more favorably. . . [situational features] that are congruent; he minimizes incongruency by devaluating those [features] that are incongruent.

3. *Selective exposure and interaction:* S maximizes engagement in congruent situations by choosing to enter and participate in situations requiring a minimum change in behavior from previous congruent. . . situations in which S had engaged.

4. *Evocation of congruent features:* S maintains congruency by developing techniques that evoke congruent [features] from [the situations he enters].

5. *Congruency by comparison:* When [the situation] confronts S with an incongruent evaluation, S may accept the evaluation but minimize the effect of incongruency by attributing the [apparent] trait to significant others [or to features of the situation]. Thus, its presence in himself is lessened by comparison: he has no more of it or no less of it than other people [or else it is attributed primarily to an external (situational) cause].

Of these five processes, we have already devoted considerable attention to the third—the individual's tendency to choose situations because of their perceived congruence with some aspect of his or her personality. Of the remaining four processes, the first, second, and fifth are related in that they define the various ways that personality can affect the individual's *construal* (i.e., cognitive representation) of the situation he or she encounters. These three cognitive processes typically mediate the influence of personality on situations in an indirect manner by affecting the individual's perceptions so that they, in

turn, affect his or her subsequent behavior within the situation. In contrast to these mediated effects, the effects of the fourth process—the evocation of congruent features—are often manifested in the individual's behavior in a more direct, unmediated way.

In the remainder of this section we consider how each of these processes can result in personality influencing the relatively nonpersonal features of the situations individuals encounter. Then, in the following section on personality and ongoing social interaction, we consider how each of these processes can result in personality influencing both the personal and interpersonal features of social situations. Examples for each case are drawn from Cervantes' *Don Quixote de la Mancha,* a book that richly illustrates the power of a romantic individual's personality to transform the situations he encounters. To supplement these literary examples and provide empirical support for the processes assumed to underlie them, we have also included citations of a few representative empirical investigations for each of the processes discussed.

Cognitive restructuring. Cervantes provides many wonderful examples of how an individual's personality can affect his perception of and behavioral reactions to the situations he confronts. Don Quixote's romantic disposition is so strong that it compels him to see a world that is congruent with his perception of himself as a knight-errant. In the Third Book, for example, Don Quixote and his squire Sancho Panza stop to rest at an inn that Don Quixote perceives to be a castle. All of the elements within this situation are cognitively redefined and restructured to conform to this perception, and all of Don Quixote's subsequent behaviors are predicated on this unique perspective. In the course of acting on his perceptions, he manages to change the situation so that, in many respects, the scene actually does come to resemble the features and activities of a medieval castle more than those of a simple country inn.

Empirical research evidence also reveals the impact of personality on the individual's cognitive restructuring of and subsequent behavioral reactions to his or her situation. For example, studies have demonstrated the influence of individual differences in field dependence (e.g., Witkin *et al.,* 1962), learned helplessness (e.g., Alloy and Abramson, 1979), locus of control (e.g., Sosis, 1974), and obesity (e.g., Schachter and Rodin, 1974) on perceptions and judgments about various objective, nonpersonal aspects of situations.

Selective evaluation. The romantic vision associated with Don Quixote's personality leads him to evaluate favorably those features of his situation that are congruent with this vision, while evaluating unfavorably those elements that are incongruent with it. Thus a barber's humble metal basin is perceived as the treasured "golden helmet of Mambrino," whereas a group of harmless windmills are perceived as menacing giants. These evaluations affect Don Quixote's behavior with regard to the elements in question, and this behavior in turn influences the situation he confronts. A number of empirical studies also demonstrate the influence of personality on an individual's selective evaluation of and response to various situational features. For example, Ickes and Layden (1978) have found that individuals with the attributional style most characteristic of high self-esteem view all situations having a negative outcome as significantly less likely to occur in their experience than do individuals with the attributional style associated with low self-esteem.

Selective exposure and interaction. Don Quixote's unique vision also leads him to enter and actively participate in situations that individuals with different temperaments and personalities would experience passively or even tend to avoid. For example, individuals of a different temperament and personality would probably not seek out opportunities to attack a flock of sheep with a lance or to engage in swordplay with a collection of wine bags. For Don Quixote, however, these situations are ideally suited to the behavioral expression of his self-perceived valor and prowess as a knight-errant. Thus he selectively chooses to enter and participate in situations that others might consider to be a waste of their time, dispositions, and energy. His participation in these situations, and the strivings for congruency that underlie his behavior, tend to alter the character of these situations in a manner reflective of his personality.

Because we have already presented, in the previous section, many empirical examples of the influence of personality on an individual's choice of situations, we will not attempt to recount them here. We should note, however, that the processes governing an individual's choice of situations and the processes governing his or her construal of situations are highly interrelated. The individual does not simply choose to enter a situation to which he or she then reacts in a completely passive manner, taking the situation at face value and going with the flow. Instead, the individual chooses to enter the situation with a set of preconceived goals and expectations already in mind. These expectations provide a context for additional cognitive assimilation and restructuring in the form of selective perception and selective evaluation of the situational features at hand. In other words, the individual's cognitive and behavioral orientation is coherently organized and directed toward a mode of engagement with the situation that is likely to reflect the impact of his or her personality on all of the interrelated processes with which we are presently concerned.

Evocation of congruent features. By acting upon his perceptions in the situations he confronts, Don Quixote frequently is able to evoke certain features or reactions from the situation that are congruent with the view of it imposed by his personality. For example, the blow that he receives from the moving arm of the windmill in his attempt to joust with it is congruent with the blow that he expected to elicit from the "giant." Similarly, in a subsequent battle with other "giants" (i.e., large bags of red wine), the "blood" that so freely flows in response to his sword thrusts is a congruent feature of the situations that his own actions again have evoked. These evoked features and reactions are, by definition, alterations of the situation that reflect the imprint of Don Quixote's personality.

The research literature also provides evidence that personality can affect situations through the evocation of congruent features. Several investigations have demonstrated the processes by which individuals evoke events that confirm and validate features of their conceptions of self and social identities (e.g., Andersen and Bem, 1981; Coyne, 1976a, 1976b; Skrypnek and Snyder, 1982; Swann, 1983; Swann and Hill, 1982; Swann and Read, 1981).

Congruency by comparison or by reattribution. In Cervantes' account, Don Quixote frequently is confronted with an incongruent evaluation of himself that he must defend against in some way. Often his mode of defense is to minimize the negative evaluation and the associated implication of a negative trait (e.g., foolishness) by attributing his behavior to a special feature of the situation that, if perceived by others, would lead them to act in the same way. For example, after Don Quixote's ill-fated attack on the sheep (which resulted in the shepherds pelting him with stones), Sancho confronts him with the discrepancy of his action by saying, "Did I not bid you, sir knight, return, and told you that you went not to invade an army of men, but a flock of sheep?'' Don Quixote's defense is to attribute to his malignant adversary the power to alter the appearance of things, so that the "enemy's squadrons" only appeared to be sheep and would soon revert to their usual appearance as men. According to this new attribution, Don Quixote's foolishness was no greater than that of anyone else who had been similarly deceived by his adversary. Empirical illustrations of congruency by comparison or by reattribution can also be found (e.g., Hakmiller, 1966; Secord, Bachman, and Eachus, 1964; Wheeler, 1966).

Having considered how each of these processes serves not only to maintain congruency between personality and situations but also to mediate the influence of personality on situations, we are now prepared to examine the operation of each of them in ongoing social interaction. As will become evident, the connections between personality and social behavior appear in their most subtle and complex forms in the context of ongoing social interaction. It is in this context, therefore, that some of the more interesting causal relationships posited by the situational strategy (and by the dynamic interactionism of which it is a part) can be identified and analyzed.

PERSONALITY AND ONGOING SOCIAL INTERACTION

In even the simplest and most prototypic type of social interaction—a dyadic encounter involving two strangers—the influences of personality on social behavior can become quite complicated. In general, the complicating factors may be stated as follows:

1. Now the influence of *two* personalities must be taken into account.

2. Each participant's personality typically constitutes an important part of the other participant's immediate situation.

3. The need of both participants to maintain congruency can precipitate a variety of interactional processes yielding different behavioral and cognitive outcomes.

4. Beliefs about the other participant's personality and dispositions may independently determine such processes and outcomes, regardless of whether or not these beliefs are really accurate.

Let us briefly elaborate on these factors. In even the simplest type of ongoing social interaction, we are forced to consider the influence of two personalities instead of one. Each participant becomes an important (indeed, perhaps the *most* important) element in the other participant's immediate situation; and, to the extent that each person's behavior is a manifestation of his or her personality, the situation each participant confronts is largely defined by the other's personality. In addition, each participant is, to some degree, motivated to achieve congruency among the three elements central to Secord and Backman's (1965) theory: a self-ascribed aspect of his or her personality, an interpretation of his or her behavior relevant to that aspect, and a perception of how the other person behaves and feels toward him or her with respect to that aspect. This need to achieve and maintain congruency may result in each participant's personality having a direct influence on his or her own behavior and cognitions, thereby having an indirect influence on the other person's behavior and cognitions as well. In other words, a true "interaction of personalities" may occur that leaves neither of the participants completely unaffected or unchanged. Moreover, to complicate matters still further, each participant's beliefs or expectations about the other's personality may independently influence the subsequent behavior of both participants, even if the original beliefs were false and without foundation. These independent influences due to one participant's beliefs about the other's personality can either augment or counteract the more direct, unmediated influences of personality on social behavior and thereby produce some rather subtle and complex effects. Finally, the resulting changes in each participant's behavior and/or cognitions may create a new congruency dynamic that in some cases may result in a relatively permanent *change* in one or both of the participants' personalities as a consequence of their having interacted with each other.

As the preceding paragraph suggests, the attempt to unravel the influences of personality in ongoing social interaction leads one inevitably to the very heart of the Gordian knot of causal relations implied by the dynamic interactional approach. To simplify and impose some structure on our attempted unravelings, let us separately consider how each of the five processes delineated by Secord and Backman (1965) operates to maintain congruency in ongoing social interaction. How, in other words, do participants' personalities influence the course and consequences of their interaction through the interrelated processes of cognitive restructuring, selective evaluation, selective exposure and interaction, the evocation of congruent features, and congruency by comparison or reattribution?

Cognitive Restructuring

In the context of ongoing social interaction, cognitive restructuring occurs whenever S misperceives O's attributes or behavior "so as to achieve congruency with aspects of his behavior and self-concept. He may also misinterpret his own attributes or behavior so as to achieve maximum congruency with an aspect of his self concept and his perception of O" (Secord and Backman, 1965, p. 97). A striking example of cognitive restructuring in Don Quixote's perception of another person can be found in his reactions to the "Asturian wench," Maritornes. As Cervantes pitilessly describes her, Maritornes is "broad-faced, flat-pated, saddle-nosed, blind of one eye, and the other almost out; . . . while her body supplied all the other defects." However, in Don Quixote's romantic view she appears to be a "princess," "a high and beautiful lady," "the goddess of love." Unfortunately for Don Quixote, however, neither Maritornes nor anyone else shares his perception of her—a lack of congruence that sets the stage for considerable interpersonal conflict later on.

Some of the early research documenting the process of cognitive restructuring in interpersonal perception has been summarized by Secord and Backman (1965, pp. 97–98). Included here are correlational studies by Miyamoto and Dornbusch (1956), Reeder, Donohue, and Biblarz (1960), Backman and Secord (1962), and Moore (1963). These studies indicate that the "correspondence between self as seen by the individual and as he thinks others see him is greater than the actual correspondence between self-concept and the views held by other persons" (Secord and Backman, 1965, p. 97). Other studies further reveal that individuals either tend to distort the evaluations they receive from others in a congruent direction (e.g., Harvey, 1962; Harvey, Kelley, and Shapiro, 1957), believe that highly incongruent evaluations are invalid (Harvey, 1962), or deny that highly incongruent evaluations were actually made (Harvey, 1962); for a review, see Shrauger and Schoeneman (1979).

More recently, studies have demonstrated the effects of individual differences in sex role identity (e.g., Bem, 1981) and of individual differences in self-schemata (e.g., Markus and Smith, 1981) on the processing and structuring of information about other people (see

also Tunnell, 1981). In addition, studies indicate that individuals attend more to self-confirmatory feedback than to self-disconfirmatory feedback, and they are motivated to encode and preferentially recall the former type of feedback more than the latter (Swann, 1983; Swann and Read, 1981). These studies are complemented by others demonstrating that feedback discrepant with individuals' self-conceptions is often dismissed as invalid (Crary, 1966; Korman, 1968; Markus, 1977). Finally, some studies have explored the possible role that reconstructive remembering of information about other people (e.g., Snyder and Cantor, 1979; Snyder and Uranowitz, 1978) and about oneself (e.g., Snyder and Skrypnek, 1981) might play in the cognitive restructuring of social situations.

A particularly encouraging note is that some of the recent theory and research on interpersonal perception has focused explicitly on dyadic interaction and has considered the implications of the congruency or incongruency of the participants' interpersonal perceptions for the success or failure of the dyad. An insightful and comprehensive theoretical perspective on these issues has been provided by Laing, Phillipson, and Lee (1966). These authors have proposed that congruency or incongruency in interpersonal perception can exist at any of three levels, defined in terms of (1) a direct perspective (e.g., S's perception of O), (2) a metaperspective (e.g., what O thinks S's perception of O is), and (3) a meta-metaperspective (e.g., what S thinks O thinks S's perception of O is). According to this formulation (Laing, Phillipson, and Lee, 1966, p. 38),

1. *understanding* can be defined as the conjunction between [i.e., congruence of] the metaperspective of one person and the direct perspective of other;

2. *being understood* is the conjunction between the meta-metaperspective of the one person and the metaperspective of the other;

3. the *feeling* of being understood is the conjunction of one's own direct perspective with one's *own* meta-metaperspective.

Laing and his colleagues have developed the Interpersonal Perception Method (IPM) as a means of assessing, within a dyadic relationship, the congruencies and incongruencies that may exist on the various levels of experience. Their administration of the IPM to groups of distressed and nondistressed married couples revealed "many fewer disjunctions [i.e., incongruencies] in all phases of the interactions" of the nondistressed couples relative to those of the distressed couples. A more recent IPM study by Knudson, Sommers, and Golding (1980) further indicates that the attempt by married couples to deal openly with conflict is associated with an increase in congruent interpersonal perceptions, whereas the attempt to avoid such conflict is associated with a decrease in congruent perceptions. These and other studies (e.g., Harvey, Wells, and Alvarez, 1978; Orvis, Kelley, and Butler, 1976; Sillars, 1981) suggest that the meshing or clashing of two personalities is mediated, at least in part, by the influence that each personality exerts on the individual's perceptions of self and partner and, thus, on the nature and magnitude of the dyadic congruencies or incongruencies resulting from these perceptions.

Selective Evaluation

In the context of ongoing social interaction, selective evaluation occurs whenever "*S* maximizes congruency by evaluating more favorably those interpersonal system components that are congruent [or minimizes] incongruency by devaluating those components that are incongruent" (Secord and Backman, 1965, p. 97). This process is nicely illustrated in Don Quixote's changeable relationship with his squire, Sancho Panza. Whenever Sancho supports his employer's conception of himself as a knight-errant—a heroic and chivalrous individual—Don Quixote commends Sancho and regards him with favor. However, whenever Sancho attempts to challenge or question his employer's professed identity, Don Quixote curses him for a fool and berates him for his stupidity. Throughout Cervantes' novel, the positivity of Don Quixote's evaluation of Sancho varies according to the degree to which Sancho's words and actions are perceived as congruent with Don Quixote's romantic conception of himself.

Secord and Backman (1965) cite a number of early studies that illustrate the various ways selective evaluation can affect interpersonal perception. Some of their own research suggests, for example, that individuals in residential groups are attracted to others whom they believe to hold congruent views of them (Backman and Secord, 1962), and that individuals who report having strong and distinct needs tend to perceive their friends as having complementary needs which the individuals' self-congruent behaviors are appropriate to meet (Secord and Backman, 1964). Other studies reveal that as another person's evaluation of the individual becomes increas-

ingly incongruent, the individual becomes more likely to devalue the other in order to minimize the need for change (Deutsch and Solomon, 1959; Harvey, 1962; Wilson, 1962). This congruency effect does not always occur, however, and often yields to a positivity effect when the other's evaluation is incongruent but in a positive direction (e.g., Deutsch and Solomon, 1959). As Secord and Backman point out, the theoretical resolution of the problem presented by these two types of effects may require "a more sophisticated view of congruency" that recognizes that an evaluation from another person may be incongruent with certain aspects of the self-concept but quite congruent with others. The same mode of theoretical resolution was later endorsed by Jones (1974) and Mettee and Aronson (1974) in their comprehensive reviews of this literature.

The effects of selective evaluation in interpersonal contexts are, of course, complicated by the fact that at least two individuals are involved, both of whom are attempting to maintain congruent relations among their self-images, their own behavior, and the behavior of their partner. And just as the individuals' personalities can affect the degree of congruency or incongruency in their perceptions of each other through the process of cognitive restructuring, so can their personalities affect the degree of congruency or incongruency in their evaluations of each other through the process of selective evaluation. Similarly, just as incongruent interpersonal perceptions typically eventuate in some form of conflict or misunderstanding, so do incongruent evaluations typically result in conflict or misunderstanding as well. Such well-known (but surprisingly little-studied) phenomena as unrequited (i.e., unreciprocated) love or other unilateral feelings (e.g., of respect, admiration, identification, pity, disgust, hatred) have their roots in the incongruency of the interactants' evaluations of each other.

Selective Interaction

Secord and Backman (1965) assert that within the social context (pp. 104–105),

> interpersonal congruency may also be maintained through selectively interacting with certain persons and not with others. An individual is most likely to interact with those persons with whom he can most readily establish a congruent state. This tendency is most directly expressed when the individual is among a group of other persons and can freely choose to interact with a select few. Selection may

also occur in a broader sense: a person may adopt social roles that call for role behavior congruent with the individual's self concept and that require role partners to behave toward him in a congruent manner.

Don Quixote's attempts to maintain congruency through selective interaction with others can easily be traced throughout his adventures. When, early in the novel, he realizes that his niece and his elderly servant will not accept his identity as a knight-errant, he decides to leave his home (and them) without even telling them that he is going. Once he has chosen not to interact any longer with people whose behavior will not support his current conception of self, he subsequently limits his company primarily to that of his horse, Rozinante, and his squire, Sancho Panza, the two beings he considers least likely to discredit his identity. His encounters with other people are typically brief, characterized by a strong imaginary component, and are generally terminated as soon as his self-concept is threatened. Apparently, the lesson Cervantes would have us draw is that isolation and increasing alienation from others may be the price of attempting to maintain a vulnerable and easily discredited conception of self.

Early studies cited by Secord and Backman indicate the utility of selective interaction in maintaining interpersonal congruency. In a study of sorority members, Backman and Secord (1962) found that individuals interacted most frequently "with those other members whom they thought perceived them in the most congruent fashion and whose perceptions actually were more congruent" (Secord and Backman, 1965, p. 104). In a conceptually related study, Broxton (1963) found that college women who requested a change of roommates perceived their new roommates to have a more congruent view of them than their old roommates had. Other studies extend these findings by indicating that selective interaction also operates to maximize the congruency of individuals' personalities and self-concepts with their chosen occupational roles (e.g., Hoe, 1962; Merenda, Musiker, and Clarke, 1960; Stern and Scanlon, 1958).

More recent findings have been concerned with the ways in which conceptions of self may influence not only one's choices of interaction partners but also the form, breadth, and scope of the interpersonal activities that follow from such choices (e.g., Snyder and Campbell, 1982). Finally, a number of clinically oriented theorists have made explicit the point that is implicit in Cervantes'

account of Don Quixote: that the maintenance of a socially deviate or consensually nonvalidated self-concept may require one to display extreme selectivity in one's interactions. Socially deviate individuals may thus require their interactions be restricted primarily to a subgroup composed of individuals who are similarly deviant or stigmatized (e.g., Goffman, 1963). Individuals whose experience is highly delusional and idiosyncratic may require that relations with others either be curtailed completely (Jones and Nisbett, 1971) or limited to a superficial, token kind of interaction in which a false social self is displayed publicly while the real self is kept hidden (Laing, 1960, 1961).

Evocation of Congruent Responses

As important as the process of selective interaction may be, it is not the only means by which individuals are able to ensure that they will be able to relate to others in ways that are not incongruent with their own personalities and self-concepts. In many cases selective interaction will operate to ensure that one's relationships will be limited to certain ideal interaction partners for whom one's own self-congruent responses will be need fulfilling and vice versa. Quite often, however, such ideal interaction partners are not available, and individuals instead must attempt to evoke congruent responses from individuals whose personalities may not predispose them to make such responses. To do so, individuals must employ behavioral techniques whose success depends on the constraining power of the general processes underlying social interaction rather than on the specific personality dispositions of their interaction partners (Goffman, 1959; Rausch, Barry, Hertel, and Swain, 1974; Schelling, 1960; Watzlawick, Beavin, and Jackson, 1967).

In an attempt to illuminate some of these more general interaction processes, Carson (1969, Chap. 4) has written a thoughtful integrative review of various theoretical formulations that have related personality to the evocation of congruent responses in interpersonal situations. Following an extensive discussion of the relevant literature, Carson proposed that the two-factor (dominance versus submission and hate versus love) circumplex model advanced by Leary (1957) and his associates could be used as an empirically defensible taxonomy of the varieties of interpersonal behavior (see Fig. 1). This model is primarily concerned with the eight categories of interpersonal behavior represented in the outermost ring of Fig. 1. According to the Leary framework (Carson, 1969, p. 112),

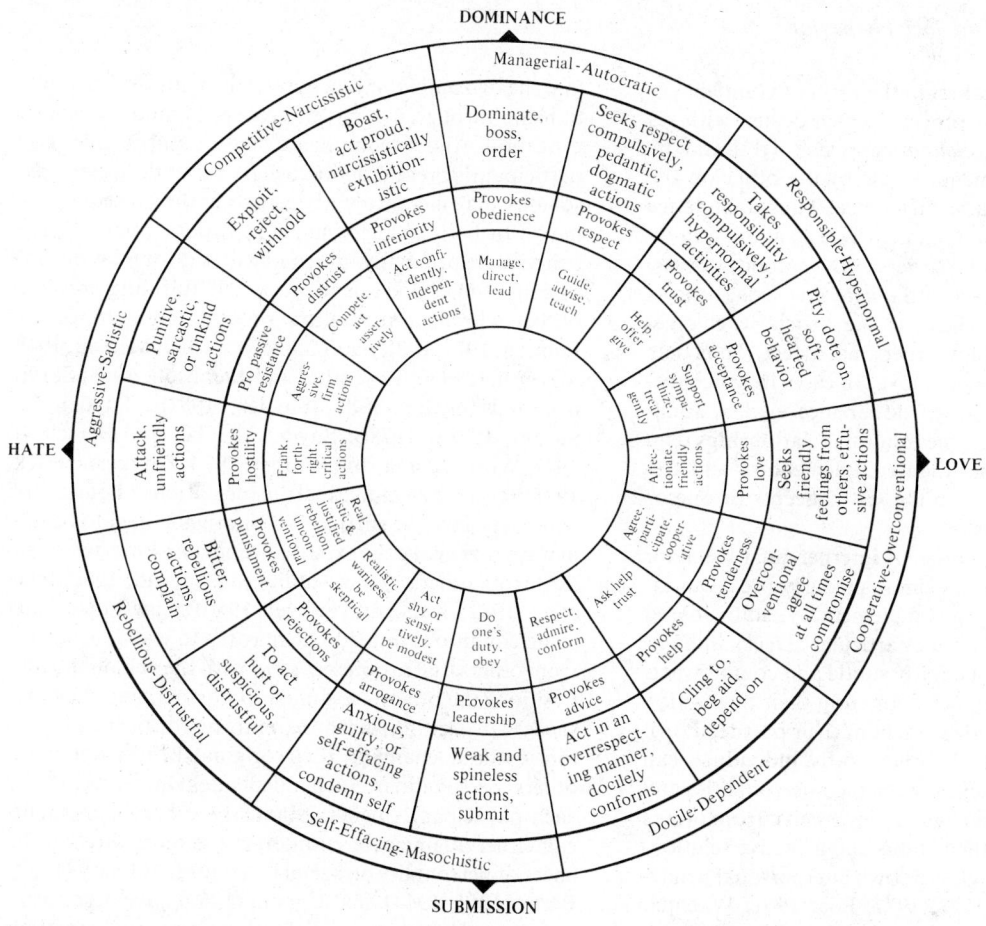

FIGURE 1
The Interpersonal Behavior Circle.

Adapted from Timothy Leary, *Interpersonal Diagnosis of Personality—A Functional Theory and Methodology for Personality Evaluation.* Copyright © 1957 The Ronald Press Company, New York.

interpersonal behaviors are viewed as being, in part, *security operations* (a Sullivanian term) employed by persons to maintain relative comfort, security, and freedom from anxiety in their interactions with others. The *purpose* of interpersonal behavior, in terms of its security-maintenance functions, is to induce from the other person behavior that is complementary to the behavior proferred. It is assumed that this induced, complementary behavior has current utility for the person inducing it, in the sense that it maximizes his momentary security. Leary

suggests that we learn how to "train" others to respond to us in security-maintaining ways by acquiring the requisite behavioral "techniques," and that each of the eight categories of interpersonal behavior may be viewed as a distinctive set of learned operations for prompting desired behavior from others.

Generally speaking, there are two major processes by which security-maintaining (i.e., self-congruent, in Secord and Backman's 1965 parlance) responses are presumably evoked from others in the form of complementary behavior. The first process, which occurs with respect to the *dominance-submission* axis, reflects the adoption of a complementary role by the other on the basis of an assumed status difference. Thus dominance on the part of one person tends to evoke submission on the part of the other and vice versa. The second process, which occurs with respect to the *hate-love* axis, reflects the operation of the reciprocity (i.e., social exchange) norm in the exchange of interpersonal affect. Thus hate evokes hate, and love evokes love. In cases in which different processes occur (e.g., dominance evokes dominance, love evokes hate), the resulting relationships tend to be antagonistic rather than complementary and frequently create instability in the self-concepts of one or both of the participants.

Because some categories of interpersonal behavior can initiate both processes simultaneously (i.e., can induce the other to adopt a complementary, status-based role as well as to reciprocate a particular affect), individuals may be able to evoke fairly subtle and complex patterns of complementary behavior from their interaction partners more or less independent of their partners' own personality dispositions. In other words, individuals can maximize the congruency between their personalities and self-concepts and the behaviors they receive from others by implicitly defining their status and affective relationships to the other through their own interpersonal behavior (see also Bowers, 1973, 1977; Foa, 1961; Wachtel, 1973). Once the nature of the relationship has been implicitly defined for the other in this way, the desired complementary behaviors are likely to be evoked. These subtle, often dimly perceived interpersonal manipulations have a gamelike quality and have been extensively analyzed from a games perspective by Berne (1961, 1964) and others. They have also been discussed by sociologists under the rubric of *altercasting processes* (e.g., Davis and Schmidt, 1977; Weinstein and Deutschberger, 1963). And the critical contributions of strategic self-presentational activities to these processes have been discussed by, most notably, Goffman (1959) and Jones and Pittman (1982).

These considerations suggest that in the context of a dyadic relationship each participant's personality will tend to define, and therefore constrain, the nature of the participants' relationship and the course of their subsequent interaction. The complicating fact that the situation now bears the imprint of two personalities requires

that the two individuals negotiate the nature of their relationship through a complex process of mutual response evocation. And to complicate matters still further, each participant's preinteraction beliefs about the other's personality may independently constrain the subsequent behavior of both participants, even if these preinteraction beliefs were originally false and without foundation. The various studies documenting the self-fulfilling prophecy or behavioral confirmation process (e.g., Jones and Panitch, 1971; Kelley and Stahelski, 1970; Merton, 1948; Rosenthal, 1966; Rosenthal and Jacobson, 1968; Skrypnek and Snyder, 1982; Snyder, 1981b; Snyder and Swann, 1978a, 1978b; Snyder, Tanke, and Berscheid, 1977; Word, Zanna, and Cooper, 1974; Zanna and Pack, 1975) reveal that individuals' expectations about others may themselves be sufficient to motivate them to behave in ways that evoke the expected behaviors (and personalities) from others. Other studies (e.g., Bond, 1972; Ickes *et al.,* 1982; Swann and Snyder, 1980) suggest that under some conditions individuals may try to evoke behaviors from others that are *inconsistent* with the personality dispositions the other is assumed to possess, and they may succeed in eliciting such apparently disconfirming behaviors without changing their original beliefs about the others' personalities. Such independent influences due to each participant's beliefs about the other's personality can either augment or counteract the more direct influences of personality on social behavior that Leary (1957), Berne (1961, 1964), and Carson (1969) have described.

In addition to the congruent-response-evoking processes just considered, Swann (1983) has proposed that individuals also use the strategic display of signs and symbols of who they are to ensure that the beliefs and behaviors of their interaction partners will validate their self-conceptions. Not only has Swann offered examples of such superficial and easily altered signs and symbols of self-identity as clothing and cosmetics, but he also has considered more dramatic alterations in body structure (e.g., through weight loss, muscle building, plastic surgery) as a means of continuing to obtain self-validating reactions from others when time (and gravity) begin to take their toll. The role of signs and symbols in the manufacturing of social identities is, of course, one that has been analyzed, with depth and insight, by Goffman (1959).

Of what consequence are the changes in each participant's behavior and/or cognitions that occur through the operation of the various response-evoking processes we have just discussed? According to a dynamic interactionist perspective, a very important potential consequence of such interaction-based change is the creation of a new congruency dynamic that in some cases may result in a relatively permanent alteration in one or both of the participants' personalities. These postinteractional changes in personality are particularly likely to occur when individuals interact with others who are effective in evoking responses from them that are congruent with the others' personalities but are incongruent with their own. If individuals are unable to reduce the discrepancy between their interaction behavior and their self-concepts through the various forms of cognitive adjustment (i.e., cognitive restructuring, selective interaction, congruency by comparison or reattribution) or through avoidance of these others in the future (i.e., selective interaction), their self-concepts and personalities may change instead to reflect the changes in their interaction behavior.

An illustration of this process can be found in Sancho Panza's relationship to Don Quixote and in the effects that this relationship has on Sancho's personality. As their relationship develops, Don Quixote becomes increasingly successful in evoking responses from Sancho that are congruent with Don Quixote's own romantic personality and worldview. The reasons for his increasing success are not too difficult to find. Because of the status difference between Sancho and Don Quixote, Sancho must follow Don Quixote's orders and be willing to act on his judgments. He must therefore be attentive to Don Quixote's point of view and give more serious regard to Don Quixote's interpretation of events than his own interpretation receives in return. Moreover, because Sancho is required to share Don Quixote's company almost constantly but has little opportunity to interact with anyone else, he is compelled to spend most of his time living out the identity that his master has bestowed on him. Thus Sancho's behavior becomes increasingly determined by Don Quixote's cognitive reconstructions, selective evaluations, and reattributions of the events that occur, while at the same time Sancho is relatively insulated (through selective interaction) from the perspective that interaction with others might provide.

As a consequence of these factors, it becomes progressively easier for Sancho to see himself in the way that Don Quixote appears to see him. And because this new self-image is more noble, romantic, and worthy of respect than the self-concept Sancho started out with, its

congruence with aspects of his ideal self probably also facilitates his acceptance of it. Thus, although Sancho's transformation into a slightly more romantic personality begins with Don Quixote's attempts to evoke responses from him congruent with Quixote's own personality, a number of other supportive and interrelated processes also operate to further this outcome. These processes reflect not only the congruency-maintaining needs of both individuals but also the congruency dynamics that emerge at the dyadic level because of the nature of their relationship.

Congruency by Comparison or Reattribution

Sancho, of course, initially resists Don Quixote's efforts to change his (Sancho's) personality through an "altercasting," desired-response-evoking process. His resistance takes the form of attributing the discrepancy between his view of himself and Don Quixote's view of him to an idiosyncratic disposition of his master. By attributing the faulty view of reality to Don Quixote rather than to himself, Sancho is able to dissociate himself from the imputation of a negative trait (i.e., being out of touch with reality) and therefore preserve his original self-concept. Sancho's continued use of this congruency-maintaining strategy throughout his travels with Don Quixote accounts for the fact that their interaction produces only a limited degree of change in Sancho's personality and self-concept. Some excellent empirical examples of congruency by comparison are provided by the work on attributional ambiguity (for a review, see Snyder and Wicklund, 1982). In one such study by Snyder *et al.,* (1979) individuals whose desire to avoid a handicapped person was incongruent with their self-image attempted to maintain congruency by reattributing their avoidance to another, non-ego-threatening aspect of the situation (here a preference to see a different movie than the one seen by the handicapped person).

As Carson (1969) has noted, the process of attributing to others those traits and dispositions that one is unwilling to see in oneself is essentially the same process of ego-defense that Freud (1928) and his followers have labeled *projection.* Empirical investigations of this form of congruency by comparison have been reported by, among others, Secord, Bachman, and Eachus (1964) and Bramel (1962).

With our discussion of the application of the theory of interpersonal congruency to understanding the role of personality in ongoing social interaction, our considerations of the impact of the individual on the social world is complete. Therefore we turn now to a critical analysis of the theoretical perspective and the methodological orientation associated with the situational strategy for the study of personality and social behavior.

ANALYSIS AND CRITIQUE OF THE SITUATIONAL STRATEGY

The core features of the situational strategy for the study of personality and social behavior are the propositions that properties of individuals (including stable traits, enduring dispositions, social attitudes, and conceptions of self) are reflected in the processes by which individuals *choose* to enter and to spend time in social situations and in the processes by which they *influence* the character of the social situations in which they find themselves. The underlying theme of the situational strategy for understanding individuals and their behavior in social contexts is the proposition that, as consequences of their transactions with their social worlds, individuals construct for themselves social worlds that are suited to expressing, maintaining, and acting upon their conceptions of self, their social attitudes, and their characteristic dispositions.

Central to the situational strategy for the study of personality and social behavior are the following:

1. Its concern with the reciprocal influences and the mutual interplay of individuals and social situations.

2. Its definition of *personality* in terms of processes that actively link individuals and their social situations.

3. Its identification of the antecedents of these processes in individuals' conceptions of self, social attitudes, and characteristic dispositions.

4. Its identification of the consequences of these processes in the structure of the social worlds within which individuals live their lives.

As we have seen in our examination of representative examples of the situational strategy in action, researchers have been able to document the manner in which properties of individuals are reflected and manifested in the choice by individuals of their social situations, in the influence of individuals on their social situations, and in the dynamics of ongoing social interaction and interpersonal relationships.

To be sure, much remains to be accomplished by the practitioners of the situational strategy for the study of personality and social behavior. For example, to our knowledge, an investigation possessing each and every one of the features of the hypothetical example that we used to illustrate the implementation of the situational strategy (i.e., the application of the strategy to the study of the social psychological phenomenon of competition; see p. 916) has yet to be conducted. Nevertheless, the converging pattern of the empirical evidence that we have surveyed leads us to suspect that the outcomes of such an investigation would fulfill the promise of the situational strategy. We should note, however, that research generated by the situational strategy has tended to focus on cases in which individuals come to live in social worlds that match their personalities (e.g., extraverts gravitate toward extraverted situations, authoritarians gravitate toward authoritarian environments) to the relative neglect of cases in which individuals come to live in social worlds that differ from features of their identities (e.g., liberals who deliberately choose to live in conservative communities for the purpose of making these communities more liberal). We hope that by having devoted some theoretical attention to the second, as well as to the first, of these cases, we will encourage researchers to devote more attention to the reciprocal influences of personalities and incongruent situations.

A major area in need of attention from users of the situational strategy is that of assessment. It follows from the basic tenets of the situational strategy that efforts to assess differences between individuals should be directed at the construction and validation of measures of the situations in which individuals live their lives. For example, consider the case of a researcher who seeks to construct a measure of individual differences in the disposition of sociability. Should that researcher construct a measure of the extent to which individuals report that they display the diverse behaviors that reflect sociability? To the extent that this researcher takes seriously the situational strategy, he or she should not construct this type of measure. Instead, his or her measure should assess the extent to which individuals report that they choose to spend time in situations that foster the expression of sociability and that they engage in activities that tend to increase the sociability of the situations they confront. To the extent that the goal of any strategy for assessing sociability is the identification of those individuals who regularly and consistently behave in sociable fashion, any strategy that focuses on the extent to which individuals are to be found in situations that foster, encourage, and promote sociable behavior would seem to possess considerable promise of being a valid assessment strategy. One readily can imagine similar assessment strategies for other dispositions, as well as for attitudes and conceptions of self.

The Situational Strategy and Dynamic Interactionism

As we have suggested, the situational strategy reflects the dynamic interactional perspective on personality and social behavior. Thus the situational strategy shares the major theoretical problem presented by dynamic interactionism: the difficulty of developing a theoretically adequate account of the complex interdependence of personality, situations, and social behavior. Because each of these elements not only influences but also is influenced by the others, theories in this tradition will have to forsake the standard simplifying assumptions of linear, unidirectional causal relationships among variables that can be unequivocally categorized as independent versus dependent. Instead, dynamic interactional models of personality and social behavior will have to deal directly with the problems of specifying the complex, co-occuring processes by which personality, situations, and social behavior are dynamically interrelated. This task is likely to present some formidable conceptual problems for the serious personality theorist.

Important theoretical complications also may arise from the role the self-concept appears to play in mediating stability and change in personality. First, the acceptability of the self-concept as a valid scientific construct has long been challenged, as Allport (1955), Gergen (1971), Epstein (1973) and others have noted. Second, the apparent differentiation (e.g., real self versus ideal self) or multidimensionality of the self-concept is, from a theoretical standpoint, both a blessing and a curse. On the one hand, such differentiation enhances the construct's explanatory potential (e.g., behavior that appears to be clearly incongruent with one aspect of the self-concept may be quite congruent with another aspect). On the other hand, it may contribute to the nonfalsifiability of research hypotheses when it is invoked *post hoc* to account for unexpected results. Third, with only a few notable exceptions (e.g., Buss, 1980; Carver and Scheier, 1981; Duval and Wicklund, 1972;

Turner, 1968; Wicklund, 1975); relatively little theoretical work has been done that attempts to specify the conditions in which certain aspects of the self-concept will become salient at the expense of others (cf. Shaver, 1976). For all of these reasons, it may be difficult to formulate a conceptually adequate account of the role of the self-concept in personality maintenance and change. Secord and Backman's (1965) congruency theory is clearly an important step in this direction, but much conceptual work remains to be done.

The primary methodological problems presented by the dynamic interactional approach are generally reflective of the theoretical problems just described. Because the assumptions of dynamic interactionism are not consistent with the assumptions underlying the use of most of the conventional statistical models, new statistical models may be required to test the implications of this approach. Some promising evidence that statistical models can be specially designed to capture the influences of individual differences in ongoing social interaction is provided by Kenny's innovative work on statistical procedures for "splitting the reciprocity coefficient" (Kenny and Nasby, 1980) and for segregating the variances associated with the individual members of interacting dyads (Kenny, 1981; Kenny and LaVoie, 1981; Warner, Kenny, and Stoto, 1979), and by the similar techniques of Mendoza and Graziano (1982) for the multivariate statistical analysis of dyadic social behavior. These statistical considerations suggest the related need for appropriate methodological frameworks, such as Ickes's unstructured dyadic interaction paradigm, in which the effects of personality on social behavior can be studied at both the between-dyad and within-dyad levels of analysis (Ickes, 1982, 1983). The importance of this level-of-analysis distinction is revealed by Ickes's (1982) observation that the effects of personality factors on social behavior are frequently more strongly evident in between-dyad comparisons of dyad types having different personality compositions than in within-dyad comparisons of dyad members who differ on the particular personality dimension being studied. In addition to these statistical and paradigmatic issues, other problems remain pertaining to the operational definition and measurement of such essential theoretical constructs as self-concept and situation. Clearly, researchers are only now beginning to recognize and address a variety of methodological problems that adherents of the dynamic interactional approach will have to confront.

Despite these various theoretical and methodological problems, the consequences of pursuing the dynamic interactional strategy are potentially quite exciting. This pursuit should not only stimulate the development of more sophisticated theory, statistics, and methodology but also yield rich insights about personality processes and their role in human social behavior. We may further expect that such insights will enhance our understanding of the disordered personality processes and their role in human social behavior. Carson (1969), for example, already has shown how Secord and Backman's (1965) congruency-maintaining processes can operate to defend an unrealistic, disordered conception of self, and Berne (1964) has written perceptively of "the games people play" in order to evoke responses from others that are congruent with their own neurotic needs and dispositions. With continued theoretical development, the dynamic interactional strategy for the study of personality and social behavior may contribute greatly to the understanding and treatment of personality disorders. It may also increase our awareness of how such disorders both affect and are affected by individuals' relationships with others (e.g., Goffman, 1961; Laing, 1961, 1969).

The Situational Strategy and the Social Psychology of Personality

Our reflections on the theoretical perspective and methodological orientation that constitute the situational strategy for the study of personality and social behavior suggest that this strategy ought to be of particular interest to social psychologists. Together, elements of the situational strategy constitute a fundamentally social psychological approach to determining the origins of the regularities and consistencies in social behavior that are thought to constitute personality. According to this social psychological interpretation of personality, regularities and consistencies in social behavior are to be understood in terms of the regularities and consistencies that individuals create in the social situations in which they live their lives.

As a fundamentally social psychological approach to determining the origins of regularities and consistencies in social behavior, the situational strategy for the study of personality and social behavior is quite compatible with sociological perspectives on the individual in society. Mead (1934), for example, emphasized the active role that individuals play in shaping their destinies and their social environments. He regarded individuals as both the causes and consequences of society. More con-temporary statements in the sociology of identity still echo Mead's message. In particular, Alexander (Alexander and Knight, 1971; Alexander and Lauderdale, 1977), Goffman (1959), McCall and Simmons (1978), Secord and Backman (1965), Stryker (1980), Turner (1968, 1975), and Weinstein (1966) all have proposed (and have offered some empirical evidence to confirm) that individuals are sensitive to the identities that they will acquire as a consequence of entering specific social situations and social roles, and that situations and roles may be chosen in the service of creating and maintaining features of identity and self-conception. In addition, the situational strategy for the study of personality and social behavior owes an obvious intellectual debt to Sullivan's interpersonal theory of psychiatry (e.g., 1953, 1964) that regarded personality as "the relatively enduring pattern of recurrent interpersonal situations which characterize a human life" (1953, p. 111) (for a useful summary of Sullivan's interactional approach to personality, see Carson, 1969, Chap. 2). Moreover, the situational strategy is compatible with contemporary assertions by personality theorists about individuals as active creators of their social worlds; e.g., "behavior partly creates the environment, and the environment influences behavior in a reciprocal fashion" (Bandura, 1974, p. 866), and "the person continuously influences the 'situations' of his life as well as being affected by them" (Mischel, 1973, p. 278). In all of these formulations, basic assumptions of the dynamic interactional approach to the study of personality and social behavior may be found.

There is yet another reason why the situational strategy for the study of personality and social behavior may prove to be of particular relevance to the concerns of social psychologists: An understanding of the influence of individuals on situations may add to the understanding of the influence of situations on individuals. By choosing and influencing their situations, individuals determine which situations will have the opportunity to influence their behavior. Thus by virtue of their choices and their subsequent actions, individuals may knowingly and willingly allow and use situations to influence their own behavior. From this perspective, whenever we witness instances of situations influencing individuals, we ought to ask, "To what extent has the individual chosen to be in that situation?" "To what extent has the individual chosen to allow that situation to influence his or her behavior?" "How might that situation facilitate the expression of real or desired attributes of that individual?" And so on. Moreover, even when individuals have *not* knowingly and willingly chosen the situations that confront them, we still may profit from asking related questions: "What actions of the individual may have unknowingly created the situation that confronts him or her?" "What characteristics of that individual might have generated those actions that produced his or her current situation?" And so on. For an elaboration of this analysis of the utility of the situational strategy for understanding not only the influence of individuals on situations but also the influence of situations on individuals, see Snyder (1981b).

CONCLUSION

We began our considerations of personality and social behavior with the proposition that an individual's behavior in a social situation is determined both by characteristics of that individual and by characteristics of that situation. Using this proposition both as a point of departure and as an organizing principle, we were able to define three strategies for the study of personality and social behavior: the dispositional strategy, the interactional strategy, and the situational strategy. These strategies differ among themselves in the extent to which they seek to identify, both theoretically and empirically, the dispositional and situational origins of regularities and consistencies (the defining features of personality) in the behavior of individuals in social contexts.

We then examined the theoretical perspectives and empirical orientations associated with each of these strategies for the study of personality and social behavior. The dispositional strategy is guided by a theoretical perspective that assumes that regularities and consistencies in social behavior can be understood in terms of stable and enduring dispositional propensities that reside within individuals, and by an empirical orientation that seeks to identify categories of individuals who characteristically and typically manifest the phenomena and processes of concern to social psychologists. The interactional strategy is guided by a theoretical perspective that seeks to understand the regularities and consistencies in social behavior in terms of the interactive contributions of dispositional and situational influences, and by an empirical orientation that seeks to identify those categories of traits, of behaviors, of people, and of situations within which regularities and consistencies in social behavior are to be found. The situational strategy is guided by a theoretical perspective that proposes that the regularities and

consistencies in social behavior are the products of regularities and consistencies in the situations within which individuals find themselves, and by an empirical orientation that seeks to understand the processes by which individuals choose and subsequently influence their social situations.

Representative illustrations of each strategy in action were presented to convey the strengths and weaknesses of each approach. As we have seen, practitioners of the dispositional strategy seek to identify individuals who typically manifest the phenomena or processes of concern to social psychologists in hopes of gaining access to the ideal candidates for investigating the social psychology of those phenomena or processes. And as our illustrative examples point out, the study of prejudiced individuals has been particularly revealing about the nature of prejudice, the study of people with high needs for social approval has been most informative about the dynamics of approval seeking, and the study of Machiavellian individuals has provided a clearer delineation of the processes of interpersonal manipulation. However, as compelling and satisfying as the portraits of social psychological phenomena that emerge from applications of the dispositional strategy may be, the extent of this strategy's ability to predict the behavior of individuals in social contexts has been a source of some concern and frustration.

Out of this concern and frustration about issues of prediction have emerged the concerted efforts of the adherents to the interactional strategy to maximize the relationships between dispositional measures as predictors and social behavior as criteria. As our illustrative examples have revealed, the search for moderating variables to answer the questions "Which traits?" "Which behaviors?" "Which people?" and "Which situations?" has yielded a set of precise specifications about those features of the predictor, the criterion, the individual, and the situation that define the boundaries of predictability in human social behavior. However, as satisfying as the improved levels of predictability that have emerged from the interactional strategy may be, the limited ability of the interactional strategy to come to grips with the nature of the intimate interplay of individuals and their social situations has been the source of concern and frustration with this approach.

Born of this concern and frustration has been the dynamic approach of the situational strategy for the study of personality and social behavior. With its theoretical and empirical analyses of the processes by which individuals actively choose and influence the social contexts and interpersonal settings of their lives, the situational strategy has promoted an appreciation of the reciprocal relationships between individuals and their social worlds. Moreover, the situational strategy, with its systematic attempts to investigate the dynamics of ongoing social interaction, has provided a vehicle for understanding the complex involvement of personality in interpersonal relationships.

Clearly, the study of personality and social behavior has seen a sequential progression from the dispositional strategy to the interactional strategy to the situational strategy. This progression has not only been one of history but also one of evolution. As a consequence of this evolutionary process, the three strategies possess much in the way of family resemblance, and themes voiced by strategies earlier in the evolutionary process are echoed by strategies later in the evolutionary process. But perhaps of greatest importance, as a consequence of this evolutionary process, not only do we have the fundamental tenet that "every psychological event depends upon the state of the person and at the same time on the environment, although their relative importance is different in different cases" (Lewin, 1936, p. 12); in addition, we have a precise set of propositions about dispositional and situational sources of regularities and consistencies in the behavior of individuals in social contexts. What has evolved has been an increasingly sophisticated theoretical and empirical understanding of the social psychology of personality and of the mutual interplay between the individual and the social world. Indeed, the emerging realization that social situations not only influence but also are influenced by the behavior of individuals may at long last stimulate attempts to answer the question (posed originally by Comte in 1852) that Allport (1968) has defined as the momentous question that provided the impetus for the conception and development of social science: How can the individual be at one and the same time the cause and the consequence of society?

REFERENCES

Abelson, R. P. (1976). Script processing in attitude formation and decision making. In J. Carroll, and J. Payne (Eds.), *Cognition and social behavior.* Hillsdale, N.J.: Erlbaum.

Adorno, T. W., E. Frenkel-Brunswik, D. J. Levinson, and R. N. Sanford (1950). *The authoritarian personality.* New York: Harper.

Ajzen, I. (1982). On behaving in accordance with one's attitudes. In M. P. Zanna, E. T. Higgins, and C. P. Herman (Eds.), *Consistency in social behavior: the Ontario symposium.* Vol. 2. Hillsdale, N.J.: Erlbaum.

Ajzen, I., C. Timko, and J. B. White (1982). Self-monitoring and the attitude-behavior relation. *J. Pers. soc. Psychol.* 42, 426–435.

Alexander, C. N., Jr., and G. W. Knight (1971). Situated identities and social psychological experimentation. *Sociometry, 34,* 65–82.

Alexander, C. N., Jr. and P. Lauderdale (1977). Situated identities and social influence. *Sociometry, 40,* 225–233.

Alker, H. A. (1972). Is personality situationally specific or intrapsychically consistent? *J. Pers., 40,* 1–16.

Alloy, L. B., and L. Y. Abramson (1979). Judgment of contingency in depressed and non-depressed students: sadder but wiser? *J. exp. Psychol.: gen., 108,* 441–485.

Allport, G. W. (1937). *Personality: a psychological interpretation.* New York: Holt, Rinehart, and Winston.

———— (1955). *Becoming.* New Haven: Yale Univ. Press.

———— (1968). The historical background of modern social psychology. In G. Lindzey, and E. Aronson (Eds.), *Handbook of social psychology* (2nd ed.). Reading, Mass.: Addison-Wesley.

Andersen, S., and S. L. Bem (1981). Sex typing and androgyny in dyadic interaction. *J. Pers. soc. Psychol., 41,* 74–86.

Argyle, M. (1969). *Social interaction.* Chicago: Aldine.

Argyle, M., and A. Furnham (1980). Who goes where, and with whom? Choice of situation as a function of relationship. Unpublished manuscript. Univ. of Oxford.

Argyle, M., and B. R. Little (1972). Do personality traits apply to social behavior? *J. Theory soc. Behav., 2,* 1–35.

Arkin, R.M., and S. Duval (1975). Focus of attention and causal attributions of actors and observers. *J. exp. soc. Psychol., 11,* 427–438.

Aronson, E., and J. M. Carlsmith (1968). Experimentation in social psychology. In G. Lindzey, and E. Aronson (Eds.), *Handbook of social psychology* (2nd ed.). Reading, Mass.: Addison-Wesley.

Atkinson, J. W. (1957). Motivational determinants of risk-taking behavior. *Psychol. Rev., 64,* 359–372.

Backman, C. W., and P. F. Secord (1962). Liking, selective interaction, and misperception in congruent interpersonal relations. *Sociometry, 25,* 321–335.

Bandura, A. (1974). Behavior therapy and the models of man. *Amer. Psychol., 29,* 859–869.

Bartlett, D. L., P. B. Drew, E. G. Fahle, and W. A. Watts (1974). Selective exposure to a presidential campaign appeal. *Publ. Opin. Quart., 38,* 264–271.

Barnes, R. D., and W. Ickes (1979). *Styles of self-monitoring: assimilative versus accommodative.* Unpublished manuscript.

Barthel, C. E. (1963). The effects of the approval motive, generalized expectancy, and situational cues upon goal setting and social defensiveness. Unpublished doctoral dissertation. Ohio State University.

Barthel, C. E., and D. P. Crowne (1962). The need for approval, task categorization, and perceptual defense. *J. consult. Psychol., 26,* 547–555.

Battie, E., and J. B. Rotter (1963). Children's feelings of personal control as related to social class and ethnic groups. *J. Pers., 31,* 482–490.

Beaman, A. L., B. Klentz, E. Diener, and S. Svanum (1979). Self-awareness and transgression in children: two field studies. *J. Pers. soc. Psychol., 37,* 1835–1846.

Becherer, R. C., and L. M. Richard (1978). Self-monitoring as a moderating variable in consumer behavior. *J. Consumer Research, 5,* 159–162.

Bem, D. J. (1972). Constructing cross-situational consistencies in behavior: some thoughts on Alker's critique of Mischel. *J. Pers., 40,* 17–26.

———— (1982). Persons, situations, and template matching: theme and variations. In M. P. Zanna, E. T. Higgins, and C. P. Herman (Eds.), *Consistency in social behavior: the Ontario symposium.* Vol. 2. Hillsdale, N.J.: Erlbaum.

Bem, D. J., and A. Allen (1974). On predicting some of the people some of the time: the search for cross-situational consistencies in behavior. *Psychol. Rev., 81,* 506–520.

Bem, D. J., and D. C. Funder (1978). Predicting more of the people more of the time: assessing the personality of situations. *Psychol. Rev., 85,* 485–501.

Bem, D. J., and C. G. Lord (1979). Template matching: a proposal for probing the ecological validity of experimental settings in social psychology. *J. Pers. soc. Psychol., 37,* 833–846.

Bem, S. L. (1974). The measurement of psychological androgyny. *J. Consult. clinic. Psychol., 42,* 155–162.

———— (1975). Sex role adaptability: one consequence of psychological androgyny. *J. Pers. soc. Psychol., 31,* 634–643.

———— (1981). Gender schema theory: a cognitive account of sex typing. *Psychol. Rev., 88,* 354–364.

Bem, S. L., and E. Lenney (1976). Sex typing and the avoidance of cross-sex behavior. *J. Pers. soc. Psychol., 33,* 48–54.

Berglas, S., and E. E. Jones (1978). Drug choice as an externalization strategy in response to noncontingent success. *J. Pers. soc. Psychol., 36,* 405–417.

Berne, E. (1961). *Transactional analysis in psychotherapy.* New York: Grove Press.

———— (1964). *Games people play.* New York: Grove Press.

Bialer, I. (1961). Conceptualization of success and failure in mentally retarded and normal children. *J. Pers., 29,* 303–320.

Bieri, J. (1955). Cognitive complexity-simplicity and predictive behavior. *J. abnorm. soc. Psychol., 51,* 263–268.

Bishop, D., and P. Witt (1970). Sources of behavioral variance during leisure time. *J. Pers. soc. Psychol., 16,* 352–360.

Blass, T., Ed. (1977). *Personality variables in social behavior.* Hillsdale, N.J.: Erlbaum.

Block, J. H. (1968). Some reasons for the apparent inconsistency of personality. *Psychol. Bull., 70,* 210–212.

———— (1971). *Lives through time.* Berkeley, Calif.: Bancroft Books.

———— (1977). Advancing the psychology of personality: paradigmatic shift or improving the quality of research. In D. Magnusson, and N. S. Endler (Eds.), *Personality at the crossroads: current issues in interactional psychology.* Hillsdale, N.J.: Erlbaum.

Block, J., and J. Block (1951). An investigation of the relationship between intolerance of ambiguity and ethnocentrism. *J. Pers., 19,* 303–311.

———— (1980). The role of ego-control and ego-resiliency in the organization of behavior. In W. A. Collins (Ed.), *Minnesota symposium on child psychology.* Hillsdale, N.J.: Erlbaum.

Bogart, K., F. L. Geis, N. Levy, and P. Zimbardo (1970). No dissonance for Machiavellians. In R. Christie, and F. L. Geis (Eds.), *Studies in Machiavellianism.* New York: Academic Press.

Bond, M. H. (1972). Effect of an impression set on subsequent behavior. *J. Pers. soc. Psychol., 24,* 301–305.

Bowers, K. S. (1973). Situationism in psychology: an analysis and critique. *Psychol. Rev., 80,* 307–336.

———— (1977). There's more to Iago than meets the eye: a clinical account of personal consistency. In D. Magnusson and N. S. Endler (Eds.), *Personality at the crossroads: current issues in interactional psychology.* Hillsdale, N.J.: Erlbaum.

Braginski, D. D. (1966). *Machiavellianism and manipulative interpersonal behavior in children: two explorative studies.* Unpublished doctoral dissertation. Univ. of Connecticut.

Bramel, D. (1962). A dissonance theory approach to defensive projection. *J. abnorm. soc. Psychol., 64,* 121–129.

Brock, T. C., and J. L. Balloun (1967). Behavioral receptivity to dissonant information. *J. Pers. soc. Psychol., 6,* 413–428.

Brockner, J. (1979). Self-esteem, self-consciousness, and task performance: replications, extensions, and possible explanations. *J. Pers. soc. Psychol., 37,* 447–461.

Brockner, J., and A. J. B. Hulton (1978). How to reverse the vicious cycle of low self-esteem: the importance of attentional focus. *J. exp. soc. Psychol., 14,* 564–578.

Brown, J. C., and B. R. Strickland (1972). Belief in internal-external control of reinforcement and reaction to frustration. *J. Pers. soc. Psychol., 25,* 35–44.

Broxton, J. A. (1963). A test of interpersonal attraction predictions derived from balance theory. *J. abnorm. soc. Psychol., 66,* 394–397.

Bryant, B., and P. Trower (1974). Social difficulty in a student sample. *Brit. J. educ. Psychol., 44,* 13–21.

Buckhout, R. (1965). Need for social approval and attitude change. *J. Psychol., 60,* 123–128.

Buss, A. H. (1980). *Self-consciousness.* San Francisco: Freeman.

Buss, A. H. and R. Plomin (1975). *A temperament theory of personality development.* New York: Wiley-Interscience.

Buss, D. M., and K. H. Craik (1980). The frequency concept of disposition: dominance and protypically dominant acts. *J. Pers., 48,* 379–392.

———— (1981). The act frequency analysis of personal dispositions: aloofness, gregariousness, dominance and submissiveness. *J. Pers., 49,* 175–192.

Buss, D. M., and M. F. Scheier (1976). Self-consciousness, self-awareness, and self-attribution. *J. Res. Pers., 10,* 463–468.

Byrne, D. (1964). Repression-sensitization as a dimension of personality. In B. A. Maher (Ed.), *Progress in experimental personality research.* Vol. 1. New York: Academic Press.

Cacioppo, J. T., and R. E. Petty (1982). The need for cognition. *J. Pers. soc. Psychol., 42,* 116–131.

Caldwell, D. F., and C. A. O'Reilly (1982). Responses to failure: the effects of choice and responsibility on impression management. *Acad. Managmnt. J., 25,* 121–136.

Campbell, D. T., and B. R. McCandless (1951). Ethnocentrism, xenophobia, and personality. *Hum. Relat., 4,* 185–192.

Campbell, D. T., and J. C. Stanley (1963). *Experimental and quasi-experimental designs for research.* Chicago: Rand McNally.

Cantor, N., and J. F. Kihlstrom (1981). Cognitive and social processes in personality: implications for behavior therapy. In C. M. Franks, and G. T. Wilson (Eds.), *Handbook of behavior therapy.* New York: Guilford Press.

Carson, R. C. (1969). *Interaction concepts of personality.* Chicago: Aldine.

Carver, C. S. (1975). Physical aggression as a function of objective self-awareness and attitudes toward punishment. *J. exp. soc. Psychol., 11,* 510–519.

_____ (1979). A cybernetic model of self-attention processes. *J. Pers. soc. Psychol., 37,* 1251–1281.

Carver, C. S., P. H. Blaney, and M. F. Scheier (1979a). Focus of attention, chronic expectancy, and responses to a feared stimulus. *J. Pers. soc. Psychol., 37,* 1186–1195.

_____ (1979b). Reassertion and giving up: the interactive role of self-directed attention and outcome expectancy. *J. Pers. soc. Psychol., 37,* 1859–1870.

Carver, C. S., and D. C. Glass (1976). The self-consciousness scale: a discriminant validity study. *J. Pers. Assessment, 40,* 169–172.

Carver, C. S., and M. F. Scheier (1978). Self-focusing effects of dispositional self-consciousness, mirror presence, and audience presence. *J. Pers. soc. Psychol., 36,* 324–332.

_____ (1981). *Attention and self-regulation: a control-theory approach to human behavior.* New York: Springer-Verlag.

Cervantes Saavedra, M. de. (1957). *Don Quixote de la Mancha.* New York: Pocket Books.

Chapko, M., and M. Lewis (1975). Authoritarianism and "All in the family." *J. Psychol., 90,* 245–248.

Charters, W., Jr., and T. Newcomb (1958). Some attitudinal effects of experimentally increased salience of a membership group. In E. Maccoby, T. Newcomb, and E. Hartley (Eds.), *Readings in social psychology.* New York: Holt.

Cheek, J. M. (1982). Aggregation, moderator variables, and the validity of personality tests: a peer-rating study. *J. Pers. soc. Psychol., 43,* 1254–1269.

Christie, R. (1978). Reconsideration: the authoritarian personality. *Hum. Nature.*

Christie, R., and P. Cook (1958). A guide to published literature relating to the authoritarian personality through 1956. *J. Psychol., 45,* 171–199.

Christie, R., and F. L. Geis (1970). *Studies in Machiavellianism.* New York: Academic Press.

Christie, R., J. Havel, and B. Seidenberg (1958). Is the F scale irreversible? *J. abnorm. soc. Psychol., 56,* 143–159.

Christie, R., and M. Jahoda, Eds. (1954). *Studies in the scope and method of "The authoritarian personality."* New York: Free Press.

Comte, A. (1875). *The positive polity.* Vol. 2. 1852. Translation, London: Longmans, Green.

Conn, L. D., and D. P. Crowne (1964). Instigation to aggression, emotional arousal, and defensive emulation. *J. Pers., 32,* 163–179.

Conolley, E. S., H. B. Gerard, and T. Kline (1978). Competitive behavior: a manifestation of motivation for ability comparison. *J. exp. soc. Psychol., 14,* 123–131.

Cook, T. D., and D. T. Campbell (1976). The design and conduct of quasi-experiments and true experiments in field settings. In M. M. Dunnette (Ed.), *Handbook of industrial and organizational research.* Chicago: Rand McNally.

Couch, A., and K. Keniston (1960). Yeasayers and naysayers: agreeing response set as a personality variable. *J. abnorm. soc. Psychol., 60,* 151–174.

Coyne, J. C. (1976a). Toward an interactional description of depression. *Psychiatry, 39,* 28–40.

_____ (1976b). Depression and the response of others. *J. abnorm. Psychol., 85,* 186–193.

Crary, W. G. (1966). Reactions to incongruent self-experience. *J. consult. Psychol., 30,* 246–252.

Crockett, W. H. (1965). Cognitive complexity and impression formation. In B. A. Maher (Ed.), *Progress in experimental personality research.* Vol. 2. New York: Academic Press.

Cronbach, L. J. (1957). The two disciplines of scientific psychology. *Amer. Psychologist, 12,* 671–684.

Crowne, D. P., and D. Marlowe (1960). A new scale of social desirability independent of psychopathology. *J. consult. Psychol., 24,* 349–354.

_____ (1964). *The approval motive.* New York: Wiley.

Crowne, D. P., and B. R. Strickland (1961). The conditioning of verbal behavior as a function of the need for social approval. *J. abnorm soc. Psychol., 63,* 395–401.

Danheiser, P. R., and W. G. Graziano (1982). Self-monitoring and cooperation as a self-presentational strategy. *J. Pers. soc. Psychol. 42,* 497–505.

Davis, J. A. (1965). *Undergraduate career decisions: correlates of occupational choice.* Chicago: Aldine.

Davis, M. S., and C. J. Schmidt (1977). The obnoxious and the nice. *Sociometry, 40,* 201–213.

Davis, W. L., and E. J. Phares (1969). Parental antecedents of internal-external control of reinforcement. *Psychol. Reports, 24,* 427–436.

Deaux, K. (1978). Sex-related patterns of social interaction. Invited paper presented at the meeting of the Midwestern Psychological Association.

Deaux, K., L. White, and E. Farris (1975). Skill versus luck: field and laboratory studies of male and female preferences. *J. Pers. soc. Psychol., 32,* 629–636.

Deutsch, M., and L. Solomon (1959). Reactions to evaluations by others as influenced by self-evaluations. *Sociometry, 22,* 93–111.

Diener, E. (1980). Deindividuation: the absence of self-awareness and self-regulation in group members. In P. Paulus (Ed.), *The psychology of group influence.* Hillsdale, N.J.: Erlbaum.

Diener, E., and T. K. Srull (1979). Self-awareness, psychological perspective, and self-reinforcement in relation to personal and social standards. *J. Pers. soc. Psychol., 37,* 413–423.

Diener, E., and M. Wallborn (1976). Effects of self-awareness on antinormative behavior. *J. Res. Pers., 10,* 107–111.

Dillehay, R. C. (1978). Authoritarianism. In H. London, and J. Exner (Eds.), *Dimensions of personality.* New York: Wiley.

Dishman, R. K., W. Ickes, and W. P. Morgan (1980). Self-motivation and adherence to habitual physical activity. *J. appl. soc. Psychol., 10,* 115–132.

Dixon, T. (1970). Experimenter approval, social desirability, and statements of self-reference. *J. Consult. clinic. Psychol., 35,* 400–405.

Duncan, S., Jr., and D. W. Fiske (1977). *Face-to-face interaction: research, methods, and theory.* Hillsdale, N.J.: Erlbaum.

Durkin, J. E. (1970). Encountering: what low Machs do. In R. Christie, and F. L. Geis, *Studies in Machiavellianism.* New York: Academic Press.

Dutton, D. G., and R. A. Lake (1973). Threat of our prejudice and reverse discrimination in interracial situations. *J. Pers. soc. Psychol., 28,* 94–100.

Duval, S. (1976). Conformity on a visual task as a function of personal novelty on attitudinal dimensions and being reminded of the object status of self. *J. exp. soc. Psychol., 12,* 87–98.

Duval, S., and R. A. Wicklund (1972). *A theory of objective self-awareness.* New York: Academic Press.

————(1973). Effects of objective self-awareness on attribution of causality. *J. exp. soc. Psychol., 9,* 17–31.

Duyvendak, J. J. L. (1928). *Kung-San Yang: the book of Lord Shang.* Translation. Chicago: Univ. of Chicago Press.

Eddy, G. L., and R. E. Sinnett (1973). Behavior settings utilization by emotionally disturbed college students. *J. Consult. clinic. Psychol., 40,* 210–216.

Edwards, A. L. (1957). *The social desirability variable in personality research.* New York: Dryden.

Elms, A. C., and S. Milgram (1966). Personality characteristics associated with obedience and defiance toward authoritative command. *J. exp. Res. Pers., 2,* 282–289.

Endler, N. S. (1973). The person versus the situation—a pseudo issue? *J. Pers., 41,* 287–343.

———— (1976). The role of person by situation interactions in personality theory. In F. Weizmann, and I. C. Uzgiris (Eds.), *The structuring of experience.* New York: Plenum.

———— (1982). Interactionism comes of age. In M. P. Zanna, E. T. Higgins, and C. P. Herman (Eds.), *Consistency in social behavior: the Ontario symposium.* Vol. 2. Hillsdale, N.J.: Erlbaum.

Endler, N. S., and D. Magnusson (1976). *International psychology and personality.* Washington, D.C.: Hemisphere.

Epstein, G. F. (1969). Machiavelli and the devil's advocate. *J. Pers. soc. Psychol., 11,* 38–41.

Epstein, S. (1973). The self-concept revisited, or a theory of a theory. *Amer. Psychologist, 28,* 404–416.

———— (1977). Traits are alive and well. In D. Magnusson, and N. S. Endler (Eds.), *Personality at the crossroads: current issues in interactional psychology.* Hillsdale, N.J.: Erlbaum.

———— (1979). The stability of behavior: I. On predicting most of the people much of the time. *J. Pers. soc. Psychol., 37,* 1097–1126.

———— (1980). The stability of behavior: II. Implications for psychological research. *Amer. Psychologist, 35,* 790–806.

Exline, R. V., J. Thibant, C. B. Hickey, and P. Gumpert (1970). Visual interaction in relation to machiavellianism and an unethical act. In R. Christie, and F. L. Geis, *Studies in Machiavellianism.* New York: Academic Press.

Eysenck, H. (1975). *Eysenck personality questionnaire manual.* Buckhurst Hill: Hodder and Stoughton.

Eysenck, H. J., and S. B. G. Eysenck (1968). *Manual for the Eysenck personality inventory.* San Diego: Educational and Industrial Testing Service.

Federoff, N. A., and J. H. Harvey (1976). Focus of attention, self-esteem, and attribution of causality. *J. Res. Pers., 10,* 336–345.

Feiler, J. (1967). Machiavellianism, dissonance and attitude change. Unpublished manuscript. New York University.

Felton, G. S. (1971). The experimenter expectancy effect examined as a function of task ambiguity and internal-external control. *J. exp. Res. Pers., 5,* 286–294.

Fenigstein, A., M. F. Scheier, and A. H. Buss (1975). Public and private self-consciousness: assessment and theory. *J. Consult. clinic Psychol., 43,* 522–527.

Festinger, L. (1954). A theory of social comparison processes. *Hum. Relat., 7,* 117–140.

Fishbein, M., and I. Ajzen (1974). Attitudes toward objects as predictors of single and multiple behavioral criteria. *Psychol. Rev., 81,* 59–74.

Fishman, C. G. (1965). Need for approval and the expression of aggression under varying conditions of frustration. *J. Pers. soc. Psychol., 2,* 805–816.

Fiske, D. W. (1974). The limits for the conventional science of personality. *J. Pers., 42,* 1–11.

Foa, U. G. (1961). Convergences in the analysis of the structure of interpersonal behavior. *Psychol. Rev., 68,* 341–353.

Forgas, J. P. (1979). *Social episodes: the study of interaction routines.* London: Academic Press.

Freedman, J. L., and A. N. Doob (1968). *Deviancy: the psychology of being different.* New York: Academic Press.

Frenkel-Brunswik, E. (1949). Intolerance of ambiguity as an emotional and perceptual personality variable. *J. Pers., 18,* 108–143.

———— (1954). Further explorations by a contributor to "The authoritarian personality." In R. Christie, and M. Jahoda (Eds.), *Studies in the scope and method of "The authoritarian personality."* New York: Free Press.

Frenkel-Brunswik, E., and J. Havel (1953). Prejudice in the interviews of children: I. Attitudes toward minority groups. *J. genetic Psychol., 82,* 91–136.

Freud, S. (1928). *The basic writings of Sigmund Freud.* (A. A. Brill Editor and translator.) New York: Random House.

Friedman, H. S., L. M. Prince, R. E. Riggio, and M. R. DiMatteo (1980). Understanding and assessing nonverbal expressiveness: the affective communication test. *J. Pers. soc. Psychol., 39,* 333–351.

Froming, W. J., K. Lopyan, and G. R. Walker (1981). *Self-awareness, individual differences, and adherence to public and private standards for behavior.* Unpublished manuscript.

Funder, D. C. (1980). The trait of ascribing traits: individual differences in personality trait ascriptions. *J. Res. Pers., 14,* 376–385.

———— (1982). On assessing social psychological theories through the study of individual differences: template matching and forced compliance. *J. Pers. soc. Psychol., 43,* 100–110.

Furnham, A. (1981). Personality and activity preference. *Brit. J. soc. clinic. Psychol., 20,* 57–68.

Geis, F. L. (1964). *Machiavellianism and success in a three-person game.* Unpublished doctoral dissertation. Columbia University.

_____ (1968). Machiavellianism in a semireal world. *Proceedings of the 76th annual convention of the American Psychological Association, 3,* 407–408.

_____ (1970). Bargaining tactics in the con game. In R. Christie, and F. L. Geis, *Studies in Machiavellianism.* New York: Academic Press.

_____ (1978). Machiavellianism. In H. London, and J. Exner (Eds.), *Dimensions of personality.* New York: Wiley.

Geis, F. L., R. Christie, and C. Nelson (1970). In search of the Machiavel. In R. Christie, and F. L. Geis, *Studies in Machiavellianism.* New York: Academic Press.

Geis, F. L., E. Krupat, and D. Berger (1965). Taking over in group discussion. Unpublished manuscript. New York University.

Geis, F. L., and T. H. Moon (1981). Machiavellianism and deception. *J. Pers. soc. Psychol., 41,* 766–775.

Geis, F. L., S. Weinheimer, and D. Berger (1970). Playing legislature: cool heads and hot issues. In R. Christie, and F. L. Geis, *Studies in Machiavellianism.* New York: Academic Press.

Gergen, K. J. (1971). *The concept of self.* New York: Holt, Rinehart, and Winston.

Gibbons, F. X. (1978). Sexual standards and reactions to pornography: enhancing behavioral consistency through self-focused attention. *J. Pers. soc. Psychol., 36,* 976–987.

Gibbons, F. X., C. S. Carver, M. F. Scheier, and S. Hormuth (1979). Self-focused attention and the placebo effect: fooling some of the people some of the time. *J. exp. soc. Psychol., 15,* 263–274.

Goffman, E. (1959). *The presentation of self in everyday life.* Garden City, N.Y.: Doubleday-Anchor.

_____ (1961). *Asylums: essays on the social situation of mental patients and other inmates.* New York: Anchor.

_____ (1963). *Stigma: notes on the management of spoiled identity.* Englewood Cliffs, N.J.: Prentice-Hall.

Goodenough, D. R. (1978). Field dependence. In H. London, and J. Exner (Eds.), *Dimensions of personality.* New York: Wiley.

Granberg, D. (1972). Authoritarianism and the assumption of similarity to self. *J. exp. Res. Pers., 6,* 1–4.

Grooms, R. R., and N. S. Endler (1960). The effect of anxiety on academic achievement. *J. educ. Psychol., 51,* 299–309.

Gruen, G. E., and D. R. Ottinger (1969). Skill and chance orientations as determiners of problem-solving behavior in lower- and middle-class children. *Psychol. Reports, 24,* 207–214.

Gurin, P., G. Gurin, R. C. Lao, and M. Beattie (1969). Internal-external control in the motivational dynamics of Negro youth. *J. soc. Issues, 25,* 29–53.

Hakmiller, K. (1966).Need for self-evaluation, perceived similarity and comparison choice. *J. exp. soc. Psychol., 1,* 49–54.

Hartshorne, H., and M. A. May (1928–30). *Studies in the nature of character.* Vol. 1. *Studies in deceit.* New York: MacMillan.

Harvey, J. H., G. Wells, and M. Alvarez (1978). Attribution in the context of conflict and separation in close relationships. In J. H. Harvey, W. Ickes, and R. F. Kidd (Eds.), *New directions in attribution research.* Vol. 2. Hillsdale, N.J.: Erlbaum.

Harvey, O. J., H. H. Kelley, and M. M. Shapiro (1957). Reactions to unfavorable evaluations of the self made by other persons. *J. Pers., 25,* 398–411.

Harvey, O. J. (1962). Personality factors on resolution of conceptual incongruities. *Sociometry, 25,* 336–352.

Higgins, J. (1965). Authoritarianism and candidate preference. *Psychol. Reports, 16,* 603–604.

Hilgard, E. R. (1973). The domain of hypnosis: with some comments on alternative paradigms. *Amer. Psychologist, 28,* 972–982.

Hoe, B. H. (1962). Occupational satisfaction as a function of self-role congruency. Unpublished master's thesis. University of Nevada, Reno.

Hogan, R. (1969). Development of an empathy scale. *J. Consult. clinic. Psychol., 33,* 307–316.

Hogan, R., and J. M. Cheek (in press). Identity, authenticity, and maturity. In T. R. Sarbin and K. E. Scheibe (Eds.), *Studies in social identity.* New York: Praeger.

Holland, J. L. (1976). Vocational preferences. In M. D. Dunnette (Ed.), *Handbook of industrial and organizational psychology.* Chicago: Rand McNally.

Horton, D. L., D. Marlowe, and D. P. Crowne (1963). The effect of instructional set and need for social approval on commonality of word association responses. *J. abnorm. soc. Psychol., 66,* 67–72.

Hoyt, M. F., and B. H. Raven (1973). Birth order and the 1971 Los Angeles earthquake. *J. Pers. soc. Psychol., 28,* 123–128.

Hull, J. G., and A. S. Levy (1979). The organizational functions of the self: an alternative to the Duval and Wicklund model of self-awareness. *J. Pers. soc. Psychol., 37,* 756–768.

Hyman, H. H., and P. B. Sheatsley (1954). "The authoritarian personality"—A methodological critique. In R. Christie, and M. Jahoda (Eds.), *Studies in the scope and method of "The authoritarian personality."* New York: Free Press. Pp. 50–122.

Ickes, W. (1978a). *The enactment of social roles in unstructured dyadic interaction.* Invited paper presented at the annual convention of the Midwestern Psychological Association, Chicago.

_____ (1978b). *The sound of one hand clapping: Isolating the influence of the individual personality in dyadic interaction.* Paper presented as part of the Symposium on the Self, annual meeting of the Society of Experimental Social Psychology, Princeton, N.J.

_____ (1981). Sex role influences in dyadic interaction: a theoretical model. In C. Mayo, and N. Henley (Eds.), *Gender and nonverbal behavior.* New York: Springer-Verlag.

_____ (1982). A basic paradigm for the study of personality, roles and social behavior. In W. Ickes and E. S. Knowles (Eds.), *Personality, roles and social behavior.* New York: Springer-Verlag.

_____ (in press a). Personality. In A. S. Bellack and M. Hersen (Eds.), *Research methods in clinical psychology.* New York: Pergamon.

_____ (In press b). Sex-role influences on compatibility in relationships. In W. Ickes (Ed.), *Compatible and incompatible relationships.* New York: Springer-Verlag.

_____ (in press c). Compositions in black and white: Determinants of interaction in interracial dyads. *J. Pers. soc. Psychol.*

Ickes, W., and R. D. Barnes (1977). The role of sex and self-monitoring in unstructured dyadic interactions. *J. Pers. soc. Psychol., 35,* 315–330.

———— (1978). Boys and girls together—and alienated: on enacting stereotyped sex roles in mixed-sex dyads. *J. Pers. soc. Psychol., 36,* 669–683.

Ickes, W., and M. A. Layden (1978). Attributional styles. In J. Harvey, W. Ickes, and R. Kidd (Eds.), *New directions in attribution research.* Vol. 2. Hillsdale, N.J.: Erlbaum.

Ickes, W., M. A. Layden, and R. D. Barnes (1978). Objective self-awareness and individuation: an empirical link. *J. Pers., 46,* 146–161.

Ickes, W., M. L. Patterson, D. W. Rajecki, and S. Tanford (1982). Behavioral and cognitive consequences of reciprocal versus compensatory responses to pre-interaction expectancies. *Social Cognition, 1,* 160–190.

Ickes, W., and E. Robertson (in press). A new paradigm for the study of personality. In O. Neumaier (Ed.), *Mind, language, and society.* Salzburg, Austria: Univ. of Salzburg Press.

Ickes, W., B. Schermer, and J. Steeno (1979). Sex and sex-role influences in same-sex dyads. *Soc. Psychol. Quart., 42,* 373–385.

Ickes, W., and M. Turner (1983). On the social advantages of having an older, opposite-sex sibling: birth order influences in mixed-sex dyads. *J. Pers. soc. Psychol., 45,* 210–222.

Ickes, W., R. A. Wicklund, and C. B. Ferris (1973). Objective self-awareness and self esteem. *J. exp. soc. Psychol., 9,* 202–219.

Izzett, R. (1971). Authoritarianism and attitudes toward the Vietnam War as reflected in behavioral and self-report measures. *J. Pers. soc. Psychol., 17,* 145–148.

Jaccard, J. J. (1974). Predicting social behavior from personality traits. *J. Res. Pers., 7,* 358–367.

———— (1977). Personality and behavioral prediction: an analysis of behavioral criterion measures. In L. Kahle, and D. Fiske (Eds.), *Methods for studying person-situation interactions.* San Francisco: Jossey-Bass.

Jellison, J. M., and W. Ickes (1974). The power of the glance: desire to see and be seen in cooperative and competitive situations. *J. exp. soc. Psychol., 10,* 444–450.

Jones, E. E. (1954). Authoritarianism as a determinant of first-impression formation. *J. Pers., 23,* 107–127.

———— (1964). *Ingratiation.* New York: Appleton-Century-Crofts.

Jones, E. E., and S. Berglas (1978). Control of attributions about the self through self-handicapping strategies: the appeal of alcohol and the role of underachievement. *Pers. soc. Psychol. Bull., 4,* 200–206.

Jones, E. E., and R. E. Nisbett (1971). *The actor and the observer: divergent perceptions of the causes of behavior.* Morristown, N.J.: General Learning Press.

Jones, E. E., and T. S. Pittman (1982). Toward a general theory of strategic self-presentation. In J. Suls (Ed.), *Psychological perspectives on the self.* Vol. 1. Hillsdale, N.J.: Erlbaum.

Jones, S. C. (1974). The psychology of interpersonal attraction. In C. Nemeth (Ed.), *Social psychology: classic and contemporary integrations.* Chicago: Rand McNally.

Jones, S. C., and D. Panitch (1971). The self-fulfilling prophecy and interpersonal attraction. *J. exp. soc. Psychol., 7,* 356–366.

Kahle, L. R. (1980). Stimulus condition self-selection by males in the interaction of locus of control and skill-chance situations. *J. pers. soc. Psychol., 38,* 50–56.

Kahle, L. R., and J. J. Berman (1979). Attitudes cause behaviors: a cross-lagged panel analysis. *J. Pers. soc. Psychol., 37,* 315–321.

Kassarjian, W. M. (1962). A study of Riesman's theory of social character. *Sociometry, 25,* 213–230.

Kelley, H. H., and A. J. Stahelski (1970). The social interaction basis of cooperators' and competitors' beliefs about others. *J. Pers. soc. Psychol., 16,* 66–91.

Kelly, G. A. (1955). *The psychology of personal constructs.* New York: Norton.

Kenny, D. A. (1981). Interpersonal perception: a multivariate round robin analysis. In M. B. Brewer, and B. E. Collins (Eds.), *Knowing and validating the social sciences: a tribute to Donald T. Campbell.* San Francisco: Jossey-Bass.

Kenny, D. A., and L. LaVoie (in press). The social relations model.

Kenny, D. A., and W. Nasby (1980). Splitting the reciprocity correlation. *J. Pers. soc. Psychol., 38,* 249–256.

Kenrick, D. T., and D. O. Stringfield (1980). Personality traits and the eye of the beholder: crossing some traditional philosophical boundaries in the search for consistency in all of the people. *Psychol. Rev., 87,* 88–104.

Kiesler, C. A. (1971). *The psychology of commitment: experiments linking behavior to belief.* New York: Academic Press.

Kiesler, C. A., R. E. Nisbett, and M. Zanna (1969). On inferring one's beliefs from one's behavior. *J. Pers. soc. Psychol., 11,* 321–327.

Kiesler, C. A., T. Roth, and M. S. Pallak (1974). The avoidance and reinterpretation of commitment and its implications. *J. Pers. soc. Psychol., 30,* 705–715.

Kirscht, J. P., and R. C. Dillehay (1967). *Dimensions of authoritarianism: a review of research and theory.* Lexington: Univ. of Kentucky Press.

Knudson, R. M., A. A. Summers, and S. L. Golding (1980). Interpersonal perception and mode of resolution in marital conflict. *J. Pers. soc. Psychol., 38,* 751–763.

Kogan, N., and M. A. Wallach (1964). *Risk-taking: a study in cognition and personality.* New York: Holt.

Korman, A. K. (1968). Task success, task popularity, and self-esteem as influences on task liking. *J. appl. Psychol. 52,* 484–490.

Kretschmer, E. (1926). *Physique and character: an investigation of the nature of constitution and of the theory of temperament.* Translated by W. J. H. Sprott. New York: Harcourt.

Kuhl, J. (1981). Action- vs. state-orientation as a mediator between motivation and action. In W. Hacker, W. Volpert, and M. von Cranach (Eds.), *Cognitive and motivational aspects of action.* Amsterdam: North Holland Publishing.

LaFrance, M., and W. Ickes (1981). Posture mirroring and interactional involvement: sex and sex-typing effects. *J. Nonverbal Behav., 5,* 139–154.

Laing, R. D. (1960). *The divided self.* New York: Pantheon.

———— (1961). *Self and others.* New York: Pantheon.

_____ (1969). *The politics of the family and other essays*. New York: Vintage Books.

Laing, R. D., H. Phillipson, and A. R. Lee (1966). *Interpersonal perception: a theory and a method of research*. New York: Harper & Row.

Lamke, L., and N. Bell (1982). *The influence of sex role orientation on initial interactions within same-sex dyads*. Unpublished manuscript.

Langer, E. (1978). Rethinking the role of thought in social interaction. In J. H. Harvey, W. J. Ickes, and R. F. Kidd (Eds.), *New directions in attribution research*. Vol. 2. Hillsdale, N.J.: Erlbaum.

Lao, R. C. (1970). Internal-external control and competent and innovative behavior among Negro college students. *J. Pers. soc. Psychol., 14,* 263–270.

Leary, T. (1957). *Interpersonal diagnosis of personality*. New York: Ronald.

Lefcourt, H. M. (1967). Effects of cue explication upon persons maintaining external control expectancies. *J. Pers. soc. Psychol., 5,* 372–378.

_____ (1972). Recent developments in the study of locus of control. In B. A. Maher (Ed.), *Progress in experimental personality research*. Vol. 6. New York: Academic Press.

_____ (1976). *Locus of control: Current trends in theory and research*. Hillsdale, N.J.: Erlbaum.

Lessing, E. E. (1969). Racial differences in indices of ego functioning relevant to academic achievement. *J. Genetic Psychol., 115,* 153–167.

Levenson, H. (1973). Perceived parental antecedents of internal, powerful others, and chance locus of control orientations. *Develop. Psychol., 9,* 268–274.

Leventhal, H., R. L. Jacobs, and N. Z. Kudirka (1964). Authoritarianism, ideology, and political candidate choice. *J. abnorm. soc. Psychol., 69,* 539–549.

Levinson, D. J., and P. E. Huffman (1955). Traditional family ideology and its relation to personality. *J. Pers., 23,* 251–273.

Lewin, K. (1936). *A dynamic theory of personaltiy*. New York: McGraw-Hill.

Lippa, R. (1976). Expressive control and the leakage of dispositional introversion—extraversion during role-played teaching. *J. Pers., 44,* 541–559.

_____ (1978a). Expressive control, expensive consistency, and the correspondence between expressive behavior and personality. *J. Pers., 46,* 438–461.

_____ (1978b). *Self-presentation and the expressive display of personality*. Paper presented at the meeting of the American Psychological Association, Toronto.

Lippa, R., and C. Beauvais (1980). Gender jeopardy: the effects of gender, assessed femininity and masculinity, and false success/failure feedback on performance in an experimental quiz game. Unpublished manuscript. California State University, Fullerton.

Lippa, R., and M. Mash (1979). *The effects of self-monitoring and self-reported consistency on the consistency of personality statements made by strangers and intimates*. Unpublished manuscript. California State University, Fullerton.

Lippa, R., E. Valdez, and A. Jolly (1979). *Self-monitoring and the consistency of masculinity-femininity cues*. Paper presented at the meetings of the American Psychological Association, New York City.

London, H., and J. Exner, Eds. (1978). *Dimensions of personality*. New York: Wiley.

Lutsky, N., P. K. Peake, and L. Wray (1978). *Inconsistencies in the search for cross-situational consistencies in behavior: a critique of the Bem and Allen study*. Paper presented at the Midwestern Psychological Association, Chicago.

Lutsky, N., W. Woodworth, and S. Clayton (1980). *Actions-attitudes-actions: a multivariate, longitudinal study of attitude-behavior consistency*. Paper presented at Midwestern Psychological Association, St. Louis, Missouri.

McCall, G. J., and J. T. Simmons (1978). *Identities and interactions* (2nd ed.). New York: Free Press.

McClelland, D. C. (1975). *Power: the inner experience*. New York: Irvington Publishers.

McClelland, D. C., J. W. Atkinson, R. A. Clark, and E. L. Lowell (1953). *The achievement motive*. New York: Appleton-Century-Crofts.

MacDonald, A. P., Jr. (1971). Internal-external locus of control: parental antecedents. *J. Consult. clinic. Psychol., 37,* 141–147.

_____ (1970). Internal-external locus of control and the practice of birth control. *Psychol. Reports, 27,* 206.

McGowan, J., and J. Gormly (1976). Validation of personality traits: a multi-criteria approach. *J. Pers. soc. Psychol., 34,* 791–795.

Machiavelli, N. (1940). *The prince. The discourses*. New York: Modern Library.

Magnusson, D., and N. S. Endler, Eds. (1977). *Personality at the crossroads: current issues in interactional psychology*. Hillsdale, N.J.: Erlbaum.

Markus, H. (1977). Self-schemas and processing information about the self. *J. Pers. soc. Psychol., 35,* 63–78.

Markus, H., and J. Smith (1981). The influence of self-schemas on the perception of others. In N. Cantor, and J. F. Kilstrom (Eds.), *Personality, cognition, and social interaction*. Hillsdale, N.J.: Erlbaum.

Marlowe, D. (1962). Need for social approval and the operant conditioning of meaningful verbal behavior. *J. consult. Psychol., 26,* 79–83.

Marlowe, D., R. S. Beecher, J. B. Cook, and A. N. Doob (1964). *The approval motive, vicarious reinforcement and verbal conditioning*. Paper read at Eastern Psychological Association, Philadelphia, Penn.

Marlowe, D., and D. P. Crowne (1961). Social desirability and response to perceived situational demands. *J. consult. Psychol., 25,* 109–115.

Marlowe, D., L. Stifler, and M. Davis (1962). *Personality correlates of primary and secondary suggestibility*. Unpublished research. Dartmouth College.

Martin, J., and F. Westie (1959). The tolerant personality. *Amer. Sociological Rev., 24,* 521–528.

Mead, G. H. (1934). *Mind, self, and society*. Chicago: Univ. of Chicago Press.

Mehrabian, A. (1972). Nonverbal communication. In J. Cole (Ed.), *Nebraska symposium on motivation*. Vol. 19. Lincoln: Univ. of Nebraska Press.

_____ (1978). Characteristic individual reactions to preferred and unpreferred environments. *J. Pers., 46,* 717–731.

Mehrabian, A., and N. A. Epstein (1972). A measure of emotional empathy. *J. Pers., 40*, 525–543.

Mehrabian, A., and J. Russell (1974). A measure of arousal seeking tendency. *Environment Behav., 5*, 315–333.

Mendoza, J., and W. G. Graziano (1982). The statistical analysis of dyadic social behavior: a multivariate approach. *Psychol. Bull., 92*, 532–540.

Merenda, P. F., H. R. Musikev, and W. V. Clarke (1960). Relation of self-concept to success in sales management. *Engineering indust. Psychol., 2*, 69–77.

Merton, R. K. (1948). The self-fulfilling prophecy. *Antioch Rev., 8*, 193–210.

Mettee, D. R., and E. Aronson (1974). Affective reactions to appraisal from others. In T. L. Huston (Ed.), *Foundations of interpersonal attraction*. New York: Academic Press.

Midlarsky, E. (1971). Aiding under stress: the effects of competence, dependency, visibility, and fatalism. *J. Pers., 39*, 132–149.

Milburn, T. W., N. Bell, and G. F. Koeske (1970). Effect of censure or praise and evaluative dependence on performance in a free-learning task. *J. Pers. soc. Psychol., 15*, 43–47.

Milham, J., and L. Jacobson (1978). The need for approval. In H. London, and J. Exner (Eds.), *Dimensions of personality*. New York: Wiley.

Miller, N., A. N. Doob, D. C. Butler, and D. Marlowe (1965). The tendency to agree: situational determinants and social desirability. *J. exp. Res. Pers., 1*, 78–83.

Mills, C., and R. Hogan (1978). A role theoretical interpretation of personality scale item responses. *J. Pers., 46*, 778–785.

Milton, O. (1952). Presidential choice and performance on a scale of authoritarianism. *Amer. Psychologist, 7*, 597–598.

Mischel, W. (1968). *Personality and assessment*. New York: Wiley.

_____ (1973). Toward a cognitive social learning reconceptualization of personality. *Psychol. Rev., 80*, 252–283.

_____ (1977). The interaction of person and situation. In D. Magnusson, and N. S. Endler (Eds.), *Personality at the crossroads: current issues in interactional psychology*. Hillsdale, N.J.: Erlbaum.

Mischel, W., E. B. Ebbesen, and A. R. Zeiss (1973). Selective attention to the self: situational and dispositional determinants. *J. Pers. soc. Psychol., 27*, 129–142.

Mischel, W., and P. K. Peake (1981). *Beyond déjà vu in the search for cross-situational consistency*. Upublished manuscript. Stanford University.

_____ (1982). In search of consistency: measure for measure. In M. P. Zanna, E. T. Higgins, and C. P. Herman (Eds.), *Consistency in social behavior: the Ontario symposium*. Vol. 2. Hillsdale, N.J.: Erlbaum.

Miyamoto, F. S., and S. M Dornbusch (1956). A test of the interactionist hypothesis of self-conception. *Amer. J. Sociol., 61*, 399–403.

Monson, T. C. (1981). *The self-selection of persons to situations and its implications for the naive psychologist's belief in traits*. Paper presented at the Society of Southeastern Social Psychologists Convention.

Monson, T. C., J. W. Hesley, and L. Chernick (1981). Specifying when personality traits can and cannot predict behavior: an alternative to abandoning the attempt to predict single-act criteria. *J. Pers. soc. Psychol., 43*, 385–399.

Monson, T. C., R. McDaniel, L. Menteer, and C. Williams (1983). *The self-selection of persons to situations: its implications for the correlation between dispositions and behavior within a situation*. Unpublished manuscript. Univ. of Texas, Arlington.

Monson, T. C., and M. Snyder (1977). Actors, observers, and the attribution process: toward a reconceptualization. *J. exp. soc. Psychol., 13*, 89–111.

Moore, J. (1963). *A further test of the interactionist hypothesis of self-conception*. Paper presented at the annual meeting of the Pacific Sociological Association, Portland, Oregon.

Morse, S., and K. Gergen (1970). Social comparison, self-consistency and the concept of self. *J. Pers. soc. Psychol., 16*, 148–156.

Mortimer, J. T., and J. Lorence (1979). Work experience and occupational value socialization: a longitudinal study. *Amer. J. Sociol., 84*, 1361–1385.

Murray, H. A. (1938). *Explorations in personality: a clinical and experimental study of fifty men of college age*. Oxford: Oxford Univ. Press.

Nachamie, S. (1969). *Machiavellianism in children: the children's Mach scale and the bluffing game*. Unpublished doctoral dissertation. Columbia University.

Neisser, U. (1967). *Cognitive psychology*. New York: Appleton-Century-Crofts.

Nisan, M. (1972). Dimension of time in relation to choice behavior and achievement orientation. *J. Pers. soc. Psychol., 21*, 175–182.

Nisbett, R. E., and T. D. Wilson (1977). Telling more than we know: verbal reports on mental processes. *Psychol. Rev., 84*, 231–279.

Novielli, J. (1968). Who persuades whom. Unpublished master's thesis. University of Delaware.

Oksenberg, L. (1964). Machiavellianism and emotionality. Unpublished master's essay. Columbia University.

Olson, J. M., and M. P. Zanna (1979). A new look at selective exposure. *J. exp. soc. Psychol., 15*, 1–15.

Olweus, D. (1977). Aggression and peer acceptance in preadolescent boys. Two short-term longitudinal studies of ratings. *Child Development, 48*, 1301–1313.

Orvis, B. K., H. H. Kelley, and D. Butler (1976). Attributional conflict in young couples. In J. H. Harvey, W. Ickes, and R. F. Kidd (Eds.), *New directions in attribution research*. Vol. 1. Hillsdale, N.J.: Erlbaum.

Pedhazur, L., and L. Wheeler (1971). Locus of perceived control and need achievement. *Percept. motor Skills, 33*, 1281–1282.

Pervin, L. A. (1967a). A twenty year study of student x college interaction using TAPE (Transactional Analysis of Personality and Environment): Rationale, reliability, and validity. *J. educ. Psychol., 58*, 290–302.

_____ (1967b). Satisfaction and perceived self-environment similarity: a semantic differential study of college-student interactions. *J. Pers., 35*, 623–634.

_____ (1968). Performances and satisfaction as a function of individual environment fit. *Psychol. Bull., 69*, 56–68.

Pervin, E. A., and D. B. Rubin (1967). Student dissatisfaction with college and the college dropout: a transactional approach. *J. soc. Psychol., 72,* 285–295.

Peterson, D. R. (1965). Scope and generality of verbally defined personality factors. *Psychol. Rev., 72,* 48–89.

———— (1968). *The clinical study of social behavior.* New York: Appleton-Century-Crofts.

Phares, E. J. (1973). *Locus of control: a personality determinant of behavior.* Morristown, N.J.: General Learning Press.

———— (1976). *Locus of control in personality.* Morristown, N.J.: General Learning Press.

Poley, W. (1974). Dimensionality in the measurement of authoritarian and political attitudes. *Canad. J. behav. Sci., 6,* 83–94.

Price, R. H. (1974). The taxonomic classification of behaviors and situations and the problem of behavior-environment congruence. *Hum. Relat., 27,* 567–585.

Price, R. H., and D. L. Bouffard (1974). Behavioral appropriateness and situational constraint as dimensions of social behavior. *J. Pers. soc. Psychol., 30,* 579–586.

Pryor, J. B., F. X. Gibbons, R. A. Wicklund, R. Fazio, and R. Hood (1977). Self-focused attention and self-report validity. *J. Pers., 45,* 513–527.

Rajecki, D. W., W. Ickes, and S. Tanford (1981). Locus of control and reactions to a stranger. *Pers. soc. Psychol. Bull., 7,* 282–289.

Rarick, D. L., G. F. Soldow, and R. S. Geizer (1976). Self-monitoring as a mediator of conformity. *Central States Speech J., 27,* 267–271.

Rausch, H. L., W. A. Barry, R. K. Hertel, and M. A. Swain (1974). *Communication, conflict and marriage.* San Francisco: Jossey-Bass.

Reeder, L. G., G. A. Donahue, and A. Biblarz (1960). Conceptions of self and others. *Amer. J. Sociol., 66,* 153–159.

Reimanis, G. (1971). Effects of experimental IE modification techniques and home environmental variables on IE. Paper presented at the annual meeting of the American Psychological Association, Washington, D.C.

Reis, H. T., J. Nezlek, and L. Wheeler (1980). Physical attractiveness in social interaction. *J. Pers. soc. Psychol., 38,* 604–617.

Robinson, J. P., and P. R. Shaver, Eds. (1973). *Measures of social psychological attitudes.* Ann Arbor, Mich.: Institute for Social Research.

Rokeach, M. (1948). Generalized mental rigidity as a factor in ethnocentrism. *J. abnorm. soc. Psychol., 43,* 259–278.

———— (1960). *The open and closed mind.* New York: Basic Books.

Rosenberg, M. (1957). *Occupations and values.* Glencoe, Ill.: Free Press.

Rosenthal, R. (1966). *Experimenter effects in behavioral research.* New York: Appleton-Century-Crofts.

Rosenthal, R., and L. Jacobson (1968). *Pygmalion in the classroom.* New York: Holt, Rinehart, and Winston.

Rotter, J. B. (1966). Generalized expectancies for internal versus external control of reinforcement. *Psychol. Monogr., 80,* (whole No. 609).

Rule, B. G., A. R. Nesdale, and R. Dyck (1975). Objective self-awareness and differing standards of aggression. *Rep. Res. soc. Psychol., 6,* 82–88.

Rushton, J. P., D. N. Jackson, and S. V. Paunonen (1981). Personality: nomothetic or idiographic? A response to Kenrick and Stringfield. *Psychol. Rev., 88,* 582–589.

Salman, A. R. (1962). *The need for approval, improvisation, and attitude change.* Unpublished master thesis. Ohio State Univ.

Sarason, I. G., R. E. Smith, and E. Diener (1975). Personality research: components of variance attributable to the person and the situation. *J. Pers. soc. Psychol., 32,* 199–204.

Satow, K. L. (1973). The role of social approval in altruistic behavior. Paper presented at the meeting of the Eastern Psychological Association, Washington, D.C.

Schachter, S. (1959). *The psychology of affiliation.* Stanford: Stanford Univ. Press.

Schachter, S., and J. Rodin (1974). *Obese humans and rats.* Potomac, Md.: Erlbaum.

Schachter, S., and J. E. Singer (1962). Cognitive, social, and physiological determinants of emotional state. *Psychol. Rev., 69,* 379–399.

Schank, R., and R. P. Abelson (1977). *Scripts, plans, goals and understanding: an inquiry into human knowledge structures.* Hillsdale, N.J.: Erlbaum.

Scheier, M. F. (1976). Self-awareness, self-consciousness, and angry aggression. *J. Pers., 44,* 627–644.

Scheier, M. F., A. H. Buss, and D. M. Buss (1978). Self-consciousness, self-report of aggressiveness and aggression. *J. Res. Pers., 12,* 133–140.

Scheier, M. F., and C. S. Carver (1977). Self-focused attention and the experience of emotion: attraction, repulsion, elation, and depression. *J. Pers. soc. Psychol., 35,* 625–636.

Scheier, M. F., C. S. Carver, and F. X. Gibbons (1981). Self-focused attention and reactions to fear. *J. Res. Pers., 15,* 1–15.

Scheier, M. F., A. Fenigstein, and A. H. Buss (1974). Self-awareness and physical aggression. *J. exp. soc. Psychol., 10,* 264–273.

Schelling, T. C. (1960). *The strategy of conflict.* New York: Oxford Univ. Press.

Schneiderman, W., W. Webb, and B. Davis (1981). *Self-monitoring and states of awareness.* Unpublished manuscript. Marshall University.

Schwartz, S. H. (1973). Normative explanations of helping behavior: a critique, proposal, and empirical test. *J. exp. soc. Psychol., 9,* 349–364.

Scodel, A., and P. Mussen (1953). Social perceptions of authoritarians and nonauthoritarians. *J. abnorm. soc. Psychol., 48,* 181–184.

Secord, P. F., and C. W. Backman (1961). Personality theory and the problem of stability and change in individual behavior: an interpersonal approach. *Psychol. Rev., 68,* 21–32.

———— (1964). Interpersonal congruency, perceived similarity, and friendship. *Sociometry, 27,* 115–127.

———— (1965). An interpersonal approach to personality. In B. Maher (Ed.), *Progress in experimental personality research.* Vol. 2. New York: Academic Press. Pp. 91–125.

Secord, P. F., C. W. Backman, and H. T. Eachus (1964). Effects of imbalance in the self-concept on the perception of persons. *J. abnorm. soc. Psychol., 68,* 442–446.

Segal, B. (1973). Sensation-seeking and anxiety: assessment of response to specific stimulus situations. *J. Consult. clinic. Psychol., 41,* 135–138.

Shaffer, D. R., J. E. Smith, and M. Tomarelli (1982). Self-monitoring as a determinant of self-disclosure reciprocity during the acquaintance process. *J. Pers. soc. Psychol., 43,* 163–175.

Shamasastry, R., Translator (1909). Kantilya's *Arthasastra.* Mygore: Wesleyan Mission Press.

Shaver, P. (1976). *Self-awareness theory: problems and prospects.* Paper presented at a meeting of the New England Social Psychological Association, Dartmouth College.

Shaw, M. E. (1971). *Group dynamics: the psychology of small group behavior.* New York: McGraw-Hill.

_____ (1977). *Group dynamics: the psychology of small group behavior* (2nd ed.). New York: McGraw-Hill.

Sheldon, W. H. (1942). *The varieties of temperament: a psychology of constitutional differences.* New York: Harper.

Sherif, M. (1937). An experimental approach to the study of attitudes. *Sociometry, 1,* 90–98.

Shore, R. E. (1967). Parental determinants of boys' internal-external control. Unpublished doctoral dissertation. Syracuse University.

Shrauger, J. S., and T. J. Schoeneman (1979). Symbolic interactionist view of self-concept: through the looking glass darkly. *Psychol. Bull., 86,* 549–573.

Sillars, A. L. (1981). Attributions and interpersonal conflict resolution. In J. H. Harvey, W. Ickes, and R. F. Kidd (Eds.), *New directions in attribution research.* Vol. 3. Hillsdale, N.J.: Erlbaum.

Simons, H. W. (1966). Authoritarianism and social perceptiveness. *J. soc. Psychol., 68,* 291–297.

Skrypnek, B. J., and M. Snyder (1982). On the self-perpetuating nature of stereotypes about women and men. *J. exp. soc. Psychol., 18,* 277–291.

Smith-Lovin, L. (1979). Behavior settings and impressions formed from social senarios. *Soc. Psychol. Quart., 42,* 31–43.

Snyder, M. (1974). The self-monitoring of expressive behavior. *J. Pers. soc. Psychol., 30,* 526–537.

_____ (1976). Attribution and behavior: social perception and social causation. In J. H. Harvey, W. J. Ickes, and R. F. Kidd (Eds.), *New directions in attribution research.* Hillsdale, N.J.: Erlbaum.

_____ (1977). Impression management. In L. S. Wrightsman, *Social psychology in the seventies.* Monterey, Calif.: Brooks/Cole.

_____ . (1979a). Cognitive, behavioral, and interpersonal consequences of self-monitoring. In P. Pliner, K. R. Blankstein, and I. M. Spigel (Eds.), *Advances in the study of communication and affect.* Vol. 5. *Perception of emotion in self and others.* New York: Plenum.

_____ (1979b). Self-monitoring processes. In L. Berkowitz (Ed.), *Advances in experimental social psychology.* Vol. 12. New York: Academic Press.

_____ (1981a). Impression management: the self in social interaction. In L. S. Wrightsman, and K. Deaux. *Social psychology in the eighties.* Monterey, Calif.: Brooks/Cole.

_____ (1981b). On the influence of individuals on situations. In N. Cantor, and J. F. Kihlstrom (Eds.), *Personality, cognition, and social interaction.* Hillsdale, N.J.: Erlbaum.

_____ (1981c). On the self-perpetuating nature of social stereotypes. In D. L. Hamilton (Ed.), *Cognitive processes in stereotyping and intergroup behavior.* Hillsdale, N.J., Erlbaum.

Snyder, M. (1982). When believing means doing: creating links between attitudes and behavior. In M. P. Zanna, E. T. Higgins, and C. P. Herman (Eds.), *Consistency in social behavior: the Ontario symposium.* Vol. 2. Hillsdale, N.J.: Erlbaum.

Snyder, M. and B. H. Campbell (1982). Self-monitoring: the self in action. In J. Suls (Ed.), *Psychological perspectives on the self.* Vol. 1. Hillsdale, N.J.: Erlbaum.

Snyder, M., and N. Cantor (1979). Testing hypotheses about other people: the use of historical knowledge. *J. exp. soc. Psychol., 15,* 330–342.

_____ (1980).Thinking about ourselves and others: self-monitoring and social knowledge. *J. Pers. soc. Psychol., 39,* 222–234.

Snyder, M., and S. Gangestad (1982). Choosing social situations: two investigations of self-monitoring processes. *J. Pers. soc. Psychol., 43,* 123–135.

Snyder, M., and D. Kendzierski (1982a). Acting on one's attitudes: procedures for linking attitude and behavior. *J. exp. soc. Psychol. 18,* 165–183.

_____ (1982b). Choosing social situations: investigating the origins of correspondence between attitudes and behavior. *J. Pers., 50,* 280–295.

Snyder, M., and T. C. Monson (1975). Persons, situations, and the control of social behavior. *J. Pers. soc. Psychol., 32,* 637–644.

Snyder, M., and B. J. Skrypnek (1981). Testing hypotheses about the self: assessments of job suitability. *J. Pers., 49,* 193–211.

Snyder, M., and W. B. Swann, Jr. (1976). When actions reflect attitudes: the politics of impression management. *J. Pers. soc. Psychol., 34,* 1034–1042.

_____ (1978a). Behavioral confirmation in social interaction: from social perception to social reality. *J. exp. soc. Psychol., 14,* 148–162.

_____ (1978b). Hypothesis-testing processes in social interaction. *J. Pers. soc. Psychol., 36,* 1202–1212.

Snyder, M., and E. D. Tanke (1976). Behavior and attitude: some people are more consistent than others. *J. Pers., 44,* 510–517.

Snyder, M., E. D. Tanke, and E. Berscheid (1977). Social perception and interpersonal behavior: on the self-fulfilling nature of social stereotypes. *J. Pers. soc. Psychol., 35,* 656–666.

Snyder, M., and S. W. Uranowitz (1978). Reconstructing the past: some cognitive consequences of person perception. *J. exp. soc. Psychol., 36,* 941–950.

Snyder, M. L., R. E. Kleck, A. Strenta, and S. J. Mentzer (1979). Avoidance of the handicapped: an attributional ambiguity analysis. *J. Pers. soc. Psychol., 37,* 2297–2306.

Snyder, M. L., and R. A. Wicklund (1981). Attribute ambiguity. In J. H. Harvey, W. Ickes, and R. F. Kidd (Eds.), *New directions in attribution research.* Vol. 3. Hillsdale, N.J.: Erlbaum. Pp. 197–221.

Sosis, R. H. (1974). Internal-external control and the perception of responsibility of another for an accident. *J. Pers. soc. Psychol., 30,* 393–399.

Spence, J. T., and R. L. Helmreich (1978). *Masculinity and femininity: their psychological dimensions, correlates, and antecedents.* Austin: Univ. of Texas Press.

Steiner, I. D., and H. Johnson (1963). Authoritarianism and "tolerance of trait inconsistency." *J. abnorm. soc. Psychol., 67,* 388–391.

Stern, G. (1969). *People in context: the measurement of environmental interaction in school and society.* New York: Wiley.

Stern, G. C., and J. C. Scanlon (1958). Pediatric lions and gynecological lambs. *J. med. Educ., 33,* Part 2, 12–18.

Stern, G., M. Stein, and B. Bloom (1956). *Methods in personality assessment: human behavior in complex social settings.* New York: Free Press.

Strickland, B. R. (1962). *The relationship of awareness to verbal conditioning and extinction.* Unpublished doctoral dissertation. Ohio State University.

_____ (1965). The prediction of social action from a dimension of internal-external control. *J. soc. Psychol., 66,* 353–358.

_____ (1965). Need approval and motor steadiness under positive and negative approval conditions. *Percept. motor Skills, 20,* 667–668.

_____ (1970). Individual differences in verbal conditioning, extinction, and awareness. *J. Pers., 38,* 364–378.

_____ (1973). Delay of gratification and internal locus of control in children. *J. Consult. clinic. Psychol., 40,* 338.

Strickland, B. R., and D. P. Crowne (1962). Conformity under conditions of simulated group pressure as a function of the need for social approval. *J. soc. Psychol., 58,* 171–181.

_____ (1963). Need for approval and the premature termination of psychotherapy. *J. consult. Psychol., 27,* 95–101.

Strickland, B. R., and O. Jenkins (1964). Simple motor performance under positive and negative approval motivation. *Percept. motor Skills, 19,* 599–605.

Stryker, S. (1980). *Symbolic interactionism: a social structural version.* Menlo Park, Calif.: Benjamin/Cummings.

Sullivan, H. S. (1953). *The interpersonal theory of psychiatry.* New York: Norton.

_____ (1964). *The fusion of psychiatry and social science.* New York: Norton.

Swann, W. B., Jr. (1983). Self-verification: bringing social reality into harmony with the self. In J. Suls, and A. Greenwald (Eds.), *Psychological perspectives on the self.* Vol. 2. Hillsdale, N.J.: Erlbaum.

Swann, W. B., Jr., and C. A. Hill (1982). When our identities are mistaken: reaffirming self-conceptions through social interaction. *J. Pers. soc. Psychol., 43,* 59–66.

Swann, W. B. Jr., and S. J. Read (1981). Self-verification processes: how we sustain our self-conceptions. *J. exp. soc. Psychol., 17,* 351–372.

Swann, W., and M. Snyder (1980). On translating beliefs into action: theories of ability and their application in an instructional setting. *J. Pers. soc. Psychol., 38,* 656–666.

Taylor, S. E., and S. T. Fiske (1975). Point of view and perceptions of causality. *J. Pers. soc. Psychol., 32,* 439–445.

_____ (1978). Salience, attention, and attribution: top of the head phenomena. In L. Berkowitz (Ed.), *Advances in experimental social psychology.* Vol. 11. New York: Academic Press.

Tellegen, A., J. Kamp, and D. Watson (1982). Recognizing individual differences in predictive structure. *Psychol. Rev., 89,* 95–105.

Thaw, J., and J. S. Efran (1967). The relationship of need for approval to defensiveness and goal setting behavior: a partial replication. *J. Psychol., 65,* 41.

Tinsley, H., T. Barrett, and R. Kass (1977). Leisure activities and need satisfaction. *J. Leisure Res., 9,* 110–120.

Tiryakian, E. A. (1968). The existential self and the person. In C. Gordon, and K. J. Gergen (Eds.), *The self in social interaction.* Volume I. *Classic and contemporary perspectives.* New York: Wiley.

Titus, H. E., and E. P. Hollander (1957). The California F Scale in psychological research. *Psychol. Bull., 54,* 47–64.

Touhey, J. C. (1974). Situated identities, attitude similarity, and interpersonal attraction. *Sociometry, 37,* 363–374.

Tryon, R. C. (1973). Basic unpredictability of individual responses to discrete stimulus presentations. *Multivariate Behav. Res., 8,* 275–295.

Tseng, M. S. (1970). Locus of control as a determinant of job proficiency, employability, and training satisfaction of vocational rehabilitation clients. *J. counsel. Psychol., 17,* 487–491.

Tunnell, G. (1980). Intraindividual consistency in personality assessment: the effect of self-monitoring. *J. Pers., 48,* 220–232.

_____ (1981). Sex role and cognitive schemata: Person perception in feminine and androgynous women. *J. Pers. soc. Pscyhol., 40,* 1126–1136.

Turner, R. G. (1978a). Consistency, self-consciousness, and the predictive validity of typical and maximal personality measures. *J. Res. Pers., 12,* 117–132.

_____ (1978b). Effects of differential request procedures and self-consciousness in trait attributions. *J. Res. Pers., 12,* 431–438.

Turner, R. G., and L. Gilliland (1979). The comparative relevance and predictive validity of subject generated trait descriptions. *J. Pers., 47,* 230–244.

Turner, R. G., M. F. Scheier, C. S. Carver, and W. Ickes (1978). Correlates of self-consciousness. *J. Pers. Assessment, 42,* 285–289.

Turner, R. H. (1968). The self-conception in social interaction. In C. Gordon, and K. J. Gergen (Eds.), *The self in social interaction.* New York: Wiley.

_____. (1975). The real self: from institution to impulse. *Amer. J. Sociol., 81,* 989–1015.

Tutko, T. A. (1962). *Need for social approval and its effect on responses to projective tests.* Unpublished doctoral dissertation. Northwestern University.

Underwood, B., and B. S. Moore (1981). Sources of behavioral consistency. *J. Pers. soc. Psychol., 40,* 780–785.

Updike, J. (1975). *Picked-up pieces.* Greenwich, Conn.: Fawcett Books.

Vallacher, R. R., and M. Solodky (1979). Objective self-awareness, standards of evaluation, and moral behavior. *J. exp. soc. Psychol., 15,* 254–262.

Vroom, V. (1964). *Work and motivation.* New York: Wiley.

Wachtel, P. (1973). Psychodynamics, behavior therapy, and the implacable experimenter: an inquiry into the consistency of personality. *J. abnorm. Psychol., 83,* 324–334.

Warner, R. M., D. A. Kenny, and M. Stoto (1979). A new round robin analysis of variance for social interaction data. *J. Pers. soc. Psychol., 37,* 1742–1757.

Watzlawick, R., J. H. Beavin, and D. D. Jackson (1967). *Pragmatics of human communication.* New York: Norton.

Wegner, D. M., and K. Finstuen (1977). Observer's focus of attention in the simulation of self-perception. *J. Pers. soc. Psychol., 35,* 56–62.

Weigel, R. H., and L. S. Newman (1976). Increasing attitude-behavior correspondence by broadening the scope of the behavioral measure. *J. Pers. soc. Psychol., 33,* 793–802.

Weiner, B. (1974). Achievement motivation as conceptualized by an attribution theorist. In B. Weiner (Ed.), *Achievement motivation and attribution theory.* Morristown, N.J.: General Learning Press.

Weinstein, E. A. (1966). Toward a theory of interpersonal tactics. In C. W. Backman, and P. E. Secord (Eds.), *Problems in social psychology.* New York: McGraw-Hill.

Weinstein, E. A., and P. Deutschberger (1963). Some dimensions of altercasting. *Sociometry, 26,* 454–466.

Werner, P. D. (1978). Personality and attitude-activism correspondence. *J. Pers. soc. Psychol., 36,* 1375–1390.

Wheeler, L. (1966). Motivation as a determinant of upward comparison. *J. exp. soc. Psychol., 1,* 27–31.

Wheeler, L., and J. Nezlek (1977). Sex differences in social participation. *J. Pers. soc. Psychol., 35,* 742–754.

Wicklund, R. A. (1975). Objective self-awareness. In L. Berkowitz (Ed.), *Advances in experimental social psychology.* Vol. 8. New York: Academic Press.

_____ (1982). Self-focused attention and the validity of self-reports. In M. P. Zanna, E. T. Higgins, and C. P. Herman (Eds.), *Consistency in social behavior: the Ontario symposium.* Vol. 2. Hillsdale, N.J.: Erlbaum.

Wicklund, R. A., and S. Duval (1971). Opinion change and performance facilitation as a result of objective self-awareness. *J. exp. soc. Psychol., 7,* 319–342.

Wicklund, R. A., and W. Ickes (1972). The effect of objective self-awareness on predecisional exposure to information. *J. exp. soc. Psychol., 8,* 378–387.

Wiener, B. (1978). Achievement strivings. In H. London, and J. Exner (Eds.), *Dimensions of personality.* New York: Wiley.

Williams, C. B., and J. B. Nickels (1969). Internal-external control dimension as related to accident and suicide proneness. *J. Consult. clinic. Psychol., 33,* 485–494.

Wilson, D. T. (1962). Ability evaluation, postdecision dissonance, and coworker attractiveness. Unpublished doctoral dissertation. University of Minnesota, Minneapolis.

Wilson G. (1978). Introversion/extraversion. In H. London, and J. Exner (Eds.), *Dimensions of personality.* New York: Wiley.

Winter, D. G. (1973). *The power motive.* New York: Free Press.

Winter, D., and A. J. Stewart (1978). The power motive. In H. London, and J. Exner (Eds.), *Dimensions of personality.* New York: Wiley.

Wish, M. (1975). Subjects' expectations about their own interpersonal communication: a multidimensional approach. *Pers. soc. Psychol. Bull., 1,* 11–20.

Wish, M., M. Deutsch, and S. J. Kaplan (1976). Perceived dimensions of interpersonal relations. *J. Pers. soc. Psychol., 33,* 409–420.

Wish, M., and S. Kaplan (1977). Toward an implicit theory of interpersonal communication. *Sociometry, 40,* 234–246.

Witkin, H. A., R. B. Dyk, H. F. Faterson, D. R. Goodenough, and S. A. Karp (1962). *Psychological differentiation.* New York: Wiley.

Word, C. O., M. P. Zanna, and J. Cooper (1974). The nonverbal mediation of self-fulfilling prophecies in interracial interaction. *J. exp. soc. Psychol., 10,* 109–120.

Wrightsman, L. S. (1960). Effects of waiting with others on changes in level of felt anxiety. *J. abnorm. soc. Psychol., 61,* 216–222.

Wrightsman, L. S. (1965). *Attitudinal and personality correlates of presidential voting preferences.* Paper presented at the meeting of the American Psychological Association, Chicago.

Wylie, R. C. (1974). *The self-concept* (2nd ed). Lincoln: Univ. of Nebraska Press.

Zanna, M. P., and J. M. Olson (1982). Individual differences in attitudinal relations. In M. P. Zanna, E. T. Higgins, and C. P. Herman (Eds.), *Consistency in social behavior: the Ontario symposium.* Vol. 2. Hillsdale, N.J.: Erlbaum.

Zanna, M. P., J. M. Olson, and R. H. Fazio (1980). Attitude-behavior consistency: an individual difference perspective. *J. Pers. soc. Psychol., 38,* 432–440.

Zanna, M. P., and S. J. Pack (1975). On the self-fulfilling nature of apparent sex differences in behavior. *J. exp. soc. Psychol., 11,* 583–591.

Zimbardo, P. G. (1969). The human choice: individuation, reason and order versus deindividuation, impulse and chaos. In W. J. Arnold, and D. Levine (Eds.), *Nebraska symposium on motivation.* Lincoln: Univ. of Nebraska Press.

Zuckerman, M. (1974). The sensation seeking motive. In B. Maher (Ed.), *Progress in experimental personality research.* (Vol. 7). New York: Academic Press.

_____ (1978). Sensation seeking. In H. London, and J. Exner (Eds.), *Dimensions of personality.* New York: Wiley.

Zuckerman, M., and H. T. Reis (1978). A comparison of three models for predicting altruistic behavior. *J. Pers. soc. Psychol., 36,* 498–510.

CHAPTER 29

Social Psychological Aspects of Environmental Psychology

John M. Darley
Princeton University

Daniel T. Gilbert
Princeton University

ORIENTATION

In this edition, for the first time, a chapter on environmental psychology appears in the *Handbook of Social Psychology*. Therefore we begin with a set of comments that attempt to position environmental psychology for the social psychologist who is the likely reader. First, a definition. In the standard definition environmental psychology is concerned with the reciprocal and interactive influences that take place between the thinking and behavior of an organism and the environment surrounding that organism. As the reader will note, it is difficult to think of an example of research in psychology that is *not* included in this definition; a rat in a Skinner box is reacting to certain aspects of the built form of his physical environment (e.g., the reinforcement schedule); a bystander's decision to aid or ignore a fallen pedestrian is affected by the information contained in and con-

cealed by his urban surroundings; a human being receiving conformity pressure is reacting to various aspects of his social environment; and so on. In practice, environmental psychologists have concentrated their efforts in a few areas that, while encompassed by this definition, have been chosen on the basis of other considerations.

We frankly admit what is widely recognized by environmental researchers: Environmental psychology is not an integrated subdiscipline within the discipline of psychology. It may be more useful to think of environmental psychology as a federation of various active research areas, within which researchers are linked by a shared set of research attitudes and metascientific concerns but do not display an integrative set of analytic techniques or theoretical postulates. Nor is it appropriate to require that they do. Environmental psychology is a problem-centered rather than a theory-centered set of activities, and it is not in the nature of such enterprises to be constrained to a single theoretical formulation.

From this fact the organization of the chapter follows. We will briefly indicate the historical and empirical origins of environmental psychology, the metascientific attitudes shared by a number of environmental researchers, and relevant research in other disciplines. Finally, we

We would like to thank Irwin Altman, Andrew Baum, Paul Stern, and Dan Stokols for helpful comments on earlier versions of this chapter.

will review selected areas of environmental psychology in three fundamental domains: the natural, the built, and the social environments. In the process we will be drawing on previously written reviews of these areas.

This book is devoted to social psychology. Therefore we will give the most coverage to topics that are of interest to social psychologists. A physiological psychologist may be fascinated by the neural mechanisms underlying the process by which high concentrations of lead in the human bloodstream lead to lowered scores on ability and achievement tests. A psychologist interested in policy formation may be fascinated by the laws governing noise levels and the feasibility of their enforcement. Still, there is relatively little of theoretical interest in these problems to a social psychologist, and in turn, the social psychologist has relatively little to say that might help solve such problems. Thus this is the sort of topic to which we will give disproportionately little coverage. As a result, the chapter will not, and does not claim to, give a balanced view of environmental psychology. The readers seeking such comprehensive coverage should complement their reading of this chapter with such reviews as Craik (1973), Stokols (1978), and Russell and Ward (1982), or the volumes on *Human Behavior and Environment* edited by Altman and Wohlwill (e.g., 1976), *Advances in Environmental Psychology* edited by Baum, Singer and Valins (e.g., 1978), and the *Handbook of Environmental Psychology* edited by Stokols and Altman (in press).

Just as the issues that form the core of environmental psychology may be important to social psychology, we will also suggest that social psychological theories can sometimes account for environmental psychological phenomena (e.g., an attributional approach to proxemics). We do so because this seems to be the way in which we can best contribute to the advancement of theoretically driven research in this field. In offering such notions, we do not wish to appear imperialistic. Very few problems exist whose solutions can be completely generated from a single theoretical position, and environmental psychology is and must remain a problem-centered discipline. Any theory we suggest to "account for" an environmental psychological phenomenon can, in reality, account only for certain aspects of the phenomenon. Therefore although this chapter may sometimes read as if we were attempting to explain complex environmental phenomena with "simple" social psychological theories, we do not intend to make any such claim.

CONCEPTUALIZING THE EFFECTS OF THE ENVIRONMENT

If we focus for a moment on the ways in which the surrounding environment can affect the encased individual, then we will remind the reader of conceptual terms that will be familiar to the working social psychologist. The environment can affect the *sensations, perceptions,* and *cognitions* of the experiencing individual. The individual may experience certain *physiological reactions* and also may evaluate and adopt *attitudes* toward the environment and the other individuals within it. His *performances* on tasks may be affected, and more generally, many of his *behaviors* in that environment may be altered. These alterations may spill over in the sense that they may appear in environments other than the ones in which they initially were developed. Occasionally, these behaviors may be of sufficient generality so that we would regard the *personality* of the individual as having been altered. In discussing various environmental phenomena, we will keep an eye toward estimating the phenomenon's impact on these various behavioral factors.

THE UBIQUITY OF DIFFERING PERSPECTIVES

We will continue to return to different instantiations of the same general realization: Physically identical or highly similar environmental circumstances will affect the persons in those circumstances very differently. In other words, different persons will have different and sometimes even contradictory reactions to the same physical setting. Some individuals may find urban living so threatening that they may, as did an elderly Bronx couple in 1976, take their own lives in desperation. Another set of individuals may find the city so exciting that they would be depressed were they to live anywhere else. While one person is enraptured by the wilderness, another finds it strange and terrifying. Several principles familiar to social psychologists frequently help to explain why these differences occur. First, any person's perceptual interpretations of people and events are to some considerable extent a product of that person's own past experiences and interpretive sets. Certainly, the same will hold true for a person's perception of environments (see Leff, 1980). Second, to use Bruner's succinct phrase, "the purpose of perception is action." This statement is acutely true and important in environmental psychology. Persons are generally in environments in order to perform various actions, and their perceptions of these environments are strongly attuned to those environmental elements that will facilitate the execution of their plans and those that may hinder them. Though the environment per se affects the individual, we will continue to suggest that its role, while unarguably *important,* is quite secondary to interpersonal, motivational, and cognitive determinants of behavior.

HISTORICAL AND EMPIRICAL ORIGINS OF ENVIRONMENTAL PSYCHOLOGY

As a recent review by Stokols (1978) points out, the research literature on environmental psychology vastly increased during the 1970s. Kenneth Craik had 280 literature citations in his 1973 review of the area; Stokols's review in 1978 contained just under 500 citations. The other inevitable signs of an academic "area" are also in evidence: Textbooks (e.g., Ittelson *et al.,* 1974; Moos, 1976; Bell, Fisher, and Loomis, 1978; Heimstra and McFarling, 1978; Holahan, 1978, 1982), collections of readings (e.g., Proshansky, Ittelson, and Rivlin, 1976; Wapner, Cohen, and Kaplan, 1976), and journals (*Environment and Behavior, Environmental Psychology and Nonverbal Behavior, Journal of Environmental Psychology*) have been published, conferences held, and environmental research societies founded. The reader will recognize the dangers inherent in attempting to single out a few psychologists who have been most involved in the shaping of the field. Still, one cannot but be struck by the work of Craik and Ittelson, of Altman and Proshansky, and of Stokols. As later parts of this chapter will show, these people have had much to do with the fact that the 1960s and 1970s were the period in which environmental psychology really began.

Earlier psychologists did occasionally recognize the importance of the environment in which human actions took place. Social psychologists will remember Lewin's distinction between the person's life space as it existed physically and as it was psychologically experienced. A study of the relationship between these two notions would have been a study in environmental psychology—more precisely, cognitive mapping—but few psychologists answered Lewin's implicit challenge to do this sort of research. In the field of perceptual psychology

Brunswik's (1969) call for more ecologically valid experimentation, in which the stimulus materials used in experiments were chosen to represent patterns as they were found in the real world, was a similar challenge that was met with a similar lack of response. In other fields of psychology authors occasionally alluded to the problems of the representations of the environment in the life space, but relatively little investigation of these problems was done. The importance of environmental and structural influences on behavior was apparently underestimated with remarkable consistency.

Three exceptions to this generalization deserve notice. The first is the field of psychology variously called human factors, human engineering, man-machine systems, or ergonomics. The second, more familiar to social psychologists, is the work of Roger Barker and his associates (e.g., 1978). The third involves disaster research.

Human Factors

Human factors psychology is concerned with the performance of the human operator of complex mechanical systems. Prior to the 1940s much of this research was done on factory workers, but with the advent of the Second World War and the influx of psychologists into the military, the research expanded to include the operation of weapons systems, particularly the airplane. Psychologists also contributed to the design of optimal displays for radar and other electronic information-summarizing systems. Note that this necessarily interdisciplinary and applied endeavor is a part of environmental psychology in which several of the area's typical characteristics are clearly seen. First, human engineering studies the interaction of aspects of the person's mechanical and spatial environment with the person's performance in that environment, thus fitting within the broad definition of environmental psychology offered earlier. Second, it has the interdisciplinary orientation and mix of applied and basic theoretical concerns characteristic of environmental psychology. Finally, it is often focused on *optimizing* performance, and this performance-optimizing concern is also a frequent hallmark of environmental psychology.

Behavioral Ecology

The work of Roger Barker and his associates will be reviewed in some detail later in this chapter. Here we simply note that the historical importance of this work lies in Barker's systematic attempt to map the physical and social environment in terms that facilitate the examination of the psychological connections between the human actions that take place within an environment and the environment itself. As well, Barker's emphasis on the ecology of action, the indivisibility of behavior sequences, has had important ramifications for modern environmental psychology's philosophical or metascientific point of view.

Disaster Research

For some years an interdisciplinary group of researchers has studied the reactions of individuals and communities to naturally occurring disasters. Modern technology has greatly facilitated this research by promoting the occurrence of a good many artificial disasters as well. Some of this work will be reviewed later in this chapter, but the conclusion to extract here is simply that historically another area of research relevant to environmental psychology existed prior to the 1960s.

RELEVANT RESEARCH IN OTHER DISCIPLINES

Disciplinary orientations sometimes expose a parochial perspective on reviewers as well as researchers. To combat this effect, we will mention developments in several other disciplines that preceded the emergence of environmental psychology, although, perhaps because of the parochial tendencies, no argument can be made that environmental psychology has been systematically built on these ideas.

American History

The single most important and original hypothesis generated by an American historian may be, in large measure, a proposition in environmental psychology. In 1896 Fredrich Jackson Turner put forth what is known as the "frontier hypothesis" (Nash, 1973, pp. 145–148). The hypothesis essentially holds that the American character structure—the personalities of Americans and therefore our social organizations—was critically influenced by the existence of the frontier. We will make more of this hypothesis in our discussion of the natural environment and, in particular, the wilderness (see Barker, 1979).

National Character Studies

Another research tradition worth mentioning in the catalogue of parallels to environmental psychological thinking that have developed in other fields is national character research (see Hunt, 1967, for an edited collection of

these studies). As others have noted, both on evidential and ideological terms, the research area is an unsettled one, but one member of the national characterologist's set of explanatory concepts is germane to environmental psychological concerns. The physical, geographical, geological, and botanical conditions of any country shape the patterns of human existence within it. Historically, in terms of our taxonomy, national character assertions have been of several sorts. First has been the assertion that physical surroundings affect the action patterns of the individuals living within them. One thinks here of the yearly life cycle of Alpine shepherds who shift their flocks down from the high mountain pastures as winter approaches. Second, and evaluatively more complex, is the suggestion that the physical surroundings interact with the cultural patterning of the possibilities for making a living that are provided by the physical surroundings to determine the social system of the inhabitants, which in turn creates a modal or typical personality structure that is characteristic of that nation (Duijker and Frijda, 1961).

Social Geography

It is an easy transition from national character studies to the concerns of social geographers. Indeed, the example we used to illustrate the national character approach is one that might be similarly used by a social geographer. Social geographers point out the qualitative understandings that arise from various kinds of topographic representations of places and would illustrate this contention by mapping the ownership patterns of the Alpine and sub-Alpine lands, for example, to demonstrate how ownership patterns bolstered and reinforced the traditional patterns of life of the Alpine shepherds. In addition, such mapping can reveal how the landownership patterns were influenced by such physical characteristics of the land as naturally occurring boundaries, its arability, and its yield. Notice here the assertion of reciprocal, rather than unidirectional, causal influences that is characteristic of environmental psychological analysis. Landownership patterns, originally perhaps a consequence of living patterns, become causal factors in perpetrating these patterns. "We shape our environment and our environment shapes us" is an underlying principle of environmental psychology that is often illustrated by the discoveries of social geographers. Maps of cities, for instance, reveal settlement patterns characterizable as low-density, single-family-unit, spatially dispersed housing that mandates a reliance on individual rather than mass transportation and guarantees a continuing high ratio of energy consumption for transportation purposes.

Patterns of the distribution of resources are often illuminating, and social geographers often reveal those patterns (Wilbanks, 1983). For example, maps of the population movements in nineteenth-century America could have been predicted by an omniscient observer with a map of the distribution of gold. Interestingly, social geographers have put forward a hypothesis that is rather like the frontier hypothesis of the historians. Briefly, they point out that the United States, compared with other countries, has been resource-rich and thus has developed an optimistic set of assumptions about what is possible, which in turn is based on assumptions about the plentifulness of resources (Potter, 1954, p. 84):

> Relative abundance is, by general consent, a basic condition of American life, . . . an influence that impinges upon all American social conditions and contributes in the most fundamental way to the shaping of the American culture and the American character.

As resources become scarce—water in the western states, oil everywhere—we are singularly ill equipped to deal with the multiple ramifications of their scarcity, because such consideration counters many of our basic assumptions. Zelinsky (1973), in a book entitled *The Cultural Geography of the United States,* suggests that the American character (note that social and cultural geographers are in the national character business here) places a high value on possibilities of mobility and change and holds an image of the world as a machine. Because of our emphasis on change, we are driven to save time, and we are willing to trade large amounts of energy and other resources for such savings or to produce mobility and change. Our view of the world as a machine implies that we can make the world behave as we wish, and so the discovery of energy shortages implies some ill functioning in our social or economic system rather than an inevitable and natural limit.

Urban Sociology

Contemporary sociologists would find odd the contention that little environmentally oriented research took place prior to 1960, for at least since the Chicago school the environmental issues of urban life have been of primary interest to sociologists (e.g., Wirth, 1938; see Burns, 1980). The extensive literature that attests to this interest within urban sociology is beyond both the scope and the purpose of this chapter, and we simply wish to point out that the themes of geographical and architectural effects on behavior were in the fore of the sociological consciousness long before they dawned on psychology. While such concerns have largely been with the environmental impact on socio-organizational rather than individual behavior (e.g., Simmel, 1950; Mumford, 1961; Fischer, 1976), the sociological influence has been keenly felt in areas such as human response to crowding, perhaps because sociology provided a ready-made literature rich in theory and description for the psychologists first interested in such problems. Again, an articulated position on environmental determinants of behavior existed prior to and outside of the social psychological literature of the 1960s.

Two conclusions can be extracted from this brief mention of environmentalist hypotheses that have been put forward in other disciplinary contexts. First, there has been a frequent occurrence and recurrence of the environmental theme in social sciences, and we would like to suggest that environmental psychologists might do well to look to these sources for possible formulations of environmental hypotheses. Otherwise, as a discipline, environmental psychology will appear—and become—insular, unscholarly, and isolated. Second, although only thinly developed in the above discussion, these hypotheses are not easy ones for psychologists to deal with in their characteristic experimental research traditions. The challenge, then, is and has been to move toward establishing a research tradition capable of addressing these problems of interest, rather than selecting problems on the basis of their goodness of fit with present methodology. It is in its eclectic empirical approach, we will later argue, that environmental psychology demonstrates both its greatest strength and its greatest weakness.

THE DELAYED APPEARANCE OF ENVIRONMENTAL PSYCHOLOGY

Psychologists are not experienced in seeing ideological or intellectual trends or in understanding their causes, yet one pattern in the above presentation is obvious. Both inside and outside the discipline of psychology, a number of research traditions of the 1950s and before created cores around which the discipline of environmental psychology could form and emerge. But it did not do so. One reason is that the methods for research in these fields were not the methods gaining widespread social acceptance in the higher-prestige field of social psychology. But the general lack of interest in environmental psychology was so great that one suspects more was at issue than simple incongruencies in research methods.

Many other writers have commented about what this "more" might be, so we make no claim to originality in putting forth some of the following suggestions. Post–World War II North America existed during a period of abundance that was perhaps unprecedented in the history of human societies. Energy sources were inexpensive and abundant, and those who looked ahead to the eventual disappearance of these sources anticipated their replacement with cheap, clean, and efficient nuclear energy. Most people did not look forward at all.

The popular magazines of the 1950s and 1960s manifested an aspect of the kind of thinking we are talking about. They contained confident predictions about the air cars of the future, stories about the weatherproofing of cities by enclosing them in giant, high-technology bubble domes, the impending development of nuclear power packs to provide all the comforts of home to remote summer cottages, and so on. Indeed, the science fiction of the 1940s appeared to have been reprinted verbatim as the popular science fact of 1961. The image that emerged was one of human beings in artificially created environments, man-made utopias but a technological stone's throw away. Our major goal was to eliminate the constraints imposed by inconvenient variations in the natural environment. Why should we be wet when we wished to be dry? Why should we be hampered by winter, by natural barriers, by the fall of night? And given this perspective, why would one study environmental psychology? One would not study what one sought to, and could soon quite easily, eliminate.

In the various editions of his history of psychology, E. G. Boring often (perhaps too often) referred to the *zeitgeist*—the spirit of the times—to explain some historical trend. Our argument here is the same. Environmental psychology was not created until forces existing outside the field of psychology (e.g., the disappointment of nuclear power, oil embargos, etc.) forced environmental concerns into the fore of the national agenda. It was to this sociopolitical shift that psychologists responded. As we will see as we survey the various fields of environmental psychology, psychologists have responded in ways that are responsive to our changing national circumstances.

Let us persist with this argument from one further angle. In his insightful discussion (Chapter 2) in this Handbook, E. E. Jones argues that the "social psychological consciousness," involving as it does the recognition of sharply different perspectives and the existence of social conflicts between groups, was connected with the urban, upper-middle-class, slightly alienated milieu in which the centers of social psychological research developed. The other side of this argument is equally striking. It is hard to think of a group of individuals who had less to do with the environment on a day-to-day basis than did the thoroughly middle-class, academic, city-dwelling opinion leaders of post–World War II social psychology.

We suspect that all of these factors were in some part responsible for the relative lack of interest in environmental concerns in psychology. We suggest that the current interest in environmental psychology is to some extent event-driven and that these critical events often take place outside psychology, forcing issues onto the national agenda (e.g., crime in housing projects or energy shortages) and motivating psychologists to work on these issues. We have already commented that this feature gives environmental psychology a problem-centered approach. Of course, exceptions to this generalization exist, for within environmental psychology one may find both basic theoretical work (e.g., cognitive representations of place) and domains descended from anthropological and ethological concerns (e.g., proxemics), none of which is necessarily problem-centered. Nonetheless, in the review that follows of various areas of environmental psychology, much of the research and theory within this discipline will reveal its intellectual origins as national issues.

THE NATURAL ENVIRONMENT

Without a doubt, most of us spend the vast majority of our lives indoors, and this basic truth is manifested in the different levels, kinds, and moreover, *amounts* of research dealing with the natural and built environments. Comparatively few studies have dealt with the perception of the natural environment and the effects of these perceptions on behavior and cognition. We will explore some of these themes in our largely descriptive section on the wilderness, but we wish here to point out the national issues origins of environmental research mentioned above. Because for most of us (and certainly for most university-employed psychologists) urban problems are most pressing and imperatively felt, the focus of environmental research has always been shifted toward the psychological aspects of built form and away from consideration of natural lands. Exceptions to this generalization are twofold. Attention has been paid to the natural environment when it has made its presence felt, that is, with the occurrence of geophysical disaster. As we will see, disaster research comprises one of the more interesting and potentially theory-rich areas of natural environmental research. Second, environmental psychologists have been quick to respond to growing threats to the natural environment's welfare and integrity, and we will touch upon some of the social psychological aspects of this burgeoning literature in our discussions of pollution and attitudes about the natural environment. Finally, we will consider the psychological aspects of the environment's threat to undermine our technological well-being in a discussion of energy conservation.

WILDERNESS

As mentioned earlier, the historian Turner (1932), in his frontier hypothesis, suggested that the American personality was influenced by the existence of large, essentially uninhabited spaces to which persons could migrate should the dissatisfactions with their current existence grow too great. Beginning around 1890 when the frontier closed, the American character gradually began to change to reflect the absence of this possibility.

This hypothesis is fascinating from a psychological perspective, for it holds that environmental conditions actually shape the personalities of those who experience the environment—no minor claim from the rather cautious perspective of the research psychologist. The frontier hypothesis claimed that not only were the characters of the frontierspeople altered by their direct experience of the frontier environment but also that the characters of those who did not live at the very edge of the settlement were affected simply by the *knowledge* of the frontier's existence. The shop clerk in Boston read newspaper accounts and novels about the frontier, the gold to be discovered and the dangers to be risked. His reactions to his New England surroundings were altered by his knowledge of these other accessible worlds, so to speak, even if he decided against experiencing them. In the vernacular of social psychology, the Boston merchant was engaged in a relationship with his environment that was influenced, as are interpersonal relations, by his comparison level for alternatives (Thibaut and Kelley, 1959); the alternative need not be chosen but simply be extant to be influential. With this notion in mind it is interesting to note the emergence of a current movement to open a new "high frontier" (O'Neill, 1977). Should the colonization

of space prove a viable alternative to terrestrial habitation, the frontier character described by Turner may be reinstated with profound effects on any number of social levels (e.g., when penal systems shift from incarceration to exile, criminals become founding fathers). An understanding of the influence of an open frontier (or the lack thereof) is therefore of current concern, and though this hypothesis is a fascinating one within environmental psychology, empirically grounded and inferentially cautious researchers are at a bit of a loss about how to test it.

A charming chapter by Barker (1979), which is little known among psychologists, attempts to specify these important psychological aspects of the frontier experience. First, the frontier was undermanned; that is, there were fewer people than were needed to operate the farms, stores, schools, and churches. Second, the living conditions imposed by geography, climate, and prevailing social conditions were novel to the pioneers. Third, the frontier environment was unfinished in the sense that many of the physical and social structures required needed to be created or completed.

Actually, over the years Americans have held shifting conceptualizations of the wilderness. A penetrating and thoughtful analysis by Nash (1973) concerns what he calls "images" of the wilderness as they were held in various historical periods. The argument, like Turner's, is a person-environment interaction hypothesis. Briefly, for earlier historical periods the wilderness represented opportunity, disorder, and danger. In the nineteenth century, for example, the wilderness was conceived of as a terrifying and evil place to be converted to farms, gardens, and towns that would be pleasing to God. Cotton Mather and others preached against it. To the American farmer of the 1860s the forest to the west of his farm was the route by which hostile Indians might attack, as well as a barrier to the expansion of his cropland. Not surprisingly, the forest seemed to warrant the treatment it frequently received, which was to burn off the underbrush, ring-cut the bark of the bigger trees so they would die, slash and burn again, and eventually clear, tame, plow, and turn the land into fields or pastureland.

As Nash (1973) documents, "the wilderness was metaphor as well as actuality" (p. 36). Prior to the 1880s the wilderness was generally seen as the villain in the drama of national development. Turner's hypothesis marked a shift in this thinking. If the frontiersman's encounters with the wilderness were responsible for his strength, self-reliance, courage, and democratic openness, then there was a sense in which these characteristics must be inherent in the wilderness. As Nash (1973) remarks, "the villain, it appeared, was as vital to the play as the hero, and, in view of the admirable qualities that contact with the wilderness was thought to produce, perhaps not so villainous as had been supposed" (p. 145). Indeed, it was a character-building paradise. One can historically trace this theme through John Muir and Theodore Roosevelt to present-day wilderness preservationists.

In the context of these images of the wilderness we can make a psychological point that seems to be a potentially rather general one. To western ranchers the national parklands surrounding them may represent a possible source of pasturage for their animals, a possible source of water, and a breeding ground for animals that prey on their herds. The lands call out for alteration and improvement. To Sierra Club members, however, they represent a natural resource, an unspoiled area, and a breeding ground for what is left of the rapidly diminishing numbers of wild animals. These lands are a resource to be treasured and preserved. What we want to emphasize here is the extent to which these images, which are in fact the products of very complex value socialization and life experiences, are experienced as perceptual phenomena. To the experienced and well-equipped camper, the vista of Canadian wilderness that *looks* beautiful and inviting is the same physical environment that to an inexperienced person *looks* terrifying. These experiences have a given quality, seeming to arise directly from our perceptual systems. The wilderness, as a complex stimulus array, seems to afford different perceivers different perceptual opportunities (Gibson, 1966). Several consequences follow from the immediate quality of our perceptions of the environment. For example, it is difficult to think that others can really see things differently. When it becomes apparent that others at least claim to see things not only differently but in contradictary ways, we generally make rather sweeping attributions about the motivations or personal characteristics that account for these differences. Other equally probative hypotheses seem to follow from this observation.

In an experimental sense, however, we still have little more than speculation of this sort to guide us in our understanding of how persons perceive and interact with the wilderness. Research has focused on recreational aspects of national park use, aesthetic aspects of various landscapes, and so on; and though the need for such research is not in question, it has not yet contributed a great deal of relevance to social psychology. Therefore we have chosen to proceed directly to what we consider a fascinating and yet relatively underexplored area within our examination of the natural environment: geophysical disaster.

DISASTER

In 1952, when it appeared certain that the next war would include thermonuclear weapons, the National Academy of Sciences National Research Council appointed a Committee on Disaster Studies to explore the social ramifications of nuclear destruction in particular and of disaster in general. This committee, and a later incarnation in 1957 as the Disaster Research Group, published nineteen reports that, until recently, constituted the bulk of the social scientific literature on human response to extreme geophysical events. With the group's dissolution in 1963 the Disaster Research Center at Ohio State University assumed responsibility for the continued investigation of social behavior in the course of disaster, but this move to Ohio also saw the exclusion of psychosocial research methods in the disaster area in favor of a strict and traditional sociological approach. Accompanying paradigmatic shifts took place, providing for greater emphasis on group than individual behavior and moving away from a psychological and toward a social organizational perspective (Quarantelli and Dynes, 1977). Recent textbooks and reviews in environmental psychology rarely do more than allude to disaster research (exceptions are Craik, 1970; Ittelson *et al.,* 1974), but we suggest that it is an important point of intellectual heritage for environmental psychology and, further, that a modern psychosocial approach to natural disaster might generate theory of importance to environmental and social psychology.

Charles Fritz's Work
The first attempt to codify disaster research was made by Charles Fritz (1961, 1968), whose work remains, to our thinking, among the most provocative of many such efforts. As Quarantelli and Dynes (1977) point out, in a quarter of a century disaster research has yet to fully explore the implications of Fritz's analyses.

Fritz began by repudiating many of the popular misconceptions of disaster behavior and initially establishing what does *not* occur during a disaster. The stereotypic picture of widespread panic, asocial and lawless behavior, emotional devastation, and hysterical flight from the disaster area gives way to a clearer understanding of behavior as goal-directed and orderly. The observer suffers from an "illusion of panic," so to speak, promoted by the divergent, uncoordinated activities of numerous small, emergent groups whose members are, in fact, responsible for the majority of rescue and recovery efforts. The confusion witnessed by the observer is often the result of convergence *onto* the disaster scene by *outsiders* offering aid, searching for family members, and seeking information. Fritz also notes that the victim's plight is one of social and informational uncertainty. In addition to life-threatening circumstances, victims may experience role conflicts (the obligations of being a paramedic versus the responsibilities of being a parent) that make it difficult for them to prioritize their responses. As a needs hierarchy suggests, familial roles usually assume primary status but—once met—are quickly subsumed by civic and professional responsibilities. Fritz observes that the disruption of normal communication channels makes it difficult for victims to acquire a realistic picture of the event and its consequences; for instance, disaster victims typically believe that the devastation has occurred only to them, and they fail to realize how pervasive and widespread the damage actually is.

Another of Fritz's unique insights is that the pressing problems inherent in a disaster situation often obscure the fact that disasters may produce therapeutic effects on social systems. The commonality of danger, the clarity of the need for common remedial actions, and the interruption of the status quo combine to eliminate status differences, encourage progressive change, and promote solidarity within the community. These unifying forces of the postdisaster phase often serve to facilitate an "amplified rebound effect" in which the reconstructed community exceeds its predisaster levels of integration, productivity, social equality, and capacity for growth.

Recent Disaster Work

In reading some of the individual reports of disasters, one gets the impression that communities ought to court the occurrence of an occasional disaster simply to enjoy these long-term beneficial effects. This may be so; that is, some disasters may have some beneficial effects. But evidence strongly indicates that serious negative effects may result from other disasters. In February 1972 in Buffalo Creek, West Virginia, a slag dam above the town gave way and released a wall of water that swept through the valley of the creek along which the town was situated. It destroyed homes, bridges, and many lives. For many reasons, not the least of which was that it was the subject of

novel litigation, this event received a great deal of publicity and scientific attention, resulting in a number of studies that are methodologically sound, conceptually thoughtful, thoroughly carried out, and that display a long-term frame of reference. Briefly, the findings (Gleser, Green, and Winget, 1981) suggest that the catastrophe had serious and measurable negative long-term effects on its victims. These effects include mood changes such as increased incidence of depression and alienation, increased pathological symptomology, more frequent sleep disorders, and an increase in patterns of substance abuse. These effects are interrelated with each other in sensible ways: They are predicted by the magnitude of loss the individual has experienced, are correlated within families, and are ameliorated if the individual has been able to carry out self-help activities. Gleser, Green, and Winget (1981) report that the Buffalo Creek victims, as a group, had symptoms that were "typical in kind and degree to patients seen in general mental health outpatient settings, but somewhat less severe than those of patients in the midst of actual life crises" (p. 141).

We are faced, then, with the conclusion that some disasters have relatively mild consequences and some have quite serious ones, while others, in fact, may actually have a positive net effect. Obviously, what we require is some taxonomy that differentiates between these sorts of disasters. One of the early sets of dimensions was proposed by Barton (1969). The four dimensions proposed are the magnitude and scope of the impact of the disaster, the speed of its onset, the duration of the disaster and its sequela, and the degree of social preparedness of the community. [These and other dimensions are also proposed by Fritz (1961, p. 656).]

Of these dimensions only the last dimension is explicitly a psychosocial one, although the others hint at underlying psychosocial processes. What might a more psychosocial set of dimensions be? Erikson's (1976) explanation for the destructive consequences of the Buffalo Creek disaster center around the loss of "feelings of community and connectedness" that it caused. Lifton and Olson (1976) relate some of the feelings of the Buffalo Creek victims to what Lifton learned from victims of Hiroshima and Nagasaki. In this regard a dimension that strikes us as quite important involves the locus of the origin of the disaster. Is it a natural disaster or a man-made disaster? One suspects that man-made disasters may be uniquely disruptive of the general relations of trust that exist within societies. Gleser, Green, and Winget (1981), in what is the most recent attempt to examine the psychosocial dimensions of disasters, list this dimension and five others. Slightly modified, these dimensions include the following:

1. The seriousness of the threat and the associated feelings of powerlessness and loss of control.

2. The degree of bereavement suffered by the victim.

3. The prolongation of the negative human consequences of the disaster over time, particularly if attempts to ameliorate these effects are ineffective.

4. Changes in the victims' life-styles or places of living.

5. The proportion of the community or group affected by the disaster and the relation of the affected group to the rest of the community.

Since the above report was written, Hohenemser, Kates, and Slovic (1983) have proposed a potentially useful taxonomy of environmental hazards (defined more broadly than in this chapter). Additionally, their factor analysis of ninety-three hazards—ranging from skateboard spills to nuclear spills—revealed five factors that account for 81 percent of the variance in hazard perception: (1) a *biocidal* factor (nonhuman mortality), (2) a *catastrophic* factor (recurrence, maximum human mortality), (3) a *delay* factor (transgenerational effects, persistence), (4) a *mortality* factor (annual human mortality), and (5) a *globality* factor (concentration, population at risk). The similarity between some of these empirically derived factors and Fritz's theoretical disaster classification system is noteworthy. The hazard classification system that these researchers report is a major contribution to further work in risk and hazard assessment, because it suggests a unified way of measuring actual and perceived hazard factors. Future research may clarify what systematic differences, if any, exist between actual and perceived hazard factors.

These dimensions seem to be appropriate ones with which to begin, and they may be refined in further studies that, for rather grim reasons, seem worth pursuing. As has been recognized, current technological and economic realities generate a great deal of interdependence between nations and individuals within those nations. One unpleasant aspect of this interdependence is that any individual or group of individuals is often capable, either accidentally or intentionally, of inflicting vast harm on large groups of people. (One thinks of building collapses, nuclear power plant malfunctions, exploding oil tankers, etc.) With the increase in the probability, psychological

or actual, of man-made disasters, it seems particularly worth determining whether man-made disasters have unique properties for deteriorating the levels of trust that previously existed within a society (e.g., see Baum *et al.,* 1981; Davidson, Baum, and Collins, 1982; Baum, Fleming, and Davidson, 1983).

Response to Disaster Warnings and Perceptions of Hazard

Since Fritz's (1961, 1968) characterization of disaster behavior, little theoretical work of a psychological nature has been done under the rubric of disaster research, and the majority of this work has focused on preimpact behavior, namely, response to disaster warnings and perception of environmental hazard. From an early, practical need to know how civilians respond to air raid warnings (Janis, 1951) grew a series of influential investigations into the nature of fear-arousing and persuasive communications (e.g., Janis and Feshbach, 1953) sparked by the disturbing observation that persons often fail to respond to warnings in their own self-interests. As Fritz (1961) notes: "Many people tend to deny or disbelieve information that danger is near at hand. They seize on any vagueness, ambiguity, or incompatibility in the warning message enabling them to...interpret signs of danger as signs of familiar, normal events" (p. 665). Early explanations of this phenomenon often invoked the debilitating character of anxiety (Janis, 1962) and, later, the need for cognitive consistency (Kates, 1962; Adams, 1973). More recently, Janis and Mann (1977) have proposed a four-step model of emergency decision making that portrays a decision maker who responds adaptively to disaster warnings only after making the proper "turn" at each of four points in a decision tree. The relative risks of responding or not responding combine with expectations of escape alternatives and the urgency of the decision to form one of five "coping patterns," of which only the vigilant pattern will produce adaptive, protection-seeking behavior.

However, as Withey (1962) points out, choice of action is also contingent upon one's estimate of the probability that the dangerous event will occur, or, in other words, one's estimate of the hazardousness of the environment. The consensual observation in this respect is that residents of hazardous environments (e.g., homeowners on the San Andreas Fault) tend to minimize their estimates of the extent of the natural hazard and minimize the uncertainty surrounding a disaster's occurrence (Burton and Kates, 1964). Such adaptations to environmental danger include attributions to fate, luck, chance, or God for disastrous events and denial of the existence of the hazard altogether. Residents of floodplains, when asked about the probability of a future flood, commonly respond, "We have no floods here, only high water." Interestingly, one of the ways in which people seem to cope with chronic hazard is by overestimating the periodicity or regular, cyclic nature of the disaster's occurrence (e.g., the 100-year flood), and this observation has prompted Slovic, Kunreuther, and White (1974) to argue that distortions in the perception of an environmental hazard are adequately explained by the mechanisms responsible for other examples of inferential bias. Drawing on the work of Tversky and Kahneman (1974), these investigators describe the means by which information-processing heuristics and biases (e.g., availability, representativeness, belief in the law of small numbers) conspire to produce for the information processor a picture of a stable, predictable, and relatively safe environment.

If indeed basic cognitive processes conspire to undermine a realistic assessment of risk, and such underestimation of hazard lessens the probability of an adaptive response to disaster warnings (or preparations for disaster such as escape routes or flood insurance), then recent outcries for the education of "naive statisticians" (Nisbett and Ross, 1980) should find an appreciative ear in the disaster area. As well as providing a useful and important potential for the application of recent developments in social cognition, disaster research may also serve to field-test many of the notions that have, to date, remained theoretical or have gotten only as far as the laboratory. In addition, we concur with Fritz (1961, p. 654), who notes:

> An experimenter cannot introduce the stresses of overwhelming threat to life and limb, of sudden loss of kin and intimates, of the destruction of home and possessions, and of seeing one's community disintegrate. Such experiments, however, are repeatedly produced by natural and man-made forces.

In conclusion, we find ourselves a bit puzzled. Although we have maintained throughout this section that the disaster area has been relatively overlooked (to the disadvantage of environmental psychology), it *has* been one of the better-researched areas in the study of natural environmental concerns. Again, we emphasize the practical basis upon which environmental psychology chooses its questions: Like a child, when the environment

misbehaves, it receives attention. It is interesting in this respect to regard disaster as abrupt and unexpected misbehavior and to note that some environmental pathologies, such as pollution, manifest themselves in a gradual, chronic fashion.

POLLUTION

In environmental science the effect of various air- or waterborne pollutants has been a central concern. One thinks of the effects of asbestos fibers on workers, various forms of poisons that have leaked into the water table, and so on. This chapter would be egregiously incomplete if it did not make some recognition of this problem. However, the contributions of environmental psychology to this issue have not been large; furthermore, it is not easy to see what illumination these problems will provide for social psychological theory or vice versa. Therefore our comments on environmental pollution will be brief and restricted to the areas of overlap between pollution considerations and social psychological theory.

The Social Psychology of Industrial Pollution

Pollution, particularly in its more serious forms, is largely caused by industries (Committee on Environmental Improvement, 1978). Asbestos fibers have been produced for household insulation, chemical companies have manufactured the kepone that poisoned the waters of the upper Chesapeake Bay, iron-mining companies are responsible for the carcinogenic mineral fibers in the waters of Lake Superior, and acid rain is largely the result of chemicals produced by companies in the midwestern states. Producing these pollutants is economically profitable in the sense that to remove them would require considerable investment; and although the social cost of the pollution, translated into dollar terms, is frequently difficult to estimate, it is almost never borne by the corporations. By and large, corporations do not reduce polluting activities unless they are legally required to do so, for it is not within the scope of economic rationality to bear immediate costs for mere moral gain. One can therefore expect that companies will resist efforts to force them to reduce pollution, and these resistances will largely be legal—delay tactics, for example, or extensive lobbying efforts opposing legislative sanction.

Within these larger social processes, however, are some of interest to environmental and social psychology. For instance, one notices that employees of such companies are in a complex and somewhat ambivalent situation. Often, because of their identification with the goals of the corporation (or at least with the wages that it pays), they may be ideologically opposed to controls on corporate polluting activity. One can expect considerable psychological bolstering of these attitudes. For instance, one can expect that corporate employees will doubt the validity or conclusiveness of the evidence demonstrating the harm of the pollution their industries produce (e.g., Festinger, 1957; Fazio, Zanna, and Cooper, 1977). While we are not aware of any such surveys, we would not be surprised to learn that the employees of cigarette manufacturers are less likely than others to believe in the carcinogenic properties of cigarette smoking. Also, given what is known about diffusion of responsibility and individuals' perceptions of personal responsibilities (Darley and Latane, 1968), we would suspect that employees at various levels often locate the responsibility for the continued polluting activities of their company at *other* levels of the corporate hierarchy. It would not be surprising were the corporate organization set up to facilitate just such an avoidance of responsibility for negative actions.

For corporate workers several considerations exist. Various chemical pollutants have an effect that is most intense at the site of production. Asbestos fibers, for example, are most concentrated within company plants, and it is therefore the worker who is likely to show the most deleterious effects of exposure. (Indeed, the phrase "mad as a hatter" has its origins in the derivatives of mercury used in the process of blocking hats. Absorbed by workers, these chemicals produced madness.) A rational analysis suggests that this result should motivate the corporate workers to push for control of the pollutants that their corporations produce. However, the psychological story may be somewhat more complicated by cognitive consistency strivings, information-processing biases, defensive attributions, and so on. The injurious effects of various chemicals are frequently only discovered after they have been produced over a course of many years; thus the senior workers in the factory will already have accumulated most of the negative effects of these chemicals. For reasons clearly addressed by social psychological theory, these workers may expend great efforts to avoid thinking about the effects of these pollutants, and they may indeed be motivated to deny such injurious effects. In addition, a distressed economy decreases the number of jobs available and thereby increases the value of each individual job. Workers who show a willingness to stand in long unemployment lines, travel hundreds of miles in order simply to submit a job

application, or risk crossing picket lines to earn a day's wage can hardly be expected to jeopardize these positions, once attained, by becoming actively vocal or by damaging the fiscal foundations upon which their employment rests. Indeed, economic and psychological realities seem to conspire to prevent those most brutally affected by industrial negligence to work toward its remedy.

We are suggesting, then, that efforts to counter an ever-growing danger—industrial pollution—may need to begin at a more fundamental level than previously believed. Current thinking about pollution often addresses the problem as one whose solution is sought by all rational individuals. The obstacle is seen to consist of ignorance (people don't know about feasible alternatives to pollution-generating activities, etc.) and motivational deficit (people do not take the initiative to alter habits, etc.). As such, the remedy has been sought in education and persuasion. Indeed, neither can *we* imagine any right-minded person who would favor asbestos poisoning or acid rain, but our point here is that psychological phenomena more subtle or complex than either a simple lack of intrinsic motivation or a degree of ignorance may be at issue here. Recognition of the problem *as* a problem must precede remedial action. We suspect that analogous to the floodplain dweller, many urbanites may be overheard to say, "We have no pollution here, only thick water." It may be reasonable then to think of everyday pollution as a geophysical risk—a slow disaster—and to begin policy-level efforts at the stage of hazard assessment [see Stern and Gardner (1981) for a review of behavior change in regard to environmental pollution].

Pollution Control by Social Science

For several reasons the problem of pollution, already significant, is likely to increase. First, with the increasing sophistication of manufacturing processes, a correlated increase in the toxicity of manufacturing by-products seems to follow. Second, as population densities increase, waste products that previously would have dissipated into relatively harmless concentrations become concentrated in toxic amounts. For these and a host of similar reasons the problem of toxic wastes grows more acute, and it becomes correspondingly useful to consider pollution control techniques that may be suggested by social science.

Frequently, if pollution is to be controlled, it is controlled with the least difficulty at or near its source. Effluents can be scrubbed out of steel plant emissions prior to emanation from the smokestack but not afterward.

Glass bottles and metal cans become pollutants in systems designed to generate heat by burning garbage; the *homeowner* can separate them from other kinds of garbage, but later separation is much more costly and difficult. Those who use dangerous chemicals in manufacturing processes can withhold them relatively easily from nearby rivers, but once they reach the river, they are extraordinarily difficult to remove. However, such immediate control at the source is generally not in effect. In many of these systems, as in other systems that social psychologists have looked at, an individual's "outflow" is pooled with that of many others, at both the individual and the corporate level. In this situation combining one's personal pollution with the communal outflow is psychologically rather easy and often technologically undetectable. The cost to the individual, even if the total system breaks down, is generally not high, and as well, responsibility cannot be easily attributed to any single "straw that broke the camel's back" (Latane, 1981). This sort of situation has been referred to by Hardin (1968) and others as "the tragedy of the commons" or the "social trap." Brechner and Linder (1981) discuss the properties of such social traps, which are defined as situations in which an individual performs some behavior for immediate gain; the long-term sum of these many individuals seeking short-term gain is disastrous for society and ultimately for the individuals themselves.

Social traps are difficult to modify. One obvious solution is monitoring the behavior of each actor and imposing higher immediate costs on the individual's destructive action. Economists have suggested that companies be able to buy "pollution rights," which would provide for limited polluting at some monetary cost. However, suppose the pollution were such as to cause a statistically reliable rise in mortality rates? Most persons find something incommensurate about trading money for lives. In addition, we have the problem of how the collection agency (presumably the state) would transfer a fair share of the profits to the injured individuals. Other analysts have suggested monetary fines or criminal sanctions for polluters, the difference here being that these fines are intended to be so large as to absolutely deter pollution activity. However, sanctions at this level often require costly due process adjudication mechanisms and motivate considerable evasive action. Too, any system that is dependent on pollution-source monitoring requires a complex and potentially fallible monitoring system. Other techniques to eliminate or reduce social traps are also possible, and Brechner and Linder (1981) suggest some of them, ranging from sample monitoring

to more social psychological techniques such as increased identification with the goals of the resource recovery group.

Here is a situation in which known social psychological theory stemming from research on cooperation might usefully be employed. At a more fundamental theoretical level it may make sense to investigate individuals' (and perhaps groups') perceptions of contingency. Do contributors to communal outflows ever become aware of the ill effects of their contributions? If so, are the input and negative outcome arranged in such a way as to ameliorate or promote a perception of contingency? Is the individual who tries to withhold his pollution from the outflow able to discern any change in the state of his environment? If not, does he become "helpless" (Seligman, 1975) or simply discouraged? We put forth these questions only to make clear the *social* nature of our current ecological crisis and to point up what we see as a potentially significant contribution to be made by social psychological theory and environmental psychological research.

ATTITUDES ABOUT THE NATURAL ENVIRONMENT

A good deal of research has been done on environmental attitudes, a topic of obvious interest to social psychologists. Because researchers have connected people's environmental attitudes to many aspects of their environmental behavior, the positioning of this section here is largely an arbitrary decision. Still, several points can be made about attitudinal environmental research that seem to us to warrant including the material in this single section rather than dispersing it among other sections.

A good many studies have been conducted that tap some aspect of what might be conceived of as environmental attitudes [see Weigel (1983) for a bibliography of many of these studies; see Olsen (1981) for a review; and see Heberlein (1981) for a cogent set of criticisms of them from a psychological perspective]. Many of the publications simply discuss the results of a single- or few-item measure of "environmental concern" and attempt to plot the advance or decline of this concern over time. Enough difficulties are associated with the assumptions behind this work for us to judge it not a particularly profitable research line to pursue. Many other researchers, interested in one aspect of the attitude-environment question, have used *ad hoc* scales created for the specific purposes of their research. This research has often been fruitful, and examples of it are discussed in other sections of this chapter. Here we will mention the work of several research teams who have set out to develop environmental attitude scales that are general in scope, useful for predictive purposes, and psychometrically respectable. Psychologists considering environmental attitude research would do well to see whether these scales would serve their specific research purposes.

Weigel and Weigel (1978) reported a sixteen-item scale that includes items that key respondents to evaluate trade-offs between, for example, the increased convenience of consumer products versus their polluting by-products or the benefits and costs of eliminating animal predators. Proenvironmental answers are summed to give a total proenvironmental attitude score. Maloney and associates (Maloney and Ward, 1973; Maloney, Ward, and Braucht, 1975) have developed an environmental attitude scale that is divided into subscales measuring *verbal commitment, actual commitment* (e.g., reports of action taken, such as joining environmental organizations), and *proenvironmental affect* (e.g., industrial pollution makes me angry). They also designed an *ecological/environmental knowledge scale* measuring knowledge of environmental systems and threats to those systems. Lounsbury and Tornatzky (1977) have made what seems to be a reasonable conceptual partition of environmental attitudes into domains including overpopulation concerns, pollution concerns, economic materialism, conservation, and environmental action concerns. Factor analyses revealed "concern for environmental degradation" and "concern for environmental action" (e.g., bottle return laws) clusters arising from response patterns. This set of scales seems of particular theoretical interest, both because it separates some logically distinct categories, such as overpopulation and pollution, and because it enables a test of several psychologically interesting hypotheses about the relations between economic materialism, conservationism, and environmentally conserving attitudes and actions.

Two other attitudinal measures seek to tap a more global and value-linked set of attitudes that approach the status of an end-state value. The value in question is perhaps best captured by the image of earth as a small, delicate, complexly interrelated network of precious resources and fragile ecological balances. This "new environmental paradigm" (Dunlap and Van Liere, 1978) is set in opposition to the older beliefs in infinitely cheap resources and the equating of economic growth with increases in people's well-being. A similar concept has emerged (perhaps not surprisingly) from a group of researchers in California. They have generated the no-

tion of "voluntary life-style simplicity," which consists of an interrelated set of attitudes and self-reports of actions involving reduced material consumption, awareness of ecological principles, and human-scale, nonenergy-intensive activity (Olsen, 1981). Some other elements of this style, such as personal growth, are less obviously connected to environmental concerns.

Intuitively, these sets of attitudes do seem to connect, in the sense that they are all held by a person we can think of, and intuitively again, a perhaps growing number of people do seem to make important life decisions on the basis of this general premise. Future research will show to what extent these sets of attitudes actually are interconnected and whether they do in fact determine behavior. From a methodological perspective we would simply point out that it will not be an empirical finding of great importance to discover that those high on a voluntary life-style simplicity scale take various environmental actions if those actions, by being included in the scale, were elements of the definition of the life-style patterns.

Research on environmental attitudes will certainly proceed in the direction most familiar to psychologists from the work of Fishbein and Ajzen (1975), who have demonstrated that attitudes, conceptualized according to their theory and measured by their procedures, can be highly predictive of behavior. The key to their approach is to make the attitudinal measures highly specific to the behaviors in question (Weigel, Vernon, and Tognacci, 1974; Heberlein and Black, 1976). Clearly, this approach is valuable when there is practical value in predicting a person's environmentally oriented behavior. What arises theoretically from this approach is more difficult to specify. We would suggest that environmental psychological theory will be most advanced by attitudinal studies that demonstrate how various environment-preserving or -destroying behaviors flow from a matrix of attitudes that are not simply statements of intentions to commit the actions in question [e.g., see Heberlein (1971) and Heberlein and Black (1976) on the prediction of littering or the purchase of lead-free gasoline; or see Becker *et al.* (1981) on the connection between the beliefs that personal health and comfort are dependent on keeping warm and the resultant high use of energy for space heating during the winter].

ENERGY CONSERVATION

Environmental psychologists have been active in seeking to persuade people to adopt energy-conserving practices and renewable energy sources such as solar heating. Although these activities are difficult to classify, energy is most often regarded as a natural resource, and therefore it makes sense to discuss energy conservation under reactions to the natural environment. Yet the ways in which people customarily use energy are through such obvious built forms as houses or automobiles, which would suggest that this section should appear in our later discussion of the built environment. Its place here is meant to highlight the ecological importance of the topic and our focus on behavior change in regard to conservation behavior.

In the past decade or more, social and environmental psychologists have flocked to the study of energy production, energy use, and energy conservation. A major reason for this sudden interest needs no great elaboration here; it stemmed from various international events, such as oil shortages, which indicated to many that our image of infinite energy sources was an incorrect one. Initially, psychologists rather naively assumed that they had a good deal to contribute to the study of energy conservation. Happily, unlike other situations, as the initial parameters of the field became clear, this assumption was generally borne out and documented. First, researchers discovered that in almost any process in which human beings used energy, savings of up to 50 percent of the energy used could be achieved without markedly degrading the processes or products involved. This conclusion came from a variety of sources, such as comparisons of similar manufacturing processes in the United States and other more energy efficient countries (see Dorf, 1978, for a review). Second, Ross and Williams (1976) carried through a very general, applied physics-based estimate of potential energy savings in numerous societal uses of energy and came to very similar conclusions. Finally, a number of analyses of specific human uses of energy have arrived at similar conclusions. For instance, Sinden (1978) reports a careful study of a set of row houses in which, not withstanding the fact that those houses are relatively modern and of good construction, it was still possible to save over 50 percent of heating and cooling energy in the houses with a variety of specifically tailored modifications.

In any particular energy-using process, there are many ways of modifying the process to produce energy conservation. Frequently, in terms of the applied physics and engineering of the problem, the energy-conserving measures are well known. That is, from one perspective the work of the physical scientist and the engineer is largely done in that there are a good many techniques available within the technological state of the art that can promote substantial energy savings. The task of the so-cial scientist, the economist, and the policy analyst, within our voluntaristic society, is to facilitate the adoption of these technological innovations by actual energy users.

A number of analyses have been done that point out areas that could potentially benefit by social science intervention. Consider the problem of transportation. Zerega (1981) reports that around 55 percent of the petroleum used in the United States is used for transportation purposes and 77 percent of that amount is used by cars and trucks. Further information points toward the conclusion that a major share of petroleum consumption is generated by private automobile use. Other perspectives also point toward the same conclusion; a one-mile, one-person trip consumes from two to ten times as much energy when made by private cars as when made by trains, buses, or subways (Zerega, 1981). Initially, and without having done the requisite behavioral studies, the government embarked on a policy of encouraging ride sharing, a policy of encouraging people to commute together. This is a typical example of our standard governmental approach to a problem. One area of low-efficiency energy consumption is identified, and that consumption is attacked by, first, a faith in market mechanisms, in which energy cost considerations are expected to modify behavior to the optimal degree; by, second, a tuning of these forces by incentives or disincentives imposed by tax laws or by legal regulatory activity (e.g., smokestack emission laws); or by, lastly (as in this case), the allocation of federal funds to facilitate the desired actions. All of these remedies have been applied in the case of facilitating car pooling: Cars with only one rider have paid disproportionately high road use fees, commuter pool lanes of highways have been set aside, and businesses have been required to take various steps to encourage commuter pooling. Politics also have not been irrelevant; changes in our administrations or pressures of political interest groups have greatly modified our national policies in this area.

All of these activities designed to facilitate more efficient use of transportation energy have been driven by economic analyses and limited by political considerations. Very little has been done in the way of establishing the social psychological parameters of the problem or people's preferences among various possible solutions. Psychologists will not be surprised to learn, therefore, that most commuter-pooling plans have had relatively little effect. Relevant psychological and sociological research on ride sharing (e.g., Dueker and Levin, 1976; Margolin and Misch, 1978) has not had a great deal of impact on programs. Reichel and Geller (1981) present a number of promising behavioral techniques for conserving transportation energy, including ways of making ride sharing more successful. One hopes that some of their suggestions will be considered in national policy decisions.

The approach to energy conservation taken by the Department of Energy has been a similar market approach. Its general principle is that as energy costs rise, the consumer, in his or her role as rational decision maker, will take all of the steps necessary to reduce his or her energy consumption. Many of the difficulties with this model are discussed in the forthcoming report of the National Academy of Science, Committee on the Social and Behavioral Aspects of Energy Consumption. Meanwhile, a good deal of behavioral research has demonstrated the utility of psychological strategies for the reduction of energy consumption. [See Winett and Neale (1979), Cook and Berrenberg (1981), and Seligman, Becker, and Darley (1981) for reviews of this literature.]

The role of feedback about energy consumption is a useful example of the application of psychological techniques to an environmental issue. Analyses of, for instance, the homeowner as a decision maker reveal that the owner has little information that indicates whether any of his or her potentially energy-conserving activity actually is effective. Providing this feedback has generally been effective in reducing homeowners' energy consumption, sometimes bringing about consumption reductions of 15 percent or more (Seligman, Becker, and Darley, 1981). These results require some qualification, and the qualifications are generally psychologically meaningful. Seligman, Becker, and Darley (1981) suggest that, first, the feedback must be credible in the sense that people need to be able to discern a relationship between their conserving actions and the feedback they receive. Second, the individual must be committed to producing the changes promoted by the feedback that is given. Finally, the feedback must be conceptualized and administered in a way that is psychologically meaningful to the participants. The understandability of the feedback is critical for its acceptance; if the feedback is comprehensible and tied to certain known actions that the consumer can use to reduce it, its exact form is not likely to be important.

Cook and Berrenberg (1981) have performed the valuable service of reviewing research on behavioral techniques to produce energy conservation and classifying the studies into general categories. They point out that attempts to encourage individuals to conserve energy have been analyzed from attitude change and behavior modification perspectives. Further subdivision of these approaches leads to eleven categories into which behavioral science studies can be grouped. The eleven categories are shown in Table 1.

Although many of the categories of the table will be familiar to social psychologists who have studied social change, a few annotating comments may be useful. The first four variables jointly or separately lead to the potential attitude changes described as attitudinal outcome variables (variable 5). Variables 6, 8, 10, and 11 are the nonattitudinal factors that facilitate or inhibit attitude-consistent behaviors. The consequences of the new behaviors (variable 11) and information about these consequences (variable 10) serve to maintain that changed pattern of behavior over time.

Questions arise about the proper psychological strategies to produce increases in energy conservation behavior. One obvious answer is information campaigns, and the reader will also recall several such campaigns during the several energy crises that have occurred. Social psychologists, for the reasons so usefully explicated in Cook and Berrenberg's (1981) table, generally would not believe that information campaigns alone would produce marked increases in energy conservation among individuals. What evidence can be brought to bear on this issue (and we ought to say that the evidence is generally complex and indirect) tends to support this conclusion. [See Seligman and Darley (1977), Winett and Neale (1979), and Olsen (1981) for comments on this issue.] This result does not mean that information campaigns are useless. On the contrary, they may lead to attitude changes that make people more favorably disposed to shifts in national policies promoting conservation or to regulation (e.g., car downsizing by manufacturers) producing conservation. But most social psychologists would argue that the uncertainties and resistances that inhibit action-pattern change require more than impersonally transmitted information to be overcome.

Here it is worth noting the complexity that exists in kinds of energy-conserving actions and decisions. Some are what can be called onetime decisions, such as buying a superinsulated refrigerator, buying an electronic-pilot light stove, or installing increased insulation in the attic. Others involve actions that are taken on a seasonal basis, such as putting on storm windows in the fall and screens in the spring. Still others, such as pulling shades on south-facing windows to keep out the heat in summer, need to be done on a daily basis. These daily actions are

TABLE 1
Conceptual Variables in Energy Conservation Research

1. *Attitude/behavior influence variables*

   Depicted severity of resource shortages and their consequences
   Specificity and feasibility of recommended actions
   Financial incentives and disincentives
   Convenience/comfort incentives and disincentives
   Symbols of social recognition
   Public commitment to conservation
   Participation in group conservation decisions
   Conservation actions by prestige models
   Conservation actions by opinion leaders

2. *Contexual environmental variables*

   Visibility of resource shortage
   Enduringness of resource shortage
   Price and rate of price change
   Reports of excess profits
   Consistency of information regarding resource shortage
   Consistency of policy toward conservation

3. *Person attributes that influence acceptance of conservation programs*

   Conservation-related attributes
      Initial conservation attitude
      Health and comfort beliefs related to conservation
      Ascription of personal responsibility for resource shortage
   Other attributes
      Financial need
      Need for social approval, status
      Beliefs regarding internal-external locus of control
      Technological optimism

4. *Perceptions relevant to the impact of attitude/behavior influence variables*

   Equitable sacrifice
   Belief/disbelief in resource crisis
   Attributions regarding motivations for conservation policies
   Impact of personal conservation efforts

5. *Attitudinal outcome variables*

6. *Variables influencing evocation of behavior consistent with pro-conservation attitudes*

   Reminders of conservation actions
   Situational salience of attitude
   Recognition of action-attitude congruence

7. *Behavioral intention outcome variables*

8. *Variables influencing actualization of pro-conservation intentions*

   Knowledge of appropriate conservation practices
   Access to appropriate conservation actions
   Anticipated consequences of conservation actions
      Financial gain/loss
      Convenience or comfort gain/loss
      Social approval gain/loss
      Satisfaction in behaving consistently with conservation values

9. *Conservation action variables*

   Compliance with conservation laws and regulations
   Conformance to national conservation standards
   Self-reported willingness to accept government constraints on resource usage
   Voluntary action
      One time action
      Continuing action
   Active support for conservation policies

10. *Variables providing information regarding the effectiveness of conservation efforts*

    Form of informational feedback
    Frequency of informational feedback
    Agent of feedback (self vs. other)

11. *Consequences of conservation behavior*

    Financial gain/loss
    Convenience or comfort gain/loss
    Social approval gain/loss
    Satisfaction of conservation values

SOURCE: Cook and Berrenberg, 1981, p. 100.

difficult to sustain, and frequently it is possible to automate them. Buying a clock thermostat, for instance, that sets back the heat on winter nights and turns it back up in the mornings can substitute for hundreds of daily individual actions by the homeowner to accomplish the same purpose. But these purchase decisions often involve significant capital outlay under conditions of uncertainty about the savings they will produce. There is some reason to believe that a homeowner's naive economic heuristics for calculating such savings tend to underestimate them.

For all of these reasons and others, social psychologists suspect that energy-conserving products and practices are underused in the sense that people could achieve more conservation than they do within the constraints of their financial, value, and comfort considerations. Several authors (Leonard-Barton and Rogers, 1979; Darley and Beniger, 1981) have suggested that a great deal of knowledge has accumulated about how these changes in pattern can be accomplished in the interdisciplinary research field of the "diffusion of innovations" (Rogers and Shoemaker, 1971). Drawing on that field, Darley and Beniger (1981) have postulated the dimensions along which energy-conserving innovations are evaluated. Because of the nature of many people's resistances to these innovations, it can be suggested that innovation-producing communications will travel along social network lines. Neighbors will tell each other what they did that really saved energy and visit each other's homes to see these innovations in action. One person will tell a working acquaintance about a thermostat that turns down the heating in the house during the middle of the day, and this device will work for both of them because they are both members of dual-career couples with empty homes while children are at school. Change strategies follow from this perspective: Persons who are attitudinally disposed to innovate can be identified and their innovations facilitated by conservation experts. The innovations of others in their social networks are made increasingly likely and can, in turn, be facilitated.

The production of energy conservation provides a natural setting for a topic that has long fascinated social psychologists, that of change in activity patterns and maintenance of that change. (Many immediately will be reminded of one of the first experiments in modern social psychology, Lewin's wartime work on persuading consumers to shift to eating less preferred cuts of meat.) For this reason many psychologists, using techniques drawn from social psychology, operant analyses, and other theoretical perspectives, have done research in the field. But two difficulties need to be pointed out.

First, undue research attention has sometimes been paid to changes that would not, in fact, contribute markedly to significant national energy savings. As is often the case when a theoretically driven research team looks at an applied area, the first problems studied are likely to be those that involve the most direct application of the theory rather than the problems that policy considerations suggest are the most important to deal with. In the initial flash of their enthusiasm researchers sometimes make exaggerated claims that are remembered unfavorably by policymakers. An article by Stern and Gardner (1981) alerts social scientists to the policy considerations in the energy field, as does the useful report edited by Stobaugh and Yergin (1979).

Second, talking in a way that implies that there is a national energy policy into which social science considerations can be fitted is unrealistic as this chapter is being written early in 1983. Energy policy, and even the need for such a policy, other than letting market forces operate, has been an issue on which successive administrators have sharply differed. One is tempted to remark that social science energy researchers, with regard to funding for their research, are something of an endangered species. This is a pity, because the research that has accumulated to date demonstrates that social psychologists can make significant contributions to producing massive reductions in energy use.

THE BUILT ENVIRONMENT

Anyone who has had an extended aerial view of this planet cannot help but conclude that humans are, above all things, builders, and this fact has not been lost on environmental psychologists. We are encapsulators, creators of enclosures, and our cognitions, behaviors, and interpersonal relationships are affected by the artificial constructions in which we perform them. A very large portion of environmental psychological research might be classified under the heading of "the built environment." This section therefore makes no claim to completeness. Instead, we have chosen to broach two major issues: environmental cognition and architectural psychology. The first issue deals with representations of the built environment and considers the built environment largely on an urban scale. The second deals with enclosures on a more immediate level, looking at factors such as ambient quality, layout, and design, and the effect of these factors on human behavior.

COGNITION AND THE BUILT ENVIRONMENT

A pressing question in modern social psychology concerns the relationship between attitudes and behavior —or, rather, the sometimes tenuous nature of their linkage. Recently, we have come to see that action is not necessarily predicated upon cognition. Nevertheless, it may still be instructive for the environmental psychologist to examine how persons think about the built environments in which they interact, keeping in mind that such cognitions do not necessarily translate directly into environmental action.

In a very real sense environmental perception is a redundancy, for all perception is necessarily environmental (unless one considers introspection to be a kind of inward perception). However, the traditional focus in perception research has been, for the most part, on the human apprehension of unitary constructs—isolated objects stripped of their context (Ittelson, 1970, 1973, 1976). Biederman's (1972) demonstration of the role played by mundane contexts in the recognition of ordinary objects testifies to the need for a perceptual psychology that addresses these issues. Most notable in this regard, of course, is the ecological perspective of James Gibson (1966, 1979), whose "theory of affordances" presupposes that properties of the environment are perceived as meaningful entities rather than distinct points and that the perception of these "invariant functional properties" conveys information directly to the organism. Although constructivist theories (Brunswik, 1969; Neisser, 1976) may ultimately do a better job of describing perception, Gibson's work is important for its molar, holistic approach.

Environmental cognition, on the other hand, has an identity quite distinct from traditional cognitive psychology in its emphasis on how human beings represent spatial features of the environment in cognitive terms, or what Downs and Stea (1977) have called "locational knowledge." The cornerstone for this activity was laid by Lynch (1960), who studied the hand-drawn "cognitive maps" of sixty residents of three major American cities. Lynch identified five fundamental features that seemed to comprise the sketch maps residents had drawn of these diverse urban areas: the channels along which persons travel are *paths,* which seem to be the predominant element in hand-drawn maps. The plazas, railroad stations, and traffic circles at which these paths intersect are *nodes.* In addition, *districts* are sections of the city possessing an identifiable character, *edges* are boundaries and barriers such as rivers and walls, and *landmarks* are visually distinct objects that provide an external point of reference for the urbanite. For Lynch these factors work together to produce a legible or illegible cityscape—one that either facilitates or resists its residents' efforts to orient themselves and navigate within it by virtue of its comprehensibility. Although Lynch's urban-planning strategies to increase the legibility of cities have been put into practice (Appleyard, 1976), there is a

great deal of debate about the validity of the sketch map methodology (see Evans, 1980, for a thorough review). Magana (1978) has provided cluster-analytic support for the five elements in Lynch's taxonomy, but a more sophisticated technique for the investigation of cognitive mapping is still needed.

Representations of the Environment

Does this discussion imply, then, that people represent their environment cartographically, literalizing the cognitive map, or is the term a simple metaphor? The answer is not at all clear, and this controversy continues to pervade environmental cognition. Propositional models (Anderson and Bower, 1973; Pylyshyn, 1973) contend that "place information" is stored in lists and that the informational nodes in this associative network are decomposed, abstracted meanings; schemas that facilitate evaluation, search, and retrieval (Neisser, 1976) are a part of this propositional network. The analogical model (Kosslyn, 1975; Shepard, 1975) holds that mental representations are stored in a roughly isomorphic correspondence to the objects they depict. The representation is thought to trigger neural processes similar to those active at the time of perception, reconstructing the image in analogical form.

As one might expect, empirical evidence can best be said to support the compromise position that both propositional *and* analogical forms are presently needed to describe human spatial memory (Kosslyn and Pomerantz, 1977; Anderson, 1978; Evans, 1980). For example, when individuals do draw sketch maps of their environments, a systematic set of incompletenesses, augmentations, and distortions occur (Downs and Stea, 1973): Long, gradual curves are straightened, paths that meet at greater or less than 90° become perpendicular, and slightly skewed paths are made parallel, implying the influence of higher-order organizational structures such as schemas (Lynch, 1960; Mandler and Parker, 1976; Byrne, 1979) or inferential aids such as alignment, rotation, and distance estimation heuristics (Sadalla and Magel, 1980; Sadalla and Staplin, 1980a, 1980b; Tversky, 1981). Norman and Rumelhart (1975), for example, found that residents of a housing complex whose balconies were oddly flush with the exterior plane of the building, drew sketch maps in which the balconies were normally extended beyond the exterior plane, as the proposition *balcony* would insist they should be. Stevens and Coupe (1978) and Wilton (1979) have shown that subjects make geographical decisions (e.g., "Which city is further west?") as though the information were stored propositionally, and Lea (1975) and Allen, Siegel, and Rosinski (1978) have utilized reaction time tasks to demonstrate that cognitively locating an object in memory as well as distance estimation tasks proceed in a list-checking fashion. However, the same chronometric procedures have been used to show that larger physical distances take longer to scan in memory (Kosslyn, Ball, and Reiser, 1978) and that, similarly, physically proximal distance discriminations elicit longer latencies (Evans and Pezdek, 1980). These latter investigators performed an interesting geographical rotation experiment, the results of which also make clear the need for inclusion of analogical models in any complete account of human spatial cognition. Summarily, both kinds of representational models appear necessary to describe the data, and the expectation of a feasible synthesis does not seem overly optimistic (e.g., Kosslyn and Pomerantz, 1977; Anderson, 1978).

Developmental Trends in Representation

Many variables have been investigated in relation to cognitive-mapping abilities (see Evans, 1980, for a review), but of these variables developmental level and familiarity seem most compatible with the emphasis of this *Handbook*. Developmental research is often divided into two broad categories: frame-of-reference research and representational research. The former focuses on the kinds of information people use in spatial orientation, while the latter concerns itself with the accuracy of spatial memory. Both areas have been largely influenced by Piagetian stage notions, which hold that children pass through three levels of spatial comprehension: the comprehension of topological, projective, and metric space (Piaget, Inhelder, and Szeminska, 1960; Piaget and Inhelder, 1967). Briefly, this transition takes the child from the simple comprehension of separation, proximity, extent of continuity, and so on, to an understanding of Euclidean space with respect to an abstract (as opposed to egocentric) set of spatial coordinates (Hart and Moore, 1973). Empirical research, though not entirely in harmony with these notions (cf. Blaut, McCleary, and Blaut, 1970; Blaut and Stea, 1974), has generally supported the Piagetian theory; children do indeed seem to begin by utilizing egocentric cues to orient themselves in space, come to use single and then multiple fixed objects (landmarks), and then finally comprehend space as a coordinate system that exists independent of the observer.

Representational research has also relied on Piagetian perspectives in its investigation of children's spatial memories. Siegel and White (1975) contend that children begin by remembering landmarks, then establish paths between them, come to organize districts, and finally will coordinate districts with one another. The investigation of these notions has entailed the use of scale model environments, and there is some doubt as to whether this procedure can accurately tap children's spatial memories (Herman and Siegel, 1978). However, on the whole, research in this domain also seems to be supportive of the Piagetian perspective (cf. Spencer and Parvizeh, 1981).

What elements of the physical environment do persons first use in learning a novel layout? This question has been of concern to environmental cognitive psychologists, and a number of studies are instructive in this regard. Lynch (1960) holds that paths are the primary structures learned in the acquisition of mental geographies and that landmarks are only later added to the cognitive atlas. In support of this notion has been the work of Appleyard (1970, 1976) and Devlin (1976), who have found that new residents emphasize paths (to the exclusion of other features) in their maps and that the depiction of landmarks increases more with residency than does the depiction of paths. These data suggest that path networks are indeed primary map components upon which other features (e.g., landmarks, districts, edges) are elaborations. However, Siegel and White (1975) and Hart and Moore (1973) claim that quite to the contrary, landmarks are learned first and interlandmark routes are added with experience. Work by Evans, Marrero, and Butler (1981) suggests that the number of paths, but not the number of landmarks, recalled increases with length of residence, and Heft (1979) reports similar findings in the laboratory.

It is interesting to note also that the accuracy of cognitive representation is increased by familiarity, and that this increase in accuracy parallels the ontogenetic acquisition of spatial concepts (Moore, 1974; Golledge, Rivizzigno, and Spector, 1976; Siegel and Schadler, 1977). More changes occur over time in metric than topological space; that is, although newcomers to and longtime residents of an area may equally well represent a number of districts and their respective features, the longtime residents are likely to have more accurate cognitive maps of the relative position of one district to another. Evans (1980) concludes that whether landmarks or paths serve as map anchors may depend, at least in part, on the physical structure of the environment to be mapped (Heft, 1979) and the relative salience of its landmarks and paths (Milgram *et al.*, 1972). We would expand this idea by suggesting that the goals of the individual in the environment (Does he wish to learn to find point X from point Y? Is this route to be used often?) as well as his general evaluation of the environment may also influence this phenomenon (see Wofsey, Rierdan, and Wapner, 1979).

Summarily, it appears as though social scientists are making some headway in their understanding of how persons come to know their environments, and environmental cognition seems to constitute environmental psychology's closest approach to basic, theory-driven research. As we have noted earlier in this chapter, one of the identifying characteristics of environmental psychology is its interactionist perspective. Humans are seen to exist within an environment that they have, at least in part, created and to which they respond, further altering its stimulus properties. In the most basic sense humans engage in a relationship with their environment, and it is this relationship rather than either of its participants with which environmental psychology is concerned. Environmental cognition research has, for the most part, upheld this promise in translating traditional cognitive paradigms into ecologically valid and environmentally relevant research. It is perhaps surprising, then, that environmental psychologists, while sometimes fulfilling and often paying dialectical tribute to this holistic approach, have more often continued the mainstream experimentalist tradition of isolating particular variables of the built environment when assessing their effects upon particular aspects of behavior. We suspect that this apparent contradiction between the real and ideal arises as a consequence of both the theoretical immaturity of the discipline and, to a greater extent, the imperfection of fit between problems in environmental psychology and social psychological research methods. As we will see, however, it is just this sort of ''variance-accounted-for'' approach to the built environment that has found its way into the applied setting.

ARCHITECTURAL CONSIDERATIONS AND ENVIRONMENTAL DESIGN

We begin by suggesting that an interior—an artificial construction that encapsulates or surrounds an occupant—influences behavior by virtue of its ambient qualities, its spatial and architectural arrangement, and its perceived purpose. The pervasiveness of such influence is clear, but its magnitude is still a matter of contention. We tend to feel, however, that human actions and interactions are relatively loosely related to their surrounds and that a tremendous amount of variability can exist between different interactions within the same physical setting. Certain environments, such as solitary-confinement cells and overcrowded mental hospitals, are perhaps exceptions to this rule and probably deserve the label of ''behavior coercive settings.'' We reiterate our belief that the environmental determinants of behavior are secondary to interpersonal and intrapersonal variables.

Though environmental research has traditionally occupied itself with aspects of the ambient environment (temperature, lighting, sound levels, etc.) and spatial layouts (seating arrangements, positioning of doors, etc.), we suggest that the single most influential force exerted by a room on its occupants is the perceived purpose of the environmental space. No architectural or ambient feature can, for example, adequately explain the silence of library patrons as well as can their knowledge of the norm ''One does not talk in libraries.'' Several libraries can differ in size, number of windows, and aesthetic appeal and yet still be identified as belonging to a common class of book-lending institutions. We assert that this identity is primarily carried not in some physical feature of the interior but in our knowledge of its use and the norms governing our behavior within it [see Proshansky's (1978) discussion of place identity]. There may be more than a germ of truth in one observer's wry contention that more people will urinate in an office marked ''bathroom'' than in a bathroom marked ''office.''

Thus environmental psychologists are less interested in how a room affects behavior per se than in how aspects of the interior facilitate or hinder the goals of the occupants. Persons are usually in a particular environment with a goal or purpose, and we may best gauge the influence of the built interior by examining the ways in which it impedes, constrains, alters, or facilitates purposive behavior. Although no design consideration can account for the library patron's silence, there may be features that remind him of his social obligation, deter his social interaction, or provide him with a measure of acoustic isolation from transgressors. How such features interact with plans, expectations, goals, and perceived function is beginning to receive some much-needed attention by environmental psychologists (e.g., Leff, 1978; Leff and Gordon, 1980; Russell and Ward, 1982), but the implications of these scattered efforts are too new to judge. Therefore our brief review of the influence of the built interior on behavior is necessarily, and perhaps revealingly, one-sided.

Ambient Factors

All built interiors possess characteristic levels of sound, illumination, and temperature, and these three aspects of the ambient environment have received a great deal of attention from environmental psychologists and ergonomicists interested in creating healthful work environments, productive school settings, therapeutic hospital surroundings, and intelligent policy decisions. The particularly quantifiable nature of these ambient factors has also allowed empirical research to address the important questions in this area without undue time spent searching for viable research methods, and from this empirical mooring, researchers have gathered extensive information about the effects of lighting (Boyce, 1975; McCormick, 1976), noise (Cohen and Weinstein, 1981), and temperature (Griffiths, 1975) on behavior. That these factors influence behavior is not a matter of contention; however, the manner in which their mediation is best construed is still much of a puzzle.

We suggest that there is a basic asymmetry in the effects of ambient factors. Fitch's (1965) characterization of the built environment as a kind of intervening force aside, ambient factors do not *facilitate* goals, but rather they either *allow* or *impede* the successful and expedient completion of purposive behavior. In this regard ambient factors are best considered as potential environmental stressors that may, under some circumstances, bring about a general state of arousal (Broadbent 1971). In attempting to explain the arousing qualities of these ambient stressors, environmental psychology has borrowed liberally from social psychological thought.

Cohen (1978, 1980) has suggested that environmental stressors place a debilitating demand upon a capacity-limited information processor, thereby diverting the focus of attention from the completion of the plans to the stressor itself. Both the interruption of the ongoing information-processing task and the organism's own attempts to cope with the interruption result in fatigue. If, indeed, the attention-grabbing properties of ambient stressors account for the annoyance level, then factors that prevent habituation (e.g., unpredictability of occurrence) should also contribute to the stressful quality of the temperature, glare, or noise. Empirical investigations have borne out this relationship (Glass and Singer, 1972), and recently the unpredictability of noise has been demonstrated to determine its debilitating effect on task performance (Matthews *et al.*, 1980). A second notion that has been influential in predicting the stressfulness of ambient factors is that of perceived control (e.g., Maier and Seligman, 1976; Abramson, Seligman, and Teasdale, 1978). Environmental studies suggest that the ability to control a stressor such as noise may at least partially eliminate its stressfulness (Glass, Reim, and Singer, 1971; Averill, 1973; Sherrod *et al.*, 1977).

Though neither the information load nor the perceived control hypotheses can fully describe the stressfulness of an ambient factor [e.g., Borsky (1969) found that noise was more annoying when subjects knew the noise-maker to be unconcerned with the welfare of others], they do seem to be compatible, and in fact, we would be surprised if both were not necessary to any comprehensive theory of environmental stress. Indeed, we will return to these very notions in our discussion of crowding stress; for our purposes now, however, it is enough to note that the ambient qualities of the built interior can have impact on mood (Mehrabian and Russell, 1974), helping behavior (Sherrod and Downs, 1974; Matthews and Canon, 1975), aggression (Geen and O'Neal, 1969; Baron and Bell, 1975; Bell and Baron, 1976, 1977; Donnerstein and Wilson, 1976), interpersonal attraction (Bell and Barnard, 1977), and health (Cohen *et al.*, 1981), to name but a few. However, the levels at which these ambient factors impede performance or influence interpersonal behavior are usually more extreme than those experienced in the normal indoor environment.

In passing, we would like to note a possible pitfall in the application of ambient factors research to environmental design, and this note is in regard to the performance-optimizing goal we earlier claimed was basic to environmental psychology. It is important to remember that those levels of any given factor that facilitate task performance may not *always* be those that are most desirable in an applied setting. For example, a lecture room that allows students to misattribute their midterm-exam anxiety to slightly uncomfortable temperatures or poor lighting may, in fact, provide an edge to its anxious occupants. Similarly, recent investigations of self-handicapping strategies (Berglas and Jones, 1978) suggest that room users may not always *choose* the optimal environment provided them by well-intentioned psychologists (cf. Newman, 1972). We are not seriously suggesting that rooms be built with gas lamps, hard wooden benches, or poor ventilation; rather, we simply wish to suggest that as we learn more about the isolated effects of ambient factors, we must apply this knowledge with careful regard to the attributional processes by which the occupant will come to view himself and his behavior within the context of the artificial environment we create.

Spatial Layout

Spatial layout refers to the ways in which objects (furniture, machinery, doors, etc.) are situated within a built environment of certain dimensions. Though research on evaluative attitudes has often linked occupant satisfaction with spatial layout (e.g., Valins and Baum, 1973; Sundstrom *et al.*, 1982), such an index is essentially a reflection of the degree to which these architectural features meet or fail to meet human needs. As relatively enduring structures, rooms possess spatial arrangements that facilitate some behaviors and constrain or prohibit others, and therefore a layout represents a compromise between the fulfillment of competing intrapersonal needs or the opposing needs of different persons. As Maslow's hierarchy suggests, such conflicts are usually resolved in favor of the most fundamental and imperatively felt need: When function and aesthetics clash, function is served; when builder and user disagree, the desires of the builder will come first. While the influence of spatial layout is difficult to characterize precisely because it is so pervasive, we would like to suggest that such influence is essentially a matter of behavior constraint, aesthetic appeal, and information regulation.

Spatial layout determines, in large part, the very identity of an interior. One may call a room "the chem lab," but unless it is equipped with ventilation hoods, chemical sinks, and carbon dioxide taps, its identity is in grave doubt. In our earlier example of the library we suggested that the perceived purpose of the environment was far more influential than its spatial layout, and we stand by this contention. However, to use Barker's (1968) phrase, an environment must be "synomorphic," or similar in form to the behavior it is designed to host. Knowledge of library norms should not, in fact, affect the behavior of persons in a room that has no books. In this sense spatial layout features serve as identification cues, which then activate social norms.

Synomorphism is not an either-or proposition, and McCormick (1976) has conceived of it as a continuum and has identified some of the spatial features that increase the degree of environment-behavior compatibility. Such observations, though, must be careful not to oversimplify the behavior-environment equation, for the environmental psychological literature explodes with instances of public-housing projects in which people refuse to live and dormitories that remain vacant year round owing to a functional malady that prohibits behaviors the users find important or fails to prohibit behaviors the users find disdainful—and that the designer simply did not imagine. It does not come as news to architects that children require playgrounds; but that parents are not satisfied with play areas that cannot be monitored from inside the home is the stuff of which empty high rises are made.

The influence of spatial arrangement on interpersonal relations has been an active research interest within social psychology at least since the publication of Festinger, Schachter, and Back's (1950) Westgate West study. Empirical verification of the role played by propinquity in regulating interpersonal attraction seemed to bring to the fore the realization that one's friends are drawn from the population of persons one has met and that meeting requires the conjoint occupation of space. More importantly, this study elevated the role of architecture as an explanation of behavior to the theoretical status of other intrapersonal and social factors. Osmond's (1957) categorization of environments as either facilitative of interpersonal relations (sociopetal) or inhibitory in this regard (sociofugal) provided some of the taxonomical underpinnings necessary to generate empirical research (e.g., Sommer and Ross, 1958). Hall's (1959, 1966) theory of proxemics—the social use of space—proved exceedingly influential and continues to draw debate and inspire a good deal of empirical research.

Quietly overlooked, however, were the other means by which spatial layout influences interpersonal behavior, and researchers, with a few exceptions, came to regard *spatial layout* and *functional distance* as synonymous when, in fact, the latter is a subset of the former. Recently, Archea (1977) has conceptualized the built environment as a mechanism that regulates information flow, and such a characterization may serve to revitalize interest in some long-ignored influences of architectual design on behavior. One need only consider the well-known plight of Kitty Genovese (Latane and Darley, 1968) to assess the impact of layout on our interpretation of social reality and therefore our behavior. Had the apartment complex design obscured, rather than highlighted, residents' views of their neighbors' windows, the unresponsive bystanders may have become Good Samaritans. We do not mean to suggest that urban planners are somehow guilty of malpractice (cf. Newman, 1972) but, rather, to underscore the importance of architecture in determining information transmission. If social behavior is truly reliant upon communication, then we would be wise not to underestimate the behavioral influence of the communications channel.

Layout serves not only to regulate communication but to communicate something of its own. We are not the first to suggest that beliefs, attitudes, and ideologies are readily revealed in the architectural use of interior space. Critics of "hard" or "inhuman" architecture (Sommer, 1974; Leff, 1978) have gone so far as to suggest that the sociopolitical structure of a nation can be seen in such designs and have rallied against traditional schools with the vigor and righteousness of a people oppressed. We prefer to take a somewhat more moderate stance; Hazard's (1962) fascinating analysis of layouts in American and Soviet courtrooms exemplifies our position. In the architectural use of this interior space, Hazard sees important clues to the relative import each legal system places on civil and criminal law, the rights of the defendant, and the hierarchical relationship between authority and the common person. Implicit in Hazard's analysis is the notion that these societal values are also communicated to the defendant, whose behavior is thus modified in congruence with his perception of his relative status within the judicial system. Similar analyses of classrooms (Richardson, 1967) and churches (Joiner, 1971) conclude that interior layout serves as a signaling system that defines roles, rights, and responsibilities (see also Konar *et al.,* 1982). Forgas (1979) describes how a businessman may use the layout of his office to define for his client the nature of the social episode, utilizing architectural props, or "sign equipment" (Goffman, 1959), to communicate information about his status, background, interests, and position.

We will discuss the interpersonal and communicatory aspects of space in our treatment of proxemics, but for now we note that spatial features provide us with information about the builders and users of environmental spaces, whether they are corporate vice presidents or societies at large. It is also worth noting that the recent "rediscovery" of gestaltist principles by social psychologists suggests that abstracting such information from an interior is not a mere academic exercise. Not only does the raised chair of the judge symbolically communicate to the defendant the relative role each is required to play in the social ritual, but it may also serve to alter the defendant's causal attributions about the proceedings by enhancing the visual salience of the judge (Taylor and Fiske, 1975, 1978; McArthur and Post, 1977). The implications of attributing greater causality to a teacher for our education or to a cleric for our moral character is left to the reader's imagination.

Aesthetics

Depending on the critic, aesthetic concerns have always occupied an unfairly powerful or inequitably inferior position in architecture. We do not intend to take sides in this form-versus-function debate, which has so faithfully provided grist for the historian's mill, but rather briefly to note the connection between aesthetic appeal and spatial layout. Berlyne's (1960, 1972, 1974) theory of environmental aesthetics suggests that the visual complexity of layout is the single most influential determinant of aesthetic appeal, and there seems to be a good deal of empirical support for this notion (see Wohlwill, 1976). Wohlwill notes, however, that although an inverted U describes evaluative or preferential aesthetic judgments (i.e., moderate levels of complexity elicit the most positive aesthetic ratings), exploratory behavior is monotonically linked to stimulus complexity. Indeed, the behavioral implications of judgments of beauty are uncertain, though the "spillover effect" (Maslow and Mintz, 1956; Mintz, 1956) suggests that perceptions of beauty or ugliness of the surroundings have their impact on a general, affective level. Scaling studies by Mehrabian and Russell (1974) and Russell and Pratt (1980) indicate that the two orthogonal dimensions best describing aesthetic judgment are affective in nature (i.e., arousing-sleepy, and unpleasant-pleasant). With regard to visual complexity it is interesting to note developments in physiological psychology that suggest that the visual complexity of the environment guides neurobiotaxis (Hubel and Wiesel, 1970). We consider this result a provocative point of departure for an interdisciplinary theory of aesthetics.

Built Form and Behavior

That the purpose, ambient qualities, and spatial arrangement of an interior affect the behavior of the occupants is, by now, a truism. More importantly, our somewhat procrustean delineation of these factors has perhaps obscured the influence of their mutual interplay: Spatial arrangement may define purpose, ambient factors may be determined by layout, and each of these may interact with another and with the physiological, affective, and cognitive state of the person. In addition, we may have overestimated the role any of these factors plays in determining the course of behavior. We find it important to temper Winston Churchill's famous dictum, that first we shape our buildings and then they shape us, with Moos's (1976) recognition of the fact that uncontrollable instances may maximize architectural effects. For reasons both methodological and practical, environmental psychologists have concentrated their investigative efforts on environments whose occupants have less than maximal choice in matters of design—namely, offices, hospitals, schools, shopping malls, and dormitories.

Environmental psychologists' attempts to apply what they have learned have resulted in the landscape office and the open-plan classroom, whose failure to be all things to all persons should only surprise those who subscribe to an overly simplistic conception of human behavior. If architecture is to become more user-friendly, more responsive to the needs of people, environmental psychologists must determine what those needs are and how the built environment satisfies or thwarts them. An understanding of architectural determinism becomes necessary for any optimistic consideration of the urban future. That buildings shape us only after we have first shaped them is to say that architecture is but a tool by which we may regulate our own behavior, and as such, it provides an acid test for the wisdom of environmental psychology.

THE SOCIAL ENVIRONMENT

Of all the section titles in this chapter, none is so ambiguous as "The Social Environment," and it is appropriate therefore to ask precisely what we mean by this phrase. In short, we intend it to recognize what one of the first social psychological experiments (Triplett, 1898) recognized: Of all the many aspects of our environment, we are most severely and most often affected by the other persons who surround us. With this definition behind us, it would be fitting to begin a complete review of the whole corpus of social psychology—but as the weight of these volumes testifies, that is a task beyond the scope of any one review or reviewer. Instead, we will attempt to touch upon those aspects of the social environment that are traditionally researched by environmental psychologists, falling victim at last to Proshansky, Ittelson, and Rivlin's (1976) definition of environmental psychology as that which environmental psychologists do (cf. Stokols, 1982). As we will see, however, what environmental psychologists "do" has been influenced by (and therefore is influential upon) social psychologists. Perhaps it is in this section that we will most clearly see the mutual interplay of these two areas, as well as the impediments to that relationship.

BARKER'S BEHAVIORAL ECOLOGY

Among the first social scientists to theorize about and conduct empirical investigations of the social environment was Roger Barker (Barker and Wright, 1955; Barker, 1960, 1963a, 1965, 1968; Barker *et al.,* 1978). Before environmental psychologists demanded intellectual autonomy—before, in fact, there were environmental psychologists to make any such demands—Barker had developed a self-contained, thorough, and unique research perspective replete with theory, methodology, and analytic concepts. In this sense Barker's behavioral ecology anticipated environmental psychology, contributed to its current outlook, and exemplified many of the characteristics that are today some of environmental psychology's hallmarks.

Foremost among these attributes is what we have variously called a holistic, interactional, or molar approach to human behavior. For Barker the partitioning of variance is a vivisection: Dismembering behavioral episodes in order to determine their underlying structure cannot be a useful method of inquiry, for the meaning of behavior lies in a gestalt whose constituents do not reflect the organizational structure of the whole. Behavior is not a hologram wherein the microcosm recapitulates the macrocosm. As Barker noted (1963b, p. 24):

> Psychology has been so busy selecting from, imposing upon, and rearranging the behavior of its subjects, that it has until recently neglected to note behavior's clear structure when it is not molested by tests, experiments, questionnaires, and interviews.

This clarion call for naturalistic methods and philosophical acknowledgment of the ecology of action has often fallen upon deaf ears, and Barker's use of somewhat ambiguous terms—such as "behavior setting"—as crucial components of his theory has left many experimental psychologists perplexed, annoyed, or, more often, unmoved. Yet even psychologists groomed in the ways of rigorous methodology have taken exception to the isolated study of behavior removed from its natural context or split into elements. Indeed, twenty years after the above statement was made, recent investigations have placed Barker's conviction in an interesting light by showing that observers agree to a large extent about the meaningful divisions of ongoing behavior, indicating that the "clear structure" is recognized by almost everyone except psychologists. The sequence called "tying his shoes" is perceptually, causally, and meaningfully distinct from "heading toward the breakfast table," and such chunks are self-evident, as are the joints or nodes that separate them (Dickman, 1963; Newtson, 1976).

The Behavior Setting

Perhaps the most notable aspect of Barker's work, however, does not lie in homage to a difficult theoretical position, with which most of us agree to some extent anyway, but in the transmutation of "ideal" to "idea." Barker's advocacy of an interactional perspective is most clearly reflected in his empirical research, in which the key notion is that of the behavior setting. A behavior setting is variously defined as a "fundamental environmental unit" (Wicker, 1973), "the ecological unit surrounding behavior episodes" (Barker, 1963b), and "a naturally occurring unit having physical, behavioral, and temporal properties" (Moos, 1976). So the reader is quite right in asking, "What is a behavior setting?" Unfortunately, definitions do little to advance our understanding of Barker's theoretical cornerstone, but descriptions often give one a feel for the concept. Consider a typical behavior setting: the worship service. Does the term *behavior setting* indicate the cleric's behavior, the assembled congregants, the arrangement of pews, or the purpose of the gathering? The answer must inevitably be, "All of these together and none of these alone," for the behavior setting is the social milieu that is irreducible to its constituent parts. Characteristically, it has standing patterns of regularly occurring behavior, it includes the physical aspects of locale and architecture, and it has clearly defined boundaries in both space and time. Most importantly, however, it is the most explicable and meaningful expression of the event that may be communicated; we would venture to guess that the phrase *worship service* brings to our readers' minds a plethora of behaviors, rules, roles, circumstances, and locales, all of which together (but none of which alone) describe the worship service. In his delivery of the Kurt Lewin Memorial Award address, Barker noted, "It is not often that a lecturer can present to his audience an example of his phenomena, whole and functioning *in situ*" (Barker, 1963b, p. 26). Indeed, Barker gave his audience the living phenomenon of the behavior setting called "the lecture." The lecture is not the room in which it happens (the ACLU meets there on Mondays), it is not the participants (these are psychologists, not lectures), and it is not the speech being read (which, when read on a street corner to no one at all, may be grounds for incarceration). It is, instead, the integral and indivisible unit comprised of all of these.

Manning Theory

Where does this conceptualization of the behavior setting lead us? In his efforts to taxonomize various behavior settings along different dimensions, Barker came to see that one crucial dimension is the number of performers required to properly operate the setting. Because settings, as we have seen, include goals and purposes, there is an optimal number of performers who may best function to most quickly, efficiently, and accurately achieve the goals implicit within the setting. When less than this optimal number are included, the setting is said to be *undermanned,* and this state of undermanning carries with it certain behavioral consequences for the performers charged with maintaining the behavior setting. Barker argued that these settings could best be viewed as ecobehavioral systems capable of generating forces necessary for their own maintenance. Because undermanning represents a threat to the system, it results in just such pressures on the performers, claiming more of each performer's time and energy and requiring the performer to function in a greater number of and more diverse settings, to feel more challenged, involved, and obligated to the setting. In addition, performers will tend to evaluate themselves and others along task-related dimensions, will be less sensitive to the differences between persons, and will place greater importance on the individual.

All these behaviors occur as a function of inadequate manning; unique here is the contention that an undermanned setting exerts force on individuals to change their behavior in order to keep the setting constant, rather than the other way about. Wicker (1973, 1979) has recently extended this conception to *overmanning* by defining a behavior setting's maintenance minimum (the fewest performers that can keep the setting operational), capacity (the most performers the setting can host), and number of applicants (those who wish to be included in the setting). When the number of applicants is greater than the behavior setting's capacity, it is said to be overmanned. The application of this concept to crowding research is, as we will see, readily evident; but as Wicker points out, whether we define a situation as crowded or overmanned will, at least in part, determine how we attempt to rectify the problem. Whereas a crowded setting may best be remedied by finding more space or reducing the number of people, an overmanned setting may change its function or goals in order to accommodate all the applicants (e.g., a chamber orchestra becomes a symphony orchestra rather than management firing string players or seeking a bigger hall). A much lengthier review would be necessary even to scratch the surface of Barker's complex theory, but it will suffice to say that its central tenets have, in the past two decades, been largely supported by empirical research (e.g., see Barker and Gump, 1964; Wicker and Mehler, 1971; Wicker, 1973). What we hope to have emphasized in this brief survey of Barker's behavioral ecology is that point with which we began this chapter, namely, that prior to the environmental revolution of the late sixties, a small federation of researchers were actively pursuing empirical research based on an interactional perspective, and that both the notion of manning and the more general ecological viewpoint have proved exceedingly influential in the years since.

PROXEMICS

The term *proxemics,* first associated with Hall's (1959, 1966) anthropological characterization of interpersonal distances, has come to more broadly describe the active use people make of the spatial context in which interaction occurs. That this context can be actively manipulated implies, of course, that such manipulation is in itself an effective determinant of behavior; in other words, spatial factors serve as both dependent and independent variables, both altering and measuring social behavior.

The "initial terminological fog in proxemics" (Russell and Ward, 1982) appears to be lifting, revealing a variety of interrelated notions of value to social psychology. As comprehensible as terms like *crowding, privacy, territoriality,* and *personal space* first appear, it was their initially undefined and occasionally interchangeable usage that hindered environmental psychology's attempts to unite them in a single theoretical whole (see Altman, 1975, as an exception). However, the assumption that these notions *can* be integrated and are in fact meaningfully related is evident both in their common grouping under the heading of "proxemics" and the considerable cross-referencing that occurs in this and other discussions of its kind; theoretical accounts of crowding research often implicate personal space as an explanatory concept, and privacy notions encompass territoriality as a regulatory mechanism.

Privacy as an Organizational Concept

Altman's (1975) influential proxemic framework makes privacy its central concept, and therefore the other concepts in proxemics may be derived from it. His "boundary model" of social interaction has provided a useful organizational outline with which to bind numerous related proxemic themes and is also one of the few truly environmental approaches to traditional social psychological concerns. In short, Altman's dialectical approach holds that privacy is the achievement of a desired level of social stimulation and as such is a negotiable, dynamic concept. Privacy as a goal implies that the individual is motivated to regulate the quantity of social interaction, and Altman suggests people use verbal, nonverbal, and paraverbal behaviors as their "boundary regulating mechanisms." What is novel here is the conceptualization of the individual as actively using proxemic control techniques to attain the momentarily appropriate level of social interaction. Altman recognizes that, in addition to managing social interaction, privacy (in the more traditional sense of "alone time") is necessary to the formation of identity and the maintenance of the self-concept (Goffman, 1959; Westin, 1967; Beardsley, 1971; Gross, 1971; Wolfe and Laufer, 1975).

Yet one might well ask why privacy—used in this broader sense of an ideal level of social stimulation—is in any way uniquely environmental, for Altman's thesis falls in the company of other psychological theories of social interaction. If, as this information regulation view suggests, opening a colleague's mail deprives her of control over the outgoing stream of information, and thereby of her privacy, then what does this model have to do with conventional environmental concerns, and how does it differ from social psychological theories?

The answer certainly lies in the organizational value of Altman's model and its unification of proxemics. Prior to Altman's thesis various works on territoriality, personal space, and crowding bore some vague resemblance to one another—enough to imply kinship but with no clearly defined interrelations. In Altman's system territorial- and personal-space-establishing behaviors are driven by privacy goals, and crowding may be seen as a reaction to the failure to fulfill them. If an individual is motivated to attain and maintain a desired level of social stimulation, then territoriality, personal spacing, and crowding can all be seen as determinants of, responses to, or factors otherwise related to the discrepancy between achieved and desired levels of privacy. It is in this sense that privacy, as a proxemic concept, is of greatest use.

If we are to accept, for at least the moment, this perspective on human spatial behavior, we are obligated to address first this assumed motivation to control social stimulation: Do people find certain levels of interaction aversive, and if so, how is such aversion dealt with? Although one might make a satisfactory case for investigating either the understimulation pole of the stimulation continuum (i.e., loneliness, isolation, etc.) or the overstimulation pole, it is the latter that has been best researched under the rubric of crowding.

Crowding

Early psychological notions of crowding grew out of both the sociologists' demographic accounts of urban life (e.g., Wirth, 1938; Simmel, 1950; Biderman, Louria, and Bacchus, 1963) and animal investigations in the ethological (Christian, Flyger, and Davis, 1960) and laboratory traditions (Calhoun, 1962a, 1962b, 1963a, 1963b). These diverse research traditions had in common the use of *population density* as the sole index of crowding, suggesting that this easily quantifiable measure of organisms per square inch defined the psychological state of crowding. These two traditions again spoke with a single voice in describing the effect of population density upon the individual and the society; each situation has its own optimal density level, the transcendence of which engenders physiological, psychological, and social pathology. That this simple measure would readily predict the disturbing "behavioral sink" fit well with the conventional wisdom of the time, and for a while it appeared as though Calhoun's pathological rats bode ill for the urban future, where density is central to the definition of city life.

However, as early as 1966, Kessler bred animals to standing-room-only conditions, without any sign of personal or social pathology, suggesting that population density was but one of many factors whose interplay described the phenomenon of crowding. Several researchers have since found reason to question early animal studies of crowding (e.g., Freedman, 1975; Freedman, Heshka, and Levy, 1975) on both methodological and conceptual grounds; this issue, combined with the inherent difficulty of extrapolating from infrahuman to

human behavior (Lloyd, 1975), has prompted a search for a replacement for the density model and a rethinking of crowding concepts.

Though not the first one to do so, Stokols (1972a, 1972b) most clearly describes the separation of crowding and density notions, defining *density* as a physical quantity that describes the number of persons in a space of particular dimensions. *Crowding,* on the other hand, is a psychoaffective state, a negative evaluation of the environmental context brought about by extreme levels of population density. In this sense density is a necessary but insufficient determinant of crowding, which should properly be renamed "perceived crowding" in order to differentiate the subjective evaluation from the objective conditions that elicit it. Rapoport (1975) argues that even density should be regarded in subjective terms and defined as the *perceived* number of persons per unit space. Stokols (1976) further suggests that social and spatial density be conceptualized separately, noting that the individual's perception of crowding as due to too many people or too little space will differentially affect his or her responses to the situation. With this idea in mind, the fundamental research challenge has become the identification of those population density factors that evoke feelings of crowdedness. What is it about high-density situations that sometimes cause one to feel crowded? Answers to this question often fall into one of two categories, variously described as input and output theories (Stockdale, 1978) or, more commonly, as cognitive overload theories and behavioral constraint theories (Schmidt and Keating, 1979).

Briefly, cognitive overload theories build upon the general conceptualization of the human being as a resource-limited information processor who, on occasion, is confronted by a greater number, variety, complexity, or intensity of stimulus inputs than he or she can efficiently manage. Implicit in the concept of density is just such an overabundance of inputs; the presence of others simply swamps the cognitive-processing mechanism, impeding concentration, diverting attention, and resulting in stress on the individual. Milgram (1970) has described the experience of city life as "a continuous set of encounters with overload...[that] deforms daily life on several levels, impinging on role performance, the evolution of social norms, cognitive functioning, and the use of facilities" (p. 1462). Milgram's emphasis is on the adaptive coping mechanisms that evolve in response to overload, noting that many of the observed behaviors of urbanites can be conceptualized as means of dealing with these chronic encounters with too much, too fast, for too long. Although this concept is intuitively plausible, it is not always clear exactly what is meant by cognitive overload. The overloaded circuitry of a machine may provide a useful metaphor for environmental cognition but not a particularly well-specified theoretical construct. And ultimately, it shifts the problem to another domain rather than addressing it directly; an overload theorist must eventually ask what it is about overload that persons find stressful.

A second group of theories focuses on the limiting of behavioral freedom (Stokols, 1976). Density limits the number or variety of behaviors in which we are able to engage and thus elicits a negative evaluation and promotes behaviors designed to reinstate our endangered freedom (Brehm, 1966). Proshansky, Ittelson, and Rivlin (1976) argue that the experience of crowding is only indirectly related to density and that it is the restriction of future behavioral options that elicits feelings of crowdedness, while other theorists (Schopler and Stockdale, 1977) emphasize interference with ongoing goal-oriented behavior. It is the preclusion of behavioral options and the interference with current activities (as well as the forced inclusion of unwanted activities, we would suppose) that causes density to be experienced as stress. It may be instructive to note that if cognitive overload forces a diversion of attention from the desired task to the demanding presence of others (Cohen, 1978), it may be conceptualized as a limiting of cognitive options. The environmental psychologist engaged in a field study of proxemic behavior is unlikely personally to find the elevator on which he or she is riding to be crowded; the manifold stimuli are those upon which he or she *wishes* his or her attention to rest. It is not entirely clear whether one can separate overload and behavioral constraint in this regard, and recent attempts to integrate these two theoretical notions (Stockdale, 1978; Schmidt and Keating, 1979) suggest that it is more useful to highlight their commonalities than to strain toward an artificial differentiation.

Such a commonality is found in the notion of personal control, which has proved to be a powerful explanatory concept within social psychology and which has similarly provided a potent conceptualization of crowding, crowding stress, and coping responses (cf. Stokols and Shumaker, 1982). As Averill (1973) notes, persons afforded a measure of behavioral, cognitive, or decisional control over a normally aversive stimulus are less adversely affected by it. High-density surroundings may

provide just such stress, and Sherrod (1974), for example, has been successful in eliminating the postexposure effects of high density on frustration tolerance by introducing a degree of personal control (see also Cohen, Glass, and Phillips, 1979). This concept of personal control has general utility in that it appears to provide a unifying theoretical underpinning for overload and constraint theories. Informational overload might be characterized by the individual's inability to control the level of incoming social information (Schmidt and Keating, 1979). Valins and Baum (1973) have found that corridor design dormitories elicit greater feelings of crowdedness than do suite design dorms, precisely because the former provide the residents with unavoidable and unwanted social contact. In other words, the inability to control the occurrence of interactions predicts self-reports of crowdedness. Langer and Saegert (1977) similarly found that subjects allowed a degree of cognitive control (i.e., a reinterpretation of the situation) perceived a high-density situation as less aversive than did subjects without such control. Behavioral constraint theories, too, hold personal control as an implicit assumption. Rodin, Solomon, and Metcalf (1978) demonstrated that subjects' feelings of crowdedness were linked to their positions in an elevator: Persons who stood by the control panel felt less crowded than did persons elsewhere in the car. Further, laboratory subjects with the option of starting and stopping group discussions found the discussion context less crowded than did subjects without such an option. Indeed, evidence suggesting that high-density environments often elicit responses identical to those elicited by exposure to uncontrollable events (Seligman, 1975; Rodin, 1976; Baum and Valins, 1977; Baum, Aiello, and Calesnick, 1978) further implicates personal control as a major determinant of perceptions of crowding.

What follows from this discussion is a picture of humans as regulators, who strive to control the amount and variety of stimuli to which they must attend, as well as the behaviors in which they will and may engage. Interference with their control of either behavior or cognition is stress producing, and when such stress follows from density-related factors, humans feel crowded and may seek to reinstate their lost freedom, may regain control over the incoming flow of information, or may suffer the cognitive and motivational consequences associated with uncontrollable outcomes.

Before closing this discussion, we will say a word about the other end of the social stimulation dimension—the pole at which persons find the *lack* of social stimulation aversive. Because cognition may take place in the absence of sensory input, cognitive underload proves an elusive concept. Psychology's closest approach seems to be in the sensory deprivation chamber (see Suedfeld, 1980, for a review), but such artificial conditions tell us almost as much about social isolation as a phone booth full of Princeton freshmen tells us about urban crowding. In addition, naturalistic observation and case study cannot help but confound isolation with personality factors (psychopathology, social deviance), occupational proclivities (hermit, forest ranger, adventurer), and situational control (incarceration). We suspect that the very real conditions of our current urban situation has biased social stimulation research toward the overstimulation end of the continuum. We only wish to note that privacy or selective-access goals often but not always imply a reduction of social interaction; we can imagine situations in which the lack of interaction is the aversive feature of the environmental milieu, and we suppose that the usefulness of much of our theorizing about crowding might be gauged by its ability to work overtime as a theory of social isolation.

All of this discussion suggests, in sum, that we are indeed strongly affected by the presence of other individuals or the lack thereof. Altman's emphasis is not as much on this point as on the mechanisms persons use to achieve the level of compresence they find most desirable. Among these many boundary-regulating mechanisms are two proxemic notions of importance to our review: territoriality and personal space.

Territoriality

With the preceding discussion in mind, we can now view territoriality—the marking of a place to communicate ownership or occupation rights and that place's defense—as a privacy-regulating mechanism. As previously detailed, spatial contexts can serve to facilitate or impede social control (Proshansky, Ittelson, and Rivlin, 1976), and such control being the desired state of affairs, a complex network of rules has evolved to ensure the usefulness of this mechanism to limit social stimulation. Retreating to our offices in order to escape observation by our students is of little practical use if our students fail to subscribe to or recognize cultural norms governing the use of territory. In this way territorial behavior is best seen as an expression of complex sociospatial norms.

That normally acculturated persons do indeed use, recognize, and respect symbolic and artifactual territory markers is one of the few well-established facts in the ter-

ritoriality literature (e.g., Sommer and Becker, 1969; Becker and Mayo, 1971; Becker, 1973; Worschel, 1978). Essentially, markers serve a communications function, delimiting space and labeling it as claimed. However, Becker and Mayo (1971), noting that territorial defense is rare in public places, question the wisdom of considering its occupancy, demarcation, and invasion as symptomatic of a territorial imperative; instead, they suggest that persons simply use markers to communicate the interactional distance they find most comfortable. Edney (1974) points out that both territorial- and personal-space factors are probably at work; and Haber (1980) has shown that territorial- and personal-space dimensions can be separated, and hence territoriality may still elicit some defensive behavior.

Altman (1975) taxonomizes territory in terms of its centrality to occupant behavior and the permanence or duration of its occupancy. Using these factors, he distinguishes primary, secondary, and public territories and notes some of the distinctive features of each. A primary territory is one most central to its occupants' lives and exclusively occupied on a permanent or semipermanent basis. Intrusion into this type of territory (a person's home or a child's room, for instance) is a serious matter, for the primary territory is often held, psychologically, to be an extention of the self, and its violation is similarly held as a personal assault (see Cooper, 1974). Secondary territory is less central, pervasive, and exclusive, and it corresponds roughly to Lyman and Scott's (1967) notion of "interactional territory." Cavan's (1963, 1966) studies of territorial behavior in a local pub indicate that such secondary territories are often reserved for regulars and that intrusion by outsiders (even though the pub is, by definition, public) is defended against. Though legal ownership does not exist, those who can use the territory and how are normatively specified. In the sense that secondary territory bridges the gap between primary territory, whose ownership and occupant rights are clear and unique to an individual or subgroup, and public territory, which is unowned and freely accessed, there is room for considerable question about and conflict over its use. Newman (1972), for example, found that in high-crime areas, places usually considered secondary territories (e.g., hallways of public housing projects, stairwells, etc.) were difficult to mark and defend and, as a result, were treated by the residents as public. Newman suggests that such secondary territories can become defensible space if architectural remedies are applied to allow for the personalization and surveillance of the areas, and hence urban crime may be partially counteracted (see Taylor, Gottfredson, and Brower, 1980, for a review of defensible space research). Along similar lines, Nelson and Paluck (1980) demonstrated that a division of a secondary territory into two primary territories increased self-esteem and feelings of adequacy in residents of an old-age home (see also Holahan and Saegert, 1973).

The third type of territory, public territory, is that whose associated rules are simply the more general norms of social behavior but to which access is not limited; these places are usually occupied for short durations and are neither personalized nor defended. Since public territory lacks ownership, it would seem that intrusion is a meaningless concept here, but Goffman (1971) has made the interesting distinction between intrusion and obtrusion, the latter denoting just such an encroachment of public space. For example, a person who spreads himself out on the extra seats during an airplane ride is intruding on public space by claiming its temporary use in excess of social norms. In this sense we can think of public territories as communally owned, and numerous hypotheses spring to mind regarding the divisions of public territories deemed equitable as a function of situations, status of persons present, individual need, and so on. Often we resent the fellow passenger who considers the middle row of the DC–10 his personal chaise, and it would be interesting to know why we begrudge him his comfort even when we do not wish to use the territory ourselves.

The current conceptualization of territoriality as a sociocultural phenomenon has been hindered by the theoretical muddling of human behaviors with those infrahuman behaviors linked to resource control, mating display, and dominance hierarchies. Research on territoriality has been scant, and theorizing has been stunted by misleading comparisons between ethological and psychological constructs, comparisons that allow for such ludicrous interpretations of enuresis in retarded adults as the marking of the bed as territory. We suggest that human research in this area might be done in a conceptually clearer way were the term *territoriality* replaced with some label less suggestive of bell birds in their leks or dogs urinating on lampposts. Indeed, just such an intelligent transition has been made in the area of personal space—a concept whose ethological roots serve as historic influences, not barriers.

Personal Space

It is not unusual to find that a friend, once close, now seems distant and aloof. Indeed, the distance-as-intimacy metaphor is so pervasive in our thinking, language, and culture that it is a most difficult task to try to extri-

cate it for examination. Nonetheless, one of the most often researched themes in proxemics is this very notion of personal space—a movable territory, so to speak, whose permanent center is the self. Although interest in interorganismic spacing, as both a dependent and an independent variable, is traced back to at least mid-century ethology (e.g., Hediger, 1955), its most notable psychological proponent has been the anthropologist E. T. Hall. His systematic account of personal space has proved exceedingly influential, and the tenets of his theory have been largely upheld in three decades of research (see Altman and Vinsel, 1977, for a critical appraisal).

In his classic work *The Hidden Dimension* (1966), Hall emphasizes the communicatory aspects of interpersonal spacing, arguing, as we have been, that the spatial context is a communications medium and, as such, regulates the amount, intensity, type, and quality of communications. Communication involves multiple sensory systems, which are differentially affected by distance: Although we can see a conversational partner at three hundred meters, with good fortune we smell him or her from no more than 3. From this communications perspective Hall found it useful to distinguish four interactional zones: intimate, personal, social, and public. Within each of these four zones a unique combination of sensory modalities operate. In the intimate zone, for example, we can see, smell, and hear another person, as well as sense his or her body heat and feel his or her breath. With so many modalities at play in this 50-centimeter range, and with the microscopic visual detail available, people situated in our intimate zones afford us a rich tapestry of communication cues, from their general state of arousal (we can hear their respiration rate, see arterial pulsations in the neck, etc.) to their general state of health (whiteness of eyes, discoloration of skin, obstruction of breathing passages). These cues virtually refuse to be ignored, although persons placed in unchosen and inappropriate proximity to one another do attempt to restrict interaction and ignore incoming stimuli (e.g., elevator behavior). As one zone becomes another, many communication modalities cease to operate, communication cues become less salient, and regulatory control, particularly over outgoing information, is regained. The point is that distance, because it determines quality and quantity of information exchange, is associated with varying levels of personal intimacy. Thus the intimacy we have (or desire to have) with another carries with it its own preferred interpersonal distance, and a mismatch between felt intimacy and physical distance is uncomfortable; an enormous literature supports this central hypothesis (see Hayduk, 1978, for a review). Yet Hall's work aside, theorizing in this regard has not kept pace with empirical work (see Evans, 1974; Patterson, 1976, 1978, for exceptions), whose main focus has been the unearthing of factors that affect personal spacing, such as gender, culture, personality, and stigmatizing conditions. Some attempts have been made (Argyle and Dean, 1965; Dosey and Meisels, 1969; Desor, 1972; Duke and Nowicki, 1972), but none has proved the theoretical structure needed to organize and explain the burgeoning literature in this area.

An Attributional Approach

Neither can we contribute any such map to the location of the grail, but we do feel that the application of a few basic attributional principles to personal distancing may prove enlightening. For example, one of the interesting findings in this area has been that adults do not find the violation of the intimate zone by small children discomforting (Fry and Willis, 1971), whereas the same intrusion by older children or adults is indeed reacted to with discomfort and engenders corrective behaviors (moving away, expulsion of intruder, etc.). This discovery promotes the realization that there cannot be a single reaction to an invasion of personal space because each invasion is different in the message it communicates.

Not only does distance determine the operating communication modalities, but it also serves to communicate something of its own. As we have seen, that something normally is intimacy; physical distance is used (and recognized) as a message regarding desired or perceived interpersonal intimacy or a desire for those actions that are initiated only from close distances (e.g., intimate physical contact but also harm-doing acts such as rape). However, because personal distance is affected by so many other functional factors (how much room is available, where the instructor has assigned us to sit, etc.), an attributional analysis is appropriate to determine whether the intruder intends to communicate his desire for intimacy by close physical actions or whether he is simply responding to constraining, situational conditions. Even in the most dense situations, however, others usually have some range of freedom within which they may position themselves in relation to us. Within this range movement from one zone to another is a meaningful communication about desired levels of personal contact. For example, in the crowded elevator car we are usually in close proximity to a number of persons with whom we

do not wish to share any degree of personal intimacy. However, the size of the car and the number of passengers does not always permit us to stand the requisite 3 meters apart, and thus the space that *is* available is taken to be the range of freedom, inside of which movement is significant. If our fellow passenger cannot be more distant than 25 centimeters, then his keeping of such a distance is not meaningful.

This situation is, of course, nothing but a simple application of the "law of noncommon effects" (Jones and Davis, 1965), suggesting that in everyday social situations we may try to understand *why* a person chooses to locate himself or herself a particular distance from us. When environmental demands are taken into account, we often find them sufficiently explanatory, and interpersonal distance is discounted as a mere functional artifact of architecture, social ritual, and so on. In these cases of external or environmental causality we need make no internal attributions to the individual, no inferences about his or her motives for standing closer to us than is generally normal. However, as normally socialized members of the cultures, we are aware that there are two general sets of reasons why another might stand close. Therefore, should the person place himself or herself a mere 10 centimeters closer than the outer limit of his or her range of freedom, we have attributional cause to believe that the person is communicating a desire for greater intimacy, and we will react accordingly (i.e., accept or reject the overture). The intruder is also aware of the possibilities of thus explosively disambiguating the situation. For this reason he or she is likely to rigidly govern his or her actions in order to avoid giving the unwanted attributional signal. The male in the crowded subway car carefully stares into space, rather than directly at the passenger crowded against him, and keeps both hands clutching his briefcase, in order that there be no suspicion of his clutching anything else (Goffman, 1963). Here the actor attempts to disambiguate the situation by sending out signals pointing to only one of the multiple causes of his closeness.

In still other situations a person may be careful *not* to disambiguate behavior that could have either environmental or internal causes. A man at a singles' bar sits on a bar stool that is the only one vacant and is next to an attractive woman. He could indicate that his real reason for taking that stool was because it was the only one vacant by turning slightly away from the woman and carefully averting his gaze. Or he could ask the woman for a date, thus demonstrating that the real reason was to make this approach. But a more sophisticated technique could involve starting up a conversation with the woman about some neutral topic. By this technique some ambiguity about his motives is preserved. He can then watch for signals of receptivity and friendliness on the part of the other. By means of this technique of alternative self-disclosure, the man minimizes the chances of an embarrassing rejection when he finally makes an unequivocal approach.

What we are suggesting is that the normal conventions of interpersonal distance, in conjunction with the physical and social environmental conditions that modify those conventions, create the possibilities of an interpersonal signaling system of considerable complexity. For instance, there are cases in which an individual who keeps the social distances that are typically normative may be seen as having some very deviant motives. Although a fellow passenger may keep a public distance by standing as far from us as possible when the elevator car is empty, he may communicate an attributionally meaningful message had he the prior choice of taking another car. Goffman (1963), in his book *Behavior in Public Places,* gives examples of many of the principles that people use to manage the attributions conveyed by personal distance. One of his most interesting observations is that people are often quite careful about potentially hurting other people's feelings by taking actions that could lead to negative attributions about the other person. An example is illuminating. I am about to get up from my seat on a crowded train, go to the end of the car to collect my baggage, and depart. Just before I do, a black man sits in the empty seat next to me. I, a white man, now face a social complexity; my departure may be taken by the black man as an insulting refusal to sit next to him. To negate the possibility of this attribution, I engage in some social ploy, such as asking the black man the name of the next stop (which I know full well) and then leaping up to get ready to get off, in order to make the noninsulting attribution clear.

All this behavior is socially complicated, and many have felt that Goffman sometimes overcomplicates the stuff of ordinary social interaction, but Snyder, Kleck, Strenta, and Mentzer (1979) have experimentally demonstrated that people actually use an equally complex social tactic in such potentially revealing situations. People are sometimes embarrassed or otherwise hesitant about closely approaching handicapped individuals, but they perceive that hesitancy as potentially insulting to the handicapped person. Snyder *et al.* arranged a dilemma

for subjects. They came into a television-viewing area in which they could take one of two seats, one in an area that included a handicapped individual or one in an area that included a normal individual. In one experimental condition the same program was on the television sets in both areas. If the subject chose to sit away from the handicapped person, it would be clear that he sought to avoid the handicapped person. Subjects in this condition tended to sit with the handicapped person. But when two different shows were being played on the TV sets, thus providing an excuse for sitting with the normal individual, subjects more frequently chose that option.

If closeness and distance are a metaphor for intimacy, and are thus used as a mode of communication about perceived and desired intimacy levels, is there any sense in talking about personal-space bubbles and space invasions? We believe that, like all metaphors, the bubble notion may be initially useful but runs the risk of being interpreted as a true picture of all of the facts, rather than as the convenience it is. Attempts to actually measure the bubble illustrate our point. We see as unproductive the asking of questions such as "How big is the bubble?" because for us this question can be rephrased as "Is there a set distance beyond which intimacy is not communicated and within which it is?" We suspect that no such set point will be found because situational factors determine the meaningfulness of personal distance. Instead, we find interesting the distance-intimacy linkage itself; can we untangle this linkage and understand why closeness has congruent psychological and physical meanings? Hall's (1966) suggestion concerning the number of operational sensory modalities is, to our thinking, a fruitful place to begin the search.

Proximity and Social Behavior

Proxemics describes the active use persons make of the spatial contexts in which interaction occurs as well as their responses to the use made by others. Research on crowding (as well as social isolation) suggests that certain levels of compresence are aversive, probably because they present too many input stimuli and restrict behavioral freedom, promoting a loss of perceived control. Therefore persons attempt to achieve a measure of selective access to the self, that is, a degree of privacy. They may do so by using any number of boundary-regulating mechanisms, including territorial behavior or the exclusive and rightful use of a particular physical setting. One such setting is the space that one occupies at any given time, that is, one's personal space, which changes in size as a result of multiple situational variables (architecture, social ritual, etc.). Entrance into the personal space of another serves to communicate something about perceived or desired intimacy or about other motives.

CONCLUSIONS

We have briefly reviewed some of the central research areas within environmental psychology, less to provide a complete and balanced overview than to present those particular areas in which a social psychologist might find the most interest or the most promise or the areas that seemed to us the most worrisome or most overlooked. We now need to attempt some conclusions, although we remind the reader of their tentativeness. It strikes us that environmental psychology must still seem an odd enterprise to a standard, research-trained, academically committed experimental social psychologist. It seems to us to be important to say why that is so. To begin, we must reaffirm our preliminary observation that environmental psychology is in no sense a single, unified area of inquiry. Rather, it is an often mismatched consortium of research questions, interests in specific social problems, and investigative techniques about which empirical and descriptive efforts have developed; these have been cast together under the heading of environmental psychology for reasons that are often more historical than logical. What, for instance, does energy conservation have to do with cognitive mapping, or personal-space maintenance with ambient lighting? All of these topics, of course, can be subsumed under the general heading of human-environment interactions; but so, as we pointed out in the introduction, can the whole of psychology—and now, we would add, significant portions of sociology, anthropology, political science, and economics. The unity provided by this definition is illusory.

In truth, problems addressed by environmental psychologists have been selected on quite other grounds than definitional purity, and this imposes certain limits on the field that are worth remarking. Because they are important social problems, environmental social psychologists are concerned with such disparate concerns and events as energy conservation, the aesthetics of architectural experience, environmental mapping, disasters, and the effects of stress on human performance. Given this commitment to speak to a broad range of problems, no single environmental theory can or will emerge; instead, there will be various theories of the middle range developed within environmental psychology (e.g., see volume 15, issue 3 of *Environment and Behavior,* 1983, edited by D. Stokols). This problem-centeredness and its consequences prohibit parsimonious theoretical elegance in the field of environmental psychology.

Environmental psychology is problem-centered in a second sense; its practitioners frequently seek to *solve* pressing social problems. That is, environmental psychologists are concerned with producing social change and with ameliorating a set of social problems, reminding those of us who go back that far of the activist wing of the group that centered around Kurt Lewin. But we ought to recognize the tension between the pure-science aspects of experimental social psychology and this more problem-focused view. If in the ordinarily experienced environment a set of causes tend to co-occur, then an environmental psychologist will be much less likely than a social psychologist to do experiments designed to unbundle that set of possible causes. Primary school classrooms generally come either informally arranged, furnished with movable furniture and other various pieces of equipment familiar to those of the open-classroom persuasion, or more formally arranged, with chairs in rows and standard readers available, all presided over by a traditional teacher. An environmental psychologist might discriminate these open and closed classrooms and do studies of the comparative learning and motivational benefits of each. He or she would be much less likely to add experimental conditions representing various of the other possible combinations of causes. This strategy, derived from an informed analysis of what in the real world can be expected to covary, is to a great extent what lies behind Proshansky's (1976) well-known criticism of the intrusion of standard social psychologists, with their classic variance-accounted-for experimental design philosophy, into the territory of environmental psychology. If these experimental designs were to become the norm, Proshansky is concerned that studies of elegant experimental design and minimal policy relevance might drive out studies of less elegance in terms of causal inference but of greater policy relevance. This is, of course, a perfectly reasonable stance, but one needs to be cautious about it. If an interrelated set of causes has been demonstrated to produce an effect, then those interpreting that effect must avoid acting as though one of those causes (or any of those causes in isolation) can be attributed a major share of the effect. The physical form of open classrooms was originally the creation of a set of teachers who had also arranged a social system and designed self-paced instructional material. But we can recall attempts to create new open classrooms that simply imposed the physical form of an open classroom on a teacher who probably didn't want it. Failure was the result. Environmental psychologists, like the rest of us, need to avoid inferential mistakes that lead to flawed policy recommendations; precisely because of their interest in making policy, environmental psychologists must be particularly wary here.

SOCIAL PSYCHOLOGY AND ENVIRONMENTAL PSYCHOLOGY

As we commented at the beginning of this chapter, environmental psychology is a new subfield of psychology. Therefore its practitioners are frequently migrants from another subfield of psychology. Those working on environmental cognition frequently have a background in cognitive psychology, and those working in energy conservation frequently came from a tradition of operant conditioning and behavioral change. But many, of course, have been trained as social psychologists. What elements of their influence can be seen within environmental psychology?

First, it does seem clear that the social psychologists have come bearing theory. Environmental psychology does draw on existing theoretical work in social psychology to explain limited aspects of many of the phenomena that it studies. One thinks here of the use of work in decision making under conditions of uncertainty in exploring perceptions of environmental risk and hazard, recent work in cognition in environmental mapping, or the applications of theories of diffusion of responsibility and perception of control to responses to accidents and disaster. Second, we have suggested that an attributional approach may illuminate a theory of interpersonal distance. Social psychological theories are clearly visible in environmental work.

TENSIONS

One might expect that any field, environmental psychology included, would provide some integrated and original image of human behavior. In our review we have seen little in environmental psychology that presents this image and little that gives us reason to be optimistic that

such an image will be forthcoming. Environmental psychology seems instead to be a compendium of research problems drawn from the peripheries of other fields.

It is interesting to follow up Stokols (1978) characterization of environmental psychology as an "undermanned setting." The reader will remember that along with various behavioral benefits to the actor, the undermanned setting specifies a lowering of role criteria; when there are not enough performers to properly produce the play, the audience must be less demanding and sometimes look the other way when an actor stumbles or forgets his lines. We would suggest that some of this is true of environmental psychology. Some of the articles in journals are not up to acceptable methodological standards. (The criterion here is not some arbitrarily imposed standard; it is simply that some of the findings do not warrant the conclusions drawn from them.) Ideas that are interesting but only vaguely developed are labeled "theories." It seems to us that environmental psychology is now ready to benefit from an increased emphasis on methodological and theoretical critiques of its work, for without critics to challenge the conventional wisdom of theory and practice and demand that rigorous conclusions be drawn from no less rigorous research, an area cannot be expected to develop a sophisticated perspective or a discriminating body of work. Without this greater emphasis on technique and concept, the important areas within environmental psychology might just as easily be returned to the parent disciplines that spawned them, and were this to happen, we suspect that there would be embarrassingly little left that is unique to environmental psychology alone.

The reader may feel that by raising these criticisms, we are suggesting that this should be the last chapter written on environmental psychology. But this is not our point. For although we have mentioned what we see as fundamental deficits within the field, we also see two aspects of the area that provide ample justification for its continued existence. First among these are the questions environmental psychology has chosen to address. We have argued that these questions are, in content, not unique and are in fact often drawn directly from other areas of psychological investigation. However, it is not clear that without the impetus from environmental researchers these questions would receive *any* attention at all. We consider the human use of spatial constructs to be an important and potentially significant addition to the psychology of social behavior. Hall's (1966) postulates are casually stated, and it has been left to environmental psychologists to generate empirical support for or disproof of these notions. And what of social isolation or crowding? With little exception these pressing social concerns have been widely ignored in the psychological community, leaving a void where a theory might have been. One can make similar cases for the study of reaction to geophysical disaster, energy conservation, and the effects of spatial layout in the built environment. In other words, environmental psychology has often taken the problem children from other areas, those questions that others of us have not seen fit to address because they do not always promise methodological clarity, theoretical neatness, or professional advancement. We grant that environmental psychologists have not always approached these problems in ways endorsed by other psychologists—but in the hands of environmental researchers they *have been* addressed. In this sense environmental psychology warrants its existence if for nothing other than the fact that it has kept many important topics from retreating into undeserved obscurity.

However, the most important aspect of environmental psychology is what we have been, during the course of this chapter, calling its holistic or interactional approach. We have suggested that environmental psychology is a list of topics rather than an integrated theoretical structure, and we will stand by that suggestion. Still, much environmental work does present psychology with a perspective that, although it is not unique, certainly is an important one. The perspective seems to us to be largely metatheoretical in that it puts forward a criterion for an acceptable theory in environmental psychology. Altman (1981), who in turn refers to the thinking of Proshansky and Ittelson, refers to the perspective as a *transactional* one in which environment and behavior are mutually defined, rather than being treated as two independent classes of variables. Altman contrasts this transactional approach to the more customary *interactive* approach in which there is some attempt to first specify the independent characteristics of persons and environments and then to study their interactions.

Altman (1981) also frankly admits that this approach has rarely been sustained in practice and that it is not a completely defined perspective. But he does suggest that it will require a system by which environments and behavioral processes are defined in essentially identical terms. He gives an example, drawn from his own research, in which he was able to use the same two dimensions (identity/community and openness/closedness) to define both home environments and social interaction processes. As psychology comes to accept this perspective, Altman suggests that as well as changing our unit of analysis, we will move to a greater emphasis on case study approaches and rely less on linear causal models.

We would agree with Altman that this perspective can be seen in some of the environmental literature and also that it has not yet been developed into a set of analytic principles. Its analytic power, or heuristic value, therefore remains to be demonstrated by sets of studies of limited scope, making good the transactional claim on a number of specific grounds. Since one of the tasks of a handbook is to point to convergences between areas, we would also mention the relevance of the transactional perspective to the debate currently raging in personality theory between trait theorists, situationalists, and interactionists. It may be that environmental and personality psychologists will have useful suggestions to make to each other about ways in which to conceptualize the environment in psychologically meaningful ways (see Craik, 1976; Craik and McKechnie, 1977; Snyder and Ickes, 1985, Chapter 28 of this book).

Environmental psychology usually emphasizes the ecology of action, the irreducibility of behavioral sequences to their component parts. Lately, under the impetus of social cognition, social psychology has moved toward the canons of natural science and looked at the cognition of an individual, while environmental psychology has continued the older social psychological tradition of interactionism. This chapter cannot even begin to describe the complexities that determine when either approach is appropriate, but we would point out that both approaches have important contributions to make. In this way environmental psychology serves as a reminder. It has not, of course, provided a means by which behavior and environment may be conceived of as a whole and still maintain the control and exactness of our variance-accounted-for laboratory experiments, but it has continued to point toward that notion as a goal—a goal toward which many of us in the experimentalist tradition have often neglected to strive. It is all too easy for cognitive psychologists to become locked in their nonsense-syllable mode and forget that such studies are undertaken because ultimately we wish to understand how persons use memory in their natural environments; social psychologists, too, may often fail to remember that their science was not meant to describe behavior as it occurs on a questionnaire in the laboratory but as it unfolds in the actual behavior setting.

This perspective should not be unfamiliar to social psychologists. Within psychology in general social psychologists have often been regarded, and have regarded themselves, as clinging to the canons of natural science with some tenuousness. That is, in the interests of continuing to focus on what they regarded as the most important problems, social psychologists positioned themselves as the investigators of human complexity, with all the attendant complex experimental designs, contrived experimental situations, and weak and fugitive effects that such commitment implies. Environmental psychologists have chosen to work on problems that seem, on the whole, to be more complex versions of the problems addressed by social psychologists and have made this commitment driven by the same underlying concern for the importance of the problems that they study. Yet to a rigorously trained experimental social psychologist, the environmental psychologist seems subject to all of the criticisms of vagueness and imprecision applied by more traditionally trained psychologists to the social area. Many social psychologists, looking at research in environmental psychology, find themselves crying for more rigor—an unusual complaint for them to be raising, but at least one to which they know the reply, since they must so frequently offer it in the defense of their own work.

This is why we chose to call this closing section "Tensions." We would simply add that these tensions are productive for both psychological science and for the social uses to which that science is to be put. The social psychologist will be moved toward more policy-relevant and more socially useful research. The environmental psychologist will be pressed to develop more unique and explicit psychological theories and will be asked to create sufficiently controllable experimental situations to put the critical elements of those theories to the test. Paradoxically, each group will gain what it most wants by heeding the urgings of the other. The environmental psychologist will be able to make more decisive and effective recommendations for social change when those recommendations are grounded in adequate theory, and the social psychologist will have a more adequate theory of human action when that theory is developed to encompass the complex performances of individuals functioning in familiar social and physical environments.

REFERENCES

Abramson, L. Y., M. E. P. Seligman, and J. D. Teasdale (1978). Learned helplessness in humans: critique and reformulation. *J. abnorm. Psychol., 87,* 49–74.

Adams, R. L. A. (1973). Uncertainty in nature, cognitive dissonance, and the perceptual distortion of environmental information: weather forecasts and New England beach trip decisions. *Econ. Geography, 49,* 287–297.

Allen, G., A. Siegel, and R. Rosinski (1978). The role of perceptual context in structuring spatial knowledge. *J. exp. Psychol.: hum. Learn. Memory, 4,* 617–630.

Altman, I. (1975). *The environment and social behavior.* Monterey, Calif.: Brooks/Cole.

——— (1981). Reflections on environmental psychology: 1981. *Hum. Environments, 2,* 5–7.

Altman, I., and A. M. Vinsel (1977). Personal space: an analysis of E. T. Hall's proxemics framework. In I. Altman, and J. Wohlwill (Eds.), *Human behavior and environment: advances in theory and research.* Vol. 2. New York: Plenum.

Anderson, J. R., and G. F. Bower (1973). *Human associative memory.* New York: Winston.

——— (1978). Arguments concerning representations for mental imagery. *Psychol. Rev., 4,* 249–277.

Appleyard, D. A. (1970). Styles and methods of structuring a city. *Environment Behav., 2,* 100–116.

——— (1976). *Planning a pluralistic city.* Cambridge, Mass.: M.I.T. Press.

Archea, J. (1977). The place of architectural features in behavioral theories of privacy. *J. soc. Issues, 33,* 116–137.

Argyle, M., and J. Dean (1965). Eye-contact, distance and affiliation. *Sociometry, 28,* 289–304.

Averill, J. (1973). Personal control over aversive stimuli and its relationship to stress. *Psychol. Bull., 80,* 286–303.

Barker, R. G. (1960). Ecology and motivation. In M. R. Jones (Ed.), *Nebraska symposium on motivation.* Lincoln: Univ. of Nebraska Press.

——— Ed. (1963a). *The stream of behavior.* New York: Appleton-Century-Crofts.

——— (1963b). On the nature of the environment. *J. soc. Issues, 4,* 17–38.

——— (1965). Explorations in ecological psychology. *Amer. Psychol., 20,* 1–14.

——— (1968). *Ecological psychology: concepts and methods for studying the environment of human behavior.* Stanford: Stanford Univ. Press.

——— (1979). The influence of frontier environments on behavior. In J. O. Steffen (Ed.), *The American West: new perspectives, new dimensions.* Tulsa: Univ. of Oklahoma Press.

Barker, R. G. and Associates (1978). *Habitats, environments, and human behavior.* San Francisco: Jossey-Bass.

Barker, R. G., and P. V. Gump (1964). *Big school, small school.* Stanford: Stanford Univ. Press.

Barker, R. G., and H. F. Wright (1955). *Midwest and its children.* New York: Harper & Row.

Baron, R. A., and P. A. Bell (1975). Aggression and heat: mediating effects of prior provocation and exposure to an aggressive model. *J. Pers. soc. Psychol., 31,* 825–832.

Barton, A. H. (1969). *Communities in disaster: a sociological analysis of collective stress situations.* New York: Doubleday.

Baum, A., J. R. Aiello, and L. E. Calesnick (1978). Crowding and personal control: social density and the development of learned helplessness. *J. Pers. soc. Psychol., 36,* 1000–1011.

Baum, A., R. Fleming, and L. M. Davidson (1983). Natural disaster and technological castastrophe. *Environment Behav., 15.*

Baum, A., R. J. Gatchel, R. Fleming, and C. R. Lane (1981). Chronic and acute stress associated with the Three Mile Island accident and decontamination: preliminary findings of a longitudinal study. Technical report to the U.S. Nuclear Regulatory Commission, Washington, D.C.

Baum, A., J. E. Singer, and S. Valins, eds. (1978). *Advances in environmental psychology.* Hillsdale, N.J.: Erlbaum.

Baum, A., and S. Valins (1977). *Architecture and social behavior: psychological studies in social density.* Hillsdale, N.J.: Erlbaum.

Beardsley, E. L. (1971). Privacy: autonomy and selective disclosure. In J. R. Pennock, and J. W. Chapman (Eds.), *Privacy.* New York: Atherton.

Becker, F. D. (1973). Study of spatial markers. *J. Pers. soc. Psychol., 26,* 439–445.

Becker, F. D., and C. Mayo (1971). Delineating personal distance and territoriality. *Environment Behav., 3,* 375–381.

Becker, L. J., C. Seligman, R. H. Fazio, and J. M. Darley (1981). Relating attitudes to residential energy use. *Environment Behav., 13,* 590–609.

Bell, P. A., and R. A. Baron (1976). Aggression and heat: the mediating role of negative affect. *J. appl. soc. Psychol., 6,* 18–30.

———— (1977). Aggression and ambient temperature: the facilitating and inhibiting effects of hot and cold environments. *Bull. psychon. Soc., 9,* 443–445.

Bell, P. A., and S. W. Barnard (1977). *Sex differences in the effects of heat and noise stress on personal space permeability.* Paper presented at the meeting of the Rocky Mountain Psychological Association, Albuquerque, N.M.

Bell, P. A., J. D. Fisher, and R. H. Loomis (1978). *Environmental psychology.* Philadelphia: Saunders.

Berglas, S., and E. E. Jones (1978). Drug choice as a self-handicapping strategy in response to noncontingent success. *J. Pers. soc. Psychol., 36,* 405–417.

Berlyne, D. E. (1960). *Conflict, arousal and curiosity.* New York: McGraw-Hill.

———— (1972). *Aesthetics and psychobiology.* New York: Appleton-Century-Crofts.

———— (1974). *Studies in the new experimental aesthetics: steps toward an objective psychology of aesthetic appreciation.* New York: Halsted Press.

Biderman, A. D., M. Louria, and J. Bacchus (1963). *Historical incidents of extreme overcrowding.* Washington, D.C.: Bureau of Social Science Research.

Biederman, I. (1972). Perceiving real-world scenes. *Science, 177,* 77–79.

Blaut, J. M., G. McCleary, and A. Blaut (1970). Environmental mapping in young children. *Environment Behav., 2,* 335–349.

Blaut, J. M., and D. Stea (1974). Mapping at the age of three. *J. Geog., 73,* 5–9.

Borsky, P. N. (1969). Effects of noise on community behavior. In W. D. Ward, and J. E. Fricke (Eds.), *Noise as a public health hazard.* Washington, D.C.: The American Speech and Hearing Association.

Boyce, P. R. (1975). The luminous environment. In D. Canter, and P. Stringer (Eds.), *Environmenal interaction: psychological approaches to our physical surroundings.* New York: International Universities Press.

Brechner, K. C., and D. E. Linder (1981). A social trap analysis of energy distribution systems. In A. Baum and J. E. Singer (Eds.), *Advances in environmental psychology.* Vol. 3. Hillsdale, N.J.: Erlbaum.

Brehm, J. W. (1966). *A theory of psychological reactance.* New York: Academic Press.

Broadbent, D. E. (1971). *Decision and stress.* New York: Academic Press.

Brunswik, E. (1969). The conceptual framework of psychology. In O. Neurath, R. Carnap, and C. Morris (Eds.), *Foundation of the unity of science: toward an international encyclopedia of unified science.* Chicago: Univ. of Chicago Press.

Burns, L. R. (1980). The Chicago school and the study of organization-environment relations. *J. Hist. behav. Sci., 16,* 342–358.

Burton, I., and R. W. Kates (1964). The perception of natural hazards in resource management. *Natural Resources J., 3,* 412–441.

Byrne, R. (1979). Memory for urban geography. *Quart. J. exp. Psychol., 31,* 147–154.

Calhoun, J. B. (1962a). A behavioral sink. In E. L. Bliss (Ed.), *Roots of behavior.* New York: Harper & Row

Calhoun, J. B. (1962b). Population density and social pathology. *Scientific Amer., 206,* 139–148.

———— (1963a). *The ecology and sociology of the Norway rat.* Publication No. 1008. Washington, D.C.: U.S. Public Health Service.

———— (1963b). The social use of space. In W. V. Mayer, and R. G. Van Gelder (Eds.), *Physiological mammalogy.* Vol. 1. New York: Academic Press. Pp. 1–187.

Cavan, S. (1963). Interaction in home territories. *Berkeley J. Sociol., 8,* 17–32.

———— (1966). *Liquor license.* Chicago: Aldine.

Christian, J. J., V. Flyger, and D. C. Davis (1960). Factors in the mass mortality of a herd of sika deer, Cervus nippon. *Chesapeake Science, 1,* 79–95.

Cohen, S. (1978). Environmental load and the allocation of attention. In A. Baum, J. E. Singer, and S. Valins (Eds.), *Advances in environmental psychology.* Vol. 1. Hillsdale, N.J.: Erlbaum.

———— (1980). Aftereffects of stress on human performance and social behavior: a review of research and theory. *Psychol. Bull., 88,* 82–108.

Cohen, S., D. C. Glass, and S. Phillips (1979). Environment and health. In H. E. Freeman, S. Levine, and L. G. Reeder (Eds.), *Handbook of medical sociology.* Englewood Cliffs, N.J.: Prentice-Hall.

Cohen, S., D. S. Krantz, G. W. Evans, and D. Stokols (1981). Cardiovascular and behavioral effects of community noise. *Amer. Scient., 69,* 528–535.

Cohen, S., and N. Weinstein (1981). Nonauditory effects of noise on behavior and health. *J. soc. Issues, 37,* 36–70.

Committee on Environmental Improvement. (1978). *Cleaning our environment: a chemical perspective.* Washington, D.C.: American Chemical Society.

Cook, S. W., and J. L. Berrenberg (1981). Approaches to encouraging conservation behavior: a review and conceptual framework. *J. soc. Issues, 37,* 73–107.

Cooper, C. (1974). The house as a symbol of the self. In J. Lang, C. Burnette, W. Moleski, and D. Vachon (Eds.), *Designing for human behavior: architecture and the behavioral sciences.* Stroudsburg, Penn.: Dowden, Hutchinson & Ross.

Craik, K. H. (1970). Environmental psychology. In K. H. Craik, B. Kleinmuntz, R. L. Rosnow, R. Rosenthal, J. R. Cheyne, and R. H. Walters (Eds.), *New directions in psychology.* Vol. 4. New York: Holt, Rinehart, and Winston.

_____ (1973). Environmental psychology. *Ann. Rev. Psychol., 24,* 403–422.

_____ (1976). The personality research paradigm in environmental psychology. In S. Wapner, S. B. Cohen, and B. Kaplan (Eds.), *Experiencing the environment.* New York: Plenum.

Craik, K. H., and G. E. McKechnie (1977). Personality and the environment. *Environment Behav., 9,* 155–168.

Darley, J. M., and J. Beniger (1981). Diffusion of energy-conserving innovations. *J. soc. Issues, 37,* 150–171.

Darley, J. M., and B. Latane (1968). Bystander intervention in emergencies: diffusion of responsibility. *J. Pers. soc. Psychol., 8,* 377–383.

Davidson, L. M., A. Baum, and D. L. Collins (1982). Stress and control-related problems at Three Mile Island. *J. appl. soc. Psychol., 12,* 349–359.

Desor, J. A. (1972). Toward a psychological theory of crowding. *J. Pers. soc. Psychol., 21,* 79–83.

Devlin, A. S. (1976). The small town cognitive map: adjusting to a new environment. In G. T. Moore, and R. G. Golledge (Eds.), *Environmental knowing.* Stroudsburg, Penn.: Dowden, Hutchinson & Ross.

Dickman, H. R. (1963). The perception of behavioral units. In R. G. Barker (Ed.), *The stream of behavior.* New York: Appleton-Century-Crofts.

Donnerstein, E., and D. Wilson (1976). Effects of noise and perceived control on ongoing, and subsequent aggressive behavior. *J. Pers. soc. Psychol., 34,* 774–781.

Dorf, R. C. (1978). *Energy resources and policy.* Reading, Mass.: Addison-Wesley.

Dosey, M. A., and M. Meisels (1969). Personal space and self-protection. *J. Pers. soc. Psychol., 11,* 93–97.

Downs, R., and D. Stea (1973). *Image and environment.* Chicago: Aldine.

_____ (1977). *Maps in minds: reflections on cognitive mapping.* New York: Harper & Row.

Dueker, K. J., and I. P. Levin (1976). *Carpooling: attitudes and participation.* Technical Report No. 81, Center for Urban Transportation Studies, Institute of Urban and Regional Research, University of Iowa.

Duijker, H. C. F., and N. H. Frijda (1961). *National character and national stereotype: a trend report prepared for the International Union of Scientific Psychology.* New York: Humanities Press.

Duke, M. P., and S. Nowicki, Jr. (1972). A new measure and social learning model for interpersonal distance. *J. exp. Res. Pers., 6,* 1–16.

_____ (1978). The new environmental paradigm: a proposed measuring instrument and preliminary results. *J. Environmental Educ., 9,* 10–19.

Edney, J. J. (1974). Human territoriality. *Psychol. Bull., 81,* 959–975.

Erikson, K. T. (1976). *Everything in its path.* New York: Simon and Schuster.

Evans, G. W. (1974). An examination of the information overload mechanism of personal space. *Man-Environment Systems, 4,* 61.

_____ (1980). Environmental cognition. *Psychol. Bull., 88,* 259–287.

Evans, G. W., and K. Pezdek (1980). Cognitive mapping: knowledge of real-world distance and location information. *J. exp. Psychol.: hum. Learn. Memory, 6,* 13–24.

Evans, G. W., D. Marrero, and P. Butler (1981). Environmental learning and cognitive mapping. *Environment Behav., 13,* 83–104.

Fazio, R. H., M. P. Zanna, and J. Cooper (1977). Dissonance and self-perception: an integrative view of each theory's proper domain of application. *J. exp. soc. Psychol., 13,* 464–479.

Festinger, L., S. Schachter, and K. Back (1950). *Social pressures in informal groups.* New York: Harper.

Festinger, L. (1957). *A theory of cognitive dissonance.* Stanford: Stanford Univ. Press.

Fischer, C. (1976). *The urban experience.* New York: Harcourt.

Fishbein, M., and I. Ajzen (1975). *Belief, attitude, intention and behavior: an introduction to theory and research.* Reading, Mass.: Addison-Wesley.

Fitch, J. M. (1965). The aesthetics of function. *Annals N.Y. Acad. Sci., 128,* Article 2, 706–714.

Forgas, J. P. (1979). *Social episodes: the study of interaction routines.* New York: Academic Press.

Freedman, J. L. (1975). *Crowding and behavior.* San Francisco: Freeman.

Freedman, J. L., S. Heshka, and A. Levy (1975). Population density and pathology: is there a relationship? *J. exp. soc. Psychol., 11,* 539–552.

Fritz, C. E. (1961). Disaster. In R. K. Merton and R. A. Nisbet (Eds.), *Contemporary social problems.* New York: Harcourt, Brace, and World.

_____ (1968). Disasters. In D. Sills (Ed.), *International encyclopedia of the social sciences.* Vol. 4. New York: Macmillan. Pp. 202–207.

Fry, A. M., and F. N. Willis (1971). Invasion of personal space as a function of the age of the invader. *Psychol. Record, 2,* 358–389.

Geen, R., and E. O'Neal (1969). Activation of cue elicited aggression by general arousal. *J. Pers. soc. Psychol., 11,* 289–292.

Gibson, J. J. (1966). *The senses considered as perceptual systems.* Boston: Houghton Mifflin.

_____ (1979). *An ecological approach to visual perception.* Boston: Houghton Mifflin.

Glass, D. C., B. Reim, and J. E. Singer (1971). Behavioral consequences of adaptation to controllable and uncontrollable noise. *J. exp. soc. Psychol., 7,* 244–257.

Glass, D. C., and J. E. Singer (1972). Behavioral aftereffects of unpredictable and uncontrollable aversive events. *Amer. Scient., 80,* 457–465.

Gleser, G. C., B. L. Green, and C. Winget (1981). *Prolonged psychosocial effects of disaster.* New York: Harcourt.

Goffman, E. (1959). *The presentation of self in everyday life.* New York: Doubleday.

_____ (1963). *Behavior in public places.* New York: Free Press.

_____ (1971). *Relations in public.* New York: Basic Books.

Golledge, R. G., V. L. Rivizzigno, and A. Spector (1976). Learning about a city: analysis by multidimensional scaling. In R. G. Golledge, and G. Rushton (Eds.), *Spatial choice and spatial behavior.* Columbus: Ohio State Press.

Griffiths, I. D. (1975). The thermal environment. In D. Canter, and P. Stringer (Eds.), *Environmental interaction: psychological approaches to our physical surroundings.* New York: International Universities Press.

Gross, H. (1971). Privacy and autonomy. In J. R. Pennock, and J. W. Chapman (Eds.), *Privacy.* New York: Atherton.

Haber, G. M. (1980). Territorial invasion in the classroom: invadee response. *Environment Behav., 12,* 17–31.

Hall, E. T. (1959). *The silent language.* New York: Doubleday.

_____ (1966). *The hidden dimension.* New York: Doubleday.

Hardin, G. (1968). The tragedy of the commons. *Science, 162,* 1243–1248.

Hart, R. A., and G. T. Moore (1973). The development of spatial cognition: a review. In R. Downs, and D. Stea (Eds.), *Image and environment.* Chicago: Aldine.

Hayduk, L. A. (1978). Personal space: an evaluative and orienting overview. *Psychol. Bull., 85,* 117–134.

Hazard, J. N. (1962). Furniture arrangement as a symbol of judicial roles. *ETC: Rev. gen. Semantics, 19,* 181–188.

Heberlein, T. A. (1971). Moral norms, threatened sanctions and littering behavior. Unpublished doctoral dissertation. Univ. of Wisconsin, Madison.

_____ (1981). Environmental attitudes. *Zeitschrift für Umweltpolitik, 2,* 241–270.

Heberlein, T. A., and J. S. Black (1976). Attitudinal specificity and the prediction of behavior in a field setting. *J. Pers. soc. Psychol., 33,* 474–479.

Hediger, H. (1955). *Studies of the psychology and behavior of captive animals in zoos and circuses.* London: Butterworth.

Heft, H. (1979). The role of environmental features in route-learning: two exploratory studies of way-finding. *Environmental Psychol. nonverbal Behav., 3,* 172–185.

Heimstra, N. W., and L. H. McFarling (1978). *Environmental psychology.* Monterey, Calif.: Brooks/Cole.

Herman, J., and A. Siegel (1978). The development of spatial representations of large-scale environments. *J. exp. child Psychol., 26,* 389–406.

Hohenemser, C., R. W. Kates, and P. Slovic (1983). The nature of technological hazard. *Science, 220,* 378–384.

Holahan, C. J. (1978). *Environment and behavior: a dynamic perspective.* New York: Plenum.

Holahan, C. J. (1982). *Environmental psychology.* New York: Random House.

Holahan, C. J., and S. Saegert (1973). Behavioral and attitudinal effects of large-scale variation in the physical environment of psychiatric wards. *J. abnorm. Psychol., 82,* 454–462.

Hubel, D. H., and T. N. Wiesel (1970). The period of susceptibility to the physiological effects of unilateral eye closure in kittens. *J. Physiology, 206,* 419–436.

Hunt, R. (1967). *Personalities and cultures: readings on psychological anthropology.* Garden City, N.Y.: The Natural History Press.

Ittelson, W. H. (1970). Perception of the large-scale environment. *Trans. N.Y. Acad. Sci., 32,* 807–815.

_____ (1973). Environmental perception and contemporary perceptual theory. In W. Ittelson (Ed.), *Environment and cognition.* New York: Seminar Press.

_____ (1976). Some issues facing a theory of environment and behavior. In H. M. Proshansky, W. H. Ittelson, and L. G. Rivlin (Eds.), *Environmental psychology: people and their physical settings.* New York: Holt, Rinehart, and Winston.

Ittelson, W. H., H. M. Proshansky, L. G. Rivlin, and G. H. Winkel (1974). *An introduction to environmental psychology.* New York: Holt, Rinehart, and Winston.

Janis, I. L. (1951). *Air war and emotional stress: psychological studies of bombing and civilian defense.* New York: McGraw-Hill.

_____ (1962). Psychological effects of warnings. In G. W. Baker and D. W. Chapman (Eds.), *Man and society in disaster.* New York: Basic Books.

Janis, I. L., and S. Feshbach (1953). Effects of fear-arousing communications. *J. abnorm. soc. Psychol., 48,* 78–92.

Janis, I. L., and L. Mann (1977). Emergency decision making: a theoretical analysis of responses to disaster warnings. *J. hum. Stress, 3,* 35–48.

Joiner, D. (1971). Social ritual and architectural space. *J. architectural Res. Teach., 3,* 11–22.

Jones, E. E., and K. E. Davis (1965). From acts to dispositions: the attribution process in person perception. In L. Berkowitz (Ed.), *Advances in experimental social psychology.* Vol. 2. New York: Academic Press.

Kates, R. W. (1962). *Hazard and choice perception in flood plain management.* Chicago: Univ. of Chicago, Department of Geography, Research Paper No. 78.

Kessler, A. (1966). *Interplay between social ecology and physiology, genetics and population dynamics of mice.* Doctoral dissertation. Rockefeller University, Ann Arbor, Mich.: University Microfilms, No. 67–9869.

Konar, E., E. Sundstrom, C. Brady, D. Mandel, and R. W. Rice (1982). Status demarcation in the office. *Environment Behav., 14,* 561–580.

Kosslyn, S. M. (1975). Information representation in visual images. *Cognit. Psychol., 7,* 341–370.

Kosslyn, S. M., T. M. Ball, and B. J. Reiser (1978). Visual images preserve metric spatial information: evidence from studies of image scanning. *J. exp. Psychol.: hum. Percept. Perform., 4,* 47–60.

Kosslyn, S. M., and J. P. Pomerantz (1977). Imagery, propositions, and the form of internal representations. *Cognit. Psychol., 9,* 52–76.

Langer, E. J., and S. Saegert (1977). Crowding and cognitive control. *J. Pers. soc. Psychol., 35,* 175–182.

Latane, B. (1981). The psychology of social impact. *Amer. Psychol., 36,* 343–356.

Latane, B., and J. M. Darley (1968). Group inhibition of bystander intervention. *J. Pers. soc. Psychol., 10,* 215–221.

Lea, G. (1975). Chronometric analysis of the method of loci. *J. exp. Psychol.: hum. Percept. Perform., 1,* 95–104.

Leff, H. L. (1978). *Experience, environment, and human potentials.* New York: Oxford Univ. Press.

Leff, H. L., and L. R. Gordon (1980). Environmental cognitive sets: a longitudinal study. *Environment Behav., 12,* 291–328.

Leonard-Barton, D., and E. Rogers (1979). Adoption of energy conservation among California homeowners. Paper presented at the International Communications Associations, Philadelphia.

Lifton, R. J., and E. Olson (1976). The human meaning of total disaster: the Buffalo Creek experience. *Psychiatry, 39,* 1–18.

Lloyd, J. A. (1975). Effects of crowding among animals: implications for man. *Sociol. Symposium, 14,* 6–23.

Lounsbury, J., and L. G. Tornatzky (1977). A scale for assessing attitudes toward environmental quality. *J. soc. Psychol., 101,* 299–305.

Lyman, S. M., and M. B. Scott (1967). Territoriality: a neglected sociological dimension. *Soc. Problems, 15,* 235–249.

Lynch, K. (1960). *The image of the city.* Cambridge, Mass.: M.I.T. Press.

McArthur, L. Z., and D. L. Post (1977). Figural emphasis and person perception. *J. exp. soc. Psychol., 13,* 520–535.

McCormick, E. J. (1976). *Human factors in engineering and design.* New York: McGraw-Hill.

Magana, J. R. (1978). An empirical and interdisciplinary test of a theory of urban perception. Doctoral dissertation. University of California, Irvine. *Dissertation Abstracts Int., 39,* 1460B. University Microfilms No. 78-15, 840.

Maier, S. F., and M. E. P. Seligman (1976). Learned helplessness: theory and evidence. *J. exp. Psychol.: Gen., 105,* 3–46.

Maloney, M. P., M. P. Ward, and G. N. Braucht (1975). A revised scale for the measurement of ecological attitudes and knowledge. *Amer. Psychol., 30,* 787–790.

Maloney, M. P., and M. P. Ward (1973). Ecology: let's hear from the people. *Amer. Psychol., 30,* 787–790.

Mandler, J. M., and R. E. Parker (1976). Memory for descriptive and spatial information in complex pictures. *J. exp. Psychol.: hum. Learn. Memory, 2,* 38–48.

Margolin, J., and M. Misch (1978). Incentives and disincentives for ride sharing, a behavioral study. Washington, D.C.: U.S. Government Printing Office.

Maslow, A. H., and N. L. Mintz (1956). Effects of esthetic surroundings: I. Initial effects of three esthetic conditions upon perceiving "energy" and "well-being" in faces. *J. Psychol., 41,* 247–254.

Matthews, K. E., and L. K. Canon (1975). Environmental noise level as a determinant of helping behavior. *J. Pers. soc. Psychol., 32,* 571–577.

Matthews, K. A., M. F. Scheier, B. I. Brunson, and B. Carducci (1980). Attention, unpredictability, and reports of physical symptoms: eliminating the benefits of predictability. *J. Pers. soc. Psychol., 38,* 525–537.

Mehrabian, A., and J. A. Russell (1974). *An approach to environmental psychology.* Cambridge, Mass.: M.I.T. Press.

Milgram, S. (1970). The experience of living in cities. *Science, 167,* 1461–1468.

Milgram, S., J. Greenwald, S. Kessler, W. McKenna, and J. Waters (1972). A psychological map of New York City. *Amer. Scient., 60,* 194–200.

Mintz, N. L. (1956). Effects of esthetic surroundings: II. Prolonged and repeated experiences in a "beautiful" and an "ugly" room. *J. Psychol., 41,* 459–466.

Moore, G. T. (1974). The development of environmental knowing: an overview of an interactional-constructivist theory and some data on within-individual development variations. In D. Canter, and T. Lee (Eds.), *Psychology and the built environment.* New York: Halsted Press.

Moos, R. H. (1976). *The human context: environmental determinants of behavior.* New York: Wiley.

Mumford, L. (1961). *The city in history.* New York: Harcourt.

Nash, R. (1973). *Wilderness and the American mind.* New Haven: Yale Univ. Press.

Neisser, U. (1976). *Cognition and reality.* San Francisco: Freeman.

Nelson, M. N., and R. J. Paluck (1980). Territorial markings, self-concept, and mental status of the institutionalized elderly. *Gerontologist, 20,* 96–98.

Newman, O. (1972). *Defensible space: crime prevention through urban design.* New York: Macmillan.

Newtson, D. (1976). The perception of on-going behavior. In J. H. Harvey, W. J. Ickes, and R. F. Kidd (Eds.), *New directions in attribution research.* Vol. 1. Hillsdale, N.J.: Erlbaum.

Nisbett, R., and L. Ross (1980). *Human inference: strategies and shortcomings of social judgment.* Englewood Cliffs, N.J.: Prentice-Hall.

Norman, D., and D. Rumelhart (1975). *Explorations in cognition.* San Francisco: Freeman.

Olsen, M. E. (1981). Consumers' attitudes toward energy conservation. *J. soc. Issues, 37,* 108–131.

O'Neill, G. K. (1977). *The high frontier.* New York: Morrow.

Osmond, H. (1957). Function as the basis of psychiatric ward design. *Mental Hospitals.* Architectural Supplement, *8,* 23–29.

Patterson, M. L. (1976). An arousal model of interpersonal intimacy. *Psychol. Rev., 83,* 235–245.

————— (1978). Arousal change and the cognitive labeling: pursuing the mediators of intimacy exchange. *Environmental Psychol. nonverbal Behav., 3,* 17–22.

Piaget, J., and B. Inhelder (1967). *The child's conception of space.* New York: Norton.

Piaget, J., B. Inhelder, and A. Szeminska (1960). *The child's conception of geometry.* New York: Basic Books.

Potter, D. M. (1954). *People of plenty.* Chicago: Chicago Univ. Press.

Proshansky, H. M. (1976). Environmental psychology and the real world. *Amer. Psychol., 31,* 303–310.

_____ (1978). The city and self-identity. *Environment Behav.,* *10,* 147–169.

Proshansky, H. M., W. H. Ittelson, and L. G. Rivlin (1976). Freedom of choice and behavior in a physical setting. In H. M. Proshansky, W. H. Ittelson, and L. G. Rivlin (Eds.), *Environmental psychology: people and their physical settings.* New York: Holt, Rinehart, and Winston.

Pylyshyn, Z. W. (1973). What the mind's eye tell the mind's brain: a critique of mental imagery. *Psychol. Bull., 80,* 1–24.

Quarantelli, E. L., and R. R. Dynes (1977). Response to social crisis and disaster. *Ann. Rev. Sociol., 3,* 23–49.

Rapoport, A. (1975). Toward a redefinition of density. *Environment Behav., 7,* 133–158.

Reichel, D., and E. S. Geller (1981). Applications of behavioral analysis for conserving transportation energy. In A. Baum, and J. Singer (Eds.), *Advances in environmental psychology.* Vol. 3. *Energy: psychological perspectives.* Hillsdale, N.J.: Erlbaum. Pp. 53–91.

Richardson, E. (1967). *The environment of learning.* New York: Weybright & Talley.

Rodin, J. (1976). Crowding, perceived choice, and response to controllable and uncontrollable outcomes. *J. exp. soc. Psychol., 12,* 564–578.

Rodin, J., S. K. Solomon, and J. Metcalf (1978). Role of control in mediating perceptions of density. *J. Pers. soc. Psychol., 36,* 988–999.

Rogers, E., and F. Shoemaker (1971). *Communication of innovations: a cross-cultural approach.* New York: Free Press.

Ross, M., and R. Williams (1976). Energy efficiency: our most overlooked energy resource. The Bulletin of Atomic Scientists. Pp. 30–38.

Russell, J. A., and G. Pratt (1980). A description of the affective quality attributed to environments. *J. Pers. soc. Psychol., 38,* 311–322.

Russell, J. A., and L. M. Ward (1982). Environmental psychology. *Ann. Rev. Psychol., 33,* 651–688.

Sadalla, E. K., and S. G. Magel (1980). The perception of traversed distance. *Environment Behav., 12,* 65–79.

Sadalla, E. K., and L. J. Staplin (1980a). An information storage model for distance cognition. *Environment Behav., 12,* 183–193.

_____ (1980b). The perception of traversed distance: interactions. *Environment Behav., 12,* 167–182.

Schmidt, D. E., and J. P. Keating (1979). Human crowding and personal control: an integration of the research. *Psychol. Bull., 86,* 680–700.

Schopler, J., and J. E. Stockdale (1977). An interference analysis of crowding. *J. environmental Psychol. nonverbal Behav., 1,* 81–88.

Seligman, C., L. J. Becker, and J. M. Darley (1981). Encouraging residential energy conservation through feedback. In A. Baum and J. E. Singer (Eds.), *Advances in environmental psychology.* Vol. 3. *Energy: psychological perspectives.* Hillsdale, N.J.: Erlbaum. Pp. 53–91.

Seligman, C., and J. M. Darley (1977). Feedback as a means of decreasing residential energy consumption. *J. appl. Psychol., 62,* 363–368.

Seligman, M. E. P. (1975). *Helplessness.* San Francisco: Freeman.

Shepard, R. N. (1975). Form, formation, and transformation of internal representation. In R. L. Solso (Ed.), *Information processing and cognition: the Loyola symposium.* Hillsdale, N.J.: Erlbaum.

Sherrod, D. R. (1974). Crowding, perceived control, and behavioral after-effects. *J. appl. soc. Psychol., 4,* 171–186.

Sherrod, D. R., and R. Downs (1974). Environmental determinants of altruism: the effects of stimulus overload and perceived control on helping. *J. exp. soc. Psychol., 10,* 468–479.

Sherrod, D. R., J. N. Hage, P. L. Halpern, and B. S. Moore (1977). Effects of personal causation and perceived control on responses to an aversive environment: the more control, the better. *J. exp. soc. Psychol., 13,* 14–27.

Siegel, A. W., and M. Schadler (1977). Young children's cognitive maps of their classroom. *Child Development, 48,* 388–394.

Siegel, A. W., and S. H. White (1975). The development of spatial representations of large-scale environments. In H. W. Reese (Ed.), *Advances in child development and behavior.* Vol. 10. New York: Academic Press.

Simmel, G. (1950). Secrecy and group communication. In K. H. Wold (Ed. and translator), *The sociology of Georg Simmel.* New York: Free Press.

Sinden, F. W. (1978). A two-thirds reduction in the space heat requirement of a Twin Rivers townhouse. *Energy and Buildings, 1,* 207–242.

Slovic, P., H. Kunreuther, and G. F. White (1974). Decision processes, rationality, and adjustment to natural hazards. In G. F. White (Ed.), *Natural hazards: local, national, global.* New York: Oxford Univ. Press.

Snyder, M., and W. Ickes (1985). Personality and social behavior. In G. Lindzey and E. Aronson (Eds.), *The handbook of social psychology* (3rd ed.). Vol. II. Reading, Mass.: Addison-Wesley.

Snyder, M. L., R. E. Kleck, A. Strenta, and J. J. Mentzer (1979). Avoidance of the handicapped: an attributional ambiguity analysis. *J. Pers. soc. Psychol., 37,* 2297–2306.

Sommer, R. (1974). *Tight spaces: hard architecture and how to humanize it.* Englewood Cliffs, N.J.: Prentice-Hall.

Sommer, R., and F. D. Becker (1969). Territorial defense and the good neighbor. *J. Pers. soc. Psychol., 11,* 85–92.

Sommer, R., and H. Ross (1958). Social interaction on a geriatrics ward. *Int. J. soc. Psychiat., 4,* 128–133.

Spencer, C., Z. Parvizeh (1981). The case for developing a cognitive psychology that does not underestimate the abilities of young children. *J. environmental Psychol., 1,* 21–31.

Stern, P. C., and G. T. Gardner (1981a). The place of behavior change in the management of environmental problems. *Zeitschrift für Umweltpolitik.* Pp. 213–240.

_____ (1981b). Psychological research and energy policy. *Amer. Psychol., 36,* 329–342.

Stevens, A., and P. Coupe (1978). Distortions in judged spatial relations. *Cognit. Psychol., 10,* 422–437.

Stobaugh, R., and D. Yergin (Eds.) (1979). *Energy future.* New York: Random House.

Stockdale, J. E. (1978). Crowding: determinants and effects. In L. Berkowitz (Ed.), *Advances in experimental social psychology.* Vol. 11. New York: Academic Press.

Stokols, D. (1972a). On the distinction between density and crowding: some implications for future research. *Psychol. Rev., 79*, 275–278.

—— (1972b). A social psychological model of human crowding phenomena. *Amer. Institute Planners J., 38*, 72–83.

—— (1976). The experience of crowding in primary and secondary environments. *Environment Behav., 8*, 49–86.

—— (1978). Environmental psychology. *Ann. Rev. Psychol., 29*, 253–295.

—— (1982). Environmental psychology: a coming of age. In A. Kraut (Ed.), *G. Stanley hall lecture series*. Vol. 2. Washington, D.C.: American Psychological Association.

—— (Ed.) (1983). *Environment Behav., 15*, 259–408.

Stokols, D., and I. Altman Eds. (In press). *Handbook of environmental psychology*. New York: Wiley.

Stokols, D., and S. A. Shumaker (1982). The psychological context of residential mobility and well-being. *J. soc. Issues, 38*, 149–171.

Suedfeld, P. (1980). *Restricted environmental stimulation*. New York: Wiley.

Sundstrom, E., J. P. Town, D. W. Brown, A. Forman, and C. McGee (1982). Physical enclosure, type of job, and privacy in the office. *Environment Behav., 14*, 543–559.

Taylor, R. B., S. D. Gottfredson, and S. Brower (1980). The defensibility of defensible space. In T. Hirschi and M. Gottfredson (Eds.), *Understanding crime*. Beverly Hills, Calif.: Sage.

Taylor, S. E., and S. T. Fiske (1975). Point of view and perceptions of causality. *J. Pers. soc. Psychol., 32*, 439–445.

—— (1978). Salience, attention, and attribution: top of the head phenomena. In L. Berkowitz (Ed.), *Advances in experimental social psychology*. Vol. 11. New York: Academic Press.

Thibaut, J. W., and H. H. Kelley (1959). *The social psychology of groups*. New York: Wiley.

Triplett, N. (1898/1960). The dynamogenic factors in pacemaking and competition. *Amer. J. Psychol., 4*, 400–408.

Turner, F. J. (1932). *The significance of sections in American history*. New York: Holt.

Tversky, A. (1981). Distortions in memory for maps, environments, and forms. *Cognit. Psychol., 13*, 407–433.

Tversky, A., and D. Kahneman (1974). Judgment under uncertainty: heuristics and biases. *Science, 185*, 1124–1131.

Valins, S., and A. Baum (1973). Residential group size, social interaction and crowding. *Environment Behav., 5*, 421–440.

Wapner, S., S. B. Cohen, and B. Kaplan (1976). *Experiencing the environment*. New York: Plenum.

Weigel, R. H. (1983). Environmental attitudes and the prediction of behavior. In N. R. Feimer and E. S. Geller (Eds.), *Environmental psychology: directions and perspectives*. New York: Praeger.

Weigel, R. H., D. Vernon, and L. Tognacci (1974). Specificity of the attitude as a determinant of attitude-behavior congruence. *J. Pers. soc. Psychol., 30*, 724–728.

Weigel, R. H., and J. Weigel (1978). Environmental concern: the development of a measure. *Environment Behav., 10*, 3–15.

Westin, A. (1967). *Privacy and freedom*. New York: Atheneum.

Wicker, A. W. (1973). Undermanning theory and research: implications for the study of psychological and behavioral effects of excess human populations. *Rep. Res. soc. Psychol., 4*, 185–206.

—— (1979). *An introduction to ecological psychology*. Monterey, Calif.: Brooks/Cole.

Wicker, A. W., and A. Mehler (1971). Assimilation of new members in a large or small church group. *J. appl. Psychol., 55*, 151–156.

Wilbanks, T. J. (1983). Geography and our energy heritage. *Materials and Society, 7*, 437–452.

Wilton, R. (1979). Knowledge of spatial relations: the specification of the information used in making inferences. *Quart. J. exp. Psychol., 31*, 133–146.

Winett, R. A., and M. S. Neale (1979). Psychological framework for energy conservation in buildings: strategies, outcomes, directions. *Energy and Buildings, 2*, 101–116.

Wirth, L. (1938). Urbanism as a way of life. *Amer. J. Sociol., 44*, 1–24.

Withey, S. (1962). Reaction to uncertain threat. In G. W. Barker and D. Chapman (Eds.), *Man and society in disaster*. New York: Basic Books.

Wofsey, E., J. Rierdan, and S. Wapner (1979). Planning to move: effects on representing the currently inhabited environment. *Environment Behav., 11*, 3–32.

Wohlwill, J. F. (1976). Environmental aesthetics: the environment as a source of affect. In I. Altman and J. F. Wohlwill (Eds.), *Human behavior and environment: advances in theory and research*. Vol. 1. New York: Plenum.

Wolfe, M., and R. S. Laufer (1975). The concept of privacy in childhood and adolescence. In D. H. Carson (Ed.), *Man-environment interactions: evaluations and applications*. Stroudsburg, Penn.: Dowden, Hutchinson & Ross.

Worchel, S. (1978). The defense of human territory. Unpublished manuscript. Univ. of Virginia, Charlottesville.

Zelinsky, W. (1973). *The cultural geography of the United States*. Englewood Cliffs, N.J.: Prentice-Hall.

Zerega, A. (1981). Transportation energy conservation policy: implications for social science research. *J. soc. Issues, 37*, 31–50.

CHAPTER 30

Cultural Psychology

D. R. Price-Williams
University of California, Los Angeles

INTRODUCTION

FIELDS

The material covered in this chapter under the general rubric of cultural psychology actually comes from two separate subdisciplines of anthropology and psychology, respectively. The first subdiscipline is known as psycho-

Although I was not always able to follow their suggestions, the following psychologists and anthropologists earn my gratitude for helpful recommendations on the extent of the content: John Berry, Erika Bourguignon, Richard Brislin, George Guthrie, Arthur Hippler, Francis Hsu, Walter Lonner, Jacques Maquet, Lee and Ruth Munroe, Sylvia Scribner, Richard Shweder, George Spindler, Melford Spiro, and Anthony Wallace. I also wish to thank my colleagues at the Neuropsychiatric Institute, UCLA, for discussions on the nature of the chapter: Robert Edgerton, Ronald Gallimore, and Lewis Langness. Harry Triandis gave me especial help in the beginning. Fred Strodtbeck and Tom Weisner were very helpful with comments on the initial drafts. My research assistant, Ceel Mairesse, owes my thanks for checking the bibliography.

Support for the work on this chapter was provided by the National Institute of Child Health and Human Development, Public Health Service Grant No. HD 11944–01, and the Mental Retardation Research Center, University of California, Los Angeles, Grant No. HD 05540–02. The UCLA School of Medicine further provided support.

logical anthropology, and the second is cross-cultural psychology. While these two subdisciplines often have quite different intents and differing methods, the rationale for merging them here is that both ascribe to the common thesis that culture and psychological phenomena are intertwined. The similarly named chapter in the second edition of this *Handbook* (De Vos and Hippler, 1969) also drew its material from both sources.

Since that time the literature from both of the principal sources has expanded considerably. This expansion can be noted from the publication of a six-volume handbook of cross-cultural psychology (Triandis and Berry, 1980; Triandis and Brislin, 1980; Triandis and Lambert, 1980; Triandis and Lonner, 1980; Triandis and Draguns, 1981; Triandis and Heron, 1981). In anthropology two new journals were started in the decade of the seventies devoted to psychological anthropology, which gives an indication of growth here too.

We cannot pretend to be able to provide a full comprehensive coverage of all this material. The intention is to provide representative examples of main directions of research and to indicate types of problems and interests. At the same time we shall have in mind what all this material means to the social psychologist, thereby discarding certain elements that might only be of direct import to the anthropologist or to the general psychologist.

DEFINITIONS

It is embarrassing to admit a lack of precision in the very building blocks of an edifice, but that in fact is what we face in this area of discourse. The key term *culture* has alternative definitions; the boundaries of both psychological anthropology and cross-cultural psychology are not easily discerned, and theories are not always strictly related to data. We can begin with the term *culture*. As is well known, Kroeber and Kluckhohn (1952) listed over one hundred fifty definitions of culture and then came up with an omnibus definition of their own (p. 180):

> Culture consists of patterns, explicit and implicit, of and for behavior acquired and transmitted by symbols, constituting the distinctive achievement of human groups, including their embodiments in artifacts; the essential core of culture consists of traditional (i.e., historically derived and selected) ideas and especially their attached values; culture systems may, on the one hand, be considered as products of action, on the other as conditioning elements of further action.

While this statement is somewhat involved, it serves the purpose of introducing the totality and interdependency aspects of culture. Indeed, in a textbook on cross-cultural psychology Segall (1979, p. 18) sees culture as a set of social stimuli:

> The concept of culture enables the psychologist to account for the fact that social stimuli do not impinge on an individual with equal probability in different places at different times. Some social stimuli are more probable than others. My children are extremely unlikely to greet me by prostrating themselves and kissing my feet. A Swiss peasant is unlikely to be passed on the street by a teenage girl in a miniskirt. A Ganda householder in his East Africa grass-thatched house is not likely to be confronted with a bowl of cornflakes for breakfast.

This account by a psychologist implies that culture and society are coterminous, and as far as the intent of cross-cultural psychology is concerned, this implication is quite appropriate. It is also in keeping with the ideas of one of the founders of anthropology, E. B. Tylor, who introduced the term into the subject with the following definition: "that complex whole which includes knowledge, belief, art, morals, law, custom, and any other capabilities and habits acquired by man as a member of

society" (Tylor, 1871, p. 1). Subsequently, the history of anthropology has tended to distinguish society from culture, particularly with the British social anthropologists who view social structure as different from culture. Nevertheless, even here the relationship between society and culture is very interlinked, as can be seen from the following quotation from Firth (1951): "If society is taken to be an aggregate of social relations, then culture is the content of those relations. Society emphasizes the human component, the aggregate of people and the relations between them. Culture emphasizes the component of accumulated resources, immaterial as well as material, which the people inherit, employ, transmute, add to, and transmit" (p. 27). The difficulty of giving a succinct definition to culture is that, as Beatrice Whiting (1976) well puts it, it is a packaged variable. By that phrase is meant that it both is embraced by and embraces other variables. Disentangling the variable from the total mass of influences is clearly difficult. Many anthropologists view culture as a system theorist might—a complex of interdependent parts. Thus changing one part changes the total unit. And while a psychologist may talk of *a* cultural variable, an anthropologist would have difficulty thinking this way, which is often the source of difficulties between the disciplines.

Culture, however it may be defined, nevertheless needs to be distinguished from types of populations. It is a common mistake among psychologists, even some cross-cultural psychologists, to identify nationality or ethnicity with culture. As anthropologists have pointed out, people are bound together by linkages other than cultural (e.g., Leach, 1954), and a sheer distinction must be made between racial and cultural [see Price-Williams (1979) for a history of this distinction both in anthropology and psychology]. While cross-cultural psychology seems in practice to gloss over the finer distinctions of culture, there is nevertheless a constancy in the use of the term; the usage now is much the same as the usage provided by Klineberg (1935) nearly half a century ago when he held that culture was a whole "way of life" that is determined by the social environment (p. 255).

In view of the difficulty encountered with *culture,* it is not surprising to find equal equivocation with the fields that use it as their key concept. Spindler (1978) confesses to the difficulty of drawing boundaries around the territory of psychological anthropology, and indeed, he says outright that there may be no field or subdiscipline in the usual sense of the word. But there is, he says, "an implict if not explicit psychological element or process in about every formulation or treatment of ostensibly social or cultural process'' (p. 10). He then goes on to say that the very word *culture* (as used in psychological anthropology) is heavily psychologically inclined and amounts to that holistic definition already cited from Tylor and Klineberg.

Furthermore, although the two subdisciplines covered overlap in many ways and equally focus on the concept of culture, as was said previously, there are differences in intent. Cross-cultural psychology takes as its starting point the descriptive categories of both general and social psychology: perception, cognition, motivation, interpersonal behavior, locus of control, and so forth. By and large the emphasis is on individual and interpersonal behavior. Psychological anthropology, on the other hand, uses the descriptive categories of its parent discipline, such as kinship, residence, and religion, and seeks clarification of them through a psychological perspective.

THEORY

Both subdisciplines represent *perspectives* embodying a particular emphasis on specific cultural factors and incorporating characteristic methods. In the range of perspectives there are theories that cover prescribed areas of investigation. These theories will emerge as we traverse the areas of discourse. Taking cross-cultural psychology independently for the moment, we can see that there is an extension of theory from mainstream psychology. For example, Piagetian methods have been extensively applied cross-culturally (Dasen, 1977), and the application has been easily assimilated into the basic theory (Piaget, 1976). Another example is Osgood's theory of meaning systems. Description of the semantic differential and its application to numerous cultures would be better discussed under the heading of psycholinguistics, but we can note here that the theory underlying it stems from mainstream psychology and was brought into cross-cultural use (see Osgood, May, and Miron, 1975). On the anthropological side, again we meet with a spectrum of theories applied to specific domains. Some theories, however, are more like a perspective than a model. One example is the evolutionary thesis, which is represented best by the sociobehavioral position discussed below. There is also an evolutionary perspective in psychoanalysis, which comes out very clearly when anthropological concerns are interpreted. Otherwise, we meet with more prescribed areas for theory.

Thus the culture and personality movement has spawned a number of theories, which more narrowly are relegated to the relationship between the individual and culture. Many anthropological contributions appear to be wholly descriptive, without being geared to any specific theory. Here we should note that ethnography can be defined as a description of cultures. Often overlooked is the fact that there may be theory underlying the description, mandating the actual choice of units described. The theory of functionalism, for example, stating that a particular cultural practice serves to maintain the entire social system, is such an underlying theory.

Nevertheless, we should not look for a grand theory as yet in cultural psychology. It is a growing area that has not yet crystallized into an overall formal theory. This lack of an overall theory may be a weakness, but often theories can be constraining, and we might anticipate for cultural psychology a major paradigmatic shift in looking at human nature.

METHODOLOGY

Triandis (1980, pp. 6–7) has remarked that perhaps cross-cultural psychology is better defined in terms of method rather than theory; Berry (1979) similarly remarks that the subject is defined primarily by method, in contrast to most areas of psychology that are defined by their content. Also of pertinence is the fact that the first contribution on cross-cultural matters to this *Handbook* was entitled ''The Cross-Cultural Method'' (Whiting, 1954), though Whiting was referring to a certain type of method used in psychological anthropology, later dubbed the holocultural approach, which we will consider presently. Actually, a plethora of methods is used in both subdisciplines, operating at different levels. Insofar as cross-cultural psychology is concerned, the subject of method has been given the sole attention of the second volume of the six-volume *Handbook of Cross-Cultural Psychology* (Triandis and Berry, 1980); in addition, there is an entire book on the subject (Brislin, Lonner, and Thorndike, 1976). We can no more than touch on some of the basic problems in these pages.

Specific problems that have arisen under the general heading of methodology cover an array of subjects: sampling, coding, observational bias, applicability of tests, translation difficulties, relevance of experimental procedures, and much more. Rather than discuss all of these specific topics, which have been well attended in the literature, we have chosen to focus on just two aspects that relate both to cross-cultural psychology and to psychological anthropology and are basic to all methodological problems.

The first concerns the question of units of study. Who or what is studied? When one compares cross-cultural psychology with psychological anthropology, there appears to be, at first sight, a significant difference in the choice of units chosen. Though individual differences are sometimes noted in anthropology, nevertheless the tendency is to study groups. Thus, as Berry has said (1969), "although both disciplines are comparative, the units of comparison are groups or modal patterns in psychological anthropology, while the units are individuals, means, and variances, in cross-cultural psychology" (p. 3). We shall need to adopt, to a certain extent, this distinction, since investigators proceed empirically on this assumption.

However, at a more fundamental level the distinction is less salient. In one of the first books on psychology and culture, Bartlett (1923) stressed that the individual must be seen as having reference to a particular set of conditions. The individual is seen in the context of a particular situation or in a given social group. Hence in the practice of cross-cultural psychology the very individuals chosen are selected just because they represent a particular cultural condition. And on the other side of psychological anthropology, anthropologists have been quite aware of the relationship of the individual to the group. Goldenweiser (1968, p. 64), for example, has gone into the various types of bonds that the individual has with the group. Early on, in the first uses of personality tests in anthropology, Wallace (1952) was concerned with sampling problems for the identification of group traits. However, the fact remains that the most repeatedly used methods in psychological anthropology are exclusively geared to group units.

Group units are used, for instance, in the so-called hologeistic method that has been identified with the cross-cultural method. An empirical base of the hologeistic method is the Human Relations Area Files, an information storage system that provides basic facts for a number of cultures coded under various headings. The original material of this set of files comes from the first-hand fieldnotes of ethnographers. Information here shows the full range of ethnography: type of economy, degree of cultural complexity, the institutions of marriage, law, family and religion, types of child-caring practices. The nature and utilization of the Human Relations Area Files has recently been well described by Barry

(1980). Studies based on this set of files, as well as on more direct surveys, come under the heading of this so-called hologeistic method. Naroll, Michik, and Naroll (1980) define this approach as a study that "tests theories by correlational analyses using data from worldwide samples of entire societies or cultures; such samples are intended as representative samples of all known human cultures (or of a defined subset of that universe)" (p. 480).These authors then go on to specify three types of hologeistic inquiry: holonational studies, which use samples from the population of nation states; holocultural studies, which use samples from the population of all known primitive cultures; and holohistorical studies, which use a sample selection from the universe of all historically known studies. We shall discuss the second type only.

It should be noted that Naroll and his associates distinguish these hologeistic studies from other types of cross-cultural research in that they use large samples of cultures. In this chapter there will be many exemplifications of this method. We note now that although this approach may seem to be very different from the methodology that utilizes individuals directly, the problems of sampling and representativeness *vis-à-vis* the larger population—the culture in its entirety—are common to both. Also, a great deal of refinement of data is done before the holocultural method is applied.

The second aspect to be considered is that of comparison itself and its concomitant problem of equivalence. This aspect, of course, relates back to the kind of units selected for study in the first place. The very first comparative study in anthropology was that of Tylor (1889), who covaried rules of residence with the custom of avoiding certain types of kin. Equivalence across cultures in an instance like this is fairly simple to apply, since rules are distinguishable. But psychological variables often run into comparative difficulties that preclude exact equivalence. For example, LeVine and Price-Williams (1974) wished to compare the understanding of family concepts among the Hausa with known results for European samples along the line of Piaget's (1928) methods. One aspect of the Piagetian questioning ran into immediate difficulty. This aspect concerns the important cognitive process of symmetrical relations. It makes sense, in English, French, and other European languages and cultures, to furnish a question based on the following proposition: If X is Y's brother, Y is also X's brother. This question could not be used with the Hausa children because in their culture they do not have symmetrical relations among siblings. They have terms that specify older brother (or sister) and younger brother (or sister). But they have no generic term for brother that would allow a sensible question for the elucidation of symmetrical kinship relations of the Piaget type. As a matter of fact, the concept of family itself, in the nuclear Western sense, has no counterpart either.

In such cases researchers settle for not exact or literal equivalence (which either is completely impossible or not relevant) but functional equivalence (Berry, 1969). Difficulty of comparability is to be found most visibly in the application of formal tests, particularly intelligence and personality tests. Segall (1979, pp. 48–54) makes two points about this aspect of comparison. First, he notes that a test may be a good index of a construct in one culture but not a good index of the same construct in another culture. Second, the same test may not even be a good measure of performance in another culture.

Among psychologists is a growing awareness that for any psychological endeavor to be meaningful in the cultural context, a good understanding of the culture in question is mandatory. This feature is manifest in Gay and Cole's (1967) study of mathematical thinking among the Kpelle of Liberia, which itemized the skill of the Kpelle in counting and related mathematical abilities. Psychological anthropologists have always been attentive to this demand.

A recent study of psychological interest is Berland's (1977) research in Pakistan, which provides the underpinning of the focal interest in psychological differentiation by describing all examples of the various skills and interests of the tribes involved in matters related to this topic. The insistence on proper context and the demand for adequate ethnographic foundation often is better served by the single case study. The distinction between a single case study and a comparative study—either of two or three cultures or the manifold hologeistic approach —is one of approximation. Recall that the Human Relations Area Files, which provide much of the ammunition for holocultural studies, are fundamentally a collection of single case studies. What makes them useful for comparative studies is the later coding that allows for comparison. In other words, single case studies and comparative studies are related. It might be strategically better to start off with a direct comparison to allow for the operationalizing of concepts, but on the other hand, the single case study allows for a wider context. As we shall note later, sometimes a concept detected by the comparative approach may not be detected in the single case study. So, there are, indeed, important differences, but the gap is not sufficiently wide to make it impossible to relate the two approaches. For this reason it is possible to array in one chapter both cross-cultural psychology and psychological anthropology. But note that the coding procedure is not without criticism within anthropological circles. The choice of categories and the necessary exclusion of contextual material are procedures that somewhat offend the traditional ethnographical method.

The subject of methodology should not be left without underlining the importance of what the anthropologists call *field method* in their work. The terminology is deceptively simple, since field work in fact incorporates a vast amount of observational and documentary techniques. Edgerton and Langness (1974) have listed a number of points that come under this heading. Equally complex is another simple-sounding term, *participant observation,* which is the hallmark of the anthropologist. Spradley (1980) has outlined the major steps of this method.

RELATIONSHIP TO GENERAL AND SOCIAL PSYCHOLOGY

There has always been an interest in cultural psychology, dating at least, as Segall (1979, p. 30) notes, from the launching of a German journal in 1860 devoted to what was then called national psychology—the *Zeitschrift fur Volkerpsychologie und Sprachwissenschaft.* A noteworthy name is Wilhelm Wundt, who sponsored interest in both the comparative method and in what can be called cultural psychology. Throughout the years we have seen a small sprinkling of papers relevant to both primitive societies and to nation states in the general psychological literature. F. C. Bartlett is another prominent psychologist who may be mentioned for the earlier time frame (1923). In more recent years have come theoretical exhortations to place the science of psychology in a historical and cultural framework (e.g., Gergen, 1973; Luria, 1976). From other directions we have noticed a renewed interest in situational psychology (Barker, 1968; Mischel, 1979).

Thus the relationship between mainstream psychology and cultural psychology is marked by a constantly shifting emphasis and realignment of boundaries. In the field of social psychology early *Readings in Social Psychology* had contributions that would now be formally tapped by the cross-cultural psychology journals. Also, a foremost publication, the *Journal of Social Psychology,* has for years had a special policy of printing cross-cultural articles. However, the emergence of a formal field, with the resultant association and conjoint journal, did not come until the late sixties. What is now new is the more deliberate focus on comparative cultural research and attendance to methodological problems.

Paying special attention to cross-cultural psychology has tended, paradoxically perhaps, to isolate it from the rest of psychology. This isolation has created a further reaction from cultural psychologists to provide a rationale for the entire endeavor. The general thrust has been to argue that psychology can enlarge its data base through including societies other than the Western industrialized communities.

Advocates of cross-cultural psychology have long recognized that the wide range of populations studied and the types of situations and conventions that are associated with such populations provide a data base that gives an adequate foundation for proper generalizations about human nature. The implication is that, by contrast, inferences about human behavior that are based on relatively limited samples of peoples indigenous to our own type of culture will be better interpreted as related to particular kinds of settings and not *ipso facto* statements about human nature in general. Whiting (1954), for example, showed that studies taking Western samples of infants indicate a linear relationship between onset of weaning and amount of emotional disturbance. This result occurs because weaning in our society rarely extends to the age of the child that is more commonly seen in non-Western cultures. When the data from these cultures are plugged into the equation, a curvilinear relationship between onset of weaning and amount of emotional disturbance is seen.

Other variables evoke more attention when stretched as a canopy across diverse cultures. Ecology, for example, while it has been given some attention in traditional psychology by theorists of perception such as Brunswik (1956), looms as a fundamental variable when perceptual and cognitive processes are studied cross-culturally (Segall, Campbell, and Herskovits, 1966; Berry, 1976). Certain substantive areas that have already been given a lot of attention by social and developmental psychologists can be viewed with a larger perspective when projected against a cross-cultural screen. For example, certain psychological conditions that are rare in our own culture—and when they do occur, are generally seen in an exclusively pathological context—are not only

frequent in other cultures but are also not necessarily interpreted in a medical framework. The instances of trance, possession, witchcraft, and sorcery are classic examples.

Jahoda (1979) has suggested that experimental social psychology is the product of a specific cultural milieu—namely, advanced industrial societies—which differ from the rest of the world on three basic parameters: literacy, an ethos of impersonality, and availability of a wide range of belief systems and attitudes. In small traditional societies all of these features are lacking. Both Jahoda's point and the preceding discussion suggest a path that can be taken in the pursuit of a selection policy. By adopting a cross-cultural or anthropological perspective, we see certain significant themes emerge. For example, Jahoda's first parameter, literacy, prompts a discussion of oral versus literate cultures that would not be salient in societies where everybody is literate. The second parameter, impersonality, is often completely lacking in non-Western cultures, which have an absence of privacy. This feature is noticeable in sleeping arrangements. The significance of sleeping patterns is not discernible in small nuclear families; it becomes only of note when nuclear families are contrasted with large extended families. Thus a full discussion of sleeping patterns is in order. Such a policy is not identical to stressing differences in cultural populations as against similarities.

It is at the point where the enlarged material spawns fresh interpretations of old material that the cultural perspective becomes more important. We have noted the different interpretation that can be placed on the relationship between weaning and emotional disturbance by inserting into the equation societies where the age of weaning is prolonged beyond the limits set by our Western groups. Another classic example concerns the Oedipus complex, which has been well discussed by Campbell and Naroll (1972, p. 437). They state that as long as the data base for this phenomenon remained in the context of the Western nuclear family, as observed early by Freud in Vienna and then by ensuing psychoanalysts in Europe and the United States, the interpretation that the male child was in rivalry with his biological father for the attention of the mother and wife could not be controverted. However, Malinowski (1927) observed the matrilineal Trobriand Islanders, who are brought up by the mother's brother (i.e., not the *genitor* but the sociological pater). In this society the child shows tension toward the mother's brother; one possible interpretation is that it is the father's role as disciplinarian that is the force at work, not necessarily the sexual rivalry.

The accretion to our knowledge of traditional psychological categories need not be so dramatic. Standard targets of inquiry can and have been amplified by extending the data base without any injury to previous suppositions. A representative case is the study of ethnocentrism, long a target of traditional social psychology. LeVine and Campbell (1972) and subsequently Brewer and Campbell (1976) investigated ethnocentrism and the related subject of stereotyping across a number of cultures. The latter study involved thirty separate cultures from East Africa, different communities in the national states of Kenya, Tanzania, and Uganda. In part, the propositions tested in this study stemmed from the theoretical position taken by Campbell previously (1967). One of his main concerns was the impact of contact between members of different groups. This issue relates to a perennial question about stereotypes, that is, whether intergroup perception is at all influenced by the degree of familiarity between the members of the different groups.

Brewer and Campbell fused the degree of familiarity with other indices: A measure of liking for specific groups and the social distance from them were fused into a single measure that they called "desirability of close interpersonal relations." Using this combined measure, they found that positive attraction between disparate groups was correlated with whether there had been traditional contact between them in the past. Similarity was an important feature: similarity in culture and similarity in language. Close geographical proximity was another factor. But the relationship between familiarity and agreement or consensus about stereotypes proved to be curvilinear. Extensive contact, associated with a variety of experiences with members from out-groups, leads to diverse stereotypic beliefs. No contact at all produces much the same reaction. However, limited contact provides a balance between accuracy and individual variation that results in better consensus.

The advantages of this cross-cultural approach lie in the variation provided by a large number of small groups and the opportunity for contact within a relatively small geographical space. This approach would be more difficult to use in continents where national states are widely separated from each other.

On the whole, cross-cultural studies on stereotyping are fairly consistent with monocultural studies. The subject has been well reviewed by Segall (1979, pp. 221–247), who maintains that the findings from cross-cultural work indicate the strength of cultural forces in shaping human behavior: "It is cultural identity that binds individuals to their own group; it is cultural similarity that permits those same individuals to accept and interact with persons from other groups" (1979, p. 245).

In another classic area of social psychology—attitude formation, attitude maintenance, and attitude change—we find again that material on these subjects has been provided by cross-cultural investigators. Most of the material has been reviewed by Davidson (1979, pp. 137–157). Here again there is not much deviation from studies done in the United States. Davidson notes that, as is the case generally, the summation and averaging models are better correlated with observed attitudes than the contiguity model. Further, as Davidson (1979, p. 154) again notes, the factors of nationality, race, and language do not need to be considered as boundary conditions in the study of attitude formation and attitude structure.

The material provided above has been introduced at this stage not so much to provide empirical findings as to indicate that many of the standard variables and processes studied in social psychology have been reintroduced into a larger cross-cultural framework without disproving former findings. We shall delve into the general issue of universals more deeply in the following section. We simply note now that rather than adopt the procedure of laboriously citing replicated studies, we shall focus on salient variables and issues that have emerged as a consequence of adopting a cross-cultural perspective, whether the result confirms a universalistic or relativistic approach.

SUMMARY AND ASSESSMENT

Both cross-cultural psychology and psychological anthropology overlap to the extent that they focus on the linkage of psychological factors with the cultural matrix. The simple term *cultural psychology* serves to identify this area of convergence. Nevertheless, there are differences in intent between the two subdisciplines, which stem from their parent disciplines. These differences give rise to the reason why certain things are studied and not others and to the kind of theory to which the inquiry is related. Despite these differences, a major common agreement between the two subdisciplines is the importance of context. Focus on context provides a further link with developments in mainstream psychology, where this is regarded as important. Another link with mainstream psychology is the replication of standard targets of inquiry in a wider perspective provided by a cross-cultural framework. This replication allows confirmation or modification of generalizations to be reached with a narrower sample of individuals and allows also for proper comparison of nonindividual factors.

Clearly, much is to be gained by the pooling of minds and resources from both cross-cultural psychology and psychological anthropology. While both of these subdisciplines are constrained to follow their own individual interests, the huge middle ground of demonstrating and analyzing how psychological and cultural factors are intertwined requires equally the explication of context so well understood by anthropology and the sophistication of method and measurement furnished in psychology. We must avoid giving the impression, articulated by one psychological anthropologist at least (Edgerton, 1974), that our two subdisciplines do not always share the same paradigm. Cross-cultural psychology has a further problem. It needs to develop its own individual style and orientation while not losing its roots in traditional psychology, particularly in social psychology. One way it can serve both purposes is to align itself both theoretically and empirically with the social psychologist who stresses the importance of the situation. For psychology as a whole the term *culture* needs to be deemphasized from its narrow connotation with national and ethnic identity and aligned with the broader meaning of style of life, background suppositions that operate on a day-to-day basis in the course of an individual's life.

UNIVERSALS AND
CULTURAL RELATIVITY

The orientation of the scholar essentially dictates whether universals are searched for or, alternatively, whether a cultural relative position is adopted. Many workers in anthropology do not strive for detecting universals or making comparisons between cultures. For those who do look for universals, the unit of description can be decided upon on a purely a priori basis. For example, sex roles are obviously to be found all over the world. A comparative scheme of sex roles is then easily constructed. Another example is the tracing of life cycles. But while there are simple examples, there are others that are more complex. In this section we shall focus on more complex examples, indicating the difficulty of unequivocally establishing

universals. Also, we shall discuss the importance of biological parameters in establishing universals, thereby touching on the somewhat controversial field of evolutionary argument. But first, we must return to the basic definitional problem.

TYPES OF UNIVERSALS

What is meant by *universals* is a key question. Two basic divisions can be made immediately. The first type of universal is one that is rooted in a phylogenetic, biological perspective, rooted in the repertoire of the organism shaped by evolution. The biosocial approach, which we shall discuss below, is of this type. Distinct from this type is the class of behavioral universals, which may or may not be interpreted phylogenetically. In turn, there are several kinds of behavioral universals. Jaynes and Bressler (1971) have in fact distinguished five kinds of behavioral universals. They name, first, simple behavioral universals, defined as single actions recognizable as the same species; facial expressions are an example. The second kind are what they call variform universals, thought of as two or more overt behaviors that share the same functional significance and also share certain common elements such as situational arousal or emotional tone. Mating behaviors are given as an example. The third style is functional universals; these are two or more behavioral configurations having similar social consequences. Jaynes and Bressler cite rites of passage, which foster group cohesion, as a good example of this kind. Diachronic universals are the fourth type; these are behavioral universals that are changed through time, like socialization behaviors. Finally, there are relational universals, which are thought of as not confined to single species.

Definitional problems aside, empirical investigations help to determine the nature of what is and what is not a universal category. Thus for a considerable period of time in the field of color perception and color naming, it was assumed that color perception was different across the world. The seminal work by Berlin and Kay (1969) then established that there were basically eleven universal foci within the color solid. They also established that although different cultures might vary in the number of colors named, these colors were named in a definite sequence. At a later date Bornstein (1973) found that within this framework there seem to be certain sensory differences in color vision. Thus what are claimed at any one time as universals may be altered at a later date.

An insightful way of looking at universals has emerged from the field of color categorization. Rosch (1975) has distinguished two kinds of representations of categories: digital and analog. Digital representations are exemplified by discrete attributes, the kind of concept that emerges with forming classes from the interaction of attributes such as shape, size, and color. Digital representation, best exemplified in the common digital wristwatch that has replaced the circular-face type, has clear boundaries and tends to be unequivocally binomial. Analog representations, best exemplified by the oscilloscope that depicts changes in electrical current, tend to focus on central or dominant tendencies and allow a gradual merging of attributes around this focus.

Rosch's main point is that there are some natural, biologically given categories that are best understood in this framework, and they operate in an analogic and not in a digital way. The classic example comes from the study of color vision. These facts are well known: that the physical properties of light are not discrete but arranged in a continuous variation; that the boundaries between color categories are not defined and thus are arbitrary in allowing codable terms for one color versus another; that some colors are better exemplars for a color term than others. Berlin and Kay (1969) introduced the idea of a focal point to refer to those places in the color space that are chosen by interlocutors as representing the best exemplars of any specific color term. Rosch's work (see Heider, 1971) has shown that such focal areas are better indicators of the color sense than using color terminology. In cross-cultural work with the Dani of New Guinea, who apparently have no terminology for chromatic colors and thus only have a two-color system, she showed that focal colors are better remembered (see Heider, 1972). Now Rosch's argument is that the identification of foci such as these, in color vision and in other behavioral contexts, is a suitable vehicle for establishing true universals. The foci or prototypes need not be always biologically given, but their identification requires an analogic way of representing these behaviors and not a digital way.

The emphasis on digital representation and the concomitant semantic problem undoubtedly is the source of confusion in establishing what is and what is not a universal behavior, as can be seen in the ethologist Eibl-Eibesfeldt's reaction (1975) to the cultural relativist argument on aggression. He argues that what are generally held up as cultural examples of nonaggressive people on closer examination could be shown to be aggressive. He cites the case of the Eskimo, and while he agrees that they

do not display aggression that leads to bloodshed, he maintains that they exhibit such behavior as verbal dueling that he considers to be nevertheless aggressive. This example, of course, shows up the further difficulty about the meaning of basic explanatory terms. Eibl-Eibesfeldt goes on to say that while the !Ko-Bushmen are undoubtedly aggressive, they are not bellicose. Indeed, their very aggressive behavior is the means by which they avoid being bellicose.

Of course, viewing any phenomenon in a universal framework does not deny the proposition that there are idiosyncratic cultural factors operating within this framework. The facial expressions of emotion represent a classic case where the varying interpretations of a pan-human tendency and cultural specificity can be dovetailed. Ever since Darwin (1872) maintained that some universal facial expressions are linked to a number of primary emotional states, like anger and fear, there has been debate whether facial expressions of emotion are thus universal or are, alternatively, linked to specific cultures. Anthropologists LaBarre (1947) and Birdwhistell (1963) have championed the culture-specific point of view.

Examining the available literature on the subject and devising specific experiments to test the notion, Ekman (1974) indicated that there are distinctive facial muscles that are linked to a number of primary states of affect, and that these states are indeed universal; but there are also certain factors that mask this universality, and these factors are culture-specific. These factors are, first, the stimuli that may elicit the same emotion but that vary from one culture to another (the same emotion of anger may be differentially elicited by various stimuli cross-culturally). Second, display rules may vary from one culture to the other. Display rules are those techniques that manage and control facial appearance: A person may be surprised, for example, but instantaneously manifest a studied expression that belies the surprise. The third factor relates to the consequence of an expressed emotion, which again will vary across cultures.

In other words, Ekman and others recognize that there is a pancultural tendency for the movement of facial expressions in the manifestation of emotion, but they also recognize that these same muscle movements are embedded in a cultural context. This point and further aspects of cross-cultural nonverbal communication are explored in Wolfgang (1979).

Despite the clear difficulty of establishing universals (without equivocation), there have been various attempts at listing behaviors that appear to cut across all cultures.

Both Kluckhohn (1953) and Murdock (1949) have produced itemized lists of pancultural traits. Murdock's list provided seventy-three items, which included such behaviors as mourning, joking, marriage, fire making, and mythologizing. The inventory approach has been simplified by reducing a long list to a small number of factors through the approximate statistical techniques. Sawyer and LeVine (1966), for example, took as their starting point certain cultural characteristics listed in Murdock's (1957) world ethnographic sample, from which they scaled anew across a sample of 565 societies. They came up with nine societal characteristics that they judged to be functional prerequisites for any society. Lomax and Berkowitz (1972) took a sample of 148 cultures, for which they found that nineteen behavioral characteristics accounted for most of the variance. On a different line of reasoning Aberle and colleagues (1950) identified nine functional requisites necessary for survival for any society. These requisites included the ability to deal effectively with the environment, the facility to make provision for sexual reproduction, a learned symbolic communication, and some form of social control against social disruptions. Whether nominated by a priori means or through empirical investigation, such lists of universals can be easily generated with varying degrees of plausibility.

Before concluding this portion on types of universals, we must return to the opening comment on the basic attitude of the investigator. A remark by an author of a textbook on psychological anthropology (Williams, 1975, p. 5) illustrates the relevance of attitude with respect to the work done on personality. Williams sees Barnouw (1973), who wrote a textbook on culture and personality, as saying that the discipline is concerned with an understanding of individual personality through an examination of cultural and social determinants. On the other side Williams sees the work of Wallace (1970), who also wrote an introductory text on culture and personality, as stating that the behavior of individuals is basically the outcome of cultural evolution, cultural change, and cultural diversity. Thus Wallace tends to dwell more on biological parameters than do scholars who adopt a less universalistic stance. The controversy in culture and personality studies is similar to the old argument in psychology of the virtues of nomothetic approaches versus ideographic outlooks. The consequence of adopting one or the other perspective does not restrict itself to pure theory or choice of data.

However, an important methodological point can arise depending on the choice of perspective. Shweder (1973) has raised the possibility that certain kinds of categories may emerge from studies that are comparative but will not be detected from studies in a single culture. Shweder took as a starting point those categories that Whiting and Whiting (1975) used in their analysis of children's behavior across six cultures. In this study the main finding was that a dimension of nurturance versus egoism was valid across all six cultures. Shweder found out that whereas this distinction was in fact consistent *across* cultures, it could not be sensibly applied within any single culture. Following the analysis of the Whitings' material with examples from other studies—making clear therefore that this finding was not simply an artifact of the six-culture study—Shweder (1973) then makes this important point (p. 543):

> Our discussion has raised the possiblity that, for reasons other than "problems of measurement," all known cultures and individuals within each of all known cultures may not differ in the same ways. Valid indications of a theoretical variable may be discovered across a representative sample of cultures without being discoverable within any of them, or may be discover*ed* within each of all cultures without being discover*able* across them.

THE EVOLUTIONARY PERSPECTIVE

A number of biological parameters have been studied on a cross-cultural basis (Munroe, Munroe, and Whiting, 1981, Part II; Thompson, 1980), but as LeVine (1974, p. 6) points out, the early approach to universals was derived from ethnographic data with little or no connection with biological data. Within the last decade there has been a renewed interest in the biological direction, best seen in the sociobiology perspective (Wilson, 1975), that has created much controversy among social scientists. What we are loosely calling the biosocial approach here (so as not to identify it exclusively with the sociobiology school) places the emphasis on evolutionary notions such as phylogenetic selection, stressing adaptational qualities to the environment, and somatic responses that have social consequences.

The study of infancy provides a good subject for identification of the biosocial approach and for cultural environmental approaches. The key term here, as elsewhere in evolutionary theory, is adaptive function, seen in a phylogenetic context. Freedman (1974) has provided one of the most cogent presentations of the evolutionary argument in the field of infancy studies. He reports (1974, pp. 145–176) systematic observations on the newborn of various ethnic groups. These groups included Navajo, Hausa infants of West Africa, and Australian aborigines, as well as mixed ethnic groups in the United States, such as Chinese-American and Afro-American. A number of infant behavioral and neurological scales were given to these populations of infants. Some of the findings are best presented in the framework of the evolutionary argument. Thus Freedman found (1974, p. 172), with his Australian aboriginal infants, that the neck, back, and legs were very much stronger at birth than were those of the infants of the Oriental and Caucasian populations. This result is attributed to the fact that the aboriginal population comes from a stock of nomadic people who "have never developed special modes of transport for infants, such as cradleboards or slings" (1974, p. 172). As Freedman points out, given this high degree of nomadic life and the absence of specialized transports for infants, it would be highly functional for the baby to be well muscled, and particularly it would be very advantageous for the head not to loll about, necessitating strong neck muscles.

On the basis of such findings, Freedman tends to reverse well-known environmental arguments. The Navajo, for example, are generally judged by observers to be emotionally subdued and passive and to display low irritability. These behaviors have sometimes been attributed to early infantile experiences with the cradleboard, the use of which restricts motility and keeps the infant pinned in for long periods. Freedman, finding that his newborn Navajo sample was the lowest of all the groups on such items as muscle tonus, vigor, and irritability, concluded that Navajo babies were more likely to *permit* the cradleboard condition than more active neonates in other samples. We note, in passing, that there have been criticisms of these findings. For an excellent review of the entire subject the article by Super (1981) should be consulted.

The biosocial approach takes into account the established fact that well over 90 percent of human history was spent in hunting and gathering societies (Washburn and McCown, 1972). As the human organism has not drastically altered for the remaining 10 percent of our history, let alone during the relatively infinitesimal two

centuries or so of industrial societies, it is inferred that the present human genes are the product of selective factors introduced during this hunting and gathering period. In turn, this inference suggests that there are evolutionary conditions appropriate to that period of human history.

Rossi (1977) has presented an argument that sexual distinctions and the care of infants are best interpreted in this evolutionary framework. She points out, for example, that human evolution has pressured a sexual dimorphism appropriate to the ecology of a hunting and gathering society. "This means that reproductive success favored females skillful in bearing and rearing their young, in small-game hunting, and in food gathering, and males skillful in large-game hunting and defense" (Rossi, 1977, p. 12). The impact of these pressures is present in the present-day chemical and physiological processes of the body. As Rossi further points out in her article, the contemporary sociological emphasis on nonbiological parameters leads one to forget that the basic functions of family life "consist in the coming together of people with physical bodies to mate, to reproduce, and to rear the young" (1977, p. 12). She goes on to cite the endocrinological literature to indicate that while both males and females obviously are oriented toward sexual activity, it is only women that have innate orientations toward reproduction—not only in the obvious sense of the ability to conceive but in the later relationship with the infant. Although this fact would not have been thought of as a social issue some years ago, the present climate of American parental and family styles necessitates the emphasis.

Much evidence indicates that there are physiological factors germane only to the female of the species that engender a special relationship with the infant. Rossi cites the relevant physiological and behavioral material. For example, infant crying stimulates the secretion of oxytocin, which stimulates uterine contractions and nipple contraction that is facilitating to and preparatory for nursing the infant. Women after childbirth nearly invariably cradle their babies in the left arm, thus facilitating the hearing of the soothing sounds of the heartbeat. This action, in turn, favors closeness with the infant in subsequent child life.

A quite important social point is raised in the article, which is relevant to our Western contemporary life and merits inclusion here. Breast feeding (in collaboration with other factors of physical proximity and a low-sugar and carbohydrate diet) keeps the body fat at a low enough threshold to inhibit ovulation. Thus a new child is not likely to be conceived for a considerable period, not until the organism is fit enough to endure the new challenge—maybe for another three years. The stress that another baby would put on an organism not physically and emotionally equipped is therefore averted. There seems to be a natural braking mechanism, initiated by breast feeding, that induces a natural spacing of babies. However, in contemporary developed societies enriched diets disturb the control that lactation otherwise would exert, and with this disturbance comes the possibility that stress on the maternal organism is reintroduced.

The related topic of parenting is discussed by Rohner (1975) in Darwinian terms. He made a global study, using 101 societies, of parental acceptance and rejection. Indications of love, warmth, and affection were taken as acceptance, and indications of hostility or indifference that resulted in the absence or withdrawal of love were taken as rejection. Rohner correlated types of subsistence economy with either acceptance or rejection. Briefly, he found that hunting societies are more likely to be accepting of their children than pastoral societies. Rohner's reasoning is that there is a built-in selective tendency in hunting societies for parents to further a certain kind of relationship with their children that fosters independence and initiative. These characteristics are the ones that active hunting groups require of their members. It is not that pastoralists actually reject their children; it is just that the demand that would generate a constant tendency does not exist.

Psychological anthropologists may adopt an evolutionary argument rather than an environmental position but not necessarily see this argument in genetic terms. A good example is LeVine's (1977) case regarding infants. LeVine has tended to be somewhat of an environmentalist in his career, but in the present case he has come out with an evolutionary argument (LeVine, 1977, pp. 13–27). He sees, in the care of the very young, standardized strategies for survival that are reflected in environmental pressures. He views this evolutionary trend as more cultural than biological, "encoded in customs rather than genes and transmitted socially rather than biologically" (1977, p. 16).

What LeVine is referring to are the various safeguards from environmental hazards that parents provide for their children, safeguards that are reflected in carrying infants on the parent's back for a relatively long period of the infant's life and in the constant physical atten-

tion that the infant receives in non-Western societies. Such practices may seem to delay the child's autonomy and limit socialization practices designed to enhance emotional life.

At this point LeVine makes an insightful remark about the use of the term *indulgence,* which is frequently used by Western observers. LeVine considers this term to be misleading for non-Western cultures since it carries with it an affective weight that actually is missing in the behavior of parents toward infants in traditional societies. LeVine notes that although there is abundant evidence of monitoring the infant's physical needs, there is less evidence of any socioemotional behavior accompanying this care, such as chatting, cooing, or smiling with eye-to-eye contact. Although this type of behavior has been traditionally interpreted as indulgent, LeVine prefers to view it as functionally adaptive behavior in a milieu that is characterized by high infant mortality and low medical technology. In other words, there are many environmental risks for the infant, such as getting burnt by the communal fire, which can only be prevented by strict monitoring by older children and adults. It is a survival matter, since the absence of effective medical help could only result in elimination of the infant. LeVine (1977) goes on to make the important point that "institutional patterns of child rearing need to be analyzed as means by which parents have responded adaptively to their experience of environmental hazards threatening the health or future welfare of their children" (pp. 26–27). Thus various customs of eliminating hazards are passed on by the generations, customs that can be viewed in evolutionary perspective if not in a genetic framework.

THE CULTURAL RELATIVITY PERSPECTIVE

The disciplines of linguistics, anthropology, and cross-cultural psychology are often forced to take into consideration the descriptive units of the people they study. We owe to Pike (1954) the behavioral interpretation of so-called *emics* and *etics,* these being the suffixes of the linguistic distinction of phonemics and phonetics. On the cultural level these suffixes have been used to distinguish terms employed by the people studied from terms stemming from the discipline of the investigator.

To take an extreme case, among the Zulu there is a state of altered consciousness called *ukuthwasa* (Lee, 1968). This word might be rendered into English and interpreted into our Western psychiatric nosology as some kind of psychosis. Whether or not this interpretation would be correct is not the point here (Lee himself thought it would be a gross oversimplification); the point is that psychosis is the *etic* term and *ukuthwasa* is the *emic* term.

Amplification of the *emic* term requires contextual treatment, a procedure that linguists and anthropologists do as a matter of form. In anthropology there has always been a traditional place for the specification of such terms toward the presentation of folk ideas and folk beliefs. There has not really been any issue in psychological anthropology about the employment of an *etic* versus an *emic* approach. It seems to have become more of a problem for cross-cultural psychology, where it has been assessed (Lonner, 1979) as one of the current major issues in the discipline. The difficulty for cross-cultural psychology stems from the fact that many of the descriptive units used in psychology as a whole turn out to be culture-specific to our own Western culture and do not make sense when applied to other cultures. When these units are embedded in a test on which comparative judgments are made, then the error is compounded, because the comparison is inclined to favor the population on which the test was constructed in the first place (accurate translation into another language is only of minimal importance in this matter). Various viewpoints in the *emic-etic* problem have surfaced in the cross-cultural literature (Berry, 1969; Price-Williams, 1975; Lonner, 1979).

Quite apart from the question of relevance, there is a place for the presentation of concepts that various folk groups entertain and act upon. In the past ten to fifteen years a sizable literature and a school of anthropology have developed this viewpoint with the help of linguistic techniques. This viewpoint will be discussed later. On the psychological side there have been parallel attempts at explicating a folk idea and relating it to existing cultural and social conditions. We can best exemplify these attempts by taking two examples of folk ideas of concepts that are meaningful to the science of psychology itself.

Intelligence tests, measuring the Western concept of intelligence, have been applied so liberally throughout the non-Western world that it may come as a surprise that scholars have felt it necessary to probe into folk concepts of the concept. A starting point is the distinction between intelligence and its opposites, like stupidity or imbecility. Is this distinction widely recognized, or is it a function of our recondite system of education and selection? Edgerton (1970) has analyzed non-Western notions of mental retardation. While recognizing that there is not anything

like definitive data regarding the perception of the retarded in so-called primitive societies, Edgerton nevertheless states that most anthropologists would be of the opinion that by and large intellectual deficit is recognized in traditional societies. Edgerton cites the available literature and notes that in a great many societies intelligence is definitely respected. He cites, for example, a study by Burrows and Spiro (1953) showing that in a small atoll in Micronesia feeblemindedness is recognized for what it is, and other studies by Margaret Mead (1953) among the Manus and Geoffrey Gorer (1938) with the Lepchas of Sikkim indicate that such groups are aware of subtle differences in intelligence. The value judgments placed on these perceptions may vary, especially when what we call feeblemindedness and idiocy are involved, but the upshot is that distinctions of intelligence, and particularly antonyms to intelligence, seem to be recognized over a wide area of the world.

More detailed analysis of folk concepts, while supporting this general finding, suggest that our own concept of intelligence, especially the *etic* definitions of scientific psychology, may differ from other cultures only in the level of differentiation from other factors. Wober (1974) tackled this question directly in Uganda. He first took two sets of villagers that actually were composed of different ethnic strains and language. He used Osgood's Semantic Differential technique in order to probe the connotational meanings around a central native term called *Obugezi*. In the dictionaries this term is freely translated into English as intelligence. Twenty-two pairs of adjectives were then given to the two ethnic Ugandan groups (the idea of scalar opposites having been previously explained to them). It was noteworthy that the groups only really differentiated significantly on two items. Both groups thought of intelligence as something that was slow, careful, and active; that was straightforward and sane; that was necessary, happy, healthy, strong, steady, and safe. Wober says that in Uganda intelligence is not unlike the Mediterranean idea of civility and *gravitas,* indicating a public-spirited orientation of the mind (Wober, 1974, p. 267). Intelligence is clearly seen as something that is extroverted, not something vectored internally.

Now while there was only a minor difference between these two groups of villagers who share the same educational level, Wober did find more distinction when he went up the educational ladder and took Ugandan teachers and medical students, plus the so-called elite of society. Again, as with the villagers, there was agreement that intelligence is a traditional entity. But the teachers did not think, as did the villagers, that intelligence was slow, stable, healthy, careful, active, or hot. And the teachers did not strongly associate intelligence with *friendly,* as did the villagers. The differences from the villagers were ones of degree, and Wober recognizes that the teachers' attitudes toward scales may be more sophisticated than the villagers'. However, the difference from the villagers is far more marked with the medical students, who were scaling the English word *intelligence* itself and not the native equivalent. These medical students did not see intelligence as a traditional entity but as a modern entity. Further, they perceived intelligence as being hurried or quick—the very opposite of what the villagers said.

Wober reviews the available literature from other parts of Africa. He notes the studies done by Barbara LeVine in Kenya (1963), Margaret Read with the Ngoni of Malawi (1959), Audrey Richards (1956) with the Bemba, and Irvine (1969) with the Shona; all verge on a common understanding regarding intelligence—namely, that it incorporates social values of obedience and wisdom, to be distinguished from mere cleverness. Also, the various native terms of these various groups in Africa agree that their respective term for intelligence means good judgment, social competence, caution, and prudence.

In analyzing this common trend, and in contrasting it with the Western idea of intelligence, Wober (1974, pp. 275–276) points out that our word *intelligence* has become separated from the arena of emotion and attitudes, as indeed is clear from the purposeful definition from the pioneers on the scientific study of the subject. Our own folk tradition has followed the scientific definitions. It seems that in many non-Western traditional societies this narrowed definition has not evolved. It also seems that the differentiation has gone hand in hand with sociological changes: The more an educational elite emerges, the more the concept of intelligence becomes separated from other components of the total personality. This result has also been noted by Olson (1970) and by Price-Williams (1975, pp. 58–59), both of whom insist that the concept of intelligence cannot be taken from the cultural medium in which it was generated.

CONCEPT OF THE SELF

If the concept of intelligence can be thought at least to have achieved some degree of scientific respectability in psychology, somewhat less can be attributed to the concept of self. Refined either arbitrarily or as an unformulated given in traditional psychology, there is clearly room for input from other cultures.

Starting points on how to study the concept of self in other cultures are themselves difficult to establish. It is commonplace to note that everybody has a public and a private side. It is also commonplace to mark that each of us has a cultural identity. The ambiguity creeps in when labels have to be attached. Goldschmidt (1966, pp. 69–70) wishes to reserve the idea of a "symbolic self" to represent that private side of the individual's meaningful universe, yet he sees even this term as imbued with culturally defined values through which the private side needs to express itself. Another approach is to accept the Western idea of self as it can be coded in a test and then to apply this idea to other cultures and see what similarities or differences emerge. Weill (1975) used this approach when applying the Tennessee Self Concept scale of Fitts to a group of Israeli adolescents. This group differed according to Oriental and occidental characteristics. Distinct differences do emerge, but the approach is not very sophisticated.

A more ambitious and difficult approach is to formulate an indigenous concept of self by using the particular culture's philosophical and sociological framework as basic parameters in order to define the self-concept. Hallowell (1974, pp. 172–182) may well be considered the pioneer of this kind of inquiry within anthropology. His analysis of the concept of self among the Ojibwa Indians has set a pattern of inquiry for what is a difficult and subtle problem. His work among the Ojibwa has been continued by Black (1977) and by Hay (1977). Further research on the nature of the self among native American groups is reflected in Straus's (1977) work among the Cheyenne. An example from another part of the world is the study among the Yoruba people of western Nigeria by Laléyê (1970), who is a Yoruba become philosopher. He was forced to forge a semantic approach through which he analyzed key Yoruba words, found both in myth and in common language. He found, in passing, that the Yoruba—wisely perhaps—do not try to fathom the essence of the self but are more interested in defining the relationships that bind the self to other things.

Establishment of what the central term *self* may mean to any given culture is probably important in understanding more complex notions of *personality*. Some anthropologists (e.g., Hsu, 1971) have recognized that the Western idea of personality is characterized by an explicit sense of separation from the society or culture in which it is embedded. In likewise fashion, a Japanese scholar (Minoura, 1979, p. 52) has noted that in American society the self or ego always seems to have a definite boundary. In contrast, for the Japanese it is the other that is anchored as the point of reference for the definition of one's own self. Also, from the reports of other Japanese scholars (e.g., Kimura, 1973, p. 154) the Japanese concept of self seems to be something different from the concept as we intuitively see it. The key term here is *jibun,* a term compounded from *ji,* representing the first person singular, and *bun,* which means, strictly, "portion, share, or fraction." However, it seems that *bun* has a more profound societal meaning (Lebra, 1976, p. 68). The difference between *jibun* then and *self,* as understood in the West, is best explained by Kimura (1973, p. 154, translated by Minoura, 1979):

> The Western concept of "self" refers essentially to the uniqueness of the individual, or the substance of the person, which has maintained its sameness and continuity over time and across situations, although it is recognized as a product of interaction with other humans. Whereas, the Japanese concept of *jibun* refers to one's sharing which is something located beyond a boundary of "self" in the Western sense.
> The amount of one's sharing varies depending upon dynamics of a situation. *Jibun* does not have a definite consistent boundary.

Doi (1973) grapples with an affiliated problem when he tries to express the Japanese equivalent of *dependence.* The Japanese translation of this term, *amae,* is clearly more involved than our term. Doi insists that *amae* is more like what the psychoanalysts would call passive love. It also has connection with *jibun;* specifically, there is a reciprocal relationship between *ama* and *jibun* in that a person who has a *jibun* is capable of checking *amae,* while a man who is at the mercy of *amae* has no *jibun.* With their deep sense of obligation and familial links, the Japanese have a sense of self that is better understood in terms of relationships and of interdependence. There is a parallel here with our Western use of *intelligence,* where (as noted previously) the term has become separate and abstracted from the emotional and attitudinal ties that it still has in other cultures. In similar fashion, it seems that many other cultures fail to have a separate sense of self and have some difficulty in separating a private idea of self from the public side, as in the case of the Mayans (Gutmann, 1967) and, appar-

ently, the Japanese. Similarly, Hsu (1971) finds, in the Chinese term *jen,* a relational meaning that is lost in its translation into English as *self.*

As soon as we depart from our Judeo-Christian ways of thinking about the self, it is very easy to get lost in a network of institutional relationships in the act of definition. The French Centre National de la Recherche Scientifique has put together a special issue concerning the notion of *personne* in Black Africa, a study comprising twenty-three indigenous societies. The introduction to the symposium noted immediately the problem of definition: that if the endeavor started out with a ready-made definition, it would imbue the specific cases with a Judeo-Christian outlook that would be foreign to African thought (Centre National, 1973, pp. 15–32). What is particularly interesting from the ensuing exemplifications is that there exist indigenous attempts to deal with what *we* would think of as unconscious factors in defining the self. Androgynous notions emerge, and so do quasi-occult ideas about the double. It seems further that in some instances there are quite complex metaphysical systems to deal with the notion of self. For example, among the Kotoko of north central Africa the self has eight elements in which one (the *sahe*) is of opposite sex to its owner; the entire concept is dependent upon a complicated cosmology (Lebeuf, 1973).

The perennial difficulties in psychology of establishing the meanings of self, ego, identity, person, and personality are thus thrown onto a larger canvas. There is evidence now of a renewed concern about the nature of the self in an anthropological context. A recent symposium on the subject was held at the American Anthropological Association (1980). Fogelson (1980) has shown that this concern with the self owes much to the brilliant, older work of Marcel Mauss (1929), and Fogelson himself presents a useful overview of what is now known about the self in a cultural framework.

SUMMARY AND ASSESSMENT

The recognition of both similarities and differences across cultures has produced a spectrum, the extremes of which are concerned with a search for universals, on the one hand, and a posture of cultural relativity, on the other hand. Both positions are affiliated with predetermining theories and methods. The universalist position tends to be associated with biological processes and further is involved with a biological evolutionary perspective. Examples can be found, though, where nonbiological parameters are used as universals and where cultural evolution is invoked rather than biological evolution. One aspect of the cultural relativity position has been to explore in depth, for any one culture, the meaning of specific psychological terms, like *intelligence* and *self*. The meaning may or may not fully accord with our own scientific ideas regarding these concepts.

The different perspectives of universalism and cultural relativity can be interpreted as just that—perspectives, seen as a distinction in the type of lens applied to behavior. If one is to make comparisons across cultures in the first place, the categories to be observed need to be salient, to have clear boundaries. It is not, perhaps, surprising that the fine-grain analysis of a single culture may lose some of the simplicity in the process. It is also not surprising that much, if not all, of the contextual material that is deemed so important by anthropologists is lost in the search for universals.

The biological evolutionary argument as expressed in the sociobiology school of thought uses an even wider-angled lens. Critics of this school have pointed to the fact that much of the behavior thought to be explained by invoking sociobiological concepts is more simply explained by reference to sociocultural notions. Undoubtedly, there is room for more biological analysis than has been used by social scientists. The jump from observation of contemporary social situations to explanations in terms of genetic heritage is too large to avoid the criticism of simplistic generalizations. Reference to the hunting and gathering stage of human evolution needs further support before being used as an explanatory construct for rather complex human behavior as witnessed in aggressive acts, for example. There are many steps to be buttressed before the full evolutionary argument can be invoked. One major step is the assessment of what is known about psychological behavior from a biological perspective. The kind of information found in the book *Psychobiology* (McGaugh, 1971) provides many of the stepping-stones necessary to furnish the sociobiological perspective with an empirical background.

Single case studies of specific cultures serve the function of providing the context in which so many of the meaningful concepts that psychology studies are embedded. The point needs to be added that much of the relevancy to psychological theory is lost if it is not recognized that this type of analysis applies equally to our own culture and to others. This statement refers not only to the recognition of subcultures but also to the recognition of the so-called mainstream culture. Both a universals

approach and a cultural relative approach do not mutually exclude the other's value. Even if they do not always agree in empirical findings, the two approaches are complementary.

CULTURAL INFLUENCES ON SOCIAL BEHAVIOR

This section is concerned with the influence of culture on specific social behaviors and social roles. For this purpose culture can be crudely divided into basic economic and subsistence factors, on the one hand, and values, roles, and statuses that we simply label as sociocultural, on the other hand. The latter group requires no prior explanation about its nature. The ecological and subsistence complex does need further description.

ECOLOGICAL AND SUBSISTENCE PATTERNS

It has already been noted that ecological and subsistence factors have been marked as being important for various kinds of behavior. Focus on early socialization has further amplified the role of these factors. John and Beatrice Whiting in anthropology have been in the forefront in emphasizing subsistence patterns that in turn are connected with varying kinds of ecology. Support for the role of ecology has also come from cross-cultural psychology, notably the work of Berry (1976), which has related the concept of psychological differentiation to varying kinds of ecological adaptations. Briefly, Berry's findings were that high psychological differentiation correlates with hunting and gathering subsistence patterns, nomadic settlement patterns, and low population density. Low psychological differentiation correlates with agricultural and sedentary communities and with high population density. He further connected these two types of communities—the nomadic, hunting and gathering versus the sedentary agricultural—with an alternate socialization emphasis: the hunting and gathering type of community emphasizing assertion, and the agricultural community demanding compliance. Ecological and subsistence patterns thus need to be considered along with socialization factors, which is also the message given by the Whiting school.

We need now to examine the model presented by Whiting and his colleagues, which is best exemplified in the outline given in the review of Harrington and Whiting (1972, p. 471):

*MAINTENANCE
SYSTEMS*

Subsistence patterns,
economy, residence
patterns, household
structure, social and
political systems and
groups

*CHILD-REARING
PRACTICES*

Time and severity of
training, methods, ini-
tiation rites, etc.

*ADULT
PERSONALITY*

Personality variables
and cognitive
processes

*CHILD
PERSONALITY*

Personality variables
and cognitive
processes

*ADULT BEHAVIOR
CULTURAL PRODUCTS*

Religion, contents of
rituals, values, arts,
etc.

*CHILD BEHAVIOR
CULTURAL
PRODUCTS*

Views of gods, games,
etc.

The model can be interpreted as showing sets of antecedent conditions, shown by maintenance systems and
child-rearing practices, that have consequents indicated
in the diagram by the adult and child behavior cultural
products. The roles of adult and child personality represent what can be thought of as intervening variables that
are anchored to the observable sets of conditions on the
antecedent and consequent sides. Although there is an
implicit, and indeed often explicit, recognition of causal
direction in this model, Harrington and Whiting (1972,
pp. 495–497) acknowledge that there are essential feedback loops. The model should not be interpreted as a simple linear process of chronological development but
more as a systems theory type of chart. Although difficult questions of directionality and of causation in general remain to be resolved, we shall focus now on the content, following the description given by Harrington and
Whiting.

Maintenance systems are defined as "economic, political, and social organization of a society surrounding
the nourishment, sheltering and protection of its members" (Whiting and Child, 1953, p. 310). The concern is
with such variables as household composition, division
of labor between the sexes, residence patterns, sleeping
arrangements in a household, and so forth. Harrington
and Whiting recognize that maintenance systems in turn
give rise to child-rearing practices, so the directionality in

the diagram should be seen as operating not only *across*
the chart but *down* it also, as far as these two units are
concerned (Harrington and Whiting, 1972, p. 472). The
explanation of child-rearing practices does not need to be
spelled out, except to indicate that they also include such
events as initiation rites, which actually play an important role in the model. Adult behavior is equally clear; a
major emphasis is on sex roles. Cultural products include
a variety of institutional systems, such as religion, art,
and games.

Maintenance systems have held much of the attention of psychological anthropologists and also of some
cross-cultural psychologists. The book by B. B. Whiting
and J. W. M. Whiting (1975), *Children of Six Cultures,*
illustrates the basic regimens for the study of maintenance systems. The full list of exemplars of this concept
includes subsistence patterns, means of production, division of labor, social structure, settlement patterns, and
systems of defense, law, and social control. Some of
these indicators go beyond the confines of ecological and
subsistence patterns as such into the domain of sociocultural parameters. The authors point out that these
maintenance systems determine to a large extent the
learning environment of the child (B. B. Whiting and J.
W. M. Whiting, 1975, p. 4):

> His play space and playmates, his teachers, the tasks
> that he is assigned, the workload of his mother, his
> opportunity to interact with his father are all
> compellingly influenced by them.

The six-culture study was comparative. The cultures
included were the following: Okinawa, Luzon island of
the Philippines, a village in northern India, agricultural
homesteads in western Kenya, Mexican families living in
the western highlands of the state of Oaxaca, and a New
England town of 5000 inhabitants. With the exception of
the New England locality, the families consisted of subsistence farmers. The wide geographical range portrayed
a variety of subsistence conditions, residential patterns,
and other indices of maintenance systems.

The dependent variables in the cross-cultural study
covered a number of social acts that spanned the behaviors of sociality, independence, nurturance, and aggression. Factor analysis reduced the various measures to two
independent dimensions. The first was characterized by a
contrast between nurturant and responsibility behaviors,
on the one hand, and dependence and dominance, on the
other. The second dimension contrasted sociable-intimate behavior with authoritative-aggressive behavior.

Apart from the factor of the complexity of the socioeconomic system, discussed below, the best predictor of children's behavior lay in the composition of the household. Briefly, the children of those families that were ideally nuclear were more sociable-intimate and less authoritarian than the children of those families that were not nuclear. "Not nuclear" included lineal families, defined as consisting of a grandmother and/or a grandfather together with one married son or daughter; extended families, defined as consisting of a grandmother and/or grandfather plus two married sons and/or daughters, or more married brothers or sisters and their children; and polygamous families.

The other predictor was the complexity of the socioeconomic system, which occasionally goes beyond the ecological and subsistence factors that we are discussing now. The maintenance systems include work specialization, settlement patterns, and the sexual division of labor, all of which bear directly on the life situation of the children of these six cultures. We will take first those children that score high on the nurturant-responsible behaviors and low on dependent-dominance behaviors. Such children came from cultures that have a relatively simple socioeconomic structure with little or no occupational specialization and no class or caste system. The settlement pattern consisted of dwellings with few or no public buildings. The authors point out that the women of these cultures have a heavy role in the work load; the corollary is that the children too are involved in the economic pursuit of the society and are involved in the maintenance of the family as caretakers for younger siblings. In contrast, those cultures in which the children scored high on egoism indices and low on nurturance were those marked by a complex sociocultural system and with occupational specialization and social stratification. In sharp opposition to the mothers in simple socioeconomic systems, the mothers of these cultures depended on their husbands for economic support and thus were free to look after the children. The children in turn were less involved in the work load and in the caretaking roles.

Further findings of the study are more complex and need to be sought in the original document. The point here is that the study has shown clearly enough that maintenance factors set the ground conditions in which social values and learning possibilities for children can be either reinforced or discouraged. Basic subsistence patterns set in motion a number of social variables that are intimately tied to these patterns.

A specific example of a maintenance system that illustrates the role of this factor in shaping early behavior

and molding relationships with others is sleeping arrangements. It has already been emphasized that household density is crucial. Hence sleeping arrangements within the household would hold similar significance. Beginning with early suggestions by Whiting, Kluckhohn, and Anthony (1958) and by Burton and Whiting (1961), a seminal study on this subject was carried out by Caudill and Plath (1966) among the Japanese. As the title of their article indicates, they asked specifically "Who sleeps by whom?" and from their findings made important generalizations to the Japanese culture as a whole. The examination of the sleeping arrangement variable indicated that it has a bearing on cultural relations in Japan. A Japanese individual can expect to co-sleep in a two-generation span for about half of his life—that is, first with a parent, then with a sibling. If we consider what happens when this same individual becomes a parent in turn, it seems that it is very rare for a Japanese individual to sleep alone. In contrast, in middle-class families in the United States, for example, the physical separation of parents and child is certainly the rule in childhood and, more often than not, even earlier in infancy. The implications of this custom for the future development of the child are various. Earlier studies had focused on the question of identification with the mother and on the wider question of sex roles, which could be influenced by the sleeping arrangements (see Harrington and Whiting, 1972, for full discussion of this aspect). Caudill and Plath (1966) took a slightly different tack and restricted their generalizations to the Japanese case. They pointed out that sleeping arrangements in Japanese families "tend to blur the distinction between generations and between the sexes, to emphasize the interdependence more than the separation of individuals, and to underplay (or largely ignore) the potentiality for the growth of conjugal intimacy between husband and wife and other matters in favor of a more general familial cohesion" (p. 146).

A related problem in the study of basic subsistence patterns is the role of mothers. It is clear that the relationship to children must differ according to whether the mother is free to interact closely with and supervise her children or, alternatively, whether the mother is so tied up with economic matters for the entire family that the role of caretaker and supervisor is largely taken over by siblings or other members of an extended family. One of the early analyses of cross-cultural socialization practices (Textor, 1967) had already noted that where women dominated subsistence activities, there was little indulgence given to the children, and further that the children showed manifest anxiety over matters concerning responsibility and obedience. An offshoot of the Whitings' six-culture study in which the spotlight was directly on the mothers (Minturn and Lambert, 1964) found that where women made a heavy economic input to the family, there was a concomitant emphasis on obedience and responsibility, thus supporting Textor's analysis.

Judith Brown (1973) has brought together all the available evidence on this point, both from the cross-cultural literature and from contemporary sociological material in the United States. The rise of the number of working mothers in the U.S. labor force pushes the implications of the study of working mothers beyond the confines of methodological anthropological inquiry into contemporary sociological problems. Brown found that employed mothers in our culture appear to rear children who do not fit into what she calls the "self-assertive, achieving mold." This finding, which is consonant with the cross-cultural material, has implications for relations between family and school and for the wider cultural relations in the United States; these relations do not concern us here but need further attention, as Brown suggests.

We turn now from discussion about input of maintenance systems to discussion of their effect on specific types of social variables. In doing so, we cite studies of single cultures as well as comparisons across cultures. We have already seen from cross-cultural information that in those cultures that have extended families living in a single household, there is more likely to be indulgence toward children. This behavior seems to be clearly related to the simple fact that there are more individuals around to care for the children. But it needed to be pinpointed more directly.

Ruth and Robert Munroe (1971) decided to check the finding more thoroughly among the Logoli people of western Kenya. They focused on attention given to infants over two time periods, between seven and thirteen months of age and between ten and sixteen months, with the same infants. The relatively small sample of a dozen infants studied (two of which were unattainable for the second time period) allowed for extremely close observational studies. In this study the independent variable was the quantity of members in the household, which ranged from two persons to ten. The dependent variables covered a variety of events and actions relating to the care of the infant. The investigators determined the location of the infant at all times during the selected observational periods; the proximity of persons to the infant; the number of persons (and their kinship relationship) who actually held the infant; and particularly the frequency of the infant's crying and the responses by others to his or her crying. The predictions of the investigators were that the greater the density of the household, the smaller would be the latency of response to crying of the infant and the smaller would be the latency of response in keeping the infant clean. In general, these predictions were upheld; in particular, the latency of response to the crying of the infant was very strongly related to household density. A surprising finding of the study was that in high-membership households the actual mother has less to do with the infant care than might have been expected. The caretaking role was assumed, among this tribe, by the older siblings of the family. Thus, in general, it is clear that higher indulgence toward the infant directly correlates with higher household density.

We will now turn to the matter of independence and compliance. Berry (1979) has pointed out that we would expect to find, in those communities that are characterized by high population density and sedentariness, a type of social responsiveness that could lead to acceptance of social influence: in a word, conformity. He further pointed out that this tendency would be reinforced by the type of family structure in that, for extended and like families, the number of individuals around would more likely than not generate social pressure.

Now the various socialization studies that have focused around this theme have found various indices of social actions, such as assertion, independence, achievement, obedience, and responsibility (see Barry, Bacon, and Child, 1957; Barry, Child, and Bacon, 1959; Minturn-Triandis and Lambert, 1961; Barry and Paxson, 1971). As Berry (1979) points out, what emerged from these early studies is a dimension of socialization that portrays a scale running from encouragement of early independence in the child to encouragement of acquiescence to social demands. If one relates this dimension to social, familial, and economic factors, there can be traced, first of all, the role of household density. This, in turn, is related to the economic functions of the family. But the sequence of events can be traced back further to the nature of the subsistence economy practiced by the culture. In the late fifties Barry, Bacon, and Child (1957) had marked food accumulation as the distinguishing variable. They argued that when either animal husbandry or subsistence agriculture is practiced, there goes along with either of these pursuits social values of strict adherence to routines and obedience to authorities; whereas in hunting and gathering societies, foraging and innovative attempts to get food are encouraged, thus reinforcing a general tendency toward independence and self-reliance.

Barry and his colleagues originally compared societies of high, medium, and low food accumulation with their respective socialization processes. When they did this on a wide cross-cultural basis, they found that there were some quite distinctive correlations. Traits such as obedience and responsibility corresponded with high-food accumulation societies (this applied to both boys and girls); traits like achievement and self-reliance correlated strongly with low–food accumulation societies.

Thus the cross-cultural evidence clearly indicates that there is an antithetical relationship between assertion or independence and conformity or compliance; moreover, this antithetical relationship covaries with the type of subsistence economy. This set of findings provided Berry (1979) with the rationale to repeat the classical Asch conformity experiments (Asch, 1956) in a cross-cultural context. With modifications of the original methodology because of the nature of the samples, Berry set out to see if judgment of lengths of lines would be influenced by group consensus. He took a number of societies that varied from nomadic and hunting groups to sedentary and agricultural communities. Berry expected to find that there would be more independent judgments, uninfluenced by group consensus, in the nomadic/hunting groups than in the stable agricultural groups, who would be anticipated to go along with the group judgment. Within traditional societies this prediction indeed was endorsed. For acculturated groups it was not. Berry (1979, p. 198) concluded:

Clearly there is a characteristic level of independence in these groups which is predictable from an examination of their cultural ecology. Consistent with the ethnographic reports, nomadic hunters tend to be independent in dealing with normative influence, while sedentary agriculturalists tend to accept such influence. Moreover, those samples which fall in the intermediate eco-cultural ranges tend to exhibit intermediate responsiveness to influence.

AGGRESSION

Further aspects of aggression will be dealt with here. There are definitional problems, which include distinctions between covert and overt aggression and distinctions of types of aggression—verbal, physical, symbolic—all of which would require an essay in its own right. Weeding out a common aggressive motive across all these distinctions is a formidable task. There are, in addition, differences from one culture to another in determining the indicators of aggression; what is commonly attributed as aggressive action in one culture is not in another, for example. Furthermore, particularly in anthropological studies, the study of aggression is embedded in the study of institutional factors of sanctions, legalities, and traditional ways of handling aggressive actions, which is not identical to the way in which psychologists might wish to study the subject. Consideration of all these points would take us too far afield; we are constrained to examining studies of aggression that fit into the topic of the present discussion.

A salient contribution here is that section of the six-culture study, previously discussed, that deals with aggression (Minturn and Lambert, 1964; Lambert, 1971). An overall finding from this study supported the idea that overcrowding is an important factor for the production of aggressive actions. In their report on the children of these six cultures, Whiting and Whiting (1975) had shown that children from extended families displayed more aggression than children from nuclear families. Lambert's more focused work (1971) on the aggression component dealt with two aspects: aggression among peers and aggression directed against the mother. For the entire population of all six cultures (a New England Baptist community, a northern Indian caste group, a Philippine barrio in northern Luzon; a village in Okinawa, a Mexican Indian village, and a rural tribal group in Kenya), the finding for peer aggression was that there were two opposing behaviors by which families handled children fighting with one another. The first cluster was composed of those families that immediately punished their children when they fought one another. This group tended to have more consistent rules against aggression and was more consistent in its demands for obedience. The second cluster actually tended to reward a child for fighting back when picked on; it had less consistent rules for aggression, and it did not follow through in its demand for obedience.

In the analysis of the specific cultures that fell into these two clusters, the researchers found that the Mexican Indian group was particularly low in aggression. The factor that seemed partially to explain this grouping was the nature of surrounding kin, that is, how many close relatives were living nearby and how interdependent the families of these close relatives were. With the Mexican families the neighboring peer children tended to be close relatives; thus peer aggression was frowned upon, since it threatened further hostility between close relatives. In the New England group there was a far wider choice of other children to play with (and thus also fight with). In this case there was therefore a far lesser chance of quarreling with kinfolk. Analysis of families *within* the individual cultures tended to support this generalization.

The other kind of aggression studied in the six-culture project was that directed against the mother specifically. Attention was given to retaliation used by the mother when her children were aggressive toward her. There were distinct differences across the cultures on this component; the Gusii tribe of Kenya was at the top of the scale of retaliation, and at the bottom were the mothers of the northern Indian caste group. The explanation again went along population grounds. Among the Gusii there were more other adults living in the same dwelling than in the case of the northern Indian mothers. The assumption is that there is a fear that aggression against the mother would generalize toward other adults unless forthrightly checked. There was another factor operating with the northern Indian mothers, namely, that the newly married Indian mother has a low family status. But basically the demographic factor was uppermost.

SOCIOCULTURAL INFLUENCES ON SOCIAL BEHAVIOR

Under this heading of sociocultural influences will be considered aspects of values, roles, and statuses, distinct behaviors laid down by institutional fiat. The material on all these factors covers a lot of territory: for present purposes we shall take as our starting point those mechanisms that are of direct interest to the psychologist. We can begin with cultural studies on competition.

Margaret Mead's *Cooperation and Competition among Primitive Peoples* (1961) had already initiated interest in this matter. Later, adopting an experimental format and taking possible cultural and subcultural differences among Anglo-Americans, Mexican Americans, and Mexicans proper as the focus of inquiry, Kagan and Madsen (1971) constructed a game in which players, working in pairs, could perform either cooperatively or competitively. The rules of the experimental game were set up such that it was actually maladaptive to display competition. Developmental differences were found first among the two age groups of four to five and seven to nine, the younger children displaying more cooperation. But what concerns us here is the cultural aspect. A clear-cut difference was shown in the three groups: Mexicans were the most cooperative, followed by the Mexican Americans, with the Anglo-Americans being the most competitive. The cultural significance of the findings were expressed by Kagan and Madsen (1971, p. 37):

> The environmental milieu in which U.S. children develop during the early school years, given the high value placed on individual achievement through competition may lead to a strong "I" orientation by age 7 which masks any potential for behaving on the basis of an autonomous morality of cooperation.

In a follow-up study Kagan and Madsen (1972) concluded that Mexican children were irrational (insofar as the experimental game was concerned) in avoiding conflict, just as Anglo-Americans were irrational in remaining in conflict.

As Segall (1979, p. 145) points out in the section of his textbook dealing with this work, these findings are confounded with rural/urban distinctions, since it turns out that the Mexican sample was from a small town while the U.S. samples were from a large urban metropolis. Indeed, subsequent work in this area suggested that confounding was indeed involved. For example, Madsen and his collaborators (Madsen and Shapira, 1977) compared children in four locations: Los Angeles, a suburb of Augsburg (a large town in west Germany), Tel Aviv, and a pair of settlements in northern Israel that were kibbutzim. Their findings indicated that it was the kibbutz children that showed the most cooperation. Again, Madsen and Yi (1975) directly compared urban and rural children in Korea. The fact that, again, it was the rural children that displayed more cooperation weighs heavily toward the argument (as the authors state) that competition is one of the inevitable concomitants of the worldwide trend toward urbanization.

In general, further investigations have supported this trend. In Canada the Indians were found to be more cooperative than their European counterparts (Miller and Thomas, 1972). In Australia the aborigines were less competitive than the European Australians (Sommerland and Bellingham, 1972). And in the South Pacific the Polynesian children of the Cook Islands and the rural Maori children displayed more cooperation than the urban children (Thomas, 1975).

While some evidence shows that it is the school that may be the carrier of values, we must go beyond the obvious fact that different societies place different premiums on competition toward a more exact focus on a specific factor or set of factors that can be thought to be the predisposing influence. This concern leads us to a discussion of achievement in general. The history of cross-cultural applications of the study of the achievement motive is now fairly long and complicated by considerations of methodology. Kornadt, Eckensberger, and Emminghaus (1980, pp. 273–297) have provided a careful examination of the subject. Cross-cultural research has raised the major question of whether different goal areas need to be differentiated from the generalized status of the achievement motive as first introduced by McClelland and his colleagues (McClelland *et al.,* 1953). Over a decade ago DeVos (1968) had already questioned the individuality aspect of the thesis, at least with respect to the Japanese. The Japanese, while undoubtedly displaying need achievement, did so with respect to the family as a whole and not to the single individual. In a similar fashion, Gallimore (1969) showed, with Hawaiians, that individual success was connected with need affiliation, the family again being the unit of endeavor. Such studies question the unitariness of the concept and imply that the emphasis on need achievement may be more appropriate to societies that are individually oriented.

At any rate the antecedents of the achievement motive, n-ach, need to be disentangled. These antecedents have been postulated on different levels. For instance, a generalized level of a philosophy of life and religious belief has been postulated. McClelland (1961) had stipulated that it was the religious spur of the Protestant ethic that sponsored economic development, a thesis that had earlier been noted by Max Weber (1930). The chain of causation was thought to be initiated in the precepts and stories told to children, which was further reinforced by society, and finally coalesced into a defined, patterned motive in adulthood. This motive would then be exhibited as entrepreneurship in the economic sphere.

McClelland supported this thesis by reference to historical evidence (McClelland, 1961), largely with respect to the generalized ethos of great cultures. An effort to focus more microscopically at this level was made by LeVine (1966) in his study of three tribal groups in Nigeria. Using recent or recurring dream reports from secondary schoolboys, instead of the customary TAT cards, LeVine analyzed the protocols for achievement imagery. He found that the Ibo had more achievement imagery than either the Yoruba or Hausa, the other two tribes studied. This result is in keeping with the reputation of the Ibo, who are renowned for their competitive spirit and entrepreneurial ability. LeVine interpreted the

sociocultural matrix of the three societies in terms of status mobility. The Hausa are a Moslem conservative group in which status and power are inherited and where there is little to no margin for individual ability. On the other hand, Ibo society is stratified along professional lines; power is decentralized. An Ibo has a greater opportunity for mobility, and an individual gains success through self-effort.

A prominent concern of the socialization and/or achievement literature is the roles of father and mother; this concern has received attention in the cross-cultural literature, and we will turn to this issue now.

The importance of the father for development of achievement motivation was noted in a study by Rosen and D'Andrade (1959), who emphasized the differential role of each of the parents for the development of achievement. In their study the mothers of high-achieving sons took the lead in stressing achievement by direct urging and emphasis on excellence. By contrast, the fathers took a backseat in a benevolent fashion. However, with low achievers a reverse pattern was seen: Authoritarian fathers were the rule, and mothers assumed a low profile. With this study as a model, workers in other cultures soon recognized that the variance in the role and importance of the father across the world could be used as a starting point for further analysis. They expected to find that in those cultures where the father has the traditional role of authority in the family, children would be relatively low achievers. These results were indeed found in Turkey (Bradburn, 1963) where male dominance is *de rigueur*. Turkish students scored lower on achievement tests against matched students from the United States. Furthermore, when Turkish students scored relatively high on achievement scores, those students had a significant separation from their father. In another study Rosen (1962) found that Brazilian authoritarian fathers had sons who showed low scores on the achievement index.

The absence of the father altogether shows up as a significant factor in a subcultural study done in the United States. In this study with northern urban blacks, Nuttall (1964) showed that those subjects whose fathers were present during childhood were high achievers; subjects with absent fathers showed only moderate achievement.

In commenting on these studies, Kornadt, Eckensberger, and Emminghaus (1980) made the following evaluation, with which we must concur: "It must remain unsettled whether the father has a positive model role which is lost when he is absent, or a negative role when he is excessively dominant and/or if this function depends on the age of the sons'' (p. 281).

The role of the mother in achievement motivation has also had attention in the cross-cultural literature (see Kornadt, Eckensberger, and Emminghaus, 1980), but only a few studies have set up the problem in direct experimental terms. One such study was carried out by Madsen and Kagan (1973), who compared mother-child pairs in Mexico and the United States. They used an experimental game involving the throwing of beanbags on squares. The mothers were given a set number of marbles with which they could reward their children after each throw of the beanbag. The mothers could give the marbles in whatever proportion they felt suitable. Thus the mother controlled the rewards for either the success or the failure of their children. Madsen and Kagan found that there was a large cultural difference in the responses of the mothers to failure. The percentage of marbles given after a performance of failure by the child was three times as much for the Mexican mother than for the U.S. mother. The two groups did not differ in their responses of rewards for success, but it was clear that the U.S. mothers chose more difficult achievement goals for their children. Moreover, they did not lower their goals following a failure, which the Mexican mothers did.

SUMMARY AND ASSESSMENT

This section has dealt with the development of a major theme in both psychological anthropology and cross-cultural psychology: the effect of ecological variables and related maintenance systems on a number of social psychological processes. Several ecological, economic, household and sociopolitical factors interrelate to form a pattern that has clear influence on specific social processes: obedience, aggression, nurturance, responsibility, and others. Working out the causal chains of this pattern has both logical and methodological problems, but the overall influence is clear, namely, that much of the behavior that is the target of social psychology can be traced back to nonpsychological conditions. Further, these nonpsychological conditions can be detailed quite specifically and not just generally related to economic and political factors.

Certain methodological problems do arise, however. Anthropologists tend to use units of description and analysis that themselves embody a number of variables that can be tackled individually. Psychologists tend to prefer to tackle these specific variables without worrying too much about their possible cohesiveness with one another, especially when experimentation is used. The problem of attributing causation to the units involved is again difficult, and it is probably better conceived in terms of systems analysis rather than a simple linear chain.

THE INDIVIDUAL AND CULTURE: MEDIATING CONCEPTS

A key problem in psychological anthropology has been to find appropriate concepts to bridge the gap between culture and the individual. This section discusses three attempts to find such concepts.

PERSONALITY

Before the term *psychological anthropology* was introduced to cover the entire psychological perspective in anthropology, the dominant term was *culture and personality*. The history of the culture and personality movement over at least four decades, with its waxing and waning interests, is too extensive to relate here (see Barnouw, 1973).

While the field has been amplified into a generalized psychological perspective covering psychological aspects other than personality, the focus and intent of utilizing the concept of personality still persists. The main function of the term, as it is used in anthropology, is to act as a mediating concept between sociocultural systems and behavior of the individual. The microcosmic world of the individual is seen as pertaining purely to the psychologist. But some unit is required that can be thought to relate to the more macrocosmic world of institutions of society yet still retain some psychological connotation. *Personality* fits this need succinctly. The role personality plays has been aptly summarized by Spiro (1972, p. 605):

> Rooted as it is in an instrumental approach to behavior, culture-and-personality necessarily looks at social systems from the perspective of ends to be achieved, functions to be served, and requirements to be satisfied. Given this perspective, its important theoretical goal is to discover the ways in which personality systems enable social and cultural systems to serve their social function.

Spiro recognizes that the personality construct, although a necessary ingredient for theory, needs to be combined with anthropological structural theory, on the one hand, and role theory, on the other hand, in order to serve its defined function of understanding human society and culture.

Now there have been varying positions regarding the relationship of culture to personality. It has been seen, for example, as a relationship in which culture is reduced to and determined by the makeup of the individual. The relationship has also been viewed as two independent systems that may be either consonant or dissonant.

Nevertheless, there has been a consistency in the kinds of questions asked. Writing at the beginning of the seventies, LeVine (1973a, pp. 10–13) reduces the field of culture and personality to three basic questions:

1. Are there psychological differences between human populations?

2. What are the causes in individual development of psychological differences between populations?

3. How are psychological differences between populations related to the sociocultural environment of those populations?

From these questions we see that LeVine views the field as more extensive than the relationship to sociocultural systems, which constitutes only one of his questions. Indeed, cross-cultural psychology is almost exclusively concerned with the first two questions, which are only partially concerned with personality. The third question has carried much of the load of personality and culture, and it is to this issue that we now turn in considering empirical work.

A comprehensive study during the past ten years, which will serve as a continuing representation of this tradition, is the study of the Tahitians by Levy (1973). Recognizing that the concept of personality is difficult to handle, Levy was concerned with those aspects of personality that were exclusively *Tahitian*. "What, if anything, do people bring to the repeated and ongoing situations...by virtue of the *commonalities* of their private experience *as Tahitians?*" (Levy, 1973, p. 489; emphasis in original).

One of the major needs for Tahitians is to find a balance between the urge for security and a desire for individual liberty. This balance calls for a successful integration of personal experience with the varying demands of the situation, and it is achieved by a number of adjust-ments. Levy sees these adjustments as dissociated in the Tahitian mind, which he prefers to interpret as alternate systems of mind rather than as repressed material. The dissociated traits involve residues of desires and reactions consequent on the dilemma between security and freedom. They consist of desires having to do with clinging to others and possession, to aspects of anger and depression resulting from separation from a mothering individual, to traces of fear of the destructive consequence of such anger, and again to fear that the desire for dependency would result in a loss of autonomy.

The most salient defense mechanism associated with this dissociated material concerns the Tahitian desire for personal freedom, so that one is not entangled either with one's own emotions or with other people. The defenses operate by means of distancing mechanisms. Undue tension in the individual is met by an urge to sleep. As one informant told Levy, "You wanted to quickly fall asleep, so that you would forget that thing. To fall asleep, and that's all, and the next morning you wouldn't remember it anymore" (Levy, 1973, p. 495). Another distancing mechanism was simply adherence to conventionality of discourse and behavior. This mechanism cut off more personalized expressions and served as a shield for individual exposure. Tahitians would refer to not caring, a posture almost amounting to a kind of stoicism, representing the need not to become emotionally involved.

In many respects Tahitian life shows a strong conformist tendency, with an associated tendency not to assert oneself individually. Levy notes mechanisms of depersonalization, a deflating of the ego that restricts the feeling of being upset by interpersonal tensions.

All such traits resonate with the Tahitians' way of life, with the interpersonal style that seems on the surface to be carefree and free of tension. A much-used term in Tahiti is *ha'ama,* which is translated as "embarrassment" or "shame." It is used in a variety of situations, some of which would be considered moral by our standards, as in feeling shamed when being observed in drunken comportment. But the term is also used in first encountering a stranger. *Ha'ama* relates to a sense of social appropriateness, to propriety in the public setting. It also portrays the pressures of conformity, as exemplified in the account that Levy (1973, p. 335) gives of a young girl who wanted to give a floral wreath to a departing schoolteacher, but she was inhibited by the fact that the other children were not doing likewise. Thus the act would draw attention to herself, and she would therefore feel *ha'ama*. The various distancing mechanisms that have been discussed are consonant with such an interpersonal norm.

Levy's methods in this research, in accord with similar investigations, rely on a combination of participant observation, field interviews, and inference based on psychoanalytic theory. The question of inference and assessment is crucial, as has been well recognized by LeVine (1973a, pp. 203-214), who gives a set of recommendations for subsequent research of this kind. One recommendation is a plea for longitudinal observation of the individual, particularly one focused on a process of directed change.

Although longitudinal research on individuals—similar to Elder's (1974) major sociological studies of people who grew up in the Depression and after—in anthropological field work is difficult and thus rare (due chiefly to pragmatic reasons), some work on culture change does relate to LeVine's proposal. It is reasonable to suggest that personality traits are predisposing agents in shaping how people adapt to social and cultural change. For example, LeVine (1973b) has argued that in many African traditional societies, relationships between family members are distanced by age and sex considerations. This mechanism presumably sets up personality traits that are adaptive to separations, as when adult men go to work or young men go to school. The separation anxiety seen in more emotionally enmeshed families is not witnessed. LeVine points out that African society puts more emphasis on material obligations and less on personal values and life-style. So taking note of personality characteristics would be important for the prediction of successful or unsuccessful culture change. It should be noted that contrary observations of African parents have been made (Super and Harkness, 1974).

A noteworthy series of studies linking cultural change with personality has been the work of George and Louise Spindler (see L. Spindler, 1978, pp. 176-200). Taking off from ideas developed by Hallowell (1952), who studied the acculturative process among Ojibwa Indians, the Spindlers analyzed culture change among the Menomini Indians of Wisconsin. Although we will discuss the work of the Spindlers under the rubric of personality, it is clear from their own analysis that they were interested in the representative manner in which their subjects perceived and responded to the world about them. Rorschach responses, for example, were analyzed not in the traditional manner of the clinical psychologist but in a new way—for expressions of perceptual structure.

The Spindlers were interested in that branch of cognition that merges with personality factors, like the early work of Witkin and associates (1954). As we shall see later, there has been a shift among anthropologists from the classic personality and culture studies that involved traits to this cognitive orientation type of world view. The work of the Spindlers foreshadows this shift, as indeed did the work of Irving Hallowell (1955) before them.

All the same the Spindlers did pay attention to more traditional treatments of personality. A new projection test was constructed to fit their specific research purposes. This test was a picture technique along the lines devised by Goldschmidt and Edgerton (1961), who used it in Africa. In the Spindlers' study the test consisted of twenty-four line drawings representing Indians engaged in activities that were germane to their life style; the drawings were given as pairs of choices of work style. A person working in a vineyard was presented along with a person working in an office. Reasons were then elicited for the given choice. Another psychological method was also invented, the Expressive Autobiographical Technique, which was a structured autobiographical method of eliciting perceived important life events of the informants.

On the basis of social and economic factors, four Indian categories were abstracted that represented "a posited continuum of cultural adaptation, running from a native-oriented, then through peyote and ungrouped 'transitional', to two acculturated groups" (Spindler and Spindler, 1976, p. 86). A white group was also chosen for control purposes. Of these groups the native-oriented one, as the name suggests, followed the traditional ways of the past, which included the traditional religious rituals. The peyote group represented an assimilation of Christian and Indian elements, as is characteristic of the Native American Church. When we come to the transitional groups, the social distance between whites and Indians is narrowed, and it is even fused when the acculturated Indians are inspected, whether they be from the elite or from the lower-status populations.

The significant part of the Spindlers' work is that their sociocultural indices and their psychological tests were independently derived. The five sets of people are as different in their psychological characteristics as they are in their sociocultural aspects. Of special note is the peyote group, which is extensively studied in the book *Dreamers Without Power* (Spindler and Spindler, 1971). As Spindler says (1978, p. 180):

It is the only Menomini category in which human movement responses exceed the animal movement responses, where introspective responses are numerous and where overt, relatively uncontrolled emotions are displayed in Rorschach responses. The Rorschach responses, the peyote ritual, and peyote belief systems are highly integrated—mutually expressive of each other.

The older culture and personality research seldom came to grips with the problem of intragroup variability [although Wallace (1952) clearly was concerned with it quite early]. Many personality tests applied cross-culturally have proved to have high specificity. So some psychological anthropologists consider the traditional approach of personality and attitude to be passé. Shweder (1980), for example, has presented basic arguments that militate against the further development of the movement. The most important argument is that linkages between personality variables and social institutional variables have proved to be more questionable than was hitherto considered. More specifically, Shweder goes over certain postulates that he claims to be at the heart of the personality and culture school and that he now questions. We shall discuss three of these.

The first postulate is the thesis that adult personality characteristics are causally attributed to child care practices—the "past in the present," as he pithily calls it. Logically, this postulate entails longitudinal research, which, as we have noted, is rare in anthropological work (for an exception, see Day, Boyer, and DeVos, 1975), but there are approximations in the cross-cultural literature that can be mentioned. Shweder himself mentions the work of Caudill and Schooler (1973) comparing Japanese caretakers and their children with American caretakers and their children. Caudill and Schooler tried to predict the children's behavior first at the age of six and then, when this experiment had failed, at the age of two and a half from the observational protocols of the caretakers' behavior when the children were infants. They failed to do so both for the age of six and for the earlier age of two and a half. Of course, this fact has long been acknowledged in the psychological literature [see Orlansky (1949) for one of the earlier formulations]. Shweder appreciates this fact but supports it from the ethnographical literature, referring to the findings from Guatemala (Kagan and Klein, 1973; Kagan, 1976) that showed that the early impairments of children there were

partially rectified in preadolescence. Kagan's work is really concerned with the question of cognitive competency, and he is at pains to point out (Kagan, 1976, p. 154) that the evidence does not imply a complete capacity for cognitive resilience. But the material does serve to undermine the deterministic past-in-the-present thesis.

Shweder's second postulate concerns the question of global personality traits and the question of intragroup variability referred to earlier. Evidence both from psychology and from psychological anthropology indicates the difficulty of generalizing across populations with a small number of personality constructs.

The third postulate, which is about the search for comparable situations, makes the point that a good deal of the behavior of individuals need not be attributed to any idea of personality at all. This postulate is in agreement with the tendency in mainstream psychology to focus on situations as such and with the pioneer work of Barker (1968) and his associates of the ecological psychology school.

A complete representation of personality and culture is now more complicated than it would have been twenty years ago or even ten years ago. Many of the processes that we have discussed in the previous section under their own name would have been formerly relegated to the rubric of personality. A kind of functional autonomy has developed to the extent that the supraordinate label has lost its unitariness. Then in the anthropological sphere many of the relevant concepts of personality that were given a decided psychological twist are now regarded sociologically. For example, in a volume that relates culture to personality, DeVos (1976, p. 349) indicates that five concepts help to summarize a number of issues raised in the field of social change. These concepts are differential socialization, selection permeability, reference group, differential role expectations, and social self-identity. Of all these only the second, selection permeability, appears to be dynamically oriented. The idea refers to the notion of ego boundaries, which allow certain experiences to penetrate and block off others. DeVos himself provides the idea of "affective dissonance," along the lines of Festinger's cognitive dissonance, to indicate a key aspect of personality that has rich cultural implications.

Basically, the sheer breakdown of the more elemental and comprehensive concept of personality is what has undermined the traditional culture and personality approach. Draguns (1979, p. 200) has put it extremely well:

The burden seems to have shifted from illustrative monocultural, qualitative studies to bilateral, multilateral, and hologeistic comparisons. While the unity of the movement for culture-personality studies has disappeared, the relationship of these topics has remained an active and productive area of investigation.

COGNITION

Shweder (1980) ends his disquisition on the morbidity of culture and personality with an appeal to the study of cognition as the new look. Anthropological approaches to cognition are complex and often appear unrelated to the set of problems that cognitive psychologists study. The anthropological approaches have been more fully discussed elsewhere (Price-Williams, 1980). Anthropologists pay attention to at least three aspects of cognition. The first and probably most important deals with forms of classification that various cultural groups use. In what follows the reader must appreciate that anthropology relies more heavily on language systems than does psychology. Indeed, it is purely through verbal interaction that the analyses of classificatory forms are discerned. Also, although some scholars recognize the problem of intragroup variability (Sanjek, 1971; Heider, 1972; Pollnac, 1975), the general tendency is to assume a commonality across the populations in the domain investigated. Hence the study of cognition has come to adopt the monocultural assumption that was assumed for the earlier personality construct.

We also note that explorations into cognition have had long and persistent attention from anthropologists and, to a very large extent, have been quite independent of what psychologists may have had to say. The French sociological school investigated classification and its relation to society in the first few years of this century (Durkheim and Mauss, 1963). In the same tradition the important dichotomy of left and right was explicated by Hertz (1909) not long afterward. Gregory Bateson (1936), through his study of New Guinea rituals, maintained that the notion of logic must be interpreted as being different from culture to culture and proposed the concept of *eidos* to cover this idea. Later, Wallace (1956) proposed the notion of "mazeway" to refer to the ideational associations behind material aspects of a culture.

It was not until the fifties and then more markedly the sixties, though, that a full-blown cognitive anthropology emerged with ready linguistic techniques of componential analysis, tree analysis, and the like, pertaining to identifiable domains of reference. Full accounts of the interpretations given to this approach, its history, and its differing domains can be found in the volume edited by Tyler (1969). It is pointed out there that the field of cognitive anthropology is concerned with how the material aspects and units of society are organized in the human mind. In this sense the focus is less on cognitive process or mechanism and more on the product. Psychologists might be interested in what strategies people use to form concepts, in concept formation and attainment for its own sake. Anthropologists are concerned with the usages of the concepts, who uses them, when they are or are not applied, and what sociological ramifications the concepts may have. In ethnographical work the primary emphasis has been on given domains of interest or activity that are of direct importance and relevance to the culture. How the culture then forms taxonomies and related questions are the proper study of cognitive anthropology. Domains have been varied; they embrace illness, types of firewood, planting practices, kinship, properties of travel across icy terrain, psychological types of people, and many others. It might be revealing to start off by citing an example from a subculture within the United States in order to convey the nature of the type of research.

Cognitive anthropologists draw their material from the communicative world of their informants. In a study of the classification of plants, for example, the taxonomy drawn up is not necessarily linnean but is reflective of the divisions and distinctions of the specific culture studied. The terminology that is given is the terminology that people use. How informants carve up the world around them is the point of the exercise. The belief is that through examination of the segment of culture that is solicited, one is seeing it through the eyes of the members of that culture. The belief is also that examining the rules and discerning the components of how people talk about things and how they use them reveals to some extent the cognitive reality of that culture.

This belief is reflected in a study of the verbal usage of tramps or hobos in our own culture (Spradley, 1970). As Spradley and McCurdy (1972, p. 63) have pointed out in their discussion of this study, hobos are quite aware of the labels that others attribute to them, such as tramps or vagrants, but adopt for themselves an entirely different terminology that presumably reflects their own self-image and their own perceived environment. These urban nomads, as Spradley calls them, identify themselves in terms of one of the cardinal features of their lifestyle, that is, how they travel. Since they are always on the move, it is not surprising that this movement is reflected in their own identifications. A *box car tramp,* for example, is one who travels in that manner; more exotically, a *ding* is a professional beggar who has no home at all. *Airedale* and *bindle stiff* are terms to refer to tramps who go about with pack and bedroll.

Homelessness is the key concept that ties all this terminology together. Mode of travel is therefore very important, but so is the necessity for bedding down for the night. Here the term *flop* is the generic label. It is verbalized into *making a flop* or *flopping out.* Kinds of flops are crucial terms, and they reflect the particular concerns that hobos have about sleeping; these concerns include not only the question of comfort and satisfaction but also anxieties about money, legalities, and the climate. In the taxonomy of flops are distinctions of paid flops, like dormitories, versus free flops, like an empty apartment or an abandoned house, which would entail legal consequences if hobos were detected inside. Or the concern is with inside versus outside, which includes places like orchards, fields, and even cemeteries. More generally, all the outside places are referred to as *weed patches.*

While one is more or less in the domain of the familiar with the case of tramps, one is quite lost with those exotic cultures that entertain belief systems quite outside one's conventional experience. In these cases the analysis of the way in which the world is broken up acts as a facilitator of entering into that world and appreciating its structures. Basso (1969) studied the discourse of the Apache tribe related to witchcraft. From the way Apaches divide the universe, we can see that religous matters are paramount. The universe is divided tripartitely: into moving things, immobile things, and holy things. What we would simply call witches, they identify as people having certain types of power, of which many are enumerated. Having elicited, learned, and appreciated these verbal distinctions, the inquiring ethnographer is at least in a more commanding position to understand the finer distinctions of Apache society and appreciate the prevailing segments of social behavior.

Although there is an implicit Sapir-Whorf hypothesis embedded in this approach, and although many anthropologists see no more in this approach than language analysis (e.g., Burling, 1964; Harris, 1968; Keesing, 1972), nevertheless the term *cognition* has stuck. Also,

many other anthropologists see in this approach a means of touching a psychological reality (e.g., Wallace, 1965).

While much effort has been spent on classificatory behavior, attention has also been paid to what justifiably can be called cognitive style. In a study with Zinacanteco shamans, Shweder (1979) devised a psychological experiment to portray the cognitive orientation of these religious specialists. He tested the idea that shamans would be more likely than nonreligious specialists to impose form on unstructured stimuli, which proved to be the case. In another area of Mexico Foster (1973) examined the dream motifs of Tzintzuntzan Indians for depiction of worldview. What Foster refers to as cognitive orientation in his paper reflects fears, anxieties, and adjustment problems that are reflected in the dream motifs.

Sometimes, reliance is placed on a formal psychological test in order to draw out cognitive distinctions. Rhoda Metraux (1976) made a study of the Iatmul people (the same group that Gregory Bateson studied) of Papua, New Guinea. She was interested in the continuities and discontinuities of cultural change. She used the Lowenfeld Mosaic Test, a nonverbal performance test that consists of over two hundred fifty plastic tiles constituted into five geometric shapes, each shape being of six colors. People are asked to arrange these tiles on a tray covered by white paper, with open-ended choices of what they would like to make. Metraux found that there was age grading in the type of design made that reflected the slowly changing mode of life. Moreover, inspection of the way in which her subjects went about making these patterns revealed that they followed the principles of symmetry and complementarity, dualistic handling that is reflected elsewhere in the culture, such as in interpersonal relations and in ceremonial themes. Metraux saw in their process of making designs the very necessities of ensuring continuity across the generations.

This study brings us to the third aspect of cognition, namely, the cognitive sets involved in belief systems. This aspect has always been a concern for anthropologists, since the kind of belief systems involved in such exotic areas as magic, sorcery, and witchcraft have seemed to presuppose some form of cognitive bias different from those in the West. It was reflection of this sort that prompted the notion of the "primitive mind" (Levy-Bruhl, 1923). Although this interpretation has been dropped (and it should be noted that Levy-Bruhl was not a field anthropologist but, rather, an armchair sociological philosopher; it was field workers like Malinowski who largely dispelled this notion), it still has to be said that puzzling anomalies remain in these very fields of magic and religion, myth and ritual, that stimulate inquiries into cognition.

The cognition here is of the nondiscursive kind, where emotion is heavily interlinked and where social parameters are closely involved. It is probably quite distant from what a contemporary cognitive psychologist would interpret as cognition, although an earlier developmental psychologist (Werner, 1957) has laid down parameters, such as global versus distinct and differentiated versus diffuse, in order precisely to establish a framework for understanding this material.

Anthropologists also have searched for categories of explanation. In a book on the subject, characteristically called *Modes of Thought* (Horton and Finnegan, 1973), the editors have indicated that polaristic explanations are mostly invoked, so that rationality is opposed to nonrationality, scientific thought is opposed to nonscientific or mistaken thought, secularism is opposed to magic, openness of thought is opposed to closure. This last distinction is reminiscent of Rokeach's earlier thesis on the nature of belief systems (1960). Despite the conceptual and obvious methodological problems involved, the implicit promise of a quasi-cognitive approach to the fields of magic, religion, and belief systems in general is still likely to attract anthropological students.

Having discussed anthropological approaches to cognition, we need to say something about the contribution of cross-cultural psychologists to the subject. The input has been considerable over the past ten to fifteen years, which is yet another example of a subject too copious to be able to analyze in a single section. The subject has been well attended to in books and review articles (Berry and Dasen, 1974; Cole and Scribner, 1974; Price-Williams, 1976; Pick, 1980). What is appropriate here is to indicate those areas that have focused on social psychological variables and are somewhat congruent with the other material in this section.

As would be anticipated from psychologists, the emphasis has been on the cognitive *process,* and the dominant method has been experimentation. What is qualitatively different from laboratory studies of cognition is the attention to context and to sociological factors that require close examination.

Two substantive areas can be immediately identified in this way. The first is the ecological approach, and the second is the emphasis on socialization. By chance, a single concept has been associated with each. This concept is the notion of psychological differentiation, with the orig-

inal laboratory studies having been performed by Witkin and his associates (1954, 1962).

In the hands of Berry (1976), psychological differentiation has been related to ecological factors that are identical with those featured in the study by Barry, Child, and Bacon (1959) discussed earlier. Berry focused on societies characterized by high– and low–food accumulation practices. High–food accumulation societies are sedentary, mainly agricultural and/or animal husbandry economies, with relatively high densities of population. In contrast, those societies that display low–food accumulation practices are nomadic or seminomadic, being hunting and gathering or fishing groups, and have a relatively low population density. Barry's thesis is that people coming from low–food accumulation societies would show high perceptual differentiation, while those from high–food accumulation societies would reveal low perceptual differentiation.

Now Witkin's concept of field dependence/independence and his more generalized concept of psychological differentiation, which subsequently subsumed the earlier field-dependence idea, has at least four independent measures that correlate significantly. These measures include, first, the Rod-and-Frame Test, where the task is to orient to the vertical a rod that varies independently of a background frame in the absence of external cues. The Embedded-Figure Test is a second measure, where the task is to detect an identifiable pattern within a complex one. A third test is one of spatial ability, measured either with the subtest in the Wechsler Intelligence Test or with Kohs's Blocks. A measurement of the way in which subjects articulate body parts in drawing a person represents the fourth measure. Rarely are all these measures employed simultaneously.

In cross-cultural work much of the burden of demonstrating psychological differentiation has fallen on the Embedded-Figure Test and/or on Kohs's Blocks. The study of three Amerindian tribes, testing the food accumulation theory, illustrates the general tendency (Berry and Annis, 1974). Three tribes, the Cree, the Carrier, and the Tsimshian, represented low–, medium–, and high–food accumulation practices, respectively, when correlated on the differentiation index. Using the analysis of spatial abilities in Kohs's Blocks, Berry and Annis demonstrated that perceptual differentiation varies with this food accumulation factor in the predicted direction.

Berry has also demonstrated this factor in other parts of the world by using other measures in addition (Berry, 1976). It is clear from his work and from others' that socialization factors and concepts of direct relevance to social psychology are bound up with the different ecologies (see Witkin and Berry, 1975, for a comprehensive review). One of the findings of the Berry and Annis study is that when they compared subgroups that displayed the old traditional values versus the modern acculturated tendencies, the index of perceptual differentiation differed accordingly.

The search for some precise index of societal regulation sponsored the study of three separate countries, Holland, Italy, and Mexico. Two villages were contrasted in each of these countries (Witkin *et al.,* 1974). The villages differed on a set of factors that was labeled "social conformity." By this term was meant a conformity to authority across a variety of social domains, such as the family and religious and political spheres. The hypothesis of the study was that children from the villages with lesser social conformity would show more development in differentiation than children in the other villages where more social conformity was displayed. Two age groups, nine to eleven and thirteen to fifteen, were chosen, both sexes being represented. Five measures of differentiation were used, the four described above plus a vocabulary index.

While the findings were, indeed, as anticipated —namely, that social settings emphasizing conformity minimized the development of psychological differentiation—the authors drew attention to the difficulty of applying this approach to whole societies or nations. The study did not attempt to compare Dutch with Italians with Mexicans (Witkin *et al.,* 1974, pp. 25–26):

> This we did not do, nor did we consider it appropriate to do, out of a feeling that when dealing with large, complex societies, of the kind represented by the nations we studied, an effort to identify "national character types" is not a very profitable or even sensible enterprise.

This study of cognition departs somewhat from the mediating function of cognition that anthropologists require. However, that social conformity, as here defined, has a cognitive aspect is a relevant finding for psychological anthropology.

If the study of cognition is to maintain the position demanded of it in psychological anthropology, at least two criteria have to be met. First, sufficient ethnographical context has to be shown in order to suitably place the cognitive material in its relevant setting. Second, cognition has to be given an analysis of process if psychological concerns are to be met.

Both of these criteria are adequately confronted in the work by Cole and his associates (1971; Laboratory of Comparative Human Cognition, 1978) and by Scribner (1975, 1976; Scribner and Cole, 1978). All have pursued experimentally and observationally the problems of learning, memory, and thinking in a cultural context. They have also examined the larger consequences of schooling and literacy. Cole (1975) particularly has pushed the necessity of placing the study of cognition in a proper ethnographic context, which necessitates methodological innovations to standard psychology inquiry. This approach has spawned original studies such as Lave's (1977), which investigated the everyday working skills of tribal tailors in Liberia. This study was pursued further by constructing an arithmetic test based on the tailors' experience in this domain, and this test, in turn, was compared with another arithmetic test drawn from a different domain. The spirit of this type of inquiry does not have to be relegated to the so-called cross-cultural; Levine, Zetlin, and Langness (1980) have utilized this approach to the trainable mentally retarded in our own culture. Analysis of the contextual arrangements is the important point.

We turn now to the third attempt at finding mediating concepts.

PSYCHOANALYSIS

With psychoanalysis we are not dealing with a single mediating concept, as with personality or with cognition, but with a *set* of constructs aimed at mediating between the disposition of individuals and involvement in diverse cultural institutions. If we trace the process of psychoanalysis throughout its connection with anthropology, two dominant themes emerge. The first is that psychoanalytical anthropology has paid attention predominantly to projective matters, which in anthropology means the areas of myth and ritual, religion and magic, dreams and certain aesthetic areas. Paralleling this theme is the focus on psychopathology. In both areas the emphasis on the interpretation of symbols is crucial.

We remark in passing that yet another new anthropological field has emerged around this subject, namely, symbolic anthropology (Firth, 1973; Dolgin, Kemnitzer, and Schneider, 1977). Although there are some exceptions (notably Lewis, 1977), the prevailing treatment of symbols in this field follows the sociological format. One should also note that the various interpretive frameworks for the study of symbols present difficulties for anthropology. Sperber (1975) has written a fine analysis of these difficulties.

Nevertheless, as far as psychoanalytical anthropology is concerned, the reliance of psychological interpretations on symbolism is heavy, and although the exclusivity on projective matters is changing, this area still provides a classical point of entry for the discipline. Implicit in the psychoanalytical discourse is a quasi-evolutionary thesis that postulates a progression of thought toward secondary-process thinking and away from dependence on primary-process thinking. Thus the thinking involved in the projective area is seen as either less advanced on some evolutionary scale of thought or downright regressive. The terms *implicit* and *quasi* have been used since the evolutionary postulate is vague and is not used in the precise sense that it is used in sociobiology. Nevertheless, the thesis needs to be kept in mind when one is evaluating psychoanalytic anthropology.

Now some observers of the anthropological scene have felt that there is no longer any great influence on the discipline from psychologists. It is probably true that psychoanalytic concepts have been so well assimilated into psychological anthropology that the imprimatur of their theoretical origin no longer bears a heavy stamp. And it may also be true that psychoanalysis no longer enjoys a monopoly, as it may have in the early personality and culture approaches. But it certainly is incorrect to state that psychoanalysis no longer has any influence. The continuing monograph series, *The Psychoanalytic Study of Society,* bears witness to sustained interest, as does a new journal that was introduced in 1978, *The Journal of Psychological Anthropology,* which has a dominant psychoanalytic emphasis and is in the process of changing its title to reflect this emphasis. LeVine (1973a pp. 205–206) has enumerated nearly twenty scholars who are either psychoanalysts or anthropologists with psychoanalytic experience who all have done field work with the precise intent of conducting psychoanalytic investigations.

Of course, there are far more scholars who do not quite fit into this tight category and yet may be interpreted as fitting into the psychoanalytic mold. Quite apart from research in the field, there are continuing debates regarding the relationship of ethnography to psychoanal-

ysis, and certain themes, which either have been given revision or new attention in psychoanalysis, are thought of as suitable candidates for cross-cultural checking. Thus the new emphasis on ego psychology begun by Anna Freud (1936) and continued by Spitz (1965) and the analysis of self, stressed by Mahler, Pine, and Bergman (1975) have aroused lively discussion by both anthropologists and clinicians (see *Journal of Psychological Anthropology,* 1978, pp. 407–416). Holter (1978) has listed ten areas of application of psychoanalytic ideas to anthropology. Some of these areas have already been given much attention, like unconscious meaning in myths and dreams. Others, like the propositions implicit in the psychoanalytic theory of normal child development, have only had limited application. Others mentioned by Holter, such as comparative psychopathology and comparisons of mode of healing, have fallen under other rubrics than the psychoanalytic and have received copious attention.

The elements of folklore, myth, and ritual have continued to be fruitful ground for psychoanalytic interpretation. The Brazilian anthropologist Carvalho-Neto (1972) has provided an introductory book on the subject that covers much of the early studies. Dundes (e.g., 1962) pursues the psychoanalytic tradition in the field of folklore, and LaBarre (1975, pp. 17–20) maintains a similar viewpoint in the field of anthropology.

A recent representative example of a psychoanalytic interpretation of a folktale is that provided by Boyer (1975). The tale came from the Apaches of the Mescalero Indian reservation. There are various versions of the tale, and it extends outside the Apaches. The essence of the tale, which is called "The Man who turned into a Water Monster," is as follows: Two brothers went out hunting. Tired of eating the customary berries and rodents, they found some large eggs. Although warned by his brother, the other brother ate the eggs and turned into a big black snake. The brother that had turned into a snake then told the first that he should return to his kin, warn the others of what happened, and inform his kinfolk that he, now the snake, could confer luck and power on all of them. When informed, the kinfolk suspected that the returning man had killed his brother, but nevertheless they went out in search of the snake. Having found the snake, they exonerated the brother. Variants of the tale had the kinfolk either finding the snake and receiving the predicted luck and power or not finding it, in which case they forgot all about the matter.

In explaining this tale, Boyer (1975) makes some pertinent introductory remarks about the role of psychoanalysis in matters of folktales (p. 127):

> As special forms of culturally condoned fantasies, oral literature helps to bring the individual into relationship with group members on the basis of common psychological needs. Oral literature helps to lessen guilt and anxiety engendered by unsecurely repressed impulses and institutes a form of adaptation to reality.

Certain aspects of Apache childhood are then referred to. The Apache child has many experiences of frustration. Longing for contact and fearing abandonment, he or she later has to compete with siblings for parental love, so rivalry develops. Boyer remarks that common to all the versions of the folktale are the symbolic expression and the resolution of anxieties pertaining to oral aggressive impulses and to fear of parental abandonment (Boyer, 1975, p. 130). The ingestion of forbidden food—the eggs in the story—is interpreted as the repressed wish to devour a part of the mother, to take her in and make her a part of one's self.

Apache socialization practices have been given attention elsewhere by Boyer (Boyer and Boyer, 1972). The conclusion of observations about the life cycle is that the young Apache is burdened with shame, guilt, and anxiety. Whereas in earlier times the aggressive drive was in harmony with the Apache life-style, being channeled into the discharge of a hunting and raiding society, ensuing reservation life has provided little or no expression for such a disposition. The observed rates of crime and drunkenness and overall anomie of the society are seen as consequences of socialization practices no longer having a functional context. Instead, there is conflict among the tribal members and an individualized feeling of malaise and failure.

One advantage of close attention to psychoanalytic dynamics in anthropology is the adoption of a methodology that views the individual over a long period of time, particularly in the context of early development and later socialization practices. Briggs (1975) focused on the way that certain Canadian Eskimo groups in the central Arctic handle their aggressive impulses. The ensuing analysis necessitates attention given to the interpersonal dynamics of the child through the important phases of the life cycle. Briggs gives an example that illustrates the Eskimo mechanism of dealing with unwanted impulses. One male Utku (Briggs, 1975, p. 144) responded to a specific situation in which his tent was burnt down, all his possessions destroyed, and his baby nearly killed, by laughing. The prevailing Eskimo principle of dealing with strong emotion is by the exercise of *ihuma,* a term that represents all the central psychological functions of mind, thought, memory, and will. As Briggs notes, laughter is the response to calamity—dictated by *ihuma.* It elicits social support in a crisis, it is not directed against others, and it does not exclude them.

Psychoanalytic attention has been given to the psychology of non-Western psychiatric syndromes, like the ghost sickness of the Kiowa-Apache (Freeman, Foulks, and Freeman, 1976) and to the Eskimo arctic hysteria (Foulks, Freeman, and Freeman, 1979). The latter authors make an important point. They indicate that earlier psychoanalytic forays into anthropology focused on somewhat arbitrary interpretations of symbolism to the point of virtual exclusiveness of the cultural context. Now, as they state (p. 42):

> Psychoanalytic fieldwork has appropriately moved from the analysis of projective systems to a more holistic method. The method involves investigating the psychology of actual individuals within the context of their cultural institutions, including projective systems.

Arctic hysteria, known indigenously as *pibloktoq,* has already been given close attention in the anthropological and psychoanalytic literature (e.g., Gussow, 1960; Wallace, 1970; Foulks, 1972; Kennedy, 1974). Thought to be related to the hysterias, it is characterized by the following behavior: frantic tearing off of clothing, wandering across the tundra, thrashing about, and glossolalia. Whereas Wallace (1970) suggested that there might be a nutritional factor involved, arctic hysteria is generally considered to be a consequence of psychogenic factors, notably a reaction to stress and the effect of strict cultural sanctions against overt aggression.

Concentrating on male arctic hysteria, Foulks and his colleagues noted that the attacks happened most frequently to individuals who were most dependent on others, particularly on their wives, or to individuals who were least individuated and who had extreme separation anxiety. "An attack is precipitated by physical separation from or by the death of the mother or the mother-substitute and/or by the loss of the special role she played in relation to the idealized image of the mother" (Foulks, Freeman, and Freeman, 1979, pp. 50–51). Childhood experience among the Eskimo consists primarily of very close contact between mother and child. The child is closeted in the mother's parka always near to hand; the infant is fed on demand and catered for whenever he or she cries. A process of affectionate teasing then sets in, which consists of holding the infant off at an awkward angle, pinching its cheeks quite hard, and rubbing its forehead. At the same time the infant is discouraged in venting his or her feelings. Control of expression is built in early and reinforced.

In later life the ambivalence is expressed by holding onto the ideal relationship with the mother, which breaks down completely when one is faced with total separation. The phenomenon of *pibloktoq* then shows up and is characterized by flight, symbolizing the escape from danger and seeking illusorily the protection of the mother out in the tundra. The behavior invites attention from others for restraint and for rescue. Tearing off the clothes is viewed as a regressive action, returning to the nakedness of childhood. The behavior of rolling in the snow and jumping into icy waters is further interpreted as a method of restoring the awareness of bodily boundaries.

The growing awareness in psychoanalytic anthropology that context is crucial is also seen in Kracke's (1979) analysis of dreaming in an Amazonian Kagwahiv Indian culture. He used free-association methods to amplify background association thoughts to the dreams. Kracke insists that there is no cultural monolithic belief about dreams; there is extreme variation, as in our own culture. Also, many of the beliefs held by certain individuals are surprisingly sophisticated. They do not at all conform to the simpleminded notion that people living in primitive technologies hold the naive belief that dreams are real perceptions of an outside reality. Some Kagwahiv people do, in fact, have this belief, but many do not.

In particular, the dreams associated with the shaman, the *pajé,* are of note. Although there is a belief that he is able to cause events through dreaming, this should not necessarily be interpreted as a belief that dreams are real perceptions. The Kagwahiv have a term, *ra'uv,* that is used for the dream appearance of a person or object and that, as Kracke points out, could well mean something like "fantasy image" or "subjective experience." Its frequent translation as "soul," Kracke maintains, does not do justice to the full meaning of the term and is misleading. More pertinently, many Kagwahiv genuinely recognize that dreams can be the fulfillment of wishes, and they also accept the idea of daytime residue phenomena from dreams.

By using free-association methods, Kracke was able to eke out more from ethnographic findings than someone without this background would have been able to. Of particular interest in his findings is that informants would *consciously* interpret traumatic dreams in a way that minimized the emotional impact. For example, if a Kagwahiv man dreams of a woman, it is interpreted as a game; if a man's penis is dreamed of, it is translated as a tapir that he would kill; if a pregnant woman turns up in the dream material, the interpretation is that the dreamer will find a nest of honeybees. As Kracke states, such interpretations reassure the dreamer by rendering the emotional material innocuous, and they allow the dreamer to go on dreaming in undistorted form. Kracke labels this phenomenon as a built-in cultural secondary elaboration.

There is little doubt that clinical Freudian theory with its more recent modifications continues to exert influence in psychological anthropology. Some cross-cultural *psychological* studies have tested Freudian hypotheses (reviewed by Kline, 1977), but they are few in number and date before the time period covered in this section. Putting Freudian theories to the test cross-culturally necessitates a deep knowledge of the culture in question. A sound knowledge of the language and the development of special psychological tests with the specific intent of checking the hypotheses are further requirements. Such studies call for a formidable array of skills and qualifications that few investigators have. It is not surprising, therefore, that few such studies are available.

SUMMARY AND ASSESSMENT

The necessity for connecting the external world of sociocultural institutions with the internal disposition of the individuals constituting those institutions has produced a number of conceptual candidates to fulfill this function. The concept of personality has served this role for over forty years. In recent years the concept of cognition has appeared as a viable alternative. In a somewhat different vein the various concepts that make up psychoanalytic theory have served the same purpose.

The tendency has been for unitary concepts to separate into their components, thereby losing their power of bonding. This separation happens particularly when operational definition is strictly demanded. The search for a suitable mediating concept makes good sense, but the demands made on this concept are stringent. It has to relate sufficiently to two quite different disciplines: psychology and anthropology. It has to be precise enough to avoid ambiguity, but not so narrow that it loses the function of connecting link. In many ways the concept of personality has been admirable for this purpose; the fact that it has persisted in this role for so long speaks to its effectiveness.

What seems to be required is a concept that connects the situational demands on an individual with his or her enduring characteristics. It is doubtful whether the concept of cognition is sufficient for this task, since the requirements entail some temperamental traits. There is no reason why scholars engaged in cultural psychology need to rely slavishly on preexistent explanatory categories, particularly if these categories were generated in a totally different context. Psychological anthropologists should feel free to invent their own language if it proves to have a better fit.

THE CULTURAL PERSPECTIVE ON ABNORMAL AND UNUSUAL BEHAVIOR

The fields of transcultural psychiatry, altered states of consciousness, and deviancy, while all related, nevertheless have each developed an individual arena of study and debate in the cultural sphere. Whereas transcultural psychiatry has been much discussed in former reviews of cultural psychology, altered states of consciousness and deviancy have been less attended to. As with previous sections of this chapter, the intention here is not to furnish a comprehensive coverage of each and every facet of these subjects but to provide characteristic examples of the cultural perspective, paying attention to relatively new fields of study.

CULTURE, MENTAL HEALTH, AND HEALING SYSTEMS

As a convenient starting point, we can examine what previous reviewers have noted on the state of the art in cultural psychiatry or psychiatric anthropology. Two such reviews (Kennedy, 1974; Dubreuil and Wittkower, 1976) were published in the midpoint of the previous decade and are thus representative of the state of the art in the latter part of the sixties and the first part of the seventies. Kennedy's review embraces five major areas: epidemiological studies, drug use (which will be discussed under the heading of deviance), cultural factors impinging on traditional nosological categories of Western psychiatry, culture-specific syndromes, and non-Western psychiatric

practices. While there have been ensuing studies in all of these areas since the time that Kennedy compiled his material, it is notable that the greatest addition has come from the last, that is, the study of non-Western psychiatric practices.

In his coverage of indigenous healing practices Kennedy (1974, pp. 1170–1172) focused mainly on the dramatic healing ritual, as in trance possession situations, and analyzed (pp. 1177–1181) the possible mechanisms involved in these rituals. In doing so, he went over familiar ground concerning the processes of faith, suggestion, group support, and catharsis, but he also focused on the dynamics of the ritual situation itself, invoking Wallace's (1966, pp. 233–242) ideas of ritual interpreted in a communicational framework. Kennedy makes the important point that the main characteristic of non-Western therapeutic techniques, as contrasted with those of the West, is the manipulation of nonverbal symbols. As he says, "Since curing is an integral part of religion in nonwestern societies, the therapeutic language is *ritual* language" (Kennedy, 1974, p. 1177).

The importance of ritual is seen very clearly when one is considering small traditional societies. But even here it is evident that other factors are connected with ritual. When we go up the scale to more complex societies, even those that are not strictly Western, we see that all kinds of social and ideational factors come into play. To study these societies, we must consider therapeutic systems in the framework of worldviews (see Jones, 1976, pp. 383–404). In traditional societies, and indeed to a lesser extent in complex societies, what we would call the religious element is a vital ingredient of this worldview. In an overview of the effectiveness of religious healing movements, Bourguignon (1976a, pp. 5–21) makes some penetrating remarks. From our customary reference point of scientific validity we tend to isolate the effectiveness of various healing techniques to agents that we accept as being beneficial, like the pharmacological attributes of certain substances. However, as Bourguignon (1976a, p. 7) says:

> To understand why a given therapeutic regime "works" in a given cultural context with a given patient, it would be nonsensical to isolate the "religious" from the empirical or pharmacological. To the contrary, we would wish to understand the cultural context of illness, diagnosis and therapy, the symbolic levels invoked at the covert as well as overt types of communication engaged in by the participants.

As Bourguignon later goes on to point out (1976a, p. 17), the big difference between scientific medicine and religious healing is that the former concentrates on symptoms and syndromes, while religious healing focuses on life-style. Taking the religious dimension into account in this way still is unsatisfying from the cultural perspective, since once again we are enforcing distinctions and boundaries that are not natural to many cultures. What is emphasized over and over again in the anthropological material is that the different institutions of traditional societies are interdependent. We still need to reformulate the perspective a little and state that while non-Western therapies can undoubtedly be viewed in a religious context, the religious context in turn is tied in with considerations of other social concerns, particularly the economic, kinship, and jural systems.

This phenomenon is best seen in the less complex societies. Studying therapy systems among the BaKongo of lower Zaire, Janzen (1978) reduces the issue to two types of consensus. First is the social consensus that permits a shared set of rules regarding relationships, and second is an ideational consensus that involves a cognitive agreement. "This consensus implies that medical ideas, values, technique and role relationships are rooted in more inclusive social, ideational and ritual orders" (Janzen, 1978, p. 224).

One crucial issue that emerges from consideration of therapy systems in the small traditional societies concerns the boundaries of the medical system. When we depart from these smaller and less complex societies to larger societies, the difficulty of forming boundaries is still apparent. Thus Leslie (1976, pp. 1–12) in his analysis of Asian medical systems sees the question of boundaries as a major issue in interpreting medical systems in that part of the world.

Leslie also dislikes the label "Western medicine," which he thinks is misleading on the grounds that scientific medicine is transcultural and not restricted to the West. He prefers the term "cosmopolitan medicine" instead. Yet he still recognizes that there is a difference between medicine practices in the West and those he is considering in Asia. The difference lies in the fact that while cosmopolitan medicine is normative in the West, in Asia there are all kinds of folk ideas, like the insistence on humoral theory (found also in traditional societies in Latin America). The position in such complex societies is pluralistic; the analysis of these medical systems needs to take into account quite distinct trends.

Elsewhere, Leslie (1977, pp. 511–517) has presented a model of the merging of two bipolar axes orthogonal to

each other that would best represent the situation as found in complex countries like India or China. One of these axes contrasts learned secular medicine—namely, our scientific medicine as taught in universities and accepted medical institutions—against learned religious medicine, or religious curing. The other axis contrasts folk medical practice as handed down orally against popular cultural medicine as communicated through advertising and as taught in schoolbooks, which nonspecialists could pick up.

Both simple societies and the larger complex civilizations present the medical anthropologist with a challenge of analysis. Scholars have differed according to their basic starting point. Some have adopted the diachronic approach, which focuses on the historical perspective; others dwell more on the synchronic aspect, preferring to view the medical emphasis within the functional mechanism of the contemporary institutions. Note that a similar ambivalence characterizes the analysis of non-Western psychotherapies. This ambivalence can be seen in the case of the Morita technique, a Buddhist-based psychotherapy used in Japan. In order to relate it to our own psychotherapies (it has affinities with Freudian theory), one must relate it to Japanese tradition, on the one hand, and to social psychological factors in contemporary Japanese society, on the other hand. Reynolds (1976, pp. 117–150) sees Morita therapy as clearly Buddhist "in its emphasis on accepting one's experience of suffering as a means of transcending misery and losing one's self in productive effort for the good of one's fellows" (1976, p. 119), although its founder, Shoma Morita, denied any strong link with Zen. But Reynolds also makes clear that the theory fits in with current social psychological elements of Japanese society, such as the emphasis on *amae,* which we have previously discussed in the section on non-Western ideas of the self.

The increase of pluralistic societies around the world plus the increase of scientific, cosmopolitan medicine among traditional societies, sensitizes the scientific therapist to cultural factors as never before. A large portion of medical anthropology is devoted to this problem. Within the smaller psychological discipline of counseling, a new field of intercultural counseling has arisen (Pedersen, Lonner, and Draguns, 1976). This new field is necessitated not only by the intermingling of quite different nationals, with their obviously different background and values, but also by ethnic groups that require a different approach. As a matter of fact, Pedersen himself (Pedersen, Lonner, and Draguns, 1976, pp. 17–41) views the values and attitudes of persons of different sex, lifestyle, and social status as requiring a cultural approach in the sense that different life-styles may be at work here. In recent years in the United States we have seen an emerging emphasis, again within the confines of clinical psychology, on the independent needs of women in therapy situations. Thus from a quite different starting point we see a leaning toward life-style as an important ingredient in therapy systems.

Focus has been centered on the transition from studies of small traditional communities to the study of cultural factors in complex societies, because this study highlights the characteristic attributes of culture. We are no longer dealing only with esoteric forms of healing but with distinct cultural and societal factors that enter into the very fabric of a differentiated field of medicine. For this reason attention has been given to the theoretical problems of distinguishing religion from medicine and social factors in general from healing.

We should further note that there is a clear mainstream of studies that now could fall squarely under the rubric of medical anthropology; these studies substantiate over and over again the interconnection of culture and healing or culture and mental disorder (Grollig and Haley, 1976; Landy, 1977). A classic research study of this nature was the study of mental disorder in an Indian village by Carstairs and Kapur (1976). In their introductory chapter the authors point out that there are two major problems that face the cross-cultural researcher. First is the problem of establishing comparable definitions of psychiatric symptoms across cultures. Second is the problem of "developing a reliable and valid method of defining a case in a non-referred population and of separating those in greater need of attention from the others" (p. 17). The study of this village on the southwestern coast of India is notable for its attention to these perennial methodological problems and to the more human problem of the need for psychiatric care in a Third World community.

ALTERNATE STATE OF CONSCIOUSNESS

Traditional healing systems have generally been handled under the rubrics of trance, possession, and shamanism. Traditionally the province of the anthropologist, in recent years the so-called altered or alternate states of consciousness have been attended to by nonanthropologists (Tart, 1969; Zinberg, 1977). While there is an admitted difficulty in specifying precisely what an altered state of consciousness is (but see attempted definitions by Ludwig, 1969; Marsh, 1977), the term has caught on in anthropology as well (Bourguignon, 1977). The idea has been easily assimilated in the discipline that is accustomed to studying the cultural relevance of hallucinogens in addition to the older established study of trance and possession. Indeed, it is from taking the last two subjects as our starting point that we can best see the anthropological approach to altered states of consciousness.

Bourguignon (1976b, pp. 1–14) has clarified much of the definitional problem of trance and possession by insisting that while trance pertains to some unusual kind of behavioral condition, possession is a concept or belief. While trance may be considered in a psychiatric framework as a behavior parallel to or even identical with dissociated states such as fugue, multiple personality, or hysteria, possession is an explanation given to such states. It can also be given to states of mind that do not involve trance at all.

A global survey of over four hundred eighty societies (Bourguignon, 1976b, pp. 42–49) looked into the characteristics of societies that entertained the notion of possession versus those who exhibited possession with trance. Clear distinctions between the two groups of societies came out of this analysis. With those societies who had possession only, the characteristics pertained to hunting, gathering, and fishing occupations. The societies were relatively nomadic, had relatively small populations, and were not too complex; also, the leadership and decision making were at the local level of the band or community. Generally, no class structure was observed. Quite opposite characteristics were observed in those societies in which possession with trance was found. These societies were of the agricultural or animal husbandry subsistence types. They were sedentary and relatively quite complex, with a hierarchical structure. Also, their decision making and leadership involved shifting to higher levels of organization.

Having established that there are, indeed, differences between those societies having possession-trance and those with just possession beliefs, what can we infer that has consequences of a social psychological nature? Bourguignon (1976b, pp. 46–49) follows the argument through to areas that have already been touched on elsewhere in this chapter. The argument concerns the concept of self and the role of maintenance systems in encouraging certain types of socialization practices. She points out that a major difference between possession belief and possession-trance behavior is that the latter involves a brief loss of identity, a replacement by another person, a will, a spiritual entity; whereas in cases of possession belief only there is no exchange of self but, rather, an increased diminution of the individual's state of health or general disposition. The self in this case is modified, not replaced.

Bourguignon then reminds us of the early finding by Barry, Child, and Bacon (1959), which showed that in subsistence societies the qualities of independence and initiative are discouraged. Obedience, reliability, and a general attitude of nurturance are engendered. This idea was discussed above. Now in this context of possession the suggestion is that it is just in those societies that encourage compliance—societies that display subsistence economies and sedentariness—that possession-trance would be more likely to be found. And in contrast, it is just in those smaller hunting and gathering and fishing societies, which encourage autonomy and a lack of compliance, that non-trance-possession would be expected. In other words, in those societies in which the individual succeeds by abdicating part or whole of his identity toward other people, one would expect to find the same pattern when it comes to dealing with supernatural entities. The same logic applies in the opposite case. Where independence, initiative, and autonomy provide the model for ordinary societal interaction, one expects to find alliance and collusion with supernatural entities and not replacement. This model leads to the role of the shaman, who is par excellence the product of the smaller nomadic, hunting and gathering type of society.

Relating possession and trance to the economy and then, in turn, to the social psychological mechanisms of a society introduces the broader question of the functional value of trance states and possession beliefs. Earlier literature had shown that in those societies where women were socially inferior, ritual possession was one channel through which they could achieve some measure of power, authority, and respect (e.g., Lewis, 1971). And many scholars have perceived possession and trance as one method of catharsis, and hence to this extent they are therapeutic. In noting such interpretations, Prince (1977), in a foreword to a book of case histories of possession, concedes that there may well be other therapeutic mechanisms at work. For example, he cites Garrison's (1977) study of possession in the Puerto Rican subculture of New York as indicating that one function of the possessing spirits, the *Espiritistas,* is that of forcing the possessed person into the realm of personal relationships—a technique that might not be advocated by indi-

vidual psychoanalysis, although it would not be unfamiliar to family therapy.

So we see that there are certain functions that ritualized possession performs. Now there is controversy over whether such instances are indeed therapeutic or represent an elaborate defense mechanism that eludes permanent resolution for the individual (see Devereux, 1961). Nonetheless, there is generally a resolution in the social sphere; the phenomenon is functional to that extent. Spiro (1967), for instance, in his analysis of Burmese supernaturalism, shows that children are socialized into a belief system of punitive spirits. This belief system helps to reduce the conflict engendered by the contrast of ideal norms regarding interpersonal relationships and the perceived hostility of the parents. More generally, Spiro (1965) refers to culturally constituted defense mechanisms that serve this general function of reducing dissonance.

Quite distinct from the functional aspects of such states is the question of their elicitation. Anthropological studies have explored several agents. In the book *Trance, Healing and Hallucination* Goodman, Henney, and Pressel (1974) describe several methods that are used to facilitate an altered state. Whirling and spinning—long known among Dervish groups—are used in Umbande, a syncretic religion in Brazil. The Shaker group in St. Vincent, an island in the Caribbean, indulge in isolated trance conditions that are analogous to sensory deprivation experiments. A dominant contribution from the anthropological literature relates to the use of drugs in order to achieve these states. The past decade has seen leading studies of this question by anthropologists (e.g., Dobkin de Rios, 1972; Furst, 1972; Harner, 1973; Myerhoff, 1974; Reichel-Dolmatoff, 1975). In this endeavor the contributions of other scholars have been fruitful. Wasson (1968), for example, has explored the historical context, showing that the mushroom ingestion ritual now found in Mexico can be traced back to very early times. Botanists and chemists (Schultes and Hofmann, 1973) have underscored the potency of such drugs by specification of the active ingredients and their distribution in plants in the natural environment.

Returning to the earlier question of trance and possession, Bourguignon (1977) has made another important distinction, namely, that the trance facilitated by drugs is different from the trance associated with possession. The former is more hallucinatory, and its performer does not carry out actions that are characteristic of the person in possession-trance. From such studies we see that a salient factor is the embedding of the drug-taking in a mythical and ritual context. Often the drug is accepted as a mythic personage, as peyote and *datura* are in Huichol society (Furst, 1972, pp. 136–184). And although the extent of it varies, a ritual context invariably has to be taken into consideration. In some cases the ritual is very extensive and elaborate, as it is with the Huichols, where there is a ritual hunt for the peyote (see Myerhoff, 1974). In other cases it may be less extensive, but it is always important. Bourguignon (1977, p. 21) again reminds us that ritual should

> be thought of as an imposition of order, a bringing under social and ideological control of what are potentially disruptive psychological states and forces. The very frequency of ritualization of ASCs suggests that in most societies many kinds of such states are so viewed, in a traditional sacred context, as well as in a modern secular one.

It is extremely difficult to state whether standard anthropological work on the nature of ritual has psychological significance. The dean of anthropological researchers on ritual, Victor Turner (1969), uses a terminology and a mode of explanation that adopts the sociological frame of reference. At the same time, in an autobiographical account Turner (1978) admits a debt to Freud. Clearly, there is room for more direct psychological application in this field.

DEVIANCE

Departures from mental health and from a customary state of consciousness are themselves deviant in the strict sense of violation or aberration from a set of norms. We should continue into other areas of so-called deviance not hitherto discussed. These areas include behaviors such as alcoholism, stealing, violence, and suicide.

Anthropology has on the whole paid very little attention to variations within cultures or to individual differences in general. During the past decade this attitude has changed to the extent that a special issue of the *American Ethnologist* (1975) was devoted entirely to intracultural variations. All the same we have much less material than we would wish on the subject of deviance. True, there have always been substantial inputs from anthropologists to the other side of the coin, that is, to studies of law, justice, and the maintenance of rules. Studies of departures from acceptable norms are rare, though.

A substantial contribution to the cultural study of deviance has been the work on alcoholism. A product of the cultural relativism perspective is that the label of alcoholism has been discarded in favor of the more neutral term *drinking pattern*. But alcoholism, as it was then still called, was the target of one of the first cross-cultural studies of the holocultural mode (Horton, 1943), the hypothesis tested in that study being the relationship between drinking and anxiety. A fuller ethnographic picture was presented in the book by McAndrew and Edgerton (1969). They stressed the cultural flexibility of alcoholic influence, indicating that a variety of factors were involved, not solely that of anxiety reduction. The role of cultural belief and expectation of the drinker is illustrated in the study of drinking in the Admiralty Islands of Melanesia (Schwartz and Romanucci-Ross, 1974). A large part of the behavior of the inebriate is dictated by ideas of how such a person should behave and what the actions themselves might mean in the native belief system.

While all these writers have focused on the culturally sanctioned aspects of drinking behavior, others have tried to tie in the behavior with the kind of social organization. In her reanalysis of Horton's original work Field (1962) showed that an increase of social organization was related to an increase in the control of drunkenness. This finding was also reported by McClelland and associates (1972), who further indicated that it is in the better organized, more settled, and hierarchical society, which provides a support system for the individual, that the individual exercises control so that he or she is less inclined to seek satisfaction from impulsive needs, such as the need for alcohol.

We shall next consider the subject of stealing, taking our information from the book on deviance by Edgerton (1976). Note that in the simpler societies theft covers a refusal to share as well as stealing. Since economic reciprocity is a common standard in folk society, abdication of it is very severe. It is particularly severe in those societies where food is short. Edgerton cites an instance of theft reported in Turnbull's (1961, 1965) studies with the Mbuti Forest Pygmies of equatorial Africa. The Mbuti people have a vehement code of not stealing from one another. Parenthetically, as in many other populations, it is quite respectable to steal from other people, like the nearby Bantu-speaking villagers, whom the Mbuti regard as animals. But stealing from one another is definitely not permitted. Hence when stealing is detected, sanctions quickly follow. Indeed, in one case reported by Turnbull, punishment was administered. But as Edgerton points out, the Pygmy people tend to put the emphasis less on what we would call justice and more on maintaining personal relationships. So a process of smoothing over the problem was followed in this case, so that the important homeostatic principle of social equilibrium was enforced.

Suicide and homicide have received more attention by anthropologists (e.g., Bohannan, 1960). With suicide an immediate cultural distinction arises. In cases like the Japanese hara-kiri or the Hindu suttee ritual, where the widow throws herself on the funeral pyre of her husband, suicide does not fall under the category of deviance at all. It is the expected and acceptable code of behavior. Edgerton (1976, p. 40) gives a far more elaborate case observed by Langness in the Bena-Bena people of Highland New Guinea. The widow of a Bena-Bena man has the right to kill herself rather than be inherited by somebody else. If she does decide to kill herself, then her own brother must assist her. He does so in an elaborate ritualistic way. She climbs on his back in order to insert her head into a noose hanging from a tree. At a given signal he simply walks away, leaving her hanging. However, not all cultures have such honorable attitudes to suicide. The Mohave Indians of the U.S. Southwest, according to Devereux (1961), probably have much the same abhorrent view of suicide as we have.

Violence in general and homicide in particular are more complicated. As Edgerton (1976, p. 46) says in his summary:

> Violence offers another view of the relativity of cultural definitions of deviance. A deviant label may be the penalty for excessive violence in one society, for the wrong use of violence in another, and far too little violence in a third.

A striking cross-cultural case allowing for different kinds of explanation—and one that we do not encounter in Western culture—is the example of twin infanticide. This practice is institutionalized in many parts of the world. Generally, the weaker member of the pair is discarded and left to die. Much of the background literature is available in Ford's *Comparative Study of Human Reproduction* (1945). Contrasting ideological and materialistic explanations have been offered to explain the incidence of this practice. On behalf of the former type of explanation, reference is usually made to su-

pernatural beliefs about twins, so that explanation is in terms of fear of the abnormal. Opposed to this explanation is the materialistic thesis that states that various ecological and economic pressures push the mother to make a choice of nourishment and need for one infant over another. We would therefore expect twin infanticide to be more often noted in societies where there are insufficient facilities for a mother to rear two children at once.

Granzberg (1973) put this hypothesis to the test, using the holographic approach of comparing those societies that did have sufficient facilities with those that did not to determine where more twin infanticide practices had been observed. Indices were constructed for measuring the amount of help available to a mother and to what degree mothers were free from work. Granzberg's findings supported the materialistic explanation; twin infanticide is indeed more likely to be found just in those societies where mothers have a heavy work load and little help at hand.

The study of more prosaic forms of murder in cross-cultural perspective plummets the student into complex questions of demography, legal definitions, and institutional channels for dealing with aggressive energy. The subject is discussed by Palmer (1970, 1975), and a brief summary has been given by Tseng and Hsu (1980). Palmer (1972, p. 30) further pursues the subject in relation to the contrasting values of cooperation and competition, which we have discussed earlier in another context. In a sample of forty nonliterate societies Palmer found a significant relationship between reciprocity and murder. Specifically, he found that those societies that were low on role reciprocity—that is, valued competition—had high murder rates. These societies were very individualistically oriented, stressing prestige differences in their members and giving a relatively high value to conflict. In contrast, the high-reciprocity, high-cooperation societies showed low murder rates. These latter societies invariably valued the group over the individual and minimized prestige ranking in individuals.

When one looks for analysis of the *process* of deviance, less anthropological literature is available. Exceptions are the studies of Theodore Graves with acculturating populations in the American Southwest (summarized in Graves and Graves, 1978). Graves worked with acculturating Spanish and Indian populations. Distinguishing high- and low-acculturating groups, he invoked the "means-goals disjunction" theory. According to this theory, when traditional means of attainment for any particular goal prove unsuccessful, traditional ethnic goals are replaced by the models of industrialized Western society, that is, material comforts such as radios, electrical gadgets, and so on. For people still living on a subsistence pattern, these new goals are unattainable, while the old traditional goals are now defunct.

Graves anticipated that for those Spanish and Indian groups that were highly acculturated and had low economic access to these new goals, deviancy would be high. Particularly, he expected to observe a heavy use of alcohol, which proved to be the case. But the traditional societies were very different with respect to deviance. A far wider spectrum of drunkenness and general deviance was observed for the traditional Indian than for the traditional Spanish, who exercised a high degree of control through the agencies of church and family. With acculturation there was a differential effect on the two groups. While the Spanish tended on the whole to lose their traditional controls, the Indians in fact became permissive in the use of alcohol and in attitudes toward deviance, since they more easily assimilated the new Western ethos.

Further information on processes underlying deviant behavior comes from cross-cultural psychological studies. An early study of group pressures on an individual and how a group reacts to a deviate was carried out in seven countries in western Europe (Schacter *et al.*, 1954). The study found distinct cultural differences in how groups of each country treated a deviant member, but the study went little beyond just noting that. As Mann (1980, pp. 164–172) points out in discussing this study and others, conformity pressures do differ across cultures. But what is perhaps of more direct relevance here is the cross-cultural work done along the lines of Piaget's early studies on the development of the concept of morality (Piaget, 1932).

Initial cross-cultural work on moral development can be traced to Kohlberg's (1958) work. Kohlberg delineated three basic moral levels, which he termed the premoral level, morality of conventional role conformity, and morality of self-accepted moral principles. Although most of his samples were from the United States, Kohlberg had previously studied children from Formosa and China. He had also compared Protestant and Catholic children, so he had a mixture of religious values also. Across all these groups Kohlberg found an invariant sequence that cut across cultures, across religions, across sex, and across socioeconomic differences. Kohlberg concluded that at first the child leans on external controls for assessment of morality, with rewards and punish-

ment constituting the guiding principles. Then an internalization gets transposed into a system of shared consensus (see Kohlberg, 1970). Given this limited data base, Kohlberg's stages of moral development, later (Kohlberg, 1969) termed preconventional, conventional, and postconventional, therefore appeared to be truly universal. However, since that time a few studies have complicated the issue.

The crucial point in Kohlberg's theory is that the stages of ethical *reasoning* are independent of the value content of the particular culture. The research of Turiel (1969) has substantiated this position. Turiel found that in those cultures where there is a wide range of moral choices, the stages of moral reasoning are passed through more rapidly.

In order to probe this issue further in a culture other than the United States, Gorsuch and Barnes (1973) investigated children from the Black Carib population of British Honduras (Belize). In order to test directly the hypothesis of diversification of choices, they collected both urban and rural samples. They also used the full range of Kohlberg's stages (six stages). In this Black Carib culture boys from ten through sixteen, which is the representative age range, never got beyond the second stage. Moreover, on the basis of less rigorous interviews with adults, the interviewers felt that the adults never got beyond the third stage. Nevertheless, the observation of the sequence of the first two stages seemed to confirm, to that extent anyhow, the validity of Kohlberg's model.

The hypothesis of the diversification of ethical choices was also supported, the urban boys being more advanced in these stages than the rural children. The apparent total absence of subsequent stages of moral reasoning provoked speculations. One interesting surmise was that this particular culture had a strong collectivist orientation. Gorsuch and Barnes point out that many of the standard stories used for testing moral development are structured individualistically. As they say, "The collectivistic orientation might not have been adequately allowed for in the individualistically oriented ethical dilemmas" (1973, p. 297).

We know from the study of Greenfield and Bruner (1969) that cultures can be thought of as being either collectively or individually oriented and that this pervading ideology influences a variety of behaviors. A graphic example from these Black Caribs illustrates the point. One of the stories presents the dilemma of a certain captain who has to decide whether or not he should send back one of his men in the face of the advancing enemy and thus to certain death in order to save the rest of his troops. The Black Carib youngsters could not adapt themselves to this individual act. They insisted that all the soldiers should have gone back, since they would help each other, and thus nobody would get killed.

Kohlberg's theory brings us to the universals versus cultural relativism argument. In assessing the available cross-cultural evidence, Edwards (1975) argued that is the lower stages only of Kohlberg's set—that is, the first three stages—that have been found to be universal. The higher or last three stages appear to be culture-specific. Edwards also makes the point that no hunter-gatherer groups have been studied. Edwards goes on to say that whereas the first three stages of moral reasoning are applicable to the life-style of traditional and isolated peasant village groups, as well as to more modern settings, the reasoning of the last three stages is really more adaptive to educated people from a more complex society. In other words, the issue is raised that a societal frame of reference is tied in with the stages of moral reasoning.

Focusing just on this last point, Edwards interviewed Kenyans who either came from a traditional tribal community or had been modernized into a cosmopolitan context in the big city. She concentrated on the transition from stage three to stage four, since this one step represented the shift from the lower three stages to the upper three stages. Her findings support the idea that the third stage would be the highest possible stage found in a small traditional society. They also support the concomitant idea that the fourth (and higher) stage would be found more frequently in university samples, such as the one she studied in urban Kenya, whose habitat is of a more complex and less face-to-face interaction. Edwards notes that these findings have been oberved in other countries such as Thailand and India (Edwards, 1975, p. 520). She makes the important observation that moral judgments should be interpreted as adaptive mechanisms and not as achievements. An urban mode of life calls for certain adaptations to moral problems that are not necessary in small face-to-face communities. Factors involving anonymity, impersonality, and heterogeneity are present in the urban complex, and they introduce moral dilemmas not seen in the rural situation.

The rural-urban distinction, however, appears to be less simplistic when a rigorous analysis is made. Weisner (1979, 1980) has reported research from Kenya that has the methodological merit of being able to sort out situational factors from nonsetting factors such as socioeconomic status, age, stage in the family developmental cycle, and modernity. He found that urban children, for example, were less sociable than rural children, and compared with rural children, they tended to act more dominantly and aggressively toward others. His study design also allowed him to determine that it is not sheer crowding or neighborhood factors that were at work here. Peer group composition, daily routines, and mobility between settings may together have constituted a more powerful influence. Weisner's findings have much relevance to the work on moral development.

SUMMARY AND ASSESSMENT

There has been an abiding interest in transcultural psychiatry and related fields for over a generation. Their continuing development was partially covered in this section. A constant concern has been the issue of separating what is medical from the surrounding social context. This concern is perhaps the main distinction of our own brands of therapy from non-Western types, although it is more probably a product of the degree of complexity of a society. The West is now seeing a reintroduction of cultural factors in medicine, particularly where large numbers of the society have different ethnic composition from the mainstream population.

The observation was made that the traditional areas of anthropology under the heading of possession and trance were now being widened and redefined in terms of altered states of consciousness, which has had a large impact on our own society. Interestingly, the distinction of societies in terms of nomadic versus sedentary, which was found to be so useful in the analysis of social variables, is now found to be of additional value in determining the occurrence of possession beliefs and trance behavior.

In following the work on cross-cultural studies of deviance, one is quickly made aware of the different levels at which the anthropologist and psychologist are working. It is one thing to determine the different value systems of cultures, to note what is considered to be normative and what is not, and even to note how the social structure may be tied in with these values. It is another thing to analyze the internalization process involved in the assimilation of values. This level is the one at which the psychologist has to work, and there is always the difficulty of connecting work at this level with the work of anthropologists. A promising start to solving this problem, which emerged from the psychoanalytic tradition, was the elucidation of the notion regarding shame versus guilt cultures by Piers and Singer (1953; reprinted 1971). And Burton and Reis (1981, p. 684) noticed that no cross-cultural surveys have explored the antecedents of shame as compared with the antecedents of guilt. There would seem to be a lacuna here for cross-cultural psychologists to explore.

CONCLUSIONS

The previous pages have been little more than an adumbration of a vast and still-growing data base. This review of the work in the previous decade constitutes a progress report, which is terminated only by the constrictions of time—specifically through 1981—and not because of any sense of closure. This reviewer is uncomfortably aware that far more has been said and continues to be said of areas that have been given only scant attention here, as, for example, the cross-cultural work on alcoholism (see Bacon, 1981) or the cultural aspects of moral judgment (see Edwards, 1981). Also, some important areas have not been discussed at all, as, for example, the relation between culture and education (see Rogoff, 1981; Jordan and Tharp, 1979; Price-Williams and Gallimore, 1980) or the cross-cultural study of play and games (Sutton-Smith and Roberts, 1981). The undeniable *embarras de richesses* of the data has presented the reviewer with a problem of selection.

Part of the problem of increasing accumulation of material is the lack of guiding, and thus constraining, theories. Another part is that what has passed for cultural psychology, and still passes for it, is a perspective that has been tacked onto already existing psychological problems and classes of problems. Thus the organization of, for example, the *Handbook of Cross-Cultural Psychology* falls into the familiar groupings of psychological issues, such as basic processes, social processes, developmental psychology, and psychopathology. Escalation of this approach moves into theoretical schemes, so that Piaget's stages, Witkin's differentiation theory, or McClelland's achievement motivation concept can all be tested with a different national or ethnic population or under cultural conditions different from our own.

Even in psychological anthropology, where culture is seen less as an experimental variable to be manipulated and more as the very fabric of existence, the tendency has been to attach psychological valences to the preexistent anthropological categories of study, such as residence, kinship, and socialization. The notable exceptions, of course, are those concepts that we discussed in the fourth section, but here preexisting *psychological*

categories (personality, cognition) are used. This trend is not to be taken as a complaint, except to mark that one might have expected by this time to see a set of emerging concepts that would characterize the individuality of the field. Perhaps this step may be more radical than might be thought, for it could entail recognizing psychological variables as being encompassed in a medium that partly, at any rate, determines them.

Working out this envelopment entails new analysis and perhaps new concepts. On the other hand, the determination of the way in which people perceive their own culture—which could be regarded as a step in the direction we are seeking—is pretty advanced in both of the fields discussed. In cross-cultural psychology Triandis and his colleagues (1972) have produced an analysis of subjective culture that merges well with the formulations of social psychology. We note in passing that whereas the field of cross-cultural psychology as a whole tends to be separated from psychology as a discipline, certain areas have been well integrated with either general or social psychological findings. Notable examples are Cole and his colleagues (1971) in the field of cognition, Triandis and colleagues (1972, 1977) in social psychology, Berry (1976) in the area of psychological differentiation, and the general Piagetian applications noted in the edited volume by Dasen (1977).

While cross-cultural psychology has been moving from a within-an-individual position to a without position, psychological anthropology has been operating in the reverse direction. The starting point here has been distinctions of basic living conditions, which are thought to influence early socialization practices, which, in turn, are thought to become internalized. The traditional distinction between hunting and gathering groups versus agricultural subsistence groups has continued to be found to relate to more specific social variables.

Relationship to the environment and complexity of the social system as factors meaningful to psychological issues are not new in psychological anthropology. Roberts's and Sutton-Smith's works on games were carried out nearly twenty years ago (1962), but the extent of the work has now expanded. It would certainly be useful for cultural psychology to be able to specify distinct social units or organizational patterns that could be considered to bear influence on psychological variables. The cross-cultural manifold of potential units is a fertile field of possibilities. One always has difficulty sorting out a complex of variables when dealing at this level, but this difficulty can be handled by correct design of observations and by statistical manipulation.

We have noted in passing quite a fresh input from the biological side. This input is welcomed, since it compensates the heavy input from the purely sociological direction. We would anticipate a growth in this tendency over the next decade and an inclination to deal with biological factors at a less simplistic level. The juxtaposition of biological and sociological factors has always been difficult for the social sciences to accommodate. It has always been so much more tantalizing to take hard positions and enter into the polemical fray than to try and work out the intricate interactions that are so obviously present. Indeed, it is just this interactionist position that is so difficult to achieve in other areas.

Sundberg (1977, p. 131) has remarked that the interaction between person and situation is most important but also most difficult to assess. The same can be said for many of the mediating concepts found in psychological anthropology. The subject is replete with interface problems, and there is not always a new conceptual armament to deal with them. So the scholar has perforce to fall back on the traditional explanations of the disciplines involved. Nevertheless, much innovation has been demonstrated in cultural psychology, as well as much enthusiasm and vigor. We should anticipate a more conservative trend, to match the times perhaps, where the more outgoing forays have to give way to consolidation and reorganization. Cultural psychology needs to realize what it already knows.

REFERENCES

Aberle, D. F., A. K. Cohen, A. K. Davis, M. J. Levy, and F. X. Sutton (1950). The functional prerequisites of a society. *Ethics, 60,* 100–111.

American Anthropological Association (1980). Ethnopersonality: assumptions, theories, and results. Symposium presented at the 79th annual meeting of the American Anthropological Association, Washington, D.C.

American Ethnologist (1975). Intra-cultural variation. Special issue, 2, No. 1.

Asch, S. E. (1956). Studies in independence and conformity I: A minority of one against a unanimous majority. *Psychol. Monogr., 70,* No. 416.

Bacon, M. K. (1981). Cross-cultural perspectives on motivations for drinking. In R. H. Munroe, R. L. Munroe, and B. B. Whiting (Eds.), *Handbook of cross-cultural human development.* New York: Garland STPM Press.

Barker, R. G. (1968). *Ecological psychology.* Stanford: Stanford Univ. Press.

Barnouw, V. (1973). *Culture and personality* (rev. ed.). Homewood, Ill.: Dorsey.

Barry, H., III (1980). Description and uses of the human relations area files. In H. C. Triandis and J. W. Berry (Eds.), *Handbook of cross-cultural psychology.* Vol. 2. *Methodology.* Boston: Allyn and Bacon. Pp. 445–478.

Barry, H., M. Bacon, and I. Child (1957). A cross-cultural survey of some sex differences in socialization. *J. abnorm. soc. Psychol., 55,* 327–332.

Barry, H., I. Child, and M. Bacon (1959). Relation of child training to subsistence economy. *Amer. Anthropologist, 61,* 51–63.

Barry, H., and L. M. Paxson (1971). Infancy and early childhood: cross-cultural codes. *Ethnology, 10,* 466–508.

Bartlett, F. C. (1923). *Psychology and primitive culture.* London: Cambridge Univ. Press.

Basso, K. H. (1969). Western Apache witchcraft. Anthropological papers of the University of Arizona, *15.*

Bateson, G. (1958). *Naven. A survey of the problems suggested by a composite picture of the culture of a New Guinea tribe drawn from three points of view* (2nd ed.). Stanford: Stanford Univ. Press. Original edition, 1936.

Berland, J. (1977). Cultural differences and psychological differentiation among Khanabadosh in Pakistan. Ph.D. dissertation. Department of Anthropology, University of Hawaii.

Berlin, B., and P. Kay (1969). *Basic color terms: their universality and evolution.* Berkeley: Univ. of California Press.

Berry, J. W. (1969). On cross-cultural comparability. *Int. J. Psychol., 4,* 119–128.

_____ (1976). *Human ecology and cognitive style.* Beverly Hills: Sage/Halsted.

_____ (1979). A cultural ecology of social behavior. In L. Berkowitz (Ed.), *Advances in experimental social psychology.* Vol. 12. New York: Academic Press.

Berry, J. W., and R. C. Annis (1974). Ecology, culture and psychological differentiation. *Int. J. Psychol., 9,* 173–193.

Berry, J. W., and P. R. Dasen, Eds. (1974). *Culture and cognition: readings in cross-cultural psychology.* London: Methuen.

Birdwhistell, R. L. (1963). The Kinesic level in the investigation of the emotions. In P. H. Knapp (Ed.), *Expression of the emotions in man.* New York: International Universities Press.

Black, M. B. (1977). Ojibwa taxonomy and percept ambiguity. *Ethos, 5,* 90–118.

Bohannan, P., Ed. (1960). *African homicide and suicide.* Princeton, N.J.: Princeton Univ. Press.

Bornstein, M. (1973). The psychophysiological component of cultural differences in color naming and illusion susceptibility. *Behav. sci. Notes, 8,* 41–101.

Bourguignon, E. (1976a). The effectiveness of religious healing movements: a review of recent literature. *Transcultural psychiatric research Review.* Vol. 13. Pp. 5–21.

_____ (1976b). *Possession.* San Francisco: Chandler and Sharp.

_____ (1977). Altered states of consciousness, myths, and rituals. In B. M. Du Toit (Ed.), *Drugs, rituals and altered states of consciousness.* Rotterdam: A. A. Balkema. Pp. 7–23.

Boyer, L. B. (1975). The man who turned into a water monster: a psychiatric contribution to folklore. In W. Muensterberger, and A. E. Esman (Eds.), *The psychoanalytic study of society.* Vol. VI. New York: International Universities Press. Pp. 100–133.

Boyer, L. B., and R. M. Boyer (1972). Effect of acculturation on the vicissitudes of the aggressive drive among the Apaches of the Mescalero Indian reservation. In W. Muensterberger, and A. E. Esman (Eds.), *The psychoanalytic study of society.* Vol. V. New York: International Universities Press. Pp. 40–82.

Bradburn, N. M. (1963). Need achievement and father dominance in Turkey. *J. abnorm. soc. Psychol., 67,* 464–468.

Brewer, M. B., and D. T. Campbell (1976). *Ethnocentrism and intergroup attitudes: East African evidence.* New York: Wiley/Halsted.

Briggs, J. L. (1975). The origins of nonviolence: aggression in two Canadian Eskimo groups. In W. Muensterberger, and A. E. Esman (Eds.), *The psychoanalytic study of society.* Vol. VI. New York: International Universities Press. Pp. 134–203.

Brislin, R. W., W. J. Lonner, and R. M. Thorndike (1976). *Cross-cultural research methods.* New York: Wiley.

Brown, J. K. (1973). The subsistence activities of women and the socialization of children. *Ethos, 1,* 413–423.

Brunswik, E. (1956). *Perception and the representative design of psychological experiments* (2nd ed.). Berkeley: Univ. of California Press.

Burling, R. (1964). Cognition and componential analysis: God's truth or hocus-pocus? *Amer. Anthropologist, 66,* 20–28.

Burrows, E. G., and M. E. Spiro (1953). *An atoll culture: ethnography of Ifaluk in the Central Carolines.* New Haven: Human Relations Area Files.

Burton, R. V., and J. Reis (1981). Internalization. In R. H. Munroe, R. L. Munroe, and B. B. Whiting (Eds.), *Handbook of cross-cultural human development.* New York and London: Garland STPM Press.

Burton, R. V., and J. W. M. Whiting (1961). The absent father and cross-sex identity. *Merrill-Palmer Quart., 7,* 85–95.

Campbell, D. T. (1967). Stereotypes and the perception of group differences. *Amer. Psychol., 22,* 817–829.

Campbell, D. T., and R. Naroll (1972). The mutual methodological relevance of anthropology and psychology. In F. L. K. Hsu (Ed.), *Psychological anthropology* (New ed.). Cambridge, Mass.: Schenkman.

Carstairs, G. M., and R. L. Kapur (1976). *The great universe of Kota: stress, change and mental disorders in an Indian village.* Berkeley: Univ. of California Press.

Carvalho-Neto, P. de (1972). *Folklore and psychoanalysis.* Translated by J. M. P. Wilson. Coral Gables, Florida: Univ. of Miami Press.

Caudill, W., and D. W. Plath (1966). Who sleeps by whom? Parent-child involvement in urban Japanese families. Reprinted in R. LeVine (Ed.), *Culture and personality.* Chicago: Aldine.

Caudill, W. A., and C. Schooler (1973). Child behavior and child rearing in Japan and the United States: an interim report. *J. Nervous mental Dis., 157,* 323–338.

Centre National de la Recherche scientifique. (1973). La notion de personne en Afrique noire. Colloques internationaux No. 544. Paris: Éditions du Centre National de la Recherche Scientifique.

Cole, M. (1975). An ethnographic psychology of cognition. In R. W. Brislin, S. Bochner, and W. J. Lonner (Eds.), *Cross-cultural perspectives on learning.* New York: Wiley.

Cole, M., J. Gay, J. A. Glick, and D. W. Sharp (1971). *The cultural context of learning and thinking.* New York: Basic Books.

Cole, M., and S. Scribner (1974). *Culture and thought: a psychological introduction.* New York: Wiley.

Darwin, C. (1872). *The expression of the emotions in man and animals.* London: Murray.

Dasen, P. Ed. (1977). *Piagetian psychology: cross-cultural contributions.* New York: Gardner Press.

Davidson, A. R. (1979). Culture and attitude structure and change. In A. J. Marsella, R. G. Tharp, and T. J. Ciborowski, (Eds.) *Perspectives on cross-cultural psychology.* New York: Academic Press.

Day, R., L. B. Boyer, and G. A. De Vos (1975). Two styles of ego development: a cross-cultural, longitudinal comparison of Apache and Anglo school children. *Ethos, 3,* 345–379.

De Rios, D. M. (1972). *Visionary vine: psychedelic healing in the Peruvian Amazon.* San Francisco: Chandler.

Devereux, G. (1961). Mohave ethnopsychiatry and suicide: the psychiatric knowledge and the psychic disturbances of an Indian tribe. Washington, D. C.: Smithsonian Institution, Bureau of American Ethnology, Bulletin 175.

De Vos, G. A. (1968). Achievement and innovation in culture and personality. In E. Norbeck, D. Price-Williams, and W. M. McCord (Eds.), *The study of personality: an interdisciplinary approach.* New York: Holt, Rinehart, and Winston. Pp. 348–370.

———— (1976). Responses to change: recurrent patterns. In G. De Vos, (Ed.), *Responses to change: society, culture and personality.* New York: Van Nostrand. Pp. 342–359.

De Vos, G. A., and A. E. Hippler (1969). Cultural psychology: comparative studies of human behavior. In G. Lindzey and E. Aronson (Eds.), *The handbook of social psychology* (2nd ed.). Vol. 4. Reading, Mass.: Addison-Wesley. Pp. 323–417.

Doi, T. (1973). *The anatomy of dependence.* Translated by John Bester. Tokyo, New York, and San Francisco: Kudansha International.

Dolgin, J. L., D. S. Kemnitzer, and D. M. Schneider, Eds. (1977). *Symbolic anthropology: a reader in the study of symbols and meaning.* New York: Columbia Univ. Press.

Draguns, J. G. (1979). Culture and personality. In A. J. Marsella, R. G. Tharp, and T. J. Ciborowski (Eds.), *Perspectives on cross-cultural psychology.* New York: Academic Press. Pp. 179–207.

Dubreuil, G., and E. D. Wittkower (1976). Psychiatric anthropology: a historical perspective. *Psychiatry, 39,* 130–141.

Dundes, A. (1962). Earth-diver: creation of the mythopoeic male. *Amer. Anthropologist, 64,* 1032–1051.

Durkheim, E., and M. Mauss (1963). De quelques formes primitives de classification. *Année Sociologique,* 1901–02, 6, 1–72. Reprinted in R. Needham (Editor and translator), *Primitive classification.* Chicago: Chicago Univ. Press.

Edgerton, R. B. (1970). Mental retardation in non-Western societies: towards a cross-cultural perspective on incompetence. In H. C. Haywood (Ed.), *Socio-cultural aspects of mental retardation.* New York: Appleton-Century-Crofts. Pp. 523–559.

_____ (1974). Cross-cultural psychology and psychological anthropology: two paradigms or not? *Rev. Anthropology, 1,* 52–64.

_____ (1976). *Deviance: a cross-cultural perspective.* Menlo Park, Calif.: Cummings.

Edgerton, R. B., and L. L. Langness (1974). *Methods and styles in the study of culture.* San Francisco: Chandler and Sharp.

Edwards, C. P. (1975). Societal complexity and moral development: a Kenyan study. *Ethos, 3,* 505–527.

_____ (1981). The comparative study of the development of moral judgment and reasoning. In R. H. Munroe, R. L. Munroe, and B. B. Whiting (Eds.), *Handbook of cross-cultural human development.* New York: Garland STPM Press.

Eibl-Eibesfeldt, I. (1975). Aggression in the !Ko-Bushmen. In T. R. Williams (Ed.), *Psychological anthropology.* The Hague: Mouton. Pp. 317–331.

Ekman, P. (1974). Universal facial expressions of emotion. In R. A. LeVine (Ed.), *Culture and personality: contemporary readings.* Chicago: Aldine. Pp. 8–15.

Elder, G. H., Jr. (1974). *Children of the great depression.* Chicago: Chicago Univ. Press.

Field, P. B. (1962). A new cross-cultural study of drunkenness. In D. J. Pittman, and C. R. Snyder (Eds.), *Society, culture and drinking.* New York: Wiley.

Firth, R. (1951). *Elements of social organization.* London: Watts.

_____ (1973). *Symbols: public and private.* Ithaca, New York: Cornell Univ. Press.

Fogelson, R. D. (1980). Person, self, and identity: some anthropological retrospects, circumspects and prospects. Unpublished manuscript.

Ford, C. S. (1945). A comparative study of human reproduction. New Haven: Yale Univ. Press.

Foster, G. M. (1973). Dreams, character and cognitive orientation in Tzintzuntzan. *Ethos, 1,* 106–121.

Foulks, E. (1972). The arctic hysterias. In D. Maybury-Lewis (Ed.), *Anthropological Studies No. 10.* Washington, D.C.: American Anthropological Association Press.

Foulks, E., D. M. A. Freeman, and P. A. Freeman (1979). Preoedipal dynamics in a case of Eskimo arctic hysteria. In W. Muensterberger, L. B. Boyer, and G. J. Rose (Eds.), *The psychoanalytic study of society.* Vol. VIII. New Haven and London: Yale Univ. Press. Pp. 41–69.

Freedman, D. G. (1974). *Human infancy: an evolutionary perspective.* Hillsdale, N.J.: Erlbaum.

Freeman, D., E. Foulks, and P. Freeman (1976). Ghost sickness and superego development in the Kiowa Apache male. In W. Muensterberger, A. E. Esman, and L. B. Boyer (Eds.), *The psychoanalytic study of society.* Vol. 7. New Haven: Yale Univ. Press. Pp. 123–171.

Freud, A. (1966). *The ego and mechanisms of defense* (rev. ed.). Originally published 1936. New York: International Universities Press.

Furst, P. T. Ed. (1972). *Flesh of the gods.* The ritual use of hallucinogens. New York: Praeger.

Gallimore, R. (1969). Variations in the motivational antecedents of achievement among Hawaii's ethnic groups. Paper read at East-West Conference on Culture and Mental Health. Social Science Research Institute, Honolulu, Hawaii.

Garrison, V. (1977). The "Puerto Rican" syndrome in psychiatry and *Espiritismo.* In V. Crapanzano and V. Garrison (Eds.), *Case studies in spirit possession.* New York: Wiley. Pp. 383–449.

Gay, J., and M. Cole (1967). *The new mathematics and an old culture: a study of learning among the Kpelle of Liberia.* New York: Holt, Rinehart, and Winston.

Gergen, K. J. (1973). Social psychology as history. *J. Pers. soc. Psychol., 26,* 309–320.

Goldenweiser, A. (1968). *History, psychology and culture.* Originally published 1933. Gloucester, Mass.: P. Smith.

Goldschmidt, W. G. (1966). *Comparative functionalism.* Berkeley: Univ. of California Press.

Goldschmidt, W., and R. Edgerton (1961). A picture technique for the study of values. *Amer. Anthropologist, 63,* 26–45.

Goodman, F. G., J. H. Henney, and E. Pressel (1974). *Trance, healing and hallucination: three field studies in religious experience.* New York: Wiley.

Gorer, G. (1938). *Himalayan village: an account of the Lepchas of Sikkim.* London: Michael Joseph.

Gorsuch, R. L., and M. L. Barnes (1973). Stages of ethical reasoning and moral norms of Carib youths. *J. cross-cultural Psychol., 41,* 283–301.

Granzberg, G. (1973). Twin infanticide a cross-cultural test of a materialistic explanation. *Ethos, 1,* 405–412.

Graves, T. D., and N. B. Graves (1978). Evolving strategies in the study of culture change. In G. D. Spindler (Ed.), *The making of psychological anthropology.* Berkeley: Univ. of California Press.

Greenfield, P. M., and J. S. Bruner (1969). Culture and cognitive growth. In D. A. Goslin (Ed.), *Handbook of socialization theory and research.* Chicago: Rand McNally. Chapter 12.

Grollig, F. X., and H. B. Haley (1976). *Medical anthropology.* The Hague: Mouton.

Gussow, Z. (1960). Pibloktoq (hysteria) among the polar Eskimo: an ethnopsychiatric study. In W. Muensterberger and S. Axelrad (Eds.), *Psychoanalysis and the social sciences, 1,* 28–36. New York: International Universities Press.

Gutmann, D. (1967). On cross-cultural studies as a naturalistic approach in psychology. *Hum. Develop., 10,* 187–198.

Hallowell, A. I. (1952). Ojibwa personality and acculturation In S. Tax (Ed.), *Acculturation in the Americas.* Proceedings and selected papers on the XXIXth International Congress of Americanists. Chicago: Univ. of Chicago Press.

_____ (1955). *Culture and experience.* Philadelphia: Univ. of Pennsylvania Press.

_____ (1974). The Ojibwa self and its behavioral environment. In A. I. Hallowell, *Culture and experience.* Philadelphia: Univ. of Pennsylvania Press. First Pennsylvania paperback edition. Pp. 75–110.

Harner, M. J. Ed. (1973). *Hallucinogens and shamanism.* London: Oxford Univ. Press.

Harrington, C., and J. W. M. Whiting (1972). Socialization process and personality, Chapter 12 of F. L. K. Hsu (Ed.), *Psychological anthropology* (new ed.). Cambridge, Mass.: Schenkman.

Harris, M. (1968). *The rise of anthropological theory*. New York: Crowell.

Hay, T. (1977). The development of some aspects of the Ojibwa self and its behavioral environment. *Ethos, 5*, 71–89.

Heider, E. R. (1971). "Focal" color areas and the development of color names. *Develop. Psychol., 4*, 447–455.

—— (1972). Probability, sampling, and ethnographic method: the case of Dani colour names. *Man, 7*, 448–466.

Hertz, R. (1973). The pre-eminence of the right hand: a study in religious polarity. La préeminence de la main droite: étude sur la polarité religieuse. *Revue Philosophique, 1909, 68*, 553–580. In R. Needham (Tr. and Ed.), *Right and left: essays on dual symbolic classification*. Chicago and London: Univ. of Chicago Press.

Holter, F. R. (1978). Psychoanalytic questions and methods in anthropological field-work. *J. psychol. Anthropology, 1*, 391–405.

Horton, D. (1943). The functions of alcohol in primitive societies: a cross-cultural study. *Quart. J. Stud. Alcohol, 4*, 199.

Horton, R., and R. Finnegan (1973). *Modes of thought: essays on thinking in western and non-western societies*. London: Faber and Faber.

Hsu, F. L. K. (1971). Psychosocial homeostasis and Jen: conceptual tools for advancing psychological anthropology. *Amer. Anthropologist, 73*, 23–43.

Irvine, S. H. (1969). Culture and mental ability. *New Scient., 42*, 230–231.

Jahoda, G. (1979). A cross-cultural perspective on experimental social psychology. *Pers. soc. Psychol. Bull., 5*, 142–148.

Janzen, J. M. (1978). *The quest for therapy in Lower Zaire*. Berkeley: Univ. of California Press.

Jaynes, J., and M. Bressler (1971). Evolutionary universals, continuities, alternatives. In J. F. Eisenberg, and W. S. Dillon (Eds.), *Man and beast: comparative social behavior*. Washington, D.C.: Smithsonian Institution Press.

Jones, W. T. (1976). World-views and Asian medical systems: some suggestions for further study. In C. Leslie (Ed.), *Asian medical systems: a comparative study*. Berkeley: Univ. of California Press. Pp. 383–404.

Jordan, C., and R. G. Tharp (1979). Culture and education. In A. J. Marsella, R. G. Tharp, and T. J. Ciborowski (Eds.), *Perspectives on cross-cultural psychology*. New York: Academic Press.

Kagan, J. (1976). Resilience in cognitive development. In T. Schwartz (Ed.), *Socialization as cultural communication*. Berkeley: Univ. of California Press. Pp. 139–155.

Kagan, J., and R. E. Klein (1973). Cross-cultural perspectives on early development. *Amer. Psychol., 28*, 947–961.

Kagan, S., and M. C. Madsen (1971). Co-operation and competition of Mexican, Mexican-American, and Anglo-American children of two ages under four instructional sets. *Develop. Psychol., 5*, 32–39.

—— (1972). Experimental analyses of cooperation and competition of Anglo-American and Mexican children. *Develop. Psychol., 6*, 49–59.

Keesing, R. (1972). Paradigms lost. *Southwestern J. Anthropology, 28*, 299–332.

Kennedy, J. G. (1974). Cultural psychiatry. In J. J. Honigmann (Ed.), *Handbook of social and cultural anthropology*. Chicago: Rand McNally. Pp. 1119–1198.

Kimura, B. (1973). *Hito to hito no aida* (In-between persons). Tokyo: Baifukan.

Kline, P. (1977). Cross-cultural studies and Freudian theory. In N. Warren (Ed.), *Studies in cross-cultural psychology*. Vol. I. London: Academic Press. Pp. 51–90.

Klineberg, O. (1935). *Race differences*. New York: Harper.

Kluckhohn, C. (1953).Universal categories of culture. In A. L. Kroeber (Ed.), *Anthropology today*. Chicago: Univ. of Chicago Press.

Kohlberg, L. (1958). The development of moral thinking and choice in the years ten to sixteen. Unpublished doctoral dissertation. Univ. of Chicago.

—— (1969). Stage and sequence: the cognitive-developmental approach to socialization. In D. A. Goslin (Ed.), *Handbook of socialization theory and research*. Chicago: Rand McNally.

—— (1970). The child as a moral philosopher. In P. Cramer (Ed.), *Readings in developmental psychology today*. Del Mar, Calif.: CRM Books. Pp. 109–115.

Kornadt, H. J., L. H. Eckensberger, and W. B. Emminghaus (1980). Cross-cultural research on motivation and its contribution to a general theory of motivation. In H. C. Triandis, and W. Lonner (Eds.), *Handbook of cross-cultural psychology*. Vol. 3. *Basic processes*. Boston: Allyn and Bacon.

Kracke, W. H. (1979). Dreaming in Kagwahiv: dream beliefs and their psychic uses in an American Indian culture. In W. Muensterberger, L. B. Boyer, and G. J. Rose (Eds.), *The psychoanalytic study of society*. Vol. 8. New Haven and London: Yale Univ. Press. Pp. 119–171.

Kroeber, A. L., and C. Kluckhohn (1952). Culture: a critical review of concepts and definitions. Papers of the Peabody Museum of American Archeology and Ethnology, *47*, No. 1.

LaBarre, W. (1947). The cultural basis of emotions and gestures. *J. Pers., 16*, 49–68.

—— (1975). Anthropological perspectives on hallucination and hallucinogens. In R. K. Siegel, and L. J. West (Eds.), *Hallucinations: behavior, experience and theory*. New York: Wiley. Pp. 9–52.

Laboratory of Comparative Human Cognition. (1978). Cognition as a residual category in anthropology. *Ann. Rev. Anthropology, 7*, 51–69.

Lalèyê, I. P. (1970). *La conception de la personne dans la pensée traditionelle Yoruba "approche phénoménologique."* Berne: Herbert Lang & Cie, SA.

Lambert, W. W. (1971). Cross-cultural backgrounds to personality development and the socialization of aggression: findings from the six culture study. In W. W. Lambert, and R. Weisbrod (Eds.), *Comparative perspectives on social psychology*. Boston: Little, Brown.

Landy, D. (1977). Culture, disease and healing. *Studies in medical anthropology*. New York: Macmillan.

Lave, J. (1977). Tailor-made experiments and evaluating the intellectual consequences of apprenticeship training. *Quart. Newsletter Institute compara. hum. Develop., 1*, 1–3.

Leach, E. R. (1954). *Political systems of highland Burma*. Boston: Beacon Press.

Lebeuf, J. P. (1973). Personne et système du monde chez les Kotoko. In Centre national de la recherche scientifique

(Ed.), *Colloques Internationaux, No. 544*. Paris: Du Centre National de La Recherche Scientifique. Pp. 373–386.

Lebra, T. S. (1976). *Japanese patterns of behavior*. Honolulu, Hawaii: Univ. Press of Hawaii.

Lee, S. G. (1968). Spirit possession among the Zulu. In J. Beattie and J. Middleton (Eds.), *Spirit mediumship and society in Africa*. London: Routledge & Kegan Paul.

Leslie, C. M., Ed. (1976). *Asian medical systems: a comparative study*. Berkeley: Univ. of California Press.

—— (1977). Pluralism and integration in the Indian and Chinese medical systems. In D. Landy (Ed.), *Culture, disease and healing: studies in medical anthropology*. New York: Macmillan. Pp. 511–517.

Levine, H. G., A. Zetlin, and L. L. Langness (1980). Everyday memory tasks in classrooms for TMR learners. *Quart. Newsletter Lab. compara. hum. Cognit., 2*, 1–6.

Le Vine, B. B. (1963). Nyansongo. In B. B. Whiting (Ed.), *Six cultures: studies of child rearing*. New York: Wiley.

Le Vine, R. A. (1966). *Dreams and deeds: achievement motivation in Nigeria*. Chicago: Univ. of Chicago Press.

—— (1973a). *Culture, behavior and personality*. Chicago: Aldine.

—— (1973b). Patterns of personality in Africa. *Ethos, 1*, 123–152.

—— Ed. (1974). *Culture and personality: contemporary readings*. Chicago: Aldine.

—— (1977). Child rearing as cultural adaptation. In P. H. Leiderman, S. R. Tulkin, and A. Rosenfeld (Eds.), *Culture and infancy: variations in the human experience*. New York: Academic Press.

Le Vine, R., and D. T. Campbell (1972). *Ethnocentrism: theories of conflict, ethnic attitudes and group behavior*. New York: Wiley.

Le Vine, R. A., and D. R. Price-Williams (1974). Children's kinship concepts: cognitive development and early experience among the Hausa. *Ethnology, 13*, 25–44.

Levy, R. I. (1973). *Tahitians: mind and experience in the Society Islands*. Chicago and London: Univ. of Chicago Press.

Lévy-Bruhl, L. (1923). *La mentalité primitive*. Paris: Alcan, 1922. Translated into English, *Primitive mentality*.

Lewis, I. M. (1971). *Ecstatic religion: an anthropological study of spirit possession*. Baltimore: Penguin Books.

—— (1977). Introduction. In I. Lewis (Ed.), *Symbols and sentiments: cross-cultural studies in symbolism*. London: Academic Press.

Lomax, A., and N. Berkowitz (1972). The evolutionary taxonomy of culture. *Science, 177*, 228–239.

Lonner, W. J. (1979). Issues in cross-cultural psychology. In A. J. Marsella, R. G. Tharp, and T. J. Ciborowski (Eds.), *Perspectives on cross-cultural psychology*. New York: Academic Press.

—— (1980). The search for psychological universals. In H. C. Triandis and W. W. Lambert (Eds.), *Handbook of cross-cultural psychology*. Vol. I. *Perspectives*. Boston: Allyn and Bacon.

Ludwig, A. (1969). Altered states of consciousness. In C. Tart (Ed.), *Altered states of consciousness*. New York: Wiley.

Luria, A. R. (1976). *Cognitive development: its cultural and social foundations*. Cambridge, Mass.: Harvard Univ. Press.

McAndrew, C., and R. B. Edgerton (1969). *Drunken comportment: a social exploration*. Chicago: Aldine.

McClelland, D. C. (1961). *The achieving society*. Princeton, N.J.: Van Nostrand.

McClelland, D. C., J. W. Atkinson, R. A. Clark, and E. L. Lowell (1953). *The achievement motive*. New York: Appleton-Century-Crofts.

McClelland, D. C., W. N. Davis, R. Kalin, and E. Wanner (1972). *The drinking man*. New York: Free Press.

McGaugh, J. L. (1971). *Psychobiology: behavior from a biological perspective*. New York, London: Academic Press.

Madsen, M. C., and S. Kagan (1973). Mother-directed achievement of children in two cultures. *J. of cross-cultural Psychol., 4*, 221–228.

Madsen, M. C., and A. Shapira (1977). Cooperation and challenge in four cultures. *J. soc. Psychol., 102*, 189–195.

Madsen, M. C., and S. Yi (1975). Cooperation and competition of urban and rural children in the republic of South Korea. *Int. J. Psychol., 10*, 269–274.

Mahler, M., F. Pine, and A. Bergman (1975). *The psychological birth of the human infant: symbiosis and individuation*. New York: Basic Books.

Malinowski, B. (1927). *Sex and repression in savage society*. London: Kegan Paul, Trench, Trubner.

Mann, L. (1980). Cross-cultural studies of small groups. In H. C. Triandis and R. W. Brislin (Eds.), *Handbook of cross-cultural psychology*. Vol. 5. Boston: Allyn and Bacon. Pp. 155–209.

Marsh, C. (1977). A framework for describing subjective states of consciousness. In N. E. Zinberg (Ed.), *Alternate states of consciousness*. New York: Free Press. Pp. 121–144.

Mauss, M. (1968). *L'âme, le nom, la personne*. Paris: Les Editions de Minuit. In *Oeuvres, 2*. Originally published 1929.

Mead, M. (1953). *Growing up in New Guinea*. New York: Mentor Books.

—— Ed. (1961). *Co-operation and competition among primitive peoples*. New York: McGraw-Hill.

Metraux, R. (1976). Eidos and change: continuity in process, discontinuity in product. In T. Schwartz (Ed.), *Socialization as cultural communication: development of a theme in the work of Margaret Mead*. Berkeley: Univ. of California Press. Pp. 201–216.

Miller, A. G., and R. Thomas (1972). Cooperation and competition among Blackfoot Indian and urban Canadian children. *Child Development, 43*, 1104–1110.

Minoura, Y. (1979). Life in-between: the acquisition of cultural identity among Japanese children living in the United States. Ph.D. dissertation (anthropology). Los Angeles: Univ. of California.

Minturn, L., and W. W. Lambert (1964). *Mothers of six cultures: antecedents of child rearing*. New York: Wiley.

Minturn-Triandis, L., and W. W. Lambert (1961). Pancultural factor analyses of reported socialization practices. *J. abnorm. soc. Psychol., 62*, 631–639.

Mischel, W. (1979). On the interface of cognition and personality: beyond the person-situation debate. *Amer. Psychol., 34*, 740–754.

Munroe, R. H., and R. L. Munroe (1971). Household density and infant care in an east African society. *J. soc. Psychol., 83*, 3–13.

Munroe, R. H., R. L. Munroe, and B. B. Whiting (1981). *Handbook of cross-cultural human development. Part II. Early experiences and growth.* New York: Garland STPM Press.

Murdock, G. P. (1949). *Social structure.* New York: Macmillan.

_____ (1957). World ethnographic sample. *Amer. Anthropologist, 59,* 664–687.

Myerhoff, B. G. (1974). *Peyote hunt: the sacred journey of the Huichol Indians.* Ithaca and London: Cornell Univ. Press.

Naroll, R., G. L. Michik, and F. Naroll (1980). Holocultural research methods. In H. C. Triandis and J. W. Berry (Eds.), *Handbook of cross-cultural psychology.* Vol. 2. *Methodology.* Boston: Allyn and Bacon.

Nuttall, R. L. (1964). Some correlates of high need for achievement among urban northern Negroes. *J. abnorm. soc. Psychol., 68,* 593–600.

Olson, D. R. (1970). *Cognitive development: the child's acquisition of diagonality.* New York: Academic Press.

Orlansky, H. (1949). Infant care and personality. *Psychol. Bull., 46,* 1.

Osgood, C. E., W. H. May, and M. S. Miron (1975). *Cross-cultural universals of affective meanings.* Champaign-Urbana: Univ. of Illinois Press.

Palmer, S. (1970). Aggression in fifty-four non-literate societies. *Annales Internationales de Criminologie* 1 er Semestre, Paris, 57–69.

_____ (1972). *The violent society.* New Haven: College and University Press.

_____ (1975). Characteristics of homicide and suicide victims in forty non-literate societies. In I. Drapkin and E. Viano (Eds.), *Victimology: a new focus.* Vol. IV. Washington, D.C.: Mason. Pp. 43–53.

Pedersen, P., W. J. Lonner, and J. G. Draguns Eds. (1976). *Counseling across cultures.* Honolulu, Hawaii: Univ. Press of Hawaii. A Cultural Learning Institute Monograph, East-West Center.

Piaget, J. (1928). *Judgment and reasoning in the child.* New York: Harcourt, Brace.

_____ (1932). *The moral judgment of the child.* London: Routledge and Kegan Paul.

_____ (1976). Need and significance of cross-cultural research in genetic psychology. In B. Inhelder, and H. H. Chipman (Eds.), *Piaget and his school: a reader in developmental psychology.* New York: Springer-Verlag. Originally published in French in the *Int. J. Psychol.,* 1966, *1,* 3–13.

Pick, A. D. (1980). Cognition: psychological perspectives. In H. C. Triandis, and W. Lonner (Eds.), *Handbook of cross-cultural psychology.* Vol. 3. *Basic Processes.* Boston: Allyn and Bacon. Pp. 117–153.

Piers, G., and M. B. Singer (1971). *Shame and guilt: a psychoanalytic and a cultural study.* Originally published by Charles C. Thomas, 1953. Reprinted, New York: Norton.

Pike, K. (1954). Language in relation to a unified theory of the structure of human behavior. Part 1. Glendale: Summer Institute of Linguistics.

Pollnac, R. B. (1975). Cognitive variability and its sociocultural correlates among the Baganda. *Ethos, 3,* 22–40.

Price-Williams, D. R. (1975). *Explorations in cross-cultural psychology.* San Francisco: Chandler and Sharp.

_____ (1976). Cross-cultural differences in cognitive development. In V. Hamilton, and M. D. Vernon (Eds.), *The development of cognitive processes.* London: Academic Press. Pp. 549–588.

_____ (1979). Modes of thought in cross-cultural psychology: an historical overview. In A. J. Marsella, R. G. Tharp, and T. J. Ciborowski (Eds.), *Perspectives on cross-cultural psychology.* New York: Academic Press.

_____ (1980). Anthropological approaches to cognition and their relevance to psychology. In H. C. Triandis, and W. Lonner (Eds.), *Handbook of cross-cultural psychology.* Vol. 3. *Basic Processes.* Boston: Allyn and Bacon.

Price-Williams, D. R., and R. Gallimore (1980). The cultural perspective. In B. K. Keogh (Ed.), *Advances in special education. A research annual.* Vol. 2. *Perspectives on applications.* Greenwich, Conn.: JAI Press.

Prince, R. (1977). Foreword in V. Crapanzano and V. Garrison (Eds.), *Case studies in spirit possession.* New York: Wiley. Pp. xi–xvi.

Read, M. (1959). *Children of their fathers.* London: Methuen.

Reichel-Dolmatoff, G. (1975). *The shaman and the jaguar.* Philadelphia: Temple Univ. Press.

Reynolds, D. K. (1976). *Morita psychotherapy.* Berkeley: Univ. of California Press.

Richards, A. I. (1956). *Chisungu: a girl's ceremony among the Bemba of Northern Rhodesia.* New York: Grove Press.

Roberts, J. M., and B. Sutton-Smith (1962). Child training and game involvement. *Ethnology, 1,* 166–185.

Rogoff, B. (1981). Schooling and the development of cognitive skills. In H. C. Triandis and A. Heron (Eds.), *Handbook of cross-cultural psychology.* Vol. 4. *Developmental psychology.* Boston: Allyn and Bacon.

Rohner, R. P. (1975). *They love me, they love me not: a worldwide study of the effects of parental acceptance and rejection.* New Haven, Conn.: H.R.A.F. Press.

Rokeach, M. (1960). *The open and closed mind: investigations into the nature of belief systems and personality systems.* New York: Basic Books.

Rosch, E. (1975). Universals and cultural specifics in human categorization. In R. W. Brislin, S. Bochner, and W. J. Lonner (Eds.) *Cross-cultural perspectives on learning: the interface between culture and learning.* New York: Wiley and Sage.

Rosen, B. C. (1962). Socialization and the achievement motivation in Brazil. *Amer. Sociol. Rev., 27,* 612–624.

Rosen, B. C., and R. D'Andrade (1959). The psychological origins of achievement motivation. *Sociometry, 22,* 185–218.

Rossi, A. (1977). A biosocial perspective on parenting. *Daedalus, J. Amer. Acad. Arts Sci., 106,* 1–31.

Sanjek, R. (1971). Brazilian racial terms: some aspects of meaning and learning. *Amer. Anthropologist, 73,* 1126–1143.

Sawyer, J., and R. A. Le Vine (1966). Cultural dimensions: a factor analysis of the world ethnographic sample. *Amer. Anthropologist, 68,* 708–731.

Schacter, S., J. Nuttin, C. DeMonchaux, P. A. Maucorps, D. Osmer, H. Duijker, R. Rommatveit, and J. Israel (1954). Cross-cultural experiments on threats and rejection. *Hum. Relat., 7,* 403–439.

Schultes, R. E., and A. Hofmann (1973). *The botany and chemistry of hallucinogens.* Springfield, Ill.: Charles C. Thomas.

Schwartz, T., and L. Romanucci-Ross (1974). Drinking and inebriate behavior in the Admiralty Islands, Melanesia. *Ethos, 2,* 213–231.

Scribner, S. (1975). Recall of classical syllogisms: a cross-cultural investigation of error on logical problems. In R. J. Falmagne (Ed.), *Reasoning, representation and process.* Hillsdale, N.J.: Erlbaum.

—— (1976). Situating the experiment in cross-cultural research. In K. Riegel and J. Meacham (Eds.), *The developing individual in a changing world.* Vol. 1. Chicago: Aldine.

Scribner, S., and M. Cole (1978). Literacy without schooling. Testing for intellectual effects. *Harvard Educ. Rev., 48,* 448–461.

Segall, M. H. (1979). *Cross-cultural psychology: human behavior in global perspective.* Monterey, Calif.: Brooks/Cole.

Segall, M. H., D. T. Campbell, and M. J. Herskovits (1966). *The influence of culture on visual perception.* Indianapolis: Bobbs-Merrill.

Shweder, R. A. (1973). The between and within of cross-cultural research. *Ethos, 1,* 531–545.

—— (1979). Aspects of cognition in Zinacanteco shamans: experimental results. In W. A. Lessa and E. Z. Vogt (Eds.). *Reader in comparative religion: an anthropological approach.* (4th ed.). New York: Harper & Row. Pp. 327–331.

—— (1980). Culture and personality theory: is it fit for survival? In R. L. Munroe, R. H. Munroe, and B. B. Whiting (Eds.), *Handbook of cross-cultural human development.* New York: Garland Publishing.

Sommerland, E., and W. P. Bellingham (1972). Cooperation-competition: a comparison of Australian European and aboriginal school children. *J. cross-cultural Psychol., 3,* 149–157.

Sperber, D. (1975). *Rethinking symbolism.* Translated by A. L. Morton. Cambridge: Cambridge Univ. Press. First published in French, 1974.

Spindler, G., and L. Spindler (1971). *Dreamers without power: the Menomini Indians.* New York: Holt, Rinehart, and Winston.

—— (1976). Adaptations to the study of change. In *Essays in honor of W. Goldschmidt.* Anthropology, UCLA, *8,* 85–97.

Spindler, L. (1978). Researching the psychology of culture change and urbanization. In G. D. Spindler (Ed.), *The making of psychological anthropology.* Berkeley: Univ. of California Press. Pp. 176–200.

Spiro, M. (1965). Religious systems as culturally constituted defense mechanisms. In M. E. Spiro (Ed.), *Context and meaning in cultural anthropology.* New York: Free Press. Pp. 100–113.

—— (1967). *Burmese supernationalism: a study in the explanation and reduction of suffering.* Englewood Cliffs, N.J.: Prentice-Hall.

—— (1972). An overview and a suggested reorientation. In F. L. K. Hsu (Ed.), *Psychological anthropology* (New ed.). Cambridge, Mass.: Schenkman. Pp. 573–607.

Spitz, R. A. (1965). *The first year of life.* New York: International Universities Press.

Spradley, J. P. (1970). *You owe yourself a drunk—an ethnography of urban nomads.* Boston: Little, Brown.

—— (1980). *Participant observation.* New York: Holt, Rinehart, and Winston.

Spradley, J. P., and D. W. McCurdy (1972). *The cultural experience: ethnography in complex society.* Chicago: Science Research Associates.

Straus, A. S. (1977). Northern Cheyenne Ethnopsychology. *Ethos, 5,* 326–357.

Sundberg, N. D. (1977). *Assessment of persons.* Englewood Cliffs, N.J.: Prentice-Hall.

Super, C. M. (1981). Behavioral developments in infancy. In R. H. Munroe, R. L. Munroe, and B. B. Whiting (Eds.), *Handbook of cross-cultural human development.* New York: Garland Press.

Super, C. M., and S. Harkness (1974). Patterns of personality in Africa. A note from the field. *Ethos, 2,* 377–381.

Sutton-Smith, B., and J. M. Roberts (1981). Play, toys, games, and sports. In H. C. Triandis, and A. Heron (Eds.), *Handbook of cross-cultural psychology.* Vol. 4. *Developmental psychology.* Boston: Allyn and Bacon.

Tart, C. Ed. (1969). *Altered states of consciousness.* New York: Wiley.

Textor, R. B. (1967). *A cross-cultural summary.* New Haven, Conn.: H.R.A.F. Press.

Thomas, D. R. (1975). Cooperation and competition among Polynesian and European children. *Child Development, 46,* 948–953.

Thompson, W. R. (1980). Cross-cultural uses of biological data and perspectives. In H. C. Triandis, and W. W. Lambert (Eds.), *Handbook of cross-cultural psychology.* Vol. 1. *Perspectives.* Boston: Allyn and Bacon.

Triandis, H. C. (1975). Social psychology and cultural analysis. *J. Theory soc. Behav., 5,* 81–106.

—— (1977). Cross-cultural social and personality psychology. *Pers. soc. Psychol. Bull., 3,* 143–158.

—— (1980). Introduction to *Handbook of cross-cultural psychology.* In H. C. Triandis and W. W. Lambert. *Handbook of cross-cultural psychology.* Vol. 1. *Perspectives.* Boston: Allyn and Bacon.

Triandis, H. C., and J. W. Berry, Eds. (1980). *Handbook of cross-cultural psychology.* Vol. 2. *Methodology.* Boston: Allyn and Bacon.

Triandis, H. C., and R. W. Brislin, Eds. (1980). *Handbook of cross-cultural psychology.* Vol. 5. *Social psychology.* Boston: Allyn and Bacon.

Triandis, H. C., and J. G. Draguns, Eds. (1981). *Handbook of cross-cultural psychology.* Vol. 6. *Psychopathology.* Boston: Allyn and Bacon.

Triandis, H. C., and A. Heron, Eds. (1981). *Handbook of cross-cultural psychology.* Vol. 4. *Developmental psychology.* Boston: Allyn and Bacon.

Triandis, H. C., and W. W. Lambert, Eds. (1980). *Handbook of cross-cultural psychology.* Vol. 1. *Perspectives.* Boston: Allyn and Bacon.

Triandis, H. C., and W. J. Lonner, Eds. (1980). *Handbook of cross-cultural psychology.* Vol. 3. *Basic processes.* Boston: Allyn and Bacon.

Triandis, H. C., V. Vassiliou, G. Vassiliou, Y. Tanaka, and A. V. Shanmugam (1972). The analysis of subjective culture. New York: Wiley.

Tseng, W.-S., and J. Hsu (1980). Minor psychological disturbances of everyday life. In H. C. Triandis, and J. G.

Draguns (1981). *Handbook of cross-cultural psychology.* Vol. 6. *Psychopathology.* Boston: Allyn and Bacon. Pp. 61–97.

Turiel, E. (1969). Developmental processes in the child's moral thinking. In P. H. Mussen, J. Langer, and M. Covington (Eds.) *Trends and issues in developmental psychology.* New York: Holt, Rinehart, and Winston.

Turnbull, C. M. (1961). *The forest people.* New York: Simon and Schuster.

——— (1965). *The wayward servants: the two worlds of the African Pygmies.* Garden City, N.Y.: Natural History Press.

Turner, V. (1969). *The ritual process.* Chicago: Aldine.

——— (1978). Encounter with Freud. The making of a comparative symbologist. In G. D. Spindler (Ed.), *The making of psychological anthropology.* Berkeley: Univ. of California Press.

Tyler, S. A. Ed. (1969). *Cognitive anthropology: readings.* New York: Holt, Rinehart, and Winston.

Tylor, E. B. (1871). *Primitive culture: researches into the development of mythology, philosophy, religion, language, art and custom.* London: J. Murray.

——— (1889). On a method of investigating the development of institutions: applied to laws of marriage and descent. *J. royal Anthropological Institute, 18,* 245–269.

Wallace, A. F. C. (1952). The modal personality of the Tuscarora Indians as revealed by the Rorschach test. Bureau of American Ethnology. *Bulletin 150.*

——— (1956). Mazeway resynthesis: a biocultural theory of religious inspiration. Transactions of the New York Academy of Sciences, *18,* 626–638.

——— (1965). The problem of the psychological validity of componential analysis. *Amer. Anthropologist, 67,* 248–299.

——— (1966). *Religion: an anthropological view.* New York: Random House.

——— (1970). *Culture and personality* (Rev. ed.). New York: Random House.

Washburn, S. L., and E. R. McCown (1972). Evolution of human behavior. *Soc. Biol., 19,* 163–170.

Wasson, R. G. (1968). *Soma: divine mushroom of immortality.* New York: Harcourt, Brace, Jovanovich.

Weber, Max (1930). *The Protestant ethic and the spirit of capitalism.* Translated by T. Parsons. (1st ed., 1904.) New York: Scribner.

Weill, G. (1975). Conception du Moi (C.M.) et facteurs socioculturels. *Ethnopsychologie, 30,* 309–325.

Weisner, T. S. (1979). Urban-rural differences in sociable and disruptive behavior of Kenya children. *Ethnology, 18,* 153–172.

——— (1980). Cities, stress and children: a review of some cross-cultural questions. In R. M. Munroe, R. L. Munroe,

and B. B. Whiting (Eds.), *Handbook of cross-cultural human development.* New York: Garland STPM Press. Pp. 783–808.

——— (1981). Cities, stress and children: a review of some cross-cultural questions. In R. H. Munroe, R. L. Munroe, and B. B. Whiting (Eds.), *Handbook of cross-cultural human development.* New York: Garland STPM Press.

Werner, H. (1957). *Comparative psychology of normal development* (Rev. ed.). New York: International Universities Press.

Whiting, B. B. (1976). The problem of the packaged variable. In K. F. Riegel, and J. A. Meacham (Eds.), *The developing individual in a changing world.* Vol. 1. Chicago: Aldine. Pp. 303–309.

Whiting, B. B., and J. W. M. Whiting (1975). *Children of six cultures.* Cambridge, Mass.: Harvard Univ. Press.

Whiting, J. W. M. (1954). The cross-cultural method. In G. Lindzey (Ed.), *Handbook of social psychology.* Vol. 1. Reading, Mass.: Addison-Wesley. Pp. 523–531.

Whiting, J. W. M., and I. Child (1953). *Child training and personality.* New Haven: Yale Univ. Press.

Whiting, J. W. M., R. Kluckhohn, and A. Anthony (1958). The function of male initiation ceremonies at puberty. In E. E. Maccoby, T. M. Newcomb, and E. L. Hartley (Eds.), *Readings in social psychology.* New York: Holt.

Williams, T. R. (1975). *Psychological anthropology.* The Hague: Mouton.

Wilson, E. O. (1975). *Sociobiology: the new synthesis.* Cambridge, Mass.: The Belknap Press of Harvard Univ. Press.

Witkin, M. A., and J. W. Berry (1975). Psychological differentiation in cross-cultural perspective. *J. cross-cultural Psychol., 6,* 4–87.

Witkin, H. A., R. B. Dyk, H. E. Faterson, D. R. Goodenough, and S. A. Karp (1962). *Psychological differentiation.* New York: Wiley.

Witkin, M. A., H. B. Lewis, M. Hertzman, K. Machover, P. B. Meissner, and S. Wapner (1954). *Personality through perception.* New York: Harper.

Witkin, H. A., D. R. Price-Williams, M. Bertini, B. Christiensen, P. K. Oltman, M. Ramirez, and J. Van Meel (1974). Social conformity and psychological differentiation. *Int. J. Psychol.,* 9, 11–29.

Wober, M. (1974). Towards an understanding of the Kiganda concept of intelligence. In J. W. Berry and P. R. Dasen (Eds.), *Culture and cognition: readings in cross-cultural psychology.* London: Methuen. Pp. 261–280.

Wolfgang, A. Ed. (1979). *Nonverbal behavior: applications and cultural implications.* New York: Academic Press.

Zinberg, N. E. Ed. (1977). *Alternate states of consciousness.* New York: Free Press.

Index

Index